COMPREHENSIVE CRIMINAL PROCEDURE

ASPEN CASEBOOK SERIES

COMPREHENSIVE CRIMINAL PROCEDURE

Third Edition

Ronald Jay Allen

John Henry Wigmore Professor of Law
Northwestern University

William J. Stuntz

Henry J. Friendly Professor of Law
Harvard University

Joseph L. Hoffmann

Harry Pratter Professor of Law
Indiana University Maurer School of Law

Debra A. Livingston

United States Circuit Judge, Second Circuit
Paul J. Kellner Professor of Law
Columbia University

Andrew D. Leipold

Edwin M. Adams Professor and Director,
Program in Criminal Law & Procedure
University of Illinois

. Wolters Kluwer

Law & Business

Published by Wolters Kluwer Law & Business in New York.

Wolters Kluwer Law & Business serves customers worldwide with CCH, Aspen Publishers, and Kluwer Law International products. (www.wolterskluwerlb.com)

To contact Customer Service, e-mail customer.service@wolterskluwer.com, call 1-800-234-1660, fax 1-800-901-9075, or mail correspondence to:

Wolters Kluwer Law & Business
Attn: Order Department
PO Box 990
Frederick, MD 21705

Printed in the United States of America.

2 3 4 5 6 7 8 9 0

ISBN 978-0-7355-8778-6

Library of Congress Cataloging-in-Publication Data

Comprehensive criminal procedure / Ronald Jay Allen . . . [et al.]. — 3rd ed.
    p. cm.
Includes bibliographical references and index.
ISBN 978-0-7355-8778-6
1. Criminal procedure—United States—Cases. 2. Criminal justice, Administration of—United States—Cases. I. Allen, Ronald J. (Ronald Jay), 1948-

KF9618.C66 2011
345.73'05—dc22

2010053400

About Wolters Kluwer Law & Business

Wolters Kluwer Law & Business is a leading global provider of intelligent information and digital solutions for legal and business professionals in key specialty areas, and respected educational resources for professors and law students. Wolters Kluwer Law & Business connects legal and business professionals as well as those in the education market with timely, specialized authoritative content and information-enabled solutions to support success through productivity, accuracy and mobility.

Serving customers worldwide, Wolters Kluwer Law & Business products include those under the Aspen Publishers, CCH, Kluwer Law International, Loislaw, Best Case, ftwilliam.com and MediRegs family of products.

CCH products have been a trusted resource since 1913, and are highly regarded resources for legal, securities, antitrust and trade regulation, government contracting, banking, pension, payroll, employment and labor, and healthcare reimbursement and compliance professionals.

Aspen Publishers products provide essential information to attorneys, business professionals and law students. Written by preeminent authorities, the product line offers analytical and practical information in a range of specialty practice areas from securities law and intellectual property to mergers and acquisitions and pension/benefits. Aspen's trusted legal education resources provide professors and students with high-quality, up-to-date and effective resources for successful instruction and study in all areas of the law.

Kluwer Law International products provide the global business community with reliable international legal information in English. Legal practitioners, corporate counsel and business executives around the world rely on Kluwer Law journals, looseleafs, books, and electronic products for comprehensive information in many areas of international legal practice.

Loislaw is a comprehensive online legal research product providing legal content to law firm practitioners of various specializations. Loislaw provides attorneys with the ability to quickly and efficiently find the necessary legal information they need, when and where they need it, by facilitating access to primary law as well as state-specific law, records, forms and treatises.

Best Case Solutions is the leading bankruptcy software product to the bankruptcy industry. It provides software and workflow tools to flawlessly streamline petition preparation and the electronic filing process, while timely incorporating ever-changing court requirements.

ftwilliam.com offers employee benefits professionals the highest quality plan documents (retirement, welfare and non-qualified) and government forms (5500/PBGC, 1099 and IRS) software at highly competitive prices.

MediRegs products provide integrated health care compliance content and software solutions for professionals in healthcare, higher education and life sciences, including professionals in accounting, law and consulting.

Wolters Kluwer Law & Business, a division of Wolters Kluwer, is headquartered in New York. Wolters Kluwer is a market-leading global information services company focused on professionals.

While it is unusual to dedicate a book to a present member of the team of authors, we dedicate this edition to Bill Stuntz in recognition of the many contributions that he has made to it and its predecessors. Since joining the third edition of the precursor to this book, *Constitutional Criminal Procedure*, Bill has influenced virtually every page of all succeeding editions, and he was critical to the evolution of that book into *Comprehensive Criminal Procedure*. Much more important, Bill's friendship and example have affected us in such innumerable and profound ways that we wished to make this small gesture of gratitude to thank him for being a part of our lives.

Summary of Contents

PART FIVE
POSTTRIAL PROCEEDINGS   1401

Contents

Chapter 2
The Idea of Due Process   81

PART TWO
THE RIGHT TO COUNSEL—THE LINCHPIN OF
CONSTITUTIONAL PROTECTION 131

Chapter 3
The Right to Counsel and Other Assistance 133

PART THREE
THE RIGHT TO BE LET ALONE—AN EXAMINATION
OF THE FOURTH AND FIFTH AMENDMENTS
AND RELATED AREAS   289

Chapter 4
The Rise and Fall of Boyd v. United States   291

Chapter 5
The Fourth Amendment   337

Chapter 7
Complex Investigations in the Fourth Amendment's Shadow

PART FOUR
THE ADJUDICATION PROCESS

Chapter 8
Bail and Pretrial Detention

Chapter 11
The Scope of the Prosecution   1055

Chapter 12
Discovery and Disclosure   1119

Chapter 13
Guilty Pleas and Plea Bargaining   1165

Chapter 14
The Jury and the Criminal Trial 1271

PART FIVE
POSTTRIAL PROCEEDINGS   1401

Chapter 15
Sentencing   1403

Chapter 16
Double Jeopardy 1491

Chapter 17
Appellate and Collateral Review 1565

Preface to the Third Edition

Comprehensive Criminal Procedure provides a set of materials suitable for any criminal procedure course beyond those that focus primarily on state law issues. Many modern American law schools provide two mainstream criminal procedure courses. One course focuses primarily on criminal investigations, including the right to counsel, the Fourth Amendment, self-incrimination, and related areas; the second course focuses primarily on adjudication, including all pretrial, trial, sentencing, and appellate issues. Other law schools offer the first but not the second of these, and some offer a single survey course combining both the investigative and the adjudicative aspects of the subject matter. This book should work well for any of these courses.

Criminal procedure is one of the most fascinating and important fields of legal study. More than any other area of law, criminal procedure determines the relationship between government and citizen, and thus defines the legal system's stance toward the demands of autonomy, privacy, and dignity. It often does so through adversarial legal processes. Thus, the study of criminal procedure leads naturally to fundamental problems of reasoning, decision making, and political and social theory, in addition to standard law school questions about the meaning of a constitutional or statutory provision, or the implications of a precedent. The subject demands, and we have tried to bring, intellectual rigor to these materials; we do not shy away from addressing intractable problems. Moreover, much of the present law reflects its past, and thus — although our emphasis is squarely on the law and practice of criminal procedure today — we have also provided, where appropriate, a full account of the relevant history.

In addition to the careful attention given to the historical roots of modern law, we develop a number of important subthemes while pursuing the overarching theme of this book — that the criminal process significantly forms the boundary between the government and the citizen. First, we draw attention to the real-world implications of alternative regulatory regimes. All too common in this field is the notion that if there is a problem, the courts should remedy it. Often courts are unable to remedy problems, and sometimes their solutions are worse than the initial problems. Second, although the subject matter of the book is criminal procedure, procedure interacts in complex and profound ways with substance. In appraising any procedural matter, especially one involving a judicial determination of a procedural right, the power of legislatures to indirectly eliminate the right through changes in substantive criminal law (or directly through statutory changes to the procedure in question) must be taken into consideration. Third, we explore throughout the book the complicated relationships, and occasional conflicts, between those institutions — primarily courts, legislatures, prosecutors, and juries — that share responsibility for processing criminal cases. Fourth, much of the modern law of criminal procedure is a direct consequence of the effort to end racial discrimination in the United States and can be understood only in that context. Fifth, in the adjudication half of the book, we address the growing concern about accuracy in criminal justice and the problem of erroneous convictions. Finally, the implications of limited resources must constantly be kept in mind. Criminal procedure is instrumental to the construction of a civilized society, and a dollar spent here is a dollar that cannot be spent somewhere else. One can have more expensive criminal procedure, or one can have more hospitals, roads, or welfare programs. One cannot, however, have it all.

The book opens with a wide-ranging set of readings about the criminal justice system, combining hard data with expert commentary. The nature of due process adjudication is then introduced, because so much of criminal procedure law either has been constitutionalized or operates within the shadow of the Constitution. With one major exception, the book then follows the processing of a criminal case more or less chronologically, from initial investigation through appeal and habeas corpus. The major exception is Chapter 3, which contains a thorough examination of the right to counsel. Counsel is the linchpin of criminal procedure, obviously so with respect to its constitutional aspects but even more critically so with respect to its statutory and common law aspects. Without adequate counsel, a suspect or defendant is, with rare exceptions, lost. The most elaborate procedural protections courts can devise are of little value to one who knows neither what those protections are nor how they can be used to best advantage.

Following the right to counsel chapter is a chapter chronicling the history of Boyd v. United States. We think it fair to say that the U.S. Supreme Court has been reacting to the *Boyd* case for more than a century, and that the present law of search and seizure and the right to be free from compelled self-incrimination cannot be understood without a grounding in *Boyd* and its aftermath. The remainder of the book then unfolds in the promised chronological order.

In this third edition of the book, we welcome to our author team Andrew D. Leipold, one of the most respected scholars working in the area of criminal procedure today. Andrew has contributed greatly to the improvements you will see herein. Those improvements include a comprehensive revision of Chapter 3, on the right to counsel; substantial refinements of Chapter 5, on the Fourth Amendment; a major reorganization of the *Miranda* portion of Chapter 6, on the Fifth Amendment; an updated Chapter 7, now titled "Complex Investigations in the Fourth Amendment's Shadow"; a new Chapter 10, on pretrial screening and the grand jury, that brings together materials previously found in separate chapters; a revised Chapter 11, on the scope of the prosecution, that not only covers speedy trial, joinder, and severance but also adds a new section on venue; up-to-the-minute presentations of *Crawford* doctrine in Chapter 14, on the jury and the criminal trial, and of *Apprendi* doctrine in Chapter 15, on sentencing; and coverage of the latest empirical research and recent policy debates about habeas corpus in Chapter 17, on appellate and collateral review.

In addition to these specific additions and changes, and the inclusion of every important criminal procedure decision in recent years, we have pursued two main goals throughout this third edition. First, we have sought to make the book more accessible for students without sacrificing any of the rigor and sophistication that we believe has been the hallmark of the book from its inception. Second, we have maintained our emphasis on keeping the book current — meaning that, wherever the theoretical or doctrinal framework of criminal procedure law has changed significantly since earlier editions, we have reworked our coverage of the relevant material to ensure that the book does not become mired in the past but instead continues to highlight the issues and the controversies of the present day.

We have endeavored to keep editing of cases at a minimum, opting at times for textual description over a series of edited excerpts. Editing is unavoidable, however. In all cases and materials reproduced here, we have kept the original footnoting sequence. Wherever our own footnotes might be confused with those of the primary material, our own footnotes are identified by the legend " — EDS." This book contains Supreme Court and lower court cases and legislative materials current through August 2010.

Ronald J. Allen
William J. Stuntz
Joseph L. Hoffmann
Debra A. Livingston
Andrew D. Leipold

December 2010

Acknowledgments

The authors would like to thank Northwestern Law School, Harvard Law School, Indiana University Maurer School of Law, Columbia Law School, and the University of Illinois College of Law for their generous support during the writing of this book. In addition, Ron Allen would like to thank his wife, Julie O'Donnell Allen, for her love and support. Bill Stuntz would like to thank his family, Ruth, Sarah, Sam, and Andy, for their generous support in every way. Joe Hoffmann would like to thank his father, George L. Hoffmann. Debra Livingston would like to thank her husband, John Merritt McEnany. And Andy Leipold would like to thank his parents, David and Ruth Leipold, for their unwavering support through the years.

We are grateful to the following sources for permission to reprint excerpts of their work:

Francis Allen, Decline of the Rehabilitative Ideal: Penal Policy and Social Purpose, pp. 60-61, 63, 65-66. Copyright © 1981 by Yale University Press. Reprinted with permission.

Ronald J. Allen & John P. Ratnaswamy, Heath v. Alabama: A Case Study of Doctrine and Rationality in the Supreme Court, 76 J. Crim. L. & Criminology 801, 807, 811-814 (1985). Reprinted by special permission of Northwestern University School of Law, Journal of Criminal Law and Criminology.

Ronald J. Allen, Melissa Luttrell, & Anne Kreeger, Clarifying Entrapment, 89 J. Crim. L. & Criminology 407, 413-414, 415-416 (1999). Reprinted by special permission of Northwestern University School of Law, Journal of Criminal Law and Criminology.

Ronald J. Allen & Ross M. Rosenberg, The Fourth Amendment and the Limits of Theory: Local Versus General Theoretical Knowledge, 72 St. John's L. Rev. 1149, 1194, 1197-1200 (1998). Reprinted with permission.

Albert W. Alschuler, Implementing the Criminal Defendant's Right to Trial: Alternatives to the Plea-Bargaining, 50 U. Chi. L. Rev. 931, 932-936, 1048-1050 (1983). Used with permission of University of Chicago Law Review from Albert W. Alschuler, Implementing the Criminal Defendant's Right to Trial: Alternatives to the Plea-Bargaining, 50 University of Chicago Law Review, 1983; permission conveyed through Copyright Clearance Center, Inc.

Akhil Reed Amar, The Future of Constitutional Criminal Procedure, 33 Am. Crim. L. Rev. 1123, 1123-1125, 1128-1129, 1132-1134 (1996). Reprinted with permission of the publisher, Georgetown University and American Criminal Law Review (1996).

Anthony G. Amsterdam, The Supreme Court and the Rights of Suspects in Criminal Cases, 45 N.Y.U. L. Rev. 785, 785-794 (1970). Reprinted with permission of the New York University Law Review.

Peter Arenella, Schmerber and the Privilege Against Self-Incrimination: A Reappraisal, 20 Am. Crim. L. Rev. 31, 37, 43-45 (1982). Arenella, Schmerber and the Privilege Against Self-Incrimination: A Reappraisal, 20 American Criminal Law Review. Copyright © 1982 by the American Bar Association. Reprinted with permission of the author.

R. Richard Banks, Beyond Profiling: Race, Policing, and the Drug War, 56 Stan. L. Rev. 571, 588-589, 602-603 (2003). Used with permission of Stanford Law Review from R. Richard Banks, Beyond Profiling: Race, Policing, and the Drug War, 56 Stanford Law Review, 2003; permission conveyed through Copyright Clearance Center, Inc.

David L. Bazelton, The Realities of Gideon and Argersinger, 64 Geo. L.J. 811 (1976). Reprinted with permission of the publisher, Georgetown Law Journal © 1976.

Sara Sun Beale & James E. Felman, The Consequences of Enlisting Federal Grand Juries in the War on Terrorism: Assessing the USA Patriot Act's Changes to Grand Jury Secrecy, 25 Harv. J.L. & Pub. Pol'y 699, 717-718 (2002). Copyright © the Harvard Journal of Law & Public Policy. Reprinted with permission.

Stephanos Bibas, Harmonizing Substantive-Criminal-Law Values and Criminal Procedure: The Case of Alford and Nolo Contendere Pleas, 88 Cornell L. Rev. 1361, 1363-1364, 1364-1366 (2003). Used with permission of the Cornell Law Review from Stephanos Bibas, Harmonizing Substantive-Criminal-Law Values and Criminal Procedure: The Case of Alford and Nolo Contendere Pleas, 88 Cornell L. Rev., 2003; permission conveyed through Copyright Clearance Center, Inc.

Stephanos Bibas, Plea Bargaining Outside the Shadow of Trial, 117 Harv. L. Rev. 2463 (2004). Used with permission of Harvard Law Review, from Stephanos Bibas, Plea Bargaining Outside the Shadow of Trial, 117 Harv. L. Rev., 2004; permission conveyed through Copyright Clearance Center, Inc.

Abraham Blumberg, The Practice of Law as Confidence Game: Organizational Cooptation of a Profession, 1 Law & Soc'y Rev. 15, 18-26, 29-31 (No. 2 1967). Copyright © 1967. Reprinted with permission of John Wiley & Sons, Inc.

Craig Bradley, Murray v. United States: The Bell Tolls for the Warrant Requirement, 64 Ind. L.J. 907, 917-918 (1989). Craig Bradley, Murray v. United States: The Bell Tolls for the Warrant Requirement, 64 Indiana Law Journal 907. Reprinted with permission.

William J. Brennan, Jr., "State Constitutions and the Protection of Individual Rights." Used with permission of Harvard Law Review, from William J. Brennan, Jr., State Constitutions and the Protection of Individual Rights, 90 Harvard Law Review, 1977; permission conveyed through Copyright Clearance Center, Inc.

Alafair S. Burke, Improving Prosecutorial Decision Making: Some Lessons of Cognitive Science, 47 Wm. & Mary L. Rev. 1587, 1610, 1611-1612 (2006).

Steven J. Burton, Comment on "Empty Ideas": Logical Positivist Analyses of Equality and Rules, 91 Yale L.J. 1136-1141, 1144-1147 (1982). Used with permission of The Yale Law Journal Company from Burton, Comment on "Empty Ideas": Logical Positivist Analyses of Equality and Rules, 91 Yale Law Journal, 1983; permission conveyed through Copyright Clearance Center, Inc.

Paul Butler, Racially Based Jury Nullification: Black Power in the Criminal Justice System, 105 Yale L.J. 677, 714 (1995). Used with permission of The Yale Law Journal Company from Paul Butler, Racially Based Jury Nullification: Black Power in the Criminal Justice System, 105 Yale Law Journal, 1995; permission conveyed through Copyright Clearance Center, Inc.

Steven E. Clark, Ryan T. Howell, & Sherrie L. Davey, Regularities in Eyewitness Identification, 32 Law & Hum. Behav. 187, 211 (2008). With kind permission from Springer Science+Business Media: Steven E. Clark, Ryan T. Howell, & Sherrie L. Davey, Regularities in Eyewitness Identification, 32 Law and Human Behavior, 2008.

Russell D. Covey, Signaling and Plea Bargaining's Innocence Problem, 66 Wash. & Lee L. Rev. 73 (2009). Reprinted with permission.

Thomas Y. Davies, Not "The Framers' Design": How the Framing-Era Ban Against Hearsay Evidence Refutes the Crawford-Davis "Testimonial" Formulation of the Scope of the Original Confrontation Clause, 15 J.L. & Pol'y 349-350 (2007). Thomas Y. Davies, Not "The Framers' Design": How the Framing-Era Ban Against Hearsay Evidence Refutes the Crawford-Davis "Testimonial" Formulation of the Scope of the Original Confrontation Clause, 15 J.L. & Pol'y. Copyright © 2007. Reprinted with permission.

Robert Dawson, Joint Trials of Defendants in Criminal Cases: An Analysis of Efficiencies and Prejudices, 77 Mich. L. Rev. 1379, 1383-1386 (1979). Reprinted from Michigan Law Review, June 1979, Vol. 77, No. 6. Copyright 1979 by The Michigan Law Review Association. Reprinted with permission of the author.

George Fisher, Plea Bargaining's Triumph, 109 Yale L.J. 857, 864-868 (2000). Used with permission of The Yale Law Journal Company from Fisher, George, Plea Bargaining's Triumph, 109 Yale Law Journal, 2000; permission conveyed through Copyright Clearance Center, Inc.

Marvin Frankel, United States District Judge for the Southern District of New York, 41 U. Cin. L. Rev. 1, 4-6, 29-31, 51 (1972).

Charles Fried, Reflections on Crime and Punishment, 30 Suffolk U. L. Rev. 681, 682-683, 685-688, 692-693, 694-695 (1997). Copyright © 1997. Reprinted with permission.

Russell Galloway, The Intruding Eye: A Status Report on the Constitutional Ban Against Paper Searches, 25 How. L.J. 367, 382-385 (1982). From 25 Howard Law Journal. Copyright © 1982 by the Howard Law Journal. Reprinted with permission.

Joseph D. Grano, Ascertaining the Truth, 77 Cornell L. Rev., 1061, 1062-1064. Copyright © 1992. Reprinted with permission.

Samuel R. Gross & Debra Livingston, Racial Profiling Under Attack, 102 Colum. L. Rev. 1413 (2002). Used with permission of Columbia Law Review, from Samuel R. Gross and Debra Livingston, Racial Profiling Under Attack, 102 Colum. L. Rev. 1413, 2002; permission conveyed through Copyright Clearance Center, Inc.

Carissa Byrne Hessick, Appellate Review of Sentencing Policy Decisions After Kimbrough, 93 Marq. L. Rev. 717, 733, 749 (2009).

Milton Heumann, Plea Bargaining: The Experiences of Prosecutors, Judges, and Defense Attorneys, pp. 49-50, 57-59, 61-63, 76-78, 89, 100-103, 105-6, University of Chicago Press, 1978. Heumann, Milton, Plea Bargaining: The Experiences of Prosecutors, Judges, and Defense Attorneys. Copyright © 1978 by the University of Chicago Press. Reprinted with permission.

Joseph L. Hoffmann, House v. Bell and the Death of Innocence, in Death Penalty Stories, John H. Blume & Jordan M. Steiker, eds. 2009. Reprinted with permission of the author.

Joseph L. Hoffmann & Nancy J. King, Rethinking the Federal Role in State Criminal Justice, 84 N.Y.U. L. Rev. 791, 806-810 (2009). Reprinted with permission of the New York University Law Review.

Pamela Karlan, Discrete and Relational Criminal Representation: The Changing Vision of the Right to Counsel, 105 Harv. L. Rev. 670, 709-710 (1992). Used with permission of Harvard Law Review, from Karlan, Discrete and Relational Criminal Representation: The Changing Vision of the Right to Counsel, 105 Harvard Law Review, 1992; permission conveyed through Copyright Clearance Center, Inc.

Randall Kennedy, Race, Crime, and the Law, pp. 158-161 (1997) Vintage Books. From Race, Crime, and the Law, by Randall Kennedy. Copyright © 1977 by Randall Kenney. Reprinted by permission of Pantheon Books, a division of Random House, Inc.

Michael Klarman, The Racial Origins of Modern Criminal Procedure, 99 Mich. L. Rev., 48, 50-52 (2000). Michael Klarman, The Racial Origins of Modern Criminal Procedure, 99 Michigan Law Review. Copyright © 2000. Reprinted with permission of the author.

Stanton D. Krauss, The Life and Times of Boyd v. United States (1886-1976), 76 Mich. L. Rev., 184, 188-189, 190, 191-195, 211-212 (1977). Krauss, The Life and Times of Boyd v. United States (1886-1976), 76 Mich. L. Rev. 184, 212 (1977). Reprinted from Michigan Law Review, 1977. Copyright 1977 by The Michigan Law Review Association. Reprinted with permission.

R. LaFountain, R. Schauffler, S. Strickland, W. Raferty, C. Bromage, C. Lee, & S. Gibson, eds., Examining the Work of State Courts, 2007: A National Perspective from the Court Statistics Project, pp. 39-46 (2008). Copyright © 2008 by National Center for State Courts. Reprinted with permission.

John H. Langbein, Understanding the Short History of Plea Bargaining, 13 Law & Soc'y Rev., Vol. 13, No. 2, pp. 261-270. John H. Langbein, Understanding the Short History of Plea Bargaining, Law & Society Review, Vol. 13, No. 2; Copyright John H. Langbein, Understanding the Short History of Plea Bargaining, Law & Society Review Vol. 13, No. 2; Copyright © 1979. Reprinted with permission of John Wiley & Sons, Inc.

Barry Latzer, Toward The Decentralization of Criminal Procedure: State Constitutional Law and Selective Incorporation, 87 J. Crim. L. & Criminology 63, 63-66, 68 (1996). Reprinted by special permission of Northwestern University School of Law, Journal of Criminal Law and Criminology.

Andrew Leipold, Why Grand Juries Do Not (and Cannot) Protect the Accused, 80 Cornell L. Rev. 260, 265-267 (1995). Copyright © 1995. Reprinted with permission.

Richard Leo, Miranda's Revenge: Police Interrogation as a Confidence Game, 30 Law & Soc'y Rev., Vol. 30, No. 2, pp. 259 (1996). Richard Leo, Miranda's Revenge: Police Interrogation as a Confidence Game, Law & Society Review, Vol. 30, No. 2; Copyright © 1996.

Lawrence Lessig, Code and Other Laws of Cyberspace, © 1999, pp. 17, 18, 20. Copyright © 2006 Lawrence Lessig. Reprinted by permission of Basic Books, a member of the Perseus Books Group.

Debra Livingston, Police, Community Caretaking and the Fourth Amendment, 1998 University of Chicago Legal Forum 261, 278, 273-274. Used with permission of University of Chicago Legal Forum from Debra Livingston, Police, Community Caretaking and the Fourth Amendment, 1998 University of Chicago Legal Forum, 1998; permission conveyed through Copyright Clearance Center, Inc.

Debra Livingston, Police Discretion and the Quality of Life in Public Places: Courts, Communities, and the New Policing, 97 Colum. L. Rev., 551, 557, 558-561,

670-671 (1997). Used with permission of Columbia Law Review, from Debra Livingston, Police Discretion and the Quality of Life in Public Places: Courts, Communities, and the New Policing, 97 Columbia Law Review, 551, 1997; permission conveyed through Copyright Clearance Center, Inc.

Debra Livingston, Gang Loitering, the Court, and Some Realism About Police Patrol, 1999 Supreme Court Review 141, 177-178 (2000).

Gary Lowenthal, Joint Representation in Criminal Cases: A Critical Appraisal, 64 Virginia Law Review 939, 941-942 (1978). Used with permission of Virginia Law Review, from Lowenthal, "Joint Representation in Criminal Cases: A Critical Appraisal," 64 Va. L. Rev., 1978; permission conveyed through Copyright Clearance Center.

Gerard E. Lynch, Screening Versus Plea Bargaining: Exactly What Are We Trading Off? 55 Stan. L. Rev. 1399, 1400-1404, 1406-1408 (2003). Used with permission of Stanford Law Review, from Gerard E. Lynch, Screening Versus Plea Bargaining: Exactly What Are We Trading Off? 55 Stan. L. Rev., 2003; permission conveyed through Copyright Clearance Center, Inc.

Gary T. Marx, Undercover: Police Surveillance in America, pp. 33-35, 47. Marx, Gary, Undercover: Police Surveillance in America, pages 22, 33-35, 47. Copyright © 1988 Twentieth Century Fund. Permission granted by the Regents of the University of California and the University of California Press.

Marc Mauer & Tracy Huling, Young Black Americans and the Criminal Justice System: Five Years Later, pp. 7-9, The Sentencing Project (1995). Reprinted with permission of The Sentencing Project.

Erin Murphy, Manufacturing Crime: Process, Pretext, and Criminal Justice, 97 Geo. L.J. 1435 (2009).

Janice Nadler, No Need to Shout: Bus Sweeps and the Psychology of Coercion, 2002 Sup. Ct. Rev. 153, 155.

Note, Formalism, Legal Realism, and Constitutionally Protected Privacy Under the Fourth and Fifth Amendments, 90 Harv. L. Rev. 945, 985-988 (1977). Used with permission of Harvard Law Review, from Note, Formalism, Legal Realism, and Constitutionally Protected Privacy Under the Fourth and Fifth Amendments, 90 Harvard Law Review, 1977; permission conveyed through Copyright Clearance Center, Inc.

Charles E. O'Hara, Fundamentals of Criminal Investigation. Used with permission of Charles C. Thomas Publisher, from Fundamentals of Criminal Investigation, O'Hara, Charles, E., 1956, pp. 99, 104-106, 112; permission conveyed through Copyright Clearance Center, Inc.

Herbert Packer, The Courts, the Police, and the Rest of Us, 57 J. Crim. L., Criminology & Police Sci., 238, 239 (1966). Reprinted by special permission of Northwestern University School of Law, Journal of Criminal Law and Criminology.

Renee Paradis, Carpe Demonstrators: Towards a Bright-Line Rule Governing Seizure in Excessive Force Claims Brought by Demonstrators, 103 Colum. L. Rev. 316, 334-339 (2003). Used with permission of Columbia Law Review, from Renee Paradis, Carpe Demonstrators: Towards a Bright-Line Rule Governing Seizure in Excessive Force Claims Brought by Demonstrators, 103 Colum. L. Rev. 316, 334-339, 2003; permission conveyed through Copyright Clearance Center, Inc.

Robert A. Pikowsky, The Need for Revisions to the Law of Wiretapping and Interception of Email, 10 Mich. Telecomm. & Tech. L. Rev. 1, 49-51 (2003). Robert A. Pikowsky, The Need for Revisions to the Law of Wiretapping and Interception of

Email, 10 Mich. Telecomm. & Tech. L. Rev. Copyright © 2003 by Michigan Telecommunications & Tech Law Review. Reprinted with permission.

Eric Rasmusen, Mezzamatto and the Economics of Self-Incrimination, 19 Cardozo L. Rev. 1541, 1551, 1552, 1559-1561. Copyright © 1998 by Cardozo Law Review. Reprinted with permission.

Frank Read, Lawyers at Lineups: Constitutional Necessity or Avoidable Extravagance? 17 UCLA L. Rev. 339, 388-393 (1969). Originally published in 17 UCLA L. Rev. 339 (1969).

Daniel Richman, Bargaining About Future Jeopardy, 49 Vand. L. Rev. 1181, 1211-1212, 1215 (1996). Richman, Daniel, Bargaining About Future Jeopardy, 49 Vanderbilt Law Review 1181, 1211-1212 (1996). Copyright © 1996 by the Vanderbilt Law Review. Reprinted with permission.

Daniel Richman, Cooperating Clients, 56 Ohio St. L.J. 69, 94-101 (1995). Originally published in 56 Ohio St. L.J. 69 (1995). Reprinted with permission of Ohio St. L.J. and the author.

Daniel C. Richman, Grand Jury Secrecy: Plugging the Leaks in an Empty Bucket, 36 Am. Crim. L. Rev. 339, 341, 355 (1999). Reprinted with permission of the publisher, Georgetown University and American Criminal Law Review © 1999.

Daniel Richman, Prosecutors and Their Agents, Agents and Their Prosecutors, 103 Colum. L. Rev. 749, 810, 815-816 (2003). Used with permission of Columbia Law Review, from Daniel Richman, Prosecutors and Their Agents, Agents and Their Prosecutors, 103 Colum. L. Rev. 749, 810, 815-816 (2003); permission conveyed through Copyright Clearance Center, Inc.

Dorothy E. Roberts, Crime, Race and Reproduction, originally published in 67 Tul. L. Rev. 1945-1977 (1993). Reprinted with the permission of the Tulane Law Review Association, which holds the copyright.

Dorothy Roberts, Foreword: Race, Vagueness, and the Social Meaning of Order-Maintenance Policing, 89 J. Crim. L. & Criminology 821, 827-828 (1999). Reprinted by special permission of Northwestern University School of Law, Journal of Criminal Law and Criminology.

William A. Schroeder, Warrantless Misdemeanor Arrests and the Fourth Amendment, 58 Mo. L. Rev. 771. Copyright © 1993 by Missouri Law Review. Reprinted with permission.

Stephen Schulhofer, Is Plea Bargaining Inevitable? 97 Harv. L. Rev. 1037, 1065-1066 (1984). Used with permission of Harvard Law Review, from Schulhofer, Is Plea Bargaining Inevitable? 97 Harvard Law Review, 1984; permission conveyed through Copyright Clearance Center, Inc.

Robert Scott & William Stuntz, Plea Bargaining as Contract, 101 Yale L.J. 1909, 1932-1934 (1992). Used with permission of The Yale Law Journal Company from Robert Scott and William Stuntz, Plea Bargaining as Contract, 101 Yale Law Journal, 1992; permission conveyed through Copyright Clearance Center, Inc.

Ryan W. Scott, Inter-Judge Sentencing Disparity After Booker: A First Look, 63 Stan. L. Rev., 1-66 (2010). Used with permission of Stanford Law Review from Ryan W. Scott, Inter-Judge Sentencing Disparity After Booker: A First Look, 63 Stanford Law Review, 2010; permission conveyed through Copyright Clearance Center, Inc.

Louis Michael Seidman, Criminal Procedure as the Servant of Politics, 12 Const. Comment. 207, 207-211. Copyright © 1995 by Constitutional Commentary. Reprinted with permission.

Louis Michael Seidman, Points of Intersection: Discontinuities at the Junction of Criminal Law and the Regulatory State, 7 J. Contemp. Legal Issues 97, 97-98, 100-102, 127 (1996). Reprinted with permission of the author.

David Sklansky, Cocaine, Race and Equal Protection, 47 Stan. L. Rev., 1283-1284, 1322 (1995). Used with permission of Stanford Law Review, from David Sklansky, Cocaine, Race and Equal Protection, 47 Stanford Law Review, 1995; permission conveyed through Copyright Clearance Center, Inc.

David Sklansky, Hearsay's Last Hurrah, [2009] Sup. Ct. Rev. 1 (2010).

Jerome H. Skolnick & David H. Bayley, The New Blue Line: Police Innovation in Six American Cities, pp. 49-52, Free Press, 1988. Reprinted with the permission of The Free Press, a Division of Simon & Schuster, Inc., from The New Blue Line: Police Innovation in Six American Cities by Jerome H. Skolnick and David H. Bayley. Copyright © 1986 by Jerome H. Skolnick and David H. Bayley. All rights reserved.

Christopher Slobogin, Why Liberals Should Chuck the Exclusionary Rule, 1999 U. Ill. L. Rev. 363. Copyright © 1999 by The Board of Trustees of the University of Illinois.

Jeffrey Standen, Plea Bargaining in the Shadow of the Guidelines, 81 Calif. L. Rev. 1471, 1506-1508, 1513 (1993). © 1993 by California Law Review, Inc. Reprinted from California Law Review, Vol. 81, No. 6, by permission of California Law Review, Inc. and the author.

Carol S. Steiker, Counter-Revolution in Constitutional Criminal Procedure? Two Audiences, Two Answers, Mich. L. Rev., 2466, 2466-2470, 2536, 2543 (1996). Reprinted from Michigan Law Review, August 1996, Vol. 94, No. 8. Copyright 1996 by The Michigan Law Review Association. Reprinted with permission of the author.

William J. Stuntz, Local Policing After the Terror, 111 Yale L.J. at 2164-2166, 2167 (2002). Used with permission of The Yale Law Journal Company from Stuntz, Local Policing After the Terror, 111 Yale Law Journal, 2002; permission conveyed through Copyright Clearance Center, Inc.

William Stuntz, Privacy's Problem and the Law of Criminal Procedure, 93 Mich. L. Rev. 1016, 1030-1034, 1050-1054 (1995). Reprinted from Michigan Law Review, March 1995, Vol. 93, No. 5. Copyright 1995 by The Michigan Law Review Association.

William J. Stuntz, Substance, Process, and the Civil-Criminal Procedure Line, 7 J. Contemp. Legal Issues I, 14-15 (1996). Reprinted with permission of the author.

William J. Stuntz, The Uneasy Relationship Between Criminal Procedure and Criminal Justice, 107 Yale L.J. 1, 1-6 (1997). Used with permission of The Yale Law Journal Company from William J. Stuntz, The Uneasy Relationship Between Criminal Procedure and Criminal Justice, 107 Yale Law Journal, 1997; permission conveyed through Copyright Clearance Center, Inc.

William Stuntz, The Virtues and Vices of the Exclusionary Rule, 20 Harv. J.L. & Pub. Pol'y 443, 445-446 (1997). William Stuntz, The Virtues and Vices of the Exclusionary Rule, 20 Harvard Journal of Law & Public Policy 443, 445-446 (1997). Copyright © the Harvard Journal of Law & Public Policy. Reprinted with permission.

William Stuntz, Warrants and Fourth Amendment Remedies, 77 Va. L. Rev. 881, 881-883 (1991). Reprinted with permission.

Scott E. Sundby, A Return to Fourth Amendment Basics: Undoing the Mischief of Camara and Terry, 72 Minn. L. Rev. 383, 388-391, 393-394 (1988). Used with permission of Minnesota Law Review from Scott E. Sundby, A Return to Fourth

Amendment Basics: Undoing the Mischief of Camara and Terry, 72 Minnesota Law Review, 1988; permission conveyed through Copyright Clearance Center, Inc.

Deanell Reece Tacha, Serving This Time: Examining the Federal Sentencing Guidelines After a Decade of Experience, 62 Mo. L. Rev. 471 (1997). Deanell Reece Tacha, U.S. Circuit Judge, U.S. Court of Appeals for the Tenth Circuit, U.S. Sentencing Commissioner 1994-1998. Reprinted with permission.

Peter Tague, Multiple Representation and Conflicts of Interest in Criminal Cases, 67 Geo. L. Rev. 1075, 1086-1087, 1094-1095 (1979). Reprinted with permission of the publisher, Georgetown University and Georgetown Law Journal © 1979.

Rodney Uphoff, The Criminal Defense Lawyer as Effective Negotiator: A Systemic Approach, 2 Clinical L. Rev., 73-94 (1995). Copyright © 1995. Reprinted with permission.

Gordon Van Kessel, European Perspectives on the Accused as a Source of Testimonial Evidence, 100 W. Va. L. Rev. 799, 802 (1998). Gordon Van Kessel, European Perspectives on the Accused as a Source of Testimonial Evidence, 100 W. Va. L. Rev. 799, 802 (1998). Copyright © 1998 by West Virginia Law Review. Reprinted with permission.

Silas Wasserstrom & Louis Michael Seidman, The Fourth Amendment as Constitutional Theory, 77 Geo. L. Rev. 19, 34-35 (1988). Reprinted with permission of the publisher, Georgetown University and Georgetown Law Journal © 1988.

Peter Westen, The Empty Idea of Equality, 95 Harv. L. Rev. 537, 539-540, 543-550 (1982). Used with permission of Harvard Law Review, from Peter Westen, The Empty Idea of Equality, 95 Harvard Law Review, 1982; permission conveyed through Copyright Clearance Center, Inc.

Peter Westen, The Three Faces of Double Jeopardy: Reflections on Government Appeals of Criminal Sentences, 78 Mich. L. Rev. 1001, 1006-1007, 1018 (1980). Reprinted with permission from Michigan Law Review, June 1980, Vol. 78, No. 7. Copyright 1980 by The Michigan Law Review Association.

Paul Wice, Chaos in the Courthouse: The Inner Workings of the Urban Criminal Courts, pp. 21-24, 63-65 (1985), Prager Publishers. Copyright © 1985 by Prager Publishers. Reproduced with permission of ABC-CLIO, LLC.

Ronald Wright & Marc Miller, The Screening/Bargaining Tradeoff, 55 Stan. L. Rev. 29, 30-35 (2002). Used with permission of Stanford Law Review, from Ronald Wright & Marc Miller, The Screening/Bargaining Tradeoff, 55 Stan. L. Rev. 29, 30-35, 2002; permission conveyed through Copyright Clearance Center, Inc.

COMPREHENSIVE CRIMINAL PROCEDURE

PART ONE

THE CRIMINAL PROCESS

Chapter 1

Introduction to the Criminal Justice "System"

A. Introduction

The system of criminal justice America uses to deal with those crimes it cannot prevent and those criminals it cannot deter is not a monolithic, or even a consistent, system. It was not designed or built in one piece at one time. Its philosophic core is that a person may be punished by the Government if, and only if, it has been proved by an impartial and deliberate process that he has violated a specific law. Around that core layer upon layer of institutions and procedures, some carefully constructed and some improvised, some inspired by principle and some by expediency, have accumulated. Parts of the system — magistrates' courts, trial by jury, bail — are of great antiquity. Other parts — juvenile courts, probation and parole, professional policemen — are relatively new. The entire system represents an adaption of the English common law to America's peculiar structure of government, which allows each local community to construct institutions that fill its special needs. Every village, town, county, city and State has its own criminal justice system, and there is a Federal one as well. All of them operate somewhat alike. No two of them operate precisely alike.

> *President's Commission on Law Enforcement and Administration of Justice,*
> *The Challenge of Crime in a Free Society 7 (1967)*

Some of the differences in operation are a result of different formal mechanisms. For example, in the federal system and in approximately two-fifths of the state systems, a defendant cannot be prosecuted for a serious crime unless a grand jury — a group usually composed of 17 to 23 citizens selected from the voter registration lists — has reviewed the evidence and decided to return an indictment or the defendant has waived the right to a grand jury indictment; in other jurisdictions, no right to a grand jury indictment exists.[1] In some jurisdictions, the authority to decide whether to proceed with a criminal prosecution rests with the local prosecutor; in others the ultimate authority, although rarely exercised, rests with the attorney general. In some jurisdictions, the prosecutor's consent is usually required for the issuance of an arrest warrant; in others it is not. However, the Supreme Court has held that a prosecutor's judgment that an arrest warrant should be issued does not satisfy

---

1. The Bill of Rights — the first ten amendments to the federal Constitution — protects citizens against certain actions by the *federal* government. Among these protections are a number of rights applicable to criminal defendants, including the Fifth Amendment right not to be prosecuted for a serious crime in the absence of a grand jury indictment. Over the years, the Supreme Court has "incorporated" most of these rights into the Due Process Clause of the Fourteenth Amendment, which restricts the actions of state governments. See Chapter 2, page 81, infra. The federal right to a grand jury indictment is one of the few rights that has not been so incorporated. Thus, states are free to adopt or reject the use of grand juries to screen criminal charges.

the "independent judicial officer" standard under the Constitution. Generally, judicial approval is required for the dismissal of a serious charge; in some jurisdictions, however, the prosecutor has unilateral discretion to dismiss.

Other, less formal differences contribute even more to variations in the operation of the criminal justice process. For example, the institutional components that constitute the criminal justice system — the police agencies, the public prosecutors, the courts, the correctional departments — each has independent functions, but the operation of each is in part dependent on the operation of the others. They interrelate differently from community to community,[2] and how they interrelate will have an impact on how the entire system operates. Thus, for the most part the prosecutors, the courts, and the correctional officials can deal only with those individuals whom the police arrest. A police officer's decision whether to arrest may in turn be influenced by how the officer believes the other institutional components of the system will respond to a situation. If an officer believes that an individual will be dealt with too leniently, the officer may arrest the individual and not press charges or perhaps not even make the arrest. Samuel Walker, Taming the System 23-24, 39-41 (1993).

Allocation of resources also affects the manner in which the system operates. Limited prosecutorial or judicial resources, for example, will force prosecutors to be more selective in choosing cases with which to proceed. Even allocation of resources within a single component of the criminal justice system has an impact on its operation. For example, at some point fairly early in the process, a member of the prosecutor's staff will review a case to determine whether it is appropriate to proceed with prosecution and, if so, on what charges. Usually, the first opportunity to make this decision will be soon after an arrest, and the decision will be based on information contained in a police report. On the one hand, if the information in the report is complete enough to permit an informed decision about prosecution, and if the prosecutor is willing to assign experienced assistants to perform this screening function, cases inappropriate for prosecution can be eliminated from the system early without incurring the cost of proceeding with preliminary hearings or presentation of evidence to the grand jury. On the other hand, if experienced prosecutors are not used for this task or if the quality of initial information from the police is not high, there may be little serious screening of cases by the prosecutor until some later stage in the proceeding.

Even within a single jurisdiction, the order in which the various steps of the criminal justice process occur will depend on how the potential defendant first becomes involved in the system. Typically, for a serious crime there will be an arrest followed by a decision to prosecute. In some situations, however, the decision to prosecute may have been made secretly by the grand jury and prosecutor prior to any attempt to arrest the defendant.[3]

---

2. And there are many communities. There are somewhere on the order of 17,000 police agencies in the United States, and more than 2,000 prosecutorial offices, all with varying resources, concerns, and objectives, and largely subject to no unifying supervision.

3. The grand jury, in addition to performing a screening function, may also act as an investigatory body. Information about an individual's criminal activity may come to light from such an investigation rather than from a citizen complaint or police investigation. On the basis of such information, the grand jury may return an indictment prior to the defendant's arrest. Indeed, the arrest may be intentionally delayed for some period of time after the indictment is returned so that the grand jury can complete its investigation without alerting a defendant's confederates.

Despite the variations in the operation of the criminal justice process, there are substantial similarities among the federal and various state criminal justice systems with respect to prosecutions for serious criminal violations. Variations both in the formal judicial structure and in the degree of informality with which cases are resolved increase when one focuses on relatively minor crimes. The prosecution of serious criminality in most jurisdictions shares the following characteristics:

1. The initial enforcement responsibility rests with police agencies that have vast discretion in deciding whether to involve individuals in the criminal justice process.

2. The decision whether formally to charge an individual with a crime is the responsibility of a public prosecutor, who also possesses vast discretion.

3. There is some mechanism for screening serious criminal charges to determine whether there is a factual basis for the charge.

4. A criminal defendant is entitled to the assistance of counsel and, if indigent, to have one appointed at public expense if incarceration will result from conviction.

5. The vast majority of defendants participate with prosecutors in negotiating a guilty plea before trial. Most criminal cases are disposed of by negotiated guilty pleas through mechanisms that facilitate negotiation between defendants and prosecutors.

6. A defendant may make various pretrial motions challenging the prosecutor's evidence and the fairness of the criminal process.

7. Successful challenges by a defendant to the prosecution's evidence are often remedied by excluding evidence at trial, particularly in the prosecution's case-in-chief. Exclusion of this evidence does not necessarily mean that the evidence may not be used at other stages of the process, such as in rebuttal or sentencing.

8. Prosecution and defense are occasionally required to share discovery of certain information prior to trial, but nowhere near to the extent found in civil cases.

9. A defendant is entitled to a trial before an impartial judge, to confront and cross-examine opposing witnesses, to present witnesses, to a trial by jury unless the charge is only a "petty offense,"[4] and to an acquittal unless the prosecutor proves each element of the offense beyond a reasonable doubt. All these rights, and others, are waived by guilty pleas.

10. A guilty defendant has the right to address the court prior to sentencing. At sentencing, judges usually have substantial discretion in setting the penalty.

11. A convicted defendant usually has the right to some form of appellate review.[5]

4. See Duncan v. Louisiana, at page 97, infra.

5. In many, but not all, jurisdictions, the decision to plead guilty is viewed as a waiver of most of the contentions that a defendant might have raised at trial. For example, if a defendant prior to trial moved to exclude a confession on the ground that it was involuntary and if the confession were admitted at the trial, the defendant on appeal could challenge the admissibility of the confession. If the defendant decided to plead guilty after receiving an unfavorable ruling on the pretrial motion to suppress, however, the defendant would not be permitted in many jurisdictions to raise the involuntariness issue on appeal. The defendant, of course, could attack the guilty plea itself as involuntary or claim ineffective assistance of counsel. See generally Lefkowitz v. Newsome, 420 U.S. 283 (1975) (describing New York procedure that permits defendant to raise constitutional claims following guilty plea and holding that existence of

The criminal justice system is, in a word, complicated. Individual systems themselves are complicated, as Figure 1.1 indicates, and in addition, there is no "criminal justice system" in the United States. Rather, there are many overlapping, competing, and conflicting, "criminal justice systems" throughout the country. Even within any particular "system," various components may be more in tension with each other than working smoothly toward uniform goals. A substantial part of the subject matter of this course is the commands of the United States Supreme Court that supposedly apply uniformly to these diverse systems, but the effect of any particular command—whether it concerns requirements of warrants, rules about presenting arrested individuals to magistrates, limits on police interrogation, or whatever—obviously will be partly contingent upon the precise contours of the particular system implementing that command. Requiring warrants, for example, will have certain implications in a low-crime, high-resource system, such as the federal system, and quite different implications in a high-crime, low-resource system, such as in many major cities. As you appraise the various opinions of the Court that you will study throughout this semester, and all the other material that is presented, keep this point well in mind.

There are additional points to keep in mind that are especially pertinent to appraising the numerous cases that you will study but that again apply much more generally. There is often a sense in which legal studies tend to focus attention on texts, whether they be cases, statutes, or regulations, and to bring to bear on those texts interpretive methodologies. You will read numerous cases, for example, and one obviously pertinent question will be the fidelity of those cases to the constitutional text. Another will be the logical implications of the various decisions, and so on. These are, to be sure, important questions, but do not neglect that the material you are about to study deals both with real-life human dramas and with the exercise of some of the more extreme forms of power that the state employs. The criminal justice process exists because of crime — people behaving in unlawful and often barbarous ways toward each other. In response to crime, the state is authorized to seize and confine people, strip them of their property and liberty, and even put them to death. And thus another important question, perhaps the single most important question for you to contemplate, is how the texts that you will read relate to these human dramas—whether their commands will be implemented in ways that appropriately respond to both the costs of crime and the costs of law enforcement.

To ask such questions is to begin to get at the heart of the "criminal justice process." The formal commands of the law emanate from social conditions, affect them, and are in turn affected by them. These interactions are much less governed by the intentions or aspirations of any court, legislature, or chief executive, or for that matter by the explicit terms of the formal commands themselves, than by the realities of human affairs. Thus, in addition to focusing on the explicit terms of the materials you will read and their logical implications, we encourage you to reflect on at least five other matters:

1. How will the formal commands of the law, whether judicial or legislative, be implemented in the real world? What will their real-life consequences be? What options are available to those affected by the formal commands to

---

such procedure precludes state from relying on guilty plea to foreclose consideration of same constitutional issues in federal habeas corpus proceedings).

Figure 1.1.   Compendium of Federal Criminal Justice Statistics (2004).[6]

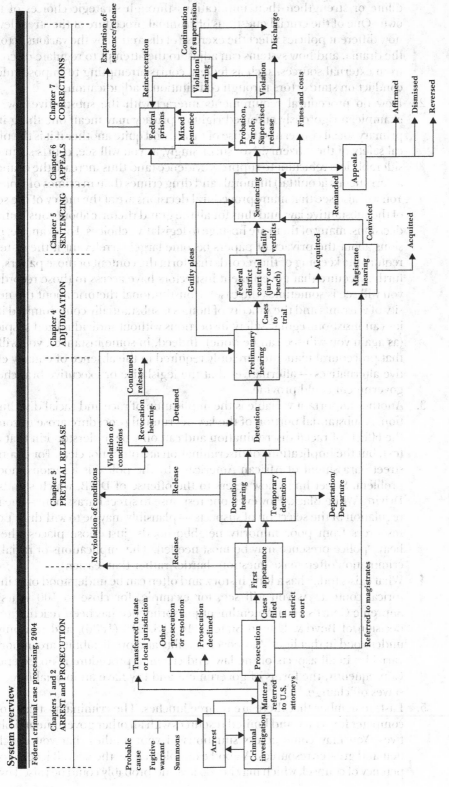

6. This graphic is from the 2004 Compendium of Federal Criminal Justice Statistics, published by the Department of Justice, Bureau of Justice Statistics. Because the publication is now produced in a different format, this graphical representation is not available for the most recent year. — Eds.

dilute or strengthen their implications through strategic choices of their own? One of the crucial questions of criminal procedure at the street level is how different policies affect the exercise of discretion by the various actors in the drama, and how systems can adjust to the attempt to regulate discretion from external sources, such as federal courts attempting to impose rules of conduct on state actors through constitutional adjudication.

2. How do procedural requirements interact with the substantive law? For example, a rigorously enforced right to privacy may mean one thing if the primary social concern is the use of drugs, and quite another if it is the physical safety of the citizenry. Not surprisingly, as you will see, courts seem considerably less reluctant to suppress evidence (and thus increase the chance of an erroneous acquittal) in morals and drug crimes than in crimes of violence. You will also see that many procedural decisions are at the mercy of the scope of the substantive law, and thus for all the grand rhetoric about constitutional decisions, many of them are hostage to legislative choices. For example, decisions about the privacy of papers become largely irrelevant if the state can require the keeping of the records that form the content of those papers, and further require that government inspectors have access to those records (as you will see is sometimes the case). Constitutional rhetoric about the necessity of warrants and the sanctity of homes is substantially compromised if cities can insist on regular safety inspections without individualized suspicion (as again you will see can be done). Indeed, in some instances, you will see that procedural mandates are only required in the absence of equally effective alternatives — alternatives that the legislative or executive branches of government could provide.

3. Another important variable is the implication of race and racial discrimination. A substantial portion of the law of criminal procedure arose to combat the effects of racial discrimination and can only be understood in that context, but the implications of discrimination are often not clear. For example, street harassment of African Americans by the police is a serious modern problem. Street lingo now refers to the offense of DWB, which stands for Driving While Black. However, one response to street harassment — heavier regulation of the selection of suspects — plausibly may be to withdraw police resources from poor minority neighborhoods, just those places where a heavy police presence may be most needed. The implications of racial discrimination often make questions harder rather than easier.

4. What exists today has a long history, and often can be understood only in historical context. As you will see, for example, for close to 100 years the Supreme Court's Fifth Amendment jurisprudence has been reacting to the decision of Boyd v. United States, 116 U.S. 616 (1886), and can only be understood in that light. Moreover, stability and predictability are important variables in all aspects of the law, and criminal procedure is no exception. Consequently, the forms of government and law have an inertial force that staves off change.

5. Last, remember that there are no free lunches. The criminal justice process competes for scarce and limited resources with all other governmental objectives. You may come across situations in your studies that you conclude demand greater resources. A good example may be the overall level of competency of counsel, which may be too low and probably could be raised by the

infusion of substantial resources. Another is that both police and prosecutorial discretion exist in substantial part because there is too much crime to
handle, given the resources, and therefore both police and prosecutors can
pick and choose how to spend their time. But, a dollar spent on providing
better counsel or more police and prosecutors is a dollar that cannot be spent
somewhere else, either within the criminal justice system, such as on providing speedier or more efficient trials, or outside the criminal justice system,
such as on programs to ease the burden of poverty, or the national infrastruc-
ture, or student loans, or whatever. Governing involves an endless series of
tragic choices in which competing demands must be traded off.

B. Lies, Damned Lies, and Statistics

We present here various statistical snapshots of aspects of the criminal justice system, first from the federal system and then from the states.

BUREAU OF JUSTICE STATISTICS, U.S. DEPARTMENT OF JUSTICE, FEDERAL JUSTICE STATISTICS SUMMARY FINDINGS

(2006)[7]

PROSECUTION

U.S. attorneys opened matters for investigation against 133,935 suspects during
2006. The number of investigations initiated by U.S. attorneys decreased by 3%
over 2005. Fifty-one percent were investigated for public-order offenses such as
regulatory (4%); immigration (26%), and weapons (10%) offenses; more than a
quarter (27%) were investigated for drug offenses; 19% for property offenses; and
4% for violent offenses such as murder, rape, assault, and robbery.

Of the 141,130 suspects in matters concluded during 2006, 79% were referred
for prosecution either before a U.S. district court judge (59%) or a U.S. magistrate
(20%). Nearly all (98%) of those investigated for immigration offenses were referred
for prosecution or disposal by U.S. magistrate.

PRETRIAL

During 2006, more than a third (37%) of defendants charged with a federal offense
were released following the initial court appearance, provided that any court-
imposed conditions were satisfied.

Most (79%) of defendants released prior to trial in 2006 completed their pretrial
release without violating the release conditions; 9% had their release revoked.
Defendants charged with weapon or drug offenses were less likely to complete
release without a violation (65% and 69%, respectively) than other defendants.

---

7. Summary text and statistical tables are available online at http://bjs.ojp.usdoj.gov/content/pub/
html/fjsst/2006/fjs06st.cfm. — EDS.

ADJUDICATION

During 2006, criminal cases were commenced against 87,650 defendants in U.S. district court. Most (89%) were charged with a felony offense. Thirty-seven percent of felony defendants were charged with a drug offense; 38% of all defendants were charged with a public-order offense — including 20% with an immigration offense and 11% with a weapons offense. Fifteen percent were charged with a property offense.

Cases were terminated against 88,094 defendants during 2006. Most (91%) defendants were convicted. Of the 79,904 defendants convicted, 76,778 (or 96%) pleaded guilty or no-contest.

SENTENCING

Of the 79,904 defendants convicted and sentenced during 2006, 80% were sentenced to a term of incarceration (either only or in conjunction with probation), 13% were sentenced to probation (either only or with incarceration), and 3% were sentenced to pay a fine alone.

The average prison sentence imposed during 2006 was 64 months. Defendants convicted of violent felonies (108 months), weapons felonies (88 months), and drug felonies (87 months) received the longest prison terms, on average.

Average incarceration sentence lengths imposed, by offense, October 1, 2005-September 30, 2006

Offense of conviction	Average sentence length
All offenses	63.7 mo
Violent offenses	108.0
Fraudulent property offenses	29.2
Other property offenses	37.3
Drug offenses	87.2
Regulatory public-order offenses	37.7
Other public-order offenses	61.4
Weapon offenses	88.4
Immigration offenses	25.9
Misdemeanors	5.1

CRIMINAL APPEALS

Of the 15,246 appeals terminated during 2006, 77% were terminated on the merits of the case; 23% were procedural terminations by the courts. Of the 11,769 appeals terminated on their merits, the appellate courts affirmed, or upheld, the district courts' decisions, at least in part, in 79% of the cases.

CORRECTIONS

During 2006 the Federal Bureau of Prisons received 61,280 inmates from U.S. district courts; an additional 17,967 inmates were received from other sources such as supervision violations; 69,557 inmates were released. As of September 30, 2006, 169,320 sentenced offenders were under the jurisdiction of the Federal Bureau of Prisons.

Offenders entering federal prison during 2003 could expect to serve about 88% of the sentence imposed compared to 65% for those who entered during 1990.

During 2006, 112,680 offenders convicted of federal offense were on community supervision. About 76% were serving a term of supervised release; 22% were serving a term of probation; and 2% were serving a term of parole on a sentence that was not imposed pursuant to the Sentencing Reform Act of 1984.

Admissions and Releases of Federal Prisoners, by Offense, October 1, 2005-September 30, 2006

Most serious original offense of conviction	All admissions	All releases	Population at year-end
All offenses	79,247	69,557	169,320
Violent offenses	5.6%	6.2%	7.6%
Property offenses	12.4	13.2	5.5
Drug offenses	37.2	35.9	54.4
Public-order offenses	7.2	6.7	5.8
Weapon offenses	12.0	10.2	14.1
Immigration offenses	23.8	25.2	11.5

Note: Percentages of offenses do not total to 100% due to offenders whose most serious offense of conviction is unknown or indeterminable.

Average Time to First Release, Standard Releases, by Offense, October 1, 2005-September 30, 2006

Most serious original offense of conviction	Mean time served
All offenses	34.5 mo
Violent offenses	66.4
Property offenses	18.6
Drug offenses	40.0
Public-order offenses	18.3
Weapon offenses	43.6
Immigration offenses	19.9

Figure 1.2. Compendium of Federal Criminal Justice Statistics (2004).[8]

Federal criminal case processing, October 1, 2003-September 30, 2004

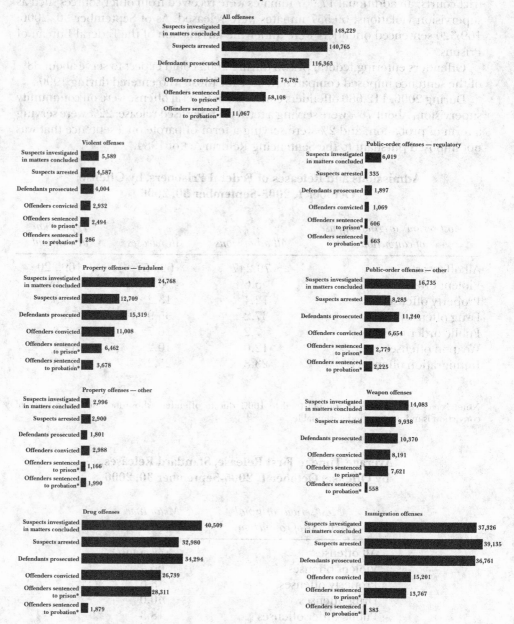

*Prison includes split, life, indeterminate, regular, and youth sentences. Offenders not shown as sentenced to prison or probation were sentenced by magistrates or received a fine-only sentence in Federal court. Probation excludes persons sentenced to prison.

8. This graphic is from the 2004 Compendium of Federal Criminal Justice Statistics, published by the Department of Justice, Bureau of Justice Statistics. Because the publication is now produced in a different format, the graphical representation above is not available for the most recent year. — EDS.

R. LAFOUNTAIN, R. SCHAUFFLER, S. STRICKLAND, W. RAFTERY,
C. BROMAGE, C. LEE, & S. GIBSON, EDITORS, EXAMINING THE
WORK OF STATE COURTS, 2007: A NATIONAL PERSPECTIVE
FROM THE COURT STATISTICS PROJECT

39-46 (2008)

The way in which criminal cases, specifically felony cases, are counted often differs from other types of cases. Most states with two-tiered systems, i.e., those with both limited and general jurisdiction courts, may hear parts of the same felony case at both levels of court and count that case as two distinct cases. For example, a felony case will often have a preliminary hearing in a limited jurisdiction court, such as a municipal court. If a judicial officer decides that the evidence against a defendant is sufficient to support the charges, the case is typically "bound over" to the court of general jurisdiction for trial. These two courts will, therefore, legitimately count the events that occurred under their purview as one filing or incoming case. Thus, the number of criminal and felony cases reported by states with two-tiered court systems may appear disproportionately higher when compared to single-tiered courts.

The [following] table shows the 2006 criminal caseloads and population-adjusted rates for 23 states. The overall rate of cases per 100,000 adults in states with a unified court ranged from a high of nearly 6,500 in California to a low of about 2,800 in Minnesota, with a median rate of about 5,400. As expected, the median rate in states with two-tiered courts, where many felony cases are counted in both the general and limited jurisdiction court, is about 50 percent higher at 7,960 cases per 100,000 adults.

Incoming Criminal Caseloads and Rates in 23 States, 2006

| | Incoming Criminal Cases | | | Criminal Cases per 100,000 Adults | | |
State	General Jurisdiction	Limited Jurisdiction	Total	General Jurisdiction	Limited Jurisdiction	Total
Unified Courts						
California	1,694,519		1,694,519	6,430		6,430
Kansas[1]	112,591	13,157	125,748	5,559	650	6,208
Illinois	546,281		546,281	5,786		5,786
Missouri	246,795		246,795	5,675		5,675
South Dakota[2]	31,034		31,034	5,377		5,377
District of Columbia	19,914		19,914	4,257		4,257
Iowa	84,277		84,277	3,785		3,785
Puerto Rico	84,656		84,656	3,024		3,024
Minnesota	105,181		105,181	2,765		2,765
Median				5,377		5,377

Incoming Criminal Caseloads and Rates in 23 States, 2006 (Continued)

	Incoming Criminal Cases			Criminal Cases per 100,000 Adults		
State	General Jurisdiction	Limited Jurisdiction	Total	General Jurisdiction	Limited Jurisdiction	Total
Two-tiered Courts						
Idaho	13,116	136,760	149,876	1,253	13,066	14,319
Michigan	70,954	975,576	1,046,530	950	13,068	14,018
Hawaii	8,024	112,857	120,881	830	11,675	12,505
Louisiana	178,809	200,163	378,972	5,796	6,489	12,285
New Hampshire	26,714	77,219	103,933	2,715	7,849	10,564
Alaska	5,851	32,992	38,843	1,241	6,997	8,238
Maryland	81,151	254,111	335,262	1,947	6,097	8,044
Kentucky	30,601	219,084	249,685	965	6,911	7,876
Washington	50,469	309,682	360,151	1,066	6,538	7,604
New Mexico	26,069	79,989	106,058	1,864	5,720	7,584
Utah	42,079	83,282	125,361	2,406	4,762	7,168
Indiana	254,932	49,092	304,024	5,459	1,051	6,510
Colorado	46,501	152,000	198,501	1,311	4,286	5,598
Rhode Island	6,233	38,726	44,959	768	4,775	5,543
Median				1,282	6,513	7,960

[1] Kansas, despite being classified as a unified court, has a municipal court with misdemeanor motor vehicle jurisdiction.

[2] South Dakota's Magistrate Court has misdemeanor jurisdiction but its caseload is counted in the general jurisdiction court.

Note: Blank cells indicate no limited jurisdiction court or no criminal jurisdiction.

Data from the 12 states able to report reopened and/or reactivated criminal caseloads indicate that 12 percent of their incoming criminal caseloads reentered the court system after an initial entry of judgment or were reactivated after a finite period of inactivity. A criminal case may be reopened after its original disposition, for example, when a defendant violates parole and the case returns to court for additional adjudication in light of that parole violation. A reactivated criminal case, on the other hand, has returned to the court's docket after a finite period of inactivity and is once again moving toward disposition. For example, if a defendant fails to appear in court, the court cannot proceed with the case, and the case is placed on inactive status. After the court issues a bench warrant and the defendant is apprehended and returned to court, the court reactivates the original case and proceeds to a disposition. Managing and counting reopened and reactivated criminal caseloads allows for more accurate calculations of the age of active pending criminal cases and the full workload associated with criminal cases.

Disaggregating the data from the . . . chart[s below] reveals the variation in reopened/reactivated caseloads in state courts. Eleven of these 12 states reported only a reopened criminal caseload; Ohio alone reported a reactivated caseload. This would suggest that many states do not place cases on inactive status, are unable to collect and report data for those cases, or do not distinguish reopened cases from reactivated cases at the state level.

Reopened/Reactivated Criminal Caseloads in Unified and General Jurisdiction Courts in 12 States, 2006

Reopened/Reactivated	New Filings	Total Incoming Criminal Caseload
204,090	1,495,853	1,699,943
12%	88%	

Reopened/Reactivated Criminal Caseloads as a Percentage of Total Criminal Caseloads in 12 States, 2006

Unified Courts	
North Dakota	24%
Illinois	2.1%
Puerto Rico	1.2%
Kansas	0.6%

General Jurisdiction Courts	
New Hampshire	41%
New Mexico	31%
Texas	23%
Virginia	22%
Pennsylvania	16%
Ohio	16%
Michigan	7%
Vermont	0.2%

Criminal caseloads, as outlined in the *State Court Guide to Statistical Reporting*, consist of felonies, misdemeanors, and certain other cases, such as criminal appeals from lower courts. The distinction between felonies and misdemeanors varies from state, to state, but, in general, misdemeanors are defined as less serious crimes punishable by up to one year in jail. Felonies are more serious crimes carrying penalties of at least one year in prison. Both types of cases can also result in fines.

Criminal Caseload Composition in 37 States, by Jurisdiction, 2006

	Felony	Misdemeanor	Other
Unified: 9 Courts	21%	78%	0.5%
General Jurisdiction: 21 Courts	69%	23%	8.0%
Limited Jurisdiction: 31 Courts	8%	91%	1.0%

As noted earlier, felonies are subject to double-counting in two-tiered courts. To mitigate these differences, a cross-state comparison should be limited to observations in courts of general jurisdiction only. Criminal caseloads and rates in unified court systems (where double-counting is not typically an issue) are more comparable to the caseloads and rates at the general jurisdiction level of two-tiered systems.

The adjacent table displays the total number of incoming felonies and population-adjusted rates of the unified and general jurisdiction courts of 34 states. Although both of these metrics clearly demonstrate variation among the states, the median population-adjusted rates are quite similar at about 1,200 felonies per 100,000 adults.

Incoming Felony Caseloads and Rates in Unified and General Jurisdiction Courts in 34 States, 2006

State	Total	Per 100,000 Adults
Unified Courts		
Missouri	100,136	2,302
North Dakota	6,644	1,390
Connecticut	35,240	1,339
Puerto Rico	35,885	1,282
District of Columbia	5,889	1,259
South Dakota	6,970	1,208
California	289,206	1,097
Illinois	99,682	1,056
Iowa	22,163	995
Kansas	19,882	982
Wisconsin	36,079	869
Minnesota	31,709	834
Median		1,153
General Jurisdiction Courts		
Virginia	131,806	2,288
Louisiana	57,862	1,876
Tennessee	85,911	1,876
New Mexico	23,245	1,662
North Carolina	109,815	1,638
Indiana	73,600	1,576
Colorado	46,501	1,311
Oregon	36,258	1,305
Alabama	43,561	1,270
Alaska	5,851	1,241
Utah	20,533	1,174
Ohio	98,126	1,147
Idaho	11,731	1,121
Washington	45,598	963
Michigan	69,933	937
Vermont	3,994	849
New Jersey	54,671	839

Incoming Felony Caseloads and Rates in Unified and General Jurisdiction Courts in 34 States, 2006 (Continued)

State	Total	Per 100,000 Adults
Rhode Island	5,961	735
Nevada	12,089	652
West Virginia	6,265	446
Hawaii	3,927	406
Massachusetts	5,534	113
Median		1,256

One way to determine whether a court is effectively managing its caseload is by calculating a clearance rate. A clearance rate is computed by dividing the number of outgoing cases during a reporting period by the number of incoming cases during the same period. A rate of 100 percent indicates that a court is keeping up with its caseload.

The general jurisdiction courts of 31 states, of which 10 are unified courts, reported incoming and outgoing felony caseloads from which clearance rates could be calculated for 2006. About one-third of these states reported at least as many outgoing cases as incoming cases, generating clearance rates of 100 percent or more. Massachusetts reported the second-highest clearance rate at 108 percent. But as shown in the [previous] chart . . . , Massachusetts also had by far the lowest population-adjusted rate of incoming felony cases (113) among the states with available data.

Felony Clearance Rates in Unified and General Jurisdiction Courts in 31 States, 2006

State	Clearance Rate
Unified Courts	
Wisconsin	114%
Puerto Rico	104%
Minnesota	101%
Kansas	99%
District of Columbia	99%
Connecticut	98%
North Dakota	97%
Missouri	97%
Illinois	96%
California	77%
Median	98%
General Jurisdiction Courts	
Massachusetts	108%
Oregon	107%
Idaho	105%
New Jersey	102%
Arkansas	102%

Felony Clearance Rates in Unified and General Jurisdiction
Courts in 31 States, 2006 (Continued)

State	Clearance Rate
Utah	101%
Michigan	101%
Alaska	100%
Colorado	99%
Ohio	99%
Rhode Island	99%
Alabama	99%
New Mexico	98%
Vermont	95%
Texas	94%
North Carolina	93%
Arizona	93%
Tennessee	92%
Indiana	89%
Washington	89%
Hawaii	76%
Median	99%

The *Guide* defines 10 distinct felony case types: person, domestic violence, property, drug, weapon, public order, motor vehicle/DUI, motor vehicle/reckless driving, motor vehicle/other, and other felony. To date, no state reports its felony caseload at that level of detail. However, five states do distinguish and report four of the most prevalent case types. The adjacent charts show the aggregate composition for the five states followed by each state's individual composition.

Property offenses dominate the aggregate felony composition of these five states. The individual compositions of Hawaii, New Mexico, and Tennessee are quite similar to one another while Kansas reported a larger proportion of person felonies. Utah's composition was unique in that the percentage of drug cases exceeded those of both property and person cases.

Felony Caseload Composition in Unified and General
Jurisdiction Courts in 5 States, 2006

State	Drug	Property	Person	Motor Vehicle	Other	Total
Utah	37%	32%	10%	9%	13%	100%
Tennessee	30%	38%	20%	3%	8%	100%
Hawaii	30%	39%	17%	2%	12%	100%
New Mexico	28%	30%	26%	7%	9%	100%
Kansas*	21%	29%	29%	8%	13%	100%
Total	29%	35%	21%	5%	10%	100%

* This state has a unified court system.

The adjacent chart shows the number of incoming misdemeanor cases and population-adjusted rates in 12 states for 2006. The number of incoming cases per 100,000 adults in these states range from a low of about 1,750 in Puerto Rico to a high of nearly 6,500 in Washington with a median rate of 3,544. Contributing to this variation in rates are law enforcement practices, charging practices, court resources, and differences in the law among these 12 states.

Incoming Misdemeanor Caseloads and Rates in 12 States, 2006

State	Total	Per 100,000 Adults
Washington	306,972	6,481
Utah	104,059	5,950
California*	1,402,584	5,322
Kansas*	103,257	5,098
Indiana	204,010	4,368
Rhode Island	30,689	3,784
Missouri*	143,750	3,305
Vermont	14,405	3,061
District of Columbia*	14,025	2,998
Iowa*	62,114	2,790
Minnesota*	73,472	1,931
Puerto Rico*	48,771	1,742
Median		3,544

The states with an * have a unified court system.

Depending upon a state's court structure, misdemeanor cases may be heard in general jurisdiction courts, limited jurisdiction courts, or some combination of the two. The [following] chart . . . shows clearance rates for misdemeanor cases in various courts in 25 states. Four of the 19 states with two-tiered systems shown here reported incoming and outgoing misdemeanor caseloads from both general and limited jurisdiction courts.

Among the six unified courts, Minnesota achieved the highest clearance rate at 100 percent. Five of 11 general jurisdiction (45 percent) and three of 12 limited jurisdiction courts (25 percent) cleared at least as many cases as were incoming in 2006.

The general jurisdiction court of Idaho reported an unusually high clearance rate for 2006. However, because of its relatively small misdemeanor caseload, only 2,035 cases needed to be disposed of to achieve its rate of 147 percent.

Misdemeanor Clearance Rates in 25 States, 2006

State	Incoming Misdemeanors	Clearance Rate
Unified Courts		
Minnesota	73,472	100%
Puerto Rico	48,771	99%
District of Columbia	14,025	96%
Missouri	143,750	94%

Misdemeanor Clearance Rates in 25 States, 2006 (Continued)

State	Incoming Misdemeanors	Clearance Rate
Kansas	103,257	91%
California	1,402,584	79%
Median		95%

General Jurisdiction Courts

Idaho	1,385	147%
New York	25,009	117%
Utah	20,777	117%
Oregon	64,132	104%
New Mexico	1,974	100%
Vermont	14,405	97%
Ohio	7,653	96%
Indiana	156,719	94%
North Carolina	18,493	92%
Tennessee	55,747	92%
Hawaii	4,097	85%
Median		97%

Limited Jurisdiction Courts

Idaho	126,800	106%
Kentucky	160,073	100%
Michigan	851,060	100%
Washington	305,106	99%
Alaska	32,992	99%
Indiana	47,291	99%
Utah	83,282	95%
New Jersey	427,577	92%
Hawaii	107,249	92%
South Carolina	917,372	91%
Rhode Island	30,689	90%
Louisiana	199,422	89%
Median		97%

Finally, consider these charts from Bureau of Justice Statistics, Sourcebook of Criminal Justice Statistics — 2007.

Arrests by Offense Charged, Sex, and Age Group, United States, 2006 and 2007

(10,565 agencies; 2006 estimated population 196,944,864; 2007 estimated population 198,239,257)

Offense charged	Male Total 2006	Male Total 2007	Percent change	Male Under 18 years of age 2006	Male Under 18 years of age 2007	Percent change	Female Total 2006	Female Total 2007	Percent change	Female Under 18 years of age 2006	Female Under 18 years of age 2007	Percent Change
Total[a]	7,117,907	7,055,371	-0.90%	1,033,632	1,009,036	-2.40%	2,255,209	2,291,715	1.60%	425,837	426,781	0.20%
Murder and nonnegligent manslaughter	7,275	7,320	0.6	735	737	0.3	912	857	-6	39	59	51.3
Forcible rape	15,710	15,030	-4.3	2,407	2,364	-1.8	205	165	-19.5	44	47	6.8
Robbery	69,562	70,271	1	19,175	18,944	-1.2	8,952	9,209	2.9	1,969	2,019	2.5
Aggravated assault	230,703	225,270	-2.4	29,683	28,544	-3.8	60,599	61,272	1.1	9,045	8,629	-4.6
Burglary	171,973	172,858	0.5	49,001	47,827	-2.4	29,817	30,422	2	6,397	6,575	2.8
Larceny-theft	451,279	473,191	4.9	112,067	115,985	3.5	276,545	318,640	15.2	77,668	88,428	13.9
Motor vehicle theft	65,668	57,100	-13	1,6443	14,122	-14.1	14,238	1,2685	-10.9	3,469	3,012	-13.2
Arson	9,228	8,903	-3.5	4,733	4,463	-5.7	1,857	1,597	-14	759	574	-24.4
Violent crime[b]	323,250	317,891	-1.7	52,000	50,589	-2.7	70,668	71,503	1.2	11,097	10,754	-3.1
Property crime[c]	698,148	712,052	2	182,244	182,397	0.1	322,457	363,344	12.7	88,293	98,589	11.7
Other assaults	640,038	645,993	0.9	108,959	105,906	-2.8	217,595	221,488	1.8	55,614	54,027	-2.9
Forgery and counterfeiting	42,675	40,028	-6.2	1,535	1,392	-9.3	28,310	25,678	-9.3	783	661	-15.6
Fraud	106,917	97,431	-8.9	3,438	3,279	-4.6	89,440	79,958	-10.6	1,799	1,870	3.9
Embezzlement	6,548	7,750	18.4	537	716	33.3	7,448	8,237	10.6	441	510	15.6
Stolen property; buying, receiving, possessing	67,396	62,948	-6.6	12,657	11,854	-6.3	15,716	15,183	-3.4	2,170	2,323	7.1
Vandalism	165,478	162,108	-2	67,899	64,979	-4.3	33,512	33,572	0.2	10,453	10,188	-2.5
Weapons; carrying, possessing, etc.	115,669	109,397	-5.4	27,088	25,224	-6.9	10,293	9,505	-7.7	3,081	2,746	-10.9
Prostitution and commercialized vice	14,152	12,339	-12.8	204	176	-13.7	25,957	26,473	2	585	585	0
Sex offenses (except forcible rape and prostitution)	50,273	48,184	-4.2	9,455	9,076	-4	3,712	3,579	-3.6	977	914	-6.4
Drug abuse violations	948,491	932,383	-1.7	102,450	102,906	0.4	228,684	224,784	-1.7	20,767	20,684	-0.4
Gambling	3,185	3,041	-4.5	439	387	-11.8	527	630	19.5	32	17	-46.9
Offenses against family and children	64,434	62,806	-2.5	2,208	2,464	11.6	20,664	20,843	0.9	1,420	1,557	9.6
Driving under the influence	749,832	749,142	-0.1	9,921	9,207	-7.2	190,420	197,974	4	2,980	2,906	-2.5
Liquor laws	309,821	305,330	-1.4	60,530	59,865	-1.1	115,879	117,916	1.8	34,381	35,758	4
Drunkenness	334,796	354,052	5.8	8,859	9,059	2.3	61,745	68,026	10.2	2,989	3,159	5.7

Arrests by Offense Charged, Sex, and Age Group, United States, 2006 and 2007 (Continued)

Disorderly conduct	345,354	340,702	-1.3	93,799	89,134	-5	127,361	126,251	-0.9	47,214	44,821	-5.1
Vagrancy	17,846	15,660	-12.2	2,426	1,951	-19.6	5,518	4,897	-11.3	1,105	829	-25
All other offenses (except traffic)	2,018,548	1,984,428	-1.7	191,928	186,769	-2.7	610,725	606,309	-0.7	71,078	68,318	-3.9
Suspicion (not included in totals)	1,153	1,042	-9.6	233	206	-11.6	304	270	-11.2	67	69	3
Curfew and loitering law violations	63,825	60,784	-4.8	63,825	60,784	-4.8	27,719	26,442	-4.6	27,719	26,442	-4.6
Runaways	31,231	30,922	-1	31,231	30,922	-1	40,859	39,123	-4.2	40,859	39,123	-4.2

Note: These data were compiled by the Federal Bureau of Investigation through the Uniform Crime Reporting (UCR) Program. On a monthly basis, law enforcement agencies report the number of offenses that become known to them in the following crime categories: murder and nonnegligent manslaughter, forcible rape, robbery, aggravated assault, burglary, larceny-theft, motor vehicle theft, and arson. Arrest statistics are compiled as part of this monthly data collection effort. Participating law enforcement agencies are instructed to count one arrest each time a person is taken into custody, notified, or cited for criminal infractions other than traffic violations. Annual arrest figures do not measure the number of individuals taken into custody because one person may be arrested several times during the year for the same type of offense or for different offenses. A juvenile is counted as a person arrested when he/she commits an act that would be a criminal offense if committed by an adult. Two offense categories, "curfew and loitering" and "runaway," are tabulated only for juveniles. Violations of local juvenile acts other than runaway and curfew and loitering law violations are included in the "all other offenses" classification (U.S. Department of Justice, Federal Bureau of Investigation, Uniform Crime Reporting Handbook, 2004, pp. 78-81 [Online]. Available: http://www.fbi.gov/ucr/handbook/ucrhandbook04.pdf). This table presents data from all law enforcement agencies submitting complete reports for 12 months in 2006 and 2007 (Source: Table 37). Population figures are estimates calculated from U.S. Census Bureau data. For definitions of offenses, see Appendix 3.

[a]Does not include suspicion.

[b]Violent crimes are offenses of murder and nonnegligent manslaughter, forcible rape, robbery, and aggravated assault.

[c]Property crimes are offenses of burglary, larceny-theft, motor vehicle theft, and arson.

Source: U.S. Department of Justice, Federal Bureau of Investigation, Crime in the United States, 2007 Table 37 [Online]. Available: http://www.fbi.gov/ucr/cius2007/data/table_37.html [Jan 3, 2009].

Arrests
by Offense Charged, Age Group, and Race, United States, 2007

(11,929 agencies; 2007 estimated population 225,477,173)

	Total arrests					Percent[a]				
Offense charged	Total	White	Black	American Indian or Alaskan Native	Asian or Pacific Islander	Total	White	Black	American Indian or Alaskan Native	Asian or Pacific Islander
Total	10,656,710	7,426,278	3,003,060	142,969	84,403	100.00%	69.70%	28.20%	1.30%	0.80%
Murder and nonnegligent manslaughter	10,067	4,789	5,078	99	101	100	47.6	50.4	1	1
Forcible rape	17,058	10,984	5,708	213	153	100	64.4	33.5	1.2	0.9
Robbery	96,584	40,573	54,774	602	635	100	42	56.7	0.6	0.7
Aggravated assault	326,277	208,762	109,985	4,374	3,156	100	64	33.7	1.3	1
Burglary	228,346	156,442	68,052	2,191	1,661	100	68.5	29.8	1	0.7
Larceny-theft	894,215	610,607	261,730	11,885	9,993	100	68.3	29.3	1.3	1.1
Motor vehicle theft	88,843	55,229	31,765	1,041	808	100	62.2	35.8	1.2	0.9

Arrests
by Offense Charged, Age Group, and Race, United States, 2007 (Continued)

Offense charged	Total	White	Black	American Indian or Alaskan Native	Asian or Pacific Islander	Total	White	Black	American Indian or Alaskan Native	Asian or Pacific Islander
Arson	11,400	8,510	2,666	119	105	100	74.6	23.4	1	0.9
Violent crime[b]	449,986	265,108	175,545	5,288	4,045	100	58.9	39	1.2	0.9
Property crime[c]	1,222,804	830,788	364,213	15,236	12,567	100	67.9	29.8	1.2	1
Other assaults	980,512	641,991	316,217	14,028	8,276	100	65.5	32.3	1.4	0.8
Forgery and counterfeiting	77,757	54,136	22,460	414	747	100	69.6	28.9	0.5	1
Fraud	184,446	127,377	54,575	1,369	1,125	100	69.1	29.6	0.7	0.6
Embezzlement	16,954	10,813	5,818	95	228	100	63.8	34.3	0.6	1.3
Stolen property; buying, receiving, possessing	91,937	57,870	32,570	735	762	100	62.9	35.4	0.8	0.8
Vandalism	220,055	166,201	48,642	3,340	1,872	100	75.5	22.1	1.5	0.9
Weapons; carrying, possessing, etc.	142,369	82,311	57,745	1,061	1,252	100	57.8	40.6	0.7	0.9
Prostitution and commercialized vice	59,307	34,190	23,251	550	1,316	100	57.6	39.2	0.9	2.2
Sex offenses (except forcible rape and prostitution)	62,586	45,961	15,372	633	620	100	73.4	24.6	1	1
Drug abuse violations	1,382,783	880,742	485,054	8,872	8,115	100	63.7	35.1	0.6	0.6
Gambling	9,141	2,199	6,805	20	117	100	24.1	74.4	0.2	1.3
Offenses against family and children	88,437	60,124	26,090	1,686	537	100	68	29.5	1.9	0.6
Driving under the influence	1,050,803	929,453	97,472	14,251	9,627	100	88.5	9.3	1.4	0.9
Liquor laws	474,726	406,221	49,434	14,422	4,649	100	85.6	10.4	3	1
Drunkenness	449,117	375,440	62,278	8,891	2,508	100	83.6	13.9	2	0.6
Disorderly conduct	537,809	342,169	183,810	8,376	3,454	100	63.6	34.2	1.6	0.6
Vagrancy	25,584	15,493	9,474	501	116	100	60.6	37	2	0.5
All other offenses (except traffic)	2,936,233	1,969,862	905,656	40,546	20,169	100	67.1	30.8	1.4	0.7
Suspicion	1,571	904	649	4	14	100	57.5	41.3	0.3	0.9
Curfew and loitering law violations	109,575	69,950	37,532	964	1,129	100	63.8	34.3	0.9	1
Runaways	82,218	56,975	22,398	1,687	1,158	100	69.3	27.2	2.1	1.4

	Arrests of persons under 18 years of age					Percent[a]				
Offense charged	Total	White	Black	American Indian or Alaskan Native	Asian or Pacific Islander	Total	White	Black	American Indian or Alaskan Native	Asian or Pacific Islander
Total	1,642,530	1,100,427	505,464	20,504	16,135	100.00%	67.00%	30.80%	1.20%	1.00%
Murder and nonnegligent manslaughter	1,011	407	580	15	9	100	40.3	57.4	1.5	0.9
Forcible rape	2,617	1,610	966	24	17	100	61.5	36.9	0.9	0.6
Robbery	26,291	8,119	17,832	122	218	100	30.9	67.8	0.5	0.8

Arrests
by Offense Charged, Age Group, and Race, United States, 2007 *(Continued)*

| | Arrests of persons 18 years of age and older | | | | | Percent[a] | | | | |
Offense charged	Total	White	Black	American Indian or Alaskan Native	Asian or Pacific Islander	Total	White	Black	American Indian or Alaskan Native	Asian or Pacific Islander
Aggravated assault	43,322	24,674	17,773	470	405	100	57	41	1.1	0.9
Burglary	61,523	40,236	20,176	605	506	100	65.4	32.8	1	0.8
Larceny-theft	228,699	152,143	70,212	2,966	3,378	100	66.5	30.7	1.3	1.5
Motor vehicle theft	22,227	12,191	9,426	339	271	100	54.8	42.4	1.5	1.2
Arson	5,397	4,123	1,148	49	77	100	76.4	21.3	0.9	1.4
Violent crime[b]	73,241	34,810	37,151	631	649	100	47.5	50.7	0.9	0.9
Property crime[c]	317,846	208,693	100,962	3,959	4,232	100	65.7	31.8	1.2	1.3
Other assaults	180,615	106,119	71,409	1,857	1,230	100	58.8	39.5	1	0.7
Forgery and counterfeiting	2,341	1,699	596	21	25	100	72.6	25.5	0.9	1.1
Fraud	5,649	3,601	1,916	77	55	100	63.7	33.9	1.4	1
Embezzlement	1,287	753	498	10	26	100	58.5	38.7	0.8	2
Stolen property; buying, receiving, possessing	16,809	9,203	7,302	127	177	100	54.8	43.4	0.8	1.1
Vandalism	84,298	66,406	16,058	1,062	772	100	78.8	19	1.3	0.9
Weapons; carrying, possessing, etc.	33,040	19,992	12,412	250	386	100	60.5	37.6	0.8	1.2
Prostitution and commercialized vice	1,156	473	670	9	4	100	40.9	58	0.8	0.3
Sex offenses (except forcible rape and prostitution)	11,526	8,139	3,239	77	71	100	70.6	28.1	0.7	0.6
Drug abuse violations	146,785	101,152	43,343	1,295	995	100	68.9	29.5	0.9	0.7
Gambling	1,584	67	1,511	1	5	100	4.2	95.4	0.1	0.3
Offenses against family and children	4,161	3,029	1,047	60	25	100	72.8	25.2	1.4	0.6
Driving under the influence	13,420	12,498	589	238	95	100	93.1	4.4	1.8	0.7
Liquor laws	105,799	96,286	5,466	2,965	1,082	100	91	5.2	2.8	1
Drunkenness	12,909	11,532	997	277	103	100	89.3	7.7	2.1	0.8
Disorderly conduct	152,817	87,683	62,490	1,602	1,042	100	57.4	40.9	1	0.7
Vagrancy	2,923	2,267	625	19	12	100	77.6	21.4	0.7	0.4
All other offenses (except traffic)	282,244	198,916	77,153	3,313	2,862	100	70.5	27.3	1.2	1
Suspicion	287	184	100	3	0	100	64.1	34.8	1	X
Curfew and loitering law violations	109,575	69,950	37,532	964	1,129	100	63.8	34.3	0.9	1
Runaways	82,218	56,975	22,398	1,687	1,158	100	69.3	27.2	2.1	1.4
Total	9,014,180	6,325,851	2,497,596	122,465	68,268	100.00%	70.20%	27.70%	1.40%	0.80%
Murder and nonnegligent manslaughter	9,056	4,382	4,498	84	92	100	48.4	49.7	0.9	1

Arrests
by Offense Charged, Age Group, and Race, United States, 2007 (Continued)

Forcible rape	14,441	9,374	4,742	189	136	100	64.9	32.8	1.3	0.9
Robbery	70,293	32,454	3,6942	480	417	100	46.2	52.6	0.7	0.6
Aggravated assault	282,955	184,088	92,212	3,904	2,751	100	65.1	32.6	1.4	1
Burglary	166,823	116,206	47,876	1,586	1,155	100	69.7	28.7	1	0.7
Larceny-theft	665,516	458,464	191,518	8,919	6,615	100	68.9	28.8	1.3	1
Motor vehicle theft	66,616	43,038	22,339	702	537	100	64.6	33.5	1.1	0.8
Arson	6,003	4,387	1,518	70	28	100	73.1	25.3	1.2	0.5
Violent crime[b]	376,745	230,298	138,394	4,657	3,396	100	61.1	36.7	1.2	0.9
Property crime[c]	904,958	622,095	263,251	11,277	8,335	100	68.7	29.1	1.2	0.9
Other assaults	799,897	535,872	244,808	12,171	7,046	100	67	30.6	1.5	0.9
Forgery and counterfeiting	75,416	52,437	21,864	393	722	100	69.5	29	0.5	1
Fraud	178,797	123,776	52,659	1,292	1,070	100	69.2	29.5	0.7	0.6
Embezzlement	15,667	10,060	5,320	85	202	100	64.2	34	0.5	1.3
Stolen property; buying, receiving, possessing	75,128	48,667	25,268	608	585	100	64.8	33.6	0.8	0.8
Vandalism	135,757	99,795	32,584	2,278	1,100	100	73.5	24	1.7	0.8
Weapons; carrying, possessing, etc.	109,329	62,319	45,333	811	866	100	57	41.5	0.7	0.8
Prostitution and commercialized vice	58,151	33,717	22,581	541	1,312	100	58	38.8	0.9	2.3
Sex offenses (except forcible rape and prostitution)	51,060	37,822	12,133	556	549	100	74.1	23.8	1.1	1.1
Drug abuse violations	1,235,998	779,590	441,711	7,577	7,120	100	63.1	35.7	0.6	0.6
Gambling	7,557	2,132	5,294	19	112	100	28.2	70.1	0.3	1.5
Offenses against family and children	84,276	57,095	25,043	1,626	512	100	67.7	29.7	1.9	0.6
Driving under the influence	1,037,383	916,955	96,883	14,013	9,532	100	88.4	9.3	1.4	0.9
Liquor laws	368,927	309,935	43,968	11,457	3,567	100	84	11.9	3.1	1
Drunkenness	436,208	363,908	61,281	8,614	2,405	100	83.4	14	2	0.6
Disorderly conduct	384,992	254,486	121,320	6,774	2,412	100	66.1	31.5	1.8	0.6
Vagrancy	22,661	13,226	8,849	482	104	100	58.4	39	2.1	0.5
All other offenses (except traffic)	2,653,989	1,770,946	828,503	37,233	17,307	100	66.7	31.2	1.4	0.7
Suspicion	1,284	720	549	1	14	100	56.1	42.8	0.1	1.1
Curfew and loitering law violations	X	X	X	X	X	X	X	X	X	X
Runaways	X	X	X	X	X	X	X	X	X	X

Note: These data were compiled by the Federal Bureau of Investigation through the Uniform Crime Reporting (UCR) Program. On a monthly basis, law enforcement agencies report the number of offenses that become known to them in the following crime categories: murder and nonnegligent manslaughter, forcible rape, robbery, aggravated assault, burglary, larceny-theft, motor vehicle theft, and arson. Arrest statistics are compiled as part of this monthly data collection effort. Participating law enforcement agencies are instructed to count one arrest each time a person is taken into custody, notified, or cited for criminal infractions other than traffic violations. Annual arrest figures do not measure the number of individuals taken into custody because one person may be arrested several times during the year for the same type of offense or for different offenses. A juvenile is counted as a person arrested when he/she commits an act that would be a criminal offense if committed by an adult. Two offense categories, "curfew and loitering" and "runaway," are tabulated only for juveniles. Violations of local juvenile acts other than runaway and curfew and loitering law violations are included in the "all other offenses" classification (U.S. Department of Justice, Federal Bureau of Investigation, Uniform Crime Reporting Handbook, 2004, pp. 78-81 [Online]. Available: http://www.fbi.gov/ucr/handbook/ucrhandbook04.pdf). Estimates by the U.S. Census Bureau indicate that on July 1, 2007, whites comprised 80.0%, blacks 12.8%, and other racial categories 7.2% of the total U.S. resident population

(U.S. Department of Commerce, U.S. Census Bureau, "Annual Estimates of the Population by Sex, Race and Hispanic or Latino Origin for the United States: April 1, 2000 to July 1, 2007" [Online]. Available: http://www.census.gov/popest/national/asrh/NC-EST2007-srh.html [Jan. 14, 2009]). For definitions of offenses, see Appendix 3.

[a]Because of rounding, percents may not add to total.

[b]Violent crimes are offenses of murder and nonnegligent manslaughter, forcible rape, robbery, and aggravated assault.

[c]Property crimes are offenses of burglary, larceny-theft, motor vehicle theft, and arson.

Source: U.S. Department of Justice, Federal Bureau of Investigation, Crime in the United States, 2007, Table 43 [Online]. Available: http://www.fbi.gov/ucr/cius2007/data/table_43.html [Jan. 14, 2009].

C.   Readings on the Criminal Justice Process

Perceptions of the criminal justice system are as varied as the system itself. Commentators, by virtue of their individual training and experience with the system, inevitably make their observations and evaluations from different perspectives. Moreover, commentators will have, if not different values, at least different priorities that they would like to see reflected in the criminal justice system. The materials in this chapter, without attempting to be comprehensive, offer some important perceptions and insights about the criminal justice system. You, of course, should approach these materials with the same questioning mind and skepticism that you bring to bear on the study of cases.

1.   Perspectives on the System as a Whole

HERBERT PACKER, THE COURTS, THE POLICE, AND THE REST OF US

57 J. Crim. L., Criminology & Police Sci. 238, 239 (1966)

[T]he kind of criminal process that we have is profoundly affected by a series of competing value choices which, consciously or unconsciously, serve to resolve tensions that arise in the system. These values represent polar extremes which, in real life, are subject to almost infinite modulation and compromise. But the extremes can be identified. The choice, basically, is between what I have termed the Crime Control and the Due Process models. The Crime Control model sees the efficient, expeditious and reliable screening and disposition of persons suspected of crime as the central value to be served by the criminal process. The Due Process model sees that function as limited by and subordinate to the maintenance of the dignity and autonomy of the individual. The Crime Control model is administrative and managerial; the Due Process model is adversary and judicial. The Crime Control model may be analogized to an assembly line, the Due Process model to an obstacle course.[9]

What we have at work today is a situation in which the criminal process as it actually operates in the large majority of cases probably approximates fairly closely the dictates of the Crime Control model. The real-world criminal process tends to be far more administrative and managerial than it does adversary and judicial. Yet, the officially prescribed norms for the criminal process, as laid down primarily by the Supreme Court, are rapidly providing a view that looks more and more like the Due Process model. This development . . . has been in the direction of "judicializing" each stage of the criminal process, of enhancing the capacity of the accused to challenge the operation of the process, and of equalizing the capacity of all persons to avail themselves of the opportunity for challenge so created. . . .

LOUIS MICHAEL SEIDMAN, CRIMINAL PROCEDURE AS THE SERVANT OF POLITICS

12 Const. Commentary 207, 207-211 (1995)

If the Constitution were doing its job, it would obstruct and destabilize our political impulses concerning crime control. Yet today, the Fourth, Fifth, and Sixth Amendments function mostly to make us satisfied with a state of affairs that should trouble us deeply.

Here are two facts about American criminal law: The United States has the most elaborate and detailed constitutional protections for criminal defendants of any country in the world. The United States also has the second highest incarceration rate of any country in the world. The relationship between these two facts (if, indeed, there is one at all) is controversial. Some critics of the Fourth, Fifth, and Sixth Amendments argue that they stymie effective law enforcement, thereby encouraging crime and requiring a high incarceration rate. Although this connection is theoretically possible, it is quite implausible. The best data available suggests that criminal procedure protections are doing very little to obstruct successful prosecutions. For example, a tiny percentage of criminal cases are lost or "no papered" because of Fourth Amendment problems. Virtually every empirical study of the impact of *Miranda* suggests that it has not reduced the rate at which suspects confess. The poor quality of criminal defense work has led some distinguished commentators to conclude that counsel now serves primarily as a barrier to the defendant's participation in his own trial. In contrast, some defenders of the Constitution's criminal procedure provisions argue that incarceration rates would be even higher if these protections were unavailable. This claim is similarly implausible. By now, the Fourth Amendment is so riddled with exceptions and limitations that it rarely prevents the police from pursuing any reasonable crime control tactic.

---

9. The *Crime Control* and *Due Process* concepts admittedly reflect different value choices, and the concepts provide a helpful way to articulate and focus on these value choices. But do they represent two different "models" of the criminal justice system? For a negative answer to this question, see Griffiths, Ideology in Criminal Procedure, or a Third "Model" of the Criminal Process, 79 Yale L.J. 359 (1970). — Eds.

Although the Supreme Court continues to insist on the ritualistic reading of *Miranda* warnings, judges have virtually gone out of the business of actually policing the voluntariness of confessions and regularly sanction the sort of coercive tactics that would have led to the suppression of evidence a half century ago. The courts have been satisfied with formal rules requiring the presence of counsel in the courtroom, while tolerating actual courtroom performances that make a mockery of the formal protections. And even when a defendant can demonstrate that the prosecution has violated minimal Fourth, Fifth, and Sixth Amendment protections, the recent evisceration of habeas corpus means that there may be no court available to entertain her claim.

It seems unlikely, then, that the criminal procedure amendments have either exacerbated our crime problem or provided an effective bulwark against police and prosecutorial overreaching. A third possibility is more plausible: constitutional protections intended to make prosecution more difficult instead serve [to] make the prosecutor's job easier.

This reversal of the historic mission of the criminal procedure amendments functions on both the individual and the global level. In individual cases, criminal procedure protections make the punishment we inflict on criminal defendants seem more acceptable. Although the amendments do little to make the prosecutor's job harder, people commonly believe that they obstruct the prosecution of dangerous criminals. Some doubt and ambivalence that might otherwise accompany the use of violent and coercive sanctions is thereby dissipated.

On the global level, criminal procedure protections serve to redirect and exacerbate the popular anger about crime. While crime rates have remained static and even declined slightly in recent years, the rate of incarceration has skyrocketed. There is no easy way to demonstrate that the crime rate would not be higher if we had incarcerated fewer people, but, at a minimum, these statistics demonstrate that the increased rate of incarceration is not caused by an increase in crime. Instead, it seems to be fed by the public perception that crime is out of control and that still more draconian punishments are necessary to deal with it.

Popular misconceptions about criminal procedure protections feed this perception. Because people believe that "legal technicalities" set large numbers of guilty and dangerous criminals free, they think that too many miscreants are escaping punishment. Because they believe that the problem could be brought under control if only the "legal technicalities" were changed, they fail to focus on the bankruptcy of mass-incarceration as a crime fighting strategy.

In the United States today, over one million people are imprisoned, the largest number in our history and the second largest percentage in the world. One out of every 193 adult Americans is behind bars, and the total inmate population is roughly equivalent to that of the city of Phoenix. Despite the absence of any evidence that these extreme measures have helped to control crime, political pressures grow for still more prisons, longer sentences, and more executions.

The criminal procedure amendments have done nothing to slow this decline into barbarism. Instead, they have contributed to an atmosphere that promotes acceptance of a situation that ought to shock us.

JOSEPH D. GRANO, ASCERTAINING THE TRUTH

77 Cornell L. Rev. 1061, 1062-1064 (1992)

Many lawyers and judges sanctimoniously defend our criminal injustice system as essential to individual freedom. Similarly academics, searching for anything or anyone to blame except the individual offenders, often applaud approaches that give offenders second, third, fourth, and even more chances to commit crimes. While these people defend the system, law abiding citizens desert the city's activities, restaurants, and retail merchants.

What accounts for the persistence of the world view illustrated by the misguided academic and judge? To a large extent, I believe it is the attitude of "there but for the grace of God go I," referring unfortunately to the offender rather than the victim. This attitude has its roots in the civil rights movement of the 1960s and in the conventional liberal ideology of the time that equated the typical criminal defendant in one courtroom with the civil rights plaintiff in another. Do not misunderstand me. . . . My argument is not with the civil rights revolution of the 1960s but rather with the distorted vision that saw, and still sees, the criminal offender not as the responsible perpetrator of an evil deed but as an unfortunate victim of a racist and oppressive society.

The view that the blame for crime lies with society rather than with the individual offender did not have much popular appeal even in the 1960s, and it has even less appeal today as crime runs rampant in our cities. Moreover, the "no responsibility" social determinists always have had to confront the rather insurmountable obstacle that the substantive criminal law is premised on a foundation of individual free will and responsibility. The common law requirement of mens rea aptly illustrates this free will foundation.

The procedural system, however, offered an attractive end run for those determined to undermine the substantive law's commitment to individual responsibility. The primary target was the basic notion that the paramount goal (I didn't say the only goal) of sound procedure should be the ascertainment of truth. Individual responsibility and accountability are not easy to achieve in a system that denigrates the importance of discovering the truth. The academics provided the underlying theory; the academics, lawyers, and judges together provided an abundance of truth-defeating procedural rules.

I am not going to review or critique the numerous truth-defeating procedural rules that plague our system. Most of us are familiar with the search and seizure exclusionary rule, with *Miranda* and *Massiah*, with the rule against prosecutorial comment on a defendant's silence, and with the effort to adopt the minority rule on entrapment, which would make the defendant's guilt or innocence irrelevant. We also are familiar with liberalism's continuing, and largely successful, effort to retain these truth-defeating rules. The latest example being the organized drive, spearheaded by the often-wrong ABA, to defeat the Bush Administration's badly needed reforms in the area of habeas corpus.

To facilitate the denigration of the search for truth, the academics who advocated these rules attacked the very concept of truth. We were told, for example, that any emphasis on "truth" must be simplistic, given the "plural forms and multi-faceted aspects of that beguiling concept." (I often have wondered what my mother's reaction would have been had I responded to a question about whether I locked my sister in the basement by saying, "Well, the truth is multifaceted and beguiling.")

DOROTHY E. ROBERTS, CRIME, RACE AND REPRODUCTION

67 Tul. L. Rev. 1945, 1945-1947 (1993)

Not only is race used to identify criminals, it is embedded in the very foundation of our criminal law. Race helps to determine who the criminals are, what conduct constitutes a crime, and which crimes society treats most seriously. Today, the states have returned to considering reproduction as a solution to crime; meanwhile, the federal government is exploring a genetic cause for criminality. Suggestions for applying reproductive techniques to punish crime have gained alarming acceptance. The racial ideology of crime increasingly enlists biology to justify the continued subordination of blacks.

THE CONSTRUCTION OF RACE AND CRIME IN AMERICA

The American criminal justice system has historically served as a means of controlling blacks. This control is accomplished through very concrete means. Local police departments patrol black neighborhoods as if they were occupied territories. The idea of local control of police in black communities seems to most Americans to be as far-fetched as the proverbial fox minding the hen house. Police serve not to protect black citizens, but to protect white citizens from black criminals. It is not surprising that many black Americans view the police with fear, anger, and distrust. The use of criminal justice as a tactic of racial domination is also manifested in the tremendous proportion of black males under correctional supervision. Two recent studies conducted by the National Center on Institutions and Alternatives (NCIA) reveal the enormity of this control. According to the NCIA, on any given day in 1991 in Washington, D.C., forty-two percent of young black males were in jail, on probation or parole, awaiting trial, or being sought on warrants for their arrest. The study suggests that seventy-five percent of black men in the city will be arrested and jailed at least once before reaching age thirty-five. A subsequent study in Baltimore, Maryland, discloses an even higher percentage—over half—of black males under supervision of the criminal justice system. The intimidation, supervision, and imprisonment of blacks in America through law enforcement is one of the most direct means of racial subordination.

The criminal justice system's control of blacks is supported on another level as well. Restraining blacks is justified by a belief system that constructs crime in terms of race and race in terms of crime. The police occupation of black communities and wholesale imprisonment of black citizens does not seem like oppression to the dominant society because it believes that these people are dangerous. It is the racial ideology of crime that sustains continued white domination of blacks in the guise of crime control.

FRANCIS ALLEN, DECLINE OF THE REHABILITATIVE IDEAL:
PENAL POLICY AND SOCIAL PURPOSE

60-61, 63, 65-66 (1981)

The last two decades of the twentieth century are not likely to bring full consensus on issues of crime and punishment. Nevertheless, one senses that in the modern decline of the rehabilitative ideal a notable turning point has been reached in American penal policy and, as in other periods of change, both perils and opportunities abound. The shift of perspective of American thought about crime and punishment does not of itself eliminate or even substantially alter the persistent and intractable obstacles to doing penal justice. . . . Much more to the point is the observation that the failures of American criminal justice in the last generation — its insensitivities, corruptions, and inefficiencies; the escalation of violence in American society; the losses in security of life, limb, and possession[—]are failures of a system that as a whole cannot be regarded in any realistic sense as rehabilitative in purpose or effect. The contributions of the rehabilitative ideal to these failures have been at most peripheral.

Much of the attack on penal rehabilitationism ultimately voices broader concerns about the performance of the institutions of criminal justice. Operating a system of pains and penalties under any guise has proved a difficult and unsatisfactory business, and dissatisfactions become increasingly acute as the times encourage doubts and criticisms of governmental action of all sorts and at all levels. Many of the problems of penal rehabilitationism have their analogues in regimes embracing competing goals: just punishment, deterrence, and incapacitation. Thus conceptual difficulties with the notion of rehabilitation are matched by those encountered in efforts to define the concept of punishment proportional to the culpability of offenders. In all regimes, however oriented, the existence, guidance, and containment of discretion is a continuing concern, and in all of them, state power tends continually to impinge on political values.

The meticulous delineation and analysis of policy options has not often characterized American political discourse during the past decade and a half. On the contrary, the political style has been largely one subjecting institutional performances to unremitting attack and articulating an impressive range of dissatisfactions and revulsions. Yet rational penal policy demands that the scrutiny of policy options proceed and that efforts be made to identify the problems characteristic of such alternatives and to inquire which of the old dilemmas are likely to persist.

In recent years, as was noted earlier, a number of groups with widely disparate motives and policy objectives united in an attack on the rehabilitative ideal. One of the strange bed-fellows is that group insisting on increasingly repressive measures in American law enforcement and penology. The extreme law-and-order advocates — the group described as adherents of the war theory of criminal justice[—]constitute one of the important and persistent realities of American political life and one of the principal limiting factors in American penal reform. Although the group rarely attempts coherent or comprehensive statements of position, and the individuals who compose it display great diversity of backgrounds and status, a few generalizations can be made. All of its members are deeply resentful of losses in the quality of American life caused by widespread criminality. Many reflect a kind of nostalgia for an earlier period of American society, real or imagined, when values were clear, the moral consensus was overwhelming, and in which the future was predictable and inviting. Typically such persons believe that modern prisons are country clubs and that American judges are involved in an inexplicable conspiracy to subvert the public order by erecting obstacles to the detection and conviction of the guilty. Repressive regimes both in the prisons and on the streets prove attractive, not only because they are seen as solutions to the crime problem, but also because they express the values of discipline, vigor, and self-confidence largely lacking in contemporary American society.

As a practical program of action the theories of extreme repression are unrealistic, even romantic in nature. Proposals of extreme repression as deliberately adopted policy ignore certain salient features of contemporary American society. Prisons and prisoners today have political constituencies in a sense that was not true in midcentury. One of the consequences of the 1960s was a democratization of punishment. Thousands of middle-class citizens have had experiences in the recent past with arrest, conviction, and incarceration as a result of war protest, civil rights activities, and narcotics offenses. The concept of prisoner-as-alien has little appeal for these groups or for the many in sympathetic association with them. Moreover, members of racial minorities, both in and out of prison, advance political interpretations of crime and punishment strongly antagonistic to policies founded on the war theory of criminal justice. Finally, the interventions of the courts and the judicial concept of prisoners' rights, however narrowly drawn, have proved radically inconsistent with penal regimes of the sort approved by extreme law-and-order advocacy. To achieve the repression proposed by such advocates would involve a significant political transformation of American society, one demanding a much higher tolerance of punitive governmental interventions throughout society than at present exists. No one can say with assurance that such transformations will not occur in the future, but nothing in the present situation, despite the current vogue of capital punishment, suggests that a political consensus supportive of extreme penal repression will soon emerge.

Nor do the prescriptions of radical criminology provide a genuine alternative to the hegemony of the rehabilitative ideal. Indeed, the dogma that the pathologies of criminal justice are the inevitable consequences of an unjust social order is a counsel of despair, at least for those persons not yet ready to man the barricades in an effort to overturn the corrupt and decadent capitalist regime. In short, the position is one that largely abandons the effort at penal reform and amelioration and seeks instead to overturn the structures of power and authority of an unjust social order.

There is, however, another strand of thought which, although rejecting the revolutionary implications of radical criminology, nevertheless associates crime with broader social pathologies — unemployment, family dissolution, bad housing, and the like — and seeks the elimination or lessening of crime by attacks on these conditions. There are probably few persons of liberal political persuasion who do not share this outlook to some degree. But appeals for general social reform do not constitute a penal policy. Indeed, such advocacy of broad social reconstruction may be employed by some as a means to avoid thinking about or involvement in the hard and disagreeable realities of crime and punishment. The advocacy of sweeping social changes primarily because they will reduce crime is rarely sensible. Minimizing crime is a good, but there are other social goals as important; and it is possible that the objectives of crime control may often prove incompatible with other desired ends. Whether and to what extent social reforms reduce the quantum of criminal behavior are far from clear. The system of criminal justice provides a very narrow base from which to launch movements of fundamental social reconstruction, and one may reasonably doubt the competence of criminologists, regardless of the disciplines in which they have been trained, to achieve the brave new world.

It is apparent, then, that one must move to other areas if acceptable options to the hegemony of the rehabilitative ideal are to be found. The weakening of penal rehabilitationism marks a new era in thought about crime and punishment, but it is an era that has as yet produced few theoretical innovations. Rather, the period is one in which old ideas about the ends and means of criminal justice are being treated with a new seriousness. Old concerns about deterring crime, the matching of penalties to culpability, and achieving social defense through the incapacitation of potentially dangerous persons have been revived, and contentions rage over which of these goals should be admitted into a modern system of penal justice and which should be given dominant expression. Disputes surround the questions of whether and how far the decriminalization of conduct now punishable should proceed and the extent penal incarceration can and ought to be avoided in a modern system of penal sanctions.

CAROL S. STEIKER, COUNTER-REVOLUTION IN CONSTITUTIONAL CRIMINAL PROCEDURE? TWO AUDIENCES, TWO ANSWERS

94 Mich. L. Rev. 2466, 2466-2470 (1996)

When Richard M. Nixon ran for president in 1968, he campaigned on a now-familiar "law and order" platform. Among other things, he pledged to appoint Justices to the Supreme Court who would combat the Warren Court's controversial constitutional decisions limiting the power of law enforcement officials to investigate and prosecute crime. When Nixon won the presidency and then almost immediately had the opportunity to replace Chief Justice Earl Warren and three Associate Justices with appointees of his own, it was widely predicted that the major innovations of the Warren Court in constitutional criminal procedure — any list would include *Mapp, Massiah*, and *Miranda* — would not long survive. In the almost thirty years since Nixon's victory, the Supreme Court's pulse-takers have offered periodic updates on the fate of the Warren Court's criminal procedure "revolution" in the Burger and Rehnquist Courts.

The voluminous body of literature formed by these assessments presents something of a puzzle. The unanimity of projection about the future of the Warren Court's criminal procedure soon gave way to widespread disagreement about the nature and extent of the response of the Burger and Rehnquist Courts. On the one hand, many commentators — usually admirers of the Warren Court's handiwork — have lamented over the years about what they view as a wholesale repudiation of the Warren Court's work; their comments are full of words like "retreat," "decline," and "counter-revolution." At the very same time, other commentators — many of them also defenders of the Warren Court — have maintained that these laments are "overstated," and "considerably exaggerated," and that the basic structure of the Warren Court's criminal procedure jurisprudence is firmly "entrenched." As one critic of the Warren Court recently has bemoaned, "The voice that continues to urge repentance [from the Warren Court's criminal procedure] today is truly '[t]he voice of him that crieth in the wilderness.'"

One could attempt to resolve (or repudiate) this puzzling conflict in a variety of ways. One could, for example, attempt to explain disagreement about the nature of change by distinguishing between levels of abstraction — between "doctrinal" and "ideological" change. Or one could note that the difficulties inherent in weighing and measuring any sort of jurisprudential shift are exacerbated greatly in the broad, diffuse, and fact-specific jungle that is constitutional criminal procedure. Or one could ascribe the debate to a dispute over semantics: just how much change, after all, is "revolutionary" or "counter-revolutionary"? Or one simply could write off the more extreme statements on either side of the divide as rhetorical flourishes offered in the spirit of academic "spin control."

I, however, want to resist these temptations to downplay or deny the conflict, because I believe that the debate over continuity and change in constitutional criminal procedure can best be accounted for in an entirely different way — a way that suggests a new kind of critique of the Burger and Rehnquist Courts' criminal procedure jurisprudence. I start with the contention that the Supreme Court has profoundly changed its approach to constitutional criminal procedure since the 1960s at least in the following fairly limited (but obviously important) sense: the Court has clearly become less sympathetic to claims of individual rights and more accommodating to assertions of the need for public order. In the last three decades, the Court has granted review to and found in favor of criminal defendants much less frequently than it did in the heyday of the Warren Court. Thus, at least in Holmes' positivist sense of law as a prediction of what courts will do in fact, the law has changed radically.

The way in which this change has occurred, however, may help explain the academic divide. My contention is that much of this change has occurred quite differently from what was predicted at the close of the Warren Court era. The Burger and Rehnquist Courts have not altered radically — and indeed, occasionally have bolstered — the Warren Court's constitutional norms regarding police practices. The edifice constructed by the Warren Court governing investigative techniques under the Fourth, Fifth, and Sixth Amendments remains surprisingly intact. Rather than redrawing in any drastic fashion the line between constitutional and unconstitutional police conduct, the Supreme Court has revolutionized the consequences of deeming conduct unconstitutional. This revolution has not taken the form of wholesale abolition of the Fourth Amendment's exclusionary rule, or the Fifth or Sixth Amendments' mandates of exclusion; rather, the Court has proliferated a variety of what I would term "inclusionary rules" — rules that permit the use at trial of admittedly unconstitutionally obtained evidence or that let stand criminal convictions based on such evidence. Examples of "inclusionary rules" are the doctrines regarding standing, the good-faith exception to the warrant requirement, the "fruit of the poisonous tree," impeachment, harmless error, and limitations on federal habeas review of criminal convictions.

Thus, for the purposes of my argument, I adapt Professor Meir Dan-Cohen's distinction (which he in turn borrowed from Jeremy Bentham) between "conduct" rules and "decision" rules. Bentham and Dan-Cohen make this distinction in the context of substantive criminal law; for their purposes, "conduct" rules are addressed to the general public in order to guide its behavior (for example, "Let no person steal") and "decision" rules are addressed to public officials in order to guide their decisionmaking about the consequences of violating conduct rules (for example, "Let the judge cause whoever is convicted of stealing to be hanged"). But as any teacher of both substantive and procedural criminal law knows, constitutional criminal procedure is a species of substantive criminal law for cops. Thus, for my purposes, "conduct" rules (my "constitutional norms") are addressed to law enforcement agents regarding the constitutional legitimacy of their investigative practices and "decision" rules (my "inclusionary rules") are addressed to courts regarding the consequences of unconstitutional conduct.

. . . My primary descriptive claim . . . is that the Supreme Court's shift in constitutional criminal procedure from the 1960s to the 1990s has occasioned much more dramatic changes in decision rules than in conduct rules. . . . This claim is qualitative rather than quantitative, and comparative rather than absolute. I do not mean to say that the Supreme Court has deployed decision rules more than conduct rules in any strict numerical sense, nor do I contend that constitutional norms have not shifted at all; rather, I argue that the Court's decision-rule cases have diverged far more from the Warren Court's starting point than have its conduct-rule cases. Thus, the dichotomy between decision rules and conduct rules helps to explain the existence of such a deep academic divide. The proponents and debunkers of the "counter-revolution" hypothesis turn out to both be right: the Burger and Rehnquist Courts have accepted to a significant extent the Warren Court's definitions of constitutional "rights" while waging counter-revolutionary war against the Warren Court's constitutional "remedies" of evidentiary exclusion and its federal review and reversal of convictions.

AKHIL REED AMAR, THE FUTURE OF CONSTITUTIONAL CRIMINAL PROCEDURE

33 Am. Crim. L. Rev. 1123, 1123-1125, 1128-1129, 1132-1134 (1996)

As a subfield of constitutional law, constitutional criminal procedure stands as an anomaly. In many other areas of constitutional law, major Marshall Court opinions stand out and continue to frame debate both in courts and beyond. In thinking about judicial review and executive power, we still look to Marbury v. Madison; in pondering the puzzle of jurisdiction-stripping, we go back to Martin v. Hunter's Lessee; in reflecting on the scope of Congress' enumerated powers, and related issues of federalism, we re-examine McCulloch v. Maryland. . . . But no comparable Marshall Court landmarks dot the plain of constitutional criminal procedure.

It is often thought that the explanation for this anomaly lies in another Marshall Court landmark, Barron v. Baltimore. Most criminal law, the argument goes, is state law; murder, rape, robbery, and the like are generally not federal crimes. Under *Barron*, the constitutional criminal procedure rules of the Bill of Rights did not apply against states, and so the Marshall Court predictably heard few cases raising issues of constitutional criminal procedure. *Barron* is indeed part of the story. . . .

Then came the Warren Court, which overruled *Barron* and began applying the Fourth, Fifth, and Sixth Amendments directly against states, under the banner of selective incorporation. With many, many more state criminal cases fueling its

docket, the Warren Court proceeded to build up, in short order, a remarkable doctrinal edifice of Fourth Amendment, Fifth Amendment, and Sixth Amendment
rules — the foundations of modern constitutional criminal procedure.

But these foundations were none too sure. On a lawyerly level, some of the Warren Court's most important criminal procedure pronouncements lacked firm
grounding in constitutional text and structure. Key rulings ran counter to early case
law both in lower federal courts and in state courts construing analogous provisions
of state constitutions. Precisely because so few Marshall Court cases existed, this
break with Founding-era understandings was less visible. On key issues, the Warren
Court seemed to contradict itself, laying down sweeping rules in some cases that it
could not quite live by in other cases. On a political level, many of the Warren
Court's constitutional criminal procedure pronouncements did not sit well with the
American electorate. The guilty too often seemed to spring free without good
reason — and by this time the guilty regularly included murderers, rapists, and robbers and not just federal income tax frauds and customs cheats. In a constitutional
democracy, the People, in the long run, usually prevail. Federal judges may be, at
times, "insulated" and "countermajoritarian," but majorities elect Presidents, and
Presidents, with the advice and consent of Senators, pick federal judges.

And so, with Earl Warren's retirement, and Richard Nixon's election on a "law
and order" platform, the Counter-Revolution began. But the foundations of this
Counter-Revolution are also none too sure. Like the Warren Court, the Burger and
Rehnquist Courts have at times paid little heed to constitutional text, history, and
structure and have mouthed rules one day only to ignore them the next. If the
Warren Court at times was too easy on the guilty, the Burger and Rehnquist Courts
at times have been too hard on the innocent.

Where does all this leave us today? At a crossroads. I submit, the present is a particularly ripe moment for a fundamental rethinking of constitutional criminal procedure, and for a choice among competing visions.

WHERE SHOULD WE GO FROM HERE? CONSTITUTIONAL METHODOLOGY

To begin with, we must distinguish constitutional criminal procedure from criminal
procedure generally. Not all sensible rules of criminal procedure can or should be
constitutionalized. The Constitution — when read in light of its text, history, and
structure, its doctrinal elaboration in precedent, the need for principled judicial
standards, and so on — simply may not speak to some issues. This is, of course, one
of the reasons we have legislatures — to make sensible policy where the Constitution
permits choice. Legislative solutions can be adjusted in the face of new facts or
changing values far more easily than can rules that have been read into the Constitution.

Textual argument is, as I have said, a proper starting point for proper constitutional analysis. Sometimes, plain-meaning textual arguments in the end must yield
to the weight of other proper constitutional arguments — from history, structure,
precedent, practicality, and so on. And so the astonishing thing is not that someone
might find the above-catalogued textual points to be outweighed at times by other
arguments. Rather, the astonishing thing is that these textual points are almost
never made, or even seen. This is true even when the text, carefully read, explains
most or all of the leading cases in a given area, or when the text resonates with obvious common sense. In virtually every other area of constitutional law, such a state of

affairs is unimaginable. I think it cannot last much longer in the area of constitutional criminal procedure. The field may have evolved as an insular ecosystem unto itself, but global changes in constitutional law discourse must soon affect the atmosphere here, too.

The Constitution seeks to protect the innocent. The guilty, in general, receive procedural protection only as an incidental and unavoidable byproduct of protecting the innocent because of their innocence. Law breaking, as such, is entitled to no legitimate expectation of privacy, and so if a search can detect only law breaking as such, it poses little threat to Fourth Amendment values. By the same token, the exclusionary rule is wrong, as a constitutional rule, precisely because it creates huge windfalls for guilty defendants but gives no direct remedy to the innocent woman wrongly searched. The guiltier you are, the more evidence the police find, the bigger the exclusionary rule windfall; but if the police know you are innocent, and just want to hassle you (because of your race, or politics, or whatever), the exclusionary rule offers exactly zero compensation or deterrence.

Truth and accuracy are vital values. A procedural system that cannot sort the innocent from the guilty will confound any set of substantive laws, however just. And so to throw out highly reliable evidence that can indeed help us separate the innocent from the guilty — and to throw it out by pointing to the Constitution, no less — is constitutional madness. A Constitution proclaimed in the name of We the People should be rooted in enduring values that Americans can recognize as our values. Truth and the protection of innocence are such values. Virtually everything in the Fourth, Fifth, and Sixth Amendments, properly read, promotes, or at least does not betray, these values.

If anyone believes that other nice-sounding, but far less intuitive, ideas are also in the Constitution, the burden of proof should be on him. Here are two examples: (1) "The Constitution requires that government must never profit from its own wrong. Hence, illegally obtained evidence must be excluded." (2) "No man should be compelled to be an instrument of his own destruction. Hence, reliable physical fruits of immunized testimony should be excluded." These sound nice, but where does the Constitution say that? And are we truly willing to live by these as constitutional rules? The first would require that the government return stolen goods to thieves, and illegal drugs to drug-dealers. But this has never been the law. The second would prevent coerced fingerprinting and DNA sampling. This, too, is almost impossible to imagine in practice. By contrast, the innocence-protection rock on which I stand, and the specific Fourth, Fifth, and Sixth Amendment derivations therefrom, are things that we can all live by, without cheating.

WILLIAM J. STUNTZ, THE UNEASY RELATIONSHIP BETWEEN CRIMINAL PROCEDURE AND CRIMINAL JUSTICE

107 Yale L.J. 1, 1-6 (1997)

Most talk about the law of criminal procedure treats that law as a self-contained universe. The picture looks something like this: The Supreme Court says that suspects and defendants have a right to be free from certain types of police or prosecutorial behavior. Police and prosecutors, for the most part, then do as they're told. When they don't, and when the misconduct is tied to criminal convictions, the courts reverse the convictions, thereby sending a message to misbehaving officials. Within the bounds of this picture there is room for a lot of debate about the wisdom or constitutional pedigree of particular doctrines, and the literature is filled with debate of that sort. There is also room for theorizing about the optimal specificity of the rules the Supreme Court creates; the literature contains some of that, though less than it should. Finally, there is room for arguing about remedies — about whether reversing criminal convictions is an appropriate means of getting the police, prosecutors, and trial judges to do what the law says they ought to do. At least in the sphere of Fourth and Fifth Amendment law, a lively debate along those lines exists. But for all their variety, these debates take for granted the same basic picture of the process, a process whose only variables are the rules themselves and the remedies for their violation.

The picture is, of course, wrong. Criminal procedure's rules and remedies are embedded in a larger system, a system that can adjust to those rules in ways other than obeying them. And the rules can in turn respond to the system in a variety of ways, not all of them pleasant. The more one focuses on that dynamic, the more problematic the law of criminal procedure seems.

The heart of the problem is the system's structure. The criminal justice system is dominated by a trio of forces: crime rates, the definition of crime (which of course partly determines crime rates), and funding decisions — how much money to spend on police, prosecutors, defense attorneys, judges, and prisons. These forces determine the ratio of crimes to prosecutors and the ratio of prosecutions to public defenders, and those ratios in turn go far toward determining what the system does and how the system does it. But the law that defines what the criminal process looks like, the law that defines defendants' rights, is made by judges and Justices who have little information about crime rates and funding decisions, and whose incentives to take account of those factors may be perverse. High crime rates make it easy for prosecutors to substitute cases without strong procedural claims for cases with such claims. Underfunding of criminal defense counsel limits the number of procedural claims that can be pressed. Both phenomena make criminal procedure doctrines seem inexpensive to the appellate judges who define those doctrines. Unsurprisingly, given that regulating the criminal justice system has seemed cheap, the courts have done a lot of regulating — more, one suspects, than they would have done in a world where defendants could afford to litigate more often and more aggressively, or where prosecutors could not so easily substitute some cases for others. Criminal procedure is thus distorted by forces its authors probably do not understand.

The distortion runs both ways. As courts have raised the cost of criminal investigation and prosecution, legislatures have sought out devices to reduce those costs. Severe limits on defense funding are the most obvious example, but not the only one. Expanded criminal liability makes it easier for the government to induce guilty pleas, as do high mandatory sentences that serve as useful threats against recalcitrant defendants. And guilty pleas avoid most of the potentially costly requirements that criminal procedure imposes. These strategies would no doubt be politically attractive anyway, but the law of criminal procedure makes them more so. Predictably, underfunding, overcriminalization, and oversentencing have increased as criminal procedure has expanded.

Nor are the law's perverse effects limited to courts and legislatures. Constitutional criminal procedure raises the cost of prosecuting wealthier defendants by giving those defendants more issues to litigate. The result, at the margin, is to steer prosecutors away from such defendants and toward poorer ones. By giving defendants other, cheaper claims to raise, constitutional criminal procedure also raises the cost to defense counsel of investigating and litigating factual claims, claims that bear directly on their clients' innocence or guilt. The result is to steer defense counsel, again at the margin, away from those sorts of claims and toward constitutional issues. More Fourth, Fifth, and Sixth Amendment claims probably mean fewer self-defense claims and mens rea arguments. This turns the standard conservative criticism of the law of criminal procedure on its head. Ever since the 1960s, the right has argued that criminal procedure frees too many of the guilty. The better criticism may be that it helps to imprison too many of the innocent.

It also does little about the concern that, more than anything else, prompted its creation. The post-1960 constitutionalization of criminal procedure arose, in large part, out of the sense that the system was treating black suspects and defendants much worse than white ones. Warren-era constitutional criminal procedure began as a kind of antidiscrimination law. But the criminal justice system is characterized by extraordinary discretion — over the definition of crimes (legislatures can criminalize as much as they wish), over enforcement (police and prosecutors can arrest and charge whom they wish), and over funding (legislatures can allocate resources as they wish). In a system so dominated by discretionary decisions, discrimination is easy, and constitutional law has surprisingly little to say about it.

To some degree, these problems are the product of a particular set of contingent circumstances. Vary the circumstances, and the problems would look quite different. For example, we may someday return to the very low crime-to-prosecutor ratios of the early 1960s, either because crime takes a nosedive or because criminal justice budgets go through the roof (or both). If that happens, prosecutorial discretion will seem less important, for prosecutors will be able to pursue all strong cases and a good number of weak ones. Guilty plea rates will fall as the proportion of contestable cases rises. More trials will mean that the cost of constitutional regulation in this area will become more visible to judges, which might lead the Supreme Court to alter the regulation in important ways. This is just one set of speculations about one possible scenario; other scenarios, pushing prosecutors and courts in very different directions, could easily be spun out. The lesson seems clear: Generalizing is dangerous, for the problems that afflict the system today are the consequence of today's facts and today's law, and both facts and law are certain to change.

Yet some cautious generalizing is still possible. In a legislatively funded system with state-paid prosecutors and defense attorneys, judge-made procedural rights are bound to have some perverse effects, pushing prosecutors and defense attorneys and legislators and even the judges themselves in uncomfortable directions. The effects are impossible to measure, and they will be larger or smaller depending on background circumstances. But they remain real, and inevitable.

It may be that the broad structure of constitutional regulation of criminal justice has it backward, that courts have been not too activist, but activist in the wrong places. The system might be better off today had Warren and his colleagues worried less about criminal procedure, and more about criminal justice.

ALAN DERSHOWITZ, THE BEST DEFENSE

xxi-xxii (1982)

In the process of litigating . . . cases, writing this book, and teaching my classes, I have discerned a series of "rules" that seem — in practice — to govern the justice game in America today. Most of the participants in the criminal justice system understand them. Although these rules never appear in print, they seem to control the realities of the process. Like all rules, they are necessarily stated in oversimplified terms. But they tell an important part of how the system operates in practice. Here are some of the key rules of the justice game:

Rule I: Almost all criminal defendants are, in fact, guilty.

Rule II: All criminal defense lawyers, prosecutors, and judges understand and believe Rule I.

Rule III: It is easier to convict guilty defendants by violating the Constitution than by complying with it, and in some cases it is impossible to convict guilty defendants without violating the Constitution.

Rule IV: Almost all police lie about whether they violated the Constitution in order to convict guilty defendants.

Rule V: All prosecutors, judges, and defense attorneys are aware of Rule IV.

Rule VI: Many prosecutors implicitly encourage police to lie about whether they violated the Constitution in order to convict guilty defendants.

Rule VII: All judges are aware of Rule VI.

Rule VIII: Most trial judges pretend to believe police officers who they know are lying.

Rule IX: All appellate judges are aware of Rule VIII, yet many pretend to believe the trial judges who pretend to believe the lying police officers.

Rule X: Most judges disbelieve defendants about whether their constitutional rights have been violated, even if they are telling the truth.

Rule XI: Most judges and prosecutors would not knowingly convict a defendant who they believe to be innocent of the crime charged (or a closely related crime).

Rule XII: Rule XI does not apply to members of organized crime, drug dealers, career criminals, or potential informers.

Rule XIII: Nobody really wants justice.

2. The Distinction Between Criminal Procedure, Civil Procedure, and Substantive Criminal Law

WILLIAM J. STUNTZ, SUBSTANCE, PROCESS, AND THE CIVIL-CRIMINAL LINE

7 J. Contemp. Legal Issues 1 (1996)

Criminal procedure is almost completely constitutionalized; civil procedure is not. Meanwhile, the substance of the law of crimes is not very heavily constitutionalized; neither is the substance of the law of everything else. Those substantive restraints that exist — for instance, the First Amendment and equal protection doctrine, not to mention the famous cases that go under the label "substantive due process" — apply, with a few exceptions, to everything the government does. That is, they apply to the civil and criminal spheres alike.

So constitutional law treats the criminal side of the civil-criminal line as special, but only when crafting procedures. When it comes to the rules that regulate primary conduct, constitutional law basically has no civil-criminal line. Legislatures decide what is and is not a crime, just as they decide what (mostly civil) rules apply to sales contracts or securities offerings. Legislatures also decide what procedures apply when civil disputes arise, though they may leave a good deal of that authority to courts as a practical matter. But courts alone decide what the law of criminal procedure looks like, since courts are the system's constitutional lawmakers and criminal procedure is the province of constitutional law.

So the constitution regulates substance in a few significant pockets, but otherwise leaves it alone, and the regulation basically spans the civil-criminal divide. There is no real substantive due process aimed specially at criminal law. Meanwhile, there is some gentle constitutional regulation of the civil process, but the regulation plainly occurs around the edges; the core is governed by non-constitutional law. Only in criminal procedure does constitutional law dominate the field.

There is a standard argument for constitutional criminal procedure's many protections. Arrest, prosecution, and criminal punishment impose huge costs on their targets. The danger is that those costs will be imposed for no reason (i.e., on the whim of some government official) or for a bad reason (e.g., the defendant's race or politics). A large portion of the law of criminal procedure addresses that danger. The requirement of probable cause to justify arrest; the requirement of magistrate review, a preliminary hearing, or grand jury screening to bring a case to trial; the right to counsel at trial and at some pretrial stages; the right to trial by jury; and the beyond-a-reasonable-doubt standard for criminal conviction — all these rights ensure that the government can punish only if it can satisfy a series of neutral decisionmakers of a high probability (increasingly high as one moves from arrest to trial to conviction) that the defendant committed a crime. If the rights work, the specter of punishment for no reason or for evil reasons vanishes.

This happy scenario depends on substantive criminal law doing a good job of separating people who deserve punishment from people who don't. Accuracy is not an end in itself; it matters only if there is something meaningful to be accurate about. The best procedures in the world cannot prevent punishment for the "crime" of being black, or a Rastafarian. In short, good procedural rules require good substantive rules in order to accomplish anything.

That much is no surprise; it is the usual relationship between procedure and substance. But at least in the criminal setting, the relationship is more problematic. Special rules of criminal procedure are not just worthless without substantive limits. The procedural rules may actually be perverse: The procedures themselves give the government an incentive to generate bad substantive rules, as a means of evading or exploiting the differences between the criminal and civil processes. This perversity takes two forms. The first arises from legal boundaries that separate criminal law enforcement from civil law enforcement, boundaries that are almost never litigated yet create important incentives. These boundary rules let the government do things to criminal suspects or defendants that it can't do to civil litigants, thereby creating some incentive to broaden the scope of criminal liability. The second arises from the many rights criminal procedure grants defendants. Safeguarding those rights is, naturally, costly to the government. And broader criminal liability allows the government to escape those costs, both by easing the burden of proving guilt and by easing the task of inducing guilty pleas.

There is a natural dynamic built into our system that leads to overcriminalization. In the absence of substantive limits, broad procedural protections for criminal defendants make that dynamic worse. Meanwhile, the same logic that legitimates constitutional criminal procedure also supports constitutional criminal substance. It follows that the current allocation of authority between constitutional law and legislative power is both unstable and contradictory.

How might the contradiction be resolved? There are two possibilities, both obvious. The system might deregulate criminal procedure, leaving it to the same forces that define criminal law. Or, the system might constitutionalize the borders of criminal law, just as it has done with criminal procedure. That is, constitutional law's line between criminal and civil might be either abolished or extended.

LOUIS MICHAEL SEIDMAN, POINTS OF INTERSECTION: DISCONTINUITIES AT THE JUNCTION OF CRIMINAL LAW AND THE REGULATORY STATE

7 J. Contemp. Legal Issues 97, 97-98, 100-102, 127 (1996)

The law of crime is special. Like an isolated, aboriginal community somehow passed over by the changes all around it, the criminal law has managed to hang onto ancient patterns of thought and behavior. Of course, there is some contact with the outside world. Emissaries from "civilization" produce disruptions when they cross the community's borders. Although these disruptions are real and serious, they remain localized and peripheral. At its core, the criminal law is a living museum that unselfconsciously preserves a rapidly receding past.

. . . . [T]he law of crime has managed to remain "formal" in a legal environment dominated by a "regulatory" perspective. Criminal law is preoccupied by discourse about rights, fault, consent, and separate private and public spheres. Much of the rest of the law, in contrast, is frankly utilitarian, regulatory, and collective.

This claim should not be overstated. Civil law is not entirely regulatory in focus, and, conversely, regulatory concepts have had some influence on the criminal law. These qualifications form an important part of my argument. Part of my aim is to demonstrate that formalism has more of a hold over the law in general than many have acknowledged. I also want to demonstrate that regulatory penetration around the peripheries of the criminal law has had a significant disruptive effect.

Still, there are important differences in degree concerning the extent to which regulatory ideas have displaced formalism in different doctrinal areas. The criminal law's central tenets are understandable only in terms of concepts that survive as no more than a deviant counter-tradition in the rest of the law. The upshot is that when standard critical techniques, developed by legal realists in the first third of this century, are applied to criminal law and procedure, they make hash out of the categories that define the doctrine.

Procedural formalism is important to the law's legitimacy because it demonstrates that when judges enforce the law, they are doing something more than simply imposing their will on others. Procedural formalism is not sufficient to legitimate the law, however. Many formalists also believe that the substantive source of law must also be impersonal and legitimate. Formalists who have thought about this substantive vision have often relied on a particular social theory grounded in classical liberalism. Although procedural formalism has had an obvious and important impact on criminal law, it is this substantive social theory that I will emphasize below.

Put crudely, the theory starts with individuals located in a preexisting private sphere — individuals who have separate and, to some degree irreconcilable, desires, life-plans, and beliefs. These individuals, in turn, form a public sphere in order to prevent a war of "all against all." This public sphere is sharply limited. In order to conform to the original bargain that created it, it must remain rigorously neutral as between conflicting individual conceptions of the good and should intervene only when necessary to protect the rights of individuals who continue to decide for themselves how to pursue their lives.

The conventional story is that this social vision was subject to withering assault by the legal realists in the first third of this century and that it collapsed when the Supreme Court effectively overruled Lochner v. New York after 1937. The realist revolt against formalism was, of course, multifaceted, but at a minimum, it entailed a rejection of the freedom of contract ideology thought to mark the boundary between private freedom and public coercion. *Lochner* reflected the view that coercion invading natural and prepolitical private space was justified only when an individual had consented to be bound. Therefore, bakers who contracted to work for longer than ten hours per day did so in an exercise of private freedom and had a right to this choice. Conversely, manufacturers who had not agreed to pay their employers a minimum wage could not be justly coerced into doing so. Because these prohibitions derived from a conception of individual rights ultimately tied to the social contract, instrumental arguments against them premised on maximizing overall welfare were simply beside the point.

The realists attacked this system on two levels. The less radical version of the critique rejected the association between freedom and the private sphere. Individual choice within this sphere was not necessarily free. Instead, it was often coerced by private forces. Government intervention therefore held the potential to increase the realm of freedom by regulating private coercion.

The more radical version rejected the very concepts of public and private or free and coerced. On this view, an antecedent state of nature in which people made free choices in a purely private sphere was a myth. What formalists called "private" was, and had always been, publicly constituted by background laws of property. What formalists called "free will" was, and had always been, situated in a social and political setting that determined the "choices" individuals made.

It followed from both the more radical and the less radical view that the wage contract was not sacrosanct. For less radical realists, it was coerced by the ability of manufacturers to withhold the means of subsistence unless their terms were accepted. On the more radical version, the very conception of a freely assumed obligation was a chimera. Because government was everywhere, choice was always determined by the legal regime, and the only relevant question was the shape of the legal regime that would determine the choice.

. . . Freed from the shackles of a priori reasoning from natural rights, policy managers could redistribute resources and manipulate incentives so as to provide socially optimal outcomes. Under the post-War implicit social contract that dominated American politics until the 1980s, this approach entailed regulation when it made sense on pragmatic grounds to alter market outcomes, social insurance that guaranteed an income floor, and modest redistribution above the floor.

The implications of all this for the criminal law are fairly obvious: Criminal law is simply another form of regulation, to be utilized when the benefits of government intervention outweigh the costs. Following Holmes, a realist's approach to criminal law would, therefore, reject individual consent as a starting point. Under the old, Kantian conception, government coercion was justified only because the criminal, by committing the crime, had freely consented to her own punishment. For realists, this "consent" is as mythical as the consent of workers to the wage contract. The "choices" made by criminals, like all other choices, are conditioned by their surroundings. It does not follow, however, that criminals should not be punished. The moral justification for punishment derives not from free choice, but from the imperatives of social welfare maximization. The key insight is that government inaction is just as likely to limit freedom as government action. The failure to criminalize or punish does not leave individuals free in a preexisting private sphere, any more than government passivity left workers free. Just as workers were coerced by their employers in the absence of government intervention, so too victims of crime are coerced by criminals.

. . . At first blush, many of the "new" rules of criminal procedure announced over the past half century seem to be regulatory in character. For example, although some have tried, it is difficult to justify the rule excluding illegally seized evidence as necessary to enforce the rights of the defendant who benefits from the exclusion. If the rule is justified at all, it is because it provides police officers with useful incentives in the future.

3. Plea Bargaining and Sentencing

ALBERT W. ALSCHULER, IMPLEMENTING THE CRIMINAL DEFENDANT'S RIGHT TO TRIAL: ALTERNATIVES TO THE PLEA BARGAINING SYSTEM

50 U. Chi. L. Rev. 931, 932-936, 1048-1050 (1983)

[P]lea bargaining has come to affect almost every aspect of our criminal justice system from the legislative drafting of substantive offenses through the efforts of correctional officials to rehabilitate convicted offenders.

Even a cursory listing of objections to this practice may consume several paragraphs. Plea bargaining makes a substantial part of an offender's sentence depend, not upon what he did or his personal characteristics, but upon a tactical decision irrelevant to any proper objective of criminal proceedings. In contested cases, it substitutes a regime of split-the-difference for a judicial determination of guilt or innocence and elevates a concept of partial guilt above the requirement that criminal responsibility be established beyond a reasonable doubt. This practice also deprecates the value of human liberty and the purposes of the criminal sanction by treating these things as commodities to be traded for economic savings — savings that, when measured against common social expenditures, usually seem minor.

Plea bargaining leads lawyers to view themselves as judges and administrators rather than as advocates; it subjects them to serious financial and other temptations to disregard their clients' interests; and it diminishes the confidence in attorney-client relationships that can give dignity and purpose to the legal profession and that [are] essential to the defendant's sense of fair treatment. In addition, this practice makes figureheads of court officials who typically prepare elaborate presentence reports only after the effective determination of sentence through prosecutorial negotiations. Indeed, it tends to make figureheads of judges, whose power over the administration of criminal justice has largely been transferred to people of less experience, who commonly lack the information that judges could secure, whose temperaments have been shaped by their partisan duties, and who have not been charged by the electorate with the important responsibilities that they have assumed. Moreover, plea bargaining perverts both the initial prosecutorial formulation of criminal charges and, as defendants plead guilty to crimes less serious than those that they apparently committed, the final judicial labeling of offenses.

The negotiation process encourages defendants to believe that they have "sold a commodity and that [they have], in a sense, gotten away with something." It sometimes promotes perceptions of corruption. It has led the Supreme Court to a hypocritical disregard of its usual standards of waiver in judging the most pervasive waiver that our criminal justice system permits. The practice of plea bargaining is inconsistent with the principle that a decent society should want to hear what an accused person might say in his defense — and with constitutional guarantees that embody this principle and other professed ideals for the resolution of criminal disputes. . . . However unjust plea bargaining may seem, it has become fashionable to contend that the process is inevitable. Indeed, scholars and practitioners proclaim that "to speak of a plea bargaining-free criminal justice system is to operate in a land of fantasy." They advance two arguments in support of this contention. First, they emphasize the extent of the demon's possession. In view of the overwhelming number of cases that currently are resolved by guilty pleas, they maintain that providing the economic resources necessary to implement the right to trial would be impracticable; their view apparently is that our nation cannot afford to give its criminal defendants their day in court. Second, they suggest that in view of the mutuality of advantage that prosecutors and defense attorneys are likely to perceive in the settlement of criminal cases, any attempt to prohibit this process would be countered by widespread subterfuge. In practice, they argue, the only choice is between a system of negotiated case resolution that is open, honest, and subject to effective regulation and one that has been driven underground.

. . . [O]ne obvious solution to today's excessive dependency on the guilty plea — spending the money necessary to implement our constitutional ideals without shortcuts. Focusing first on felony prosecutions, it argues that the United States could provide three-day jury trials to all felony defendants who reach the trial stage by adding no more than an estimated $850 million to annual criminal justice expenditures. Moreover, it contends that the actual cost of implementing a plea bargaining prohibition would be less than this amount, in part because most cases now resolved through plea bargaining could be tried in less than three days and, even more importantly, because many defendants would plead guilty without bargaining.

. . . [T]he Anglo-American legal system afforded defendants an unfettered right to trial during most of its history and . . . most legal systems of the world apparently survive without plea bargaining today. Nevertheless, every legal system that has managed without plea bargaining has employed a much more expeditious trial procedure than ours.

The impediments to implementation of a plea bargaining prohibition are not worth a fraction of the paralysis that they have prompted. Americans certainly could afford full implementation of the right to jury trial in both felony and misdemeanor prosecutions. Moreover, without additional expenditures, they could allocate existing resources more effectively by simplifying the trial process and making trials more available. Finally, states could easily substitute jury waiver bargaining for plea bargaining. Observers who proclaim that implementation of the right to trial is impossible have perpetrated a remarkable myth — one whose effectiveness depends largely on the "outsider's" fear of being thought naive or utopian and one that any glance outside our own legal system destroys.

At the end of a long investigation of plea bargaining, I confess to some bafflement concerning the insistence of most lawyers and judges that plea bargaining is inevitable and desirable. Perhaps I am wrong in thinking that a few simple precepts of criminal justice should command the unqualified support of fair-minded people:

— that it is important to hear what someone may be able to say in his defense before convicting him of crime;

— that, when he denies his guilt, it is also important to try to determine on the basis of all the evidence whether he is guilty;

— that it is wrong to punish a person, not for what he did, but for asking that the evidence be heard (and wrong deliberately to turn his sentence in significant part on his strategies rather than on his crime);

— and, finally, that it is wrong to alibi departures from these precepts by saying that we do not have the time and money to listen, that most defendants are guilty anyway, that trials are not perfect, that it is all an inevitable product of organizational interaction among stable courtroom work groups, and that any effort to listen would merely drive our failure to listen underground.

From my viewpoint, it is difficult to understand why these precepts are controversial; what is more, I do not understand why the legal profession, far from according them special reverence, apparently values them less than the public in general does. Daniel Webster thought it a matter of definition that "law" would hear before it condemned, proceed upon inquiry, and render judgment only after trial. Apparently the legal profession has lost sight of Webster's kind of law, and, for all the pages that I have written about plea bargaining, the issue in the end may be that simple.

RONALD WRIGHT & MARC MILLER, THE SCREENING/BARGAINING TRADEOFF

55 Stan. L. Rev. 29, 30-35 (2002)

When it comes to plea bargaining, we have created a false dilemma. The dilemma grows out of the central reality of criminal adjudication in the United States. The vast majority of criminal cases are resolved through guilty pleas rather than trials. Most of those guilty pleas result from negotiations between prosecution and defense.

Scholars, judges, prosecutors, defense lawyers, and politicians have offered only two basic responses to the fact that guilt is mostly resolved through negotiated guilty pleas: They take it or they leave it.

Some take the system more or less as it is. They accept negotiated pleas in the ordinary course of events, either because such a system produces good results or because it is inevitable. They might identify some exceptional cases that create an intolerable risk of convicting innocent defendants, or unusual cases where there are special reasons to doubt the knowing and voluntary nature of the defendant's plea. But the mine run of cases, in this view, must be resolved with a heavy dose of plea bargains and a sprinkling of trials.

Then there are those who leave it, arguing that our system's reliance on negotiated guilty pleas is fundamentally mistaken. Some call for a complete ban. . . . Others, doubting that an outright ban is feasible, still encourage a clear shift to more short trials to resolve criminal charges. Restoring the criminal trial to its rightful place at the center of criminal justice might require major changes in public spending, and it might take a lifetime, but these critics say the monstrosity of the current system demands such a change.

This dilemma about plea bargaining — take it or leave it — is a false one. It is based on a false dichotomy. It errs in assuming that criminal trials are the only alternative to plea bargains. In this erroneous view, fewer plea bargains lead inexorably to more trials; indeed, the whole point in limiting plea bargains is to produce more trials.

[There is] a different choice . . . prosecutorial "screening" as the principal alternative to plea bargains. Of course all prosecutors "screen" when they make any charging decision. By prosecutorial screening we mean a far more structured and reasoned charge selection process than is typical in most prosecutors' offices in this country. The prosecutorial screening system we describe has four interrelated features, all internal to the prosecutor's office: early assessment, reasoned selection, barriers to bargains, and enforcement.

First, the prosecutor's office must make an early and careful assessment of each case, and demand that police and investigators provide sufficient information before the initial charge is filed. Second, the prosecutor's office must file only appropriate charges. Which charges are "appropriate" is determined by several factors. A prosecutor should only file charges that the office would generally want to result in a criminal conviction and sanction. In addition, appropriate charges must reflect reasonably accurately what actually occurred. They are charges that the prosecutor can very likely prove in court. Third, and critically, the office must severely restrict all plea bargaining, and most especially charge bargains. Prosecutors should also recognize explicitly that the screening process is the mechanism that makes such restrictions possible. Fourth, the kind of prosecutorial screening we advocate must include sufficient training, oversight, and other internal enforcement mechanisms to ensure reasonable uniformity in charging and relatively few changes to charges after they have been filed. . . .

Intense prosecutorial screening may produce a small increase in the number of trials, but the more substantial change would likely be an increase in the number of "open" pleas — defendants pleading guilty as charged without any prior negotiated agreement with the prosecutor. . . .

Jurisdictions that implement the screening/bargaining tradeoff will be more honest and more accessible. In hard screening systems, prosecutors will be less likely to "overcharge" or "undercharge." The weakest cases exit early, while those remaining should stand up at trial. A screening-based system should also be more accessible than a system of negotiated pleas, because the public (especially the victims of alleged crimes) will receive clearer and more accurate signals about how the system adjudicates and punishes crimes. The charge is declared publicly from the outset and is easy to evaluate. . . .

We know this practice is viable because it is now operating in a few American jurisdictions, without much controversy and without attracting the attention it deserves. For instance, over the last three decades New Orleans District Attorney Harry Connick has emphasized early screening of cases and has actively discouraged any changes of criminal charges as a result of negotiations after the charges are filed. . . .

[O]ur study of the New Orleans data . . . confirms that a prosecutor can invest serious resources in early evaluation of cases and maintain this practice over the long run. This screening leads to relatively high rates of declination (that is, refusals to prosecute a case after the police recommend charges). When combined with policies discouraging reductions in charges once they are filed, the results are lower levels of negotiated pleas, slightly higher rates of trial, and notably higher rates of open guilty pleas than in typical American jurisdictions. . . .

The screening/bargaining tradeoff should . . . become part of the public, political dialogue about the justice system, especially at election time. The interesting public question should not be the "conviction rate," but rather the "as charged conviction rate." . . . [T]he higher the ratio of "as charged convictions" to "convictions," the more readily a prosecutor should be praised and reelected. A ratio near one — where most convictions are "as charged," *whether they result from guilty pleas or trials* — is the best sign of a healthy, honest, and tough system. The lower the ratio of "as charged convictions" to "convictions" (approaching zero), the more the prosecutor should be criticized for sloppiness, injustice, and obfuscation. A lower ratio might also reflect a prosecutor's undue leniency. . . .

GERARD E. LYNCH, SCREENING VERSUS PLEA BARGAINING: EXACTLY WHAT ARE WE TRADING OFF?

55 Stan. L. Rev. 1399, 1400-1404, 1406-1408 (2003)

In questioning "the traditional plea bargaining/trial tradeoff," and seeking to replace it with a model in which the proper tradeoff is seen as one between plea bargaining and prosecutorial screening, Wright and Miller rather tellingly start with plea bargaining as the baseline system, and ask which of their two alternatives, trials or screening, can best serve as a viable substitute for it. The question seems to be: Can we eliminate plea bargaining without incurring the burden and expense of a vastly increased trial docket? Putting aside for the moment other questions about this formulation, it is readily apparent that asking the question in this way avoids the real reason that plea bargaining is traditionally seen as in opposition to trial: It is the *trial* that is the official baseline system, proclaimed in the Constitution, in all state and federal variations of criminal procedure rules, and in the popular imagination as educated in civics classes and entertained by American media. . . .

Thus, there is a tradeoff between plea bargaining and trials, not merely in the practical sense that (as some have argued and as Wright and Miller dispute) we might not be able to reduce plea bargaining without increasing the number of trials, but in the deeper sense that plea bargaining (and variant systems of agreed disposition) exists in the first place as an alternative to the expense and uncertainty of trials. It is in this sense that I would argue that plea bargaining is best seen as an alternative to a trial system, and that the screening system that appears to operate in New Orleans is simply a variant or refinement of a system of disposition in which the prosecutor, rather than a judge or jury, is the principal adjudicator of guilt and punishment, and the defendant's role is to acquiesce in that determination, rather than to contest it before a neutral adjudicator. . . .

In what sense, then, does the screening system eliminate the defects of a plea bargaining regime? Wright and Miller seem to focus on *bargaining* as the key negative characteristic of adjudication by guilty plea. . . .

. . . "Plea bargaining" is a loaded term. . . . Substantively, it suggests that defendants receive "bargains" — in the sense of discounts — from the presumptively appropriate charge or penalty for their crimes. . . . It is not clear, however, why we should privilege the sentences received by the tiny minority of defendants who go to trial as the "correct" sentences, from which the sentences received by defendants who plead represent an unduly lenient departure. . . . Where almost no one pays the "manufacturer's suggested retail price," and almost everyone buys the item at a "discounted" price, no one really gets a "bargain," and the product's real price is what is actually charged in the marketplace. . . .

But even if we assume for the sake of argument that giving lesser sentences to induce guilty pleas results in sentences that are unduly lenient, Wright and Miller notably do not suggest that defendants who plead guilty in New Orleans receive the same sentences as similar defendants convicted after trial. . . . If . . . defendants who plead guilty receive an imprecise, unannounced, yet roughly predictable sentencing discount from judges in exchange for their waiver of rights, the elimination of "plea bargaining" by prosecutors seems much less significant. There may be reasons why an implicit bargain between defendants and judges who are understood to reward guilty pleas with leniency is preferable to express bargaining with defendants by prosecutors to accomplish the same end. But I suspect few critics of plea bargaining would consider substituting the former system for the latter a major accomplishment.

Procedurally, plea "bargaining" suggests an inappropriate *process* of adjudication, by implying that guilt and punishment are determined by some form of mercantile haggling rather than objective inquiry. But the process of negotiating pleas, in my experience, is not accurately regarded as one of "bargaining," if by that one imagines some simplistic model of haggling over prices. Wright and Miller at times seem implicitly to adopt this model: The prosecutor sets the bid artificially high by overcharging at the outset; the defendant balks and proposes that the charges be dismissed; the parties then settle on a compromise somewhere between these two extremes. The authors . . . seem to regard any reduction from the charged offense as either a sell-out by the prosecutor or an admission that the original charge was merely a bargaining chip. Most plea negotiations, in fact, are primarily discussions of the merits of the case, in which defense attorneys point out legal, evidentiary, or practical weaknesses in the prosecutor's case, or mitigating circumstances that merit mercy, and argue based on these considerations that the defendant is entitled to a more lenient disposition than that originally proposed. . . .

To me, the essence of this practice, and what radically distinguishes it from the adversarial litigation model embodied in textbooks . . . is that the *prosecutor*, rather than a judge or jury, is the central adjudicator of facts (as well as replacing the judge as arbiter of most legal issues and of the appropriate sentence to be imposed). Potential defenses are presented by the defendant and his counsel not in a court, but to a prosecutor, who assesses their factual accuracy and likely persuasiveness to a hypothetical judge or jury, and then decides the charge of which the defendant should be adjudged guilty. Mitigating information, similarly, is argued not to the judge, but to the prosecutor. . . .

. . . Instituting an aggressive screening procedure may significantly improve that process, but only if it implies that prosecutors will reach a more accurate and more just decision, rather than automatically adopting the police view of the appropriate charge or instituting excessive charges in order to bring pressure on defendants to plead. But it hardly constitutes a radical alternative to plea bargaining as actually practiced, and in important ways it merely ratifies and entrenches (or at least, assumes the inevitability of) that practice. . . .

Moreover, certain aspects of the New Orleans screening program endorsed by Wright and Miller . . . may have negative effects on the justice of outcomes. The authors seem to assume, in my opinion unjustifiably, that the charge determined by the prosecutors at an early stage of the case should normally be the charge to which the defendant pleads guilty or that is tried. If the prosecutor is essentially determining guilt, operating as a kind of inquisitorial, administrative adjudicator of the merits of cases, it becomes critical to provide a fair opportunity, within the internal administration process, for the defendant to present evidence, challenge the prosecutor's case, and argue defenses and mitigating circumstances. It is difficult to see how such an opportunity can be provided at the typical screening stage between arrest and charge, before defense counsel can possibly have an adequate opportunity to investigate the case. . . .

. . . The great benefit of Wright and Miller's . . . article is to focus our attention not on lamenting the absence of trials, but on improving the administrative adjudication system (mislabeled plea bargaining) so that it functions better and more fairly. Serious prosecutorial screening to eliminate unjustifiable charges can be a real improvement in the system. Reducing the opportunity for defendants to have meaningful input into the disposition has the opposite effect.

CHARLES FRIED, REFLECTIONS ON CRIME AND PUNISHMENT

30 Suffolk U. L. Rev. 681, 682-683, 685-688, 692-693, 694-695 (1997)

It appears for a number of reasons, including some that do great credit to our commitment to the rule of law and to individual rights, that the United States makes it more difficult than other decent, reasonable democracies to prevent crimes and to apprehend and convict those whose crimes we do not prevent. Once a criminal is convicted in the United States, however, our system subjects the offender to longer sentences in a sometimes degrading regime which is hurtful to criminals and society alike. I do not suggest that prison food, medical care, or amenities are inhumane. . . . In fact, some of our prisons may appear quite astonishingly luxurious to authorities from other countries. Rather, I am more concerned by the failure of some American prison systems to assure the physical safety of [their] inmates and by the widespread regime of intimidation by stronger, organized inmates against the weaker or less experienced inmates. What we cannot blink away is the astonishing prevalence and tolerance of sexual violence and subjugation particularly among male prisoners. These conditions must be evaluated in the context of the very long sentences served by criminals who will eventually be allowed to leave prison. In short, prison life is too often a terrifying and degrading experience endured by prisoners for unimaginably long periods of time — six, ten, twenty years — after which society expects the released individuals to lead self-sufficient, constructive, and law-abiding lives.

. . . [S]tudies and findings from Florida, Texas, Pennsylvania, Louisiana and Connecticut . . . demonstrate that rape is endemic in the American prison population. In fact, one corrections officer stated that a young inmate's chances of avoiding rape are "almost zero. . . . He'll get raped within the first twenty-four to forty-eight hours. That's almost standard." Furthermore, an investigator observed that ten years ago, when the prison population was far smaller than it is today, there were as many as "eighteen adult males raped every minute" of every day. Moreover, it is common knowledge that an exceptionally large proportion of male prisoners engage in regular homosexual activity, and rape simply becomes the violent alternative to sexual submission. Feminist scholars, including Dworkin, Estrich and MacKinnon, have raised our consciousness about the prevalence of heterosexual rape and the degrading impact that it has upon women. Surely, the homosexual rape prevalent in so many prisons is no less destructive of the souls of its victims. One of the most distressing features of this infernal system is that the prison authorities are aware of the prevalence of prison rape, yet sometimes choose not to intervene and actually discourage complaints. In effect, some prison guards tolerate rape and sexual coercion as a means of making the prison population, particularly the more aggressive and troublesome segment, more manageable.

Thus, the one institution in which we have the almost unlimited right to control the lives of our fellow citizens and which is intended to represent the ultimate commitment to order and personal security, is too often deeply disorderly and ultimately insecure. The lesson for the individuals subjected to this system — including their friends, family members, and everyone else close enough to feel it breathing down their necks — is that our commitment to the moral values of order, lawfulness and security are mere hypocrisy. . . .

This condition of long prison sentences served in often undisciplined, dangerous and degrading circumstances may perhaps be related to the earlier part of our
criminal justice system which consists of the methods and procedures by which we
seek to prevent crimes, to catch those who commit crimes, and to determine the
guilt and punishment of those we catch. The two features I mention make up a system. The United States has elaborate — surely the most elaborate — procedures for
determining who will be punished, and yet we also have by far the largest prison
population of any industrialized country to which we would care to compare ourselves.

If there is a connection between these two aspects of the system, then it may be
seen as an enactment of Cesare Beccaria's formula that the efficacy of punishment
is a function of its severity, its swiftness and its certainty. On that hypothesis, if the
American criminal justice system has made punishment seem cumbersome, slow
and uncertain, then it is only by increasing the severity of the punishment that the
public feels that it will get the measure of deterrence to which it merits. I shall call
this the Beccaria hypothesis. Such a relationship between the two aspects of the system would also be dynamic, because one effect of such greater severity of penalty
would be even greater deployment of those procedures designed to assure the punishment was truly deserved and fairly imposed. . . . These procedural safeguards
then contribute to further delays and uncertainties, which only increases the public
pressure for severity.

4.   Some Distributional Consequences of the Criminal Justice System — Race and Drugs

MARC MAUER, YOUNG BLACK AMERICANS AND THE CRIMINAL JUSTICE SYSTEM: FIVE YEARS LATER

7-9 (1995)

We have documented the dramatically high rates of criminal justice control for
young black men. In many respects it would be quite surprising if these rates were
not high, given the social and economic circumstances and crime rates in their communities.

The growth of the criminal justice system in the past twenty years has coincided
with a host of economic disruptions and changes in social policy that have had profound effects on income distribution, employment and family structure. Since the
1970s, many urban areas have witnessed the decline of manufacturing, the expansion of low-wage service industries and the loss of a significant part of the middle
class tax base. Real wages have declined for most Americans during this period, with
a widening of the gap between rich and poor beginning in the 1980s. For black male
high school dropouts in their twenties, annual earnings fell by a full 50 percent from
1973 to 1989. Social service benefits such as mental health services and other supports have generally declined while the social problems that they address have been
exacerbated.

The impact of these changes on the African American community has resulted
from the intersection of race and class effects. Since African Americans are disproportionately represented in low-income urban communities, the effects of these

social ills are intensified. As Douglas Massey and Nancy Denton have illustrated, the persistence of housing segregation exacerbates the difficult life circumstances of these communities, contributing to extremely high rates of unemployment, poor schooling, and high crime rates. Over the years many researchers have examined the extent to which racial disparity within the criminal justice system can be explained by higher crime rates among blacks or other relevant factors. Historically, there can be little doubt about the prominent role played by race in criminal justice processing, given the history of lynching in the South, the development of chain gangs, and the well documented racial patterns involved in the imposition of the death penalty.

More recently, though, researchers have found that the evidence on these issues is mixed. While some studies have documented specific cases of racially unwarranted outcomes, much research has concluded that, with one significant exception, race plays a relatively minor role in sentencing and incarceration. Michael Tonry's review, for example, concludes that "for nearly a decade there has been a near consensus among scholars and policy analysts that most of the black punishment disproportions result not from racial bias or discrimination within the system but from patterns of black offending and of blacks' criminal records." Similarly, Alfred Blumstein's research has concluded that 76 percent of the racial disparity in prison populations is explained by higher rates of offending among blacks for serious offenses.

But both authors find, as Tonry indicates, that "Drug law enforcement is the conspicuous exception. Blacks are arrested and confined in numbers grossly out of line with their use or sale of drugs." Blumstein concludes that for drug offenses, fully half of the racial disproportions in prison are not explained by higher arrest rates.

While scholars will continue to study the relative influence of race within the criminal justice system, several key issues should not go unaddressed in explaining these disparities. First, as noted above, it is difficult to isolate the relative influence of race and class in public policy and decisionmaking. That is, to the extent that African Americans are overrepresented in the criminal justice system, to what degree is this a function of their being disproportionately low-income?

In its comprehensive examination of the problem of violence, the National Research Council reviewed existing studies of homicide victimization and class. The Council found that among low-income populations blacks had much higher rates of homicide victimization than whites but that among higher income groups, there was essentially no difference. The Council suggests that the more concentrated effects of inner-city poverty may contribute to a more serious breakdown of family and community support than in other low-income neighborhoods.

Studies of sentencing practices reveal that the current offense and the offender's prior record are the most significant factors determining a prison sentence. But if low-income youth are more subject to police scrutiny and have fewer counseling and treatment resources available to them than middle class adolescents, their youthful criminal activities will more likely result in a criminal record that will affect their chances of going to prison later on.

DAVID A. SKLANSKY, COCAINE, RACE AND EQUAL PROTECTION

47 Stan. L. Rev. 1283-1284, 1322 (1995)

Thousands of federal prisoners, including a few I helped prosecute, are currently serving long mandatory sentences for trafficking in crack cocaine. Nine out of ten of them are black. They were sentenced under laws that treat crack offenders far more harshly than the predominantly nonblack defendants caught with the more common, powder form of cocaine. Indeed, since 1986 federal crack defendants have received by law the same sentences imposed on defendants convicted of trafficking in one hundred times as much cocaine powder. Almost without exception, constitutional claims of unequal treatment raised by the crack defendants have been rejected out of hand. . . . What it tells us, I argue, is that there are certain important dimensions of racial injustice our law does not see.

There are many ways to evaluate a set of legal rules, in part because there are many things we want the law to do. The assumption underlying my approach is that one thing we should want legal rules to do is to take into account the important aspects of the situations they address. A set of rules that satisfies this requirement may yet be unfair, unworkable, or otherwise undesirable, but at least it will not be blind to its own major shortcomings. Nor will it tend to blind those who apply it.

These modest boasts, I suggest, cannot be made for equal protection doctrine in its current form. . . . I argue that the crack sentences raise troubling issues of fairness that we should want equal protection doctrine to address. These issues arise, I contend, even under the relatively narrow, process-oriented conception of equality that has dominated equal protection discussions in recent years.

Federal appellate courts have uniformly rejected these challenges, based on a largely mechanical application of the equal protection rules developed by the Supreme Court. I suggest that those rules systematically ignore, and lead judges and others to ignore, much of what is most troubling about the crack sentences: the evidence of at least unconscious racism on the part of Congress, the severity of the disparity between the average sentences imposed on black defendants and those imposed on whites, and the special need to avoid racial bias when meting out criminal punishment.

I offer some tentative thoughts about how equal protection doctrine became so feeble-sighted, and how it could be made more perceptive. Much of the problem . . . may arise from a doctrinal discussion carried out at too high a level of generality. For at least the past two decades the Supreme Court, along with many of its critics, has tended to assume that equal protection doctrine should remain relatively uniform regardless of factual context: the test for unconstitutional inequality in criminal sentencing, for example, should be the same as in civil service promotions. This universalist approach has strong theoretical advantages for constructing equal protection rules for an ideal society. In our real and imperfect society, however, the universalist approach has proved disastrous. It has blocked consideration of equal protection claims that should be taken seriously, and it has stifled the development of our collective understanding of equality.

Inequality tends, notoriously, to be accompanied and sustained by ways of thinking that render it imperceptible to those it benefits, and sometimes also to those it burdens. Many of these ways of thinking have been and remain jurisprudential. But law need not obscure more than it reveals. Indeed, one of the most important functions served on occasion by equal protection law has also been the simplest: identifying inequality and helping to deny it the protection of invisibility.

5. The Police

HERBERT PACKER, THE LIMITS OF THE CRIMINAL SANCTION

283-284 (1968)

The aggressively interventionist character of much of our criminal law thrusts the police into the role of snoopers and harassers. There is simply no way for the police to provide so much as a semblance of enforcement of laws against prostitution, sexual deviance, gambling, narcotics, and the like without widespread and visible intrusion into what people regard as their private lives. . . .

There are three generic types of police investigatory conduct that are so at odds with values of privacy and human dignity that we should resort to them only under the most exigent circumstances. They are physical intrusion, electronic surveillance, and the use of decoys. Although there arguably are circumstances under which each of the three can justifiably be employed, it is safe to say that any use of the criminal sanction that requires consistent use to be made of any of them should be suspect.

JEROME H. SKOLNICK & DAVID H. BAYLEY, COMMUNITY POLICING: ISSUES AND PRACTICES AROUND THE WORLD

49-52 (1988)

One way of comprehending a police department is through a table of organization. Such tables do offer useful, indeed indispensable, information. . . . But however indispensable they might be, tables of organization are limited in the information they offer — they don't tell us anything about the human side of the landscape they describe. The most significant features of police departments — their attitudes, internal divisions, belief systems, traditions, values — cannot be captured by the labelled boxes of a table of organization. . . .

How police officers learn to see the world around them and their role in it has come to be acknowledged by all scholars of police as an indispensable key to understanding the behavior and attitudes of police. "It is a commonplace of the now voluminous sociological literature on police operations and discretion," writes Robert Reiner, "that the rank-and-file officer is the primary determinant of policing where it really counts — on the street."[1] Moreover, . . . there are identifiable commonalities in police culture. . . .

[There is] the perception of *danger* which, although real, is typically magnified. Police officers are sometimes shot at and killed, of course. But the first line of defense against anticipated danger is *suspicion*, the development of a cognitive map of the social world to protect against signs of trouble, offense, and potential threat.

---

1. Robert Reiner, The Politics of the Police (Sussex, England: Wheatsheaf Books, 1985), p. 85.

The combination of danger and suspicion leads to a third feature of police culture, namely solidarity or *brotherhood*. Most police tend to socialize with other police. . . . There are any number of reasons for police solidarity. One is that police do not work normal hours. As emergency service workers, they often find themselves in the position of having to work nights, weekends, and other odd hours. Police work time is one of the major stresses of police work. When one's days off are Wednesday and Thursday, one becomes a deviant in the social world and is drawn to socialize with others who are similarly situated.

Another reason is that cops don't feel they fit into many worlds they might occupy. Every cop has a story about how they were stared at or otherwise adversely noted at a party or social occasion. This has been a special problem for young police in the 1970s and 1980s, when many of their peers might light up a joint and pass it around at a festive occasion. When faced with this dilemma, young police will find new friends — among police.

A third reason is the policeman's felt need for support from other police. Police are in fact in dangerous or potentially dangerous situations. When cops, looking for drug dealers, walk through a pool hall occupied by unfriendly young men, they depend on their partners for cover and assistance. But, as Mark Baker comments:

> The real reason most police officers socialize exclusively with other police officers is that they just don't trust the people they police — which is everybody who is not a cop. They know the public generally resents their authority and is fickle in its support of police policy and individual police officers. Older officers teach younger ones that it is best to avoid civilians. Civilians will try to "hurt" the cop in the end, they say.[2] . . .
>
> Students of the police have frequently noted the *machismo* qualities in the world of policing.[3]

Those who are attracted to the occupation are often very young, in chronological age and in maturity of temperament and judgment. . . . Recruits typically have athletic backgrounds, are sports minded, and are trained in self-defense. It is not uncommon for trainees to bulk the upper body — like football players, through weight lifting — so as to offer a more formidable appearance as a potential adversary in street encounters. They are also trained to handle a variety of offensive weapons, including deadly weapons. They are taught how to disable and kill people with their bare hands. No matter how many warnings may be offered by superiors about limitations on the use of force, its possible use is a central feature of the police role, and of the policemen's perceptions of themselves.

The training and permission in the use of force combined with the youth of police can well inhibit the capacity of a police officer to empathize with the situation of those being policed in ethnically diverse and low-income neighborhoods. . . . Senior officers are . . . less likely to be macho. . . .

When scholars write about the culture of policing, they usually have in mind the street-wise cop who follows a blue code of solidarity with fellow officers. Street-wise officers are likely to be cynical, tough, skeptical of innovation within management. By contrast, management cops tend to project a vision of policing that is more

2. Mark Baker, Cops: Their Lives in Their Own Words (New York: Fawcett, 1985), p. 211.
3. See Robert Reiner, The Politics of the Police, p. 99.

acceptable to the general public. This concept of two contrasting cultures of policing grew out of research conducted in New York City by Ianni and Ianni (1983), who developed a distinction between "street cops" and "management cops."

The "street-wise" cop is apt to approve of cutting corners, of throwing weight around on the street, of expressing the qualities of in-group solidarity referred to above. Management cops tend to be more legalistic, rule oriented, rational. . . . [S]ome street cops are hard-boiled cynics who deride innovations in policing as needless and unworkable incursions into the true and eternal role of the cop — the one they were socialized into as recruits by a sometimes venerated field training officer. These "street-wise" police, instead of gradually developing a broader perspective, taking advanced degrees in management, law, or criminal justice and so forth, reinforce their post-recruit identity. Unfortunately, this reinforcement sometimes develops into a lifelong occupational vision rooted in an abiding, even growing, bitterness that seems impervious to any sort of hope for change or new ideas.

The cynicism typifying these officers may of course also be present at higher levels of management — after all, . . . all American police begin their career as street cops, and the learning that takes place on the street is never outgrown by many. . . . The innovative management cop employs prior street experience to overcome the resistance of the street cop. By contrast, the self-conception of the traditional street cop remains firmly rooted in his earliest training experiences.

Elizabeth Ruess-Ianni summarizes the difference between the two cultures as follows, based on her study of the New York City Police Department:

> In a sense, the management cop culture represents those police who have decided that the old way of running a police department is finished (for a variety of external reasons, such as social pressures, economic realities of the city, increased visibility, minority recruitment, and growth in size that cannot be managed easily in the informal fashion of the old days) and they are "going to get in on the ground floor of something new." They do not, like the street cops, regard community relations, for example, as "Mickey Mouse bullshit," but as something that must be done for politically expedient reasons if not for social ones.[4]

DEBRA LIVINGSTON, POLICE DISCRETION AND THE QUALITY OF LIFE IN PUBLIC PLACES: COURTS, COMMUNITIES, AND THE NEW POLICING

97 Colum. L. Rev. 551, 557, 558-561, 670-671 (1997)

On the whole . . . legal scholars have paid inadequate attention to the reemergence of statutes, ordinances, and law enforcement measures aimed at public conduct and, more broadly, the quality of life in public spaces. Moreover, they have virtually ignored the implications of this new focus on quality-of-life concerns for a subject that it profoundly affects — namely, the scope of police discretion in street encounters. This inattention is surprising. After all, the aspiration to constrain police discretion on the street was in large part what prompted legal scholars over thirty years ago to mount a constitutional attack on the vagueness that characterized

---

4. Elizabeth Ruess-Ianni, The Two Cultures of Policing: Street Cops and Management Cops (Brunswick, N.J.: Transaction Books, New Brunswick, 1983), p. 121.

broadly-worded vagrancy, loitering, breach of peace, and disorderly conduct statutes and ordinances. This scholarly attack helped prompt the judicial invalidation
of many such laws and left police departments with considerably less authority to
intervene in street-order problems than citizens often assumed to be the case.

The ongoing transformation in the philosophy of American policing, from professional policing to community and problem-oriented policing, will likely continue
to fuel interest, among these scholars, in the "order maintenance" activities of
police. Such activities are aimed at preserving what might be termed the "neighborhood commons": both tangible community resources like parks, streets, play-
grounds, parking lots, and libraries, and the associated intangible interactions
among people, both organized and spontaneous, that take place around these
resources. Proponents of these new policing strategies have increasingly asserted, as
did Jane Jacobs over thirty years ago, that preservation of the neighborhood commons is essential to the vitality and well-being of American cities. . . .

For legal scholars, this new focus on addressing concerns with the quality of life
in public places raises anew the tension between traditional rule of law concepts and
the order maintenance activities of police. Police intervention to address neighborhood disorder is different, in kind, from the straightforward investigation, arrest,
and prosecution of those who have committed serious crimes. First, problems of disorder stem not so much from isolated behaviors as from the coming together of certain conditions: the congruence of behavior, its location and circumstances, its
frequency, its intent, and others' reactions. The behavior appropriate in a St.
Patrick's Day parade may thus be disruptive on a quiet, residential street. And while
a single person loitering on a street corner is unlikely to threaten neighborhood life,
a street on which many loiter to complete drug transactions, even apart from their
success, is likely to experience decline — to be seen by many as a place where children should not play, and where those with adequate resources should choose not to
live. But can the police be authorized to intervene on such a street by dispersing or
arresting those loiterers seemingly intent upon the narcotics trade? And can they be
trusted to identify those contexts in which intervention is appropriate — that is, to
distinguish the quiet residential Sunday morning from St. Patrick's Day on Main
Street? Second, police intervention to address neighborhood order is often invisible
to formal legal processes, since intervention often begins — and ends — with an
admonition to "knock it off" or requests to "quiet down" or "move along." Should
police intervene in this way? Should they intervene except by employing their
resources to enforce laws against serious crime?

Contrary to the implications of some scholarship in the police literature, the
police cannot perform substantial order maintenance tasks without legal authority.
At the same time, the many new laws addressing problems of public disorder, even
those laws that are far more specific than ones struck down in the 1960s and 1970s,
raise many of the same concerns that led courts of that period to invalidate public
order laws for vagueness. Courts have thus been tempted to invoke the open texture
of vagueness review to facially invalidate even reasonably specific public order
laws — a temptation that, when not resisted, retards positive changes in American
policing. While it plays an important role in pruning the legal code of outright del-
egations of authority to police to maintain public order as they deem appropriate,
the void-for-vagueness doctrine is itself an inadequate and even potentially destructive mechanism for constraining police discretion in the performance of order

maintenance tasks. Courts cannot "solve" the problem of police discretion by invalidating reasonably specific public order laws — as some have attempted — without seriously impairing legitimate community efforts to enhance the quality of neighborhood life. Nevertheless, because the recent legislative trend does raise many of the same concerns that led courts of the 1960s and 1970s to invalidate vague laws, there is a need for renewed focus upon those political, administrative, and other "subconstitutional" controls that might assist in constraining arbitrary police enforcement. The philosophies of community and problem-oriented policing posit a new way of thinking about police and about the exercise of police discretion that themselves suggest ways in which these controls might work.

Policing, like judging, is a complex task, and the prospects and promise of the new policing reforms must at this juncture be deemed uncertain. Policing is not the simple enforcement of law, though law is important to the police role; policing that ignores the ebb and flow of community life does so only at grave peril to both police and the people for whom they work. But there are real and serious questions here. Can police departments identify those among their number "inclined toward self-directed information gathering and analysis, capable of inventive planning, and motivated to work for long-range solutions," and then use such personnel in problem solving? Can departments walk the tightrope between responsiveness to community concerns and outright deterioration in the ideal of evenhanded enforcement associated with the rule of law? "Perhaps it is better in the long run," as one scholar recently put it, "to say that the law should be equally enforced — even though equal enforcement is often unrealistic — than to say that the law should be used by the police to maintain order acceptable to local communities[.]" But if there is promise in these policing reforms, there is also peril.

Courts have little capacity — very little capacity — to constrain police and to control the discretion that they inevitably exercise on streets, in neighborhoods, in the precincts where patrol officers are given their tours of duty, and in the administrative offices in which police enforcement policies are hammered out. The reforms of the 1960s and 1970s established principles from which no thoughtful person now seeks retreat: that police cannot be delegated authority to maintain order as they see fit and that rules governing the conduct of citizens on the street must set forth intelligible limits on enforcement authority. These reforms, however, could not eliminate the significant discretion that police have in order maintenance tasks, nor could they promote the beneficial exercise of that discretion in ways that might enhance rather than imperil the public life of a community. Interpreted too broadly, the open texture of these constitutional reforms could threaten public order by invalidating the reasonable efforts of communities to regulate matters like unreasonable noise, aggressive panhandling, or loitering on a street corner to solicit customers for the sale of drugs. At the same time, the reforms could not ensure that police departments acted fairly, with restraint, and with an abiding respect for the rights of individuals and for constitutional values. The reforms could not solve the problem of police discretion.

Nor can neighborhoods and their police. But perhaps communities and police departments, prompted by the problems that beset them and the new philosophies that point in a different direction, might take up the task — an ongoing one — of better managing police discretion. . . . There is a dense complexity to the problem of public order with which communities are now grappling and to the enduring problem of controlling the police. Perhaps some views from the bottom up — views that begin with the recognition that neighborhoods and police departments will succeed or fail in their efforts to deal with local problems at the local level, in communities and in neighborhoods, where laws are passed and police policies are pursued — might be in order.

6. The Lawyers and the Trial Courts

PAUL B. WICE, CHAOS IN THE COURTHOUSE: THE INNER WORKINGS OF THE URBAN CRIMINAL COURTS

21-24, 63-65 (1985)

The first problem faced by all cities visited[10] was inadequate staffing. Although particular agencies or institutions within each city's criminal justice system may have differing levels of understaffing, all were handicapped in some degree by personnel shortages. . . . These shortages were documented by federal commission studies in 1967 and 1973.[2] . . .

. . . The judges appeared to be most understaffed at the earlier stages of the adjudicative process — initial appearance, preliminary hearing and arraignment. The arraignment court may also be responsible for deciding pretrial motions, scheduling trials, and conducting pre-sentencing hearings in addition to accepting guilty pleas. By the trial stage, the staffing shortages had generally abated to a tolerable level in most cities. . . .

Closely related to the staffing problems, is the serious backlog of cases. . . . The most common method criminal courts utilize in dealing with their caseload and delay problems is the practice of plea bargaining. Despite the negative connotations of this term, it describes a negotiating process which has been taking place within our nation's court systems . . . for many decades. A *plea bargain* is simply an agreement between the defendant (with the advice of his attorney) and the prosecutor, that in exchange for a plea of guilty, he will receive favorable consideration by the court. This consideration usually takes the form of being charged with a less serious crime, which will usually result in a lighter sentence or receiving the minimum punishment allowable for the originally-charged offense. The rationale behind this exchange of favors is that the defendant is given the lesser sentence because of his cooperation with the court in choosing not to go to trial and thereby saving the city a great deal of time and expense. . . .

. . . Various studies have indicated that approximately 75 percent of all defendants indicted for felonies plead guilty.[5] . . .

Since nearly two thirds of all defendants accused of committing a felony are indigent, the state is constitutionally obligated to provide the overwhelming majority of

---

10. This book is based on the study of criminal courts in 15 major jurisdictions over a 12-year period. Chaos in the Courthouse 1. — EDS.

2. President's Commission on Law Enforcement and the Administration of Justice, Task Force Report: The Courts (Washington, D.C.: Government Printing Office, 1967); National Advisory Commission on Criminal Justice Goals and Standards, Courts (Washington, D.C.: Government Printing Office, 1973).

5. Pasqual DeVito. An Experiment in the Use of Court Statistics, Judicature. 56 (August/September, 1972), p. 56.

defendants with assistance of counsel. In nearly every city visited, the local courts decided to establish a public defender program in order to meet this mandate. . . .

The two alternatives to the public defender plan, for indigent defendants, are either to rely entirely upon an assigned counsel system — privately-appointed members of the bar who are typically paid on a per hour basis — or a mixed system in which the courts have decided to limit the percentage of cases which the local public defender can handle, and reserve the sizable remainder for private attorneys through an assigned counsel system. Large cities rarely find the assigned counsel system cost-effective (although it is most popular in small cities and rural areas). . . .

In most cities, the defendant first notifies the judge of his indigent status and desire to have a court-appointed lawyer at his initial appearance. . . . The judge rarely inquires into the financial capabilities of the defendant. . . . Most judges seem to feel that if a defendant is willing to settle for a public defender, then he is not likely to be in possession of the funds necessary to hire a private attorney. Rarely is a representative from the public defender's office present at this initial appearance, except in an administrative capacity to commence the paperwork. . . .

Two of the major frustrations facing the indigent defendant who is being represented by a public defender are apparent very early in the process. The first, and for many defendants, the most disheartening, is the absence of choice of attorney. . . .

The second frustration, exacerbating the already noted absence of choice, is the assembly-line system of defense in which the indigent defendant may be assisted by a different attorney at nearly every stage of the proceedings up to the arraignment. This means that the indigent will briefly meet with three or four different public defenders for a few minutes before each of his pretrial proceedings. It is also likely that interviews and meetings outside of court may be with an assortment of different public defenders. . . .

For many defendants, the assembly-line style of operation is another indication that the public defender's office is simply an uncaring bureaucracy which is both financially and emotionally subservient to the criminal court judiciary. . . .

Although I am sure that their clientele would vociferously disagree, I do not believe that the quality of public defender services has suffered. After conducting national studies of both public defender programs and private criminal lawyers, I am in agreement with the findings of nearly all of the empirical research which concluded that the ultimate case dispositions are not significantly affected by the type of defense.[31] I still concur with the personal conclusions reached in 1978 that

> although the middle 50 percent of public defenders and private attorneys were operating at similar levels of ability and achieving nearly identical results, there were marked differences at the extremes. Thus it was generally agreed by the criminal lawyers that the top 25 percent of private attorneys were clearly superior to the best public defenders, while the bottom 25 percent of the public defenders were believed to be significantly better than the bottom group of private attorneys. [Paul Wice, Criminal Lawyers: An Endangered Species. Beverly Hills, Sage Publications, 1978, p. 201.]

. . . [T]he public defender office may even offer some distinct advantages unavailable to certain private practitioners. Most public defenders have access to

---

31. Jean Taylor et al., An Analysis of Defense Counsel in the Processing of Felony Defendants in San Diego, Denver Law Journal (1972), p. 233.

their own law libraries, as well as limited use of investigators. Additionally, the public defender is clearly a criminal law specialist. Finally, because of his continual involvement with the prosecutors and judiciary, the public defender can frequently develop a positive working relationship in which the exchange of favors, so necessary to greasing the squeaky wheel of justice, can directly benefit the indigent defendant.

BRUCE JACKSON, LAW AND DISORDER: CRIMINAL JUSTICE IN AMERICA

81 (1984)

Private counsel retained by wealthy clients may assume their clients are innocent, civil rights lawyers representing defendants in politically motivated cases may assume their clients are innocent, but most public defender and court-appointed attorneys — and they handle the greatest bulk of the criminal cases — assume their clients are guilty. "If he's not guilty of this one, he's guilty of one just like it," one public defense lawyer said to me. "He knows it and I know it. Why go up there and argue? Almost everybody in these tanks is guilty of something. Everybody knows that. My job is to see that these people get out of here with as little jail time as possible. You don't win anything in this job because none of these clients are winners." The only time a defendant without funds gets extensive trial and appeal representation is when his case has political aspects and it is picked up by an organization willing to fund it or by an attorney who is not concerned with money. There are not many such organizations and there are not many such attorneys.

Most criminal justice lawyers work as partners with the court and the prosecutors, not as unequivocal representatives of the defendants. The defendants come and go, but the attorney's relationships with the other officers of the court continue for years.

ABRAHAM S. BLUMBERG, THE PRACTICE OF LAW AS CONFIDENCE GAME: ORGANIZATIONAL CO-OPTATION OF A PROFESSION

1 Law & Soc'y Rev. 15, 18-26, 29-31 (No. 2, 1967)

The overwhelming majority of convictions in criminal cases (usually over 90 percent) are not the product of a combative, trial-by-jury process at all, but instead merely involve the sentencing of the individual after a negotiated, bargained-for plea of guilty has been entered. . . .

Organizational goals and discipline impose a set of demands and conditions of practice on the respective professions in the criminal court, to which they respond by abandoning their ideological and professional commitments to the accused client, in the service of these higher claims of the court organization. All court personnel, including the accused's own lawyer, tend to be co-opted to become agent-mediators who help the accused redefine his situation and restructure his perceptions concomitant with a plea of guilty.

Of all the occupational roles in the court the only private individual who is officially recognized as having a special status and concomitant obligations is the lawyer. His legal status is that of "an officer of the court" and he is held to a standard of ethical performance and duty to his client as well as to the court. This obligation is thought to be far higher than that expected of ordinary individuals occupying the various occupational statuses in the court community. However, lawyers, whether privately retained or of the legal-aid, public defender variety, have close and continuing relations with the prosecuting office and the court itself through discreet relations with the judges via their law secretaries or "confidential" assistants. Indeed, lines of communication, influence and contact with those offices, as well as with the Office of the Clerk of the court, Probation Division, and with the press, are essential to present and prospective requirements of criminal law practice. Similarly, the subtle involvement of the press and other mass media in the court's organizational network is not readily discernible to the casual observer. Accused persons come and go in the court system schema, but the structure and its occupational incumbents remain to carry on their respective career, occupational and organizational enterprises. The individual stridencies, tensions, and conflicts a given accused person's case may present to all the participants are overcome, because the formal and informal relations of all the groups in the court setting require it. The probability of continued future relations and interaction must be preserved at all costs.

This is particularly true of the "lawyer regulars," i.e., those defense lawyers, who by virtue of their continuous appearances in behalf of defendants, tend to represent the bulk of a criminal court's non-indigent case workload, and those lawyers who are not "regulars," who appear almost casually in behalf of an occasional client. Some of the "lawyer regulars" are highly visible as one moves about the major urban centers of the nation, their offices line the back streets of the courthouses, at times sharing space with bondsmen. Their political "visibility" in terms of local club house ties, reaching into the judge's chambers and prosecutor's office, are also deemed essential to successful practitioners. . . .

. . . The accused's lawyer has far greater professional, economic, intellectual and other ties to the various elements of the court system than he does to his own client. In short, the court is a closed community.

This is more than just the case of the usual "secrets" of bureaucracy which are fanatically defended from an outside view. Even all elements of the press are zealously determined to report on that which will not offend the board of judges, the prosecutor, probation, legal-aid, or other officials, in return for privileges and courtesies granted in the past and to be granted in the future. Rather than any view of the matter in terms of some variation of a "conspiracy" hypothesis, the simple explanation is one of an ongoing system handling delicate tensions, managing the trauma produced by law enforcement and administration, and requiring almost pathological distrust of "outsiders" bordering on group paranoia.

The hostile attitude toward "outsiders" is in large measure engendered by a defensiveness itself produced by the inherent deficiencies of assembly line justice, so characteristic of our major criminal courts. Intolerably large caseloads of defendants which must be disposed of in an organizational context of limited resources and personnel, potentially subject the participants in the court community to harsh scrutiny from appellate courts, and other public and private sources of condemnation. As a consequence, an almost irreconcilable conflict is posed in terms of intense pressures to process large numbers of cases on the one hand, and the stringent ideological and legal requirements of "due process of law," on the other hand. A rather tenuous resolution of the dilemma has emerged in the shape of a large variety of bureaucratically ordained and controlled "work crimes," short cuts, deviations, and outright rule violations adopted as court practice in order to meet production norms. Fearfully anticipating criticism on ethical as well as legal grounds, all the significant participants in the court's social structure are bound into an organized system of complicity. This consists of a work arrangement in which the patterned, covert, informal breaches, and evasions of "due process" are institutionalized, but are, nevertheless, denied to exist.

These institutionalized evasions will be found to occur to some degree, in all criminal courts. Their nature, scope and complexity are largely determined by the size of the court, and the character of the community in which it is located, e.g., whether it is a large, urban institution, or a relatively small rural county court. In addition, idiosyncratic, local conditions may contribute to a unique flavor in the character and quality of the criminal law's administration in a particular community. However, in most instances a variety of stratagems are employed — some subtle, some crude, in effectively disposing of what are often too large caseloads. A wide variety of coercive devices are employed against an accused-client, couched in a depersonalized, instrumental, bureaucratic version of due process of law, and which are in reality a perfunctory obeisance to the ideology of due process. These include some very explicit pressures which are exerted in some measure by all court personnel, including judges, to plead guilty and avoid trial. In many instances the sanction of a potentially harsh sentence is utilized as the visible alternative to pleading guilty, in the case of recalcitrants. Probation and psychiatric reports are "tailored" to organizational needs, or are at least responsive to the court organization's requirements for the refurbishment of a defendant's social biography, consonant with his new status. A resourceful judge can, through his subtle domination of the proceedings, impose his will on the final outcome of a trial. Stenographers and clerks, in their function as record keepers, are on occasion pressed into service in support of a judicial need to "rewrite" the record of a courtroom event. Bail practices are usually employed for purposes other than simply assuring a defendant's presence on the date of a hearing in connection with his case. Too often, the discretionary power as to bail is part of the arsenal of weapons available to collapse the resistance of an accused person. The foregoing is a most cursory examination of some of the more prominent "short cuts" available to any court organization. . . .

The real key to understanding the role of defense counsel in a criminal case is to be found in the area of the fixing of the fee to be charged and its collection. The problem of fixing and collecting the fee tends to influence to a significant degree the criminal court process itself, and not just the relationship of the lawyer and his client. In essence, a lawyer-client "confidence game" is played. . . . Legal service lends itself particularly well to confidence games. . . .

. . . [M]uch legal activity, whether it is at the lowest or highest "white shoe" law firm levels, is of the brokerage, agent, sales representative, lobbyist type of activity, in which the lawyer acts for someone else in pursuing the latter's interests and designs. The service is intangible. . . .

. . . Defense lawyers condition even the most obtuse clients to recognize that there is a firm interconnection between fee payment and the zealous exercise of professional expertise, secret knowledge, and organizational "connections" in their behalf. Lawyers, therefore, seek to keep their clients in a proper state of tension, and to arouse in them the precise edge of anxiety which is calculated to encourage prompt fee payment. Consequently, the client attitude in the relationship between defense counsel and an accused is in many instances a precarious admixture of hostility, mistrust, dependence, and sycophancy. By keeping his client's anxieties aroused to the proper pitch, and establishing a seemingly causal relationship between a requested fee and the accused's ultimate extrication from his onerous difficulties, the lawyer will have established the necessary preliminary groundwork to assure a minimum of haggling over the fee and its eventual payment.

In varying degrees, as a consequence, all law practice involves a manipulation of the client and a stage management of the lawyer-client relationship so that at least an *appearance* of help and service will be forthcoming. This is accomplished in a variety of ways, often exercised in combination with each other. At the outset, the lawyer-professional employs with suitable variation a measure of sales-puff which may range from an air of unbounding self-confidence, adequacy, and dominion over events, to that of complete arrogance. This will be supplemented by the affectation of a studied, faultless mode of personal attire. In the larger firms, furnishings and office trappings will serve as the backdrop to help in impression management and client intimidation. In all firms, solo or large scale, an access to secret knowledge, and to the seats of power and influence is inferred, or presumed to a varying degree as the basic vendible commodity of the practitioners. . . .

The fee is often collected in stages, each installment usually payable prior to a necessary court appearance required during the course of an accused's career journey. At each stage, in his interviews and communications with the accused, or in addition, with members of his family, if they are helping with the fee payment, the lawyer employs an air of professional confidence and "inside-dopesterism" in order to assuage anxieties on all sides. He makes the necessary bland assurances, and in effect manipulates his client, who is usually willing to do and say the things, true or not, which will help his attorney extricate him. Since the dimensions of what he is essentially selling, organizational influence and expertise, are not technically and precisely measurable, the lawyer can make extravagant claims of influence and secret knowledge with impunity. Thus, lawyers frequently claim to have inside knowledge in connection with information in the hands of the D.A., police, probation officials or to have access to these functionaries. Factually, they often do, and need only to exaggerate the nature of their relationships with them to obtain the desired effective impression upon the client. But, as in the genuine confidence game, the victim who has participated is loathe to do anything which will upset the lesser plea which his lawyer has "conned" him into accepting.

In effect, in his role as double agent, the criminal lawyer performs an extremely vital and delicate mission for the court organization and the accused. Both principals are anxious to terminate the litigation with a minimum of expense and damage to each other. There is no other personage or role incumbent in the total court structure more strategically located, who by training and in terms of his own requirements, is more ideally suited to do so than the lawyer. In recognition of this, judges will cooperate with attorneys in many important ways. For example, they will adjourn the case of an accused in jail awaiting plea or sentence if the attorney requests such action. While explicitly this may be done for some innocuous and seemingly valid reason, the tacit purpose is that pressure is being applied by the attorney for the collection of his fee, which he knows will probably not be forthcoming if the case is concluded. Judges are aware of this tactic on the part of lawyers, who, by requesting an adjournment, keep an accused incarcerated a while longer as a not too subtle method of dunning a client for payment. However, the judges will go along with this, on the ground that important ends are being served. Often, the only end served is to protect a lawyer's fee.

The judge will help an accused's lawyer in still another way. He will lend the official aura of his office and courtroom so that a lawyer can stage manage an impression of an "all out" performance for the accused in justification of his fee. The judge and other court personnel will serve as a backdrop for a scene charged with dramatic fire, in which the accused's lawyer makes a stirring appeal in his behalf. With a show of restrained passion, the lawyer will intone the virtues of the accused and recite the social deprivations which have reduced him to his present state. The speech varies somewhat, depending on whether the accused has been convicted after trial or has pleaded guilty. In the main, however, the incongruity, superficiality, and ritualistic character of the total performance is underscored by a visibly impassive, almost bored reaction on the part of the judge and other members of the court retinue.

Afterward, there is a hearty exchange of pleasantries between the lawyer and district attorney, wholly out of context in terms of the supposed adversary nature of the preceding events. The fiery passion in defense of his client is gone, and the lawyers for both sides resume their offstage relations, chatting amiably and perhaps including the judge in their restrained banter. No other aspect of their visible conduct so effectively serves to put even a casual observer on notice, that these individuals have claims upon each other. These seemingly innocuous actions are indicative of continuing organizational and informal relations, which, in their intricacy and depth, range far beyond any priorities or claims a particular defendant may have. . . .

RODNEY J. UPHOFF, THE CRIMINAL DEFENSE LAWYER AS EFFECTIVE NEGOTIATOR: A SYSTEMIC APPROACH

2 Clinical L. Rev. 73-94 (1995)

I. Understanding the Context: The Pressure to Plea Bargain

A. Systemic Pressures to Plead Guilty . . .

Blumberg undoubtedly is correct that there are criminal defense lawyers of limited ability, zeal or professional commitment who do manipulate their clients into ill-advised plea bargains. Some lawyers do promote their own interests at the expense of their client's best interest. Moreover, Blumberg's analysis highlights the substantial systemic pressures on criminal defense lawyers to behave in a cooperative, non-adversarial manner. And yet, Blumberg's condemnation of criminal defense lawyers as double agents sweeps too broadly. There are simply too many dedicated defense lawyers, too much litigation and too many other variables affecting client decisionmaking to conclude that manipulative, complicitous criminal defense lawyers are the cause of most plea bargaining. . . .

2. The Pressures on Defendants to Plead Guilty

The decision of many defendants to plead guilty is the product of a number of individual forces and systemic factors which have little to do with the behavior of criminal defense lawyers. Indeed, the zeal or even the availability of counsel may have little [effect] on the defendant's decision. Simply put, a significant number of defendants just want to plead guilty. Few criminal defendants, even those who are innocent, actually want to go to trial. Many who are accused of a crime do not even consider going to trial a viable option.

Criminal defendants offer a variety of reasons to explain their reluctance to go to trial and their interest in a plea bargain. Internal as well as external pressures may shape the defendant's attitude. For many defendants, the prospect of actually going through a trial and having to take the witness stand is very intimidating. Fear, embarrassment, or the risk of adverse publicity drives some defendants to negotiate and to avoid trial. Unquestionably, the risk of a jail sentence or the prospects of a harsher sentence also deters many defendants from viewing a trial as a desirable alternative to pleading guilty. For some, a pessimistic or fatalistic mind-set dampens any enthusiasm for going to trial. Standing up to the state by taking a case to trial is similar to taking on city hall, a Sisyphean task few are willing to readily embrace.

Some defendants, of course, have been through the system before and these prior experiences significantly influence their attitude toward plea bargaining. For some, especially defendants of color, their perception that the system is heavily stacked against them adversely affects their view of a trial as a viable option. For other defendants, many criminal cases just do not seem to be "that big a deal" or are "nothing really to worry about." For these defendants, the time and trouble it would take to fight a particular charge is outweighed by the inconvenience the defendant feels. It is easier and quicker simply to plead guilty and to get the matter resolved rather than spend time going to trial even if the charge is baseless or the prosecution's evidence is very weak. Thus, the defendant's attitude about the charge, his or her other responsibilities and time commitments, financial resources, past experiences and perceptions about the criminal justice system all affect the defendant's ability to resist the pressure to enter a negotiated plea.

Some defendants readily admit their guilt and are reluctant to do anything other than acknowledge responsibility for the crime or crimes committed. Sometimes this reaction is fed by the defendant's religious or moral feelings. In other instances, the defendant's "get it over with" attitude is spurred on by concerns that contesting a charge will have a negative effect on the defendant's family, financial situation or employment status. Such defendants may be unaware of or fail to consider the long-term consequences of a hasty decision to plead guilty. . . .

Many defendants, especially those who have already been through the system, recognize that the criminal justice system encourages the resolution of cases through plea bargaining. The prospect of securing a more lenient sentence, in fact, drives many defendants to want to plead guilty. The defendant who received a significant break in an earlier case may be particularly anxious to enter into a plea bargain. Or the defendant may be savvy enough to know that it is advantageous to deal quickly with the police or prosecutor before other potential defendants or coconspirators do. Indeed, a lawyer bent on finding the facts in an initial interview may be brusquely instructed or directed by a seasoned defendant just to "cut a deal." . . .

Notwithstanding counsel's advice, it is often the defendant, not the so-called "double agent" defense lawyer, who is insistent on working out a plea bargain. In many cases defendants simply recognize that our overburdened criminal justice system has been structured to discourage them from going to trial. Too few criminal defendants can really afford to pay the cost of mounting an effective defense. In some jurisdictions, access to appointed counsel, the quality of indigent defenders and the resources provided to support the defense of the indigent affect the extent to which defendants have a meaningful right to go to trial. The unrepresented defendant or the accused able to scrape up only a minimal retainer faces substantial pressure to plead guilty. Take, for example, the defendant who has used his last $500 to bail himself out and to retain counsel. His lawyer threatens to withdraw unless the defendant pays an additional $2,000 for a trial. Rather than fight the charge, the defendant pleads guilty to save the $2,000 fee. Or he accepts the proffered plea bargain because he simply cannot raise any more money. Thus, economic pressures often eliminate the criminal defendant's right to trial as a viable option.

Those pressures intensify for the defendant who is held in jail unable to make bail. Many defendants, especially first offenders, will agree to almost anything to get out of jail. It is all too common for defendants to enter a guilty plea merely as the quickest means to secure their release from jail. Accordingly, defense counsel's ability to secure her client's release on bond is likely to minimize pressure on the defendant to agree to a poor plea bargain, thereby significantly improving counsel's negotiating position.

3. Judicial and Prosecutorial Pressures

Both trial judges and appellate courts contribute to the systemic pressure on defendants to plea bargain. Judges are increasingly under fire by the public and state legislators who clamor for tougher sentences and an end to the "coddling" of criminals. Trial judges, many of whom are elected, cannot grant defendants too many sentencing concessions without being labeled "soft on crime." Yet, overflowing court dockets and prison overcrowding create conflicting pressure on judges to move cases efficiently while still imposing tough sentences. Plea bargaining enables trial judges to resolve large numbers of cases in an orderly, timely fashion that would not be possible if more cases actually went to trial.

Criminal defendants also are discouraged from challenging questionable rulings on suppression issues or taking marginal cases to trial because appellate review often is a lengthy process in which defendants enjoy only limited success. In addition, the expanded application of the harmless error doctrine, the diminution of the exclusionary rule, the narrowing of the scope of federal habeas corpus relief and the difficulty of showing ineffective assistance of counsel also encourage defendants to settle their cases. The message sent to defendants and defense lawyers, whether intended or not, is to cooperate and not litigate.

Trial judges send a similar message to defendants contemplating a trial: go to trial and if you lose, you will get a stiffer sentence. Even if the defendant is initially unaware of this reality, defense counsel when discussing the defendant's options usually will raise this consideration. The uncertainty of success at trial, combined with the real prospect of a harsher penalty should the defendant lose, makes the trial option for many defendants a risky gamble. Thus, the defendant's fear of jail not only may seriously undercut counsel's ability to project a credible threat to go to trial, but also cripple the client's will to hold out for a better bargain.

Like their indigent defender counterparts, most prosecutors' offices lack sufficient resources to adequately investigate, prepare and try many cases. Prosecutors, therefore, also are subject to considerable pressure to settle the vast majority of cases. Unlike defense lawyers, however, prosecutors retain considerable power and discretion in determining when cases are brought, which cases are dismissed or pushed and how cases are ultimately settled. Courts have given prosecutors broad latitude both in the charging decision and in the bargaining process. The prosecutor often can select from a wide range of potential charges growing out of any criminal episode, which permits the prosecutor to charge one or multiple counts. In addition, prosecutors generally are free to offer concessions or to threaten additional punishment to force defendants to accept some negotiated deal. Prosecutors are well aware of the allure of a "no jail" recommendation and use it frequently to entice a defendant into a guilty plea in a marginal case, especially if the offer includes a reduction to a misdemeanor charge. Because a prosecutor's sentencing recommendations are readily accepted by most judges and the prosecutor is vested with virtually unfettered charging discretion, it is the prosecutor who really is in the position to dictate the level of punishment meted out to most defendants. . . .

B. RESISTING THE PRESSURE TO CONFORM

The culture in any particular criminal justice system ultimately influences how plea bargaining is conducted in that jurisdiction and how many cases actually go to trial. If in a particular jurisdiction few defense lawyers file motions or take cases to trial, the pressure on other defense lawyers and defendants to follow suit is much greater than in a jurisdiction in which defendants regularly exercise their right to go to trial. A defense lawyer in a jurisdiction in which prosecutors rarely have to make any concessions because few cases are tried may find it more difficult to extract reasonable concessions from the prosecutor, even though the state's case is weak, than defense counsel in a county with a vigorous defense bar. The prosecutor in a county with a timid defense bar may single out the more zealous defense lawyer and refuse to provide her clients the kind of concessions generally provided the more pliant defense lawyers. Defense counsel who stands up to fight in one case may be concerned that the prosecutor will take it out on her other clients. . . .

Thus, the conscientious defense lawyer is often in a precarious position. Defense counsel must attempt to provide zealous representation in a system geared to the efficient resolution of cases which, for the most part, means entering into negotiated settlements. It is the criminal defense lawyer who vigorously investigates the facts, researches the law, raises appropriate and creative motions, demonstrates a willingness to go to trial and competently handles the trial who is providing the representation demanded by the ethical rules and ABA Standards. Yet, counsel who seeks to gain an advantage for her client in the plea bargaining process by engaging in legitimate tactics — such as filing and aggressively litigating discovery motions, suppression motions, requests for jury instructions, and the like — runs the risk of alienating judges and prosecutors primarily concerned about efficiently disposing of the mass of cases on their crowded dockets. Similarly, a good defense lawyer may want to respond to a prosecutor's inappropriate or unjustified threats in the plea bargaining process by refusing to continue to negotiate and going to trial. She may want to do so not only to secure justice for her individual client but also to demonstrate her willingness to go to trial rather than accept a poor plea bargain. Defense counsel may find herself, however, forced to agree to a poor plea bargain despite her efforts, recommendations and desires because ultimately the choice of accepting a proffered settlement is the client's.

It is important to recognize, then, that it is the defendant's interests, attitude and desires, together with various systemic pressures, that frequently put criminal defense lawyers in a difficult and frustrating position. Defense lawyers all too often find themselves representing an unsympathetic defendant with a lengthy criminal record in a case without any apparent defense. The zealous advocate with a case in which the defendant has little or no leverage confronts a daunting challenge. Many defense lawyers have endured the unpleasant task of going to negotiate on behalf of an unemployed recidivist who simply wants to plead guilty and "bargaining" with a particularly hard-headed prosecutor who is perfectly aware that the state's case is virtually unassailable. In such a case, defense counsel may feel more like a beggar than a bargainer, left with little more than the unenviable chore of imploring a mean-spirited prosecutor to be fair or reasonable. . . .

7. The Supreme Court

ANTHONY AMSTERDAM, THE SUPREME COURT AND THE RIGHTS OF SUSPECTS IN CRIMINAL CASES

45 N.Y.U. L. Rev. 785, 785-794 (1970)

The impression is widespread that decisions of the Supreme Court of the United States during the past decade have vastly enlarged the rights of criminal suspects and defendants. That impression is not wholly unfounded, but the broad form in which it is generally entertained ignores very significant limitations upon what the Supreme Court can do, and what it has in fact done, to create and enforce such rights. . . .

According to Par Lagerkvist,[1] the role of the Pythia or priestess of the Oracle at Delphi was of incomparable grandeur and futility. This young maiden was periodically lashed to a tripod above a noisome abyss, where her god dwelt and from which nauseating odors rose and assaulted her. There, the god entered her body and soul, so that she thrashed madly and uttered inspired, incomprehensible cries. The cries were interpreted by the corps of professional priests of the Oracle, and their interpretations were, of course, for mere mortals the words of the god. The Pythia experienced incalculable ecstasy and degradation; she was viewed with utmost reverence and abhorrence; to her every utterance, enormous importance attached; but, from the practical point of view, what she said did not matter much.

On its tripod atop the system of American criminal justice, the Supreme Court of the United States performs in remarkably Pythian fashion. Occasional ill-smelling cases are wafted up to it by the fortuities of litigation, evoking its inspired and spasmodic reaction. Neither the records nor the issues presented by these cases give the Court a comprehensive view — or even a reliably representative view — of the

1. P. Lagerkvist, The Sibyl (N. Walford transl., 1958).

doings in the dark pit in which criminal suspects, police and the functionaries of the criminal courts wrestle with each other in the sightless ooze. It is not surprising, then, that in these cases the Court should be incapable of announcing judgments which respond coherently to the real problems of the pit. No matter. The significance of the Court's pronouncements—their power to shake the assembled faithful with awful tremors of exultation and loathing—does not depend upon their correspondence with reality. Once uttered, these pronouncements will be interpreted by arrays of lower appellate courts, trial judges, magistrates, commissioners and police officials. *Their* interpretation of the Pythia, for all practical purposes, will become the word of god.

To some extent this Pythian metaphor describes the Supreme Court's functioning in all the fields of law with which the Court deals. But the metaphor has special cogency with regard to the field of criminal procedure and particularly procedure that regulates the rights of suspects in their dealings with police prior to the time of the suspect's first court appearance. Let me explain why this is so and some of the implications of that fact.

First, the Supreme Court, like any other court, lacks the sort of supervisory power over the practices of the police that is possessed by the chief of police or the district attorney. The Court can only review those practices, and thus can only define the rights of suspects subject to those practices, when the practices become an issue in a lawsuit. There are several ways in which police practices may become the subject of a lawsuit. An individual who thinks that he has been mistreated by the police may file a civil action for damages or, in limited circumstances, for an injunction, complaining of false arrest or false imprisonment or assault or the violation of his constitutional rights. But such lawsuits are very rare, and until recently were so rare as to be insignificant, because the obstacles to their maintenance are formidable. Most persons mistreated by the police are marginal types who are quite happy, once out of police clutches, to let well enough alone. Few have the knowledge or resources to obtain the services of a lawyer. Many lawyers who might otherwise be available to them cannot afford to tangle with the police because these lawyers depend upon the good will of the police in other cases (e.g., to protect a divorce client who is being badgered by her estranged husband or to reduce charges against a criminal client) or upon police testimony in other cases (e.g., motor vehicle accident cases) or upon more dubious police services (e.g., referrals).

Juries are not sympathetic to suits against the police; policemen are seldom sufficiently solvent to make verdicts against them worth the trouble to obtain; even fairly solid citizens who sue policemen may have to fear reprisals in the form of traffic tickets, refusals to give needed aid and similar harassments. As a result, civil suits seldom bring police practices under judicial scrutiny. And for reasons too obvious to detail, criminal charges against policemen for mistreatment of citizens are even rarer than civil suits.

So, to date the Supreme Court has had occasion to review the conduct of police almost exclusively in criminal cases where the defendant is the asserted victim of police misconduct. The way in which the issue of police misconduct is presented in such cases almost invariably involves the application of the "exclusionary rule"—that is, an evidentiary rule which disallows the admission against a criminal defendant, at his trial, of certain kinds of evidence obtained in violation of his rights. This exclusionary rule, whose scope and utility in enforcing various constitutional guarantees has been considerably expanded by the Supreme Court in the past decade, is today the principal instrument of judicial control of the police and the principal vehicle for announcement by the courts of the rights of suspects in their dealings with the police.

This last point, in itself, has important implications. Certain police practices (for example, the "booking" and "mugging" of suspects and the assorted minor or major indignities that attend station-house detention of suspects, ranging from the taking of a suspect's belt and shoelaces to vicious beatings) will virtually never become the subjects of judicial scrutiny because they virtually never produce evidence against the suspect. Since there can arise no exclusionary rule challenges to these practices, there have been no significant judicial decisions concerning them; and since (as I shall develop shortly) judicial decisions are almost the only source of legal rights of suspects, suspects do not now have legal rights against or in connection with such practices.

Other police practices (for example, refusing arrested suspects the right to use the telephone or detaining them in pig-sty cells) may or may not come under judicial consideration, depending upon whether they do or do not produce evidentiary consequences such as confessions. For several reasons, judicial control of the latter practices and judicial definition of a suspect's rights in connection with those practices must remain an imprecise, haphazard business. Under the exclusionary rule, judicial attention is focused upon an evidentiary product of the practices rather than upon the practices themselves. For example, a confession will ordinarily be the product of several such practices and of other adventitious circumstances such as the suspect's age and psychological makeup, the nature of police interrogation, etc. Consequently, a judicial ruling admitting or excluding it will seldom give occasion for a clear-cut pronouncement concerning the legality of any one of the underlying practices. Moreover, because these practices themselves are not the focus of the litigation, they will usually be imperfectly explained and explored in the record made before the courts. Courts which pass judgment on them may do so half-sightedly; or, realizing this danger, the courts may strive to avoid passing judgment upon practices that they know they do not understand. The result, once again, is that courts are unable to speak clearly concerning any particular or specific rights of a criminal suspect. Still less are they able to develop systematically any comprehensive canon or register of suspects' rights in the context of the entire range of police practices that affect the suspect.

Second, the Supreme Court of the United States is uniquely unable to take a comprehensive view of the subject of suspects' rights. In part its inability is simply a function of the Court's workload. Saddled with a back-breaking docket and properly occupied with other matters of grave national importance, the Court can only hear three or four cases a year involving the treatment of criminal suspects by the police.

Workload is not the Court's only problem. I have said earlier that fortuities determine which criminal cases reach the Supreme Court. Because police practices are ordinarily challengeable only through the exclusionary rule and because the exclusionary rule ordinarily comes into play only at trial following a plea of not guilty, police treatment of a suspect is effectively insulated against Supreme Court review in that large percentage of criminal convictions (as many as 90 percent in some jurisdictions) that rest upon a guilty plea.

Guilty pleas may be entered for many reasons in cases that involve serious questions of violations of a suspect's rights in the precourt phases. The arguable violations may have had no evidentiary consequences. The prosecution may have sufficient evidence for conviction apart from that obtained through the arguable violations. The defendant may be detained pending trial in default of bail on a charge for which a probationary or "time-served" sentence is likely, so that he will be imprisoned longer awaiting trial on a plea of not guilty than he would as a result of a quick guilty plea. The prosecutor may offer an attractive plea bargain, or the known sentencing practices of the trial judge may promise similar consideration for a guilty plea. Obviously, these factors that determine the entry of a guilty plea do not systematically send to trial a selection of cases which present the courts with any comprehensive set of issues relative to suspects' rights.

Additional selective factors prevent many of the cases that are tried from being appealed or from being carried all the way to the Supreme Court. Factual findings by the trial judge concerning contested police conduct frequently obscure or entirely obstruct the presentation to appellate courts of issues relating to that conduct. A convicted defendant cannot challenge on appeal any treatment by the police that the trial court, crediting incredible police denials, finds did not occur. (For example, suspects invariably "trip" and strike their heads while entering their cells; they are never shoved against the bars by police.) Also, the trial court may admit the police conduct but credit incredible explanations of it. (For example, the humiliating anal examinations to which some suspects are subjected in police stations are justified as "weapons searches" on police testimony that such suspects are known to conceal razor blades between their buttocks.) Finally, the trial court may admit and resolve against the defendant an issue relating to the legality of police conduct, then sentence him so lightly that an appeal is not worthwhile. (Some trial judges will impose light sentences in cases in which they have made dubious evidentiary rulings, thereby "buying off" appeals.) In any event the presentation of a convicted defendant's appeal — still more, the taking of his case to the Supreme Court — depends upon the energy, dedication and painstaking care of his lawyer, commodities understandably scarce on the part of overworked public defenders or private lawyers conscripted without compensation to represent the indigents who constitute the bulk of convicted persons.

For these reasons, the Supreme Court simply never gets to see many of the police practices that raise the most pervasive and significant issues of suspects' rights. The cases which do come to the Court are selected by a process that can only be described as capricious insofar as it may be relied upon to present the Court any opportunity for systematic development of a body of legal rights of individuals in the police, or precourt, phases of criminal proceedings. Therefore, the Court's ability to serve as architect of such a body of rights is woefully slight.

Third, the Court is further disabled by the fact that almost the only law relating to police practices or to suspects' rights is the law that the Court itself makes by its judicial decisions. Statutes and administrative regulations governing these matters are virtually nonexistent. The ubiquitous lack of legislative and executive attention to the problems of police treatment of suspects both forces the Court into the role of lawmaker in this area and makes it virtually impossible for the Court effectively to play that role.

This point has been largely ignored by the Court's conservative critics. The judicial "activism" that they deplore, usually citing the Court's "handcuffing" of the police, has been the almost inevitable consequence of the failure of other agencies of law to assume responsibility for regulating police practices. In most areas of constitutional law the Supreme Court of the United States plays a backstopping role, reviewing the ultimate permissibility of dispositions and policies guided in the first instance by legislative enactments, administrative rules or local common-law traditions. In the area of controls upon the police, a vast abnegation of responsibility at the level of each of these ordinary sources of legal rulemaking has forced the Court to construct *all* the law regulating the everyday functioning of the police. Of course, the Court has responded by being "activist"; it has had to. Its decisions have seemed wildly "liberal" because the only other body of principles operating in the field, against which the Court's principles may be measured, are the principles under which individual policemen act in the absence of any legal restraint.

This same subconstitutional lawlessness which forces the Court to act also prevents it from acting informedly. When the Court reviews the operation of legislation or of administrative regulations or of common-law rules governing, for example, criminal trial procedure, its consideration of the constitutional issues raised is informed and greatly assisted by the very fact that it *is* legislation or a regulation or a rule of some sort that is in question. Because the rule is articulated in more or less general terms, its contour is more or less visible; its relations and interactions with the rules are more or less perceptible, and some of the judgments and policies that underlie or oppose its acceptance are more or less intelligible. However, when the Court reviews conduct, such as police conduct, that is essentially rule-less, it is seriously impeded in understanding the nature, purposes and effects of what it is reviewing. Its view of the questioned conduct is limited to the appearance of the conduct on a particular trial record or records — records which may not even isolate or focus precisely upon that conduct. The Court cannot know whether the conduct before it is typical or atypical, unconnected or connected with a set of other practices or — if there is some connection — what is the comprehensive shape of the set of practices involved, what are their relations, their justifications, their consequences.

Operating thus darkly, the Court is obviously deprived of the ability to make any coherent response to, or to develop any organized regulation of, police conduct. Nor can the Court predict or understand the implications of any rule of constitutional law that it may itself project into this well of shadows. If the Court announces a decision striking down or modifying, for example, some rule of criminal trial practice, it can reasonably foresee how a trial will be conducted following its decision since the decision will operate within a system governed by other visible and predictable rules. But if the Court strikes down a police practice, announces a "right" of a criminal suspect in his dealings with the police, God only knows what the result will be.[11] Out there in the formless void, some adjustment will undoubtedly be made to accommodate the new "right," but what the product of this whole exercise will be remains unfathomable. So, again, the Court is effectively disarmed.

Fourth, when and if the Supreme Court ventures to announce some constitutional right of a suspect, that "right" filters down to the level of flesh and blood suspects only through the refracting layers of lower courts, trial judges, magistrates and police officials. All pronouncements of the Supreme Court undergo this filtering

---

11. One possible result is that prosecutors may offer greater concessions to defendants during plea bargaining. If a bargain is too good to refuse, the defendant may forgo the opportunity to challenge a police practice or assert a constitutional right. To the extent that this occurs, "what the due process revolution will have gained is simply shorter sentences." D. Oaks & W. Lehman, A Criminal Justice System and the Indigent 80 (1968). — EDS.

process, but in few other areas of law are the filters as opaque as in the area of suspects' rights.

Let there be no mistake about it. To a mind-staggering extent — to an extent that conservatives and liberals alike who are not criminal trial lawyers simply cannot conceive — the entire system of criminal justice below the level of the Supreme Court of the United States is solidly massed against the criminal suspect. Only a few appellate judges can throw off the fetters of their middle-class backgrounds — the dimly remembered, friendly face of the school crossing guard, their fear of a crowd of "toughs," their attitudes engendered as lawyers before their elevation to the bench by years of service as prosecutors or as private lawyers for honest, respectable business clients — and identify with the criminal suspect instead of with the policeman or with the putative victim of the suspect's theft, mugging, rape or murder. Trial judges still more, and magistrates beyond belief, are functionally and psychologically allied with the police, their co-workers in the unending and scarifying work of bringing criminals to book.

These trial judges and magistrates are the human beings that must find the "facts" when cases involving suspects' rights go into court (that is, when police treatment of a suspect is not conclusively masked behind a guilty plea or ignored by a defense lawyer too overworked or undercompensated to develop the issues adequately). Their factual findings resolve the inevitable conflict between the testimony of the police and the testimony of the suspect — usually a down-and-outer or a bad type, and often a man with a record. The result is about what one would expect. Even when the cases go to court, a suspect's rights as announced by the Supreme Court are something he has, not something he gets.

But, of course, for the reasons mentioned previously, most cases do not go to court. In these cases, the "rights" of the suspect are defined by how the police are willing to treat him. With regard to matters of treatment that have no evidentiary consequences and hence will not be judicially reviewable in exclusionary rule proceedings, the police have no particular reason to obey the law, even if the Supreme Court has had occasion to announce it. With regard to police practices that may have evidentiary consequences, the police are motivated to obey the law only to the extent that (1) they are more concerned with securing a conviction than with some other police purpose which is served by disobeying the law (in this connection, it is worth noting that police departments almost invariably measure their own efficiency in terms of "clearances by arrest," not by conviction), and (2) they think that they can secure the evidence necessary for conviction within the law.

Police work is hard work; it is righteous work; it is combative work, and competitive. Policemen are undereducated, they are scandalously underpaid, and their personal advancement lies in producing results according to the standards of the police ethic. When they go to the commander's office or to court, their conformity to this ethic is almost always vindicated. Neither their superiors nor the judges whom they know nor the public find it necessary to impede the performance of their duties with fettering rules respecting rights of suspects. If the Supreme Court finds this necessary, it must be that the Court is out of step. So its decisions — which are difficult to understand anyway — cannot really be taken seriously.

This concludes my observations concerning the Supreme Court's power to guarantee rights of criminal suspects in any other than an unworldly sense. The idealist would conclude from what I have said that the priests surrounding the Pythia are unfaithful to their priesthood. The cynic would conclude that the whole damned system is corrupt. I forgo such judgments and conclude only that Supreme Court power to enlarge the rights of suspects is very, very limited. . . .

. . . I do not mean to suggest that Supreme Court decisions respecting suspects' and defendants' rights are unimportant. Like the Pythia's cries, they have vast mystical significance. They state our aspirations. They give a few good priests something to work with. They give some of the faithful the courage to carry on and reason to improve the priesthood instead of tearing down the temple.

Also, they have *some* practical significance. With the Pythia shrieking underground, the priests may pervert the word of god, but they cannot ignore it entirely, nor entirely silence those who offer interpretations of it different from their own. Indeed, fear lest these alternative explanations gain popular support may cause the priests to bend a little in their direction.

So it is worth the effort to examine what the Supreme Court has pronounced concerning suspects' and defendants' rights. . . .[12]

8.   The Role of State Constitutions and State Constitutional Law

WILLIAM J. BRENNAN, JR., STATE CONSTITUTIONS AND THE PROTECTION OF INDIVIDUAL RIGHTS

90 Harv. L. Rev. 489-497 (1977)

Reaching the biblical summit of three score and ten seems the occasion — or the excuse — for looking back. Forty-eight years ago I entered law school and forty-four years ago was admitted to the New Jersey Bar. In those days of innocence, the preoccupation of the profession, bench and bar, was with questions usually answered by *application* of state common law principles or state statutes. Any necessity to consult federal law was at best episodic. But those were also the grim days of the Depression, and its cure was dramatically to change the face of American law. The year 1933 witnessed the birth of a plethora of new federal laws and new federal agencies developing and enforcing those laws; ones that were to affect profoundly the daily lives of every person in the nation.

In recent years, however, another variety of federal law — that fundamental law protecting all of us from the use of governmental powers in ways inconsistent with American conceptions of human liberty — has dramatically altered the grist of the state courts. Over the past two decades, decisions of the Supreme Court of the United States have returned to the fundamental promises wrought by the blood of those who fought our War between the States, promises which were thereafter embodied in our fourteenth amendment — that the citizens of all our states are also and no less citizens of our United States, that this birthright guarantees our federal

---

12. For more on the relationship between Supreme Court decision making and the operation of the criminal justice system, see Weisberg, Foreword: Criminal Procedure Doctrine: Some Versions of the Skeptical, 76 J. Crim. L. & Criminology 832 (1985). For differing perspectives on the role of the Burger Court in adjudicating the rights of criminal defendants, compare Whitebread, The Burger Court's Counter-Revolution in Criminal Procedure: The Recent Criminal Decisions of the United States Supreme Court, 24 Washburn L.J. 471 (1985), with Israel, Criminal Procedure, the Burger Court, and the Legacy of the Warren Court, 75 Mich. L. Rev. 1319 (1977). See also O'Neill, The Good, The Bad, and the Burger Court: Victim's Rights and a New Model of Criminal Review, 75 J. Crim. L. & Criminology 363 (1984). — Eds.

constitutional liberties against encroachment by governmental action at any level of our federal system, and that each of us is entitled to due process of law and the equal protection of the laws from our state governments no less than from our national one. Although courts do not today substitute their personal economic beliefs for the judgments of our democratically elected legislatures, Supreme Court decisions under the fourteenth amendment have significantly affected virtually every other area, civil and criminal, of state action. And while these decisions have been accompanied by the enforcement of federal rights by federal courts, they have significantly altered the work of state court judges as well. This is both necessary and desirable under our federal system — state courts no less than federal are and ought to be the guardians of our liberties.

But the point I want to stress here is that state courts cannot rest when they have afforded their citizens the full protections of the federal Constitution. State constitutions, too, are a font of individual liberties, their protections often extending beyond those required by the Supreme Court's interpretation of federal law. The legal revolution which has brought federal law to the fore must not be allowed to inhibit the independent protective force of state law — for without it, the full realization of our liberties cannot be guaranteed.

Of late, however, more and more state courts are construing state constitutional counterparts of provisions of the Bill of Rights as guaranteeing citizens of their states even more protection than the federal provisions, even those identically phrased. This is surely an important and highly significant development for our constitutional jurisprudence and for our concept of federalism. I suppose it was only natural that when during the 1960s our rights and liberties were in the process of becoming increasingly federalized, state courts saw no reason to consider what protections, if any, were secured by state constitutions. It is not easy to pinpoint why state courts are now beginning to emphasize the protections of their states' own bills of rights. It may not be wide of the mark, however, to suppose that these state courts discern, and disagree with, a trend in recent opinions of the United States Supreme Court to pull back from, or at least suspend for the time being, the enforcement of the *Boyd* principle with respect to application of the federal Bill of Rights and the restraints of the due process and equal protection clauses of the fourteenth amendment.

The essential point I am making, of course, is not that the United States Supreme Court is necessarily wrong in its interpretation of the federal Constitution, or that ultimate constitutional truths invariably come prepackaged in the dissents, including my own, from decisions of the Court. It is simply that the decisions of the Court are not, and should not be, dispositive of questions regarding rights guaranteed by counterpart provisions of state law. Accordingly, such decisions are not mechanically applicable to state law issues, and state court judges and the members of the bar seriously err if they so treat them. Rather, state court judges, and also practitioners, do well to scrutinize constitutional decisions by federal courts, for only if they are found to be logically persuasive and well-reasoned, paying due regard to precedent and the policies underlying specific constitutional guarantees, may they properly claim persuasive weight as guide-posts when interpreting counterpart state guarantees. I suggest to the bar that, although in the past it might have been safe for counsel to raise only federal constitutional issues in state courts, plainly it would be most unwise these days not also to raise the state constitutional questions.

BARRY LATZER, TOWARD THE DECENTRALIZATION OF
CRIMINAL PROCEDURE: STATE CONSTITUTIONAL LAW
AND SELECTIVE INCORPORATION

87 J. Crim. L. & Criminology 63, 63-66, 68 (1996)

When one surveys the growing body of criminal procedure cases in which the decision is grounded in a state constitutional provision, a rather startling trend becomes manifest. It is increasingly evident that at some time during the early years of the next century virtually every significant federal constitutional criminal procedure right will have been duplicated or expanded as a matter of state law by the appellate courts of most of the states. That is, the *same* rights that *defendants* now enjoy as a *result of* United States Supreme Court cases construing the federal Bill of Rights, or an even broader state-law-based version of those rights, will be established in most of the states by cases construing state bills of rights. Little if any thought has been given to the implications of this development for constitutional law in the United States, or on the relations between state courts and the United States Supreme Court.

For openers, consider this question: if defendants' rights are protected by state law, why is there a need for redundant federal law? Why provide federal protections where state rights exist, especially in light of the fact that the state rights are as broad or broader? This is in part, of course, a question about the Supreme Court's incorporation policy by which federal rights have been applied to the states through the Fourteenth Amendment Due Process Clause. The stock answer is that together, the federal rights established through incorporation and the rights established through interpretation of state constitutions afford a double-barreled protection for individual rights in America, and we all benefit from such dual assurances. Upon close examination, however, rights-redundancy has distinct disadvantages.

There can be little question that incorporation forced the states to adopt uniform procedures without regard to local needs. In the decades since the 1960s, when the Supreme Court "selectively" incorporated nearly all of the criminal procedure rights in the Bill of Rights, the state courts have had little choice but to give force to these federal procedures (absent broader state rights). No matter how costly, no matter how inefficient, no matter how difficult to implement, no matter how much injustice they might cause, and no matter how inappropriate to local circumstances they might be, the state courts have had to give effect to these federal procedural rights. These disadvantages of incorporation were acknowledged even in the 1960s, but they were believed to be outweighed by one important value: equality. Whatever the disadvantages in stifling state uniqueness, independence, and freedom to experiment, the advantage of uniform treatment of defendants throughout the United States, at least with respect to the fundamental rights of the Bill of Rights, seemed to justify incorporation.

But let us be candid. Incorporation was also predicated upon an assumption — a very negative assumption — about the states, and especially about state courts. The assumption was that some state courts were chronically, and virtually all state courts were occasionally, backward. Without the Supreme Court to stand over them, ready to review and reverse, the state *courts* would fail to provide the minimal rights that all defendants were entitled to at all times. In short, incorporation was motivated by the Mississippi Problem: the assumption that the state bench was, at its worst racist and incompetent, and merely competent most of the time. . . .

[T]he Mississippi Problem is history. . . . [T]he state courts are no longer rights-antediluvians, and . . . therefore an entire set of assumptions underlying incorporation has eroded. The proof of the change in the state courts lies in their eagerness to protect federal constitutional rights, but even more, in the development of state constitutional law. State constitutionalism has not only created rights-redundancy, it has undermined the very reasons for that redundancy. It gives the lie to the assumption that the state bench is rights-backward. Unlike federal constitutional law, which is imposed upon the state courts, state constitutional law is a matter of choice. Whereas state courts must enforce federal procedural rights incorporated into due process, they need not provide equivalent state constitutional rights. State constitutional rights need not be as protective as comparable federal rights, and they certainly do not have to be more protective, as they so often are. State constitutional law epitomizes the change in the attitude and orientation of state judges. It shows that state courts are now every bit as rights-sensitive as the United States Supreme Court, if not more so.

. . . [O]nly those procedures that are both fundamental and required by the Bill of Rights, or are at least demonstrably essential to the implementation of a fundamental right in the Bill of Rights, may be imposed upon the states. Where a procedure is none of the above it is not a proper part of due process and the Supreme Court has no authority to compel the state courts to adopt it. Where a previously incorporated procedure is challenged and it cannot be proven essential to a fundamental right, it should be disincorporated, by which I mean that the incorporation decision should be reversed and the procedure should no longer be required by the Fourteenth Amendment Due Process Clause.

Chapter 2
The Idea of Due Process

One of the defining characteristics of the modern state is its monopoly on criminal law enforcement. Government officials, not private individuals, investigate, apprehend, try, and punish criminals. Much of this business is routine and bureaucratic, but some of it is terrifying, and it can be brutal. Suspects' homes and cars must be searched (and the searches can be rough); arrests must be made, sometimes by force; defendants must be incarcerated. Giving the government a monopoly on that kind of power may be necessary, but it is also very dangerous — consider the use of the phrase "police state" to describe less-than-free societies. Police, prosecutors, and the courts can do enormous good: They are the difference between a decent society and an unlivable one. But they can also do enormous harm.

The basic goal of the law of criminal procedure is to limit the harm without too severely limiting the good. In our system, the entity that does most of the limiting is courts. Most of the law of criminal procedure is constitutional, and American constitutional law is largely judge-defined. Which means that judges — and, especially, Supreme Court Justices — are the primary generators of rules for regulating the behavior of police, prosecutors, defense attorneys, and the other actors who administer the criminal process. That explains why books like this one devote so much space to Supreme Court opinions: Those opinions define what Henry Friendly properly labeled our constitutional code of criminal procedure.[1]

All this constitutional regulation begins with the idea of due process: When the state uses its coercive machinery to catch and punish criminals, it must treat people fairly, even the people it wishes to punish. That idea probably underlies the law of criminal procedure in all free societies. In ours, the connection is particularly clear, since the law of criminal procedure begins not only with the idea but with the phrase, "due process of law." The Fifth Amendment bars the federal government from depriving anyone of "life, liberty, or property" without it; the Fourteenth Amendment applies that same prohibition to the states. Since the criminal justice system is in the business of depriving people of liberty and property (and occasionally deprives them of life itself), those constitutional bans naturally have their most frequent application to criminal procedure.

That last point deserves emphasis. An enormous amount of ink has been spilled debating the proper meaning of the Due Process Clauses of the Fifth and Fourteenth Amendments — the subject is central to most constitutional law courses. Those debates usually focus on things like economic regulation (see Lochner v. New York, 198 U.S. 45 (1905)) and birth control (see Griswold v. Connecticut, 381 U.S. 479

---

1. See Henry J. Friendly, The Bill of Rights as a Code of Criminal Procedure, 53 Cal. L. Rev. 929 (1965). It should be noted that Friendly thought this constitutional code was a bad development — that it risked stifling reform efforts by other, nonjudicial actors.

(1965)), abortion (see Roe v. Wade, 410 U.S. 113 (1973)) and gay rights (see Bowers v. Hardwick, 478 U.S. 186 (1986)). But the Due Process Clauses have had their greatest impact not in these places, but in criminal procedure. As of summer 2009, over 2.3 million people were incarcerated in the United States. The legal system that put them there is filled with rules that have their origins in the Fourteenth Amendment's Due Process Clause. And the question whether those rules ensure fair punishment begins with the idea of due process.

A Brief History

The relationship between that idea and the American criminal justice system has a long and strange history. Broadly speaking, the history has three phases. The first phase lasts from independence to the passage of the Fourteenth Amendment; the second extends to the 1960s; the third runs to the present.

The first phase is when the criminal justice system as we know it came into being. In 1776 (or 1787 or 1791 — the choice of starting date does not matter here),[2] career public prosecutors basically didn't exist; prosecution was either the crime victim's job, the constable's job, or the job of some private lawyer serving as a temporary public advocate. Police forces didn't exist either; constables and sheriffs performed their law enforcement task largely through the aid of private parties.[3] There seems to have been no plea bargaining — the best history of that topic to date puts its origins in the early nineteenth century.[4] Criminal law, the body of rules that define the elements of crimes, had little meaning, since juries could decide what the law was on an ad hoc basis.[5] And imprisonment for crime was rare; penitentiaries were still a half-century in the future.[6] Many of the most basic, taken-for-granted features of contemporary criminal justice were absent at the time of the Founding — indeed, they were unimaginable.

By 1868, the year the Fourteenth Amendment was ratified, all that had changed, and changed dramatically. Public prosecutors, police forces, plea bargains, and prisons were all common. Criminal law was defined by a mix of courts and legislatures, just as it is today. The criminal justice system of 1868 — an interlocking set of public institutions that managed large numbers of cases and administered punishment to large numbers of people — would be quite recognizable to us today, for the system then and the system now share most basic features.

In other words, when the Constitution (including the Bill of Rights) was written, no criminal justice system in the modern sense existed. Constitutional norms came first; the system came later. Given that timing, it would hardly be surprising if there was some tension between the norms and the system.

---

2. Independence was declared in 1776, the convention that produced our Constitution was held in 1787, and the Bill of Rights was ratified in 1791. Whichever of these is the relevant date, the statements in the text hold true.

3. See generally Peter Charles Hoffer, Law and People in Colonial America 80-89 (1992).

4. See George Fisher, Plea Bargaining's Triumph, 109 Yale L.J. 857 (2000).

5. See, e.g., William E. Nelson, The Eighteenth-Century Background of John Marshall's Constitutional Jurisprudence, 76 Mich. L. Rev. 904 (1978).

6. At the time of the Founding, penitentiaries were first being used in England. See George Fisher, The Birth of the Prison Retold, 104 Yale L.J. 1235 (1994). The widespread use of incarceration in America began only in the 1820s and 1830s. See David J. Rothman, Perfecting the Prison: United States, 1789-1865, in The Oxford History of the Prison 100 (Norval Morris & David J. Rothman eds., 1998).

All the more so, since the criminal justice system evolved in the nineteenth century with basically no input from constitutional law. The Bill of Rights included a number of rules that were specifically about criminal procedure — the Fifth Amendment's ban on double jeopardy, requirement of indictment by grand jury, and privilege against self-incrimination, the Sixth Amendment's rights to counsel and trial by jury, the Eighth Amendment's ban on cruel and unusual punishments. But like the rest of the Bill of Rights, those criminal procedure rules applied only to the federal government. See Barron v. Baltimore, 32 U.S. 243 (1833). And the federal government did very, very little in the way of criminal law enforcement — as late as 1904, the federal government incarcerated only 1,641 people, a mere 3 percent of the number of state prisoners. See Margaret Werner Cahalan, Historical Corrections Statistics in the United States, 1850-1984, at 29 tbl. 3-2 (1986). State constitutions seem not to have played any particular role either, perhaps because criminal appeals were still so unusual.[7] The criminal justice system that emerged in the nineteenth century was generated from the bottom up, not from the top down; institutions like public prosecutors and police forces sprang up locally without any overall design and without any constitutional regulation. The same was true of practices like plea bargaining.

Enter the Fourteenth Amendment. The Fourteenth Amendment's ban on deprivations of life, liberty, or property without due process of law, unlike the similar ban in the Fifth Amendment, applied to the *states*. Then as now, the states are the locus of the huge majority of criminal law enforcement. Thus, though there is no reason to believe its authors viewed it this way, the Fourteenth Amendment's Due Process Clause amounted to a textual invitation to courts to define some limits on the newly emerged criminal justice system, by defining what a fair criminal process must entail.

Beginning with Hurtado v. California, 110 U.S. 516 (1884), reprinted at page 84, infra, the Supreme Court began accepting that invitation; for the next 75 years, the Court engaged in the business of placing constitutional limits on the criminal process, with the limits anchored in due process. The results are described in the notes following *Hurtado*. For now, it is enough to note that the limits were both few and vague. By 1960, there were at most a handful of things state criminal justice systems were clearly not allowed to do — they could not run mob-dominated trials;[8] they could not pay judges by the conviction;[9] they could not beat confessions out of suspects[10] — but otherwise, they were subject only to the amorphous notion that whatever they did had to comply with "fundamental fairness," which seemed to permit anything that did not "shock the conscience" of the judiciary. What any of that meant was a mystery, apparently even to the Justices, but what it did *not* mean was a substantial body of law regulating the criminal process. There was a law of due process in 1960, but it barely deserved the label "law," and it hardly ensured a fair process.

---

7. See, e.g., Francis A. Allen, *Griffin v. Illinois*: Antecedents and Aftermath, 25 U. Chi. L. Rev. 151, 154 (1957) (calling criminal appeals "a modern innovation"). For an argument that appeals in criminal cases were more widespread in the eighteenth and nineteenth centuries, see Marc M. Arkin, Rethinking the Constitutional Right to a Criminal Appeal, 39 UCLA L. Rev. 503 (1992).

8. Moore v. Dempsey, 261 U.S. 86 (1923).

9. Tumey v. Ohio, 273 U.S. 510 (1927).

10. Brown v. Mississippi, 297 U.S. 278 (1936).

The 1960s at least remedied the first of those two deficiencies: At the end of that decade, we had, for the first time, a large law of constitutional criminal procedure. The 1960s saw a series of major reforms in the criminal justice system, and the reforms were both based on federal constitutional law and driven by the Supreme Court. But these reforms had a different constitutional basis than the sporadic limits the Court had imposed between 1884 and 1960. For the most part, as it sought to rein in what it saw as an abusive criminal justice system, Earl Warren's Supreme Court relied not on due process but on the Bill of Rights. Limits on search and seizure and police interrogation, the right to counsel, the privilege against self-incrimination, the ban on double jeopardy, the right to jury trial — these became the foundations of American criminal procedure, and each has spawned its own elaborate body of law. These bodies of law will occupy the bulk of this large book. But the words "due process" rarely appear in the cases that define these constitutional rules; instead, the relevant piece of constitutional text comes from the Fourth, Fifth, or Sixth Amendments. In effect, the Supreme Court decided that defining due process was impossible, so it turned to the enterprise of defining the more specific guarantees of the Bill of Rights. But the point of those guarantees is itself due process; the goal remains to define criminal procedure in a way that ensures fair treatment for the millions of people who pass through the criminal justice system's large net. The basic question that so bothered the Court from 1884 to 1960 — What are the conditions of a fair criminal process? — has not so much been answered as recast, and perhaps avoided.

In short, for roughly its first century, our nation had no law of constitutional criminal procedure. For roughly the next 80 years, the Supreme Court tried, and largely failed, to define a law of criminal procedure built on the phrase "due process of law." For the 40 years after that, down to the present, the phrase "due process of law" has faded in importance; a huge, nearly comprehensive law of criminal procedure has been built on the various provisions of the Bill of Rights. But the idea of due process still lurks in the background, posing the basic question any criminal process must face: Is this fair?

A. *Defining Due Process*

HURTADO v. CALIFORNIA

Writ of Error to the Supreme Court of California
110 U.S. 516 (1884)

MR. JUSTICE MATTHEWS delivered the opinion of the Court. [Hurtado was charged and convicted of first-degree murder. He was charged by information, not indictment; that is, no grand jury ever considered his case. He argued that the absence of grand jury indictment for a serious crime violated the Fourteenth Amendment's guarantee of due process.]

. . . The proposition of law we are asked to affirm is that an indictment or presentment by a grand jury, as known to the common law of England, is essential to that "due process of law," when applied to prosecutions for felonies, which is secured and guaranteed by [the Fourteenth Amendment to] the Constitution of the United States, and which accordingly it is forbidden to the States respectively to dispense with in the administration of criminal law. . . .

. . . [I]t is maintained on behalf of the plaintiff in error that the phrase "due process of law" is equivalent to "law of the land," as found in the 29th chapter of Magna Charta; that by immemorial usage it has acquired a fixed, definite, and technical meaning; that it refers to and includes, not only the general principles of public liberty and private right, which lie at the foundation of all free government, but the very institutions which, venerable by time and custom, have been tried by experience and found fit and necessary for the preservation of those principles. . . .

This, it is argued, furnishes an indispensable test of what constitutes "due process of law"; that any proceeding otherwise authorized by law, which is not thus sanctioned by usage, or which supersedes and displaces one that is, cannot be regarded as due process of law.

But this inference is unwarranted. The real [principle] is, that a process of law, which is not otherwise forbidden, must be taken to be due process of law, if it can show the sanction of settled usage both in England and in this country; but it by no means follows that nothing else can be due process of law. . . . [T]o hold that such a characteristic is essential to due process of law, would be to deny every quality of the law but its age, and to render it incapable of progress or improvement. It would be to stamp upon our jurisprudence the unchangeableness attributed to the laws of the Medes and Persians. . . .

The Constitution of the United States was ordained, it is true, by descendants of Englishmen, who inherited the traditions of English law and history; but it was made for an undefined and expanding future, and for a people gathered and to be gathered from many nations and of many tongues. . . . There is nothing in Magna Charta, rightly construed as a broad charter of public right and law, which ought to exclude the best ideas of all systems and of every age; and as it was the characteristic principle of the common law to draw its inspiration from every fountain of justice, we are not to assume that the sources of its supply have been exhausted. On the contrary, we should expect that the new and various experiences of our own situation and system will mould and shape it into new and not less useful forms. . . .

We are to construe this phrase in the Fourteenth Amendment by the [usage] of the Constitution itself. The same words are contained in the Fifth Amendment. That article makes specific and express provision for perpetuating the institution of the grand jury, so far as relates to prosecutions for the more aggravated crimes under the laws of the United States. It declares that:

> No person shall be held to answer for a capital or otherwise infamous crime, unless on a presentment or indictment of a grand jury, except in cases arising in the land or naval forces, or in the militia when in actual service in time of war or public danger; nor shall any person be subject for the same offence to be twice put in jeopardy of life or limb; nor shall he be compelled in any criminal case to be a witness against himself. [It then immediately adds]: Nor be deprived of life, liberty, or property, without due process of law.

According to a recognized canon of interpretation, especially applicable to formal and solemn instruments of constitutional law, we are forbidden to assume, without clear reason to the contrary, that any part of this most important amendment is superfluous. The natural and obvious inference is, that in the sense of the Constitution, "due process of law" was not meant or intended to include . . . the institution and procedure of a grand jury in any case. The conclusion is equally irresistible, that when the same phrase was employed in the Fourteenth Amendment to restrain the action of the States, it was used in the same sense and with no greater extent; and that if in the adoption of that amendment it had been part of its purpose to perpetuate the institution of the grand jury in all the States, it would have embodied, as did the Fifth Amendment, express declarations to that effect. Due process of law in the latter refers to that law of the land which derives its authority from the legislative powers conferred upon Congress by the Constitution of the United States, exercised within the limits therein prescribed, and interpreted according to the principles of the common law. In the Fourteenth Amendment, by parity of reason, it refers to that law of the land in each State, which derives its authority from the inherent and reserved powers of the State, exerted within the limits of those fundamental principles of liberty and justice which lie at the base of all our civil and political institutions, and the greatest security for which resides in the right of the people to make their own laws, and alter them at their pleasure. . . .

But it is not to be supposed that these legislative powers are absolute and despotic, and that the amendment prescribing due process of law is too vague and indefinite to operate as a practical restraint. It is not every act, legislative in form, that is law. Law is something more than mere will exerted as an act of power. It must be not a special rule for a particular person or a particular case, but, in the language of Mr. Webster, in his familiar definition, "the general law, a law which hears before it condemns, which proceeds upon inquiry, and renders judgment only after trial," so "that every citizen shall hold his life, liberty, property and immunities under the protection of the general rules which govern society," and thus excluding, as not due process of law, acts of attainder, bills of pains and penalties, acts of confiscation, acts reversing judgments, and acts directly transferring one man's estate to another, legislative judgments and decrees, and other similar special, partial and arbitrary exertions of power under the forms of legislation. Arbitrary power, enforcing its edicts to the injury of the persons and property of its subjects, is not law, whether manifested as the decree of a personal monarch or of an impersonal multitude. . . . The enforcement of these limitations by judicial process is the device of self-governing communities to protect the rights of individuals and minorities, as well against the power of numbers, as against the violence of public agents transcending the limits of lawful authority, even when acting in the name and wielding the force of the government. . . .

It follows that any legal proceeding enforced by public authority, whether sanctioned by age and custom, or newly devised in the discretion of the legislative power, in furtherance of the general public good, which regards and preserves these principles of liberty and justice, must be held to be due process of law. . . .

Tried by these principles, we are unable to say that the substitution for a presentment or indictment by a grand jury of the proceeding by information, after examination and commitment by a magistrate, certifying to the probable guilt of the defendant, with the right on his part to the aid of counsel, and to the cross-examination of the witnesses produced for the prosecution, is not due process of law. . . .

MR. JUSTICE HARLAN, dissenting.

. . . [I]t is said that the framers of the Constitution did not suppose that due process of law necessarily required for a capital offence the institution and procedure of a grand jury, else they would not in the same amendment prohibiting the deprivation of life, liberty, or property, without due process of law, have made specific and express provision for a grand jury where the crime is capital or otherwise infamous. . . .

This line of argument, it seems to me, would lead to results which are inconsistent with the vital principles of republican government. If the presence in the Fifth Amendment of a specific provision for grand juries in capital cases, alongside the provision for due process of law . . . is held to prove that "due process of law" did not . . . require a grand jury in capital cases, inexorable logic would require it to be, likewise, held that the right not to be put twice in jeopardy of life and limb for the same offence, nor compelled in a criminal case to testify against one's self — rights and immunities also specifically recognized in the Fifth Amendment — were not protected by that [same] due process of law. . . . More than that, other amendments of the Constitution proposed at the same time, expressly recognize the right of persons to just compensation for private property taken for public use; their right, when accused of crime, to be informed of the nature and cause of the accusation against them, and to a speedy and public trial, by an impartial jury of the State and district wherein the crime was committed; to be confronted by the witnesses against them; and to have compulsory process for obtaining witnesses in their favor. Will it be claimed that these rights were not secured by the "law of the land" or by "due process of law," as declared and established at the foundation of our government? Are they to be excluded from the enumeration of the fundamental principles of liberty and justice, and, therefore, not embraced by "due process of law"? If the argument of my brethren be sound, those rights — although universally recognized at the establishment of our institutions as secured by that due process of law which for centuries had been the foundation of Anglo-Saxon liberty — were not deemed by our fathers as essential in the due process of law prescribed by our Constitution; because — such seems to be the argument — had they been regarded as involved in due process of law they would not have been specifically and expressly provided for. . . .

Still further, it results from the doctrines of the opinion — if I do not misapprehend its scope — that the clause of the Fourteenth Amendment forbidding the deprivation of life or liberty without due process of law, would not be violated by a State regulation, dispensing with petit juries in criminal cases, and permitting a person charged with a crime involving life to be tried before a single judge, or even a justice of the peace, upon a rule to show cause why he should not be hanged. . . .

. . . My sense of duty constrains me to dissent from this interpretation of the supreme law of the land.

MR. JUSTICE FIELD did not take part in the decision of this case.

NOTES ON THE MEANING OF "DUE PROCESS OF LAW" IN CRIMINAL CASES

1. *Hurtado* was the Supreme Court's first extended discussion of what "due process of law" means for criminal procedure. How well did the Court do? Do the majority and dissenting opinions reflect the kinds of concerns you would expect to see? Do the opinions make you think better or worse of the idea of giving the Supreme Court the power to define the rules that govern the criminal process?

In answering these questions, it helps to have some more information about the issue in *Hurtado*. The question before the Court was whether California was required to proceed by indictment in capital cases. To translate, the question was whether murder defendants like Hurtado (and perhaps defendants in other felony cases) were constitutionally entitled to a judgment by a grand jury that they should be charged, as a prerequisite to going to trial. How one answers that question, in turn, might plausibly depend on one's sense of what grand juries do, how they function. Consider the following description of contemporary grand jury practice in federal cases:[11]

> The operation of a typical federal grand jury is straightforward. A pool of citizens is summoned at random from the judicial district where the jury will sit. From the group of qualified people who appear, twenty-three are chosen to serve on the jury. The jurors sit for an indefinite period not to exceed eighteen months; the number of days per month when they must actually appear depends on the prosecutor's case load. A district court judge administers the oath and gives the jurors general instructions about their duties. This marks the end of the judge's formal involvement in the process. From that point forward, the prosecutor dictates the course of the proceedings.
>
> The most striking feature of grand jury hearings is their secrecy. The press and public are barred from the proceedings, as are suspects and their counsel. Even judges are not allowed in the grand jury room; attendance is limited to the prosecutor, the jurors, the court reporter, and the single witness being questioned. Those who participate in the hearing are sworn to secrecy, and the court may use its contempt powers to ensure that this silence is maintained even after the case is resolved.
>
> Once in session, the grand jury's primary task is to review the cases presented to it by the government. The prosecutor calls and questions witnesses, and presents documentary evidence related to the crime in question. Unlike trial jurors, grand jurors may ask questions of the witness and may discuss the case with the prosecutor as evidence is submitted. After the case is presented, the prosecutor asks the jurors to vote to return an indictment accusing the defendant of a specific crime that the prosecutor believes is supported by the evidence. The jurors then deliberate in private. If at least twelve agree that there is probable cause to believe that the suspect committed the crime, the grand jury returns a "true bill" that, when signed by the prosecutor, becomes the indictment. If the grand jury concludes that the evidence is insufficient, it returns a "no bill" (or "no true bill"), and any preliminary charges filed against the suspect are dismissed.
>
> By traditional trial standards, a grand jury is allowed to consider a surprising, even shocking, mix of evidence. . . . The Rules of Evidence do not apply, so the prosecutor can ask leading questions and pursue matters that would be considered irrelevant if presented at trial. The decision of which evidence to present is also in the prosecutor's hands: the suspect has no right to testify in his own defense, and if he does testify, is not allowed to bring counsel with him into the grand jury room. The suspect may not put on contrary evidence, is not given access to the testimony of his accusers until the trial begins, and indeed, may not even be told he is being investigated. The result . . . is that grand jurors hear only what the prosecution wants them to hear. . . .

Andrew Leipold, Why Grand Juries Do Not (and Cannot) Protect the Accused, 80 Cornell L. Rev. 260, 265-267 (1995) (footnotes omitted). As the title of Leipold's article suggests, it is not clear how this process protects criminal defendants. On the contrary, its chief use today seems to be as a device the government uses to obtain

---

11. This description is reprinted at page 991, infra, as part of the consideration of grand juries as screening devices.

information — hence the widespread use of grand jury subpoenas in white-collar criminal investigations.

Of course, white-collar criminal practice was well in the future when *Hurtado* was decided, and grand jury practice was no doubt different in some respects in 1884 than it is today. But the essential point — prosecutorial control over the information grand jurors receive — would have been true then as now. Given that point, is there any serious argument for constitutionally requiring grand juries? What could Justice Harlan have been worrying about?

2. Both Justice Matthews and Justice Harlan offered coherent, fairly well-developed interpretations of due process. Justice Matthews construes "due process of law" with special emphasis on the words "of law"; the result is a constitutional requirement of legality and nonarbitrariness. Justice Harlan sees due process as incorporating the list of protections that appear in the Bill of Rights; the result of this view is to transfer interpretive questions from the Fourteenth Amendment to the more particular guarantees of the Fourth, Fifth, and Sixth Amendments. Though these positions competed with each other in *Hurtado*, each has prevailed in its own sphere over the years. (Harlan's argument has won the greater victory, as the next main case shows.) In addition to these two interpretations, two other views of due process in criminal cases have won judicial favor from time to time. Some cases treat due process as a guarantee of accurate procedures, meaning procedures that minimize the risk that innocent defendants will be convicted of crime. And some cases define "due process" as "fundamental fairness," which turns out to be a term defined more by judicial intuition than by any analytic structure.

Each of these four strands — due process as the rule of law, due process as the Bill of Rights, due process as accuracy, and due process as "fundamental fairness" — survives in the law of due process today. Oddly, none of the four views seems to have much to do with any of the others. That strange fact has its origins in cases from early in the twentieth century. In the decades following *Hurtado*, the Supreme Court saw a wide range of cases challenging one or another aspect of state criminal procedure, but as it decided those cases the Court did not follow a consistent path. Rather, the Court seized on whichever of the four approaches mentioned in the preceding paragraph seemed most applicable to the issue at hand (and whichever was able to attract a majority of the Court). Cases taking one approach usually made no mention of cases taking another, and at some times the Court seemed unaware that some of the approaches even existed. The upshot is that today, there are (at least) four meanings of due process in criminal cases, and there is no obvious answer to the question why one meaning prevails in one kind of case and another in a different kind of case.

The material that follows briefly traces the development of each of those four meanings. As you read it, ask yourself whether one or another of these approaches seems clearly superior to the others, or (alternatively) whether the law is better off with strands of each.

The Rule of Law.   The following passage in Justice Matthews's opinion in *Hurtado* offers a good summary of what is meant by the "rule of law":

> It is not every act, legislative in form, that is law. Law is something more than mere will exerted as an act of power. It must be not a special rule for a particular person or a particular case, but, in the language of Mr. Webster, in his familiar definition, "the general

law, a law which hears before it condemns, which proceeds upon inquiry, and renders judgment only after trial," . . . and thus excluding, as not due process of law, acts of attainder, bills of pains and penalties, acts of confiscation, acts reversing judgments, and acts directly transferring one man's estate to another, legislative judgments and decrees, and other similar special, partial and arbitrary exertions of power under the forms of legislation. Arbitrary power, enforcing its edicts to the injury of the persons and property of its subjects, is not law, whether manifested as the decree of a personal monarch or of an impersonal multitude. . . .

For a good contemporary statement of the same principle, see John C. Jeffries, Jr., Legality, Vagueness, and the Construction of Penal Statutes, 71 Va. L. Rev. 189, 212 (1985):

The rule of law signifies the constraint of arbitrariness in the exercise of government power. In the context of the penal law, it means that the agencies of official coercion should, to the extent feasible, be guided by rules — that is, by openly acknowledged, relatively stable, and generally applicable statements of proscribed conduct. The evils to be retarded are caprice and whim, the misuse of government power for private ends, and the unacknowledged reliance on illegitimate criteria of selection. The goals to be advanced are regularity and evenhandedness in the administration of justice and accountability in the use of government power.

This idea of ensuring that criminal punishment is according to law and not "mere will" requires, at the least, that crimes be defined generally rather than (as Matthews put it) as a "special rule for a particular person or a particular case." That much is easy. Legislatures cannot make it a crime to *be* Hurtado, nor can they wait until Hurtado acts and then criminalize whatever he has done.

More importantly as a practical matter, the rule-of-law idea might be thought to require that legislatures define crimes with some specificity, that vague criminal statutes be deemed unconstitutional. Jeffries states the basic argument well:

The power to define a vague law is effectively left to those who enforce it, and those who enforce the penal law characteristically operate in settings of secrecy and informality, often punctuated by a sense of emergency, and rarely constrained by self-conscious generalization of standards. In such circumstances, the wholesale delegation of discretion naturally invites its abuse, and an important first step in constraining that discretion is the invalidation of indefinite laws.

Id., at 215.

For a long period following *Hurtado*, this idea lay mostly dormant. Vagueness doctrine existed, but it was mostly used as an adjunct to First Amendment law, a way to invalidate laws that might chill protected speech. See Note, The Void-for-Vagueness Doctrine in the Supreme Court, 109 U. Pa. L. Rev. 67 (1960). Beginning in the early 1970s, though, the Supreme Court began to apply vagueness doctrine to strike down statutes that seemed to criminalize ordinary street behavior. Thus, in Coates v. Cincinnati, 402 U.S. 611 (1971), the Court invalidated an ordinance that forbade conduct "annoying to persons passing by." In Papachristou v. Jacksonville, 405 U.S. 156 (1972), the Court struck down a vagrancy law that criminalized, inter alia, "rogues and vagabonds," "habitual loafers," and "persons wandering or strolling around from place to place without any lawful purpose or object." More recently, in Chicago v. Morales, 527 U.S. 41 (1999), the Court invalidated a local ordinance that prohibited loitering by two or more people, at least one of whom was a "street gang member." *Morales* is excerpted at page 586, infra.

Cases like *Coates, Papachristou,* and *Morales* are all applications of Justice Matthews's rule-of-law view of due process. Are the applications sound? Does the rule-of-law idea go farther? Suppose a given jurisdiction forbids knowing possession of marijuana. Suppose further that there have been no prosecutions for this offense for several years and that marijuana possession is fairly common in some communities. Under these circumstances, would an arrest or prosecution for marijuana possession violate the rule of law? Does the answer depend on why the defendant was selected for arrest and prosecution? Is that something courts will be able to uncover?

More generally, is the rule-of-law ideal a good basis for constitutional regulation of the criminal justice system generally? Consider how one might apply the ideal to, say, police brutality. Is the problem with excessive police violence that the violence is lawless? Or is it something else?

The Bill of Rights. The Fourth Amendment forbids unreasonable searches and seizures. The Fifth Amendment requires indictment by grand jury for "capital, or otherwise infamous crime[s]," and bans double jeopardy and compelled self-incrimination. The Sixth Amendment grants defendants "the right to a speedy and public trial, by an impartial jury," as well as the right to be informed of the charges, to be confronted with opposing witnesses, to have "compulsory process for obtaining witnesses in his favor," and to have "the Assistance of Counsel for his defence."

As Justice Harlan's dissent in *Hurtado* shows, one longstanding reading of due process in criminal cases is that it incorporates all these rights. That position was rejected in *Hurtado* and for a long time afterward: In 1908, the Court declined to incorporate the privilege against self-incrimination into due process, see Twining v. New Jersey, 211 U.S. 78 (1908); three decades later, the Court similarly declined to incorporate the prohibition against double jeopardy into due process. See Palko v. Connecticut, 302 U.S. 319 (1937). But beginning in the middle of the twentieth century, the Court reversed course. In Wolf v. Colorado, 338 U.S. 25 (1949), the Court concluded that the Fourth Amendment's ban on unreasonable searches and seizures applied to the states through the Due Process Clause. (Though the Court waited until 1961 to apply the exclusionary rule to the states. See Mapp v. Ohio, 367 U.S. 643 (1961), reprinted at page 340.) And in the 1960s, a series of decisions incorporated every one of the rights listed in the preceding paragraph except for the right to a grand jury. *Hurtado* still stands, but today it stands alone — everywhere else, the argument of the first Justice Harlan has prevailed. Duncan v. Louisiana, the next main case, discusses this development.

There is a lively debate about the historical accuracy of incorporation — about the question whether the authors and ratifiers of the Fourteenth Amendment intended to apply the Bill of Rights to state and local governments. For the classic arguments on each side, see Charles Fairman, Does the Fourteenth Amendment Incorporate the Bill of Rights? The Original Understanding, 2 Stan. L. Rev. 5 (1949) (against incorporation); William Winslow Crosskey, Charles Fairman, "Legislative History," and the Constitutional Limitations on State Authority, 22 U. Chi. L. Rev. 1 (1954) (for incorporation). That debate is, to say the least, not easily summarized. The tide seems to be shifting among the historians toward the conclusion that there is substantial evidence indicating that the Due Process Clause was designed in part to make the Bill of Rights enforceable against the states, although more through action of Congress than the judiciary. For a thorough airing, see the symposium, The Fourteenth Amendment and the Bill of Rights, 18 J. of Cont. Legal Issues 1-533 (2009). In the most recent case to reach the issue, the Supreme Court, relying almost entirely on an historical analysis, concluded that the Second Amendment is incorporated into the Due Process Clause. McDonald v. City of Chicago, IL 561 U.S. _____ (2010). For more on *McDonald*, see note 5, infra.

Putting historical questions aside, what is the case, either principled or pragmatic, for reading "due process" as meaning, roughly, "that process which complies with the Bill of Rights"? One possible answer is that compliance with the Bill of Rights will generate a fair criminal process. But it would be surprising if that were true. Recall that the Bill of Rights arose out of a legal system that had none of the basic institutions of contemporary American criminal justice. For the Framers to have accurately anticipated the conditions of a fair criminal process today, they would have to have accurately anticipated district attorneys' offices and police forces, plea bargaining and prison systems. That kind of foresight seems, literally, incredible. It seems more likely that some Bill of Rights protections improve the criminal process, others make that process worse, and still others make no real difference. That hardly sounds like a recipe for sound constitutional regulation.

And there is another difficulty. One might imagine that due process of law flows out of some principle, that constitutional regulation of the criminal process is in pursuit of some definable goal. The rule of law is a plausible candidate for such a goal or principle, as is accuracy. But the Bill of Rights is not. There is no obvious unifying principle to the disparate set of protections in the Fourth, Fifth, and Sixth Amendments. That makes it hard to see how the phrase "due process of law" has room to hold all those protections.

Accuracy (and Race).   In a series of decisions in the 1920s and 1930s, the Supreme Court overturned convictions of black defendants in Southern state courts in circumstances where there was good reason to believe the defendants were innocent. Michael Klarman describes four such cases:

> . . . [All of the cases] involved southern black criminal defendants convicted and sentenced to death after egregiously unfair trials. In Moore v. Dempsey,[5] the Supreme Court interpreted the Due Process Clause of the Fourteenth Amendment to forbid criminal convictions obtained through mob-dominated trials. In Powell v. Alabama,[6] the Court ruled that the Due Process Clause requires state appointment of counsel in capital cases and overturned convictions where defense counsel had been appointed the morning of trial. In Norris v. Alabama,[7] the Court reversed a conviction under the Equal Protection Clause where blacks had been intentionally excluded from juries. To reach that result, the Court had to revise the critical "subconstitutional"[8] rules that previously had made such claims nearly impossible to prove. In Brown v. Mississippi,[9] the

---

5. 261 U.S. 86 (1923).
6. 287 U.S. 45 (1932).
7. 294 U.S. 587 (1935).
8. By "subconstitutional" rules, I mean not the substantive liability standards, but rather the all-important rules bearing on standards of proof, standards of appellate review, and access to federal court. For a fuller discussion, see Michael J. Klarman, The *Plessy* Era, 1998 Sup. Ct. Rev. 303, 376-378.
9. 297 U.S. 278 (1936).

Court construed the Due Process Clause to forbid criminal convictions based on confessions extracted through torture.

These four decisions arose from three distinct episodes. In *Moore*, six black defendants appealed death sentences imposed for a murder allegedly committed in connection with the infamous race riot in Phillips County, Arkansas in the fall of 1919.[10] Phillips was a typical deep South cotton county with a black majority of approximately three-to-one. According to the local black community, the cause of the racial altercation that culminated in the *Moore* litigation was the brutal suppression by whites of an effort by black sharecroppers after World War I to form a tenant farmers' union and to seek legal redress for their landlords' peonage practices. The white community, on the contrary, charged that the cause of the conflagration was a black conspiracy to murder white planters throughout the county. An initial altercation in which whites shot into a black union meeting at a church and blacks returned the gunfire, killing a white man, quickly escalated into mayhem. Marauding whites, some of whom flocked to Phillips County from adjoining states and enjoyed the assistance of federal troops ostensibly employed to quell the disturbance, went on a rampage against blacks, tracking them down through the rural county, and killing (on one estimate) as many as 250 of them. Seventy-nine blacks (and no whites) were prosecuted as a result of the riot; twelve received the death penalty for murder; and six were involved in the appeal to the United States Supreme Court in Moore v. Dempsey. The Court reversed their convictions on the ground that mob-dominated trial proceedings violated the Due Process Clause.

The second and third race-based criminal procedure cases of the interwar period, Powell v. Alabama and Norris v. Alabama, both arose out of the famous Scottsboro Boys episode.[11] Nine black youths, ranging in age from thirteen to twenty, impoverished, illiterate, and transient, were charged with raping two young white women, alleged to be prostitutes, on a freight train in northern Alabama in the spring of 1931. They were tried in a mob-dominated atmosphere, and eight of the defendants received the death penalty. The state supreme court reversed one of these death sentences on the ground that the defendant was too young to be executed under state law and affirmed the other seven. The United States Supreme Court twice reversed the Scottsboro Boys' convictions — the first time on the ground that they had been denied the right to counsel, and the second time on the ground that blacks had been intentionally excluded from the grand jury that indicted them and the trial jury that convicted them.

Fourth and finally, in Brown v. Mississippi the Supreme Court reversed the death sentences of three black sharecroppers convicted of murdering their white landlord.[12] The principal evidence against the defendants was their own confessions, extracted through torture. The Supreme Court ruled that convictions so obtained violated the Due Process Clause of the Fourteenth Amendment.

These four cases arose out of three quite similar episodes. Southern black defendants were charged with serious crimes against whites — either rape or murder. All three sets of defendants nearly were lynched before their cases could be brought to trial. In all three episodes, mobs comprised of hundreds or even thousands of whites surrounded the courthouse during the trial, demanding that the defendants be turned over for a swift execution. No change of venue was granted in these cases (except in the retrial of the Scottsboro Boys). Lynchings were avoided only through the presence of

10. The most detailed treatment of *Moore* is Richard C. Cortner, A Mob Intent on Death: The NAACP and the Arkansas Riot Cases (1988). A briefer description appears in O. A. Rogers, Jr., The Elaine Race Riots of 1919, 19 Ark. Hist. Q. 142 (1960).

11. For extensive treatment of the Scottsboro Boys episode, see Dan T. Carter, Scottsboro: A Tragedy of the American South (rev. ed. 1979) and James Goodman, Stories of Scottsboro (1994).

12. The most complete treatment is Richard C. Cortner, A "Scottsboro" Case in Mississippi: The Supreme Court and *Brown v. Mississippi* (1986).

state militiamen armed with machine guns surrounding the courthouse. There was a serious doubt — not just with the aid of historical hindsight, but at the time of the trial — as to whether any of the defendants was in fact guilty of the crime charged. The defendants in *Moore* and *Brown* were tortured into confessing. In all three cases, defense lawyers were appointed either the day of or the day preceding trial, with no adequate opportunity to consult with their clients, to interview witnesses, or to prepare a defense strategy. Trials took place quickly after the alleged crimes in order to avoid a lynching — less than a week afterwards in *Brown*, twelve days in *Powell*, and a month in *Moore*. The trials were completed within a matter of hours (forty-five minutes in *Moore*), and the juries, from which blacks were intentionally excluded in all three cases, deliberated for only a matter of minutes before imposing death sentences.[13]

Michael J. Klarman, The Racial Origins of Modern Criminal Procedure, 99 Mich. L. Rev. 48, 50-52 (2000). For a more general treatment of the role of race in Supreme Court adjudication, see Michael J. Klarman, From Jim Crow to Civil Rights: The Supreme Court and the Struggle for Racial Equality (2004).

As Klarman argues in his article, these cases are as much about race as about criminal procedure. But they gave rise to an idea that goes beyond race — the idea that due process should ensure accurate procedures, procedures that would prevent conviction of innocent defendants. Thus, the problem with the mob-dominated trial in *Moore*, with the absence of any real defense counsel in *Powell*, and with the beating-induced confession in *Brown* was the same: All tended to lead to conviction and punishment without regard to whether the defendants were guilty.

From roughly 1940 to 1960, this strand of due process produced two major lines of cases. First, indigent criminal defendants were entitled to appointed counsel if there were "special circumstances" that made it impossible for them to represent themselves. See Betts v. Brady, 316 U.S. 455 (1942). Obviously, this standard required a good deal of ad hoc evaluation of the nature of the case in order to decide whether appointed counsel was really necessary. The second line of cases held, following Brown v. Mississippi, that involuntary confessions were inadmissible. That standard prompted a good deal of litigation in the 1940s and 1950s; one of the themes running through those cases was the need to ensure that confessions were truthful. See, e.g., Stein v. New York, 346 U.S. 156, 182 (1953) ("The tendency of the innocent . . . to risk remote results of a false confession rather than suffer immediate pain is so strong that judges long ago found it necessary to . . . treat[ ] any confession made concurrently with torture or threat of brutality as too untrustworthy to be received as evidence of guilt.").

Since 1960, due-process-as-accuracy has produced a variety of doctrines. Under Brady v. Maryland, 373 U.S. 83 (1963), and its progeny, the prosecution must turn

---

13. On Scottsboro, see Carter, supra note 11, chs. 1-2; Goodman, supra note 11, chs. 1-2. On *Moore*, see Cortner, *Mob*, supra note 10, ch. 1. On *Brown*, see Cortner, *Brown*, supra note 12, chs. 1-2. The Scottsboro Boys certainly were innocent of the crimes charged, as revealed in a subsequent recantation by one of the alleged victims. Their innocence should have been reasonably clear at the trial both from the medical evidence and from the conflicting testimony of the prosecution's witnesses. See Brief for Petitioners at 28-30, Powell v. Alabama, 287 U.S. 45 (1932) (Nos. 98-100), reprinted in 27 Landmark Briefs and Arguments of the Supreme Court of the United States: Constitutional Law 291, 324-326 (Philip B. Kurland & Gerhard Casper eds., 1975); Carter, supra, at 27-30, 227-228, 232. The *Brown* defendants possibly were innocent, and the State surely lacked sufficient evidence to convict them apart from their tortured [confessions]. See Brown v. State, 161 So. 465, 471 (Miss. 1935) (Griffith, J., dissenting). The *Moore* defendants at most were guilty of being present when the lethal shots were fired, and not even clearly of this. See Cortner, *Mob*, supra note 10, 124-125. . . .

over exculpatory evidence to the defense. (This requirement is discussed in Chapter 11.) Under Drope v. Missouri, 420 U.S. 162 (1975), defendants cannot be made to stand trial unless they are competent to assist in their own defense. (This line of cases is discussed in Medina v. California, at page 104, infra.) Ake v. Oklahoma, 470 U.S. 168 (1985), holds that in some cases the court must appoint a mental health expert to assist in the preparation of a defendant's insanity claim.

Are these rules adequate to ensure a fair process? Is there anything beyond accuracy that needs constitutional protection?

"Fundamental Fairness."   The last of the four strands is the hardest to describe, because it boils down to little more than judicial intuition. In a series of cases going back to the first decade of the twentieth century, the Supreme Court has decided whether due process requires a given practice by asking whether the practice is somehow basic to a decent criminal justice system — whether it is the sort of protection any free society ought to provide. The Court has used different phrases to capture this approach at different times; today the phrase of choice is "fundamental fairness." What is meant by that phrase (or by its earlier substitutes) is not clear; it seems to be a stand-in for a generalized sense that some kinds of government conduct are outrageous (never mind why) or that some procedures are essential (never mind for what).

An early example of this approach is Twining v. New Jersey, 211 U.S. 78 (1908). Twining's jury was told it could draw adverse inferences from his failure to take the witness stand; Twining's claim was that this violated the privilege against self-incrimination, which, he argued, applied to New Jersey through the Fourteenth Amendment's Due Process Clause. The Court's analysis is captured by the following strange sentence: "We have to consider whether the right is so fundamental in due process that a refusal of the right is a denial of due process." Id., at 107. The Court's answer was no. In Palko v. Connecticut, 302 U.S. 319 (1937), the Court gave the same answer when asked whether the prohibition against double jeopardy was sufficiently "fundamental." (Palko was tried and convicted of second-degree murder; he successfully appealed the conviction; the state then retried him and this time convicted him of capital murder and sentenced him to death.) Justice Cardozo, speaking for the majority, explained the line between those procedures required by due process and those not:

> There emerges the perception of a rationalizing principle which gives . . . a proper order and coherence. The right to trial by jury and the immunity from prosecution except as the result of an indictment may have value and importance. Even so, they are not of the very essence of a scheme of ordered liberty. To abolish them is not to violate a "principle of justice so rooted in the traditions and conscience of our people as to be ranked as fundamental." Snyder v. Massachusetts, [291 U.S. 97,] 105. Few would be so narrow or provincial as to maintain that a fair and enlightened system of justice would be impossible without them. What is true of jury trials and indictments is true also, as the cases show, of the immunity from compulsory self-incrimination. Twining v. New Jersey, supra. This too might be lost, and justice still be done. . . . Justice . . . would not perish if the accused were subject to a duty to respond to orderly inquiry. . . .
>
>   . . . Is that kind of double jeopardy to which the statute has subjected [the defendant] a hardship so acute and shocking that our polity will not endure it? Does it violate those "fundamental principles of liberty and justice which lie at the base of all our

civil and political institutions"? Hebert v. Louisiana, [272 U.S. 312]. The answer surely must be "no."

One is tempted to ask, "Why not?"

This sort of analysis reached its nadir in Rochin v. California, 342 U.S. 165 (1952). The Court recounted the facts in *Rochin* as follows:

> Having "some information that [the petitioner here] was selling narcotics," three deputy sheriffs of the County of Los Angeles, on the morning of July 1, 1949, made for the two-story dwelling house in which Rochin lived with his mother, common-law wife, brothers and sisters. Finding the outside door open, they entered and then forced open the door to Rochin's room on the second floor. Inside they found petitioner sitting partly dressed on the side of the bed, upon which his wife was lying. On a "night stand" beside the bed the deputies spied two capsules. When asked "Whose stuff is this?" Rochin seized the capsules and put them in his mouth. A struggle ensued, in the course of which the three officers "jumped upon him" and attempted to extract the capsules. The force they applied proved unavailing against Rochin's resistance. He was hand-cuffed and taken to a hospital. At the direction of one of the officers a doctor forced an emetic solution through a tube into Rochin's stomach against his will. This "stomach pumping" produced vomiting. In the vomited matter were found two capsules which proved to contain morphine.

In a stunningly uninformative opinion by Justice Frankfurter, the Court concluded that the stomach pumping violated due process:

> The vague contours of the Due Process Clause do not leave judges at large. We may not draw on our merely personal and private notions and disregard the limits that bind judges in their judicial function. Even though the concept of due process of law is not final and fixed, these limits are derived from considerations that are fused in the whole nature of our judicial process. These are considerations deeply rooted in reason and in the compelling traditions of the legal profession. The Due Process Clause places upon this Court the duty of exercising a judgment, within the narrow confines of judicial power in reviewing State convictions, upon interests of society pushing in opposite directions. . . .
>
> . . . [T]hat does not make due process of law a matter of judicial caprice. The fac-ulties of the Due Process Clause may be indefinite and vague, but the mode of their ascertainment is not self-willed. In each case "due process of law" requires an evalua-tion based on a disinterested inquiry pursued in the spirit of science, on a balanced order of facts exactly and fairly stated, on the detached consideration of conflicting claims, on a judgment not ad hoc and episodic but duly mindful of reconciling the needs both of continuity and of change in a progressive society.
>
> Applying these general considerations to the circumstances of the present case, we are compelled to conclude that the proceedings by which this conviction was obtained do more than offend some fastidious squeamishness or private sentimentalism about combatting crime too energetically. This is conduct that shocks the conscience. Ille-gally breaking into the privacy of the petitioner, the struggle to open his mouth and remove what was there, the forcible extraction of his stomach's contents — this course of proceeding by agents of government to obtain evidence is bound to offend even hardened sensibilities. They are methods too close to the rack and the screw to permit of constitutional differentiation.

342 U.S., at 170-172. Is Justice Frankfurter saying anything more than that he thinks the police behaved very badly? Does he say why?

Rochin-style due process analysis survives today, at least in a few outposts. A good modern example is Darden v. Wainwright, 477 U.S. 168 (1986). *Darden* was a capital murder case; in his closing argument, the prosecutor called the defendant an "animal," said "he shouldn't be out of his cell unless he has a leash on him," and expressed the wish that someone could have "blown his head off" before he had committed the crime. The Court held that the argument was improper, but not improper enough to amount to a violation of due process:

> . . . The relevant question is whether the prosecutors' comments "so infected the trial with unfairness as to make the resulting conviction a denial of due process." Donnelly v. DeChristoforo, 416 U.S. 637 (1974). . . .
>
> Under this standard of review, we agree with the reasoning of every court to consider these comments that they did not deprive petitioner of a fair trial. The prosecutors' argument did not manipulate or misstate the evidence, nor did it implicate other specific rights of the accused such as the right to counsel or the right to remain silent. . . . The trial court instructed the jurors several times that their decision was to be made on the basis of the evidence alone, and that the arguments of counsel were not evidence. The weight of the evidence against petitioner was heavy . . . [reducing] the likelihood that the jury's decision was influenced by argument. . . . For these reasons, we agree with the District Court below that "Darden's trial was not perfect — few are — but neither was it fundamentally unfair."

477 U.S., at 181-183. So the search in *Rochin* was shocking, while the prosecutor's argument in *Darden* was not (though it was close). Why are some things shocking and others not? Is there any content to these cases? Does the idea of fundamental fairness seem empty?

B. *Incorporation*

DUNCAN v. LOUISIANA

Appeal from the Supreme Court of Louisiana
391 U.S. 145 (1968)

MR. JUSTICE WHITE delivered the opinion of the Court. Appellant, Gary Duncan, was convicted of simple battery in the Twenty-fifth Judicial District Court of Louisiana. Under Louisiana law simple battery is a misdemeanor, punishable by a maximum of two years' imprisonment and a $300 fine. Appellant sought trial by jury, but because the Louisiana Constitution grants jury trials only in cases in which capital punishment or imprisonment at hard labor may be imposed, the trial judge denied the request. Appellant was convicted and sentenced to serve 60 days in the parish prison and pay a fine of $150. [The conviction was affirmed on appeal.] . . .

Appellant was 19 years of age when tried. While driving on Highway 23 in Plaquemines Parish on October 18, 1966, he saw two younger cousins engaged in a conversation by the side of the road with four white boys. Knowing his cousins, Negroes who had recently transferred to a formerly all-white high school, had reported the occurrence of racial incidents at the school, Duncan stopped the car, got out, and approached the six boys. At trial the white boys and a white onlooker testified, as did appellant and his cousins. The testimony was in dispute on many points, but the witnesses agreed that appellant and the white boys spoke to each other, that appellant encouraged his cousins to break off the encounter and enter his car, and that appellant was about to enter the car himself for the purpose of driving away with his cousins. The whites testified that just before getting in the car appellant slapped Herman Landry, one of the white boys, on the elbow. The Negroes testified that appellant had not slapped Landry, but had merely touched him. The trial judge concluded that the State had proved beyond a reasonable doubt that Duncan had committed simple battery, and found him guilty.

The Fourteenth Amendment denies the States the power to "deprive any person of life, liberty, or property, without due process of law." In resolving conflicting claims concerning the meaning of this spacious language, the Court has looked increasingly to the Bill of Rights for guidance; many of the rights guaranteed by the first eight Amendments to the Constitution have been held to be protected against state action by the Due Process Clause of the Fourteenth Amendment. That clause now protects the right to compensation for property taken by the State;[4] the rights of speech, press, and religion covered by the First Amendment;[5] the Fourth Amendment rights to be free from unreasonable searches and seizures and to have excluded from criminal trials any evidence illegally seized;[6] the right guaranteed by the Fifth Amendment to be free of compelled self-incrimination;[7] and the Sixth Amendment rights to counsel,[8] to a speedy[9] and public[10] trial, to confrontation of opposing witnesses,[11] and to compulsory process for obtaining witnesses.[12]

The test for determining whether a right extended by the Fifth and Sixth Amendments with respect to federal criminal proceedings is also protected against state action by the Fourteenth Amendment has been phrased in a variety of ways in the opinions of this Court. The question has been asked whether a right is among those "fundamental principles of liberty and justice which lie at the base of all our civil and political institutions," Powell v. Alabama, 287 U.S. 45, 67 (1932); whether it is "basic in our system of jurisprudence," In re Oliver, 333 U.S. 257, 273 (1948); and whether it is "a fundamental right, essential to a fair trial," Gideon v. Wainwright, 372 U.S. 335, 343-344 (1963). The claim before us is that the right to trial by jury guaranteed by the Sixth Amendment meets these tests. The position of Louisiana, on the other hand, is that the Constitution imposes upon the States no duty to give a jury trial in any criminal case, regardless of the seriousness of the crime or the size of the punishment which may be imposed. Because we believe that trial by jury in criminal cases is fundamental to the American scheme of justice, we hold that the Fourteenth Amendment guarantees a right of jury trial in all criminal cases which — were they

4. Chicago, B. & Q. R. Co. v. Chicago, 166 U.S. 226 (1897).
5. See, e.g., Fiske v. Kansas, 274 U.S. 380 (1927).
6. See Mapp v. Ohio, 367 U.S. 643 (1961).
7. Malloy v. Hogan, 378 U.S. 1 (1964).
8. Gideon v. Wainwright, 372 U.S. 335 (1963).
9. Klopfer v. North Carolina, 386 U.S. 213 (1967).
10. In re Oliver, 333 U.S. 257 (1948).
11. Pointer v. Texas, 380 U.S. 400 (1965).
12. Washington v. Texas, 388 U.S. 14 (1967).

to be tried in a federal court — would come within the Sixth Amendment's guarantee.[14] Since we consider the appeal before us to be such a case, we hold that the Constitution was violated when appellant's demand for jury trial was refused.

The history of trial by jury in criminal cases has been frequently told. It is sufficient for present purposes to say that by the time our Constitution was written, jury trial in criminal cases had been in existence in England for several centuries and carried impressive credentials traced by many to Magna Carta. Its preservation and proper operation as a protection against arbitrary rule were among the major objectives of the revolutionary settlement which was expressed in the Declaration and Bill of Rights of 1689. . . . Jury trial came to America with English colonists, and received strong support from them. Royal interference with the jury trial was deeply resented. . . . The Declaration of Independence stated solemn objections to the King's . . . "depriving us in many cases, of the benefits of Trial by Jury." . . . The Constitution itself, in Art. III, §2, commanded: "The Trial of all Crimes, except in Cases of Impeachment, shall be by Jury; and such Trial shall be held in the State where the said Crimes shall have been committed." . . .

The constitutions adopted by the original States guaranteed jury trial. Also, the constitution of every State entering the Union thereafter in one form or another protected the right to jury trial in criminal cases. Even such skeletal history is impressive support for considering the right to jury trial in criminal cases to be fundamental to our system of justice. . . .

Jury trial continues to receive strong support. The laws of every State guarantee a right to jury trial in serious criminal cases; no State has dispensed with it; nor are there significant movements under way to do so. . . .

14. In one sense recent cases applying provisions of the first eight Amendments to the States represent a new approach to the "incorporation" debate. Earlier the Court can be seen as having asked, when inquiring into whether some particular procedural safeguard was required of a State, if a civilized system could be imagined that would not accord the particular protection. For example, Palko v. Connecticut, 302 U.S. 319, 325 (1937), stated: "The right to trial by jury and the immunity from prosecution except as the result of an indictment may have value and importance. Even so, they are not of the very essence of a scheme of ordered liberty. . . . Few would be so narrow or provincial as to maintain that a fair and enlightened system of justice would be impossible without them." The recent cases, on the other hand, have proceeded upon the valid assumption that state criminal processes are not imaginary and theoretical schemes but actual systems bearing virtually every characteristic of the common-law system that has been developing contemporaneously in England and in this country. The question thus is whether given this kind of system a particular procedure is fundamental — whether, that is, a procedure is necessary to an Anglo-American regime of ordered liberty. It is this sort of inquiry that can justify the conclusions that state courts must exclude evidence seized in violation of the Fourth Amendment, Mapp v. Ohio, 367 U.S. 643 (1961); that state prosecutors may not comment on a defendant's failure to testify, Griffin v. California, 380 U.S. 609 (1965); and that criminal punishment may not be imposed for the status of narcotics addiction, Robinson v. California, 370 U.S. 660 (1962). Of immediate relevance for this case are the Court's holdings that the States must comply with certain provisions of the Sixth Amendment, specifically that the States may not refuse a speedy trial, confrontation of witnesses, and the assistance, at state expense if necessary, of counsel. See cases cited in nn. 8-12, supra. Of each of these determinations that a constitutional provision originally written to bind the Federal Government should bind the States as well it might be said that the limitation in question is not necessarily fundamental to fairness in every criminal system that might be imagined but is fundamental in the context of the criminal processes maintained by the American States.

. . . A criminal process which was fair and equitable but used no juries is easy to imagine. It would make use of alternative guarantees and protections which would serve the purposes that the jury serves in the English and American systems. Yet no American State has undertaken to construct such a system. Instead, every American State, including Louisiana, uses the jury extensively, and imposes very serious punishments only after a trial at which the defendant has a right to a jury's verdict. In every State, including Louisiana, the structure and style of the criminal process — the supporting framework and the subsidiary procedures — are of the sort that naturally complement jury trial, and have developed in connection with and in reliance upon jury trial.

. . . The guarantees of jury trial in the Federal and State Constitutions reflect a profound judgment about the way in which law should be enforced and justice administered. A right to jury trial is granted to criminal defendants in order to prevent oppression by the Government. Those who wrote our constitutions knew from history and experience that it was necessary to protect against unfounded criminal charges brought to eliminate enemies and against judges too responsive to the voice of higher authority. . . . Providing an accused with the right to be tried by a jury of his peers gave him an inestimable safeguard against the corrupt or overzealous prosecutor and against the compliant, biased, or eccentric judge. If the defendant preferred the common-sense judgment of a jury to the more tutored but perhaps less sympathetic reaction of the single judge, he was to have it. Beyond this, the jury trial provisions in the Federal and State Constitutions reflect a fundamental decision about the exercise of official power — a reluctance to entrust plenary powers over the life and liberty of the citizen to one judge or to a group of judges. . . . The deep commitment of the Nation to the right of jury trial in serious criminal cases as a defense against arbitrary law enforcement qualifies for protection under the Due Process Clause of the Fourteenth Amendment, and must therefore be respected by the States.

. . . We are aware of the long debate, especially in this century, among those who write about the administration of justice, as to the wisdom of permitting untrained laymen to determine the facts in civil and criminal proceedings. . . . [A]t the heart of the dispute have been express or implicit assertions that juries are incapable of adequately understanding evidence or determining issues of fact, and that they are unpredictable, quixotic, and little better than a roll of dice. Yet, the most recent and exhaustive study of the jury in criminal cases concluded that juries do understand the evidence and come to sound conclusions in most of the cases presented to them and that when juries differ with the result at which the judge would have arrived, it is usually because they are serving some of the very purposes for which they were created and for which they are now employed.[26]

The State of Louisiana urges that holding that the Fourteenth Amendment assures a right to jury trial will cast doubt on the integrity of every trial conducted without a jury. Plainly, this is not the import of our holding. . . . We would not assert . . . that every criminal trial — or any particular trial — held before a judge alone is unfair or that a defendant may never be as fairly treated by a judge as he would be by a jury. Thus we hold no constitutional doubts about the practices, common in both federal and state courts, of accepting waivers of jury trial and prosecuting petty crimes without extending a right to jury trial. However, the fact is that in most places more trials for serious crimes are to juries than to a court alone; a great many defendants prefer the judgment of a jury to that of a court. Even where defendants are satisfied with bench trials, the right to a jury trial very likely serves its intended purpose of making judicial or prosecutorial unfairness less likely.

Louisiana's final contention is that even if it must grant jury trials in serious criminal cases, the conviction before us is valid and constitutional because here the petitioner was tried for simple battery and was sentenced to only 60 days in the parish prison. . . . It is doubtless true that there is a category of petty crimes or offenses which is not subject to the Sixth Amendment jury trial provision and should not be subject to the Fourteenth Amendment jury trial requirement here applied to the

---

26. [Citing Harry Kalven, Jr. & Hans Zeisel, The American Jury (1966).]

States. . . . In the case before us the Legislature of Louisiana has made simple battery a criminal offense punishable by imprisonment for up to two years and a fine. The question, then, is whether a crime carrying such a penalty is an offense which Louisiana may insist on trying without a jury. . . .

. . . In the federal system, petty offenses are defined as those punishable by no more than six months in prison and a $500 fine. In 49 of the 50 States crimes subject to trial without a jury, which occasionally include simple battery, are punishable by no more than one year in jail. Moreover, in the late 18th century in America crimes triable without a jury were for the most part punishable by no more than a six-month prison term, although there appear to have been exceptions to this rule. We need not, however, settle in this case the exact location of the line between petty offenses and serious crimes. It is sufficient for our purposes to hold that a crime punishable by two years in prison is, based on past and contemporary standards in this country, a serious crime and not a petty offense. Consequently, appellant was entitled to a jury trial and it was error to deny it. . . .

[The concurring opinion of Justice Black, joined by Justice Douglas, and the dissenting opinion of Justice Harlan, joined by Justice Stewart, are omitted.]

NOTES ON *DUNCAN* AND THE INCORPORATION OF THE BILL OF RIGHTS

1. *Duncan*'s facts, at least as the Court recounts them, suggest a racially rigged proceeding, do they not? In this respect, *Duncan* looks like Moore v. Dempsey, 261 U.S. 86 (1923), Powell v. Alabama, 287 U.S. 45 (1932), and Brown v. Mississippi, 297 U.S. 278 (1936) — earlier cases in which the Court overturned convictions of black defendants in proceedings that seemed racially rigged. (*Moore, Powell,* and *Brown* are discussed at pages 93-94, supra.)

In none of these cases did the Court treat the legal issue as one of race discrimination. Instead, the Court's rulings were general, mandating or prohibiting certain procedures across the board — no mob-dominated trials in *Moore*, no uncounseled convictions in capital cases in *Powell*, no involuntary confessions in *Brown*, no denial of jury trial in *Duncan*. This has been a longstanding pattern in the law of constitutional criminal procedure. A great deal of the law covered in books like this one arises out of cases like *Duncan* — cases in which the real concern seems to be race-based injustice. Yet the law almost always deals with that concern indirectly, by regulating procedures that have little to do with race.

Why the indirection? Why not say *Duncan*'s conviction was discriminatory, and leave it at that? One answer is that regulating discrimination directly would have led the Court, and the judiciary, into some very large and complex thickets. Suppose in a given jurisdiction, black Americans constitute 10 percent of the population but 25 percent of those arrested and convicted of crimes. Does that suggest discrimination? It might. But it might mean instead that the black population of that jurisdiction is disproportionately poor, and hence disproportionately involved in (and victimized by) crime. Indeed, the *absence* of a racial disproportion might be a sign of discrimination. Consider: In South Carolina in 1950 — the deep South, during the heyday of Jim Crow — the imprisoned felon population was slightly *whiter* than the population as a whole. Compare Federal Bureau of Prisons, National Prisoner Statistics: Prisoners in State and Federal Institutions — 1950, at 55 tbl. 21 (1954) (prison population nearly two-thirds white) with U.S. Department of Commerce, Statistical Abstract of the United States — 1953, at 36 tbl. 25 (overall population 61 percent white). South Carolina in 1950 was not running a color-blind criminal justice system. The more plausible possibility is that local police forces and local prosecutors were neglecting to investigate and prosecute crimes *against* blacks. Since most crime is intraracial, that tendency would naturally lead to fewer black prisoners. For a good discussion of this two-sided nature of discrimination in the criminal justice system, see Randall Kennedy, Race, Crime, and the Law (1997). All of which means that it is much harder than one might think to draw the line between racist law enforcement and law enforcement that is trying as best it can to advance the interests of the communities it serves.

Spotting clear cases of discrimination, like *Duncan*, may be easy. But once the easy cases are put aside, discrimination becomes much more subtle — which is not to say it is less real or less substantial — and much harder for courts to identify. Should the focus be on discrimination against black suspects? Black crime victims? Should courts be in the business of allocating police and prosecutorial resources across different racial communities? These questions, and others equally hard, would have to be faced if the Court sought to attack the criminal justice system's race problems directly.

None of this is to say that the Court's approach in *Duncan*, or in earlier cases like *Moore*, *Powell*, and *Brown*, was right. Perhaps we would be better off if race were addressed more directly in the law of criminal procedure. Whatever the right answer to that question is, the Supreme Court's usual strategy has been to sidestep — and to regulate procedures aggressively on *non*-racial grounds.

2. Notice one key difference between *Duncan* and most of the pre-incorporation due process cases. In the older due process cases, the Court almost always responded to apparent injustices with standards that required case-by-case development and application. Brown v. Mississippi, 297 U.S. 278 (1936), barred the use of involuntary confessions, but left open what voluntariness meant. Betts v. Brady, 316 U.S. 455 (1942), required use of appointed counsel where special circumstances suggested a particular need, but left undefined what those circumstances were. In *Duncan*, by contrast, the Court established a hard-and-fast rule. At the least, the Court said, any crime punishable by two years in prison triggers the right to a jury; the Court hinted that any crime punishable by more than six months would do so as well. (The hint was soon confirmed by Baldwin v. New York, 399 U.S. 66 (1970).) Why the shift from standards to rules? What would a standard (as opposed to a rule) look like in *Duncan*?

3. The move from standards to rules is one of the most important effects of incorporation; in one area after another, the Court of the 1960s and 1970s created a large body of detailed legal rules where previously constitutional law had said little more than "be fair." Examples include the right to jury trial in *Duncan*, covered in more detail in Chapter 14, the detailed rules governing the Fourth Amendment's warrant requirement (and exceptions thereto) covered in Chapter 5, the rules governing application of the Fifth Amendment's privilege against self-incrimination to police interrogation, covered in Chapter 6, or the rules defining the ban on double jeopardy, the subject of Chapter 16. In each of these areas, pre-incorporation constitutional law either said nothing at all or offered only a vague prohibition of extreme misconduct. Constitutional law today says a great deal, and a great deal of it is in the form of rules.

As that description suggests, there are two other changes that went alongside the move from standards to rules. Before incorporation, constitutional law regulated the criminal process very lightly. After incorporation, it regulates much more extensively. Constitutional law today goes far toward defining the criminal process — it is not a marginal presence in criminal procedure; on the contrary, it *dominates* criminal procedure. So constitutional regulation has become much more intrusive — much larger — as it has become much more rulelike. The last of these three changes is the most obvious. Incorporation shifts the constitutional focus from the Due Process Clause to the various criminal procedure provisions of the Bill of Rights. Instead of construing the phrase "due process of law," courts today are more likely to be interpreting phrases like "the assistance of counsel," or "compelled to be a witness against himself," or "unreasonable searches and seizures."

These three changes — from standards to rules, from light regulation to heavy regulation, from due process to the Bill of Rights — happened together. Is that anything more than an accident? Couldn't the Supreme Court have crafted a law of due process that was more rule-like? That regulated criminal procedure more extensively? As you study subsequent chapters in this book, consider this question: How might the law differ if it were based on due process and not on some provision of the Fourth, Fifth, or Sixth Amendment?

4. One common complaint about pre-incorporation due process cases is the absence of any clear, agreed-upon value being advanced. In some cases, the Court seemed concerned with ensuring accurate trials; in other cases, it was more concerned with preserving the rule of law; in still others, it was concerned with something the Justices found impossible to articulate, capturing it in labels like "fundamental fairness" or "shocks the conscience." Incorporation seems, at first blush, to solve that problem, by anchoring the Court's criminal procedure decisions in more definite pieces of constitutional text. The right to a jury, the right to counsel, the privilege against self-incrimination — all these things seem clearer than "due process of law."

But that clarity may be an illusion. Think about *Duncan* and the right to jury trial. What is the point of that right? There are several possible answers. Juries could be designed to ensure accuracy — the idea here would be that a single judge is more likely to convict an innocent defendant than are 12 citizens. Or juries could be designed as a democratic check on the judiciary. Here, the image is of juries as mini-legislatures, supervising the behavior of police, prosecutors, and judges. Yet a third possibility is suggested by the facts in *Duncan*: Juries could be a way to ensure that racial or ethnic minorities are punished with the consent of their peers. That might translate into juries that always have black or Latino members when judging black or Latino defendants.

These possibilities lead to very different visions of the right. If accuracy is the point, the right to a jury ought to be available, at the least, for all serious crimes — as *Duncan* holds. If preserving a democratic check on the courts is the point, perhaps juries ought to be required in *all* criminal trials (and perhaps *trials* should be required, since plea bargains are hidden from the public). If ensuring minority representation is the point, maybe the right to a jury ought to be available to black defendants like Duncan, but not to the white teenagers with whom Duncan was allegedly fighting.

In short, the Court must, at least tacitly, decide what the right to a jury is *about* in order to decide what that right entails. Answering that question may be no easier than answering the question of what due process is about. And with incorporation, the question is repeated for every Bill of Rights provision. What is the point of banning "unreasonable searches and seizures"? Privacy protection? Protecting against police coercion? Something else? What about the privilege against self-incrimination — is it a protection for the guilty, or for the innocent? Does it protect freedom of thought, or does it only limit the government's ability to twist people's arms? Is the right to counsel a means of ensuring equality between rich and poor defendants, or a tool for generating accurate results? Because of incorporation, the law of criminal procedure must answer all these questions. And the questions are just as difficult as the question the Due Process Clause poses: What does it mean to treat people fairly?

5. As mentioned above, McDonald v. City of Chicago, IL, 561 U.S. _____ (2010), is the most recent incorporationist case concluding that the Second Amendment is implicit in the Due Process Clause of the Fourteenth Amendment. In a somewhat stunning development, the positions of the various justices were completely reversed from that of their intellectual precursors on the Court. Incorporationist theory was employed by the "liberal" wing of the Court throughout the Warren era, and steadfastly resisted by "conservative" wing. In *McDonald*, by contrast, Justice Alito wrote for a plurality that included Chief Justice Roberts and Justices Kennedy and Scalia. Justice Thomas concurred with the result on the ground that the Privileges and Immunities Clause, not the Due Process Clause, does the work here, and the last 60 years or so of constitutional development should be rethought. Justices Stevens, Breyer, Ginsburg, and Sotomayor dissented. After *McDonald*, only four of the specific provisions of the Bill of Rights are not incorporated into Due Process: the Third Amendment's protection against the quartering of soldiers; the grand jury provision dealt with in *Hurtado*; the right to a civil jury in the Seventh Amendment; and the excessive fines provision in the Eighth Amendment. We leave it to you to determine what you think the implications of this development might be.

C.   The Residual Due Process Clause

What is left of due process in criminal cases apart from the Bill of Rights? Consider the following case.

MEDINA v. CALIFORNIA

Certiorari to the Supreme Court of California
505 U.S. 437 (1992)

JUSTICE KENNEDY delivered the opinion of the Court.

It is well established that the Due Process Clause of the Fourteenth Amendment prohibits the criminal prosecution of a defendant who is not competent to stand trial. Drope v. Missouri, 420 U.S. 162 (1975); Pate v. Robinson, 383 U.S. 375 (1966). The issue in this case is whether the Due Process Clause permits a State to require a defendant who alleges incompetence to stand trial to bear the burden of proving so by a preponderance of the evidence.

In 1984, petitioner Teofilo Medina, Jr., stole a gun from a pawnshop in Santa Ana, California. In the weeks that followed, he held up two gas stations, a drive-in dairy, and a market, murdered three employees of those establishments, attempted to rob a fourth employee, and shot at two passers-by who attempted to follow his get-away car. Petitioner was . . . charged with a number of criminal offenses, including three counts of first-degree murder. Before trial, petitioner's counsel moved for a competency hearing . . . on the ground that he was unsure whether petitioner had the ability to participate in the criminal proceedings against him.

Under California law, "[a] person cannot be tried or adjudged to punishment while such person is mentally incompetent." Cal. Penal Code Ann. §1367 (West 1982). A defendant is mentally incompetent "if, as a result of mental disorder or developmental disability, the defendant is unable to understand the nature of the criminal proceedings or to assist counsel in the conduct of a defense in a rational manner." Ibid. The statute establishes a presumption that the defendant is competent, and the party claiming incompetence bears the burden of proving that the defendant is incompetent by a preponderance of the evidence. . . .

The trial court granted the motion for a hearing and the preliminary issue of petitioner's competence to stand trial was tried to a jury. Over the course of the 6-day hearing, in addition to lay testimony, the jury heard conflicting expert testimony about petitioner's mental condition. The Supreme Court of California gives this summary:

> Dr. Gold, a psychiatrist who knew defendant while he was in the Arizona prison system, testified that defendant was a paranoid schizophrenic and was incompetent to assist his attorney at trial. Dr. Echeandia, a clinical psychologist at the Orange County jail, doubted the accuracy of the schizophrenia diagnosis, and could not express an opinion on defendant's competence to stand trial. Dr. Sharma, a psychiatrist, likewise expressed doubts regarding the schizophrenia diagnosis and leaned toward a finding of competence. Dr. Pierce, a psychologist, believed defendant was schizophrenic, with impaired memory and hallucinations, but nevertheless was competent to stand trial. Dr. Sakurai, a jail psychiatrist, opined that although defendant suffered from depression, he was competent, and that he may have been malingering. Dr. Sheffield, who treated defendant for knife wounds he incurred in jail, could give no opinion on the competency issue.

51 Cal. 3d 870, 880, 799 P.2d 1282, 1288 (1990).

During the competency hearing, petitioner engaged in several verbal and physical outbursts. On one of these occasions, he overturned the counsel table.

. . . The jury found petitioner competent to stand trial. A new jury was empaneled for the criminal trial, and . . . found [petitioner] guilty of all three counts of first-degree murder and a number of lesser offenses. . . . A sanity hearing was held, and the jury found that petitioner was sane at the time of the offenses. At the penalty phase, the jury found that the murders were premeditated and deliberate and returned a verdict of death. The trial court imposed the death penalty for the murder convictions and sentenced petitioner to a prison term for the remaining offenses. . . . [The California Supreme Court affirmed.]

Petitioner argues that our decision in Mathews v. Eldridge, 424 U.S. 319 (1976), provides the proper analytical framework for determining whether California's allocation of the burden of proof in competency hearings comports with due process. We disagree. In *Mathews*, we articulated a three-factor test for evaluating procedural due process claims which requires a court to consider first, the private interest that will be affected by the official action; second, the risk of an erroneous deprivation of such interest through the procedures used, and the probable value, if any, of additional or substitute procedural safeguards; and finally, the Government's interest, including the function involved and the fiscal and administrative burdens that the additional or substitute procedural requirement would entail.

Id., at 335.

In our view, the *Mathews* balancing test does not provide the appropriate framework for assessing the validity of state procedural rules which, like the one at bar, are part of the criminal process. . . .

In the field of criminal law, we "have defined the category of infractions that violate 'fundamental fairness' very narrowly" based on the recognition that, "beyond the specific guarantees enumerated in the Bill of Rights, the Due Process Clause has limited operation." Dowling v. United States, 493 U.S. 342, 352 (1990). The Bill of Rights speaks in explicit terms to many aspects of criminal procedure, and the expansion of those constitutional guarantees under the open-ended rubric of the Due Process Clause invites undue interference with both considered legislative judgments and the careful balance that the Constitution strikes between liberty and order. As we said in Spencer v. Texas, 385 U.S. 554, 564 (1967), "it has never been thought that [decisions under the Due Process Clause] establish this Court as a rule-making organ for the promulgation of state rules of criminal procedure."

Mathews itself involved a due process challenge to the adequacy of administrative procedures established for the purpose of terminating Social Security disability benefits, and the *Mathews* balancing test was first conceived to address due process claims arising in the context of administrative law. . . .

The proper analytical approach, and the one that we adopt here, is that set forth in Patterson v. New York, 432 U.S. 197 (1977), which was decided one year after *Mathews*. In *Patterson*, we rejected a due process challenge to a New York law which placed on a criminal defendant the burden of proving the affirmative defense of extreme emotional disturbance. Rather than relying upon the *Mathews* balancing test, however, we reasoned that a narrower inquiry was more appropriate:

> It goes without saying that preventing and dealing with crime is much more the business of the States than it is of the Federal Government, and that we should not lightly construe the Constitution so as to intrude upon the administration of justice by the individual States. Among other things, it is normally "within the power of the State to regulate procedures under which its laws are carried out, including the burden of producing evidence and the burden of persuasion," and its decision in this regard is not subject to proscription under the Due Process Clause unless "it offends some principle of justice so rooted in the traditions and conscience of our people as to be ranked as fundamental." Speiser v. Randall, 357 U.S. 513, 523 (1958).

Patterson v. New York, 432 U.S., at 201-202.

As *Patterson* suggests, because the States have considerable expertise in matters of criminal procedure and the criminal process is grounded in centuries of common-law tradition, it is appropriate to exercise substantial deference to legislative judgments in this area. The analytical approach endorsed in *Patterson* is thus far less intrusive than that approved in *Mathews*.

Based on our review of the historical treatment of the burden of proof in competency proceedings, the operation of the challenged rule, and our precedents, we cannot say that the allocation of the burden of proof to a criminal defendant to prove incompetence "offends some principle of justice so rooted in the traditions and conscience of our people as to be ranked as fundamental." Patterson v. New York, 432 U.S., at 202 (internal quotation marks omitted). Historical practice is probative of whether a procedural rule can be characterized as fundamental. See In re Winship, 397 U.S. 358, 361 (1970). The rule that a criminal defendant who is incompetent should not be required to stand trial has deep roots in our common-law heritage. Blackstone acknowledged that a defendant "who became 'mad' after the commission of an offense should not be arraigned for it 'because he is not able to plead to it with that advice and caution that he ought,'" and "if he became 'mad' after pleading, he should not be tried, 'for how can he make his defense?'" Drope v. Missouri, 420 U.S., at 171 (quoting 4 W. Blackstone, Commentaries *24); accord, 1 M. Hale, Pleas of the Crown *34-*35.

By contrast, there is no settled tradition on the proper allocation of the burden of proof in a proceeding to determine competence. . . . Contemporary practice, while of limited relevance to the due process inquiry, demonstrates that there remains no settled view of where the burden of proof should lie. . . . Some States have enacted statutes that, like §1369(f), place the burden of proof on the party raising the issue. E.g., Conn. Gen. Stat. §54-56d(b) (1991); Pa. Stat. Ann., Tit. 50, §7403(a) (Purdon Supp. 1991). A number of state courts have said that the burden of proof may be placed on the defendant to prove incompetence. E.g., Wallace v. State, 248 Ga. 255, 258-259, 282 S.E.2d 325, 330 (1981); State v. Aumann, 265 N.W.2d 316, 319-320 (Iowa 1978); State v. Chapman, 104 N.M. 324, 327-328, 721 P.2d 392, 395-396 (1986); Barber v. State, 757 S.W.2d 359, 362-363 (Tex. Crim. App. 1988) (en banc). Still other state courts have said that the burden rests with the prosecution. E.g., Diaz v. State, 508 A.2d 861, 863-864 (Del. 1986); Commonwealth v. Crowley, 393 Mass. 393, 400-401, 471 N.E.2d 353, 357-358 (1984); State v. Bertrand, 123 N.H. 719, 727-728, 465 A.2d 912, 916 (1983); State v. Jones, 406 N.W.2d 366, 369-370 (S.D. 1987).

Discerning no historical basis for concluding that the allocation of the burden of proving incompetence to the defendant violates due process, we turn to consider whether the rule transgresses any recognized principle of "fundamental fairness" in operation. . . .

Under California law, the allocation of the burden of proof to the defendant will affect competency determinations only in a narrow class of cases where the evidence is in equipoise; that is, where the evidence that a defendant is competent is just as strong as the evidence that he is incompetent. Our cases recognize that a defendant has a constitutional right "not to be tried while legally incompetent," and that a State's "failure to observe procedures adequate to protect a defendant's right not to be tried or convicted while incompetent to stand trial deprives him of his due process right to a fair trial." Drope v. Missouri, 420 U.S., at 172, 173. Once a State provides a defendant access to procedures for making a competency evaluation, however, we perceive no basis for holding that due process further requires the State to assume the burden of vindicating the defendant's constitutional right by persuading the trier of fact that the defendant is competent to stand trial.

Petitioner relies upon federal-and state-court decisions which have said that the allocation of the burden of proof to the defendant in these circumstances is inconsistent with the rule of Pate v. Robinson, 383 U.S., at 384, where we held that a defendant whose competence is in doubt cannot be deemed to have waived his right to a competency hearing. . . . In our view, the question whether a defendant whose competence is in doubt may waive his right to a competency hearing is quite different from the question whether the burden of proof may be placed on the defendant once a hearing is held. The rule announced in *Pate* was driven by our concern that it is impossible to say whether a defendant whose competence is in doubt has made a knowing and intelligent waiver of his right to a competency hearing. Once a competency hearing is held, however, the defendant is entitled to the assistance of counsel, and psychiatric evidence is brought to bear on the question of the defendant's mental condition. Although an impaired defendant might be limited in his ability to assist counsel in demonstrating incompetence, the defendant's inability to assist counsel can, in and of itself, constitute probative evidence of incompetence, and defense counsel will often have the best-informed view of the defendant's ability to participate in his defense. While reasonable minds may differ as to the wisdom of placing the burden of proof on the defendant in these circumstances, we believe that a State may take such factors into account in making judgments as to the allocation of the burden of proof. . . .

Petitioner argues that psychiatry is an inexact science, and that placing the burden of proof on the defendant violates due process because it requires the defendant to "bear the risk of being forced to stand trial as a result of an erroneous finding of competency." Brief for Petitioner 8. . . . The Due Process Clause does not, however, require a State to adopt one procedure over another on the basis that it may produce results more favorable to the accused. See, e.g., Patterson v. New York, 432 U.S., at 208 ("Due process does not require that every conceivable step be taken, at whatever cost, to eliminate the possibility of convicting an innocent person"). Consistent with our precedents, it is enough that the State affords the criminal defendant on whose behalf a plea of incompetence is asserted a reasonable opportunity to demonstrate that he is not competent to stand trial.

Petitioner further contends that the burden of proof should be placed on the State because we have allocated the burden to the State on a variety of other issues that implicate a criminal defendant's constitutional rights. E.g., Colorado v. Connelly, 479 U.S. 157, 168-169 (1986) (waiver of *Miranda* rights); Nix v. Williams, 467 U.S. 431, 444-445, n. 5 (1984) (inevitable discovery of evidence obtained by unlawful means); United States v. Matlock, 415 U.S. 164, 177-178, n. 14 (1974) (voluntariness of consent to search); Lego v. Twomey, 404 U.S. 477, 489 (1972) (voluntariness of confession). The decisions upon which petitioner relies, however, do not control the result here, because they involved situations where the government sought to introduce inculpatory evidence obtained by virtue of a waiver of, or in violation of, a defendant's constitutional rights. In such circumstances, allocating the burden of proof to the government furthers the objective of "deterring lawless conduct by police and prosecution." Ibid. No such purpose is served by allocating the burden of proof to the government in a competency hearing.

In light of our determination that the allocation of the burden of proof to the defendant does not offend due process, it is not difficult to dispose of petitioner's challenge to the presumption of competence imposed by §1369(f). . . . [I]n essence, the challenged presumption is a restatement of the burden of proof, and it follows from what we have said that the presumption does not violate the Due Process Clause.

Nothing in today's decision is inconsistent with our long-standing recognition that the criminal trial of an incompetent defendant violates due process. Rather, our rejection of petitioner's challenge to §1369(f) is based on a determination that the California procedure is "constitutionally adequate" to guard against such results, Drope v. Missouri, 420 U.S., at 172, and reflects our considered view that "traditionally, due process has required that only the most basic procedural safeguards be observed; more subtle balancing of society's interests against those of the accused has been left to the legislative branch," Patterson v. New York, 432 U.S., at 210. . . .

JUSTICE O'CONNOR, with whom JUSTICE SOUTER joins, concurring in the judgment.

I concur in the judgment of the Court, but I reject its intimation that the balancing of equities is inappropriate in evaluating whether state criminal procedures amount to due process. . . . The balancing of equities that Mathews v. Eldridge [, 424 U.S. 319 (1976),] outlines remains a useful guide in due process cases.

In *Mathews*, however, we did not have to address the question of how much weight to give historical practice; in the context of modern administrative procedures, there was no historical practice to consider. . . . While I agree with the Court that historical pedigree can give a procedural practice a presumption of constitutionality, the presumption must surely be rebuttable.

. . . Against the historical status quo, I read the Court's opinion to allow some weight to be given countervailing considerations of fairness in operation, considerations much like those we evaluated in *Mathews*. Any less charitable reading of the Court's opinion would put it at odds with many of our criminal due process cases, in which we have required States to institute procedures that were neither required at common law nor explicitly commanded by the text of the Constitution. See, e.g., Griffin v. Illinois [, 351 U.S. 12 (1956)] (due process right to trial transcript on appeal); Brady v. Maryland, 373 U.S. 83 (1963) (due process right to discovery of exculpatory evidence); Sheppard v. Maxwell, 384 U.S. 333 (1966) (due process right to protection from prejudicial publicity and courtroom disruptions); Chambers v. Mississippi, 410 U.S. 284 (1973) (due process right to introduce certain evidence); Gagnon v. Scarpelli, 411 U.S. 778 (1973) (due process right to hearing and counsel before probation revoked); Ake v. Oklahoma [, 470 U.S. 68 (1985)] (due process right to psychiatric examination when sanity is significantly in question).

In determining whether the placement of the burden of proof is fundamentally unfair, relevant considerations include: whether the government has superior access to evidence; whether the defendant is capable of aiding in the garnering and evaluation of evidence on the matter to be proved; and whether placing the burden of proof on the government is necessary to help enforce a further right, such as the right to be presumed innocent, the right to be free from self-incrimination, or the right to be tried while competent.

After balancing the equities in this case, I agree with the Court that the burden of proof may constitutionally rest on the defendant. . . . [T]he competency determination is based largely on the testimony of psychiatrists. The main concern of the prosecution, of course, is that a defendant will feign incompetence in order to avoid trial. If the burden of proving competence rests on the government, a defendant will have less incentive to cooperate in psychiatric investigations, because an inconclusive examination will benefit the defense, not the prosecution. A defendant may also be less cooperative in making available friends or family who might have information about the defendant's mental state. States may therefore decide that a more complete picture of a defendant's competence will be obtained if the defense has the incentive to produce all the evidence in its possession. The potentially greater over-all access to information provided by placing the burden of proof on the defense may outweigh the danger that, in close cases, a marginally incompetent defendant is brought to trial. Unlike the requirement of a hearing or a psychiatric examination, placing the burden of proof on the government will not necessarily increase the reliability of the proceedings. The equities here, then, do not weigh so much in petitioner's favor as to rebut the presumption of constitutionality that the historical toleration of procedural variation creates. . . .

[The dissenting opinion of Justice Blackmun, joined by Justice Stevens, is omitted.]

NOTES AND QUESTIONS

1. The Supreme Court first held, squarely, that due process requires a hearing on the defendant's competence to stand trial in cases where competence is plausibly at issue in Pate v. Robinson, 383 U.S. 375 (1966). In that case, the state conceded the existence of the legal right but argued that the defendant had waived it. The Court rejected the argument out of hand, saying only that "it is contradictory to argue that a defendant may be incompetent, and yet knowingly or intelligently 'waive' his right to have the court determine his capacity to stand trial." Id., at 384. Is that right? Does the presence of competent defense counsel affect the waiver issue?

Pate left the law of competence to stand trial in an uncertain state. Drope v. Missouri, 420 U.S. 162 (1975), resolved some of the uncertainty. The defendant in *Drope* had a history of mental illness. During his rape trial, he tried unsuccessfully to kill himself; the trial court ruled that the trial could continue in the defendant's absence, and he was convicted. No inquiry into the defendant's competence to stand trial was conducted. A unanimous Court concluded that due process was violated:

> It has long been accepted that a person whose mental condition is such that he lacks the capacity to understand the nature and object of the proceedings against him, to consult with counsel, and to assist in preparing his defense may not be subjected to a trial. Thus, Blackstone wrote that one who became "mad" after the commission of an offense should not be arraigned for it "because he is not able to plead to it with that advice and caution that he ought." Similarly, if he became "mad" after pleading, he should not be tried, "for how can he make his defense?" 4 W. Blackstone, Commentaries *24. . . . Accordingly, as to federal cases, we have approved a test of incompetence which seeks to ascertain whether a criminal defendant "has sufficient present ability to consult with his lawyer with a reasonable degree of rational understanding — and whether he has a rational as well as factual understanding of the proceedings against him," Dusky v. United States, 362 U.S., at 402.
>
> In Pate v. Robinson, 383 U.S. 375 (1966), we held that the failure to observe procedures adequate to protect a defendant's right not to be tried or convicted while incompetent to stand trial deprives him of his due process right to a fair trial. . . . [T]he Court did not prescribe a general standard with respect to the nature or quantum of evidence necessary to require resort to an adequate procedure. Rather, it noted that under the Illinois statute a hearing was required where the evidence raised a "bona fide doubt" as to a defendant's competence, and the Court concluded "that the evidence introduced on Robinson's behalf entitled him to a hearing on this issue." 383 U.S., at 385. . . .

In the present case . . . , [the question is] whether, in light of what was then known, the failure to make further inquiry into petitioner's competence to stand trial, denied him a fair trial. . . .

Notwithstanding the difficulty of making evaluations of the kind required in these circumstances, we conclude that the record reveals a failure to give proper weight to the information suggesting incompetence which came to light during trial. . . .

The import of our decision in Pate v. Robinson is that evidence of a defendant's irrational behavior, his demeanor at trial, and any prior medical opinion on competence to stand trial are all relevant in determining whether further inquiry is required, but that even one of these factors standing alone may, in some circumstances, be sufficient. There are, of course, no fixed or immutable signs which invariably indicate the need for further inquiry to determine fitness to proceed; the question is often a difficult one in which a wide range of manifestations and subtle nuances are implicated. That they are difficult to evaluate by the varying opinions trained psychiatrists can entertain on the same facts.

. . . Petitioner's absence [from much of his trial] bears on the analysis in two ways: first, it was due to an act which suggests a rather substantial degree of mental instability contemporaneous with the trial; second, as a result of petitioner's absence the trial judge and defense counsel were no longer able to observe him in the context of the trial and to gauge from his demeanor whether he was able to cooperate with his attorney and to understand the nature and object of the proceedings against him.

Even when a defendant is competent at the commencement of his trial, a trial court must always be alert to circumstances suggesting a change that would render the accused unable to meet the standards of competence to stand trial. Whatever the relationship between mental illness and incompetence to stand trial, in this case the bearing of the former on the latter was sufficiently likely that, in light of the evidence of petitioner's behavior including his suicide attempt, and there being no opportunity without his presence to evaluate that bearing in fact, the correct course was to suspend the trial until such an evaluation could be made. . . .

420 U.S., at 172-175, 179-181. *Drope* was an easy case: Defense counsel had moved for a hearing on competence prior to trial, and moved for a continuance when his client attempted suicide. What if no such motion is made?

The question is not merely hypothetical. The usual consequence of a finding of incompetence to stand trial is not that the defendant goes free — rather, the state is likely to initiate some form of civil commitment proceeding. Civil commitment statutes generally authorize holding defendants in custody as long as they are a danger to themselves or to others. For some defendants, that may mean a de facto life sentence, which may be considerably worse than the prison term the defendant faces if he is convicted of a crime. Notice what this means: Competence to stand trial is unlike most criminal procedure issues. Ordinarily, defendants have a strong incentive to raise valid procedural claims. In the case of competence, a rational defendant may wish to ignore the issue. Of course, if the defendant is arguably incompetent, he is not likely to *be* rational. But his lawyer is. What should defense counsel do if her client (i) may well be incompetent to stand trial, (ii) faces a brief prison term if convicted, and (iii) faces a long stay in a state-run mental institution if civilly committed? How does your answer to this question bear on the burden-of-proof issue in *Medina*?

2. During the same Term as *Medina*, the Court decided Riggins v. Nevada, 504 U.S. 127 (1992). In *Riggins*, following a sparse evidentiary hearing, the trial court permitted the forced medication of the defendant with an antipsychotic drug. The

trial court's order "gave no indication of the court's rationale." In reversing, the
Court, per Justice O'Connor, opined:

> Although we have not had occasion to develop substantive standards for judging
> forced administration of such drugs in the trial or pretrial settings, Nevada certainly
> would have satisfied due process if the prosecution had demonstrated and the District
> Court had found that treatment with antipsychotic medication was medically appropri-
> ate and, considering less intrusive alternatives, essential for the sake of Riggins' own
> safety or the safety of others. Similarly, the State might have been able to justify medi-
> cally appropriate, involuntary treatment with the drug by establishing that it could not
> obtain an adjudication of Riggins' guilt or innocence by using less intrusive means.
>   . . . We have no occasion to finally prescribe such substantive standards . . . , since
> the District Court allowed the administration of Mellaril to continue without making
> *any* determination of the need for this course or *any* findings about reasonable alter-
> natives. The court's laconic order denying Riggins' motion did not adopt the State's
> view, which was that continued administration of Mellaril was required to ensure that
> the defendant could be tried; in fact, the hearing testimony casts considerable doubt
> on that argument. Nor did the order indicate a finding that safety considerations or
> other compelling concerns outweighed Riggins' interest in freedom from unwanted
> antipsychotic drugs.

504 U.S., at 135-136. Is *Riggins* consistent with *Medina*?

3. In Cooper v. Oklahoma, 517 U.S. 348 (1996), the Court confronted a state statute that required defendants to prove incompetence by clear and convincing evidence. The Court found that rule, unlike the burden-of-proof rule in *Medina*,
violated due process:

> The question we address today is quite different from the question posed in *Medina*.
> Petitioner's claim requires us to consider whether a State may proceed with a criminal
> trial after the defendant has demonstrated that he is more likely than not incompetent.
> Oklahoma does not contend that it may require the defendant to prove incompetence
> beyond a reasonable doubt. The State maintains, however, that the clear and convinc-
> ing standard provides a reasonable accommodation of the opposing interests of the
> State and the defendant. We are persuaded, by both traditional and modern practice
> and the importance of the constitutional interest at stake, that the State's argument
> must be rejected.
>   "Historical practice is probative of whether a procedural rule can be characterized
> as fundamental," *Medina*, 505 U.S., at 446. In this case, unlike in *Medina*, there is no
> indication that the rule Oklahoma seeks to defend has any roots in prior practice.
> Indeed, it appears that a rule significantly more favorable to the defendant has had a
> long and consistent application. . . .
>   [The Court then discussed a series of cases suggesting that the traditional common
> law rule required only proof of incompetence by a preponderance of the evidence.]
>   Contemporary practice demonstrates that the vast majority of jurisdictions remain
> persuaded that the heightened standard of proof imposed on the accused in Okla-
> homa is not necessary to vindicate the State's interest in prompt and orderly disposi-
> tion of criminal cases. Only 4 of the 50 States presently require the criminal defendant
> to prove his incompetence by clear and convincing evidence. None of the remaining
> 46 jurisdictions imposes such a heavy burden on the defendant. Indeed, a number of
> States place no burden on the defendant at all, but rather require the prosecutor to
> prove the defendant's competence to stand trial once a question about competency has
> been credibly raised. The situation is no different in federal court. Congress has

directed that the accused in a federal prosecution must prove incompetence by a preponderance of the evidence. 18 U.S.C. §4241. . . .

The near-uniform application of a standard that is more protective of the defendant's rights than Oklahoma's clear and convincing evidence rule supports our conclusion that the heightened standard offends a principle of justice that is deeply "rooted in the traditions and conscience of our people." *Medina*, 505 U.S., at 445 (internal quotation marks omitted).

517 U.S., at 355-356, 360-362. After *Cooper*, states may force defendants to prove incompetence, but not by more than a preponderance. Does this seem like a sensible splitting of the difference, or like an arbitrary splitting of constitutional hairs?

Perhaps *Medina* and *Cooper*, taken together, represent a sound pragmatic judgment — that defendants are better able to gather evidence of incompetence than the government is to prove competence, *but* that a "clear and convincing" burden would risk too many incompetent defendants going to trial. But is there any principled basis for drawing the line where *Medina* and *Cooper* draw it?

This is a persistent problem in criminal procedure. Protections for defendants' rights constantly involve questions of degree — infinite protection is impossible, so protection must be rationed, graded. And there is rarely any obvious reason to choose this degree of protection rather than something a little more, or a little less. More than most areas of law, criminal procedure may be in the business of splitting differences, and splitting differences rarely seems principled.

4. Notice the *Medina* Court's statement that the Mathews v. Eldridge test for due process, the test used in civil cases, is not to be used in criminal procedure. Instead, the Court says in *Medina*, "because the States have considerable expertise in matters of criminal procedure and the criminal process is grounded in centuries of common-law tradition, it is appropriate to exercise substantial deference to legislative judgments in this area."

Does this statement seem strange? One would ordinarily think of criminal procedure as deserving greater constitutional regulation than the civil process. Yet the *Medina* Court seems to flip the two categories. Why?

The reason, the Court says, is the Bill of Rights: "The Bill of Rights speaks in explicit terms to many aspects of criminal procedure, and the expansion of those constitutional guarantees under the open-ended rubric of the Due Process Clause invites undue interference with both considered legislative judgments and the careful balance that the Constitution strikes between liberty and order." The idea resembles a kind of constitutional displacement, with the Bill of Rights occupying the relevant constitutional space, leaving very little space left over for an expansive reading of due process.

What do you think of that idea? Does it affect your view of incorporation? Decisions like *Duncan* plainly offered greater protection to criminal defendants in some respects; the reasoning in *Medina* suggests those decisions may have led to reduced protection in other areas.

5. The Court reentered the thicket of freestanding Due Process analysis in the context of the "war on terror." Consider:

HAMDI v. RUMSFELD

Certiorari to the United States Court of Appeals for the Fourth Circuit
542 U.S. 507 (2004)

JUSTICE O'CONNOR announced the judgment of the Court and delivered an opinion, in which CHIEF JUSTICE REHNQUIST, JUSTICE KENNEDY, and JUSTICE BREYER join.

At this difficult time in our Nation's history, we are called upon to consider the legality of the Government's detention of a United States citizen on United States soil as an "enemy combatant" and to address the process that is constitutionally owed to one who seeks to challenge his classification as such. . . .

I

On September 11, 2001, the al Qaeda terrorist network used hijacked commercial airliners to attack prominent targets in the United States. Approximately 3,000 people were killed in those attacks. One week later, in response to these "acts of treacherous violence," Congress passed a resolution authorizing the President to "use all necessary and appropriate force against those nations, organizations, or persons he determines planned, authorized, committed, or aided the terrorist attacks" or "harbored such organizations or persons, in order to prevent any future acts of international terrorism against the United States by such nations, organizations, or persons." Authorization for Use of Military Force ("the AUMF"), 115 Stat 224. Soon thereafter, the President ordered United States Armed Forces to Afghanistan, with a mission to subdue al Qaeda and quell the Taliban regime that was known to support it.

This case arises out of the detention of a man whom the Government alleges took up arms with the Taliban during this conflict. His name is Yaser Esam Hamdi. Born an American citizen in Louisiana in 1980, Hamdi moved with his family to Saudi Arabia as a child. By 2001, the parties agree, he resided in Afghanistan. At some point that year, he was seized by members of the Northern Alliance, a coalition of military groups opposed to the Taliban government, and eventually was turned over to the United States military. The Government asserts that it initially detained and interrogated Hamdi in Afghanistan before transferring him to the United States Naval Base in Guantanamo Bay in January 2002. In April 2002, upon learning that Hamdi is an American citizen, authorities transferred him to a naval brig in Norfolk, Virginia, where he remained until a recent transfer to a brig in Charleston, South Carolina. The Government contends that Hamdi is an "enemy combatant," and that this status justifies holding him in the United States indefinitely — without formal charges or proceedings — unless and until it makes the determination that access to counsel or further process is warranted.

In June 2002, Hamdi's father, Esam Fouad Hamdi, filed the present petition for a writ of habeas corpus under 28 U.S.C. §2241 in the Eastern District of Virginia, naming as petitioners his son and himself as next friend. The elder Hamdi alleges in the petition that he has had no contact with his son since the Government took custody of him in 2001, and that the Government has held his son "without access to legal counsel or notice of any charges pending against him." . . . The habeas petition asks that the court, among other things, (1) appoint counsel for Hamdi; (2)

order respondents to cease interrogating him; (3) declare that he is being held in violation of the Fifth and Fourteenth Amendments; (4) "[t]o the extent Respondents contest any material factual allegations in this Petition, schedule an evidentiary hearing, at which Petitioners may adduce proof in support of their allegations"; and (5) order that Hamdi be released from his "unlawful custody." Although his habeas petition provides no details with regard to the factual circumstances surrounding his son's capture and detention, Hamdi's father has asserted in documents found elsewhere in the record that his son went to Afghanistan to do "relief work," and that he had been in that country less than two months before September 11, 2001, and could not have received military training. The 20-year-old was traveling on his own for the first time, his father says, and "[b]ecause of his lack of experience, he was trapped in Afghanistan once that military campaign began."

The District Court . . . appointed the federal public defender as counsel for the petitioners, and ordered that counsel be given access to Hamdi. The United States Court of Appeals for the Fourth Circuit reversed that order, holding that the District Court had failed to extend appropriate deference to the Government's security and intelligence interests. 296 F.3d 278, 279, 283 (2002). It directed the District Court to consider "the most cautious procedures first," id., at 284, and to conduct a deferential inquiry into Hamdi's status, id., at 283. It opined that "if Hamdi is indeed an 'enemy combatant' who was captured during hostilities in Afghanistan, the government's present detention of him is a lawful one." Ibid.

On remand, the Government filed a response and a motion to dismiss the petition. It attached to its response a declaration from one Michael Mobbs (hereinafter "Mobbs Declaration"), who identified himself as Special Advisor to the Under Secretary of Defense for Policy. Mobbs indicated that in this position, he has been "substantially involved with matters related to the detention of enemy combatants in the current war against the al Qaeda terrorists and those who support and harbor them (including the Taliban)." . . . Mobbs . . . set forth what remains the sole evidentiary support that the Government has provided to the courts for Hamdi's detention. The declaration states that Hamdi "traveled to Afghanistan" in July or August 2001, and that he thereafter "affiliated with a Taliban military unit and received weapons training." It asserts that Hamdi "remained with his Taliban unit following the attacks of September 11" and that, during the time when Northern Alliance forces were "engaged in battle with the Taliban," "Hamdi's Taliban unit surrendered" to those forces, after which he "surrender[ed] his Kalishnikov assault rifle" to them. The Mobbs Declaration also states that, because al Qaeda and the Taliban "were and are hostile forces engaged in armed conflict with the armed forces of the United States," "individuals associated with" those groups "were and continue to be enemy combatants." Mobbs states that Hamdi was labeled an enemy combatant "[b]ased upon his interviews and in light of his association with the Taliban." According to the declaration, a series of "U.S. military screening team[s]" determined that Hamdi met "the criteria for enemy combatants," and "a subsequent interview of Hamdi has confirmed that he surrendered and gave his firearm to Northern Alliance forces, which supports his classification as an enemy combatant."

After the Government submitted this declaration, the Fourth Circuit directed the District Court to proceed in accordance with its earlier ruling and, specifically, to "consider the sufficiency of the Mobbs Declaration as an independent matter before proceeding further." 316 F.3d 450, 462 (2003). The District Court found that the Mobbs Declaration fell "far short" of supporting Hamdi's detention. . . . It ordered the Government to turn over numerous materials for *in camera* review, including copies of all of Hamdi's statements and the notes taken from interviews with him that related to his reasons for going to Afghanistan and his activities therein; a list of all interrogators who had questioned Hamdi and their names and addresses; statements by members of the Northern Alliance regarding Hamdi's surrender and capture; a list of the dates and locations of his capture and subsequent detentions; and the names and titles of the United States Government officials who made the determinations that Hamdi was an enemy combatant and that he should be moved to a naval brig. . . .

The Government sought to appeal the production order, and the District Court certified the question of whether the Mobbs Declaration, "standing alone, is sufficient as a matter of law to allow meaningful judicial review of [Hamdi's] classification as an enemy combatant." 316 F.3d, at 462. The Fourth Circuit reversed, but did not squarely answer the certified question. It instead stressed that, because it was "undisputed that Hamdi was captured in a zone of active combat in a foreign theater of conflict," no factual inquiry or evidentiary hearing allowing Hamdi to be heard or to rebut the Government's assertions was necessary or proper. Id., at 459. Concluding that the factual averments in the Mobbs Declaration, "if accurate," provided a sufficient basis upon which to conclude that the President had constitutionally detained Hamdi pursuant to the President's war powers, it ordered the habeas petition dismissed. Id., at 473. . . .

II

The threshold question before us is whether the Executive has the authority to detain citizens who qualify as "enemy combatants." There is some debate as to the proper scope of this term, and the Government has never provided any court with the full criteria that it uses in classifying individuals as such. It has made clear, however, that, for purposes of this case, the "enemy combatant" that it is seeking to detain is an individual who, it alleges, was "part of or supporting forces hostile to the United States or coalition partners" in Afghanistan and who "engaged in an armed conflict against the United States" there. Brief for Respondents 3. We therefore answer only the narrow question before us: whether the detention of citizens falling within that definition is authorized. . . .

The Government . . . maintains that [18 U.S.C.] §4001(a)[12] is satisfied, because Hamdi is being detained "pursuant to an Act of Congress"—the AUMF. Id., at 21-22. . . . [W]e conclude that the AUMF is explicit congressional authorization for the detention of individuals in the narrow category we describe (assuming, without deciding, that such authorization is required), and that the AUMF satisfied §4001(a)'s requirement that a detention be "pursuant to an Act of Congress" (assuming, without deciding, that §4001(a) applies to military detentions). . . .

There is no bar to this Nation's holding one of its own citizens as an enemy combatant. In [Ex parte Quirin, 317 U.S. 1 (1942)], one of the detainees, Haupt, alleged that he was a naturalized United States citizen. 317 U.S., at 20. We held that "[c]itizens who associate themselves with the military arm of the enemy government, and with its aid, guidance and direction enter this country bent on hostile acts, are

---

12. "No citizen shall be imprisoned or otherwise detained by the United States except pursuant to an Act of Congress." — EDS.

enemy belligerents within the meaning of . . . the law of war." Id., at 37-38. While Haupt was tried for violations of the law of war, nothing in *Quirin* suggests that his citizenship would have precluded his mere detention for the duration of the relevant hostilities. See id., at 30-31. . . . . A citizen, no less than an alien, can be "part of or supporting forces hostile to the United States or coalition partners" and "engaged in an armed conflict against the United States," Brief for Respondents 3; such a citizen, if released, would pose the same threat of returning to the front during the ongoing conflict. . . . .

Hamdi objects, nevertheless, that Congress has not authorized the *indefinite* detention to which he is now subject. . . . We take Hamdi's objection to be not to the lack of certainty regarding the date on which the conflict will end, but to the substantial prospect of perpetual detention. We recognize that the national security underpinnings of the "war on terror," although crucially important, are broad and malleable. As the Government concedes, given its unconventional nature, the current conflict is unlikely to end with a formal cease-fire agreement. The prospect Hamdi raises is therefore not far-fetched. If the Government does not consider this unconventional war won for two generations, and if it maintains during that time that Hamdi might, if released, rejoin forces fighting against the United States, then the position it has taken throughout the litigation of this case suggests that Hamdi's detention could last for the rest of his life. . . . .

. . . . Certainly, we agree that indefinite detention for the purpose of interrogation is not authorized. Further, we understand Congress' grant of authority for the use of "necessary and appropriate force" to include the authority to detain for the duration of the relevant conflict, and our understanding is based on longstanding law-of-war principles. If the practical circumstances of a given conflict are entirely unlike those of the conflicts that informed the development of the law of war, that understanding may unravel. But that is not the situation we face as of this date. Active combat operations against Taliban fighters apparently are ongoing in Afghanistan-. . . . The United States may detain, for the duration of these hostilities, individuals legitimately determined to be Taliban combatants who "engaged in an armed conflict against the United States." If the record establishes that United States troops are still involved in active combat in Afghanistan, those detentions are part of the exercise of "necessary and appropriate force," and therefore are authorized by the AUMF. . . .

III

Even in cases in which the detention of enemy combatants is legally authorized, there remains the question of what process is constitutionally due to a citizen who disputes his enemy-combatant status. Hamdi argues that he is owed a meaningful and timely hearing and that "extra-judicial detention [that] begins and ends with the submission of an affidavit based on third-hand hearsay" does not comport with the Fifth and Fourteenth Amendments. Brief for Petitioners 16. The Government counters that any more process than was provided below would be both unworkable and "constitutionally intolerable." Brief for Respondents 46. Our resolution of this dispute requires a careful examination both of the writ of habeas corpus, which Hamdi now seeks to employ as a mechanism of judicial review, and of the Due Process Clause, which informs the procedural contours of that mechanism in this instance. . . .

The Government [argues] that further factual exploration is unwarranted and inappropriate in light of the extraordinary constitutional interests at stake. Under the Government's most extreme rendition of this argument, "[r]espect for separation of powers and the limited institutional capabilities of courts in matters of military decision-making in connection with an ongoing conflict" ought to eliminate entirely any individual process, restricting the courts to investigating only whether legal authorization exists for the broader detention scheme. Brief for Respondents 26. At most, the Government argues, courts should review its determination that a citizen is an enemy combatant under a very deferential "some evidence" standard. Id., at 34. Under this review, a court would assume the accuracy of the Government's articulated basis for Hamdi's detention, as set forth in the Mobbs Declaration, and assess only whether that articulated basis was a legitimate one. Brief for Respondents 36. . . .

In response, Hamdi emphasizes that this Court consistently has recognized that an individual challenging his detention may not be held at the will of the Executive without recourse to some proceeding before a neutral tribunal to determine whether the Executive's asserted justifications for that detention have basis in fact and warrant in law. See, e.g., Zadvydas v. Davis, 533 U.S. 678, 690 (2001); Addington v. Texas, 441 U.S. 418, 425-427 (1979). He argues that the Fourth Circuit inappropriately "ceded power to the Executive during wartime to define the conduct for which a citizen may be detained, judge whether that citizen has engaged in the proscribed conduct, and imprison that citizen indefinitely," Brief for Petitioners 21, and that due process demands that he receive a hearing in which he may challenge the Mobbs Declaration and adduce his own counter evidence. The District Court, agreeing with Hamdi, apparently believed that the appropriate process would approach the process that accompanies a criminal trial. It therefore disapproved of the hearsay nature of the Mobbs Declaration and anticipated quite extensive discovery of various military affairs. Anything less, it concluded, would not be "meaningful judicial review."

Both of these positions highlight legitimate concerns. And both emphasize the tension that often exists between the autonomy that the Government asserts is necessary in order to pursue effectively a particular goal and the process that a citizen contends he is due before he is deprived of a constitutional right. The ordinary mechanism that we use for balancing such serious competing interests, and for determining the procedures that are necessary to ensure that a citizen is not "deprived of life, liberty, or property, without due process of law," U.S. Const., Amdt. 5, is the test that we articulated in Mathews v. Eldridge, 424 U.S. 319 (1976). *Mathews* dictates that the process due in any given instance is determined by weighing "the private interest that will be affected by the official action" against the Government's asserted interest, "including the function involved" and the burdens the Government would face in providing greater process. 424 U.S., at 335. The *Mathews* calculus then contemplates a judicious balancing of these concerns, through an analysis of "the risk of an erroneous deprivation" of the private interest if the process were reduced and the "probable value, if any, of additional or substitute safeguards." Ibid. . . .

It is beyond question that substantial interests lie on both sides of the scale in this case. Hamdi's "private interest . . . affected by the official action," ibid., is the most elemental of liberty interests — the interest in being free from physical detention by one's own government. . . .

On the other side of the scale are the weighty and sensitive governmental interests in ensuring that those who have in fact fought with the enemy during a war do not return to battle against the United States. . . .

The Government also argues at some length that its interests in reducing the process available to alleged enemy combatants are heightened by the practical difficulties that would accompany a system of trial-like process. In its view, military officers who are engaged in the serious work of waging battle would be unnecessarily and dangerously distracted by litigation half a world away, and discovery into military operations would both intrude on the sensitive secrets of national defense and result in a futile search for evidence buried under the rubble of war. Brief for Respondents 46-49. To the extent that these burdens are triggered by heightened procedures, they are properly taken into account in our due process analysis.

Striking the proper constitutional balance here is of great importance to the Nation during this period of ongoing combat. But it is equally vital that our calculus not give short shrift to the values that this country holds dear or to the privilege that is American citizenship. It is during our most challenging and uncertain moments that our Nation's commitment to due process is most severely tested; and it is in those times that we must preserve our commitment at home to the principles for which we fight abroad. . . .

With due recognition of these competing concerns, we believe that neither the process proposed by the Government nor the process apparently envisioned by the District Court below strikes the proper constitutional balance when a United States citizen is detained in the United States as an enemy combatant. That is, "the risk of erroneous deprivation" of a detainee's liberty interest is unacceptably high under the Government's proposed rule, while some of the "additional or substitute procedural safeguards" suggested by the District Court are unwarranted in light of their limited "probable value" and the burdens they may impose on the military in such cases. *Mathews*, 424 U.S., at 335.

We therefore hold that a citizen-detainee seeking to challenge his classification as an enemy combatant must receive notice of the factual basis for his classification, and a fair opportunity to rebut the Government's factual assertions before a neutral decisionmaker. . . . These essential constitutional promises may not be eroded.

At the same time, the exigencies of the circumstances may demand that, aside from these core elements, enemy combatant proceedings may be tailored to alleviate their uncommon potential to burden the Executive at a time of ongoing military conflict. Hearsay, for example, may need to be accepted as the most reliable available evidence from the Government in such a proceeding. Likewise, the Constitution would not be offended by a presumption in favor of the Government's evidence, so long as that presumption remained a rebuttable one and fair opportunity for rebuttal were provided. Thus, once the Government puts forth credible evidence that the habeas petitioner meets the enemy-combatant criteria, the onus could shift to the petitioner to rebut that evidence with more persuasive evidence that he falls outside the criteria. A burden-shifting scheme of this sort would meet the goal of ensuring that the errant tourist, embedded journalist, or local aid worker has a chance to prove military error while giving due regard to the Executive once it has put forth meaningful support for its conclusion that the detainee is in fact an enemy combatant. In the words of *Mathews*, process of this sort would sufficiently address the "risk of erroneous deprivation" of a detainee's liberty interest while eliminating certain procedures that have questionable additional value in light of the burden on the Government. 424 U.S., at 335. . . .

In sum, while the full protections that accompany challenges to detentions in other settings may prove unworkable and inappropriate in the enemy-combatant setting, the threats to military operations posed by a basic system of independent review are not so weighty as to trump a citizen's core rights to challenge meaningfully the Government's case and to be heard by an impartial adjudicator.

In so holding, we necessarily reject the Government's assertion that separation of powers principles mandate a heavily circumscribed role for the courts in such circumstances. Indeed, the position that the courts must forgo any examination of the individual case and focus exclusively on the legality of the broader detention scheme cannot be mandated by any reasonable view of separation of powers, as this approach serves only to *condense* power into a single branch of government. . . . Thus, while we do not question that our due process assessment must pay keen attention to the particular burdens faced by the Executive in the context of military action, it would turn our system of checks and balances on its head to suggest that a citizen could not make his way to court with a challenge to the factual basis for his detention by his government, simply because the Executive opposes making available such a challenge. Absent suspension of the writ [of habeas corpus] by Congress, a citizen detained as an enemy combatant is entitled to this process. . . .

There remains the possibility that the standards we have articulated could be met by an appropriately authorized and properly constituted military tribunal. . . . In the absence of such process, however, a court that receives a petition for a writ of habeas corpus from an alleged enemy combatant must itself ensure that the minimum requirements of due process are achieved. . . . We have no reason to doubt that courts faced with these sensitive matters will pay proper heed both to the matters of national security that might arise in an individual case and to the constitutional limitations safeguarding essential liberties that remain vibrant even in times of security concerns.

IV

Hamdi asks us to hold that the Fourth Circuit also erred by denying him immediate access to counsel upon his detention and by disposing of the case without permitting him to meet with an attorney. Brief for Petitioners 19. Since our grant of certiorari in this case, Hamdi has been appointed counsel, with whom he has met for consultation purposes on several occasions, and with whom he is now being granted unmonitored meetings. He unquestionably has the right to access to counsel in connection with the proceedings on remand. No further consideration of this issue is necessary at this stage of the case.

The judgment of the United States Court of Appeals for the Fourth Circuit is vacated, and the case is remanded for further proceedings. . . .

JUSTICE SOUTER, with whom JUSTICE GINSBURG joins, concurring in part, dissenting in part, and concurring in the judgment.

. . . The Government [argues] that Hamdi's incommunicado imprisonment as an enemy combatant seized on the field of battle falls within the President's power as Commander in Chief under the laws and usages of war, and is in any event authorized by two statutes. Accordingly, the Government contends that Hamdi has no basis for any challenge by petition for habeas except to his own status as an enemy combatant; and even that challenge may go no further than to enquire whether "some evidence" supports Hamdi's designation, see Brief for Respondents 34-36; if there is "some evidence," Hamdi should remain locked up at the discretion of the Executive. . . .

The plurality rejects any such limit on the exercise of habeas jurisdiction and so far I agree with its opinion. The plurality does, however, accept the Government's position that if Hamdi's designation as an enemy combatant is correct, his detention (at least as to some period) is authorized by an Act of Congress as required by §4001(a). . . . Here, I disagree and respectfully dissent. The Government has failed to demonstrate that the Force Resolution authorizes the detention complained of here even on the facts the Government claims. If the Government raises nothing further than the record now shows, . . . Hamdi [should] be released. . . .

Because I find Hamdi's detention forbidden by §4001(a) and unauthorized by the Force Resolution, I would not reach any questions of what process he may be due in litigating disputed issues in a proceeding under the habeas statute or prior to the habeas enquiry itself. For me, it suffices that the Government has failed to justify holding him in the absence of a further Act of Congress, criminal charges, a showing that the detention conforms to the laws of war, or a demonstration that §4001(a) is unconstitutional. I would therefore vacate the judgment of the Court of Appeals and remand for proceedings consistent with this view.

Since this disposition does not command a majority of the Court, however, the need to give practical effect to the conclusions of eight members of the Court rejecting the Government's position calls for me to join with the plurality in ordering remand on terms closest to those I would impose. Although I think litigation of Hamdi's status as an enemy combatant is unnecessary, the terms of the plurality's remand will allow Hamdi to offer evidence that he is not an enemy combatant, and he should at the least have the benefit of that opportunity.

It should go without saying that in joining with the plurality to produce a judgment, I do not adopt the plurality's resolution of constitutional issues that I would not reach. It is not that I could disagree with the plurality's determinations (given the plurality's view of the Force Resolution) that someone in Hamdi's position is entitled at a minimum to notice of the Government's claimed factual basis for holding him, and to a fair chance to rebut it before a neutral decision maker; nor, of course, could I disagree with the plurality's affirmation of Hamdi's right to counsel. On the other hand, I do not mean to imply agreement that the Government could claim an evidentiary presumption casting the burden of rebuttal on Hamdi, or that an opportunity to litigate before a military tribunal might obviate or truncate enquiry by a court on habeas.

Subject to these qualifications, I join with the plurality in a judgment of the Court vacating the Fourth Circuit's judgment and remanding the case.

JUSTICE SCALIA, with whom JUSTICE STEVENS joins, dissenting.
. . . Where the Government accuses a citizen of waging war against it, our constitutional tradition has been to prosecute him in federal court for treason or some other crime. Where the exigencies of war prevent that, the Constitution's Suspension Clause, Art. I, §9, cl. 2, allows Congress to relax the usual protections temporarily. Absent suspension, however, the Executive's assertion of military exigency

has not been thought sufficient to permit detention without charge. No one contends that the congressional Authorization for Use of Military Force, on which the Government relies to justify its actions here, is an implementation of the Suspension Clause. Accordingly, I would reverse the decision below.

I

. . . The gist of the Due Process Clause, as understood at the founding and since, was to force the Government to follow those common-law procedures traditionally deemed necessary before depriving a person of life, liberty, or property. When a citizen was deprived of liberty because of alleged criminal conduct, those procedures typically required committal by a magistrate followed by indictment and trial. 3 J. Story, Commentaries on the Constitution of the United States §1783, p. 661 (1833) (hereinafter Story) (equating "due process of law" with "due presentment or indictment, and being brought in to answer thereto by due process of the common law"). The Due Process Clause "in effect affirms the right of trial according to the process and proceedings of the common law." Ibid. See also T. Cooley, General Principles of Constitutional Law 224 (1880) ("When life and liberty are in question, there must in every instance be judicial proceedings; and that requirement implies an accusation, a hearing before an impartial tribunal, with proper jurisdiction, and a conviction and judgment before the punishment can be inflicted" (internal quotation marks omitted)). . . .

These due process rights have historically been vindicated by the writ of habeas corpus. . . . The writ of habeas corpus was preserved in the Constitution — the only common-law writ to be explicitly mentioned. See Art. I, §9, cl. 2. Hamilton lauded "the establishment of the writ of habeas corpus" in his Federalist defense as a means to protect against "the practice of arbitrary imprisonments . . . in all ages, [one of] the favourite and most formidable instruments of tyranny." The Federalist No. 84. . . .

II

The allegations here, of course, are no ordinary accusations of criminal activity. Yaser Esam Hamdi has been imprisoned because the Government believes he participated in the waging of war against the United States. The relevant question, then, is whether there is a different, special procedure for imprisonment of a citizen accused of wrongdoing *by aiding the enemy in wartime*.

Justice O'Connor, writing for a plurality of this Court, asserts that captured enemy combatants (other than those suspected of war crimes) have traditionally been detained until the cessation of hostilities and then released. That is probably an accurate description of wartime practice with respect to enemy *aliens*. The tradition with respect to American citizens, however, has been quite different. Citizens aiding the enemy have been treated as traitors subject to the criminal process. . . .

The modern treason statute is 18 U.S.C. §2381; it basically tracks the language of the constitutional provision. Other provisions of Title 18 criminalize various acts of warmaking and adherence to the enemy. See, e.g., §32 (destruction of aircraft or aircraft facilities), §2332a (use of weapons of mass destruction), §2332b (acts of terrorism transcending national boundaries), §2339A (providing material support to terrorists), §2339B (providing material support to certain terrorist organizations), §2382 (misprision of treason), §2383 (rebellion or insurrection), §2384 (seditious conspiracy), §2390 (enlistment to serve in armed hostility against the United States). See also 31 CFR §595.204 (2003) (prohibiting the "making or receiving of any contribution of funds, goods, or services" to terrorists); 50 U.S.C. §1705(b) (criminalizing violations of 31 CFR §595.204). The only citizen other than Hamdi known to be imprisoned in connection with military hostilities in Afghanistan against the United States *was* subjected to criminal process and convicted upon a guilty plea. See United States v. Lindh, 212 F. Supp. 2d 541 (ED Va. 2002) (denying motions for dismissal); Seelye, N.Y. Times, Oct. 5, 2002, p. A1, col. 5.

There are times when military exigency renders resort to the traditional criminal process impracticable. English law accommodated such exigencies by allowing legislative suspension of the writ of habeas corpus for brief periods. Blackstone explained:

> And yet sometimes, when the state is in real danger, even this [i.e., executive detention] may be a necessary measure. But the happiness of our constitution is, that it is not left to the executive power to determine when the danger of the state is so great, as to render this measure expedient. For the parliament only, or legislative power, whenever it sees proper, can authorize the crown, by suspending the habeas corpus act for a short and limited time, to imprison suspected persons without giving any reason for so doing. . . . In like manner this experiment ought only to be tried in case of extreme emergency; and in these the nation parts with it[s] liberty for a while, in order to preserve it for ever.

1 Blackstone 132.

Where the Executive has not pursued the usual course of charge, committal, and conviction, it has historically secured the Legislature's explicit approval of a suspension. In England, Parliament on numerous occasions passed temporary suspensions in times of threatened invasion or rebellion. . . .

Our Federal Constitution contains a provision explicitly permitting suspension, but limiting the situations in which it may be invoked: "The privilege of the Writ of Habeas Corpus shall not be suspended, unless when in Cases of Rebellion or Invasion the public Safety may require it." Art. I, §9, cl. 2. Although this provision does not state that suspension must be effected by, or authorized by, a legislative act, it has been so understood, consistent with English practice and the Clause's placement in Article I. See Ex parte Merryman, 17 F. Cas. 144, 151-152 (CD Md. 1861) (Taney, C. J., rejecting Lincoln's unauthorized suspension); 3 Story §1336, at 208-209.

The Suspension Clause was by design a safety valve, the Constitution's only "express provision for exercise of extraordinary authority because of a crisis," Youngstown Sheet & Tube Co. v. Sawyer, 343 U.S. 579, 650 (1952) (Jackson, J., concurring). . . .

III

. . . President Lincoln, when he purported to suspend habeas corpus without congressional authorization during the Civil War, apparently did not doubt that suspension was required if the prisoner was to be held without criminal trial. In his famous message to Congress on July 4, 1861, he argued only that he could suspend the writ, not that even without suspension, his imprisonment of citizens without criminal trial was permitted. . . .

The proposition that the Executive lacks indefinite wartime detention authority over citizens is consistent with the Founders' general mistrust of military power permanently at the Executive's disposal. In the Founders' view, the "blessings of liberty" were threatened by "those military establishments which must gradually poison its very fountain." The Federalist No. 45, p. 238 (J. Madison). No fewer than 10 issues of the Federalist were devoted in whole or part to allaying fears of oppression from the proposed Constitution's authorization of standing armies in peacetime. Many safeguards in the Constitution reflect these concerns. Congress's authority "[t]o raise and support Armies" was hedged with the proviso that "no Appropriation of Money to that Use shall be for a longer Term than two Years." U.S. Const., Art. 1, §8, cl. 12. Except for the actual command of military forces, all authorization for their maintenance and all explicit authorization for their use is placed in the control of Congress under Article I, rather than the President under Article II. . . . A view of the Constitution that gives the Executive authority to use military force rather than the force of law against citizens on American soil flies in the face of the mistrust that engendered these provisions. . . .

V

It follows from what I have said that Hamdi is entitled to a habeas decree requiring his release unless (1) criminal proceedings are promptly brought, or (2) Congress has suspended the writ of habeas corpus. A suspension of the writ could, of course, lay down conditions for continued detention, similar to those that today's opinion prescribes under the Due Process Clause. Cf. Act of Mar. 3, 1863, 12 Stat. 755. But there is a world of difference between the people's representatives' determining the need for that suspension (and prescribing the conditions for it) and this Court's doing so.

The plurality finds justification for Hamdi's imprisonment in the Authorization for Use of Military Force, 115 Stat. 224, which provides:

> That the President is authorized to use all necessary and appropriate force against those nations, organizations, or persons he determines planned, authorized, committed, or aided the terrorist attacks that occurred on September 11, 2001, or harbored such organizations or persons, in order to prevent any future acts of international terrorism against the United States by such nations, organizations or persons.

§2(a).

This is not remotely a congressional suspension of the writ, and no one claims that it is. Contrary to the plurality's view, I do not think this statute even authorizes detention of a citizen with the clarity necessary to satisfy the interpretive canon that statutes should be construed so as to avoid grave constitutional concerns, . . . or with the clarity necessary to overcome the statutory prescription that "[n]o citizen shall be imprisoned or otherwise detained by the United States except pursuant to an Act of Congress." 18 U.S.C. §4001(a). But even if it did, I would not permit it to overcome Hamdi's entitlement to habeas corpus relief. The Suspension Clause of the Constitution, which carefully circumscribes the conditions under which the writ can be withheld, would be a sham if it could be evaded by congressional prescription of requirements *other than the common-law requirement of committal for criminal prosecution* that render the writ, though available, unavailing. If the Suspension Clause does not guarantee the citizen that he will either be tried or released, unless the conditions for suspending the writ exist and the grave action of suspending the writ has been taken; if it merely guarantees the citizen that he will not be detained unless Congress by ordinary legislation says he can be detained; it guarantees him very little indeed.

It should not be thought, however, that the plurality's evisceration of the Suspension Clause augments, principally, the power of Congress. As usual, the major effect of its constitutional improvisation is to increase the power of the Court. Having found a congressional authorization for detention of citizens where none clearly exists; and having discarded the categorical procedural protection of the Suspension Clause; the plurality then proceeds, under the guise of the Due Process Clause, to prescribe what procedural protections it thinks appropriate. It "weigh[s] the private interest . . . against the Government's asserted interest," and — just as though writing a new Constitution — comes up with an unheard-of system in which the citizen rather than the Government bears the burden of proof, testimony is by hearsay rather than live witnesses, and the presiding officer may well be a "neutral" military officer rather than judge and jury. It claims authority to engage in this sort of "judicious balancing" from Mathews v. Eldridge, 424 U.S. 319 (1976), a case involving . . . . *the withdrawal of disability benefits!* Whatever the merits of this technique when newly recognized property rights are at issue (and even there they are questionable), it has no place where the Constitution and the common law already supply an answer. . . .

There is a certain harmony of approach in the plurality's making up for Congress's failure to invoke the Suspension Clause and its making up for the Executive's failure to apply what it says are needed procedures — an approach that reflects what might be called a Mr. Fix-it Mentality. The plurality seems to view it as its mission to Make Everything Come Out Right, rather than merely to decree the consequences, as far as individual rights are concerned, of the other two branches' actions and omissions. Has the Legislature failed to suspend the writ in the current dire emergency? Well, we will remedy that failure by prescribing the reasonable conditions that a suspension should have included. And has the Executive failed to live up to those reasonable conditions? Well, we will ourselves make that failure good, so that this dangerous fellow (if he is dangerous) need not be set free. The problem with this approach is not only that it steps out of the courts' modest and limited role in a democratic society; but that by repeatedly doing what it thinks the political branches ought to do it encourages their lassitude and saps the vitality of government by the people. . . .

VI

Several limitations give my views in this matter a relatively narrow compass. They apply only to citizens, accused of being enemy combatants, who are detained within the territorial jurisdiction of a federal court. This is not likely to be a numerous group; currently we know of only two, Hamdi and Jose Padilla. Where the citizen is captured outside and held outside the United States, the constitutional requirements may be different. Moreover, even within the United States, the accused citizen-enemy combatant may lawfully be detained once prosecution is in progress or in contemplation. See, e.g., County of Riverside v. McLaughlin, 500 U.S. 44 (1991) (brief detention pending judicial determination after warrantless arrest); United States v. Salerno, 481 U.S. 739 (1987) (pretrial detention under the Bail Reform Act). The Government has been notably successful in securing conviction, and hence long-term custody or execution, of those who have waged war against the state.

I frankly do not know whether these tools are sufficient to meet the Government's security needs, including the need to obtain intelligence through interrogation. It is far beyond my competence, or the Court's competence, to determine that. But it is not beyond Congress's. If the situation demands it, the Executive can ask Congress to authorize suspension of the writ — which can be made subject to whatever conditions Congress deems appropriate, including even the procedural novelties invented by the plurality today. To be sure, suspension is limited by the Constitution to cases of rebellion or invasion. But whether the attacks of September 11, 2001, constitute an "invasion," and whether those attacks still justify suspension several years later, are questions for Congress rather than this Court. If civil rights are to be curtailed during wartime, it must be done openly and democratically, as the Constitution requires, rather than by silent erosion through an opinion of this Court. . . .

JUSTICE THOMAS, dissenting. The Executive Branch, acting pursuant to the powers vested in the President by the Constitution and with explicit congressional approval, has determined that Yaser Hamdi is an enemy combatant and should be detained. This detention falls squarely within the Federal Government's war powers, and we lack the expertise and capacity to second-guess that decision. As such, petitioners' habeas challenge should fail, and there is no reason to remand the case. . . .

Although the President very well may have inherent authority to detain those arrayed against our troops, I agree with the plurality that we need not decide that question because Congress has authorized the President to do so. The Authorization for Use of Military Force (AUMF), 115 Stat. 224, authorizes the President to "use all necessary and appropriate force against those nations, organizations, or persons he determines planned, authorized, committed, or aided the terrorist attacks" of September 11, 2001. Indeed, the Court has previously concluded that language materially identical to the AUMF authorizes the Executive to "make the ordinary use of the soldiers . . . ; that he may kill persons who resist and, of course, that he may use the milder measure of seizing [and detaining] the bodies of those whom he considers to stand in the way of restoring peace." Moyer v. Peabody, 212 U.S. 78, 84 (1909). . . .

I agree with the plurality that the Federal Government has power to detain those that the Executive Branch determines to be enemy combatants. But I do not think that the plurality has adequately explained the breadth of the President's authority to detain enemy combatants, an authority that includes making virtually conclusive factual findings. . . . In my view, . . . we lack the capacity and responsibility to second-guess this determination. . . .

The Government's asserted authority to detain an individual that the President has determined to be an enemy combatant, at least while hostilities continue, comports with the Due Process Clause. . . . [T]he Executive's decision that a detention is necessary to protect the public need not and should not be subjected to judicial second-guessing. Indeed, at least in the context of enemy-combatant determinations, this would defeat the unity, secrecy, and dispatch that the Founders believed to be so important to the warmaking function. . . .

Accordingly, I conclude that the Government's detention of Hamdi as an enemy combatant does not violate the Constitution. By detaining Hamdi, the President, in the prosecution of a war and authorized by Congress, has acted well within his authority. Hamdi thereby received all the process to which he was due under the circumstances. I therefore believe that this is no occasion to balance the competing interests, as the plurality unconvincingly attempts to do. . . .

Although I do not agree with the plurality that the balancing approach of Mathews v. Eldridge, 424 U.S. 319 (1976), is the appropriate analytical tool with which to analyze this case,[5] I cannot help but explain that the plurality misapplies its chosen framework, one that if applied correctly would probably lead to the result I have reached. . . . In *Moyer*, the Court recognized the paramount importance of the Governor's interest in the tranquility of a Colorado town. At issue here is the far more significant interest of the security of the Nation. The Government seeks to further that interest by detaining an enemy soldier not only to prevent him from rejoining the ongoing fight. Rather, as the Government explains, detention can serve to gather critical intelligence regarding the intentions and capabilities of our adversaries, a function that the Government avers has become all the more important in the war on terrorism.

Additional process, the Government explains, will destroy the intelligence gathering function. Brief for Respondents 43-45. It also does seem quite likely that, under the process envisioned by the plurality, various military officials will have to take time to litigate this matter. And though the plurality does not say so, a meaningful ability to challenge the Government's factual allegations will probably require the Government to divulge highly classified information to the purported enemy combatant, who might then upon release return to the fight armed with our most closely held secrets. . . .

Undeniably, Hamdi has been deprived of a serious interest, one actually protected by the Due Process Clause. Against this, however, is the Government's overriding interest in protecting the Nation. If a deprivation of liberty can be justified by the need to protect a town, the protection of the Nation, *a fortiori*, justifies it. . . .

NOTES AND QUESTIONS

1. As Justice Scalia's opinion emphasizes, *Hamdi* isn't a criminal case. But the various opinions in *Hamdi* sound a number of themes that run through much of the law of criminal procedure: the role of the Founders' understandings in interpreting the Constitution, the role of open-ended interest balancing in deciding on the scope of proper procedures, the boundaries (if any) of enforcement discretion by the executive branch, the relevance of public safety needs to a sound interpretation of constitutional restrictions on government power, the relevance of the government's need to gather information — and its need to avoid *disclosing* information — to a sound interpretation of those restrictions, and the list could go on. Though not itself

5. Evidently, neither do the parties, who do not cite *Mathews* even once.

a part of the law of criminal procedure, *Hamdi* is a window on that law, a way of look-ing at the most fundamental debates in the field in a different context than the ones that dominate this book.

One of those debates, one that is central to the decision in *Hamdi*, concerns the nature and meaning of due process. Notice the different approaches Justices O'Connor, Scalia, and Thomas take to that basic question. Justice O'Connor seems to see due process as a question for the courts, to be decided by a common-law pro-cess, with interest balancing as the appropriate method of decision. Justice Scalia uses a different interpretive method — a mix of textualism and originalism — to reach a very different conclusion: In his preferred world, the key player in defining the process for prisoners like Hamdi is the legislative branch, not the judiciary. Jus-tice Thomas deploys the same interpretive method as Justice Scalia, but comes to yet another conclusion: It is the executive branch that should decide what process Hamdi should receive. Which branch is best suited to defining due process? The executive? The legislature? The courts? How much should courts defer to the defi-nitions the political branches use?

2. The *Hamdi* plurality approves a set of procedures that is significantly less pro-tective than those used in criminal trials. It follows that it is a good deal easier for the government to detain suspected terrorists — even when they are American citizens — than it is to detain other suspected criminals. One might reasonably won-der about the incentives that procedural gap creates. If the government finds it more procedurally convenient to fight the war on terrorism with military and intel-ligence agencies than with criminal law enforcement agencies, what effect will that have on civil liberties? What effect will it have on the progress of the fight against terrorism?

Perhaps the answer is "not much." After all, Hamdi belongs to a very small class of people: American citizens (allegedly) fighting American armed forces in a for-eign country. On the other hand, the logic of the Court's position — is it even pos-sible to say what that is, given the fractured decision in *Hamdi*? — might apply to suspected terrorists found *within* the United States. Does it?

3. *Hamdi* is part of a substantial legal tradition, one you will encounter a number of times in this book. The essence of the tradition is this: Often, the government wishes to justify detention that looks a lot like criminal punishment without using the procedures that generally attend criminal punishment. In general, the Supreme Court has been quite receptive to government claims of this sort. The usual legal jus-tification is that, for one or another reason, the relevant detention is something other than "punishment." Thus pretrial detention of criminal defendants is autho-rized based on much less protective procedures than those used in criminal trials because the detention is "regulatory" rather than punitive. See United States v. Sal-erno, 481 U.S. 739 (1987). (*Salerno* is excerpted in Chapter 8, at page 946.) The long-term incarceration of sex offenders can be authorized with less than the usual processes in criminal cases, as long as the incarceration can be seen as a response to the offenders' mental abnormality rather than punishment for their wrongful con-duct. See Kansas v. Hendricks, 521 U.S. 346 (1997). (*Hendricks* is noted in Chapter 16, at page 1562.) There are other examples.

Cases like *Salerno*, *Hendricks*, and *Hamdi* raise the following question: What does, and doesn't, count as criminal punishment for purposes of defining appropriate procedures? How is the question to be answered? One approach would be to look at the nature of the harm to the claimant. Under that approach, whenever a prisoner is detained in circumstances that seem similar to the detention of prison or jail inmates, criminal procedure protections would be triggered. Another approach would be to allow legislatures to classify detention as punitive or not, and defer to their classification. Under that approach, legislative labels would decide such cases. Yet another approach would be to decide whether a given detention is or isn't "punishment" based on the strength of the government's interest in more flexible procedures than those used in criminal litigation. (Arguably, the last is the approach taken by the *Hamdi* plurality.) Each of these approaches has support in the case law. Which is best?

4. The government claims that its interest in detaining Hamdi justifies special — and, from the government's point of view, specially favorable — procedures. Assume for the moment that the government's claim has substantial merit. (A majority of the Justices so assumed.) Should the government get especially favorable procedures when it prosecutes serial killers? After all, there is a very strong social interest in catching and punishing murderers, especially those who keep killing until they are caught. Should that interest be weighed in the balance when deciding what murder defendants' procedural rights should include? If not, why not?

Speaking of interest balancing, Justice O'Connor's plurality opinion relied on Mathews v. Eldridge, 424 U.S. 319 (1976), to determine how much process to grant Hamdi; *Mathews* requires weighing both sides' interests as the means by which courts decide what process is due in particular cases. It would seem to follow that whatever process the Court deems necessary represents, at least in the Justices' view, the optimal accommodation of the competing interests. That is not the usual method by which criminal procedure rights are defined. Should it be? Presumably, everyone wants optimal procedures. Why not perform a *Mathews*-style balance throughout the criminal process? Do the opinions in *Hamdi* suggest an answer?

5. Much of the debate in *Hamdi* concerns the proper balance between legislative and executive power. In the criminal justice system, those two sources of government power are usually allies, not competitors. Legislatures draft broad criminal statutes and allow police and prosecutors nearly total discretion in deciding when, how, and against whom to enforce those statutes. As a general matter, legislative power has not been a check on executive-branch agencies — more like a blank check, authorizing the executive to do pretty much what it pleases. Courts, not legislatures, are the source of most restrictions on executive power to enforce the criminal law. How does that affect your view of the arguments in Justice Scalia's dissent? How do you suppose he would respond?

6. The Supreme Court reentered the fray of the rights of enemy combatants in Boumediene v. Bush, 553 U.S. 723 (2008), in holding that they had the right to file a habeas corpus petition in federal court challenging their continued detention, which in turn could result in further Due Process rulings of their rights. *Boumediene* is considered further in Chapter 17.

7. Return to the interpretive question that lies at the heart of *Hamdi, Medina, Duncan, Hurtado*, and a host of other due process cases: What values does due process protect? In criminal cases, one's answer probably begins with accuracy: Above all else, the criminal process should be designed to ensure that innocent defendants are not convicted and punished. How well does American criminal procedure protect against punishment of innocent defendants? Perhaps not very well:

. . . As the scope of various constitutional protections has continued to expand [in the years since incorporation], judicial review targeted at potential errors on the merits — at cases where the wrong person was convicted — has been surprisingly muted. When, for example, the Supreme Court established constitutional sufficiency-of-the-evidence review in 1979, Justice Stevens predicted that federal judges would be swamped by the resulting additional work. The flood of new work never materialized, in part because appellate treatment of the relevant claims has been so perfunctory. Ineffective assistance doctrine, created in the 1970s and 1980s, has regulated conflicts of interest much more rigorously than it has regulated attorney decisions not to make plausible factual arguments. The Court's 1985 decision in Ake v. Oklahoma, requiring appointment of mental health experts to assist in preparing a criminal defense, has had few ripple effects, remaining basically restricted to the very small pool of insanity defense claims that go to trial.

Most strikingly, as the Supreme Court and lower appellate courts have developed standards of review for different kinds of constitutional claims, the courts consistently have adopted more favorable standards of review for non-guilt-related claims than for those claims most likely to be tied to guilt and innocence. The erroneous denial of Fourth Amendment and Miranda claims must be harmless beyond a reasonable doubt for the government to escape reversal on appeal. But a defendant making an ineffective-assistance-of-counsel claim (again, outside of conflicts of interest, which may be least tied to guilt or innocence and which require no showing of prejudice at all) must show a reasonable probability — substantially more than a reasonable doubt — that counsel's error or errors caused the defendant's conviction. The same tougher standard applies to claims that the government wrongfully withheld material exculpatory evidence. Nonconstitutional claims of newly discovered evidence . . . must meet an even tougher standard: The new evidence must not only have been unavailable at the time of trial but must also prove that the result reached at trial was probably wrong.

William J. Stuntz, The Uneasy Relationship Between Criminal Procedure and Criminal Justice, 107 Yale L.J. 1, 61-62 (1997). Perhaps incorporation of the Bill of Rights has yielded not so much *expansion* of defendants' rights as the *displacement* of some rights by others. Is the trade worth it? Has the Bill of Rights distracted attention from the system's central job: separation of the guilty from the innocent? Or is that not the system's central job?

PART TWO

THE RIGHT TO COUNSEL—THE LINCHPIN OF CONSTITUTIONAL PROTECTION

Chapter 3

The Right to Counsel and Other Assistance

A. The Constitutional Requirements

1. The Right to the Assistance of Counsel at Trial

> In all criminal prosecutions, the accused shall enjoy the right . . . to have the Assistance of Counsel for his defence.
>
> *U.S. Const. amend. VI*

> It never has been doubted by this court, or any other so far as we know, that notice and hearing are preliminary steps essential to the passing of an enforceable judgment, and that they, together with a legally competent tribunal having jurisdiction of the case, constitute basic elements of the constitutional requirement of due process of law. . . .
>
> What, then, does a hearing include? Historically and in practice, in our own country at least, it has always included the right to the aid of counsel when desired and provided by the party asserting the right. The right to be heard would be, in many cases, of little avail if it did not comprehend the right to be heard by counsel. Even the intelligent and educated layman has small and sometimes no skill in the science of law. If charged with crime, he is incapable, generally, of determining for himself whether the indictment is good or bad. He is unfamiliar with the rules of evidence. Left without the aid of counsel he may be put on trial without a proper charge, and convicted upon incompetent evidence, or evidence irrelevant to the issue or otherwise inadmissible. He lacks both the skill and knowledge adequately to prepare his defense, even though he have a perfect one. He requires the guiding hand of counsel at every step in the proceedings against him. Without it, though he be not guilty, he faces the danger of conviction because he does not know how to establish his innocence. If that be true of men of intelligence, how much more true is it of the ignorant and illiterate, or those of feeble intellect. If in any case, civil or criminal, a state or federal court were arbitrarily to refuse to hear a party by counsel, employed by and appearing for him, it reasonably may not be doubted that such a refusal would be a denial of a hearing, and, therefore, of due process in the constitutional sense.
>
> *Justice Sutherland, for the Court, in Powell v. Alabama,*
> *287 U.S. 45, 68-69 (1932)*

The meaning and scope of the Sixth Amendment right to counsel in criminal proceedings have been contested, for the most part, in the context of the right of an indigent to have counsel appointed and financed by the state. As the preceding quotation from *Powell* indicates, the right to be heard by retained counsel has never been seriously questioned in the United States. Quite early in our history, we rejected the English common law that denied accused felons the right to the assistance of retained counsel. For a discussion of the history of the right to counsel, see Note, An Historical Argument for the Right to Counsel during Police Interrogation, 73 Yale L.J. 1000, 1018-1034 (1964).

However, we proved to be much less solicitous of the plight of the indigent. In capital cases, federal law has always required the appointment of counsel, 1 Stat. 118 (1790), and a number of states followed a similar path. Nonetheless, it was not until *Powell* that the Supreme Court held that in capital cases Fourteenth Amendment due process is violated by state action that in effect denied a defendant access to effective assistance of counsel. Moreover, *Powell* appeared to be limited to those cases in which the defendant is "incapable adequately of making his own defense because of ignorance, feeble-mindedness, illiteracy, or the like." *Powell*, 287 U.S., at 71. The Court did hold, however, that the state's "duty is not discharged by an assignment [of counsel] at such a time or under such circumstances as to preclude the giving of effective aid in the preparation and trial of the case." Ibid.

Powell, in essence, created a *special circumstances rule* — effective assistance, or an adequate opportunity to obtain it, must be provided in capital cases if defendants are unable to represent themselves adequately. By 1961, this special circumstances rule had been transmuted into a "flat" requirement of counsel in capital cases, Hamilton v. Alabama, 368 U.S. 52 (1961), in large measure due to the awesome finality of capital punishment. See Yale Kamisar, Betts v. Brady Twenty Years Later: The Right to Counsel and Due Process Values, 61 Mich. L. Rev. 219, 255 (1962). But see id., at 255-260 (arguing that sentence should be immaterial to need for counsel).

In noncapital cases, a special circumstances rule also developed that required the appointment of counsel only when the absence of counsel would result in a "trial . . . offensive to the common and fundamental ideas of fairness and right." Betts v. Brady, 316 U.S. 455, 473 (1942). In *Betts*, the Court, over a sharp and prescient dissent by Justice Black, held that due process does not demand the appointment of counsel for indigent defendants in every state case because "the furnishing of counsel in all cases whatever" is *not* "dictated by natural, inherent and fundamental principles of justice." Id., at 464.

Four years prior to *Betts*, the Supreme Court held that the Sixth Amendment required the appointment of counsel in all noncapital federal criminal prosecutions. In doing so, the Court commented:

> The Sixth Amendment stands as a constant admonition that if the constitutional safeguards it provides be lost, justice will not "still be done." It embodies a realistic recognition of the obvious truth that the average defendant does not have the professional legal skill to protect himself when brought before a tribunal with power to take his life or liberty, wherein the prosecution is presented by experienced and learned counsel. That which is simple, orderly and necessary to the lawyer, to the untrained layman may appear intricate, complex and mysterious.

Johnson v. Zerbst, 304 U.S. 458, 462-463 (1938).

But if "justice cannot be done" in all federal prosecutions and in state capital cases without the assistance of counsel, and if, in state noncapital cases, the right to counsel "when desired and provided by the party asserting the right" is something that the party "requires . . . at every step," in order to minimize the chance of an erroneous conviction,[1] how could the *Betts* "special circumstances rule" be maintained? How could it be that justice *could* be done in a state prosecution, but not in a federal one, when an indigent is tried without counsel? And how does the absence of wealth minimize the need for counsel's guiding hand, whether in a capital or a noncapital case? Prior to *Gideon*, in short, had not the Court *already concluded*, even if it had still to be articulated, that the absence of counsel was itself a "special circumstance"?[2]

GIDEON v. WAINWRIGHT

Certiorari to the Supreme Court of Florida
372 U.S. 335 (1963)

MR. JUSTICE BLACK delivered the opinion of the Court.

Petitioner was charged in a Florida state court with having broken and entered a poolroom with intent to commit a misdemeanor. This offense is a felony under Florida law. Appearing in court without funds and without a lawyer, petitioner asked the court to appoint counsel for him, whereupon the following colloquy took place:

> *The Court:* Mr. Gideon, I am sorry, but I cannot appoint Counsel to represent you in this case. Under the laws of the State of Florida, the only time the Court can appoint Counsel to represent a Defendant is when that person is charged with a capital offense. I am sorry, but I will have to deny your request to appoint Counsel to defend you in this case.
>
> *The Defendant:* The United States Supreme Court says I am entitled to be represented by Counsel.

Put to trial before a jury, Gideon conducted his defense about as well as could be expected from a layman. He made an opening statement to the jury, cross-examined the State's witnesses, presented witnesses in his own defense, declined to testify himself, and made a short argument "emphasizing his innocence to the charge contained in the Information filed in this case." The jury returned a verdict of guilty, and petitioner was sentenced to serve five years in the state prison. . . . Since 1942, when Betts v. Brady, 316 U.S. 455, was decided by a divided Court, the problem of a defendant's federal constitutional right to counsel in a state court has been a continuing source of controversy and litigation in both state and federal courts. To give this problem another review here, we granted certiorari. Since Gideon was proceeding in forma pauperis, we appointed counsel to represent him and requested both sides to discuss in their briefs and oral arguments the following: "Should this Court's holding in Betts v. Brady . . . be reconsidered?" . . .

---

1. Indeed, the Supreme Court had gone so far as to say that a defendant's right to be heard by retained counsel was "unqualified." Chandler v. Fretag, 348 U.S. 3, 9 (1954). The reason for this conclusion surely was the Court's recognition of the significance of counsel. Id., at 9-10. But the very same "significance" that results in a conclusion of an unqualified right to be heard by retained counsel obviously highlights the untenable plight of the indigent unable to obtain counsel. This, too, appears to have contributed to the Court's willingness to reconsider *Betts*.

2. From 1950 until *Gideon*, the Supreme Court found a "special circumstance" requiring the appointment of counsel in every case that it heard that raised the issue. By 1962, the standard had apparently become "potential prejudice," a standard that will virtually always be met. Chewning v. Cunningham, 368 U.S. 443 (1962).

I

The facts upon which Betts claimed that he had been unconstitutionally denied the right to have counsel appointed to assist him are strikingly like the facts upon which Gideon here bases his federal constitutional claim. Betts was indicted for robbery in a Maryland state court. On arraignment, he told the trial judge of his lack of funds to hire a lawyer and asked the court to appoint one for him. Betts was advised that it was not the practice in that county to appoint counsel for indigent defendants except in murder and rape cases. He then pleaded not guilty, had witnesses summoned, cross-examined the State's witnesses, examined his own, and chose not to testify himself. He was found guilty by the judge, sitting without a jury, and sentenced to eight years in prison. Like Gideon, Betts sought release by habeas corpus, alleging that he had been denied the right to assistance of counsel in violation of the Fourteenth Amendment. Betts was denied any relief, and on review this Court affirmed. It was held that a refusal to appoint counsel for an indigent defendant charged with a felony did not necessarily violate the Due Process Clause of the Fourteenth Amendment, which for reasons given the Court deemed to be the only applicable federal constitutional provision. The Court said:

> Asserted denial [of due process] is to be tested by an appraisal of the totality of facts in a given case. That which may, in one setting, constitute a denial of fundamental fairness, shocking to the universal sense of justice, may, in other circumstances, and in the light of other considerations, fall short of such denial. [316 U.S., at 462.]

Treating due process as "a concept less rigid and more fluid than those envisaged in other specific and particular provisions of the Bill of Rights," the Court held that refusal to appoint counsel under the particular facts and circumstances in the Betts case was not so "offensive to the common and fundamental ideas of fairness" as to amount to a denial of due process. Since the facts and circumstances of the two cases are so nearly indistinguishable, we think the Betts v. Brady holding if left standing would require us to reject Gideon's claim that the Constitution guarantees him the assistance of counsel. Upon full reconsideration we conclude that Betts v. Brady should be overruled.

II

The Sixth Amendment provides, "In all criminal prosecutions, the accused shall enjoy the right . . . to have the Assistance of Counsel for his defence." We have construed this to mean that in federal courts counsel must be provided for defendants unable to employ counsel unless the right is competently and intelligently waived.[3] Betts argued that this right is extended to indigent defendants in state courts by the Fourteenth Amendment. In response the Court stated that, while the Sixth Amendment laid down "no rule for the conduct of the States, the question recurs whether the constraint laid by the Amendment upon the national courts expresses a rule so fundamental and essential to a fair trial, and so, to due process of law, that it is made obligatory upon the States by the Fourteenth Amendment." 316 U.S., at 465. In order to decide whether the Sixth Amendment's guarantee of counsel is of this fundamental nature, the court in *Betts* set out and considered "[r]elevant data on the

---

3. Johnson v. Zerbst, 304 U.S. 458 (1938).

subject . . . afforded by constitutional and statutory provisions subsisting in the colonies and the States prior to the inclusion of the Bill of Rights in the national Constitution, and in the constitutional, legislative, and judicial history of the States to the present date." 316 U.S., at 465. On the basis of this historical data the Court concluded that "appointment of counsel is not a fundamental right, essential to a fair trial." 316 U.S., at 471. It was for this reason the *Betts* Court refused to accept the contention that the Sixth Amendment's guarantee of counsel for indigent federal defendants was extended to or, in the words of that Court, "made obligatory upon the States by the Fourteenth Amendment." Plainly, had the Court concluded that appointment of counsel for an indigent criminal defendant was "a fundamental right, essential to a fair trial," it would have held that the Fourteenth Amendment requires appointment of counsel in a state court, just as the Sixth Amendment requires in a federal court.

We think the Court in *Betts* had ample precedent for acknowledging that those guarantees of the Bill of Rights which are fundamental safeguards of liberty immune from federal abridgment are equally protected against state invasion by the Due Process Clause of the Fourteenth Amendment. This same principle was recognized, explained, and applied in Powell v. Alabama, 287 U.S. 45 (1932), a case upholding the right of counsel, where the Court held that despite sweeping language to the contrary in Hurtado v. California, 110 U.S. 516 (1884), the Fourteenth Amendment "embraced" those "fundamental principles of liberty and justice which lie at the base of all our civil and political institutions," even though they had been "specifically dealt with in another part of the federal Constitution." 287 U.S., at 67. In many cases other than *Powell* and *Betts*, this Court has looked to the fundamental nature of original Bill of Rights guarantees to decide whether the Fourteenth Amendment makes them obligatory on the States. Explicitly recognized to be of this "fundamental nature" and therefore made immune from state invasion by the Fourteenth, or some part of it, are the First Amendment's freedoms of speech, press, religion, assembly, association, and petition for redress of grievances. For the same reason, though not always in precisely the same terminology, the Court has made obligatory on the States the Fifth Amendment's command that private property shall not be taken for public use without just compensation, the Fourth Amendment's prohibition of unreasonable searches and seizures, and the Eighth's ban on cruel and unusual punishment. On the other hand, this Court in Palko v. Connecticut, 302 U.S. 319 (1937), refused to hold that the Fourteenth Amendment made the double jeopardy provision of the Fifth Amendment obligatory on the States. In so refusing, however, the Court, speaking through Mr. Justice Cardozo, was careful to emphasize that "immunities that are valid as against the federal government by force of the specific pledges of particular amendments have been found to be implicit in the concept of ordered liberty, and thus, through the Fourteenth Amendment, become valid as against the states" and that guarantees "in their origin . . . effective against the federal government alone" had by prior cases "been taken over from the earlier articles of the federal bill of rights and brought within the Fourteenth Amendment by a process of absorption." 302 U.S., at 324-325, 326.

We accept Betts v. Brady's assumption, based as it was on our prior cases, that a provision of the Bill of Rights which is "fundamental and essential to a fair trial" is made obligatory upon the States by the Fourteenth Amendment. We think the Court in *Betts* was wrong, however, in concluding that the Sixth Amendment's guarantee of counsel is not one of these fundamental rights. Ten years before Betts v.

Brady, this Court, after full consideration of all the historical data examined in *Betts*, had unequivocally declared that "the right to the aid of counsel is of this fundamental character." Powell v. Alabama, 287 U.S. 25, 68 (1932). . . . And again in 1938 this Court said:

> [The assistance of counsel] is one of the safeguards of the Sixth Amendment deemed necessary to insure fundamental human rights of life and liberty. . . . The Sixth Amendment stands as a constant admonition that if the constitutional safeguards it provides be lost, justice will not "still be done." [Johnson v. Zerbst, 304 U.S. 458, 462 (1938).] . . .

In light of these and many other prior decisions of this Court, it is not surprising that the *Betts* Court, when faced with the contention that "one charged with crime, who is unable to obtain counsel, must be furnished counsel by the State," conceded that "[e]xpressions in the opinions of this court lend color to the argument. . . . " 316 U.S., at 462-463. The fact is that in deciding as it did — that "appointment of counsel is not a fundamental right, essential to a fair trial" — the Court in Betts v. Brady made an abrupt break with its own well-considered precedents. In returning to these old precedents, sounder we believe than the new, we but restore constitutional principles established to achieve a fair system of justice. Not only these precedents but also reason and reflection require us to recognize that in our adversary system of criminal justice, any person haled into court, who is too poor to hire a lawyer, cannot be assured a fair trial unless counsel is provided for him. This seems to us to be an obvious truth. Governments, both state and federal, quite properly spend vast sums of money to establish machinery to try defendants accused of crime. Lawyers to prosecute are everywhere deemed essential to protect the public's interest in an orderly society. Similarly, there are few defendants charged with crime, few indeed, who fail to hire the best lawyers they can get to prepare and present their defenses. That government hires lawyers to prosecute and defendants who have the money hire lawyers to defend are the strongest indications of the widespread belief that lawyers in criminal courts are necessities, not luxuries. The right of one charged with crime to counsel may not be deemed fundamental and essential to fair trials in some countries, but it is in ours. From the very beginning, our state and national constitutions and laws have laid great emphasis on procedural and substantive safeguards designed to assure fair trials before impartial tribunals in which every defendant stands equal before the law. This noble idea cannot be realized if the poor man charged with crime has to face his accusers without a lawyer to assist him. . . . The Court in Betts v. Brady departed from the sound wisdom upon which the Court's holding in Powell v. Alabama rested. Florida, supported by two other States, has asked that Betts v. Brady be left intact. Twenty-two states, as friends of the Court, argue that *Betts* was "an anachronism when handed down" and that it should now be overruled. We agree.

Reversed.

MR. JUSTICE DOUGLAS, concurring.

While I join the opinion of the Court, a brief historical resume of the relation between the Bill of Rights and the first section of the Fourteenth Amendment seems pertinent. Since the adoption of that Amendment, ten Justices have felt that it protects from infringement by the States the privileges, protections, and safeguards granted by the Bill of Rights. . . . Unfortunately it has never commanded a Court. Yet, happily, all constitutional questions are always open. And what we do today does not foreclose the matter.

My Brother Harlan is of the view that a guarantee of the Bill of Rights that is made applicable to the States by reason of the Fourteenth Amendment is a lesser version of that same guarantee as applied to the Federal Government. Mr. Justice Jackson shared that view. But that view has not prevailed and rights protected against state invasion by the Due Process Clause of the Fourteenth Amendment are not watered-down versions of what the Bill of Rights guarantees.

MR. JUSTICE CLARK, concurring in the result.

That the Sixth Amendment requires appointment of counsel in "all criminal prosecutions" is clear, both from the language of the Amendment and from this Court's interpretation. . . . It is equally clear . . . that the Fourteenth Amendment requires such appointment in all prosecutions for capital crimes. The Court's decision today, then, does no more than erase a distinction which has no basis in logic and an increasingly eroded basis in authority. . . .

. . . [T]he Constitution makes no distinction between capital and noncapital cases. The Fourteenth Amendment requires due process of law for the deprival of "liberty" just as for deprival of "life," and there cannot constitutionally be a difference in the quality of the process based merely upon a supposed difference in the sanction involved. How can the Fourteenth Amendment tolerate a procedure which it condemns in capital cases on the ground that deprival of liberty may be less onerous than deprival of life — a value judgment not universally accepted — or that only the latter deprival is irrevocable? I can find no acceptable rationalization for such a result, and I therefore concur in the judgment of the Court.

MR. JUSTICE HARLAN, concurring.

I agree that Betts v. Brady should be overruled, but consider it entitled to a more respectful burial than has been accorded, at least on the part of those of us who were not on the Court when that case was decided.

I cannot subscribe to the view that Betts v. Brady represented "an abrupt break with its own well-considered precedents." . . . In 1932, in Powell v. Alabama, . . . a capital case, this Court declared that under the particular facts there presented — "the ignorance and illiteracy of the defendants, their youth, the circumstances of public hostility . . . and above all that they stood in deadly peril of their lives" (287 U.S., at 71) — the state court had a duty to assign counsel for the trial as a necessary requisite of due process of law. It is evident that these limiting facts were not added to the opinion as an afterthought; they were repeatedly emphasized, see 287 U.S., at 52, 57-58, 71, and were clearly regarded as important to the result.

Thus when this Court, a decade later, decided Betts v. Brady, it did no more than to admit of the possible existence of special circumstances in noncapital as well as capital trials, while at the same time insisting that such circumstances be shown in order to establish a denial of due process. The right to appointed counsel had been recognized as being considerably broader in federal prosecutions, see Johnson v. Zerbst, 304 U.S. 458, but to have imposed these requirements on the States would indeed have been "an abrupt break" with the almost immediate past. The declaration that the right to appointed counsel in state prosecutions, as established in Powell v. Alabama, was not limited to capital cases was in truth not a departure from, but an extension of, existing precedent. The principles declared in *Powell* and in *Betts*, however, have had a troubled journey throughout the years that have followed first the one case and then the other. Even by the time of the *Betts* decision, dictum in at least one of the Court's opinions had indicated that there was an absolute right to the services of counsel in the trial of state capital cases.[1] Such dicta continued to appear in subsequent decisions,[2] and any lingering doubts were finally eliminated by the holding of Hamilton v. Alabama, 368 U.S. 52.

In noncapital cases, the "special circumstances" rule has continued to exist in form while its substance has been substantially and steadily eroded. In the first decade after *Betts*, there were cases in which the Court found special circumstances to be lacking, but usually by a sharply divided vote. However, no such decision has been cited to us, and I have found none, [since] 1950. At the same time, there have been not a few cases in which special circumstances were found in little or nothing more than the "complexity" of the legal questions presented, although those questions were often of only routine difficulty. The Court has come to recognize, in other words, that the mere existence of a serious criminal charge constituted in itself special circumstances requiring the services of counsel at trial. In truth the Betts v. Brady rule is no longer a reality.

This evolution, however, appears not to have been fully recognized by many state courts, in this instance charged with the front-line responsibility for the enforcement of constitutional rights. To continue a rule which is honored by this Court only with lip service is not a healthy thing and in the long run will do disservice to the federal system.

The special circumstances rule has been formally abandoned in capital cases, and the time has now come when it should be similarly abandoned in noncapital cases, at least as to offenses which, as the one involved here, carry the possibility of a substantial prison sentence. (Whether the rule should extend to *all* criminal cases need not now be decided.) This indeed does no more than to make explicit something that has long since been foreshadowed in our decisions.

In agreeing with the Court that the right to counsel in a case such as this should now be expressly recognized as a fundamental right embraced in the Fourteenth Amendment, I wish to make a further observation. When we hold a right or immunity, valid against the Federal Government, to be "implicit in the concept of ordered liberty" and thus valid against the States, I do not read our past decisions to suggest that by so holding, we automatically carry over an entire body of federal law and apply it in full sweep to the States. Any such concept would disregard the frequently wide disparity between the legitimate interests of the States and of the Federal Government, the divergent problems that they face, and the significantly different consequences of their actions.

. . . In what is done today I do not understand the Court to depart from the principles laid down in Palko v. Connecticut, 302 U.S. 319, or to embrace the concept that the Fourteenth Amendment "incorporates" the Sixth Amendment as such.

On these premises I join in the judgment of the Court.

---

1. Avery v. Alabama, 308 U.S. 444, 445.
2. E.g., Bute v. Illinois, 333 U.S. 640, 674; Uveges v. Pennsylvania, 335 U.S. 437, 441.

NOTES AND QUESTIONS

1. In one sense, the result in *Gideon* appears to have been inevitable. Even if there are cases that could be tried fairly without defense counsel, one cannot determine from the record in uncounseled cases which ones would have benefited from counsel. Records that look good on appeal might have looked quite different had counsel been present. Indeed, *Betts* is such a case. Each court that reviewed the record in *Betts* concluded that Betts had not been prejudiced by the absence of counsel. In an insightful analysis of the factual setting of *Betts*, Professor Kamisar demonstrated quite forcefully that a competent lawyer may very well have had an impact on the outcome of the trial. Yale Kamisar, The Right to Counsel and the Fourteenth Amendment: A Dialogue on "The Most Pervasive Right" of an Accused, 30 U. Chi. L. Rev. 1, 42-56 (1962). For example, one of the trial witnesses, Bollinger, identified Betts at the jailhouse, as well as a coat, dark glasses, and a handkerchief allegedly worn by Betts during the robbery. *But*:

> *What* coat? *Whose* dark glasses and handkerchief? . . .
> Is it possible that the coat Bollinger "identified" at the jail was simply one the police procured from somebody other than Betts — pursuant to Bollinger's own description of the dark gray, bagged-pocketed coat the man wore who robbed him?
> Even if a coat were offered in evidence, "objects or things offered in evidence do not generally identify themselves." The object must be shown to have some connection with Betts. Not only was this not done; no coat was ever offered in evidence. . . .
> As for the other items, there was testimony by the state that "smoked glasses were put on Betts' eyes and a handkerchief around his neck like the man was supposed to have had that did the holding up." But once again, no handkerchief or glasses were offered in evidence. Presumably, Betts owned a handkerchief or two, but once again, the state failed to establish that he even owned a pair of dark glasses. One alibi witness who was asked about this on cross simply did "not know," and the matter was dropped.

Why did the state fail to offer any of these items in evidence? Why was one of Betts' own witnesses cross-examined, albeit casually, about the defendant's ownership of a dark gray overcoat and smoked glasses? If the state had possessed these items, why would it have asked such questions? Although the matter is not free from doubt — because neither trial judge nor prosecutor seemed to care much, and Betts evidently failed to realize how this would weaken the state's case — it is difficult to avoid the conclusion that the following "bootstraps" operation occurred: Bollinger described to the police the various items the robber was supposed to have worn; the police simply went out, begged or borrowed the requisite coat, glasses, and handkerchief, and slapped them on Betts; Bollinger then made his identification, based largely on the coat, glasses, and handkerchief the police had put on Betts.

2. Even if it is true that defense counsel normally is of value, does it follow that the result in *Gideon* is constitutionally mandated? There is no requirement that the state provide everything that is useful or of value to defendants. Thus, there must be some other criteria that determine what the state must provide. To what extent, for example, should constitutional analysis be informed by general practice in the states? By the "intent of the Framers" of the relevant constitutional provisions? By the cost to government of a decision one way or the other? By what is "fair" or "just"? If notions of fairness or justice are to play a role, how does one determine what those words mean?

3. Regardless of the scope of words such as "fairness" or "justice," there probably would be general agreement that any practice that generated a relatively high risk of erroneous convictions is "unfair," as the absence of counsel most likely does. Why was that not emphasized more in *Gideon*? Justice Black's opinion for the Court in *Gideon* primarily asserted that *Betts* was an abrupt change from its precedents and thus was wrong, although the excerpt from *Powell* at the beginning of this section was quoted but not developed. Is that adequate? If a court decides to overrule a case, how can it go about it? How *should* it go about it, or does it matter? See Jerold Israel, Gideon v. Wainwright: The "Art" of Overruling, [1963] Sup. Ct. Rev. 211. Does the method employed in the majority opinion explain, at least in part, why the concurrences were written to what was a unanimous judgment?

4. What are *Gideon*'s consequences? At one level, the answer seems easy: Presumably, the system functions better and more accurately when defendants have lawyers than when they must fend for themselves. But the answer may be more complicated than first appears. Defense lawyers make criminal trials more elaborate and hence more expensive. The state presumably must bear that cost. Yet the state need not hold a trial in order to obtain a conviction: Most convictions — in the neighborhood of 90 percent by most estimates — are the result of guilty pleas, not criminal trials. And the more costly trials are to the state, the more the state may be willing to pay, in the form of reduced charges or sentences, in order to get the defendant to plead guilty. These "payments" are, of course, the centerpiece of plea bargaining. The point is that *Gideon*, like other defense rights that raise the expense of criminal prosecution, may significantly improve the criminal trial process, but it may also lead to a system in which fewer defendants actually use that process. Which is better — a careful and expensive trial process coupled with lots of guilty pleas, or a more casual trial process that is used by more defendants?

NOTES ON THE *GIDEON* RIGHT TO COUNSEL AS APPLIED TO MISDEMEANORS

1. What was the judgment in *Gideon*, apart from the overruling of *Betts*? What, in other words, is the scope of the right to counsel imposed on the states by *Gideon*? Must counsel be appointed in every criminal case? Every felony? What about trials of misdemeanors with a jury, or when a somewhat complicated issue may be contested? The Supreme Court first faced that question in Argersinger v. Hamlin, 407 U.S. 25 (1972):

> Petitioner, an indigent, was charged in Florida with carrying a concealed weapon, an offense punishable by imprisonment up to six months, a $1,000 fine, or both. The trial was to a judge, and petitioner was unrepresented by counsel. He was sentenced to serve 90 days in jail, and brought this habeas corpus action in the Florida Supreme Court, alleging that, being deprived of his right to counsel, he was unable as an indigent layman properly to raise and present to the trial court good and sufficient defenses to the charge for which he stands convicted. The Florida Supreme Court by a four-to-three decision, in ruling on the right to counsel, followed the line we marked out in Duncan v. Louisiana, 391 U.S. 145, 159, as respects the right to trial by jury and held that the right to court-appointed counsel extends only to trials "for non-petty offenses punishable by more than six months imprisonment." . . . We reverse.

In rejecting the analogy to trial by jury, the Court noted:

> The right to trial by jury, also guaranteed by the Sixth Amendment by reason of the
> Fourteenth, was limited by Duncan v. Louisiana to trials where the potential punish-
> ment was imprisonment for six months or more. But . . . the right to trial by jury has a
> different genealogy and is brigaded with a system of trial to a judge alone. . . .
>
> While there is historical support for limiting the "deep commitment" to trial by jury
> to "serious criminal cases,"[2] there is no such support for a similar limitation on the
> right to assistance of counsel:
>
>> Originally, in England, a person charged with treason or felony was denied the aid of coun-
>> sel, except in respect of legal questions which the accused himself might suggest. At the
>> same time parties in civil cases and persons accused of misdemeanors were entitled to the
>> full assistance of counsel. . . . [It] appears that in at least twelve of the thirteen colonies the
>> rule of the English common law, in the respect now under consideration, had been defini-
>> tively rejected and the right to counsel fully recognized in all criminal prosecutions, save
>> that in one or two instances the right was limited to capital offenses or to the more serious
>> crimes. . . . [Powell v. Alabama, 287 U.S. 45, 60 and 64-65.]
>
> The Sixth Amendment thus extended the right to counsel beyond its common-law
> dimensions. But there is nothing in the language of the Amendment, its history, or in
> the decisions of this Court, to indicate that it was intended to embody a retraction of
> the right in petty offenses wherein the common law previously did require that counsel
> be provided. . . .
>
> We reject, therefore, the premise that since prosecutions for crimes punishable by
> imprisonment for less than six months may be tried without a jury, they may also be
> tried without a lawyer. . . .
>
> The requirement of counsel may well be necessary for a fair trial even in a petty-
> offense prosecution. We are by no means convinced that legal and constitutional ques-
> tions involved in a case that actually leads to imprisonment even for a brief period are
> any less complex than when a person can be sent off for six months or more. . . .
>
> We hold, therefore, that absent a knowing and intelligent waiver, no person may be
> imprisoned for any offense, whether classified as petty, misdemeanor, or felony, unless
> he was represented by counsel at his trial. . . .

Justice Powell concurred in the result, but expressed doubts about the breadth of
the decision.

> . . . Due process, perhaps the most fundamental concept in our law, embodies prin-
> ciples of fairness rather than immutable line drawing as to every aspect of a criminal
> trial. While counsel is often essential to a fair trial, this is by no means a universal fact.
> Some petty offense cases are complex; others are exceedingly simple. As a justification
> for furnishing counsel to indigents accused of felonies, the Court noted, "That govern-
> ment hires lawyers to prosecute and defendants who have the money hire lawyers to
> defend are the strongest indications of the widespread belief that lawyers in criminal
> courts are necessities, not luxuries."[12] Yet government often does not hire lawyers to
> prosecute petty offenses; instead the arresting police officer presents the case. Nor
> does every defendant who can afford to do so hire lawyers to defend petty charges.
> Where the possibility of a jail sentence is remote and the probable fine seems small, or
> where the evidence of guilt is overwhelming, the costs of assistance of counsel may

---

2. See Felix Frankfurter & Thomas G. Corcoran, Petty Offenses and the Constitutional Guaranty of
Trial by Jury, 39 Harv. L. Rev. 917, 980-982 (1926). . . .

12. Gideon v. Wainwright, 372 U.S., at 344.

exceed the benefits. It is anomalous that the Court's opinion today will extend the right of appointed counsel to indigent defendants in cases where the right to counsel would rarely be exercised by nonindigent defendants. . . .

There are thousands of statutes and ordinances which authorize imprisonment for six months or less, usually as an alternative to a fine. These offenses include some of the most trivial of misdemeanors, ranging from spitting on the sidewalk to certain traffic offenses. They also include a variety of more serious misdemeanors. This broad spectrum of petty-offense cases daily floods the lower criminal courts. The rule laid down today will confront the judges of each of these courts with an awkward dilemma. If counsel is not appointed or knowingly waived, no sentence of imprisonment for any duration may be imposed. The judge will therefore be forced to decide in advance of trial — and without hearing the evidence — whether he will forgo entirely his judicial discretion to impose some sentence of imprisonment and abandon his responsibility to consider the full range of punishments established by the legislature. His alternatives, assuming the availability of counsel, will be to appoint counsel and retain the discretion vested in him by law, or to abandon this discretion in advance and proceed without counsel. . . .

I would hold that the right to counsel in petty-offense cases is not absolute but is one to be determined by the trial courts exercising a judicial discretion on a case-by-case basis. The determination should be made before the accused formally pleads; many petty cases are resolved by guilty pleas in which the assistance of counsel may be required.

Why does Justice Powell wish to resurrect the *Betts* special circumstances rule? Are you convinced or unpersuaded? Note his assertion that "Due Process . . . embodies principles of fairness rather than immutable line drawing." How helpful is that? How do you determine what is "fair" without "drawing a line" between that and what is "unfair"?

2. What is the holding in *Argersinger*? Does *Argersinger* supplement, or modify, *Gideon*? Does counsel need to be appointed in a felony case in which the judge determines before trial not to sentence the defendant to a term of imprisonment? If so, why? What is the significance of labeling one offense a felony and another a misdemeanor? How do aggravated misdemeanors fit into the taxonomy? See, e.g., Iowa Crim. Code §903.1 (aggravated misdemeanor punishable by two-year imprisonment).

The Court in Scott v. Illinois, 440 U.S. 367 (1979), addressed some of these issues:

We granted certiorari in this case to resolve a conflict among state and lower federal courts regarding the proper application of our decision in Argersinger v. Hamlin. . . . Scott was convicted of theft and fined $50 after a bench trial in the Circuit Court of Cook County, Ill. . . . The applicable Illinois statute set the maximum penalty for such an offense at a $500 fine or one year in jail, or both. The petitioner argues that a line of this Court's cases culminating in Argersinger v. Hamlin, . . . requires state provision of counsel whenever imprisonment is an authorized penalty. . . .

Although the intentions of the *Argersinger* Court are not unmistakably clear from its opinion, we conclude today that *Argersinger* did indeed delimit the constitutional right to appointed counsel in state criminal proceedings. Even were the matter res nova, we believe that the central premise of *Argersinger* — that actual imprisonment is a penalty different in kind from fines or the mere threat of imprisonment — is eminently sound and warrants adoption of actual imprisonment as the line defining the constitutional right to appointment of counsel. *Argersinger* has proved workable, whereas any extension would create confusion and impose unpredictable, but necessarily substantial, costs on 50 quite diverse States.[5] We therefore hold that the Sixth and Fourteenth Amendments to the United States Constitution require only that no indigent criminal defendant be sentenced to a term of imprisonment unless the State has afforded him the right to assistance of appointed counsel in his defense. The judgement of the Supreme Court of Illinois is accordingly affirmed.

Justice Brennan dissented:

In my view petitioner could prevail in this case without extending the right to counsel beyond what was assumed to exist in *Argersinger*. Neither party in that case questioned the existence of the right to counsel in trials involving "non-petty" offenses punishable by more than six months in jail. The question the Court addressed was whether the right applied to some "petty" offenses to which the right to jury trial did not extend. The Court's reasoning in applying the right to counsel in the case before it — that the right to counsel is more fundamental to a fair proceeding than the right to jury trial and that the historical limitations on the jury trial right are irrelevant to the right to counsel — certainly cannot support a standard for the right to counsel that is more restrictive than the standard for granting a right to jury trial. . . . *Argersinger* thus established a "two dimensional" test for the right to counsel: the right attaches to any "non-petty" offense punishable by more than six months in jail and in addition to any offense where actual incarceration is likely regardless of the maximum authorized penalty. See Duke, The Right to Appointed Counsel: *Argersinger* and Beyond, 12 Am. Crim. L. Rev. 601 (1975).

. . . Not only is the "actual imprisonment" standard unprecedented as the exclusive test, but also the problems inherent in its application demonstrate the superiority of an "authorized imprisonment" standard that would require the appointment of counsel for indigents accused of any offense for which imprisonment for any time is authorized.

First, the "authorized imprisonment" standard more faithfully implements the principles of the Sixth Amendment identified in *Gideon*. The procedural rules established by state statutes are geared to the nature of the potential penalty for an offense, not to the actual penalty imposed in particular cases. The authorized penalty is also a better predictor of the stigma and other collateral consequences that attach to conviction of an offense. . . .

Second, the "authorized imprisonment" test presents no problems of administration. It avoids the necessity for time-consuming consideration of the likely sentence in each individual case before trial and the attendant problems of inaccurate predictions, unequal treatment, and apparent and actual bias. . . .

Finally, the "authorized imprisonment" test ensures that courts will not abrogate legislative judgments concerning the appropriate range of penalties to be considered for each offense. . . .

The apparent reason for the Court's adoption of the "actual imprisonment" standard for all misdemeanors is concern for the economic burden that an "authorized imprisonment" standard might place on the States. But, with all respect, that concern is both irrelevant and speculative.

5. Unfortunately, extensive empirical work has not been done. That which exists suggests that the requirements of *Argersinger* have not proved to be unduly burdensome. See, e.g., B. Ingraham, The Impact of *Argersinger* — One Year Later, 8 Law & Soc. Rev. 615 (1974). That some jurisdictions have had difficulty implementing *Argersinger* is certainly not an argument for extending it. S. Krantz, C. Smith, D. Rossman, P. Froyd, & J. Hoffman, Right to Counsel in Criminal Cases 1-18 (1976).

This Court's role in enforcing constitutional guarantees for criminal defendants cannot be made dependent on the budgetary decisions of state governments. . . .

3. *Argersinger* referred explicitly to "the trial of a misdemeanor," thus apparently leaving intact the general understanding that *Gideon* requires the appointment of counsel for indigents in all felony cases. Is that understanding consistent with *Scott*? If the only constitutional criterion is actual imprisonment, then presumably it should apply to misdemeanors and felonies alike. Nevertheless, lower courts have mostly assumed, even after *Scott*, that felonies are governed by *Gideon*'s across-the-board requirement of appointment of counsel. In an offhand statement in a footnote, the Supreme Court has accepted that view. Nichols v. United States, 511 U.S. 738, 743 n. 9 (1994) ("In felony cases, in contrast to misdemeanor charges, the Constitution requires that an indigent defendant be offered appointed counsel unless that right is intelligently and competently waived.") (citing *Gideon*).

4. In Lewis v. United States, 518 U.S. 322 (1996), the Court concluded that a defendant does not have a constitutional right to trial by jury when prosecuted in a single proceeding for multiple petty offenses, even if the possible aggregate prison term exceeds six months. In an interesting passage, however, the Court suggested that other factors may be relevant to determining whether an offense is "petty" for purposes of the Sixth Amendment: "An offense carrying a maximum prison term of six months or less is presumed petty, unless the legislature has authorized additional statutory penalties so severe as to indicate that the legislature considered the offense serious." For a critical analysis of *Lewis*, see Colleen P. Murphy, The Narrowing of the Entitlement to Criminal Jury Trial, [1997] Wis. L. Rev. 133.

5. If you read *Scott* broadly, it fundamentally reworks the meaning of the Sixth Amendment, but can it also be read more narrowly, as essentially refining *Argersinger*'s treatment of less serious criminal cases? Read more narrowly, would the aftermath of *Scott* contain a series of principles, any one of which would be adequate to require counsel in any particular case? What are those principles? In this regard, consider the implications of United States v. Nachtigal, 507 U.S. 1 (1993), in which the court of appeals held that a jury trial was required even though maximum punishment did not exceed six months. The Court summarily reversed but in doing so emphasized the importance of Blanton v. North Las Vegas, 489 U.S. 538 (1989), which implies that factors other than length of sentence may be relevant to the right to a jury trial. If that is so, can factors other than imprisonment also be relevant to the right to counsel?

6. How cogent is the majority's emphasis on imprisonment as the controlling factor? Criminal conviction apparently has a stigmatizing effect on the defendant, and there are other, more tangible collateral consequences that can follow from conviction, such as the loss of various kinds of licenses or of the right to vote. Did the Court adequately address these kinds of consequences? Indeed, did the Court address them at all? How should they be addressed?

7. The most serious collateral consequence that can flow from a criminal conviction is a dramatically increased sentence for a subsequent criminal conviction. In Baldasar v. Illinois, 446 U.S. 222 (1980), the Court reviewed the constitutionality of a statute that converted a second conviction for misdemeanor theft (property worth less than $150) into a felony with enhanced punishment. Baldasar was convicted of the first offense without counsel, and the question before the Court was whether the uncounseled conviction could trigger the enhancement provisions after the second,

counseled conviction. By a 5-4 vote, the Court said no, though no single opinion commanded a majority.

In Nichols v. United States, 511 U.S. 738 (1994), the Court returned to this issue. In 1983, Nichols was convicted of driving under the influence, a misdemeanor, for which he was fined but not jailed. He was not represented in the DUI proceeding. In 1990, Nichols was convicted on federal drug charges, and under the federal sentencing guidelines, the earlier, uncounseled DUI conviction led to an addition of roughly two years to his federal prison sentence. The Court upheld the sentence. In an opinion by Chief Justice Rehnquist, one of the dissenters in *Baldasar*, the Court concluded that *Baldasar* should be overruled, and that uncounseled convictions can be used to enhance sentences for subsequent crimes. The Court reasoned that this was the only position "consistent with the traditional understanding of the sentencing process, which we have often recognized as less exacting than the process of establishing guilt":

> As a general proposition, a sentencing judge "may appropriately conduct an inquiry broad in scope, largely unlimited either as to the kind of information he may consider, or the source from which it may come." (U.S. v. Tucker, 404 U.S. 443, 448) . . . "Traditionally, sentencing judges have considered a wide variety of factors in addition to evidence of guilt in determining what sentence to impose on a convicted defendant." (Wisconsin v. Mitchell, 508 U.S. 476, 485) . . . One such important factor . . . is a defendant's prior convictions. Sentencing courts have not only taken into consideration a defendant's prior convictions, but have also considered a defendant's past criminal behavior, even if no conviction resulted from that behavior. We have upheld the constitutionality of considering such previous conduct in Williams v. New York, 337 U.S. 241 (1949). . . . [And] in McMillan v. Pennsylvania, 477 U.S. 79 (1986) . . . we held that the state could consider, as a sentence enhancement factor, visible possession of a firearm during the felonies of which defendant was found guilty.
>
> Thus, consistently with due process, petitioner in the present case could have been sentenced more severely based simply on evidence of the underlying conduct which gave rise to the previous DUI offense. And the state need prove such conduct only by a preponderance of the evidence. Surely, then, it must be constitutionally permissible to consider a prior uncounseled misdemeanor conviction based on the same conduct where that conduct must be proven beyond a reasonable doubt.

511 U.S. 747-748. Justice Blackmun, joined by Justices Stevens and Ginsburg, dissented, arguing that *Scott* stands for the proposition that Nichols's uncounseled DUI conviction may not be "used as the basis for any incarceration, not even a 1-day jail sentence," id., at 754, much less the two years of additional time Nichols had to serve.

Which position in *Nichols* is more faithful to *Scott*? Which position is more faithful to *Gideon*? What you are beginning to see is that such questions are often quite difficult to answer. Constitutional principles can arise in cases in virtually limitless ways. Any single case applies those principles to the facts of that case, but their applicability to some other case with different facts can be unpredictable. The right to counsel area is a good example of this because of the enormous complexity involved in the various ways that states can sanction offenders, and the numerous variables that can affect the decision to sanction. One sees in the path forward from *Gideon* the implications of this dynamic. Rather than laying down immutable principles to then be faithfully applied in a straightforward fashion, the Court is engaged in a common law process of building up a system of precedent sensitive to the factual nuances of the cases that arise. This may be generally true with respect to the Court's constitutional criminal procedure jurisprudence. See, e.g., Ronald J. Allen & Ross M. Rosenberg, The Fourth Amendment and the Limits of Theory: Local Versus General Theoretical Knowledge, 72 St. John's L. Rev. 1149 (1998); Ronald J. Allen & M. Kristin Mace, The Self-Incrimination Clause Explained and Its Future Predicted, 94 J. Crim. L. & Criminology 243 (2004); Craig M. Bradley, The Uncertainty Principle in the Supreme Court, 1986 Duke L.J. 1.

ALABAMA v. SHELTON

Certiorari to the Alabama Supreme Court
535 U.S. 654 (2002)

JUSTICE GINSBURG delivered the opinion of the Court.

. . . Defendant-respondent LeReed Shelton, convicted of third-degree assault, was sentenced to a jail term of 30 days, which the trial court immediately suspended, placing Shelton on probation for two years. The question presented is whether the Sixth Amendment right to appointed counsel, as delineated in *Argersinger* and *Scott*, applies to a defendant in Shelton's situation. We hold that a suspended sentence that may "end up in the actual deprivation of a person's liberty" may not be imposed unless the defendant was accorded "the guiding hand of counsel" in the prosecution for the crime charged. *Argersinger*, 407 U.S., at 40.

I

After representing himself at a bench trial in the District Court of Etowah County, Alabama, Shelton was convicted of third-degree assault, a class A misdemeanor carrying a maximum punishment of one year imprisonment and a $2000 fine. He invoked his right to a new trial before a jury in Circuit Court, where he again appeared without a lawyer and was again convicted. The court repeatedly warned Shelton about the problems self-representation entailed, but at no time offered him assistance of counsel at state expense.

The Circuit Court sentenced Shelton to serve 30 days in the county prison. As authorized by Alabama law, however, the court suspended that sentence and placed Shelton on two years' unsupervised probation, conditioned on his payment of court costs, a $500 fine, reparations of $25, and restitution in the amount of $516.69.

Shelton appealed his conviction and sentence on Sixth Amendment grounds. . . . A suspended sentence, the [Alabama Court of Criminal Appeals] concluded, does not trigger the Sixth Amendment right to appointed counsel unless there is "evidence in the record that the [defendant] has actually been deprived of liberty." Because Shelton remained on probation, the court held that he had not been denied any Sixth Amendment right at trial.

The Supreme Court of Alabama reversed the Court of Criminal Appeals in relevant part. . . . In the Alabama high court's view, a suspended sentence constitutes a "term of imprisonment" within the meaning of *Argersinger* and *Scott* even though incarceration is not immediate or inevitable. And because the State is constitutionally barred from activating the conditional sentence, the Alabama court concluded, "the threat itself is hollow and should be considered a nullity." Accordingly, the court affirmed Shelton's conviction and the monetary portion of his punishment, but invalidated "that aspect of his sentence imposing 30 days of suspended jail time." By reversing Shelton's suspended sentence, the State informs us, the court also vacated the two-year term of probation.

Courts have divided on the Sixth Amendment question presented in this case. Some have agreed with the decision below that appointment of counsel is a constitutional prerequisite to imposition of a conditional or suspended prison sentence. . . . Others have rejected that proposition. . . . We granted certiorari to resolve the conflict.

II

. . . Applying the "actual imprisonment" rule to the case before us, we take up first the [following] question . . . : Where the State provides no counsel to an indigent defendant, does the Sixth Amendment permit activation of a suspended sentence upon the defendant's violation of the terms of probation? We conclude that it does not. A suspended sentence is a prison term imposed for the offense of conviction. Once the prison term is triggered, the defendant is incarcerated not for the probation violation, but for the underlying offense. The uncounseled conviction at that point "results in imprisonment," Nichols [v. United States, 511 U.S. 738, 746 (1994)]; it "ends up in the actual deprivation of a person's liberty," *Argersinger*, 407 U.S., at 40. This is precisely what the Sixth Amendment, as interpreted in *Argersinger* and *Scott*, does not allow.

Amicus[3] resists this reasoning primarily on two grounds. First, he attempts to align this case with our decisions in *Nichols* and Gagnon v. Scarpelli, 411 U.S. 778 (1973). . . .

Nichols presented the question whether the Sixth Amendment barred consideration of a defendant's prior uncounseled misdemeanor conviction in determining his sentence for a subsequent felony offense. 511 U.S., at 740. [We concluded that] "an uncounseled misdemeanor conviction, valid under *Scott* because no prison term was imposed, is also valid when used to enhance punishment at a subsequent conviction." Id., at 749. In *Gagnon*, the question was whether the defendant, who was placed on probation pursuant to a suspended sentence for armed robbery, had a due process right to representation by appointed counsel at a probation revocation hearing. 411 U.S., at 783. We held that counsel was not invariably required in parole or probation revocation proceedings; we directed, instead, a "case-by-case approach" turning on the character of the issues involved. Id., at 788-791.

Considered together, amicus contends, *Nichols* and *Gagnon* establish this principle: Sequential proceedings must be analyzed separately for Sixth Amendment purposes, and only those proceedings "resulting in *immediate* actual imprisonment" trigger the right to state-appointed counsel, id., at 13 (emphasis added). Thus, the defendant in *Nichols* had no right to appointed counsel in the DUI proceeding because he was not immediately imprisoned at the conclusion of that proceeding. The uncounseled DUI, valid when imposed, did not later become invalid because it was used to enhance the length of imprisonment that followed a separate and subsequent felony proceeding. Just so here, amicus contends: Shelton had no right to

---

3. Oddly, when this case got to the Supreme Court, Alabama refused to defend its own statute, so the Court appointed Professor Charles Fried as amicus to defend that position. — Eds.

appointed counsel in the Circuit Court because he was not incarcerated immediately after trial; his conviction and suspended sentence were thus valid and could serve as proper predicates for actual imprisonment at a later hearing to revoke his probation.

Gagnon and *Nichols* do not stand for the broad proposition amicus would extract from them. The dispositive factor in those cases was not whether incarceration occurred immediately or only after some delay. Rather, the critical point was that the defendant had a recognized right to counsel when adjudicated guilty of the felony offense for which he was imprisoned. . . . Unlike this case, in which revocation of probation would trigger a prison term imposed for a misdemeanor of which Shelton was found guilty without the aid of counsel, the sentences imposed in *Nichols* and *Gagnon* were for felony convictions — a federal drug conviction in *Nichols*, and a state armed robbery conviction in *Gagnon* — for which the right to counsel is unquestioned. . . .

Thus, neither *Nichols* nor *Gagnon* altered or diminished *Argersinger*'s command that "no person may be imprisoned *for any offense* . . . unless he was represented by counsel at his trial," 407 U.S., at 37 (emphasis added). Far from supporting amicus' position, *Gagnon* and *Nichols* simply highlight that the Sixth Amendment inquiry trains on the stage of the proceedings corresponding to Shelton's Circuit Court trial, where his guilt was adjudicated, eligibility for imprisonment established, and prison sentence determined. . . .

Amicus also contends that "practical considerations clearly weigh against" the extension of the Sixth Amendment appointed-counsel right to a defendant in Shelton's situation. He cites figures suggesting that although conditional sentences are commonly imposed, they are rarely activated. Tr. of Oral Arg. 20-21 (speculating that "hundreds of thousands" of uncounseled defendants receive suspended sentences, but only "thousands" of that large number are incarcerated upon violating the terms of their probation). Based on these estimations, amicus argues that a rule requiring appointed counsel in every case involving a suspended sentence would unduly hamper the States' attempts to impose effective probationary punishment. A more "workable solution," he contends, would permit imposition of a suspended sentence on an uncounseled defendant and require appointment of counsel, if at all, only at the probation revocation stage, when incarceration is imminent.

. . . [But] the sole issue at the [probation revocation] hearing . . . is whether the defendant breached the terms of probation. . . . The validity or reliability of the underlying conviction is beyond attack. . . .

We think it plain that a hearing so timed and structured cannot compensate for the absence of trial counsel, for it does not even address the key Sixth Amendment inquiry: whether the adjudication of guilt corresponding to the prison sentence is sufficiently reliable to permit incarceration. Deprived of counsel when tried, convicted, and sentenced, and unable to challenge the original judgment at a subsequent probation revocation hearing, a defendant in Shelton's circumstances faces incarceration on a conviction that has never been subjected to "the crucible of meaningful adversarial testing," United States v. Cronic, 466 U.S. 648, 656 (1984). The Sixth Amendment does not countenance this result.

In a variation on amicus' position, the dissent would limit review in this case to the question whether the *imposition* of Shelton's suspended sentence required appointment of counsel, answering that question "plainly no" because such a step "does not deprive a defendant of his personal liberty." Only if the sentence is later activated, the dissent contends, need the Court "ask whether the procedural safeguards attending the imposition of [Shelton's] sentence comply with the Constitution."

Severing the analysis in this manner makes little sense. One cannot assess the constitutionality of imposing a suspended sentence while simultaneously walling off the procedures that will precede its activation. The dissent imagines a set of safeguards Alabama might provide at the probation revocation stage sufficient to cure its failure to appoint counsel prior to sentencing, including, perhaps, "complete retrial of the misdemeanor violation with assistance of counsel." But there is no cause for speculation about Alabama's procedures; they are established by Alabama statute and decisional law, and they bear no resemblance to those the dissent invents in its effort to sanction the prospect of Shelton's imprisonment on an uncounseled conviction. Assessing the issue before us in light of actual circumstances, we do not comprehend how the procedures Alabama in fact provides at the probation revocation hearing could bring Shelton's sentence within constitutional bounds.

. . . Most jurisdictions already provide a state-law right to appointed counsel more generous than that afforded by the Federal Constitution. All but 16 States, for example, would provide counsel to a defendant in Shelton's circumstances, either because he received a substantial fine or because state law authorized incarceration for the charged offense or provided for a maximum prison term of one year. There is thus scant reason to believe that a rule conditioning imposition of a suspended sentence on provision of appointed counsel would affect existing practice in the large majority of the States. And given the current commitment of most jurisdictions to affording court-appointed counsel to indigent misdemeanants while simultaneously preserving the option of probationary punishment, we do not share amicus' concern that other States may lack the capacity and resources to do the same.

Moreover, even if amicus is correct that "some courts and jurisdictions at least cannot bear" the costs of the rule we confirm today, those States need not abandon probation or equivalent measures as viable forms of punishment. Although they may not attach probation to an imposed and suspended prison sentence, States unable or unwilling routinely to provide appointed counsel to misdemeanants in Shelton's situation are not without recourse to another option capable of yielding a similar result.

That option is pretrial probation, employed in some form by at least 23 States. . . . Under such an arrangement, the prosecutor and defendant agree to the defendant's participation in a pretrial rehabilitation program, which includes conditions typical of post-trial probation. The adjudication of guilt and imposition of sentence for the underlying offense then occur only if and when the defendant breaches those conditions. . . .

Like the regime urged by amicus, this system reserves the appointed-counsel requirement for the "small percentage" of cases in which incarceration proves necessary, thus allowing a State to "supervise a course of rehabilitation" without providing a lawyer every time it wishes to pursue such a course, *Gagnon*, 411 U.S., at 784. Unlike amicus' position, however, pretrial probation also respects the constitutional imperative that "no person may be imprisoned for any offense . . . unless he was represented by counsel at his trial," *Argersinger*, 407 U.S., at 37. . . .

Satisfied that Shelton is entitled to appointed counsel at the critical stage when his guilt or innocence of the charged crime is decided and his vulnerability to imprisonment is determined, we affirm the judgment of the Supreme Court of Alabama.

It is so ordered.

JUSTICE SCALIA, with whom THE CHIEF JUSTICE, JUSTICE KENNEDY, and JUSTICE THOMAS join, dissenting.

. . . Respondent's 30-day suspended sentence, and the accompanying 2-year term of probation, are invalidated for lack of appointed counsel even though respondent has not suffered, and may never suffer, a deprivation of liberty. The Court holds that the suspended sentence violates respondent's Sixth Amendment right to counsel because it "*may* 'end up in the actual deprivation of [respondent's] liberty,'" ante (emphasis added), *if* he someday violates the terms of probation, *if* a court determines that the violation merits revocation of probation, and *if* the court determines that no other punishment will "adequately protect the community from further criminal activity" or "avoid depreciating the seriousness of the violation," Ala. Code §15-22-54(d)(4). And to all of these contingencies there must yet be added, before the Court's decision makes sense, an element of rank speculation. Should all these contingencies occur, the Court speculates, the Alabama Supreme Court would mechanically apply its decisional law applicable to routine probation revocation (which establishes procedures that the Court finds inadequate) rather than adopt special procedures for situations that raise constitutional questions in light of *Argersinger* and *Scott*. . . .

But that question is not the one before us, and the Court has no business offering an advisory opinion on its answer. We are asked to decide whether "imposition of a suspended or conditional sentence in a misdemeanor case invoke[s] a defendant's Sixth Amendment right to counsel." Pet. for Cert. i. Since *imposition* of a suspended sentence does not deprive a defendant of his personal liberty, the answer to that question is plainly no. In the future, *if and when* the State of Alabama seeks to imprison respondent on the previously suspended sentence, we can ask whether the procedural safeguards attending the imposition of that sentence comply with the Constitution. But that question is *not* before us now. . . .

. . . Surely the procedures attending reimposition of a suspended sentence would be adequate if they required, upon the defendant's request, complete retrial of the misdemeanor violation with assistance of counsel. By what right does the Court deprive the State of that option? It may well be a sensible option, since most defendants will be induced to comply with the terms of their probation by the mere threat of a retrial that could send them to jail, and since the expense of those rare, counseled retrials may be much less than the expense of providing counsel initially in all misdemeanor cases that bear a possible sentence of imprisonment. And it may well be that, in some cases, even procedures short of complete retrial will suffice.

. . . [The Court's] observation that "[a]ll but 16 States" already appoint counsel for *defendants like respondent*, is interesting but quite irrelevant, since today's holding is not confined to defendants like respondent. Appointed counsel must henceforth be offered before *any* defendant can be awarded a suspended sentence, no matter how short. Only 24 States have announced a rule of this scope.[4] Thus, the Court's

---

4. Ten of the thirty-four States cited by the Court do not offer appointed counsel in all cases where a misdemeanor defendant might suffer a suspended sentence. Six States guarantee counsel only when the authorized penalty is at least three or six months' imprisonment. [Justice Scalia then explained in detail the exceptions that apply in the other four states. — EDS.] . . .

decision imposes a large, new burden on a majority of the States, including some of the poorest. . . . That burden consists not only of the cost of providing state-paid counsel in cases of such insignificance that even financially prosperous defendants sometimes forgo the expense of hired counsel, but also the cost of enabling courts and prosecutors to respond to the "over-lawyering" of minor cases. Nor should we discount the burden placed on the minority 24 States that currently provide counsel: that they keep their current disposition forever in place, however imprudent experience proves it to be.

Today's imposition upon the States finds justification neither in the text of the Constitution, nor in the settled practices of our people, nor in the prior jurisprudence of this Court. I respectfully dissent.

NOTES AND QUESTIONS

1. The subject of *Shelton* is the scope of the *Gideon* right to state-paid counsel for indigent defendants. The Court decided that the scope of that right is broad — broader, by some measures, than most states previously provided. Why? Is there a rationale for the *Gideon* right that explains *Shelton*, but that also explains why the right does not extend to misdemeanor cases where neither incarceration nor the threat of it is part of the defendant's sentence?

2. Why isn't it good enough, as the dissenters suggest, to give Shelton an elaborate process, *with* counsel, if and when his probation is revoked? What do you think about the majority's asserted justification for precluding Alabama from trying to develop such a process, if and when it is needed?

3. In the Supreme Court, Alabama also argued for an alternative, creative way around the Sixth Amendment problem: Enforce the conditions of probation through contempt proceedings for failure to abide by those conditions, which could in turn lead to jail or prison as long as defense counsel is provided at the time of the contempt proceeding. The Court did not address this argument, as it had not been presented below.

If the state's contempt argument loses, *Shelton* has potentially huge effects on the prosecution of low-grade misdemeanors. At least in a few states, it is common to prosecute such cases, and impose probation or a suspended sentence, without offering counsel to defendants. This amounts to an order to the defendant to keep his nose clean — if he fails to do so, he can go to jail; otherwise, his conviction will carry no significant penalty. Most defendants faced with that threat do keep their noses clean; only a very small minority of suspended sentences are ever imposed and a similarly small minority of probations are revoked. After *Shelton*, though, the state must provide counsel in all these cases, even the ones (the great majority) where the defendant is never incarcerated — or else the state must abandon its threat. Perhaps

---

The Court asserts that the burden of today's decision on these jurisdictions is small because the "circumstances in which [they] currently allow prosecution of misdemeanors without appointed counsel are quite *narrow*." (emphasis added). But the narrowness of the range of circumstances covered says nothing about the number of suspended-sentence cases covered. Misdemeanors punishable by less than six months' imprisonment may be a narrow category, but it may well include the vast majority of cases in which (precisely *because* of the minor nature of the offense) a suspended sentence is imposed. There is simply nothing to support the Court's belief that few offenders are prosecuted for crimes in which counsel is not already provided. . . .

the state will do just that. But abandoning the threat of jail might make the misdemeanor proceeding pointless: Remember that we're talking about indigent defendants (other defendants can, of course, hire counsel for themselves), so significant fines are not available as a deterrent to further crimes. The obvious alternative is to see that many more misdemeanor defendants get lawyers — but also that many more misdemeanor defendants go directly to jail.

2. The Right to the Assistance of Counsel Before and After Trial

The cases in the preceding section all deal with one particular aspect of the scope of the Sixth Amendment right to counsel: To what criminal cases does that right apply? All criminal cases, or only some kinds of criminal cases? The Court's focus in *Gideon*, *Argersinger*, *Scott*, *Nichols*, and *Shelton* is on the application of the right to counsel to the "main event" in each case: the trial (or its functional equivalent, the plea hearing).

In this section, we take up a different aspect: In any particular criminal case to which the Sixth Amendment right to counsel *does* apply, exactly when in the case does that right "attach," or begin? When does it end? And, along the way, to what particular legal proceedings, or stages of the case, does the right apply?

a. When Does the Right to Counsel Begin?

ROTHGERY v. GILLESPIE COUNTY, TEXAS, 554 U.S. 191 (2008): Although petitioner Walter Rothgery has never been convicted of a felony, a criminal background check disclosed an erroneous record that he had been, and on July 15, 2002, Texas police officers relied on this record to arrest him as a felon in possession of a firearm. The officers . . . promptly brought Rothgery before a magistrate judge, as required by [Texas law]. Texas law has no formal label for this initial appearance before a magistrate, which is sometimes called the "article 15.17 hearing"; it combines the Fourth Amendment's required probable-cause determination with the setting of bail, and is the point at which the arrestee is formally apprised of the accusation against him, see Tex. Crim. Proc. Code Ann., Art. 15.17(a).

Rothgery's article 15.17 hearing followed routine. The arresting officer submitted a sworn "Affidavit Of Probable Cause" that described the facts supporting the arrest and "charge[d] that . . . Rothgery . . . commit[ted] the offense of unlawful possession of a firearm by a felon . . . ." After reviewing the affidavit, the magistrate judge "determined that probable cause existed for the arrest." The magistrate judge informed Rothgery of the accusation, set his bail at $5,000, and committed him to jail, from which he was released after posting a surety bond. The bond, which the Gillespie County deputy sheriff signed, stated that "Rothgery stands charged by complaint duly filed . . . with the offense of a . . . felony, to wit: Unlawful Possession of a Firearm by a Felon." . . .

Rothgery had no money for a lawyer and made several oral and written requests for appointed counsel, which went unheeded.[1] The following January, he was

---

1. Rothgery also requested counsel at the article 15.17 hearing itself, but the magistrate judge informed him that the appointment of counsel would delay setting bail (and hence his release from jail).

indicted by a Texas grand jury for unlawful possession of a firearm by a felon, resulting in rearrest the next day, and an order increasing bail to $15,000. When he could not post it, he was put in jail and remained there for three weeks.

On January 23, 2003, six months after the article 15.17 hearing, Rothgery was finally assigned a lawyer, who promptly obtained a bail reduction (so Rothgery could get out of jail), and assembled the paperwork confirming that Rothgery had never been convicted of a felony. Counsel relayed this information to the district attorney, who in turn filed a motion to dismiss the indictment, which was granted.

[Rothgery filed a §1983 federal civil rights lawsuit, claiming that Gillespie County's "unwritten policy" of denying appointed counsel to indigent defendants out on bond, prior to entry of an information or indictment, violated his Sixth Amendment right to counsel and caused him to be erroneously indicted, rearrested, and jailed for three weeks. The District Court granted summary judgment to the County, holding that the right to counsel had not attached at the relevant time because no prosecutor had been assigned to the case. (Apparently, no prosecutor was even aware of the case at the time of the article 15.17 hearing.) The Fifth Circuit affirmed, and the Supreme Court granted certiorari. — EDS.]

. . . [W]e have twice held that the right to counsel attaches at the initial appearance before a judicial officer, see [Michigan v. Jackson, 475 U.S. 625, 629, n. 3 (1986); Brewer v. Williams, 430 U.S. 387, 399 (1977)]. This first time before a court, also known as the "preliminary arraignment" or "arraignment on the complaint," see 1 W. LaFave, J. Israel, N. King, & O. Kerr, Criminal Procedure §1.4(g), p. 135 (3d ed. 2007), is generally the hearing at which "the magistrate informs the defendant of the charge in the complaint, and of various rights in further proceedings," and "determine[s] the conditions for pretrial release," ibid. Texas's article 15.17 hearing is an initial appearance: Rothgery was taken before a magistrate judge, informed of the formal accusation against him, and sent to jail until he posted bail. *Brewer* and *Jackson* control.

The *Brewer* defendant surrendered to the police after a warrant was out for his arrest on a charge of abduction. He was then "arraigned before a judge . . . on the outstanding arrest warrant," and at the arraignment, "[t]he judge advised him of his Miranda [v. Arizona, 384 U.S. 436 (1966)] rights and committed him to jail." *Brewer*, 430 U.S., at 391. After this preliminary arraignment, and before an indictment on the abduction charge had been handed up, police elicited incriminating admissions that ultimately led to an indictment for first-degree murder. Because neither of the defendant's lawyers had been present when the statements were obtained, the Court found it "clear" that the defendant "was deprived of . . . the right to the assistance of counsel." Id., at 397-398. In plain terms, the Court said that "[t]here can be no doubt in the present case that judicial proceedings had been initiated" before the defendant made the incriminating statements. Id., at 399. Although it noted that the State had conceded the issue, the Court nevertheless held that the defendant's right had clearly attached for the reason that "[a] warrant had been issued for his arrest, he had been arraigned on that warrant before a judge in a . . . courtroom, and he had been committed by the court to confinement in jail." Ibid.

Given the choice of proceeding without counsel or remaining in custody, Rothgery waived the right to have appointed counsel present at the hearing. See 491 F.3d at 295, n. 2.

In *Jackson*, the Court was asked to revisit the question whether the right to counsel attaches at the initial appearance, and we had no more trouble answering it the second time around. *Jackson* was actually two consolidated cases, and although the State conceded that respondent Jackson's arraignment "represented the initiation of formal legal proceedings," 475 U.S., at 629, n. 3, it argued that the same was not true for respondent Bladel. In briefing us, the State explained that "[i]n Michigan, any person charged with a felony, after arrest, must be brought before a Magistrate or District Court Judge without unnecessary delay for his initial arraignment." Brief for Petitioner in Michigan v. Bladel, O. T. 1985, No. 84-1539, p. 24. The State noted that "[w]hile [Bladel] had been arraigned . . . , there is also a second arraignment in Michigan procedure . . . , at which time defendant has his first opportunity to enter a plea in a court with jurisdiction to render a final decision in a felony case." Id., at 25. The State contended that only the latter proceeding . . . should trigger the Sixth Amendment right. . . .

We flatly rejected the distinction between initial arraignment and arraignment on the indictment, the State's argument being "untenable" in light of the "clear language in our decisions about the significance of arraignment." *Jackson*, supra, at 629, n. 3. The conclusion was driven by the same considerations the Court had endorsed in *Brewer*: by the time a defendant is brought before a judicial officer, is informed of a formally lodged accusation, and has restrictions imposed on his liberty in aid of the prosecution, the State's relationship with the defendant has become solidly adversarial. And that is just as true when the proceeding comes before the indictment (in the case of the initial arraignment on a formal complaint) as when it comes after it (at an arraignment on an indictment). . . .

We think the County is wrong both about the clarity of our cases and the substance that we find clear. Certainly it is true that the Court in *Brewer* and *Jackson* saw no need for lengthy disquisitions on the significance of the initial appearance, but that was because it found the attachment issue an easy one. . . .

If, indeed, the County had simply taken the cases at face value, it would have avoided the mistake of merging the attachment question (whether formal judicial proceedings have begun) with the distinct "critical stage" question (whether counsel must be present at a postattachment proceeding unless the right to assistance is validly waived). Attachment occurs when the government has used the judicial machinery to signal a commitment to prosecute as spelled out in *Brewer* and *Jackson*. Once attachment occurs, the accused at least[15] is entitled to the presence of appointed counsel during any "critical stage" of the postattachment proceedings; what makes a stage critical is what shows the need for counsel's presence. Thus, counsel must be appointed within a reasonable time after attachment to allow for adequate representation at any critical stage before trial, as well as at trial itself.

The County thus makes an analytical mistake in its assumption that attachment necessarily requires the occurrence or imminence of a critical stage. . . . On the contrary, it is irrelevant to attachment that the presence of counsel at an article 15.17 hearing, say, may not be critical, just as it is irrelevant that counsel's presence may not be critical when a prosecutor walks over to the trial court to file an information.

---

15. We do not here purport to set out the scope of an individual's postattachment right to the presence of counsel. It is enough for present purposes to highlight that the enquiry into that right is a different one from the attachment analysis.

As we said in *Jackson*, "[t]he question whether arraignment signals the initiation of adversary judicial proceedings . . . is distinct from the question whether the arraignment itself is a critical stage requiring the presence of counsel." 475 U.S., at 60. Texas's article 15.17 hearing plainly signals attachment, even if it is not itself a critical stage.[17]

Our holding is narrow. . . . We merely reaffirm what we have held before and what an overwhelming majority of American jurisdictions understand in practice: a criminal defendant's initial appearance before a judicial officer, where he learns the charge against him and his liberty is subject to restriction, marks the start of adversary judicial proceedings that trigger attachment of the Sixth Amendment right to counsel. Because the Fifth Circuit came to a different conclusion on this threshold issue, its judgment is vacated, and the case is remanded for further proceedings consistent with this opinion.

[Chief Justice Roberts's concurring opinion is omitted.]

JUSTICE ALITO, joined by CHIEF JUSTICE ROBERTS and JUSTICE SCALIA, concurring.

I join the Court's opinion because I do not understand it to hold that a defendant is entitled to the assistance of appointed counsel as soon as his Sixth Amendment right attaches. As I interpret our precedents, the term "attachment" signifies nothing more than the beginning of the defendant's prosecution. It does not mark the beginning of a substantive entitlement to the assistance of counsel. . . .

The Sixth Amendment provides in pertinent part that "[i]n all criminal prosecutions, the accused shall enjoy the right . . . to have the Assistance of Counsel for his defence." The Amendment thus defines the scope of the right to counsel in three ways: It provides *who* may assert the right ("the accused"); *when* the right may be asserted ("[i]n all criminal prosecutions"); and *what* the right guarantees ("the right . . . to have the Assistance of Counsel for his defence").

It is in the context of interpreting the Amendment's answer to the second of these questions — when the right may be asserted — that we have spoken of the right "attaching." In Kirby v. Illinois, 406 U.S. 682, 688 (1972), a plurality of the Court explained that "a person's Sixth and Fourteenth Amendment right to counsel attaches only at or after the time that adversary judicial proceedings have been initiated against him." A majority of the Court elaborated on that explanation in Moore v. Illinois, 434 U.S. 220 (1977):

> In Kirby v. Illinois, the plurality opinion made clear that the right to counsel . . . attaches only to corporeal identifications conducted at or after the initiation of adversary judicial criminal proceedings — whether by way of formal charge, preliminary hearing, indictment, information, or arraignment. This is so because the initiation of such proceedings marks the commencement of the 'criminal prosecutions' to which alone the explicit guarantees of the Sixth Amendment are applicable. Thus, in *Kirby* the

---

17. The dissent likewise anticipates an issue distinct from attachment when it claims Rothgery has suffered no harm the Sixth Amendment recognizes. Post, at ___. Whether the right has been violated and whether Rothgery has suffered cognizable harm are separate questions from when the right attaches, the sole question before us.

plurality held that the prosecution's evidence of a robbery victim's one-on-one station-house identification of an uncounseled suspect shortly after the suspect's arrest was admissible because adversary judicial criminal proceedings had not yet been initiated.

Id., at 226-227.

When we wrote in *Kirby* and *Moore* that the Sixth Amendment right had "attached," we evidently meant nothing more than that a "criminal prosecutio[n]" had begun. . . .

Because pretrial criminal procedures vary substantially from jurisdiction to jurisdiction, there is room for disagreement about when a "prosecution" begins for Sixth Amendment purposes. As the Court, notes, however, we have previously held that "arraignments" that were functionally indistinguishable from the Texas magistration marked the point at which the Sixth Amendment right to counsel "attached."

It does not follow, however, and I do not understand the Court to hold, that the county had an obligation to appoint an attorney to represent petitioner within some specified period after his [appearance]. To so hold, the Court would need to do more than conclude that petitioner's criminal prosecution had begun. It would also need to conclude that the assistance of counsel in the wake of the Texas magistration is part of the substantive guarantee of the Sixth Amendment. That question lies beyond our reach, petitioner having never sought our review of it. . . . [W]e have been asked to address only the *when* question, not the *what* question. Whereas the temporal scope of the right is defined by the words "[i]n all criminal prosecutions," the right's substantive guarantee flows from a different textual font: the words "Assistance of Counsel for his defence."

In interpreting this latter phrase, we have held that "defence" means defense at trial, not defense in relation to other objectives that may be important to the accused. See [United States v. Gouveia, 467 U.S. 180,] 190 (1985) ("[T]he right to counsel exists to protect the accused during trial-type confrontations with the prosecutor . . ."); United States v. Ash, 413 U.S. 300, 309 (1973) ("[T]he core purpose of the counsel guarantee was to assure 'Assistance' at trial . . .")]. We have thus rejected the argument that the Sixth Amendment entitles the criminal defendant to the assistance of appointed counsel at a probable cause hearing. See Gerstein v. Pugh, 420 U.S. 103, 122-123 (1975) (observing that the Fourth Amendment hearing "is addressed only to pretrial custody" and has an insubstantial effect on the defendant's trial rights). More generally, we have rejected the notion that the right to counsel entitles the defendant to a "preindictment private investigator." *Gouveia*, supra, at 191.

. . . I interpret the Sixth Amendment to require the appointment of counsel only after the defendant's prosecution has begun, and then only as necessary to guarantee the defendant effective assistance at trial. . . . Texas counties need only appoint counsel as far in advance of trial, and as far in advance of any pretrial "critical stage," as necessary to guarantee effective assistance at trial. . . .

[The dissenting opinion of Justice Thomas is omitted.]

NOTES AND QUESTIONS

1. Are you persuaded by the Court's opinion? Or by Justice Alito's concurrence? What does it mean to say that Rothgery's right to counsel had "attached," but that

he may not actually have had the right either to have a lawyer appointed to represent him or to meet with a lawyer to assist him in the relevant proceeding?

2. Beyond its obvious practical impact on states like Texas that previously did not provide appointed counsel for first appearances, *Rothgery* is also potentially important in both doctrinal and theoretical terms. See Note, Leading Case, 122 Harv. L. Rev. 306 (2008). Doctrinally speaking, it settles — once and for all — the question of when the right to counsel formally "attaches." Prior case law was somewhat vague on this point; *Rothgery* makes clear that the right attaches at the first judicial proceeding where a defendant learns of the charges against him and is subject to restraints on his liberty, no matter what that proceeding is labeled, and no matter whether the prosecutor is involved. Theoretically speaking, *Rothgery* uncouples the "attachment" issue from the "critical stage" issue (in Justice Alito's terms, separating the "temporal" from the "substantive" scope of the Sixth Amendment) to an extent not previously seen — especially with respect to a formal court procedure like Texas's article 15.17 hearing.

After *Rothgery*, what approach should courts use to decide whether such a proceeding is a "critical stage," signifying that defendants are entitled to appointed counsel? The term has previously been used to refer to any formal interaction between the defendant and the state that could adversely affect the defendant's ability to exercise effectively a legal right. Thus, preliminary hearings, Coleman v. Alabama, 399 U.S. 1 (1970); initial appearances, Brewer v. Williams, 430 U.S. 387 (1977); and arraignments, Hamilton v. Alabama, 368 U.S. 52 (1961), have all been held to be "critical stages" of a criminal case, but certain ex parte proceedings such as warrant hearings (discussed in Chapter 5) are not. The concept of a "critical stage" has also been extended to any *informal* meeting between the defendant and a representative of the state that is designed or is likely to elicit incriminating information from the defendant (discussed in Chapter 6). In *Rothgery*, however, Justice Alito suggests that counsel must be provided "only as necessary to guarantee the defendant effective assistance *at trial*"; does that mean that, henceforth, the defendant's interest in such matters as prompt pretrial release (i.e., bail) should no longer be part of the "critical stage" calculus?

3. Notice a curious feature of the law in this area. One might expect that the definition of when formal adversary proceedings — and thus the right to counsel — begins would involve some form of adjudication. That fits the model Justice Alito suggests: The "assistance of counsel" is needed at those proceedings at which the defendant must formally defend himself. Actually, however, most of the relevant Supreme Court decisions arise from police investigations, not from judicial proceedings. *Jackson* and *Brewer*, the two cases on which the majority relies, are classic examples. In both cases, the police questioned the defendant after his first appearance in court. In both cases, the issue was whether the Sixth Amendment right to counsel had been violated by the police in the course of the questioning. (Incidentally, *Jackson* itself is no longer good law — the Court overruled its primary holding with respect to police interrogations in Montejo v. Louisiana, 556 U.S. _____ (2009), see Chapter 6, at page 894 — but that does not affect the specific part of *Jackson* relevant here.) Similarly, *Kirby*, *Moore*, and *Ash* — the main cases cited in Justice Alito's concurrence — all raise the question whether eyewitness identifications obtained by the police violated the Sixth Amendment right to counsel. The subject of all five cases, in other words, is police evidence gathering.

Rothgery, of course, does involve a form of adjudication: Thanks to the judge's ruling at his second bail hearing, the defendant spent three weeks in jail. That ruling was in error, due to the kind of mistake that a competent defense lawyer would immediately spot. In other words, *Rothgery* looks like precisely the sort of case in which the presence of defense counsel would help to ensure more accurate adjudication. But that is not necessarily true in police interrogation cases like *Jackson* and *Brewer*, nor is it true in most eyewitness identification cases like *Kirby*, *Moore*, and *Ash*. Should this difference matter?

NOTES ON THE RIGHT TO COUNSEL AT LINEUPS, SHOW-UPS, AND PHOTO ARRAYS

1. In 1967, the Supreme Court decided three companion cases involving constitutional challenges to pretrial eyewitness identification procedures. The lead case, United States v. Wade, 388 U.S. 218 (1967), as well as one companion case, Gilbert v. California, 388 U.S. 263 (1967), involved postindictment lineups conducted in the absence of defense counsel at which eyewitnesses identified the respective defendants as the perpetrators of the crimes. In both cases, the same eyewitnesses later identified the defendant, at trial, as the perpetrator of the crime; in *Gilbert*, the eyewitnesses also testified that they had previously identified the defendant at the pretrial lineup. The other companion case, Stovall v. Denno, 388 U.S. 293 (1967), involved a "show-up," in which the defendant alone was shown to the eyewitness, who identified him as the perpetrator, again in the absence of defense counsel; the same eyewitness later identified the defendant in court, and also testified about the prior "show-up" identification.

In *Wade*, the Court held that postindictment lineups and show-ups are "critical stages" of the case at which the defendant's Sixth Amendment right to counsel applies:

> [T]he confrontation compelled by the State between the accused and the victim or witnesses to a crime to elicit identification evidence is peculiarly riddled with innumerable dangers and variable factors which might seriously, even crucially, derogate from a fair trial. The vagaries of eyewitness identification are well-known; the annals of criminal law are rife with instances of mistaken identification. . . . A major factor contributing to the high incidence of miscarriage of justice from mistaken identification has been the degree of suggestion inherent in the manner in which the prosecution presents the suspect to witnesses for pretrial identification. A commentator has observed that "[t]he influence of improper suggestion upon identifying witnesses probably accounts for more miscarriages of justice than any other single factor — perhaps it is responsible for more such errors than all other factors combined." Patrick M. Wall, Eye-Witness Identification in Criminal Cases 26. Suggestion can be created intentionally or unintentionally in many subtle ways. And the dangers for the suspect are particularly grave when the witness' opportunity for observation was insubstantial, and thus his susceptibility to suggestion the greatest.
>
> Moreover, "[i]t is a matter of common experience that, once a witness has picked out the accused at the line-up, he is not likely to go back on his word later on, so that in practice the issue of identity may (in the absence of other relevant evidence) for all practical purposes be determined there and then, before the trial."[8]

---

8. Glanville Williams & H. A. Hammelmann, Identification Parades, Part I, [1963] Crim. L. Rev. 479, 482.

The pretrial confrontation for purpose of identification may take the form of a lineup, . . . as in the present case, or presentation of the suspect alone to the witness, as in Stovall v. Denno. It is obvious that risks of suggestion attend either form of confrontation and increase the dangers inhering in eyewitness identification. But as is the case with secret interrogations, there is serious difficulty in depicting what transpires at lineups and other forms of identification confrontations. . . . [T]he defense can seldom reconstruct the manner and mode of lineup identification for judge or jury at trial. Those participating in a lineup with the accused may often be police officers; in any event, the participants' names are rarely recorded or divulged at trial. The impediments to an objective observation are increased when the victim is the witness. Lineups are prevalent in rape and robbery prosecutions and present a particular hazard that a victim's understandable outrage may excite vengeful or spiteful motives. In any event, neither witnesses nor lineup participants are apt to be alert for conditions prejudicial to the suspect. And if they were, it would likely be of scant benefit to the suspect since neither witnesses nor lineup participants are likely to be schooled in the detection of suggestive influences.[13] Improper influences may go undetected by a suspect, guilty or not, who experiences the emotional tension which we might expect in one being confronted with potential accusers. Even when he does observe abuse, if he has a criminal record he may be reluctant to take the stand and open up the admission of prior convictions. Moreover, any protestations by the suspect of the fairness of the lineup made at trial are likely to be in vain; the jury's choice is between the accused's unsupported version and that of the police officers present. In short, the accused's inability to reconstruct at trial any unfairness that occurred at the lineup may deprive him of his only opportunity meaningfully to attack the credibility of the witness' courtroom identification. . . .

The Court held that Wade's right to counsel was violated because he neither was represented by nor had waived counsel for purposes of the lineup. However, the Court remanded the case to give the prosecution a chance to try to prove (by "clear and convincing evidence") that the in-court eyewitness identifications were "based upon observations of the suspect other than the lineup identification," in which instance the in-court IDs would be independent of the constitutional violation and the conviction could therefore be upheld. In *Gilbert*, the Court went a step further, imposing a per se exclusionary rule with respect to the in-court testimony of the eyewitnesses specifically mentioning the unconstitutional lineup. And in *Stovall*, the Court held that *Wade* and *Gilbert* applied only to lineups or show-ups occurring *after* those Court decisions, but that *prior* lineups could still be evaluated as to whether they were "so unnecessarily suggestive and conducive to irreparable mistaken identification" as to violate due process. On the specific facts of *Stovall*, which involved an "imperative" need to show the defendant to an eyewitness who was seriously injured during the crime and about to undergo major surgery, the Court found no due process violation.

---

13. An additional impediment to the detection of such influences by participants, including the suspect, is the physical conditions often surrounding the conduct of the lineup. In many, lights shine on the stage in such a way that the suspect cannot see the witness. See Gilbert v. United States, 366 F.2d 923 (C.A. 9th Cir. 1966). In some a one-way mirror is used and what is said on the witness' side cannot be heard. . . .

2. What about preindictment lineups and show-ups? One might think that they should be governed by the same rules announced in *Wade* and *Gilbert*; after all, the existence of an indictment would seem irrelevant to the particular dangers identified in *Wade*. The Court first addressed such issues just five years after *Wade* in Kirby v. Illinois, 406 U.S. 682 (1972),[4] which involved a preindictment show-up:

> In a line of constitutional cases in this Court stemming back to the Court's landmark opinion in Powell v. Alabama, it has been firmly established that a person's Sixth and Fourteenth Amendment right to counsel attaches only at or after the time that adversary judicial proceedings have been initiated against him. . . .
>
> This is not to say that a defendant in a criminal case has a constitutional right to counsel only at the trial itself. The *Powell* case makes clear that the right attaches at the time of arraignment, and the Court has recently held that it exists also at the time of a preliminary hearing. Coleman v. Alabama. . . . But the point is that, while members of the Court have differed as to existence of the right to counsel in the contexts of some of the above cases, *all* of those cases have involved points of time at or after the initiation of adversary judicial criminal proceedings — whether by way of formal charge, preliminary hearing, indictment, information, or arraignment. . . .
>
> The initiation of judicial criminal proceedings is far from a mere formalism. It is the starting point of our whole system of adversary criminal justice. For it is only then that the government has committed itself to prosecute, and only then that the adverse positions of government and defendant have solidified. It is then that a defendant finds himself faced with the prosecutorial forces of organized society, and immersed in the intricacies of substantive and procedural criminal law. It is this point, therefore, that marks the commencement of the "criminal prosecutions" to which alone the explicit guarantees of the Sixth Amendment are applicable. . . .
>
> In this case we are asked to import into a routine police investigation an absolute constitutional guarantee historically and rationally applicable only after the onset of formal prosecutorial proceedings. We decline to do so. Less than a year after *Wade* and *Gilbert* were decided, the Court explained the rule of those decisions as follows: "The rationale of those cases was that an accused is entitled to counsel at any 'critical stage of the *prosecution*,' and that a post-indictment lineup is such a 'critical stage.'" (Emphasis supplied.) We decline to depart from that rationale today by imposing a per se exclusionary rule upon testimony concerning an identification that took place long before the commencement of any prosecution whatever.
>
> . . . What has been said is not to suggest that there may not be occasions during the course of a criminal investigation when the police do abuse identification procedures. Such abuses are not beyond the reach of the Constitution. As the Court pointed out in *Wade* itself, it is always necessary to "scrutinize *any* pretrial confrontation. . . ." The Due Process Clause of the Fifth and Fourteenth Amendments forbids a lineup that is unnecessarily suggestive and conducive to irreparable mistaken identification. When a person has not been formally charged with a criminal offense, *Stovall* strikes the appropriate constitutional balance between the right of a suspect to be protected from prejudicial procedures and the interest of society in the prompt and purposeful investigation of an unsolved crime.

The *Kirby* dissenters made the obvious point that *Wade* and *Kirby* are impossible to reconcile on *Wade*'s rationale. Of course, the cases are easy to reconcile on *Kirby*'s

---

4. Although *Kirby* was technically a plurality opinion (Justice Powell concurred only in the result), a majority of the Court subsequently has cited and relied upon it. See, e.g., Brewer v. Williams, 430 U.S. 387, 398 (1997).

rationale. Which strikes you as more persuasive, as more rational, as more appropriate?

3. What if the criminal case against the defendant does not originate with an indictment? Does that render *Wade* inapplicable? In Moore v. Illinois, 434 U.S. 220 (1977), the defendant was identified by the complaining witness at a preliminary hearing at which he was not represented by counsel. The defendant was convicted and appealed on the grounds that the preliminary-hearing identification violated *Wade*. The Court of Appeals was unpersuaded, but the Supreme Court reversed:

> . . . The prosecution in this case was commenced under Illinois law when the victim's complaint was filed in court. The purpose of the preliminary hearing was to determine whether there was probable cause to bind petitioner over to the grand jury and to set bail. Petitioner had the right to oppose the prosecution at that hearing by moving to dismiss the charges and to suppress the evidence against him. He faced counsel for the State, who elicited the victim's identification, summarized the State's other evidence against petitioner, and urged that the State be given more time to marshal its evidence. It is plain that "the government ha[d] committed itself to prosecute," and that petitioner found "himself faced with the prosecutorial forces of organized society, and immersed in the intricacies of substantive and procedural criminal law." *Kirby*. The State candidly concedes that this preliminary hearing marked the "initiation of adversary judicial criminal proceedings" against petitioner, . . . and it hardly could contend otherwise. The Court of Appeals therefore erred in holding that petitioner's rights under *Wade* and *Gilbert* had not yet attached at the time of the preliminary hearing. . . .
>
> If the court believed that petitioner did not have a right to counsel at this identification procedure because it was conducted in the course of a judicial proceeding, we do not agree. The reasons supporting *Wade*'s holding that a corporeal identification is a critical stage of a criminal prosecution for Sixth Amendment purposes apply with equal force to this identification. It is difficult to imagine a more suggestive manner in which to present a suspect to a witness for their critical first confrontation than was employed in this case. The victim, who had seen her assailant for only 10 to 15 seconds, was asked to make her identification after she was told that she was going to view a suspect, after she was told his name and heard it called as he was led before the bench, and after she heard the prosecutor recite the evidence believed to implicate petitioner. Had petitioner been represented by counsel, some or all of this suggestiveness could have been avoided.[5] . . .

Id., at 228-230.

4. How do the principles of *Wade* and *Kirby* apply to photo arrays (where the witness is presented with a set of photos of possible suspects and asked to identify the photo of the perpetrator)? That question was addressed in United States v. Ash, 413 U.S. 300 (1973):

---

5. For example, counsel could have requested that the hearing be postponed until a lineup could be arranged at which the victim would view petitioner in a less suggestive setting. Short of that, counsel could have asked that the victim be excused from the courtroom while the charges were read and the evidence against petitioner was recited, and that petitioner be seated with other people in the audience when the victim attempted an identification. Counsel might have sought to cross-examine the victim to test her identification before it hardened. Because it is in the prosecution's interest as well as the accused's that witnesses' identifications remain untainted, we cannot assume that such requests would have been in vain. Such requests ordinarily are addressed to the sound discretion of the court; we express no opinion as to whether the preliminary hearing court would have been required to grant any such requests.

. . . [T]he test utilized by the Court [to determine whether a particular event is a "critical stage" for purposes of the Sixth Amendment] has called for examination of the event in order to determine whether the accused required aid in coping with legal problems or assistance in meeting his adversary. . . .

A substantial departure from the historical test would be necessary if the Sixth Amendment were interpreted to give Ash a right to counsel at the photographic identification in this case. Since the accused himself is not present at the time of the photographic display, and asserts no right to be present, no possibility arises that the accused might be misled by his lack of familiarity with the law or overpowered by his professional adversary. Similarly, the counsel guarantee would not be used to produce equality in a trial-like adversary confrontation. . . .

Even if we were willing to view the counsel guarantee in broad terms as a generalized protection of the adversary process, we would be unwilling to go so far as to extend the right to a portion of the prosecutor's trial-preparation interviews with witnesses. Although photography is relatively new, the interviewing of witnesses before trial is a procedure that predates the Sixth Amendment. In England in the 16th and 17th centuries counsel regularly interviewed witnesses before trial. 9 W. Holdsworth, History of English Law 226-228 (1926). The traditional counterbalance in the American adversary system for these interviews arises from the equal ability of defense counsel to seek and interview witnesses himself.

That adversary mechanism remains as effective for a photographic display as for other parts of pretrial interviews. No greater limitations are placed on defense counsel in constructing displays, seeking witnesses, and conducting photographic identifications than those applicable to the prosecution.[11] Selection of the picture of a person other than the accused, or the inability of a witness to make any selection, will be useful to the defense in precisely the same manner that the selection of a picture of the defendant would be useful to the prosecution. In this very case, for example, the initial tender of the photographic display was by [defense] counsel, who sought to demonstrate that the witness had failed to make a photographic identification. Although we do not suggest that equality of access to photographs removes all potential for abuse, it does remove any inequality in the adversary process itself and thereby fully satisfies the historical spirit of the Sixth Amendment's counsel guarantee.

Pretrial photographic identifications . . . are hardly unique in offering possibilities for the actions of the prosecutor unfairly to prejudice the accused. Evidence favorable to the accused may be withheld; testimony of witnesses may be manipulated; the results of laboratory tests may be contrived. In many ways the prosecutor, by accident or by design, may improperly subvert the trial. The primary safeguard against abuses of this kind is the ethical responsibility of the prosecutor,[16] who, as so often has been said, may "strike hard blows" but not "foul ones." If that safeguard fails, review remains available under due process standards. . . .

Id., at 313-321. Justices Brennan, Marshall, and Douglas dissented:

11. We do not suggest, of course, that defense counsel has any greater freedom than the prosecution to abuse the photographic identification. Evidence of photographic identifications conducted by the defense may be excluded as unreliable under the same standards that would be applied to unreliable identifications conducted by the Government.

16. Throughout a criminal prosecution the prosecutor's ethical responsibility extends, of course, to supervision of any continuing investigation of the case. By prescribing procedures to be used by his agents and by screening the evidence before trial with a view to eliminating unreliable identifications, the prosecutor is able to minimize abuse in photographic displays even if they are conducted in his absence.

. . . [W]e have expressly recognized that "a corporeal identification . . . is normally more accurate" than a photographic identification. Simmons v. United States[, 390 U.S. 377 (1968)]. Thus, in this sense at least, the dangers of misidentification are even greater at a photographic display than at a lineup.

Moreover, as in the lineup situation, the possibilities for impermissible suggestion in the context of a photographic display are manifold. Such suggestion, intentional, or unintentional, may derive from three possible sources. First, the photographs themselves might tend to suggest which of the pictures is that of the suspect. For example, differences in age, pose, or other physical characteristics of the persons represented, and variations in the mounting, background, lighting, or markings of the photographs all might have the effect of singling out the accused.

Second, impermissible suggestion may inhere in the manner in which the photographs are displayed to the witness. . . .

Third, gestures or comments of the prosecutor at the time of the display may lead an otherwise uncertain witness to select the "correct" photograph. For example, the prosecutor might "indicate to the witness that [he has] other evidence that one of the persons pictured committed the crime,"[11] and might even point to a particular photograph and ask whether the person pictured "looks familiar." More subtly, the prosecutor's inflection, facial expressions, physical motions, and myriad other almost imperceptible means of communication might tend, intentionally or unintentionally, to compromise the witness' objectivity. . . .

Finally, and *unlike* the lineup situation, the accused himself is not even present at the photographic identification, thereby reducing the likelihood that irregularities in the procedures will ever come to light. . . . [T]he difficulties of reconstructing at trial an uncounseled photographic display are at least equal to, and possibly greater than, those involved in reconstructing an uncounseled lineup.[15] . . . As a result, both photographic and corporeal identifications create grave dangers that an innocent defendant might be convicted simply because of his inability to expose a tainted identification. This being so, considerations of logic, consistency, and, indeed, fairness compel the conclusion that a pretrial photographic identification, like a pretrial corporeal identification, is a "critical stage of the prosecution. . . ."

Id., at 332-338.

5. *Ash* holds that the Sixth Amendment right to counsel does not apply to photo arrays; as in *Stovall* and *Kirby*, however, this does not preclude finding a due process violation. In Manson v. Brathwaite, 432 U.S. 98 (1977), the defendant's photo was shown to an undercover police officer who identified him as the perpetrator. When the case reached the Supreme Court, the prosecution argued for a "totality of the circumstances" approach to the due process question, focusing on the reliability of the challenged evidence, as in *Stovall* and Neil v. Biggers, 409 U.S. 183 (1972). The

---

11. Simmons v. United States, supra, at 383.

15. The Court's assertion, . . . that these difficulties of reconstruction are somehow minimized because the defense can "duplicate" a photographic identification reflects a complete misunderstanding of the issues in this case. . . . Due to the "freezing effect" recognized in *Wade*, once suggestion has tainted the identification, its mark is virtually indelible. For once a witness has made a mistaken identification, "he is not likely to go back on his word later on." United States v. Wade. As a result, any effort of the accused to "duplicate" the initial photographic display will almost necessarily lead to a reaffirmation of the initial misidentification.

The Court's related assertion, that "equality of access" to the results of a Government conducted photographic display "remove[s] any inequality in the adversary process," . . . is similarly flawed. For due to the possibilities for suggestion, intentional or unintentional, the so-called "equality of access" is, in reality, skewed sharply in favor of the prosecution.

defendant, however, advocated a per se rule requiring "exclusion of the out-of-court identification evidence, without regard to reliability, whenever it has been obtained through unnecessarily [suggestive] confrontation procedures." According to the Court:

> There are, of course, several interests to be considered and taken into account. The driving force behind *Wade, Gilbert,* and *Stovall* . . . was the Court's concern with the problems of eyewitness identification. Usually the witness must testify about an encounter with a total stranger under circumstances of emergency or emotional stress. The witness' recollection of the stranger can be distorted easily by the circumstances or by later actions of the police. Thus, *Wade* and its companion cases reflect the concern that the jury not hear eyewitness testimony unless that evidence has aspects of reliability. It must be observed that both approaches before us are responsive to this concern. The per se rule, however, goes too far since its application automatically and peremptorily, and without consideration of alleviating factors, keeps evidence from the jury that is reliable and relevant.
>
> The second factor is deterrence. Although the per se approach has the more significant deterrent effect, the totality approach also has an influence on police behavior. The police will guard against unnecessarily suggestive procedures under the totality rule, as well as the per se one, for fear that their actions will lead to the exclusion of identifications as unreliable.
>
> The third factor is the effect on the administration of justice. Here the per se approach suffers serious drawbacks. Since it denies the trier reliable evidence, it may result, on occasion, in the guilty going free. Also, because of its rigidity, the per se approach may make error by the trial judge more likely than the totality approach. And in those cases in which the admission of identification evidence is error under the per se approach but not under the totality approach — cases in which the identification is reliable despite an unnecessarily suggestive identification procedure — reversal is a Draconian sanction. Certainly, inflexible rules of exclusion that may frustrate rather than promote justice have not been viewed recently by this Court with unlimited enthusiasm. . . .
>
> The standard, after all, is that of fairness as required by the Due Process Clause of the Fourteenth Amendment. . . . *Stovall*, with its reference to "the totality of the circumstances," and *Biggers*, with its continuing stress on the same totality, did not, singly or together, establish a strict exclusionary rule or new standard of due process.
>
> We therefore conclude that reliability is the linchpin in determining the admissibility of identification testimony. . . . The factors to be considered are set out in *Biggers*. These include the opportunity of the witness to view the criminal at the time of the crime, the witness' degree of attention, the accuracy of his prior description of the criminal, the level of certainty demonstrated at the confrontation, and the time between the crime and the confrontation. Against these factors is to be weighed the corrupting effect of the suggestive identification itself.

Id., at 111-114.

6. The *Wade* Court, in a separate passage not reproduced above, stated that "[l]egislative or other regulations . . . which eliminate the risks of abuse and unintentional suggestion at lineup proceedings and the impediments to meaningful confrontation at trial may also remove the basis for regarding the stage as 'critical.'" 388 U.S., at 239. In response, Professor Frank Read proposed the following Model Regulation:

Proposed Regulation of Eyewitness Identification Procedures

(1) *Restrictions on Identification*

(a) Restrictions on Police. No law enforcement officer shall conduct a lineup or otherwise attempt, by having a witness view or hear the voice of an arrested person, to secure the identification of an arrested person as a person involved in a crime unless such identification procedure is authorized by this regulation. . . .

(b) Restrictions on Witnesses. No witness at trial shall hereafter be permitted to identify a criminal defendant as the person involved in a crime unless the prosecution has first shown, to the Court's satisfaction, and in the absence of the jury:

(1) That the witness was sufficiently acquainted with the defendant before the alleged offense to make recognition then likely; or

(2) That the witness' recognition of the defendant arose from an independent origin or source under circumstances other than that the police or other authorities were attempting to elicit identification; or

(3) That all pertinent provisions of this regulation were followed by police in conducting eyewitness confrontation or lineup identification procedures. . . .

(2) *Required Procedures*

A lineup or identification procedure is authorized only if there has been compliance with the following rules:

(a) No person participating in any police lineup or other identification procedure and no person present at such lineup or identification procedure shall do any act or say any thing which shall directly, indirectly, or impliedly suggest to or influence any identifying witness to make or not to make a particular identification, or which suggests to or influences any identifying witness to believe or suspect that any member or members of the group standing [in] the lineup has been arrested for the offense in question or for any offense.

(b) The officer conducting any police lineup or identification proceeding shall take all steps necessary to guarantee that any identification or failure to identify shall be the product of the free choice of the identifying witness based on the independent recollection or recognition of such witness. . . .

(c) All police lineups or identification proceedings shall be composed of a minimum of five persons, in addition to the suspect, and these additional five or more persons shall be of the same general age, sex, race and general physical characteristics as the suspect and be required to wear clothing similar to that worn by the suspect. . . .

(d) All body movements, gestures or verbal statements that may be necessary shall be done one time only by each person participating in the lineup and shall be repeated only at the express request of the identifying witness. . . .

(e) The suspect may select his own position in any police lineup or identification procedure and may change his position after each identifying witness has completed his viewing. . . .

(f) Under no circumstances shall any identifying witness be allowed to see a suspect or any member of the lineup in custody or otherwise prior to the lineup or identification procedure and no interrogation of the suspect or any member of the lineup group shall occur in the presence of an identifying witness. . . .

(g) Two (2) or more identifying witnesses shall not view the same lineup or identification procedure in each other's presence nor shall they be permitted to communicate with each other before completion of all attempted identifications by all witnesses. . . .

(h) Prior to viewing the lineup, an identifying witness shall be required to give a description of the person or persons responsible for the crime in question and such description shall be written and signed or otherwise verified and a copy of such description and all other descriptions that may have been given to the police prior to the lineup shall be made available to defense counsel. . . .

(i) Any identifying witness may remain unseen or masked when viewing the lineup or identification procedure. . . .

(j) The officer conducting any police lineup or identification proceeding shall record the names and addresses of persons participating in the lineup or identification, including the suspect or defendant, the others standing in the lineup group with the suspect or defendant, the police officers present, any person representing the suspect, and any independent observers; provided however, that names of identifying witnesses shall not be required to be disclosed; a copy of said list of names and addresses so recorded shall be furnished to defense counsel.

(k) A full record of all statements made by the identifying witness regarding the identification shall be made by voice recording, or, if no such recording equipment is available, a complete transcript of all statements made by the identifying witness regarding the identification shall be made; a copy of such voice recording or transcript shall be made available to defense counsel.

(l) A visual recording of the conduct of the lineup or identification procedure shall be made by videotape or other appropriate moving picture-type process, or, if no such videotape or moving picture type equipment is available, a minimum of one good quality color photograph of the entire group included in the lineup which was viewed by the identifying witness shall be taken and a copy of such photograph shall be made available to defense counsel. . . .

(3) *Urgent Necessity*

In cases of urgent necessity, as where a witness is dying at the scene of the crime, an identification confrontation shall be lawful with only such compliance with subsections a, b, j, k, and l of section 2, above, as may be reasonable under the circumstances. . . .

Frank T. Read, Lawyers at Lineups: Constitutional Necessity or Avoidable Extravagance? 17 UCLA L. Rev. 339, 388-393 (1969). Prof. Read's proposal anticipated work that would be done by research psychologists decades later.

In the 1980s, some defense lawyers proposed to assist the jury by employing experts — usually psychologists — to testify to the limits of human perception, memory, etc., as well as to the potential for suggestiveness that lineups and similar procedures possess. The courts were not very receptive to such evidence, although a few courts admitted it, and a few appellate cases held that exclusion of such expert testimony was an abuse of discretion. See, e.g., People v. McDonald, 37 Cal. 3d 351 (1984). By the 1990s, it could be said that "the admission of expert psychological testimony on eyewitness memory appears to be the exception rather than the rule." Steven Penrod, Solomon M. Fulero, & Brian L. Cutler, Expert Psychological Testimony on Eyewitness Reliability before and after *Daubert*: The State of the Law and the Science 229, 230 (1995). This judicial reluctance was largely for two reasons. First, science had not produced the kind of clear-cut answers most amenable to judicial use. See Rogers Elliott, Expert Testimony about Eyewitness Identification, 17 L. & Hum. Behav. 423 (1993). Second, the critical empirical question is not the extent of human foibles in eyewitness identification but whether expert testimony will positively contribute to accurate verdicts, a proposition not easy to establish. See Michael McCloskey & Howard E. Egeth, Eyewitness Identification: What Can a Psychologist Tell a Jury? 38 Am. Psychol. 550 (1983).

In the late 1990s, growing national concern over false confessions — prompted by highly publicized DNA exonerations — generated a new round of psychology research on the operation of memory and the ability of individuals to make reliable identifications. See Jim Dwyer, Peter Neufeld, & F. Barry Scheck, Actual Innocence: Five Days to Execution and Other Dispatches from the Wrongly Convicted (2000) (false identifications often play a role in erroneous convictions). One study found that eyewitness identifications made during events "personally relevant, highly stressful, and realistic in nature" are prone to "substantial error" — even when the eyewitness views the target for more than 30 minutes. Charles A. Morgan III, Gary Hazlett, Anthony Doran, Stephan Garrett, Gary Hoyt, Paul Thomas, Madelon Baranoski, & Steven Southwicket, Accuracy of Eyewitness Memory for Persons Encountered During Exposure to Highly Intense Stress, 27 Intl. J.L. & Psychiatry 265 (2004). Cross-racial identifications, which are systematically harder to make than own-race identifications, pose a special problem. Christian A. Meissner & John C. Brigham, Eyewitness Identification: Thirty Years of Investigating the Own-Race Bias in Memory for Faces: A Meta-Analytic Review, 7 Psychol. Pub. Pol'y & L. 3 (2001). And identifications by children are often influenced by their susceptibility to suggestiveness. M. Bruck & J. Ceci, The Description of Children's Suggestibility, in Nancy L. Stein et al. (eds.), Memory for Everyday and Emotional Events (1997).

One group of researchers, led by Gary Wells, suggested the following:

1. The person conducting a lineup should not know who is accused;
2. The person making an identification should be told that perhaps the suspect is not in the lineup;
3. The suspect should look like everyone else in the lineup; and
4. Statements of confidence from those identifying should be obtained.

Gary L. Wells, Mark Small, Steven Penrod, Roy S. Malpass, Solomon M. Fulero, & C. A. E. Brimacombe, Eyewitness Identification Procedures: Recommendations for Lineups and Photospreads, 22 Law & Hum. Behav. 603 (1998). Based largely on Wells's research, and similar work done by the National Institute of Justice,[5] a strong push was made in some states to replace traditional simultaneous lineups (where the suspect appears together with other persons) with double-blind sequential lineups (where neither the eyewitness nor the person administering the lineup knows in advance the suspect's position in the lineup; the eyewitness is advised that the suspect may not even be in the lineup; the eyewitness must view the lineup one person at a time; and the eyewitness must answer "yes" or "no" for each person in the lineup before moving on to the next person). These new procedures were implemented in New Jersey, Boston, and Hennepin County, Minnesota. See Kate Zernike, Questions Raised over New Trend in Police Lineups, N.Y. Times, Apr. 19, 2006, at A1.

In Illinois, similar new lineup procedures were proposed for all homicide cases by Governor George Ryan's Commission on Capital Punishment[6] in 2002, and thereafter became the subject of a controversial pilot study by police departments that purported to show an overall *decrease* in accuracy under the new procedures.

5. See Technical Working Group for Eyewitness Evidence, "Eyewitness Evidence: A Guide for Law Enforcement" (NIJ, U.S. Department of Justice, October 1999).

6. The Commission did not propose to make the new procedures mandatory, due to concerns about the practicalities of implementation. The Committee's Report is available at http://www.idoc.state.il.us/ccp/ccp/reports/commission_report/complete_report.pdf.

See Zack L. Winzeler, Whoa, Whoa, Whoa . . . One at a Time: Examining the
Responses to the Illinois Study on Double-Blind Sequential Lineup Procedures,
2008 Utah L. Rev. 1595; Jack King, NACDL News: NACDL Files Suit over Illinois
"Lineup" Report, 31 Champion 6 (2007) (detailing ongoing effort by National
Association of Criminal Defense Lawyers to challenge the validity of the Illinois
pilot study).

In 2008, Steven Clark, Ryan Howell, and Sherrie Davey reviewed the psychology
literature, including 94 prior studies, in an effort to find the common ground and
also to explain variations in experimental results on eyewitness lineup identifications. They concluded:

> An identification of the suspect is diagnostic and therefore evidence of the suspect's
> guilt. However, the present analyses suggest that a suspect identification is less infor-
> mative if the lineup is biased. The present analyses also suggest that in a biased lineup,
> suspect identifications have less probative value in a simultaneous lineup than in a
> sequential lineup. . . . [W]e would add that the probative value of a suspect identifica-
> tion is undermined as well if lineup instructions increase the witness's willingness to
> make an identification. A general principle that emerges from these analyses is that a
> suspect identification has greater probative value to the extent that it is based on the
> witness's memory, and less probative value to the extent that it is due to lineup com-
> position or an increase in the witness's conformity, willingness, or desire to make an
> identification.
>
> Nonidentifications also are straightforward. They are diagnostic of the suspect's
> innocence. . . . [N]onidentifications are not merely "failures" to identify the suspect,
> but rather carry important information whose value should not be overlooked. It is
> important to note as well that lineup rejections carry a different meaning than don't
> know responses. The distinction between don't know and reject responses is important.
> In contrast to the witness who responds don't know, the witness who rejects the lineup
> may be more clearly stating "I *do* know — that the culprit is *not* in the lineup."
>
> The least straightforward case is for foil identifications[, in which the eyewitness
> identifies someone in the lineup other than the suspect]. What does a foil identifica-
> tion bring to the question of the suspect's guilt? Wells and Olson, based on their analy-
> ses, concluded that foil identifications were indicators of the suspect's innocence. [See
> Gary L. Wells & E. A. Olson, Eyewitness Identification: Information Gain from Incrimi-
> nating and Exonerating Behaviors, 8 J. Exp. Psychol. Appl. 155 (2002).] Our analysis
> suggests that this may be true if the lineup foils are selected based on their match to the
> witness's description of the perpetrator, but not if the foils are selected based on their
> match to the suspect. In the suspect-matched case, foil identifications appear either to
> have no probative value, or to be indicative of the suspect's guilt.

Steven E. Clark, Ryan T. Howell, & Sherrie L. Davey, Regularities in Eyewitness
Identification, 32 Law & Hum. Behav. 187, 211 (2008). With respect to the probative value of expert testimony based on psychology research, the authors noted that
"[t]he present results show that through what might appear as very inconsistent,
highly variable results, consistent response patterns and consistent, predictable
variations in those response patterns, emerge." Id., at 211-212. Finally, they suggested that further research be done on two important yet relatively understudied
matters: (1) the accuracy of lineups involving foils selected on the basis of their similarity to the suspect (the most common lineup technique actually used by the police)
and (2) the relative accuracy of simultaneous and sequential lineups (this question

has been studied, but most of the studies used lineups that also contained other sources of bias). Id., at 212.

In an interesting follow-up article, Clark and Ryan Godfrey attempted to analyze the "innocence risk," or the risk of producing a wrongful conviction, of various eyewitness identification procedures. They concluded:

> Unbiased instructions, sequential lineups, and the use of plausible foils were all shown to reduce innocence risk, because reductions in false identification rates were proportionally larger than reductions in correct identification rates. . . . However, since there are few cases in which one procedure dominates another [i.e., produces measurable benefits without imposing measurable costs], policy decisions must address the question of how much cost (decrease in correct identifications) is acceptable in exchange for how much benefit (decrease in false identifications).

See Steven E. Clark & Ryan D. Godfrey, Eyewitness Identification Evidence and Innocence Risk, 16 Psychonomic Bull. & Rev. 22, 38 (2009).

7. Another possible response to the problem of eyewitness identification is to provide for special jury instructions. See State v. Green, 86 N.J. 281, 430 A.2d 914 (1981), reversing for the failure of the trial court to give such instructions. In Joseph D. Grano, *Kirby, Biggers,* and *Ash*: Do Any Constitutional Safeguards Remain Against the Danger of Convicting the Innocent? 72 Mich. L. Rev. 717, 796-797 (1974), Professor Grano suggests the following instruction:

> Because of the scientifically proven dangers of mistaken identification, the law has established certain rules for the conduct of identification procedures. One of the most significant dangers is that the identification procedure will itself mislead the witness into identifying the wrong person. For example, when the police present only one person to the witness, they magnify the risk of mistake. The witness, though perfectly honest, is likely to be misled into believing that the police must have captured the right person if they are presenting him . . . for identification. A much safer procedure is to conduct a lineup, where the witness is tested by being forced to pick the defendant from a group of men. Because lineups are much more reliable, . . . the police [should not] conduct . . . one-man showups when a lineup can be held. In this case, the police, without justifiable excuse, [did so]. In doing this, they unnecessarily increased the risk of mistaken identification. In evaluating the identification evidence in this case, you should consider this . . . and the unnecessary risk it caused.

8. In this area, as in others, state courts of last resort have extended procedural protections to defendants as a matter of state law that exceed the federal constitutional requirements. See, e.g., State v. Dubose, 699 N.W.2d 582 (Wis. 2005) (per se exclusion of all out-of-court show-up identifications unless necessary); Commonwealth v. Johnson, 650 N.E.2d 1257 (Mass. 1995) (per se exclusion of identification evidence resulting from unnecessarily suggestive show-ups); State v. Ramirez, 817 P.2d 774 (Utah 1991) (expanding *Biggers* criteria for evaluating reliability, and thus admissibility, of identification evidence); People v. Adams, 440 N.Y.S.2d 902 (N.Y. 1981) (forbidding the admission of testimony concerning an unnecessarily suggestive identification, but also applying harmless-error analysis); People v. Bustamonte, 634 P.2d 927, 177 Cal. Rptr. 576 (1981) (extending right to counsel to preindictment lineups).

b. When Does the Right to Counsel End?

Once the Sixth Amendment right to counsel "attaches," the right continues to apply to all "critical stages" until the final determination by the trial judge of the sentence to be imposed. Mempa v. Rhay, 389 U.S. 128 (1967) (right to counsel applicable at probation revocation hearing at which judge imposed sentence). But the Sixth Amendment right does not apply past the point of sentencing. In Morrissey v. Brewer, 408 U.S. 471 (1972), the Court held that parole revocation is not a part of a criminal prosecution but that due process nonetheless mandates certain procedural protections. In Gagnon v. Scarpelli, 411 U.S. 778 (1973), the Court held that one of those protections is right to counsel at parole or probation revocation proceedings where, unlike *Mempa*, sentence was not imposed at the hearing and where there are "special circumstances." The special circumstances calling for counsel exist whenever the probationer or parolee makes a request for counsel, based on a timely and colorable claim (i) that he has not committed the alleged violation of the conditions upon which he is at liberty; or (ii) that, even if the violation is a matter of public record and is uncontested, there are substantial reasons that justified or mitigated the violation and make revocation inappropriate, and that the reasons are complex or otherwise difficult to develop or present. Id., at 790. The Court has also determined that a prisoner has a right to be heard in prison disciplinary hearings that could adversely affect his liberty interests, but not necessarily with the assistance of counsel. Wolff v. McDonnell, 418 U.S. 539 (1974). For a discussion, see David A. Harris, The Constitution and Truth Seeking: A New Theory on Expert Services for Indigent Defendants, 83 J. Crim. L. & Criminology 469 (1992). Curiously enough, the Court in *Gagnon* made a point of emphasizing that it was *not* deciding anything about the scope of the right to be heard by retained counsel in revocation proceedings. 411 U.S., at 783 n. 6. Counsel need not be appointed for inmates placed in administrative segregation as a result of crimes committed while incarcerated, unless adversary judicial proceedings are initiated against the inmates. United States v. Gouveia, 467 U.S. 180 (1984).

Even if the Sixth Amendment right to counsel does not apply beyond sentencing, might there be another constitutional source for a right to appointed counsel in appellate proceedings?

HALBERT v. MICHIGAN

Supreme Court of the United States
545 U.S. 605 (2005)

JUSTICE GINSBURG delivered the opinion of the Court.

In 1994, Michigan voters approved a proposal amending the State Constitution to provide that "an appeal by an accused who pleads guilty or nolo contendere shall be by leave of the court." Mich. Const., Art. 1, §20. Thereafter, "several Michigan state judges began to deny appointed appellate counsel to indigents" convicted by plea. Kowalski v. Tesmer, 543 U.S. 125, 127 (2004). Rejecting challenges based on the Equal Protection and Due Process Clauses of the Fourteenth Amendment to the Federal Constitution, the Michigan Supreme Court upheld this practice. . . .

Petitioner Antonio Dwayne Halbert, convicted on his plea of *nolo contendere*, sought the appointment of counsel to assist him in applying for leave to appeal to the Michigan Court of Appeals. The state trial court and the Court of Appeals denied Halbert's requests for appointed counsel, and the Michigan Supreme Court declined review.

Michigan Court of Appeals review of an application for leave to appeal, Halbert contends, ranks as a first-tier appellate proceeding requiring appointment of counsel under Douglas v. California, 372 U.S. 353 (1963). Michigan urges that appeal to the State Court of Appeals is discretionary and, for an appeal of that order, Ross v. Moffitt, 417 U.S. 600 (1974), holds counsel need not be appointed. . . . Today, we . . . conclude that Halbert's case is properly ranked with *Douglas* rather than *Ross*. Accordingly, we hold that the Due Process and Equal Protection Clauses require the appointment of counsel for defendants, convicted on their pleas, who seek access to first-tier review in the Michigan Court of Appeals.

I

The Federal Constitution imposes on the States no obligation to provide appellate review of criminal convictions. McKane v. Durston, 153 U.S. 684, 687 (1894). Having provided such an avenue, however, a State may not "bolt the door to equal justice" to indigent defendants. Griffin v. Illinois, 351 U.S. 12, 24 (1956) (Frankfurter, J., concurring in judgment); see id., at 23 (same) ("[W]hen a State deems it wise and just that convictions be susceptible to review by an appellate court, it cannot by force of its exactions draw a line which precludes convicted indigent persons . . . from securing such . . . review."). *Griffin* held that, when a State conditions an appeal from a conviction on the provision of a trial transcript, the State must furnish free transcripts to indigent defendants who seek to appeal. Id., at 16-20 (plurality opinion). *Douglas* relied on *Griffin*'s reasoning to hold that, in first appeals as of right, States must appoint counsel to represent indigent defendants. 372 U.S., at 357. *Ross* held, however, that a State need not appoint counsel to aid a poor person in discretionary appeals to the State's highest court, or in petitioning for review in this Court. 417 U.S., at 610-612, 615-618.

. . . [B]arriers [to appeal] encountered by persons unable to pay their own way, we have observed, "cannot be resolved by resort to easy slogans or pigeonhole analysis." M.L.B. v. S.L.J., 519 U.S. 102, 120 (1996) (internal quotation marks omitted). Our decisions in point reflect "both equal protection and due process concerns." Ibid. "The equal protection concern relates to the legitimacy of fencing out would-be appellants based solely on their inability to pay core costs," while "[t]he due process concern homes in on the essential fairness of the state-ordered proceedings." Ibid.

Two considerations were key to our decision in *Douglas* that a State is required to appoint counsel for an indigent defendant's first-tier appeal as of right. First, such an appeal entails an adjudication on the "merits." 372 U.S., at 357. Second, first-tier review differs from subsequent appellate stages "at which the claims have once been presented by [appellate counsel] and passed upon by an appellate court." Id., at 356. Under the California system at issue in *Douglas*, the first-tier appellate court independently examined the record to determine whether to appoint counsel. Id., at 355. When a defendant able to retain counsel pursued an appeal, the *Douglas* Court observed, "the appellate court passe[d] on the merits of [the] case only after having the full benefit of written briefs and oral argument by counsel." Id., at 356. In contrast, when a poor person appealed, "the appellate court [wa]s forced to prejudge the merits [of the case] before it c[ould] even determine whether counsel should be provided." Ibid.

In *Ross*, we explained why the rationale of *Douglas* did not extend to the appointment of counsel for an indigent seeking to pursue a second-tier discretionary appeal to the North Carolina Supreme Court or, thereafter, certiorari review in this Court. The North Carolina Supreme Court, in common with this Court we perceived, does not sit as [a court of error correction.] 417 U.S., at 615. Principal criteria for state high court review, we noted, included "whether the subject matter of the appeal has significant public interest, whether the cause involves legal principles of major significance to the jurisprudence of the State, [and] whether the decision below is in probable conflict" with the court's precedent. Ibid. (internal quotation marks omitted). Further, we pointed out, a defendant who had already benefited from counsel's aid in a first-tier appeal as of right would have, "at the very least, a transcript or other record of trial proceedings, a brief on his behalf in the Court of Appeals setting forth his claims of error, and in many cases an opinion by the Court of Appeals disposing of his case." Ibid.

II

Michigan has a two-tier appellate system comprising the State Supreme Court and the intermediate Court of Appeals. The Michigan Supreme Court hears appeals by leave only. Mich. Comp. Laws Ann. §770.3(6). Prior to 1994, the Court of Appeals adjudicated appeals as of right from all criminal convictions. To reduce the workload of the Court of Appeals, a 1994 amendment to the Michigan Constitution changed the process for appeals following plea-based convictions. As amended, the State Constitution provides: "In every criminal prosecution, the accused shall have the right . . . to have an appeal as a matter of right, except as provided by law an appeal by an accused who pleads guilty or nolo contendere shall be by leave of the court." Mich. Const., Art. 1, §20.

A defendant convicted by plea who seeks review in the Michigan Court of Appeals must now file an application for leave to appeal pursuant to Mich. Ct. Rule 7.205. In response, the Court of Appeals may, among other things, "grant or deny the application; enter a final decision; [or] grant other relief." Rule 7.205(D)(2). If the court grants leave, "the case proceeds as an appeal of right." Rule 7.205(D)(3). The parties agree that the Court of Appeals, in its orders denying properly filed applications for leave, uniformly cites "lack of merit in the grounds presented" as the basis for its decision. See Tr. of Oral Arg. 21-22, 24, 39.

Under Michigan law, most indigent defendants convicted by plea must proceed pro se in seeking leave to appeal. Michigan Comp. Laws Ann. §770.3a provides, in relevant part, that a "defendant who pleads guilty, guilty but mentally ill, or nolo contendere shall not have appellate counsel appointed for review of the defendant's conviction or sentence," [with certain exceptions not relevant to the instant case.]

In People v. Bulger, [614 N.W.2d 103 (Mich. S. Ct. 2000)], the Michigan Supreme Court . . . concluded that appointment of counsel is not required for several reasons: Court of Appeals review following plea-based convictions is by leave and is thus "discretionary," id., at 506-508, 519; "[p]lea proceedings are . . . shorter, simpler, and more routine than trials," id., at 517; and by entering a plea, a defendant "accede[s] to the state's fundamental interest in finality," ibid. . . .

Petitioner Halbert pleaded *nolo contendere* to two counts of second-degree criminal sexual conduct. During Halbert's plea colloquy, the trial court asked Halbert, "You understand if I accept your plea you are giving up or waiving any claim of an appeal as of right," and Halbert answered, "Yes, sir." The court then advised Halbert of certain instances in which, although the appeal would not be as of right, the court nevertheless "must" or "may" appoint appellate counsel. The court did not tell Halbert, however, that it could not appoint counsel in any other circumstances, including Halbert's own case:

> THE COURT: You understand if I accept your plea and you are financially unable to retain a lawyer to represent you on appeal, the Court must appoint an attorney for you if the sentence I impose exceeds the sentencing guidelines or you seek leave to appeal a conditional plea or the prosecutor seeks leave to appeal or the Court of Appeals or Supreme Court grants you leave to appeal. Under those conditions I must appoint an attorney, do you understand that?
> THE DEFENDANT: Yes, sir.
> THE COURT: Further, if you are financially unable to retain a lawyer to represent you on appeal, the Court may appoint an attorney for you if you allege an improper scoring of the sentencing guidelines, you object to the scoring at the time of the sentencing and the sentence I impose exceeds the sentencing guidelines as you allege it should be scored. Under those conditions I may appoint an attorney for you, do you understand that?
> THE DEFENDANT: Yes, sir.

At Halbert's sentencing hearing, defense counsel requested that the sentences for the two counts run concurrently, but urged no error in the determination of Halbert's exposure under the Michigan sentencing guidelines. The trial court set Halbert's sentences to run consecutively. Halbert submitted a handwritten motion to withdraw his plea the day after sentencing. Denying the motion, the trial court stated that Halbert's "proper remedy is to appeal to the Michigan Court of Appeals."

Twice thereafter and to no avail, Halbert asked the trial court to appoint counsel to help him prepare an application for leave to appeal to the intermediate appellate court. He submitted his initial request on a form provided by the State. The trial court denied the request. Halbert next sent the trial court a letter and accompanying motion, again seeking appointed counsel. Halbert stated that his sentence had been misscored and that he needed the aid of counsel to preserve the issue before undertaking an appeal. Halbert also related that he had "required special education due to learning disabilities," and was "mentally impaired." To prepare his pro se filings, he noted, he was obliged to rely on the assistance of fellow inmates. The trial court denied Halbert's motion; citing *Bulger*, the court stated that Halbert "does not have a constitutional . . . right to appointment of appellate counsel to pursue a discretionary appeal."

Again using a form supplied by the State and acting pro se, Halbert filed an application for leave to appeal. He asserted claims of sentencing error and ineffective assistance of counsel, and sought remand for appointment of appellate counsel and resentencing. In a standard form order, the Court of Appeals denied Halbert's application "for lack of merit in the grounds presented."

The State Supreme Court, dividing 5 to 2, denied Halbert's application for leave to appeal to that court. . . . We granted certiorari to consider whether the denial of appointed counsel to Halbert violated the Fourteenth Amendment. We now vacate the judgment of the Michigan Court of Appeals.

III

Petitioner Halbert's case is framed by two prior decisions of this Court concerning state-funded appellate counsel, *Douglas* and *Ross*. The question before us is essentially one of classification: With which of those decisions should the instant case be aligned? We hold that *Douglas* provides the controlling instruction. Two aspects of the Michigan Court of Appeals' process following plea-based convictions lead us to that conclusion. First, in determining how to dispose of an application for leave to appeal, Michigan's intermediate appellate court looks to the merits of the claims made in the application. Second, indigent defendants pursuing first-tier review in the Court of Appeals are generally ill equipped to represent themselves.

A defendant who pleads guilty or *nolo contendere* in a Michigan court does not thereby forfeit all opportunity for appellate review. Although he relinquishes access to an appeal as of right, he is entitled to apply for leave to appeal, and that entitlement is officially conveyed to him. Of critical importance, the tribunal to which he addresses his application, the Michigan Court of Appeals, unlike the Michigan Supreme Court, sits [to correct errors].[3]

The Court of Appeals may respond to a leave application in a number of ways. It "may grant or deny the application; enter a final decision; grant other relief; request additional material from the record; or require a certified concise statement of proceedings and facts from the court . . . whose order is being appealed." Mich. Ct. Rule 7.205(D)(2). When the court denies leave using the stock phrase "for lack of merit in the grounds presented," its disposition may not be equivalent to a "final decision" on the merits, *i.e.*, the disposition may simply signal that the court found the matters asserted unworthy of the expenditure of further judicial resources. But the court's response to the leave application by any of the specified alternatives—including denial of leave—necessarily entails some evaluation of the merits of the applicant's claims.

Michigan urges that review in the Court of Appeals following a plea-based conviction is as "discretionary" as review in the Michigan Supreme Court because both require an application for leave to appeal. See *Bulger*, 614 N.W.2d, at 108, 113. Therefore, Michigan maintains, *Ross* is dispositive. . . . The Court in *Ross*, however, recognized that leave-granting determinations by North Carolina's Supreme Court turned on considerations other than the commission of error by a lower court, *e.g.*, the involvement of a matter of "significant public interest." See 417 U.S., at 611.

---

3. Both the majority and the dissent in People v. Bulger, 614 N.W.2d 103 (Mich. S.Ct. 2000), described the State's intermediate appellate court's function as error correction. Compare id., at 112-113 (in the majority's view, the Court of Appeals could perform its review function, despite the defendant's lack of representation, because plea-convicted defendants have ample aid for preservation of their claims in the trial court and ineffective assistance of counsel should be readily apparent to the Court of Appeals from the record), with id., 125 (Cavanagh, J., dissenting) ("[T]he function of our Court of Appeals is reviewing the merits and correcting errors made by the lower courts.").

Michigan's Supreme Court, too, sits not to correct errors in individual cases, but to decide matters of larger public import. By contrast, the Michigan Court of Appeals . . . is guided in responding to leave to appeal applications by the merits of the particular defendant's claims, not by the general importance of the questions presented.

Whether formally categorized as the decision of an appeal or the disposal of a leave application, the Court of Appeals' ruling on a plea-convicted defendant's claims provides the first, and likely the only, direct review the defendant's conviction and sentence will receive. Parties like Halbert, however, are disarmed in their endeavor to gain first-tier review. As the Court in *Ross* emphasized, a defendant seeking State Supreme Court review following a first-tier appeal as of right earlier had the assistance of appellate counsel. The attorney appointed to serve at the intermediate appellate court level will have reviewed the trial court record, researched the legal issues, and prepared a brief reflecting that review and research. 417 U.S., at 615. The defendant seeking second-tier review may also be armed with an opinion of the intermediate appellate court addressing the issues counsel raised. A first-tier review applicant, forced to act pro se, will face a record unreviewed by appellate counsel, and will be equipped with no attorney's brief prepared for, or reasoned opinion by, a court of review.

The *Bulger* court concluded that "a pro se defendant seeking discretionary review" in the Court of Appeals is adequately armed because he "will have the benefit of a transcript, trial counsel's framing of the issues in [a] motion to withdraw, and the trial court's ruling on the motion." 614 N.W.2d, at 113. But we held in Swenson v. Bosler, 386 U.S. 258 (1967) (per curiam), that comparable materials prepared by trial counsel are no substitute for an appellate lawyer's aid. There, the Missouri court reviewing an indigent's post-trial appeal had before it a transcript plus trial counsel's "notice of appeal and . . . motion for new trial which specifically designated the issues which could be considered on direct appeal." Id., at 259. The absence of counsel in these circumstances, *Bosler* held, "violated [the defendant's] Fourteenth Amendment rights, as defined in *Douglas*." Ibid. Adhering to *Douglas*, we explained that "[t]he assistance of appellate counsel in preparing and submitting a brief to the appellate court which defines the legal principles upon which the claims of error are based and which designates and interprets the relevant portions of the [record] may well be of substantial benefit to the defendant [and] may not be denied . . . solely because of his indigency." 386 U.S., at 259. Although *Bosler* involved a post-trial rather than post-plea appeal, the Court recognized that a transcript and motion by trial counsel are not adequate stand-ins for an appellate lawyer's review of the record and legal research. Without guides keyed to a court of review, a pro se applicant's entitlement to seek leave to appeal to Michigan's intermediate court may be more formal than real.

Persons in Halbert's situation are particularly handicapped as self-representatives. As recounted earlier this Term, "[a]pproximately 70% of indigent defendants represented by appointed counsel plead guilty, and 70% of those convicted are incarcerated." *Kowalski*, 543 U.S., at 140 (Ginsburg, J., dissenting). "[Sixty-eight percent] of the state prison populatio[n] did not complete high school, and many lack the most basic literacy skills." Ibid. (citation omitted). "[S]even out of ten inmates fall in the lowest two out of five levels of literacy — marked by an inability to do such basic tasks as write a brief letter to explain an error on a credit card bill, use a bus schedule, or state in writing an argument made in a lengthy newspaper article." Ibid. Many, Halbert among them, have learning disabilities and mental impairments.

Navigating the appellate process without a lawyer's assistance is a perilous endeavor for a layperson, and well beyond the competence of individuals, like Halbert, who have little education, learning disabilities, and mental impairments. See Gideon v. Wainwright, 372 U.S. 335, 345 (1963) ("Even the intelligent and educated layman has small and sometimes no skill in the science of law."). Appeals by defendants convicted on their pleas may involve "myriad and often complicated" substantive issues, *Kowalski*, 543 U.S., at 145 (Ginsburg, J., dissenting). . . . One who pleads guilty or *nolo contendere* may still raise on appeal

> constitutional defects that are irrelevant to his factual guilt, double jeopardy claims requiring no further factual record, jurisdictional defects, challenges to the sufficiency of the evidence at the preliminary examination, preserved entrapment claims, mental competency claims, factual basis claims, claims that the state had no right to proceed in the first place, including claims that a defendant was charged under an inapplicable statute, and claims of ineffective assistance of counsel.

Bulger, 614 N.W.2d, at 133-134 (Cavanagh, J., dissenting).

Michigan's very procedures for seeking leave to appeal after sentencing on a plea, moreover, may intimidate the uncounseled. Michigan Ct. Rule 7.205(A) requires the applicant to file for leave to appeal within 21 days after the trial court's entry of judgment. The defendant must submit five copies of the application "stating the date and nature of the judgment or order appealed from; concisely reciting the appellant's allegations of error and the relief sought; [and] setting forth a concise argument . . . in support of the appellant's position on each issue." Rule 7.205(B)(1). . . . [This task] "would not be onerous for an applicant familiar with law school examinations, but it is a tall order for a defendant of marginal literacy." *Kowalski*, 543 U.S., at 142 (Ginsburg, J., dissenting).

While the State has a legitimate interest in reducing the workload of its judiciary, providing indigents with appellate counsel will yield applications easier to comprehend. Michigan's Court of Appeals would still have recourse to summary denials of leave applications in cases not warranting further review. And when a defendant's case presents no genuinely arguable issue, appointed counsel may so inform the court. See Anders v. California, 386 U.S. 738, 744 (1967) ("[I]f counsel finds [the] case to be wholly frivolous, after a conscientious examination of it, he should so advise the court and request permission to withdraw," filing "a brief referring to anything in the record that might arguably support the appeal.").

Michigan contends that, even if Halbert had a constitutionally guaranteed right to appointed counsel for first-level appellate review, he waived that right by entering a plea of *nolo contendere*. We disagree. At the time he entered his plea, Halbert, in common with other defendants convicted on their pleas, had no recognized right to appointed appellate counsel he could elect to forgo. Moreover, . . . the trial court did not tell Halbert, simply and directly, that in his case, there would be no access to appointed counsel. Cf. Iowa v. Tovar, 541 U.S. 77, 81 (2004) ("Waiver of the right to counsel, as of constitutional rights in the criminal process generally, must be a knowing, intelligent ac[t] done with sufficient awareness of the relevant circumstances.").

For the reasons stated, we vacate the judgment of the Michigan Court of Appeals and remand the case for further proceedings not inconsistent with this opinion.

JUSTICE THOMAS, with whom [CHIEF JUSTICE ROBERTS and] JUSTICE SCALIA join, dissenting.

Petitioner Antonio Halbert pleaded no contest to charges that he sexually assaulted his stepdaughter and another young girl. Michigan law did not provide Halbert — as a defendant convicted by a plea of guilty or no contest — an appointed attorney to help him prepare an application for leave to appeal to the Michigan Court of Appeals. The Court holds Michigan's law unconstitutional as applied to Halbert. It fails, however, to ground its analysis in any particular provision of the Constitution or in this Court's precedents. . . .

The majority . . . finds that all plea-convicted indigent defendants have the right to appellate counsel when seeking leave to appeal. The majority does not say where in the Constitution that right is located — the Due Process Clause, the Equal Protection Clause, or some purported confluence of the two. Nor does the majority attempt to anchor its holding in the history of those Clauses. . . .

Instead, the majority pins its hopes on a single case: Douglas v. California, 372 U.S. 353 (1963). Douglas, however, does not support extending the right to counsel to any form of discretionary review, as Ross v. Moffitt, 417 U.S. 600 (1974), and later cases make clear. Moreover, Michigan has not engaged in the sort of invidious discrimination against indigent defendants that Douglas condemns. Michigan has done no more than recognize the undeniable difference between defendants who plead guilty and those who maintain their innocence, in an attempt to divert resources from largely frivolous appeals to more meritorious ones. . . .

In Douglas, California granted an initial appeal as of right to all convicted criminal defendants. 372 U.S., at 356. However, the California Court of Appeal appointed counsel for indigent defendants only after determining whether counsel would be useful to the defendant or the court. Thus the California appellate court was "forced to prejudge the merits" of indigent defendants' appeals, while it judged the merits of other defendants' appeals only after briefing and oral argument. Ibid.

In previous cases, this Court had considered state-imposed conditions like transcript and filing fees that prevented indigent criminal defendants from obtaining any appellate review. Ross, supra, at 606-607 (discussing Griffin v. Illinois, 351 U.S. 12 (1956), and its progeny). By contrast, in Douglas, California provided appellate review to all criminal defendants, but it did not provide a state subsidy for indigent defendants whose claims appeared unlikely to benefit from counsel's assistance. This Court nevertheless held that when States provide a first appeal as of right, they must supply indigent defendants with counsel. In Ross, however, this Court declined to extend Douglas' right to counsel beyond initial appeals as of right. States need not appoint counsel for indigent defendants who seek discretionary review in a State's highest court or this Court. Ross, supra, at 616-618.

. . . Like the defendant in Douglas, Halbert requests appointed counsel for an initial appeal before an intermediate appellate court. But like the defendant in Ross, Halbert requests appointed counsel for an appeal that is discretionary, not as of right. Crucially, however, Douglas noted that its decision extended only to initial appeals *as of right* — and later cases have repeatedly reaffirmed that understanding.[1] This Court has never required States to appoint counsel for discretionary review. And an appeal permitted only "by leave of the court," Mich. Const., Art. 1, §20, is discretionary — as the Michigan Supreme Court has recognized, *Bulger*, 614 N.W.2d, at 113. Neither *Douglas* nor any other decision of this Court warrants extending the right to counsel to discretionary review, even on a defendant's initial appeal.

Just as important, the rationale of *Douglas* does not support extending the right to counsel to this particular form of discretionary review. Admittedly, the precise rationale for the *Griffin/Douglas* line of cases has never been made explicit. Those cases, however, have a common theme. States may not impose financial barriers that preclude indigent defendants from securing appellate review altogether. *Griffin*, 351 U.S., at 17-18 (plurality opinion); id., at 22 (Frankfurter, J., concurring in judgment). Nor may States create "unreasoned distinctions" among defendants, [M.L.B. v. S.L.J., 519 U.S. 102, 111 (1996)]; *Douglas*, supra, at 356, that "arbitrarily cut off appeal rights for indigents while leaving open avenues of appeals for more affluent persons," *Ross*, supra, at 607.

Far from being an "arbitrary" or "unreasoned" distinction, Michigan's differentiation between defendants convicted at trial and defendants convicted by plea is sensible. . . . In *Douglas*, California preliminarily denied counsel to all indigent defendants, regardless of whether they maintained their innocence at trial or conceded their guilt by plea. Here, Michigan preliminarily denies paid counsel only to indigent defendants who admit or do not contest their guilt. . . . When a defendant pleads in open court, there is less need for counsel to develop the record and refine claims to present to an appellate court. These are . . . "[r]easoned distinctions" between defendants convicted by trial and those convicted by their own plea. *M.L.B.*, 519 U.S., at 111.

The brief history of Michigan's system confirms this. When Michigan voters amended the State Constitution to establish the current system, roughly 13,000 civil and criminal appeals per year clogged the Michigan Court of Appeals' docket. Of those, nearly a third were appeals by criminal defendants who had pleaded guilty or no contest. Even though at the time plea-convicted defendants were appointed paid appellate counsel, few of these defendants were granted relief on appeal. Simply put, Michigan's bar and bench were devoting a substantial portion of their scarce resources to thousands of cases with little practical effect. Reallocating resources was not "invidious discrimination" against criminal defendants, indigent or otherwise. *Douglas*, 372 U.S., at 356. It was an attempt to ensure "that frivolous appeals [were] not subsidized and public moneys not needlessly spent." *Griffin*, supra, at 24 (Frankfurter, J., concurring in judgment).

Today's decision will therefore do no favors for indigent defendants in Michigan — at least, indigent defendants with nonfrivolous claims. While defendants who admit their guilt will receive more attention, defendants who maintain their innocence will receive less. . . . Holding Michigan's resources constant (since we have no control over the State's bar or budget), the majority's policy choice to

---

1. *Douglas*, 372 U.S., at 357; *Ross*, 417 U.S., at 608 ("[*Douglas*] extended only to initial appeals as of right"); Evitts v. Lucey, 469 U.S. 387, 394 (1985) (*Douglas* "is limited to the first appeal as of right"); Pennsylvania v. Finley, 481 U.S. 551, 555 (1987) ("[T]he right to appointed counsel extends to the first appeal of right, and no further"). . . .

redistribute the State's limited resources only harms those most likely to have worth-while claims. . . . Then, too, Michigan is under no constitutional obligation to provide appeals for plea-convicted defendants. Ante, at 610 (citing McKane v. Durston, 153 U.S. 684 (1894)). Michigan may decline to provide an appellate process altogether (since the Court's ruling increases the cost of having a system of appellate review). Surely plea-convicted defendants would prefer appeals with limited access to counsel than no appeals at all. . . .

Today the Court confers on defendants convicted by plea a right nowhere to be found in the Constitution or this Court's cases. It does so at the expense of defendants whose claims are, on average, likely more meritorious. . . . I respectfully dissent.

NOTES AND QUESTIONS

1. *Halbert* was not the first time the Court was called upon to assess Michigan's system of providing — and not providing — counsel to indigent criminal defendants who plead guilty. In Kowalski v. Tesmer, 543 U.S. 125 (2004), a pair of lawyers sued various government officials, raising the same constitutional claims at issue in *Halbert* on behalf of future indigent defendants who would be adversely affected by the relevant Michigan rule. The lawyer-plaintiffs in *Kowalski* sought to enjoin the state to provide the kind of legal assistance that *Halbert* later required. But the *Kowalski* plaintiffs lost, because six of the nine Justices — all save Justices Ginsburg, Stevens, and Souter — found that the plaintiffs lacked standing to raise the claims of what the Court called "as yet unascertained Michigan criminal defendants." 543 U.S., at 130. Those defendants, Chief Justice Rehnquist's majority opinion held, had to raise their own claims for themselves.

What is the best way to raise claims like the one in *Halbert*: in criminal prosecutions, or in civil suits like *Kowalski*? The answer might seem obvious: Criminal prosecutions give courts concrete cases in which to decide on the procedures that should govern all such cases. But civil injunction actions have an important advantage too. In successful civil suits raising constitutional claims, plaintiffs' lawyers eventually get paid by the government agencies or officials they sue. Those attorneys' fees may be substantial enough to finance serious litigation, the kind of litigation that produces a significant factual record — not just the facts of a single case, but the overall nature of a procedural system that decides thousands of cases. Criminal procedure opinions usually pay little attention to the effects of the rules they craft on the justice *system*, perhaps because those opinions are written in cases like *Halbert* — not in cases like *Kowalski*. Maybe that's a good thing. Then again, maybe it isn't.

2. According to Justice Thomas's dissent, one effect of the *Halbert* ruling will be to divert scarce state funds from cases that are more likely have problems worthy of judicial attention (cases involving convictions following trials) to those that more likely do not (convictions based on pleas of guilty). That can't be a good thing, can it?

3. When Douglas v. California, 372 U.S. 353 (1963), was decided, the guilty plea rate was roughly 60 percent, meaning that roughly three-fifths of all felony convictions were obtained by plea. See Lee Silverstein, Defense of the Poor in Criminal Cases in American State Courts: A Field Study and Report 22-23 (1965) (study of 22 counties finding a plea rate of 74 percent in cases in which defendants received

appointed counsel and 48 percent in cases with privately retained counsel). Today, that figure is 95 percent. See Online Sourcebook, tbl. 5.57.2002, available at http://www.albany.edu/sourcebook/pdf/t557.pdf. Does the change in the plea rate affect the decision in *Halbert*? Should it?

4. Another large legal change over the last generation might affect *Halbert*: the rise of determinate sentencing. Before the mid-1970s, criminal sentencing was a matter of judicial discretion; criminal statutes specified wide sentencing ranges, and trial judges chose some sentence within the relevant range. The sentencing judge was not required to justify her sentence, nor was the sentence subject to appellate review, so long as it fell within the statutory range. Over the last 30 years, roughly half the states and the federal government have adopted sentencing guidelines — elaborate sets of legal rules governing the amount of prison time dispensed in felony cases. Even in non-guidelines states, mandatory minimum sentences are often specified by statute in gun and drug cases. Thirty years ago, only a tiny fraction of felony sentences were decided by the application of legal rules. Today, a large fraction of felony sentences are so decided.

Given that fact, and given also the sharp increase in the guilty plea rate over the last 40 years, the consequences of *Halbert* might be considerable. Had Justice Thomas's position prevailed, the vast majority of criminal defendants in guidelines states like Michigan would likely be unable to challenge their sentences. After all, sentences are imposed after conviction — meaning, in the many cases in which defendants plead guilty, after those pleas are entered. If, as Michigan argued, a guilty plea effectively waives the right to state-paid counsel on appeal, post-plea sentences are not subject to appellate review in cases in which defendants are poor enough to receive state-paid counsel. That might be a small matter in a system in which sentencing is purely discretionary — sentencing appeals are pointless in such a system. But criminal sentencing is no longer purely discretionary.

5. In *Halbert*, all nine Justices agree that there is no constitutional right to appellate review; Justices Ginsburg and Thomas cite McKane v. Durston, 153 U.S. 684 (1894), for that proposition. All states do, in fact, provide opportunity for appellate review of criminal convictions, and have long done so. Why would the Court insist that they need not do so? And *McKane* is a strange case to cite for that strange proposition, since the petitioner in that case — John Y. McKane, a New York politician — *did* appeal his conviction, and a court heard his appeal. McKane complained not of the absence of appellate review and certainly not of the denial of counsel (he could afford the best lawyers); rather, he claimed that the Constitution entitled him to be free on bail while his appeal was pending. New York law said otherwise. In *McKane*, Justice Harlan found the relevant state law constitutional.

The story behind *McKane* is interesting. John McKane was the late-nineteenth-century political boss of Coney Island. He made his living by requiring local businesses to pay protection money in order to receive police services and through kickbacks from friends to whom he sold valuable public land for below-market prices. The kickbacks and extortion not only lined McKane's pockets but also paid for the local police force. A court order mandated the monitoring of an 1893 election in McKane's town; when the monitors showed up with the order in hand, McKane said, "Injunctions don't go here" — and then ordered the monitors beaten and jailed. One of them escaped and told his story to a Brooklyn newspaper. McKane's dismissive words made national headlines. He was tried and convicted of state election law violations and sentenced to six years at Sing Sing — a remarkably severe sentence for that time. By the time he got out of prison, Coney Island and its environs had been annexed by Brooklyn, then the second-largest city in the United States, and McKane was not on good terms with Brooklyn's leading politicians. His power base was gone; he never returned to public office.

In criminal procedure as elsewhere, it is exceedingly rare for the Supreme Court to rest some important legal proposition on the authority of a more-than-century-old decision. Yet *McKane* continues to be cited with approval. Why? Perhaps the answer is that the legal proposition for which *McKane* now stands is less well-settled than first appears. All 50 states *do* provide appellate review — so no one really knows how the Justices would respond if a state suddenly chose to stop doing so. If that ever happens, *McKane*'s authority may prove less substantial than first appears, which is pretty much what happened to John McKane.

6. In a portion of his dissent that is not excerpted above, Justice Thomas argues that, even assuming Halbert had a valid Sixth Amendment claim to state-paid counsel on appeal, he waived that claim by pleading guilty. The majority dismisses the argument with the following footnote:

> We are unpersuaded by the suggestion that, because a defendant may be able to waive his right to appeal entirely, Michigan can consequently exact from him a waiver of the right to government-funded appellate counsel. . . . [I]f Michigan were to require defendants to waive all forms of appeal as a condition of entering a plea, that condition would operate against moneyed and impoverished defendants alike. A required waiver of the right to appointed counsel's assistance when applying for leave to appeal to the Michigan Court of Appeals, however, would accomplish the very result worked by Mich. Comp. Laws Ann. §770.3a: It would leave indigents without access to counsel in that narrow range of circumstances in which, our decisions hold, the State must affirmatively ensure that poor defendants receive the legal assistance necessary to provide meaningful access to the judicial system. See *Douglas*, 372 U.S., at 357-358.

545 U.S., at 624 n. 8. What does this language mean? Often, indigent defendants are under enormous pressure to plead guilty: Their lawyers' docket pressure makes it impossible to take more than a small fraction of cases to trial. Rich defendants feel no such pressure — yet that fact does not render most guilty pleas unconstitutional. Why is Michigan's argument different?

7. It seems reasonable to suppose that some line must be drawn between proceedings for which the state is required to pay for counsel for indigent defendants, and proceedings in which no such requirement applies. Where should the line be drawn? Before *Halbert*, the general understanding was that proceedings to which all defendants were legally entitled — a trial or guilty plea, an appeal "as of right" (meaning, an appeal to which all defendants are entitled under the relevant state or federal law) — were on one side of that line, and discretionary proceedings were on the other. That fits the line drawn in Ross v. Moffitt, 417 U.S. 600 (1974), which is cited and discussed in both opinions in *Halbert* (and below as well). Where is the line drawn now? When does the right to appointed counsel cease to apply?

NOTES AND QUESTIONS ON FAIRNESS, EQUALITY, AND THE RIGHT TO COUNSEL

Both Justice Ginsburg's majority opinion and Justice Thomas's dissent agree that *Halbert* is essentially "bracketed" by two prior Court decisions: Douglas v. California and Ross v. Moffitt. *Douglas* held the right to appointed counsel applicable to first appeals as of right, while *Ross* held the same right inapplicable to discretionary appeals and applications for certiorari review in the Supreme Court. In *Halbert*, Ginsburg finds *Douglas* controlling, and describes that case as having been based on both the Equal Protection Clause and the Due Process Clause; she explains that the equal protection concern "relates to the legitimacy of fencing out would-be appellants based solely on their inability to pay core costs," while the due process concern "homes in on the essential fairness of the state-ordered proceedings." Thomas, meanwhile, complains that the Court never clearly states which constitutional provision underlies either *Douglas* or *Halbert*; he concludes that *Ross* controls *Halbert*, and that Michigan's rule is constitutionally valid because it does not create an "unreasoned distinction" that "arbitrarily" treats indigent defendants differently from nonindigent ones.

The same debate, involving the same paired concepts of equal protection and due process, can be traced through the entire line of Sixth Amendment cases beginning with *Douglas* and culminating in *Halbert*. *Douglas* was decided on the same day as *Gideon*, but the real story of *Douglas* began seven years earlier. In Griffin v. Illinois, 351 U.S. 12 (1956), the Court struck down an Illinois statute that denied free transcripts of trial proceedings to indigents in circumstances in which a transcript was necessary for an appeal under Illinois law. A four-person plurality, with Justice Frankfurter concurring, concluded that the Constitution prohibits a state from structuring an appellate process that has the effect of denying an effective review to indigents while permitting it to those with financial means.

If all *Griffin* stood for is that a state may not deny access to an important legal process on the basis of wealth, it still would have been an important decision interpreting the due process requirement of fundamental fairness in the criminal process, but not a particularly startling one. The plurality, however, did not stop at that point. Instead, the plurality suggested that the real issue in *Griffin* was not access but any discrimination at all between the rich and the poor. Indeed, the opinion went so far as to say: "There can be no equal justice when the kind of trial a man gets depends on the amount of money he has."[4] Were that to be taken literally, fundamental changes in the criminal process would have to be made, for surely a defendant of means is better off in myriad ways than an indigent one.

Douglas gave the appearance of beginning to take literally the dicta of *Griffin*. Petitioners in *Douglas* were convicted and appealed as of right to the California

---

4. See also the Report of the Attorney General's Committee on Poverty and Administration of Criminal Justice at pages 8-11 (1963): "One of the prime objectives of the civilized administration of justice is to render the poverty of the litigant an irrelevancy. While this is true of the entire range of judicial administration, the interests involved make the attainment of this objective peculiarly urgent in the administration of criminal justice. . . . When government chooses to exert its powers in the criminal area, its obligation is surely no less than that of taking reasonable measures to eliminate those factors that are irrelevant to just administration of the law but which, nevertheless, may occasionally affect determinations of the accused's liability or penalty. While government may not be required to relieve the accused of his poverty, it may properly be required to minimize the influence of poverty on its administration of justice."

Court of Appeal. On appeal, petitioners requested, and were denied, the assistance of appellate counsel. However, the denial came only after the court of appeal, following the applicable California rule of criminal procedure, made an independent investigation of the record to determine whether the assistance of counsel would be helpful to the petitioner or the court. Thus, petitioners were not denied access to the appellate process; they were only denied state-financed assistance after a determination was made that such assistance would be futile. Nonetheless, the Court found the California procedure unconstitutional, in large part on the basis of *Griffin*. Consequently, *Griffin*, as modified by *Douglas*, no longer appeared to be limitable to questions of access (if indeed it ever was).

The limits of *Douglas*, however, were always unclear. Read broadly, it would seem to require the extirpation of all differences resulting from the financial condition of defendants. However, it was difficult to tell from the opinions in *Douglas* how broadly to read it, because the underlying rationale of the decision was never adequately specified. As in *Griffin*, the decision could have been based either upon some notion of fairness that was now seen to extend beyond mere questions of access or, by contrast, upon the requirement of equal treatment. The greater the reliance on equal treatment as the operative principle, however, the more difficult it became to draw any limits on the reach of *Douglas*. And, indeed, as time went by, the Court appeared to interpret *Douglas* as establishing an equality principle that was then extended in a series of cases, with each succeeding case heightening the perceived tension between the equality principle and the other possible explanation for *Douglas* — fundamental fairness.

This process culminated in Ross v. Moffitt. In *Ross*, the defendant challenged North Carolina's procedures for the appeal of criminal cases not involving either a death sentence or life imprisonment. Under those rules, all such cases were appealable as of right to the North Carolina Court of Appeals (where indigent defendants were entitled, under *Douglas*, to appointed counsel to represent them); if the defendant lost and thereafter sought discretionary review in the North Carolina Supreme Court, however, no further right to appointed counsel was recognized. Justice Rehnquist wrote the majority opinion in *Ross*:

> The precise rationale for the *Griffin* and *Douglas* lines of cases has never been explicitly stated, some support being derived from the Equal Protection Clause of the Fourteenth Amendment, and some from the Due Process Clause of that Amendment.[8] Neither Clause by itself provides an entirely satisfactory basis for the result reached, each depending on a different inquiry which emphasizes different factors. "Due process" emphasizes fairness between the State and the individual dealing with the State, regardless of how other individuals in the same situation may be treated. "Equal protection," on the other hand, emphasizes disparity in treatment by a State between classes of individuals whose situations are arguably indistinguishable. . . .

---

8. The Court of Appeals in this case, for example, examined both possible rationales, stating: "If the holding [in *Douglas*] be grounded on the equal protection clause, inequality in the circumstances of these cases is as obvious as it was in the circumstances of *Douglas*. If the holding in *Douglas* were grounded on the Due Process Clause, and Mr. Justice Harlan in dissent thought the discourse should have been in those terms, due process encompasses elements of equality. There simply cannot be due process of the law to a litigant deprived of all professional assistance when other litigants, similarly situated, are able to obtain professional assistance and to be benefited by it. The same concepts of fairness and equality, which require counsel in a first appeal of right, require counsel in other and subsequent discretionary appeals." 483 F.2d, at 655.

Recognition of the due process rationale in *Douglas* is found both in the Court's opinion and in the dissenting opinion of Mr. Justice Harlan. The Court in *Douglas* stated that "[w]hen an indigent is forced to run this [gauntlet] of a preliminary showing of merit, the right to appeal does not comport with fair procedure." 372 U.S., at 357. Mr. Justice Harlan thought that the due process issue in *Douglas* was the only one worthy of extended consideration, remarking: "The real question in this case, I submit, and the only one that permits of satisfactory analysis, is whether or not the state rule, as applied in this case, is consistent with the requirements of fair procedure guaranteed by the Due Process Clause." Id., at 363.

We do not believe that the Due Process Clause requires North Carolina to provide respondent with counsel on his discretionary appeal to the State Supreme Court. At the trial stage of a criminal proceeding, the right of an indigent defendant to counsel is fundamental and binding upon the States by virtue of the Sixth and Fourteenth Amendments. Gideon v. Wainwright, 372 U.S. 335 (1963). But there are significant differences between the trial and appellate stages of a criminal proceeding. The purpose of the trial stage from the State's point of view is to convert a criminal defendant from a person presumed innocent to one found guilty beyond a reasonable doubt. To accomplish this purpose, the State employs a prosecuting attorney who presents evidence to the court, challenges any witnesses offered by the defendant, argues rulings of the court, and makes direct arguments to the court and jury seeking to persuade them of the defendant's guilt. Under these circumstances "reason and reflection require us to recognize that in our adversary system of criminal justice, any person haled into court, who is too poor to hire a lawyer, cannot be assured a fair trial unless counsel is provided for him." Id., at 344.

By contrast, it is ordinarily the defendant, rather than the State, who initiates the appellate process, seeking not to fend off the efforts of the State's prosecutor but rather to overturn a finding of guilt made by a judge or jury below. The defendant needs an attorney on appeal not as a shield to protect him against being "haled into court" by the State and stripped of his presumption of innocence, but rather as a sword to upset the prior determination of guilt. This difference is significant for, while no one would agree that the State may simply dispense with the trial stage of proceedings without a criminal defendant's consent, it is clear that the State need not provide any appeal at all. McKane v. Durston, 153 U.S. 684 (1894). The fact that an appeal *has* been provided does not automatically mean that a State then acts unfairly by refusing to provide counsel to indigent defendants at every stage of the way. Douglas v. California, supra. Unfairness results only if indigents are singled out by the State and denied meaningful access to the appellate system because of their poverty. That question is more profitably considered under an equal protection analysis.

Language invoking equal protection notions is prominent both in *Douglas* and in other cases treating the rights of indigents on appeal. The Court in *Douglas*, for example, stated: "[W]here the merits of *the one and only appeal* an indigent has as of right are decided without benefit of counsel, we think an unconstitutional line has been drawn between rich and poor." 372 U.S., at 357. (Emphasis in original.) . . .

. . . Despite the tendency of all rights "to declare themselves absolute to their logical extreme,"[9] there are obviously limits beyond which the equal protection analysis may not be pressed without doing violence to principles recognized in other decisions of this Court. The Fourteenth Amendment "does not require absolute equality or precisely equal advantages," San Antonio Independent School District v. Rodriguez, 411 U.S. 1, 24 (1973), nor does it require the State to "equalize economic conditions." Griffin v. Illinois, 351 U.S., at 23 (Frankfurter, J., concurring). It does require that the state appellate system be "free of unreasoned distinctions," Rinaldi v. Yeager, 384 U.S. 305,

---

9. Hudson County Water Co. v. McCarter, 209 U.S. 349, 355 (1908).

310 (1966), and that indigents have an adequate opportunity to present their claims fairly within the adversary system. Griffin v. Illinois, supra; Draper v. Washington, 372 U.S. 487 (1963). The State cannot adopt procedures which leave an indigent defendant "entirely cut off from any appeal at all," by virtue of his indigency, Lane v. Brown, 372 U.S., at 481, or extend to such indigent defendants merely a "meaningless ritual" while others in better economic circumstances have a "meaningful appeal." Douglas v. California, supra, at 358. The question is not one of absolutes, but one of degrees. In this case we do not believe that the Equal Protection Clause, when interpreted in the context of these cases, requires North Carolina to provide free counsel for indigent defendants seeking to take discretionary appeals to the North Carolina Supreme Court, or to file petitions for certiorari in this Court.

The facts show that respondent . . . received the benefit of counsel in examining the record of his trial and in preparing an appellate brief on his behalf for the state Court of Appeals. Thus, prior to his seeking discretionary review in the State Supreme Court, his claims had "once been presented by a lawyer and passed upon by an appellate court." Douglas v. California, 372 U.S., at 356. We do not believe that it can be said, therefore, that a defendant in respondent's circumstances is denied meaningful access to the North Carolina Supreme Court simply because the State does not appoint counsel to aid him in seeking review in that court. At that stage he will have, at the very least, a transcript or other record of trial proceedings, a brief on his behalf in the Court of Appeals setting forth his claims of error, and in many cases an opinion by the Court of Appeals disposing of his case. These materials, supplemented by whatever submission respondent may make pro se, would appear to provide the Supreme Court of North Carolina with an adequate basis for its decision to grant or deny review.

We are fortified in this conclusion by our understanding of the function served by discretionary review in the North Carolina Supreme Court. The critical issue in that court, as we perceive it, is not whether there has been "a correct adjudication of guilt" in every individual case, see Griffin v. Illinois, 351 U.S., at 18, but rather whether "the subject matter of the appeal has significant public interest," whether "the cause involves legal principles of major significance to the jurisprudence of the State," or whether the decision below is in probable conflict with a decision of the Supreme Court. The Supreme Court may deny certiorari even though it believes that the decision of the Court of Appeals was incorrect, see Peaseley v. Virginia Iron, Coal & Coke Co., 282 N.C. 585, 194 S.E.2d 133 (1973), since a decision which appears incorrect may nevertheless fail to satisfy any of the criteria discussed above. Once a defendant's claims of error are organized and presented in a lawyerlike fashion to the Court of Appeals, the justices of the Supreme Court of North Carolina who make the decision to grant or deny discretionary review should be able to ascertain whether his case satisfies the standards established by the legislature for such review.

This is not to say, of course, that a skilled lawyer, particularly one trained in the somewhat arcane art of preparing petitions for discretionary review, would not prove helpful to any litigant able to employ him. An indigent defendant seeking review in the Supreme Court of North Carolina is therefore somewhat handicapped in comparison with a wealthy defendant who has counsel assisting him in every conceivable manner at every stage in the proceeding. But both the opportunity to have counsel prepare an initial brief in the Court of Appeals and the nature of discretionary review in the Supreme Court of North Carolina make this relative handicap far less than the handicap borne by the indigent defendant denied counsel on his initial appeal as of right in *Douglas*. And the fact that a particular service might be of benefit to an indigent defendant does not mean that the service is constitutionally required. The duty of the State under our cases is not to duplicate the legal arsenal that may be privately retained by a criminal defendant in a continuing effort to reverse his conviction, but only to assure the indigent defendant an adequate opportunity to present his claims fairly in the context of the State's appellate process. We think respondent was given that opportunity under the existing North Carolina system.

Much of the discussion in the preceding section is equally relevant to the question of whether a State must provide counsel for a defendant seeking review of his conviction in this Court. North Carolina will have provided counsel for a convicted defendant's only appeal as of right, and the brief prepared by that counsel together with one and perhaps two North Carolina appellate opinions will be available to this Court in order that it may decide whether or not to grant certiorari. This Court's review, much like that of the Supreme Court of North Carolina, is discretionary and depends on numerous factors other than the perceived correctness of the judgment we are asked to review.

There is also a significant difference between the source of the right to seek discretionary review in the Supreme Court of North Carolina and the source of the right to seek discretionary review in this Court. The former is conferred by the statutes of the State of North Carolina, but the latter is granted by statute enacted by Congress. Thus the argument relied upon in the *Griffin* and *Douglas* cases, that the State having once created a right of appeal must give all persons an equal opportunity to enjoy the right, is by its terms inapplicable. The right to seek certiorari in this Court is not granted by any State, and exists by virtue of federal statute with or without the consent of the State whose judgment is sought to be reviewed.

The suggestion that a State is responsible for providing counsel to one petitioning this Court simply because it initiated the prosecution which led to the judgment sought to be reviewed is unsupported by either reason or authority. It would be quite as logical under the rationale of *Douglas* and *Griffin*, and indeed perhaps more so, to require that the Federal Government or this Court furnish and compensate counsel for petitioners who seek certiorari here to review state judgments of conviction. Yet this Court has followed a consistent policy of denying applications for appointment of counsel by persons seeking to file jurisdictional statements or petitions for certiorari in this Court. See, e.g., Drumm v. California, 373 U.S. 947 (1963). . . . In the light of these authorities, it would be odd, indeed, to read the Fourteenth Amendment to impose such a requirement on the States, and we decline to do so. . . .

Id., at 608-617.

Assuming that it is helpful to try to distinguish "fairness" from "equality," what does "fairness" seem to mean to the Court in the context of *Ross*? What are the word's parameters and, more important, how were they reached? Can the Court be serious, for example, when it says "unfairness results only if indigents are singled out by the State and denied meaningful access to the appellate system because of their poverty"? Why should access be the sole criterion of fairness? What role should other values play, such as reliability in factfinding or concern for basic notions of human dignity? Indeed, if access is the primary criterion, does *Ross* substantially undercut *Douglas*? If not, what does the word "access" mean, and why isn't that meaning just as applicable to the petitioner in *Ross* as it was to those in *Douglas*?

Maybe the real problem is not with the meaning of "access" or "fairness," but instead with the meaning of "equality." Do "fairness" and "access" differ from "equality" in any meaningful or useful way? Consider the following exchange.

PETER WESTEN, THE EMPTY IDEA OF EQUALITY, 95 HARV. L. REV. 537, 539-540, 543-545, 545-550 (1982): Equality is commonly perceived to differ from rights and liberties. . . .

I believe that this contrasting of rights and equality is fundamentally misconceived. It is based on a misunderstanding, both in law and in morals, about the role of equality in ethical discourse. To avoid possible misunderstanding, let me emphasize what I mean by equality and rights. By "equality" I mean the proposition in law and morals that "people who are alike should be treated alike" and its correlative, that "people who are unalike should be treated unalike." Equality thus includes all statements to the effect that the reason one person should be treated in a certain way is that he is "like" or "equal to" or "similar to" or "identical to" or "the same as" another who receives such treatment. "Rights," by contrast, means all claims that can justly be made by or on behalf of an individual or group of individuals to some condition or power — except claims that "people who are alike be treated alike." . . .

The proposition that "likes should be treated alike" is said to be a universal moral truth — a truth that can "be intuitively known with perfect clearness and certainty." Why? What is the connection between the fact that people are alike and the normative conclusion that they ought to be treated alike? How can one move from an "is" to an "ought"?

The answer can be found in the component parts of the equality formula. The formula "people who are alike should be treated alike" involves two components: (1) a determination that two people are alike; and (2) a moral judgment that they ought to be treated alike. The determinative component is the first. Once one determines that two people are alike for purposes of the equality principle, one knows how they ought to be treated. To understand why this is so — that is, to understand how (1) works — one must understand what kind of determination (1) is. One must know precisely what it means to say for purposes of equality that two persons are alike.

First, "people who are alike" might mean people who are alike in every respect. The trouble is that no two people are alike in every respect. The only things that are completely alike in every respect are immaterial symbols and forms, such as ideal numbers and geometric figures, which are not themselves the subject of morals.

Second, "people who are alike" may mean people, who, though not alike in every respect, are alike in some respects. Unfortunately, while the previous definition excludes every person in the world, the present definition includes every person and thing because all people and things are alike in some respect; and one is left with the morally absurd proposition that "all people and things should be treated alike."

Third, "people who are alike" may refer to people who are *morally* alike in a certain respect. The latter interpretation successfully avoids the philosophical hurdle of deriving an "ought" from an "is." It starts with a normative determination that two people are alike in a morally significant respect and moves to a normative conclusion that the two should be treated alike. Instead of deriving an "ought" from an "is," it derives an "ought" from an "ought." However, categories of morally alike objects do not exist in nature; moral alikeness is established only when people define categories. To say that people are morally alike is therefore to articulate a moral standard of treatment — a standard or rule specifying certain treatment for certain people — by reference to which they are, and thus are to be treated, alike. . . . Just as no categories of "like" people exist in nature, neither do categories of "like" treatment exist; treatments can be alike only in reference to some moral rule. Thus, to say that people who are morally alike in a certain respect "should be treated alike" means that they should be treated in accord with the moral rule by which they are determined to be alike. Hence "likes should be treated alike" means that people for whom a certain treatment is prescribed by a standard should all be given the treatment prescribed by the standard. Or, more simply, people who by a rule should be treated alike should by the rule be treated alike.

So there it is: Equality is entirely "[c]ircular." It tells us to treat like people alike; but when we ask who "like people" are, we are told they are "people who should be treated alike." Equality is an empty vessel with no substantive moral content of its own. Without moral standards, equality remains meaningless, a formula that can have nothing to say about how we should act. With such standards, equality becomes superfluous, a formula that can do nothing but repeat what we already know. As Bernard Williams observed, "when the statement of equality ceases to claim more than is warranted, it rather rapidly reaches the point where it claims less than is interesting." . . . Relationships of equality (and inequality) are derivative, secondary relationships; they are logically posterior, not anterior, to rights. To say that two persons are the same in a certain respect is to presuppose a rule — a prescribed standard for treating them — that both fully satisfy. Before such a rule is established, no standard of comparison exists. After such a rule is established, equality between them is a "logical consequence" of the established rule. They are then "equal" in respect of the rule because that is what equal means: "Equally" means "according to one and the same rule." They are also then entitled to equal treatment under the rule because that is what possessing a rule means: "To conform to a rule is (tautologically) to apply it to the cases to which it applies." To say that two people are "equal" and entitled to be treated "equally" is to say that they both fully satisfy the criteria of a governing rule of treatment. It says nothing at all about the content or wisdom of the governing rule. . . .

It might be thought that, while relationships of equality logically follow substantive definitions of right, equality may also precede definitions of right. Thus, it might be thought that a substantive right of persons to be treated with human respect is itself a product of an antecedent judgment that all persons are equal. That is not so. To see why, consider how one would go about deciding whether monstrously deformed neonates or human embryos or stroke victims in irreversible comas should be treated as "persons" for purposes of the right to respect. In trying to make the decision, one gets nowhere by intoning that all persons are equal, because the very question is whether the three candidates are indeed "persons" within the meaning of the rule. Nor does it do any good to say that likes should be treated alike, because the very question is whether the three candidates are indeed alike for purposes of human respect. Rather, one must first identify the trait that entitles anyone to be treated with respect and then ascertain empirically whether the trait appears in one or more of the three candidates.[40] If the candidates possess the relevant trait, they become "persons" within the meaning of the rule and hence

40. The issue of the empirical basis for moral traits has caused some confusion. Some commentators, believing that relationships of equality must be grounded in some verifiable traits, tend to conclude that equality is entirely empirical. . . . others, believing that an "ought" cannot be inferred from an "is," tend to conclude that moral notions of equality have no empirical basis. . . . In fact, both contending camps are correct. Statements of moral and legal equality do have an empirical base, because otherwise one would have no way of distinguishing those creatures who are equal from those who are not. . . . Yet at the same time, statements of moral or legal equality also presuppose a normative element. . . . In short, statements of equality presuppose the presence of empirical traits that we decide ought to carry certain moral consequences.

entitled to respect. If they lack the relevant trait, they are not "persons," not equal to persons, and not to be treated like persons for purposes of the rule.

STEVEN BURTON, COMMENT ON "EMPTY IDEAS": LOGICAL POSITIVIST ANALYSES OF EQUALITY AND RULES, 91 YALE L.J. 1136-1141, 1144-1147 (1982): In a recent article in the Harvard Law Review, Professor Peter Westen directs his considerable capacity for logical analysis at the idea of equality. Professor Westen asserts and defends "two propositions: (1) that statements of equality logically entail (and necessarily collapse into) simpler statements of rights; and (2) that the additional step of transforming simple statements of rights into statements of equality not only involves unnecessary work but also engenders profound conceptual confusion." Therefore, he says, equality is an "empty idea" that "should be banished from moral and legal discourse as an explanatory norm."

Many, no doubt, will wish to defend equality as a concept with independent content, at least in some situations. This Comment takes a different tack. "Statements of rights" (rules) are the heroes of Professor Westen's story, though they are spared the scrutiny lavished on equality. He seems to regard rules as suitable norms for explanatory moral and legal discourse — norms that in themselves are independent of equality, imbued with content, and comparatively simple to apply without confusion.[4] Using methods of logical analysis similar to those Westen used to criticize equality, this Comment will demonstrate that rules collapse into equality and also are empty, in the sense that Westen regards equality as empty. By the logical positivist method of analysis, both equality and rules must be banished from explanatory legal and moral discourse, a move that would render such discourse impossible. The alternative is to reject that method of analysis because it proves too much, and to retain both equality and rules as instruments of thought and argument. . . .

Now the assumption seems to be that "the terms of the rule *dictate* that it be applied," and that they do so by an intellectual process that does not depend of necessity on considerations of equality, or on other norms that are vulnerable to the criticisms made of equality.[13] Though Professor Westen did not undertake to analyze the logic of rules in his paper, such an analysis is necessary to the soundness of his thesis, which appeals to the meaningfulness and analytical simplicity of rules as contrasted with equality. We would have two choices if the idea of substantive rights, determined by

4. . . . Professor Westen might regard substantive rights as empty ideas analytically, but useful ones nonetheless. Cf. Westen at 579 n. 147. ("Some formal concepts [such as rights] are quite handy, even indispensible [*sic*].") He argues that equality as a form of analysis is not useful, id., at 577-592, largely because "people do not realize that [equality] is derivative [from substantive rights], and not realizing it, they allow equality to distort the substance of their decisionmaking." Id., at 592. It would seem to be at least equally so that "people" often do not realize that statements of substantive rights themselves are empty of content in the same sense, and allow the so-called plain meanings of such statements to distort their decision making. Westen offers no empirical grounds for concluding that equality causes more confusion than rules. Cf. infra Note 14 (such grounds might support Westen's position if rights did not collapse into equality); Note 50 (like equality, rules hide their incompleteness).

13. To summarize, the principal criticisms were (1) that statements of equality have no substantive content *of their own*, but depend on norms outside equality *itself*, id., at 553, 566, 571-572, 574, 577-778, 580-881; (2) that equality is a wholly normative concept, lacking the identification of empirical traits, the presence of which would entitle a person to the treatment claimed, id., at 544-547, 549; and (3) that application of the equality norm requires logically illicit moves between "is" and "ought," id., at 544-545. To justify banishing equality while retaining rules requires at least that rules be different from and better than equality by the same criteria.

the language of rules, were as empty as, and collapsed into, the idea of equality. We could conclude that rules also should be "banished from moral and legal discourse as an explanatory norm," or that neither concept should be banished because the method of analysis yielding such an absurd result is inappropriate. . . .

It is simply wrong, however, to suggest that substantive rights can be determined in any case without reference to a person's normative relationship to other rights-holders, at least if the statement is meant to convey what is involved in legal reasoning. Let us consider the right of free speech. The general terms of the First Amendment appear on their face to be simple to apply: "Congress shall make no law . . . abridging the freedom of speech. . . ." We will apply this general proscription to two particular cases, which will serve as illustrations throughout the remainder of this Part.

Imagine that a state has made it a crime to hang the Governor in effigy, and that a state has made it a crime to hang any person, including the Governor. It will be seen that the Supreme Court could not reach conclusions as to the validity of these laws without considering the normative relationship of (1) hanging the Governor or (2) hanging the Governor in effigy to other activities that enjoy (or do not enjoy) First Amendment protection. The Court must determine whether hanging the Governor in effigy or in the flesh is in some important aspect "like" such other activities — for example, (3) making a public speech criticizing the Governor or (4) hanging one's spouse. Because "the terms of the rule" do not "dictate" which aspect of each activity is *important*, arguments based on the rule collapse into arguments by analogy, which themselves are claims to equal treatment under the law. . . .

. . . In the analysis of reasoning, analogies necessarily appeal to the principle that "like cases should be treated alike" — the equality principle — and are vulnerable to the criticisms Westen makes of equality, to the same extent. . . .

To separate rules from equality completely, one who would adopt Professor Westen's position seems forced to regard legal reasoning as fundamentally deductive, rather than purposive, inductive, or analogical in character. Only a logical positivist model of legal reasoning can purport to explain rules and rights independently of equality or other similarly vulnerable norms. Thus, in the hypothetical free speech cases, a statement of the state's general duty of behavior (the rule) would stand as the major premise of a syllogism. A statement of the state's treatment of the person (the facts) would stand as the minor premise. Whether the state acted in accord with its duty would depend on whether the rule logically entailed the facts.

That this is Professor Westen's view of all defensible legal reasoning seems a fair interpretation of his expressions in this work, despite the facial implausibility of such a mechanical model. To repeat, he says that "[t]o decide whether a person's speech rights are violated, one *juxtaposes* the state's general duty of behavior against the state's particular treatment of the person to determine whether the state treats the person in *accord* with its prescribed duty." He emphasizes that equality between two persons "is a 'logical consequence' of the established rule." Thus, "[r]elationships of equality are derivative, secondary relationships; they are logically posterior, not anterior, to rights." . . .

I suggest that the two Governor-hanging cases are clear because we engage in analogical reasoning. We posit a clear case of protected speech (a lecture criticizing the Governor's policies) and a clear case of murder (killing one's spouse). In the light of the values underlying the First Amendment, we regard hanging the Governor in effigy as more like the first case, and hanging the Governor as more like the second. And we regard all four cases as easy ones. Of course, no two of the four cases are alike in all respects, and all four cases are alike in some respects. We make a normative judgment as to what respects are the important ones.

That judgment, however, is not a logical consequence of the terms of the First Amendment, which cannot be applied in a particular case without recourse to such analogies. For example, all four cases are "expression" in some respect, while none of the four cases is "expression" in all respects; and all are "anti-social behaviors" in some but not all respects. To apply the rule, we must make judgments about which respects are important in each case. The judgment of importance in applying a rule, like the judgment of similarity in using an analogy, depends on unspecified values outside the rule itself, and involves us in analytical problems of moving from "ought" to "is" when we apply the rule. Professor Westen therefore errs in stating that the conclusions are the "logical consequences" of the rule — not normative judgments but logically deduced from a "given." Where are the "given" rules that distinguish the Governor-hanging cases?

To test the point further, let us posit some rules (really meta-rules) that stand on a different logical plane and tell us how to apply the enacted rules: (1) The First Amendment shall not invalidate state statutes if the statutes are necessary to protect a compelling state interest; and (2) a constitutional provision shall be construed according to the intention of the Framers or according to its purpose. It should be observed that both of the meta-rules are judge-made and consequently partake of the problems of common-law rules, making the process of applying enacted rules wholly dependent on analogical reasoning in the same manner. But let us pass over that problem and inquire whether these rules can be applied without engaging in reasoning by analogy — without using the equality principle to determine substantive rights.

The logic of the so-called "compelling state interest" test is fairly transparent. To say that the First Amendment invalidates a state statute unless the statute is necessary to protect a compelling state interest is logically reducible to saying something like: Freedom of expression is more important than a state statute unless the state statute is more important than freedom of expression. Again, what do we mean by "important"? Surely nothing follows as a "logical consequence" in any real-world case from "important" as the key term in the major premise of a syllogism. Neither "compelling state interest" nor "importance" are things that exist in nature (observables), nor can they be reduced analytically to necessary and sufficient conditions that are observable without deriving an "is" from an "ought." They are normative concepts. As such, they beg the question whether application of a state murder statute to one who hung the Governor, or a state statute against hanging the Governor in effigy, should be invalidated by the First Amendment: It should if it should. One might offer another rule to tell us, as a "logical consequence," what a compelling state interest is — a meta-meta-rule — but it should be apparent that this tack leads to an infinite regress of no small significance.

The logic of construing a constitutional provision according to the intention of the Framers or according to its purpose could lead us into a similar regress. Neither "intention" nor "purpose" are observables, if we state them in the abstract. We can say that the Framers intended the First Amendment to protect "expression" or "political expression," though they said "speech" or that this was the purpose of the text. The problems of knowing such things, with the assurance necessary to exclude de novo normative judgments, are well-known. And even if we knew that the Framers had such an intention or purpose, we still do not know that hanging the Governor in effigy and in the flesh are not both "expression," or neither "expression," or one "expression" and the other not, or the other "expression" and the one not, so far as the logical consequences of the meta-rule take us. Again, we need a meta-meta-rule and are off into the darkness of a regress.

Alternatively, the purpose or intention (of "freedom of speech" or of "compelling state interest") can be stated in the particular. To do so, however, is to state a case, be it hypothetical or historical. To say merely that the evil before the minds of the Framers was, for example, suppression of the political opposition is again abstract, a negative version of the statement analyzed in the preceding paragraph. We must have a *case*, such as what happened to Zenger, or what Zenger did. As "general propositions do not decide concrete cases," however, "[c]oncrete decisions do not make law." What Zenger did can be described in narrow terms and limited to the press, or in broad terms and expanded to cover all thought and action. Another meta-meta-rule seems necessary to tell us what the rule of the Zenger case is, unless we break the regress by shifting from deduction to analogy. Then, we might say, hanging the Governor in effigy is like what Zenger did but hanging the Governor is not, and all might agree.

Of course, shifting from deduction to analogy (equality) does not solve our problems as analysts of legal reasoning. The problem identified by Professor Westen and others — identifying normative grounds for purposes of determining whether cases are alike or unalike — is no small problem. It is not solved, however, by shifting from equality to rules, which also depend on unspecified values outside the rules themselves. Thus, if rules are given the same kind of intensive logical analysis that Westen gives to equality, they too stand empty and collapse into equality. This logical analysis of rules and equality drives us back and forth between the two in a regress, as when we stand between the barber's mirrors. . . .

_____

The debate over the nature of equality has a long philosophical history, but it also has an immediate practical significance. The notion that like cases should be treated alike has a strong rational and emotional pull; but without substantive determinations of what counts in determining "like cases," the commitment to treating like cases alike appears empty. Consider a concrete example. What does it mean to provide equal medical insurance to males and females? Does it violate equality to cover pregnancy, since that provides a benefit that only females can take advantage of? Or does it violate equality by excluding a major health issue from coverage, and where no analogous issue is excluded for males? Or consider pension benefits on the assumption that the life expectancy of males is shorter than females. Should males and females be paid the same monthly benefits or instead an amount that actuarially will result in equal payouts over the lives of both? These examples point out what is at stake in the Weston/Burton debate: Before one can analyze "equality," one needs to know what counts for the analysis. For an extended development of this idea, see Amartya Sen, Inequality Reexamined (1992).

Return to the criminal procedure battleground on which this debate is fought: the scope of the right to counsel and other assistance. One consequence of granting the right to state-paid counsel and other forms of assistance, whether at trial or on appeal or anywhere else, is to reduce the likelihood of errors that favor the state. Innocent Gideons are less likely to be convicted in a regime that gives them help. The flip side of this proposition is equally clear: Denying state assistance raises the risk of errors that favor the state. The decision to extend or contract the *Gideon* right is a decision about whether to tolerate a higher risk of error in the state's favor. And of course it is also a decision about how much lowering the risk of wrongful conviction is worth.

Your views about that decision — and thus your views about the equality versus fairness debate explored above — might depend on just what issues are on the table. If the question is whether Gideon in fact broke into the poolroom as the state charged, there would be widespread agreement that any substantial risk of error in the state's favor is unacceptable. But suppose the question is whether a police officer read the *Miranda* warnings correctly before questioning the defendant, or whether an officer had probable cause to search the trunk of the defendant's car, or whether the prosecutor's peremptory challenges were prompted by racial stereotypes. Should the system be willing to tolerate a higher risk of error for questions like these than for issues that bear more directly on guilt and innocence? In practice, it does: The burden of persuasion on issues of the sort just mentioned is usually a preponderance of the evidence, while guilt must be proved beyond a reasonable doubt. Errors on some issues are treated as less important than errors on others.

Perhaps this divide, between issues on which errors in the state's favor are seen as intolerable and issues for which that is not so, suggests why the Court's right-to-counsel jurisprudence might be unsatisfying. The right to counsel, like burdens of persuasion, is in part about allocating the risk of error. With burden-of-proof law, we allocate that risk issue by issue; the burden can be assigned differently on different issues in the same proceeding. The right to counsel cannot work that way as a practical matter. Defendants either receive state-paid counsel on discretionary state appeals or they do not: No one suggests giving defendants counsel with respect to sufficiency-of-the-evidence claims but not with respect to challenges to evidentiary rulings. The result may be that the right to counsel must always go too far or not far enough, since wherever the right is granted (or denied), it affects a range of issues, some of which are more important to resolve correctly than others.

What do you think?

NOTES AND QUESTIONS ABOUT OTHER FORMS OF ASSISTANCE

1. Recall that *Douglas* held that a criminal defendant has the right to counsel — under the Fourteenth Amendment, not the Sixth Amendment — on his first appeal as of right. Evitts v. Lucey, 469 U.S. 387 (1985), addressed the related question "whether the Due Process Clause of the Fourteenth Amendment guarantees the criminal defendant the effective assistance of counsel on such an appeal." In other words, does the right to counsel carry with it the corresponding right to have that counsel perform to a minimally acceptable level? At trial, where the *Gideon* right to counsel applies, the answer is clearly yes, as we will explore later in this

chapter. What about on appeal? In *Evitts*, the Court, in an opinion by Justice Brennan, held that the answer to this question is also yes:

Almost a century ago, the Court held that the Constitution does not require States to grant appeals as of right to criminal defendants seeking to review alleged trial court errors. McKane v. Durston, 153 U.S. 684 (1894). Nonetheless, if a State has created appellate courts as "an integral part of the . . . system for finally adjudicating the guilt or innocence of a defendant," Griffin v. Illinois, 351 U.S., at 18, the procedures used in deciding appeals must comport with the demands of the Due Process and Equal Protection Clauses of the Constitution. . . .

The two lines of cases . . . recognizing the right to counsel on a first appeal as of right and . . . recognizing that the right to counsel at trial includes a right to effective assistance of counsel . . . are dispositive of respondent's claim. In bringing an appeal as of right from his conviction, a criminal defendant is attempting to demonstrate that the conviction, and the consequent drastic loss of liberty, is unlawful. To prosecute the appeal, a criminal appellant must face an adversary proceeding that — like a trial — is governed by intricate rules that to a layperson would be hopelessly forbidding. An unrepresented appellant — like an unrepresented defendant at trial — is unable to protect the vital interests at stake. . . .

A first appeal as of right therefore is not adjudicated in accord with due process of law if the appellant does not have the effective assistance of an attorney.[7] . . .

The right to an appeal would be unique among state actions if it could be withdrawn without consideration of applicable due process norms. For instance, although a State may choose whether it will institute any given welfare program, it must operate whatever programs it does establish subject to the protections of the Due Process Clause. See Goldberg v. Kelly, 397 U.S. 254, 262 (1970). . . . In short, when a State opts to act in a field where its action has significant discretionary elements, it must nonetheless act in accord with the dictates of the Constitution — and, in particular, in accord with the Due Process Clause. . . .

According to the petitioners, the constitutional requirements recognized in *Griffin*, *Douglas*, and the cases that followed had their source in the Equal Protection Clause, and not the Due Process Clause, of the Fourteenth Amendment. In support of this contention, petitioners point out that all of the cases in the *Griffin* line have involved claims by indigent defendants that they have the same right to a decision on the merits of their appeal as do wealthier defendants who are able to afford lawyers, transcripts, or the other prerequisites of a fair adjudication on the merits. As such, petitioners claim, the cases all should be understood as equal protection cases challenging the constitutional validity of the distinction made between rich and poor criminal defendants. Petitioners conclude that if the Due Process Clause permits criminal appeals as of right to be forfeited because the appellant has no transcript or no attorney, it surely permits such appeals to be forfeited when the appellant has an attorney who is unable to assist in prosecuting the appeal.

Petitioners' argument rests on a misunderstanding of the diverse sources of our holdings in this area. In Ross v. Moffitt, we held that "[t]he precise rationale for the *Griffin* and *Douglas* lines of cases has never been explicitly stated, some support being derived from the Equal Protection Clause of the Fourteenth Amendment, and some from the Due Process Clause of that Amendment." This rather clear statement in *Ross* that the Due Process Clause played a significant role in prior decisions is well supported by the cases themselves. . . .

---

7. As Ross v. Moffitt, 417 U.S. 600 (1974), held, the considerations governing a discretionary appeal are somewhat different. Of course, the right to effective assistance of counsel is dependent on the right to counsel itself. . . .

Justice Rehnquist, in dissent, responded:

> There is no constitutional requirement that a State provide an appeal at all. . . . McKane v. Durston, 153 U.S. 684, 687 (1894). If a State decides to confer a right of appeal, it is free to do so "upon such terms as in its wisdom may be deemed proper." Id., at 687-688. . . . Proper analysis of our precedents would indicate that apart from the Equal Protection Clause, which respondent has not invoked in this case, there cannot be a constitutional right to *counsel* on appeal, and that, therefore, even under the logic of the Court there cannot be derived a constitutional right to *effective assistance of counsel* on appeal.

According to Justice Rehnquist, in other words, the defendant must take the "bitter with the sweet" — having no constitutional right to an appeal at all, due process cannot be violated when the state chooses to give him an appeal, but then precludes him from complaining about his appellate lawyer's alleged ineffectiveness. Nor can this possibly be an equal protection violation, because the state's rule applies to all appellate lawyers — whether retained or appointed — the same way.

2. Can *Ross* and *Evitts* be reconciled? Compare *Evitts*, in turn, with the per curiam decision in Wainwright v. Torna, 455 U.S. 586 (1982), refusing to extend the right to the effective assistance of counsel to petitions for discretionary review:

> Respondent is in custody pursuant to several felony convictions. The Florida Supreme Court dismissed an application for a writ of certiorari, on the ground that the application was not filed timely. . . . A petition for rehearing and clarification was later denied. . . .
>
> In Ross v. Moffitt, . . . this Court held that a criminal defendant does not have a constitutional right to counsel to pursue discretionary state appeals or applications for review in this Court. Respondent does not contest the finding of the District Court that he had no absolute right to appeal his convictions to the Florida Supreme Court. Since respondent had no constitutional right to counsel, he could not be deprived of the effective assistance of counsel by his retained counsel's failure to file the application timely.[4] The District Court was correct in dismissing the petition.

Id., at 586-587. The Court subsequently held that there is no constitutional right to counsel at all in habeas corpus/collateral review proceedings (which are discussed in Chapter 17, infra). See Pennsylvania v. Finley, 481 U.S. 551 (1987) (Sixth Amendment right not applicable on habeas); Murray v. Giarratano, 492 U.S. 1, 10 (1989) (no due process right to counsel on "access to courts" theory in habeas).

3. Mayer v. City of Chicago, 404 U.S. 189 (1971), held that a state must provide an indigent defendant, free of charge, with a record of sufficient completeness to permit proper consideration of his claims on appeal, even though such a record is *not*, unlike in *Griffin*, a condition precedent for an appeal.

One interesting aspect of *Mayer* was the state's argument that *Griffin* should not be extended to cases in which the relevant sentence is a fine rather than imprisonment. The Court, per Justice Brennan, responded:

---

4. Respondent was not denied due process of law by the fact that counsel deprived him of his right to petition the Florida Supreme Court for review. Such deprivation — even if implicating a due process interest — was caused by his counsel, and not by the State. Certainly, the actions of the Florida Supreme Court in dismissing an application for review that was not filed timely did not deprive respondent of due process of law.

The city of Chicago urges another distinction to set this case apart from *Griffin* and its progeny. The city notes that the defendants in all the transcript cases previously decided by this Court were sentenced to some term of confinement. Where the accused, as here, is not subject to imprisonment, but only a fine, the city suggests that his interest in a transcript is outweighed by the State's fiscal and other interests in not burdening the appellate process. This argument misconceives the principle of *Griffin*. . . . *Griffin* does not represent a balance between the needs of the accused and the interests of society; its principle is a flat prohibition against pricing indigent defendants out of as effective an appeal as would be available to others able to pay their own way. The invidiousness of the discrimination that exists when criminal procedures are made available only to those who can pay is not erased by any differences in the sentences that may be imposed. The State's fiscal interest is, therefore, irrelevant.

We add that even approaching the problem in the terms the city suggests hardly yields the answer the city tenders. The practical effects of conviction of even petty offenses of the kind involved here are not to be minimized. A fine may bear as heavily on an indigent accused as forced confinement. The collateral consequences of conviction may be even more serious, as when (as was apparently a possibility in this case) the impecunious medical student finds himself barred from the practice of medicine because of a conviction he is unable to appeal for lack of funds. Moreover, the State's long-term interest would not appear to lie in making access to appellate processes from even its most inferior courts depend upon the defendant's ability to pay. It has been aptly said: "[F]ew citizens ever have contact with the higher courts. In the main, it is the police and the lower court Bench and Bar that convey the essence of our democracy to the people. Justice, if it can be measured, must be measured by the experience the average citizen has with the police and the lower courts."[7] Arbitrary denial of appellate review of proceedings of the State's lowest trial courts may save the State some dollars and cents, but only at the substantial risk of generating frustration and hostility toward its courts among the most numerous consumers of justice. . . .

Id., at 196-199.

4. The Supreme Court has extended, in certain respects, the same analysis developed in the *Griffin/Douglas* line of cases to civil suits. In M.L.B. v. S.L.J., 519 U.S. 102 (1996), a Mississippi Chancery Court terminated a mother's parental rights, and the mother appealed. Her appeal was dismissed because she could not pay the record preparation fees as required by a Mississippi statute. The Court held that the statute violated the Equal Protection and Due Process Clauses of the Fourteenth Amendment: "[J]ust as a state may not block an indigent petty offender's access to an appeal afforded others [see *Mayer*,] so Mississippi may not deny M.L.B. because of her poverty, appellate review of the sufficiency of the evidence on which the trial court found her unfit to remain a parent." This is the furthest extension of *Mayer* to date. In *M.L.B.*, Justice Thomas in a strong dissent argues that *Mayer* was wrongly decided and should be overruled.

Other examples of civil cases applying *Griffin/Douglas* include Boddie v. Connecticut, 401 U.S. 371 (1971), where the Court struck down a state filing fee that restricted the access of indigents to a divorce proceeding. In Little v. Streater, 452 U.S. 1 (1981), the Court held that the appellant, the putative father in a paternity suit, was denied due process when the state refused to fund potentially dispository blood-grouping tests that the appellant could not afford. However, on the same day

---

7. Patrick V. Murphy, The Role of the Police in Our Modern Society, 26 The Record of the Association of the Bar of the City of New York 292, 293 (1971).

Little was decided, the Court held in Lassiter v. Department of Social Services of Durham County, 452 U.S. 18 (1981), that failure to appoint counsel for indigent parents in a state-initiated proceeding to terminate parental status did not violate due process. For a discussion, see The Supreme Court, 1980 Term: Indigents' Rights to State Funding in Civil Actions, 95 Harv. L. Rev. 132 (1981). For a discussion of the general problem of providing indigents access to legal services, see Note, Court Appointment of Attorneys in Civil Cases: The Constitutionality of Uncompensated Legal Assistance, 81 Colum. L. Rev. 366 (1981).

5. Statutes in various jurisdictions provide for the furnishing of aid to indigents, other than counsel and transcripts, that may assist in the preparation for trial or be useful at trial itself (e.g., investigative aids or expert evaluation and testimony). In federal litigation, the relevant statute is 18 U.S.C. §3006A, which also provides for the appointment of counsel on habeas "in the interests of justice" in cases not involving the death penalty.[7]

In Ake v. Oklahoma, 470 U.S. 68 (1985), the Court held that when an indigent defendant "demonstrates to the trial judge that his sanity at the time of the offense is to be a significant factor at trial, the State must, at a minimum, assure the defendant access to a competent psychiatrist who will conduct an appropriate examination and assist in evaluation, preparation, and presentation of the defense." 470 U.S., at 83. In emphasizing that a defendant must have access to the "basic tools of an adequate defense," id., at 77, the Court further held that a defendant must have access to psychiatric expertise if his future dangerousness is relevant as an aggravating factor in a capital sentencing proceeding.

B.   *Effective Assistance of Counsel*

1.   The Meaning of Effective Assistance

The mere appointment of counsel does not satisfy the constitutional guarantee of right to counsel. Indeed, the trial court in Powell v. Alabama appointed counsel but in such a way as to preclude the giving of effective aid in the preparation and trial of the case. The concern for effectiveness has been a consistent thread running through the Supreme Court's cases, as evidenced by the rhetoric in McMann v. Richardson, 397 U.S. 759 (1970) ("if the right to counsel guaranteed by the Constitution

---

7. As for death penalty cases, the Anti-Drug Abuse Act of 1988, 21 U.S.C.A. §§848(q) and 848(r) (West 1994 & Supp. 1998), requires the appointment of counsel for indigent prisoners seeking to set aside a death sentence in federal habeas corpus proceedings (under either 28 U.S.C. §2254, for state prisoners, or 28 U.S.C. §2255, for federal prisoners). The Supreme Court, in McFarland v. Scott, 512 U.S. 849 (1994), held that appointment of counsel under this statute can be made prior to the actual filing of the habeas corpus petition (i.e., upon the prisoner's filing of a motion seeking counsel to help with the preparation of a habeas corpus petition). In the Anti-Terrorism and Effective Death Penalty Act of 1996 (AEDPA), Congress added a section to the federal habeas corpus statute that allows states to "opt in" to a new system providing accelerated habeas procedures for capital cases. The qualifications include the requirement that the state must provide qualified counsel in state postconviction proceedings for indigent prisoners seeking to set aside a death sentence. See 28 U.S.C. §2261. The statute further provides: "The ineffectiveness or incompetence of counsel during State or Federal post-conviction proceedings in a capital case shall not be a ground for relief in a [federal habeas corpus] proceeding arising under section 2254." See 28 U.S.C. §2261(e). In short, under the "opt-in" part of AEDPA, death-row inmates get a broader statutory right to appointed counsel, but cannot challenge counsel's effectiveness. The Court has not yet ruled on this provision's constitutionality.

is to serve its purpose, defendants cannot be left to the mercies of incompetent counsel," id., at 771).

To ensure the basic conditions under which effective assistance is likely to be obtained, the Supreme Court has rendered a series of decisions prohibiting certain forms of interference with the attorney-client relationship. An attorney may not be prohibited from conferring with the client during an overnight recess that falls between direct examination and cross-examination. Geders v. United States, 425 U.S. 80 (1976). A lawyer may not be denied the right to give a closing summation in a nonjury trial. Herring v. New York, 422 U.S. 853 (1975). The state may not prohibit the attorney from eliciting the client's testimony on direct examination, Ferguson v. Georgia, 365 U.S. 570 (1961), nor may the state restrict the attorney's choice as to when to put the defendant on the stand, Brooks v. Tennessee, 406 U.S. 605 (1972). There are limits on the Court's solicitude for criminal defendants, however. In Perry v. Leeke, 488 U.S. 272 (1989), the Court held that the trial court did not err by ordering the defendant not to consult with his lawyer during a 15-minute recess that immediately followed his direct examination and preceded cross-examination.

Outside of these, and similar, relatively narrow areas, during much of the nation's history the lower courts almost uniformly adopted the "mockery of justice" standard to test claims of ineffectiveness under which ineffectiveness was found only in such shocking circumstances as to reduce the trial to a farce or charade. Even inebriated counsel often was insufficient cause to find lack of effectiveness.

The mockery of justice standard seems inordinately low, but there are some justifications for it. The higher the level of scrutiny, the greater is the impetus on the part of the trial judge to intervene in derogation of basic premises of the adversary system. Moreover, intervention may occur at a point of what appears to be problematic action by counsel but in fact is an integral part of a trial strategy known only to counsel. Also, the more active trial judges become, the more they are implicitly or explicitly critical of the bar that practices before them; and the more active appellate courts become, the more critical they become of the trial judges.

Beginning around 1970, a large proportion of the states, and most of the federal circuits, replaced the mockery of justice standard with one that requires counsel to possess and exercise the legal competence customarily found in the jurisdiction. For an early and influential example, see Moore v. United States, 432 F.2d 730 (3d Cir. 1970). Two developments stimulated this change. The first was the Supreme Court's legitimation of plea bargaining in 1970. See Chapter 13, infra. If pleas were now to receive greater protection against challenge, then the legal advice received by an accused assumes greater importance. Moreover, one of the challenges to a guilty plea that could not be deemed waived by it is the very advice that led to the plea in the first instance, which has the effect of focusing greater attention on the competency of counsel throughout the plea negotiations. The second development that stimulated a greater concern for the competency of counsel was the Supreme Court's tightening of the rules of habeas corpus (recently furthered by Congress). See Chapter 17, infra. As most avenues to relief for habeas petitioners have narrowed, the incentive to relitigate those closed avenues under the alternative rubric of the right to counsel has grown.

The Supreme Court finally turned to these issues in:

STRICKLAND v. WASHINGTON

Certiorari to the United States Court of Appeals for the Eleventh Circuit
466 U.S. 668 (1984)

JUSTICE O' CONNOR delivered the opinion of the Court.

This case requires us to consider the proper standards for judging a criminal defendant's contention that the Constitution requires a conviction or death sentence to be set aside because counsel's assistance at the trial or sentencing was ineffective.

I

A

During a ten-day period in September 1976, respondent planned and committed three groups of crimes, which included three brutal stabbing murders, torture, kidnapping, severe assaults, attempted murders, attempted extortion, and theft. After his two accomplices were arrested, respondent surrendered to police and voluntarily gave a lengthy statement confessing to the third of the criminal episodes. The State of Florida indicted respondent for kidnapping and murder and appointed an experienced criminal lawyer to represent him.

Counsel actively pursued pretrial motions and discovery. He cut his efforts short, however, and he experienced a sense of hopelessness about the case, when he learned that, against his specific advice, respondent had also confessed to the first two murders. By the date set for trial, respondent was subject to indictment for three counts of first degree murder and multiple counts of robbery, kidnapping for ransom, breaking and entering and assault, attempted murder, and conspiracy to commit robbery. Respondent waived his right to a jury trial, again acting against counsel's advice, and pleaded guilty to all charges, including the three capital murder charges.

In the plea colloquy, respondent told the trial judge that, although he had committed a string of burglaries, he had no significant prior criminal record and that at the time of his criminal spree he was under extreme stress caused by his inability to support his family. . . . He also stated, however, that he accepted responsibility for the crimes. . . . The trial judge told respondent that he had "a great deal of respect for people who are willing to step forward and admit their responsibility" but that he was making no statement at all about his likely sentencing decision. . . .

Counsel advised respondent to invoke his right under Florida law to an advisory jury at his capital sentencing hearing. Respondent rejected the advice and waived the right. He chose instead to be sentenced by the trial judge without a jury recommendation.

In preparing for the sentencing hearing, counsel spoke with respondent about his background. He also spoke on the telephone with respondent's wife and mother, though he did not follow up on the one unsuccessful effort to meet with them. He did not otherwise seek out character witnesses for respondent. . . . Nor did he request a psychiatric examination, since his conversations with his client gave no indication that respondent had psychological problems. . . .

Counsel decided not to present and hence not to look further for evidence concerning respondent's character and emotional state. That decision reflected trial counsel's sense of hopelessness about overcoming the evidentiary effect of respondent's confessions to the gruesome crimes. . . . It also reflected the judgment that it was advisable to rely on the plea colloquy for evidence about respondent's background and about his claim of emotional stress: The plea colloquy communicated sufficient information about these subjects, and by [forgoing] the opportunity to present new evidence on these subjects, counsel prevented the State from cross-examining respondent on his claim and from putting on psychiatric evidence of its own. . . .

Counsel also excluded from the sentencing hearing other evidence he thought was potentially damaging. He successfully moved to exclude respondent's "rap sheet." . . . Because he judged that a presentence report might prove more detrimental than helpful, as it would have included respondent's criminal history and thereby undermined the claim of no significant history of criminal activity, he did not request that one be prepared. . . .

At the sentencing hearing, counsel's strategy was based primarily on the trial judge's remarks at the plea colloquy as well as on his reputation as a sentencing judge who thought it important for a convicted defendant to own up to his crime. Counsel argued that respondent's remorse and acceptance of responsibility justified sparing him from the death penalty. . . . Counsel also argued that respondent had no history of criminal activity and that respondent committed the crimes under extreme mental or emotional disturbance, thus coming within the statutory list of mitigating circumstances. He further argued that respondent should be spared death because he had surrendered, confessed, and offered to testify against a co-defendant and because respondent was fundamentally a good person who had briefly gone badly wrong in extremely stressful circumstances. The State put on evidence and witnesses largely for the purpose of describing the details of the crimes. Counsel did not cross-examine the medical experts who testified about the manner of death of respondent's victims. . . .

. . . The trial judge found numerous aggravating circumstances and no (or a single comparatively insignificant) mitigating circumstance. With respect to each of the three convictions for capital murder, the trial judge concluded: "A careful consideration of all matters presented to the court impels the conclusion that there are insufficient mitigating circumstances . . . to outweigh the aggravating circumstances." He therefore sentenced respondent to death on each of the three counts of murder and to prison terms for the other crimes. The Florida Supreme Court upheld the convictions and sentences on direct appeal. . . .

C

Respondent next filed a petition for a writ of habeas corpus in the United States District Court for the Southern District of Florida.

The District Court held an evidentiary hearing to inquire into trial counsel's efforts to investigate and to present mitigating circumstances. Respondent offered the affidavits and reports he had submitted in the state collateral proceedings; he also called his trial counsel to testify. The State of Florida, over respondent's objection, called the trial judge to testify. [The court denied the petition for a writ of habeas corpus.]

On appeal, . . . the Court of Appeals stated that the Sixth Amendment right to assistance of counsel accorded criminal defendants a right to "counsel reasonably likely to render and rendering reasonably effective assistance given the totality of the circumstances." . . . Summarily rejecting respondent's claims other than ineffectiveness of counsel, the court . . . reversed the judgment of the District Court and remanded the case. . . .

D

Petitioners, who are officials of the State of Florida, filed a petition for a writ of certiorari seeking review of the decision of the Court of Appeals. The petition presents a type of Sixth Amendment claim that this Court has not previously considered in any generality. . . . With the exception of Cuyler v. Sullivan [see page 206, infra — EDS.] which involved a claim that counsel's assistance was rendered ineffective by a conflict of interest, the Court has never directly and fully addressed a claim of "actual ineffectiveness" of counsel's assistance in a case going to trial. . . .

II

. . . In giving meaning to the requirement [of effective assistance of counsel,] we must take its purpose — to ensure a fair trial — as the guide. The benchmark for judging any claim of ineffectiveness must be whether counsel's conduct so undermined the proper functioning of the adversarial process that the trial cannot be relied on as having produced a just result.

The same principle applies to a capital sentencing proceeding such as that provided by Florida law. We need not consider the role of counsel in an ordinary sentencing, which may involve informal proceedings and standardless discretion in the sentencer, and hence may require a different approach to the definition of constitutionally effective assistance. . . .

III

A convicted defendant's claim that counsel's assistance was so defective as to require reversal of a conviction or death sentence has two components. First, the defendant must show that counsel's performance was deficient. This requires showing that counsel made errors so serious that counsel was not functioning as the "counsel" guaranteed the defendant by the Sixth Amendment. Second, the defendant must show that the deficient performance prejudiced the defense. This requires showing that counsel's errors were so serious as to deprive the defendant of a fair trial, a trial whose result is reliable. Unless a defendant makes both showings, it cannot be said that the conviction or death sentence resulted from a breakdown in the adversary process that renders the result unreliable.

A

As all the Federal Courts of Appeals have now held, the proper standard for attorney performance is that of reasonably effective assistance. . . . When a convicted defendant complains of the ineffectiveness of counsel's assistance, the defendant must show that counsel's representation fell below an objective standard of reasonableness.

More specific guidelines are not appropriate. The Sixth Amendment refers simply to "counsel," not specifying particular requirements of effective assistance. It relies instead on the legal profession's maintenance of standards sufficient to justify the law's presumption that counsel will fulfill the role in the adversary process that the Amendment envisions. . . . The proper measure of attorney performance remains simply reasonableness under prevailing professional norms.

Representation of a criminal defendant entails certain basic duties. Counsel's function is to assist the defendant, and hence counsel owes the client a duty of loyalty, a duty to avoid conflicts of interest. . . . From counsel's function as assistant to the defendant derive the overarching duty to advocate the defendant's cause and the more particular duties to consult with the defendant on important decisions and to keep the defendant informed of important developments in the course of the prosecution. Counsel also has a duty to bring to bear such skill and knowledge as will render the trial a reliable adversarial testing process. . . .

These basic duties neither exhaustively define the obligations of counsel nor form a checklist for judicial evaluation of attorney performance. In any case presenting an ineffectiveness claim, the performance inquiry must be whether counsel's assistance was reasonable considering all the circumstances. Prevailing norms of practice as reflected in American Bar Association standards and the like, e.g., ABA Standards for Criminal Justice 4-1.1 to 4-8.6 (2d ed. 1980) ("The Defense Function"), are guides to determining what is reasonable, but they are only guides. No particular set of detailed rules for counsel's conduct can satisfactorily take account of the variety of circumstances faced by defense counsel or the range of legitimate decisions regarding how best to represent a criminal defendant. Any such set of rules would interfere with the constitutionally protected independence of counsel and restrict the wide latitude counsel must have in making tactical decisions. . . . Indeed, the existence of detailed guidelines for representation could distract counsel from the overriding mission of vigorous advocacy of the defendant's cause. Moreover, the purpose of the effective assistance guarantee of the Sixth Amendment is not to improve the quality of legal representation, although that is a goal of considerable importance to the legal system. The purpose is simply to ensure that criminal defendants receive a fair trial.

Judicial scrutiny of counsel's performance must be highly deferential. It is all too tempting for a defendant to second-guess counsel's assistance after conviction or adverse sentence, and it is all too easy for a court, examining counsel's defense after it has proved unsuccessful, to conclude that a particular act or omission of counsel was unreasonable. . . . A fair assessment of attorney performance requires that every effort be made to eliminate the distorting effects of hindsight, to reconstruct the circumstances of counsel's challenged conduct, and to evaluate the conduct from counsel's perspective at the time. Because of the difficulties inherent in making the evaluation, a court must indulge a strong presumption that counsel's conduct falls within the wide range of reasonable professional assistance. . . . There are countless ways to provide effective assistance in any given case. Even the best criminal defense attorneys would not defend a particular client in the same way. See Gary Goodpaster, The Trial for Life: Effective Assistance of Counsel in Death Penalty Cases, 58 N.Y.U. L. Rev. 299, 343 (1983).

The availability of intrusive post-trial inquiry into attorney performance or of detailed guidelines for its evaluation would encourage the proliferation of ineffectiveness challenges. Criminal trials resolved unfavorably to the defendant would increasingly come to be followed by a second trial, this one of counsel's unsuccessful defense. Counsel's performance and even willingness to serve could be adversely affected. Intensive scrutiny of counsel and rigid requirements for acceptable assistance could dampen the ardor and impair the independence of defense counsel, discourage the acceptance of assigned cases, and undermine the trust between attorney and client.

Thus, a court deciding an actual ineffectiveness claim must judge the reasonableness of counsel's challenged conduct on the facts of the particular case, viewed as of the time of counsel's conduct. A convicted defendant making a claim of ineffective assistance must identify the acts or omissions of counsel that are alleged not to have been the result of reasonable professional judgment. The court must then determine whether, in light of all the circumstances, the identified acts or omissions were outside the wide range of professionally competent assistance. In making that determination, the court should keep in mind that counsel's function, as elaborated in prevailing professional norms, is to make the adversarial testing process work in the particular case. At the same time, the court should recognize that counsel is strongly presumed to have rendered adequate assistance and made all significant decisions in the exercise of reasonable professional judgment.

These standards require no special amplification in order to define counsel's duty to investigate, the duty at issue in this case. As the Court of Appeals concluded, strategic choices made after thorough investigation of law and facts relevant to plausible options are virtually unchallengeable; and strategic choices made after less than complete investigation are reasonable precisely to the extent that reasonable professional judgments support the limitations on investigation. In other words, counsel has a duty to make reasonable investigations or to make a reasonable decision that makes particular investigations unnecessary. In any ineffectiveness case, a particular decision not to investigate must be directly assessed for reasonableness in all the circumstances, applying a heavy measure of deference to counsel's judgments.

The reasonableness of counsel's actions may be determined or substantially influenced by the defendant's own statements or actions. Counsel's actions are usually based, quite properly, on informed strategic choices made by the defendant and on information supplied by the defendant. In particular, what investigation decisions are reasonable depends critically on such information. For example, when the facts that support a certain potential line of defense are generally known to counsel because of what the defendant has said, the need for further investigation may be considerably diminished or eliminated altogether. And when a defendant has given counsel reason to believe that pursuing certain investigations would be fruitless or even harmful, counsel's failure to pursue those investigations may not later be challenged as unreasonable. In short, inquiry into counsel's conversations with the defendant may be critical to a proper assessment of counsel's investigation decisions, just as it may be critical to a proper assessment of counsel's other litigation decisions. . . .

B

An error by counsel, even if professionally unreasonable, does not warrant setting aside the judgment of a criminal proceeding if the error had no effect on the judgment. . . . The purpose of the Sixth Amendment guarantee of counsel is to ensure that a defendant has the assistance necessary to justify reliance on the outcome of the proceeding. Accordingly, any deficiencies in counsel's performance must be prejudicial to the defense in order to constitute ineffective assistance under the Constitution.

In certain Sixth Amendment contexts, prejudice is presumed. Actual or constructive denial of the assistance of counsel altogether is legally presumed to result in prejudice. So are various kinds of state interference with counsel's assistance. . . . Prejudice in these circumstances is so likely that case by case inquiry into prejudice is not worth the cost. Moreover, such circumstances involve impairments of the Sixth Amendment right that are easy to identify and, for that reason and because the prosecution is directly responsible, easy for the government to prevent.

One type of actual ineffectiveness claim warrants a similar, though more limited, presumption of prejudice. In Cuyler v. Sullivan, 446 U.S., at 345-350, the Court held that prejudice is presumed when counsel is burdened by an actual conflict of interest. In those circumstances, counsel breaches the duty of loyalty, perhaps the most basic of counsel's duties. . . .

Conflict of interest claims aside, actual ineffectiveness claims alleging a deficiency in attorney performance are subject to a general requirement that the defendant affirmatively prove prejudice. The government is not responsible for, and hence not able to prevent, attorney errors that will result in reversal of a conviction or sentence. Attorney errors come in an infinite variety and are as likely to be utterly harmless in a particular case as they are to be prejudicial. They cannot be classified according to likelihood of causing prejudice. Nor can they be defined with sufficient precision to inform defense attorneys correctly just what conduct to avoid. Representation is an art, and an act or omission that is unprofessional in one case may be sound or even brilliant in another. Even if a defendant shows that particular errors of counsel were unreasonable, therefore, the defendant must show that they actually had an adverse effect on the defense.

It is not enough for the defendant to show that the errors had some conceivable effect on the outcome of the proceeding. Virtually every act or omission of counsel would meet that test, . . . and not every error that conceivably could have influenced the outcome undermines the reliability of the result of the proceeding. Respondent suggests requiring a showing that the errors "impaired the presentation of the defense." That standard, however, provides no workable principle. Since any error, if it is indeed an error, "impairs" the presentation of the defense, the proposed standard is inadequate because it provides no way of deciding what impairments are sufficiently serious to warrant setting aside the outcome of the proceeding.

On the other hand, we believe that a defendant need not show that counsel's deficient conduct more likely than not altered the outcome in the case. This outcome-determinative standard has several strengths. It defines the relevant inquiry in a way familiar to courts, though the inquiry, as is inevitable, is anything but precise. The standard also reflects the profound importance of finality in criminal proceedings. Moreover, it comports with the widely used standard for assessing motions for new trial based on newly discovered evidence. . . . Nevertheless, the standard is not quite appropriate.

Even when the specified attorney error results in the omission of certain evidence, the newly discovered evidence standard is not an apt source from which to draw a prejudice standard for ineffectiveness claims. The high standard for newly discovered evidence claims presupposes that all the essential elements of a presumptively accurate and fair proceeding were present in the proceeding whose result is challenged. . . . An ineffective assistance claim asserts the absence of one of the crucial assurances that the result of the proceeding is reliable, so finality concerns are somewhat weaker and the appropriate standard of prejudice should be somewhat lower. The result of a proceeding can be rendered unreliable, and hence the proceeding itself unfair, even if the errors of counsel cannot be shown by a preponderance of the evidence to have determined the outcome.

Accordingly, the appropriate test for prejudice finds its roots in the test for materiality of exculpatory information not disclosed to the defense by the prosecution, United States v. Agurs, 427 U.S., at 104, 112-113, and in the test for materiality of testimony made unavailable to the defense by Government deportation of a witness, United States v. Valenzuela-Bernal, 458 U.S., at 872-874. The defendant must show that there is a reasonable probability that, but for counsel's unprofessional errors, the result of the proceeding would have been different. A reasonable probability is a probability sufficient to undermine confidence in the outcome.

In making the determination whether the specified errors resulted in the required prejudice, a court should presume, absent challenge to the judgment on grounds of evidentiary insufficiency, that the judge or jury acted according to law. An assessment of the likelihood of a result more favorable to the defendant must exclude the possibility of arbitrariness, whimsy, caprice, "nullification," and the like. A defendant has no entitlement to the luck of a lawless decisionmaker, even if a lawless decision cannot be reviewed. The assessment of prejudice should proceed on the assumption that the decisionmaker is reasonably, conscientiously, and impartially applying the standards that govern the decision. It should not depend on the idiosyncracies of the particular decisionmaker, such as unusual propensities toward harshness or leniency. Although these factors may actually have entered into counsel's selection of strategies and, to that limited extent, may thus affect the performance inquiry, they are irrelevant to the prejudice inquiry. Thus, evidence about the actual process of decision, if not part of the record of the proceeding under review, and evidence about, for example, a particular judge's sentencing practices, should not be considered in the prejudice determination.

The governing legal standard plays a critical role in defining the question to be asked in assessing the prejudice from counsel's errors. When a defendant challenges a conviction, the question is whether there is a reasonable probability that, absent the errors, the fact-finder would have had a reasonable doubt respecting guilt. When a defendant challenges a death sentence such as the one at issue in this case, the question is whether there is a reasonable probability that, absent the errors, the sentencer — including an appellate court, to the extent it independently reweighs the evidence — would have concluded that the balance of aggravating and mitigating circumstances did not warrant death.

In making this determination, a court hearing an ineffectiveness claim must consider the totality of the evidence before the judge or jury. Some of the factual findings will have been unaffected by the errors, and factual findings that were affected will have been affected in different ways. Some errors will have had a pervasive effect on the inferences to be drawn from the evidence, altering the entire evidentiary picture, and some will have had an isolated, trivial effect. Moreover, a verdict or conclusion only weakly supported by the record is more likely to have been affected by the errors than one with overwhelming record support. Taking the unaffected findings as a given, and taking due account of the effect of the errors on the remaining findings, a court making the prejudice inquiry must ask if the defendant has met the burden of showing that the decision reached would reasonably likely have been different absent the errors.

IV

A number of practical considerations are important for the application of the standards we have outlined. Most important, in adjudicating a claim of actual ineffectiveness of counsel, a court should keep in mind that the principles we have stated do not establish mechanical rules. Although those principles should guide the process of decision, the ultimate focus of inquiry must be on the fundamental fairness of the proceeding whose result is being challenged. In every case the court should be concerned with whether, despite the strong presumption of reliability, the result of the particular proceeding is unreliable because of a breakdown in the adversarial process that our system counts on to produce just results. . . .

Although we have discussed the performance component of an ineffectiveness claim prior to the prejudice component, there is no reason for a court deciding an ineffective assistance claim to approach the inquiry in the same order or even to address both components of the inquiry if the defendant makes an insufficient showing on one. In particular, a court need not determine whether counsel's performance was deficient before examining the prejudice suffered by the defendant as a result of the alleged deficiencies. The object of an ineffectiveness claim is not to grade counsel's performance. If it is easier to dispose of an ineffectiveness claim on the ground of lack of sufficient prejudice, which we expect will often be so, that course should be followed. Courts should strive to ensure that ineffectiveness claims not become so burdensome to defense counsel that the entire criminal justice system suffers as a result.

The principles governing ineffectiveness claims should apply in federal collateral proceedings as they do on direct appeal or in motions for a new trial. As indicated by the "cause and prejudice" test for overcoming procedural waivers of claims of error, the presumption that a criminal judgment is final is at its strongest in collateral attacks on that judgment. . . . An ineffectiveness claim, however, as our articulation of the standards that govern decision of such claims makes clear, is an attack on the fundamental fairness of the proceeding whose result is challenged. Since fundamental fairness is the central concern of the writ of habeas corpus, . . . no special standards ought to apply to ineffectiveness claims made in habeas proceedings.

Finally, in a federal habeas challenge to a state criminal judgment, a state court conclusion that counsel rendered effective assistance is not a finding of fact binding on the federal court to the extent stated by 28 U.S.C. §2254(d). Ineffectiveness is not a question of "basic, primary, or historical fac[t]." Rather, like the question whether multiple representation in a particular case gave rise to a conflict of interest, it is a mixed question of law and fact. . . . Although state court findings of fact made in the course of deciding an ineffectiveness claim are subject to the deference requirement of §2254(d), and although District Court findings are subject to the clearly erroneous standard of Fed. R. Civ. Proc. 52(a), both the performance and prejudice components of the ineffectiveness inquiry are mixed questions of law and fact.

V . . .

Application of the governing principles is not difficult in this case. The facts as described above, . . . make clear that the conduct of respondent's counsel at and before respondent's sentencing proceeding cannot be found unreasonable. They also make clear that, even assuming the challenged conduct of counsel was unreasonable, respondent suffered insufficient prejudice to warrant setting aside his death sentence.

With respect to the performance component, the record shows that respondent's counsel made a strategic choice to argue for the extreme emotional distress mitigating circumstance and to rely as fully as possible on respondent's acceptance of responsibility for his crimes. Although counsel understandably felt hopeless about respondent's prospects, . . . nothing in the record indicates, as one possible reading of the District Court's opinion suggests . . . that counsel's sense of hopelessness distorted his professional judgment. Counsel's strategy choice was well within the range of professionally reasonable judgments, and the decision not to seek more character or psychological evidence than was already in hand was likewise reasonable.

The trial judge's views on the importance of owning up to one's crimes were well known to counsel. The aggravating circumstances were utterly overwhelming. Trial counsel could reasonably surmise from his conversations with respondent that character and psychological evidence would be of little help. Respondent had already been able to mention at the plea colloquy the substance of what there was to know about his financial and emotional troubles. Restricting testimony on respondent's character to what had come in at the plea colloquy ensured that contrary character and psychological evidence and respondent's criminal history, which counsel had successfully moved to exclude, would not come in. On these facts, there can be little question, even without application of the presumption of adequate performance, that trial counsel's defense, though unsuccessful, was the result of reasonable professional judgment.

With respect to the prejudice component, the lack of merit of respondent's claim is even more stark. The evidence that respondent says his trial counsel should have offered at the sentencing hearing would barely have altered the sentencing profile presented to the sentencing judge. As the state courts and District Court found, at most this evidence shows that numerous people who knew respondent thought he was generally a good person and that a psychiatrist and a psychologist believed he was under considerable emotional stress that did not rise to the level of extreme disturbance. Given the overwhelming aggravating factors, there is no reasonable probability that the omitted evidence would have changed the conclusion that the aggravating circumstances outweighed the mitigating circumstances and, hence, the sentence imposed. Indeed, admission of the evidence respondent now offers might even have been harmful to his case: his "rap sheet" would probably have been admitted into evidence, and the psychological reports would have directly contradicted respondent's claim that the mitigating circumstance of extreme emotional disturbance applied to his case.

Our conclusions on both the prejudice and performance components of the ineffectiveness inquiry do not depend on the trial judge's testimony at the District Court hearing. We therefore need not consider the general admissibility of that testimony, although, as noted . . . , that testimony is irrelevant to the prejudice inquiry. Moreover, the prejudice question is resolvable, and hence the ineffectiveness claim can be rejected, without regard to the evidence presented at the District Court hearing. The state courts properly concluded that the ineffectiveness claim was meritless without holding an evidentiary hearing.

Failure to make the required showing of either deficient performance or sufficient prejudice defeats the ineffectiveness claim. Here there is a double failure. More generally, respondent has made no showing that the justice of his sentence was rendered unreliable by a breakdown in the adversary process caused by deficiencies in counsel's assistance. Respondent's sentencing proceeding was not fundamentally unfair.

We conclude, therefore, that the District Court properly declined to issue a writ of habeas corpus. The judgment of the Court of Appeals is accordingly reversed.

JUSTICE MARSHALL, dissenting. . . .

I

The opinion of the Court revolves around two holdings. First, the majority ties the constitutional minima of attorney performance to a simple "standard of reasonableness." . . . Second, the majority holds that only an error of counsel that has sufficient impact on a trial to "undermine confidence in the outcome" is grounds for overturning a conviction. . . . I disagree with both of these rulings.

A

My objection to the performance standard adopted by the Court is that it is so malleable that, in practice, it will either have no grip at all or will yield excessive variation in the manner in which the Sixth Amendment is interpreted and applied by different courts. To tell lawyers and the lower courts that counsel for a criminal defendant must behave "reasonably" and must act like "a reasonably competent attorney," . . . is to tell them almost nothing. In essence, the majority has instructed judges called upon to assess claims of ineffective assistance of counsel to advert to their own intuitions regarding what constitutes "professional" representation, and has discouraged them from trying to develop more detailed standards governing the performance of defense counsel. In my view, the Court has thereby not only abdicated its own responsibility to interpret the Constitution, but also impaired the ability of the lower courts to exercise theirs.

The debilitating ambiguity of an "objective standard of reasonableness" in this context is illustrated by the majority's failure to address important issues concerning the quality of representation mandated by the Constitution. It is an unfortunate but undeniable fact that a person of means, by selecting a lawyer and paying him enough to ensure he prepares thoroughly, usually can obtain better representation than that available to an indigent defendant, who must rely on appointed counsel, who, in turn, has limited time and resources to devote to a given case. Is a "reasonably competent attorney" a reasonably competent adequately paid retained lawyer or a reasonably competent appointed attorney? It is also a fact that the quality of representation available to ordinary defendants in different parts of the country varies significantly. Should the standard of performance mandated by the Sixth Amendment vary by locale? The majority offers no clues as to the proper responses to these questions. . . .

The opinion of the Court of Appeals in this case represents one sound attempt to develop particularized standards designed to ensure that all defendants receive effective legal assistance. . . . By refusing to address the merits of these proposals, and indeed suggesting that no such effort is worthwhile, the opinion of the Court, I fear, will stunt the development of constitutional doctrine in this area.

B

I object to the prejudice standard adopted by the Court for two independent reasons. *First*, it is often very difficult to tell whether a defendant convicted after a trial in which he was ineffectively represented would have fared better if his lawyer had been competent. Seemingly impregnable cases can sometimes be dismantled by good defense counsel. On the basis of a cold record, it may be impossible for a reviewing court confidently to ascertain how the government's evidence and arguments would have stood up against rebuttal and cross-examination by a shrewd, well prepared lawyer. The difficulties of estimating prejudice after the fact are exacerbated by the possibility that evidence of injury to the defendant may be missing from the record precisely because of the incompetence of defense counsel. In view of all these impediments to a fair evaluation of the probability that the outcome of a trial was affected by ineffectiveness of counsel, it seems to me senseless to impose on a defendant whose lawyer has been shown to have been incompetent the burden of demonstrating prejudice.

Second and more fundamentally, the assumption on which the Court's holding rests is that the only purpose of the constitutional guarantee of effective assistance of counsel is to reduce the chance that innocent persons will be convicted. In my view, the guarantee also functions to ensure that convictions are obtained only through fundamentally fair procedures. The majority contends that the Sixth Amendment is not violated when a manifestly guilty defendant is convicted after a trial in which he was represented by a manifestly ineffective attorney. I cannot agree. Every defendant is entitled to a trial in which his interests are vigorously and conscientiously advocated by an able lawyer. A proceeding in which the defendant does not receive meaningful assistance in meeting the forces of the state does not, in my opinion, constitute due process. . . .

III

The majority suggests that, "[f]or purposes of describing counsel's duties," a capital sentencing proceeding "need not be distinguished from an ordinary trial." I cannot agree.

The Court has repeatedly acknowledged that the Constitution requires stricter adherence to procedural safeguards in a capital case than in other cases. . . .

In my view, a person on death row, whose counsel's performance fell below constitutionally acceptable levels, should not be compelled to demonstrate a "reasonable probability" that he would have been given a life sentence if his lawyer had been competent . . . ; if the defendant can establish a significant chance that the outcome would have been different, he surely should be entitled to a redetermination of his fate. . . .

IV

The views expressed in the preceding section oblige me to dissent from the majority's disposition of the case before us. It is undisputed that respondent's trial counsel made virtually no investigation of the possibility of obtaining testimony from respondent's relatives, friends, or former employers pertaining to respondent's character or background. Had counsel done so, he would have found several persons willing and able to testify that, in their experience, respondent was a responsible, nonviolent man, devoted to his family, and active in the affairs of his church. . . . Respondent contends that his lawyer could have and should have used that testimony to "humanize" respondent, to counteract the impression conveyed by the trial that he was little more than a cold-blooded killer. Had this evidence been admitted, respondent argues, his chances of obtaining a life sentence would have been significantly better.

Measured against the standards outlined above, respondent's contentions are substantial. Experienced members of the death-penalty bar have long recognized the crucial importance of adducing evidence at a sentencing proceeding that establishes the defendant's social and familial connections. . . . The State makes a colorable — though in my view not compelling — argument that defense counsel in this case might have made a reasonable "strategic" decision not to present such evidence at the sentencing hearing on the assumption that an unadorned acknowledgement of respondent's responsibility for his crimes would be more likely to appeal to the trial judge, who was reputed to respect persons who accepted responsibility for their actions. But however justifiable such a choice might have been after counsel had fairly assessed the potential strength of the mitigating evidence available to him, counsel's failure to make any significant effort to find out what evidence might be garnered from respondent's relatives and acquaintances surely cannot be described as "reasonable." Counsel's failure to investigate is particularly suspicious in light of his candid admission that respondent's confessions and conduct in the course of the trial gave him a feeling of "hopelessness" regarding the possibility of saving respondent's life. . . .

That the aggravating circumstances implicated by respondent's criminal conduct were substantial . . . does not vitiate respondent's constitutional claim; judges and juries in cases involving behavior at least as egregious have shown mercy, particularly when afforded an opportunity to see other facets of the defendant's personality and life. Nor is respondent's contention defeated by the possibility that the material his counsel turned up might not have been sufficient to establish a *statutory* mitigating circumstance under Florida law; Florida sentencing judges and the Florida Supreme Court sometimes refuse to impose death sentences in cases "in which, even though *statutory* mitigating circumstances do not outweigh statutory aggravating circumstances, the addition of nonstatutory mitigating circumstances tips the scales in favor of life imprisonment." Barclay v. Florida, 463 U.S. 939, 964 (Stevens, J., concurring in the judgment) (emphasis in original).

If counsel had investigated the availability of mitigating evidence, he might well have decided to present some such material at the hearing. If he had done so, there is a significant chance that respondent would have been given a life sentence. In my view, those possibilities, conjoined with the unreasonableness of counsel's failure to investigate, are more than sufficient to establish a violation of the Sixth Amendment and to entitle respondent to a new sentencing proceeding.

I respectfully dissent.

NOTES AND QUESTIONS

1. On the same day as *Strickland*, the Court also decided the companion case of United States v. Cronic, 466 U.S. 648 (1984), in which the defendant was convicted of mail fraud in connection with a "check kiting" scheme.[9] Shortly before trial, Cronic's defense counsel withdrew; the trial judge "appointed a young lawyer with a real estate practice to represent [Cronic], but allowed him only 25 days for pretrial preparation, even though it had taken the Government over four and one-half years to investigate the case and it had reviewed thousands of documents during that investigation." Id., at 652. At trial, the prosecution introduced extensive testimony from two co-conspirators who had entered into plea bargains; Cronic declined to take the stand due to concerns about his prior convictions being introduced against him. Cronic's lawyer presented no defense, but did cross-examine the prosecution's witnesses with some success. Cronic was convicted on 11 out of 13 counts, and received a 25-year sentence; he appealed on the grounds, inter alia, that his trial counsel was constitutionally ineffective. The Tenth Circuit did not find specific flaws in defense counsel's performance, but reversed the convictions nevertheless, holding that the Sixth Amendment was violated because the circumstances of the case created an "inference" that defense counsel could not perform effectively; this inference was based on: "(1) [T]he time afforded for investigation and preparation; (2) the experience of counsel; (3) the gravity of the charge; (4) the complexity of possible defenses; and (5) the accessibility of witnesses to counsel." 675 F.2d 1126, 1129 (10th Cir. 1982).

The Supreme Court, in an opinion by Justice Stevens, held unanimously (Justice Marshall concurred in the judgment) that no such "inference" of constitutional ineffectiveness arose from the facts of the *Cronic* case:

---

9. "Check kiting" involves writing a series of checks from different bank accounts in order to take advantage of the "float," or delay in cashing the checks, in order to hide a lack of sufficient funds to cover the checks.

[T]he adversarial process protected by the Sixth Amendment requires that the accused have "counsel acting in the role of an advocate." Anders v. California, 386 U.S. 738, 743 (1967). The right to the effective assistance of counsel is thus the right of the accused to require the prosecution's case to survive the crucible of meaningful adversarial testing. When a true adversarial criminal trial has been conducted — even if defense counsel may have made demonstrable errors — the kind of testing envisioned by the Sixth Amendment has occurred. But if the process loses its character as a confrontation between adversaries, the constitutional guarantee is violated. . . .

. . . [T]he right to the effective assistance of counsel is recognized not for its own sake, but because of the effect it has on the ability of the accused to receive a fair trial. Absent some effect of challenged conduct on the reliability of the trial process, the Sixth Amendment guarantee is generally not implicated. Moreover, because we presume that the lawyer is competent to provide the guiding hand that the defendant needs, . . . the burden rests on the accused to demonstrate a constitutional violation. There are, however, circumstances that are so likely to prejudice the accused that the cost of litigating their effect in a particular case is unjustified.

Most obvious, of course, is the complete denial of counsel. The presumption that counsel's assistance is essential requires us to conclude that a trial is unfair if the accused is denied counsel at a critical stage of his trial. Similarly, if counsel entirely fails to subject the prosecution's case to meaningful adversarial testing, then there has been a denial of Sixth Amendment rights that makes the adversary process itself presumptively unreliable. No specific showing of prejudice was required in Davis v. Alaska, 415 U.S. 308 (1974), because the petitioner had been "denied the right of effective cross-examination" which "would be constitutional error of the first magnitude, and no amount of showing of want of prejudice would cure it." Id., at 318.

Circumstances of that magnitude may be present on some occasions when, although counsel is available to assist the accused during trial, the likelihood that any lawyer, even a fully competent one, could provide effective assistance is so small that a presumption of prejudice is appropriate without inquiry into the actual conduct of the trial. Powell v. Alabama, 287 U.S. 45 (1932), was such a case.

The defendants had been indicted for a highly publicized capital offense. Six days before trial, the trial judge appointed "all the members of the bar" for purposes of arraignment. . . . On the day of trial, a lawyer from Tennessee appeared on behalf of persons "interested" in the defendants, but stated that he had not had an opportunity to prepare the case or to familiarize himself with local procedure, and therefore was unwilling to represent the defendants on such short notice. The problem was resolved when the court decided that the Tennessee lawyer would represent the defendants, with whatever help the local bar could provide.

"The defendants, young, ignorant, illiterate, surrounded by hostile sentiment, haled back and forth under guard of soldiers, charged with an atrocious crime regarded with especial horror in the community where they were to be tried, were thus put in peril of their lives within a few moments after counsel for the first time charged with any degree of responsibility began to represent them." Id., at 57-58.

This Court held that "such designation of counsel as was attempted was either so indefinite or so close upon the trial as to amount to a denial of effective and substantial aid in that regard." Id., at 53. . . . *Powell* was thus a case in which the surrounding circumstances made it so unlikely that any lawyer could provide effective assistance that ineffectiveness was properly presumed without inquiry into actual performance at trial.

But every refusal to postpone a criminal trial will not give rise to such a presumption. In Avery v. Alabama, 308 U.S. 444 (1940), counsel was appointed in a capital case only three days before trial, and the trial court denied counsel's request for additional time to prepare. Nevertheless, the Court held that, since evidence and witnesses were easily accessible to defense counsel, the circumstances did not make it unreasonable to expect that counsel could adequately prepare for trial during that period of time, id., at 450-453. Thus, only when surrounding circumstances justify a presumption of ineffectiveness can a Sixth Amendment claim be sufficient without inquiry into counsel's actual performance at trial. . . .

The five factors listed in the Court of Appeals' opinion are relevant to an evaluation of a lawyer's effectiveness in a particular case, but neither separately nor in combination do they provide a basis for concluding that competent counsel was not able to provide this respondent with the guiding hand that the Constitution guarantees. . . .

This case is not one in which the surrounding circumstances make it unlikely that the defendant could have received the effective assistance of counsel. The criteria used by the Court of Appeals do not demonstrate that counsel failed to function in any meaningful sense as the Government's adversary. Respondent can therefore make out a claim of ineffective assistance only by pointing to specific errors made by trial counsel. . . .

466 U.S., at 656-666.

2. In *Strickland*, the Court exempted several categories of cases from the requirement that the defendant, in order to win on an ineffective-assistance-of-counsel claim, must show prejudice as a result of counsel's specific errors of performance:[5] (1) actual or constructive denial of counsel (as in *Gideon* or *Powell*); (2) certain kinds of state interference with counsel (e.g., refusing to allow counsel to meet with the defendant during an overnight recess, see Geders v. United States, 425 U.S. 80 (1976)); and (3) some situations involving attorney conflicts of interest, see Cuyler v. Sullivan, 446 U.S. 335 (1980), discussed infra, at page 206. *Cronic* adds one more category of "presumed prejudice": where "counsel failed to function in any meaningful sense as the government's adversary."

The *Cronic* category potentially could have become very significant, at least in terms of opening up floodgates of litigation, but in actuality its scope has turned out to be quite limited. In Bell v. Cone, 535 U.S. 685 (2002), the defendant was convicted of robbery and capital murder and sentenced to death. At the sentencing proceeding, the defense counsel cross-examined government witnesses but called no defense witnesses, referring instead to the evidence introduced at trial in support of the defendant's insanity claim. The defense counsel also waived the closing argument, ostensibly to avoid giving the prosecutor a chance to argue in rebuttal. The defendant argued that this amounted to a "fail[ure] to subject the prosecution's case to meaningful adversarial testing," and so amounted to ineffective assistance of counsel without regard to whether there was any prejudice. With only Justice Stevens dissenting, the Court disagreed:

. . . When we spoke in *Cronic* of the possibility of presuming prejudice based on an attorney's failure to test the prosecutor's case, we indicated that the attorney's failure must be complete. . . . Here, respondent's argument is not that his counsel failed to oppose the prosecution throughout the sentencing proceeding as a whole, but that his counsel failed to do so at specific points. For purposes of distinguishing between the rule of *Strickland* and that of *Cronic*, this difference is not of degree but of kind. . . .

---

5. A few brief terminological notes about *Strickland*: Ineffective assistance of counsel claims are often referred to as "IAC" claims. The two requirements to establish a *Strickland* violation are usually called the "performance prong" and the "prejudice prong." Finally, notice that the case probably should be called *Washington*, not *Strickland* — after all, the defendant was Washington. Universal custom, however — including within the Supreme Court itself — long ago decided that the case would be called *Strickland*, and we must abide. — EDS.

We hold, therefore, that the state correctly identified the principles announced in *Strickland* as those governing the analysis of respondent's claim.

Id., at 697. Given the analysis in *Bell*, one suspects that successful *Cronic* claims will be rare. Lower-court cases generally confirm this observation: The number of reported *Strickland* claims is enormous — *Strickland* claims are probably the single largest category of criminal procedure claims in post-trial litigation — while the number of *Cronic* claims is very small.

3. The majority and dissent in *Strickland* disagree on the role of the defendant's probable guilt and whether the purported error likely would have affected the outcome. What do you think of the dissenters' argument that these factors are largely irrelevant? What is the significance of these two points? Is all well that ends well, or not? Does the majority's position overestimate the value of stability and finality, or does the minority's underestimate it?

4. Note that the *Strickland* majority has a complicated view of the question whether hindsight is appropriate in these cases. The Court states explicitly that attorney performance must *not* be judged in hindsight; lawyers' judgments are to be assessed according to how those judgments appeared at the time they were made. But the prejudice standard is applied with hindsight: The defendant cannot obtain relief unless he shows it is reasonably likely that his attorney's errors altered the outcome. This two-pronged approach rules out two kinds of claims. The first was mentioned in the preceding note: a claim by a defendant whose lawyer behaved incompetently but who would have been convicted (or, as in *Strickland*, sentenced to death) regardless. The second is a claim by a defendant whose lawyer made a reasonable (or perhaps only marginally negligent) mistake that cost her client the case. Justice Marshall's dissent in *Strickland* essentially argues that the defendant in the first case should get relief. Doesn't the second case deserve relief even more? What does that say about the relationship between attorney incompetence and prejudice, and about the role of the ineffective-assistance doctrine?

5. In Cuyler v. Sullivan, 446 U.S. 335 (1980), the aforementioned leading case on attorney conflicts of interest (discussed further at page 206, infra), the Court also held that ineffective assistance by *retained* counsel can violate the Sixth Amendment right to counsel, thus disposing of the issue whether there is "state action" in such circumstances. Nonetheless, whatever the "state action" may be in criminal cases generally, it is not enough to permit an indigent to sue appointed counsel under 42 U.S.C. §1983 for damages resulting from allegedly ineffective assistance in derogation of the defendant's right to counsel. In Polk County v. Dodson, 454 U.S. 312 (1981), the Court held that an attorney representing a client does not act "under color of state law." Therefore, §1983 is not applicable.

ROMPILLA v. BEARD

Certiorari to the United States Court of Appeals for the Third Circuit
545 U.S. 374 (2005)

JUSTICE SOUTER delivered the opinion of the Court.

This case calls for specific application of the standard of reasonable competence required on the part of defense counsel by the Sixth Amendment. We hold that even when a capital defendant's family members and the defendant himself have suggested that no mitigating evidence is available, his lawyer is bound to make reasonable efforts to obtain and review material that counsel knows the prosecution will probably rely on as evidence of aggravation at the sentencing phase of trial.

I

On the morning of January 14, 1988, James Scanlon was discovered dead in a bar he ran in Allentown, Pennsylvania, his body having been stabbed repeatedly and set on fire. Rompilla was indicted for the murder and related offenses, and the Commonwealth gave notice of intent to ask for the death penalty. Two public defenders were assigned to the case.

The jury at the guilt phase of trial found Rompilla guilty on all counts, and during the ensuing penalty phase, the prosecutor sought to prove three aggravating factors to justify a death sentence: that the murder was committed in the course of another felony; that the murder was committed by torture; and that Rompilla had a significant history of felony convictions indicating the use or threat of violence. See 42 Pa. Cons. Stat. §§9711(d)(6), (8), (9) (2002). The Commonwealth presented evidence on all three aggravators, and the jury found all proven. Rompilla's evidence in mitigation consisted of relatively brief testimony: five of his family members argued in effect for residual doubt, and beseeched the jury for mercy, saying that they believed Rompilla was innocent and a good man. Rompilla's 14-year-old son testified that he loved his father and would visit him in prison. The jury acknowledged this evidence to the point of finding, as two factors in mitigation, that Rompilla's son had testified on his behalf and that rehabilitation was possible. But the jurors assigned the greater weight to the aggravating factors, and sentenced Rompilla to death. The Supreme Court of Pennsylvania affirmed both conviction and sentence.

In December 1995, with new lawyers, Rompilla filed claims . . . including ineffective assistance by trial counsel in failing to present significant mitigating evidence about Rompilla's childhood, mental capacity and health, and alcoholism. The [state habeas] court found that trial counsel had done enough to investigate the possibilities of a mitigation case, and the Supreme Court of Pennsylvania affirmed the denial of relief.

Rompilla then petitioned for a writ of habeas corpus under 28 U.S.C. §2254 in Federal District Court. . . . The District Court found that the State Supreme Court had unreasonably applied Strickland v. Washington, 466 U.S. 668 (1984), as to the penalty phase of the trial, and granted relief for ineffective assistance of counsel. . . .

A divided Third Circuit panel reversed. Rompilla v. Horn, 355 F.3d 233 (2004). The majority found nothing unreasonable in the state court's application of *Strickland*, given defense counsel's efforts to uncover mitigation material, which included interviewing Rompilla and certain family members, as well as consultation with three mental health experts. Although the majority noted that the lawyers did not unearth the "useful information" to be found in Rompilla's "school, medical, police, and prison records," it thought the lawyers were justified in failing to hunt through these records when their other efforts gave no reason to believe the search would yield anything helpful. 355 F.3d at 252. The panel thus distinguished Rompilla's case from Wiggins v. Smith, 539 U.S. 510 (2003). Whereas Wiggins's counsel failed to investigate adequately, to the point even of ignoring the leads their limited enquiry yielded, the Court of Appeals saw the Rompilla investigation as going far enough to leave counsel with reason for thinking further efforts would not be a wise use of the limited resources they had. But Judge Sloviter's dissent stressed that trial counsel's failure to obtain relevant records on Rompilla's background was owing to the lawyers' unreasonable reliance on family members and medical experts to tell them what records might be useful. . . .

II

. . . Ineffective assistance under *Strickland* is deficient performance by counsel resulting in prejudice, 466 U.S., at 687, with performance being measured against an "objective standard of reasonableness," id., at 688, "under prevailing professional norms." Ibid. This case, like some others recently, looks to norms of adequate investigation in preparing for the sentencing phase of a capital trial, when defense counsel's job is to counter the State's evidence of aggravated culpability with evidence in mitigation. . . .

A

A standard of reasonableness applied as if one stood in counsel's shoes spawns few hard-edged rules, and the merits of a number of counsel's choices in this case are subject to fair debate. This is not a case in which defense counsel simply ignored their obligation to find mitigating evidence, and their workload as busy public defenders did not keep them from making a number of efforts, including interviews with Rompilla and some members of his family, and examinations of reports by three mental health experts who gave opinions at the guilt phase. None of the sources proved particularly helpful.

Rompilla's own contributions to any mitigation case were minimal. Counsel found him uninterested in helping, as on their visit to his prison to go over a proposed mitigation strategy, when Rompilla told them he was "bored being here listening" and returned to his cell. App. 668. To questions about childhood and schooling, his answers indicated they had been normal, ibid., save for quitting school in the ninth grade, id., at 677. There were times when Rompilla was even actively obstructive by sending counsel off on false leads. Id., at 663-664.

The lawyers also spoke with five members of Rompilla's family (his former wife, two brothers, a sister-in-law, and his son), id., at 494, and counsel testified that they developed a good relationship with the family in the course of their representation. Id., at 669. The state postconviction court found that counsel spoke to the relatives in a "detailed manner," attempting to unearth mitigating information, id., at 264, although the weight of this finding is qualified by the lawyers' concession that "the overwhelming response from the family was that they didn't really feel as though they knew him all that well since he had spent the majority of his adult years and some of his childhood years in custody," id., at 495; see also id., at 669. Defense counsel also said that because the family was "coming from the position that [Rompilla] was innocent . . . they weren't looking for reasons for why he might have done this." Id., at 494.

The third and final source tapped for mitigating material was the cadre of three mental health witnesses who were asked to look into Rompilla's mental state as of the time of the offense and his competency to stand trial, id., at 473-474, 476, but their reports revealed "nothing useful" to Rompilla's case, id., at 1358, and the lawyers consequently did not go to any other historical source that might have cast light on Rompilla's mental condition.

When new counsel entered the case to raise Rompilla's postconviction claims, however, they identified a number of likely avenues the trial lawyers could fruitfully have followed in building a mitigation case [, including school records and] records of Rompilla's juvenile and adult incarcerations. . . . And while counsel knew from police reports provided in pretrial discovery that Rompilla had been drinking heavily at the time of his offense, Lodging to App. 111-120 (hereinafter Lodging), and although one of the mental health experts reported that Rompilla's troubles with alcohol merited further investigation, App. 723-724, counsel did not look for evidence of a history of dependence on alcohol that might have extenuating significance.

Before us, trial counsel and the Commonwealth respond to these unexplored possibilities by emphasizing this Court's recognition that the duty to investigate does not force defense lawyers to scour the globe on the off-chance something will turn up; reasonably diligent counsel may draw a line when they have good reason to think further investigation would be a waste. See Wiggins v. Smith, 539 U.S., at 525 (further investigation excusable where counsel has evidence suggesting it would be fruitless); Strickland v. Washington, supra, at 699 (counsel could "reasonably surmise . . . that character and psychological evidence would be of little help"); Burger v. Kemp, 483 U.S. 776, 794 (1987) (limited investigation reasonable because all witnesses brought to counsel's attention provided predominantly harmful information). The Commonwealth argues that the information trial counsel gathered from Rompilla and the other sources gave them sound reason to think it would have been pointless to spend time and money on . . . additional investigation . . . , and we can say that there is room for debate about trial counsel's obligation to follow at least some of those potential lines of enquiry. There is no need to say more, however, for a further point is clear and dispositive: the lawyers were deficient in failing to examine the court file on Rompilla's prior conviction.

B

There is an obvious reason that the failure to examine Rompilla's prior conviction file fell below the level of reasonable performance. Counsel knew that the Commonwealth intended to seek the death penalty by proving Rompilla had a significant history of felony convictions indicating the use or threat of violence, an aggravator under state law. Counsel further knew that the Commonwealth would attempt to establish this history by proving Rompilla's prior conviction for rape and assault, and would emphasize his violent character by introducing a transcript of the rape victim's testimony given in that earlier trial. App. 665-666. . . . It is also undisputed that the prior conviction file was a public document, readily available for the asking at the very courthouse where Rompilla was to be tried.

It is clear, however, that defense counsel did not look at any part of that file, including the transcript, until warned by the prosecution [twice]. . . . [C]rucially, even after obtaining the transcript of the victim's testimony on the eve of the sentencing hearing, counsel apparently examined none of the other material in the file.

. . . [I]t is difficult to see how counsel could have failed to realize that without examining the readily available file they were seriously compromising their opportunity to respond to a case for aggravation. The prosecution was going to use the dramatic facts of a similar prior offense, and Rompilla's counsel had a duty to make all reasonable efforts to learn what they could about the offense. Reasonable efforts certainly included obtaining the Commonwealth's own readily available file on the prior conviction to learn what the Commonwealth knew about the crime, to discover any mitigating evidence the Commonwealth would downplay and to anticipate the details of the aggravating evidence the Commonwealth would emphasize.[4] . . . The obligation to get the file was particularly pressing here owing to the similarity of the violent prior offense to the crime charged and Rompilla's sentencing strategy stressing residual doubt. Without making efforts to learn the details and rebut the relevance of the earlier crime, a convincing argument for residual doubt was certainly beyond any hope. . . .

At argument the most that Pennsylvania (and the United States as *amicus*) could say was that defense counsel's efforts to find mitigating evidence by other means excused them from looking at the prior conviction file. Tr. of Oral Arg. 37-39, 45-46. . . .

We think this [is] . . . an objectively unreasonable conclusion. It flouts prudence to deny that a defense lawyer should try to look at a file he knows the prosecution will cull for aggravating evidence, let alone when the file is sitting in the trial courthouse, open for the asking. No reasonable lawyer would forgo examination of the file thinking he could do as well by asking the defendant or family relations whether they recalled anything helpful or damaging in the prior victim's testimony. . . . Questioning a few more family members and searching for old records can promise less than looking for a needle in a haystack, when a lawyer truly has reason to doubt there is any needle there. But looking at a file the prosecution says it will use is a sure bet: whatever may be in that file is going to tell defense counsel something about what the prosecution can produce.

The dissent thinks this analysis creates a "rigid, *per se*" rule that requires defense counsel to do a complete review of the file on any prior conviction introduced, but that is a mistake. Counsel fell short here because they failed to make reasonable efforts to review the prior conviction file, despite knowing that the prosecution intended to introduce Rompilla's prior conviction not merely by entering a notice of conviction into evidence but by quoting damaging testimony of the rape victim in that case. The unreasonableness of attempting no more than they did was heightened by the easy availability of the file at the trial courthouse, and the great risk that testimony about a similar violent crime would hamstring counsel's chosen defense of residual doubt. . . . Other situations, where a defense lawyer is not charged with knowledge that the prosecutor intends to use a prior conviction in this way, might well warrant a different assessment.

---

4. The ease with which counsel could examine the entire file makes application of this standard correspondingly easy. Suffice it to say that when the State has warehouses of records available in a particular case, review of counsel's performance will call for greater subtlety.

C

Since counsel's failure to look at the file fell below the line of reasonable practice, there is a further question about prejudice, that is, whether "there is a reasonable probability that, but for counsel's unprofessional errors, the result of the proceeding would have been different." 466 U.S., at 694. . . . We think Rompilla has shown beyond any doubt that counsel's lapse was prejudicial. . . .

If the defense lawyers had looked in the file on Rompilla's prior conviction, it is uncontested they would have found a range of mitigation leads that no other source had opened up. In the same file with the transcript of the prior trial were the records of Rompilla's imprisonment on the earlier conviction, which defense counsel testified she had never seen. The prison files pictured Rompilla's childhood and mental health very differently from anything defense counsel had seen or heard. An evaluation by a corrections counselor states that Rompilla was "reared in the slum environment of Allentown, Pa. vicinity. He early came to the attention of juvenile authorities, quit school at 16, [and] started a series of incarcerations in and out Penna. often of assaultive nature and commonly related to over-indulgence in alcoholic beverages." Lodging 40. The same file discloses test results that the defense's mental health experts would have viewed as pointing to schizophrenia and other disorders, and test scores showing a third grade level of cognition after nine years of schooling. Id., at 32-35.

. . . The accumulated entries would have destroyed the benign conception of Rompilla's upbringing and mental capacity defense counsel had formed from talking with Rompilla himself and some of his family members, and from the reports of the mental health experts. With this information, counsel . . . would unquestionably have gone further to build a mitigation case. Further effort would presumably have unearthed much of the material postconviction counsel found, including testimony from several members of Rompilla's family whom trial counsel did not interview. Judge Sloviter summarized this evidence:

> Rompilla's parents were both severe alcoholics who drank constantly. His mother drank during her pregnancy with Rompilla, and he and his brothers eventually developed serious drinking problems. His father, who had a vicious temper, frequently beat Rompilla's mother, leaving her bruised and black-eyed, and bragged about his cheating on her. His parents fought violently, and on at least one occasion his mother stabbed his father. He was abused by his father who beat him when he was young with his hands, fists, leather straps, belts and sticks. All of the children lived in terror. There were no expressions of parental love, affection or approval. Instead, he was subjected to yelling and verbal abuse. His father locked Rompilla and his brother Richard in a small wire mesh dog pen that was filthy and excrement filled. He had an isolated background, and was not allowed to visit other children or to speak to anyone on the phone. They had no indoor plumbing in the house, he slept in the attic with no heat, and the children were not given clothes and attended school in rags.

355 F.3d at 279 (citations omitted) (dissenting opinion).

The jury never heard any of this and neither did the mental health experts who examined Rompilla before trial. While they found "nothing helpful to [Rompilla's] case," *Rompilla*, 554 Pa., at 385, 721 A.2d, at 790, their postconviction counterparts, alerted by information from school, medical, and prison records that trial counsel never saw, found plenty of "red flags" pointing up a need to test further. 355 F.3d at

279 (Sloviter, J., dissenting). When they tested, they found that Rompilla "suffers from organic brain damage, an extreme mental disturbance significantly impairing several of his cognitive functions." Ibid. They also said that "Rompilla's problems relate back to his childhood, and were likely caused by fetal alcohol syndrome [and that] Rompilla's capacity to appreciate the criminality of his conduct or to conform his conduct to the law was substantially impaired at the time of the offense." Id., at 280 (Sloviter, J., dissenting). . . .

. . . [A]lthough we suppose it is possible that a jury could have heard [all this evidence] and still have decided on the death penalty, that is not the test. It goes without saying that the undiscovered "mitigating evidence, taken as a whole, 'might well have influenced the jury's appraisal' of [Rompilla's] culpability," *Wiggins*, 539 U.S., at 538 (quoting Williams v. Taylor, 529 U.S., at 398), and the likelihood of a different result if the evidence had gone in is "sufficient to undermine confidence in the outcome" actually reached at sentencing, *Strickland*, 466 U.S., at 694.

The judgment of the Third Circuit is reversed, and Pennsylvania must either retry the case on penalty or stipulate to a life sentence.

JUSTICE O'CONNOR, concurring.

I write separately to put to rest one concern. The dissent worries that the Court's opinion "imposes on defense counsel a rigid requirement to review all documents in what it calls the 'case file' of any prior conviction that the prosecution might rely on at trial." But the Court's opinion imposes no such rule. Rather, today's decision simply applies our longstanding case-by-case approach to determining whether an attorney's performance was unconstitutionally deficient under Strickland v. Washington, 466 U.S. 668 (1984). Trial counsel's performance in Rompilla's case falls short under that standard, because the attorneys' behavior was not "reason-able considering all the circumstances." Id., at 688. In particular, there were three circumstances which made the attorneys' failure to examine Rompilla's prior conviction file unreasonable.

First, Rompilla's attorneys knew that their client's prior conviction would be at the very heart of the *prosecution's* case. The prior conviction went not to a collateral matter, but rather to one of the aggravating circumstances making Rompilla eligible for the death penalty. The prosecutors intended not merely to mention the fact of prior conviction, but to read testimony about the details of the crime. That crime, besides being quite violent in its own right, was very similar to the murder for which Rompilla was on trial, and Rompilla had committed the murder at issue a mere three months after his release from prison on the earlier conviction. In other words, the prosecutor clearly planned to use details of the prior crime as powerful evidence that Rompilla was a dangerous man for whom the death penalty would be both appropriate punishment and a necessary means of incapacitation. This was evidence the defense should have been prepared to meet. . . .

Second, the prosecutor's planned use of the prior conviction threatened to eviscerate one of the *defense's* primary mitigation arguments. Rompilla was convicted on the basis of strong circumstantial evidence. His lawyers structured the entire mitigation argument around the hope of convincing the jury that residual doubt about Rompilla's guilt made it inappropriate to impose the death penalty. In announcing an intention to introduce testimony about Rompilla's similar prior offense, the prosecutor put Rompilla's attorneys on notice that the prospective defense on mitigation likely would be ineffective and counterproductive. . . . Such a scenario called for further investigation, to determine whether circumstances of the prior case gave any hope of saving the residual doubt argument, or whether the best strategy instead would be to jettison that argument so as to focus on other, more promising issues.

Third, the attorneys' decision not to obtain Rompilla's prior conviction file was not the result of an informed tactical decision about how the lawyers' time would best be spent. . . . Rompilla's attorneys did not ignore the prior case file in order to spend their time on other crucial leads. They did not determine that the file was so inaccessible or so large that examining it would necessarily divert them from other trial-preparation tasks they thought more promising. They did not learn at the 11th hour about the prosecution's intent to use the prior conviction, when it was too late for them to change plans. Rather, their failure to obtain the crucial file "was the result of inattention, not reasoned strategic judgment." Wiggins v. Smith, 539 U.S. 510, 534 (2003). As a result, their conduct fell below constitutionally required standards. See id., at 533 ("Strategic choices made after less than complete investigation are reasonable' only to the extent that 'reasonable professional judgments support the limitations on investigation" (quoting *Strickland*, 466 U.S., at 690-691)). . . .

JUSTICE KENNEDY, with whom CHIEF JUSTICE REHNQUIST, JUSTICE SCALIA, and JUSTICE THOMAS join, dissenting.

Today the Court brands two committed criminal defense attorneys as ineffective — "outside the wide range of professionally competent counsel," Strickland v. Washington, 466 U.S. 668, 690 (1984) — because they did not look in an old case file and stumble upon something they had not set out to find. . . .

Rompilla was represented at trial by Fredrick Charles, the chief public defender for Lehigh County at the time, and Maria Dantos, an assistant public defender. Charles and Dantos were assisted by John Whispell, an investigator in the public defender's office. Rompilla's defense team sought to develop mitigating evidence from various sources. First, they questioned Rompilla extensively about his upbringing and background. App. 668-669. . . . Second, Charles and Dantos arranged for Rompilla to be examined by three experienced mental health professionals. . . . Finally, Rompilla's attorneys questioned his family extensively in search of any information that might help spare Rompilla the death penalty. . . .

The Court acknowledges the steps taken by Rompilla's attorneys in preparation for sentencing but finds fault nonetheless. "The lawyers were deficient," the Court says, "in failing to examine the court file on Rompilla's prior conviction." . . .

The majority . . . disregards the sound strategic calculation supporting the decisions made by Rompilla's attorneys. Charles and Dantos were "aware of [Rompilla's] priors" and "aware of the circumstances" surrounding these convictions. Id., at 507. At the postconviction hearing, Dantos also indicated that she had reviewed documents relating to the prior conviction. Ibid. Based on this information, as well as their numerous conversations with Rompilla and his family, Charles and Dantos reasonably could conclude that reviewing the full prior conviction case file was not the best allocation of resources.

The majority concludes otherwise only by ignoring *Strickland*'s command that "judicial scrutiny of counsel's performance must be highly deferential." 466 U.S., at 689. According to the Court, the Constitution required nothing less than a full review of the prior conviction case file by Rompilla's attorneys. Even with the benefit of hindsight the Court struggles to explain how the file would have proved helpful, offering only the vague speculation that Rompilla's attorneys might have discovered "circumstances that extenuated the behavior described by the [rape] victim." What the Court means by "circumstances" is a mystery. If the Court is referring to details on Rompilla's mental fitness or upbringing, surely Rompilla's attorneys were more likely to discover such information through the sources they consulted: Rompilla, his family, and the three mental health experts that examined him.

Perhaps the circumstances to which the majority refers are the details of Rompilla's 1974 crimes. Charles and Dantos, however, had enough information about the prior convictions to determine that reviewing the case file was not the most effective use of their time. Rompilla had been convicted of breaking into the residence of Josephine Macrenna, who lived in an apartment above the bar she owned. App. 56-89. After Macrenna gave him the bar's receipts for the night, Rompilla demanded that she disrobe. When she initially resisted, Rompilla slashed her left breast with a knife. Rompilla then held Macrenna at knifepoint while he raped her for over an hour. Charles and Dantos were aware of these circumstances of the prior conviction and the brutality of the crime. Id., at 507. It did not take a review of the case file to know that quibbling with the Commonwealth's version of events was a dubious trial strategy. At sentencing Dantos fought vigorously to prevent the Commonwealth from introducing the details of the 1974 crimes, id., at 16-40, but once the transcript was admitted there was nothing that could be done. Rompilla was unlikely to endear himself to the jury by arguing that his prior conviction for burglary, theft, and rape really was not as bad as the Commonwealth was making it out to be. Recognizing this, Rompilla's attorneys instead devoted their limited time and resources to developing a mitigation case. That those efforts turned up little useful evidence does not make the ex ante strategic calculation of Rompilla's attorneys constitutionally deficient.

One of the primary reasons this Court has rejected a checklist approach to effective assistance of counsel is that each new requirement risks distracting attorneys from the real objective of providing vigorous advocacy as dictated by the facts and circumstances in the particular case. The Court's rigid requirement that counsel always review the case files of convictions the prosecution seeks to use at trial will be just such a distraction. Capital defendants often have a history of crime. . . . If the prosecution relies on these convictions as aggravators, the Court has now obligated defense attorneys to review the boxes of documents that come with them.

In imposing this new rule, the Court states that counsel in this case could review the "entire file" with "ease." There is simply no support in the record for this assumption. Case files often comprise numerous boxes. The file may contain, among other things, witness statements, forensic evidence, arrest reports, grand jury transcripts, testimony and exhibits relating to any pretrial suppression hearings, trial transcripts, trial exhibits, post-trial motions and presentence reports. Full review of even a single prior conviction case file could be time consuming, and many of the documents in a file are duplicative or irrelevant. The Court, recognizing the flaw in its analysis, suggests that cases involving "warehouses of records" "will call for greater subtlety." Yet for all we know, this is such a case. . . .

Even accepting the Court's misguided analysis of the adequacy of representation by Rompilla's trial counsel, Rompilla is still not entitled to habeas relief. *Strickland* assigns the defendant the burden of demonstrating prejudice, 466 U.S., at 692. Rompilla cannot satisfy this standard. . . .

The Court's theory of prejudice rests on serendipity. Nothing in the old case file diminishes the aggravating nature of the prior conviction. The only way Rompilla's attorneys could have minimized the aggravating force of the earlier rape conviction was through Dantos' forceful, but ultimately unsuccessful, fight to exclude the transcript at sentencing. The Court, recognizing this problem, instead finds prejudice through chance. If Rompilla's attorneys had reviewed the case file of his prior rape and burglary conviction, the Court says, they would have stumbled across "a range of mitigation leads."

The range of leads to which the Court refers is in fact a handful of notations within a single 10-page document. The document, an "Initial Transfer Petition," appears to have been prepared by the Pennsylvania Department of Corrections after Rompilla's conviction to facilitate his initial assignment to one of the Commonwealth's maximum-security prisons. Lodging 31-40.

Rompilla cannot demonstrate prejudice because nothing in the record indicates that Rompilla's trial attorneys would have discovered the transfer petition, or the clues contained in it, if they had reviewed the old file. The majority faults Rompilla's attorneys for failing to "learn what the Commonwealth knew about the crime," "discover any mitigating evidence the Commonwealth would downplay," and "anticipate the details of the aggravating evidence the Commonwealth would emphasize." Yet if Rompilla's attorneys had reviewed the case file with these purposes in mind, they almost surely would have attributed no significance to the transfer petition following only a cursory review. The petition, after all, was prepared by the Bureau of Correction after Rompilla's conviction for the purpose of determining Rompilla's initial prison assignment. It contained no details regarding the circumstances of the conviction. Reviewing the prior conviction file for information to counter the Commonwealth, counsel would have looked first at the transcript of the trial testimony, and perhaps then to probative exhibits or forensic evidence. There would have been no reason for counsel to read, or even to skim, this obscure document. . . .

The majority thus finds itself in a bind. If counsel's alleged deficiency lies in the failure to review the file for the purposes the majority has identified, then there is no prejudice: for there is no reasonable probability that review of the file for those purposes would have led counsel to accord the transfer petition enough attention to discover the leads the majority cites. Prejudice could only be demonstrated if the deficiency in counsel's performance were to be described not as the failure to perform a purposive review of the file, but instead as the failure to accord intense scrutiny to every single page of every single document in that file, regardless of the purpose motivating the review. . . . Surely, however, the Court would not require defense counsel to look at every document, no matter how tangential, included in the prior conviction file on the off chance that some notation therein might provide a lead, which in turn might result in the discovery of useful information. The Constitution does not mandate that defense attorneys perform busy work. . . .

Strickland anticipated the temptation "to second-guess counsel's assistance after conviction or adverse sentence" and cautioned that "[a] fair assessment of attorney performance requires that every effort be made to eliminate the distorting effects of hindsight, to reconstruct the circumstances of counsel's challenged conduct, and to evaluate the conduct from counsel's perspective at the time." 466 U.S., at 689.

Today, the Court succumbs to the very temptation that *Strickland* warned against. In the process, the majority imposes on defense attorneys a rigid requirement that finds no support in our cases or common sense.

I would affirm the judgment of the Court of Appeals.

NOTES AND QUESTIONS

1. Compare *Rompilla* to *Strickland*. Both are capital cases; in both, the government had strong evidence of aggravating factors that would make the defendant eligible for the death penalty. And both defendants claimed that their defense counsel failed to do enough to uncover mitigating evidence to avoid the death penalty. There are differences, of course — but some of those differences make Washington's claim look much stronger than Rompilla's. For example: Washington's lawyer basically did nothing to come up with an argument in mitigation. Rompilla's lawyers did quite a lot. It is hard to explain why Washington's lawyer passed *Strickland*'s performance standard, while Rompilla's lawyers flunked that same standard.

Was the standard really the same? Is Justice Souter's majority opinion in *Rompilla* consistent with Justice O'Connor's majority opinion in *Strickland*? Judging from her *Rompilla* concurrence, Justice O'Connor seems to think so. Is she right?

2. Consider another potentially relevant factual difference between *Rompilla* and *Strickland*. Even the most comprehensive investigation would have turned up little in *Strickland*, because there wasn't much of a mitigating case to be made. Washington had killed three people (a fourth died later) — a college student, a minister, and an elderly woman — because he was upset that he had lost his job. (In the words of one psychiatric report, he was "chronically frustrated and depressed because of his economic dilemma." *Strickland*, 466 U.S., at 676.) Even in the hands of the most skillful defense lawyer, that is not a winning argument. Rompilla's lawyers, by contrast, had a much stronger case on sentencing to begin with: Rompilla was charged with one murder rather than three, and his key prior conviction was decades old. If they managed to find it, they also had a mother lode of mitigating evidence. Where Washington was "chronically frustrated and depressed," Rompilla may have been schizophrenic. Add to that the hellish childhood described by Judge Sloviter in the passage quoted by the majority opinion, and you have a substantial case for mitigation. One can easily imagine that a jury confronted with that evidence and argument would decide that Rompilla should be incarcerated, not executed.

3. In the end, what exactly did Rompilla's lawyers do wrong? Whatever it was, did it look wrong at the time or only in hindsight?

The preceding two notes suggest that the main difference between *Rompilla* and *Strickland* might be the following: In *Strickland*, on the one hand, the Court evaluated the defense attorney's performance from the perspective of the lawyer *at the time he made his decisions* about what to do or what not to do. In *Rompilla*, on the other hand, the Court seems to have evaluated the defense attorney's performance with the benefit of hindsight. In other words, the *Rompilla* Court seems to have judged performance based on what eventually came to light (i.e., the fact that there actually existed helpful mitigating evidence that never was presented to the jury). To put it another way, *Strickland*'s performance analysis was ex ante, whereas *Rompilla*'s was ex post.

Is this a good idea? An ex post approach to evaluating defense attorney performance results in something like strict liability — no matter how reasonable the attorney's decisions may have been at the time, those decisions will be found constitutionally ineffective if it turns out that something truly helpful was missed. This essentially conflates the "prejudice" and "performance" prongs of Strickland. Such a conflated analysis means that a very small number of defendants will obtain judicial relief, at great cost to society, in a manner that seems highly unlikely to produce an effective and comprehensive solution to the general problem of ineffective defense representation.

4. Maybe the real problem with trying to reconcile *Rompilla* with *Strickland* is that — like virtually all ineffective-assistance cases litigated pursuant to *Strickland* — the IAC issues in each case are so inherently and heavily fact-bound that no meaningful comparisons are possible. In other words, a search for the kind of consistency that can be translated into a clearly articulable and applicable legal rule may be doomed from the start.

Think about the daunting task that faced the Court in *Strickland*. The Court clearly (and no doubt correctly) perceived serious problems with the quality of defense representation in the state courts — especially for indigent defendants. Such problems were well documented at the time in lower-court decisions as well as in national research reports. See, e.g., ABA, Gideon Undone: The Crises in Indigent Defense Funding (John Thomas Moran ed. 1982). Many of the problems were (and still remain) structural, in the sense that they resulted from chronic underfunding of defense services by financially strapped states and localities.[6]

But what to do about these serious problems? If the Court were an executive or a legislature, it might try to design a new federal program to improve the quality of defense lawyering. Indeed, a well-known proposal for such a program has been kicking around for many years; the American Bar Association first rolled out the proposal back in 1979,[7] and it was introduced into Congress later that same year.[8] The ABA proposal — which would have included federal matching funds to help the states accomplish necessary reforms — remains viable today,[9] and continues to attract scholarly attention. See, e.g., Joseph L. Hoffmann & Nancy J. King, Rethinking the Federal Role in State Criminal Justice, 84 N.Y.U. L. Rev. 791 (2009) (advocating cutbacks in federal habeas corpus review of state criminal cases combined with adoption and funding of a new Federal Center for Defense Services, modeled on the ABA proposal).

As a judicial institution, however, the Court in *Strickland* had fewer good options. It could try to create, by judicial fiat, a new and comprehensive set of *ex ante* prophylactic rules, enforcible by courts, to try to prevent or reduce the prevalence of defense attorney errors. But that undoubtedly would have enmeshed the lower courts in highly controversial administrative and supervisory roles. And it would

---

6. A 1982 study by the ABA found, among other things, that "The financing of criminal defense services for indigents is generally inadequate, constituting only 1.5% of total expenditures for criminal justice matters by state and local governments." See Norman Lefstein, In Search of Gideon's Promise: Lessons from England and the Need for Federal Help, 55 Hastings L.J. 835, 838 n. 15 (2004).

7. See ABA Standing Committee on Legal Aid and Indigent Defendants, ABA Principal Indigent Defense Resolution No. 121, Report to the House of Delegates, at 3 (1979), available at http://www.abanet.org/legalservices/downloads/sclaid/121.pdf.

8. See Center for Defense Services Act, S. 2170, 96th Cong. 4(a), 5(a) (1979) (cosponsored by Senators Dennis DeConcini (R-Ariz.) and Robert F. Kennedy (D-Mass.).

9. The ABA reconfirmed its support for the proposal in 1998, and again in 2005.

have opened up the Court itself to serious criticism for overreaching the scope of its legitimate judicial powers.

Or the Court could do instead what it actually did in *Strickland*, which was to authorize post hoc, fact-based, case-by-case litigation about the deficient performance of defense counsel and its prejudicial effects on the individual defendant. The Court undoubtedly recognized that such issues must be decided primarily by the trial courts that observed the proceedings in the first instance — no appellate or habeas court could ever successfully reconstruct, in sufficient detail, the factual context within which the defense attorney acted (or failed to act). So the Court's role in *Strickland* was largely limited to laying out an exhortatory standard that would at least allow appellate and habeas courts to remedy the most obvious injustices (such as drunk, drugged, or sleeping lawyers), and then leaving the matter primarily to the trial courts to enforce.

That is probably the main reason why the legal rules declared in *Strickland* have not changed one iota for more than 25 years. The Court occasionally returns to the subject of ineffective assistance, to address a novel fact pattern or to send signals that the lower courts should become either more or less aggressive in policing defense attorney performance. But the post hoc regulatory system created by *Strickland* remains completely intact — for better or for worse.

Do you find this account of *Strickland* disturbing or just depressing? If so, can you think of a better approach to solving the problems of inadequate defense representation?

5. What, if anything, does a decision like *Rompilla* mean for noncapital cases? So far, the Supreme Court seems to have limited the ex post performance analysis of *Rompilla* to the special context of capital cases. In general, noncapital defendants have had little success in making *Strickland* claims based on their lawyers' inaction. Perhaps not coincidentally, inaction by defense lawyers is the norm in most criminal cases. One study of appointed counsel in New York City in the mid-1980s found that counsel filed written motions in 26 percent of homicide cases and 11 percent of other felony cases, interviewed witnesses in 21 percent of homicides and 4 percent of other felonies, employed experts in 17 percent of homicides and 2 percent of other felonies, and visited the crime scene in 12 percent of homicides and 4 percent of other felonies. See Michael McConville & Chester L. Mirsky, Criminal Defense of the Poor in New York City, 15 N.Y.U. Rev. L. & Soc. Change 581, 762-767 (1986-87).

6. The practical meaning of the right to counsel depends on how indigent defendants are given lawyers and on how those lawyers are paid. There are several different methods. Most densely populated areas use public defender offices. These offices consist of full-time attorneys who do nothing but indigent defense; the offices are usually funded by annual appropriations from local (or, less frequently, state) governments. If the appropriation is low and the number of criminal cases high, the results can be staggering: In 2004, one public defender sought an opinion from the Ethics Advisory Committee of the South Carolina Bar because he was burdened with a crushing caseload of more than 1,000 felonies.[10] Where public defender offices do not exist, indigent defendants are assigned private counsel from a list of those who are willing (however grudgingly) and able to serve. The pay scale

10. See Norman Lefstein & Georgia Vagenas, Restraining Excessive Defender Caseloads: The ABA Ethics Committee Requires Action, The Champion, at 16 (Dec. 2006) (available at http://www.abanet.org/legalservices/sclaid/defender/downloads/ABA_ethicsp10-22.pdf).

is typically low, although there have been significant improvements in many juris-dictions over the past decade.

What is the proper judicial response to inadequate funding for defense services? Should courts ratchet up Sixth Amendment standards to try to force states and localities to provide greater resources for indigent defense? Would that work? There have been some challenges to the constitutionality of defense representation sys-tems, but not many successful ones. For a notable exception, see State v. Peart, 621 So. 2d 780 (La. 1993). In *Peart*, the Louisiana Supreme Court concluded that indi-gent defendants in New Orleans were frequently being deprived of effective assis-tance of counsel due to the extremely high caseloads that public defenders were required to carry. Id., at 788-790. The court held that, henceforth, defendants in that district would have a rebuttable presumption that counsel was ineffective, at least until the funding problem was rectified. Id., at 790-792. *Peart* was decided under Louisiana law, though the content of Louisiana's requirement of effective assistance was not obviously different from the content of the federal law require-ment.

It seems a truism to say that the right to state-provided counsel can't mean much unless the state appropriates an adequate amount to pay for it. See Note, Effectively Ineffective: The Failure of Courts to Address Underfunded Indigent Defense Sys-tems, 118 Harv. L. Rev. 1731 (2005).[11] Yet in the 41 years since *Gideon* was decided, the Supreme Court has made no move to require adequate funding as a constitu-tional imperative. Why not?

The answer may have more to do with timing than with any constitutional prin-ciple. If adequate funding for indigent defense were to arise out of litigation, the liti-gation would likely have to take the form of a class action lawsuit by criminal defendants (or perhaps by their lawyers), seeking to enjoin the state both to provide an appropriate level of resources to local public defenders' offices and to offer an appropriate pay scale to separately appointed counsel. In 1963, when *Gideon* was decided, the era of large-scale institutional injunction litigation had not yet begun. No one even imagined the kind of lawsuits just described.

The late 1960s and 1970s saw a boom in class actions seeking complex injunc-tions against government agencies (they became known as "structural injunctions"). Plaintiffs in a number of these cases succeeded — meaning that a number of federal courts issued injunctions that directed government officials to manage their agen-cies in particular ways; most of those edicts also required the expenditure of large amounts of money. But those cases were brought by parents of public-school chil-dren seeking the busing of students to achieve racial balance, or by inmates of state prisons or local jails seeking improvements in the conditions of their incarceration. No similar suits were brought by criminal defendants seeking better funding for defense counsel. By the time *those* claims began to arise, in the late 1980s and 1990s, structural injunctions had gone out of fashion; the Supreme Court had cut back on judges' authority to issue broad orders to government agencies — especially when the orders required those agencies to spend large sums of money. For the classic example of this new, more restrictive attitude, see Missouri v. Jenkins, 515 U.S. 70 (1995), where the Court overturned a broad injunctive order aimed at reforming

---

11. See also The Spangenberg Group, Rates of Compensation Paid to Court-Appointed Counsel in Non-Capital Felony Cases at Trial: A State-by-State Overview (Aug. 2003) (available at http://www.abanet.org/legalservices/downloads/sclaid/indigentdefense/compensationratesnoncapital2003.pdf).

the Kansas City school system. Given that attitude, it is not exactly surprising that Sixth Amendment funding claims have not enjoyed much success.

In other words, underfunding-of-indigent-defense claims may have simply arrived at the courthouse too late. If those claims had arisen in 1970 or 1975, they might have won the day: States might have been required to establish the kinds of institutional arrangements and budget practices that would ensure adequate provision of defense counsel to indigents. But because structural injunctions were tried elsewhere — schools and prisons — and found wanting, courts have been loath to use them to enforce Sixth Amendment rights.

7. Especially in light of all of the above, what would be wrong with courts instead articulating a checklist of basic obligations for defense counsel and then enforcing it in an appropriate manner? The first such proposal was made by Professor Joseph D. Grano, The Right to Counsel: Collateral Issues Affecting Due Process, 54 Minn. L. Rev. 1175, 1248 (1970). Judge David L. Bazelon later developed Grano's suggestion in his article, The Realities of Gideon and Argersinger, 64 Geo. L.J. 811 (1976). Consider a part of his proposed checklist, id., at 837-838:

PRELIMINARY HEARING   _____

                                                        Date

_____

Comments

_____

_____

_____

_____

Official Records	*Obtained**
1. Complaint	_____
2. Bail Agency form	_____
3. Narcotics Treatment Ad. Report	_____
4. Arrest warrant (affidavit)	_____
5. Search warrant (affidavit)	_____
6. Defendant's record	_____
7. PD 251	_____
8. PD 252, 253, 254	_____
9. PD 163	_____
10. Other_____	_____

Statements	*Obtained**
1. Written	_____
2. Oral	_____
3. Co-defendant	_____

Scientific Exams	AUSA Requested	Obtained*
1. Mental		
2. Fingerprints		
3. Blood		
4. Semen		
5. Hair		
6. Fiber		
7. Pathologist		
8. Ballistics		
9. Chemist report		
10. Handwriting		
11. Other		

Police Officer Witnesses	Name & Precinct	Interview Obtained*
1. Arresting Officer		
2. Mobile Crime Lab		
3. Invest. Officer		
4. Line-Up Officer		
5. Search Officer		
6. Confession Officer		

Other Witnesses	Name & Address	Interview Obtained*
1. Victim		
2. Eyewitnesses		
3. Other		

Motions to Be Filed (check)   Comments

_____ 1. Suppression of Tangible Object _____

_____ 2. Suppression of Statements _____

_____ 3. Identification _____

_____ 4. Severance _____

_____ 5. Notice of Alibi _____

_____ 6. Notice of Insanity Defense _____

_____7. Mental Competency Exam _____
       _____

_____8. Bond Review _____
       _____

_____9. Other _____
       _____

Defendant's Version of Events _____
_____
_____
_____
_____

   I hereby certify that the case referred to in the above work-sheet has been completely investigated and information contained therein and attached thereto is
accurate to the best of my knowledge.

   Date _____   *Attorney's Signature* _____

* Attached is a copy of all statements, oral or written, obtained by counsel, all documents, reports, interviews, and other materials received in the preparation of this case. A completed time sheet is also to be
maintained for purposes of administrative records.

Do you see any problems with the so-called "checklist" approach to defense lawyering? Would defendants universally benefit from such an approach? Why or why not?
What about unintended collateral consequences? Might the checklist approach
indirectly undermine the goals of *Strickland*, by discouraging bright young lawyers
from pursuing a career in defense representation?
   The Court in *Strickland* specifically rejected the idea of adopting a checklist like
the one above. Instead, the Court adopted a more general reasonableness standard.
But "reasonableness" in this context seems to mean something other than ordinary
negligence: The Court's discussion in *Strickland* suggests something more like a
gross negligence standard. Why such a deferential approach? Why not hold defense
counsel to a tougher standard? What would be the consequences of doing so for the
independence of defense counsel, the attorney-client relationship, and the functions of an adversary system?

NOTES AND QUESTIONS ON THE APPLICATION OF *STRICKLAND*

   1. What is a defense lawyer's responsibility when dealing with possibly perjurious
testimony? In Nix v. Whiteside, 475 U.S. 157 (1986), the defendant (Whiteside) was
charged with murder. Initially, he told his court-appointed lawyer (Robinson) that
he stabbed the victim while the victim was reaching for a gun. Upon further questioning, however, he admitted that he had not actually seen a gun. No gun was found

at the crime scene, and none of the other witnesses reported seeing a gun. About one week before the trial, Whiteside told Robinson that he had seen something "metallic" in the victim's hand. He added, "If I don't say I saw a gun I'm dead." Robinson informed Whiteside that this would be perjury, and that he would not assist in it. Robinson told Whiteside that if he insisted on perjuring himself, Robinson would advise the trial court about the perjury, impeach Whiteside's testimony, and withdraw from Whiteside's representation.

The Court split 5-4 on the application of *Strickland*'s performance prong to Robinson's conduct, with the dissent critical of Robinson for essentially "judging" his own client, but the majority found Robinson's conduct acceptable under prevailing professional norms:

> . . . Considering Robinson's representation of respondent in light of the accepted norms of professional conduct, we discern no failure to adhere to reasonable professional standards that would in any sense make out a deprivation of the Sixth Amendment right to counsel. Whether Robinson's conduct is seen as a successful attempt to dissuade his client from committing the crime of perjury, or whether seen as a "threat" to withdraw from representation and disclose the illegal scheme, Robinson's representation of Whiteside falls well within accepted standards of professional conduct and the range of reasonable professional conduct acceptable under *Strickland*. . . .
>
> Whatever the scope of a constitutional right to testify, it is elementary that such a right does not extend to testifying *falsely*. In Harris v. New York, we assumed the right of an accused to testify "in his own defense, or to refuse to do so" and went on to hold that "that privilege cannot be construed to include the right to commit perjury. Having voluntarily taken the stand, petitioner was under an obligation to speak truthfully. . . ." 401 U.S., at 225. In *Harris* we held the defendant could be impeached by prior contrary statements which had been ruled inadmissible under Miranda v. Arizona. *Harris* and other cases make it crystal clear that there is no right whatever — constitutional or otherwise — for a defendant to use false evidence. . . .
>
> Robinson's admonitions to his client can in no sense be said to have forced respondent into an *impermissible* choice between his right to counsel and his right to testify as he proposed for there was no *permissible* choice to testify falsely. For defense counsel to take steps to persuade a criminal defendant to testify truthfully, or to withdraw, deprives the defendant of neither his right to counsel nor the right to testify truthfully. In United States v. Havens we made clear that "when defendants testify, they must testify truthfully or suffer the consequences." When an accused proposes to resort to perjury or to produce false evidence, one consequence is the risk of withdrawal of counsel.

All nine Justices agreed, however, that whether or not Robinson's performance was adequate, Whiteside could not have suffered "prejudice," within the meaning of *Strickland*. According to the majority:

> We hold that, as a matter of law, counsel's conduct complained of here cannot establish the prejudice required for relief under the second strand of the *Strickland* inquiry. . . . The *Strickland* Court noted that the "benchmark" of an ineffective assistance claim is the fairness of the adversary proceeding, and that in judging prejudice and the likelihood of a different outcome, "[a] defendant has no entitlement to the luck of a lawless decisionmaker." . . .
>
> In his attempt to evade the prejudice requirement of *Strickland*, Whiteside relies on cases involving conflicting loyalties of counsel. [See, e.g.,] Cuyler v. Sullivan, 446 U.S. 335 (1980). . . . Here, there was indeed a "conflict," but of a quite different kind; it was

one imposed on the attorney by the client's proposal to commit the crime of fabricating testimony without which, as he put it, "I'm dead." . . . If a "conflict" between a client's proposal and counsel's ethical obligation gives rise to a presumption that counsel's assistance was prejudicially ineffective, every guilty criminal's conviction would be suspect if the defendant had sought to obtain an acquittal by illegal means. Can anyone doubt what practices and problems would be spawned by such a rule and what volumes of litigation it would generate?

Whether he was persuaded or compelled to desist from perjury, Whiteside has no valid claim that confidence in the result of his trial has been diminished by his desisting from the contemplated perjury. Even if we were to assume that the jury might have believed his perjury, it does not follow that Whiteside was prejudiced. . . .

Whiteside's attorney treated Whiteside's proposed perjury in accord with professional standards, and since Whiteside's truthful testimony could not have prejudiced the result of his trial, the Court of Appeals was in error to direct the issuance of a writ of habeas corpus and must be reversed.

Id., at 171-176.

What effect does *Whiteside* have on the meaning of *Strickland*'s "prejudice" requirement? The one proposition that all nine Justices agreed upon in *Whiteside* was that the failure to use perjured testimony cannot satisfy that requirement. Why not? Preventing client perjury can of course affect the outcome of a case — indeed, affecting the outcome is presumably the entire point of the perjury. Yet all the Justices were prepared to hold that even if attorney Robinson's performance violated constitutional standards, and apparently even if his performance led to Whiteside's conviction, Whiteside suffered no Sixth Amendment prejudice. This position suggests that *Strickland* prejudice requires more than that attorney ineffectiveness have an effect on the outcome of the case; it requires the *right kind* of outcome effect. What kind of outcome effect counts? The idea seems to be that preventing perjured testimony by the defendant is not the sort of thing that leads to an unjust result, regardless of what one thinks of defense counsel's conduct. But what does "unjust" mean in this context? Must a defendant show a reasonable probability that he is innocent?

2. Lockhart v. Fretwell, 506 U.S. 364 (1993), was a capital case in which Fretwell's defense counsel failed to object to one of the aggravating circumstances that was used to authorize the death penalty. Under binding Eighth Circuit precedent, the objection surely would have succeeded, and the defendant almost surely would have avoided the death sentence. By the time the issue was raised in Fretwell's federal habeas corpus petition, however, an intervening Supreme Court decision had reversed the Eighth Circuit's prior precedent. Reviewing Fretwell's ineffective-assistance claim, the Court held that he suffered no "prejudice" under *Strickland*, because the outcome in his case was "neither unfair nor unreliable"; avoiding the death sentence based on erroneous precedent would have been a "windfall to which the law does not entitle" Fretwell. Id., at 366.

3. In Williams v. Taylor, 529 U.S. 362 (2000), the Court tried to explain the relationship among *Strickland*, *Lockhart*, and *Whiteside*:

The Virginia Supreme Court erred in holding that our decision in Lockhart v. Fretwell modified or in some way supplanted the rule set down in *Strickland*. It is true that while the *Strickland* test provides sufficient guidance for resolving virtually all ineffective-assistance-of-counsel claims, there are situations in which the overriding focus on fundamental fairness may affect the analysis. Thus, on the one hand, as *Strickland* itself explained, there are a few situations in which prejudice may be presumed. And, on the other hand, there are also situations in which it would be unjust to characterize the like-lihood of a different outcome as legitimate "prejudice." Even if a defendant's false tes-timony might have persuaded the jury to acquit him, it is not fundamentally unfair to conclude that he was not prejudiced by counsel's interference with his intended per-jury. Nix v. Whiteside.

Similarly, in [*Fretwell,*] we concluded that, given the overriding interest in funda-mental fairness, the likelihood of a different outcome attributable to an incorrect inter-pretation of the law should be regarded as a potential "windfall" to the defendant rather than the legitimate "prejudice" contemplated by our opinion in *Strickland*. . . . Because the ineffectiveness of Fretwell's counsel had not deprived him of any sub-stantive or procedural right to which the law entitled him, we held that his claim did not satisfy the "prejudice" component of the *Strickland* test.

Cases such as Nix v. Whiteside and Lockhart v. Fretwell do not justify a departure from a straightforward application of *Strickland* when the ineffectiveness of counsel does deprive the defendant of a substantive or procedural right to which the law entitles him. In the instant case, it is undisputed that Williams had a right — indeed, a constitutionally protected right — to provide the jury with the mitigating evidence that his trial counsel either failed to discover or failed to offer.

Id., at 391-393.[12] Are *Whiteside* and *Fretwell* now limited to their facts?

4. In Hill v. Lockhart, 477 U.S. 52 (1985), the defendant alleged that his guilty plea was involuntary as a result of ineffective assistance of counsel because he received erroneous information about his parole eligibility from his counsel. Coun-sel advised the defendant that he would have to serve one-third of his time before he would be eligible for parole, whereas in fact he had to serve one-half of his time as a result of a previous conviction, of which counsel was apparently not informed by the defendant. In applying *Strickland* to this case, the Court concluded that "in order to satisfy the 'prejudice' requirement, the defendant must show that there is a reasonable probability that, but for counsel's errors, he would not have pleaded guilty and would have insisted on going to trial."

Hill says that *Strickland*'s prejudice standard means the same thing in guilty plea cases as in cases that go to trial. But there is a particular kind of outcome effect in guilty plea cases that has no analogue for cases that go to trial. Many, perhaps most, guilty pleas are the product of plea bargaining. It is likely that, in many of these cases, attorney errors will not affect whether the defendant will plead guilty, but *will* affect the terms of the plea agreement — the charge, the prosecutor's sentencing recommendation, possibly (in states where such bargains are allowed) the actual sentence to be imposed by the judge, and so forth. Under *Hill*, those sorts of out-come effects apparently don't count, because the defendant cannot show that but for the attorney error he "would not have pleaded guilty and would have insisted on going to trial." Is that the right result? Is it consistent with *Strickland*? *Hill* is consid-ered in greater detail in Chapter 13, infra.

5. *Hill* addressed the application of the *prejudice* prong of *Strickland* to guilty pleas. In Padilla v. Kentucky, 130 S. Ct. 1473 (2010), by contrast, the Court con-cluded that a defense attorney's failure to fully advise the defendant concerning one special consequence of pleading guilty was ineffective *performance*. Counsel did not inform Padilla, a noncitizen who had resided lawfully in the United States for 40

12. The issues posed by Williams v. Taylor and related cases are discussed further at page 238, infra.

years and had served with honor in Vietnam, that his plea of guilty to a drug charge
would render him automatically removable and further told him that he need not
worry about the immigration consequences of the plea. The prior law had been
reasonably clear that, at most, the right to effective assistance extended to advice
concerning the direct consequences of a plea, and not to collateral consequences.
The effect of a conviction on immigration status had largely been viewed as
collateral. However, the Court concluded that the effect on Padilla was so
dramatic — automatic deportation after having spent 40 years in the United
States — that the direct/collateral distinction was blurred, and that, in any event, a
reasonably competent lawyer would have advised of such a clear and dramatic consequence. Justice Scalia dissented on the ground that the Court's opinion impermissibly breached the direct/collateral divide, leaving a highly ambiguous
admonition in its place that would lead to further instability in pleas and to substantial litigation.

The Court remanded for a determination of whether or not Padilla suffered
Strickland prejudice as a result of his attorney's mistaken advice. How do you think
that issue should be resolved in light of *Hill*?

6. Compare *Hill* with Glover v. United States, 531 U.S. 198 (2001), where in a
unanimous opinion delivered by Justice Kennedy, the Court considered the kinds
of errors in sentencing proceedings that might be deemed prejudicial enough to
support an ineffective-assistance claim:

> The issue presented rests upon the initial assumption, which we accept for analytic
> purposes, that the trial court erred in a Sentencing Guidelines determination after
> petitioner's conviction of a federal offense. [The petitioner was sentenced by the trial
> court to 84 months in prison. — Eds.] The legal error, petitioner alleges, increased his
> prison sentence by at least 6 months and perhaps by 21 months. We must decide
> whether this would be "prejudice" under Strickland v. Washington, 466 U.S. 668
> (1984). The Government is not ready to concede error in the sentencing determina-
> tion but now acknowledges that if an increased prison term did flow from an error the
> petitioner has established *Strickland* prejudice. In agreement with the Government and
> petitioner on this point, we reverse and remand for further proceedings. . . .
> [After his conviction was final, the defendant filed a motion to correct his sentence,
> alleging ineffective assistance of counsel as the reason for the error]. The District Court
> denied Glover's motion [for resentencing], determining that under Seventh Circuit
> precedent an increase of 6 to 21 months in a defendant's sentence was not significant
> enough to amount to prejudice for purposes of Strickland v. Washington. . . .
> It appears the Seventh Circuit drew the substance of its no-prejudice rule from our
> opinion in Lockhart v. Fretwell[, 506 U.S. 364 (1993)]. *Fretwell* holds that in some cir-
> cumstances a mere difference in outcome will not suffice to establish prejudice. The
> Seventh Circuit extracted from this holding the rule at issue here, which denies relief
> when the increase in sentence is said to be not so significant as to render the outcome
> of sentencing unreliable or fundamentally unfair. The Court explained last Term that
> our holding in *Fretwell* does not supplant the *Strickland* analysis. The Seventh Circuit
> was incorrect to rely on *Fretwell* to deny relief to persons attacking their sentence who
> might show deficient performance in counsel's failure to object to an error of law affect-
> ing the calculation of a sentence because the sentence increase does not meet some
> baseline standard of prejudice. Authority does not suggest that a minimal amount of
> additional time in prison cannot constitute prejudice. Quite to the contrary, our juris-
> prudence suggests that any amount of actual jail time has Sixth Amendment signifi-
> cance. Compare Argersinger v. Hamlin, 407 U.S. 25 (1972) (holding that the assistance

of counsel must be provided when a defendant is tried for a crime that results in a sentence of imprisonment), with Scott v. Illinois, 440 U.S. 367 (1979) (holding that a criminal defendant has no Sixth Amendment right to counsel when his trial does not result in a sentence of imprisonment). Our decisions on the right to jury trial in a criminal case do not suggest that there is no prejudice in the circumstances here. Those cases have limited the right to jury trial to offenses where the potential punishment was imprisonment for six months or more. See *Argersinger*, supra, at 29 (citing Duncan v. Louisiana, 391 U.S. 145 (1968)). But they do not control the question whether a showing of prejudice, in the context of a claim for ineffective assistance of counsel, requires a significant increase in a term of imprisonment.

The Seventh Circuit's rule is not well considered in any event, because there is no obvious dividing line by which to measure how much longer a sentence must be for the increase to constitute substantial prejudice. Indeed, it is not even clear if the relevant increase is to be measured in absolute terms or by some fraction of the total authorized sentence. Although the amount by which a defendant's sentence is increased by a particular decision may be a factor to consider in determining whether counsel's performance in failing to argue the point constitutes ineffective assistance, under a determinate system of constrained discretion such as the Sentencing Guidelines it cannot serve as a bar to a showing of prejudice. We hold that the Seventh Circuit erred in engrafting this additional requirement onto the prejudice branch of the *Strickland* test. This is not a case where trial strategies, in retrospect, might be criticized for leading to a harsher sentence. Here we consider the sentencing calculation itself, a calculation resulting from a ruling which, if it had been error, would have been correctable on appeal. We express no opinion on the ultimate merits of Glover's claim because the question of deficient performance is not before us, but it is clear that prejudice flowed from the asserted error in sentencing. . . .

Id., at 198-701.

Hill held that defendants who plead guilty may not claim *Strickland* prejudice based on the notion that a minimally competent defense attorney would have gotten them a better sentencing deal; only a showing that the defendant would have rejected the prosecution's plea bargain altogether will suffice. Based on *Glover*, however, it would appear that *any* effect on the length of a prison or jail term — even an effect as small as 6 to 21 months — can constitute *Strickland* prejudice. Does that mean that *Glover* effectively overrules *Hill*? If not, how would you reconcile the two cases?

How does the result in *Glover* square with the way trial errors are analyzed? Suppose defense counsel in *Glover* had made a mistake at Glover's trial; suppose further that the mistake had raised the odds of Glover's conviction by, say, 1 percent. Glover was then convicted. Presumably, counsel's error would not satisfy *Strickland*'s prejudice prong, because it did not raise a "reasonable probability" that, but for the error, the outcome would have been different.

Now suppose Glover's counsel's error cost Glover one extra month in prison — i.e., but for the error, Glover would have been sentenced to 83 months, instead of the 84-month sentence he actually received. Why does that extra month amount to prejudice, when adding 1 percent to the odds of a conviction doesn't? And if the latter premise is wrong — if even a small increase in the odds of a conviction *does* amount to prejudice — then what is left of the "reasonable probability" standard?

Perhaps these questions misconceive what is really at stake in these cases. Perhaps the right question to ask is whether a change in the probability of guilt plausibly could affect the conclusion of guilt beyond a reasonable doubt. If so, the error would be prejudicial; if not, it would not be. This harmonizes *Glover* with *Strickland*, although it is by no means clear that this is what the Court had in mind.

Note, incidentally, that *Glover*-type ineffectiveness claims would seem to be plausible only where the defendant is deprived, as a result of his lawyer's mistake, of a particular sentence (or sentencing range) to which he is legally entitled. This, in turn, is likely to be true only where the sentence is determinate, as opposed to broadly discretionary. Otherwise, it would be very difficult for the reviewing court to say that the lawyer's mistake made a "reasonable probability" of a difference in the sentencing outcome. For more on determinate sentencing and its consequences, see infra, Chapter 15.

7. In Roe v. Flores-Ortega, 528 U.S. 470 (2000), the Court considered the implications of *Strickland* for postsentencing advice concerning the right to appeal and the necessity for the timely filing of a notice of appeal. The filing deadline passed, and the facts were ambiguous as to whether counsel had ever consulted with the client about the appellate process or advised him of his need to file the notice of appeal. The Court held that the *Strickland* standards applied, and that, with respect to the performance prong, flat rules concerning consultation were not constitutionally justifiable. Nonetheless, the Court opined that "[I]f counsel has consulted with the defendant, the question of deficient performance is easily answered: Counsel performs in a professionally unreasonable manner only by failing to follow the defendant's express instructions with respect to an appeal." What if counsel had *not* consulted with the client? Again, no flat rules exist, according to the Court, but: "We instead hold that counsel has a constitutionally imposed duty to consult with the defendant about an appeal where there is reason to think either (1) that a rational defendant would want to appeal (for example, because there are nonfrivolous grounds for appeal, or (2) that this particular defendant reasonably demonstrated to counsel that he was interested in appealing." As to prejudice, if the failure to consult deprives an individual of the right to appeal, prejudice will be presumed if the defendant demonstrates "that there is a reasonable probability that, but for counsel's deficient failure to consult with him about an appeal, he would have timely appealed."

NOTES ON INEFFECTIVE ASSISTANCE, HABEAS CORPUS, AND THE DEATH PENALTY

Like most of the Supreme Court's key ineffective assistance cases — Strickland v. Washington, 466 U.S. 668 (1984), Nix v. Whiteside, 475 U.S. 157 (1986), Williams v. Taylor, 529 U.S. 362 (2000), Bell v. Cone, 535 U.S. 685 (2002), and Wiggins v. Smith, 539 U.S. 510 (2003), are all examples — *Rompilla* is a federal habeas corpus decision. That is no accident. Ineffective assistance claims are usually first raised after the defendant has lost both at trial *and* on direct appeal. This is for two separate reasons: (1) defendant's trial counsel, who usually handles the direct appeal as well, is unlikely to raise his own ineffectiveness as an appellate issue; and (2) most appellate courts lack the authority (and the capacity) to hold evidentiary hearings, which are usually required to flesh out the details of an IAC claim. So, instead, most defendants first raise their IAC claims pro se in a separate proceeding in the state trial court, after losing on appeal. That separate proceeding, which all state court systems provide (with some variations as to procedural details), is usually referred to as "state post-conviction" or "state habeas corpus."[13] In all the cases cited at the beginning of this paragraph, the defendant's IAC claim was first rejected in state habeas, after which the defendant then filed the claim in federal district court under the *federal* habeas statute.

In the Anti-Terrorism and Effective Death Penalty Act of 1996 (AEDPA), Congress established a deferential standard of review for federal habeas decisions. Federal courts are to grant relief and overturn state-court decisions only when they are "contrary to, or involved an unreasonable application of, clearly established Federal law, as determined by the Supreme Court of the United States." 28 U.S.C. §2254(d)(1). The Court has stressed that "an *unreasonable* application of federal law is different from an *incorrect* application of federal law." Williams v. Taylor, 529 U.S. 362, 410-411 (2000) (emphasis in original).

Recall that in *Strickland*, the Court emphasized that, when judging ineffective assistance claims, courts should defer to the decision making of defense counsel. AEDPA requires similar deference to state court judges who deny IAC claims. The result, when deference is piled upon deference, is a tall mountain for defendants to climb. To prevail in federal court, the defendant (now called a "habeas petitioner") must show that trial counsel behaved so unreasonably that it was unreasonable — and not merely incorrect — for the state habeas court to deny relief. (Got that?) If AEDPA means what it says, then federal habeas is an exceedingly unfriendly environment for ineffective assistance claims.

That is the harsh reality for most ineffective assistance litigation. A recent study of more than 2,300 federal habeas corpus petitions filed since AEDPA showed that the overall success rate in noncapital cases was less than one-third of 1 percent; the study also found that, although about half of the petitions studied contained an IAC claim, *not one* of those claims ultimately led to a grant of relief. See Nancy J. King, Fred L. Cheesman II, & Brian J. Ostrom, Final Technical Report: Habeas Litigation in U.S. District Courts, 52, 58 (2007), available at http://www.ncjrs.gov/pdffiles1/nij/grants/219559.pdf.

But the story is a little different in capital cases. In Williams v. Taylor, for example, a capital defendant claimed that his counsel was ineffective for failing to raise various mitigating arguments; on state habeas, the Virginia Supreme Court rejected the claim. Notwithstanding the language quoted above, the Supreme Court *granted* relief. Another example is Wiggins v. Smith, 539 U.S. 510 (2003). Again, a capital defendant claimed that his counsel failed to raise appropriate mitigating arguments; again, the state habeas courts rejected the claim. And once again, the Supreme Court *granted* relief, notwithstanding AEDPA. *Rompilla* was yet another in this line of capital habeas cases. Tellingly, Justice Souter's majority opinion barely mentioned AEDPA or Williams v. Taylor, except for the bottom line that the state court's decision was "objectively unreasonable." Justice O'Connor's concurrence was even more cryptic:

---

13. One important variation, seen today in a number of states, is the "consolidated appeal," in which the functions of the direct appeal and the state postconviction proceeding are combined into a single procedural stage.

> In the particular circumstances of this case, the attorneys' failure to obtain and review the case file from their client's prior conviction did not meet standards of "reasonable professional judgment." [*Strickland*, 466 U.S.], at 691. Because the Court's opinion is consistent with the "case-by-case examination of the evidence" called for under our cases, Williams v. Taylor, 529 U.S. 362, 391 (2000), I join the opinion.

Id., at 396. That does not sound much like deference to the state courts. Evidently, AEDPA's reasonableness standard meant little in *Rompilla*.

At the least, *Williams*, *Wiggins*, and *Rompilla* stand for the proposition that the reasonableness standards in *Strickland*'s performance prong and in AEDPA are applied more generously when reviewing defense counsel's performance *in capital sentencing proceedings*. Why would the Court treat such cases differently? Perhaps the answer is simply that the death penalty is different from all other punishments. But is it different in a way that relates specifically to ineffective assistance claims? Should defense lawyers at capital sentencing hearings be held to a higher standard than at criminal trials in general? See Stephen B. Bright, Counsel for the Poor: The Death Sentence Not for the Worst Crime but for the Worst Lawyer, 103 Yale L.J. 1835 (1994); and Welsh S. White, Effective Assistance of Counsel in Capital Cases: The Evolving Standard of Care, [1993] U. Ill. L. Rev. 323 (both answering "yes").

But maybe the real point of cases like *Williams*, *Wiggins*, and *Rompilla* isn't that ineffective assistance standards apply differently in death penalty cases. Maybe it's that the Court *feels* differently about death penalty cases. Maybe the Court simply wants to regulate capital cases more closely than other state criminal cases — and ineffective assistance doctrine provides a useful method for doing so. Indeed, it may be one of the *only* remaining methods for doing so — precisely because AEDPA, together with many of the Court's own modern decisions restricting access to federal habeas, has largely taken away from the federal courts the power to reverse state criminal convictions and sentences on most federal constitutional grounds. Today, just about the only constitutional claims that still get relatively full federal review are ineffective assistance claims and *Brady* claims (i.e., claims that the prosecution withheld helpful evidence from the defense — see Chapter 12, infra). Not surprisingly, IAC claims and *Brady* claims tend to dominate federal habeas litigation.

There remain some limits on the use of ineffective assistance doctrine to regulate capital cases. In Schriro v. Landrigan, 550 U.S. 465 (2007), the defendant refused to allow his defense counsel to present mitigating evidence at capital sentencing, and indeed told the trial judge that he did not want to have such evidence introduced, preferring instead to "bring on" the death penalty. The Court, by 5-4, held that the Ninth Circuit erroneously ordered a federal district court to hold an evidentiary hearing on the defendant's ineffective assistance claim, finding instead that the denial of the evidentiary hearing was within the district court's discretion in light of the defendant's own actions.

Schriro suggests that, at least in some cases, a capital defendant will be held to the negative consequences of his own decisions. In light of this, should a defense lawyer always be required to secure the defendant's prior consent before conceding guilt at trial and focusing his efforts entirely on arguing for leniency at capital sentencing? If the lawyer concedes guilt without the defendant's consent, is this the kind of "fail[ure] to subject the prosecution's case to meaningful adversarial testing," that triggers the *Cronic* presumption of prejudice? In Florida v. Nixon, 543 U.S. 175 (2004), the Supreme Court unanimously answered "no" to both questions

(Chief Justice Rehnquist was ill and did not participate). According to the Court, the decision to concede guilt in a capital case is not the same as entering a guilty plea or waiving basic trial rights (both of which would have to be done with the defendant's express consent). Nixon's defense lawyer discussed his choice of strategy with Nixon on several occasions, explaining the pros and cons thereof, but Nixon repeatedly refused to respond: "Given Nixon's constant resistance to answering inquiries put to him by counsel and court, . . . [his lawyer] was not additionally required to gain express consent before conceding Nixon's guilt." Moreover, the Court held, any review of the lawyer's decision to concede guilt must be conducted pursuant to the traditional *Strickland* standards of "performance" and "prejudice," rather than under the *Cronic* approach.

2. Multiple Representation

A special problem of effective assistance arises in cases in which a lawyer represents more than one client in either joint or separate proceedings. The difficulty results from the potential conflict of interest among the defendants. In separate trials of accomplices, for example, a lawyer will have to choose whether to call certain potentially exculpating witnesses at the first trial. On the one hand, if the lawyer chooses not to call the witnesses, the defense in the present case will be impaired in order to protect the defense in the later trial. On the other hand, if the witnesses are called, the defense at the first trial will be bolstered at the cost to the defense at the second trial of exposing to the prosecution the contents of the defendant's case. Moreover, it is the lawyer, who owes the duty of essentially undivided allegiance to the client, who will have to make the choices. Obviously, the necessity of making such choices compromises the faithful discharge of the duty and may impact adversely on the client's interests.

The problems are exacerbated in joint proceedings. Consider the following true story, recounted in Gary T. Lowenthal, Joint Representation in Criminal Cases: A Critical Appraisal, 64 Va. L. Rev. 939, 941-942 (1978):

> An attorney appeared in a municipal court for the purpose of requesting a reduction of bail for four defendants jointly charged with possession of a large cache of drugs seized from a communal house. Referring to the first of his clients, the lawyer stated: "This defendant should be released on his own recognizance, Your Honor, because he has no rap sheet. Obviously he is not a hardened criminal and should not be locked up with others who are." When the second defendant's case was called, counsel argued: "No drugs were found in this defendant's bedroom, Your Honor. His chance for an acquittal is great and consequently it is highly likely that he will show up for trial." On behalf of the third defendant, the lawyer began to argue that his client had lived in the area all of his life. The judge interrupted the lawyer, asking him if any drugs had been seized from the bedroom of defendant number three. The lawyer responded. "No comment, Your Honor." The judge countered with the remark: "I suppose that this client also has a prior record, making him a hardened criminal," evoking the response that although the defendant had a prior record, he certainly was not a hardened criminal. The fourth

defendant then interrupted the proceedings by eagerly requesting to be represented by the public defender.[11] . . .

The episode related above illustrates a circumstance of the criminal process that is essential to an understanding of joint representation in practice. Decisionmakers exercise considerable discretion in evaluating and comparing defendants at every stage of a criminal case. The government, for example, has substantial leeway in determining which charges, if any, to file against an accused; a judge or magistrate may consider a broad range of factors when predicting whether a defendant will appear in court if released on bail; the prosecutor's discretion in plea bargaining is almost unlimited in most jurisdictions; a trier of fact is free to ignore the evidence in acquitting the defendant; and a judge or jury is expected to differentiate among convicted offenders to arrive at an appropriate sentence for each. At each step in the process, a defendant's appearance, attitude, and background, as well as the extent of his culpability, will influence decisionmakers. As a result, a lawyer's effectiveness in representing a client will depend in virtually every case on how well he can manipulate these factors to the advantage of the client. Thus the lawyer must differentiate his client from others charged with the same or similar conduct and emphasize those attributes of his client that will have a favorable effect on the prosecutor, judge, or jury.

As Professor Lowenthal explains, the ability of a lawyer to distinguish one client from another is greatly compromised in cases of joint representation. Yet joint representation may offer some advantages, including efficiency as well as the possibility of discouraging codefendants from turning on each other. The question thus arises whether there are circumstances that render joint representation — either at the request, or over the objection, of the codefendants — so defective as to violate the right to counsel.

CUYLER v. SULLIVAN

Certiorari to the United States Court of Appeals for the Third Circuit
446 U.S. 335 (1980)

MR. JUSTICE POWELL delivered the opinion of the Court.

I

Respondent John Sullivan was indicted with Gregory Carchidi and Anthony DiPasquale for the first-degree murders of John Gorey and Rita Janda. The victims, a labor official and his companion, were shot to death in Gorey's second-story office at the Philadelphia headquarters of Teamsters' Local 107. Francis McGrath, a janitor, saw the three defendants in the building just before the shooting. They appeared to be awaiting someone, and they encouraged McGrath to do his work on another day. McGrath ignored their suggestions. Shortly afterward, Gorey arrived

---

11. This incident occurred in March 1972, before Judge Jacqueline Taber in Department Six of the Oakland-Piedmont Municipal Court, Oakland, California, when I was an Assistant Public Defender for Alameda County, California. See Letter from Judge Jacqueline Taber to Gary T. Lowenthal (Oct. 23, 1978) (copy on file with the Virginia Law Review Association). It is the most vivid of many such incidents that prompted me to write this article.

and went to his office. McGrath then heard what sounded like firecrackers exploding in rapid succession. Carchidi, who was in the room where McGrath was working, abruptly directed McGrath to leave the building and to say nothing. McGrath hastily complied. When he returned to the building about 15 minutes later, the defendants were gone. The victims' bodies were discovered the next morning.

Two privately retained lawyers, G. Fred DiBona and A. Charles Peruto, represented all three defendants throughout the state proceedings that followed the indictment. Sullivan had different counsel at the medical examiner's inquest, but he thereafter accepted representation from the two lawyers retained by his codefendants because he could not afford to pay his own lawyer.[1] At no time did Sullivan or his lawyers object to the multiple representation. Sullivan was the first defendant to come to trial. The evidence against him was entirely circumstantial, consisting primarily of McGrath's testimony. At the close of the Commonwealth's case, the defense rested without presenting any evidence. The jury found Sullivan guilty and fixed his penalty at life imprisonment. . . . Sullivan's codefendants, Carchidi and DiPasquale, were acquitted at separate trials.

Sullivan then petitioned for collateral relief. . . . He alleged, among other claims, that he had been denied effective assistance of counsel because his defense lawyers represented conflicting interests. In five days of hearings, the Court of Common Pleas heard evidence from Sullivan, Carchidi, Sullivan's lawyers, and the judge who presided at Sullivan's trial.

DiBona and Peruto had different recollections of their roles at the trials of the three defendants. DiBona testified that he and Peruto had been "associate counsel" at each trial. . . . Peruto recalled that he had been chief counsel for Carchidi and DiPasquale, but that he merely had assisted DiBona in Sullivan's trial. DiBona and Peruto also gave conflicting accounts of the decision to rest Sullivan's defense. DiBona said he had encouraged Sullivan to testify even though the Commonwealth had presented a very weak case. Peruto remembered that he had not "want[ed] the defense to go on because I thought we would only be exposing the [defense] witnesses for the other two trials that were coming up." . . . Sullivan testified that he had deferred to his lawyers' decision not to present evidence for the defense. But other testimony suggested that Sullivan preferred not to take the stand because cross-examination might have disclosed an extramarital affair. Finally, Carchidi claimed he would have appeared at Sullivan's trial to rebut McGrath's testimony about Carchidi's statement at the time of the murders.

The Court of Common Pleas . . . did not pass directly on the claim that defense counsel had a conflict of interest, but it found that counsel fully advised Sullivan about his decision not to testify. . . . All other claims for collateral relief were rejected or reserved for consideration in the new appeal.

The Pennsylvania Supreme Court affirmed both Sullivan's original conviction and the denial of collateral relief. . . .

Having exhausted his state remedies, Sullivan sought habeas corpus relief in the United States District Court for the Eastern District of Pennsylvania. The petition was referred to a Magistrate, who found that Sullivan's defense counsel had represented conflicting interests. The District Court, however, accepted the Pennsylvania

---

1. DiBona and Peruto were paid in part with funds raised by friends of the three defendants. The record does not disclose the source of the balance of their fee, but no part of the money came from either Sullivan or his family.

Supreme Court's conclusion that there had been no multiple representation. The court also found that, assuming there had been multiple representation, the evidence adduced in the state postconviction proceeding revealed no conflict of interest. . . .

The Court of Appeals for the Third Circuit reversed. . . . We granted certiorari to consider recurring issues left unresolved by Holloway v. Arkansas, 435 U.S. 475 (1978). We now vacate and remand. . . .

IV

We come . . . to Sullivan's claim that he was denied the effective assistance of counsel guaranteed by the Sixth Amendment because his lawyers had a conflict of interest. The claim raises two issues expressly reserved in Holloway v. Arkansas, [Id.] at 483-484. The first is whether a state trial judge must inquire into the propriety of multiple representation even though no party lodges an objection. The second is whether the mere possibility of a conflict of interest warrants the conclusion that the defendant was deprived of his right to counsel.

A

In *Holloway*, a single public defender represented three defendants at the same trial. The trial court refused to consider the appointment of separate counsel despite the defense lawyer's timely and repeated assertions that the interests of his clients conflicted. This Court recognized that a lawyer forced to represent codefendants whose interests conflict cannot provide the adequate legal assistance required by the Sixth Amendment. Given the trial court's failure to respond to timely objections, however, the Court did not consider whether the alleged conflict actually existed. It simply held that the trial court's error unconstitutionally endangered the right to counsel.

Holloway requires state trial courts to investigate timely objections to multiple representation. But nothing in our precedents suggests that the Sixth Amendment requires state courts themselves to initiate inquiries into the propriety of multiple representation in every case.[10] Defense counsel have an ethical obligation to avoid conflicting representations and to advise the court promptly when a conflict of interest arises during the course of trial. Absent special circumstances, therefore, trial courts may assume either that multiple representation entails no conflict or that the lawyer and his clients knowingly accept such risk of conflict as may exist. Indeed, as the Court noted in *Holloway*, trial courts necessarily rely in large measure upon the good faith and good judgment of defense counsel. "An 'attorney representing two defendants in a criminal matter is in the best position professionally and

---

10. In certain cases, proposed Federal Rule of Criminal Procedure 44(c) provides that the federal district courts "shall promptly inquire with respect to . . . joint representation and shall personally advise each defendant of his right to the effective assistance of counsel, including separate representation." See also ABA Project on Standards for Criminal Justice, Function of the Trial Judge §3.4(b) (App. Draft 1972).

Several Courts of Appeals already invoke their supervisory power to require similar inquiries. As our promulgation of Rule 44(c) suggests, we view such an exercise of the supervisory power as a desirable practice. See generally William W. Schwarzer, Dealing with Incompetent Counsel — The Trial Judge's Role, 93 Harv. L. Rev. 633, 653-654 (1980). . . .

ethically to determine when a conflict of interest exists or will probably develop in the course of a trial.'" Unless the trial court knows or should have known that a particular conflict exists, the court need not initiate an inquiry.

Nothing in the circumstances of this case indicates that the trial court had a duty to inquire whether there was a conflict of interest. The provision of separate trials for Sullivan and his codefendants significantly reduced the potential for a divergence in their interests. No participant in Sullivan's trial ever objected to the multiple representation. DiBona's opening argument for Sullivan outlined a defense compatible with the view that none of the defendants was connected with the murders. . . . The opening argument also suggested that counsel was not afraid to call witnesses whose testimony might be needed at the trials of Sullivan's codefendants. . . . Finally, as the Court of Appeals noted, counsel's critical decision to rest Sullivan's defense was on its face a reasonable tactical response to the weakness of the circumstantial evidence presented by the prosecutor. On these facts, we conclude that the Sixth Amendment imposed upon the trial court no affirmative duty to inquire into the propriety of multiple representation.

B

Holloway reaffirmed that multiple representation does not violate the Sixth Amendment unless it gives rise to a conflict of interest. Since a possible conflict inheres in almost every instance of multiple representation, a defendant who objects to multiple representation must have the opportunity to show that potential conflicts impermissibly imperil his right to a fair trial. But unless the trial court fails to afford such an opportunity, a reviewing court cannot presume that the possibility for conflict has resulted in ineffective assistance of counsel. Such a presumption would preclude multiple representation even in cases where "[a] common defense . . . gives strength against a common attack." Id., at 482-483, quoting Glasser v. United States, 315 U.S. 60, 92 (Frankfurter, J., dissenting).

In order to establish a violation of the Sixth Amendment, a defendant who raised no objection at trial must demonstrate that an actual conflict of interest adversely affected his lawyer's performance. In Glasser v. United States, for example, the record showed that defense counsel failed to cross-examine a prosecution witness whose testimony linked Glasser with the crime, and failed to resist the presentation of arguably inadmissible evidence. The Court found that both omissions resulted from counsel's desire to diminish the jury's perception of a codefendant's guilt. Indeed, the evidence of counsel's "struggle to serve two masters [could not] seriously be doubted." Since this actual conflict of interest impaired Glasser's defense, the Court reversed his conviction.

Dukes v. Warden, 406 U.S. 250 (1972), presented a contrasting situation. Dukes pleaded guilty on the advice of two lawyers, one of whom also represented Dukes' codefendants on an unrelated charge. Dukes later learned that this lawyer had sought leniency for the codefendants by arguing that their cooperation with the police induced Dukes to plead guilty. Dukes argued in this Court that his lawyer's conflict of interest had infected his plea. We found "nothing in the record . . . which would indicate that the alleged conflict resulted in ineffective assistance of counsel and did in fact render the plea in question involuntary and unintelligent." Since Dukes did not identify an actual lapse in representation, we affirmed the denial of habeas corpus relief.

Glasser established that unconstitutional multiple representation is never harmless error. Once the Court concluded that Glasser's lawyer had an actual conflict of
interest, it refused "to indulge in nice calculations as to the amount of prejudice"
attributable to the conflict. The conflict itself demonstrated a denial of the "right to
have the effective assistance of counsel." 315 U.S., at 76. Thus, a defendant who
shows that a conflict of interest actually affected the adequacy of his representation
need not demonstrate prejudice in order to obtain relief. But until a defendant
shows that his counsel actively represented conflicting interests, he has not established the constitutional predicate for his claim of ineffective assistance. . . .

C

The Court of Appeals granted Sullivan relief because he had shown that the multiple representation in this case involved a possible conflict of interest. We hold that
the possibility of conflict is insufficient to impugn a criminal conviction. In order to
demonstrate a violation of his Sixth Amendment rights, a defendant must establish
that an actual conflict of interest adversely affected his lawyer's performance. Sullivan believes he should prevail even under this standard. He emphasizes Peruto's
admission that the decision to rest Sullivan's defense reflected a reluctance to
expose witnesses who later might have testified for the other defendants. The petitioner, on the other hand, points to DiBona's contrary testimony and to evidence
that Sullivan himself wished to avoid taking the stand. Since the Court of Appeals
did not weigh these conflicting contentions under the proper legal standard, its
judgment is vacated and the case is remanded for further proceedings consistent
with this opinion.

So ordered.

MR. JUSTICE MARSHALL, concurring in part and dissenting in part. . . .

I believe . . . that the potential for conflict of interest in representing multiple
defendants is "so grave," see ABA Project on Standards for Criminal Justice,
Defense Function, Standard 4-3.5(b) (App. Draft, 2d ed. 1979), that whenever two
or more defendants are represented by the same attorney the trial judge must make
a preliminary determination that the joint representation is the product of the
defendants' informed choice. I therefore [think] . . . that the trial court has a duty
to inquire whether there is multiple representation, to warn defendants of the possible risks of such representation, and to ascertain that the representation is the
result of the defendants' informed choice.

I dissent from the Court's formulation of the proper standard for determining
whether multiple representation has violated the defendant's right to the effective
assistance of counsel. The Court holds that in the absence of an objection at trial,
the defendant must show "that an actual conflict of interest adversely affected his
lawyer's performance." . . . If the Court's holding would require a defendant to
demonstrate that his attorney's trial performance differed from what it would have
been if the defendant had been the attorney's only client, I believe it is inconsistent
with our previous cases. Such a test is not only unduly harsh, but incurably speculative as well. The appropriate question under the Sixth Amendment is whether an
actual, relevant conflict of interests existed during the proceedings. If it did, the
conviction must be reversed. Since such a conflict was present in this case, I would
affirm the judgment of the Court of Appeals.

Our cases make clear that every defendant has a constitutional right to "the assistance of an attorney unhindered by a conflict of interests." Holloway v. Arkansas, 435 U.S. 475, 483, n. 5 (1978). "[T]he 'assistance of counsel' guaranteed by the Sixth Amendment contemplates that such assistance be untrammeled and unimpaired by a court order requiring that one lawyer shall simultaneously represent conflicting interests." Glasser v. United States, 315 U.S. 60, 70 (1942). If "[t]he possibility of the inconsistent interests of [the clients] was brought home to the court" by means of an objection at trial, id., at 71, the court may not require joint representation. But if no objection was made at trial, the appropriate inquiry is whether a conflict actually existed during the course of the representation.

Because it is the simultaneous representation of conflicting interests against which the Sixth Amendment protects a defendant, he need go no further than to show the existence of an actual conflict. An actual conflict of interests negates the unimpaired loyalty a defendant is constitutionally entitled to expect and receive from his attorney.

Moreover, a showing that an actual conflict adversely affected counsel's performance is not only unnecessary, it is often an impossible task. As the Court emphasized in *Holloway*:

> [I]n a case of joint representation of conflicting interests the evil — it bears repeating — is in what the advocate finds himself compelled to *refrain* from doing. . . . It may be possible in some cases to identify from the record the prejudice resulting from an attorney's failure to undertake certain trial tasks, but even with a record of the sentencing hearing available it would be difficult to judge intelligently the impact of a conflict on the attorney's representation of a client. And to assess the impact of a conflict of interests on the attorney's options, tactics, and decisions in plea negotiations would be virtually impossible. 435 U.S., at 490-491.

Accordingly, in *Holloway* we emphatically rejected the suggestion that a defendant must show prejudice in order to be entitled to relief. For the same reasons, it would usually be futile to attempt to determine how counsel's conduct would have been different if he had not been under conflicting duties. . . .

NOTES AND QUESTIONS

1. What does it mean to say that "a defendant who shows that a conflict of interest actually affected the adequacy of his representation need not demonstrate prejudice in order to obtain relief"?

2. In Burger v. Kemp, 483 U.S. 776 (1987), the Court held that an actual conflict of interest was not present in the following circumstances: Two law partners represented two codefendants in a capital murder case. One of the partners wrote the appellate briefs for both defendants. The brief filed on Burger's behalf did not make a "lesser culpability" argument (i.e., argue that Burger was the less culpable of the killers); Burger argued that that omission showed an actual conflict that adversely affected counsel's representation. The Court concluded that the "decision to forgo this [argument] had a sound strategic basis," and found that if there were any conflict, it had not affected the representation Burger received.

3. The *Holloway* case, cited and discussed in *Sullivan*, is a prime example of what can go wrong when a trial judge is insensitive to the potential problems of joint

representation. Public defender Harold Hall, appointed to represent three code-fendants charged with robbery and rape, moved twice before trial for separate counsel based on conflict of interest, but the trial judge denied both motions. Here is what happened next:

On the second day of trial, after the prosecution had rested its case, Hall advised the court that, against his recommendation, all three defendants had decided to testify. He then stated:

> Now, since I have been appointed, I had previously filed a motion asking the Court to appoint a separate attorney for each defendant because of a possible conflict of interest. This conflict will probably be now coming up since each one of them wants to testify.

> *The Court:* That's all right; let them testify. There is no conflict of interest. Every time I try more than one person in this court each one blames it on the other one.
>
> *Mr. Hall:* I have talked to each one of these defendants, and I have talked to them individually, not collectively.
>
> *The Court:* Now talk to them collectively.

The court then indicated satisfaction that each petitioner understood the nature and consequences of his right to testify on his own behalf, whereupon Hall observed:

> I am in a position now where I am more or less muzzled as to any cross-examination.

> *The Court:* You have no right to cross-examine your own witness.
>
> *Mr. Hall:* Or to examine them.
>
> *The Court:* You have a right to examine them, but have no right to cross-examine them. The prosecuting attorney does that.
>
> *Mr. Hall:* If one [defendant] takes the stand, somebody needs to protect the other two's interest while that one is testifying, and I can't do that since I have talked to each one individually.
>
> *The Court:* Well, you have talked to them, I assume, individually and collectively, too. They all say they want to testify. I think it's perfectly alright [*sic*] for them to testify if they want to, or not. It's their business. . . . Each defendant said he wants to testify, and there will be no cross-examination of these witnesses, just a direct examination by you.
>
> *Mr. Hall:* Your Honor, I can't even put them on direct examination because if I ask them —
>
> *The Court:* (Interposing) You can just put them on the stand and tell the Court that you have advised them of their rights and they want to testify; then you tell the man to go ahead and relate what he wants to. That's all you need to do.

Holloway took the stand on his own behalf, testifying that during the time described as the time of the robbery, he was at his brother's home. His brother had previously given similar testimony. When Welch, a codefendant, took the witness stand, the record shows Hall advised him, as he had Holloway, that "I cannot ask you any questions that might tend to incriminate any one of the three of you. . . . Now, the only thing I can say is tell these ladies and gentlemen of the jury what you know about this case." Welch responded that he did not "have any kind of speech ready for the jury or anything. I thought I was going to be questioned." When Welch denied, from the witness stand, that he was at the restaurant the night of the robbery, Holloway interrupted, asking:

Your Honor, are we allowed to make an objection?

The Court: No, sir. Your counsel will take care of any objections.

Mr. Hall: Your Honor, that is what I am trying to say. I can't cross-examine them.

The Court: You proceed like I tell you to, Mr. Hall. You have no right to cross-examine your own witness anyhow.

Id., at 478-480. The Court reversed Holloway's convictions:

> Here trial counsel, by the pretrial motions . . . and by his accompanying representations, made as an officer of the court, focused explicitly on the probable risk of a conflict of interests. The judge then failed either to appoint separate counsel or to take adequate steps to ascertain whether the risk was too remote to warrant separate counsel. We hold that the failure, in the face of the representations made by counsel weeks before trial and again before the jury was empaneled, deprived petitioners of the guarantee of "assistance of counsel."

Id., at 484. The Court also concluded that "whenever a trial court improperly requires joint representation over timely objection reversal is automatic." Id., at 488.

After *Sullivan*, and taking *Holloway* into account, what are the consequences of making, as compared to not making, a pretrial objection to joint representation?

4. In *Sullivan*, the trial judge had no good reason to suspect the potential conflict. What should the standard of effective assistance be if the trial judge was, or should have been, aware of a potential conflict? Should there be a duty to inquire, even if nobody objects? In the absence of judicial inquiry, should prejudice be presumed if counsel has any conflict whatsoever? Does *Sullivan* apply to every conflict of interest or only to those involving multiple representations? Ought there be different standards for "active" representation of conflicted interests as compared to the kind of conflict that may emerge from the prior representation of a different person?

MICKENS v. TAYLOR, 535 U.S. 162 (2002): In 1993, a Virginia jury convicted petitioner Mickens of the premeditated murder of Timothy Hall during or following the commission of an attempted forcible sodomy. Finding the murder outrageously and wantonly vile, it sentenced petitioner to death. In June 1998, Mickens filed a petition for writ of habeas corpus . . . in the United States District Court for the Eastern District of Virginia, alleging, inter alia, that he was denied effective assistance of counsel because one of his court-appointed attorneys had a conflict of interest at trial. Federal habeas counsel had discovered that petitioner's lead trial attorney, Bryan Saunders, was representing Hall (the victim) on assault and concealed-weapons charges at the time of the murder. Saunders had been appointed to represent Hall, a juvenile, on March 20, 1992, and had met with him once for 15 to 30 minutes some time the following week. Hall's body was discovered on March 30, 1992, and four days later a juvenile court judge dismissed the charges against him, noting on the docket sheet that Hall was deceased. The one-page docket sheet also listed Saunders as Hall's counsel. On April 6, 1992, the same judge appointed Saunders to represent petitioner. Saunders did not disclose to the court, his co-counsel, or petitioner that he had previously represented Hall. Under Virginia law, juvenile case files are confidential and may not generally be disclosed without a court order, but petitioner learned about Saunders' prior representation when a clerk mistakenly produced Hall's file to federal habeas counsel. . . .

The District Court held an evidentiary hearing and denied petitioner's habeas petition. . . . [The en banc Fourth Circuit] assumed that the juvenile court judge had neglected a duty to inquire into a potential conflict, but rejected petitioner's argument that this failure either mandated automatic reversal of his conviction or relieved him of the burden of showing that a conflict of interest adversely affected his representation. . . . Concluding that petitioner had not demonstrated adverse effect, it affirmed. . . .

Petitioner's proposed rule of automatic reversal when there existed a conflict that did not affect counsel's performance, but the trial judge failed to make the *Sullivan*-mandated inquiry, makes little policy sense. . . . [T]he rule applied when the trial judge is not aware of the conflict (and thus not obligated to inquire) is that prejudice will be presumed only if the conflict has significantly affected counsel's performance — thereby rendering the verdict unreliable, even though *Strickland* prejudice cannot be shown. The trial court's awareness of a potential conflict neither renders it more likely that counsel's performance was significantly affected nor in any other way renders the verdict unreliable. Nor does the trial judge's failure to make the *Sullivan*-mandated inquiry often make it harder for reviewing courts to determine conflict and effect, particularly since those courts may rely on evidence and testimony whose importance only becomes established at the trial.

Nor, finally, is automatic reversal simply an appropriate means of enforcing *Sullivan*'s mandate of inquiry. Despite [the dissent's] belief that there must be a threat of sanction (to-wit, the risk of conferring a windfall upon the defendant) in order to induce "resolutely obdurate" trial judges to follow the law, we do not presume that judges are as careless or as partial as those police officers who need the incentive of the exclusionary rule. And in any event, the *Sullivan* standard, which requires proof of effect upon representation but (once such effect is shown) presumes prejudice, already creates an "incentive" to inquire into a potential conflict. In those cases where the potential conflict is in fact an actual one, only inquiry will enable the judge to avoid all possibility of reversal by either seeking waiver or replacing a conflicted attorney. We doubt that the deterrence of "judicial dereliction" that would be achieved by an automatic reversal rule is significantly greater.

Since this was not a case in which (as in *Holloway*) counsel protested his inability simultaneously to represent multiple defendants; and since the trial court's failure to make the *Sullivan*-mandated inquiry does not reduce the petitioner's burden of proof; it was at least necessary, to void the conviction, for petitioner to establish that the conflict of interest adversely affected his counsel's performance. The Court of Appeals having found no such effect, the denial of habeas relief must be affirmed. . . .

Lest today's holding be misconstrued, we note that the only question presented was the effect of a trial court's failure to inquire into a potential conflict upon the *Sullivan* rule that deficient performance of counsel must be shown. The case was presented and argued on the assumption that (absent some exception for failure to inquire) *Sullivan* would be applicable. . . . That assumption was not unreasonable in light of the holdings of Courts of Appeals, which . . . have invoked the Sullivan standard not only when (as here) there is a conflict rooted in counsel's obligations to *former* clients, but even when representation of the defendant somehow implicates counsel's personal or financial interests, including a book deal, a job with the prosecutor's office, the teaching of classes to Internal Revenue Service agents, a romantic "entanglement" with the prosecutor, or fear of antagonizing the trial judge.

It must be said, however, that the language of *Sullivan* itself does not clearly establish, or indeed even support, such expansive application. "[U]ntil," it said, "a defendant shows that his counsel *actively represented* conflicting interests, he has not established the constitutional predicate for his claim of ineffective assistance." 446 U.S., at 350 (emphasis added). Both *Sullivan* itself, and *Holloway*, stressed the high probability of prejudice arising from multiple concurrent representation, and the difficulty of proving that prejudice. . . . Not all attorney conflicts present comparable difficulties. Thus, the Federal Rules of Criminal Procedure treat concurrent representation and prior representation differently, requiring a trial court to inquire into the likelihood of conflict whenever jointly charged defendants are represented by a single attorney (Rule 44(c)), but not when counsel previously represented another defendant in a substantially related matter, even where the trial court is aware of the prior representation.

JUSTICE KENNEDY, joined by JUSTICE O'CONNOR, concurring:

. . . The constitutional question must turn on whether trial counsel had a conflict of interest that hampered the representation, not on whether the trial judge should have been more assiduous in taking prophylactic measures. If it were otherwise, the judge's duty would not be limited to cases where the attorney is suspected of harboring a conflict of interest. The Sixth Amendment protects the defendant against an ineffective attorney, as well as a conflicted one. . . . It would be a major departure to say that the trial judge must step in every time defense counsel appears to be providing ineffective assistance, and indeed, there is no precedent to support this proposition. As the Sixth Amendment guarantees the defendant the assistance of counsel, the infringement of that right must depend on a deficiency of the lawyer, not of the trial judge. . . .

[Justice Stevens and Justice Breyer, joined by Justice Ginsburg, dissented based on (1) the risk of prejudice arising from the conflict present in this case, and (2) the perception that — especially in a capital case — the "appearance of justice" was not satisfied. — EDS.]

JUSTICE SOUTER, dissenting:

. . . The different burdens on the *Holloway* and *Sullivan* defendants are consistent features of a coherent scheme for dealing with the problem of conflicted defense counsel; a prospective risk of conflict subject to judicial notice is treated differently from a retrospective claim that a completed proceeding was tainted by conflict, although the trial judge had not been derelict in any duty to guard against it. When the problem comes to the trial court's attention before any potential conflict has become actual, the court has a duty to act prospectively to assess the risk and, if the risk is not too remote, to eliminate it or to render it acceptable through a defendant's knowing and intelligent waiver. This duty is something more than the general responsibility to rule without committing legal error; it is an affirmative obligation to investigate a disclosed possibility that defense counsel will be unable to act with uncompromised loyalty to his client. It was the judge's failure to fulfill that duty of care to enquire further and do what might be necessary that the *Holloway* Court remedied by vacating the defendant's subsequent conviction. The error occurred when the judge failed to act, and the remedy restored the defendant to the position he would have occupied if the judge had taken reasonable steps to fulfill his obligation. But when the problem of conflict comes to judicial attention not prospectively, but only after the fact, the defendant must show an actual conflict with adverse consequence to him in order to get relief. Fairness requires nothing more, for no judge was at fault in allowing a trial to proceed even though fraught with hidden risk.

In light of what the majority holds today, it bears repeating that, in this coherent scheme established by *Holloway* and *Sullivan*, there is nothing legally crucial about an objection by defense counsel to tell a trial judge that conflicting interests may impair the adequacy of counsel's representation. Counsel's objection in *Holloway* was important as a fact sufficient to put the judge on notice that he should enquire. In most multiple-representation cases, it will take just such an objection to alert a trial judge to prospective conflict, and the *Sullivan* Court reaffirmed that the judge is obliged to take reasonable prospective action whenever a timely objection is made. But the Court also indicated that an objection is not required as a matter of law: "Unless the trial court knows or reasonably should know that a particular conflict exists, the court need not initiate an enquiry." The Court made this clear beyond cavil 10 months later when Justice Powell, the same Justice who wrote the *Sullivan* opinion, explained in Wood v. Georgia[, 450 U.S. 261 (1981),] that *Sullivan* "*mandates* a reversal when the trial court has failed to make an inquiry even though it 'knows or reasonably should know that a particular conflict exists.'" [Id.] at 272, n. 18 (emphasis in original).

Since the District Court in this case found that the state judge was on notice of a prospective potential conflict, this case calls for nothing more than the application of the prospective notice rule announced and exemplified by *Holloway* and confirmed in *Sullivan* and *Wood*. The remedy for the judge's dereliction of duty should be an order vacating the conviction and affording a new trial.

NOTES AND QUESTIONS

1. Justice Souter's reliance on Wood v. Georgia is a bit peculiar, as the actual holding in *Wood* sent the case back to the district court to make the *Sullivan* "adverse effect" inquiry. In a passage unremarked by Justice Souter, the *Wood* Court stated: "On the record before us, we cannot be sure whether counsel was influenced in his basic strategic decisions by the interests of his employer who hired him. If this was the case, the due process rights of petitioners were not respected." 450 U.S., at 272.

Regardless who wins the game of parsing prior opinions, what should the respective burdens be in cases like this? If a defendant makes no objection to his representation, why should there be any after-the-fact review that does not, at a minimum, focus on whether the defendant was actually harmed? For that matter, why shouldn't the defendant meet the *Strickland* burden of showing a reasonable probability that the conflicted representation might have affected the outcome in the case? Why is it the trial court's, or the prosecutor's, responsibility to police the relationship between defense counsel and client?

Reversals of reliable convictions impose substantial costs. A plausibly erroneous, or just different, outcome may justify such costs, but do you think the "appearance of justice" does? And what, exactly, is the "appearance of justice"? Wouldn't Justice Souter's proposed approach create perverse incentives for a defendant to proceed with conflicted representation? If he gets acquitted, the case is over; if he gets convicted, he may well obtain a reversal and a second bite at the apple. Bear in mind that there are other possible means of regulating cases like this, including sanctions against the lawyer. After all, it is the lawyer and the client who create these problems; shouldn't they have some incentive to correct them, rather than to benefit from them?

2. What result under *Sullivan* if a defendant, in full knowledge of a potential conflict, waives the right not to have separate counsel, and subsequently the potential conflict is actualized? In this regard, consider Rule 44(c) of the Federal Rules of Criminal Procedure (which was cited in footnote 10 of *Sullivan*, and which has (with some stylistic changes) since gone into effect:

Rule 44. Right to and Appointment of Counsel

(a) Right to Appointed Counsel. A defendant who is unable to obtain counsel is entitled to have counsel appointed to represent the defendant at every stage of the proceeding from initial appearance through appeal, unless the defendant waives this right.

(b) Appointment Procedure. Federal law and local court rules govern the procedure for implementing the right to counsel.

(c) Inquiry Into Joint Representation.

(1) Joint Representation. Joint representation occurs when:

(A) two or more defendants have been charged jointly under Rule 8(b) or have been joined for trial under Rule 13; and

(B) the defendants are represented by the same counsel, or counsel who are associated in law practice.

(2) Court's Responsibilities in Cases of Joint Representation. The court must promptly inquire about the propriety of joint representation and must personally advise each defendant of the right to the effective assistance of counsel, including separate representation. Unless there is good cause to believe that no conflict of interest is likely to arise, the court must take appropriate measures to protect each defendant's right to counsel.

In an insightful analysis of Rule 44(c) prior to its effective date, Professor Tague commented:

If the rule values the assistance of conflict-free representation above the right to choose one's attorney, it has three distressing omissions. First, the rule orders the "court" to make an inquiry about possible conflicts whenever defendants "are charged pursuant to Rule 8(b) or have been joined for trial pursuant to Rule 13." Does the rule apply only after the defendants have been indicted or an information has been filed in district court? Is there then no obligation to inquire at any earlier stage, such as at the presentment or the preliminary hearing? The rule's reference to the "court" [and not the "magistrate"] as the inquiring entity supports this apparent restriction. . . . Indeed, the Advisory Committee implies that separate counsel need not be initially appointed for each defendant. This limitation is unfortunate. . . . Many defendants seek to plead guilty before they are indicted, because the defendants frequently obtain a more favorable plea bargain if they plead early in the process. A guilty plea might bury a glaring conflict that infected the plea bargaining for the codefendants.

Second, the rule does not appear to cover cases like Dukes v. Warden, in which a defendant, charged alone in one proceeding, is a codefendant in a second proceeding and one attorney represents defendants in both proceedings. The rule's reference to Rules 8(b) and 13 suggests that the court is not under any obligation even if it knows of the separate indictments. The rule also would appear to apply if the codefendants are severed under Rule 14.

Third, the rule fails to provide adequate guidelines for review of a postconviction attack based on conflict. The Committee indicates that although a trial court's failure to make a Rule 44(c) inquiry will not necessarily result in reversal, an appellate court is more likely to find that a conflict existed in this instance. Further, because conflicts that were not apparent initially may surface later in the proceeding, even an adequate initial inquiry does not preclude reversal on conflict grounds. If the trial court makes an inadequate inquiry or none at all, the appellate court would still face the problem of defining and allocating the burden of proving the existence of a conflict. The proposed rule thus fails to solve one of the major problems of multiple representation.

Peter Tague, Multiple Representation and Conflicts of Interest in Criminal Cases, 67 Geo. L.J. 1075, 1094-1095 (1979). Professor Tague concluded that the Rule should require (1) the appointment of separate counsel for all indigents; (2) that nonindigents must at least discuss the matter with separate counsel; and (3) that if defendants insist on joint representation, they should have to establish an intelligent waiver. Others have argued for a flat prohibition against joint representation. Gary T. Lowenthal, Joint Representation in Criminal Cases: A Critical Appraisal, 64 Va. L. Rev. 939, 986 (1978). How would you work out these conflicting concerns of autonomy and procedural fairness?

3. The general view seems to be that a client may waive the right to conflict-free representation. See, e.g., United States v. Curcio, 680 F.2d 881 (2d Cir. 1982). However, in Wheat v. United States, 486 U.S. 153 (1988), the Court held that trial courts are not required to accept defendants' waivers of conflict-free representation, notwithstanding the presumption in favor of counsel of choice. In part, the Court was motivated by the fact that the courts of appeals have been willing to entertain ineffective-assistance-of-counsel claims even from defendants who have specifically waived the right to conflict-free representation.

4. What about the *government's* interest in separate counsel? Consider the following:

In *Wheat*, there are two reasons why the coconspirators might have wished to use Iredale [the defendants' attorney] as common counsel. The first, offered by the defendants, is unobjectionable: The defendants believed Iredale to be a very good attorney, better than the likely alternatives. But the second is troubling. If the three defendants in question were guilty, they may well have faced a classic prisoners' dilemma: It may have been in each individual's interest to "sell out" to the government and implicate his colleagues, but may have been far better for all if all either lied or remained silent. Common counsel may have removed the dilemma by facilitating the enforcement of an agreement not to finger each other. Obtaining the testimony of one conspirator against others may require careful negotiation with the would-be witness. If all the conspirators have the same lawyer, the government is, in effect, able to deal with one defendant only by dealing with all.

William J. Stuntz, Waiving Rights in Criminal Procedure, 75 Va. L. Rev. 761, 798-799 (1989). But if the government's interests do count, what is to prevent the government from objecting to common counsel solely in order to get an unusually strong defense lawyer out of the case, at least with respect to some of the defendants? There is some reason to believe that that is exactly what happened in *Wheat*. See Pamela S. Karlan, Discrete and Relational Criminal Representation: The Changing Vision of the Right to Counsel, 105 Harv. L. Rev. 670, 687 n. 79 (1992) (noting that Iredale was reportedly an exceptionally good lawyer). See also Bruce A. Green, "Through a Glass, Darkly": How the Court Sees Motions to Disqualify Criminal Defense Lawyers, 89 Colum. L. Rev. 1201 (1989) (criticizing *Wheat*).

Are there any situations in which defendants should simply be barred from proceeding with conflicted counsel? Some courts have said "yes." For example, in United States v. Fulton, 5 F.3d 605 (2d Cir. 1993), during trial the government disclosed that a government witness presently on the stand had alleged that he had illegally imported heroin for Fulton's defense counsel. The court informed the defendant that this injected the defense counsel's interests into the trial, and further that counsel would not be able to cross-examine the witness on these matters, because to do so would reveal confidences of a former client. The client nonetheless wished to proceed with counsel and to waive the conflict. The court of appeals reversed the ensuing conviction on the ground that "no rational defendant would knowingly and intelligently be represented by a lawyer whose conduct was guided largely by a desire for self-preservation." How could the court know what "largely" guided defense counsel? What do you think of the equation of this choice with the inability to make a knowing and intelligent waiver? More important, why, absent a showing of prejudice, should a defendant be insulated from the consequences of such choices, even if you think such a choice is problematic? For that matter, is even prejudice sufficient to require reversal? Unless the defendant is truly incompetent, and did not just make a decision that ex post looks like it didn't work out, why shouldn't the defendant be stuck with the consequences of his or her choices? Had Fulton been acquitted, he would have walked, regardless of his lack of a "knowing and intelligent" waiver. Following a conviction, what justifies forcing the state to go through the time, expense, and risk, of another trial?

The Second Circuit extended the *Fulton* holding in the infamous case of United States v. Schwarz, 283 F.3d 76 (2d Cir. 2002), which dealt with two police officers, Schwarz and Bruder, who were charged with crimes in connection with a brutal assault on Abner Louima at a police station in Brooklyn. Following two jury trials, the defendants were convicted, and Schwarz appealed on the ground that his defense counsel had unwaivable conflicts. Schwarz's defense counsel, Stephen Worth, worked for the same law firm as Stuart London, who represented Bruder. In addition, the same law firm had been paid a $10 million retainer as counsel for the Policeman's Benevolent Association; the police union was a codefendant in a civil suit filed by Louima for conspiracy, and negligent failure to supervise and monitor, in connection with the assault. The government strenuously raised these potential conflicts with the judge before trial, arguing that they "cannot be waived," but both Worth and London, as well as defendants Schwarz and Bruder themselves, told the judge that they did not want any substitutions of counsel. The judge then held a pretrial hearing at which he personally informed Schwartz and Bruder about some of the possible conflicts that could arise. After the hearing, the judge appointed independent counsel to further advise each of the codefendants about the risks of joint representation, and also barred Worth's and London's law firm from representing the PBA in the civil suit. At the next court hearing on the matter, the following colloquy ensued:

> *The Court:* Mr. Schwarz, tell me what you see here as inconsistencies between your case and Mr. Bruder's case.
>
> *Defendant Schwarz:* I understand that with this case, there may be some potential conflicts of interest, one being that my attorney and Mr. Bruder's attorney are now with the same firm. This is a conflict in that one defendant may receive a better defense at the expense of the other defendant.
>
> I'm also aware of the contract that my attorney has with the PBA. I know that there's another conflict with that, in that the government may call other police officers who are a member of the PBA or even PBA officials. There's a concern that possibly my attorney may have another agenda and may not be vigorous in his cross-examination of these witnesses.
>
> I'm also aware of in the calling of witnesses with this potential conflict, with the two lawyers in the same firm. If they call a witness who — my lawyer may be reluctant to call a witness who may be able to help me but who in his testimony may be harmful to the other defendant. I understand that there could be a conflict in that.
>
> Other conflict issues were if the government were to offer some type of plea to one defendant, that would probably be harmful to the other defendant. Also, if there were a guilty conviction, another conflict may be that my attorney may be reluctant, if he was trying to plead for some type of leniency, he may be reluctant to try to shift blame on to the other defendant in this case. . . .
>
> *The Court:* Do you want to keep your lawyer?
>
> *Defendant Schwarz:* Yes, sir.

After the independent counsel for Schwarz told the court that he had also advised Schwarz of all of these conflicts and believed Schwarz understood them, the court accepted Schwarz's waiver of the right to conflict-free counsel and permitted Worth to continue representing Schwarz; Worth's partner, London, was permitted to continue representing Bruder.

In a peculiar opinion on the issue of waiver of conflict, the Second Circuit said:

> The waiver given by Schwarz . . . would defeat his claim of ineffective assistance of counsel unless it is determined that (1) the conflict with respect to the PBA retainer was so severe as to be unwaivable, or (2) the . . . waiver by Schwarz was not knowing and intelligent with respect to the specific conflict that led to the lapse in Worth's representation. We need not decide whether Schwarz's waiver was knowing and intelligent because we conclude that the actual conflict that Schwarz's attorney faced was unwaivable. . . .
>
> . . . *Fulton*'s rationale with respect to when an attorney's self-interest renders a conflict unwaivable is equally applicable to the unusual facts of this case. As noted above, Worth's representation of Schwarz was in conflict not only with his ethical obligation to the PBA as his client, but also with his own substantial self-interest in the two-year, $10 million retainer agreement his newly formed firm had entered into with the PBA. Like the conflict in *Fulton*, Worth's conflict "so permeate[d] the defense that no meaningful waiver could be obtained." *Fulton*, 5 F.3d at 613. We must assume that, under such circumstances, the distinct possibility existed that, at each point the conflict was felt, Worth would sacrifice Schwarz's interests for those of the PBA. Indeed, we think it likely

that these very concerns motivated the government to argue to the district court . . . that the conflict created by the PBA retainer could not be waived. Thus, we conclude that the conflict between Worth's representation of Schwarz, on the one hand, and his ethical obligation to the PBA as his client and his self interest in the PBA retainer, on the other, was so severe that no rational defendant in Schwarz's position would have knowingly and intelligently desired Worth's representation. . . .

In sum, we hold that Schwarz's counsel suffered an actual conflict, that the conflict adversely affected his counsel's representation, and that the conflict was unwaivable. Accordingly, we are required to vacate Schwarz's conviction in the first trial and remand for a new trial.

Id., at 95-98.

"In sum," hasn't the court essentially held that it needn't decide if the waiver in this case was knowing and intelligent because under these facts, it could never be knowing and intelligent? Review the colloquy with the defendant reproduced above. Did the Second Circuit take this peculiar tack because plainly this *was* a knowing and intelligent waiver? Why sacrifice the interests in effective law enforcement through a reversal of a conviction in a case like this rather than sanction the lawyers — if indeed there is any problem at all?

C.   *Some Implications of the Right to Counsel*

1.   The Right to Proceed Pro Se

Somewhat counterintuitively, possessing a right does not necessarily mean that one also possesses the right to dispense with that right. The right to trial by jury, for example, does not mean that a defendant has a right to a bench trial; the prosecution has an interest as well, and the trial judge has some discretion whether or not to proceed with a bench trial. And as we have just seen, the right to conflict-free counsel does not necessarily engender a right to proceed with conflicted counsel. The Court dealt with the right to forgo counsel altogether — the right to proceed pro se — in the following case.

FARETTA v. CALIFORNIA

Certiorari to the Court of Appeal of California, Second Appellate District
422 U.S. 806 (1975)

MR. JUSTICE STEWART delivered the opinion of the Court.

The question before us now is whether a defendant in a state criminal trial has a constitutional right to proceed *without* counsel when he voluntarily and intelligently elects to do so. Stated another way, the question is whether a State may constitutionally hale a person into its criminal courts and there force a lawyer upon him, even when he insists that he wants to conduct his own defense. It is not an easy question, but we have concluded that a State may not constitutionally do so.

I

Anthony Faretta was charged with grand theft in an information filed in the Superior Court of Los Angeles County, Cal. At the arraignment, the Superior Court Judge assigned to preside at the trial appointed the public defender to represent Faretta. Well before the date of trial, however, Faretta requested that he be permitted to represent himself. Questioning by the judge revealed that Faretta had once represented himself in a criminal prosecution, that he had a high school education, and that he did not want to be represented by the public defender because he believed that the office was "very loaded down with . . . a heavy case load." The judge responded that he believed Faretta was "making a mistake" and emphasized that in further proceedings Faretta would receive no special favors. Nevertheless, after establishing that Faretta wanted to represent himself and did not want a lawyer, the judge, in a "preliminary ruling," accepted Faretta's waiver of the assistance of counsel. The judge indicated, however, that he might reverse this ruling if it later appeared that Faretta was unable adequately to represent himself.

Several weeks thereafter, but still prior to trial, the judge sua sponte held a hearing to inquire into Faretta's ability to conduct his own defense, and questioned him specifically about both the hearsay rule and the state law governing the challenge of potential jurors. After consideration of Faretta's answers, and observation of his demeanor, the judge ruled that Faretta had not made an intelligent and knowing waiver of his right to the assistance of counsel, and also ruled that Faretta had no constitutional right to conduct his own defense. The judge, accordingly, reversed his earlier ruling permitting self-representation and again appointed the public defender to represent Faretta. Faretta's subsequent request for leave to act as cocounsel was rejected, as were his efforts to make certain motions in his own behalf.[5] Throughout the subsequent trial, the judge required that Faretta's defense be conducted only through the appointed lawyer from the public defender's office. At the conclusion of the trial, the jury found Faretta guilty as charged, and the judge sentenced him to prison.

The California Court of Appeal . . . affirmed the trial judge's ruling that Faretta had no federal or state constitutional right to represent himself.[7] Accordingly, the appellate court affirmed Faretta's conviction. . . . We granted certiorari.

II

In the federal courts, the right of self-representation has been protected by statute since the beginnings of our Nation. Section 35 of the Judiciary Act of 1789, 1 Stat. 73, 92, enacted by the First Congress and signed by President Washington one day before the Sixth Amendment was proposed, provided that "in all the courts of the United States, the parties may plead and manage their own causes personally or by the assistance of . . . counsel." The right is currently codified in 28 U.S.C. §1654.

With few exceptions, each of the several States also accords a defendant the right to represent himself in any criminal case. The Constitutions of 36 States explicitly

5. Faretta also urged without success that he was entitled to counsel of his choice, and three times moved for the appointment of a lawyer other than the public defender. These motions, too, were denied.

7. The Court of Appeal also held that the trial court had not "abused its discretion in concluding that Faretta had not made a knowing and intelligent waiver of his right to be represented by counsel," since "Faretta did not appear aware of the possible consequences of waiving the opportunity for skilled and experienced representation at trial."

confer that right. Moreover, many state courts have expressed the view that the right is also supported by the Constitution of the United States.

This Court has more than once indicated the same view. In Adams v. United States ex rel. McCann, 317 U.S. 269, 279, the Court recognized that the Sixth Amendment right to the assistance of counsel implicitly embodies a "correlative right to dispense with a lawyer's help." [The Court explained that] "an accused, in the exercise of a free and intelligent choice, and with the considered approval of the court, may waive trial by jury, and so likewise may he competently and intelligently waive his Constitutional right to assistance of counsel." Id., at 275.

The *Adams* case does not, of course, necessarily resolve the issue before us. It held only that "the Constitution does not force a lawyer upon a defendant." Id., at 279.[12] Whether the Constitution forbids a State from forcing a lawyer upon a defendant is a different question. But the Court in *Adams* did recognize, albeit in dictum, an affirmative right of self-representation:

> The right to assistance of counsel and the *correlative right to dispense with a lawyer's help* are not legal formalisms. They rest on considerations that go to the substance of an accused's position before the law. . . .
> . . . What were contrived as protections for the accused should not be turned into fetters. . . . To deny an accused a choice of procedure in circumstances in which he, though a layman, is as capable as any lawyer of making an intelligent choice, is to impair the worth of great Constitutional safeguards by treating them as empty verbalisms.
> . . . When the administration of the criminal law . . . is hedged about as it is by the Constitutional safeguards for the protection of an accused, to deny him in the exercise of his free choice the right to dispense with some of these safeguards . . . is to imprison a man in his privileges and call it the Constitution.

In other settings as well, the Court has indicated that a defendant has a constitutionally protected right to represent himself in a criminal trial. For example, in Snyder v. Massachusetts, 291 U.S. 97, the Court held that the Confrontation Clause of the Sixth Amendment gives the accused a right to be present at all stages of the proceedings where fundamental fairness might be thwarted by his absence. This right to "presence" was based upon the premise that the "defense may be made easier if the accused is permitted to be present at the examination of jurors or the summing up of counsel, *for it will be in his power*, if present, to give advice or suggestion or *even to supersede his lawyers altogether and conduct the trial himself*." Id., at 106 (emphasis added). And in Price v. Johnston, 334 U.S. 266, the Court, in holding that a convicted person had no absolute right to argue his own appeal, said this holding was in "sharp contrast" to his "recognized privilege of conducting his own defense at the trial."

The United States Courts of Appeals have repeatedly held that the right of self-representation is protected by the Bill of Rights. . . .

---

12. The holding of *Adams* was reaffirmed in a different context in Carter v. Illinois, 329 U.S. 173, 174-175, where the Court again adverted to the right of self-representation: "Neither the historic conception of Due Process nor the vitality it derives from progressive standards of justice denies a person *the right to defend himself* or to confess guilt. Under appropriate circumstances the Constitution requires that counsel be tendered; it does not require that under all circumstances counsel be forced upon a defendant." (Emphasis added.) See also Moore v. Michigan, 355 U.S. 155, 161.

This Court's past recognition of the right of self-representation, the federal-court authority holding the right to be of constitutional dimension, and the state constitutions pointing to the right's fundamental nature form a consensus not easily ignored. "[T]he mere fact that a path is a beaten one," Mr. Justice Jackson once observed, "is a persuasive reason for following it."[13] We confront here a nearly universal conviction, on the part of our people as well as our courts, that forcing a lawyer upon an unwilling defendant is contrary to his basic right to defend himself if he truly wants to do so.

III

This consensus is soundly premised. The right of self-representation finds support in the structure of the Sixth Amendment, as well as in the English and colonial jurisprudence from which the Amendment emerged.

A . . .

The Sixth Amendment does not provide merely that a defense shall be made for the accused; it grants to the accused personally the right to make his defense. It is the accused, not counsel, who must be "informed of the nature and cause of the accusation," who must be "confronted with the witnesses against him," and who must be accorded "compulsory process for obtaining witnesses in his favor." Although not stated in the Amendment in so many words, the right to self-representation — to make one's own defense personally — is thus necessarily implied by the structure of the Amendment.[15] The right to defend is given directly to the accused; for it is he who suffers the consequences if the defense fails.

The counsel provision supplements this design. It speaks of the "assistance" of counsel, and an assistant, however expert, is still an assistant. The language and spirit of the Sixth Amendment contemplate that counsel, like the other defense tools guaranteed by the Amendment, shall be an aid to a willing defendant — not an organ of the State interposed between an unwilling defendant and his right to

---

13. Robert H. Jackson, Full Faith and Credit — The Lawyer's Clause of the Constitution, 45 Col. L. Rev. 1, 26 (1945).

15. This Court has often recognized the constitutional stature of rights that, though not literally expressed in the document, are essential to due process of law in a fair adversary process. It is now accepted, for example, that an accused has a right to be present at all stages of the trial where his absence might frustrate the fairness of the proceedings, Snyder v. Massachusetts, 291 U.S. 97; to testify on his own behalf, see Harris v. New York, 401 U.S. 222, 225; and to be convicted only if his guilt is proved beyond a reasonable doubt, In re Winship, 397 U.S. 358 . . .

The inference of rights is not, of course, a mechanical exercise. In Singer v. United States, 380 U.S. 24, the Court held that an accused has no right to a bench trial, despite his capacity to waive his right to a jury trial. In so holding, the Court stated that "[t]he ability to waive a constitutional right does not ordinarily carry with it the right to insist upon the opposite of that right." Id., at 34-35. But that statement was made only *after* the Court had concluded that the Constitution does not affirmatively protect any right to be tried by a judge. Recognizing that an implied right must arise independently from the design and history of the constitutional text, the Court searched for, but could not find, any "indication that the colonists considered the ability to waive a jury trial to be [of] equal importance to the right to demand one." Id., at 26. Instead, the Court could locate only "isolated instances" of a right to trial by judge, and concluded that these were "clear departures from the common law." Ibid.

We follow the approach of *Singer* here. Our concern is with an independent right of self-representation. We do not suggest that this right arises mechanically from a defendant's power to waive the right to the assistance of counsel. See supra, at 814-815. On the contrary, the right must be independently found in the structure and history of the constitutional text.

defend himself personally. To thrust counsel upon the accused, against his considered wish, thus violates the logic of the Amendment. In such a case, counsel is not an assistant, but a master;[16] and the right to make a defense is stripped of the personal character upon which the Amendment insists. It is true that when a defendant chooses to have a lawyer manage and present his case, law and tradition may allocate to the counsel the power to make binding decisions of trial strategy in many areas. . . . This allocation can only be justified, however, by the defendant's consent, at the outset, to accept counsel as his representative. An unwanted counsel "represents" the defendant only through a tenuous and unacceptable legal fiction. Unless the accused has acquiesced in such representation, the defense presented is not the defense guaranteed him by the Constitution, for, in a very real sense, it is not *his* defense.

B

The Sixth Amendment, when naturally read, thus implies a right of self-representation. This reading is reinforced by the Amendment's roots in English legal history. [The Court reviewed the history, concluding that the "common law rule has evidently always been that 'no person charged with a criminal offense can have counsel forced upon him against his will.'"]

C

In the American Colonies the insistence upon a right of self-representation was, if anything, more fervent than in England. . . . [After a lengthy examination of the colonial experience, the Court concluded that] there is no evidence that the colonists and the Framers ever doubted the right of self-representation, or imagined that this right might be considered inferior to the right of assistance of counsel. To the contrary, the colonists and the Framers, as well as their English ancestors, always conceived of the right to counsel as an "assistance" for the accused, to be used at his option, in defending himself. The Framers selected in the Sixth Amendment a form of words that necessarily implies the right of self-representation. That conclusion is supported by centuries of consistent history.

IV

There can be no blinking the fact that the right of an accused to conduct his own defense seems to cut against the grain of this Court's decisions holding that the Constitution requires that no accused can be convicted and imprisoned unless he has been accorded the right to the assistance of counsel. . . . For it is surely true that the basic thesis of those decisions is that the help of a lawyer is essential to assure the defendant a fair trial. And a strong argument can surely be made that the whole

---

16. Such a result would sever the concept of counsel from its historic roots. The first lawyers were personal friends of the litigant, brought into court by him so that he might "take 'counsel' with them" before pleading. 1 F. Pollock & F. Maitland, The History of English Law 211 (2d ed. 1909). Similarly, the first "attorneys" were personal agents, often lacking any professional training, who were appointed by those litigants who had secured royal permission to carry on their affairs through a representative, rather than personally. Id., at 212-213.

thrust of those decisions must inevitably lead to the conclusion that a State may constitutionally impose a lawyer upon even an unwilling defendant.

But it is one thing to hold that every defendant, rich or poor, has the right to the assistance of counsel, and quite another to say that a State may compel a defendant to accept a lawyer he does not want. The value of state-appointed counsel was not unappreciated by the Founders, yet the notion of compulsory counsel was utterly foreign to them. And whatever else may be said of those who wrote the Bill of Rights, surely there can be no doubt that they understood the inestimable worth of free choice.

It is undeniable that in most criminal prosecutions defendants could better defend with counsel's guidance than by their own unskilled efforts. But where the defendant will not voluntarily accept representation by counsel, the potential advantage of a lawyer's training and experience can be realized, if at all, only imperfectly. To force a lawyer on a defendant can only lead him to believe that the law contrives against him. Moreover, it is not inconceivable that in some rare instances, the defendant might in fact present his case more effectively by conducting his own defense. Personal liberties are not rooted in the law of averages. The right to defend is personal. The defendant, and not his lawyer or the State, will bear the personal consequences of a conviction. It is the defendant, therefore, who must be free personally to decide whether in his particular case counsel is to his advantage. And although he may conduct his own defense ultimately to his own detriment, his choice must be honored out of "that respect for the individual which is the lifeblood of the law." Illinois v. Allen, 397 U.S. 337, 350-351 (Brennan, J., concurring).[46]

V

When an accused manages his own defense, he relinquishes, as a purely factual matter, many of the traditional benefits associated with the right to counsel. For this reason, in order to represent himself, the accused must "knowingly and intelligently" [forgo] those relinquished benefits. Johnson v. Zerbst, 304 U.S., at 464-465. Although a defendant need not himself have the skill and experience of a lawyer in order competently and intelligently to choose self-representation, he should be made aware of the dangers and disadvantages of self-representation, so that the record will establish that "he knows what he is doing and his choice is made with eyes open." Adams v. United States ex rel. McCann, 317 U.S., at 279.

Here, weeks before trial, Faretta clearly and unequivocally declared to the trial judge that he wanted to represent himself and did not want counsel. The record affirmatively shows that Faretta was literate, competent, and understanding, and that he was voluntarily exercising his informed free will. The trial judge had warned

46. We are told that many criminal defendants representing themselves may use the courtroom for deliberate disruption of their trials. But the right of self-representation has been recognized from our beginnings by federal law and by most of the States, and no such result has thereby occurred. Moreover, the trial judge may terminate self-representation by a defendant who deliberately engages in serious and obstructionist misconduct. See Illinois v. Allen, 397 U.S. 337. Of course, a State may — even over objection by the accused — appoint a "standby counsel" to aid the accused if and when the accused requests help, and to be available to represent the accused in the event that termination of the defendant's self-representation is necessary. See United States v. Dougherty, 473 F.2d 1113, 1124-1126 (D.C. Cir.).

The right of self-representation is not a license to abuse the dignity of the courtroom. Neither is it a license not to comply with relevant rules of procedural and substantive law. Thus, whatever else may or may not be open to him on appeal, a defendant who elects to represent himself cannot thereafter complain that the quality of his own defense amounted to a denial of "effective assistance of counsel."

Faretta that he thought it was a mistake not to accept the assistance of counsel, and that Faretta would be required to follow all the "ground rules" of trial procedure. We need make no assessment of how well or poorly Faretta had mastered the intricacies of the hearsay rule and the California code provisions that govern challenges of potential jurors on voir dire. For his technical legal knowledge, as such, was not relevant to an assessment of his knowing exercise of the right to defend himself.

In forcing Faretta, under these circumstances, to accept against his will a state-appointed public defender, the California courts deprived him of his constitutional right to conduct his own defense. Accordingly, the judgment before us is vacated, and the case is remanded for further proceedings not inconsistent with this opinion.

It is so ordered.

MR. CHIEF JUSTICE BURGER, with whom MR. JUSTICE BLACKMUN and MR. JUSTICE REHNQUIST join, dissenting.

This case . . . is another example of the judicial tendency to constitutionalize what is thought "good." That effort fails on its own terms here, because there is nothing desirable or useful in permitting every accused person, even the most uneducated and inexperienced, to insist upon conducting his own defense to criminal charges. Moreover, there is no constitutional basis for the Court's holding, and it can only add to the problems of an already malfunctioning criminal justice system. I therefore dissent.

I

The most striking feature of the Court's opinion is that it devotes so little discussion to the matter which it concedes is the core of the decision, that is, discerning an independent basis in the Constitution for the supposed right to represent oneself in a criminal trial.[2] . . . Its ultimate assertion that such a right is tucked between the lines of the Sixth Amendment is contradicted by the Amendment's language and its consistent judicial interpretation.

As the Court seems to recognize . . . the conclusion that the rights guaranteed by the Sixth Amendment are "personal" to an accused reflects nothing more than the obvious fact that it is he who is on trial and therefore has need of a defense. But neither that nearly trivial proposition nor the language of the Amendment, which speaks in uniformly mandatory terms, leads to the further conclusion that the right to counsel is merely supplementary and may be dispensed with at the whim of the accused. Rather, this Court's decisions have consistently included the right to counsel as an integral part of the bundle making up the larger "right to a defense as we know it." . . .

The reason for this hardly requires explanation. The fact of the matter is that in all but an extraordinarily small number of cases an accused will lose whatever defense he may have if he undertakes to conduct the trial himself. . . . Obviously, [the necessity of counsel to guarantee a fair trial does] not vary depending upon whether the accused actively desires to be represented by counsel or wishes to proceed pro se. Nor is it accurate to suggest, as the Court seems to later in its opinion, that the quality of his representation at trial is a matter with which only the accused

2. The Court deliberately, and in my view properly, declines to characterize this case as one in which the defendant was denied a fair trial. . . .

is legitimately concerned. . . . Although we have adopted an adversary system of criminal justice, . . . the prosecution is more than an ordinary litigant, and the trial judge is not simply an automaton who insures that technical rules are adhered to. Both are charged with the duty of insuring that justice, in the broadest sense of that term, is achieved in every criminal trial. . . . That goal is ill-served, and the integrity of and public confidence in the system are undermined, when an easy conviction is obtained due to the defendant's ill-advised decision to waive counsel. The damage thus inflicted is not mitigated by the lame explanation that the defendant simply availed himself of the "freedom" "to go to jail under his own banner. . . ." United States ex rel. Maldonado v. Denno, 348 F.2d 12, 15 (C.A.2 1965). The system of criminal justice should not be available as an instrument of self-destruction.

In short, both the "spirit and the logic" of the Sixth Amendment are that every person accused of crime shall receive the fullest possible defense; in the vast majority of cases this command can be honored only by means of the expressly guaranteed right to counsel, and the trial judge is in the best position to determine whether the accused is capable of conducting his defense. True freedom of choice and society's interest in seeing that justice is achieved can be vindicated only if the trial court retains discretion to reject any attempted waiver of counsel and insist that the accused be tried according to the Constitution. This discretion is as critical an element of basic fairness as a trial judge's discretion to decline to accept a plea of guilty. See Santobello v. New York, 404 U.S. 257, 262 (1971).

II

The Court's attempt to support its result by collecting dicta from prior decisions is no more persuasive than its analysis of the Sixth Amendment. Considered in context, the cases upon which the Court relies to "beat its path" either lead it nowhere or point in precisely the opposite direction.

In Adams v. United States ex rel. McCann, 317 U.S. 269 (1942), and Carter v. Illinois, 329 U.S. 173 (1946), the defendants had competently waived counsel but later sought to renounce actions taken by them while proceeding pro se. . . . The language which the Court so carefully excises from those opinions relates, not to an affirmative right of self-representation, but to the consequences of waiver. . . .

. . . Thus, although *Adams* and *Carter* support the Court's conclusion that a defendant who represents himself may not thereafter disaffirm his deliberate trial decisions, . . . they provide it no comfort regarding the primary issue in this case. . . .

In short, what the Court represents as a well-traveled road is in reality a constitutional trail which it is blazing for the first time today, one that has not even been hinted at in our previous decisions. . . .

III

. . . Piecing together shreds of English legal history and early state constitutional and statutory provisions, without a full elaboration of the context in which they occurred or any evidence that they were relied upon by the drafters of our Federal Constitution, creates more questions than it answers and hardly provides the firm foundation upon which the creation of new constitutional rights should rest. . . .

As if to illustrate this point, the single historical fact cited by the Court which would appear truly relevant to ascertaining the meaning of the Sixth Amendment proves too much. As the Court points out, . . . §35 of the Judiciary Act of 1789 provided a statutory right to self-representation in federal criminal trials. The text of the Sixth Amendment, which expressly provides only for a right to counsel, was proposed the day after the Judiciary Act was signed. It can hardly be suggested that the Members of the Congress of 1789, then few in number, were unfamiliar with the Amendment's carefully structured language, which had been under discussion since the 1787 Constitutional Convention. And it would be most remarkable to suggest, had the right to conduct one's own defense been considered so critical as to require constitutional protection, that it would have been left to implication. Rather, under traditional canons of construction, inclusion of the right in the Judiciary Act and its *omission* from the constitutional amendment drafted at the same time by many of the same men, supports the conclusion that the omission was intentional.

There is no way to reconcile the idea that the Sixth Amendment impliedly guaranteed the right of an accused to conduct his own defense with the contemporaneous action of the Congress in passing a statute explicitly giving that right. If the Sixth Amendment created a right to self-representation it was unnecessary for Congress to enact any statute on the subject at all. In this case, therefore, history ought to lead judges to conclude that the Constitution leaves to the judgment of legislatures, and the flexible process of statutory amendment, the question whether criminal defendants should be permitted to conduct their trials pro se.

. . . And the fact that we have not hinted at a contrary view for 185 years is surely entitled to some weight in the scales.[6] . . .

IV

. . . [T]he Court blandly assumes that once an accused has elected to defend himself he will be bound by his choice and not be heard to complain of it later. . . . This assumption ignores the role of appellate review, for the reported cases are replete with instances of a convicted defendant being relieved of a deliberate decision even when made *with the advice of counsel*. See Silber v. United States, 370 U.S. 717 (1962). It is totally unrealistic, therefore, to suggest that an accused will always be held to the consequences of a decision to conduct his own defense. Unless, as may be the case, most persons accused of crime have more wit than to insist upon the dubious benefit that the Court confers today, we can expect that many expensive and good-faith prosecutions will be nullified on appeal for reasons that trial courts are now deprived of the power to prevent.[7]

MR. JUSTICE BLACKMUN, with whom THE CHIEF JUSTICE and MR. JUSTICE REHNQUIST join, dissenting.

. . . Although the Court indicates that a pro se defendant necessarily waives any claim he might otherwise make of ineffective assistance of counsel, . . . the opinion leaves open a host of other procedural questions. Must every defendant be advised

---

6. The fact that Congress has retained a statutory right to self-representation suggests that it has also assumed that the Sixth Amendment does not guarantee such a right. See 28 U.S.C. §1654.

7. Some of the damage we can anticipate from a defendant's ill-advised insistence on conducting his own defense may be mitigated by appointing a qualified lawyer to sit in the case as the traditional "friend of the court." The Court does not foreclose this option. . . .

of his right to proceed pro se? If so, when must that notice be given? Since the right
to assistance of counsel and the right to self-representation are mutually exclusive,
how is the waiver of each right to be measured? If a defendant has elected to exercise his right to proceed pro se, does he still have a constitutional right to assistance
of standby counsel? How soon in the criminal proceeding must a defendant decide
between proceeding by counsel or pro se? Must he be allowed to switch in midtrial?
May a violation of the right to self-representation ever be harmless error? Must the
trial court treat the pro se defendant differently than it would professional counsel?
I assume that many of these questions will be answered with finality in due course.
Many of them, however, such as the standards of waiver and the treatment of the pro
se defendant, will haunt the trial of every defendant who elects to exercise his right
to self-representation. The procedural problems spawned by an absolute right to
self-representation will far outweigh whatever tactical advantage the defendant may
feel he has gained by electing to represent himself.

If there is any truth to the old proverb that "one who is his own lawyer has a fool
for a client," the Court by its opinion today now bestows a *constitutional* right on one
to make a fool of himself.

NOTES AND QUESTIONS

1. Who wins the historical argument in *Faretta* centering on the intent of the framers of the Sixth Amendment? Which way does the statutory history cut?

2. If a defendant's right to proceed pro se is violated, what should be the remedy?

3. Pro se representation is uncommon, and thus is not a large practical problem
for the legal system. Moreover, those few defendants who elect to proceed pro se are
systematically convicted in short order, largely because, precisely as the *Faretta* dissenters predicted, such individuals typically are incompetent to conduct their own
defense. One famous case involved Colin Ferguson, the "Long Island Railroad
Shooter," who entered a commuter rail car and began shooting passengers, killing
6 and wounding 19 more. He proceeded pro se, causing much anguish by cross-
examining the surviving victims, and was quickly convicted. People v. Ferguson, 670
N.Y.S.2d 327 (N.Y.A.D. 2 Dept. 1998).

Another such case involved the so-called "twentieth hijacker," Zacarias Moussaoui, who was accused of involvement in the plot to destroy the World Trade Center on Sept. 11, 2001. He, too, exercised his right to proceed pro se, but in a curious
twist, the decision worked temporarily to his advantage. This is because he insisted
on interviewing other terrorism-related prisoners held by the United States whom
he asserted might provide exculpatory evidence. The U.S. government objected on
national security grounds. The district court initially ordered that adequate access
be provided to Moussaoui (acting as his own lawyer), but the Fourth Circuit later
ruled that in-person meetings were not required. See United States v. Moussaoui,
365 F.3d 292 (4th Cir. 2004); 382 F.3d 453 (4th Cir. 2004). Moussaoui eventually
pleaded guilty to six counts of conspiracy, and was sentenced to six terms of life
imprisonment without possibility of parole.

4. For another good example of the dangers (and maybe the benefits?) of self-
representation, consider the case of Adam Martin, accused — along with two of his
brothers — of robbing several banks along I-35 in Austin, Texas. Adam chose to represent himself. At a pretrial hearing, he subpoenaed his brother, Michael (who was

already serving time after pleading guilty to one of the robberies), and asked him to state whether Adam had committed any crimes. To which Michael replied: "Yeah. You were with me on four different bank robberies, Adam, you know that."

At trial, things did not get better for Adam. His cross-examination of Michael (by now, a prosecution witness) included bizarre questions about Michael's nicknames, his religion, and the time the brothers spent together in jail. At one point, Adam asked Michael, "Do you fear me in any way?" Michael responded, "I've seen you do people bad ways," and related how Adam had attacked people with knives and was once involved with organized crime. When Adam noted that "I haven't been convicted of it," Michael replied, "That doesn't mean it's not true."

Adam was convicted on all charges. Afterward, he explained: "The right to defend yourself in this country is one of the greatest rights you have." He also said that he considered disrupting the trial, but decided not to do so because he feared it might jeopardize the rights of future pro se litigants. See Steven Kreytak, "Eldest of Three Bank-Robbing Brothers Guilty; 'I-35 Robber,' Who Acted as Own Attorney, Not Surprised at Verdict," Austin American-Statesman, August 19, 2004, p. A1.

5. In McCaskle v. Wiggins, 465 U.S. 168 (1984), the Court fleshed out the concept of "standby counsel" mentioned in footnote 46 of *Faretta*. The defendant, Wiggins, initially exercised his *Faretta* right of self-representation and objected to the appointment of standby counsel, but over the course of two separate trials on the same charges he repeatedly changed his mind about whether or not he truly wanted to go it alone (the Court aptly described Wiggins's position regarding appointed counsel as "volatile"). As the second trial approached, Wiggins requested appointment of not one but two standby counsel (Samples and Graham). According to the Court, here is what happened next:

> The trial began . . . and shortly thereafter Wiggins interrupted his cross-examination of a witness to consult with Graham off the record. Still later, Wiggins expressly agreed to allow Graham to conduct voir dire of another witness.
>
> Wiggins started the next day of trial . . . with a request that the trial not proceed in Samples' absence from the courtroom. Later that morning Wiggins requested that counsel not be allowed to assist or interrupt, but a short while after Wiggins interrupted his own cross-examination of a witness to confer with Samples off the record. When the trial reconvened in the afternoon, Wiggins agreed to proceed in Samples' absence. After Samples returned, however, Wiggins again interrupted his own cross-examination of a witness to confer with him. Later Wiggins insisted that counsel should not initiate private consultations with Wiggins. Before the end of the day Wiggins once again found occasion to interrupt his own examination of a witness to confer with Samples.
>
> On the following day, . . . Wiggins agreed that Graham would make Wiggins' opening statement to the jury. [The next day], Wiggins was once again willing to have the trial proceed in the absence of one of his standby counsel. Following his conviction, Wiggins moved for a new trial. . . . Wiggins denounced the services standby counsel had provided. He insisted that they had unfairly interfered with his presentation of his defense.

Id., at 173-174. The Court held that Wiggins's *Faretta* rights were not violated:

> In determining whether a defendant's *Faretta* rights have been respected, the primary focus must be on whether the defendant had a fair chance to present his case in

his own way. *Faretta* itself dealt with the defendant's affirmative right to participate, not with the limits on standby counsel's additional involvement. The specific rights to make his voice heard that Wiggins was plainly accorded, form the core of a defendant's right of self-representation.

We recognize, nonetheless, that the right to speak for oneself entails more than the opportunity to add one's voice to a cacophony of others. . . . [T]he objectives underlying the right to proceed pro se may be undermined by unsolicited and excessively intrusive participation by standby counsel. In proceedings before a jury the defendant may legitimately be concerned that multiple voices "for the defense" will confuse the message the defendant wishes to convey, thus defeating *Faretta*'s objectives.[7] Accordingly, the *Faretta* right must impose some limits on the extent of standby counsel's unsolicited participation.[8]

First, the pro se defendant is entitled to preserve actual control over the case he chooses to present to the jury. This is the core of the *Faretta* right. If standby counsel's participation over the defendant's objection effectively allows counsel to make or substantially interfere with any significant tactical decisions, or to control the questioning of witnesses, or to speak *instead* of the defendant on any matter of importance, the *Faretta* right is eroded.

Second, participation by standby counsel without the defendant's consent should not be allowed to destroy the jury's perception that the defendant is representing himself. The defendant's appearance in the status of one conducting his own defense is important in a criminal trial, since the right to appear pro se exists to affirm the accused's individual dignity and autonomy. . . . From the jury's perspective, the message conveyed by the defense may depend as much on the messenger as on the message itself. From the defendant's own point of view, the right to appear pro se can lose much of its importance if only the lawyers in the courtroom know that the right is being exercised.

Participation by standby counsel outside the presence of the jury engages only the first of these two limitations. . . . *Faretta* rights are adequately vindicated in proceedings outside the presence of the jury if the pro se defendant is allowed to address the court freely on his own behalf and if disagreements between counsel and the pro se defendant are resolved in the defendant's favor whenever the matter is one that would normally be left to the discretion of counsel.

Participation by standby counsel in the presence of the jury is more problematic. It is here that the defendant may legitimately claim that excessive involvement by counsel will destroy the appearance that the defendant is acting pro se. This, in turn, may erode the dignitary values that the right to self-representation is intended to promote and may undercut the defendant's presentation to the jury of his own most effective defense. . . .

The record in this case reveals that Wiggins' pro se efforts were undermined primarily by his own, frequent changes of mind regarding counsel's role. . . . In these circumstances it is very difficult to determine how much of counsel's participation was in fact contrary to Wiggins' desires of the moment.

Faretta does not require a trial judge to permit "hybrid" representation of the type Wiggins was actually allowed. But if a defendant is given the opportunity and elects to

---

7. A pro se defendant must generally accept any unsolicited help or hindrance that may come from the judge who chooses to call and question witnesses, from the prosecutor who faithfully exercises his duty to present evidence favorable to the defense, from the plural voices speaking "for the defense" in a trial of more than one defendant, or from an amicus counsel appointed to assist the court, see Brown v. United States, 264 F.2d 363, 369 (C.A.D.C. 1959) (Judge Burger, concurring in part).

8. Since the right of self-representation is a right that when exercised usually increases the likelihood of a trial outcome unfavorable to the defendant, its denial is not amenable to "harmless error" analysis. The right is either respected or denied; its deprivation cannot be harmless. . . .

have counsel appear before the court or jury, his complaints concerning counsel's subsequent unsolicited participation lose much of their force. A defendant does not have a constitutional right to choreograph special appearances by counsel. Once a pro se defendant invites or agrees to any substantial participation by counsel, subsequent appearances by counsel must be presumed to be with the defendant's acquiescence, at least until the defendant expressly and unambiguously renews his request that standby counsel be silenced. . . .

[W]e make explicit today what is already implicit in *Faretta*: A defendant's Sixth Amendment rights are not violated when a trial judge appoints standby counsel—even over the defendant's objection—to relieve the judge of the need to explain and enforce basic rules of courtroom protocol or to assist the defendant in overcoming routine obstacles that stand in the way of the defendant's achievement of his own clearly indicated goals. Participation by counsel to steer a defendant through the basic procedures of trial is permissible even in the unlikely event that it somewhat undermines the pro se defendant's appearance of control over his own defense. . . .

Faretta affirmed the defendant's constitutional right to appear on stage at his trial. We recognize that a pro se defendant may wish to dance a solo, not a pas de deux. Standby counsel must generally respect that preference. But counsel need not be excluded altogether, especially when the participation is outside the presence of the jury or is with the defendant's express or tacit consent. The defendant in this case was allowed to make his own appearances as he saw fit. In our judgment counsel's unsolicited involvement was held within reasonable limits.

Id., at 168-188.

6. May counsel "waive" the honor of representing an indigent defendant? The problem arises primarily after conviction, when counsel believes that an appeal would be fruitless. In Anders v. California, 386 U.S. 738 (1967), the Court held that an attorney who wishes to withdraw from a case after conviction on the grounds that an appeal would be wholly frivolous may request permission to do so but must file a brief referring to anything in the record that might support an appeal. The court must then to decide whether to permit withdrawal. Requiring counsel to write a brief in support of what counsel believes to be a wholly frivolous appeal may seem curious, but there are cases in which such briefs have led to reversals. See Paul D. Carrington, Daniel J. Meador, & Maurice Rosenberg, Justice on Appeal 77 (1976).

The Court reaffirmed *Anders* in Penson v. Ohio, 488 U.S. 75 (1988), holding that it was error to fail to appoint counsel to brief and argue any claim that a court of appeals finds to be colorable, even if problematic. The Court also held that *Strickland* does not apply in this context, for otherwise *Anders* would be effectively overruled. But the states still retain some flexibility in complying with *Anders*. In McCoy v. Court of Appeals of Wisconsin, District 1, 486 U.S. 429 (1988), the Court upheld a Wisconsin statute requiring *Anders* briefs to include a discussion of why the issues raised in the brief lacked merit. And in Smith v. Robbins, 528 U.S. 259 (2000), the Court upheld California's rule, which differed slightly from *Anders* as follows:

Unlike under the *Anders* procedure, counsel . . . . neither explicitly states that his review has led him to conclude that an appeal would be frivolous (although that is considered implicit) nor requests leave to withdraw. Instead, he is silent on the merits of the case and expresses his availability to brief any issues on which the court might desire briefing.

In Pennsylvania v. Finley, 481 U.S. 551 (1987), the Supreme Court concluded that an indigent has neither an equal protection nor a due process right to appointed counsel in postconviction proceedings, and thus has no right to insist that *Anders* be followed whenever the state nonetheless has provided counsel. The Court rejected the argument that whenever a state supplies counsel, due process demands the *Anders* procedures.

7. The Court has protected the access of prisoners to postconviction judicial review in other ways. In Johnson v. Avery, 393 U.S. 483 (1969), the Court held that prisoners without counsel could not be denied the aid of literate prisoners in filing habeas corpus petitions. Similarly, in Bounds v. Smith, 430 U.S. 817 (1977), the Court held that a state must provide prisoners with either adequate law libraries or adequate legal assistance to facilitate their requests for postconviction relief. In Murray v. Giarratano, 492 U.S. 1 (1989), however, the Court ruled that death row inmates do not have a special constitutional right to counsel in postconviction proceedings; the plurality declared *Finley* applicable to capital as well as noncapital cases, and rejected the argument that *Bounds* should be extended to provide a right to counsel under certain circumstances. And in Lewis v. Casey, 518 U.S. 343 (1996), the Court limited *Bounds* to protecting the right of access to the courts, disavowing the suggestion in *Bounds* that prisoners must also be able to discover grievances and to litigate effectively once in court.

8. In the context of trial representation, it is a given that the ultimate decision on defense strategy belongs to the defendant (although good defense attorneys probably rarely, if ever, have much difficulty persuading a defendant to go along with the lawyer's view of sound strategy). But on appeal, there are limits to the defendant's ability to control counsel. In Jones v. Barnes, 463 U.S. 745 (1983), the Court rejected the defendant's assertion that "counsel has a constitutional duty to raise every non-frivolous issue requested by the defendant":

> Experienced advocates since time beyond memory have emphasized the importance of winnowing out weaker arguments on appeal and focusing on one central issue if possible, or at most on a few key issues. Justice Jackson, after observing appellate advocates for many years, stated:
>
> One of the first tests of a discriminating advocate is to select the question, or questions, that he will present orally. Legal contentions, like the currency, depreciate through overissue. The mind of an appellate judge is habitually receptive to the suggestion that a lower court committed an error. But receptiveness declines as the number of assigned errors increases. Multiplicity hints at lack of confidence in any one. . . . [E]xperience on the bench convinces me that multiplying assignments of error will dilute and weaken a good case and will not save a bad one. [Jackson, Advocacy Before the United States Supreme Court, 25 Temple L.Q. 115, 119 (1951).]
>
> . . . There can hardly be any question about the importance of having the appellate advocate examine the record with a view to selecting the most promising issues for review. This has assumed a greater importance in an era when oral argument is strictly limited in most courts — often to as little as 15 minutes — and when page limits on briefs are widely imposed. Even in a court that imposes no time or page limits, however, . . . [a] brief that raises every colorable issue runs the risk of burying good arguments — those that, in the words of the great advocate John W. Davis, "go for the jugular," Davis, The Argument of an Appeal, 26 A.B.A.J. 895, 897 (1940) — in a verbal mound made up of strong and weak contentions. . . .

. . . For judges to second-guess reasonable professional judgments and impose on appointed counsel a duty to raise every "colorable" claim suggested by a client would disserve the very goal of vigorous and effective advocacy that underlies *Anders*. Nothing in the Constitution or our interpretation of that document requires such a standard.[7]

Jones was reaffirmed in Knowles v. Mirzayance, 129 S. Ct. 1411 (2009). Mirzayance was charged with first-degree murder. He pleaded both "not guilty" and "not guilty by reason of insanity." This necessitated a two-phase jury trial: one phase to determine guilt, which the prosecution had to prove "beyond a reasonable doubt," and a second phase to decide the insanity issue, which the defense had to prove by a "preponderance of the evidence." At the first phase, the defense introduced all of the available evidence of insanity in order to show lack of mens rea, but Mirzayance was convicted. Before phase two, defense counsel advised Mirzayance to drop his "not guilty by reason of insanity" plea because the insanity claim had already been rejected under a more favorable burden of persuasion. The Court of Appeals held that it was ineffective assistance to advise dropping the only possible defense, even if it was essentially hopeless. The Supreme Court reversed, concluding that neither prong of *Strickland* could be established. Counseling withdrawal of a hopeless claim did not fall below an objective standard of reasonableness. Moreover, Mirzayance could not possibly demonstrate prejudice, given that the jury had already concluded that the available evidence did not raise even a reasonable doubt about his sanity.

9. Interestingly, given the general parameters of Sixth Amendment doctrine, a convicted defendant does not have the right to dispense with the assistance of counsel on appeal. In Martinez v. Court of Appeal of California, 528 U.S. 152 (2000), the Court said:

> We are not aware of any historical consensus establishing a right of self-representation on appeal. We might, nonetheless, paraphrase *Faretta* and assert: No State or Colony ever forced counsel upon a convicted appellant, and no spokesman ever suggested that such a practice would be tolerable or advisable. Such negative historical evidence was meaningful to the *Faretta* Court, because the fact that the "[dog] had not barked" arguably demonstrated that early lawmakers intended to preserve the "long-respected right of self-representation" at trial. Historical silence, however, has no probative force in the appellate context because there simply was no long-respected right of self-representation on appeal. In fact, the right of appeal itself is of relatively recent origin.
>
> Appeals as of right in federal courts were nonexistent for the first century of our Nation, and appellate review of any sort was rarely allowed. The States, also, did not generally recognize an appeal as of right until Washington became the first to constitutionalize the right explicitly in 1889. There was similarly no right to appeal in criminal cases at common law, and appellate review of any sort was "limited" and "rarely used." Thus, unlike the inquiry in *Faretta*, the historical evidence does not provide any support for an affirmative constitutional right to appellate self-representation.

---

7. The only question presented by this case is whether a criminal defendant has a constitutional right to have appellate counsel raise every nonfrivolous issue that the defendant requests. The availability of federal habeas corpus to review claims that counsel declined to raise is not before us, and we have no occasion to decide whether counsel's refusal to raise requested claims would constitute "cause" for a petitioner's default within the meaning of Wainwright v. Sykes, 433 U.S. 72 (1977). . . .

The *Faretta* majority's reliance on the structure of the Sixth Amendment is also not relevant. The Sixth Amendment identifies the basic rights that the accused shall enjoy in "all criminal prosecutions." They are presented strictly as rights that are available in preparation for trial and at the trial itself. The Sixth Amendment does not include any right to appeal. . . .

Finally, the *Faretta* majority found that the right to self-representation at trial was grounded in part in a respect for individual autonomy. This consideration is, of course, also applicable to an appellant seeking to manage his own case. As we explained in *Faretta*, at the trial level "[t]o force a lawyer on a defendant can only lead him to believe that the law contrives against him." On appellate review, there is surely a similar risk that the appellant will be skeptical of whether a lawyer, who is employed by the same government that is prosecuting him, will serve his cause with undivided loyalty. Equally true on appeal is the related observation that it is the appellant personally who will bear the consequences of the appeal.

In light of our conclusion that the Sixth Amendment does not apply to appellate proceedings, any individual right to self-representation on appeal based on autonomy principles must be grounded in the Due Process Clause. Under the practices that prevail in the Nation today, however, we are entirely unpersuaded that the risk of either disloyalty or suspicion of disloyalty is a sufficient concern to conclude that a constitutional right of self-representation is a necessary component of a fair appellate proceeding. We have no doubt that instances of disloyal representation are rare. In both trials and appeals there are, without question, cases in which counsel's performance is ineffective. Even in those cases, however, it is reasonable to assume that counsel's performance is more effective than what the unskilled appellant could have provided for himself.

No one, including Martinez and the *Faretta* majority, attempts to argue that as a rule pro se representation is wise, desirable or efficient.[10] Although we found in *Faretta* that the right to defend oneself at trial is "fundamental" in nature, 422 U.S., at 817, it is clear that it is representation by counsel that is the standard, not the exception. See Patterson v. Illinois, 487 U.S. 285, 307 (1988) (noting the "strong presumption against" waiver of right to counsel). Our experience has taught us that "a pro se defense is usually a bad defense, particularly when compared to a defense provided by an experienced criminal defense attorney."[11]

. . . Even at the trial level . . . , the government's interest in ensuring the integrity and efficiency of the trial at times outweighs the defendant's interest in acting as his own lawyer. . . . In the appellate context, the balance between the two competing interests surely tips in favor of the State. The status of the accused defendant, who retains a presumption of innocence throughout the trial process, changes dramatically when a jury returns a guilty verdict. . . . In the words of the *Faretta* majority, appellate proceedings are simply not a case of "hal[ing] a person into its criminal courts."

Id., at 159-162. Note that *Martinez* was a 9-0 decision, with eight Justices joining the majority opinion. Does some of the language in *Martinez* suggest that a Court majority may be ready to rethink the balance that was struck in *Faretta* between autonomy and the fairness of the trial?

10. Some critics argue that the right to proceed pro se at trial in certain cases is akin to allowing the defendant to waive his right to a fair trial. See, e.g., United States v. Farhad, 190 F.3d 1097, 1106-1107 (CA9 1999) (Reinhardt, J., concurring specially).

11. Decker, The Sixth Amendment Right to Shoot Oneself in the Foot: An Assessment of the Guarantee of Self-Representation Twenty Years After *Faretta*, 6 Seton Hall Const. L. J. 483, 598 (1996).

NOTES ON COMPETENCY AND WAIVER

1. Is there, or ought there to be, a requirement of competency to waive counsel, separate from the issues of competency to proceed to trial and an intelligent waiver? The New York Court of Appeals answered the question negatively in the aptly named case of People v. Reason, 37 N.Y.2d 351 (1975). According to the court, "it would be difficult to say that a standard which was designed to determine whether a defendant was capable of defending himself, is inadequate when he chooses to conduct his own defense." Id., at 354. Bearing in mind the limits of anecdotal data, consider the decision in *Reason* in light of the following excerpts from Mr. Reason's opening and closing to the jury:

The Court: The order of business before the Court now, Mr. Reason, is your opening statement. Will you proceed and make it properly?

The Defendant: I will try to prove the existence of the dead, reincarnation of the realm of Todis, . . . Hays, . . . Hell, the underworld and the hushed truth of society based upon the entities of which our way of life is based. Fighting among themselves even for possession of the living and the dead and the association of whatever rationality or religion.

I will prove an angel, demon, a devil and a soul. Paradoxically I will introduce proof of police corruption, political control of government, criminal affairs according to certain arbitrations, abiding the way of life for a particular entity of homage of their dues for the bargaining of their souls. . . .

I will prove or I will disprove Christ as our God, saints, the devil and let these entities of the power to take human life and due — there is many deeply religious people that say it was the will of God who in many instances — it isn't always the will of God, but the will of other entities or as we read at the bottom of insurance contracts except by acts of God, sometimes by those acts of men too, by means of what may be considered a spiritual sort seemingly to have been of natural causes and often some that would have died by the cause of another is used as an instrument to die; that the other would be subject to the instrument of society such as fate, destiny, pre-destiny. But history is an accepted fact as disorderly as it may be which I will also attempt to prove, and historically men have proved, prayed to something of a greater competency, to Jehovah, Brahma, Ghatama, God and others. They believe, practice and perform rituals of sorcery, Budabo, witchcraft, Christianity, black magic, occult, Bubanza, . . . soothsayers, fortune tellers and priests. . . .

I will introduce the defendant's bad character to show his good intention or expose his entire criminal record, acts of his criminal importance, accomplishments, activities and disciplinary reports be considered. . . .

[In closing, the defendant argued in part:]

The issue of the dead belonged to God. It's in the bible. Each of the dead belong to God. God seeks the past. Life gives birth to time, time is passed, just passed, time passed, just passed. Anticipate time. Time is past. Hour has already been. I wrote right here, I would like to repeat that and I would, I would like to repeat that.

A long time ago, anticipating this, I would like to repeat that.

The issue of the dead belong of God. God seeks what is passed. Life gives birth to time. Time is past. We set time ahead of us confusing time and motion with duration. We are towards a delusion, perhaps, create illusion of a present that don't really exist; create instantaneous occurring successions on the same pattern offset by the evolving sun as time though it made difference to the sun how fast — (Unintelligible).

Now, look at that, you people. I wrote it for you people. Memorized the whole thing if I had the time. This is not only pedantics, I quote Corinthian, Chapter 13, 8th Verse. . . .

2. In Godinez v. Moran, 509 U.S. 389 (1993), the Supreme Court held that the constitutional standard for competency to waive the right to counsel, as well as to plead guilty, is no higher than the constitutional standard for competency to stand trial. That standard was established in Dusky v. United States, 420 U.S. 162 (1960): whether the defendant has "sufficient present ability to consult with his lawyer with a reasonable degree of rational understanding" and has "a rational as well as factual understanding of the proceedings against him." The *Moran* Court added:

> A finding that a defendant is competent to stand trial, however, is not all that is necessary before he may be permitted to plead guilty or waive his right to counsel. In addition to determining that a defendant who seeks to plead guilty or waive counsel is competent, a trial court must satisfy itself that the waiver of his constitutional rights is knowing and voluntary. Parke v. Raley, 506 U.S. 20, 28-29 (1992) (guilty plea); *Faretta*, supra, at 835 (waiver of counsel). In this sense there is a "heightened" standard for pleading guilty and for waiving the right to counsel, but it is not a heightened standard of *competence*.[12]
>
> This two-part inquiry is what we had in mind in [Westbrook v. Arizona, 384 U.S. 150 (1966) (per curiam)]. When we distinguished between "competence to stand trial" and "competence to waive [the] constitutional right to the assistance of counsel," 384 U.S., at 150, we were using "competence to waive" as a shorthand for the "intelligent and competent waiver" requirement of Johnson v. Zerbst. . . . Thus, *Westbrook* stands only for the unremarkable proposition that when a defendant seeks to waive his right to counsel, a determination that he is competent to stand trial is not enough; the waiver must also be intelligent and voluntary before it can be accepted.

Id., at 400-402. The Court also noted that states could choose to impose a higher standard of competency to stand trial than the one constitutionally mandated, under due process, by *Dusky*.

Some states, perhaps taking a hint from *Moran*, imposed restrictions on waiving the right to counsel that went beyond the bare-bones minimum of *Faretta*. One such state-law restriction reached the Court in the following case.

INDIANA v. EDWARDS, 554 U.S. 164 (2008): This case focuses upon a criminal defendant whom a state court found mentally competent to stand trial if represented by counsel but not mentally competent to conduct that trial himself. We must decide whether in these circumstances the Constitution forbids a State from insisting that the defendant proceed to trial with counsel, the State thereby denying the defendant the right to represent himself. . . . We conclude that the Constitution does not forbid a State so to insist.

---

12. The focus of a competency inquiry is the defendant's mental capacity; the question is whether he has the ability to understand the proceedings. . . . The purpose of the "knowing and voluntary" inquiry, by contrast, is to determine whether the defendant actually does understand the significance and consequences of a particular decision and whether the decision is uncoerced. . . .

. . . [I]n our view, a right of self-representation at trial will not "affirm the dignity" of a defendant who lacks the mental capacity to conduct his defense without the assistance of counsel. *Wiggins*, 465 U.S., at 176-177 ("Dignity" and "autonomy" of individual underlie self-representation right). To the contrary, given defendant's uncertain mental state, the spectacle that could well result from his self-representation at trial is at least as likely to prove humiliating as ennobling. Moreover, insofar as a defendant's lack of capacity threatens an improper conviction or sentence, self-representation in that exceptional context undercuts the most basic of the Constitution's criminal law objectives, providing a fair trial. As Justice Brennan put it, "[t]he Constitution would protect none of us if it prevented the courts from acting to preserve the very processes that the Constitution itself prescribes." *Illinois v. Allen*, 397 U.S., at 350 (concurring opinion). See *Martinez*, 528 U.S., at 162 ("Even at the trial level . . . the government's interest in ensuring the integrity and efficiency of the trial at times outweighs the defendant's interest in acting as his own lawyer"). . . .

Further, proceedings must not only be fair, they must "appear fair to all who observe them." *Wheat v. United States*, 486 U.S. 153, 160. . . . An amicus brief reports one psychiatrist's reaction to having observed a patient (a patient who had satisfied *Dusky*) try to conduct his own defense: "[H]ow in the world can our legal system allow an insane man to defend himself?" Brief for Ohio et al. as Amici Curiae 24. . . . The application of *Dusky*'s basic mental competence standard can help in part to avoid this result. But given the different capacities needed to proceed to trial without counsel, there is little reason to believe that *Dusky* alone is sufficient. At the same time, the trial judge, particularly one such as the trial judge in this case, who presided over one of Edwards' competency hearings and his two trials, will often prove best able to make more fine-tuned mental capacity decisions, tailored to the individualized circumstances of a particular defendant.

We consequently conclude that . . . the Constitution permits States to insist upon representation by counsel for those competent enough to stand trial under *Dusky* but who still suffer from severe mental illness to the point where they are not competent to conduct trial proceedings by themselves.

Indiana has also asked us to adopt . . . a more specific standard that would "deny a criminal defendant the right to represent himself at trial where the defendant cannot communicate coherently with the court or a jury." Brief for Petitioner 20 (emphasis deleted). We are sufficiently uncertain, however, as to how that particular standard would work in practice to refrain from endorsing it as a federal constitutional standard here. We need not now, and we do not, adopt it. . . .

JUSTICE SCALIA, dissenting:

Beyond [forbidding a defendant to disrupt the courtroom], we have never constrained the ability of a defendant to retain "actual control over the case he chooses to present to the jury" — what we have termed "the core of the *Faretta* right." *Wiggins*, supra, at 178. . . .

. . . I would not adopt an approach to the right of self-representation that we have squarely rejected for other rights — allowing courts to disregard the right when doing so serves the purposes for which the right was intended. But if I were to adopt such an approach, I would remain in dissent, because I believe the Court's assessment of the purposes of the right of self-representation is inaccurate to boot. While there is little doubt that preserving individual "dignity" (to which the Court refers), is paramount among those purposes, there is equally little doubt that the loss of "dignity" the right is designed to prevent is not the defendant's making a fool of himself by presenting an amateurish or even incoherent defense. Rather, the dignity at issue is the supreme human dignity of being master of one's fate rather than a ward of the State — the dignity of individual choice. . . . In sum, if the Court is to honor the particular conception of "dignity" that underlies the self-representation right, it should respect the autonomy of the individual by honoring his choices knowingly and voluntarily made.

A further purpose that the Court finds is advanced by denial of the right of self-representation is the purpose of assuring that trials "appear fair to all who observe them." To my knowledge we have never denied a defendant a right simply on the ground that it would make his trial appear less "fair" to outside observers, and I would not inaugurate that principle here. But were I to do so, I would not apply it to deny a defendant the right to represent himself when he knowingly and voluntarily waives counsel. When Edwards stood to say that "I have a defense that I would like to represent or present to the Judge," it seems to me the epitome of both actual and apparent unfairness for the judge to say, I have heard "your desire to proceed by yourself and I've denied your request, so your attorney will speak for you from now on."

. . . The facts of this case illustrate this point with the utmost clarity. Edwards wished to take a self-defense case to the jury. His counsel preferred a defense that focused on lack of intent. Having been denied the right to conduct his own defense, Edwards was convicted without having had the opportunity to present to the jury the grounds he believed supported his innocence. I do not doubt that he likely would have been convicted anyway. But to hold that a defendant may be deprived of the right to make legal arguments for acquittal simply because a state-selected agent has made different arguments on his behalf is, as Justice Frankfurter wrote in *Adams*, supra, at 280, to "imprison a man in his privileges and call it the Constitution." In singling out mentally ill defendants for this treatment, the Court's opinion does not even have the questionable virtue of being politically correct. At a time when all society is trying to mainstream the mentally impaired, the Court permits them to be deprived of a basic constitutional right — for their own good.

NOTES AND QUESTIONS

1. After *Edwards*, apparently a state may permit a severely mentally ill defendant to commit judicial suicide but may also decline to do so. As interesting as this conclusion is the manner in which the Court reached it. *Faretta* is best understood as an exegesis on the significance of autonomy — the right to control oneself and one's decisions — for understanding the Sixth Amendment. Autonomy is one of three concepts that often are intermingled under the terms of the other two — privacy and dignity. Privacy refers to the right to control information about yourself, and dignity to the manner in which others must treat you. As can be seen in both *Wiggins* and *Edwards*, autonomy and dignity can be at odds with each other. Indeed, to some extent, *Wiggins* foreshadowed *Edwards* by suggesting that *Faretta*'s strong focus on autonomy must give way under the pressure of pragmatism to a focus on dignitary interests. This change allowed the Court ostensibly to protect *Faretta* rights while simultaneously protecting incompetent defendants from themselves.

2. Now consider the dissent. Isn't Justice Scalia right to be outraged by the notion that a state may hale a person into court to answer for a serious crime (because he *is* competent enough to stand trial), and also may force that person to be represented in court by a lawyer whom he doesn't want (because he *isn't* competent enough to represent himself)? How many defendants are likely to fall into that gap? And what do you think about Justice Scalia's argument that the defendant was actually deprived of the ability to make what he believed was his best defense?

3. Beyond the issue of competency, what does it mean that a waiver of counsel must be "knowing and intelligent"? Is that phrase internally inconsistent? If not, what are its referents? The Court in *Faretta* asserts that "technical knowledge" is not even relevant to the inquiry and implies that on being convicted a technically incompetent individual may not assert ineffectiveness as a grounds for relief. How realistic is that? How would you react as a judge to a case in which an untrained person unknowingly forewent a potentially dispositive defense? If you believed that pro se representation had caused a false conviction, but recognized that no other legally adequate ground for reversal existed, would you feel bound by *Faretta*'s admonition that pro se litigants cannot claim error due to ineffectiveness? Might you be tempted to stretch other legal rules to reach the right result?

That is exactly what a number of courts have done, according to Sarah L. Allen, Faretta: Self-Representation, or Legal Misrepresentation? 90 Iowa L. Rev. 1553 (2005). The author searched for cases involving pro se representation that involved reversals of convictions, and in which there were dissents, the idea being that dissents might signal a majority stretching the law. A number of such cases were found with majority opinions fairly plainly stretching other legal rules to compensate for the inability to reverse on competency grounds.

4. Should a waiver of the Sixth Amendment right to counsel ever be allowed without first appointing counsel to discuss the matter with the defendant?

What if a defendant seeks to waive his right to counsel and plead guilty without the advice of counsel? Does the Constitution require that such a defendant be informed specifically by the trial judge, prior to entering the plea, that by virtue of waiving his right to counsel (1) he may wind up overlooking a viable defense, and (2) he may make an unwise decision about entering the plea? In Iowa v. Tovar, 541 U.S. 77 (2004), the Court rejected the claim that such warnings are essential to an intelligent and knowing waiver of the right to counsel, holding that in such a situation the Constitution requires knowledge of only the nature of charges, the right to be counseled about the plea, and the range of allowable punishments.

2. The Right to Counsel of One's Choice

Throughout this chapter, there have been intimations that the Sixth Amendment provides some protection for the right to counsel of one's choice, so long as either the defendant can afford an attorney or the attorney is otherwise willing to serve without reimbursement from the state for services provided. That issue came before the Court in the following case:

UNITED STATES v. GONZALEZ-LOPEZ

Certiorari to the United States Court of Appeals for the Eighth Circuit
548 U.S. 140 (2006)

JUSTICE SCALIA delivered the opinion of the Court.

We must decide whether a trial court's erroneous deprivation of a criminal defendant's choice of counsel entitles him to a reversal of his conviction.

I

Respondent Cuauhtemoc Gonzalez-Lopez was charged in the Eastern District of Missouri with conspiracy to distribute more than 100 kilograms of marijuana. His family hired attorney John Fahle to represent him. After the arraignment, respondent called a California attorney, Joseph Low, to discuss whether Low would represent him, either in addition to or instead of Fahle. Low flew from California to meet with respondent, who hired him. . . .

The following week, respondent informed Fahle that he wanted Low to be his only attorney. Low then filed an application for admission *pro hac vice*. The District Court denied his application without comment. A month later, Low filed a second application, which the District Court again denied without explanation. . . .

The case proceeded to trial, and Dickhaus represented respondent. Low again moved for admission and was again denied. The Court also denied Dickhaus's request to have Low at counsel table with him and ordered Low to sit in the audience and to have no contact with Dickhaus during the proceedings. To enforce the Court's order, a United States Marshal sat between Low and Dickhaus at trial. Respondent was unable to meet with Low throughout the trial, except for once on the last night. The jury found respondent guilty. . . .

Respondent appealed, and the Eighth Circuit vacated the conviction. The Court . . . held that the District Court erred in . . . its denials of [Low's] . . . motions, and violated respondent's Sixth Amendment right to paid counsel of his choosing. The court then concluded that this Sixth Amendment violation was not subject to harmless-error review. We granted certiorari.

II

. . . The Government here agrees, as it has previously, that "the Sixth Amendment guarantees the defendant the right to be represented by an otherwise qualified attorney whom that defendant can afford to hire, or who is willing to represent the defendant even though he is without funds." Caplin & Drysdale, Chartered v. United States, 491 U.S. 617, 624-625 (1989). To be sure, the right to counsel of choice "is circumscribed in several important respects." But the Government does not dispute the Eighth Circuit's conclusion in this case that the District Court erroneously deprived respondent of his counsel of choice.

The Government contends, however, that the Sixth Amendment violation is not "complete" unless the defendant can show that substitute counsel was ineffective within the meaning of Strickland v. Washington — i.e., that substitute counsel's performance was deficient and the defendant was prejudiced by it. In the alternative, the Government contends that the defendant must at least demonstrate that his counsel of choice would have pursued a different strategy that would have created a "reasonable probability that . . . the result of the proceedings would have been different," — in other words, that he was prejudiced within the meaning of *Strickland* by the denial of his counsel of choice even if substitute counsel's performance was not constitutionally deficient.[1] To support these propositions, the Government points to our prior cases, which note that the right to counsel "has been accorded . . . not for its own sake, but for the effect it has on the ability of the accused to receive a fair trial." Mickens v. Taylor, 535 U.S. 162, 166 (2002). A trial is not unfair and thus the Sixth Amendment is not violated, the Government reasons, unless a defendant has been prejudiced.

Stated as broadly as this, the Government's argument in effect reads the Sixth Amendment as a more detailed version of the Due Process Clause — and then proceeds to give no effect to the details. It is true enough that the purpose of the rights set forth in that Amendment is to ensure a fair trial; but it does not follow that the rights can be disregarded so long as the trial is, on the whole, fair. . . .

. . . [T]he Sixth Amendment right to counsel of choice . . . commands, not that a trial be fair, but that a particular guarantee of fairness be provided — to wit, that the accused be defended by the counsel he believes to be best. "The Constitution guarantees a fair trial through the Due Process Clauses, but it defines the basic elements of a fair trial largely through the several provisions of the Sixth Amendment, including the Counsel Clause." *Strickland*, supra, at 684-685. In sum, the right at stake here is the right to counsel of choice, not the right to a fair trial; and that right was violated because the deprivation of counsel was erroneous. No additional showing of prejudice is required to make the violation "complete."

The cases the Government relies on involve the right to the effective assistance of counsel, the violation of which generally requires a defendant to establish prejudice. The earliest case generally cited for the proposition that "the right to counsel is the right to the effective assistance of counsel," McMann v. Richardson, 397 U.S. 759, 771 (1970), was based on the Due Process Clause rather than on the Sixth Amendment. And even our recognition of the right to effective counsel within the Sixth Amendment was a consequence of our perception that representation by counsel "is critical to the ability of the adversarial system to produce just results." *Strickland*, supra, at 685. Having derived the right to effective representation from the purpose of ensuring a fair trial, we have, logically enough, also derived the limits of that right from that same purpose. The requirement that a defendant show prejudice in effective representation cases arises from the very nature of the specific element of the right to counsel at issue there — *effective* (not mistake-free) representation. Counsel cannot be "ineffective" unless his mistakes have harmed the defense (or, at least, unless it is reasonably likely that they have). Thus, a violation of the Sixth Amendment right to *effective* representation is not "complete" until the defendant is prejudiced.

---

1. The dissent proposes yet a third standard — viz., that the defendant must show "an identifiable difference in the quality of representation between the disqualified counsel and the attorney who represents the defendant at trial." (opinion of ALITO, J.). That proposal suffers from the same infirmities (outlined later in text) that beset the Government's positions. In addition, however, it greatly impairs the clarity of the law. How is a lower-court judge to know what an "identifiable difference" consists of? Whereas the Government at least appeals to *Strickland* and the case law under it, the most the dissent can claim by way of precedential support for its rule is that it is "consistent with" cases that never discussed the issue of prejudice.

The right to select counsel of one's choice, by contrast, has never been derived from the Sixth Amendment's purpose of ensuring a fair trial.[3] It has been regarded as the root meaning of the constitutional guarantee. Where the right to be assisted by counsel of one's choice is wrongly denied, therefore, it is unnecessary to conduct an ineffectiveness or prejudice inquiry to establish a Sixth Amendment violation. Deprivation of the right is "complete" when the defendant is erroneously prevented from being represented by the lawyer he wants, regardless of the quality of the representation he received. To argue otherwise is to confuse the right to counsel of choice—which is the right to a particular lawyer regardless of comparative effectiveness—with the right to effective counsel—which imposes a baseline requirement of competence on whatever lawyer is chosen or appointed.

III

Having concluded, in light of the Government's concession of erroneous deprivation, that the trial court violated respondent's Sixth Amendment right to counsel of choice, we must consider whether this error is subject to review for harmlessness . . . [NOTE — The general subject of harmless error is discussed infra, in Chapter 17. — EDS.]

We have little trouble concluding that erroneous deprivation of the right to counsel of choice, "with consequences that are necessarily unquantifiable and indeterminate, unquestionably qualifies as 'structural error'" [not subject to harmless error review.] Different attorneys will pursue different strategies with regard to investigation and discovery, development of the theory of defense, selection of the jury, presentation of the witnesses, and style of witness examination and jury argument. And the choice of attorney will affect whether and on what terms the defendant cooperates with the prosecution, plea bargains, or decides instead to go to trial. In light of these myriad aspects of representation, the erroneous denial of counsel bears directly on the "framework within which the trial proceeds," — or indeed on whether it proceeds at all. It is impossible to know what different choices the rejected counsel would have made, and then to quantify the impact of those different choices on the outcome of the proceedings. Many counseled decisions, including those involving plea bargains and cooperation with the government, do not even concern the conduct of the trial at all. Harmless-error analysis in such a context would be a speculative inquiry into what might have occurred in an alternate universe.

The Government acknowledges that the deprivation of choice of counsel pervades the entire trial, but points out that counsel's ineffectiveness may also do so and yet we do not allow reversal of a conviction for that reason without a showing of prejudice. But the requirement of showing prejudice in ineffectiveness claims stems from the very definition of the right at issue; it is not a matter of showing that the violation was harmless, but of showing that a violation of the right to effective representation *occurred*. A choice-of-counsel violation occurs *whenever* the defendant's

---

3. In Wheat v. United States, 486 U.S. 153 (1988), where we formulated the right to counsel of choice and discussed some of the limitations upon it, we took note of the overarching purpose of fair trial in holding that the trial court has discretion to disallow a first choice of counsel that would create serious risk of conflict of interest. It is one thing to conclude that the right to counsel of choice may be limited by the need for fair trial, but quite another to say that the right does not exist unless its denial renders the trial unfair.

choice is wrongfully denied. Moreover, if and when counsel's ineffectiveness "pervades" a trial, it does so (to the extent we can detect it) through identifiable mistakes. We can assess how those mistakes affected the outcome. To determine the effect of wrongful denial of choice of counsel, however, we would not be looking for mistakes committed by the actual counsel, but for differences in the defense that would have been made by the rejected counsel — in matters ranging from questions asked on *voir dire* and cross-examination to such intangibles as argument style and relationship with the prosecutors. We would have to speculate upon what matters the rejected counsel would have handled differently — or indeed, would have handled the same but with the benefit of a more jury — pleasing courtroom style or a longstanding relationship of trust with the prosecutors. And then we would have to speculate upon what effect those different choices or different intangibles might have had. The difficulties of conducting the two assessments of prejudice are not remotely comparable.[5]

IV

Nothing we have said today casts any doubt or places any qualification upon our previous holdings that limit the right to counsel of choice and recognize the authority of trial courts to establish criteria for admitting lawyers to argue before them. As the dissent too discusses, the right to counsel of choice does not extend to defendants who require counsel to be appointed for them. Nor may a defendant insist on representation by a person who is not a member of the bar, or demand that a court honor his waiver of conflict-free representation. We have recognized a trial court's wide latitude in balancing the right to counsel of choice against the needs of fairness, and against the demands of its calendar. The court has, moreover, an "independent interest in ensuring that criminal trials are conducted within the ethical standards of the profession and that legal proceedings appear fair to all who observe them." None of these limitations on the right to choose one's counsel is relevant here. This is not a case about a court's power to enforce rules or adhere to practices that determine which attorneys may appear before it, or to make scheduling and other decisions that effectively exclude a defendant's first choice of counsel. However broad a court's discretion may be, the Government has conceded that the District Court here erred when it denied respondent his choice of counsel. Accepting that premise, we hold that the error violated respondent's Sixth Amendment right to counsel of choice and that this violation is not subject to harmless-error analysis.

* * *

The judgment of the Court of Appeals is affirmed, and the case is remanded for further proceedings consistent with this opinion.

JUSTICE ALITO, with whom CHIEF JUSTICE ROBERTS, JUSTICE KENNEDY, and JUSTICE THOMAS join, dissenting.

5. In its discussion of the analysis that would be required to conduct harmless-error review, the dissent focuses on which counsel was "better." This focus has the effect of making the analysis look achievable, but it is fundamentally inconsistent with the principle (which the dissent purports to accept for the sake of argument) that the Sixth Amendment can be violated without a showing of harm to the quality of representation. By framing its inquiry in these terms and expressing indignation at the thought that a defendant may receive a new trial when his actual counsel was at least as effective as the one he wanted, the dissent betrays its misunderstanding of the nature of the right to counsel of choice and its confusion of this right with the right to effective assistance of counsel.

I disagree with the Court's conclusion that a criminal conviction must automatically be reversed whenever a trial court errs in applying its rules regarding *pro hac vice* admissions and as a result prevents a defendant from being represented at trial by the defendant's first-choice attorney. Instead, a defendant should be required to make at least *some* showing that the trial court's erroneous ruling adversely affected the quality of assistance that the defendant received. In my view, the majority's contrary holding is based on an incorrect interpretation of the Sixth Amendment and a misapplication of harmless-error principles. I respectfully dissent.

I

The majority makes a subtle but important mistake at the outset in its characterization of what the Sixth Amendment guarantees. The majority states that the Sixth Amendment protects "the right of a defendant who does not require appointed counsel to choose who will represent him." What the Sixth Amendment actually protects, however, is the right to have *the assistance* that the defendant's counsel of choice is able to provide. It follows that if the erroneous disqualification of a defendant's counsel of choice does not impair the assistance that a defendant receives at trial, there is no violation of the Sixth Amendment.

The language of the Sixth Amendment supports this interpretation. The Assistance of Counsel Clause focuses on what a defendant is entitled to receive ("Assistance"), rather than on the identity of the provider. The background of the adoption of the Sixth Amendment points in the same direction. The specific evil against which the Assistance of Counsel Clause was aimed was the English common-law rule severely limiting a felony defendant's ability to be assisted by counsel. . . .

There is no doubt, of course, that the right "to have the Assistance of Counsel" carries with it a limited right to be represented by counsel of choice. At the time of the adoption of the Bill of Rights, when the availability of appointed counsel was generally limited, that is how the right inevitably played out: A defendant's right to have the assistance of counsel necessarily meant the right to have the assistance of whatever counsel the defendant was able to secure. But from the beginning, the right to counsel of choice has been circumscribed.

For one thing, a defendant's choice of counsel has always been restricted by the rules governing admission to practice before the court in question. . . .

The right to counsel of choice is also limited by conflict-of-interest rules. Even if a defendant is aware that his or her attorney of choice has a conflict, and even if the defendant is eager to waive any objection, the defendant has no constitutional right to be represented by that attorney.

Similarly, the right to be represented by counsel of choice can be limited by mundane case-management considerations. If a trial judge schedules a trial to begin on a particular date and defendant's counsel of choice is already committed for other trials until some time thereafter, the trial judge has discretion under appropriate circumstances to refuse to postpone the trial date and thereby, in effect, to force the defendant to forgo counsel of choice.

These limitations on the right to counsel of choice are tolerable because the focus of the right is the quality of the representation that the defendant receives, not the identity of the attorney who provides the representation. Limiting a defendant to those attorneys who are willing, available, and eligible to represent the defendant still leaves a defendant with a pool of attorneys to choose from — and, in most jurisdictions today, a large and diverse pool. Thus, these restrictions generally have no adverse effect on a defendant's ability to secure the best assistance that the defendant's circumstances permit.

Because the Sixth Amendment focuses on the quality of the assistance that counsel of choice would have provided, I would hold that the erroneous disqualification of counsel does not violate the Sixth Amendment unless the ruling diminishes the quality of assistance that the defendant would have otherwise received. This would not require a defendant to show that the second-choice attorney was constitutionally ineffective within the meaning of Strickland v. Washington. Rather, the defendant would be entitled to a new trial if the defendant could show "an identifiable difference in the quality of representation between the disqualified counsel and the attorney who represents the defendant at trial."

II

But even accepting, as the majority holds, that the erroneous disqualification of counsel of choice always violates the Sixth Amendment, it still would not follow that reversal is required in all cases. The Constitution, by its terms, does not mandate any particular remedy for violations of its own provisions. Instead, we are bound in this case by Federal Rule of Criminal Procedure 52(a), which instructs federal courts to "disregar[d]" "[a]ny error . . . which does not affect substantial rights." The only exceptions we have recognized to this rule have been for "a limited class of fundamental constitutional errors that 'defy analysis by "harmless error" standards.'" Neder v. United States, 527 U.S. 1, 7 (1999).

Thus, in *Neder*, we rejected the argument that the omission of an element of a crime in a jury instruction "*necessarily* render[s] a criminal trial fundamentally unfair or an unreliable vehicle for determining guilt or innocence." In fact, in that case, "quite the opposite [was] true: Neder was tried before an impartial judge, under the correct standard of proof and with the assistance of counsel; a fairly selected, impartial jury was instructed to consider all of the evidence and argument in respect to Neder's defense. . . ."

Neder's situation — with an impartial judge, the correct standard of proof, assistance of counsel, and a fair jury — is much like respondent's. Fundamental unfairness does not inexorably follow from the denial of first-choice counsel. The "decision to retain a particular lawyer" is "often uninformed"; a defendant's second-choice lawyer may thus turn out to be better than the defendant's first-choice lawyer. More often, a defendant's first- and second-choice lawyers may be simply indistinguishable. These possibilities would not justify violating the right to choice of counsel, but they do make me hard put to characterize the violation as "*always* render[ing] a trial unfair." Fairness may not limit the right, but it does inform the remedy.

Nor is it always or nearly always impossible to determine whether the first choice would have provided better representation than the second choice. There are undoubtedly cases in which the prosecution would have little difficulty showing that the second-choice attorney was better qualified than or at least as qualified as the defendant's initial choice, and there are other cases in which it will be evident to the trial judge that any difference in ability or strategy could not have possibly affected the outcome of the trial.

Requiring a defendant to fall back on a second-choice attorney is not comparable to denying a defendant the right to be represented by counsel at all. Refusing to permit a defendant to receive the assistance of any counsel is the epitome of fundamental unfairness, and as far as the effect on the outcome is concerned, it is much more difficult to assess the effect of a complete denial of counsel than it is to assess the effect of merely preventing representation by the defendant's first-choice attorney. To be sure, when the effect of an erroneous disqualification is hard to gauge, the prosecution will be unable to meet its burden of showing that the error was harmless beyond a reasonable doubt. But that does not justify eliminating the possibility of showing harmless error in all cases. . . .

III

Either of the two courses outlined above — requiring at least some showing of prejudice, or engaging in harmless-error review — would avoid the anomalous and unjustifiable consequences that follow from the majority's two-part rule of error without prejudice followed by automatic reversal.

Under the majority's holding, a defendant who is erroneously required to go to trial with a second-choice attorney is automatically entitled to a new trial even if this attorney performed brilliantly. By contrast, a defendant whose attorney was ineffective in the constitutional sense . . . cannot obtain relief without showing prejudice.

Under the majority's holding, a trial court may adopt rules severely restricting *pro hac vice* admissions, but if it adopts a generous rule and then errs in interpreting or applying it, the error automatically requires reversal of any conviction, regardless of whether the erroneous ruling had any effect on the defendant.

Under the majority's holding, some defendants will be awarded new trials even though it is clear that the erroneous disqualification of their first-choice counsel did not prejudice them in the least. Suppose, for example, that a defendant is initially represented by an attorney who previously represented the defendant in civil matters and who has little criminal experience. Suppose that this attorney is erroneously disqualified and that the defendant is then able to secure the services of a nationally acclaimed and highly experienced criminal defense attorney who secures a surprisingly favorable result at trial — for instance, acquittal on most but not all counts. Under the majority's holding, the trial court's erroneous ruling automatically means that the Sixth Amendment was violated — even if the defendant makes no attempt to argue that the disqualified attorney would have done a better job. In fact, the defendant would still be entitled to a new trial on the counts of conviction even if the defendant publicly proclaimed after the verdict that the second attorney had provided better representation than any other attorney in the country could have possibly done. . . .

Because I believe that some showing of prejudice is required to establish a violation of the Sixth Amendment, I would vacate and remand to let the Court of Appeals determine whether there was prejudice. However, assuming for the sake of argument that no prejudice is required, I believe that such a violation, like most constitutional violations, is amenable to harmless-error review. . . .

NOTES AND QUESTIONS

1. The majority opinion purports to be a straightforward application of the literal command of the Sixth Amendment, but is it? Where in the Amendment does it refer to the counsel the defendant "believes to be best"?

2. The dissent is surely correct that there is a critical distinction between right and remedy that the majority elides. But what about the dissent's view of the correct remedy? There is a certain intuitive appeal to the dissent's position that the focus should be on whether the disallowed counsel would have been better, but what exactly does that mean and how could it be implemented in fact? For example, how could it be shown that some other counsel might have been more effective in cross-examining a witness or making a closing argument? One cannot simply rely on reputation here; one needs evidence, but where would that evidence come from? If trial counsel were so bad as to meet the ineffectiveness standard, that would be one thing, but then the holding in *Gonzalez-Lopez* would be unnecessary.

Perhaps more troublesome, suppose trial counsel *did* botch a cross-examination. What about all the other examinations and cross-examinations counsel conducted? What if they were spectacularly effective? The measure of the quality of assistance is based not just on one discrete moment at trial, but on the trial as a whole. But if that is true, then the dissent implicitly calls for a complex comparison of how this trial actually went with how some counter-factual trial would have gone. Is that possible? Sensible?

3. On the one hand, given the curious linguistic difficulties of the majority's opinion and the practical difficulties of the dissent's, should the Court have simply focused on whether the defendant received constitutionally adequate representation and been done with it? On the other hand, wouldn't that approach (as the majority points out) effectively turn the Sixth Amendment's right to counsel into a mere bit player in support of the defendant's due process right to a fair trial? As we have seen throughout this chapter, one of the recurring themes in right to counsel cases is the effort to identify the core values that the Sixth Amendment serves: If it is about something more than fairness, what else is it about? Equality? Accuracy? Autonomy?

4. What effect, if any, will *Gonzalez-Lopez* have on substantive decisions concerning the right to counsel? The government conceded that the decision to deny Low's motions to represent the defendant was erroneous. Does the case increase the pressure on courts to find to the contrary simply to avoid automatic reversal?

5. If defendants who can afford counsel enjoy at least a limited right to counsel of their choice, and if *all* individuals have the right to proceed pro se as an implication of basic values of autonomy and dignity, should an indigent defendant also have the right to choose who is appointed to represent him? The general view is that there is no such right, the leading case being Drumgo v. Superior Court, 506 P.2d 1007, 106 Cal. Rptr. 631 (1973). Four years after *Drumgo*, the California Supreme Court held that failure to respect an indigent's choice of counsel may amount to an abuse of discretion by the trial court when there are objective circumstances making the defendant's request reasonable. Harris v. Superior Court, 19 Cal. 3d 786, 567 P.2d 750,

140 Cal. Rptr. 318 (1977).[14] The objective circumstances in *Harris* were that the counsel the defendants wanted also represented them in related matters and were intimately acquainted with factual and legal matters likely to be relevant to the present litigation. Moreover, counsel appointed by the trial court were essentially ignorant of the case.

In Morris v. Slappy, 461 U.S. 1 (1983), the Supreme Court held that the Sixth Amendment does not guarantee a "meaningful relationship" between attorney and client. Therefore, it was not error to refuse to grant a continuance to allow one public defender, whom the defendant desired as counsel, rather than another to try the case. The primary issue, according to the Court, was whether the attorney who actually tried the case did so competently.

Does *Gonzalez-Lopez* in any way affect the holding in Morris v. Slappy? Should it?

NOTES ON FORFEITURE STATUTES AND THE RIGHT TO COUNSEL

1. In Caplin & Drysdale, Chartered v. United States, 491 U.S. 617 (1989), a well-known D.C. law firm sued the U.S. government for legal fees that it did not receive for defending one Charles Reckmeyer on charges of running a massive illegal drug operation. The reason the law firm did not get its money is that the government first "froze" it (before trial) and then "seized" it (after trial, at which Reckmeyer was convicted) through forfeiture, as authorized by the particular criminal statute under which Reckmeyer was charged. The law firm argued that this (1) effectively denied Reckmeyer (or, more precisely, would deny any future Reckmeyer) his Sixth Amendment right to counsel of choice; (2) violated due process, by allowing the prosecution to abuse its power and upset the "balance of forces" with the defense; and (3) created untenable conflicts of interest between Reckmeyer and his attorneys (e.g., because the attorneys had an incentive to encourage Reckmeyer to take any plea bargain that would include more prison time but avoid forfeiture).

The Court did not agree. Justice White, writing for a narrow 5-4 majority, found that Reckmeyer's right to counsel of choice was not infringed, mostly because the forfeited money was never really Reckmeyer's to begin with. Under "long-recognized and lawful practice," legal title to the "ill-gotten gains" vested in the government "at the time of the criminal act." This "relation-back" doctrine meant that Reckmeyer was basically in the same position as a bank robber seeking to use the bank's money to pay for his defense lawyer. And any future Reckmeyer who might prove unable to persuade paid counsel to take his case, due to the risk of forfeiture, would simply have to make do with court-appointed counsel — just like most other criminal defendants already do, even in complex cases. On the due process claim, the Court acknowledged the possibility of prosecutorial abuse, but left it up to the lower courts to police such problems on a case-by-case basis. And the Court dismissed the conflict of interest arguments in a footnote as largely theoretical and speculative, also pointing out that *Strickland* remains available to deal with any such scenario, should it ever occur.

---

14. The case involved William and Emily Harris, two leaders of the Symbionese Liberation Army, a radical left-wing organization responsible for a string of notorious crimes in California that included murder, bank robbery, and the kidnapping of newspaper heiress Patty Hearst.

Leaving aside the irony of *Caplin & Drysdale* using Reckmeyer's plight as grounds to seek almost $200,000 in legal fees from the government, what is the real issue in *Caplin & Drysdale*? Is it that the Reckmeyers of the world must (at least in the future) suffer the indignity of being represented by appointed counsel (or, maybe even worse, the public defender)? Or is it that prosecutors now have a potent new weapon in cases involving forfeiture statutes — namely, the ability to assert control over the defendant's choice of counsel? As Justice Blackmun argued, in dissent, "[t]he Government will be ever tempted to use the forfeiture weapon against a defense attorney who is particularly talented or aggressive on the client's behalf. . . ."

2. Does *Caplin & Drysdale* differ from most of the other cases in this chapter? Consider the following argument:

> One might view the ability to purchase lawyers' services as very much like the ability to acquire any other market commodity. Just as we strip Reckmeyer . . . of the ability to buy fancy houses, so, too, we deny [him] the right to hire fancy lawyers.
>
> But there is an alternative conception . . . under which lawyers are a very different kind of good. Under this conception, economic power serves as an *instrumentality* of criminal activity as well as a *proceed* from it. The complex criminal enterprise's wealth gives the enterprise opportunities for criminal activity that poorer entities do not have and gives it opportunities to evade liability that less affluent criminals lack. If the outcome of a criminal proceeding is positively correlated to the caliber of counsel appearing on a defendant's behalf, and if the caliber of counsel is positively related to the ability to retain the best counsel money can buy — both common assumptions — then the economic power acquired by a complex enterprise may enable the enterprise to stay in business by avoiding convictions and forfeitures. Economic power not only constitutes a *benefit* to the criminal; it also lessens her *costs* (because it lowers the probability that she will be detected or successfully prosecuted). The power to buy fancy lawyers may in fact be *worse* than the power to buy fancy houses, because the latter does not facilitate the commission of further crimes as the former can.

Pamela S. Karlan, Discrete and Relational Criminal Representation: The Changing Vision of the Right to Counsel, 105 Harv. L. Rev. 670, 709-710 (1992). If Professor Karlan is right, does that mean Sixth Amendment law should treat lawyers in organized crime cases differently than in more run-of-the-mill criminal cases?

3. In *Caplin & Drysdale*, the Court also rejected the argument (made by the American Bar Association as amicus curiae) that forcing defendants to use appointed counsel in complex criminal cases is a form of per se ineffective assistance. In the words of the Court, "we cannot say that the Sixth Amendment's guarantee of effective assistance of counsel is a guarantee of a privately-retained counsel in every complex case, irrespective of a defendant's ability to pay."

Why not? Remember that the *Caplin & Drysdale* problem is much more likely to arise in conspiracy and large-scale drug distribution cases (where forfeiture statutes are common) than in cases of ordinary "street crime" (where they are not). Such cases are likely to be expensive and time-consuming — perhaps a great deal more so than the average criminal case. Might the low pay, fee caps, and high caseloads of appointed defense counsel have a greater impact on the quality of representation in conspiracy-type cases than in run-of-the-mill criminal cases?

4. Most forfeiture statutes contain an "innocent owner" provision designed to protect those who engage in good-faith transactions with a person subsequently convicted of crimes involving forfeiture. But the courts have not been terribly forgiving.

See, e.g., United States v. 1977 Porsche Carrera 911 VIN 9117201924 License No. 459 DWR, 748 F. Supp. 1180 (W.D. Texas 1990):

> If a lawyer receives property under suspicious circumstances, he has a duty to investigate further into the origin of the property in order to establish that he has not been "willfully blind" as to the illegal nature of the property. This Court is of the opinion that even in a case in which a lawyer is truly ignorant of any wrongdoing at the precise moment of acquisition of the property, but subsequently learns within a reasonable period . . . that the property is proceeds or has been used to facilitate a crime, that lawyer should not be considered an "innocent owner" . . . .
>
> The Court is aware of the hardships this may impose on criminal defense lawyers, but such burden is contemplated by the asset forfeiture provisions, which aim to prevent criminals from using the proceeds of their illegal activities to obtain "the best defense counsel that money can buy." . . .

5. If requiring the forfeiture of assets that would have been used to pay for counsel does not violate any of the defendant's rights, what about searching a lawyer pursuant to a warrant while the lawyer's client is testifying before a grand jury? Not a due process violation, said the Court in Conn v. Gabbert, 526 U.S. 286 (1999). Whether such a search might be unreasonable under the Fourth Amendment was not decided.

What about charging the attorney with a crime? The line between receiving legitimate fees and illegal money laundering may not always be clear. And defense attorneys have been indicted for their alleged involvement in criminal conspiracies based on allegations of money laundering. See, e.g., United States v. Abbell, 963 F. Supp. 1178 (S.D. Fla. 1997).

PART THREE

THE RIGHT TO BE LET ALONE—AN EXAMINATION OF THE FOURTH AND FIFTH AMENDMENTS AND RELATED AREAS

Chapter 4

The Rise and Fall of Boyd v. United States

. . . Boyd v. United States [is] a case that will be remembered as long as civil liberty lives in the United States.

Justice Brandeis, dissenting, in
Olmstead v. United States,
277 U.S. 438, at 474 (1928)

. . . *Boyd* is dead.

Stanton D. Krauss, The Life and Times of
Boyd v. United States (1886-1976),
76 Mich. L. Rev. 184, 212 (1977)
(hereinafter cited as Krauss)

It is a trivial exercise in two different senses to learn what the law "is." Law is in a constant state of change. Thus, to "know" the law is to know only what was, not what is. Similarly, legal principles are in large measure conclusions or labels applied to a synthesis of competing interests, considerations, and developments that themselves change over time. To understand the principles, one must understand their etiologies and implications, not just their logical relationships. As Oliver Wendell Holmes put it in The Common Law (1881):

It is something to show that the consistency of a system requires a particular result, but it is not all. The life of the law has not been logic: it has been experience. The felt necessities of the time, the prevalent moral and political theories, intuitions of public policy, avowed or unconscious, even the prejudices which judges share with their fellow-men, have had a good deal more to do than the syllogism in determining the rules by which men should be governed. The law embodies the story of a nation's development through many centuries, and it cannot be dealt with as if it contained only the axioms and corollaries of a book of mathematics. In order to know what it is, we must know what it has been, and what it tends to become. We must alternately consult history and existing theories of legislation. But the most difficult labor will be to understand the combination of the two into new products at every stage. The substance of the law at any given time pretty nearly corresponds, so far as it goes, with what is then understood to be convenient; but its form and machinery, and the degree to which it is able to work out desired results, depend very much upon its past. . . .

. . . In [using history to explicate legal principles, however,] there are two errors equally to be avoided both by writer and reader. One is that of supposing, because an idea seems very familiar and natural to us, that it has always been so. Many things which we take for granted have had to be laboriously fought out or thought out in past times. The other mistake is the opposite one of asking too much of history. We start with man full grown. It may be assumed that the earliest barbarian whose practices are to be considered, had a good many of the same feelings and passions as ourselves.

Id., at 1-2.

The necessity of understanding the source of contemporary developments in order to understand, and more important to evaluate, the developments themselves is nowhere more evident than in the areas of the Fourth and Fifth amendments. The starting point is the following case.

BOYD v. UNITED STATES

Error to the United States District Court for the Southern District of New York
116 U.S. 616 (1886)

MR. JUSTICE BRADLEY delivered the opinion of the Court.

This was an information filed by the District Attorney of the United States in the District Court for the Southern District of New York, in July, 1884, in a cause of seizure and forfeiture of property, against thirty-five cases of plate glass, seized by the collector as forfeited to the United States, under §12 of the "Act to amend the customs revenue laws, and to repeal moieties," passed June 22, 1874, 18 Stat. 186.

It is declared by that section that any owner, importer, consignee, &c., who shall, with intent to defraud the revenue, make, or attempt to make, any entry of imported merchandise, by means of any fraudulent or false invoice, affidavit, letter or paper, or by means of any false statement, written or verbal, or who shall be guilty of any wilful act or omission by means whereof the United States shall be deprived of the lawful duties, or any portion thereof, accruing upon the merchandise, or any portion thereof, embraced or referred to in such invoice, affidavit, letter, paper, or statement, or affected by such act or omission, shall for each offence be fined in any sum not exceeding $5000 nor less than $50, or be imprisoned for any time not exceeding two years, or both; and, in addition to such fine, such merchandise shall be forfeited.

The charge was that the goods in question were imported into the United States to the port of New York, subject to the payment of duties; and that the owners or agents of said merchandise, or other person unknown, committed the alleged fraud, which was described in the words of the statute. The plaintiffs in error entered a claim for the goods, and pleaded that they did not become forfeited in manner and form as alleged. On the trial of the cause it became important to show the quantity and value of the glass contained in twenty-nine cases previously imported. To do this the district attorney offered in evidence an order made by the District Judge under §5 of the same act of June 22, 1874, directing notice under seal of the court to be given to the claimants, requiring them to produce the invoice of the twenty-nine cases. The claimants, in obedience to the notice, but objecting to its validity and to the constitutionality of the law, produced the invoice; and when it was offered in evidence by the district attorney they objected to its reception on the ground that, in a suit for forfeiture, no evidence can be compelled from the claimants themselves, and also that the statute, so far as it compels production of evidence to be used against the claimants is unconstitutional and void.

The evidence being received, and the trial closed, the jury found a verdict for the United States, condemning the thirty-five cases of glass which were seized, and judgment of forfeiture was given. This judgment was affirmed by the Circuit Court, and the decision of that court is now here for review. . . .

The 5th section of the act of June 22, 1874, under which this order was made, is in the following words, to wit:

In all suits and proceedings other than criminal arising under any of the revenue laws of the United States, the attorney representing the government, whenever in his belief any business book, invoice, or paper belonging to, or under the control of, the defendant or claimant, will tend to prove any allegation made by the United States, may make a written motion, particularly describing such book, invoice, or paper, and setting forth the allegation which he expects to prove; and thereupon the court in which suit or proceeding is pending may, at its discretion, issue a notice to the defendant or claimant to produce such book, invoice, or paper in court, at a day and hour to be specified in said notice, which, together with a copy of said motion, shall be served formally on the defendant or claimant by the United States marshal by delivering to him a certified copy thereof, or otherwise serving the same as original notices of suit in the same court are served; and if the defendant or claimant shall fail or refuse to produce such book, invoice, or paper in obedience to such notice, the allegations stated in the said motion shall be taken as confessed, unless his failure or refusal to produce the same shall be explained to the satisfaction of the court. And if produced the said attorney shall be permitted, under the direction of the court, to make examination (at which examination the defendant, or claimant, or his agent, may be present) of such entries in said book, invoice, or paper as relate to or tend to prove the allegation aforesaid, and may offer the same in evidence on behalf of the United States. But the owner of said books and papers, his agent or attorney, shall have, subject to the order of the court, the custody of them, except pending their examination in court as aforesaid.

This section was passed in lieu of the 2d section of the act of March 2, 1867, . . . which section of said last-mentioned statute authorized the district judge, on complaint and affidavit that any fraud on the revenue had been committed by any person interested or engaged in the importation of merchandise, to issue his warrant to the marshal to enter any premises where any invoices, books, or papers were deposited relating to such merchandise, and take possession of such books and papers and produce them before said judge, to be subject to his order, and allowed to be examined by the collector, and to be retained as long as the judge should deem necessary.

The section last recited was passed in lieu of the 7th section of the act of March 3, 1863, . . . 12 Stat. 737. The 7th section of this act was in substance the same as the 2d section of the act of 1867, except that the warrant was to be directed to the collector instead of the marshal. It was the first legislation of the kind that ever appeared on the statute book of the United States, and, as seen from its date, was adopted at a period of great national excitement, when the powers of the government were subjected to a severe strain to protect the national existence.

The clauses of the Constitution, to which it is contended that these laws are repugnant, are the Fourth and Fifth Amendments. The Fourth declares, "The right of the people to be secure in their persons, houses, papers, and effects, against unreasonable searches and seizures, shall not be violated, and no warrants shall issue, but upon probable cause, supported by oath or affirmation, and particularly describing the place to be searched, and the persons or things to be seized." The Fifth Article, amongst other things, declares that no person "shall be compelled in any criminal case to be a witness against himself."

But, in regard to the Fourth Amendment, it is contended that, whatever might have been alleged against the constitutionality of the acts of 1863 and 1867, that of 1874, under which the order in the present case was made, is free from constitutional objection, because it does not authorize the search and seizure of books and papers, but only requires the defendant or claimant to produce them. That is so; but it declares that if he does not produce them, the allegations which it is affirmed they will prove shall be taken as confessed. This is tantamount to compelling their production; for the prosecuting attorney will always be sure to state the evidence expected to be derived from them as strongly as the case will admit of. It is true that certain aggravating incidents of actual search and seizure, such as forcible entry into a man's house and searching amongst his papers, are wanting, and to this extent the proceeding under the act of 1874 is a mitigation of that which was authorized by the former acts; but it accomplishes the substantial object of those acts in forcing from a party evidence against himself. It is our opinion, therefore, that a compulsory production of a man's private papers to establish a criminal charge against him, or to forfeit his property, is within the scope of the Fourth Amendment to the Constitution, in all cases in which a search and seizure would be; because it is a material ingredient, and effects the sole object and purpose of search and seizure.

The principal question, however, remains to be considered. Is a search and seizure, or, what is equivalent thereto, a compulsory production of a man's private papers, to be used in evidence against him in a proceeding to forfeit his property for alleged fraud against the revenue laws — is such a proceeding for such a purpose an "*unreasonable* search and seizure" within the meaning of the Fourth Amendment of the Constitution? [O]r, is it a legitimate proceeding? It is contended by the counsel for the government, that it is a legitimate proceeding, sanctioned by long usage, and the authority of judicial decision. No doubt long usage, acquiesced in by the courts, goes a long way to prove that there is some plausible ground or reason for it in the law, or in the historical facts which have imposed a particular construction of the law favorable to such usage. . . . But we do not find any long usage, or any contemporary construction of the Constitution, which would justify any of the acts of Congress now under consideration. As before stated, the act of 1863 was the first act in this country, and, we might say, either in this country or in England, so far as we have been able to ascertain, which authorized the search and seizure of a man's private papers, or the compulsory production of them, for the purpose of using them in evidence against him in a criminal case, or in a proceeding to enforce the forfeiture of his property. Even the act under which the obnoxious writs of assistance were issued did not go as far as this, but only authorized the examination of ships and vessels, and persons found therein, for the purpose of finding goods prohibited to be imported or exported, or on which the duties were not paid, and to enter into and search any suspected vaults, cellars, or warehouses for such goods. The search for and seizure of stolen or forfeited goods, or goods liable to duties and concealed to avoid the payment thereof, are totally different things from a search for and seizure of a man's private books and papers for the purpose of obtaining information therein contained, or of using them as evidence against him. The two things differ *toto coelo*. In the one case, the government is entitled to the possession of the property; in the other it is not. The seizure of stolen goods is authorized by the common law; and the seizure of goods forfeited for a breach of the revenue laws, or concealed to avoid the duties payable on them, has been authorized by English statutes for at least two centuries past; and the like seizures have been authorized by our own revenue acts from the commencement of the government. The first statute passed by Congress to regulate the collection of duties, the act of July 31, 1789, 1 Stat. 29, 43, contains provisions to this effect. As this act was passed by the same Congress which proposed for adoption the original amendments to the Constitution, it is clear that the members of that body did not regard searches and seizures of this kind as "unreasonable," and they are not embraced within the prohibition of the amendment. So, also, the supervision authorized to be exercised by officers of the revenue over the manufacture or custody of excisable articles, and the entries thereof in books required by law to be kept for their inspection, are necessarily excepted out of the category of unreasonable searches and seizures. So, also, the laws which provide for the search and seizure of articles and things which it is unlawful for a person to have in his possession for the purpose of issue or disposition, such as counterfeit coin, lottery tickets, implements of gambling, &c., are not within this category. Many other things of this character might be enumerated. The entry upon premises, made by a sheriff or other officer of the law, for the purpose of seizing goods and chattels by virtue of a judicial writ, such as an attachment, a sequestration, or an execution, is not within the prohibition of the Fourth or Fifth Amendment, or any other clause of the Constitution; nor is the examination of a defendant under oath after an ineffectual execution, for the purpose of discovering secreted property or credits, to be applied to the payment of a judgment against him, obnoxious to those amendments.

But, when examined with care, it is manifest that there is a total unlikeness of these official acts and proceedings to that which is now under consideration. In the case of stolen goods, the owner from whom they were stolen is entitled to their possession; and in the case of excisable or dutiable articles, the government has an interest in them for the payment of the duties thereon, and until such duties are paid has a right to keep them under observation, or to pursue and drag them from concealment; and in the case of goods seized on attachment or execution, the creditor is entitled to their seizure in satisfaction of his debt; and the examination of a defendant under oath to obtain a discovery of concealed property or credits is a proceeding merely civil to effect the ends of justice, and is no more than what the court of chancery would direct on a bill for discovery. Whereas, by the proceeding now under consideration, the court attempts to extort from the party his private books and papers to make him liable for a penalty or to forfeit his property.

In order to ascertain the nature of the proceedings intended by the Fourth Amendment to the Constitution under the terms "unreasonable searches and seizures," it is only necessary to recall the contemporary or then recent history of the controversies on the subject, both in this country and in England. The practice had obtained in the colonies of issuing writs of assistance to the revenue officers, empowering them, in their discretion, to search suspected places for smuggled goods, which James Otis pronounced "the worst instrument of arbitrary power, the most destructive of English liberty, and the fundamental principles of law, that ever was found in an English law book"; since they placed "liberty of every man in the hands of every petty officer."* This was in February, 1761, in Boston, and the famous

---

* Note by the Court. — Cooley's Constitutional Limitations, 301-303, (5th ed. 368, 369). A very full and interesting account of this discussion will be found in the works of John Adams, vol. 2, Appendix A, pp. 523-525; vol. 10, pp. 183, 233, 244, 256, &c., and in Quincy's Reports, pp. 469-482: and see Paxton's Case, do. 51-57, which was argued in November of the same year (1761). An elaborate history of the writs

debate in which it occurred was perhaps the most prominent event which inaugurated the resistance of the colonies to the oppressions of the mother country. "Then and there," said John Adams, "then and there was the first scene of the first act of opposition to the arbitrary claims of Great Britain. Then and there the child Independence was born."

These things, and the events which took place in England immediately following the argument about writs of assistance in Boston, were fresh in the memories of those who achieved our independence and established our form of government. . . . Prominent and principal among these was the practice of issuing general warrants by the Secretary of State, for searching private houses for the discovery and seizure of books and papers that might be used to convict their owner of the charge of libel. . . . The case . . . which will always be celebrated as being the occasion of Lord Camden's memorable discussion of the subject, was that of Entick v. Carrington and Three Other King's Messengers, reported at length in 19 Howell's State Trials, 1029.[1] The action was trespass for entering the plaintiff's dwelling-house in November, 1762, and breaking open his desks, boxes, &c., and searching and examining his papers. The jury rendered a special verdict, and the case was twice solemnly argued at the bar. Lord Camden pronounced the judgment of the court in Michaelmas Term, 1765, and the law as expounded by him has been regarded as settled from that time to this, and his great judgment on that occasion is considered as one of the landmarks of English liberty. It was welcomed and applauded by the lovers of liberty in the colonies as well as in the mother country. It is regarded as one of the permanent monuments of the British Constitution, and is quoted as such by the English authorities on that subject down to the present time.

As every American statesman, during our revolutionary and formative period as a nation, was undoubtedly familiar with this monument of English freedom, and considered it as the true and ultimate expression of constitutional law, it may be confidently asserted that its propositions were in the minds of those who framed the Fourth Amendment to the Constitution, and were considered as sufficiently explanatory of what was meant by unreasonable searches and seizures. We think, therefore, it is pertinent to the present subject of discussion to quote somewhat largely from this celebrated judgment.

After describing the power claimed by the Secretary of State for issuing general search warrants, and the manner in which they were executed, Lord Camden says:

> Such is the power, and, therefore, one would naturally expect that the law to warrant it should be clear in proportion as the power is exorbitant. If it is law, it will be found in our books; if it is not to be found there, it is not law.
>
> The great end for which men entered into society was to secure their property. That right is preserved sacred and incommunicable in all instances where it has not been taken away or abridged by some public law for the good of the whole. The cases where this right of property is set aside by positive law are various. Distresses, executions, forfeitures, taxes, &c., are all of this description, wherein every man by common consent gives up that right for the sake of justice and the general good. By the laws of England, every invasion of private property, be it ever so minute, is a trespass. No man can set his

---

of assistance is given in the Appendix to Quincy's Reports, above referred to, written by Horace Gray, Jr., Esq., now a member of this court.

1. For a discussion of *Entick* and its background, see Russell W. Galloway, Jr., The Intruding Eye: A Status Report on the Constitutional Ban against Paper Searches, 25 How. L.J. 367 (1982). — EDS.

foot upon my ground without my license, but he is liable to an action though the damage be nothing; which is proved by every declaration in trespass where the defendant is called upon to answer for bruising the grass and even treading upon the soil. If he admits the fact, he is bound to show, by way of justification, that some positive law has justified or excused him. The justification is submitted to the judges, who are to look into the books, and see if such a justification can be maintained by the text of the statute law, or by the principles of the common law. If no such excuse can be found or produced, the silence of the books is an authority, against the defendant, and the plaintiff must have judgment. According to this reasoning, it is now incumbent upon the defendants to show the law by which this seizure is warranted. If that cannot be done, it is a trespass.

Papers are the owner's goods and chattels; they are his dearest property; and are so far from enduring a seizure, that they will hardly bear an inspection; and though the eye cannot by the laws of England be guilty of a trespass, yet where private papers are removed and carried away the secret nature of those goods will be an aggravation of the trespass, and demand more considerable damages in that respect. Where is the written law that gives any magistrate such a power? I can safely answer, there is none; and, therefore, it is too much for us, without such authority, to pronounce a practice legal which would be subversive of all the comforts of society.

But though it cannot be maintained by any direct law, yet it bears a resemblance, as was urged, to the known case of search and seizure for stolen goods. I answer that the difference is apparent. In the one, I am permitted to seize my own goods, which are placed in the hands of a public officer, till the felon's conviction shall entitle me to restitution. In the other, the party's own property is seized before and without conviction, and he has no power to reclaim his goods, even after his innocence is declared by acquittal. . . .

Then, after showing that these general warrants for search and seizure of papers originated with the Star Chamber, and never had any advocates in Westminster Hall except Chief Justice Scroggs and his associates, Lord Camden proceeds to add:

Lastly, it is urged as an argument of utility, that such a search is a means of detecting offenders by discovering evidence. I wish some cases had been shown, where the law forceth evidence out of the owner's custody by process. There is no process against papers in civil causes. It has been often tried, but never prevailed. Nay, where the adversary has by force or fraud got possession of your own proper evidence, there is no way to get it back but by action. In the criminal law such a proceeding was never heard of; and yet there are some crimes, such, for instance, as murder, rape, robbery, and housebreaking, to say nothing of forgery and perjury, that are more atrocious than libelling. But our law has provided no paper-search in these cases to help forward the conviction. Whether this proceedeth from the gentleness of the law towards criminals, or from a consideration that such a power would be more pernicious to the innocent than useful to the public, I will not say. It is very certain that the law obligeth no man to accuse himself; because the necessary means of compelling self-accusation, falling upon the innocent as well as the guilty, would be both cruel and unjust; and it would seem, that search for evidence is disallowed upon the same principle. Then, too, the innocent would be confounded with the guilty.

After a few further observations, his Lordship concluded thus: "I have now taken notice of everything that has been urged upon the present point; and upon the whole we are all of opinion, that the warrant to seize and carry away the party's papers in the case of a seditious libel, is illegal and void."*

The principles laid down in this opinion affect the very essence of constitutional liberty and security. They reach farther than the concrete form of the case then before the court, with its adventitious circumstances; they apply to all invasions on the part of the government and its employees of the sanctity of a man's home and the privacies of life. It is not the breaking of his doors, and the rummaging of his drawers, that constitutes the essence of the offence; but it is the invasion of his indefeasible right of personal security, personal liberty and private property, where that right has never been forfeited by his conviction of some public offence, — it is the invasion of this sacred right which underlies and constitutes the essence of Lord Camden's judgment. Breaking into a house and opening boxes and drawers are circumstances of aggravation; but any forcible and compulsory extortion of a man's own testimony or of his private papers to be used as evidence to convict him of crime or to forfeit his goods, is within the condemnation of that judgment. In this regard the Fourth and Fifth Amendments run almost into each other.

Can we doubt that when the Fourth and Fifth Amendments to the Constitution of the United States were penned and adopted, the language of Lord Camden was relied on as expressing the true doctrine on the subject of searches and seizures, and as furnishing the true criteria of the reasonable and "unreasonable" character of such seizures? Could the men who proposed those amendments, in the light of Lord Camden's opinion, have put their hands to a law like those of March 3, 1863, and March 2, 1867, before recited? If they could not, would they have approved the 5th section of the act of June 22, 1874, which was adopted as a substitute for the previous laws? It seems to us that the question cannot admit of a doubt. They never would have approved of them. The struggles against arbitrary power in which they had been engaged for more than twenty years, would have been too deeply engraved in their memories to have allowed them to approve of such insidious disguises of the old grievance which they had so deeply abhorred. . . .

Reverting then to the peculiar phraseology of this act, and to the information in the present case, which is founded on it, we have to deal with an act which expressly excludes criminal proceedings from its operation (though embracing civil suits for penalties and forfeitures), and with an information not technically a criminal proceeding, and neither, therefore, within the literal terms of the Fifth Amendment to the Constitution any more than it is within the literal terms of the Fourth. Does this relieve the proceedings or the law from being obnoxious to the prohibitions of either? We think not; we think they are within the spirit of both.

We have already noticed the intimate relation between the two amendments. They throw great light on each other. For the "unreasonable searches and seizures" condemned in the Fourth Amendment are almost always made for the purpose of compelling a man to give evidence against himself, which in criminal cases is condemned in the Fifth Amendment; and compelling a man "in a criminal case to be a witness against himself," which is condemned in the Fifth Amendment, throws light

---

* Note by the Court. — See further as to searches and seizures, Story on the Constitution, §§1901, 1902, and notes; Cooley's Constitutional Limitations, 299, (5th ed. 365); Sedgwick on Stat. and Const. Law, 2d ed. 498; Wharton Com. on Amer. Law, §560; Robinson v. Richardson, 13 Gray, 454.

on the question as to what is an "unreasonable search and seizure" within the meaning of the Fourth Amendment. And we have been unable to perceive that the seizure of a man's private books and papers to be used in evidence against him is substantially different from compelling him to be a witness against himself. We think it is within the clear intent and meaning of those terms. We are also clearly of opinion that proceedings instituted for the purpose of declaring the forfeiture of a man's property by reason of offences committed by him, though they may be civil in form, are in their nature criminal. In this very case, the ground of forfeiture as declared in the 12th section of the act of 1874, on which the information is based, consists of certain acts of fraud committed against the public revenue in relation to imported merchandise, which are made criminal by the statute; and it is declared, that the offender shall be fined not exceeding $5000 nor less than $50, or be imprisoned not exceeding two years, or both; and in addition to such fine such merchandise shall be forfeited. These are the penalties affixed to the criminal acts; the forfeiture sought by this suit being one of them. If an indictment had been presented against the claimants, upon conviction the forfeiture of the goods could have been included in the judgment. If the government prosecutor elects to waive an indictment, and to file a civil information against the claimants — that is, civil in form — can he by this device take from the proceeding its criminal aspect and deprive the claimants of their immunities as citizens, and extort from them a production of their private papers, or, as an alternative, a confession of guilt? This cannot be. The information, though technically a civil proceeding, is in substance and effect a criminal one. . . . As, therefore, suits for penalties and forfeitures incurred by the commission of offences against the law, are of this quasi-criminal nature, we think that they are within the reason of criminal proceedings for all the purposes of the Fourth Amendment of the Constitution, and of that portion of the Fifth Amendment which declares that no person shall be compelled in any criminal case to be a witness against himself; and we are further of opinion that a compulsory production of the private books and papers of the owner of goods sought to be forfeited in such a suit is compelling him to be a witness against himself, within the meaning of the Fifth Amendment to the Constitution, and is the equivalent of a search and seizure — and an unreasonable search and seizure — within the meaning of the Fourth Amendment. Though the proceeding in question is divested of many of the aggravating incidents of actual search and seizure, yet, as before said, it contains their substance and essence, and effects their substantial purpose. It may be that it is the obnoxious thing in its mildest and least repulsive form; but illegitimate and unconstitutional practices get their first footing in that way, namely, by silent approaches and slight deviations from legal modes of procedure. This can only be obviated by adhering to the rule that constitutional provisions for the security of person and property should be liberally construed. A close and literal construction deprives them of half their efficacy, and leads to gradual depreciation of the right, as if it consisted more in sound than in substance. It is the duty of courts to be watchful for the constitutional rights of the citizen, and against any stealthy encroachments thereon. Their motto should be *obsta principiis*. We have no doubt that the legislative body is actuated by the same motives; but the vast accumulation of public business brought before it sometimes prevents it on a first presentation, from noticing objections which become developed by time and the practical application of the objectionable law. . . .

We think that the notice to produce the invoice in this case, the order by virtue of which it was issued, and the law which authorized the order, were unconstitutional and void, and that the inspection by the district attorney of said invoice, when produced in obedience to said notice, and its admission in evidence by the court, were erroneous and unconstitutional proceedings. We are of opinion, therefore, that

The judgment of the Circuit Court should be reversed, and the cause remanded, with directions to award a new trial.

MR. JUSTICE MILLER, with whom was THE CHIEF JUSTICE, concurring. I concur in the judgment of the court, reversing that of the Circuit Court, and in so much of the opinion of this court as holds the 5th section of the act of 1874 void as applicable to the present case.

I am of opinion that this is a criminal case within the meaning of that clause of the Fifth Amendment to the Constitution of the United States which declares that no person "shall be compelled in any criminal case to be a witness against himself."

And I am quite satisfied that the effect of the act of Congress is to compel the party on whom the order of the court is served to be a witness against himself. The order of the court under the statute is in effect a subpoena duces tecum, and, though the penalty for the witness's failure to appear in court with the criminating papers is not fine and imprisonment, it is one which may be made more severe, namely, to have charges against him of a criminal nature, taken for confessed, and made the foundation of the judgment of the court. That this is within the protection which the Constitution intended against compelling a person to be a witness against himself, is, I think, quite clear.

But this being so, there is no reason why this court should assume that the action of the court below, in requiring a party to produce certain papers as evidence on the trial, authorizes an unreasonable search or seizure of the house, papers, or effects of that party.

There is in fact no search and no seizure authorized by the statute. No order can be made by the court under it which requires or permits anything more than service of notice on a party to the suit. . . .

Nothing in the nature of a search is here hinted at. Nor is there any seizure, because the party is not required at any time to part with the custody of the papers. They are to be produced in court, and, when produced, the United States attorney is permitted, under the direction of the court, to make examination in presence of the claimant, and may offer in evidence such entries in the books, invoices, or papers as relate to the issue. The act is careful to say that "the owner of said books and papers, his agent or attorney, shall have, subject to the order of the court, the custody of them, except pending their examination in court as aforesaid." . . .

The things . . . forbidden [by the Fourth Amendment] are two — search and seizure. And not all searches nor all seizures are forbidden, but only those that are unreasonable. Reasonable searches, therefore, may be allowed, and if the thing sought be found, it may be seized.

But what search does this statute authorize? If the mere service of a notice to produce a paper to be used as evidence, which the party can obey or not as he chooses is a search, then a change has taken place in the meaning of words, which has not come within my reading, and which I think was unknown at the time the Constitution was made. The searches meant by the Constitution were such as led to seizure when the search was successful. But the statute in this case uses language carefully framed to forbid any seizure under it, as I have already pointed out.

While the framers of the Constitution had their attention drawn, no doubt, to the abuses of this power of searching private houses and seizing private papers, as practiced in England, it is obvious that they only intended to restrain the abuse, while they did not abolish the power. Hence it is only *unreasonable* searches and seizures that are forbidden, and the means of securing this protection was by abolishing searches under warrants, which were called general warrants, because they authorized searches in any place, for any thing.

This was forbidden, while searches founded on affidavits, and made under warrants which described the thing to be searched for, the person and place to be searched, are still permitted.

I cannot conceive how a statute aptly framed to require the production of evidence in a suit by mere service of notice on the party, who has that evidence in his possession, can be held to authorize an unreasonable search or seizure, when no seizure is authorized or permitted by the statute.

I am requested to say that The Chief Justice concurs in this opinion.

NOTES AND QUESTIONS

1. Does *Boyd* rest on concerns of privacy, a desire to protect a person's papers, or an expansive view of the incriminating pressures that are inappropriate for a government to bring to bear on an individual? To what extent do these concerns interrelate? Does it matter which concern *Boyd* primarily is based on?

Thirty-five years after *Boyd*, the Court in Gouled v. United States, 255 U.S. 298 (1921), returned to these issues. *Gouled* applied *Boyd* to a search and seizure pursuant to a warrant that produced documents of the defendant, later used at trial over objection. In finding that the Fourth Amendment was violated by the search and seizure, and the use of the evidence at trial in violation of the Fifth, the Court said:

> Although search warrants have thus been used in many cases ever since the adoption of the Constitution, and although their use has been extended from time to time to meet new cases within the old rules, nevertheless it is clear that, at common law and as the result of . . . *Boyd* . . . , they may not be used as a means of gaining access to a man's house or office and papers solely for the purpose of making search to secure evidence to be used against him in a criminal or penal proceeding, but that they may be resorted to only when a primary right to such search and seizure may be found in the interest which the public or the complainant may have in the property to be seized, or in the right to the possession of it, or when a valid exercise of the police power renders possession of the property by the accused unlawful and provides that it may be taken. *Boyd Case*, pp. 623, 624.
>
> There is no special sanctity in papers, as distinguished from other forms of property, to render them immune from search and seizure, if only they fall within the scope of the principles of the cases in which other property may be seized, and if they be adequately described in the affidavit and warrant. . . .

Is the Court's last sentence about the lack of "special sanctity in papers" significant? Consider the following passage:

This passing remark, which was not without support in *Boyd*, reflected the common-sense judgment that, if the government's appropriation of an individual's documents as mere evidence is wrongful because it makes him "the unwilling source" of incrimination evidence, the same must be true of the seizure of any of his other possessions. Its effect, however, was to transform the paper-search rule of *Boyd* into a broader rule under which the search for or seizure of any item as "mere evidence" was proscribed. In this roundabout way, the fourth amendment in fact became the protector of privacy.

Krauss, page 291, supra, at 190.

2. What is the significance of property for the "intimate relationship" of the Fourth and Fifth amendments that is so important to *Boyd*? Consider the following passage:

Justice Bradley offered no positive definition of "the indefeasible right of personal security, personal liberty and private property" that he considered to be at the core of the intimate relation between the two amendments. It is clear, however, that confidentiality was not the interest that the Court sought to protect. Whether the Boyds had kept the invoice a secret to the world or whether they had made its contents a matter of public knowledge was irrelevant; either way, the government's action was illegal. But, perhaps because the opinion was couched in such sweeping language, the positive nature of the fundamental right was unclear.

Later courts[20] interpreted *Boyd* as identifying the privilege against self-incrimination as the concept at the heart of the intimate relation. Viewing an individual's papers as an extension of his "self," adherents of this view treated the unreasonable search clause of the fourth amendment as an extension of the fifth amendment. On this theory, the amendments, taken together, define the ultimate scope of each person's right not to be compelled to serve as the source of evidence against himself.

But this guarantee that a person's papers are free from official inspection was absolute only in theory. The *Boyd* majority had to reconcile its doctrine with traditional practices. Historically, the government had been allowed to require recordkeeping with regard to certain goods, such as those subject to duties, in which it had some property interest, and those records had always been deemed seizable. The Court in *Boyd* incorporated this tradition into its constitutional theory by proclaiming the seizure of documents to be inherently unconstitutional only when they were taken as mere evidence and by granting that, on the basis of its property interest in such goods, the government had a superior right to the corresponding records. Because any such record did not truly belong to the accused, it could not be viewed as an extension of his "self"; thus, its use against him did not constitute a compelled self-incrimination. This accommodation to tradition did not seem to compromise the general paper-search rule significantly. The rule attached to all documents in an individual's possession to which he had a superior claim of right. Consequently, although it was not viewed as having been designed to protect property rights per se, the scope of the privilege embodied in the unreasonable search clause came to be defined in terms of the law of property. In that respect, the doctrine contained the seeds of its own destruction.

Krauss, page 291, supra, at 188-189.

20. See, e.g., Olmstead v. United States, 277 U.S. 438 (1928), . . . Brown v. Walker, 161 U.S. 591 (1896). In holding that an individual who has been granted immunity may be compelled to testify against himself, the majority in *Brown* must have concluded that *Boyd* had been solely concerned with protecting the individual from compelled self-incrimination. The four dissenting justices cited *Boyd* in support of the proposition that, because the Constitution grants the individual an *absolute* right to remain silent, testimony compelled under a grant of immunity is subject to constitutional attack.

3. The initial stage of the assault on *Boyd* is accurately summarized by Krauss, supra, at 191-195:

Over the years, the Court grew increasingly dissatisfied with interpreting the unreasonable search clause in terms of property interests. This dissatisfaction had several possible sources. Traditional views of the sanctity of property were quickly giving way to the demand for increasing governmental control over its ownership, use, and disposition. The view that a fundamental right to privacy exists, espoused in the famous article by Brandeis and Warren,[35] was gaining acceptance. This concept was defined in terms of a basic right "to be left alone,"[36] rather than in terms of the technicalities of English property law. Finally, perhaps the Court simply was not content with the results that would have been entailed by strict adherence to the mere evidence rule as it had been propounded in *Boyd* and expanded by *Gouled*.

Where strict adherence would not interfere with governmental regulation of economic activity, the rule was duly applied. . . .

Where the mere evidence rule interfered with governmental regulation of economic activity, however, it was modified or "refined." In a group of cases involving subpoenas directed to business organizations, the Court refused to include such associations within the class of entities protected by the fifth amendment privilege. In Hale v. Henkel,[38] the Court held that the privilege does not apply to corporations. Thus, an agent cannot refuse to answer questions or to comply with a subpoena duces tecum[39] on the ground that the corporation might be incriminated. Moreover, because the documents are in the custody of and are being subpoenaed from the corporate entity rather than from the agent, the agent cannot refuse to comply on the ground that compliance might incriminate him.[40] . . . Of the decisions that considered *Boyd* during this period of retreat, perhaps Shapiro v. United States[43] had the greatest impact on the individual's ability to shield the details of his life from the government. In that case the Court enunciated the "required records" doctrine, under which no person can invoke the fourth or fifth amendment to justify refusal to comply with a facially valid subpoena compelling the production of records that the person is legally required to keep. This decision represented a complete rejection of the fundamental limitations that the Court in *Boyd* had placed on the government's power to compel the production of records kept pursuant to its command. The Court in effect recognized the power of the legislature to acquire any and all information it wants from an individual.[44]

---

35. Warren & Brandeis, The Right to Privacy, 4 Harv. L. Rev. 193 (1890).

36. Olmstead v. United States, 277 U.S. 438, 478 (1928) (Brandeis, J., dissenting).

38. 201 U.S. 43 (1906).

39. The order involved in the *Boyd* case differed from a subpoena duces tecum only in the penalty imposed for noncompliance. *Hale* held that the paper-search rule enunciated in *Boyd* applied as well to subpoenas duces tecum.

40. In Wilson v. United States, 221 U.S. 361 (1911), the writ was directed to the corporation. In Dreier v. United States, 221 U.S. 394 (1911), it was directed to the agent. In both cases the Court held that the self-incrimination clause did not allow the agent to refuse to comply with the subpoena. It was later held, however, that the custodian of an organization's "missing" documents can refuse to answer questions about their whereabouts when to do so would incriminate him. Curcio v. United States, 354 U.S. 118, 125 (1957).

43. 335 U.S. 1 (1948).

44. Congress eventually exercised this authority to require the keeping of records to aid its fight against crime, as well as its regulation of economic activity. On the basis of this "required records" doctrine, the Court has sanctioned congressional enactments that have intruded substantially upon personal privacy. See United States v. Miller, 425 U.S. 435, 447 (1976) (Brennan, J., dissenting); California Bankers Assn. v. Shultz, 416 U.S. 21, 93 (1974) (Marshall, J., dissenting). But see Grosso v. United States, 390 U.S. 62 (1968); Marchetti v. United States, 390 U.S. 39 (1968).

The Court also narrowed the scope of the protection provided by the mere evidence rule in Marron v. United States.[45] In that case the Court distinguished between property that is merely evidence of a crime and property used in the commission of a crime.[46] Whereas *Gouled* had allowed the seizure of an instrumentality of a crime only insofar as it was contraband, *Marron* allowed the seizure of *any* such instrumentality. Because even papers can be characterized as instrumentalities of crime,[47] *Marron* represented a serious threat to the zone of protection established by *Boyd* and broadened by *Gouled*.[48]

To the extent that the decisions following *Boyd* and *Gouled* reduced the obstacles to governmental seizure of an individual's property, they also narrowed his effective zone of privacy. A conflict arose within the Court over this development. Although the dispute concerned the fundamental nature of the rights protected by the Fourth and Fifth Amendments, it took the form of a debate over the "real" meaning of *Boyd*. On the one hand, proponents of the traditional interpretation of *Boyd* believed that the core of the "intimate relation" between the Amendments was the privilege against self-incrimination. Since the key question to these Justices was whether the evidence belonged to the defendant, they found the government's increasing power to intrude into the life of the individual to be constitutionally permissible so long as the exercise of that power was consistent with the rules of property law. On the other hand, advocates of a revisionist interpretation of *Boyd* argued that the true concern of the framers of the Fourth and Fifth Amendments was the protection of a fundamental right of privacy. . . .

This revisionist interpretation of the "intimate relation" first appeared as a fully articulated doctrine in Justice Brandeis' dissent in Olmstead v. United States.[52] That case concerned the applicability of the Fourth Amendment to warrantless wiretapping by government agents. The majority, which was as eager to facilitate the government's efforts to combat crime as it had been a year earlier in *Marron*, analyzed the issue in terms of the privilege against self-incrimination,[53] whose parameters were determined by property law. Finding that speech is not property within the context of the Fourth Amendment, they concluded that wiretapping infringed upon an interest protected by the Fourth Amendment, and thereby the Fifth, only if it involved trespassing upon the accused's tangible property. Justice Brandeis' dissent, however, argued that the majority opinion was based on the false premise that the Fourth Amendment had been designed either to perpetuate antiquated notions of English property law or to bolster the privilege against self-incrimination.[54] In Justice Brandeis' view, at the heart of *Entick*, *Boyd*, and *Gouled* was the premise that the Amendment had been designed to protect a fundamental "right to be left alone":[55] "Every unjustifiable intrusion by the Government upon the private life of the individual, whatever the means employed, must be deemed a violation of the Fourth Amendment. And the use, as evidence in a criminal proceeding, of facts ascertained by such intrusion must be deemed a violation

---

45. 275 U.S. 192 (1927).

46. The Court in *Marron* did not attempt to explain its holding in terms of a superior title theory. A possible rationale for the decision is that, by using an object to commit a crime, the criminal has forfeited it to the state.

47. In *Marron*, the Court treated records maintained in an establishment where liquor was sold as instrumentalities. *Gouled* had also recognized that papers might be used as instrumentalities of crime. See 255 U.S., at 309.

48. For a discussion of the ingenuity of prosecutors in characterizing different types of property as instrumentalities, see Comment, The Search and Seizure of Private Papers: Fourth and Fifth Amendment Considerations, 6 Loy. L.A. L. Rev. 274, 282-283 (1973).

52. 277 U.S. 438 (1928).

53. See 277 U.S., at 462-463.

54. Justice Brandeis advocated a privacy rationale for the Fifth Amendment, also. See text at n. 56, infra.

55. 277 U.S., at 478.

of the Fifth."[56] Although Justice Brandeis had lost the battle in *Olmstead*, by the second half of the twentieth century he had won the war. The theory that his dissenting opinion espoused eventually became the official position of the Court.[57] Moreover, during this period it became clear that the mere evidence rule had outlived its usefulness. The criteria for determining whether an object was immune from seizure had become so structured that the rule no longer served as a bulwark for the privilege against self-incrimination. Furthermore, the rule was at odds with public opinion, as it frustrated the popular demand for law and order that was increasing along with the crime rate. Although Justice Brandeis had identified the right of privacy as the basic interest to be protected, he had indicated neither the manner in which this protection would be ensured nor the extent to which the law derived from *Boyd* would have to be repudiated. The Court undertook this task in three cases decided three decades after *Olmstead*: Schmerber v. California,[58] Warden v. Hayden,[59] and Berger v. New York.[60] . . .

SCHMERBER v. CALIFORNIA

Certiorari to the Appellate Department of the Superior Court of California,
County of Los Angeles
384 U.S. 757 (1966)

MR. JUSTICE BRENNAN delivered the opinion of the Court.

Petitioner was convicted in Los Angeles Municipal Court of the criminal offense of driving an automobile while under the influence of intoxicating liquor. He had been arrested at a hospital while receiving treatment for injuries suffered in an accident involving the automobile that he had apparently been driving. At the direction of a police officer, a blood sample was then withdrawn from petitioner's body by a physician at the hospital. The chemical analysis of this sample revealed a percent by weight of alcohol in his blood at the time of the offense which indicated intoxication, and the report of this analysis was admitted in evidence at the trial. Petitioner objected to receipt of this evidence of the analysis on the ground that the blood had been drawn despite his refusal, on the advice of his counsel, to consent to the test. He contended that in that circumstance the withdrawal of the blood and the admission of the analysis in evidence denied him due process of law under the Fourteenth Amendment, as well as specific guarantees of the Bill of Rights secured against the States by that Amendment: his privilege against self-incrimination under the Fifth Amendment; his right to counsel under the Sixth Amendment; and his right not to be subjected to unreasonable searches and seizures in violation of the Fourth Amendment. The Appellate Department of the California Superior Court rejected these contentions and affirmed the conviction. . . .

56. 277 U.S., at 478-479.

57. Regarding the Fourth Amendment, see, e.g., Wolf v. Colorado, 338 U.S. 25, 27 (1949) ("The security of one's privacy against arbitrary intrusion by the police . . . is at the core of the Fourth Amendment."). Regarding the Fifth Amendment, see, e.g., Griswold v. Connecticut, 381 U.S. 479, 484 (1965) ("The Fifth Amendment in its Self-Incrimination Clause enables the citizen to create a zone of privacy which government may not force him to surrender to his detriment.").

58. 384 U.S. 757 (1966).

59. 387 U.S. 294 (1967). [Other aspects of *Warden* are discussed in Chapter 5 infra. — EDS.]

60. 388 U.S. 41 (1967). [Other aspects of *Berger* are considered in Chapter 7 infra. — EDS.]

II.   The Privilege Against Self-Incrimination Claim

. . . We . . . must now decide whether the withdrawal of the blood and admission in evidence of the analysis involved in this case violated petitioner's privilege. We hold that the privilege protects an accused only from being compelled to testify against himself, or otherwise provide the State with evidence of a testimonial or communicative nature,[5] and that the withdrawal of blood and use of the analysis in question in this case did not involve compulsion to these ends.

It could not be denied that in requiring petitioner to submit to the withdrawal and chemical analysis of his blood the State compelled him to submit to an attempt to discover evidence that might be used to prosecute him for a criminal offense. He submitted only after the police officer rejected his objection and directed the physician to proceed. The officer's direction to the physician to administer the test over petitioner's objection constituted compulsion for the purposes of the privilege. The critical question, then, is whether petitioner was thus compelled "to be a witness against himself."[6]

If the scope of the privilege coincided with the complex of values it helps to protect, we might be obliged to conclude that the privilege was violated. Miranda v. Arizona [discussed in Chapter 6, infra], the Court said of the interests protected by the privilege:

> All these policies point to one overriding thought: the constitutional foundation underlying the privilege is the respect a government — state or federal — must accord to the dignity and integrity of its citizens. To maintain a "fair state-individual balance," to require the government "to shoulder the entire load," . . . to respect the inviolabilty of the human personality, our accusatory system of criminal justice demands that the government seeking to punish an individual produce the evidence against him by its own independent labors, rather than by the cruel, simple expedient of compelling it from his own mouth.

The withdrawal of blood necessarily involves puncturing the skin for extraction, and the percent by weight of alcohol in that blood, as established by chemical analysis, is evidence of criminal guilt. Compelled submission fails on one view to respect the "inviolability of the human personality." Moreover, since it enables the State to rely on evidence forced from the accused, the compulsion violates at least one meaning

---

5. A dissent suggests that the report of the blood test was "testimonial" or "communicative," because the test was performed in order to obtain the testimony of others, communicating to the jury facts about petitioner's condition. Of course, all evidence received in court is "testimonial" or "communicative" if these words are thus used. But the Fifth Amendment relates only to acts on the part of the person to whom the privilege applies, and we use these words subject to the same limitations. A nod or head-shake is as much a "testimonial" or "communicative" act in this sense as are spoken words. But the terms as we use them do not apply to evidence of acts noncommunicative in nature as to the person asserting the privilege, even though, as here, such acts are compelled to obtain the testimony of others.

6. Many state constitutions, including those of most of the original Colonies, phrase the privilege in terms of compelling a person to give "evidence" against himself. But our decision cannot turn on the Fifth Amendment's use of the word "witness." "[A]s the manifest purpose of the constitutional provisions, both of the States and of the United States, is to prohibit the compelling of testimony of a self-incriminating kind from a party or a witness, the liberal construction which must be placed upon constitutional provisions for the protection of personal rights would seem to require that the constitutional guaranties, however differently worded, should have as far as possible the same interpretation. . . ." Counselman v. Hitchcock, 142 U.S. 547, 584-585. 8 Wigmore, Evidence §2252 (McNaughton rev. 1961). Miranda v. Arizona [discussed in Chapter 6, infra], the Court said of the interests protected by the privilege.

of the requirement that the State procure the evidence against an accused "by its own independent labors."

As the passage in *Miranda* implicitly recognizes, however, the privilege has never been given the full scope which the values it helps to protect suggest. History and a long line of authorities in lower courts have consistently limited its protection to situations in which the State seeks to submerge those values by obtaining the evidence against an accused through "the cruel, simple expedient of compelling it from his own mouth. . . . In sum, the privilege is fulfilled only when the person is guaranteed the right 'to remain silent unless he chooses to speak in the unfettered exercise of his own will.'" Ibid. The leading case in this Court is Holt v. United States, 218 U.S. 245. There the question was whether evidence was admissible that the accused, prior to trial and over his protest, put on a blouse that fitted him. It was contended that compelling the accused to submit to the demand that he model the blouse violated the privilege. Mr. Justice Holmes, speaking for the Court, rejected the argument as "based upon an extravagant extension of the Fifth Amendment," and went on to say:

> [T]he prohibition of compelling a man in a criminal court to be witness against himself is a prohibition of the use of physical or moral compulsion to extort communications from him, not an exclusion of his body as evidence when it may be material. The objection in principle would forbid a jury to look at a prisoner and compare his features with a photograph in proof.

It is clear that the protection of the privilege reaches an accused's communications, whatever form they might take, and the compulsion of responses which are also communications, for example, compliance with a subpoena to produce one's papers. Boyd v. United States, 116 U.S. 616. On the other hand, both federal and state courts have usually held that it offers no protection against compulsion to submit to fingerprinting, photographing, or measurements, to write or speak for identification, to appear in court, to stand, to assume a stance, to walk, or to make a particular gesture. The distinction which has emerged, often expressed in different ways, is that the privilege is a bar against compelling "communications" or "testimony," but that compulsion which makes a suspect or accused the source of "real or physical evidence" does not violate it.

Although we agree that this distinction is a helpful framework for analysis, we are not to be understood to agree with past applications in all instances. There will be many cases in which such a distinction is not readily drawn. Some tests seemingly directed to obtain "physical evidence," for example, lie detector tests measuring changes in body function during interrogation, may actually be directed to eliciting responses which are essentially testimonial. To compel a person to submit to testing in which an effort will be made to determine his guilt or innocence on the basis of physiological responses, whether willed or not, is to evoke the spirit and history of the Fifth Amendment. Such situations call to mind the principle that the protection of the privilege "is as broad as the mischief against which it seeks to guard."

In the present case, however, no such problem of application is presented. Not even a shadow of testimonial compulsion upon or enforced communication by the accused was involved either in the extraction or in the chemical analysis. Petitioner's testimonial capacities were in no way implicated; indeed, his participation, except as a donor, was irrelevant to the results of the test, which depend on chemical analysis and on that alone.[9] Since the blood test evidence, although an incriminating product of compulsion, was neither petitioner's testimony nor evidence relating to some communicative act or writing by the petitioner, it was not inadmissible on privilege grounds.

III. THE RIGHT TO COUNSEL CLAIM

This conclusion also answers petitioner's claim that, in compelling him to submit to the test in face of the fact that his objection was made on the advice of counsel, he was denied his Sixth Amendment right to the assistance of counsel. Since petitioner was not entitled to assert the privilege, he has no greater right because counsel erroneously advised him that he could assert it. His claim is strictly limited to the failure of the police to respect his wish, reinforced by counsel's advice, to be left inviolate. No issue of counsel's ability to assist petitioner in respect of any rights he did possess is presented. The limited claim thus made must be rejected.

IV. THE SEARCH AND SEIZURE CLAIM . . .

The overriding function of the Fourth Amendment is to protect personal privacy and dignity against unwarranted intrusion by the State. . . .

The values protected by the Fourth Amendment thus substantially overlap those the Fifth Amendment helps to protect. History and precedent have required that we today reject the claim that the Self-Incrimination Clause of the Fifth Amendment requires the human body in all circumstances to be held inviolate against state expeditions seeking evidence of crime. But if compulsory administration of a blood test does not implicate the Fifth Amendment, it plainly involves the broadly conceived reach of a search and seizure under the Fourth Amendment. That Amendment expressly provides that "[t]he right of the people to be secure in their *persons*, houses, papers, and effects, against unreasonable searches and seizures, shall not be violated. . . ." (Emphasis added.) It could not reasonably be argued, and indeed respondent does not argue, that the administration of the blood test in this case was free of the constraints of the Fourth Amendment. Such testing procedures plainly constitute searches of "persons," within the meaning of that Amendment.

Because we are dealing with intrusions into the human body rather than with state interferences with property relationships or private papers — "houses, papers, and effects" — we write on a clean slate. Limitations on the kinds of property which may be seized under warrant,[10] as distinct from the procedures for search and the permissible scope of search,[11] are not instructive in this context. We begin with the

9. This conclusion would not necessarily govern had the State tried to show that the accused had incriminated himself when told that he would have to be tested. Such incriminating evidence may be an unavoidable by-product of the compulsion to take the test, especially for an individual who fears the extraction or opposes it on religious grounds. If it wishes to compel persons to submit to such attempts to discover evidence, the State may have to forgo the advantage of any *testimonial* products of administering the test — products which would fall within the privilege. Indeed, there may be circumstances in which the pain, danger, or severity of an operation would almost inevitably cause a person to prefer confession to undergoing the "search," and nothing we say today should be taken as establishing the permissibility of compulsion in that case. But no such situation is presented in this case. . . .

10. See, e.g., Gouled v. United States, 255 U.S. 298; Boyd v. United States, 116 U.S. 616; contra, People v. Thayer, 63 Cal. 2d 635, 408 P.2d 108 (1965); State v. Bisaccia, 45 N.J. 504, 213 A.2d 185 (1965); Note, Evidentiary Searches: The Rule and the Reason, 54 Geo. L.J. 593 (1966).

11. See, e.g., Silverman v. United States, 365 U.S. 505; Abel v. United States, 362 U.S. 217, 235; United States v. Rabinowitz, 339 U.S. 56.

assumption that once the privilege against self-incrimination has been found not to bar compelled intrusions into the body for blood to be analyzed for alcohol content, the Fourth Amendment's proper function is to constrain, not against all intrusions as such, but against intrusions which are not justified in the circumstances, or which are made in an improper manner. In other words, the questions we must decide in this case are whether the police were justified in requiring petitioner to submit to the blood test, and whether the means and procedures employed in taking his blood respected relevant Fourth Amendment standards of reasonableness.

In this case, as will often be true when charges of driving under the influence of alcohol are pressed, these questions arise in the context of an arrest made by an officer without a warrant. Here, there was plainly probable cause for the officer to arrest petitioner and charge him with driving an automobile while under the influence of intoxicating liquor. The police officer who arrived at the scene shortly after the accident smelled liquor on petitioner's breath, and testified that petitioner's eyes were "bloodshot, watery, sort of a glassy appearance." The officer saw petitioner again at the hospital, within two hours of the accident. There he noticed similar symptoms of drunkenness. He thereupon informed petitioner "that he was under arrest and that he was entitled to the services of an attorney, and that he could remain silent, and that anything that he told me would be used against him in evidence." . . .

Although the facts which established probable cause to arrest in this case also suggested the required relevance and likely success of a test of petitioner's blood for alcohol, the question remains whether the arresting officer was permitted to draw these inferences himself, or was required instead to procure a warrant before proceeding with the test. Search warrants are ordinarily required for searches of dwellings, and, absent an emergency, no less could be required where intrusions into the human body are concerned. . . . The importance of informed, detached and deliberate determinations of the issue whether or not to invade another's body in search of evidence of guilt is indisputable and great.

The officer in the present case, however, might reasonably have believed that he was confronted with an emergency, in which the delay necessary to obtain a warrant, under the circumstances, threatened "the destruction of evidence," Preston v. United States, 376 U.S. 364, 367. We are told that the percentage of alcohol in the blood begins to diminish shortly after drinking stops, as the body functions to eliminate it from the system. Particularly in a case such as this, where time had to be taken to bring the accused to a hospital and to investigate the scene of the accident, there was no time to seek out a magistrate and secure a warrant. Given these special facts, we conclude that the attempt to secure evidence of blood-alcohol content in this case was an appropriate incident to petitioner's arrest.

Similarly, we are satisfied that the test chosen to measure petitioner's blood-alcohol level was a reasonable one. Extraction of blood samples for testing is a highly effective means of determining the degree to which a person is under the influence of alcohol. . . .

Finally, the record shows that the test was performed in a reasonable manner. Petitioner's blood was taken by a physician in a hospital environment according to accepted medical practices. We are thus not presented with the serious questions which would arise if a search involving use of a medical technique, even of the most rudimentary sort, were made by other than medical personnel or in other than a medical environment — for example, if it were administered by police in the privacy of the stationhouse. To tolerate searches under these conditions might be to invite an unjustified element of personal risk of infection and pain.

We thus conclude that the present record shows no violation of petitioner's right under the Fourth and Fourteenth Amendments to be free of unreasonable searches and seizures. It bears repeating, however, that we reach this judgment only on the facts of the present record. The integrity of an individual's person is a cherished value of our society. That we today hold that the Constitution does not forbid the States minor intrusions into an individual's body under stringently limited conditions in no way indicates that it permits more substantial intrusions, or intrusions under other conditions.

Affirmed. . . .

MR. CHIEF JUSTICE WARREN, dissenting.

While there are other important constitutional issues in this case, I believe it is sufficient for me to reiterate my dissenting opinion in Breithaupt v. Abram, 352 U.S. 432, 440, [which upheld a conviction based in part on an analysis of blood extracted from an unconscious suspect] as the basis on which to reverse this conviction.

MR. JUSTICE BLACK with whom MR. JUSTICE DOUGLAS joins, dissenting.

I would reverse petitioner's conviction. . . . I disagree with the Court's holding that California did not violate petitioner's constitutional right against self-incrimination when it compelled him, against his will, to allow a doctor to puncture his blood vessels in order to extract a sample of blood and analyze it for alcoholic content, and then used that analysis as evidence to convict petitioner of a crime.

The Court admits that "the State compelled [petitioner] to submit to an attempt to discover evidence [in his blood] that might be [and was] used to prosecute him for a criminal offense." To reach the conclusion that compelling a person to give his blood to help the State convict him is not equivalent to compelling him to be a witness against himself strikes me as quite an extraordinary feat. The Court, however, overcomes what had seemed to me to be an insuperable obstacle to its conclusion by holding that

> . . . the privilege protects an accused only from being compelled to testify against himself, or otherwise provide the State with evidence of a testimonial or communicative nature, and that the withdrawal of blood and use of the analysis in question in this case did not involve compulsion to these ends.

I cannot agree that this distinction and reasoning of the Court justify denying petitioner his Bill of Rights' guarantee that he must not be compelled to be a witness against himself.

In the first place it seems to me that the compulsory extraction of petitioner's blood for analysis so that the person who analyzed it could give evidence to convict him had both a "testimonial" and a "communicative nature." The sole purpose of this project which proved to be successful was to obtain "testimony" from some person to prove that petitioner had alcohol in his blood at the time he was arrested. And the purpose of the project was certainly "communicative" in that the analysis of the blood was to supply information to enable a witness to communicate to the court and jury that petitioner was more or less drunk.

I think it unfortunate that the Court rests so heavily for its very restrictive reading of the Fifth Amendment's privilege against self-incrimination on the words "testimonial" and "communicative." These words are not models of clarity and precision as the Court's rather labored explication shows. Nor can the Court, so far as I know, find precedent in the former opinions of this Court for using these particular words to limit the scope of the Fifth Amendment's protection. . . .

It concedes, as it must so long as Boyd v. United States stands, that the Fifth Amendment bars a State from compelling a person to produce papers he has that might tend to incriminate him. It is a strange hierarchy of values that allows the State to extract a human being's blood to convict him of a crime because of the blood's content but proscribes compelled production of his lifeless papers. Certainly there could be few papers that would have any more "testimonial" value to convict a man of drunken driving than would an analysis of the alcoholic content of a human being's blood introduced in evidence at a trial for driving while under the influence of alcohol. In such a situation blood, of course, is not oral testimony given by an accused but it can certainly "communicate" to a court and jury the fact of guilt.

The Court itself . . . expresses its own doubts, if not fears, of its own shadowy distinction between compelling "physical evidence" like blood which it holds does not amount to compelled self-incrimination, and "eliciting responses which are essentially testimonial." And in explanation of its fears the Court goes on to warn that

> To compel a person to submit to testing [by lie detectors, for example] in which an effort will be made to determine his guilt or innocence on the basis of physiological responses, whether willed or not, is to evoke the spirit and history of the Fifth Amendment. Such situations call to mind the principle that the protection of the privilege "is as broad as the mischief against which it seeks to guard." Counselman v. Hitchcock, 142 U.S. 547, 562.
>
> A basic error in the Court's holding and opinion is its failure to give the Fifth Amendment's protection against compulsory self-incrimination the broad and liberal construction that *Counselman* and other opinions of this Court have declared it ought to have.

The liberal construction given the Bill of Rights' guarantee in Boyd v. United States, supra, . . . makes that one among the greatest constitutional decisions of this Court. . . . The Court today departs from the teachings of *Boyd*. Petitioner Schmerber has undoubtedly been compelled to give his blood "to furnish evidence against himself," yet the Court holds that this is not forbidden by the Fifth Amendment. With all deferences I must say that the Court here gives the Bill of Rights' safeguard against compulsory self-incrimination a construction that would generally be considered too narrow and technical even in the interpretation of an ordinary commercial contract. . . . How can it reasonably be doubted that the blood test evidence was not in all respects the actual equivalent of "testimony" taken from petitioner when the result of the test was offered as testimony, was considered by the jury as testimony, and the jury's verdict of guilt rests in part on that testimony? The refined, subtle reasoning and balancing process used here to narrow the scope of the Bill of Rights' safeguard against self-incrimination provides a handy instrument for further narrowing of that constitutional protection, as well as others, in the future. Believing with the Framers that these constitutional safeguards broadly construed by independent tribunals of justice provide our best hope for keeping our people free from governmental oppression, I deeply regret the Court's holding. . . .

MR. JUSTICE DOUGLAS, dissenting.

I adhere to the views of The Chief Justice in his dissent in Breithaupt v. Abram, 352 U.S. 432, 440, and to the views I stated in my dissent in that case (id., 442) and add only a word. We are dealing with the right of privacy which, since the *Breithaupt* case, we have held to be within the penumbra of some specific guarantees of the Bill of Rights. Griswold v. Connecticut, 381 U.S. 479. Thus, the Fifth Amendment marks "a zone of privacy" which the Government may not force a person to surrender. Id., 484. Likewise the Fourth Amendment recognizes that right when it guarantees the right of the people to be secure "in their persons." Ibid. No clearer invasion of this right of privacy can be imagined than forcible bloodletting of the kind involved here.

MR. JUSTICE FORTAS, dissenting.

I would reverse. In my view, petitioner's privilege against self-incrimination applies. I would add that, under the Due Process Clause, the State, in its role as prosecutor, has no right to extract blood from an accused or anyone else, over his protest. As prosecutor, the State has no right to commit any kind of violence upon the person, or to utilize the results of such a tort, and the extraction of blood, over protest, is an act of violence. Cf. Chief Justice Warren's dissenting opinion in Breithaupt v. Abram, 352 U.S. 432, 440.

WARDEN, MARYLAND PENITENTIARY v. HAYDEN

Certiorari to the United States Court of Appeals for the Fourth Circuit
387 U.S. 294 (1967)

MR. JUSTICE BRENNAN delivered the opinion of the Court.

We review in this case the validity of the proposition that there is under the Fourth Amendment a "distinction between merely evidentiary materials, on the one hand, which may not be seized either under the authority of a search warrant or during the course of a search incident to arrest, and on the other hand, those objects which may validly be seized including the instrumentalities and means by which a crime is committed, the fruits of crime such as stolen property, weapons by which escape of the person arrested might be effected, and property the possession of which is a crime."[1]

A Maryland court sitting without a jury convicted respondent of armed robbery. Items of his clothing, a cap, jacket, and trousers, among other things, were seized during a search of his home, and were admitted in evidence without objection. After unsuccessful state court proceedings, he sought and was denied federal habeas corpus relief in the District Court for Maryland. A divided panel of the Court of Appeals for the Fourth Circuit reversed. The Court of Appeals believed that Harris v. United States, 331 U.S. 145, 154, sustained the validity of the search, but held that respondent was correct in his contention that the clothing seized was improperly admitted in evidence because the items had "evidential value only" and therefore were not lawfully subject to seizure. We granted certiorari. We reverse. . . .

1. Harris v. United States, 331 U.S. 145, 154; see also Gouled v. United States, 255 U.S. 298; United States v. Lefkowitz, 285 U.S. 452, 465-466; United States v. Rabinowitz, 339 U.S. 56, 64, n. 6; Abel v. United States, 362 U.S. 217, 234-235.

[The Court disposed of the validity of the search. For a discussion, see pages 211-212, supra.]

We come, then, to the question whether, even though the search was lawful, the Court of Appeals was correct in holding that the seizure and introduction of the items of clothing violated the Fourth Amendment because they are "mere evidence." The distinction made by some of our cases between seizure of items of evidential value only and seizure of instrumentalities, fruits, or contraband has been criticized by courts and commentators. The Court of Appeals, however, felt "obligated to adhere to it." We today reject the distinction as based on premises no longer accepted as rules governing the application of the Fourth Amendment.[8] . . .

Nothing in the language of the Fourth Amendment supports the distinction between "mere evidence" and instrumentalities, fruits of crime, or contraband. On its face, the provision assures the "right of the people to be secure in their persons, houses, papers, and effects . . . ," without regard to the use to which any of these things are applied. This "right of the people" is certainly unrelated to the "mere evidence" limitation. Privacy is disturbed no more by a search directed to a purely evidentiary object than it is by a search directed to an instrumentality, fruit, or contraband. A magistrate can intervene in both situations, and the requirements of probable cause and specificity can be preserved intact. Moreover, nothing in the nature of the property seized as evidence renders it more private than property seized, for example, as an instrumentality; quite the opposite may be true. Indeed, the distinction is wholly irrational, since, depending on the circumstances, the same "papers and effects" may be "mere evidence" in one case and "instrumentality" in another.

In Gouled v. United States, the Court said that search warrants "may not be used as a means of gaining access to a man's house or office and papers solely for the purpose of making search to secure evidence to be used against him in a criminal or penal proceeding. . . ." The Court derived from Boyd v. United States, supra, the proposition that warrants "may be resorted to only when a primary right to such search and seizure may be found in the interest which the public or the complainant may have in the property to be seized, or in the right to the possession of it, or when a valid exercise of the police power renders possession of the property by the accused unlawful and provides that it may be taken," 255 U.S., at 309; that is, when the property is an instrumentality or fruit of crime, or contraband. Since it was "impossible to say, on the record . . . that the Government had any interest" in the papers involved "other than as evidence against the accused . . . ," "to permit them to be used in evidence would be, in effect, as ruled in the *Boyd Case*, to compel the defendant to become a witness against himself." Id., at 311.

The items of clothing involved in this case are not "testimonial" or "communicative" in nature, and their introduction therefore did not compel respondent to become a witness against himself in violation of the Fifth Amendment. This case thus does not require that we consider whether there are items of evidential value whose very nature precludes them from being the object of a reasonable search and seizure.

8. This Court has approved the seizure and introduction of items having only evidential value without, however, considering the validity of the distinction rejected today. See Schmerber v. California, 384 U.S. 757; Cooper v. California, 386 U.S. 58.

The Fourth Amendment ruling in *Gouled* was based upon the dual, related premises that historically the right to search for and seize property depended upon the
assertion by the Government of a valid claim of superior interest, and that it was not
enough that the purpose of the search and seizure was to obtain evidence to use in
apprehending and convicting criminals. . . .

The premise that property interests control the right of the Government to
search and seize has been discredited. Searches and seizures may be "unreasonable"
within the Fourth Amendment even though the Government asserts a superior
property interest at common law. We have recognized that the principal object of the
Fourth Amendment is the protection of privacy rather than property, and have
increasingly discarded fictional and procedural barriers rested on property concepts. . . . And with particular relevance here, we have given recognition to the
interest in privacy despite the complete absence of a property claim by suppressing
the very items which at common law could be seized with impunity: stolen goods,
Henry v. United States, 361 U.S. 98; instrumentalities, Beck v. Ohio, 379 U.S. 89;
McDonald v. United States, supra; and contraband, Trupiano v. United States, 334
U.S. 699; Aguilar v. Texas, 378 U.S. 108.

The premise in *Gouled* that government may not seize evidence simply for the
purpose of proving crime has likewise been discredited. The requirement that the
Government assert in addition some property interest in material it seizes has long
been a fiction,[11] obscuring the reality that government has an interest in solving
crime. *Schmerber* settled the proposition that it is reasonable, within the terms of the
Fourth Amendment, to conduct otherwise permissible searches for the purpose of
obtaining evidence which would aid in apprehending and convicting criminals. The
requirements of the Fourth Amendment can secure the same protection of privacy
whether the search is for "mere evidence" or for fruits, instrumentalities or contraband. . . .

The rationale most frequently suggested for the rule preventing the seizure of
evidence is that "limitations upon the fruit to be gathered tend to limit the quest
itself." But privacy "would be just as well served by a restriction on search to the
even-numbered days of the month. . . . And it would have the extra advantage of
avoiding hair-splitting questions. . . ." Kaplan, [Search and Seizure: A No-Man's
Land in the Criminal Law, 49 Cal. L. Rev. 474,] at 479. The "mere evidence" limitation has spawned exceptions so numerous and confusion so great, in fact, that it is
questionable whether it affords meaningful protection. But if its rejection does
enlarge the area of permissible searches, the intrusions are nevertheless made after
fulfilling the probable cause and particularity requirements of the Fourth Amendment and after the intervention of "a neutral and detached magistrate. . . ." The

---

11. At common law the Government did assert a superior property interest when it searched lawfully
for stolen property, since the procedure then followed made it necessary that the true owner swear that
his goods had been taken. But no such procedure need be followed today; the Government may demonstrate probable cause and lawfully search for stolen property even though the true owner is unknown
or unavailable to request and authorize the Government to assert his interest. As to instrumentalities, the
Court in *Gouled* allowed their seizure, not because the Government had some property interest in them
(under the ancient, fictitious forfeiture theory), but because they could be used to perpetrate further
crime. 255 U.S., at 309. The same holds true, of course, for "mere evidence"; the prevention of crime is
served at least as much by allowing the Government to identify and capture the criminal, as it is by allowing the seizure of his instrumentalities. Finally, contraband is indeed property in which the Government
holds a superior interest, but only because the Government decides to vest such an interest in itself. And
while there may be limits to what may be declared contraband, the concept is hardly more than a form
through which the Government seeks to prevent and deter crime.

Fourth Amendment allows intrusions upon privacy under these circumstances, and there is no viable reason to distinguish intrusions to secure "mere evidence" from intrusions to secure fruits, instrumentalities, or contraband.

The judgment of the Court of Appeals is reversed.

MR. JUSTICE BLACK concurs in the result.

MR. JUSTICE FORTAS, with whom THE CHIEF JUSTICE joins, concurring.

While I agree that the Fourth Amendment should not be held to require exclusion from evidence of the clothing as well as the weapons and ammunition found by the officers during the search, I cannot join in the majority's broad — and in my judgment, totally unnecessary — repudiation of the so-called "mere evidence" rule.

Our Constitution envisions that searches will ordinarily follow procurement by police of a valid search warrant. Such warrants are to issue only on probable cause, and must describe with particularity the persons or things to be seized. There are exceptions to this rule. Searches may be made incident to a lawful arrest, and — as today's decision indicates — in the course of "hot pursuit." But searches under each of these exceptions have, until today, been confined to those essential to fulfill the purpose of the exception: that is, we have refused to permit use of articles the seizure of which could not be strictly tied to and justified by the exigencies which excused the warrantless search. The use in evidence of weapons seized in a "hot pursuit" search or search incident to arrest satisfies this criterion because of the need to protect the arresting officers from weapons to which the suspect might resort. The search for and seizure of fruits are, of course, justifiable on independent grounds: The fruits are an object of the pursuit or arrest of the suspect, and should be restored to their true owner. The seizure of contraband has been justified on the ground that the suspect has not even a bare possessory right to contraband. . . .

In the present case, the articles of clothing admitted into evidence are not within any of the traditional categories which describe what materials may be seized, either with or without a warrant. The restrictiveness of these categories has been subjected to telling criticism, and although I believe that we should approach expansion of these categories with the diffidence which their imposing provenance commands, I agree that the use of identifying clothing worn in the commission of a crime and seized during "hot pursuit" is within the spirit and intendment of the "hot pursuit" exception to the search-warrant requirement. That is because the clothing is pertinent to identification of the person hotly pursued as being, in fact, the person whose pursuit was justified by connection with the crime. I would frankly place the ruling on that basis. I would not drive an enormous and dangerous hole in the Fourth Amendment to accommodate a specific and, I think, reasonable exception.

As my Brother Douglas notes, post, opposition to general searches is a fundamental of our heritage and of the history of Anglo-Saxon legal principles. Such searches, pursuant to "writs of assistance," were one of the matters over which the American Revolution was fought. The very purpose of the Fourth Amendment was to outlaw such searches, which the Court today sanctions. I fear that in gratuitously striking down the "mere evidence" rule, which distinguished members of this Court have acknowledged as essential to enforce the Fourth Amendment's prohibition against general searches, the Court today needlessly destroys, root and branch, a basic part of liberty's heritage.

MR. JUSTICE DOUGLAS, dissenting.

We start with the Fourth Amendment. . . . This constitutional guarantee, . . . has been thought, until today, to have two faces of privacy:

(1)   One creates a zone of privacy that may not be invaded by the police through raids, by the legislators through laws, or by magistrates through the issuance of warrants.

(2)   A second creates a zone of privacy that may be invaded either by the police in hot pursuit or by a search incident to arrest or by a warrant issued by a magistrate on a showing of probable cause. . . .

This is borne out by what happened in the Congress. In the House the original draft read as follows:

> The right of the people to be secured in their persons, houses, papers, and effects, shall not be violated by warrants issuing without probable cause, supported by oath or affirmation, and not particularly describing the place to be searched and the persons or things to be seized. 1 Annals of Cong. 754.

That was amended to read "The right of the people to be secured in their persons, houses, papers, and effects, against unreasonable seizures and searches," etc. Ibid. Mr. Benson, Chairman of a Committee of Three to arrange the amendments, objected to the words "by warrants issuing" and proposed to alter the amendment so as to read "and no warrant shall issue." Ibid. But Benson's amendment was defeated. Ibid. And if the story had ended there, it would be clear that the Fourth Amendment touched only the form of the warrants and the manner of their issuance. But when the Benson Committee later reported the Fourth Amendment to the House, it was in the form he had earlier proposed and was then accepted. 1 Annals of Cong. 779. The Senate agreed. Senate Journal August 25, 1789.

Thus it is clear that the Fourth Amendment has two faces of privacy, a conclusion emphasized by Nelson B. Lasson, The History and Development of the Fourth Amendment to the United States Constitution 103 (1937):

> As reported by the Committee of Eleven and corrected by Gerry, the Amendment was a one-barrelled affair, directed apparently only to the essentials of a valid warrant. The general principle of freedom from unreasonable search and seizure seems to have been stated only by way of premise, and the positive inhibition upon action by the Federal Government limited consequently to the issuance of warrants without probable cause, etc. That Benson interpreted it in this light is shown by his argument that although the clause was good as far as it went, *it was not sufficient*, and by the change which he advocated to obviate this objection. The provision as he proposed it contained *two* clauses. The general right of security from unreasonable search and seizure was given a sanction of its own and the amendment thus intentionally given a broader scope. That the prohibition against "unreasonable searches" was intended, accordingly, to cover something other than the form of the warrant is a question no longer left to implication to be derived from the phraseology of the Amendment. . . .

. . . Our question is whether the Government, though armed with a proper search warrant or though making a search incident to an arrest, may seize, and use at the trial, testimonial evidence, whether it would otherwise be barred by the Fifth

Amendment or would be free from such strictures. The teaching of *Boyd* is that such evidence, though seized pursuant to a lawful search, is inadmissible. . . .

We have, to be sure, breached that barrier, Schmerber v. California, 384 U.S. 757, being a conspicuous example. But I dissented then and renew my opposing view at this time. That which is taken from a person without his consent and used as testimonial evidence violates the Fifth Amendment.

That was the holding in *Gouled*; and that was the line of authority followed by Judge Simon Sobeloff, writing for the Court of Appeals for reversal in this case. 363 F.2d 647. As he said, even if we assume that the search was lawful, the articles of clothing seized were of evidential value only and under *Gouled* could not be used at the trial against petitioner. As he said, the Fourth Amendment guarantees the right of the people to be secure "in their persons, houses, papers, and effects, against unreasonable searches and seizures." Articles of clothing are covered as well as papers. Articles of clothing may be of evidential value as much as documents or papers. Judge Learned Hand stated a part of the philosophy of the Fourth Amendment in United States v. Poller, 43 F.2d 911, 914:

> [I]t is only fair to observe that the real evil aimed at by the Fourth Amendment is the search itself, that invasion of a man's privacy which consists in rummaging about among his effects to secure evidence against him. If the search is permitted at all, perhaps it does not make so much difference what is taken away, since the officers will ordinarily not be interested in what does not incriminate, and there can be no sound policy in protecting what does. Nevertheless, limitations upon the fruit to be gathered tend to limit the quest itself. . . .

The right of privacy protected by the Fourth Amendment relates in part of course to the precincts of the home or the office. But it does not make them sanctuaries where the law can never reach. . . . A policeman in "hot pursuit" or an officer with a search warrant can enter any house, any room, any building, any office. The privacy of those *places* is of course protected against invasion except in limited situations. The full privacy protected by the Fourth Amendment is, however, reached when we come to books, pamphlets, papers, letters, documents, and other personal effects. Unless they are contraband or instruments of the crime, they may not be reached by any warrant nor may they be lawfully seized by the police who are in "hot pursuit." By reason of the Fourth Amendment the police may not rummage around among these personal effects, no matter how formally perfect their authority may appear to be. They may not seize them. If they do, those articles may not be used in evidence. Any invasion whatsoever of those personal effects is "unreasonable" within the meaning of the Fourth Amendment. That is the teaching of Entick v. Carrington, Boyd v. United States, and Gouled v. United States. . . .

The constitutional philosophy is, I think, clear. The personal effects and possessions of the individual (all contraband and the like excepted) are sacrosanct from prying eyes, from the long arm of the law, from any rummaging by police. Privacy involves the choice of the individual to disclose or to reveal what he believes, what he thinks, what he possesses. The article may be a nondescript work of art, a manuscript of a book, a personal account book, a diary, invoices, personal clothing, jewelry, or whatnot. Those who wrote the Bill of Rights believed that every individual needs both to communicate with others and to keep his affairs to himself. That dual aspect of privacy means that the individual should have the freedom to select for himself the time and circumstances when he will share his secrets with others and decide the extent of that sharing. This is his prerogative not the States'. The Framers, who were as knowledgeable as we, knew what police surveillance meant and how the practice of rummaging through one's personal effects could destroy freedom. . . . The third case in which the Court considered the extent to which "the law derived from *Boyd* would have to be repudiated" was Berger v. New York, 388 U.S. 41 (1967):

We . . . turn to New York's statute to determine the basis of the search and seizure authorized by it upon the order of a state supreme court justice, a county judge or general sessions judge of New York County. Section 813-a authorizes the issuance of an "ex parte order for eavesdropping" upon "oath or affirmation of a district attorney, or of the attorney-general or of an officer above the rank of sergeant of any police department of the state or of any political subdivision thereof. . . ." The oath must state "that there is reasonable ground to believe that evidence of crime may be thus obtained, and particularly describing the person or persons whose communications, conversations or discussions are to be overheard or recorded and the purpose thereof, and . . . identifying the particular telephone number or telegraph line involved." The judge "may examine on oath the applicant and any other witness he may produce and shall satisfy himself of the existence of reasonable grounds for the granting of such application." The order must specify the duration of the eavesdrop — not exceeding two months unless extended — and "(a)ny such order together with the papers upon which the application was based, shall be delivered to and retained by the applicant as authority for the eavesdropping authorized therein." . . .

The Fourth Amendment commands that a warrant issue not only upon probable cause supported by oath or affirmation, but also "particularly describing the place to be searched, and the persons or things to be seized." New York's statute lacks this particularization. It merely says that a warrant may issue on reasonable ground to believe that evidence of crime may be obtained by the eavesdrop. It lays down no requirement for particularity in the warrant as to what specific crime has been or is being committed, nor "the place to be searched," or "the persons or things to be seized" as specifically required by the Fourth Amendment. The need for particularity and evidence of reliability in the showing required when judicial authorization of a search is sought is especially great in the case of eavesdropping. By its very nature eavesdropping involves an intrusion on privacy that is broad in scope. As was said in Osborn v. United States, 385 U.S. 32 (1966), the "indiscriminate use of such devices in law enforcement raises grave constitutional questions under the Fourth and Fifth Amendments," and imposes "a heavier responsibility on this Court in its supervision of the fairness of procedures. . . ." At 329, n. 7. There, two judges acting jointly authorized the installation of a device on the person of a prospective witness to record conversations between him and an attorney for a defendant then on trial in the United States District Court. The judicial authorization was based on an affidavit of the witness setting out in detail previous conversations between the witness and the attorney concerning the bribery of jurors in the case. The recording device was, as the Court said, authorized "under the most precise and discriminate circumstances, circumstances which fully met the 'requirement of particularity'" of the Fourth Amendment. The Court was asked to exclude the evidence of the recording of the conversations seized pursuant to the order on constitutional grounds, Weeks v. United States, 232 U.S. 383 (1914), or in the exercise of supervisory power, McNabb v. United States, 318 U.S. 332 (1943). The Court refused to do so finding that the recording, although an invasion of the privacy protected by the Fourth Amendment, was admissible because of the authorization of the judges, based upon "a detailed factual affidavit alleging the commission of a specific criminal offense directly and immediately affecting the administration of justice . . .

for the narrow and particularized purpose of ascertaining the truth of the affidavit's allegations." The invasion was lawful because there was sufficient proof to obtain a search warrant to make the search for the limited purpose outlined in the order of the judges. Through these "precise and discriminate" procedures the order authorizing the use of the electronic device afforded similar protections to those that are present in the use of conventional warrants authorizing the seizure of tangible evidence. Among other safeguards, the order described the type of conversation sought with particularity, thus indicating the specific objective of the Government in entering the constitutionally protected area and the limitations placed upon the officer executing the warrant. Under it the officer could not search unauthorized areas; likewise, once the property sought, and for which the order was issued, was found the officer could not use the order as a passkey to further search. In addition, the order authorized one limited intrusion rather than a series or a continuous surveillance. And, we note that a new order was issued when the officer sought to resume the search and probable cause was shown for the succeeding one. Moreover, the order was executed by the officer with dispatch, not over a prolonged and extended period. In this manner no greater invasion of privacy was permitted than was necessary under the circumstances. Finally the officer was required to and did make a return on the order showing how it was executed and what was seized. Through these strict precautions the danger of an unlawful search and seizure was minimized.

By contrast, New York's statute lays down no such "precise and discriminate" requirements. Indeed, it authorizes the "indiscriminate use" of electronic devices as specifically condemned in *Osborn*. "The proceeding by search warrant is a drastic one," Sgro v. United States, 287 U.S. 206 (1932), and must be carefully circumscribed so as to prevent unauthorized invasions of "the sanctity of a man's home and the privacies of life." Boyd v. United States, 116 U.S. 616, 630. New York's broadside authorization rather than being "carefully circumscribed" so as to prevent unauthorized invasions of privacy actually permits general searches by electronic devices, the truly offensive character of which was first condemned in Entick v. Carrington, 19 How. St. Tr. 1029, and which were then known as "general warrants." The use of the latter was a motivating factor behind the Declaration of Independence. In view of the many cases commenting on the practice it is sufficient here to point out that under these "general warrants" customs officials were given blanket authority to conduct general searches for goods imported to the Colonies in violation of the tax laws of the Crown. The Fourth Amendment's requirement that a warrant "particularly describ(e) the place to be searched, and the persons or things to be seized," repudiated these general warrants and "makes general searches . . . impossible and prevents the seizure of one thing under a warrant describing another. As to what is to be taken, nothing is left to the discretion of the officer executing the warrant." Marron v. United States, 275 U.S. 192, 196 (1927).

We believe the statute here is equally offensive. First, as we have mentioned, eavesdropping is authorized without requiring belief that any particular offense has been or is being committed; nor that the "property" sought, the conversations, be particularly described. The purpose of the probable cause requirement of the Fourth Amendment, to keep the state out of constitutionally protected areas until it has reason to believe that a specific crime has been or is being committed, is thereby wholly aborted. Likewise the statute's failure to describe with particularity the conversations sought gives the officer a roving commission to "seize" any and all conversations. It is true that the statute requires the naming of "the person or persons whose communications, conversations or discussions are to be overheard or recorded. . . ." But this does no more than identify the person whose constitutionally protected area is to be invaded rather than "particularly describing" the communications, conversations, or discussions to be seized. As with general warrants this leaves too much to the discretion of the officer executing the order. Secondly, authorization of eavesdropping for a two-month period is the equivalent of a series of intrusions, searches, and seizures pursuant to a single showing of probable cause. Prompt execution is also avoided. During such a long and continuous (24 hours a day) period the conversations of any and all persons coming into the area covered by the device will be seized indiscriminately and without regard to their connection with the crime under investigation. Moreover, the statute permits, and there were authorized here, extensions of the original two-month period — presumably for two months each — on a mere showing that such extension is "in the public interest." Apparently the original grounds on which the eavesdrop order was initially issued also form the basis of the renewal. This we believe insufficient without a showing of present probable cause for the continuance of the eavesdrop. Third, the statute places no termination date on the eavesdrop once the conversation sought is seized. This is left entirely in the discretion of the officer. Finally, the statute's procedure, necessarily because its success depends on secrecy, has no requirement for notice as do conventional warrants, nor does it overcome this defect by requiring some showing of special facts. On the contrary, it permits uncontested entry without any showing of exigent circumstances. Such a showing of exigency, in order to avoid notice would appear more important in eavesdropping, with its inherent dangers, than that required when conventional procedures of search and seizure are utilized. Nor does the statute provide for a return on the warrant thereby leaving full discretion in the officer as to the use of seized conversations of innocent as well as guilty parties. In short, the statute's blanket grant of permission to eavesdrop is without adequate judicial supervision or protective procedures.

NOTES AND QUESTIONS

1. What is left of the theoretical underpinnings of *Boyd* and *Gouled* after *Schmerber*, *Hayden*, and *Berger*? Is it conceivable that the "paper search" component of *Boyd* survived these cases? Is the seizure of spoken words in any crucial respect different from the seizure of private papers? Is it true that the "mere evidence" rule is insupportable? Consider the following passage from Russell W. Galloway, Jr., The Intruding Eye: A Status Report on the Constitutional Ban against Paper Searches, 25 How. L.J. 367, 382-385 (1982):

[T]he mere evidence rule was a rational method for protecting privacy. When searches and seizures are limited to contraband, fruits and instrumentalities, the only persons who may be searched, in most instances, are criminals. Normally, only the criminals themselves possess contraband, fruits or instrumentalities. In contrast, innocent people (so-called "third parties") frequently possess evidence that may tie some *other* person to a crime. Thus, the mere evidence rule ensures that the government will not be able to invade the privacy of innocent third parties. Moreover, evidence searches often result in much more serious invasions of personal privacy. Rarely will a person's private papers contain contraband, fruits or instrumentalities. Yet searches for evidence of crime lead easily and directly into private paper where descriptions of prior acts and statements may be recorded side by side with the most intimate details of private life and thought. A search for a stolen television, for example, will normally be far less intrusive than a search for written statements concerning the suspect's whereabouts on the night the television was stolen. For reasons such as these, Learned Hand described the policy underlying the mere evidence rule as follows: "Limitations upon the fruit to be gathered tend to limit the quest itself."[70] . . .

The reasons given for the repudiation of the mere evidence rule are unconvincing. The absence of explicit reference to the mere evidence rule in the fourth amendment means little in light of the Court's insistence that *Entick* was in the forefront of the framers' minds when they banned unreasonable searches.[78] The Court's assurances notwithstanding, evidence searches tend to disturb privacy *much more deeply* than searches for contraband, fruits and instrumentalities. One need only consider, for example, that neither extended electronic surveillance, one of the most insidious invasions of privacy, nor the reading of most private papers would be possible if the mere evidence rule had been retained. The mere evidence rule was definitely not an irrational restriction like "a restriction on search to even-numbered days." The mere evidence rule was a rational limitation which operated to restrict searches of innocent third parties and to ban the most intrusive invasions of private papers and conversations.

Boyd continues to generate favorable commentary. See, e.g., Richard A. Nagareda, "Compulsion to Be a Witness" and the Resurrection of *Boyd*, 74 N.Y.U. L. Rev. 1575 (1999); Eric Schnapper, Unreasonable Searches and Seizures of Papers, 71 Va. L. Rev. 869 (1985). But see Samuel A. Alito, Jr., Documents and the Privilege against Self Incrimination, 48 U. Pitt. L. Rev. 27 (1986).

2. Although the Court struck down the statute in *Berger*, did it essentially write its replacement? Is that replacement statute true to the message of *Boyd*? Should it have been? These and other issues are considered in Chapter 5, infra.

3. The Court continued its reconstruction of *Boyd* in Fisher v. United States, 425 U.S. 391 (1976), and Andresen v. Maryland, 427 U.S. 463 (1976). In *Fisher*, the Court upheld a summons that directed the defendants' attorneys to produce documents prepared by defendants' accountants and turned over to the attorneys for purposes of obtaining legal advice. After determining that the materials would be privileged in the hands of the attorney, as a result of the attorney-client privilege, only if the Fifth Amendment protected the materials when they were in the possession of the client, the Court proceeded to discuss its understanding of the Fourth and the Fifth Amendments:

> It is true that the Court has often stated that one of the several purposes served by the constitutional privilege against compelled testimonial self-incrimination is that of protecting personal privacy. . . . But the Court has never suggested that every invasion of privacy violates the privilege. Within the limits imposed by the language of the Fifth Amendment, which we necessarily observe, the privilege truly serves privacy interests; but the Court has never on any ground, personal privacy included, applied the Fifth Amendment to prevent the otherwise proper acquisition or use of evidence which, in the Court's view, did not involve compelled testimonial self-incrimination of some sort.[5]

70. United States v. Poller, 43 F.2d 911, 914 (2d Cir. 1930).

78. See, e.g., Boyd v. United States, 116 U.S. 616, 626-627 (1886), which stated: "As every American statesm[a]n, during our revolutionary and formative period as a nation, was undoubtedly familiar with [Entick v. Carrington] . . . , and considered it as the true and ultimate expression of constitutional law, it may be confidently asserted that its propositions were in the minds of those who framed the Fourth Amendment to the Constitution, and were considered as sufficiently explanatory of what was meant by unreasonable searches and seizures."

5. There is a line of cases in which the Court stated that the Fifth Amendment was offended by the use in evidence of documents or property seized in violation of the Fourth Amendment. . . . In any event the predicate for those cases, lacking here, was a violation of the Fourth Amendment.

The proposition that the Fifth Amendment protects private information obtained without compelling self-incriminating testimony is contrary to the clear statements of this Court that under appropriate safeguards private incriminating statements of an accused may be overheard and used in evidence, if they are not compelled at the time they were uttered, . . . Berger v. New York; . . . and that disclosure of private information may be compelled if immunity removes the risk of incrimination. If the Fifth Amendment protected generally against the obtaining of private information from a man's mouth or pen or house, its protections would presumably not be lifted by probable cause and a warrant or by immunity. The privacy invasion is not mitigated by immunity; and the Fifth Amendment's strictures, unlike the Fourth's, are not removed by showing reasonableness. The Framers addressed the subject of personal privacy directly in the Fourth Amendment. They struck a balance so that when the State's reason to believe incriminating evidence will be found becomes sufficiently great, the invasion of privacy becomes justified and a warrant to search and seize will issue. They did not seek in still another Amendment — the Fifth — to achieve a general protection of privacy but to deal with the more specific issue of compelled self-incrimination.

We cannot cut the Fifth Amendment completely loose from the moorings of its language, and make it serve as a general protector of privacy — a word not mentioned in its text and a concept directly addressed in the Fourth Amendment. We adhere to the view that the Fifth Amendment protects against "compelled self-incrimination, not [the disclosure of] private information." United States v. Nobles, 422 U.S. 225, 233 n. 7 (1975).

Insofar as private information not obtained through compelled self-incriminating testimony is legally protected, its protection stems from other sources[6] — the Fourth Amendment's protection against seizures without warrant or probable cause and against subpoenas which suffer from "too much indefiniteness or breadth in the things required to be 'particularly described,'" Oklahoma Press Pub. Co. v. Walling, 327 U.S. 186, 208 (1946); or evidentiary privileges such as the attorney-client privilege.[7]

425 U.S., at 399-401.

In light of its general understanding of the amendments, the only Fifth Amendment problem the Court could see with a summons to produce documents prepared by someone else (here the accountants) had to do with the testimonial components of production itself.

A subpoena served on a taxpayer requiring him to produce an accountant's workpapers in his possession without doubt involves substantial compulsion. But it does not compel oral testimony; nor would it ordinarily compel the taxpayer to restate, repeat, or affirm the truth of the contents of the documents sought. Therefore, the Fifth Amendment would not be violated by the fact alone that the papers on their face might incriminate the taxpayer, for the privilege protects a person only against being incriminated by his own compelled testimonial communications. Schmerber v. California,

6. In Couch v. United States, 409 U.S. 322 (1973), on which taxpayers rely for their claim that the Fifth Amendment protects their "legitimate expectation of privacy," the Court differentiated between the things protected by the Fourth and Fifth Amendments. "We hold today that no Fourth or Fifth Amendment claim can prevail where, as in this case, there exists no legitimate expectation of privacy and no semblance of governmental compulsion against the person of the accused." Id., at 336.

7. The taxpayers and their attorneys have not raised arguments of a Fourth Amendment nature before this Court and could not be successful if they had. The summonses are narrowly drawn and seek only documents of unquestionable relevance to the tax investigation. Special problems of privacy which might be presented by subpoena of a personal diary, United States v. Bennett, 409 F.2d 888, 897 (CA2 1969) (Friendly, J.), are not involved here.

First Amendment values are also plainly not implicated in these cases.

supra. . . . The accountant's workpapers are not the taxpayer's. They were not prepared by the taxpayer, and they contain no testimonial declarations by him. Furthermore, as far as this record demonstrates, the preparation of all of the papers sought in
these cases was wholly voluntary, and they cannot be said to contain compelled testimonial evidence, either of the taxpayers or of anyone else.[11] The taxpayer cannot
avoid compliance with the subpoena merely by asserting that the item of evidence
which he is required to produce contains incriminating writing, whether his own or that
of someone else.

The act of producing evidence in response to a subpoena nevertheless has communicative aspects of its own, wholly aside from the contents of the papers produced.
Compliance with the subpoena tacitly concedes the existence of the papers demanded
and their possession or control by the taxpayer. It also would indicate the taxpayer's
belief that the papers are those described in the subpoena. Curcio v. United States, 354
U.S. 118, 125 (1957). The elements of compulsion are clearly present, but the more difficult issues are whether the tacit averments of the taxpayer are both "testimonial" and
"incriminating" for purposes of applying the Fifth Amendment. These questions perhaps do not lend themselves to categorical answers; their resolution may instead
depend on the facts and circumstances of particular cases or classes thereof. In light of
the records now before us, we are confident that however incriminating the contents of
the accountant's workpapers might be, the act of producing them — the only thing
which the taxpayer is compelled to do — would not itself involve testimonial self-
incrimination.

It is doubtful that implicitly admitting the existence and possession of the papers
rises to the level of testimony within the protection of the Fifth Amendment. The
papers belong to the accountant, were prepared by him, and are the kind usually prepared by an accountant working on the tax returns of his client. Surely the Government
is in no way relying on the "truthtelling" of the taxpayer to prove the existence of or his
access to the documents. 8 Wigmore §2264, p. 380. The existence and location of the
papers are a foregone conclusion and the taxpayer adds little or nothing to the sum
total of the Government's information by conceding that he in fact has the papers.
Under these circumstances by enforcement of the summons "no constitutional rights
are touched. The question is not of testimony but of surrender." In re Harris, 221 U.S.
274, 279 (1911). . . .

As for the possibility that responding to the subpoena would authenticate the workpapers, production would express nothing more than the taxpayer's belief that the
papers are those described in the subpoena. The taxpayer would be no more competent to authenticate the accountant's workpapers or reports by producing them than
he would be to authenticate them if testifying orally. The taxpayer did not prepare the
papers and could not vouch for their accuracy. The documents would not be admissible
in evidence against the taxpayer without authenticating testimony. Without more,
responding to the subpoena in the circumstances before us would not appear to represent a substantial threat of self-incrimination. Moreover, in [a series of cases] the custodian of corporate, union, or partnership books or those of a bankrupt business was
ordered to respond to a subpoena for the business' books even though doing so

11. The fact that the documents may have been written by the person asserting the privilege is insufficient to trigger the privilege, Wilson v. United States, 221 U.S. 361, 378 (1911). And, unless the Government has compelled the subpoenaed person to write the document, cf. Marchetti v. United States, 390
U.S. 39 (1968); Grosso v. United States, 390 U.S. 62 (1968), the fact that it was written by him is not controlling with respect to the Fifth Amendment issue. Conversations may be seized and introduced in evidence under proper safeguards, . . . Berger v. New York, 388 U.S. 41 (1967); . . . if not compelled. In
the case of a documentary subpoena the only thing compelled is the act of producing the document and
the compelled act is the same as the one performed when a chattel or document not authored by the pro-
ducer is demanded. McCormick §128, p. 269.

involved a "representation that documents produced are those demanded by the sub-poena," Curcio v. United States, 354 U.S., at 125.

425 U.S., at 409-413.

Justice Brennan concurred, but made the point that the Fifth Amendment, in his view, would protect against the production of private papers that were unrelated to the defendant's business activities. Justice Marshall also concurred, primarily on the ground that *Fisher* would not modify the scope of the protections previously afforded by the Court's decisions:

> I am hopeful that the Court's new theory, properly understood and applied, will pro-vide substantially the same protection as our prior focus on the contents of the docu-ments. The Court recognizes, as others have argued, that the act of production can verify the authenticity of the documents produced. But the promise of the Court's theory lies in its innovative discernment that production may also verify the docu-ments' very existence and present possession by the producer. This expanded recog-nition of the kinds of testimony inherent in production not only rationalizes the cases, but seems to me to afford almost complete protection against compulsory production of our most private papers.
>
> Thus, the Court's rationale provides a persuasive basis for distinguishing between the corporate document cases and those involving the papers of private citizens. Since the existence of corporate record books is seldom in doubt, the verification of their existence, inherent in their production, may fairly be termed not testimonial at all. On the other hand, there is little reason to assume the present existence and possession of most private papers, and certainly not those Mr. Justice Brennan places at the top of his list of documents that the privilege should protect. . . . Indeed, there would appear to be a precise inverse relationship between the private nature of the document and the permissibility of assuming its existence. Therefore, under the Court's theory, the admission through production that one's diary, letters, prior tax returns, personally maintained financial records, or cancelled checks exist would ordinarily provide sub-stantial testimony. The incriminating nature of such an admission is clear, for while it may not be criminal to keep a diary, or write letters or checks, the admission that one does and that those documents are still available may quickly — or simultaneously — lead to incriminating evidence. If there is a "real danger" of such a result, that is enough under our cases to make such testimony subject to the claim of privilege. Thus, in practice, the Court's approach should still focus upon the private nature of the papers subpoenaed and protect those about which *Boyd* and its progeny were most concerned.
>
> The Court's theory will also limit the prosecution's ability to use documents secured through a grant of immunity. If authentication that the document produced is the document demanded were the only testimony inherent in production, immunity would be a useful tool for obtaining written evidence. So long as a document obtained under an immunity grant could be authenticated through other sources, as would often be possible, reliance on the immunized testimony — the authentication — and its fruits would not be necessary, and the document could be introduced. The Court's recogni-tion that the act of production also involves testimony about the existence and posses-sion of the subpoenaed documents mandates a different result. Under the Court's theory, if the document is to be obtained the immunity grant must extend to the testi-mony that the document is presently in existence. Such a grant will effectively shield the contents of the document, for the contents are a direct fruit of the immunized testimony — that the document exists — and cannot usually be obtained without reli-ance on that testimony. Accordingly, the Court's theory offers substantially the same

protection against procurement of documents under grant of immunity that our prior cases afford.

In short, while the Court sacrifices our pragmatic, if somewhat ad hoc, content analysis for what might seem an unduly technical focus on the act of production itself, I am far less pessimistic than Mr. Justice Brennan that this new approach signals the end of Fifth Amendment protection for documents we have long held to be privileged. I am not ready to embrace the approach myself, but I am confident in the ability of the trial judges who must apply this difficult test in the first instance to act with sensitivity to our traditional concerns in this uncertain area. . . .

425 U.S., at 432-434.

In *Andresen*, the Court dealt with the issue left open in *Fisher* — the production of a person's private papers — but approached it from a different perspective. The defendant was convicted on various counts of fraud. At trial, the government relied on personal business papers of the defendant that were seized under the authority of a search warrant. Some of the documents seized included memoranda handwritten by the defendant. According to the Court, this raised "the issue whether the introduction into evidence of a person's business records, seized during a search of his offices, violates the Fifth Amendment's command."

The question . . . is whether the seizure of these business records, and their admission into evidence at his trial, compelled petitioner to testify against himself in violation of the Fifth Amendment. This question may be said to have been reserved in Warden v. Hayden . . . .

In the very recent case of Fisher v. United States, the Court held that an attorney's production, pursuant to a lawful summons, of his client's tax records in his hands did not violate the Fifth Amendment privilege of the taxpayer "because enforcement against a taxpayer's lawyer would not 'compel' the taxpayer to do anything — and certainly would not compel him to be a 'witness' against himself." . . .[7]

Similarly, in this case, petitioner was not asked to say or to do anything. The records seized contained statements that petitioner had voluntarily committed to writing. The search for and seizure of these records were conducted by law enforcement personnel. Finally, when these records were introduced at trial, they were authenticated by a handwriting expert, not by petitioner. Any compulsion of petitioner to speak, other than the inherent psychological pressure to respond at trial to unfavorable evidence, was not present.

This case thus falls within the principle stated by Mr. Justice Holmes: "A party is privileged from producing the evidence but not from its production." Johnson v. United States, 228 U.S. 457, 458 (1913). This principle recognizes that the protection afforded by the Self-Incrimination Clause of the Fifth Amendment "adheres basically to the person, not to information that may incriminate him." Couch v. United States, 409 U.S., at 328. Thus, although the Fifth Amendment may protect an individual from complying with a subpoena for the production of his personal records in his possession because the very act of production may constitute a compulsory authentication of incriminating information, see Fisher v. United States, supra, a seizure of the same materials by law enforcement officers differs in a crucial respect — the individual

7. Petitioner relies on the statement in *Couch* that "possession bears the closest relationship to personal compulsion forbidden by the Fifth Amendment," 409 U.S., at 331, in support of his argument that possession of incriminating evidence itself supplies the predicate for invocation of the privilege. *Couch*, of course, was concerned with the production of documents pursuant to a summons directed to the accountant where there might have been a possibility of compulsory self-incrimination by the principal's implicit or explicit "testimony" that the documents were those identified in the summons. The risk of authentication is not present where the documents are seized pursuant to a search warrant.

against whom the search is directed is not required to aid in the discovery, production, or authentication of incriminating evidence. . . .

We find a useful analogy to the Fifth Amendment question in those cases that deal with the "seizure" of oral communications. As the Court has explained, "[t]he constitutional privilege against self-incrimination . . . is designed to prevent the use of legal process to force from the lips of the accused individual the evidence necessary to convict him or to force him to produce and authenticate any personal documents or effects that might incriminate him." Bellis v. United States, 417 U.S., at 88. The significant aspect of this principle was apparent and applied in Hoffa v. United States, where the Court rejected the contention that an informant's "seizure" of the accused's conversation with him, and his subsequent testimony at trial concerning that conversation, violated the Fifth Amendment. The rationale was that, although the accused's statements may have been elicited by the informant for the purpose of gathering evidence against him, they were made voluntarily. We see no reasoned distinction to be made between the compulsion upon the accused in that case and the compulsion in this one. In each, the communication, whether oral or written, was made voluntarily. The fact that seizure was contemporaneous with the communication in *Hoffa* but subsequent to the communication here does not affect the question whether the accused was compelled to speak.

Finally we do not believe that permitting the introduction into evidence of a person's business records seized during an otherwise lawful search would offend or undermine any of the policies undergirding the privilege. Murphy v. Waterfront Comm'n, 378 U.S. 52, 55 (1964).[8]

In this case, petitioner, at the time he recorded his communication, at the time of the search, and at the time the records were admitted at trial, was not subjected to "the cruel trilemma of self-accusation, perjury or contempt." Indeed, he was never required to say or to do anything under penalty of sanction. Similarly, permitting the admission of the records in question does not convert our accusatorial system of justice into an inquisitorial system. "The requirement of specific charges, their proof beyond a reasonable doubt, the protection of the accused from confessions extorted through whatever form of police pressures, the right to a prompt hearing before a magistrate, the right to assistance of counsel, to be supplied by government when circumstances make it necessary, the duty to advise an accused of his constitutional rights — these are all characteristics of the accusatorial system and manifestations of its demands." Watts v. Indiana, 338 U.S. 49, 54 (1949). None of these attributes is endangered by the introduction of business records "independently secured through skillful investigation." Ibid. Further, the search for and seizure of business records pose no danger greater than that inherent in every search that evidence will be "elicited by inhumane treatment and abuses." 378 U.S., at 55. In this case, the statements seized were voluntarily committed to paper before the police arrived to search for them, and petitioner was not treated discourteously during the search. Also, the "good cause" to "disturb," ibid., petitioner was independently determined by the judge who issued the warrants; and the State bore the burden of executing them. Finally, there is no chance, in this case, of

---

8. "The privilege against self-incrimination . . . reflects many of our fundamental values and most noble aspirations: our unwillingness to subject those suspected of crime to the cruel trilemma of self-accusation, perjury or contempt; our preference for an accusatorial rather than an inquisitorial system of criminal justice; our fear that self-incriminating statements will be elicited by inhumane treatment and abuses; our sense of fair play which dictates 'a fair state-individual balance by requiring the government to leave the individual alone until good cause is shown for disturbing him and by requiring the government in its contest with the individual to shoulder the entire load' . . . ; our respect for the inviolability of the human personality and of the right of each individual 'to a private enclave where he may lead a private life' . . . ; our distrust of self-deprecatory statements; and our realization that the privilege, while sometimes 'a shelter to the guilty,' is often 'a protection to the innocent.'"

petitioner's statements being self-deprecatory and untrustworthy because they were extracted from him — they were already in existence and had been made voluntarily.

We recognize, of course, that the Fifth Amendment protects privacy to some extent. However, "the Court has never suggested that every invasion of privacy violates the privilege." Fisher v. United States, 425 U.S., at 399. Indeed, we recently held that unless incriminating testimony is "compelled," any invasion of privacy is outside the scope of the Fifth Amendment's protection, saying that "the Fifth Amendment protects against 'compelled self-incrimination, not [the disclosure of] private information.'" Id., at 401. Here, as we have already noted, petitioner was not compelled to testify in any manner.

Accordingly, we hold that the search of an individual's office for business records, their seizure, and subsequent introduction into evidence do not offend the Fifth Amendment's proscription that "[n]o person . . . shall be compelled in any criminal case to be a witness against himself."

427 U.S., at 471-477.

4. What does *Fisher* protect? Frankly, the answer to that question is not altogether clear. Some of its opacity is eliminated by recognizing that, generally speaking, production of any tangible item may communicate two different types of information. The item may speak for itself, as writings do, and as other kinds of items may (a gun that can be tested by ballistics experts, for example). This is precisely the kind of information that the Court found not to be protected by the Fifth Amendment because its creation was not compelled. The second type of information communicated by the act of production has to do with the object itself rather than its contents. By producing an object, one admits that it exists, that it is genuine, and that one believes it to be the item requested by the government. By admitting such matters, the person producing the object would provide the government sufficient information to authenticate it under normal evidentiary rules. Unlike the contents, this information is compelled and thus is protected by the Fifth Amendment.

The difficulty is that the two aspects of information discussed above are paradigm cases, but in the real world they exist as variables. Sometimes the government knows what is in a writing and who possesses it, and sometimes the government possesses virtually no information on either score. How the "act of production" rationale is supposed to apply in the complex manifestations of these two variables that are generated in real life is unclear.

Fisher may seem to be indifferent to whether the government knows the contents of a writing. After all, that is just what the Court said is not protected by the Fifth Amendment. Nonetheless, there is an intimate connection between knowing the contents and knowing of the existence of a document, a matter that the Court found to be protected. Indeed, in one sense, only if the government already knows of the contents of a document can it know of the existence of the document. If the government does not know the contents of a document, producing it admits that it exists and contains — whatever it contains — information that the government would not previously have possessed. And of course, if the government already knew what the document contains, in many cases the government would not need it. There is thus often tension between the government's claim that it knows of the existence of a document and that it needs it. How the "act of production" rationale resolves this tension is not clear.

5. After *Fisher* and *Andresen*, may the state obtain, in any fashion, a diary that it has probable cause to believe would incriminate the diary's owner and possessor? Should it be able to do so? Consider the following passage from Note, Formalism,

Legal Realism, and Constitutionally Protected Privacy under the Fourth and Fifth
Amendments, 90 Harv. L. Rev. 945, 985-988 (1977):

> The conclusion that the fourth and fifth amendments should protect absolutely a
> core of one's expressions and effects is impelled by the moral and symbolic need to rec-
> ognize and defend the private aspect of personality.
>
> Belief in the uniqueness of each individual is one of the fundamental moral tenets
> of Western society. Such uniqueness inheres in being human and is not an entitlement
> to be granted or withheld by the state. In fact, one of the primary purposes of law is to
> ensure respect for this belief by preserving each person's right to a private life free from
> unwanted intrusion and disclosure. Justice Brandeis saw this as the purpose underly-
> ing the fourth amendment:
>
> > The makers of our Constitution undertook to secure conditions favorable to the pursuit of
> > happiness. They recognized the significance of man's spiritual nature, of his feelings and
> > of his intellect. . . . They sought to protect Americans in their beliefs, their thoughts, their
> > emotions and their sensations. They conferred, as against the Government, the right to be
> > let alone. . . .[247]
>
> A record of one's private beliefs and emotions tells a good deal about the person. Simi-
> larly, when one intimately and privately shares such thoughts and feelings with others
> he reveals much of the inner person he is.[248] Such experiences may include the
> exchange of letters, tapes, or phone conversations as well as actual gathering and con-
> versation. Just as recognition of the relationship between private reflection, socializa-
> tion, and personality has led the Court to block legislative attempts to control intimate
> private conduct,[249] interference with the private life by search or subpoena should be
> proscribed under the fourth and fifth amendments rather than tolerated as a necessary
> incident of criminal law enforcement. The privacy value should not suffer abridgement
> simply because there is reason to believe a person is involved in criminal activity.

Consider the following excerpt that proposes that the "paper search" rule of *Boyd*
can be seen to survive *Fisher* as a function of the First Amendment. If that point is
recognized, the author suggests, the present state of the law provides reasonable
protection for the central concerns expressed in *Boyd*.

> Properly read, Fisher v. United States stands for the proposition that no defendant may
> be compelled to authenticate evidence. Although this holding narrows the application
> of the self-incrimination clause, it adequately protects the rights of criminal defendants
> if the prohibitions of other amendments and evidentiary rules are properly applied.
> The implicit authentication doctrine of the fifth amendment prevents defendants from
> being forced to verify the case against them. The protection of the fourth amendment
> applicable to subpoenas duces tecum prohibits authorities from wholesale rummaging
> through a citizen's papers. Finally, the first amendment can prevent the government
> from probing into a defendant's most personal papers. Specific amendments answer
> specific concerns. Drawing on all of them, courts can forge a broad constitutional pro-
> tection for all citizens' rights.

247. Olmstead v. United States, 277 U.S. 438, 478 (1928) (Brandeis, J., dissenting).
248. Charles Fried, Privacy, 77 Yale L.J. 475, 477-478 (1968). See also Griswold v. Connecticut, 381
U.S. 479, 486 (1965).
249. Roe v. Wade, 410 U.S. 113 (1973) (abortion); Eisenstadt v. Baird, 405 U.S. 438 (1972) (contra-
ceptives for unmarried persons); Stanley v. Georgia, 394 U.S. 557 (1969) (private possession of obscene
material); Griswold v. Connecticut, 381 U.S. 479 (1965) (right of marital privacy).

Note, The Rights of Criminal Defendants and the Subpoena Duces Tecum: The Aftermath of *Fisher v. United States*, 95 Harv. L. Rev. 683, 701, 702 (1982).

The author of the Krauss quotation at the beginning of the chapter, page 291, supra, although not considering the First Amendment issue, views the state of the law considerably less sanguinely:

> In light of *Andresen* and *Fisher*, *Boyd* is dead. No zone of privacy now exists that the government cannot enter to take an individual's property for the purpose of obtaining incriminating information. In most cases, the zone can be entered by the issuance of a subpoena; in the rest, it can be breached by a search warrant. . . . The words of the Constitution can legitimately be understood in many ways. Precedent and history can be used to support divergent readings. Ultimately, the difference between the various interpretations given to the Constitution can be traced to disagreements on policy.
>
> So it is with *Boyd*. That case reflected the belief of a majority of the Justices then constituting the Supreme Court that the individual's interest in the rights that the privilege against self-incrimination was designed to safeguard was more important than the government's interest in convicting criminals. The Court protected those rights as completely as possible, though it could have read the Constitution as compelling less. At least seven members of that Court shared the views expressed in the *Boyd* opinion:
>
>> Though the proceeding in question is divested of many of the aggravating effects of actual search and seizure, yet, as before said, it contains their substance and essence, and effects their essential purpose. It may be that it is the obnoxious thing in its mildest and least repulsive form, but illegitimate and unconstitutional practices get their first footing in that way, namely, by silent approaches and slight deviations from legal modes of procedure. This can only be obviated by adhering to the rule that constitutional provisions for the security of person and property should be liberally construed. A close and literal construction of them deprives them of half their efficacy, and leads to gradual depreciation of the right, as if it consisted more in sound than in substance. It is the duty of courts to be watchful for the constitutional rights of the citizen, and guard against any stealthy encroachments thereon. Their motto should be *obsta principiis*.[138]
>
> The Burger Court has rejected *Boyd* because it no longer considers those values to be paramount; it is more impressed by the government's interest in combatting crime. In *Couch*, Justice Powell captured the spirit of the current Court: "It is important, in applying constitutional principles, to interpret them in light of the fundamental interests of personal liberty they were meant to serve. Respect for these principles is eroded when they leap their proper bounds to interfere with the legitimate interest of society in enforcement of its laws and collection of the revenues."[139] Accordingly, *Boyd* is dead. But the Court refuses to take the final step of overruling it.
>
> Justice Brandeis once called *Boyd* "a case that will be remembered as long as civil liberty lives in the United States."[140] At least it deserves a decent burial.

Krauss, 76 Mich. L. Rev., at 211-212.

To which view do you subscribe, and why? The trend is to permit even diaries to be seized by the government. A juvenile was convicted of murder on the basis of her diary, for example. See "Dear Diary" teen convicted of murder, Chicago Tribune, Sunday, June 12, 1993, sec. 1, at 8. The possible demise of *Boyd* has not been universally decried. See Robert S. Gerstein, The Demise of *Boyd*: Self-Incrimination and Private Papers in the Burger Court, 27 UCLA L. Rev. 343 (1979), arguing that *Boyd* obscured the rationale of the Fifth Amendment's concern for autonomy, and

---

138. 116 U.S., at 635.
139. Couch v. United States, 409 U.S. 322, 336 (1973).
140. Olmstead v. United States, 277 U.S. 438, 474 (Brandeis, J., dissenting).

Henry J. Friendly, The Fifth Amendment Tomorrow: The Case for Constitutional Change, 37 U. Cin. L. Rev. 671 (1968), arguing that *Boyd* should be overruled.

The law is not entirely settled on whether the Fifth Amendment puts some private papers beyond the reach of the subpoena power. Several circuits have said that private papers are not entitled to special treatment, and that just like business records, the documents may only be withheld if the contents were themselves compelled or the act of production would be incriminating. See, e.g., In re Grand Jury Subpoena Duces Tecum, 1 F.3d 87, 93 (2d Cir. 1993); In re Sealed Case, 877 F.2d 83, 84 (D.C. Cir. 1989); In re Grand Jury Proceedings, 759 F.2d 1418 (9th Cir. 1985). At least one court has indicated that there remains some protection for private papers. In re Grand Jury Proceedings, 55 F.3d 1012, 1013-14 (5th Cir. 1995) (per curiam). Still a third group says that because the Court has not specifically overruled *Boyd*, the status of private papers remains an open question. In re Grand Jury Investigation U.S. Attorney Matter No. 89-4-8881-J, 921 F.2d 1184 (11th Cir. 1991). See also In re Steinberg, 837 F.2d 527, 531 (1st Cir. 1988) ("If the contents of private papers are protected at all — a matter as to which we express no opinion today — it is only in rare situations, where compelled disclosure would break 'the heart of our sense of privacy.'" (citation omitted)).

6. In light of *Schmerber* and the other cases we have been considering, the Court has held that individuals can be required to give voice exemplars, United States v. Wade, page 160, supra; and handwriting exemplars, Gilbert v. California, page 160, supra. In such cases, an individual is normally subpoenaed to appear. The Court has held that subpoenas do not need to meet the probable cause standard of the Fourth Amendment. Rather, they must call for relevant material and not be unduly burdensome. The author argues that one solution for fears of overly broad subpoenas, as well as for fears concerning the demise of *Boyd*, is to require a higher than normal standard for obtaining private papers. There are, however, due process limits on the extraction of evidence from a suspect's body. In Rochin v. California, 342 U.S. 165 (1952), the Court reversed a conviction for possession of drugs that was based in part on evidentiary use of morphine tablets obtained by forcibly injecting an emetic into the defendant, over his objection, causing him to vomit up the capsules.

In Pennsylvania v. Muniz, 496 U.S. 582 (1990), the Court concluded that the incriminating inferences from a suspect's inability to perform sobriety tests were admissible on the *Wade/Gilbert* ground that there was no testimonial compulsion. *Muniz* is excerpted in Chapter 6, at pages 744-746.

7. If the defendant can be forced to yield information concerning his or her physical characteristics, should the defendant have the right to present such information in the defense case without waiving Fifth Amendment rights? Yes, say most courts. See, e.g., United States v. Bay, 748 F.2d 1344 (9th Cir. 1984).

8. Has the Supreme Court finally buried *Boyd*? Perhaps the reports of its demise are premature. In United States v. Doe, 465 U.S. 605 (1984), the Court concluded that "the Fifth Amendment privilege against compelled self-incrimination applies to the business records of a sole proprietorship," including *Fisher*'s authentication/ act of production doctrine, and affirmed the lower courts' findings that the act of production in this case would be incriminating.

By contrast, in a curious opinion in Braswell v. United States, 487 U.S. 99 (1988), a five-to-four majority of the Court addressed the question whether the custodian of corporate records may resist a subpoena for such records on the ground that the act of production would incriminate him in violation of the Fifth Amendment. We conclude that he may not. . . .

There is no question but that the contents of the subpoenaed business records are not privileged. See *Doe*, supra; Fisher v. United States. Similarly, petitioner asserts no self-incrimination claim on behalf of the corporations; it is well established that such artificial entities are not protected by the Fifth Amendment. Petitioner instead relies solely upon the argument that his act of producing the documents has independent testimonial significance, which would incriminate him individually, and that the Fifth Amendment prohibits government compulsion of that act. The bases for this argument are extrapolated from the decisions of this Court in *Fisher* and *Doe*. . . .

Had petitioner conducted his business as a sole proprietorship, *Doe* would require that he be provided the opportunity to show that his act of production would entail testimonial self-incrimination. But petitioner has operated his business through the corporate form, and we have long recognized that for purposes of the Fifth Amendment, corporations and other collective entities are treated differently from individuals. This doctrine — known as the collective entity rule — has a lengthy and distinguished pedigree [which the Court proceeded to discuss, citing cases such as Wilson v. United States, 221 U.S. 361 (1911), United States v. White, 322 U.S. 694 (1944), and Bellis v. United States, 417 U.S. 85 (1974)]. . . .

The plain mandate of these decisions is that without regard to whether the subpoena is addressed to the corporation, or as here, to the individual in his capacity as a custodian, a corporate custodian such as petitioner may not resist a subpoena for corporate records on Fifth Amendment grounds. Petitioner argues, however, that this rule falls in the wake of Fisher v. United States, and United States v. Doe. In essence, petitioner's argument is as follows: In response to Boyd v. United States, with its privacy rationale shielding personal books and records, the Court developed the collective entity rule, which declares simply that corporate records are not private and therefore are not protected by the Fifth Amendment. The collective entity decisions were concerned with the contents of the documents subpoenaed, however, and not with the act of production. In *Fisher* and *Doe*, the Court moved away from the privacy based collective entity rule, replacing it with a compelled testimony standard under which the contents of business documents are never privileged but the act of producing the documents may be. Under this new regime, the act of production privilege is available without regard to the entity whose records are being sought. . . .

To be sure, the holding in *Fisher* — later reaffirmed in *Doe* — embarked upon a new course of Fifth Amendment analysis. We cannot agree, however, that it rendered the collective entity rule obsolete. The agency rationale undergirding the collective entity decisions, in which custodians asserted that production of entity records would incriminate them personally, survives. . . . [T]he Court has consistently recognized that the custodian of corporate or entity records holds those documents in a representative rather than a personal capacity. Artificial entities such as corporations may act only through their agents, and a custodian's assumption of his representative capacity leads to certain obligations, including the duty to produce corporate records on proper demand by the Government. Under those circumstances, the custodian's act of production is not deemed a personal act, but rather an act of the corporation. Any claim of Fifth Amendment privilege asserted by the agent would be tantamount to a claim of privilege by the corporation — which of course possesses no such privilege. . . .

Although a corporate custodian is not entitled to resist a subpoena on the ground that his act of production will be personally incriminating, we do think certain consequences flow from the fact that the custodian's act of production is one in his representative rather than personal capacity. Because the custodian acts as a representative, the act is deemed one of the corporation and not the individual. Therefore, the Government concedes, as it must, that it may make no evidentiary use of the "individual act" against the individual. For example, in a criminal prosecution against the custodian, the Government may not introduce into evidence before the jury the fact that the subpoena was served upon and the corporation's documents were delivered by one particular individual, the custodian. The Government has the right, however, to use the corporation's act of production against the custodian. The Government may offer testimony — for example, from the process server who delivered the subpoena and from the individual who received the records — establishing that the corporation produced the records subpoenaed. The jury may draw from the corporation's act of production the conclusion that the records in question are authentic corporate records, which the corporation possessed, and which it produced in response to the subpoena. And if the defendant held a prominent position within the corporation that produced the records, the jury may, just as it would had someone else produced the documents, reasonably infer that he had possession of the documents or knowledge of their contents. Because the jury is not told that the defendant produced the records, any nexus between the defendant and the documents results solely from the corporation's act of production and other evidence in the case.[11] . . .

NOTES AND QUESTIONS ON *BRASWELL*

1. What do you think of a jurisprudence that gives details of enterprise law substantial constitutional significance? Perhaps the problem lies in *Fisher*. Does it stand for something too complicated to be administered? Professor Heidt thinks perhaps so. Robert Heidt, The Fifth Amendment Privilege and Documents — Cutting *Fisher*'s Tangled Line, 49 Mo. L. Rev. 439 (1984). See also Kevin R. Reitz, Clients, Lawyers and the Fifth Amendment: The Need for a Projected Privilege, 41 Duke L.J. 572 (1991). For other literature that examines the relationship between the Fifth Amendment and demands for the production of documents, see, e.g., Aaron M. Clemens, The Pending Reinvigoration of Boyd: Personal Papers are Protected by the Privilege Against Self-Incrimination, 25 N. Ill. U. L. Rev. 75 (2004); Robert P. Mosteller, Simplifying Subpoena Law: Taking the Fifth Amendment Seriously, 73 Va. L. Rev. 1 (1987).

2. The corporation in *Braswell* was basically a one-man operation, much like the sole proprietorship in *Doe*. Yet the Fifth Amendment applies to the subpoena in *Doe* but not to the one in *Braswell*. Why, exactly? Does the *Braswell* Court offer a satisfying answer?

Consider a different answer. Suppose the privilege *did* apply to subpoenas for corporate documents. Now suppose that the government issues a subpoena for documents in a corporate vice president's file cabinet. The documents technically incriminate the corporate vice president, but only technically. But if they come to

---

11. We reject the suggestion that the limitation on the evidentiary use of the custodian's act of production is the equivalent of constructive use immunity barred under our decision in *Doe*, 465 U.S., at 616-617. Rather, the limitation is a necessary concomitant of the notion that a corporate custodian acts as an agent and not an individual when he produces corporate records in response to a subpoena addressed to him in his representative capacity.

We leave open the question whether the agency rationale supports compelling a custodian to produce corporate records when the custodian is able to establish, by showing for example that he is the sole employee and officer of the corporation, that the jury would inevitably conclude that he produced the records.

light, the documents are sure to send the CEO to prison. Might the vice president be tempted to decline to produce the documents, allegedly on the ground that they incriminate him (but really in order to save the CEO's hide)? Such assertions of the privilege, nominally due to fear of self-incrimination but actually designed to avoid incriminating someone else, would be very common indeed if corporate documents were covered by the privilege. As for the application of the collective entity to one-person corporations like the one in *Braswell*: If *Braswell* came out the other way, how would courts draw the line between corporations that count as corporations for purposes of the privilege and corporations that are treated like sole proprietorships?

3. Reread the last of the quoted paragraphs from the *Braswell* majority opinion. Before that paragraph, the Court had explained that Braswell did not enjoy any Fifth Amendment protection when responding to a subpoena for corporate documents. But then, the Court goes on to say that, maybe, Braswell's act of producing the documents could not be used against him personally — which suggests that he does enjoy Fifth Amendment protection after all. What gives?

4. Why can individuals be required to turn over but not to testify about documents? According to the *Fisher* line of cases, the act of production is, or at least can be, testimonial. If any particular act is testimonial, what coherent theory allows that form of testimony to be compelled but provides protection for some other form of testimony? If a rose by any other name would smell as sweet, why isn't testimony protected no matter what the label?

5. Reconsider note 6, page 330, supra. Why doesn't the act of production rationale apply to such matters as voice and handwriting exemplars?

6. *Doe* and *Braswell* are important criminal procedure cases, but they are more than that: Because the scope of the subpoena power is so important to the administration of a variety of regulatory statutes, they have an impact on the law that undergirds the regulatory state. What difference do you think that makes in the Court's reasoning, and its results?

The point may be broader. If there is one constant in the modern state, it is the need for information. Whether on tax forms, in OSHA or EPA inspections, in SEC investigations, or through the various ways government employers monitor their employees, the government is constantly inspecting otherwise private places or requiring citizens to produce (or to step aside and let the government uncover) otherwise private information. Presumably, the privacy value that underlies *Boyd* applies to information gathering *outside* the criminal process — after all, the privacy intrusion does not depend on whether it is a police officer or an IRS agent who is doing the looking. Does this mean that any attempt to seriously protect privacy would place severe limits on government activities that we have come to accept as routine? Does that explain *Boyd*'s checkered history? Does it imply that constitutional protection of individual privacy is necessarily linked with pro-"laissez-faire" constitutional law? The answer to each of these questions is "yes," according to William J. Stuntz, Privacy's Problem and the Law of Criminal Procedure, 93 Mich. L. Rev. 1016, 1030-1034, 1050-1054 (1995):

> Law enforcement, civil or criminal, depends on information. That information is often "private" in the sense that it rests in the hands of someone who would like it kept secret. This description fits almost all incriminating evidence in the hands of a criminal defendant, information that sometimes cannot be extracted due to the Fifth Amendment. Much of the information the system needs is also "private" in a more

meaningful sense. It is of a type that many people, not just a particular litigant, might care about keeping secret. A cocaine dealer may be convicted because of drugs found in his bedroom closet; even those who comply with the drug laws wish to keep people out of their bedroom closets. A fraud conviction may depend on evidence of a large bank deposit on a given date; even wholly honest citizens value the secrecy of their bank transactions.

Fourth Amendment law purports to protect most information that is private in this second sense. . . .

If one starts with this definition of private, protecting private information outside the criminal context would have huge substantive effects, especially if the information is protected absolutely — without any provision for disclosure in response to a showing of relevance or need or cause. . . . [I]n any system that seeks to do more than pro forma regulation of business or finance or that tries to police the distribution of guns or drugs, absolute protection of private information is unacceptable unless private is defined so narrowly as to make the enterprise pointless. Much criminal law enforcement, and an even larger category of civil regulation, would be impossible. . . .

That, in a nutshell, is the substantive problem with protecting the kinds of privacy interests we claim to protect in search and seizure cases. Wherever the regulatory state engages in any form of compelled information gathering (and it does so everywhere), there is an enormous cost to taking privacy interests seriously: doing so requires judicial judgments about whether one regulatory path is more reasonable than another. That sounds uncomfortably close to the regime that the Supreme Court sought to bury a half-century ago [as it began the process of limiting *Boyd*'s reach]. . . .

Had the cases continued along the path [of a broad reading of *Boyd*], *Boyd* might have come to play much the same role in constitutional law, and perhaps the same villain's role in constitutional theory, that Lochner v. New York and its ilk came to play. Government regulation required lots of information, and *Boyd* came dangerously close to giving regulated actors a blanket entitlement to nondisclosure. It is hard to see how modern health, safety, environmental, or economic regulation would be possible in such a regime.

As it happened, the cases did not continue along *Boyd*'s path. Beginning in the first decade of this century, *Boyd* was effectively cabined, so much so that its implications for the world outside criminal justice have been largely forgotten. Hale v. Henkel held that corporations have no privilege against self-incrimination and receive only slight protection against unreasonable searches and seizures. Marron v. United States held that instrumentalities of crime could be seized without violating the Fourth or Fifth Amendments, and also that documents could be instrumentalities. Shapiro v. United States held that the privilege was not violated by asking someone to produce "required records" — meaning any records that the government ordered him to keep — no matter how incriminating the records' contents might be. These cases left *Boyd* largely inapplicable to the burgeoning world of government regulation. The records in *Boyd* itself were probably instrumentalities under *Marron*, and the documents sought in the various ICC cases of the 1890s might well have been judged "required records" by the standards used a half-century later.

The Court did not explain its position in these cases in privacy terms. By and large, it justified the outcomes by political necessity. *Hale*, which arose out of a grand jury investigation of antitrust violations, is the clearest example. The argument for a corporate privilege was strong: Wigmore, then the foremost expert on the privilege's scope and meaning, thought it applied to corporations as it did to individuals. That was the position the Court had taken with respect to the Due Process Clause, and like that clause the Fifth Amendment privilege applied to "any person." Moreover, the privacy interest in corporate documents was at least as plausible as *Boyd*'s privacy interest in his invoices. Even if a corporation could not "feel" privacy intrusions, its shareholders and employees could; as with due process claims, corporate assertion of the privilege against self-incrimination was a way of protecting the flesh-and-blood people whose money and labor made the corporation run. *Hale* rejected all these arguments in a peremptory paragraph, stating that "the privilege claimed would practically nullify" the Sherman Act.

In other words, *Boyd*-style privacy protection was not compatible with activist government, because government cannot be very activist if it cannot force people to tell it things. Cases like *Hale* resolved the conflict by yielding ground — preserving privacy protection, but only within boundaries that themselves had nothing whatever to do with privacy. Privacy's substantive shadow was kept within acceptable bounds, but only by fiat.

Professor Stuntz both accurately captures the consistent reduction in the significance of the *Boyd* case and identifies its cause in the demands of the modern bureaucratic state.

7. Perhaps the most remarkable aspect of *Boyd*'s demise has been its consistency. With the exception of a few ambiguous paragraphs scattered throughout the cases on the potential scope of immunity following responses to subpoenas, the Supreme Court has consistently cut back the potential scope of *Boyd*-like claims — at least until United States v. Hubbell, 530 U.S. 27 (2000).

In *Hubbell*, the Office of the Independent Counsel (OIC) was investigating Webster Hubbell, a former high-ranking official in the Justice Department, for obstructing justice. As part of its investigation, the OIC issued a broad grand jury subpoena, seeking voluminous personal and business records directly from Hubbell, who resisted on the ground that the act of producing these documents would incriminate him — that is, he claimed that the production of the documents would "testify" that the documents existed, that Hubbell had them within his control, and that the documents were authentic. The OIC then granted Hubbell immunity for the act of production, and Hubbell collected and produced the subpoenaed documents to the grand jury.

After reviewing the documents, the OIC concluded that Hubbell had actually committed tax crimes, and indicted him despite the prior grant of immunity. The OIC argued that it was not making prohibited use of Hubbell's immunized testimony about the existence, control, and authenticity of the documents, because it had no plans to use the physical production to inform the jury of any of these facts. Instead, said the OIC, the government had simply used the contents of the documents to further its investigation, and since no one had compelled Hubbell to create the documents, the Fifth Amendment was not implicated.

The Court disagreed, ruling that because the OIC was not aware of the documents in question before issuing the subpoena, it was in fact making improper use of Hubbell's "testimony" that the documents existed. While the Court agreed that the physical act of producing the documents — like the act of putting on a shirt or providing a voice exemplar — did not implicate the Fifth Amendment, Hubbell's actions were different, because "[i]t was unquestionably necessary for respondent to make extensive use of 'the contents of his own mind' in identifying the hundreds of documents responsive to the requests in the subpoena." 530 U.S., at 43. In addition, said the Court, "[t]he assembly of those documents was like telling an inquisitor the combination to a wall safe, not like being forced to surrender the key to a strongbox." Id. Thus, any information the government learned as a result of that act of production, including the information contained in the documents themselves, was impermissible.

The precise impact of *Hubbell* is unclear. Does it matter whether "extensive use" of the contents of the mind is required rather than only minimal use, or is it any use of the contents of the mind that matters? What, exactly, is the difference between surrendering a key to a strongbox and disclosing the combination to a safe? It cannot simply be the difference between an act and a statement. That is precisely the distinction the Court rejected in *Hubbell* when it asserted that the assembling of the documents called for by the subpoena was the "functional equivalent of the preparation of an answer to either a detailed written interrogatory or a series of oral questions at a discovery deposition" and therefore within the protections of the Fifth Amendment. Id., at 41-42.

For one effort to answer these various questions, see Ronald J. Allen & Kristin Mace, The Fifth Amendment Explained and Its Future Predicted, 94 J. Crim. L. & Criminology 243-294 (2004), who argue that the future of the Fifth Amendment prong of *Boyd* will be determined by how the tension between *Hubbell* and *Fisher* is resolved. *Fisher* seemed to indicate that the contents and makeup of papers turned over were not derivative fruits of the act of production and that merely responding to a subpoena was not necessarily incriminating for the purposes of the Fifth Amendment. *Hubbell* casts doubt on both propositions. Thus, future cases will need to resolve the scope of the derivative fruits doctrine and whether any cognition at all in responding to a subpoena triggers the Fifth Amendment, or instead whether "extensive" cognition is required.

8. Whatever the meaning of *Hubbell* turns out to be, remember that the case deals only with the Fifth Amendment branch of the *Boyd* jurisprudence; the Fourth Amendment branch remains untouched. Thus, if a search warrant could have been issued for these same documents, the government would have had an alternative route to obtaining them. As you shall see, that depends on whether the government had probable cause to seize the documents as evidence of some crime and whether they could be described with sufficient "particularity" to satisfy the Fourth Amendment. One cannot tell from the case itself whether either requirement could have been satisfied. It is interesting, but by no means dispositive of these matters, to note that what Hubbell was eventually indicted for had nothing to do with the investigation that generated the subpoena in the first place.

Whether *Boyd* should be extolled or vilified, its ideal continues to exert a powerful hold on the legal imagination. As the following chapters show, the goal of privacy protection is far from dead in the law of criminal procedure. Notwithstanding the repeated claims of its demise, *Boyd* still casts a large shadow.

Chapter 5

The Fourth Amendment

The Fourth Amendment plays two key roles in the American legal order. First, it is the law's chief source of privacy protection. The Fourth Amendment's domain extends to "all invasions on the part of the government and its employees of the sanctity of a man's home and the privacies of life" — so the Supreme Court said in 1886: four years *before* Samuel Warren and Louis Brandeis penned the essay widely credited with making privacy a central concept in American law. See Boyd v. United States, 116 U.S. 616, 630 (1886); Samuel D. Warren & Louis D. Brandeis, The Right of Privacy, 4 Harv. L. Rev. 193 (1890). For most of American history, that privacy protection was aspirational only; it had little practical relevance. Only federal officials were bound by *Boyd* to respect the sanctity of homes and "the privacies of life," since the Fourth Amendment applied only to the federal government — and the federal government's criminal law enforcement apparatus was quite small. Local police agencies were much more likely to invade individual privacy, and those agencies were subject to no serious legal regulation, constitutional or otherwise. That state of affairs changed in 1961, when the Supreme Court held that the Fourth Amendment's exclusionary rule applied in state and federal cases alike. Mapp v. Ohio, 367 U.S. 643 (1961). *Mapp* gave Fourth Amendment law its teeth. *Boyd* ensured that the law *Mapp* enforced was grounded in privacy.

The second role Fourth Amendment law plays concerns not the interests being protected but rather the actors being regulated. The Fourth Amendment applies to all government actors, but it is almost always enforced against police officers. It is not too much to say that the Fourth Amendment functions as a kind of tort law for the police, the chief source of legal regulation of criminal law enforcement. Since there are more than 13 million arrests each year, and 750,000 police officers working for local, state, or federal governments, the task of regulating police is obviously important — indeed, *some* regulation of policing is essential to any free society.

And legal regulation of police searches and arrests consists mostly of Fourth Amendment regulation. There is a state law of search and seizure, but until the last generation it was very thin; the number of reported state cases discussing search and seizure claims before 1961 was trivially small. Today, most state-law search and seizure cases arise under state constitutional provisions that parallel the federal Fourth Amendment; the arguments and holdings in those cases tend to track arguments that appear in Fourth Amendment cases. And police training programs, which once (again, before 1961) ignored training in the law, now offer elaborate instruction in legal rules — mostly Fourth Amendment rules.

This is quite different from the state of affairs that prevails elsewhere in federal constitutional law. Most of constitutional law defines outer bounds within which the government may operate; the rules that define ordinary government operations are nonconstitutional. For the people who run public schools or government hospitals, constitutional law has little to do with the day-to-day business of those institutions. For police, Fourth Amendment law is the primary source of legal restraint; it regulates ordinary, run-of-the-mill interactions between officers and suspects.

These two roles — protecting privacy and regulating the police — may be more important in the twenty-first century than ever before. Advances in information technology place privacy at greater risk than in an age when police used eyes and ears rather than electronics to monitor suspects. Yet, in an age of terrorism, police *need* to do a lot of monitoring: The costs of regulating the police badly may be measured in lives lost, perhaps thousands of them. One question you should keep in mind, as you study the materials in this chapter, is whether the law regulates wisely — whether privacy is adequately protected without disabling the police from guarding public safety.

Text and History

One of the large stories of the past generation in constitutional law is the revival of attention to the constitutional text and the original intent of the men who wrote and ratified it. This revival has been less pronounced in Fourth Amendment law than in some other areas; even so, text-and-history arguments appear frequently in the materials that follow.

The text of the Fourth Amendment is uncomplicated:

> The right of the people to be secure in their persons, houses, papers, and effects, against unreasonable searches and seizures, shall not be violated, and no warrants shall issue, but upon probable cause, supported by oath or affirmation, and particularly describing the place to be searched, and the persons or things to be seized.

Notice that the first clause of the Amendment defines the prohibition — no "unreasonable searches and seizures." The second clause places some restrictions on the issuance of warrants, the most important being the requirement of probable cause. The relationship between the two clauses is, on the face of the text, unclear; it will be explored in detail in Section C, infra. For now, it is enough to say that one conventional reading of the text, the one adopted in nearly all Supreme Court opinions in the years after *Mapp*, treats probable cause and a warrant as defining the usual conditions for a "reasonable" search or seizure. Today, however, the Supreme Court more usually treats reasonableness as a freestanding concept, not necessarily anchored to warrants or probable cause. The results of that trend are explored in Section D, infra.

This relatively simple text has a relatively simple history. Although there are serious debates about some aspects of the story, most scholars agree on the basic outlines. The Fourth Amendment arose out of a trio of famous eighteenth-century cases, two from England and one from the colonies. The less famous of the two English cases was Entick v. Carrington, 19 Howell's State Trials 1029 (C.P. 1765), which is discussed at length in Boyd v. United States, page 296, supra. Entick was an English pamphleteer critical of the King's ministers. As part of a seditious libel investigation, a warrant was issued authorizing Entick's arrest and the seizure of all his books and papers. The warrant was carried out; Entick sued for trespass, and he won a verdict of 300 pounds. The other English case was Wilkes v. Wood, 19 Howell's State Trials 1153 (C.P. 1763). Wilkes was likewise a pamphleteer, and also a well-known Member of Parliament, perhaps the most popular man in England in his day. He too was a critic of the government, and he too was rewarded with arrest, search of his home, and the seizure of his books and papers (some 49 of Wilkes's friends received the same treatment). All these searches and seizures were made pursuant to a warrant that neither named suspects nor specified places to be searched. Like Entick, Wilkes and a number of his friends sued for trespass and won; in Wilkes's case, the verdict was 1,000 pounds, a considerable sum at the time. Both *Entick* and *Wilkes* won renown in the American colonies in the years leading up to the American Revolution; the judge who presided over both their trials, Lord Camden, was a colonial hero for whom a number of American cities and counties were named.

The third case arose in colonial Massachusetts, where customs inspectors were seeking to crack down on the smuggling that dominated Boston's economy. To aid them in that task, inspectors used "writs of assistance," which were issued by the King and which authorized the inspectors both to draft assistance (hence the name of the writs) and to search any place where smuggled goods might be concealed. In 1761 in *The Writs of Assistance Case*, James Otis argued, on behalf of some of the smugglers, that these writs conveyed no legal authority. Otis lost, but according to John Adams, his argument was the beginning of the Revolution — in Adams's words, "Then and there was the child Independence born."

Whatever else the Fourth Amendment was about, it was probably designed to enact the results in *Entick* and *Wilkes* and to overturn the result in *The Writs of Assistance Case*. Notice that none of the three cases involved a typical instance of criminal law enforcement: These were not investigations of murders, rapes, or robberies. Indeed, two of the three cases — *Entick* and *Wilkes* — arose out of investigations that could not happen today, because they would be clear violations of the *First* Amendment. Notice too that the officials who conducted the searches in these cases were not ordinary police officers — in *Entick* and *Wilkes*, they were "messengers," special agents of the Crown; in *The Writs of Assistance Case*, they were customs inspectors. That is no accident; ordinary police officers did not exist, either in eighteenth-century England or in the colonies. The first police force was established in London in 1829; American police forces were born, one by one, between that date and about 1870. Thus, the Fourth Amendment — the prime source of legal restraint for the police — was written before the police existed, at least in anything like the form they take today. That fact should make us cautious when seeking to determine the "original understanding" of contemporary Fourth Amendment issues.

Remedy and Right

Today, Fourth Amendment litigation overwhelmingly involves challenges to searches and seizures conducted by the police in the course of investigating or enforcing ordinary criminal prohibitions — homicide, rape, theft, and, especially, drug violations. The large majority of those challenges occur in criminal cases, as defendants seek to suppress evidence they claim the police seized in violation of the Fourth Amendment.

There are other remedies for Fourth Amendment violations — they are explored in Section A.2, infra — but the dominant one, the one that is invoked most often by far, is the exclusionary rule. Motions to suppress illegally seized physical evidence are filed in 5 percent of criminal cases (defendants win 17 percent of those motions). See Peter F. Nardulli, The Societal Cost of the Exclusionary Rule: An Empirical Assessment, [1983] Am. Bar Found. Res. J. 595, 595-596. Even if only a quarter of all arrests produce a criminal case, that would mean roughly 175,000 suppression motions per year, nationwide. The number of civil lawsuits against police for Fourth Amendment violations is, at most, a few thousand per year. The number of criminal prosecutions of the police who violate the Fourth Amendment is a few dozen.

That may have a large effect on the substance of Fourth Amendment law. The exclusionary rule shapes the kinds of Fourth Amendment cases judges see. All exclusionary rule claims seek to suppress incriminating evidence; if no incriminating evidence is found, there is nothing for the defendant to exclude. Thus, judges see the cases where the police find cocaine in the car, not the cases where they find nothing. Perhaps that affects the way judges think about car searches. You should consider, as you read the cases that follow, how the presence of the exclusionary rule might have affected judicial perceptions about different kinds of searches, and how those perceptions might have affected the Fourth Amendment doctrines those cases discuss.

We begin the chapter with a brief consideration of the exclusionary rule and some of its possible alternatives, because the rule is so important to so many features of Fourth Amendment law. The chapter then turns to the substance of Fourth Amendment law — what the Fourth Amendment requires of the police or the other officials — and then returns, in Section F, to a more detailed consideration of the exclusionary rule and its scope.

A. Remedies

1. The Exclusionary Rule

MAPP v. OHIO

Appeal from the Supreme Court of Ohio
367 U.S. 643 (1961)

MR. JUSTICE CLARK delivered the opinion of the Court.

Appellant stands convicted of knowingly having had in her possession and under her control certain lewd and lascivious books, pictures, and photographs in violation of §2905.34 of Ohio's Revised Code.[2] . . . [T]he Supreme Court of Ohio found that her conviction was valid though "based primarily upon the introduction in evidence of lewd and lascivious books and pictures unlawfully seized during an unlawful search of defendant's home. . . ."

On May 23, 1957, three Cleveland police officers arrived at appellant's residence in that city pursuant to information that "a person [was] hiding out in the home, who was wanted for questioning in connection with a recent bombing, and that there

2. The statute provides in pertinent part that

No person shall knowingly . . . have in his possession or under his control an obscene, lewd, or lascivious book [or] . . . , picture. . . .

Whoever violates this section shall be fined not less than two hundred nor more than two thousand dollars or imprisoned not less than one nor more than seven years, or both.

was a large amount of policy paraphernalia being hidden in the home." Miss Mapp and her daughter by a former marriage lived on the top floor of the two-family dwelling. Upon their arrival at that house, the officers knocked on the door and demanded entrance but appellant, after telephoning her attorney, refused to admit them without a search warrant. They advised their headquarters of the situation and undertook a surveillance of the house.

The officers again sought entrance some three hours later when four or more additional officers arrived on the scene. When Miss Mapp did not come to the door immediately, at least one of the several doors to the house was forcibly opened[3] and the policemen gained admittance. Meanwhile Miss Mapp's attorney arrived, but the officers, having secured their own entry, and continuing in their defiance of the law, would permit him neither to see Miss Mapp nor to enter the house. It appears that Miss Mapp was halfway down the stairs from the upper floor to the front door when the officers, in this highhanded manner, broke into the hall. She demanded to see the search warrant. A paper, claimed to be a warrant, was held up by one of the officers. She grabbed the "warrant" and placed it in her bosom. A struggle ensued in which the officers recovered the piece of paper and as a result of which they handcuffed appellant because she had been "belligerent" in resisting their official rescue of the "warrant" from her person. Running rough-shod over appellant, a policeman "grabbed" her, "twisted [her] hand," and she "yelled [and] pleaded with him" because "it was hurting." Appellant, in handcuffs, was then forcibly taken upstairs to her bedroom where the officers searched a dresser, a chest of drawers, a closet and some suitcases. They also looked into a photo album and through personal papers belonging to the appellant. The search spread to the rest of the second floor including the child's bedroom, the living room, the kitchen and a dinette. The basement of the building and a trunk found therein were also searched. The obscene materials for possession of which she was ultimately convicted were discovered in the course of that widespread search.

At the trial no search warrant was produced by the prosecution, nor was the failure to produce one explained or accounted for. At best, "There is, in the record, considerable doubt as to whether there ever was any warrant for the search of defendant's home." 170 Ohio St., at 430, 166 N.E.2d, at 389. The Ohio Supreme Court believed a "reasonable argument" could be made that the conviction should be reversed "because the 'methods' employed to obtain the [evidence] . . . were such as to offend a sense of justice," but the court found determinative the fact that the evidence had not been taken "from defendant's person by the use of brutal or offensive physical force against defendant."

The State says that even if the search were made without authority, or otherwise unreasonably, it is not prevented from using the unconstitutionally seized evidence at trial, citing Wolf v. Colorado, 338 U.S. 25 (1949), in which this Court did indeed hold "that in a prosecution in a State court for a State crime the Fourteenth Amendment does not forbid the admission of evidence obtained by an unreasonable search and seizure." On this appeal, . . . it is urged once again that we review that holding.[4]

---

3. A police officer testified that "we did pry the screen door to gain entrance"; the attorney on the scene testified that a policeman "tried . . . to kick in the door" and then "broke the glass in the door and somebody reached in and opened the door and let them in"; the appellant testified that "The back door was broken."

4. Other issues have been raised on this appeal but, in the view we have taken of the case, they need not be decided. Although appellant chose to urge what may have appeared to be the surer ground for

Seventy-five years ago, in Boyd v. United States, 116 U.S. 616, 630 (1886), considering the Fourth and Fifth Amendments as running "almost into each other" on the facts before it, this Court held that the doctrines of those Amendments "apply to all invasions on the part of the government and its employees of the sanctity of a man's home and the privacies of life." . . . The Court noted that "constitutional provisions for the security of person and property should be liberally construed. . . . It is the duty of courts to be watchful for the constitutional rights of the citizen, and against any stealthy encroachments thereon." . . . Less than 30 years after *Boyd*, this Court, in Weeks v. United States, 232 U.S. 383 (1914), stated that "the Fourth Amendment . . . put the courts of the United States and Federal officials, in the exercise of their power and authority, under limitations and restraints." . . . Specifically dealing with the use of the evidence unconstitutionally seized, the Court concluded:

> If letters and private documents can thus be seized and held and used in evidence against a citizen accused of an offense, the protection of the Fourth Amendment declaring his right to be secure against such searches and seizures is of no value, and, so far as those thus placed are concerned, might as well be *stricken from* the Constitution. . . .

Finally, the Court in that case clearly stated that use of the seized evidence involved "a denial of the constitutional rights of the accused." . . .

In 1949, 35 years after *Weeks* was announced, this Court, in Wolf v. Colorado, supra, . . . discussed the effect of the Fourth Amendment upon the States through the operation of the Due Process Clause of the Fourteenth Amendment. . . . [A]fter declaring that the "security of one's privacy against arbitrary intrusion by the police" is "implicit in 'the concept of ordered liberty' and as such enforceable against the States through the Due Process Clause," and announcing that it "stoutly adhere[d]" to the *Weeks* decision, the Court decided that the *Weeks* exclusionary rule would not then be imposed upon the States as "an essential ingredient of the right." The Court's reasons for not considering essential to the right to privacy, as a curb imposed upon the States by the Due Process Clause, that which decades before had been posited as part and parcel of the Fourth Amendment's limitation upon federal encroachment of individual privacy, were bottomed on factual considerations. . . .

The Court in *Wolf* first stated that "the contrariety of views of the States" on the adoption of the exclusionary rule of *Weeks* was "particularly impressive"; and, in this connection, that it could not "brush aside the experience of States which deem the incidence of such conduct by the police too slight to call for a deterrent remedy . . . by overriding the [States'] relevant rules of evidence." While in 1949, prior to the *Wolf* case, almost two-thirds of the States were opposed to the use of the exclusionary rule, now, despite the *Wolf* case, more than half of those since passing upon it, by their own legislative or judicial decision, have wholly or partly adopted or adhered to the *Weeks* rule. Significantly, among those now following the rule is California, which, according to its highest court, was "compelled to reach that conclusion because other remedies have completely failed to secure compliance with the constitutional provisions. . . ." People v. Cahan, 44 Cal. 2d 434, 445, 282 P.2d 905, 911 (1955). In connection with this California case, we note that the second basis

---

favorable disposition and did not insist that *Wolf* be overruled, the amicus curiae, who was also permitted to participate in the oral argument, did urge the Court to overrule *Wolf*.

elaborated in *Wolf* in support of its failure to enforce the exclusionary doctrine against the States was that "other means of protection" have been afforded "the right to privacy." 338 U.S., at 30. The experience of California that such other remedies have been worthless and futile is buttressed by the experience of other States. . . .

Likewise, time has set its face against what *Wolf* called the "weighty testimony" of People v. Defore, 242 N.Y. 13, 150 N.E. 585 (1926). There Justice (then Judge) Cardozo, rejecting adoption of the *Weeks* exclusionary rule in New York, had said that "the Federal rule as it stands is either too strict or too lax." 242 N.Y., at 22, 150 N.E., at 588. However, the force of that reasoning has been largely vitiated by later decisions of this Court. These include the recent discarding of the "silver platter" doctrine which allowed federal judicial use of evidence seized in violation of the Constitution by state agents, Elkins v. United States, [364 U.S. 206 (1960)]; the relaxation of the formerly strict requirements as to standing to challenge the use of evidence thus seized, so that now the procedure of exclusion . . . is available to anyone even "legitimately on [the] premises" unlawfully searched, Jones v. United States, 362 U.S. 257, 266-267 (1960); and, finally, the formulation of a method to prevent state use of evidence unconstitutionally seized by federal agents, Rea v. United States, 350 U.S. 214 (1956). . . .

It, therefore, plainly appears that the factual considerations supporting the failure of the *Wolf* Court to include the *Weeks* exclusionary rule when it recognized the enforceability of the right to privacy against the States in 1949, while not basically relevant to the constitutional consideration, could not, in any analysis, now be deemed controlling.

. . . Today we once again examine *Wolf*'s constitutional documentation of the right to privacy free from unreasonable state intrusion, and, after its dozen years on our books, are led by it to close the only courtroom door remaining open to evidence secured by official lawlessness in flagrant abuse of that basic right, reserved to all persons as a specific guarantee against that very same unlawful conduct. We hold that all evidence obtained by searches and seizures in violation of the Constitution is, by that same authority, inadmissible in a state court.

Since the Fourth Amendment's right of privacy has been declared enforceable against the States through the Due Process Clause of the Fourteenth, it is enforceable against them by the same sanction of exclusion as is used against the Federal Government. Were it otherwise, then just as without the *Weeks* rule the assurance against unreasonable federal searches and seizures would be "a form of words," valueless and undeserving of mention in a perpetual charter of inestimable human liberties, so too, without that rule the freedom from state invasions of privacy would be so ephemeral and so neatly severed from its conceptual nexus with the freedom from all brutish means of coercing evidence as not to merit this Court's high regard as a freedom "implicit in the concept of ordered liberty." . . . [T]he admission of the new constitutional right by *Wolf* could not consistently tolerate denial of its most important constitutional privilege, namely, the exclusion of the evidence which an accused had been forced to give by reason of the unlawful seizure. To hold otherwise is to grant the right but in reality to withhold its privilege and enjoyment. Only last year the Court itself recognized that the purpose of the exclusionary rule "is to deter — to compel respect for the constitutional guaranty in the only effectively available way — by removing the incentive to disregard it." Elkins v. United States, supra, at 217. . . .

Moreover, our holding that the exclusionary rule is an essential part of both the Fourth and Fourteenth Amendments is not only the logical dictate of prior cases, but it also makes very good sense. There is no war between the Constitution and common sense. Presently, a federal prosecutor may make no use of evidence illegally seized, but a State's attorney across the street may, although he supposedly is operating under the enforceable prohibitions of the same Amendment. Thus the State, by admitting evidence unlawfully seized, serves to encourage disobedience to the Federal Constitution which it is bound to uphold. Moreover, as was said in *Elkins*, "the very essence of a healthy federalism depends upon the avoidance of needless conflict between state and federal courts." 364 U.S., at 221. . . . In nonexclusionary States, federal officers, being human, were . . . invited to and did, as our cases indicate, step across the street to the State's attorney with their unconstitutionally seized evidence. Prosecution on the basis of that evidence was then had in a state court in utter disregard of the enforceable Fourth Amendment. If the fruits of an unconstitutional search had been inadmissible in both state and federal courts, this inducement to evasion would have been sooner eliminated. . . .

There are those who say, as did Justice (then Judge) Cardozo, that under our constitutional exclusionary doctrine "the criminal is to go free because the constable has blundered." People v. Defore, 242 N.Y., at 21, 150 N.E., at 587. In some cases this will undoubtedly be the result. But, as was said in *Elkins*, "there is another consideration — the imperative of judicial integrity." 364 U.S., at 222. The criminal goes free, if he must, but it is the law that sets him free. Nothing can destroy a government more quickly than its failure to observe its own laws, or worse, its disregard of the charter of its own existence. As Mr. Justice Brandeis, dissenting, said in Olmstead v. United States, 277 U.S. 438, 485 (1928): "Our Government is the potent, the omnipresent teacher. For good or for ill, it teaches the whole people by its example. . . . If the Government becomes a lawbreaker, it breeds contempt for law; it invites every man to become a law unto himself; it invites anarchy." Nor can it lightly be assumed that, as a practical matter, adoption of the exclusionary rule fetters law enforcement. Only last year this Court expressly considered that contention and found that "pragmatic evidence of a sort" to the contrary was not wanting. Elkins v. United States, supra, at 218. The Court noted that

> The federal courts themselves have operated under the exclusionary rule of *Weeks* for almost half a century; yet it has not been suggested either that the Federal Bureau of Investigation has thereby been rendered ineffective, or that the administration of criminal justice in the federal courts has thereby been disrupted. Moreover, the experience of the states is impressive. . . . The movement towards the rule of exclusion has been halting but seemingly inexorable.

Id., at 218-219.

The ignoble shortcut to conviction left open to the State tends to destroy the entire system of constitutional restraints on which the liberties of the people rest. Having once recognized that the right to privacy embodied in the Fourth Amendment is enforceable against the States, and that the right to be secure against rude invasions of privacy by state officers is, therefore, constitutional in origin, we can no longer permit that right to remain an empty promise. Because it is enforceable in the same manner and to like effect as other basic rights secured by the Due Process Clause, we can no longer permit it to be revocable at the whim of any police officer who, in the name of law enforcement itself, chooses to suspend its enjoyment. Our decision, founded on reason and truth, gives to the individual no more than that which the Constitution guarantees him, to the police officer no less than that to which honest law enforcement is entitled, and, to the courts, that judicial integrity so necessary in the true administration of justice. . . .

MR. JUSTICE BLACK, concurring.

. . . I am . . . not persuaded that the Fourth Amendment, standing alone, would be enough to bar the introduction into evidence against an accused of papers and effects seized from him in violation of its commands. For the Fourth Amendment does not itself contain any provision expressly precluding the use of such evidence, and I am extremely doubtful that such a provision could properly be inferred from nothing more than the basic command against unreasonable searches and seizures. . . . [But] when the Fourth Amendment's ban against unreasonable searches and seizures is considered together with the Fifth Amendment's ban against compelled self-incrimination, a constitutional basis emerges which not only justifies but actually requires the exclusionary rule.

The close interrelationship between the Fourth and Fifth Amendments, as they apply to this problem, has long been recognized and, indeed, was expressly made the ground for this Court's holding in Boyd v. United States. There the Court fully discussed this relationship and declared itself "unable to perceive that the seizure of a man's private books and papers to be used in evidence against him is substantially different from compelling him to be a witness against himself." . . . In the final analysis, it seems to me that the *Boyd* doctrine, though perhaps not required by the express language of the Constitution strictly construed, is amply justified from an historical standpoint, soundly based in reason, and entirely consistent with what I regard to be the proper approach to interpretation of our Bill of Rights. . . .

MR. JUSTICE DOUGLAS, concurring.

. . . This criminal proceeding started with a lawless search and seizure. The police entered a home forcefully, and seized documents that were later used to convict the occupant of a crime. . . .

The only remaining remedy, if exclusion of the evidence is not required, is an action of trespass by the homeowner against the offending officer. . . . The truth is that trespass actions against officers who make unlawful searches and seizures are mainly illusory remedies.

Without judicial action making the exclusionary rule applicable to the States, Wolf v. Colorado in practical effect reduced the guarantee against unreasonable searches and seizures to "a dead letter," as Mr. Justice Rutledge said in his dissent. See 338 U.S., at 47.

[*Wolf*] was decided in 1949. The immediate result was a storm of constitutional controversy which only today finds its end. I believe that this is an appropriate case in which to put an end to the asymmetry which *Wolf* imported into the law. It is an appropriate case because the facts it presents show — as would few other cases — the casual arrogance of those who have the untrammelled power to invade one's home and to seize one's person. . . .

Memorandum of MR. JUSTICE STEWART.

. . . I express no view as to the merits of the constitutional issue which the Court today decides. I would, however, reverse the judgment in this case, because I am persuaded that the provision of §2905.34 of the Ohio Revised Code, upon which the petitioner's conviction was based, is, in the words of Mr. Justice Harlan, not "consistent with the rights of free thought and expression assured against state action by the Fourteenth Amendment."

MR. JUSTICE HARLAN, whom MR. JUSTICE FRANKFURTER and MR. JUSTICE WHITTAKER join, dissenting.

In overruling the *Wolf* case the Court, in my opinion, has forgotten the sense of judicial restraint which, with due regard for stare decisis, is one element that should enter into deciding whether a past decision of this Court should be overruled. Apart from that I also believe that the *Wolf* rule represents sounder Constitutional doctrine than the new rule which now replaces it. . . .

At the heart of the majority's opinion in this case is the following syllogism: (1) the rule excluding in federal criminal trials evidence which is the product of an illegal search and seizure is "part and parcel" of the Fourth Amendment; (2) *Wolf* held that the "privacy" assured against federal action by the Fourth Amendment is also protected against state action by the Fourteenth Amendment; and (3) it is therefore "logically and constitutionally necessary" that the *Weeks* exclusionary rule should also be enforced against the States.

This reasoning ultimately rests on the unsound premise that because *Wolf* carried into the States, as part of "the concept of ordered liberty" embodied in the Fourteenth Amendment, the principle of "privacy" underlying the Fourth Amendment, it must follow that whatever configurations of the Fourth Amendment have been developed in the particularizing federal precedents are likewise to be deemed a part of "ordered liberty," and as such are enforceable against the States. For me, this does not follow at all. . . .

I would not impose upon the States this federal exclusionary remedy. The reasons given by the majority for now suddenly turning its back on *Wolf* seem to me notably unconvincing.

First, it is said that "the factual grounds upon which *Wolf* was based" have since changed, in that more States now follow the *Weeks* exclusionary rule than was so at the time *Wolf* was decided. While that is true, a recent survey indicates that at present one-half of the States still adhere to the common-law non-exclusionary rule, and one, Maryland, retains the rule as to felonies. But in any case surely all this is beside the point, as the majority itself indeed seems to recognize. Our concern here, as it was in *Wolf*, is not with the desirability of that rule but only with the question whether the States are Constitutionally free to follow it or not as they may themselves determine, and the relevance of the disparity of views among the States on this point lies simply in the fact that the judgment involved is a debatable one. . . .

The preservation of a proper balance between state and federal responsibility in the administration of criminal justice demands patience on the part of those who might like to see things move faster among the States in this respect. Problems of criminal law enforcement vary widely from State to State. One State, in considering the totality of its legal picture, may conclude that the need for embracing the *Weeks* rule is pressing because other remedies are unavailable or inadequate to secure compliance with the substantive Constitutional principle involved. Another, though equally solicitous of Constitutional rights, may choose to pursue one purpose at a time, allowing all evidence relevant to guilt to be brought into a criminal trial, and dealing with Constitutional infractions by other means. Still another may consider the exclusionary rule too rough-and-ready a remedy, in that it reaches only unconstitutional intrusions which eventuate in criminal prosecution of the victims. Further, a State after experimenting with the *Weeks* rule for a time may, because of unsatisfactory experience with it, decide to revert to a non-exclusionary rule. And so on. . . .

[W]e are told that imposition of the *Weeks* rule on the States makes "very good sense," in that it will promote recognition by state and federal officials of their "mutual obligation to respect the same fundamental criteria" in their approach to law enforcement, and will avoid "needless conflict between state and federal courts." . . .

An approach which regards the issue as one of achieving procedural symmetry or of serving administrative convenience surely disfigures the boundaries of this Court's functions in relation to the state and federal courts. . . . Here we review state procedures whose measure is to be taken not against the specific substantive commands of the Fourth Amendment but under the flexible contours of the Due Process Clause. I do not believe that the Fourteenth Amendment empowers this Court to mould state remedies effectuating the right to freedom from "arbitrary intrusion by the police" to suit its own notions of how things should be done, as, for instance, the California Supreme Court did in People v. Cahan, 44 Cal. 2d 434, 282 P.2d 905, with reference to procedures in the California courts or as this Court did in *Weeks* for the lower federal courts.

A state conviction comes to us as the complete product of a sovereign judicial system. Typically a case will have been tried in a trial court, tested in some final appellate court, and will go no further. In the comparatively rare instance when a conviction is reviewed by us on due process grounds we deal then with a finished product in the creation of which we are allowed no hand, and our task, far from being one of over-all supervision, is, speaking generally, restricted to a determination of whether the prosecution was Constitutionally fair. The specifics of trial procedure, which in every mature legal system will vary greatly in detail, are within the sole competence of the States. I do not see how it can be said that a trial becomes unfair simply because a State determines that evidence may be considered by the trier of fact, regardless of how it was obtained, if it is relevant to the one issue with which the trial is concerned, the guilt or innocence of the accused. Of course, a court may use its procedures as an incidental means of pursuing other ends than the correct resolution of the controversies before it. Such indeed is the *Weeks* rule, but if a State does not choose to use its courts in this way, I do not believe that this Court is empowered to impose this much-debated procedure on local courts, however efficacious we may consider the *Weeks* rule to be as a means of securing Constitutional rights. . . .

I regret that I find so unwise in principle and so inexpedient in policy a decision motivated by the high purpose of increasing respect for Constitutional rights. But in the last analysis I think this Court can increase respect for the Constitution only if it rigidly respects the limitations which the Constitution places upon it, and respects as well the principles inherent in its own processes. In the present case I think we exceed both, and that our voice becomes only a voice of power, not of reason.

NOTES AND QUESTIONS

1. *Mapp* has an unusual history. It was litigated as a *First* Amendment case; the Fourth Amendment was barely mentioned in the parties' briefs and in the oral argument. The First Amendment question was whether Ohio could criminalize possession of obscene materials in one's home — a serious question that potentially involved both the bounds of obscenity and the question of whether criminal law must distinguish between conduct inside and outside one's dwelling. Mapp's First Amendment argument prevailed eight years later, in Stanley v. Georgia, 394 U.S. 557 (1969), in which the Court struck down a Georgia statute similar to the Ohio statute under which Mapp was convicted.

Does Mapp's First Amendment claim strengthen her Fourth Amendment argument? Does the exclusionary rule seem more palatable in cases in which the crime is substantively questionable? Recall that the Fourth Amendment arose out of seditious libel investigations, which would be unconstitutional today and might have seemed substantively questionable even in the eighteenth century. For an extended discussion of this point, see William J. Stuntz, The Substantive Origins of Criminal Procedure, 105 Yale L.J. 393 (1995).

2. If the nature of the crime in *Mapp* strengthens the argument for an exclusionary rule, might a more serious crime offer a reason for limiting the rule? Why not hold that illegally seized evidence is inadmissible — unless the evidence was seized in a homicide investigation, or in an investigation of terrorist networks?

3. What is the relationship between the exclusionary remedy and the Fourth Amendment right? Is the remedy *part of* the right? Or is it merely a means by which the right is protected? Justice Clark's opinion for the Court in *Mapp* was ambiguous on these questions. Not so Justice Black — notice the emphasis he places on Boyd v. United States, 116 U.S. 616 (1886), which married the Fourth Amendment to the Fifth Amendment's privilege against self-incrimination. The exclusionary rule was, in a sense, the progeny of that marriage. The use of compelled self-incriminating testimony in court was and is a clear violation of the privilege — the privilege was not merely a ban on the compulsion, but also on *the evidentiary use* of that compulsion. If the Fourth Amendment is seen as a kind of adjunct of the Fifth, then the exclusionary rule is a natural part of the Fourth Amendment right.

4. But the Fourth Amendment's text reads differently than the text of the Fifth Amendment. Which leads to one of the most common criticisms of *Mapp*: that the Court's decision runs contrary to the text, since the Fourth Amendment nowhere states that it is to be enforced by an exclusionary rule. See, e.g., Akhil Reed Amar, Fourth Amendment First Principles, 107 Harv. L. Rev. 757 (1994). Of course, the Fourth Amendment does not say anything about other remedies, either. One of the problems the Court faced in *Weeks* and *Wolf* and *Mapp* was how to enforce a prohibition that specifies no means of enforcement. One possibility is to use tort suits, which was roughly the approach the common law took at the time the Fourth Amendment was ratified. But as Justice Douglas's opinion notes, these common law remedies were, in practice, close to nonexistent at the time of *Mapp*: One nationwide survey of judges, prosecutors, defense lawyers, and police chiefs found that 76 percent were unaware of *any* civil suits against police officers for illegal searches or

seizures. See Stuart S. Nagel, Law and Society: Testing the Effects of Excluding Illegally Seized Evidence, [1965] Wis. L. Rev. 283. Should the Court be bound by common law remedies in that setting, or should it be free to craft appropriate remedies of its own?

5. Consider the arguments in the majority opinion. One is that differences in federal and state rules were an invitation to evasion by police at both levels of government. The idea is that local police would search illegally and then hand the evidence over to federal agents, and federal agents would return the favor in other cases. Yet that problem is surely solvable without *Mapp*. Indeed, the Court had already solved it, by holding both that federal prosecutors could not use evidence illegally obtained by state officials, Elkins v. United States, 364 U.S. 206 (1960), and that federal agents could not hand over to state prosecutors the fruits of the agents' illegal searches, Rea v. United States, 350 U.S. 214 (1956).

6. Another reason the majority gave for the result in *Mapp* was "the imperative of judicial integrity." In what sense does admission of illegally obtained evidence conflict with judicial integrity? Might judicial integrity actually cut the other way? Imagine a robbery case in which the stolen goods were found on the defendant immediately after the robbery but suppressed because the search that uncovered them was unconstitutional. At trial, the prosecution puts on testimony of witnesses who placed the defendant near the scene of the robbery, but no one can actually identify the defendant as the robber. The defense, naturally, points out the weaknesses in the government's case. The judge, prosecutor, defense attorney, and defendant all know the defendant was caught red-handed. But the jury doesn't. And the defense is, at least indirectly, striving to persuade the jury that the defendant didn't rob the store, while the defendant, both lawyers, and the judge know he did. Is that process characterized by integrity?

This point highlights a basic problem with the exclusionary rule, and with the Court's integrity argument. On the one hand, one can say, with Justice Clark, that admitting illegally obtained evidence seems to condone the illegality. On the other hand, suppressing it produces a kind of fraud on the fact finder. At the least, concern for the system's integrity seems to be present on both sides of the scale, does it not?

7. The integrity of the system is at issue in another respect. The exclusionary rule is enforced in suppression hearings, in which the most common witnesses are the defendant and the police officer(s) who conducted the search. Defendants tend not to be the most credible of witnesses, because they have a strong motive to lie, in order to exclude the incriminating evidence. The more serious the crime, the stronger that motive, and hence the less credible the defendant. The officer, meanwhile, will tend to be more credible: He may have some incentive to lie as well, but that incentive is less strong than the defendant's, and the officer, unlike the defendant, is not seeking to suppress incriminating evidence. This swearing match creates both the opportunity and the temptation for police perjury.

Morgan Cloud summarizes the evidence on police perjury as follows:

> The empirical studies on the subject suggest that perjured testimony is common, particularly in drug prosecutions. These studies indicate that police officers commit perjury most often to avoid suppression of evidence and to fabricate probable cause, knowing that judges "may 'wink' at obvious police perjury in order to admit incriminating evidence." . . .

Of course, this does not mean that all police officers lie under oath, or that most officers lie, or that even some officers lie all the time. But these empirical studies substantiate the subjective belief common among lawyers, judges, and police officers that police perjury occurs — and frequently enough to be a significant problem for the justice system. We know it exists, but it is impossible to determine with any precision how often it occurs, or how often officers "get away with it."

Morgan Cloud, The Dirty Little Secret, 43 Emory L.J. 1311, 1312-1313 (1994). As Christopher Slobogin notes, the exclusionary rule is at least partly responsible:

The most obvious explanation for all of this lying is a desire to see the guilty brought to "justice." As law enforcement officers, the police do not want a person they know to be a criminal to escape conviction simply because of a "technical" violation of the Constitution [or] a procedural formality.

Christopher Slobogin, Testilying: Police Perjury and What to Do About It, 67 U. Colo. L. Rev. 1037, 1044 (1996). Is this a persuasive argument against the exclusionary rule, or is it merely an argument that the legal system should do a better job of judging the credibility of police testimony?

8. A third argument the Court makes for the exclusionary rule is deterrence. Though this argument was not dominant in *Mapp*, it has become the dominant argument for the exclusionary rule; over the past three decades, the Supreme Court has repeatedly stated that the rule exists *solely* in order to deter violations of the Fourth Amendment. See, e.g., United States v. Leon, 468 U.S. 897 (1984). (*Leon* is reprinted at page 658, infra.) There is a large literature on the subject. For a good summary, see Christopher Slobogin, Why Liberals Should Chuck the Exclusionary Rule, [1999] U. Ill. L. Rev. 363. Slobogin concludes that the evidence is mixed, and not terribly informative:

No one is going to win the empirical debate over whether the exclusionary rule deters the police from committing a significant number of illegal searches and seizures. Most of the studies of the rule suggest that it forces police to pay more attention to the Fourth Amendment than they would without any sanction for illegal searches. At the same time, virtually all the studies also suggest that, for many police officers, concern over the rule is not a significant influence when contemplating a search or seizure. In short, we do not know how much the rule deters.

We probably never will. . . . Observations of police in action, interviews, and questionnaires are probably the best source of data we have. Even here, however, there are significant problems. Observational studies to date have been anecdotal in nature, interviews may be tainted by underreporting of misbehavior, and conclusions drawn from hypothetical questions [e.g., asking police officers whether they would search in a given fact situation] are plagued by the external validity problem familiar to all social scientists who try to draw generalizations . . . from laboratory studies.

. . . [T]hus, one is left with two plausible points of view. . . . Those who favor the rule can reasonably assert that officers who know illegally seized evidence will be excluded cannot help but try to avoid illegal searches because they will have nothing to gain from them. . . . Just as reasonably, those who oppose the rule can point out that its most direct consequence is imposed on the prosecutor rather than the cop, that police know and count on the fact that the rule is rarely applied (for both legal and not-so-legal reasons), and that the rule cannot affect searches and seizures the police believe will not result in prosecution.

Id., at 368-372.

As Slobogin rightly notes, the exclusionary rule matters only if (i) incriminating evidence is found, and (ii) the government wishes to charge the defendant with a crime that the evidence tends to prove. When the police know beforehand that one or both these conditions will be absent, they have no reason to fear application of the exclusionary rule.

That is no small point. Twenty-seven percent of felony arrestees are never convicted of anything, usually because the charges against them were voluntarily dismissed. Sourcebook of Criminal Justice Statistics — 2002, at tbl. 5.57 (available at www.albany.edu/sourcebook). Another 20 percent are convicted (usually by guilty plea) but serve no prison or jail time. See id., at tbl. 5.59. Keep in mind that these are *felony* arrestees; the percentages are higher for misdemeanor arrests. In that kind of world, officers will often care little about evidence to be used in formal adjudications; rather, they will search in order to seize drugs and guns and dispose of them, or to harass or inconvenience suspects, or to "send a message" to gang members on the street, or for some other reason having nothing to do with criminal prosecution. The exclusionary rule provides no deterrent to those kinds of searches. And those may be the kinds of searches that most need deterring.

Plus, of course, when the police behave violently, when they strike or shoot suspects, they are typically not searching for evidence. Consequently, excessive police use of force rarely gives rise to an exclusionary rule claim. The exclusionary rule thus does not contribute to the deterrence of excessive force; other remedies must do that job. All of which says that the exclusionary rule's deterrent benefits are limited, at best.

9. But then, the exclusionary rule's costs seem fairly low. In United States v. Leon, 468 U.S. 897 (1984), the Supreme Court noted studies showing that only 1 or 2 percent of felony arrestees escape punishment because of the exclusionary rule (the figure rises to between 3 and 7 percent when one considers only felony drug arrests). See id., at 907, n. 6.

10. Oddly, one of the exclusionary rule's great virtues may be that it does not deter too *much*. The idea here is that some sort of damages remedy (the usual alternative to exclusion) would overdeter, and that the exclusionary rule solves that overdeterrence problem:

> Police are paid on salary, not by the arrest or search. This is a good thing: Given the enormous scope of criminal liability in our system, we rely heavily on the police to exercise discretion not to search and arrest. This system of payment, coupled with this degree of discretion, is a recipe for overdeterrence. Officers gain little from the marginal legal search, so if they lose something substantial from the marginal illegal one, they may choose simply to search much less often and thereby reduce their exposure.
>
> . . . [Similarly, if] an officer faces serious loss whenever he makes a bad arrest, he will make fewer bad arrests, but also many fewer good ones. The same is true, only more so, if the law threatens the officer with jail for constitutional violations. The social costs of this overdeterrence are surely high: they can be measured by murders and rapes and drug deals that would not have happened if their perpetrators had been put away.
>
> The temptation is to solve this problem by making the government, rather than the individual police officer, bear the immediate costs of legal liability. Unfortunately, that move solves nothing. Most police work for local governments, and most local governments operate under serious budget constraints. The effect of governmental damages

liability for police misconduct mimics the effect of making individual officers pay damages: the locality has an incentive to reduce its liability by reducing the level of policing. And police work is redistributive. Because crime tends to be concentrated in poor neighborhoods, the people who get the biggest benefits from police work do not pay the biggest tax bills. So the government cannot respond to a rise in the cost of police services (which is what broader damages liability means) by charging the beneficiaries of those services more. Just as a government faced with large damages liability for running a municipal pool, which serves poor residents but is paid for by rich ones, may simply close the pool, a government faced with large damages liability for the police may simply reduce the police presence in areas likeliest to give rise to lawsuits. This is overdeterrence writ large.

In a system faced with these problems, suppressing evidence looks like a godsend. Suppression is restitutionary: the officer loses the very thing he gained from the illegal search, and no more. That largely takes care of overdeterrence. And because the rule does not seriously overdeter, courts need not reserve it for the worst constitutional violations. Instead, the exclusionary rule can be applied across the board to the mass of illegal searches and seizures, without fear that doing so will lead officers to stop searching altogether. This gives courts the chance to define just where the constitutional line falls, to develop a working body of law in this area that tells police [what] they should and should not do. These virtues — the ability to deter without overdeterring, coupled with the ability to define the law — are very substantial indeed.

William J. Stuntz, The Virtues and Vices of the Exclusionary Rule, 20 Harv. J.L. & Pub. Pol'y 443, 445-446 (1997). For a contrary argument, suggesting that carefully crafted damages remedies against local governments would work better than the exclusionary rule, see Slobogin, Why Liberals Should Chuck the Exclusionary Rule, 1999 U. Ill. L. Rev. 363, discussed in Note 8, supra.

11. Although Mapp says that "all evidence obtained by searches and seizures in violation of the Constitution is, by that same authority, inadmissible," 367 U.S., at 655, that language should be read with caution. As discussed in Section F of this chapter, in later cases the Court retreats from this sweeping pronouncement, and applies the exclusionary rule in a far more measured — some would say miserly — fashion. See, e.g., Hudson v. Michigan, 547 U.S. 586 (2006) ("Suppression of evidence . . . has always been our last resort, not our first impulse.").

2.   Other Remedies

The exclusionary rule has been a part of the law and popular culture for so long that it is tempting to believe that it has always been a feature of the legal system. But this is not the case. For most of our history, Fourth Amendment rights were enforced chiefly through civil suits for damages, although lawsuits were extremely rare. As a practical matter, before Mapp v. Ohio, 367 U.S. 643 (1961), the Fourth Amendment was not enforced at all — at least not against local police, who perform the vast majority of searches and seizures in the United States. *Mapp* changed that state of affairs by applying the exclusionary rule, previously limited to federal criminal cases, in state criminal cases. Ever since, exclusion of illegally seized evidence has been the primary remedy for Fourth Amendment violations.

In this section, we briefly consider other possible remedies for Fourth Amendment violations. As you read this material, consider what the best mix of remedies might be. What form of relief best compensates victims of illegal searches and arrests? What remedy best deters violations? And importantly, what remedy or remedies pose the least danger of stifling *good* police work?

a. Damages

There are a number of damages actions that are potentially available to people whose Fourth Amendment rights are violated. Unconstitutional searches and seizures may give rise to state tort claims such as false arrest or trespass, or to claims under state constitutions. In addition, 42 U.S.C. §1983 gives plaintiffs a cause of action in federal or state court when their federal constitutional rights have been violated by persons acting under color of state law.[1] In Bivens v. Six Unknown Named Agents of Federal Bureau of Narcotics, 403 U.S. 388 (1971), the Supreme Court recognized a parallel federal common law claim against federal officials. Finally, the Federal Tort Claims Act makes the federal government liable for specified torts of its law enforcement officers, some of which may involve violations of the Fourth Amendment. Consider the following notes on the pros and cons of a civil damage remedy.

1. Federal civil rights claims present some distinct advantages for plaintiffs, including the possibility of class actions and the recovery of attorneys' fees for prevailing litigants. There are, however, substantial obstacles to such claims. The typical Fourth Amendment case — say, a gratuitous frisk or car search — does not involve the kind of physical injury or property damage that would translate into significant money damages, even assuming liability can be established. Particularly if the plaintiffs are unsympathetic (as many criminal suspects are), juries may be unwilling to impose liability or to award more than nominal amounts in such cases, making lawsuits seem not worth the trouble. Even a cursory survey of reported §1983 cases bears out this intuition. Very few involve the automobile, briefcase, or pocket searches common in exclusionary rule litigation. Claims of illegal arrest and police brutality are more common.

2. Another major obstacle is doctrinal: The courts have created a variety of immunity doctrines that limit government damages liability. Liability against a state or local government for state-law torts may only be obtained when sovereign immunity has been waived. States often limit the circumstances in which a suit may be brought against a government agency, while various forms of official immunity may shield its officers. Under the Eleventh Amendment and §1983, meanwhile, states and state agencies are absolutely immune from damages liability for constitutional violations. That immunity does not extend to local governments — or to local police departments — but another one does: Local governments are liable under §1983 only if the relevant constitutional violation was caused by an official policy or custom. Monell v. Department of Social Services, 436 U.S. 658, 694 (1978).

---

1. Section 1983 provides as follows:

Every person who, under color of any statute, ordinance, regulation, custom, or usage of any State or Territory, subjects, or causes to be subjected, any citizen of the United States or any other person within the jurisdiction thereof to the deprivation of any rights, privileges, or immunities secured by the Constitution and laws, shall be liable to the party injured in an action at law, suit in equity, or other proper proceeding for redress.

3. That leaves the question of damages liability for individual police officers. The key doctrine here is qualified immunity — a constitutional fault standard that applies whenever government officials are sued for damages under either §1983 or *Bivens*. In Anderson v. Creighton, 483 U.S. 635 (1987), the Court ruled that damages are available against a police officer who has violated the Fourth Amendment only when he has behaved with something akin to gross negligence — when the governing law and its application to the circumstances facing the officer are clear, and he has nevertheless disregarded them.

Why limit recovery in this way? After all, a large number of people whose Fourth Amendment rights have been violated will receive no compensation under this regime, thus depriving the damages remedy of one of its chief virtues over exclusion — namely, that it will compensate the *innocent* victim.

4. The intersection of the qualified immunity doctrine and the substantive Fourth Amendment claim can be tricky. The plaintiff in Saucier v. Katz, 533 U.S. 194 (2001), was an animal-rights protester who was attending a speech by then-Vice President Al Gore. When Katz began to unfurl a cloth banner he was carrying, two officers grabbed him and led him away; one of the officers shoved Katz into a waiting police van. Katz sued, claiming that the shove constituted excessive use of force in violation of the Fourth Amendment. The Court found that Graham v. Connor, 490 U.S. 386 (1990), governed Katz's claim; under *Graham*, officers may use only that level of force which is reasonable under all the circumstances. Katz contended that qualified immunity must mean the same thing as the underlying Fourth Amendment doctrine — in other words, that unreasonable behavior as a matter of Fourth Amendment law was also sufficient to strip the officers of their qualified immunity, since two layers of "reasonableness" would make no sense. Citing Anderson v. Creighton, supra, the Court rejected the argument:

> Officers can have reasonable, but mistaken, beliefs as to the facts establishing the existence of probable cause or exigent circumstances, . . . and in those situations courts will not hold that they have violated the Constitution. Yet, even if a court were to hold that the officer violated the Fourth Amendment by conducting an unreasonable, warrantless search, *Anderson* still operates to grant officers immunity for reasonable mistakes as to the legality of their actions. The same analysis is applicable in excessive force cases, where in addition to the deference officers receive on the underlying constitutional claim, qualified immunity can apply in the event the mistaken belief was reasonable.

533 U.S., at 206.

5. Perhaps the limits placed on compensating victims in *Anderson* speak to a larger problem with the damages remedy — specifically, that in furthering the goal of compensating individual victims, the remedy may have the effect of deterring socially desirable (and constitutional) enforcement activity. Consider the following:

> Property damage aside, the injury [from a typical Fourth Amendment violation] consists of the victim's humiliation and loss of privacy, and the more diffuse harm to society's sense of security. Harms such as these cannot be priced by the legal system with any accuracy. Yet, accurate pricing is essential to a well-functioning damages system. The actors (police officers) receive no tangible reward for the marginal legal search or arrest, and are usually free to avoid acting altogether — that is, to avoid performing the search or making the arrest — without suffering substantial sanctions. Under these

circumstances, if damages are imposed for illegal action (and if, as is probably the case in all legal systems, the standards that determine what is legal are somewhat vague), there is the serious danger that society will not only get fewer illegal searches and seizures, but will also get many fewer legal ones. This activity-level effect is exacerbated if the relevant damages are overestimated — and the risk of such overestimates is likely to be high, given that the harms in question are both socially sensitive and irreducibly subjective.

Saul Levmore & William J. Stuntz, Remedies and Incentives in Private and Public Law: A Comparative Essay, [1990] Wis. L. Rev. 483, 490. Do the difficulties in "pricing" Fourth Amendment damages justify denying compensation to people whose rights have been violated?

b. Injunctions

Damages are backward-looking, designed to compensate a person for a harm that has already been caused by the Fourth Amendment violation. Normally, this is the best we can do, because police officers who conduct an unreasonable search or seizure would say, if asked, that they have no plans to repeat their (presumably) aberrant behavior, and so prospective relief is a nonissue.

But what if the police do plan to repeat their behavior? Some questionable police practices, especially those involving the use of force, are a part of the officers' training and may well be legitimate in some circumstances but excessive or unreasonable in other settings. In such a case, can the courts enjoin the police from engaging in future behavior that might run afoul of the Fourth Amendment? Consider the following notes.

1. Courts generally have the power to enjoin future constitutional violations, but there are significant barriers to enjoining police practices. In Los Angeles v. Lyons, 461 U.S. 95 (1983), a man sued the city of Los Angeles and four of its police officers, claiming that the police had, without justification, used a "chokehold" on him during an arrest. The suit sought money damages, and also a preliminary and permanent injunction against the city barring the future use of the chokeholds. But a 5-4 Supreme Court rejected the argument, finding that the claim for future relief failed to raise an "actual case or controversy," because there were no grounds to believe that *this* particular claimant — Mr. Lyons — would in the future be subjected to a chokehold. To properly maintain a suit for injunctive relief, said the Court, Mr. Lyons "would have had not only to allege that he would have another encounter with the police but also to make the incredible assertion either, (1) that all police officers in Los Angeles always choke any citizen with whom they happen to have an encounter, whether for the purpose of arrest, issuing a citation or for questioning or, (2) that the City ordered or authorized police officers to act in such manner." Id., at 105-106.

Was the Court correct to require a showing that Mr. Lyons *personally* was likely to be put in a chokehold in the future in order to obtain an injunction? If not, should anyone (or perhaps, anyone subject to the jurisdiction of the Los Angeles police) be able to move for injunctive relief, even if they had not been subject to the police technique? Then again, assuming that the chokehold violated the Fourth Amendment prohibition on unreasonable seizures,[2] would *any* plaintiff have standing to bring an action for injunctive relief against the LAPD after *Lyons*?

2. Cases like *Lyons* have not prevented plaintiffs from successfully seeking federal injunctions against police in some cases. But the effect of *Lyons* and similar Court opinions, "if not their overt strategy, is to push claimants toward damages actions and away from systematic relief against cities and police departments." Paul Chevigny, Edge of the Knife 110 (1995). Given that damages awards do not always prompt timely reform in police operations — partly because the damages rarely come out of police budgets — is this result wise? Do principles of federalism support it? Justice Marshall argued in his *Lyons* dissent that while district courts should be mindful that federal court intervention into the daily operations of a police department is undesirable and to be avoided whenever possible, the injunctive relief requested there — simply a prohibition on the use of chokeholds absent the threat of deadly force — "does not implicate the federalism concerns" that arise when a federal court undertakes to supervise the running of a police department. 461 U.S., at 133-134. Do you agree?

3. In 1994, Congress enacted 42 U.S.C. §14141, which prohibits governmental authorities or those acting on their behalf from engaging in "a pattern or practice of conduct by law enforcement officials" that deprives persons of "rights, privileges, or immunities secured or protected by the Constitution or laws of the United States." Whenever the Attorney General has reasonable cause to believe that a violation has occurred, the Justice Department is authorized to sue for equitable and declaratory relief "to eliminate the pattern or practice." The Justice Department's Civil Rights Division has investigated a number of police agencies to determine whether to bring §14141 litigation; it has instituted suits against several others.

For a positive assessment of the approach to police reform reflected in these decrees, see Samuel Walker, The New Paradigm of Police Accountability: The U.S. Justice Department "Pattern or Practice" Suits in Context, 22 St. Louis U. Pub. L. Rev. 3 (2003). Professor Walker argues that §14141 consent decrees are evidence of significant progress in promoting police accountability. The organizational reforms mandated in these consent decrees, he notes, "were not developed by the Justice Department itself but were drawn from recognized 'best practices' related to accountability already in place in other more progressive police departments." Id., at 6. These "best practices" include: "(a) a comprehensive use-of-force reporting system, (b) an open and accessible citizen complaint system, (c) an early intervention (or warning) system to identify potential 'problem' officers, and (d) the collection of data on traffic stops for the purpose of curbing racial profiling." Id., at 6-7. Walker suggests that the consent decrees reflect a new paradigm with regard to police accountability, one that "focus[es] on organizational change rather than individual officers or discrete police problems (e.g., use of deadly force)." Id., at 51. And this new paradigm might, Walker argues, "achieve a life of its own, independent of future §14141 litigation by the Justice Department," as police departments pursue a best-practices approach on their own. Id.

___

2. The LAPD was virtually alone among big-city departments at this time in instructing officers that chokeholds were pain compliance techniques, rather than a form of deadly force. The LAPD reclassified the carotid control hold as a type of deadly force during the *Lyons* litigation. See Jerome Skolnick & James J. Fyfe, Above the Law 42 (1993).

c. Criminal Prosecution

Some violations of the Fourth Amendment can lead to criminal prosecution of the police officer. Consider:

- 18 U.S.C. §242 makes it a crime for a person under color of law to willfully to deprive citizens of their constitutional rights. The punishment for violating this section is up to one year in prison unless bodily injury results, in which case up to ten years is authorized.
- 18 U.S.C. §2234 says that if an officer executing a search warrant "willfully exceeds his authority or exercises it with unnecessary severity," he shall be punished by a fine and up to one year in prison.
- 18 U.S.C. §2235 says an officer who "maliciously and without probable cause procures a search warrant to be issued and executed" shall be punished by a fine and up to one year in prison.
- 18 U.S.C. §2236 provides that any federal law enforcement official who "searches any private dwelling used and occupied as such dwelling without a warrant directing such search, or maliciously and without reasonable cause searches any other building or property without a search warrant," shall be fined for a first offense, and subject to a fine up to a year in prison for a subsequent offense.

While this array of statutes suggests a seriousness about pursuing police officers who violate the Fourth Amendment, prosecutions for these crimes are relatively rare. In fiscal year 2008, for example, there were about 60 cases filed charging a violation of §242, and none filed alleging a violation of §§2234-2236, the laws specific to illegal searches.

A significant percentage of the cases that are filed charge police officers with excessive use of force against suspects. Consider the prosecutions of Sergeant Stacey Koon and LAPD officers Laurence Powell, Timothy Wind, and Ted Briseno in connection with the beating of Rodney King in 1991. Justice Kennedy recounted the facts in Koon v. United States, 518 U.S. 81, 85-87 (1996):

> On the evening of March 2, 1991, Rodney King and two of his friends sat in King's wife's car in Altadena, California, a city in Los Angeles County, and drank malt liquor for a number of hours. Then, with King driving, they left Altadena via a major freeway. King was intoxicated.
>
> California Highway Patrol officers observed King's car traveling at a speed they estimated to be in excess of 100 m.p.h. The officers followed King with red lights and sirens activated and ordered him by loudspeaker to pull over, but he continued to drive. The Highway Patrol officers called on the radio for help. Units of the Los Angeles Police Department joined in the pursuit, one of them manned by petitioner Laurence Powell and his trainee, Timothy Wind.
>
> King left the freeway, and after a chase of about eight miles, stopped at an entrance to a recreation area. The officers ordered King and his two passengers to exit the car and to assume a felony prone position — that is, to lie on their stomachs with legs spread and arms behind their backs. King's two friends complied. King, too, got out of the car but did not lie down. Petitioner Stacey Koon arrived, at once followed by Ted Briseno and Roland Solano. All were officers of the Los Angeles Police Department, and as sergeant, Koon took charge. The officers again ordered King to assume the

felony prone position. King got on his hands and knees but did not lie down. Officers Powell, Wind, Briseno and Solano tried to force King down, but King resisted and became combative, so the officers retreated. Koon then fired taser darts (designed to stun a combative suspect) into King.

The events that occurred next were captured on videotape by a bystander. As the videotape begins, it shows that King rose from the ground and charged toward Officer Powell. Powell took a step and used his baton to strike King on the side of his head. King fell to the ground. From the 18th to the 30th second on the videotape, King attempted to rise, but Powell and Wind each struck him with their batons to prevent him from doing so. From the 35th to the 51st second, Powell administered repeated blows to King's lower extremities; one of the blows fractured King's leg. At the 55th second, Powell struck King on the chest, and King rolled over and lay prone. At that point, the officers stepped back and observed King for about 10 seconds. Powell began to reach for his handcuffs. . . .

At one-minute-five-seconds (1:05) on the videotape, Briseno, in the District Court's words, "stomped" on King's upper back or neck. King's body writhed in response. At 1:07, Powell and Wind again began to strike King with a series of baton blows, and Wind kicked him in the upper thoracic or cervical area six times until 1:26. At about 1:29, King put his hands behind his back and was handcuffed. . . .

Powell radioed for an ambulance. He sent two messages over a communications network to the other officers that said "ooops" and "I havent [*sic*] beaten anyone this bad in a long time." Koon sent a message to the police station that said: "U[nit] just had a big time use of force. . . . Tased and beat the suspect of CHP pursuit big time."

King was taken to a hospital where he was treated for a fractured leg, multiple facial fractures, and numerous bruises and contusions. Learning that King worked at Dodger Stadium, Powell said to King: "We played a little ball tonight, didn't we, Rodney?"

Koon, Powell, Briseno, and Wind were tried in state court on charges of assault with a deadly weapon and excessive use of force by a police officer. The trial resulted in acquittals on all charges, with the exception of one assault charge against Powell on which the jury hung. The verdicts sparked one of the largest civil disorders in American history. More than 40 people were killed in the rioting, more than 2,000 were injured, and nearly $1 billion in property was destroyed.

A federal grand jury subsequently indicted the four officers under 18 U.S.C. §242, charging them with violating King's constitutional rights under color of law. The second jury convicted Koon and Powell but acquitted Wind and Briseno.

The history of Koon v. United States illustrates the importance of vindicating constitutional rights through the mechanism of criminal prosecution in appropriate cases. But doesn't it also speak to the range of factors that have led many scholars to conclude that "[c]riminal law is . . . not a system of 'discipline' for police misconduct . . ."? Paul Chevigny, Edge of the Knife 101 (1995). Consider Professor Chevigny's analysis of the reasons why criminal prosecution cannot be expected to be a major vehicle for reform in the area of excessive force:

Criminal prosecution is the most cumbersome tool for the accountability of officials. As an instrument for policy, it presents the difficulties with disciplinary proceedings writ large: the charges are made after the fact; it is a matter of hazard which cases can be proved and which cannot; and because the burden of proof is extremely high, the likelihood of success is small. Prosecutions are brought in the few cases where the evidence happens to be available, and the results thus create a patchy deterrent; they may have no effect on police policy at all if police executives do not agree with the decision to prosecute. Furthermore, the standards of the criminal law usually cannot delineate what is good police work that will minimize the unnecessary use of force — that must be shaped by police regulations, training, and practice. Police standards for the use of firearms, for example, are commonly more restrictive than the criminal law of justification, because a shooting may be "wrong" in the sense that there was a better way to handle the situation, without being "wrong" in the sense of a flagrantly offensive act that ought to be punished as a crime. The state prosecution in California for the Rodney King beating presents a rather complex example of the problems. The police who beat King were first prosecuted in state court for felony assault and were acquitted; one of their defenses was that they believed King was a threat to them and that they responded as they claimed they had been taught to respond. Thus, within limits, poor police practices throughout a department can aid the defense of a criminal case by suggesting that there is not criminal intent on the part of a police defendant.

Id., at 98-99. Despite this analysis, Professor Chevigny emphasizes that "[i]t is very important . . . to prosecute acts that are clearly criminal, whether deliberate or reckless," and that with regard to the use of force, such prosecutions "do have a broad deterrent effect, making officers aware that the lawful use of force is always at the border of actions that may be criminal." Id., at 99. In what circumstances do you think criminal prosecution may play a role in remedying Fourth Amendment harms?

d. Administrative and Political Remedies

Police regulation and discipline are generally directed at deterring police misconduct rather than compensating victims. Similarly, police training aims at avoiding Fourth Amendment violations before they occur. These internal administrative functions, however, should not be overlooked in any discussion of minimizing Fourth Amendment harms:

> Given the decentralized and dispersed nature of police organizations, it is utterly hopeless to attempt to control police conduct other than by making the administrative system work. No court or specially constituted civilian body, based outside the police agency, can possibly provide the kind of day-to-day direction that is essential if the behavior of police officers at the operating level is to be effectively controlled. This means that even in the most acute situations, when administrators and supervisors are either unwilling or incapable of asserting themselves, there is simply no way to work around them.

Herman Goldstein, Policing a Free Society 174 (1977). At the same time, "there is widespread recognition that police departments have failed to develop adequate methods of accountability. In particular, there has been a failure both to identify and punish chronic misconduct and to reward good conduct." Samuel Walker, The Police in America 289 (2d ed. 1992). This may be particularly true in the context of illegal searches and seizures, where misconduct can occur in the normal course of law enforcement and may be condoned by police managers and tolerated by prosecutors.

There are external influences on these internal controls, of course, and these should also be considered in the context of controlling Fourth Amendment abuses. Consider the role of local politics on police operations:

. . . In those communities where top police officials are still popularly elected, political control [of the police function] is direct. And even when police chiefs or police commissioners are appointed, they are today accountable to elected officials in all major American cities. "At the municipal level a police chief who is by legislation required to function under the direction of an elected mayor and who is appointed by the mayor, is obviously considered responsible to the mayor for all aspects of police operations." Police departments are also at least theoretically accountable to local legislative bodies, since these bodies perform an oversight function that . . . might be enhanced: "[A]ccountability might be increased by regular reporting and discussion in city council meetings or council committee meetings of the kinds of problems police are dealing with in the community and how they are handling them. . . ."

There is reason, however, to be less than sanguine about the role that both formal and informal mechanisms of political control can play in holding police managers and their departments accountable. . . . The historical effort to wrest control of policing from local ward politicians resulted in broad dissemination of the ideas associated with reform era policing. . . . These ideas, like faith in police professionalism and in neutral law enforcement in lieu of potentially corrupting political controls, have sometimes been interpreted to condemn as corrupt *any* political oversight of the police. . . . "[I]t is not uncommon for mayors running for reelection to brag about the degree of independence they allowed their police departments." Politicians also have their own reasons for disclaiming much of their responsibility for monitoring police operations. Policing is a risky business, and distance between politicians and the police helps the former avoid blame when the latter become ensnared in controversy. Police "are not autonomous; the sensitive function they perform in our society requires that they be accountable, through the political process, to the community." Achieving this accountability, however, is no small feat.

Debra Livingston, Police Discretion and the Quality of Life in Public Places: Courts, Communities, and the New Policing, 97 Colum. L. Rev. 551, 654, 656-657 (1997) (footnotes omitted).

Local political agitation in many cities has resulted in the creation of various forms of "citizen review" boards to monitor police. Indeed, the establishment of citizen complaint review procedures has been a primary political objective of many civil rights and civil liberties advocates in recent years. In cities that have adopted one or another version of "citizen review," citizens share responsibility with police for the review of complaints brought against individual police officers. In some places, agencies independent of the police department investigate and review such complaints, thereafter making recommendations about the discipline of officers found to have engaged in misconduct. Many big cities currently have at least a hybrid complaint system in which police may investigate complaints, but civilians sit on the board that recommends discipline. See Paul Chevigny, Edge of the Knife 88 (1995). These boards could come to play an important role in monitoring police departments for Fourth Amendment violations. But they have not as yet emerged as a principal form of redress for such violations, nor as a significant vehicle for police reform: "To date, most such boards have focused narrowly on the performance of individual police officers rather than on broader questions about the quality of police services or the overall acceptability of particular policing practices within local neighborhoods." Livingston, supra, at 665. See also, Debra Livingston, The Unfulfilled Promise of Citizen Review, 1 Ohio St. J. of Crim. L. 653, 658-659 (2004).

Given these observations, is there a way that administrative and political controls over police might be strengthened so as to increase their effectiveness in addressing

Fourth Amendment harms? More generally, might these regulatory mechanisms, if given broader scope, serve as a substitute for *judicial* regulation of police misconduct?

B. The Scope of the Fourth Amendment

1. The Meaning of "Searches"

a. The Relationship Between Privacy and Property

KATZ v. UNITED STATES

Certiorari to the United States Court of Appeals for the Ninth Circuit
389 U.S. 347 (1967)

MR. JUSTICE STEWART delivered the opinion of the Court.

The petitioner was convicted in the District Court for the Southern District of California under an eight-count indictment charging him with transmitting wagering information by telephone from Los Angeles to Miami and Boston in violation of a federal statute. At trial the Government was permitted, over the petitioner's objection, to introduce evidence of the petitioner's end of telephone conversations, overheard by FBI agents who had attached an electronic listening and recording device to the outside of the public telephone booth from which he had placed his calls. In affirming his conviction, the Court of Appeals rejected the contention that the recordings had been obtained in violation of the Fourth Amendment, because "[t]here was no physical entrance into the area occupied by [the petitioner]." We granted certiorari in order to consider the constitutional questions thus presented.

The petitioner has phrased those questions as follows:

"A. Whether a public telephone booth is a constitutionally protected area so that evidence obtained by attaching an electronic listening recording device to the top of such a booth is obtained in violation of the right to privacy of the user of the booth.

"B. Whether physical penetration of a constitutionally protected area is necessary before a search and seizure can be said to be violative of the Fourth Amendment to the United States Constitution."

We decline to adopt this formulation of the issues. In the first place the correct solution of Fourth Amendment problems is not necessarily promoted by incantation of the phrase "constitutionally protected area." Secondly, the Fourth Amendment cannot be translated into a general constitutional "right to privacy." That Amendment protects individual privacy against certain kinds of governmental intrusion, but its protections go further, and often have nothing to do with privacy at all.[4] Other provisions of the Constitution protect personal privacy from other

___

4. "The average man would very likely not have his feelings soothed any more by having his property seized openly than by having it seized privately and by stealth. . . . And a person can be just as much, if not more, irritated, annoyed and injured by an unceremonious public arrest by a policeman as he is by a

forms of governmental invasion.[5] But the protection of a person's *general* right to privacy — his right to be let alone by other people — is, like the protection of his property and of his very life, left largely to the law of the individual States.

Because of the misleading way the issues have been formulated, the parties have attached great significance to the characterization of the telephone booth from which the petitioner placed his calls. The petitioner has strenuously argued that the booth was a "constitutionally protected area." The Government has maintained with equal vigor that it was not.[8] But this effort to decide whether or not a given "area," viewed in the abstract, is "constitutionally protected" deflects attention from the problem presented by this case.[9] For the Fourth Amendment protects people, not places. What a person knowingly exposes to the public, even in his own home or office, is not a subject of Fourth Amendment protection. But what he seeks to preserve as private, even in an area accessible to the public, may be constitutionally protected. The Government stresses the fact that the telephone booth from which the petitioner made his calls was constructed partly of glass, so that he was as visible after he entered it as he would have been if he had remained outside. But what he sought to exclude when he entered the booth was not the intruding eye — it was the uninvited ear. He did not shed his right to do so simply because he made his calls from a place where he might be seen. No less than an individual in a business office, in a friend's apartment, or in a taxicab, a person in a telephone booth may rely upon the protection of the Fourth Amendment. One who occupies it, shuts the door behind him, and pays the toll that permits him to place a call is surely entitled to assume that the words he utters into the mouthpiece will not be broadcast to the world. To read the Constitution more narrowly is to ignore the vital role that the public telephone has come to play in private communication.

The Government contends, however, that the activities of its agents in this case should not be tested by Fourth Amendment requirements, for the surveillance technique they employed involved no physical penetration of the telephone booth from which the petitioner placed his calls. It is true that the absence of such penetration was at one time thought to foreclose further Fourth Amendment inquiry, Olmstead v. United States, 277 U.S. 438, 457, 464, 466; Goldman v. United States, 316 U.S. 129, 134-136, for that Amendment was thought to limit only searches and seizures of tangible property.[13] But "[t]he premise that property interests control the right of the Government to search and seize has been discredited." Warden v. Hayden, 387

---

seizure in the privacy of his office or home." Griswold v. State of Connecticut, 381 U.S. 479, 509 (dissenting opinion of Mr. Justice Black).

5. The First Amendment, for example, imposes limitations upon governmental abridgment of "freedom to associate and privacy in one's associations." NAACP v. State of Alabama, 357 U.S. 449, 462. The Third Amendment's prohibition against the unconsented peacetime quartering of soldiers protects another aspect of privacy from governmental intrusion. To some extent, the Fifth Amendment too "reflects the Constitution's concern for . . . '. . . the right of each individual "to a private enclave where he may lead a private life."'" Tehan v. Shott, 382 U.S. 406, 416. Virtually every governmental action interferes with personal privacy to some degree. The question in each case is whether that interference violates a command of the United States Constitution.

8. In support of their respective claims, the parties have compiled competing lists of "protected areas" for our consideration. It appears to be common ground that a private home is such an area but that an open field is not.

9. It is true that this Court has occasionally described its conclusions in terms of "constitutionally protected areas," but we have never suggested that this concept can serve as a talismanic solution to every Fourth Amendment problem.

13. We do not deal in this case with the law of detention or arrest under the Fourth Amendment.

U.S. 294, 304. Thus, although a closely divided Court supposed in *Olmstead* that surveillance without any trespass and without the seizure of any material object fell outside the ambit of the Constitution, we have since departed from the narrow view on which that decision rested. Indeed, we have expressly held that the Fourth Amendment governs not only the seizure of tangible items, but extends as well to the recording of oral statements, overheard without any "technical trespass under . . . local property law." Silverman v. United States, 365 U.S. 505, 511. Once this much is acknowledged, and once it is recognized that the Fourth Amendment protects people — and not simply "areas" — against unreasonable searches and seizures, it becomes clear that the reach of that Amendment cannot turn upon the presence or absence of a physical intrusion into any given enclosure.

We conclude that the underpinnings of *Olmstead* and *Goldman* have been so eroded by our subsequent decisions that the "trespass" doctrine there enunciated can no longer be regarded as controlling. The Government's activities in electronically listening to and recording the petitioner's words violated the privacy upon which he justifiably relied while using the telephone booth and thus constituted a "search and seizure" within the meaning of the Fourth Amendment. The fact that the electronic device employed to achieve that end did not happen to penetrate the wall of the booth can have no constitutional significance.

The question remaining for decision, then, is whether the search and seizure conducted in this case complied with constitutional standards. In that regard, the Government's position is that its agents acted in an entirely defensible manner: They did not begin their electronic surveillance until investigation of the petitioner's activities had established a strong probability that he was using the telephone in question to transmit gambling information to persons in other States, in violation of federal law. Moreover, the surveillance was limited, both in scope and in duration, to the specific purpose of establishing the contents of the petitioner's unlawful telephonic communications. The agents confined their surveillance to the brief periods during which he used the telephone booth,[14] and they took great care to overhear only the conversations of the petitioner himself.[15]

Accepting this account of the Government's actions as accurate, it is clear that this surveillance was so narrowly circumscribed that a duly authorized magistrate, properly notified of the need for such investigation, specifically informed of the basis on which it was to proceed, and clearly apprised of the precise intrusion it would entail, could constitutionally have authorized, with appropriate safeguards, the very limited search and seizure that the Government asserts in fact took place. . . .

. . . Yet the inescapable fact is that this restraint was imposed by the agents themselves, not by a judicial officer. They were not required, before commencing the search, to present their estimate of probable cause for detached scrutiny by a neutral magistrate. They were not compelled, during the conduct of the search itself, to observe precise limits established in advance by a specific court order. Nor were they

14. Based upon their previous visual observations of the petitioner, the agents correctly predicted that he would use the telephone booth for several minutes at approximately the same time each morning. The petitioner was subjected to electronic surveillance only during this predetermined period. Six recordings, averaging some three minutes each, were obtained and admitted in evidence. They preserved the petitioner's end of conversations concerning the placing of bets and the receipt of wagering information.

15. On the single occasion when the statements of another person were inadvertently intercepted, the agents refrained from listening to them.

directed, after the search had been completed, to notify the authorizing magistrate in detail of all that had been seized. In the absence of such safeguards, this Court has never sustained a search upon the sole ground that officers reasonably expected to find evidence of a particular crime and voluntarily confined their activities to the least intrusive means consistent with that end. Searches conducted without warrants have been held unlawful "notwithstanding facts unquestionably showing probable cause," Agnello v. United States, 269 U.S. 20, 33, for the Constitution requires "that the deliberate, impartial judgment of a judicial officer . . . be interposed between the citizen and the police. . . ." Wong Sun v. United States, 371 U.S. 471, 481-482. "Over and again this Court has emphasized that the mandate of the [Fourth] Amendment requires adherence to judicial processes," United States v. Jeffers, 342 U.S. 48, 51, and that searches conducted outside the judicial process, without prior approval by judge or magistrate, are per se unreasonable under the Fourth Amendment — subject only to a few specifically established and well-delineated exceptions.

It is difficult to imagine how any of those exceptions could ever apply to the sort of search and seizure involved in this case. . . .

The Government does not question these basic principles. Rather, it urges the creation of a new exception to cover this case. It argues that surveillance of a telephone booth should be exempted from the usual requirement of advance authorization by a magistrate upon a showing of probable cause. We cannot agree. Omission of such authorization

> bypasses the safeguards provided by an objective predetermination of probable cause, and substitutes instead the far less reliable procedure of an after-the-event justification for the . . . search, too likely to be subtly influenced by the familiar shortcomings of hindsight judgment.

Beck v. State of Ohio, 379 U.S. 89, 96.

And bypassing a neutral predetermination of the *scope* of a search leaves individuals secure from Fourth Amendment violations "only in the discretion of the police." Id., at 97.

These considerations do not vanish when the search in question is transferred from the setting of a home, an office, or a hotel room to that of a telephone booth. Wherever a man may be, he is entitled to know that he will remain free from unreasonable searches and seizures. The government agents here ignored "the procedure of antecedent justification . . . that is central to the Fourth Amendment," a procedure that we hold to be a constitutional precondition of the kind of electronic surveillance involved in this case. Because the surveillance here failed to meet that condition, and because it led to the petitioner's conviction, the judgment must be reversed.

It is so ordered.

MR. JUSTICE MARSHALL took no part in the consideration or decision of this case. [The concurring opinions of Justice Douglas and Justice White are omitted.]

MR. JUSTICE HARLAN, concurring.

I join the opinion of the Court, which I read to hold only (a) that an enclosed telephone booth is an area where, like a home, and unlike a field, a person has a constitutionally protected reasonable expectation of privacy; (b) that electronic as well as physical intrusion into a place that is in this sense private may constitute a violation of the Fourth Amendment; and (c) that the invasion of a constitutionally protected area by federal authorities is, as the Court has long held, presumptively unreasonable in the absence of a search warrant.

As the Court's opinion states, "the Fourth Amendment protects people, not places." The question, however, is what protection it affords to those people. Generally, as here, the answer to that question requires reference to a "place." My understanding of the rule that has emerged from prior decisions is that there is a twofold requirement, first that a person have exhibited an actual (subjective) expectation of privacy and, second, that the expectation be one that society is prepared to recognize as "reasonable." Thus a man's home is, for most purposes, a place where he expects privacy, but objects, activities, or statements that he exposes to the "plain view" of outsiders are not "protected" because no intention to keep them to himself has been exhibited. On the other hand, conversations in the open would not be protected against being overheard, for the expectation of privacy under the circumstances would be unreasonable.

The critical fact in this case is that "[o]ne who occupies [a telephone booth], shuts the door behind him, and pays the toll that permits him to place a call is surely entitled to assume" that his conversation is not being intercepted. The point is not that the booth is "accessible to the public" at other times, but that it is a temporarily private place whose momentary occupants' expectations of freedom from intrusion are recognized as reasonable.

In Silverman v. United States, 365 U.S. 505, we held that eavesdropping accomplished by means of an electronic device that penetrated the premises occupied by petitioner was a violation of the Fourth Amendment. That case established that interception of conversations reasonably intended to be private could constitute a "search and seizure," and that the examination or taking of physical property was not required. This view of the Fourth Amendment was followed in Wong Sun v. United States, 371 U.S. 471, at 485, and Berger v. New York, 388 U.S. 41, at 51. In *Silverman* we found it unnecessary to re-examine Goldman v. United States, 316 U.S. 129, which had held that electronic surveillance accomplished without the physical penetration of petitioner's premises by a tangible object did not violate the Fourth Amendment. This case requires us to reconsider *Goldman*, and I agree that it should now be overruled.* Its limitation on Fourth Amendment protection is, in the present day, bad physics as well as bad law, for reasonable expectations of privacy may be defeated by electronic as well as physical invasion. . . .

MR. JUSTICE BLACK, dissenting. . . .

My basic objection is twofold: (1) I do not believe that the words of the Amendment will bear the meaning given them by today's decision, and (2) I do not believe that it is the proper role of this Court to rewrite the Amendment in order "to bring it into harmony with the times" and thus reach a result that many people believe to be desirable.

While I realize that an argument based on the meaning of words lacks the scope, and no doubt the appeal, of broad policy discussions and philosophical discourses on such nebulous subjects as privacy, for me the language of the Amendment is the

---

* I also think that the course of development evinced by *Silverman*, supra, *Wong Sun*, supra, *Berger*, supra, and today's decision must be recognized as overruling Olmstead v. United States, 277 U.S. 438, which essentially rested on the ground that conversations were not subject to the protection of the Fourth Amendment.

crucial place to look in construing a written document such as our Constitution.
. . . The first clause protects "persons, houses, papers, and effects, against unreasonable searches and seizures. . . ." These words connote the idea of tangible things
with size, form, and weight, things capable of being searched, seized, or both. The
second clause of the Amendment still further establishes its Framers' purpose to
limit its protection to tangible things by providing that no warrants shall issue but
those "particularly describing the place to be searched, and the persons or things to
be seized." A conversation overheard by eavesdropping, whether by plain snooping
or wiretapping, is not tangible and, under the normally accepted meanings of the
words, can neither be searched nor seized. In addition the language of the second
clause indicates that the Amendment refers not only to something tangible so it can
be seized but to something already in existence so it can be described. Yet the
Court's interpretation would have the Amendment apply to overhearing future
conversations which by their very nature are nonexistent until they take place. How
can one "describe" a future conversation, and, if one cannot, how can a magistrate
issue a warrant to eavesdrop one in the future? It is argued that information showing what is expected to be said is sufficient to limit the boundaries of what later can
be admitted into evidence; but does such general information really meet the specific language of the Amendment which says "particularly describing"? Rather than
using language in a completely artificial way, I must conclude that the Fourth
Amendment simply does not apply to eavesdropping.

Tapping telephone wires, of course, was an unknown possibility at the time the
Fourth Amendment was adopted. But eavesdropping (and wiretapping is nothing
more than eavesdropping by telephone) was . . . "an ancient practice which at common law was condemned as a nuisance. 4 Blackstone, Commentaries 168. . . ."
[Berger v. New York], 388 U.S., at 45. There can be no doubt that the Framers were
aware of this practice, and if they had desired to outlaw or restrict the use of evidence obtained by eavesdropping, I believe that they would have used the appropriate language to do so in the Fourth Amendment. They certainly would not have
left such a task to the ingenuity of language-stretching judges. . . .

The first case to reach this Court which actually involved a clear-cut test of the
Fourth Amendment's applicability to eavesdropping through a wiretap was, of
course, *Olmstead*, supra. In holding that the interception of private telephone conversations by means of wiretapping was not a violation of the Fourth Amendment,
this Court, speaking through Mr. Chief Justice Taft, examined the language of the
Amendment and found, just as I do now, that the words could not be stretched to
encompass overheard conversations:

> The Amendment itself shows that the search is to be of material things — the per
> son, the house, his papers or his effects. The description of the warrant necessary to
> make the proceeding lawful, is that it must specify the place to be searched and the per
> son or *things* to be seized. . . .
> Justice Bradley in the *Boyd* case [116 U.S. 616 (1886)] and Justice Clark[e] in
> [Gouled v. United States, 255 U.S. 298 (1921)] said that the Fifth Amendment and the
> Fourth Amendment were to be liberally construed to effect the purpose of the framers
> of the Constitution in the interest of liberty. But that can not justify enlargement of the
> language employed beyond the possible practical meaning of houses, persons, papers,
> and effects, or so to apply the words search and seizure as to forbid hearing or sight.

[277 U.S., at 464-465.]

Goldman v. United States, 316 U.S. 129, is an even clearer example of this Court's traditional refusal to consider eavesdropping as being covered by the Fourth Amendment. There federal agents used a detectaphone, which was placed on the wall of an adjoining room, to listen to the conversation of a defendant carried on in his private office and intended to be confined within the four walls of the room. This Court, referring to *Olmstead*, found no Fourth Amendment violation. . . .

Since I see no way in which the words of the Fourth Amendment can be construed to apply to eavesdropping, that closes the matter for me. In interpreting the Bill of Rights, I willingly go as far as a liberal construction of the language takes me, but I simply cannot in good conscience give a meaning to words which they have never before been thought to have and which they certainly do not have in common ordinary usage. I will not distort the words of the Amendment in order to "keep the Constitution up to date" or "to bring it into harmony with the times." It was never meant that this Court have such power, which in effect would make us a continuously functioning constitutional convention.

With this decision the Court has completed, I hope, its rewriting of the Fourth Amendment, which started only recently when the Court began referring incessantly to the Fourth Amendment not so much as a law against *unreasonable* searches and seizures as one to protect an individual's privacy. By clever word juggling the Court finds it plausible to argue that language aimed specifically at searches and seizures of things that can be searched and seized may, to protect privacy, be applied to eavesdropped evidence of conversations that can neither be searched nor seized. Few things happen to an individual that do not affect his privacy in one way or another. Thus, by arbitrarily substituting the Court's language, designed to protect privacy, for the Constitution's language, designed to protect against unreasonable searches and seizures, the Court has made the Fourth Amendment its vehicle for holding all laws violative of the Constitution which offend the Court's broadest concept of privacy. . . .

The Fourth Amendment protects privacy only to the extent that it prohibits unreasonable searches and seizures of "persons, houses, papers, and effects." No general right is created by the Amendment so as to give this Court the unlimited power to hold unconstitutional everything which affects privacy. Certainly the Framers, well acquainted as they were with the excesses of governmental power, did not intend to grant this Court such omnipotent lawmaking authority as that. The history of governments proves that it is dangerous to freedom to repose such powers in courts.

For these reasons I respectfully dissent.

NOTES AND QUESTIONS

1. *Katz* is the leading case on the question what constitutes a "search" for Fourth Amendment purposes. Notice that the immediate effect of *Katz* was to expand the Fourth Amendment by rejecting the notions: (1) that the Amendment is concerned only with the search or seizure of tangible property; and (2) that the Amendment only applies to surveillance techniques involving the physical penetration of protected spaces. Broadly, *Katz* continued the reconstruction of Boyd v. United States,

116 U.S. 616 (1886), detailed in the last chapter. But notice that even as it reworked the very scope of the Amendment, *Katz* offered no comprehensive test of Fourth Amendment coverage, nor any general theory by which questions of coverage might be resolved. As one scholar puts it: "In the end, the basis of the *Katz* decision seems to be that the fourth amendment protects those interests that may justifiably claim fourth amendment protection." Anthony G. Amsterdam, Perspectives on the Fourth Amendment, 58 Minn. L. Rev. 349, 385 (1974). Is this a fair characterization, or does the Court's broadening of the Amendment as described above contain more substance than Amsterdam suggests?

2. Justice Stewart's opinion did not long define the law in this area; Justice Harlan's two-prong formula soon became the Court's test for determining whether a "search" had taken place: "My understanding of the rule that has emerged from prior decisions is that there is a twofold requirement, first that a person have exhibited an actual (subjective) expectation of privacy and second, that the expectation be one that society is prepared to recognize as 'reasonable.'" If a search takes place only when the government intrudes on an individual's reasonable expectation of privacy, it would seem that some animating theory of privacy is necessary — if only to ground questions about the Fourth Amendment's scope. What might this theory of privacy be?

3. Perhaps the lack of a privacy theory in *Katz* is a virtue rather than a vice. Consider the argument in Ronald J. Allen & Ross M. Rosenberg, The Fourth Amendment and the Limits of Theory: Local Versus General Theoretical Knowledge, 72 St. John's L. Rev. 1149 (1998). Allen and Rosenberg draw on the distinction, made famous by Friederich Hayek, between "made" and "grown" orders. "Made" orders are created by some plan or design. "Grown" orders, by contrast, arise spontaneously without central coordination. Allen and Rosenberg argue that Fourth Amendment law, a "grown" order, is ill-suited to overarching theory but that it more properly evolves incrementally, in a process not unlike the evolution of the common law:

> Made orders usually possess a limited number of variables, and thus those variables may be manipulated in order to produce predictable outcomes. If the woodlot suffers a drought, watering will promote growth. If the soil becomes too acidic, it can be treated. . . . Spontaneous orders are extremely complex; introducing reforms into spontaneous systems leads to much more unpredictable consequences. Introducing a new vine as ground cover around the periphery of the forest may result in the forest's destruction as the vine, freed from its natural enemies, grows out of control and chokes out all other plant forms. Unintended, unanticipated consequences are much more likely to result from the introduction of change into a spontaneous order. . . .
>
> In essence, the Fourth Amendment is . . . a grown, spontaneous system. . . . [I]t has too many variables to yield its essence to logical analysis designed to generate decision algorithms. Its subject matter encompasses virtually every human action and interaction imaginable, . . . from public statements to private thoughts recorded in a secret diary, from the affairs of the homeless to those of Dow Chemical, from participating in illegal [drug] markets . . . to illegal restraints of trade. . . . The beliefs of the [academic] commentators, in short, that . . . the Fourth Amendment or privacy will reduce to simple variables, a simple theory, is unjustified. Some things are just more complicated than that.
>
> Are we, then, simply at the mercy of an uncontrollable monster? No. . . . [C]autious, incremental change, with a sensitive awareness of the need for close monitoring and adjustment can be done with a reasonable prospect of favorable outcomes — as the

common law demonstrates so well. Adjustments can come from other sources besides the courts, of course. Whatever the sources, we suggest this is the path to take. . . .

Id., at 1197-1200 (footnotes omitted). If Allen and Rosenberg are right, questions of the Fourth Amendment's coverage might best be approached incrementally, and without the aid of any overly articulated theory of what constitutes the privacy subject to Fourth Amendment regulation. Perhaps incrementalism ensures that the Court's conception of privacy can adapt to changes in culture and technology — the sorts of change evident in *Katz* itself, where the Court grapples with a surveillance technique unknown to the Framers.

4. While the holding in *Katz* expanded the scope of the Fourth Amendment's concerns, numerous commentators have observed that its methodology may have led the Court to restrict the definition of "searches" in subsequent cases. Professor Colb has argued, for instance, that since *Katz* was decided, the Court's overall methodology for defining the Fourth Amendment search has "steadily eroded privacy in specific cases, and conceptually promise[s] to eliminate it altogether." Sherry F. Colb, What Is a Search? Two Conceptual Flaws in Fourth Amendment Doctrine and Some Hints of a Remedy, 55 Stan. L. Rev. 119, 121 (2002). If Colb is right (a question you will be better able to answer after considering *Katz*'s progeny), would a more developed theory of Fourth Amendment privacy have helped avoid this result? Was (and is) the Supreme Court situated to provide such a theory?

5. Be aware that one issue lurking just beneath the surface in *Katz* is the degree to which Fourth Amendment regulation should be uniform, with a single set of legal requirements to govern all searches and seizures, or graduated, with greater or lesser regulation depending on the nature and degree of the privacy intrusion at stake. Until fairly recently, Fourth Amendment law followed the first, "all-or-nothing" approach to the regulation of policing. Thus, if a particular police action constituted a "search" or a "seizure," then (at least presumptively) it had to be based on probable cause and authorized by a judicial warrant. As Professor Amsterdam noted some years ago, this approach to the Fourth Amendment strains the process of drawing the Amendment's boundary lines: "Police practices that cry for some form of constitutional control but not the control of a warrant or a probable cause requirement must be dubbed 'searches' and overrestricted or dubbed something other than searches and left completely unrestricted." It would be both

> easier and more likely for a court to say that a patrolman's shining of a flashlight into the interior of a parked car was a "search" if that conclusion did not encumber the flashlight with a warrant requirement but simply required, for example, that the patrolman "be able to point to specific and articulable facts" supporting a reasonable inference that something in the car required his attention.

Amsterdam, Perspectives on the Fourth Amendment, 58 Minn. L. Rev., at 393. But does this mean that a "graduated approach" to the Fourth Amendment — an approach in which the Amendment would impose lesser or greater restraints on searches and seizures in proportion to their intrusiveness or the nature of the interests they invade — would be preferable? We take up this question in more detail later. For now, consider Professor Amsterdam's famous conclusion that despite the advantages such an approach would have for the process of defining the Fourth Amendment's coverage

. . . the graduated model . . . [would] convert[ ] the fourth amendment into one
immense Rorschach blot. . . . [P]resent law is a positive paragon of simplicity compared to what a graduated fourth amendment would produce. The varieties of police
behavior and of the occasions that call it forth are so innumerable that their reflection
in a general sliding scale approach could only produce more slide than scale.

Id., at 393-394.

6. *Katz* determined that a physical trespass is not *necessary* to invoke Fourth
Amendment protections. But as it turns out, neither is a trespass automatically *sufficient* to ensure that a given police activity constitutes a search. Long before *Katz*, the
Court established an "open fields" doctrine, which held that police entry and search
of open fields involves no Fourth Amendment intrusion even if officers intrude on
privately owned land. Hester v. United States, 265 U.S. 57 (1924). This doctrine was
reaffirmed post-*Katz* in Oliver v. United States, 466 U.S. 170 (1984). Oliver and
Thornton were charged with cultivating marijuana. Oliver was growing marijuana
on his farm, in a field located more than a mile from his house; Thornton's marijuana was growing in two patches in the woods behind his house. Both locations
were highly secluded, and both were posted with "No Trespassing" signs. In each
case, police officers discovered the marijuana as the result of a warrantless entry
onto and inspection of the property. Justice Powell wrote the opinion for the Court,
concluding that the officers' trespass did not constitute a search:

> The rule announced in Hester v. United States was founded upon the explicit lan-
> guage of the Fourth Amendment. That Amendment indicates with some precision the
> places and things encompassed by its protections. As Justice Holmes explained for the
> Court in his characteristically laconic style: "[T]he special protection accorded by
> the Fourth Amendment to the people in their 'persons, houses, papers, and effects,' is
> not extended to the open fields. The distinction between the latter and the house is as
> old as the common law." . . .
>   This interpretation of the Fourth Amendment's language is consistent with the
> understanding of the right to privacy expressed in our Fourth Amendment jurispru-
> dence. Since Katz v. United States, 389 U.S. 347 (1967), the touchstone of Amendment
> analysis has been the question whether a person has a "constitutionally protected rea-
> sonable expectation of privacy." Id., at 360 (Harlan, J., concurring). . . .
>   No single factor determines whether an individual legitimately may claim under the
> Fourth Amendment that a place should be free of government intrusion not authorized
> by warrant. In assessing the degree to which a search infringes upon individual privacy,
> the Court has given weight to such factors as the intention of the Framers . . . , the uses
> to which the individual has put a location, and our societal understanding that certain
> areas deserve the most scrupulous protection from government invasion. . . .
>   In this light, the rule of Hester v. United States, supra, that we reaffirm today, may
> be understood as providing that an individual may not legitimately demand privacy for
> activities conducted out of doors in fields, except in the area immediately surrounding
> the home. This rule is true to the conception of the right to privacy embodied in the
> Fourth Amendment. The Amendment reflects the recognition of the Framers that cer-
> tain enclaves should be free from arbitrary government interference. For example, the
> Court since the enactment of the Fourth Amendment has stressed "the overriding
> respect for the sanctity of the home that has been embedded in our traditions since the
> origins of the Republic." Payton v. New York, [445 U.S. 573, 601 (1980)].
>   In contrast, open fields do not provide the setting for those intimate activities that
> the Amendment is intended to shelter from government interference or surveillance.

There is no societal interest in protecting the privacy of those activities, such as the cultivation of crops, that occur in open fields. Moreover, as a practical matter these lands usually are accessible to the public and the police in ways that a home, an office, or commercial structure would not be. . . .

Nor is the government's intrusion upon an open field a "search" in the constitutional sense because that intrusion is a trespass at common law. The existence of a property right is but one element in determining whether expectations of privacy are legitimate. . . .

Id., at 176-179, 183.

Is Justice Powell's textual argument persuasive in light of *Katz*? Justice Marshall, joined by Justices Brennan and Stevens, dissented in *Oliver*, noting that neither the telephone booth in *Katz* nor the conversation conducted therein could fairly be described as a "person, house, paper, or effect" — and yet the *Katz* Court held the Fourth Amendment to apply. But setting this problem aside, what about the majority's analysis of the privacy interests at stake in open fields? The Court rejected a case-by-case approach to the open fields doctrine, noting that police officers should not have to guess before every intrusion "whether landowners had erected fences sufficiently high, posted a sufficient number of warning signs, or located contraband in an area sufficiently secluded to establish a right of privacy." Id., at 181. But is it so clear that even such marked efforts to protect privacy in land outside the immediate confines of the home should be inadequate to establish a Fourth Amendment interest? What happened to the first prong of Justice Harlan's two-prong test? See William C. Heffernan, Fourth Amendment Privacy Interests, 92 J. Crim. L. & Criminology 1, 36 (2001/2002).

7. The open fields doctrine distinguishes between open fields and "curtilage" — the area surrounding the home where reasonable privacy expectations receive Fourth Amendment protection. In United States v. Dunn, 480 U.S. 294 (1987), the Court considered this distinction and concluded that a barn located approximately 50 yards from a fence surrounding the defendant's residence was outside the curtilage and in an open field. In *Dunn*, Drug Enforcement Administration agents had to cross several barbed-wire fences on the defendant's 200-acre ranch to reach the barn. They also had to pass through a wooden fence that enclosed the front portion of the barn in order to get close enough to look inside and observe what appeared to be a drug laboratory. The agents entered the ranch several times before eventually obtaining a warrant, searching the barn, and seizing amphetamines and materials used in the manufacture of controlled substances. The Court concluded that these warrantless entries did not violate Dunn's Fourth Amendment rights because the officers had entered only on open fields, not the curtilage.[3]

The Court reasoned that "curtilage questions should be resolved with particular reference to four factors: the proximity of the area claimed to be curtilage to the home, whether the area is included within an enclosure surrounding the home, the nature of the uses to which the area is put and the steps taken by the resident to protect the area from observations by the people passing by." Id., at 301. The Court rejected the government's argument that it should adopt a bright-line rule that the

---

3. The Court assumed without deciding that Dunn had a protectable interest in the barn itself, but reasoned that prior to obtaining the warrant, the officers never intruded on this interest because they did not enter the barn, but only "stood outside the curtilage of the house and in the open fields upon which the barn was constructed, and peered into the barn's open front." Id., at 304.

curtilage extends no farther than the nearest fence surrounding a fenced house, noting that "[a]pplication of the Government's 'first fence rule' might lead to diminished Fourth Amendment protection in those cases where a structure lying outside a home's enclosed fence" is nevertheless used for those intimate activities associated with the home. Id., at 301, n. 4. Does this mean police after *Dunn* must, in every case, guess how far the curtilage extends? Isn't this precisely the sort of inquiry the Court sought to avoid in *Oliver*? If so, why are questions about the extent of the home's curtilage treated differently from questions about whether a given tract of land constitutes an open field?

8. Police do not always inspect open fields (not to mention curtilage) by walking across them. Sometimes they fly. In California v. Ciraolo, 476 U.S. 207 (1986), police inspected the backyard of a house while flying in a fixed-wing aircraft at 1,000 feet. They discovered marijuana growing there. While recognizing that the yard was within the curtilage of the home and that a fence shielded the yard from street observation, the Court nevertheless held that the aerial surveillance did not constitute a search: "In an age where private and commercial flight in the public airways is routine, it is unreasonable for respondent to expect that his marijuana plants were constitutionally protected from being observed with the naked eye from an altitude of 1,000 feet." Id., at 215. *Ciraolo* set the stage for the next case, where the Justices further explored what constitutes a reasonable expectation of privacy when police officers fly overhead.

FLORIDA v. RILEY

Certiorari to the Supreme Court of Florida
488 U.S. 445 (1989)

JUSTICE WHITE announced the judgment of the Court and delivered an opinion, in which THE CHIEF JUSTICE, JUSTICE SCALIA, and JUSTICE KENNEDY joined.

On certification to it by a lower state court, the Florida Supreme Court addressed the following question: "Whether surveillance of the interior of a partially covered greenhouse in a residential backyard from the vantage point of a helicopter located 400 feet above the greenhouse constitutes a 'search' for which a warrant is required under the Fourth Amendment. . . ." 511 So. 2d 282 (1987). The court answered the question in the affirmative, and we granted the State's petition for certiorari challenging that conclusion.

Respondent Riley lived in a mobile home located on five acres of rural property. A greenhouse was located 10 to 20 feet behind the mobile home. Two sides of the greenhouse were enclosed. The other two sides were not enclosed but the contents of the greenhouse were obscured from view from surrounding property by trees, shrubs, and the mobile home. The greenhouse was covered by corrugated roofing panels, some translucent and some opaque. At the time relevant to this case, two of the panels, amounting to approximately 10% of the roof area, were missing. A wire fence surrounded the mobile home and the greenhouse, and the property was posted with a "DO NOT ENTER" sign.

This case originated with an anonymous tip to the Pasco County Sheriff's office that marijuana was being grown on respondent's property. When an investigating officer discovered that he could not see the contents of the greenhouse from the road, he circled twice over respondent's property in a helicopter at the height of 400 feet. With his naked eye, he was able to see through the openings in the roof and one or more of the open sides of the greenhouse and to identify what he thought was marijuana growing in the structure. A warrant was obtained based on these observations, and the ensuing search revealed marijuana growing in the greenhouse. Respondent was charged with possession of marijuana under Florida law. . . .

We agree with the State's submission that our decision in California v. Ciraolo, 476 U.S. 207 (1986), controls this case. There, acting on a tip, the police inspected the backyard of a particular house while flying in a fixed-wing aircraft at 1,000 feet. With the naked eye the officers saw what they concluded was marijuana growing in the yard. A search warrant was obtained on the strength of this airborne inspection, and marijuana plants were found. . . . We [held] that the inspection was not a search subject to the Fourth Amendment. We recognized that the yard was within the curtilage of the house, that a fence shielded the yard from observation from the street, and that the occupant had a subjective expectation of privacy. We held, however, that such an expectation was not reasonable and not one "that society is prepared to honor." Id., at 214. . . . "In an age where private and commercial flight in the public airways is routine, it is unreasonable for respondent to expect that his marijuana plants were constitutionally protected from being observed with the naked eye from an altitude of 1,000 feet. The Fourth Amendment simply does not require the police traveling in the public airways at this altitude to obtain a warrant in order to observe what is visible to the naked eye." Id., at 215.

We arrive at the same conclusion in the present case. In this case, as in *Ciraolo*, the property surveyed was within the curtilage of respondent's home. Riley no doubt intended and expected that his greenhouse would not be open to public inspection, and the precautions he took protected against ground-level observation. Because the sides and roof of his greenhouse were left partially open, however, what was growing in the greenhouse was subject to viewing from the air. . . .

Nor on the facts before us, does it make a difference for Fourth Amendment purposes that the helicopter was flying at 400 feet when the officer saw what was growing in the greenhouse through the partially open roof and sides of the structure. We would have a different case if flying at that altitude had been contrary to law or regulation. But helicopters are not bound by the lower limits of the navigable airspace allowed to other aircraft. Any member of the public could legally have been flying over Riley's property in a helicopter at the altitude of 400 feet and could have observed Riley's greenhouse. The police officer did no more. This is not to say that an inspection of the curtilage of a house from an aircraft will always pass muster under the Fourth Amendment simply because the plane is within the navigable airspace specified by law. But it is of obvious importance that the helicopter in this case was *not* violating the law, and there is nothing in the record or before us to suggest that helicopters flying at 400 feet are sufficiently rare in this country to lend substance to respondent's claim that he reasonably anticipated that his greenhouse would not be subject to observation from that altitude. Neither is there any intimation here that the helicopter interfered with respondent's normal use of the greenhouse or of other parts of the curtilage. As far as this record reveals, no intimate details connected with the use of the home or curtilage were observed, and there was no undue noise, and no wind, dust, or threat of injury. In these circumstances, there was no violation of the Fourth Amendment. . . .

JUSTICE O'CONNOR, concurring in the judgment. . . .

Observations of curtilage from helicopters at very low altitudes are not perfectly analogous to ground-level observations from public roads or sidewalks. While in both cases the police may have a legal right to occupy the physical space from which their observations are made, the two situations are not necessarily comparable in terms of whether expectations of privacy from such vantage points should be considered reasonable. Public roads, even those less traveled by, are clearly demarked public thoroughfares. Individuals who seek privacy can take precautions, tailored to the location of the road, to avoid disclosing private activities to those who pass by. They can build a tall fence, for example, and thus ensure private enjoyment of the curtilage without risking public observation from the road or sidewalk. If they do not take such precautions, they cannot reasonably expect privacy from public observation. In contrast, even individuals who have taken effective precautions to ensure against ground-level observations cannot block off all conceivable aerial views of their outdoor patios and yards without entirely giving up their enjoyment of those areas. . . . The fact that a helicopter could conceivably observe the curtilage at virtually any altitude or angle, without violating FAA regulations, does not in itself mean that an individual has no reasonable expectation of privacy from such observation.

In determining whether Riley had a reasonable expectation of privacy from aerial observation, the relevant inquiry after *Ciraolo* is not whether the helicopter was where it had a right to be under FAA regulations. Rather, consistent with *Katz*, we must ask whether the helicopter was in the public airways at an altitude at which members of the public travel with sufficient regularity that Riley's expectation of privacy from aerial observation was not "one that society is prepared to recognize as 'reasonable.'" Katz [v. United States, 389 U.S. 347, 361 (1967)]. . . .

In my view, the defendant must bear the burden of proving that his expectation of privacy was a reasonable one, and thus that a "search" within the meaning of the Fourth Amendment even took place. . . .

Because there is reason to believe that there is considerable public use of airspace at altitudes of 400 feet and above, and because Riley introduced no evidence to the contrary before the Florida courts, I conclude that Riley's expectation that his curtilage was protected from naked-eye aerial observation from that altitude was not a reasonable one. However, public use of altitudes lower than that — particularly public observations from helicopters circling over the curtilage of a home — may be sufficiently rare that police surveillance from such altitudes would violate reasonable expectations of privacy, despite compliance with FAA air safety regulations.

JUSTICE BRENNAN, with whom JUSTICE MARSHALL and JUSTICE STEVENS, join, dissenting. . . .

. . . Under the plurality's exceedingly grudging Fourth Amendment theory, the expectation of privacy is defeated if a single member of the public could conceivably position herself to see into the area in question without doing anything illegal. It is defeated whatever the difficulty a person would have in so positioning herself, and however infrequently anyone would in fact do so. In taking this view the plurality ignores the very essence of *Katz*. . . .

In California v. Ciraolo, 476 U.S. 207 (1986), we held that whatever might be observed from the window of an airplane flying at 1,000 feet could be deemed unprotected by any reasonable expectation of privacy. That decision was based on the belief that airplane traffic at that altitude was sufficiently common that no expectation of privacy could inure in anything on the ground observable with the naked eye from so high. . . . Seizing on a reference in *Ciraolo* to the fact that the police officer was in a position "where he ha[d] a right to be," ibid., today's plurality professes to find this case indistinguishable because FAA regulations do not impose a minimum altitude requirement on helicopter traffic; thus, the officer in this case too made his observations from a vantage point where he had a right to be.

It is a curious notion that the reach of the Fourth Amendment can be so largely defined by administrative regulations issued for purposes of flight safety. It is more curious still that the plurality relies to such an extent on the legality of the officer's act, when we have consistently refused to equate police violation of the law with infringement of the Fourth Amendment.[3] But the plurality's willingness to end its inquiry when it finds that the officer was in a position he had a right to be in is misguided for an even more fundamental reason. Finding determinative the fact that the officer was where he had a right to be is, at bottom, an attempt to analogize surveillance from a helicopter to surveillance by a police officer standing on a public road and viewing evidence of crime through an open window or a gap in a fence. In such a situation, the occupant of the home may be said to lack any reasonable expectation of privacy in what can be seen from that road — even if, in fact, people rarely pass that way.

The police officer positioned 400 feet above Riley's backyard was not, however, standing on a public road. The vantage point he enjoyed was not one any citizen could readily share. His ability to see over Riley's fence depended on his use of a very expensive and sophisticated piece of machinery to which few ordinary citizens have access. In such circumstances it makes no more sense to rely on the legality of the officer's position in the skies than it would to judge the constitutionality of the wiretap in *Katz* by the legality of the officer's position outside the telephone booth. . . . The question before us must be not whether the police were where they had a right to be, but whether public observation of Riley's curtilage was so commonplace that Riley's expectation of privacy in his backyard could not be considered reasonable. . . .

What separates me from Justice O'Connor is essentially an empirical matter concerning the extent of public use of the airspace at that altitude, together with the question of how to resolve that issue. I do not think the constitutional claim should fail simply because "there is reason to believe" that there is "considerable" public flying this close to earth or because Riley "introduced no evidence to the contrary before the Florida courts." . . .

If, however, we are to resolve the issue by considering whether the appropriate party carried its burden of proof, I again think that Riley must prevail. Because the State has greater access to information concerning customary flight patterns and because the coercive power of the State ought not be brought to bear in cases in which it is unclear whether the prosecution is a product of an unconstitutional, warrantless search, the burden of proof properly rests with the State and not with the individual defendant. The State quite clearly has not carried this burden. . . .

---

3. In Oliver v. United States, 466 U.S. 170 (1984), for example, we held that police officers who trespassed upon posted and fenced private land did not violate the Fourth Amendment, despite the fact that their action was subject to criminal sanctions. We noted that the interests vindicated by the Fourth Amendment were not identical with those served by the common law of trespass.

JUSTICE BLACKMUN, dissenting.

The question before the Court is whether the helicopter surveillance over Riley's property constituted a "search" within the meaning of the Fourth Amendment. Like Justice Brennan, Justice Marshall, Justice Stevens, and Justice O'Connor, I believe that answering this question depends upon whether Riley has a "reasonable expectation of privacy" that no such surveillance would occur, and does not depend upon the fact that the helicopter was flying at a lawful altitude under FAA regulations. A majority of this Court thus agrees to at least this much. . . .

[B]ecause I believe that private helicopters rarely fly over curtilages at an altitude of 400 feet, I would impose upon the prosecution the burden of proving contrary facts necessary to show that Riley lacked a reasonable expectation of privacy. Indeed, I would establish this burden of proof for any helicopter surveillance case in which the flight occurred below 1,000 feet — in other words, for any aerial surveillance case not governed by the Court's decision in California v. Ciraolo, 476 U.S. 207 (1986).

In this case, the prosecution did not meet this burden of proof, as Justice Brennan notes. This failure should compel a finding that a Fourth Amendment search occurred. But because our prior cases gave the parties little guidance on the burden of proof issue, I would remand this case to allow the prosecution an opportunity to meet this burden.

NOTES AND QUESTIONS

1. The plurality doesn't quite say that the question of whether Riley had a reasonable expectation of privacy in his greenhouse turns solely on the applicable FAA regulations; indeed, Justice White specifically rejects that position. But doesn't the plurality's methodology suggest that the mere *possibility* of lawful public observation, rather than its frequency or its likelihood, can render a subjective expectation of privacy unreasonable? As Professor Simmons points out, "Although it is now possible for law enforcement officials — or the general public — to fly in the air and observe the activities in private backyards, the practice is hardly considered routine and commonplace." Ric Simmons, From *Katz* to *Kyllo*: A Blueprint for Adapting the Fourth Amendment to Twenty-First Century Technologies, 53 Hastings L.J. 1303, 1333 (2002). Moreover, shouldn't the reasonableness of Riley's privacy expectation be determined, not by the prevalence of helicopters nationwide, but by the situation in his own rural community? But then, do we want a body of Fourth Amendment law in which the very meaning of a search might vary from place to place?

2. Because of *Riley* and *Ciraolo*, most aerial surveillance of a home's curtilage is outside the scope of Fourth Amendment concern, while physical invasion of the curtilage is still likely to be held a "search." Does this make any sense? After all, if the Fourth Amendment protects reasonable expectations of privacy, what difference does the police method of intrusion make, so long as equivalent personal information is (or is not) disclosed? See id., at 1306 (arguing that courts should disregard the method of search in applying the *Katz* test and consider "only the result of the search — the type of information that was acquired.") In this connection, consider Bond v. United States, 529 U.S. 334 (2000). In *Bond*, a Border Patrol official who had boarded a bus to check the immigration status of its passengers squeezed the soft luggage that passengers had placed in overhead storage as he walked the bus aisle.

His suspicions aroused by a "brick-like" object that he felt in one of the bags, the officer eventually obtained consent to open the bag and discovered a "brick" of methamphetamine. Chief Justice Rehnquist, writing for the Court, concluded that the officer's manipulation of the exterior of the bag constituted a search:

> . . . [T]he Government asserts that by exposing his bag to the public, petitioner lost a reasonable expectation that his bag would not be physically manipulated. The Government relies on our decisions in California v. Ciraolo, [476 U.S. 207 (1986)], and Florida v. Riley, 488 U.S. 445 (1989), for the proposition that matters open to public observation are not protected by the Fourth Amendment. . . .
>
> But *Ciraolo* and *Riley* are different from this case because they involved only visual, as opposed to tactile, observation. Physically invasive inspection is simply more intrusive than purely visual inspection. . . .
>
> Our Fourth Amendment analysis embraces two questions. First, we ask whether the individual, by his conduct, has exhibited an actual expectation of privacy. . . . Here, petitioner sought to preserve privacy by using an opaque bag and placing that bag directly above his seat. Second, we inquire whether the individual's expectation of privacy is "one that society is prepared to recognize as reasonable." When a bus passenger places a bag in an overhead bin, he expects that other passengers or bus employees may move it for one reason or another. . . . He does not expect that other passengers or bus employees will, as a matter of course, feel the bag in an exploratory manner. But this is exactly what the agent did here.

529 U.S., at 337-339. Is the animating vision of privacy in *Katz* starting to look a little complicated? After all, as Justice Breyer pointed out in a dissent joined by Justice Scalia, it is hardly unusual for overhead luggage to be pushed, pulled, prodded, and squeezed by people attempting to make room for another parcel. Indeed, "[t]he comparative likelihood that strangers will give bags in an overhead compartment a hard squeeze" does seem far greater than the likelihood that strangers will look down at fenced-in property from an aircraft. 529 U.S., at 341.

Does the majority capture anything fundamental with its distinction between "physically invasive" and "purely visual" inspections? Wasn't it irrelevant in *Katz* that the telephone booth was partly constructed of glass? Contrary to the majority's analysis, the dissent contended that "[w]hether tactile manipulation (say, of the exterior of luggage) is more intrusive or less intrusive than visual observation (say, through a lighted window) necessarily depends on the particular circumstances." Isn't this correct?

3. Finally, consider United States v. Place, 462 U.S. 695 (1983). Federal narcotics agents suspected that two suitcases in the possession of Raymond Place, a deplaning passenger at LaGuardia Airport, contained narcotics. The officers exposed the suitcases to a "sniff test" by a narcotics detection dog. When the dog reacted positively to one of the suitcases, the officers obtained a search warrant for the bag and discovered cocaine. The Supreme Court, in an opinion by Justice O'Connor, determined that the "sniff test" was not a Fourth Amendment search:

> A "canine sniff" by a well-trained narcotics detection dog . . . does not require opening the luggage. It does not expose noncontraband items that otherwise would remain hidden from public view, as does, for example, an officer's rummaging through the contents of the luggage. Thus, the manner in which information is obtained through this investigative technique is much less intrusive than a typical search. Moreover, the sniff discloses only the presence or absence of narcotics, a contraband item. Thus,

despite the fact that the sniff tells the authorities something about the contents of the luggage, the information obtained is limited.

In these respects, the canine sniff is sui generis. We are aware of no other investigative procedure that is so limited both in the manner in which the information is obtained and in the content of the information revealed by the procedure.

Id., at 707. What notion of privacy is at work in *Place*? After all, physical manipulation of the exterior of a suitcase likewise reveals a limited amount of information; is it obvious that the "search" in *Bond* was more intrusive than the dog sniff in *Place*? Is the need for Fourth Amendment regulation of police activity more apparent in one case than in the other?

4. Twenty years after the Supreme Court's decision in *Place*, the Court returned to the subject of "sniff tests" in Illinois v. Caballes, 543 U.S. 405 (2005). Caballes was stopped for speeding. While one officer on the scene was writing a ticket, another walked his narcotics-detection dog around Caballes's car. When the dog alerted at the trunk, officers searched it and found marijuana. The majority assumed that if Caballes's traffic stop had been prolonged beyond the time needed reasonably required to issue a warning ticket so that officers, without any reason to suspect Caballes of drug possession, could conduct a dog sniff of his car, any subsequent discovery of contraband would have been the result of an unconstitutional seizure. Because the dog sniff in *Caballes* did not prolong the legitimate traffic stop, however, the Court determined that the approach in *Place* was still the proper one:

> [T]he use of a well-trained narcotics-detection dog — one that "does not expose noncontraband items that otherwise would remain hidden from public view," *Place*, 462 U.S., at 707 — during a lawful traffic stop, generally does not implicate legitimate privacy interests. In this case, the dog sniff was performed on the exterior of respondent's car while he was lawfully seized for a traffic violation. Any intrusion on respondent's privacy expectations does not rise to the level of a constitutionally cognizable infringement.

543 U.S., at 409.

Reread the first sentence of the quote above. What do you think the majority meant by its use of the word *generally*? Would it have made a difference if the dog in *Caballes* had been given access to the interior of the car? At oral argument, Justice Souter, who dissented in *Caballes*, asked the Illinois Attorney General whether adhering to the approach in *Place* means that "nothing prevents the police from taking the dogs through every municipal garage in the United States and . . . from taking the dogs up to any homeowner's door, ringing the bell, and seeing if the dog[s] get[ ] a sniff of something when the door is opened." After *Caballes*, are police free to use sniffing dogs wherever they wish?

5. Should the purpose of a dog sniff make a difference to whether it constitutes a search? Justice Ginsburg, who dissented in *Caballes*, would have held that the police violated Caballes' Fourth Amendment rights when they conducted a dog sniff of his car without cause to suspect him of drug possession. At the same time, however, she said that a dog sniff for explosives, dangerous chemicals or biological weapons "would be an entirely different matter" on which she reserved judgment. Does this make any sense? Should the purpose for which a dog sniff is conducted count in the determination whether a sniff is a search or merely in the determination whether the "search" is reasonable?

6. A final thought on Fourth Amendment privacy. As it turns out, much law enforcement investigation involves seeking out the cooperation of witnesses. A suspect's friends and neighbors may be located and interviewed. Perhaps an employer or a relative has relevant information. Most of these witnesses work cooperatively with police; such interactions rarely involve "searches," as Fourth Amendment law construes the term. Yet police investigation of this sort can raise enormous privacy concerns — at least insofar as we conceive of privacy (which can mean many things) as the safeguarding of personal information. Is it a problem that police investigation of this type falls largely outside of Fourth Amendment control? You may want to reconsider this question after you have examined the materials in the next subsection.

b.   "Knowingly Expose[d] to the Public"

Recall the *Katz* majority's admonition that "[w]hat a person knowingly exposes to the public, even in his own home or office, is not a subject of Fourth Amendment protection." Katz v. United States, 389 U.S., at 351. This idea has played a central role in shaping the Court's post-*Katz* decision making — and in a direction that some view as placing too much police investigative activity outside Fourth Amendment constraints. The Court's critics may be right or wrong. But to understand the case law and how it is developed, it is centrally important to grapple with this idea of "knowing exposure."

We begin with the sensitive subject of undercover agents and informants. Prior to *Katz*, the Court decided several cases involving the Fourth Amendment's application to the use of undercover agents and informants who engaged in communications with suspects, some of which were either secretly recorded or transmitted to back-up law enforcement personnel. In Hoffa v. United States, 385 U.S. 293, 302 (1966), the Court held that the successful efforts of an informant to obtain the confidence of a suspect and to elicit statements from him involved only "a wrongdoer's misplaced belief that a person to whom he voluntarily confide[d] his wrongdoing [would] not reveal it" — and so "no interest legitimately protected by the Fourth Amendment." Accord, Lewis v. United States, 385 U.S. 206 (1966). The Court had earlier held that neither the recording of statements elicited by an undercover agent, see Lopez v. United States, 373 U.S. 427 (1963), nor the transmission of a suspect's statements to a nearby police officer via a secret microphone hidden on an informant's person, see On Lee v. United States, 343 U.S. 747 (1952), violated the Fourth Amendment. In the next case, the Court addressed the question whether its decision in *Katz* — with its newfound focus on reasonable expectations of privacy — affected these results.

UNITED STATES v. WHITE

Certiorari to the United States Court of Appeals for the Seventh Circuit
401 U.S. 745 (1971)

MR. JUSTICE WHITE announced the judgment of the Court and an opinion in which the CHIEF JUSTICE, MR. JUSTICE STEWART, and MR. JUSTICE BLACKMUN joined.

In 1966, respondent James A. White was tried and convicted under two consolidated indictments charging various illegal transactions in narcotics . . . . The issue before us is whether the Fourth Amendment bars from evidence the testimony of governmental agents who related certain conversations which had occurred between defendant White and a government informant, Harvey Jackson, and which the agents overheard by monitoring the frequency of a radio transmitter carried by Jackson and concealed on his person. On four occasions the conversations took place in Jackson's home; each of these conversations was overheard by an agent concealed in a kitchen closet with Jackson's consent and by a second agent outside the house using a radio receiver. Four other conversations — one in respondent's home, one in a restaurant, and two in Jackson's car — were overheard by the use of radio equipment. The prosecution was unable to locate and produce Jackson at the trial and the trial court overruled objections to the testimony of the agents who conducted the electronic surveillance. The jury returned a guilty verdict and defendant appealed. . . .

Our problem is not what the privacy expectations of particular defendants in particular situations may be or the extent to which they may in fact have relied on the discretion of their companions. Very probably, individual defendants neither know nor suspect that their colleagues have gone or will go to the police or are carrying recorders or transmitters. Otherwise, conversation would cease and our problem with these encounters would be nonexistent or far different from those now before us. Our problem, in terms of the principles announced in *Katz*, is what expectations of privacy are constitutionally "justifiable" — what expectations the Fourth Amendment will protect in the absence of a warrant. So far, the law permits the frustration of actual expectations of privacy by permitting authorities to use the testimony of those associates who for one reason or another have determined to turn to the police, as well as by authorizing the use of informants in the manner exemplified by *Hoffa* and *Lewis*.[4] If the law gives no protection to the wrongdoer whose trusted accomplice is or becomes a police agent, neither should it protect him when that same agent has recorded or transmitted the conversations which are later offered in evidence to prove the State's case.

Inescapably, one contemplating illegal activities must realize and risk that his companions may be reporting to the police. If he sufficiently doubts their trustworthiness, the association will very probably end or never materialize. But if he has no doubts, or allays them, or risks what doubt he has, the risk is his. In terms of what his course will be, what he will or will not do or say, we are unpersuaded that he would distinguish between probable informers on the one hand and probable informers with transmitters on the other. Given the possibility or probability that one of his colleagues is cooperating with the police, it is only speculation to assert that the defendant's utterances would be substantially different or his sense of security any less if he also thought it possible that the suspected colleague is wired for sound. At least there is no persuasive evidence that the difference in this respect between the

_____

4. Justice White described *Hoffa* and *Lewis* earlier in the opinion as follows:

Hoffa . . . , which was left undisturbed by *Katz*, held that however strongly a defendant may trust an apparent colleague, his expectations in this respect are not protected by the Fourth Amendment when it turns out that the colleague is a government agent regularly communicating with the authorities. . . . No warrant to "search and seize" is required in such circumstances, nor is it when the Government sends to defendant's home a secret agent who conceals his identity and makes a purchase of narcotics from the accused, *Lewis*. . . . — EDS.

electronically equipped and the unequipped agent is substantial enough to require discrete constitutional recognition, particularly under the Fourth Amendment which is ruled by fluid concepts of "reasonableness."

Nor should we be too ready to erect constitutional barriers to relevant and probative evidence which is also accurate and reliable. An electronic recording will many times produce a more reliable rendition of what a defendant has said than will the unaided memory of a police agent. It may also be that with the recording in existence it is less likely that the informant will change his mind, less chance that threat or injury will suppress unfavorable evidence and less chance that cross-examination will confound the testimony. Considerations like these obviously do not favor the defendant, but we are not prepared to hold that a defendant who has no constitutional right to exclude the informer's unaided testimony nevertheless has a Fourth Amendment privilege against a more accurate version of the events in question.

It is thus untenable to consider the activities and reports of the police agent himself, though acting without a warrant, to be a "reasonable" investigative effort and lawful under the Fourth Amendment but to view the same agent with a recorder or transmitter as conducting an "unreasonable" and unconstitutional search and seizure. Our opinion is currently shared by Congress and the Executive Branch, Title III, Omnibus Crime Control and Safe Streets Act of 1968, 82 Stat. 212, 18 U.S.C. §2510 et seq. (1964 ed., Supp. V), and the American Bar Association. Project on Standards for Criminal Justice, Electronic Surveillance §4.1 (Approved Draft 1971). It is also the result reached by prior cases in this Court. . . .

The judgment of the Court of Appeals is reversed.[5]

MR. JUSTICE BLACK concurs in the judgment of the Court for the reasons set forth in his dissent in Katz v. United States.

[The concurring opinion of Justice Brennan is omitted.]

MR. JUSTICE DOUGLAS, dissenting.

The issue in this case is clouded and concealed by the very discussion of it in legalistic terms. What the ancients knew as "eavesdropping," we now call "electronic surveillance"; but to equate the two is to treat man's first gunpowder on the same level as the nuclear bomb. Electronic surveillance is the greatest leveler of human privacy ever known. How most forms of it can be held "reasonable" within the meaning of the Fourth Amendment is a mystery. To be sure, the Constitution and Bill of Rights are not to be read as covering only the technology known in the 18th century. Otherwise its concept of "commerce" would be hopeless when it comes to the management of modern affairs. At the same time the concepts of privacy which the Founders enshrined in the Fourth Amendment vanish completely when we slavishly allow an all-powerful government, proclaiming law and order, efficiency, and other benign purposes, to penetrate all the walls and doors which men need to shield them from the pressures of a turbulent life around them and give them the health and strength to carry on. . . .

---

5. The Court had earlier held in Desist v. United States, 394 U.S. 244 (1969), that *Katz* would not be applied retroactively to electronic surveillance predating the *Katz* decision. Since the activity in *White* occurred prior to that decision, Justice White's plurality opinion relied on *Desist* as an independent basis for affirming the conviction. Justice Brennan believed that *Katz* required overruling both *On Lee* and *Lopez* but concurred with the four-justice plurality on the retroactivity issue. — EDS.

Monitoring, if prevalent, certainly kills free discourse and spontaneous utterances. Free discourse — a First Amendment value — may be frivolous or serious, humble or defiant, reactionary or revolutionary, profane or in good taste; but it is not free if there is surveillance. Free discourse liberates the spirit, though it may produce only froth. The individual must keep some facts concerning his thoughts within a small zone of people. At the same time he must be free to pour out his woes or inspirations or dreams to others. He remains the sole judge as to what must be said and what must remain unspoken. This is the essence of the idea of privacy implicit in the First and Fifth Amendments as well as in the Fourth. . . .

MR. JUSTICE HARLAN, dissenting. . . .

The plurality opinion . . . [adopts] the following reasoning: if A can relay verbally what is revealed to him by B (as in *Lewis* and *Hoffa*), or record and later divulge it (as in *Lopez*), what difference does it make if A conspires with another to betray B by contemporaneously transmitting to the other all that is said? The contention is, in essence, an argument that the distinction between third-party monitoring and *other* undercover techniques is one of form and not substance. The force of the contention depends on the evaluation of two separable but intertwined assumptions: first, that there is no greater invasion of privacy in the third-party situation, and, second, that uncontrolled consensual surveillance in an electronic age is a tolerable technique of law enforcement, given the values and goals of our political system.

The first of these assumptions takes as a point of departure the so-called "risk analysis" approach of *Lewis*, and *Lopez*, and to a lesser extent *On Lee*, or the expectations approach of *Katz*. While these formulations represent an advance over the unsophisticated trespass analysis of the common law, they too have their limitations and can, ultimately, lead to the substitution of words for analysis. The analysis must, in my view, transcend the search for subjective expectations or legal attribution of assumptions of risk. Our expectations, and the risks we assume, are in large part reflections of laws that translate into rules the customs and values of the past and present.

Since it is the task of the law to form and project, as well as mirror and reflect, we should not, as judges, merely recite the expectations and risks without examining the desirability of saddling them upon society. The critical question, therefore, is whether under our system of government, as reflected in the Constitution, we should impose on our citizens the risks of the electronic listener or observer without at least the protection of a warrant requirement.

This question must, in my view, be answered by assessing the nature of a particular practice and the likely extent of its impact on the individual's sense of security balanced against the utility of the conduct as a technique of law enforcement. For those more extensive intrusions that significantly jeopardize the sense of security which is the paramount concern of Fourth Amendment liberties, I am of the view that more than self-restraint by law enforcement officials is required and at the least warrants should be necessary.

The impact of the practice of third-party bugging, must, I think, be considered such as to undermine that confidence and sense of security in dealing with one another that is characteristic of individual relationships between citizens in a free society. It goes beyond the impact on privacy occasioned by the ordinary type of "informer" investigation upheld in *Lewis* and *Hoffa*. The argument of the plurality opinion, to the effect that it is irrelevant whether secrets are revealed by the mere tattletale or the transistor, ignores the differences occasioned by third-party monitoring and recording which insures full and accurate disclosure of all that is said, free of the possibility of error and oversight that inheres in human reporting.

Authority is hardly required to support the proposition that words would be measured a good deal more carefully and communication inhibited if one suspected his conversations were being transmitted and transcribed. Were third-party bugging a prevalent practice, it might well smother that spontaneity — reflected in frivolous, impetuous, sacrilegious, and defiant discourse — that liberates daily life. Much offhand exchange is easily forgotten and one may count on the obscurity of his remarks, protected by the very fact of a limited audience, and the likelihood that the listener will either overlook or forget what is said, as well as the listener's inability to reformulate a conversation without having to contend with a documented record.[24] All these values are sacrificed by a rule of law that permits official monitoring of private discourse limited only by the need to locate a willing assistant. . . .

Finally, it is too easy to forget — and, hence, too often forgotten — that the issue here is whether to interpose a search warrant procedure between law enforcement agencies engaging in electronic eavesdropping and the public generally. By casting its "risk analysis" solely in terms of the expectations and risks that "wrongdoers" or "one contemplating illegal activities" ought to bear, the plurality opinion, I think, misses the mark entirely. *On Lee* does not simply mandate that criminals must daily run the risk of unknown eavesdroppers prying into their private affairs; it subjects each and every law-abiding member of society to that risk. The very purpose of interposing the Fourth Amendment warrant requirement is to redistribute the privacy risks throughout society in a way that produces the results the plurality opinion ascribes to the *On Lee* rule. Abolition of *On Lee* would not end electronic eavesdropping. It would prevent public officials from engaging in that practice unless they first had probable cause to suspect an individual of involvement in illegal activities and had tested their version of the facts before a detached judicial officer. . . .

[The dissenting opinion of Justice Marshall is omitted.]

NOTES AND QUESTIONS

1. According to the plurality opinion in *White*, it makes no sense to recognize a Fourth Amendment privilege against the use at trial of an accurate version of one's conversation — a version secretly tape-recorded or transmitted by an informant —

---

24. From the same standpoint it may also be thought that electronic recording by an informer of a face-to-face conversation with a criminal suspect, as in *Lopez*, should be differentiated from third-party monitoring, as in *On Lee* and the case before us, in that the latter assures revelation to the Government by obviating the possibility that the informer may be tempted to renege in his undertaking to pass on to the Government all that he has learned. While the continuing vitality of *Lopez* is not drawn directly into question by this case, candor compels me to acknowledge that the views expressed in this opinion may impinge upon that part of the reasoning in *Lopez* which suggested that a suspect has no right to anticipate unreliable testimony. I am now persuaded that such an approach misconceives the basic issue, focusing, as it does, on the interests of a particular individual rather than evaluating the impact of a practice on the sense of security that is the true concern of the Fourth Amendment's protection of privacy. Distinctions do, however, exist between *Lopez*, where a known Government agent uses a recording device, and this case which involves third-party overhearing. However unlikely that the participant recorder will not play his tapes, the fact of the matter is that in a third-party situation the intrusion is instantaneous. Moreover, differences in the prior relationship between the investigator and the suspect may provide a focus for future distinctions.

when there is no Fourth Amendment privilege barring the informant from testifying to his recollection of the conversation. But this argument begs the question
whether the Court took a wrong turn in *Hoffa* and *Lewis*. The basis for the holdings
in these "unbugged agent" cases was that persons assume the risk that their trusted
colleagues may be or may become government agents. But should we have to
assume this risk? At least when the government places a covert agent in our midst to
cajole us into talking, isn't it "constitutionally justifiable" to impose the requirement
of a warrant based on probable cause?

In part, the answer may depend on which metaphor one chooses. Current doctrine tends to emphasize the comparison between the undercover agent and a gossipy friend, the idea being that, just as we all bear the risk that our friends will repeat
things they've heard us say, so suspects bear the risk that people they trust (including successful undercover agents) will betray that trust. An alternative comparison
is between the undercover agent and a spy. Like spies (and unlike gossipy friends),
undercover agents are not who they pretend to be — they are not friends who talk
too much but rather are more like enemies who pretend to be friends. Do we really
bear the risk of spies in our ordinary lives? If not, should we bear the risk of police
spies? Why should the Fourth Amendment reach a transmitting device placed on a
telephone booth but not one placed on a person charged with following the suspect
and eliciting potentially incriminating statements?

2. Perhaps the results in cases like *Hoffa*, *Lewis*, and *White* stem from the recognition that certain crimes cannot be investigated effectively without using covert
agents and that the warrant and probable cause requirements would unduly frustrate their use. Professor Philip Heymann has argued that undercover operations
are most important to the investigation of crimes that cannot be readily observed
and reported by witnesses and that will not be reported by participants or victims.
See Philip Heymann, Understanding Criminal Investigations, 22 Harv. J. Legis.
315, 325-327, 331-334 (1985). Narcotics trafficking and the bribery of public officials, for instance, involve willing participants and infrequently produce victims who
notice they have been harmed. Similarly, the intimidation of witnesses makes it difficult to investigate crimes like loan sharking or extortion. Requiring an overly rigorous form of factual justification prior to use of a covert agent "could altogether
eliminate the use of undercover operations in even the most pressing situations."
Id., at 332.

Assume for the moment that Heymann is right. (He probably is.) How much
weight should courts give this kind of government need? If the investigation of
some but not all crimes requires covert methods, should Fourth Amendment law
differ according to the kinds of crime police investigate? Whatever the best answer
in theory, historically Fourth Amendment law does seem to have responded to law
enforcement needs, and law enforcement needs are, in part, a function of what
crimes the police investigate. For now, note three points: First, some crimes by their
nature require much more in the way of privacy intrusion to investigate than
others. Second, as Heymann's article emphasizes, those crimes often (though not
always) involve consensual transactions. Third and finally, our society devotes a
great deal of energy and resources to attacking drug crime, which primarily
consists of consensual transactions. Given those three points, perhaps the outcome
in *White* is unsurprising.

3. The plurality opinion in *White* cites Title III of the Omnibus Crime Control
and Safe Streets Act of 1968, which is treated in more detail in Chapter 7. In the
wake of *Katz* and Berger v. New York, 388 U.S. 41 (1967), which held New York's

wiretap statute to be unconstitutional,[6] Congress enacted Title III to establish procedures for the use of electronic eavesdropping by law enforcement that would be consistent with the Court's holdings. After its enactment, most states passed their own statutes patterned on Title III's provisions. Today, Title III and similar state statutes, along with subsequently enacted laws, such as the Electronic Communications Privacy Act of 1986, regulate not only the use of traditional wiretaps and the electronic surveillance of oral communications, but also the interception of electronic communications such as e-mail. Most of these statutes, however, do not apply to the recording or third-party surveillance of a communication when one of the parties to the communication consents — hence, they play only a small role in regulating police use of undercovers and informants.

4. Finally, notice that by the time *White* was decided, Justice Harlan, the author of the "reasonable expectations" approach, was already expressing reservations about any analytic framework for Fourth Amendment coverage questions — including his own — that might lead to the "substitution of words for analysis." Whatever you think about the result in *White*, doesn't it suggest that Justice Harlan's caution may be well taken? Does *White*'s methodology amount to a conclusion that the "knowing exposure" of one's words to another forfeits the protections of the Fourth Amendment if that other elects to betray us? Is this approach to defining the Fourth Amendment's scope consistent with any robust account of the privacy interests that the Amendment should protect? Ponder the *Katz* Court's statement that "[w]hat a person knowingly exposes to the public" cannot be the subject of Fourth Amendment protection as you read the following case. Is the next case an example of how a legal formula can take on a life of its own?

CALIFORNIA v. GREENWOOD

Certiorari to the Court of Appeal of California, Fourth Appellate District
486 U.S. 35 (1988)

JUSTICE WHITE delivered the opinion of the Court. . . .

In early 1984, Investigator Jenny Stracner of the Laguna Beach Police Department received information indicating that respondent Greenwood might be engaged in narcotics trafficking. . . . On April 6, 1984, Stracner asked the neighborhood's regular trash collector to pick up the plastic garbage bags that Greenwood had left on the curb in front of his house and to turn the bags over to her without mixing their contents with garbage from other houses. The trash collector cleaned his truck bin of other refuse, collected the garbage bags from the street in front of Greenwood's house, and turned the bags over to Stracner. The officer searched through the rubbish and found items indicative of narcotics use. She recited the information that she had gleaned from the trash search in an affidavit in support of a warrant to search Greenwood's home.

Police officers encountered both respondents at the house later that day when they arrived to execute the warrant. The police discovered quantities of cocaine and hashish during their search of the house. Respondents were arrested on felony narcotics charges. They subsequently posted bail.

---

6. *Berger* is discussed in Chapter 4, at pages 318-320.

The police continued to receive reports of many late-night visitors to the Greenwood house. On May 4, Investigator Robert Rahaeuser obtained Greenwood's garbage from the regular trash collector in the same manner as had Stracner. The garbage again contained evidence of narcotics use.

Rahaeuser secured another search warrant for Greenwood's home based on the information from the second trash search. The police found more narcotics and evidence of narcotics trafficking when they executed the warrant. Greenwood was again arrested.

The Superior Court dismissed the charges against respondents on the authority of People v. Krivda, 5 Cal. 3d 357 (1971), which held that warrantless trash searches violate the Fourth Amendment. . . . The court found that the police would not have had probable cause to search the Greenwood home without the evidence obtained from the trash searches.

The Court of Appeal affirmed. . . .

The California Supreme Court denied the State's petition for review of the Court of Appeal's decision. We granted certiorari, and now reverse.

The warrantless search and seizure of the garbage bags left at the curb outside the Greenwood house would violate the Fourth Amendment only if respondents manifested a subjective expectation of privacy in their garbage that society accepts as objectively reasonable. Respondents do not disagree with this standard.

They assert, however, that they had, and exhibited, an expectation of privacy with respect to the trash that was searched by the police: The trash, which was placed on the street for collection at a fixed time, was contained in opaque plastic bags, which the garbage collector was expected to pick up, mingle with the trash of others, and deposit at the garbage dump. The trash was only temporarily on the street, and there was little likelihood that it would be inspected by anyone.

It may well be that respondents did not expect that the contents of their garbage bags would become known to the police or other members of the public. An expectation of privacy does not give rise to Fourth Amendment protection, however, unless society is prepared to accept that expectation as objectively reasonable.

Here, we conclude that respondents exposed their garbage to the public sufficiently to defeat their claim to Fourth Amendment protection. It is common knowledge that plastic garbage bags left on or at the side of a public street are readily accessible to animals, children, scavengers, snoops,[4] and other members of the public. Moreover, respondents placed their refuse at the curb for the express purpose of conveying it to a third party, the trash collector, who might himself have sorted through respondents' trash or permitted others, such as the police, to do so. . . .

[A]s we have held, the police cannot reasonably be expected to avert their eyes from evidence of criminal activity that could have been observed by any member of the public. Hence, "[w]hat a person knowingly exposes to the public, even in his own home or office, is not a subject of Fourth Amendment protection." Katz v. United States. . . .

4. Even the refuse of prominent Americans has not been invulnerable. In 1975, for example, a reporter for a weekly tabloid seized five bags of garbage from the sidewalk outside the home of Secretary of State Henry Kissinger. Washington Post, July 9, 1975, p. A1, col. 8. A newspaper editorial criticizing this journalistic "trashpicking" observed that "[e]vidently . . . 'everybody does it.'" Washington Post, July 10, 1975, p. A18, col. 1. We of course do not, as the dissent implies, "bas[e] [our] conclusion" that individuals have no reasonable expectation of privacy in their garbage on this "sole incident." Post, at 51.

The judgment of the California Court of Appeal is therefore reversed. . . . It is so ordered.

JUSTICE KENNEDY took no part in the consideration or decision of this case.

JUSTICE BRENNAN, with whom JUSTICE MARSHALL joins, dissenting.

Every week for two months, and at least once more a month later, the Laguna Beach police clawed through the trash that respondent Greenwood left in opaque, sealed bags on the curb outside his home. Complete strangers minutely scrutinized their bounty, undoubtedly dredging up intimate details of Greenwood's private life and habits. The intrusions proceeded without a warrant, and no court before or since has concluded that the police acted on probable cause to believe Greenwood was engaged in any criminal activity. . . .

The Framers of the Fourth Amendment understood that "unreasonable searches" of "paper[s] and effects" — no less than "unreasonable searches" of "person[s] and houses" — infringe privacy. . . . [S]o long as a package is "closed against inspection," the Fourth Amendment protects its contents, "wherever they may be," and the police must obtain a warrant to search it just "as is required when papers are subjected to search in one's own household." . . .

Our precedent . . . leaves no room to doubt that had respondents been carrying their personal effects in opaque, sealed plastic bags — identical to the ones they placed on the curb — their privacy would have been protected from warrantless police intrusion. . . .

Respondents deserve no less protection just because Greenwood used the bags to discard rather than to transport his personal effects. Their contents are not inherently any less private, and Greenwood's decision to discard them, at least in the manner in which he did, does not diminish his expectation of privacy.

A trash bag, like [other containers we have addressed,] "is a common repository for one's personal effects" and, even more than many of them, is "therefore . . . inevitably associated with the expectation of privacy." . . . A single bag of trash testifies eloquently to the eating, reading, and recreational habits of the person who produced it. A search of trash, like a search of the bedroom, can relate intimate details about sexual practices, health, and personal hygiene. Like rifling through desk drawers or intercepting phone calls, rummaging through trash can divulge the target's financial and professional status, political affiliations and inclinations, private thoughts, personal relationships, and romantic interests. It cannot be doubted that a sealed trash bag harbors telling evidence of the "intimate activity associated with the 'sanctity of a man's home and the privacies of life,'" which the Fourth Amendment is designed to protect.

The Court properly rejects the State's attempt to distinguish trash searches from other searches on the theory that trash is abandoned and therefore not entitled to an expectation of privacy. As the author of the Court's opinion observed last Term, a defendant's "property interest [in trash] does not settle the matter for Fourth Amendment purposes, for the reach of the Fourth Amendment is not determined by state property law." [California v. Rooney, 483 U.S. 307, 320 (1987)] (White, J., dissenting). In evaluating the reasonableness of Greenwood's expectation that his sealed trash bags would not be invaded, the Court has held that we must look to "understandings that are recognized and permitted by society." Most of us, I believe, would be incensed to discover a meddler — whether a neighbor, a reporter, or a detective — scrutinizing our sealed trash containers to discover some detail of our personal lives. That was, quite naturally, the reaction to the sole incident on which the Court bases its conclusion that "snoops" and the like defeat the expectation of privacy in trash. When a tabloid reporter examined then-Secretary of State Henry Kissinger's trash and published his findings, Kissinger was "really revolted" by the intrusion and his wife suffered "grave anguish." N.Y. Times, July 9, 1975, p. A1, col. 8. The public response roundly condemning the reporter demonstrates that society not only recognized those reactions as reasonable, but shared them as well. . . .

That is not to deny that isolated intrusions into opaque, sealed trash containers occur. When, acting on their own, "animals, children, scavengers, snoops, [or] other members of the public," *actually* rummage through a bag of trash and expose its contents to plain view, "police cannot reasonably be expected to avert their eyes from evidence of criminal activity that could have been observed by any member of the public." . . .

Had Greenwood flaunted his intimate activity by strewing his trash all over the curb for all to see, or had some nongovernmental intruder invaded his privacy and done the same, I could accept the Court's conclusion that an expectation of privacy would have been unreasonable. Similarly, had police searching the city dump run across incriminating evidence that, despite commingling with the trash of others, still retained its identity as Greenwood's, we would have a different case. But all that Greenwood "exposed . . . to the public," were the exteriors of several opaque, sealed containers. . . .

The mere *possibility* that unwelcome meddlers *might* open and rummage through the containers does not negate the expectation of privacy in their contents any more than the possibility of a burglary negates an expectation of privacy in the home; or the possibility of a private intrusion negates an expectation of privacy in an unopened package; or the possibility that an operator will listen in on a telephone conversation negates an expectation of privacy in the words spoken on the telephone. "What a person . . . seeks to preserve as private, *even in an area accessible to the public*, may be constitutionally protected." *Katz*, 389 U.S., at 351-352. We have therefore repeatedly rejected attempts to justify a State's invasion of privacy on the ground that the privacy is not absolute. See Chapman v. United States, 365 U.S. 610, 616-617 (1961) (search of a house invaded tenant's Fourth Amendment rights even though landlord had authority to enter house for some purposes); Stoner v. California, 376 U.S. 483, 487-490 (1964) (implicit consent to janitorial personnel to enter motel room does not amount to consent to police search of room); O'Connor v. Oretega, 480 U.S. 709, 717 (1987) (a government employee has a reasonable expectation of privacy in his office, even though "it is the nature of government offices that others — such as fellow employees, supervisors, consensual visitors, and the general public — may have frequent access to an individual's office"). . . .

Nor is it dispositive that "respondents placed their refuse at the curb for the express purpose of conveying it to a third party, . . . who might himself have sorted through respondents' trash or permitted others, such as the police, to do so." In the first place, Greenwood can hardly be faulted for leaving trash on his curb when a county ordinance commanded him to do so, Orange County Code §4-3-45(a) (1986) (must "remov[e] from the premises at least once each week" all "solid waste created, produced or accumulated in or about [his] dwelling house"), and prohibited him from disposing of it in any other way, see Orange County Code §3-3-85

(1988) (burning trash is unlawful). . . . More importantly, even the voluntary relinquishment of possession or control over an effect does not necessarily amount to a relinquishment of a privacy expectation in it. Were it otherwise, a letter or package would lose all Fourth Amendment protection when placed in a mailbox or other depository with the "express purpose" of entrusting it to the postal officer or a private carrier; those bailees are just as likely as trash collectors (and certainly have greater incentive) to "sor[t] through" the personal effects entrusted to them, "or permi[t] others, such as police to do so." Yet, it has been clear for at least 110 years that the possibility of such an intrusion does not justify a warrantless search by police in the first instance.

In holding that the warrantless search of Greenwood's trash was consistent with the Fourth Amendment, the Court paints a grim picture of our society. It depicts a society in which local authorities may command their citizens to dispose of their personal effects in the manner least protective of the "sanctity of [the] home and the privacies of life," Boyd v. United States, 116 U.S., at 630, and then monitor them arbitrarily and without judicial oversight — a society that is not prepared to recognize as reasonable an individual's expectation of privacy in the most private of personal effects sealed in an opaque container and disposed of in a manner designed to commingle it imminently and inextricably with the trash of others. The American society with which I am familiar . . . is more dedicated to individual liberty and more sensitive to intrusions on the sanctity of the home than the Court is willing to acknowledge.

I dissent.

NOTES AND QUESTIONS

1. What do you think? Does *Greenwood* represent a defensible approach to privacy protection, or does it, as Justice Harlan cautioned in *White*, substitute words for analysis? Be aware that the Court has invoked the concept of "knowing exposure" in a number of cases to limit the Fourth Amendment's coverage. Thus, a bank depositor has no protectible Fourth Amendment interest in the bank's microfilms of his checks, deposit slips, and other financial records related to his account because he "takes the risk, in revealing his affairs to another, that the information will be conveyed by that person to the Government." United States v. Miller, 424 U.S. 435, 443 (1976). Similarly, the telephone company's installation at its offices, pursuant to police request, of a pen register to record the numbers dialed on an individual's telephone raises no Fourth Amendment concern because individuals "voluntarily convey[ ] numerical information to the telephone company and 'expose[ ]' that information . . . in the ordinary course of business." Smith v. Maryland, 442 U.S. 735, 744 (1979).

2. Whether these results are defensible, there are a number of questions about the Court's approach in these and similar cases. As Professor Heffernan has said, the cases seem to suggest that we have privacy expectations only in contexts where we demonstrate "eternal vigilance" against others: "[E]ven the slightest exposure of an item to the public can defeat a privacy claim." William C. Heffernan, Fourth Amendment Privacy Interests, 92 J. Crim. L. & Criminology 1, 38-40 (2001/2002). But Heffernan argues that our actual experiences with what is "public" and what is "private" don't lead us to be eternally vigilant against the scrutiny of others, but

instead to rely on "an expectation that outsiders will exercise forbearance with respect to personal matters." Think of all our limited, special-purpose revelations of private information: "[P]eople who take steps to ensure that the public does not have access to their financial records nonetheless routinely rely on bank officials to process their checks and deposits." Id., at 39. If we expose things to others all the time on the expectation that these others will respect our privacy, does this suggest a problem with the Court's framework?

3. For that matter, do we have any choice but to make such special-purpose revelations? We may "knowingly" reveal our deposit information to the bank, the numbers we dial to the telephone company, and the e-mails we send to the Internet service provider, but are such revelations in any sense voluntary? Note Justice Brennan's observation that Greenwood was required by law to leave his garbage at the curb. Shouldn't the law entitle Greenwood to rely on the garbage collector's rectitude about personal information that his garbage might disclose — particularly given his limited options for trash disposal?

4. Cases like *Greenwood*, *Miller*, and *Smith*, some scholars have argued, reflect a narrow, individualistic conception of privacy that is deeply contrary to reality: "Much of what is important in human life takes place in a situation of shared privacy. The important events in our lives are shared with a chosen group of others; they do not occur in isolation, nor are they open to the entire world." Mary I. Coombs, Shared Privacy and the Fourth Amendment, or the Rights of Relationships, 75 Cal. L. Rev. 1593 (1987). Though the Court has viewed such "sharing" as proof of the absence of reasonable privacy expectations, it is not clear that citizens view privacy in the same way. The survey participants in one empirical study, for instance, considered the government perusal of bank records to be highly intrusive. See Christopher Slobogin & Joseph E. Schumacher, Reasonable Expectations of Privacy and Autonomy in Fourth Amendment Cases: An Empirical Look at "Understandings Recognized and Permitted by Society," 42 Duke L.J. 727, 740 (1993).

c.   Privacy and Technology

When the Fourth Amendment was written and ratified, the chief tools used for "searches" were the constable's eyes and a lantern. Today, a great many searches are still performed by the unaided eyes and ears of a police officer. But a great many make use of surveillance techniques and technologies that no one imagined in 1791. You have already encountered some of those technologies: telephones and "bugs" in *Katz*, the helicopter in *Riley*, the wire worn by the informant in *White*. What happens when the technology is more advanced? In the years since *Katz*, the Supreme Court has made plain that anything that a suspect "knowingly exposes" to the public is exposed to the police as well. But how are courts to measure what is, and isn't, "exposed"? Is it anything any member of the public could see or hear with the most advanced surveillance technology available? Anything the *police* can see or hear with the most advanced technology available to *them*?

We begin with electronic tracking devices. In United States v. Knotts, 460 U.S. 276 (1983), the Court held that no search took place when police monitored a beeper attached to a drum of chloroform, a chemical commonly used for the manufacture of illegal drugs, to track the movements of a car they knew to be carrying the drum. The Court concluded that a person traveling in a car on public thoroughfares has no reasonable expectation of privacy in his movements from one place to the next because he "voluntarily convey[s] to anyone who want[s] to look the fact that he [is] travelling over particular roads in a particular direction, the fact of whatever stops he ma[kes], and the fact of his final destination when he exit[s] from public roads onto private property." Id., at 281-282. Is this a sound application of the "knowingly exposed" principle? Does it seem right that we have no reasonable expectation of privacy in our movements from place to place? Or do we reasonably possess some measure of privacy in public places — if only by virtue of our anonymity and the inattention of others? The next case, also involving the use of an electronic tracking device, provided the Court with a second opportunity to pursue this and related issues only one year after *Knotts* was decided.

UNITED STATES v. KARO

Certiorari to the United States Court of Appeals for the Tenth Circuit
468 U.S. 705 (1984)

JUSTICE WHITE delivered the opinion of the Court.

In United States v. Knotts, 460 U.S. 276 (1983), we held that the warrantless monitoring of an electronic tracking device ("beeper") inside a container of chemicals did not violate the Fourth Amendment when it revealed no information that could not have been obtained through visual surveillance. In this case, we are called upon to address two questions left unresolved in *Knotts*: (1) whether installation of a beeper in a container of chemicals with the consent of the original owner constitutes a search or seizure within the meaning of the Fourth Amendment when the container is delivered to a buyer having no knowledge of the presence of the beeper, and (2) whether monitoring of a beeper falls within the ambit of the Fourth Amendment when it reveals information that could not have been obtained through visual surveillance.

In August 1980 Agent Rottinger of the Drug Enforcement Administration (DEA) learned that respondents James Karo, Richard Horton, and William Harley had ordered 50 gallons of ether from Government informant Carl Muehlenweg of Graphic Photo Design in Albuquerque, N.M. Muehlenweg told Rottinger that the ether was to be used to extract cocaine from clothing that had been imported into the United States. . . . With Muehlenweg's consent, agents substituted their own can containing a beeper for one of the cans in the shipment and then had all 10 cans painted to give them a uniform appearance.

On September 20, 1980, agents saw Karo pick up the ether from Muehlenweg. They then followed Karo to his house using visual and beeper surveillance. At one point later that day, agents determined by using the beeper that the ether was still inside the house, but they later determined that it had been moved undetected to Horton's house, where they located it using the beeper. . . . Two days later, agents discovered that the ether had once again been moved, and, using the beeper, they located it at the residence of Horton's father. The next day, the beeper was no longer transmitting from Horton's father's house, and agents traced the beeper to a commercial storage facility. . . .

Using the beeper, agents traced the beeper can to another self-storage facility three days later. Agents detected the smell of ether coming from locker 15 and learned from the manager that Horton and Harley had rented that locker using an alias the same day that the ether had been removed from the first storage facility. The agents . . . obtained consent from the manager of the facility to install a closed-circuit video camera in a locker that had a view of locker 15. On February 6, 1981, agents observed, by means of the video camera, Gene Rhodes and an unidentified woman removing the cans from the locker and loading them onto the rear bed of Horton's pickup truck. Using both visual and beeper surveillance agents tracked the truck to Rhodes' residence where it was parked in the driveway. Agents then observed Rhodes and a woman bringing boxes and other items from inside the house and loading the items into the trunk of an automobile. Agents did not see any cans being transferred from the pickup.

At about 6 p.m. on February 6, the car and the pickup left the driveway and traveled along public highways to Taos. During the trip, the two vehicles were under both physical and electronic surveillance. When the vehicles arrived at a house in Taos rented by Horton, Harley, and Michael Steele, the agents did not maintain tight surveillance for fear of detection. When the vehicles left the Taos residence, agents determined, using the beeper monitor, that the beeper can was still inside the house. Again on February 7, the beeper revealed that the ether can was still on the premises. At one point, agents noticed that the windows of the house were wide open on a cold windy day, leading them to suspect that the ether was being used. On February 8, the agents applied for and obtained a warrant to search the Taos residence based in part on information derived through use of the beeper. The warrant was executed on February 10, 1981, and Horton, Harley, Steele, and Evan Roth were arrested, and cocaine and laboratory equipment were seized. . . .

. . . It is clear that the actual placement of the beeper into the can violated no one's Fourth Amendment rights. The can into which the beeper was placed belonged at the time to the DEA, and by no stretch of the imagination could it be said that respondents then had any legitimate expectation of privacy in it. The ether and the original 10 cans, on the other hand, belonged to, and were in the possession of, Muehlenweg, who had given his consent to any invasion of those items that occurred. Thus, even if there had been no substitution of cans and the agents had placed the beeper into one of the original 10 cans, Muehlenweg's consent was sufficient to validate the placement of the beeper in the can.

The Court of Appeals . . . did not hold that the actual placement of the beeper into the ether can violated the Fourth Amendment. Instead, it held that the violation occurred at the time the beeper-laden can was transferred to Karo. . . .

Not surprisingly, the Court of Appeals did not describe the transfer as either a "search" or a "seizure," for plainly it is neither. . . . The mere transfer to Karo of a can containing an unmonitored beeper infringed no privacy interest. It conveyed no information that Karo wished to keep private, for it conveyed no information at all. To be sure, it created a *potential* for an invasion of privacy, but we have never held that potential, as opposed to actual, invasions of privacy constitute searches for purposes of the Fourth Amendment. . . .

We likewise do not believe that the transfer of the container constituted a seizure. . . . Although the can may have contained an unknown and unwanted foreign object, it cannot be said that anyone's possessory interest was interfered with in a meaningful way. At most, there was a technical trespass on the space occupied by the beeper. The existence of a physical trespass is only marginally relevant to the question of whether the Fourth Amendment has been violated, however, for an actual trespass is neither necessary nor sufficient to establish a constitutional violation. . . .

Here, there is no gainsaying that the beeper was used to locate the ether in a specific house in Taos, N.M., and that that information was in turn used to secure a warrant for the search of the house. . . . This case thus presents the question whether the monitoring of a beeper in a private residence, a location not open to visual surveillance, violates the Fourth Amendment rights of those who have a justifiable interest in the privacy of the residence. . . . [W]e think that it does.

At the risk of belaboring the obvious, private residences are places in which the individual normally expects privacy free of governmental intrusion not authorized by a warrant, and that expectation is plainly one that society is prepared to recognize as justifiable . . . In this case, had a DEA agent thought it useful to enter the Taos residence to verify that the ether was actually in the house and had he done so surreptitiously and without a warrant, there is little doubt that he would have engaged in an unreasonable search within the meaning of the Fourth Amendment. For purposes of the Amendment, the result is the same where, without a warrant, the Government surreptitiously employs an electronic device to obtain information that it could not have obtained by observation from outside the curtilage of the house. The beeper tells the agent that a particular article is actually located at a particular time in the private residence and is in the possession of the person or persons whose residence is being watched. Even if visual surveillance has revealed that the article to which the beeper is attached has entered the house, the later monitoring not only verifies the officers' observations but also establishes that the article remains on the premises. . . .

The monitoring of an electronic device such as a beeper is, of course, less intrusive than a full-scale search, but it does reveal a critical fact about the interior of the premises that the Government is extremely interested in knowing and that it could not have otherwise obtained without a warrant. The case is thus not like *Knotts*, for there the beeper told the authorities nothing about the interior of Knotts' cabin. . . .

We cannot accept the Government's contention that it should be completely free from the constraints of the Fourth Amendment to determine by means of an electronic device, without a warrant and without probable cause or reasonable suspicion, whether a particular article — or a person, for that matter — is in an individual's home at a particular time. Indiscriminate monitoring of property that has been withdrawn from public view would present far too serious a threat to privacy interests in the home to escape entirely some sort of Fourth Amendment oversight. . . .

[B]y maintaining the beeper the agents verified that the ether was actually located in the Taos house and that it remained there while the warrant was sought. This information was obtained without a warrant and would therefore be inadmissible at trial against those with privacy interests in the house. . . . That information, which was included in the warrant affidavit, would also invalidate the warrant for the search of the house if it proved to be critical to establishing probable cause for the issuance of the warrant. . . .

It requires only a casual examination of the warrant affidavit . . . to conclude that the officers could have secured the warrant without relying on the beeper to locate the ether in the house sought to be searched. The affidavit recounted the months-long tracking of the evidence, including the visual and beeper surveillance of Horton's pickup on its trip from Albuquerque to the immediate vicinity of the Taos residence; its departure a short time later without the ether; its later return to the residence; and the visual observation of the residence with its windows open on a cold night.

This leaves the question whether any part of this additional information contained in the warrant affidavit was itself the fruit of a Fourth Amendment violation. . . .

. . . On the initial leg of its journey, the ether came to rest in Karo's house where it was monitored; it then moved in succession to two other houses . . . before it was moved first to a locker in one public warehouse and then to a locker in another. . . . On September 6, the ether was removed from the second storage facility and transported to Taos.

Assuming for present purposes that prior to its arrival at the second warehouse the beeper was illegally used to locate the ether . . . we are confident that such use of the beeper does not taint its later use in locating the ether and tracking it to Taos. The movement of the ether from the first warehouse was undetected, but by monitoring the beeper the agents discovered that it had been moved to the second storage facility. No prior monitoring of the beeper contributed to this discovery; using the beeper for this purpose was thus untainted by any possible prior illegality. Furthermore, the beeper informed the agents only that the ether was somewhere in the warehouse; it did not identify the specific locker in which the ether was located. Monitoring the beeper revealed nothing about the contents of the locker . . . and hence was not a search of that locker. The locker was identified only when agents traversing the public parts of the facility found that the smell of ether was coming from a specific locker.

The agents set up visual surveillance of that locker, and on September 6, they observed Rhodes and a female remove the ether and load it into Horton's pickup truck. The truck moved over the public streets and was tracked by beeper to Rhodes' house, where it was temporarily parked. At about 6 p.m. the truck was observed departing and was tracked visually and by beeper to the vicinity of the house in Taos. Because locating the ether in the warehouse was not an illegal search — and because the ether was seen being loaded into Horton's truck, which then traveled the public highways — it is evident that under *Knotts* there was no violation of the Fourth Amendment. . . . Under these circumstances, it is clear that the warrant affidavit, after striking the facts about monitoring the beeper while it was in the Taos residence, contained sufficient untainted information to furnish probable cause for the issuance of the search warrant. . . .

The judgment of the Court of Appeals is accordingly reversed.

[Justice O'Connor's opinion, joined by Justice Rehnquist, concurring in part and concurring in the judgment, is omitted.]

JUSTICE STEVENS, with whom JUSTICE BRENNAN and JUSTICE MARSHALL join, concurring in part and dissenting in part.

The beeper is a species of radio transmitter. Mounted inside a container, it has much in common with a microphone mounted on a person. It reveals the location of the item to which it is attached — the functional equivalent of a radio transmission saying "Now I am at _____ ."

. . . In my opinion the surreptitious use of a radio transmitter — whether it contains a microphone or merely a signalling device — on an individual's personal property is both a seizure and a search within the meaning of the Fourth Amendment. . . .

[T]he Court correctly concludes that when beeper surveillance reveals the location of property that has been concealed from public view, it constitutes a "search" within the meaning of the Fourth Amendment. . . . However, I find it necessary to write separately because I believe the Fourth Amendment's reach is somewhat broader. . . .

The attachment of the beeper, in my judgment, constituted a "seizure." The owner of property, of course, has a right to exclude from it all the world, including the Government, and a concomitant right to use it exclusively for his own purposes. When the Government attaches an electronic monitoring device to that property, it infringes that exclusionary right. . . . Surely such an invasion is an "interference" with possessory rights; the right to exclude, which attached as soon as the can respondents purchased was delivered, had been infringed. That interference is also "meaningful"; the character of the property is profoundly different when infected with an electronic bug than when it is entirely germ free. . . .

The Court has developed a relatively straightforward test for determining what expectations of privacy are protected by the Fourth Amendment with respect to the possession of personal property. If personal property is in the plain view of the public, the possession of the property is in no sense "private" and hence is unprotected . . . : When a person's property is concealed from public view, however, then the fact of his possession is private and the subject of Fourth Amendment protection.

United States v. Knotts, 460 U.S. 276 (1983), illustrates this approach. There, agents watched as a container of chloroform in which they had placed a beeper was delivered to Knotts' codefendant and placed in his car. They then used the beeper to track the car's movements on a single trip through a public place. Used in this way the beeper did not disclose that the codefendant was in possession of the property; the agents already knew that. It revealed only the route of a trip through areas open to the public, something that was hardly concealed from public view.

In this case, the beeper enabled the agents to learn facts that were not exposed to public view. In *Knotts* the agents already saw the codefendant take possession of chloroform, and therefore the beeper accomplished no more than following the codefendant without the aid of the beeper would have. Here, once the container went into Karo's house, the agents thereafter learned who had the container and where it was only through use of the beeper. The beeper alone told them when the container was taken into private residences and storage areas, and when it was transported from one place to another.

The Court recognizes that concealment of personal property from public view gives rise to Fourth Amendment protection when it writes: "Indiscriminate monitoring of property that has been withdrawn from public view would present far too serious a threat to privacy interests in the home to escape entirely some sort of Fourth Amendment oversight." This protection is not limited to times when the beeper was in a home. The beeper also revealed when the can of ether had been moved. When a person drives down a public thoroughfare in a car with a can of ether concealed in the trunk, he is not exposing to public view the fact that he is in possession of a can of ether; the can is still "withdrawn from public view" and hence its location is entitled to constitutional protection. . . . In this case it was only the beeper that enabled the agents to discover where the can was once it had been concealed in Karo's house. . . .

The agents did not know who was in possession of the property or where it was once it entered Karo's house. From that moment on it was concealed from view. Because the beeper enabled the agents to learn the location of property otherwise concealed from public view, it infringed a privacy interest protected by the Fourth Amendment. . . .

Accordingly, I respectfully dissent.

NOTES AND QUESTIONS

1. The *Karo* Court distinguishes between the use of a beeper to obtain information that at least in theory could have been obtained by an officer's visual observations from a lawful vantage point, and the use of a beeper to obtain information from within a private residence that could not have been so observed. We will explore privacy interests in the home in some detail in the next case. For now, what about the principle established in *Knotts* and followed in *Karo*? Does the Court shortchange the privacy interests we have in our public movements — privacy interests that may today be at risk with the development of new technologies? "Intelligent transportation systems" that rely on features like electronic toll collection have already added to the information available to law enforcement about the movement of people in public spaces. Professor Weisberg has opined that various automatic tracking systems may one day "permit the state to know everywhere you have driven and when — every road you have taken, every toll you have paid, every gas station you have patronized." Robert Weisberg, IVHS, Legal Privacy, and the Legacy of Dr. Faustus, 11 Santa Clara Computer & High Tech. L.J. 75, 76 (1995). Granted, the Court noted in *Knotts* that if the 24-hour surveillance of citizens by law enforcement authorities ever becomes a problem, "there will be time enough then to determine whether different constitutional principles may be applicable." United States v. Knotts, 460 U.S. 276, 284 (1983). But developing technology may have brought us closer to this possibility than the Court ever deemed likely in the 1980s, when *Knotts* and *Karo* were decided.

2. In fact, we may be there already. Think about the growing use of surveillance cameras in this country — cameras that record the faces we have "knowingly exposed" in the name of reassuring us about the safety of public places. Consider the British experience with such cameras. In the 1990s, fears of terrorism prompted the British to install cameras in public places on a wide scale — so that by one estimate, there are at least 4.2 million surveillance cameras in the United Kingdom, each keeping a watchful public eye. Professor Rosen recently described the prevalence of these cameras in the city of London:

> As I filed through customs at Heathrow Airport, there were cameras concealed in domes in the ceiling. There were cameras pointing at the ticket counters, at the escalators, and at the tracks as I waited for the Heathrow Express to Paddington Station. When I got out at Paddington, there were cameras on the platform and cameras on the pillars in the main terminal. Cameras followed me as I walked from the main station to the underground, and there were cameras at each of the stations on the way to King's Cross. Outside King's Cross, there were cameras trained on the bus stand and the taxi

stand and the sidewalk, and still more cameras in the station. There were cameras on the backs of buses to record people who crossed into the wrong traffic lane. Throughout Britain today, there are speed cameras and red-light cameras, cameras in lobbies and elevators, in hotels and restaurants, in nursery schools and high schools. There are even cameras in hospitals. . . . By one estimate, the average Briton is now photographed by more than 300 separate cameras from 30 separate CCTV networks in a single day.

Jeffrey Rosen, The Naked Crowd 36-37 (2004). According to Rosen, the British cameras, though initially justified as a counterterrorism measure, have come to serve a variety of other purposes. They provide the record supporting the ban of disorderly persons from shopping malls. They monitor and deter "unconventional" behavior in public places. See id., at 38. Already there is evidence that the close monitoring of young men, especially young men of color, has produced a backlash: "CCTV is far less popular among black men than among British men as a whole." Id., at 49. Rosen argues that the cameras in Britain are "a powerful inducement toward social conformity." They represent "ways of putting people in their place, of deciding who gets in and who stays out"—as when the one-time shoplifter or miscreant finds herself permanently barred from a public establishment. In this way, Rosen says, the cameras "are in tension with values of equality. They are ways of . . . limiting people's movement and restricting their opportunities." Id., at 51.

In the wake of the September 11, 2001, terrorist attacks, there are many who claim that greater use of such technology is important in the United States. Does this possibility raise Fourth Amendment privacy concerns that suggest a need to depart from the approach of cases like *Knotts* and *Karo*? Or is this about privacy at all? Note that at least part of Rosen's argument against such cameras is that they are in tension with American society's supposed openness to perpetual reinvention of the self. New digital technologies may make it possible for people to be "followed throughout life by their past misdeeds," see id., at 52—to be instantly identified as a check bouncer, for instance, on entry into a supermarket. But should this be a Fourth Amendment concern?

However, we probably *do* expect some degree of anonymity in public, as we walk into a bar or an AA meeting, or as we pick out a video or order deli food. See Christopher Slobogin, Public Privacy: Camera Surveillance of Public Places and the Right to Anonymity, 72 Miss. L.J. 213, 238-239 (2002) (making this point). See also Daniel J. Solove, Digital Dossiers and the Dissipation of Fourth Amendment Privacy, 75 S. Cal. L. Rev. 1083, 1095 (2002) (noting that technological advance has made possible near-instant access to "a horde of aggregated bits of information combined to reveal a portrait of who we are based on what we buy, the organizations we belong to, how we navigate the Internet, and which shows and videos we watch").

3. Even the use of a precision aerial mapping camera that enhances what the eye alone can see will not necessarily render police surveillance of outdoor movements subject to Fourth Amendment constraints. In Dow Chemical Co. v. United States, 476 U.S. 227, 238 (1986), the Court observed that "surveillance of private property by using highly sophisticated surveillance equipment not generally available to the public, such as satellite technology, might be constitutionally proscribed absent a warrant." Noting that the area subject to surveillance in the case before it was more like an open field than the curtilage of a home, however, the Court concluded that the use of an aerial mapping camera to take photographs of the open areas of a

chemical plant from altitudes of 1,200, 3,000, and 12,000 feet did not bring Fourth Amendment protections into play. See id., at 239.

4. The now ubiquitous global positioning system (GPS) capabilities of cell phones and of tracking, mapping, and other devices far exceed the bleat-like "beep" of the radio transmitters in *Karo* and *Knotts*, the movements and location of which could not be determined without (i) contemporaneous operation (ii) by investigating agents (iii) of a directional radio locator (iv) within the beeper's transmission range. In contrast, a GPS device, once installed, can independently determine and record for subsequent retrieval weeks and months of movement, completely unconstrained by the otherwise not insignificant costs of real-time surveillance. Does the ability to so effortlessly reconstruct a subject's trips on the public thoroughfare "to the psychiatrist, the plastic surgeon, the abortion clinic, the AIDS treatment center, the strip club, the criminal defense attorney, the by-the-hour motel, the union meeting, the mosque, synagogue or church, the gay bar and on and on" (see People v. Weaver, 12 N.Y.3d 433, 441-442 (2009)) call now for imposition of the constraint of the warrant requirement that was not considered necessary when *Knotts* and *Karo* looked at tracking beepers a quarter century ago? *Weaver* says yes, under the New York State constitution; compare United States v. Garcia, 474 F.3d 994 (7th Cir. 2007) (Posner, J.) (GPS tracking, although more sophisticated than the beeper, remains on the same side of the Fourth Amendment divide as surveillance cameras and satellite imaging), with United States v. Maynard, 615 F.3d 544 (D.C. Cir. 2010) (Ginsburg, J.) (placement of GPS device on car was a search because it defeated the subject's reasonable expectation of privacy).

As *Karo* itself illustrates, the Court has sharply distinguished between the use of technology to track public movements and its use to glean information from inside the home. Consider whether this sharp distinction makes sense as you read the following case.

KYLLO v. UNITED STATES

Certiorari to the United States Court of Appeals for the Ninth Circuit
533 U.S. 27 (2001)

JUSTICE SCALIA delivered the opinion of the Court. . . .

In 1991 Agent William Elliott of the United States Department of the Interior came to suspect that marijuana was being grown in the home belonging to petitioner Danny Kyllo, part of a triplex on Rhododendron Drive in Florence, Oregon. Indoor marijuana growth typically requires high-intensity lamps. In order to determine whether an amount of heat was emanating from petitioner's home consistent with the use of such lamps, at 3:20 a.m. on January 16, 1992, Agent Elliott and Dan Haas used an Agema Thermovision 210 thermal imager to scan the triplex. Thermal imagers detect infrared radiation, which virtually all objects emit but which is not visible to the naked eye. The imager converts radiation into images based on relative warmth — black is cool, white is hot, shades of gray connote relative differences; in that respect, it operates somewhat like a video camera showing heat images. The scan of Kyllo's home took only a few minutes and was performed from the passenger seat of Agent Elliott's vehicle across the street from the front of the house and also from the street in back of the house. The scan showed that the roof over the garage and a side wall of petitioner's home were relatively hot compared to the rest of the home and substantially warmer than neighboring homes in the triplex. Agent Elliott concluded that petitioner was using halide lights to grow marijuana in his house, which indeed he was. Based on tips from informants, utility bills, and the thermal imaging, a Federal Magistrate Judge issued a warrant authorizing a search of petitioner's home, and the agents found an indoor growing operation involving more than 100 plants. Petitioner was indicted on one count of manufacturing marijuana. . . .

He unsuccessfully moved to suppress the evidence seized from his home and then entered a conditional guilty plea.

The Court of Appeals for the Ninth Circuit remanded the case for an evidentiary hearing regarding the intrusiveness of thermal imaging. On remand the District Court found that the Agema 210 "is a non-intrusive device which emits no rays or beams and shows a crude visual image of the heat being radiated from the outside of the house"; it "did not show any people or activity within the walls of the structure"; "[t]he device used cannot penetrate walls or windows to reveal conversations or human activities"; and "[n]o intimate details of the home were observed." Based on these findings, the District Court upheld the validity of the warrant that relied in part upon the thermal imaging, and reaffirmed its denial of the motion to suppress. A divided Court of Appeals initially reversed, but that opinion was withdrawn and the panel (after a change in composition) affirmed. . . .

The present case involves officers on a public street engaged in more than nakedeye surveillance of a home. We have previously reserved judgment as to how much technological enhancement of ordinary perception from such a vantage point, if any, is too much. While we upheld enhanced aerial photography of an industrial complex in *Dow Chemical*, we noted that we found "it important that this is *not* an area immediately adjacent to a private home, where privacy expectations are most heightened," 476 U.S., at 237, n. 4 (emphasis in original).

It would be foolish to contend that the degree of privacy secured to citizens by the Fourth Amendment has been entirely unaffected by the advance of technology. For example . . . the technology enabling human flight has exposed to public view (and hence, we have said, to official observation) uncovered portions of the house and its curtilage that once were private. See *Ciraolo*, [476 U.S.], at 215. The question we confront today is what limits there are upon this power of technology to shrink the realm of guaranteed privacy.

The *Katz* test — whether the individual has an expectation of privacy that society is prepared to recognize as reasonable — has often been criticized as circular, and hence subjective and unpredictable. While it may be difficult to refine *Katz* when the search of areas such as telephone booths . . . or even the curtilage and uncovered portions of residences is at issue, in the case of the search of the interior of homes — the prototypical and hence most commonly litigated area of protected privacy — there is a ready criterion, with roots deep in the common law, of the minimal expectation of privacy that *exists*, and that is acknowledged to be *reasonable*. . . . We think that obtaining by sense-enhancing technology any information regarding the interior of the home that could not otherwise have been obtained without physical "intrusion into a constitutionally protected area" constitutes a search — at least where (as here) the technology in question is not in general public use. This assures preservation of that degree of privacy against government that existed when the Fourth Amendment was adopted. On the basis of this criterion, the information obtained by the thermal imager in this case was the product of a search.

The Government maintains, however, that the thermal imaging must be upheld because it detected "only heat radiating from the external surface of the house." The dissent makes this its leading point, contending that there is a fundamental difference between what it calls "off-the-wall" observations and "through-the-wall surveillance." But just as a thermal imager captures only heat emanating from a house, so also a powerful directional microphone picks up only sound emanating from a house — and a satellite capable of scanning from many miles away would pick up only visible light emanating from a house. We rejected such a mechanical interpretation of the Fourth Amendment in *Katz*, where the eavesdropping device picked up only sound waves that reached the exterior of the phone booth. Reversing that approach would leave the homeowner at the mercy of advancing technology — including imaging technology that could discern all human activity in the home. While the technology used in the present case was relatively crude, the rule we adopt must take account of more sophisticated systems that are already in use or in development. . . .

The Government also contends that the thermal imaging was constitutional because it did not "detect private activities occurring in private areas." It points out that in *Dow Chemical* we observed that the enhanced aerial photography did not reveal any "intimate details." 476 U.S., at 238. *Dow Chemical*, however, involved enhanced aerial photography of an industrial complex, which does not share the Fourth Amendment sanctity of the home. . . . In the home, our cases show, *all* details are intimate details, because the entire area is held safe from prying government eyes.

Limiting the prohibition of thermal imaging to "intimate details" would not only be wrong in principle; it would be impractical in application. . . . To begin with, there is no necessary connection between the sophistication of the surveillance equipment and the "intimacy" of the details that it observes — which means that one cannot say (and the police cannot be assured) that use of the relatively crude equipment at issue here will always be lawful. The Agema Thermovision 210 might disclose, for example, at what hour each night the lady of the house takes her daily sauna and bath — a detail that many would consider "intimate"; and a much more sophisticated system might detect nothing more intimate than the fact that someone left a closet light on. We could not, in other words, develop a rule approving only that through-the-wall surveillance which identifies objects no smaller than 36 by 36 inches, but would have to develop a jurisprudence specifying which home activities are "intimate" and which are not. And even when (if ever) that jurisprudence were fully developed, no police officer would be able to know *in advance* whether his through-the-wall surveillance picks up "intimate" details — and thus would be unable to know in advance whether it is constitutional. . . .

We have said that the Fourth Amendment draws "a firm line at the entrance to the house." That line, we think, must be not only firm but also bright — which requires clear specification of those methods of surveillance that require a warrant. While it is certainly possible to conclude from the videotape of the thermal imaging that occurred in this case that no "significant" compromise of the homeowner's privacy has occurred, we must take the long view, from the original meaning of the Fourth Amendment forward. . . . Where, as here, the Government uses a device that is not in general public use, to explore details of the home that would previously have been unknowable without physical intrusion, the surveillance is a "search" and is presumptively unreasonable without a warrant. . . .

JUSTICE STEVENS, with whom THE CHIEF JUSTICE, JUSTICE O'CONNOR, and JUSTICE KENNEDY join, dissenting. . . .

While the Court "take[s] the long view" and decides this case based largely on the potential of yet-to-be-developed technology that might allow "through-the-wall surveillance," this case involves nothing more than off-the-wall surveillance by law enforcement officers to gather information exposed to the general public from the outside of petitioner's home. All that the infrared camera did in this case was passively measure heat emitted from the exterior surfaces of petitioner's home; all that those measurements showed were relative differences in emission levels, vaguely indicating that some areas of the roof and outside walls were warmer than others. . . . [N]o details regarding the interior of petitioner's home were revealed. . . .

Indeed, the ordinary use of the senses might enable a neighbor or passerby to notice the heat emanating from a building, particularly if it is vented, as was the case here. Additionally, any member of the public might notice that one part of a house is warmer than another part or a nearby building if, for example, rainwater evaporates or snow melts at different rates across its surfaces. . . .

Thus, the notion that heat emissions from the outside of a dwelling are a private matter implicating the protections of the Fourth Amendment (the text of which guarantees the right of the people "to be secure *in* their . . . houses" against unreasonable searches and seizures (emphasis added)) is not only unprecedented but also quite difficult to take seriously. Heat waves, like aromas that are generated in a kitchen, or in a laboratory or opium den, enter the public domain if and when they leave a building. A subjective expectation that they would remain private is not only implausible but also surely not "one that society is prepared to recognize as 'reasonable.'" *Katz*, 389 U.S., at 361 (Harlan, J., concurring).

To be sure, the homeowner has a reasonable expectation of privacy concerning what takes place within the home, and the Fourth Amendment's protection against physical invasions of the home should apply to their functional equivalent. But the equipment in this case did not penetrate the walls of petitioner's home, and while it did pick up "details of the home" that were exposed to the public, it did not obtain "any information regarding the *interior* of the home." In the Court's own words, based on what the thermal imager "showed" regarding the outside of petitioner's home, the officers "concluded" that petitioner was engaging in illegal activity inside the home. It would be quite absurd to characterize their thought processes as "searches," regardless of whether they inferred (rightly) that petitioner was growing marijuana in his house, or (wrongly) that "the lady of the house [was taking] her daily sauna and bath." . . . For the first time in its history, the Court assumes that an inference can amount to a Fourth Amendment violation.

Notwithstanding the implications of today's decision, there is a strong public interest in avoiding constitutional litigation over the monitoring of emissions from homes, and over the inferences drawn from such monitoring. . . . [P]ublic officials should not have to avert their senses or their equipment from detecting emissions in the public domain such as excessive heat, traces of smoke, suspicious odors, odorless gases, airborne particulates, or radioactive emissions, any of which could identify hazards to the community. In my judgment, monitoring such emissions with "sense-enhancing technology," and drawing useful conclusions from such monitoring, is an entirely reasonable public service.

On the other hand, the countervailing privacy interest is at best trivial. After all, homes generally are insulated to keep heat in, rather than to prevent the detection of heat going out, and it does not seem to me that society will suffer from a rule requiring the rare homeowner who both intends to engage in uncommon activities that produce extraordinary amounts of heat, and wishes to conceal that production from outsiders, to make sure that the surrounding area is well insulated. . . .

Instead of trying to answer the question whether the use of the thermal imager in this case was even arguably unreasonable, the Court has fashioned a rule that is intended to provide essential guidance for the day when "more sophisticated systems" gain the "ability to 'see' through walls and other opaque barriers."

. . . In my judgment, the Court's new rule is at once too broad and too narrow, and is not justified by the Court's explanation for its adoption. . . .

Despite the Court's attempt to draw a line that is "not only firm but also bright," the contours of its new rule are uncertain because its protection apparently dissipates as soon as the relevant technology is "in general public use." Yet how much use is general public use is not even hinted at by the Court's opinion, which makes the somewhat doubtful assumption that the thermal imager used in this case does not satisfy that criterion. In any event, putting aside its lack of clarity, this criterion is somewhat perverse because it seems likely that the threat to privacy will grow, rather than recede, as the use of intrusive equipment becomes more readily available. . . .

The application of the Court's new rule to "any information regarding the interior of the home," is also unnecessarily broad. If it takes sensitive equipment to detect an odor that identifies criminal conduct and nothing else, the fact that the odor emanates from the interior of a home should not provide it with constitutional protection. The criterion, moreover, is too sweeping in that information "regarding" the interior of a home apparently is not just information obtained through its walls, but also information concerning the outside of the building that could lead to (however many) inferences "regarding" what might be inside. Under that expansive view, I suppose, an officer using an infrared camera to observe a man silently entering the side door of a house at night carrying a pizza might conclude that its interior is now occupied by someone who likes pizza, and by doing so the officer would be guilty of conducting an unconstitutional "search" of the home.

Because the new rule applies to information regarding the "interior" of the home, it is too narrow as well as too broad. Clearly, a rule that is designed to protect individuals from the overly intrusive use of sense-enhancing equipment should not be limited to a home. If such equipment did provide its user with the functional equivalent of access to a private place — such as, for example, the telephone booth involved in *Katz*, or an office building — then the rule should apply to such an area as well as to a home. See *Katz*, 389 U.S., at 351 ("[T]he Fourth Amendment protects people, not places"). . . .

The two reasons advanced by the Court as justifications for the adoption of its new rule are both unpersuasive. First, the Court suggests that its rule is compelled by our holding in *Katz*, because in that case, as in this, the surveillance consisted of nothing more than the monitoring of waves emanating from a private area into the public domain. Yet there are critical differences between the cases. In *Katz*, the electronic listening device attached to the outside of the phone booth allowed the officers to pick up the content of the conversation inside the booth, making them the functional equivalent of intruders because they gathered information that was otherwise available only to someone inside the private area; it would be as if, in this case, the thermal imager presented a view of the heat-generating activity inside petitioner's home. By contrast, the thermal imager here disclosed only the relative amounts of heat radiating from the house; it would be as if, in *Katz*, the listening device disclosed only the relative volume of sound leaving the booth, which presumably was discernible in the public domain. Surely, there is a significant difference between the general and well-settled expectation that strangers will not have direct access to the contents of private communications, on the one hand, and the rather theoretical expectation that an occasional homeowner would even care if anybody noticed the relative amounts of heat emanating from the walls of his house, on the other. It is pure hyperbole for the Court to suggest that refusing to extend the holding of *Katz* to this case would leave the homeowner at the mercy of "technology that could discern all human activity in the home."

Second, the Court argues that the permissibility of "through-the-wall surveillance" cannot depend on a distinction between observing "intimate details" such as "the lady of the house [taking] her daily sauna and bath," and noticing only "the nonintimate rug on the vestibule floor" or "objects no smaller than 36 by 36 inches." This entire argument assumes, of course, that the thermal imager in this case could or did perform "through-the-wall surveillance" that could identify any detail "that would previously have been unknowable without physical intrusion." In fact, the device could not and did not enable its user to identify either the lady of the house, the rug on the vestibule floor, or anything else inside the house, whether smaller or larger than 36 by 36 inches. Indeed, the vague thermal images of petitioner's home that are reproduced in the Appendix were submitted by him to the District Court as part of an expert report raising the question whether the device could even take "accurate, consistent infrared images" of the *outside* of his house. But even if the device could reliably show extraordinary differences in the amounts of heat leaving his home, drawing the inference that there was something suspicious occurring inside the residence — a conclusion that officers far less gifted than Sherlock Holmes would readily draw — does not qualify as "through-the-wall surveillance," much less a Fourth Amendment violation.

Although the Court is properly and commendably concerned about the threats to privacy that may flow from advances in the technology available to the law enforcement profession, it has unfortunately failed to heed the tried and true counsel of judicial restraint. Instead of concentrating on the rather mundane issue that is actually presented by the case before it, the Court has endeavored to craft an all-encompassing rule for the future. It would be far wiser to give legislators an unimpeded opportunity to grapple with these emerging issues rather than to shackle them with prematurely devised constitutional constraints.

I respectfully dissent.

NOTES AND QUESTIONS

1. Does the distinction between "through-the-wall" and "off-the-wall" surveillance sound familiar? Is the majority correctly declining to resurrect a version of the trespass requirement so soundly rejected in *Katz*?

2. Maybe so. But at the same time, the majority's emphasis on the location of the police activity — on the special sanctity of the home — seems in tension with the *Katz* Court's admonition that "the Fourth Amendment protects people, not places." Professor Sklansky has pointed out that *Katz* "seemed to promise a Fourth Amendment that was less tied to specific locations, and therefore somehow more modern."

The Justices in the years since *Katz*, "keep renewing that promise, but . . . have never figured out how to make good on it." David A. Sklansky, Back to the Future: *Kyllo*, *Katz*, and Common Law, 72 Miss. L.J. 143, 160 (2002). From this perspective, *Kyllo* is but one of a number of more recent cases in which the Court, with Justice Scalia in the lead, has looked to the past in an effort to anchor Fourth Amendment law — to free it from the indeterminacy that characterizes its efforts to answer the question, "What is a search?"

3. To be clear, the *Kyllo* Court's emphasis on the special sanctity of the home is in no way unique. But do heightened protections for the home make sense? Consider the following:

> Of course there are costs to treating the home differently than other places. If privacy receives more protection in the home than elsewhere, it necessarily follows that leaving one's home means losing some privacy — that the price of full privacy is not going out. That price might impair rather than foster a free and vibrant society. Moreover, the price is not visited equally on everyone, because not all homes are equivalent. . . . [R]ich people have bigger and more comfortable homes than poor people; it is therefore much easier for rich people than for poor people to stay home when engaged in activities they wish to keep private. Granting homes more privacy than other places therefore tilts Fourth Amendment protection in favor of the rich and against the poor. . . .

Sklansky, 72 Miss. L.J. at 192. Of course, as Professor Sklansky goes on to say, all this is not to suggest that advocates for greater privacy need necessarily view the result in *Kyllo* negatively: "[T]here is little reason to believe that erasing the boundary between the home and the street would give streets as much privacy as homes, instead of giving homes as little privacy as streets." Id., at 193. But *Kyllo*'s emphasis on the privacy interest in homes may give short shrift to other places (including cyberspace) where privacy interests are high and the Court has not yet developed a Fourth Amendment framework for dealing with new technologies.

4. Consider another angle on the search in *Kyllo*. *Kyllo* is an example of what one might call "white-collar drug investigations" — police investigation of drug networks that cater to middle- or upper-class customers. Most drug arrests and drug prosecutions fall into a different category; they occur not on places like Rhododendron Drive in Florence, Oregon, but on rough street corners in high-crime urban neighborhoods. And note one other important fact about these "blue-collar" drug cases: Disproportionately, the search targets, arrestees, and defendants those cases generate are African Americans.

Kyllo makes white-collar drug investigations a little more costly than they otherwise might be. At the margin, that is likely to shift police resources away from those investigations and toward more blue-collar drug cases. In other words, part of the cost of increased privacy protection for homes is that police attention will tend to be diverted elsewhere, to spaces where Fourth Amendment regulation is more lax — like urban street corners. See William J. Stuntz, The Distribution of Fourth Amendment Privacy, 67 Geo. Wash. L. Rev. 1265, 1274-1287 (1999). Is that wise criminal justice policy?

5. What about the Court's approach to advancing technology? Should Fourth Amendment analysis turn on whether "the technology in question is not in general public use"? And how is "general public use" to be determined? Presumably, if the device in question is available in the local Wal-Mart, its use does not trigger the

Fourth Amendment. What about an Internet catalogue? As publicly available technology advances, constitutionally protected privacy will diminish. Is that result right as a matter of constitutional law?

6. Suppose technological advances produced a wholly unobtrusive, noninvasive scanner that could detect from the street whether explosives or chemical weapons were being unlawfully stored in a home, without revealing anything else — would the use of such a device violate the test enunciated in *Kyllo*? Recall the discussion of the dog sniffs in *Place* and *Caballes*, which can be found at pages 377 and 378. The Court in *Caballes* affirmed that "any interest in possessing contraband cannot be deemed 'legitimate,' and thus, governmental conduct that *only* reveals the possession of contraband 'compromises no legitimate privacy interest.'" *Caballes* was about the dog sniff of a car, and perhaps the Court would qualify this statement in the context of a home. But if not, presumably a scanner that only detected illegal explosives would not implicate the Fourth Amendment, even if the scan penetrated the walls of a home.

But scanners that would only detect *illegal* items in a home may be unrealistic. Suppose a scanner could reveal the presence of certain chemicals in buildings. Possession of such chemicals is most commonly associated with the manufacture of explosive devices or illegal drugs, but the chemicals are not unlawful to possess and have other purposes — albeit purposes not usually associated with the home. Should it make a difference for Fourth Amendment purposes whether the scanner reveals, narrowly, the presence of explosives or, more generally, the presence of chemicals that might be used to produce explosives but that might also have some other legal uses?

7. Your view of the majority's approach in *Kyllo* might depend on the consequences of subjecting a given law enforcement activity to Fourth Amendment regulation. Recall the discussion in Note 5 on page 369 about whether Fourth Amendment law follows the graduated or "all-or-nothing" approach to the regulation of police activity. In a graduated regime, it may not matter so much that use of a noninvasive scanner that might detect chemical weapons is covered by the Fourth Amendment, provided that law enforcement agents acting consistently with the Amendment's requirements can nevertheless employ the scanner in most circumstances. If the consequence of Fourth Amendment regulation is essentially to render the scanner useless for the detection of such activity, however (if subjecting the scanner to Fourth Amendment constraints means deciding that it can be used only when a warrant for physical entry into the home could also be obtained), that might be a different matter.

2. The Meaning of "Seizures"

UNITED STATES v. DRAYTON

Certiorari to the United States Court of Appeals for the Eleventh Circuit
536 U.S. 194 (2002)

JUSTICE KENNEDY delivered the opinion of the Court.

The Fourth Amendment permits police officers to approach bus passengers at random to ask questions and to request their consent to searches, provided a reasonable person would understand that he or she is free to refuse. Florida v. Bostick, 501 U.S. 429 (1991). This case requires us to determine whether officers must advise bus passengers during these encounters of their right not to cooperate.

On February 4, 1999, respondents Christopher Drayton and Clifton Brown, Jr., were traveling on a Greyhound bus en route from Ft. Lauderdale, Florida, to Detroit, Michigan. The bus made a scheduled stop in Tallahassee, Florida. The passengers were required to disembark so the bus could be refueled and cleaned. As the passengers reboarded, the driver checked their tickets and then left to complete paperwork inside the terminal. As he left, the driver allowed three members of the Tallahassee Police Department to board the bus as part of a routine drug and weapons interdiction effort. The officers were dressed in plain clothes and carried concealed weapons and visible badges.

Once onboard Officer Hoover knelt on the driver's seat and faced the rear of the bus. He could observe the passengers and ensure the safety of the two other officers without blocking the aisle or otherwise obstructing the bus exit. Officers Lang and Blackburn went to the rear of the bus. Blackburn remained stationed there, facing forward. Lang worked his way toward the front of the bus, speaking with individual passengers as he went. He asked the passengers about their travel plans and sought to match passengers with luggage in the overhead racks. To avoid blocking the aisle, Lang stood next to or just behind each passenger with whom he spoke.

According to Lang's testimony, passengers who declined to cooperate with him or who chose to exit the bus at any time would have been allowed to do so without argument. In Lang's experience, however, most people are willing to cooperate. Some passengers go so far as to commend the police for their efforts to ensure the safety of their travel. Lang could recall five to six instances in the previous year in which passengers had declined to have their luggage searched. It also was common for passengers to leave the bus for a cigarette or a snack while the officers were on board. Lang sometimes informed passengers of their right to refuse to cooperate. On the day in question, however, he did not.

Respondents were seated next to each other on the bus. Drayton was in the aisle seat, Brown in the seat next to the window. Lang approached respondents from the rear and leaned over Drayton's shoulder. He held up his badge long enough for respondents to identify him as a police officer. With his face 12-to-18 inches away from Drayton's, Lang spoke in a voice just loud enough for respondents to hear:

> I'm Investigator Lang with the Tallahassee Police Department. We're conducting bus interdiction [sic], attempting to deter drugs and illegal weapons being transported on the bus. Do you have any bags on the bus?

Both respondents pointed to a single green bag in the overhead luggage rack. Lang asked, "Do you mind if I check it?" and Brown responded, "Go ahead." Lang handed the bag to Officer Blackburn to check. The bag contained no contraband.

Officer Lang noticed that both respondents were wearing heavy jackets and baggy pants despite the warm weather. In Lang's experience drug traffickers often use baggy clothing to conceal weapons or narcotics. The officer thus asked Brown if he had any weapons or drugs in his possession. And he asked Brown: "Do you mind if I check your person?" Brown answered, "Sure," and cooperated by leaning up in his seat, pulling a cell phone out of his pocket, and opening up his jacket. Lang reached across Drayton and patted down Brown's jacket and pockets, including his waist area, sides, and upper thighs. In both thigh areas, Lang detected hard objects similar to drug packages detected on other occasions. Lang arrested and hand-cuffed Brown. Officer Hoover escorted Brown from the bus.

Lang then asked Drayton, "Mind if I check you?" Drayton responded by lifting his hands about eight inches from his legs. Lang conducted a patdown of Drayton's thighs and detected hard objects similar to those found on Brown. He arrested Drayton and escorted him from the bus. A further search revealed that respondents had duct-taped plastic bundles of powder cocaine between several pairs of their boxer shorts. . . .

The District Court determined that the police conduct was not coercive and respondents' consent to the search was voluntary. . . .

The Court of Appeals for the Eleventh Circuit reversed and remanded with instructions to grant respondents' motions to suppress. The court held that this dis-position was compelled by its previous decisions in United States v. Washington, 151 F.3d 1354 (1998), and United States v. Guapi, 144 F.3d 1393 (1998). Those cases had held that bus passengers do not feel free to disregard police officers' requests to search absent "some positive indication that consent could have been refused."

We granted certiorari. The respondents, we conclude, were not seized and their consent to the search was voluntary; and we reverse. . . .

The Court has addressed on a previous occasion the specific question of drug interdiction efforts on buses. . . .

. . . [Florida v. Bostick, 501 U.S. 429 (1991)] first made it clear that for the most part per se rules are inappropriate in the Fourth Amendment context. The proper inquiry necessitates a consideration of "all the circumstances surrounding the encounter." The Court noted next that the traditional rule, which states that a sei-zure does not occur so long as a reasonable person would feel free "to disregard the police and go about his business," California v. Hodari D., 499 U.S. 621, 628 (1991), is not an accurate measure of the coercive effect of a bus encounter. . . . The proper inquiry "is whether a reasonable person would feel free to decline the officers' requests or otherwise terminate the encounter." Finally, the Court rejected Bostick's argument that he must have been seized because no reasonable person would con-sent to a search of luggage containing drugs. The reasonable person test, the Court explained, is objective and "presupposes an *innocent* person."

In light of the limited record, *Bostick* refrained from deciding whether a seizure occurred. The Court, however, identified two factors "particularly worth noting" on remand. First, although it was obvious that an officer was armed, he did not remove the gun from its pouch or use it in a threatening way. Second, the officer advised the passenger that he could refuse consent to the search.

Relying upon this latter factor, the Eleventh Circuit has adopted what is in effect a per se rule that evidence obtained during suspicionless drug interdiction efforts aboard buses must be suppressed unless the officers have advised passengers of their right not to cooperate and to refuse consent to a search. . . .

. . . The Court of Appeals erred in adopting this approach. Applying the *Bostick* framework to the facts of this particular case, we conclude that the police did not seize respondents when they boarded the bus and began questioning passengers. The officers gave the passengers no reason to believe that they were required to answer the officers' questions. When Officer Lang approached respondents, he did not brandish a weapon or make any intimidating movements. He left the aisle free so that respondents could exit. He spoke to passengers one by one and in a polite, quiet voice. Nothing he said would suggest to a reasonable person that he or she was barred from leaving the bus or otherwise terminating the encounter.

There were ample grounds for the District Court to conclude that "everything that took place between Officer Lang and [respondents] suggests that it was cooperative" and that there "was nothing coercive [or] confrontational" about the encounter. There was no application of force, no intimidating movement, no overwhelming show of force, no brandishing of weapons, no blocking of exits, no threat, no command, not even an authoritative tone of voice. It is beyond question that had this encounter occurred on the street, it would be constitutional. The fact that an encounter takes place on a bus does not on its own transform standard police questioning of citizens into an illegal seizure. . . .

Respondents make much of the fact that Officer Lang displayed his badge. In Florida v. Rodriguez, 469 U.S., at 5-6, however, the Court rejected the claim that the defendant was seized when an officer approached him in an airport, showed him his badge, and asked him to answer some questions. Likewise, in INS v. Delgado, 466 U.S. 210, 212-213 (1984), the Court held that Immigration and Naturalization Service (INS) agents' wearing badges and questioning workers in a factory did not constitute a seizure. And while neither Lang nor his colleagues were in uniform or visibly armed, those factors should have little weight in the analysis. Officers are often required to wear uniforms and in many circumstances this is cause for assurance, not discomfort. Much the same can be said for wearing sidearms. That most law enforcement officers are armed is a fact well known to the public. The presence of a holstered firearm thus is unlikely to contribute to the coerciveness of the encounter absent active brandishing of the weapon.

Officer Hoover's position at the front of the bus also does not tip the scale in respondents' favor. Hoover did nothing to intimidate passengers, and he said nothing to suggest that people could not exit and indeed he left the aisle clear. . . .

Finally, the fact that in Officer Lang's experience only a few passengers have refused to cooperate does not suggest that a reasonable person would not feel free to terminate the bus encounter. In Lang's experience it was common for passengers to leave the bus for a cigarette or a snack while the officers were questioning passengers. And of more importance, bus passengers answer officers' questions and otherwise cooperate not because of coercion but because the passengers know that their participation enhances their own safety and the safety of those around them. "While most citizens will respond to a police request, the fact that people do so, and do so without being told they are free not to respond, hardly eliminates the consensual nature of the response." *Delgado*, supra, at 216.

Drayton contends that even if Brown's cooperation with the officers was consensual, Drayton was seized because no reasonable person would feel free to terminate the encounter with the officers after Brown had been arrested. The Court of Appeals did not address this claim; and in any event the argument fails. The arrest of one person does not mean that everyone around him has been seized by police. If anything, Brown's arrest should have put Drayton on notice of the consequences of continuing the encounter by answering the officers' questions. . . .

We turn now from the question whether respondents were seized to whether they were subjected to an unreasonable search, i.e., whether their consent to the suspicionless search was involuntary. In circumstances such as these, where the question of voluntariness pervades both the search and seizure inquiries, the respective analyses turn on very similar facts. And, as the facts above suggest, respondents' consent to the search of their luggage and their persons was voluntary. Nothing Officer Lang said indicated a command to consent to the search. Rather, when respondents informed Lang that they had a bag on the bus, he asked for their permission to check it. And when Lang requested to search Brown and Drayton's persons, he asked first if they objected, thus indicating to a reasonable person that he or she was free to refuse. . . .

The Court has rejected in specific terms the suggestion that police officers must always inform citizens of their right to refuse when seeking permission to conduct a warrantless consent search. "While knowledge of the right to refuse consent is one factor to be taken into account, the government need not establish such knowledge as the sine qua non of an effective consent." Nor do this Court's decisions suggest that even though there are no per se rules, a presumption of invalidity attaches if a citizen consented without explicit notification that he or she was free to refuse to cooperate. . . .

In a society based on law, the concept of agreement and consent should be given a weight and dignity of its own. Police officers act in full accord with the law when they ask citizens for consent. It reinforces the rule of law for the citizen to advise the police of his or her wishes and for the police to act in reliance on that understanding. When this exchange takes place, it dispels inferences of coercion. . . .

JUSTICE SOUTER, with whom JUSTICE STEVENS and JUSTICE GINSBURG join, dissenting.

Anyone who travels by air today submits to searches of the person and luggage as a condition of boarding the aircraft. It is universally accepted that such intrusions are necessary to hedge against risks that, nowadays, even small children understand. The commonplace precautions of air travel have not, thus far, been justified for ground transportation, however, and no such conditions have been placed on passengers getting on trains or buses. There is therefore an air of unreality about the Court's explanation that bus passengers consent to searches of their luggage to "enhanc[e] their own safety and the safety of those around them." Nor are the other factual assessments underlying the Court's conclusion in favor of the Government more convincing.

The issue we took to review is whether the police's examination of the bus passengers, including respondents, amounted to a suspicionless seizure under the Fourth Amendment. If it did, any consent to search was plainly invalid as a product of the illegal seizure.

Florida v. Bostick, 501 U.S. 429 (1991), established the framework for determining whether the bus passengers were seized in the constitutional sense. . . .

Before applying the standard in this case, it may be worth getting some perspective from different sets of facts. A perfect example of police conduct that supports no colorable claim of seizure is the act of an officer who simply goes up to a pedestrian on the street and asks him a question. A pair of officers questioning a pedestrian, without more, would presumably support the same conclusion. Now consider three officers, one of whom stands behind the pedestrian, another at his side toward the open sidewalk, with the third addressing questions to the pedestrian a foot or two from his face. Finally, consider the same scene in a narrow alley. On such barebones facts, one may not be able to say a seizure occurred, even in the last case, but one can say without qualification that the atmosphere of the encounters differed significantly from the first to the last examples. In the final instance there is every reason to believe that the pedestrian would have understood, to his considerable discomfort, what Justice Stewart described as the "threatening presence of several officers," United States v. Mendenhall, 446 U.S. 544, 554 (1980) (opinion of Stewart, J.). The police not only carry legitimate authority but also exercise power free from immediate check, and when the attention of several officers is brought to bear on one civilian the imbalance of immediate power is unmistakable. We all understand this, as well as we understand that a display of power rising to Justice Stewart's "threatening" level may overbear a normal person's ability to act freely, even in the absence of explicit commands or the formalities of detention. As common as this understanding is, however, there is little sign of it in the Court's opinion. . . .

[F]or reasons unexplained, the driver with the tickets entitling the passengers to travel had yielded his custody of the bus and its seated travelers to three police officers, whose authority apparently superseded the driver's own. The officers took control of the entire passenger compartment, one stationed at the door keeping surveillance of all the occupants, the others working forward from the back. With one officer right behind him and the other one forward, a third officer accosted each passenger at quarters extremely close and so cramped that as many as half the passengers could not even have stood to face the speaker. None was asked whether he was willing to converse with the police or to take part in the enquiry. Instead the officer said the police were "conducting bus interdiction," in the course of which they "would like . . . cooperation." The reasonable inference was that the "interdiction" was not a consensual exercise, but one the police would carry out whatever the circumstances; that they would prefer "cooperation" but would not let the lack of it stand in their way. There was no contrary indication that day, since no passenger had refused the cooperation requested, and there was no reason for any passenger to believe that the driver would return and the trip resume until the police were satisfied. The scene was set and an atmosphere of obligatory participation was established by this introduction. Later requests to search prefaced with "Do you mind . . ." would naturally have been understood in the terms with which the encounter began.

It is very hard to imagine that either Brown or Drayton would have believed that he stood to lose nothing if he refused to cooperate with the police, or that he had any free choice to ignore the police altogether. No reasonable passenger could have believed that, only an uncomprehending one. . . . While I am not prepared to say that no bus interrogation and search can pass the *Bostick* test without a warning that passengers are free to say no, the facts here surely required more from the officers than a quiet tone of voice. A police officer who is certain to get his way has no need to shout. . . .

NOTES AND QUESTIONS

1. What role does the meaning of "seizures" play in the protection of Fourth Amendment privacy? At first blush, doesn't a governmental seizure suggest that *liberty* — not privacy — is at stake? But if privacy is the "right to be let alone," as Justice Brandeis famously said, then perhaps privacy is more at issue than might first appear to be the case. After all, what is more basic to the right to be let alone than the right not to have a police officer in your face?

2. But does the Court's concept of seizure adequately protect this right? *Drayton* was the second of two bus interdiction cases the Court has considered. In the first,

Florida v. Bostick, 501 U.S. 429, 434 (1991), decided 11 years earlier, the Court said the following:

> Our cases make clear that a seizure does not occur simply because a police officer approaches an individual and asks a few questions. So long as a reasonable person would feel free "to disregard the police and go about his business," the encounter is consensual.

But when does a reasonable person feel free to terminate a police encounter? In an earlier case, United States v. Mendenhall, 446 U.S. 544 (1980), Justice Stewart gave examples of factors the presence of which might suggest that a given police-citizen exchange constitutes a "seizure" for Fourth Amendment purposes. These factors include "the threatening presence of several officers, the display of a weapon by an officer, some physical touching of the person of the citizen, or the use of language or tone of voice indicating that compliance with the officer's request might be compelled." Id., at 554. Yet even if none of the factors just listed is present, does the average person, when approached by a police officer, feel free to terminate the encounter — whether or not it occurs on a bus? Isn't the seizure test in fact a legal fiction premised on the view that effective law enforcement requires that police be entitled to trade upon the pressure to cooperate that citizens feel?

3. Perhaps that last question is unfair. Some police-citizen encounters are surely voluntary. The friendly cop on the beat doesn't exist solely in fiction, and many people do in fact *want* to cooperate with the police. The legal problem is distinguishing consensual encounters from the nonconsensual kind. But if this is the problem, why isn't the solution the one rejected in *Drayton* — namely, imposing a requirement that police advise citizens of their right to go about their business by ending the conversation? What is the source of the Court's hostility to this per se rule — at least in the context of bus encounters? Note that in the oral argument in *Drayton*, the government asserted that police activity of the type in *Drayton* is particularly important "in today's environment with respect to the protection of passengers in the Nation's public transportation system." How big a role might such considerations have played in the result in this case, which was argued just seven months after the terrorists attacks of September 11, 2001?

4. According to the *Drayton* Court, consensual police-citizen encounters are those that a reasonable person in the citizen's shoes would feel free to terminate. Should race factor into this "reasonable person" test? Professor Maclin has argued that "the dynamics surrounding an encounter between a police officer and a black male are quite different from those that surround an encounter between an officer and the so-called average, reasonable person." Tracey Maclin, "Black and Blue Encounters" — Some Preliminary Thoughts about Fourth Amendment Seizures: Should Race Matter? 26 Val. U. L. Rev. 243, 250 (1991). He contends that the race of the individual stopped should be considered in assessing the coerciveness of a police encounter:

> My position simply recognizes that, for most black men, the typical police confrontation is not a consensual encounter. Black men simply do not trust police officers to respect their rights. Although many black men *know* of their right to walk away from a police encounter, I submit that most do not trust the police to respect their decision to do so.

Id., at 272. A reasonable person test that does not take account of race, in Maclin's view, "runs the risk that majoritarian values and perceptions of police practices will go unchallenged." Id., at 274. Do you agree?

5. In Brower v. County of Inyo, 489 U.S. 593, 594 (1989), the Court dealt with the question whether police officers had "seized" Brower when the stolen car he was driving crashed into a police roadblock that was set up to stop him, resulting in his death. *Brower* was a federal civil rights action brought by Brower's heirs, who claimed that the use of the roadblock violated Brower's Fourth Amendment rights. According to the complaint:

> [R]espondents (1) caused an 18-wheel tractor-trailer to be placed across both lanes of a two-lane highway in the path of Brower's flight, (2) "effectively concealed" this road-block by placing it behind a curve and leaving it unilluminated, and (3) positioned a police car, with its headlights on, between Brower's oncoming vehicle and the truck, so that Brower would be "blinded" on his approach.

The Ninth Circuit affirmed the district court's dismissal of the plaintiffs' Fourth Amendment claim, concluding that there had been no "seizure." The Supreme Court reversed. After observing that the Fourth Amendment is not implicated when a suspect being chased by the police suddenly loses control of his car and crashes, Justice Scalia's opinion for the Court stated:

> Violation of the Fourth Amendment requires an intentional acquisition of physical control. A seizure occurs even when an unintended person or thing is the object of the detention or taking, but the detention or taking itself must be wilful. This is implicit in the word "seizure," which can hardly be applied to an unknowing act. . . .
>
> Thus, if a parked and unoccupied police car slips its brake and pins a passenger against a wall, it is likely that a tort has occurred, but not a violation of the Fourth Amendment. And the situation would not change if the passerby happened, by lucky chance, to be a serial murderer for whom there was an outstanding arrest warrant — even if, at the time he was pinned, he was in the process of running away from two pursuing constables. It is clear, in other words, that a Fourth Amendment seizure does not occur whenever there is a governmentally caused termination of an individual's freedom of movement (the innocent passerby), nor even whenever there is a governmentally caused and governmentally *desired* termination of an individual's freedom of movement (the fleeing felon), but only when there is a governmental termination of freedom of movement *through means intentionally applied*. . . .
>
> [It is not] possible in determining whether there has been a seizure in a case such as this, to distinguish between a roadblock that is designed to give the oncoming driver the option of a voluntary stop (e.g., one at the end of a long straightaway), and a roadblock that is designed precisely to produce a collision (e.g., one located just around a bend). In determining whether the means that terminates the freedom of movement is the very means that the government intended we cannot draw too fine a line, or we will be driven to saying that one is not seized who has been stopped by the accidental discharge of a gun with which he was meant only to be bludgeoned, or by a bullet in the heart that was meant only for the leg. We think it enough for a seizure that a person be stopped by the very instrumentality set in motion or put in place in order to achieve that result. . . .
>
> This is not to say that the precise character of the roadblock is irrelevant. . . . [For §1983 liability], the seizure must be "unreasonable." Petitioners can claim the right to

recover for Brower's death only because the unreasonableness they allege consists precisely of setting up the roadblock in such manner as to be likely to kill him. This should be contrasted with the situation that would obtain if the sole claim of unreasonableness were that there was no probable cause for the stop. In that case, if Brower had had the opportunity to stop voluntarily at the roadblock, but had negligently or intentionally driven into it, then, because of lack of proximate causality, respondents, though responsible for depriving him of his freedom of movement, would not be liable for his death. Thus, the circumstances of this roadblock, including the allegation that the headlights were used to blind the oncoming driver, may yet determine the outcome of this case.

Id., at 596-599 (emphasis in original).

6. The Court's decision in *Brower* involved unusual circumstances. Soon thereafter, however, *Brower*'s reasoning was invoked by the Court in the context of a factual scenario that arises much more frequently. California v. Hodari D., 499 U.S. 621 (1991), concerned the Fourth Amendment's application to a case in which a suspect seeks to avoid an encounter with the police by running away. Consider how *Brower* was used to help answer the question whether a suspect who attempts to run away from police is seized when police pursue him:

CALIFORNIA v. HODARI D.

Certiorari to the California Supreme Court
499 U.S. 621 (1991)

JUSTICE SCALIA delivered the opinion of the Court.

Late one evening in April 1988, Officers Brian McColgin and Jerry Pertoso were on patrol in a high-crime area of Oakland, California. They were dressed in street clothes but wearing jackets with "Police" embossed on both front and back. Their unmarked car proceeded west on Foothill Boulevard, and turned south onto 63rd Avenue. As they rounded the corner, they saw four or five youths huddled around a small red car parked at the curb. When the youths saw the officers' car approaching they apparently panicked, and took flight. The respondent here, Hodari D., and one companion ran west through an alley; the others fled south. The red car also headed south, at a high rate of speed.

The officers were suspicious and gave chase. McColgin remained in the car and continued south on 63rd Avenue; Pertoso left the car, ran back north along 63rd, then west on Foothill Boulevard, and turned south on 62nd Avenue. Hodari, meanwhile, emerged from the alley onto 62nd and ran north. Looking behind as he ran, he did not turn and see Pertoso until the officer was almost upon him, whereupon he tossed away what appeared to be a small rock. A moment later, Pertoso tackled Hodari, handcuffed him, and radioed for assistance. Hodari was found to be carrying $130 in cash and a pager; and the rock he had discarded was found to be crack cocaine.

As this case comes to us, the only issue presented is whether, at the time he dropped the drugs, Hodari had been "seized" within the meaning of the Fourth Amendment. If so, respondent argues, the drugs were the fruit of that seizure and the evidence concerning them was properly excluded. If not, the drugs were abandoned by Hodari and lawfully recovered by the police, and the evidence should have been admitted.

We have long understood that the Fourth Amendment's protection against "unreasonable . . . seizures" includes seizure of the person. From the time of the founding to the present, the word "seizure" has meant a "taking possession," 2 N. Webster, An American Dictionary of the English Language 67 (1828); 2 J. Bouvier, A Law Dictionary 510 (6th ed. 1856); Webster's Third New International Dictionary 2057 (1981). For most purposes at common law, the word connoted not merely grasping, or applying physical force to, the animate or inanimate object in question, but actually bringing it within physical control. A ship still fleeing, even though under attack, would not be considered to have been seized as a war prize. Cf. *The Josefa Segunda*, 10 Wheat. 312, 325-326, 6 L. Ed. 320 (1825). A res capable of manual delivery was not seized until "tak[en] into custody." Pelham v. Rose, 9 Wall. 103, 106, 19 L. Ed. 602 (1870). To constitute an arrest, however — the quintessential "seizure of the person" under our Fourth Amendment jurisprudence — the mere grasping or application of physical force with lawful authority, whether or not it succeeded in subduing the arrestee, was sufficient. See, e.g., Whitehead v. Keyes, 85 Mass. 495, 501 (1862) ("[A]n officer effects an arrest of a person whom he has authority to arrest, by laying his hand on him for the purpose of arresting him, though he may not succeed in stopping and holding him").

To say that an arrest is effected by the slightest application of physical force, despite the arrestee's escape, is not to say that for Fourth Amendment purposes there is a *continuing* arrest during the period of fugitivity. If, for example, Pertoso had laid his hands upon Hodari to arrest him, but Hodari had broken away and had *then* cast away the cocaine, it would hardly be realistic to say that that disclosure had been made during the course of an arrest. The present case, however, is even one step further removed. It does not involve the application of any physical force; Hodari was untouched by Officer Pertoso at the time he discarded the cocaine. His defense relies instead upon the proposition that a seizure occurs "when the officer, by means of physical force *or show of authority*, has in some way restrained the liberty of a citizen." Terry v. Ohio, 392 U.S. 1, 19, n. 16 (1968) (emphasis added). Hodari contends (and we accept as true for purposes of this decision) that Pertoso's pursuit qualified as a "show of authority" calling upon Hodari to halt. The narrow question before us is whether, with respect to a show of authority as with respect to application of physical force, a seizure occurs even though the subject does not yield. We hold that it does not.

The language of the Fourth Amendment, of course, cannot sustain respondent's contention. The word "seizure" readily bears the meaning of a laying on of hands or application of physical force to restrain movement, even when it is ultimately unsuccessful. ("She seized the purse-snatcher, but he broke out of her grasp.") It does not remotely apply, however, to the prospect of a policeman yelling "Stop, in the name of the law!" at a fleeing form that continues to flee. That is no seizure. Nor can the result respondent wishes to achieve be produced — indirectly, as it were — by suggesting that Pertoso's uncomplied-with show of authority was a common-law arrest, and then appealing to the principle that all common-law arrests are seizures. An arrest requires *either* physical force (as described above) *or*, where that is absent, *submission* to the assertion of authority. . . .

We do not think it desirable, even as a policy matter, to stretch the Fourth Amendment beyond its words and beyond the meaning of arrest, as respondent urges. Street pursuits always place the public at some risk, and compliance with police orders to stop should therefore be encouraged. Only a few of those orders, we must presume, will be without adequate basis, and since the addressee has no ready means of identifying the deficient ones it almost invariably is the responsible course to comply. Unlawful orders will not be deterred, moreover, by sanctioning through the exclusionary rule those of them that are *not* obeyed. Since policemen do not command "Stop!" expecting to be ignored, or give chase hoping to be outrun, it fully suffices to apply the deterrent to their genuine, successful seizures.

Respondent contends that his position is sustained by the so-called *Mendenhall* test, formulated by Justice Stewart's opinion in United States v. Mendenhall, 446 U.S. 544, 554 (1980), and adopted by the Court in later cases: "[A] person has been 'seized' within the meaning of the Fourth Amendment only if, in view of all the circumstances surrounding the incident, a reasonable person would have believed that he was not free to leave." 446 U.S., at 554. In seeking to rely upon that test here, respondent fails to read it carefully. It says that a person has been seized "only if," not that he has been seized "whenever"; it states a *necessary*, but not a *sufficient*, condition for seizure — or, more precisely, for seizure effected through a "show of authority." *Mendenhall* establishes that the test for existence of a "show of authority" is an objective one: not whether the citizen perceived that he was being ordered to restrict his movement, but whether the officer's words and actions would have conveyed that to a reasonable person. . . .

Quite relevant to the present case, however, was our decision in Brower v. Inyo County, 489 U.S. 593, 596 (1989). In that case, police cars with flashing lights had chased the decedent for 20 miles — surely an adequate "show of authority" — but he did not stop until his fatal crash into a police-erected blockade. The issue was whether his death could be held to be the consequence of an unreasonable seizure in violation of the Fourth Amendment. We did not even consider the possibility that a seizure could have occurred during the course of the chase because, as we explained, that "show of authority" did not produce his stop. Id., at 597. . . .

In sum, assuming that Pertoso's pursuit in the present case constituted a "show of authority" enjoining Hodari to halt, since Hodari did not comply with that injunction he was not seized until he was tackled. The cocaine abandoned while he was running was in this case not the fruit of a seizure, and his motion to exclude evidence of it was properly denied. . . .

NOTES AND QUESTIONS

1. What do you make of the Court's use of the common law to define the meaning of a seizure for the purpose of the Fourth Amendment? In a dissent joined by Justice Marshall, Justice Stevens argued that the Court's reliance on common law precedents in *Hodari D.* was at odds with the Court's approach in *Katz:* "Significantly, in the *Katz* opinion, the Court repeatedly used the word 'seizure' to describe the process of recording sounds that could not possibly have been the subject of a common-law seizure." 499 U.S., at 634. Is there any more reason to rely on common law precedents in one context than the other?

2. How much should the Court be influenced in its approach to defining what a seizure is for Fourth Amendment purposes by the reality discussed at the start of this chapter — namely, that Fourth Amendment law functions as a chief source of legal regulation of police? The *Hodari D.* dissenters also argued that by hinging the timing of a seizure accomplished by show of authority on the citizen's reaction, rather than on the officer's conduct, the majority deprives an officer of the ability to determine in advance whether his conduct implicates the Fourth Amendment — presumably undercutting the ability to fashion appropriate training around the legal standard. Because of the range of possible responses to a police show of authority and the time that may elapse between a show of authority (like the sound of sirens accompanied by a patrol car's flashing lights) and the complete submission of the citizen, the dissenters further contended that the majority's approach "can only create uncertainty and generate litigation." Id., at 643-644. Do you agree with these criticisms? If so, what weight should factors such as these have in the Court's approach to Fourth Amendment interpretation?

3. *Brower*'s emphasis on seizure as the "intentional acquisition of physical control" and *Hodari D.*'s distinction between "seizure by physical force" and by "show of authority plus submission" may raise as many questions as they answer. Consider one discussion of the problems inherent in applying seizure standards developed in criminal investigations in a very different context — namely, in civil litigation in which protestors seek damages for allegedly unconstitutional police conduct in the course of confrontations with police:

> [A]t large-scale public street demonstrations police are acting in their public order function and are not primarily concerned with making arrests. Dozens or hundreds of officers confront hundreds or thousands of demonstrators. . . . Where force is used, it is usually in service of a dispersal order. . . . Rarely are all or even most demonstrators actually arrested for failing to disperse; police intent in using force is to clear the streets quickly by making demonstrators leave, rather than to detain and arrest them.
>
> . . . [M]any of the methods used by police in handling recent large-scale demonstrations present added difficulties in determining when their use constitutes a seizure of their targets. . . . [W]eaponry includes less-lethal munitions such as rubber, plastic, foam, and wooden bullets and bean bag rounds; chemical irritants such as tear gas and pepper spray; and other assorted devices, including concussion grenades, more colorfully known as "flash-bang devices." . . .
>
> . . . [I]t is unclear whether less-lethal munitions that do not hit their mark will implicate *Hodari D.*'s per se physical force rule, or instead constitute a show of authority. . . .
>
> Chemical irritants such as mace and pepper spray present two difficulties: Does use of these gaseous agents constitute a "touching" of citizens by police . . . ? If so, are only direct targets of the irritant "touched," or are members of a crowd over whom the gas merely "wafted" also touched? . . .
>
> Those demonstrators who cannot avail themselves of *Hodari D.*'s per se rule for physical force must proceed under a theory of show of authority, and face a difficult road to seizure. . . .
>
> If courts were to . . . hold that police use of less-lethal weapons against demonstrators to enforce a dispersal order constitutes a show of police authority sufficient to seize, demonstrators would still need to "submit" to that authority to be seized under California v. Hodari D. What would submission look like in such a case? Holding one's ground? Running away as quickly as possible — i.e., doing precisely what Hodari D. did, but also what police want demonstrators to do? . . .

Hodari D.'s statement that the slightest touching with lawful authority constitutes an arrest currently represents the best chance of demonstrators . . . to establish seizure and receive Fourth Amendment review of police action against them. If *Hodari D.* is taken at its word, it seems likely that demonstrators who were directly touched by rubber bullets and chemical irritants were seized. . . . *Hodari D.*'s word, however, is relatively untested, and the Court's earlier decision in Brower v. County of Inyo and subsequent lower court readings of *Hodari D.* that identify a requirement of officer intent to arrest cast into further doubt its viability.

In *Brower* the Court held that a seizure by physical force is "an intentional acquisition of physical control." . . . *Brower* and similar formulations of seizure can be read to indicate that where one avenue of movement is denied to a citizen, she is not seized, but where all avenues of movement are denied to her, she is. Whereas touching a suspect is usually an attempt or a prelude to denying freedom of movement to the suspect, in the case of demonstrators, the touching is an attempt to deny only one avenue of movement — e.g., continuing a march, or remaining in a particular area. . . .

. . . This is essentially the overarching problem demonstrators face under current law: whereas arrest, the "quintessential 'seizure of the person,'" involves an attempt to subdue and detain the subject, a dispersal order involves an attempt to mobilize the subject by force. . . . It is uncertain whether a touching without intent to seize will be a seizure, or the targets of force not touched by the force will be seized.

Renee Paradis, Carpe Demonstrators: Towards a Bright-Line Rule Governing Seizure in Excessive Force Claims Brought by Demonstrators, 103 Colum. L. Rev. 316, 334-339 (2003). Should the definition of "seizures" be context-specific? Does the same definition work in *Hodari D.*, *Brower*, and police dispersal of a public demonstration? Does the difficulty of defining "seizures" cast doubt on the enterprise of using Fourth Amendment law as the primary tool for regulating the police?

4. *Drayton*, *Hodari D.*, and *Brower* all explore a timing question: When — at what point in an encounter between officers and an individual suspect — does the Fourth Amendment apply? The public demonstration example raises a different problem: not *when* the Fourth Amendment applies, but *to whom*. Suppose, for example, that the police stopped Drayton's bus with all the passengers inside just as it was leaving the bus station and heading toward the highway. Who, if anyone, has been "seized"?

The answer appears to be: both the driver and all the passengers. Brendlin v. California, 551 U.S. 249 (2007), raised a variant of the hypothetical just posed. In *Brendlin*, the police stopped a car, not a bus, and the car held two people, not two dozen. The police stopped the car to check on a possibly expired registration — even though the car had a valid registration tag posted. Once the car was stopped, one of the officers recognized the passenger as a parole violator with an outstanding arrest warrant. The passenger was then placed under arrest; a subsequent search turned up various items used to manufacture methamphetamine. The California Supreme Court held that Brendlin (the passenger) was not "seized" when the car was first stopped, but only when the officer placed him under arrest. The Supreme Court unanimously disagreed:

California defends the State Supreme Court's ruling . . . by citing our cases holding that seizure requires a purposeful, deliberate act of detention. But [Michigan v. Chesternut, 486 U.S. 567 (1988)], answers that argument. The intent that counts under the Fourth Amendment is the "intent [that] has been conveyed to the person confronted," id., at 575, n. 7, and the criterion of willful restriction on freedom of movement is no invitation to look to subjective intent when determining who is seized. . . . Nor is

[Brower v. County of Inyo, 489 U.S. 593 (1989)], to the contrary, where it was dispositive that "Brower was meant to be stopped by the physical obstacle of the roadblock — and that he was so stopped." Id., at 599. California reads this language to suggest that for a specific occupant of the car to be seized he must be the motivating target of an officer's show of authority, as if the thrust of our observation were that Brower, and not someone else, was "meant to be stopped." But our point was not that Brower alone was the target but that officers detained him "through means intentionally applied"; if the car had had another occupant, it would have made sense to hold that he too had been seized when the car collided with the roadblock. . . .

. . . [T]he Supreme Court of California assumed that Brendlin, "as the passenger, had no ability to submit to the deputy's show of authority" because only the driver was in control of the moving vehicle. But what may amount to submission depends on what a person was doing before the show of authority: a fleeing man is not seized until he is physically overpowered, but one sitting in a chair may submit to authority by not getting up to run away. Here, Brendlin had no effective way to signal submission while the car was still moving on the roadway, but once it came to a stop he could, and apparently did, submit by staying inside.

551 U.S., at 260-261 *Brendlin* suggests that, when the police detain a number of people in order to investigate one, *all* members of the group have been "seized."

C.   *Probable Cause and Warrants*

The last section dealt with the Fourth Amendment's scope. Some kinds of police observation amount to "searches," and some don't. In some police-citizen encounters the citizen is "seized," and in some he isn't. If no "search" or "seizure" has taken place, the Fourth Amendment does not apply.

What happens when the Fourth Amendment *does* apply? That question breaks down into two others: (1) To what standard are the police held — in other words, how much or what kind of justification must they have in order to search or seize? (2) And who decides whether that justification is present — a magistrate in a warrant proceeding before the search or seizure takes place, or a trial judge in a suppression hearing after the fact? Fourth Amendment law has a traditional answer to each of these questions. The presumptive standard that applies to police searches and seizures is probable cause. The presumptive decision maker is a neutral magistrate, in advance of the search or seizure. Sometimes these two requirements are relaxed, but the strong presumption, again according to Fourth Amendment tradition, is that searches and seizures must be supported by probable cause and must be authorized by a warrant.

Notice that these two requirements are different and separable. Probable cause is a substantive standard: It defines the level of suspicion police must have before they search or seize someone or some thing. The warrant requirement is a rule of procedure: It determines the method by which probable cause or some other substantive standard is to be applied. One could have searches supported by probable cause but without a warrant; one could also have searches authorized by a warrant but without probable cause — in fact, both these scenarios exist in Fourth Amendment law (though the second is rare). But the classical starting point for Fourth Amendment analysis joins the two; unless the case falls within one or another recognized exception, the police must meet both the substantive hurdle and the procedural one.

Most Fourth Amendment decisions take the probable cause requirement for granted, as though its justification were too obvious to bother spelling out. But probable cause has not always been the dominant standard in Fourth Amendment cases. Under Boyd v. United States, 116 U.S. 616 (1886), it appeared that in most cases, there was no standard at all — if the Fourth Amendment applied, the police conduct was forbidden. (*Boyd*'s rise and fall are described in Chapter 4.) That sounds extreme, and perhaps it is. But it is the surest way to protect individual privacy: Define a zone of private life, and declare that the government may not invade it. The probable cause standard presupposes that the government *can* invade one's privacy — as long as it has a good enough reason. Strangely, there is no developed body of literature defending the proposition that probable cause *is* a good enough reason.

The warrant requirement has received a good deal more attention, from judges and academics alike. The standard justification was best and most famously put by Justice Jackson in Johnson v. United States, 333 U.S. 10, 13-14 (1948):

> The point of the Fourth Amendment, which often is not grasped by zealous officers, is not that it denies law enforcement the support of the usual inferences which reasonable men draw from evidence. Its protection consists in requiring that those inferences be drawn by a neutral and detached magistrate instead of being judged by the officer engaged in the often competitive enterprise of ferreting out crime. Any assumption that evidence sufficient to support a magistrate's disinterested determination to issue a search warrant will justify the officers in making a search without a warrant would reduce the Amendment to a nullity and leave the people's homes secure only in the discretion of police officers.

Notwithstanding this stirring language, the presumption that police must have a warrant before searching was never as strong as it appeared. There have always been enough exceptions that a large fraction, probably a large majority, of searches and seizures have fallen outside the scope of the warrant requirement, and a smaller but still substantial fraction fall outside the requirement of probable cause as well. Nevertheless, courts continue to talk as though both probable cause and a warrant are presumptively required — though that talk is much less frequent than it once was — so it makes sense to start with the meaning of those two requirements.

The Text (Again)

The idea that Fourth Amendment analysis begins with the probable cause and warrant requirements is long-standing, but it has also long been under attack. One line of attack stems from the Fourth Amendment's text:

> The right of the people to be secure in their persons, houses, papers, and effects, against unreasonable searches and seizures, shall not be violated, and no warrants shall issue, but upon probable cause, supported by oath or affirmation, and particularly describing the place to be searched, and the persons or things to be seized.

Notice that the first clause, which contains the basic prohibition of "unreasonable searches and seizures," mentions neither probable cause nor warrants. The second clause mentions both, but it expressly *requires* only that "no warrants shall issue, but upon probable cause." Nowhere does the text say that warrants themselves are ever required. Nor does it say that probable cause is to be the ordinary standard for searches and seizures.

In an influential discussion that surveyed the background and historical development of Fourth Amendment law, Telford Taylor — his chief reputation was as a prosecutor at the Nuremberg war crimes trials — argued that this text was plainly designed to limit warrants, not to require them. Telford Taylor, Two Studies in Constitutional Interpretation 23-50 (1969). Taylor noted that in the eighteenth century cases that gave rise to the Fourth Amendment, general warrants (including, in the colonies, the infamous writs of assistance) were used as a means of authorizing searches that would have been illegal under the common law. Accordingly, Taylor argued, the Framers sought to limit this abuse of warrants. By requiring warrants and probable cause, Taylor maintained, the Supreme Court had "stood the Fourth Amendment on its head."[7]

Taylor's argument suggests that neither the warrant process nor the probable cause standard ought to govern in ordinary search and seizure cases. Five years after Taylor's argument, Anthony Amsterdam offered the following response:

> The Court's construction of the amendment as embodying an overriding preference for search warrants is supportable, in my view, because the Court is obliged to give an internally coherent reading to the unreasonableness clause and the warrant clause as expressions of repudiation of the general warrant. In this view, the fourth amendment condemns searches conducted under general warrants and writs of assistance as "unreasonable." It also forbids unreasonable warrantless searches. That is all the amendment says about warrantless searches, and the word "unreasonable" is hardly self-illuminating. Surely then the Court has done right to seek some part of the meaning of an "unreasonable" warrantless search by asking what the condemnation of general warrants and writs implies about the nature of "unreasonable" searches and seizures. . . .
>
> The framers of the fourth amendment accepted specific warrants as reasonable: the second clause of the amendment tells us so. Therefore, the objectionable feature of general warrants and writs must be their indiscriminate character. Warrants are not to issue indiscriminately: that is the office of the probable cause requirement. Nor may indiscriminate searches be made under them: that is why particularity of description of the persons or things to be seized is demanded. . . .
>
> Indiscriminate searches or seizures might be thought to be bad for either or both of two reasons. The first is that they expose people and their possessions to interferences by government when there is no good reason to do so. The concern here is against *unjustified* searches and seizures. . . . The second is that indiscriminate searches and

---

7. Taylor, supra, at 23-24. Akhil Amar has expanded on Taylor's historical analysis, reaching the same basic conclusion: that the Fourth Amendment was intended to be read as requiring neither probable cause nor warrants (Taylor's chief focus was the warrant requirement, but his, and Amar's, argument applies to both). See Akhil Reed Amar, Fourth Amendment First Principles, 107 Harv. L. Rev. 757 (1994). More recently, some scholars have suggested that the history is more complicated than Taylor and Amar believed — and that warrants may have been used in the eighteenth century as they are today, as a tool for protecting individuals from unjustified searches. See Thomas Y. Davies, Recovering the Original Fourth Amendment, 98 Mich. L. Rev. 547 (1999); Morgan Cloud, Searching Through History; Searching for History, 63 U. Chi. L. Rev. 1707 (1996); Tracey Maclin, The Central Meaning of the Fourth Amendment, 35 Wm. & Mary L. Rev. 197 (1993).

seizures are conducted at the discretion of executive officials, who may act despotically and capriciously in the exercise of the power to search and seize. This latter concern runs against *arbitrary* searches and seizures. . . .

Anthony G. Amsterdam, Perspectives on the Fourth Amendment, 58 Minn. L. Rev. 349, 410-411 (1974). The best way to protect against arbitrary and unjustified searches, Amsterdam maintained, is to require probable cause and a warrant whenever feasible.

Regarding the choice between these two readings — Taylor's, with its focus on reasonableness, with probable cause and warrants a kind of textual afterthought; and Amsterdam's, with probable cause and warrants serving to define what reasonableness means — the Supreme Court in recent years has clearly shifted in Taylor's direction. Yet many canonical cases were decided within the "probable cause and warrant" framework, and many students of the Fourth Amendment continue to believe that it offers a better approach to Fourth Amendment interpretation. The merits of the choice between these two approaches obviously depend, in part, on what the warrant process entails and what probable cause means.

The next two subsections take up those two issues. Subsection 3 then deals with cases in which probable cause is the governing standard but warrants are not required. Section D, in turn, takes up those cases in which the probable cause and warrant requirements have both been held inapplicable, and a (usually softer) "reasonableness" standard applies instead.

1.   The Warrant "Requirement"

The Supreme Court has so often expressed a preference for searches and seizures pursuant to warrant that the superiority of warrants over after-the-fact review and sanctions for Fourth Amendment violations is widely taken for granted. In fact, the Fourth Amendment's warrant "requirement" is something of a puzzle:

> First, its very existence seems odd. Legal standards are usually enforced through after-the-fact review. . . . Potential tortfeasors do not ordinarily seek judicial permission to engage in risky conduct; they decide how to behave in light of the governing law and (if things work out badly) defend themselves in litigation later. It is not clear why search and seizure law should work differently. Suppression hearings and damages actions offer readily available means of reviewing police decisions after the fact. And there is no obvious reason why police officers cannot both understand the legal signals these decisions provide and translate those signals into behavior on the street. Finally, after-the-fact review in suppression hearings or damage suits is both adversarial and in-depth, while review of warrant applications by magistrates is ex parte and cursory, so that one would expect that the ex post decisions better protect individuals' interests. . . .
>
> The Supreme Court . . . claims that the warrant requirement is the centerpiece of the law of search and seizure, and that pre-screening by neutral and detached magistrates is the heart of citizens' protection against police overreaching. But the same Court regularly narrows the range of cases to which the warrant requirement applies. . . . [T]he critics are, if anything worse. On the one hand, they argue that the Court should substantially broaden the scope of the warrant requirement, in order to protect citizens' privacy in the many cases that are now left to the supposed vagaries of after-the-fact review. But the same critics often contend that magistrates are rubber stamps

who cannot be trusted to do a sound job of deciding whether probable cause exists in particular cases, and hence should receive little deference from district courts in suppression hearings. This position seems odd, to say the least: if magistrates do a poor job of deciding whether probable cause exists, it is unclear why anyone should want them to do so more often, or indeed at all.

William J. Stuntz, Warrants and Fourth Amendment Remedies, 77 Va. L. Rev. 881, 881-883 (1991).

Stuntz argues that in an exclusionary rule system, the preference for warrants may address two problems: that judges' after-the-fact probable cause determinations may be biased by knowledge that incriminating evidence has been found, and that police in suppression hearings may subvert Fourth Amendment standards by testifying falsely — something they are less able to do when required to state the relevant facts before evidence is found. This still leaves the puzzle, however, as to why *magistrates* review warrant applications:

> The [warrant] requirement is premised on the assumption that officials engaged in the "often competitive enterprise of ferreting out crime" cannot be relied upon to give appropriate weight to privacy costs. But there is surely no a priori reason that police officers must necessarily be unconcerned about the legal protection of fourth amendment rights. Conversely, there is no a priori reason why magistrates, who are also law enforcement officers of a sort, should be especially sensitive to such rights. . . .
>
> Imagine a police department in which a senior, well-respected officer is told that his function is to review warrants to ensure that they are supported by probable cause.
>
> Is there reason to doubt that, once informed of his role, he would do a less effective job than a magistrate? . . .
>
> Of course, modern police departments do not have such officers. Ironically, this failure is attributable, at least in part, to the Court's insistence that they cannot assign officers to this role. The Court's pessimistic assumptions about police behavior thus become self-fulfilling prophecies.

Silas J. Wasserstrom & Louis Michael Seidman, The Fourth Amendment as Constitutional Theory, 77 Geo. L.J. 19, 34-35 (1988).

Thus, the arguments for a warrant preference rule may be both more subtle and more complicated than is sometimes assumed. Returning to the Fourth Amendment's text for a moment, however, it clearly contemplates the existence of some warrant process. Indeed, the text goes to some lengths to impose conditions on the issuance of warrants beyond the basic probable cause requirement. Thus, probable cause must be "supported by Oath or affirmation." Warrants must particularly describe "the place to be searched, and the persons or things to be seized." The Court has added that the magistrate who issues a warrant must be "neutral and detached." Johnson v. United States, 333 U.S. 10, 14 (1946). In addition, state and federal statutes, local codes, and local rules of court commonly specify procedures for warrants — requiring that search warrants be executed within a specified period of time, for instance, or mandating daytime execution in the absence of special reasons for proceeding at night. All this may suggest a high degree of formality in the warrant process, but don't be fooled — in fact, there is considerably less formality in the process than one might suppose.

The Oath or Affirmation Requirement

The oath or affirmation requirement is often satisfied by specifying the facts giving rise to probable cause in a police officer's affidavit that is attached to the warrant application — though oral statements may also be sworn. In some places, affiant police officers appear personally before the magistrate. Other places expressly authorize telephonic search warrant procedures that dispense with any personal appearance requirement.

It is important that the circumstances giving rise to probable cause be adequately presented to the magistrate. In Whiteley v. Warden, 401 U.S. 560, 565, n. 8 (1971), the Court concluded that facially insufficient affidavits "cannot be rehabilitated by testimony concerning information possessed by the affiant when he sought the warrant but not disclosed to the issuing magistrate." A defendant may challenge a facially *sufficient* affidavit after the fact, moreover, when it is shown to contain false statements. "Negligent" or "innocent" falsehoods will not invalidate a warrant. But if a defendant can establish that the affidavit contained perjured statements or false statements made in reckless disregard of their truth, and provided the affidavit's remaining content is not sufficient to establish probable cause, the search warrant will be voided and the fruits of the search excluded. Franks v. Delaware, 438 U.S. 154, 155-156 (1978).

One study sponsored by the National Center for State Courts in the early 1980s examined the search warrant application process in seven cities and found that in most places, warrant affidavits "were often barely distinguishable from one another: extensive and critical portions of many affidavits were rendered in 'boilerplate' recitations of informant reliability, information trustworthiness, and probable cause to believe certain specified contraband was in the possession of the accused at the place indicated." L. Paul Sutton, Getting Around the Fourth Amendment, in Carl B. Klockars & Stephen D. Mastrofski eds., Thinking About Police 433, 440-441 (2d ed. 1991). This raises the question how seriously officers take the warrant preparation process. One magistrate interviewed in connection with the study recounted the following exchange stemming from the magistrate's having asked an officer/affiant about a specific statement in the affidavit that contradicted a statement the officer made orally:

> *Officer:*   Well, I didn't write that statement.
> *Magistrate:*   But you signed it! And that concerns me. You know, you could potentially open yourself up to a nice lawsuit if you're going to issue warrants that you haven't read and you don't know what's contained within the four corners of those warrants.
> *Officer:*   All I'm doing is relying on my best information and belief.
> *Magistrate:*   But your best information and belief is more than what's in here!

Id., at 442. One way to avoid scenarios like this is to use prosecutors to screen warrant applications, in the hope that those applications will then be more informative and contain fewer errors. From the perspective of the police officer, however, prosecutorial screening may simply mean more needless delay.

The time and resources required to obtain a warrant are no small matter. Police often have to move quickly to secure evidence that may be moved or destroyed, and the more obstacles there are to obtaining a warrant, the more likely it is that evidence will be lost because of the process. More pointedly, we might suspect that bureaucratic delays in obtaining the warrant will encourage police to avoid the warrant process entirely, and hope that they will be able to argue later that the search was justified by exigent circumstances, or by some other exception to the warrant requirement discussed below. As a partial response to this concern, the Federal Rules of Criminal Procedure provide for a process by which the police can obtain a search warrant via telephone, hoping to avoid the sometimes considerable delay caused by having to appear before a magistrate judge in person. See Rule 41(d)(3), (e)(3).

The Magistrate

The Supreme Court has had several occasions to interpret the "neutral and detached magistrate" requirement. In Coolidge v. New Hampshire, 403 U.S. 443 (1971), the Court found the requirement to be violated by a procedure in which a state attorney general issued a search warrant in the course of a murder investigation that he was conducting. The Court has also refused to uphold a warrant process in which the magistrate received a fee for issuing warrants but not for refusing them. See Connally v. Georgia, 429 U.S. 245 (1977). In the view of some commentators, however, the Court may have done little else to ensure that the review of warrant applications by magistrates is meaningful:

> The validity of the Court's procedural structure rests on the empirical claim that "neutral and detached" magistrates do a better job of assessing the law enforcement/privacy tradeoff than do police officers. But the "rubber stamp" quality of magistrate review of warrant applications is an open scandal, and the Court has done little to show that it takes its own procedures seriously. On the contrary, it has failed to impose minimal standards to ensure that magistrates understand the meaning of probable cause.

Silas J. Wasserstrom & Louis Michael Seidman, The Fourth Amendment as Constitutional Theory, 77 Geo. L.J. 19, 34 (1988). In Shadwick v. City of Tampa, 407 U.S. 345, 350-352 (1972), the Court upheld a warrant process in which clerks without law degrees were permitted to issue arrest warrants for municipal ordinance violations, noting that "[c]ommunities may have sound reasons for delegating the responsibility of issuing warrants to competent personnel other than judges or lawyers."

The process by which warrants are issued, moreover, can be quite perfunctory. Consider again what the NCSC team heard from interested parties during its study:

> In virtually every jurisdiction we studied, representatives of all perspectives (police, judiciary, prosecution, and defense) suggested that at least some of the judges with whom they had contact were sometimes remiss in their review of warrant applications. Characterizations of this delinquency ranged from sympathetic concern (usually on the part of law enforcement) to biting sarcasm (on the part of the offending party's judicial brethren). We must have been told by at least one person in each of the jurisdictions studied that "There are some judges who will sign anything."

L. Paul Sutton, Getting Around the Fourth Amendment, in Carl B. Klockars & Stephen D. Mastrofski eds., Thinking About Police 433, 439 (2d ed. 1991).

Officers interviewed for the study also noted "considerable variation . . . not only in terms of judges' interpretation of the evidence required to meet the probable cause standard but also in terms of judges' attitudes about whether certain crimes ought even to be enforced." Id., at 436. In the words of one law enforcement official:

> If [the judge] feels comfortable with the area of law — say narcotics law — [then he] doesn't treat you like a pain. . . . He will show some desire, some willingness to work [with you], look at the thing, ask you some questions, professionally discuss the thing. [Conversely,] there are those judges obviously who don't believe that strongly in taking a hard-line approach to narcotics enforcement. I think that is reflected in their attitudes when we come in to get search warrants.

Id., at 437.

Perfunctory review of warrant applications by some magistrates and variation among magistrates in the standards they apply to such review create opportunities for "judge shopping" by police. Such opportunities in turn might suggest that the warrant application process imposes few real restraints on law enforcement. Lest you too easily conclude from all this that the process is not meaningful, however, it's worth recalling that searches pursuant to warrants usually uncover evidence — over 90 percent of the time, according to the NCSC research. See page 446, below. This figure at least suggests that police often target the right places in their warrant applications. Do you think this is a consequence of the warrant process? Or is it merely coincident with it? For an argument that the key benefit of the warrant process may be the inconvenience it poses for the police — that searches pursuant to warrants tend to succeed because police officers don't want to spend time preparing the papers and waiting to see a magistrate only to engage in a fruitless search — see Donald Dripps, Living with *Leon*, 95 Yale L.J. 906 (1986).

The Particularity Requirement

The Fourth Amendment's text requires that warrants "particularly describ[e] the place to be searched, and the persons or things to be seized." With respect to the place searched, the Supreme Court has said that the description should be particular enough to permit an officer "with reasonable effort [to] ascertain and identify the place intended." Steele v. United States, 267 U.S. 498, 503 (1925). When a seemingly adequate description of the premises turns out to be so ambiguous that police have no idea which premises to search, the particularity requirement is not satisfied and police may not proceed. If police possess information that clarifies the ambiguity or if it is reasonably clear what portion of the warrant description is in error, however, a search of the "proper" premises may be permitted.

What if the police search the wrong place? In Maryland v. Garrison, 480 U.S. 79 (1987), police had probable cause to search the third-floor apartment of Lawrence McWebb. Without realizing that the third floor contained two apartments, they obtained a warrant to search "the premises known as 2036 Park Avenue third floor apartment." The police entered the wrong apartment and seized contraband there before discovering their error. The Court first determined that the warrant was valid when issued, based on the information that the police disclosed to the magistrate, or had a duty to discover and disclose. The validity of the search of the apartment "depend[ed] on whether the officers' failure to realize the over-breadth of the warrant was objectively reasonable"; after reviewing the facts, the Court determined that the officers' mistake satisfied this standard. Id., at 88.

The particularity requirement for items sought to be seized serves several purposes. First, it supports the probable cause requirement: If the police cannot specify what they are looking for, the factual basis for their suspicions is likely weak. Second, it limits the legitimate scope of searches both spatially and temporally. (Thus, if police are searching only for stolen paintings, they may not look in desk drawers or other places too small to contain them. Once the paintings are found, the search must end.) Finally, the particularity requirement helps to ensure that people will not be wrongly deprived of their property. Note, however, that in Andresen v. Maryland, 427 U.S. 463 (1976), the Court upheld warrants that, after listing a long series of specific documents to be seized, also authorized the seizure of "other fruits, instrumentalities and evidence of crime at (this) time unknown." The Court construed the phrase to refer to the specific crime under investigation and held that so construed, its inclusion did not render the warrants fatally general. Note, too, that the particularity requirement does not mean that police are absolutely precluded from seizing other items not mentioned in the warrant application. See pages 465-475, infra, for a discussion of the plain view doctrine.

The Execution of Warrants

Not only do warrants and warrant applications raise Fourth Amendment issues; so does the manner in which warrants are "executed." That is, the Fourth Amendment regulates the manner of warrant-based searches, not just the question whether those searches may happen.

This point requires some explanation. Nearly all the cases you have read in this chapter — and the large majority of the cases that follow — address one of two questions: First, does the Fourth Amendment apply to this encounter? Katz doctrine and the cases defining "seizures" deal with this question. Second, did the police have a sufficient justification for searching the relevant place or seizing the relevant person? The cases defining "probable cause" address this question. Remarkably few Fourth Amendment cases deal with a third question: Did the police carry out the search or seizure in an unreasonably intrusive manner?

The exclusionary rule explains that strange fact. Because most Fourth Amendment claims are raised by motions to suppress physical evidence, judges are regularly required to ask whether the police had sufficiently good reason for looking in this place or listening to that conversation. But when officers carry out searches in an unusually violent or degrading manner, the violence and degradation itself rarely leads to the discovery of evidence. So motions to suppress rarely challenge those kinds of police conduct, and judges have fewer opportunities to define the legal standards that protect against such harms.

What little Fourth Amendment law exists on the subject tends to fall into two categories: doctrines that restrict police violence — the use of deadly and nondeadly force — and doctrines that govern the execution of warrants to search homes. The cases on police use of force are covered below, at pages 630-640. The notes here, dealing first with the "knock and announce" requirement, concern the second category of cases.

NOTES ON WARRANT EXECUTION

1. In Wilson v. Arkansas, 514 U.S. 927 (1995), a unanimous Supreme Court held that absent some law enforcement interest establishing the reasonableness of an unannounced intrusion, the Fourth Amendment requires police to knock and announce themselves before entering premises to execute a warrant. Richards v. Wisconsin, 520 U.S. 385 (1997), raised the question whether *Wilson* mandated a case-by-case inquiry, or whether courts might categorically permit "no-knock" entries in some types of cases. The Wisconsin Supreme Court had ruled that such entries were automatically permissible whenever police executed search warrants in felony drug investigations. Writing for the Court, Justice Stevens rejected this per se rule:

> [T]he Wisconsin rule contains considerable overgeneralization. For example, while drug investigation frequently does pose special risks to officer safety and the preservation of evidence, not every drug investigation will pose these risks to a substantial degree. For example, a search could be conducted at a time when the only individuals present in a residence have no connection with the drug activity and thus will be unlikely to threaten officers or destroy evidence. Or the police could know that the drugs being searched for were of a type or in a location that made them impossible to destroy quickly. . . . Wisconsin's blanket rule impermissibly insulates these cases from judicial review.

Id., at 393. Justice Stevens' opinion concluded that "[i]n order to justify a 'no-knock' entry, the police must have a reasonable suspicion that knocking and announcing their presence, under the particular circumstances, would be dangerous or futile, or that it would inhibit the effective investigation of the crime by, for example, allowing the destruction of evidence."

2. In United States v. Ramirez, 523 U.S. 65 (1998), the Court made clear that this "reasonable suspicion" standard is sufficient to justify an unannounced entry even when the officers must damage property — for instance, by breaking down a door — to make the entry. Chief Justice Rehnquist's opinion for the Court cautioned, however, that "[t]he general touchstone of reasonableness . . . governs the method of execution of the warrant. Excessive or unnecessary destruction of property in the course of a search may violate the Fourth Amendment, even though the entry itself is lawful and the fruits of the search not subject to suppression." Id., at 71. (Consider again what remedies other than suppression might be available.)

3. The Court revisited the "knock and announce" requirement in United States v. Banks, 540 U.S. 31 (2003). In *Banks*, officers executing a warrant to search for cocaine in Banks's two-bedroom apartment knocked and announced their authority, but waited only 15 to 20 seconds before using a battering ram to break open the front door. Banks was in the shower at the time, and testified that he heard nothing until the crash. The search of his home produced weapons, crack cocaine, and other evidence of drug dealing. The Court concluded that this entry was constitutionally permissible because the officers entered after a reasonable suspicion of exigency had ripened:

The Fourth Amendment says nothing specific about formalities in exercising a warrant's authorization, speaking to the manner of searching as well as to the legitimacy of searching at all simply in terms of the right to be "secure . . . against unreasonable searches and seizures." Although the notion of reasonable execution must therefore be fleshed out, we have done that case by case, largely avoiding categories and protocols for searches. . . .

In Wilson v. Arkansas, 514 U.S. 927 (1995), we held that the common law knock-and-announce principle is one focus of the reasonableness enquiry; and we subsequently decided that although the standard generally requires the police to announce their intent to search before entering closed premises, the obligation gives way when officers "have a reasonable suspicion that knocking and announcing their presence, under the particular circumstances, would be dangerous or futile, or . . . would inhibit the effective investigation of the crime by, for example, allowing the destruction of evidence," Richards v. Wisconsin, 520 U.S. 385, 394 (1997). . . .

Since most people keep their doors locked, entering without knocking will normally do some damage, a circumstance too common to require a heightened justification when a reasonable suspicion of exigency already justifies an unwarned entry. We have accordingly held that police in exigent circumstances may damage premises so far as necessary for a no-knock entrance without demonstrating the suspected risk in any more detail than the law demands for an unannounced intrusion simply by lifting the latch. United States v. Ramirez, 523 U.S. 65, 70-71 (1998). Either way, it is enough that the officers had a reasonable suspicion of exigent circumstances.

. . . Although the police concededly arrived at Banks's door without reasonable suspicion of facts justifying a no-knock entry, they argue that announcing their presence started the clock running toward the moment of apprehension that Banks would flush away the easily disposable cocaine, prompted by knowing the police would soon be coming in. . . .

Banks does not, of course, deny that exigency may develop in the period beginning when officers with a warrant knock to be admitted, and the issue comes down to whether it was reasonable to suspect imminent loss of evidence after the 15 to 20 seconds the officers waited prior to forcing their way. Though . . . this call is a close one, we think that after 15 or 20 seconds without a response, police could fairly suspect that cocaine would be gone if they were reticent any longer. . . .

[E]ach of [Banks's] reasons for saying that 15 to 20 seconds was too brief rests on a mistake about the relevant enquiry: the fact that he was actually in the shower and did not hear the officers is not to the point, and the same is true of the claim that it might have taken him longer than 20 seconds if he had heard the knock and headed straight for the door. As for the shower, it is enough to say that the facts known to the police are what count in judging reasonable waiting time, and there is no indication that the police knew that Banks was in the shower. . . .

And the argument that 15 to 20 seconds was too short for Banks to have come to the door ignores the very risk that justified prompt entry. True, if the officers were to justify their timing here by claiming that Banks's failure to admit them fairly suggested a refusal to let them in, Banks could at least argue that no such suspicion can arise until an occupant has had time to get to the door, a time that will vary with the size of the establishment, perhaps five seconds to open a motel room door, or several minutes to move through a townhouse. In this case, however, the police claim exigent need to enter, and the crucial fact in examining their actions is not time to reach the door but the particular exigency claimed. On the record here, what matters is the opportunity to get rid of cocaine, which a prudent dealer will keep near a commode or kitchen sink. . . . That is, when circumstances are exigent because a pusher may be near the point of putting his drugs beyond reach, it is imminent disposal, not travel time to the entrance, that governs when the police may reasonably enter; since the bathroom and kitchen are usually in the interior of a dwelling, not the front hall, there is no reason generally to peg the travel time to the location of the door, and no reliable basis for giving the proprietor of a mansion a longer wait than the resident of a bungalow, or an apartment like Banks's. And 15 to 20 seconds does not seem an unrealistic guess about the time someone would need to get in a position to rid his quarters of cocaine.

4. Compare *Banks* to *Richards*. In *Richards*, the Court rejected a per se rule allowing no-knock entries in all felony drug cases. The officers in *Banks* had no reasonable suspicion of facts justifying a no-knock entry at the time they arrived on the scene. But 15 seconds after knocking (even if it takes longer than that to get to the door) they are permitted to break in, due principally to the ease with which narcotics may be disposed of. Are these results — both reached unanimously — consistent?

5. Although the Justices were in agreement about the contours of the knock and announce requirement — all four of the Supreme Court decisions that established and defined it were unanimous — when the time came to define a remedy, the consensus crumbled. In Hudson v. Michigan, 547 U.S. 586, 591 (2006), a five-member majority concluded that when the police violated the Fourth Amendment by failing to properly knock and announce their presence, the exclusionary rule did *not* apply — that is, the evidence seized as a result of the improperly initiated search did not have to be suppressed. Civil remedies and other checks on police behavior, said the Court, were sufficient to deter the police. Hudson is discussed in much more detail in Section F of this chapter.

6. The Court's knock-and-announce cases recognize that law enforcement interests might establish the reasonableness of an unannounced entry. What about an unannounced and *covert* entry in which notice of the search is delayed? Conventional search warrants are executed "overtly." A resident may be present during the search; in any event, notice of the search is left behind. Courts have recognized circumstances, however, in which "sneak-and-peek" warrants may be upheld. See, e.g., United States v. Villegas, 899 F.2d 1324, 1337 (2d Cir. 1990) (permitting delayed notice upon "good reason").

The USA PATRIOT Act (United and Strengthening America by Providing Appropriate Tools Required to Intercept and Obstruct Terrorism Act) of 2001, Pub. L. No. 107-56, 115 Stat. 272, enacted in the wake of the September 11 terrorist attacks for the stated purposed of enabling government officials to protect against similar attacks, included a uniform statutory standard for the issuance of delayed notice search warrants, or so-called "sneak-and-peek" warrants, in *all* federal cases — not just those involving terrorism. 18 U.S.C. §3103a(b) now provides that as to search warrants

> to search for or seize any property or material that constitutes evidence of a criminal offense in violation of the laws of the United States, any notice required, or that may be required, to be given may be delayed if (1) the court finds reasonable cause to believe that providing immediate notification of the execution of the warrant may have an adverse result; (2) the warrant prohibits the seizure of any tangible property . . . except where the court finds reasonable necessity for the seizure; and (3) the warrant provides for the giving of such notice within a reasonable period not to exceed 30 days after the date of its execution, or on a later date certain if the facts of the case justify a longer period of delay.

Pursuant to this provision, courts have authorized brief delays in notice of the execution of a warrant but also delays of longer duration in some cases. They have found that "sneak-and-peek" *seizures* were necessary for a variety of reasons, including the protection of the safety of a confidential informant and the prevention of evidence destruction. Do so-called "sneak-and-peek" warrants raise special concerns beyond those associated with the normal warrant procedure? Why or why not?

7. Sometimes the execution of a warrant raises *First* Amendment concerns. Zurcher v. Stanford Daily, 436 U.S. 547 (1978), raised the question whether such concerns limit the use of warrants to search newspaper offices. Officers had probable cause to believe that a photographer with the *Stanford Daily* had taken photographs of demonstrators who had attacked police. The officers sought and received a warrant to search the student newspaper's office, and the search was carried out. The Court refused to impose special limits on the use of warrants in this context, noting that "if the requirements of specificity and reasonableness are properly applied, policed, and observed," no occasion would arise for officers "to rummage at large in newspaper files or to intrude into or to deter normal editorial and publication decisions." Id., at 566. Do you agree?

8. Challenges to the method of executing a warrant are not limited to knock and announce cases. In Wilson v. Layne, 526 U.S. 603 (1999), the Court addressed the Fourth Amendment propriety of "media ride-alongs" in which reporters accompany police as they perform their duties. Officers went to the home of Charles and Geraldine Wilson with an arrest warrant for the Wilson's son, Dominic. They invited a reporter and a photographer from the *Washington Post* to accompany them. The Court concluded that while the officers had a warrant and were "undoubtedly entitled to enter the Wilson home in order to execute the arrest warrant for Dominic Wilson," they violated the Fourth Amendment by bringing members of the media into the home:

> In Horton v. California, 496 U.S. 128, 140 (1990), we held "[i]f the scope of the search exceeds that permitted by the terms of a validly issued warrant . . . the subsequent seizure is unconstitutional without more." While this does not mean that every police action while inside a home must be explicitly authorized by the text of the warrant, the Fourth Amendment does require that police actions in execution of a warrant be related to the objectives of the authorized intrusion. . . .
>
> This is not a case in which the presence of the third parties directly aided in the execution of the warrant. Where the police enter a home under the authority of a warrant to search for stolen property, the presence of third parties for the purpose of identifying the stolen property has long been approved by this Court and our common-law tradition.
>
> Respondents argue that the presence of the Washington Post reporters in the Wilsons' home nonetheless served a number of legitimate law enforcement purposes. They first assert that officers should be able to exercise reasonable discretion about when it would "further their law enforcement mission to permit members of the news media to accompany them in executing a warrant." But this claim ignores the importance of the right of residential privacy at the core of the Fourth Amendment. It may well be that media ride-alongs further the law enforcement objectives of the police in a general sense, but that is not the same as furthering the purposes of the search. . . .
>
> Respondents next argue that the presence of third parties could serve the law enforcement purpose of publicizing the government's efforts to combat crime, and facilitate accurate reporting on law enforcement activities. There is certainly language in our opinions interpreting the First Amendment which points to the importance of

"the press" in informing the general public about the administration of criminal justice. . . . But the Fourth Amendment also protects a very important right, and in the present case it is in terms of that right that the media ride-alongs must be judged. . . .

Finally, respondents argue that the presence of third parties could serve in some situations to minimize police abuses and protect suspects, and also to protect the safety of the officers. While it might be reasonable for police officers to themselves videotape home entries as part of a "quality control" effort to ensure that the rights of homeowners are being respected, or even to preserve evidence, such a situation is significantly different from the media presence in this case. The Washington Post reporters in the Wilsons' home were working on a story for their own purposes. They were not present for the purpose of protecting the officers, much less the Wilsons. . . .

We hold that it is a violation of the Fourth Amendment for police to bring members of the media or other third parties into a home during the execution of a warrant when the presence of the third parties in the home was not in aid of the execution of the warrant.

9. The Supreme Court in *Wilson* stressed the requirement that police actions in executing a warrant must be related to the objective of the intrusion that the warrant authorizes. Even when police honor this precept, however, the people on the scene where a warrant is executed — who themselves may be uninvolved in criminal activity — may well suffer serious inconvenience. In Michigan v. Summers, 452 U.S. 692, 705 (1981), the Supreme Court held that officers executing a search warrant for contraband have the authority "to detain the occupants of the premises while a proper search is conducted." Such detentions prevent flight in the event that incriminating evidence is found; minimize the risk of harm to officers; and facilitate the orderly carrying out of the search. In Muehler v. Mena, 544 U.S. 93 (2005), the Court concluded that a two- to three-hour handcuff detention was constitutionally reasonable given that the warrant being executed authorized a search for both weapons and a wanted gang member, who was believed to reside on the premises: "In such inherently dangerous situations, the use of handcuffs minimizes the risk of harm to both officers and occupants."

Consider also Los Angeles County v. Rettele, 550 U.S. 609 (2007). The Los Angeles County Sheriff's office was conducting an investigation of fraud and identity theft; one of the suspects had a registered handgun, a fact that plainly affected the nature of the subsequent search. Deputies obtained a warrant to search two houses where various public records indicated the suspects lived. Unbeknownst to the police, one of the two houses had recently been sold to plaintiff Max Rettele, who lived there with his girlfriend and her teenage son. When the police arrived at Rettele's door at 7:15 a.m., here is what transpired:

Watters and six other deputies knocked on the door and announced their presence. Chase Hall [the teenage son] answered. The deputies entered the house after ordering Hall to lie face down on the ground.

The deputies' announcement awoke Rettele and Sadler. The deputies entered their bedroom with guns drawn and ordered them to get out of their bed and to show their hands. They protested that they were not wearing clothes. Rettele stood up and attempted to put on a pair of sweatpants, but deputies told him not to move. Sadler also stood up and attempted, without success, to cover herself with a sheet. Rettele and Sadler were held at gun-point for one to two minutes before Rettele was allowed to retrieve a robe for Sadler. He was then permitted to dress. Rettele and Sadler left the bedroom within three to four minutes to sit on the couch in the living room.

By that time the deputies realized they had made a mistake. They apologized to Rettele and Sadler, thanked them for not becoming upset, and left within five minutes. They proceeded to the other house the warrant authorized them to search, where they found three suspects. Those suspects were arrested and convicted.

550 U.S., at 611-612. Rettele sued, claiming that, even if the warrant was legally valid, the search was conducted in an unreasonable manner. The Supreme Court disagreed, unanimously:

The orders by the police to the occupants, in the context of this lawful search, were permissible, and perhaps necessary, to protect the safety of the deputies. Blankets and bedding can conceal a weapon, and one of the suspects was known to own a firearm, factors which underscore this point. The Constitution does not require an officer to ignore the possibility that an armed suspect may sleep with a weapon within reach. The reports are replete with accounts of suspects sleeping close to weapons. . . .

The deputies needed a moment to secure the room and ensure that other persons were not close by or did not present a danger. Deputies were not required to turn their backs to allow Rettele and Sadler to retrieve clothing or to cover themselves with the sheets. Rather, "the risk of harm to both the police and the occupants is minimized if the officers routinely exercise unquestioned command of the situation." [Michigan v. Summers, 452 U.S. 692, 702-703 (1981).]

This is not to say, of course, that the deputies were free to force Rettele and Sadler to remain motionless and standing for any longer than necessary. We have recognized that "special circumstances, or possibly a prolonged detention" might render a search unreasonable. See id., at 705, n. 21. There is no accusation that the detention here was prolonged. The deputies left the home less than 15 minutes after arriving. The detention was shorter and less restrictive than the 2- to 3-hour handcuff detention upheld in *Mena*. And there is no allegation that the deputies prevented Sadler and Rettele from dressing longer than necessary to protect their safety. Sadler was unclothed for no more than two minutes, and Rettele for only slightly more time than that. Sadler testified that once the police were satisfied that no immediate threat was presented, "they wanted us to get dressed and they were pressing us really fast to hurry up and get some clothes on."

The Fourth Amendment allows warrants to issue on probable cause, a standard well short of absolute certainty. Valid warrants will issue to search the innocent, and people like Rettele and Sadler unfortunately bear the cost. Officers executing search warrants on occasion enter a house when residents are engaged in private activity; and the resulting frustration, embarrassment, and humiliation may be real, as was true here. When officers execute a valid warrant and act in a reasonable manner to protect themselves from harm, however, the Fourth Amendment is not violated.

550 U.S., at 614-616. Do you agree? Who is likely to make wiser judgments about the objective reasonableness of police conduct in executing search warrants — juries determining whether to award damages, or appellate courts reviewing their decisions?

2.   The Probable Cause Standard

Courts have had trouble finding a working definition of probable cause. In Brinegar v. United States, 338 U.S. 160 (1949), the Supreme Court said, unhelpfully, that a police officer has probable cause to arrest when "the facts and circumstances within [the officers'] knowledge and of which they had reasonably trustworthy information [are] sufficient in themselves to warrant a man of reasonable caution in the belief that an offense has been or is being committed." Id., at 175-176 (quotation omitted). What that definition means depends, obviously, on how it is applied. And in the Supreme Court, it has been applied most often in cases involving the police use of informants. Consider the facts and holdings of the following three cases, the first involving a police officer's bare hunch, the second and third involving informants' tips.

In Nathanson v. United States, 290 U.S. 41 (1933), a police officer, in support of an application for a search warrant for illegal liquor, swore out an affidavit that stated simply that the officer "has cause to suspect and does believe that certain merchandise," namely illegal liquor, "is now deposited and contained within the premises of J.J. Nathanson." Id., at 44. The warrant was issued and the search carried out. The Court unanimously found the search illegal, saying:

> Under the Fourth Amendment, an officer may not properly issue a warrant to search a private dwelling unless he can find probable cause therefore from facts or circumstances presented to him under oath or affirmation. Mere affirmance of belief or suspicion is not enough.

Id., at 47.

In Draper v. United States, 358 U.S. 307 (1958), an informant named Hereford "from time to time gave information" to federal agent Marsh about narcotics violations; "Hereford was paid small sums of money" for the information. According to Marsh, these tips had consistently been accurate.

> . . . Hereford told Marsh that James Draper . . . recently had taken up abode at a stated address in Denver and "was peddling narcotics to several addicts" in that city. Four days later, on September 7, Hereford told Marsh "that Draper had gone to Chicago the day before . . . by train [and] that he was going to bring back three ounces of heroin [and] that he would return to Denver either on the morning of the 8th of September or the morning of the 9th of September also by train." Hereford also gave Marsh a detailed physical description of Draper and of the clothing he was wearing, and said that he would be carrying "a tan zipper bag," and that he habitually "walked real fast."
>
> On the morning of September 8, Marsh and a Denver police officer went to the Denver Union Station and kept watch over all incoming trains from Chicago, but they did not see anyone fitting the description that Hereford had given. Repeating the process on the morning of September 9, they saw a person, having the exact physical attributes and wearing the precise clothing described by Hereford, alight from an incoming Chicago train and start walking "fast" toward the exit. He was carrying a tan zipper bag in his right hand and the left was thrust in his raincoat pocket. Marsh, accompanied by the police officer, . . . stopped and arrested him. They then searched him and found . . . two "envelopes containing heroin" clutched in his left hand in his raincoat pocket, and found [a] syringe in the tan zipper bag.

Id., at 309-310. The Supreme Court found that Marsh had probable cause to support the arrest; the accompanying search was a permissible search incident to arrest. (See Section C.3.e, below, for a discussion of searches incident to arrest.)

In Spinelli v. United States, 393 U.S. 410 (1969), FBI agents obtained a warrant to search the defendant's apartment based on an affidavit containing these allegations:

1. The FBI had kept track of Spinelli's movements on five days during the month of August 1965. On four of these occasions, Spinelli was seen crossing one of two bridges leading from Illinois into St. Louis, Missouri, between 11 a.m. and 12:15 p.m. On four of the five days, Spinelli was also seen parking his car in a lot used by residents of an apartment house at 1108 Indian Circle Drive in St. Louis, between 3:30 p.m. and 4:45 p.m. On one day, Spinelli was followed further and seen to enter a particular apartment in the building.
2. An FBI check with the telephone company revealed that this apartment contained two telephones listed under the name of Grace P. Hagen, and carrying the numbers WYdown 4-0029 and WYdown 4-0136.
3. The application stated that "William Spinelli is known to this affiant and to federal law enforcement agents and local law enforcement agents as a bookmaker, an associate of bookmakers, a gambler, and an associate of gamblers."
4. Finally, it was stated that the FBI "has been informed by a confidential reliable informant that William Spinelli is operating a handbook and accepting wagers and disseminating wagering information by means of the telephones which have been assigned the numbers WYdown 4-0029 and WYdown 4-0136."

Id., at 413-414. Writing for the Court, Justice Harlan analyzed the affidavit as follows:

> There can be no question that the last item mentioned, detailing the informant's tip, has a fundamental place in this warrant application. Without it, probable cause could not be established. The first two items reflect only innocent-seeming activity and data. Spinelli's travels to and from the apartment building and his entry into a particular apartment on one occasion could hardly be taken as bespeaking gambling activity; and there is surely nothing unusual about an apartment containing two separate telephones. Many a householder indulges himself in this petty luxury. Finally, the allegation that Spinelli was "known" to the affiant and to other federal and local law enforcement officers as a gambler and an associate of gamblers is but a bald and unilluminating assertion of suspicion that is entitled to no weight in appraising the magistrate's decision. Nathanson v. United States, 290 U.S. 41, 46 (1933).

Id., at 414. Justice Harlan went on to note the circular quality of the government's argument: "[T]he Government claims that the informant's tip gives a suspicious color to the FBI's reports detailing Spinelli's innocent-seeming conduct and that, conversely, the FBI's surveillance corroborates the informant's tip, thereby entitling it to more weight." He rejected that "totality of the circumstances" approach, in favor of "a more precise analysis" of informants' tips that emphasizes both the informant's reliability and the basis of his knowledge:

> Applying these principles to the present case, we first consider the weight to be given the informer's tip when it is considered apart from the rest of the affidavit. It is clear that a Commissioner could not credit it without abdicating his constitutional function. Though the affiant swore that his confidant was "reliable," he offered the magistrate

no reason in support of this conclusion. Perhaps even more important is the fact that . . . [t]he tip does not contain a sufficient statement of the underlying circumstances from which the informer concluded that Spinelli was running a bookmaking operation. We are not told how the FBI's source received his information — it is not alleged that the informant personally observed Spinelli at work or that he had ever placed a bet with him. Moreover, if the informant came by the information indirectly, he did not explain why his sources were reliable. In the absence of a statement detailing the manner in which the information was gathered, it is especially important that the tip describe the accused's criminal activity in sufficient detail that the magistrate may know that he is relying on something more substantial than a casual rumor circulating in the underworld or an accusation based merely on an individual's general reputation.

. . . Such an inference cannot be made in the present case. Here, the only facts supplied were that Spinelli was using two specified telephones and that these phones were being used in gambling operations. This meager report could easily have been obtained from an offhand remark heard at a neighborhood bar. . . .

We conclude, then, that in the present case the informant's tip — even when corroborated to the extent indicated — was not sufficient to provide the basis for a finding of probable cause. This is not to say that the tip was so insubstantial that it could not properly have counted in the magistrate's determination. Rather, it needed some further support. When we look to the other parts of the application, however, we find nothing alleged which would permit the suspicions engendered by the informant's report to ripen into a judgment that a crime was probably being committed. As we have already seen, the allegations detailing the FBI's surveillance of Spinelli and its investigation of the telephone company records contain no suggestion of criminal conduct when taken by themselves — and they are not endowed with an aura of suspicion by virtue of the informer's tip. Nor do we find that the FBI's reports take on a sinister color when read in light of common knowledge that bookmaking is often carried on over the telephone and from premises ostensibly used by others for perfectly normal purposes. . . . All that remains to be considered is the flat statement that Spinelli was "known" to the FBI and others as a gambler. But just as a simple assertion of police suspicion is not itself a sufficient basis for a magistrate's finding of probable cause, we do not believe it may be used to give additional weight to allegations that would otherwise be insufficient.

Id., at 416-419.

Draper and *Spinelli* seemed to point in opposite directions. The next case appeared to resolve the tension.

ILLINOIS v. GATES

Certiorari to the Supreme Court of Illinois
462 U.S. 213 (1983)

JUSTICE REHNQUIST delivered the opinion of the Court.

Respondents Lance and Susan Gates were indicted for violation of state drug laws after police officers, executing a search warrant, discovered marihuana and other contraband in their automobile and home. Prior to trial the Gateses moved to suppress evidence seized during this search. . . .

II

. . . A chronological statement of events usefully introduces the issues at stake. Bloomingdale, Ill., is a suburb of Chicago located in Du Page County. On May 3, 1978, the Bloomingdale Police Department received by mail an anonymous hand-written letter which read as follows:

> This letter is to inform you that you have a couple in your town who strictly make their living on selling drugs. They are Sue and Lance Gates, they live on Greenway, off Bloomingdale Rd. in the condominiums. Most of their buys are done in Florida. Sue his wife drives their car to Florida, where she leaves it to be loaded up with drugs, then Lance flys down and drives it back. Sue flys back after she drops the car off in Florida. May 3 she is driving down there again and Lance will be flying down in a few days to drive it back. At the time Lance drives the car back he has the trunk loaded with over $100,000.00 in drugs. Presently they have over $100,000.00 worth of drugs in their basement.
>
> They brag about the fact they never have to work, and make their entire living on pushers.
>
> I guarantee if you watch them carefully you will make a big catch. They are friends with some big drugs dealers, who visit their house often.
>
> Lance & Susan Gates
Greenway in Condominiums

The letter was referred by the Chief of Police of the Bloomingdale Police Department to Detective Mader, who decided to pursue the tip. Mader learned, from the office of the Illinois Secretary of State, that an Illinois driver's license had been issued to one Lance Gates, residing at a stated address in Bloomingdale. He contacted a confidential informant, whose examination of certain financial records revealed a more recent address for the Gateses, and he also learned from a police officer assigned to O'Hare Airport that "L. Gates" had made a reservation on Eastern Airlines Flight 245 to West Palm Beach, Fla., scheduled to depart from Chicago on May 5 at 4:15 p.m.

Mader then made arrangements with an agent of the Drug Enforcement Administration for surveillance of the May 5 Eastern Airlines flight. The agent later reported to Mader that Gates had boarded the flight, and that federal agents in Florida had observed him arrive in West Palm Beach and take a taxi to the nearby Holiday Inn. They also reported that Gates went to a room registered to one Susan Gates and that, at 7 o'clock the next morning, Gates and an unidentified woman left the motel in a Mercury bearing Illinois license plates and drove northbound on an interstate highway frequently used by travelers to the Chicago area. In addition, the DEA agent informed Mader that the license plate number on the Mercury was registered to a Hornet station wagon owned by Gates. The agent also advised Mader that the driving time between West Palm Beach and Bloomingdale was approximately 22 to 24 hours.

Mader signed an affidavit setting forth the foregoing facts, and submitted it to a judge of the Circuit Court of Du Page County, together with a copy of the anonymous letter. The judge of that court thereupon issued a search warrant for the Gateses' residence and for their automobile. . . .

At 5:15 a.m. on March 7, only 36 hours after he had flown out of Chicago, Lance Gates, and his wife, returned to their home in Bloomingdale, driving the car in which they had left West Palm Beach some 22 hours earlier. The Bloomingdale police were awaiting them, searched the trunk of the Mercury, and uncovered approximately 350 pounds of marihuana. A search of the Gateses' home revealed marihuana, weapons, and other contraband. The Illinois Circuit Court ordered suppression of all these items, on the ground that the affidavit submitted to the Circuit Judge failed to support the necessary determination of probable cause to believe that the Gateses' automobile and home contained the contraband in question. This decision was affirmed in turn by the Illinois Appellate Court, and by a divided vote of the Supreme Court of Illinois.

The Illinois Supreme Court concluded — and we are inclined to agree — that, standing alone, the anonymous letter sent to the Bloomingdale Police Department would not provide the basis for a magistrate's determination that there was probable cause to believe contraband would be found in the Gateses' car and home. The letter provides virtually nothing from which one might conclude that its author is either honest or his information reliable; likewise, the letter gives absolutely no indication of the basis for the writer's predictions regarding the Gateses' criminal activities. Something more was required, then, before a magistrate could conclude that there was probable cause to believe that contraband would be found in the Gateses' home and car.

. . . In holding that the affidavit in fact did not contain sufficient additional information to sustain a determination of probable cause, the Illinois court applied a "two-pronged test," derived from our decision in Spinelli v. United States, 393 U.S. 410 (1969). The Illinois Supreme Court . . . understood *Spinelli* as requiring that the anonymous letter satisfy each of two independent requirements before it could be relied on. According to this view, the letter, as supplemented by Mader's affidavit, first had to adequately reveal the "basis of knowledge" of the letterwriter — the particular means by which he came by the information given in his report. Second, it had to provide facts sufficiently establishing either the "veracity" of the affiant's informant, or, alternatively, the "reliability" of the informant's report in this particular case.

. . . [T]he "veracity" prong was not satisfied because, "[there] was simply no basis [for] conclud[ing] that the anonymous person [who wrote the letter to the Bloomingdale Police Department] was credible." . . . In addition, the letter gave no indication of the basis of its writer's knowledge of the Gateses' activities. . . . Thus, [the court] concluded that no showing of probable cause had been made.

We agree with the Illinois Supreme Court that an informant's "veracity," "reliability," and "basis of knowledge" are all highly relevant in determining the value of his report. We do not agree, however, that these elements should be understood as entirely separate and independent requirements to be rigidly exacted in every case. . . . Rather, as detailed below, they should be understood simply as closely intertwined issues that may usefully illuminate the common-sense, practical question whether there is "probable cause" to believe that contraband or evidence is located in a particular place.

III

. . . Perhaps the central teaching of our decisions bearing on the probable-cause standard is that it is a "practical, nontechnical conception." Brinegar v. United States, 338 U.S. 160, 176 (1949). "In dealing with probable cause, . . . as the very name implies, we deal with probabilities. These are not technical; they are the factual and practical considerations of everyday life on which reasonable and prudent men, not legal technicians, act." Id., at 175. . . .

As these comments illustrate, probable cause is a fluid concept — turning on the assessment of probabilities in particular factual contexts — not readily, or even usefully, reduced to a neat set of legal rules. Informants' tips doubtless come in many shapes and sizes from many different types of persons. . . .

. . . [T]he "two-pronged test" directs analysis into two largely independent channels — the informant's "veracity" or "reliability" and his "basis of knowledge." There are persuasive arguments against according these two elements such independent status. Instead, they are better understood as relevant considerations in the totality-of-the-circumstances analysis that traditionally has guided probable-cause determinations: a deficiency in one may be compensated for, in determining the overall reliability of a tip, by a strong showing as to the other, or by some other indicia of reliability.

If, for example, a particular informant is known for the unusual reliability of his predictions of certain types of criminal activities in a locality, his failure, in a particular case, to thoroughly set forth the basis of his knowledge surely should not serve as an absolute bar to a finding of probable cause based on his tip. Likewise, if an unquestionably honest citizen comes forward with a report of criminal activity — which if fabricated would subject him to criminal liability — we have found rigorous scrutiny of the basis of his knowledge unnecessary. Adams v. Williams, [407 U.S. 143 (1972)]. Conversely, even if we entertain some doubt as to an informant's motives, his explicit and detailed description of alleged wrongdoing, along with a statement that the event was observed firsthand, entitles his tip to greater weight than might otherwise be the case. . . .

As early as Locke v. United States, 7 Cranch 339, 348 (1813), Chief Justice Marshall observed, in a closely related context: "[The] term 'probable cause,' according to its usual acceptation, means less than evidence which would justify condemnation. . . . It imports a seizure made under circumstances which warrant suspicion." More recently, we said that "the *quanta* . . . of proof" appropriate in ordinary judicial proceedings are inapplicable to the decision to issue a warrant. *Brinegar*, 338 U.S., at 173. Finely tuned standards such as proof beyond a reasonable doubt or by a preponderance of the evidence, useful in formal trials, have no place in the magistrate's decision. While an effort to fix some general, numerically precise degree of certainty corresponding to "probable cause" may not be helpful, it is clear that "only the probability, and not a prima facie showing, of criminal activity is the standard of probable cause." *Spinelli*, 393 U.S., at 419. . . .

Finally, . . . [t]he strictures that inevitably accompany the "two-pronged test" cannot avoid seriously impeding the task of law enforcement. If, as the Illinois Supreme Court apparently thought, that test must be rigorously applied in every case, anonymous tips would be of greatly diminished value in police work. Ordinary citizens, like ordinary witnesses, generally do not provide extensive recitations of the basis of their everyday observations. Likewise, as the Illinois Supreme Court observed in this case, the veracity of persons supplying anonymous tips is by hypothesis largely unknown, and unknowable. As a result, anonymous tips seldom could survive a rigorous application of either of the *Spinelli* prongs. Yet, such tips, particularly when supplemented by independent police investigation, frequently contribute to the solution of otherwise "perfect crimes." While a conscientious assessment of the basis for crediting such tips is required by the Fourth Amendment, a standard that leaves virtually no place for anonymous citizen informants is not.

For all these reasons, we conclude that it is wiser to abandon the "two-pronged test" established by . . . *Spinelli*.[11] In its place we reaffirm the totality-of-the-circumstances analysis that traditionally has informed probable-cause determinations. The task of the issuing magistrate is simply to make a practical, common-sense decision whether, given all the circumstances set forth in the affidavit before him, including the "veracity" and "basis of knowledge" of persons supplying hearsay information, there is a fair probability that contraband or evidence of a crime will be found in a particular place. And the duty of a reviewing court is simply to ensure that the magistrate had a "substantial basis for . . . conclud[ing]" that probable cause existed. Jones v. United States, 362 U.S., at 271. . . .

Our earlier cases illustrate the limits beyond which a magistrate may not venture in issuing a warrant. A sworn statement of an affiant that "he has cause to suspect and does believe" that liquor illegally brought into the United States is located on certain premises will not do. Nathanson v. United States, 290 U.S. 41 (1933). . . . An officer's statement that "[a]ffiants have received reliable information from a credible person and do believe" that heroin is stored in a home, is likewise inadequate. Aguilar v. Texas, 378 U.S. 108 (1964). As in *Nathanson*, this is a mere conclusory statement that gives the magistrate virtually no basis at all for making a judgment regarding probable cause. Sufficient information must be presented to the magistrate to allow that official to determine probable cause; his action cannot be a mere ratification of the bare conclusions of others. In order to ensure that such an abdication of the magistrate's duty does not occur, courts must continue to conscientiously review the sufficiency of affidavits on which warrants are issued. But when we move beyond the "bare bones" affidavits present in cases such as *Nathanson* and *Aguilar*, this area simply does not lend itself to a prescribed set of rules, like that which had developed from *Spinelli*. Instead, the flexible, common-sense standard articulated [above] better serves the purposes of the Fourth Amendment's probable-cause requirement.

IV

Our decisions applying the totality-of-the-circumstances analysis outlined above have consistently recognized the value of corroboration of details of an informant's tip by independent police work. . . .

Our decision in Draper v. United States, 358 U.S. 307 (1959), . . . is the classic case on the value of corroborative efforts of police officials. There, an informant named Hereford reported that Draper would arrive in Denver on a train from Chicago on one of two days, and that he would be carrying a quantity of heroin. The informant also supplied a fairly detailed physical description of Draper, and predicted that he would be wearing a light colored raincoat, brown slacks, and black

---

11. . . . Whether the allegations submitted to the magistrate in *Spinelli* would, under the view we now take, have supported a finding or probable cause, we think it would not be profitable to decide. There are so many variables in the probable-cause equation that one determination will seldom be a useful "precedent" for another. Suffice it to say that while we in no way abandon *Spinelli*'s concern for the trustworthiness of informers and for the principle that it is the magistrate who must ultimately make a finding of probable cause, we reject the rigid categorization suggested by some of its language.

shoes, and would be walking "real fast." Id., at 309. Hereford gave no indication of the basis for his information.[12]

On one of the stated dates police officers observed a man matching this description exit a train arriving from Chicago; his attire and luggage matched Hereford's report and he was walking rapidly. We explained in *Draper* that, by this point in his investigation, the arresting officer "had personally verified every facet of the information given him by Hereford except whether petitioner had accomplished his mission and had the three ounces of heroin on his person or in his bag. And surely, with every other bit of Hereford's information being thus personally verified, [the officer] had 'reasonable grounds' to believe that the remaining unverified bit of Hereford's information — that Draper would have the heroin with him — was likewise true," id., at 313.

The showing of probable cause in the present case was fully as compelling as that in *Draper*. Even standing alone, the facts obtained through the independent investigation of Mader and the DEA at least suggested that the Gateses were involved in drug trafficking. In addition to being a popular vacation site, Florida is well known as a source of narcotics and other illegal drugs. Lance Gates' flight to West Palm Beach, his brief, overnight stay in a motel, and apparent immediate return north to Chicago in the family car, conveniently awaiting him in West Palm Beach, is as suggestive of a prearranged drug run, as it is of an ordinary vacation trip.

In addition, the judge could rely on the anonymous letter, which had been corroborated in major part by Mader's efforts — just as had occurred in *Draper*.[13] The Supreme Court of Illinois reasoned that *Draper* involved an informant who had given reliable information on previous occasions, while the honesty and reliability of the anonymous informant in this case were unknown to the Bloomingdale police. While this distinction might be an apt one at the time the Police Department received the anonymous letter, it became far less significant after Mader's independent investigative work occurred. The corroboration of the letter's predictions that the Gateses' car would be in Florida, that Lance Gates would fly to Florida in the next day or so, and that he would drive the car north toward Bloomingdale all indicated, albeit not with certainty, that the informant's other assertions also were true. "[B]ecause an informant is right about some things, he is more probably right about other facts," *Spinelli*, 393 U.S., at 427 (White, J., concurring) — including the claim regarding the Gateses' illegal activity. This may well not be the type of "reliability" or "veracity" necessary to satisfy some views of the "veracity prong" of *Spinelli*, but we think it suffices for the practical, common-sense judgment called for in making a probable-cause determination. . . .

---

12. The tip in *Draper* might well not have survived the rigid application of the "two-pronged test" that developed following *Spinelli*. The only reference to Hereford's reliability was that he had "been engaged as a 'special employee' of the Bureau of Narcotics at Denver for about six months, and from time to time gave information to [the police for] small sums of money, and that [the officer] had always found the information given by Hereford to be accurate and reliable." 358 U.S., at 309. Likewise, the tip gave no indication of how Hereford came by his information. At most, the detailed and accurate predictions in the tip indicated that, however Hereford obtained his information, it was reliable.

13. The Illinois Supreme Court thought that the verification of details contained in the anonymous letter in this case amounted only to "[t]he corroboration of innocent activity," and that this was insufficient to support a finding of probable cause. We are inclined to agree, however, with the observation of Justice Moran in his dissenting opinion that "[i]n this case, just as in *Draper*, seemingly innocent activity became suspicious in light of the initial tip." And it bears noting that *all* of the corroborating detail established in *Draper* was of entirely innocent activity . . . .

Finally, the anonymous letter contained a range of details relating not just to easily obtained facts and conditions existing at the time of the tip, but to future actions of third parties ordinarily not easily predicted. The letterwriter's accurate information as to the travel plans of each of the Gateses was of a character likely obtained only from the Gateses themselves, or from someone familiar with their not entirely ordinary travel plans. If the informant had access to accurate information of this type a magistrate could properly conclude that it was not unlikely that he also had access to reliable information of the Gateses' alleged illegal activities. Of course, the Gateses' travel plans might have been learned from a talkative neighbor or travel agent. . . . But, as discussed previously, probable cause does not demand the certainty we associate with formal trials. It is enough that there was a fair probability that the writer of the anonymous letter had obtained his entire story either from the Gateses or someone they trusted. And corroboration of major portions of the letter's predictions provides just this probability. It is apparent, therefore, that the judge issuing the warrant had a "substantial basis for . . . conclud[ing]" that probable cause to search the Gateses' home and car existed. . . .

JUSTICE WHITE, concurring in the judgment.

. . . Abandoning the "two-pronged test" of . . . Spinelli v. United States, 393 U.S. 410 (1969), the Court upholds the validity of the warrant under a new "totality of the circumstances" approach. Although I agree that the warrant should be upheld, I reach this conclusion in accordance with [*Spinelli*'s] framework.

For present purposes, the . . . *Spinelli* rules can be summed up as follows. First, an affidavit based on an informant's tip, standing alone, cannot provide probable cause for issuance of a warrant unless the tip includes information that apprises the magistrate of the informant's basis for concluding that the contraband is where he claims it is (the "basis of knowledge" prong), *and* the affiant informs the magistrate of his basis for believing that the informant is credible (the "veracity" prong). *Spinelli*, supra, at 412-413, 416. Second, if a tip fails under either or both of the two prongs, probable cause may yet be established by independent police investigatory work that corroborates the tip to such an extent that it supports "both the inference that the informer was generally trustworthy and that he made his charge . . . on the basis of information obtained in a reliable way." *Spinelli*, supra, at 417. . . .

In the present case, it is undisputed that the anonymous tip, by itself, did not furnish probable cause. The question is whether those portions of the affidavit describing the results of the police investigation of the respondents, when considered in light of the tip, "would permit the suspicions engendered by the informant's report to ripen into a judgment that a crime was probably being committed." *Spinelli*, supra, at 418. . . .

[T]he proper focus should be on whether the actions of the suspects, whatever their nature, give rise to an inference that the informant is credible and that he obtained his information in a reliable manner.

Thus, in Draper v. United States, 358 U.S. 307 (1959), an informant stated on September 7 that Draper would be carrying narcotics when he arrived by train in Denver on the morning of September 8 or September 9. The informant also provided the police with a detailed physical description of the clothes Draper would be wearing when he alighted from the train. The police observed Draper leaving a train on the morning of September 9, and he was wearing the precise clothing described by the informant. The Court held that the police had probable cause to arrest Draper at this point, even though the police had seen nothing more than the totally innocent act of a man getting off a train carrying a briefcase. . . . The fact that the informant was able to predict, two days in advance, the exact clothing Draper would be wearing dispelled the possibility that his tip was just based on rumor . . . . Probably Draper had planned in advance to wear these specific clothes so that an accomplice could identify him. A clear inference could therefore be drawn that the informant was either involved in the criminal scheme himself or that he otherwise had access to reliable, inside information.

As in *Draper*, the police investigation in the present case satisfactorily demonstrated that the informant's tip was as trustworthy as one that would alone satisfy [*Spinelli*]. The tip predicted that Sue Gates would drive to Florida, that Lance Gates would fly there a few days after May 3, and that Lance would then drive the car back. After the police corroborated these facts,[23] the judge could reasonably have inferred, as he apparently did, that the informant, who had specific knowledge of these unusual travel plans, did not make up his story and that he obtained his information in a reliable way. It is theoretically possible, as respondents insist, that the tip could have been supplied by a "vindictive travel agent" and that the Gateses' activities, although unusual, might not have been unlawful. But [our cases] do not require that certain guilt be established before a warrant may properly be issued. . . .

The Court agrees that the warrant was valid, but, in the process of reaching this conclusion, it overrules the [*Spinelli* test] and replaces [it] with a "totality of the circumstances" standard. . . . [B]ecause I am inclined to believe that, when applied properly, the [*Spinelli*] rules play an appropriate role in probable-cause determinations, and because the Court's holding may foretell an evisceration of the probable-cause standard, I do not join the Court's holding.

The Court reasons that the "veracity" and "basis of knowledge" tests are not independent, and that a deficiency as to one can be compensated for by a strong showing as to the other. Thus, a finding of probable cause may be based on a tip from an informant "known for the unusual reliability of his predictions" or from "an unquestionably honest citizen," even if the report fails thoroughly to set forth the basis upon which the information was obtained. If this is so, then it must follow a fortiori that the "affidavit of an officer, known by the magistrate to be honest and experienced, stating that [contraband] is located in a certain building" must be acceptable. *Spinelli*, 393 U.S., at 424 (White, J., concurring). It would be quixotic if a similar statement from an honest informant, but not one from an honest officer, could furnish probable cause. But we have repeatedly held that the unsupported assertion or belief of an officer does not satisfy the probable-cause requirement. See, e.g., Nathanson v. United States, 290 U.S. 41 (1933). Thus, this portion of today's holding can be read as implicitly rejecting the teachings of these prior holdings.

[Justice Brennan's dissenting opinion, joined by Justice Marshall, is omitted.]

JUSTICE STEVENS, with whom JUSTICE BRENNAN joins, dissenting.

The fact that Lance and Sue Gates made a 22-hour nonstop drive from West Palm Beach, Florida, to Bloomingdale, Illinois, only a few hours after Lance had flown to Florida provided persuasive evidence that they were engaged in illicit activity. That

---

23. Justice Stevens is correct that one of the informant's predictions proved to be inaccurate. However, . . . an informant need not be infallible.

fact, however, was not known to the judge when he issued the warrant to search their home.

What the judge did know at that time was that the anonymous informant had not been completely accurate in his or her predictions. The informant had indicated that "Sue . . . drives their car to Florida *where she leaves it to be loaded up with drugs. . . . Sue fl[ies] back after she drops the car off in Florida.*" Yet Detective Mader's affidavit reported that she "left the West Palm Beach area driving the Mercury northbound."

The discrepancy between the informant's predictions and the facts known to Detective Mader is significant for three reasons. First, it cast doubt on the informant's hypothesis that the Gates already had "over [$100,000] worth of drugs in their basement." The informant had predicted an itinerary that always kept one spouse in Bloomingdale, suggesting that the Gates did not want to leave their home unguarded because something valuable was hidden within. That inference obviously could not be drawn when it was known that the pair was actually together over a thousand miles from home.

Second, the discrepancy made the Gates' conduct seem substantially less unusual than the informant had predicted it would be. It would have been odd if, as predicted, Sue had driven down to Florida on Wednesday, left the car, and flown right back to Illinois. But the mere facts that Sue was in West Palm Beach with the car, that she was joined by her husband at the Holiday Inn on Friday, and that the couple drove north together the next morning[3] are neither unusual nor probative of criminal activity.

Third, the fact that the anonymous letter contained a material mistake undermines the reasonableness of relying on it as a basis for making a forcible entry into a private home. . . .

NOTES AND QUESTIONS

1. Some aspects of the Court's decision in *Gates* bear on the warrant process, but for the most part, the opinion is about the meaning of probable cause. At least officially, probable cause means the same thing in warrant and nonwarrant cases. Keep that in mind as you read the notes that follow; except where otherwise noted, the questions and comments apply whether or not the officer got a warrant.

2. For every search or arrest where the probable cause standard applies, the question arises: What must the police have probable cause to believe?

For arrests, the answer is: that the defendant committed a crime. For searches, the answer is: that the police will find evidence of crime in the place being searched. Nominally, the standard does not vary according to the seriousness of the crime. Note that in *Gates*, there is no language to the effect that, because the police were looking for marijuana rather than for evidence of, say, multiple murders, a higher level of probability is needed to justify the search. On the contrary, as far as the

---

3. Detective Mader's affidavit hinted darkly that the couple had set out upon "that interstate highway commonly used by travelers to the Chicago area." But the same highway is also commonly used by travelers to Disney World, Sea World, and Ringling Brothers and Barnum and Bailey Circus World. It is also the road to Cocoa Beach, Cape Canaveral, and Washington, D.C. I would venture that each year dozens of perfectly innocent people fly to Florida, meet a waiting spouse, and drive off together in the family car.

Supreme Court is concerned, probable cause appears to mean the same thing regardless of what crime the police are investigating.

Why should that be so? Doesn't the state have a much stronger interest in investigating some crimes than others? The Gateses had a great deal of marijuana in their basement, but it was, after all, marijuana, not a set of plans to blow up a public building. Shouldn't that matter to the governing Fourth Amendment standard?

It probably does matter, at least in practice. Magistrates likely apply at least slightly different standards when issuing warrants to search for evidence of different sorts of crimes (imagine if the police in *Gates* had been asking to search for a few marijuana cigarettes instead of the large quantities at issue). But those differences go unacknowledged in the doctrine, and presumably they vary from courthouse to courthouse and crime to crime.

3. Variation in the practical meaning of "probable cause" is especially likely given the way *Gates* defines the standard. The Court in *Gates* rejects *Spinelli*'s two-part test in part because it was too technical, too legally complicated; in the place of *Spinelli* the Court puts a consider-all-the-circumstances, "commonsense" inquiry. That amounts to a decision not to have a detailed law of probable cause, with different tests for different sorts of cases, and with some fact patterns resolved categorically either in favor of or against the police. Probable cause, after *Gates*, seems to be fact-specific, not susceptible to detailed legal analysis. (Note that Ornelas v. United States, 517 U.S. 690 (1996), discussed at Note 9 below, may modify this conclusion slightly.) Is that sensible?

4. One consequence of keeping the law of probable cause to a minimum is that it permits local variation. This makes more likely a system in which probable cause is applied more stringently in a given city than in its suburbs (or vice versa) — just as negligence in personal injury litigation is likely to mean different things to juries in neighboring jurisdictions. The more this sort of thing happens, the more Fourth Amendment law amounts to a series of local liability rules, rather than one standard to which police must adhere everywhere.

Second, keeping the law of probable cause to a minimum reduces the power of appellate courts. Under *Spinelli*, state and federal appellate courts decided a host of probable cause cases, developing variations and permutations on the famous two-part test. Since *Gates*, the appellate case law has been less substantial. Appellate judges seem to have less power over the meaning of probable cause, while magistrates and trial judges have more. Is *that* sensible?

Perhaps so. It is often hard to tell whether a given set of facts creates a probability that evidence of crime will be found in a given place; as with many things, experience in making and observing such decisions will likely produce better decisions. Magistrates and trial judges, who must decide on warrant applications and suppression hearings, frequently make such decisions, while appellate judges do not. Perhaps the probable cause standard is in safer hands after *Gates* than before it.

5. Much of what the Court has had to say about the meaning of probable cause has come in cases involving informants' tips. Why would that be so?

It would *not* be so if informants could easily be brought before the magistrate for questioning. Presumably they cannot, because they are unwilling to disclose their identities other than to the officers with whom they deal. One author of a leading study of warrants noted that magistrates very rarely insist on disclosure of the informant's identity. The same author notes: "In each of the cases in which the court [did order] that the informant be produced, the prosecution dismissed the charges, rather than comply." L. Paul Sutton, Getting Around the Fourth Amendment, in Carl B. Klockars & Stephen D. Mastrofski eds., Thinking About Police 433, 441 (2d ed. 1991).

If informants cannot be made to submit to questioning, magistrates and judges have two choices: decide to believe them or decide not to. How should that choice be made? Consider the following four scenarios:

1. Anonymous Informant tells Officer that once a week, Suspect flies to Florida, loads up a trailer with bags of white powder, and then drives the trailer to Suspect's house in Illinois, where he unloads the contents of the trailer into his basement. Officer then observes Suspect do the things Anonymous Informant described.

2. Anonymous Informant tells Officer that Suspect will, at 7:30 p.m. next Tuesday, be standing at a particular intersection downtown, that Suspect will be wearing a blue suit, red polka-dot tie, black tasseled loafers, and a tan trench coat and will be carrying a briefcase. Anonymous Informant further tells Officer that the briefcase will contain cocaine. Officer confirms that Suspect is indeed in the place described, wearing the clothes described, carrying a briefcase, on Tuesday at 7:30 p.m.

3. Anonymous Informant tells Officer that Suspect has cocaine in his house. Anonymous Informant has always supplied good information in the past — his tips have always been right. But the officer provides no supporting data.

4. There is no informant. Officer tells Magistrate that Suspect has cocaine in his house. Officer says he can't explain why he believes this, but he reminds Magistrate that he (Officer) has never been wrong about such things in the past.

In the first scenario, the information supplied suggests guilt; the officer's observations confirm the information, so it makes no difference whether the informant is trustworthy or not. The second scenario resembles *Draper*: The informant has supplied information with plenty of detail, but none of the information gives rise to a substantial inference of crime. The case for finding probable cause rests on the tip, which is to say it rests on trusting the informant. The argument for trusting the informant is, roughly, this: Since he knew so much about the details of Suspect's movements and choice of clothing, he must have known about Suspect's illegal activities. Since he was right about the former, he must be right about the latter. *Gates* approves of findings of probable cause based on that sort of reasoning.

Scenario #3 is a case that would have failed under *Spinelli*, but might succeed after *Gates*. (Should it?) The strong track record presumably suggests that the informant is highly credible, and *Gates* suggests that a strong showing of either credibility or basis of the informant's knowledge can compensate for a weak showing of the other.

Which leads to scenario #4. Here, there is no probable cause under *Nathanson*. Why? If informants with good track records are trustworthy, why aren't officers with good track records? After all, the informants are themselves likely involved with crime; the officers aren't (one hopes). Is there any principled way to answer this question without doing away with informants?

6. Given that the law does, in some circumstances, trust informants but not police officers, might that tempt some officers to concoct phony "informants"? What, if anything, can the law do to minimize that temptation?

7. Very little data exists on the success rate of police searches. Data on warrantless searches is close to nonexistent, and the best data on warrants probably comes from a study sponsored by the National Center for State Courts in the early 1980s. See Richard Van Duizend, L. Paul Sutton, & Charlotte A. Carter, The Search Warrant Process: Preconceptions, Perceptions, Practices (1985). The NCSC study showed two things that might bear on one's evaluation of *Gates*, and of how the law should treat informants' tips. First, informants' tips seem to be closely tied to drug investigations. Warrant applications that rely on informants' tips overwhelmingly arise in drug cases — in the seven jurisdictions studied, the percentages range from 55 to 96; five of the seven percentages were 75 or higher. See id., at 33 tbl. 14. And, on the other side of the coin, warrant applications in drug investigations overwhelmingly rely on informants' tips — those percentages range from 44 to 93, with six of the seven jurisdictions exceeding 70 percent. See id., at 34 tbl. 15. These numbers suggest, unsurprisingly, that informants' tips may be particularly important to the penetration of drug markets; such tips may matter a good deal less when investigating other crimes.

Second, searches pursuant to warrants usually uncover evidence: In the cases covered by the NCSC study, evidence was seized more than 90 percent of the time, and at least some evidence listed in the warrant was seized 86 percent of the time. See id., at 38 tbl. 21. (The authors of the study note skeptically: "The reader is reminded that these percentages are probably inflated for at least some of the cities" because of the failure to keep consistent records of searches that do not turn up evidence. Id., at 38.) The data do not answer the question whether informants' tips make warrant applications more accurate, though it is worth noting that the jurisdiction where police relied on informants' tips most frequently (71 percent of warrants were based on them) also had the lowest success rate (76 percent of searches uncovered evidence listed in the warrant). See id., at 33 tbl. 13, 38 tbl. 21.

8. In a portion of *Gates* not excerpted above, the Court emphasized the deference that appellate courts are to give decisions by magistrates to issue warrants:

A magistrate's "determination of probable cause should be paid great deference by reviewing courts." *Spinelli*, supra, at 419. "A grudging or negative attitude by reviewing courts toward warrants," [United States v. Ventresca, 380 U.S. 102, 108 (1965)], is inconsistent with the Fourth Amendment's strong preference for searches conducted pursuant to a warrant; "courts should not invalidate warrant[s] by interpreting affidavit[s] in a hypertechnical, rather than a commonsense, manner." Id., at 109.

If the affidavits submitted by police officers are subjected to the type of scrutiny some courts have deemed appropriate, police might well resort to warrantless searches, with the hope of relying on consent or some other exception to the Warrant Clause that might develop at the time of the search. In addition, the possession of a warrant by officers conducting an arrest or search greatly reduces the perception of unlawful or intrusive police conduct, by assuring "the individual whose property is searched or seized of the lawful authority of the executing officer, his need to search, and the limits of his power to search." United States v. Chadwick, 433 U.S. 1, 9 (1977). Reflecting this preference for the warrant process, the traditional standard for review of an issuing magistrate's probable-cause determination has been that so long as the magistrate had a "substantial basis for . . . conclud[ing]" that a search would uncover evidence of wrongdoing, the Fourth Amendment requires no more. Jones v. United States, 362 U.S. 257, 271 (1960).

This language suggests that deference is reserved for warrants — that in cases where police conduct a warrantless search, the trial judge's decision on the defendant's subsequent motion to suppress need not receive deference.

9. This suggestion was confirmed, at least partly, in Ornelas v. United States, 517 U.S. 690 (1996). In *Ornelas*, a detective in the Milwaukee County Sheriff's Department conducting drug interdiction surveillance in the early morning in 1992 noticed a 1981 two-door Oldsmobile with California plates in a motel parking lot. The officer was aware that such cars are often used by drug couriers because it is easy to hide things in them. Police thereafter took a series of steps that eventually led them to dismantle a panel above the right rear passenger armrest of the Oldsmobile, behind which they found two kilograms of cocaine. The Supreme Court rejected the Court of Appeals' determination that the district court's finding of probable cause to search should be reviewed deferentially and held that the question of whether probable cause existed to make a warrantless search should be reviewed de novo on appeal:

> The Court of Appeals . . . reasoned that de novo review for warrantless searches would be inconsistent with the "great deference" paid when reviewing a decision to issue a warrant, see Illinois v. Gates, 462 U.S. 213 (1983). We cannot agree. The Fourth Amendment demonstrates a "strong preference for searches conducted pursuant to a warrant," *Gates*, supra, at 236, and the police are more likely to use the warrant process if the scrutiny applied to a magistrate's probable-cause determination to issue a warrant is less than that for warrantless searches. Were we to eliminate this distinction, we would eliminate the incentive.
>
> We therefore hold that as a general matter determinations of . . . probable cause should be reviewed de novo on appeal. Having said this, we hasten to point out that a reviewing court should take care both to review findings of historical fact only for clear error and to give due weight to inferences drawn from those facts by resident judges and local law enforcement officers.
>
> A trial judge views the facts of a particular case in light of the distinctive features and events of the community; likewise, a police officer views the facts through the lens of his police experience and expertise.

Id., at 698-699.

10. Is *Ornelas* an important case? On the one hand, given the definition of probable cause offered by *Gates*, there's an argument that the standard of review doesn't matter very much. If probable cause determinations are always fact-specific, appellate decisions are unlikely to have broad legal implications. And if probable cause determinations almost always rest on credibility judgments (and deference is still owed to district court findings of fact, including credibility judgments), there will rarely be reason for reversal.

On the other hand, perhaps the standard of review matters, but in a more subtle fashion than one might think. Consider the following argument:

> Ornelas and his codefendant won in the Supreme Court, and the case was widely reported as a victory for criminal defendants. But the matter is not so simple.

. . . Immediately after holding that determinations of probable cause . . . should generally receive de novo review, the Court in *Ornelas* "hasten[ed] to point out" that appellate courts "should take care . . . to give due weight to the inferences drawn by resident judges and local law enforcement officers." This instruction is not simply inconsistent with true de novo review; it is inconsistent in a way that gives the prosecution a leg up. A deferential standard of review like "clear error," the standard initially applied by the court of appeals in *Ornelas*, gives weight to the judgments of the trial court, but not to those of the officers involved in the case. By rejecting a "clear error" standard in favor of a "de novo with due weight" standard, the Court in effect declared that police officers should receive as much deference as trial judges. Taken as a whole, then, *Ornelas* may make appellate review of suppression rulings appreciably more hospitable to law enforcement.

David A. Sklansky, Traffic Stops, Minority Motorists, and the Future of the Fourth Amendment, 1997 Sup. Ct. Rev. 271, 300-301.

11. The probable cause determination in *Ornelas* rested heavily on an officer's observation that the suspect panel in the 1981 Oldsmobile was loose, leading him to suspect that it had been removed and replaced. Notice that the significance of that loose panel depends on a pair of empirical questions: How many similarly loose panels hide drugs? How many don't? Hard data on those questions do not exist; the best one can do is to draw inferences from one's own experience and intuitions and from the testimony of police witnesses. Whose inferences are likely to be more accurate — the trial judge's, or the appellate panel's?

Perhaps trial judges do a better job of making such determinations — after all, the trial judge is more likely to have seen similar cases before than is the appellate court — but it may be that *neither* trial *nor* appellate judges have the knowledge base necessary to do a good job of making determinations like the one in *Ornelas*. If so, probable cause determinations like that one boil down to the question whether the judge should trust the police officer. The "due weight" language in the Court's opinion (see the preceding notes) suggests that the legally correct answer to that question is ordinarily yes.

12. Trusting police officers does not sound like a recipe for careful judicial review. But what is the alternative? If courts undertake a searching, careful review of officers' testimony in cases like *Ornelas*, police officers might respond by embellishing, by adding "facts" until probable cause becomes clear. Courts are not necessarily in a good position to combat this tactic, for just as they may not know what inferences to draw from a loose panel in an automobile, they may not know when officers are embellishing and when they are telling the truth.

And from the officers' perspective, embellishment — perjury — may seem more defensible than one might first suspect. Consider Jerome Skolnick's account of the following episode, involving an officer who sees a "known addict" on the street.

When approached, . . . the suspect turned around and backed off to the police car, with his left hand closed. The officer asked the man to open his fist. Instead, the man quickly brought his hand to his mouth . . . .

Jerome Skolnick, Justice Without Trial 210 (3d ed. 1994). Did the officer have probable cause at this point? The officer thought so, though he also thought a judge would likely disagree. Skolnick's account continues:

As the police officer said:

> It's awfully hard to explain to a judge what I mean when I testify that I saw a furtive movement. . . . I can testify as to the character of the neighborhood, my knowledge that the man was an addict, and all that stuff, but what I mean is that when I see a hype move the way that guy moved, I *know* he's trying to get rid of something. [Emphasis supplied by the speaker.]

> I asked the police officer if he had ever been wrong in this kind of judgment, and he replied that he had but felt that he was right often enough to justify a search, even when lacking evidence to arrest the suspect.

Id., at 211. In the incident just described, the officer in Skolnick's account was right: The suspect swallowed a marijuana cigarette.

Police officers will often be better at identifying criminal behavior than at analyzing or explaining how the identification process works. The result may be that judges — or at least some judges — undervalue police hunches. Would it be surprising if even ordinarily honest officers tended to exaggerate or twist the facts in response? Yet if judges respond by deferring to officers' hunches, what is left of the probable cause standard? Is there any way out of this box?

3. "Exceptions" to the Warrant "Requirement"

We next take up a series of exceptions to the warrant requirement — circumstances in which probable cause is the governing standard, but warrants are not required. Katz v. United States, 389 U.S. 347, 357 (1967), describes the scope of the warrant requirement this way: "[S]earches conducted outside the judicial process, without prior approval by judge or magistrate, are per se unreasonable under the Fourth Amendment — subject only to a few specifically established and well-delineated exceptions." As this language suggests, when courts decide whether a warrant is or is not required, the issue usually is framed in terms of the bounds of one or another exception to the warrant requirement. Taken individually, these exceptions may seem narrow enough. Cumulatively, the exceptions may be the rule — and warrants the real exception.

a. *Exigent Circumstances*

MINCEY v. ARIZONA

Certiorari to the Supreme Court of Arizona
437 U.S. 385 (1978)

MR. JUSTICE STEWART delivered the opinion of the Court.

On the afternoon of October 28, 1974, undercover police officer Barry Headricks of the Metropolitan Area Narcotics Squad knocked on the door of an apartment in Tucson, Ariz., occupied by the petitioner, Rufus Mincey. Earlier in the day, Officer Headricks had allegedly arranged to purchase a quantity of heroin from Mincey and had left, ostensibly to obtain money. On his return he was accompanied by nine other plainclothes policemen and a deputy county attorney. The door was opened by John Hodgman, one of three acquaintances of Mincey who were in the living room of the apartment. Officer Headricks slipped inside and moved quickly into the bedroom. Hodgman attempted to slam the door in order to keep the other officers from entering, but was pushed back against the wall. As the police entered the apartment, a rapid volley of shots was heard from the bedroom. Officer Headricks emerged and collapsed on the floor. When other officers entered the bedroom they found Mincey lying on the floor, wounded and semiconscious. Officer Headricks died a few hours later in the hospital.

The petitioner was indicted for murder, assault, and three counts of narcotics offenses. He was tried at a single trial and convicted on all the charges. At his trial and on appeal, he contended that evidence used against him had been unlawfully seized from his apartment without a warrant. . . . The Arizona Supreme Court . . . held that the warrantless search of a homicide scene is permissible under the Fourth and Fourteenth Amendments. . . .

The first question presented is whether the search of Mincey's apartment was constitutionally permissible. After the shooting, the narcotics agents, thinking that other persons in the apartment might have been injured, looked about quickly for other victims. They found a young woman wounded in the bedroom closet and Mincey apparently unconscious in the bedroom, as well as Mincey's three acquaintances (one of whom had been wounded in the head) in the living room. Emergency assistance was requested, and some medical aid was administered to Officer Headricks. But the agents refrained from further investigation, pursuant to a Tucson Police Department directive that police officers should not investigate incidents in which they are involved. They neither searched further nor seized any evidence; they merely guarded the suspects and the premises.

Within 10 minutes, however, homicide detectives who had heard a radio report of the shooting arrived and took charge of the investigation. They supervised the removal of Officer Headricks and the suspects, trying to make sure that the scene was disturbed as little as possible, and then proceeded to gather evidence. Their search lasted four days, during which period the entire apartment was searched, photographed, and diagrammed. The officers opened drawers, closets, and cupboards, and inspected their contents; they emptied clothing pockets; they dug bullet fragments out of the walls and floors; they pulled up sections of the carpet and removed them for examination. Every item in the apartment was closely examined and inventoried, and 200 to 300 objects were seized. In short, Mincey's apartment was subjected to an exhaustive and intrusive search. No warrant was ever obtained.

The petitioner's pretrial motion to suppress the fruits of this search was denied after a hearing. Much of the evidence introduced against him at trial (including photographs and diagrams, bullets and shell casings, guns, narcotics, and narcotics paraphernalia) was the product of the four-day search of his apartment. On appeal, the Arizona Supreme Court reaffirmed previous decisions in which it had held that the warrantless search of the scene of a homicide is constitutionally permissible. . . .

We cannot agree. The Fourth Amendment proscribes all unreasonable searches and seizures, and it is a cardinal principle that "searches conducted outside the judicial process, without prior approval by judge or magistrate, are per se unreasonable under the Fourth Amendment — subject only to a few specifically established and well-delineated exceptions." Katz v. United States, 389 U.S. 347, 357. The Arizona Supreme Court did not hold that the search of the petitioner's apartment fell within any of the exceptions to the warrant requirement previously recognized by this Court, but rather that the search of a homicide scene should be recognized as an additional exception.

Several reasons are advanced by the State to meet its "burden . . . to show the existence of such an exceptional situation" as to justify creating a new exception to the warrant requirement. See Vale v. Louisiana, [399 U.S. 30,] 34. None of these reasons, however, persuades us of the validity of the generic exception delineated by the Arizona Supreme Court.

The first contention is that the search of the petitioner's apartment did not invade any constitutionally protected right of privacy. See Katz v. United States, supra. This argument appears to have two prongs. On the one hand, the State urges that by shooting Officer Headricks, Mincey forfeited any reasonable expectation of privacy in his apartment. . . . [T]his reasoning would impermissibly convict the suspect even before the evidence against him was gathered. On the other hand, the State contends that the police entry to arrest Mincey was so great an invasion of his privacy that the additional intrusion caused by the search was constitutionally irrelevant. But this claim is hardly tenable in light of the extensive nature of this search. . . .

The State's second argument in support of its categorical exception to the warrant requirement is that a possible homicide presents an emergency situation demanding immediate action. We do not question the right of the police to respond to emergency situations. Numerous state and federal cases have recognized that the Fourth Amendment does not bar police officers from making warrantless entries and searches when they reasonably believe that a person within is in need of immediate aid. Similarly, when the police come upon the scene of a homicide they may make a prompt warrantless search of the area to see if there are other victims or if a killer is still on the premises. . . .

But a warrantless search must be "strictly circumscribed by the exigencies which justify its initiation," Terry v. Ohio, [392 U.S. 1,] 25-26, and it simply cannot be contended that this search was justified by any emergency threatening life or limb. All the persons in Mincey's apartment had been located before the investigating homicide officers arrived there and began their search. And a four-day search that included opening dresser drawers and ripping up carpets can hardly be rationalized in terms of the legitimate concerns that justify an emergency search.

Third, the State points to the vital public interest in the prompt investigation of the extremely serious crime of murder. No one can doubt the importance of this goal. But the public interest in the investigation of other serious crimes is comparable. If the warrantless search of a homicide scene is reasonable, why not the warrantless search of the scene of a rape, a robbery, or a burglary? "No consideration relevant to the Fourth Amendment suggests any point of rational limitation of such a doctrine." Chimel v. California, [395 U.S. 752, 766 (1969)].

Moreover, the mere fact that law enforcement may be made more efficient can never by itself justify disregard of the Fourth Amendment. The investigation of crime would always be simplified if warrants were unnecessary. But the Fourth Amendment reflects the view of those who wrote the Bill of Rights that the privacy of a person's home and property may not be totally sacrificed in the name of maximum simplicity in enforcement of the criminal law. For this reason, warrants are generally required to search a person's home or his person unless "the exigencies of the situation" make the needs of law enforcement so compelling that the warrant-less search is objectively reasonable under the Fourth Amendment. McDonald v. United States, 335 U.S. 451, 456. See, e.g., Warden v. Hayden, 387 U.S. 294, 298-300 ("hot pursuit" of fleeing suspect); Schmerber v. California, 384 U.S. 757, 770-771 (imminent destruction of evidence).

Except for the fact that the offense under investigation was a homicide, there were no exigent circumstances in this case. . . . There was no indication that evidence would be lost, destroyed, or removed during the time required to obtain a search warrant. Indeed, the police guard at the apartment minimized that possibility. And there is no suggestion that a search warrant could not easily and conveniently have been obtained. We decline to hold that the seriousness of the offense under investigation itself creates exigent circumstances of the kind that under the Fourth Amendment justify a warrantless search. . . .

It may well be that the circumstances described by the Arizona Supreme Court would usually be constitutionally sufficient to warrant a search of substantial scope. But the Fourth Amendment requires that this judgment in each case be made in the first instance by a neutral magistrate. . . .

In sum, we hold that the "murder scene exception" created by the Arizona Supreme Court is inconsistent with the Fourth and Fourteenth Amendments — that the warrantless search of Mincey's apartment was not constitutionally permissible simply because a homicide had recently occurred there. . . .

[The concurring opinion of Justice Marshall, joined by Justice Brennan, and the opinion by Justice Rehnquist concurring in part and dissenting in part, are omitted.]

NOTES ON EXIGENT CIRCUMSTANCES

1. *Mincey* was reaffirmed in Flippo v. West Virginia, 528 U.S. 11 (1999) (per curiam). The facts in *Flippo* are as follows:

> One night in 1996, petitioner and his wife were vacationing at a cabin in a state park. After petitioner called 911 to report that they had been attacked, the police arrived to find petitioner waiting outside the cabin, with injuries to his head and legs. After questioning him, an officer entered the building and found the body of petitioner's wife, with fatal head wounds. The officers closed off the area, took petitioner to the hospital, and searched the exterior and environs of the cabin for footprints or signs of forced entry. When a police photographer arrived at about 5:30 a.m., the officers reentered the building and proceeded to "process the crime scene." Brief in Opposition 5. For over 16 hours, they took photographs, collected evidence, and searched through the contents of the cabin. According to the trial court, "at the crime scene, the investigating officers found on a table in Cabin 13, among other things, a briefcase, which they, in the ordinary course of investigating a homicide, opened, wherein they found and seized various photographs and negatives."

The Court unanimously concluded that the contents of the briefcase should be suppressed.

What is accomplished by insisting that the officers in *Mincey* or *Flippo* get a warrant? There is not the slightest doubt that a warrant would have been issued; indeed, there is not the slightest doubt that a warrant to search the scene of a homicide would *always* be issued. Is requiring a warrant therefore a waste of time?

2. The basic idea of exigent circumstances is easy: Officers should not be required to get a warrant when they can't feasibly do so. That simple principle gives rise to at least four kinds of cases. *Mincey* and *Flippo* are one: In those cases, the officers were legally in the defendant's dwelling without a warrant — they had exigent circumstances enough to justify entry — but their warrantless searches lasted too long. *Mincey* and *Flippo* stand for the proposition that the warrantless search must end, roughly, when the exigency ends. The other three kinds of exigent circumstances claims arise more often than the issue in *Mincey* and *Flippo*; the next three notes deal with each in turn.

3. *Fleeing suspects.* The facts in Warden v. Hayden, 387 U.S. 294 (1967), illustrate this category:

> About 8 a.m. on March 17, 1962, an armed robber entered the business premises of the Diamond Cab Company in Baltimore, Maryland. He took some $363 and ran. Two cab drivers in the vicinity, attracted by shouts of "Holdup," followed the man to 2111 Cocoa Lane. One driver notified the company dispatcher by radio that the man was a Negro about 5' 8" tall, wearing a light cap and dark jacket, and that he had entered the house on Cocoa Lane. The dispatcher relayed the information to police who were proceeding to the scene of the robbery. Within minutes, police arrived at the house in a number of patrol cars.

Id., at 297. The officers proceeded to search the house, finding the man, two guns, and the jacket and cap the man had been wearing. The Court concluded that this was a valid warrantless search:

> The Fourth Amendment does not require police officers to delay in the course of an investigation if to do so would gravely endanger their lives or the lives of others. Speed here was essential, and only a thorough search of the house for persons and weapons could have insured that Hayden was the only man present and that the police had control of all weapons which could be used against them or to effect an escape.

Id., at 298-299.

4. *Destruction of evidence.* Perhaps the most common kind of exigent circumstance is the fear that, if officers do not search immediately, evidence will be destroyed. In U.S. v. Elkins, 300 F.3d 638 (6th Cir. 2002), the police found drugs inside a building that they had entered without a warrant. The police claimed that exigent circumstances justified the entry, including: (a) they had seen marijuana plants in the building through a hole in the wall; (b) they had reason to think that the defendant was aware of the police interest in the building, because just before the search the police had detained a person outside the building in connection with the drugs; and (c) the police had seen a man enter the building shortly after he observed the police detaining his colleague outside. The court agreed, finding that these facts gave ample reason to think that the evidence could be destroyed if the police did not enter the building immediately. And while the court acknowledged that part of the exigency was created by the police themselves when they detained the person outside the building, that fact was not dispositive. "As long as police refrain from unreasonably tipping off suspects, they may use normal investigative and law enforcement measures in the vicinity of a suspected crime location without forfeiting their ability

to perform a warrantless search to secure evidence if exigent circumstances arise." The court cited with approval circuit precedent saying "[T]he created-exigency cases have typically required some showing of deliberate conduct on the part of the police evincing an effort intentionally to evade the warrant requirement." Id., at 655 (citation and internal quotation marks omitted).

In light of *Elkins,* consider the "knock and talk" procedure followed by police in Milwaukee:

> [I]n a "knock and talk," the police approach a house or apartment in which they suspect drug dealing is occurring. They listen outside the door for a brief period of time, and then they knock on the door and attempt to persuade whoever answers to give them permission to enter. If consent is forthcoming, they enter and interview the occupants of the place; if it is not, they try to see from their vantage point at the door whether drug paraphernalia or contraband is in plain view. If it is, then they make a warrantless entry.

United States v. Johnson, 170 F.3d 908 (7th Cir. 1999). Is the warrantless entry justified? Not in *Johnson*. There, the police went to an apartment door and listened for a brief time; just when the officers were about to knock on the door, the defendant opened it. They asked consent to enter the apartment, and the defendant refused. One of the officers claimed he saw a woman throw down a crack pipe inside the apartment, but that testimony was disbelieved by the trial court. The officers then frisked the defendant (still standing in the doorway) and entered the apartment, where they found two guns and small quantities of cocaine. The Seventh Circuit Court of Appeals found, over a spirited dissent by Judge Easterbrook, that the frisk and entry were illegal — though the court went out of its way to state: "We do not hold today that the 'knock and talk' technique is automatically unconstitutional."

When would a "knock and talk" entry be permissible? If the officer's testimony about the crack pipe in *Johnson* were believable, would *that* entry be permissible?

5. *"Community caretaking."*[8] Sometimes police need to enter a home or building quickly, with no time to obtain a warrant, for reasons that have nothing to do with catching criminals or finding evidence:

> Police routinely receive calls from friends, neighbors, relatives, and employers expressing concern about people who have not been heard from over a period of time. These people are often elderly and the callers are often fearful that the missing person may be ill or even dead. Police must respond to such calls, but absent unusual circumstances, they in no way conceive of them as implicating law enforcement objectives. Patrol officers typically visit the person's residence (often after some delay) and they knock on the door. All is well if the person answers. But what if there is no response?

Debra Livingston, Police, Community Caretaking, and the Fourth Amendment, 1998 U. Chi. Legal F. 261, 278. Suppose, in such a case, the police enter, find no one inside, but discover a large quantity of drugs. Are the drugs admissible? The same issue arises in cases in which the police seek to protect not personal safety but property: Neighbors report a possible burglary, the police show up and find a window or door open but no one home, and they enter and find evidence of crime by the homeowners.

8. This phrase is taken from Cady v. Dombrowski, 413 U.S. 433, 441 (1973).

As Livingston's article recounts, courts have been fairly quick to find exigent circumstances in such cases. But as the scenarios just described suggest, sometimes the
issue is not just exigency but probable cause as well. Officers entering the house of
an elderly couple at the instigation of concerned neighbors may have no reason to
believe they will uncover evidence of crime inside. Officers checking out the scene
of a burglary may have some suspicion that the burglar is still inside, but that suspicion may fall far short of probable cause. Should the officers be permitted to
enter — and, if they find anything, to use it — anyway? Livingston says yes:

> Community caretaking intrusions are unlike searches and seizures for the purpose
> of locating evidence or suspects in several important ways. First, the absence of a law
> enforcement motive often mitigates the harms associated with intrusions on privacy for
> the purpose of criminal investigation. Thus, when police enter the home of an elderly
> woman to ensure that she is not injured within, their "search" does not "damage repu-
> tation or manifest official suspicion." Nor is it as intrusive as the normal search for
> evidence on such premises — a search which criminal investigators will pursue
> throughout the home until the evidence is found or determined not to be present.
>
>   Similarly, the potential for overzealousness is often reduced when police serve com-
> munity caretaking, as opposed to law enforcement ends. Motivated by the desire to
> make felony arrests, police may be tempted to search a warehouse based on mere sus-
> picion that evidence will be found within. This temptation is less likely to be present,
> however, when police answer complaints about noxious odors or barking dogs. . . .

Id., at 273-274. Are you persuaded? Consider the question again in light of the following case.

WELSH v. WISCONSIN

Certiorari to the Supreme Court of Wisconsin
466 U.S. 740 (1984)

MR. JUSTICE BRENNAN delivered the opinion of the Court.
Shortly before 9 o'clock on the rainy night of April 24, 1978, a lone witness,
Randy Jablonic, observed a car being driven erratically. After changing speeds and
veering from side to side, the car eventually swerved off the road and came to a stop
in an open field. No damage to any person or property occurred. Concerned about
the driver and fearing that the car would get back on the highway, Jablonic drove
his truck up behind the car so as to block it from returning to the road. Another passerby also stopped at the scene, and Jablonic asked her to call the police. Before the
police arrived, however, the driver of the car emerged from his vehicle, approached
Jablonic's truck, and asked Jablonic for a ride home. Jablonic instead suggested that
they wait for assistance in removing or repairing the car. Ignoring Jablonic's suggestion, the driver walked away from the scene.
A few minutes later, the police arrived and questioned Jablonic. He told one
officer what he had seen, specifically noting that the driver was either very inebriated or very sick. The officer checked the motor vehicle registration of the abandoned car and learned that it was registered to the petitioner, Edward G. Welsh. In
addition, the officer noted that the petitioner's residence was a short distance from
the scene, and therefore easily within walking distance.

Without securing any type of warrant, the police proceeded to the petitioner's home, arriving about 9 p.m. When the petitioner's stepdaughter answered the door, the police gained entry into the house.[1] Proceeding upstairs to the petitioner's bedroom, they found him lying naked in bed. At this point, the petitioner was placed under arrest for driving or operating a motor vehicle while under the influence of an intoxicant. . . .

It is axiomatic that the "physical entry of the home is the chief evil against which the wording of the Fourth Amendment is directed." And a principal protection against unnecessary intrusions into private dwellings is the warrant requirement imposed by the Fourth Amendment on agents of the government who seek to enter the home for purposes of search or arrest. It is not surprising, therefore, that the Court has recognized, as "a 'basic principle of Fourth Amendment law[,]' that searches and seizures inside a home without a warrant are presumptively unreasonable." Payton v. New York, 445 U.S. [573,] 586 [(1980)] ("a search or seizure carried out on a suspect's premises without a warrant is per se unreasonable, unless the police can show . . . the presence of 'exigent circumstances'").

Consistently with these long-recognized principles, the Court decided in Payton v. New York, supra, that warrantless felony arrests in the home are prohibited by the Fourth Amendment, absent probable cause and exigent circumstances. 445 U.S., at 583-590. At the same time, the Court declined to consider the scope of any exception for exigent circumstances that might justify warrantless home arrests, id., at 583, thereby leaving to the lower courts the initial application of the exigent-circumstances exception. Prior decisions of this Court, however, have emphasized that exceptions to the warrant requirement are "few in number and carefully delineated," and that the police bear a heavy burden when attempting to demonstrate an urgent need that might justify warrantless searches or arrests. . . .

Our hesitation in finding exigent circumstances, especially when warrantless arrests in the home are at issue, is particularly appropriate when the underlying offense for which there is probable cause to arrest is relatively minor. Before agents of the government may invade the sanctity of the home, the burden is on the government to demonstrate exigent circumstances that overcome the presumption of unreasonableness that attaches to all warrantless home entries. See Payton v. New York, supra, 445 U.S., at 586. When the government's interest is only to arrest for a minor offense, that presumption of unreasonableness is difficult to rebut, and the government usually should be allowed to make such arrests only with a warrant issued upon probable cause by a neutral and detached magistrate. . . .

Consistently with this approach, the lower courts have looked to the nature of the underlying offense as an important factor to be considered in the exigent-circumstances calculus. . . .

We . . . conclude that the common-sense approach utilized by most lower courts is required by the Fourth Amendment prohibition on "unreasonable searches and seizures," and hold that an important factor to be considered when determining whether any exigency exists is the gravity of the underlying offense for which the arrest is being made. Moreover, although no exigency is created simply because

---

1. The state trial court never decided whether there was consent to the entry because it deemed decision of that issue unnecessary in light of its finding that exigent circumstances justified the warrantless arrest. . . . For purposes of this decision, . . . we assume that there was no valid consent to enter the petitioner's home.

there is probable cause to believe that a serious crime has been committed, application of the exigent-circumstances exception in the context of a home entry should rarely be sanctioned when there is probable cause to believe that only a minor offense, such as the kind at issue in this case, has been committed.

Application of this principle to the facts of the present case is relatively straightforward. The petitioner was arrested in the privacy of his own bedroom for a noncriminal, traffic offense. The State attempts to justify the arrest by relying on the hot-pursuit doctrine, on the threat to public safety, and on the need to preserve evidence of the petitioner's blood-alcohol level. On the facts of this case, however, the claim of hot pursuit is unconvincing because there was no immediate or continuous pursuit of the petitioner from the scene of a crime. Moreover, because the petitioner had already arrived home, and had abandoned his car at the scene of the accident, there was little remaining threat to the public safety. Hence, the only potential emergency claimed by the State was the need to ascertain the petitioner's blood-alcohol level.

Even assuming, however, that the underlying facts would support a finding of this exigent circumstance, mere similarity to other cases involving the imminent destruction of evidence is not sufficient. The State of Wisconsin has chosen to classify the first offense for driving while intoxicated as a noncriminal, civil forfeiture offense for which no imprisonment is possible. This is the best indication of the State's interest in precipitating an arrest, and is one that can be easily identified both by the courts and by officers faced with a decision to arrest. Given this expression of the State's interest, a warrantless home arrest cannot be upheld simply because evidence of the petitioner's blood-alcohol level might have dissipated while the police obtained a warrant. To allow a warrantless home entry on these facts would be to approve unreasonable police behavior that the principles of the Fourth Amendment will not sanction.

The Supreme Court of Wisconsin let stand a warrantless, nighttime entry into the petitioner's home to arrest him for a civil traffic offense. Such an arrest, however, is clearly prohibited by the special protection afforded the individual in his home by the Fourth Amendment. The petitioner's arrest was therefore invalid, the judgment of the Supreme Court of Wisconsin is vacated, and the case is remanded for further proceedings not inconsistent with this opinion. . . .

THE CHIEF JUSTICE would dismiss the writ as having been improvidently granted and defer resolution of the question presented to a more appropriate case.

[Justice Blackmun's concurring opinion is omitted.]

JUSTICE WHITE, with whom JUSTICE REHNQUIST joins, dissenting. . . .

A test under which the existence of exigent circumstances turns on the perceived gravity of the crime would significantly hamper law enforcement and burden courts with pointless litigation concerning the nature and gradation of various crimes. . . . The decision to arrest without a warrant typically is made in the field under less-than-optimal circumstances; officers have neither the time nor the competence to determine whether a particular offense . . . is serious enough to justify a warrantless home entry to prevent the imminent destruction or removal of evidence. . . .

Even if the Court were correct in concluding that the gravity of the offense is an important factor to consider in determining whether a warrantless in-home arrest is justified by exigent circumstances, it has erred in assessing the seriousness of the civil-forfeiture offense for which the officers thought they were arresting Welsh. As the Court observes, the statutory scheme in force at the time of Welsh's arrest provided that the first offense for driving under the influence of alcohol involved no potential incarceration. Nevertheless, this Court has long recognized the compelling state interest in highway safety, the Supreme Court of Wisconsin identified a number of factors suggesting a substantial and growing governmental interest in apprehending and convicting intoxicated drivers and in deterring alcohol-related offenses, and recent actions of the Wisconsin Legislature evince its "belief that significant benefits, in the reduction of the costs attributable to drunk driving, may be achieved by the increased apprehension and conviction of even first time . . . offenders." Note, 1983 Wis. L. Rev. 1023, 1053. . . .

In short, the fact that Wisconsin has chosen to punish the first offense for driving under the influence with a fine rather than a prison term does not demand the conclusion that the State's interest in punishing first offenders is insufficiently substantial to justify warrantless in-home arrests under exigent circumstances. As the Supreme Court of Wisconsin observed, "[t]his is a model case demonstrating the urgency involved in arresting the suspect in order to preserve evidence of the statutory violation." We have previously recognized that "the percentage of alcohol in the blood begins to diminish shortly after drinking stops, as the body functions to eliminate it from the system." Schmerber v. California, 384 U.S. 757, 770 (1966). Moreover, a suspect could cast substantial doubt on the validity of a blood or breath test by consuming additional alcohol upon arriving at his home. In light of the promptness with which the officers reached Welsh's house, therefore, I would hold that the need to prevent the imminent and ongoing destruction of evidence of a serious violation of Wisconsin's traffic laws provided an exigent circumstance justifying the warrantless in-home arrest. . . .

NOTES AND QUESTIONS

1. Is *Welsh* a proper application of exigent circumstances analysis? It seems clear that the police had probable cause to believe Welsh guilty of driving while intoxicated. It seems equally clear that evidence of that crime would dissipate if the police waited to obtain a warrant before examining Welsh. Why, then, was the entry into Welsh's home improper?

2. The answer, apparently, is that the offense in question was not sufficiently serious to justify the intrusion. In effect, *Welsh* creates an exception to the exigent circumstances exception to the warrant requirement (got that?) for minor crimes, although it gives little guidance on how we might separate the minor from the major offenses.

That may be a sensible principle — though its application to *Welsh* is surely contestable, given that drunk drivers kill thousands of Americans every year. If it *is* sensible to restrict police authority to enter private homes to enforce minor crimes, though, presumably it is also sensible to restrict other kinds of police authority to enforce minor crimes. Suppose, for example, the police had encountered Welsh before he entered his house. Could they arrest Welsh, take him back to the police station, "book" him, and put him in a holding cell? The answer is yes. See Atwater v. Lago Vista, 532 U.S. 318 (2001); *Atwater* is excerpted infra, at page 503. Why should the police be allowed to make full-custody arrests in cases in which they would not be permitted to enter the defendant's home without a warrant?

3. Is exigency really the issue in *Welsh*? The most likely effect of the Court's decision, after all, is that police in Wisconsin forget about gathering blood-alcohol evidence in cases where a suspect has returned home. In the time it takes to obtain a warrant, such evidence loses its value; police won't bother to seek it. The Court seems to be ruling, sub silentio, that the forcible entry into a home to obtain evidence of this type is simply unreasonable — with or without a warrant. Assume for the moment that the police in *Welsh* had immediate access to a magistrate so that they might have obtained a warrant before the evidence lost its value. Should this magistrate take into account that under Wisconsin law drunk driving is only a "noncriminal civil forfeiture offense"? For an incisive argument that *Welsh* is best understood in such terms, see Silas J. Wasserstrom, The Court's Turn Toward a General Reasonableness Interpretation of the Fourth Amendment, 27 Am. Crim. L. Rev. 119, 133 (1989).

4. What if the officers in *Welsh* had actually been in hot pursuit of the defendant? Should it make a difference to the exigent circumstances analysis if a suspect like Welsh flees from police before entering his house?

5. Consider United States v. Rohrig, 98 F.3d 1506 (6th Cir. 1996). In that case, two Canton, Ohio, police officers responded in the early morning hours to a complaint about loud music emanating from a private home. Police first heard the music from a block away. When they drove up, several pajama-clad neighbors came out to complain. The officers banged on the front door of the house from which the music was blaring, tapped on the first floor windows, and repeatedly shouted out their presence, but to no avail. So the police opened an unlocked screen door and went inside. They walked through the house, continuing loudly to call for an occupant, before locating the offending stereo and turning down the volume. In the same room, they found the defendant Rohrig asleep on the floor.

What were the police doing in *Rohrig*? Were they enforcing a law against making unreasonable noise? Or were they abating a nuisance? Either way, do you think police were justified in entering Rohrig's home without a warrant? If so, how do you square that result with *Welsh*, given that police were presumably enforcing a local noise ordinance? It may be worth noting that, while looking for Rohrig's stereo (and Rohrig), the officers stumbled upon "wall-to-wall" marijuana plants in a basement equipped with fans and running water — evidence that was subsequently introduced against Rohrig in his trial on federal drug charges.

6. One era's trivial offense is another era's major crime. *Welsh* is an example: In many places, driving under the influence of alcohol was once treated like driving a few miles an hour over the speed limit. Drivers paid a small fine and went on with their lives. Today, it is taken a lot more seriously. Does that change your view of the Court's analysis in *Welsh*? Are appellate courts likely to do a good job of assessing which crimes are serious and which ones aren't?

7. Finally, what if the officers in *Welsh* were not seeking evidence of crime, but to determine whether Welsh was ill? Recall that the witness on the scene told police that Welsh was either very inebriated *or* very sick. One possible concern in "community caretaking" cases — and imagine if Welsh had been argued this way — is that police might pretend to be seeking to help victims in order to establish exigency or even to exempt themselves from the probable cause requirement. In the next case, the Supreme Court unanimously concludes that motive isn't the question — that

whether police may enter a home to offer assistance to an occupant depends on an objective test.

BRIGHAM CITY v. STUART

Certiorari to the Utah Supreme Court
547 U.S. 398 (2006)

CHIEF JUSTICE ROBERTS delivered the opinion of the Court.

In this case we consider whether police may enter a home without a warrant when they have an objectively reasonable basis for believing that an occupant is seriously injured or imminently threatened with such injury. We conclude that they may.

I

This case arises out of a melee that occurred in a Brigham City, Utah, home in the early morning hours of July 23, 2000. At about 3 a.m., four police officers responded to a call regarding a loud party at a residence. Upon arriving at the house, they heard shouting from inside, and proceeded down the driveway to investigate. There, they observed two juveniles drinking beer in the backyard. They entered the backyard, and saw — through a screen door and windows — an altercation taking place in the kitchen of the home. According to the testimony of one of the officers, four adults were attempting, with some difficulty, to restrain a juvenile. The juvenile eventually "broke free, swung a fist and struck one of the adults in the face." 2005 UT 13, ¶2. The officer testified that he observed the victim of the blow spitting blood into a nearby sink. App. 40. The other adults continued to try to restrain the juvenile, pressing him up against a refrigerator with such force that the refrigerator began moving across the floor. At this point, an officer opened the screen door and announced the officers' presence. Amid the tumult, nobody noticed. The officer entered the kitchen and again cried out, and as the occupants slowly became aware that the police were on the scene, the altercation ceased.

The officers subsequently arrested respondents and charged them with contributing to the delinquency of a minor, disorderly conduct, and intoxication. In the trial court, respondents filed a motion to suppress all evidence obtained after the officers entered the home, arguing that the warrantless entry violated the Fourth Amendment. The court granted the motion, and the Utah Court of Appeals affirmed.

Before the Supreme Court of Utah, Brigham City argued that although the officers lacked a warrant, their entry was nevertheless reasonable on either of two grounds. The court rejected both contentions and, over two dissenters, affirmed. First, the court held that the injury caused by the juvenile's punch was insufficient to trigger the so-called "emergency aid doctrine" because it did not give rise to an "objectively reasonable belief that an unconscious, semi-conscious, or missing person feared injured or dead [was] in the home." 122 P.3d, at 513 (internal quotation marks omitted). Furthermore, the court suggested that the doctrine was inapplicable because the officers had not sought to assist the injured adult, but instead had acted "exclusively in their law enforcement capacity." Ibid.

The court also held that the entry did not fall within the exigent circumstances exception to the warrant requirement. This exception applies, the court explained, where police have probable cause and where "a reasonable person [would] believe that the entry was necessary to prevent physical harm to the officers or other persons." Id., at 514 (internal quotation marks omitted). Under this standard, the court stated, the potential harm need not be as serious as that required to invoke the emergency aid exception. Although it found the case "a close and difficult call," the court nevertheless concluded that the officers' entry was not justified by exigent circumstances. Id., at 515.

We granted certiorari in light of differences among state courts and the Courts of Appeals concerning the appropriate Fourth Amendment standard governing warrantless entry by law enforcement in an emergency situation.

II

It is a "basic principle of Fourth Amendment law that searches and seizures inside a home without a warrant are presumptively unreasonable." Groh v. Ramirez, 540 U.S. 551, 559 (2004) (quoting Payton v. New York, 445 U.S. 573, 586 (1980) (some internal quotation marks omitted)). Nevertheless, because the ultimate touchstone of the Fourth Amendment is "reasonableness," the warrant requirement is subject to certain exceptions. Flippo v. West Virginia, 528 U.S. 11, 13 (1999) (per curiam); Katz v. United States, 389 U.S. 347, 357 (1967). We have held, for example, that law enforcement officers may make a warrantless entry onto private property to fight a fire and investigate its cause, Michigan v. Tyler, 436 U.S. 499, 509 (1978), to prevent the imminent destruction of evidence, Ker v. California, 374 U.S. 23, 40 (1963), or to engage in "hot pursuit" of a fleeing suspect, United States v. Santana, 427 U.S. 38, 42-43 (1976). "[W]arrants are generally required to search a person's home or his person unless 'the exigencies of the situation' make the needs of law enforcement so compelling that the warrantless search is objectively reasonable under the Fourth Amendment." Mincey v. Arizona, 437 U.S. 385, 393-394 (1978).

One exigency obviating the requirement of a warrant is the need to assist persons who are seriously injured or threatened with such injury. "The need to protect or preserve life or avoid serious injury is justification for what would be otherwise illegal absent an exigency or emergency." Id., at 392 (quoting Wayne v. United States, 318 F.2d 205, 212 (CADC 1963) (Burger, J.)); see also Tyler, supra, at 509. Accordingly, law enforcement officers may enter a home without a warrant to render emergency assistance to an injured occupant or to protect an occupant from imminent injury. Mincey, supra, at 392.

Respondents do not take issue with these principles, but instead advance two reasons why the officers' entry here was unreasonable. First, they argue that the officers were more interested in making arrests than quelling violence. They urge us to consider, in assessing the reasonableness of the entry, whether the officers were "indeed motivated primarily by a desire to save lives and property." Brief for Respondents 3; see also Brief for National Association of Criminal Defense Lawyers as Amicus Curiae 6 (entry to render emergency assistance justifies a search "only when the searching officer is acting outside his traditional law-enforcement capacity"). The Utah Supreme Court also considered the officers' subjective motivations relevant. See 122 P.3d, at 513 (search under the "emergency aid doctrine" may not be "primarily motivated by intent to arrest and seize evidence" (internal quotation marks omitted)).

Our cases have repeatedly rejected this approach. An action is "reasonable" under the Fourth Amendment, regardless of the individual officer's state of mind, "as long as the circumstances, viewed *objectively*, justify [the] action." Scott v. United States, 436 U.S. 128, 138 (1978) (emphasis added). The officer's subjective motivation is irrelevant. See Bond v. United States, 529 U.S. 334, 338, n. 2 (2000) ("The parties properly agree that the subjective intent of the law enforcement officer is irrelevant in determining whether that officer's actions violate the Fourth Amendment . . . ; the issue is not his state of mind, but the objective effect of his actions"); Whren v. United States, 517 U.S. 806, 813 ("[W]e have been unwilling to entertain Fourth Amendment challenges based on the actual motivations of individual officers"); Graham v. Connor, 490 U.S. 386, 397 (1989) ("[O]ur prior cases make clear" that "the subjective motivations of the individual officers . . . ha[ve] no bearing on whether a particular seizure is 'unreasonable' under the Fourth Amendment"). It therefore does not matter here — even if their subjective motives could be so neatly unraveled — whether the officers entered the kitchen to arrest respondents and gather evidence against them or to assist the injured and prevent further violence.

As respondents note, we have held in the context of programmatic searches conducted without individualized suspicion — such as checkpoints to combat drunk driving or drug trafficking — that "an inquiry into *programmatic* purpose" is sometimes appropriate. Indianapolis v. Edmond, 531 U.S. 32, 46 (2000) (emphasis added); see also Florida v. Wells, 495 U.S. 1, 4 (1990) (an inventory search must be regulated by "standardized criteria" or "established routine" so as not to "be a ruse for a general rummaging in order to discover incriminating evidence"). But this inquiry is directed at ensuring that the purpose behind the program is not "ultimately indistinguishable from the general interest in crime control." *Edmond*, 531 U.S., at 44. It has nothing to do with discerning what is in the mind of the individual officer conducting the search. Id., at 48.

Respondents further contend that their conduct was not serious enough to justify the officers' intrusion into the home. They rely on Welsh v. Wisconsin, 466 U.S. 740, 753 (1984), in which we held that "an important factor to be considered when determining whether any exigency exists is the gravity of the underlying offense for which the arrest is being made." This contention, too, is misplaced. *Welsh* involved a warrantless entry by officers to arrest a suspect for driving while intoxicated. There, the "only potential emergency" confronting the officers was the need to preserve evidence (i.e., the suspect's blood-alcohol level) — an exigency that we held insufficient under the circumstances to justify entry into the suspect's home. Ibid. Here, the officers were confronted with ongoing violence occurring within the home. *Welsh* did not address such a situation.

We think the officers' entry here was plainly reasonable under the circumstances. The officers were responding, at 3 o'clock in the morning, to complaints about a loud party. As they approached the house, they could hear from within "an altercation occurring, some kind of a fight." App. 29. "It was loud and it was tumultuous." Id., at 33. The officers heard "thumping and crashing" and people yelling "stop, stop" and "get off me." Id., at 28, 29. As the trial court found, "it was obvious that . . . knocking on the front door" would have been futile. Id., at 92. The noise seemed to be coming from the back of the house; after looking in the front window and seeing nothing, the officers proceeded around back to investigate further. They found two juveniles drinking beer in the backyard. From there, they could see that a fracas was taking place inside the kitchen. A juvenile, fists clenched, was being held back by several adults. As the officers watch, he breaks free and strikes one of the adults in the face, sending the adult to the sink spitting blood.

In these circumstances, the officers had an objectively reasonable basis for believing both that the injured adult might need help and that the violence in the kitchen was just beginning. Nothing in the Fourth Amendment required them to wait until another blow rendered someone "unconscious" or "semi-conscious" or worse before entering. The role of a peace officer includes preventing violence and restoring order, not simply rendering first aid to casualties; an officer is not like a boxing (or hockey) referee, poised to stop a bout only if it becomes too one-sided.

The manner of the officers' entry was also reasonable. After witnessing the punch, one of the officers opened the screen door and "yelled in police." Id., at 40. When nobody heard him, he stepped into the kitchen and announced himself again. Only then did the tumult subside. The officer's announcement of his presence was at least equivalent to a knock on the screen door. Indeed, it was probably the only option that had even a chance of rising above the din. Under these circumstances, there was no violation of the Fourth Amendment's knock-and-announce rule. Furthermore, once the announcement was made, the officers were free to enter; it would serve no purpose to require them to stand dumbly at the door awaiting a response while those within brawled on, oblivious to their presence.

Accordingly, we reverse the judgment of the Supreme Court of Utah, and remand the case for further proceedings not inconsistent with this opinion.

It is so ordered.

[Justice Stevens' concurring opinion is omitted.]

NOTES ON PUNITIVE AND PROTECTIVE POLICING

1. In a concurring opinion, Justice Stevens observed as follows:

> This is an odd flyspeck of a case. The charges that have been pending against respondents for the past six years are minor offenses — intoxication, contributing to the delinquency of a minor, and disorderly conduct — two of which could have been proved by evidence that was gathered by the responding officers before they entered the home. The maximum punishment for these crimes ranges between 90 days and 6 months in jail. And the Court's unanimous opinion restating well-settled rules of federal law is so clearly persuasive that it is hard to imagine the outcome was ever in doubt.
>
> Under these circumstances, the only difficult question is which of the following is the most peculiar: (1) that the Utah trial judge, the intermediate state appellate court, and the Utah Supreme Court all found a Fourth Amendment violation on these facts; (2) that the prosecution chose to pursue this matter all the way to the United States Supreme Court; or (3) that this Court voted to grant the petition for a writ of certiorari.

Justice Stevens noted that a possible explanation for the Utah state court rulings was that suppression was deemed correct as a matter of Utah law, and that neither trial counsel nor the trial judge bothered to identify the Utah Constitution as an independent basis for decision. Assume Justice Stevens is correct. Should police motive be considered in deciding on the reasonableness of a warrantless entry in cases like this? Whether or not it should, it often is: A number of state courts have elaborated emergency doctrines that do take police motive into account in settings like the one in *Stuart*.

2. The Chief Justice is careful not to say that the police entry was legal because the officers' intent was to protect victims, not to punish offenders. Likewise, the Court's opinion characterizes the case as an easy one, calling the police conduct "plainly reasonable." But while the bottom line may be clear, the rationale is not. Here is the key sentence in Chief Justice Roberts' opinion: "In these circumstances, the officers had an objectively reasonable basis for believing both that the injured adult might need help and that the violence in the kitchen was just beginning." Notice what is missing from that sentence. There is no mention of probable cause or reasonable suspicion. As Roberts puts it, "[t]he role of a peace officer includes preventing violence and restoring order, not simply rendering first aid to casualties." The idea that the officers had good reason to suspect that they would find evidence of crime inside the house, and that the evidence might be destroyed if they sought a warrant — the core justification for warrantless entries into private homes — is nowhere to be found in *Stuart*.

Presumably, Chief Justice Roberts avoided the words "probable cause" in the sentences just quoted for a reason. If probable cause isn't the standard, what should be?

3. *Stuart* is a particular instance of a more general problem. Nearly all Fourth Amendment law was designed for situations in which the police and search targets are adversaries — the police are trying to gather evidence that can be used in court to convict suspects of crimes. But, as *Stuart* illustrates, the police and those whose privacy they infringe often are *not* adversaries. Police officers often enter private homes in order to protect people, not to punish them. It would seem strange to say that officers must not protect citizens from harm unless they have good reason to suspect those same citizens of wrongdoing.

It seems obvious, then, that different rules should apply to protective policing than to the punitive kind. If one accepts that proposition, two questions follow. What limits should be placed on police exercise of their protective function? And how should the line between protective and punitive policing be drawn?

4. The answers to both questions may turn on intent — either the intent of the private citizens involved, or the intent of the officers. Consider first the limits on police authority to protect. There is obviously a danger in the idea that police can enter any dwelling anytime so long as they claim to be offering help rather than trying to bring the law's hammer down on those inside. The idea is a good deal less dangerous if one important limit is added: The party being protected *wanted* the police assistance. Sometimes, as in *Stuart*, it isn't possible to freeze the situation and ask everyone involved whether they wish to invite police officers inside. But it seems reasonable to assume that, if asked, victims of domestic violence would say "yes." That alone seems to make the entry in this case reasonable.

Or does it? Often protecting one person may mean arresting and punishing another. It's a fair guess that while those victimized by violence in private homes might want outside intervention, those doing the violence don't. Whose wishes should control? *Stuart* hints that the answer is that victims' wishes control. In another case decided during the same Term, the Court held — over a strong dissent by Chief Justice Roberts — that the consent of one spouse to police entry was not enough to override the nonconsent of the other. See Georgia v. Randolph, 547 U.S. 103 (2006). (*Randolph* is discussed in Section E, below.) Which answer is right?

5. Assuming that the law places appropriate limits on protective policing, there is still a need to separate it from more traditional, and more adversarial, kinds of

policing. One obvious way to do that is to look to police officers' intent: If the officers were trying to gather evidence, the usual rules apply; if they were trying to assist those in need of assistance, different rules apply. The Court rejects that approach in *Stuart*, but it has not always done so — as the Chief Justice's opinion acknowledges. Indianapolis v. Edmond, 531 U.S. 32 (2000) (discussed in Section D.3.a below), barred a police roadblock designed to catch and punish drug crime. But the Court left standing precedents permitting police roadblocks with a "primary purpose" that was something other than "detect[ing] evidence of ordinary criminal wrongdoing." Id., at 37.

6. In both cases — both with respect to private citizens' desire for assistance and police officers' desire to provide it — the law may consider intent without having cases turn on the thoughts of particular police officers or litigants. In a case like *Stuart*, one might ask whether a reasonable person in the circumstances of the adult spitting blood in the kitchen sink would welcome police intervention. Similarly, one might ask whether a reasonable officer would have believed the need for assistance was strong enough to justify entry without express permission. Such objective indicators of intent may be what the Court is describing when it says that "'an inquiry into *programmatic* purpose' is sometimes appropriate."

7. Judicial power to define the bounds of police searches and seizures is sometimes justified by the need to protect the interests of those unable to protect themselves through politics. Criminal suspects are not exactly a powerful political lobby — one might fear that, if courts do not look out for their interests, no one will. Does the same proposition hold true of people in need of police protection? Are there good reasons why Supreme Court Justices should define the boundaries of police authority in settings like *Stuart*? Perhaps Justice Stevens was right to complain that the Court chose to hear and decide the case — not because it was "a flyspeck," but because it deals with issues that other institutions can resolve better than the Justices can.

b.   Plain View

When he was stopped by New York City police officers, Benigno Class was driving over the speed limit in a car with a cracked windshield — both traffic violations under state law. After the car was stopped, Class got out and one of the officers opened the car door to look for the Vehicle Identification Number (VIN), which is found on the left doorjamb in older cars. When the officer did not find the VIN on the door jamb, he reached into the car to move some papers that obscured the area of the dashboard where the VIN is located on later-model automobiles. In so doing, the officer saw the handle of a gun protruding from underneath the driver's seat. The officer seized the gun. Class was later charged and convicted of a state-law weapons offense.

In New York v. Class, 475 U.S. 106 (1986), the Supreme Court determined that Class had no reasonable expectation of privacy in the VIN, which is required by federal law to be placed in the plain view of someone outside the automobile. Because the officer could not see the VIN from outside the car and because the driver had exited the vehicle, it was constitutionally permissible for the officer to enter the car to the limited extent necessary to uncover the VIN. Of course, "[t]he evidence that [Class] sought to have suppressed was not the VIN, . . . but a gun, the handle of which the officer saw from the interior of the car while reaching for the papers that covered the VIN." Id., at 114. The officer was allowed to seize the gun, the Court found, because of the plain view doctrine, since the officer in *Class* saw the gun from a position he was authorized to be and from which he could legally gain physical control over it. Consider what "plain view" means as you read the following case — involving not a VIN, but the serial numbers on some stereo components.

ARIZONA v. HICKS

Certiorari to the Court of Appeals of Arizona
480 U.S. 321 (1987)

JUSTICE SCALIA delivered the opinion of the Court. . . .

On April 18, 1984, a bullet was fired through the floor of respondent's apartment, striking and injuring a man in the apartment below. Police officers arrived and entered respondent's apartment to search for the shooter, for other victims, and for weapons. They found and seized three weapons, including a sawed-off rifle, and in the course of their search also discovered a stocking-cap mask.

One of the policemen, Officer Nelson, noticed two sets of expensive stereo components, which seemed out of place in the squalid and otherwise ill-appointed four-room apartment. Suspecting that they were stolen, he read and recorded their serial numbers — moving some of the components, including a Bang and Olufsen turntable, in order to do so — which he then reported by phone to his headquarters. On being advised that the turntable had been taken in an armed robbery, he seized it immediately. It was later determined that some of the other serial numbers matched those on other stereo equipment taken in the same armed robbery, and a warrant was obtained and executed to seize that equipment as well. Respondent was subsequently indicted for the robbery. . . .

The state trial court granted respondent's motion to suppress. . . . The Court of Appeals of Arizona affirmed. . . . The Arizona Supreme Court denied review, and the State filed this petition.

As an initial matter, the State argues that Officer Nelson's actions constituted neither a "search" nor a "seizure" within the meaning of the Fourth Amendment. We agree that the mere recording of the serial numbers did not constitute a seizure. To be sure, that was the first step in a process by which respondent was eventually deprived of the stereo equipment. In and of itself, however, it did not "meaningfully interfere" with respondent's possessory interest in either the serial numbers or the equipment, and therefore did not amount to a seizure.

Officer Nelson's moving of the equipment, however, did constitute a "search" separate and apart from the search for the shooter, victims, and weapons that was the lawful objective of his entry into the apartment. Merely inspecting those parts of the turntable that came into view during the latter search would not have constituted an independent search, because it would have produced no additional invasion of respondent's privacy interest. But taking action, unrelated to the objectives of the authorized intrusion, which exposed to view concealed portions of the apartment or its contents, did produce a new invasion of respondent's privacy unjustified by the exigent circumstance that validated the entry. . . . It matters not that the search uncovered nothing of any great personal value to respondent — serial numbers rather than (what might conceivably have been hidden behind or under the equipment) letters or photographs. A search is a search, even if it happens to disclose nothing but the bottom of a turntable.

The remaining question is whether the search was "reasonable" under the Fourth Amendment. . . .

. . . . "It is well established that under certain circumstances the police may *seize* evidence in plain view without a warrant," Coolidge v. New Hampshire, 403 U.S. [443], 465 [1971] (plurality opinion) (emphasis added). Those circumstances include situations "[w]here the initial intrusion that brings the police within plain view of such [evidence] is supported . . . by one of the recognized exceptions to the warrant requirement," ibid., such as the exigent-circumstances intrusion here. It would be absurd to say that an object could lawfully be seized and taken from the premises, but could not be moved for closer examination. It is clear, therefore, that the search here was valid if the "plain view" doctrine would have sustained a seizure of the equipment.

There is no doubt it would have done so if Officer Nelson had probable cause to believe that the equipment was stolen. The State has conceded, however, that he had only a "reasonable suspicion," by which it means something less than probable cause. We have not ruled on the question whether probable cause is required in order to invoke the "plain view" doctrine. . . .

We now hold that probable cause is required. To say otherwise would be to cut the "plain view" doctrine loose from its theoretical and practical moorings. The theory of that doctrine consists of extending to nonpublic places such as the home, where searches and seizures without a warrant are presumptively unreasonable, the police's longstanding authority to make warrantless seizures in public places of such objects as weapons and contraband. And the practical justification for that extension is the desirability of sparing police, whose viewing of the object in the course of a lawful search is as legitimate as it would have been in a public place, the inconvenience and the risk — to themselves or to preservation of the evidence — of going to obtain a warrant. Dispensing with the need for a warrant is worlds apart from permitting a lesser standard of *cause* for the seizure than a warrant would require, i.e., the standard of probable cause. No reason is apparent why an object should routinely be seizable on lesser grounds, during an unrelated search and seizure, than would have been needed to obtain a warrant for that same object if it had been known to be on the premises.

We do not say, of course, that a seizure can never be justified on less than probable cause. We have held that it can — where, for example, the seizure is minimally intrusive and operational necessities render it the only practicable means of detecting certain types of crime. See, e.g., United States v. Cortez, 449 U.S. 411 (1981) (investigative detention of vehicle suspected to be transporting illegal aliens); United States v. Place, 462 U.S. 696, 709, and n. 9 (1983) (dictum) (seizure of suspected drug dealer's luggage at airport to permit exposure to specially trained dog). No special operational necessities are relied on here, however — but rather the mere fact that the items in question came lawfully within the officer's plain view. That alone cannot supplant the requirement of probable cause.

The same considerations preclude us from holding that, even though probable cause would have been necessary for a *seizure*, the *search* of objects in plain view that occurred here could be sustained on lesser grounds. A dwelling-place search, no less than a dwelling-place seizure, requires probable cause, and there is no reason in theory or practicality why application of the "plain view" doctrine would supplant that requirement. . . .

Justice O'Connor's dissent suggests that we uphold the action here on the ground that it was a "cursory inspection" rather than a "full-blown search," and could therefore be justified by reasonable suspicion instead of probable cause. As already noted, a truly cursory inspection — one that involves merely looking at what is already exposed to view, without disturbing it — is not a "search" for Fourth Amendment purposes, and therefore does not even require reasonable suspicion. We are unwilling to send police and judges into a new thicket of Fourth Amendment law, to seek a creature of uncertain description that is neither a "plain view" inspection nor yet a "full-blown search." . . .

Justice Powell's dissent reasonably asks what it is we would have had Officer Nelson do in these circumstances. The answer depends, of course, upon whether he had probable cause to conduct a search. . . . If he had, then he should have done precisely what he did. If not, then he should have followed up his suspicions, if possible, by means other than a search — just as he would have had to do if, while walking along the street, he had noticed the same suspicious stereo equipment sitting inside a house a few feet away from him, beneath an open window. It may well be that, in such circumstances, no effective means short of a search exist. But there is nothing new in the realization that the Constitution sometimes insulates the criminality of a few in order to protect the privacy of us all. . . .

For the reasons stated, the judgment of the Court of Appeals of Arizona is Affirmed.

[The concurring opinion of Justice White is omitted.]

JUSTICE POWELL, with whom THE CHIEF JUSTICE and JUSTICE O'CONNOR join, dissenting. . . .

It is fair to ask what Officer Nelson should have done in these circumstances. Accepting the State's concession that he lacked probable cause, he could not have obtained a warrant to seize the stereo components. Neither could he have remained on the premises and forcibly prevented their removal. . . .

The Court holds that there was an unlawful search of the turntable. It agrees that the "mere recording of the serial numbers did not constitute a seizure." Thus, if the computer had identified as stolen property a component with a visible serial number, the evidence would have been admissible. But the Court further holds that "Officer Nelson's moving of the equipment . . . did constitute a 'search . . .'" It perceives a constitutional distinction between reading a serial number on an object and moving or picking up an identical object to see its serial number. . . . With all respect, this distinction between "looking" at a suspicious object in plain view and "moving" it even a few inches trivializes the Fourth Amendment. The Court's new rule will cause uncertainty, and could deter conscientious police officers from lawfully obtaining evidence necessary to convict guilty persons. . . . Accordingly, I dissent.

JUSTICE O'CONNOR, with whom THE CHIEF JUSTICE and JUSTICE POWELL join, dissenting.

The Court today gives the right answer to the wrong question. The Court asks whether the police must have probable cause before either seizing an object in plain view or conducting a full-blown search of that object, and concludes that they must.

I agree. In my view, however, this case presents a different question: whether police must have probable cause before conducting a cursory inspection of an item in plain view. . . . I conclude that such an inspection is reasonable if the police are aware of facts or circumstances that justify a reasonable suspicion that the item is evidence of a crime. . . .

. . . If an officer could indiscriminately search every item in plain view, a search justified by a limited purpose — such as exigent circumstances — could be used to eviscerate the protections of the Fourth Amendment. In order to prevent such a general search, therefore, we require that the relevance of the item be "immediately apparent." . . .

Thus, I agree with the Court that even under the plain-view doctrine, probable cause is required before the police seize an item, or conduct a full-blown search of evidence in plain view. . . . This is not to say, however, that even a mere inspection of a suspicious item must be supported by probable cause. When a police officer makes a cursory inspection of a suspicious item in plain view in order to determine whether it is indeed evidence of a crime, there is no "exploratory rummaging." Only those items that the police officer "reasonably suspects" as evidence of a crime may be inspected, and perhaps more importantly, the scope of such an inspection is quite limited . . .

This distinction between searches based on their relative intrusiveness . . . is entirely consistent with our Fourth Amendment jurisprudence. We have long recognized that searches can vary in intrusiveness, and that some brief searches "may be so minimally intrusive of Fourth Amendment interests that strong countervailing governmental interests will justify a [search] based only on specific articulable facts" that the item in question is contraband or evidence of a crime. United States v. Place, 462 U.S. 696, 706 (1983). . . .

In my view, the balance of the governmental and privacy interests strongly supports a reasonable-suspicion standard for the cursory examination of items in plain view. The additional intrusion caused by an inspection of an item in plain view for its serial number is minuscule. . . .

Weighed against this minimal additional invasion of privacy are rather major gains in law enforcement. The use of identification numbers in tracing stolen property is a powerful law enforcement tool. Serial numbers are far more helpful and accurate in detecting stolen property than simple police recollection of the evidence. Cf. New York v. Class, 475 U.S. 106, 111 (1986) (observing importance of vehicle identification numbers). . . .

Unfortunately, in its desire to establish a "bright-line" test, the Court has taken a step that ignores a substantial body of precedent and that places serious roadblocks to reasonable law enforcement practices. . . . The theoretical advantages of the "search is a search" approach adopted by the Court today are simply too remote to justify the tangible and severe damage it inflicts on legitimate and effective law enforcement. . . .

NOTES ON "PLAIN VIEW" DOCTRINE

1. In many Fourth Amendment cases, the issue is whether the police were behaving legally when they first saw the evidence in question. It is important to understand that *that* question is not a matter of plain view doctrine at all. For example,

suppose a police officer standing on a public street sees a drug transaction through an open window in a nearby house. Plain view doctrine does not justify entry into the house; indeed, plain view doctrine does not even come into play. The officer can enter the house if what he saw gives him both probable cause and exigent circumstances or if he obtains a valid warrant, but not otherwise. Plain view doctrine deals with a different sort of question: Assuming the officer was behaving legally when he *saw* the evidence in question, and also assuming that he is legally in a place where he can gain physical control over the evidence, can he *seize* it? *Hicks* says yes, if the officer has probable cause. But short of probable cause, even the most cursory "search" to confirm one's suspicions is invalid.

2. Speaking of probable cause, was the state wise to concede that the police lacked probable cause to believe the stereos were stolen in *Hicks*? In Justice O'Connor's dissent, she expressed "little doubt" that this standard was satisfied. Had the concession not been made, how should the issue have been resolved? Would the presence of expensive electronic equipment in a "squalid and otherwise ill-appointed" apartment have been enough for a magistrate to issue a search warrant?

3. Consider the following discussion of the majority's approach in *Hicks*:

> Having concluded that a search did occur, Justice Scalia asserts that the "remaining question" is whether the search was reasonable under the fourth amendment. However, not a single word of the Court's opinion is directed to this question. Instead, Justice Scalia focuses exclusively on the fact that the officer lacked probable cause to believe that the turntable was stolen and that, in the absence of probable cause, the doctrine authorizing warrantless searches and seizures of items in "plain view" was not applicable.
>
> The Court's treatment of the constitutional problem posed by *Hicks* is puzzling in two respects. First, there is a startling disjunction between the requirements imposed by the text of the fourth amendment and those imposed by the Court in the name of the text. . . . There was no claim in *Hicks* that the kind of warrant outlawed by the second clause of the amendment had been issued and . . . the opinion did not inquire into whether the police action was "unreasonable."
>
> These deficiencies might be understandable if the requirements the Court imposed were associated with the policy concerns that, according to the Court, lie behind the fourth amendment. But a second puzzling aspect of the opinion is how little of the Court's reasoning relates to these concerns. Although one can imagine other substantive goals, the Court seems to have settled on using the fourth amendment to balance personal privacy against effective law enforcement. . . . Even when measured against the Court's own goals, however, the analysis in *Hicks* fares poorly.
>
> Thus, the Court virtually concedes that the marginal privacy loss when Officer Nelson picked up the turntable was de minimis. The Court also appears to concede that the loss to law enforcement created by the rule it announces might be considerable. Yet despite these concessions, which to the uninitiated might appear to establish that the officer's conduct was "reasonable," the Court slavishly adheres to a series of rules relating to warrants and probable cause that have no basis in constitutional text.

Silas J. Wasserstrom & Louis Michael Seidman, The Fourth Amendment as Constitutional Theory, 77 Geo. L.J. 19, 23-25 (1988). Do you agree? Does *Hicks* represent a strong argument for less focus on probable cause and warrants and more focus on reasonableness as the touchstone of Fourth Amendment interpretation? Or is there more to the majority's approach?

4. Consider the relationship between *Hicks* and Mincey v. Arizona, page 449, supra. In *Mincey*, the police conducted "an exhaustive and intrusive search" without a warrant of the defendant's apartment in the wake of a shooting, and the Court held that the search lasted longer than exigent circumstances would justify. In *Hicks* too, the police entered the defendant's apartment based on probable cause and exigent circumstances — and as in *Mincey*, the Court held that the police exceeded their legal authority once inside. Both exigent circumstances doctrine in *Mincey* and plain view doctrine in *Hicks* serve to limit police officers' ability to conduct wide-ranging searches of private dwellings in the absence of a warrant.

That sounds sensible. But plain view doctrine does not, by its terms, differ for warrant-based and warrantless searches — if the officers had been in Hicks' apartment pursuant to a warrant to search for weapons, the plain view issue should be analyzed precisely the same as in the actual case. Is *that* sensible?

5. Justice O'Connor suggests that the *Hicks* majority is fixated on establishing a bright-line test for plain view doctrine. Does the majority achieve this goal? If you think the answer is no, how would you craft a standard that would tell police how much they can "look around" when they are otherwise legitimately in a place?

6. Notice that when *Hicks* was decided, at least some of the Justices were of the view that there were three requirements for a plain view search or seizure: (1) that the police must lawfully be in a position from which they can view particular items and gain physical custody over them, (2) that it must be "immediately apparent" to the police that the items they observe are subject to seizure, and (3) that these items are discovered "inadvertently" — that the police weren't looking for what they stumbled upon. *Hicks* elaborated on the second of these requirements. The next case focused on whether the third "requirement" is an aspect of plain view doctrine at all.

HORTON v. CALIFORNIA

Certiorari to the Court of Appeal of California, Sixth Appellate District
496 U.S. 128 (1990)

JUSTICE STEVENS delivered the opinion of the Court.

In this case we revisit . . . [the question whether] the warrantless seizure of evidence of crime in plain view is prohibited by the Fourth Amendment if the discovery of the evidence was not inadvertent. We conclude that even though inadvertence is a characteristic of most legitimate "plain-view" seizures, it is not a necessary condition.

Petitioner was convicted of the armed robbery of Erwin Wallaker, the treasurer of the San Jose Coin Club. When Wallaker returned to his home after the Club's annual show, he entered his garage and was accosted by two masked men, one armed with a machine gun and the other with an electrical shocking device, sometimes referred to as a "stun gun." The two men shocked Wallaker, bound and handcuffed him, and robbed him of jewelry and cash. During the encounter sufficient conversation took place to enable Wallaker subsequently to identify petitioner's distinctive voice. His identification was partially corroborated by a witness who saw the robbers leaving the scene, and by evidence that petitioner had attended the coin shows.

Sergeant LaRault . . . investigated the crime and determined that there was probable cause to search petitioner's home for the proceeds of the robbery and for the weapons used by the robbers. His affidavit for a search warrant referred to police reports that described the weapons as well as the proceeds, but the warrant issued by the Magistrate only authorized a search for the proceeds, including three specifically described rings.

Pursuant to the warrant, LaRault searched petitioner's residence, but he did not find the stolen property. During the course of the search, however, he discovered the weapons in plain view and seized them. Specifically, he seized an Uzi machine gun, a .38 caliber revolver, two stun guns, a handcuff key, a San Jose Coin Club advertising brochure, and a few items of clothing identified by the victim. LaRault testified that while he was searching for the rings, he also was interested in finding other evidence connecting petitioner to the robbery. Thus, the seized evidence was not discovered "inadvertently."

The trial court refused to suppress the evidence found in petitioner's home and, after a jury trial, petitioner was found guilty and sentenced to prison. The California Court of Appeal affirmed[, rejecting] petitioner's argument that . . . suppression of the seized evidence that had not been listed in the warrant [was required] because its discovery was not inadvertent. . . .

. . . The "plain view" doctrine is often considered an exception to the general rule that warrantless searches are presumptively unreasonable, but this characterization overlooks the important difference between searches and seizures. If an article is already in plain view, neither its observation nor its seizure would involve any invasion of privacy. A seizure of the article, however, would obviously invade the owner's possessory interest. If "plain view" justifies an exception from an otherwise applicable warrant requirement, therefore, it must be an exception that is addressed to the concerns that are implicated by seizures rather than by searches.

The criteria that generally guide "plain view" seizures were set forth in Coolidge v. New Hampshire, 403 U.S. 443 (1971). The Court held that [the seizure of] two automobiles parked in plain view on the defendant's driveway in the course of arresting the defendant, violated the Fourth Amendment. Accordingly, particles of gunpowder that had been subsequently found in vacuum sweepings from one of the cars could not be introduced in evidence against the defendant. The State endeavored to justify the seizure of the automobiles, and their subsequent search at the police station, on four different grounds, including the "plain-view" doctrine. The scope of that doctrine as it had developed in earlier cases was fairly summarized in . . . Justice Stewart's opinion. . . . Justice Stewart . . . described the two limitations on the doctrine that he found implicit in its rationale: First, "that plain view *alone* is never enough to justify the warrantless seizure of evidence," id., at 468; and second, "that the discovery of evidence in plain view must be inadvertent." Id., at 469.

Justice Stewart's analysis of the "plain view" doctrine did not command a majority[9] . . . .

It is, of course, an essential predicate to any valid warrantless seizure of incriminating evidence that the officer did not violate the Fourth Amendment in arriving

---

9. The portion of Justice Stewart's opinion in *Coolidge* that discussed plain view was joined by Justices Douglas, Brennan, and Marshall. Justice Harlan was the fifth vote in *Coolidge*; his opinion did not mention plain view. — Eds.

at the place from which the evidence could be plainly viewed. There are, moreover, two additional conditions that must be satisfied to justify [a] warrantless seizure. First, not only must the item be in plain view, its incriminating character must also be "immediately apparent." Id., at 466; see also Arizona v. Hicks, 480 U.S., at 326-327. Thus, in *Coolidge*, the cars were obviously in plain view, but their probative value remained uncertain until after the interiors were swept and examined microscopically. Second, not only must the officer be lawfully located in a place from which the object can be plainly seen, but he or she must also have a lawful right of access to the object itself. . . . [I]n *Coolidge* . . . the seizure of the cars was accomplished by means of a warrantless trespass on the defendant's property. . . . [W]e are satisfied that the absence of inadvertence was not essential to the Court's rejection of the State's "plain-view" argument in *Coolidge*.

Justice Stewart concluded that the inadvertence requirement was necessary to avoid a violation of the express constitutional requirement that a valid warrant must particularly describe the things to be seized. He explained:

> The rationale of the exception to the warrant requirement, as just stated, is that a plain-view seizure will not turn an initially valid (and therefore limited) search into a "general" one, while the inconvenience of procuring a warrant to cover an inadvertent discovery is great. But where the discovery is anticipated, where the police know in advance the location of the evidence and intend to seize it, the situation is altogether different. The requirement of a warrant to seize imposes no inconvenience whatever, or at least none which is constitutionally cognizable in a legal system that regards warrantless searches as "per se unreasonable" in the absence of "exigent circumstances."
>
> If the initial intrusion is bottomed upon a warrant that fails to mention a particular object, though the police know its location and intend to seize it, then there is a violation of the express constitutional requirement of "Warrants . . . particularly describing . . . [the] things to be seized."

403 U.S., at 469-471.

We find two flaws in this reasoning. First, evenhanded law enforcement is best achieved by the application of objective standards of conduct, rather than standards that depend upon the subjective state of mind of the officer. The fact that an officer is interested in an item of evidence and fully expects to find it in the course of a search should not invalidate its seizure if the search is confined in area and duration by the terms of a warrant or a valid exception to the warrant requirement. If the officer has knowledge approaching certainty that the item will be found, we see no reason why he or she would deliberately omit a particular description of the item to be seized from the application for a search warrant. Specification of the additional item could only permit the officer to expand the scope of the search. On the other hand, if he or she has a valid warrant to search for one item and merely a suspicion concerning the second, whether or not it amounts to probable cause, we fail to see why that suspicion should immunize the second item from seizure if it is found during a lawful search for the first. The hypothetical case put by Justice White in his concurring and dissenting opinion in *Coolidge* is instructive:

> Let us suppose officers secure a warrant to search a house for a rifle. While staying well within the range of a rifle search, they discover two photographs of the murder victim, both in plain sight in the bedroom. Assume also that the discovery of the one photograph was inadvertent but finding the other was anticipated. The Court would

permit the seizure of only one of the photographs. But in terms of the "minor" peril to Fourth Amendment values there is surely no difference between these two photographs: the interference with possession is the same in each case and the officers' appraisal of the photograph they expected to see is no less reliable than their judgment about the other. And in both situations the actual inconvenience and danger to evidence remain identical if the officers must depart and secure a warrant.

Id., at 516.

Second, the suggestion that the inadvertence requirement is necessary to prevent the police from conducting general searches, or from converting specific warrants into general warrants, is not persuasive because that interest is already served by the requirements that no warrant issue unless it "particularly describ[es] the place to be searched and the persons or things to be seized," see Maryland v. Garrison, 480 U.S. 79, 84 (1987), and that a warrantless search be circumscribed by the exigencies which justify its initiation. See, e.g., Mincey v. Arizona, 437 U.S. 385, 393 (1978). Scrupulous adherence to these requirements serves the interests in limiting the area and duration of the search that the inadvertence requirement inadequately protects. Once those commands have been satisfied and the officer has a lawful right of access, however, no additional Fourth Amendment interest is furthered by requiring that the discovery of evidence be inadvertent. . . .

In this case, the scope of the search was not enlarged in the slightest by the omission of any reference to the weapons in the warrant. Indeed, if the three rings and other items named in the warrant had been found at the outset — or petitioner had them in his possession and had responded to the warrant by producing them immediately — no search for weapons could have taken place. Again, Justice White's concurring and dissenting opinion in *Coolidge* is instructive:

> Police with a warrant for a rifle may search only places where rifles might be and must terminate the search once the rifle is found; the inadvertence rule will in no way reduce the number of places into which they may lawfully look.

403 U.S., at 517. . . .

[T]he items seized from petitioner's home were discovered during a lawful search authorized by a valid warrant. When they were discovered, it was immediately apparent to the officer that they constituted incriminating evidence. He had probable cause, not only to obtain a warrant to search for the stolen property, but also to believe that the weapons and handguns had been used in the crime he was investigating. The search was authorized by the warrant; the seizure was authorized by the "plain view" doctrine. The judgment is affirmed. . . .

[The dissenting opinion of Justice Brennan, joined by Justice Marshall, is omitted.]

If *Horton* had come out the other way, what incentives would plain view doctrine create for police? Imagine two suspects, Smith and Jones. Smith is suspected of a series of robberies and rapes. Jones is suspected of being Smith's accomplice in one of the robberies; the police do not believe Jones is involved in any other crimes. The police have enough evidence to give them probable cause to search both suspects' homes for evidence of the one robbery; they lack probable cause with respect to the rest of Smith's possible crimes. It is easy for the police to search Jones's home, assuming they can get a warrant to do so. Smith is another matter. If the police submit their evidence on the one robbery to a magistrate, get a warrant, and then find evidence linking Smith to other crimes, they might effectively immunize Smith for those other crimes. That is what an inadvertence requirement would mean.

Of course, the police could always submit everything they had to the magistrate. But why should they have to do that? At the least, it would make the warrant process more costly for magistrates and police officers alike. And notice where the extra cost arises — in investigations of suspects like Smith, who are suspected of committing not one crime but several. Surely it doesn't make sense to have an inadvertence requirement that would benefit primarily repeat criminals. Or does it?

c.   *Automobiles*

As technology evolves and both shapes and changes American society, it tends to shape Fourth Amendment law as well. Arguably the most important single technological advance of the twentieth century was the automobile. There are more than 250 million vehicles[10] registered in the United States for an adult population 232 million,[11] making cars and trucks one of the most commonly owned items in America, and surely one of the most important for many individuals and businesses.

As one might expect, the Fourth Amendment law relating to automobiles has evolved significantly in response to the automobile's increasing ubiquity. The starting point of this evolution was the Supreme Court's decision in Carroll v. United States, 267 U.S. 132 (1925). In *Carroll*, federal prohibition agents (together with a state police officer) encountered a car, on the highway between Detroit and Grand Rapids, whose occupants they believed (based on "reasonably trustworthy information") to be bootleggers. The agents stopped the car and searched it without a warrant, and found 68 bottles of whiskey and gin stuffed inside the hollowed-out upholstery.[12] The Court upheld the search, concluding that the traditional Fourth Amendment warrant requirement was unsuited to the search of "a ship, motor boat, wagon or automobile, for contraband goods, where it is not practicable to secure a warrant because the vehicle can be quickly moved out of the locality or jurisdiction in which the warrant must be sought." This led the Court to recognize what came to be called the "automobile exception" to the warrant requirement: For searches and seizures of cars stopped along the road, if obtaining a warrant is not "reasonably practicable," then "[t]he measure of legality . . . . is that the seizing officer shall have reasonable or probable cause for believing that the automobile which he stops and seizes has contraband liquor therein which is being illegally transported."

Even in its day, *Carroll* was a controversial decision. America was in the midst of its first war on drugs — the drug in question was alcohol, not heroin or cocaine — and as in later drug wars, many people worried that Fourth Amendment freedoms were giving way to the convenience of police seeking to enforce a criminal prohibition that was widely violated. Justices McReynolds and Sutherland captured

---

10. This is a 2008 estimate from the Bureau of Transportation Statistics. See National Transportation Statistics at http://www.bts.gov/publications, tbl. 1-11.

11. This is a 2009 estimate from the U.S. Census Bureau, http://factfinder.census.gov/servlet/ QTTable?_bm=y&-qr_name=PEP_2009_EST_DP1&-geo_id=01000US&-ds_name=PEP_2009_EST&-_ lang=en&-format=&-CONTEXT=qt.

12. The agents had to rip open the upholstery to find the liquor. See United States v. Ross, 456 U.S. 798, 817-818 (1982).

that concern in their *Carroll* dissent when they noted that "[t]he damnable character of the 'bootlegger's' business should not close our eyes to the mischief which will surely follow any attempt to destroy it by unwarranted methods." Id., at 163 (McReynolds, J., dissenting). Later in the decade, the Court would respond differently to that concern; Fourth Amendment restrictions on federal agents enforcing Prohibition were ratcheted up in the late 1920s and early 1930s. See Kenneth M. Murchison, Prohibition and the Fourth Amendment: A New Look at Some Old Cases, 73 J. Crim. L. & Criminology 471 (1982). But in 1925, the law still favored the agents, not the bootleggers.

On this somewhat shaky foundation, the Supreme Court slowly built an elaborate body of law governing warrantless searches of automobiles and their contents. The scope of police authority in that body of law was expanded in Chambers v. Maroney, 399 U.S. 42 (1970), where the police stopped a car based on probable cause that its occupants had just committed a late-night armed robbery. The police arrested the suspects and drove the car to the police station, where a thorough warrantless search of the car was conducted, producing two handguns and other evidence of the crime. The issue in *Chambers* was whether the "automobile exception" of *Carroll* applied to the search of a car in police custody, at the police station, rather than along the road. The Court noted that, under *Carroll*, the car could have been searched immediately upon being stopped. The car also could have been immobilized while the police awaited issuance of a search warrant, but the Court found "little to choose in terms of practical consequences" between that option and an immediate warrantless search. The decision to move the car to the police station before conducting the search was "not unreasonable," because it would have been potentially dangerous for the police (and perhaps inconvenient for the car's owner) to conduct the search on a dark street in the middle of the night. Because the police had probable cause to conduct the search, and because they behaved reasonably in dealing with the car's mobility, the search was valid under the Fourth Amendment.

After *Carroll* and *Chambers*, it was clear that, as a general matter, the search of a car (including its integral parts, such as the glove compartment and trunk) could be based solely on probable cause to believe that the car contained evidence or contraband, and did not require a warrant. Indeed, in Cardwell v. Lewis, 417 U.S. 583 (1974), a plurality of the Court found it permissible for officers acting with probable cause but without a warrant to take paint scrapings from an automobile seized from a public parking lot — a constitutionally permissible confiscation and destruction of the owner's property. The Court next turned its attention to the subsidiary, but hugely important, issue of the warrantless search of containers that happened to be located within cars. The first three such cases, United States v. Chadwick, 433 U.S. 1 (1977), Arkansas v. Sanders, 442 U.S. 753 (1979), and Robbins v. California, 435 U.S. 420 (1981) (plurality opinion), all were decided against the police.

In *Chadwick*, federal agents had probable cause to believe that a locked footlocker being transported by a train passenger contained marijuana. They waited until the suspect disembarked the train and placed the footlocker in the trunk of a car. Then — before the car's engine even was started — they arrested the suspect and his traveling companion, as well as the driver of the car. The car and footlocker were brought to a federal building, and subsequently searched without a warrant, revealing a "large quantity" of marijuana.[13] The Court rejected the government's argument that the rationale of the *Carroll-Chambers* "automobile exception" also should apply to luggage. According to the Court, the "automobile exception" is based only in part on the "inherent mobility" of automobiles; an additional, important basis for the exception is the "diminished expectation of privacy which surrounds the automobile." Cars are registered with, and heavily regulated by, the state, including (in many states) a periodic inspection requirement. None of these characteristics applies to a footlocker, which is "intended as a repository of personal effects," and in which "expectations of privacy . . . are substantially greater than in an automobile." Moreover, as compared to cars, smaller containers can be secured more easily while awaiting issuance of a warrant. The Court held that the police should have maintained custody of the footlocker until they could obtain a warrant to search it.

In *Sanders*, police had probable cause to believe that a green suitcase being transported by an airline passenger contained marijuana. They waited until the suspect put the suitcase in the trunk of a taxicab and left the airport before giving chase. The police stopped the taxicab a few blocks from the airport and immediately searched the suitcase, finding 9.3 pounds of marijuana. The Court found the search invalid. It was unimpressed by the government's argument that, unlike in *Chadwick*, the police waited to act until the car was moving; "the exigency of mobility must be assessed at the point immediately before the search — after the police have seized the object to be searched and have it securely within their control." Nor did the suitcase have a "diminished expectation of privacy" simply because it was seized from the trunk of a car. The "automobile exception" therefore did not apply to the suitcase.

In *Robbins*, police stopped a car for erratic driving, and noticed the odor of marijuana wafting from the car. They arrested the driver and conducted a warrantless search of the car. In a recessed luggage compartment, they found two "bricks" covered with green opaque plastic, which they unwrapped. The packages contained 30 pounds of marijuana. The Court concluded that this search, too, violated the Fourth Amendment, although there was no majority opinion. A four-Justice plurality based the result on the fact that the "bricks" were in a "closed, opaque container" that was indistinguishable from the foot-locker in *Chadwick* and the suitcase in *Sanders*. The fact that the kind of container in *Robbins* was not the kind normally used to transport "personal effects" did not matter; "[w]hat one person may put into a suitcase, another person may put into a paper bag."

Justice Powell, in concurrence, found that Robbins had manifested a "reasonable expectation of privacy" by carefully wrapping the "bricks," and thus was entitled to the protection of the warrant requirement, but he disagreed with the plurality's extension of the *Chadwick-Sanders* rule to other "insubstantial containers" that did not reflect such an expectation. Powell noted in passing that, arguably, neither *Chadwick* nor *Sanders* really was an "automobile case" at all, because the probable cause in both cases attached to the respective containers "before either came near an automobile." But he declined to rely on that argument in *Robbins*, because the parties had not argued or briefed it.

13. The court did not say exactly how much marijuana was inside, but the footlocker weighed 200 pounds, and it took three persons to lift it into the trunk of the car.

Only a few years later, the Court shifted course and handed the police a major victory. In United States v. Ross, 456 U.S. 798 (1982), police had probable cause to believe that Ross was selling narcotics out of the trunk of his maroon Chevy Malibu. They found the car, but did not see Ross nearby, so they kept circling the neighborhood. A few minutes later, they saw Ross driving the Malibu, stopped the car, and arrested Ross. They conducted a warrantless search of the car, including the trunk, where they found a "closed brown paper bag." Inside the bag were "a number of glassine bags containing a white powder," which turned out to be heroin.

The Court upheld the search in Ross. Noting the importance of "striving for clarification in this area of the law," which affected "countless" police-citizen encounters every day, the Court reviewed the entire line of cases recounted above. The key aspect in Ross, according to the Court, was the same one that had been noted (but not relied upon) by Justice Powell in Robbins — that the police in Ross, as in Robbins, had probable cause that extended to the entire car, rather than being limited (as in Chadwick and Sanders) to a particular container that happened to be located in the car. "A lawful search of fixed premises generally extends to the entire area in which the object of the search may be found and is not limited by the possibility that separate acts of entry or opening may be required to complete the search. . . . When a legitimate search is underway, . . . nice distinctions . . . between glove compartments, upholstered seats, trunks, and wrapped packages . . . must give way to the interest in the prompt and efficient completion of the task at hand." Without such a rule, the "practical consequences" of Carroll would be "nullified."

The Ross Court agreed with the Robbins plurality that the same rule must apply equally to all containers, from a "paper bag" to a "locked attache case." The Court concluded: "The scope of a warrantless search of an automobile thus is not defined by the nature of the container in which the contraband is secreted. Rather, it is defined by the object of the search and the places in which there is probable cause to believe that it may be found."

After the decision in Ross, the legality of warrantless searches of containers in cars generally depended on whether the probable cause possessed by the police was "container-specific" (in which case the Chadwick-Sanders rule applied) or "car-general" (in which case the Ross rule applied). But Ross did not put an end to litigation about searches of containers in cars, as the following two cases demonstrate.

CALIFORNIA v. ACEVEDO

Certiorari to the Court of Appeal of California, Fourth Appellate District
500 U.S. 565 (1991)

JUSTICE BLACKMUN delivered the opinion of the Court.

This case requires us once again to consider the so-called "automobile exception" to the warrant requirement of the Fourth Amendment and its application to the search of a closed container in the trunk of a car.

On October 28, 1987, Officer Coleman of the Santa Ana, Cal., Police Department received a telephone call from a federal drug enforcement agent in Hawaii. The agent informed Coleman that he had seized a package containing marijuana which was to have been delivered to the Federal Express Office in Santa Ana and which was addressed to J. R. Daza at 805 West Stevens Avenue in that city. The agent arranged to send the package to Coleman instead. Coleman then was to take the package to the Federal Express office and arrest the person who arrived to claim it.

Coleman received the package on October 29, verified its contents, and took it to the Senior Operations Manager at the Federal Express office. At about 10:30 a.m. on October 30, a man, who identified himself as Jamie Daza, arrived to claim the package. He accepted it and drove to his apartment on West Stevens. He carried the package into the apartment.

At 11:45 a.m., officers observed Daza leave the apartment and drop the box and paper that had contained the marijuana into a trash bin. Coleman at that point left the scene to get a search warrant. About 12:05 p.m., the officers saw Richard St. George leave the apartment carrying a blue knapsack which appeared to be half full. The officers stopped him as he was driving off, searched the knapsack, and found 1½ pounds of marijuana.

At 12:30 p.m., respondent Charles Steven Acevedo arrived. He entered Daza's apartment, stayed for about 10 minutes, and reappeared carrying a brown paper bag that looked full. The officers noticed that the bag was the size of one of the wrapped marijuana packages sent from Hawaii. Acevedo walked to a silver Honda in the parking lot. He placed the bag in the trunk of the car and started to drive away. Fearing the loss of evidence, officers in a marked police car stopped him. They opened the trunk and the bag, and found marijuana.[1]

Respondent was charged in state court with possession of marijuana for sale. . . . He moved to suppress the marijuana found in the car. The motion was denied. He then pleaded guilty but appealed the denial of the suppression motion.

The California Court of Appeal, Fourth District, concluded that the marijuana found in the paper bag in the car's trunk should have been suppressed. The court concluded that the officers had probable cause to believe that the paper bag contained drugs but lacked probable cause to suspect that Acevedo's car, itself, otherwise contained contraband. Because the officers' probable cause was directed specifically at the bag, the court held that the case was controlled by United States v. Chadwick, 433 U.S. 1 (1977), rather than by United States v. Ross, 456 U.S. 798 (1982). Although the court agreed that the officers could seize the paper bag, it held that, under Chadwick, they could not open the bag without first obtaining a warrant for that purpose. The court then recognized "the anomalous nature" of the dichotomy between the rule in Chadwick and the rule in Ross. That dichotomy dictates that if there is probable cause to search a car, then the entire car — including any closed container found therein — may be searched without a warrant, but if there is probable cause only as to a container in the car, the container may be held but not searched until a warrant is obtained.

The Supreme Court of California denied the State's petition for review. . . .

We granted certiorari to reexamine the law applicable to a closed container in an automobile, a subject that has troubled courts and law enforcement officers since it was first considered in Chadwick.

The Fourth Amendment protects the "right of the people to be secure in their persons, houses, papers, and effects, against unreasonable searches and seizures."

---

1. When Officer Coleman returned with a warrant, the apartment was searched and bags of marijuana were found there. We are here concerned, of course, only with what was discovered in the automobile.

Contemporaneously with the adoption of the Fourth Amendment, the First Congress, and, later, the Second and Fourth Congresses, distinguished between the need for a warrant to search for contraband concealed in "a dwelling house or similar place" and the need for a warrant to search for contraband concealed in a movable vessel. See Carroll v. United States, 267 U.S. 132, 151 (1925). See also Boyd v. United States, 116 U.S. 616, 623-624 (1886). In *Carroll*, this Court established an exception to the warrant requirement for moving vehicles, for it recognized

> a necessary difference between a search of a store, dwelling house or other structure in respect of which a proper official warrant readily may be obtained, and a search of a ship, motor boat, wagon or automobile, for contraband goods, where it is not practicable to secure a warrant because the vehicle can be quickly moved out of the locality or jurisdiction in which the warrant must be sought. 267 U.S., at 153.

It therefore held that a warrantless search of an automobile, based upon probable cause to believe that the vehicle contained evidence of crime in the light of an exigency arising out of the likely disappearance of the vehicle, did not contravene the Warrant Clause of the Fourth Amendment. See id., at 158-159.

The Court refined the exigency requirement in Chambers v. Maroney, 399 U.S. 42 (1970), when it held that the existence of exigent circumstances was to be determined at the time the automobile is seized. The car search at issue in *Chambers* took place at the police station, where the vehicle was immobilized, some time after the driver had been arrested. Given probable cause and exigent circumstances at the time the vehicle was first stopped, the Court held that the later warrantless search at the station passed constitutional muster. . . .

In United States v. Ross, 456 U.S. 798, decided in 1982, we held that a warrantless search of an automobile under the *Carroll* doctrine could include a search of a container or package found inside the car when such a search was supported by probable cause. The warrantless search of Ross' car occurred after an informant told the police that he had seen Ross complete a drug transaction using drugs stored in the trunk of his car. The police stopped the car, searched it, and discovered in the trunk a brown paper bag containing drugs. We decided that the search of Ross' car was not unreasonable under the Fourth Amendment: "The scope of a warrantless search based on probable cause is no narrower — and no broader — than the scope of a search authorized by a warrant supported by probable cause." Id., at 823. Thus, "[i]f probable cause justifies the search of a lawfully stopped vehicle, it justifies the search of every part of the vehicle and its contents that may conceal the object of the search." Id., at 825. In *Ross*, therefore, we clarified the scope of the *Carroll* doctrine as properly including a "probing search" of compartments and containers within the automobile so long as the search is supported by probable cause. Id., at 800.

In addition to this clarification, *Ross* distinguished the *Carroll* doctrine from the separate rule that governed the search of closed containers. See 456 U.S., at 817. The Court had announced this separate rule, unique to luggage and other closed packages, bags, and containers, in United States v. Chadwick, 433 U.S. 1 (1977). In *Chadwick*, federal narcotics agents had probable cause to believe that a 200-pound double-locked footlocker contained marijuana. The agents tracked the locker as the defendants removed it from a train and carried it through the station to a waiting car. As soon as the defendants lifted the locker into the trunk of the car, the agents arrested them, seized the locker, and searched it. In this Court, the United States did not contend that the locker's brief contact with the automobile's trunk sufficed to make the *Carroll* doctrine applicable. Rather, the United States urged that the search of movable luggage could be considered analogous to the search of an automobile. 433 U.S., at 11-12.

The Court rejected this argument because, it reasoned, a person expects more privacy in his luggage and personal effects than he does in his automobile. Id., at 13. Moreover, it concluded that as "may often not be the case when automobiles are seized," secure storage facilities are usually available when the police seize luggage. Id., at 13, n. 7.

In Arkansas v. Sanders, 442 U.S. 753 (1979), the Court extended *Chadwick's* rule to apply to a suitcase actually being transported in the trunk of a car. In *Sanders*, the police had probable cause to believe a suitcase contained marijuana. They watched as the defendant placed the suitcase in the trunk of a taxi and was driven away. The police pursued the taxi for several blocks, stopped it, found the suitcase in the trunk, and searched it. Although the Court had applied the *Carroll* doctrine to searches of integral parts of the automobile itself, (indeed, in *Carroll*, contraband whiskey was in the upholstery of the seats, see 267 U.S., at 136), it did not extend the doctrine to the warrantless search of personal luggage "merely because it was located in an automobile lawfully stopped by the police." 442 U.S., at 765. Again, the *Sanders* majority stressed the heightened privacy expectation in personal luggage and concluded that the presence of luggage in an automobile did not diminish the owner's expectation of privacy in his personal items. Id., at 764-765.

In *Ross*, the Court endeavored to distinguish between *Carroll*, which governed the *Ross* automobile search, and *Chadwick*, which governed the *Sanders* automobile search. It held that the *Carroll* doctrine covered searches of automobiles when the police had probable cause to search an entire vehicle, but that the *Chadwick* doctrine governed searches of luggage when the officers had probable cause to search only a container within the vehicle. Thus, in a *Ross* situation, the police could conduct a reasonable search under the Fourth Amendment without obtaining a warrant, whereas in a *Sanders* situation, the police had to obtain a warrant before they searched. . . .

III

The facts in this case closely resemble the facts in *Ross*. In *Ross*, the police had probable cause to believe that drugs were stored in the trunk of a particular car. See 456 U.S., at 800. Here, the California Court of Appeal concluded that the police had probable cause to believe that respondent was carrying marijuana in a bag in his car's trunk. . . .

. . . We now must decide the question deferred in *Ross*: whether the Fourth Amendment requires the police to obtain a warrant to open the sack in a movable vehicle simply because they lack probable cause to search the entire car. We conclude that it does not.

IV

. . . [A] container found after a general search of the automobile and a container found in a car after a limited search for the container are equally easy for the police to store and for the suspect to hide or destroy. In fact, we see no principled distinction in terms of either the privacy expectation or the exigent circumstances between the paper bag found by the police in *Ross* and the paper bag found by the police here. Furthermore, by attempting to distinguish between a container for which the police are specifically searching and a container which they come across in a car, we have provided only minimal protection for privacy and have impeded effective law enforcement.

The line between probable cause to search a vehicle and probable cause to search a package in that vehicle is not always clear, and separate rules that govern the two objects to be searched may enable the police to broaden their power to make warrantless searches and disserve privacy interests. We noted this in *Ross* in the context of a search of an entire vehicle. Recognizing that under *Carroll*, the "entire vehicle itself . . . could be searched without a warrant," we concluded that "prohibiting police from opening immediately a container in which the object of the search is most likely to be found and instead forcing them first to comb the entire vehicle would actually exacerbate the intrusion on privacy interests." 456 U.S., at 821, n. 28. At the moment when officers stop an automobile, it may be less than clear whether they suspect with a high degree of certainty that the vehicle contains drugs in a bag or simply contains drugs. If the police know that they may open a bag only if they are actually searching the entire car, they may search more extensively than they otherwise would in order to establish the general probable cause required by *Ross*. . . .

To the extent that the *Chadwick-Sanders* rule protects privacy, its protection is minimal. Law enforcement officers may seize a container and hold it until they obtain a search warrant. *Chadwick*, 433 U.S., at 13. "Since the police, by hypothesis, have probable cause to seize the property, we can assume that a warrant will be routinely forthcoming in the overwhelming majority of cases." *Sanders*, 442 U.S., at 770 (dissenting opinion). . . .

Finally, the search of a paper bag intrudes far less on individual privacy than does the incursion sanctioned long ago in *Carroll*. In that case, prohibition agents slashed the upholstery of the automobile. This Court nonetheless found their search to be reasonable under the Fourth Amendment. If destroying the interior of an automobile is not unreasonable, we cannot conclude that looking inside a closed container is. In light of the minimal protection to privacy afforded by the *Chadwick-Sanders* rule, and our serious doubt whether that rule substantially serves privacy interests, we now hold that the Fourth Amendment does not compel separate treatment for an automobile search that extends only to a container within the vehicle.

V

The *Chadwick-Sanders* rule not only has failed to protect privacy but also has confused courts and police officers and impeded effective law enforcement. . . . One leading authority on the Fourth Amendment, after comparing *Chadwick* and *Sanders* with *Carroll* and its progeny, observed: "These two lines of authority cannot be completely reconciled, and thus how one comes out in the container-in-the-car situation depends upon which line of authority is used as a point of departure." 3 W. LaFave, Search and Seizure 53 (2d ed. 1987).

The discrepancy between the two rules has led to confusion for law enforcement officers. For example, when an officer, who has developed probable cause to believe that a vehicle contains drugs, begins to search the vehicle and immediately discovers a closed container, which rule applies? The defendant will argue that the fact that the officer first chose to search the container indicates that his probable cause extended only to the container and that *Chadwick* and *Sanders* therefore require a warrant. On the other hand, the fact that the officer first chose to search in the most obvious location should not restrict the propriety of the search. The *Chadwick* rule, as applied in *Sanders*, has devolved into an anomaly such that the more likely the police are to discover drugs in a container, the less authority they have to search it. We have noted the virtue of providing "clear and unequivocal guidelines to the law enforcement profession." Minnick v. Mississippi, 498 U.S. 146, 151 (1990). The *Chadwick-Sanders* rule is the antithesis of a "clear and unequivocal guideline." . . .

Although we have recognized firmly that the doctrine of stare decisis serves profoundly important purposes in our legal system, this Court has overruled a prior case on the comparatively rare occasion when it has bred confusion or been a derelict or led to anomalous results. *Sanders* was explicitly undermined in *Ross*, 456 U.S., at 824, and the existence of the dual regimes for automobile searches that uncover containers has proved as confusing as the *Chadwick* and *Sanders* dissenters predicted. We conclude that it is better to adopt one clear-cut rule to govern automobile searches and eliminate the warrant requirement for closed containers set forth in *Sanders*.

VI

The interpretation of the *Carroll* doctrine set forth in *Ross* now applies to all searches of containers found in an automobile. In other words, the police may search without a warrant if their search is supported by probable cause. The Court in *Ross* put it this way:

> The scope of a warrantless search of an automobile . . . is not defined by the nature of the container in which the contraband is secreted. Rather, it is defined by the object of the search and the places in which there is probable cause to believe that it may be found. 456 U.S., at 824.

It went on to note: "Probable cause to believe that a container placed in the trunk of a taxi contains contraband or evidence does not justify a search of the entire cab." Ibid. We reaffirm that principle. In the case before us, the police had probable cause to believe that the paper bag in the automobile's trunk contained marijuana. That probable cause now allows a warrantless search of the paper bag. The facts in the record reveal that the police did not have probable cause to believe that contraband was hidden in any other part of the automobile and a search of the entire vehicle would have been without probable cause and unreasonable under the Fourth Amendment.

Our holding today neither extends the *Carroll* doctrine nor broadens the scope of the permissible automobile search delineated in *Carroll*, *Chambers*, and *Ross*. It remains a "cardinal principle that 'searches conducted outside the judicial process, without prior approval by judge or magistrate, are per se unreasonable under the Fourth Amendment — subject only to a few specifically established and well-delineated exceptions.'" Mincey v. Arizona, 437 U.S. 385, 390 (1978), quoting Katz v. United States, 389 U.S. 347, 357 (1967). We held in *Ross*: "The exception recognized in *Carroll* is unquestionably one that is 'specifically established and well delineated.'" 456 U.S., at 825.

Until today, this Court has drawn a curious line between the search of an automobile that coincidentally turns up a container and the search of a container that coincidentally turns up in an automobile. The protections of the Fourth Amendment must not turn on such coincidences. We therefore interpret *Carroll* as providing one rule to govern all automobile searches. The police may search an automobile and the containers within it where they have probable cause to believe contraband or evidence is contained.

The judgment of the California Court of Appeal is reversed. . . .

JUSTICE SCALIA, concurring in the judgment.

I agree with the dissent that it is anomalous for a briefcase to be protected by the "general requirement" of a prior warrant when it is being carried along the street, but for that same briefcase to become unprotected as soon as it is carried into an automobile. On the other hand, I agree with the Court that it would be anomalous for a locked compartment in an automobile to be unprotected by the "general requirement" of a prior warrant, but for an unlocked briefcase within the automobile to be protected. I join in the judgment of the Court because I think its holding is more faithful to the text and tradition of the Fourth Amendment, and if these anomalies in our jurisprudence are ever to be eliminated that is the direction in which we should travel.

The Fourth Amendment does not by its terms require a prior warrant for searches and seizures; it merely prohibits searches and seizures that are "unreasonable." What it explicitly states regarding warrants is by way of limitation upon their issuance rather than requirement of their use. For the warrant was a means of insulating officials from personal liability assessed by colonial juries. An officer who searched or seized without a warrant did so at his own risk; he would be liable for trespass, including exemplary damages, unless the jury found that his action was "reasonable." Amar, The Bill of Rights as a Constitution, 100 Yale L.J. 1131, 1178-1180 (1991); Huckle v. Money, 2 Wils. 205, 95 Eng. Rep. 768 (K.B. 1763). If, however, the officer acted pursuant to a proper warrant, he would be absolutely immune. See Bell v. Clapp, 10 Johns. 263 (N.Y. 1813); 4 W. Blackstone, Commentaries 288 (1769). By restricting the issuance of warrants, the Framers endeavored to preserve the jury's role in regulating searches and seizures. Amar, supra; Posner, Rethinking the Fourth Amendment, 1981 S. Ct. Rev. 49, 72-73; see also T. Taylor, Two Studies in Constitutional Interpretation 41 (1969).

Although the Fourth Amendment does not explicitly impose the requirement of a warrant, it is of course textually possible to consider that implicit within the requirement of reasonableness. For some years after the (still continuing) explosion in Fourth Amendment litigation that followed our announcement of the exclusionary rule in Weeks v. United States, 232 U.S. 383 (1914), our jurisprudence lurched back and forth between imposing a categorical warrant requirement and looking to reasonableness alone. (The opinions preferring a warrant involved searches of structures.) By the late 1960s, the preference for a warrant had won out, at least rhetorically. See Chimel [v. California, 395 U.S. 752 (1969)]; Coolidge v. New Hampshire, 403 U.S. 443 (1971).

The victory was illusory. Even before today's decision, the "warrant requirement" had become so riddled with exceptions that it was basically unrecognizable. In 1985, one commentator cataloged nearly 20 such exceptions, including "searches incident to arrest . . . automobile searches . . . border searches . . . administrative searches of regulated businesses . . . exigent circumstances . . . search[es] incident to nonarrest when there is probable cause to arrest . . . boat boarding for document checks . . . welfare searches . . . inventory searches . . . airport searches . . . school search[es]. . . ." Bradley, Two Models of the Fourth Amendment, 83 Mich. L. Rev. 1468, 1473-1474. Since then, we have added at least two more. California v. Carney, 471 U.S. 386 (1985) (searches of mobile homes); O'Connor v. Ortega, 480 U.S. 709 (1987) (searches of offices of government employees). Our intricate body of law regarding "reasonable expectation of privacy" has been developed largely as a means of creating these exceptions, enabling a search to be denominated not a Fourth Amendment "search" and therefore not subject to the general warrant requirement.

Unlike the dissent, therefore, I do not regard today's holding as some momentous departure, but rather as merely the continuation of an inconsistent jurisprudence that has been with us for years. Cases like United States v. Chadwick, 433 U.S. 1 (1977), and Arkansas v. Sanders, 442 U.S. 753 (1979), have taken the "preference for a warrant" seriously, while cases like United States v. Ross, 456 U.S. 798 (1982), and Carroll v. United States, 267 U.S. 132 (1925), have not. There can be no clarity in this area unless we make up our minds, and unless the principles we express comport with the actions we take.

In my view, the path out of this confusion should be sought by returning to the first principle that the "reasonableness" requirement of the Fourth Amendment affords the protection that the common law afforded. I have no difficulty with the proposition that that includes the requirement of a warrant, where the common law required a warrant; and it may even be that changes in the surrounding legal rules (for example, elimination of the common-law rule that reasonable, good-faith belief was no defense to absolute liability for trespass), may make a warrant indispensable to reasonableness where it once was not. But the supposed "general rule" that a warrant is always required does not appear to have any basis in the common law, and confuses rather than facilitates any attempt to develop rules of reasonableness in light of changed legal circumstances, as the anomaly eliminated and the anomaly created by today's holding both demonstrate. . . .

I would reverse the judgment in the present case, not because a closed container carried inside a car becomes subject to the "automobile" exception to the general warrant requirement, but because the search of a closed container, outside a privately owned building, with probable cause to believe that the container contains contraband, and when it in fact does contain contraband, is not one of those searches whose Fourth Amendment reasonableness depends upon a warrant. For that reason I concur in the judgment of the Court.

[Justice White's dissenting opinion is omitted.]

JUSTICE STEVENS, with whom JUSTICE MARSHALL joins, dissenting.

. . . The Fourth Amendment is a restraint on Executive power. The Amendment constitutes the Framers' direct constitutional response to the unreasonable law enforcement practices employed by agents of the British Crown. See Boyd v. United States, 116 U.S. 616, 624-625 (1886). Over the years — particularly in the period immediately after World War II and particularly in opinions authored by Justice Jackson after his service as a special prosecutor at the Nuremburg trials — the Court has recognized the importance of this restraint as a bulwark against police practices that prevail in totalitarian regimes. See, e.g., United States v. Di Re, 332 U.S. 581, 595 (1948); Johnson v. United States, 333 U.S. 10, 17 (1948).

This history is, however, only part of the explanation for the warrant requirement. The requirement also reflects the sound policy judgment that, absent exceptional circumstances, the decision to invade the privacy of an individual's personal effects should be made by a neutral magistrate rather than an agent of the Executive. . . .

The Court does not attempt to identify any exigent circumstances that would justify its refusal to apply the general rule against warrantless searches. Instead, it advances these three arguments: First, the rules identified in the foregoing cases are confusing and anomalous. Second, the rules do not protect any significant interest in privacy. And, third, the rules impede effective law enforcement. None of these arguments withstands scrutiny. . . .

The Court summarizes the alleged "anomaly" created by the coexistence of *Ross*, *Chadwick*, and *Sanders* with the statement that "the more likely the police are to discover drugs in a container, the less authority they have to search it." This juxtaposition is only anomalous, however, if one accepts the flawed premise that the degree to which the police are likely to discover contraband is correlated with their authority to search *without a warrant*. Yet, even proof beyond a reasonable doubt will not justify a warrantless search that is not supported by one of the exceptions to the warrant requirement. And, even when the police have a warrant or an exception applies, once the police possess probable cause, the extent to which they are more or less certain of the contents of a container has no bearing on their authority to search it.

To the extent there was any "anomaly" in our prior jurisprudence, the Court has "cured" it at the expense of creating a more serious paradox. For surely it is anomalous to prohibit a search of a briefcase while the owner is carrying it exposed on a public street yet to permit a search once the owner has placed the briefcase in the locked trunk of his car. One's privacy interest in one's luggage can certainly not be diminished by one's removing it from a public thoroughfare and placing it — out of sight — in a privately owned vehicle. Nor is the danger that evidence will escape increased if the luggage is in a car rather than on the street. In either location, if the police have probable cause, they are authorized to seize the luggage and to detain it until they obtain judicial approval for a search. Any line demarking an exception to the warrant requirement will appear blurred at the edges, but the Court has certainly erred if it believes that, by erasing one line and drawing another, it has drawn a clearer boundary.

The Court's statement that *Chadwick* and *Sanders* provide only "minimal protection to privacy" is also unpersuasive. Every citizen clearly has an interest in the privacy of the contents of his or her luggage, briefcase, handbag or any other container that conceals private papers and effects from public scrutiny. That privacy interest has been recognized repeatedly in cases spanning more than a century.

Under the Court's holding today, the privacy interest that protects the contents of a suitcase or a briefcase from a warrantless search when it is in public view simply vanishes when its owner climbs into a taxicab. Unquestionably the rejection of the *Sanders* line of cases by today's decision will result in a significant loss of individual privacy. . . .

The Court's suggestion that *Chadwick* and *Sanders* have created a significant burden on effective law enforcement is unsupported, inaccurate, and, in any event, an insufficient reason for creating a new exception to the warrant requirement.

Despite repeated claims that *Chadwick* and *Sanders* have "impeded effective law enforcement," the Court cites no authority for its contentions. Moreover, all evidence that does exist points to the contrary conclusion. In the years since *Ross* was decided, the Court has heard argument in 30 Fourth Amendment cases involving narcotics. In all but one, the government was the petitioner. All save two involved a search or seizure without a warrant or with a defective warrant. And, in all except three, the Court upheld the constitutionality of the search or seizure. . . .

Even if the warrant requirement does inconvenience the police to some extent, that fact does not distinguish this constitutional requirement from any other procedural protection secured by the Bill of Rights. It is merely a part of the price that our society must pay in order to preserve its freedom. . . .

NOTES AND QUESTIONS

1. In California v. Carney, 471 U.S. 386 (1985), the Court faced the question whether the automobile exception applies to a mobile home. It does. Chief Justice Burger's majority opinion justifies this conclusion by reference to "the lesser expectation of privacy resulting from its use as a readily mobile vehicle." Id., at 391. That lesser privacy expectation, in turn, "derive[s] . . . from the pervasive regulation of vehicles capable of traveling on the public highways." Id., at 392. What does that mean? How, precisely, does traffic regulation reduce one's privacy interest in the contents of one's car?

2. *Carney* raises a basic question about the automobile exception: What is its point? Is it exigency? Or is it reduced privacy expectations? Language in cases like *Carroll* suggests exigency is the problem — automobiles can move. But in *Chambers*, also discussed in *Acevedo*, the Court applied the automobile exception even though the police had already impounded the car when the search took place — the car was in police custody, and hence no longer mobile. And, of course, in *Acevedo* itself, the police clearly could have seized and held the paper bag pending the outcome of a warrant application. Exigency seems absent.

3. Which leads to the rationale the Court used in *Carney* — reduced privacy expectations. The extent of the privacy interest in cars is surely contestable, but assume for the moment the Court is right to conclude that this interest is weaker than the privacy interest in, say, houses and apartments. What does that have to do with warrants? The question whether to require a warrant is a question about *process*; the same substantive standard — probable cause — applies either way. It seems easy to understand why one would want to vary the substantive standard based on the seriousness of the privacy interest at stake. But why vary the process?

Perhaps the answer is that process determines substance — that requiring warrants effectively means mandating a tougher probable cause standard. Judges decide suppression motions after the search has happened; such motions are filed only in cases in which incriminating evidence was found. It would be natural for judges to "tilt" toward finding probable cause in such cases. After all, the police officer's suspicion was justified — he found the evidence. By contrast, magistrates decide on warrant applications before the search has taken place; they are in a better position to evaluate the officer's suspicion neutrally. Maybe, then, we actually have two probable cause standards — "probable cause plus" in warrant cases, and "probable cause minus" in nonwarrant cases. For a detailed argument along these lines, see William J. Stuntz, Warrants and Fourth Amendment Remedies, 77 Va. L. Rev. 881 (1991).

4. Imagine four searches. In the first, police search a house. In the second, police search a bag of the sort at issue in *Acevedo*, but on the street outside a car. In the third, police search the same bag, now inside a car. In the fourth, police search the glove compartment of a car.

Fourth Amendment law could, of course, treat all four searches the same, and apply the warrant requirement to each (with an exception for exigent circumstances). Or it could apply the warrant requirement to the searches that involve the more serious privacy intrusions, and exempt the police from having to get a warrant where the privacy interest is less serious. If the law chose the latter option, where would the line be drawn among these four searches?

The answer seems clear: Houses would get extra protection, and the other three searches would not. Yet that position does not win in *any* of the cases discussed here — indeed, the one time the government took that position, in *Chadwick*, the Supreme Court unanimously rejected it. And note — though the Court explicitly overrules *Sanders*, it does not overrule *Chadwick*: A warrant is still required to search Chadwick's footlocker.

5. One thing the automobile exception does is to lower the cost of searching cars. Police need not go through the hassles and incur the administrative costs of impounding containers or whole cars while waiting for a magistrate to rule on a warrant application. If they are confident of their probable cause judgment, they can search on the spot and take their chances that a judge in a suppression hearing will disagree. All of which will naturally lead police to do what they did in *Acevedo*: search the car. What would happen if the rule were otherwise — if there were no automobile exception to the warrant requirement? That would *raise* the cost of car searches, which would presumably lead police to search cars less frequently. It would also lower the relative cost of other searches — if the police have to wait for a warrant to search Acevedo's car, they might conclude that they may as well seek a warrant to search Acevedo's house as well assuming that they are uncertain where the evidence is located. Fewer car searches thus might mean more house searches. In this sense, a more protective Fourth Amendment rule for cars might actually lead to greater privacy intrusions overall.

This is a particular instance of a general point. If the police are resource constrained, anything that lowers the cost of some police tactics raises the relative cost of some others. *Acevedo*, together with other Court decisions that make searches outside homes easier to justify, may have the effect of limiting the number of searches of homes.

WYOMING v. HOUGHTON

Certiorari to the Supreme Court of Wyoming
526 U.S. 295 (1999)

JUSTICE SCALIA delivered the opinion of the Court.

This case presents the question whether police officers violate the Fourth Amendment when they search a passenger's personal belongings inside an automobile that they have probable cause to believe contains contraband.

In the early morning hours of July 23, 1995, a Wyoming Highway Patrol officer stopped an automobile for speeding and driving with a faulty brake light. There were three passengers in the front seat of the car: David Young (the driver), his girl-friend, and respondent. While questioning Young, the officer noticed a hypodermic syringe in Young's shirt pocket. He left the occupants under the supervision of two backup officers as he went to get gloves from his patrol car. Upon his return, he instructed Young to step out of the car and place the syringe on the hood. The officer then asked Young why he had a syringe; with refreshing candor, Young replied that he used it to take drugs.

At this point, the backup officers ordered the two female passengers out of the car and asked them for identification. Respondent falsely identified herself as "San-dra James" and stated that she did not have any identification. Meanwhile, in light of Young's admission, the officer searched the passenger compartment of the car for contraband. On the back seat, he found a purse, which respondent claimed as hers. He removed from the purse a wallet containing respondent's driver's license, identifying her properly as Sandra K. Houghton. When the officer asked her why she had lied about her name, she replied: "In case things went bad."

Continuing his search of the purse, the officer found a brown pouch and a black wallet-type container. Respondent denied that the former was hers, and claimed ignorance of how it came to be there; it was found to contain drug paraphernalia and a syringe with 60 ccs of methamphetamine. Respondent admitted ownership of the black container, which was also found to contain drug paraphernalia, and a syringe (which respondent acknowledged was hers) with 10 ccs of methamphetamine — an amount insufficient to support the felony conviction at issue in this case. The officer also found fresh needle-track marks on respondent's arms. He placed her under arrest.

The State of Wyoming charged respondent with felony possession of metham-phetamine in a liquid amount greater than three-tenths of a gram. After a hearing, the trial court denied her motion to suppress all evidence obtained from the purse as the fruit of a violation of the Fourth and Fourteenth Amendments. The court held that the officer had probable cause to search the car for contraband, and, by exten-sion, any containers therein that could hold such contraband. A jury convicted respondent as charged.

The Wyoming Supreme Court, by divided vote, reversed the conviction and announced the following rule:

> Generally, once probable cause is established to search a vehicle, an officer is entitled to search all containers therein which may contain the object of the search. However, if the officer knows or should know that a container is the personal effect of a passenger who is not suspected of criminal activity, then the container is outside the scope of the search unless someone had the opportunity to conceal the contraband within the personal effect to avoid detection. 956 P.2d 363, 372 (1998).

The court held that the search of respondent's purse violated the Fourth and Four-teenth Amendments because the officer "knew or should have known that the purse did not belong to the driver, but to one of the passengers," and because "there was no probable cause to search the passengers' personal effects and no reason to believe that contraband had been placed within the purse." Ibid. . . .

The Fourth Amendment protects "[t]he right of the people to be secure in their persons, houses, papers, and effects, against unreasonable searches and seizures." In determining whether a particular governmental action violates this provision, we inquire first whether the action was regarded as an unlawful search or seizure under the common law when the Amendment was framed. See Wilson v. Arkansas, 514 U.S. 927, 931 (1995); California v. Hodari D., 499 U.S. 621, 624 (1991). Where that inquiry yields no answer, we must evaluate the search or seizure under traditional standards of reasonableness by assessing, on the one hand, the degree to which it intrudes upon an individual's privacy and, on the other, the degree to which it is needed for the promotion of legitimate governmental interests.

It is uncontested in the present case that the police officers had probable cause to believe there were illegal drugs in the car. Carroll v. United States, 267 U.S. 132 (1925), similarly involved the warrantless search of a car that law enforcement officials had probable cause to believe contained contraband — in that case, bootleg liquor. The Court concluded that the Framers would have regarded such a search as reasonable in light of legislation enacted by Congress from 1789 through 1799 — as well as subsequent legislation from the founding era and beyond — that empowered customs officials to search any ship or vessel without a warrant if they had probable cause to believe that it contained goods subject to a duty. Id., at 150-153. Thus, the Court held that "contraband goods concealed and illegally transported in an automobile or other vehicle may be searched for without a warrant" where probable cause exists. *Carroll*, supra, at 153.

We have furthermore read the historical evidence to show that the Framers would have regarded as reasonable (if there was probable cause) the warrantless search of containers *within* an automobile. In [United States v. Ross, 456 U.S. 798 (1982)], we upheld as reasonable the warrantless search of a paper bag and leather pouch found in the trunk of the defendant's car by officers who had probable cause to believe that the trunk contained drugs. Justice Stevens, writing for the Court, observed:

> It is noteworthy that the early legislation on which the Court relied in *Carroll* concerned the enforcement of laws imposing duties on imported merchandise. . . . Presumably such merchandise was shipped then in containers of various kinds, just as it is today. Since Congress had authorized warrantless searches of vessels and beasts for imported merchandise, it is inconceivable that it intended a customs officer to obtain a warrant for every package discovered during the search; certainly Congress intended customs officers to open shipping containers when necessary and not merely to examine the exterior of cartons or boxes in which smuggled goods might be concealed. During virtually the entire history of our country — whether contraband was transported in a horse-drawn carriage, a 1921 roadster, or a modern automobile — it has been assumed that a lawful search of a vehicle would include a search of any container that might conceal the object of the search. Id., at 820, n. 26.

. . . To be sure, there was no passenger in *Ross*, and it was not claimed that the package in the trunk belonged to anyone other than the driver. Even so, if the rule of law that *Ross* announced were limited to contents belonging to the driver, or contents other than those belonging to passengers, one would have expected that substantial limitation to be expressed. And, more importantly, one would have expected that limitation to be apparent in the historical evidence that formed the basis for *Ross*'s holding. In fact, however, nothing in the statutes *Ross* relied upon, or in the practice under those statutes, would except from authorized warrantless search packages belonging to passengers on the suspect ship, horse-drawn carriage, or automobile.

Finally, we must observe that the analytical principle underlying the rule announced in *Ross* is fully consistent — as respondent's proposal is not — with the balance of our Fourth Amendment jurisprudence. *Ross* concluded from the historical evidence that the permissible scope of a warrantless car search "is defined by the object of the search and the places in which there is probable cause to believe that it may be found." 456 U.S., at 824. The same principle is reflected in an earlier case involving the constitutionality of a search warrant directed at premises belonging to one who is not suspected of any crime: "The critical element in a reasonable search is not that the owner of the property is suspected of crime but that there is reasonable cause to believe that the specific 'things' to be searched for and seized are located on the property to which entry is sought." Zurcher v. Stanford Daily, 436 U.S. 547, 556 (1978). This statement was illustrated by citation and description of *Carroll,* 267 U.S., at 158-159, 167.

In sum, neither *Ross* itself nor the historical evidence it relied upon admits of a distinction among packages or containers based on ownership. When there is probable cause to search for contraband in a car, it is reasonable for police officers — like customs officials in the founding era — to examine packages and containers without a showing of individualized probable cause for each one. A passenger's personal belongings, just like the driver's belongings or containers attached to the car like a glove compartment, are "in" the car, and the officer has probable cause to search for contraband *in* the car.

Even if the historical evidence . . . were thought to be equivocal, we would find that the balancing of the relative interests weighs decidedly in favor of allowing searches of a passenger's belongings. Passengers, no less than drivers, possess a reduced expectation of privacy with regard to the property that they transport in cars, which "trave[l] public thoroughfares," Cardwell v. Lewis, 417 U.S. 583, 590 (1974), "seldom serv[e] as . . . the repository of personal effects," ibid., are subjected to police stop and examination to enforce "pervasive" governmental controls "[a]s an everyday occurrence," South Dakota v. Opperman, 428 U.S. 364, 368 (1976), and, finally, are exposed to traffic accidents that may render all their contents open to public scrutiny.

In this regard — the degree of intrusiveness upon personal privacy and indeed even personal dignity — the two cases the Wyoming Supreme Court found dispositive differ substantially from the package search at issue here. United States v. Di Re, 332 U.S. 581 (1948), held that probable cause to search a car did not justify a body search of a passenger. And Ybarra v. Illinois, 444 U.S. 85 (1979), held that a search warrant for a tavern and its bartender did not permit body searches of all the bar's patrons. These cases turned on the unique, significantly heightened protection afforded against searches of one's person. "Even a limited search of the outer clothing . . . constitutes a severe, though brief, intrusion upon cherished personal security, and it must surely be an annoying, frightening, and perhaps humiliating experience." Terry v. Ohio, 392 U.S. 1, 24-25 (1968). Such traumatic consequences are not to be expected when the police examine an item of personal property found in a car.

Whereas the passenger's privacy expectations are, as we have described, considerably diminished, the governmental interests at stake are substantial. Effective law enforcement would be appreciably impaired without the ability to search a passenger's personal belongings when there is reason to believe contraband or evidence of criminal wrongdoing is hidden in the car. As in all car-search cases, the "ready mobility" of an automobile creates a risk that the evidence or contraband will be permanently lost while a warrant is obtained. California v. Carney, 471 U.S. 386, 390 (1985). In addition, a car passenger—unlike the unwitting tavern patron in *Ybarra*—will often be engaged in a common enterprise with the driver, and have the same interest in concealing the fruits or the evidence of their wrongdoing. A criminal might be able to hide contraband in a passenger's belongings as readily as in other containers in the car—perhaps even surreptitiously, without the passenger's knowledge or permission. (This last possibility provided the basis for respondent's defense at trial; she testified that most of the seized contraband must have been placed in her purse by her traveling companions at one or another of various times, including the time she was "half asleep" in the car.)

To be sure, these factors favoring a search will not always be present, but the balancing of interests must be conducted with an eye to the generality of cases. To require that the investigating officer have positive reason to believe that the passenger and driver were engaged in a common enterprise, or positive reason to believe that the driver had time and occasion to conceal the item in the passenger's belongings, surreptitiously or with friendly permission, is to impose requirements so seldom met that a "passenger's property" rule would dramatically reduce the ability to find and seize contraband and evidence of crime. Of course these requirements would not attach (under the Wyoming Supreme Court's rule) until the police officer knows or has reason to know that the container belongs to a passenger. But once a "passenger's property" exception to car searches became widely known, one would expect passenger-confederates to claim everything as their own. And one would anticipate a bog of litigation—in the form of both civil lawsuits and motions to suppress in criminal trials—involving such questions as whether the officer should have believed a passenger's claim of ownership, whether he should have inferred ownership from various objective factors, whether he had probable cause to believe that the passenger was a confederate, or to believe that the driver might have introduced the contraband into the package with or without the passenger's knowledge. When balancing the competing interests, our determinations of "reasonableness" under the Fourth Amendment must take account of these practical realities. We think they militate in favor of the needs of law enforcement, and against a personal-privacy interest that is ordinarily weak. . . .

We hold that police officers with probable cause to search a car may inspect passengers' belongings found in the car that are capable of concealing the object of the search. The judgment of the Wyoming Supreme Court is reversed.

[Justice Breyer's concurring opinion is omitted.]

JUSTICE STEVENS, with whom JUSTICE SOUTER and JUSTICE GINSBURG join, dissenting.

. . . In all of our prior cases applying the automobile exception to the Fourth Amendment's warrant requirement, either the defendant was the operator of the vehicle and in custody of the object of the search, or no question was raised as to the defendant's ownership or custody. In the only automobile case confronting the search of a passenger defendant—United States v. Di Re, 332 U.S. 581 (1948)—the Court held that the exception to the warrant requirement did not apply. Id., at 583-587 (addressing searches of the passenger's pockets and the space between his shirt and underwear, both of which uncovered counterfeit fuel rations). In *Di Re*, as here, the information prompting the search directly implicated the driver, not the passenger. . . . Moreover, unlike the Court, I think it quite plain that the search of a passenger's purse or briefcase involves an intrusion on privacy that may be just as serious as was the intrusion in *Di Re*. . . .

Nor am I persuaded that the mere spatial association between a passenger and a driver provides an acceptable basis for presuming that they are partners in crime or for ignoring privacy interests in a purse. Whether or not the Fourth Amendment required a warrant to search Houghton's purse, at the very least the trooper in this case had to have probable cause to believe that her purse contained contraband. The Wyoming Supreme Court concluded that he did not.

Finally, in my view, the State's legitimate interest in effective law enforcement does not outweigh the privacy concerns at issue.[3] I am as confident in a police officer's ability to apply a rule requiring a warrant or individualized probable cause to search belongings that are — as in this case — obviously owned by and in the custody of a passenger as is the Court in a "passenger-confederate[']s" ability to circumvent the rule. Certainly the ostensible clarity of the Court's rule is attractive. But that virtue is insufficient justification for its adoption. Moreover, a rule requiring a warrant or individualized probable cause to search passenger belongings is every bit as simple as the Court's rule; it simply protects more privacy. . . .

NOTES AND QUESTIONS

1. After California v. Acevedo, supra, authority to search an automobile includes authority to search containers found within the automobile. *Houghton* asks what happens when this rule is applied to containers that are attached to people.

Can an officer search your jacket pockets if you're a passenger in a car and the officer is entitled to search the car? Does the answer depend on whether you're wearing the jacket at the time the car is stopped? In United States v. Di Re, 332 U.S. 581 (1948), a case cited by both the *Houghton* majority and dissent, the Court held that searches of a passenger's clothing were not included within a lawful car search. In *Houghton*, the Court holds that a search of a passenger's purse *is* included within a lawful car search. Apparently, the hypothetical jacket pocket search *does* turn on whether the passenger is wearing the jacket. If the purse is slung around the passenger's shoulder, does that change the result in *Houghton*? If a passenger is holding a paper bag in his lap, is the bag treated like an article of clothing (because it is attached to the passenger) or like a container? Does Houghton tell the police how to answer these questions?

2. Does *Houghton* make sense? Surely the privacy interest in purses or jacket pockets is the same whether or not those articles are being worn by passengers when they

---

3. To my knowledge, we have never restricted ourselves to a two-step Fourth Amendment approach wherein the privacy and governmental interests at stake must be considered only if 18th-century common law "yields no answer." . . . In a later discussion, the Court does attempt to address the contemporary privacy and governmental interests at issue in cases of this nature. Either the majority is unconvinced by its own recitation of the historical materials, or it has determined that considering additional factors is appropriate in any event. The Court does not admit the former; and of course the latter, standing alone, would not establish uncertainty in the common law as the prerequisite to looking beyond history in Fourth Amendment cases.

are searched. Then again, does any *other* line make sense? As the majority notes, it would be hard for the police to have to make judgments about what belonged to whom whenever a car with several passengers is searched.

3. The most important thing about *Houghton* may be the Court's methodology. Justice Scalia, speaking for a Court majority, states that Fourth Amendment analysis follows two steps: First, one asks "whether the action was regarded as an unlawful search or seizure under the common law when the Amendment was framed." Only if that inquiry yields no clear answer does one go to the second step, which consists of the familiar balance of individual privacy and law enforcement need. Does this sound like the analysis followed in other Fourth Amendment cases? Should a similar analysis apply to the question whether the Fourth Amendment should be enforced through an exclusionary rule — a remedy unknown to the common law in 1791? If not, why not?

Houghton is one more piece of evidence of a growing judicial interest in the original understanding as a guide to decision in search and seizure cases. What are the merits of that approach here?

4. A final thought. Could the officers in *Houghton* have arrested Houghton even before searching her purse? Recall that it was uncontested in *Houghton* that the police had probable cause to believe there were illegal drugs in the car. Now consider Maryland v. Pringle, 540 U.S. 366 (2003). In this case, a Baltimore police officer stopped a Nissan Maxima for speeding. There were three occupants in the vehicle, including Pringle, who was the front-seat passenger. When the driver, one Partlow, opened the glove compartment to retrieve the vehicle registration, the officer noticed a large amount of rolled-up money inside the glove compartment. Partlow consented to a search of the car, which yielded $763 from the glove compartment and five plastic glassine baggies containing cocaine. The officer questioned all three men at the scene about the ownership of the drugs, but the men offered no information. All three were arrested.

At the station house, Pringle confessed that the cocaine belonged to him. He later argued that his confession should be suppressed because the officer who had arrested him lacked probable cause. The Supreme Court unanimously disagreed:

> In this case, Pringle was one of three men riding in a Nissan Maxima at 3:16 a.m. There was $763 of rolled-up cash in the glove compartment directly in front of Pringle. Five plastic glassine baggies of cocaine were behind the back-seat armrest and accessible to all three men. Upon questioning, the three men failed to offer any information with respect to the ownership of the cocaine or the money.
>
> We think it an entirely reasonable inference from these facts that any or all three of the occupants had knowledge of, and exercised dominion and control over, the cocaine. Thus a reasonable officer could conclude that there was probable cause to believe Pringle committed the crime of possession of cocaine, either solely or jointly.
>
> Pringle's attempt to characterize this case as a guilt-by-association case is unavailing. His reliance on Ybarra v. Illinois, [444 U.S. 85 (1979)] . . . is misplaced. In *Ybarra*, police officers obtained a warrant to search a tavern and its bartender for evidence of possession of a controlled substance. Upon entering the tavern, the officers conducted patdown searches of the customers present in the tavern, including Ybarra. Inside a cigarette pack retrieved from Ybarra's pocket, an officer found six tinfoil packets containing heroin. We stated:
>
> > [A] person's mere propinquity to others independently suspected of criminal activity does not, without more, give rise to probable cause to search that person. Where the standard is

> probable cause, a search or seizure of a person must be supported by probable cause particularized with respect to that person. This requirement cannot be undercut or avoided by simply pointing to the fact that coincidentally there exists probable cause to search or seize another or to search the premises where the person may happen to be.

444 U.S., at 91.

We held that the search warrant did not permit body searches of all of the tavern's patrons and that the police could not pat down the patrons for weapons, absent individualized suspicion. Id., at 92.

This case is quite different from *Ybarra*. Pringle and his two companions were in a relatively small automobile, not a public tavern. In Wyoming v. Houghton, 526 U.S. 295 (1999), we noted that "a car passenger — unlike the unwitting tavern patron in *Ybarra* —will often be engaged in a common enterprise with the driver, and have the same interest in concealing the fruits or the evidence of their wrongdoing." Id., at 304-305. Here we think it was reasonable for the officer to infer a common enterprise among the three men. The quantity of drugs and cash in the car indicated the likelihood of drug dealing, an enterprise to which a dealer would be unlikely to admit an innocent person with the potential to furnish evidence against him.

Do you think, similarly, that the officers in *Houghton* had probable cause to believe she possessed the drugs in the car — even before they searched her purse? Why or why not?

d. Arrests

The central object of the Fourth Amendment is to protect the individual's "right to be let alone — the most comprehensive of rights and the right most valued by civilized men." Olmsted v. United States, 277 U.S. 438, 478 (1928) (Brandeis, J., dissenting). It would seem to follow that, of all the police behaviors that Fourth Amendment law regulates, arrests should be subject to the most stringent legal standards. "The invasion and disruption of a man's life and privacy which stem from his arrest are ordinarily far greater than the relatively minor intrusions attending a search of his premises." Chimel v. California, 395 U.S. 752, 776 (1969) (White, J., dissenting). The arrest is likely to be an "awesome and frightening" experience for the arrestee. See ALI Model Code of Pre-Arraignment Procedure, section 120.1, Commentary at 290-291 (1975). Professor Schroeder has described some of the reasons:

> Any arrest has a profound and long-lasting effect on the arrestee. Even if an arrest is for a minor offense, and charges against the arrestee are ultimately dropped or the arrestee is acquitted, the records of the arrest probably will be retained and disseminated. Moreover, widespread public feeling that "where there's smoke, there's fire" often leaves a cloud of suspicion hanging over an arrestee even if no conviction follows. The result will often be lost employment opportunities and future law enforcement scrutiny.
>
> A custodial arrest is an especially "awesome and frightening" experience. The arrestee is abruptly constrained and usually searched, even if the arrest is for a minor offense. He is then forcibly taken to an unfamiliar place, booked, fingerprinted, photographed, searched more extensively, and held in jail, possibly under unsanitary and unsafe conditions, until, and unless, he can obtain his release. The arrestee may suffer emotional distress and public humiliation, and may lose contact with family and friends. He may lose time from work and will probably be required to retain an attorney

and spend money on bail. . . . Because the consequences of an arrest are so severe, substantial civil damages have been awarded to persons improperly arrested for minor offenses.

William A. Schroeder, Warrantless Misdemeanor Arrests and the Fourth Amendment, 58 Mo. L. Rev. 771 (1993) (footnote omitted).

The legal rules that govern arrests historically have been derived from three distinct but related sources: the common law, statutes, and the Constitution. A complete understanding of arrests thus requires an examination of all three sources. At common law, arrests for misdemeanors generally were prohibited without a warrant. The main exception was for breaches of the peace[14] committed in the arrestor's[15] presence,[16] as long as the arrest was made at the time of or shortly after the offense. For felonies, the common law rule was broader: Warrantless arrests were generally allowed, so long as the arrestor had "reasonable grounds" to believe that a felony had been committed and that the arrestee had committed it. "Reasonable grounds" meant something very much like the modern concept of "probable cause." See Draper v. United States, 358 U.S. 307, 310, n. 3 (1959).

Over time, statutes gradually expanded the common law rules of arrest, at least as applied to arrests made by police officers.[17] For misdemeanors, most modern statutes authorize arrests without a warrant whenever the offense is committed within the officer's presence, or for certain offenses even when committed outside the officer's presence (such as domestic abuse or violations of protective orders), or for any misdemeanor offenses under certain factual circumstances (such as when the suspect is attempting to flee or to destroy evidence). This authority to arrest without a warrant for misdemeanors generally is not limited to breaches of the peace, although such arrests still must be made promptly after the offense. For felonies, most modern statutes generally reflect the common law rule and authorize arrests regardless whether the crime was committed in the officer's presence.

As far as the Constitution is concerned, the first and most important rule is that all custodial arrests must be based on probable cause. See Dunaway v. New York, 442 U.S. 200 (1979). The constitutional rule with respect to warrants, however, is not so clear. In at least some situations, police officers may arrest without a warrant. The leading case is United States v. Watson, 423 U.S. 411 (1976). Federal postal inspectors received a reliable tip that Watson was in possession of stolen credit cards. The inspectors persuaded the tipster (who had worked with Watson in the past to profit from such credit cards) to arrange a meeting with Watson at a restaurant. At the restaurant, the tipster signaled the inspectors that Watson did, indeed, possess stolen

14. But see Atwater v. Lago Vista, 532 U.S. 318 (2001), infra, in which the Court concludes that the common law rule for misdemeanor arrests was not strictly limited to breaches of the peace.

15. Notice that the "arrestor" could be an ordinary citizen as well as a police officer. Indeed, these common law rules of arrest developed at a time when police forces did not yet exist.

16. "In the arrestor's presence" generally meant that the arrestor must have learned of the offense through one or more of the senses. Some jurisdictions also allowed a police officer to rely on sensory knowledge acquired by another police officer.

17. Today, many statutes continue to authorize arrests by private persons in at least some situations. Such authority often has been expanded beyond its common-law scope, although it is still generally less extensive than the authority granted to police officers. See, e.g., 725 Ill. Comp. Stat. Ann. §5/107-3 (Smith-Hurd 1993) ("Any person may arrest another when he has reasonable grounds to believe that an offense other than an ordinance violation is being committed."); Utah Code Ann. §77-7-3 (1990) ("A private person may arrest another: (1) For a public offense committed or attempted in his presence; or (2) When a felony has been committed and he has reasonable cause to believe the person arrested has committed it.").

credit cards. The inspectors moved in and arrested Watson without a warrant (as they were authorized to do by the relevant statutes and regulations of the U.S. Postal Service), but they found no credit cards on Watson's person. After receiving Watson's consent to search his nearby car, the police found two stolen credit cards under the car's floor mat. Watson was convicted of two counts of possessing stolen mail, and subsequently challenged, under the Fourth Amendment, the admission into evidence of the credit cards.[18]

According to the Court in *Watson*:

> Contrary to the Court of Appeals' view, Watson's arrest was not invalid because executed without a warrant. Title 18 U.S.C. §3061(a)(3) expressly empowers the Board of Governors of the Postal Service to authorize Postal Service officers and employees "performing duties related to the inspection of postal matters" to "make arrests without warrant for felonies cognizable under the laws of the United States if they have reasonable grounds to believe that the person to be arrested has committed or is committing such a felony." . . .
>
> . . . Section 3061 represents a judgment by Congress that it is not unreasonable under the Fourth Amendment for postal inspectors to arrest without a warrant provided they have probable cause to do so. This was not an isolated or quixotic judgment of the legislative branch. Other federal law enforcement officers have been expressly authorized by statute for many years to make felony arrests on probable cause but without a warrant. This is true of United States marshals, 18 U.S.C. §3053, and of agents of the Federal Bureau of Investigation, 18 U.S.C. §3052; the Drug Enforcement Administration, 84 Stat. 1273, 21 U.S.C. §878; the Secret Service, 18 U.S.C. §3056(a); and the Customs Service, 26 U.S.C. §7607.
>
> Because there is a "strong presumption of constitutionality due to an Act of Congress, especially when it turns on what is 'reasonable,'" "[o]bviously the Court should be reluctant to decide that a search thus authorized by Congress was unreasonable and that the Act was therefore unconstitutional." United States v. Di Re, 332 U.S. 581, 585 (1948). . . .
>
> The cases construing the Fourth Amendment . . . reflect the ancient common-law rule that a peace officer was permitted to arrest without a warrant for a misdemeanor or felony committed in his presence as well as for a felony not committed in his presence if there was reasonable ground for making the arrest. 10 Halsbury's Laws of England 344-345 (3d ed. 1955); 4 W. Blackstone, Commentaries *292; 1 J. Stephen, A History of the Criminal Law of England 193 (1883); 2 M. Hale, Pleas of the Crown *72-74; Wilgus, Arrest Without a Warrant, 22 Mich. L. Rev. 541, 547-550, 686-688 (1924); Samuel v. Payne, 1 Doug. 359, 99 Eng. Rep. 230 (K.B. 1780); Beckwith v. Philby, 6 Barn. & Cress. 635, 108 Eng. Rep. 585 (K.B. 1827). . . .
>
> The balance struck by the common law in generally authorizing felony arrests on probable cause, but without a warrant, has survived substantially intact. It appears in almost all of the States in the form of express statutory authorization. In 1963, the American Law Institute undertook the task of formulating a model statute governing

---

18. The Court of Appeals' opinion in *Watson* did not state clearly whether the Fourth Amendment was implicated because the credit cards were the "fruits" of an illegal arrest, or because the illegal arrest tainted Watson's subsequent consent to the search of his car. The Supreme Court concluded that this ambiguity was immaterial, since the outcome of the case — under either theory — turned on the constitutionality of the arrest.

Incidentally, Watson represents the typical way that issues involving arrest warrants get litigated. Even if an arrest is improperly made without a warrant, the custody itself is not unlawful, and the resulting conviction therefore does not become invalid. See United States v. Crews, 445 U.S. 463 (1980); Gerstein v. Pugh, 420 U.S. 103 (1975). But a person who has been improperly arrested without a warrant may be able to challenge the admission of any evidence that was obtained as a result of the arrest.

police powers and practice in criminal law enforcement and related aspects of pretrial procedure. In 1975, after years of discussion, A Model Code of Pre-arraignment Procedure was proposed. Among its provisions was §120.1 which authorizes an officer to take a person into custody if the officer has reasonable cause to believe that the person to be arrested has committed a felony, or has committed a misdemeanor or petty misdemeanor in his presence. The commentary to this section said: "The Code thus adopts the traditional and almost universal standard for arrest without a warrant."

This is the rule Congress has long directed its principal law enforcement officers to follow. Congress has plainly decided against conditioning warrantless arrest power on proof of exigent circumstances. Law enforcement officers may find it wise to seek arrest warrants where practicable to do so, and their judgments about probable cause may be more readily accepted where backed by a warrant issued by a magistrate. But we decline to transform this judicial preference into a constitutional rule when the judgment of the Nation and Congress has for so long been to authorize warrantless public arrests on probable cause rather than to encumber criminal prosecutions with endless litigation with respect to the existence of exigent circumstances, whether it was practicable to get a warrant, whether the suspect was about to flee, and the like. . . .

Because our judgment is that Watson's arrest comported with the Fourth Amendment, Watson's consent to the search of his car was not the product of an illegal arrest. To the extent that the issue of the voluntariness of Watson's consent was resolved on the premise that his arrest was illegal, the Court of Appeals was also in error.

Justice Powell, in concurrence, noted the "anomaly" created by the Court's decision:

Since the Fourth Amendment speaks equally to both searches and seizures, and since an arrest, the taking hold of one's person, is quintessentially a seizure, it would seem that the constitutional provision should impose the same limitations upon arrests that it does upon searches. Indeed, as an abstract matter an argument can be made that the restrictions upon arrest perhaps should be greater. A search may cause only annoyance and temporary inconvenience to the law-abiding citizen, assuming more serious dimension only when it turns up evidence of criminality. An arrest, however, is a serious personal intrusion regardless of whether the person seized is guilty or innocent. Although an arrestee cannot be held for a significant period without some neutral determination that there are grounds to do so, see [Gerstein v. Pugh, 420 U.S. 103, 113 (1975)], no decision that he should go free can come quickly enough to erase the invasion of his privacy that already will have occurred. Logic therefore would seem to dictate that arrests be subject to the warrant requirement at least to the same extent as searches.

But logic sometimes must defer to history and experience. . . . There is no historical evidence that the Framers or proponents of the Fourth Amendment, outspokenly opposed to the infamous general warrants and writs of assistance, were at all concerned about warrantless arrests by local constables and other peace officers. . . .

Moreover, a constitutional rule permitting felony arrests only with a warrant or in exigent circumstances could severely hamper effective law enforcement. Good police practice often requires postponing an arrest, even after probable cause has been established, in order to place the suspect under surveillance or otherwise develop further evidence necessary to prove guilt to a jury. Under the holding of the Court of Appeals such additional investigative work could imperil the entire prosecution. Should the officers fail to obtain a warrant initially, and later be required by unforeseen circumstances to arrest immediately with no chance to procure a last-minute warrant, they would risk a court decision that the subsequent exigency did not excuse their failure to get a warrant in the interim since they first developed probable cause. If the officers attempted to meet such a contingency by procuring a warrant as soon as they had probable cause and then merely held it during their subsequent investigation, they would risk a court decision that the warrant had grown stale by the time it was used.[5] Law enforcement personnel caught in this squeeze could ensure validity of their arrests only by obtaining a warrant and arresting as soon as probable cause existed, thereby foreclosing the possibility of gathering vital additional evidence from the suspect's continued actions.

Justice Marshall wrote the dissent:

The Court . . . relies on the English common-law rule of arrest and the many state and federal statutes following it. There are two serious flaws in this approach. First, as a matter of factual analysis, the substance of the ancient common-law rule provides no support for the far-reaching modern rule that the Court fashions on its model. Second, as a matter of doctrine, the longstanding existence of a Government practice does not immunize the practice from scrutiny under the mandate of our Constitution.

The common-law rule was indeed as the Court states it: "[A] peace officer was permitted to arrest without a warrant for a misdemeanor or felony committed in his presence as well as for a felony not committed in his presence if there was reasonable ground for making the arrest." To apply the rule blindly today, however, makes as much sense as attempting to interpret Hamlet's admonition to Ophelia, "Get thee to a nunnery, go," without understanding the meaning of Hamlet's words in the context of their age.[3] For the fact is that a felony at common law and a felony today bear only slight resemblance, with the result that the relevance of the common-law rule of arrest to the modern interpretation of our Constitution is minimal.

. . . Only the most serious crimes were felonies at common law, and many crimes now classified as felonies under federal or state law were treated as misdemeanors. [NOTE — This includes, among many others, such crimes as assault with intent to murder or rape, escape from lawful arrest, kidnapping, mayhem, obstructing justice, and perjury. — EDS.] . . . To make an arrest for any of these crimes at common law, the police officer was required to obtain a warrant, unless the crime was committed in his presence. Since many of these same crimes are commonly classified as felonies today, however, under the Court's holding a warrant is no longer needed to make such arrests, a result in contravention of the common law.

Thus the lesson of the common law, and those courts in this country that have accepted its rule, is an ambiguous one. Applied in its original context, the common-law rule would allow the warrantless arrest of some, but not all, of those we call felons today. Accordingly, the Court is simply historically wrong when it tells us that "[t]he balance struck by the common law in generally authorizing felony arrests on probable cause, but without a warrant, has survived substantially intact." . . . Indeed, the only clear lesson of history is contrary to the one the Court draws: the common law considered the arrest warrant far more important than today's decision leaves it.

I do not mean by this that a modern warrant requirement should apply only to arrests precisely analogous to common-law misdemeanors, and be inapplicable to analogues of common-law felonies. Rather, the point is simply that the Court's unblinking

5. The probable cause to support issuance of an arrest warrant normally would not grow stale as easily as that which supports a warrant to search a particular place for particular objects. This is true because once there is probable cause to believe that someone is a felon the passage of time often will bring new supporting evidence. But in some cases the original grounds supporting the warrant could be disproved by subsequent investigation that at the same time turns up wholly new evidence supporting probable cause on a different theory. In those cases the warrant could be stale because based upon discredited information.

3. Nunnery was Elizabethan slang for house of prostitution. 7 Oxford English Dictionary 264 (1933).

literalism cannot replace analysis of the constitutional interests involved. While we can learn from the common law, the ancient rule does not provide a simple answer directly transferable to our system. . . .

My Brother Powell concludes: "Logic . . . would seem to dictate that arrests be subject to the warrant requirement at least to the same extent as searches." I agree. . . .

Surely there is no reason to place greater trust in the partisan assessment of a police officer that there is probable cause for an arrest than in his determination that probable cause exists for a search. . . .

We come then to the [question] whether a warrant requirement would unduly burden legitimate law enforcement interests. . . .

The Government's assertion that a warrant requirement would impose an intolerable burden stems, in large part, from the specious supposition that procurement of an arrest warrant would be necessary as soon as probable cause ripens. [But t]here is no requirement that a search warrant be obtained the moment police have probable cause to search. The rule is only that present probable cause be shown and a warrant obtained before a search is undertaken. The same rule should obtain for arrest warrants, where it may even make more sense. Certainly, there is less need for prompt procurement of a warrant in the arrest situation. Unlike probable cause to search, probable cause to arrest, once formed, will continue to exist for the indefinite future, at least if no intervening exculpatory facts come to light.

This sensible approach obviates most of the difficulties that have been suggested with an arrest warrant rule. Police would not have to cut their investigation short the moment they obtain probable cause to arrest, nor would undercover agents be forced suddenly to terminate their work and forfeit their covers. Moreover, if in the course of the continued police investigation exigent circumstances develop that demand an immediate arrest, the arrest may be made without fear of unconstitutionality, so long as the exigency was unanticipated and not used to avoid the arrest warrant requirement. Likewise, if in the course of the continued investigation police uncover evidence tying the suspect to another crime, they may immediately arrest him for that crime if exigency demands it, and still be in full conformity with the warrant rule. This is why the arrest in this case was not improper. Other than where police attempt to evade the warrant requirement, the rule would invalidate an arrest only in the obvious situation: where police, with probable cause but without exigent circumstances, set out to arrest a suspect. Such an arrest must be void, . . . otherwise the warrant requirement would be reduced to a toothless prescription. . . .

Thus, the practical reasons marshaled against an arrest warrant requirement are unimpressive. If anything, the virtual nonexistence of a staleness problem suggests that such a requirement would be less burdensome for police than the search warrant rule. . . . Thus, I believe the proper result is application of the warrant requirement, as it has developed in the search context, to all arrests.

NOTES ON THE SCOPE OF THE ARREST POWER

1. In County of Riverside v. McLaughlin, 500 U.S. 44 (1991), the Court held that a defendant arrested without a warrant and held in custody must receive, within 48 hours, a judicial determination of whether his arrest met the probable cause standard. The Court added:

This is not to say that the probable cause determination in a particular case passes constitutional muster simply because it is provided within 48 hours. Such a hearing may nonetheless violate [the Fourth Amendment] if the arrested individual can prove that his or her probable cause determination was delayed unreasonably. Examples of unreasonable delay are delays for the purpose of gathering additional evidence to justify the arrest, a delay motivated by ill will against the arrested individual, or delay for delay's sake. In evaluating whether the delay in a particular case is unreasonable, however, courts must allow a substantial degree of flexibility. Courts cannot ignore the often unavoidable delays in transporting arrested persons from one facility to another, handling late-night bookings where no magistrate is readily available, obtaining the presence of an arresting officer who may be busy processing other suspects or securing the premises of an arrest, and other practical realities.

Id., at 56-57. *Watson* raises potentially serious concerns about police arresting defendants without any judicial review. Does *McLaughlin* put those concerns to rest?

2. Justice Powell's concurrence and Justice Marshall's dissent debate the administrability of a warrant requirement for arrests. Who wins the debate? Staleness seems a nonissue: Either the suspect committed the crime or he didn't; that fact will not change — unlike searches, for the location of evidence *can* change while police are waiting to search. As Justice Marshall notes, precisely because of this point a warrant requirement would seem *more* administrable in arrest cases than in search cases.

So why not require arrest warrants? Aren't arrests at least as important as, say, house searches? Perhaps *Watson* suggests that, in the eyes of the law, the answer is no. Certainly, after *Watson*, it seems fair to say that privacy interests receive more Fourth Amendment protection than liberty interests. At the least, that hierarchy of protection is contestable. And it may have significant distributive implications:

> Privacy, in Fourth Amendment terms, is something that exists only in certain types of spaces; not surprisingly, the law protects it only where it exists. Rich people have more access to those spaces than poor people; they therefore enjoy more legal protection. That is not true of some other interests Fourth Amendment law protects. Thus, to the extent the law focuses on privacy rather than, say, the interest in avoiding police harassment or discrimination, it shifts something valuable — legal protection — from poorer suspects to wealthier ones.

William J. Stuntz, The Distribution of Fourth Amendment Privacy, 67 Geo. Wash. L. Rev. 1265, 1266-1267 (1999). Is this an argument for overturning *Watson*?

3. At one point in *Watson*, the Court suggests that a contrary rule would "encumber criminal prosecutions with endless litigation with respect to the existence of exigent circumstances, whether it was practicable to get a warrant, whether the suspect was about to flee, and the like." This may be a serious concern. If exigent circumstances were a condition of a valid warrantless arrest, there would presumably be a great deal of litigation about just what circumstances are exigent — much more than one now sees, if only because there are vastly more warrantless arrests than there are warrantless searches where the government relies on exigency. Courts might find themselves swamped — there are roughly 14 million arrests each year, see Sourcebook of Criminal Justice Statistics Online, tbl. 4.1.2008, http://www.albany.edu/sourcebook/), and the large majority of them happen outside homes.

4. *Watson* plainly allows warrantless arrests outside homes. What about arrests *inside* homes? Four years after *Watson*, in Payton v. New York, 445 U.S. 573 (1980), the Court struck down a New York statute that authorized warrantless entries into private homes for the purpose of making felony arrests. The Court concluded that,

if warrants were necessary to look for property in a private home, warrants should be necessary to look for people as well:

> The simple language of the Amendment applies equally to seizures of persons and to seizures of property. Our analysis in this case may therefore properly commence with rules that have been well established in Fourth Amendment litigation involving tangible items. As the Court reiterated just a few years ago, the "physical entry of the home is the chief evil against which the wording of the Fourth Amendment is directed." United States v. United States District Court, 407 U.S. 297, 313. And we have long adhered to the view that the warrant procedure minimizes the danger of needless intrusions of that sort.

Id., at 585-586. Interestingly, the Court did *not* require the use of *search* warrants:

> . . . [W]e note the State's suggestion that only a search warrant based on probable cause to believe the suspect is at home at a given time can adequately protect the privacy interests at stake, and since such a warrant requirement is manifestly impractical, there need be no warrant of any kind. We find this ingenious argument unpersuasive. It is true that an arrest warrant requirement may afford less protection than a search warrant requirement, but it will suffice to interpose the magistrate's determination of probable cause between the zealous officer and the citizen. If there is sufficient evidence of a citizen's participation in a felony to persuade a judicial officer that his arrest is justified, it is constitutionally reasonable to require him to open his doors to the officers of the law. Thus, for Fourth Amendment purposes, an arrest warrant founded on probable cause implicitly carries with it the limited authority to enter a dwelling in which the suspect lives when there is reason to believe the suspect is within.

Id., at 602-603. Note the last clause: Presumably, police cannot get an arrest warrant, wait until the suspect has left home, and then break into and search the home, using the warrant as authority for the entry.

5. Steagald v. United States, 451 U.S. 204 (1981), involved a twist on *Payton*. In *Steagald*, officers had an arrest warrant for one Ricky Lyons; an informant's tip had reported that Lyons could be found at Steagald's house. Officers went to Steagald's house and searched it; they did not find Lyons but did find a substantial quantity of cocaine. The question was whether an arrest warrant justified the search of the home of someone other than the arrestee. The Court held that it did not:

> . . . [W]hether the arrest warrant issued in this case adequately safeguarded the interests protected by the Fourth Amendment depends upon what the warrant authorized the agents to do. To be sure, the warrant embodied a judicial finding that there was probable cause to believe that Ricky Lyons had committed a felony, and the warrant therefore authorized the officers to seize Lyons. However, the agents sought to do more than use the warrant to arrest Lyons in a public place or in his home; instead, they relied on the warrant as legal authority to enter the home of a third person based on their belief that Ricky Lyons might be a guest there. Regardless of how reasonable this belief might have been, it was never subjected to the detached scrutiny of a judicial officer. Thus, while the warrant in this case may have protected Lyons from an unreasonable seizure, it did absolutely nothing to protect petitioner's privacy interest in being free from an unreasonable invasion and search of his home. . . .
>
> In sum, two distinct interests were implicated by the search at issue here — Ricky Lyons' interest in being free from an unreasonable seizure and petitioner's interest in

being free from an unreasonable search of his home. Because the arrest warrant for Lyons addressed only the former interest, the search of petitioner's home was no more reasonable from petitioner's perspective than it would have been if conducted in the absence of any warrant. Since warrantless searches of a home are impermissible absent consent or exigent circumstances, we conclude that the instant search violated the Fourth Amendment. . . .

. . . [T]o render the instant search reasonable under the Fourth Amendment, a search warrant was required.

Id., at 213-214, 216, 222.

Both *Payton* and *Steagald* contained long discussions of common-law history. In both cases, the Court concluded that the history was inconclusive. In both cases, dissenting opinions argued forcefully, and persuasively, that the weight of the historical evidence counseled against requiring a warrant, that warrantless felony arrests in the felon's home were both common and generally permissible at common law. See *Steagald*, 451 U.S., at 227-230 (Rehnquist, J., dissenting); *Payton*, 445 U.S., at 604-613 (White, J., dissenting). Was the Court's discussion of history in *Watson* a smokescreen? Or should the Court have stuck to its historical guns and permitted warrantless arrests in homes in *Payton* and *Steagald*? Only in *Payton*?

6. Two decades after *Steagald*, the Supreme Court again addressed the scope of the arrest power. This time, the warrant requirement was not at issue.

ATWATER v. LAGO VISTA

Certiorari to the United States Court of Appeals for the Fifth Circuit
532 U.S. 318 (2001)

JUSTICE SOUTER delivered the opinion of the Court. The question is whether the Fourth Amendment forbids a warrantless arrest for a minor criminal offense, such as a misdemeanor seatbelt violation punishable only by a fine. We hold that it does not.

I

In Texas, if a car is equipped with safety belts, a front-seat passenger must wear one, Tex. Tran. Code Ann. §545.413(a) (1999), and the driver must secure any small child riding in front, §545.413(b). Violation of either provision is "a misdemeanor punishable by a fine not less than $25 or more than $50." §545.413(d). Texas law expressly authorizes "[a]ny peace officer [to] arrest without warrant a person found committing a violation" of these seatbelt laws, §543.001, although it permits police to issue citations in lieu of arrest, §§543.003-543.005.

In March 1997, Petitioner Gail Atwater was driving her pickup truck in Lago Vista, Texas, with her 3-year-old son and 5-year-old daughter in the front seat. None of them was wearing a seatbelt. Respondent Bart Turek, a Lago Vista police officer at the time, observed the seatbelt violations and pulled Atwater over. According to Atwater's complaint (the allegations of which we assume to be true for present purposes), Turek approached the truck and "yelled" something to the effect of "we've met before" and "you're going to jail."[1] He then called for backup and asked to see Atwater's driver's license and insurance documentation, which state law required her to carry. When Atwater told Turek that she did not have the papers because her purse had been stolen the day before, Turek said that he had "heard that story two-hundred times."

Atwater asked to take her "frightened, upset, and crying" children to a friend's house nearby, but Turek told her, "you're not going anywhere." As it turned out, Atwater's friend learned what was going on and soon arrived to take charge of the children. Turek then handcuffed Atwater, placed her in his squad car, and drove her to the local police station, where booking officers had her remove her shoes, jewelry, and eyeglasses, and empty her pockets. Officers took Atwater's "mug shot" and placed her, alone, in a jail cell for about one hour, after which she was taken before a magistrate and released on $310 bond.

Atwater was charged with driving without her seatbelt fastened, failing to secure her children in seatbelts, driving without a license, and failing to provide proof of insurance. She ultimately pleaded no contest to the misdemeanor seatbelt offenses and paid a $50 fine; the other charges were dismissed.

Atwater and her husband, petitioner Michael Haas, filed suit . . . under 42 U.S.C. §1983 against Turek and respondents City of Lago Vista and Chief of Police Frank Miller. So far as concerns us, petitioners (whom we will simply call Atwater) alleged that respondents (for simplicity, the City) had violated Atwater's Fourth Amendment "right to be free from unreasonable seizure," App. 23, and sought compensatory and punitive damages.

. . . Given Atwater's admission that she had "violated the law" and the absence of any allegation "that she was harmed or detained in any way inconsistent with the law," the District Court ruled the Fourth Amendment claim "meritless" and granted the City's summary judgment motion. A panel of the United States Court of Appeals for the Fifth Circuit reversed. 165 F.3d 380 (1999). It concluded that "an arrest for a first-time seat belt offense" was an unreasonable seizure within the meaning of the Fourth Amendment, id., at 387, and held that Turek was not entitled to qualified immunity, id., at 389.

Sitting en banc, the Court of Appeals vacated the panel's decision and affirmed the District Court's summary judgment for the City. 195 F.3d 242 (CA5 1999). . . . [T]he en banc court observed that, although the Fourth Amendment generally requires a balancing of individual and governmental interests, where "an arrest is based on probable cause then 'with rare exceptions . . . the result of that balancing is not in doubt.'" 195 F.3d, at 244 (quoting [Whren v. United States, 517 U.S. 806, 817 (1996)]). Because "neither party disputed that Officer Turek had probable cause to arrest Atwater," and because "there [was] no evidence in the record that Officer Turek conducted the arrest in an 'extraordinary manner, unusually harmful' to Atwater's privacy interests," the en banc court held that the arrest was not unreasonable for Fourth Amendment purposes. 195 F.3d at 245-246 (quoting Whren, supra, at 818). . . .

---

1. Turek had previously stopped Atwater for what he had thought was a seatbelt violation, but had realized that Atwater's son, although seated on the vehicle's armrest, was in fact belted in. Atwater acknowledged that her son's seating position was unsafe, and Turek issued a verbal warning.

II

The Fourth Amendment safeguards "[t]he right of the people to be secure in their persons, houses, papers, and effects, against unreasonable searches and seizures." In reading the Amendment, we are guided by "the traditional protections against unreasonable searches and seizures afforded by the common law at the time of the framing," Wilson v. Arkansas, 514 U.S. 927, 931 (1995). . . . Thus, the first step here is to assess Atwater's claim that peace officers' authority to make warrantless arrests for misdemeanors was restricted at common law (whether "common law" is understood strictly as law judicially derived or, instead, as the whole body of law extant at the time of the framing). Atwater's specific contention is that "founding era common-law rules" forbade peace officers to make warrantless misdemeanor arrests except in cases of "breach of the peace," a category she claims was then understood narrowly as covering only those nonfelony offenses "involving or tending toward violence." Brief for Petitioners 13. Although her historical argument is by no means insubstantial, it ultimately fails.

We begin with the state of pre-founding English common law and find that, even after making some allowance for variations in the common-law usage of the term "breach of the peace," the "founding-era common-law rules" were not nearly as clear as Atwater claims; on the contrary, the common-law commentators (as well as the sparsely reported cases) reached divergent conclusions with respect to officers' warrantless misdemeanor arrest power. Moreover, in the years leading up to American independence, Parliament repeatedly extended express warrantless arrest authority to cover misdemeanor-level offenses not amounting to or involving any violent breach of the peace. . . .

[Justice Souter characterized English treatises and case law as inconclusive.]

A second, and equally serious, problem for Atwater's historical argument is posed by the "divers Statutes," M. Dalton, Country Justice ch. 170, §4, p. 582 (1727), enacted by Parliament well before this Republic's founding that authorized warrantless misdemeanor arrests without reference to violence or turmoil. . . . [T]he legal background of any conception of reasonableness the Fourth Amendment's Framers might have entertained would have included English statutes, some centuries old, authorizing peace officers (and even private persons) to make warrantless arrests for all sorts of relatively minor offenses unaccompanied by violence. The so-called "nightwalker" statutes are perhaps the most notable examples. From the enactment of the Statute of Winchester in 1285, through its various readoptions and until its repeal in 1827, night watchmen were authorized and charged "as . . . in Times past" to "watch the Town continually all Night, from the Sun-setting unto the Sun-rising" and were directed that "if any Stranger do pass by them, he shall be arrested until Morning. . . ." 13 Edw. I, ch. 4, §§5-6, 1 Statutes at Large 232-233. . . . [A]ccording to Blackstone, these watchmen had virtually limitless warrantless nighttime arrest power: "Watchmen, either those appointed by the statute of Winchester . . . or such as are merely assistants to the constable, may *virtute officii* arrest all offenders, and particularly nightwalkers, and commit them to custody till the morning." 4 Blackstone 289. . . .

Nor were the nightwalker statutes the only legislative sources of warrantless arrest authority absent real or threatened violence. . . . On the contrary, following the Edwardian legislation and throughout the period leading up to the framing, Parliament repeatedly extended warrantless arrest power to cover misdemeanor-level offenses not involving any breach of the peace. [Such statutes included a

16th-century statute authorizing warrantless arrests for persons playing "unlawful games," as well as those "haunting" the places where such games were played; a 17th-century act applicable to any "hawker, pedlar, petty chapman, or other trading person" found selling without a license; and 18th-century statutes authorizing warrantless arrests of "rogues, vagabonds, beggars, and other idle and disorderly persons"; "horrid" persons who "profanely swear or curse"; those who obstruct "publick streets, lanes or open passages" with "pipes, butts, barrels, casks or other vessels" or an "empty cart, car, dray or other carriage";] and, most significantly of all given the circumstances of the case before us, negligent carriage drivers, 27 Geo. II, ch. 16, §7, 21 Statutes at Large 188 (1754).

. . . [T]hese early English statutes . . . riddle Atwater's supposed common-law rule with enough exceptions to unsettle any contention that the law of the mother country would have left the Fourth Amendment's Framers of a view that it would necessarily have been unreasonable to arrest without warrant for a misdemeanor unaccompanied by real or threatened violence.

An examination of specifically American evidence is to the same effect. Neither the history of the framing era nor subsequent legal development indicates that the Fourth Amendment was originally understood, or has traditionally been read, to embrace Atwater's position.

To begin with, Atwater has cited no particular evidence that those who framed and ratified the Fourth Amendment sought to limit peace officers' warrantless misdemeanor arrest authority to instances of actual breach of the peace. . . . Nor have we found in any of the modern historical accounts of the Fourth Amendment's adoption any substantial indication that the Framers intended such a restriction. Indeed, to the extent these modern histories address the issue, their conclusions are to the contrary. See [J. Landynski, Search and Seizure and the Supreme Court 45 (1966)] (Fourth Amendment arrest rules are "based on common-law practice," which "dispensed with" a warrant requirement for misdemeanors "committed in the presence of the arresting officer").

The evidence of actual practice also counsels against Atwater's position. During the period leading up to and surrounding the framing of the Bill of Rights, colonial and state legislatures, like Parliament before them, regularly authorized local peace officers to make warrantless misdemeanor arrests without conditioning statutory authority on breach of the peace. [Here, Justice Souter cited numerous state statutes from the late 1700s that authorized warrantless arrests of drunks, gamblers, vagrants, prostitutes, "night-walkers," fortune-tellers, profane swearers, Sabbath-breakers, and others. — EDS.]

. . . Given the early state practice, it is likewise troublesome for Atwater's view that just one year after the ratification of the Fourth Amendment, Congress vested federal marshals with "the same powers in executing the laws of the United States, as sheriffs and their deputies in the several states have by law, in executing the laws of their respective states." Act of May 2, 1792, ch. 28, §9, 1 Stat. 265. Thus, as we have said before in only slightly different circumstances, the Second Congress apparently "saw no inconsistency between the Fourth Amendment and legislation giving United States marshals the same power as local peace officers" to make warrantless arrests. United States v. Watson, 423 U.S. 411, 420 (1976).

The record thus supports Justice Powell's observation that "there is no historical evidence that the Framers or proponents of the Fourth Amendment, outspokenly opposed to the infamous general warrants and writs of assistance, were at all concerned about warrantless arrests by local constables and other peace officers." Id., at 429 (concurring opinion). We simply cannot conclude that the Fourth Amendment, as originally understood, forbade peace officers to arrest without a warrant for misdemeanors not amounting to or involving breach of the peace.

Nor does Atwater's argument from tradition pick up any steam from the historical record as it has unfolded since the framing. . . . The story, on the contrary, is of two centuries of uninterrupted (and largely unchallenged) state and federal practice permitting warrantless arrests for misdemeanors not amounting to or involving breach of the peace. . . .

[Justice Souter's opinion proceeds to survey Supreme Court cases, state cases, and commentaries spanning the nineteenth and twentieth centuries.]

Small wonder, then, that today statutes in all 50 States and the District of Columbia permit warrantless misdemeanor arrests by at least some (if not all) peace officers without requiring any breach of the peace, as do a host of congressional enactments. The American Law Institute has long endorsed the validity of such legislation, see American Law Institute, Code of Criminal Procedure §21(a), p. 28 (1930); American Law Institute, Model Code of Pre-Arraignment Procedure §120.1(1)(c), p. 13 (1975), and the consensus, as stated in the current literature, is that statutes "remov[ing] the breach of the peace limitation and thereby permitt[ing] arrest without warrant for *any* misdemeanor committed in the arresting officer's presence" have "never been successfully challenged and stand as the law of the land." 3 W. LaFave, Search and Seizure §5.1(b), pp. 13-14, and n. 76 (1996) (citation omitted). This, therefore, simply is not a case in which the claimant can point to "a clear answer [that] existed in 1791 and has been generally adhered to by the traditions of our society ever since." County of Riverside v. McLaughlin, 500 U.S. 44, 60 (1991) (Scalia, J., dissenting).

III

. . . Atwater does not wager all on history. Instead, she asks us to mint a new rule of constitutional law on the understanding that when historical practice fails to speak conclusively to a claim grounded on the Fourth Amendment, courts are left to strike a current balance between individual and societal interests by subjecting particular contemporary circumstances to traditional standards of reasonableness. Atwater accordingly argues for a modern arrest rule, one not necessarily requiring violent breach of the peace, but nonetheless forbidding custodial arrest, even upon probable cause, when conviction could not ultimately carry any jail time and when the government shows no compelling need for immediate detention.

If we were to derive a rule exclusively to address the uncontested facts of this case, Atwater might well prevail. She was a known and established resident of Lago Vista with no place to hide and no incentive to flee, and common sense says she would almost certainly have buckled up as a condition of driving off with a citation. In her case, the physical incidents of arrest were merely gratuitous humiliations imposed by a police officer who was (at best) exercising extremely poor judgment. Atwater's claim to live free of pointless indignity and confinement clearly outweighs anything the City can raise against it specific to her case.

But we have traditionally recognized that a responsible Fourth Amendment balance is not well served by standards requiring sensitive, case-by-case determinations of government need, lest every discretionary judgment in the field be converted into an occasion for constitutional review. Often enough, the Fourth Amendment has to be applied on the spur (and in the heat) of the moment, and the object in implementing its command of reasonableness is to draw standards sufficiently clear and simple to be applied with a fair prospect of surviving judicial second-guessing months and years after an arrest or search is made. Courts attempting to strike a reasonable Fourth Amendment balance thus credit the government's side with an essential interest in readily administrable rules.

At first glance, Atwater's argument may seem to respect the values of clarity and simplicity, so far as she claims that the Fourth Amendment generally forbids warrantless arrests for minor crimes not accompanied by violence or some demonstrable threat of it. . . . But the claim is not ultimately so simple, nor could it be, for complications arise the moment we begin to think about . . . the several criteria Atwater proposes for drawing a line between minor crimes with limited arrest authority and others not so restricted.

One line, she suggests, might be between "jailable" and "fine-only" offenses. . . . The trouble with this distinction, of course, is that an officer on the street might not be able to tell. It is not merely that we cannot expect every police officer to know the details of frequently complex penalty schemes, but that penalties for ostensibly identical conduct can vary on account of facts difficult (if not impossible) to know at the scene of an arrest. Is this the first offense or is the suspect a repeat offender? Is the weight of the marijuana a gram above or a gram below the fine-only line? Where conduct could implicate more than one criminal prohibition, which one will the district attorney ultimately decide to charge? And so on.

But Atwater's refinements would not end there. She represents that if the line were drawn at nonjailable traffic offenses, her proposed limitation should be qualified by a proviso authorizing warrantless arrests where "necessary for enforcement of the traffic laws or when [an] offense would otherwise continue and pose a danger to others on the road." Brief for Petitioners 46. (Were the line drawn at misdemeanors generally, a comparable qualification would presumably apply.) The proviso only compounds the difficulties. Would, for instance, either exception apply to speeding? At oral argument, Atwater's counsel said that "it would not be reasonable to arrest a driver for speeding unless the speeding rose to the level of reckless driving." Tr. of Oral Arg. 16. But is it not fair to expect that the chronic speeder will speed again despite a citation in his pocket, and should that not qualify as showing that the "offense would . . . continue" under Atwater's rule? And why, as a constitutional matter, should we assume that only reckless driving will "pose a danger to others on the road" while speeding will not?

There is no need for more examples to show that Atwater's general rule and limiting proviso promise very little in the way of administrability. It is no answer that the police routinely make judgments on grounds like risk of immediate repetition; they surely do and should. But there is a world of difference between making that judgment in choosing between the discretionary leniency of a summons in place of a clearly lawful arrest, and making the same judgment when the question is the lawfulness of the warrantless arrest itself. It is the difference between no basis for legal action challenging the discretionary judgment, on the one hand, and the prospect of evidentiary exclusion or (as here) personal §1983 liability for the misapplication of a constitutional standard, on the other. Atwater's rule therefore would not only place police in an almost impossible spot but would guarantee increased litigation over many of the arrests that would occur. For all these reasons, Atwater's various distinctions between permissible and impermissible arrests for minor crimes strike us as "very unsatisfactory line[s]" to require police officers to draw on a moment's notice. Carroll v. United States, [267 U.S. 132, 157 (1925)]. . . .

Just how easily the costs could outweigh the benefits may be shown by asking, as one Member of this Court did at oral argument, "how bad the problem is out there." Tr. of Oral Arg. 20. The very fact that the law has never jelled the way Atwater would have it leads one to wonder whether warrantless misdemeanor arrests need constitutional attention. . . . So far as such arrests might be thought to pose a threat to the probable-cause requirement, anyone arrested for a crime without formal process, whether for felony or misdemeanor, is entitled to a magistrate's review of probable cause within 48 hours, County of Riverside v. McLaughlin, 500 U.S., at 55-58, and there is no reason to think the procedure in this case atypical in giving the suspect a prompt opportunity to request release, see Tex. Tran. Code Ann. §543.002 (1999) (persons arrested for traffic offenses to be taken "immediately" before a magistrate). Many jurisdictions, moreover, have chosen to impose more restrictive safeguards through statutes limiting warrantless arrests for minor offenses. It is of course easier to devise a minor-offense limitation by statute than to derive one through the Constitution, simply because the statute can let the arrest power turn on any sort of practical consideration without having to subsume it under a broader principle. . . . Finally, and significantly, under current doctrine the preference for categorical treatment of Fourth Amendment claims gives way to individualized review when a defendant makes a colorable argument that an arrest, with or without a warrant, was "conducted in an extraordinary manner, unusually harmful to [his] privacy or even physical interests." Whren v. United States, 517 U.S., at 818; see also Graham v. Connor, 490 U.S. 386, 395-396 (1989) (excessive force actionable under §1983).

The upshot of all these influences, combined with the good sense (and, failing that, the political accountability) of most local lawmakers and law-enforcement officials, is a dearth of horribles demanding redress. Indeed, when Atwater's counsel was asked at oral argument for any indications of comparably foolish, warrantless misdemeanor arrests, he could offer only one.[23] We are sure that there are others,[24] but just as surely the country is not confronting anything like an epidemic of unnecessary minor-offense arrests. . . .

Accordingly, we confirm today what our prior cases have intimated: the standard of probable cause "applie[s] to all arrests, without the need to 'balance' the interests and circumstances involved in particular situations." Dunaway v. New York, 442 U.S. 200, 208 (1979). If an officer has probable cause to believe that an individual has committed even a very minor criminal offense in his presence, he may, without violating the Fourth Amendment, arrest the offender.

---

23. He referred to a newspaper account of a girl taken into custody for eating french fries in a Washington, D.C., subway station. Tr. of Oral Arg. 20-21; see also Washington Post, Nov. 16, 2000, p. A1 (describing incident). Not surprisingly, given the practical and political considerations discussed in text, the Washington Metro Transit Police recently revised their "zero-tolerance" policy to provide for citation in lieu of custodial arrest of subway snackers. Washington Post, Feb. 27, 2001, at B1.

24. One of Atwater's amici described a handful in its brief. Brief for American Civil Liberties Union et al. as Amici Curiae 7-8 (reporting arrests for littering, riding a bicycle without a bell or gong, operating a business without a license, and "walking as to create a hazard").

IV

Atwater's arrest satisfied constitutional requirements. There is no dispute that Officer Turek had probable cause to believe that Atwater had committed a crime in his presence. She admits that neither she nor her children were wearing seatbelts . . . Turek was accordingly authorized (not required, but authorized) to make a custodial arrest without balancing costs and benefits or determining whether or not Atwater's arrest was in some sense necessary.

Nor was the arrest made in an "extraordinary manner, unusually harmful to [her] privacy or . . . physical interests." Whren v. United States, 517 U.S., at 818. As our citations in *Whren* make clear, the question whether a search or seizure is "extraordinary" turns, above all else, on the manner in which the search or seizure is executed. See id., at 818 (citing Tennessee v. Garner, 471 U.S. 1 (1985) ("seizure by means of deadly force"), Wilson v. Arkansas, 514 U.S. 927 (1995) ("unannounced entry into a home"), Welsh v. Wisconsin, 466 U.S. 740 (1984) ("entry into a home without a warrant"), and Winston v. Lee, 470 U.S. 753 (1985) ("physical penetration of the body")). Atwater's arrest was surely "humiliating," as she says in her brief, but it was no more "harmful to . . . privacy or . . . physical interests" than the normal custodial arrest. She was handcuffed, placed in a squad car, and taken to the local police station, where officers asked her to remove her shoes, jewelry, and glasses, and to empty her pockets. They then took her photograph and placed her in a cell, alone, for about an hour, after which she was taken before a magistrate, and released on $310 bond. The arrest and booking were inconvenient and embarrassing to Atwater, but not so extraordinary as to violate the Fourth Amendment. . . .

JUSTICE O'CONNOR, with whom JUSTICE STEVENS, JUSTICE GINSBURG, and JUSTICE BREYER join, dissenting.

. . . The majority . . . acknowledges that "Atwater's claim to live free of pointless indignity and confinement clearly outweighs anything the City can raise against it specific to her case." But instead of remedying this imbalance, the majority allows itself to be swayed by the worry that "every discretionary judgment in the field [will] be converted into an occasion for constitutional review." It therefore mints a new rule that "[i]f an officer has probable cause to believe that an individual has committed even a very minor criminal offense in his presence, he may, without violating the Fourth Amendment, arrest the offender." This rule . . . runs contrary to the principles that lie at the core of the Fourth Amendment. . . .

. . . [W]e have held that the existence of probable cause is a necessary condition for an arrest. And in the case of felonies punishable by a term of imprisonment, we have held that the existence of probable cause is also a sufficient condition for an arrest. See United States v. Watson, 423 U.S. 411, 416-417 (1976). In *Watson*, however, there was a clear and consistently applied common law rule permitting warrantless felony arrests. See id., at 417-422. Accordingly, our inquiry ended there and we had no need to assess the reasonableness of such arrests by weighing individual liberty interests against state interests.

Here, however, we have no such luxury. The Court's thorough exegesis makes it abundantly clear that warrantless misdemeanor arrests were not the subject of a clear and consistently applied rule at common law. We therefore must engage in the balancing test required by the Fourth Amendment. See Wyoming v. Houghton, [526 U.S. 295,] 299-300 [(1995)]. While probable cause is surely a necessary condition for warrantless arrests for fine-only offenses, any realistic assessment of the interests implicated by such arrests demonstrates that probable cause alone is not a sufficient condition. . . .

A custodial arrest exacts an obvious toll on an individual's liberty and privacy, even when the period of custody is relatively brief. The arrestee is subject to a full search of her person and confiscation of her possessions. United States v. Robinson, [414 U.S. 218 (1973)]. If the arrestee is the occupant of a car, the entire passenger compartment of the car, including packages therein, is subject to search as well. See New York v. Belton, 453 U.S. 454 (1981). The arrestee may be detained for up to 48 hours without having a magistrate determine whether there in fact was probable cause for the arrest. See County of Riverside v. McLaughlin, 500 U.S. 44 (1991). Because people arrested for all types of violent and nonviolent offenses may be housed together awaiting such review, this detention period is potentially dangerous. And once the period of custody is over, the fact of the arrest is a permanent part of the public record. . . .

. . . Giving police officers constitutional carte blanche to effect an arrest whenever there is probable cause to believe a fine-only misdemeanor has been committed is irreconcilable with the Fourth Amendment's command that seizures be reasonable. Instead, I would require that when there is probable cause to believe that a fine-only offense has been committed, the police officer should issue a citation unless the officer is "able to point to specific and articulable facts which, taken together with rational inferences from those facts, reasonably warrant [the additional] intrusion" of a full custodial arrest. Terry v. Ohio, [392 U.S. 1, 21 (1968)].

The majority insists that a bright-line rule focused on probable cause is necessary to vindicate the State's interest in easily administrable law enforcement rules. Probable cause itself, however, is not a model of precision. "The quantum of information which constitutes probable cause — evidence which would 'warrant a man of reasonable caution in the belief' that a [crime] has been committed — must be measured by the facts of the particular case." Wong Sun v. United States, 371 U.S. 471, 479 (1963). The rule I propose — which merely requires a legitimate reason for the decision to escalate the seizure into a full custodial arrest — thus does not undermine an otherwise "clear and simple" rule. . . .

The record in this case makes it abundantly clear that Ms. Atwater's arrest was constitutionally unreasonable. . . .

There is no question that Officer Turek's actions severely infringed Atwater's liberty and privacy. Turek was loud and accusatory from the moment he approached Atwater's car. Atwater's young children were terrified and hysterical. Yet when Atwater asked Turek to lower his voice because he was scaring the children, he responded by jabbing his finger in Atwater's face and saying, "You're going to jail." . . .

Atwater asked if she could at least take her children to a friend's house down the street before going to the police station. But Turek — who had just castigated Atwater for not caring for her children — refused and said he would take the children into custody as well. Only the intervention of neighborhood children who had witnessed the scene and summoned one of Atwater's friends saved the children from being hauled to jail with their mother.

With the children gone, Officer Turek handcuffed Ms. Atwater with her hands behind her back, placed her in the police car, and drove her to the police station. Ironically, Turek did not secure Atwater in a seat belt for the drive. At the station, Atwater was forced to remove her shoes, relinquish her possessions, and wait in a holding cell for about an hour. A judge finally informed Atwater of her rights and the charges against her, and released her when she posted bond. Atwater returned to the scene of the arrest, only to find that her car had been towed.

Ms. Atwater ultimately pleaded no contest to violating the seatbelt law and was fined $50. Even though that fine was the maximum penalty for her crime, Tex. Tran. Code Ann. §545.413(d) (1999), and even though Officer Turek has never articulated any justification for his actions, the city contends that arresting Atwater was constitutionally reasonable because it advanced two legitimate interests: "the enforcement of child safety laws and encouraging [Atwater] to appear for trial." Brief for Respondents 15.

It is difficult to see how arresting Atwater served either of these goals any more effectively than the issuance of a citation. With respect to the goal of law enforcement generally, Atwater did not pose a great danger to the community. She had been driving very slowly — approximately 15 miles per hour — in broad daylight on a residential street that had no other traffic. Nor was she a repeat offender; until that day, she had received one traffic citation in her life — a ticket, more than 10 years earlier, for failure to signal a lane change. Although Officer Turek had stopped Atwater approximately three months earlier because he thought that Atwater's son was not wearing a seatbelt, Turek had been mistaken. Moreover, Atwater immediately accepted responsibility and apologized for her conduct. Thus, there was every indication that Atwater would have buckled herself and her children in had she been cited and allowed to leave. . . .

Respondents also contend that the arrest was necessary to ensure Atwater's appearance in court. Atwater, however, was far from a flight risk. A 16-year resident of Lago Vista, population 2,486, Atwater was not likely to abscond. Although she was unable to produce her driver's license because it had been stolen, she gave Officer Turek her license number and address. In addition, Officer Turek knew from their previous encounter that Atwater was a local resident. . . .

The Court's error, however, does not merely affect the disposition of this case. The per se rule that the Court creates has potentially serious consequences for the everyday lives of Americans. A broad range of conduct falls into the category of fine-only misdemeanors. In Texas alone, for example, disobeying any sort of traffic warning sign is a misdemeanor punishable only by fine, see Tex. Tran. Code Ann. §472.022 (1999 and Supp. 2000-2001), as is failing to pay a highway toll, see §284.070, and driving with expired license plates, see §502.407. Nor are fine-only crimes limited to the traffic context. In several States, for example, littering is a criminal offense punishable only by fine. See, e.g., Cal. Penal Code Ann. §374.7 (West 1999); Ga. Code Ann. §16-7-43 (1996); Iowa Code §§321.369, 805.8(2)(af) (Supp. 2001). . . .

Such unbounded discretion carries with it grave potential for abuse. The majority takes comfort in the lack of evidence of "an epidemic of unnecessary minor-offense arrests." But the relatively small number of published cases dealing with such arrests proves little and should provide little solace. Indeed, as the recent debate over racial profiling demonstrates all too clearly, a relatively minor traffic infraction may often serve as an excuse for stopping and harassing an individual. . . .

The Court neglects the Fourth Amendment's express command in the name of administrative ease. In so doing, it cloaks the pointless indignity that Gail Atwater suffered with the mantle of reasonableness. I respectfully dissent.

NOTES AND QUESTIONS

1. In Whren v. United States, 517 U.S. 806 (1996), the Court held that a police officer's motive for making a traffic stop (and accompanying brief detention) does not affect the constitutionality of the stop, so long as there was probable cause to believe that the traffic violation had occurred. (*Whren* is excerpted infra, at page 576.) Along the way, the Court stated that probable cause is the sole constitutional requirement for arrests, save when the arrest is "conducted in an extraordinary manner, unusually harmful to an individual's privacy or . . . physical interests." Id., at 818. Justice Souter quoted this language in support of his position in *Atwater*. Was he right to do so? Was Atwater treated "in an extraordinary manner"? Not if "ordinary" is defined by the treatment of arrestees as a whole. But if only those persons stopped for seat belt violations are considered, Atwater's treatment surely *was* "extraordinary." Why should Atwater be treated like a felon rather than like other traffic offenders? Doesn't *that* seem "extraordinary"?

2. Justice Souter's extended discussion of pre-1791 cases and statutes may be another piece of evidence for the ascendancy of originalism in Fourth Amendment law. For an interesting and sometimes scathing discussion of what that ascendancy might mean, see David A. Sklansky, The Fourth Amendment and Common Law, 100 Colum. L. Rev. 1739 (2000). Sklansky maintains that neither the Fourth Amendment's text nor its history support the idea that the Fourth Amendment incorporates the eighteenth-century common law of search and seizure. He also argues that the common law as the Framers knew it was too vague and too varied to answer many of the questions the Court asks of it. (*Atwater* seems a nice example of this point.) But, he contends, the kind of originalism one sees in Fourth Amendment cases may have large consequences for the long-range shape of the law:

> . . . [T]he rhetoric of the new Fourth Amendment originalism legitimizes some outcomes more easily than others and is relatively uncongenial to certain broad uses to which the Fourth Amendment might otherwise be put. The problem is not so much the answers provided by eighteenth-century common law — those are rare — but rather the limited range of the questions it asked.
>
> To take perhaps the most obvious example, of late the Supreme Court has studiously avoided considerations of equality in assessing the reasonableness of searches and seizures. . . . [C]onsiderations of race, class, and gender equity . . . are difficult to read into the common law of 1791. Indeed, . . . eighteenth-century rules of search and seizure, far from reflecting a broad commitment to equality, systematically codified class privilege.

100 Colum. L. Rev. at 1772-1773. Are you persuaded? Should evidence of the sort discussed in part II of Justice Souter's opinion affect outcomes in cases like *Atwater*?

3. Consider Justice Souter's claim that the doctrine proposed by the dissent is not administrable. At first blush, the argument seems powerful. Substantive distinctions of the sort Souter mentions — whether a suspect is a first-time or repeat offender, whether the weight of the drugs the suspect possesses are over or under the jailable line, which crime or crimes the prosecutor's office will want to charge — would surely be difficult, perhaps impossible, to sort out at the time of arrest. Yet if the seriousness of the crime determines the scope of the arrest power, police would *have* to make such distinctions. But this administrability argument may not be as strong as

it seems. The alternative to the Court's bright-line rule is (as is always the case with bright-line rules) a standard: Officers should behave reasonably, considering all the circumstances — including the circumstance that some circumstances are harder for the arresting officer to discern than others. Arrests are presumptively reasonable when the crime is serious; not so when the crime isn't. That seems to be, roughly, what Justice O'Connor's dissent argues for. Why, precisely, would that be unadministrable?

The answer comes down to a claim about the unique needs of the police. Regulated actors are often subject to vague standards like negligence; courts don't assume that such standards are unworkable elsewhere. If they are unworkable here, it must be because, as the Court seems to believe, police *uniquely* need clear rules to do their jobs. Perhaps they do: Certainly police officers must make many quick decisions based on limited information; they often lack the time to calculate their actions carefully. But perhaps they don't: Unlike most regulated actors, police officers receive fairly detailed legal training and are frequently in court, so they can see how the relevant standards are applied by local magistrates. As Justice O'Connor suggests, that is why the probable cause standard works reasonably well: Over time, police officers come to know what "probable cause" means to the magistrates in their jurisdictions. Perhaps the same would be true of a standard like "crime serious enough to justify a full custodial arrest."

4. Justice Souter noted in *Atwater* that many jurisdictions have limited police authority to arrest in the context of minor offenses. He concluded that the "upshot" of this and related measures, "combined with the good sense (and, failing that, the political accountability) of most local lawmakers and law-enforcement officials," is a "dearth of horribles" involving warrantless arrests for trivial crimes. In Virginia v. Moore, 128 S. Ct. 1598 (2008), the Court reiterated this conclusion in holding that even when officers violate a state law requiring them to issue a summons instead of arresting, this provides no basis for concluding that the Fourth Amendment has similarly been violated. Moore was arrested for driving on a suspended license when he should have been issued a summons. A search incident to arrest of his person uncovered crack cocaine. Moore moved to suppress, stating his Fourth Amendment rights had been violated. The Court disagreed:

> Incorporating state-law arrest limitations into the Constitution would produce a constitutional regime no less vague and unpredictable than the one we rejected in *Atwater*. The constitutional standard would be only as easy to apply as the underlying state law, and state law can be complicated indeed. The Virginia statute in this case, for example, calls on law enforcement officers to weigh just the sort of case-specific factors that *Atwater* said would deter legitimate arrests if made part of the constitutional inquiry . . . . *Atwater* differs from this case in only one significant respect: It considered (and rejected) federal constitutional remedies for *all* minor-misdemeanor arrests; Moore seeks them in only that subset of minor-misdemeanor arrests in which there is the least to be gained — that is, where the State has already acted to constrain officers' discretion and prevent abuse. Here we confront fewer horribles than in *Atwater*, and less of a need for redress. . . .
>
> We conclude that warrantless arrests for crimes committed in the presence of an arresting officer are reasonable under the Constitution and that while States are free to regulate such arrests however they desire, state restrictions do not alter the Fourth Amendment's protections.

Do you agree? Is the Court correct that the Fourth Amendment should avoid being tied to state law, which it says "can be complicated indeed?" But then, what does an arrest based on probable cause mean except for an arrest based on a fair probability that the arrestee has violated a law — a *state* law, in Moore's case? And if the relevant state holds that it is not reasonable to arrest based simply on cause to believe that one of its laws has been violated, what sense does it make for Fourth Amendment doctrine to hold that an arrest is nonetheless reasonable?

5. In some cases, the arrest power may apply even without probable cause to believe the arrestee has committed a crime. Consider United States v. Awadallah, 349 F.3d 42 (2d Cir. 2003). In that case, a Second Circuit panel rejected a Fourth Amendment challenge to a detention based on the federal material witness statute, 18 U.S.C. §3144, the current version of which reads:

> If it appears from an affidavit filed by a party that the testimony of a person is material in a criminal proceeding, and if it is shown that it may become impracticable to secure the presence of the person by subpoena, a judicial officer may order the arrest of the person. . . . Release of a material witness may be delayed for a reasonable period of time until the deposition of the witness can be taken pursuant to the Federal Rules of Criminal Procedure.

Federal agents had evidence that the defendant, Osama Awadallah, had been in contact with two of the September 11 hijackers in the days immediately before the attacks on the Pentagon and the World Trade Center. Awadallah was taken into custody and interviewed extensively; three weeks later, he testified before a federal grand jury investigating the attacks. Awadallah was charged and convicted of false statements he made during that testimony. He claimed that those statements were the fruit of an unconstitutional arrest.

Judge Jacobs's opinion "conclude[d] that §3144 sufficiently limits [the] infringement [on individual liberty] and reasonably balances it against the government's countervailing interests." 349 F.3d at 49. The Court acknowledged that the several-week detention "constitute[d] a significant intrusion on liberty," but found that under the circumstances, "Awadallah's detention was not unreasonably prolonged." Id., at 58.

Is *Awadallah* correct as a matter of Fourth Amendment law? Should courts pay attention to the seriousness of the crime under investigation when evaluating material witness detentions? Would that approach be contrary to *Atwater*?

e. *Searches Incident to Arrest*

When a person is validly arrested, should the arresting officer also be allowed to search the person of the arrestee without first obtaining a search warrant? Can the officer search the place where the arrest is made? These questions have long vexed the Supreme Court, with the pendulum of precedent swinging first one way and then the other for the past 80 years.

The modern "search incident to arrest" doctrine has its origins in the following dictum from Weeks v. United States, 232 U.S. 383, 392 (1914):

> What then is the present case? Before answering that inquiry specifically, it may be well by a process of exclusion to state what it is not. It is not an assertion of the right on

the part of the Government, always recognized under English and American law, to search the person of the accused when legally arrested to discover and seize the fruits or evidences of crime. . . .

In Carroll v. United States, 267 U.S. 132 (1925), the first car-search case, the Court suggested that the rule alluded to in *Weeks* includes "whatever is found upon [the arrestee's] person or in his control which it is unlawful for him to have and which may be used to prove the offense." In Agnello v. United States, 269 U.S. 20 (1925), the Court went even further, stating that the rule also encompasses "the place where the arrest is made in order to find and seize things connected with the crime as its fruits or as the means by which it was committed, as well as weapons and other things to effect an escape from custody. . . ." And in Marron v. United States, 275 U.S. 192 (1927), the Court specifically relied upon *Weeks* to uphold a search that was conducted pursuant to a warrant, but that clearly exceeded the scope of the warrant; the Court explained that the search-incident authority "extended to all parts of the premises used for the unlawful purpose."

The next two search-incident cases, Go-Bart Importing Co. v. United States, 282 U.S. 344 (1931), and United States v. Lefkowitz, 285 U.S. 452 (1932), cut back on the developing doctrine. In *Go-Bart*, the Court held that the search of a desk, safe, and other parts of an office was unlawful, in part because the arresting police "had an abundance of information and time" to obtain a search warrant. And in *Lefkowitz*, the Court invalidated the warrantless search of desk drawers and a cabinet, despite the fact that the search was conducted pursuant to a valid arrest.

In Harris v. United States, 331 U.S. 145 (1947), police arrested the defendant in the living room of his apartment, on a forgery charge, and proceeded to search the entire apartment for forged checks. Instead, they found (and seized) altered Selective Service documents. The Court upheld the search in *Harris* as "incident to arrest." Only one year later, however, in Trupiano v. United States, 334 U.S. 699 (1948), the Court found a Fourth Amendment violation when police officers arrested a bootlegger in the act of distilling illegal liquor, and proceeded to seize (without a warrant) the still. Finally, in United States v. Rabinowitz, 339 U.S. 56 (1950), federal agents obtained a warrant to arrest the defendant for forgery of stamps. The warrant was served at the defendant's one-room business office. The agents then conducted a 90-minute search, including a desk, safe, and file cabinets, and seized 573 forged stamps. The Court upheld the search, citing *Harris*, and finding that the agents had "the right to search the place where the arrest is made in order to find and seize things connected with the crime."

As you can see, the Court's early search-incident-to-arrest decisions were marked by "shifting constitutional standards" and "remarkable instability." See Chimel v. California, 395 U.S. 752 (1969) (White, J., dissenting). And the beat goes on . . .

CHIMEL v. CALIFORNIA

Certiorari to the Supreme Court of California
395 U.S. 752 (1969)

JUSTICE STEWART delivered the opinion of the Court.

. . . Late in the afternoon of September 13, 1965, three police officers arrived at the Santa Ana, California, home of the petitioner with a warrant authorizing his arrest for the burglary of a coin shop. The officers knocked on the door, identified themselves to the petitioner's wife, and asked if they might come inside. She ushered them into the house, where they waited 10 or 15 minutes until the petitioner returned home from work. When the petitioner entered the house, one of the officers handed him the arrest warrant and asked for permission to "look around." The petitioner objected, but was advised that "on the basis of the lawful arrest," the officers would nonetheless conduct a search. No search warrant had been issued.

Accompanied by the petitioner's wife, the officers then looked through the entire three-bedroom house, including the attic, the garage, and a small workshop. In some rooms the search was relatively cursory. In the master bedroom and sewing room, however, the officers directed the petitioner's wife to open drawers and "to physically move contents of the drawers from side to side so that [they] might view any items that would have come from [the] burglary." After completing the search, they seized numerous items — primarily coins, but also several medals, tokens, and a few other objects. The entire search took between 45 minutes and an hour.

At the petitioner's subsequent state trial on two charges of burglary, the items taken from his house were admitted into evidence against him, over his objection that they had been unconstitutionally seized. He was convicted, and the judgments of conviction were affirmed by both the California Court of Appeal, 61 Cal. Rptr. 714, and the California Supreme Court, 68 Cal. 2d 436, 439 P. 2d 333. Both courts accepted the petitioner's contention that the arrest warrant was invalid because the supporting affidavit was set out in conclusory terms, but held that since the arresting officers had procured the warrant "in good faith," and since in any event they had had sufficient information to constitute probable cause for the petitioner's arrest, that arrest had been lawful. From this conclusion the appellate courts went on to hold that the search of the petitioner's home had been justified, despite the absence of a search warrant, on the ground that it had been incident to a valid arrest. We granted certiorari in order to consider the petitioner's substantial constitutional claims.

Without deciding the question, we proceed on the hypothesis that the California courts were correct in holding that the arrest of the petitioner was valid under the Constitution. This brings us directly to the question whether the warrantless search of the petitioner's entire house can be constitutionally justified as incident to that arrest. The decisions of this Court bearing upon that question have been far from consistent, as even the most cursory review makes evident.

[Here, Justice Stewart reviewed the history of the search-incident-to-arrest doctrine as described above. — EDS.]

Rabinowitz has come to stand for the proposition, inter alia, that a warrantless search "incident to a lawful arrest" may generally extend to the area that is considered to be in the "possession" or under the "control" of the person arrested. And it was on the basis of that proposition that the California courts upheld the search of the petitioner's entire house in this case. That doctrine, however, at least in the broad sense in which it was applied by the California courts in this case, can withstand neither historical nor rational analysis.

Even limited to its own facts, the *Rabinowitz* decision was, as we have seen, hardly founded on an unimpeachable line of authority. As Mr. Justice Frankfurter commented in dissent in that case, the "hint" contained in *Weeks* was, without persuasive justification, "loosely turned into dictum and finally elevated to a decision." 339 U.S., at 75. And the approach taken in cases such as *Go-Bart*, *Lefkowitz*, and *Trupiano* was essentially disregarded by the *Rabinowitz* Court.

Nor is the rationale by which the State seeks here to sustain the search of the petitioner's house supported by a reasoned view of the background and purpose of the Fourth Amendment. Mr. Justice Frankfurter wisely pointed out in his *Rabinowitz* dissent that the Amendment's proscription of "unreasonable searches and seizures" must be read in light of "the history that gave rise to the words" — a history of "abuses so deeply felt by the Colonies as to be one of the potent causes of the Revolution. . . ." 339 U.S., at 69. The Amendment was in large part a reaction to the general warrants and warrantless searches that had so alienated the colonists and had helped speed the movement for independence.[5] In the scheme of the Amendment, therefore, the requirement that "no Warrants shall issue, but upon probable cause," plays a crucial part. As the Court put it in McDonald v. United States, 335 U.S. 451:

> We are not dealing with formalities. The presence of a search warrant serves a high function. Absent some grave emergency, the Fourth Amendment has interposed a magistrate between the citizen and the police. This was done not to shield criminals nor to make the home a safe haven for illegal activities. It was done so that an objective mind might weigh the need to invade that privacy in order to enforce the law. The right of privacy was deemed too precious to entrust to the discretion of those whose job is the detection of crime and the arrest of criminals. . . . And so the Constitution requires a magistrate to pass on the desires of the police before they violate the privacy of the home. We cannot be true to that constitutional requirement and excuse the absence of a search warrant without a showing by those who seek exemption from the constitutional mandate that the exigencies of the situation made that course imperative.

Id., at 455-456. . . .

Only last Term in Terry v. Ohio, 392 U.S. 1, we emphasized that "the police must, whenever practicable, obtain advance judicial approval of searches and seizures through the warrant procedure," id., at 20, and that "the scope of [a] search must be 'strictly tied to and justified by' the circumstances which rendered its initiation permissible." Id., at 19. The search undertaken by the officer in that "stop and frisk" case was sustained under that test, because it was no more than a "protective . . . search for weapons." Id., at 29. . . .

A similar analysis underlies the "search incident to arrest" principle, and marks its proper extent. When an arrest is made, it is reasonable for the arresting officer to search the person arrested in order to remove any weapons that the latter might seek to use in order to resist arrest or effect his escape. Otherwise, the officer's safety might well be endangered, and the arrest itself frustrated. In addition, it is entirely reasonable for the arresting officer to search for and seize any evidence on the arrestee's person in order to prevent its concealment or destruction. And the area into which an arrestee might reach in order to grab a weapon or evidentiary items must, of course, be governed by a like rule. A gun on a table or in a drawer in front of one who is arrested can be as dangerous to the arresting officer as one concealed in the clothing of the person arrested. There is ample justification, therefore, for a search of the arrestee's person and the area "within his immediate control" — construing that phrase to mean the area from within which he might gain possession of a weapon or destructible evidence.

---

5. See generally Boyd v. United States, 116 U.S. 616, 624-625. . . .

There is no comparable justification, however, for routinely searching any room other than that in which an arrest occurs — or, for that matter, for searching through all the desk drawers or other closed or concealed areas in that room itself. Such searches, in the absence of well-recognized exceptions, may be made only under the authority of a search warrant. The "adherence to judicial processes" mandated by the Fourth Amendment requires no less. . . .

It is argued in the present case that it is "reasonable" to search a man's house when he is arrested in it. But that argument is founded on little more than a subjective view regarding the acceptability of certain sorts of police conduct, and not on considerations relevant to Fourth Amendment interests. Under such an unconfined analysis, Fourth Amendment protection in this area would approach the evaporation point. It is not easy to explain why, for instance, it is less subjectively "reasonable" to search a man's house when he is arrested on his front lawn — nor just down the street — than it is when he happens to be in the house at the time of arrest. . . .

It would be possible, of course, to draw a line between *Rabinowitz* and *Harris* on the one hand, and this case on the other. For *Rabinowitz* involved a single room, and *Harris* a four-room apartment, while in the case before us an entire house was searched. But such a distinction would be highly artificial. The rationale that allowed the searches and seizures in *Rabinowitz* and *Harris* would allow the searches and seizures in this case. No consideration relevant to the Fourth Amendment suggests any point of rational limitation, once the search is allowed to go beyond the area from which the person arrested might obtain weapons or evidentiary items. The only reasoned distinction is one between a search of the person arrested and the area within his reach on the one hand, and more extensive searches on the other.[12]

The petitioner correctly points out that one result of decisions such as *Rabinowitz* and *Harris* is to give law enforcement officials the opportunity to engage in searches not justified by probable cause, by the simple expedient of arranging to arrest suspects at home rather than elsewhere. We do not suggest that the petitioner is necessarily correct in his assertion that such a strategy was utilized here,[13] but the fact remains that had he been arrested earlier in the day, at his place of employment rather than at home, no search of his house could have been made without a search

12. It is argued in dissent that so long as there is probable cause to search the place where an arrest occurs, a search of that place should be permitted even though no search warrant has been obtained. This position seems to be based principally on two premises: first, that once an arrest has been made, the additional invasion of privacy stemming from the accompanying search is "relatively minor"; and second, that the victim of the search may "shortly thereafter" obtain a judicial determination of whether the search was justified by probable cause. With respect to the second premise, one may initially question whether all of the States in fact provide the speedy suppression procedures the dissent assumes. More fundamentally, however, we cannot accept the view that Fourth Amendment interests are vindicated so long as "the rights of the criminal" are "protect[ed] . . . against introduction of evidence seized without probable cause." The Amendment is designed to prevent, not simply to redress, unlawful police action. In any event, we cannot join in characterizing the invasion of privacy that results from a top-to-bottom search of a man's house as "minor." And we can see no reason why, simply because some interference with an individual's privacy and freedom of movement has lawfully taken place, further intrusions should automatically be allowed despite the absence of a warrant that the Fourth Amendment would otherwise require.

13. Although the warrant was issued at 10:39 a.m. and the arrest was not made until late in the afternoon, the State suggests that the delay is accounted for by normal police procedures and by the heavy workload of the officer in charge. In addition, that officer testified that he and his colleagues went to the petitioner's house "to keep from approaching him at his place of business to cause him any problem there."

warrant. In any event, even apart from the possibility of such police tactics, the general point so forcefully made by Judge Learned Hand in United States v. Kirschenblatt, 16 F.2d 202, remains:

> After arresting a man in his house, to rummage at will among his papers in search of whatever will convict him, appears to us to be indistinguishable from what might be done under a general warrant; indeed, the warrant would give more protection, for presumably it must be issued by a magistrate. True, by hypothesis the power would not exist, if the supposed offender were not found on the premises; but it is small consolation to know that one's papers are safe only so long as one is not at home.

Id., at 203.

Rabinowitz and *Harris* have been the subject of critical commentary for many years, and have been relied upon less and less in our own decisions. It is time, for the reasons we have stated, to hold that on their own facts, and insofar as the principles they stand for are inconsistent with those that we have endorsed today, they are no longer to be followed.

Application of sound Fourth Amendment principles to the facts of this case produces a clear result. The search here went far beyond the petitioner's person and the area from within which he might have obtained either a weapon or something that could have been used as evidence against him. There was no constitutional justification, in the absence of a search warrant, for extending the search beyond that area. The scope of the search was, therefore, "unreasonable" under the Fourth and Fourteenth Amendments, and the petitioner's conviction cannot stand.

Reversed.

[The concurring opinion of Justice Harlan is omitted.]

JUSTICE WHITE, with whom JUSTICE BLACK joins, dissenting.

. . . The [Fourth] Amendment does not proscribe "warrantless searches" but instead it proscribes "unreasonable searches" and this Court has never held nor does the majority today assert that warrantless searches are necessarily unreasonable.

Applying this reasonableness test to the area of searches incident to arrests, one thing is clear at the outset. Search of an arrested man and of the items within his immediate reach must in almost every case be reasonable. There is always a danger that the suspect will try to escape, seizing concealed weapons with which to overpower and injure the arresting officers, and there is a danger that he may destroy evidence vital to the prosecution. Circumstances in which these justifications would not apply are sufficiently rare that inquiry is not made into searches of this scope, which have been considered reasonable throughout.

The justifications which make such a search reasonable obviously do not apply to the search of areas to which the accused does not have ready physical access. This is not enough, however, to prove such searches unconstitutional. The Court has always held, and does not today deny, that when there is probable cause to search and it is "impracticable" for one reason or another to get a search warrant, then a warrantless search may be reasonable. This is the case whether an arrest was made at the time of the search or not.

This is not to say that a search can be reasonable without regard to the probable cause to believe that seizable items are on the premises. But when there are exigent circumstances, and probable cause, then the search may be made without a warrant, reasonably. An arrest itself may often create an emergency situation making it impracticable to obtain a warrant before embarking on a related search. Again assuming that there is probable cause to search premises at the spot where a suspect is arrested, it seems to me unreasonable to require the police to leave the scene in order to obtain a search warrant when they are already legally there to make a valid arrest, and when there must almost always be a strong possibility that confederates of the arrested man will in the meanwhile remove the items for which the police have probable cause to search. This must so often be the case that it seems to me as unreasonable to require a warrant for a search of the premises as to require a warrant for search of the person and his very immediate surroundings. . . .

[W]here as here the existence of probable cause is independently established and would justify a warrant for a broader search for evidence, I would follow past cases and permit such a search to be carried out without a warrant, since the fact of arrest supplies an exigent circumstance justifying police action before the evidence can be removed, and also alerts the suspect to the fact of the search so that he can immediately seek judicial determination of probable cause in an adversary proceeding, and appropriate redress.

This view, consistent with past cases, would not authorize the general search against which the Fourth Amendment was meant to guard, nor would it broaden or render uncertain in any way whatsoever the scope of searches permitted under the Fourth Amendment. The issue in this case is not the breadth of the search, since there was clearly probable cause for the search which was carried out. No broader search than if the officers had a warrant would be permitted. The only issue is whether a search warrant was required as a precondition to that search. It is agreed that such a warrant would be required absent exigent circumstances. I would hold that the fact of arrest supplies such an exigent circumstance, since the police had lawfully gained entry to the premises to effect the arrest and since delaying the search to secure a warrant would have involved the risk of not recovering the fruits of the crime.

. . . Without more basis for radical change than the Court's opinion reveals, I would not upset the balance of these interests which has been struck by the former decisions of this Court.

NOTES AND QUESTIONS

1. *Chimel* clarified the scope of a permissible search incident to arrest in the arrestee's home. What about the arrestee's person? In United States v. Robinson, 414 U.S. 218 (1973), a D.C. police officer stopped a 1965 Cadillac based on reliable information that the driver's operating license had been revoked. All three occupants exited the car, and the officer arrested the driver, Robinson. (The Court assumed that Robinson's full-custody arrest was valid.) The officer proceeded to search Robinson and felt a package whose contents the officer could not immediately identify. Upon removing the package — a crumpled cigarette packet — and opening it, the officer discovered "14 gelatin capsules of white powder" that turned

out to be heroin. In an opinion by then-Justice Rehnquist, the Court upheld the search:

> It is well settled that a search incident to a lawful arrest is a traditional exception to the warrant requirement of the Fourth Amendment. This general exception has historically been formulated into two distinct propositions. The first is that a search may be made of the *person* of the arrestee by virtue of the lawful arrest. The second is that a search may be made of the area within the control of the arrestee.
>
> Examination of this Court's decisions shows that these two propositions have been treated quite differently. The validity of the search of a person incident to a lawful arrest has been regarded as settled from its first enunciation, and has remained virtually unchallenged until the present case. The validity of the second proposition, while likewise conceded in principle, has been subject to differing interpretations as to the extent of the area which may be searched. . . .
>
> The Court of Appeals in effect determined that the *only* reason supporting the authority for a *full* search incident to lawful arrest was the possibility of discovery of evidence or fruits. . . .
>
> [But the] justification or reason for the authority to search incident to a lawful arrest rests quite as much on the need to disarm the suspect in order to take him into custody as it does on the need to preserve evidence on his person for later use at trial. The standards traditionally governing a search incident to lawful arrest are not, therefore, [altered] . . . by the absence of probable fruits or further evidence of the particular crime for which the arrest is made.
>
> Nor are we inclined, on the basis of what seems to us to be a rather speculative judgment, to qualify the breadth of the general authority to search incident to a lawful custodial arrest on an assumption that persons arrested for the offense of driving while their licenses have been revoked are less likely to possess dangerous weapons than are those arrested for other crimes.[5] It is scarcely open to doubt that the danger to an officer is far greater in the case of the extended exposure which follows the taking of a suspect into custody and transporting him to the police station than in the case of the relatively fleeting contact resulting from the typical [street] stop. This is an adequate basis for treating all custodial arrests alike for purposes of search justification.
>
> But quite apart from these distinctions, our more fundamental disagreement with the Court of Appeals arises from its suggestion that there must be litigated in each case the issue of whether or not there was present one of the reasons supporting the authority for a search of the person incident to a lawful arrest. We do not think the long line of authorities of this Court . . . or what we can glean from the history of practice in this country and in England, requires such a case-by-case adjudication. A police officer's determination as to how and where to search the person of a suspect whom he has arrested is necessarily a quick ad hoc judgment which the Fourth Amendment does not require to be broken down in each instance into an analysis of each step in the search. The authority to search the person incident to a lawful custodial arrest, while based upon the need to disarm and to discover evidence, does not depend on what a court

---

5. Such an assumption appears at least questionable in light of the available statistical data concerning assaults on police officers who are in the course of making arrests. The danger to the police officer flows from the fact of the arrest, and its attendant proximity, stress, and uncertainty, and not from the grounds for arrest. One study concludes that approximately 30% of the shootings of police officers occur when an officer stops a person in an automobile. Bristow, Police Officer Shootings — A Tactical Evaluation, 54 J. Crim. L.C. & P.S. 93 (1963). The Government in its brief notes that the Uniform Crime Reports, prepared by the Federal Bureau of Investigation, indicate that a significant percentage of murders of police officers occurs when the officers are making traffic stops. Those reports indicate that during January-March 1973, 35 police officers were murdered; 11 of those officers were killed while engaged in making traffic stops.

may later decide was the probability in a particular arrest situation that weapons or evidence would in fact be found upon the person of the suspect. A custodial arrest of a suspect based on probable cause is a reasonable intrusion under the Fourth Amendment; that intrusion being lawful, a search incident to the arrest requires no additional justification. It is the fact of the lawful arrest which establishes the authority to search, and we hold that in the case of a lawful custodial arrest a full search of the person is not only an exception to the warrant requirement of the Fourth Amendment, but is also a "reasonable" search under that Amendment.

. . . Since it is the fact of custodial arrest which gives rise to the authority to search, it is of no moment that Jenks did not indicate any subjective fear of the respondent or that he did not himself suspect that respondent was armed. Having in the course of a lawful search come upon the crumpled package of cigarettes, he was entitled to inspect it; and when his inspection revealed the heroin capsules, he was entitled to seize them as "fruits, instrumentalities, or contraband" probative of criminal conduct.

414 U.S., at 224, 233-236.

Justice Marshall wrote a sharp dissent joined by Justices Douglas and Brennan. Marshall argued that the majority's decision would facilitate pretextual arrests: police officers arresting suspects for minor traffic infractions in order to search those suspects for drugs. He also contended that, even if the rest of the search was permissible, opening the crumpled cigarette pack was another story: "[E]ven were we to assume, arguendo, that it was reasonable for Jenks to remove the object he felt in respondent's pocket, clearly there was no justification consistent with the Fourth Amendment which would authorize his opening the package and looking inside." Id., at 255-256 (Marshall, J., dissenting). He continued:

One wonders if the result in this case would have been the same were respondent a businessman who was lawfully taken into custody for driving without a license and whose wallet was taken from him by the police. Would it be reasonable for the police officer, because of the possibility that a razor blade was hidden somewhere in the wallet, to open it, remove all the contents, and examine each item carefully? Or suppose a lawyer lawfully arrested for a traffic offense is found to have a sealed envelope on his person. Would it be permissible for the arresting officer to tear open the envelope in order to make sure that it did not contain a clandestine weapon — perhaps a pin or a razor blade?

Id., at 257. How would you respond to the hypotheticals in Justice Marshall's dissent? Are those searches legal under *Robinson*?

2. Which way does history cut in *Robinson*? The conventional — though contested — wisdom among historians is that there has long been broad authority for police officers to search incident to arrest. The leading discussion is Telford Taylor, Two Studies in Constitutional Interpretation 23-50 (1969). For the best and most detailed version of the contrary argument, see Thomas Y. Davies, Recovering the Original Fourth Amendment, 98 Mich. L. Rev. 547 (1999). But even if the conventional wisdom is correct, the historical search-incident-to-arrest doctrine also included a search of the arrestee's house, if the arrest occurred there. See Taylor, supra, at 29 ("Neither in the reported cases nor the legal literature is there any indication that search of the person of an arrestee, *or the premises in which he was taken*, was ever challenged in England until the end of the nineteenth century") (emphasis added). Recall that in *Chimel*, the Court expressly rejected *that* rule. Does it make sense for the Court to follow the historical practice in *Robinson* but not in *Chimel*?

3. In Maryland v. Buie, 494 U.S. 325 (1990), the Court addressed the question whether police may conduct a "protective sweep" through a home when executing an arrest warrant there. The Court determined that officers may "as a precautionary matter and without probable cause or reasonable suspicion, look in closets and other spaces immediately adjoining the place of arrest from which an attack could be immediately launched." Id., at 334. But, relying on Terry v. Ohio, 392 U.S. 1 (1968), the *Buie* majority also concluded that to look in additional areas not immediately adjoining the scene, there must be articulable suspicion that the area swept harbors an individual posing a danger to those present. (*Terry* is excerpted infra, at page 539.) The Court emphasized that "a protective sweep, aimed at protecting the arresting officers, . . . may extend only to a cursory inspection of those spaces where a person may be found." Id., at 335.

4. *Chimel*, *Robinson*, and *Buie* all involve a basic choice: whether to define the scope of police authority with a rule or with a standard. Broadly speaking, *Chimel* and *Buie* opted for standards: Police may search the areas from which the suspect might grab a weapon, or may look for accomplices in places from which an attack could be quickly launched. *Robinson* chose a rule: All suspects who may be arrested may be searched, along with items found on their persons at the time of arrest. Are these decisions consistent? Are they wise? For the leading argument in support of rules in this context, see Wayne R. LaFave, "Case-by-Case Adjudication" versus "Standardized Procedures": The *Robinson* Dilemma, 1974 Sup. Ct. Rev. 127, 141-143. For the leading argument in favor of standards, see Albert W. Alschuler, Bright Line Fever and the Fourth Amendment, 45 U. Pitt. L. Rev. 227 (1984).

5. The Court issued another rulelike decision in New York v. Belton, 453 U.S. 454 (1981). Belton was pulled over for speeding; when the officer saw a small quantity of marijuana on the floor of Belton's car, he arrested Belton for possession of marijuana. The officer then searched the passenger compartment of the car and, inside the pocket of a jacket on the back seat, found cocaine. The Court held that "when a policeman has made a lawful custodial arrest of the occupant of an automobile, he may, as a contemporaneous incident of that arrest, search the passenger compartment of that automobile," id., at 460 — including examining the contents of any containers found there.

Notice that, for many cases, *Belton* does no more than replicate a portion of the authority police are given by California v. Acevedo, page 478, supra. *Acevedo* authorizes a search of the whole car, including the contents of containers, if the police have probable cause to believe evidence will be found there. *Belton* was decided a decade earlier than *Acevedo*; had it been decided later, the Court would probably have found the search permissible under the automobile exception, and search-incident-to-arrest doctrine would have been unaffected.

Belton nevertheless mattered a great deal in the many cases where the offense for which the defendant is arrested is not one for which evidence is likely to be found in the car. Suppose, for example, that the officer had arrested Belton not for marijuana possession but for speeding — a crime in some states, though only a civil violation in others. The search of the car would still have been permissible under *Belton*, but not under *Acevedo*? Can you articulate why?

6. Critics of *Belton* (and there were many) argued that it provided police an incentive to make traffic arrests in order to make drug searches — one of the problems Justice Marshall raised in his *Robinson* dissent. In Thornton v. United States, 541

U.S. 615 (2004), it appeared that the Supreme Court itself was in some disagreement over *Belton*'s scope. The majority reaffirmed the *Belton* rule, holding it to apply even when an officer does not make contact with an arrestee until this person has already left a recently occupied vehicle. Justices Stevens and Souter dissented from this extension of *Belton*. Justice Scalia concurred only in the judgment, offering a new approach:

When petitioner's car was searched in this case, he was neither in, nor anywhere near, the passenger compartment of his vehicle. Rather, he was handcuffed and secured in the back of the officer's squad car. The risk that he would nevertheless "grab a weapon or evidentiary item" from his car was remote in the extreme. The Court's effort to apply our current doctrine to this search stretches it beyond its breaking point, and for that reason I cannot join the Court's opinion.

I see three reasons why the search in this case might have been justified to protect officer safety or prevent concealment or destruction of evidence. None ultimately persuades me.

The first is that, despite being handcuffed and secured in the back of a squad car, petitioner might have escaped and retrieved a weapon or evidence from his vehicle—a theory that calls to mind Judge Goldberg's reference to the mythical arrestee "possessed of the skill of Houdini and the strength of Hercules." United States v. Frick, 490 F.2d 666, 673 (CA5 1973) (opinion concurring in part and dissenting in part). . . .

The second defense of the search in this case is that, since the officer could have conducted the search at the time of arrest (when the suspect was still near the car), he should not be penalized for having taken the sensible precaution of securing the suspect in the squad car first. . . . The weakness of this argument is that it assumes that, one way or another, the search must take place. But conducting a *Chimel* search is not the Government's right; it is an exception—justified by necessity—to a rule that would otherwise render the search unlawful. If "sensible police procedures" require that suspects be handcuffed and put in squad cars, then police should handcuff suspects, put them in squad cars, and not conduct the search. . . .

The third defense of the search is that, even though the arrestee posed no risk here, *Belton* searches in general are reasonable, and the benefits of a bright-line rule justify upholding that small minority of searches that, on their particular facts, are not reasonable. The validity of this argument rests on the accuracy of *Belton*'s claim that the passenger compartment is "in fact generally, even if not inevitably," within the suspect's immediate control. 453 U.S., at 460. By the United States' own admission, however, "the practice of restraining an arrestee on the scene before searching a car that he just occupied is so prevalent that holding that *Belton* does not apply in that setting would . . . largely render *Belton* a dead letter." Brief for United States 36-37. Reported cases involving this precise factual scenario—a motorist handcuffed and secured in the back of a squad car when the search takes place—are legion. . . .

If *Belton* searches are justifiable, it is not because the arrestee might grab a weapon or evidentiary item from his car, but simply because the car might contain evidence relevant to the crime for which he was arrested. . . .

. . . There is nothing irrational about broader police authority to search for evidence when and where the perpetrator of a crime is lawfully arrested. The fact of prior lawful arrest distinguishes the arrestee from society at large, and distinguishes a search for evidence of *his* crime from general rummaging. Moreover, it is not illogical to assume that evidence of a crime is most likely to be found where the suspect was apprehended. . . .

. . . But if we are going to continue to allow *Belton* searches on stare decisis grounds, we should at least be honest about why we are doing so. *Belton* cannot reasonably be explained as a mere application of *Chimel*. Rather, it is a return to the broader sort of search incident to arrest that we allowed before *Chimel* — limited, of course, to searches of motor vehicles, a category of "effects" which give rise to a reduced expectation of privacy and heightened law enforcement needs.

Justice Scalia concurred in the judgment in *Thornton* because Thornton was lawfully arrested for a drug offense, and so it was reasonable for the officer "to believe that further contraband or similar evidence relevant to the crime for which he had been arrested might be found in the vehicle from which he had just alighted. . . ." Justice Ginsburg joined in Justice Scalia's opinion, and Justice O'Connor's concurrence all but announced that she would take the same position as Justice Scalia in future cases, but that she was reluctant to adopt it in *Thornton*, because the parties had not addressed it. That suggested five votes to rethink *Belton*, at least as it had come to apply to contexts where neither officer safety nor evidence destruction concerns were present. That rethinking occurred a few years later:

ARIZONA v. GANT

Certiorari to the Arizona Supreme Court
129 S. Ct. 1710 (2009)

JUSTICE STEVENS delivered the opinion of the Court.

After Rodney Gant was arrested for driving with a suspended license, handcuffed, and locked in the back of a patrol car, police officers searched his car and discovered cocaine in the pocket of a jacket on the backseat. Because Gant could not have accessed his car to retrieve weapons or evidence at the time of the search, the Arizona Supreme Court held that the search-incident-to-arrest exception to the Fourth Amendment's warrant requirement, as defined in Chimel v. California, 395 U.S. 752 (1969), and applied to vehicle searches in New York v. Belton, 453 U.S. 454 (1981), did not justify the search in this case. We agree with that conclusion.

Under *Chimel*, police may search incident to arrest only the space within an arrestee's "immediate control," meaning "the area from within which he might gain possession of a weapon or destructible evidence." 395 U.S., at 763. The safety and evidentiary justifications underlying *Chimel*'s reaching-distance rule determine *Belton*'s scope. Accordingly, we hold that *Belton* does not authorize a vehicle search incident to a recent occupant's arrest after the arrestee has been secured and cannot access the interior of the vehicle. Consistent with the holding in Thornton v. United States, 541 U.S. 615, and following the suggestion in Justice Scalia's opinion concurring in the judgment in that case, id., at 632, we also conclude that circumstances unique to the automobile context justify a search incident to arrest when it is reasonable to believe that evidence of the offense of arrest might be found in the vehicle.

I

On August 25, 1999, acting on an anonymous tip that the residence at 2524 North Walnut Avenue was being used to sell drugs, Tucson police officers Griffith and Reed knocked on the front door and asked to speak to the owner. Gant answered the door and, after identifying himself, stated that he expected the owner to return later. The officers left the residence and conducted a records check, which revealed that Gant's driver's license had been suspended and there was an outstanding warrant for his arrest for driving with a suspended license.

When the officers returned to the house that evening, they found a man near the back of the house and a woman in a car parked in front of it. After a third officer arrived, they arrested the man for providing a false name and the woman for possessing drug paraphernalia. Both arrestees were handcuffed and secured in separate patrol cars when Gant arrived. The officers recognized his car as it entered the driveway, and Officer Griffith confirmed that Gant was the driver by shining a flashlight into the car as it drove by him. Gant parked at the end of the driveway, got out of his car, and shut the door. Griffith, who was about 30 feet away, called to Gant, and they approached each other, meeting 10-to-12 feet from Gant's car. Griffith immediately arrested Gant and handcuffed him.

Because the other arrestees were secured in the only patrol cars at the scene, Griffith called for backup. When two more officers arrived, they locked Gant in the backseat of their vehicle. After Gant had been handcuffed and placed in the back of a patrol car, two officers searched his car: One of them found a gun, and the other discovered a bag of cocaine in the pocket of a jacket on the backseat.

Gant was charged with two offenses-possession of a narcotic drug for sale and possession of drug paraphernalia (i.e., the plastic bag in which the cocaine was found). . . .

After protracted state-court proceedings, the Arizona Supreme Court concluded that the search of Gant's car was unreasonable within the meaning of the Fourth Amendment. . . .

The chorus that has called for us to revisit *Belton* includes courts, scholars, and Members of this Court who have questioned that decision's clarity and its fidelity to Fourth Amendment principles. We therefore granted the State's petition for certiorari. . . .

II

In *Chimel*, we held that a search incident to arrest may only include "the arrestee's person and the area 'within his immediate control' — construing that phrase to mean the area from within which he might gain possession of a weapon or destructible evidence." Ibid. That limitation, which continues to define the boundaries of the exception, ensures that the scope of a search incident to arrest is commensurate with its purposes of protecting arresting officers and safeguarding any evidence of the offense of arrest that an arrestee might conceal or destroy. . . .

In *Belton*, we considered *Chimel*'s application to the automobile context. . . .

[W]e held that when an officer lawfully arrests "the occupant of an automobile, he may, as a contemporaneous incident of that arrest, search the passenger compartment of the automobile" and any containers therein. *Belton*, 453 U.S., at 460 (footnote omitted). That holding was based in large part on our assumption "that articles inside the relatively narrow compass of the passenger compartment of an automobile are in fact generally, even if not inevitably, within 'the area into which an arrestee might reach.'" Ibid.

The Arizona Supreme Court read our decision in *Belton* as merely delineating "the proper scope of a search of the interior of an automobile" incident to an arrest, id., at 459. That is, *when* the passenger compartment is within an arrestee's reaching distance, *Belton* supplies the generalization that the entire compartment and any containers therein may be reached. On that view of *Belton*, the state court concluded that the search of Gant's car was unreasonable because Gant clearly could not have accessed his car at the time of the search. . . .

III

Despite the textual and evidentiary support for the Arizona Supreme Court's reading of *Belton*, our opinion has been widely understood to allow a vehicle search incident to the arrest of a recent occupant even if there is no possibility the arrestee could gain access to the vehicle at the time of the search. . . .

Under this broad reading of *Belton*, a vehicle search would be authorized incident to every arrest of a recent occupant notwithstanding that in most cases the vehicle's passenger compartment will not be within the arrestee's reach at the time of the search. To read *Belton* as authorizing a vehicle search incident to every recent occupant's arrest would thus untether the rule from the justifications underlying the *Chimel* exception — a result clearly incompatible with our statement in *Belton* that it "in no way alters the fundamental principles established in the *Chimel* case regarding the basic scope of searches incident to lawful custodial arrests." 453 U.S., at 460, n. 3. Accordingly, we reject this reading of *Belton* and hold that the *Chimel* rationale authorizes police to search a vehicle incident to a recent occupant's arrest only when the arrestee is unsecured and within reaching distance of the passenger compartment at the time of the search.

Although it does not follow from *Chimel*, we also conclude that circumstances unique to the vehicle context justify a search incident to a lawful arrest when it is "reasonable to believe evidence relevant to the crime of arrest might be found in the vehicle." *Thornton*, 541 U.S., at 632 (Scalia, J., concurring in judgment). In many cases, as when a recent occupant is arrested for a traffic violation, there will be no reasonable basis to believe the vehicle contains relevant evidence. See, e.g., Atwater v. Lago Vista, 532 U.S. 318, 324 (2001); Knowles v. Iowa, 525 U.S. 113, 118 (1998). But in others, including *Belton* and *Thornton*, the offense of arrest will supply a basis for searching the passenger compartment of an arrestee's vehicle and any containers therein.

Neither the possibility of access nor the likelihood of discovering offense-related evidence authorized the search in this case. . . . Because police could not reasonably have believed either that Gant could have accessed his car at the time of the search or that evidence of the offense for which he was arrested might have been found therein, the search in this case was unreasonable.

IV

The State does not seriously disagree with the Arizona Supreme Court's conclusion that Gant could not have accessed his vehicle at the time of the search, but it nevertheless asks us to uphold the search of his vehicle under the broad reading of *Belton* discussed above. The State argues that *Belton* searches are reasonable regardless of the possibility of access in a given case because that expansive rule correctly balances law enforcement interests, including the interest in a bright-line rule, with an arrestee's limited privacy interest in his vehicle.

For several reasons, we reject the State's argument. First, the State seriously undervalues the privacy interests at stake. Although we have recognized that a motorist's privacy interest in his vehicle is less substantial than in his home, see New York v. Class, 475 U.S. 106, 112-113 (1986), the former interest is nevertheless important and deserving of constitutional protection, see *Knowles*, 525 U.S., at 117. It is particularly significant that *Belton* searches authorize police officers to search not just the passenger compartment but every purse, briefcase, or other container within that space. A rule that gives police the power to conduct such a search whenever an individual is caught committing a traffic offense, when there is no basis for believing evidence of the offense might be found in the vehicle, creates a serious and recurring threat to the privacy of countless individuals. Indeed, the character of that threat implicates the central concern underlying the Fourth Amendment-the concern about giving police officers unbridled discretion to rummage at will among a person's private effects.

At the same time as it undervalues these privacy concerns, the State exaggerates the clarity that its reading of *Belton* provides. Courts that have read *Belton* expansively are at odds regarding how close in time to the arrest and how proximate to the arrestee's vehicle an officer's first contact with the arrestee must be to bring the encounter within *Belton*'s purview and whether a search is reasonable when it commences or continues after the arrestee has been removed from the scene. . . .

Contrary to the State's suggestion, a broad reading of *Belton* is also unnecessary to protect law enforcement safety and evidentiary interests. Under our view, *Belton* and *Thornton* permit an officer to conduct a vehicle search when an arrestee is within reaching distance of the vehicle or it is reasonable to believe the vehicle contains evidence of the offense of arrest. Other established exceptions to the warrant requirement authorize a vehicle search under additional circumstances when safety or evidentiary concerns demand. . . .

V

Our dissenting colleagues argue that the doctrine of *stare decisis* requires adherence to a broad reading of *Belton* even though the justifications for searching a vehicle incident to arrest are in most cases absent. The doctrine of stare decisis is of course "essential to the respect accorded to the judgments of the Court and to the stability of the law," but it does not compel us to follow a past decision when its rationale no longer withstands "careful analysis." Lawrence v. Texas, 539 U.S. 558, 577 (2003). . . .

The experience of the 28 years since we decided *Belton* has shown that the generalization underpinning the broad reading of that decision is unfounded. We now know that articles inside the passenger compartment are rarely "within 'the area into which an arrestee might reach,'" 453 U.S., at 460, and blind adherence to *Belton*'s faulty assumption would authorize myriad unconstitutional searches. The doctrine of stare decisis does not require us to approve routine constitutional violations.

VI

Police may search a vehicle incident to a recent occupant's arrest only if the arrestee is within reaching distance of the passenger compartment at the time of the search or it is reasonable to believe the vehicle contains evidence of the offense of arrest.

When these justifications are absent, a search of an arrestee's vehicle will be unreasonable unless police obtain a warrant or show that another exception to the warrant requirement applies. The Arizona Supreme Court correctly held that this case involved an unreasonable search. Accordingly, the judgment of the State Supreme Court is affirmed.

JUSTICE SCALIA, concurring.

To determine what is an "unreasonable" search within the meaning of the Fourth Amendment, we look first to the historical practices the Framers sought to preserve; if those provide inadequate guidance, we apply traditional standards of reasonableness. Since the historical scope of officers' authority to search vehicles incident to arrest is uncertain, see Thornton v. United States, 541 U.S. 615, 629-631 (Scalia, J., concurring in judgment), traditional standards of reasonableness govern. It is abundantly clear that those standards do not justify what I take to be the rule set forth in New York v. Belton, 453 U.S. 454 (1981), and *Thornton*: that arresting officers may always search an arrestee's vehicle in order to protect themselves from hidden weapons. When an arrest is made in connection with a roadside stop, police virtually always have a less intrusive and more effective means of ensuring their safety-and a means that is virtually always employed: ordering the arrestee away from the vehicle, patting him down in the open, handcuffing him, and placing him in the squad car. . . .

Justice Stevens acknowledges that an officer-safety rationale cannot justify all vehicle searches incident to arrest, but asserts that that is not the rule *Belton* and *Thornton* adopted. (As described above, I read those cases differently). Justice Stevens would therefore retain the application of Chimel v. California, 395 U.S. 752 (1969), in the car-search context but would apply in the future what he believes our cases held in the past: that officers making a roadside stop may search the vehicle so long as the "arrestee is within reaching distance of the passenger compartment at the time of the search." I believe that this standard fails to provide the needed guidance to arresting officers and also leaves much room for manipulation, inviting officers to leave the scene unsecured (at least where dangerous suspects are not involved) in order to conduct a vehicle search. In my view we should simply abandon the *Belton-Thornton* charade of officer safety and overrule those cases. I would hold that a vehicle search incident to arrest is ipso facto "reasonable" only when the object of the search is evidence of the crime for which the arrest was made, or of another crime that the officer has probable cause to believe occurred. Because respondent was arrested for driving without a license (a crime for which no evidence could be expected to be found in the vehicle), I would hold in the present case that the search was unlawful. . . .

Justice Alito argues that there is no reason to adopt a rule limiting automobile-arrest searches to those cases where the search's object is evidence of the crime of arrest. I disagree. This formulation of officers' authority both preserves the outcomes of our prior cases and tethers the scope and rationale of the doctrine to the triggering event. *Belton*, by contrast, allowed searches precisely when its exigency-based rationale was least applicable: The fact of the arrest in the automobile context makes searches on exigency grounds *less* reasonable, not more. . . .

No other Justice, however, shares my view that application of *Chimel* in this context should be entirely abandoned. It seems to me unacceptable for the Court to come forth with a 4-to-1-to-4 opinion that leaves the governing rule uncertain. I am therefore confronted with the choice of either leaving the current understanding of *Belton* and *Thornton* in effect, or acceding to what seems to me the artificial narrowing of those cases adopted by Justice Stevens. The latter, as I have said, does not provide the degree of certainty I think desirable in this field; but the former opens the field to what I think are plainly unconstitutional searches — which is the greater evil. I therefore join the opinion of the Court.

[Justice Breyer's dissenting opinion is omitted.]

JUSTICE ALITO, with whom CHIEF JUSTICE ROBERTS and JUSTICE KENNEDY join, and with whom JUSTICE BREYER joins except as to Part II-E, dissenting.

Twenty-eight years ago, in New York v. Belton, 453 U.S. 454, 460 (1981), this Court held that "when a policeman has made a lawful custodial arrest of the occupant of an automobile, he may, as a contemporaneous incident of that arrest, search the passenger compartment of that automobile." (Footnote omitted.) Five years ago, in Thornton v. United States, 541 U.S. 615 (2004) — a case involving a situation not materially distinguishable from the situation here — the Court not only reaffirmed but extended the holding of *Belton*, making it applicable to recent occupants. Today's decision effectively overrules those important decisions. . . .

II

Because the Court has substantially overruled *Belton* and *Thornton*, the Court must explain why its departure from the usual rule of stare decisis is justified. . . . [T]he Court has said that a constitutional precedent should be followed unless there is a "special justification" for its abandonment. Dickerson v. United States, 530 U.S. 428, 443 (2000). Relevant factors identified in prior cases include whether the precedent has engendered reliance, id., at 442, whether there has been an important change in circumstances in the outside world, Randall v. Sorrell, 548 U.S. 230, 244 (2006) (plurality opinion); Burnet v. Coronado Oil & Gas Co., 285 U.S. 393, 412 (1932) (Brandeis, J., dissenting), whether the precedent has proved to be unworkable, Vieth v. Jubelirer, 541 U.S. 267, 306 (2004) (plurality opinion) (citing *Payne*, supra, at 827), whether the precedent has been undermined by later decisions, see, e.g., Patterson v. McLean Credit Union, 491 U.S. 164, 173-174 (1989), and whether the decision was badly reasoned. *Vieth*, supra, at 306 (plurality opinion). These factors weigh in favor of retaining the rule established in *Belton*.

A

Reliance. . . . The opinion of the Court recognizes that "*Belton* has been widely taught in police academies and that law enforcement officers have relied on the rule in conducting vehicle searches during the past 28 years." But for the Court, this seemingly counts for nothing. The Court states that "[w]e have never relied on stare decisis to justify the continuance of an unconstitutional police practice," but of course the Court routinely relies on decisions sustaining the constitutionality of police practices without doing what the Court has done here — sua sponte considering whether those decisions should be overruled. And the Court cites no authority for the proposition that stare decisis may be disregarded or provides only lesser protection when the precedent that is challenged is one that sustained the constitutionality of a law enforcement practice. . . .

B

Changed circumstances. Abandonment of the *Belton* rule cannot be justified on the ground that the dangers surrounding the arrest of a vehicle occupant are different today than they were 28 years ago. The Court claims that "[w]e now know that articles inside the passenger compartment are rarely within 'the area into which an arrestee might reach,'" but surely it was well known in 1981 that a person who is taken from a vehicle, handcuffed, and placed in the back of a patrol car is unlikely to make it back into his own car to retrieve a weapon or destroy evidence.

C

Workability. The *Belton* rule has not proved to be unworkable. On the contrary, the rule was adopted for the express purpose of providing a test that would be relatively easy for police officers and judges to apply. The Court correctly notes that even the *Belton* rule is not perfectly clear in all situations. Specifically, it is sometimes debatable whether a search is or is not contemporaneous with an arrest, but that problem is small in comparison with the problems that the Court's new two-part rule will produce.

The first part of the Court's new rule — which permits the search of a vehicle's passenger compartment if it is within an arrestee's reach at the time of the search — reintroduces the same sort of case-by-case, fact-specific decisionmaking that the *Belton* rule was adopted to avoid. . . .

Even more serious problems will also result from the second part of the Court's new rule, which requires officers making roadside arrests to determine whether there is reason to believe that the vehicle contains evidence of the crime of arrest. What this rule permits in a variety of situations is entirely unclear.

D

Consistency with later cases. The *Belton* bright-line rule has not been undermined by subsequent cases. On the contrary, that rule was reaffirmed and extended just five years ago in *Thornton.*

E

Bad reasoning. The Court is harshly critical of *Belton*'s reasoning, but the problem that the Court perceives cannot be remedied simply by overruling *Belton*. *Belton* represented only a modest-and quite defensible-extension of *Chimel*, as I understand that decision.

Prior to *Chimel*, the Court's precedents permitted an arresting officer to search the area within an arrestee's "possession" and "control" for the purpose of gathering evidence. See 395 U.S., at 759-760. Based on this "abstract doctrine," id., at 760, n. 4, the Court had sustained searches that extended far beyond an arrestee's grabbing area. See United States v. Rabinowitz, 339 U.S. 56 (1950) (search of entire office); Harris v. United States, 331 U.S. 145 (1947) (search of entire apartment).

The *Chimel* Court, in an opinion written by Justice Stewart, overruled these cases. Concluding that there are only two justifications for a warrantless search incident to arrest — officer safety and the preservation of evidence — the Court stated that such a search must be confined to "the arrestee's person" and "the area from within which he might gain possession of a weapon or destructible evidence." 395 U.S., at 762-763.

Unfortunately, *Chimel* did not say whether "the area from within which [an arrestee] might gain possession of a weapon or destructible evidence" is to be measured at the time of the arrest or at the time of the search, but unless the *Chimel* rule was meant to be a specialty rule, applicable to only a few unusual cases, the Court must have intended for this area to be measured at the time of arrest.

This is so because the Court can hardly have failed to appreciate the following two facts. First, in the great majority of cases, an officer making an arrest is able to handcuff the arrestee and remove him to a secure place before conducting a search incident to the arrest. Second, because it is safer for an arresting officer to secure an arrestee before searching, it is likely that this is what arresting officers do in the great majority of cases. (And it appears, not surprisingly, that this is in fact the prevailing practice.) Thus, if the area within an arrestee's reach were assessed, not at the time of arrest, but at the time of the search, the *Chimel* rule would rarely come into play.

Moreover, if the applicability of the *Chimel* rule turned on whether an arresting officer chooses to secure an arrestee prior to conducting a search, rather than searching first and securing the arrestee later, the rule would "create a perverse incentive for an arresting officer to prolong the period during which the arrestee is kept in an area where he could pose a danger to the officer." United States v. Abdul-Saboor, 85 F.3d 664, 669 (CADC 1996). If this is the law, the D.C. Circuit observed, "the law would truly be, as Mr. Bumble said, 'a ass.'" Ibid.

I do not think that this is what the *Chimel* Court intended. Handcuffs were in use in 1969. The ability of arresting officers to secure arrestees before conducting a search — and their incentive to do so — are facts that can hardly have escaped the Court's attention. I therefore believe that the *Chimel* Court intended that its new rule apply in cases in which the arrestee is handcuffed before the search is conducted.

The *Belton* Court, in my view, proceeded on the basis of this interpretation of *Chimel*. . . . Viewing *Chimel* as having focused on the time of arrest, *Belton*'s only new step was to eliminate the need to decide on a case-by-case basis whether a particular person seated in a car actually could have reached the part of the passenger compartment where a weapon or evidence was hidden. For this reason, if we are going to reexamine *Belton*, we should also reexamine the reasoning in *Chimel* on which *Belton* rests.

F

The Court, however, does not reexamine *Chimel* and thus leaves the law relating to searches incident to arrest in a confused and unstable state. The first part of the Court's new two-part rule — which permits an arresting officer to search the area within an arrestee's reach at the time of the search — applies, at least for now, only to vehicle occupants and recent occupants, but there is no logical reason why the same rule should not apply to all arrestees.

The second part of the Court's new rule, which the Court takes uncritically from Justice Scalia's separate opinion in *Thornton*, raises doctrinal and practical problems that the Court makes no effort to address. Why, for example, is the standard for this type of evidence-gathering search "reason to believe" rather than probable cause? And why is this type of search restricted to evidence of the offense of arrest?

It is true that an arrestee's vehicle is probably more likely to contain evidence of the crime of arrest than of some other crime, but if reason-to-believe is the governing standard for an evidence-gathering search incident to arrest, it is not easy to see why an officer should not be able to search when the officer has reason to believe that the vehicle in question possesses evidence of a crime other than the crime of arrest.

Nor is it easy to see why an evidence-gathering search incident to arrest should be restricted to the passenger compartment. The *Belton* rule was limited in this way because the passenger compartment was considered to be the area that vehicle occupants can generally reach, 453 U.S., at 460, but since the second part of the new rule is not based on officer safety or the preservation of evidence, the ground for this limitation is obscure.

III

. . . In this case, I would simply apply *Belton* and reverse the judgment below.

NOTES AND QUESTIONS

1. How is *Gant* consistent with the holding in *Thornton*, as the majority proclaims? Presumably because in *Thornton*, unlike *Gant*, the officer who performed the search had reason to believe that additional contraband or other evidence relevant to Thornton's drug offense might be found in the car. But what is the Fourth Amendment rationale for permitting *any* search of the car's interior, once an arrestee has been secured? In *Thornton*, Justice Scalia suggested that it is reasonable to permit searches for evidence related to the crime for which a car's occupant has been arrested, due in part to the reduced expectation of privacy associated with cars. But the majority takes pains to emphasize the importance of our privacy interest in vehicles. So what is the rationale?

2. Does the absence of one suggest, as the dissent contends, that *Gant* has unsettled not just *Belton* and *Thornton*, but also *Chimel*? It may seem obvious *Gant* will restrict police authority to search the passenger compartment of vehicles as incident to arrest. But the same argument might also *expand* police authority to search homes. Suppose, for example, Justice Scalia and his colleagues applied his *Thornton* argument to cases like *Chimel*. As long as the crime was one that made discovery of evidence reasonably likely, the police might have the power to search the arrestee's entire home. (The law allowed precisely that before *Chimel* limited such searches to the area within the arrestee's reach.) So Justice Scalia's position might mean narrower search authority with respect to cars, but broader search authority with respect to homes. Would this be a good result?

3. Who has the better argument with regard to the workability of the new rule, as opposed to the old? Do you agree with Justice Alito that while *Belton* and *Thornton* produced some uncertainty as to whether a passenger compartment search is incident to an arrest, *Gant* is likely to produce considerably more uncertainty?

4. Consider the following. In *Thornton*, Justice Scalia concluded that because Thornton had been arrested for a drug offense, "it was reasonable for Officer Nichols to believe that further contraband or similar evidence relevant to the crime for which he had been arrested might be found in the vehicle. . . ." Thornton was

carrying drugs on his person when arrested. Should the same passenger compartment search rule apply when a drug kingpin is arrested after a four-month investigation, and he happens to be driving his car? Would it be reasonable to believe that an investment advisor who has been defrauding clients might be carrying relevant evidence in his briefcase when he is arrested in his car?

5. The defendant in Colorado v. Bertine, 479 U.S. 367 (1987), was arrested for driving under the influence of alcohol. Shortly before a tow truck arrived to take the defendant's van to the police impoundment lot, the police "inventoried" the contents of the van. The Court held this inventory search permissible, and summarized its rationale as follows: "[I]nventory procedures serve to protect an owner's property while it is in the custody of the police, to insure against claims of lost, stolen, or vandalized, property, and to guard the police from danger." Id., at 372. Note the use of the phrase "inventory procedures" — language in earlier inventory search cases had suggested that the police must follow regular procedures in order to take advantage of this particular doctrine. See Illinois v. Lafayette, 462 U.S. 640 (1983); South Dakota v. Opperman, 428 U.S. 364 (1976). *Bertine* seemed less concerned with regular procedures:

> Bertine . . . argues that the inventory search of his van was unconstitutional because departmental regulations gave the police officers discretion to choose between impounding his van and parking and locking it in a public parking place. . . . [W]e reject [this argument]. Nothing in *Opperman* or *Lafayette* prohibits the exercise of police discretion so long as that discretion is exercised according to standard criteria and on the basis of something other than suspicion of evidence of criminal activity. Here, the discretion afforded the Boulder police was exercised in light of standardized criteria, related to the feasibility and appropriateness of parking and locking a vehicle rather than impounding it.

Id., at 375-376.

It seems fair to see inventory search doctrine as an adjunct to search-incident-to-arrest doctrine: Both are triggered by a decision to take the defendant into custody, and under both the police have something close to blanket authority to search anything the defendant has with him at the time of arrest. Consider how these doctrines change the meaning of arrests. Not only are arrests the means by which the police gain physical control over criminal defendants; not only are they a mechanism for triggering more formal criminal proceedings. Arrests are also a powerful means of gathering evidence. Which means that *both* liberty *and* privacy are at stake in arrests. Inventory search doctrine may also mean that cases like *Gant* have small practical consequences: If the police may not search at the time of arrest, they may impound the car and inventory its contents, plus the contents of any items the defendant is carrying on his person, later at the police station. Given the breadth of inventory search authority, why must we carefully calibrate the appropriate scope of the search incident to arrest as it applies to cars? Isn't this a fundamental point distinguishing cars from houses, and the *Belton-Thornton-Gant* line of cases from *Chimel*?

D. Reasonableness

To this point, the materials have shown two approaches that the Court has taken to protect the "privacies of life" that it praised in Boyd v. United States, 116 U.S. 616,

630 (1886). One approach — the one adopted in *Boyd* — was to make the protection absolute: The invoices in that case were simply free from official inspection, whatever the means employed. In contrast, Katz v. United States, 389 U.S. 347 (1967), offered conditional privacy protection: Given a warrant based on probable cause, the intrusion on the suspect's privacy is permissible. Many of the cases in the preceding section then added a qualification to *Katz*-style protection: Given an appropriate exception to the warrant requirement, probable cause alone is enough to justify a Fourth Amendment intrusion.

There is a third way to approach privacy protection, and this third way is increasingly coming to dominate Fourth Amendment case law: Privacy is not protected absolutely, nor by the warrant and probable cause requirements. Instead, privacy protection is rooted in the constitutional command that searches and seizures be reasonable.

This section takes up cases in which the Supreme Court has employed an open-ended "reasonableness" standard to judge the propriety of Fourth Amendment intrusions. This approach has the virtue of permitting courts to consider factors not formally taken into account in the more traditional warrant-and-probable-cause formula. The seriousness of the crime under investigation, the importance of evidence sought by the government, and the extent of the government's privacy invasion, for instance, might be deemed relevant in determining whether a given search or seizure or category of searches and seizures should be permitted, and upon what showing.

Notice that reasonableness need not mean less stringent limits on police searches and seizures. Fourth Amendment reasonableness could be *more* demanding — a point demonstrated by Winston v. Lee, 470 U.S. 753 (1985). In *Winston*, a shopkeeper was wounded during an attempted robbery but, being armed, also wounded his assailant in the left side as the assailant fled. The defendant, who was suffering from a gunshot wound to his left chest area, was found shortly after the crime about eight blocks away from the scene. The issue in *Winston* involved a proposed "search" for the shopkeeper's bullet. The Court determined that on the facts before it, searching for the evidence — even with probable cause and advance judicial authorization — would be unreasonable, given that the bullet was lodged in the suspect's body and could only be retrieved through surgery requiring general anesthesia.

Despite cases like *Winston*, however, many commentators have worried that any sliding scale, balancing, or "all circumstances considered" approach to Fourth Amendment interpretation inevitably means in practice that

> . . . appellate courts [will] defer to trial courts and trial courts . . . to the police. What other results should we expect? If there are no fairly clear rules telling the policeman what he may and may not do, courts are seldom going to say that what he did was unreasonable.

Anthony G. Amsterdam, Perspectives on the Fourth Amendment, 58 Minn. L. Rev. 349, 394 (1974). Carol Steiker has warned that "[j]udgments couched in terms of 'reasonableness' slide very easily into the familiar constitutional rubric of 'rational basis' review — a level of scrutiny that has proven to be effectively no scrutiny at all." Carol S. Steiker, Second Thoughts About First Principles, 107 Harv. L. Rev. 820, 855 (1994). And if reasonableness is decided case by case, with the propriety of each

Fourth Amendment intrusion judged in light of its particular facts, it is worth wondering whether this approach can provide adequate guidance to police as they decide when to search or seize, and when not to.

Perhaps it can. Professor Alschuler has argued that the case for bright-line Fourth Amendment rules has been overstated, and that the desire for such rules has needlessly complicated the case law. He urges courts to reconsider the virtues of the case-by-case approach:

> [C]ourts sometimes can give law enforcement officers significant guidance within a framework of case-by-case adjudication by establishing subordinate, presumptive rules for the resolution of recurring fourth amendment issues. . . . In addition, every ruling in a system of case-by-case adjudication becomes part of a dialogue between judges and law enforcement officers. This dialogue can — and has in fact — established standards that may not be subject to precise verbalization. . . . [Nevertheless,] [o]ur traditional regime of case-by-case adjudication plainly does communicate.

Albert W. Alschuler, Bright Line Fever and the Fourth Amendment, 45 U. Pitt. L. Rev. 227, 256 (1984).

Whatever the merits of these arguments, consider-all-the-circumstances reasonableness has played an important role in Fourth Amendment doctrine — a role that has only increased in recent years. Interestingly, the early cases using this approach fell outside the traditional concerns of criminal investigation. In Camara v. Municipal Court, 387 U.S. 523 (1967), and See v. City of Seattle, 387 U.S. 541 (1967), the Court took up the question of Fourth Amendment constraints on fire, health, and housing code inspection programs, overruling Franks v. Maryland, 359 U.S. 360 (1959), which had deemed such programs to be at the periphery of Fourth Amendment concerns. Suspicionless government inspections to enforce safety code regulations posed a problem for the then-prevailing approach to Fourth Amendment interpretation, with its emphasis on probable cause and search warrants. Consider Professor Sundby's account:

> Because requiring a warrant based on probable cause would have precluded suspicionless government inspections, the Court did not extend the amendment's coverage very far beyond the context of criminal arrests and searches. When the fourth amendment governed, therefore, it provided the full protections of the warrant clause — but the protections generally did not apply to government intrusions other than criminal investigations.
>
> The Court's warrant clause emphasis and corresponding reluctance to expand fourth amendment protections beyond criminal investigations largely explain its holding in Frank v. Maryland. In *Frank* the Court addressed the issue whether the defendant's conviction for resisting a warrantless inspection of his house violated the fourth amendment. Upholding the conviction and fine, the *Frank* majority espoused the traditional view that if inspections like those at issue were subject to full fourth amendment protections, the search would have to satisfy the warrant requirement. Yet requiring a warrant based on probable cause for housing inspections would defeat the inspections' objective of maintaining community health . . . .
>
> [T]he *Frank* majority . . . argued that because Frank's asserted privacy interest did not concern a criminal investigation, his claim, at most, touched "upon the periphery" of the important fourth amendment interests protected against invasion by government officials. Stressing that the housing inspection was not a search for criminal evidence, Justice Frankfurter argued that the Constitution's prohibition against official

invasion arose almost entirely from the individual's fundamental right to be secure from evidentiary searches made in connection with criminal prosecutions. . . . Consequently, the majority concluded that any legitimate liberty interest Frank had was overwhelmed by the government's need for inspection and the desirability of not tampering with the fourth amendment's rigorous protections.

Scott E. Sundby, A Return to Fourth Amendment Basics: Undoing the Mischief of *Camara* and *Terry*, 72 Minn. L. Rev. 383, 388-391 (1988).

Camara and *See* rejected the *Frank*'s conclusion that regulatory inspections lie at the periphery of Fourth Amendment concerns: "We may agree that a routine inspection of the physical condition of private property is a less hostile intrusion than the typical policeman's search for the fruits and instrumentalities of crime. But we cannot agree that the Fourth Amendment interests at stake in these inspections are merely 'peripheral.' It is surely anomalous to say that the individual and his private property are fully protected by the Fourth Amendment only when the individual is suspected of criminal behavior." *Camara*, 387 U.S., at 530. But the Court brought both the housing inspection in *Camara* and the commercial warehouse inspection in *See* into the core of Fourth Amendment concerns only by redefining the warrant procedure and the concept of probable cause:

> In cases in which the Fourth Amendment requires that a warrant to search be obtained, "probable cause" is the standard by which a particular decision to search is tested against the constitutional mandate of reasonableness. To apply this standard, it is obviously necessary first to focus upon the governmental interest which allegedly justifies official intrusion upon the constitutionally protected interests of the private citizen. . . .
>
> Unlike the search pursuant to a criminal investigation, the inspection programs at issue here are aimed at securing city-wide compliance with minimum physical standards for private property. The primary governmental interest at stake is to prevent even the unintentional development of conditions which are hazardous to public health and safety. . . . In determining whether a particular inspection is reasonable — and thus in determining whether there is probable cause to issue a warrant for that inspection — the need for the inspection must be weighed in terms of these reasonable goals of code enforcement. . . .
>
> . . . [T]here can be no ready test for determining reasonableness other than by balancing the need to search against the invasion which the search entails. But we think that a number of persuasive factors combine to support the reasonableness of area code-enforcement inspections. First, such programs have a long history of judicial and public acceptance. Second, the public interest demands that all dangerous conditions be prevented or abated, yet it is doubtful that any other canvassing technique would achieve acceptable results. . . . Finally, because the inspections are neither personal in nature nor aimed at the discovery of evidence of crime, they involve a relatively limited invasion of the urban citizen's privacy. . . .
>
> Having concluded that the area inspection is a "reasonable" search of private property within the meaning of the Fourth Amendment, it is obvious that "probable cause" to issue a warrant to inspect must exist if reasonable legislative or administrative standards for conducting an area inspection are satisfied with respect to a particular dwelling. Such standards . . . may be based upon the passage of time, the nature of the building . . . , or the condition of the entire area, but they will not necessarily depend upon specific knowledge of the condition of the particular dwelling. . . . The warrant procedure is designed to guarantee that a decision to search private property is justified by a reasonable governmental interest. But reasonableness is still the ultimate standard. . . .

Id., at 534-539. The Court thus redefined the probable cause necessary for issuance of a warrant in terms of the reasonableness of the inspection program. As Professor Sundby has argued:

> Ironically, in redefining probable cause as a flexible concept, the Court's effort to satisfy the warrant clause gave reasonableness a foot in the door as an independent factor in fourth amendment analysis. Prior to *Camara* the warrant clause had dictated the meaning of the reasonableness clause. A search or arrest was reasonable only when a warrant based on probable cause issued. *Camara*, in contrast, reversed the roles of probable cause and reasonableness. Instead of probable cause defining a reasonable search, after *Camara*, reasonableness, in the form of a balancing test, defined probable cause.

Sundby, 72 Minn. L. Rev. at 393-394.

1. Stops and Frisks

Within a year of the decisions in *Camara* and *See*, the Court had extended the balancing methodology they employed into a context very familiar to the criminal process — the street encounter between a police officer and a citizen. Terry v. Ohio, 392 U.S. 1 (1968), arose in a turbulent political context. As one of Chief Justice Earl Warren's law clerks recalled some 30 years later, the period leading up to *Terry* was a time of rioting in urban ghettoes and protest over the Vietnam War: "It was the decade of the long, hot summers. . . . Only two months before *Terry* was handed down, there was a major outbreak of rioting in many cities, including Washington, D.C., in the wake of the assassination of Dr. Martin Luther King, Jr." Earl C. Dudley, Jr., Terry v. Ohio, The Warren Court, and the Fourth Amendment: A Law Clerk's Perspective, 72 St. John's L. Rev. 891, 892 (1998). Crime was skyrocketing, and with spiraling crime came increased criticism of the Court:

> [T]he Supreme Court had come under heavy fire for its decisions enforcing the constitutional claims of those accused of crimes. In 1964 the Court's criminal procedure decisions were for the first time a major target of the Republican presidential campaign, and similar attacks were to be expected in the upcoming 1968 election.

Id. To compound the problems, in 1968 many urban police forces were nearly all white, and charges of police racism were both common and credible. In that charged context, the Court took up the question whether probable cause was the right standard for street stops — or whether *Camara*-style reasonableness should rule.

TERRY v. OHIO
Certiorari to the Supreme Court of Ohio
392 U.S. 1 (1968)

MR. CHIEF JUSTICE WARREN delivered the opinion of the Court. . . .

Petitioner Terry was convicted of carrying a concealed weapon and sentenced to the statutorily prescribed term of one to three years in the penitentiary. Following the denial of a pretrial motion to suppress, the prosecution introduced in evidence two revolvers and a number of bullets seized from Terry and a codefendant, Richard Chilton, by Cleveland Police Detective Martin McFadden. At the hearing on the motion to suppress this evidence, Officer McFadden testified that while he was patrolling in plain clothes in downtown Cleveland at approximately 2:30 in the afternoon of October 31, 1963, his attention was attracted by two men, Chilton and Terry, standing on the corner of Huron Road and Euclid Avenue. He had never seen the two men before, and he was unable to say precisely what first drew his eye to them. However, he testified that he had been a policeman for 39 years and a detective for 35 and that he had been assigned to patrol this vicinity of downtown Cleveland for shoplifters and pickpockets for 30 years. He explained that he had developed routine habits of observation over the years and that he would "stand and watch people or walk and watch people at many intervals of the day." He added "Now, in this case when I looked over they didn't look right to me at the time."

His interest aroused, Officer McFadden took up a post of observation in the entrance to a store 300 to 400 feet away from the two men. "I get more purpose to watch them when I seen their movements," he testified. He saw one of the men leave the other one and walk southwest on Huron Road, past some stores. The man paused for a moment and looked in a store window, then walked on a short distance, turned around and walked back toward the corner, pausing once again to look in the same store window. He rejoined his companion at the corner, and the two conferred briefly. Then the second man went through the same series of motions, strolling down Huron Road, looking in the same window, walking on a short distance, turning back, peering in the store window again, and returning to confer with the first man at the corner. The two men repeated this ritual alternately between five and six times apiece — in all, roughly a dozen trips. At one point, while the two were standing together on the corner, a third man approached them and engaged them briefly in conversation. This man then left the two others and walked west on Euclid Avenue. Chilton and Terry resumed their measured pacing, peering and conferring. After this had gone on for 10 to 12 minutes, the two men walked off together, heading west on Euclid Avenue, following the path taken earlier by the third man.

By this time Officer McFadden had become thoroughly suspicious. He testified that after observing their elaborately casual and oft-repeated reconnaissance of the store window on Huron Road, he suspected the two men of "casing a job, a stick-up," and that he considered it his duty as a police officer to investigate further. He added that he feared "they may have a gun." Thus, Officer McFadden followed Chilton and Terry and saw them stop in front of Zucker's store to talk to the same man who had conferred with them earlier on the street corner. Deciding that the situation was ripe for direct action, Officer McFadden approached the three men, identified himself as a police officer and asked for their names. At this point his knowledge was confined to what he had observed. He was not acquainted with any of the three men by name or by sight, and he had received no information concerning them from any other source. When the men "mumbled something" in response to his inquiries, Officer McFadden grabbed petitioner Terry, spun him around so that they were facing the other two, with Terry between McFadden and the others, and patted down the outside of his clothing. In the left breast pocket of Terry's overcoat Officer McFadden felt a pistol. He reached inside the overcoat pocket, but was unable to remove the gun. At this point, keeping Terry between himself and the others, the officer ordered all three men to enter Zucker's store. As they went in, he removed Terry's overcoat completely, removed a .38-caliber revolver from the pocket and ordered all three men to face the wall with their hands raised. Officer McFadden proceeded to pat down the outer clothing of Chilton and the third man, Katz. He discovered another revolver in the outer pocket of Chilton's overcoat, but no weapons were found on Katz. The officer testified that he only patted the men down to see whether they had weapons, and that he did not put his hands beneath the outer garments of either Terry or Chilton until he felt their guns. So far as appears from the record, he never placed his hands beneath Katz' outer garments. Officer McFadden seized Chilton's gun, asked the proprietor of the store to call a police wagon, and took all three men to the station, where Chilton and Terry were formally charged with carrying concealed weapons. . . .

I

. . . Unquestionably petitioner was entitled to the protection of the Fourth Amendment as he walked down the street in Cleveland. The question is whether in all the circumstances of this on-the-street encounter, his right to personal security was violated by an unreasonable search and seizure.

We would be less than candid if we did not acknowledge that this question thrusts to the fore difficult and troublesome issues regarding a sensitive area of police activity — issues which have never before been squarely presented to this Court. Reflective of the tensions involved are the practical and constitutional arguments pressed with great vigor on both sides of the public debate over the power of the police to "stop and frisk" — as it is sometimes euphemistically termed — suspicious persons.

On the one hand, it is frequently argued that in dealing with the rapidly unfolding and often dangerous situations on city streets the police are in need of an escalating set of flexible responses, graduated in relation to the amount of information they possess. For this purpose it is urged that distinctions should be made between a "stop" and an "arrest" (or a "seizure" of a person), and between a "frisk" and a "search." Thus, it is argued, the police should be allowed to "stop" a person and detain him briefly for questioning upon suspicion that he may be connected with criminal activity. Upon suspicion that the person may be armed, the police should have the power to "frisk" him for weapons. If the "stop" and the "frisk" give rise to probable cause to believe that the suspect has committed a crime, then the police should be empowered to make a formal "arrest" and a full incident "search" of the person. This scheme is justified in part upon the notion that a "stop" and a "frisk" amount to a mere "minor inconvenience and petty indignity," which can properly be imposed upon the citizen in the interest of effective law enforcement on the basis of a police officer's suspicion.

On the other side the argument is made that the authority of the police must be strictly circumscribed by the law of arrest and search as it has developed to date in the traditional jurisprudence of the Fourth Amendment. It is contended with some force that there is not — and cannot be — a variety of police activity which does not depend solely upon the voluntary cooperation of the citizen and yet which stops short of an arrest based upon probable cause to make such an arrest. The heart of the Fourth Amendment, the argument runs, is a severe requirement of specific justification for any intrusion upon protected personal security, coupled with a highly developed system of judicial controls to enforce upon the agents of the State the commands of the Constitution. Acquiescence by the courts in the compulsion inherent in the field interrogation practices at issue here, it is urged, would constitute an abdication of judicial control over, and indeed an encouragement of, substantial interference with liberty and personal security by police officers whose judgment is necessarily colored by their primary involvement in "the often competitive enterprise of ferreting out crime." This, it is argued, can only serve to exacerbate police-community tensions in the crowded centers of our Nation's cities.

In this context we approach the issues in this case mindful of the limitations of the judicial function in controlling the myriad daily situations in which policemen and citizens confront each other on the street. . . . Ever since its inception, the rule excluding evidence seized in violation of the Fourth Amendment has been recognized as a principal mode of discouraging lawless police conduct. . . . A ruling admitting evidence in a criminal trial, we recognize, has the necessary effect of legitimizing the conduct which produced the evidence, while an application of the exclusionary rule withholds the constitutional imprimatur.

The exclusionary rule has its limitations, however, as a tool of judicial control. It cannot properly be invoked to exclude the products of legitimate police investigative techniques on the ground that much conduct which is closely similar involves unwarranted intrusions upon constitutional protections. Moreover, in some contexts the rule is ineffective as a deterrent. Street encounters between citizens and police officers are incredibly rich in diversity. They range from wholly friendly exchanges of pleasantries or mutually useful information to hostile confrontations of armed men involving arrests, or injuries, or loss of life. Moreover, hostile confrontations are not all of a piece. Some of them begin in a friendly enough manner, only to take a different turn upon the injection of some unexpected element into the conversation. Encounters are initiated by the police for a wide variety of purposes, some of which are wholly unrelated to a desire to prosecute for crime.[9] Doubtless some police "field interrogation" conduct violates the Fourth Amendment. But a stern refusal by this Court to condone such activity does not necessarily render it responsive to the exclusionary rule. Regardless of how effective the rule may be where obtaining convictions is an important objective of the police, it is powerless to deter invasions of constitutionally guaranteed rights where the police either have no interest in prosecuting or are willing to forgo successful prosecution in the interest of serving some other goal.

Proper adjudication of cases in which the exclusionary rule is invoked demands a constant awareness of these limitations. The wholesale harassment by certain elements of the police community, of which minority groups, particularly Negroes, frequently complain,[11] will not be stopped by the exclusion of any evidence from any

9. See L. Tiffany, D. McIntyre, & D. Rotenberg, Detection of Crime: Stopping and Questioning, Search and Seizure, Encouragement and Entrapment 18-56 (1967). This sort of police conduct may, for example, be designed simply to help an intoxicated person find his way home, with no intention of arresting him unless he becomes obstreperous. Or the police may be seeking to mediate a domestic quarrel which threatens to erupt into violence. They may accost a woman in an area known for prostitution as part of a harassment campaign designed to drive prostitutes away without the considerable difficulty involved in prosecuting them. Or they may be conducting a dragnet search of all teenagers in a particular section of the city for weapons because they have heard rumors of an impending gang fight.

11. The President's Commission on Law Enforcement and Administration of Justice found that "[i]n many communities, field interrogations are a major source of friction between the police and minority groups." President's Commission on Law Enforcement and Administration of Justice, Task Force Report: The Police 183 (1967). It was reported that the friction caused by "[m]isuse of field interrogations" increases "as more police departments adopt 'aggressive patrol' in which officers are encouraged routinely to stop and question persons on the street who are unknown to them, who are suspicious, or whose purpose for being abroad is not readily evident." Id., at 184. While the frequency with which "frisking" forms a part of field interrogation practice varies tremendously with the locale, the objective of the interrogation, and the particular officer, see Tiffany, McIntyre & Rotenberg, supra, n. 9, at 47-48, it cannot

criminal trial. Yet a rigid and unthinking application of the exclusionary rule, in futile protest against practices which it can never be used effectively to control, may exact a high toll in human injury and frustration of efforts to prevent crime. No judicial opinion can comprehend the protean variety of the street encounter, and we can only judge the facts of the case before us. Nothing we say today is to be taken as indicating approval of police conduct outside the legitimate investigative sphere. Under our decision, courts still retain their traditional responsibility to guard against police conduct which is overbearing or harassing, or which trenches upon personal security without the objective evidentiary justification which the Constitution requires. When such conduct is identified, it must be condemned by the judiciary and its fruits must be excluded from evidence in criminal trials. And, of course, our approval of legitimate and restrained investigative conduct undertaken on the basis of ample factual justification should in no way discourage the employment of other remedies than the exclusionary rule to curtail abuses for which that sanction may prove inappropriate.

. . . [W]e turn our attention to the quite narrow question posed by the facts before us: whether it is always unreasonable for a policeman to seize a person and subject him to a limited search for weapons unless there is probable cause for an arrest. . . .

II

. . . There is some suggestion in the use of such terms as "stop" and "frisk" that such police conduct is outside the purview of the Fourth Amendment because neither action rises to the level of a "search" or "seizure" within the meaning of the Constitution. We emphatically reject this notion. It is quite plain that the Fourth Amendment governs "seizures" of the person which do not eventuate in a trip to the station house and prosecution for crime — "arrests" in traditional terminology. It must be recognized that whenever a police officer accosts an individual and restrains his freedom to walk away, he has "seized" that person. And it is nothing less than sheer torture of the English language to suggest that a careful exploration of the outer surfaces of a person's clothing all over his or her body in an attempt to find weapons is not a "search." Moreover, it is simply fantastic to urge that such a procedure performed in public by a policeman while the citizen stands helpless, perhaps facing a wall with his hands raised, is a "petty indignity."[13] It is a serious intrusion upon the sanctity of the person, which may inflict great indignity and arouse strong resentment, and it is not to be undertaken lightly.

The danger in the logic which proceeds upon distinctions between a "stop" and an "arrest," or "seizure" of the person, and between a "frisk" and a "search" is twofold. It seeks to isolate from constitutional scrutiny the initial stages of the contact between the policeman and the citizen. And by suggesting a rigid all or-nothing model of justification and regulation under the Amendment, it obscures the utility

---

help but be a severely exacerbating factor in police-community tensions. This is particularly true in situations where the "stop and frisk" of youths or minority group members is "motivated by the officers' perceived need to maintain the power image of the beat officer, an aim sometimes accomplished by humiliating anyone who attempts to undermine police control of the streets." Ibid.

13. Consider the following apt description: "[T]he officer must feel with sensitive fingers every portion of the prisoner's body. A thorough search must be made of the prisoner's arms and armpits, waistline and back, the groin and area about the testicles, and entire surface of the legs down to the feet." Priar & Martin, Searching and Disarming Criminals, 45 J. Crim. L.C. & P.S. 481 (1954).

of limitations upon the scope, as well as the initiation, of police action as a means of constitutional regulation. . . .

In this case there can be no question, then, that Officer McFadden "seized" petitioner and subjected him to a "search" when he took hold of him and patted down the outer surfaces of his clothing. We must decide whether at that point it was reasonable for Officer McFadden to have interfered with petitioner's personal security as he did.[16] And in determining whether the seizure and search were "unreasonable" our inquiry is a dual one — whether the officer's action was justified at its inception, and whether it was reasonably related in scope to the circumstances which justified the interference in the first place.

III

If this case involved police conduct subject to the Warrant Clause of the Fourth Amendment, we would have to ascertain whether "probable cause" existed to justify the search and seizure which took place. However, that is not the case. We do not retreat from our holdings that the police must, whenever practicable, obtain advance judicial approval of searches and seizures through the warrant procedure, or that in most instances failure to comply with the warrant requirement can only be excused by exigent circumstances. But we deal here with an entire rubric of police conduct — necessarily swift action predicated upon the on-the-spot observations of the officer on the beat — which historically has not been, and as a practical matter could not be, subjected to the warrant procedure. Instead, the conduct involved in this case must be tested by the Fourth Amendment's general proscription against unreasonable searches and seizures.

Nonetheless, the notions which underlie both the warrant procedure and the requirement of probable cause remain fully relevant in this context. In order to assess the reasonableness of Officer McFadden's conduct as a general proposition, it is necessary "first to focus upon the governmental interest which allegedly justifies official intrusion upon the constitutionally protected interests of the private citizen," for there is "no ready test for determining reasonableness other than by balancing the need to search [or seize] against the invasion which the search [or seizure] entails." Camara v. Municipal Court, 387 U.S. 523, 534-535, 536-537 (1967). And in justifying the particular intrusion the police officer must be able to point to specific and articulable facts which, taken together with rational inferences from those facts, reasonably warrant that intrusion. The scheme of the Fourth Amendment becomes meaningful only when it is assured that at some point the conduct of those charged with enforcing the laws can be subjected to the more detached, neutral scrutiny of a judge who must evaluate the reasonableness of a particular search or seizure in light of the particular circumstances. And in making that assessment it is imperative that the facts be judged against an objective standard: would the facts available to the officer at the moment of the seizure or the search "warrant a man of

---

16. We thus decide nothing today concerning the constitutional propriety of an investigative "seizure" upon less than probable cause for purposes of "detention" and/or interrogation. Obviously, not all personal intercourse between policemen and citizens involves "seizures" of persons. Only when the officer, by means of physical force or show of authority, has in some way restrained the liberty of a citizen may we conclude that a "seizure" has occurred. We cannot tell with any certainty upon this record whether any such "seizure" took place here prior to Officer McFadden's initiation of physical contact for purposes of searching Terry for weapons, and we thus may assume that up to that point no intrusion upon constitutionally protected rights had occurred.

reasonable caution in the belief" that the action taken was appropriate? Anything less would invite intrusions upon constitutionally guaranteed rights based on nothing more substantial than inarticulate hunches, a result this Court has consistently refused to sanction. . . .

Applying these principles to this case, we consider first the nature and extent of the governmental interests involved. One general interest is of course that of effective crime prevention and detection; it is this interest which underlies the recognition that a police officer may in appropriate circumstances and in an appropriate manner approach a person for purposes of investigating possibly criminal behavior even though there is no probable cause to make an arrest. It was this legitimate investigative function Officer McFadden was discharging when he decided to approach petitioner and his companions. He had observed Terry, Chilton, and Katz go through a series of acts, each of them perhaps innocent in itself, but which taken together warranted further investigation. There is nothing unusual in two men standing together on a street corner, perhaps waiting for someone. Nor is there anything suspicious about people in such circumstances strolling up and down the street, singly or in pairs. Store windows, moreover, are made to be looked in. But the story is quite different where, as here, two men hover about a street corner for an extended period of time, at the end of which it becomes apparent that they are not waiting for anyone or anything; where these men pace alternately along an identical route, pausing to stare in the same window roughly 24 times; where each completion of this route is followed immediately by a conference between the two men on the corner; where they are joined in one of these conferences by a third man who leaves swiftly; and where the two men finally follow the third and rejoin him a couple of blocks away. It would have been poor police work indeed for an officer of 30 years' experience in the detection of thievery from stores in this same neighborhood to have failed to investigate this behavior further.

The crux of this case, however, is not the propriety of Officer McFadden's taking steps to investigate petitioner's suspicious behavior, but rather, whether there was justification for McFadden's invasion of Terry's personal security by searching him for weapons in the course of that investigation. We are now concerned with more than the governmental interest in investigating crime; in addition, there is the more immediate interest of the police officer in taking steps to assure himself that the person with whom he is dealing is not armed with a weapon that could unexpectedly and fatally be used against him. Certainly it would be unreasonable to require that police officers take unnecessary risks in the performance of their duties. American criminals have a long tradition of armed violence, and every year in this country many law enforcement officers are killed in the line of duty, and thousands more are wounded. Virtually all of these deaths and a substantial portion of the injuries are inflicted with guns and knives.

In view of these facts, we cannot blind ourselves to the need for law enforcement officers to protect themselves and other prospective victims of violence in situations where they may lack probable cause for an arrest. When an officer is justified in believing that the individual whose suspicious behavior he is investigating at close range is armed and presently dangerous to the officer or to others, it would appear to be clearly unreasonable to deny the officer the power to take necessary measures to determine whether the person is in fact carrying a weapon and to neutralize the threat of physical harm.

We must still consider, however, the nature and quality of the intrusion on individual rights which must be accepted if police officers are to be conceded the right
to search for weapons in situations where probable cause to arrest for crime is lacking. Even a limited search of the outer clothing for weapons constitutes a severe,
though brief, intrusion upon cherished personal security, and it must surely be an
annoying, frightening, and perhaps humiliating experience. Petitioner contends
that such an intrusion is permissible only incident to a lawful arrest. . . .

There are two weaknesses in this line of reasoning, however. First, it . . . recognizes no distinction in purpose, character, and extent between a search incident to
an arrest and a limited search for weapons. The former, although justified in part by
the acknowledged necessity to protect the arresting officer from assault with a concealed weapon, is also justified on other grounds and can therefore involve a relatively extensive exploration of the person. A search for weapons in the absence of
probable cause to arrest, however, must, like any other search, be strictly circumscribed by the exigencies which justify its initiation. Thus it must be limited to that
which is necessary for the discovery of weapons which might be used to harm the
officer or others nearby, and may realistically be characterized as something less
than a "full" search, even though it remains a serious intrusion.

A second, and related, objection to petitioner's argument is that it assumes that
the law of arrest has already worked out the balance between the particular interests
involved here — the neutralization of danger to the policeman in the investigative
circumstance and the sanctity of the individual. But this is not so. An arrest is a
wholly different kind of intrusion upon individual freedom from a limited search for
weapons, and the interests each is designed to serve are likewise quite different. An
arrest is the initial stage of a criminal prosecution. It is intended to vindicate society's interest in having its laws obeyed, and it is inevitably accompanied by future
interference with the individual's freedom of movement, whether or not trial or
conviction ultimately follows. The protective search for weapons, on the other hand,
constitutes a brief, though far from inconsiderable, intrusion upon the sanctity of
the person. . . .

Our evaluation of the proper balance that has to be struck in this type of case
leads us to conclude that there must be a narrowly drawn authority to permit a reasonable search for weapons for the protection of the police officer, where he has reason to believe that he is dealing with an armed and dangerous individual, regardless
of whether he has probable cause to arrest the individual for a crime. The officer
need not be absolutely certain that the individual is armed; the issue is whether a
reasonably prudent man in the circumstances would be warranted in the belief that
his safety or that of others was in danger. And in determining whether the officer
acted reasonably in such circumstances, due weight must be given, not to his inchoate and unparticularized suspicion or "hunch," but to the specific reasonable inferences which he is entitled to draw from the facts in light of his experience.

IV

We must now examine the conduct of Officer McFadden in this case to determine
whether his search and seizure of petitioner were reasonable, both at their inception
and as conducted. . . . We think on the facts and circumstances Officer McFadden
detailed before the trial judge a reasonably prudent man would have been warranted in believing petitioner was armed and thus presented a threat to the officer's

safety while he was investigating his suspicious behavior. The actions of Terry and Chilton were consistent with McFadden's hypothesis that these men were contemplating a daylight robbery — which, it is reasonable to assume, would be likely to involve the use of weapons — and nothing in their conduct from the time he first noticed them until the time he confronted them and identified himself as a police officer gave him sufficient reason to negate that hypothesis. . . .

We need not develop at length in this case . . . the limitations which the Fourth Amendment places upon a protective seizure and search for weapons. These limitations will have to be developed in the concrete factual circumstances of individual cases. Suffice it to note that such a search, unlike a search without a warrant incident to a lawful arrest, is not justified by any need to prevent the disappearance or destruction of evidence of crime. The sole justification of the search in the present situation is the protection of the police officer and others nearby, and it must therefore be confined in scope to an intrusion reasonably designed to discover guns, knives, clubs, or other hidden instruments for the assault of the police officer.

The scope of the search in this case presents no serious problem in light of these standards. . . . Officer McFadden confined his search strictly to what was minimally necessary to learn whether the men were armed and to disarm them once he discovered the weapons. He did not conduct a general exploratory search for whatever evidence of criminal activity he might find.

V

We conclude that the revolver seized from Terry was properly admitted in evidence against him. . . . Each case of this sort will, of course, have to be decided on its own facts. We merely hold today that where a police officer observes unusual conduct which leads him reasonably to conclude in light of his experience that criminal activity may be afoot and that the persons with whom he is dealing may be armed and presently dangerous, where in the course of investigating this behavior he identifies himself as a policeman and makes reasonable inquiries, and where nothing in the initial stages of the encounter serves to dispel his reasonable fear for his own or others' safety, he is entitled for the protection of himself and others in the area to conduct a carefully limited search of the outer clothing of such persons in an attempt to discover weapons which might be used to assault him. Such a search is a reasonable search under the Fourth Amendment, and any weapons seized may properly be introduced in evidence against the person from whom they were taken. Affirmed.

[The concurring opinion of Mr. Justice Black is omitted.]

MR. JUSTICE HARLAN, concurring.

While I unreservedly agree with the Court's ultimate holding in this case, I am constrained to fill in a few gaps. . . .

. . . [I]f the frisk is justified in order to protect the officer during an encounter with a citizen, the officer must first have constitutional grounds to insist on an encounter, to make a *forcible* stop. Any person, including a policeman, is at liberty to avoid a person he considers dangerous. If and when a policeman has a right instead to disarm such a person for his own protection, he must first have a right not to avoid him but to be in his presence. That right must be more than the liberty (again, possessed by every citizen) to address questions to other persons, for ordinarily the person addressed has an equal right to ignore his interrogator and walk away; he certainly need not submit to a frisk for the questioner's protection. . . .

Where such a stop is reasonable, however, the right to frisk must be immediate and automatic if the reason for the stop is, as here, an articulable suspicion of a crime of violence. Just as a full search incident to a lawful arrest requires no additional justification, a limited frisk incident to a lawful stop must often be rapid and routine. There is no reason why an officer, rightfully but forcibly confronting a person suspected of a serious crime, should have to ask one question and take the risk that the answer might be a bullet. . . .

I would affirm this conviction for what I believe to be the same reasons the Court relies on. I would, however, make explicit what I think is implicit in affirmance on the present facts. Officer McFadden's right to interrupt Terry's freedom of movement and invade his privacy arose only because circumstances warranted forcing an encounter with Terry in an effort to prevent or investigate a crime. Once that forced encounter was justified, however, the officer's right to take suitable measures for his own safely followed automatically.

Upon the foregoing premises, I join the opinion of the Court.

MR. JUSTICE WHITE, concurring. . . .

. . . I think an additional word is in order concerning the matter of interrogation during an investigative stop. There is nothing in the Constitution which prevents a policeman from addressing questions to anyone on the streets. Absent special circumstances, the person approached may not be detained or frisked but may refuse to cooperate and go on his way. However, given the proper circumstances, such as those in this case, it seems to me the person may be briefly detained against his will while pertinent questions are directed to him. Of course, the person stopped is not obliged to answer, answers may not be compelled, and refusal to answer furnishes no basis for an arrest, although it may alert the officer to the need for continued observation. In my view, it is temporary detention, warranted by the circumstances, which chiefly justifies the protective frisk for weapons. Perhaps the frisk itself, where proper, will have beneficial results whether questions are asked or not. If weapons are found, an arrest will follow. If none are found, the frisk may nevertheless serve preventive ends because of its unmistakable message that suspicion has been aroused. But if the investigative stop is sustainable at all, constitutional rights are not necessarily violated if pertinent questions are asked and the person is restrained briefly in the process.

MR. JUSTICE DOUGLAS, dissenting. . . .

The opinion of the Court disclaims the existence of "probable cause." . . . Had a warrant been sought, a magistrate would, therefore, have been unauthorized to issue one, for he can act only if there is a showing of "probable cause." We hold today that the police have greater authority to make a "seizure" and conduct a "search" than a judge has to authorize such action. We have said precisely the opposite over and over again.

. . . The term "probable cause" rings a bell of certainty that is not sounded by phrases such as "reasonable suspicion." Moreover, the meaning of "probable cause" is deeply imbedded in our constitutional history. . . .

The infringement on personal liberty of any "seizure" of a person can only be "reasonable" under the Fourth Amendment if we require the police to possess "probable cause" before they seize him. Only that line draws a meaningful distinction between an officer's mere inkling and the presence of facts within the officer's personal knowledge which would convince a reasonable man that the person seized has committed, is committing, or is about to commit a particular crime. . . .

To give the police greater power than a magistrate is to take a long step down the totalitarian path. Perhaps such a step is desirable to cope with modern forms of lawlessness. But if it is taken, it should be the deliberate choice of the people through a constitutional amendment. . . .

There have been powerful hydraulic pressures throughout our history that bear heavily on the Court to water down constitutional guarantees and give the police the upper hand. That hydraulic pressure has probably never been greater than it is today.

Yet if the individual is no longer to be sovereign, if the police can pick him up whenever they do not like the cut of his jib, if they can "seize" and "search" him in their discretion, we enter a new regime. The decision to enter it should be made only after a full debate by the people of this country.

NOTES AND QUESTIONS

1. What was Officer McFadden doing when he approached Terry and his companions? In many respects, McFadden did exactly what we want the police to do: He used his professional experience and good judgment to intervene and prevent a serious crime before it was ever committed. The traditional Fourth Amendment approach — with its heavy reliance on probable cause, subject to advance review by a neutral magistrate — may make sense in the context of investigating past crimes, but it seems completely ill-suited to the kind of proactive, preventive policing that was practiced in *Terry*.

The same might be said of police investigations of so-called "victimless" crimes — in particular, drug crimes. Even after these crimes have occurred, there's usually no victim who is willing to complain and provide information to the police about the crime or its perpetrator. This makes it difficult for the police to satisfy traditional standards of probable cause, both with respect to whether a crime actually happened and with respect to who committed it. Thus, police in these types of cases must engage in the type of prospective policing that gave rise to *Terry* if they are to combat the offense effectively. Perhaps it should not be surprising that most of the Court's "reasonableness" cases (like *Terry*) have involved either preventive policing or drug offenses.

Notice some implications of the differences between these two kinds of police activity. Whatever its benefits, proactive crime prevention by police, in which police select the targets of their attention and attempt to intervene to disrupt possible criminal activity, "presents heightened risks of discriminatory law enforcement and inappropriate police involvement in community life and private affairs" — at least as compared to a reactive style of policing in which police mobilize in response to serious crimes that have already taken place. Debra Livingston, Police Discretion

and the Quality of Life in Public Places: Courts, Communities, and the New Policing, 97 Colum. L. Rev. 551, 578 (1997). As the Terry opinion noted in footnote 11,
this general problem can become acute in the area of stop and frisk. Do the risks
associated with proactive, preventive strategies argue in favor of more reactive strategies, where police departments principally respond to citizen complaints? Perhaps
not:

> The philosophical choice is deceptively simple, with reactive policing appearing to
> be far more democratic than proactive policing. What could be more egalitarian than
> to give all citizens an equal right to pick the targets of police crime control? Yet absent
> an equal willingness to use that right, reactive policing becomes anything but egalitar-
> ian.
>   Enormous "selection bias" . . . afflicts every choice of police targets by citizens.
> Many crime victims never call the police . . . for reasons ranging from fear of retalia-
> tion to lack of homeowner's insurance. Other people falsely accuse enemies and rela-
> tives, using police as a tool for private disputes. Reactive policing is completely
> vulnerable to racial, class, religious, sexual, and ethnic prejudices in citizen decisions
> to complain about other citizens.

Lawrence W. Sherman, Attacking Crime: Police and Crime Control, in Modern
Policing: 15 Crime and Justice, 159, 173 (M. Tonry & N. Morris eds. 1992).

Notice, finally, that at least with regard to terrorist activity, prevention has
become the watchword for *federal* law enforcement over the last decade. In the words
of one former Justice Department official: "We cannot afford to wait for them to
execute their plans; the death toll is too high; the consequences too great. . . . The
overriding goal is to prevent and disrupt terrorist activity by questioning, investigating, and arresting those who violate the law and threaten our national security." Viet
D. Dinh, Freedom and Security After September 11, 25 Harv. J.L. &. Pub. Pol'y 399,
401 (2002). Today, terrorism prevention occupies a large fraction of the FBI's
resources: Agents who once investigated reports of federal crimes now focus their
energies on preventing further attacks.

2. *Terry* contained all the seeds that eventually grew into modern stop-and-frisk
doctrine. The results reached in *Terry* and its progeny have been often defended as
practical, reasonable, and necessary. Consider Professor Saltzburg:

> The common sense of *Terry* is that law enforcement officers should not be required to
> wait to act until a crime is complete, whereby society suffers a criminal injury, if they
> have reasonable grounds to suspect that criminal activity is under way and the ability to
> establish quickly whether their suspicion is correct . . . As a result of *Terry*, officers are
> not compelled to make a Hobson's choice between waiting for suspicious activity to
> play out in terms of completed crimes, and prematurely intervening to arrest suspects
> who may be innocent. *Terry* permits an intermediate approach. . . .

Stephen A. Saltzburg, Terry v. Ohio, A Practically Perfect Doctrine, 72 St. John's L.
Rev. 911, 952 (1998). But did that "intermediate approach" adequately address
longstanding concerns with racial and ethnic discrimination? Proactive and preventive policing means that the police are choosing where to put officers, and
when — and against whom — to intervene. That greater police discretion may give
rise to discrimination. Consider the following:

Terry v. Ohio . . . may be the Court's single most important Fourth Amendment case in terms of its role in constituting a legal environment broadly supportive of the street-level discretion of officers on patrol. . . . [D]etentions and frisks take place without prior judicial authorization. In the great majority of cases, moreover, there is no subsequent judicial review of the officer's judgment about the propriety of his actions.

No one could deny that patrol officers employ significant street-level discretion in this context, nor that the proper exercise of this discretion is of tremendous importance both to communities and to police. Indiscriminate street stops and searches, after all, were blamed by the Kerner Commission for helping to foster the "deep hostility between police and ghetto communities" that contributed to numerous tragic riots between 1964 and 1968. And even when properly employed, aggressive use of stop and frisk can alienate and estrange communities in ways that ultimately detract from, rather than contribute to, the maintenance of a vibrant civil order.

But these considerations have not led the Court to attempt more stringently to regulate the area of stop and frisk. The Court has found both street detentions and frisks based on reasonable suspicion to be consistent with Fourth Amendment principles despite its recognition that such encounters are not trivial, but are often "annoying," "frightening," and even "humiliating" to the persons involved. The Court has upheld the stop-and-frisk authority even though police departments vary widely in the degree to which they train and oversee officers so as to minimize its abuse.

Debra Livingston, Gang Loitering, The Court, and Some Realism About Police Patrol, 1999 Supreme Court Review 141, 177-178 (2000).

Actually, *Terry* is one of the very few of the Court's Fourth Amendment cases that explicitly discuss issues of race. But does the Court address these issues in a meaningful way? For an argument that the Court should have taken facts about racial impact more seriously in delineating the scope of the stop-and-frisk power, see Adina Schwartz, "Just Take Away Their Guns": The Hidden Racism of Terry v. Ohio, 23 Fordham Urb. L.J. 317 (1996).

3. Let's return to *Terry*'s impact on Fourth Amendment law. Professor Amar has argued that "in place of the misguided notions that every search or seizure always requires a warrant, and always requires probable cause," *Terry* properly insisted "that the Fourth Amendment means what it says and says what it means: All searches and seizures must be reasonable." Akhil Reed Amar, *Terry* and Fourth Amendment First Principles, 72 St. John's L. Rev. 1097, 1098 (1997). He goes on to contend that *Terry* accurately identified some of the basic components of Fourth Amendment reasonableness:

Reasonable intrusions must be *proportionate* to legitimate governmental purposes — more intrusive government action requires more justification. Reasonableness must focus not only on privacy and secrecy but also on *bodily integrity* and *personal dignity*; Cops act unreasonably not just when they paw through my pockets without good reason, but also when they beat me up for fun or toy with me for sport. Reasonableness also implicates *race* — a complete Fourth Amendment analysis must be sensitive to the possibility of racial oppression and harassment.

Id. Amar correctly identifies aspects of what a reasonableness approach to Fourth Amendment interpretation should encompass. But what about the merits of adopting such an approach in the first place? *Terry* significantly changed existing law by employing a balancing test to hold that the police could subject criminal suspects to a Fourth Amendment intrusion without probable cause. Others have suggested that the case thus "unwittingly cracked the door for a decline in the role of traditional probable cause," thus jeopardizing "the foundation of Fourth Amendment safeguards." See Scott E. Sundby, An Ode to Probable Cause, 72 St. John's L. Rev. 1133, 1134 (1997).

4. Under what circumstances should a particular police practice qualify for assessment under *Terry*'s balancing test? The Court made clear that some types of police intrusion would *not* qualify for such consideration in Dunaway v. New York, 442 U.S. 200 (1979). The defendant, a murder suspect, was taken into custody without probable cause, and "although he was not told he was under arrest, he would have been physically restrained if he had attempted to leave." He was questioned while in custody and made incriminating statements that were used against him at his murder trial. The Court ruled that the statements were the fruits of an illegal seizure:

> Respondent State now urges the Court to apply a balancing test, rather than the general rule, to custodial interrogations, and to hold that "seizures" such as that in this case may be justified by mere "reasonable suspicion." *Terry* and its progeny clearly do not support such a result. The narrow intrusions involved in those cases were judged by a balancing test rather than by the general principle that Fourth Amendment seizures must be supported by the "long-prevailing standards" of probable cause only because these intrusions fell far short of the kind of intrusion associated with an arrest. . . .
>
> . . . [T]he detention of petitioner was in important respects indistinguishable from a traditional arrest. Petitioner was not questioned briefly where he was found. Instead, he was taken from a neighbor's home to a police car, transported to a police station, and placed in an interrogation room. He was never informed that he was "free to go"; indeed, he would have been physically restrained if he had refused to accompany the officers or had tried to escape their custody. The application of the Fourth Amendment's requirement of probable cause does not depend on whether an intrusion of this magnitude is termed an "arrest" under state law. The mere facts that petitioner was not told he was under arrest, was not "booked," and would not have had an arrest record if the interrogation had proved fruitless, obviously do not make petitioner's seizure even roughly analogous to the narrowly defined intrusions involved in *Terry*, and its progeny. Indeed, any "exception" that could cover a seizure as intrusive as that in this case would threaten to swallow the general rule that Fourth Amendment seizures are "reasonable" only if based on probable cause.

Id., at 211-212.

5. *Dunaway* refused to extend *Terry*'s balancing test to cover all seizures falling short of a technical arrest. It's important to note, however, that by the time *Dunaway* was decided, the *Terry* "progeny" to which it referred had already considerably expanded *Terry*'s scope along the lines suggested in Justice Harlan's concurrence. Thus, although the *Terry* Court carefully refrained from lending a constitutional imprimatur to the investigative "stop" (meaning the temporary detention of an individual for investigative purposes), later decisions upheld such detentions so long as police had some articulable basis for suspecting criminal activity.

These later cases also made clear that the suspected criminal activity legitimating an investigative stop need not involve a potential armed robbery, as in *Terry*. Indeed, by the 1990s, the more routine fact pattern to be found in "*Terry* stop" cases before the Court involved the detention of people passing through airports and suspected of being drug couriers. The Court addressed one such airport confrontation in Florida v. Royer, 460 U.S. 491 (1983):

On January 3, 1978, Royer was observed at Miami International Airport by two plain-clothes detectives of the Dade County, Florida, Public Safety Department assigned to the county's Organized Crime Bureau, Narcotics Investigation Section. Detectives Johnson and Magdalena believed that Royer's appearance, mannerisms, luggage, and actions fit the so-called "drug courier profile." Royer, apparently unaware of the attention he had attracted, purchased a one-way ticket to New York City and checked his two suitcases, placing on each suitcase an identification tag bearing the name "Holt" and the destination, "LaGuardia." As Royer made his way to the concourse which led to the airline boarding area, the two detectives approached him, identified themselves as policemen working out of the sheriff's office, and asked if Royer had a "moment" to speak with them; Royer said "Yes."

Upon request, but without oral consent, Royer produced for the detectives his airline ticket and his driver's license. The airline ticket, like the baggage identification tags, bore the name "Holt," while the driver's license carried respondent's correct name, "Royer." When the detectives asked about the discrepancy, Royer explained that a friend had made the reservation in the name of "Holt." Royer became noticeably more nervous during this conversation, whereupon the detectives informed Royer that they were in fact narcotics investigators and that they had reason to suspect him of transporting narcotics.

Id., at 493-494. Without returning his airline ticket or identification, the detectives asked Royer to accompany them to a room about 40 feet away. The detectives then retrieved Royer's suitcases, brought them to the room, and asked for Royer's permission to search them — a process that took about 15 minutes.

The *Royer* plurality concluded that the drugs recovered in the resulting search should have been suppressed because at the time Royer produced a key to his luggage, his detention had already escalated from the type of stop authorized by the *Terry* line of cases into "a more serious intrusion . . . than is allowable on mere suspicion of criminal activity." Id., at 502. The plurality emphasized Royer's removal to a police interrogation room and also the conclusion that the officers' conduct was more intrusive than necessary — that police could have asked Royer for consent to search his bags on the concourse, or that they might have exposed the bags to a narcotics detection dog, confirming or dispelling their suspicions more expeditiously.

Royer raises a number of interesting questions about *Terry* stops. Can a person ever be moved to another location in the midst of a legitimate *Terry* detention? Would imposing what amounts to a "least intrusive alternative" requirement on the circumstances surrounding a stop and frisk be a good idea? Would such a requirement be defensible as a matter of Fourth Amendment interpretation? *Royer* is also noteworthy for what it illustrates about the development of *Terry* doctrine. None of the Justices questioned the authority of the officers to conduct a *Terry*-style detention to pursue their suspicions that Royer was carrying narcotics once officers had ascertained that he was traveling under an alias, paid cash for a one-way ticket, and had evaluated Royer's appearance and conduct.

6. *Terry*'s usefulness as a tool in the investigation of drug crimes was further extended when its reasoning was held to have application not only to the detention of persons, but also in at least some circumstances to property. Recall United States v. Place, 462 U.S. 695 (1983), first discussed supra, at pages 377-378. Federal narcotics officers had articulable suspicion to believe that two suitcases in the possession of a deplaning passenger at LaGuardia Airport contained narcotics. Raymond Place, the passenger, refused to consent to a search. The officers thereafter seized the suitcases and took them to Kennedy Airport. When the suitcases were subjected

to a "sniff test" by a narcotics detection dog approximately 90 minutes after their initial seizure, the dog reacted positively to one suitcase. The officers obtained a search warrant for the bag and discovered it to contain cocaine. Place was charged and eventually convicted of possession with intent to distribute.

The Supreme Court, in an opinion by Justice O'Connor, held that the cocaine found in Place's luggage should have been suppressed because the 90-minute retention of the suitcases without probable cause violated the Fourth Amendment. The Court recognized, however, that "when an officer's observations lead him reasonably to believe that a traveler is carrying luggage that contains narcotics, the principles of *Terry* and its progeny would permit the officer to detain the luggage briefly to investigate the circumstances that aroused his suspicion, provided that the investigative detention is properly limited in scope." Id., at 706.

Do you agree that special law enforcement needs associated with the interdiction of drugs in airports are sufficient to invoke the *Terry* balancing test? Why wasn't the option of temporary seizure available in Arizona v. Hicks, 480 U.S. 321 (1987), at page 466, supra?

NOTES ON THE REFINEMENT OF "STOP AND FRISK"

1. The basic requirements of *Terry* are plainly standards rather than rules, but the standard that separates *Terry* stops from the more substantial seizures that require probable cause is not very precise. Consider in this connection United States v. Sharpe, 470 U.S. 675 (1985). In *Sharpe*, a DEA agent and a highway patrolman, in separate cars, attempted to stop a Pontiac and a blue pickup with an attached camper on suspicion that the vehicles, which were traveling in tandem, were transporting contraband. Highway Patrol Officer Thrasher pulled alongside the Pontiac, which was driven by the defendant Sharpe, and signaled for the driver to stop. As Sharpe pulled to the side of the road, the defendant Savage drove his pickup truck between Officer Thrasher and Sharpe, nearly hitting the trooper's car, and proceeded down the road. DEA Agent Cooke remained with Sharpe while Officer Thrasher pursued the pickup and stopped it a half mile down the highway.

DEA Agent Cooke radioed the local police to assist him with Sharpe. After they arrived, he joined Officer Thrasher, who had removed Savage from the pickup and was waiting for Cooke's arrival. Upon detecting the odor of marijuana emanating from the camper attached to Savage's truck, Agent Cooke subjected the vehicle to a search and recovered a large quantity of marijuana.

Twenty minutes had elapsed between the initial stop of Savage and this search.[19] The government argued that the length of this detention did not exceed the permissible scope of a *Terry* seizure, that the odor of marijuana detected by Agent Cooke thereafter provided probable cause for the search, and that the automobile exception justified dispensing with the warrant requirement.

Chief Justice Burger, in an opinion for the Court, upheld the legality of the stop:

> Obviously, if an investigative stop continues indefinitely, at some point it can no longer
> be justified as an investigative stop. But our cases impose no rigid time limitation on
> *Terry* stops. While it is clear that "the brevity of the invasion of the individual's Fourth

---

19. Defendant Sharpe was obviously detained for a longer period, but as the Court noted, there was no causal connection between this detention and discovery of the contraband. 470 U.S., at 683.

Amendment interests is an important factor in determining whether the seizure is so minimally intrusive as to be justifiable on reasonable suspicion," we have emphasized the need to consider the law enforcement purposes to be served by the stop as well as the time reasonably needed to effectuate those purposes. Much as a "bright line" rule would be desirable, in evaluating whether an investigative detention is unreasonable, common sense and ordinary human experience must govern over rigid criteria. . . .

In assessing whether a detention is too long in duration to be justified as an investigative stop, we consider it appropriate to examine whether the police diligently pursued a means of investigation that was likely to confirm or dispel their suspicions quickly, during which time it was necessary to detain the defendant. A court making this assessment should take care to consider whether the police are acting in a swiftly developing situation, and in such cases the court should not indulge in unrealistic second-guessing. . . . The question is not simply whether some other alternative was available, but whether the police acted unreasonably in failing to recognize and pursue it.

We readily conclude that, given the circumstances facing him, Agent Cooke pursued his investigation in a diligent and reasonable manner.

Id., at 685-687. Does this language give Officer Thrasher and Agent Cook sufficient guidance to help them decide in the next case how long a *Terry* stop can last?

2. The Court has been more willing to adopt bright-line rules in the context of *Terry*-style interactions when such rules are urged as necessary to officer safety. Consider Pennsylvania v. Mimms, 434 U.S. 105 (1977) (per curiam). There, the defendant was lawfully stopped for driving with an expired license plate and was ordered out of his car. As the defendant emerged from the automobile, the officer noticed a large bulge under his sports jacket. A frisk revealed the bulge to be a .38 caliber revolver. The issue arising from the defendant's trial on concealed weapons charges was whether the officer had acted properly under *Terry* in commanding the defendant to exit his vehicle:

[W]e look first to that side of the balance which bears the officer's interest in taking the action that he did. The State freely concedes the officer had no reason to suspect foul play from the particular driver at the time of the stop, there having been nothing unusual or suspicious about his behavior. It was apparently his practice to order all drivers out of their vehicles as a matter of course whenever they had been stopped for a traffic violation. The State argues that this practice was adopted as a precautionary measure to afford a degree of protection to the officer and that it may be justified on that ground. Establishing a face-to-face confrontation diminishes the possibility, otherwise substantial, that the driver can make unobserved movements; this, in turn, reduces the likelihood that the officer will be the victim of an assault.

We think it too plain for argument that the State's proffered justification — the safety of the officer — is both legitimate and weighty. . . .

The hazard of accidental injury from passing traffic to an officer standing on the driver's side of the vehicle may also be appreciable in some situations. Rather than conversing while standing exposed to moving traffic, the officer prudently may prefer to ask the driver of the vehicle to step out of the car and off onto the shoulder of the road where the inquiry may be pursued with greater safety to both.

Against this important interest we are asked to weigh the intrusion into the driver's personal liberty occasioned not by the initial stop of the vehicle, which was admittedly justified, but by the order to get out of the car. We think this additional intrusion can only be described as de minimis.

Id., at 109-111.

3. In Maryland v. Wilson, 519 U.S. 408 (1997), the Court applied a similar analysis to passengers, concluding that once a stop was properly made, the police could legitimately require the passengers to exit the car as well. Then, once the riders were out of the car, the next step was to decide whether officer safety justified a Terry frisk of the passengers who the police had reason to think created a risk to officer safety, even if the police had no reason to believe that the passengers had or were about to violate any laws.

In Arizona v. Johnson, 129 S. Ct. 781 (2009), three members of Arizona's gang task force stopped a car in Tucson after a license plate check revealed that the car's registration had been suspended for an insurance-related civil violation. The officers were patrolling near a neighborhood associated with Crips activity, but they had no reason to suspect anyone in the car of gang-related conduct. As the other officers approached the driver and the front seat passenger, Officer Trevizo engaged Johnson, who was in the backseat. Trevizo had noticed that Johnson looked back and kept his eyes on the officers when they approached. She observed that Johnson was wearing clothing consistent with Crips membership and that he carried a scanner that could be used to evade police. Johnson had no identification, but volunteered that he had served time in prison for burglary and that he was from Eloy, Arizona, which the officer knew to be the home of a Crips gang. Officer Trevizo, who wanted to pose some questions to Johnson about gang membership, asked him to get out of the car and patted him down. During the patdown, she discovered a gun near Johnson's waist.

The Supreme Court unanimously upheld the search, concluding that when a driver or a passenger is lawfully detained in connection with a traffic stop, the police may pat down the person whenever they have reasonable suspicion that the person is armed and dangerous, regardless whether police also have cause to believe the vehicle's occupant is involved in criminal activity:

> A lawful roadside stop begins when a vehicle is pulled over for investigation of a traffic violation. The temporary seizure of driver and passengers ordinarily continues, and remains reasonable, for the duration of the stop. Normally, the stop ends when the police have no further need to control the scene, and inform the driver and passengers they are free to leave. An officer's inquiries into matters unrelated to the justification for the traffic stop . . . do not convert the encounter into something other than a lawful seizure, so long as those inquiries do not measurably extend the duration of the stop.
>
> In sum . . . a traffic stop of a car communicates to a reasonable passenger that he or she is not free to terminate the encounter with the police and move about at will. Nothing occurred in this case that would have conveyed to Johnson that, prior to the frisk, the traffic stop had ended or that he was otherwise free "to depart without police permission." Officer Trevizo surely was not constitutionally required to give Johnson an opportunity to depart the scene after he exited the vehicle without first ensuring that, in so doing, she was not permitting a dangerous person to get behind her.

How persuasive is the Court's assessment of the relative interests at stake? The majority in *Mimms* cited a study to the effect that 30 percent of all shootings of police occur when a police officer approaches a suspect seated in an automobile. Even acknowledging serious officer safety concerns, however, routine traffic stops may not seem so routine when a car's occupants are ordered out of the car by police and then frisked for weapons. Do *Mimms*, *Wilson*, and *Johnson* support a bright-line rule giving officers the discretion to so order a car's occupants to exit a vehicle and to raise their hands above their heads while a traffic summons is issued? If officers are left to choose whether to employ such methods in a routine traffic stop, in what circumstances are they likely to exercise this authority?

4. Michigan v. Long, 463 U.S. 1032 (1983), further attests to the Court's deference to law enforcement in the face of plausible claims that officer safety is at stake:

> Deputies Howell and Lewis were on patrol in a rural area one evening when, shortly after midnight, they observed a car traveling erratically and at excessive speed. The officers observed the car turning down a side road, where it swerved off into a shallow ditch. The officers stopped to investigate. Long, the only occupant of the automobile, met the deputies at the rear of the car, which was protruding from the ditch onto the road. The door on the driver's side of the vehicle was left open.
>
> Deputy Howell requested Long to produce his operator's license, but he did not respond. After the request was repeated, Long produced his license. Long again failed to respond when Howell requested him to produce the vehicle registration. After another repeated request, Long, whom Howell thought "appeared to be under the influence of something," turned from the officers and began walking toward the open door of the vehicle. The officers followed Long and both observed a large hunting knife on the floorboard of the driver's side of the car. The officers then stopped Long's progress and subjected him to a *Terry* protective pat-down, which revealed no weapons.
>
> Long and Deputy Lewis then stood by the rear of the vehicle while Deputy Howell shined his flashlight into the interior of the vehicle, but did not actually enter it. The purpose of Howell's action was "to search for other weapons." The officer noticed that something was protruding from under the armrest on the front seat. He knelt in the vehicle and lifted the armrest. He saw an open pouch on the front seat, and upon flashing his light on the pouch, determined that it contained what appeared to be marijuana. After Deputy Howell showed the pouch and its contents to Deputy Lewis, Long was arrested for possession of marijuana.

Id., at 1035-1036.

In an opinion by Justice O'Connor, the Court noted that "investigative detentions involving suspects in vehicles are especially fraught with danger to police officers." Even though the suspect may be outside the car at the time it is searched, because a stop is a temporary intrusion, the suspect "will be permitted to reenter his automobile, and he will then have access to any weapons inside." The Court held that Deputy Howell's search of the passenger compartment of Long's vehicle was a permissible *Terry*-type search: "[T]he search of the passenger compartment of an automobile, limited to those areas in which a weapon may be placed or hidden, is permissible if the police . . . [have reasonable suspicion to believe] that the suspect is dangerous and . . . may gain immediate control of the weapons." Id., at 1049.

Justice Brennan argued in dissent that the officers could have pursued a less intrusive but equally effective means of ensuring their safety by continuing to detain Long outside his car, while asking him to tell them where his registration was and then retrieving the registration themselves. Do you agree that this approach would have been preferable? Would it have been more protective of Long's privacy? Equally effective at ensuring the officer's safety?

5. Officer safety concerns pervade the Court's opinion in *Terry*. But have such concerns taken the frisk authority too far? David Harris argues that lower courts

have inappropriately made categorical judgments that frisks are permissible in certain situations — for instance, in stops involving drug offenses, even when only small-time street corner sales are involved, or in cases involving the companions of arrested people, whether or not there is any reason to believe these bystanders pose a threat. David A. Harris, Particularized Suspicion, Categorical Judgments: Supreme Court Rhetoric Versus Lower Court Reality under Terry v. Ohio, 72 St. John's L. Rev. 975, 1001-1012 (1998). Courts generally see cases challenging the propriety of a frisk, of course, when the frisk has resulted in the seizure of evidence — most commonly some weapon. Is it surprising given this context that judges have been generous in upholding police officers' judgments?

For that matter, is this an area where judicial rulings are likely to have all that much effect on officer behavior anyway? Consider Professor Skolnick's observation that a preoccupation with danger is a central element of the police officer's "working personality" and that the perception of danger "undermines the judicious use of authority." Jerome H. Skolnick, Justice Without Trial 43 (3d ed. 1994). Is it realistic to think that an officer making a nighttime stop in a poorly lit place and facing a suspect who is wearing clothing that could easily conceal a weapon will *not* frisk — regardless of any individualized suspicion? See Stephen A. Saltzburg, Terry v. Ohio: A Practically Perfect Doctrine, 72 St. John's L. Rev., at 970 (arguing that self-protective frisks of this type should be permitted). Indeed, if an officer truly believes that his life is in danger, is there *any* legal rule that is likely to prevent a frisk?

6. Despite the consideration shown to law enforcement interests in cases like *Mimms*, *Wilson*, *Johnson*, and *Long*, the Court has been considerably less willing to tolerate elaborations on the stop-and-frisk authority in the absence of officer safety concerns. This holds true even when such elaborations involve relatively minor additional intrusions on privacy. Thus, in Minnesota v. Dickerson, 508 U.S. 366 (1993), the Court considered what happens when an officer during a *Terry* frisk feels an item that he believes may be contraband. Just as there is a "plain view" exception to the warrant requirement, the Court said, there is a "plain feel" exception. But a plain feel seizure, like a plain view seizure, must be based on probable cause. Moreover, the "feel" that leads to probable cause is narrowly circumscribed. In *Dickerson*, the officer concluded that the object he felt in the defendant's pocket was not a weapon. The officer then squeezed and manipulated the object in an effort to ascertain its character. The squeezing and manipulating provided the officer with probable cause to believe that the item was a lump of crack cocaine in a plastic bag, but because that activity exceeded the scope of a legitimate frisk for weapons, the Court held that the seizure was illegal. Is *Dickerson* an example of sensible line-drawing, or foolish hair-splitting?

One might expect that the issue in *Dickerson* would arise constantly — that officers would regularly be confronted with unidentified lumps in pockets that might be anything from drugs to a pair of eyeglasses. Judging from reported decisions, though, such cases are rare. Why would that be so? Perhaps officers do a very good job of identifying what they feel during the course of a *Terry* frisk, so doubtful cases like *Dickerson* simply don't occur. Or perhaps officers have learned, through decisions like *Dickerson*, to say they felt something that could have been a weapon. And perhaps courts, hearing such testimony, usually approve the frisk.

NOTE ON THE MEANING OF REASONABLE SUSPICION

Though the majority opinion in *Terry* never used the phrase, "reasonable suspicion" has come to define the legal standard applied to *Terry*-style encounters. Like the probable cause standard, the "reasonable" or "articulable suspicion" standard has never been given a precise definition. It is yet another of those "consider-all-the-circumstances" inquiries found throughout Fourth Amendment case law.

The Court discussed the standard in the context of anonymous tips in Alabama v. White, 496 U.S. 325 (1990). The case involved a tip that one Vanessa White would be leaving 235-C Lynwood Terrace Apartments at a particular time in a brown Plymouth station wagon with the right taillight lens broken, that she would be going to Dobey's Motel, and that she would be in possession of about an ounce of cocaine inside a brown attache case. After observing a woman leave the 235 building at the proper time, enter a station wagon matching the tipster's description, and travel the route to the highway on which the motel was located, police stopped the vehicle. The Court noted that "[r]easonable suspicion is a less demanding standard than probable cause not only in the sense that reasonable suspicion can be established with information that is different in quantity or content than that required to establish probable cause, but also in the sense that reasonable suspicion can arise from information that is less reliable than that required to show probable cause." Id., at 330. While emphasizing that it was a close case, the Court held that "under the totality of the circumstances the anonymous tip, as corroborated, exhibited sufficient indicia of reliability to justify the investigatory stop of respondent's car." Id., at 332. The Court revisited *White* — and the meaning of reasonable suspicion — in the following case.

FLORIDA v. J.L.

Certiorari to the Supreme Court of Florida
529 U.S. 266 (2000)

JUSTICE GINSBURG delivered the opinion for a unanimous Court. The question presented in this case is whether an anonymous tip that a person is carrying a gun is, without more, sufficient to justify a police officer's stop and frisk of that person. We hold that it is not.

On October 13, 1995, an anonymous caller reported to the Miami-Dade Police that a young black male standing at a particular bus stop and wearing a plaid shirt was carrying a gun. So far as the record reveals, there is no audio recording of the tip, and nothing is known about the informant. Sometime after the police received the tip — the record does not say how long — two officers were instructed to respond. They arrived at the bus stop about six minutes later and saw three black males "just hanging out [there]." One of the three, respondent J.L., was wearing a plaid shirt. Apart from the tip, the officers had no reason to suspect any of the three of illegal conduct. The officers did not see a firearm, and J.L. made no threatening or otherwise unusual movements. One of the officers approached J.L., told him to put his hands up on the bus stop, frisked him, and seized a gun from J.L.'s pocket. The second officer frisked the other two individuals, against whom no allegations had been made, and found nothing. J.L., who was at the time of the frisk "10 days shy of his 16th birth[day]," was charged under state law with carrying a concealed firearm without a license and possessing a firearm while under the age of 18. He moved to suppress the gun as the fruit of an unlawful search. . . .

In the instant case, the officers' suspicion that J.L. was carrying a weapon arose not from any observations of their own but solely from a call made from an unknown location by an unknown caller. Unlike a tip from a known informant whose reputation can be assessed and who can be held responsible if her allegations turn out to be fabricated, "an anonymous tip alone seldom demonstrates the informant's basis of knowledge or veracity," Alabama v. White, 496 U.S. [325], 329 [1990]. As we have recognized, however, there are situations in which an anonymous tip, suitably corroborated, exhibits "sufficient indicia of reliability to provide reasonable suspicion to make the investigatory stop." Id., at 327. The question we here confront is whether the tip pointing to J.L. had those indicia of reliability.

In *White*, the police received an anonymous tip asserting that a woman was carrying cocaine and predicting that she would leave an apartment building at a specified time, get into a car matching a particular description, and drive to a named motel. Standing alone, the tip would not have justified a *Terry* stop. Only after police observation showed that the informant had accurately predicted the woman's movements . . . did it become reasonable to think the tipster had inside knowledge about the suspect and therefore to credit his assertion about the cocaine. Although the Court held that the suspicion in *White* became reasonable after police surveillance, we regarded the case as borderline. Knowledge about a person's future movements indicates some familiarity with that person's affairs, but having such knowledge does not necessarily imply that the informant knows, in particular, whether that person is carrying hidden contraband. We accordingly classified *White* as a "close case."

The tip in the instant case lacked the moderate indicia of reliability present in *White* and essential to the Court's decision in that case. The anonymous call concerning J.L. provided no predictive information and therefore left the police without means to test the informant's knowledge or credibility. . . . All the police had to go on in this case was the bare report of an unknown, unaccountable informant who neither explained how he knew about the gun nor supplied any basis for believing he had inside information about J.L. If *White* was a close case on the reliability of anonymous tips, this one surely falls on the other side of the line.

Florida contends that the tip was reliable because its description of the suspect's visible attributes proved accurate: There really was a young black male wearing a plaid shirt at the bus stop. The United States as amicus curiae makes a similar argument, proposing that a stop and frisk should be permitted "when (1) an anonymous tip provides a description of a particular person at a particular location illegally carrying a concealed firearm, (2) police promptly verify the pertinent details of the tip except the existence of the firearm, and (3) there are no factors that cast doubt on the reliability of the tip. . . ." These contentions misapprehend the reliability needed for a tip to justify a *Terry* stop.

An accurate description of a subject's readily observable location and appearance is of course reliable in this limited sense: It will help the police correctly identify the person whom the tipster means to accuse. Such a tip, however, does not show that the tipster has knowledge of concealed criminal activity. The reasonable suspicion here at issue requires that a tip be reliable in its assertion of illegality, not just in its tendency to identify a determinate person.

A second major argument advanced by Florida and the United States as amicus is, in essence, that the standard *Terry* analysis should be modified to license a "firearm exception." Under such an exception, a tip alleging an illegal gun would justify a stop and frisk even if the accusation would fail standard pre-search reliability testing. We decline to adopt this position.

Firearms are dangerous, and extraordinary dangers sometimes justify unusual precautions. Our decisions recognize the serious threat that armed criminals pose to public safety; *Terry*'s rule, which permits protective police searches on the basis of reasonable suspicion rather than demanding that officers meet the higher standard of probable cause, responds to this very concern. But an automatic firearm exception to our established reliability analysis would rove too far. Such an exception would enable any person seeking to harass another to set in motion an intrusive, embarrassing police search of the targeted person simply by placing an anonymous call falsely reporting the target's unlawful carriage of a gun. . . .

[T]he Fourth Amendment is not so easily satisfied. The facts of this case do not require us to speculate about the circumstances under which the danger alleged in an anonymous tip might be so great as to justify a search even without a showing of reliability. We do not say, for example, that a report of a person carrying a bomb need bear the indicia of reliability we demand for a report of a person carrying a firearm before the police can constitutionally conduct a frisk. Nor do we hold that public safety officials in quarters where the reasonable expectation of Fourth Amendment privacy is diminished, such as airports and schools, cannot conduct protective searches on the basis of information insufficient to justify searches elsewhere.

Finally, the requirement that an anonymous tip bear standard indicia of reliability in order to justify a stop in no way diminishes a police officer's prerogative, in accord with *Terry*, to conduct a protective search of a person who has already been legitimately stopped. We speak in today's decision only of cases in which the officer's authority to make the initial stop is at issue. . . .

The judgment of the Florida Supreme Court is affirmed.

[Justice Kennedy's concurring opinion, joined by Chief Justice Rehnquist, is omitted.]

NOTES AND QUESTIONS

1. Does the Court really address the issue here? After *J.L.*, what is a police officer to do when he receives an anonymous tip that a person of a given description is unlawfully carrying a weapon in a specified public place? Is he supposed to approach this person but not to seize him? If so, is it realistic to believe that an officer will engage in a face-to-face encounter with such a person *without* conducting a frisk — and therefore seizing him? Is it reasonable for courts to instruct police to behave in this way? Perhaps the Justices are implicitly saying that an officer receiving such information should place the suspect under observation, but not approach. Such observation might add to the information from the tipster if the officer, for instance, observes a bulge or sees that the suspect's coat is weighted down in a way consistent with carrying a weapon. But what if the officer observes nothing to add to the information she has already received? Should she be on her way?

2. The unanimous Court in *J.L.* suggests that reasonable suspicion is not a single standard — or at least that the evidence needed to satisfy it may differ, depending on whether the matter at issue is a report of a person carrying a bomb or a firearm. Commentators have long noted that both reasonable suspicion and probable cause vary in their practical meaning depending on the circumstances in which these standards are invoked. But do cases like *J.L.* and *Gates*, see pages 435-443, supra, both stressing the flexibility in their respective standards, go a step further? Do they in effect treat reasonable suspicion and probable cause as a general requirement that officers behave reasonably in the circumstances? For an incisive argument to this effect, see Silas J. Wasserstrom, The Court's Turn Toward a General Reasonableness Interpretation of the Fourth Amendment, 27 Am. Crim. L. Rev. 119, 129-130 (1989).

3. *J.L.* was decided before the war on terror had begun; in this regard, its allusion to anonymous tips about bombs and other great dangers sounds strangely prophetic. Now consider United States v. Arvizu, 534 U.S. 266 (2002). A border patrol agent in southern Arizona stopped a minivan with two adults and three children; the agent suspected that the van might contain drugs. (The agent was right, and a consent search of the van yielded over a hundred pounds of marijuana.) The government's claim of reasonable suspicion was based on the following facts: (1) the vehicle "was a minivan, a type of automobile that [the agent] knew smugglers used"; (2) the van was driving along a dirt road sometimes used by drug smugglers (though it was also sometimes used by vacationers); (3) the trip "coincided with the point when agents begin heading back to the checkpoint for a shift change, which leaves the area unpatrolled"; (4) when the van's driver saw the agent, the van slowed down considerably; (5) the driver of the van "appeared stiff and his posture very rigid"; (6) the children in the back of the van waved at the agent "in an abnormal pattern . . . as if the children were being instructed"; (7) the children's knees seemed to be propped up on something in the back of the van; (8) the van was registered to an address near the Mexican border, in an area "notorious for alien and narcotics smuggling." The Ninth Circuit found stop of the van invalid as a matter of law, but a unanimous Supreme Court reversed, finding that the reasonable suspicion standard was satisfied

Arvizu was argued in November 2001, two months after the terrorist attacks on the World Trade Center and the Pentagon. Terrorism was in no way at issue in the case, but Justice O'Connor made several thinly veiled references to the September 11 attacks during oral argument. Speaking to Arvizu's lawyer, Justice O'Connor noted that "we live in perhaps a more dangerous age today than we did when this event took place," confessed concern that "the Ninth Circuit opinion seemed to be a little more rigid than . . . common sense would dictate today," and noted that "it may become very important to us" to preserve the flexibility of the reasonable suspicion standard. Linda Greenhouse, Court Rules on Police Search of Motorists, N.Y. Times, Jan. 16, 2002, at A17. One wonders whether the Court might have viewed the stop with a more critical eye *before* September 11.

4. How should a suspect's flight on sight of the police be factored into the reasonable suspicion equation? Consider the following case.

ILLINOIS v. WARDLOW

Certiorari to the Supreme Court of Illinois
528 U.S. 119 (2000)

CHIEF JUSTICE REHNQUIST delivered the opinion of the Court.

. . . On September 9, 1995, Officers Nolan and Harvey were working as uniformed officers in the special operations section of the Chicago Police Department. The officers were driving the last car of a four car caravan converging on an area known for heavy narcotics trafficking in order to investigate drug transactions. . . .

As the caravan passed 4035 West Van Buren, Officer Nolan observed respondent Wardlow standing next to the building holding an opaque bag. Respondent looked in the direction of the officers and fled. Nolan and Harvey turned their car southbound, watched him as he ran through the gangway and an alley, and eventually cornered him on the street. Nolan then exited his car and stopped respondent. He immediately conducted a protective pat-down search for weapons because in his experience it was common for there to be weapons in the near vicinity of narcotics transactions. During the frisk, Officer Nolan squeezed the bag respondent was carrying and felt a heavy, hard object similar to the shape of a gun. The officer then opened the bag and discovered a .38-caliber handgun with five live rounds of ammunition. The officers arrested Wardlow. . . .

This case, involving a brief encounter between a citizen and a police officer on a public street, is governed by the analysis we first applied in *Terry*. In *Terry*, we held that an officer may, consistent with the Fourth Amendment, conduct a brief, investigatory stop when the officer has a reasonable, articulable suspicion that criminal activity is afoot. While "reasonable suspicion" is a less demanding standard than probable cause and requires a showing considerably less than preponderance of the evidence, the Fourth Amendment requires at least a minimal level of objective justification for making the stop. The officer must be able to articulate more than an "inchoate and unparticularized suspicion or 'hunch'" of criminal activity.

Nolan and Harvey were among eight officers in a four-car caravan that was converging on an area known for heavy narcotics trafficking, and the officers anticipated encountering a large number of people in the area, including drug customers and individuals serving as lookouts. It was in this context that Officer Nolan decided to investigate Wardlow after observing him flee. An individual's presence in an area of expected criminal activity, standing alone, is not enough to support a reasonable, particularized suspicion that the person is committing a crime. But officers are not required to ignore the relevant characteristics of a location in determining whether the circumstances are sufficiently suspicious to warrant further investigation. Accordingly, we have previously noted the fact that the stop occurred in a "high crime area" among the relevant contextual considerations in a *Terry* analysis. Adams v. Williams, 407 U.S. 143, 144, and 147-148 (1972).

In this case, moreover, it was not merely respondent's presence in an area of heavy narcotics trafficking that aroused the officers' suspicion but his unprovoked flight upon noticing the police. Our cases have also recognized that nervous, evasive behavior is a pertinent factor in determining reasonable suspicion. Headlong flight — wherever it occurs — is the consummate act of evasion: It is not necessarily indicative of wrongdoing, but it is certainly suggestive of such. In reviewing the propriety of an officer's conduct, courts do not have available empirical studies dealing with inferences drawn from suspicious behavior, and we cannot reasonably demand scientific certainty from judges or law enforcement officers where none exists. Thus, the determination of reasonable suspicion must be based on commonsense judgments and inferences about human behavior. We conclude Officer Nolan was justified in suspecting that Wardlow was involved in criminal activity, and, therefore, in investigating further.

Such a holding is entirely consistent with our decision in Florida v. Royer, 460 U.S. 491 (1983), where we held that when an officer, without reasonable suspicion or probable cause, approaches an individual, the individual has a right to ignore the police and go about his business. And any "refusal to cooperate, without more, does not furnish the minimal level of objective justification needed for a detention or seizure." Florida v. Bostick, 501 U.S. 429, 437 (1991). But unprovoked flight is simply not a mere refusal to cooperate. Flight, by its very nature, is not "going about one's business"; in fact, it is just the opposite. Allowing officers confronted with such flight to stop the fugitive and investigate further is quite consistent with the individual's right to go about his business or to stay put and remain silent in the face of police questioning.

Respondent and amici also argue that there are innocent reasons for flight from police and that, therefore, flight is not necessarily indicative of ongoing criminal activity. This fact is undoubtedly true, but does not establish a violation of the Fourth Amendment. Even in *Terry*, the conduct justifying the stop was ambiguous and susceptible of an innocent explanation. The officer observed two individuals pacing back and forth in front of a store, peering into the window and periodically conferring. All of this conduct was by itself lawful, but it also suggested that the individuals were casing the store for a planned robbery. *Terry* recognized that the officers could detain the individuals to resolve the ambiguity.

In allowing such detentions, *Terry* accepts the risk that officers may stop innocent people. Indeed, the Fourth Amendment accepts that risk in connection with more drastic police action; persons arrested and detained on probable cause to believe they have committed a crime may turn out to be innocent. The *Terry* stop is a far more minimal intrusion, simply allowing the officer to briefly investigate further. If the officer does not learn facts rising to the level of probable cause, the individual must be allowed to go on his way. . . .

JUSTICE STEVENS, with whom JUSTICE SOUTER, JUSTICE GINSBURG, and JUSTICE BREYER join, concurring in part and dissenting in part.

The State of Illinois asks this Court to announce a "bright-line rule" authorizing the temporary detention of anyone who flees at the mere sight of a police officer. Respondent counters by asking us to adopt the opposite per se rule — that the fact that a person flees upon seeing the police can never, by itself, be sufficient to justify a temporary investigative stop of the kind authorized by Terry v. Ohio, 392 U.S. 1 (1968). . . .

Although I agree with the Court's rejection of the per se rules proffered by the parties, unlike the Court, I am persuaded that in this case the brief testimony of the officer who seized respondent does not justify the conclusion that he had reasonable suspicion to make the stop. . . .

The question in this case concerns "the degree of suspicion that attaches to" a person's flight — or, more precisely, what "commonsense conclusions" can be drawn respecting the motives behind that flight. A pedestrian may break into a run for a variety of reasons — to catch up with a friend a block or two away, to seek shelter from an impending storm, to arrive at a bus stop before the bus leaves, to get home in time for dinner, to resume jogging after a pause for rest, to avoid contact with a bore or a bully, or simply to answer the call of nature — any of which might coincide with the arrival of an officer in the vicinity. A pedestrian might also run because he or she has just sighted one or more police officers. In the latter instance, the State properly points out "that the fleeing person may be, inter alia, (1) an escapee from jail; (2) wanted on a warrant; (3) in possession of contraband, (i.e. drugs, weapons, stolen goods, etc.); or (4) someone who has just committed another type of crime." In short, there are unquestionably circumstances in which a person's flight is suspicious, and undeniably instances in which a person runs for entirely innocent reasons.[3]

Given the diversity and frequency of possible motivations for flight, it would be profoundly unwise to endorse either per se rule. The inference we can reasonably draw about the motivation for a person's flight, rather, will depend on a number of different circumstances. Factors such as the time of day, the number of people in the area, the character of the neighborhood, whether the officer was in uniform, the way the runner was dressed, the direction and speed of the flight, and whether the person's behavior was otherwise unusual might be relevant in specific cases. This number of variables is surely sufficient to preclude either a bright-line rule that always justifies, or that never justifies, an investigative stop based on the sole fact that flight began after a police officer appeared nearby.

Still, Illinois presses for a per se rule regarding "unprovoked flight upon seeing a clearly identifiable police officer." The phrase "upon seeing," as used by Illinois, apparently assumes that the flight is motivated by the presence of the police officer. Illinois contends that unprovoked flight is "an extreme reaction," because innocent people simply do not "flee at the mere sight of the police." To be sure, Illinois concedes, an innocent person — even one distrustful of the police — might "avoid eye contact or even sneer at the sight of an officer," and that would not justify a *Terry* stop or any sort of per se inference. But, Illinois insists, unprovoked flight is altogether different. Such behavior is so "aberrant" and "abnormal" that a per se inference is justified.

Even assuming we know that a person runs because he sees the police, the inference to be drawn may still vary from case to case. Flight to escape police detection, we have said, may have an entirely innocent motivation:

> [I]t is a matter of common knowledge that men who are entirely innocent do sometimes fly from the scene of a crime through fear of being apprehended as the guilty parties, or from an unwillingness to appear as witnesses. Nor is it true as an accepted axiom of criminal law that the "wicked flee when no man pursueth, but the righteous are as bold as a lion." Innocent men sometimes hesitate to confront a jury — not necessarily because they fear that the jury will not protect them, but because they do not wish their names to appear in connection with criminal acts, are humiliated at being obliged to incur the popular odium of an arrest and trial, or because they do not wish to be put to the annoyance or expense of defending themselves.

---

3. Compare, e.g., Proverbs 28:1 ("The wicked flee when no man pursueth: but the righteous are as bold as a lion") with Proverbs 22:3 ("A shrewd man sees trouble coming and lies low; the simple walk into it and pay the penalty"). . . .

Alberty v. United States, 162 U.S. 499, 511 (1896).

In addition to these concerns, a reasonable person may conclude that an officer's sudden appearance indicates nearby criminal activity. And where there is criminal activity there is also a substantial element of danger — either from the criminal or from a confrontation between the criminal and the police. These considerations can lead to an innocent and understandable desire to quit the vicinity with all speed.

Among some citizens, particularly minorities and those residing in high crime areas, there is also the possibility that the fleeing person is entirely innocent, but, with or without justification, believes that contact with the police can itself be dangerous, apart from any criminal activity associated with the officer's sudden presence.[7] For such a person, unprovoked flight is neither "aberrant" nor "abnormal."[8] Moreover, these concerns and fears are known to the police officers themselves,[9] and are validated by law enforcement investigations into their own practices.[10]

7. See Johnson, Americans' Views on Crime and Law Enforcement: Survey Findings, National Institute of Justice Journal 13 (Sept. 1997) (reporting study by the Joint Center for Political and Economic Studies in April 1996, which found that 43% of African Americans consider "police brutality and harassment of African-Americans a serious problem" in their own community); President's Comm'n on Law Enforcement and Administration of Justice, Task Force Report: The Police 183-184 (1967) (documenting the belief, held by many minorities, that field interrogations are conducted "indiscriminately" and "in an abusive . . . manner," and labeling this phenomenon a "principal problem" causing "friction" between minorities and the police) (cited in *Terry*, 392 U.S., at 14, n. 11); see also Casimir, Minority Men: We Are Frisk Targets, N.Y. Daily News, Mar. 26, 1999, p. 34 (informal survey of 100 young black and Hispanic men living in New York City; 81 reported having been stopped and frisked by police at least once; none of the 81 stops resulted in arrests); Brief for NAACP Legal Defense & Educational Fund as Amicus Curiae 17-19 (reporting figures on disproportionate street stops of minority residents in Pittsburgh and Philadelphia, Pennsylvania, and St. Petersburg, Florida); U.S. Dept. of Justice, Bureau of Justice Statistics, S. Smith, Criminal Victimization and Perceptions of Community Safety in 12 Cities 25 (June 1998) (African-American residents in 12 cities are more than twice as likely to be dissatisfied with police practices than white residents in same community).

8. See, e.g., Kotlowitz, Hidden Casualties: Drug War's Emphasis on Law Enforcement Takes a Toll on Police, Wall Street Journal, Jan. 11, 1991, p. A2, col. 1 ("Black leaders complained that innocent people were picked up in the drug sweeps. . . . Some teenagers were so scared of the task force they ran even if they weren't selling drugs"). . . .

9. The Chief of the Washington, D.C., Metropolitan Police Department, for example, confirmed that "sizeable percentages of Americans today — especially Americans of color — still view policing in the United States to be discriminatory, if not by policy and definition, certainly in its day-to-day application." P. Verniero, Attorney General of New Jersey, Interim Report of the State Police Review Team Regarding Allegations of Racial Profiling 46 (Apr. 20, 1999) (hereinafter Interim Report). And a recent survey of 650 Los Angeles Police Department officers found that 25% felt that "racial bias (prejudice) on the part of officers toward minority citizens currently exists and contributes to a negative interaction between police and the community." Report of the Independent Comm'n on the Los Angeles Police Department 69 (1991); see also 5 United States Comm'n on Civil Rights, Racial and Ethnic Tensions in American Communities: Poverty, Inequality and Discrimination, The Los Angeles Report 26 (June 1999).

10. New Jersey's Attorney General, in a recent investigation into allegations of racial profiling on the New Jersey Turnpike, concluded that "minority motorists have been treated differently [by New Jersey State Troopers] than non-minority motorists during the course of traffic stops on the New Jersey Turnpike." "[T]he problem of disparate treatment is real — not imagined," declared the Attorney General. Not surprisingly, the report concluded that this disparate treatment "engender[s] feelings of fear, resentment, hostility, and mistrust by minority citizens." See Interim Report 4, 7. . . .

Likewise, the Massachusetts Attorney General investigated similar allegations of egregious police conduct toward minorities. The report stated:

We conclude that Boston police officers engaged in improper, and unconstitutional, conduct in the 1989-90 period with respect to stops and searches of minority individuals. . . . Although we cannot say with precision how widespread this illegal conduct was, we believe that it was sufficiently common to justify changes in certain Department practices.

Perhaps the most disturbing evidence was that the *scope* of a number of *Terry* searches went far beyond anything authorized by that case and indeed, beyond anything that we believe would be acceptable under the federal and state constitutions even where probable cause existed to conduct a full search incident to an arrest. Forcing young men to lower their trousers, or otherwise

Accordingly, the evidence supporting the reasonableness of these beliefs is too pervasive to be dismissed as random or rare, and too persuasive to be disparaged as inconclusive or insufficient. In any event, just as we do not require "scientific certainty" for our commonsense conclusion that unprovoked flight can sometimes indicate suspicious motives, neither do we require scientific certainty to conclude that unprovoked flight can occur for other, innocent reasons.[12]

The probative force of the inferences to be drawn from flight is a function of the varied circumstances in which it occurs. Sometimes those inferences are entirely consistent with the presumption of innocence, sometimes they justify further investigation, and sometimes they justify an immediate stop and search for weapons. These considerations have led us to avoid categorical rules concerning a person's flight and the presumptions to be drawn therefrom. . . .

Guided by [the] totality-of-the-circumstances test, the Court concludes that Officer Nolan had reasonable suspicion to stop respondent. In this respect, my view differs from the Court's. The entire justification for the stop is articulated in the brief testimony of Officer Nolan. . . .

Respondent Wardlow was arrested a few minutes after noon on September 9, 1995. Nolan was part of an eight-officer, four-car caravan patrol team. The officers were headed for "one of the areas in the 11th District [of Chicago] that's high [in] narcotics traffic." The reason why four cars were in the caravan was that "[n]ormally in these different areas there's an enormous amount of people, sometimes lookouts, customers." Officer Nolan testified that he was in uniform on that day, but he did not recall whether he was driving a marked or an unmarked car.

Officer Nolan and his partner were in the last of the four patrol cars that "were all caravanning eastbound down Van Buren." Nolan first observed respondent "in front of 4035 West Van Buren." Wardlow "looked in our direction and began fleeing." Nolan then "began driving southbound down the street observing [respondent] running through the gangway and the alley southbound," and observed that Wardlow was carrying a white, opaque bag under his arm. After the car turned south and intercepted respondent as he "ran right towards us," Officer Nolan stopped him and conducted a "protective search," which revealed that the bag under respondent's arm contained a loaded handgun.

This terse testimony is most noticeable for what it fails to reveal. Though asked whether he was in a marked or unmarked car, Officer Nolan could not recall the answer. He was not asked whether any of the other three cars in the caravan were marked, or whether any of the other seven officers were in uniform. Though he explained that the size of the caravan was because "[n]ormally in these different areas there's an enormous amount of people, sometimes lookouts, customers," Officer Nolan did not testify as to whether *anyone* besides Wardlow was nearby 4035 West Van Buren. Nor is it clear that that address was the intended destination of the

---

searching inside their underwear, on public streets or in public hallways, is so demeaning and invasive of fundamental precepts of privacy that it can only be condemned in the strongest terms. The fact that not only the young men themselves, but independent witnesses complained of strip searches, should be deeply alarming to all members of this community.

J. Shannon, Attorney General of Massachusetts, Report of the Attorney General's Civil Rights Division on Boston Police Department Practices 60-61 (Dec. 18, 1990).

12. As a general matter, local courts often have a keener and more informed sense of local police practices and events that may heighten these concerns at particular times or locations. Thus, a reviewing court may accord substantial deference to a local court's determination that fear of the police is especially acute in a specific location or at a particular time.

caravan. As the Appellate Court of Illinois interpreted the record, "it appears that the officers were simply driving by, on their way to some unidentified location, when they noticed defendant standing at 4035 West Van Buren." Officer Nolan's testimony also does not reveal how fast the officers were driving. It does not indicate whether he saw respondent notice the other patrol cars. And it does not say whether the caravan, or any part of it, had already passed Wardlow by before he began to run.

Indeed, the Appellate Court thought the record was even "too vague to support the inference that . . . . defendant's flight was related to his expectation of police focus on him." Presumably, respondent did not react to the first three cars, and we cannot even be sure that he recognized the occupants of the fourth as police officers. The adverse inference is based entirely on the officer's statement: "He looked in our direction and began fleeing."

No other factors sufficiently support a finding of reasonable suspicion. Though respondent was carrying a white, opaque bag under his arm, there is nothing at all suspicious about that. Certainly the time of day—shortly after noon—does not support Illinois' argument. Nor were the officers "responding to any call or report of suspicious activity in the area." Officer Nolan did testify that he expected to find "an enormous amount of people," including drug customers or lookouts, and the Court points out that "[i]t was in this context that Officer Nolan decided to investigate Wardlow after observing him flee." This observation, in my view, lends insufficient weight to the reasonable suspicion analysis; indeed, in light of the absence of testimony that anyone else was nearby when respondent began to run, this observation points in the opposite direction.

The State, along with the majority of the Court, relies as well on the assumption that this flight occurred in a high crime area. Even if that assumption is accurate, it is insufficient because even in a high crime neighborhood unprovoked flight does not invariably lead to reasonable suspicion. On the contrary, because many factors providing innocent motivations for unprovoked flight are concentrated in high crime areas, the character of the neighborhood arguably makes an inference of guilt less appropriate, rather than more so. Like unprovoked flight itself, presence in a high crime neighborhood is a fact too generic and susceptible to innocent explanation to satisfy the reasonable suspicion inquiry.

It is the State's burden to articulate facts sufficient to support reasonable suspicion. In my judgment, Illinois has failed to discharge that burden. I am not persuaded that the mere fact that someone standing on a sidewalk looked in the direction of a passing car before starting to run is sufficient to justify a forcible stop and frisk. . . .

NOTES AND QUESTIONS

1. Is there a problem here that the Court ignores? Flight may give rise to reasonable suspicion that a suspect is involved in crime of some sort, at least in certain circumstances. But flight alone—or even flight in a high-crime area—does not provide reasonable suspicion that a suspect is engaged in any *particular* crime, does it? Yet in other Fourth Amendment settings—in arresting individuals, or in searching in specific places—we require a certain level of probability that a particular crime has been committed or that evidence of a particular crime will be found. No

one would argue that police can arrest someone for "crime in general." How and why is the *Terry* context different?

2. What type of evidence should courts consider in drawing the conclusion that a particular neighborhood lies within a "high-crime area"? Officers relying upon this claim to help justify a stop typically offer testimony about a given neighborhood's reputation in the precinct or in the community, or about their own experiences with crime in that neighborhood. Such testimony has probative value, but precisely what weight should be afforded to it? Professor Harris asserts that judges credit conclusory statements by police that a suspect was observed in a "high crime" or "high drug-trafficking" area. David A. Harris, Particularized Suspicion, Categorical Judgments: Supreme Court Rhetoric Versus Lower Court Reality Under Terry v. Ohio, 72 St. John's L. Rev. 975, 998 (1998). Is there anything wrong with affording *some* weight to such statements?

3. Consider the following: "Those who live in high crime areas will likely be poor and members of minority groups, and these very same people may also have strong reasons to avoid the police, given their past experiences. Thus, if the law allows stops based on membership in just these two categories, it effectively allows police nearly complete discretion to stop African Americans who live in crime-prone urban neighborhoods." Id., at 1000.

2. Police Discretion and Profiling

As we have seen, police officers enjoy considerable discretion. That is true even under the traditional Fourth Amendment approach, with its preference for warrants and probable cause. It is still more true under the "reasonableness" approach of *Terry* and its progeny. Officers every day decide to intervene or ignore suspicious circumstances, applying broad legal standards like probable cause or reasonable suspicion, often without prior or subsequent judicial supervision. They may arrest, or choose to treat an infraction in some other way. One of the principal questions in Fourth Amendment law is how strictly or loosely police discretion should be regulated. This broad question lurks behind a host of issues we have already addressed: the warrant requirement, for instance, and the propriety of departing from it; the meaning of "searches" and "seizures"; the boundaries of "stops" and "frisks."

One way police exercise their discretionary power is through the use of profiles: sets of characteristics that may (or may not) be correlated to particular kinds of criminal activity. Consider drug courier profiles. Such profiles list characteristics said to be commonly found among people engaged in drug trafficking. In United States v. Sokolow, 490 U.S. 1 (1989), DEA agents using a "drug courier profile" stopped the defendant at the Honolulu International Airport. The Supreme Court upheld the legality of this *Terry* stop, which was based on the following information:

(1) [The defendant] paid $2,100 for two airplane tickets from a roll of $20 bills;
(2) he traveled under a name that did not match the name under which his telephone number was listed;
(3) his original destination was Miami, a source city for illicit drugs;
(4) he stayed in Miami for only 48 hours, even though a round-trip flight from Honolulu to Miami takes 20 hours;

(5) he appeared nervous during his trip; and

(6) he checked none of his luggage.

Id., at 3. The Court did not rely on the drug courier profile in concluding that there was reasonable suspicion for the stop. But neither did it condemn the use of such profiles:

> A court sitting to determine the existence of reasonable suspicion must require the agent to articulate the factors leading to that conclusion, but the fact that these factors may be set forth in a "profile" does not somehow detract from their evidentiary significance as seen by a trained agent.

Id., at 10.

Justice Marshall, in a dissenting opinion joined by Justice Brennan, disagreed that the DEA agents' use of a drug courier profile to focus attention on suspects was benign:

> It is highly significant that the DEA agents stopped Sokolow because he matched one of the DEA's "profiles" of a paradigmatic drug courier. In my view, a law enforcement officer's mechanistic application of a formula of personal and behavioral traits in deciding whom to detain can only dull the officer's ability and determination to make sensitive and fact-specific inferences "in light of his experience," *Terry*, [392 U.S., at 27], particularly in ambiguous or borderline cases. Reflexive reliance on a profile of drug courier characteristics runs a far greater risk than does ordinary, case-by-case police work, of subjecting innocent individuals to unwarranted police harassment and detention.

490 U.S., at 13 (Marshall, J., dissenting).

> When officers use race or ethnicity as an element of suspicion in the profiles they employ, the stakes are even higher — implicating not just Fourth Amendment, but equal protection concerns. But racial profiling, like profiling in general, . . . depends on police discretion in choosing suspects. At one end of the continuum, racial profiling is impossible once the police are looking for a particular person — the victim's partner, the woman in the surveillance video, Osama bin Laden — although it may be a factor at an earlier stage, in determining who to look for. At the other extreme, racial profiling can flourish in proactive investigations in which the police scan large numbers of people in search of culprits in crimes that have not been reported or have not yet occurred.

Samuel R. Gross & Katherine Y. Barnes, Road Work: Racial Profiling and Drug Interdiction on the Highway, 101 Mich. L. Rev. 651, 655 (2002).

"Racial profiling" is a term that has no fixed legal meaning. It began appearing in published opinions only in the 1990s. Yet today it represents a central issue in law enforcement — and one that bears dramatically on the question of how closely Fourth Amendment law should regulate police discretion in choosing among suspects. We take up two cases in this section — Whren v. United States, 517 U.S. 806 (1996), a leading Fourth Amendment case, and Chicago v. Morales, 527 U.S. 41 (1999), a case addressing due process limits on the scope of substantive criminal law. The cases implicate different legal doctrines, but both involve a kind of regulatory strategy for addressing profiling. Before turning to these cases, however, consider the following analyses of the uses — and misuses — of profiles.

RANDALL L. KENNEDY, RACE, CRIME AND THE LAW
158-161 (1997)

When a Mexican-American motorist is selected for questioning in part on the basis of his perceived ancestry, he is undoubtedly being burdened more heavily at that moment on account of his race than his white Anglo counterpart. He is being made to pay a type of racial tax for the campaign against illegal immigration that whites, blacks, and Asians escape. Similarly, a young black man selected for questioning by police as he alights from an airplane or drives a car is being made to pay a type of racial tax for the war against drugs that whites and other groups escape. That tax is the cost of being subjected to greater scrutiny than others. But is that tax illegitimate?

One defense of it is that, under the circumstances, people of other races are simply not in a position to pay the tax effectively. In contrast to apparent Mexican ancestry, neither apparent white nor black nor Asian ancestry appreciably raises the risk that a person near the Mexican border is illegally resident in the United States. Similarly, the argument would run that in contrast to the young black man, the young white man is not as likely to be a courier of illicit drugs. The defense could go on to say that, in this context, race is *not* being used invidiously. It is not being used as a marker to identify people to harm through enslavement, or exclusion, or segregation. Rather, race is being used merely as a signal that facilitates efficient law enforcement. In this context, apparent Mexican ancestry or blackness is being used for unobjectionable ends in the same way that whiteness is used in the affirmative action context: as a marker that has the effect, though not the purpose, of burdening a given racial group. Whereas whites are made to pay a racial tax for the purpose of opening up opportunities for people of color in education and employment, Mexican-Americans and blacks are made to pay a racial tax for the purpose of more efficient law enforcement.

We need to pause here to consider the tremendous controversy that has surrounded affirmative action policies aimed at helping racial minorities. Many of the same arguments against race-based affirmative action are applicable as well in the context of race-based police stops. With affirmative action, many whites claim that they are victims of racial discrimination. With race-based police stops, many people of color complain that they are victims of racial discrimination. With affirmative action, many adversely affected whites claim that they are *innocent* victims of a policy that penalizes them for the misconduct of others who also happened to have been white. With race-based police stops, many adversely affected people of color maintain that they are *innocent* victims of a policy that penalizes them for the misconduct of others who also happen to be colored. . . .

Whatever one thinks of the conclusions drawn by the Court with respect to affirmative action, at least it begins at the correct starting point for analysis — that race-dependent decisions by officials call for more than ordinary justification. With respect to race-dependent policing, however, the Court, mirroring public opinion, has made the terrible error of permitting race-dependent decisionmaking to become a normal part of police practice.

Many of those who defend the current regime of race-dependent policing speak as if there existed no sensible alternative. But there is an alternative: spending more on other means of enforcement to make up for any diminution in crime control caused by the reform I seek: prohibiting officers (except in absolutely extraordinary circumstances) from using race as a proxy for increased risk of criminality. Instead of placing a racial tax on blacks, Mexican-Americans, and other colored people, governments should, if necessary, increase taxes across the board. More specifically, rather than authorizing police to count apparent Mexican ancestry or apparent blackness as negative proxies, states and the federal government should be forced either to hire more officers or to inconvenience everyone at checkpoints by subjecting all motorists and passengers to questioning (or to the same chance at random questioning). . . .

The law should authorize police to engage in racially discriminatory investigative conduct only on atypical, indeed extraordinary, occasions in which the social need is absolutely compelling: weighty, immediate, and incapable of being addressed sensibly by any other means. I have in mind a real emergency, a situation . . . in which there is clear reason to believe that a violent crime has been or is about to be committed and that the reported characteristics of the perpetrator are such that using racial criteria to narrow the pool of potential suspects clearly increases the ability of the police to apprehend the criminal quickly. This formulation is by no means foolproof. Recall *Korematsu*. Implemented properly, however, this proposal would prohibit officers from using racial criteria as a *routine* element of patrolling. . . .

SAMUEL R. GROSS AND DEBRA LIVINGSTON, RACIAL PROFILING UNDER ATTACK

102 Colum. L. Rev. 1413 (2002)

We had just reached a consensus on racial profiling. By September 10, 2001, virtually everyone, from Jesse Jackson to Al Gore to George W. Bush to John Ashcroft, agreed that racial profiling was very bad. We also knew what racial profiling was: Police officers would stop, question, and search African American and Hispanic citizens disproportionately, because of their race or ethnicity, in order to try to catch common criminals. All this has changed in the wake of the September 11 attacks on the World Trade Center and the Pentagon. Now racial profiling is more likely to mean security checks or federal investigations that target Muslim men from Middle Eastern countries, in order to try to catch terrorists. And now lots of people are for it. In the fall of 1999, 81% of respondents in a national poll said they disapproved of "racial profiling," which was defined as the practice by some police officers of stopping "motorists of certain racial or ethnic groups because the officers believe that these groups are more likely than others to commit certain types of crimes." Two years later, 58% said they favored "requiring Arabs, including those who are U.S. citizens, to undergo special, more intrusive security checks before boarding airplanes in the U.S." . . .

As we use the term, "racial profiling" occurs whenever a law enforcement officer questions, stops, arrests, searches, or otherwise investigates a person because the officer believes that members of that person's racial or ethnic group are more likely than the population at large to commit the sort of crime the officer is investigating. The essence of racial profiling is a global judgment that the targeted group—before September 11, usually African Americans or Hispanics—is more prone to commit crime in general, or to commit a particular type of crime, than other racial or ethnic groups. If the officer's conduct is based at least in part on such a general racial or ethnic judgment, it does not matter if she uses other criteria as well in deciding on her course of action. It is racial profiling to target young black men on the basis of a belief that they are more likely than others to commit crimes, even though black women and older black men are not directly affected.

. . . In November 2001, the Department of Justice began efforts to interview "more than 5,000 people nationwide—the majority Middle Eastern men ages eighteen to thirty-three who came here within the last two years on non-immigrant visas—in search of information on terrorist organizations such as al Qaeda." . . . The Department said that these men [were] not suspected of crimes but "might, either wittingly or unwittingly, be in the same circles, communities, or social groups as those engaged in terrorist activities." . . .

Is the Justice Department's interview campaign an ethnic profiling program? Some civil libertarians, Arab American organizations, and local police departments say it is; the Department of Justice says it is not. Who is right? And would answering this question tell us whether the Justice Department's program is appropriate? . . .

. . . By our definition, [even assuming that ethnicity was a central factor in the selection of subjects], it is not ethnic profiling for officers to focus their attention on people of a given ethnicity because the police have information that the specific crime they are investigating was committed by someone of that ethnic group. There is plenty of information that Middle Eastern men, some of whom remain at large, engaged in a conspiracy to commit acts of mass terror in the United States on September 11, 2001. Granted, the concept of a "specific crime" grows somewhat hazy when the crime at issue is an ongoing conspiracy of indeterminate size—and one that potentially involves not just Middle Eastern men, but also others, from different racial or ethnic groups. Nevertheless, if the sole purpose for this interview program was to determine whether any of the thousands to be interviewed was involved in this conspiracy, or had information that might lead to those who were, this would not be ethnic profiling. (Which is not to say that such a broad brush investigation would be unproblematic; that's a different question, as we will see.) . . .

The range of things the government can do on the basis of racial or ethnic information is enormous. If mass imprisonment defines the high end (short of torture or execution), paying close attention may define the low end. After September 11, nobody could seriously complain about the FBI paying more attention to reports of suspicious behavior by Saudi men than to similar reports about Hungarian women—even though as a consequence many more Saudi men will set off false alarms. In between there are infinite gradations, as the government's conduct becomes increasingly intrusive, disruptive, frightening, and humiliating. There are, however, two important questions that cut across the terrain.

The first separates out a class of cases near the bottom of the slope: Did the investigators impinge on the suspect by confronting him, or by covertly invading his privacy? If not—if, in the clearest case, the authorities did no more than gather information at a distance, from public sources—the worst consequences will be minimal. . . .

The second question is more important because it affects the experience of people who do know what is being done to them: Is the subject treated as one of *us* or as one of *them*, as a law abiding person to be checked out or as a criminal to be caught and punished? Security checkpoints are democratic; everybody must go through them, so no stigma is attached to the process. Some people these days get angry if they are *not* checked carefully enough, but even those who are asked to open their bags or scanned by hand are treated essentially like ordinary members of the public. The operating assumption for any individual, Muslim or Presbyterian, is that she will clear security and rejoin the crowd. On the other hand, a passenger who is kicked off an airliner (for good reasons or bad) is treated as a presumptive terrorist. Not only are his plans disrupted, but he is singled out and humiliated in public. . . .

Those of us who have not been through this sort of experience probably underestimate its impact. To be treated as a criminal is a basic insult to a person's self image and to his position in society. It cannot easily be shrugged off. Of course, many victims of racial profiling are not surprised by this treatment. They know why they were stopped — which makes it worse. It's bad enough to have the accidental misfortune of being mistaken for a bad guy; it's worse to feel that you are assumed to be a criminal because of your race. Short of imprisonment, intimidation, or physical abuse, most of the pain of racial profiling is caused by treating law abiding people like criminals. . . .

To return to the Justice Department's program: Does the plan to interview thousands of Middle Eastern men who came here within the last two years on nonimmigrant visas constitute ethnic profiling? The answer turns out to be draw. It is ethnic profiling to the extent that the FBI is operating on a general assumption that Middle Eastern men are more likely than others to commit acts of terror; it is not to the extent that the agents are pursuing case-specific information about the September 11 attacks, albeit in a dragnet fashion. . . .

We also think that neither the question nor the answer is all-important. . . . The Justice Department's program may or may not fall within our definitional line. Its wisdom and morality, however, do not depend on the pigeonhole in which it is placed but on what the Justice Department in fact does. Are the interviews conducted respectfully, in a manner designed to seek out relevant information from those who are willing to give it? If so, the program is acceptable; it may even be an example of good investigative work. On the other hand, if the "voluntary" character of these interviews is merely a ruse — if men against whom there is no evidence are treated as suspects and demeaned — then the program is an intolerable form of ethnic discrimination. . . .

Is all this to suggest that racial and ethnic profiling is less troubling than we once thought? Not at all. It is certainly true that other race-based practices by Government can be as bad, or worse, in criminal investigations as elsewhere. Nonetheless we should be deeply suspicious of racial profiling, however mild the government's actions and however justified they may appear. Investigative choices that are made on the basis of global assumptions about the criminal propensities of racial or ethnic groups are stigmatizing. They reinforce the negative stereotypes on which they are based because investigators are more likely to detect criminal behavior in groups they target than in the groups they overlook. This is dangerous both because it may be misleading, and because it is humiliating to the targeted group. It is a substantial cost of the Justice Department's interview program — whether or not it is ethnic profiling — that many Arab Americans see it as a slap in the face of their entire ethnic group. . . .

U.S. DEPARTMENT OF JUSTICE, CIVIL RIGHTS DIVISION GUIDANCE REGARDING THE USE OF RACE BY FEDERAL LAW ENFORCEMENT AGENCIES

June 2003

In his February 27, 2001, Address to a Joint Session of Congress, President George W. Bush declared that racial profiling is "wrong and we will end it in America." He directed the Attorney General to review the use by Federal law enforcement authorities of race as a factor in conducting stops, searches and other law enforcement investigative procedures. The Attorney General, in turn, instructed the Civil Rights Division to develop guidance for Federal officials to ensure an end to racial profiling in law enforcement. . . .

The use of race as the basis for law enforcement decision-making clearly has a terrible cost, both to the individuals who suffer invidious discrimination and to the Nation, whose goal of "liberty and justice for all" recedes with every act of discrimination. For this reason, this guidance in many cases imposes more restrictions on the consideration of race and ethnicity in Federal law enforcement than the Constitution requires. . . .

I. TRADITIONAL LAW ENFORCEMENT ACTIVITIES.

Two standards in combination should guide use by Federal law enforcement authorities of race or ethnicity in law enforcement activities:

- In making routine or spontaneous law enforcement decisions, such as ordinary traffic stops, Federal law enforcement officers may not use race or ethnicity to any degree, except that officers may rely on race and ethnicity in a specific suspect description. . . .
- In conducting activities in connection with a specific investigation, Federal law enforcement officers may consider race and ethnicity only to the extent that there is trustworthy information, relevant to the locality or time frame, that links persons of a particular race or ethnicity to an identified criminal incident, scheme, or organization. . . .

II. NATIONAL SECURITY AND BORDER INTEGRITY.

The above standards do not affect current Federal policy with respect to law enforcement activities and other efforts to defend and safeguard against threats to national security or the integrity of the Nation's borders, to which the following applies:

- In investigating or preventing threats to national security or other catastrophic events (including the performance of duties related to air transportation security), or in enforcing laws protecting the integrity of the Nation's borders, Federal law enforcement officers may not consider race or ethnicity except to the extent permitted by the Constitution and laws of the United States.

Suppose an FBI agent receives credible information from several informants that a gang composed primarily of Asian males is engaged in narcotics trafficking in a given neighborhood. Does the Justice Department's Guideline permit this agent to consider race as a factor adding to the suspicion that a young Asian man standing on a street corner in the neighborhood is a member of the gang? What is the agent authorized to do, based on this suspicion? What does the Guideline say about taking race or ethnicity into account in connection with the prevention of terrorist incidents? Is it permissible to consider ethnicity in enforcing the traffic laws around a nuclear power plant? Consider this question again after you have looked at the following case.

WHREN v. UNITED STATES

Certiorari to the United States Court of Appeals for the District of Columbia Circuit
517 U.S. 806 (1996)

JUSTICE SCALIA delivered the opinion of the Court.

In this case we decide whether the temporary detention of a motorist who the police have probable cause to believe has committed a civil traffic violation is inconsistent with the Fourth Amendment's prohibition against unreasonable seizures unless a reasonable officer would have been motivated to stop the car by a desire to enforce the traffic laws.

On the evening of June 10, 1993, plainclothes vice-squad officers of the District of Columbia Metropolitan Police Department were patrolling a "high drug area" of the city in an unmarked car. Their suspicions were aroused when they passed a dark Pathfinder truck with temporary license plates and youthful occupants waiting at a stop sign, the driver looking down into the lap of the passenger at his right. The truck remained stopped at the intersection for what seemed an unusually long time — more than 20 seconds. When the police car executed a U-turn in order to head back toward the truck, the Pathfinder turned suddenly to its right, without signalling, and sped off at an "unreasonable" speed. The policemen followed, and in a short while overtook the Pathfinder when it stopped behind other traffic at a red light. They pulled up alongside, and Officer Ephraim Soto stepped out and approached the driver's door, identifying himself as a police officer and directing the driver, petitioner Brown, to put the vehicle in park. When Soto drew up to the driver's window, he immediately observed two large plastic bags of what appeared to be crack cocaine in petitioner Whren's hands. Petitioners were arrested, and quantities of several types of illegal drugs were retrieved from the vehicle.

Petitioners were charged in a four-count indictment with violating various federal drug laws. . . . At a pretrial suppression hearing, they challenged the legality of the stop and the resulting seizure of the drugs. They argued that the stop had not been justified by probable cause to believe, or even reasonable suspicion, that petitioners were engaged in illegal drug-dealing activity; and that Officer Soto's asserted ground for approaching the vehicle — to give the driver a warning concerning traffic violations — was pretextual. The District Court denied the suppression motion. . . .

Petitioners were convicted of the counts at issue here. The Court of Appeals affirmed the convictions, holding with respect to the suppression issue that, "regardless of whether a police officer subjectively believes that the occupants of an automobile may be engaging in some other illegal behavior, a traffic stop is permissible as long as a reasonable officer in the same circumstances *could have* stopped the car for the suspected traffic violation." We granted certiorari. . . .

Petitioners accept that Officer Soto had probable cause to believe that various provisions of the District of Columbia traffic code had been violated. See 18 D.C. Mun. Regs. §§2213.4 (1995) ("An operator shall . . . give full time and attention to the operation of the vehicle"); 2204.3 ("No person shall turn any vehicle . . . without giving an appropriate signal"); 2200.3 ("No person shall drive a vehicle . . . at a speed greater than is reasonable and prudent under the conditions"). They argue, however, that "in the unique context of civil traffic regulations" probable cause is not enough. Since, they contend, the use of automobiles is so heavily and minutely regulated that total compliance with traffic and safety rules is nearly impossible, a police officer will almost invariably be able to catch any given motorist in a technical violation. This creates the temptation to use traffic stops as a means of investigating other law violations, as to which no probable cause or even articulable suspicion exists. Petitioners, who are both black, further contend that police officers might decide which motorists to stop based on decidedly impermissible factors, such as the race of the car's occupants. To avoid this danger, they say, the Fourth Amendment test for traffic stops should be, not the normal one . . . of whether probable cause existed to justify the stop; but rather, whether a police officer, acting reasonably, would have made the stop for the reason given.

Petitioners contend that the standard they propose is consistent with our past cases' disapproval of police attempts to use valid bases of action against citizens as pretexts for pursuing other investigatory agendas. We are reminded . . . that in Colorado v. Bertine, 479 U.S. 367, 372 (1987), in approving an inventory search, we apparently thought it significant that there had been "no showing that the police, who were following standardized procedures, acted in bad faith or for the sole purpose of investigation"; and that in New York v. Burger, 482 U.S. 691, 716-717, n. 27 (1987), we observed, in upholding the constitutionality of a warrantless administrative inspection, that the search did not appear to be "a 'pretext' for obtaining evidence of . . . violation of . . . penal laws." But only an undiscerning reader would regard these cases as endorsing the principle that ulterior motives can invalidate police conduct that is justifiable on the basis of probable cause to believe that a violation of law has occurred. In each case we were addressing the validity of a search conducted in the *absence* of probable cause. Our quoted statements simply explain that the exemption from the need for probable cause (and warrant), which is accorded to searches made for the purpose of inventory or administrative regulation, is not accorded to searches that are *not* made for those purposes. . . .

. . . Petitioners' difficulty is not simply a lack of affirmative support for their position. Not only have we never held, outside the context of inventory search or administrative inspection (discussed above), that an officer's motive invalidates objectively justifiable behavior under the Fourth Amendment; but we have repeatedly held and asserted the contrary. In United States v. Villamonte-Marquez, 462 U.S. 579, 584, n. 3 (1983), we held that an otherwise valid warrantless boarding of a vessel by customs officials was not rendered invalid "because the customs officers were accompanied by a Louisiana state policeman, and were following an informant's tip that a vessel in the ship channel was thought to be carrying marihuana." We flatly dismissed the idea that an ulterior motive might serve to strip the agents of their legal justification. In United States v. Robinson, 414 U.S. 218 (1973), we held that a traffic-violation arrest (of the sort here) would not be rendered invalid by the fact that it was "a mere pretext for a narcotics search," id., at 221, n. 1; and that a lawful postarrest search of the person would not be rendered invalid by the fact that it was not motivated by the officer-safety concern that justifies such searches, see id., at 236. . . .

We think these cases foreclose any argument that the constitutional reasonableness of traffic stops depends on the actual motivations of the individual officers involved. We of course agree with petitioners that the Constitution prohibits selective enforcement of the law based on considerations such as race. But the constitutional basis for objecting to intentionally discriminatory application of laws is the Equal Protection Clause, not the Fourth Amendment. Subjective intentions play no role in ordinary, probable-cause Fourth Amendment analysis.

Recognizing that we have been unwilling to entertain Fourth Amendment challenges based on the actual motivations of individual officers, petitioners disavow any intention to make the individual officer's subjective good faith the touchstone of "reasonableness." They insist that the standard they have put forward — whether the officer's conduct deviated materially from usual police practices, so that a reasonable officer in the same circumstances would not have made the stop for the reasons given — is an "objective" one.

But although framed in empirical terms, this approach is plainly and indisputably driven by subjective considerations. Its whole purpose is to prevent the police from doing under the guise of enforcing the traffic code what they would like to do for different reasons. Petitioners' proposed standard may not use the word "pretext," but it is designed to combat nothing other than the perceived "danger" of the pretextual stop, albeit only indirectly and over the run of cases. Instead of asking whether the individual officer had the proper state of mind, the petitioners would have us ask, in effect, whether (based on general police practices) it is plausible to believe that the officer had the proper state of mind.

Why one would frame a test designed to combat pretext in such fashion that the court cannot take into account *actual and admitted pretext* is a curiosity that can only be explained by the fact that our cases have foreclosed the more sensible option. If those cases were based only upon the evidentiary difficulty of establishing subjective intent, petitioners' attempt to root out subjective vices through objective means might make sense. But they were not based only upon that, or indeed even principally upon that. Their principal basis — which applies equally to attempts to reach subjective intent through ostensibly objective means — is simply that the Fourth Amendment's concern with "reasonableness" allows certain actions to be taken in certain circumstances, *whatever* the subjective intent. See, e.g., *Robinson*, supra, at 236 ("Since it is the fact of custodial arrest which gives rise to the authority to search, it is of no moment that [the officer] did not indicate any subjective fear of the [arrestee] or that he did not himself suspect that [the arrestee] was armed") (footnotes omitted). But even if our concern had been only an evidentiary one, petitioners' proposal would by no means assuage it. Indeed, it seems to us somewhat easier to figure out the intent of an individual officer than to plumb the collective consciousness of law enforcement in order to determine whether a "reasonable officer" would have been moved to act upon the traffic violation. While police manuals and standard procedures may sometimes provide objective assistance, ordinarily one would be reduced to speculating about the hypothetical reaction of a hypothetical constable — an exercise that might be called virtual subjectivity.

Moreover, police enforcement practices, even if they could be practicably assessed by a judge, vary from place to place and from time to time. We cannot accept that the search and seizure protections of the Fourth Amendment are so variable, and can be made to turn upon such trivialities. The difficulty is illustrated by petitioners' arguments in this case. Their claim that a reasonable officer would not have made this stop is based largely on District of Columbia police regulations which permit plainclothes officers in unmarked vehicles to enforce traffic laws "only in the case of a violation that is so grave as to pose an *immediate threat* to the safety of others." This basis of invalidation would not apply in jurisdictions that had a different practice. And it would not have applied even in the District of Columbia, if Officer Soto had been wearing a uniform or patrolling in a marked police cruiser. . . .

In what would appear to be an elaboration on the "reasonable officer" test, petitioners argue that the balancing inherent in any Fourth Amendment inquiry requires us to weigh the governmental and individual interests implicated in a traffic stop such as we have here. That balancing, petitioners claim, does not support investigation of minor traffic infractions by plainclothes police in unmarked vehicles. . . .

It is of course true that in principle, every Fourth Amendment case, since it turns upon a "reasonableness" determination, involves a balancing of all relevant factors. With rare exceptions not applicable here, however, the result of that balancing is not in doubt where the search or seizure is based upon probable cause. . . .

Petitioners urge as an extraordinary factor in this case that the "multitude of applicable traffic and equipment regulations" is so large and so difficult to obey perfectly that virtually everyone is guilty of violation, permitting the police to single out almost whomever they wish for a stop. But we are aware of no principle that would allow us to decide at what point a code of law becomes so expansive and so commonly violated that infraction itself can no longer be the ordinary measure of the lawfulness of enforcement. And even if we could identify such exorbitant codes, we do not know by what standard (or what right) we would decide, as petitioners would have us do, which particular provisions are sufficiently important to merit enforcement.

For the run-of-the-mine case, which this surely is, we think there is no realistic alternative to the traditional common-law rule that probable cause justifies a search and seizure. . . .

NOTES AND QUESTIONS

1. Racial profiling is a means of exercising police discretion. The broader the discretion, the greater the opportunity to profile. One obvious way to limit police discretion is to ban the use of pretexts — i.e., to require that, if the police target a suspect due to suspicion of drug crime, the police must have sufficient cause to believe evidence of *that same crime* is present before stopping or searching the suspect. *Whren* rejects that position as a matter of Fourth Amendment law. Why? Is the Court's reasoning persuasive?

2. On the surface, *Whren* looks like an easy case. The police made a U-turn, which plainly did not amount to a "search" or a "seizure." The defendants then turned and sped away, committing a traffic violation for which, naturally, they could be pulled

over. What the police saw when they caught up with the defendants was in plain view, and hence was the fruit of a legal seizure. Underneath that simple fact pattern, though, lies a complex issue: the proper relationship between the Fourth Amendment and substantive criminal law. That relationship is, surprisingly, almost never discussed in the cases and rarely explored in the literature. It nevertheless is both important and a little unusual.

For most searches and seizures, the Fourth Amendment requires probable cause. That standard has no independent meaning; it necessarily incorporates the contents of the relevant criminal law. Thus, if a court concludes that a police officer had probable cause to believe a suspect had just committed a burglary, the court has determined that (1) based on the information available at the time, there was a fair probability (2) that the suspect had engaged in the behavior defined by the state's criminal code as "burglary." The first of these two parts of Fourth Amendment standards — the part that refers to the level of probability — is constitutionally required. No state legislature or local police department could decide, for example, to authorize arrests based on something *less* than probable cause that the suspect had committed a crime. But the second part — the part that refers to the crime the suspect is thought to have committed — is completely within the state's control.

This obviously creates an opportunity from the state's point of view. If the state defines driving 56 miles per hour or more as a crime, and if virtually every driver on the highway drives at least 56 miles per hour, then the police will have probable cause to arrest virtually every driver on the highway. In that event, Fourth Amendment law does not really do any work — by defining "crime" broadly, the state no longer needs to worry about probable cause, for it will always exist. *Whren* holds, unanimously, that this is not a problem — that the Fourth Amendment ordinarily has nothing to say about the content of criminal law, even though the content of criminal law determines what Fourth Amendment standards mean.

3. Does that holding make sense? If the point of the Fourth Amendment is to ensure that the police have a good reason before searching or seizing someone, shouldn't the Fourth Amendment place some limits on the state's ability to define innocuous conduct as a crime? One response is that the only alternative to the position the Court took in *Whren* is to look to police officers' motivations. Justice Scalia suggests this when he says that the defendants' proposed objective standard is "plainly and indisputably driven by subjective considerations." But that raises a different question: What is so wrong with a standard "driven by subjective considerations"? A good deal of constitutional law, including a number of doctrines covered in this book, turns on the subjective motives of government officials. Why are police motives distinctively problematic?

4. *Whren* reaffirms the proposition that there is no "pretext search" or "pretext seizure" doctrine in Fourth Amendment law — that the legality of a search or seizure does not depend on why the officer carried it out. The defense argued that this proposition creates an enormous potential for discrimination — that it leaves the police free to engage in racial profiling, stopping black motorists under circumstances where they would not stop whites. The Court responded, in effect, by saying that this is a problem for equal protection doctrine, not for the Fourth Amendment.

In evaluating this conclusion, you might consider what equal protection doctrine requires in this setting. In order to make out an equal protection claim, a defendant would have to show that the police intentionally discriminated against him based on a protected characteristic like race. How would the defendant go about making that showing? Successful equal protection claims against the police are extremely rare. Is that surprising?

5. For a rare example of a successful equal protection challenge to a police intervention — in a case that did not involve any allegations of race discrimination — see People v. Kail, 501 N.E.2d 969 (Ill. App. 1986). Kail was a suspected prostitute; she was arrested not for prostitution but for violating an obscure local ordinance requiring all bicycles to be equipped with bells. The arrest stemmed from a police-department policy requiring strict enforcement of all laws against suspected prostitutes. (The arresting officer testified that she had seen hundreds if not thousands of bicycles without bells during her career, but had never arrested anyone before for that offense.) Kail eventually was convicted of a drug offense when a post-arrest inventory search turned up a small quantity of marijuana. The Illinois Court of Appeals reversed, finding — even under a "rational basis" approach (since suspected prostitutes are not a "suspect class") — that the arrest was a violation of equal protection.

The dissent in *Kail* argued that the majority's position would bar, for example, prosecuting Al Capone for tax evasion, since the government was primarily interested in other, unrelated offenses Capone had allegedly committed. Is that right? It bears noting that there is a long legal tradition of permitting pretextual prosecutions like the one in the Capone case — prosecutions for crimes other than the ones that attracted the government's interest. Should the standards for pretextual searches and seizures by police be the same?

6. Police discrimination in traffic stops has received a good deal of attention, with frequent claims that police are much more likely to stop black motorists than white ones. See, e.g., David A. Harris, The Stories, the Statistics, and the Law: Why "Driving While Black" Matters, 84 Minn. L. Rev. 265 (1999); Wesley MacNeil Oliver, With an Evil Eye and an Unequal Hand: Pretextual Stops and Doctrinal Remedies to Racial Profiling, 74 Tul. L. Rev. 1409 (2000). Those claims find support in work by John L. Lamberth, a psychology professor at Temple University. A government report summarizes Lamberth's findings as follows:

> An analysis . . . of motorists traveling along a segment of the New Jersey Turnpike found the following: (1) 14 percent of the cars traveling the roadway had an African American driver or other occupant; (2) 15 percent of cars exceeding the speed limit by at least 6 miles per hour had an African American driver or other occupant; (3) of stops where race was noted by police, 44 percent of the individuals in one section of the roadway and 35 percent of the individuals in this section and a larger section combined were African American. Lamberth also reported that 98 percent of all drivers violated the speed limit by at least 6 miles per hour. . . .
>
> In a similar analysis of motorists traveling along a segment of Interstate 95 in northeastern Maryland, Lamberth found the following: (1) 17 percent of the cars had an African American driver; (2) 18 percent of cars exceeding the speed limit by at least 1 mile per hour or violating another traffic law had an African American driver; (3) 29 percent of the motorists stopped by the Maryland State Police were African American. This study also found that 92 percent of all motorists were violating the speeding law, [and] 2 percent were violating another traffic law. . . .

United States General Accounting Office, Racial Profiling: Limited Data Available on Motorists Stops 8-9 (Mar. 2000) (footnotes omitted). As the GAO report noted, the data do not indicate the racial breakdown of drivers who violate the speed limit by a large margin. Id., at 1 and n. 1. Still, the percentages cited above do suggest discrimination by the New Jersey and Maryland state police, and it is widely believed that similar patterns exist in many other states.

Assume the suggestion is accurate. How might a different result in *Whren* affect that state of affairs? Could a court find that any stop of a motorist going only six miles per hour over the speed limit on the New Jersey Turnpike is constitutionally unreasonable, since 98 percent of the drivers go at least that fast? If so, presumably the court would have to determine what speed is fast enough to justify a stop. How would that determination be made? Is it feasible for courts to be in the business of defining traffic rules?

Another possible means of redressing the kind of discrimination suggested by Lamberth's work would involve the exclusionary rule. The Supreme Court has steadfastly avoided using Fourth Amendment exclusion prophylactically — excluding evidence even when the police behaved properly in order to give the police the right incentives. Might such an approach make sense in the *Whren* context? Suppose the law required suppression of any evidence of nontraffic offenses found during the course of a traffic stop. Would that requirement reduce the racial disparity in traffic stops? Would it be a wise use of the exclusionary rule?

7. Now consider the following argument:

> The strategic brilliance of the campaign against racial profiling is that it reduces complex issues of race, policing, and the drug war to the simple and arresting image of the irrational and racially discriminatory investigation of innocent, middle-class people. But the appeal of the means should not seduce us into mistaking it for the end.

R. Richard Banks, Beyond Profiling: Race, Policing, and the Drug War, 56 Stan. L. Rev. 571, 602 (2003). Professor Banks argues that "efforts to prove racial profiling will founder on empirical findings that invite contrary interpretations." He notes that the elimination of racial profiling might not solve many problems commonly associated with the practice: "Such problems may persist in the absence of racial profiling or be remedied without eliminating racial profiling." He also warns that remedial efforts may be "futile or counterproductive":

> [N]o simple prohibition of racial profiling will suffice. If racial profiling helps officers to apprehend drug traffickers, then officers will have a powerful incentive to use racial profiling, no matter what the rules say. . . . Indeed, recent findings from New Jersey and Maryland, jurisdictions that have sought to end racial profiling, are consistent with its continued use by state troopers.
>
> In any event, the absence of proof of racial profiling by individual officers or against individual citizens precludes individualized remedies. Remedies must take the form of broad prophylactic measures, such as monitoring, or the elimination of discretionary actions. . . . Although such reforms will narrow the opportunities for racial profiling, they may also prompt officers to conceal their racial profiling. Moreover, limitations on officer discretion might influence the behavior of other actors within the criminal justice system. Because the discretion that enables racial profiling is also integral to effective law enforcement, remedies that constrain discretion should be evaluated based on the full scope of their consequences, not simply whether they would diminish racial profiling.

Id., at 588-589. Banks argues that given these problems, "policymakers should abandon efforts to ferret out and eliminate racial profiling in drug interdiction," and should focus instead on race-related consequences of the drug war, regardless of whether these consequences flow from profiling:

> Analyses should fully assess the consequences of the drug war, prominent among them the astoundingly high level of incarceration of disadvantaged racial minorities. Analyses of policing practices more generally should confront law enforcement officers' mistreatment of racial minorities and minorities' distrust of the criminal justice system and their perception of injustice. Reform should aim to generate effective and practical solutions. . . .
>
> My primary purpose . . . [is] to counter the tendency to reduce questions of race, policing, and the drug war to questions of racial profiling. However politically appealing that approach, it may obscure rather than clarify potential remedies for problems that deserve immediate attention.

Id., at 602-603. Is Banks' analysis sound? Is it consistent with the Court's decision in *Whren*?

NOTES ON POLICE DISCRETION AND SUBSTANTIVE CRIMINAL LAW

1. *Whren* rules out regulating police use of profiles by banning police use of pretexts. And the practical obstacles of proving impermissible police motives rule out the Equal Protection Clause as a viable regulatory tool. The chief alternative is to limit the criminal prohibitions that give police officers their discretionary power.

That means limiting the range of "public order" offenses that provide a large portion of that discretionary power: loitering laws, curfews, anti-noise ordinances, anti-"cruising" ordinances, anti-gang laws, and the like. In the 1960s and 1970s, an older generation of such laws — chiefly loitering and vagrancy statutes — were widely held to be unconstitutionally vague; the leading case was Papachristou v. Jacksonville, 405 U.S. 156 (1972). But public order offenses made a comeback in the 1980s and 1990s, partly due to an argument by social scientists James Q. Wilson and George L. Kelling. See Broken Windows, Atlantic Monthly, Mar. 1982, at 29. Wilson and Kelling maintained that public disorder — they used broken windows that go unrepaired as an example; hence their article's title — signals law-abiding citizens to steer clear of the streets, which in turn promotes more disorder, signaling would-be criminals that the streets are safe for criminal enterprises. Police intervention to address disorder, they suggested, might be critically important to enhance citizens' quality of life in public places and to shore up the sense of security in neighborhoods under threat. For a more detailed exposition of the argument, see George L. Kelling & Catherine M. Coles, Fixing Broken Windows (1996).

The "broken windows" thesis was implemented, at least to some degree, in New York and in some other large cities with some success. Most famously, a crackdown on subway vandalism and turnstile jumping in the New York City subway system led to a sharp drop in other, more serious crime in the subways. That success has been disputed; some scholars have claimed that the data do not support the "broken windows" thesis. For the leading argument, see Bernard Harcourt, Illusion of Order:

The False Promise of Broken Windows Policing (2001). Nevertheless, a large fraction of police agencies have adopted the principle that enforcing *minor* crimes is a useful way to reduce the incidence of *major* crimes.

2. Even if the particulars of the "broken windows" thesis are wrong, it is possible that the courts, and the Court, went too far in the many *Papachristou*-era decisions striking down criminal statutes and ordinances designed to help the police keep order on the streets. For an argument along these lines, see Robert C. Ellickson, Controlling Chronic Misconduct in City Spaces: Of Panhandlers, Skid Rows, and Public-Space Zoning, 105 Yale L.J. 1165, 1247-1248 (1996):

> Unchecked street misconduct creates an ambience of unease, and for some, of menace. Pedestrians can sense that even minor disorder in public spaces tends to encourage more severe crime. City dwellers who perceive that their streets are out of control are apt to take defensive measures. They may use sidewalks and parks less, or favor architectural designs that discourage leisurely stays in public spaces. In particular, they may relocate to more inviting locales. . . .
>
> Since about 1965, federal constitutional decisions have limited the power of cities to control panhandling, bench squatting, public drunkenness, and other minor street nuisances. By allowing the denizens of Skid Rows to spend more time in the central business district, these decisions contributed to the demise of Skid Rows. These constitutional rulings, in combination with the attenuation of informal social controls and the increase in the size of the urban underclass, also made American downtowns much more disorderly. . . .

Elsewhere in his article, Ellickson argues that cities should be able to authorize their police to enforce different standards of street behavior in different parts of town — to keep downtown business districts free of panhandlers and bench squatters, while allowing freer rein to such behavior in "skid row"-type areas.

3. Partly out of a desire to expand police authority on the street, a number of legislatures have passed identification statutes. The Supreme Court addressed the constitutionality of one such statute in Hiibel v. Sixth Judicial District Court of Nevada, 124 S. Ct. 2451 (2004). The sheriff's department in Humboldt County, Nevada, received a telephone call in which the caller reported seeing a man assault a woman in a red and silver GMC truck on Grass Valley Road. A deputy sheriff arrived to find the truck parked on the side of the road with a man standing next to it and a young woman sitting inside. The officer observed skid marks in the gravel behind the vehicle, leading him to believe the truck had come to a sudden stop.

The officer approached the man, who appeared to be intoxicated, and asked him if he had any identification. The man refused to identify himself and became agitated. After repeated requests for identification and repeated refusals, the man began to taunt the officer by putting his hands behind his back and daring the officer to arrest him. After a final warning that he would be arrested if he continued to refuse to comply, the officer placed the man, subsequently identified as Hiibel, under arrest. Hiibel was charged with obstructing the officer in discharging his duties by refusing to comply with Nevada's "stop and identify" statute. Hiibel argued that arresting someone for refusing to give his name violated the Fourth Amendment. The Court disagreed:

> [T]he Fourth Amendment does not impose obligations on the citizen but instead provides rights against the government. As a result, the Fourth Amendment itself cannot

require a suspect to answer questions. This case concerns a different issue, however. Here, the source of the legal obligation arises from Nevada state law, not the Fourth Amendment. . . .

The principles of *Terry* permit a State to require a suspect to disclose his name in the course of a *Terry* stop. The reasonableness of a seizure under the Fourth Amendment is determined "by balancing its intrusion on the individual's Fourth Amendment interests against its promotion of legitimate government interests." Delaware v. Prouse, 440 U.S. 648, 654 (1979). The Nevada statute satisfies that standard. The request for identity has an immediate relation to the purpose, rationale, and practical demands of a *Terry* stop. . . . [T]he Nevada statute does not alter the nature of the stop itself: it does not change its duration, or its location. A state law requiring a suspect to disclose his name in the course of a valid *Terry* stop is consistent with Fourth Amendment prohibitions against unreasonable searches and seizures.

Petitioner argues that the Nevada statute circumvents the probable cause requirement, in effect allowing an officer to arrest a person for being suspicious. According to petitioner, this creates a risk of arbitrary police conduct that the Fourth Amendment does not permit.

. . . Petitioner's concerns are met by the requirement that a *Terry* stop must be justified at its inception and "reasonably related in scope to the circumstances which justified" the initial stop. 392 U.S., at 20. . . . It is clear in this case that the request for identification was "reasonably related in scope to the circumstances which justified" the stop. The officer's request was a commonsense inquiry, not an effort to obtain an arrest for failure to identify after a *Terry* stop yielded insufficient evidence.

Id., at 2459-2460. Notice that the deputy sheriff clearly had reasonable suspicion to stop Hiibel in connection with the reported assault. The statutory obligation to identify himself did not arise until Hiibel was already suspected of criminal activity.

That is the primary difference between *Hiibel* and the Court's previous stop-and-identify cases: In those earlier decisions, the legality of the stop rested on the identification requirement. So, in Brown v. Texas, 443 U.S. 47 (1979), the Court invalidated a conviction for violating a Texas stop and identify statute on Fourth Amendment grounds — ruling that the initial stop was not based on reasonable suspicion and that absent that factual basis for detaining the defendant, the risk of arbitrary and abusive police practices was too great. (In *Brown*, one of the arresting officers explained the stop by saying that "we had never seen that subject in that area before.") *Hiibel* thus appears to be no more than a modest extension, perhaps even a straightforward application, of *Terry*.

4. Or perhaps *Hiibel* is about the change in climate that the terrorist attacks of September 11 produced. Since those attacks, there has been an ongoing public debate about the merits of a mandatory national identification card, which all Americans would be required to carry when in public. Would such a requirement, coupled with a requirement that the card be produced whenever a police officer had reasonable suspicion to justify a stop, violate the Fourth Amendment? Presumably not, after *Hiibel*. Now imagine a federal statute requiring that individuals produce their identity cards whenever a federal agent (but only a federal agent) requests. Would that statute violate the Fourth Amendment? Would your answer change if the federal government defended the statute as a necessary tool in the war on terrorism?

5. As "public order" offenses have proliferated, legislatures have sought to cure the constitutional defects that caused courts to strike down loitering laws in earlier

decades. And police departments have sought to use these newer, more targeted loitering laws to attack urban gangs. The next case involves the intersection of these two trends.

CHICAGO v. MORALES

Certiorari to the Supreme Court of Illinois
527 U.S. 41 (1999)

JUSTICE STEVENS announced the judgment of the Court and delivered the opinion of the Court with respect to Parts I, II, and V, and an opinion with respect to Parts III, IV, and VI, in which JUSTICE SOUTER and JUSTICE GINSBURG join.

In 1992, the Chicago City Council enacted the Gang Congregation Ordinance, which prohibits "criminal street gang members" from "loitering" with one another or with other persons in any public place. The question presented is whether the Supreme Court of Illinois correctly held that the ordinance violates the Due Process Clause of the Fourteenth Amendment to the Federal Constitution.

I

. . . The ordinance creates a criminal offense punishable by a fine of up to $500, imprisonment for not more than six months, and a requirement to perform up to 120 hours of community service. Commission of the offense involves four predicates. First, the police officer must reasonably believe that at least one of the two or more persons present in a "public place" is a "criminal street gang member." Second, the persons must be "loitering," which the ordinance defines as "remaining in any one place with no apparent purpose." Third, the officer must then order "all" of the persons to disperse and remove themselves "from the area." Fourth, a person must disobey the officer's order. If any person, whether a gang member or not, disobeys the officer's order, that person is guilty of violating the ordinance.[2]

Two months after the ordinance was adopted, the Chicago Police Department promulgated General Order 92-4 to provide guidelines to govern its enforcement.

---

2. The ordinance states in pertinent part:

(a) Whenever a police officer observes a person whom he reasonably believes to be a criminal street gang member loitering in any public place with one or more other persons, he shall order all such persons to disperse and remove themselves from the area. Any person who does not promptly obey such an order is in violation of this section.

(b) It shall be an affirmative defense to an alleged violation of this section that no person who was observed loitering was in fact a member of a criminal street gang.

(c) As used in this Section:

(1) "Loiter" means to remain in any one place with no apparent purpose.

(2) "Criminal street gang" means any ongoing organization, association in fact or group of three or more persons, whether formal or informal, having as one of its substantial activities the commission of one or more of the criminal acts enumerated in paragraph (3), and whose members individually or collectively engage in or have engaged in a pattern of criminal gang activity. . . .

(5) "Public place" means the public way and any other location open to the public, whether publicly or privately owned. . . .

(e) Any person who violates this Section is subject to a fine of not less than $100 and not more than $500 for each offense, or imprisonment for not more than six months, or both.

In addition to or instead of the above penalties, any person who violates this section may be required to perform up to 120 hours of community service pursuant to section 1-4-120 of this Code.

Chicago Municipal Code §8-4-015 (added June 17, 1992).

That order purported to establish limitations on the enforcement discretion of police officers "to ensure that the anti-gang loitering ordinance is not enforced in an arbitrary or discriminatory way." Chicago Police Department, General Order 92-4. The limitations confine the authority to arrest gang members who violate the ordinance to sworn "members of the Gang Crime Section" and certain other designated officers, and establish detailed criteria for defining street gangs and membership in such gangs. In addition, the order directs district commanders to "designate areas in which the presence of gang members has a demonstrable effect on the activities of law abiding persons in the surrounding community," and provides that the ordinance "will be enforced only within the designated areas." The city, however, does not release the locations of these "designated areas" to the public.

II

During the three years of its enforcement, the police issued over 89,000 dispersal orders and arrested over 42,000 people for violating the ordinance. In the ensuing enforcement proceedings, 2 trial judges upheld the constitutionality of the ordinance, but 11 others ruled that it was invalid. In respondent Youkhana's case, the trial judge held that the "ordinance fails to notify individuals what conduct is prohibited, and it encourages arbitrary and capricious enforcement by police."

The Illinois Appellate Court affirmed the trial court's ruling in the *Youkhana* case, consolidated and affirmed other pending appeals in accordance with *Youkhana*, and reversed the convictions of respondents Gutierrez, Morales, and others. . . .

The Illinois Supreme Court affirmed. . . . We granted certiorari, and now affirm. Like the Illinois Supreme Court, we conclude that the ordinance enacted by the city of Chicago is unconstitutionally vague.

III

The basic factual predicate for the city's ordinance is not in dispute. As the city argues in its brief, "the very presence of a large collection of obviously brazen, insistent, and lawless gang members and hangers-on on the public ways intimidates residents, who become afraid even to leave their homes and go about their business. That, in turn, imperils community residents' sense of safety and security, detracts from property values, and can ultimately destabilize entire neighborhoods." The findings in the ordinance explain that it was motivated by these concerns. We have no doubt that a law that directly prohibited such intimidating conduct would be constitutional,[17] but this ordinance broadly covers a significant amount of additional activity. Uncertainty about the scope of that additional coverage provides the basis for respondents' claim that the ordinance is too vague. . . .

. . . [T]he freedom to loiter for innocent purposes is part of the "liberty" protected by the Due Process Clause of the Fourteenth Amendment. We have expressly identified this "right to remove from one place to another according to inclination" as "an attribute of personal liberty" protected by the Constitution. Williams v. Fears,

17. In fact the city already has several laws that serve this purpose. See, e.g., Ill. Comp. Stat. ch. 720 §§5/12-6 (1998) (intimidation); 570/405.2 (streetgang criminal drug conspiracy); 147/1 et seq. (Illinois Streetgang Terrorism Omnibus Prevention Act); 5/25-1 (mob action). . . .

179 U.S. 270, 274 (1900); see also Papachristou v. Jacksonville, 405 U.S. 156, 164 (1972). Indeed, it is apparent that an individual's decision to remain in a public place of his choice is as much a part of his liberty as the freedom of movement inside frontiers that is "a part of our heritage," Kent v. Dulles, 357 U.S. 116, 126 (1958), or the right to move "to whatsoever place one's own inclination may direct" identified in Blackstone's Commentaries. 1 W. Blackstone, Commentaries on the Laws of England 130 (1765).

There is no need, however, to decide whether the impact of the Chicago ordinance on constitutionally protected liberty alone would suffice to support a facial challenge under the overbreadth doctrine. For it is clear that the vagueness of this enactment makes a facial challenge appropriate. This is not an ordinance that "simply regulates business behavior and contains a scienter requirement." See Hoffman Estates v. Flipside, Hoffman Estates, Inc., 455 U.S. 489, 499 (1982). It is a criminal law that contains no mens rea requirement, and infringes on constitutionally protected rights. When vagueness permeates the text of such a law, it is subject to facial attack.

Vagueness may invalidate a criminal law for either of two independent reasons. First, it may fail to provide the kind of notice that will enable ordinary people to understand what conduct it prohibits; second, it may authorize and even encourage arbitrary and discriminatory enforcement. Accordingly, we first consider whether the ordinance provides fair notice to the citizen and then discuss its potential for arbitrary enforcement.

IV

. . . The Illinois Supreme Court recognized that the term "loiter" may have a common and accepted meaning, but the definition of that term in this ordinance — "to remain in any one place with no apparent purpose" — does not. It is difficult to imagine how any citizen of the city of Chicago standing in a public place with a group of people would know if he or she had an "apparent purpose." If she were talking to another person, would she have an apparent purpose? If she were frequently checking her watch and looking expectantly down the street, would she have an apparent purpose?

Since the city cannot conceivably have meant to criminalize each instance a citizen stands in public with a gang member, the vagueness that dooms this ordinance is not the product of uncertainty about the normal meaning of "loitering," but rather about what loitering is covered by the ordinance and what is not. . . .

The city's principal response to this concern about adequate notice is that loiterers are not subject to sanction until after they have failed to comply with an officer's order to disperse. . . . We find this response unpersuasive for at least two reasons.

First, . . . [a]lthough it is true that a loiterer is not subject to criminal sanctions unless he or she disobeys a dispersal order, the loitering is the conduct that the ordinance is designed to prohibit. If the loitering is in fact harmless and innocent, the dispersal order itself is an unjustified impairment of liberty. . . . Because an officer may issue an order only after prohibited conduct has already occurred, it cannot provide the kind of advance notice that will protect the putative loiterer from being ordered to disperse. Such an order cannot retroactively give adequate warning of the boundary between the permissible and the impermissible applications of the law.

Second, the terms of the dispersal order compound the inadequacy of the notice afforded by the ordinance. It provides that the officer "shall order all such persons to disperse and remove themselves from the area." This vague phrasing raises a host of questions. After such an order issues, how long must the loiterers remain apart? How far must they move? If each loiterer walks around the block and they meet again at the same location, are they subject to arrest or merely to being ordered to disperse again? . . .

V

The broad sweep of the ordinance also violates "the requirement that a legislature establish minimal guidelines to govern law enforcement." Kolender v. Lawson, 461 U.S., at 358. There are no such guidelines in the ordinance. In any public place in the city of Chicago, persons who stand or sit in the company of a gang member may be ordered to disperse unless their purpose is apparent. . . . It matters not whether the reason that a gang member and his father, for example, might loiter near Wrigley Field is to rob an unsuspecting fan or just to get a glimpse of Sammy Sosa leaving the ballpark; in either event, if their purpose is not apparent to a nearby police officer, she may — indeed, she "shall" — order them to disperse.

Recognizing that the ordinance does reach a substantial amount of innocent conduct, we turn, then, to its language to determine if it "necessarily entrusts lawmaking to the moment-to-moment judgment of the policeman on his beat." Kolender v. Lawson, 461 U.S., at 359 (internal quotation marks omitted). As we discussed in the context of fair notice, the principal source of the vast discretion conferred on the police in this case is the definition of loitering as "to remain in any one place with no apparent purpose."

As the Illinois Supreme Court interprets that definition, it "provides absolute discretion to police officers to determine what activities constitute loitering." 177 Ill. 2d, at 457. We have no authority to construe the language of a state statute more narrowly than the construction given by that State's highest court. . . .

It is true, as the city argues, that the requirement that the officer reasonably believe that a group of loiterers contains a gang member does place a limit on the authority to order dispersal. That limitation would no doubt be sufficient if the ordinance only applied to loitering that had an apparently harmful purpose or effect, or possibly if it only applied to loitering by persons reasonably believed to be criminal gang members. But this ordinance . . . requires no harmful purpose and applies to non-gang members as well as suspected gang members. . . . Friends, relatives, teachers, counselors, or even total strangers might unwittingly engage in forbidden loitering if they happen to engage in idle conversation with a gang member. . . .

Finally, in its opinion striking down the ordinance, the Illinois Supreme Court refused to accept the general order issued by the police department as a sufficient limitation on the "vast amount of discretion" granted to the police in its enforcement. We agree. That the police have adopted internal rules limiting their enforcement to certain designated areas in the city would not provide a defense to a loiterer who might be arrested elsewhere. Nor could a person who knowingly loitered with a well-known gang member anywhere in the city safely assume that they would not be ordered to disperse no matter how innocent and harmless their loitering might be.

VI

In our judgment, the Illinois Supreme Court correctly concluded that the ordinance does not provide sufficiently specific limits on the enforcement discretion of the police "to meet constitutional standards for definiteness and clarity." 177 Ill. 2d, at 459. . . .

JUSTICE O'CONNOR, with whom JUSTICE BREYER joins, concurring in part and concurring in the judgment. . . .

As it has been construed by the [Illinois Supreme Court], Chicago's gang loitering ordinance is unconstitutionally vague because it lacks sufficient minimal standards to guide law enforcement officers. In particular, it fails to provide police with any standard by which they can judge whether an individual has an "*apparent* purpose." Indeed, because any person standing on the street has a general "purpose" — even if it is simply to stand — the ordinance permits police officers to choose which purposes are *permissible*. . . .

This vagueness consideration alone provides a sufficient ground for affirming the Illinois court's decision, and I agree with Part V of the Court's opinion, which discusses this consideration. . . . Accordingly, there is no need to consider the other issues briefed by the parties and addressed by the plurality. I express no opinion about them.

It is important to courts and legislatures alike that we characterize more clearly the narrow scope of today's holding. . . . [T]here remain open to Chicago reasonable alternatives to combat the very real threat posed by gang intimidation and violence. For example, the Court properly and expressly distinguishes the ordinance from laws that require loiterers to have a "harmful purpose," from laws that target only gang members, and from laws that incorporate limits on the area and manner in which the laws may be enforced. . . .

In my view, the gang loitering ordinance could have been construed more narrowly. The term "loiter" might possibly be construed in a more limited fashion to mean "to remain in any one place with no apparent purpose other than to establish control over identifiable areas, to intimidate others from entering those areas, or to conceal illegal activities." Such a definition would be consistent with the Chicago City Council's findings and would avoid the vagueness problems of the ordinance as construed by the Illinois Supreme Court. . . .

The Illinois Supreme Court did not choose to give a limiting construction to Chicago's ordinance. . . . Accordingly, I join Parts I, II, and V of the Court's opinion and concur in the judgment.

JUSTICE KENNEDY, concurring in part and concurring in the judgment. I join Parts I, II, and V of the Court's opinion and concur in the judgment. I also share many of the concerns Justice Stevens expressed in Part IV. . . . As interpreted by the Illinois Supreme Court, the Chicago ordinance would reach a broad range of innocent conduct. For this reason it is not necessarily saved by the requirement that the citizen must disobey a police order to disperse before there is a violation.

We have not often examined these types of orders. It can be assumed, however, that some police commands will subject a citizen to prosecution for disobeying whether or not the citizen knows why the order is given. Illustrative examples include when the police tell a pedestrian not to enter a building and the reason is to avoid impeding a rescue team, or to protect a crime scene, or to secure an area for the protection of a public official. It does not follow, however, that any unexplained police order must be obeyed without notice of the lawfulness of the order. The predicate of an order to disperse is not, in my view, sufficient to eliminate doubts regarding the adequacy of notice under this ordinance. A citizen, while engaging in a wide array of innocent conduct, is not likely to know when he may be subject to a dispersal order based on the officer's own knowledge of the identity or affiliations of other persons with whom the citizen is congregating; nor may the citizen be able to assess what an officer might conceive to be the citizen's lack of an apparent purpose.

[Justice Breyer's opinion, concurring in part and concurring in the judgment, is omitted.]

JUSTICE SCALIA, dissenting.

The citizens of Chicago were once free to drive about the city at whatever speed they wished. At some point Chicagoans (or perhaps Illinoisans) decided this would not do, and imposed prophylactic speed limits designed to assure safe operation by the average (or perhaps even subaverage) driver with the average (or perhaps even subaverage) vehicle. This infringed upon the "freedom" of all citizens, but was not unconstitutional.

Similarly, the citizens of Chicago were once free to stand around and gawk at the scene of an accident. At some point Chicagoans discovered that this obstructed traffic and caused more accidents. They did not make the practice unlawful, but they did authorize police officers to order the crowd to disperse, and imposed penalties for refusal to obey such an order. Again, this prophylactic measure infringed upon the "freedom" of all citizens, but was not unconstitutional.

Until the ordinance that is before us today was adopted, the citizens of Chicago were free to stand about in public places with no apparent purpose — to engage, that is, in conduct that appeared to be loitering. In recent years, however, the city has been afflicted with criminal street gangs. . . . Many residents of the inner city felt that they were prisoners in their own homes. Once again, Chicagoans decided that to eliminate the problem it was worth restricting some of the freedom that they once enjoyed. The means they took was similar to the second, and more mild, example given above rather than the first: Loitering was not made unlawful, but when a group of people occupied a public place without an apparent purpose and in the company of a known gang member, police officers were authorized to order them to disperse, and the failure to obey such an order was made unlawful. The minor limitation upon the free state of nature that this prophylactic arrangement imposed upon all Chicagoans seemed to them (and it seems to me) a small price to pay for liberation of their streets. . . .

Respondents' consolidated appeal presents a facial challenge to the Chicago ordinance on vagueness grounds. When a facial challenge is successful, the law in question is declared to be unenforceable in *all* its applications, and not just in its particular application to the party in suit. . . .

. . . When our normal criteria for facial challenges are applied, it is clear that the Justices in the majority have transposed the burden of proof. Instead of requiring the respondents, who are challenging the ordinance, to show that it is invalid in all its applications, they have required the petitioner to show that it is valid in all its applications. . . .

The plurality's explanation for its departure from the usual rule governing facial challenges is seemingly contained in the following statement: "[This] is a criminal law that . . . infringes on constitutionally protected rights . . . When vagueness permeates the text of *such* a law, it is subject to facial attack." (emphasis added) . . .

. . . I turn first to the support for the proposition that there is a constitutionally protected right to loiter — or, as the plurality more favorably describes it, for a person to "remain in a public place of his choice." The plurality thinks much of this Fundamental Freedom to Loiter, which it contrasts with such lesser, constitutionally *un*protected, activities as doing (ugh!) *business*: "This is not an ordinance that simply regulates business behavior and contains a scienter requirement. . . . It is a criminal law that contains no mens rea requirement . . . and infringes on constitutionally protected rights." Ante, at 55 (internal quotation marks omitted). . . .

Of course every activity, even scratching one's head, can be called a "constitutional right" if one means by that term nothing more than the fact that the activity is covered (as all are) by the Equal Protection Clause, so that those who engage in it cannot be singled out without "rational basis." But using the term in that sense utterly impoverishes our constitutional discourse. We would then need a new term for those activities — such as political speech or religious worship — that cannot be forbidden even *with* rational basis.

The plurality tosses around the term "constitutional right" in this renegade sense, because there is not the slightest evidence for the existence of a genuine constitutional right to loiter. Justice Thomas recounts the vast historical tradition of criminalizing the activity. It is simply not maintainable that the right to loiter would have been regarded as an essential attribute of liberty at the time of the framing or at the time of adoption of the Fourteenth Amendment. . . .

It would be unfair, however, to criticize the plurality's failed attempt to establish that loitering is a constitutionally protected right while saying nothing of the concurrences. The plurality at least makes an attempt. The concurrences, on the other hand, make no pretense at attaching their broad "vagueness invalidates" rule to a liberty interest. As far as appears from Justice O'Connor's and Justice Breyer's opinions, *no* police officer may issue *any* order, affecting *any* insignificant sort of citizen conduct (except, perhaps, an order addressed to the unprotected class of "gang members") unless the standards for the issuance of that order are precise. No modern urban society — and probably none since London got big enough to have sewers — could function under such a rule. There are innumerable reasons why it may be important for a constable to tell a pedestrian to "move on" — and even if it were possible to list in an ordinance all of the reasons that are known, many are simply unpredictable. Hence the (entirely reasonable) Rule of the City of New York which reads: "No person shall fail, neglect or refuse to comply with the lawful direction or command of any Police Officer, Urban Park Ranger, Parks Enforcement Patrol Officer or other [Parks and Recreation] Department employee, indicated verbally, by gesture or otherwise." 56 RCNY §1-03(c)(1) (1996). . . . [T]o say that such a general ordinance permitting "lawful orders" is void *in all its applications* demands more than a safe and orderly society can reasonably deliver. . . .

[The portion of Justice Scalia's opinion arguing that the ordinance is not unconstitutionally vague is omitted.]

. . . The citizens of Chicago have decided that depriving themselves of the freedom to "hang out" with a gang member is necessary to eliminate pervasive gang crime and intimidation — and that the elimination of the one is worth the deprivation of the other. This Court has no business second-guessing either the degree of necessity or the fairness of the trade. . . .

JUSTICE THOMAS, with whom THE CHIEF JUSTICE and JUSTICE SCALIA join, dissenting. . . .

The human costs exacted by criminal street gangs are inestimable. In many of our Nation's cities, gangs have "[v]irtually overtak[en] certain neighborhoods, contributing to the economic and social decline of these areas and causing fear and lifestyle changes among law-abiding residents." U.S. Dept. of Justice, Office of Justice Programs, Bureau of Justice Assistance, Monograph: Urban Street Gang Enforcement 3 (1997). . . .

The city of Chicago has suffered the devastation wrought by this national tragedy. Last year, in an effort to curb plummeting attendance, the Chicago Public Schools hired dozens of adults to escort children to school. The youngsters had become too terrified of gang violence to leave their homes alone. Martinez, Parents Paid to Walk Line Between Gangs and School, Chicago Tribune, Jan. 21, 1998, p. 1. The children's fears were not unfounded. In 1996, the Chicago Police Department estimated that there were 132 criminal street gangs in the city. Illinois Criminal Justice Information Authority, Research Bulletin: Street Gangs and Crime 4 (Sept. 1996). Between 1987 and 1994, these gangs were involved in 63,141 criminal incidents, including 21,689 nonlethal violent crimes and 894 homicides. Id., at 4-5. Many of these criminal incidents and homicides result from gang "turf battles," which take place on the public streets and place innocent residents in grave danger.

Before enacting its ordinance, the Chicago City Council held extensive hearings on the problems of gang loitering. Concerned citizens appeared to testify poignantly as to how gangs disrupt their daily lives. Ordinary citizens like Ms. D'Ivory Gordon explained that she struggled just to walk to work:

> When I walk out my door, these guys are out there. . . .
> They watch you. . . . They know where you live. They know what time you leave, what time you come home. I am afraid of them. I have even come to the point now that I carry a meat cleaver to work with me . . .
> . . . I don't want to hurt anyone, and I don't want to be hurt. We need to clean these corners up. Clean these communities up and take it back from them.

Transcript of Proceedings before the City Council of Chicago, Committee on Police and Fire 66-67 (May 15, 1992).

Eighty-eight-year-old Susan Mary Jackson echoed her sentiments, testifying, "We used to have a nice neighborhood. We don't have it anymore. . . . I am scared to go out in the daytime. . . . You can't pass because they are standing. I am afraid to go to the store. I don't go to the store because I am afraid. . . ." Id., at 93-95. . . .

Following these hearings, the council found that "criminal street gangs establish control over identifiable areas . . . by loitering in those areas and intimidating others from entering those areas." App. to Pet. for Cert. 60a-61a. It further found that the mere presence of gang members "intimidate[s] many law abiding citizens" and "creates a justifiable fear for the safety of persons and property in the area." It is the product of this democratic process — the council's attempt to address these social ills — that we are asked to pass judgment upon today.

. . . The [Chicago] ordinance does nothing more than confirm the well-established principle that the police have the duty and the power to maintain the public peace, and, when necessary, to disperse groups of individuals who threaten it. The plurality, however, concludes that the city's commonsense effort to combat gang loitering fails constitutional scrutiny for two separate reasons — because it infringes upon gang members' constitutional right to "loiter for innocent purposes," and because it is vague on its face. A majority of the Court endorses the latter conclusion. I respectfully disagree. . . .

The plurality's sweeping conclusion that this ordinance infringes upon a liberty interest protected by the Fourteenth Amendment's Due Process Clause withers when exposed to the relevant history: Laws prohibiting loitering and vagrancy have been a fixture of Anglo-American law at least since the time of the Norman Conquest. See generally C. Ribton-Turner, A History of Vagrants and Vagrancy and Beggars and Begging (reprint 1972) (discussing history of English vagrancy laws); see also Papachristou v. Jacksonville, 405 U.S. 156, 161-162 (1972) (recounting history of vagrancy laws). The American colonists enacted laws modeled upon the English vagrancy laws, and at the time of the founding, state and local governments customarily criminalized loitering and other forms of vagrancy. Vagrancy laws were common in the decades preceding the ratification of the Fourteenth Amendment, and remained on the books long after. . . .

The Court concludes that the ordinance is also unconstitutionally vague because it fails to provide adequate standards to guide police discretion and because, in the plurality's view, it does not give residents adequate notice of how to conform their conduct to the confines of the law. I disagree on both counts.

. . . Far from according officers too much discretion, the ordinance merely enables police officers to fulfill one of their traditional functions. Police officers are not, and have never been, simply enforcers of the criminal law. They wear other hats — importantly, they have long been vested with the responsibility for preserving the public peace. . . .

In their role as peace officers, the police long have had the authority and the duty to order groups of individuals who threaten the public peace to disperse. . . . The authority to issue dispersal orders continues to play a commonplace and crucial role in police operations, particularly in urban areas. . . .

In order to perform their peace-keeping responsibilities satisfactorily, the police inevitably must exercise discretion. . . . That is not to say that the law should not provide objective guidelines for the police, but simply that it cannot rigidly constrain their every action. By directing a police officer not to issue a dispersal order unless he "observes a person whom he reasonably believes to be a criminal street gang member loitering in any public place," Chicago's ordinance strikes an appropriate balance between those two extremes. Just as we trust officers to rely on their experience and expertise in order to make spur-of-the-moment determinations about amorphous legal standards such as "probable cause" and "reasonable suspicion," so we must trust them to determine whether a group of loiterers contains individuals (in this case members of criminal street gangs) whom the city has determined threaten the public peace. . . .

Today, the Court focuses extensively on the "rights" of gang members and their companions. It can safely do so — the people who will have to live with the consequences of today's opinion do not live in our neighborhoods. Rather, the people who will suffer from our lofty pronouncements are people like Ms. Susan Mary Jackson; people who have seen their neighborhoods literally destroyed by gangs and violence and drugs. They are good, decent people who must struggle to overcome their desperate situation, against all odds, in order to raise their families, earn a living, and remain good citizens. As one resident described, "There is only about maybe one or two percent of the people in the city causing these problems maybe, but it's keeping 98 percent of us in our houses and off the streets and afraid to shop." By focusing exclusively on the imagined "rights" of the two percent, the Court today has denied our most vulnerable citizens the very thing that Justice Stevens elevates above all else — the "freedom of movement." And that is a shame. I respectfully dissent.

NOTES AND QUESTIONS

1. *Morales* was litigated and decided as a due process case, not a Fourth Amendment case. But it raises issues that go to the heart of Fourth Amendment law: How much discretion should police have when dealing with suspects on the street? What is a proper basis for police intervention? Does the answer change if the intervention takes the form of an "order to disperse"?

2. Maybe it does, for reasons that build on Justice Thomas's dissent. Police, Justice Thomas notes, are not simply enforcers of criminal law; they also are keepers of public order. It follows that police must be able, in some settings, to search or seize people — to intrude on places in which people have a reasonable expectation of privacy, or to command people to leave places they are otherwise permitted to be — even when there is no suspicion of crime. We have already seen in our discussion of the "community caretaking" cases, see pages 454-465, supra, that police sometimes enter homes or other private places not expecting to find evidence of crime, but instead responding to illness, missing person reports, and the like. Justice Scalia offers us the example of a traffic accident with a crowd of onlookers. Surely, he says, the officer can order the onlookers to leave. Or take Justice Kennedy's example of a police officer telling pedestrians not to enter a public building where a crime scene is being investigated. Such police commands are common, and it is commonly assumed that the commands are legitimate and must be obeyed.

These examples might suggest that police authority to "search" or "seize" does not always depend on suspicion of crime. Or perhaps in hypotheticals like Justice Scalia's and Justice Kennedy's, no "seizure" has taken place: recall the discussion of "seizure" doctrine and public demonstrations at pages 416-417, supra. Do examples like these mean that *Morales* was wrongly decided?

3. Is facial invalidation the right way to deal with the potential for racial discrimination in the enforcement of laws like Chicago's gang loitering ordinance? Professors Meares and Kahan argue that the vagueness cases from the era of Papachristou v. Jacksonville, 405 U.S. 156 (1972), were "decided against the background of institutionalized racism," in a context in which law enforcement was a key instrument of racial repression. Tracey L. Meares & Dan M. Kahan, The Wages of Antiquated Procedural Thinking: A Critique of Chicago v. Morales, [1998] U. Chi. Legal F. 197, 205. They urge that the distrust of community-based policing and the skepticism about even guided police discretion reflected in these cases, while appropriate to

the 1960s and 1970s, do not map well onto the contemporary scene, in which members of minority communities in the inner city have sometimes been in the forefront of the push for the enactment of laws like Chicago's gang loitering ordinance:

> The anti-community and anti-discretion principles that animate *Papachristou* address problems that no longer characterize American political life. Given the emergence of African American political power in the inner cities, it is no longer plausible to presume that all law enforcement policies adopted by local institutions are designed to oppress minority citizens. These new conditions require a new conception of rights — one that assures that the individuals who have the most at stake make the difficult choices anti-loitering provisions and the like present.

Id., at 209. It is true that Chicago's gang loitering ordinance received significant support among the city's black and Latino aldermen — though the proposed ordinance "drew both support and opposition from Chicago citizens of all backgrounds." Brief of Chicago Alliance for Neighborhood Safety, et al., as Amici Curiae in Support of Respondents, p. 4. Alderman Ed Smith, an African American representing a heavily minority district with severe crime problems, was particularly outspoken in the ordinance's defense: "This doesn't allow the police to go hog wild. But we're tired of seeing the rights of gangbangers get protected when . . . a mother can't send her children outside for fear of them getting shot to death in a drive-by shooting." John Kass, Old Tactic Sought in Crime War, Chi. Trib., at A1 (May 15, 1992).

But is all this relevant to the constitutional issues at stake in *Morales*? Professor Roberts argues that contemporary loitering laws, like those of the 1960s and 1970s, involve "expansive and ambiguous allocations of police discretion [that] are likely to unjustly burden members of unpopular or minority groups." Dorothy E. Roberts, Foreword: Race, Vagueness, and the Social Meaning of Order-Maintenance Policing, 89 J. Crim. L. & Criminology 775, 783 (1999). She responds to Meares and Kahan as follows:

> Kahan and Meares . . . correctly observe that racial politics are more complicated today than at the time liberal criminal procedure doctrines were instituted. But the increase in Black political participation and shift from de jure discrimination to other forms of institutional inequality does not erase the need for these constitutional protections. To the contrary, the changed conditions of American social and political life require a constitutional jurisprudence that recognizes how seemingly color blind laws continue to produce glaring racial inequities in the criminal justice system. . . .
>
> Even if it could be proven that a majority of Black inner-city residents endorse [Chicago's] loitering law, what relevance would that support have to the law's constitutionality? . . .
>
> . . . The gang loitering ordinance was passed by the predominantly white Chicago City Council, not an inner-city political body. Elected officials of white districts enacted the ordinance while minority communities were disproportionately subjected to the violations of liberty it imposed. . . . Although Black citizens certainly influence politics in cities like Chicago, they do not (yet) determine, design, or implement the law enforcement policies that govern their communities.

Id., at 821, 827-828. Should the Court in *Morales* have confronted these issues more directly? Do you think the majority's holding is important one way or the other to the issue of racial discrimination in law enforcement? To addressing the often strained relationship between police and minority communities?

3. "Special Needs"

The Court often has used an interest-balancing approach, similar to the one in *Terry*, to uphold administrative inspections, regulatory searches, and other kinds of governmental action involving "special needs" beyond those to be found in the typical law enforcement context. The basic methodology was outlined in Brown v. Texas, 443 U.S. 47 (1979):

> The reasonableness of seizures that are less intrusive than a traditional arrest, see Dunaway v. New York, 442 U.S. 200, 209-210 (1979); Terry v. Ohio, 392 U.S. 1, 20 (1968), depends "on a balance between the public interest and the individual's right to personal security free from arbitrary interference by law officers." Pennsylvania v. Mimms, 434 U.S. 106, 109 (1977). Consideration of the constitutionality of such seizures involves a weighing of the gravity of the public concerns served by the seizure, the degree to which the seizure advances the public interest, and the severity of the interference with individual liberty.

Id., at 50.

The first case to refer to "special needs" in so many words was New Jersey v. T.L.O., 469 U.S. 325 (1985), where the Court considered the Fourth Amendment's application to the search of a student's purse by an assistant vice principal enforcing anti-smoking rules (the search uncovered marijuana as well as cigarettes.) The Court determined that neither the warrant nor probable cause requirements were suitable to "maintenance of the swift and informal disciplinary procedures needed in the school." Id., at 340. Instead, the Court concluded that "the legality of a search of a student should depend simply on [its] reasonableness, under all the circumstances." Id., at 341. In his concurrence, Justice Blackmun noted that "exceptional circumstances" may at times arise "in which special needs, beyond the normal need for law enforcement, make the warrant and probable-cause requirement impracticable." Id., at 351.

Since *T.L.O.*, the Court has invoked the "special needs" rationale repeatedly. In Griffin v. Wisconsin, 483 U.S. 868 (1987), for instance, the Court concluded that a Wisconsin regulation permitting probation officers to engage in warrantless searches of their probationers' homes on "reasonable grounds" (meaning, less than probable cause) to believe contraband was present satisfied the Fourth Amendment's reasonableness requirement. The warrant and probable cause requirements would, among other things, prevent probation officers from responding quickly to evidence of misconduct and interfere with officers' judgment about how close the supervision of a probationer should be. They were thus deemed inconsistent with the state's "special need" in this context to supervise the probationer. Similarly, O'Connor v. Ortega, 480 U.S. 709 (1987), involved a doctor employed by a government hospital who was suspected by hospital administrators of mismanaging a psychiatric residency program. Citing the "special needs" associated with the proper operation of the workplace, a plurality concluded that the test for whether a public employer's work-related search of its employee's office, desk, or file cabinet comports with the Fourth Amendment should be simply the "reasonableness" of the search, under all the circumstances.

How can such results be explained? After all, the privacy interest in a student's purse, a probationer's home, and an employee's desk certainly do not vary depending on whether a school principal, a probation officer, a boss, or a police officer is performing the search. Indeed, why shouldn't the "special need" to solve or prevent violent crimes justify searches outside the warrant and probable cause framework? Isn't the need to stop criminal violence as important as the need to enforce a no-smoking rule in a junior high school? Why should the less important interest receive more Fourth Amendment deference?

Keep these questions in mind as you read the materials that follow. Below, we examine two kinds of "special needs" cases. The first deals with vehicle roadblocks, which the government often tries to justify under the Brown v. Texas interest-balancing approach. The second deals with searches conducted by persons other than police officers, such as regulatory agency officials or public-school administrators.

a. Roadblocks

Terry is generally seen as a major doctrinal innovation. In one respect, however, *Terry* was quite traditional: The Court required individualized suspicion of criminal activity to justify an intrusion on Fourth Amendment interests. Roadblocks raise the question whether the police may seize a group of drivers and passengers — all those who pass a particular point on a particular roadway during the time when the roadblock is in place — without any reason to believe that any one driver or passenger is violating the law. As you read the cases that follow, consider these questions. What could be the justification for this police tactic? Why dispense with probable cause and reasonable suspicion? Is it because of the strength of the government's interest? The weakness of the individuals' privacy and autonomy interests? The presence of alternative constraints on police abuse? Something else?

A few years after *Terry*, the Court approved the suspicionless stopping of vehicles at a permanent checkpoint on a highway leading away from the Mexican border. See United States v. Martinez-Fuerte, 428 U.S. 543 (1976). The theory of *Martinez-Fuerte* was interest balancing: "[T]he need to make routine checkpoint stops is great, [and] the consequent intrusion on Fourth Amendment rights is quite limited." Id., at 557. In Delaware v. Prouse, 440 U.S. 648 (1979), the Court declined to permit random, suspicionless police stops of automobiles to check drivers' licenses and registrations. But the *Prouse* Court noted that it was not preventing states "from developing methods for spot checks that involve less intrusion or that do not involve the unconstrained exercise of discretion." The Court expanded on that idea in Michigan Department of State Police v. Sitz, 496 U.S. 444 (1990), where it faced a challenge to roadblocks used to check for drunk drivers. As in *Martinez-Fuerte* and *Prouse*, the police had no reason to suspect any of the drivers stopped in *Sitz* before the stop itself. Nevertheless, the Court held that these suspicionless roadblock stops were permissible, due to the "magnitude of the drunken driving problem [and] the States' interest in eradicating it," as well as the fact that, unlike the random stops in *Prouse*, *all* cars were stopped at the roadblocks in *Sitz*.

These cases raised the possibility that, at least within the narrow sphere of vehicle stops, the police might be able to stop *anyone* as long as they stopped *everyone* — that seizures of many motorists were permissible absent suspicion of any of them. The next case cast serious doubt on that possibility.

INDIANAPOLIS v. EDMOND

Certiorari to the United States Court of Appeals for the Seventh Circuit
531 U.S. 32 (2000)

JUSTICE O'CONNOR delivered the opinion of the Court.

... In August 1998, the city of Indianapolis began to operate vehicle check-points on Indianapolis roads in an effort to interdict unlawful drugs. The city conducted six such roadblocks between August and November that year, stopping 1,161 vehicles and arresting 104 motorists. Fifty-five arrests were for drug-related crimes, while 49 were for offenses unrelated to drugs. The overall "hit rate" of the program was thus approximately nine percent. The parties stipulated to the facts concerning the operation of the checkpoints.

... At each checkpoint location, the police stop a predetermined number of vehicles. Approximately 30 officers are stationed at the checkpoint. Pursuant to written directives issued by the chief of police, at least one officer approaches the vehicle, advises the driver that he or she is being stopped briefly at a drug check-point, and asks the driver to produce a license and registration. The officer also looks for signs of impairment and conducts an open-view examination of the vehicle from the outside. A narcotics-detection dog walks around the outside of each stopped vehicle.

The directives instruct the officers that they may conduct a search only by consent or based on the appropriate quantum of particularized suspicion. The officers must conduct each stop in the same manner until particularized suspicion develops, and the officers have no discretion to stop any vehicle out of sequence. The city agreed in the stipulation to operate the checkpoints in such a way as to ensure that the total duration of each stop, absent reasonable suspicion or probable cause, would be five minutes or less.

The affidavit of Indianapolis Police Sergeant Marshall DePew, although it is technically outside the parties' stipulation, provides further insight concerning the operation of the checkpoints. According to Sergeant DePew, checkpoint locations are selected weeks in advance based on such considerations as area crime statistics and traffic flow. The checkpoints are generally operated during daylight hours and are identified with lighted signs reading, "NARCOTICS CHECKPOINT ___ MILE AHEAD, NARCOTICS K-9 IN USE, BE PREPARED TO STOP." Once a group of cars has been stopped, other traffic proceeds without interruption until all the stopped cars have been processed or diverted for further processing. Sergeant DePew also stated that the average stop for a vehicle not subject to further processing lasts two to three minutes or less.

Respondents James Edmond and Joell Palmer were each stopped at a narcotics checkpoint in late September 1998. Respondents then filed a lawsuit on behalf of themselves and the class of all motorists who had been stopped or were subject to being stopped in the future at the Indianapolis drug checkpoints. Respondents claimed that the roadblocks violated the Fourth Amendment of the United States

Constitution and the search and seizure provision of the Indiana Constitution. Respondents requested declaratory and injunctive relief for the class, as well as damages and attorney's fees for themselves.

Respondents then moved for a preliminary injunction. . . . The United States District Court for the Southern District of Indiana . . . denied the motion for a preliminary injunction, holding that the checkpoint program did not violate the Fourth Amendment. Edmond v. Goldsmith, 38 F. Supp. 2d 1016 (1998). A divided panel of the United States Court of Appeals for the Seventh Circuit reversed, holding that the checkpoints contravened the Fourth Amendment. 183 F.3d 659 (1999). . . . We granted certiorari, and now affirm.

The Fourth Amendment requires that searches and seizures be reasonable. A search or seizure is ordinarily unreasonable in the absence of individualized suspicion of wrongdoing. While such suspicion is not an "irreducible" component of reasonableness, [United States v. Martinez-Fuerte, 428 U.S. 543, 561 (1976)], we have recognized only limited circumstances in which the usual rule does not apply. . . .

We have . . . upheld brief, suspicionless seizures of motorists at a fixed Border Patrol checkpoint designed to intercept illegal aliens, *Martinez-Fuerte*, supra, and at a sobriety checkpoint aimed at removing drunk drivers from the road, Michigan Dept. of State Police v. Sitz, 496 U.S. 444 (1990). In addition, in Delaware v. Prouse, 440 U.S. 648 (1979), we suggested that a similar type of roadblock with the purpose of verifying drivers' licenses and vehicle registrations would be permissible. In none of these cases, however, did we indicate approval of a checkpoint program whose primary purpose was to detect evidence of ordinary criminal wrongdoing.

In *Martinez-Fuerte*, we entertained Fourth Amendment challenges to stops at two permanent immigration checkpoints located on major United States highways less than 100 miles from the Mexican border. We noted at the outset the particular context in which the constitutional question arose, describing in some detail the "formidable law enforcement problems" posed by the northbound tide of illegal entrants into the United States. 428 U.S., at 551-554. . . . [W]e found that the balance tipped in favor of the Government's interests in policing the Nation's borders. 428 U.S., at 561-564. In so finding, we emphasized the difficulty of effectively containing illegal immigration at the border itself. 428 U.S., at 556. We also stressed the impracticality of the particularized study of a given car to discern whether it was transporting illegal aliens, as well as the relatively modest degree of intrusion entailed by the stops. 428 U.S., at 556-564. . . .

In *Sitz*, we evaluated the constitutionality of a Michigan highway sobriety checkpoint program. The *Sitz* checkpoint involved brief, suspicionless stops of motorists so that police officers could detect signs of intoxication and remove impaired drivers from the road. 496 U.S., at 447-448. Motorists who exhibited signs of intoxication were diverted for a license and registration check and, if warranted, further sobriety tests. 496 U.S., at 447. This checkpoint program was clearly aimed at reducing the immediate hazard posed by the presence of drunk drivers on the highways, and there was an obvious connection between the imperative of highway safety and the law enforcement practice at issue. The gravity of the drunk driving problem and the magnitude of the State's interest in getting drunk drivers off the road weighed heavily in our determination that the program was constitutional. See 496 U.S., at 451.

In *Prouse*, we invalidated a discretionary, suspicionless stop for a spot check of a motorist's driver's license and vehicle registration. The officer's conduct in that case was unconstitutional primarily on account of his exercise of "standardless and unconstrained discretion." 440 U.S., at 661. We nonetheless acknowledged the States' "vital interest in ensuring that only those qualified to do so are permitted to operate motor vehicles, that these vehicles are fit for safe operation, and hence that licensing, registration, and vehicle inspection requirements are being observed." 440 U.S., at 658. Accordingly, we suggested that "questioning of all oncoming traffic at roadblock-type stops" would be a lawful means of serving this interest in highway safety. 440 U.S., at 663. . . .

. . . [W]hat principally distinguishes [the Indianapolis] checkpoints from those we have previously approved is their primary purpose.

As petitioners concede, the Indianapolis checkpoint program unquestionably has the primary purpose of interdicting illegal narcotics. In their stipulation of facts, the parties repeatedly refer to the checkpoints as "drug checkpoints" and describe them as "being operated by the City of Indianapolis in an effort to interdict unlawful drugs in Indianapolis." App. to Pet. for Cert. 51a-52a. In addition, the first document attached to the parties' stipulation is entitled "DRUG CHECKPOINT CONTACT OFFICER DIRECTIVES BY ORDER OF THE CHIEF OF POLICE." Id., at 53a. These directives instruct officers to "advise the citizen that they are being stopped briefly at a drug checkpoint." Ibid. . . .

We have never approved a checkpoint program whose primary purpose was to detect evidence of ordinary criminal wrongdoing. Rather, our checkpoint cases have recognized only limited exceptions to the general rule that a seizure must be accompanied by some measure of individualized suspicion. We suggested in *Prouse* that we would not credit the "general interest in crime control" as justification for a regime of suspicionless stops. 440 U.S., at 659, n. 18. Consistent with this suggestion, each of the checkpoint programs that we have approved was designed primarily to serve purposes closely related to the problems of policing the border or the necessity of ensuring roadway safety. Because the primary purpose of the Indianapolis narcotics checkpoint program is to uncover evidence of ordinary criminal wrongdoing, the program contravenes the Fourth Amendment.

Petitioners propose several ways in which the narcotics-detection purpose of the instant checkpoint program may instead resemble the primary purposes of the checkpoints in *Sitz* and *Martinez-Fuerte*. Petitioners state that the checkpoints in those cases had the same ultimate purpose of arresting those suspected of committing crimes. Securing the border and apprehending drunk drivers are, of course, law enforcement activities, and law enforcement officers employ arrests and criminal prosecutions in pursuit of these goals. If we were to rest the case at this high level of generality, there would be little check on the ability of the authorities to construct roadblocks for almost any conceivable law enforcement purpose. Without drawing the line at roadblocks designed primarily to serve the general interest in crime control, the Fourth Amendment would do little to prevent such intrusions from becoming a routine part of American life.

Petitioners also emphasize the severe and intractable nature of the drug problem as justification for the checkpoint program. There is no doubt that traffic in illegal narcotics creates social harms of the first magnitude. The law enforcement problems that the drug trade creates likewise remain daunting and complex, particularly in light of the myriad forms of spin-off crime that it spawns. The same can be said of various other illegal activities, if only to a lesser degree. But the gravity of the threat alone cannot be dispositive of questions concerning what means law enforcement officers may employ to pursue a given purpose. Rather, in determining whether individualized suspicion is required, we must consider the nature of the interests threatened and their connection to the particular law enforcement practices at issue. We are particularly reluctant to recognize exceptions to the general rule of individualized suspicion where governmental authorities primarily pursue their general crime control ends.

Nor can the narcotics-interdiction purpose of the checkpoints be rationalized in terms of a highway safety concern similar to that present in *Sitz*. The detection and punishment of almost any criminal offense serves broadly the safety of the community, and our streets would no doubt be safer but for the scourge of illegal drugs. Only with respect to a smaller class of offenses, however, is society confronted with the type of immediate, vehicle-bound threat to life and limb that the sobriety checkpoint in *Sitz* was designed to eliminate.

Petitioners also liken the anticontraband agenda of the Indianapolis checkpoints to the antismuggling purpose of the checkpoints in *Martinez-Fuerte*. Petitioners cite this Court's conclusion in *Martinez-Fuerte* that the flow of traffic was too heavy to permit "particularized study of a given car that would enable it to be identified as a possible carrier of illegal aliens," 428 U.S., at 557, and claim that this logic has even more force here. The problem with this argument is that the same logic prevails any time a vehicle is employed to conceal contraband or other evidence of a crime. . . . [T]he Indianapolis checkpoints are far removed from the border context that was crucial in *Martinez-Fuerte*. While the difficulty of examining each passing car was an important factor in validating the law enforcement technique employed in *Martinez-Fuerte*, this factor alone cannot justify a regime of suspicionless searches or seizures. Rather, we must look more closely at the nature of the public interests that such a regime is designed principally to serve.

The primary purpose of the Indianapolis narcotics checkpoints is in the end to advance "the general interest in crime control," *Prouse*, 440 U.S., at 659, n. 18. We decline to suspend the usual requirement of individualized suspicion where the police seek to employ a checkpoint primarily for the ordinary enterprise of investigating crimes. We cannot sanction stops justified only by the generalized and ever-present possibility that interrogation and inspection may reveal that any given motorist has committed some crime.

Of course, there are circumstances that may justify a law enforcement checkpoint where the primary purpose would otherwise, but for some emergency, relate to ordinary crime control. For example, ... the Fourth Amendment would almost certainly permit an appropriately tailored roadblock set up to thwart an imminent terrorist attack or to catch a dangerous criminal who is likely to flee by way of a particular route. The exigencies created by these scenarios are far removed from the circumstances under which authorities might simply stop cars as a matter of course to see if there just happens to be a felon leaving the jurisdiction. While we do not limit the purposes that may justify a checkpoint program to any rigid set of categories, we decline to approve a program whose primary purpose is ultimately indistinguishable from the general interest in crime control.[1]

---

1. The Chief Justice's dissent erroneously characterizes our opinion as resting on the application of a "non-law-enforcement primary purpose test." Post, at 6. Our opinion nowhere describes the purposes of the *Sitz* and *Martinez-Fuerte* checkpoints as being "not primarily related to criminal law enforcement." Post, at 3. Rather, our judgment turns on the fact that the primary purpose of the Indianapolis checkpoints is to advance the general interest in crime control. . . .

Petitioners argue that our prior cases preclude an inquiry into the purposes of the checkpoint program. For example, they cite Whren v. United States, 517 U.S. 806 (1996) . . . to support the proposition that "where the government articulates and pursues a legitimate interest for a suspicionless stop, courts should not look behind that interest to determine whether the government's 'primary purpose' is valid." Brief for Petitioners 34. [That case], however, [does] not control the instant situation.

In Whren, we held that an individual officer's subjective intentions are irrelevant to the Fourth Amendment validity of a traffic stop that is justified objectively by probable cause to believe that a traffic violation has occurred. . . . In so holding, we expressly distinguished cases where we had addressed the validity of searches conducted in the absence of probable cause. See 517 U.S., at 811-812 (distinguishing Florida v. Wells, 495 U.S. 1, 4 (1990) (stating that "an inventory search must not be a ruse for a general rummaging in order to discover incriminating evidence") [and] Colorado v. Bertine, 479 U.S. 367, 372 (1987) (suggesting that the absence of bad faith and the lack of a purely investigative purpose were relevant to the validity of an inventory search)).

Whren therefore reinforces the principle that, while "subjective intentions play no role in ordinary, probable-cause Fourth Amendment analysis," 517 U.S., at 813, programmatic purposes may be relevant to the validity of Fourth Amendment intrusions undertaken pursuant to a general scheme without individualized suspicion. . . .

Petitioners argue that the Indianapolis checkpoint program is justified by its lawful secondary purposes of keeping impaired motorists off the road and verifying licenses and registrations. If this were the case, however, law enforcement authorities would be able to establish checkpoints for virtually any purpose so long as they also included a license or sobriety check. For this reason, we examine the available evidence to determine the primary purpose of the checkpoint program. While we recognize the challenges inherent in a purpose inquiry, courts routinely engage in this enterprise in many areas of constitutional jurisprudence as a means of sifting abusive governmental conduct from that which is lawful. As a result, a program driven by an impermissible purpose may be proscribed while a program impelled by licit purposes is permitted, even though the challenged conduct may be outwardly similar. . . .[2]

It goes without saying that our holding today does nothing to alter the constitutional status of the sobriety and border checkpoints that we approved in Sitz and Martinez-Fuerte, or of the type of traffic checkpoint that we suggested would be lawful in Prouse. The constitutionality of such checkpoint programs still depends on a balancing of the competing interests at stake and the effectiveness of the program. See Sitz, 496 U.S., at 450-455; Martinez-Fuerte, 428 U.S., at 556-564. When law enforcement authorities pursue primarily general crime control purposes at checkpoints such as here, however, stops can only be justified by some quantum of individualized suspicion.

---

2. Because petitioners concede that the primary purpose of the Indianapolis checkpoints is narcotics detection, we need not decide whether the State may establish a checkpoint program with the primary purpose of checking licenses or driver sobriety and a secondary purpose of interdicting narcotics. Specifically, we express no view on the question whether police may expand the scope of a license or sobriety checkpoint seizure in order to detect the presence of drugs in a stopped car.

Our holding also does not affect the validity of border searches or searches at places like airports and government buildings, where the need for such measures to ensure public safety can be particularly acute. Nor does our opinion speak to other intrusions aimed primarily at purposes beyond the general interest in crime control. . . .

CHIEF JUSTICE REHNQUIST, with whom [JUSTICE SCALIA and] JUSTICE THOMAS join[], . . . dissenting.

. . . As it is nowhere to be found in the Court's opinion, I begin with blackletter roadblock seizure law. "The principal protection of Fourth Amendment rights at checkpoints lies in appropriate limitations on the scope of the stop." United States v. Martinez-Fuerte, 428 U.S. 543, 566-567 (1976). Roadblock seizures are consistent with the Fourth Amendment if they are "carried out pursuant to a plan embodying explicit, neutral limitations on the conduct of individual officers." Brown v. Texas, 443 U.S. 47, 51 (1979). Specifically, the constitutionality of a seizure turns upon "a weighing of the gravity of the public concerns served by the seizure, the degree to which the seizure advances the public interest, and the severity of the interference with individual liberty." 443 U.S., at 50-51.

We first applied these principles in Martinez-Fuerte, supra, which approved highway checkpoints for detecting illegal aliens. In Martinez-Fuerte, we balanced the United States' formidable interest in checking the flow of illegal immigrants against the limited "objective" and "subjective" intrusion on the motorists. The objective intrusion — the stop itself, the brief questioning of the occupants, and the visual inspection of the car — was considered "limited" because "neither the vehicle nor its occupants [were] searched." 428 U.S., at 558. Likewise, the subjective intrusion, or the fear and surprise engendered in law-abiding motorists by the nature of the stop, was found to be minimal because the "regularized manner in which [the] established checkpoints [were] operated [was] visible evidence, reassuring to law-abiding motorists, that the stops [were] duly authorized and believed to serve the public interest." 428 U.S., at 559. . . . And although the decision in Martinez-Fuerte did not turn on the checkpoints' effectiveness, the record in one of the consolidated cases demonstrated that illegal aliens were found in 0.12 percent of the stopped vehicles. See 428 U.S., at 554.

In Michigan Dept. of State Police v. Sitz, 496 U.S. 444 (1990), we upheld the State's use of a highway sobriety checkpoint. . . . There, we recognized the gravity of the State's interest in curbing drunken driving and found the objective intrusion of the approximately 25-second seizure to be "slight." 496 U.S., at 451. Turning to the subjective intrusion, we noted that the checkpoint was selected pursuant to guidelines and was operated by uniformed officers. See 496 U.S., at 453. Finally, we concluded that the program effectively furthered the State's interest because the checkpoint resulted in the arrest of two drunk drivers, or 1.6 percent of the 126 drivers stopped. See 496 U.S., at 455-456.

This case follows naturally from Martinez-Fuerte and Sitz. Petitioners acknowledge that the "primary purpose" of these roadblocks is to interdict illegal drugs, but this fact should not be controlling. . . . The District Court found that another "purpose of the checkpoints is to check driver's licenses and vehicle registrations," App. to Pet. for Cert. 44a, and the written directives state that the police officers are to "look for signs of impairment." Id., at 53a. The use of roadblocks to look for signs of impairment was validated by Sitz, and the use of roadblocks to check for driver's licenses and vehicle registrations was expressly recognized in Delaware v. Prouse, 440 U.S. 648, 663 (1979). That the roadblocks serve these legitimate state interests cannot be seriously disputed, as the 49 people arrested for offenses unrelated to drugs can attest. Edmond v. Goldsmith, 183 F.3d 659, 661 (CA7 1999). And it would be speculative to conclude — given the District Court's findings, the written directives, and the actual arrests — that petitioners would not have operated these road-blocks but for the State's interest in interdicting drugs. . . .

JUSTICE THOMAS, dissenting.

Taken together, our decisions in Michigan Dept. of State Police v. Sitz, 496 U.S. 444 (1990), and United States v. Martinez-Fuerte, 428 U.S. 543 (1976), stand for the proposition that suspicionless roadblock seizures are constitutionally permissible if conducted according to a plan that limits the discretion of the officers conducting the stops. I am not convinced that Sitz and Martinez-Fuerte were correctly decided. Indeed, I rather doubt that the Framers of the Fourth Amendment would have considered "reasonable" a program of indiscriminate stops of individuals not suspected of wrongdoing.

Respondents did not, however, advocate the overruling of Sitz and Martinez-Fuerte, and I am reluctant to consider such a step without the benefit of briefing and argument. For the reasons given by the Chief Justice, I believe that those cases compel upholding the program at issue here. I, therefore, join his opinion.

NOTES AND QUESTIONS

1. Why does the "primary purpose" of the Indianapolis checkpoints matter? Would the drivers' liberty have been any less invaded had the purpose been to check for drunk drivers? For illegal aliens? For licenses and registrations? Would the state's interest have been stronger in those cases?

2. The answer to the last question is probably no. The state's interest in stopping motorists — or, to be more precise, the law enforcement gain from stopping motorists — is a function of two things: the importance of the violations the police are detecting or deterring, and the number of violations detected or deterred. Consider these factors one at a time.

It is not obvious how to rank order drunk driving (the harm in Sitz), evading immigration law (the harm in Martinez-Fuerte), unlicensed driving (the harm the Court thought sufficient in dicta in Prouse), and illegal drug possession. Still, the Edmond goal of detecting drug possession is surely not the least important, and some jurisdictions might plausibly conclude that it is the most important item on that list. Besides, couldn't Indianapolis plausibly claim that its roadblocks had multiple purposes, that while the chief goal may have been to catch drug violations, subsidiary goals included catching unlicensed or intoxicated drivers? The fact that 49 non-drug arrests were made suggests that those other purposes were in fact advanced by the roadblocks. Does that mean Indianapolis is being punished for the 55 drug arrests? Why?

With regard to the other factor in the law enforcement side of the balance in Edmond — the number of violations caught or deterred — consider the success rates in the roadblocks in Martinez-Fuerte (0.12 percent), Sitz (1.6 percent), and Edmond (4.7 percent for drug violations alone, 9.0 percent counting all arrests). Isn't it odd that the Court approved the two less successful roadblock programs, and disapproved the most successful one?

3. Consider the other side of the balance: the individual privacy and liberty interests at stake in roadblocks. Here the *state*'s argument is a little odd: Stopping a lot of people is less of an intrusion than stopping a few. Justice Rehnquist, dissenting in *Delaware v. Prouse*, 440 U.S. 648 (1979), noted the irony:

> The Court holds, in successive sentences, that absent an articulable, reasonable suspicion of unlawful conduct, a motorist may not be subjected to a random license check, but that the States are free to develop "methods for spot checks that . . . do not involve the unconstrained exercise of discretion," such as "[q]uestioning . . . all oncoming traffic at roadblock-type stops. . . ." Because motorists, apparently like sheep, are much less likely to be "frightened" or "annoyed" when stopped en masse, a highway patrolman needs neither probable cause nor articulable suspicion to stop *all* motorists on a particular thoroughfare, but he cannot without articulable suspicion stop *less* than all motorists. The Court thus elevates the adage "misery loves company" to a novel role in Fourth Amendment jurisprudence.

Id., at 664. Does he have a point? Or do constraints (or the lack thereof) on police discretion really change the nature of the harm individuals suffer from searches and seizures? Perhaps an isolated seizure is stigmatizing, even humiliating, in a way that a group seizure is not. For an argument along these lines, see Sherry F. Colb, Innocence, Privacy, and Targeting in Fourth Amendment Jurisprudence, 96 Colum. L. Rev. 1456 (1996). Colb maintains that individuals suffer a cognizable Fourth Amendment injury she calls "targeting harm" when they are "singled out from others through an exercise of official discretion that is not based on an adequate evidentiary foundation." Id., at 1487. If that is right, it would seem to follow that "[w]hen the police stop fifty people, they do not cause fifty times the injury inflicted when they stop one. On the contrary, they are likely to cause a small fraction of the injury inflicted by stopping the same fifty people one by one." William J. Stuntz, Local Policing After the Terror, 111 Yale L.J. 2137, 2166 (2002). Perhaps cases like *Martinez-Fuerte* and *Sitz* rest on the idea not that misery loves company, but that group seizures inflict less misery than individual ones.

4. Suppose there really is a reduced harm suffered when a group of people are seized together; suppose further that that reduced harm is part of the justification for approving the roadblocks designed to catch drunk drivers in *Sitz*. Is the harm any different in *Edmond*? Is being stopped at a drug checkpoint a qualitatively different experience from being stopped at a drunk driving checkpoint? Perhaps so. But the most obvious difference between the stops in *Sitz* and the stops in *Edmond* has to do with the use of drug-sniffing dogs in *Edmond*—a difference the Court expressly stated does not affect its result.

5. Note that the roadblock program in *Edmond*—whatever else might be its pros and cons—at least minimized the aforementioned problem of police discretion, with all of the concomitant opportunities for abuse. At least as long as the roadblocks are not situated in a discriminatory manner, one big advantage of a roadblock program is that it affects all motorists—no matter what their race, ethnicity, or socioeconomic class—equally. All motorists are in the same boat (so to speak), which means that all motorists have the same motivation to invoke the political

process to regulate or even eliminate such roadblocks, should they become overly intrusive. Because the political process might be expected to work pretty well to regulate roadblocks, perhaps the courts need not worry so much about regulating them.

The *Edmond* Court nevertheless struck down Indianapolis's nondiscriminatory approach to proactive policing. At the same time, the Court consistently has approved the alternative, discretionary approach to proactive policing typified by *Terry* and, even worse, *Whren* (in which the Court upheld a concededly pretextual automobile stop) — despite the fact that such a discretionary approach seems tailor-made for discriminatory application.

Do these results seem backward? Think about the following argument:

> Consider why constitutional regulation of searches and seizures is necessary in the first place. Police are in the business of imposing costs on suspects. Stops, frisks, arrests, detentions, questioning — these things are generally unpleasant and can be seriously harmful. The benefits of this sort of activity are diffused among the local population. The costs, at least the nonmonetary sort (which are more severe than the monetary costs), are concentrated; they are felt primarily by those whom the police target. Anytime the government does something that has concentrated costs but diffused benefits, there is a danger that it will do too much — harming one voter to please ten is generally thought to be a good deal from the point of view of politically accountable decision-makers. That is the theory behind the Takings Clause, which requires compensation as a condition of seizing one person's property for the benefit of the larger public. Law enforcement presents what looks like a recurring takings problem. . . . That is the strongest case for constitutional regulation of law enforcement. Some kind of regulation is needed, and political checks will not do the job, given politicians' natural tendency to worry too little about those who bear the nonmonetary cost of police work.
>
> Notice that the argument concerns police searches and seizures of *individuals*. When the police stop large groups of people, the story is quite different. Law enforcement's costs are spread more broadly; the effect is to convert searches and seizures from takings, burdening only isolated individuals, into taxes, burdening classes of people. And when groups are searched or seized, the burdens are more visible — a larger slice of the population can see and hear them. These differences mean that political checks are much more likely to function. If the police treat individual arrestees badly, there may be no pressure brought to bear to treat them well, but if they treat groups of citizens badly, the bad treatment is likely to have political costs. To put it another way, spreading the cost of policing through a larger slice of the population (which is what things like roadblocks and security checkpoints do) reduces the odds of voters demanding harsh and intrusive police tactics secure in the knowledge that those tactics will be applied only to others.
>
> The point is not that searching and seizing groups is always better than the alternatives. Usually, it isn't. Police work generally involves differentiating people, not lumping them together, and the law neither can nor should change that. Rather, the point is that with across-the-board search procedures — police work that taxes instead of takes — those who enforce the law tend to take account of both the benefits and the costs of their tactics. With individual searches, the costs tend to be externalized. It follows that when police officers *want* to deal with suspects wholesale rather than retail, the law should encourage them to do so. In terms of regulatory strategy, group searches and seizures are an opportunity, not a problem.

Stuntz, Local Policing After the Terror, 111 Yale L.J. at 2164-2166. This argument might apply to more than roadblocks:

. . . Suppose the police officers investigating drug trafficking in a poor African-American neighborhood have to choose between two tactics — street sweeps, with everyone in the vicinity of a supposed drug market stopped and questioned, or targeted individual stops. Both tactics may involve a species of discrimination, since in white neighborhoods the tactics may be different, and the number and severity of the stops smaller. But the sweeps have a large advantage: transparency. The more people who see a police raid and feel its effects, the more people who are in a position to complain if police tactics are needlessly harsh, and in a position to counter false police testimony if the need arises. (How likely is it that Rodney King would have become a cause célèbre without the famous videotape? How likely is it that Officer Koon and his friends would have behaved so brutally had they been dealing with a dozen citizens instead of three?) Discriminatory street sweeps and discriminatory street stops are both discriminatory, but the first kind of discrimination is more likely to occasion public complaint, and hence less likely to involve the kind of behavior that prompts complaint, than the second. The idea is much the same as the one behind requiring public trials: Visibility is a powerful regulatory tool. The ban on group seizures gets that idea backward.

Id., at 2167. Is *Edmond* right? Is *Sitz*? When, if ever, should the police be able to target groups rather than individuals?

6. What about roadblocks that are designed to elicit information, not about a crime that is still in progress (as in *Martinez-Fuerte*, *Sitz*, and *Edmond*), but about one that occurred in the past? The next case addresses this question.

ILLINOIS v. LIDSTER

Certiorari to the Supreme Court of Illinois
540 U.S. 419 (2004)

JUSTICE BREYER delivered the opinion of the Court. This Fourth Amendment case focuses upon a highway checkpoint where police stopped motorists to ask them for information about a recent hit-and-run accident. We hold that the police stops were reasonable, hence, constitutional.

I

The relevant background is as follows: On Saturday, August 23, 1997, just after midnight, an unknown motorist traveling eastbound on a highway in Lombard, Illinois, struck and killed a 70-year-old bicyclist. The motorist drove off without identifying himself. About one week later at about the same time of night and at about the same place, local police set up a highway checkpoint designed to obtain more information about the accident from the motoring public.

Police cars with flashing lights partially blocked the eastbound lanes of the highway. The blockage forced traffic to slow down, leading to lines of up to 15 cars in each lane. As each vehicle drew up to the checkpoint, an officer would stop it for 10 to 15 seconds, ask the occupants whether they had seen anything happen there the previous weekend, and hand each driver a flyer. The flyer said "ALERT . . . FATAL HIT & RUN ACCIDENT" and requested "assistance in identifying the vehicle and driver in this accident which killed a 70 year old bicyclist." App. 9.

Robert Lidster, the respondent, drove a minivan toward the checkpoint. As he approached the checkpoint, his van swerved, nearly hitting one of the officers. The officer smelled alcohol on Lidster's breath. He directed Lidster to a side street where another officer administered a sobriety test and then arrested Lidster. Lidster was tried and convicted in Illinois state court of driving under the influence of alcohol.

Lidster challenged the lawfulness of his arrest and conviction on the ground that the government had obtained much of the relevant evidence through use of a checkpoint stop that violated the Fourth Amendment. The trial court rejected that challenge. But an Illinois appellate court reached the opposite conclusion. 319 Ill. App. 3d 825, 747 N.E.2d 419, 254 Ill. Dec. 379 (2001). The Illinois Supreme Court agreed with the appellate court. It held (by a vote of 4 to 3) that our decision in Indianapolis v. Edmond, 531 U.S. 32 (2000), required it to find the stop unconstitutional. 202 Ill. 2d 1, 779 N.E.2d 855, 269 Ill. Dec. 1 (2002). . . . We now reverse the Illinois Supreme Court's determination.

II

The Illinois Supreme Court basically held that our decision in *Edmond* governs the outcome of this case. We do not agree. *Edmond* involved a checkpoint at which police stopped vehicles to look for evidence of drug crimes committed by occupants of those vehicles. After stopping a vehicle at the checkpoint, police would examine (from outside the vehicle) the vehicle's interior; they would walk a drug-sniffing dog around the exterior; and, if they found sufficient evidence of drug (or other) crimes, they would arrest the vehicle's occupants. 531 U.S., at 35. We found that police had set up this checkpoint primarily for general "crime control" purposes, i.e., "to detect evidence of ordinary criminal wrongdoing." Id., at 41. We noted that the stop was made without individualized suspicion. And we held that the Fourth Amendment forbids such a stop, in the absence of special circumstances. Id., at 44.

The checkpoint stop here differs significantly from that in *Edmond*. The stop's primary law enforcement purpose was *not* to determine whether a vehicle's occupants were committing a crime, but to ask vehicle occupants, as members of the public, for their help in providing information about a crime in all likelihood committed by others. The police expected the information elicited to help them apprehend, not the vehicle's occupants, but other individuals.

Edmond's language, as well as its context, makes clear that the constitutionality of this latter, information-seeking kind of stop was not then before the Court. *Edmond* refers to the subject matter of its holding as "stops justified only by the generalized and ever-present possibility that interrogation and inspection may reveal that *any given motorist has committed some crime.*" Ibid. (emphasis added). We concede that *Edmond* describes the law enforcement objective there in question as a "general interest in crime control," but it specifies that the phrase "general interest in crime control" does not refer to every "law enforcement" objective. Id., at 44, n. 1. We must read this and related general language in *Edmond* as we often read general language in judicial opinions — as referring in context to circumstances similar to the circumstances then before the Court and not referring to quite different circumstances that the Court was not then considering.

Neither do we believe, *Edmond* aside, that the Fourth Amendment would have us apply an *Edmond*-type rule of automatic unconstitutionality to brief, information-seeking highway stops of the kind now before us. For one thing, the fact that such

stops normally lack individualized suspicion cannot by itself determine the constitutional outcome. As in *Edmond*, the stop here at issue involves a motorist. The
Fourth Amendment does not treat a motorist's car as his castle. See, e.g., New York
v. Class, 475 U.S. 106, 112-113 (1986); United States v. Martinez-Fuerte, 428 U.S.
543, 561 (1976). And special law enforcement concerns will sometimes justify highway stops without individualized suspicion. See Michigan Dept. of State Police v.
Sitz, 496 U.S. 444 (1990) (sobriety checkpoint); *Martinez-Fuerte*, supra (Border
Patrol checkpoint). Moreover, unlike *Edmond*, the context here (seeking information
from the public) is one in which, by definition, the concept of individualized suspicion has little role to play. Like certain other forms of police activity, say, crowd control or public safety, an information-seeking stop is not the kind of event that
involves suspicion, or lack of suspicion, of the relevant individual.

For another thing, information-seeking highway stops are less likely to provoke
anxiety or to prove intrusive. The stops are likely brief. The police are not likely to
ask questions designed to elicit self-incriminating information. And citizens will
often react positively when police simply ask for their help as "responsible citizen[s]" to "give whatever information they may have to aid in law enforcement."
Miranda v. Arizona, 384 U.S. 436, 477-478 (1966).

Further, the law ordinarily permits police to seek the voluntary cooperation of
members of the public in the investigation of a crime. "[L]aw enforcement officers
do not violate the Fourth Amendment by merely approaching an individual on the
street or in another public place, by asking him if he is willing to answer some
questions, [or] by putting questions to him if the person is willing to listen." Florida
v. Royer, 460 U.S. 491, 497 (1983). See also ALI, Model Code of Pre-Arraignment
Procedure §110.1(1) (1975) ("[L]aw enforcement officer may . . . request any
person to furnish information or otherwise cooperate in the investigation or
prevention of crime"). That, in part, is because voluntary requests play a vital role
in police investigatory work. See, e.g., Haynes v. Washington, 373 U.S. 503, 515
(1963) ("[I]nterrogation of witnesses . . . is undoubtedly an essential tool in
effective law enforcement"); U.S. Dept. of Justice, Eyewitness Evidence: A Guide
for Law Enforcement 14-15 (1999) (instructing law enforcement to gather information from witnesses near the scene).

The importance of soliciting the public's assistance is offset to some degree by
the need to stop a motorist to obtain that help — a need less likely present where a
pedestrian, not a motorist, is involved. The difference is significant in light of our
determinations that such an involuntary stop amounts to a "seizure" in Fourth
Amendment terms. E.g., *Edmond*, 531 U.S., at 40. That difference, however, is not
important enough to justify an *Edmond*-type rule here. After all, as we have said, the
motorist stop will likely be brief. Any accompanying traffic delay should prove no
more onerous than many that typically accompany normal traffic congestion. And
the resulting voluntary questioning of a motorist is as likely to prove important for
police investigation as is the questioning of a pedestrian. Given these considerations, it would seem anomalous were the law (1) ordinarily to allow police freely to
seek the voluntary cooperation of pedestrians but (2) ordinarily to forbid police to
seek similar voluntary cooperation from motorists.

Finally, we do not believe that an *Edmond*-type rule is needed to prevent an unreasonable proliferation of police checkpoints. . . . Practical considerations — namely,
limited police resources and community hostility to related traffic tieups — seem
likely to inhibit any such proliferation. See Fell, Ferguson, Williams, & Fields, Why

Aren't Sobriety Checkpoints Widely Adopted as an Enforcement Strategy in the United States? 35 Accident Analysis & Prevention 897 (Nov. 2003) (finding that sobriety checkpoints are not more widely used due to the lack of police resources and the lack of community support). And, of course, the Fourth Amendment's normal insistence that the stop be reasonable in context will still provide an important legal limitation on police use of this kind of information-seeking checkpoint.

These considerations, taken together, convince us that an *Edmond*-type presumptive rule of unconstitutionality does not apply here. That does not mean the stop is automatically, or even presumptively, constitutional. It simply means that we must judge its reasonableness, hence, its constitutionality, on the basis of the individual circumstances. And as this Court said in Brown v. Texas, 443 U.S. 47, 51 (1979), in judging reasonableness, we look to "the gravity of the public concerns served by the seizure, the degree to which the seizure advances the public interest, and the severity of the interference with individual liberty." . . .

III

We now consider the reasonableness of the checkpoint stop before us in light of the factors just mentioned. . . . We hold that the stop was constitutional.

The relevant public concern was grave. Police were investigating a crime that had resulted in a human death. No one denies the police's need to obtain more information at that time. And the stop's objective was to help find the perpetrator of a specific and known crime, not of unknown crimes of a general sort. Cf. *Edmond*, supra, at 44.

The stop advanced this grave public concern to a significant degree. The police appropriately tailored their checkpoint stops to fit important criminal investigatory needs. The stops took place about one week after the hit-and-run accident, on the same highway near the location of the accident, and at about the same time of night. And police used the stops to obtain information from drivers, some of whom might well have been in the vicinity of the crime at the time it occurred. See App. 28-29 (describing police belief that motorists routinely leaving work after night shifts at nearby industrial complexes might have seen something relevant).

Most importantly, the stops interfered only minimally with liberty of the sort the Fourth Amendment seeks to protect. Viewed objectively, each stop required only a brief wait in line — a very few minutes at most. Contact with the police lasted only a few seconds. Cf. *Martinez-Fuerte*, 428 U.S., at 547 (upholding stops of three-to-five minutes); *Sitz*, 496 U.S., at 448 (upholding delays of 25 seconds). Police contact consisted simply of a request for information and the distribution of a flyer. Cf. *Martinez-Fuerte*, supra, at 546 (upholding inquiry as to motorists' citizenship and immigration status); *Sitz*, supra, at 447 (upholding examination of all drivers for signs of intoxication). Viewed subjectively, the contact provided little reason for anxiety or alarm. The police stopped all vehicles systematically. And there is no allegation here that the police acted in a discriminatory or otherwise unlawful manner while questioning motorists during stops.

For these reasons we conclude that the checkpoint stop was constitutional.

The judgment of the Illinois Supreme Court is reversed.

JUSTICE STEVENS, with whom JUSTICE SOUTER and JUSTICE GINSBURG join, concurring in part and dissenting in part.

There is a valid and important distinction between seizing a person to determine whether she has committed a crime and seizing a person to ask whether she has any information about an unknown person who committed a crime a week earlier. I therefore join Parts I and II of the Court's opinion explaining why our decision in Indianapolis v. Edmond, 531 U.S. 32 (2000), is not controlling in this case. However, I find the issue discussed in Part III of the opinion closer than the Court does and believe it would be wise to remand the case to the Illinois state courts to address that issue in the first instance.

In contrast to pedestrians, who are free to keep walking when they encounter police officers handing out flyers or seeking information, motorists who confront a roadblock are required to stop, and to remain stopped for as long as the officers choose to detain them. Such a seizure may seem relatively innocuous to some, but annoying to others who are forced to wait for several minutes when the line of cars is lengthened — for example, by a surge of vehicles leaving a factory at the end of a shift. Still other drivers may find an unpublicized roadblock at midnight on a Saturday somewhat alarming.

On the other side of the equation, the likelihood that questioning a random sample of drivers will yield useful information about a hit-and-run accident that occurred a week earlier is speculative at best. To be sure, the sample in this case was not entirely random: The record reveals that the police knew that the victim had finished work at the Post Office shortly before the fatal accident, and hoped that other employees of the Post Office or the nearby industrial park might work on similar schedules and, thus, have been driving the same route at the same time the previous week. That is a plausible theory, but there is no evidence in the record that the police did anything to confirm that the nearby businesses in fact had shift changes at or near midnight on Saturdays, or that they had reason to believe that a roadblock would be more effective than, say, placing flyers on the employees' cars.

In short, the outcome of the multifactor test prescribed in Brown v. Texas, 443 U.S. 47 (1979), is by no means clear on the facts of this case. Because the Illinois Appellate Court and the State Supreme Court held that the Lombard roadblock was per se unconstitutional under Indianapolis v. Edmond, neither court attempted to apply the *Brown* test. . . . We should be especially reluctant to abandon our role as a court of review in a case in which the constitutional inquiry requires analysis of local conditions and practices more familiar to judges closer to the scene. I would therefore remand the case to the Illinois courts to undertake the initial analysis of the issue that the Court resolves in Part III of its opinion. To that extent, I respectfully dissent.

NOTES AND QUESTIONS

1. In *Edmond*, the Court rejects Indianapolis's use of roadblocks to deal with the difficult problem of drug crimes — precisely the kind of proactive policing to which *Terry*-style reasonableness analysis often applies. But in *Lidster* the Court upholds the use of a roadblock to investigate a known past crime — precisely the kind of situation to which traditional Fourth Amendment analysis (with its reliance on probable cause and warrants) usually applies. Do these results seem backward? Is there a reasonable explanation for them?

2. What happened to the idea, expressed so forcefully in *Edmond*, that exceptions to the requirement of individualized suspicion should not be approved "where the police seek to employ a checkpoint primarily for the ordinary enterprise of investigating crimes"? Isn't that exactly what the police were doing in *Lidster*? In *Edmond*, the Court seemed to be saying that the interest-balancing approach applies only when the government's "primary purpose" lies outside of traditional crime control—i.e., when it is a so-called "special need." Why, then, did the *Lidster* Court—unanimously, on this issue—decide to use the interest-balancing approach? Is crime investigation now a "special need"?

3. Notice the Court's emphasis on the fact that the police in *Lidster* were chiefly looking for witnesses, not suspects. Why should that fact matter? If the Indianapolis police had printed up a flyer asking for citizens' cooperation in gathering information about local drug distribution networks, would *Edmond* have been decided differently?

4. The legal status of most roadblocks may be uncertain after *Edmond* and *Lidster*. But *Martinez-Fuerte* seems to be on stable ground. Courts have traditionally regarded certain types of searches and seizures at an international border (or its functional equivalent) as reasonable, and have required neither reasonable suspicion nor constraints on officer discretion to justify them. Routine luggage inspections upon entering the country are the most common example. Detention of travelers beyond the scope of a routine customs search requires more in the way of justification, but the government is still afforded broad authority in this context. Consider United States v. Montoya de Hernandez, 473 U.S. 531 (1985). There, customs officials had reasonable suspicion to believe that the defendant, who had traveled from Colombia, was smuggling contraband in her alimentary canal. After she refused to submit to an X-ray, Montoya de Hernandez remained in detention for 16 hours before customs officials obtained a court order for a medical examination that ultimately revealed narcotics. The Supreme Court held that though the length of her detention exceeded any other it had approved on reasonable suspicion, it was nonetheless acceptable, noting that the defendant herself had contributed to this time period by attempting to avoid a bowel movement. The Fourth Amendment balance of interests, the Court said, "leans heavily to the Government" at an international border:

> At the border, customs officials have more than merely an investigative law enforcement role. They are also charged, along with immigration officials, with protecting this Nation from entrants who bring anything harmful into this country, whether that be communicable diseases, narcotics, or explosives. In this regard, the detention of a suspected alimentary canal smuggler at the border is analogous to the detention of a suspected tuberculosis carrier at the border; both are detained until their bodily processes dispel the suspicion that they will introduce a harmful agent into this country.

Id., at 543-544.

The Court reaffirmed the government's broad authority to conduct border searches in United States v. Flores-Montano, 541 U.S. 149 (2004). The gas tank of Flores-Montano's 1987 Ford Taurus station wagon was removed, disassembled, and searched when Flores-Montano attempted to enter the United States at the Otay Mesa Port of Entry in southern California. Customs officials seized 37 kilograms of marijuana from the tank. The Ninth Circuit, relying on language from *Montoya de*

Hernandez to the effect that *routine* searches of persons and effects at the border are not subject to any requirement of reasonable suspicion, probable cause, or warrant, had earlier determined that the search of a vehicle's gas tank is not a routine border search and must be supported by reasonable suspicion. The Supreme Court disagreed:

> The Court of Appeals took the term "routine," fashioned a new balancing test, and extended it to searches of vehicles. But the reasons that might support a requirement of some level of suspicion in the case of highly intrusive searches of the person — dignity and privacy interests of the person being searched — simply do not carry over to vehicles. Complex balancing tests to determine what is a "routine" search of a vehicle, as opposed to a more "intrusive" search of a person, have no place in border searches of vehicles.

Id., at 1585. The Court noted that it was hard to conceive how the search of a gas tank, "which should be solely a repository for fuel, could be more of an invasion of privacy than the search of an automobile's passenger compartment" — a search commonly performed in the context of border inspections. The Justices unanimously concluded that while it might be true that some searches of property at the border are so destructive as to require more in the way of justification, the government's general authority to conduct suspicionless border inspections "includes the authority to remove, disassemble, and reassemble a vehicle's fuel tank." Id., at 1587.

b. Non-Police Searches

Many "special needs" cases involve actions that would require probable cause and a warrant if they were undertaken by police officers in the course of traditional law enforcement, but that may require far less — such as reasonable suspicion, or even no individualized suspicion at all — if the relevant actors are not police officers. For example, the aforementioned case in which the term "special needs" was first used, New Jersey v. T.L.O., 469 U.S. 325 (1985), involved the search of a student's purse by the assistant vice principal of a public school. The Court approved the search based on a test of "reasonableness, under all the circumstances," which generally means that school officials must have "reasonable grounds for suspecting" that the student to be searched is violating (or has violated) the law or the rules of the school, and must also limit the scope of the search so that it is not "excessively intrusive." Id., at 341-342.

In Board of Education of Independent School District No. 92 of Pottawatomie County v. Earls, 536 U.S. 822 (2002), the Court again relied on the "special needs" of public schoolteachers and administrators to uphold a program of suspicionless drug-testing of students who wished to participate in competitive extracurricular activities:

> The Court has . . . held that a warrant and finding of probable cause are unnecessary in the public school context because such requirements "would unduly interfere with the maintenance of the swift and informal disciplinary procedures [that are] needed."

. . . Significantly, this Court has previously held that "special needs" inhere in the public school context [citing *T.L.O.*]. While schoolchildren do not shed their constitutional rights when they enter the schoolhouse, Fourth Amendment rights . . . are different in public schools than elsewhere; the reasonableness' inquiry cannot disregard the schools custodial and tutelary responsibility for children. In particular, a finding of individualized suspicion may not be necessary when a school conducts drug testing.

Id., at 828-830 (internal quotation marks and citations omitted). On the facts, the Court concluded that the students' privacy interest at school was limited, especially given the students' voluntary choice to participate in extracurricular activities; that the degree of intrusion caused by the collection of a urine sample was minimal; and that the school's interest in combating the drug problem was sufficiently great to make the practice constitutional.

Of course, the search of students must still be reasonable, not only in its justification but in its scope. Later the Court would find that a strip search of a 13-year-old girl by a school nurse to find contraband pain killers was unreasonable, even though school officials had reasonable suspicion that the student was distributing the drugs. In finding that the search stepped over the Fourth Amendment line, the Court considered the age and sex of the student, the intrusiveness of the search, and the minimal threat the alleged drugs presented to the school. Safford Unified School Dist. No. 1 v. Redding, 129 S. Ct. 2633 (2009). (The Court also found, however, that the school officials were entitled to qualify immunity from a civil claim, as the law regarding students searches was not clearly established at the time.)

The *Pottawatomie County* case is but one of several "special needs" cases in which the Court has sustained suspicionless drug-testing programs as reasonable under the Fourth Amendment. See Treasury Employees v. Von Raab, 489 U.S. 656 (1989) (drug tests for United States Customs Service employees who seek transfer or promotion to positions directly involving drug interdiction or requiring the employee to carry a firearm); Skinner v. Railway Labor Executives' Assn., 489 U.S. 602 (1989) (drug and alcohol tests for railway employees involved in train accidents or violating particular safety rules).

In Chandler v. Miller, 520 U.S. 305 (1997), however, the Court made it clear that suspicionless drug testing will not always pass constitutional muster. *Chandler* involved a Georgia law requiring that candidates for designated state offices pass a drug test. The procedures at issue were relatively unintrusive, compared to the earlier cases: A candidate was permitted to provide a urine specimen in the office of a personal physician and the test results were first given to the candidate, who controlled their further dissemination. The Court nevertheless found the law invalid, noting that "the proffered special need for drug testing must be substantial—important enough to override the individual's acknowledged privacy interest, sufficiently vital to suppress the Fourth Amendment's normal requirement of individualized suspicion." Id., at 318. The majority observed that nothing in the record suggested that there was a real problem with drug use among Georgia's office holders and noted that, at any rate, the challenged drug testing scheme, permitting candidates to schedule their own test dates, could hardly be defended as a credible means of deterring drug use or ferreting it out. The Court concluded that the need served by Georgia's drug testing scheme was "symbolic, not 'special,' as that term draws meaning from our case law." Id., at 322.

The fact patterns in all of these cases seem fairly far removed from criminal law enforcement. Some "special needs" cases, however, do involve situations where law enforcement officials may foreseeably obtain evidence of criminal wrongdoing as a result of a non-police search and, indeed, may even participate in it. What difference should this make to the "special needs" analysis? The Court considered the problem of "entanglement" with law enforcement in the following case:

FERGUSON v. CHARLESTON

Certiorari to the United States Court of Appeals for the Fourth Circuit
532 U.S. 67 (2001)

JUSTICE STEVENS delivered the opinion of the Court.

I

In the fall of 1988, staff members at the public hospital operated in the city of Charleston by the Medical University of South Carolina (MUSC) became concerned about an apparent increase in the use of cocaine by patients who were receiving pre-natal treatment. In response to this perceived increase, as of April 1989, MUSC began to order drug screens to be performed on urine samples from maternity patients who were suspected of using cocaine. If a patient tested positive, she was then referred by MUSC staff to the county substance abuse commission for counsel-ing and treatment. However, despite the referrals, the incidence of cocaine use among the patients at MUSC did not appear to change.

Some four months later, Nurse Shirley Brown, the case manager for the MUSC obstetrics department, heard a news broadcast reporting that the police in Green-ville, South Carolina, were arresting pregnant users of cocaine on the theory that such use harmed the fetus and was therefore child abuse. Nurse Brown discussed the story with MUSC's general counsel, Joseph C. Good, Jr., who then contacted Charleston Solicitor Charles Condon in order to offer MUSC's cooperation in pros-ecuting mothers whose children tested positive for drugs at birth.[3]

After receiving Good's letter, Solicitor Condon took the first steps in developing the policy at issue in this case. He organized the initial meetings, decided who would participate, and issued the invitations, in which he described his plan to prosecute women who tested positive for cocaine while pregnant. The task force that Condon formed included representatives of MUSC, the police, the County Substance Abuse Commission and the Department of Social Services. Their deliberations led to MUSC's adoption of a 12-page document entitled "POLICY M-7," dealing with the subject of "Management of Drug Abuse During Pregnancy." App. to Pet. for Cert. A-53.

The first three pages of Policy M-7 set forth the procedure to be followed by the hospital staff to "identify/assist pregnant patients suspected of drug abuse." Id., at A-53 to A-56. The first section, entitled the "Identification of Drug Abusers," pro-vided that a patient should be tested for cocaine through a urine drug screen if she

---

3. In his letter dated August 23, 1989, Good wrote: "Please advise us if your office is anticipating future criminal action and what if anything our Medical Center needs to do to assist you in this matter." App. to Pet. for Cert. A-67.

met one or more of nine criteria.[4] . . . The policy also provided for education and referral to a substance abuse clinic for patients who tested positive. Most important, it added the threat of law enforcement intervention that "provided the necessary 'leverage' to make the [p]olicy effective." Brief for Respondents 8. . . .

The threat of law enforcement involvement was set forth in two protocols, the first dealing with the identification of drug use during pregnancy, and the second with identification of drug use after labor. Under the latter protocol, the police were to be notified without delay and the patient promptly arrested. Under the former, after the initial positive drug test, the police were to be notified (and the patient arrested) only if the patient tested positive for cocaine a second time or if she missed an appointment with a substance abuse counselor.[5] In 1990, however, the policy was modified at the behest of the solicitor's office to give the patient who tested positive during labor, like the patient who tested positive during a prenatal care visit, an opportunity to avoid arrest by consenting to substance abuse treatment.

The last six pages of the policy contained forms for the patients to sign, as well as procedures for the police to follow when a patient was arrested. The policy also prescribed in detail the precise offenses with which a woman could be charged, depending on the stage of her pregnancy. If the pregnancy was 27 weeks or less, the patient was to be charged with simple possession. If it was 28 weeks or more, she was to be charged with possession and distribution to a person under the age of 18 — in this case, the fetus. If she delivered "while testing positive for illegal drugs," she was also to be charged with unlawful neglect of a child. App. to Pet. for Cert. A-62. Under the policy, the police were instructed to interrogate the arrestee in order "to ascertain the identity of the subject who provided illegal drugs to the suspect." Id., at A-63. Other than the provisions describing the substance abuse treatment to be offered to women who tested positive, the policy made no mention of any change in the prenatal care of such patients, nor did it prescribe any special treatment for the newborns.

II

Petitioners are 10 women who received obstetrical care at MUSC and who were arrested after testing positive for cocaine. Four of them were arrested during the initial implementation of the policy; they were not offered the opportunity to receive drug treatment as an alternative to arrest. The others were arrested after the policy was modified in 1990; they either failed to comply with the terms of the drug treatment program or tested positive for a second time. . . .

---

4. Those criteria were as follows:

    1. No prenatal care
    2. Late prenatal care after 24 weeks gestation
    3. Incomplete prenatal care
    4. Abruptio placentae
    5. Intrauterine fetal death
    6. Preterm labor "of no obvious cause"
    7. IUGR [intrauterine growth retardation] "of no obvious cause"
    8. Previously known drug or alcohol abuse
    9. Unexplained congenital anomalies.

Id., at A-53 to A-54.

5. Despite the conditional description of the first category, when the policy was in its initial stages, a positive test was immediately reported to the police, who then promptly arrested the patient.

Petitioners' complaint challenged the validity of the policy under various theories, including the claim that warrantless and nonconsensual drug tests conducted for criminal investigatory purposes were unconstitutional searches. Respondents advanced two principal defenses to the constitutional claim: (1) that, as a matter of fact, petitioners had consented to the searches; and (2) that, as a matter of law, the searches were reasonable, even absent consent, because they were justified by special non-law-enforcement purposes. The District Court rejected the second defense because the searches in question "were not done by the medical university for independent purposes. [Instead,] the police came in and there was an agreement reached that the positive screens would be shared with the police." App. 1248-1249. Accordingly, the District Court submitted the factual defense to the jury with instructions that required a verdict in favor of petitioners unless the jury found consent.[6] The jury found for respondents.

Petitioners appealed, arguing that the evidence was not sufficient to support the jury's consent finding. The Court of Appeals for the Fourth Circuit affirmed, but without reaching the question of consent. Disagreeing with the District Court, the majority of the appellate panel held that the searches were reasonable as a matter of law under our line of cases recognizing that "special needs" may, in certain exceptional circumstances, justify a search policy designed to serve non-law-enforcement ends. On the understanding "that MUSC personnel conducted the urine drug screens for medical purposes wholly independent of an intent to aid law enforcement efforts," the majority applied the balancing test used in Treasury Employees v. Von Raab, 489 U.S. 656 (1989), and Vernonia School Dist. 47J v. Acton, 515 U.S. 646 (1995), and concluded that the interest in curtailing the pregnancy complications and medical costs associated with maternal cocaine use outweighed what the majority termed a minimal intrusion on the privacy of the patients. . . .

We granted certiorari to review the appellate court's holding on the "special needs" issue. Because we do not reach the question of the sufficiency of the evidence with respect to consent, we necessarily assume for purposes of our decision — as did the Court of Appeals — that the searches were conducted without the informed consent of the patients. We conclude that the judgment should be reversed and the case remanded for a decision on the consent issue.

III

Because MUSC is a state hospital, the members of its staff are government actors, subject to the strictures of the Fourth Amendment. Moreover, the urine tests conducted by those staff members were indisputably searches within the meaning of the Fourth Amendment. Skinner v. Railway Labor Executives' Assn., 489 U.S. 602, 617 (1989). Neither the District Court nor the Court of Appeals concluded that any of the nine criteria used to identify the women to be searched provided either probable cause to believe that they were using cocaine, or even the basis for a reasonable suspicion of such use. Rather, the District Court and the Court of Appeals viewed the case as one involving MUSC's right to conduct searches without warrants or

---

6. . . . Under the judge's instructions, in order to find that the plaintiffs had consented to the searches, it was necessary for the jury to find that they had consented to the taking of the samples, to the testing for evidence of cocaine, and to the possible disclosure of the test results to the police. Respondents have not argued, as Justice Scalia does, that it is permissible for members of the staff of a public hospital to use diagnostic tests "deceivingly" to obtain incriminating evidence from their patients.

probable cause. Furthermore, given the posture in which the case comes to us, we must assume for purposes of our decision that the tests were performed without the informed consent of the parties.

Because the hospital seeks to justify its authority to conduct drug tests and to turn the results over to law enforcement agents without the knowledge or consent of the patients, this case differs from the four previous cases in which we have considered whether comparable drug tests "fit within the closely guarded category of constitutionally permissible suspicionless searches." Chandler v. Miller, 520 U.S. 305, 309 (1997). In three of those cases, we sustained drug tests for railway employees involved in train accidents, Skinner v. Railway Labor Executives' Assn., 489 U.S. 602 (1989), for United States Customs Service employees seeking promotion to certain sensitive positions, Treasury Employees v. Von Raab, 489 U.S. 656 (1989), and for high school students participating in interscholastic sports, Vernonia School Dist. 47J v. Acton, 515 U.S. 646. In the fourth case, we struck down such testing for candidates for designated state offices as unreasonable. Chandler v. Miller, 520 U.S. 305 (1997).

In each of those cases, we employed a balancing test that weighed the intrusion on the individual's interest in privacy against the "special needs" that supported the program. As an initial matter, we note that the invasion of privacy in this case is far more substantial than in those cases. In the previous four cases, there was no misunderstanding about the purpose of the test or the potential use of the test results, and there were protections against the dissemination of the results to third parties. The use of an adverse test result to disqualify one from eligibility for a particular benefit, such as a promotion or an opportunity to participate in an extracurricular activity, involves a less serious intrusion on privacy than the unauthorized dissemination of such results to third parties. The reasonable expectation of privacy enjoyed by the typical patient undergoing diagnostic tests in a hospital is that the results of those tests will not be shared with nonmedical personnel without her consent. In none of our prior cases was there any intrusion upon that kind of expectation.[14]

The critical difference between those four drug-testing cases and this one, however, lies in the nature of the "special need" asserted as justification for the warrantless searches. In each of those earlier cases, the "special need" that was advanced as a justification for the absence of a warrant or individualized suspicion was one divorced from the State's general interest in law enforcement.[15] . . . In this case, however, the central and indispensable feature of the policy from its inception was the use of law enforcement to coerce the patients into substance abuse treatment. This fact distinguishes this case from circumstances in which physicians or psychologists, in the course of ordinary medical procedures aimed at helping the patient herself, come across information that under rules of law or ethics is subject to reporting requirements, which no one has challenged here. See, e.g., Council on Ethical and Judicial Affairs, American Medical Association, PolicyFinder, Current Opinions E-5.05 (2000) (requiring reporting where "a patient threatens to inflict serious

14. In fact, we have previously recognized that an intrusion on that expectation may have adverse consequences because it may deter patients from receiving needed medical care. Whalen v. Roe, 429 U.S. 589, 599-600 (1977).

15. . . . In other special needs cases, we have tolerated suspension of the Fourth Amendment's warrant or probable-cause requirement in part because there was no law enforcement purpose behind the searches in those cases, and there was little, if any, entanglement with law enforcement. . . .

bodily harm to another person or to him or herself and there is a reasonable probability that the patient may carry out the threat"); Ark. Code Ann. §12-12-602 (1999) (requiring reporting of intentionally inflicted knife or gunshot wounds); Ariz. Rev. Stat. Ann. §13-3620 (Supp. 2000) (requiring "any . . . person having responsibility for the care or treatment of children" to report suspected abuse or neglect to a peace officer or child protection agency).

Respondents argue in essence that their ultimate purpose — namely, protecting the health of both mother and child — is a beneficent one. . . . [A] review of the M-7 policy plainly reveals that the purpose actually served by the MUSC searches "is ultimately indistinguishable from the general interest in crime control." Indianapolis v. Edmond, 531 U.S. 32, 44 (2000).

In looking to the programmatic purpose, we consider all the available evidence in order to determine the relevant primary purpose. See, e.g., id., at 45-47. In this case, as Judge Blake put it in her dissent below, "it . . . is clear from the record that an initial and continuing focus of the policy was on the arrest and prosecution of drug-abusing mothers. . . ." Tellingly, the document codifying the policy incorporates the police's operational guidelines. It devotes its attention to the chain of custody, the range of possible criminal charges, and the logistics of police notification and arrests. Nowhere, however, does the document discuss different courses of medical treatment for either mother or infant, aside from treatment for the mother's addiction.

Moreover, throughout the development and application of the policy, the Charleston prosecutors and police were extensively involved in the day-to-day administration of the policy. Police and prosecutors decided who would receive the reports of positive drug screens and what information would be included with those reports. Law enforcement officials also helped determine the procedures to be followed when performing the screens. In the course of the policy's administration, they had access to Nurse Brown's medical files on the women who tested positive, routinely attended the substance abuse team's meetings, and regularly received copies of team documents discussing the women's progress. Police took pains to coordinate the timing and circumstances of the arrests with MUSC staff, and, in particular, Nurse Brown.

While the ultimate goal of the program may well have been to get the women in question into substance abuse treatment and off of drugs, the immediate objective of the searches was to generate evidence *for law enforcement purposes* in order to reach that goal. The threat of law enforcement may ultimately have been intended as a means to an end, but the direct and primary purpose of MUSC's policy was to ensure the use of those means. In our opinion, this distinction is critical. Because law enforcement involvement always serves some broader social purpose or objective, under respondents' view, virtually any nonconsensual suspicionless search could be immunized under the special needs doctrine by defining the search solely in terms of its ultimate, rather than immediate, purpose. Such an approach is inconsistent with the Fourth Amendment. Given the primary purpose of the Charleston program, which was to use the threat of arrest and prosecution in order to force women into treatment, and given the extensive involvement of law enforcement officials at every stage of the policy, this case simply does not fit within the closely guarded category of "special needs."

The fact that positive test results were turned over to the police does not merely provide a basis for distinguishing our prior cases applying the "special needs" balancing approach to the determination of drug use. It also provides an affirmative reason for enforcing the strictures of the Fourth Amendment. While state hospital employees, like other citizens, may have a duty to provide the police with evidence of criminal conduct that they inadvertently acquire in the course of routine treatment, when they undertake to obtain such evidence from their patients *for the specific purpose of incriminating those patients*, they have a special obligation to make sure that the patients are fully informed about their constitutional rights, as standards of knowing waiver require.[24] Cf. Miranda v. Arizona, 384 U.S. 436 (1966).

As respondents have repeatedly insisted, their motive was benign rather than punitive. Such a motive, however, cannot justify a departure from Fourth Amendment protections, given the pervasive involvement of law enforcement with the development and application of the MUSC policy. The stark and unique fact that characterizes this case is that Policy M-7 was designed to obtain evidence of criminal conduct by the tested patients that would be turned over to the police and that could be admissible in subsequent criminal prosecutions. While respondents are correct that drug abuse both was and is a serious problem, "the gravity of the threat alone cannot be dispositive of questions concerning what means law enforcement officers may employ to pursue a given purpose." Indianapolis v. Edmond, 531 U.S., at 42-43. The Fourth Amendment's general prohibition against non-consensual, warrantless, and suspicionless searches necessarily applies to such a policy.

Accordingly, the judgment of the Court of Appeals is reversed, and the case is remanded for further proceedings consistent with this opinion.

JUSTICE KENNEDY, concurring in the judgment.

I agree that the search procedure in issue cannot be sustained under the Fourth Amendment. My reasons for this conclusion differ somewhat from those set forth by the Court, however, leading to this separate opinion.

The Court does not dispute that the search policy at some level serves special needs, beyond those of ordinary law enforcement, such as the need to protect the health of mother and child when a pregnant mother uses cocaine. Instead, the majority characterizes these special needs as the "ultimate goal[s]" of the policy, as distinguished from the policy's "immediate purpose," the collection of evidence of drug use, which, the Court reasons, is the appropriate inquiry for the special needs analysis.

The majority views its distinction between the ultimate goal and immediate purpose of the policy as critical to its analysis. The distinction the Court makes, however, lacks foundation in our special needs cases. All of our special needs cases have turned upon what the majority terms the policy's ultimate goal. For example, in Skinner v. Railway Labor Executives' Assn., 489 U.S. 602 (1989), had we employed the majority's distinction, we would have identified as the relevant need the collection of evidence of drug and alcohol use by railway employees. Instead, we identified the relevant need as "[t]he Government's interest in regulating the conduct of

---

24. . . . The dissent . . . mischaracterizes our opinion as holding that "material which a person voluntarily entrusts to someone else cannot be given by that person to the police, and used for whatever evidence it may contain." But, as we have noted elsewhere, given the posture of the case, we must assume for purposes of decision that the patients did *not* consent to the searches, and we leave the question of consent for the Court of Appeals to determine. . . .

railroad employees to ensure [railroad] safety." Id., at 620. In Treasury Employees v. Von Raab, 489 U.S. 656 (1989), the majority's distinction should have compelled us to isolate the relevant need as the gathering of evidence of drug abuse by would-be drug interdiction officers. Instead, the special needs the Court identified were the necessities "to deter drug use among those eligible for promotion to sensitive positions within the [United States Customs] Service and to prevent the promotion of drug users to those positions." Id., at 666. In Vernonia School Dist. 47J v. Acton, 515 U.S. 646 (1995), the majority's distinction would have required us to identify the immediate purpose of gathering evidence of drug use by student-athletes as the relevant "need" for purposes of the special needs analysis. Instead, we sustained the policy as furthering what today's majority would have termed the policy's ultimate goal: "[d]eterring drug use by our Nation's schoolchildren," and particularly by student-athletes, because "the risk of immediate physical harm to the drug user or those with whom he is playing his sport is particularly high." Id., at 661-662.

It is unsurprising that in our prior cases we have concentrated on what the majority terms a policy's ultimate goal, rather than its proximate purpose. By very definition, in almost every case the immediate purpose of a search policy will be to obtain evidence. The circumstance that a particular search, like all searches, is designed to collect evidence of some sort reveals nothing about the need it serves. Put a different way, although procuring evidence is the immediate result of a successful search, until today that procurement has not been identified as the special need which justifies the search.

While the majority's reasoning seems incorrect in the respects just discussed, I agree with the Court that the search policy cannot be sustained. As the majority demonstrates and well explains, there was substantial law enforcement involvement in the policy from its inception. None of our special needs precedents has sanctioned the routine inclusion of law enforcement, both in the design of the policy and in using arrests, either threatened or real, to implement the system designed for the special needs objectives. . . . The traditional warrant and probable-cause requirements are waived in our previous cases on the explicit assumption that the evidence obtained in the search is not intended to be used for law enforcement purposes. Most of those tested for drug use under the policy at issue here were not brought into direct contact with law enforcement. This does not change the fact, however, that, as a systemic matter, law enforcement was a part of the implementation of the search policy in each of its applications. Every individual who tested positive was given a letter explaining the policy not from the hospital but from the solicitor's office. Everyone who tested positive was told a second positive test or failure to undergo substance abuse treatment would result in arrest and prosecution. As the Court holds, the hospital acted, in some respects, as an institutional arm of law enforcement for purposes of the policy. . . .

In my view, it is necessary and prudent to be explicit in explaining the limitations of today's decision. The beginning point ought to be to acknowledge the legitimacy of the State's interest in fetal life and of the grave risk to the life and health of the fetus, and later the child, caused by cocaine ingestion. . . . There should be no doubt that South Carolina can impose punishment upon an expectant mother who has so little regard for her own unborn that she risks causing him or her lifelong damage and suffering. The State, by taking special measures to give rehabilitation and training to expectant mothers with this tragic addiction or weakness, acts well within its powers and its civic obligations.

The holding of the Court, furthermore, does not call into question the validity of mandatory reporting laws such as child abuse laws which require teachers to report evidence of child abuse to the proper authorities, even if arrest and prosecution is the likely result. That in turn highlights the real difficulty. As this case comes to us, and as reputable sources confirm, see K. Farkas, Training Health Care and Human Services Personnel in Perinatal Substance Abuse, in Drug & Alcohol Abuse Reviews, Substance Abuse During Pregnancy and Childhood, 13, 27-28 (R. Watson ed. 1995); U.S. Dept. of Health and Human Services, Substance Abuse and Mental Health Services Administration, Pregnant, Substance-Using Women 48 (1993), we must accept the premise that the medical profession can adopt acceptable criteria for testing expectant mothers for cocaine use in order to provide prompt and effective counseling to the mother and to take proper medical steps to protect the child. If prosecuting authorities then adopt legitimate procedures to discover this information and prosecution follows, that ought not to invalidate the testing. One of the ironies of the case, then, may be that the program now under review, which gives the cocaine user a second and third chance, might be replaced by some more rigorous system. . . .

An essential, distinguishing feature of the special needs cases is that the person searched has consented, though the usual voluntariness analysis is altered because adverse consequences, (e.g., dismissal from employment or disqualification from playing on a high school sports team), will follow from refusal. The person searched has given consent, as defined to take into account that the consent was not voluntary in the full sense of the word. The consent, and the circumstances in which it was given, bear upon the reasonableness of the whole special needs program.

Here, on the other hand, the question of consent, even with the special connotation used in the special needs cases, has yet to be decided. Indeed, the Court finds it necessary to take the unreal step of assuming there was no voluntary consent at all. Thus, we have erected a strange world for deciding the case.

My discussion has endeavored to address the permissibility of a law enforcement purpose in this artificial context. The role played by consent might have affected our assessment of the issues. . . . Had we the prerogative to discuss the role played by consent, the case might have been quite a different one. All are in agreement, of course, that the Court of Appeals will address these issues in further proceedings on remand.

With these remarks, I concur in the judgment.

JUSTICE SCALIA, with whom THE CHIEF JUSTICE and JUSTICE THOMAS join as to Part II, dissenting. . . .

I

The first step in Fourth Amendment analysis is to identify the search or seizure at issue. What petitioners, the Court, and to a lesser extent the concurrence really object to is not the urine testing, but the hospital's reporting of positive drug-test results to police. But the latter is obviously not a search. . . . There is only one act that could conceivably be regarded as a search of petitioners in the present case: the *taking* of the urine sample. I suppose the *testing* of that urine for traces of unlawful drugs could be considered a search of sorts, but the Fourth Amendment protects only against searches of citizens' "persons, houses, papers, and effects"; and it is entirely unrealistic to regard urine as one of the "effects" (i.e., part of the property) of the person who has passed and abandoned it. Cf. California v. Greenwood, 486 U.S. 35 (1988) (garbage left at curb is not property protected by the Fourth Amendment). Some would argue, I suppose, that testing of the urine is prohibited by some generalized privacy right "emanating" from the "penumbras" of the Constitution (a question that is not before us); but it is not even arguable that the testing of urine that has been lawfully obtained is a Fourth Amendment search. (I may add that, even if it were, the factors legitimizing the taking of the sample, which I discuss below, would likewise legitimize the testing of it.)

It is rudimentary Fourth Amendment law that a search which has been consented to is not unreasonable. There is no contention in the present case that the urine samples were extracted forcibly. The only conceivable bases for saying that they were obtained without consent are the contentions (1) that the consent was coerced by the patients' need for medical treatment, (2) that the consent was uninformed because the patients were not told that the tests would include testing for drugs, and (3) that the consent was uninformed because the patients were not told that the results of the tests would be provided to the police. . . .

Under our established Fourth Amendment law, the last two contentions would not suffice, even without reference to the special-needs doctrine. The Court's analogizing of this case to Miranda v. Arizona, 384 U.S. 436 (1966), and its claim that "standards of knowing waiver" apply, are flatly contradicted by our jurisprudence, which shows that using lawfully (but deceivingly) obtained material for purposes other than those represented, and giving that material or information derived from it to the police, is not unconstitutional. In Hoffa v. United States, 385 U.S. 293 (1966), "[t]he argument [was] that [the informant's] failure to disclose his role as a government informant vitiated the consent that the petitioner gave" for the agent's access to evidence of criminal wrongdoing, id., at 300. We rejected that argument, because "the Fourth Amendment [does not protect] a wrongdoer's misplaced belief that a person to whom he voluntarily confides his wrongdoing will not reveal it." Id., at 302. Because the defendant had voluntarily provided access to the evidence, there was no reasonable expectation of privacy to invade. . . .

Until today, we have *never* held — or even suggested — that material which a person voluntarily entrusts to someone else cannot be given by that person to the police, and used for whatever evidence it may contain. Without so much as discussing the point, the Court today opens a hole in our Fourth Amendment jurisprudence, the size and shape of which is entirely indeterminate. Today's holding would be remarkable enough if the confidential relationship violated by the police conduct were at least one protected by state law. It would be surprising to learn, for example, that in a State which recognizes a spousal evidentiary privilege the police cannot use evidence obtained from a cooperating husband or wife. But today's holding goes even beyond that, since there does not exist any physician-patient privilege in South Carolina. See, e.g., Peagler v. Atlantic Coast R.R. Co., 232 S.C. 274 (1958). Since the Court declines even to discuss the issue, it leaves law enforcement officials entirely in the dark as to when they can use incriminating evidence obtained from "trusted" sources. Presumably the lines will be drawn in the case-by-case development of a whole new branch of Fourth Amendment jurisprudence, taking yet another social judgment (which confidential relationships ought not be invaded by the police) out of democratic control, and confiding it to the uncontrolled judgment of this Court — uncontrolled because there is no common-law precedent to guide it. I would adhere to our established law, which says that information obtained through violation of a relationship of trust is obtained consensually, and is hence not a search.[4]

There remains to be considered the first possible basis for invalidating this search, which is that the patients were coerced to produce their urine samples by their necessitous circumstances, to-wit, their need for medical treatment of their pregnancy. If that was coercion, it was not coercion applied by the government — and if such nongovernmental coercion sufficed, the police would never be permitted to use the ballistic evidence obtained from treatment of a patient with a bullet wound. And the Fourth Amendment would invalidate those many state laws that require physicians to report gunshot wounds, evidence of spousal abuse, and (like the South Carolina law relevant here, see S.C. Code Ann. §20-7-510 (2000)) evidence of child abuse.

II

I think it clear, therefore, that there is no basis for saying that obtaining of the urine sample was unconstitutional. The special-needs doctrine is thus quite irrelevant, since it operates only to validate searches and seizures that are otherwise unlawful. In the ensuing discussion, however, I shall assume (contrary to legal precedent) that the taking of the urine sample was (either because of the patients' necessitous circumstances, or because of failure to disclose that the urine would be tested for drugs, or because of failure to disclose that the results of the test would be given to the police) coerced. Indeed, I shall even assume (contrary to common sense) that the testing of the urine constituted an unconsented search of the patients' effects. On those assumptions, the special-needs doctrine *would* become relevant; and, properly applied, would validate what was done here.

The conclusion of the Court that the special-needs doctrine is inapplicable rests upon its contention that respondents "undert[ook] to obtain [drug] evidence from their patients" not for any medical purpose, but *"for the specific purpose of incriminating those patients."* Ante, at 85 (emphasis in original). In other words, the purported medical rationale was merely a pretext; there was no special need. This contention contradicts the District Court's finding of fact that the goal of the testing policy "was not to arrest patients but to facilitate their treatment and protect both the mother

4. The Court contends that I am "mischaracteriz[ing]" its opinion, since the Court is merely "assum-[ing] for purposes of decision that the patients did *not* consent to the searches, and [leaves] the question of consent for the Court of Appeals to determine." That is not responsive. The "question of consent" that the Court leaves open is whether the patients consented, not merely to the taking of the urine samples, but to the drug testing in particular, and to the provision of the results to the police. Consent to the taking of the samples alone — or even to the taking of the samples *plus* the drug testing — does not suffice. The Court's contention that the question of the sufficiency of that more limited consent is not before us because respondents did not raise it is simply mistaken. Part II of respondents' brief, entitled "The Petitioners consented to the searches," argues that "Petitioners . . . freely and voluntarily . . . provided the urine samples"; that "each of the Petitioners signed a consent to treatment form which authorized the MUSC medical staff to conduct all necessary tests of those urine samples — including drug tests"; and that "[t]here is no precedent in this Court's Fourth Amendment search and seizure jurisprudence which imposes any . . . requirement that the searching agency inform the consenting party that the results of the search will be turned over to law enforcement." Brief for Respondent 38-39. . . .

In sum, I think it clear that the Court's disposition requires the holding that violation of a relationship of trust constitutes a search. . . .

and unborn child." This finding is binding upon us unless clearly erroneous, see Fed. Rule Civ. Proc. 52(a). Not only do I find it supportable; I think any other finding would have to be overturned.

The cocaine tests started in April 1989, *neither at police suggestion nor with police involvement*. Expectant mothers who tested positive were referred by hospital staff for substance-abuse treatment — an obvious health benefit to both mother and child. See App. 43 (testimony that a single use of cocaine can cause fetal damage). And, since "[i]nfants whose mothers abuse cocaine during pregnancy are born with a wide variety of physical and neurological abnormalities," ante, at 89 (Kennedy, J., concurring in judgment), which require medical attention, see Brief in Opposition A76-A77, the tests were of additional medical benefit in predicting needed postnatal treatment for the child. Thus, in their origin — before the police were in any way involved — the tests had an immediate, not merely an "ultimate," purpose of improving maternal and infant health. Several months after the testing had been initiated, a nurse discovered that local police were arresting pregnant users of cocaine for child abuse, the hospital's general counsel wrote the county solicitor to ask "what, if anything, our Medical Center needs to do to assist you in this matter," App. 499 (South Carolina law requires child abuse to be reported, see S.C. Code Ann. §20-7-510), the police suggested ways to avoid tainting evidence, and the hospital and police in conjunction used the testing program as a means of securing what the Court calls the "ultimate" health benefit of coercing drug-abusing mothers into drug treatment. Why would there be any reason to believe that, once this policy of using the drug tests for their "ultimate" health benefits had been adopted, use of them for their original, *immediate*, benefits somehow disappeared, and testing somehow became in its entirety nothing more than a "pretext" for obtaining grounds for arrest? On the face of it, this is incredible. The only evidence of the exclusively arrest-related purpose of the testing adduced by the Court is that the police-cooperation policy *itself* does not describe how to care for cocaine-exposed infants. But *of course* it does not, since that policy, adopted months after the cocaine testing was initiated, had as its only health object the "ultimate" goal of inducing drug treatment through threat of arrest. Does the Court really believe (or even *hope*) that, once invalidation of the program challenged here has been decreed, drug testing will cease?

In sum, there can be no basis for the Court's purported ability to "distinguis[h] this case from circumstances in which physicians or psychologists, in the course of ordinary medical procedures aimed at helping the patient herself, come across information that . . . is subject to reporting requirements," ante, at 80-81, unless it is this: That the *addition* of a law-enforcement-related purpose *to* a legitimate medical purpose destroys applicability of the "special-needs" doctrine. But that is quite impossible, since the special-needs doctrine was developed, and is ordinarily employed, precisely to enable searches *by law enforcement officials* who, of course, ordinarily have a law enforcement objective. Thus, in Griffin v. Wisconsin, 483 U.S. 868 (1987), a probation officer received a tip from a detective that petitioner, a felon on parole, possessed a firearm. Accompanied by police, he conducted a warrantless search of petitioner's home. The weapon was found and used as evidence in the probationer's trial for unlawful possession of a firearm. Affirming denial of a motion to suppress, we concluded that the "special need" of assuring compliance with terms of release justified a warrantless search of petitioner's home. Notably, we observed that a probation officer is not the police officer who normally conducts searches against the ordinary citizen. He is an employee of the State Department of Health and Social Services who, while assuredly charged with protecting the public interest, is also supposed to have in mind the welfare of the probationer. . . . In such a setting, we think it reasonable to dispense with the warrant requirement.

Id., at 876-877.

Like the probation officer, the doctors here do not "ordinarily conduc[t] searches against the ordinary citizen," and they are "supposed to have in mind the welfare of the [mother and child]." That they have in mind in addition the provision of evidence to the police should make no difference. The Court suggests that if police involvement in this case was in some way incidental and after-the-fact, that would make a difference in the outcome. But in *Griffin*, even more than here, police were involved in the search from the very beginning; indeed, the initial tip about the gun came from a detective. Under the factors relied upon by the Court, the use of evidence approved in *Griffin* would have been permitted only if the parole officer had been untrained in chain-of-custody procedures, had not known of the possibility a gun was present, and had been unaccompanied by police when he simply happened upon the weapon. Why any or all of these is constitutionally significant is baffling.

Petitioners seek to distinguish *Griffin* by observing that probationers enjoy a lesser expectation of privacy than does the general public. That is irrelevant to the point I make here, which is that the presence of a law enforcement purpose does not render the special-needs doctrine inapplicable. In any event, I doubt whether Griffin's reasonable expectation of privacy in his home was any less than petitioners' reasonable expectation of privacy in their urine taken, or in the urine tests performed, in a hospital — especially in a State such as South Carolina, which recognizes no physician-patient testimonial privilege and requires the physician's duty of confidentiality to yield to public policy, see McCormick v. England, 328 S.C. 627, 633, 640-642 (Ct. App. 1997); and which requires medical conditions that indicate a violation of the law to be reported to authorities, see, e.g., S.C. Code Ann. §20-7-510 (2000) (child abuse). . . .

[I]t is not the function of this Court — at least not in Fourth Amendment cases — to weigh petitioners' privacy interest against the State's interest in meeting the crisis of "crack babies" that developed in the late 1980s. I cannot refrain from observing, however, that the outcome of a wise weighing of those interests is by no means clear. The initial goal of the doctors and nurses who conducted cocaine-testing in this case was to refer pregnant drug addicts to treatment centers, and to prepare for necessary treatment of their possibly affected children. When the doctors and nurses agreed to the program providing test results to the police, they did so because (in addition to the fact that child abuse was required by law to be reported) they wanted to use the sanction of arrest as a strong incentive for their addicted patients to undertake drug-addiction treatment. And the police themselves used it for that benign purpose, as is shown by the fact that only 30 of 253 women testing positive for cocaine were ever arrested, and only 2 of those prosecuted. It would not be unreasonable to conclude that today's judgment, authorizing the assessment of damages against the county solicitor and individual doctors and nurses who participated in the program, proves once again that no good deed goes unpunished. . . .

NOTES AND QUESTIONS

1. What if the hospital's policy did not require positive test results to be provided to police, but these results were subpoenaed by a grand jury? Would such a subpoena raise any Fourth Amendment concerns?

2. Does *Ferguson* reprise certain problems in the analysis the Court employed in Indianapolis v. Edmond, supra, at page 599? Recall that in that case, the Court held that a checkpoint program violated the Fourth Amendment because the "primary purpose" of the roadblocks was to uncover evidence of crime — there, narcotics violations. The Court distinguished earlier checkpoint cases, including the sobriety checkpoint it had approved in Michigan Dept. of State Police v. Sitz, 496 U.S. 444 (1990), on the ground that in those cases, the primary purpose served was not the detection of evidence of criminal violations. (The Court distinguished *Sitz* on the ground that, though the sobriety checkpoint program was used by police to identify drunk drivers, the principal aim of the program was highway safety rather than criminal investigation.)

In *Ferguson*, the Court tries to draw a similar line between medical procedures that may incidentally produce evidence of crime (like the examination of a battered child that reveals abuse that must then be reported) and procedures whose aim is to produce such evidence (supposedly the case in *Ferguson*). But how does the Court discern the "primary purpose" behind programs like the ones at issue in these cases? As Justice Scalia suggests in dissent, excessive "entanglement" with law enforcement cannot be the test — for surely the probation officer who received a tip from police before conducting a search of a probationer's home in *Griffin* was acting closely in concert with law enforcement authorities. And think for a moment about *Ferguson*. If gathering evidence of criminal wrongdoing was the primary purpose of the program there, it's not apparent that *using* such evidence to prosecute drug offenders was a paramount goal: As the dissent points out, only two of the 253 women who tested positive for cocaine were ever prosecuted. In either the checkpoint or special needs cases, is a test premised on purpose likely to prove workable in practice? Will such a test adequately safeguard privacy interests?

3. What about Justice Scalia's argument that this case involves no Fourth Amendment event at all — a proposition for which he is the single vote? What distinguishes this case from *Hoffa*, *White*, and the other "misplaced confidence" cases discussed beginning on page 379?

4. Various administrative inspections of closely regulated businesses have been upheld as "reasonable" for Fourth Amendment purposes — without requiring probable cause or warrants. See, e.g., Donovan v. Dewey, 452 U.S. 594 (1981) (warrantless inspections of mines and stone quarries to ensure compliance with health and safety standards); United States v. Biswell, 406 U.S. 311 (1972) (warrantless inspection of pawnshop licensed to sell sporting weapons for compliance with gun control laws). Of these cases, New York v. Burger, 482 U.S. 691 (1987), most clearly illustrates the degree to which the Court sometimes is willing to recognize "special needs" in settings where law enforcement interests clearly are also present. *Burger* involved a New York statute that required the owners of automobile junkyards and related businesses to maintain records of cars and major parts in their possession and to make these records, as well as the automobiles and components listed in them, available for warrantless inspection by police during regular business hours. These inspections were for the purpose of deterring motor vehicle theft. (The

police in *Burger* had inspected a junkyard pursuant to the statute, found evidence of stolen vehicles, and arrested the owner.)

The Court observed that the warrantless inspection of premises in a "closely regulated" industry is reasonable when three criteria are met. First, there must be a "substantial" government interest informing the regulatory scheme pursuant to which the inspection is made. Second, warrantless inspections must be necessary to further the regulatory scheme. And third, the inspection program must provide a "constitutionally adequate substitute" for a warrant (by informing proprietors that regular inspections of a defined type take place pursuant to law in this industry and by placing appropriate limits on the time, place, and scope of inspections). The Court found the New York statute met these criteria. The fact that the regulatory goals in *Burger* — separating legitimate dealers in used auto parts from "chop shops" that "fenced" parts from stolen cars, and ensuring that stolen cars and parts could be traced — overlapped with purposes in the penal laws did not render the regulatory scheme invalid. "Nor do we think," the Court continued, "that this administrative scheme is unconstitutional simply because, in the course of enforcing it, an inspecting officer may discover evidence of crimes, besides violations of the scheme itself." Id., at 716.

5. Is there any justification for the relaxed Fourth Amendment standards to be found in all of these "special needs" cases? Consider how the government might behave if its authority to search were more limited: if, say, the probable cause and warrant requirements applied. The state might pass regulations extensive enough that probable cause to search regulated businesses would be easily established, or enact intrusive record-keeping and reporting requirements and gather information that way. School principals told they cannot search students' purses for cigarettes might simply impose punishments on the best available information, or create a system of hall passes and monitors that leaves students with less privacy than they would otherwise have. Government employers barred from searching their employees' file cabinets might remove the cabinets, and put all files in public areas. And if probation officers could not easily search probationers, those probationers might serve longer prison terms. In all these settings, the power to search is just one aspect of the government's regulatory power — and limiting search authority risks pushing the government to exercise its power in other ways. Search targets might be better off with broad search authority. For elaboration, see William J. Stuntz, Implicit Bargains, Government Power, and the Fourth Amendment, 44 Stan. L. Rev. 553 (1992).

Is that rationale sound? Is it consistent with the "special needs" cases? With the way Fourth Amendment law regulates ordinary police investigation of crime?

6. The forebear of the "special needs" cases was a Warren Court decision that aimed at extending, not relaxing, Fourth Amendment protections. In Camara v. Municipal Court of San Francisco, 387 U.S. 523 (1967) (also discussed supra, at page 537), the Court overturned an earlier decision, Frank v. Maryland, 359 U.S. 360 (1959), which permitted a municipal health inspector to perform a home inspection without a warrant. The *Camara* Court held that a warrant was necessary for such inspections. Noting that the routine periodic inspection of all structures was the only way to achieve universal compliance with health and safety codes, however, the Court redefined the probable cause needed for such an "administrative warrant." It concluded that in the housing inspection context, probable cause exists to issue a warrant to inspect if reasonable legislative or administrative standards for

conducting area inspections are satisfied — even though these standards do not require specific knowledge that code violations exist in a particular dwelling.

Does requiring an "administrative warrant" in the absence of traditional probable cause protect Fourth Amendment values? Should the Court require such warrants more frequently in its special needs cases? Or does the crafting of a new kind of warrant instead endanger the integrity of the probable-cause-and-warrant framework?

4. Reasonableness and Police Use of Force

TENNESSEE v. GARNER

Certiorari to the United States Court of Appeals for the Sixth Circuit
471 U.S. 1 (1985)

JUSTICE WHITE delivered the opinion of the Court.

This case requires us to determine the constitutionality of the use of deadly force to prevent the escape of an apparently unarmed suspected felon. We conclude that such force may not be used unless it is necessary to prevent the escape and the officer has probable cause to believe that the suspect poses a significant threat of death or serious physical injury to the officer or others.

I

At about 10:45 p.m. on October 3, 1974, Memphis Police Officers Elton Hymon and Leslie Wright were dispatched to answer a "prowler inside call." Upon arriving at the scene they saw a woman standing on her porch and gesturing toward the adjacent house. She told them she had heard glass breaking and that "they" or "someone" was breaking in next door. While Wright radioed the dispatcher to say that they were on the scene, Hymon went behind the house. He heard a door slam and saw someone run across the backyard. The fleeing suspect, who was appellee respondent's decedent, Edward Garner, stopped at a 6-feet-high chain link fence at the edge of the yard. With the aid of a flashlight, Hymon was able to see Garner's face and hands. He saw no sign of a weapon, and, though not certain, was "reasonably sure" and "figured" that Garner was unarmed. He thought Garner was 17 or 18 years old and about 5' 5" or 5' 7" tall.[2] While Garner was crouched at the base of the fence, Hymon called out "police, halt" and took a few steps toward him. Garner then began to climb over the fence. Convinced that if Garner made it over the fence he would elude capture, Hymon shot him. The bullet hit Garner in the back of the head. Garner was taken by ambulance to a hospital, where he died on the operating table. Ten dollars and a purse taken from the house were found on his body.

In using deadly force to prevent the escape, Hymon was acting under the authority of a Tennessee statute and pursuant to Police Department policy. . . .

Garner's father . . . brought this action . . . seeking damages under 42 U.S.C. §1983 for asserted violations of Garner's constitutional rights. . . . After a 3-day bench trial, the District Court entered judgment for all defendants. . . .

---

2. In fact, Garner, an eighth-grader, was 15. He was 5' 4" tall and weighed somewhere around 100 or 110 pounds.

The Court of Appeals reversed and remanded. . . .

II

. . . [T]here can be no question that apprehension by the use of deadly force is a seizure subject to the reasonableness requirement of the Fourth Amendment.

A police officer may arrest a person if he has probable cause to believe that person committed a crime. Petitioners and appellant argue that if this requirement is satisfied the Fourth Amendment has nothing to say about *how* that seizure is made. This submission ignores the many cases in which this Court, by balancing the extent of the intrusion against the need for it, has examined the reasonableness of the manner in which a search or seizure is conducted. . . . Because one of the factors is the extent of the intrusion, it is plain that reasonableness depends on not only when a seizure is made, but also how it is carried out. . . .

. . . [N]otwithstanding probable cause to seize a suspect, an officer may not always do so by killing him. The intrusiveness of a seizure by means of deadly force is unmatched. The suspect's fundamental interest in his own life need not be elaborated upon. The use of deadly force also frustrates the interest of the individual, and of society, in judicial determination of guilt and punishment. Against these interests are ranged governmental interests in effective law enforcement. It is argued that overall violence will be reduced by encouraging the peaceful submission of suspects who know that they may be shot if they flee. Effectiveness in making arrests requires the resort to deadly force, or at least the meaningful threat thereof. "Being able to arrest such individuals is a condition precedent to the state's entire system of law enforcement." Brief for Petitioners 14.

Without in any way disparaging the importance of these goals, we are not convinced that the use of deadly force is a sufficiently productive means of accomplishing them to justify the killing of nonviolent suspects. . . . [W]hile the meaningful threat of deadly force might be thought to lead to the arrest of more live suspects by discouraging escape attempts, the presently available evidence does not support this thesis. The fact is that a majority of police departments in this country have forbidden the use of deadly force against nonviolent suspects. If those charged with the enforcement of the criminal law have abjured the use of deadly force in arresting nondangerous felons, there is a substantial basis for doubting that the use of such force is an essential attribute of the arrest power in all felony cases. Petitioners and appellant have not persuaded us that shooting nondangerous fleeing suspects is so vital as to outweigh the suspect's interest in his own life.

The use of deadly force to prevent the escape of all felony suspects, whatever the circumstances, is constitutionally unreasonable. It is not better that all felony suspects die than that they escape. Where the suspect poses no immediate threat to the officer and no threat to others, the harm resulting from failing to apprehend him does not justify the use of deadly force to do so. It is no doubt unfortunate when a suspect who is in sight escapes, but the fact that the police arrive a little late or are a little slower afoot does not always justify killing the suspect. A police officer may not seize an unarmed, nondangerous suspect by shooting him dead. . . .

. . . Where the officer has probable cause to believe that the suspect poses a threat of serious physical harm, either to the officer or to others, it is not constitutionally unreasonable to prevent escape by using deadly force. Thus, if the suspect threatens the officer with a weapon or there is probable cause to believe that he has committed a crime involving the infliction or threatened infliction of serious physical harm, deadly force may be used if necessary to prevent escape, and if, where feasible, some warning has been given. . . .

III

It is insisted that the Fourth Amendment must be construed in light of the common-law rule, which allowed the use of whatever force was necessary to effect the arrest of a fleeing felon, though not a misdemeanant. . . .

The State and city argue that because this was the prevailing rule at the time of the adoption of the Fourth Amendment and for some time thereafter, and is still in force in some States, use of deadly force against a fleeing felon must be "reasonable." It is true that this Court has often looked to the common law in evaluating the reasonableness, for Fourth Amendment purposes, of police activity. On the other hand, it "has not simply frozen into constitutional law those law enforcement practices that existed at the time of the Fourth Amendment's passage." Because of sweeping change in the legal and technological context, reliance on the common-law rule in this case would be a mistaken literalism that ignores the purposes of a historical inquiry.

It has been pointed out many times that the common-law rule is best understood in light of the fact that it arose at a time when virtually all felonies were punishable by death. . . . Courts have also justified the common-law rule by emphasizing the relative dangerousness of felons.

Neither of these justifications makes sense today. Almost all crimes formerly punishable by death no longer are or can be. . . . Many crimes classified as misdemeanors, or nonexistent, at common law are now felonies. . . . [N]umerous misdemeanors involve conduct more dangerous than many felonies.

There is an additional reason why the common-law rule cannot be directly translated to the present day. The common-law rule developed at a time when weapons were rudimentary. Deadly force could be inflicted almost solely in a hand-to-hand struggle during which, necessarily, the safety of the arresting officer was at risk. Handguns were not carried by police officers until the latter half of the last century. Only then did it become possible to use deadly force from a distance as a means of apprehension. As a practical matter, the use of deadly force under the standard articulation of the common-law rule has an altogether different meaning — and harsher consequences — now than in past centuries. . . .

In evaluating the reasonableness of police procedures under the Fourth Amendment, we have also looked to prevailing rules in individual jurisdictions. [Of the states in which the rule is relatively clear, 21 follow the fleeing felon rule, and 23 limit the right to use deadly force to apprehend a fleeing felon.] . . .

It cannot be said that there is a constant or overwhelming trend away from the common-law rule. In recent years, some States have reviewed their laws and expressly rejected abandonment of the common-law rule. Nonetheless, the long-term movement has been away from the rule that deadly force may be used against any fleeing felon, and that remains the rule in less than half the States.

This trend is more evident and impressive when viewed in light of the policies adopted by the police departments themselves. Overwhelmingly, these are more restrictive than the common-law rule. The Federal Bureau of Investigation and the New York City Police Department, for example, both forbid the use of firearms except when necessary to prevent death or grievous bodily harm. For accreditation by the Commission on Accreditation for Law Enforcement Agencies, a department must restrict the use of deadly force to situations where "the officer reasonably believes that the action is in defense of human life . . . or in defense of any person in immediate danger of serious physical injury." . . . Overall, only 7.5% of departmental and municipal policies explicitly permit the use of deadly force against any felon; 86.8% explicitly do not. . . .

Actual departmental policies are important for an additional reason. We would hesitate to declare a police practice of long standing "unreasonable" if doing so would severely hamper effective law enforcement. But the indications are to the contrary. There has been no suggestion that crime has worsened in any way in jurisdictions that have adopted, by legislation or departmental policy, rules similar to that announced today. . . .

Nor do we agree with petitioners and appellant that the rule we have adopted requires the police to make impossible, split-second evaluations of unknowable facts. We do not deny the practical difficulties of attempting to assess the suspect's dangerousness. However, similarly difficult judgments must be made by the police in equally uncertain circumstances. See, e.g., Terry v. Ohio, 392 U.S., at 20, 27. Nor is there any indication that in States that allow the use of deadly force only against dangerous suspects, the standard has been difficult to apply or has led to a rash of litigation involving inappropriate second-guessing of police officers' split-second decisions. . . .

IV

The District Court concluded that . . . Garner appeared to be unarmed, though Hymon could not be certain that was the case. Restated in Fourth Amendment terms, this means Hymon had no articulable basis to think Garner was armed.

. . . [T]he fact that Garner was a suspected burglar could not, without regard to the other circumstances, automatically justify the use of deadly force. Hymon did not have probable cause to believe that Garner, whom he correctly believed to be unarmed, posed any physical danger to himself or others.

The dissent argues that the shooting was justified by the fact that Officer Hymon had probable cause to believe that Garner had committed a nighttime burglary. While we agree that burglary is a serious crime, we cannot agree that it is so dangerous as automatically to justify the use of deadly force. The FBI classifies burglary as a "property" rather than a "violent" crime. Although the armed burglar would present a different situation, the fact that an unarmed suspect has broken into a dwelling at night does not automatically mean he is physically dangerous. This case demonstrates as much. In fact, the available statistics demonstrate that burglaries only rarely involve physical violence. During the 10-year period from 1973-1982, only 3.8% of all burglaries involved violent crime. Bureau of Justice Statistics, Household Burglary 4 (1985).[23]

---

23. The dissent points out that three-fifths of all rapes in the home, three-fifths of all home robberies, and about a third of home assaults are committed by burglars. These figures mean only that if one knows that a suspect committed a rape in the home, there is a good chance that the suspect is also a burglar. That has nothing to do with the question here, which is whether the fact that someone has committed a burglary indicates that he has committed, or might commit, a violent crime.

V

. . . We hold that the [Tennessee] statute is invalid insofar as it purported to give Hymon the authority to act as he did. . . .

The judgment of the Court of Appeals is affirmed, and the case is remanded for further proceedings consistent with this opinion. . . .

[The dissenting opinion of Justice O'Connor, joined by Chief Justice Burger and Justice Rehnquist, is omitted.]

NOTES AND QUESTIONS

1. *Garner* is yet another "reasonableness" case in which the Court employs a free-wheeling balancing methodology to arrive at its result. But *Garner* is different from the other cases in this section. Usually, reasonableness and interest balancing mean less Fourth Amendment protection: The sliding scale slides only in one direction. In *Garner*, the Court crafts a test for police use of deadly force that is *more* stringent than the ordinary probable cause requirement.

Perhaps this should be unsurprising. There is nothing about interest balancing that automatically yields results favorable to the police. Yet the pattern of the Court's cases is striking. The largest category of "reasonableness" cases involve street stops and frisks, where the standard is explicitly lower than probable cause, and where warrants are never required. Why should the balance tilt so consistently in the government's favor? As is often the case, the circumstances of the question tend to determine the answer. The Court turned to the Fourth Amendment's reasonableness clause, and to consider-all-the-circumstances balancing, in cases where the probable cause and warrant requirements seemed too stringent. A brief street stop is less intrusive than an arrest; a pat-down of the suspect's outer clothing invades privacy less than a top-to-bottom house search. Naturally, interest-balancing would tend to produce a less stringent standard for such cases — which is how we ended up with *Terry* doctrine. Similar stories might be told about the "special needs" cases or drunk driving checkpoints. Meanwhile, cases where the probable cause standard seems too *low*, where the intrusiveness of the relevant police conduct is higher than in house searches or full-custody arrests — cases like *Garner* — are rare. The methodology is neutral; it neither favors the police nor criminal suspects. But the cases to which the methodology is applied tend to cluster at one end of the spectrum. That is why the government wins so often where "reasonableness" is the test.

Are you persuaded? Is the balance struck appropriately in *Garner*?

2. As the Court's opinion points out, many police departments, particularly those in big cities, had moved to deadly force policies more restrictive than the fleeing felon rule long before the decision in *Garner*. The results of efforts by police departments to define more narrowly the circumstances in which the use of deadly force is permitted have been positive:

The dissent also points out that this 3.8% adds up to 2.8 million violent crimes over a 10-year period, as if to imply that today's holding will let loose 2.8 million violent burglars. The relevant universe is, of course, far smaller. At issue is only that tiny fraction of cases where violence has taken place and an officer who has no other means of apprehending the suspect is unaware of its occurrence.

In sum, the empirical research suggests with remarkable unanimity . . . that restrictive policies seem to have worked well where they have been tried. Their adoption usually is followed by marked decreases in shootings by police, increases in the proportion of the shootings that are responses to serious criminal activity, greater or unchanged officer safety, and no resultant adverse impact on crime levels or arrest aggressiveness.

William A. Geller & Michael S. Scott, Deadly Force: What We Know, in Carl B. Klockars & Stephen D. Mastrofski, Thinking About Police 446, 465 (2d ed. 1991). This is particularly true in places that have combined restrictive shooting policies with the institution of administrative review of shooting incidents within the police department. (In New York City, for instance, a Firearms Discharge Review Board was created in 1972 to review each and every incident in which a shot is fired by an NYPD officer; shootings by police were reduced significantly.) Some researchers have concluded that "continuing administrative pressure [of this type] is an essential supplement to a restrictive written policy." Id., at 466. If this is true, should municipal liability for Fourth Amendment violations involving police shootings turn, in part, on whether the relevant police department had adequate procedures in place for administrative review of shooting incidents? Consider in this connection Canton v. Harris, 489 U.S. 378, 388 (1989), which held that municipalities may be liable for inadequately training police pursuant to §1983 "only where the failure to train amounts to deliberate indifference to the rights of persons with whom the police come into contact."

3. A few police departments forbid the use of firearms except strictly in the defense of life. Others impose a requirement that officers reasonably believe that a suspect poses an *imminent* threat to the officer or to others. Does *Garner* do either of these things? Precisely what is the *Garner* standard?

4. One thing it is not: a set of preconditions that apply whenever an officer's actions constitute "deadly force." In Scott v. Harris, 550 U.S. 372 (2007), the Court considered a high-speed chase, captured on videotape, in which Deputy Timothy Scott rammed a fleeing motorist's car from behind in an effort to stop the motorist's reckless and public-endangering flight. As a result, the motorist lost control of his vehicle, crashed, and was rendered a quadriplegic. He thereafter brought suit, charging that his Fourth Amendment rights had been violated. The Court disagreed:

Respondent urges us to analyze this case as we analyzed *Garner*. We must first decide, he says, whether the actions Scott took constituted "deadly force." . . . If so, respondent claims that *Garner* prescribes certain preconditions that must be met before Scott's actions can survive Fourth Amendment scrutiny: (1) The suspect must have posed an immediate threat of serious physical harm to the officer or others; (2) deadly force must have been necessary to prevent escape; and (3) where feasible, the officer must have given the suspect some warning. See Brief for Respondent 17-18 (citing *Garner*, 471 U.S., at 9-12). Since these *Garner* preconditions for using deadly force were not met in this case, Scott's actions were *per se* unreasonable.

Respondent's argument falters at its first step; *Garner* did not establish a magical on/off switch that triggers rigid preconditions whenever an officer's actions constitute "deadly force." *Garner* was simply an application of the Fourth Amendment's "reasonableness" test to the use of a particular type of force in a particular situation. *Garner* held that it was unreasonable to kill a "young, slight, and unarmed" burglary suspect, 471 U.S., at 21, by shooting him "in the back of the head" while he was running away on foot, id., at 4, and when the officer "could not reasonably have believed that [the suspect] . . . posed any threat," and "never attempted to justify his actions on any basis other than the need to prevent an escape," id., at 21. Whatever *Garner* said about the factors that *might have* justified shooting the suspect in that case, such "preconditions" have scant applicability to this case, which has vastly different facts. . . . Although respondent's attempt to craft an easy-to-apply legal test in the Fourth Amendment context is admirable, in the end we must still slosh our way through the factbound morass of "reasonableness." Whether or not Scott's actions constituted application of "deadly force," all that matters is whether Scott's actions were reasonable.

[I]n judging whether Scott's actions were reasonable, we must consider the risk of bodily harm that Scott's actions posed to respondent in light of the threat to the public that Scott was trying to eliminate. Although there is no obvious way to quantify the risks on either side, it is clear from the videotape that respondent posed an actual and imminent threat to the lives of any pedestrians who might have been present, to other civilian motorists, and to the officers involved in the chase. It is equally clear that Scott's actions posed a high likelihood of serious injury or death to respondent — though not the near *certainty* of death posed by, say, shooting a fleeing felon in the back of the head. . . . So how does a court go about weighing the perhaps lesser probability of injuring or killing numerous bystanders against the perhaps larger probability of injuring or killing a single person? We think it appropriate in this process to take into account not only the number of lives at risk, but also their relative culpability. It was respondent, after all, who intentionally placed himself and the public in danger. . . . We have little difficulty in concluding it was reasonable for Scott to take the action that he did . . .

But wait, says respondent: Couldn't the innocent public equally have been protected, and the tragic accident entirely avoided, if the police had simply ceased their pursuit? We think the police need not have taken that chance and hoped for the best. . . .

[W]e are loath to lay down a rule requiring the police to allow fleeing suspects to get away whenever they drive *so recklessly* that they put other people's lives in danger. It is obvious the perverse incentives such a rule would create . . . . Instead, we lay down a more sensible rule: A police officer's attempt to terminate a dangerous high-speed car chase that threatens the lives of innocent bystanders does not violate the Fourth Amendment, even when it places the fleeing motorist at risk of serious injury or death.

5. Does *Scott* change the standard to be applied in more ordinary deadly force cases? Before *Scott*, *Garner* was not usually seen as an instance of the Court "slosh-[ing] its ways through the fact-bound morass of reasonableness." But that is the way Justice Scalia, writing for the majority in *Scott*, describes it.

One of the intriguing features of *Scott* is that the Court did not have to rely on the parties' descriptions of what happened — the car chase was videotaped, and the Court was explicitly influence by what it saw. See id., at 378 ("The videotape quite clearly contradicts the version of the story told by respondent and adopted by the Court of Appeals.") And in response to Justice Steven's suggestion in dissent that the majority's characterization of the chase was inaccurate, the Court invites readers to watch the video themselves. Id., at n. 5. Although the majority provides a link to the video, it is easier to look it up on YouTube (www.youtube.com). Search for "Scott v Harris chase."

After *Scott*, the *Garner* test (Is there such a thing anymore?) seems more "factbound" than it did before. That may mean that cases involving deadly force are not so distinct from cases involving force generally. Consider that possibility as you read the following case.

GRAHAM v. CONNOR

Certiorari to the United States Court of Appeals for the Fourth Circuit
490 U.S. 386 (1989)

CHIEF JUSTICE REHNQUIST delivered the opinion of the Court.

This case requires us to decide what constitutional standard governs a free citizen's claim that law enforcement officials used excessive force in the course of making an arrest, investigatory stop, or other "seizure" of his person. . . .

In this action under 42 U.S.C. §1983, petitioner Dethorne Graham seeks to recover damages for injuries allegedly sustained when law enforcement officers used physical force against him during the course of an investigatory stop. Because the case comes to us from a decision of the Court of Appeals affirming the entry of a directed verdict for respondents, we take the evidence hereafter noted in the light most favorable to petitioner. On November 12, 1984, Graham, a diabetic, felt the onset of an insulin reaction. He asked a friend, William Berry, to drive him to a nearby convenience store so he could purchase some orange juice to counteract the reaction. Berry agreed, but when Graham entered the store, he saw a number of people ahead of him in the checkout line. Concerned about the delay, he hurried out of the store and asked Berry to drive him to a friend's house instead.

Respondent Connor, an officer of the Charlotte, North Carolina, Police Department, saw Graham hastily enter and leave the store. The officer became suspicious that something was amiss and followed Berry's car. About one-half mile from the store, he made an investigative stop. Although Berry told Connor that Graham was simply suffering from a "sugar reaction," the officer ordered Berry and Graham to wait while he found out what, if anything, had happened at the convenience store. When Officer Connor returned to his patrol car to call for backup assistance, Graham got out of the car, ran around it twice, and finally sat down on the curb, where he passed out briefly.

In the ensuing confusion, a number of other Charlotte police officers arrived on the scene in response to Officer Connor's request for backup. One of the officers rolled Graham over on the sidewalk and cuffed his hands tightly behind his back, ignoring Berry's pleas to get him some sugar. Another officer said: "I've seen a lot of people with sugar diabetes that never acted like this. Ain't nothing wrong with the M.F. but drunk. Lock the S.B. up." Several officers then lifted Graham up from behind, carried him over to Berry's car, and placed him face down on its hood. Regaining consciousness, Graham asked the officers to check in his wallet for a diabetic decal that he carried. In response, one of the officers told him to "shut up" and shoved his face down against the hood of the car. Four officers grabbed Graham and threw him headfirst into the police car. A friend of Graham's brought some orange juice to the car, but the officers refused to let him have it. Finally, Officer Connor received a report that Graham had done nothing wrong at the convenience store, and the officers drove him home and released him.

At some point during his encounter with the police, Graham sustained a broken foot, cuts on his wrists, a bruised forehead, and an injured shoulder; he also claims to have developed a loud ringing in his right ear that continues to this day. He commenced this action under 42 U.S.C. §1983 against the individual officers involved in the incident . . . alleging that they had used excessive force in making the investigatory stop, in violation of "rights secured to him under the Fourteenth Amendment to the United States Constitution and 42 U.S.C. §1983." The case was tried before a jury. At the close of petitioner's evidence, respondents moved for a directed verdict. In ruling on that motion, the District Court considered the following four factors, which it identified as "[t]he factors to be considered in determining when the excessive use of force gives rise to a cause of action under §1983": (1) the need for the application of force; (2) the relationship between that need and the amount of force that was used; (3) the extent of the injury inflicted; and (4) "[w]hether the force was applied in a good faith effort to maintain and restore discipline or maliciously and sadistically for the very purpose of causing harm." Finding that the amount of force used by the officers was "appropriate under the circumstances," that "[t]here was no discernable injury inflicted," and that the force used "was not applied maliciously or sadistically for the very purpose of causing harm," but in "a good faith effort to maintain or restore order in the face of a potentially explosive situation," the District Court granted respondents' motion for a directed verdict.

A divided panel of the Court of Appeals for the Fourth Circuit affirmed. . . . We granted certiorari, and now reverse.

Fifteen years ago, in Johnson v. Glick, 481 F.2d 1028 (1973), the Court of Appeals for the Second Circuit addressed a §1983 damages claim filed by a pre-trial detainee who claimed that a guard had assaulted him without justification. In evaluating the detainee's claim, Judge Friendly applied neither the Fourth Amendment nor the Eighth, the two most textually obvious sources of constitutional protection against physically abusive governmental conduct. Instead, he looked to "substantive due process," holding that "quite apart from any 'specific' provisions of the Bill of Rights, application of undue force by law enforcement officers deprives a suspect of liberty without due process of law." 481 F.2d, at 1032. . . . Judge Friendly went on to set forth four factors to guide courts in determining "whether the constitutional line has been crossed" by a particular use of force — the same four factors relied upon by the courts below in this case. . . .

We reject this notion that all excessive force claims brought under §1983 are governed by a single generic standard. . . . In addressing an excessive force claim brought under §1983, analysis begins by identifying the specific constitutional right allegedly infringed by the challenged application of force. . . .

Where, as here, the excessive force claim arises in the context of an arrest or investigatory stop of a free citizen, it is most properly characterized as one invoking the protections of the Fourth Amendment, which guarantees citizens the right "to be secure in their persons . . . against unreasonable . . . seizures" of the person. This much is clear from our decision in Tennessee v. Garner[, 471 U.S. 1 (1985)]. In Garner, . . . [t]hough the complaint alleged violations of both the Fourth Amendment and the Due Process Clause, we analyzed the constitutionality of the challenged application of force solely by reference to the Fourth Amendment's prohibition against unreasonable seizures of the person, holding that the "reasonableness" of a particular seizure depends not only on when it is made, but also on how it is carried out. Today we make explicit what was implicit in Garner's analysis, and hold that all claims that law enforcement officers have used excessive force — deadly or not — in the course of an arrest, investigatory stop, or other "seizure" of a free citizen should be analyzed under the Fourth Amendment and its "reasonableness" standard, rather than under a "substantive due process" approach. . . .

Determining whether the force used to effect a particular seizure is "reasonable" under the Fourth Amendment requires a careful balancing of "the nature and quality of the intrusion on the individual's Fourth Amendment interests" against the countervailing governmental interests at stake. [471 U.S.] at 8, quoting United States v. Place, 462 U.S. 696, 703 (1983). Our Fourth Amendment jurisprudence has long recognized that the right to make an arrest or investigatory stop necessarily carries with it the right to use some degree of physical coercion or threat thereof to effect it. See Terry v. Ohio, 392 U.S., at 22-27. Because "[t]he test of reasonableness under the Fourth Amendment is not capable of precise definition or mechanical application," Bell v. Wolfish, 441 U.S. 520, 559 (1979), however, its proper application requires careful attention to the facts and circumstances of each particular case, including the severity of the crime at issue, whether the suspect poses an immediate threat to the safety of the officers or others, and whether he is actively resisting arrest or attempting to evade arrest by flight. See Tennessee v. Garner, 471 U.S., at 8-9 (the question is "whether the totality of the circumstances justifie[s] a particular sort of . . . seizure").

The "reasonableness" of a particular use of force must be judged from the perspective of a reasonable officer on the scene, rather than with the 20/20 vision of hindsight. The Fourth Amendment is not violated by an arrest based on probable cause, even though the wrong person is arrested, nor by the mistaken execution of a valid search warrant on the wrong premises. With respect to a claim of excessive force, the same standard of reasonableness at the moment applies: "Not every push or shove, even if it may later seem unnecessary in the peace of a judge's chambers," Johnson v. Glick, 481 F.2d, at 1033, violates the Fourth Amendment. The calculus of reasonableness must embody allowance for the fact that police officers are often forced to make split-second judgments — in circumstances that are tense, uncertain, and rapidly evolving — about the amount of force that is necessary in a particular situation.

As in other Fourth Amendment contexts, however, the "reasonableness" inquiry in an excessive force case is an objective one: the question is whether the officers' actions are "objectively reasonable" in light of the facts and circumstances confronting them, without regard to their underlying intent or motivation. An officer's evil intentions will not make a Fourth Amendment violation out of an objectively reasonable use of force; nor will an officer's good intentions make an objectively unreasonable use of force constitutional.

Because petitioner's excessive force claim is one arising under the Fourth Amendment, the Court of Appeals erred in analyzing it under the four-part Johnson v. Glick test. That test, which requires consideration of whether the individual officers acted in "good faith" or "maliciously and sadistically for the very purpose of causing harm," is incompatible with a proper Fourth Amendment analysis. . . . The Fourth Amendment inquiry is one of "objective reasonableness" under the circumstances, and subjective concepts like "malice" and "sadism" have no proper place in that inquiry.

Because the Court of Appeals reviewed the District Court's ruling on the motion for directed verdict under an erroneous view of the governing substantive law, its judgment must be vacated and the case remanded to that court for reconsideration of that issue under the proper Fourth Amendment standard. . . .

[Justice Blackmun's opinion, joined by Justice Brennan and Justice Marshall, concurring in part and concurring in the judgment, is omitted.]

NOTES AND QUESTIONS

1. *Graham* squarely rejects using officers' subjective intent as part of Fourth Amendment analysis in excessive force cases. Is that sensible? What difference, if any, does it make?

2. Compare the legal standard *Graham* establishes with the standards the Court has established in many other Fourth Amendment areas. *Graham*'s standard seems unusually vague and open-ended, does it not? Why would that be? How would one go about constructing a more definite rule structure, something that would give police officers greater guidance when it comes to the police use of force? If more definite rules are not possible, what does that say about the ability of courts to regulate police violence effectively?

3. In the one passage of its opinion that seems designed to give some content to its reasonableness standard for excessive force claims, the Court says attention must be paid to "the severity of the crime at issue, whether the suspect poses an immediate threat to the safety of the officers or others, and whether he is actively resisting arrest or attempting to evade arrest by flight." What if these factors cut in different directions? Suppose, for example, a defendant is suspected of a minor and nonviolent crime but is "attempting to evade arrest by flight." Can the police use (nondeadly) force to apprehend him?

4. The *Graham* Court cautions that Fourth Amendment reasonableness in the context of use of force "must embody allowance for the fact that police officers are often forced to make split-second judgments — in circumstances that are tense, uncertain, and rapidly evolving — about the amount of force that is necessary in a particular situation." But consider what one use-of-force expert has to say about what he terms the "split-second syndrome":

> [S]hould police receive a report of an armed robbery in a crowded supermarket, [the split-second syndrome holds that] they should be granted great leeway in their manner of response, because no two armed-robbery calls are precisely alike. If, in the course of responding, they decide that, to prevent the robber from escaping, the best course of action is to confront him immediately in the midst of a crowd of shoppers, they should not be told they should have acted otherwise. When they do challenge the alleged robber and he suddenly reacts to their calls from behind by turning on them with a shiny object in his hand, the only issue to be decided by those who subsequently review police actions is whether, at that instant, the suspect's actions were sufficiently provocative to justify their shooting him. That is so regardless of how the prior actions of the police may have contributed to their peril; regardless of how predictable it was that the suspect would be alarmed and would turn toward the police when they shouted to him; regardless of how many innocent bystanders were hit by bullets; and regardless of whether the reported armed robber was in fact an unhappy customer who, with pen in hand to complete a check for his purchase, had been engaged in a loud argument with a clerk. . . .

James J. Fyfe, The Split-Second Syndrome and Other Determinants of Police Violence, in Violent Transactions 207, 218 (Anne Campbell & John Gibbs eds. 1986). Professor Fyfe urges that this approach to the analysis of use of force condones unnecessary violence and encourages an operating style among police "that eschews advance diagnosis, planning and training." Was the Court in *Graham* too lenient?

E.   *Consent Searches*

SCHNECKLOTH v. BUSTAMONTE

Certiorari to the United States Court of Appeals for the Ninth Circuit
412 U.S. 218 (1973)

JUSTICE STEWART delivered the opinion of the Court.

. . . [O]ne of the specifically established exceptions to the requirements of both a warrant and probable cause is a search that is conducted pursuant to consent. The constitutional question in the present case concerns the definition of "consent" in this Fourth and Fourteenth Amendment context.

The respondent was brought to trial in a California court upon a charge of possessing a check with intent to defraud. He moved to suppress the introduction of certain material as evidence against him on the ground that the material had been acquired through an unconstitutional search and seizure. . . .

While on routine patrol in Sunnyvale, California, at approximately 2:40 in the morning, Police Officer James Rand stopped an automobile when he observed that one headlight and its license plate light were burned out. Six men were in the vehicle. Joe Alcala and the respondent, Robert Bustamonte, were in the front seat with Joe Gonzales, the driver. Three older men were seated in the rear. When, in response to the policeman's question, Gonzales could not produce a driver's license, Officer Rand asked if any of the other five had any evidence of identification. Only Alcala produced a license, and he explained that the car was his brother's. After the six occupants had stepped out of the car at the officer's request and after two additional policemen had arrived, Officer Rand asked Alcala if he could search the car. Alcala replied, "Sure, go ahead." Prior to the search no one was threatened with arrest and, according to Officer Rand's uncontradicted testimony, it "was all very congenial at this time." Gonzales testified that Alcala actually helped in the search of the car, by opening the trunk and glove compartment. In Gonzales' words: "[T]he police officer asked Joe [Alcala], he goes, 'Does the trunk open?' And Joe said, 'Yes.' He went to the car and got the keys and opened up the trunk." Wadded up under the left rear seat, the police officers found three checks that had previously been stolen from a car wash.

The trial judge denied the motion to suppress, and the checks in question were admitted in evidence at Bustamonte's trial. On the basis of this and other evidence he was convicted, and the California Court of Appeal for the First Appellate District affirmed the conviction. . . .

Thereafter, the respondent sought a writ of habeas corpus in a federal district court. It was denied. On appeal, the Court of Appeals for the Ninth Circuit . . . set aside the District Court's order. . . .

. . . [T]he State concedes that "[w]hen a prosecutor seeks to rely upon consent to justify the lawfulness of a search, he has the burden of proving that the consent was, in fact, freely and voluntarily given."

The precise question in this case, then, is what must the prosecution prove to demonstrate that a consent was "voluntarily" given. . . . The Court of Appeals for the Ninth Circuit concluded that it is an essential part of the State's initial burden to prove that a person knows he has a right to refuse consent. The California courts have followed the rule that voluntariness is a question of fact to be determined from the totality of all the circumstances, and that the state of a defendant's knowledge is only one factor to be taken into account in assessing the voluntariness of a consent.

The most extensive judicial exposition of the meaning of "voluntariness" has been developed in those cases in which the Court has had to determine the "voluntariness" of a defendant's confession for purposes of the Fourteenth Amendment. . . .

Those cases yield no talismanic definition of "voluntariness," mechanically applicable to the host of situations where the question has arisen. "The notion of 'voluntariness,'" Mr. Justice Frankfurter once wrote, "is itself an amphibian." Culombe v. Connecticut, 367 U.S. 568, 604-605. It cannot be taken literally to mean a "knowing" choice. "Except where a person is unconscious or drugged or otherwise lacks capacity for conscious choice, all incriminating statements — even those made under brutal treatment — are 'voluntary' in the sense of representing a choice of alternatives. On the other hand, if 'voluntariness' incorporates notions of 'but-for' cause, the question should be whether the statement would have been made even absent inquiry or other official action. Under such a test, virtually no statement would be voluntary because very few people give incriminating statements in the absence of official action of some kind."[7] It is thus evident that neither linguistics nor epistemology will provide a ready definition of the meaning of "voluntariness."

Rather, "voluntariness" has reflected an accommodation of the complex of values implicated in police questioning of a suspect. . . .

". . . Is the confession the product of an essentially free and unconstrained choice by its maker? If it is, if he has willed to confess, it may be used against him. If it is not, if his will has been overborne and his capacity for self-determination critically impaired, the use of his confession offends due process." [Culombe v. Connecticut, 367 U.S. 568, 602 (1961).]

In determining whether a defendant's will was overborne in a particular case, the Court has assessed the totality of all the surrounding circumstances — both the characteristics of the accused and the details of the interrogation. . . .

[None of this Court's voluntary confession cases] . . . turned on the presence or absence of a single controlling criterion. . . .

Similar considerations lead us to agree with the courts of California that the question whether a consent to a search was in fact "voluntary" or was the product of duress or coercion, express or implied, is a question of fact to be determined from the totality of all the circumstances. While knowledge of the right to refuse consent is one factor to be taken into account, the government need not establish such knowledge as the sine qua non of an effective consent. As with police questioning, two competing concerns must be accommodated in determining the meaning of a "voluntary" consent — the legitimate need for such searches and the equally important requirement of assuring the absence of coercion.

In situations where the police have some evidence of illicit activity, but lack probable cause to arrest or search, a search authorized by a valid consent may be the only means of obtaining important and reliable evidence. . . . And in those cases where there is probable cause to arrest or search, but where the police lack a warrant, a consent search may still be valuable. If the search is conducted and proves fruitless, that in itself may convince the police that an arrest with its possible

7. Bator & Vorenberg, Arrest, Detention, Interrogation and the Right to Counsel: Basic Problems and Possible Legislative Solutions, 66 Col. L. Rev. 62, 72-73. . . .

stigma and embarrassment is unnecessary, or that a far more extensive search pursuant to a warrant is not justified. In short, a search pursuant to consent may result in considerably less inconvenience for the subject of the search, and, properly conducted, is a constitutionally permissible and wholly legitimate aspect of effective police activity.

But the Fourth and Fourteenth Amendments require that a consent not be coerced, by explicit or implicit means, by implied threat or covert force. For, no matter how subtly the coercion was applied, the resulting "consent" would be no more than a pretext for the unjustified police intrusion against which the Fourth Amendment is directed. . . .

The problem of reconciling the recognized legitimacy of consent searches with the requirement that they be free from any aspect of official coercion cannot be resolved by any infallible touchstone. . . . In examining all the surrounding circumstances to determine if in fact the consent to search was coerced, account must be taken of subtly coercive police questions, as well as the possibly vulnerable subjective state of the person who consents. . . .

. . . [The Court of Appeals'] ruling, that the State must affirmatively prove that the subject of the search knew that he had a right to refuse consent, would, in practice, create serious doubt whether consent searches could continue to be conducted. There might be rare cases where it could be proved from the record that a person in fact affirmatively knew of his right to refuse. . . . But more commonly where there was no evidence of any coercion, explicit or implicit, the prosecution would nevertheless be unable to demonstrate that the subject of the search in fact had known of his right to refuse consent. . . .

One alternative that would go far toward proving that the subject of a search did know he had a right to refuse consent would be to advise him of that right before eliciting his consent. That, however, is a suggestion that has been almost universally repudiated by both federal and state courts, and, we think, rightly so. For it would be thoroughly impractical to impose on the normal consent search the detailed requirements of an effective warning. Consent searches are part of the standard investigatory techniques of law enforcement agencies. They normally occur on the highway, or in a person's home or office, and under informal and unstructured conditions. The circumstances that prompt the initial request to search may develop quickly or be a logical extension of investigative police questioning. The police may seek to investigate further suspicious circumstances or to follow up leads developed in questioning persons at the scene of a crime. These situations are a far cry from the structured atmosphere of a trial where, assisted by counsel if he chooses, a defendant is informed of his trial rights. And, while surely a closer question, these situations are still immeasurably far removed from "custodial interrogation" where, in Miranda v. Arizona, [384 U.S. 436 (1966)], we found that the Constitution required certain now familiar warnings as a prerequisite to police interrogation. . . .

It is said, however, that a "consent" is a "waiver" of a person's rights under the Fourth and Fourteenth Amendments. The argument is that by allowing the police to conduct a search, a person "waives" whatever right he had to prevent the police from searching. It is argued that under the doctrine of Johnson v. Zerbst, 304 U.S. 458, 464 [(1938)], to establish such a "waiver" the State must demonstrate "an intentional relinquishment or abandonment of a known right or privilege."

But these standards were enunciated in *Johnson* in the context of the safeguards of a fair criminal trial. Our cases do not reflect an uncritical demand for a knowing and intelligent waiver in every situation where a person has failed to invoke a constitutional protection. . . .

Almost without exception, the requirement of a knowing and intelligent waiver has been applied only to those rights which the Constitution guarantees to a criminal defendant in order to preserve a fair trial. Hence, . . . the standard of a knowing and intelligent waiver has most often been applied to test the validity of a waiver of counsel, either at trial, or upon a guilty plea. And the Court has also applied the *Johnson* criteria to assess the effectiveness of a waiver of other trial rights such as the right to confrontation, to a jury trial, and to a speedy trial, and the right to be free from twice being placed in jeopardy. Guilty pleas have been carefully scrutinized to determine whether the accused knew and understood all the rights to which he would be entitled at trial, and that he had intentionally chosen to forgo them. . . .

The guarantees afforded a criminal defendant at trial also protect him at certain stages before the actual trial, and any alleged waiver must meet the strict standard of an intentional relinquishment of a "known" right. But the "trial" guarantees that have been applied to the "pretrial" stage of the criminal process are similarly designed to protect the fairness of the trial itself. . . .

There is a vast difference between those rights that protect a fair criminal trial and the rights guaranteed under the Fourth Amendment. . . .

The protections of the Fourth Amendment . . . have nothing whatever to do with promoting the fair ascertainment of truth at a criminal trial. Rather, as Justice Frankfurter's opinion for the Court put it in Wolf v. Colorado, 338 U.S. 25, 27, the Fourth Amendment protects the "security of one's privacy against arbitrary intrusion by the police." . . .

Nor can it even be said that a search, as opposed to an eventual trial, is somehow "unfair" if a person consents to a search. While the Fourth and Fourteenth Amendments limit the circumstances under which the police can conduct a search, there is nothing constitutionally suspect in a person's voluntarily allowing a search. . . . Rather, the community has a real interest in encouraging consent, for the resulting search may yield necessary evidence for the solution and prosecution of crime, evidence that may insure that a wholly innocent person is not wrongly charged with a criminal offense.

. . . It would be unrealistic to expect that in the informal, unstructured context of a consent search, a policeman, upon pain of tainting the evidence obtained, could make the detailed type of examination demanded by *Johnson*. And, if for this reason a diluted form of "waiver" were found acceptable, that would itself be ample recognition of the fact that there is no universal standard that must be applied in every situation where a person forgoes a constitutional right.

Similarly, a "waiver" approach to consent searches would be thoroughly inconsistent with our decisions that have approved "third party consents." . . . Frazier v. Cupp, 394 U.S. 731, 740, held that evidence seized from the defendant's duffel bag in a search authorized by his cousin's consent was admissible at trial. We found that the defendant had assumed the risk that his cousin, with whom he shared the bag, would allow the police to search it. . . .

Much of what has already been said disposes of the argument that the Court's decision in the *Miranda* case requires the conclusion that knowledge of a right to refuse is an indispensable element of a valid consent. The considerations that informed the Court's holding in *Miranda* are simply inapplicable in the present case. In *Miranda* the Court found that the techniques of police questioning and the nature of custodial surroundings produce an inherently coercive situation. . . .

In this case, there is no evidence of any inherently coercive tactics — either from the nature of the police questioning or the environment in which it took place. Indeed, since consent searches will normally occur on a person's own familiar territory, the specter of incommunicado police interrogation in some remote station house is simply inapposite. . . .

It is also argued that the failure to require the Government to establish knowledge as a prerequisite to a valid consent, will relegate the Fourth Amendment to the special province of "the sophisticated, the knowledgeable and the privileged." We cannot agree. The traditional definition of voluntariness we accept today has always taken into account evidence of minimal schooling, low intelligence, and the lack of any effective warnings to a person of his rights; and the voluntariness of any statement taken under those conditions has been carefully scrutinized to determine whether it was in fact voluntarily given.

Our decision today is a narrow one. We hold only that when the subject of a search is not in custody and the State attempts to justify a search on the basis of his consent, the Fourth and Fourteenth Amendments require that it demonstrate that the consent was in fact voluntarily given, and not the result of duress or coercion, express or implied. Voluntariness is a question of fact to be determined from all the circumstances, and while the subject's knowledge of a right to refuse is a factor to be taken into account, the prosecution is not required to demonstrate such knowledge as a prerequisite to establishing a voluntary consent. Because the California court followed these principles in affirming the respondent's conviction, and because the Court of Appeals for the Ninth Circuit in remanding for an evidentiary hearing required more, its judgment must be reversed.

It is so ordered. [The concurring opinions of Justice Blackmun and Justice Powell and the dissenting opinions of Justice Douglas and Justice Brennan are omitted.]

JUSTICE MARSHALL, dissenting. . . . If consent to search means that a person has chosen to forgo his right to exclude the police from the place they seek to search, it follows that his consent cannot be considered a meaningful choice unless he knew that he could in fact exclude the police. The Court appears, however, to reject even the modest proposition that, if the subject of a search convinces the trier of fact that he did not know of his right to refuse assent to a police request for permission to search, the search must be held unconstitutional. For it says only that "knowledge of the right to refuse consent is one factor to be taken into account." I find this incomprehensible. I can think of no other situation in which we would say that a person agreed to some course of action if he convinced us that he did not know that there was some other course he might have pursued. I would therefore hold, at a minimum, that the prosecution may not rely on a purported consent to search if the subject of the search did not know that he could refuse to give consent. . . .

If one accepts this view, the question then is a simple one: must the Government show that the subject knew of his rights, or must the subject show that he lacked such knowledge?

I think that any fair allocation of the burden would require that it be placed on the prosecution. On this question, the Court indulges in what might be called the "straw man" method of adjudication. The Court responds to this suggestion by overinflating the burden. And, when it is suggested that the *prosecution*'s burden of proof could be easily satisfied if the police informed the subject of his rights, the Court responds by refusing to require the *police* to make a "detailed" inquiry. If the

Court candidly faced the real question of allocating the burden of proof, neither of these maneuvers would be available to it.

If the burden is placed on the defendant, all the subject can do is to testify that he did not know of his rights. And I doubt that many trial judges will find for the defendant simply on the basis of that testimony. Precisely because the evidence is very hard to come by, courts have traditionally been reluctant to require a party to prove negatives such as the lack of knowledge.

In contrast, there are several ways by which the subject's knowledge of his rights may be shown. The subject may affirmatively demonstrate such knowledge by his responses at the time the search took place. . . . . Denials of knowledge may be disproved by establishing that the subject had, in the recent past, demonstrated his knowledge of his rights, for example, by refusing entry when it was requested by the police. The prior experience or training of the subject might in some cases support an inference that he knew of his right to exclude the police.

The burden on the prosecutor would disappear, of course, if the police, at the time they requested consent to search, also told the subject that he had a right to refuse consent and that his decision to refuse would be respected. The Court's assertions to the contrary notwithstanding, there is nothing impractical about this method of satisfying the prosecution's burden of proof. . . .

The Court contends that if an officer paused to inform the subject of his rights, the informality of the exchange would be destroyed. I doubt that a simple statement by an officer of an individual's right to refuse consent would do much to alter the informality of the exchange, except to alert the subject to a fact that he surely is entitled to know. It is not without significance that for many years the agents of the Federal Bureau of Investigation have routinely informed subjects of their right to refuse consent, when they request consent to search. . . .

The proper resolution of this case turns, I believe, on a realistic assessment of the nature of the interchange between citizens and the police, and of the practical import of allocating the burden of proof in one way rather than another. The Court seeks to escape such assessments by escalating its rhetoric to unwarranted heights, but no matter how forceful the adjectives the Court uses, it cannot avoid being judged by how well its image of these interchanges accords with reality. . . .

NOTES AND QUESTIONS

1. *Schneckloth* is a strange decision, is it not? If the search target does not know he may refuse consent, it would seem to follow that any "consent" was fictive, since the target believed he had no choice. Yet the Court holds that knowledge of the right to refuse is only one of many factors that goes into an analysis of voluntary consent. What does "voluntary" mean in this context? More generally, why would a suspect ever voluntarily consent to a search that the suspect knows will reveal incriminating evidence? If you were a judge deciding a suppression motion, would you assume such consent was probably voluntary, or would you assume the opposite?

2. Both the majority and the dissent in *Schneckloth* seem to think that warnings would have a large effect on suspects' behavior. The truth may be otherwise. Professor Nadler has examined the Court's consent doctrine in light of evidence about the psychology of compliance and consent. She points out that "empirical studies over the last several decades on the social psychology of compliance, conformity, social

influence, and politeness have all converged on a single conclusion: the extent to which people feel free to refuse to comply is extremely limited under situationally induced pressures" of the sort common to many police-citizen encounters. Janice Nadler, No Need to Shout: Bus Sweeps and the Psychology of Coercion, 2002 Sup. Ct. Rev. 153, 155. Consider the following:

> . . . [T]he majority in *Schneckloth* appears to have assumed that if warnings were required, virtually all citizens would refuse to consent to a search.
>
> That assumption turns out to be mistaken, at least in instances where it has been explicitly examined. A study of all Ohio highway stops conducted between 1995 and 1997 found no decrease in consent rates after police were required to advise motorists of their right to refuse to cooperate with a request for consent to search. In fact, the same number of citizens consent with the warnings as without the warnings. Apparently, people are unaffected by the warnings because they do not believe them — they feel that they will be searched regardless of whether or not they consent. Why would people who are told by police that they have a right to refuse to consent to search persist in believing that they have no choice and will be searched anyway? Many . . . factors . . . come into play here: we comply with the police not because we make a deliberate conscious choice to respond in a particular way, but rather because we mindlessly respond in a manner consistent with social roles; just as we do not hear "May I see your license and registration please?" as a genuine question, we do not hear "You have the right to refuse to consent" as a genuine option; under time pressure we respond to requests of authorities in the same way we usually do, by automatically complying. In this way, the experimental research suggests generally what the survey of motorists finds explicitly: people who are targeted for a search by police and informed that they have a right to refuse nonetheless feel intense pressure to comply and feel that refusal is not a genuine option.
>
> [T]here is no reason to think that police advising citizens that they have a right not to cooperate with their request for consent to search will significantly reduce coercion experienced by citizens in this situation. In this sense the issue of police warnings in consensual search situations . . . is something of a red herring and should be put aside. This issue simply diverts attention away from the real question — whether citizens who are approached and searched in these situations have consented freely or perceived themselves as having no choice.

Id., at 204-206.

3. Note that despite the Court's assurance that the voluntariness of consent to search is "carefully scrutinized" by courts in light of subjective factors that would draw it into question, there is scant evidence that such searching inquiries commonly take place. Professor Cole cites one study based on a review of all cases involving consent searches decided by the United States Court of Appeals for the District of Columbia Circuit from January 1, 1989, to April 15, 1995. In each case in which the validity of consent was challenged, the court found the consent voluntary. "In most of the cases, the courts did not even discuss the subjective factors that the Supreme Court . . . said would be relevant in determining voluntariness." David Cole, No Equal Justice 32 (1999). Professor Cole goes on to charge that the voluntariness doctrine enunciated in *Schneckloth* in practice creates a race- and class-based double standard:

> Because a consent search requires no objective individualized suspicion, it is more likely to be directed at poor young black men than wealthy white elderly women. In

addition, those who are white and wealthy are more likely to know their rights and to feel secure in asserting them.

Id., at 31. Professor Thomas has argued, further, that "[t]he consent search doctrine is the handmaiden of racial profiling. . . . If police are routinely rewarded with consent, they have little incentive to develop individualized probable cause. . . ." George C. Thomas III, Terrorism, Race and a New Approach to Consent Searches, 73 Miss. L.J. 525, 542 (2003). Does this argue for rethinking the Court's approach?

4. Why is a warrantless and suspicionless consent search consistent with the Fourth Amendment — even assuming that consent is "voluntary"? Granted, constitutional rights can generally be waived. But as the Court points out in *Schneckloth*, the waiver approach cannot explain "third-party consent" doctrine. This doctrine permits police to search based on the consent of someone other than the suspect, provided that this third person has common authority over the area searched. In *Schneckloth*, the Court treated the third-party cases as "assumption of risk" cases in which the defendant against whom evidence is proffered had assumed the risk that police would be permitted to search areas in which he had granted joint access and control to another. See also United States v. Matlock, 415 U.S. 164 (1974) (where people mutually use property and have joint access or control for most purposes, "it is reasonable to recognize that any of the co-inhabitants has the right to permit the inspection in his own right and that the others have assumed the risk that one of their number might permit the common area to be searched"). In Illinois v. Rodriguez, 497 U.S. 177 (1990), however, the Court further extended the doctrine — to intrusions based on the consent of a third party whom the police *reasonably believed* to possess common authority over the premises, even when no such authority existed.

Justice Scalia, writing for the *Rodriguez* majority, addressed both the third-party consent doctrine and the underlying rationale for consent searches:

> On July 26, 1985, police were summoned to the residence of Dorothy Jackson on South Wolcott in Chicago. They were met by Ms. Jackson's daughter, Gail Fischer, who showed signs of a severe beating. She told the officers that she had been assaulted by respondent Edward Rodriguez earlier that day in an apartment on South California Avenue. Fischer stated that Rodriguez was then asleep in the apartment, and she consented to travel there with the police in order to unlock the door with her key so that officers could enter and arrest him. During this conversation, Fischer several times referred to the apartment on South California as "our" apartment, and said that she had clothes and furniture there. It is unclear whether she indicated that she currently lived at the apartment, or only that she used to live there. . . .
>
> [When the officers and Fischer arrived at the apartment, she unlocked the door and gave the officers permission to enter. Police arrested Rodriguez and also seized narcotics in plain view. The state courts held that the narcotics were not admissible against Rodriguez because Fisher, who in fact was not currently residing in the apartment, did not have authority to consent to the search. They also ruled as a matter of law that the officers' reasonable belief in Fisher's authority would not validate the search.]
>
>   . . . What [the defendant] is assured by the Fourth Amendment . . . is not that no government search of his house will occur unless he consents; but that no such search will occur that is "unreasonable." There are various elements, of course, that can make a search of a person's house "reasonable" — one of which is the consent of the person or his cotenant. The essence of respondent's argument is that we should impose upon

this element a requirement that we have not imposed upon other elements that regularly compel government officers to exercise judgment regarding the facts: namely, the requirement that their judgment be not only responsible but correct.

The fundamental objective that alone validates all unconsented government searches is, of course, the seizure of persons who have committed or are about to commit crimes, or of evidence related to crimes. But "reasonableness," with respect to this necessary element, does not demand that the government be factually correct in its assessment that that is what a search will produce. Warrants need only be supported by "probable cause." . . . If a magistrate, based upon seemingly reliable but factually inaccurate information, issues a warrant for the search of a house in which the sought-after felon is not present, has never been present, and was never likely to have been present, the owner of that house suffers one of the inconveniences we all expose ourselves to as the cost of living in a safe society; he does not suffer a violation of the Fourth Amendment. . . .

[I]n order to satisfy the "reasonableness" requirement of the Fourth Amendment, what is generally demanded of the many factual determinations that must regularly be made by agents of the government — whether the magistrate issuing a warrant, the police officer executing a warrant, or the police officer conducting a search or seizure under one of the exceptions to the warrant requirement — is not that they always be correct, but that they always be reasonable. . . .

We see no reason to depart from this general rule with respect to facts bearing upon the authority to consent to a search. . . .

497 U.S., at 179-186.

5. Do you find Justice Scalia's perspective on third-party consents persuasive? In the following case the Court took up the question whether one occupant can consent to the search of a home as against the objection of another occupant who is present at the scene and expressly refuses to consent. Is it reasonable in *these* circumstances for police to proceed?

GEORGIA v. RANDOLPH

Certiorari to the Georgia Supreme Court
547 U.S. 103 (2006)

JUSTICE SOUTER delivered the opinion of the Court.

The Fourth Amendment recognizes a valid warrantless entry and search of premises when police obtain the voluntary consent of an occupant who shares, or is reasonably believed to share, authority over the area in common with a co-occupant who later objects to the use of evidence so obtained. Illinois v. Rodriguez, 497 U.S. 177 (1990); United States v. Matlock, 415 U.S. 164 (1974). The question here is whether such an evidentiary seizure is likewise lawful with the permission of one occupant when the other, who later seeks to suppress the evidence, is present at the scene and expressly refuses to consent. We hold that, in the circumstances here at issue, a physically present co-occupant's stated refusal to permit entry prevails, rendering the warrantless search unreasonable and invalid as to him.

I

Respondent Scott Randolph and his wife, Janet, separated in late May 2001, when she left the marital residence in Americus, Georgia, and went to stay with her parents in Canada, taking their son and some belongings. In July, she returned to the Americus house with the child. . . .

On the morning of July 6, she complained to the police that after a domestic dispute her husband took their son away, and when officers reached the house she told them that her husband was a cocaine user whose habit had caused financial troubles. She mentioned the marital problems and said that she and their son had only recently returned after a stay of several weeks with her parents. Shortly after the police arrived, Scott Randolph returned and explained that he had removed the child to a neighbor's house out of concern that his wife might take the boy out of the country again; he denied cocaine use, and countered that it was in fact his wife who abused drugs and alcohol.

One of the officers, Sergeant Murray, went with Janet Randolph to reclaim the child, and when they returned she not only renewed her complaints about her husband's drug use, but also volunteered that there were "items of drug evidence" in the house. Sergeant Murray asked Scott Randolph for permission to search the house, which he unequivocally refused.

The sergeant turned to Janet Randolph for consent to search, which she readily gave. She led the officer upstairs to a bedroom that she identified as Scott's, where the sergeant noticed a section of a drinking straw with a powdery residue he suspected was cocaine. He then left the house to get an evidence bag from his car and to call the district attorney's office, which instructed him to stop the search and apply for a warrant. When Sergeant Murray returned to the house, Janet Randolph withdrew her consent. The police took the straw to the police station, along with the Randolphs. After getting a search warrant, they returned to the house and seized further evidence of drug use, on the basis of which Scott Randolph was indicted for possession of cocaine.

He moved to suppress the evidence . . . . The trial court denied the motion, ruling that Janet Randolph had common authority to consent to the search. The Court of Appeals of Georgia reversed, and was itself sustained by the State Supreme Court . . . .

II

To the Fourth Amendment rule ordinarily prohibiting the warrantless entry of a person's house as unreasonable per se, one "jealously and carefully drawn" exception, Jones v. United States, 357 U.S. 493, 499 (1958), recognizes the validity of searches with the voluntary consent of an individual possessing authority, *Rodriguez*, 497 U.S., at 181. . . . [T]he exception for consent extends even to entries and searches with the permission of a co-occupant whom the police reasonably, but erroneously, believe to possess shared authority as an occupant, *Rodriguez*, supra, at 186. None of our co-occupant consent-to-search cases, however, has presented the further fact of a second occupant physically present and refusing permission to search, and later moving to suppress evidence so obtained.

The defendant in [*Matlock*] was arrested in the yard of a house where he lived with a Mrs. Graff and several of her relatives, and was detained in a squad car parked nearby. When the police went to the door, Mrs. Graff admitted them and consented to a search of the house. In resolving the defendant's objection to use of the evidence taken in the warrantless search, we said that "the consent of one who possesses common authority over premises or effects is valid as against the absent, nonconsenting person with whom that authority is shared." Id., at 170. Consistent with our prior understanding that Fourth Amendment rights are not limited by the law of property, cf. Katz v. United States, 389 U.S. 347, 352-353 (1967), we explained that the third party's "common authority" is not synonymous with a technical property interest. . . .

The constant element in assessing Fourth Amendment reasonableness in the consent cases, then, is the great significance given to widely shared social expectations, which are naturally enough influenced by the law of property, but not controlled by its rules. *Matlock* accordingly not only holds that a solitary co-inhabitant may sometimes consent to a search of shared premises, but stands for the proposition that the reasonableness of such a search is in significant part a function of commonly held understanding about the authority that co-inhabitants may exercise in ways that affect each other's interests. . . .

Although we have not dealt directly with the reasonableness of police entry in reliance on consent by one occupant subject to immediate challenge by another, we took a step toward the issue in an earlier case dealing with the Fourth Amendment rights of a social guest arrested at premises the police entered without a warrant or the benefit of any exception to the warrant requirement. Minnesota v. Olson, 495 U.S. 91 (1990), held that overnight houseguests have a legitimate expectation of privacy in their temporary quarters because "it is unlikely that [the host] will admit someone who wants to see or meet with the guest over the objection of the guest," id., at 99. If that customary expectation of courtesy or deference is a foundation of Fourth Amendment rights of a houseguest, it presumably should follow that an inhabitant of shared premises may claim at least as much, and it turns out that the co-inhabitant naturally has an even stronger claim.

To begin with, it is fair to say that a caller standing at the door of shared premises would have no confidence that one occupant's invitation was a sufficiently good reason to enter when a fellow tenant stood there saying, "stay out." Without some very good reason, no sensible person would go inside under those conditions. . . .

The visitor's reticence . . . would show not timidity but a realization that when people living together disagree over the use of their common quarters, a resolution must come through voluntary accommodation, not by appeals to authority. . . .

Since the co-tenant wishing to open the door to a third party has no recognized authority in law or social practice to prevail over a present and objecting co-tenant, his disputed invitation, without more, gives a police officer no better claim to reasonableness in entering than the officer would have in the absence of any consent at all. . . .

[T]his case has no bearing on the capacity of the police to protect domestic victims. . . . No question has been raised, or reasonably could be, about the authority of the police to enter a dwelling to protect a resident from domestic violence; so long as they have good reason to believe such a threat exists, it would be silly to suggest that the police would commit a tort by entering, say, to give a complaining tenant the opportunity to collect belongings and get out safely, or to determine whether violence (or threat of violence) has just occurred or is about to (or soon will) occur, however much a spouse or other co-tenant objected. . . . Thus, the question whether the police might lawfully enter over objection in order to provide any protection that might be reasonable is easily answered yes. The undoubted right of the police to enter in order to protect a victim, however, has nothing to do with the question in this case, whether a search with the consent of one co-tenant is good against another, standing at the door and expressly refusing consent. . . .

The dissent's red herring aside, we know, of course, that alternatives to disputed consent will not always open the door to search for evidence that the police suspect is inside. The consenting tenant may simply not disclose enough information, or information factual enough, to add up to a showing of probable cause, and there may be no exigency to justify fast action. But nothing in social custom or its reflection in private law argues for placing a higher value on delving into private premises to search for evidence in the face of disputed consent, than on requiring clear justification before the government searches private living quarters over a resident's objection. We therefore hold that a warrantless search of a shared dwelling for evidence over the express refusal of consent by a physically present resident cannot be justified as reasonable as to him on the basis of consent given to the police by another resident. . . .

. . . Although the *Matlock* defendant was not present with the opportunity to object, he was in a squad car not far away; the *Rodriguez* defendant was actually asleep in the apartment, and the police might have roused him with a knock on the door before they entered with only the consent of an apparent co-tenant. If those cases are not to be undercut by today's holding, we have to admit that we are drawing a fine line; if a potential defendant with self-interest in objecting is in fact at the door and objects, the co-tenant's permission does not suffice for a reasonable search, whereas the potential objector, nearby but not invited to take part in the threshold colloquy, loses out.

This is the line we draw, and we think the formalism is justified. So long as there is no evidence that the police have removed the potentially objecting tenant from the entrance for the sake of avoiding a possible objection, there is practical value in the simple clarity of complementary rules, one recognizing the co-tenant's permission when there is no fellow occupant on hand, the other according dispositive weight to the fellow occupant's contrary indication when he expresses it. . . .

. . . Scott Randolph's refusal is clear, and nothing in the record justifies the search on grounds independent of Janet Randolph's consent. . . . The judgment of the Supreme Court of Georgia is therefore affirmed.

JUSTICE ALITO took no part in the consideration or decision of this case.

[Justice Stevens' and Justice Breyer's concurring opinions are omitted.]

CHIEF JUSTICE ROBERTS, with whom JUSTICE SCALIA joins, dissenting.

. . . The correct approach to the question presented is clearly mapped out in our precedents: The Fourth Amendment protects privacy. If an individual shares information, papers, *or places* with another, he assumes the risk that the other person will in turn share access to that information or those papers *or places* with the government. And just as an individual who has shared illegal plans or incriminating documents with another cannot interpose an objection when that other person turns the information over to the government, just because the individual happens to be present at the time, so too someone who shares a place with another cannot interpose an objection when that person decides to grant access to the police, simply because the objecting individual happens to be present. . . .

. . . One element that can make a warrantless government search of a home "reasonable" is voluntary consent. [United States v. Matlock, 415 U.S. 164, 184 (1974)]. Proof of voluntary consent "is not limited to proof that consent was given by the defendant," but the government "may show that permission to search was obtained from a third party who possessed common authority over or other sufficient relationship to the premises." *Matlock*, supra, at 171. Today's opinion creates an exception to this otherwise clear rule . . . .

This exception is based on what the majority describes as "widely shared social expectations" that "when people living together disagree over the use of their common quarters, a resolution must come through voluntary accommodation." But this fundamental predicate to the majority's analysis gets us nowhere: Does the objecting cotenant accede to the consenting cotenant's wishes, or the other way around? The majority's assumption about voluntary accommodation simply leads to the common stalemate of two gentlemen insisting that the other enter a room first.

Nevertheless, the majority is confident in assuming—confident enough to incorporate its assumption into the Constitution—that an invited social guest who arrives at the door of a shared residence, and is greeted by a disagreeable co-occupant shouting "stay out," would simply go away. . . .

The fact is that a wide variety of differing social situations can readily be imagined, giving rise to quite different social expectations. A relative or good friend of one of two feuding roommates might well enter the apartment over the objection of the other roommate. . . . A guest who came to celebrate an occupant's birthday, or one who had traveled some distance for a particular reason, might not readily turn away simply because of a roommate's objection. The nature of the place itself is . . . pertinent: Invitees may react one way if the feuding roommates share one room, differently if there are common areas from which the objecting roommate could readily be expected to absent himself. Altering the numbers might well change the social expectations: Invitees might enter if two of three co-occupants encourage them to do so, over one dissenter.

The possible scenarios are limitless, and slight variations in the fact pattern yield vastly different expectations about whether the invitee might be expected to enter or to go away. Such shifting expectations are not a promising foundation on which to ground a constitutional rule . . . .

And in fact the Court has not looked to such expectations to decide questions of consent under the Fourth Amendment, but only to determine when a search has occurred and whether a particular person has standing to object to a search. . . .

The majority suggests that "widely shared social expectations" are a "constant element in assessing Fourth Amendment reasonableness," but that is not the case; the Fourth Amendment precedents the majority cites refer instead to a "legitimate expectation of *privacy*." Whatever social expectation the majority seeks to protect, it is not one of privacy. The very predicate giving rise to the question in cases of shared information, papers, containers, or places is that privacy has been shared with another. Our common social expectations may well be that the other person will not, in turn, share what we have shared with them with another—including the police—but that is the risk we take in sharing . . . .

Our cases reflect this understanding. In United States v. White, [401 U.S. 745 (1971)], we held that one party to a conversation can consent to government eavesdropping, and statements made by the other party will be admissible at trial. 401 U.S., at 752. This rule is based on privacy: "Inescapably, one contemplating illegal activities must realize and risk that his companions may be reporting to the police . . . . [I]f he has no doubts, or allays them, or risks what doubt he has, the risk is his." Ibid.

The Court has applied this same analysis to objects and places as well. In Frazier v. Cupp, 394 U.S. 731 (1969), a duffel bag "was being used jointly" by two cousins. Id., at 740. The Court held that the consent of one was effective to result in the seizure of evidence used against both: "[I]n allowing [his cousin] to use the bag and in leaving it in his house, [the defendant] must be taken to have assumed the risk that [his cousin] would allow someone else to look inside." Ibid. . . .

In Coolidge v. New Hampshire, 403 U.S. 443 (1971), Mrs. Coolidge retrieved four of her husband's guns and the clothes he was wearing the previous night and handed them over to police. We held that these items were properly admitted at trial because "when Mrs. Coolidge of her own accord produced the guns and clothes for inspection, . . . it was not incumbent on the police to stop her or avert their eyes." Id., at 489.

Even in our most private relationships, our observable actions and possessions are private at the discretion of those around us. A husband can request that his wife not tell a jury about contraband that she observed in their home or illegal activity to which she bore witness, but it is she who decides whether to invoke the testimonial marital privilege. Trammel v. United States, 445 U.S. 40, 53 (1980). . . .

There is no basis for evaluating physical searches of shared space in a manner different from how we evaluated the privacy interests in the foregoing cases, and in fact the Court has proceeded along the same lines in considering such searches. In *Matlock*, police arrested the defendant in the front yard of a house and placed him in a squad car, and then obtained permission from Mrs. Graff to search a shared bedroom for evidence of Matlock's bank robbery. 415 U.S., at 166. Police certainly could have assumed that Matlock would have objected were he consulted as he sat handcuffed in the squad car outside. And in *Rodriguez*, where Miss Fischer offered to facilitate the arrest of her sleeping boyfriend by admitting police into an apartment she apparently shared with him, 497 U.S., at 179, police might have noted that this entry was undoubtedly contrary to Rodriguez's social expectations. Yet both of these searches were reasonable under the Fourth Amendment because Mrs. Graff had authority, and Miss Fischer apparent authority, to admit others into areas over which they exercised control, despite the almost certain wishes of their present co-occupants. . . .

The majority states its rule as follows: "[A] warrantless search of a shared dwelling for evidence over the express refusal of consent by a physically present resident cannot be justified as reasonable as to him on the basis of consent given to the police by another resident."

Just as the source of the majority's rule is not privacy, so too the interest it protects cannot reasonably be described as such. That interest is not protected if a co-owner happens to be absent when the police arrive, in the backyard gardening, asleep in the next room, or listening to music through earphones so that only his co-occupant hears the knock on the door. That the rule is so random in its application confirms that it bears no real relation to the privacy protected by the Fourth

Amendment. . . . We should not embrace a rule at the outset that its *sponsors* appreciate will result in drawing fine, formalistic lines. . . .

While the majority's rule protects something random, its consequences are particularly severe. The question presented often arises when innocent cotenants seek to disassociate or protect themselves from ongoing criminal activity. See, e.g., United States v. Hendrix, 595 F.2d 883, 884 (CADC 1979) (wife asked police "to get her baby and take [a] sawed-off shotgun out of her house"); People v. Cosme, 48 N.Y.2d 286, 288-289, 293 (1979) (woman asked police to remove cocaine and a gun from a shared closet). Under the majority's rule, there will be many cases in which a consenting co-occupant's wish to have the police enter is overridden by an objection from another present co-occupant. What does the majority imagine will happen, in a case in which the consenting co-occupant is concerned about the other's criminal activity, once the door clicks shut? . . .

Perhaps the most serious consequence of the majority's rule is its operation in domestic abuse situations, a context in which the present question often arises. . . .

The majority acknowledges these concerns, but dismisses them on the ground that its rule can be expected to give rise to exigent situations, and police can then rely on an exigent circumstances exception to justify entry. This is a strange way to justify a rule, and the fact that alternative justifications for entry might arise does not show that entry pursuant to consent is unreasonable. In addition, it is far from clear that an exception for emergency entries suffices to protect the safety of occupants in domestic disputes. See, e.g., United States v. Davis, 290 F.3d 1239, 1240-1241 (CA10 2002) (finding no exigent circumstances justifying entry when police responded to a report of domestic abuse, officers heard no noise upon arrival, defendant told officers that his wife was out of town, and wife then appeared at the door seemingly unharmed but resisted husband's efforts to close the door).

Rather than give effect to a consenting spouse's authority to permit entry into her house to avoid such situations, the majority again alters established Fourth Amendment rules to defend giving veto power to the objecting spouse. In response to the concern that police might be turned away under its rule before entry can be justified based on exigency, the majority creates a new rule: A "good reason" to enter, coupled with one occupant's consent, will ensure that a police officer is "lawfully in the premises." As support for this "consent plus a good reason" rule, the majority cites a treatise, which itself refers only to emergency entries. For the sake of defending what it concedes are fine, formalistic lines, the majority spins out an entirely new framework for analyzing exigent circumstances. Police may now enter with a "good reason" to believe that "violence (or threat of violence) has just occurred or is about to (or soon will) occur." And apparently a key factor allowing entry with a "good reason" short of exigency is the very consent of one co-occupant the majority finds so inadequate in the first place. . . .

* * *

Our third-party consent cases have recognized that a person who shares common areas with others "assume[s] the risk that one of their number might permit the common area to be searched." *Matlock*, 415 U.S., at 171, n. 7. The majority reminds us, in high tones, that a man's home is his castle, but even under the majority's rule, it is not his castle if he happens to be absent, asleep in the keep, or otherwise engaged when the constable arrives at the gate. Then it is his co-owner's castle. And, of course, it is not his castle if he wants to consent to entry, but his co-owner objects.

Rather than constitutionalize such an arbitrary rule, we should acknowledge that a decision to share a private place, like a decision to share a secret or a confidential document, necessarily entails the risk that those with whom we share may in turn choose to share — for their own protection or for other reasons — with the police.

I respectfully dissent.

[The dissenting opinions of Justice Scalia and Justice Thomas are omitted.]

NOTES AND QUESTIONS

1. Don't the dissenters have a point here? What interest is served by safeguarding the right of a home's occupant to override any consent to search given by his co-occupant — if, but only if, the objecting party happens to be at the door when the search is to take place? Is there any principled way to square the result in *Randolph* with the Court's decision in United States v. Matlock, 415 U.S. 164 (1974)? Suppose the two cases had arisen in the opposite order: Imagine that the Court had decided in *Randolph* that the search target's objection was decisive, notwithstanding his spouse's consent — and some years later, *Matlock* arose, forcing the Court to decide whether police could evade *Randolph* by taking the search target to a nearby police car and only *then* asking the consent of another occupant of the target's house. Could one persuasively argue that the police conduct in *Matlock* was constitutionally reasonable, even in the absence of affirmative evidence that the officers were seeking to avoid an objection?

If the answer is no — if these two decisions are contradictory — why didn't the Court simply overrule *Matlock*?

2. What do you think of the dissent's argument that the Court's decision will seriously complicate police responses to domestic violence? Police are often called to a home by one or more of the home's occupants, usually in circumstances that lead some members of the household to fear violence from other members of the household. Naturally, in such circumstances, some residents want to invite the police inside the home, and other residents object to any police entry. How are police officers supposed to respond? Might *Randolph* lead officers to underrate that threat?

3. Are you persuaded by the majority's evaluation of our widely shared social expectations regarding settings in which roommates, spouses, or family members disagree about admitting a visitor? Or have you had the experience of helping one feuding roommate pack up and move out over the objection of the other? Whether you agree with the majority's analysis regarding shared social expectations, are you persuaded that this is the right way to define the contours of consent search doctrine?

4. Chief Justice Roberts argues that search targets assume the risk that those who share their homes may allow police to enter those homes when the targets would prefer that they chose differently. Is *that* the right way to define the contours of consent search doctrine? The defendant in United States v. White, 401 U.S. 745 (1971), assumed the risk that the informant in that case was an informant, just as the defendant in California v. Greenwood, 486 U.S. 35 (1988), assumed the risk that sanitation workers would turn over his garbage to the police. Are those risks more readily assumable? Is *Randolph* consistent with *White* and *Greenwood*?

5. Finally, consider Florida v. Jimeno, 500 U.S. 248 (1991), the leading case on the permissible scope of a consent search. In that case, Officer Frank Trujillo over-heard a telephone conversation in which Jimeno appeared to be arranging a drug transaction. Suspecting that Jimeno was in possession of narcotics, he began to fol-low Jimeno's car. When Jimeno failed to stop at a red light, Officer Trujillo pulled him over and obtained his consent to search the car. The officer discovered cocaine in a folded brown paper bag located on the floorboard. The Florida Supreme Court held that the cocaine was properly suppressed on the ground that the consent did not extend to the search of the paper bag. The Supreme Court, in an opinion by Chief Justice Rehnquist, disagreed:

> . . . The Fourth Amendment is satisfied when, under the circumstances, it is objectively reasonable for the officer to believe that the scope of the suspect's consent permitted him to open a particular container within the automobile. . . .
>
> . . . The standard for measuring the scope of a suspect's consent under the Fourth Amendment is that of "objective" reasonableness — what would the typical reasonable person have understood by the exchange between the officer and the suspect? The question before us, then, is whether it is reasonable for an officer to consider a suspect's general consent to a search of his car to include consent to examine a paper bag lying on the floor of the car. We think that it is.
>
> . . . Trujillo had informed Jimeno that he believed Jimeno was carrying narcotics, and that he would be looking for narcotics in the car. We think that it was objectively reasonable for the police to conclude that the general consent to search respondent's car included consent to search containers within the car which might bear drugs. . . .
>
> The facts of this case are . . . different from those in State v. Wells, [539 So. 2d 464 (Fla. 1989)], on which the Supreme Court of Florida relied in affirming the suppres-sion order in this case. There the Supreme Court of Florida held that consent to search the trunk of a car did not include authorization to pry open a locked briefcase found inside the trunk. It is very likely unreasonable to think that a suspect, by consenting to the search of his trunk, has agreed to the breaking open of a locked briefcase within the trunk, but it is otherwise with respect to a closed paper bag.
>
> Respondent argues . . . , that if the police wish to search closed containers within a car they must separately request permission to search each container. But we see no basis for adding this sort of superstructure to the Fourth Amendment's basic test of objective reasonableness. A suspect may of course delimit as he chooses the scope of the search to which he consents. But if his consent would reasonably be understood to extend to a particular container, the Fourth Amendment provides no grounds for requiring a more explicit authorization.

500 U.S., at 249, 251-252. Isn't *Jimeno* something of a reprise on the container search issue that *Acevedo*, see page 478, supra, supposedly put to rest — at least for containers in automobiles? The *Jimeno* Court might have considered a bright-line rule for the consent search of an automobile similar to the one it adopted in *Acevedo* — authority to search an automobile includes the authority to search con-tainers. To the extent that the Court in *Jimeno* declined to offer police such a rule, is it more appropriate in this context to leave them to act at their peril?

F. The Scope of the Exclusionary Rule

1. The "Good Faith" Exception

UNITED STATES v. LEON

Certiorari to the United States Court of Appeals for the Ninth Circuit
468 U.S. 897 (1984)

JUSTICE WHITE delivered the opinion of the Court.

This case presents the question whether the Fourth Amendment exclusionary rule should be modified so as not to bar the use in the prosecution's case in chief of evidence obtained by officers acting in reasonable reliance on a search warrant. . . .

In August 1981, a confidential informant of unproven reliability informed an officer of the Burbank Police Department that two persons known to him as "Armando" and "Patsy" were selling large quantities of cocaine and methaqualone from their residence at 620 Price Drive in Burbank, Cal. The informant also indicated that he had witnessed a sale of methaqualone by "Patsy" at the residence approximately five months earlier and had observed at that time a shoebox containing a large amount of cash that belonged to "Patsy." He further declared that "Armando" and "Patsy" generally kept only small quantities of drugs at their residence and stored the remainder at another location in Burbank.

On the basis of this information, the Burbank police initiated an extensive investigation. . . . Cars parked at the Price Drive residence were determined to belong to respondents Armando Sanchez, who had previously been arrested for possession of marihuana, and Patsy Stewart, who had no criminal record. During the course of the investigation, officers observed an automobile belonging to respondent Ricardo Del Castillo, who had previously been arrested for possession of 50 pounds of marihuana, arrive at the Price Drive residence. The driver of that car entered the house, exited shortly thereafter carrying a small paper sack, and drove away. A check of Del Castillo's probation records led the officers to respondent Alberto Leon, whose telephone number Del Castillo had listed as his employer's. Leon had been arrested in 1980 on drug charges, and a companion had informed the police at that time that Leon was heavily involved in the importation of drugs into this country. Before the current investigation began, the Burbank officers had learned that an informant had told a Glendale police officer that Leon stored a large quantity of methaqualone at his residence in Glendale. During the course of this investigation, the Burbank officers learned that Leon was living at 716 South Sunset Canyon in Burbank.

Subsequently, the officers observed several persons, at least one of whom had prior drug involvement, arriving at the Price Drive residence and leaving with small packages [and] observed a variety of other material activity at the two residences. . . . Based on these and other observations summarized in the affidavit, Officer Cyril Rombach of the Burbank Police Department, an experienced and well-trained narcotics investigator, prepared an application for a warrant to search 620 Price Drive [and] 716 South Sunset Canyon, . . . and automobiles registered to each of the respondents for an extensive list of items believed to be related to respondents' drug-trafficking activities. Officer Rombach's extensive application was reviewed by several Deputy District Attorneys.

A facially valid search warrant was issued in September 1981 by a State Superior Court Judge. The ensuing searches produced large quantities of drugs at the . . . Sunset Canyon [address] and a small quantity at the Price Drive residence. Other evidence was discovered at each of the residences and in Stewart's and Del Castillo's automobiles. Respondents were indicted by a grand jury in the District Court for the Central District of California and charged with conspiracy to possess and distribute cocaine and a variety of substantive counts.

The respondents then filed motions to suppress the evidence seized pursuant to the warrant. The District Court held an evidentiary hearing and, while recognizing that the case was a close one, granted the motions to suppress in part. It concluded that the affidavit was insufficient to establish probable cause, but did not suppress all of the evidence as to all of the respondents because none of the respondents had standing to challenge all of the searches. In response to a request from the Government, the court made clear that Officer Rombach had acted in good faith. . . .

[A] divided panel of the Court of Appeals for the Ninth Circuit affirmed. . . . The Government's petition for certiorari expressly declined to seek review of the lower courts' determinations that the search warrant was unsupported by probable cause and presented only the question "[whether] the Fourth Amendment exclusionary rule should be modified so as not to bar the admission of evidence seized in reasonable, good-faith reliance on a search warrant that is subsequently held to be defective." We granted certiorari to consider the propriety of such a modification. Although it undoubtedly is within our power to consider the question whether probable cause existed under the "totality of the circumstances" test announced last Term in Illinois v. Gates, 462 U.S. 213 (1983), that question has not been briefed or argued; and it is also within our authority, which we choose to exercise, to take the case as it comes to us, accepting the Court of Appeals' conclusion that probable cause was lacking under the prevailing legal standards.

We have concluded that . . . the exclusionary rule can be modified somewhat without jeopardizing its ability to perform its intended functions. Accordingly, we reverse the judgment of the Court of Appeals. . . .

The Fourth Amendment contains no provision expressly precluding the use of evidence obtained in violation of its commands, and an examination of its origin and purposes makes clear that the use of fruits of a past unlawful search or seizure "[works] no new Fourth Amendment wrong." United States v. Calandra, 414 U.S. 338, 354 (1974). The wrong condemned by the Amendment is "fully accomplished" by the unlawful search or seizure itself, ibid., and the exclusionary rule is neither intended nor able to "cure the invasion of the defendant's rights which he has already suffered." Stone v. Powell, [428 U.S. 465,] 540 [(1976)] (White, J., dissenting). The rule thus operates as "a judicially created remedy designed to safeguard Fourth Amendment rights generally through its deterrent effect, rather than a personal constitutional right of the party aggrieved." United States v. Calandra, supra, at 348.

Whether the exclusionary sanction is appropriately imposed in a particular case, our decisions make clear, is "an issue separate from the question whether the Fourth Amendment rights of the party seeking to invoke the rule were violated by police conduct." Illinois v. Gates, supra, at 223. Only the former question is currently before us, and it must be resolved by weighing the costs and benefits of preventing the use in the prosecution's case in chief of inherently trustworthy tangible evidence obtained in reliance on a search warrant issued by a detached and neutral magistrate that ultimately is found to be defective.

The substantial social costs exacted by the exclusionary rule for the vindication of Fourth Amendment rights have long been a source of concern. "Our cases have consistently recognized that unbending application of the exclusionary sanction to enforce ideals of governmental rectitude would impede unacceptably the truth-finding functions of judge and jury." United States v. Payner, 447 U.S. 727, 734 (1980). An objectionable collateral consequence of this interference with the criminal justice system's truth-finding function is that some guilty defendants may go free or receive reduced sentences as a result of favorable plea bargains.[6] Particularly when law enforcement officers have acted in objective good faith or their transgressions have been minor, the magnitude of the benefit conferred on such guilty defendants offends basic concepts of the criminal justice system . . . . Accordingly, "[as] with any remedial device, the application of the rule has been restricted to those areas where its remedial objectives are thought most efficaciously served." United States v. Calandra, supra, at 348.

Close attention to those remedial objectives has characterized our recent decisions concerning the scope of the Fourth Amendment exclusionary rule. . . . [There follows a discussion of contexts in which the Court has declined to apply the exclusionary rule, including grand jury proceedings, see *Calandra*, supra; habeas corpus litigation, see Stone v. Powell, supra; and civil tax proceedings, see United States v. Janis, 428 U.S. 433 (1976). The opinion then goes on to note the significant limits imposed on the exclusionary rule by standing doctrine and by fruit-of-the-poisonous-tree doctrine.]

As yet, we have not recognized any form of good-faith exception to the Fourth Amendment exclusionary rule. But the balancing approach that has evolved during the years of experience with the rule provides strong support for the modification currently urged upon us. . . .

. . . Reasonable minds frequently may differ on the question whether a particular affidavit establishes probable cause, and we have thus concluded that the preference for warrants is most appropriately effectuated by according "great

6. Researchers have only recently begun to study extensively the effects of the exclusionary rule on the disposition of felony arrests. One study suggests that the rule results in the nonprosecution or nonconviction of between 0.6% and 2.35% of individuals arrested for felonies. Davies, A Hard Look at What We Know (and Still Need to Learn) About the "Costs" of the Exclusionary Rule: The NIJ Study and Other Studies of "Lost" Arrests, 1983 A.B.F. Res. J. 611, 621. The estimates are higher for particular crimes the prosecution of which depends heavily on physical evidence. Thus, the cumulative loss due to nonprosecution or nonconviction of individuals arrested on felony drug charges is probably in the range of 2.8% to 7.1%. Id., at 680. Davies' analysis of California data suggests that screening by police and prosecutors results in the release because of illegal searches or seizures of as many as 1.4% of all felony arrestees, id., at 650, that 0.9% of felony arrestees are released, because of illegal searches or seizures, at the preliminary hearing or after trial, id., at 653, and that roughly 0.05% of all felony arrestees benefit from reversals on appeal because of illegal searches. Id., at 654. See also National Institute of Justice, The Effects of the Exclusionary Rule: A Study in California 1-2 (1982); Nardulli, The Societal Cost of the Exclusionary Rule: An Empirical Assessment, 1983 A.B.F. Res. J. 585, 600. . . .

Many of these researchers have concluded that the impact of the exclusionary rule is insubstantial, but the small percentages with which they deal mask a large absolute number of felons who are released because the cases against them were based in part on illegal searches or seizures. "[Any] rule of evidence that denies the jury access to clearly probative and reliable evidence must bear a heavy burden of justification, and must be carefully limited to the circumstances in which it will pay its way by deterring official unlawfulness." Illinois v. Gates, 462 U.S., at 257-258 (White, J., concurring in judgment). Because we find that the rule can have no substantial deterrent effect in the sorts of situations under consideration in this case, we conclude that it cannot pay its way in those situations.

deference" to a magistrate's determination. Spinelli v. United States, 393 U.S., at 419. See Illinois v. Gates, 462 U.S., at 236. Deference to the magistrate, however, is not boundless. It is clear, first, that the deference accorded to a magistrate's finding of probable cause does not preclude inquiry into the knowing or reckless falsity of the affidavit on which that determination was based. Franks v. Delaware, 438 U.S. 154 (1978). Second, . . . [a] magistrate failing to "manifest that neutrality and detachment demanded of a judicial officer when presented with a warrant application" and who acts instead as "an adjunct law enforcement officer" cannot provide valid authorization for an otherwise unconstitutional search. Lo-Ji Sales, Inc. v. New York, 442 U.S. 319, 326-327 (1979).

Third, reviewing courts will not defer to a warrant based on an affidavit that does not "provide the magistrate with a substantial basis for determining the existence of probable cause." Illinois v. Gates, 462 U.S., at 239. . . . Even if the warrant application was supported by more than a "bare bones" affidavit, a reviewing court may properly conclude that, notwithstanding the deference that magistrates deserve, the warrant was invalid because the magistrate's probable-cause determination reflected an improper analysis of the totality of the circumstances. . . .

Only in the first of these three situations, however, has the Court set forth a rationale for suppressing evidence obtained pursuant to a search warrant; in the other areas, it has simply excluded such evidence without considering whether Fourth Amendment interests will be advanced. To the extent that proponents of exclusion rely on its behavioral effects on judges and magistrates in these areas, their reliance is misplaced. First, the exclusionary rule is designed to deter police misconduct rather than to punish the errors of judges and magistrates. Second, there exists no evidence suggesting that judges and magistrates are inclined to ignore or subvert the Fourth Amendment or that lawlessness among these actors requires application of the extreme sanction of exclusion.

Third, and most important, we discern no basis, and are offered none, for believing that exclusion of evidence seized pursuant to a warrant will have a significant deterrent effect on the issuing judge or magistrate . . . Judges and magistrates are not adjuncts to the law enforcement team; as neutral judicial officers, they have no stake in the outcome of particular criminal prosecutions. The threat of exclusion thus cannot be expected significantly to deter them. . . .

If exclusion of evidence obtained pursuant to a subsequently invalidated warrant is to have any deterrent effect, therefore, it must alter the behavior of individual law enforcement officers or the policies of their departments. One could argue that applying the exclusionary rule in cases where the police failed to demonstrate probable cause in the warrant application deters future inadequate presentations or "magistrate shopping" and thus promotes the ends of the Fourth Amendment. Suppressing evidence obtained pursuant to a technically defective warrant supported by probable cause also might encourage officers to scrutinize more closely the form of the warrant and to point out suspected judicial errors. We find such arguments speculative and conclude that suppression of evidence obtained pursuant to a warrant should be ordered only on a case-by-case basis and only in those unusual cases in which exclusion will further the purposes of the exclusionary rule.

We have frequently questioned whether the exclusionary rule can have any deterrent effect when the offending officers acted in the objectively reasonable belief that their conduct did not violate the Fourth Amendment. "No empirical researcher, proponent or opponent of the rule, has yet been able to establish with any assurance whether the rule has a deterrent effect. . . ." United States v. Janis, 428 U.S., at 452, n. 22. But even assuming that the rule effectively deters some police misconduct and provides incentives for the law enforcement profession as a whole to conduct itself in accord with the Fourth Amendment, it cannot be expected, and should not be applied, to deter objectively reasonable law enforcement activity. . . .

This is particularly true, we believe, when an officer acting with objective good faith has obtained a search warrant from a judge or magistrate and acted within its scope. In most such cases, there is no police illegality and thus nothing to deter. It is the magistrate's responsibility to determine whether the officer's allegations establish probable cause and, if so, to issue a warrant comporting in form with the requirements of the Fourth Amendment. In the ordinary case, an officer cannot be expected to question the magistrate's probable-cause determination or his judgment that the form of the warrant is technically sufficient . . . Penalizing the officer for the magistrate's error, rather than his own, cannot logically contribute to the deterrence of Fourth Amendment violations.

We conclude that the marginal or nonexistent benefits produced by suppressing evidence obtained in objectively reasonable reliance on a subsequently invalidated search warrant cannot justify the substantial costs of exclusion. We do not suggest, however, that exclusion is always inappropriate in cases where an officer has obtained a warrant and abided by its terms. . . . [T]he officer's reliance on the magistrate's probable-cause determination and on the technical sufficiency of the warrant he issues must be objectively reasonable, and it is clear that in some circumstances the officer will have no reasonable grounds for believing that the warrant was properly issued.

Suppression therefore remains an appropriate remedy if the magistrate or judge in issuing a warrant was misled by information in an affidavit that the affiant knew was false or would have known was false except for his reckless disregard of the truth. Franks v. Delaware, 438 U.S. 154 (1978). The exception we recognize today will also not apply in cases where the issuing magistrate wholly abandoned his judicial role in the manner condemned in Lo-Ji Sales, Inc. v. New York, 442 U.S. 319 (1979); in such circumstances, no reasonably well trained officer should rely on the warrant. Nor would an officer manifest objective good faith in relying on a warrant based on an affidavit "so lacking in indicia of probable cause as to render official belief in its existence entirely unreasonable." Brown v. Illinois, 422 U.S., at 610-611 (Powell, J., concurring in part). Finally, depending on the circumstances of the particular case, a warrant may be so facially deficient — i.e., in failing to particularize the place to be searched or the things to be seized — that the executing officers cannot reasonably presume it to be valid.

In so limiting the suppression remedy, we leave untouched the probable-cause standard and the various requirements for a valid warrant. Other objections to the modification of the Fourth Amendment exclusionary rule we consider to be insubstantial. The good-faith exception for searches conducted pursuant to warrants is not intended to signal our unwillingness strictly to enforce the requirements of the Fourth Amendment, and we do not believe that it will have this effect. . . .

Nor are we persuaded that application of a good-faith exception to searches conducted pursuant to warrants will preclude review of the constitutionality of the search or seizure, deny needed guidance from the courts, or freeze Fourth Amendment law in its present state. There is no need for courts to adopt the inflexible practice of always deciding whether the officers' conduct manifested objective good faith before turning to the question whether the Fourth Amendment has been violated. . . .

If the resolution of a particular Fourth Amendment question is necessary to guide future action by law enforcement officers and magistrates, nothing will prevent reviewing courts from deciding that question before turning to the good-faith issue. Indeed, it frequently will be difficult to determine whether the officers acted reasonably without resolving the Fourth Amendment issue. . . .

When the principles we have enunciated today are applied to the facts of this case, it is apparent that the judgment of the Court of Appeals cannot stand. . . . Officer Rombach's application for a warrant clearly was supported by much more than a "bare bones" affidavit. The affidavit related the results of an extensive investigation and, as the opinions of the divided panel of the Court of Appeals make clear, provided evidence sufficient to create disagreement among thoughtful and competent judges as to the existence of probable cause. Under these circumstances, the officers' reliance on the magistrate's determination of probable cause was objectively reasonable, and application of the extreme sanction of exclusion is inappropriate. . . .

JUSTICE BLACKMUN, concurring.

. . . As the Court's opinion in this case makes clear, the Court has narrowed the scope of the exclusionary rule because of an empirical judgment that the rule has little appreciable effect in cases where officers act in objectively reasonable reliance on search warrants. Because I share the view that the exclusionary rule is not a constitutionally compelled corollary of the Fourth Amendment itself, I see no way to avoid making an empirical judgment of this sort, and I am satisfied that the Court has made the correct one on the information before it. . . .

What must be stressed, however, is that any empirical judgment about the effect of the exclusionary rule in a particular class of cases necessarily is a provisional one. By their very nature, the assumptions on which we proceed today cannot be cast in stone. To the contrary, they now will be tested in the real world of state and federal law enforcement, and this Court will attend to the results. If it should emerge from experience that, contrary to our expectations, the good-faith exception to the exclusionary rule results in a material change in police compliance with the Fourth Amendment, we shall have to reconsider what we have undertaken here. . . .

JUSTICE BRENNAN, with whom JUSTICE MARSHALL joins, dissenting.

. . . At bottom, the Court's decision turns on the proposition that the exclusionary rule is merely a "judicially created remedy designed to safeguard Fourth Amendment rights generally through its deterrent effect, rather than a personal constitutional right." This reading of the Amendment implies that its proscriptions are directed solely at those government agents who may actually invade an individual's constitutionally protected privacy. The courts are not subject to any direct constitutional duty to exclude illegally obtained evidence, because the question of the admissibility of such evidence is not addressed by the Amendment. This view of the scope of the Amendment relegates the judiciary to the periphery. Because the only constitutionally cognizable injury has already been "fully accomplished" by the police by the time a case comes before the courts, the Constitution is not itself violated if the judge decides to admit the tainted evidence. Indeed, the most the judge can do is wring his hands and hope that perhaps by excluding such evidence he can deter future transgressions by the police.

Such a reading appears plausible, because, as critics of the exclusionary rule never tire of repeating, the Fourth Amendment makes no express provision for the exclusion of evidence secured in violation of its commands. A short answer to this claim, of course, is that many of the Constitution's most vital imperatives are stated in general terms and the task of giving meaning to these precepts is therefore left to subsequent judicial decisionmaking in the context of concrete cases. The nature of our Constitution, as Chief Justice Marshall long ago explained, "requires that only its great outlines should be marked, its important objects designated, and the minor ingredients which compose those objects be deduced from the nature of the objects themselves." McCulloch v. Maryland, 4 Wheat. 316, 407 (1819).

A more direct answer may be supplied by recognizing that the Amendment, like other provisions of the Bill of Rights, restrains the power of the government as a whole; it does not specify only a particular agency and exempt all others. The judiciary is responsible, no less than the executive, for ensuring that constitutional rights are respected.

When that fact is kept in mind, the role of the courts and their possible involvement in the concerns of the Fourth Amendment comes into sharper focus. Because seizures are executed principally to secure evidence, and because such evidence generally has utility in our legal system only in the context of a trial supervised by a judge, it is apparent that the admission of illegally obtained evidence implicates the same constitutional concerns as the initial seizure of that evidence. Indeed, by admitting unlawfully seized evidence, the judiciary becomes a part of what is in fact a single governmental action prohibited by the terms of the Amendment. Once that connection between the evidence-gathering role of the police and the evidence-admitting function of the courts is acknowledged, the plausibility of the Court's interpretation becomes more suspect. . . . The Amendment therefore must be read to condemn not only the initial unconstitutional invasion of privacy — which is done, after all, for the purpose of securing evidence — but also the subsequent use of any evidence so obtained. . . .

For my part, "[the] right of the people to be secure in their persons, houses, papers, and effects, against unreasonable searches and seizures" comprises a personal right to exclude all evidence secured by means of unreasonable searches and seizures. The right to be free from the initial invasion of privacy and the right of exclusion are coordinate components of the central embracing right to be free from unreasonable searches and seizures. . . .

By remaining within its redoubt of empiricism and by basing the [exclusionary] rule solely on the deterrence rationale, the Court has robbed the rule of legitimacy. A doctrine that is explained as if it were an empirical proposition but for which there is only limited empirical support is both inherently unstable and an easy mark for critics. The extent of this Court's fidelity to Fourth Amendment requirements, however, should not turn on such statistical uncertainties. . . .

Even if I were to accept the Court's general approach to the exclusionary rule, I could not agree with today's result. There is no question that in the hands of the present Court the deterrence rationale has proved to be a powerful tool for confining the scope of the rule. In *Calandra*, for example, the Court concluded that the "speculative and undoubtedly minimal advance in the deterrence of police misconduct," was insufficient to outweigh the "expense of substantially impeding the role of the grand jury." 414 U.S., at 351-352. In Stone v. Powell, the Court found that "the additional contribution, if any, of the consideration of search-and-seizure claims of state prisoners on collateral review is small in relation to the costs." 428 U.S., at 493. In United States v. Janis, 428 U.S. 433 (1976), the Court concluded that "exclusion from federal civil proceedings of evidence unlawfully seized by a state criminal enforcement officer has not been shown to have a sufficient likelihood of deterring the conduct of the state police so that it outweighs the societal costs imposed by the exclusion." Id., at 454. And in an opinion handed down today, the Court finds that the "balance between costs and benefits comes out against applying the exclusionary rule in civil deportation hearings held by the [Immigration and Naturalization Service]." INS v. Lopez-Mendoza, [468 U.S.], at 1050.

Thus, in this bit of judicial stagecraft, while the sets sometimes change, the actors always have the same lines. Given this well-rehearsed pattern, one might have predicted with some assurance how the present case would unfold. First there is the ritual incantation of the "substantial social costs" exacted by the exclusionary rule, followed by the virtually foreordained conclusion that, given the marginal benefits, application of the rule in the circumstances of these cases is not warranted. Upon analysis, however, such a result cannot be justified even on the Court's own terms.

. . . [A]s the Court acknowledges, see ante, at n. 6, recent studies have demonstrated that the "costs" of the exclusionary rule — calculated in terms of dropped prosecutions and lost convictions — are quite low. Contrary to the claims of the rule's critics that exclusion leads to "the release of countless guilty criminals," Bivens v. Six Unknown Federal Narcotics Agents, 403 U.S. 388, 416 (1971) (Burger, C.J., dissenting), these studies have demonstrated that federal and state prosecutors very rarely drop cases because of potential search and seizure problems. For example, a 1979 study prepared at the request of Congress by the General Accounting Office reported that only 0.4% of all cases actually declined for prosecution by federal prosecutors were declined primarily because of illegal search problems. Report of the Comptroller General of the United States, Impact of the Exclusionary Rule on Federal Criminal Prosecutions 14 (1979). If the GAO data are restated as a percentage of all arrests, the study shows that only 0.2% of all felony arrests are declined for prosecution because of potential exclusionary rule problems. See Davies, A Hard Look at What We Know (and Still Need to Learn) About the "Costs" of the Exclusionary Rule: The NIJ Study and Other Studies of "Lost" Arrests, 1983 A.B.F. Res. J. 611, 635.[11] Of course, these data describe only the costs attributable to

11. In a series of recent studies, researchers have attempted to quantify the actual costs of the rule. A recent National Institute of Justice study based on data for the 4-year period 1976-1979 gathered by the California Bureau of Criminal Statistics showed that 4.8% of all cases that were declined for prosecution by California prosecutors were rejected because of illegally seized evidence. National Institute of Justice, Criminal Justice Research Report — The Effects of the Exclusionary Rule: A Study in California 1 (1982). However, if these data are calculated as a percentage of all arrests, they show that only 0.8% of all arrests were rejected for prosecution because of illegally seized evidence. See Davies, 1983 A.B.F. Res. J., at 619.

In another measure of the rule's impact — the number of prosecutions that are dismissed or result in acquittals in cases where evidence has been excluded — the available data again show that the Court's past assessment of the rule's costs has generally been exaggerated. For example, a study based on data from nine midsized counties in Illinois, Michigan, and Pennsylvania reveals that motions to suppress physical evidence were filed in approximately 5% of the 7,500 cases studied, but that such motions were successful in only 0.7% of all these cases. Nardulli, The Societal Cost of the Exclusionary Rule: An Empirical Assessment, 1983 A.B.F. Res. J. 585, 596. The study also shows that only 0.6% of all cases resulted in acquittals because evidence had been excluded. Id., at 600. In the GAO study, suppression motions were filed in 10.5% of all federal criminal cases surveyed, but of the motions filed, approximately 80-90% were denied. GAO Report, at 8, 10. Evidence was actually excluded in only 1.3% of the cases studied, and only

the exclusion of evidence in all cases; the costs due to the exclusion of evidence in the narrower category of cases where police have made objectively reasonable mistakes must necessarily be even smaller. . . .

When the public, as it quite properly has done in the past as well as in the present, demands that those in government increase their efforts to combat crime, it is all too easy for those government officials to seek expedient solutions. In contrast to such costly and difficult measures as building more prisons, improving law enforcement methods, or hiring more prosecutors and judges to relieve the overburdened court systems in the country's metropolitan areas, the relaxation of Fourth Amendment standards seems a tempting, costless means of meeting the public's demand for better law enforcement. In the long run, however, we as a society pay a heavy price for such expediency, because . . . [o]nce lost, such rights are difficult to recover. There is hope, however, that in time this or some later Court will restore these precious freedoms to their rightful place as a primary protection for our citizens against overreaching officialdom.

[Justice Stevens's dissenting opinion is omitted.]

NOTES AND QUESTIONS

1. Reexamine the facts in *Leon*. Did the police have probable cause?

2. When will it be unreasonable for the police to rely on a warrant? Presumably when the magistrate's decision to issue it was obviously wrong. Merely "wrong on further review" is not enough; magistrates must get the benefit of close calls. When will a magistrate's decision to issue a warrant be overturned on appeal, given the deference due to such decisions under *Gates*? Again, presumably when the decision was obviously wrong. So if the warrant will already be upheld under *Gates* on review in close cases, and if *Leon*'s good-faith exception does not cover police who rely on obviously wrong warrants, is *Leon* really necessary? Stated differently, can you describe a case where a reviewing court would find no probable cause under *Gates*, but that the police nonetheless relied on the warrant in good faith?

3. At the time it was decided, *Leon* was thought to matter a lot — for warrant*less* search cases. Imagine, for example, a case in which the permissible scope of a search incident to arrest was at issue. The government argues that, even if the search was not constitutional, it was at least close enough that a reasonable officer could have *believed* it was constitutional. The Court's argument in *Leon* would seem to apply fairly readily to such a case. The result would be a vast expansion in the scope of warrantless searches, as each of the many exceptions to the warrant requirement would be expanded to include close calls. It might not be much of an exaggeration to say that the warrant requirement might disappear altogether.

That is what *Leon*'s critics thought the case would mean. More than a quarter century later, it hasn't happened: The good-faith exception has remained fairly cabined. Why might that be so? Is it a sign that the Court has rethought its position in

---

0.7% of all cases resulted in acquittals or dismissals after evidence was excluded. Id., at 9-11. See Davies, supra, at 660. And in another study based on data from cases during 1978 and 1979 in San Diego and Jacksonville, it was shown that only 1% of all cases resulting in nonconviction were caused by illegal searches. F. Feeney, F. Dill, & A. Weir, Arrests Without Conviction: How Often They Occur and Why (National Institute of Justice 1983).

Leon? Or is it a sign that the good-faith exception has less merit for warrantless searches than for searches pursuant to warrants?

4. There have been some legislative proposals to broaden the good-faith exception. In 1995, the House of Representatives passed a measure that purported to eliminate the exclusionary rule in federal courts for all searches conducted in good faith, whether with or without a warrant. (The measure died in the Senate.) See Exclusionary Rule Reform Act of 1995, H.R. 666 (Feb. 8, 1995). Are such proposals constitutional?

The answer turns on what, precisely, the exclusionary rule's constitutional status is, a point on which the majority and dissent in Mapp strongly disagreed. On the one hand, the Court states clearly that the rule is not constitutionally compelled. On the other hand, the Court regularly overturns state-court convictions based on the rule — that is, if a state court fails to suppress evidence that ought to be suppressed under the exclusionary rule, the Supreme Court will reverse the state-court decision. Needless to say, the Supreme Court has no authority to reverse state-court decisions unless those decisions violate federal law. There is no federal *statute* that requires state courts to have an exclusionary rule, and the exclusionary rule would not seem to be part of some binding general federal common law. So its only possible source is the federal constitution — which the Court says doesn't require it. Where does that leave things?

Perhaps the answer is that the exclusionary rule is a species of "constitutional common law." For the classic discussion of this much-contested category, see Henry Monaghan, The Supreme Court, 1974 Term — Foreword: Constitutional Common Law, 89 Harv. L. Rev. 1 (1975). Assuming it is, there would seem to be two possibilities. First, it may be that legislatures could simply overturn the exclusionary rule if they wished. On this theory, the exclusionary rule is a kind of constitutional law that is subject to legislative definition; courts have no interpretive primacy in this sphere. Second, legislatures may not have the power simply to do away with the exclusionary rule, but they may have the power to replace it with another, equally effective remedy. If the first possibility is correct, the House Republican proposal was constitutional; if the second possibility is correct, it wasn't.

A preview: In Chapter 6 of this book, there is a discussion of whether the famous "Miranda warnings" (from Miranda v. Arizona, 384 U.S. 436 (1966)) that the police must give before interrogating a suspect in custody are constitutionally required or are simply judicially created rules that Congress can overturn. The Court resolved this issue for *Miranda* purposes in Dickerson v. United States, 530 U.S. 428 (2000), holding that "*Miranda* is a constitutional decision" and thus cannot be legislatively overturned. When you study *Miranda*, think back to the exclusionary rule and see if the arguments for its constitutional status are the same or distinguishable in this context.

5. *Leon* has yet to be extended to warrantless searches generally, but it *has* been extended in some other respects. In Illinois v. Krull, 480 U.S. 340 (1987), the Court applied the good-faith exception to a search pursuant to an unconstitutional state statute. The defendants operated a junkyard that housed old automobiles and automobile parts. An Illinois statute authorized police inspection of records and vehicles at such places at the discretion of the police, without the need for probable cause or reasonable suspicion. During the course of such an inspection, police discovered several stolen vehicles. In separate litigation, the Illinois statute was declared unconstitutional, on the ground that it vested police with too much discretionary

power. (Note: In New York v. Burger, 482 U.S. 691 (1987), a similar state statute was upheld, on the ground that there were "special needs" for the government's regulatory authority.) The Supreme Court nevertheless declined to suppress the stolen cars:

> Unless a statute is clearly unconstitutional, an officer cannot be expected to question the judgment of the legislature that passed the law. If the statute is subsequently declared unconstitutional, excluding evidence obtained pursuant to it prior to such a judicial declaration will not deter future Fourth Amendment violations by an officer who has simply fulfilled his responsibility to enforce the statute as written. To paraphrase the Court's comment in Leon: "Penalizing the officer for the [legislature's] error, rather than his own, cannot logically contribute to the deterrence of Fourth Amendment violations."

Krull, 480 U.S., at 349-350.

6. *Leon* and *Krull* indicate that when the source of the error that led to the Fourth Amendment violation was someone other than law enforcement, there is no deterrent value to the police in suppressing the evidence. This idea was reaffirmed in Arizona v. Evans, 514 U.S. 1 (1995), where the police made a traffic stop, entered the defendant's name into a computer terminal in the police car, and learned that there was an outstanding warrant for the defendant's arrest. The officers proceeded to arrest the defendant, and during the course of a search incident to arrest found drugs.

It turned out that there was no outstanding arrest warrant; the information in the police computer was the result of an error in the court clerk's office. In an opinion by Chief Justice Rehnquist, the Court nevertheless held that the drugs found during the search incident to the mistaken arrest were admissible:

> If court employees were responsible for the erroneous computer record, the exclusion of evidence at trial would not sufficiently deter future errors so as to warrant such a severe sanction. First, as we noted in *Leon*, the exclusionary rule was historically designed as a means of deterring police misconduct, not mistakes by court employees. Second, respondent offers no evidence that court employees are inclined to ignore or subvert the Fourth Amendment or that lawlessness among these actors requires application of the extreme sanction of exclusion. . . .
>
> Finally, and most important, there is no basis for believing that application of the exclusionary rule in these circumstances will have a significant effect on court employees. . . . Because court clerks are not adjuncts to the law enforcement team engaged in the often competitive enterprise of ferreting out crime, they have no stake in the outcome of particular criminal prosecutions. The threat of exclusion of evidence could not be expected to deter such individuals. . . .
>
> If it were indeed a court clerk who was responsible for the erroneous entry on the police computer, application of the exclusionary rule also could not be expected to alter the behavior of the arresting officer. As the trial court in this case stated: "I think the police officer [was] bound to arrest. I think he would [have been] derelict in his duty if he failed to arrest."

Id., at 14-16.

7. But what if the source of the error is the police themselves? Consider the following case:

HERRING v. UNITED STATES

Certiorari to the United States Court of Appeals for the Eleventh Circuit
129 S. Ct. 695 (2009)

CHIEF JUSTICE ROBERTS delivered the opinion of the Court.

The Fourth Amendment forbids "unreasonable searches and seizures," and this usually requires the police to have probable cause or a warrant before making an arrest. What if an officer reasonably believes there is an outstanding arrest warrant, but that belief turns out to be wrong because of a negligent bookkeeping error by another police employee? The parties here agree that the ensuing arrest is still a violation of the Fourth Amendment, but dispute whether contraband found during a search incident to that arrest must be excluded in a later prosecution.

Our cases establish that such suppression is not an automatic consequence of a Fourth Amendment violation. Instead, the question turns on the culpability of the police and the potential of exclusion to deter wrongful police conduct. Here the error was the result of isolated negligence attenuated from the arrest. We hold that in these circumstances the jury should not be barred from considering all the evidence.

I

On July 7, 2004, Investigator Mark Anderson learned that Bennie Dean Herring had driven to the Coffee County Sheriff's Department to retrieve something from his impounded truck. Herring was no stranger to law enforcement, and Anderson asked the county's warrant clerk, Sandy Pope, to check for any outstanding warrants for Herring's arrest. When she found none, Anderson asked Pope to check with Sharon Morgan, her counterpart in neighboring Dale County. After checking Dale County's computer database, Morgan replied that there was an active arrest warrant for Herring's failure to appear on a felony charge. Pope relayed the information to Anderson and asked Morgan to fax over a copy of the warrant as confirmation. Anderson and a deputy followed Herring as he left the impound lot, pulled him over, and arrested him. A search incident to the arrest revealed methamphetamine in Herring's pocket, and a pistol (which as a felon he could not possess) in his vehicle.

There had, however, been a mistake about the warrant. The Dale County sheriff's computer records are supposed to correspond to actual arrest warrants, which the office also maintains. But when Morgan went to the files to retrieve the actual warrant to fax to Pope, Morgan was unable to find it. She called a court clerk and learned that the warrant had been recalled five months earlier. Normally when a warrant is recalled the court clerk's office or a judge's chambers calls Morgan, who enters the information in the sheriff's computer database and disposes of the physical copy. For whatever reason, the information about the recall of the warrant for Herring did not appear in the database. Morgan immediately called Pope to alert her to the mixup, and Pope contacted Anderson over a secure radio. This all unfolded in 10 to 15 minutes, but Herring had already been arrested and found with the gun and drugs, just a few hundred yards from the sheriff's office.

[Herring] moved to suppress the evidence. . . . The Magistrate Judge recommended denying the motion because the arresting officers had acted in a good-faith belief that the warrant was still outstanding. . . . The District Court adopted the Magistrate Judge's recommendation, and the Court of Appeals for the Eleventh Circuit affirmed.

We now affirm the Eleventh Circuit's judgment.

II

For purposes of deciding this case . . . we accept the parties' assumption that there was a Fourth Amendment violation. The issue is whether the exclusionary rule should be applied.

A

The Fourth Amendment protects "[t]he right of the people to be secure in their persons, houses, papers, and effects, against unreasonable searches and seizures," but "contains no provision expressly precluding the use of evidence obtained in violation of its commands," Arizona v. Evans, 514 U.S. 1, 10 (1995). Nonetheless, our decisions establish an exclusionary rule that, when applicable, forbids the use of improperly obtained evidence at trial. We have stated that this judicially created rule is "designed to safeguard Fourth Amendment rights generally through its deterrent effect." United States v. Calandra, 414 U.S. 338, 348 (1974).

The Coffee County officers did nothing improper. Indeed, the error was noticed so quickly because Coffee County requested a faxed confirmation of the warrant.

The Eleventh Circuit concluded, however, that somebody in Dale County should have updated the computer database to reflect the recall of the arrest warrant. The court also concluded that this error was negligent, but did not find it to be reckless or deliberate. That fact is crucial to our holding that this error is not enough by itself to require "the extreme sanction of exclusion." [United States v. Leon, 468 U.S. 897, 916 (1984)].

B

1. The fact that a Fourth Amendment violation occurred — i.e., that a search or arrest was unreasonable — does not necessarily mean that the exclusionary rule applies. Illinois v. Gates, 462 U.S. 213, 223 (1983). Indeed, exclusion "has always been our last resort, not our first impulse," Hudson v. Michigan, 547 U.S. 586, 591 (2006).

First, the exclusionary rule is not an individual right and applies only where it "result[s] in appreciable deterrence." *Leon*, supra, at 909 (quoting United States v. Janis, 428 U.S. 433, 454 (1976)).

In addition, the benefits of deterrence must outweigh the costs. *Leon*, supra, at 910. . . . The principal cost of applying the rule is, of course, letting guilty and possibly dangerous defendants go free — something that "offends basic concepts of the criminal justice system." *Leon*, supra, at 908.

2. The extent to which the exclusionary rule is justified by these deterrence principles varies with the culpability of the law enforcement conduct.

An error that arises from nonrecurring and attenuated negligence is . . . far removed from the core concerns that led us to adopt the rule in the first place. And in fact since *Leon*, we have never applied the rule to exclude evidence obtained in violation of the Fourth Amendment, where the police conduct was no more intentional or culpable than this.

3. To trigger the exclusionary rule, police conduct must be sufficiently deliberate that exclusion can meaningfully deter it, and sufficiently culpable that such deterrence is worth the price paid by the justice system. As laid out in our cases, the exclusionary rule serves to deter deliberate, reckless, or grossly negligent conduct, or in some circumstances recurring or systemic negligence. The error in this case does not rise to that level.

4. We do not suggest that all recordkeeping errors by the police are immune from the exclusionary rule. In this case, however, the conduct at issue was not so objectively culpable as to require exclusion. . . .

If the police have been shown to be reckless in maintaining a warrant system, or to have knowingly made false entries to lay the groundwork for future false arrests, exclusion would certainly be justified under our cases should such misconduct cause a Fourth Amendment violation. We said as much in *Leon*, explaining that an officer could not "obtain a warrant on the basis of a 'bare bones' affidavit and then rely on colleagues who are ignorant of the circumstances under which the warrant was obtained to conduct the search." Id., at 923, n. 24 (citing Whiteley v. Warden, Wyo. State Penitentiary, 401 U.S. 560, 568 (1971)).

In a case where systemic errors were demonstrated, it might be reckless for officers to rely on an unreliable warrant system. See *Evans*, 514 U.S., at 17 (O'Connor, J., concurring) ("Surely it would *not* be reasonable for the police to rely . . . on a recordkeeping system . . . that *routinely* leads to false arrests" (second emphasis added)); *Hudson*, 547 U.S., at 604 (Kennedy, J., concurring) ("If a *widespread pattern* of violations were shown . . . there would be reason for grave concern" (emphasis added)). But there is no evidence that errors in Dale County's system are routine or widespread.

Petitioner's claim that police negligence automatically triggers suppression cannot be squared with the principles underlying the exclusionary rule, as they have been explained in our cases. In light of our repeated holdings that the deterrent effect of suppression must be substantial and outweigh any harm to the justice system, e.g., *Leon*, 468 U.S., at 909-910, we conclude that when police mistakes are the result of negligence such as that described here, rather than systemic error or reckless disregard of constitutional requirements, any marginal deterrence does not "pay its way." Id., at 907-908, n. 6 (internal quotation marks omitted). In such a case, the criminal should not "go free because the constable has blundered." People v. Defore, 242 N.Y. 13, 21 (1926) (opinion of the Court by Cardozo, J.).

The judgment of the Court of Appeals for the Eleventh Circuit is affirmed.

JUSTICE GINSBURG, with whom JUSTICE STEVENS, JUSTICE SOUTER, and JUSTICE BREYER join, dissenting.

The exclusionary rule provides redress for Fourth Amendment violations by placing the government in the position it would have been in had there been no unconstitutional arrest and search. The rule thus strongly encourages police compliance with the Fourth Amendment in the future. The Court, however, holds the rule inapplicable because careless recordkeeping by the police — not flagrant or deliberate misconduct — accounts for Herring's arrest. . . .

Others have described "a more majestic conception" of the Fourth Amendment and its adjunct, the exclusionary rule. [Arizona v. Evans, 514 U.S. 1, 18 (1995)] (Stevens, J., dissenting). . . . I share that vision of the Amendment.

Beyond doubt, a main objective of the rule "is to deter — to compel respect for the constitutional guaranty in the only effectively available way — by removing the incentive to disregard it." Elkins v. United States, 364 U.S. 206, 217 (1960). But the rule also serves other important purposes: It "enabl[es] the judiciary to avoid the taint of partnership in official lawlessness," and it "assur[es] the people — all potential victims of unlawful government conduct — that the government would not profit from its lawless behavior, thus minimizing the risk of seriously undermining popular trust in government." United States v. Calandra, 414 U.S. 338, 357 (1974) (Brennan, J., dissenting).

The Court maintains that Herring's case is one in which the exclusionary rule could have scant deterrent effect and therefore would not "pay its way." I disagree.

Electronic databases form the nervous system of contemporary criminal justice operations. In recent years, their breadth and influence have dramatically expanded. Police today can access databases that include not only the updated National Crime Information Center (NCIC), but also terrorist watchlists, the Federal Government's employee eligibility system, and various commercial databases. Moreover, States are actively expanding information sharing between jurisdictions. As a result, law enforcement has an increasing supply of information within its easy electronic reach.

The risk of error stemming from these databases is not slim. . . . Inaccuracies in expansive, interconnected collections of electronic information raise grave concerns for individual liberty. "The offense to the dignity of the citizen who is arrested, handcuffed, and searched on a public street simply because some bureaucrat has failed to maintain an accurate computer data base" is evocative of the use of general warrants that so outraged the authors of our Bill of Rights. Evans, 514 U.S., at 23 (Stevens, J., dissenting).

The Court assures that "exclusion would certainly be justified" if "the police have been shown to be reckless in maintaining a warrant system, or to have knowingly made false entries to lay the groundwork for future false arrests." This concession provides little comfort.

First, by restricting suppression to bookkeeping errors that are deliberate or reckless, the majority leaves Herring, and others like him, with no remedy for violations of their constitutional rights. There can be no serious assertion that relief is available under 42 U.S.C. §1983. The arresting officer would be sheltered by qualified immunity, see Harlow v. Fitzgerald, 457 U.S. 800 (1982), and the police department itself is not liable for the negligent acts of its employees, see Monell v. New York City Dept. of Social Servs., 436 U.S. 658 (1978). Moreover, identifying the department employee who committed the error may be impossible.

Second, I doubt that police forces already possess sufficient incentives to maintain up-to-date records. The Government argues that police have no desire to send officers out on arrests unnecessarily, because arrests consume resources and place officers in danger. The facts of this case do not fit that description of police motivation. Here the officer wanted to arrest Herring and consulted the Department's records to legitimate his predisposition.

Third, even when deliberate or reckless conduct is afoot, the Court's assurance will often be an empty promise: How is an impecunious defendant to make the required showing?

Negligent recordkeeping errors by law enforcement threaten individual liberty, are susceptible to deterrence by the exclusionary rule, and cannot be remedied effectively through other means. Such errors present no occasion to further erode the exclusionary rule. The rule "is needed to make the Fourth Amendment something real; a guarantee that does not carry with it the exclusion of evidence obtained by its violation is a chimera." *Calandra*, 414 U.S., at 361 (Brennan, J., dissenting).

For the reasons stated, I would reverse the judgment of the Eleventh Circuit.

[Justice Breyer's dissenting opinion, in which Justice Souter joined, is omitted.]

NOTES AND QUESTIONS

1. Are you persuaded by the majority's analysis? In a portion of the dissent not excerpted here, Justice Ginsburg charged that the majority was ignoring a "foundational premise of tort law — that liability for negligence, i.e., lack of due care, creates an incentive to act with greater care." Do you agree that by suppressing evidence in circumstances such as this, courts encourage police policymakers and systems managers better to monitor their recordkeeping systems and the people who operate them? Is there any reason to question this assumption? Do we need the exclusionary rule to make sure police forces have adequate incentives to keep their recordkeeping systems up to date?

2. How would a defendant like Mr. Herring show that the police error that led to his arrest was the result of "systemic error or reckless disregard of constitutional requirements," as the majority opinion requires? Will a future criminal defendant in Herring's situation be entitled to discovery into a department's recordkeeping system, so that he might establish that the injury he suffered was the result of recklessness or grossly negligent conduct? Is there a reason to think civil plaintiffs might be better positioned to pursue such matters?

3. Justice Ginsburg writes that there is a more majestic conception of the exclusionary rule's purposes — that the rule provides a means for the judiciary to avoid the taint of official lawlessness and assures the public that the government will not profit from its lawless behavior. But how are such concerns implicated in this case — where, as Chief Justice Roberts says, the officer involved did nothing improper? Does Justice Ginsburg have a stronger argument based on deterrence or based on this majestic conception of the exclusionary rule?

2. Standing

One basic question about the exclusionary rule is who gets to invoke it. As a threshold matter, it is undisputed that the person seeking the exclusion must be the defendant in a criminal action. If the police illegally search my house and find evidence that implicates my brother, only my brother can seek to exclude the evidence; I may have a civil or other remedy against the police, but I have no standing to seek exclusion.

Being a defendant against whom the illegal evidence is to be used is necessary for standing, but it is not sufficient. As a matter of first principles, we might conclude that any defendant can challenge any improper evidence, regardless of where it was found. After all, the defendant is surely harmed by the putative illegal search, and he has the greatest incentive to discover and expose illegal police practices — the reward for his monitoring may be the exclusion of critical evidence that may lead in turn to an acquittal. And of course, if the exclusionary rule is designed to deter the police, allowing the broadest group of defendants to challenge police practices will bring about the maximum deterrent effect.

The Supreme Court, however, has never embraced such an expansive view. In Jones v. United States, 362 U.S. 257, 261 (1960), the Court seemed to adopt a "target theory" of standing, by which a defendant could seek exclusion of evidence if the search or seizure was "directed" at him, even if the search took place in someone else's home. Later, in Alderman v. United States, 394 U.S. 165, 174 (1969), the Court appeared to reject that theory, stating that "Fourth Amendment rights are personal rights which, like some other constitutional rights, may not be vicariously asserted." Reading *Jones* and *Alderman* together left Fourth Amendment standing doctrine in a state of confusion.

In Rakas v. Illinois, 439 U.S. 128 (1978), the Court imposed a measure of order on the chaos. The facts in *Rakas* were as follows:

> A police officer on a routine patrol received a radio call notifying him of a robbery of a [nearby] clothing store . . . and describing the getaway car. Shortly thereafter, the officer spotted an automobile which he thought might be the getaway car. After following the car for some time and after the arrival of assistance, he and several other officers stopped the vehicle. The occupants of the automobile, petitioners and two female companions, were ordered out of the car and, after the occupants had left the car, two officers searched the interior of the vehicle. They discovered a box of rifle shells in the glove compartment, which had been locked, and a sawed-off rifle under the front passenger seat. After discovering the rifle and the shells, the officers took petitioners to the station and placed them under arrest.

Id., at 130. Rakas and his codefendant conceded that they did not own the car. Nor, apparently, did they own the shells or the rifle.

In an opinion by then-Justice Rehnquist, the Court concluded that Rakas lacked standing to complain about the car search. Rehnquist began by dismissing the target theory, on the ground that it empowers defendants to seek relief for searches that did not infringe any protected privacy interest of theirs:

> A person who is aggrieved by an illegal search and seizure only through the introduction of damaging evidence secured by a search of a third person's premises or property has not had any of his Fourth Amendment rights infringed. And since the exclusionary rule is an attempt to effectuate the guarantees of the Fourth Amendment, it is proper to permit only defendants whose Fourth Amendment rights have been violated to benefit from the rule's protections.

Id., at 134. In addition, Rehnquist argued that the target theory imposed serious administrative burdens on courts, for it required findings about police officers' motivations when searching. Instead, he (and the Court) concluded, standing "is more properly subsumed under substantive Fourth Amendment doctrine." Id., at 139. Rehnquist stated the rule as follows: "[T]he question is whether the challenged search and seizure violated the Fourth Amendment rights of a criminal defendant who seeks to exclude the evidence obtained during it." Id., at 140.

Another source of confusion — created, once again, by the *Jones* opinion — concerned the effect on standing if the defendant admitted to owning or possessing the items seized in the allegedly illegal search. The Court in *Rakas* found it significant that the defendant did not claim ownership of the gun and the shells seized by the police. But if they had claimed ownership, would that be sufficient to confer standing?

In Rawlings v. Kentucky, 448 U.S. 98 (1980), the defendant and others were being detained in the home of a third party while the police were conducting a search. The police emptied the handbag of a woman who had been seated next to the defendant, and found illegal drugs. Defendant promptly claimed ownership of the drugs, and later moved to suppress, arguing that the search of the handbag was illegal. The Court found that defendant lacked standing to challenge the search. It noted that defendant had known the woman who owned the purse for only a few days, had apparently placed the drugs in the purse just before the police arrived, perhaps without the woman's consent, and had never sought or had been given access to the purse in the past. These factors, said the Court, showed that the defendant had no "reasonable expectation of privacy" in the purse, and thus, did not suffer any Fourth Amendment harm. Mere ownership of the evidence itself, as opposed to a privacy interest in the place searched, was insufficient.

What these rules mean in practice, and especially what they mean for searches of dwellings, is the subject of the next case.

MINNESOTA v. CARTER

Certiorari to the Supreme Court of Minnesota

525 U.S. 83 (1998)

CHIEF JUSTICE REHNQUIST delivered the opinion of the Court.

Respondents and the lessee of an apartment were sitting in one of its rooms, bagging cocaine. While so engaged they were observed by a police officer, who looked through a drawn window blind. The Supreme Court of Minnesota held that the officer's viewing was a search which violated respondents' Fourth Amendment rights. We hold that no such violation occurred.

James Thielen, a police officer in the Twin Cities' suburb of Eagan, Minnesota, went to an apartment building to investigate a tip from a confidential informant. The informant said that he had walked by the window of a ground-floor apartment and had seen people putting a white powder into bags. The officer looked in the same window through a gap in the closed blind and observed the bagging operation for several minutes. He then notified headquarters, which began preparing affidavits for a search warrant while he returned to the apartment building. When two men left the building in a previously identified Cadillac, the police stopped the car. Inside were respondents Carter and Johns. As the police opened the door of the car to let Johns out, they observed a black zippered pouch and a handgun, later determined to be loaded, on the vehicle's floor. Carter and Johns were arrested, and a later police search of the vehicle the next day discovered pagers, a scale, and 47 grams of cocaine in plastic sandwich bags.

After seizing the car, the police returned to Apartment 103 and arrested the occupant, Kimberly Thompson, who is not a party to this appeal. A search of the apartment pursuant to a warrant revealed cocaine residue on the kitchen table and plastic baggies similar to those found in the Cadillac. Thielen identified Carter, Johns, and Thompson as the three people he had observed placing the powder into baggies. The police later learned that while Thompson was the lessee of the apartment, Carter and Johns lived in Chicago and had come to the apartment for the sole purpose of packaging the cocaine. Carter and Johns had never been to the apartment before and were only in the apartment for approximately 2 hours. In return for the use of the apartment, Carter and Johns had given Thompson one-eighth of an ounce of the cocaine.

Carter and Johns . . . moved to suppress all evidence obtained from the apartment and the Cadillac, as well as to suppress several post-arrest incriminating statements they had made. They argued that Thielen's initial observation of their drug packaging activities was an unreasonable search in violation of the Fourth Amendment and that all evidence obtained as a result of this unreasonable search was inadmissible as fruit of the poisonous tree. The Minnesota trial court held that since, unlike the defendant in Minnesota v. Olson, 495 U.S. 91 (1990), Carter and Johns were not overnight social guests but temporary out-of-state visitors, they were not entitled to claim the protection of the Fourth Amendment against the government intrusion into the apartment. . . .

A divided Minnesota Supreme Court reversed, holding that respondents had "standing" to claim the protection of the Fourth Amendment because they had "a legitimate expectation of privacy in the invaded place." The court noted that even though "society does not recognize as valuable the task of bagging cocaine, we conclude that society does recognize as valuable the right of property owners or leaseholders to invite persons into the privacy of their homes to conduct a common task, be it legal or illegal activity." . . . We granted certiorari, and now reverse.

The Minnesota courts analyzed whether respondents had a legitimate expectation of privacy under the rubric of "standing" doctrine, an analysis which this Court expressly rejected 20 years ago in [Rakas v. Illinois, 439 U.S. 128 (1978)]. In that case, we held that automobile passengers could not assert the protection of the Fourth Amendment against the seizure of incriminating evidence from a vehicle where they owned neither the vehicle nor the evidence. Ibid. Central to our analysis was the idea that in determining whether a defendant is able to show the violation of his (and not someone else's) Fourth Amendment rights, the "definition of those rights is more properly placed within the purview of substantive Fourth Amendment law than within that of standing." 439 U.S., at 140. Thus, we held that in order to claim the protection of the Fourth Amendment, a defendant must demonstrate that he personally has an expectation of privacy in the place searched, and that his expectation is reasonable. . . .

The Fourth Amendment . . . protects persons against unreasonable searches of "their persons [and] houses" and thus indicates that the Fourth Amendment is a personal right that must be invoked by an individual. See Katz v. United States, 389 U.S. 347, 351 (1967) ("The Fourth Amendment protects people, not places"). But the extent to which the Fourth Amendment protects people may depend upon where those people are. We have held that "capacity to claim the protection of the Fourth Amendment depends . . . upon whether the person who claims the protection of the Amendment has a legitimate expectation of privacy in the invaded place." Rakas, supra, at 143.

The text of the Amendment suggests that its protections extend only to people in "their" houses. But we have held that in some circumstances a person may have a legitimate expectation of privacy in the house of someone else. In Minnesota v. Olson, 495 U.S. 91 (1990), for example, we decided that an overnight guest in a house had the sort of expectation of privacy that the Fourth Amendment protects. We said:

> To hold that an overnight guest has a legitimate expectation of privacy in his host's home merely recognizes the every day expectations of privacy that we all share. Staying overnight in another's home is a long-standing social custom that serves functions recognized as valuable by society. We stay in others' homes when we travel to a strange city for business or pleasure, we visit our parents, children, or more distant relatives out of town, when we are in between jobs, or homes, or when we house-sit for a friend. . . .
>
> From the overnight guest's perspective, he seeks shelter in another's home precisely because it provides him with privacy, a place where he and his possessions will not be disturbed by anyone but his host and those his host allows inside. We are at our most vulnerable when we are asleep because we cannot monitor our own safety or the security of our belongings. It is for this reason that, although we may spend all day in public places, when we cannot sleep in our own home we seek out another private place to sleep, whether it be a hotel room, or the home of a friend. 495 U.S., at 98-99.

In Jones v. United States, 362 U.S. 257, 259 (1960), the defendant seeking to exclude evidence resulting from a search of an apartment had been given the use of the apartment by a friend. He had clothing in the apartment, had slept there "maybe a night," and at the time was the sole occupant of the apartment. But while the holding of *Jones* — that a search of the apartment violated the defendant's Fourth Amendment rights — is still valid, its statement that "anyone legitimately on the premises where a search occurs may challenge its legality," id., at 267, was expressly repudiated in Rakas v. Illinois, 439 U.S. 128 (1978). Thus an overnight guest in a home may claim the protection of the Fourth Amendment, but one who is merely present with the consent of the householder may not.

Respondents here were obviously not overnight guests, but were essentially present for a business transaction and were only in the home a matter of hours. There is no suggestion that they had a previous relationship with Thompson, or that there was any other purpose to their visit. Nor was there anything similar to the overnight guest relationship in *Olson* to suggest a degree of acceptance into the household. While the apartment was a dwelling place for Thompson, it was for these respondents simply a place to do business. . . .

If we regard the overnight guest in Minnesota v. Olson as typifying those who may claim the protection of the Fourth Amendment in the home of another, and one merely "legitimately on the premises" as typifying those who may not do so, the present case is obviously somewhere in between. But the purely commercial nature of the transaction engaged in here, the relatively short period of time on the premises, and the lack of any previous connection between respondents and the householder, all lead us to conclude that respondents' situation is closer to that of one simply permitted on the premises. We therefore hold that any search which may have occurred did not violate their Fourth Amendment rights.

Because we conclude that respondents had no legitimate expectation of privacy in the apartment, we need not decide whether the police officer's observation constituted a "search." The judgment of the Supreme Court of Minnesota is accordingly reversed, and the cause is remanded for proceedings not inconsistent with this opinion.

JUSTICE SCALIA, with whom JUSTICE THOMAS joins, concurring.

I join the opinion of the Court because I believe it accurately applies our recent case law, including Minnesota v. Olson, 495 U.S. 91 (1990). I write separately to express my view that that case law — like the submissions of the parties in this case — gives short shrift to the text of the Fourth Amendment, and to the well and long understood meaning of that text. Specifically, it leaps to apply the fuzzy standard of "legitimate expectation of privacy" — a consideration that is often relevant to whether a search or seizure covered by the Fourth Amendment is "unreasonable" — to the threshold question whether a search or seizure covered by the Fourth Amendment has occurred. If that latter question is addressed first and analyzed under the text of the Constitution as traditionally understood, the present case is not remotely difficult.

The Fourth Amendment protects "the right of the people to be secure in their persons, houses, papers, and effects, against unreasonable searches and seizures. . . ." U.S. Const., Amdt. 4. It must be acknowledged that the phrase "their . . . houses" in this provision is, in isolation, ambiguous. It could mean "their respective houses," so that the protection extends to each person only in his own house. But it could also mean "their respective and each other's houses," so that each person would be protected even when visiting the house of someone else. As today's opinion for the Court suggests, however, it is not linguistically possible to give the provision the latter, expansive interpretation with respect to "houses" without giving it the same interpretation with respect to the nouns that are parallel to "houses" — "persons, . . . papers, and effects" — which would give me a constitutional right not to have your person unreasonably searched. This is so absurd that it has to my knowledge never been contemplated. The obvious meaning of the provision is that each person has the right to be secure against unreasonable searches and seizures in his own person, house, papers, and effects.

The Founding-era materials that I have examined confirm that this was the understood meaning. (Strangely, these materials went unmentioned by the State and its amici — unmentioned even in the State's reply brief, even though respondents had thrown down the gauntlet: "In briefs totaling over 100 pages, the State of Minnesota, the amici 26 attorneys general, and the Solicitor General of the United States of America have not mentioned one word about the history and purposes of the Fourth Amendment or the intent of the framers of that amendment." Brief for Respondents 12, n. 4.) Like most of the provisions of the Bill of Rights, the Fourth Amendment was derived from provisions already existing in state constitutions. Of the four of those provisions that contained language similar to that of the Fourth Amendment, two used the same ambiguous "their" terminology. See Pa. Const., Art. X (1776) ("That the people have a right to hold themselves, their houses, papers, and possessions free from search and seizure . . ."); Vt. Const., ch. I, §XI (1777) ("That the people have a right to hold themselves, their houses, papers, and possessions free from search or seizure . . ."). The other two, however, avoided the ambiguity by using the singular instead of the plural. See Mass. Const., pt. I, Art. XIV (1780) ("Every subject has a right to be secure from all unreasonable searches, and seizures of his person, his houses, his papers, and all his possessions"); N.H. Const. §XIX (1784) ("Every subject hath a right to be secure from all unreasonable searches and seizures of his person, his houses, his papers, and all his possessions"). The New York Convention that ratified the Constitution proposed an amendment that would have given every freeman "a right to be secure from all unreasonable searches and seizures of his person, his papers or his property," 4 B. Schwartz, The Roots of the Bill of Rights 913 (1980) (reproducing New York proposed amendments, 1778), and the Declaration of Rights that the North Carolina Convention demanded prior to its ratification contained a similar provision protecting a freeman's right against "unreasonable searches and seizures of his person, his papers and property," id., at 968 (reproducing North Carolina proposed Declaration of Rights, 1778). There is no indication anyone believed that the Massachusetts, New Hampshire, New York, and North Carolina texts, by using the word "his" rather than "their," narrowed the protections contained in the Pennsylvania and Vermont Constitutions.

That "their . . . houses" was understood to mean "their respective houses" would have been clear to anyone who knew the English and early American law of arrest and trespass that underlay the Fourth Amendment. The people's protection against unreasonable search and seizure in their "houses" was drawn from the English common-law maxim, "A man's home is his castle." As far back as Semayne's Case of 1604, the leading English case for that proposition . . . the King's Bench proclaimed that "the house of any one is not a castle or privilege but for himself, and shall not extend to protect any person who flies to his house." Semayne v. Gresham, 5 Co. Rep. 91a, 93a, 77 Eng. Rep. 194, 198 (K.B. 1604). . . .

Of course this is not to say that the Fourth Amendment protects only the Lord of the Manor who holds his estate in fee simple. People call a house "their" home when legal title is in the bank, when they rent it, and even when they merely occupy it rent-free — so long as they actually live there. That this is the criterion of the people's protection against government intrusion into "their" houses is established by the leading American case of Oystead v. Shed, 13 Mass. 520 (1816), which held it a trespass for the sheriff to break into a dwelling to capture a boarder who lived there. The court reasoned that the "inviolability of dwelling houses" . . . extends to "the occupier or any of his family . . . who have their domicile or ordinary residence there," including "a boarder or a servant" "who have made the house their home." Id., at 523. But, it added, "the house shall not be made a sanctuary" for one such as "a stranger, or perhaps a visitor," who "upon a pursuit, takes refuge in the house of another," for "the house is not his castle; and the officer may break open the doors or windows in order to execute his process." Ibid.

Thus, in deciding the question presented today we write upon a slate that is far from clean. The text of the Fourth Amendment, the common-law background against which it was adopted, and the understandings consistently displayed after its adoption make the answer clear. We were right to hold in Chapman v. United States, 365 U.S. 610 (1961), that the Fourth Amendment protects an apartment tenant against an unreasonable search of his dwelling, even though he is only a leaseholder. And we were right to hold in Bumper v. North Carolina, 391 U.S. 543

(1968), that an unreasonable search of a grandmother's house violated her resident grandson's Fourth Amendment rights because the area searched "was his home," id., at 548, n. 11. We went to the absolute limit of what text and tradition permit in Minnesota v. Olson, 495 U.S. 91 (1990), when we protected a mere overnight guest against an unreasonable search of his hosts' apartment. But whereas it is plausible to regard a person's overnight lodging as at least his "temporary" residence, it is entirely impossible to give that characterization to an apartment that he uses to package cocaine. Respondents here were not searched in "their . . . house" under any interpretation of the phrase that bears the remotest relationship to the well understood meaning of the Fourth Amendment. . . .

The dissent may be correct that a person invited into someone else's house to engage in a common business (even common monkey-business, so to speak) ought to be protected against government searches of the room in which that business is conducted; and that persons invited in to deliver milk or pizza (whom the dissent dismisses as "classroom hypotheticals," as opposed, presumably, to flesh-and-blood hypotheticals) ought not to be protected against government searches of the rooms that they occupy. I am not sure of the answer to those policy questions. But I am sure that the answer is not remotely contained in the Constitution, which means that it is left — as many, indeed most, important questions are left — to the judgment of state and federal legislators. We go beyond our proper role as judges in a democratic society when we restrict the people's power to govern themselves over the full range of policy choices that the Constitution has left available to them.

JUSTICE KENNEDY, concurring.

I join the Court's opinion, for its reasoning is consistent with my view that almost all social guests have a legitimate expectation of privacy, and hence protection against unreasonable searches, in their host's home. . . .

. . . I would expect that most, if not all, social guests legitimately expect that, in accordance with social custom, the homeowner will exercise her discretion to include or exclude others for the guests' benefit. As we recognized in Minnesota v. Olson, 495 U.S. 91 (1990), where these social expectations exist — as in the case of an overnight guest — they are sufficient to create a legitimate expectation of privacy, even in the absence of any property right to exclude others. In this respect, the dissent must be correct that reasonable expectations of the owner are shared, to some extent, by the guest. This analysis suggests that, as a general rule, social guests will have an expectation of privacy in their host's home. That is not the case before us, however.

In this case respondents have established nothing more than a fleeting and insubstantial connection with Thompson's home. For all that appears in the record, respondents used Thompson's house simply as a convenient processing station, their purpose involving nothing more than the mechanical act of chopping and packing a substance for distribution. There is no suggestion that respondents engaged in confidential communications with Thompson about their transaction. Respondents had not been to Thompson's apartment before, and they left it even before their arrest. The Minnesota Supreme Court, which overturned respondents' convictions, acknowledged that respondents could not be fairly characterized as Thompson's "guests."

If respondents here had been visiting twenty homes, each for a minute or two, to drop off a bag of cocaine and were apprehended by a policeman wrongfully present in the nineteenth home; or if they had left the goods at a home where they were not staying and the police had seized the goods in their absence, we would have said that *Rakas* compels rejection of any privacy interest respondents might assert. So it does here, given that respondents have established no meaningful tie or connection to the owner, the owner's home, or the owner's expectation of privacy. . . .

JUSTICE BREYER, concurring in the judgment.

I agree with Justice Ginsburg that respondents can claim the Fourth Amendment's protection. Petitioner, however, raises a second question, whether under the circumstances Officer Thielen's observation made "from a public area outside the curtilage of the residence" violated respondents' Fourth Amendment rights. See Pet. for Cert. i. In my view, it did not.

I would answer the question on the basis of the following factual assumptions, derived from the evidentiary record presented here: (1) On the evening of May 15, 1994, an anonymous individual approached Officer Thielen, telling him that he had just walked by a nearby apartment window through which he had seen some people bagging drugs; (2) the apartment in question was a garden apartment that was partly below ground level; (3) families frequently used the grassy area just outside the apartment's window for walking or for playing; (4) members of the public also used the area just outside the apartment's window to store bicycles; (5) in an effort to verify the tipster's information, Officer Thielen walked to a position about 1 to 1½ feet in front of the window; (6) Officer Thielen stood there for about 15 minutes looking down through a set of Venetian blinds; (7) what he saw, namely, people putting white powder in bags, verified the account he had heard; and (8) he then used that information to help obtain a search warrant. [Following is a long series of citations to the record.]

The trial court concluded that persons then within Ms. Thompson's kitchen "did not have an expectation of privacy from the location where Officer Thielen made his observations . . . ," because Officer Thielen stood outside the apartment's "curtilage" when he made his observations. And the Minnesota Supreme Court, while finding that Officer Thielen had violated the Fourth Amendment, did not challenge the trial court's curtilage determination; indeed, it assumed that Officer Thielen stood outside the apartment's curtilage. 569 N.W.2d 169, 177, and n. 10 (1987) (stating "it is plausible that Thielen's presence just outside the apartment window was legitimate").

Officer Thielen, then, stood at a place used by the public and from which one could see through the window into the kitchen. The precautions that the apartment's dwellers took to maintain their privacy would have failed in respect to an ordinary passerby standing in that place. Given this Court's well-established case law, I cannot say that the officer engaged in what the Constitution forbids, namely, an "unreasonable search." See, e.g., Florida v. Riley, 488 U.S. 445, 448 (1989) (finding observation of greenhouse from helicopters in public airspace permissible, even though owners had enclosed greenhouse on two sides, relied on bushes blocking ground-level observations through remaining two sides, and covered 90% of roof); California v. Ciraolo, 476 U.S. 207, 209 (1986) (finding observation of backyard from plane in public airspace permissible despite 6-foot outer fence and 10-foot inner fence around backyard).

The Minnesota Supreme Court reached a different conclusion in part because it believed that Officer Thielen had engaged in unusual activity, that he "climbed over some bushes, crouched down and placed his face 12 to 18 inches from the window," and in part because he saw into the apartment through "a small gap" in blinds that were drawn. 569 N.W.2d at 177-178. But I would not here determine whether the crouching and climbing or "placing his face" makes a constitutional difference because the record before us does not contain support for those factual conclusions. That record indicates that Officer Thielen would not have needed to, and did not, climb over bushes or crouch. [Following are citations to Officer Thielen's testimony and to a photograph of the apartment complex.] And even though the primary evidence consists of Officer Thielen's own testimony, who else could have known? Given the importance of factual nuance in this area of constitutional law, I would not determine the constitutional significance of factual assertions that the record denies.

Neither can the matter turn upon "gaps" in drawn blinds. Whether there were holes in the blinds or they were simply pulled the "wrong way" makes no difference. One who lives in a basement apartment that fronts a publicly traveled street, or similar space, ordinarily understands the need for care lest a member of the public simply direct his gaze downward.

Putting the specific facts of this case aside, there is a benefit to an officer's decision to confirm an informant's tip by observing the allegedly illegal activity from a public vantage point. Indeed, there are reasons why Officer Thielen stood in a public place and looked through the apartment window. He had already received information that a crime was taking place in the apartment. He intended to apply for a warrant. He needed to verify the tipster's credibility. He might have done so in other ways, say, by seeking general information about the tipster's reputation and then obtaining a warrant and searching the apartment. But his chosen method — observing the apartment from a public vantage point — would more likely have saved an innocent apartment dweller from a physically intrusive, though warrant-based, search if the constitutionally permissible observation revealed no illegal activity.

For these reasons, while agreeing with Justice Ginsburg, I also concur in the Court's judgment reversing the Minnesota Supreme Court.

JUSTICE GINSBURG, with whom JUSTICE STEVENS and JUSTICE SOUTER join, dissenting.

The Court's decision undermines not only the security of short-term guests, but also the security of the home resident herself. In my view, when a homeowner or lessor personally invites a guest into her home to share in a common endeavor, whether it be for conversation, to engage in leisure activities, or for business purposes licit or illicit, that guest should share his host's shelter against unreasonable searches and seizures. . . .

. . . . [E]ven within the home itself, the position to which I would adhere would not permit "a casual visitor who has never seen, or been permitted to visit, the basement of another's house to object to a search of the basement if the visitor happened to be in the kitchen of the house at the time of the search." *Rakas*, 439 U.S., at 142. Further, I would here decide only the case of the homeowner who chooses to share the privacy of her home and her company with a guest, and would not reach classroom hypotheticals like the milkman or pizza deliverer.

My concern centers on an individual's choice to share her home and her associations there with persons she selects. Our decisions indicate that people have a reasonable expectation of privacy in their homes in part because they have the prerogative to exclude others. See id., at 149 (legitimate expectation of privacy turns in large part on ability to exclude others from place searched). The power to exclude implies the power to include.

Through the host's invitation, the guest gains a reasonable expectation of privacy in the home. Minnesota v. Olson, 495 U.S. 91 (1990), so held with respect to an overnight guest. The logic of that decision extends to shorter term guests as well. . . . Visiting the home of a friend, relative, or business associate, whatever the time of day, "serves functions recognized as valuable by society." Olson, 495 U.S., at 98. One need not remain overnight to anticipate privacy in another's home, "a place where [the guest] and his possessions will not be disturbed by anyone but his host and those his host allows inside." Id., at 99. In sum, when a homeowner chooses to share the privacy of her home and her company with a short-term guest, the two-fold requirement "emerging from prior decisions" has been satisfied: Both host and guest "have exhibited an actual (subjective) expectation of privacy"; that "expectation [is] one [our] society is prepared to recognize as 'reasonable.'" Katz v. United States, 389 U.S. 347, 361 (1967) (Harlan, J., concurring).[2]

. . . [T]he illegality of the host-guest conduct, the fact that they were partners in crime, would not alter the analysis. In Olson, for example, the guest whose security this Court's decision shielded stayed overnight while the police searched for him. 495 U.S., at 93-94. The Court held that the guest had Fourth Amendment protection against a warrantless arrest in his host's home despite the guest's involvement in grave crimes (first-degree murder, armed robbery, and assault).

Indeed, it must be this way. If the illegality of the activity made constitutional an otherwise unconstitutional search, such Fourth Amendment protection, reserved for the innocent only, would have little force in regulating police behavior toward either the innocent or the guilty.

NOTES AND QUESTIONS

1. Is Justice Breyer right? Regardless of the identity of the persons Officer Thielen saw through the apartment window, was anyone "searched" within the meaning of the Fourth Amendment?

2. When evaluating the privacy interests of houseguests, consider the following possibility. On the one hand, a houseguest is likely to have no significant privacy interest in things that can be found in his host's home: They are, after all, his host's things. On the other hand, a guest may have a considerable — and quite reasonable,

---

2. In his concurring opinion, Justice Kennedy maintains that respondents here lacked "an expectation of privacy that society recognizes as reasonable," because they "established nothing more than a fleeting and insubstantial connection" with the host's home. As the Minnesota Supreme Court reported, however, the stipulated facts showed that respondents were inside the apartment with the host's permission, remained inside for at least 2 hours, and, during that time, engaged in concert with the host in a collaborative venture. These stipulated facts . . . securely demonstrate that the host intended to share her privacy with respondents. . . . I think it noteworthy that five Members of the Court would place under the Fourth Amendment's shield, at least, "almost all social guests." (Kennedy, J., concurring).

in the ordinary sense of that word — expectation of privacy in the guest's own activities, in what the guest is doing while in the host's home. Should this distinction matter for purposes of Fourth Amendment doctrine? Does it?

3. Some of the language in Chief Justice Rehnquist's opinion suggests the problem with Carter's and Johns's claim is that they were engaged in illegal activity in Thompson's apartment — packaging cocaine — and they can have no legitimate expectation of privacy in such behavior. It is hard to take this language seriously. After all, if Carter has no claim because he was packaging cocaine when Officer Thielen saw him, then Carter would have no claim even if he had been packaging cocaine *in his own apartment.* Virtually every motion to suppress drugs would fail, because no one can have a legitimate expectation of privacy in illegal drug possession.

Of course, the Court does not carry the point nearly so far. But this suggests a problem with the analysis in *Carter*, and in *Rakas*. Both of those cases emphasize that a defendant can base his Fourth Amendment claim only on the violation of his own privacy interests. But in a system with an exclusionary rule, the Fourth Amendment claims of defendants like Carter and Johns protect the privacy interests of law-abiding citizens — by making it harder to search apartments for drugs, the Fourth Amendment makes it harder to search apartments where no drugs will be found. One might say that all exclusionary rule litigation involves a form of third-party standing, where the claimant is permitted to raise his claim in order to protect other parties not before the court. The theory underlying *Rakas* and *Carter* seems inconsistent with the primary remedy the Court uses to enforce the Fourth Amendment.

4. Recall the facts of Wyoming v. Houghton, page 488, supra. There the defendant was a passenger in someone else's car; the police stopped and searched the car, including the defendant's purse, which was found sitting on the back seat. The Court assumed that the defendant had standing to challenge the search of her purse. In Rakas v. Illinois, 439 U.S. 128 (1978), the defendant was likewise a passenger in someone else's car. There, the Court held that the defendant lacked standing to challenge the search of the car's glove compartment. Is the line between *Rakas* and *Houghton* obvious? Is it right?

5. The defendant in United States v. Payner, 447 U.S. 727 (1980), was charged with falsifying his income tax return; among other things, the government claimed that the defendant had a foreign bank account that he denied having. In the course of the government's investigation, federal agents lured a bank officer to dinner, while other agents entered the bank officer's hotel room, removed his briefcase, and photographed documents found there. Those documents were in turn used against the defendant. The Court found that the defendant lacked standing, because the hotel room, briefcase, and documents had belonged to the bank officer, not to him.

There is some reason to believe the search in *Payner* was strategic. As Carol Steiker reports,

> In testimony before the District Court in [*Payner*], it came to light that a Mr. Hyatt, an attorney with the Department of Justice, explicitly had instructed the I.R.S. agents in the case that the bank officer whose briefcase was stolen to obtain information against the defendant would be the only individual to have standing to object to the blatantly illegal search and that he was not a target of the investigation.

Carol S. Steiker, Counter-Revolution in Constitutional Criminal Procedure? Two Audiences, Two Answers, 94 Mich. L. Rev. 2466, 2536 (1996). Steiker argues that this sort of behavior is natural given the state of standing doctrine. The problem, she suggests, is this: Standing rules are "decision rules" whose proper audience is the courts. Ideally, the police should be unaware of them. The rules the police should pay attention to are the Fourth Amendment's many "conduct rules," the doctrines that define what searches and seizures the police may or may not undertake. But decision rules like standing doctrine cannot be kept from the police, and the police cannot be expected to ignore such rules once they know about them. As Steiker puts it,

> As for the police, [what] ought to concern us is the likelihood that . . . decision rules will, in effect, become conduct rules. Where the police "hear" the Court's decision rules and thus are able to predict the likely legal consequences of their unconstitutional behavior, they may see little reason to continue to obey conduct rules that are consistently unenforced. . . . [C]hanges in decision rules will necessarily change compliance with conduct rules.

Id., at 2543. What does Steiker's argument imply for standing doctrine? Should the Court grant everyone standing, to avoid the kind of strategic behavior that appears in *Payner*? Or should standing simply be made less predictable, so that police would find it harder to anticipate who would and who wouldn't be able to object to any given illegal search? Might standing be one area of Fourth Amendment doctrine where standards rather than rules are appropriate?

3. "Fruit of the Poisonous Tree" Doctrine

WONG SUN v. UNITED STATES

Certiorari to the United States Court of Appeals for the Ninth Circuit
371 U.S. 471 (1963)

MR. JUSTICE BRENNAN delivered the opinion of the Court.

The petitioners were tried without a jury in the District Court for the Northern District of California under a two-count indictment for violation of the Federal Narcotics Laws. They were acquitted under the first count which charged a conspiracy, but convicted under the second count which charged the substantive offense of fraudulent and knowing transportation and concealment of illegally imported heroin. The Court of Appeals for the Ninth Circuit, one judge dissenting, affirmed the convictions. 288 F.2d 366. We granted certiorari.

About 2 a.m. on the morning of June 4, 1959, federal narcotics agents in San Francisco, after having had one Hom Way under surveillance for six weeks, arrested him and found heroin in his possession. Hom Way, who had not before been an informant, stated after his arrest that he had bought an ounce of heroin the night before from one known to him only as "Blackie Toy," proprietor of a laundry on Leavenworth Street.

About 6 a.m. that morning six or seven federal agents went to a laundry at 1733 Leavenworth Street. The sign above the door of this establishment said "Oye's

Laundry." It was operated by the petitioner James Wah Toy. There is, however, nothing in the record which identifies James Wah Toy and "Blackie Toy" as the same person. The other federal officers remained nearby out of sight while Agent Alton Wong, who was of Chinese ancestry, rang the bell. When petitioner Toy appeared and opened the door, Agent Wong told him that he was calling for laundry and dry cleaning. Toy replied that he didn't open until 8 o'clock and told the agent to come back at that time. Toy started to close the door. Agent Wong thereupon took his badge from his pocket and said, "I am a federal narcotics agent." Toy immediately "slammed the door and started running" down the hallway through the laundry to his living quarters at the back where his wife and child were sleeping in a bedroom. Agent Wong and the other federal officers broke open the door and followed Toy down the hallway to the living quarters and into the bedroom. Toy reached into a nightstand drawer. Agent Wong thereupon drew his pistol, pulled Toy's hand out of the drawer, placed him under arrest and handcuffed him. There was nothing in the drawer and a search of the premises uncovered no narcotics.

One of the agents said to Toy ". . . [Hom Way] says he got narcotics from you." Toy responded, "No, I haven't been selling any narcotics at all. However, I do know somebody who has." When asked who that was, Toy said, "I only know him as Johnny. I don't know his last name." . . . Toy described a house on Eleventh Avenue where he said Johnny lived; he also described a bedroom in the house where he said "Johnny kept about a piece"[2] of heroin, and where he and Johnny had smoked some of the drug the night before. The agents left immediately for Eleventh Avenue and located the house. They entered and found one Johnny Yee in the bedroom. After a discussion with the agents, Yee took from a bureau drawer several tubes containing in all just less than one ounce of heroin, and surrendered them. Within the hour Yee and Toy were taken to the Office of the Bureau of Narcotics. Yee there stated that the heroin had been brought to him some four days earlier by petitioner Toy and another Chinese known to him only as "Sea Dog."

Toy was questioned as to the identity of "Sea Dog" and said that "Sea Dog" was Wong Sun. Some agents, including Agent Alton Wong, took Toy to Wong Sun's neighborhood where Toy pointed out a multifamily dwelling where he said Wong Sun lived. Agent Wong rang a downstairs door bell and a buzzer sounded, opening the door. The officer identified himself as a narcotics agent to a woman on the landing and asked "for Mr. Wong." The woman was the wife of petitioner Wong Sun. She said that Wong Sun was "in the back room sleeping." Alton Wong and some six other officers climbed the stairs and entered the apartment. One of the officers went into the back room and brought petitioner Wong Sun from the bedroom in handcuffs. A thorough search of the apartment followed, but no narcotics were discovered.

Petitioner Toy and Johnny Yee were arraigned . . . on June 4 on a complaint charging [narcotics violations]. Later that day, each was released on his own recognizance. Petitioner Wong Sun was arraigned on a similar complaint filed the next day and was also released on his own recognizance. Within a few days, both petitioners and Yee were interrogated at the office of the Narcotics Bureau by Agent William Wong, also of Chinese ancestry. The agent advised each of the three of his right to withhold information which might be used against him, and stated to each that he was entitled to the advice of counsel, though it does not appear that any attorney was present during the questioning of any of the three. The officer also explained to

2. A "piece" is approximately one ounce.

each that no promises or offers of immunity or leniency were being or could be made.

The agent interrogated each of the three separately. After each had been interrogated the agent prepared a statement in English from rough notes. The agent read petitioner Toy's statement to him in English and interpreted certain portions of it for him in Chinese. Toy also read the statement in English aloud to the agent, said there were corrections to be made, and made the corrections in his own hand. Toy would not sign the statement, however. . . . Wong Sun had considerable difficulty understanding the statement in English and the agent restated its substance in Chinese. Wong Sun refused to sign the statement although he admitted the accuracy of its contents.

. . . The Government's evidence tending to prove the petitioners' possession (the petitioners offered no exculpatory testimony) consisted of four items which the trial court admitted over timely objections that they were inadmissible as "fruits" of unlawful arrests or of attendant searches: (1) the statements made orally by petitioner Toy in his bedroom at the time of his arrest; (2) the heroin surrendered to the agents by Johnny Yee; (3) petitioner Toy's pretrial unsigned statement; and (4) petitioner Wong Sun's similar statement. The dispute below and here has centered around the correctness of the rulings of the trial judge allowing these items in evidence.

The Court of Appeals held that the arrests of both petitioners were illegal because not based on "'probable cause' within the meaning of the Fourth Amendment." . . . The Court of Appeals nevertheless held that the four items of proof were not the "fruits" of the illegal arrests and that they were therefore properly admitted in evidence. . . .

We believe that significant differences between the cases of the two petitioners require separate discussion of each. We shall first consider the case of petitioner Toy.

I

The Court of Appeals found there was neither reasonable grounds nor probable cause for Toy's arrest. Giving due weight to that finding, we think it is amply justified by the facts clearly shown on this record. . . . The quantum of information which constitutes probable cause — evidence which would "warrant a man of reasonable caution in the belief" that a felony has been committed — must be measured by the facts of the particular case. The history of the use, and not infrequent abuse, of the power to arrest cautions that a relaxation of the fundamental requirements of probable cause would "leave law-abiding citizens at the mercy of the officers' whim or caprice." Brinegar v. United States, 338 U.S. 160, 176.

Whether or not the requirements of reliability and particularity of the information on which an officer may act are more stringent where an arrest warrant is absent, they surely cannot be less stringent than where an arrest warrant is obtained. . . . The threshold question in this case, therefore, is whether the officers could, on the information which impelled them to act, have procured a warrant for the arrest of Toy. We think that no warrant would have issued on evidence then available.

The narcotics agents had no basis in experience for confidence in the reliability of Hom Way's information; he had never before given information. And yet they acted upon his imprecise suggestion that a person described only as "Blackie Toy," the proprietor of a laundry somewhere on Leavenworth Street, had sold one ounce of heroin. We have held that identification of the suspect by a reliable informant may constitute probable cause for arrest where the information given is sufficiently accurate to lead the officers directly to the suspect. Draper v. United States, 358 U.S. 307. That rule does not, however, fit this case. For aught that the record discloses, Hom Way's accusation merely invited the officers to roam the length of Leavenworth Street (some 30 blocks) in search of one "Blackie Toy's" laundry — and whether by chance or other means (the record does not say) they came upon petitioner Toy's laundry, which bore not his name over the door, but the unrevealing label "Oye's." Not the slightest intimation appears on the record . . . to suggest that the agents had information giving them reason to equate "Blackie" Toy and James Wah Toy.

The Government contends, however, that any defects in the information which somehow took the officers to petitioner Toy's laundry were remedied by events which occurred after they arrived. Specifically, it is urged that Toy's flight down the hall when the supposed customer at the door revealed that he was a narcotics agent adequately corroborates the suspicion generated by Hom Way's accusation.

[I]n Miller v. United States, 357 U.S. 301, . . . [w]e held that when an officer insufficiently or unclearly identifies his office or his mission, the occupant's flight from the door must be regarded as ambiguous conduct. . . . Agent Wong did eventually disclose that he was a narcotics officer. However, he affirmatively misrepresented his mission at the outset, by stating that he had come for laundry and dry cleaning. And before Toy fled, the officer never adequately dispelled the misimpression engendered by his own ruse.

Toy's refusal to admit the officers and his flight down the hallway thus signified a guilty knowledge no more clearly than it did a natural desire to repel an apparently unauthorized intrusion.

A contrary holding here would mean that a vague suspicion could be transformed into probable cause for arrest by reason of ambiguous conduct which the arresting officers themselves have provoked. That result would have the same essential vice as a proposition we have consistently rejected — that a search unlawful at its inception may be validated by what it turns up. Byars v. United States, 273 U.S. 28; United States v. Di Re, 332 U.S. 581, 595. Thus we conclude that the Court of Appeals' finding that the officers' uninvited entry into Toy's living quarters was unlawful and that the bedroom arrest which followed was likewise unlawful, was fully justified on the evidence. It remains to be seen what consequences flow from this conclusion.

II

It is conceded that Toy's declarations in his bedroom are to be excluded if they are held to be "fruits" of the agents' unlawful action.

In order to make effective the fundamental constitutional guarantees of sanctity of the home and inviolability of the person, Boyd v. United States, 116 U.S. 616, this Court held nearly half a century ago that evidence seized during an unlawful search could not constitute proof against the victim of the search. Weeks v. United States, 232 U.S. 383. The exclusionary prohibition extends as well to the indirect as the direct products of such invasions. Silverthorne Lumber Co. v. United States, 251 U.S. 385. Mr. Justice Holmes, speaking for the Court in that case, in holding that the Government might not make use of information obtained during an unlawful search to subpoena from the victims the very documents illegally viewed, expressed succinctly the policy of the broad exclusionary rule:

> The essence of a provision forbidding the acquisition of evidence in a certain way is that not merely evidence so acquired shall not be used before the Court but that it shall not be used at all. Of course this does not mean that the facts thus obtained become sacred and inaccessible. If knowledge of them is gained from an independent source they may be proved like any others, but the knowledge gained by the Government's own wrong cannot be used by it in the way proposed.

251 U.S., at 392.

The exclusionary rule has traditionally barred from trial physical, tangible materials obtained either during or as a direct result of an unlawful invasion. It follows from our holding in Silverman v. United States, 365 U.S. 505, that the Fourth Amendment may protect against the overhearing of verbal statements as well as against the more traditional seizure of "papers and effects." Similarly, testimony as to matters observed during an unlawful invasion has been excluded in order to enforce the basic constitutional policies. Thus, verbal evidence which derives so immediately from an unlawful entry and an unauthorized arrest as the officers' action in the present case is no less the "fruit" of official illegality than the more common tangible fruits of the unwarranted intrusion. Nor do the policies underlying the exclusionary rule invite any logical distinction between physical and verbal evidence. Either in terms of deterring lawless conduct by federal officers, or of closing the doors of the federal courts to any use of evidence unconstitutionally obtained, the danger in relaxing the exclusionary rules in the case of verbal evidence would seem too great to warrant introducing such a distinction.

The Government argues that Toy's statements to the officers in his bedroom, although closely consequent upon the invasion which we hold unlawful, were nevertheless admissible because they resulted from "an intervening independent act of a free will." This contention, however, takes insufficient account of the circumstances. Six or seven officers had broken the door and followed on Toy's heels into the bedroom where his wife and child were sleeping. He had been almost immediately handcuffed and arrested. Under such circumstances it is unreasonable to infer that Toy's response was sufficiently an act of free will to purge the primary taint of the unlawful invasion.

III

We now consider whether the exclusion of Toy's declarations requires also the exclusion of the narcotics taken from Yee, to which those declarations led the police. The prosecutor candidly told the trial court that "we wouldn't have found those drugs except that Mr. Toy helped us to." Hence this is not the case envisioned by this Court where the exclusionary rule has no application because the Government learned of the evidence "from an independent source," Silverthorne Lumber Co. v. United States, 251 U.S. 385, 392; nor is this a case in which the connection between the lawless conduct of the police and the discovery of the challenged evidence has "become so attenuated as to dissipate the taint." Nardone v. United States, 308 U.S. 338, 341. We need not hold that all evidence is "fruit of the poisonous tree" simply because it would not have come to light but for the illegal actions of the police. Rather, the more apt question in such a case is "whether, granting establishment of the primary illegality, the evidence to which instant objection is made has been come at by exploitation of that illegality or instead by means sufficiently distinguishable to be purged of the primary taint." Maguire, Evidence of Guilt, 221 (1959). We think it clear that the narcotics were "come at by the exploitation of that illegality" and hence that they may not be used against Toy.

IV

It remains only to consider Toy's unsigned statement. We need not decide whether, in light of the fact that Toy was free on his own recognizance when he made the statement, that statement was a fruit of the illegal arrest. Since we have concluded that his declarations in the bedroom and the narcotics surrendered by Yee should not have been admitted in evidence against him, the only proofs remaining to sustain his conviction are his and Wong Sun's unsigned statements. Without scrutinizing the contents of Toy's ambiguous recitals, we conclude that no reference to Toy in Wong Sun's statement constitutes admissible evidence corroborating any admission by Toy. We arrive at this conclusion upon two clear lines of decisions which converge to require it. One line of our decisions establishes that criminal confessions and admissions of guilt require extrinsic corroboration; the other line of precedents holds that an out-of-court declaration made after arrest may not be used at trial against one of the declarant's partners in crime.

. . . Thus as to Toy the only possible source of corroboration is removed and his conviction must be set aside for lack of competent evidence to support it.

V

We turn now to the case of the other petitioner, Wong Sun. We have no occasion to disagree with the finding of the Court of Appeals that his arrest, also, was without probable cause or reasonable grounds. At all events no evidentiary consequences turn upon that question. For Wong Sun's unsigned confession was not the fruit of that arrest, and was therefore properly admitted at trial. On the evidence that Wong Sun had been released on his own recognizance after a lawful arraignment, and had returned voluntarily several days later to make the statement, we hold that the connection between the arrest and the statement had "become so attenuated as to dissipate the taint." Nardone v. United States, 308 U.S. 338, 341. The fact that the statement was unsigned, whatever bearing this may have upon its weight and credibility, does not render it inadmissible; Wong Sun understood and adopted its substance, though he could not comprehend the English words. The petitioner has never suggested any impropriety in the interrogation itself which would require the exclusion of this statement.

We must then consider the admissibility of the narcotics surrendered by Yee. Our holding that this ounce of heroin was inadmissible against Toy does not compel a like result with respect to Wong Sun. The exclusion of the narcotics as to Toy was required solely by their tainted relationship to information unlawfully obtained from Toy, and not by any official impropriety connected with their surrender by Yee. The seizure of this heroin invaded no right of privacy of person or premises which would entitle Wong Sun to object to its use at his trial.

However, for the reasons that Wong Sun's statement was incompetent to corroborate Toy's admissions contained in Toy's own statement, any references to Wong Sun in Toy's statement were incompetent to corroborate Wong Sun's admissions. Thus, the only competent source of corroboration for Wong Sun's statement was the heroin itself. We cannot be certain, however, on this state of the record, that the trial judge may not also have considered the contents of Toy's statement as a source of corroboration.

We intimate no view one way or the other as to whether the trial judge might have found in the narcotics alone sufficient evidence to corroborate Wong Sun's admissions that he delivered heroin to Yee and smoked heroin at Yee's house around the date in question. But because he might, as the factfinder, have found insufficient corroboration from the narcotics alone, we cannot be sure that the scales were not tipped in favor of conviction by reliance upon the inadmissible Toy statement. . . .

. . . We therefore hold that petitioner Wong Sun is also entitled to a new trial. . . .

[The concurring opinion of Justice Douglas, and the dissenting opinion of Justice Clark, joined by Justices Harlan, Stewart, and White, are omitted.]

NOTES ON *WONG SUN*

1. It is important to follow the chain of events in *Wong Sun*. Federal agents first got a tip from Hom Way, then proceeded to Toy's laundry. Toy answered the door and then fled; agents followed him inside and arrested him in his bedroom. Toy made various incriminating statements at the scene of his arrest, which led the police to Johnny Yee's home. The police found heroin in Yee's bedroom; shortly afterward, Yee made statements that incriminated Wong Sun. Later, some time after Toy and Wong Sun had both been arraigned, agents interrogated both men; both made various incriminating statements during the course of those interrogations.

2. As that description suggests, the chief potential "poisonous tree" in *Wong Sun* is Toy's arrest. If Toy's arrest were legal, then Toy's contemporaneous statements and the heroin found in Yee's bedroom would both be admissible against him. Why *wasn't* the arrest legal? The Court explains that Hom Way's identification was not detailed enough to amount to probable cause by itself, which sounds right. But Toy's flight upon hearing Agent Wong identify himself suggested that Hom Way's tip was correct — that Toy was indeed "Blackie Toy" and that he was involved in heroin trafficking. The Court concludes otherwise, on the ground that Toy's flight was "ambiguous," because Agent Wong never "adequately dispelled the misimpression" he created when he said, initially, that he was there to pick up some laundry. Does *that* sound right? It's hard to believe that Toy ran because he thought Wong was an angry customer; it is much easier to believe that he ran because he thought Wong was there to arrest him. In short, the "fruit of the poisonous tree" analysis in *Wong Sun* depends on the probable cause analysis — and the probable cause analysis looks seriously flawed.

3. There is also a standing issue in *Wong Sun*. On that score, Justice Brennan's analysis is more conventional. Notice that the drugs taken from Yee could not be used against Toy, since the search of Yee's bedroom was the fruit of Toy's illegal arrest. But those same drugs *could* be used against Wong Sun, because Wong Sun had no standing to complain of Toy's illegal arrest. (And, of course, neither Toy nor

Wong Sun had any standing to complain about any aspect of Yee's arrest.) All of those conclusions would hold true under current standing doctrine just as they did in 1963.

4. Which leads to the "fruit of the poisonous tree" aspect of *Wong Sun*. The Court's opinion offers three key "fruits" holdings. First, Toy's statements at the scene of his own arrest were the fruit of that arrest. Second, the drugs found in Yee's bedroom were also the fruit of Toy's arrest. And third, Wong Sun's statement, given several days after his arraignment, was *not* the fruit of Wong Sun's illegal arrest. Do those holdings make sense? Is *Wong Sun* a wise application of the exclusionary rule?

NOTES ON "FRUIT OF THE POISONOUS TREE" DOCTRINE

1. To answer those questions, it helps to step back from the factual tangles in *Wong Sun* and consider the basic issue underlying "fruit of the poisonous tree" doctrine. The exclusionary rule obviously requires the suppression of illegally seized evidence — when the police illegally search a suspect's home and find heroin, the heroin must be suppressed at that suspect's trial. That obvious principle resolves most, but not all cases. Sometimes, criminal defendants claim that a given piece of evidence is inadmissible not because it was illegally seized, but because it was the "fruit" of — i.e., its discovery was caused by — an illegal search or seizure.

Why not suppress *only* illegally seized evidence? One possible answer is that the government should not benefit from its own wrongdoing — that is the point of Justice Holmes' language in *Silverthorne Lumber*, quoted in *Wong Sun*. To avoid an illegitimate benefit, the government must forgo use of all evidence obtained because of police illegality, not just evidence obtained at the scene of the illegal search. Another, more conventional answer would be that if the police know they can still use the fruits of illegal searches, they will have an incentive to search illegally. So to eliminate the incentive to violate the Fourth Amendment, the exclusionary rule must make sure that police gain nothing from violations, and the only way to do that is to suppress all evidence obtained *because of* the violations.

The response to these arguments goes as follows: Suppressing reliable evidence is a bad thing, because it takes criminal trials further from the truth. The law should therefore suppress evidence only when it must do so to ensure an acceptable level of compliance with the Fourth Amendment. And suppressing fruits of illegal searches is not necessary to reach that level of compliance. It is hard enough for police to know what evidence they will find when they search. Surely it is much harder still for police to anticipate evidence that they will find sometime down the road *because of* the search. When the police in *Wong Sun* arrested Hom Way or followed James Wah Toy into his bedroom, they had no idea what other evidence (and which other suspects) they might uncover as a result. On this account, the incentive problem is simply not worth worrying about; it is enough to tell the police that they cannot use any evidence found in the course of — not because of — an illegal search.

Which side is right depends, at least in part, on empirical judgments. How often do police search in order to find evidence other than the evidence at the scene of the search? How well do police anticipate later discoveries when making earlier ones? Reliable answers to those questions do not exist; courts must make educated guesses.

Perhaps that explains why the law has basically split the difference. Along with many other cases, *Wong Sun* holds that when evidence is obtained because of an illegal search, it must be suppressed unless the "taint" of the illegal search has somehow "dissipated." But then, as discussed above, no defendant can complain of an illegal search of someone else — meaning (to use the facts of *Wong Sun*) that if the police search Toy's bedroom illegally, Yee cannot complain of *that* illegality when the police later wind up in Yee's bedroom. The upshot of these two rules is that some fruits of illegal searches are suppressed, and some are not. Standing doctrine and fruit-of-the-poisonous-tree doctrine deal with the same problem — a given illegal search produces other evidence, or leads to other suspects — but they resolve that problem very differently. The other evidence might be suppressed, but not against the other suspects. Does this strike you as a sensible compromise?

2. The basic concept underlying the fruit of the poisonous tree doctrine is causation. Whenever the law deals with causation, the inquiry divides into two questions: "But for" this event, would that event have happened? And if not, was the first event *responsible* for the second one? In tort law, the first question is dealt with under the doctrinal heading of "cause in fact," sometimes called "but-for cause." The second question is the subject of "proximate cause" doctrine.

Fruit of the poisonous tree doctrine uses the same division and the same concepts, but different labels. As in torts, one must ask whether, but for the illegal search, the evidence in question would have been found. In Fourth Amendment law, that question turns into two other questions: Was the evidence at issue obtained through an "independent source"? If so, it is not suppressible, because the illegal search did not cause the police to find it. Alternatively, would the evidence inevitably have been discovered? Again, if so, it is not suppressible, because the illegal search did not cause the police to discover it. Only if the evidence was neither obtained through an independent source nor inevitably discovered can it be suppressed.

This means that "but-for cause" is, in Fourth Amendment law, dealt with through two doctrines — independent source and inevitable discovery — and those doctrines define the cases where cause in fact is not satisfied. We will take up those doctrines in the next main case.

3. What about proximate cause? There, the Fourth Amendment analogue is the concept of attenuation. Notice that the Court in *Wong Sun* referred to whether the "taint" of the illegal search had "dissipated." The idea is the same as in proximate cause cases: Sometimes, the chain of causation is sufficiently long or complicated that one can say that a particular earlier link should not be deemed responsible for a later one.

Like proximate cause, attenuation is hard to define. In *Wong Sun*, the Court says it is "clear" that the drugs taken from Yee were not too attenuated a result of the illegal search of Toy's bedroom. Yet the Court holds, with little explanation, that Wong Sun's statement several days after his arrest *was* too attenuated a result of his arrest. Are these conclusions right? Can they be justified, or is the Court's conclusory treatment unavoidable?

The Court tried, not entirely successfully, to define the concept of attenuation a little more fully in United States v. Ceccolini, 435 U.S. 268 (1978). The illegal search in *Ceccolini* took place in the defendant's flower shop; Officer Biro, who was involved in an ongoing investigation of various gambling activities, opened an envelope behind the cash register and saw policy slips. Biro returned the envelope before the search was noticed, and he told his superiors what he had found. Four months later, relying in part on Biro's report, another officer interviewed one Lois Hennessey, a clerk at the same flower shop. Hennessey, in turn, supplied critical testimony at the defendant's later perjury trial, and the defendant was convicted. The defendant argued that Hennessey's testimony was the fruit of the illegal search of the envelope. The Court disagreed:

> [We] reject the Government's suggestion that we adopt what would in practice amount to a per se rule that the testimony of a live witness should not be excluded at trial no matter how close and proximate the connection between it and a violation of the Fourth Amendment. We also reaffirm the holding of *Wong Sun* that "verbal evidence which derives so immediately from an unlawful entry and an unauthorized arrest as the officers' action in the present case is no less the 'fruit' of official illegality than the more common tangible fruits of the unwarranted intrusion." We are of the view, however, that cases decided since *Wong Sun* significantly qualify its further observation that "the policies underlying the exclusionary rule [do not] invite any logical distinction between physical and verbal evidence." . . .
>
>   The greater the willingness of the witness to freely testify, the greater the likelihood that he or she will be discovered by legal means and, concomitantly, the smaller the incentive to conduct an illegal search to discover the witness. Witnesses are not like guns or documents which remain hidden from view until one turns over a sofa, or opens a filing cabinet. Witnesses can, and often do, come forward and offer evidence entirely of their own volition. And evaluated properly, the degree of free will necessary to dissipate the taint will very likely be found more often in the case of live-witness testimony than other kinds of evidence. . . .
>
>   . . . The evidence indicates overwhelmingly that the testimony given by the witness was an act of her own free will in no way coerced or even induced by official authority as a result of Biro's discovery of the policy slips. Nor were the slips themselves used in questioning Hennessey. Substantial periods of time elapsed between the time of the illegal search and the initial contact with the witness, on the one hand, and between the latter and the testimony at trial on the other. . . .
>
>   There is, in addition, not the slightest evidence to suggest that Biro . . . entered the shop and searched [the envelope] with the intent of finding a willing and knowledgeable witness to testify against respondent. Application of the exclusionary rule in this situation could not have the slightest deterrent effect on the behavior of an officer such as Biro. . . .
>
>   Obviously no mathematical weight can be assigned to any of the factors which we have discussed, but just as obviously they all point to the conclusion that the exclusionary rule should be invoked with much greater reluctance where the claim is based on a causal relationship between a constitutional violation and the discovery of a live witness than when a similar claim is advanced to support suppression of an inanimate object.

Id., at 274-280. Is the definition clear now?

MURRAY v. UNITED STATES

Certiorari to the United States Court of Appeals for the First Circuit
487 U.S. 533 (1988)

JUSTICE SCALIA delivered the opinion of the Court.

. . . Based on information received from informants, federal law enforcement agents had been surveilling petitioner Murray and several of his co-conspirators. At about 1:45 p.m. on April 6, 1983, they observed Murray drive a truck and Carter drive a green camper, into a warehouse in South Boston. When the petitioners drove the vehicles out about 20 minutes later, the surveilling agents saw within the warehouse two individuals and a tractor-trailer rig bearing a long, dark container. Murray and Carter later turned over the truck and camper to other drivers, who were in turn followed and ultimately arrested, and the vehicles lawfully seized. Both vehicles were found to contain marijuana.

After receiving this information, several of the agents converged on the South Boston warehouse and forced entry. They found the warehouse unoccupied, but observed in plain view numerous burlap-wrapped bales that were later found to contain marijuana. They left without disturbing the bales, kept the warehouse under surveillance, and did not reenter it until they had a search warrant. In applying for the warrant, the agents did not mention the prior entry, and did not rely on any observations made during that entry. When the warrant was issued — at 10:40 p.m., approximately eight hours after the initial entry — the agents immediately reentered the warehouse and seized 270 bales of marijuana and notebooks listing customers for whom the bales were destined.

Before trial, petitioners moved to suppress the evidence found in the warehouse. The District Court denied the motion, rejecting petitioners' arguments that the warrant was invalid because the agents did not inform the Magistrate about their prior warrantless entry, and that the warrant was tainted by that entry. The First Circuit affirmed. . . .

The exclusionary rule prohibits introduction into evidence of tangible materials seized during an unlawful search, and of testimony concerning knowledge acquired during an unlawful search. Beyond that, the exclusionary rule also prohibits the introduction of derivative evidence, both tangible and testimonial, that is the product of the primary evidence, or that is otherwise acquired as an indirect result of the unlawful search, up to the point at which the connection with the unlawful search becomes "so attenuated as to dissipate the taint," Nardone v. United States, 308 U.S. 338, 341 (1939). See Wong Sun v. United States, 371 U.S. 471, 484-485 (1963). Almost simultaneously with our development of the exclusionary rule, in the first quarter of this century, we also announced what has come to be known as the "independent source" doctrine. See Silverthorne Lumber Co. v. United States, 251 U.S. 385, 392 (1920). That doctrine, which has been applied to evidence acquired not only through Fourth Amendment violations but also through Fifth and Sixth Amendment violations, has recently been described as follows:

> [T]he interest of society in deterring unlawful police conduct and the public interest in having juries receive all probative evidence of a crime are properly balanced by putting the police in the same, not a worse, position that they would have been in if no police error or misconduct had occurred. . . . When the challenged evidence has an independent source, exclusion of such evidence would put the police in a worse position than they would have been in absent any error or violation. Nix v. Williams, 467 U.S. 431, 443 (1984).

The dispute here is over the scope of this doctrine. Petitioners contend that it applies only to evidence obtained for the first time during an independent lawful search. The Government argues that it applies also to evidence initially discovered during, or as a consequence of, an unlawful search, but later obtained independently from activities untainted by the initial illegality. We think the Government's view has better support in both precedent and policy. Our cases have used the concept of "independent source" in a more general and a more specific sense. The more general sense identifies all evidence acquired in a fashion untainted by the illegal evidence-gathering activity. Thus, where an unlawful entry has given investigators knowledge of facts x and y, but fact z has been learned by other means, fact z can be said to be admissible because derived from an "independent source." This is how we used the term in Segura v. United States, 468 U.S. 796 (1984). In that case, agents unlawfully entered the defendant's apartment and remained there until a search warrant was obtained. The admissibility of what they discovered while waiting in the apartment was not before us, id., at 802-803, n. 4, but we held that the evidence found for the first time during the execution of the valid and untainted search warrant was admissible because it was discovered pursuant to an "independent source," id., at 813-814.

The original use of the term, however, and its more important use for purposes of these cases, was more specific. It was originally applied in the exclusionary rule context, by Justice Holmes, with reference to that particular category of evidence acquired by an untainted search which is identical to the evidence unlawfully acquired — that is, in the example just given, to knowledge of facts x and y derived from an independent source:

> The essence of a provision forbidding the acquisition of evidence in a certain way is that not merely evidence so acquired shall not be used before the Court but that it shall not be used at all. Of course this does not mean that the facts thus obtained become sacred and inaccessible. If knowledge of them is gained from an independent source they may be proved like any others. Silverthorne Lumber, supra, at 392.

. . . We recently assumed this application of the independent source doctrine (in the Sixth Amendment context) in Nix v. Williams, supra. There incriminating statements obtained in violation of the defendant's right to counsel had led the police to the victim's body. The body had not in fact been found through an independent source as well, and so the independent source doctrine was not itself applicable. We held, however, that evidence concerning the body was nonetheless admissible because a search had been under way which would have discovered the body, had it not been called off because of the discovery produced by the unlawfully obtained statements. This "inevitable discovery" doctrine obviously assumes the validity of the independent source doctrine as applied to evidence initially acquired unlawfully. It would make no sense to admit the evidence because the independent search, had it not been aborted, would have found the body, but to exclude the evidence if the search had continued and had in fact found the body. The inevitable discovery doctrine, with its distinct requirements, is in reality an extrapolation from the independent source doctrine: Since the tainted evidence would be admissible if in fact discovered through an independent source, it should be admissible if it inevitably would have been discovered. Petitioners' asserted policy basis for excluding evidence which is initially discovered during an illegal search, but is subsequently acquired through an independent and lawful source, is that a contrary rule will remove all deterrence to, and indeed positively encourage, unlawful police searches. As petitioners see the incentives, law enforcement officers will routinely enter without a warrant to make sure that what they expect to be on the premises is in fact there. If it is not, they will have spared themselves the time and trouble of getting a warrant; if it is, they can get the warrant and use the evidence despite the unlawful entry. We see the incentives differently. An officer with probable cause sufficient to obtain a search warrant would be foolish to enter the premises first in an unlawful manner. By doing so, he would risk suppression of all evidence on the premises, both seen and unseen, since his action would add to the normal burden of convincing a magistrate that there is probable cause the much more onerous burden of convincing a trial court that no information gained from the illegal entry affected either the law enforcement officers' decision to seek a warrant or the magistrate's decision to grant it. Nor would the officer without sufficient probable cause to obtain a search warrant have any added incentive to conduct an unlawful entry, since whatever he finds cannot be used to establish probable cause before a magistrate. . . .

To apply what we have said to the present cases: Knowledge that the marijuana was in the warehouse was assuredly acquired at the time of the unlawful entry. But it was also acquired at the time of entry pursuant to the warrant, and if that later acquisition was not the result of the earlier entry there is no reason why the independent source doctrine should not apply. Invoking the exclusionary rule would put the police (and society) not in the same position they would have occupied if no violation occurred, but in a worse one. See Nix v. Williams, 467 U.S., at 443. . . .

The ultimate question, therefore, is whether the search pursuant to warrant was in fact a genuinely independent source of the information and tangible evidence at issue here. This would not have been the case if the agents' decision to seek the warrant was prompted by what they had seen during the initial entry, or if information obtained during that entry was presented to the Magistrate and affected his decision to issue the warrant. . . .

. . . The District Court found that the agents did not reveal their warrantless entry to the Magistrate, and that they did not include in their application for a warrant any recitation of their observations in the warehouse. It did not, however, explicitly find that the agents would have sought a warrant if they had not earlier entered the warehouse. . . . Accordingly, we vacate the judgment and remand these cases to the Court of Appeals with instructions that it remand to the District Court for determination whether the warrant-authorized search of the warehouse was an independent source of the challenged evidence in the sense we have described.

[The dissenting opinion of Justice Marshall, joined by Justice Stevens and Justice O'Connor, is omitted.]

NOTES ON THE "INDEPENDENT SOURCE" AND "INEVITABLE DISCOVERY" DOCTRINES

1. No one argues that the exclusionary rule should extend to *more than* evidence obtained because of the illegal search or seizure. It would seem to follow that evidence obtained through some independent legal source should be admissible, as should evidence that would have been discovered, "inevitably" or otherwise, even if the illegal search had never taken place. Both independent source doctrine and inevitable discovery doctrine seem not only right, but obvious.

2. But if the doctrines are easy in principle, they may be very hard indeed in application, as Craig Bradley's discussion of *Murray* illustrates:

Consider the position of the rational police officer. Assume that it is true, as the Court avers, that if he has ample probable cause and ample time, he will go ahead and get a warrant in order to avoid the additional explanations that a warrantless search will entail. But suppose, as is frequently the case, that his probable cause is shaky or non-existent. *Murray* positively encourages him to proceed with an illegal search. If he finds nothing, he simply shrugs his shoulders and walks away. If he finds evidence, he leaves his partner to watch over it, repairs to the magistrate, and reports that "an anonymous reliable informant who has given information on three occasions in the past that has led to convictions called to tell me that he had just seen bales of marijuana stored at a warehouse at 123 Elm Street." The warrant issues and the marijuana is seized. Before trial (assuming that the defense has found out about the illegal search), the officer admits it, chalks it up to a fear that the evidence would be lost if the warehouse were not immediately secured, apologizes for being wrong in this assessment, and introduces the warrant affidavit to demonstrate an independent source. . . .

Of course, it has always been the case that the police could make up the existence of "Old Reliable," the informant, and use his fictitious "tip" as the basis for a search warrant. The problem with this tactic is that, if the police are wrong and no evidence is found, they are forced to return to the magistrate empty-handed. This is embarrassing to the police department and would only have to happen a few times before the magistrates and defense attorneys would realize that the police were liars. After *Murray*, there is no such fear, because the fictitious "Old Reliable" will always be right! His "tip" will always lead to evidence because the police will have found it in advance.

Craig M. Bradley, Murray v. United States: The Bell Tolls for the Warrant Requirement, 64 Ind. L.J. 907, 917-918 (1989).

Bradley's point is that figuring out what sources are truly "independent" may be impossible; given *Murray*, it will often be easy for officers to turn a run-of-the-mill illegal search into a plausible "independent source" search. Of course, this assumes that police officers will be willing to lie. Should the law so assume? Is police perjury any more of a problem here than in an ordinary warrantless search case in which a dishonest officer could concoct a set of facts that made the search legal?

3. Causation in "independent source" cases like *Murray* may be hard because of concerns about the trustworthiness of police testimony. Causation in inevitable discovery cases is hard, period. The defendant in Nix v. Williams, 467 U.S. 431 (1984) (discussed in *Murray*) was subjected to police questioning that violated his Sixth Amendment right to counsel. In response to the questioning, the defendant led the police to the body of a ten-year-old girl; the defendant was later charged with the girl's murder. The defendant sought to suppress evidence obtained from the girl's body on the ground that all such evidence constituted fruits of the illegal questioning. The state responded that the body would inevitably have been found without the illegal questioning.

The body was found "in a ditch beside a gravel road." Id., at 436. At the time it was found, multiple police search teams were looking for the missing girl; the closest search team was two-and-one-half miles away. Id. The trial court concluded, and the Supreme Court agreed, that the search teams probably would have found the girl's body fairly soon had the search not been called off once the defendant showed police to the right spot.

How accurate do you think such conclusions are? In some cases, the issue is easy: Suppose, for example, the search team had only been a hundred yards away when the body was found. But in cases like *Nix* itself, the inquiry involves an enormous amount of speculation. How long would the search have gone on? What directions would it have moved? How far? The questions are, if anything, even harder when the case involves a less sensational crime. On the one hand, when a young girl is murdered and her body is missing, the police will invest a great deal in finding the body and catching the killer. For an investigation of a convenience store robbery, on the other hand, the police may much more quickly conclude that the investigation is going nowhere, and drop it. Thus, the "inevitable discovery" question turns into this: Had the police not illegally discovered the evidence in question, would they have kept investigating long enough to find it legally? Again, how accurately can courts answer that question?

4. Can inevitable discovery doctrine apply to warrant cases? Suppose, in *Murray*, the officers seize the marijuana when they first enter the warehouse illegally. The defendant moves to suppress, on the ground that the police failed to get a warrant and lack exigent circumstances. The government concedes that the search was illegal but argues that the marijuana would inevitably have been discovered. The reasoning goes as follows: The police had probable cause and so could have gotten a warrant had they tried to do so. Had they not searched illegally, they would have applied for a warrant, gotten one, searched, and found the marijuana. All of which adds up to inevitable discovery.

This argument seems entirely natural, does it not? Yet if it works, the police never need to get a warrant again — and they also do not need to lie to a magistrate in order to prevail; see Note 2. It would seem to follow that a special rule must apply in warrant cases and that inevitable discovery doctrine simply cannot apply there. Is that consistent with *Murray*?

5. The Court continued to wrestle with the meaning of attenuation, independent source, the effect of a warrant, and other related matters in a case involving a very different type of Fourth Amendment violation — the failure of the police to knock and announce their presence when executing a warrant.

HUDSON v. MICHIGAN

Certiorari to the Michigan Court of Appeals
547 U.S. 586 (2006)

JUSTICE SCALIA delivered the opinion of the Court with respect to Parts I, II, and III, and an opinion with respect to Part IV, in which CHIEF JUSTICE ROBERTS, JUSTICE THOMAS, and JUSTICE ALITO joined.

We decide whether violation of the "knock-and-announce" rule requires the suppression of all evidence found in the search.

I

Police obtained a warrant authorizing a search for drugs and firearms at the home of petitioner Booker Hudson. They discovered both. Large quantities of drugs were found, including cocaine rocks in Hudson's pocket. A loaded gun was lodged between the cushion and armrest of the chair in which he was sitting. Hudson was charged under Michigan law with unlawful drug and firearm possession.

This case is before us only because of the method of entry into the house. When the police arrived to execute the warrant, they announced their presence, but waited only a short time — perhaps "three to five seconds" — before turning the knob of the unlocked front door and entering Hudson's home. Hudson moved to suppress all the inculpatory evidence, arguing that the premature entry violated his Fourth Amendment rights.

The Michigan trial court granted his motion. On interlocutory review, the Michigan Court of Appeals reversed . . . . The Michigan Supreme Court denied leave to appeal. Hudson was convicted of drug possession. He renewed his Fourth Amendment claim on appeal, but the Court of Appeals rejected it and affirmed the conviction. The Michigan Supreme Court again declined review. We granted certiorari.

II

The common-law principle that law enforcement officers must announce their presence and provide residents an opportunity to open the door is an ancient one. See Wilson v. Arkansas, 514 U.S. 927, 931-932 (1995). Since 1917, when Congress passed the Espionage Act, this traditional protection has been part of federal statutory law, and is currently codified at 18 U.S.C. §3109. . . . [I]in *Wilson*, we were asked whether the rule was also a command of the Fourth Amendment. Tracing its origins in our English legal heritage, we concluded that it was.

We recognized that the new constitutional rule we had announced is not easily applied. *Wilson* and cases following it have noted the many situations in which it is not necessary to knock and announce. It is not necessary when "circumstances presen[t] a threat of physical violence," or if there is "reason to believe that evidence would likely be destroyed if advance notice were given," id., at 936, or if knocking and announcing would be "futile," Richards v. Wisconsin, 520 U.S. 385, 394 (1997). We require only that police "have a reasonable suspicion . . . under the particular circumstances" that one of these grounds for failing to knock and announce exists, and we have acknowledged that "[t]his showing is not high." Ibid.

When the knock-and-announce rule does apply, it is not easy to determine precisely what officers must do. How many seconds' wait are too few? Our "reasonable wait time" standard, see United States v. Banks, 540 U.S. 31, 41 (2003), is necessarily vague. . . . [I]t is unsurprising that, ex ante, police officers about to encounter someone who may try to harm them will be uncertain how long to wait.

Happily, these issues do not confront us here. From the trial level onward, Michigan has conceded that the entry was a knock-and-announce violation. The issue here is remedy.

III

A

Suppression of evidence . . . has always been our last resort, not our first impulse. The exclusionary rule generates "substantial social costs," United States v. Leon, 468 U.S. 897, 907 (1984), which sometimes include setting the guilty free and the dangerous at large. . . . We have rejected "[i]ndiscriminate application" of the rule, *Leon*, supra, at 908, and have held it to be applicable only "where its remedial objectives are thought most efficaciously served," United States v. Calandra, 414 U.S. 338, 348 (1974) — that is, "where its deterrence benefits outweigh its 'substantial social costs,'" [Pennsylvania Bd. of Probation v. Scott, 524 U.S. 357, 363 (1998) (quoting *Leon*, supra)].

We did not always speak so guardedly. Expansive dicta in Mapp [v. Ohio, 367 U.S. 643 (1961)], for example, suggested wide scope for the exclusionary rule. See, e.g., 367 U.S., at 655 ("[A]ll evidence obtained by searches and seizures in violation of the Constitution is, by that same authority, inadmissible in a state court"). . . . But we have long since rejected that approach.

[E]xclusion may not be premised on the mere fact that a constitutional violation was a "but-for" cause of obtaining evidence. Our cases show that but-for causality is only a necessary, not a sufficient, condition for suppression. In this case, of course, the constitutional violation of an illegal manner of entry was not a but-for cause of obtaining the evidence. Whether that preliminary misstep had occurred or not, the police would have executed the warrant they had obtained, and would have discovered the gun and drugs inside the house. But even if the illegal entry here could be characterized as a but-for cause of discovering what was inside, we have "never held that evidence is 'fruit of the poisonous tree' simply because 'it would not have come to light but for the illegal actions of the police.'" Segura v. United States, 468 U.S. 796, 815 (1984). Rather, but-for cause, or "causation in the logical sense alone," United States v. Ceccolini, 435 U.S. 268, 274 (1978), can be too attenuated to justify exclusion.

Attenuation can occur, of course, when the causal connection is remote. Attenuation also occurs when, even given a direct causal connection, the interest protected by the constitutional guarantee that has been violated would not be served by suppression of the evidence obtained. . . .

For this reason, cases excluding the fruits of unlawful warrantless searches say nothing about the appropriateness of exclusion to vindicate the interests protected by the knock-and-announce requirement. Until a valid warrant has issued, citizens are entitled to shield "their persons, houses, papers, and effects," U.S. Const., Amdt. 4, from the government's scrutiny. Exclusion of the evidence obtained by a warrantless search vindicates that entitlement. The interests protected by the knock-and-announce requirement are quite different — and do not include the shielding of potential evidence from the government's eyes.

One of those interests is the protection of human life and limb, because an unannounced entry may provoke violence in supposed self-defense by the surprised resident. Another interest is the protection of property. . . . The knock-and-announce rule gives individuals "the opportunity to comply with the law and to avoid the destruction of property occasioned by a forcible entry." *Richards*, 520 U.S., at 393, n. 5. And thirdly, the knock-and-announce rule protects those elements of privacy and dignity that can be destroyed by a sudden entrance. . . . In other words, it assures the opportunity to collect oneself before answering the door.

What the knock-and-announce rule has never protected, however, is one's interest in preventing the government from seeing or taking evidence described in a warrant. Since the interests that were violated in this case have nothing to do with the seizure of the evidence, the exclusionary rule is inapplicable.

B

Quite apart from the requirement of unattenuated causation, the exclusionary rule has never been applied except "where its deterrence benefits outweigh its 'substantial social costs,'" *Scott*, 524 U.S., at 363 (quoting *Leon*, 468 U.S., at 907). The costs here are considerable. In addition to the grave adverse consequence that exclusion of relevant incriminating evidence always entails (viz., the risk of releasing dangerous criminals into society), imposing that massive remedy for a knock-and-announce violation would generate a constant flood of alleged failures to observe the rule, and claims that any asserted *Richards* justification for a no-knock entry, see 520 U.S., at 394, had inadequate support. The cost of entering this lottery would be small, but the jackpot enormous: suppression of all evidence, amounting in many cases to a get-out-of-jail-free card. Courts would experience as never before the reality that "[t]he exclusionary rule frequently requires extensive litigation to determine whether particular evidence must be excluded." *Scott*, supra, at 366. Unlike the warrant or *Miranda* requirements, compliance with which is readily determined (either there was or was not a warrant; either the *Miranda* warning was given, or it was not), what constituted a "reasonable wait time" in a particular case, *Banks*, supra, at 41 (or, for that matter, how many seconds the police in fact waited), or whether there was "reasonable suspicion" of the sort that would invoke the *Richards* exceptions, is difficult for the trial court to determine and even more difficult for an appellate court to review.

Another consequence of the incongruent remedy Hudson proposes would be police officers' refraining from timely entry after knocking and announcing. As we have observed, the amount of time they must wait is necessarily uncertain. If the consequences of running afoul of the rule were so massive, officers would be inclined to wait longer than the law requires — producing preventable violence against officers in some cases, and the destruction of evidence in many others.

Next to these "substantial social costs" we must consider the deterrence benefits, existence of which is a necessary condition for exclusion. . . . To begin with, the value of deterrence depends upon the strength of the incentive to commit the forbidden act. Viewed from this perspective, deterrence of knock-and-announce violations is not worth a lot. Violation of the warrant requirement sometimes produces incriminating evidence that could not otherwise be obtained. But ignoring knock-and-announce can realistically be expected to achieve absolutely nothing except the prevention of destruction of evidence and the avoidance of life-threatening resistance by occupants of the premises — dangers which, if there is even "reasonable suspicion" of their existence, suspend the knock-and-announce requirement anyway. Massive deterrence is hardly required.

It seems to us not even true, as Hudson contends, that without suppression there will be no deterrence of knock-and-announce violations at all. Of course even if this assertion were accurate, it would not necessarily justify suppression. Assuming (as the assertion must) that civil suit is not an effective deterrent, one can think of many forms of police misconduct that are similarly "undeterred." When, for example, a confessed suspect in the killing of a police officer, arrested (along with incriminating evidence) in a lawful warranted search, is subjected to physical abuse at the station house, would it seriously be suggested that the evidence must be excluded, since that is the only "effective deterrent"? And what, other than civil suit, is the "effective deterrent" of police violation of an already-confessed suspect's Sixth Amendment rights by denying him prompt access to counsel? Many would regard these violated rights as more significant than the right not to be intruded upon in one's nightclothes — and yet nothing but "ineffective" civil suit is available as a deterrent.

We cannot assume that exclusion in this context is necessary deterrence simply because we found that it was necessary deterrence in different contexts and long ago. That would be forcing the public today to pay for the sins and inadequacies of a legal regime that existed almost half a century ago. Dollree Mapp could not turn to 42 U.S.C. §1983 for meaningful relief; Monroe v. Pape, 365 U.S. 167 (1961), which began the slow but steady expansion of that remedy, was decided the same Term as *Mapp*.

Hudson complains that "it would be very hard to find a lawyer to take a case such as this," but 42 U.S.C. §1988(b) answers this objection. Since some civil-rights violations would yield damages too small to justify the expense of litigation, Congress has authorized attorney's fees for civil-rights plaintiffs. This remedy was unavailable in the heydays of our exclusionary-rule jurisprudence, because it is tied to the availability of a cause of action.

Hudson points out that few published decisions to date announce huge awards for knock-and-announce violations. But this is an unhelpful statistic. Even if we thought that only large damages would deter police misconduct (and that police somehow are deterred by "damages" but indifferent to the prospect of large §1988 attorney's fees), we do not know how many claims have been settled, or indeed how many violations have occurred that produced anything more than nominal injury. It is clear, at least, that the lower courts are allowing colorable knock-and-announce suits to go forward, unimpeded by assertions of qualified immunity. As far as we know, civil liability is an effective deterrent here, as we have assumed it is in other contexts.

Another development over the past half-century that deters civil-rights violations is the increasing professionalism of police forces, including a new emphasis on internal police discipline. . . . Numerous sources are now available to teach officers and their supervisors what is required of them under this Court's cases, how to respect constitutional guarantees in various situations, and how to craft an effective regime for internal discipline. Failure to teach and enforce constitutional requirements exposes municipalities to financial liability. Moreover, modern police forces are staffed with professionals; it is not credible to assert that internal discipline, which can limit successful careers, will not have a deterrent effect. There is also evidence that the increasing use of various forms of citizen review can enhance police accountability.

In sum, the social costs of applying the exclusionary rule to knock-and-announce violations are considerable; the incentive to such violations is minimal to begin with, and the extant deterrences against them are substantial — incomparably greater than the factors deterring warrantless entries when *Mapp* was decided. Resort to the massive remedy of suppressing evidence of guilt is unjustified.

IV

. . . For the foregoing reasons we affirm the judgment of the Michigan Court of Appeals.

[The opinion of Justice Kennedy, concurring in part and concurring in the judgment, is omitted.]

JUSTICE BREYER, with whom JUSTICE STEVENS, JUSTICE SOUTER, and JUSTICE GINSBURG join, dissenting. . . .

Reading our knock-and-announce cases in light of . . . foundational Fourth Amendment case law, it is clear that the exclusionary rule should apply. For one thing, elementary logic leads to that conclusion. We have held that a court must "conside[r]" whether officers complied with the knock-and-announce requirement "in assessing the reasonableness of a search or seizure." Wilson [v. Arkansas, 514 U.S. 927, 934 (1995)]. The Fourth Amendment insists that an unreasonable search or seizure is, constitutionally speaking, an illegal search or seizure. And ever since [Weeks v. United States, 232 U.S. 383 (1914)] (in respect to federal prosecutions) and [Mapp v. Ohio, 367 U.S. 643 (1961)] (in respect to state prosecutions), "the use of evidence secured through an illegal search and seizure" is "barred" in criminal trials. Wolf [v. Colorado, 338 U.S. 25, 28 (1949)] (citing *Weeks*); see *Mapp*, supra, at 655.

For another thing, the driving legal purpose underlying the exclusionary rule, namely, the deterrence of unlawful government behavior, argues strongly for suppression. . . . Without such a rule, as in *Mapp*, police know that they can ignore the Constitution's requirements without risking suppression of evidence discovered after an unreasonable entry. . . .

The cases reporting knock-and-announce violations are legion. . . . Yet the majority . . . has failed to cite a single reported case in which a plaintiff has collected more than nominal damages solely as a result of a knock-and-announce violation. . . .

To argue, as the majority does, that new remedies, such as 42 U.S.C. §1983 actions or better trained police, make suppression unnecessary is to argue that *Wolf*, not *Mapp*, is now the law. . . . Neither can the majority justify its failure to respect the need for deterrence . . . through its claim of "substantial social costs" — at least if it means that those "social costs" are somehow special here. The only costs it mentions are those that typically accompany any use of the Fourth Amendment's exclusionary principle. . . .

The majority . . . argues that "the constitutional violation of an illegal manner of entry was not a but-for cause of obtaining the evidence." But taking causation as it is commonly understood in the law, I do not see how that can be so. Although the police might have entered Hudson's home lawfully, they did not in fact do so. Their unlawful behavior inseparably characterizes their actual entry; that entry was a necessary condition of their presence in Hudson's home; and their presence in Hudson's home was a necessary condition of their finding and seizing the evidence.

The Court nonetheless accepts Michigan's argument that the requisite but-for causation is not satisfied in this case because, whether or not the constitutional violation occurred (what the Court refers to as a "preliminary misstep"), "the police would have executed the warrant they had obtained, and would have discovered the gun and drugs inside the house." As support for this proposition, Michigan rests on this Court's inevitable discovery cases.

This claim, however, misunderstands the inevitable discovery doctrine. Justice Holmes in [Silverthorne Lumber Co. v. United States, 251 U.S. 385 (1920)], in discussing an "independent source" exception, set forth the principles underlying the inevitable discovery rule. That rule does not refer to discovery that would have taken place if the police behavior in question had (contrary to fact) been lawful. The doctrine does not treat as critical what hypothetically could have happened had the police acted lawfully in the first place. Rather, "independent" or "inevitable" discovery refers to discovery that did occur or that would have occurred (1) despite (not simply in the absence of) the unlawful behavior and (2) independently of that unlawful behavior. The government cannot, for example, avoid suppression of evidence seized without a warrant (or pursuant to a defective warrant) simply by showing that it could have obtained a valid warrant had it sought one.

[T]he Court's opinion reflects a misunderstanding of what "inevitable discovery" means when it says, "[i]n this case, of course, the constitutional violation of an illegal manner of entry was not a but-for cause of obtaining the evidence." The majority rests this conclusion on its next statement: "Whether that preliminary misstep has occurred or not, the police . . . would have discovered the gun and the drugs inside the house." Despite the phrase "of course," neither of these statements is correct. It is not true that, had the illegal entry not occurred, "police would have discovered the guns and drugs inside the house." Without that unlawful entry they would not have been inside the house; so there would have been no discovery.

Of course, had the police entered the house lawfully, they would have found the gun and drugs. But that fact is beside the point. The question is not what police might have done had they not behaved unlawfully. The question is what they did do. Was there set in motion an independent chain of events that would have inevitably led to the discovery and seizure of the evidence despite, and independent of, that behavior? The answer here is "no." . . .

The majority . . . says that evidence should not be suppressed once the causal connection between unlawful behavior and discovery of the evidence becomes too "attenuated." But the majority then makes clear that it is not using the word "attenuated" to mean what this Court's precedents have typically used that word to mean, namely, that the discovery of the evidence has come about long after the unlawful behavior or in an independent way.

Rather, the majority gives the word "attenuation" a new meaning . . . . "Attenuation," it says, "also occurs when, even given a direct causal connection, the interest protected by the constitutional guarantee that has been violated would not be served by suppression of the evidence obtained." . . .

There are three serious problems with this argument. First, it does not fully describe the constitutional values, purposes, and objectives underlying the knock-and-announce requirement. That rule does help to protect homeowners from damaged doors; it does help to protect occupants from surprise. But it does more than that. It protects the occupants' privacy by assuring them that government agents will not enter their home without complying with those requirements . . . that diminish the offensive nature of any such intrusion. . . .

Second, whether the interests underlying the knock-and-announce rule are implicated in any given case is, in a sense, beside the point. As we have explained, failure to comply with the knock-and-announce rule renders the related search unlawful. And where a search is unlawful, the law insists upon suppression of the evidence consequently discovered . . . .

Third, the majority's interest-based approach departs from prior law. Ordinarily a court will simply look to see if the unconstitutional search produced the evidence. . . .

Leaving aside what I believe are invalid arguments based on precedent or the majority's own estimate that suppression is not necessary to deter constitutional violations, one is left with a simple unvarnished conclusion, namely, that in this kind of case, a knock-and-announce case, "[r]esort to the massive remedy of suppressing evidence of guilt is unjustified." Why is that judicial judgment, taken on its own, inappropriate? Could it not be argued that the knock-and-announce rule, a subsidiary Fourth Amendment rule, is simply not important enough to warrant a suppression remedy? Could the majority not simply claim that the suppression game is not worth the candle?

The answer, I believe, is "no." That "no" reflects history, a history that shows the knock-and-announce rule is important. That "no" reflects precedent, precedent that shows there is no pre-existing legal category of exceptions to the exclusionary rule into which the knock-and-announce cases might fit. That "no" reflects empirical fact, experience that provides confirmation of what common sense suggests: Without suppression there is little to deter knock-and-announce violations.

NOTES AND QUESTIONS

1. Is *Hudson* primarily about remedies, or is it primarily about rights? The majority notes that the knock-and-announce rule is a recent addition to Fourth Amendment doctrine — the Court confirmed its existence only in 1995 — and that the rule is both vague and costly to apply. Those might be seen as reasons not to enforce the rule. Are they good reasons?

2. Perhaps they are. One might plausibly argue that the knock-and-announce principle should be folded into the broader requirement that searches be carried out reasonably: the same requirement that yields limits on police use of force against criminal suspects. Or, one might say that the rule amounts to a wise principle of policing that is best left out of Fourth Amendment litigation — because courts are poorly equipped to decide when no-knock entries are appropriate, and how long police should wait for a response when they aren't. But those arguments aren't obviously right. Fourth Amendment law focuses a great deal of attention on small distinctions involving what police officers saw and heard: Think of Arizona v. Hicks, 480 U.S. 321 (1987), which turned on the fact that a police officer had to turn over a piece of stereo equipment to see its serial number. Perhaps that is as it should be: A detailed constitutional law of privacy is bound to draw fine lines. But if the law is to pay close attention to what officers see and hear, it may be even more important to pay close attention to what officers *do* — to the fear and indignity and violence that sometimes accompany police searches. That is what knock-and-announce doctrine is about. Why should that doctrine merit less stringent enforcement than other Fourth Amendment doctrines?

4.   Impeachment

UNITED STATES v. HAVENS

Certiorari to the United States Court of Appeals for the Fifth Circuit
446 U.S. 620 (1980)

MR. JUSTICE WHITE delivered the opinion of the Court.

The petition for certiorari filed by the United States in this criminal case presented a single question: whether evidence suppressed as the fruit of an unlawful search and seizure may nevertheless be used to impeach a defendant's false trial testimony, given in response to proper cross-examination, where the evidence does not squarely contradict the defendant's testimony on direct examination. . . .

Respondent was convicted of importing, conspiring to import, and intentionally possessing a controlled substance, cocaine. According to the evidence at his trial, Havens and John McLeroth, both attorneys from Ft. Wayne, Ind., boarded a flight from Lima, Peru, to Miami, Fla. In Miami, a customs officer searched McLeroth and found cocaine sewed into makeshift pockets in a T-shirt he was wearing under his outer clothing. McLeroth implicated respondent, who had previously cleared customs and who was then arrested. His luggage was seized and searched without a warrant. The officers found no drugs but seized a T-shirt from which pieces had been cut that matched the pieces that had been sewn to McLeroth's T-shirt. The T-shirt and other evidence seized in the course of the search were suppressed on motion prior to trial.

Both men were charged in a three-count indictment, but McLeroth pleaded guilty to one count and testified against Havens. Among other things, he asserted that Havens had supplied him with the altered T-shirt and had sewed the makeshift pockets shut. Havens took the stand in his own defense and denied involvement in smuggling cocaine. His direct testimony included the following:

> Q. And you heard Mr. McLeroth testify earlier as to something to the effect that this material was taped or draped around his body and so on, you heard that testimony?
> A. Yes, I did.
> Q. Did you ever engage in that kind of activity with Mr. McLeroth and Augusto or Mr. McLeroth and anyone else on that fourth visit to Lima, Peru?
> A. I did not.

On cross-examination, Havens testified as follows:

> Q. Now, on direct examination, sir, you testified that on the fourth trip you had absolutely nothing to do with the wrapping of any bandages or tee shirts or anything involving Mr. McLeroth; is that correct?
> A. I don't — I said I had nothing to do with any wrapping or bandages or anything, yes. I had nothing to do with anything with McLeroth in connection with this cocaine matter. . . .
> Q. And your testimony is that you had nothing to do with the sewing of the cotton swatches to make pockets on that tee shirt?
> A. Absolutely not. . . .
> Q. On that day, sir, did you have in your luggage a Size 38-40 medium man's tee shirt with swatches of clothing missing from the tail of that tee shirt?
> A. Not to my knowledge.
> Q. Mr. Havens, I'm going to hand you what is Government's Exhibit 9 for identification and ask you if this tee shirt was in your luggage on October 2nd, 1975 [sic]?
> A. Not to my knowledge. No. [Id., at 46.]

Respondent Havens also denied having told a Government agent that the T-shirts found in his luggage belonged to McLeroth.

On rebuttal, a Government agent testified that Exhibit 9 had been found in respondent's suitcase and that Havens claimed the T-shirts found in his bag, including Exhibit 9, belonged to McLeroth. Over objection, the T-shirt was then admitted into evidence, the jury being instructed that the rebuttal evidence should be considered only for impeaching Havens' credibility. . . .

In Walder v. United States, [437 U.S. 62 (1954)], the use of evidence obtained in an illegal search and inadmissible in the Government's case in chief was admitted to impeach the direct testimony of the defendant. This Court approved, saying that it would pervert the [federal exclusionary rule] to hold otherwise. Similarly, in Harris v. New York, 401 U.S. 222 (1971), and Oregon v. Hass, 420 U.S. 714 (1975), statements taken in violation of Miranda v. Arizona, 384 U.S. 436 (1966), and unusable by the prosecution as part of its own case, were held admissible to impeach statements made by the defendant in the course of his direct testimony. . . .

These cases were understood by the Court of Appeals to hold that tainted evidence, inadmissible when offered as part of the Government's main case, may not be used as rebuttal evidence to impeach a defendant's credibility unless the evidence is offered to contradict a particular statement made by a defendant during his direct examination; a statement made for the first time on cross-examination may not be so impeached. This approach required the exclusion of the T-shirt taken from Havens' luggage because, as the Court of Appeals read the record, Havens was asked nothing on his direct testimony about the incriminating T-shirt or about the contents of his luggage; the testimony about the T-shirt, which the Government desired to impeach first appeared on cross-examination, not on direct. . . .

There is no gainsaying that arriving at the truth is a fundamental goal of our legal system. We have repeatedly insisted that when defendants testify, they must testify truthfully or suffer the consequences. . . . It is essential, therefore, to the proper functioning of the adversary system that when a defendant takes the stand, the government be permitted proper and effective cross-examination in an attempt to elicit the truth. The defendant's obligation to testify truthfully is fully binding on him when he is cross-examined. His privilege against self-incrimination does not shield him from proper questioning. He would unquestionably be subject to a perjury prosecution if he knowingly lies on cross-examination. In terms of impeaching a defendant's seemingly false statements with his prior inconsistent utterances or with other reliable evidence available to the government, we see no difference of constitutional magnitude between the defendant's statements on direct examination and his answers to questions put to him on cross-examination that are plainly within the scope of the defendant's direct examination. Without this opportunity, the normal function of cross-examination would be severely impeded.

We also think that the policies of the exclusionary rule no more bar impeachment here than they did in *Walder*, *Harris*, and *Hass*. In those cases, the ends of the exclusionary rules were thought adequately implemented by denying the government the use of the challenged evidence to make out its case in chief. The incremental furthering of those ends by forbidding impeachment of the defendant who testifies was deemed insufficient to permit or require that false testimony go unchallenged, with the resulting impairment of the integrity of the factfinding goals of the criminal trial. We reaffirm this assessment of the competing interests, and hold that a defendant's statements made in response to proper cross-examination reasonably suggested by the defendant's direct examination are subject to otherwise proper impeachment by the government, albeit by evidence that has been illegally obtained and that is inadmissible on the government's direct case, or otherwise, as substantive evidence of guilt. . . .

[The dissenting opinion of Justice Brennan, joined by Justice Stewart, Justice Marshall, and Justice Stevens, is omitted.]

NOTES AND QUESTIONS

1. One strong piece of conventional wisdom is that juries tend to believe defendants guilty if they don't testify. Knowing that a piece of damning evidence will come out on cross-examination is presumably a strong disincentive to testify. This is likely the biggest effect of *Havens*: It decreases the likelihood, perhaps substantially, that defendants who were the victims of illegal searches will take the witness stand. Doesn't that seriously undermine the exclusionary rule?

2. But if *Havens* came out the other way, that would create large opportunities for defendant perjury. Can the legal system, or the public, be expected to tolerate that? Is there any way out of this box?

3. In Illinois v. James, 493 U.S. 307 (1990), the Court faced the question whether *Havens* applies not just to defendants but to all defense witnesses. Defendant James was a teenager suspected of involvement in a shooting. At the time of his arrest, James had curly black hair. Shortly afterward, James told the police that he had changed his hair color and style — that at the time of the shooting, James admitted, his hair was reddish-brown, straight, and combed back. The trial judge suppressed James' post-arrest statements to the police on the ground that those statements were the fruit of an illegal arrest. At trial, James put on a witness who claimed that James had had curly black hair at the time of the shooting. The prosecution introduced James's statements to the police in order to impeach that defense witness.

Speaking for a five-vote majority (himself plus Justices White, Marshall, Blackmun, and Stevens), Justice Brennan concluded that the statements should not have been admitted into evidence, that *Havens* applies only to defendants:

> The previously recognized [impeachment] exception penalizes defendants for committing perjury by allowing the prosecution to expose their perjury through impeachment using illegally obtained evidence. . . . But the exception leaves defendants free to testify truthfully on their own behalf; they can offer probative and exculpatory evidence to the jury without opening the door to impeachment by carefully avoiding any statements that directly contradict the suppressed evidence. The exception thus generally discourages perjured testimony without discouraging truthful testimony.
>
> . . . [E]xpanding the impeachment exception to encompass the testimony of all defense witnesses would not have the same beneficial effects. First, the mere threat of a subsequent criminal prosecution for perjury is far more likely to deter a witness from intentionally lying on a defendant's behalf than to deter a defendant, already facing conviction for the underlying offense, from lying on his own behalf. . . .
>
> More significantly, expanding the impeachment exception to encompass the testimony of all defense witnesses likely would chill some defendants from presenting their best defense — and sometimes any defense at all — through the testimony of others. Whenever police obtained evidence illegally, defendants would have to assess prior to trial the likelihood that the evidence would be admitted to impeach the otherwise favorable testimony of any witness they call. Defendants might reasonably fear that one or more of their witnesses, in a position to offer truthful and favorable testimony, would also make some statement in sufficient tension with the tainted evidence to allow the prosecutor to introduce that evidence for impeachment. . . . As a result, an expanded

impeachment exception likely would chill some defendants from calling witnesses who would otherwise offer probative evidence. . . .

Id., at 314-317. Are you persuaded?

4. Are *James* and *Havens* consistent? Most of the Justices didn't think so. Six Justices — Brennan, White, Marshall, Blackmun, Rehnquist, and Stevens — voted in both cases. Five of those six supported the same result in both cases. Justices Brennan, Marshall, Blackmun, and Stevens all thought that the exclusionary rule barred use of illegally obtained evidence to impeach *either* defendants *or* other defense witnesses. Justice (later Chief Justice) Rehnquist thought the exclusionary rule should permit the use of illegally obtained evidence to impeach *all* defense witnesses. Only Justice White thought some line should be drawn between defendants and other witnesses.

What is the proper result in such a case? One might argue that an appropriate respect for precedent should have required the *Havens* dissenters (Justices Brennan, Marshall, Blackmun, and Stevens) to support whatever result in *James* was most consistent with *Havens*. Had they done so, it seems likely that the result in *James* would be different. What should a Justice do in such situations? Vote his conscience, and precedent be damned? Honor precedent that he thinks foolish? Something else?

5. The impeachment issue in *Havens* and *James* is a variant on the question posed by the standing and fruit-of-the-poisonous-tree doctrines. In all three settings, the police conduct an illegal search; in all three settings, the illegal search produces some collateral benefit — it leads the police to evidence against other suspects (standing), it leads them to further evidence against the same suspect (fruit of the poisonous tree), or it keeps the suspect or some other defense witness from taking the witness stand at a later criminal trial (impeachment). And in all three settings, there is a common set of arguments. Defendants argue that the police will search illegally in order to obtain the collateral benefit — that unless the law takes away all gains from illegal searches, too many illegal searches will happen. The government argues that the collateral benefit is not foreseeable — that, for example, officers were not thinking about Havens taking the witness stand when they searched his luggage — and that police will not conduct illegal searches in order to get such unforeseeable benefits. As you have seen, the argument is basically resolved in the government's favor in standing doctrine, mostly resolved in the defendants' favor in fruit-of-the-poisonous-tree doctrine, while impeachment doctrine splits the difference.

Does that set of results make sense?

Chapter 6

The Fifth Amendment

The Fifth Amendment privilege against self-incrimination is a doctrine in search of a theory. With respect to most constitutional rights, there is broad agreement about the right's basic purpose. Freedom of speech protects some combination of artistic expression and political argument. The right to equal protection of the laws protects against official discrimination. Fourth Amendment law protects individual privacy. There are, of course, complications and exceptions, but the basic vision behind these rights is widely and well understood.

The privilege is not like that. There is no agreement on the privilege's purpose; indeed, some writers challenge the idea that it should exist at all. Our legal system (for that matter, any legal system) regularly compels witnesses to turn over documents and give testimony when they would prefer not to do those things. Why make an exception for one whose testimony would incriminate him? As Judge Henry Friendly famously argued:

> No parent would teach such a doctrine to his children; the lesson parents preach is that while a misdeed, even a serious one, will generally be forgiven, a failure to make a clean breast of it will not be. Every hour of the day people are being asked to explain their conduct to parents, employers and teachers. Those who are questioned consider themselves to be morally bound to respond, and the questioners believe it proper to take action if they do not.

Henry J. Friendly, The Fifth Amendment Tomorrow: The Case for Constitutional Change, 37 U. Cin. L. Rev. 671, 680 (1968). And the privilege is puzzling in another respect. In general, the law of criminal procedure seems designed to grant broader legal protection to innocent citizens than to criminals. For example, Fourth Amendment law holds that the police may search private spaces only if they have good reason (probable cause or reasonable suspicion) to believe the search will uncover evidence of crime. The greater the risk of incrimination, the smaller the legal protection — and the broader the authority granted to police. The privilege against self-incrimination tilts in the opposite direction. If the government asks a witness a question and the answer cannot possibly provide evidence that the witness is guilty of a crime, the witness must answer — even if the question intrudes grievously on the witness's privacy. The greater the risk of incrimination, the *broader* the legal protection — and the narrower the authority that is granted to the government. Why do we have this odd right?

Text and History

Begin with the text. The Fifth Amendment contains several different constitutional protections: the ban on double jeopardy, the requirement of a grand jury in federal cases, the right to due process of law (again, in federal cases — the due process requirement in state cases comes from the Fourteenth Amendment), and, of course, the privilege. The privilege's text is spare: "No person . . . shall be compelled in any criminal case to be a witness against himself." From this text come the privilege's three basic elements: compulsion, incrimination, and testimony. But what are those elements designed to protect?

Like most provisions of the Bill of Rights, the privilege against self-incrimination was picked up from English common law, where it arose out of two sorts of cases: heresy and sedition. The English High Commission of the late sixteenth and early seventeenth centuries forced suspected heretics to swear an oath to answer questions honestly before being informed of the nature of any charges against them; questioning usually went to the content of the witnesses' religious beliefs and the identities of their fellow believers. Some of these alleged heretics claimed that the questioning was unlawful on the ground that no one should be forced to give testimony against himself; to do so would be to "put the conscience upon the racke." Leonard W. Levy, Origins of the Fifth Amendment 177 (1968) (quoting a statement made around 1591 by Thomas Cartwright and eight Puritan colleagues). Political dissidents made a similar argument. John Lilburne, a popular English pamphleteer and political gadfly of the mid-seventeenth century, was charged with authoring various items critical of those in power. When asked about his authorship, Lilburne refused to answer. He was acquitted, and the privilege against self-incrimination was born.

Its incorporation into the Fifth Amendment was not the subject of much debate, either in the Congress that wrote the Bill of Rights or in the states' ratification processes. Criminal defendants in the eighteenth century had no right to testify — parties in civil and criminal cases alike were forbidden to testify under oath — so a right not to testify seemed unimportant. Besides, defense lawyers were rare in eighteenth-century American criminal trials, and without counsel, defendants were forced to speak (albeit not under oath) on their own behalf. That state of affairs changed gradually during the course of the nineteenth century. The rise of professional prosecutors and the increasingly common use of defense counsel made criminal litigation into something like the lawyers' battle that we know today. And the common law soon adopted the notion that litigants, including criminal defendants, could testify under oath if they wished, giving new meaning to a legal right to avoid giving testimony. The privilege slowly became a staple of the criminal trial process.

When the Supreme Court decided Boyd v. United States, 116 U.S. 616 (1886), the privilege became something else as well: a constitutional guarantee of individual privacy. Boyd was a glass importer. Suspecting customs fraud, the government initiated a civil forfeiture action against some shipments of glass; in the course of that proceeding, a subpoena was issued ordering Boyd to produce the invoices for those shipments. He challenged the subpoena, claiming that it was both an unreasonable search in violation of the Fourth Amendment and compelled self-incrimination in violation of the Fifth. The Supreme Court agreed, holding that that the two prohibitions covered "any forcible and compulsory extortion of a man's own testimony or of his private papers to be used as evidence to convict him of crime or to forfeit his goods." The Court added: "In this regard the Fourth and Fifth Amendments run almost into each other." *Boyd* is excerpted and discussed in Chapter 4, at page 292.

This privacy-based privilege has had its ups and downs, as the balance of this chapter will show. Other, competing theories have risen to the fore. And sometimes, the Supreme Court has restricted the privilege's scope not because of any theory, but as a pragmatic accommodation to the government's need to gather evidence and information in order to govern. This last point is particularly important. On the one hand, if the government can never obtain incriminating evidence from suspects, the criminal justice system may be unable to do its job. On the other hand, if the government can obtain whatever information it likes whenever it likes, the privacy and autonomy values underlying the privilege might become a practical nullity. This may be one area of constitutional law where the conflict between individual rights and government needs is especially stark.

The balance of this chapter deals with the ways in which Fifth Amendment law manages that conflict. In Section A, we explore the underlying purposes of the privilege, using the history of Fifth Amendment immunity as a vehicle. Section B turns to the privilege's basic doctrinal structure, which is built around three portions of constitutional text: compulsion ("No person . . . shall be compelled"), incrimination ("in any criminal case"), and testimony ("to be a witness against himself"). Section C deals with the ways in which the Supreme Court has limited the privilege's scope in deference to the government's interest in regulation. Section D then turns to police interrogation, where the "right to remain silent" has acquired a special meaning, and a large and intricate body of law supports and surrounds (some would say undermines) it. As you read these materials, it is wise to keep two questions in mind. First, what theory of the privilege best explains the cases? And second, how do courts — and how does the Supreme Court — negotiate the tension between the individual's right to keep silent and the government's interest in gathering evidence?

A. The Fifth Amendment Privilege Against Self-Incrimination and Its Justifications

The earliest interpretation of the Fifth Amendment by a sitting Supreme Court Justice gave the privilege very broad scope. The case was the trial of Aaron Burr in 1807, and the justice was Chief Justice John Marshall. A witness was called before the grand jury considering the Burr case; the witness was asked whether, on Burr's orders, he had copied a particular document. The witness refused to answer, on the ground that his answer might be incriminating. The Chief Justice heard argument on the question whether the witness's assertion of the privilege was proper. Using (typically, for Marshall) sweeping language, he upheld the witness's claim:

> When a question is propounded, it belongs to the court to consider and to decide whether any direct answer to it can implicate the witness. If this be decided in the negative, then he may answer it without violating the privilege which is secured to him by law. If a direct answer to it may criminate himself, then he must be the sole judge what his answer would be. The court cannot participate with him in this judgment;

because they cannot decide on the effect of his answer without knowing what it would be; and a disclosure of that fact to the judges would strip him of the privileges which the law allows, and which he claims. It follows, necessarily, then, from this state of things, that if the question be of such a description that an answer to it may or may not criminate the witness, according to the purport of that answer, it must rest with himself, who alone can tell what it would be, to answer the question or not. If, in such a case, he say, upon his oath, that his answer would criminate himself, the court can demand no other testimony of the fact. If the declaration be untrue, it is in conscience and in law as much a perjury as if he had declared any other untruth upon his oath; as it is one of those cases in which the rule of law must be abandoned, or the oath of the witness be received. The counsel for the United States have also laid down this rule, according to their understanding of it, but they appear to the court to have made it as much too narrow as the counsel for the witness have made it too broad. According to their statement, a witness can never refuse to answer any question, unless that answer, unconnected with other testimony, would be sufficient to convict him of a crime. This would be rendering the rule almost perfectly worthless. Many links frequently compose that chain of testimony which is necessary to convict any individual of a crime. It appears to the court to be the true sense of the rule that no witness is compellable to furnish any one of them against himself. It is certainly not only a possible, but a probable, case, that a witness, by disclosing a single fact, may complete the testimony against himself, and to every effectual purpose accuse himself as entirely as he would by stating every circumstance which would be required for his conviction. That fact of itself might be unavailing; but all other facts without it might be insufficient. While that remains concealed within his own bosom he is safe; but draw it from thence, and he is exposed to a prosecution. The rule which declares that no man is compelled to accuse himself, would most obviously be infringed by compelling a witness to disclose a fact of this description. What testimony may be possessed, or is attainable, against any individual, the court can never know. It would seem, then, that the court ought never to compel a witness to give an answer which discloses a fact that might form a necessary and essential part of a crime, which is punishable by the laws. . . . In such a case, the witness must himself judge what his answer will be; and if he say, on oath, that he cannot answer without accusing himself, he cannot be compelled to answer.

1 Burr's Trial, 244, 245, quoted in Brown v. Walker, 161 U.S. 591, 612-615 (1896) (Shiras, J., dissenting).

Predictably, the government found Marshall's literal interpretation of the Fifth Amendment too confining, and in the century following Aaron Burr's trial, state and federal governments alike passed statutes providing witnesses with various types of immunity from prosecution in order to compel testimony over an otherwise legitimate invocation of the privilege. These statutes were premised on the view that a witness could hardly be seen as incriminating himself if he was given immunity from prosecution with respect to the acts testified to or, alternatively, if the state was not allowed to use the compelled testimony against the witness. When the Court first reviewed the constitutionality of one of these statues, it relied heavily on Chief Justice Marshall's opinion in the Burr trial, and on the then-recent case of Boyd v. United States, 116 U.S. 616 (1886), in striking down the statute.

COUNSELMAN v. HITCHCOCK, 142 U.S. 547, 560-561, 562-564, 585-586 (1892): [The federal statute in question in *Counselman* provided:] ". . . No pleading of a party, nor any discovery or evidence obtained from a party or witness by means of a judicial proceeding in this or any foreign country, shall be given in evidence, or in any manner used against him or his property or estate, in any court of the United States, in any criminal proceeding, or for the enforcement of any penalty or forfeiture: *Provided*, That this section shall not exempt any party or witness from prosecution and punishment for perjury committed in discovering or testifying as aforesaid. . . ."

[In finding it unconstitutional, the Court first held that the Fifth Amendment is not limited to testimony given at the trial of a criminal case:]

It is broadly contended on the part of the appellee that a witness is not entitled to plead the privilege of silence, except in a criminal case against himself; but such is not the language of the Constitution. Its provision is that no person shall be compelled in any criminal case to be a witness against himself. This provision must have a broad construction in favor of the right which it was intended to secure. The matter under investigation by the grand jury in this case was a criminal matter, to inquire whether there had been a criminal violation of the Interstate Commerce Act. If Counselman had been guilty of the matters inquired of in the questions which he refused to answer, he himself was liable to criminal prosecution under the act. The case before the grand jury was, therefore, a criminal case. The reason given by Counselman for his refusal to answer the questions was that his answers might tend to criminate him, and showed that his apprehension was that, if he answered the questions truly and fully (as he was bound to do if he should answer them at all), the answers might show that he had committed a crime against the Interstate Commerce Act, for which he might be prosecuted. His answers, therefore, would be testimony against himself, and he would be compelled to give them in a criminal case.

It is impossible that the meaning of the constitutional provision can only be, that a person shall not be compelled to be a witness against himself in a criminal prosecution against himself. It would doubtless cover such cases; but it is not limited to them. The object was to insure that a person should not be compelled, when acting as a witness in any investigation, to give testimony which might tend to show that he himself had committed a crime. The privilege is limited to criminal matters, but it is as broad as the mischief against which it seeks to guard.

It is argued for the appellee that the investigation before the grand jury was not a criminal case, but was solely for the purpose of finding out whether a crime had been committed, or whether any one should be accused of an offence, there being no accuser and no parties plaintiff or defendant, and that a case could arise only when an indictment should be returned. In support of this view reference is made to article 6 of the amendments to the Constitution of the United States, which provides that in all criminal prosecutions the accused shall enjoy the right to a speedy and public trial by an impartial jury, to be confronted with the witnesses against him, to have compulsory process for witnesses, and the assistance of counsel for his defence.

But this provision distinctly means a criminal prosecution against a person who is accused and who is to be tried by a petit jury. A criminal prosecution under article 6 of the amendments, is much narrower than a "criminal case," under article 5 of the amendments. It is entirely consistent with the language of article 5, that the privilege of not being a witness against himself is to be exercised in a proceeding before a grand jury. . . .

It is an ancient principle of the law of evidence, that a witness shall not be compelled, in any proceeding, to make disclosures or to give testimony which will tend to criminate him or subject him to fines, penalties or forfeitures. . . .

The relations of Counselman to the subject of inquiry before the grand jury, as shown by the questions put to him, in connection with the provisions of the Interstate Commerce Act, entitled him to invoke the protection of the Constitution. . . .

[The Court then proceeded to determine whether the immunity provided in the statute was sufficient to protect Counselman's rights:]

It remains to consider whether §860 of the Revised Statutes removes the protection of the constitutional privilege of Counselman. That section must be construed as declaring that no evidence obtained from a witness by means of a judicial proceeding shall be given in evidence, or in any manner used against him or his property or estate, in any court of the United States, in any criminal proceeding, or for the enforcement of any penalty or forfeiture. It follows, that any evidence which might have been obtained from Counselman by means of his examination before the grand jury could not be given in evidence or used against him or his property in any court of the United States, in any criminal proceeding, or for the enforcement of any penalty or forfeiture. This, of course, protected him against the use of his testimony against him or his property in any prosecution against him or his property, in any criminal proceeding, in a court of the United States. But it had only that effect. It could not, and would not, prevent the use of his testimony to search out other testimony to be used in evidence against him or his property, in a criminal proceeding in such court. It could not prevent the obtaining and the use of witnesses and evidence which should be attributable directly to the testimony he might give under compulsion, and on which he might be convicted, when otherwise, and if he had refused to answer, he could not possibly have been convicted. . . .

We are clearly of opinion that no statute which leaves the party or witness subject to prosecution after he answers the criminating question put to him, can have the effect of supplanting the privilege conferred by the Constitution of the United States. Section 860 of the Revised Statutes does not supply a complete protection from all the perils against which the constitutional prohibition was designed to guard, and is not a full substitute for that prohibition. In view of the constitutional provision, a statutory enactment, to be valid, must afford absolute immunity against future prosecution for the offence to which the question relates. In this respect, . . . we consider that the ruling of this court in Boyd v. United States . . . supports the view we take. Section 860, moreover, affords no protection against that use of compelled testimony which consists in gaining therefrom a knowledge of the details of a crime, and of sources of information which may supply other means of convicting the witness or party. . . .

From a consideration of the language of the constitutional provision, and of all the authorities referred to, we are clearly of opinion that the appellant was entitled to refuse, as he did, to answer. The judgment of the Circuit Court must, therefore, be Reversed, and the case remanded to that court, with a direction to discharge the appellant from custody, on the writ of habeas corpus.

Congress responded to the Court's decision in *Counselman* by enacting a broader immunity statute. The new law stated that no person shall be excused from attending and testifying or from producing books, papers, tariffs, contracts, agreements and documents before the Interstate Commerce Commission, or in obedience to the subpoena of the Commission, . . . on the ground or for the reason that the testimony or evidence, documentary or otherwise, required of him, may tend to criminate him or subject him to a penalty or forfeiture. But no person shall be prosecuted or subjected to any penalty or forfeiture for or on account of any transaction, matter or thing, concerning which he may testify, or produce evidence, documentary or otherwise, before said Commission, or in obedience to its subpoena, or the subpoena of either of them, or in any such case or proceeding.

In Brown v. Walker, 161 U.S. 591 (1896), the Court upheld this new, transactional immunity statute:

> The clause of the Constitution in question is obviously susceptible of two interpretations. If it be construed literally, as authorizing the witness to refuse to disclose any fact which might tend to incriminate, disgrace or expose him to unfavorable comments, then as he must necessarily to a large extent determine upon his own conscience and responsibility whether his answer to the proposed question will have that tendency, . . . the practical result would be, that no one could be compelled to testify to a material fact in a criminal case, unless he chose to do so. . . . If, upon the other hand, the object of the provision be to secure the witness against a criminal prosecution, which might be aided directly or indirectly by his disclosure, then, if no such prosecution be possible — in other words, if his testimony operate as a complete pardon for the offence to which it relates — a statute absolutely securing to him such immunity from prosecution would satisfy the demands of the clause in question. . . .
>
> The maxim nemo tenetur seipsum accusare had its origin in a protest against the inquisitorial and manifestly unjust methods of interrogating accused persons, which has long obtained in the continental system, and, until the expulsion of the Stuarts from the British throne in 1688, and the erection of additional barriers for the protection of the people against the exercise of arbitrary power, was not uncommon even in England. While the admissions or confessions of the prisoner, when voluntarily and freely made, have always ranked high in the scale of incriminating evidence, if an accused person be asked to explain his apparent connection with a crime under investigation, the ease with which the questions put to him may assume an inquisitorial character, the temptation to press the witness unduly, to browbeat him if he be timid or reluctant, to push him into a corner, and to entrap him into fatal contradictions, which is so painfully evident in many of the earlier state trials, notably in those of Sir Nicholas Throckmorton, and Udal, the Puritan minister, made the system so odious as to give rise to a demand for its total abolition. The change in the English criminal procedure in that particular seems to be founded upon no statute and no judicial opinion, but upon a general and silent acquiescence of the courts in a popular demand. But, however adopted, it has become firmly embedded in English, as well as in American jurisprudence. So deeply did the iniquities of the ancient system impress themselves upon the minds of the American colonists that the States, with one accord, made a denial of the right to question an accused person a part of their fundamental law, so that a maxim, which in England was a mere rule of evidence, became clothed in this country with the impregnability of a constitutional enactment.
>
> Stringent as the general rule is, however, certain classes of cases have always been treated as not falling within the reason of the rule. . . . When examined, these cases will all be found to be based upon the idea that, if the testimony sought cannot possibly be used as a basis for, or in aid of, a criminal prosecution against the witness, the rule ceases to apply. . . .

1. Thus, if the witness himself elects to waive his privilege, as he may doubtless do, since the privilege is for his protection and not for that of other parties, and discloses his criminal connections, he is not permitted to stop, but must go on and make a full disclosure. . . . So, under modern statutes permitting accused persons to take the stand in their own behalf, they may be subjected to cross-examination upon their statements. . . .

2. For the same reason if a prosecution for a crime, concerning which the witness is interrogated, is barred by the statute of limitations, he is compellable to answer. . . .

3. If the answer of the witness may have a tendency to disgrace him or bring him into disrepute [but not to incriminate him], and the proposed evidence be material to the issue on trial, the great weight of authority is that he may be compelled to answer. . . . The extent to which the witness is compelled to answer such questions as do not fix upon him a criminal culpability is within the control of the legislature. . . .

4. . . . [I]f the witness has already received a pardon, he cannot longer set up his privilege, since he stands with respect to such offence as if it had never been committed. . . .

The danger of extending the principle announced in Counselman v. Hitchcock is that the privilege may be put forward for a sentimental reason, or for a purely fanciful protection of the witness against an imaginary danger, and for the real purpose of securing immunity to some third person, who is interested in concealing the facts to which he would testify. Every good citizen is bound to aid in the enforcement of the law, and has no right to permit himself, under the pretext of shielding his own good name, to be made the tool of others, who are desirous of seeking shelter behind his privilege. . . .

It is entirely true that the statute does not purport . . . to shield the witness from the personal disgrace or opprobrium attaching to the exposure of his crime; but . . . the authorities are numerous and very nearly uniform to the effect that, if the proposed testimony is material to the issue on trial, the fact that the testimony may tend to degrade the witness in public estimation does not exempt him from the duty of disclosure. A person who commits a criminal act is bound to contemplate the consequences of exposure to his good name and reputation, and ought not to call upon the courts to protect that which he has himself esteemed to be of such little value. The safety and welfare of an entire community should not be put into the scale against the reputation of a self-confessed criminal, who ought not, either in justice or in good morals, to refuse to disclose that which may be of great public utility, in order that his neighbors may think well of him. The design of the constitutional privilege is not to aid the witness in vindicating his character, but to protect him against being compelled to furnish evidence to convict him of a criminal charge. If he secure legal immunity from prosecution, the possible impairment of his good name is a penalty which it is reasonable he should be compelled to pay for the common good. . . .

If, as was justly observed in the opinion of the court below, witnesses standing in Brown's position were at liberty to set up an immunity from testifying, the enforcement of the Interstate Commerce law or other analogous acts, wherein it is for the interest of both parties to conceal their misdoings, would become impossible, since it is only from the mouths of those having knowledge of the inhibited contracts that the facts can be ascertained. While the constitutional provision in question is justly regarded as one of the most valuable prerogatives of the citizen, its object is fully accomplished by the statutory immunity, and we are, therefore, of opinion that the witness was compellable to answer, and that the judgment of the court below must be affirmed.

161 U.S., at 595-606, 610. In dicta, the Court expressed the view that the statutory immunity would extend to state criminal prosecutions — that immunized witnesses could not be criminally punished by any American jurisdiction for any of the conduct about which they testified. Notwithstanding the breadth of this immunity, four Justices (Field, Shiras, Gray, and White) took the position that it was not broad enough to overcome the privilege. The following excerpts from Justice Field's dissent capture their argument:

The [Fifth Amendment] . . . protects [the witness] from all compulsory testimony which would expose him to infamy and disgrace, though the facts disclosed might not lead to a criminal prosecution. It is contended, indeed, that it was not the object of the constitutional safeguard to protect the witness against infamy and disgrace. It is urged that its sole purpose was to protect him against incriminating testimony with reference to the offence under prosecution. But I do not agree that such limited protection was all that was secured. As stated by counsel of the appellant,

it is entirely possible, and certainly not impossible, that the framers of the Constitution reasoned that in bestowing upon witnesses in criminal cases the privilege of silence when in danger of self-incrimination, they would at the same time save him in all such cases from the shame and infamy of confessing disgraceful crimes and thus preserve to him some measure of self-respect. . . .

It is true, as counsel observes, that

both the safeguard of the Constitution and the common law rule spring alike from that sentiment of *personal self-respect, liberty, independence and dignity* which has inhabited the breasts of English speaking peoples for centuries, and to save which they have always been ready to sacrifice many governmental facilities and conveniences. In scarcely anything has that sentiment been more manifest than in the abhorrence felt at the legal compulsion upon witnesses to make concessions which must cover the witness with lasting shame and leave him degraded both in his own eyes and those of others. What can be more abhorrent . . . than to compel a man who has fought his way from obscurity to dignity and honor to reveal crimes of which he had repented and of which the world was ignorant? . . .

The essential and inherent cruelty of compelling a man to expose his own guilt is obvious to every one, and needs no illustration. It is plain to every person who gives the subject a moment's thought . . . .

Id., at 631-632, 637. Interestingly, Justice Field also noted in passing that "[t]he Fourth Amendment . . . is equally encroached upon by the act in question." Id., at 636.

As Counselman v. Hitchcock and Brown v. Walker indicate, the analytic foundation of Fifth Amendment law rests on three dependent variables: (1) the policies that inform the privilege; (2) the appropriate scope of the privilege in light of those policies; and (3) the extent of immunity necessary to satisfy those policies. As you think about *Counselman, Brown*, and the cases that follow, try to assess each variable separately and then in relation to the other two.

Consider the possibility that, depending on what the relevant policies are, the privilege might apply differently to different crimes. Both *Counselman* and *Brown* involved the enforcement of the Interstate Commerce Act, which regulated railroad shipping practices. Does that affect your view of the proper construction of the Fifth Amendment in those cases? How? Recall the *Brown* Court's statement that such regulatory legislation would be unenforceable in the absence of some provision for compelled, immunized testimony. And notice that Justice Field, whose dissent in *Brown* advanced a broad theory of the privilege, was famous for his opinions invalidating state and federal legislation regulating business and economic affairs. The privacy-autonomy right that Field defends so strongly was, in practice, closely tied to a particular vision of *property* rights — a vision that is, to say the least, not widely accepted today.

Whatever the merits of Justice Field's position, at least since *Brown* the privilege has been unavailable unless the witness's testimony could lead to some kind of punishment. Why should the threat of punishment obviate the need to testify truthfully?

As Professor Dolinko notes, our society forces people to testify in a number of other circumstances where testifying would be painful: Witnesses must testify notwithstanding threats of reprisal; they can also be forced to testify against close friends or (for the most part) family members. See David Dolinko, Is There a Rationale for the Privilege against Self-Incrimination? 33 UCLA L. Rev. 1063, 1093-1095 (1986). Is there any way to square these practices with the privilege?

This question arose again in Ullmann v. United States, 350 U.S. 422 (1956). The petitioner in *Ullmann* was given a grant of immunity and called to testify before a grand jury about "attempts to endanger the national security by espionage and conspiracy to commit espionage." The petitioner refused to testify, notwithstanding the immunity grant, and was held in contempt. The Court reaffirmed Brown v. Walker, including the congressional power to extend immunity to state offenses, and rejected the petitioner's attempt to distinguish it:

> Petitioner . . . argues that this case is different from Brown v. Walker because the impact of the disabilities imposed by federal and state authorities and the public in general — such as loss of job, expulsion from labor unions, state registration and investigation statutes, passport eligibility, and general public opprobrium — is so oppressive that the statute does not give him true immunity. This, he alleges, is significantly different from the impact of testifying on the auditor in Brown v. Walker, who could the next day resume his job with reputation unaffected. But, as this Court has often held, the immunity granted need only remove those sanctions which generate the fear justifying invocation of the privilege: "The interdiction of the Fifth Amendment operates only where a witness is asked to incriminate himself — in other words, to give testimony which may possibly expose him to a criminal charge. But if the criminality has already been taken away, the Amendment ceases to apply." Hale v. Henkel, 201 U.S. 43, 67. Here, since the Immunity Act protects a witness who is compelled to answer to the extent of his constitutional immunity, he has of course, when a particular sanction is sought to be imposed against him, the right to claim that it is criminal in nature. . . .

Id., at 430-431. Justices Douglas and Black dissented, in an opinion that struck many of the same notes as Justice Field's dissent in Brown v. Walker:

> The "mischief" to be prevented [by the Fifth Amendment] falls under at least three heads.
>   (1) One "mischief" is not only the risk of conviction but the risk of prosecution. . . .
>   [T]he statute protects the accused only on account of the "transaction, matter, or thing" concerning which he is compelled to testify and bars the use as evidence of the "testimony so compelled." The forced disclosure may open up vast new vistas for the prosecutor. . . . What related offenses may be disclosed by leads furnished by the confession? How remote need the offense be before the immunity ceases to protect it? . . .

It is, for example, a crime for a person who is a member of a Communist organization registered under the Subversive Activities Control Act, 64 Stat. 987, 50 U.S.C. §781, to be employed by the United States, to be employed in any defense facility, to hold office or employment with any labor organization, §5(a)(1), or to apply for a passport or to use a passport. §6(a). The crime under that Act is the application for a passport, the use of a passport, or employment by one of the named agencies, as the case may be. Are those crimes included within the "transaction, matter, or thing" protected by the Immunity Act? . . .

(2) The guarantee against self-incrimination contained in the Fifth Amendment is not only a protection against conviction and prosecution but a safeguard of conscience and human dignity and freedom of expression as well. My view is that the Framers put it beyond the power of Congress to compel anyone to confess his crimes. The evil to be guarded against was partly self-accusation under legal compulsion. But that was only a part of the evil. The conscience and dignity of man were also involved. So too was his right to freedom of expression guaranteed by the First Amendment. The Framers, therefore, created the federally protected right of silence and decreed that the law could not be used to pry open one's lips and make him a witness against himself.

A long history and a deep sentiment lay behind this decision. Some of those who came to these shores were Puritans who had known the hated oath ex officio used both by the Star Chamber and the High Commission. See Mary Hume Maguire, Attack of the Common Lawyers on the Oath Ex Officio as Administered in the Ecclesiastical Courts in England, Essays in History and Political Theory (1936), c. VII. They had known the great rebellion of Lilburn, Cartwright and others against those instruments of oppression. . . .

(3) . . . The Fifth Amendment was designed to protect the accused against infamy as well as against prosecution. . . . The history of infamy as a punishment was notorious. Luther had inveighed against excommunication. The Massachusetts Body of Liberties of 1641 had provided in Article 60: "No church censure shall degrade or depose any man from any Civill dignitie, office, or Authoritie he shall have in the Commonwealth." Loss of office, loss of dignity, loss of face were feudal forms of punishment. Infamy was historically considered to be punishment as effective as fine and imprisonment.

The Beccarian attitude toward infamy was a part of the background of the Fifth Amendment. The concept of infamy was explicitly written into it. We need not guess as to that. For the first Clause of the Fifth Amendment contains the concept in haec verba: "No person shall be held to answer for a capital, or otherwise *infamous* crime, unless on a presentment or indictment of a Grand Jury. . . ." (Italics added.) And the third Clause, the one we are concerned with here — "No person . . . shall be compelled in any criminal case to be a witness against himself . . ." — also reflects the revulsion of society at infamy imposed by the State. . . .

. . . The critical point is that the Constitution places the right of silence *beyond the reach of government*. The Fifth Amendment stands between the citizen and his government. When public opinion casts a person into the outer darkness, as happens today when a person is exposed as a Communist, the government brings infamy on the head of the witness when it compels disclosure. That is precisely what the Fifth Amendment prohibits.

Id., at 443-454 (Douglas, J., dissenting).

Justice Douglas suggests that the privilege should be available whenever the witness would be subject to "infamy." What does that mean? If his position were adopted, would courts need to develop a body of doctrine defining what sorts of questioning might produce infamous answers, or would witnesses simply be able to claim the privilege whenever they were asked questions they preferred not to answer? Recall Chief Justice Marshall's ruling in the *Burr* case, quoted at page 713, supra.

Notice the way Justice Douglas's opinion links the Fifth Amendment privilege with First Amendment values. That link has a long history. The Puritans who were forced to testify before the English High Commission were being persecuted for their faith, just as John Lilburne was being persecuted for his politics. Indeed, the preconstitutional history of the privilege against self-incrimination reads like a catalogue of religious and political persecution. See Leonard W. Levy, The Origins of the Fifth Amendment (2d ed. 1986). *Ullmann* arguably falls in the same tradition. Is this the right role for the privilege? Should rules for ordinary criminal cases be made with an eye toward protecting against McCarthyite harassment of political dissidents? For an argument in the affirmative, see Erwin Griswold, The Fifth Amendment Today (1955). For a thorough review of the history of the self-incrimination clause, see Richard H. Helmholz et al., The Privilege against Self-Incrimination (1997).

Today the privilege is rarely invoked in cases with free speech overtones, which may be why the dissenters' argument in *Ullmann* seems to have fallen out of favor. The next case has more to do with criminal conduct than with free speech — though the subject matter was politically charged: The defendants refused to answer questions concerning fraudulent medical deferments in a grand jury investigation of Vietnam War-era violations of the selective service laws.

KASTIGAR v. UNITED STATES

Certiorari to the United States Court of Appeals for the Ninth Circuit
406 U.S. 441 (1972)

MR. JUSTICE POWELL delivered the opinion of the Court.

This case presents the question whether the United States Government may compel testimony from an unwilling witness, who invokes the Fifth Amendment privilege against compulsory self-incrimination, by conferring on the witness immunity from use of the compelled testimony in subsequent criminal proceedings, as well as immunity from use of evidence derived from the testimony.

Petitioners were subpoenaed to appear before a United States grand jury in the Central District of California on February 4, 1971. . . .

Petitioners appeared but refused to answer questions, asserting their privilege against compulsory self-incrimination. They were brought before the District Court, and each persisted in his refusal to answer the grand jury's questions, notwithstanding the grant of immunity. The court found both in contempt, and committed them to the custody of the Attorney General until either they answered the grand jury's questions or the term of the grand jury expired. The Court of Appeals for the Ninth Circuit affirmed. Stewart v. United States, 440 F.2d 954 (CA9 1971). This Court granted certiorari to resolve the important question whether testimony may be compelled by granting immunity from the use of compelled testimony and evidence derived therefrom ("use and derivative use" immunity), or whether it is necessary to grant immunity from prosecution for offenses to which compelled testimony relates ("transactional" immunity). . . .

III

Petitioners' . . . contention is that the scope of immunity provided by the federal witness immunity statute, 18 U.S.C. §6002, is not coextensive with the scope of the Fifth Amendment privilege against compulsory self-incrimination, and therefore is not sufficient to supplant the privilege and compel testimony over a claim of the privilege. The statute provides that when a witness is compelled by district court order to testify over a claim of the privilege:

> the witness may not refuse to comply with the order on the basis of his privilege against self-incrimination; but no testimony or other information compelled under the order (or any information directly or indirectly derived from such testimony or other information) may be used against the witness in any criminal case, except a prosecution for perjury, giving a false statement, or otherwise failing to comply with the order.

The constitutional inquiry, rooted in logic and history, as well as in the decisions of this Court, is whether the immunity granted under this statute is coextensive with the scope of the privilege. . . .

Petitioners draw a distinction between statutes that provide transactional immunity and those that provide, as does the statute before us, immunity from use and derivative use. They contend that a statute must at a minimum grant full transactional immunity in order to be coextensive with the scope of the privilege. . . .

The statute's explicit proscription of the use in any criminal case of "testimony or other information compelled under the order (or any information directly or indirectly derived from such testimony or other information)" is consonant with Fifth Amendment standards. We hold that such immunity from use and derivative use is coextensive with the scope of the privilege against self-incrimination, and therefore is sufficient to compel testimony over a claim of the privilege. While a grant of immunity must afford protection commensurate with that afforded by the privilege, it need not be broader. Transactional immunity, which accords full immunity from prosecution for the offense to which the compelled testimony relates, affords the witness considerably broader protection than does the Fifth Amendment privilege. The privilege has never been construed to mean that one who invokes it cannot subsequently be prosecuted. Its sole concern is to afford protection against being "forced to give testimony leading to the infliction of 'penalties affixed to . . . criminal acts.'"[38] Immunity from the use of compelled testimony, as well as evidence derived directly and indirectly therefrom, affords this protection. It prohibits the prosecutorial authorities from using the compelled testimony in *any* respect, and it therefore insures that the testimony cannot lead to the infliction of criminal penalties on the witness. . . .

In Murphy v. Waterfront Commn., 378 U.S. 52 (1964), the Court carefully considered immunity from use of compelled testimony and evidence derived therefrom. The *Murphy* petitioners were subpoenaed to testify at a hearing conducted by the Waterfront Commission of New York Harbor. After refusing to answer certain questions on the ground that the answers might tend to incriminate them, petitioners were granted immunity from prosecution under the laws of New Jersey and New York. They continued to refuse to testify, however, on the ground

---

38. Ullmann v. United States, 350 U.S., at 438-439, quoting Boyd v. United States, 116 U.S., at 634.

that their answers might tend to incriminate them under federal law, to which the immunity did not purport to extend. They were adjudged in civil contempt, and that judgment was affirmed by the New Jersey Supreme Court.

The issue before the Court in *Murphy* was whether New Jersey and New York could compel the witnesses, whom these States had immunized from prosecution under their laws, to give testimony that might then be used to convict them of a federal crime. Since New Jersey and New York had not purported to confer immunity from federal prosecution, the Court was faced with the question what limitations the Fifth Amendment privilege imposed on the prosecutorial powers of the Federal Government, a nonimmunizing sovereign. After undertaking an examination of the policies and purposes of the privilege, the Court overturned the rule that one jurisdiction within our federal structure may compel a witness to give testimony which could be used to convict him of a crime in another jurisdiction.[42] The Court held that the privilege protects state witnesses against incrimination under federal as well as state law, and federal witnesses against incrimination under state as well as federal law. Applying this principle to the state immunity legislation before it, the Court held the constitutional rule to be that:

> [A] state witness may not be compelled to give testimony which may be incriminating under federal law unless the compelled testimony and its fruits cannot be used in any manner by federal officials in connection with a criminal prosecution against him. We conclude, moreover, that in order to implement this constitutional rule and accommodate the interests of the State and Federal Governments in investigating and prosecuting crime, the Federal Government must be prohibited from making any such use of compelled testimony and its fruits.

The Court emphasized that this rule left the state witness and the federal government, against which the witness had immunity only from the *use* of the compelled testimony and evidence derived therefrom, "in substantially the same position as if the witness had claimed his privilege in the absence of a state grant of immunity." Ibid. . . .

IV

. . . Petitioners argue that use and derivative-use immunity will not adequately protect a witness from various possible incriminating uses of the compelled testimony: for example, the prosecutor or other law enforcement officials may obtain leads, names of witnesses, or other information not otherwise available that might result in a prosecution. It will be difficult and perhaps impossible, the argument goes, to identify . . . the subtle ways in which the compelled testimony may disadvantage a witness. . . .

This argument presupposes that the statute's prohibition will prove impossible to enforce. The statute provides a sweeping proscription of any use, direct or indirect, of the compelled testimony and any information derived therefrom: "[N]o

42. Reconsideration of the rule that the Fifth Amendment privilege does not protect a witness in one jurisdiction against being compelled to give testimony that could be used to convict him in another jurisdiction was made necessary by the decision in Malloy v. Hogan, 378 U.S. 1 (1964), in which the Court held the Fifth Amendment privilege applicable to the States through the Fourteenth Amendment. Murphy v. Waterfront Commn., 378 U.S., at 57.

testimony or other information compelled under the order (or any information directly or indirectly derived from such testimony or other information) may be used against the witness in any criminal case." This total prohibition on use provides a comprehensive safeguard, barring the use of compelled testimony as an "investigatory lead,"[50] and also barring the use of any evidence obtained by focusing investigation on a witness as a result of his compelled disclosures.

A person accorded this immunity under 18 U.S.C. §6002, and subsequently prosecuted, is not dependent for the preservation of his rights upon the integrity and good faith of the prosecuting authorities. As stated in *Murphy*: "Once a defendant demonstrates that he has testified, under a state grant of immunity, to matters related to the federal prosecution, the federal authorities have the burden of showing that their evidence is not tainted by establishing that they had an independent, legitimate source for the disputed evidence." 378 U.S., at 79, n. 18. This burden of proof, which we reaffirm as appropriate, is not limited to a negation of taint; rather, it imposes on the prosecution the affirmative duty to prove that the evidence it proposes to use is derived from a legitimate source wholly independent of the compelled testimony. . . .

The statutory [immunity] is analogous to the Fifth Amendment requirement in cases of coerced confessions. A coerced confession, as revealing of leads as testimony given in exchange for immunity, is inadmissible in a criminal trial, but it does not bar prosecution. . . .

There can be no justification in reason or policy for holding that the Constitution requires an amnesty grant where, acting pursuant to statute and accompanying safeguards, testimony is compelled in exchange for immunity from use and derivative use when no such amnesty is required where the government, acting without colorable right, coerces a defendant into incriminating himself.

We conclude that the immunity provided by 18 U.S.C. §6002 leaves the witness and the prosecutorial authorities in substantially the same position as if the witness had claimed the Fifth Amendment privilege. The immunity therefore is coextensive with the privilege and suffices to supplant it. The judgment of the Court of Appeals for the Ninth Circuit accordingly is affirmed.

MR. JUSTICE BRENNAN and MR. JUSTICE REHNQUIST took no part in the consideration or decision of this case.

MR. JUSTICE MARSHALL, dissenting.

Today the Court holds that the United States may compel a witness to give incriminating testimony, and subsequently prosecute him for crimes to which that testimony relates. I cannot believe the Fifth Amendment permits that result.

The Fifth Amendment gives a witness an absolute right to resist interrogation, if the testimony sought would tend to incriminate him. A grant of immunity may strip the witness of the right to refuse to testify, but only if it is broad enough to eliminate all possibility that the testimony will in fact operate to incriminate him. It must put him in precisely the same position, vis-à-vis the government that has compelled his testimony, as he would have been in had he remained silent in reliance on the privilege. . . .

---

50. See, e.g., Albertson v. Subversive Activities Control Board, 382 U.S., at 80.

The Court recognizes that an immunity statute must be tested by that standard. . . . I assume, moreover, that in theory that test would be met by a complete ban on the use of the compelled testimony, including all derivative use, however remote and indirect. But I cannot agree that a ban on use will in practice be total, if it remains open for the government to convict the witness on the basis of evidence derived from a legitimate independent source. The Court asserts that the witness is adequately protected by a rule imposing on the government a heavy burden of proof if it would establish the independent character of evidence to be used against the witness. But in light of the inevitable uncertainties of the factfinding process, a greater margin of protection is required. . . . That margin can be provided only by immunity from prosecution for the offenses to which the testimony relates, i.e., transactional immunity.

I do not see how it can suffice merely to put the burden of proof on the government. . . . A witness who suspects that his compelled testimony was used to develop a lead will be hard pressed indeed to ferret out the evidence necessary to prove it. And of course it is no answer to say he need not prove it, for though the Court puts the burden of proof on the government, the government will have no difficulty in meeting its burden by mere assertion if the witness produces no contrary evidence. The good faith of the prosecuting authorities is thus the sole safeguard of the witness' rights. . . . [And] even their good faith is not a sufficient safeguard. For the paths of information through the investigative bureaucracy may well be long and winding, and even a prosecutor acting in the best of faith cannot be certain that somewhere in the depths of his investigative apparatus, often including hundreds of employees, there was not some prohibited use of the compelled testimony. The Court today sets out a loose net to trap tainted evidence and prevent its use against the witness, but it accepts an intolerably great risk that tainted evidence will in fact slip through that net. . . .

[The dissenting opinion of Justice Douglas is omitted.]

NOTES AND QUESTIONS

1. The Court consistently asserts that for an immunity grant to displace the privilege, it must be "co-extensive" with the privilege. What does that mean? Consider the arguments raised by Justice Field's dissent in *Brown* (page 719, supra) and Justice Douglas's dissent in *Ullmann* (page 720, supra) as well as Justice Marshall's dissent in *Kastigar*.

2. Justice Marshall argued that, in practice, the kind of immunity the *Kastigar* Court approved would leave defendants in a worse position than before their immunized testimony: The government would use the immunized testimony to generate new leads and to identify new witnesses, and courts would be unable to separate what *was* the fruit of immunized testimony from what was *not*.

Two Court of Appeals cases from the early 1990s raise the question whether Justice Marshall's prediction has proved accurate. The first is United States v. North, 910 F.2d 843, *modified*, 920 F.2d 940 (D.C. Cir. 1990). Defendant Oliver North gave immunized testimony on the Iran-Contra affair before a congressional committee on national television. North's prosecutor made no direct use of the testimony; indeed, the prosecution took elaborate steps to ensure that his staff avoided all exposure to the immunized testimony. At trial, the independent counsel relied on witnesses who had testified before the grand jury prior to North's immunized congressional testimony. But because the trial witnesses were found to have been exposed to North's immunized testimony, the court of appeals remanded to the district court with instructions to analyze the government's case "line by line" to ensure that neither its content nor the source of the testimony was derived from North's testimony. That being an impossible task, the charges were ultimately dismissed.

The second is United States v. Helmsley, 941 F.2d 71 (2d Cir. 1991). In *Helmsley*, a newspaper article covering the defendant's immunized state testimony prompted a reporter to investigate the possibility that Helmsley had misappropriated corporate funds for her own use. The resulting article contributed to a subsequent federal prosecution for tax fraud. The court of appeals found the relationship between the immunized testimony and the subsequent prosecution to be too attenuated to violate the Fifth Amendment.

Are *North* and *Helmsley* consistent? If not, which approach do you prefer?

3. Notice how thoroughly Justice Douglas's position in *Ullmann* has been rejected. Both the *Kastigar* majority and Justice Marshall's dissent seem to agree that all the privilege requires is to keep the government from forcing people to testify and then somehow using that testimony to help convict them of crime. Compelling people to talk about the crimes they've committed is perfectly permissible as long as their statements do not advantage the government in any subsequent criminal prosecution of the witness. What does this say about the values that the privilege now serves? One common argument for the privilege is that it is wrong for the state to force an individual to pass judgment on himself. See Robert S. Gerstein, The Demise of *Boyd*: Self-Incrimination and Private Papers in the Burger Court, 27 UCLA L. Rev. 343 (1979); R. Kent Greenawalt, Silence as a Moral and Constitutional Right, 23 Wm. & Mary L. Rev. 15 (1981). Isn't a defendant passing judgment on himself anytime he confesses to crime, whether or not the confession is immunized?

4. In Murphy v. Waterfront Commission of New York Harbor, 378 U.S. 52 (1964), discussed in *Kastigar*, Justice Goldberg's opinion for the Court addressed the policies then perceived to underlie the privilege:

> The privilege against self-incrimination "registers an important advance in the development of our liberty — 'one of the great landmarks in man's struggle to make himself civilized.'" Ullmann v. United States, 350 U.S. 422, 426.[4] It reflects many of our fundamental values and most noble aspirations: our unwillingness to subject those suspected of crime to the cruel trilemma of self-accusation, perjury or contempt; our preference for an accusatorial rather than an inquisitorial system of criminal justice; our fear that self-incriminating statements will be elicited by inhumane treatment and abuses; our sense of fair play which dictates "a fair state-individual balance by requiring the government to leave the individual alone until good cause is shown for disturbing him and by requiring the government in its contest with the individual to shoulder the entire load," 8 Wigmore, Evidence (McNaughton rev., 1961), 317; our respect for the inviolability of the human personality and of the right of each individual "to a private enclave where he may lead a private life," United States v. Grunewald, 233 F.2d 556, 581-582 (Frank, J., dissenting), rev'd 353 U.S. 391; our distrust of self-deprecatory statements; and our realization that the privilege, while

4. The quotation is from Erwin N. Griswold, The Fifth Amendment Today 7 (1955).

sometimes "a shelter to the guilty," is often "a protection to the innocent." Quinn v. United States, 349 U.S. 155, 162.

Consider Professor Arenella's analysis of Justice Goldberg's effort to articulate the policies of the privilege:

An examination of Justice Goldberg's fundamental values reveals three obvious points. First, some of them seem to overlap with each other (e.g., numbers two and four; or numbers one, three, and six). Second, many of these values are stated so abstractly that they can be used to justify almost any result. For example, what does it mean to speak of "our preference for an accusatorial rather than an inquisitorial system" (number two)? What criteria should a court use to determine whether state practices have upset a fair state-individual balance (number four)? Finally, this list of fundamental values suggests that the privilege against self-incrimination protects both *substantive values* (e.g., privacy, human dignity, and moral autonomy) and *accusatorial process norms* (e.g., a fair state-individual balance of advantage and adversarial determination of guilt) whose applicability may vary with the procedural context involved and whose significance may depend on the countervailing state interests at stake. Thus, when the Court confronts procedural contexts and state objectives not envisioned by the Constitution's framers, it must first identify which fifth amendment values are implicated and what state interests are at stake that might justify some impairment of these values. In other words, the Court must inevitably engage in a balancing analysis of these competing interests before it can interpret fifth amendment concepts like "compulsion" or "to be a witness against himself."

Peter Arenella, *Schmerber* and the Privilege against Self-Incrimination: A Reappraisal, 20 Am. Crim. L. Rev. 31, 37 (1982).

5. United States v. Balsys, 542 U.S. 666 (1998), addressed *Murphy*'s list of policies underlying the privilege. In *Balsys*, the Court held that the Fifth Amendment does not extend to the risk of prosecution by a foreign nation. In the course of his opinion for the Court, Justice Souter wrote:

The *Murphy* majority opens its discussion with a catalog of "Policies of the Privilege." . . . Some of the policies listed would seem to point no further than domestic arrangements and so raise no basis for any privilege looking beyond fear of domestic prosecution. Others however, might suggest a concern broad enough to encompass foreign prosecutions and accordingly to support a more expansive theory of the privilege . . .

. . . The most general of *Murphy*'s policy items ostensibly suggesting protection as comprehensive as that sought by Balsys is listed in the opinion as "the inviolability of the human personality and . . . the right of each individual to a private enclave where he may lead a private life." . . . If in fact these values were reliable guides to the actual scope of protection under the Clause, they would be seen to demand a very high degree of protection indeed: "inviolability" is, after all, an uncompromising term, and we know as well from Fourth Amendment law as from a layman's common sense that breaches of privacy are complete at the moment of illicit intrusion, whatever use may or may not later be made of their fruits.

The Fifth Amendment tradition, however, offers no such degree of protection. If the Government is ready to provide the requisite use and derivative use immunity, the protection goes no further: no violation of personality is recognized and no claim of privilege will avail. One might reply that the choice of the word "inviolability" was just unfortunate; while testimonial integrity may not be inviolable, it is sufficiently served by requiring the Government to pay a price in the form of use (and derivative use) immunity before a refusal to testify will be overruled. But that answer overlooks the fact that when a witness's response will raise no fear of criminal penalty, there is no protection for testimonial privacy at all.

Thus, what we find in practice is not the protection of personal testimonial inviolability, but a conditional protection of testimonial privacy subject to basic limits recognized before the framing and refined through immunity doctrine in the intervening years. Since the Judiciary could not recognize fear of foreign prosecution and at the same time preserve the Government's existing rights to seek testimony in exchange for immunity (because domestic courts could not enforce the immunity abroad), it follows that extending protection as Balsys requests would change the balance of private and governmental interests that has seemingly been accepted for as long as there has been Fifth Amendment doctrine. . . .

For a discussion of self-incrimination in the international context, see Diane Marie Amann, A Whipsaw Cuts Both Ways: The Privilege against Self-Incrimination in an International Court, 45 UCLA L. Rev. 1201 (1998).

6. Perhaps because the Court has not plainly specified what value or values it is trying to advance in its Fifth Amendment cases, a large and constantly growing literature seeks to explain why we have a privilege against self-incrimination. For a sampling, see Robert S. Gerstein, Privacy and Self-Incrimination, 80 Ethics 87 (1970) (privilege protects individual privacy and autonomy); R. Kent Greenawalt, Silence as a Moral and Constitutional Right, 23 Wm. & Mary L. Rev. 15 (1981) (privilege protects against forced self-judgment); Stephen J. Schulhofer, Some Kind Words for the Privilege against Self-Incrimination, 26 Val. U. L. Rev. 311 (1991) (privilege protects innocent defendants); Louis Michael Seidman, Rubashov's Question: Self-Incrimination and the Problem of Coerced Preferences, 2 Yale J.L. & Human. 149 (1990) (privilege prevents government from coercing "consent" to punishment); William J. Stuntz, Self-Incrimination and Excuse, 88 Colum. L. Rev. 1227 (1988) (privilege bars compelled testimony where ordinary person would likely lie); George C. Thomas III & Marshall D. Bilder, Aristotle's Paradox and the Self-Incrimination Puzzle, 82 J. Crim. L. & Criminology 243 (1991) (privilege protects free choice). See also David Dolinko, Is There a Rationale for the Privilege against Self-Incrimination? 33 UCLA L. Rev. 1063 (1986) (criticizing all major theories of the privilege); Donald A. Dripps, Self-Incrimination and Self-Preservation: A Skeptical View, 1991 U. Ill. L. Rev. 329 (criticizing theories of the privilege based on self-preservation); Ronald J. Allen, The Simpson Affair, Reform of the Criminal Justice Process, and Magic Bullets, 67 U. Colo. L. Rev. 989 (1996).

B.   The Contours of the Privilege Against Self-Incrimination

In order to make out a claim that the privilege against self-incrimination was violated, a claimant must satisfy the privilege's three elements, which track its three clauses: compulsion ("no person . . . shall be compelled"), incrimination ("in any criminal case"), and testimony ("to be a witness against himself"). The claimant must also explicitly claim the privilege — save only for three exceptions: police interrogation, considered in Section D, infra; a peculiar and rarely used exception that excuses statutory reporting requirements for "inherently suspect classes," considered in Section C, infra; and cases in which exercising one's rights would be penalized. See, e.g., Garrity v. New Jersey, 385 U.S. 493 (1967). Apart from these exceptions, a witness must invoke the Fifth Amendment on being questioned, and a failure to do so is deemed a waiver. Moreover, once a witness answers a question, the witness cannot refuse to be examined further concerning the general area of the answer — "Disclosure of a fact waives the privilege as to details." Rogers v. United States, 340 U.S. 367, 373 (1951). As to each subsequent question asked, the issue is whether the answer might subject the witness to a "real danger of further crimination," id., at 379, beyond that contained in the original answer. The *Rogers* test is not easy to apply, however, as the trial judge must make very refined appraisals of the effect of any admission as well as the potential effect of any subsequent statements. The lower courts have also required subsequent disclosure where an answer to a question would result in a distortion of truth. For a discussion, see Note, Testimonial Waiver of the Privilege against Self Incrimination, 92 Harv. L. Rev. 1752 (1979).

1. "No Person . . . Shall Be Compelled": The Meaning of Compulsion

The paradigmatic case of Fifth Amendment compulsion is sworn testimony under threat of legal penalty. A person called as a witness at a trial is required to testify by a state actor — the judge — and will be held in contempt if he or she refuses to answer questions. The same analysis applies to the many administrative or legislative settings in which witnesses are ordered to respond to questions or face legal sanctions.

Fifth Amendment compulsion extends beyond these obvious cases. As we will see in Section D below, the Supreme Court has found that jailhouse interrogation is sufficiently coercive to amount to compulsion, even though the police have no formal authority to require a suspect to speak. And in Lefkowitz v. Turley, 414 U.S. 70 (1973), the Court struck down a New York statute that conditioned all state contracts on contractors' willingness to waive their Fifth Amendment rights if asked to testify about the subject matter of their contracts. According to the Court, the rule in *Lefkowitz* constituted Fifth Amendment compulsion. So did a state statute decreeing that government employees should lose their jobs if they invoked their Fifth Amendment rights in response to questions within the scope of their employment. See Garrity v. New Jersey, 385 U.S. 493 (1967). And so did the threat of disbarment for a lawyer. See Spevack v. Klein, 385 U.S. 511 (1967).

Perhaps unsurprisingly, compulsion receives its broadest construction when the witness in question is the defendant at a criminal trial. In Griffin v. California, 380 U.S. 609 (1965), the Court forbade the prosecutor from commenting to the jury on the defendant's failure to take the stand. Such comment had been common in a number of jurisdictions for as long as criminal defendants had been permitted to testify under oath. Nevertheless, the Court held that prosecutorial comment on the defendant's silence impermissibly penalizes the defendant's exercise of his Fifth Amendment rights — and the threat of such comments puts pressure on the defendant to testify, hence to waive those rights. In Carter v. Kentucky, 450 U.S. 288 (1981), the Court concluded that defendants who choose not to testify also have the right to have their juries instructed *not* to draw inferences from their silence. It is not clear how much difference the rules in *Griffin* and *Carter* make. If the prosecution has put on a reasonably strong case, everyone in the courtroom, jurors included, knows who is in the best position to rebut it. A reasonably strong case that goes unanswered by the defendant almost always leads to a conviction, no matter how often or how strongly the jury is admonished not to infer guilt from silence. Perhaps the chief effect of the cautionary instructions *Griffin* and *Carter* require is to undermine jurors' faith in judges' instructions.

Outside of defendants in criminal trials, the person who wishes to claim the privilege may be examined, and the privilege must be invoked in response to the relevant questions. Adverse inferences from the refusal to testify are permissible. See, e.g., Baxter v. Palmigiano, 425 U.S. 308 (1976) (prison authorities are entitled to draw adverse inferences from silence in prison disciplinary proceedings). Such proceedings do not "compel" testimony, under the Court's cases. In Ohio Adult Parole Authority v. Woodward, 523 U.S. 272 (1998), the Court considered whether Ohio's clemency proceedings for inmates under sentence of death violated the Fifth Amendment:

> Respondent . . . presses on us the Court of Appeals' conclusion that the provision of a voluntary inmate interview, without the benefit of counsel or a grant of immunity . . . , implicates the inmate's Fifth and Fourteenth Amendment right not to incriminate himself. . . . In our opinion, the procedures of the Authority do not under any view violate the Fifth Amendment privilege. . . .
>
> Assuming . . . that the Authority will draw adverse inferences from respondent's refusal to answer questions — which it may do in a civil proceeding without offending the Fifth Amendment — we do not think that respondent's testimony at a clemency interview would be "compelled" within the meaning of the Fifth Amendment. It is difficult to see how a voluntary interview could "compel" respondent to speak. He merely faces a choice quite similar to the sorts of choices that a criminal defendant must make in the course of criminal proceedings, none of which has ever been held to violate the Fifth Amendment.
>
> Long ago we held that a defendant who took the stand in his own defense could not claim the privilege against self-incrimination when the prosecution sought to cross-examine. . . .
>
> A defendant whose motion for acquittal at the close of the Government's case is denied must then elect whether to stand on his motion or to put on a defense, with the accompanying risk that in doing so he will augment the Government's case against him. In each of these situations, there are undoubted pressures — generated by the strength of the Government's case against him — pushing the criminal defendant to testify. But it has never been suggested that such pressures constitute "compulsion" for Fifth Amendment purposes.

Id., at 285-287. The Court went on to discuss its holding in Williams v. Florida, 399 U.S. 78 (1970). Florida law required defendants to give notice prior to trial that they planned to raise an alibi defense; the defendant in *Williams* claimed such mandatory notice amounted to compelled self-incrimination. The Court disagreed, reasoning that the pressure involved was no different than the kind of pressure that defendants often bear in a criminal trial process due to the strength of the government's evidence and arguments. The pressure to testify in the clemency proceeding in *Woodard*, the Court concluded, was similar.

With *Woodard* and *Williams*, compare McKune v. Lile, 536 U.S. 24 (2002). The facts in *McKune* were as follows:

In 1982, respondent lured a high school student into his car as she was returning home from school. At gunpoint, respondent forced the victim to perform oral sodomy on him and then drove to a field where he raped her. After the sexual assault, the victim went to her school, where, crying and upset, she reported the crime. The police arrested respondent and recovered on his person the weapon he used to facilitate the crime. Although respondent maintained that the sexual intercourse was consensual, a jury convicted him of rape, aggravated sodomy, and aggravated kidnaping. . . .

In 1994, a few years before respondent was scheduled to be released, prison officials ordered him to participate in a Sexual Abuse Treatment Program (SATP). As part of the program, participating inmates are required to complete and sign an "Admission of Responsibility" form, in which they discuss and accept responsibility for the crime for which they have been sentenced. Participating inmates also are required to complete a sexual history form, which details all prior sexual activities, regardless of whether such activities constitute uncharged criminal offenses. A polygraph examination is used to verify the accuracy and completeness of the offender's sexual history.

While information obtained from participants advances the SATP's rehabilitative goals, the information is not privileged. Kansas leaves open the possibility that new evidence might be used against sex offenders in future criminal proceedings. In addition, Kansas law requires the SATP staff to report any uncharged sexual offenses involving minors to law enforcement authorities. Although there is no evidence that incriminating information has ever been disclosed under the SATP, the release of information is a possibility.

Department officials informed respondent that if he refused to participate in the SATP, his privilege status would be reduced from Level III to Level I. As part of this reduction, respondent's visitation rights, earnings, work opportunities, ability to send money to family, canteen expenditures, access to a personal television, and other privileges automatically would be curtailed. In addition, respondent would be transferred to a maximum-security unit, where his movement would be more limited, he would be moved from a two-person to a four-person cell, and he would be in a potentially more dangerous environment.

Id., at 29-30. By a 5-4 vote, the Supreme Court held that these facts did not constitute Fifth Amendment compulsion. Justice Kennedy, speaking for himself, Chief Justice Rehnquist, and Justices Scalia and Thomas, stressed the large degree of control prison officials have over prisoners:

The SATP does not compel prisoners to incriminate themselves in violation of the Constitution. . . . The consequences in question here — a transfer to another prison where television sets are not placed in each inmate's cell, where exercise facilities are not readily available, and where work and wage opportunities are more limited — are not ones that compel a prisoner to speak about his past crimes despite a desire to remain silent. The fact that these consequences are imposed on prisoners, rather than ordinary citizens, moreover, is important in weighing respondent's constitutional claim. . . .

In the present case, respondent's decision not to participate in the Kansas SATP did not extend his term of incarceration. Nor did his decision affect his eligibility for good-time credits or parole. Respondent instead complains that if he remains silent about his past crimes, he will be transferred from the medium-security unit — where the program is conducted — to a less desirable maximum-security unit.

No one contends, however, that the transfer is intended to punish prisoners for exercising their Fifth Amendment rights. Rather, the limitation on these rights is incidental to Kansas' legitimate penological reason for the transfer: Due to limited space, inmates who do not participate in their respective programs will be moved out of the facility where the programs are held to make room for other inmates. As the Secretary of Corrections has explained, "it makes no sense to have someone who's not participating in a program taking up a bed in a setting where someone else who may be willing to participate in a program could occupy that bed and participate in a program." App. 99.

Respondent also complains that he will be demoted from Level III to Level I status as a result of his decision not to participate. This demotion means the loss of his personal television; less access to prison organizations and the gym area; a reduction in certain pay opportunities and canteen privileges; and restricted visitation rights. An essential tool of prison administration, however, is the authority to offer inmates various incentives to behave. The Constitution accords prison officials wide latitude to bestow or revoke these perquisites as they see fit. . . . [B]y virtue of their convictions, inmates must expect significant restrictions, inherent in prison life, on rights and privileges free citizens take for granted.

. . . [R]elying on the so-called penalty cases, respondent treats the fact of his incarceration as if it were irrelevant. See, e.g., Garrity v. New Jersey, 385 U.S. 493 (1967); Spevack v. Klein, 385 U.S. 511 (1967). Those cases, however, involved free citizens given the choice between invoking the Fifth Amendment privilege and sustaining their economic livelihood. See, e.g., id., at 516 ("Threat of disbarment and the loss of professional standing, professional reputation, and of livelihood are powerful forms of compulsion"). Those principles are not easily extended to the prison context, where inmates surrender upon incarceration their rights to pursue a livelihood and to contract freely with the State, as well as many other basic freedoms. The persons who asserted rights in *Garrity* and *Spevack* had not been convicted of a crime. It would come as a surprise if *Spevack* stands for the proposition that when a lawyer has been disbarred by reason of a final criminal conviction, the court or agency considering reinstatement of the right to practice law could not consider that the disbarred attorney has admitted his guilt and expressed contrition. Indeed, this consideration is often given dispositive weight by this Court itself on routine motions for reinstatement. The current case is more complex, of course, in that respondent is also required to discuss other criminal acts for which he might still be liable for prosecution. On this point, however, there is still a critical distinction between the instant case and *Garrity* or *Spevack*. Unlike those cases, respondent here is asked to discuss other past crimes as part of a legitimate rehabilitative program conducted within prison walls.

To reject out of hand these considerations would be to ignore the State's interests in offering rehabilitation programs and providing for the efficient administration of its prisons. There is no indication that the SATP is an elaborate attempt to avoid the protections offered by the privilege against compelled self-incrimination. Rather, the program serves an important social purpose. It would be bitter medicine to treat as irrelevant the State's legitimate interests and to invalidate the SATP on the ground that it incidentally burdens an inmate's right to remain silent. . . .

Id., at 35-41 (plurality opinion).

Justice O'Connor provided the fifth vote for the result in *McKune*. She concluded that Fifth Amendment compulsion was broader than Justice Kennedy's opinion would have it—but not broad enough to encompass the situation in *McKune*.

. . . Our precedents establish that certain types of penalties are capable of coercing incriminating testimony: termination of employment, Uniformed Sanitation Men Assn., Inc. v. Commissioner of Sanitation of City of New York, 392 U.S. 280 (1968), the loss of a professional license, Spevack v. Klein, 385 U.S. 511 (1967), ineligibility to receive government contracts, Lefkowitz v. Turley, 414 U.S. 70 (1973), and the loss of the right to participate in political associations and to hold public office, Lefkowitz v. Cunningham, 431 U.S. 801 (1977). All of these penalties, however, are far more significant than those facing respondent here.

The first three of these so-called "penalty cases" involved the potential loss of one's livelihood, either through the loss of employment, loss of a professional license essential to employment, or loss of business through government contracts. In *Lefkowitz* we held that the loss of government contracts was constitutionally equivalent to the loss of a profession because "[a government contractor] lives off his contracting fees just as surely as a state employee lives off his salary." 414 U.S., at 83. To support oneself in one's chosen profession is one of the most important abilities a person can have. A choice between incriminating oneself and being deprived of one's livelihood is the very sort of choice that is likely to compel someone to be a witness against himself. The choice presented in the last case, *Cunningham*, implicated not only political influence and prestige, but also the First Amendment right to run for office and to participate in political associations. 431 U.S., at 807-808. In holding that the penalties in that case constituted compulsion for Fifth Amendment purposes, we properly referred to those consequences as "grave." Id., at 807.

I do not believe the consequences facing respondent in this case are serious enough to compel him to be a witness against himself. These consequences involve a reduction in incentive level, and a corresponding transfer from a medium-security to a maximum-security part of the prison. In practical terms, these changes involve restrictions on the personal property respondent can keep in his cell, a reduction in his visitation privileges, a reduction in the amount of money he can spend in the canteen, and a reduction in the wage he can earn through prison employment. These changes in living conditions seem to me minor. Because the prison is responsible for caring for respondent's basic needs, his ability to support himself is not implicated by the reduction in wages he would suffer as a result. While his visitation is reduced as a result of his failure to incriminate himself, he still retains the ability to see his attorney, his family, and members of the clergy. The limitation on the possession of personal items, as well as the amount that respondent is allowed to spend at the canteen, may make his prison experience more unpleasant, but seems very unlikely to actually compel him to incriminate himself.

Id., at 49-51 (O'Connor, J., concurring in the judgment).

Both the plurality and concurring opinions in *McKune* emphasize the fact that people in the claimant's position—prison inmates—regularly face burdens similar to those imposed for failure to participate in the prison's rehabilitation program for sexual offenders. But does that fact really distinguish *McKune* from the so-called "penalty cases" Justices Kennedy and O'Connor cite? After all, employees regularly face the risk of losing their jobs, in settings that have nothing to do with the privilege against self-incrimination. Why isn't that risk the same as the risk of being assigned to a maximum security prison?

There is an argument that the Court's cases have it backward—that the threat of losing one's government job should *not* amount to Fifth Amendment compulsion, but the threat of assignment to a more unpleasant prison *should*. Consider: The Fifth Amendment claimants in Garrity v. New Jersey were police officers; they were asked to testify about taking bribes in the course of an investigation of police corruption. State law required that they testify in such circumstances or else lose their jobs. That threat amounted to compulsion, in the Court's view. But suppose the *Garrity* claimants had been private security guards and the corruption investigation was being run by their employer, a private corporation. Plainly, the private-sector employer could fire any security guards who refused to answer the employer's questions. Equally plainly, the security guards would have no valid Fifth Amendment claim on these facts. Why should government employees be treated differently? Shouldn't a police department have as much right to weed out corrupt or brutal officers as a private security company? Notice that no such argument can be made in *McKune*. There is no private-sector analogue to the penalties imposed on the prisoner in *McKune*, because private actors are not allowed to incarcerate people: The state has a monopoly on criminal punishment. It has no such monopoly on employment. Why doesn't Fifth Amendment compulsion treat disabilities only the state can impose more seriously than disabilities that private employers can (and do) impose?

At least one lower court has held, notwithstanding *McKune*, that a probation condition requiring disclosure of prior sex crimes (without a grant of immunity from prosecution for those crimes) cannot be enforced. In United States v. Antelope, 395 F.3d 1128 (9th Cir. 2005), the Ninth Circuit concluded that revocation of the defendant's probation was "more than merely hypothetical" (the government actually had pursued such revocation twice, based on Antelope's repeated refusal to disclose), and effectively "extend[ed the defendant's] term of incarceration," thus distinguishing the case from *McKune* on both counts. The court went on to state in dictum that Antelope should be entitled to immunity from prosecution based on any statements he might make in response to the "compulsion" of the probation revocation. The court rejected the government's argument that Chavez v. Martinez, 538 U.S. 760 (2003), see infra, at pages 740-741 and 881-882, left the defendant without Fifth Amendment protection unless and until actually prosecuted based on his statements; according to the court, "the holding of *Chavez* is tightly bound to its §1983 context," and does not alter the scope or application of immunity in the context of a criminal proceeding.

2. "In Any Criminal Case": The Meaning of Incrimination

The Fifth Amendment states that no one "shall be compelled *in any criminal case* to be a witness against himself" (emphasis added). The phrase "in any criminal case" is most naturally read to refer to the procedural setting in which the testimony takes place. Historically, that is not how the phrase has been construed. Rather, "in any criminal case" refers not to the timing or context of the question but to the consequences of a truthful answer. If the witness's answer poses a sufficiently serious risk of criminal punishment (and if the other two elements — compulsion and testimony — are satisfied), the privilege applies. If not, it doesn't. That is the basic meaning of "incrimination" in Fifth Amendment law.

That definition gives rise to two basic questions: What counts as criminal punishment? And how serious must the risk of criminal punishment be in order to trigger the privilege? On the first question, the courts have been less than consistent. There is a long doctrinal tradition, going back to Boyd v. United States, 116 U.S. 616 (1886), holding that various sorts of civil forfeiture proceedings should be deemed criminal for purposes of Fifth Amendment law. In more recent cases, however, the Court has emphasized the primary importance of legislative intent when classifying penalties as civil or criminal under the Fifth Amendment. United States v. Ward, 448 U.S. 242 (1980), involved a statute requiring any ship or facility that spilled oil into navigable waters to report to the relevant federal authorities. The statute gave the reported information "use immunity" from criminal prosecution, but a different subsection allowed the imposition of a "civil" monetary fine for the relevant conduct. Coincidentally, an 1899 statute made the same conduct a crime. The Court rejected Ward's contention that the statute's reporting requirements violated the Fifth Amendment if used to support the civil penalty.

UNITED STATES v. WARD, 448 U.S. 242, 248-256 (1980): This Court has often stated that the question whether a particular statutorily-defined penalty is civil or criminal is a matter of statutory construction. See, e.g., One Lot Emerald Cut Stones v. United States, 409 U.S. 232, 237 (1972). . . . Our inquiry in this regard has traditionally proceeded on two levels. First, we have set out to determine whether Congress, in establishing the penalizing mechanism, indicated either expressly or impliedly a preference for one label or the other. See [id.], at 236-237. Second, where Congress has indicated an intention to establish a civil penalty, we have inquired further whether the statutory scheme was so punitive either in purpose or effect as to negate that intention. See Flemming v. Nestor, 363 U.S. 603, 617-621 (1960). In regard to this latter inquiry, we have noted that "only the clearest proof could suffice to establish the unconstitutionality of a statute on such a ground." Id., at 617. See also Rex Trailer Co. v. United States, 350 U.S. 148, 154 (1956).

As for our first inquiry in the present case, we believe it quite clear that Congress intended to impose a civil penalty upon persons in Ward's position. Initially, and importantly, Congress labeled the sanction authorized in §311(b)(6) a "civil penalty," a label that takes on added significance given its juxtaposition with the criminal penalties set forth in the immediately preceding subparagraph, §311(b)(5). Thus, we have no doubt that Congress intended to allow imposition of penalties under §311(b)(6) without regard to the procedural protections and restrictions available in criminal prosecutions.

We turn then to consider whether Congress, despite its manifest intention to establish a civil, remedial mechanism, nevertheless provided for sanctions so punitive as to "transfor[m] what was clearly intended as a civil remedy into a criminal penalty." Rex Trailer Co. v. United States, supra, at 154. In making this determination, both the District Court and the Court of Appeals found it useful to refer to the seven considerations listed in Kennedy v. Mendoza-Martinez, [372 U.S. 144,] at 168-169. This list of considerations, while certainly neither exhaustive nor dispositive, . . . provides some guidance in the present case.[7]

Without setting forth here our assessment of each of the seven *Mendoza-Martinez* factors, we think only one, the fifth, aids respondent. That is a consideration of whether "the behavior to which [the penalty] applies is already a crime." 372 U.S., at 168-169. In this regard, respondent contends that §13 of the Rivers and Harbors Appropriation Act of 1899, 33 U.S.C. §407, makes criminal the precise conduct penalized in the present case. Moreover, respondent points out that at least one

---

7. The standards set forth were "[w]hether the sanction involves an affirmative disability or restraint, whether it has historically been regarded as a punishment, whether it comes into play only on a finding of scienter, whether its operation will promote the traditional aims of punishment — retribution and deterrence, whether the behavior to which it applies is already a crime, whether an alternative purpose to which it may rationally be connected is assignable for it, and whether it appears excessive in relation to the alternative purpose assigned. . . ." 372 U.S., at 168-169 (footnotes omitted).

federal court has held that §13 of the Rivers and Harbors Appropriation Act defines a "strict liability crime," for which the Government need prove no scienter. See United States v. White Fuel Corp., 498 F.2d 619 (1st Cir. 1974). According to respondent, this confirms the lower court's conclusion that this fifth factor "falls clearly in favor of a finding that [§311(b)(6)] is criminal in nature." 598 F.2d, at 1193.

While we agree that this consideration seems to point toward a finding that §311(b)(6) is criminal in nature, that indication is not as strong as it seems at first blush. We have noted on a number of occasions that "Congress may impose both a criminal and a civil sanction in respect to the same act or omission." . . . One Lot Emerald Cut Stones v. United States, supra, at 235. Moreover, in Helvering [v. Mitchell, 303 U.S. 391 (1938)] where we held a 50% penalty for tax fraud to be civil, we found it quite significant that "the Revenue Act of 1928 contains two separate and distinct provisions imposing sanctions," and that "these appear in different parts of the statute. . . ." 303 U.S., at 404. See also One Lot Emerald Cut Stones v. United States, supra, at 236-237. To the extent that we found significant the separation of civil and criminal penalties within the same statute, we believe that the placement of criminal penalties in one statute and the placement of civil penalties in another statute enacted 70 years later tends to dilute the force of the fifth *Mendoza-Martinez* criterion in this case.

In sum, we believe that the factors set forth in *Mendoza-Martinez*, while neither exhaustive nor conclusive on the issue, are in no way sufficient to render unconstitutional the congressional classification of the penalty established in §311(b)(6) as civil. Nor are we persuaded by any of respondent's other arguments that he has offered the "clearest proof" that the penalty here in question is punitive in either purpose or effect. . . .

Our conclusion that §311(b)(6) does not trigger all the protections afforded by the Constitution to a criminal defendant does not completely dispose of this case. Respondent asserts that, even if the penalty imposed upon him was not sufficiently criminal in nature to trigger other guarantees, it was "quasi-criminal," and therefore sufficient to implicate the Fifth Amendment's protection against compulsory self-incrimination. He relies primarily in this regard upon Boyd v. United States, 116 U.S. 616 (1886), and later cases quoting its language.

In *Boyd*, [the] . . . Court found the Fifth Amendment applicable, even though the action in question was one contesting the forfeiture of certain goods. According to the Court: "We are . . . clearly of opinion that proceedings instituted for the purpose of declaring the forfeiture of a man's property by reason of offences committed by him, though they may be civil in form, are in their nature criminal." Id., at 633-634. While at this point in its opinion, the Court seemed to limit its holding to proceedings involving the forfeiture of property, shortly after the quoted passage it broadened its reasoning in a manner that might seem to apply to the present case:

> As, therefore, suits for *penalties and forfeitures* incurred by the commission of offences against the law, are of this quasi-criminal nature, we think that they are within the reason of criminal proceedings for all the purposes of the Fourth Amendment of the Constitution, and of that portion of the Fifth Amendment which declares that no person shall be compelled in any criminal case to be a witness against himself. . . .

Id., at 634 (emphasis added).

. . . Read broadly, *Boyd* might control the present case. This Court has declined, however, to give full scope to the reasoning and dicta in *Boyd*, noting on at least one occasion that "[s]everal of *Boyd*'s express or implicit declarations have not stood the test of time." Fisher v. United States, 425 U.S. 391, 407 (1976). . . .

The question before us, then, is whether the penalty imposed in this case, although clearly not "criminal" enough to trigger the protections of the Sixth Amendment, the Double Jeopardy Clause of the Fifth Amendment, or the other procedural guarantees normally associated with criminal prosecutions, is nevertheless "so far criminal in [its] nature" as to trigger the Self-Incrimination Clause of the Fifth Amendment. Initially, we note that the penalty and proceeding considered in *Boyd* were quite different from those considered in this case. *Boyd* dealt with forfeiture of property, a penalty that had absolutely no correlation to any damages sustained by society or to the cost of enforcing the law. . . . Here the penalty is much more analogous to traditional civil damages. Moreover, the statute under scrutiny in *Boyd* listed forfeiture along with fine and imprisonment as one possible punishment for customs fraud, a fact of some significance to the *Boyd* Court. See 116 U.S., at 634. Here, as previously stated, the civil remedy and the criminal remedy are contained in separate statutes enacted 70 years apart. The proceedings in *Boyd* also posed a danger that the appellants would prejudice themselves in respect to later criminal proceedings. Here, respondent is protected by §311(b)(5), which expressly provides that "[n]otification received pursuant to this paragraph or information obtained by the exploitation of such notification shall not be used against any such person in any criminal case, except [for] prosecution for perjury or for giving a false statement." 33 U.S.C. §1321(b)(5).

More importantly, however, we believe that in the light of what we have found to be overwhelming evidence that Congress intended to create a penalty civil in all respects and quite weak evidence of any countervailing punitive purpose or effect it would be quite anomalous to hold that §311(b)(6) created a criminal penalty for the purposes of the Self-Incrimination Clause but a civil penalty for all other purposes. We do not read *Boyd* as requiring a contrary conclusion. . . .

NOTES ON THE MEANING OF INCRIMINATION

1. What does the phrase "civil penalty" mean?
2. In Allen v. Illinois, 478 U.S. 364 (1986), the Court held that the Illinois Sexually Dangerous Persons Act was civil rather than criminal in nature and thus that the Fifth Amendment does not apply to it. The Court based its conclusion on the state's assertion of its civil nature and the statute's "benign purpose" of providing treatment rather than punishment. As the dissent pointed out, however, the statute could be triggered only by a related criminal proceeding, could be initiated only by the state, required proof beyond reasonable doubt as well as the establishment of a criminal offense, and resulted in incarceration in the state's penal system.

Cases like *Ward* and *Allen* seem to leave the definition of "incrimination" in the hands of state legislatures and Congress. Is that appropriate? Should legislatures have the power to opt out of the Fifth Amendment by declaring that a given penalty is civil rather than criminal? Is this consistent with the Court's definition of Fifth Amendment compulsion?

3. *Ward* and *Allen* address the question whether the threat of a given penalty qualifies as incriminating for purposes of the privilege. A separate question is how great must the risk be in order for a witness to invoke the privilege. There too, the Court has spoken inconsistently. In Brown v. Walker, 161 U.S. 591 (1896), the Court stated that Fifth Amendment claimants must show

> reasonable ground to apprehend danger to the witness from his being compelled to answer. . . . The danger to be apprehended must be real and appreciable, with reference to the ordinary operation of law in the ordinary course of things — not a danger of an imaginary and unsubstantial character, having reference to some extraordinary and barely possible contingency, so improbable that no reasonable man would suffer it to influence his conduct.

Id., at 599-600. Hoffman v. United States, 341 U.S. 479, 487 (1951), describes the relevant standard more leniently:

> The privilege afforded not only extends to answers that would in themselves support a conviction under a federal criminal statute but likewise embraces those which would furnish a link in the chain of evidence needed to prosecute the claimant for a federal crime. . . . To sustain the privilege, it need only be evident from the implications of the question, in the setting in which it is asked, that a responsive answer to the question or an explanation of why it cannot be answered might be dangerous because injurious disclosure could result.

In Hiibel v. Sixth Judicial District Court of Nevada, 542 U.S. 177 (2004), the Court repeatedly quoted *Hoffman*'s "link in the chain of evidence" language — but did not quote the portion of the above passage stating that "it need only be evident . . . that a responsive answer . . . *might* be dangerous because injurious disclosure *could* result" (emphasis added). Instead, Justice Kennedy's opinion for the Court in *Hiibel* contained the quoted passage from Brown v. Walker, emphasizing that Fifth Amendment incrimination did not include "imaginary and unsubstantial" risks that "no reasonable man" would credit. If adjectives in Supreme Court opinions matter, *Hiibel* may signal a change in the meaning of incrimination.

Whether or not adjectives matter, context certainly does. *Hiibel* arose out of a police stop. The police had received a phone call reporting an assault, and describing the truck the perpetrator was driving. The officer stopped Hiibel because his truck fit the description. At the scene, the officer asked Hiibel for identification, which he refused to provide. At no time did he expressly invoke his Fifth Amendment privilege. Hiibel was arrested and charged with "willfully resisting, delaying, or obstructing a public officer in discharging or attempting to discharge any legal duty of his office" in violation of Nevada law. According to the charging documents, the "legal duty" that Hiibel obstructed was defined by Nev. Rev. Stat. §171.123, which provides that:

> 1. Any peace officer may detain any person whom the officer encounters under circumstances which reasonably indicate that the person has committed, is committing or is about to commit a crime. . . .
> 3. The officer may detain the person pursuant to this section only to ascertain his identity and the suspicious circumstances surrounding his presence abroad. Any person so detained shall identify himself, but may not be compelled to answer any other inquiry of any peace officer.

Hiibel claimed that this stop-and-identify statute violated the Fifth Amendment. The Court rejected the claim out of hand, while reserving the question whether disclosing one's identity might sometimes be sufficiently incriminating to trigger the privilege:

> In this case petitioner's refusal to disclose his name was not based on any articulated real and appreciable fear that his name would be used to incriminate him. . . . As best we can tell, petitioner refused to identify himself only because he thought his name was none of the officer's business. Even today, petitioner does not explain how the disclosure of his name could have been used against him in a criminal case. While we recognize petitioner's strong belief that he should not have to disclose his identity, the Fifth Amendment does not override the Nevada Legislature's judgment to the contrary absent a reasonable belief that the disclosure would tend to incriminate him.
>
> The narrow scope of the disclosure requirement is also important. One's identity is, by definition, unique; yet it is, in another sense, a universal characteristic. Answering a request to disclose a name is likely to be so insignificant in the scheme of things as to be incriminating only in unusual circumstances. . . . In every criminal case, it is known and must be known who has been arrested and who is being tried. Even witnesses who plan to invoke the Fifth Amendment privilege answer when their names are called to take the stand. Still, a case may arise where there is a substantial allegation that furnishing identity at the time of a stop would have given the police a link in the chain of evidence needed to convict the individual of a separate offense. In that case, the court can then consider whether the privilege applies, and, if the Fifth Amendment has been violated, what remedy must follow. We need not resolve those questions here. . . .

542 U.S., at 190-91. The second of the two paragraphs just quoted suggests that claims like Hiibel's are not likely to succeed, even on more favorable facts — notice the reference to witnesses in court answering when their names are called. Is that the right answer? Surely one's name may sometimes provide a link in an incriminating chain of evidence. Indeed, that must be true in a large fraction of criminal prosecutions. Why should identity be treated differently than other potentially incriminating information?

4. The doctrine that has the greatest practical effect on the meaning of incrimination deals with immunity. See Kastigar v. United States, supra, at page 722. Under *Kastigar*, the government may compel testimony if it immunizes the witness; in any subsequent criminal prosecution of that witness, the government bears the burden of proving that neither the immunized testimony nor its fruits were used against the defendant. Section A, supra, discusses the evolution of Fifth Amendment immunity and its implications for the privilege's rationale.

5. Return to the relevant constitutional language: "no person . . . shall be compelled in any criminal case to be a witness against himself." The preceding cases all treat the phrase "in any criminal case" as referring to the consequences of answering the relevant questions. In Chavez v. Martinez, 538 U.S. 760 (2003), four Justices asserted that that phrase also refers to the setting in which the compelled testimony is used. *Chavez* was a civil damages action brought by Oliverio Martinez, who claimed that Officer Chavez had interrogated him while he was in extreme physical pain, in violation of both due process and Miranda v. Arizona, 384 U.S. 436 (1966). A fractured Court concluded that section 1983 does not establish a cause of action for damages for *Miranda* violations, and remanded to the Court of

Appeals for the Ninth Circuit to determine whether Martinez had a valid cause of action under the Fourteenth Amendment's Due Process Clause. Justice Thomas, speaking for himself, Chief Justice Rehnquist, and Justices O'Connor and Scalia, concluded that Martinez's Fifth Amendment rights were not violated by Chavez's questioning — no matter how coercive that questioning was — because Martinez's statements were never used against him in a criminal trial. Only when testimony is introduced "in [a] criminal case" is the Fifth Amendment violated.

The other five Justices declined to adopt Justice Thomas's position. Had they done so, the meaning of incrimination — and the application of the privilege to a host of out-of-court conversations between state officials and criminal suspects — would be quite different than it has been in the past. *Chavez*'s implications for police interrogation doctrine are addressed below, at page 881.

3. "To Be a Witness Against Himself": The Meaning of Testimony

In order to make out a valid Fifth Amendment claim, the claimant must show that he was compelled to "be a witness" — in other words, to give testimony. In most cases, this requirement is easy, because most Fifth Amendment claims involve spoken questions that call for spoken answers, as with testimony given by witnesses in court. Problems arise when the evidence in question consists of something other than oral statements. Recall that in Schmerber v. California, 384 U.S. 757 (1966), the Supreme Court held that blood taken from a defendant (for the purpose of testing the defendant's blood alcohol content — breathalyzers did not yet exist) was not "testimonial," and hence did not trigger Fifth Amendment protection. *Schmerber* appears in Chapter 4, at page 305; you may wish to reread it now.

Schmerber suggests that physical evidence is not covered by the privilege, on the ground that it is not communicative in the way that oral testimony is. The same logic has been applied to requirements that a defendant stand in a lineup while wearing particular clothing, that he furnish a voice sample, or that he furnish a handwriting sample — even when the "sample" is used to authorize production of clearly incriminating evidence. For example, the defendant in Doe v. United States, 487 U.S. 201 (1988), was ordered to sign a form authorizing foreign banks to turn over his account records; the defendant was not asked either to identify any accounts or to verify their existence but only to sign the form. Relying on *Schmerber*, the Court held that this process did not compel Fifth Amendment testimony:

> . . . [I]n order to be testimonial, an accused's communication must itself, explicitly or implicitly, relate a factual assertion or disclose information.[9] Only then is a person compelled to be a "witness" against himself.
>
> This understanding is perhaps most clearly revealed in those cases in which the Court has held that certain acts, though incriminating, are not within the privilege.

---

9. We do not disagree with the dissent that "[t]he expression of the contents of an individual's mind" is testimonial communication for purposes of the Fifth Amendment. We simply disagree with the dissent's conclusion that the execution of the consent directive at issue here forced petitioner to express the contents of his mind. In our view, such compulsion is more like [in the words of the dissent] "be[ing] forced to surrender a key to a strong box containing incriminating documents," than it is like "be[ing] compelled to reveal the combination to [petitioner's] wall safe."

Thus, a suspect may be compelled to furnish a blood sample, *Schmerber*; to provide a handwriting exemplar, Gilbert [v. California, 388 U.S. 263 (1967)], or a voice exemplar, United States v. Dionisio, 410 U.S. 1, 7 (1973); to stand in a lineup, [United States v. Wade, 388 U.S. 218 (1967)]; and to wear particular clothing, Holt v. United States, 218 U.S. 245, 252-253 (1910). These decisions are grounded on the proposition that "the privilege protects an accused only from being compelled to testify against himself, or otherwise provide the State with evidence of a testimonial or communicative nature." *Schmerber*, 384 U.S., at 761. The Court accordingly held that the privilege was not implicated in each of those cases, because the suspect was not required "to disclose any knowledge he might have," or "to speak his guilt," *Wade*, 388 U.S., at 222-223. It is the "extortion of information from the accused," Couch v. United States, 409 U.S., at 328, the attempt to force him "to disclose the contents of his own mind," Curcio v. United States, 354 U.S. 118, 128 (1957), that implicates the Self-Incrimination Clause.[10] It is consistent with the history of and the policies underlying the Self-Incrimination Clause to hold that the privilege may be asserted only to resist compelled explicit or implicit disclosures of incriminating information. . . . These policies are served when the privilege is asserted to spare the accused from having to reveal, directly or indirectly, his knowledge of facts relating him to the offense or from having to share his thoughts and beliefs with the Government.[11]

487 U.S., at 210-213.

Justice Stevens' dissent in *Doe* sought to distinguish *Schmerber*:

A defendant can be compelled to produce material evidence that is incriminating. Fingerprints, blood samples, voice exemplars, handwriting specimens or other items of physical evidence may be extracted from a defendant against his will. But can he be compelled to use his mind to assist the prosecution in convicting him of a crime? I

10. Petitioner's reliance on a statement in this Court's decision in *Schmerber* for the proposition that all verbal statements sought for their content are testimonial is misplaced. In *Schmerber*, the Court stated that the privilege extends to "an accused's communications, whatever form they might take," but it did so in the context of clarifying that the privilege may apply not only to verbal communications, as was once thought, but also to physical communications. Contrary to petitioner's urging, the *Schmerber* line of cases does not draw a distinction between unprotected evidence sought for its physical characteristics and protected evidence sought for its content. Rather, the Court distinguished between the suspect's being compelled himself to serve as evidence and the suspect's being compelled to disclose or communicate information or facts that might serve as or lead to incriminating evidence. . . . In order to be privileged, it is not enough that the compelled communication is sought for its content. The content itself must have testimonial significance.

11. Petitioner argues that at least some of these policies would be undermined unless the Government is required to obtain evidence against an accused from sources other than his compelled statements, whether or not the statements make a factual assertion or convey information. Petitioner accordingly maintains that the policy of striking an appropriate balance between the power of the Government and the sovereignty of the individual precludes the Government from compelling an individual to utter or write words that lead to incriminating evidence. Even if some of the policies underlying the privilege might support petitioner's interpretation of the privilege, "it is clear that the scope of the privilege does not coincide with the complex of values it helps to protect. Despite the impact upon the inviolability of the human personality, and upon our belief in an adversary system of criminal justice in which the Government must produce the evidence against an accused through its own independent labors, the prosecution is allowed to obtain and use . . . evidence which although compelled is generally speaking not 'testimonial,' Schmerber v. California, 384 U.S. 757, 761." Grosso v. United States, 390 U.S. 62, 72-73 (1968) (Brennan, J., concurring). If the societal interests in privacy, fairness, and restraint of governmental power are not unconstitutionally offended by compelling the accused to have his body serve as evidence that leads to the development of highly incriminating testimony, as *Schmerber* and its progeny make clear, it is difficult to understand how compelling a suspect to make a nonfactual statement that facilitates the production of evidence by someone else offends the privilege.

think not. He may in some cases be forced to surrender a key to a strong box containing incriminating documents, but I do not believe he can be compelled to reveal the combination to his wall safe — by word or deed.

The document the Government seeks to extract from John Doe purports to order third parties to take action that will lead to the discovery of incriminating evidence. The directive itself may not betray any knowledge petitioner may have about the circumstances of the offenses being investigated by the Grand Jury, but it nevertheless purports to evidence a reasoned decision by Doe to authorize action by others. The forced execution of this document differs from the forced production of physical evidence just as human beings differ from other animals.[1]

Id., at 219 (Stevens, J., dissenting).

The disagreement between the Court and Justice Stevens in *Doe* is a disagreement about the applicable theory of the Fifth Amendment. Both sides agree that the Fifth Amendment applies to compelled, self-incriminating testimony. Both agree that physical evidence, like the blood sample in *Schmerber*, falls outside the definition of "testimony." But the two sides use different definitions. Justice Stevens believes that no one may be "compelled to use his mind to assist the prosecution in convicting him of a crime." Doe, in his view, was forced to use his mind when he signed his name; that mental exercise plainly "assist[ed] the prosecution in convicting him of a crime," since it led to the production of incriminating bank records.

The Court, by contrast, holds that "the accused's communication must itself, explicitly or implicitly, relate a factual assertion or disclose information" in order to qualify as Fifth Amendment testimony. The reason for this definition is not entirely clear in *Doe*, but it does appear in some other Supreme Court opinions. Consider the choice the defendant faced in *Schmerber*. When the government told Schmerber to extend his arm so blood could be drawn, he had no choice to make as long as the privilege did not apply. Schmerber could not by an act of will change the alcohol

---

1. The forced production of physical evidence, which we have condoned involves no intrusion upon the contents of the mind of the accused. See *Schmerber*, 384 U.S., at 765 (forced blood test permissible because it does not involve "even a shadow of testimonial compulsion upon or enforced communication by the accused"). The forced execution of a document that purports to convey the signer's authority, however, does invade the dignity of the human mind; it purports to communicate a deliberate command. The intrusion on the dignity of the individual is not diminished by the fact that the document does not reflect the true state of the signer's mind. Indeed, that the assertions petitioner is forced to utter by executing the document are false causes an even greater violation of human dignity. For the same reason a person cannot be forced to sign a document purporting to authorize the entry of judgment against himself, cf. Brady v. United States, 397 U.S. 742, 748 (1970), I do not believe he can be forced to sign a document purporting to authorize the disclosure of incriminating evidence. In both cases the accused is being compelled "to be a witness against himself"; indeed, here he is being compelled to bear false witness against himself.

The expression of the contents of an individual's mind falls squarely within the protection of the Fifth Amendment. Justice Holmes' observation that "the prohibition of compelling a man in a criminal court to be witness against himself is a prohibition of the use of physical or moral compulsion to extort communications from him," Holt v. United States, 218 U.S., at 252-253, manifests a recognition that virtually any communication reveals the contents of the mind of the speaker. Thus the Fifth Amendment privilege is fulfilled only when the person is guaranteed the right "'to remain silent unless he chooses to speak in the unfettered exercise of his own will.'" Miranda v. Arizona, 384 U.S. 436, 460 (1966) (quoting Malloy v. Hogan, 378 U.S. 1, 8 (1964)). The deviation from this principle can only lead to mischievous abuse of the dignity the Fifth Amendment commands the Government afford its citizens. The instant case is illustrative. In allowing the Government to compel petitioner to execute the directive, the Court permits the Government to compel petitioner to speak against his will in answer to the question "Do you consent to the release of these documents?" Beyond this affront, however, the Government is being permitted also to demand that the answer be "yes."

content of his blood, and if he refused to comply, the government could presumably strap him down and take the blood test anyway. That makes *Schmerber* quite
different from the paradigmatic case where the privilege *does* apply: the guilty
defendant ordered to take the witness stand and say whether he committed the
crime. The defendant on the witness stand has a choice to confess, to lie, or to
remain silent and face contempt sanctions. Perhaps the nature of that choice is the
key to what is (and what isn't) testimonial.

That is the implication of the many references in Fifth Amendment cases to the
"cruel trilemma": the three-pronged choice a guilty witness would face if forced to
answer questions about his crime; such a witness could confess crime and send
himself to prison, he could lie and risk a perjury prosecution, or he could keep
quiet and be held in contempt. Whatever else the privilege bars, it plainly bars the
government from putting witnesses to that choice. On the prevailing view, the
concept of "testimony" is really a stand-in for the presence or absence of that
choice. Justice Brennan (author of the Court's opinion in *Schmerber*) articulated
this position most clearly:

> . . . Whatever else it may include, . . . the definition of "testimonial" evidence articu-
> lated in *Doe* must encompass all responses to questions that, if asked of a sworn suspect
> during a criminal trial, could place the suspect in the "cruel trilemma." This conclu-
> sion is consistent with our recognition in *Doe* that "the vast majority of verbal state-
> ments thus will be testimonial" because "there are very few instances in which a verbal
> statement, either oral or written, will not convey information or assert facts." 487
> U.S., at 213. Whenever a suspect is asked for a response requiring him to communi-
> cate an express or implied assertion of fact or belief, the suspect confronts the
> "trilemma" of truth, falsity, or silence and hence the response . . . contains a testimo-
> nial component.
>
> This approach accords with each of our post-*Schmerber* cases finding that a particu-
> lar oral or written response to express or implied questioning was nontestimonial; the
> questions presented in these cases did not confront the suspects with this trilemma. As
> we noted in *Doe*, 487 U.S., at 210-211, the cases upholding compelled writing and
> voice exemplars did not involve situations in which suspects were asked to communi-
> cate any personal beliefs or knowledge of facts, and therefore the suspects were not
> forced to choose between truthfully or falsely revealing their thoughts. We carefully
> noted in Gilbert v. California, 388 U.S. 263 (1967), for example, that a "mere hand-
> writing exemplar, in contrast to the content of what is written, like the voice or body
> itself, is an identifying physical characteristic outside [the privilege's] protection." Id.,
> at 266-267. . . . And in *Doe*, the suspect was asked merely to sign a consent form waiv-
> ing a privacy interest in foreign bank records. Because the consent form spoke in the
> hypothetical and did not identify any particular banks, accounts, or private records,
> the form neither "communicated any factual assertions, implicit or explicit, nor con-
> veyed any information to the Government." 487 U.S., at 215. . . .

Pennsylvania v. Muniz, 496 U.S. 582, 596-598 (1990) (plurality opinion).

On that theory, did *Doe* reach the right result? It may well be that Doe's signature
communicated nothing more than the fact that he could sign his name, which the
government presumably knew and which he would presumably concede. Still, he
could have refused to sign — he could have forced federal agents to wrap his hand
around the pen and move it along the page. Or, he could have lied: perhaps by
signing some other name, or signing in a way that did not match the signature on
file with the bank. Was his choice really so different from the paradigmatic "cruel

trilemma"? For a discussion concluding that the choice theory does not very well explain the Fifth Amendment cases, see Ronald J. Allen & Kristin Mace, The Fifth Amendment Explained and Its Future Predicted, 94 J. Crim. L. & Crim. 243 (2004). Allen and Mace demonstrate that the cases cannot be reconciled by whether the use of "mind" is somehow compelled, either. Instead, the cases are consistent with forbidding the government to use the substantive results of cognition created by government action (such as asking questions, giving orders, serving subpoenas). One plainly employs one's "mind" in putting on a shirt, signing a document, or turning over an object, but will is different from cognition, which is the critical distinction Justice Stevens neglected. Allen and Mace do not claim that the Court has ever explicitly adopted this theory, but do claim that it is the best explanation of the actual results in the cases.

The Justices in *Muniz* (the case just quoted) referred liberally to the cruel trilemma theory, though they disagreed about how to apply the theory to the facts. The police picked up Muniz for drunk driving and brought him back to the police station. There, in the course of filling out some forms, an officer asked Muniz eight questions: his name, address, height, weight, eye color, date of birth, current age, and the date of his sixth birthday. Both questions and answers were videotaped. Muniz's answers were obviously slurred, and he responded to what the Court referred to as "the sixth birthday question" by saying that he did not remember.

Justice Marshall concluded that all aspects of Muniz's answers were testimonial and hence protected by the privilege. Justice Brennan, joined by Justices O'Connor, Scalia, and Kennedy, concluded that the slurred speech was not "testimonial," because it communicated only physical characteristics (indeed, the same physical characteristic that Schmerber's blood communicated). However, Justice Brennan and his colleagues decided that the nonresponse to the sixth birthday question *was* testimonial:

> In contrast, the sixth birthday question in this case required a testimonial response. When Officer Hosterman asked Muniz if he knew the date of his sixth birthday and Muniz . . . could not remember or calculate that date, he was confronted with the trilemma. By hypothesis, the inherently coercive environment created by the custodial interrogation precluded the option of remaining silent. Muniz was left with the choice of incriminating himself by admitting that he did not then know the date of his sixth birthday, or answering untruthfully by reporting a date that he did not then believe to be accurate (an incorrect guess would be incriminating as well as untruthful). The content of his truthful answer supported an inference that his mental faculties were impaired, because his assertion (he did not know the date of his sixth birthday) was different from the assertion . . . that the trier of fact might reasonably have expected a lucid person to provide. Hence, the incriminating inference of impaired mental faculties stemmed, not just from the fact that Muniz slurred his response, but also from a testimonial aspect of that response.

496 U.S., at 598-599. Chief Justice Rehnquist, joined by Justices White, Blackmun, and Stevens — *Muniz* produced an odd lineup of Justices — accepted the premise but disputed the conclusion:

> The sixth birthday question here was an effort on the part of the police to check how well Muniz was able to do a simple mathematical exercise. . . . Muniz may be required to perform a "horizontal gaze nystagmus" test, the "walk and turn" test, and

the "one leg stand" test, all of which are designed to test a suspect's physical coordination. If the police may require Muniz to use his body in order to demonstrate the level of his physical coordination, there is no reason why they should not be able to require him to speak or write in order to determine his mental coordination. That was all that was sought here. Since it was permissible for the police to extract and examine a sample of Schmerber's blood to determine how much that part of his system had been affected by alcohol, I see no reason why they may not examine the functioning of Muniz' mental processes for the same purpose.

Surely if it were relevant, a suspect might be asked to take an eye examination in the course of which he might have to admit that he could not read the letters on the third line of the chart. At worst, he might utter a mistaken guess. Muniz likewise might have attempted to guess the correct response to the sixth birthday question instead of attempting to calculate the date or answer "I don't know." But the potential for giving a bad guess does not subject the suspect to the truth-falsity-silence predicament that renders a response testimonial and, therefore, within the scope of the Fifth Amendment privilege.

Id., at 607-608 (Rehnquist, C.J., concurring in part and dissenting in part).

Which side was right in *Muniz*? In *Doe*? In *Schmerber*? Is the so-called "cruel trilemma" a helpful way to think about these questions, or a distraction? After all, the "trilemma" is "cruel" only because the defendant's past conduct makes honesty a painful option; it is not clear why this is a form of "cruelty" that deserves sympathy, much less constitutional protection. Besides, honesty is often painful for reasons that have nothing to do with criminal liability. On a regular basis, our legal system requires witnesses to testify truthfully when they would rather not. Is that cruel? If not, is there a better way to think about what is and isn't testimonial? One possible answer is that the Fifth Amendment is an adjunct to the Fourth: Where the latter protects privacy interests in physical items and spaces, the former protects "mental privacy," the privacy of one's mind. For an extended argument along these lines, written partly as a defense of *Schmerber*, see Peter Arenella, *Schmerber* and the Privilege against Self-Incrimination: A Reappraisal, 20 Am. Crim. L. Rev. 31 (1982). Of course, if privacy is the reigning theory of the privilege, it is hard to explain the "incrimination" requirement: Testimony about even the most private matters can be compelled if the witness is immunized.

C.   Limiting the Privilege?

In most Fifth Amendment cases, courts apply the standard compulsion-incrimination-testimony model outlined in Section B. Sometimes, though, that model yields very substantial restrictions on the government's ability to gather information — which, in turn, substantially restricts the government's ability to regulate a wide range of behavior. When that happens — when standard application of the privilege against self-incrimination appears to pose some danger to the regulatory state's ability to regulate — the Supreme Court often limits the privilege. As you read the cases and notes below, consider the question whether the limits conform to any coherent rationale, aside from a desire not to have a privilege against self-incrimination that costs the government too much.

One way to limit the privilege's cost is to limit the conduct the privilege can be used to shield. The most common limit has to do with misrepresentation. Virtually all immunity statutes contain an exception that permits the use of immunized testimony in prosecutions for perjury or false statements. The Court cast some doubt on the constitutionality of those exceptions in New Jersey v. Portash, 440 U.S. 450 (1979). Portash gave immunized testimony to a grand jury; he was subsequently charged with extortion. The government asked for and received permission to use Portash's immunized testimony to impeach him if he testified at his criminal trial, and if his trial testimony was inconsistent with his statements to the grand jury. The threatened use of his immunized testimony kept Portash from taking the stand, and he was convicted. The Supreme Court held that the Fifth Amendment barred this procedure:

> Testimony given in response to a grant of legislative immunity is the essence of coerced testimony. In such cases there is no question whether physical or psychological pressures overrode the defendant's will; the witness is told to talk or face the government's coercive sanctions, notably, a conviction for contempt. The information given in response to a grant of immunity may well be more reliable than information beaten from a helpless defendant, but it is no less compelled. The Fifth and Fourteenth Amendments provide a privilege against *compelled* self-incrimination, not merely against unreliable self-incrimination. . . . Here . . . we deal with the constitutional privilege against compulsory self-incrimination in its most pristine form.
>
> . . . [A] person's testimony before a grand jury under a grant of immunity cannot constitutionally be used to impeach him when he is a defendant in a later criminal trial.

Id., at 459-460.

The form of the privilege seemed a bit less pristine in United States v. Apfelbaum, 445 U.S. 115 (1980). The federal immunity statute, 18 U.S.C. §6002, provides that when a witness is compelled to testify over his claim of a Fifth Amendment privilege, "no testimony or other information compelled under the order (or any information directly or indirectly derived from such testimony or other information) may be used against the witness in any criminal case, except a prosecution for perjury, giving a false statement, or otherwise failing to comply with the order." The question before the Court was whether the statute was constitutional, given that it "makes no distinction between truthful and untruthful statements made during the course of the immunized testimony. Rather, it creates a blanket exemption from the bar against the use of immunized testimony in cases in which the witness is subsequently prosecuted for making false statements." The Court found that there is "no doctrine of 'anticipatory perjury'" and thus upheld the statute.

In Brogan v. United States, 522 U.S. 398 (1998), the Court addressed the question whether a defendant can be held criminally liable when, instead of claiming his right to remain silent, he falsely denies some form of misconduct; the denial is known as an "exculpatory no." The Court concluded that an "exculpatory no" can be criminally punished, just like any other misrepresentation:

> The second line of defense that petitioner invokes for the "exculpatory no" doctrine is inspired by the Fifth Amendment. He argues that a literal reading of [18 U.S.C. §1001, criminalizing false statements to federal investigators] violates the "spirit" of the Fifth Amendment because it places a "cornered suspect" in the "cruel trilemma" of admitting guilt, remaining silent, or falsely denying guilt. This "trilemma" is wholly of the

guilty suspect's own making, of course. An innocent person will not find himself in a similar quandary (as one commentator has put it, the innocent person lacks even a "lemma," Allen, The Simpson Affair, Reform of the Criminal Justice Process, and Magic Bullets, 67 U. Colo. L. Rev. 989, 1016 (1996)). And even the honest and contrite guilty person will not regard the third prong of the "trilemma" (the blatant lie) as an available option. . . . In order to validate the "exculpatory no," the elements of this "cruel trilemma" have now been altered — ratcheted up, as it were, so that the right to remain silent, which was the liberation from the original trilemma, is now itself a cruelty. We are not disposed to write into our law this species of compassion inflation.

Whether or not the predicament of the wrongdoer run to ground tugs at the heart strings, neither the text nor the spirit of the Fifth Amendment confers a privilege to lie. "[P]roper invocation of the Fifth Amendment privilege against compulsory self-incrimination allows a witness to remain silent, but not to swear falsely." United States v. Apfelbaum, 445 U.S. 115, 117 (1980). Petitioner contends that silence is an "illusory" option because a suspect may fear that his silence will be used against him later, or may not even know that silence is an available option. As to the former: It is well established that the fact that a person's silence can be used against him — either as substantive evidence of guilt or to impeach him if he takes the stand — does not exert a form of pressure that exonerates an otherwise unlawful lie. And as for the possibility that the person under investigation may be unaware of his right to remain silent: In the modern age of frequently dramatized "*Miranda*" warnings, that is implausible. . . .

522 U.S., at 404-405.

Apfelbaum and *Brogan* suggest that the privilege does not protect lies. (Except, *Portash* suggests, when it does.) A second means of limiting the privilege's coverage is to limit the parties who can invoke it. At the beginning of the twentieth century, it was widely believed that the privilege against self-incrimination could be claimed by corporations — just as corporations had been deemed "persons" for purposes of the Fourteenth Amendment's Due Process Clause. See Santa Clara County v. Southern Pacific R.R., 118 U.S. 394 (1886). Nevertheless, in Hale v. Henkel, 201 U.S. 43 (1906), the Court held that only natural persons could assert the privilege; corporations have no Fifth Amendment rights. The rationale for this rule was simple government necessity: "Of what use would it be for the legislature to declare these combinations unlawful [the reference is to antitrust conspiracies; *Hale* arose out of a Sherman Act investigation] if the judicial power may close the door of access to every available source of information upon the subject?" Id., at 70.

Limiting the privilege to natural persons was essential to extensive government regulation of economic affairs. So was a more obscure exception to the privilege's coverage known as the "required records" doctrine. The key case is Shapiro v. United States, 335 U.S. 1 (1948). Shapiro was a fruit wholesaler. In the course of an investigation of violations of federal price controls, he was asked to turn over various invoices and other business records. He claimed the privilege. The Court denied Shapiro's claim, both because the law required him to keep the records in question, and because the records were used not merely for criminal law enforcement but in service of a civil regulatory regime:

It may be assumed at the outset that there are limits which the Government cannot constitutionally exceed in requiring the keeping of records which may be inspected by an administrative agency and may be used in prosecuting statutory violations committed by the recordkeeper himself. But no serious misgiving that those bounds have been overstepped would appear to be evoked when there is a sufficient relation between the activity sought to be regulated and the public concern so that the Government can constitutionally regulate or forbid the basic activity concerned, and can constitutionally require the keeping of particular records. . . .

Id., at 32.

Shapiro seemed to give the government broad authority to require any disclosures it wished, but the authority turned out to be less broad than first appeared. The defendant in Marchetti v. United States, 390 U.S. 39 (1968), was a professional gambler. A federal statute required gamblers to register and pay an occupational tax — notwithstanding that their "profession" was a crime. That took the "required records" concept too far, in the Court's view. It distinguished *Shapiro* as follows:

> Each of the three principal elements of the doctrine, as it is described in *Shapiro*, is absent from this situation. *First*, petitioner Marchetti was not, by the provisions now at issue, obliged to keep and preserve records "of the same kind as he has customarily kept"; he was required simply to provide information, unrelated to any records which he may have maintained, about his wagering activities. This requirement is not significantly different from a demand that he provide oral testimony. *Second*, whatever "public aspects" there were to the records at issue in *Shapiro*, there are none to the information demanded from Marchetti. The Government's anxiety to obtain information known to a private individual does not without more render that information public; if it did, no room would remain for the application of the constitutional privilege. Nor does it stamp information with a public character that the Government has formalized its demands in the attire of a statute; if this alone were sufficient, the constitutional privilege could be entirely abrogated by any Act of Congress. *Third*, the requirements at issue in *Shapiro* were imposed in "an essentially non-criminal and regulatory area of inquiry" while those here are directed to a "selective group inherently suspect of criminal activities." Cf. Albertson v. Subversive Activities Control Board, 382 U.S. 70, 79. The United States' principal interest is evidently the collection of revenue, and not the punishment of gamblers; but the characteristics of the activities about which information is sought, and the composition of the groups to which inquiries are made, readily distinguish this situation from that in *Shapiro*. There is no need to explore further the elements and limitations of *Shapiro* and the cases involving public papers; these points of difference in combination preclude any appropriate application of those cases to the present one.

390 U.S., at 56-57. Notice that Marchetti did not have to assert his privilege; the Court concluded that any such assertion would have been incriminating under the circumstances.

Yet another way to limit the privilege's scope is to require some balancing of interests in Fifth Amendment cases, with the autonomy and privacy interests the privilege protects weighed against the government's interest in regulating the relevant conduct. As should be clear by now, ordinary Fifth Amendment analysis does not involve that kind of balancing. *Fourth* Amendment law does: Probable cause and reasonable suspicion, the two leading standards for Fourth Amendment "searches," are both ways of establishing the government's need to conduct the search. *Fifth* Amendment law works differently: Regardless of how great is the government's suspicion or need for the defendant's testimony, if that testimony would be incriminating, the government cannot force the defendant to provide it.

Except sometimes. California v. Byers, 402 U.S. 424 (1971), raised the question whether California's hit-and-run statute—every state has one; such statutes require those involved in traffic accidents to remain at the scene of the accident and to identify themselves when the police arrive—violated the Fifth Amendment. A four-Justice plurality held that the compelled conduct, staying at the scene and identifying oneself, was neither testimonial nor incriminating. See id., at 425-434 (opinion of Burger, C.J.). Four Justices dissented, arguing that such conduct was as testimonial and as incriminating as the compelled registration in *Marchetti*. See id., at 459-464 (Black, J., dissenting); id., at 464-478 (Brennan, J., dissenting). Justice Harlan's was the deciding vote. In Harlan's view, remaining at the scene of an accident and identifying oneself communicated vital information in cases where the accident involved criminal conduct, and the information was plainly incriminating. Thus, ordinary Fifth Amendment analysis would suggest that the hit-and-run statutes were unconstitutional. But Harlan refused to extend the privilege that far, because of the cost to the government's interest in civil regulation of traffic accidents:

. . . [T]he public regulation of driving behavior through a pattern of laws which includes compelled self-reporting to ensure financial responsibility for accidents and criminal sanctions to deter dangerous driving entails genuine risks of self-incrimination from the driver's point of view. The conclusion that the Fifth Amendment extends to this regulatory scheme will impair the capacity of the State to pursue these objectives simultaneously. For compelled self-reporting is a necessary part of an effective scheme of assuring personal financial responsibility for automobile accidents. Undoubtedly, it can be argued that self-reporting is at least as necessary to an effective scheme of criminal law enforcement in this area. The fair response to that latter contention may be that the purpose of the Fifth Amendment is to compel the State to opt for the less efficient methods of an "accusatorial" system. . . . But it would not follow that the constitutional values protected by the "accusatorial" system . . . are of such overriding significance that they compel substantial sacrifices in the efficient pursuit of other governmental objectives in all situations where the pursuit of those objectives requires the disclosure of information which will undoubtedly significantly aid in criminal law enforcement. . . .

These values are implicated by government compulsion to disclose information about driving behavior as part of a regulatory scheme including criminal sanctions. . . . It is also true that, unlike the ordinary civil lawsuit context, special governmental interests in addition to the deterrence of antisocial behavior by use of criminal sanctions are affected by extension of the privilege to this regulatory context. If the privilege is extended to the circumstances of this case, it must, I think, be potentially available in every instance where the government relies on self-reporting. And the considerable risks to efficient government of a self-executing claim of privilege will require acceptance of, at the very least, a use restriction of unspecified dimensions. Technological progress creates an ever-expanding need for governmental information about individuals. If the individual's ability in any particular case to perceive a genuine risk of self-incrimination is to be a sufficient condition for imposition of use restrictions on the government in all self-reporting contexts, then the privilege threatens the capacity of the government to respond to societal needs with a realistic mixture of criminal sanctions and other regulatory devices. To the extent that [*Marchetti*] appears to suggest that the presence of perceivable risks of incrimination in and of itself justifies imposition of a use restriction on the information gained by the Government through compelled self-reporting, I think that [case] should be explicitly limited by this Court.

Id., at 448-452 (Harlan, J., concurring in the judgment).

Is this sort of open-ended interest balancing an appropriate way to define the boundaries of the privilege? See whether your answer is affected by the next case.

BALTIMORE CITY DEPARTMENT OF SOCIAL SERVICES v. BOUKNIGHT

Certiorari to Maryland Court of Appeals
493 U.S. 549 (1990)

JUSTICE O'CONNOR delivered the opinion of the Court.

In this action, we must decide whether a mother, the custodian of a child pursuant to a court order, may invoke the Fifth Amendment privilege against self-incrimination to resist an order of the Juvenile Court to produce the child. We hold that she may not.

I

Petitioner Maurice M. is an abused child. When he was three months old, he was hospitalized with a fractured left femur, and examination revealed several partially healed bone fractures and other indications of severe physical abuse. In the hospital, respondent Bouknight, Maurice's mother, was observed shaking Maurice, dropping him in his crib despite his spica cast, and otherwise handling him in a manner inconsistent with his recovery and continued health. Hospital personnel notified Baltimore City Department of Social Services (BCDSS) of suspected child abuse. In February 1987, BCDSS secured a court order removing Maurice from Bouknight's control and placing him in shelter care. Several months later, the shelter care order was inexplicably modified to return Maurice to Bouknight's custody temporarily. Following a hearing held shortly thereafter, the Juvenile Court declared Maurice to be a "child in need of assistance," thus asserting jurisdiction over Maurice and placing him under BCDSS's continuing oversight. BCDSS agreed that Bouknight could continue as custodian of the child, but only pursuant to extensive conditions set forth in a court-approved protective supervision order. The order required Bouknight to "co-operate with BCDSS," "continue in therapy," participate in parental aid and training programs, and "refrain from physically punishing [Maurice]." The order's terms were "all subject to the further Order of the Court." Bouknight's attorney signed the order, and Bouknight in a separate form set forth her agreement to each term.

Eight months later, fearing for Maurice's safety, BCDSS returned to Juvenile Court. BCDSS caseworkers related that Bouknight would not cooperate with them and had in nearly every respect violated the terms of the protective order. BCDSS states that Maurice's father had recently died in a shooting incident and that Bouknight, in light of the results of a psychological examination and her history of drug use, could not provide adequate care for the child. On April 20, 1988, the Court granted BCDSS's petition to remove Maurice from Bouknight's control for placement in foster care. BCDSS officials also petitioned for judicial relief from Bouknight's failure to produce Maurice or reveal where he could be found. The petition recounted that on two recent visits by BCDSS officials to Bouknight's home, she had refused to reveal the location of the child or had indicated that the child was with an aunt whom she would not identify. The petition further asserted that inquiries of Bouknight's known relatives had revealed that none of them had recently seen Maurice and that BCDSS had prompted the police to issue a missing persons report and referred the case for investigation by the police homicide division. Also on April 20, the Juvenile Court, upon a hearing on the petition, cited Bouknight for violating the protective custody order and for failing to appear at the hearing. Bouknight had indicated to her attorney that she would appear with the child, but also expressed fear that if she appeared the State would "snatch the child." The court issued an order to show cause why Bouknight should not be held in civil contempt for failure to produce the child.

Expressing concern that Maurice was endangered or perhaps dead, the court issued a bench warrant for Bouknight's appearance.

Maurice was not produced at subsequent hearings. At a hearing one week later, Bouknight claimed that Maurice was with a relative in Dallas. Investigation revealed that the relative had not seen Maurice. The next day, following another hearing at which Bouknight again declined to produce Maurice, the Juvenile Court found Bouknight in contempt for failure to produce the child as ordered. There was and has been no indication that she was unable to comply with the order. The court directed that Bouknight be imprisoned until she "purge[d] herself of contempt by either producing [Maurice] before the court or revealing to the court his exact whereabouts."

The Juvenile Court rejected Bouknight's subsequent claim that the contempt order violated the Fifth Amendment's guarantee against self-incrimination. The court stated that the production of Maurice would purge the contempt and that "[t]he contempt is issued not because she refuse[d] to testify in any proceeding . . . [but] because she had failed to abide by the Order of this Court mainly [for] the production of Maurice M." While that decision was being appealed, Bouknight was convicted of theft and sentenced to 18 months' imprisonment in separate proceedings. The Court of Appeals of Maryland vacated the Juvenile Court's judgment upholding the contempt order. The Court of Appeals found that the contempt order unconstitutionally compelled Bouknight to admit through the act of production "a measure of continuing control and dominion over Maurice's person" in circumstances in which "Bouknight has a reasonable apprehension that she will be prosecuted." We granted certiorari, and we now reverse.

II

. . . The courts below concluded that Bouknight could comply with the order through the unadorned act of producing the child, and we thus address that aspect of the order. When the government demands that an item be produced, "the only thing compelled is the act of producing the [item]." Fisher [v. United States, 425 U.S. 391, 410, n. 11 (1976)]. The Fifth Amendment's protection may nonetheless be implicated because the act of complying with the government's demand testifies to the existence, possession, or authenticity of the things produced. But a person may not claim the Amendment's protection based upon the incrimination that may result from the contents or nature of the thing demanded. Bouknight therefore cannot claim the privilege based upon anything that examination of Maurice might reveal, nor can she assert the privilege upon the theory that compliance would assert that the child produced is in fact Maurice (a fact the State could readily establish, rendering any testimony regarding existence of authenticity insufficiently incriminating). Rather, Bouknight claims the benefit of the privilege because the act of production would amount to testimony regarding her control over and possession of Maurice. Although the State could readily introduce evidence of Bouknight's continuing control over the child — e.g., the custody order, testimony of relatives, and Bouknight's own statements to Maryland officials before invoking the privilege — her implicit communication of control over Maurice at the moment of production might aid the State in prosecuting Bouknight.

The possibility that a production order will compel testimonial assertions that may prove incriminating does not, in all contexts, justify invoking the privilege to resist production. Even assuming that this limited testimonial assertion is sufficiently incriminating and "sufficiently testimonial for purposes of the privilege," *Fisher*, supra, at 411, Bouknight may not invoke the privilege to resist the production order because she has assumed custodial duties related to production and because production is required as part of a noncriminal regulatory regime.

The Court has on several occasions recognized that the Fifth Amendment privilege may not be invoked to resist compliance with a regulatory regime constructed to effect the State's public purposes unrelated to the enforcement of its criminal laws. In Shapiro v. United States, 335 U.S. 1 (1948), the Court considered an application of the Emergency Price Control Act and a regulation issued thereunder which required licensed businesses to maintain records and make them available for inspection by administrators. The Court indicated that no Fifth Amendment protection attached to production of the "required records," which the "'defendant was required to keep, not for his private uses, but for the benefit of the public, and for public inspection.'" Id., at 17-18 (quoting Wilson v. United States, 221 U.S. 361, 381 (1911)). . . .

The Court has since [defined] limits to the government's authority to gain access to items or information vested with this public character. The Court has noted that "the requirements at issue in *Shapiro* were imposed in "an essentially non-criminal and regulatory area of inquiry," and that *Shapiro*'s reach is limited where requirements "are directed to a 'selective group inherently suspect of criminal activities,'" Marchetti v. United States, 390 U.S. 39, 57 (1968) (quoting Albertson v. Subversive Activities Control Board, 382 U.S. 70, 79 (1965)). . . .

California v. Byers confirms that the ability to invoke the privilege may be greatly diminished when invocation would interfere with the effective operation of a generally applicable, civil regulatory requirement. . . .

When a person assumes control over items that are the legitimate object of the government's non-criminal regulatory powers, the ability to invoke the privilege is reduced. . . . In *Shapiro*, the Court interpreted this principle as extending well beyond the corporate context, and emphasized that Shapiro had assumed and retained control over documents in which the government had a direct and particular regulatory interest. Indeed, it was in part Shapiro's custody over items having this public nature that allowed the Court in *Marchetti* . . . to distinguish the measures considered in those cases from the regulatory requirement at issue in *Shapiro*. These principles readily apply to this case. Once Maurice was adjudicated a child in need of assistance, his care and safety became the particular object of the State's regulatory interests. . . . Maryland first placed Maurice in shelter care, authorized placement in foster care, and then entrusted responsibility for Maurice's care to Bouknight. By accepting care of Maurice subject to the custodial order's conditions (including requirements that she cooperate with BCDSS, follow a prescribed training regime, and be subject to further court orders), Bouknight submitted to the routine operation of the regulatory system and agreed to hold Maurice in a manner consonant with the State's regulatory interests and subject to inspection by BCDSS. In assuming the obligations attending custody, Bouknight "has accepted the incident obligation to permit inspection." *Wilson*, 221 U.S., at 382. The State imposes and enforces that obligation as part of a broadly directed, noncriminal regulatory regime governing children cared for pursuant to custodial orders.

Persons who care for children pursuant to a custody order, and who may be subject to a request for access to the child, are hardly a "selective group inherently suspect of criminal activities." The Juvenile Court may place a child within its jurisdiction with social service officials or "under supervision in his own home or in the custody or under the guardianship of a relative or other fit person, upon terms the court deems appropriate." Md. Cts. & Jud. Proc. Code Ann. §3-820(c)(1)(i) (Supp. 1989). Children may be placed, for example, in foster care, in homes of relatives, or in the care of state officials. Even when the court allows a parent to retain control of a child within the court's jurisdiction, that parent is not one singled out for criminal conduct, but rather has been deemed to be, without the State's assistance, simply "unable or unwilling to give proper care and attention to the child and his problems." Md. Cts. & Jud. Proc. Code Ann. §3-801(e) (Supp. 1989).

Similarly, BCDSS's efforts to gain access to children, as well as judicial efforts to the same effect, do not "focu[s] almost exclusively on conduct which was criminal." *Byers*, 402 U.S., at 454 (Harlan, J., concurring in judgment). Many orders will arise in circumstances entirely devoid of criminal conduct. Even when criminal conduct may exist, the court may properly request production and return of the child, and enforce that request through exercise of the contempt power, for reasons related entirely to the child's well-being and through measures unrelated to criminal law enforcement or investigation. This case provides an illustration: concern for the child's safety underlay the efforts to gain access to and then compel production of Maurice. Finally, production in the vast majority of cases will embody no incriminating testimony, even if in particular cases the act of production may incriminate the custodian through an assertion of possession, the existence, or the identity of the child. These orders to produce children cannot be characterized as efforts to gain some testimonial component of the act of production. The government demands production of the very public charge entrusted to a custodian, and makes the demand for compelling reasons unrelated to criminal law enforcement and as part of a broadly applied regulatory regime. In these circumstances, Bouknight cannot invoke the privilege to resist the order to produce Maurice.

We are not called upon to define the precise limitations that may exist upon the State's ability to use the testimonial aspects of Bouknight's act of production in subsequent criminal proceedings. But we note that imposition of such limitations is not foreclosed. The same custodial role that limited the ability to resist the production order may give rise to corresponding limitations upon the direct and indirect use of that testimony. See *Braswell*, 487 U.S., at 118, and n. 11. The State's regulatory requirement in the usual case may neither compel incriminating testimony nor aid a criminal prosecution, but the Fifth Amendment protections are not thereby necessarily unavailable to the person who complies with the regulatory requirement after invoking the privilege and subsequently faces prosecution. See *Marchetti*, 390 U.S., at 58-59 (the "attractive and apparently practical" course of subsequent use restriction not appropriate where a significant element of the regulatory requirement is to aid law enforcement). In a broad range of contexts, the Fifth Amendment limits prosecutors' ability to use testimony that has been compelled. . . .

III

The judgment of the Court of Appeals of Maryland is reversed, and the cases are remanded to that court for further proceedings not inconsistent with this opinion.

JUSTICE MARSHALL, with whom JUSTICE BRENNAN joins, dissenting.

Although the Court assumes that respondent's act of producing her child would be testimonial and could be incriminating, it nonetheless concludes that she cannot invoke her privilege against self-incrimination and refuse to reveal her son's current location. Neither of the reasons the Court articulates to support its refusal to permit respondent to invoke her constitutional privilege justifies its decision. I therefore dissent.

The Court correctly assumes that Bouknight's production of her son to the Maryland court would be testimonial because it would amount to an admission of Bouknight's physical control over her son. The Court also assumes that Bouknight's act of production would be self-incriminating. I would not hesitate to hold explicitly that Bouknight's admission of possession or control presents a "real and appreciable" threat of self-incrimination. Marchetti v. United States, 390 U.S. 39, 48 (1968). Bouknight's ability to produce the child would conclusively establish her actual and present physical control over him, and thus might "prove a significant 'link in a chain' of evidence tending to establish [her] guilt."

Indeed, the stakes for Bouknight are much greater than the Court suggests. Not only could she face criminal abuse and neglect charges for her alleged mistreatment of Maurice, but she could also be charged with causing his death. The State acknowledges that it suspects that Maurice is dead, and the police are investigating his case as a possible homicide. In these circumstances, the potentially incriminating aspects to Bouknight's act of production are undoubtedly significant.

Notwithstanding the real threat of self-incrimination, the Court holds that "Bouknight may not invoke the privilege to resist the production order because she has assumed custodial duties related to production and because production is required as part of a noncriminal regulatory regime." In characterizing Bouknight as Maurice's "custodian," and in describing the relevant Maryland juvenile statutes as part of a noncriminal regulatory regime, the Court relies on two distinct lines of Fifth Amendment precedent, neither of which applies to this case.

The Court's first line of reasoning turns on its view that Bouknight has agreed to exercise on behalf of the State certain custodial obligations with respect to her son, obligations that the Court analogizes to those of a custodian of the records of a collective entity. This characterization is baffling. . . .

. . . . [T]he rationale for denying a corporate custodian Fifth Amendment protection for acts done in her representative capacity . . . rests on the well-established principle that a collective entity, unlike a natural person, has no Fifth Amendment privilege against self-incrimination. Because an artificial entity can act only through its agents, a custodian of such an entity's documents may not invoke her personal privilege to resist producing documents. . . . Jacqueline Bouknight is not the agent for an artificial entity that possesses no Fifth Amendment privilege. Her role as Maurice's parent is very different from the role of a corporate custodian who is merely the instrumentality through whom the corporation acts. I am unwilling to extend the collective entity doctrine into a context where it denies individuals, acting in their personal rather than representative capacities, their constitutional privilege against self-incrimination.

The Court's decision rests as well on cases holding that "the ability to invoke the privilege may be greatly diminished when invocation would interfere with the effective operation of a generally applicable, civil regulatory requirement." The cases the Court cites have two common features: they concern civil regulatory systems not primarily intended to facilitate criminal investigations, and they target the general public. See California v. Byers, 402 U.S. 424, 430-431 (1971) (determining that a "hit and run" statute that required a driver involved in an accident to stop and give certain information was primarily civil). In contrast, regulatory regimes that are directed at a "'selective group inherently suspect of criminal activities,'" Marchetti, 390 U.S., at 57 (quoting Albertson v. Subversive Activities Control Board, 382 U.S. 70, 79 (1965)), do not result in a similar diminution of the Fifth Amendment privilege.

. . . In contrast to Marchetti, the Court here disregards the practical implications of the civil scheme and holds that the juvenile protection system does not "'focu[s] almost exclusively on conduct which was criminal'" (quoting Byers, supra, at 454 (Harlan, J., concurring in judgment)). I cannot agree. . . . The State's goal of protecting children from abusive environments through its juvenile welfare system cannot be separated from criminal provisions that serve the same goal. When the conduct at which a civil statute aims — here, child abuse and neglect — is frequently the same conduct subject to criminal sanction, it strikes me as deeply problematic to dismiss the Fifth Amendment concerns by characterizing the civil scheme as "unrelated to criminal law enforcement investigation." A civil scheme that *inevitably* intersects with criminal sanctions may not be used to coerce, on pain of contempt, a potential criminal defendant to furnish evidence crucial to the success of her own prosecution.

The Court's approach includes a second element; it holds that a civil regulatory scheme cannot override Fifth Amendment protection unless it is targeted at the general public. . . . Maryland's juvenile welfare scheme clearly is *not* generally applicable. A child is considered in need of assistance because "[h]e is mentally handicapped or is not receiving ordinary and proper care and attention, and . . . [h]is parents . . . are unable or unwilling to give proper care and attention to the child and his problems." The juvenile court has jurisdiction only over children who are alleged to be in need of assistance, not over all children in the State. . . . In other words, the regulatory scheme that the Court describes as "broadly directed," is actually narrowly targeted at parents who through abuse or neglect deny their children the minimal reasonable level of care and attention. Not all such abuse or neglect rises to the level of criminal child abuse, but parents of children who have been so seriously neglected or abused as to warrant allegations that the children are in need of state assistance are clearly "a selective group inherently suspect of criminal activities." . . .

Although I am disturbed by the Court's willingness to apply inapposite precedent to deny Bouknight her constitutional right against self-incrimination, especially in light of the serious allegations of homicide that accompany this civil proceeding, I take some comfort in the Court's recognition that the State may be prohibited from using any testimony given by Bouknight in subsequent criminal proceedings.[2] Because I am not content to deny Bouknight the constitutional protection required by the Fifth Amendment now in the hope that she will not be convicted later on the basis of her own testimony, I dissent.

NOTES AND QUESTIONS

1. Bouknight remained in prison until 1995, refusing to disclose Maurice's location. After she was released, there were further proceedings in the case but they were closed to the public. For a procedural history, see Baltimore Sun Company v. Maryland, 340 Md. 437, 667 A.2d 166 (1995).

2. It was reasonable to suspect that Bouknight had either murdered or seriously injured Maurice, and was refusing to report on his whereabouts because doing so would lead to criminal liability. That sounds like a straightforward claim of the privilege, does it not? If a murder suspect were ordered to take the police to the victim's dead body and the suspect refused, invoking his Fifth Amendment privilege, any court would hold that the privilege applied and the state's investigators would have to find the body on their own. Why should the conclusion be different in *Bouknight*?

3. Justice O'Connor's answer is: There are civil regulatory interests at stake — the same answer that Justice Harlan gave (in response to the same argument) in California v. Byers. Think about that argument in the context of *Bouknight*. If the state were certain that Maurice was dead, the civil regulatory interests would disappear; the state's only goal would be to prosecute and convict Maurice's killer. In that event, Bouknight would be able to assert the privilege and keep quiet. But because Maurice might be alive, the story is different — Bouknight must talk, or else face an indeterminate prison sentence for contempt (she ended up sitting in prison for seven years). Does this seem odd? Bouknight has more of a privilege if she is a murderer than if she is "merely" guilty of child abuse and aggravated assault. Is that a sensible application of the principles underlying the privilege? Does it seem sensible to weigh the government's interest in regulating child custody more heavily than its interest in prosecuting people who murder children?

4. One might defend the Court's approach by noting that if Maurice were alive, the state would have a serious interest in protecting him *in the future* — not just an interest in punishing past crimes against him. That argument suggests that the privilege should yield to important interests in protecting public safety. Today, the

---

2. I note, with both exasperation and skepticism about the bona fide nature of the State's intentions, that the State may be able to grant Bouknight use immunity under a recently enacted immunity statute, even though it has thus far failed to do so. See 1989 Md. Laws, Ch. 288 (amending §9-123). Although the statute applies only to testimony "in a criminal prosecution or a proceeding before a grand jury of the State," Md. Cts. & Jud. Proc. Code Ann. §9-123(b)(1) (Supp. 1989), the State represented to this Court that "[a]s a matter of law, [granting limited use immunity for the testimonial aspects of Bouknight's compliance with the production order] would now be possible," Tr. of Oral Arg. 10. If such a grant of immunity has been possible since July 1989 and the State has refused to invoke it so that it can litigate Bouknight's claim of privilege, I have difficulty believing that the State is sincere in its protestations of concern for Maurice's well-being.

government is regularly seeking information about terrorist plans to kill Americans, which sounds like an important public safety interest. Should the privilege yield to *that* interest? Should the government be able to compel suspected terrorists to answer questions about their activities and their associates? Does your answer change if the suspected terrorists are American citizens on American soil? If so, why?

5. What is the significance of the last paragraph of Justice O'Connor's opinion? After a long and elaborate argument for the proposition that the privilege does not protect Bouknight, Justice O'Connor reminds us that "[i]n a broad range of contexts, the Fifth Amendment limits prosecutors' ability to use testimony that has been compelled" — and hints that such limits may apply even in cases like *Bouknight*. (Notice the last paragraph of Justice Marshall's dissent, where he refers to this passage.) What is the purpose of the hint?

Here is one possible answer: Like the other cases discussed in this section, *Bouknight* arises at the borders of the Fifth Amendment privilege. Bouknight's claim is plausible, even powerful in conventional Fifth Amendment terms, but granting that claim would impose serious and difficult-to-calibrate costs on the government. One response to that phenomenon is to split the difference: to grant Bouknight's claim while hinting that similar claims may be denied in future cases, or to deny Bouknight's claim while hinting that similar claims may be granted in the future. In *Marchetti*, the Court chose the former option; in *Byers*, Justice Harlan chose the latter, and in *Bouknight*, Justice O'Connor followed Justice Harlan's lead. Bouknight herself lost, but Justice O'Connor's opinion gives room to some future Court majority to award victory to some future Bouknight-like claimant, perhaps at a time when the social costs of the privilege seem less substantial than they did in 1990.

How should such a case be resolved today? On the one hand, the years since 1990 have seen serious nondrug crime fall by more than 40 percent. That fact suggests that the government's interest in gathering information is perhaps less urgent than it was when *Bouknight* was decided. On the other hand, the rise of terrorism means that the situation in *Bouknight* — a suspect has information that might save innocent lives — probably arises more frequently today than it did in 1990. If interest balancing is the proper way to resolve these cases, which way does the balance tilt now?

6. In *Bouknight*, the Court's analysis begins with Fisher v. United States, 425 U.S. 391 (1976). *Fisher* dealt with the Fifth Amendment law relating to subpoenas (i.e., judicial orders to testify or to produce some piece of evidence). In *Bouknight*, the "evidence" was a child — or, the police feared, the child's body. Most subpoenas are more mundane; they order the production of documents, usually financial records and related correspondence.

Document production is a small matter in most criminal cases. Murders and drug deals do not usually leave paper trails. Physical evidence and live witnesses tend to be the keys to solving those crimes, and police tend to gather that evidence through searches and seizures and interrogation of witnesses and suspects. White-collar criminal investigations, however, are different. The police cannot feasibly search through hundreds of file cabinets looking for a single piece of paper. And pieces of paper are critical to the proof of crime in white-collar cases. So the government requires suspects (or witnesses, or custodians of relevant corporate documents) to do the work of searching through the file cabinets and assembling the relevant pieces of paper.

Modern case law on subpoenas and the Fifth Amendment is, to say the least, complex. The subpoena cases squarely raise the same question that animates *Bouknight*, *Byers*, and *Marchetti*: When application of ordinary Fifth Amendment analysis would make government regulation difficult, what should yield — the government regulation, or the Fifth Amendment? The Court's answers have not always been completely consistent. In *Fisher*, for example, the Court held that a suspect's act of producing tax documents in response to a summons "testified" only to the existence of the documents, their authenticity, and the fact that the suspect had custody of them — all of which were "foregone conclusion[s]," and none of which were therefore sufficient to trigger the Fifth Amendment privilege. But in United States v. Hubbell, 530 U.S. 27 (2000), the Court concluded that a subpoena — aptly described as a "fishing expedition" that resulted in the submission of 13,230 pages of documents — required the suspect to "make extensive use of 'the contents of his own mind' in identifying the hundreds of documents responsive to the [prosecution's] requests," thus violating the suspect's Fifth Amendment rights. *Fisher*, *Hubbell*, and the other subpoena cases are discussed at length infra, at Chapter 10, pages 1024-1034.

As in *Bouknight*, *Byers*, and *Marchetti*, the Court's decisions in the subpoena cases appear to represent a bit of a compromise. The Court seems to take the general position that the Fifth Amendment privilege must be protected, even at some cost to the government — but not if the cost turns out to be too high. These decisions may be unsatisfying to those seeking intellectual or theoretical consistency, but may instead reflect a deliberately pragmatic approach to dealing with the conflicting individual and societal interests at stake — an approach that preserves the Court's flexibility to deal with changing social conditions.

D. Police Interrogation

1. The *Miranda* Revolution

Since earliest recorded times, officialdom has interrogated individuals suspected of or charged with criminality. In more barbaric times, the questioning was often accompanied by physical abuse or torture, and a confession resulting from such methods, no matter the extent of the physical coercion applied to the suspect, could form part of the basis of a conviction. Nonetheless, the factual accuracy of statements made under extreme duress is obviously problematic where the only means of halting an interrogation is to assent to the views of the interrogator. Thus, there developed the view that a person ought not to face coercive interrogation designed to yield self-incriminating responses.

The opposition to coercive interrogation gained support from the opposition to the practices of the High Commission and the Court of Star Chamber in England — in particular, the use of the oath ex officio, which required those called before the court to swear to answer truthfully all questions, on pain of perjury, without being informed of the subject matter of the inquiry and prior to any official allegation of criminality. The resistance to the practices of the High Commission and the Star Chamber, while initially resting on the common law principle that a person could not be compelled to answer questions under oath regarding charges that had not been formally made, came to rest on the moral ground that it was unfair for the state to attempt to coerce an individual to contribute to his or her own conviction. These interrelated concerns about trustworthiness, the developing view of the requirements of fairness, and the demands for privacy and autonomy, discussed in Section A, supra, at page 713 and in Chapter 4, supra, at page 303, together seem to have formed the basis of the Fifth Amendment privilege.[1]

Nonetheless, the applicability of the Fifth Amendment to pretrial interrogation was not generally accepted at an early date in this country. Notwithstanding the periodic recognition of the abuses of pretrial interrogation similar to those that gave rise in part to the Fifth Amendment,[2] confessions were excluded only if they were untrustworthy, see, e.g., Hopt v. Utah, 110 U.S. 574 (1884), although one important determinant of trustworthiness was the nature of the interrogation process that led to the incriminating statements. In 1897, however, the Supreme Court, in a remarkable opinion, appeared to bring pretrial interrogation within the scope of the Fifth Amendment in a fashion that unified the Court's treatment of the various issues underlying the Fourth and Fifth Amendments.

The case was Bram v. United States, 168 U.S. 532 (1897). Bram was first officer on a ship bound from Boston to South America; he and a shipmate were charged with killing the ship's master.

> On reaching port, these two suspected persons were delivered to the custody of the police authorities of Halifax and were there held in confinement awaiting the action of the United States consul, which was to determine whether the suspicions which had caused the arrest justified the sending of one or both of the prisoners into the United States for formal charge and trial. Before this examination had taken place the police detective caused Bram to be brought from jail to his private office, and when there alone with the detective he was stripped of his clothing, and either whilst the detective was in the act of so stripping him, or after he was denuded, the conversation offered as a confession took place. The detective repeats what he said to the prisoner, whom he had thus stripped, as follows:
>
>> When Mr. Bram came into my office I said to him: "Bram, we are trying to unravel this horrible mystery." I said: "Your position is rather an awkward one. I have had Brown in this office, and he made a statement that he saw you do the murder." He said: "He could not have seen me. Where was he?" I said: "He states he was at the wheel." "Well," he said, "he could not see me from there."

Id., at 561-562. On these facts, the Court concluded that

> the situation of the accused, and the nature of the communication made to him by the detective, necessarily overthrows any possible implication that his reply to the detective could have been the result of a purely voluntary mental action; that is to say, when all the surrounding circumstances are considered in their true relations, not only is the claim that the statement was voluntary overthrown, but the impression is irresistibly

---

1. For discussions of these developments, see Leonard W. Levy, The Origins of the Fifth Amendment (1968); Richard H. Helmholz et al., The Privilege against Self-Incrimination (1997). The constitutional debates over the Fifth Amendment are peculiarly unenlightening — thus, the word "seem" in the text. Modern scholarship has called into question the conventional understanding of the origins of the right to be free from compelled self-incrimination. In a very interesting article, John Langbein argues that the origins of the privilege lie in the latter part of the eighteenth century — in particular, the introduction of defense counsel. John Langbein, The Historical Origins of the Privilege against Self-Incrimination at Common Law, 92 Mich. L. Rev. 1047 (1994).

2. See, e.g., National Commission on Law Observance and Enforcement, Report on Lawlessness in Law Enforcement (1931) (often referred to as the Wickersham Commission).

produced that it must necessarily have been the result of either hope or fear, or both, operating on the mind.

Id., at 562. "Either hope or fear, or both" failed the constitutional standard, which the Court defined in expansive terms:

> In criminal trials, in the courts of the United States, wherever a question arises whether a confession is incompetent because not voluntary, the issue is controlled by that portion of the Fifth Amendment to the Constitution of the United States, commanding that no person "shall be compelled in any criminal case to be a witness against himself." The legal principle by which the admissibility of the confession of an accused person is to be determined is expressed in the textbooks.
>
> > In 3 Russell on Crimes, (6th ed.) 478, it is stated as follows:
> >
> > But a confession, in order to be admissible, must be free and voluntary: that is, must not be extracted by any sort of threats or violence, nor obtained by any direct or implied promises, however slight, nor by the exertion of any improper influence. . . . A confession can never be received in evidence where the prisoner has been influenced by any threat or promise; for the law cannot measure the force of the influence used, or decide upon its effect upon the mind of the prisoner, and therefore excludes the declaration if any degree of influence has been exerted. . . .

Id., at 542. On that standard, *Bram* was an easy case: "A plainer violation as well of the letter as of the spirit and purpose of the constitutional immunity could scarcely be conceived of." Id., at 564. The Court's opinion continued:

> Moreover, aside from the natural result arising from the situation of the accused and the communication made to him by the detective, the conversation conveyed an express intimation rendering the confession involuntary within the rule laid down by the authorities. What further was said by the detective? "Now, look here, Bram, I am satisfied that you killed the captain from all I have heard from Mr. Brown. But, 'I said,' some of us here think you could not have done all that crime alone. If you had an accomplice, you should say so, and not have the blame of this horrible crime on your own shoulders." But how could the weight of the whole crime be removed from the shoulders of the prisoner as a consequence of his speaking, unless benefit as to the crime and its punishment was to arise from his speaking? Conceding that, closely analyzed, the hope of benefit which the conversation suggested was that of the removal from the conscience of the prisoner of the merely moral weight resulting from concealment, and therefore would not be an inducement, we are to consider the import of the conversation, not from a mere abstract point of view, but by the light of the impression that it was calculated to produce on the mind of the accused, situated as he was at the time the conversation took place. Thus viewed, the weight to be removed by speaking naturally imported a suggestion of some benefit as to the crime and its punishment as arising from making a statement. . . .

Id., at 564-565.

The *Bram* decision proved remarkably prescient; 70 years later, the Court and commentators would debate police interrogation in terms that coincide almost exactly with the Court's opinion. Yet, just as remarkably, *Bram* had little immediate impact. Two facts contributed to its unimportance. First, it was not until 1964 that the Supreme Court ruled that the Fifth Amendment privilege was applicable to the states. Malloy v. Hogan, 378 U.S. 1 (1964). Thus, *Bram* was limited to federal cases — and the vast majority of prosecutions for ordinary street crime, hence the vast majority of police interrogation sessions, are litigated in state courts. Second, although *Bram* invoked the Fifth Amendment, the standard the Court actually employed was the common law's voluntariness standard.

Roughly 40 years after *Bram* was decided, the Supreme Court held that a constitutional voluntariness requirement applied to state courts as well as federal courts. But that voluntariness standard rested on due process, not on the Fifth Amendment. And it was a good deal less rigorous, as the notes below illustrate.

NOTES ON THE DUE PROCESS VOLUNTARINESS TEST

1. The case that inaugurated the voluntariness requirement for state cases was Brown v. Mississippi, 297 U.S. 278 (1936). Chief Justice Hughes drew his chilling statement of facts from a dissenting opinion in the state court below:

> . . . On Sunday night, . . . the same deputy, accompanied by a number of white men, one of whom was also an officer, and by the jailer, came to the jail, and [defendants Ed Brown and Henry Shields] were made to strip and they were laid over chairs and their backs were cut to pieces with a leather strap with buckles on it, and they were likewise made by the said deputy definitely to understand that the whipping would be continued unless and until they confessed, and not only confessed, but confessed in every matter of detail as demanded by those present; and in this manner the defendants confessed the crime, and as the whippings progressed and were repeated, they changed or adjusted their confession in all particulars of detail so as to conform to the demands of their torturers. When the confessions had been obtained in the exact form and contents as desired by the mob, they left with the parting admonition and warning that, if the defendants changed their story at any time in any respect from that last stated, the perpetrators of the outrage would administer the same or equally effective treatment. . . .

Id., at 282 (citation omitted). The state argued that the admission of these confessions into evidence violated no federal right, citing Twining v. New Jersey, 211 U.S. 78 (1908), which had held that the Fifth Amendment's privilege against self-incrimination did not bind state courts. Hughes responded:

> . . . [T]he question of the right of the State to withdraw the privilege against self-incrimination is not here involved. The compulsion to which the quoted statements [in *Twining*] refer is that of the processes of justice by which the accused may be called as a witness and required to testify. Compulsion by torture to extort a confession is a different matter.
>
> The State is free to regulate the procedure of its courts in accordance with its own conceptions of policy, unless in so doing it "offends some principle of justice so rooted in the traditions and conscience of our people as to be ranked as fundamental." Snyder v. Massachusetts, [291 U.S. 97 (1933)]. The State may abolish trial by jury. It may dispense with indictment by a grand jury and substitute complaint or information. But the freedom of the State in establishing its policy is the freedom of constitutional government and is limited by the requirement of due process of law. Because a State may dispense with a jury trial, it does not follow that it may substitute trial by ordeal. The rack and torture chamber may not be substituted for the witness stand. . . . It would be difficult to conceive of methods more revolting to the sense of justice than those taken to procure the confessions of these petitioners, and the use of

the confessions thus obtained as the basis for conviction and sentence was a clear denial of due process.

297 U.S., at 285-286.

The torture in *Brown* was not hidden; the police officers and their accomplices did not fear any court declaration that the confessions were involuntary and hence inadmissible, because no such federal doctrine existed. After *Brown*, voluntariness cases were more complicated. Some aspects of compelled questioning, such as the timing of the relevant events, were uncontested; as to other facts, the parties rarely agreed. Defendants often claimed physical brutality. The police generally denied it. Whether or not the Justices believed the denial was often critical to the Court's decisions — though opinions rarely said so.

2. The facts in Ashcraft v. Tennessee, 322 U.S. 143 (1944), were typical:

> . . . It appears that the officers placed Ashcraft at a table in this room on the fifth floor of the county jail with a light over his head and began to quiz him. They questioned him in relays until the following Monday morning, June 16, 1941, around nine-thirty or ten o'clock. It appears that Ashcraft from Saturday evening at seven o'clock until Monday morning at approximately nine-thirty never left this homicide room on the fifth floor.
>
> Testimony of the officers shows that the reason they questioned Ashcraft "in relays" was that they became so tired they were compelled to rest. But from 7:00 Saturday evening until 9:30 Monday morning Ashcraft had no rest. . . .
>
> As to what happened in the fifth-floor jail room during this thirty-six hour secret examination the testimony follows the usual pattern and is in hopeless conflict. Ashcraft swears that . . . during the course of the examination he was threatened and abused in various ways; and that as the hours passed his eyes became blinded by a powerful electric light, his body became weary, and the strain on his nerves became unbearable. The officers, on the other hand, swear that throughout the questioning they were kind and considerate. . . . [T]he officers declare that . . . Ashcraft was "cool," "calm," "collected," "normal"; that his vision was unimpaired and his eyes not bloodshot; and that he showed no outward signs of being tired or sleepy.

Id., at 149-151. Ashcraft claimed that he never confessed; the police contended that he did. The Court concluded that

> if Ashcraft made a confession it was not voluntary but compelled. We reach this conclusion from facts which are not in dispute at all. . . . We think a situation such as that here shown by uncontradicted evidence is so inherently coercive that its very existence is irreconcilable with the possession of mental freedom by a lone suspect against whom its full coercive force is brought to bear. It is inconceivable that any court of justice in the land, conducted as our courts are, open to the public, would permit prosecutors serving in relays to keep a defendant witness under continuous cross-examination for thirty-six hours without rest or sleep in an effort to extract a "voluntary" confession. Nor can we, consistently with Constitutional due process of law, hold voluntary a confession where prosecutors do the same thing away from the restraining influences of a public trial in an open court room.

Id., at 153-154. Justices Jackson, Roberts, and Frankfurter dissented, arguing that the Court was overturning state court findings of fact without good cause. Jackson added: "[D]oes the Constitution prohibit use of all confessions made after arrest because questioning, while one is deprived of freedom, is 'inherently coercive'? The Court does not quite say so, but it is moving far and fast in that direction." Id., at 161 (Jackson, J., dissenting).

3. In Watts v. Indiana, 338 U.S. 49 (1949),

> . . . [The police] took [petitioner] from the county jail to State Police Headquarters, where he was questioned by officers in relays from about 11:30 that night [the date was November 12] until sometime between 2:30 and 3 o'clock the following morning. The same procedure of persistent interrogation from about 5:30 in the afternoon until about 3 o'clock the following morning, by a relay of six to eight officers, was pursued on Thursday the 13th, Friday the 14th, Saturday the 15th, Monday the 17th. Sunday was a day of rest from interrogation. About 3 o'clock on Tuesday morning, November 18, the petitioner made an incriminating statement after continuous questioning since 6 o'clock of the preceding evening. . . .
>
> Until his inculpatory statements were secured, the petitioner was a prisoner in the exclusive control of the prosecuting authorities. He was kept for the first two days in solitary confinement in a cell aptly enough called "the hole" in view of its physical conditions as described by the State's witnesses. . . . Although the law of Indiana required that petitioner be given a prompt preliminary hearing before a magistrate, . . . the petitioner was not only given no hearing during the entire period of interrogation but was without friendly or professional aid and without advice as to his constitutional rights. Disregard of rudimentary needs of life — opportunities for sleep and a decent allowance of food — are also relevant, not as aggravating elements of petitioner's treatment, but as part of the total situation out of which his confessions came and which stamped their character.

Id., at 52-53. Justice Frankfurter wrote for the Court:

> . . . A statement to be voluntary of course need not be volunteered. But if it is the product of sustained pressure by the police it does not issue from a free choice. . . . We would have to shut our minds to the plain significance of what here transpired to deny that this was a calculated endeavor to secure a confession through the pressure of unrelenting interrogation. The very relentlessness of such interrogation implies that it is better for the prisoner to answer than to persist in the refusal of disclosure which is his constitutional right. To turn the detention of an accused into a process of wrenching from him evidence which could not be extorted in open court with all its safeguards, is so grave an abuse of the power of arrest as to offend the procedural standards of due process.

Id., at 53-54.

Justice Jackson again dissented in *Watts* — two companion cases were decided the same day; Jackson dissented in one and concurred in the other — and offered the following criticism of the Court's path:

> These three cases, from widely separated states, present essentially the same problem. Its recurrence suggests that it has roots in some condition fundamental and general to our criminal system.
>
> In each case police were confronted with one or more brutal murders which the authorities were under the highest duty to solve. Each of these murders was unwitnessed, and the only positive knowledge on which a solution could be based was possessed by the killer. In each there was reasonable ground to *suspect* an individual but not enough legal evidence to *charge* him with guilt. In each the police attempted to

meet the situation by taking the suspect into custody and interrogating him. This extended over varying periods. In each, confessions were made and received in evidence at the trial. Checked with external evidence, they are inherently believable, and were not shaken as to truth by anything that occurred at the trial. Each confessor was convicted by a jury and state courts affirmed. This Court sets all three convictions aside.

The seriousness of the Court's judgment is that no one suggests that any course held promise of solution of these murders other than to take the suspect into custody for questioning. The alternative was to close the books on the crime and forget it, with the suspect at large. This is a grave choice for a society in which two-thirds of the murders already are closed out as insoluble. . . .

Others would strike down these confessions because of conditions which they say make them "involuntary." In this, on only a printed record, they pit their judgment against that of the trial judge and the jury. Both, with the great advantage of hearing and seeing the confessor and also the officers whose conduct and bearing toward him is in question, have found that the confessions were voluntary. In addition, the majority overrule in each case one or more state appellate courts, which have the same limited opportunity to know the truth that we do.

Amid much that is irrelevant or trivial, one serious situation seems to me to stand out in these cases. The suspect neither had nor was advised of his right to get counsel. This presents a real dilemma in a free society. To subject one without counsel to questioning which may and is intended to convict him, is a real peril to individual freedom. To bring in a lawyer means a real peril to solution of the crime, because, under our adversary system, he deems that his sole duty is to protect his client — guilty or innocent — and that in such a capacity he owes no duty whatever to help society solve its crime problem. Under this conception of criminal procedure, any lawyer worth his salt will tell the suspect in no uncertain terms to make no statement to police under any circumstances.

If the State may arrest on suspicion and interrogate without counsel, there is no denying the fact that it largely negates the benefits of the constitutional guaranty of the right to assistance of counsel. Any lawyer who has ever been called into a case after his client has "told all" and turned any evidence he has over to the Government, knows how helpless he is to protect his client against the facts thus disclosed.

I suppose the view one takes will turn on what one thinks should be the right of an accused person against the State. Is it his right to have the judgment on the facts? Or is it his right to have a judgment based on only such evidence as he cannot conceal from the authorities, who cannot compel him to testify in court and also cannot question him before? Our system comes close to the latter by any interpretation, for the defendant is shielded by such safeguards as no system of law except the Anglo-American concedes to him.

Of course, no confession that has been obtained by any form of physical violence to the person is reliable and hence no conviction should rest upon one obtained in that manner. Such treatment not only breaks the will to conceal or lie, but may even break the will to stand by the truth. Nor is it questioned that the same result can sometimes be achieved by threats, promises, or inducements, which torture the mind but put no scar on the body. If the opinion of Mr. Justice Frankfurter in the *Watts* case were based solely on the State's admissions as to the treatment of Watts, I should not disagree. But if ultimate quest in a criminal trial is the truth and if the circumstances indicate no violence or threats of it, should society be deprived of the suspect's help in solving a crime merely because he was confined and questioned when uncounseled?

We must not overlook that, in these as in some previous cases, once a confession is obtained it supplies ways of verifying its trustworthiness. In these cases before us the verification is sufficient to leave me in no doubt that the admissions of guilt were genuine and truthful. Such corroboration consists in one case of finding a weapon where the accused has said he hid it, and in others that conditions which could only have been known to one who was implicated correspond with his story. It is possible, but it is rare, that a confession, if repudiated on the trial, standing alone will convict unless there is external proof of its verity.

In all such cases, along with other conditions criticized, the continuity and duration of the questioning is invoked and it is called an "inquiry," "inquest" or "inquisition," depending mainly on the emotional state of the writer. But as in some of the cases here, if interrogation is permissible at all, there are sound reasons for prolonging it — which the opinions here ignore. The suspect at first perhaps makes an effort to exculpate himself by alibis or other statements. These are verified, found false, and he is then confronted with his falsehood. Sometimes (though such cases do not reach us) verification proves them true or credible and the suspect is released. Sometimes, as here, more than one crime is involved. The duration of an interrogation may well depend on the temperament, shrewdness and cunning of the accused and the competence of the examiner. But, assuming a right to examine at all, the right must include what is made reasonably necessary by the facts of the particular case.

If the right of interrogation be admitted, then it seems to me that we must leave it to trial judges and juries and state appellate courts to decide individual cases, unless they show some want of proper standards of decision. I find nothing to indicate that any of the courts below in these cases did not have a correct understanding of the Fourteenth Amendment, unless this Court thinks it means absolute prohibition of interrogation while in custody before arraignment.

I suppose no one would doubt that our Constitution and Bill of Rights, grounded in revolt against the arbitrary measures of George III and in the philosophy of the French Revolution, represent the maximum restrictions upon the power of organized society over the individual that are compatible with the maintenance of organized society itself. They were so intended and should be so interpreted. It cannot be denied that, even if construed as these provisions traditionally have been, they contain an aggregate of restrictions which seriously limit the power of society to solve such crimes as confront us in these cases. Those restrictions we should not for that reason cast aside, but that is good reason for indulging in no unnecessary expansion of them.

I doubt very much if they require us to hold that the State may not take into custody and question one suspected reasonably of an unwitnessed murder. If it does, the people of this country must discipline themselves to seeing their police stand by helplessly while those suspected of murder prowl about unmolested. Is it a necessary price to pay for the fairness which we know as "due process of law"? And if not a necessary one, should it be demanded by this Court? I do not know the ultimate answer to these questions; but, for the present, I should not increase the handicap on society.

338 U.S., at 57-62 (Jackson, J., dissenting).

4. The debate in *Watts* continued for another 15 years. Judging from case results, Justice Jackson's position did poorly: The Court reversed convictions based on involuntary confessions with growing frequency in the 1950s and early 1960s. The fact patterns of the cases began to change; allegations of physical brutality were replaced with the kind of psychological brutality found in Payne v. Arkansas, 356 U.S. 560 (1958), where an African American defendant with a fifth-grade education was told that a white mob would be waiting for him unless he confessed. The Court's focus began to change as well; the opinions devoted less space to the question whether the suspect's will was "overborne" (what do you suppose that means?) and more to the question whether the police conduct was unacceptable in a free society. Usually, the Court concluded that it was.

Another trend in the cases is harder to document but clear to everyone who followed the law's development in this area: More and more, the Justices distrusted state-court factfinding processes. Plainly, if the state courts could not be counted on to do a conscientious job of applying constitutional mandates, a fact-bound test like voluntariness would not do. A court not wishing to apply the test could simply manipulate its factual findings to reach whatever result it desired. For excellent discussions of this phenomenon and the Court's response to it, see Anthony G. Amsterdam, The Supreme Court and the Rights of Suspects in Criminal Cases, 45 N.Y.U. L. Rev. 785 (1970); Geoffrey R. Stone, The *Miranda* Doctrine in the Burger Court, [1977] Sup. Ct. Rev. 99. This skepticism on the Court's part made it even harder for lower courts — or the police — to tell what the governing legal standard for confessions was; by the early 1960s, it was not clear to anyone what it would take to render a confession voluntary.

Increasing dissatisfaction with the voluntariness approach, growing distrust of state factfinding procedures, the Court's practical inability to act as an effective court of error over the state criminal process, and the fact that the implications of habeas corpus had not yet been fully recognized — all these forces drove the Justices to seek out alternatives to the voluntariness test. They found one in the right to counsel, as is indicated in the next case.[3]

MASSIAH v. UNITED STATES

Certiorari to the United States Court of Appeals for the Second Circuit
377 U.S. 201 (1964)

MR. JUSTICE STEWART delivered the opinion of the Court.

The petitioner was indicted for violating the federal narcotics laws. He retained a lawyer, pleaded not guilty, and was released on bail. While he was free on bail a federal agent succeeded by surreptitious means in listening to incriminating statements made by him. Evidence of these statements was introduced against the petitioner at his trial over his objection. He was convicted, and the Court of Appeals affirmed. We granted certiorari to consider whether, under the circumstances here presented, the prosecution's use at the trial of evidence of the petitioner's own incriminating statements deprived him of any right secured to him under the Federal Constitution. . . .

The petitioner, a merchant seaman, was in 1958 a member of the crew of the S.S. Santa Maria. In April of that year federal customs officials in New York received information that he was going to transport a quantity of narcotics aboard that ship from South America to the United States. As a result of this and other information, the agents searched the Santa Maria upon its arrival in New York and found in the afterpeak of the vessel five packages containing about three and a half pounds of cocaine. They also learned of circumstances, not here relevant, tending to connect

---

3. The Court toyed with another alternative in two federal cases, McNabb v. United States, 318 U.S. 332 (1943), and Mallory v. United States, 354 U.S. 449 (1957). Together, the cases structured what has come to be known as the McNabb-Mallory Rule, which excludes confessions obtained in violation of Fed. R. Crim. P. 5(a)'s requirement that an arrested person be taken without unnecessary delay to the nearest community officer. The Court invoked its supervisory power over the federal courts as the basis for the rule, and it never applied the rule to the states through the Fourteenth Amendment.

the petitioner with the cocaine. He was arrested, promptly arraigned, and subsequently indicted for possession of narcotics aboard a United States vessel. In July a superseding indictment was returned, charging the petitioner and a man named Colson with the same substantive offense, and in separate counts charging the petitioner, Colson, and others with having conspired to possess narcotics aboard a United States vessel, and to import, conceal, and facilitate the sale of narcotics. The petitioner, who had retained a lawyer, pleaded not guilty and was released on bail, along with Colson.

A few days later, and quite without the petitioner's knowledge, Colson decided to cooperate with the government agents in their continuing investigation of the narcotics activities in which the petitioner, Colson, and others had allegedly been engaged. Colson permitted an agent named Murphy to install a Schmidt radio transmitter under the front seat of Colson's automobile, by means of which Murphy, equipped with an appropriate receiving device, could overhear from some distance away conversations carried on in Colson's car.

On the evening of November 19, 1959, Colson and the petitioner held a lengthy conversation while sitting in Colson's automobile, parked on a New York street. By prearrangement with Colson, and totally unbeknown to the petitioner, the agent Murphy sat in a car parked out of sight down the street and listened over the radio to the entire conversation. The petitioner made several incriminating statements during the course of this conversation. At the petitioner's trial these incriminating statements were brought before the jury through Murphy's testimony, despite the insistent objection of defense counsel. The jury convicted the petitioner of several related narcotics offenses, and the convictions were affirmed by the Court of Appeals.

The petitioner argues that it was an error of constitutional dimensions to permit the agent Murphy at the trial to testify to the petitioner's incriminating statements which Murphy had overheard under the circumstances disclosed by this record. This argument is based upon two distinct and independent grounds. First, we are told that Murphy's use of the radio equipment violated the petitioner's rights under the Fourth Amendment, and, consequently, that all evidence which Murphy thereby obtained was, under the rule Weeks v. United States, 232 U.S. 383, inadmissible against the petitioner at the trial. Secondly, it is said that the petitioner's Fifth and Sixth Amendment rights were violated by the use in evidence against him of incriminating statements which government agents had deliberately elicited from him after he had been indicted and in the absence of his retained counsel. Because of the way we dispose of the case, we do not reach the Fourth Amendment issue.

In Spano v. New York, 360 U.S. 315, this Court reversed a state criminal conviction because a confession had been wrongly admitted into evidence against the defendant at his trial. In that case the defendant had already been indicted for first-degree murder at the time he confessed. The Court held that the defendant's conviction could not stand under the Fourteenth Amendment. While the Court's opinion relied upon the totality of the circumstances under which the confession had been obtained, four concurring justices pointed out that the Constitution required reversal of the conviction upon the sole and specific ground that the confession had been deliberately elicited by the police after the defendant had been indicted, and therefore at a time when he was clearly entitled to a lawyer's help. It was pointed out that under our system of justice the most elemental concepts of due process of law contemplate that an indictment be followed by a trial, "in an orderly courtroom, presided over by a judge, open to the public, and protected by all the procedural safeguards of the law." 360 U.S., at 327 (Stewart, J., concurring). It was said that a Constitution which guarantees a defendant the aid of counsel at such a trial could surely vouchsafe no less to an indicted defendant under interrogation by the police in a completely extrajudicial proceeding. Anything less, it was said, might deny a defendant "effective representation by counsel at the only stage when legal aid and advice would help him." 360 U.S., at 326 (Douglas, J., concurring). . . .

This view no more than reflects a constitutional principle established as long ago as Powell v. Alabama, 287 U.S. 45, where the Court noted that ". . . during perhaps the most critical period of the proceedings . . . that is to say, from the time of their arraignment until the beginning of their trial, when consultation, thoroughgoing investigation and preparation [are] vitally important, the defendants . . . [are] as much entitled to such aid [of counsel] during that period as at the trial itself." Id., at 57. And since the *Spano* decision the same basic constitutional principle has been broadly reaffirmed by this Court. Hamilton v. Alabama, 368 U.S. 52; White v. Maryland, 373 U.S. 59. See Gideon v. Wainwright, 372 U.S. 335. Here we deal not with a state court conviction, but with a federal case, where the specific guarantee of the Sixth Amendment directly applies. Johnson v. Zerbst, 304 U.S. 458. We hold that the petitioner was denied the basic protections of that guarantee when there was used against him at his trial evidence of his own incriminating words, which federal agents had deliberately elicited from him after he had been indicted and in the absence of his counsel. It is true that in the *Spano* case the defendant was interrogated in a police station, while here the damaging testimony was elicited from the defendant without his knowledge while he was free on bail. But, as Judge Hays pointed out in his dissent in the Court of Appeals, "if such a rule is to have any efficacy it must apply to indirect and surreptitious interrogations as well as those conducted in the jailhouse. In this case, Massiah was more seriously imposed upon . . . because he did not even know that he was under interrogation by a government agent." 307 F.2d, at 72-73.

The Solicitor General, in his brief and oral argument, has strenuously contended that the federal law enforcement agents had the right, if not indeed the duty, to continue their investigation of the petitioner and his alleged criminal associates even though the petitioner had been indicted. He points out that the Government was continuing its investigation in order to uncover not only the source of narcotics found on the S.S. Santa Maria, but also their intended buyer. He says that the quantity of narcotics involved was such as to suggest that the petitioner was part of a large and well-organized ring, and indeed that the continuing investigation confirmed this suspicion, since it resulted in criminal charges against many defendants. Under these circumstances the Solicitor General concludes that the government agents were completely "justified in making use of Colson's cooperation by having Colson continue his normal associations and by surveilling them."

We may accept and, at least for present purposes, completely approve all that this argument implies, Fourth Amendment problems to one side. We do not question that in this case, as in many cases, it was entirely proper to continue an investigation of the suspected criminal activities of the defendant and his alleged confederates, even though the defendant had already been indicted. All that we hold is that the defendant's own incriminating statements, obtained by federal agents under the circumstances here disclosed, could not constitutionally be used by the prosecution as evidence against *him* at his trial. Reversed.

MR. JUSTICE WHITE, with whom MR. JUSTICE CLARK and MR. JUSTICE HARLAN join, dissenting. . . .

It is . . . a rather portentous occasion when a constitutional rule is established barring the use of evidence which is relevant, reliable and highly probative of the issue which the trial court has before it — whether the accused committed the act with which he is charged. Without the evidence, the quest for truth may be seriously impeded and in many cases the trial court, although aware of proof showing defendant's guilt, must nevertheless release him because the crucial evidence is deemed inadmissible. This result is entirely justified in some circumstances because exclusion serves other policies of overriding importance, as where evidence seized in an illegal search is excluded, not because of the quality of the proof, but to secure meaningful enforcement of the Fourth Amendment. Weeks v. United States, 232 U.S. 383; Mapp v. Ohio, 367 U.S. 643. But this only emphasizes that the soundest of reasons is necessary to warrant the exclusion of evidence otherwise admissible and the creation of another area of privileged testimony. With all due deference, I am not at all convinced that the additional barriers to the pursuit of truth which the Court today erects rest on anything like the solid foundations which decisions of this gravity should require.

The importance of the matter should not be underestimated, for today's rule promises to have wide application well beyond the facts of this case. The reason given for the result here — the admissions were obtained in the absence of counsel — would seem equally pertinent to statements obtained at any time after the right to counsel attaches, whether there has been an indictment or not; to admissions made prior to arraignment, at least where the defendant has counsel or asks for it; to the fruits of admissions improperly obtained under the new rule; to criminal proceedings in state courts; and to defendants long since convicted upon evidence including such admissions. The new rule will immediately do service in a great many cases.

Whatever the content or scope of the rule may prove to be, I am unable to see how this case presents an unconstitutional interference with Massiah's right to counsel. Massiah was not prevented from consulting with counsel as often as he wished. No meetings with counsel were disturbed or spied upon. Preparation for trial was in no way obstructed. It is only a sterile syllogism — an unsound one, besides — to say that because Massiah had a right to counsel's aid before and during the trial, his out-of-court conversations and admissions must be excluded if obtained without counsel's consent or presence. The right to counsel has never meant as much before, . . . and its extension in this case requires some further explanation, so far unarticulated by the Court.

Since the new rule would exclude all admissions made to the police, no matter how voluntary and reliable, the requirement of counsel's presence or approval would seem to rest upon the probability that counsel would foreclose any admissions at all. This is nothing more than a thinly disguised constitutional policy of minimizing or entirely prohibiting the use in evidence of voluntary out-of-court admissions and confessions made by the accused. Carried as far as blind logic may compel some to go, the notion that statements from the mouth of the defendant should not be used in evidence would have a severe and unfortunate impact upon the great bulk of criminal cases. . . .

Applying the new exclusionary rule is peculiarly inappropriate in this case. At the time of the conversation in question, petitioner was not in custody but free on bail. He was not questioned in what anyone could call an atmosphere of official coercion. What he said was said to his partner in crime who had also been indicted. There was no suggestion or any possibility of coercion. What petitioner did not know was that Colson had decided to report the conversation to the police. Had there been no prior arrangements between Colson and the police, had Colson simply gone to the police after the conversation had occurred, his testimony relating Massiah's statements would be readily admissible at the trial, as would a recording which he might have made of the conversation. In such event, it would simply be said that Massiah risked talking to a friend who decided to disclose what he knew of Massiah's criminal activities. But if, as occurred here, Colson had been cooperating with the police prior to his meeting with Massiah, both his evidence and the recorded conversation are somehow transformed into inadmissible evidence despite the fact that the hazard to Massiah remains precisely the same — the defection of a confederate in crime.

Reporting criminal behavior is expected or even demanded of the ordinary citizen. Friends may be subpoenaed to testify about friends, relatives about relatives and partners about partners. I therefore question the soundness of insulating Massiah from the apostasy of his partner in crime and of furnishing constitutional sanctions for the strict secrecy and discipline of criminal organizations. Neither the ordinary citizen nor the confessed criminal should be discouraged from reporting what he knows to the authorities and from lending his aid to secure evidence of crime. Certainly after this case the Colsons will be few and far between; and the Massiahs can breathe much more easily, secure in the knowledge that the Constitution furnishes an important measure of protection against faithless compatriots and guarantees sporting treatment for sporting peddlers of narcotics. . . .

Undoubtedly, the evidence excluded in this case would not have been available but for the conduct of Colson in cooperation with Agent Murphy, but is it this kind of conduct which should be forbidden to those charged with law enforcement? It is one thing to establish safeguards against procedures fraught with the potentiality of coercion and to outlaw "easy but self-defeating ways in which brutality is substituted for brains as an instrument of crime detection." McNabb v. United States, 318 U.S. 332, 344. But here there was no substitution of brutality for brains, no inherent danger of police coercion justifying the prophylactic effect of another exclusionary rule. Massiah was not being interrogated in a police station, was not surrounded by numerous officers or questioned in relays, and was not forbidden access to others. Law enforcement may have the elements of a contest about it, but it is not a game. McGuire v. United States, 273 U.S. 95, 99. Massiah and those like him receive ample protection from the long line of precedents in this Court holding that confessions may not be introduced unless they are voluntary. In making these determinations the courts must consider the absence of counsel as one of several factors by which voluntariness is to be judged.

. . . This is a wiser rule than the automatic rule announced by the Court, which requires courts and juries to disregard voluntary admissions which they might well find to be the best possible evidence in discharging their responsibility for ascertaining truth. . . .

The meaning of *Massiah* was not altogether clear, however. For example, did it matter whether the defendant had been indicted? Been arraigned? Obtained counsel? The Court returned to these matters a year later in Escobedo v. Illinois. In *Escobedo*, the defendant had been arrested but not charged and had invoked his right to counsel (presuming he had one), his lawyer was present at the station house but not allowed to see his client, and the defendant was subject to interrogation during which incriminating statements were made. Over a sharp dissent, the Court, in a schizoid opinion marked by an uneasy relationship between sweeping assertion and narrow holding, held that the defendant's constitutional rights had been violated. The curious progression of the opinion can be seen in the following excerpt.

ESCOBEDO V. ILLINOIS, 378 U.S. 478, 488-491 (1964): It is argued that if the right to counsel is afforded prior to indictment, the number of confessions obtained by the police will diminish significantly, because most confessions are obtained during the period between arrest and indictment, and "any lawyer worth his salt will tell the suspect in no uncertain terms to make no statement to police under any circumstances." Watts v. Indiana, 338 U.S. 49, 59 (Jackson, J., concurring in part and dissenting in part). This argument, of course, cuts two ways. The fact that many confessions are obtained during this period points up its critical nature as a "stage when legal aid and advice" are surely needed. . . . The right to counsel would indeed be hollow if it began at a period when few confessions were obtained. There is necessarily a direct relationship between the importance of a stage to the police in their quest for a confession and the criticalness of that stage to the accused in his need for legal advice. Our Constitution, unlike some others, strikes the balance in favor of the right of the accused to be advised by his lawyer of his privilege against self-incrimination. . . .

We have learned the lesson of history, ancient and modern, that a system of criminal law enforcement which comes to depend on the "confession" will, in the long run, be less reliable and more subject to abuses than a system which depends on extrinsic evidence independently secured through skillful investigation. As Dean Wigmore so wisely said:

> [A]ny system of administration which permits the prosecution to trust habitually to compulsory self-disclosure as a source of proof must itself suffer morally thereby. The inclination develops to rely mainly upon such evidence, and to be satisfied with an incomplete investigation of the other sources. The exercise of the power to extract answers begets a forgetfulness of the just limitations of that power. The simple and peaceful process of questioning breeds a readiness to resort to bullying and to physical force and torture. If there is a right to an answer, there soon seems to be a right to the expected answer — that is, to a confession of guilt. Thus the legitimate use grows into the unjust abuse; ultimately, the innocent are jeopardized by the encroachments of a bad system. Such seems to have been the course of experience in those legal systems where the privilege was not recognized.

8 Wigmore, Evidence (3d ed. 1940), 309. (Emphasis in original.)

This Court also has recognized that "history amply shows that confessions have often been extorted to save law enforcement officials the trouble and effort of obtaining valid and independent evidence. . . ." Haynes v. Washington, 373 U.S. 503, 519.

We have also learned the companion lesson of history that no system of criminal justice can, or should, survive if it comes to depend for its continued effectiveness on the citizens' abdication through unawareness of their constitutional rights. No system worth preserving should have to *fear* that if an accused is permitted to consult with a lawyer, he will become aware of, and exercise, these rights.[13] If the exercise of constitutional rights will thwart the effectiveness of a system of law enforcement then there is something very wrong with that system.

We hold, therefore, that where, as here, the investigation is no longer a general inquiry into an unsolved crime but has begun to focus on a particular suspect, the suspect has been taken into police custody, the police carry out a process of interrogations that lends itself to eliciting incriminating statements, the suspect has requested and been denied an opportunity to consult with his lawyer, and the police have not effectively warned him of his absolute constitutional right to remain silent, the accused has been denied "the Assistance of Counsel" in violation of the Sixth Amendment to the Constitution as "made obligatory upon the States by the Fourteenth Amendment," Gideon v. Wainwright, 372 U.S., at 342, and that no statement elicited by the police during the interrogation may be used against him at a criminal trial. . . .

_____

Was *Escobedo* a simple application of *Massiah*? Was it a harbinger of the complete elimination of confessions, or at least of police interrogation as then conceived? Or was it an example of a Court realizing that it was breaking new ground, but not altogether sure of the way to proceed or of the implications of its actions? Some of these questions were answered two years later in the *Miranda* case.

MIRANDA v. ARIZONA

Certiorari to the Supreme Court of Arizona
384 U.S. 436 (1966)

MR. CHIEF JUSTICE WARREN delivered the opinion of the Court.

The cases before us raise questions which go to the roots of our concepts of American criminal jurisprudence: the restraints society must observe consistent with the Federal Constitution in prosecuting individuals for crime. More specifically, we deal with the admissibility of statements obtained from an individual who

13. Cf. Report of Attorney General's Committee on Poverty and the Administration of Federal Criminal Justice (1963), 10-11:

> The survival of our system of criminal justice and the values which it advances depends upon a constant, searching, and creative questioning of official decisions and assertions of authority at all stages of the process. . . . Persons [denied access to counsel] are incapable of providing the challenges that are indispensable to satisfactory operation of the system. The loss to the interests of accused individuals, occasioned by these failures, are great and apparent. It is also clear that a situation in which persons are required to contest a serious accusation but are denied access to the tools of contest is offensive to fairness and equity. Beyond these considerations, however, is the fact that [this situation is] detrimental to the proper functioning of the system of justice and that the loss in vitality of the adversary system, thereby occasioned, significantly endangers the basic interests of a free community.

is subjected to custodial police interrogation and the necessity for procedures which assure that the individual is accorded his privilege under the Fifth Amendment to the Constitution not to be compelled to incriminate himself. We dealt with certain phases of this problem recently in Escobedo v. Illinois, 378 U.S. 478 (1964). . . .

Our holding will be spelled out with some specificity in the pages which follow but briefly stated it is this: the prosecution may not use statements, whether exculpatory or inculpatory, stemming from custodial interrogation of the defendant unless it demonstrates the use of procedural safeguards effective to secure the privilege against self-incrimination. By custodial interrogation, we mean questioning initiated by law enforcement officers after a person has been taken into custody or otherwise deprived of his freedom of action in any significant way.[4] As for the procedural safeguards to be employed, unless other fully effective means are devised to inform accused persons of their right of silence and to assure a continuous opportunity to exercise it, the following measures are required. Prior to any questioning, the person must be warned that he has a right to remain silent, that any statement he does make may be used as evidence against him, and that he has a right to the presence of an attorney, either retained or appointed. The defendant may waive effectuation of these rights, provided the waiver is made voluntarily, knowingly and intelligently. If, however, he indicates in any manner and at any stage of the process that he wishes to consult with an attorney before speaking there can be no questioning. Likewise, if the individual is alone and indicates in any manner that he does not wish to be interrogated, the police may not question him. The mere fact that he may have answered some questions or volunteered some statements on his own does not deprive him of the right to refrain from answering any further inquiries until he has consulted with an attorney and thereafter consents to be questioned.

I

. . . An understanding of the nature and setting of this in-custody interrogation is essential to our decisions today. The difficulty in depicting what transpires at such interrogations stems from the fact that in this country they have largely taken place incommunicado. From extensive factual studies undertaken in the early 1930s, including the famous Wickersham Report to Congress by a Presidential Commission, it is clear that police violence and the "third degree" flourished at that time. In a series of cases decided by this Court long after these studies, the police resorted to physical brutality — beating, hanging, whipping — and to sustained and protracted questioning incommunicado in order to extort confessions. . . . The use of physical brutality and violence is not, unfortunately, relegated to the past or to any part of the country. Only recently in Kings County, New York, the police brutally beat, kicked and placed lighted cigarette butts on the back of a potential witness under interrogation for the purpose of securing a statement incriminating a third party. People v. Portelli, 15 N.Y. 2d 235, 205 N.E.2d 857 (1965).[7]

4. This is what we meant in Escobedo when we spoke of an investigation which had focused on an accused.

7. In addition, see People v. Wakat, 415 Ill. 610, 114 N.E.2d 706 (1953); Wakat v. Harlib, 253 F.2d 59 (C.A. 7th Cir. 1958) (defendant suffering from broken bones, multiple bruises and injuries sufficiently serious to require eight months' medical treatment after being manhandled by five policemen). . . .

The examples given above are undoubtedly the exception now, but they are sufficiently widespread to be the object of concern. Unless a proper limitation upon custodial interrogation is achieved — such as these decisions will advance — there can be no assurance that practices of this nature will be eradicated in the foreseeable future. . . .

. . . [T]he modern practice of in-custody interrogation is psychologically rather than physically oriented. . . . Interrogation still takes place in privacy. Privacy results in secrecy and this in turn results in a gap in our knowledge as to what in fact goes on in the interrogation rooms. A valuable source of information about present police practices, however, may be found in various police manuals and texts which document procedures employed with success in the past, and which recommend various other effective tactics.[8] These texts are used by law enforcement agencies themselves as guides. It should be noted that these texts professedly present the most enlightened and effective means presently used to obtain statements through custodial interrogation. By considering these texts and other data, it is possible to describe procedures observed and noted around the country.

The officers are told by the manuals that the "principal psychological factor contributing to a successful interrogation is *privacy* — being alone with the person under interrogation."[10] The efficacy of this tactic has been explained as follows:

> If at all practicable, the interrogation should take place in the investigator's office or at least in a room of his own choice. The subject should be deprived of every psychological advantage. In his own home he may be confident, indignant, or recalcitrant. He is more keenly aware of his rights and more reluctant to tell of his indiscretions or criminal behavior within the walls of his home. Moreover his family and other friends are nearby, their presence lending moral support. In his own office, the investigator possesses all the advantages. The atmosphere suggests the invincibility of the forces of the law.[11]

To highlight the isolation and unfamiliar surroundings, the manuals instruct the police to display an air of confidence in the suspect's guilt and from outward appearance to maintain only an interest in confirming certain details. The guilt of the subject is to be posited as a fact. The interrogator should direct his comments toward the reasons why the subject committed the act, rather than court failure by asking the subject whether he did it. Like other men, perhaps the subject has had a bad family life, had an unhappy childhood, had too much to drink, had an unrequited desire for women. The officers are instructed to minimize the moral seriousness of the offense,[12] to cast blame on the victim or on society.[13] These tactics are designed to put the subject in a psychological state where his story is but an elaboration of what the police purport to know already — that he is guilty. Explanations to the contrary are dismissed and discouraged.

8. The manuals quoted in the text following are the most recent and representative of the texts currently available. Material of the same nature appears in Kidd, Police Interrogation (1940); Mulbar, Interrogation (1951); Dienstein, Technics for the Crime Investigator 97-115 (1952). . . .

10. Inbau & Reid, Criminal Interrogation and Confessions (1962), at 1.

11. O'Hara, [Fundamentals of Criminal Investigation (1956),] at 99.

12. Inbau & Reid, supra, at 34-43, 87. For example, in Leyra v. Denno, 347 U.S. 556 (1954), the interrogator-psychiatrist told the accused, "We do sometimes things that are not right, but in a fit of temper or anger we sometimes do things we aren't really responsible for," id., at 562, and again, "We know that morally you were just in anger. Morally, you are not to be condemned," id., at 582.

13. Inbau & Reid, supra, at 43-55.

The texts thus stress that the major qualities an interrogator should possess are patience and perseverance. One writer describes the efficacy of these characteristics in this manner:

> In the preceding paragraphs emphasis has been placed on kindness and stratagems. The investigator will, however, encounter many situations where the sheer weight of his personality will be the deciding factor. Where emotional appeals and tricks are employed to no avail, he must rely on an oppressive atmosphere of dogged persistence. He must interrogate steadily and without relent, leaving the subject no prospect of surcease. He must dominate his subject and overwhelm him with his inexorable will to obtain the truth. He should interrogate for a spell of several hours pausing only for the subject's necessities in acknowledgment of the need to avoid a charge of duress that can be technically substantiated. In a serious case, the interrogation may continue for days, with the required intervals for food and sleep, but with no respite from the atmosphere of domination. It is possible in this way to induce the subject to talk without resorting to duress or coercion. The method should be used only when the guilt of the subject appears highly probable.[14]

The manuals suggest that the suspect be offered legal excuses for his actions in order to obtain an initial admission of guilt. Where there is a suspected revenge-killing, for example, the interrogator may say:

> Joe, you probably didn't go out looking for this fellow with the purpose of shooting him. My guess is, however, that you expected something from him and that's why you carried a gun — for your own protection. You knew him for what he was, no good. Then when you met him he probably started using foul, abusive language and he gave some indication that he was about to pull a gun on you, and that's when you had to act to save your own life. That's about it, isn't it Joe?[15]

Having then obtained the admission of shooting, the interrogator is advised to refer to circumstantial evidence which negates the self-defense explanation. This should enable him to secure the entire story. One text notes that "Even if he fails to do so, the inconsistency between the subject's original denial of the shooting and his present admission of at least doing the shooting will serve to deprive him of a self-defense 'out' at the time of trial."[16]

When the techniques described above prove unavailing, the texts recommend they be alternated with a show of some hostility. One ploy often used has been termed the "friendly-unfriendly" or the "Mutt and Jeff" act:

> . . . In this technique, two agents are employed. Mutt, the relentless investigator, who knows the subject is guilty and is not going to waste any time. He's sent a dozen men away for this crime and he's going to send the subject away for the full term. Jeff, on the other hand, is obviously a kindhearted man. He has a family himself. He has a brother who was involved in a little scrape like this. He disapproves of Mutt and his tactics and will arrange to get him off the case if the subject will cooperate. He can't hold Mutt off for very long. The subject would be wise to make a quick decision. The technique is applied by having both investigators present while Mutt acts out his role.

14. O'Hara, supra, at 112.
15. Inbau & Reid, supra, at 40.
16. Ibid.

Jeff may stand by quietly and demur at some of Mutt's tactics. When Jeff makes his plea for cooperation, Mutt is not present in the room.[17]

The interrogators sometimes are instructed to induce a confession out of trickery. The technique here is quite effective in crimes which require identification or which run in series. In the identification situation, the interrogator may take a break in his questioning to place the subject among a group of men in a line-up. "The witness or complainant (previously coached, if necessary) studies the line-up and confidently points out the subject as the guilty party."[18] Then the questioning resumes "as though there were now no doubt about the guilt of the subject." A variation on this technique is called the "reverse line-up":

> The accused is placed in a line-up, but this time he is identified by several fictitious witnesses or victims who associated him with different offenses. It is expected that the subject will become desperate and confess to the offense under investigation in order to escape from the false accusations.[19]

The manuals also contain instructions for police on how to handle the individual who refuses to discuss the matter entirely, or who asks for an attorney or relatives. The examiner is to concede him the right to remain silent. "This usually has a very undermining effect. First of all, he is disappointed in his expectation of an unfavorable reaction on the part of the interrogator. Secondly, a concession of this right to remain silent impresses the subject with the apparent fairness of his interrogator."[20] After this psychological conditioning, however, the officer is told to point out the incriminating significance of the suspect's refusal to talk:

> Joe, you have a right to remain silent. That's your privilege and I'm the last person in the world who'll try to take it away from you. If that's the way you want to leave this, O.K. But let me ask you this. Suppose you were in my shoes and I were in yours and you called me in to ask me about this and I told you, "I don't want to answer any of your questions." You'd think I had something to hide, and you'd probably be right in thinking that. That's exactly what I'll have to think about you, and so will everybody else. So let's sit here and talk this whole thing over.[21]

Few will persist in their initial refusal to talk, it is said, if this monologue is employed correctly.

In the event that the subject wishes to speak to a relative or an attorney, the following advice is tendered:

---

17. O'Hara, supra, at 104, Inbau & Reid, supra, at 58-59. See Spano v. New York, 360 U.S. 315 (1959). A variant on the technique of creating hostility is one of engendering fear. This is perhaps best described by the prosecuting attorney in Malinski v. New York, 324 U.S. 401, 407 (1945): "Why this talk about being undressed? Of course, they had a right to undress him to look for bullet scars, and keep the clothes off him. That was quite proper police procedure. That is some more psychology — let him sit around with a blanket on him, humiliate him there for a while; let him sit in the corner, let him think he is going to get a shellacking."

18. O'Hara, supra, at 105-106.

19. Id., at 106.

20. Inbau & Reid, supra, at 111.

21. Ibid.

[T]he interrogator should respond by suggesting that the subject first tell the truth to the interrogator himself rather than get anyone else involved in the matter. If the request is for an attorney, the interrogator may suggest that the subject save himself or his family the expense of any such professional service, particularly if he is innocent of the offense under investigation. The interrogator may also add, "Joe, I'm only looking for the truth, and if you're telling the truth, that's it. You can handle this by yourself."[22] . . .

Even without employing brutality, the "third degree" or the specific stratagems described above, the very fact of custodial interrogation exacts a heavy toll on individual liberty and trades on the weakness of individuals. This fact may be illustrated simply by referring to three confession cases decided by this Court in the Term immediately preceding our *Escobedo* decision. In Townsend v. Sain, 372 U.S. 293 (1963), the defendant was a 19-year-old heroin addict, described as a "near mental defective," id., at 307-310. The defendant in Lynumn v. Illinois, 372 U.S. 528 (1963), was a woman who confessed to the arresting officer after being importuned to "cooperate" in order to prevent her children from being taken by relief authorities. This Court as in those cases reversed the conviction of a defendant in Haynes v. Washington, 373 U.S. 503 (1963), whose persistent request during his interrogation was to phone his wife or attorney. In other settings, these individuals might have exercised their constitutional rights. In the incommunicado police-dominated atmosphere, they succumbed.

In the cases before us today, . . . we might not find the defendant's statements to have been involuntary in traditional terms. Our concern for adequate safeguards to protect precious Fifth Amendment rights is, of course, not lessened in the slightest. In each of the cases, the defendant was thrust into an unfamiliar atmosphere and run through menacing police interrogation procedures. The potentiality for compulsion is forcefully apparent, for example, in *Miranda*, where the indigent Mexican defendant was a seriously disturbed individual with pronounced sexual fantasies, and in *Stewart*, in which the defendant was an indigent Los Angeles Negro who had dropped out of school in the sixth grade. To be sure, the records do not evince overt physical coercion or patent psychological ploys. The fact remains that in none of these cases did the officers undertake to afford appropriate safeguards at the outset of the interrogation to insure that the statements were truly the product of free choice.

It is obvious that such an interrogation environment is created for no purpose other than to subjugate the individual to the will of his examiner. This atmosphere carries its own badge of intimidation. To be sure, this is not physical intimidation, but it is equally destructive of human dignity.[26] The current practice of incommunicado interrogation is at odds with one of our Nation's most cherished

---

22. Inbau & Reid, supra, at 112.

26. The absurdity of denying that a confession obtained under these circumstances is compelled is aptly portrayed by an example in Professor Sutherland's recent article, Crime and Confession, 79 Harv. L. Rev. 21, 37 (1965):

Suppose a well-to-do testatrix says she intends to will her property to Elizabeth. John and James want her to bequeath it to them instead. They capture the testatrix, put her in a carefully designed room, out of touch with everyone but themselves and their convenient "witness," keep her secluded there for hours while they make insistent demands, weary her with contradictions of her assertions that she wants to leave her money to Elizabeth, and finally induce her to execute the will in their favor. Assume that John and James are deeply and correctly convinced that Elizabeth is unworthy and will make base use of the property if she gets her hands on it, whereas John

principles — that the individual may not be compelled to incriminate himself. Unless adequate protective devices are employed to dispel the compulsion inherent in custodial surroundings, no statement obtained from the defendant can truly be the product of his free choice.

From the foregoing, we can readily perceive an intimate connection between the privilege against self-incrimination and police custodial questioning. It is fitting to turn to history and precedent underlying the Self-Incrimination Clause to determine its applicability in this situation.

II

. . . The question in these cases is whether the privilege is fully applicable during a period of custodial interrogation. In this Court, the privilege has consistently been accorded a liberal construction. . . . We are satisfied that all the principles embodied in the privilege apply to informal compulsion exerted by law enforcement officers during in-custody questioning. An individual swept from familiar surroundings into police custody, surrounded by antagonistic forces, and subjected to the techniques of persuasion described above cannot be otherwise than under compulsion to speak. As a practical matter, the compulsion to speak in the isolated setting of the police station may well be greater than in courts or other official investigations, where there are often impartial observers to guard against intimidation or trickery.

This question, in fact, could have been taken as settled in federal courts almost 70 years ago, when, in Bram v. United States, 168 U.S. 532, 542 (1897), this Court held:

> In criminal trials, in the courts of the United States, wherever a question arises whether a confession is incompetent because not voluntary, the issue is controlled by that portion of the Fifth Amendment . . . commanding that no person "shall be compelled in any criminal case to be a witness against himself." . . .

In addition to the expansive historical development of the privilege and the sound policies which have nurtured its evolution, judicial precedent thus clearly establishes its application to incommunicado interrogation. . . .

III

Today, then, there can be no doubt that the Fifth Amendment privilege is available outside of criminal court proceedings and serves to protect persons in all settings in which their freedom of action is curtailed in any significant way from being compelled to incriminate themselves. We have concluded that without proper safeguards the process of in-custody interrogation of persons suspected or accused of crime contains inherently compelling pressures which work to undermine the individual's will to resist and to compel him to speak where he would not otherwise do so freely. In order to combat these pressures and to permit a full opportunity to exercise the privilege against self-incrimination, the accused must be adequately and effectively apprised of his rights and the exercise of those rights must be fully honored.

---

and James have the noblest and most righteous intentions. Would any judge of probate accept the will so procured as the "voluntary" act of the testatrix?

It is impossible for us to foresee the potential alternatives for protecting the privilege which might be devised by Congress or the States in the exercise of their creative rule-making capacities. Therefore we cannot say that the Constitution necessarily requires adherence to any particular solution for the inherent compulsions of the interrogation process as it is presently conducted. Our decision in no way creates a constitutional straitjacket which will handicap sound efforts at reform, nor is it intended to have this effect. We encourage Congress and the States to continue their laudable search for increasingly effective ways of protecting the rights of the individual while promoting efficient enforcement of our criminal laws. However, unless we are shown other procedures which are at least as effective in apprising accused persons of their right of silence and in assuring a continuous opportunity to exercise it, the following safeguards must be observed.

At the outset, if a person in custody is to be subjected to interrogation, he must first be informed in clear and unequivocal terms that he has the right to remain silent. For those unaware of the privilege, the warning is needed simply to make them aware of it — the threshold requirement for an intelligent decision as to its exercise. More important, such a warning is an absolute prerequisite in overcoming the inherent pressures of the interrogation atmosphere. It is not just the subnormal or woefully ignorant who succumb to an interrogator's imprecations, whether implied or expressly stated, that the interrogation will continue until a confession is obtained or that silence in the face of accusation is itself damning and will bode ill when presented to a jury. Further, the warning will show the individual that his interrogators are prepared to recognize his privilege should he choose to exercise it.

The Fifth Amendment privilege is so fundamental to our system of constitutional rule and the expedient of giving an adequate warning as to the availability of the privilege so simple, we will not pause to inquire in individual cases whether the defendant was aware of his rights without a warning being given. Assessments of the knowledge the defendant possessed, based on information as to his age, education, intelligence, or prior contact with authorities, can never be more than speculation; a warning is a clearcut fact. More important, whatever the background of the person interrogated, a warning at the time of the interrogation is indispensable to overcome its pressures and to insure that the individual knows he is free to exercise the privilege at that point in time.

The warning of the right to remain silent must be accompanied by the explanation that anything said can and will be used against the individual in court. This warning is needed in order to make him aware not only of the privilege, but also of the consequences of forgoing it. It is only through an awareness of these consequences that there can be any assurance of real understanding and intelligent exercise of the privilege. Moreover, this warning may serve to make the individual more acutely aware that he is faced with a phase of the adversary system — that he is not in the presence of persons acting solely in his interest.

The circumstances surrounding in-custody interrogation can operate very quickly to overbear the will of one merely made aware of his privilege by his interrogators. Therefore, the right to have counsel present at the interrogation is indispensable to the protection of the Fifth Amendment privilege under the system we delineate today. Our aim is to assure that the individual's right to choose between silence and speech remains unfettered throughout the interrogation process. A once-stated warning, delivered by those who will conduct the interrogation, cannot itself suffice to that end among those who most require knowledge of their rights. A mere warning given by the interrogators is not alone sufficient to accomplish that end. . . . Even preliminary advice given to the accused by his own attorney can be swiftly overcome by the secret interrogation process. . . . Thus, the need for counsel to protect the Fifth Amendment privilege comprehends not merely a right to consult with counsel prior to questioning, but also to have counsel present during any questioning if the defendant so desires. . . .

Accordingly we hold that an individual held for interrogation must be clearly informed that he has the right to consult with a lawyer and to have the lawyer with him during interrogation under the system for protecting the privilege we delineate today. As with the warnings of the right to remain silent and that anything stated can be used in evidence against him, this warning is an absolute prerequisite to interrogation. No amount of circumstantial evidence that the person may have been aware of this right will suffice to stand in its stead. Only through such a warning is there ascertainable assurance that the accused was aware of this right. . . .

In order fully to apprise a person interrogated of the extent of his rights under this system . . . , it is necessary to warn him not only that he has the right to consult with an attorney, but also that if he is indigent a lawyer will be appointed to represent him. Without this additional warning, the admonition of the right to consult with counsel would often be understood as meaning only that he can consult with a lawyer if he has one or has the funds to obtain one. The warning of a right to counsel would be hollow if not couched in terms that would convey to the indigent — the person most often subjected to interrogation — the knowledge that he too has a right to have counsel present. As with the warnings of the right to remain silent and of the general right to counsel, only by effective and express explanation to the indigent of this right can there be assurance that he was truly in a position to exercise it.

Once warnings have been given, the subsequent procedure is clear. If the individual indicates in any manner, at any time prior to or during questioning, that he wishes to remain silent, the interrogation must cease. At this point he has shown that he intends to exercise his Fifth Amendment privilege; any statement taken after the person invokes his privilege cannot be other than the product of compulsion, subtle or otherwise. Without the right to cut off questioning, the setting of in-custody interrogation operates on the individual to overcome free choice in producing a statement after the privilege has been once invoked. If the individual states that he wants an attorney, the interrogation must cease until an attorney is present. At that time, the individual must have an opportunity to confer with the attorney and to have him present during any subsequent questioning. If the individual cannot obtain an attorney and he indicates that he wants one before speaking to police, they must respect his decision to remain silent. This does not mean, as some have suggested, that each police station must have a "station house lawyer" present at all times to advise prisoners. It does mean, however, that if police propose to interrogate a person they must make known to him that he is entitled to a lawyer and that if he cannot afford one, a lawyer will be provided for him prior to any interrogation. If authorities conclude that they will not provide counsel during a reasonable period of time in which investigation in the field is carried out, they may refrain from doing so without violating the person's Fifth Amendment privilege so long as they do not question him during that time.

If the interrogation continues without the presence of an attorney and a statement is taken, a heavy burden rests on the government to demonstrate that the defendant knowingly and intelligently waived his privilege against self-incrimination and his right to retained or appointed counsel. Escobedo v. Illinois, 378 U.S. 478, 490, n.14. This Court has always set high standards of proof for the waiver of constitutional rights, Johnson v. Zerbst, 304 U.S. 458 (1938), and we re-assert these standards as applied to in-custody interrogation. Since the State is responsible for establishing the isolated circumstances under which the interrogation takes place and has the only means of making available corroborated evidence of warnings given during incommunicado interrogation, the burden is rightly on its shoulders.

An express statement that the individual is willing to make a statement and does not want an attorney followed closely by a statement could constitute a waiver. But a valid waiver will not be presumed simply from the silence of the accused after warnings are given or simply from the fact that a confession was in fact eventually obtained. . . . Moreover, where in-custody interrogation is involved, there is no room for the contention that the privilege is waived if the individual answers some questions or gives some information on his own prior to invoking his right to remain silent when interrogated.

Whatever the testimony of the authorities as to waiver of rights by an accused, the fact of lengthy interrogation or incommunicado incarceration before a statement is made is strong evidence that the accused did not validly waive his rights. In these circumstances the fact that the individual eventually made a statement is consistent with the conclusion that the compelling influence of the interrogation finally forced him to do so. It is inconsistent with any notion of a voluntary relinquishment of the privilege. Moreover, any evidence that the accused was threatened, tricked, or cajoled into a waiver will, of course, show that the defendant did not voluntarily waive his privilege. The requirement of warnings and waiver of rights is a fundamental with respect to the Fifth Amendment privilege and not simply a preliminary ritual to existing methods of interrogation.

The warnings required and the waiver necessary in accordance with our opinion today are, in the absence of a fully effective equivalent, prerequisites to the admissibility of any statement made by a defendant. No distinction can be drawn between statements which are direct confessions and statements which amount to "admissions" of part or all of an offense. The privilege against self-incrimination protects the individual from being compelled to incriminate himself in any manner; it does not distinguish degrees of incrimination. . . .

The principles announced today deal with the protection which must be given to the privilege against self-incrimination when the individual is first subjected to police interrogation while in custody at the station or otherwise deprived of his freedom of action in any significant way. It is at this point that our adversary system of criminal proceedings commences, distinguishing itself at the outset from the inquisitorial system recognized in some countries. Under the system of warnings we delineate today or under any other system which may be devised and found effective, the safeguards to be erected about the privilege must come into play at this point.

Our decision is not intended to hamper the traditional function of police officers in investigating crime. . . . When an individual is in custody on probable cause, the police may, of course, seek out evidence in the field to be used at trial against him. Such investigation may include inquiry of persons not under restraint. General on-the-scene questioning as to facts surrounding a crime or other general questioning of citizens in the fact-finding process is not affected by our holding. It is an act of responsible citizenship for individuals to give whatever information they may have to aid in law enforcement. In such situations the compelling atmosphere inherent in the process of in-custody interrogation is not necessarily present.

In dealing with statements obtained through interrogation, we do not purport to find all confessions inadmissible. Confessions remain a proper element in law enforcement. Any statement given freely and voluntarily without any compelling influences is, of course, admissible in evidence. The fundamental import of the privilege while an individual is in custody is not whether he is allowed to talk to the police without the benefit of warnings and counsel, but whether he can be interrogated. There is no requirement that police stop a person who enters a police station and states that he wishes to confess to a crime, or a person who calls the police to offer a confession or any other statement he desires to make. Volunteered statements of any kind are not barred by the Fifth Amendment and their admissibility is not affected by our holding today. . . .

IV

A recurrent argument made in these cases is that society's need for interrogation outweighs the privilege. . . .

Over the years the Federal Bureau of Investigation has compiled an exemplary record of effective law enforcement while advising any suspect or arrested person, at the outset of an interview, that he is not required to make a statement, that any statement may be used against him in court, that the individual may obtain the services of an attorney of his own choice and, more recently, that he has a right to free counsel if he is unable to pay. . . .

The practice of the FBI can readily be emulated by state and local enforcement agencies. The argument that the FBI deals with different crimes than are dealt with by state authorities does not mitigate the significance of the FBI experience. . . .

V

Because of the nature of the problem and because of its recurrent significance in numerous cases, we have to this point discussed the relationship of the Fifth Amendment privilege to police interrogation without specific concentration on the facts of the cases before us. We turn now to these facts to consider the application to these cases of the constitutional principles discussed above. In each instance, we have concluded that statements were obtained from the defendant under circumstances that did not meet constitutional standards for protection of the privilege.

NO. 759. MIRANDA V. ARIZONA

On March 13, 1963, petitioner, Ernesto Miranda, was arrested at his home and taken in custody to a Phoenix police station. He was there identified by the complaining witness. The police then took him to "Interrogation Room No. 2" of the detective bureau. There he was questioned by two police officers. The officers admitted at trial that Miranda was not advised that he had a right to have an attorney present. Two hours later, the officers emerged from the interrogation room with a written confession signed by Miranda. At the top of the statement was a typed paragraph stating that the confession was made voluntarily, without threats or promises of immunity and "with full knowledge of my legal rights, understanding any statement I make may be used against me."[67]

At his trial before a jury, the written confession was admitted into evidence over the objection of defense counsel, and the officers testified to the prior oral confession made by Miranda during the interrogation. Miranda was found guilty of kidnapping and rape. . . .

We reverse. From the testimony of the officers and by the admission of respondent, it is clear that Miranda was not in any way apprised of his right to consult with an attorney and to have one present during the interrogation, nor was his right not to be compelled to incriminate himself effectively protected in any other manner. Without these warnings the statements were inadmissible. The mere fact that he signed a statement which contained a typed-in clause stating that he had "full knowledge" of his "legal rights" does not approach the knowing and intelligent waiver required to relinquish constitutional rights.

NO. 760. VIGNERA V. NEW YORK

[Vignera was interrogated by a detective about the robbery of a Brooklyn dress shop, and he admitted the crime. Hours later, an assistant district attorney also questioned Vignera, and his statement was transcribed. At trial, the judge did not allow Vignera's defense lawyer to ask the detective whether he ever warned Vignera about his right to counsel; the transcribed statement did not mention any warnings. Both the oral and transcribed statements were admitted, and Vignera was convicted. The Supreme Court reversed, because the record indicated that Vignera was not warned of his rights prior to questioning. — EDS.]

NO. 761. WESTOVER V. UNITED STATES

[Westover was arrested in Kansas City as a suspect in two local robberies as well as a felony crime in California. He was held for over 14 hours and interrogated at length by Kansas City police, who apparently did not warn him about his rights. Westover was then turned over to the FBI. After two and a half hours of further questioning, Westover signed confessions to two separate robberies in California. An FBI agent testified at trial that Westover was warned that he did not have to make a statement, that any statements made could be used against him, and that he had the right to a lawyer. Westover's signed confessions also contained language to the same effect. At trial in federal court, Westover's confessions were admitted, and he was convicted of the California robberies. The Supreme Court reversed, holding that, due to the initial custody and lengthy interrogation by Kansas City police, as well as the lack of an "articulated waiver of rights" before the FBI interrogation, "we cannot find that Westover knowingly and intelligently waived his rights to remain silent and his right to consult with counsel." — EDS.]

---

67. One of the officers testified that he read this paragraph to Miranda. Apparently, however, he did not do so until after Miranda had confessed orally.

NO. 584. CALIFORNIA V. STEWART

[Stewart was arrested, at his own house, as a suspect in a series of purse-snatchings, one of which caused the victim's death. An officer asked if he could search the house, and Stewart said, "Go ahead." The search found items taken in the robberies. Stewart was then taken to the police station and questioned nine separate times, mostly in isolation, over five days. During the ninth interrogation, Stewart admitted that he robbed the dead victim, but said he did not intend to hurt her. The record did not indicate whether Stewart was ever advised of his rights, and the officers who testified at trial did not say that he had been so advised. Stewart was convicted of robbery and first-degree murder and sentenced to death. The California Supreme Court reversed, based on *Escobedo*. The Supreme Court affirmed, stating "we will not presume" either effective warnings or a "knowing and intelligent" waiver "on a silent record." — EDS.]

[Mr. Justice Clark's opinion, dissenting in Nos. 759, 760, and 761, and concurring in the result in No. 584, is omitted.]

MR. JUSTICE HARLAN, whom MR. JUSTICE STEWART and MR. JUSTICE WHITE join, dissenting.

. . . The Court's opening contention, that the Fifth Amendment governs police station confessions, is perhaps not an impermissible extension of the law but it has little to commend itself in the present circumstances. Historically, the privilege against self-incrimination did not bear at all on the use of extra-legal confessions, for which distinct standards evolved; indeed, "the *history* of the two principles is wide apart, differing by one hundred years in origin, and derived through separate lines of precedents. . . ." 8 Wigmore, Evidence §2266, at 401 (McNaughton rev. 1961). Practice under the two doctrines has also differed in a number of important respects.[6] Even those who would readily enlarge the privilege must concede some linguistic difficulties since the Fifth Amendment in terms proscribes only compelling any person "in any criminal case to be a witness against himself."

. . . Having decided that the Fifth Amendment privilege does apply in the police station, the Court reveals that the privilege imposes more exacting restrictions than does the Fourteenth Amendment's voluntariness test. It then emerges . . . that the Fifth Amendment requires for an admissible confession that it be given by one distinctly aware of his right not to speak and shielded from "the compelling atmosphere" of interrogation. . . . From these key premises, the Court finally develops the safeguards of warning, counsel, and so forth. I do not believe these premises are sustained by precedents under the Fifth Amendment.

The more important premise is that pressure on the suspect must be eliminated though it be only the subtle influence of the atmosphere and surroundings. The Fifth Amendment, however, has never been thought to forbid *all* pressure to incriminate one's self in the situations covered by it. On the contrary, it has been held that failure to incriminate one's self can result in denial of removal of one's case from state to federal court, Maryland v. Soper, 270 U.S. 9; in refusal of a

---

6. Among the examples given in 8 Wigmore, Evidence §2266, at 401 (McNaughton rev. 1961), are these: the privilege applies to any witness, civil or criminal, but the confession rule protects only criminal defendants; the privilege deals only with compulsion, while the confession rule may exclude statements obtained by trick or promise; and where the privilege has been nullified — as by the English Bankruptcy Act — the confession rule may still operate.

military commission, Orloff v. Willoughby, 345 U.S. 83; in denial of a discharge in bankruptcy, Kaufman v. Hurwitz, 176 F.2d 210; and in numerous other adverse consequences. . . . This is not to say that short of jail or torture any sanction is permissible in any case; policy and history alike may impose sharp limits. See, e.g., Griffin v. California, 380 U.S. 609. However, the Court's unspoken assumption that *any* pressure violates the privilege is not supported by the precedents and it has failed to show why the Fifth Amendment prohibits that relatively mild pressure the Due Process Clause permits.

The Court appears similarly wrong in thinking that precise knowledge of one's rights is a settled prerequisite under the Fifth Amendment to the loss of its protections. . . . No Fifth Amendment precedent is cited for the Court's contrary view. . . .

A closing word must be said about the Assistance of Counsel Clause of the Sixth Amendment, which is never expressly relied on by the Court but whose judicial precedents turn out to be linchpins of the confession rules announced today. . . . While the Court finds no pertinent difference between judicial proceedings and police interrogation, I believe the differences are so vast as to disqualify wholly the Sixth Amendment precedents as suitable analogies in the present cases.

The only attempt in this Court to carry the right to counsel into the station house occurred in *Escobedo*, the Court repeating several times that that stage was no less "critical" than trial itself. See 378 U.S., 485-488. This is hardly persuasive when we consider that a grand jury inquiry, the filing of a certiorari petition, and certainly the purchase of narcotics by an undercover agent from a prospective defendant may all be equally "critical" yet provision of counsel and advice on that score have never been thought compelled by the Constitution in such cases. The sound reason why this right is so freely extended for a criminal trial is the severe injustice risked by confronting an untrained defendant with a range of technical points of law, evidence, and tactics familiar to the prosecutor but not to himself. This danger shrinks markedly in the police station where indeed the lawyer in fulfilling his professional responsibilities of necessity may become an obstacle to truthfinding. . . .

Examined as an expression of public policy, the Court's new regime proves so dubious that there can be no due compensation for its weakness in constitutional law. . . .

Without at all subscribing to the generally black picture of police conduct painted by the Court, I think it must be frankly recognized at the outset that police questioning allowable under due process precedents may inherently entail some pressure on the suspect and may seek advantage in his ignorance or weaknesses. The atmosphere and questioning techniques, proper and fair though they be, can in themselves exert a tug on the suspect to confess, and in this light "[t]o speak of any confessions of crime made after arrest as being 'voluntary' or 'uncoerced' is somewhat inaccurate, although traditional. A confession is wholly and incontestably voluntary only if a guilty person gives himself up to the law and becomes his own accuser." Ashcraft v. Tennessee, 322 U.S. 143, 161 (Jackson, J., dissenting). Until today, the role of the Constitution has been only to sift out *undue* pressure, not to assure spontaneous confessions. . . .

What the Court largely ignores is that its rules impair, if they will not eventually serve wholly to frustrate, an instrument of law enforcement that has long and quite reasonably been thought worth the price paid for it. There can be little doubt that the Court's new code would markedly decrease the number of confessions. To warn the suspect that he may remain silent and remind him that his confession may be used in court are minor obstructions. To require also an express waiver by the suspect and an end to questioning whenever he demurs must heavily handicap questioning. And to suggest or provide counsel for the suspect simply invites the end of the interrogation. . . .

While passing over the costs and risks of its experiment, the Court portrays the evils of normal police questioning in terms which I think are exaggerated. . . . [I]nterrogation is no doubt often inconvenient and unpleasant for the suspect. However, it is no less so for a man to be arrested and jailed, to have his house searched, or to stand trial in court, yet all this may properly happen to the most innocent given probable cause, a warrant, or an indictment. Society has always paid a stiff price for law and order, and peaceful interrogation is not one of the dark moments of the law.

This brief statement of the competing considerations seems to me ample proof that the Court's preference is highly debatable at best and therefore not to be read into the Constitution. However, it may make the analysis more graphic to consider the actual facts of one of the four cases reversed by the Court. Miranda v. Arizona serves best, being neither the hardest nor easiest of the four under the Court's standards.

On March 3, 1963, an 18-year-old girl was kidnapped and forcibly raped near Phoenix, Arizona. Ten days later, on the morning of March 13, petitioner Miranda was arrested and taken to the police station. At this time Miranda was 23 years old, indigent, and educated to the extent of completing half the ninth grade. He had "an emotional illness" of the schizophrenic type, according to the doctor who eventually examined him; the doctor's report also stated that Miranda was "alert and oriented as to time, place, and person," intelligent within normal limits, competent to stand trial, and sane within the legal definition. At the police station, the victim picked Miranda out of a lineup, and two officers then took him into a separate room to interrogate him, starting about 11:30 a.m. Though at first denying his guilt, within a short time Miranda gave a detailed oral confession and then wrote out in his own hand and signed a brief statement admitting and describing the crime. All this was accomplished in two hours or less without any force, threats or promises and — I will assume this though the record is uncertain . . . — without any effective warnings at all.

Miranda's oral and written confessions are now held inadmissible under the Court's new rules. One is entitled to feel astonished that the Constitution can be read to produce this result. These confessions were obtained during brief, daytime questioning conducted by two officers and unmarked by any of the traditional indicia of coercion. They assured a conviction for a brutal and unsettling crime. . . . There was, in sum, a legitimate purpose, no perceptible unfairness, and certainly little risk of injustice in the interrogation. Yet the resulting confessions, and the responsible course of police practice they represent, are to be sacrificed to the Court's own finespun conception of fairness. . . .

MR. JUSTICE WHITE, with whom MR. JUSTICE HARLAN and MR. JUSTICE STEWART join, dissenting. . . .

. . . To reach the result announced on the grounds it does, the Court must stay within the confines of the Fifth Amendment, which forbids self-incrimination only if *compelled*. . . . [T]he Court concedes that it cannot truly know what occurs during custodial questioning, because of the innate secrecy of such proceedings. It extrapolates a picture of what it conceives to be the norm from police investigatorial manuals, published in 1959 and 1962 or earlier, without any attempt to allow for adjustments in police practices that may have occurred in the wake of more recent decisions of state appellate tribunals or this Court. But even if the relentless application of the described procedures could lead to involuntary confessions, it most assuredly does not follow that each and every case will disclose this kind of interrogation or this kind of consequence.[2] Insofar as appears from the Court's opinion, it has not examined a single transcript of any police interrogation, let alone the interrogation that took place in any one of these cases which it decides today. Judged by any of the standards for empirical investigation utilized in the social sciences the factual basis for the Court's premise is patently inadequate.

Although in the Court's view in-custody interrogation is inherently coercive, the Court says that the spontaneous product of the coercion of arrest and detention is still to be deemed voluntary. An accused, arrested on probable cause, may blurt out a confession which will be admissible despite the fact that he is alone and in custody, without any showing that he had any notion of his right to remain silent or of the consequences of his admission. Yet, under the Court's rule, if the police ask him a single question such as "Do you have anything to say?" or "Did you kill your wife?" his response, if there is one, has somehow been compelled, even if the accused has been clearly warned of his right to remain silent. Common sense informs us to the contrary. . . .

Today's result would not follow even if it were agreed that to some extent custodial interrogation is inherently coercive. . . . The test has been whether the totality of circumstances deprived the defendant of a "free choice to admit, to deny, or to refuse to answer," Lisenba v. California, 314 U.S. 219, 241, and whether physical or psychological coercion was of such a degree that "the defendant's will was overborne at the time he confessed," Haynes v. Washington, 373 U.S. 503, 513; Lynumn v. Illinois, 372 U.S. 528, 534. The duration and nature of incommunicado custody, the presence or absence of advice concerning the defendant's constitutional rights, and the granting or refusal of requests to communicate with lawyers, relatives or friends have all been rightly regarded as important data bearing on the basic inquiry. . . . But it has never been suggested, until today, that such questioning was so coercive and accused persons so lacking in hardihood that the very first response to the very first question following the commencement of custody must be conclusively presumed to be the product of an overborne will. . . .

On the other hand, even if one assumed that there was an adequate factual basis for the conclusion that all confessions obtained during in-custody interrogation are the product of compulsion, the rule propounded by the Court would still be irrational, for, apparently, it is only if the accused is also warned of his right to counsel and waives both that right and the right against self-incrimination that the inherent compulsiveness of interrogation disappears. But if the defendant may not

---

2. In fact, the type of sustained interrogation described by the Court appears to be the exception rather than the rule. A survey of 399 cases in one city found that in almost half of the cases the interrogation lasted less than 30 minutes. Barrett, Police Practices and the Law — From Arrest to Release or Charge, 50 Calif. L. Rev. 11, 41-45 (1962). Questioning tends to be confused and sporadic and is usually concentrated on confrontations with witnesses or new items of evidence, as these are obtained by officers conducting the investigation. See generally LaFave, Arrest: The Decision to Take a Suspect into Custody 386 (1965); ALI, A Model Code of Pre-Arraignment Procedure, Commentary §5.01, at 17, n. 4 (Tent. Draft No. 1, 1966).

answer without a warning a question such as "Where were you last night?" without having his answer be a compelled one, how can the Court ever accept his negative answer to the question of whether he wants to consult his retained counsel or counsel whom the court will appoint? And why if counsel is present and the accused nevertheless confesses, or counsel tells the accused to tell the truth, and that is what the accused does, is the situation any less coercive insofar as the accused is concerned? The Court apparently realizes its dilemma of foreclosing questioning without the necessary warnings but at the same time permitting the accused, sitting in the same chair in front of the same policemen, to waive his right to consult an attorney. It expects, however, that the accused will not often waive the right; and if it is claimed that he has, the State faces a severe, if not impossible burden of proof. . . .

In sum, for all the Court's expounding on the menacing atmosphere of police interrogation procedures, it has failed to supply any foundation for the conclusions it draws or the measures it adopts.

. . . The obvious underpinning of the Court's decision is a deep-seated distrust of all confessions. As the Court declares that the accused may not be interrogated without counsel present, absent a waiver of the right to counsel, and as the Court all but admonishes the lawyer to advise the accused to remain silent, the result adds up to a judicial judgment that evidence from the accused should not be used against him in any way, whether compelled or not. This is the not so subtle overtone of the opinion — that it is inherently wrong for the police to gather evidence from the accused himself. . . . I see nothing wrong or immoral, and certainly nothing unconstitutional, in the police's asking a suspect whom they have reasonable cause to arrest whether or not he killed his wife or in confronting him with the evidence on which the arrest was based, at least where he has been plainly advised that he may remain completely silent. . . .

Much of the trouble with the Court's new rule is that it will operate indiscriminately in all criminal cases, regardless of the severity of the crime or the circumstances involved. It applies to every defendant, whether the professional criminal or one committing a crime of momentary passion who is not part and parcel of organized crime. It will slow down the investigation and the apprehension of confederates in those cases where time is of the essence, . . . and some of those involving organized crime. In the latter context the lawyer who arrives may also be the lawyer for the defendant's colleagues and can be relied upon to insure that no breach of the organization's security takes place even though the accused may feel that the best thing he can do is to cooperate. . . .

Applying the traditional standards to the cases before the Court, I would hold these confessions voluntary.

NOTES AND QUESTIONS

1. Compare *Bram* and *Miranda*. Which, in your view, is "better" and why? Which is more realistic? Which better relates the remedy provided to the wrong done? Which provides more serious protections for the accused? In this regard, consider the contemporary role of plea bargaining, in which the accused and the state negotiate a plea where the accused "trades" his procedural protections for sentencing or charging concessions by the state. The normal outcome is a plea of guilty that is

generally tantamount to a legally binding confession. The Supreme Court has legitimized this practice, Brady v. United States, 397 U.S. 742 (1970), but how would it have fared under *Bram*? How *should* it fare today?

2. Chief Justice Warren begins his argument in *Miranda* with a discussion of the ongoing problem of physical brutality in police interrogation. Does that problem justify the Court's holding? It would seem more natural to conclude that physical force and psychological ploys are substitutes for one another — the more the police rely on one, the less they are likely to rely on the other. Physical force was already illegal before *Miranda*; Warren's opinion seems designed to make psychological ploys illegal as well. Is that likely to diminish police brutality, or to increase its frequency?

3. One of the motivating factors in *Miranda* appears to have been the Court's concern that police interrogation practices were something of a mystery. Assuming the concern was valid, what was the proper response? Why not require video- and/ or audiotaping of interrogation sessions rather than the Court's warnings and waiver restrictions? See, e.g., Paul G. Cassell, *Miranda*'s Social Cost: An Empirical Assessment, 90 Nw. U. L. Rev. 387, 486 (1996) (making this proposal). Indeed, if trial judges were unable to uncover the truth about police interrogation before *Miranda*, why should one assume that they could uncover the truth about *Miranda* waivers afterward?

Alaska and Minnesota have required the taping of interrogations by court decision. Stephen v. State, 711 P.2d 1156 (Alaska 1985); State v. Scales, 518 N.W.2d 587 (Minn. 1994). Illinois requires it by statute for certain crimes (mostly homicides). Ill. Comp. Stat. Ann. §5/103-2.1. And an increasing number of police agencies tape interrogations on their own. According to Cassell, most officers with experience with videotaping approve of the practice, and England apparently has had success with videotaping.

4. Speaking of *Miranda* waivers, consider Justice White's argument: All the same factors that make police interrogation "inherently coercive" must apply equally to the suspect who waives his *Miranda* rights. Does it follow that *Miranda* waivers should be almost impossible to show? In practice, that has not been the case: Something in the vicinity of 80 percent of suspects routinely waive their *Miranda* rights and talk to the police. See Richard A. Leo, The Impact of *Miranda* Revisited, 86 J. Crim. L. & Criminology 621, 653 (1996). Is that statistic evidence for the proposition that *Miranda* has not proved very costly, or does it suggest that courts do not rigorously enforce *Miranda*'s requirements?

5. The Court suggests that the standards it is imposing on the states are not that burdensome, as proven by the fact that the FBI has labored successfully under similar restrictions for years. As Justice Harlan pointed out, in a portion of his dissent not excerpted above, the Court was not quite right about the analogy: The FBI's pre-*Miranda* practice was not to require waivers, and whenever suspects invoked their rights, agents were free to try to persuade them to change their minds. Putting these differences to one side, how cogent is the Court's analogy? The FBI does not deal with routine street crimes; that is the job of local police departments. Meanwhile, the FBI does deal with organized crime and white-collar crime, areas in which suspects are likely to be more sophisticated than those whom local police must interrogate. How do these differences play out when it comes to a proper analysis of police interrogation?

6. If *Miranda* is sound policy for domestic police interrogation, is it also sound policy for military interrogation of suspected terrorists? Terrorists are different from most criminal suspects: smarter than the average street criminal, and vastly more committed to their enterprise. If *Miranda*'s rules are applied to them, the Jose Padillas of the world will ask for a lawyer sometime soon after questioning begins — whereupon questioning will cease, if *Miranda*'s rules are followed. That may make men like Padilla (an American citizen accused of conspiring with fellow Al Qaeda members to set off a "dirty bomb" in an American city, and eventually convicted of conspiracy to support terrorism — he is now serving a 17-year prison sentence) unconvictable. Worse, it may make their crimes unpreventable. And by holding the government to that standard, we risk encouraging precisely the kind of game-playing we saw in Padilla's case — shortly after his arrest, he was reclassified as an enemy combatant in order to evade various domestic criminal procedure doctrines. Finally, interrogators facing such suspects, if barred from using fraud and deceit to get what they want, may be tempted to use force.

Are these claims simply rationalizations for an "anything goes" policy — the sort of policy that produced the interrogation abuses at Abu Ghraib prison in Iraq? Or are these sound arguments for restricting *Miranda*? Might these same arguments apply to some categories of domestic criminals? Note Justice White's complaint that the Court's formula takes no account of differences among crimes, or differences among criminals. Should police interrogation rules be different for murder suspects than for securities fraud suspects? Which group should receive more legal protection?

7. *Miranda* is not the only legal doctrine that requires police officers to warn detained suspects of their rights prior to questioning them. Under Article 36 of the Vienna Convention on Consular Relations, which the United States ratified in 1969, police must notify officials in the relevant foreign consulate when they arrest a foreign national, and must inform the arrestee that he has a right to have officials in his consulate notified of his detention. In Sanchez-Llamas v. Oregon, 548 U.S. 331 (2006), however, the Court ruled that a violation of these requirements does *not* require exclusion of the evidence obtained. As Chief Justice Roberts wrote:

> . . . The exclusionary rule as we know it is an entirely American legal creation. More than 40 years after the drafting of the Convention, the automatic exclusionary rule applied in our courts is still "universally rejected" by other countries. Bradley, *Mapp Goes Abroad*, 52 Case W. Res. L. Rev. 375, 399-400 (2001). It is implausible that other signatories to the Convention thought it to require a remedy that nearly all refuse to recognize as a matter of domestic law. . . .

548 U.S., at 343. Justice Breyer's dissent conceded that "a *Miranda*-style automatic exclusionary rule" would be inappropriate, but argued for a *discretionary* rule of exclusion rule like the one that applies in many other countries.

8. Though *Miranda* displaced the due process voluntariness test as the primary constitutional limit on police interrogation, voluntariness still matters in two distinct ways. Waivers of the *Miranda* right must be, among other things, voluntary. (*Miranda* waivers are discussed below, at pages 828-856.) And the due process requirement of voluntariness continues to apply to confessions — in addition to *Miranda*, and in addition to the Sixth Amendment right granted by Massiah v. United States, 377 U.S. 201 (1964). (*Massiah* is excerpted supra, at pages 767-771.)

In the wake of *Miranda*, some wondered whether the due process voluntariness requirement might extend more broadly than *Miranda*'s elaborate rule structure, in the following respect: Plainly, *Miranda* was limited to police conduct; its rules do not apply to questioning by private parties. That conclusion is not as obvious with respect to voluntariness. If the key to the voluntariness requirement is ensuring that admissible confessions are not the product of "overborne" wills, one might imagine that the requirement would apply regardless of the source of the pressure that overpowered the defendant.

The Supreme Court faced this question in Colorado v. Connelly, 479 U.S. 157 (1986). The defendant in *Connelly* approached a Denver, Colorado police officer and confessed to a murder. The officer to whom this confession was made immediately gave the defendant his *Miranda* warnings, whereupon he confessed again. The confession was thoroughly corroborated; there was no doubt as to its accuracy. The day after he delivered this confession, the defendant "stated that 'voices' had told him to come to Denver and that he had followed the directions of these voices in confessing." Id., at 161. Later, the defendant described what he heard as "the voice of God." He was examined by a psychiatrist and diagnosed as a schizophrenic.

The defendant claimed that these voices rendered his confession involuntary. (Ask yourself: Could anything be more coercive than the "voice of God" ordering someone to confess to a crime?) The Supreme Court held otherwise:

> . . . [T]he cases considered by this Court over the 50 years since Brown v. Mississippi [, 297 U.S. 278 (1936),] have focused upon the crucial element of police overreaching. While each confession case has turned on its own set of factors justifying the conclusion that police conduct was oppressive, all have contained a substantial element of coercive police conduct. Absent police conduct causally related to the confession, there is simply no basis for concluding that any state actor has deprived a criminal defendant of due process of law. Respondent correctly notes that as interrogators have turned to more subtle forms of psychological persuasion, courts have found the mental condition of the defendant a more significant factor in the "voluntariness" calculus. But this fact does not justify a conclusion that a defendant's mental condition, by itself and apart from its relation to official coercion, should ever dispose of the inquiry into constitutional "voluntariness."

479 U.S., at 163-164.

9. Is there a middle ground between the dictates of *Miranda* and the awkwardness of the *Bram* voluntariness test to judge the admissibility of confessions obtained through pretrial interrogation? Note that in *Miranda* the Court said that equally effective procedures to ensure the Fifth Amendment's protections could supplant the Court's requirements. Yet before "equally effective" procedures can be provided, one must know the answer to this question: "Equally effective" as to what?

The answer to that question *cannot* be to protect the unfettered exercise of the suspect's "free will." Every time a person provides incriminating statements, there is *some* reason for doing so that acts on the defendant's "will." To be sure, some distinctions can be made. There are, for example, many reasons why we do not countenance the use of serious physical abuse to induce statements, but does it follow from that proposition that *no* incentive to speak should ever be brought to bear on the suspect by the state? If you think it does *not* follow, again you must try to construct what *does*. In that regard, consider the following short excerpt from a remarkable article written over 70 years ago by Professor Kauper. Bear in mind that Professor Kauper was writing prior to the "criminal procedure revolution," and also that his focus was to eliminate brutal police practices. Nonetheless, consider whether his proposal has any relevance to contemporary society.

KAUPER, JUDICIAL EXAMINATION OF THE ACCUSED — A REMEDY FOR THE THIRD DEGREE, 30 MICH. L. REV. 1224, 1239-1241 (1932): The remedy proposed consists of two essentials:

(1) That the accused be promptly produced before a magistrate for interrogation; and,

(2) That the interrogation be supported by the threat that refusal to answer questions of the magistrate will be used against the accused at the trial.

It is submitted that the two features of the proposed plan must be linked together. The magistrate must have power to interrogate the prisoner. The present system which allows the accused an opportunity to make a statement but denies the magistrate power to ask questions is not effective for the purpose of securing information. And the power to interrogate must be supported by some compulsion to answer questions; otherwise it will be rendered impotent. Neither is the compulsion afforded by the right to comment on *failure to testify at the trial* sufficient. The comment must be upon the prisoner's *refusal to answer questions at the interrogation*. It is true that some writers have asserted that the problem of the police third degree would be solved if the judge and prosecutor were given the right to comment on the prisoner's failure to testify at his trial. But analysis of that proposition makes the conclusion appear to be a non sequitur. The possibility that at the trial an inference of guilt may be drawn from the accused's silence is hardly equivalent in the eyes of the police to a confession or other valuable information obtained shortly after arrest. In other words, making criminal procedure at the trial more effective against the accused does not satisfy police motives that demand interrogation immediately upon arrest. . . .

The plan proposed of requiring prompt interrogation by a magistrate supported by the threat of comment on failure to answer carries considerable promise. The plan necessarily involves prompt production of the accused before a magistrate. This is a sine qua non in the mitigation of third degree abuses, for so long as prisoners are in the control of officers there is a temptation to resort to third degree practices.

The plan provides an *immediate* opportunity for questioning the accused while the pursuit is still hot and the clues are yet fresh. By warning the accused that the whole record of the interrogation will go to the trial court, so that his silence in refusing to answer questions or make explanations will be used with telling effect against him before the jury, a strong psychic pressure will induce him to break his silence. Nor should it be forgotten that the larger number of those who are arrested are willing to speak and answer questions.[82] Even the fact of a false statement made

---

82. "In Washtenaw County, Michigan, of the 312 judgments of the county court in criminal cases in one year, 305 were on pleas of guilty. The prosecuting attorney's explanation of his success in obtaining so many confessions of guilt was his practice of himself interviewing every person arrested on a felony charge immediately after the arrest while he was still excited and before he had opportunity to consult

by a prisoner after arrest in order to cover his guilt can be used against him at the trial often with as much effectiveness as a truthful incriminating statement. Questioned immediately upon arrest, the accused does not have time to work out a coherent fabricated story or defense alibi. From the viewpoint of police psychology it appears that inauguration of a scheme of magisterial interrogation will greatly weaken the police motive for private interrogation since that motive will find vicarious expression in a substituted device. Viewing the problem historically, Dean Pound ascribes the extra-legal development of the "unhappy system of police examination" in the United States to the sloughing off by justices of the peace of their police powers, including examination of the accused, thereby leaving "a gap which in practice had to be filled outside of the law."[83] The proposed plan would fill the gap which resulted from the differentiation in function between magistrate and police with the effect of forcing the police to adopt the system of extra-legal interrogation. It would vest the power of interrogation in officers who are better qualified to exercise the power of interrogation fairly and effectively. . . .

2. The Scope of *Miranda*

Miranda held that incriminating statements made in response to custodial interrogation were presumptively "compelled" for purposes of the Fifth Amendment privilege, and hence inadmissible. But the compulsion is only presumptive, not automatic — plainly, Chief Justice Warren's majority opinion contemplated that some suspects would waive their *Miranda* rights.

Some, but probably not many. The language in Warren's opinion suggested that valid *Miranda* waivers would be rare. Consider:

> In dealing with custodial interrogation, we will not presume that a defendant has been effectively apprised of his rights and that his privilege against self-incrimination has been adequately safeguarded on a record that does not show that any warnings have been given or that any effective alternative has been employed. Nor can a knowing and intelligent waiver of these rights be assumed on a silent record.

Id., at 498.

The *Miranda* majority also indicated that the state would have to meet a "heavy burden" to demonstrate waiver:

> An express statement that the individual is willing to make a statement and does not want an attorney followed closely by a statement could constitute a waiver. But a valid waiver will not be presumed simply from the silence of the accused after warnings are given or simply from the fact that a confession was in fact eventually obtained.

Id., at 475.

---

with a lawyer. In that way, the prosecutor said, he got the truth. None of the confessions were repudiated in court nor did any of the 305 defendants make allegations of mistreatment. If all be as it appears, that prompt interrogation produced justice." John Barker Waite, 30 Mich. L. Rev. 54 at 59 (1931).

83. Criminal Justice in America 88 (1930). See also Wickersham Comm. Rep. No. 8, pp. 9, 10 (1930).

> [T]he fact of lengthy interrogation or incommunicado incarceration before a state-
> ment is made is strong evidence that the accused did not validly waive his
> rights. . . . Moreover, any evidence that the accused was threatened, tricked, or
> cajoled into a waiver will, of course, show that the defendant did not voluntarily waive
> his privilege.

Id., at 476.

Given such language, it seemed natural to assume that *Miranda* waivers (and consequently, police station confessions) would not be common. But they *are* common. The best study to date appears in Richard A. Leo, The Impact of *Miranda* Revisited, 86 J. Crim. L. & Criminology 621 (1996). Of 182 interrogations observed in three California jurisdictions, only 38 suspects — 21 percent — invoked their *Miranda* rights; the rest waived their rights and agreed to talk to the police. (Interestingly, only two of the 38 invocations came after questioning had begun. The rest occurred immediately after the suspect received his *Miranda* warnings.) See id., at 653. Other studies have generated similar numbers. See, e.g., Paul G. Cassell & Bret S. Hayman, Police Interrogation in the 1990s: An Empirical Study of the Effects of *Miranda*, 43 UCLA L. Rev. 839 (1996). As you read the material that follows, ask yourself what those numbers mean. Is *Miranda* working as it should? Is it a sham? Whom does it protect? Who is left unprotected?

a.   *"Custody"*

Miranda has consistently been interpreted to apply only to custodial interrogations, but "custody" has been given a functional definition. For example, in Orozco v. Texas, 394 U.S. 324 (1969), the Court applied *Miranda* to the questioning of a suspect in his bedroom at 4:00 a.m. by four police. The Court also applied *Miranda* to the testimony of a psychiatrist at the penalty stage of a capital case based on his psychiatric examination of the defendant where the defendant was not given the *Miranda* warnings prior to the examination. Estelle v. Smith, 451 U.S. 454 (1981). In contrast, the Court found no violation of *Miranda* in Oregon v. Mathiason, 429 U.S. 492 (1977), and California v. Beheler, 463 U.S. 1121 (1983), where the defendants voluntarily went to the station houses, were not under arrest, and gave confessions there. Nor has it been applied to grand jury witnesses. United States v. Mandujano, 425 U.S. 564 (1976). Nor is *Miranda* applicable when an investigation has focused on a suspect but the police have not yet made an arrest. Beckwith v. United States, 425 U.S. 341 (1976).

These cases left the meaning of "custody" uncertain. Berkemer v. McCarty, 468 U.S. 420 (1984), offered some clarification. The facts in *Berkemer* were as follows:

> . . . On the evening of March 31, 1980, Trooper Williams of the Ohio State Highway
> Patrol observed respondent's car weaving in and out of a lane on Interstate Highway
> 270. After following the car for two miles, Williams forced respondent to stop and
> asked him to get out of the vehicle. When respondent complied, Williams noticed that
> he was having difficulty standing. At that point, "Williams concluded that [respon-
> dent] would be charged with a traffic offense and, therefore, his freedom to leave the
> scene was terminated." However, respondent was not told that he would be taken into
> custody. Williams then asked respondent to perform a field sobriety test, commonly
> known as a "balancing test." Respondent could not do so without falling.

While still at the scene of the traffic stop, Williams asked respondent whether he had been using intoxicants. Respondent replied that "he had consumed two beers and had smoked several joints of marijuana a short time before." Respondent's speech was slurred, and Williams had difficulty understanding him. Williams thereupon formally placed respondent under arrest and transported him in the patrol car to the Franklin County Jail.

468 U.S., at 423. By an 8-1 vote (Justice Stevens did not reach the issue), the Court concluded that these facts do not amount to "custody" for purposes of *Miranda*:

Two features of an ordinary traffic stop mitigate the danger that a person questioned will be induced "to speak where he would not otherwise do so freely," Miranda v. Arizona, 384 U.S., at 467. First, detention of a motorist pursuant to a traffic stop is presumptively temporary and brief. The vast majority of roadside detentions last only a few minutes. A motorist's expectations, when he sees a policeman's light flashing behind him, are that he will be obliged to spend a short period of time answering questions and waiting while the officer checks his license and registration, that he may then be given a citation, but that in the end he most likely will be allowed to continue on his way. In this respect, questioning incident to an ordinary traffic stop is quite different from stationhouse interrogation, which frequently is prolonged, and in which the detainee often is aware that questioning will continue until he provides his interrogators the answers they seek. See id., at 451.

Second, circumstances associated with the typical traffic stop are not such that the motorist feels completely at the mercy of the police. To be sure, the aura of authority surrounding an armed, uniformed officer and the knowledge that the officer has some discretion in deciding whether to issue a citation, in combination, exert some pressure on the detainee to respond to questions. But other aspects of the situation substantially offset these forces. Perhaps most importantly, the typical traffic stop is public, at least to some degree. Passersby, on foot or in other cars witness the interaction of officer and motorist. This exposure to public view both reduces the ability of an unscrupulous policeman to use illegitimate means to elicit self-incriminating statements and diminishes the motorist's fear that, if he does not cooperate, he will be subjected to abuse. The fact that the detained motorist typically is confronted by only one or at most two policemen further mutes his sense of vulnerability. In short, the atmosphere surrounding an ordinary traffic stop is substantially less "police dominated" than that surrounding the kinds of interrogation at issue in *Miranda* itself, see 384 U.S., at 445, 491-498. . . .

In both of these respects, the usual traffic stop is more analogous to a so-called "*Terry* stop," see Terry v. Ohio, 392 U.S. 1 (1968), than to a formal arrest. Under the Fourth Amendment, we have held, a policeman who lacks probable cause but whose "observations lead him reasonably to suspect" that a particular person has committed, is committing, or is about to commit a crime, may detain that person briefly in order to "investigate the circumstances that provoke suspicion." United States v. Brignoni-Ponce, 422 U.S. 873, 881 (1975). "[The] stop and inquiry must be 'reasonably related in scope to the justification for their initiation.'" Ibid. (quoting Terry v. Ohio, supra, at 29.) Typically, this means that the officer may ask the detainee a moderate number of questions to determine his identity and to try to obtain information confirming or dispelling the officer's suspicions. But the detainee is not obliged to respond. And, unless the detainee's answers provide the officer with probable cause to arrest him, he must then be released. The comparatively nonthreatening character of detentions of this sort explains the absence of any suggestion in our opinions that *Terry* stops are subject to the dictates of *Miranda*. The similarly noncoercive aspect of ordinary traffic stops prompts us to hold that persons temporarily detained pursuant to such stops are not "in custody" for the purposes of *Miranda*.

468 U.S., at 437-440. Elsewhere in his opinion for the Court in *Berkemer*, Justice Marshall made clear that once a suspect is arrested, *Miranda*'s restrictions apply — no matter how minor the crime that prompts the arrest.

After *Berkemer*, *Terry* stops (although they *are* "seizures" under the Fourth Amendment) do not implicate *Miranda*, while arrests do. Note the practical importance of this line: A great many encounters between police officers and citizens begin with a *Terry* stop and "ripen" into an arrest as the officer obtains incriminating information, often through conversation with the suspect. If *Miranda* applied whenever a suspect was "seized," those encounters might look very different: The officer would have to precede any conversation (and presumably any request for consent to search) with the *Miranda* warnings. *Berkemer* means that these street encounters will continue to be governed solely by a fairly flexible body of Fourth Amendment law, without any interference from Fifth Amendment doctrine.

Is this the right answer? Are brief street stops really "comparatively nonthreatening"? What does this test mean in other contexts? Consider Minnesota v. Murphy, 465 U.S. 420 (1984):

In 1974, Marshall Murphy was twice questioned by Minneapolis Police concerning the rape and murder of a teenage girl. No charges were then brought. In 1980, in connection with a prosecution for criminal sexual conduct arising out of an unrelated incident, Murphy pleaded guilty to a reduced charge of false imprisonment. He was sentenced to a prison term of 16 months, which was suspended, and three years' probation. The terms of Murphy's probation required, among other things, that he participate in a treatment program for sexual offenders at Alpha House, report to his probation officer as directed, and be truthful with the probation officer "in all matters." Failure to comply with these conditions, Murphy was informed, could result in his return to the sentencing court for a probation revocation hearing.

Murphy met with his probation officer at her office approximately once a month, and his probation continued without incident until July 1981, when the officer learned that he had abandoned the treatment program. The probation officer then wrote to Murphy and informed him that failure to set up a meeting would "result in an immediate request for a warrant." . . . At a meeting in late July, the officer agreed not to seek revocation of probation for nonparticipation in the treatment program since Murphy was employed and doing well in other areas.

In September 1981, an Alpha House counselor informed the probation officer that, during the course of treatment, Murphy had admitted to a rape and murder in 1974. After discussions with her superior, the officer determined that the police should have this information. She then wrote to Murphy and asked him to contact her to discuss a treatment plan for the remainder of his probationary period. Although she did not contact the police before the meeting, the probation officer knew in advance that she would report any incriminating statements.

Upon receipt of the letter, Murphy arranged to meet with his probation officer in her office on September 28, 1981. The officer opened the meeting by telling Murphy about the information she had received from the Alpha House counselor and expressing her belief that this information evinced his continued need for treatment. Murphy became angry about what he considered to be a breach of his confidences and stated that he "felt like calling a lawyer." The probation officer replied that Murphy would have to deal with that problem outside the office; for the moment, their primary concern was the relationship between the crimes that Murphy had admitted to the Alpha House counselor and the incident that led to his conviction for false imprisonment.

During the course of the meeting, Murphy denied the false imprisonment charge, admitted that he had committed the rape and murder, and attempted to persuade the probation officer that further treatment was unnecessary because several extenuating circumstances explained the prior crimes. At the conclusion of the meeting, the officer told Murphy that she had a duty to relay the information to the authorities and encouraged him to turn himself in. Murphy then left the office. Two days later, Murphy called his probation officer and told her that he had been advised by counsel not to surrender himself to the police. The officer then procured the issuance of an arrest and detention order from the judge who had sentenced Murphy on the false imprisonment charge. On October 29, 1981, a State grand jury returned an indictment charging Murphy with first-degree murder.

465 U.S., at 422-425. The Court found *Miranda* inapplicable:

> . . . [I]t is clear that Murphy was not "in custody" for purposes of receiving *Miranda* protection since there was no "'formal arrest or restraint on freedom of movement' of the degree associated with a formal arrest." California v. Beheler, 463 U.S. 1121, 1125 (1983) (per curiam) (quoting Oregon v. Mathiason, 429 U.S., at 495). . . .
>
> Even a cursory comparison of custodial interrogation and probation interviews reveals the inaptness of the . . . analogy to *Miranda*. Custodial arrest is said to convey to the suspect a message that he has no choice but to submit to the officers' will and to confess. Miranda v. Arizona, 384 U.S., at 456-457. It is unlikely that a probation interview, arranged by appointment at a mutually convenient time, would give rise to a similar impression. Moreover, custodial arrest thrusts an individual into "an unfamiliar atmosphere" or "an interrogation environment . . . created for no purpose other than to subjugate the individual to the will of his examiner." Id., at 457. Many of the psychological ploys discussed in *Miranda* capitalize on the suspect's unfamiliarity with the officers and the environment. Murphy's regular meetings with his probation officer should have served to familiarize him with her and her office and to insulate him from psychological intimidation that might overbear his desire to claim the privilege. Finally, the coercion inherent in custodial interrogation derives in large measure from an interrogator's insinuations that the interrogation will continue until a confession is obtained. Id., at 468. Since Murphy was not physically restrained and could have left the office, any compulsion he might have felt from the possibility that terminating the meeting would have led to revocation of probation was not comparable to the pressure on a suspect who is painfully aware that he literally cannot escape a persistent custodial interrogator.
>
> We conclude, therefore, that Murphy cannot claim the benefit of the [*Miranda*] exception to the general rule that the Fifth Amendment privilege is not self-executing. . . .

465 U.S., at 430-434.

Does the presence or absence of "custody" depend, at least in part, on the intent of the police? A unanimous Supreme Court said no in Stansbury v. California, 511 U.S. 318 (1994). In *Stansbury*, police officers investigating a homicide went to the defendant's home late at night and when the defendant answered the door, the officers "told him [they] were investigating a homicide to which Stansbury was a possible witness and asked if he would accompany them to the police station to answer some questions." Id., at 320. After he got to the police station, Stansbury made several incriminating statements. Only then did the police give him *Miranda* warnings and tell him he was under arrest. The California Supreme Court had concluded that Stansbury was not in custody at the time he made the statements because the officers investigating the case had not considered him their prime suspect. The Court reversed, stating that the officers' intent was irrelevant, and remanded for a new "custody" determination.

b. "Interrogation"

RHODE ISLAND v. INNIS

Certiorari to the Rhode Island Supreme Court
446 U.S. 291 (1980)

MR. JUSTICE STEWART delivered the opinion of the Court. . . .

I

On the night of January 12, 1975, John Mulvaney, a Providence, R.I., taxicab driver, disappeared after being dispatched to pick up a customer. His body was discovered four days later buried in a shallow grave in Coventry, R.I. He had died from a shotgun blast aimed at the back of his head.

On January 17, 1975, shortly after midnight, the Providence police received a telephone call from Gerald Aubin, also a taxicab driver, who reported that he had just been robbed by a man wielding a sawed-off shotgun. Aubin further reported that he had dropped off his assailant near Rhode Island College in a section of Providence known as Mount Pleasant. While at the Providence police station waiting to give a statement, Aubin noticed a picture of his assailant on a bulletin board. Aubin so informed one of the police officers present. The officer prepared a photo array, and again Aubin identified a picture of the same person. That person was the respondent. Shortly thereafter, the Providence police began a search of the Mount Pleasant area.

At approximately 4:30 a.m. on the same date, Patrolman Lovell, while cruising the streets of Mount Pleasant in a patrol car, spotted the respondent standing in the street facing him. When Patrolman Lovell stopped his car, the respondent walked towards it. Patrolman Lovell then arrested the respondent, who was unarmed, and advised him of his so-called *Miranda* rights. While the two men waited in the patrol car for other police officers to arrive, Patrolman Lovell did not converse with the respondent other than to respond to the latter's request for a cigarette.

Within minutes, Sergeant Sears arrived at the scene of the arrest, and he also gave the respondent the *Miranda* warnings. Immediately thereafter, Captain Leyden and other police officers arrived. Captain Leyden advised the respondent of his *Miranda* rights. The respondent stated that he understood those rights and wanted to speak with a lawyer. Captain Leyden then directed that the respondent be placed in a "caged wagon," a four-door police car with a wire screen mesh between the front and rear seats, and be driven to the central police station. Three officers, Patrolmen Gleckman, Williams, and McKenna, were assigned to accompany the respondent to the central station. They placed the respondent in the vehicle and shut the doors. Captain Leyden then instructed the officers not to question the respondent or intimidate or coerce him in any way. The three officers then entered the vehicle, and it departed.

While en route to the central station, Patrolman Gleckman initiated a conversation with Patrolman McKenna concerning the missing shotgun.[1] As Patrolman Gleckman later testified:

A. At this point, I was talking back and forth with Patrolman McKenna stating that I frequent this area while on patrol and [that because a school for handicapped children is located nearby,] there's a lot of handicapped children running around in this area, and God forbid one of them might find a weapon with shells and they might hurt themselves.

Patrolman McKenna apparently shared his fellow officer's concern:

A. I more or less concurred with him [Gleckman] that it was a safety factor and that we should, you know, continue to search for the weapon and try to find it.

While Patrolman Williams said nothing, he overheard the conversation between the two officers:

A. He [Gleckman] said it would be too bad if the little — I believe he said a girl — would pick up the gun, maybe kill herself.

The respondent then interrupted the conversation, stating that the officers should turn the car around so he could show them where the gun was located. At this point, Patrolman McKenna radioed back to Captain Leyden that they were returning to the scene of the arrest, and that the respondent would inform them of the location of the gun. At the time the respondent indicated that the officers should turn back, they had traveled no more than a mile, a trip encompassing only a few minutes.

The police vehicle then returned to the scene of the arrest where a search for the shotgun was in progress. There, Captain Leyden again advised the respondent of his *Miranda* rights. The respondent replied that he understood those rights but that he "wanted to get the gun out of the way because of the kids in the area in the school." The respondent then led the police to a nearby field, where he pointed out the shotgun under some rocks by the side of the road. . . .

We granted certiorari to address for the first time the meaning of "interrogation" under Miranda v. Arizona.

II . . .

A

The starting point for defining "interrogation" in this context is, of course, the Court's *Miranda* opinion. There the Court observed that "[b]y custodial interrogation, we mean *questioning* initiated by law enforcement officers after a person has been taken into custody or otherwise deprived of his freedom of action in any significant way." Id., at 444 (emphasis added). This passage and other references throughout the opinion to "questioning" might suggest that the *Miranda* rules were

---

1. Although there was conflicting testimony about the exact seating arrangements, it is clear that everyone in the vehicle heard the conversation.

to apply only to those police interrogation practices that involve express questioning of a defendant while in custody.

We do not, however, construe the *Miranda* opinion so narrowly. The concern of the Court in *Miranda* was that the "interrogation environment" created by the interplay of interrogation and custody would "subjugate the individual to the will of his examiner" and thereby undermine the privilege against compulsory self-incrimination. Id., at 457-458. The police practices that evoked this concern included several that did not involve express questioning. For example, one of the practices discussed in *Miranda* was the use of lineups in which a coached witness would pick the defendant as the perpetrator. This was designed to establish that the defendant was in fact guilty as a predicate for further interrogation. Id., at 453. A variation on this theme discussed in *Miranda* was the so-called "reverse line-up" in which a defendant would be identified by coached witnesses as the perpetrator of a fictitious crime, with the object of inducing him to confess to the actual crime of which he was suspected in order to escape the false prosecution. Ibid. The Court in *Miranda* also included in its survey of interrogation practices the use of psychological ploys, such as to "posi[t]" "the guilt of the subject," to "minimize the moral seriousness of the offense," and "to cast blame on the victim or on society." Id., at 450. It is clear that these techniques of persuasion, no less than express questioning, were thought, in a custodial setting, to amount to interrogation.[3]

This is not to say, however, that all statements obtained by the police after a person has been taken into custody are to be considered the product of interrogation. . . . [T]he special procedural safeguards outlined in *Miranda* are required not where a suspect is simply taken into custody, but rather where a suspect in custody is subjected to interrogation. "Interrogation," as conceptualized in the *Miranda* opinion, must reflect a measure of compulsion above and beyond that inherent in custody itself.

We conclude that the *Miranda* safeguards come into play whenever a person in custody is subjected to either express questioning or its functional equivalent. That is to say, the term "interrogation" under *Miranda* refers not only to express questioning, but also to any words or actions on the part of the police (other than those normally attendant to arrest and custody) that the police should know are reasonably likely to elicit an incriminating response from the suspect.[6] The latter portion of this definition focuses primarily upon the perceptions of the suspect, rather than the intent of the police. This focus reflects the fact that the *Miranda* safeguards were designed to vest a suspect in custody with an added measure of protection against coercive police practices, without regard to objective proof of the underlying intent of the police. A practice that the police should know is reasonably likely to evoke an incriminating response from a suspect thus amounts to interrogation.[7] But, since

---

3. To limit the ambit of *Miranda* to express questioning would "place a premium on the ingenuity of the police to devise methods of indirect interrogation, rather than to implement the plain mandate of *Miranda*." Commonwealth v. Hamilton, 445 Pa. 292, 297, 285 A.2d 172, 175.

6. One of the dissenting opinions seems totally to misapprehend this definition in suggesting that it "will almost certainly exclude every statement [of the police] that is not punctuated with a question mark."

7. This is not to say that the intent of the police is irrelevant, for it may well have a bearing on whether the police should have known that their words or actions were reasonably likely to evoke an incriminating response. In particular, where a police practice is designed to elicit an incriminating response from the accused, it is unlikely that the practice will not also be one which the police should have known was reasonably likely to have that effect.

the police surely cannot be held accountable for the unforeseeable results of their words or actions, the definition of interrogation can extend only to words or actions on the part of police officers that they should have known were reasonably likely to elicit an incriminating response.[8]

B

Turning to the facts of the present case, we conclude that the respondent was not "interrogated" within the meaning of *Miranda*. It is undisputed that the first prong of the definition of "interrogation" was not satisfied, for the conversation between Patrolmen Gleckman and McKenna included no express questioning of the respondent. Rather, that conversation was, at least in form, nothing more than a dialogue between the two officers to which no response from the respondent was invited.

Moreover, it cannot be fairly concluded that the respondent was subjected to the "functional equivalent" of questioning. It cannot be said, in short, that Patrolmen Gleckman and McKenna should have known that their conversation was reasonably likely to elicit an incriminating response from the respondent. There is nothing in the record to suggest that the officers were aware that the respondent was peculiarly susceptible to an appeal to his conscience concerning the safety of handicapped children. Nor is there anything in the record to suggest that the police knew that the respondent was unusually disoriented or upset at the time of his arrest.[9]

The case thus boils down to whether, in the context of a brief conversation, the officers should have known that the respondent would suddenly be moved to make a self-incriminating response. Given the fact that the entire conversation appears to have consisted of no more than a few offhand remarks, we cannot say that the officers should have known that it was reasonably likely that Innis would so respond. This is not a case where the police carried on a lengthy harangue in the presence of the suspect. Nor does the record support the respondent's contention that, under the circumstances, the officers' comments were particularly "evocative." It is our view, therefore, that the respondent was not subjected by the police to words or actions that the police should have known were reasonably likely to elicit an incriminating response from him.

The Rhode Island Supreme Court erred, in short, in equating "subtle compulsion" with interrogation. That the officers' comments struck a responsive chord is readily apparent. Thus, it may be said, as the Rhode Island Supreme Court did say, that the respondent was subjected to "subtle compulsion." But that is not the end of the inquiry. It must also be established that a suspect's incriminating response was the product of words or actions on the part of the police that they should have

---

8. Any knowledge the police may have had concerning the unusual susceptibility of a defendant to a particular form of persuasion might be an important factor in determining whether the police should have known that their words or actions were reasonably likely to elicit an incriminating response from the suspect.

9. The record in no way suggests that the officers' remarks were *designed* to elicit a response. See n. 7, supra. It is significant that the trial judge, after hearing the officers' testimony, concluded that it was "entirely understandable that [the officers] would voice their concern [for the safety of the handicapped children] to each other."

known were reasonably likely to elicit an incriminating response.[10] This was not established in the present case.

For the reasons stated, the judgment of the Supreme Court of Rhode Island is vacated, and the case is remanded to that court for further proceedings not inconsistent with this opinion.

JUSTICE STEVENS, dissenting.

[I]n order to give full protection to a suspect's right to be free from any interrogation at all, the definition of "interrogation" must include any police statement or conduct that has the same purpose or effect as a direct question. Statements that appear to call for a response from the suspect, as well as those that are designed to do so, should be considered interrogation. By prohibiting only those relatively few statements or actions that a police officer should know are likely to elicit an incriminating response, the Court today accords a suspect considerably less protection. Indeed, since I suppose most suspects are unlikely to incriminate themselves even when questioned directly, this new definition will almost certainly exclude every statement that is not punctuated with a question mark from the concept of "interrogation."

The difference between the approach required by a faithful adherence to *Miranda* and the stinted test applied by the Court today can be illustrated by comparing three different ways in which Officer Gleckman could have communicated his fears about the possible dangers posed by the shotgun to handicapped children. He could have:

(1) directly asked Innis:
Will you please tell me where the shotgun is so we can protect handicapped schoolchildren from danger?
(2) announced to the other officers in the wagon:
If the man sitting in the back seat with me should decide to tell us where the gun is, we can protect handicapped children from danger.
or
(3) stated to the other officers:
It would be too bad if a little handicapped girl would pick up the gun that this man left in the area and maybe kill herself.

In my opinion, all three of these statements should be considered interrogation because all three appear to be designed to elicit a response from anyone who in fact knew where the gun was located.[12] Under the Court's test, on the other hand, the form of the statements would be critical. The third statement would not be

10. By way of example, if the police had done no more than to drive past the site of the concealed weapon while taking the most direct route to the police station, and if the respondent, upon noticing for the first time the proximity of the school for handicapped children, had blurted out that he would show the officers where the gun was located, it could not seriously be argued that this "subtle compulsion" would have constituted "interrogation" within the meaning of the *Miranda* opinion.

12. See Welsh S. White, Rhode Island v. Innis: The Significance of a Suspect's Assertion of His Right to Counsel, 17 Am. Crim. L. Rev. 53, 68 (1979), where the author proposes the same test and applies it to the facts of this case, stating: "Under the proposed objective standard, the result is obvious. Since the conversation indicates a strong desire to know the location of the shotgun, any person with knowledge of the weapon's location would be likely to believe that the officers wanted him to disclose its location. Thus, a reasonable person in Innis's position would believe that the officers were seeking to solicit precisely the type of response that was given."

interrogation because in the Court's view there was no reason for Officer Gleckman to believe that Innis was susceptible to this type of an implied appeal, . . . therefore, the statement would not be reasonably likely to elicit an incriminating response. Assuming that this is true, . . . then it seems to me that the first two statements, which would be just as unlikely to elicit such a response, should also not be considered interrogation. But, because the first statement is clearly an express question, it *would* be considered interrogation under the Court's test. The second statement, although just as clearly a deliberate appeal to Innis to reveal the location of the gun, would presumably not be interrogation because (a) it was not in form a direct question and (b) it does not fit within the "reasonably likely to elicit an incriminating response" category that applies to indirect interrogation.

As this example illustrates, the Court's test creates an incentive for police to ignore a suspect's invocation of his rights in order to make continued attempts to extract information from him. If a suspect does not appear to be susceptible to a particular type of psychological pressure, the police are apparently free to exert that pressure on him despite his request for counsel, so long as they are careful not to punctuate their statements with question marks. And if, contrary to all reasonable expectations, the suspect makes an incriminating statement, that statement can be used against him at trial. The Court thus turns *Miranda*'s unequivocal rule against any interrogation at all into a trap in which unwary suspects may be caught by police deception. . . .

[Chief Justice Burger's and Justice White's concurring opinions are omitted, as is Justice Marshall's dissent, in which Justice Brennan joined.]

NOTES AND QUESTIONS

1. Would *Innis* have come out differently if the officer's remarks had been directed at Innis? If they had been directed at him in the form of a question? If so, what is the point of imposing a "reasonable likelihood of success" limitation on what actually occurred? Is it because possibly the *Miranda* rules already go too far and an arbitrary limitation is better than extending them further still?

2. Suppose an individual is arrested for murder, is given his *Miranda* warnings, and refuses to speak to the police. Suppose further that the suspect's wife is being interrogated by the police and insists on seeing her husband. The police attempt to dissuade her from talking with her husband, but she insists. The police accede to her demand, but inform the couple that a police officer will be present during the meeting and their conversation will be tape-recorded. During the meeting of husband and wife, a conversation occurs that is subsequently admitted at the husband's trial to demonstrate that he was not insane at the time of the alleged event. Assuming that the police knew that there was a substantial risk that incriminating statements would be made, does the husband have a legitimate claim that his Fifth Amendment rights have been violated?

No, according to the Court in a 5-to-4 decision in Arizona v. Mauro, 481 U.S. 421 (1987). Although the police knew that there was a substantial likelihood that incriminating material would be obtained, the police attempted to discourage the wife from seeing her husband. Thus, this was not a "psychological ploy that properly could be treated as the functional equivalent of interrogation," a conclusion bolstered in the Court's view by the fact that there was "no evidence that the officers sent Mrs. Mauro in to see her husband for the purpose of eliciting incriminating statements."

What do you think of the wisdom of incorporating the subjective state of mind of the police into the definition of "interrogation"? How could a suspect's will possibly be overborne merely because the police consciously constructed a ruse analogous to the facts of *Mauro*, but not overborne in the actual *Mauro* case? From *Mauro's* point of view, what is the significance of whether the police (1) had no idea what would occur during the meeting, (2) hoped an incriminating conversation would occur, (3) intended for it to occur, or (4) urged the wife to bring about such a conversation? If these four possibilities cannot be distinguished in terms of their effect on Mauro, should they all be allowed or all disallowed? *Innis* suggests the first two are acceptable and the last two are violations of *Miranda*. Is the problem with *Innis* or with *Miranda*? Moreover, why should the state of mind of the police matter to the issue of "interrogation," but not (according to *Stansbury*, see page 798, supra) to the issue of "custody"?

Three years after *Mauro*, the Court returned to the question whether police officers' intent determines whether "interrogation" has taken place.

ILLINOIS v. PERKINS

Certiorari to the Appellate Court of Illinois
496 U.S. 292 (1990)

JUSTICE KENNEDY delivered the opinion of the Court.

An undercover government agent was placed in the cell of respondent Perkins, who was incarcerated on charges unrelated to the subject of the agent's investigation. Respondent made statements that implicated him in the crime that the agent sought to solve. Respondent claims that the statements should be inadmissible because he had not been given *Miranda* warnings by the agent. We hold that the statements are admissible. *Miranda* warnings are not required when the suspect is unaware that he is speaking to a law enforcement officer and gives a voluntary statement.

I

In November 1984, Richard Stephenson was murdered in a suburb of East St. Louis, Illinois. The murder remained unsolved until March 1986, when one Donald Charlton told police that he had learned about a homicide from a fellow inmate at the Graham Correctional Facility, where Charlton had been serving a sentence for burglary. The fellow inmate was Lloyd Perkins, who is the respondent here. Charlton told police that, while at Graham, he had befriended respondent, who told him in detail about a murder that respondent had committed in East St. Louis. On hearing Charlton's account, the police recognized details of the Stephenson murder that were not well known, and so they treated Charlton's story as a credible one.

By the time the police heard Charlton's account, respondent had been released from Graham, but police traced him to a jail in Montgomery County, Illinois, where he was being held pending trial on a charge of aggravated battery, unrelated to the Stephenson murder. The police wanted to investigate further respondent's connection to the Stephenson murder, but feared that the use of an eavesdropping device would prove impracticable and unsafe. They decided instead to place an undercover agent in the cellblock with respondent and Charlton. The plan was for Charlton and undercover agent John Parisi to pose as escapees from a work release program who had been arrested in the course of a burglary. Parisi and Charlton were instructed to engage respondent in casual conversation and report anything he said about the Stephenson murder.

Parisi, using the alias "Vito Bianco," and Charlton, both clothed in jail garb, were placed in the cellblock with respondent at the Montgomery County jail. The cellblock consisted of 12 separate cells that opened onto a common room. Respondent greeted Charlton who, after a brief conversation with respondent, introduced Parisi by his alias. Parisi told respondent that he "wasn't going to do any more time," and suggested that the three of them escape. Respondent replied that the Montgomery County jail was "rinky-dink" and that they could "break out." The trio met in respondent's cell later that evening, after the other inmates were asleep, to refine their plan. Respondent said that his girlfriend could smuggle in a pistol. Charlton said: "Hey, I'm not a murderer, I'm a burglar. That's your guys' profession." After telling Charlton that he would be responsible for any murder that occurred, Parisi asked respondent if he had ever "done" anybody. Respondent said that he had, and proceeded to describe at length the events of the Stephenson murder. Parisi and respondent then engaged in some casual conversation before respondent went to sleep. Parisi did not give respondent *Miranda* warnings before the conversations.

Respondent was charged with the Stephenson murder. Before trial, he moved to suppress the statements made to Parisi in the jail. The trial court granted the motion to suppress, and the State appealed. The Appellate Court of Illinois affirmed, holding that Miranda v. Arizona prohibits all undercover contacts with incarcerated suspects which are reasonably likely to elicit an incriminating response.

We granted certiorari to decide whether an undercover law enforcement officer must give *Miranda* warnings to an incarcerated suspect before asking him questions that may elicit an incriminating response. We now reverse.

II

In Miranda v. Arizona, the Court held that the Fifth Amendment privilege against self-incrimination prohibits admitting statements given by a suspect during "custodial interrogation" without a prior warning. Custodial interrogation means "questioning initiated by law enforcement officers after a person has been taken into custody. . . ." "Fidelity to the doctrine announced in *Miranda* requires that it be enforced strictly, but only in those types of situations in which the concerns that powered the decision are implicated." Berkemer v. McCarty, 468 U.S. 420, 437 (1984).

Conversations between suspects and undercover agents do not implicate the concerns underlying *Miranda*. The essential ingredients of a "police-dominated atmosphere" and compulsion are not present when an incarcerated person speaks freely to someone that he believes to be a fellow inmate. Coercion is determined from the perspective of the suspect. When a suspect considers himself in the company of cellmates and not officers, the coercive atmosphere is lacking. There is no empirical basis for the assumption that a suspect speaking to those whom he assumes are not officers will feel compelled to speak by the fear of reprisal for remaining silent or in the hope of more lenient treatment should he confess.

It is the premise of *Miranda* that the danger of coercion results from the interaction of custody and official interrogation. We reject the argument that *Miranda* warnings are required whenever a suspect is in custody in a technical sense and converses with someone who happens to be a government agent. Questioning by captors, who appear to control the suspect's fate, may create mutually reinforcing pressures that the Court has assumed will weaken the suspect's will, but where a suspect does not know that he is conversing with a government agent, these pressures do not exist. The State Court here mistakenly assumed that because the suspect was in custody, no undercover questioning could take place. When the suspect has no reason to think that the listeners have official power over him, it should not be assumed that his words are motivated by the reaction he expects from his listeners. "[W]hen the agent carries neither badge nor gun and wears not 'police blue,' but the same prison gray" as the suspect, there is no "interplay between police interrogation and police custody." Yale Kamisar, Brewer v. Williams, *Massiah* and *Miranda*: What Is "Interrogation"? When Does It Matter? 67 Geo. L.J. 1, 67, 63 (1978).

Miranda forbids coercion, not mere strategic deception by taking advantage of a suspect's misplaced trust in one he supposes to be a fellow prisoner. As we recognized in *Miranda*, "[c]onfessions remain a proper element in law enforcement. Any statement given freely and voluntarily without any compelling influences is, of course, admissible in evidence." 384 U.S., at 478. Ploys to mislead a suspect or lull him into a false sense of security that do not rise to the level of compulsion or coercion to speak are not within *Miranda*'s concerns.

Miranda was not meant to protect suspects from boasting about their criminal activities in front of persons whom they believe to be their cellmates. This case is illustrative. Respondent had no reason to feel that undercover agent Parisi had any legal authority to force him to answer questions or that Parisi could affect respondent's future treatment. Respondent viewed the cellmate-agent as an equal and showed no hint of being intimidated by the atmosphere of the jail. In recounting the details of the Stephenson murder, respondent was motivated solely by the desire to impress his fellow inmates. He spoke at his own peril. . . .

We hold that an undercover law enforcement officer posing as a fellow inmate need not give *Miranda* warnings to an incarcerated suspect before asking questions that may elicit an incriminating response. The statements at issue in this case were voluntary, and there is no federal obstacle to their admissibility at trial. We now reverse and remand for proceedings not inconsistent with our opinion.

JUSTICE BRENNAN, concurring in the judgment.

The Court holds that Miranda v. Arizona does not require suppression of a statement made by an incarcerated suspect to an undercover agent. Although I do not subscribe to the majority's characterization of *Miranda* in its entirety, I do agree that when a suspect does not know that his questioner is a police agent, such questioning does not amount to "interrogation" in an "inherently coercive" environment so as to require application of *Miranda*. Since the only issue raised at this stage of the litigation is the applicability of *Miranda*, I concur in the judgment of the Court.

This is not to say that I believe the Constitution condones the method by which the police extracted the confession in this case. To the contrary, the deception and manipulation practiced on respondent raise a substantial claim that the confession was obtained in violation of the Due Process Clause. . . .

The method used to elicit the confession in this case deserves close scrutiny. The police devised a ruse to lure respondent into incriminating himself when he was in jail on an unrelated charge. A police agent, posing as a fellow inmate and proposing a sham escape plot, tricked respondent into confessing that he had once committed a murder, as a way of proving that he would be willing to do so again should the need arise during the escape. The testimony of the undercover officer and a police informant at the suppression hearing reveal the deliberate manner in which the two elicited incriminating statements from respondent. We have recognized that "the mere fact of custody imposes pressures on the accused; confinement may bring into play subtle influences that will make him particularly susceptible to the ploys of undercover Government agents." United States v. Henry, 447 U.S. 264, 274 (1980). As Justice Marshall points out [in dissent], the pressures of custody make a suspect more likely to confide in others and to engage in "jailhouse bravado." The State is in a unique position to exploit this vulnerability because it has virtually complete control over the suspect's environment. Thus, the State can ensure that a suspect is barraged with questions from an undercover agent until the suspect confesses. The testimony in this case suggests the State did just that.

The deliberate use of deception and manipulation by the police appears to be incompatible "with a system that presumes innocence and assures that a conviction will not be secured by inquisitorial means," Miller [v. Fenton, 474 U.S. 104, 116 (1985)], and raises serious concerns that respondent's will was overborne. It is open to the lower court on remand to determine whether, under the totality of the circumstances, respondent's confession was elicited in a manner that violated the Due Process Clause. That the confession was not elicited through means of physical torture, or overt psychological pressure, does not end the inquiry. "[A]s law enforcement officers become more responsible, and the methods used to extract confessions more sophisticated, [a court's] duty to enforce federal constitutional protections does not cease. It only becomes more difficult because of the more delicate judgments to be made." Spano [v. New York, 360 U.S. 315, 321 (1959)].

JUSTICE MARSHALL, dissenting.

. . . The Court does not dispute that the police officer here conducted a custodial interrogation of a criminal suspect. Perkins was incarcerated in county jail during the questioning at issue here; under these circumstances, he was in custody as that term is defined in *Miranda*. The Solicitor General argues that Perkins was not in custody for purpose of *Miranda* because he was familiar with the custodial environment as a result of being in jail for two days and previously spending time in prison. Perkins' familiarity with confinement, however, does not transform his incarceration into some sort of noncustodial arrangement. Cf. Orozco v. Texas, 394 U.S. 324 (1969) (holding that suspect who had been arrested in his home and then questioned in his bedroom was in custody, notwithstanding his familiarity with the surroundings).

While Perkins was confined, an undercover police officer, with the help of a police informant, questioned him about a serious crime. . . .

Because Perkins was interrogated by police while he was in custody, *Miranda* required that the officer inform him of his rights. In rejecting that conclusion, the Court finds that "conversations" between undercover agents and suspects are devoid of the coercion inherent in stationhouse interrogations conducted by law enforcement officials who openly represent the State. *Miranda* was not, however, concerned solely with police coercion. It dealt with any police tactics that may operate to compel a suspect in custody to make incriminating statements without full awareness of his constitutional rights. . . . Thus, when a law enforcement agent structures a custodial interrogation so that a suspect feels compelled to reveal incriminating information, he must inform the suspect of his constitutional rights and give him an opportunity to decide whether or not to talk.

The compulsion proscribed by *Miranda* includes deception by the police. See *Miranda*, supra, at 453 (indicting police tactics "to induce a confession out of trickery," such as using fictitious witnesses or false accusations); Berkemer v. McCarty, 468 U.S. 420, 433 (1984) ("The purposes of the safeguards prescribed by *Miranda* are to ensure that the police do not coerce or trick captive suspects into confessing"). Cf. Moran v. Burbine, 475 U.S. 412, 421 (1986) ("[T]he relinquishment of the right [protected by the *Miranda* warnings] must have been voluntary in the sense that it was the product of a free and deliberate choice rather than intimidation, coercion, or deception"). Although the Court did not find trickery by itself sufficient to constitute compulsion in Hoffa v. United States, the defendant in that case was not in custody. Perkins, however, was interrogated while incarcerated. As the Court has acknowledged in the Sixth Amendment context: "[T]he mere fact of custody imposes pressures on the accused; confinement may bring into play subtle influences that will make him particularly susceptible to the ploys of undercover Government agents." United States v. Henry, 447 U.S. 264, 274 (1980). . . .

Custody works to the State's advantage in obtaining incriminating information. The psychological pressures inherent in confinement increase the suspect's anxiety, making him likely to seek relief by talking with others. . . . The inmate is thus more susceptible to efforts by undercover agents to elicit information from him. Similarly, where the suspect is incarcerated, the constant threat of physical danger peculiar to the prison environment may make him demonstrate his toughness to other inmates by recounting or inventing past violent acts. "Because the suspect's ability to select people with whom he can confide is completely within their control, the police have a unique opportunity to exploit the suspect's vulnerability. In short, the police can insure that if the pressures of confinement lead the suspect to confide in anyone, it will be a police agent." Welsh S. White, Police Trickery in Inducing Confessions, 127 U. Pa. L. Rev. 581, 605 (1979). In this case, the police deceptively took advantage of Perkins' psychological vulnerability by including him in a sham escape plot, a situation in which he would feel compelled to demonstrate his willingness to shoot a prison guard by revealing his past involvement in a murder. . . .

Thus, the pressures unique to custody allow the police to use deceptive interrogation tactics to compel a suspect to make an incriminating statement. The compulsion is not eliminated by the suspect's ignorance of his interrogator's true identity. The Court therefore need not inquire past the bare facts of custody and interrogation to determine whether *Miranda* warnings are required. . . .

I dissent.

NOTES AND QUESTIONS

1. Perkins was unquestionably in custody at the time of the conversations with his cellmate. And the government unquestionably intended to use the cellmate/ undercover agent to get information out of Perkins. Why doesn't that add up to custodial interrogation under *Innis*? Does *Perkins* mean that police officers' subjective intent really doesn't matter after all?

2. One hidden problem in *Perkins* is the relationship between Fifth Amendment doctrine and Fourth Amendment doctrine. The use of undercover agents is largely unregulated by Fourth Amendment law; under United States v. White, 401 U.S. 745 (1971), conversations with undercover agents, even agents wearing wires, are not "searches." Thus, if *Perkins* had come out differently, undercover agents would be almost totally unregulated before arrest, but forbidden after arrest. (If undercover agents had to give *Miranda* warnings, they obviously couldn't be undercover agents; treating what happened in *Perkins* as custodial interrogation is therefore the same as abolishing the use of police agents as cellmates.) Is there any reason to draw such a line? Does the law's tolerance of police deception *before* arrest logically require the same posture *after*?

3. Note that the use of undercover agents to get information from suspects in custody can still run into constitutional problems. For example, if the suspect is actually a *defendant* — i.e., he has been indicted for, or otherwise formally charged with, the crime about which information is being sought — the practice violates the Sixth Amendment. See United States v. Henry, 447 U.S. 264 (1980). It can also violate the Due Process Clause. In Arizona v. Fulminante, 499 U.S. 279 (1991), the defendant, while incarcerated, made friends with an FBI informer masquerading as an organized crime figure. The defendant was apparently subjected to threats of assault from other inmates; the informant offered to protect him if he would tell the informant what happened in a rumored murder. The defendant confessed to the murder, and the informant passed the confession along to the police. The Court held that the confession was involuntary and hence inadmissible. For an argument suggesting that *Fulminante* leaves too much room for the use of prison informants, see Welsh S. White, Regulating Prison Informers under the Due Process Clause, [1991] Sup. Ct. Rev. 4. Professor White suggests that prison informants raise especially great concerns with reliability and that a focus on voluntariness does not sufficiently address those concerns.

4. *Perkins* seems a clear signal that trickery is an appropriate means of obtaining incriminating statements from criminal suspects. Is that the right signal to send to police? Is it the signal Earl Warren tried to send in his majority opinion in *Miranda*? For a vigorous argument that the answer to those last two questions is "no," see Welsh S. White, Police Trickery in Inducing Confessions, 127 U. Pa. L. Rev. 581 (1979). Notice that the permissibility (or not) of police trickery arises in two settings. The first is *Perkins*: Police use deceptive tactics to avoid *Miranda*'s restrictions. Second, the police may mislead the suspect in an effort to induce him to waive his *Miranda* rights. Deception and *Miranda* waivers are discussed below, at pages 829-841.

5. The same year the Court decided *Perkins*, it also decided Pennsylvania v. Muniz, 496 U.S. 582 (1990). The defendant in *Muniz* was arrested for drunk driving; he was taken back to the police station, where he was asked a series of questions by a police officer who was doing the paperwork incident to the defendant's arrest.

The state argued that these administrative questions—about the defendant's name, address, height, weight, eye color, date of birth, and current age—did not constitute "interrogation" within the meaning of *Miranda*. A four-Justice plurality disagreed, but found the questions fell within a "routine booking exception" to *Miranda*:

> We disagree with the Commonwealth's contention that Officer Hosterman's first seven questions regarding Muniz' name, address, height, weight, eye color, date of birth, and current age do not qualify as custodial interrogation as we defined the term in *Innis*, merely because the questions were not intended to elicit information for investigatory purposes. As explained above, the *Innis* test focuses primarily upon the perspective of the suspect. We agree with amicus United States, however, that Muniz' answers to these first seven questions are nonetheless admissible because the questions fall within a "routine booking question" exception which exempts from *Miranda*'s coverage questions to secure the "biographical data necessary to complete booking or pretrial services." Brief for the United States as Amicus Curiae 12. The state court found that the first seven questions were "requested for record-keeping purposes only," and therefore the questions appear reasonably related to the police's administrative concerns.[14] In this context, therefore, the first seven questions asked at the Booking Center fall outside the protections of *Miranda* and the answers thereto need not be suppressed.

496 U.S., at 601-602. Another four Justices concluded that the defendant's responses to the "booking" questions were not testimonial, and hence that the Fifth Amendment did not apply to the case. Id., at 608 (Rehnquist, C.J., concurring in part and dissenting in part). The "testimony" issue in *Muniz* is discussed supra, at pages 744-746.

c. *Warnings*

If the required *Miranda* warnings have not been given, a *Miranda* waiver is clearly impossible; the presumption of police coercion is irrebuttable. That aspect of *Miranda* remains good law. Which means that police must know what the required warnings are. The Court in *Miranda* listed four essential warnings:

> He must be warned prior to any questioning that he has the right to remain silent, that anything he says can be used against him in a court of law, that he has the right to the presence of an attorney, and that if he cannot afford an attorney one will be appointed for him prior to any questioning if he so desires.

384 U.S., at 479.

Despite the fact that the *Miranda* warnings have become part of American popular culture, police still occasionally fail to give the warnings in the precise language specified in *Miranda*. The Court has proven to be rather flexible. For example, in California v. Prysock, 453 U.S. 355 (1981), the Court upheld a conviction where the

---

14. As amicus United States explains, "[r]ecognizing a 'booking exception' to *Miranda* does not mean, of course, that any question asked during the booking process falls within that exception. Without obtaining a waiver of the suspect's *Miranda* rights, the police may not ask questions, even during booking, that are designed to elicit incriminatory admissions." Brief for United States as Amicus Curiae 13.

warnings given the suspect did not expressly state that an attorney would be made available prior to interrogation. And in Duckworth v. Eagan, 492 U.S. 195 (1989), an Indiana case, the Court held that the following statement of rights satisfied *Miranda*:

> Before we ask you any questions, you must understand your rights. You have the right to remain silent. Anything you say can be used against you in court. You have a right to talk to a lawyer for advice before we ask you any questions, and to have him with you during questioning. You have this right to the advice and the presence of a lawyer even if you cannot afford to hire one. We have no way of giving you a lawyer, but one will be appointed for you, if you wish, if and when you go to court. If you wish to answer questions now without a lawyer present, you have the right to stop answering questions at any time. You also have the right to stop answering at any time until you've talked to a lawyer.

The *Eagan* dissent argued that a suspect might construe these warnings as providing a right to counsel before questioning only to those who can afford to pay for it. In the dissent's view, "It poses no great burden on law enforcement officers to eradicate confusion stemming from the 'if and when' caveat." The majority, however, concluded that the "if and when" language accurately described Indiana's procedure, and anticipated a suspect's natural question concerning when counsel might actually be appointed.

Note that if the warnings given in *Eagan* seem confusing, this confusion may be due to *Miranda* itself, not the police. *Miranda* required the police to tell the suspect that he could have a lawyer if he wished; the clear implication is that the government would get the suspect a lawyer immediately — i.e., at the police station. But *Miranda* does *not* actually require that suspects be given lawyers *immediately*. Instead, *Miranda* requires only that, if suspects "invoke" their right to counsel, the police must immediately stop questioning them. (See supra, at pages 814-828.) The police do *not* have to provide station-house lawyers for all indigent suspects; instead, those suspects who want appointed counsel will obtain such counsel when they eventually go to court — exactly as the police explained to Eagan.

In Florida v. Powell, 130 S. Ct. 1195 (2010), police in Tampa, Florida, warned Powell as follows:

> You have the right to remain silent. If you give up the right to remain silent, anything you say can be used against you in court. You have the right to talk to a lawyer before answering any of our questions. If you cannot afford to hire a lawyer, one will be appointed for you without cost and before any questioning. You have the right to use any of these rights at any time you want during this interview.

Powell argued (and the Florida Supreme Court agreed) that these warnings failed to specify that he had not only the right to consult with counsel *before* questioning, but also the right to have counsel present *during* questioning. The Court, in a 7-2 decision authored by Justice Ginsburg, held that the warnings given to Powell were constitutionally adequate:

> The four warnings *Miranda* requires are invariable, but this Court has not dictated the words in which the essential information must be conveyed. . . .

. . . The Tampa officers did not "entirely omi[t]," post, at 9, any information *Miranda* required them to impart. They informed Powell that he had "the right to talk to a lawyer before answering any of [their] questions" and "the right to use any of [his] rights at any time [he] want[ed] during th[e] interview." App. 3. The first statement communicated that Powell could consult with a lawyer before answering any particular question, and the second statement confirmed that he could exercise that right while the interrogation was underway. In combination, the two warnings reasonably conveyed Powell's right to have an attorney present, not only at the outset of interrogation, but at all times.

To reach the opposite conclusion, i.e., that the attorney would not be present throughout the interrogation, the suspect would have to imagine an unlikely scenario: To consult counsel, he would be obliged to exit and reenter the interrogation room between each query. A reasonable suspect in a custodial setting who has just been read his rights, we believe, would not come to the counterintuitive conclusion that he is obligated, or allowed, to hop in and out of the holding area to seek his attorney's advice. Instead, the suspect would likely assume that he must stay put in the interrogation room and that his lawyer would be there with him the entire time.

The Florida Supreme Court found the warning misleading because it believed the temporal language — that Powell could "talk to a lawyer before answering any of [the officers'] questions" — suggested Powell could consult with an attorney only before the interrogation started. In context, however, the term "before" merely conveyed when Powell's right to an attorney became effective — namely, before he answered any questions at all. Nothing in the words used indicated that counsel's presence would be restricted after the questioning commenced. Instead, the warning communicated that the right to counsel carried forward to and through the interrogation: Powell could seek his attorney's advice before responding to "*any* of [the officers'] questions" and "*at any time . . . during* th[e] interview." App. 3 (emphasis added). Although the warnings were not the *clearest possible* formulation of *Miranda*'s right-to-counsel advisement, they were sufficiently comprehensive and comprehensible when given a commonsense reading.

Pursuing a different line of argument, Powell points out that most jurisdictions in Florida and across the Nation expressly advise suspects of the right to have counsel present both before and during interrogation. If we find the advice he received adequate, Powell suggests, law enforcement agencies, hoping to obtain uninformed waivers, will be tempted to end-run *Miranda* by amending their warnings to introduce ambiguity. Brief for Respondent 50-53. But as the United States explained as *amicus curiae* in support of the State of Florida, "law enforcement agencies have little reason to assume the litigation risk of experimenting with novel *Miranda* formulations," Brief for United States as *Amicus Curiae* 6; instead, it is "desirable police practice" and "in law enforcement's own interest" to state warnings with maximum clarity, id., at 12. See also id., at 11 ("By using a conventional and precise formulation of the warnings, police can significantly reduce the risk that a court will later suppress the suspect's statement on the ground that the advice was inadequate.").

For these reasons, "all . . . federal law enforcement agencies explicitly advise . . . suspect[s] of the full contours of each [*Miranda*] right, including the right to the presence of counsel during questioning." Id., at 12. The standard warnings used by the Federal Bureau of Investigation are exemplary. They provide, in relevant part: "You have the right to talk to a lawyer for advice before we ask you any questions. You have the right to have a lawyer with you during questioning." Ibid., n. 3 (internal quotation marks omitted). This advice is admirably informative, but we decline to declare its precise formulation necessary to meet *Miranda*'s requirements. Different words were used in the advice Powell received, but they communicated the same essential message.

Id., at 1204-1206.

d. Invocations

The *Miranda* Court placed special emphasis on protecting suspects who, having been warned of their rights, choose to invoke them:

> If, however, he indicates in any manner and at any stage of the process that he wishes to consult with an attorney before speaking there can be no questioning. Likewise, if the individual is alone and indicates in any manner that he does not wish to be interrogated, the police may not question him.

384 U.S., at 444-445.

> Once warnings have been given, the subsequent procedure is clear. If the individual indicates in any manner, at any time prior to or during questioning, that he wishes to remain silent, the interrogation must cease. At this point he has shown that he intends to exercise his Fifth Amendment privilege; any statement taken after the person invokes his privilege cannot be other than the product of compulsion.

Id., at 473-474.

> If the individual states that he wants an attorney, the interrogation must cease until an attorney is present. At that time, the individual must have an opportunity to confer with the attorney and to have him present during any subsequent questioning. . . . If the interrogation continues without the presence of an attorney and a statement is taken, a heavy burden rests on the government to demonstrate that the defendant knowingly and intelligently waived his privilege against self-incrimination and his right to retained or appointed counsel.

Id., at 474-475.

These words have occasioned more litigation than any other passage of the Court's opinion. An early example of such litigation involved a defendant named Richard Mosley. Mosley was arrested in connection with certain robberies, was briefly interrogated, and then invoked his right to remain silent (but not his right to counsel), at which point the interrogation ceased. Some time later a different police officer interrogated Mosley about an unrelated homicide. The second officer advised Mosley of his rights, obtained a waiver, and secured incriminating information. The Court found no violation of Mosley's rights:

MICHIGAN v. MOSLEY, 423 U.S. 96, 101-107 (1975): [*Miranda*] could be literally read to mean that a person who has invoked his "right to silence" can never again be subjected to custodial interrogation by any police officer at any time or place on any subject. Another possible construction of the passage would characterize "any statement taken after the person invokes his privilege" as "the product of compulsion" and would therefore mandate its exclusion from evidence, even if it were volunteered by the person in custody without any further interrogation whatever. Or the passage could be interpreted to require only the immediate cessation of questioning and to permit a resumption of interrogation after a momentary respite.

It is evident that any of these possible literal interpretations would lead to absurd and unintended results. To permit the continuation of custodial interrogation after a momentary cessation would clearly frustrate the purposes of *Miranda* by allowing repeated rounds of questioning to undermine the will of the person being questioned. At the other extreme, a blanket prohibition against the taking of voluntary statements or a permanent immunity from further interrogation, regardless of the circumstances, would transform the *Miranda* safeguards into wholly irrational obstacles to legitimate police investigative activity, and deprive suspects of an opportunity to make informed and intelligent assessments of their interests. Clearly, therefore, . . . the *Miranda* opinion can[not] sensibly be read to create a per se proscription of indefinite duration upon any further questioning by any police officer on any subject, once the person in custody has indicated a desire to remain silent.

A reasonable and faithful interpretation of the *Miranda* opinion must rest on the intention of the Court in that case to adopt "fully effective means . . . to notify the person of his right of silence and to assure that the exercise of the right will be scrupulously honored. . . ." 384 U.S., at 479. The critical safeguard identified in the passage at issue is a person's "right to cut off questioning." Id., at 474. Through the exercise of his option to terminate questioning he can control the time at which questioning occurs, the subjects discussed and the duration of the interrogation. The requirement that law enforcement authorities must respect a person's exercise of that option counteracts the coercive pressures of the custodial setting. We therefore conclude that the admissibility of statements obtained after the person in custody has decided to remain silent depends under *Miranda* on whether his "right to cut off questioning" was "scrupulously honored."

A review of the circumstances leading to Mosley's confession reveals that his "right to cut off questioning" was fully respected in this case. Before his initial interrogation, Mosley was carefully advised that he was under no obligation to answer any questions and could remain silent if he wished. He orally acknowledged that he understood the *Miranda* warnings and then signed a printed notification of rights form. When Mosley stated that he did not want to discuss the robberies, Detective Cowie immediately ceased the interrogation and did not try either to resume the questioning or in any way to persuade Mosley to reconsider his position. After an interval of more than two hours, Mosley was questioned by another police officer at another location about an unrelated holdup murder. He was given full and complete *Miranda* warnings at the outset of the second interrogation. He was thus reminded again that he could remain silent and could consult with a lawyer, and was carefully given a full and fair opportunity to exercise these options. The subsequent questioning did not undercut Mosley's previous decision not to answer Detective Cowie's inquiries. Detective Hill did not resume the interrogation about the White Tower Restaurant robbery or inquire about the Blue Goose Bar robbery, but instead focused exclusively on the Leroy Williams homicide, a crime different in nature and in time and place of occurrence from the robberies for which Mosley had been arrested and interrogated by Detective Cowie. Although it is not clear from the record how much Detective Hill knew about the earlier interrogation, his questioning of Mosley about an unrelated homicide was quite consistent with a reasonable interpretation of Mosley's earlier refusal to answer any questions about the robberies.

This is not a case, therefore, where the police failed to honor a decision of a person in custody to cut off questioning, either by refusing to discontinue the interrogation upon request or by persisting in repeated efforts to wear down his resistance and make him change his mind. In contrast to such practices, the police here immediately ceased the interrogation, resumed questioning only after the passage of a significant period of time and the provision of a fresh set of warnings, and restricted the second interrogation to a crime that had not been a subject of the earlier interrogation.

The Michigan Court of Appeals viewed this case as factually similar to Westover v. United States, 384 U.S. 436, a companion case to *Miranda*. But the controlling facts of the two cases are strikingly different.

In *Westover*, the petitioner was arrested by the Kansas City police at 9:45 p.m. and taken to the police station. Without giving any advisory warnings of any kind to Westover, the police questioned him that night and throughout the next morning about various local robberies. At noon, three FBI agents took over, gave advisory warnings to Westover, and proceeded to question him about two California bank robberies. After two hours of questioning, the petitioner confessed to the California crimes. The Court held that the confession obtained by the FBI was inadmissible because the interrogation leading to the petitioner's statement followed on the heels of prolonged questioning that was commenced and continued by the Kansas City police without preliminary warnings to Westover of any kind. The Court found that "the federal authorities were the beneficiaries of the pressure applied by the local in-custody interrogation" and that the belated warnings given by the federal officers were "not sufficient to protect" Westover because from his point of view "the warnings came at the end of the interrogation process." 384 U.S., at 496-497.

Here, by contrast, the police gave full "*Miranda* warnings" to Mosley at the very outset of each interrogation, subjected him to only a brief period of initial questioning, and suspended questioning entirely for a significant period before beginning the interrogation that led to his incriminating statement. The cardinal fact of *Westover* — the failure of the police officers to give any warnings whatever to the person in their custody before embarking on an intense and prolonged interrogation of him — was simply not present in this case. The Michigan Court of Appeals was mistaken, therefore, in believing that Detective Hill's questioning of Mosley was "not permitted" by the *Westover* decision. 51 Mich. 105, 108, 214 N.W.2d 564, 566.

Are you convinced by the *Mosley* Court's treatment of *Westover*? Compare *Mosley* to the next case.

EDWARDS v. ARIZONA, 451 U.S. 477, 478-487 (1981): On January 19, 1976, a sworn complaint was filed against Edwards in Arizona state court charging him with robbery, burglary, and first-degree murder. . . . Edwards was arrested at his home later that same day. At the police station, he was informed of his rights as required by Miranda v. Arizona, 384 U.S. 436 (1966). Petitioner stated that he understood his rights, and was willing to submit to questioning. After being told that another suspect already in custody had implicated him in the crime, Edwards denied involvement and gave a taped statement presenting an alibi defense. He then sought to "make a deal." The interrogating officer told him that he wanted a statement, but that he did not have the authority to negotiate a deal. The officer provided Edwards with the number of a county attorney. Petitioner made the call, but hung up after a few moments. Edwards then said, "I want an attorney before making a deal." At that point, questioning ceased and Edwards was taken to county jail.

At 9:15 the next morning, two detectives, colleagues of the officer who had interrogated Edwards the previous night, came to the jail and asked to see Edwards. When the detention officer informed Edwards that the detectives wished to speak with him, he replied that he did not want to talk to anyone. The guard told him that "he had" to talk and then took him to meet with the detectives. The officers identified themselves, stated they wanted to talk to him and informed him of his *Miranda* rights. Edwards was willing to talk, but he first wanted to hear the taped statement of the alleged accomplice who had implicated him. After listening to the tape for several minutes, petitioner said that he would make a statement so long as it was not tape recorded. The detectives informed him that the recording was irrelevant since they could testify in court concerning whatever he said. Edwards replied: "I'll tell you anything you want to know, but I don't want it on tape." He thereupon implicated himself in the crime. . . .

Miranda . . . declared that an accused has a Fifth and Fourteenth Amendment right to have counsel present during custodial interrogation. Here, the critical facts . . . are that Edwards asserted his right to counsel and his right to remain silent on January 19, but that the police, without furnishing him counsel, returned the next morning to confront him and as a result of the meeting secured incriminating oral admissions. . . . Edwards insists that having exercised his right on the 19th to have counsel present during interrogation, he did not validly waive that right on the 20th. For the following reasons, we agree.

First, the Arizona Supreme Court applied an erroneous standard for determining waiver where the accused has specifically invoked his right to counsel. It is reasonably clear under our cases that waivers of counsel must not only be voluntary, but constitute a knowing and intelligent relinquishment or abandonment of a known right or privilege, a matter which depends in each case "upon the particular facts and circumstances surrounding that case, including the background, experience and conduct of the accused." Johnson v. Zerbst, 304 U.S. 458, 464 (1938). . . .

Considering the proceedings in the state courts in the light of this standard, we note that in denying petitioner's motion to suppress, the trial court found the admission to have been "voluntary" . . . without separately focusing on whether Edwards had knowingly and intelligently relinquished his right to counsel. The Arizona Supreme Court, in a section of its opinion entitled "Voluntariness of Waiver," stated that in Arizona, confessions are prima facie involuntary and that the State had the burden of showing by a preponderance of the evidence that the confession was freely and voluntarily made. The court stated that the issue of voluntariness should be determined based on the totality of the circumstances as it related to whether an accused's action was "knowing and intelligent and whether his will was overborne." Once the trial court determines that "the confession is voluntary, the finding will not be upset on appeal absent clear and manifest error."

. . . The court then upheld the trial court's finding that the "waiver and confession were voluntarily and knowingly made." . . .

In referring to the necessity to find Edwards' confession knowing and intelligent, the State Supreme Court cited Schneckloth v. Bustamonte, 412 U.S. 218, 226 (1973). Yet, it is clear that *Schneckloth* does not control the issue presented in this case. The issue in *Schneckloth* was under what conditions an individual could be found to have consented to a search and thereby waived his Fourth Amendment rights. The Court declined to impose the "intentional relinquishment or abandonment of a known right or privilege" standard and required only that the consent be voluntary under the totality of the circumstances. The Court specifically noted that the right to counsel was a prime example of those rights requiring the special protection of the knowing and intelligent waiver standard, id., at 241, but held that "[t]he considerations that informed the Court's holding in *Miranda* are simply inapplicable in the present case." 412 U.S., at 246. *Schneckloth* itself thus emphasized that the voluntariness of a consent or an admission on the one hand, and a knowing and intelligent waiver on the other, are discrete inquiries. Here, however sound the conclusion of the state courts as to the voluntariness of Edwards' admission may be, neither the trial court nor the Arizona Supreme Court undertook to focus on whether Edwards understood his right to counsel and intelligently and knowingly relinquished it. It is thus apparent that the decision below misunderstood the requirement for finding a valid waiver of the right to counsel, once invoked.

Second, although we have held that after initially being advised of his *Miranda* rights, the accused may himself validly waive his rights and respond to interrogation, see North Carolina v. Butler, 441 U.S., at 372-376, the Court has strongly indicated that additional safeguards are necessary when the accused asks for counsel; and we now hold that when an accused has invoked his right to have counsel present during custodial interrogation, a valid waiver of that right cannot be established by showing only that he responded to further police-initiated custodial interrogation even if he has been advised of his rights. We further hold that an accused, such as Edwards, having expressed his desire to deal with the police only through counsel, is not subject to further interrogation by the authorities until counsel has been made available to him, unless the accused himself initiates further communication, exchanges or conversations with the police.

Miranda itself indicated that the assertion of the right to counsel was a significant event and that once exercised by the accused, "interrogation must cease until an attorney is present." 384 U.S., at 474. Our later cases have not abandoned that view. In Michigan v. Mosley, 423 U.S. 96 (1975), the Court noted that *Miranda* had distinguished between the procedural safeguards triggered by a request to remain silent and a request for an attorney and had required that interrogation cease until an attorney was present only if the individual stated that he wanted counsel. In Fare v. Michael C., 442 U.S., at 719, the Court referred to *Miranda*'s "rigid rule that an accused's request for an attorney is per se an invocation of his Fifth Amendment rights, requiring that all interrogation cease." And just last Term, in a case where a suspect in custody had invoked his *Miranda* right to counsel, the Court again referred to the "undisputed right" under *Miranda* to remain silent and to be free of interrogation "until he had consulted with a lawyer." Rhode Island v. Innis, 446 U.S. 291, 298 (1980). We reconfirm these views and to lend them substance, emphasize that it is inconsistent with *Miranda* and its progeny for the authorities, at their instance, to reinterrogate an accused in custody if he has clearly asserted his right to counsel.

In concluding that the fruits of the interrogation initiated by the police on January 20 could not be used against Edwards, we do not hold or imply that Edwards was powerless to countermand his election or that the authorities could in no event use any incriminating statements made by Edwards prior to his having access to counsel. Had Edwards initiated the meeting on January 20, nothing in the

Fifth and Fourteenth Amendments would prohibit the police from merely listening to his voluntary, volunteered statements and using them against him at the trial. The Fifth Amendment right identified in *Miranda* is the right to have counsel present at any custodial interrogation. Absent such interrogation, there would have been no infringement of the right that Edwards invoked and there would be no occasion to determine whether there had been a valid waiver. Rhode Island v. Innis, supra, makes this sufficiently clear. 446 U.S., at 298, n. 2.[9]

But this is not what the facts of this case show. Here, the officers conducting the interrogation on the evening of January 19, ceased interrogation when Edwards requested counsel as he had been advised he had the right to do. The Arizona Supreme Court was of the opinion that this was a sufficient invocation of his *Miranda* rights, and we are in accord. It is also clear that without making counsel available to Edwards, the police returned to him the next day. This was not at his suggestion or request. Indeed, Edwards informed the detention officer that he did not want to talk to anyone. At the meeting, the detectives told Edwards that they wanted to talk to him and again advised him of his *Miranda* rights. Edwards stated that he would talk, but what prompted this action does not appear. He listened at his own request to part of the taped statement made by one of his alleged accomplices and then made an incriminating statement, which was used against him at his trial. We think it is clear that Edwards was subjected to custodial interrogation on January 20 within the meaning of Rhode Island v. Innis, supra, and that this occurred at the instance of the authorities. His statement made without having had access to counsel, did not amount to a valid waiver and hence was inadmissible.

Accordingly, the holding of the Arizona Supreme Court that Edwards had waived his right to counsel was infirm and the judgment of that court is reversed....

NOTES AND QUESTIONS

1. Can *Mosley* and *Edwards* be reconciled? Remember that the whole point of this exercise is supposed to be protection of the accused's right to remain silent. The *Miranda* right to counsel is given in order to help protect that right. Yet after *Edwards* and *Mosley*, invocation of the right to counsel gets greater protection than invocation of the right to remain silent. Why? What's going on here?

2. *Edwards* holds that the police may not seek to interrogate a suspect who has previously invoked his right to counsel, unless that suspect "initiates further communication" with the police. This makes the definition of "invocation" extremely important: Once the suspect "invokes," the police may have no more chances to talk to him.

In Davis v. United States, 512 U.S. 452 (1994), the Court addressed "how law enforcement officers should respond when a suspect makes a reference to counsel that is insufficiently clear to invoke the *Edwards* prohibition on further questioning":

---

9. If, as frequently would occur in the course of a meeting initiated by the accused, the conversation is not wholly one-sided, it is likely that the officers will say or do something that clearly would be "interrogation." In that event, the question would be whether a valid waiver of the right to counsel and the right to silence had occurred, that is, whether the purported waiver was knowing and intelligent and found to be so under the totality of the circumstances, including the necessary fact that the accused, not the police, reopened the dialogue with the authorities. . . .

[I]f a suspect makes a reference to an attorney that is ambiguous or equivocal in that a reasonable officer in light of the circumstances would have understood only that the suspect might be invoking the right to counsel, our precedents do not require the cessation of questioning. . . . Rather, the suspect must unambiguously request counsel. Although a suspect need not "speak with the discrimination of an Oxford don," he must articulate his desire to have counsel present sufficiently clearly that a reasonable police officer in the circumstances would understand the statement to be a request for an attorney. If the statement fails to meet the requisite level of clarity, *Edwards* does not require that the officers stop questioning the suspect. . . . We decline petitioner's invitation to extend *Edwards* and require law enforcement officers to cease questioning immediately upon the making of an ambiguous or equivocal reference to an attorney. The rationale underlying *Edwards* is that the police must respect a suspect's wishes regarding his right to have an attorney present during custodial interrogation. But when the officers conducting the questioning reasonably do not know whether or not the suspect wants a lawyer, a rule requiring the immediate cessation of questioning "would transform the *Miranda* safeguards into wholly irrational obstacles to legitimate police investigative activity," Michigan v. Mosley, 423 U.S. 96, 102 (1975), because it would needlessly prevent the police from questioning a suspect in the absence of counsel even if the suspect did not wish to have a lawyer present. Nothing in *Edwards* requires the provision of counsel to a suspect who consents to answer questions without the assistance of a lawyer.

Id., at 459-460.

In evaluating *Davis*, it is helpful to consider the facts of some of the Court's earlier invocation cases. In Smith v. Illinois, 469 U.S. 91 (1984) (per curiam), the Court held (over a sharp dissent) that the following facts and "interrogation" violated *Miranda* and *Edwards*:

Shortly after his arrest, 18-year-old Steven Smith was taken to an interrogation room at the Logan County Safety Complex for questioning by two police detectives. The session began as follows:

Q. Steve, I want to talk with you in reference to the armed robbery that took place at McDonald's restaurant on the morning of the 19th. Are you familiar with this?
A. Yeah. My cousin Greg was.
Q. Okay. But before I do that I must advise you of your rights. Okay? You have a right to remain silent. You do not have to talk to me unless you want to do so. Do you understand that?
A. Uh. She told me to get my lawyer. She said you guys would railroad me.
Q. Do you understand that as I gave it to you, Steve?
A. Yeah.
Q. If you do want to talk to me I must advise you that whatever you say can and will be used against you in court. Do you understand that?
A. Yeah.
Q. You have a right to consult with a lawyer and to have a lawyer present with you when you're being questioned. Do you understand that?
A. Uh, yeah, I'd like to do that.
Q. Okay.

Instead of terminating the questioning at this point, the interrogating officers proceeded to finish reading Smith his *Miranda* rights and then pressed him again to answer their questions:

Q. .... If you want a lawyer and you're unable to pay for one a lawyer will be appointed to represent you free of cost, do you understand that?

A. Okay.

Q. Do you wish to talk to me at this time without a lawyer being present?

A. Yeah and no, uh, I don't know what's what really.

Q. Well. You either have to talk to me this time without a lawyer being present and if you do agree to talk with me without a lawyer being present you can stop at any time you want to.

A. All right. I'll talk to you then.

Smith then told the detectives that he knew in advance about the planned robbery, but contended that he had not been a participant. After considerable probing by the detectives, Smith confessed that "I committed it," but he then returned to his earlier story that he had only known about the planned crime. Upon further questioning, Smith again insisted that "I wanta get a lawyer." This time the detectives honored the request and terminated the interrogation.

In a curious linguistic exercise, the Court held "only that, under the logical force of settled precedent, an accused's responses to further interrogation after his request for counsel may not be used to cast retrospective doubt on the clarity of the initial request itself. Such subsequent statements are relevant only to the distinct question of waiver." Id., at 495. As the dissent pointed out, it is not clear why informing a suspect of the remainder of his rights amounts to "interrogation," nor is it clear why subsequent events that may shed light on prior ones should be ignored in attempting to determine the exact nature of those prior events.

Another case extensively cited in *Davis* is Connecticut v. Barrett, 479 U.S. 523 (1987). In *Barrett*, the defendant agreed to talk to the police, but he refused to make a written statement without counsel present. According to the Court, this did not amount to a generalized assertion of counsel sufficient to invoke the implications of *Edwards*. In *Edwards* itself, the defendant said, "I want an attorney before making a deal." Is there any way to explain why the Court found that *Edwards* had invoked his right to counsel but *Barrett* had not? How would these cases be decided under the standard announced in *Davis*?

3. In his opinion concurring in the judgment in *Davis* (the opinion is not excerpted above), Justice Souter argued that some defendants may respond hesitantly to the police, so that the only invocation they will give is conditional or tentative. If such responses do not trigger the *Edwards* rule, as a practical matter those defendants may be effectively forced to talk to the police—the very outcome *Edwards* is designed to prevent. For an argument that this is precisely the problem faced by criminal suspects generally and by female suspects in particular, see Janet E. Ainsworth, In a Different Register: The Pragmatics of Powerlessness in Police Interrogation, 103 Yale L.J. 259 (1993).

In light of Justice Souter's and Professor Ainsworth's argument, consider one final invocation case. In Fare v. Michael C., 442 U.S. 707 (1979), a juvenile was interrogated about a murder. After being given his rights, he asked, "Can I have my probation officer here?" The police officer said that he was not going to call the probation officer and "If you want to talk to us without an attorney present, you can. If you don't want to, you don't have to." The juvenile agreed to talk and made incriminating statements. The Court found the statements admissible, on the grounds that *Miranda* had not adequately been invoked and that attorneys play a unique role in the criminal justice system. Note that *Michael C.* was decided after *Mosley* but before *Edwards*.

4. Assuming a suspect has "invoked" his right to counsel, the police must leave him alone unless he "initiates" further communication. The Court addressed the issue of "initiating" in Oregon v. Bradshaw, 462 U.S. 1039 (1983), in a badly splintered decision:

> [R]espondent was placed under arrest for furnishing liquor to Reynolds, a minor, and again advised of his *Miranda* rights. A police officer then told respondent the officer's theory of how the traffic accident that killed Reynolds occurred; a theory which placed respondent behind the wheel of the vehicle. Respondent again denied his involvement, and said "I do want an attorney before it goes very much further." . . . The officer immediately terminated the conversation.
>
> Sometime later respondent was transferred from the Rockaway Police Station to the Tillamook County jail, a distance of some ten or fifteen miles. Either just before, or during, his trip from Rockaway to Tillamook, respondent inquired of a police officer, "Well, what is going to happen to me now?" The officer answered by saying: "You do not have to talk to me. You have requested an attorney and I don't want you talking to me unless you so desire because anything you say — because — since you have requested an attorney, you know, it has to be at your own free will." App. 16. . . . Respondent said he understood. There followed a discussion between respondent and the officer concerning where respondent was being taken and the offense with which he would be charged. The officer suggested that respondent might help himself by taking a polygraph examination. Respondent agreed to take such an examination, saying that he was willing to do whatever he could to clear up the matter.
>
> The next day, following another reading to respondent of his *Miranda* rights, and respondent's signing a written waiver of those rights, the polygraph was administered. At its conclusion, the examiner told respondent that he did not believe respondent was telling the truth. Respondent then recanted his earlier story, admitting that he had been at the wheel of the vehicle in which Reynolds was killed, that he had consumed a considerable amount of alcohol, and that he had passed out at the wheel before the vehicle left the roadway and came to rest in the creek.

Id., at 1041-1042 (opinion of Rehnquist, J.). On these facts, was *Edwards* violated? The plurality — Justice Rehnquist was joined by Chief Justice Burger and Justices White and O'Connor — thought not:

> There can be no doubt in this case that in asking, "Well, what is going to happen to me now?," respondent "initiated" further conversation in the ordinary dictionary sense of that word. While we doubt that it would be desirable to build a superstructure of legal refinements around the word "initiate" in this context, there are undoubtedly situations where a bare inquiry by either a defendant or by a police officer should not be held to "initiate" any conversation or dialogue. There are some inquiries, such as a request for a drink of water or a request to use a telephone that are so routine that they cannot be fairly said to represent a desire on the part of an accused to open up a more generalized discussion relating directly or indirectly to the investigation. Such inquiries or statements, by either an accused or a police officer, relating to routine incidents of the custodial relationship, will not generally "initiate" a conversation in the sense in which that word was used in *Edwards*.
>
> Although ambiguous, the respondent's question in this case as to what was going to happen to him evinced a willingness and a desire for a generalized discussion about the investigation; it was not merely a necessary inquiry arising out of the incidents of

the custodial relationship. It could reasonably have been interpreted by the officer as relating generally to the investigation. That the police officer so understood it is apparent from the fact that he immediately reminded the accused that "you do not have to talk to me," and only after the accused told him that he "understood" did they have a generalized conversation. On these facts we believe that there was not a violation of the *Edwards* rule.

Id., at 1045-1046. Justice Powell provided the fifth vote for the state in *Bradshaw*; he declined to apply the strict rule of *Edwards*, finding only that Bradshaw's waiver was valid on these facts. Id., at 1047-1051 (Powell, J., concurring in the judgment).

Justice Marshall, joined by Justices Brennan, Blackmun, and Stevens, believed that *Edwards* barred the conversation in *Bradshaw*:

> I agree with the plurality that, in order to constitute "initiation" under *Edwards*, an accused's inquiry must demonstrate a desire to discuss the subject matter of the criminal investigation. . . . I am baffled, however, at the plurality's application of that standard to the facts of this case. The plurality asserts that respondent's question, "What is going to happen to me now?," evinced both "a willingness and a desire for a generalized discussion about the investigation." . . . If respondent's question had been posed by Jean-Paul Sartre before a class of philosophy students, it might well have evinced a desire for a "generalized" discussion. But under the circumstances of this case, it is plain that respondent's only "desire" was to find out where the police were going to take him. As the Oregon Court of Appeals stated, respondent's query came only minutes after his invocation of the right to counsel and was simply "a normal reaction to being taken from the police station and placed in a police car, obviously for transport to some destination." 54 Or. App., at 949, 636 P.2d, at 1013.[3] On these facts, I fail to see how respondent's question can be considered "initiation" of a conversation about the subject matter of the criminal investigation.
>
> To hold that respondent's question in this case opened a dialogue with the authorities flies in the face of the basic purpose of the *Miranda* safeguards. When someone in custody asks, "What is going to happen to me now?," he is surely responding to his custodial surroundings. The very essence of custody is the loss of control over one's freedom of movement. The authorities exercise virtually unfettered control over the accused. To allow the authorities to recommence an interrogation based on such a question is to permit them to capitalize on the custodial setting. Yet *Miranda*'s procedural protections were adopted precisely in order "to dispel the compulsion inherent in custodial surrounding." 384 U.S., at 458.

Id., at 1055-1056 (Marshall, J., dissenting).

5. Does a different waiver standard apply in cases where the suspect has invoked his *Miranda* right to counsel, but then "initiates" further communication with the police? The answer appears to be "no." In Wyrick v. Fields, 459 U.S. 42 (1982) (per curiam), the suspect, Fields, invoked his right to counsel and later "initiated"

---

3. The plurality seems to place some reliance on the police officer's reaction to respondent's question. The officer described his response as follows. "I says, 'You do not have to talk to me. You have requested an attorney and I don't want you talking to me unless you so desire because anything you say — because — since you have requested an attorney, you know, it has to be at your own free will.' I says, 'I can't prevent you from talking, but you understand where your place — you know, where your standing is here?' and he agreed. He says 'I understand.'" As the officer's testimony indicates, respondent's statement was at best ambiguous. In any event, as the Oregon Court of Appeals noted, the officer clearly took advantage of respondent's inquiry to commence once again his questioning — a practice squarely at odds with *Edwards*. See 54 Or. App., at 953, 636 P.2d, at 1013.

communication by requesting a polygraph examination. Before the polygraph, Fields was given new *Miranda* warnings. After the polygraph, the examiner told Fields that his answers had not been true and asked him "if he could explain why his answers were bothering him." Fields proceeded to make several incriminating statements. The Court of Appeals for the Eighth Circuit held that the examiner should have given Fields still another set of *Miranda* warnings at the close of the polygraph, before asking him any further questions. The Supreme Court reversed:

> In reaching [its] result, the Court of Appeals did not consider the "totality of the circumstances," as *Edwards* requires. Fields did not merely initiate a "meeting." By requesting a polygraph examination, he initiated interrogation. That is, Fields waived not only his right to be free of contact with the authorities in the absence of an attorney, but also his right to be free of interrogation about the crime of which he was suspected. Fields validly waived his right to have counsel present at "post-test" questioning, unless the circumstances changed so seriously that his answers no longer were voluntary, or unless he no longer was making a "knowing and intelligent relinquishment or abandonment" of his rights.

459 U.S., at 47.

6. In Arizona v. Roberson, 486 U.S. 675 (1988), the defendant was arrested for burglary and given *Miranda* warnings, and he said that he "wanted a lawyer before answering any questions." Three days later, a different police officer questioned Roberson about a different burglary; Roberson was again advised of his rights and this time agreed to talk. The Supreme Court held that Roberson's statements were inadmissible under *Edwards*. *Mosley* was distinguished on the ground that it involved an invocation of the right to remain silent, not of the right to counsel.

7. In Minnick v. Mississippi, 498 U.S. 146 (1990), the Court considered whether *Edwards* is satisfied when a suspect invokes his right to counsel, is allowed to consult with his counsel, and is thereafter re-Mirandized and interrogated. The Court held that this scenario violates *Edwards*:

> In our view, a fair reading of *Edwards* and subsequent cases demonstrates that we have interpreted the rule to bar police-initiated interrogation unless the accused has counsel with him at the time of questioning. Whatever the ambiguities of our earlier cases on this point, we now hold that when counsel is requested, interrogation must cease, and officials may not reinitiate interrogation without counsel present, whether or not the accused has consulted with his attorney.
>
> We consider our ruling to be an appropriate and necessary application of the *Edwards* rule. A single consultation with an attorney does not remove the suspect from persistent attempts by officials to persuade him to waive his rights, or from the coercive pressures that accompany custody and that may increase as custody is prolonged. The case before us well-illustrates the pressures, and abuses, that may be concomitants of custody. Petitioner testified that though he resisted, he was required to submit to both the F.B.I. and the Denham interviews. In the latter instance, the compulsion to submit to interrogation followed petitioner's unequivocal request during the F.B.I. interview that questioning cease until counsel was present. The case illustrates also that consultation is not always effective in instructing the suspect of his rights. One plausible interpretation of the record is that petitioner thought he could keep his admissions out of evidence by refusing to sign a formal waiver of rights. If the authorities had complied with Minnick's request to have counsel present during interrogation, the attorney could have corrected Minnick's misunderstanding or indeed

counseled him that he need not make a statement at all. We decline to remove protection from police-initiated questioning based on isolated consultation with counsel who is absent when the interrogation resumes.

Id., at 153-154. Justice Scalia, joined by Chief Justice Rehnquist, dissented:

Today's extension of the *Edwards* prohibition is the latest stage of prophylaxis built upon prophylaxis, producing a veritable fairyland castle of imagined Constitutional restrictions upon law enforcement. This newest tower, according to the court, is needed to avoid inconsistency with the purpose of *Edwards*'s prophylactic rule, which was needed to protect *Miranda*'s prophylactic right to have counsel present, which was needed to protect the right against compelled self-incrimination found (at last!) in the Constitution.

It seems obvious to me that, even in *Edwards* itself but surely in today's decision, we have gone far beyond any genuine concern about suspects who do not know their right to remain silent, or who have been coerced to abandon it. Both holdings are explicable, in my view, only as an effort to protect suspects against what is regarded as their own folly. The sharp-witted criminal would know better than to confess; why should the dull-witted suffer for his lack of mental endowment? Providing him with an attorney at every stage where he might be induced or persuaded (though not coerced) to incriminate himself will even the odds. Apart from the fact that this protective enterprise is beyond our authority under the Fifth Amendment or any other provision of the Constitution, it is unwise. The procedural protections of the Constitution protect the guilty as well as the innocent. But it is not their objective to set the guilty free. That some clever criminals may employ those protections to their advantage is poor reason to allow criminals who have not done so to escape justice.

Thus, even if I were to concede that an honest confession is a foolish mistake, I would welcome rather than reject it; a rule that foolish mistakes do not count would leave most offenders not only unconvicted but undetected. More fundamentally, however, it is wrong, and subtly corrosive of our criminal justice system, to regard an honest confession as a "mistake." While every person is entitled to stand silent, it is more virtuous for the wrongdoer to admit his offense and accept the punishment he deserves. Not only for society, but for the wrongdoer himself, "admission of guilt . . . , if not coerced, [is] inherently desirable," because it advances the goals of both "justice *and* rehabilitation" . . . . We should, then, rejoice at an honest confession, rather than pity the "poor fool" who has made it; and we should regret the attempted retraction of that good act, rather than seek to facilitate and encourage it. To design our laws on premises contrary to these is to abandon belief in either personal responsibility or the moral claim of just government to obedience. Today's decision is misguided, it seems to me, in so readily exchanging, for marginal, super-*Zerbst* protection against genuinely compelled testimony, investigators' ability to urge, or even ask, a person in custody to do what is right.

Id., at 166-167 (internal citations omitted).

8. What if the police interrogate a suspect who is already in long-term custody — either pending trial or after conviction for a different crime — and the suspect invokes his right to counsel? After *Roberson* and *Minnick*, the police must immediately stop questioning the suspect, and cannot seek to question him again even after he has consulted with counsel (unless, of course, the suspect "initiates" further communication). How long does this prohibition last? For as long as the suspect remains in custody?

This issue was addressed in Maryland v. Shatzer, 130 S. Ct. 1213 (2010). Shatzer was interrogated on August 7, 2003, about allegations that he had sexually abused his three-year-old son. At the time, Shatzer was already serving a prison sentence for an unrelated crime of sexual abuse of a child. Shatzer was read, and signed a waiver of, his *Miranda* rights. Shortly thereafter, Shatzer told the interrogating officer that he did not want to speak without an attorney. The officer ended the interrogation, and Shatzer was returned to the general prison population.

On March 2, 2006, more than two and a half years later, a different detective obtained new information from Shatzer's son about the sexual abuse he had suffered. The detective went to the prison where Shatzer had since been transferred and sought to interview Shatzer. Shatzer expressed surprise because he thought the investigation had been closed, but the detective explained that they had reopened it. The detective read Shatzer his *Miranda* warnings, and obtained a written waiver. Shatzer then admitted to performing sexual acts in front of his son. Five days later, on March 7, Shatzer—after again receiving and again waiving his *Miranda* rights—confessed to sexual abuse of his son. Shatzer was convicted at trial of sexual child abuse.

The question before the Court was whether *Edwards* rendered Shatzer's March 2006 statements inadmissible. All nine Justices agreed that it did not. Justice Scalia, writing for seven Justices, engaged in explicit cost-benefit analysis to conclude that *Edwards* should not reach so far:

> When, unlike what happened in [*Edwards, Roberson,* and *Minnick*], a suspect has been released from his pretrial custody and has returned to his normal life for some time before the later attempted interrogation, there is little reason to think that his change of heart regarding interrogation without counsel has been coerced. He has no longer been isolated. He has likely been able to seek advice from an attorney, family members, and friends. And he knows from his earlier experience that he need only demand counsel to bring the interrogation to a halt; and that investigative custody does not last indefinitely. In these circumstances, it is far fetched to think that a police officer's asking the suspect whether he would like to waive his *Miranda* rights will any more "wear down the accused," Smith v. Illinois, 469 U.S. 91, 98 (1984) (per curiam), than did the first such request at the original attempted interrogation—which is of course not deemed coercive. His change of heart is less likely attributable to "badgering" than it is to the fact that further deliberation in familiar surroundings has caused him to believe (rightly or wrongly) that cooperating with the investigation is in his interest. Uncritical extension of *Edwards* to this situation would not significantly increase the number of genuinely coerced confessions excluded. . . .
>
> At the same time that extending the *Edwards* rule yields diminished benefits, extending the rule also increases its costs: the in-fact voluntary confessions it excludes from trial, and the voluntary confessions it deters law enforcement officers from even trying to obtain. Voluntary confessions are not merely "a proper element in law enforcement," *Miranda*, supra, at 478, they are an "unmitigated good," McNeil [v. Wisconsin], 501 U.S. [171], 181 [(1991)], "'essential to society's compelling interest in finding, convicting, and punishing those who violate the law,'" ibid. (quoting Moran v. Burbine, 475 U.S. 412, 426 (1986)).
>
> The only logical endpoint of *Edwards* disability is termination of *Miranda* custody and any of its lingering effects. Without that limitation—and barring some purely arbitrary time-limit—every *Edwards* prohibition of custodial interrogation of a particular suspect would be eternal. The prohibition applies, of course, when the subsequent interrogation pertains to a different crime, *Roberson,* supra, when it is conducted

by a different law enforcement authority, *Minnick*, 498 U.S. 146, and even when the suspect has met with an attorney after the first interrogation, ibid. And it not only prevents questioning *ex ante*; it would render invalid *ex post*, confessions invited and obtained from suspects who (unbeknownst to the interrogators) have acquired *Edwards* immunity previously in connection with any offense in any jurisdiction. In a country that harbors a large number of repeat offenders, this consequence is disastrous.

Id., at 1221-1222. In a separate part of the opinion joined by eight Justices, Scalia also concluded that Shatzer's return to the general prison population after the August 2003 invocation of his right to counsel represented a break in "custody," noting that it placed Shatzer back into his usual prison routine and removed him from the direct control of the interrogating officer.

Finally, Scalia declared it "impractical" to leave "for clarification in future case-by-case adjudication" the issue of just how long a break in custody might be required to terminate the *Edwards* protection:

> [L]aw enforcement officers need to know, with certainty and beforehand, when renewed interrogation is lawful. . . .
>
> . . . We think it appropriate to specify a period of time. . . . It seems to us that period is 14 days. That provides plenty of time for the suspect to get reacclimated to his normal life, to consult with friends and counsel, and to shake off any residual coercive effects of his prior custody.
>
> The 14-day limitation meets Shatzer's concern that a break-in-custody rule lends itself to police abuse. He envisions that once a suspect invokes his *Miranda* right to counsel, the police will release the suspect briefly (to end the *Edwards* presumption) and then promptly bring him back into custody for reinterrogation. But once the suspect has been out of custody long enough (14 days) to eliminate its coercive effect, there will be nothing to gain by such gamesmanship — nothing, that is, except the entirely appropriate gain of being able to interrogate a suspect who has made a valid waiver of his *Miranda* rights.

Id., at 1222-1223. The Court reserved, for another day, the question whether mere passage of time, without a break in custody, might likewise end the *Edwards* protection. Id., at 1222, n. 4. Justice Thomas concurred in the judgment because he believed that *Edwards* protection should not necessarily last for even 14 days after a break in "custody," and Justice Stevens concurred in the judgment because he believed that *Edwards* protection should not necessarily expire at the end of 14 days after a break in "custody."

Keep in mind — for whatever it's worth — that *Shatzer* affects *only* the prophylactic protection of *Edwards*. Suspects like Shatzer may still argue that their subsequent *Miranda* waivers are involuntary in fact and thus invalid.

9. Does *Shatzer* limit the duration of *Mosley*, as well as *Edwards*, protection? On the one hand, *Mosley* protection has always been more limited than *Edwards* protection. On the other hand, *Shatzer* seems to depend at least in part on the fact that a 14-day break in "custody" allows the suspect ample time to consult with others, including his defense attorney. *Mosley* cases, by contrast, involve suspects who have chosen to deal with the police on their own (rather than through their defense attorneys). Does this mean that a 14-day release from custody is likely worth less to a *Mosley* suspect than to an *Edwards* suspect?

10. The prophylactic protections of both *Edwards* and *Mosley* — even after *Shatzer* — provide police officers with a strong incentive to avoid *Miranda* invocations. This means that the police will want to avoid the kinds of coercive questioning that might cause suspects to invoke their *Miranda* rights. But that happy conclusion holds only if suspects do, in fact, invoke their *Miranda* rights in response to coercive questioning. They may not. Professor Leo's data on *Miranda* waivers and invocations reveal that, while 21 percent of suspects invoke their rights, only 1 percent invoke their rights after questioning has actually begun. The other 20 percent invoke right away, when the warnings are first given — for them, *Miranda* is not a right to be free of coercive questioning; it is a right to opt out of police questioning altogether.

e.   Waivers

What happens if a suspect does *not* invoke his *Miranda* rights? *Miranda* holds that, as a threshold matter, the police must obtain a waiver of those rights before they may proceed with an interrogation. And the standards for such a waiver, as expressed in *Miranda*, are demanding:

> This Court has always set high standards of proof for the waiver of constitutional rights, Johnson v. Zerbst, 304 U.S. 458 (1938), and we re-assert these standards as applied to in-custody interrogation. Since the State is responsible for establishing the isolated circumstances under which the interrogation takes place and has the only means of making available corroborated evidence of warnings given during incommunicado interrogation, the burden is rightly on its shoulders.
>
> An express statement that the individual is willing to make a statement and does not want an attorney followed closely by a statement could constitute a waiver. But a valid waiver will not be presumed simply from the silence of the accused after warnings are given or simply from the fact that a confession was in fact eventually obtained. . . .
>
> Whatever the testimony of the authorities as to waiver of rights by an accused, the fact of lengthy interrogation or incommunicado incarceration before a statement is made is strong evidence that the accused did not validly waive his rights. In these circumstances the fact that the individual eventually made a statement is consistent with the conclusion that the compelling influence of the interrogation finally forced him to do so. It is inconsistent with any notion of a voluntary relinquishment of the privilege. Moreover, any evidence that the accused was threatened, tricked, or cajoled into a waiver will, of course, show that the defendant did not voluntarily waive his privilege. The requirement of warnings and waiver of rights is a fundamental with respect to the Fifth Amendment privilege and not simply a preliminary ritual to existing methods of interrogation.

Id., at 475-476.

This language suggests that, in many cases, a suspect who has not "invoked" his *Miranda* rights may not have "waived" those rights, either. In other words, there appears to be at least some "space" between *Miranda* invocations and *Miranda* waivers. What legal rule governs within this "space"? The problem can arise in two ways. First, the suspect may *say* that he wants to waive his rights (and perhaps even sign a statement to that effect), but the validity of the waiver may later be called into question. Second, the suspect may respond ambiguously, neither expressly invoking nor expressly waiving his rights.

As to the first scenario, cases like *Prysock, Eagan,* and *Powell* (discussed supra, at pages 811-813) establish that the police need not use the precise language of *Miranda* to warn suspects about their *Miranda* rights. Does the spirit of *Miranda* suggest that, in at least some circumstances, the police are required to go *beyond* the four essential warnings, and that a subsequent *Miranda* waiver should be held invalid unless the suspect is provided with additional information? For example, what if the police fail to inform the suspect that a defense lawyer is trying to contact him? (Recall that this was one of the key issues in *Escobedo*.) The next case addresses this question, in the context of deciding what constitutes a "knowing and intelligent" *Miranda* waiver.

MORAN v. BURBINE

Certiorari to the United States Court of Appeals for the First Circuit
475 U.S. 412 (1986)

JUSTICE O'CONNOR delivered the opinion of the Court.

After being informed of his rights pursuant to Miranda v. Arizona, and after executing a series of written waivers, respondent confessed to the murder of a young woman. At no point during the course of the interrogation, which occurred prior to arraignment, did he request an attorney. While he was in police custody, his sister attempted to retain a lawyer to represent him. The attorney telephoned the police station and received assurances that respondent would not be questioned further until the next day. In fact, the interrogation session that yielded the inculpatory statements began later that evening. The question presented is whether either the conduct of the police or respondent's ignorance of the attorney's efforts to reach him taints the validity of the waivers and therefore requires exclusion of the confessions.

I

On the morning of March 3, 1977, Mary Jo Hickey was found unconscious in a factory parking lot in Providence, Rhode Island. Suffering from injuries to her skull apparently inflicted by a metal pipe found at the scene, she was rushed to a nearby hospital. Three weeks later she died from her wounds.

Several months after her death, the Cranston, Rhode Island, police arrested respondent and two others in connection with a local burglary. Shortly before the arrest, Detective Ferranti of the Cranston police force had learned from a confidential informant that the man responsible for Ms. Hickey's death lived at a certain address and went by the name of "Butch." Upon discovering that respondent lived at that address and was known by that name, Detective Ferranti informed respondent of his *Miranda* rights. When respondent refused to execute a written waiver, Detective Ferranti spoke separately with the two other suspects arrested on the breaking and entering charge and obtained statements further implicating respondent in Ms. Hickey's murder. At approximately 6 p.m., Detective Ferranti telephoned the police in Providence to convey the information he had uncovered. An hour later, three officers from that department arrived at the Cranston headquarters for the purpose of questioning respondent about the murder.

That same evening, at about 7:45 p.m., respondent's sister telephoned the Public Defender's Office to obtain legal assistance for her brother. Her sole concern was the breaking and entering charge, as she was unaware that respondent was then under suspicion for murder. She asked for Richard Casparian, who had been scheduled to meet with respondent earlier that afternoon to discuss another charge unrelated to either the break-in or the murder. As soon as the conversation ended, the attorney who took the call attempted to reach Mr. Casparian. When those efforts were unsuccessful, she telephoned Allegra Munson, another Assistant Public Defender, and told her about respondent's arrest and his sister's subsequent request that the office represent him.

At 8:15 p.m., Ms. Munson telephoned the Cranston police station and asked that her call be transferred to the detective division. In the words of the Supreme Court of Rhode Island . . . the conversation proceeded as follows:

> A male voice responded with the word "Detectives." Ms. Munson identified herself and asked if Brian Burbine was being held; the person responded affirmatively. Ms. Munson explained to the person that Burbine was represented by attorney Casparian who was not available; she further stated that she would act as Burbine's legal counsel in the event that the police intended to place him in a lineup or question him. The unidentified person told Ms. Munson that the police would not be questioning Burbine or putting him in a lineup and that they were through with him for the night. Ms. Munson was not informed that the Providence Police were at the Cranston police station or that Burbine was a suspect in Mary's murder.

At all relevant times, respondent was unaware of his sister's efforts to retain counsel and of the fact and contents of Ms. Munson's telephone conversation.

Less than an hour later, the police brought respondent to an interrogation room and conducted the first of a series of interviews concerning the murder. Prior to each session, respondent was informed of his *Miranda* rights, and on three separate occasions he signed a written form acknowledging that he understood his right to the presence of an attorney and explicitly indicating that he "[did] not want an attorney called or appointed for [him]" before he gave a statement. Uncontradicted evidence at the suppression hearing indicated that at least twice during the course of the evening, respondent was left in a room where he had access to a telephone, which he apparently declined to use. Eventually, respondent signed three written statements fully admitting to the murder.

Prior to trial, respondent moved to suppress the statements. The court denied the motion, finding that respondent had received the *Miranda* warnings and had "knowingly, intelligently, and voluntarily waived his privilege against self-incrimination [and] his right to counsel." . . . The jury found respondent guilty of murder in the first degree, and he appealed to the Supreme Court of Rhode Island. A divided court rejected his contention that the Fifth and Fourteenth Amendments to the Constitution required the suppression of the inculpatory statements and affirmed the conviction. . . . After unsuccessfully petitioning the United States District Court for the District of Rhode Island for a writ of habeas corpus, respondent appealed to the Court of Appeals for the First Circuit. That court reversed.

We granted certiorari to decide whether a prearraignment confession preceded by an otherwise valid waiver must be suppressed either because the police misinformed an inquiring attorney about their plans concerning the suspect or because they failed to inform the suspect of the attorney's efforts to reach him. We now reverse.

II

. . . Respondent does not dispute that the Providence police followed [the *Miranda*] procedures with precision. . . . Nor does respondent contest the Rhode Island courts' determination that he at no point requested the presence of a lawyer. He contends instead that the confessions must be suppressed because the police's failure to inform him of the attorney's telephone call deprived him of information essential to his ability to knowingly waive his Fifth Amendment rights. In the alternative, he suggests that to fully protect the Fifth Amendment values served by *Miranda*, we should extend that decision to condemn the conduct of the Providence police. We address each contention in turn.

A

Echoing the standard first articulated in Johnson v. Zerbst, 304 U.S. 458, 464 (1938), *Miranda* holds that "[t]he defendant may waive effectuation" of the rights conveyed in the warnings "provided the waiver is made voluntarily, knowingly and intelligently." The inquiry has two distinct dimensions. First, the relinquishment of the right must have been voluntary in the sense that it was the product of a free and deliberate choice rather than intimidation, coercion, or deception. Second, the waiver must have been made with a full awareness of both the nature of the right being abandoned and the consequences of the decision to abandon it. Only if the "totality of the circumstances surrounding the interrogation" reveals both an uncoerced choice and the requisite level of comprehension may a court properly conclude that the *Miranda* rights have been waived.

Under this standard, we have no doubt that respondent validly waived his right to remain silent and to the presence of counsel. The voluntariness of the waiver is not at issue. As the Court of Appeals correctly acknowledged, the record is devoid of any suggestion that police resorted to physical or psychological pressure to elicit the statements. Indeed it appears that it was respondent, and not the police, who spontaneously initiated the conversation that led to the first and most damaging confession. Nor is there any question about respondent's comprehension of the full panoply of rights set out in the *Miranda* warnings and of the potential consequences of a decision to relinquish them. Nonetheless, the Court of Appeals believed that the "[d]eliberate or reckless" conduct of the police, in particular their failure to inform respondent of the telephone call, fatally undermined the validity of the otherwise proper waiver. We find this conclusion untenable as a matter of both logic and precedent.

Events occurring outside of the presence of the suspect and entirely unknown to him surely can have no bearing on the capacity to comprehend and knowingly relinquish a constitutional right. Under the analysis of the Court of Appeals, the same defendant, armed with the same information and confronted with precisely the same police conduct, would have knowingly waived his *Miranda* rights had a lawyer not telephoned the police station to inquire about his status. Nothing in any of our waiver decisions or in our understanding of the essential components of a valid waiver requires so incongruous a result. No doubt the additional information would have been useful to respondent; perhaps even it might have affected his decision to confess. But we have never read the Constitution to require that the police supply a suspect with a flow of information to help him calibrate his self-interest in deciding whether to speak or stand by his rights. Once it is determined that a suspect's decision not to rely on his rights was uncoerced, that he at all times knew he could stand mute and request a lawyer, and that he was aware of the State's intention to use his statements to secure a conviction, the analysis is complete and the waiver is valid as a matter of law. The Court of Appeals' conclusion to the contrary was in error.

Nor do we believe that the level of the police's culpability in failing to inform respondent of the telephone call has any bearing on the validity of the waivers. In light of the state-court findings that there was no "conspiracy or collusion" on the part of the police, we have serious doubts about whether the Court of Appeals was free to conclude that their conduct constituted "deliberate or reckless irresponsibility." 753 F.2d, at 185. But whether intentional or inadvertent, the state of mind of the police is irrelevant to the question of the intelligence and voluntariness of respondent's election to abandon his rights. Although highly inappropriate, even deliberate deception of an attorney could not possibly affect a suspect's decision to waive his *Miranda* rights unless he were at least aware of the incident. Compare Escobedo v. Illinois (excluding confession where police incorrectly told the suspect that his lawyer "'didn't want to see' him"). Nor was the failure to inform respondent of the telephone call the kind of "trick[ery]" that can vitiate the validity of a waiver. *Miranda*, 384 U.S., at 476. Granting that the "deliberate or reckless" withholding of information is objectionable as a matter of ethics, such conduct is only relevant to the constitutional validity of a waiver if it deprives a defendant of knowledge essential to his ability to understand the nature of his rights and the consequences of abandoning them. Because respondent's voluntary decision to speak was made with full awareness and comprehension of all the information *Miranda* requires the police to convey, the waivers were valid.

B

At oral argument respondent acknowledged that a constitutional rule requiring the police to inform a suspect of an attorney's efforts to reach him would represent a significant extension of our precedents. He contends, however, that the conduct of the Providence police was so inimical to the Fifth Amendment values *Miranda* seeks to protect that we should read that decision to condemn their behavior. Regardless of any issue of waiver, he urges, the Fifth Amendment requires the reversal of a conviction if the police are less than forthright in their dealings with an attorney or if they fail to tell a suspect of a lawyer's unilateral efforts to contact him. Because the proposed modification ignores the underlying purposes of the *Miranda* rules and because we think that the decision as written strikes the proper balance . . . , we decline the invitation to further extend *Miranda*'s reach.

At the outset, while we share respondent's distaste for the deliberate misleading of an officer of the court, reading *Miranda* to forbid police deception of an attorney would cut [the decision] completely loose from its own explicitly stated rationale. As is now well established, "[t]he . . . *Miranda* warnings are 'not themselves rights protected by the Constitution but [are] instead measures to insure that the [suspect's] right against compulsory self-incrimination [is] protected.'" New York v. Quarles, 467 U.S. 649, 654 (1984), quoting Michigan v. Tucker, 417 U.S. 433, 444 (1974). Their objective is not to mold police conduct for its own sake. Nothing in the Constitution vests in us the authority to mandate a code of behavior for state officials wholly unconnected to any federal right or privilege. The purpose of the

Miranda warnings instead is to dissipate the compulsion inherent in custodial interrogation and, in so doing, guard against abridgment of the suspect's Fifth Amendment rights. Clearly, a rule that focuses on how the police treat an attorney —
conduct that has no relevance at all to the degree of compulsion experienced by the
defendant during interrogation — would ignore both *Miranda*'s mission and its
only source of legitimacy. . . . [The Court also expressed concerns about adding
unnecessary complexity to the *Miranda* rules.]

Moreover, problems of clarity to one side, reading *Miranda* to require the police
in each instance to inform a suspect of an attorney's efforts to reach him would
work a substantial and, we think, inappropriate shift in the subtle balance struck in
that decision. Custodial interrogations implicate two competing concerns. On the
one hand, the need for police questioning as a tool for effective enforcement of
criminal laws cannot be doubted. Admissions of guilt are more than merely "desirable"; they are essential to society's compelling interest in finding, convicting, and
punishing those who violate the law. On the other hand, the Court has recognized
that the interrogation process is "inherently coercive" and that, as a consequence,
there exists a substantial risk that the police will inadvertently traverse the fine line
between legitimate efforts to elicit admissions and constitutionally impermissible
compulsion. *Miranda* attempted to reconcile these opposing concerns by giving the
defendant the power to exert some control over the course of the interrogation.
Declining to adopt the more extreme position that the actual presence of a lawyer
was necessary to dispel the coercion inherent in custodial interrogation, the Court
found that the suspect's Fifth Amendment rights could be adequately protected by
less intrusive means. Police questioning, often an essential part of the investigatory
process, could continue in its traditional form, the Court held, but only if the suspect clearly understood that, at any time, he could bring the proceeding to a halt
or, short of that, call in an attorney to give advice and monitor the conduct of his
interrogators.

The position urged by respondent would upset this carefully drawn approach in
a manner that is both unnecessary for the protection of the Fifth Amendment privilege and injurious to legitimate law enforcement. Because, as *Miranda* holds, full
comprehension of the rights to remain silent and request an attorney are sufficient
to dispel whatever coercion is inherent in the interrogation process, a rule requiring the police to inform the suspect of an attorney's efforts to contact him would
contribute to the protection of the Fifth Amendment privilege only incidentally, if
at all. This minimal benefit, however, would come at a substantial cost to society's
legitimate and substantial interest in securing admissions of guilt. Indeed, the very
premise of the Court of Appeals was not that awareness of Ms. Munson's phone call
would have dissipated the coercion of the interrogation room, but that it might
have convinced respondent not to speak at all. Because neither the letter nor purposes of *Miranda* require this additional handicap on otherwise permissible investigatory efforts, we are unwilling to expand the *Miranda* rules to require the police
to keep the suspect abreast of the status of his legal representation.

III

[The Court rejected the defendant's separate argument that the Sixth Amendment
applies in these circumstances. This part of the Court's opinion is reproduced
below, at pages 894-896. — EDS.]

IV

Finally, respondent contends that the conduct of the police was so offensive as to deprive him of the fundamental fairness guaranteed by the Due Process Clause of the Fourteenth Amendment. Focusing primarily on the impropriety of conveying false information to an attorney, he invites us to declare that such behavior should be condemned as violative of canons fundamental to the "traditions and conscience of our people." We do not question that on facts more egregious than those presented here police deception might rise to a level of a due process violation. Accordingly, Justice Stevens' apocalyptic suggestion that we have approved any and all forms of police misconduct is demonstrably incorrect. We hold only that, on these facts, the challenged conduct falls short of the kind of misbehavior that so shocks the sensibilities of civilized society as to warrant a federal intrusion into the criminal processes of the States.

We hold therefore that the Court of Appeals erred in finding that the Federal Constitution required the exclusion of the three inculpatory statements. Accordingly, we reverse and remand for proceedings consistent with this opinion.

JUSTICE STEVENS, with whom JUSTICE BRENNAN and JUSTICE MARSHALL join, dissenting.

This case poses fundamental questions about our system of justice. As this Court has long recognized, and reaffirmed only weeks ago, "ours is an accusatorial and not an inquisitorial system." Miller v. Fenton, 474 U.S. 104, 110 (1985). The Court's opinion today represents a startling departure from that basic insight.

The Court concludes that the police may deceive an attorney by giving her false information about whether her client will be questioned, and that the police may deceive a suspect by failing to inform him of his attorney's communications and efforts to represent him. For the majority, this conclusion, though "distaste[ful]," is not even debatable. The deception of the attorney is irrelevant because the attorney has no right to information, accuracy, honesty, or fairness in the police response to her questions about her client. The deception of the client is acceptable, because, although the information would affect the client's assertion of his rights, the client's actions in ignorance of the availability of his attorney are voluntary, knowing, and intelligent; additionally, society's interest in apprehending, prosecuting, and punishing criminals outweighs the suspect's interest in information regarding his attorney's efforts to communicate with him. Finally, even mendacious police interference in the communications between a suspect and his lawyer does not violate any notion of fundamental fairness because it does not shock the conscience of the majority. . . .

II

Well-settled principles of law lead inexorably to the conclusion that the failure to inform Burbine of the call from his attorney makes the subsequent waiver of his constitutional rights invalid. Analysis should begin with an acknowledgment that the burden of proving the validity of a waiver of constitutional rights is always on the government. When such a waiver occurs in a custodial setting, that burden is an especially heavy one because custodial interrogation is inherently coercive, because disinterested witnesses are seldom available to describe what actually happened, and because history has taught us that the danger of overreaching during incommunicado interrogation is so real. . . .

In this case it would be perfectly clear that Burbine's waiver was invalid if, for example, Detective Ferranti had "threatened, tricked, or cajoled" Burbine in their private pre-confession meeting — perhaps by misdescribing the statements obtained from DiOrio and Sparks — even though, under the Court's truncated analysis of the issue, Burbine fully understood his rights. For *Miranda* clearly condemns threats or trickery that cause a suspect to make an unwise waiver of his rights even though he fully understands those rights. In my opinion there can be no constitutional distinction — as the Court appears to draw — between a deceptive misstatement and the concealment by the police of the critical fact that an attorney retained by the accused or his family has offered assistance, either by telephone or in person.

Thus, the Court's truncated analysis, which relies in part on a distinction between deception accomplished by means of an omission of a critically important fact and deception by means of a misleading statement, is simply untenable. If, as the Court asserts, "the analysis is at an end" as soon as the suspect is provided with enough information to have the capacity to understand and exercise his rights, I see no reason why the police should not be permitted to make the same kind of misstatements to the suspect that they are apparently allowed to make to his lawyer. *Miranda*, however, clearly establishes that both kinds of deception vitiate the suspect's waiver of his right to counsel. . . .

III

The Court makes the alternative argument that requiring police to inform a suspect of his attorney's communications to and about him is not required because it would upset the careful "balance" of *Miranda*. . . .

The Court's balancing approach is profoundly misguided. The cost of suppressing evidence of guilt will always make the value of a procedural safeguard appear "minimal," "marginal," or "incremental." Indeed, the value of any trial at all seems like a "procedural technicality" when balanced against the interest in administering prompt justice to a murderer or a rapist caught red-handed. The individual interest in procedural safeguards that minimize the risk of error is easily discounted when the fact of guilt appears certain beyond doubt.

What is the cost of requiring the police to inform a suspect of his attorney's call? It would decrease the likelihood that custodial interrogation will enable the police to obtain a confession. This is certainly a real cost, but it is the same cost that this Court has repeatedly found necessary to preserve the character of our free society and our rejection of an inquisitorial system. . .

If the Court's cost-benefit analysis were sound, it would justify a repudiation of the right to a warning about counsel itself. There is only a difference in degree between a presumption that advice about the immediate availability of a lawyer would not affect the voluntariness of a decision to confess, and a presumption that every citizen knows that he has a right to remain silent and therefore no warnings of any kind are needed. In either case, the withholding of information serves precisely the same law enforcement interests. And in both cases, the cost can be described as nothing more than an incremental increase in the risk that an individual will make an unintelligent waiver of his rights.

In cases like *Escobedo* [and] *Miranda*, the Court has viewed the balance from a much broader perspective. In these cases — indeed, whenever the distinction between an inquisitorial and an accusatorial system of justice is implicated — the law enforcement interest served by incommunicado interrogation has been weighed against the interest in individual liberty that is threatened by such practices. The balance has never been struck by an evaluation of empirical data of the kind submitted to legislative decisionmakers — indeed, the Court relies on no such data today. Rather, the Court has evaluated the quality of the conflicting rights and interests. In the past, that kind of balancing process has led to the conclusion that the police have no right to compel an individual to respond to custodial interrogation, and that the interest in liberty that is threatened by incommunicado interrogation is so precious that special procedures must be followed to protect it. The Court's contrary conclusion today can only be explained by its failure to appreciate the value of the liberty that an accusatorial system seeks to protect. . . .

V

At the time attorney Munson made her call to the Cranston police station, she was acting as Burbine's attorney. Under ordinary principles of agency law the deliberate deception of Munson was tantamount to deliberate deception of her client. If an attorney makes a mistake in the course of her representation of her client, the client must accept the consequences of that mistake. It is equally clear that when an attorney makes an inquiry on behalf of her client, the client is entitled to a truthful answer. Surely the client must have the same remedy for a false representation to his lawyer that he would have if he were acting pro se and had propounded the question himself. The majority brushes aside the police deception involved in the misinformation of attorney Munson. It is irrelevant to the Fifth Amendment analysis, concludes the majority, because that right is personal.

In my view, as a matter of law, the police deception of Munson was tantamount to deception of Burbine himself. It constituted a violation of Burbine's right to have an attorney present during the questioning that began shortly thereafter. The existence of that right is undisputed. Whether the source of that right is the Sixth Amendment, the Fifth Amendment, or a combination of the two is of no special importance, for I do not understand the Court to deny the existence of the right.

The pertinent question is whether police deception of the attorney is utterly irrelevant to that right. In my judgment, it blinks at reality to suggest that misinformation which prevented the presence of an attorney has no bearing on the protection and effectuation of the right to counsel in custodial interrogation. . . .

The possible reach of the Court's opinion is stunning. For the majority seems to suggest that police may deny counsel all access to a client who is being held. At least since Escobedo v. Illinois, it has been widely accepted that police may not simply deny attorneys access to their clients who are in custody. This view has survived the recasting of *Escobedo* from a Sixth Amendment to a Fifth Amendment case that the majority finds so critically important. That this prevailing view is shared by the police can be seen in the state-court opinions detailing various forms of police deception of attorneys. For, if there were no obligation to give attorneys access, there would be no need to take elaborate steps to avoid access, such as shuttling the suspect to a different location, or taking the lawyer to different locations; police could simply refuse to allow the attorneys to see the suspects. But the law enforcement profession has apparently believed, quite rightly in my view, that denying lawyers access to their clients is impermissible. The Court today seems to assume that this view was error — that, from the federal constitutional perspective, the lawyer's access is, as a question from the Court put it in oral argument, merely "a matter of prosecutorial grace." Certainly, nothing in the Court's . . . analysis acknowledges that there is any federal constitutional bar to an absolute denial of lawyer access to a suspect who is in police custody. . . .

VI

The Court devotes precisely five sentences to its conclusion that the police interference in the attorney's representation of Burbine did not violate the Due Process Clause. In the majority's view, the due process analysis is a simple "shock the conscience" test. Finding its conscience troubled, but not shocked, the majority rejects the due process challenge. . . .

In my judgment, police interference in the attorney-client relationship is the type of governmental misconduct on a matter of central importance to the administration of justice that the Due Process Clause prohibits. Just as the police cannot impliedly promise a suspect that his silence will not be used against him and then proceed to break that promise, so too police cannot tell a suspect's attorney that they will not question the suspect and then proceed to question him. Just as the government cannot conceal from a suspect material and exculpatory evidence, so too the government cannot conceal from a suspect the material fact of his attorney's communication.

Police interference with communications between an attorney and his client violates the due process requirement of fundamental fairness. Burbine's attorney was given completely false information about the lack of questioning; moreover, she was not told that her client would be questioned regarding a murder charge about which she was unaware. Burbine, in turn, was not told that his attorney had phoned and that she had been informed that he would not be questioned. . . .

The majority does not "question that on facts more egregious than those presented here police deception might rise to a level of a due process violation." In my view, the police deception disclosed by this record plainly does rise to that level.

VII

This case turns on a proper appraisal of the role of the lawyer in our society. If a lawyer is seen as a nettlesome obstacle to the pursuit of wrongdoers — as in an inquisitorial society — then the Court's decision today makes a good deal of sense. If a lawyer is seen as an aid to the understanding and protection of constitutional rights — as in an accusatorial society — then today's decision makes no sense at all. . . .

NOTES AND QUESTIONS

1. Justice O'Connor's opinion for the Court and Justice Stevens' dissent in Moran v. Burbine read a good deal like the opinions in *Miranda* itself. But the roles are now reversed. It is Justice O'Connor's majority opinion that reminds us of law

enforcement needs and the important role station house confessions play in solving crimes, just as Justices Harlan and White reminded us of those factors in their *Miranda* dissents. And it is Justice Stevens' dissent that stresses the importance of rational, informed decisionmaking by suspects, and that emphasizes the role defense lawyers play in protecting that interest — just as Earl Warren did in his opinion for the Court. What explains this role reversal? What does it mean for *Miranda* waivers? If the *Burbine* majority accepted the principles of the *Miranda* dissenters, why did it leave *Miranda* in place?

2. The *Burbine* Court assumed, for purposes of its decision, that the officers lied to Burbine's lawyer (although the Court was careful to hedge about whether the lie was "deliberate"). Does Illinois v. Perkins, 496 U.S. 292 (1990), apply here? (*Perkins* is excerpted supra, at pages 805-809.) Recall that in *Perkins*, the police put an undercover agent in the defendant's jail cell; the Court found no *Miranda* "interrogation." Justice Stevens' dissent in *Burbine* seems to assume that lying to the suspect himself would be impermissible — yet *Perkins* plainly permitted lying to the suspect. Is lying to the suspect's lawyer worse than lying to the suspect himself? Is it worse when a police officer, acting as a police officer, lies than when an undercover police agent does so?

3. The relationship between police deception and *Miranda* waivers is complex. Consider Miller v. Fenton, 796 F.2d 598 (3d Cir. 1986), in which a divided Court of Appeals panel found a valid *Miranda* waiver on these facts:

> At the outset of our analysis, it is essential that we review the salient features of the interrogation. Because the state police taped the interrogation, we have had an opportunity actually to hear Detective Boyce's questions and Miller's responses. A significant portion of the questioning was in the typical police interrogation mode, developing chronologically Miller's whereabouts on the day in question, confronting him with the identification of his car, asking him point-blank whether he committed the crime, challenging his answers, and attempting to discover the details of the crime. This element of the interrogation is unexceptionable and unchallenged. We shall therefore focus primarily on the features of the interrogation that are at issue.
>
> It is clear that Boyce made no threats and engaged in no physical coercion of Miller. To the contrary, throughout the interview, Detective Boyce assumed a friendly, understanding manner and spoke in a soft tone of voice. He repeatedly assured Miller that he was sympathetic to him and wanted to help him unburden his mind. As the following excerpts demonstrate, the Detective's statements of sympathy at times approached the maudlin:
>
> > *Boyce*:   Now listen to me, Frank. This hurts me more than it hurts you, because I love people. . . .
> >
> > *Boyce*:   Let it come out, Frank. I'm here, I'm here with you now. I'm on your side, I'm on your side, Frank. I'm your brother, you and I are brothers, Frank. We are brothers, and I want to help my brother. . . .
> >
> > *Boyce*:   We have, we have a relationship, don't we? Have I been sincere with you, Frank?
>
> Boyce also gave Miller certain factual information, some of which was untrue. At the beginning of the interrogation, for example, Boyce informed Miller that the victim was still alive; this was false. During the interview, Boyce told Miller that Ms. Margolin had just died, although in fact she had been found dead several hours earlier.

Detective Boyce's major theme throughout the interrogation was that whoever had committed such a heinous crime had mental problems and was desperately in need of psychological treatment. From early in the interview, Detective Boyce led Miller to understand that he believed that Miller had committed the crime and that Miller now needed a friend to whom he could unburden himself. The Detective stated several times that Miller was not a criminal who should be punished, but a sick individual who should receive help. He assured Miller that he (Detective Boyce) was sincerely understanding and that he wished to help him with his problem. The following excerpts from the transcript of the interrogation provide examples of the statements about Miller's having psychological problems, as well as of the assurances of help:

Boyce: [L]et's forget this incident, [l]et's talk about your problem. This is what, this is what I'm concerned with, Frank, your problem.

Miller: Right.

Boyce: If I had a problem like your problem, I would want you to help me with my problem.

Miller: Uh, huh.

Boyce: Now, you know what I'm talking about.

Miller: Yeah.

Boyce: And I know, and I think that, uh, a lot of other people know. You know what I'm talking about. I don't think you're a criminal, Frank.

Miller: No, but you're trying to make me one.

Boyce: No I'm not, no I'm not, but I want you to talk to me so we can get this thing worked out. . . .

Boyce: I want you to talk to me. I want you to tell me what you think. I want you to tell me how you think about this, what you think about this.

Miller: What I think about it?

Boyce: Yeah.

Miller: I think whoever did it really needs help.

Boyce: And that's what I think and that's what I know. They don't, they don't need punishment, right? Like you said, they need help.

Miller: Right.

Boyce: They don't need punishment. They need help, good medical help.

Miller: That's right.

Boyce: [T]o rectify their problem. Putting them in, in a prison isn't going to solve it, is it?

Miller: No, sir. I know, I was in there for three and a half years. . . .

Boyce: You can see it Frank, you can feel it, you can feel it but you are not responsible. This is what I'm trying to tell you, but you've got to come forward and tell me. Don't, don't, don't let it eat you up, don't, don't fight it. You've got to rectify it, Frank. We've got to get together on this thing, or I, I mean really, you need help, you need proper help, and you know it, my God, you know, in God's name, you, you, you know it. You are not a criminal, you are not a criminal.

Boyce also appealed to Miller's conscience and described the importance of Miller's purging himself of the memories that must be haunting him. This aspect of the interrogation is exemplified in the preceding passage — "Don't, don't, don't let it eat you up, don't, don't fight it. You've got to rectify it, Frank." The following excerpts are representative of Boyce's arguments along this line:

Boyce: Frank, listen to me, honest to God, I'm, I'm telling you, Frank, (inaudible). I know, it's going to bother you, Frank, it's going to bother you. It's there, it's not going to go away, it's there. It's right in front of you, Frank. Am I right or wrong?

Miller: Yeah. . . .

Boyce: Honest, Frank. It's got to come out. You can't leave it in. It's hard for you, I realize that, how hard it is, how difficult it is, I realize that, but you've got to help yourself before anybody else can help you. . . .

Boyce: First thing we have to do is let it all come out. Don't fight it because it's worse, Frank, it's worse. It's hurting me because I feel it. I feel it wanting to come out, but it's hurting me, Frank. . . .

Boyce: No, listen to me, Frank, please listen to me. The issue now is what happened. The issue now is truth. Truth is the issue now. You've got to believe this, and the truth prevails in the end, Frank. You have to believe that and I'm sincere when I'm saying it to you. You've got to be truthful with yourself. . . .

Boyce: That's the most important thing, not, not what has happened, Frank. The fact that you were truthful, you came forward and you said, look I have a problem. I didn't mean to do what I did. I have a problem, this is what's important, Frank. This is very important, I got, I, I got to get closer to you, Frank, I got to make you believe this and I'm, and I'm sincere when I tell you this. You got to tell me exactly what happened, Frank. That's very important. I know how you feel inside, Frank, it's eating you up, am I right? It's eating you up, Frank. You've got to come forward. You've got to do it for yourself, for your family, for your father, this is what's important, the truth, Frank.

When Miller at last confessed, he collapsed in a state of shock. He slid off his chair and onto the floor with a blank stare on his face. The police officers sent for a first aid squad that took him to the hospital.

796 F.2d at 601-603. Are some kinds of deception more coercive than others? Was the deception in Miller v. Fenton coercive? Is your conclusion affected by the last three sentences quoted above? If so, why?

4. In Colorado v. Spring, 479 U.S. 564 (1987), the Supreme Court held a *Miranda* waiver valid even though the defendant was not apprised of every alleged crime with respect to which the police intended to interrogate him. Even if the police deliberately failed to inform Spring that they intended to interrogate him about another crime, the Court "has never held that mere silence by law enforcement officials as to the subject matter of an interrogation is 'trickery' sufficient to invalidate a suspect's waiver of *Miranda* rights, and we expressly decline so to hold today. Once *Miranda* warnings are given, it is difficult to see how official silence could cause a suspect to misunderstand the nature of his constitutional right . . . to refuse to answer any question which might incriminate him. . . . Here, the additional information could affect only the wisdom of a . . . waiver, not its essential voluntary and knowing nature." The dissent, by contrast, accused the majority of letting the state "take unfair advantage of the suspect's psychological state, as the unexpected questions cause the compulsive pressures [of custodial interrogation] suddenly to reappear."

5. The status of police trickery issue depends in part on the meaning of the words "knowing" and "intelligent." The *Burbine* Court found that the waiver was made "knowingly and intelligently." Is that finding correct? If Burbine had fully understood the practical implications of talking to the police as opposed to waiting to see a lawyer, do you think he would have talked? One might fairly argue that virtually no police station confessions are "knowing" or "intelligent" in the ordinary sense of those words because a well-informed suspect who is thinking would almost certainly keep quiet. So what do "knowing" and "intelligent" really mean in this context?

6. How does *Burbine* differ from *Escobedo*? Would the case have come out differently if the lawyer had been at the station house? If Burbine had asked if "anybody" had tried to contact him? If his lawyer had done so? Would it make any difference whether the police were truthful or dishonest in responding to such questions? In People v. McCauley, 645 N.E.2d 923 (Ill. 1994), the Supreme Court of Illinois concluded that "[r]egardless of the United States Supreme Court's current views on waiver of the right to counsel under the Federal Constitution, the law in Illinois [where *Escobedo* took place] remains that when police, prior to or during custodial interrogation, refuse an attorney appointed or retained to assist a suspect access to the suspect, there can be no knowing waiver of the right to counsel if the suspect has not been informed that the attorney was present and seeking to consult with him." Some other state supreme courts agree. See State v. Stoddard, 537 A.2d 446 (Conn. 1988); Haliburton v. State, 514 So. 2d 1088 (Fla. 1987).

7. *Escobedo*, *Burbine*, and *Spring* all dealt with situations where the suspect clearly made (and clearly articulated) a decision to *waive* his *Miranda* rights and speak to the police; the question was whether the waiver was valid. On the flip side, *Edwards* and *Mosley*, discussed in the preceding section, established that an *invocation* of *Miranda* rights has serious consequences, often making it much more difficult for the police to obtain information from the suspect.

What about cases where it is difficult (or impossible) to know exactly what the suspect wants to do? What if the suspect himself does not know? How large (or how small) is the "space" between invocation and waiver? These questions place the Court squarely on the horns of the fundamental dilemma posed by *Miranda*: How should the individual rights of crime suspects be balanced with the legitimate needs of law enforcement?

BERGHUIS v. THOMPKINS

Certiorari to United States Court of Appeals for the Sixth Circuit
130 S. Ct. 2250 (2010)

JUSTICE KENNEDY delivered the opinion of the Court.

I

A

On January 10, 2000, a shooting occurred outside a mall in Southfield, Michigan. Among the victims was Samuel Morris, who died from multiple gunshot wounds. The other victim, Frederick France, recovered from his injuries and later testified. Thompkins, who was a suspect, fled. About one year later he was found in Ohio and arrested there.

Two Southfield police officers traveled to Ohio to interrogate Thompkins, then awaiting transfer to Michigan. The interrogation began around 1:30 p.m. and lasted about three hours. The interrogation was conducted in a room that was 8 by 10 feet, and Thompkins sat in a chair that resembled a school desk (it had an arm on it that swings around to provide a surface to write on). App. 144a-145a. At the beginning of the interrogation, one of the officers, Detective Helgert, presented Thompkins with a form derived from the *Miranda* rule. It stated:

NOTIFICATION OF CONSTITUTIONAL RIGHTS AND STATEMENT

1. You have the right to remain silent.

2. Anything you say can and will be used against you in a court of law.

3. You have a right to talk to a lawyer before answering any questions and you have the right to have a lawyer present with you while you are answering any questions.

4. If you cannot afford to hire a lawyer, one will be appointed to represent you before any questioning, if you wish one.

5. You have the right to decide at any time before or during questioning to use your right to remain silent and your right to talk with a lawyer while you are being questioned.

Brief for Petitioner 60 (some capitalization omitted).

Helgert asked Thompkins to read the fifth warning out loud. App. 8a. Thompkins complied. Helgert later said this was to ensure that Thompkins could read, and Helgert concluded that Thompkins understood English. Helgert then read the other four *Miranda* warnings out loud and asked Thompkins to sign the form to demonstrate that he understood his rights. Thompkins declined to sign the form. The record contains conflicting evidence about whether Thompkins then verbally confirmed that he understood the rights listed on the form. Compare id., at 9a (at a suppression hearing, Helgert testified that Thompkins verbally confirmed that he understood his rights), with id., at 148a (at trial, Helgert stated, "I don't know that I orally asked him" whether Thompkins understood his rights).

Officers began an interrogation. At no point during the interrogation did Thompkins say that he wanted to remain silent, that he did not want to talk with the police, or that he wanted an attorney. Thompkins was "[l]argely" silent during the interrogation, which lasted about three hours. He did give a few limited verbal responses, however, such as "yeah," "no," or "I don't know." And on occasion he communicated by nodding his head. Thompkins also said that he "didn't want a peppermint" that was offered to him by the police and that the chair he was "sitting in was hard." Id., at [19a], 152a.

About 2 hours and 45 minutes into the interrogation, Helgert asked Thompkins, "Do you believe in God?" Thompkins made eye contact with Helgert and said "Yes," as his eyes "well[ed] up with tears." Helgert asked, "Do you pray to God?" Thompkins said "Yes." Helgert asked, "Do you pray to God to forgive you for shooting that boy down?" Thompkins answered "Yes" and looked away. Thompkins refused to make a written confession, and the interrogation ended about 15 minutes later. Id., at 11a[, 153a].

Thompkins was charged with first-degree murder, assault with intent to commit murder, and certain firearms-related offenses. He moved to suppress the statements made during the interrogation. He argued that he had invoked his Fifth Amendment right to remain silent, requiring police to end the interrogation at once, see Michigan v. Mosley, 423 U.S. 96, 103 (1975) (citing *Miranda*, 384 U.S., at 474), that he had not waived his right to remain silent, and that his inculpatory statements were involuntary. The trial court denied the motion.

. . . The jury found Thompkins guilty on all counts. He was sentenced to life in prison without parole.

B

[On appeal, the Michigan Court of Appeals affirmed, and the Michigan Supreme Court denied review. Thompkins then filed a federal habeas corpus petition. The district court held that Thompkins did not invoke his *Miranda* right to silence, and was not coerced into confessing. The district court also held that, under the governing habeas corpus standard, 28 U.S.C. §2254(d), the Michigan Court of Appeals made a "reasonable" decision that Thompkins had waived his right to silence. The Sixth Circuit reversed, granting the habeas petition on the grounds that the state court's waiver decision was "unreasonable." — EDS.]

III

The *Miranda* Court formulated a warning that must be given to suspects before they can be subjected to custodial interrogation. The substance of the warning still must be given to suspects today. . . . All concede that the warning given in this case was in full compliance with these requirements. The dispute centers on the response — or nonresponse — from the suspect.

A

Thompkins makes various arguments that his answers to questions from the detectives were inadmissible. He first contends that he "invoke[d] his privilege" to remain silent by not saying anything for a sufficient period of time, so the interrogation should have "cease[d]" before he made his inculpatory statements. [*Miranda*, 383 U.S.,] at 474; see *Mosley*, 423 U.S., at 103 (police must "'scrupulously hono[r]'" this "critical safeguard" when the accused invokes his or her "'right to cut off questioning'" (quoting *Miranda*, supra, at 474, 479)).

This argument is unpersuasive. In the context of invoking the *Miranda* right to counsel, the Court in Davis v. United States, 512 U.S. 452, 459 (1994), held that a suspect must do so "unambiguously." If an accused makes a statement concerning the right to counsel "that is ambiguous or equivocal" or makes no statement, the police are not required to end the interrogation, ibid., or ask questions to clarify whether the accused wants to invoke his or her *Miranda* rights, 512 U.S., at 461-462.

The Court has not yet stated whether an invocation of the right to remain silent can be ambiguous or equivocal, but there is no principled reason to adopt different standards for determining when an accused has invoked the *Miranda* right to remain silent and the *Miranda* right to counsel at issue in *Davis*. See, e.g., Solem v. Stumes, 465 U.S. 638, 648 (1984) ("[M]uch of the logic and language of [*Mosley*]," which discussed the *Miranda* right to remain silent, "could be applied to the invocation of the [*Miranda* right to counsel]"). Both protect the privilege against compulsory self-incrimination, *Miranda*, supra, at 467-473, by requiring an interrogation to cease when either right is invoked, *Mosley*, supra, at 103 (citing *Miranda*, supra, at 474); Fare v. Michael C., 442 U.S. 707, 719 (1979).

There is good reason to require an accused who wants to invoke his or her right to remain silent to do so unambiguously. A requirement of an unambiguous invocation of *Miranda* rights results in an objective inquiry that "avoid[s] difficulties of proof and . . . provide[s] guidance to officers" on how to proceed in the face of ambiguity. *Davis*, 512 U.S., at 458-459. If an ambiguous act, omission, or statement could require police to end the interrogation, police would be required to make difficult decisions about an accused's unclear intent and face the consequence of suppression "if they guess wrong." Id., at 461. Suppression of a voluntary confession in these circumstances would place a significant burden on society's interest in prosecuting criminal activity. See id., at 459-461; Moran v. Burbine, 475 U.S. 412, 427 (1986). Treating an ambiguous or equivocal act, omission, or statement as an invocation of *Miranda* rights "might add marginally to *Miranda*'s goal of dispelling the compulsion inherent in custodial interrogation." *Burbine*, 475 U.S., at 425. But "as *Miranda* holds, full comprehension of the rights to remain silent and request an attorney are sufficient to dispel whatever coercion is inherent in the interrogation process." Id., at 427; see *Davis*, supra, at 460.

Thompkins did not say that he wanted to remain silent or that he did not want to talk with the police. Had he made either of these simple, unambiguous statements, he would have invoked his "'right to cut off questioning.'" *Mosley*, supra, at 103 (quoting *Miranda*, supra, at 474). Here he did neither, so he did not invoke his right to remain silent.

B

We next consider whether Thompkins waived his right to remain silent. Even absent the accused's invocation of the right to remain silent, the accused's statement during a custodial interrogation is inadmissible at trial unless the prosecution can establish that the accused "in fact knowingly and voluntarily waived [*Miranda*] rights" when making the statement. [North Carolina v.] Butler, 441 U.S. [369,] 373 [(1979)]. The waiver inquiry "has two distinct dimensions": waiver must be "voluntary in the sense that it was the product of a free and deliberate choice rather than intimidation, coercion, or deception," and "made with a full awareness of both the nature of the right being abandoned and the consequences of the decision to abandon it." *Burbine*, supra, at 421.

Some language in *Miranda* could be read to indicate that waivers are difficult to establish absent an explicit written waiver or a formal, express oral statement. *Miranda* said "a valid waiver will not be presumed simply from the silence of the accused after warnings are given or simply from the fact that a confession was in fact eventually obtained." 384 U.S., at 475 . . . In addition, the *Miranda* Court stated that "a heavy burden rests on the government to demonstrate that the defendant knowingly and intelligently waived his privilege against self-incrimination and his right to retained or appointed counsel." Id., at 475.

The course of decisions since *Miranda*, informed by the application of *Miranda* warnings in the whole course of law enforcement, demonstrates that waivers can be established even absent formal or express statements of waiver that would be expected in, say, a judicial hearing to determine if a guilty plea has been properly entered. Cf. Fed. Rule Crim. Proc. 11. The main purpose of *Miranda* is to ensure that an accused is advised of and understands the right to remain silent and the right to counsel. See *Davis*, supra, at 460; *Burbine*, supra, at 427. Thus, "[i]f anything, our subsequent cases have reduced the impact of the *Miranda* rule on legitimate law enforcement while reaffirming the decision's core ruling that unwarned statements may not be used as evidence in the prosecution's case in chief." Dickerson v. United States, 530 U.S. 428, 443-444 (2000).

One of the first cases to decide the meaning and import of *Miranda* with respect to the question of waiver was North Carolina v. Butler. The *Butler* Court, after discussing some of the problems created by the language in *Miranda*, established certain important propositions. *Butler* interpreted the *Miranda* language concerning the "heavy burden" to show waiver, 384 U.S., at 475, in accord with usual principles of determining waiver, which can include waiver implied from all the circumstances. See *Butler*, supra, at 373, 376. And in a later case, the Court stated that this "heavy burden" is not more than the burden to establish waiver by a preponderance of the evidence. Colorado v. Connelly, 479 U.S. 157, 168 (1986).

The prosecution therefore does not need to show that a waiver of *Miranda* rights was express. An "implicit waiver" of the "right to remain silent" is sufficient to admit a suspect's statement into evidence. *Butler*, supra, at 376. *Butler* made clear that a waiver of *Miranda* rights may be implied through "the defendant's silence, coupled with an understanding of his rights and a course of conduct indicating waiver." 441 U.S., at 373. The Court in *Butler* therefore "retreated" from the "language and tenor of the *Miranda* opinion," which "suggested that the Court would require that a waiver . . . be 'specifically made.'" Connecticut v. Barrett, 479 U.S. 523, 531-532 (1987) (Brennan, J., concurring in judgment).

If the State establishes that a *Miranda* warning was given and the accused made an uncoerced statement, this showing, standing alone, is insufficient to demonstrate "a valid waiver" of *Miranda* rights. *Miranda*, supra, at 475. The prosecution must make the additional showing that the accused understood these rights. See Colorado v. Spring, 479 U.S. 564, 573-575 (1987); *Barrett*, supra, at 530; *Burbine*, supra, at 421-422. Cf. Tague v. Louisiana, 444 U.S. 469, 469, 471 (1980) (per curiam) (no evidence that accused understood his *Miranda* rights); Carnley v. Cochran, 369 U.S. 506, 516 (1962) (government could not show that accused "understandingly" waived his right to counsel in light of "silent record"). Where the prosecution shows that a *Miranda* warning was given and that it was understood by the accused, an accused's uncoerced statement establishes an implied waiver of the right to remain silent.

Although *Miranda* imposes on the police a rule that is both formalistic and practical when it prevents them from interrogating suspects without first providing them with a *Miranda* warning, see *Burbine*, 475 U.S., at 427, it does not impose a formalistic waiver procedure that a suspect must follow to relinquish those rights. As a general proposition, the law can presume that an individual who, with a full understanding of his or her rights, acts in a manner inconsistent with their exercise has made a deliberate choice to relinquish the protection those rights afford. See, e.g., *Butler*, supra, at 372-376; *Connelly*, supra, at 169-170 ("There is obviously no reason to require more in the way of a 'voluntariness' inquiry in the *Miranda* waiver context than in the [due process] confession context"). The Court's cases have recognized that a waiver of *Miranda* rights need only meet the standard of Johnson v. Zerbst, 304 U.S. 458, 464 (1938). See *Butler*, supra, at 374-375; *Miranda*, supra, at 475-476 (applying *Zerbst* standard of intentional relinquishment of a known right). As *Butler* recognized, 441 U.S., at 375-376, *Miranda* rights can therefore be waived through means less formal than a typical waiver on the record in a courtroom, cf. Fed. Rule Crim. Proc. 11, given the practical constraints and necessities of interrogation and the fact that *Miranda*'s main protection lies in advising defendants of their rights, see *Davis*, 512 U.S., at 460; *Burbine*, 475 U.S., at 427.

The record in this case shows that Thompkins waived his right to remain silent. There is no basis in this case to conclude that he did not understand his rights; and on these facts it follows that he chose not to invoke or rely on those rights when he did speak. First, there is no contention that Thompkins did not understand his rights; and from this it follows that he knew what he gave up when he spoke. See id., at 421. There was more than enough evidence in the record to conclude that Thompkins understood his *Miranda* rights. Thompkins received a written copy of the *Miranda* warnings; Detective Helgert determined that Thompkins could read and understand English; and Thompkins was given time to read the warnings. Thompkins, furthermore, read aloud the fifth warning, which stated that "you have the right to decide at any time before or during questioning to use your right to remain silent and your right to talk with a lawyer while you are being questioned." Brief for Petitioner 60 (capitalization omitted). He was thus aware that his right to remain silent would not dissipate after a certain amount of time and that police would have to honor his right to be silent and his right to counsel during the whole course of interrogation. Those rights, the warning made clear, could be asserted at any time. Helgert, moreover, read the warnings aloud.

Second, Thompkins's answer to Detective Helgert's question about whether Thompkins prayed to God for forgiveness for shooting the victim is a "course of conduct indicating waiver" of the right to remain silent. *Butler*, supra, at 373. If Thompkins wanted to remain silent, he could have said nothing in response to Helgert's questions, or he could have unambiguously invoked his *Miranda* rights and ended the interrogation. The fact that Thompkins made a statement about three hours after receiving a *Miranda* warning does not overcome the fact that he engaged in a course of conduct indicating waiver. Police are not required to rewarn suspects from time to time. Thompkins's answer to Helgert's question about praying to God for forgiveness for shooting the victim was sufficient to show a course of conduct indicating waiver. This is confirmed by the fact that before then Thompkins had given sporadic answers to questions throughout the interrogation.

Third, there is no evidence that Thompkins's statement was coerced. See *Burbine*, supra, at 421. Thompkins does not claim that police threatened or injured him during the interrogation or that he was in any way fearful. The interrogation was conducted in a standard-sized room in the middle of the afternoon. It is true that apparently he was in a straight-backed chair for three hours, but there is no authority for the proposition that an interrogation of this length is inherently coercive. Indeed, even where interrogations of greater duration were held to be improper, they were accompanied, as this one was not, by other facts indicating coercion, such as an incapacitated and sedated suspect, sleep and food deprivation, and threats. Cf. *Connelly*, 479 U.S., at 163-164, n. 1. The fact that Helgert's question referred to Thompkins's religious beliefs also did not render Thompkins's statement involuntary. "[T]he Fifth Amendment privilege is not concerned 'with moral and psychological pressures to confess emanating from sources other than official coercion.'" Id., at 170 (quoting Oregon v. Elstad, 470 U.S. 298, 305 (1985)). In these circumstances, Thompkins knowingly and voluntarily made a statement to police, so he waived his right to remain silent.

C

Thompkins next argues that, even if his answer to Detective Helgert could constitute a waiver of his right to remain silent, the police were not allowed to question him until they obtained a waiver first. *Butler* forecloses this argument. The *Butler* Court held that courts can infer a waiver of *Miranda* rights "from the actions and words of the person interrogated." 441 U.S., at 373. This principle would be inconsistent with a rule that requires a waiver at the outset. The *Butler* Court thus rejected the rule proposed by the *Butler* dissent, which would have "requir[ed] the police to obtain an express waiver of [*Miranda* rights] before proceeding with interrogation." Id., at 379 (Brennan, J., dissenting). This holding also makes sense given that "the primary protection afforded suspects subject[ed] to custodial interrogation is the *Miranda* warnings themselves." *Davis*, 512 U.S., at 460. The *Miranda* rule and its requirements are met if a suspect receives adequate *Miranda* warnings, understands them, and has an opportunity to invoke the rights before giving any answers or admissions. Any waiver, express or implied, may be contradicted by an invocation at any time. If the right to counsel or the right to remain silent is invoked at any point during questioning, further interrogation must cease.

Interrogation provides the suspect with additional information that can put his or her decision to waive, or not to invoke, into perspective. As questioning commences and then continues, the suspect has the opportunity to consider the choices he or she faces and to make a more informed decision, either to insist on silence or to cooperate. When the suspect knows that *Miranda* rights can be invoked at any time, he or she has the opportunity to reassess his or her immediate and long-term interests. Cooperation with the police may result in more favorable treatment for the suspect; the apprehension of accomplices; the prevention of continuing injury and fear; beginning steps towards relief or solace for the victims; and the beginning of the suspect's own return to the law and the social order it seeks to protect.

In order for an accused's statement to be admissible at trial, police must have given the accused a *Miranda* warning. See *Miranda*, 384 U.S., at 471. If that condition is established, the court can proceed to consider whether there has been an express or implied waiver of *Miranda* rights. Id., at 476. In making its ruling on the admissibility of a statement made during custodial questioning, the trial court, of course, considers whether there is evidence to support the conclusion that, from the whole course of questioning, an express or implied waiver has been established. Thus, after giving a *Miranda* warning, police may interrogate a suspect who has neither invoked nor waived his or her *Miranda* rights. On these premises, it follows the police were not required to obtain a waiver of Thompkins's *Miranda* rights before commencing the interrogation.

D

In sum, a suspect who has received and understood the *Miranda* warnings, and has not invoked his *Miranda* rights, waives the right to remain silent by making an uncoerced statement to the police. Thompkins did not invoke his right to remain silent and stop the questioning. Understanding his rights in full, he waived his right to remain silent by making a voluntary statement to the police. The police, moreover, were not required to obtain a waiver of Thompkins's right to remain silent before interrogating him. The state court's decision rejecting Thompkins's

Miranda claim was thus correct under de novo review and therefore necessarily reasonable under the more deferential AEDPA standard of review, 28 U.S.C. §2254(d). . . .

* * *

The judgment of the Court of Appeals is reversed, and the case is remanded with instructions to deny the petition.

JUSTICE SOTOMAYOR, with whom JUSTICE STEVENS, JUSTICE GINSBURG, and JUSTICE BREYER join, dissenting.

The Court concludes today that a criminal suspect waives his right to remain silent if, after sitting tacit and uncommunicative through nearly three hours of police interrogation, he utters a few one-word responses. The Court also concludes that a suspect who wishes to guard his right to remain silent against such a finding of "waiver" must, counterintuitively, speak—and must do so with sufficient precision to satisfy a clear-statement rule that construes ambiguity in favor of the police. Both propositions mark a substantial retreat from the protection against compelled self-incrimination that Miranda v. Arizona, 384 U.S. 436 (1966), has long provided during custodial interrogation. . . .

I

. . . The strength of Thompkins' *Miranda* claims depends in large part on the circumstances of the 3-hour interrogation, at the end of which he made inculpatory statements later introduced at trial. The Court's opinion downplays record evidence that Thompkins remained almost completely silent and unresponsive throughout that session. One of the interrogating officers, Detective Helgert, testified that although Thompkins was administered *Miranda* warnings, the last of which he read aloud, Thompkins expressly declined to sign a written acknowledgment that he had been advised of and understood his rights. There is conflicting evidence in the record about whether Thompkins ever verbally confirmed understanding his rights. The record contains no indication that the officers sought or obtained an express waiver.

As to the interrogation itself, Helgert candidly characterized it as "very, very one-sided" and "nearly a monologue." Thompkins was "[p]eculiar," "[s]ullen," and "[g]enerally quiet." Helgert and his partner "did most of the talking," as Thompkins was "not verbally communicative" and "[l]argely" remained silent. To the extent Thompkins gave any response, his answers consisted of "a word or two. A 'yeah,' or a 'no,' or 'I don't know.' . . . And sometimes . . . he simply sat down . . . with [his] head in [his] hands looking down. Sometimes . . . he would look up and make eye-contact would be the only response." After proceeding in this fashion for approximately 2 hours and 45 minutes, Helgert asked Thompkins three questions relating to his faith in God. The prosecution relied at trial on Thompkins' one-word answers of "yes." See [App.] at 10a-11a[, 17a, 19a, 23a-24a, and 149a].

Thompkins' nonresponsiveness is particularly striking in the context of the officers' interview strategy, later explained as conveying to Thompkins that "this was his opportunity to explain his side [of the story]" because "[e]verybody else, including [his] co-[d]efendants, had given their version." . . . Yet, Helgert confirmed that the "*only* thing [Thompkins said] relative to his involvement [in the shooting]" occurred near the end of the interview—i.e., in response to the questions about God. Id., at 10a-11a, [21a] (emphasis added). . . . Nevertheless, the Michigan court concluded on this record that Thompkins had not invoked his right to remain silent because "he continued to talk with the officer, albeit sporadically," and that he voluntarily waived that right. App. to Pet. for Cert. 75a. . . .

The question whether a suspect has validly waived his right is "entirely distinct" as a matter of law from whether he invoked that right. Smith v. Illinois, 469 U.S. 91, 98 (1984) (per curiam). The questions are related, however, in terms of the practical effect on the exercise of a suspect's rights. A suspect may at any time revoke his prior waiver of rights — or, closer to the facts of this case, guard against the possibility of a future finding that he implicitly waived his rights — by invoking the rights and thereby requiring the police to cease questioning.

II

A

Like the Sixth Circuit, I begin with the question whether Thompkins waived his right to remain silent. Even if Thompkins did not invoke that right, he is entitled to relief because Michigan did not satisfy its burden of establishing waiver.

. . . Rarely do this Court's precedents provide clearly established law so closely on point with the facts of a particular case. Together, *Miranda* and *Butler* establish that a court "must presume that a defendant did not waive his right[s]"; the prosecution bears a "heavy burden" in attempting to demonstrate waiver; the fact of a "lengthy interrogation" prior to obtaining statements is "strong evidence" against a finding of valid waiver; "mere silence" in response to questioning is "not enough"; and waiver may not be presumed "simply from the fact that a confession was in fact eventually obtained." *Miranda*, supra, at 475-476; *Butler*, supra, at 372-373.[3]

It is undisputed here that Thompkins never expressly waived his right to remain silent. His refusal to sign even an acknowledgment that he understood his *Miranda* rights evinces, if anything, an intent not to waive those rights. Cf. United States v. Plugh, 576 F.3d 135, 142 (CA2 2009) (suspect's refusal to sign waiver-of-rights form "constituted an unequivocally negative answer to the question . . . whether he was willing to waive his rights"). That Thompkins did not make the inculpatory statements at issue until after approximately 2 hours and 45 minutes of interrogation serves as "strong evidence" against waiver. *Miranda* and *Butler* expressly preclude the possibility that the inculpatory statements themselves are sufficient to establish waiver.

In these circumstances, Thompkins' "actions and words" preceding the inculpatory statements simply do not evidence a "course of conduct indicating waiver" sufficient to carry the prosecution's burden. See *Butler*, supra, at 373.

3. Likely reflecting the great weight of the prosecution's burden in proving implied waiver, many contemporary police training resources instruct officers to obtain a waiver of rights prior to proceeding at all with an interrogation. See, e.g., F. Inbau, J. Reid, J. Buckley, & B. Jayne, Criminal Interrogation and Confessions 491 (4th ed. 2004) (hereinafter Inbau) ("Once [a] waiver is given, the police may proceed with the interrogation"); D. Zulawski & D. Wicklander, Practical Aspects of Interview and Interrogation 55 (2d ed. 2002) ("Only upon the waiver of th[e] [*Miranda*] rights by the suspect can an interrogation occur"); see also Brief for National Association of Criminal Defense Lawyers et al. as *Amici Curiae* 11-12 (hereinafter NACDL brief) (collecting authorities).

Although the Michigan court stated that Thompkins "sporadically" participated in the interview, App. to Pet. for Cert. 75a, that court's opinion and the record before us are silent as to the subject matter or context of even a single question to which Thompkins purportedly responded, other than the exchange about God and the statements respecting the peppermint and the chair. Unlike in *Butler*, Thompkins made no initial declaration akin to "I will talk to you." See also 547 F.3d at 586-587 (case below) (noting that the case might be different if the record showed Thompkins had responded affirmatively to an invitation to tell his side of the story or described any particular question that Thompkins answered). Indeed, Michigan and the United States concede that no waiver occurred in this case until Thompkins responded "yes" to the questions about God. See Tr. of Oral Arg. 7, 30. I believe it is objectively unreasonable under our clearly established precedents to conclude the prosecution met its "heavy burden" of proof on a record consisting of three one-word answers, following 2 hours and 45 minutes of silence punctuated by a few largely nonverbal responses to unidentified questions.

B

. . . The Court concludes that when *Miranda* warnings have been given and understood, "an accused's uncoerced statement establishes an implied waiver of the right to remain silent." More broadly still, the Court states that, "[a]s a general proposition, the law can presume that an individual who, with a full understanding of his or her rights, acts in a manner inconsistent with their exercise has made a deliberate choice to relinquish the protection those rights afford."

These principles flatly contradict our longstanding views that "a valid waiver will not be presumed . . . simply from the fact that a confession was in fact eventually obtained," *Miranda*, 384 U.S., at 475, and that "[t]he courts must presume that a defendant did not waive his rights," *Butler*, 441 U.S., at 373. Indeed, we have in the past summarily reversed a state-court decision that inverted *Miranda*'s antiwaiver presumption, characterizing the error as "readily apparent." *Tague*, 444 U.S., at 470-471. At best, the Court today creates an unworkable and conflicting set of presumptions that will undermine *Miranda*'s goal of providing "concrete constitutional guidelines for law enforcement agencies and courts to follow," 384 U.S., at 442. At worst, it overrules *sub silentio* an essential aspect of the protections *Miranda* has long provided for the constitutional guarantee against self-incrimination.

The Court's conclusion that Thompkins' inculpatory statements were sufficient to establish an implied waiver finds no support in *Butler*. *Butler* itself distinguished between a sufficient "course of conduct" and inculpatory statements, reiterating *Miranda*'s admonition that "'a valid waiver will not be presumed simply from . . . the fact that a confession was in fact eventually obtained.'" *Butler*, supra, at 373 (quoting *Miranda*, supra, at 475). Michigan suggests Butler's silence "'when advised of his right to the assistance of a lawyer,'" combined with our remand for the state court to apply the implied-waiver standard, shows that silence followed by statements can be a "'course of conduct.'" Brief for Petitioner 26 (quoting *Butler*, supra, at 371). But the evidence of implied waiver in *Butler* was worlds apart from the evidence in this case, because Butler unequivocally said "I will talk to you" after having been read *Miranda* warnings. Thompkins, of course, made no such statement.

The Court also relies heavily on *Burbine* in characterizing the scope of the prosecution's burden in proving waiver. Consistent with *Burbine*, the Court observes, the prosecution must prove that waiver was "'voluntary in the sense that it was the product of a free and deliberate choice rather than intimidation'" and "'made with a full awareness of both the nature of the right being abandoned and the consequences of the decision to abandon it.'" (quoting 475 U.S., at 421). I agree with the Court's statement, so far as it goes. What it omits, however, is that the prosecution also bears an antecedent burden of showing there was, in fact, either an express waiver or a "course of conduct" sufficiently clear to support a finding of implied waiver. Nothing in *Burbine* even hints at removing that obligation. The question in that case, rather, was whether a suspect's multiple express waivers of his rights were invalid because police "misinformed an inquiring attorney about their plans concerning the suspect or because they failed to inform the suspect of the attorney's efforts to reach him." Id., at 420; see also Colorado v. Spring, 479 U.S. 564, 573 (1987). The Court's analysis in *Burbine* was predicated on the existence of waiver-in-fact.

Today's dilution of the prosecution's burden of proof to the bare fact that a suspect made inculpatory statements after *Miranda* warnings were given and understood takes an unprecedented step away from the "high standards of proof for the waiver of constitutional rights" this Court has long demanded. *Miranda*, supra, at 475; cf. Brewer v. Williams, 430 U.S. 387, 404 (1977) ("[C]ourts indulge in every reasonable presumption against waiver"); *Zerbst*, 304 U.S., at 464. When waiver is to be inferred during a custodial interrogation, there are sound reasons to require evidence beyond inculpatory statements themselves. *Miranda* and our subsequent cases are premised on the idea that custodial interrogation is inherently coercive. See 384 U.S., at 455 ("Even without employing brutality, the 'third degree' or [other] specific strategems . . . the very fact of custodial interrogation exacts a heavy toll on individual liberty and trades on the weakness of individuals"); Dickerson v. United States, 530 U.S. 428, 435 (2000). Requiring proof of a course of conduct beyond the inculpatory statements themselves is critical to ensuring that those statements are voluntary admissions and not the dubious product of an overborne will. . . .

III

Thompkins separately argues that his conduct during the interrogation invoked his right to remain silent, requiring police to terminate questioning. Like the Sixth Circuit, I would not reach this question because Thompkins is in any case entitled to relief as to waiver. But even if Thompkins would not prevail on his invocation claim . . . , I cannot agree with the Court's much broader ruling that a suspect must clearly invoke his right to silence by speaking. Taken together with the Court's reformulation of the prosecution's burden of proof as to waiver, today's novel clear-statement rule for invocation invites police to question a suspect at length — notwithstanding his persistent refusal to answer questions — in the hope of eventually obtaining a single inculpatory response which will suffice to prove waiver of rights. Such a result bears little semblance to the "fully effective" prophylaxis, 384 U.S., at 444, that *Miranda* requires. . . .

B

The Court . . . extend[s] [Davis v. United States, 512 U.S. 452 (1994)] to hold that police may continue questioning a suspect until he unambiguously invokes his right to remain silent. Because Thompkins neither said "he wanted to remain silent" nor said "he did not want to talk with the police," the Court concludes, he did not clearly invoke his right to silence.

I disagree with this novel application of *Davis*. Neither the rationale nor holding of that case compels today's result. *Davis* involved the right to counsel, not the right to silence. . . . *Miranda* itself "distinguished between the procedural safeguards triggered by a request to remain silent and a request for an attorney." *Mosley*, supra, at 104, n. 10; accord, *Edwards*, supra, at 485. *Mosley* upheld the admission of statements when police immediately stopped interrogating a suspect who invoked his right to silence, but reapproached him after a 2-hour delay and obtained inculpatory responses relating to a different crime after administering fresh *Miranda* warnings. The different effects of invoking the rights are consistent with distinct standards for invocation. To the extent *Mosley* contemplates a more flexible form of prophylaxis than *Edwards* — and, in particular, does not categorically bar police from reapproaching a suspect who has invoked his right to remain silent — *Davis'* concern about "wholly irrational obstacles" to police investigation applies with less force.

In addition, the suspect's equivocal reference to a lawyer in *Davis* occurred only *after* he had given express oral and written waivers of his rights. *Davis'* holding is explicitly predicated on that fact. See 512 U.S., at 461 ("We therefore hold that, after a knowing and voluntary waiver of the *Miranda* rights, law enforcement officers may continue questioning until and unless the suspect clearly requests an attorney"). The Court ignores this aspect of *Davis*, as well as the decisions of numerous federal and state courts declining to apply a clear-statement rule when a suspect has not previously given an express waiver of rights. . . .

In my mind, a more appropriate standard for addressing a suspect's ambiguous invocation of the right to remain silent is the constraint *Mosley* places on questioning a suspect who has invoked that right: The suspect's "right to cut off questioning" must be "scrupulously honored." See 423 U.S., at 104. Such a standard is necessarily precautionary and fact specific. The rule would acknowledge that some statements or conduct are so equivocal that police may scrupulously honor a suspect's rights without terminating questioning — for instance, if a suspect's actions are reasonably understood to indicate a willingness to listen before deciding whether to respond. But other statements or actions — in particular, when a suspect sits silent throughout prolonged interrogation, long past the point when he could be deciding whether to respond — cannot reasonably be understood other than as an invocation of the right to remain silent. Under such circumstances, "scrupulous" respect for the suspect's rights will require police to terminate questioning under *Mosley*.[8]

___

8. Indeed, this rule appears to reflect widespread contemporary police practice. Thompkins' *amici* collect a range of training materials that instruct police not to engage in prolonged interrogation after a suspect has failed to respond to initial questioning. See NACDL Brief 32-34. One widely used police manual, for example, teaches that a suspect who "indicates," "even by silence itself," his unwillingness to answer questions "has obviously exercised his constitutional privilege against self-incrimination." Inbau 498.

To be sure, such a standard does not provide police with a bright-line rule. But, as we have previously recognized, *Mosley* itself does not offer clear guidance to police about when and how interrogation may continue after a suspect invokes his rights. . . . Given that police have for nearly 35 years applied *Mosley*'s fact-specific standard in questioning suspects who have invoked their right to remain silent; that our cases did not during that time resolve what statements or actions suffice to invoke that right; and that neither Michigan nor the Solicitor General have provided evidence in this case that the status quo has proved unworkable, I see little reason to believe today's clear-statement rule is necessary to ensure effective law enforcement.

Davis' clear-statement rule is also a poor fit for the right to silence. Advising a suspect that he has a "right to remain silent" is unlikely to convey that he must speak (and must do so in some particular fashion) to ensure the right will be protected. Cf. Soffar v. Cockrell, 300 F.3d 588, 603 (CA5 2002) (en banc) (DeMoss, J., dissenting) ("What in the world must an individual do to exercise his constitutional right to remain silent beyond actually, in fact, remaining silent?"). By contrast, telling a suspect "he has the right to the presence of an attorney, and that if he cannot afford an attorney one will be appointed for him prior to any questioning if he so desires," *Miranda*, 384 U.S., at 479, implies the need for speech to exercise that right. . . .

. . . If a suspect makes an ambiguous statement or engages in conduct that creates uncertainty about his intent to invoke his right, police can simply ask for clarification. See *Davis*, 512 U.S., at 467 (Souter, J., concurring in judgment). It is hardly an unreasonable burden for police to ask a suspect, for instance, "Do you want to talk to us?" The majority in *Davis* itself approved of this approach as protecting suspects' rights while "minimiz[ing] the chance of a confession [later] being suppressed." Id., at 461. . . . Police may well prefer not to seek clarification of an ambiguous statement out of fear that a suspect will invoke his rights. But "our system of justice is not founded on a fear that a suspect will exercise his rights. 'If the exercise of constitutional rights will thwart the effectiveness of a system of law enforcement, then there is something very wrong with that system.'" *Burbine*, 475 U.S., at 458 (Stevens, J., dissenting) (quoting Escobedo v. Illinois, 378 U.S. 478, 490 (1964)).

The Court asserts in passing that treating ambiguous statements or acts as an invocation of the right to silence will only "marginally" serve *Miranda*'s goals. Experience suggests the contrary. In the 16 years since *Davis* was decided, ample evidence has accrued that criminal suspects often use equivocal or colloquial language in attempting to invoke their right to silence. A number of lower courts that have (erroneously, in my view) imposed a clear-statement requirement for invocation of the right to silence have rejected as ambiguous an array of statements whose meaning might otherwise be thought plain.[9] At a minimum, these decisions suggest that

9. See United States v. Sherrod, 445 F.3d 980, 982 (CA7 2006) (suspect's statement "I'm not going to talk about nothin'" was ambiguous, "as much a taunt — even a provocation — as it [was] an invocation of the right to remain silent"); Burket v. Angelone, 208 F.3d 172, 200 (CA4 2000) (upholding on [habeas] review a state court's conclusion that "I just don't think that I should say anything" was not a clear request to remain silent); State v. Jackson, 839 N.E.2d 362, 373 [(Ohio S. Ct. 2006)] (finding ambiguous "I don't even like talking about it man . . . I told you . . . what happened, man . . . I mean, I don't even want to, you know what I'm saying, discuss no more about it, man"); . . . State v. Deen, 953 So. 2d 1057, 1058-1060 [(La. App. 2007)] ("Okay, if you're implying that I've done it, I wish to not say any more. I'd like to be done with this. Cause that's just ridiculous. I wish I'd . . . don't wish

differentiating "clear" from "ambiguous" statements is often a subjective inquiry. Even if some of the cited decisions are themselves in tension with *Davis'* admonition that a suspect need not "speak with the discrimination of an Oxford don" to invoke his rights, 512 U.S., at 459, they demonstrate that today's decision will significantly burden the exercise of the right to silence. Notably, when a suspect "understands his (expressed) wishes to have been ignored . . . in contravention of the 'rights' just read to him by his interrogator, he may well see further objection as futile and confession (true or not) as the only way to end his interrogation." Id., at 472-473.

For these reasons, I believe a precautionary requirement that police "scrupulously hono[r]" a suspect's right to cut off questioning is a more faithful application of our precedents than the Court's awkward and needless extension of *Davis*.

* * *

Today's decision turns *Miranda* upside down. Criminal suspects must now unambiguously invoke their right to remain silent — which, counterintuitively, requires them to speak. At the same time, suspects will be legally presumed to have waived their rights even if they have given no clear expression of their intent to do so. Those results, in my view, find no basis in *Miranda* or our subsequent cases and are inconsistent with the fair-trial principles on which those precedents are grounded. . . . I respectfully dissent.

NOTES AND QUESTIONS

1. The *Thompkins* Court (and dissent) relied heavily on North Carolina v. Butler, 441 U.S. 369 (1979). Here are the facts in *Butler*:

> . . . Agent Martinez testified that at the time of the arrest he fully advised the respondent of the rights delineated in the *Miranda* case. According to the uncontroverted testimony of Martinez, the agents then took the respondent to the FBI office in nearby New Rochelle, N.Y. There, after the agents determined that the respondent had an 11th grade education and was literate, he was given the Bureau's "Advice of Rights" form which he read. When asked if he understood his rights, he replied that he did. The respondent refused to sign the waiver at the bottom of the form. He was told that he need neither speak nor sign the form, but that the agents would like him to talk to them. The respondent replied: "I will talk to you but I am not signing any form." He then made inculpatory statements. Agent Martinez testified that the respondent said nothing when advised of his right to the assistance of a lawyer. At no time did the respondent request counsel or attempt to terminate the agents' questioning.

Id., at 370-371. The Court found a valid *Miranda* waiver:

> An express written or oral statement of waiver of the right to remain silent or of the right to counsel is usually strong proof of the validity of that waiver, but is not inevitably either necessary or sufficient to establish waiver. . . . The courts must presume that

---

to answer any more questions" ambiguous because conditioned on officer's implication that suspect committed specific assault). . . . See generally Strauss, The Sounds of Silence: Reconsidering the Invocation of the Right to Remain Silent under *Miranda*, 17 Wm. & Mary Bill Rights J. 773, 788-802 (2009) (surveying cases).

a defendant did not waive his rights; . . . but in at least some cases waiver can be clearly inferred from the actions and words of the person interrogated.

Id., at 373.

2. Before *Thompkins*, some of the most difficult questions surrounding *Miranda* involved the "space" between clear invocations and clear waivers. See, e.g., *Butler*; *Davis*; *Smith*; *Barrett*; and *Michael C.*; see also the several lower-court cases cited in footnote 9 of Justice Sotomayor's *Thompkins* dissent). These kinds of cases posed two key doctrinal challenges: What does it take to make a legally valid invocation or a legally valid waiver of *Miranda* rights? And if a particular situation falls somewhere between the two, what legal standard governs the behavior of the police?

Thompkins appears to solve the problem by essentially eliminating the "space" itself. Until the moment when a suspect clearly invokes one of his *Miranda* rights, the police may continue to seek a waiver of those rights — and, even absent a clear waiver, as soon as the suspect says anything to the police he will be held to have impliedly waived his rights (as long as the police can show that they gave him proper warnings, that he understood those warnings, and that his statement was not coerced).

After *Thompkins*, are there any cases remaining that would fall into the "space" between *Miranda* invocations and *Miranda* waivers? What about cases like *Burbine* and *Spring* — if, that is, the suspect in those cases had been held *not* to have validly waived his rights?

3. If *Burbine* is arguably inconsistent with the spirit of *Miranda*, can *Thompkins* even be reconciled with its letter? In *Thompkins*, the Court says:

> Where the prosecution shows that a *Miranda* warning was given and that it was understood by the accused, an accused's uncoerced statement establishes an implied waiver of the right to remain silent. . . .
>
> The record in this case shows that Thompkins waived his right to remain silent. There is no basis in this case to conclude that he did not understand his rights; and on these facts it follows that he chose not to invoke or rely on those rights when he did speak. . . .
>
> [T]here is no evidence that Thompkins's statement was coerced. . . . In these circumstances, Thompkins knowingly and voluntarily made a statement to police, so he waived his right to remain silent.

Whatever happened to the "heavy burden" on the prosecution to show a waiver of *Miranda* rights? After *Thompkins*, how much (if anything) is left of *Miranda*'s fundamental principle that custodial interrogation involves inherent coercion — and that waivers will not be inferred from a suspect's silence?

3. It is natural to think about cases like *Burbine* and *Thompkins* in terms of protecting the defendant's *Miranda* rights. But what about the defendant's right to waive *Miranda*? Shouldn't that right be protected as well? How much protection does it need? Compare this issue to Faretta v. California, Chapter 3, page 257, supra, where the Court granted defendants the right to represent themselves in criminal litigation — i.e., the right to forgo the right to counsel *at trial*.

4. As you think about the question of *Miranda* waivers, should it matter whether the suspect is already represented by counsel? In New York it does. The New York Court of Appeals has rendered a series of decisions that do not permit the police to approach the suspect after the police are aware that the suspect is represented by

counsel. See, e.g., People v. Arthur, 22 N.Y.2d 325, 239 N.E.2d 537 (1968); People v. Rogers, 48 N.Y.2d 167, 397 N.E.2d 709 (1979). The New York rule presumably gives an advantage to suspects who already have lawyers when they are arrested — presumably a more sophisticated category than unrepresented suspects. Is that fair?

For an argument that the New York rule does not go far enough, see Charles J. Ogletree, Are Confessions Really Good for the Soul?: A Proposal to Mirandize *Miranda*, 100 Harv. L. Rev. 1826 (1987). Professor Ogletree argues that suspects should be given a nonwaivable right to consult with counsel before any questioning takes place, since this is the only way to prevent waivers based on ignorance, lack of information, or police deception. Is that what *Miranda* is about?

NOTE ON *MIRANDA*'S EFFECTS

How should a case like *Miranda* be appraised? By its aspirational content? By its symbolism? By its practical effects? And if its practical effects, which ones count? Its real effects on criminal justice, such as on police practices, the ability of interrogated suspects to exercise their right to remain silent, the conditions of interrogated suspects more generally, the number (absolute or relative) of inculpatory statements made, the rate at which police solve crimes (the "clearance" rate), the conviction rate? All the above? And what about the effect of *Miranda* on innocent people wrongly charged with an offense? Might the restrictions on interrogation actually result in wrongful convictions if the police cannot learn through interrogating one person that someone else has been wrongly accused? These issues, and many more, have been the subject of an astonishingly rich literature. For representative samples, see Joseph D. Grano, Confessions, Truth and the Law (1993); Richard Leo & George C. Thomas III, The *Miranda* Debate: Law Justice, and Policing (1998) (containing excerpts from numerous articles debating the merits of *Miranda*); Akhil Reed Amar & Renee Lettow, Fifth Amendment First Principles: The Self-Incrimination Clause, 93 Mich. L. Rev. 857 (1995); Dialogue on *Miranda* (with a debate between, on the one hand, George C. Thomas III and, on the other, Paul G. Cassell and Bret S. Hayman), 43 UCLA L. Rev. 821 (1996). The Grano book and the Amar and Lettow article have, in turn, generated a cottage industry of critique and response.

Most of the published material is analytical or rhetorical. There have been two recent efforts to investigate empirically various aspects of the *Miranda* regime. The first is by two sociologists, Richard Leo and Richard Ofshe. In a series of articles, they have put forward a theoretical model of police interrogation and the results of Professor Leo's observations of real interrogation practices over a nine-month period (involving more than 500 hours of fieldwork). Professor Leo observed 122 interrogations personally and observed another 60 on videotape. For descriptions of the theoretical model and Leo's field observations, see Richard Leo, *Miranda*'s Revenge: Police Interrogation as a Confidence Game, 30 Law & Soc. Rev. 259 (1996); Richard Leo, Inside the Interrogation Room, 86 J. Crim. L. & Criminology 266 (1996); Richard Leo, The Impact of *Miranda* Revisited, 86 J. Crim. L. & Criminology 621 (1996); Richard Ofshe & Richard Leo, The Social Psychology of Police Interrogation: The Theory and Classification of True and False Confessions, 16 Stud. L., Pol. & Soc'y 189 (1997). Leo's findings are quite remarkable. Using a broad definition of "coercion," he found that in only 4 of the 182 cases examined was there anything that rose to the level of "coercion"; and in those 4 cases, none involved physical coercion. Moreover, only about a quarter of warned suspects invoked their rights after being warned, and approximately 65 percent of those interrogated following warnings and waivers made incriminating statements. Why do so many people act so self-destructively? Was this just what *Miranda* was supposed to stop, or was it only supposed to stop physical and psychological terrorism? Whatever it was supposed to stop, it seems to have affected only the latter. According to Leo, "[P]olice have successfully adapted their practices to the legal requirements of *Miranda* by using conditioning, deemphasizing [guilt], and persuasive strategies to orchestrate consent to custodial questioning in most cases. In addition, in response to *Miranda*, police have developed increasingly specialized, sophisticated, and effective interrogation techniques with which to elicit statements from suspects during interrogation." 86 J. Crim. L. & Criminology at 675. Moreover:

These new methods appear to be just as effective as the earlier ones that they have replaced. That contemporary American police interrogation resembles the structure and sequence of a classic confidence game helps us understand not only why custodial suspects waive their *Miranda* rights and admit to wrongdoing in such high numbers but also how police power is exercised in the interrogation room. As we have seen, contemporary interrogation strategies are based fundamentally on the manipulation and betrayal of trust. Like confidence men, police interrogators attempt to induce compliance from their suspects by offering them the hope of a better situation in exchange for incriminating information. The interrogator exercises power through his ability to frame the suspect's definition of the situation, exploiting the suspect's ignorance to create the illusion of a relationship that is symbiotic rather than adversarial. In the exercise of his power, the interrogator relies on a series of appeals that mystify both the true nature of the detective's relationship to the suspect and the true extent of his influence with other actors in the criminal justice system. . . .

Miranda's revenge . . . has been to transform police power inside the interrogation room without undermining its effectiveness. Not only have *Miranda* warnings exercised little or no effect on confession rates, but police have also embraced *Miranda* as a legitimating symbol of their professionalism. *Miranda* warnings symbolically declare that police take individual rights seriously. At the same time, *Miranda* inspired police to create more sophisticated interrogation strategies, effectively giving them the license to act as confidence men and develop their skills in human manipulation and deception. In ways not captured by doctrinal analysis, *Miranda* has changed profoundly both the psychological context and the moral ordering of the police interrogation. Driven by careful strategic considerations, police interrogators exercise power by manipulating custodial suspects' definition of the situation and of their role; by creating the appearance of a symbiotic rather than an adversarial relationship; by appealing to their insider knowledge and expertise; and by exploiting the suspects' ignorance, fear and trust. . . . That contemporary police interrogation resembles both the method and substance of a classic confidence game — and thus has become manipulative and deceptive to its very core — may be *Miranda*'s most enduring legacy.

30 Law & Soc'y Rev. 259 (1996). Professor Leo and Professor White added to this literature with an extended discussion of the ways in which police turn *Miranda* to their advantage. See Richard Leo & Welsh S. White, Adapting to *Miranda*: Modern Interrogators' Strategies for Dealing with the Obstacles Posed by *Miranda*, 84

Minn. L. Rev. 397 (1999). A journalistic account of a reporter following a shift of detectives for a year throughout their responsibilities, including observing interrogations, which paints a harsher picture of the police/*Miranda* relationship, is contained in David Simon, Homicide: A Year on the Killing Streets (1991).

What is objectionable about exploiting a "suspect's ignorance, fear and trust" when there is very good reason to believe he has committed a heinous crime? Is it carrying appeals to sentiment a bit too far to look only at the police/suspect interaction and not at the events that give rise to such interactions — serious criminality? One answer obviously is that not all suspects are guilty and that the tactics of police may pry false confessions out of innocent suspects. For just such an argument, see Richard Leo & Richard Ofshe, The Consequences of False Confessions: Deprivations of Liberty and Miscarriages of Justice in the Age of Psychological Interrogation, 88 Nw. U. L. Rev. 429 (1998). The authors also demonstrate that individuals who made incriminating statements are systematically worse off throughout the criminal justice process.

How frequent are false confessions? It is hard to know, because most suspects who confess to crimes end up with convictions whose factual basis never gets further investigated. There are, however, notable exceptions. After numerous inmates on Illinois's Death Row were proven to have been wrongly convicted — some on the basis of false confessions — then-Governor George Ryan commuted all existing Illinois death sentences in early 2003. In 2009, Rob Warden and Steven A. Drizen (codirectors of Northwestern University School of Law's Center on Wrongful Convictions) edited a book, "True Stories of False Confessions" (Northwestern U. Press), containing accounts of 39 cases of false confessions. And in early 2010, Lisa Black and Steve Mills, award-winning Chicago Tribune reporters who had previously helped publicize the problems on Illinois's Death Row, wrote about the recent cases of two Illinois fathers who falsely confessed to murdering their own children; the authors quoted several "experts" on the subject of false confessions who said that they occur "far more often than most people believe":

> Trauma, lack of sleep and highly manipulative interrogation techniques are a few factors that can cause the most level-headed people to falsely confess to a crime — even one as heinous as a child's murder, according to experts. Researchers believe that false confessions lead to about 25 percent of wrongful convictions, a statistic underscored by the increasingly sophisticated use of DNA evidence.

See Black & Mills, "What Causes People to Give False Confessions?" http://articles .chicagotribune.com/2010-07-11/news/ct-met-forced-confessions-20100711_1_ confess-dna-evidence-interrogation. Still, according to another commentator, the total number of false confessions is minuscule. See Paul G. Cassell, Protecting the Innocent from False Confessions and Lost Confessions — and from *Miranda*, 88 Nw. U. L. Rev. 497 (1988). Moreover, according to Cassell, the decision whether to eliminate this risk by eliminating or reducing the effectiveness of interrogation must also take into account the total cost of proposed changes, such as the loss of true confessions as well.

In a second empirical development, Professor Cassell has taken head-on the assertion of Leo, Ofshe, and others, such as Professor Schulhofer, that *Miranda* has not had a dramatic impact on clearance and conviction rates. He has engaged in a running debate, involving data collection and analysis and reanalysis of previous studies, over the impact of *Miranda* on the rate of confessions and the resultant effect on clearance and conviction rates. In addition to the articles cited above, the main contributions to this debate have been Paul G. Cassell, *Miranda*'s Social Costs: An Empirical Assessment, 90 Nw. U. L. Rev. 387 (1996); Stephen J. Schulhofer, *Miranda*'s Practical Effect: Substantial Benefits and Vanishingly Small Social Costs, id., at 500; Paul G. Cassell, All Benefits, No Costs: The Grand Illusion of *Miranda*'s Defenders, id., at 1084; Stephen J. Schulhofer, *Miranda* and Clearance Rates, 91 Nw. U. L. Rev. 278 (1996); Paul G. Cassell, *Miranda*'s "Negligible" Effect on Law Enforcement: Some Skeptical Observations, 20 Harv. J.L. & Pub. Pol'y 327 (1997); Paul G. Cassell & Richard Fowles, Handcuffing the Cops? A Thirty-Year Perspective on *Miranda*'s Harmful Effects on Law Enforcement, 50 Stan. L. Rev. 1055 (1998); John Donohue III, Did *Miranda* Diminish Police Effectiveness? id., at 1147; Paul G. Cassell & Richard Fowles, Falling Clearance Rates after *Miranda*: Coincidence or Consequence? id., at 1181. According to Professor Cassell, the data show that *Miranda* has had a noticeable effect on all the FBI index crimes except murder and rape. His efforts have been systematically attacked by the supporters of the decision, such as Professor Schulhofer. And, indeed, the task that Cassell has undertaken is decidedly difficult. He is attempting to sort out one variable — the *Miranda* decision — from all the other variables that affected social change from the mid-1960s to the present, and doing so in the absence of the ability to run any controlled tests of the relevant phenomenon. Still, a number of the critiques of Cassell's efforts have an other-worldly quality about them. They appear to be defending *Miranda* in part on the basis of the argument that it has had little effect on crime enforcement. To the extent this is true, and to the extent that Professor Leo's description of actual interrogation practices is both accurate and troubling, is it time to replace *Miranda* with some alternative? Like what? And to solve exactly what problem? It should be noted that the most dispassionate of the responses to Cassell, the analysis of Professor John Donohue, concludes that a drop in some clearance rates following *Miranda* occurred that is not easy to explain, and thus possibly attributable to *Miranda*. Professor Donohue does not think the magnitude of this drop is as large as Cassell and Fowles suggest, but he reaches that conclusion through a reanalysis of the data involving certain adjustments that Cassell and Fowles plausibly argue should not be adopted. When those adjustments are not made, Donohue's analysis comes out quite similarly to Cassell's and Fowles's, although the question whether to attribute the results to *Miranda* or some other unspecified cause is not easily answerable.

Professor Schulhofer recognizes the "otherworldliness" of some of the criticisms of Cassell, including some of his own, or as he puts it: "Underlying my analysis is a paradox that will trouble many readers, whether they are inclined to support *Miranda* or oppose it. If *Miranda* really has so little impact on confessions and conviction rates, why bother defending it? Isn't *Miranda* simply a hollow promise for civil libertarians and an inconvenient nuisance for law enforcement?" No, says Professor Schulhofer, for a number of reasons. First, the symbolic purpose is not irrelevant; second, it is a great leap forward to substitute psychological ploys for physical abuse; and third, were *Miranda* overruled, the road back to physical abuse is cleared of its major hurdle. 90 Nw. U.L. Rev., at 561-562.

3.   The Consequences of a *Miranda* Violation

At the time of the Court's decision, the common understanding was that *Miranda* was a piece of conventional constitutional law, a set of requirements that flowed from the Fifth Amendment, imposed on the states through the Due Process Clause of the Fourteenth Amendment — with the corresponding consequence that a *Miranda* violation generally would require reversal of the defendant's conviction. That conventional wisdom did not hold for long.

The defendant in Michigan v. Tucker, 417 U.S. 433 (1974), was questioned before *Miranda* was decided. The police obeyed the law as it existed at the time of the questioning — they even gave Tucker some of what later became the *Miranda* warnings — but they did not tell Tucker that he had a right to state-appointed counsel. The Court ruled against Tucker, and had some interesting things to say about *Miranda*'s relationship with the Fifth Amendment:

> The [*Miranda*] Court recognized that these procedural safeguards were not themselves rights protected by the Constitution but were instead measures to insure that the right against compulsory self-incrimination was protected. As the Court remarked: "We cannot say that the Constitution necessarily requires adherence to any particular solution for the inherent compulsions of the interrogation process as it is presently conducted." [Miranda v. Arizona, 382 U.S. 436, 467 (1966)]. The suggested safeguards were not intended to "create a constitutional straitjacket," ibid., but rather to provide practical reinforcement for the right against compulsory self-incrimination.
>
> A comparison of the facts in this case with the historical circumstances underlying the privilege against compulsory self-incrimination strongly indicates that the police conduct here did not deprive respondent of his privilege against compulsory self-incrimination as such, but rather failed to make available to him the full measure of procedural safeguards associated with that right since *Miranda*.

417 U.S., at 444.

The defendant in New York v. Quarles, 467 U.S. 649 (1984), was arrested in a supermarket after a police pursuit. When he was arrested, the defendant was wearing an empty shoulder holster. The arresting officer asked the defendant where the gun was, and the defendant told him. Only then was the defendant given his *Miranda* warnings. The defendant was charged and convicted of a gun offense; the question before the Court was whether the gun itself was admissible. The Court held that it was, pursuant to a "public safety exception" to *Miranda*:

> The police in this case, in the very act of apprehending a suspect, were confronted with the immediate necessity of ascertaining the whereabouts of a gun which they had every reason to believe the suspect had just removed from his empty holster and discarded in the supermarket. So long as the gun was concealed somewhere in the supermarket, with its actual whereabouts unknown, it obviously posed more than one danger to the public safety: an accomplice might make use of it, a customer or employee might later come upon it.
>
> In such a situation, if the police are required to recite the familiar *Miranda* warnings before asking the whereabouts of the gun, suspects in Quarles' position might well be deterred from responding. Procedural safeguards which deter a suspect from responding were deemed acceptable in *Miranda* in order to protect the Fifth Amendment privilege; when the primary social cost of those added protections is the possibility of fewer convictions, the *Miranda* majority was willing to bear that cost. Here,

had *Miranda* warnings deterred Quarles from responding to Officer Kraft's question about the whereabouts of the gun, the cost would have been something more than merely the failure to obtain evidence useful in convicting Quarles. Officer Kraft needed an answer to his question not simply to make his case against Quarles but to insure that further danger to the public did not result from the concealment of the gun in a public area.

. . . [T]he need for answers to questions in a situation posing a threat to the public safety outweighs the need for the prophylactic rule protecting the Fifth Amendment's privilege against self-incrimination.

467 U.S., at 657. Notice that the Court's decision in *Quarles* obviated the need to decide on the admissibility of the fruits of *Miranda* violations. Notice, too, the Court's characterization of *Miranda* as a "prophylactic rule protecting the Fifth Amendment's privilege against self-incrimination." Then-Justice Rehnquist wrote the Court opinions in both *Tucker* and *Quarles*, and in both cases he went out of his way to describe *Miranda* as something other than, and presumably less than, a piece of conventional constitutional law. See, for example, the following passage from *Quarles*:

> The *Miranda* Court . . . presumed that interrogation in certain custodial circum-
> stances is inherently coercive and held that statements made under those circum-
> stances are inadmissible unless the suspect is specifically informed of his *Miranda*
> rights and freely decides to forgo those rights. The prophylactic *Miranda* warnings
> therefore are "not themselves rights protected by the Constitution but [are] instead
> measures to insure that the right against compulsory self-incrimination [is] pro-
> tected." Michigan v. Tucker, 417 U.S. 433, 444 (1974). Requiring *Miranda* warnings
> before custodial interrogation provides "practical reinforcement" for the Fifth
> Amendment right. [Id.]

467 U.S., at 654. The Court made the same point even more explicitly in Oregon v. Elstad, 470 U.S. 298 (1985):

> The *Miranda* exclusionary rule . . . serves the Fifth Amendment and sweeps more
> broadly than the Fifth Amendment itself. It may be triggered even in the absence of a
> Fifth Amendment violation. The Fifth Amendment prohibits use by the prosecution in
> its case in chief only of compelled testimony. Failure to administer *Miranda* warnings
> creates a presumption of compulsion. Consequently, unwarned statements that are
> otherwise voluntary within the meaning of the Fifth Amendment must nevertheless be
> excluded from evidence under *Miranda*. Thus, in the individual case, *Miranda*'s pre-
> ventive medicine provides a remedy even to the defendant who has suffered no iden-
> tifiable constitutional harm.

Id., at 306-07.

Miranda's awkward constitutional status raised an important question about the status of a piece of nonconstitutional federal law. In 1968, as part of the Omnibus Crime Control and Safe Streets Act, Congress purported to overrule *Miranda*, at least in federal cases. "In any criminal prosecution brought by the United States or by the District of Columbia, a confession . . . shall be admissible in evidence if it is voluntarily given." 18 U.S.C. §3501(a). In determining voluntariness, courts were directed to take account of all the circumstances, and they were specifically directed not to regard the giving or withholding of warnings as dispositive. 18 U.S.C.

§3501(b). Surprisingly, this provision was almost completely ignored by the federal judiciary for the next 30 years. The government never raised arguments that relied on §3501, and federal courts consequently paid no attention to it. Given the Court's language in *Tucker*, *Quarles*, and *Elstad*, however, there was some reason to believe that §3501 would be deemed constitutional if ever the federal courts considered the issue. In 2000, the Supreme Court finally ruled on the status of §3501 — and on *Miranda*'s constitutional status as well.

UNITED STATES v. DICKERSON, 530 U.S. 428 (2000): In Miranda v. Arizona, 384 U.S. 436 (1966), we held that certain warnings must be given before a suspect's statement made during custodial interrogation could be admitted in evidence. In the wake of that decision, Congress enacted 18 U.S.C. §3501, which in essence laid down a rule that the admissibility of such statements should turn only on whether or not they were voluntarily made. We hold that *Miranda*, being a constitutional decision of this Court, may not be in effect overruled by an Act of Congress, and we decline to overrule *Miranda* ourselves. We therefore hold that *Miranda* and its progeny in this Court govern the admissibility of statements made during custodial interrogation in both state and federal courts. . . .

. . . Congress may not legislatively supersede our decisions interpreting and applying the Constitution. This case therefore turns on whether the *Miranda* Court announced a constitutional rule or merely exercised its supervisory authority to regulate evidence in the absence of congressional direction. . . . Relying on the fact that we have created several exceptions to *Miranda*'s warnings requirement and that we have repeatedly referred to the *Miranda* warnings as "prophylactic," and "not themselves rights protected by the Constitution," the Court of Appeals concluded that the protections announced in *Miranda* are not constitutionally required.

We disagree with the Court of Appeals' conclusion, although we concede that there is language in some of our opinions that supports the view taken by that court. But first and foremost of the factors on the other side — that *Miranda* is a constitutional decision — is that both *Miranda* and two of its companion cases applied the rule to proceedings in state courts — to wit, Arizona, California, and New York. Since that time, we have consistently applied *Miranda*'s rule to prosecutions arising in state courts. It is beyond dispute that we do not hold a supervisory power over the courts of the several States. . . . With respect to proceedings in state courts, our "authority is limited to enforcing the commands of the United States Constitution." Mu'Min v. Virginia, 500 U.S. 415, 422 (1991). . . .

Additional support for our conclusion that *Miranda* is constitutionally based is found in the *Miranda* Court's invitation for legislative action to protect the constitutional right against coerced self-incrimination. . . . [In *Miranda*,] the Court emphasized that it could not foresee "the potential alternatives for protecting the privilege which might be devised by Congress or the States," and it accordingly opined that the Constitution would not preclude legislative solutions that differed from the prescribed *Miranda* warnings but which were "at least as effective in apprising accused persons of their right of silence and in assuring a continuous opportunity to exercise it."

. . . The dissent argues that it is judicial overreaching for this Court to hold §3501 unconstitutional unless we hold that the *Miranda* warnings are required by the Constitution, in the sense that nothing else will suffice to satisfy constitutional requirements. But we need not go farther than *Miranda* to decide this case. In *Miranda*, the Court noted that reliance on the traditional totality-of-the-circumstances test raised a risk of overlooking an involuntary custodial confession, a risk that the Court found unacceptably great when the confession is offered in the case in chief to prove guilt. The Court therefore concluded that something more than the totality test was necessary. As discussed above, §3501 reinstates the totality test as sufficient. Section 3501 therefore cannot be sustained if *Miranda* is to remain the law.

Whether or not we would agree with *Miranda*'s reasoning and its resulting rule, were we addressing the issue in the first instance, the principles of stare decisis weigh heavily against overruling it now. While "stare decisis is not an inexorable command," particularly when we are interpreting the Constitution, "even in constitutional cases, the doctrine carries such persuasive force that we have always required a departure from precedent to be supported by some 'special justification.'" United States v. International Business Machines Corp., 517 U.S. 843, 856 (1996).

We do not think there is such justification for overruling *Miranda*. *Miranda* has become embedded in routine police practice to the point where the warnings have become part of our national culture. While we have overruled our precedents when subsequent cases have undermined their doctrinal underpinnings, we do not believe that this has happened to the *Miranda* decision. If anything, our subsequent cases have reduced the impact of the *Miranda* rule on legitimate law enforcement while reaffirming the decision's core ruling that unwarned statements may not be used as evidence in the prosecution's case in chief.

The disadvantage of the *Miranda* rule is that statements which may be by no means involuntary, made by a defendant who is aware of his "rights," may nonetheless be excluded and a guilty defendant go free as a result. But experience suggests that the totality-of-the-circumstances test which §3501 seeks to revive is more difficult than *Miranda* for law enforcement officers to conform to, and for courts to apply in a consistent manner. . . .

In sum, we conclude that *Miranda* announced a constitutional rule that Congress may not supersede legislatively. Following the rule of stare decisis, we decline to overrule *Miranda* ourselves. The judgment of the Court of Appeals is therefore Reversed.

JUSTICE SCALIA, with whom JUSTICE THOMAS joins, dissenting.

Marbury v. Madison, 1 Cranch 137 (1803), held that an Act of Congress will not be enforced by the courts if what it prescribes violates the Constitution of the United States. That was the basis on which *Miranda* was decided. One will search today's opinion in vain, however, for a statement (surely simple enough to make) that what 18 U.S.C. §3501 prescribes — the use at trial of a voluntary confession, even when a *Miranda* warning or its equivalent has failed to be given — violates the Constitution. The reason the statement does not appear is not only (and perhaps not so much) that it would be absurd, inasmuch as §3501 excludes from trial precisely what the Constitution excludes from trial, viz., compelled confessions; but also that Justices whose votes are needed to compose today's majority are on record as believing that a violation of *Miranda* is not a violation of the Constitution. See Davis v. United States, 512 U.S. 452, 457-458 (1994) (opinion of the Court, in which Kennedy, J., joined); Duckworth v. Eagan, 492 U.S. 195, 203 (1989) (opinion of the Court, in which Kennedy, J., joined); Oregon v. Elstad, 470 U.S. 298 (1985) (opinion of the Court by O'Connor, J.); New York v. Quarles, 467 U.S. 649 (1984) (opinion of the Court by Rehnquist, J.). And so, to justify today's agreed-upon result, the Court must adopt a significant new, if not entirely comprehensible, principle of constitutional law. As the Court chooses to describe that principle, statutes of Congress can be disregarded, not only when what they prescribe violates the Constitution, but when what they prescribe contradicts a decision of this Court that "announced a constitutional rule." . . . [T]he only thing that can possibly mean in the context of this case is that this Court has the power, not merely to apply the Constitution but to expand it, imposing what it regards as useful "prophylactic" restrictions upon Congress and the States. That is an immense and frightening antidemocratic power, and it does not exist.

It takes only a small step to bring today's opinion out of the realm of power-judging and into the mainstream of legal reasoning: The Court need only go beyond its carefully couched iterations that "*Miranda* is a constitutional decision," that "*Miranda* is constitutionally based," that *Miranda* has "constitutional underpinnings," and come out and say quite clearly: "We reaffirm today that custodial interrogation that is not preceded by *Miranda* warnings or their equivalent violates the Constitution of the United States." It cannot say that, because a majority of the Court does not believe it. The Court therefore acts in plain violation of the Constitution when it denies effect to this Act of Congress.

. . . It was once possible to characterize the so-called *Miranda* rule as resting (however implausibly) upon the proposition that what the statute here before us permits — the admission at trial of un-Mirandized confessions — violates the Constitution. That is the fairest reading of the *Miranda* case itself. . . .

So understood, *Miranda* was objectionable for innumerable reasons . . . There is, for example, simply no basis in reason for concluding that a response to the very first question asked, by a suspect who already knows all of the rights described in the *Miranda* warning, is anything other than a volitional act. And even if one assumes that the elimination of compulsion absolutely requires informing even the most knowledgeable suspect of his right to remain silent, it cannot conceivably require the right to have counsel present. . . . The only good reason for having counsel there is that he can be counted on to advise the suspect that he should not speak.

. . . [W]hat is most remarkable about the *Miranda* decision — and what made it unacceptable as a matter of straightforward constitutional interpretation in the *Marbury* tradition — is its palpable hostility toward the act of confession per se, rather than toward what the Constitution abhors, compelled confession. The Constitution is not, unlike the *Miranda* majority, offended by a criminal's commendable qualm of conscience or fortunate fit of stupidity.

. . . [T]he Court asserts that *Miranda* must be a "constitutional decision" announcing a "constitutional rule," and thus immune to congressional modification, because we have since its inception applied it to the States. If this argument is meant as an invocation of stare decisis, it fails because, though it is true that our cases applying *Miranda* against the States must be reconsidered if *Miranda* is not required by the Constitution, it is likewise true that our cases based on the principle that *Miranda* is not required by the Constitution will have to be reconsidered if it is. So the stare decisis argument is a wash. If, on the other hand, the argument is meant as an appeal to logic rather than stare decisis, it is a classic example of begging the question: Congress's attempt to set aside *Miranda*, since it represents an assertion that violation of *Miranda* is not a violation of the Constitution, also represents an assertion that the Court has no power to impose *Miranda* on the States. To answer this assertion — not by showing why violation of *Miranda* is a violation of the Constitution — but by asserting that *Miranda* does apply against the States, is to assume precisely the point at issue. In my view, our continued application of the *Miranda* code to the States despite our consistent statements that running afoul of its dictates does not necessarily — or even usually — result in an actual constitutional violation, represents not the source of *Miranda*'s salvation but rather evidence of its ultimate illegitimacy. . . .

. . . Petitioner and the United States contend that there is nothing at all exceptional, much less unconstitutional, about the Court's adopting prophylactic rules to buttress constitutional rights, and enforcing them against Congress and the States. Indeed, the United States argues that "[p]rophylactic rules are now and have been for many years a feature of this Court's constitutional adjudication." That statement is not wholly inaccurate, if by "many years" one means since the mid-1960s. However, in their zeal to validate what is in my view a lawless practice, the United States and petitioner greatly overstate the frequency with which we have engaged in it. . . .

[W]hat the Court did in *Miranda* (assuming, as later cases hold, that *Miranda* went beyond what the Constitution actually requires) is in fact extraordinary. . . . Where the Constitution has wished to lodge in one of the branches of the Federal Government some limited power to supplement its guarantees, it has said so. See Amdt. 14, §5 ("The Congress shall have power to enforce, by appropriate legislation, the provisions of this article"). The power with which the Court would endow itself under a "prophylactic" justification for *Miranda* goes far beyond what it has permitted Congress to do under authority of that text. Whereas we have insisted that congressional action under §5 of the Fourteenth Amendment must be "congruent" with, and "proportional" to, a constitutional violation, see City of Boerne v. Flores, 521 U.S. 507, 520 (1997), the *Miranda* nontextual power to embellish confers authority to prescribe preventive measures against not only constitutionally prohibited compelled confessions, but also (as discussed earlier) foolhardy ones.

I applaud, therefore, the refusal of the Justices in the majority to enunciate this boundless doctrine of judicial empowerment as a means of rendering today's decision rational. In nonetheless joining the Court's judgment, however, they overlook two truisms: that actions speak louder than silence, and that (in judge-made law at least) logic will out. Since there is in fact no other principle that can reconcile today's judgment with the post-*Miranda* cases that the Court refuses to abandon, what today's decision will stand for, whether the Justices can bring themselves to say it or not, is the power of the Supreme Court to write a prophylactic, extraconstitutional Constitution, binding on Congress and the States. . . .

Today's judgment converts *Miranda* from a milestone of judicial overreaching into the very Cheops' Pyramid (or perhaps the Sphinx would be a better analogue) of judicial arrogance. In imposing its Court-made code upon the States, the original opinion at least asserted that it was demanded by the Constitution. Today's decision does not pretend that it is — and yet still asserts the right to impose it against the will of the people's representatives in Congress. Far from believing that stare decisis compels this result, I believe we cannot allow to remain on the books even a celebrated decision — especially a celebrated decision — that has come to stand for the proposition that the Supreme Court has power to impose extraconstitutional constraints upon Congress and the States. This is not the system that was established by the Framers, or that would be established by any sane supporter of government by the people.

I dissent from today's decision, and, until §3501 is repealed, will continue to apply it in all cases where there has been a sustainable finding that the defendant's confession was voluntary.

NOTES AND QUESTIONS

1. The majority opinion in *Dickerson* was written by none other than Chief Justice Rehnquist. What's up with that? Did he change his mind after the time he wrote the majority opinions in *Tucker* and *Quarles*?

2. Reread the last sentence of Justice Scalia's dissent. Is it proper for a Supreme Court Justice to announce that he will not follow binding precedent?

3. Justice Scalia argues that, because *Miranda* cannot be justified by the Fifth Amendment privilege against self-incrimination, it amounts to "a prophylactic, extraconstitutional Constitution, binding on Congress and the States." Might *Miranda* instead be justified as an application of the Fifth and Fourteenth Amendments' Due Process Clauses? Recall that, for 30 years prior to *Miranda*, the Court had struggled to draw lines between voluntary and involuntary confessions; the failure of that enterprise was the key factor precipitating the Court's decision in *Miranda*. Perhaps the real problem with *Miranda* was that the Court relied on the wrong piece of constitutional language. After all, if voluntariness is a constitutional requirement (a proposition that the Court and Justice Scalia both accept) and if voluntariness is difficult to determine after the fact (which seems hard to deny), courts presumably have the authority to craft legal rules that will ensure that only voluntary confessions are admitted into evidence. Might *Miranda*'s rules fit that description? Most suspects continue to talk to the police, but they do so after being informed that they may remain silent, as Justice Scalia would agree they may.

And current *Miranda* doctrine clearly aims at preventing coercive police interrogation tactics — the same aim that motivates voluntariness doctrine. Illinois v. Perkins, 496 U.S. 292 (1990), holds that if a police officer pretends to be something other than a police officer and thereby induces a suspect to talk, the conversation falls outside of *Miranda*. Moran v. Burbine, 475 U.S. 412 (1986), seems to permit *Miranda* waivers in the face of deceptive police questioning. Whatever the *Miranda* Court intended, *Miranda* doctrine today serves as a kind of indirect voluntariness doctrine.

4. But if *Miranda* guards primarily against involuntary confessions, then the current warnings and the current invocation rules are hard to justify, are they not? A due process-based *Miranda* rule might better justify warnings like these: "You have the right to remain silent. I have the right to ask you questions. If you do not wish to answer, you do not have to. And if you want questioning to stop, it will stop — for awhile." Would that be a better regime?

5. Even after the terrorist attacks of September 11, 2001, there is broad political support for civil liberties in the United States — broader in most respects than in

the 1960s. And recent scandals involving military interrogation of prisoners in Iraq would seem to indicate that the public generally supports protections against the abuse of suspects and defendants. In light of these realities, should police interrogation be left to Congress and state legislatures to regulate?

6. In Harris v. New York, 401 U.S. 222 (1971), the Court held that voluntary statements obtained in violation of *Miranda* may be used to impeach a defendant's trial testimony:

> . . . Petitioner's testimony in his own behalf concerning the events of January 7 contrasted sharply with what he told the police shortly after his arrest. The impeachment process here undoubtedly provided valuable aid to the jury in assessing petitioner's credibility, and the benefits of this process should not be lost, in our view, because of the speculative possibility that impermissible police conduct will be encouraged thereby. Assuming that the exclusionary rule has a deterrent effect on proscribed police conduct, sufficient deterrence flows when the evidence in question is made unavailable to the prosecution in its case in chief.
>
> . . . The shield provided by *Miranda* cannot be perverted into a license to use perjury by way of a defense, free from the risk of confrontation with prior inconsistent utterances. We hold, therefore, that petitioner's credibility was appropriately impeached by use of his earlier conflicting statements.

Id., at 225-226.

7. In Doyle v. Ohio, 426 U.S. 610 (1976), two defendants charged with sale of marijuana testified at trial that they had been framed by the government informant who had allegedly made the purchase. On cross-examination, each defendant was questioned about why he didn't give his exculpatory story to the police at the time of arrest. Before the Supreme Court, the state attempted to justify this line of questioning on the theory that the defendants' postarrest silence was inconsistent with their trial testimony and thus admissible to impeach their credibility. The Court disagreed and held that the impeachment use of the defendants' postarrest silence following *Miranda* warnings violated their right to due process:

> Silence in the wake of these warnings may be nothing more than an arrestee's exercise of these *Miranda* rights. Thus, every post-arrest silence is insolubly ambiguous because of what the State is required to advise the person arrested. Moreover, while it is true that the *Miranda* warnings contain no express assurance that silence will carry no penalty, such assurance is implicit to any person who receives the warnings. In such circumstances, it would be fundamentally unfair . . . to allow the arrested person's silence to be used to impeach an explanation subsequently offered at trial.

Id., at 617-618. In Jenkins v. Anderson, 447 U.S. 231 (1980), where a murder defendant testified at trial that the killing was in self-defense, the Court found no constitutional barrier to questions on cross-examination about why the defendant had remained silent and not reported the matter to the police during the two weeks between the killing and the time that he turned himself in to the authorities. According to the Court, "In this case, no governmental action induced petitioner to remain silent before arrest. The failure to speak occurred before the petitioner was taken into custody and given *Miranda* warnings. Consequently, the fundamental unfairness present in *Doyle* is not present in this case." Id., at 240.

Are *Doyle* and *Jenkins* consistent with *Harris*?

8. Oregon v. Elstad, 470 U.S. 298 (1985) — one of the cases in which the Court expressly declared that *Miranda* was something other than a constitutional mandate — raised the question whether the fruits of *Miranda* violations were admissible. The defendant in *Elstad* made incriminating statements to the police prior to receiving *Miranda* warnings; subsequently, he was warned and gave the police a written confession. Reasoning that "a careful and thorough administration of *Miranda* warnings serves to cure the condition that rendered the unwarned statement inadmissible," id., at 310-311, the Court found Elstad's confession admissible. Almost 20 years later, the Court returned to the status of the fruits of *Miranda* violations.

MISSOURI v. SEIBERT

Certiorari to the Supreme Court of Missouri
542 U.S. 600 (2004)

JUSTICE SOUTER announced the judgment of the Court and delivered an opinion, in which JUSTICE STEVENS, JUSTICE GINSBURG, and JUSTICE BREYER join.

This case tests a police protocol for custodial interrogation that calls for giving no warnings of the rights to silence and counsel until interrogation has produced a confession. . . .

Respondent Patrice Seibert's 12-year-old son Jonathan had cerebral palsy, and when he died in his sleep she feared charges of neglect because of bedsores on his body. In her presence, two of her teenage sons and two of their friends devised a plan to conceal the facts surrounding Jonathan's death by incinerating his body in the course of burning the family's mobile home, in which they planned to leave Donald Rector, a mentally ill teenager living with the family, to avoid any appearance that Jonathan had been unattended. Seibert's son Darian and a friend set the fire, and Donald died.

Five days later, the police awakened Seibert at 3 a.m. at a hospital where Darian was being treated for burns. In arresting her, Officer Kevin Clinton followed instructions from Rolla, Missouri, officer Richard Hanrahan that he refrain from giving *Miranda* warnings. After Seibert had been taken to the police station and left alone in an interview room for 15 to 20 minutes, Hanrahan questioned her without *Miranda* warnings for 30 to 40 minutes, squeezing her arm and repeating "Donald was also to die in his sleep." After Seibert finally admitted she knew Donald was meant to die in the fire, she was given a 20-minute coffee and cigarette break. Officer Hanrahan then turned on a tape recorder, gave Seibert the *Miranda* warnings, and obtained a signed waiver of rights from her. He resumed the questioning with "'Ok,' Trice, we've been talking for a little while about what happened on Wednesday the twelfth, haven't we?," and confronted her with her prewarning statements:

> *Hanrahan*: "Now, in discussion you told us, you told us that there was an understanding about Donald."
> *Seibert*: "Yes."
> *Hanrahan*: "Did that take place earlier that morning?"
> *Seibert*: "Yes."
> *Hanrahan*: "And what was the understanding about Donald?"

> *Seibert*: "If they could get him out of the trailer, to take him out of the trailer."
> *Hanrahan*: "And if they couldn't?"
> *Seibert*: "I, I never even thought about it. I just figured they would."
> *Hanrahan*: "'Trice, didn't you tell me that he was supposed to die in his sleep?"
> *Seibert*: "If that would happen, 'cause he was on that new medicine, you know. . . ."
> *Hanrahan*: "The Prozac? And it makes him sleepy. So he was supposed to die in his sleep?"
> *Seibert*: "Yes."

After being charged with first-degree murder for her role in Donald's death, Seibert sought to exclude both her prewarning and postwarning statements. At the suppression hearing, Officer Hanrahan testified that he made a "conscious decision" to withhold *Miranda* warnings, thus resorting to an interrogation technique he had been taught: question first, then give the warnings, and then repeat the question "until I get the answer that she's already provided once." He acknowledged that Seibert's ultimate statement was "largely a repeat of information . . . obtained" prior to the warning.

The trial court suppressed the prewarning statement but admitted the responses given after the *Miranda* recitation. A jury convicted Seibert of second-degree murder. On appeal, the Missouri Court of Appeals affirmed, treating this case as indistinguishable from Oregon v. Elstad, 470 U.S. 298 (1985).

The Supreme Court of Missouri reversed, holding that "in the circumstances here, where the interrogation was nearly continuous, . . . the second statement, clearly the product of the invalid first statement, should have been suppressed." 93 S.W.3d 700, 701 (2002). . . .

We granted certiorari . . . . We now affirm.

. . . *Miranda* conditioned the admissibility at trial of any custodial confession on warning a suspect of his rights: failure to give the prescribed warnings and obtain a waiver of rights before custodial questioning generally requires exclusion of any statements obtained. Conversely, giving the warnings and getting a waiver has generally produced a virtual ticket of admissibility; maintaining that a statement is involuntary even though given after warnings and voluntary waiver of rights requires unusual stamina, and litigation over voluntariness tends to end with the finding of a valid waiver. See Berkemer v. McCarty, 468 U.S. 420, 433, n. 20 (1984) ("Cases in which a defendant can make a colorable argument that a self-incriminating statement was 'compelled' despite the fact that the law enforcement authorities adhered to the dictates of *Miranda* are rare"). . . . [T]his common consequence would not be common at all were it not that *Miranda* warnings are customarily given under circumstances allowing for a real choice between talking and remaining silent.

There are those, of course, who preferred the old way of doing things, giving no warnings and litigating the voluntariness of any statement in nearly every instance. In the aftermath of *Miranda*, Congress even passed a statute seeking to restore that old regime, 18 U.S.C. §3501, although the Act lay dormant for years until finally invoked and challenged in Dickerson v. United States, [530 U.S. 428 (2000)]. *Dickerson* reaffirmed *Miranda* and held that its constitutional character prevailed against the statute.

The technique of interrogating in successive, unwarned and warned phases raises a new challenge to *Miranda*. Although we have no statistics on the frequency of this practice, it is not confined to Rolla, Missouri. An officer of that police department testified that the strategy of withholding *Miranda* warnings until after interrogating and drawing out a confession was promoted not only by his own department, but by a national police training organization and other departments in which he had worked. Consistently with the officer's testimony, the Police Law Institute, for example, instructs that "officers may conduct a two-stage interrogation. . . . At any point during the pre-*Miranda* interrogation, usually after arrestees have confessed, officers may then read the *Miranda* warnings and ask for a waiver. If the arrestees waive their *Miranda* rights, officers will be able to repeat any subsequent incriminating statements later in court." Police Law Institute, Illinois Police Law Manual 83 (Jan. 2001-Dec. 2003).[2] The upshot of all this advice is a question-first practice of some popularity. . . .

. . . *Miranda* addressed "interrogation practices . . . likely . . . to disable [an individual] from making a free and rational choice" about speaking, 384 U.S., at 464-465, and held that a suspect must be "adequately and effectively" advised of the choice the Constitution guarantees, id., at 467. The object of question-first is to render *Miranda* warnings ineffective by waiting for a particularly opportune time to give them, after the suspect has already confessed.

Just as "no talismanic incantation [is] required to satisfy [*Miranda*'s] strictures," California v. Prysock, 453 U.S. 355, 359 (1981) (per curiam), it would be absurd to think that mere recitation of the litany suffices to satisfy *Miranda* in every conceivable circumstance. "The inquiry is simply whether the warnings reasonably 'convey to [a suspect] his rights as required by *Miranda*.'" Duckworth v. Eagan, 492 U.S. 195, 203 (1989) (quoting *Prysock*, supra, at 361). The threshold issue when interrogators question first and warn later is thus whether it would be reasonable to find that in these circumstances the warnings could function "effectively" as *Miranda* requires. Could the warnings effectively advise the suspect that he had a real choice about giving an admissible statement at that juncture? Could they reasonably convey that he could choose to stop talking even if he had talked earlier? For unless the warnings could place a suspect who has just been interrogated in a position to make such an informed choice, there is no practical justification for accepting the formal warnings as compliance with *Miranda*, or for treating the second stage of interrogation as distinct from the first, unwarned and inadmissible segment.[4]

2. Emphasizing the impeachment exception to the *Miranda* rule approved by this Court, Harris v. New York, 401 U.S. 222 (1971), some training programs advise officers to omit *Miranda* warnings altogether or to continue questioning after the suspect invokes his rights. See, e.g., Police Law Manual 83 ("There is no need to give a *Miranda* warning before asking questions if . . . the answers given . . . will not be required by the prosecutor during the prosecution's case-in-chief"). . . . This training is reflected in the reported cases involving deliberate questioning after invocation of *Miranda* rights. See, e.g., California Attorneys for Criminal Justice v. Butts, 195 F.3d 1039, 1042-1044 (CA9 2000); People v. Neal, 72 P.3d 280, 282 (Cal. S. Ct. 2003). Scholars have noted the growing trend of such practices. See, e.g., Leo, Questioning the Relevance of *Miranda* in the Twenty-First Century, 99 Mich. L. Rev. 1000, 1010 (2001); Weisselberg, In the Stationhouse After *Dickerson*, 99 Mich. L. Rev. 1121, 1123-1154 (2001). . . .

4. Respondent Seibert argues that her second confession should be excluded from evidence under the doctrine known by the metaphor of the "fruit of the poisonous tree," developed in the Fourth Amendment context in Wong Sun v. United States, 371 U.S. 471 (1963): evidence otherwise admissible but discovered as a result of an earlier violation is excluded as tainted, lest the law encourage future violations. But the Court in *Elstad* rejected the *Wong Sun* fruits doctrine for analyzing the admissibility of a subsequent warned confession following "an initial failure . . . to administer the warnings required by *Miranda*." *Elstad*, 470 U.S., at 300 . . . *Elstad* held that "a suspect who has once responded to unwarned yet uncoercive questioning is not thereby disabled from waiving his rights and confessing after he has been given the requisite *Miranda* warnings." Id., at 318. In a sequential confession case, clarity is served if the later confession is approached by asking whether in the circumstances the *Miranda* warnings given

There is no doubt about the answer that proponents of question-first give to this question about the effectiveness of warnings given only after successful interrogation, and we think their answer is correct. By any objective measure, applied to circumstances exemplified here, it is likely that if the interrogators employ the technique of withholding warnings until after interrogation succeeds in eliciting a confession, the warnings will be ineffective in preparing the suspect for successive interrogation, close in time and similar in content. After all, the reason that question-first is catching on is as obvious as its manifest purpose, which is to get a confession the suspect would not make if he understood his rights at the outset; the sensible underlying assumption is that with one confession in hand before the warnings, the interrogator can count on getting its duplicate, with trifling additional trouble. Upon hearing warnings only in the aftermath of interrogation and just after making a confession, a suspect would hardly think he had a genuine right to remain silent, let alone persist in so believing once the police began to lead him over the same ground again. A more likely reaction on a suspect's part would be perplexity about the reason for discussing rights at that point, bewilderment being an unpromising frame of mind for knowledgeable decision. . . . By the same token, it would ordinarily be unrealistic to treat two spates of integrated and proximately conducted questioning as independent interrogations subject to independent evaluation simply because *Miranda* warnings formally punctuate them in the middle.

Missouri argues that a confession repeated at the end of an interrogation sequence envisioned in a question-first strategy is admissible on the authority of Oregon v. Elstad, 470 U.S. 298 (1985), but the argument disfigures that case. In *Elstad*, the police went to the young suspect's house to take him into custody on a charge of burglary. Before the arrest, one officer spoke with the suspect's mother, while the other one joined the suspect in a "brief stop in the living room," where the officer said he "felt" the young man was involved in a burglary. The suspect acknowledged he had been at the scene. This Court noted that the pause in the living room "was not to interrogate the suspect but to notify his mother of the reason for his arrest," and described the incident as having "none of the earmarks of coercion." The Court, indeed, took care to mention that the officer's initial failure to warn was an "oversight" that "may have been the result of confusion as to whether the brief exchange qualified as 'custodial interrogation' or . . . may simply have reflected . . . reluctance to initiate an alarming police procedure before [an officer] had spoken with respondent's mother." At the outset of a later and systematic station house interrogation going well beyond the scope of the laconic prior admission, the suspect was given *Miranda* warnings and made a full confession. In holding the second statement admissible and voluntary, *Elstad* rejected the "cat out of the bag" theory that any short, earlier admission, obtained in arguably innocent neglect of *Miranda*, determined the character of the later, warned confession; on the facts of that case, the Court thought any causal connection between the first and second responses to the police was "speculative and attenuated." Although the *Elstad* Court expressed no explicit conclusion about either officer's state of mind, it

---

could reasonably be found effective. If yes, a court can take up the standard issues of voluntary waiver and voluntary statement; if no, the subsequent statement is inadmissible for want of adequate *Miranda* warnings, because the earlier and later statements are realistically seen as parts of a single, unwarned sequence of questioning.

is fair to read *Elstad* as treating the living room conversation as a good-faith *Miranda* mistake, not only open to correction by careful warnings before systematic questioning in that particular case, but posing no threat to warn-first practice generally. [*Elstad*, 470 U.S., at 311-316.] . . .

The contrast between *Elstad* and this case reveals a series of relevant facts that bear on whether *Miranda* warnings delivered midstream could be effective enough to accomplish their object: the completeness and detail of the questions and answers in the first round of interrogation, the overlapping content of the two statements, the timing and setting of the first and the second, the continuity of police personnel, and the degree to which the interrogator's questions treated the second round as continuous with the first. In *Elstad*, it was not unreasonable to see the occasion for questioning at the station house as presenting a markedly different experience from the short conversation at home; since a reasonable person in the suspect's shoes could have seen the station house questioning as a new and distinct experience, the *Miranda* warnings could have made sense as presenting a genuine choice whether to follow up on the earlier admission.

At the opposite extreme are the facts here, which by any objective measure reveal a police strategy adapted to undermine the *Miranda* warnings. The unwarned interrogation was conducted in the station house, and the questioning was systematic, exhaustive, and managed with psychological skill. When the police were finished there was little, if anything, of incriminating potential left unsaid. The warned phase of questioning proceeded after a pause of only 15 to 20 minutes, in the same place as the unwarned segment. . . . [T]he same officer who had conducted the first phase recited the *Miranda* warnings . . . [T]he police did not advise that her prior statement could not be used.[7] . . . [A]ny uncertainty on her part about a right to stop talking about matters previously discussed would only have been aggravated by the way Officer Hanrahan set the scene by saying "we've been talking for a little while about what happened on Wednesday the twelfth, haven't we?" The impression that the further questioning was a mere continuation of the earlier questions and responses was fostered by references back to the confession already given. It would have been reasonable to regard the two sessions as parts of a continuum, in which it would have been unnatural to refuse to repeat at the second stage what had been said before. These circumstances must be seen as challenging the comprehensibility and efficacy of the *Miranda* warnings to the point that a reasonable person in the suspect's shoes would not have understood them to convey a message that she retained a choice about continuing to talk.[8]

Strategists dedicated to draining the substance out of *Miranda* cannot accomplish by training instructions what *Dickerson* held Congress could not do by statute. Because the question-first tactic effectively threatens to thwart *Miranda*'s purpose of reducing the risk that a coerced confession would be admitted, and because the facts here do not reasonably support a conclusion that the warnings given could have served their purpose, Seibert's postwarning statements are inadmissible. . . .

---

7. We do not hold that a formal addendum warning that a previous statement could not be used would be sufficient to change the character of the question-first procedure to the point of rendering an ensuing statement admissible, but its absence is clearly a factor that blunts the efficacy of the warnings and points to a continuing, not a new, interrogation.

8. Because we find that the warnings were inadequate, there is no need to assess the actual voluntariness of the statement.

JUSTICE BREYER, concurring.

In my view, the following simple rule should apply to the two-stage interrogation technique: Courts should exclude the "fruits" of the initial unwarned questioning unless the failure to warn was in good faith. Cf. Oregon v. Elstad, 470 U.S. 298, 309, 318, n. 5 (1985); United States v. Leon, 468 U.S. 897 (1984). I believe this is a sound and workable approach to the problem this case presents. Prosecutors and judges have long understood how to apply the "fruits" approach, which they use in other areas of law. See Wong Sun v. United States, 371 U.S. 471 (1963). And in the workaday world of criminal law enforcement the administrative simplicity of the familiar has significant advantages over a more complex exclusionary rule.

I believe the plurality's approach in practice will function as a "fruits" test. The truly "effective" *Miranda* warnings on which the plurality insists will occur only when certain circumstances — a lapse in time, a change in location or interrogating officer, or a shift in the focus of the questioning — intervene between the unwarned questioning and any postwarning statement. . . .

I consequently join the plurality's opinion in full. I also agree with Justice Kennedy's opinion insofar as it is consistent with this approach and makes clear that a good-faith exception applies.

JUSTICE KENNEDY, concurring in the judgment.

. . . The *Miranda* rule has become an important and accepted element of the criminal justice system. At the same time, not every violation of the rule requires suppression of the evidence obtained. Evidence is admissible when the central concerns of *Miranda* are not likely to be implicated and when other objectives of the criminal justice system are best served by its introduction. Thus, we have held that statements obtained in violation of the rule can be used for impeachment, so that the truth finding function of the trial is not distorted by the defense, see Harris v. New York, 401 U.S. 222 (1971); that there is an exception to protect countervailing concerns of public safety, see New York v. Quarles, 467 U.S. 649 (1984); and that physical evidence obtained in reliance on statements taken in violation of the rule is admissible, see United States v. Patane, [542 U.S. 630 (2004)]. These cases, in my view, are correct. They recognize that admission of evidence is proper when it would further important objectives without compromising *Miranda*'s central concerns. Under these precedents, the scope of the *Miranda* suppression remedy depends on a consideration of those legitimate interests and on whether admission of the evidence under the circumstances would frustrate *Miranda*'s central concerns and objectives.

Oregon v. Elstad, 470 U.S. 298 (1985), reflects this approach. In *Elstad*, a suspect made an initial incriminating statement at his home. The suspect had not received a *Miranda* warning before making the statement, apparently because it was not clear whether the suspect was in custody at the time. The suspect was taken to the station house, where he received a proper warning, waived his *Miranda* rights, and made a second statement. He later argued that the postwarning statement should be suppressed because it was related to the unwarned first statement, and likely induced or caused by it. The Court held that, although a *Miranda* violation made the first statement inadmissible, the postwarning statements could be introduced against the accused because "neither the general goal of deterring improper police conduct nor the Fifth Amendment goal of assuring trustworthy evidence would be served by suppression" given the facts of that case. *Elstad*, supra, at 308.

In my view, *Elstad* was correct in its reasoning and its result. *Elstad* reflects a balanced and pragmatic approach to enforcement of the *Miranda* warning. An officer may not realize that a suspect is in custody and warnings are required. The officer may not plan to question the suspect or may be waiting for a more appropriate time. Skilled investigators often interview suspects multiple times, and good police work may involve referring to prior statements to test their veracity or to refresh recollection. In light of these realities it would be extravagant to treat the presence of one statement that cannot be admitted under *Miranda* as sufficient reason to prohibit subsequent statements preceded by a proper warning. . . .

This case presents different considerations. The police used a two-step questioning technique based on a deliberate violation of *Miranda*. The *Miranda* warning was withheld to obscure both the practical and legal significance of the admonition when finally given. As Justice Souter points out, the two-step technique permits the accused to conclude that the right not to respond did not exist when the earlier incriminating statements were made. The strategy is based on the assumption that *Miranda* warnings will tend to mean less when recited midinterrogation, after inculpatory statements have already been obtained. This tactic relies on an intentional misrepresentation of the protection that *Miranda* offers and does not serve any legitimate objectives that might otherwise justify its use.

Further, the interrogating officer here relied on the defendant's prewarning statement to obtain the postwarning statement used against her at trial. The postwarning interview resembled a cross-examination. The officer confronted the defendant with her inadmissible prewarning statements and pushed her to acknowledge them. See App. 70 ("'Trice, didn't you tell me that he was supposed to die in his sleep?"). This shows the temptations for abuse inherent in the two-step technique. Reference to the prewarning statement was an implicit suggestion that the mere repetition of the earlier statement was not independently incriminating. The implicit suggestion was false.

 . . . The plurality concludes that whenever a two-stage interview occurs, admissibility of the postwarning statement should depend on "whether the *Miranda* warnings delivered midstream could have been effective enough to accomplish their object" given the specific facts of the case. This test envisions an objective inquiry from the perspective of the suspect, and applies in the case of both intentional and unintentional two-stage interrogations. In my view, this test cuts too broadly. *Miranda*'s clarity is one of its strengths, and a multifactor test that applies to every two-stage interrogation may serve to undermine that clarity. I would apply a narrower test applicable only in the infrequent case, such as we have here, in which the two-step interrogation technique was used in a calculated way to undermine the *Miranda* warning.

The admissibility of postwarning statements should continue to be governed by the principles of *Elstad* unless the deliberate two-step strategy was employed. If the deliberate two-step strategy has been used, postwarning statements that are related to the substance of prewarning statements must be excluded unless curative measures are taken before the postwarning statement is made. Curative measures should be designed to ensure that a reasonable person in the suspect's situation would understand the import and effect of the *Miranda* warning and of the *Miranda* waiver. For example, a substantial break in time and circumstances between the prewarning statement and the *Miranda* warning may suffice in most circumstances, as it allows the accused to distinguish the two contexts and appreciate that the interrogation has taken a new turn. Alternatively, an additional warning that explains the likely inadmissibility of the prewarning custodial statement may be sufficient. No curative steps were taken in this case, however, so the postwarning statements are inadmissible and the conviction cannot stand. . . .

JUSTICE O'CONNOR, with whom CHIEF JUSTICE REHNQUIST, JUSTICE SCALIA, and JUSTICE THOMAS join, dissenting.

. . . On two preliminary questions I am in full agreement with the plurality. First, the plurality appropriately follows [Oregon v. Elstad, 470 U.S. 298 (1985)] in concluding that Seibert's statement cannot be held inadmissible under a "fruit of the poisonous tree" theory. Ante, at [fn. 4]. Second, the plurality correctly declines to focus its analysis on the subjective intent of the interrogating officer. . . .

Although the analysis the plurality ultimately espouses examines the same facts and circumstances that a "fruits" analysis would consider (such as the lapse of time between the two interrogations and change of questioner or location), it does so for entirely different reasons. The fruits analysis would examine those factors because they are relevant to the balance of deterrence value versus the "drastic and socially costly course" of excluding reliable evidence. Nix v. Williams, 467 U.S. 431, 442443 (1984). The plurality, by contrast, looks to those factors to inform the psychological judgment regarding whether the suspect has been informed effectively of her right to remain silent. The analytical underpinnings of the two approaches are thus entirely distinct, and they should not be conflated just because they function similarly in practice.

The plurality's rejection of an intent-based test is also, in my view, correct. Freedom from compulsion lies at the heart of the Fifth Amendment, and requires us to assess whether a suspect's decision to speak truly was voluntary. Because voluntariness is a matter of the suspect's state of mind, we focus our analysis on the way in which suspects experience interrogation. . . .

Thoughts kept inside a police officer's head cannot affect that experience. See Moran v. Burbine, 475 U.S. 412, 422 (1986). . . .

The same principle applies here. A suspect who experienced the exact same interrogation as Seibert, save for a difference in the undivulged, subjective intent of the interrogating officer when he failed to give *Miranda* warnings, would not experience the interrogation any differently. . . .

Because the isolated fact of Officer Hanrahan's intent could not have had any bearing on Seibert's "capacity to comprehend and knowingly relinquish" her right to remain silent, it could not by itself affect the voluntariness of her confession. Moreover, recognizing an exception to *Elstad* for intentional violations would require focusing constitutional analysis on a police officer's subjective intent, an unattractive proposition that we all but uniformly avoid. . . .

For these reasons, I believe that the approach espoused by Justice Kennedy is ill advised.

Justice Kennedy would extend *Miranda*'s exclusionary rule to any case in which the use of the "two-step interrogation technique" was "deliberate" or "calculated." This approach untethers the analysis from facts knowable to, and therefore having any potential directly to affect, the suspect. Far from promoting "clarity," the approach will add a third step to the suppression inquiry. In virtually every two-stage interrogation case, in addition to addressing the standard *Miranda* and voluntariness questions, courts will be forced to conduct the kind of difficult, state-of-mind inquiry that we normally take pains to avoid.

The plurality's adherence to *Elstad*, and mine to the plurality, end there. Our decision in *Elstad* rejected two lines of argument advanced in favor of suppression. The first was based on the "fruit of the poisonous tree" doctrine, discussed above. The second was the argument that the "lingering compulsion" inherent in a defendant's having let the "cat out of the bag" required suppression. 470 U.S., at 311. The Court of Appeals of Oregon, in accepting the latter argument, had endorsed a theory indistinguishable from the one today's plurality adopts: "The coercive impact of the unconstitutionally obtained statement remains, because in a defendant's mind it has sealed his fate. It is this impact that must be dissipated in order to make a subsequent confession admissible." 658 P.2d 552, 554 (Ore. Ct. App. 1983).

We rejected this theory outright. We did so not because we refused to recognize the "psychological impact of the suspect's conviction that he has let the cat out of the bag," but because we refused to "endow" those "psychological effects" with "constitutional implications." 470 U.S., at 311. . . . The plurality might very well think that we struck the balance between Fifth Amendment rights and law enforcement interests incorrectly in *Elstad*; but that is not normally a sufficient reason for ignoring the dictates of stare decisis.

I would analyze the two-step interrogation procedure under the voluntariness standards central to the Fifth Amendment and reiterated in *Elstad*. *Elstad* commands that if Seibert's first statement is shown to have been involuntary, the court must examine whether the taint dissipated through the passing of time or a change in circumstances. . . . In addition, Seibert's second statement should be suppressed if she showed that it was involuntary despite the *Miranda* warnings. Although I would leave this analysis for the Missouri courts to conduct on remand, I note that, unlike the officers in *Elstad*, Officer Hanrahan referred to Seibert's unwarned statement during the second part of the interrogation when she made a statement at odds with her unwarned confession. App. 70 ("'Trice, didn't you tell me that he was supposed to die in his sleep?'"); cf. *Elstad*, supra, at 316 (officers did not "exploit the unwarned admission to pressure respondent into waiving his right to remain silent"). Such a tactic may bear on the voluntariness inquiry. . . .

Because I believe that the plurality gives insufficient deference to *Elstad* and that Justice Kennedy places improper weight on subjective intent, I respectfully dissent.

UNITED STATES v. PATANE

Certiorari to the United States Court of Appeals for the Tenth Circuit
542 U.S. 630 (2004)

JUSTICE THOMAS announced the judgment of the Court and delivered an opinion, in which CHIEF JUSTICE REHNQUIST and JUSTICE SCALIA join.

. . . In June 2001, respondent, Samuel Francis Patane, was arrested for harassing his ex-girlfriend, Linda O'Donnell. He was released on bond, subject to a temporary restraining order that prohibited him from contacting O'Donnell. Respondent apparently violated the restraining order by attempting to telephone O'Donnell. On June 6, 2001, Officer Tracy Fox of the Colorado Springs Police

Department began to investigate the matter. On the same day, a county probation officer informed an agent of the Bureau of Alcohol, Tobacco, and Firearms (ATF), that respondent, a convicted felon, illegally possessed a .40 Glock pistol. The ATF relayed this information to Detective Josh Benner, who worked closely with the ATF. Together, Detective Benner and Officer Fox proceeded to respondent's residence.

After reaching the residence . . . Officer Fox arrested respondent for violating the restraining order. Detective Benner attempted to advise respondent of his *Miranda* rights but got no further than the right to remain silent. At that point, respondent interrupted, asserting that he knew his rights, and neither officer attempted to complete the warning.

Detective Benner then asked respondent about the Glock. Respondent was initially reluctant to discuss the matter, stating: "I am not sure I should tell you anything about the Glock because I don't want you to take it away from me." Detective Benner persisted, and respondent told him that the pistol was in his bedroom. Respondent then gave Detective Benner permission to retrieve the pistol. Detective Benner found the pistol and seized it.

A grand jury indicted respondent for possession of a firearm by a convicted felon, in violation of 18 U.S.C. §922(g)(1). The District Court granted respondent's motion to suppress the firearm, reasoning that the officers lacked probable cause to arrest respondent for violating the restraining order. It therefore declined to rule on respondent's alternative argument that the gun should be suppressed as the fruit of an unwarned statement.

The Court of Appeals reversed the District Court's ruling with respect to probable cause but affirmed the suppression order on respondent's alternative theory. . . .

As we explain below, the *Miranda* rule is a prophylactic employed to protect against violations of the Self-Incrimination Clause. The Self-Incrimination Clause, however, is not implicated by the admission into evidence of the physical fruit of a voluntary statement. Accordingly, there is no justification for extending the *Miranda* rule to this context. And just as the Self-Incrimination Clause primarily focuses on the criminal trial, so too does the *Miranda* rule. The *Miranda* rule is not a code of police conduct, and police do not violate the Constitution (or even the *Miranda* rule, for that matter) by mere failures to warn. For this reason, the exclusionary rule articulated in cases such as Wong Sun [v. United States, 371 U.S. 471 (1963)] does not apply. . . .

The Self-Incrimination Clause provides: "No person . . . shall be compelled in any criminal case to be a witness against himself." U.S. Const., Amdt. 5. We need not decide here the precise boundaries of the Clause's protection. For present purposes, it suffices to note that the core protection afforded by the Self-Incrimination Clause is a prohibition on compelling a criminal defendant to testify against himself at trial. See, e.g., Chavez v. Martinez, 538 U.S. 760, 764-768 (2003) (plurality opinion); id., at 777-779 (Souter, J., concurring in judgment). The Clause cannot be violated by the introduction of nontestimonial evidence obtained as a result of voluntary statements. . . .

To be sure, the Court has recognized and applied several prophylactic rules designed to protect the core privilege against self-incrimination. For example, although the text of the Self-Incrimination Clause at least suggests that "its coverage [is limited to] compelled testimony that is used against the defendant in the trial itself," [United States v. Hubbell, 530 U.S. 27, 37 (2000)], potential suspects may, at times, assert the privilege in proceedings in which answers might be used to incriminate them in a subsequent criminal case. We have explained that "the natural concern which underlies [these] decisions is that an inability to protect the right at one stage of a proceeding may make its invocation useless at a later stage." [Michigan v. Tucker, 417 U.S. 433, 440-441 (1974)].

Similarly, in *Miranda*, the Court concluded that the possibility of coercion inherent in custodial interrogations unacceptably raises the risk that a suspect's privilege against self-incrimination might be violated. 384 U.S., at 467. To protect against this danger, the *Miranda* rule creates a presumption of coercion, in the absence of specific warnings, that is generally irrebuttable for purposes of the prosecution's case in chief.

But because these prophylactic rules (including the *Miranda* rule) necessarily sweep beyond the actual protections of the Self-Incrimination Clause, any further extension of these rules must be justified by its necessity for the protection of the actual right against compelled self-incrimination. . . .

It is for these reasons that statements taken without *Miranda* warnings (though not actually compelled) can be used to impeach a defendant's testimony at trial, see Harris v. New York, 401 U.S. 222 (1971), though the fruits of actually compelled testimony cannot, see New Jersey v. Portash, 440 U.S. 450, 458-459 (1979). More generally, the *Miranda* rule "does not require that the statements [taken without complying with the rule] and their fruits be discarded as inherently tainted," [Oregon v. Elstad, 470 U.S. 298, 307 (1985)]. Such a blanket suppression rule could not be justified by reference to the "Fifth Amendment goal of assuring trustworthy evidence" or by any deterrence rationale, id., at 308, and would therefore fail our close-fit requirement.

Furthermore, the Self-Incrimination Clause contains its own exclusionary rule. It provides that "no person . . . shall be compelled in any criminal case to be a witness against himself." Unlike the Fourth Amendment's bar on unreasonable searches, the Self-Incrimination Clause is self-executing. We have repeatedly explained "that those subjected to coercive police interrogations have an automatic protection from the use of their involuntary statements (or evidence derived from their statements) in any subsequent criminal trial." *Chavez*, 538 U.S., at 769 (plurality opinion). This explicit textual protection supports a strong presumption against expanding the *Miranda* rule any further.

Finally, nothing in Dickerson [v. United States, 530 U.S. 428 (2000)], including its characterization of *Miranda* as announcing a constitutional rule, 530 U.S., at 444, changes any of these observations. Indeed, in *Dickerson*, the Court specifically noted that the Court's "subsequent cases have reduced the impact of the *Miranda* rule on legitimate law enforcement while reaffirming [*Miranda*]'s core ruling that unwarned statements may not be used as evidence in the prosecution's case in chief." Id., at 443-444. This description of *Miranda*, especially the emphasis on the use of "unwarned statements . . . in the prosecution's case in chief," makes clear our continued focus on the protections of the Self-Incrimination Clause. . . .

Our cases also make clear the related point that a mere failure to give *Miranda* warnings does not, by itself, violate a suspect's constitutional rights or even the *Miranda* rule. So much was evident in many of our pre-*Dickerson* cases, and we have adhered to this view since *Dickerson*. See *Chavez*, supra, at 772-773 (plurality opinion) (holding that a failure to read *Miranda* warnings did not violate the respondent's constitutional rights); 538 U.S., at 789 (Kennedy, J., concurring in part and dissenting in part) (agreeing "that failure to give a *Miranda* warning does not, without more, establish a completed violation when the unwarned interrogation ensues"). . . .

It follows that police do not violate a suspect's constitutional rights (or the *Miranda* rule) by negligent or even deliberate failures to provide the suspect with the full panoply of warnings prescribed by *Miranda*. Potential violations occur, if at all, only upon the admission of unwarned statements into evidence at trial. And, at that point, "the exclusion of unwarned statements . . . is a complete and sufficient remedy" for any perceived *Miranda* violation. *Chavez*, supra, at 790.

Thus, unlike unreasonable searches under the Fourth Amendment or actual violations of the Due Process Clause or the Self-Incrimination Clause, there is, with respect to mere failures to warn, nothing to deter. There is therefore no reason to apply the "fruit of the poisonous tree" doctrine of *Wong Sun*, 371 U.S., at 488. It is not for this Court to impose its preferred police practices on either federal law enforcement officials or their state counterparts.

In the present case, the Court of Appeals, relying on *Dickerson*, wholly adopted the position that the taking of unwarned statements violates a suspect's constitutional rights. 304 F.3d at 1028-1029. And, of course, if this were so, a strong deterrence-based argument could be made for suppression of the fruits.

But *Dickerson*'s characterization of *Miranda* as a constitutional rule does not lessen the need to maintain the closest possible fit between the Self-Incrimination Clause and any judge-made rule designed to protect it. And there is no such fit here. Introduction of the nontestimonial fruit of a voluntary statement, such as respondent's Glock, does not implicate the Self-Incrimination Clause. The admission of such fruit presents no risk that a defendant's coerced statements (however defined) will be used against him at a criminal trial. . . . There is simply no need to extend (and therefore no justification for extending) the prophylactic rule of *Miranda* to this context. . . .

. . . And although it is true that the Court requires the exclusion of the physical fruit of actually coerced statements, it must be remembered that statements taken without sufficient *Miranda* warnings are presumed to have been coerced only for certain purposes and then only when necessary to protect the privilege against self-incrimination. For the reasons discussed above, we decline to extend that presumption further. . . .

JUSTICE KENNEDY, with whom JUSTICE O'CONNOR joins, concurring in the judgment.

In Oregon v. Elstad, 470 U.S. 298 (1985), New York v. Quarles, 467 U.S. 649 (1984), and Harris v. New York, 401 U.S. 222 (1971), evidence obtained following an unwarned interrogation was held admissible. This result was based in large part on our recognition that the concerns underlying the Miranda v. Arizona, 384 U.S. 436 (1966), rule must be accommodated to other objectives of the criminal justice system. I agree with the plurality that Dickerson v. United States, 530 U.S. 428 (2000), did not undermine these precedents and, in fact, cited them in support. Here, it is sufficient to note that the Government presents an even stronger case for admitting the evidence obtained as the result of Patane's unwarned statement. Admission of nontestimonial physical fruits (the Glock in this case), even more so than the postwarning statements to the police in *Elstad* and Michigan v. Tucker, 417

U.S. 433 (1974), does not run the risk of admitting into trial an accused's coerced incriminating statements against himself. In light of the important probative value of reliable physical evidence, it is doubtful that exclusion can be justified by a deterrence rationale sensitive to both law enforcement interests and a suspect's rights during an in-custody interrogation. Unlike the plurality, however, I find it unnecessary to decide whether the detective's failure to give Patane the full *Miranda* warnings should be characterized as a violation of the *Miranda* rule itself, or whether there is "anything to deter" so long as the unwarned statements are not later introduced at trial.

With these observations, I concur in the judgment of the Court.

JUSTICE SOUTER, with whom JUSTICE STEVENS and JUSTICE GINSBURG join, dissenting.

The majority repeatedly says that the Fifth Amendment does not address the admissibility of nontestimonial evidence, an overstatement that is beside the point. The issue actually presented today is whether courts should apply the fruit of the poisonous tree doctrine lest we create an incentive for the police to omit *Miranda* warnings before custodial interrogation. In closing their eyes to the consequences of giving an evidentiary advantage to those who ignore *Miranda*, the majority adds an important inducement for interrogators to ignore the rule in that case.

Miranda rested on insight into the inherently coercive character of custodial interrogation and the inherently difficult exercise of assessing the voluntariness of any confession resulting from it. Unless the police give the prescribed warnings meant to counter the coercive atmosphere, a custodial confession is inadmissible, there being no need for the previous time-consuming and difficult enquiry into voluntariness. That inducement to forestall involuntary statements and troublesome issues of fact can only atrophy if we turn around and recognize an evidentiary benefit when an unwarned statement leads investigators to tangible evidence. There is, of course, a price for excluding evidence, but the Fifth Amendment is worth a price, and in the absence of a very good reason, the logic of *Miranda* should be followed: a *Miranda* violation raises a presumption of coercion, Oregon v. Elstad, 470 U.S. 298, 306-307 (1985), and the Fifth Amendment privilege against compelled self-incrimination extends to the exclusion of derivative evidence, see United States v. Hubbell, 530 U.S. 27, 37-38 (2000) (recognizing "the Fifth Amendment's protection against the prosecutor's use of incriminating information derived directly or indirectly from . . . [actually] compelled testimony"). That should be the end of this case.

The fact that the books contain some exceptions to the *Miranda* exclusionary rule carries no weight here. In Harris v. New York, 401 U.S. 222 (1971), it was respect for the integrity of the judicial process that justified the admission of unwarned statements as impeachment evidence. But Patane's suppression motion can hardly be described as seeking to "pervert" *Miranda* "into a license to use perjury" or otherwise handicap the "traditional truth-testing devices of the adversary process." 401 U.S., at 225-226. Nor is there any suggestion that the officers' failure to warn Patane was justified or mitigated by a public emergency or other exigent circumstance, as in New York v. Quarles, 467 U.S. 649 (1984). And of course the premise of Oregon v. Elstad, supra, is not on point; although a failure to give *Miranda* warnings before one individual statement does not necessarily bar the admission of a subsequent statement given after adequate warnings, cf. Missouri v.

Seibert, [542 U.S. 600 (2004)] (plurality opinion), that rule obviously does not apply to physical evidence seized once and for all.

There is no way to read this case except as an unjustifiable invitation to law enforcement officers to flout *Miranda* when there may be physical evidence to be gained. The incentive is an odd one, coming from the Court on the same day it decides Missouri v. Seibert. I respectfully dissent.

JUSTICE BREYER, dissenting.

For reasons similar to those set forth in Justice Souter's dissent and in my concurring opinion in Missouri v. Seibert, I would extend to this context the "fruit of the poisonous tree" approach, which I believe the Court has come close to adopting in *Seibert*. Under that approach, courts would exclude physical evidence derived from unwarned questioning unless the failure to provide *Miranda* warnings was in good faith. Because the courts below made no explicit finding as to good or bad faith, I would remand for such a determination.

NOTES AND QUESTIONS

1. What rule can one infer from *Seibert* and *Patane*? In both cases, Justice Kennedy's opinion seems decisive. In *Seibert*, Justice Kennedy finds the defendant's statements inadmissible because the *Miranda* violation was intentional and the police took no steps to cure it. Kennedy's position in *Patane* is harder to understand. He seems to adopt the plurality's rule — no exclusion of physical fruits of a voluntary statement — but without the plurality's rationale. What is Justice Kennedy's rationale? Why treat physical fruits differently than testimonial fruits?

2. Why not instead draw a line between intentional violations of *Miranda* and unintentional ones? Doesn't Justice Breyer's position — exclude the fruits of intentional *Miranda* violations, but not the fruits of good-faith violations — have a good deal of common sense to it?

3. Suppose a case like *Seibert* — an intentional violation of *Miranda* — where the violation leads the police to discover physical evidence: say, a gun. Is the gun admissible? How will Justice Kennedy vote in such a case? His *Seibert* opinion emphasizes the intentional nature of the *Miranda* violation. His *Patane* opinion emphasizes the lesser protection that (in his view) should be afforded to physical evidence, as opposed to testimony. What happens when those concerns cut in opposite directions?

4. Is it clear that there was even a violation in *Patane*? Reread the statement of facts in Justice Thomas's opinion in the case. Should a suspect have the right not to hear the *Miranda* warnings if that is his preference? At the very least, any violation in *Patane* seems likely to have been in good faith — something that cannot be said of the police conduct at issue in *Seibert*.

5. What do you think of the *Patane* plurality's theory? Your answer may depend on your view of another recent Supreme Court decision: Chavez v. Martinez, 538 U.S. 760 (2003). *Chavez* was a civil case arising under 42 U.S.C. §1983; plaintiff Martinez had been questioned by police officers in the emergency room of a local hospital. The interrogating officer never delivered the *Miranda* warnings. Martinez sued, seeking damages for this alleged violation of his Fifth Amendment rights. A divided Supreme Court found for the defendant. The plurality opinion by Justice

Thomas (joined by Chief Justice Rehnquist and Justices O'Connor and Scalia) maintained that there could be no Fifth Amendment violation in *Chavez*, because Martinez's statements were never used against him in any criminal case. Justices Souter and Breyer did not go quite so far. They concluded that the constitutional violation in this case was "outside the Fifth Amendment's core," id., at 778 (Souter, J., concurring in the judgment), and so did not justify providing the protection of civil liability. Is *Chavez* right? Is *Patane*?

4. The Right to Counsel Reconsidered

Miranda is not the only constitutional limit on police interrogation. The voluntariness requirement of the Due Process Clause still matters. And what about the Sixth Amendment? *Massiah* and *Escobedo* suggested the Sixth Amendment right to counsel would play a large role in regulating police questioning. Were those cases superseded by *Miranda*? Or do they carry independent weight? Consider the next case.

BREWER v. WILLIAMS

Certiorari to the Eighth Circuit Court of Appeals
430 U.S. 387 (1977)

MR. JUSTICE STEWART delivered the opinion of the Court.

An Iowa trial jury found the respondent, Robert Williams, guilty of murder. The judgment of conviction was affirmed in the Iowa Supreme Court by a closely divided vote. In a subsequent habeas corpus proceeding a Federal District Court ruled that under the United States Constitution Williams is entitled to a new trial, and a divided Court of Appeals for the Eighth Circuit agreed. The question before us is whether the District Court and the Court of Appeals were wrong.

On the afternoon of December 24, 1968, a 10-year-old girl named Pamela Powers went with her family to the YMCA in Des Moines, Iowa, to watch a wrestling tournament in which her brother was participating. When she failed to return from a trip to the washroom, a search for her began. The search was unsuccessful.

Robert Williams, who had recently escaped from a mental hospital, was a resident of the YMCA. Soon after the girl's disappearance Williams was seen in the YMCA lobby carrying some clothing and a large bundle wrapped in a blanket. He obtained help from a 14-year-old boy in opening the street door of the YMCA and the door to his automobile parked outside. When Williams placed the bundle in the front seat of his car the boy "saw two legs in it and they were skinny and white." Before anyone could see what was in the bundle Williams drove away. His abandoned car was found the following day in Davenport, Iowa, roughly 160 miles east of Des Moines. A warrant was then issued in Des Moines for his arrest on a charge of abduction.

On the morning of December 26, a Des Moines lawyer named Henry McKnight went to the Des Moines police station and informed the officers present that he had just received a long-distance call from Williams, and that he had advised Williams to turn himself in to the Davenport police. Williams did surrender that morning to the police in Davenport, and they booked him on the charge specified in the arrest warrant and gave him the warnings required by Miranda v. Arizona, 384 U.S. 436. The Davenport police then telephoned their counterparts in Des Moines to inform them that Williams had surrendered. McKnight, the lawyer, was still at the Des Moines police headquarters, and Williams conversed with McKnight on the telephone. In the presence of the Des Moines chief of police and a police detective named Leaming, McKnight advised Williams that Des Moines police officers would be driving to Davenport to pick him up, that the officers would not interrogate him or mistreat him, and that Williams was not to talk to the officers about Pamela Powers until after consulting with McKnight upon his return to Des Moines. As a result of these conversations, it was agreed between McKnight and the Des Moines police officials that Detective Leaming and a fellow officer would drive to Davenport to pick up Williams, that they would bring him directly back to Des Moines, and that they would not question him during the trip.

In the meantime Williams was arraigned before a judge in Davenport on the outstanding arrest warrant. The judge advised him of his *Miranda* rights and committed him to jail. Before leaving the courtroom, Williams conferred with a lawyer named Kelly, who advised him not to make any statements until consulting with McKnight back in Des Moines.

Detective Leaming and his fellow officer arrived in Davenport about noon to pick up Williams and return him to Des Moines. Soon after their arrival they met with Williams and Kelly, who, they understood, was acting as Williams' lawyer. Detective Leaming repeated the *Miranda* warnings, and told Williams: "[W]e both know that you're being represented here by Mr. Kelly and you're being represented by Mr. McKnight in Des Moines, and . . . I want you to remember this because we'll be visiting between here and Des Moines." Williams then conferred again with Kelly alone, and after this conference Kelly reiterated to Detective Leaming that Williams was not to be questioned about the disappearance of Pamela Powers until after he had consulted with McKnight back in Des Moines. When Leaming expressed some reservations, Kelly firmly stated that the agreement with McKnight was to be carried out — that there was to be no interrogation of Williams during the automobile journey to Des Moines. Kelly was denied permission to ride in the police car back to Des Moines with Williams and two officers.

The two detectives, with Williams in their charge, then set out on the 160-mile drive. At no time during the trip did Williams express a willingness to be interrogated in the absence of an attorney. Instead, he stated several times that "[w]hen I get to Des Moines and see Mr. McKnight, I am going to tell you the whole story." Detective Leaming knew that Williams was a former mental patient, and knew also that he was deeply religious.

The detective and his prisoner soon embarked on a wide-ranging conversation covering a variety of topics, including the subject of religion. Then, not long after leaving Davenport and reaching the interstate highway, Detective Leaming delivered what has been referred to in the briefs and oral arguments as the "Christian burial speech." Addressing Williams as "Reverend," the detective said:

> I want to give you something to think about while we're traveling down the road. . . . Number one, I want you to observe the weather conditions, it's raining, it's sleeting, it's freezing, driving is very treacherous, visibility is poor, it's going to be dark early this evening. They are predicting several inches of snow for tonight, and I feel that you yourself are the only person that knows where this little girl's body is, that you

yourself have only been there once, and if you get a snow on top of it you yourself may be unable to find it. And, since we will be going right past the area on the way into Des Moines, I feel that we could stop and locate the body, that the parents of this little girl should be entitled to a Christian burial for the little girl who was snatched away from them on Christmas [E]ve and murdered. And I feel we should stop and locate it on the way in rather than waiting until morning and trying to come back out after a snow storm and possibly not being able to find it at all.

Williams asked Detective Leaming why he thought their route to Des Moines would be taking them past the girl's body, and Leaming responded that he knew the body was in the area of Mitchellville — a town they would be passing on the way to Des Moines.[1] Leaming then stated: "I do not want you to answer me. I don't want to discuss it any further. Just think about it as we're riding down the road."

As the car approached Grinnell, a town approximately 100 miles west of Davenport, Williams asked whether the police had found the victim's shoes. When Detective Leaming replied that he was unsure, Williams directed the officers to a service station where he said he had left the shoes; a search for them proved unsuccessful. As they continued towards Des Moines, Williams asked whether the police had found the blanket, and directed the officers to a rest area where he said he had disposed of the blanket. Nothing was found. The car continued towards Des Moines, and as it approached Mitchellville, Williams said that he would show the officers where the body was. He then directed the police to the body of Pamela Powers.

Williams was indicted for first-degree murder. Before trial, his counsel moved to suppress all evidence relating to or resulting from any statements Williams had made during the automobile ride from Davenport to Des Moines. After an evidentiary hearing the trial judge denied the motion. He found that "an agreement was made between defense counsel and the police officials to the effect that the Defendant was not to be questioned on the return trip to Des Moines," and that the evidence in question had been elicited from Williams during "a critical stage in the proceedings requiring the presence of counsel on his request." The judge ruled, however, that Williams had "waived his right to have an attorney present during the giving of such information."

II. . . .

B

[T]he District Court based its judgment in this case on three independent grounds. The Court of Appeals appears to have affirmed the judgment on two of those grounds. We have concluded that only one of them need be considered here.

Specifically, there is no need to review in this case the doctrine of Miranda v. Arizona, a doctrine designed to secure the constitutional privilege against compulsory self-incrimination, Michigan v. Tucker, 417 U.S. 433, 438-439. It is equally unnecessary to evaluate the ruling of the District Court that Williams' self-incriminating statements were, indeed, involuntarily made. Cf. Spano v. New York, 360 U.S. 315. For it is clear that the judgment before us must in any event be affirmed upon the ground that Williams was deprived of a different constitutional right — the right to the assistance of counsel. . . .

1. The fact of the matter, of course, was that Detective Leaming possessed no such knowledge.

There can be no doubt in the present case that judicial proceedings had been initiated against Williams before the start of the automobile ride from Davenport to Des Moines. A warrant had been issued for his arrest, he had been arraigned on that warrant before a judge in a Davenport courtroom, and he had been committed by the court to confinement in jail. The State does not contend otherwise.

There can be no serious doubt, either, that Detective Leaming deliberately and designedly set out to elicit information from Williams just as surely as — and perhaps more effectively than — if he had formally interrogated him. Detective Leaming was fully aware before departing for Des Moines that Williams was being represented in Davenport by Kelly and in Des Moines by McKnight. Yet he purposely sought during Williams' isolation from his lawyers to obtain as much incriminating information as possible. Indeed, Detective Leaming conceded as much when he testified at Williams' trial:

> Q: In fact, Captain, whether he was a mental patient or not, you were trying to get all the information you could before he got to his lawyer, weren't you?
> A: I was sure hoping to find out where that little girl was, yes sir. . . .
> Q: Well, I'll put it this way: You was [sic] hoping to get all the information you could before Williams got back to McKnight, weren't you?
> A: Yes, sir.[6]

The state courts clearly proceeded upon the hypothesis that Detective Leaming's "Christian burial speech" had been tantamount to interrogation. Both courts recognized that Williams had been entitled to the assistance of counsel at the time he made the incriminating statements. Yet no such constitutional protection would have come into play if there had been no interrogation.

The circumstances of this case are thus constitutionally indistinguishable from those presented in Massiah v. United States, supra. . . .

That the incriminating statements were elicited surreptitiously in the *Massiah* case, and otherwise here, is constitutionally irrelevant. . . . Rather, the clear rule of *Massiah* is that once adversary proceedings have commenced against an individual, he has a right to legal representation when the government interrogates him.[8] It thus requires no wooden or technical application of the *Massiah* doctrine to conclude that Williams was entitled to the assistance of counsel guaranteed to him by the Sixth and Fourteenth Amendments.

---

6. Counsel for petitioner, in the course of oral argument in this Court, acknowledged that the "Christian burial speech" was tantamount to interrogation:

> Q: But isn't the point, really, Mr. Attorney General, what you indicated earlier, and that is that the officer wanted to elicit information from Williams —
> A: Yes, sir.
> Q: — by whatever techniques he used, I would suppose a lawyer would consider that he were pursuing interrogation.
> A: It is, but it was very brief. [Tr. of Oral Arg. 17.]

8. The only other significant factual difference between the present case and *Massiah* is that here the police had agreed that they would not interrogate Williams in the absence of his counsel. This circumstance plainly provides petitioner with no argument for distinguishing away the protection afforded by *Massiah*. It is argued that this agreement may not have been an enforceable one. But we do not deal here with notions of offer, acceptance, consideration, or other concepts of the law of contracts. We deal with constitutional law. And every court that has looked at this case has found an "agreement" in the sense of a commitment made by the Des Moines police officers that Williams would not be questioned about Pamela Powers in the absence of his counsel.

III

The Iowa courts recognized that Williams had been denied the constitutional right to the assistance of counsel. They held, however, that he had waived that right during the course of the automobile trip from Davenport to Des Moines. . . .

In the federal habeas corpus proceeding the District Court, believing that the issue of waiver was not one of fact but of federal law, held that the Iowa courts had "applied the wrong constitutional standards" in ruling that Williams had waived the protections that were his under the Constitution. 375 F. Supp., at 182. The court held "that it is the *government* which bears a heavy burden . . . but that is the burden which explicitly was placed on [Williams] by the state courts." Ibid. (emphasis in original). . . .

The Court of Appeals approved the reasoning of the District Court. . . .

The District Court and the Court of Appeals were correct in the view that the question of waiver was not a question of historical fact, but one which, in the words of Mr. Justice Frankfurter, requires "application of constitutional principles to the facts as found. . . ." Brown v. Allen, 344 U.S. 443, 507 (separate opinion). . . .

The District Court and the Court of Appeals were also correct in their understanding of the proper standard to be applied in determining the question of waiver as a matter of federal constitutional law — that it was incumbent upon the State to prove "an intentional relinquishment or abandonment of a known right or privilege." Johnson v. Zerbst, 304 U.S., at 464. . . .

We conclude . . . that the Court of Appeals was correct in holding that, judged by these standards, the record in this case falls far short of sustaining petitioner's burden. It is true that Williams had been informed of and appeared to understand his right to counsel. But waiver requires not merely comprehension but relinquishment, and Williams' consistent reliance upon the advice of counsel in dealing with the authorities refutes any suggestion that he waived that right. He consulted McKnight by long-distance telephone before turning himself in. He spoke with McKnight by telephone again shortly after being booked. After he was arraigned, Williams sought out and obtained legal advice from Kelly. Williams again consulted with Kelly after Detective Leaming and his fellow officer arrived in Davenport. Throughout, Williams was advised not to make any statements before seeing McKnight in Des Moines, and was assured that the police had agreed not to question him. His statements while in the car that he would tell the whole story after seeing McKnight in Des Moines were the clearest expressions by Williams himself that he desired the presence of an attorney before any interrogation took place. But even before making these statements, Williams had effectively asserted his right to counsel by having secured attorneys at both ends of the automobile trip, both of whom, acting as his agents, had made clear to the police that no interrogation was to occur during the journey. Williams knew of that agreement and, particularly in view of his consistent reliance on counsel, there is no basis for concluding that he disavowed it.

Despite Williams' express and implicit assertions of his right to counsel, Detective Leaming proceeded to elicit incriminating statements from Williams. Leaming did not preface this effort by telling Williams that he had a right to the presence of a lawyer, and made no effort at all to ascertain whether Williams wished to relinquish that right. The circumstances of record in this case thus provide no reasonable basis for finding that Williams waived his right to the assistance of counsel.

The Court of Appeals did not hold, nor do we, that under the circumstances of this case Williams *could not*, without notice to counsel, have waived his rights under the Sixth and Fourteenth Amendments. It only held, as do we, that he did not.

IV

The crime of which Williams was convicted was senseless and brutal, calling for swift and energetic action by the police to apprehend the perpetrator and gather evidence with which he could be convicted. No mission of law enforcement officials is more important. Yet "[d]isinterested zeal for the public good does not assure either wisdom or right in the methods it pursues." Haley v. Ohio, 332 U.S. 596, 605 (Frankfurter, J., concurring in judgment). Although we do not lightly affirm the issuance of a writ of habeas corpus in this case, so clear a violation of the Sixth and Fourteenth Amendments as here occurred cannot be condoned. The pressures on state executive and judicial officers charged with the administration of the criminal law are great, especially when the crime is murder and the victim a small child. But it is precisely the predictability of those pressures that makes imperative a resolute loyalty to the guarantees that the Constitution extends to us all.

The judgment of the Court of Appeals is affirmed.[12]

[The concurring opinions of Justice Marshall, Justice Powell, and Justice Stevens are omitted.]

MR. CHIEF JUSTICE BURGER, dissenting.

The result in this case ought to be intolerable in any society which purports to call itself an organized society. It continues the Court — by the narrowest margin — on the much-criticized course of punishing the public for the mistakes and misdeeds of law enforcement officers, instead of punishing the officer directly, if in fact he is guilty of wrongdoing. It mechanically and blindly keeps reliable evidence from juries whether the claimed constitutional violation involves gross police misconduct or honest human error.

Williams is guilty of the savage murder of a small child; no member of the Court contends he is not. While in custody, and after no fewer than five warnings of his rights to silence and to counsel, he led police to the concealed body of his victim. The Court concedes Williams was not threatened or coerced and that he spoke and acted voluntarily and with full awareness of his constitutional rights. In the face of all this, the Court now holds that because Williams was prompted by the detective's statement — not interrogation but a statement — the jury must not be told how the police found the body.

---

12. The District Court stated that its decision "does not touch upon the issue of what evidence, if any, beyond the incriminating statements themselves must be excluded as 'fruit of the poisonous tree.'" 375 F. Supp. 170, 185. We, too, have no occasion to address this issue, and in the present posture of the case there is no basis for the view of our dissenting Brethren . . . that any attempt to retry the respondent would probably be futile. While neither Williams' incriminating statements themselves nor any testimony describing his having led the police to the victim's body can constitutionally be admitted into evidence, evidence of where the body was found and of its condition might well be admissible on the theory that the body would have been discovered in any event, even had incriminating statements not been elicited from Williams. Cf. Killough v. United States, 336 F.2d 929. In the event that a retrial is instituted, it will be for the state courts in the first instance to determine whether particular items of evidence may be admitted.

Today's holding fulfills Judge (later Mr. Justice) Cardozo's grim prophecy that someday some court might carry the exclusionary rule to the absurd extent that its operative effect would exclude evidence relating to the body of a murder victim because of the means by which it was found.[1] In so ruling the Court regresses to playing a grisly game of "hide and seek," once more exalting the sporting theory of criminal justice which has been experiencing a decline in our jurisprudence. With Justices White, Blackmun, and Rehnquist, I categorically reject the remarkable notion that the police in this case were guilty of unconstitutional misconduct, or any conduct justifying the bizarre result reached by the Court. Apart from a brief comment on the merits, however, I wish to focus on the irrationality of applying the increasingly discredited exclusionary rule to this case.

(1) THE COURT CONCEDES WILLIAMS' DISCLOSURES WERE VOLUNTARY

Under well-settled precedents which the court freely acknowledges, it is very clear that Williams had made a valid waiver of his Fifth Amendment right to silence and his Sixth Amendment right to counsel when he led police to the child's body. Indeed, even under the Court's analysis I do not understand how a contrary conclusion is possible.

The Court purports to apply as the appropriate constitutional waiver standard the familiar "intentional relinquishment or abandonment of a known right or privilege" test of Johnson v. Zerbst, 304 U.S. 458, 464 (1938). . . . The Court assumes, without deciding, that Williams' conduct and statements were voluntary. It concedes, as it must, . . . that Williams had been informed of and fully understood his constitutional rights and the consequences of their waiver. Then, having either assumed or found every element necessary to make out a valid waiver under its own test, the Court reaches the astonishing conclusion that no valid waiver has been demonstrated. . . .

The evidence is uncontradicted that Williams had abundant knowledge of his right to have counsel present and of his right to silence. Since the Court does not question his mental competence, it boggles the mind to suggest that Williams could not understand that leading police to the child's body would have other than the most serious consequences. All of the elements necessary to make out a valid waiver are shown by the record and acknowledged by the Court; we thus are left to guess how the Court reached its holding. . . .

In any case, the Court assures us . . . that a valid waiver was possible in these circumstances, but was not quite made. Here, of course, Williams did not confess to the murder in so many words; it was his conduct in guiding police to the body, not his words, which incriminated him. And the record is replete with evidence that Williams knew precisely what he was doing when he guided police to the body. The human urge to confess wrongdoing is, of course, normal in all save hardened, professional criminals, as psychiatrists and analysts have demonstrated. T. Reik, The Compulsion to Confess (1972).

---

1. "The criminal is to go free because the constable has blundered. . . . A room is searched against the law, and the body of a murdered man is found. . . . The privacy of the home has been infringed, and the murderer goes free." People v. Defore, 242 N.Y. 13, 21, 23-24, 150 N.E. 585, 587, 588 (1926). . . .

(2) THE EXCLUSIONARY RULE SHOULD NOT BE APPLIED TO
NON-EGREGIOUS POLICE CONDUCT . . .

[I]t is striking that the Court fails even to consider whether the benefits secured by application of the exclusionary rule in this case outweigh its obvious social costs. Perhaps the failure is due to the fact that this case arises not under the Fourth Amendment, but under Miranda v. Arizona and the Sixth Amendment right to counsel. The Court apparently perceives the function of the exclusionary rule to be so different in these varying contexts that it must be mechanically and uncritically applied in all cases arising outside the Fourth Amendment.[5]

But this is demonstrably not the case where police conduct collides with *Miranda*'s procedural safeguards rather than with the Fifth Amendment privilege against compulsory self-incrimination. Involuntary and coerced admissions are suppressed because of the inherent unreliability of a confession wrung from an unwilling suspect by threats, brutality, or other coercion. . . . We can all agree on "[t]he abhorrence of society to the use of involuntary confessions," Linkletter v. Walker, [381 U.S.] at 638, and the need to preserve the integrity of the human personality and individual free will. . . .

But use of Williams' disclosures and their fruits carries no risk whatever of unreliability, for the body was found where he said it would be found. Moreover, since the Court makes no issue of voluntariness, no dangers are posed to individual dignity or free will. *Miranda*'s safeguards are premised on presumed unreliability long associated with confessions extorted by brutality or threats; they are not personal constitutional rights, but are simply judicially created prophylactic measures. Michigan v. Tucker, 417 U.S. 433 (1974). . . .

Thus, in cases where incriminating disclosures are voluntarily made without coercion, and hence not violative of the Fifth Amendment, but are obtained in violation of one of the *Miranda* prophylaxes, suppression is no longer automatic. Rather, we weigh the deterrent effect on unlawful police conduct, together with the normative Fifth Amendment justifications for suppression, against "the strong interest under any system of justice of making available to the trier of fact all concededly relevant and trustworthy evidence which either party seeks to adduce. . . . We also 'must consider society's interest in the effective prosecution of criminals. . . .'" Michigan v. Tucker, supra, at 450.[6] This individualized consideration or balancing process with respect to the exclusionary sanction is possible in this case, as in others, because Williams' incriminating disclosures are not infected with any element of compulsion the Fifth Amendment forbids; nor, as noted earlier, does this evidence pose any danger of unreliability to the factfinding process. In short, there is no reason to exclude this evidence.

Similarly, the exclusionary rule is not uniformly implicated in the Sixth Amendment, particularly its pretrial aspects. We have held that "the core purpose of the counsel guarantee was to assure 'Assistance' at trial, when the accused was confronted with both the intricacies of the law and the advocacy of the public prosecutor." United States v. Ash, 413 U.S. 300, 309 (1973). Thus, the right to counsel is

5. Indeed, if this were a Fourth Amendment case our course would be clear; only last Term, in Stone v. Powell, [428 U.S. 465 (1976), we held that application of the exclusionary rule in federal habeas corpus has such a minimal deterrent effect on law enforcement officials that habeas relief should not be granted on the ground that unconstitutionally seized evidence was introduced at trial. . . .

6. Statements obtained in violation of *Miranda* have long been used for impeachment purposes. Oregon v. Hass, 420 U.S. 714 (1975); Harris v. New York, 401 U.S. 222 (1971). . . .

fundamentally a "trial" right necessitated by the legal complexities of a criminal prosecution and the need to offset, to the trier of fact, the power of the State as prosecutor. See Schneckloth v. Bustamonte, supra, at 241. . . .

In any event, the fundamental purpose of the Sixth Amendment is to safeguard the fairness of the trial and the integrity of the factfinding process.[7] In this case, where the evidence of how the child's body was found is of unquestioned reliability, and since the Court accepts Williams' disclosures as voluntary and uncoerced, there is no issue either of fairness or evidentiary reliability to justify suppression of truth. It appears suppression is mandated here for no other reason than the Court's general impression that it may have a beneficial effect on future police conduct; indeed, the Court fails to say even that much in defense of its holding.

Thus, whether considered under *Miranda* or the Sixth Amendment, there is no more reason to exclude the evidence in this case than there was in Stone v. Powell [428 U.S. 465 (1976)];[8] that holding was premised on the utter reliability of evidence sought to be suppressed, the irrelevancy of the constitutional claim to the criminal defendant's factual guilt or innocence, and the minimal deterrent effect of habeas corpus on police misconduct. . . . Relevant factors in this case are thus indistinguishable from those in *Stone*, and from those in other Fourth Amendment cases suggesting a balancing approach toward utilization of the exclusionary sanction. Rather than adopting a formalistic analysis varying with the constitutional provision invoked, we should apply the exclusionary rule on the basis of its benefits and costs, at least in those cases where the police conduct at issue is far from being outrageous or egregious. . . .

[The dissenting opinions of Justice White, joined by Justices Blackmun and Rehnquist, and Justice Blackmun, joined by Justices White and Rehnquist, are omitted.]

NOTES AND QUESTIONS

1. Williams was retried on remand. The body was admitted at trial on the theory that it would have been inevitably discovered, and the Supreme Court ultimately approved of its admission. Nix v. Williams, 467 U.S. 431 (1984).

2. Although *Massiah* and *Miranda* apparently are premised on differing policies, the concerns of the cases are strikingly similar. Both elaborate when state may elicit information from a person suspected of criminality. Still, the conditions precedent for the application of each case do differ. The adversarial process must be initiated before the Sixth Amendment rights discussed in *Massiah* come into play, and custody is not directly relevant to the analysis. The Fifth Amendment rights

---

7. Indeed, we determine whether pretrial proceedings are "critical" by asking whether counsel is there needed to protect the fairness of the trial. See United States v. Ash, 413 U.S. 300, 322 (1973) (Stewart, J., concurring); Schneckloth v. Bustamonte, 412 U.S. 218, 239 (1973). It is also clear that the danger of actual error was the moving force behind the counsel guarantee in such cases as United States v. Wade, 388 U.S. 218 (1967) (post-indictment lineups).

8. This is a far cry from Massiah v. United States, 377 U.S. 201 (1964). Massiah's statements had no independent indicia of reliability as do respondent's. Moreover, Massiah was unaware that he was being interrogated by ruse and had not been advised of his right to counsel. Here, as Mr. Justice Blackmun has noted, there was no interrogation of Williams in the sense that term was used in *Massiah*, Escobedo v. Illinois, 378 U.S. 478 (1964), or *Miranda*. That the detective's statement appealed to Williams' conscience is not a sufficient reason to equate it to a police station grilling. It could well be that merely driving on the road and passing the intersection where he had turned off to bury the body might have produced the same result without suggestive comments.

discussed in *Miranda*, by contrast, are relevant only at the point of custodial interrogation, and the initiation of formal proceedings is irrelevant.

The significance of these distinctions was demonstrated by United States v. Henry, 447 U.S. 264 (1980). In *Henry*, an informant was planted in a cell with Henry, who had previously been indicted. The informant apparently initiated conversations with Henry, who made incriminating comments later used against him. The Court held that this violated Henry's Sixth Amendment rights. Once formal proceedings have begun, the government may not "deliberately elicit" information from a suspect without first obtaining a waiver of rights. *Henry* was important for two reasons. First, it revived *Massiah*, indicating that *Massiah* had avoided *Escobedo*'s fate. Second, it suggested that merely planting an informant, even if the informant remained passive and did not initiate any conversations, would violate the Sixth Amendment: By "intentionally creating a situation likely to induce Henry to make incriminating statements without the assistance of counsel, the government violated the Sixth Amendment right to counsel."

The broad implications of this language did not long survive, however. In Kuhlmann v. Wilson, 477 U.S. 436 (1986), the defendant had been placed in a cell with a police informant named Lee:

[T]he trial court found that [Lee's superior] had instructed Lee "to ask no questions of [the defendant] about the crime but merely to listen as to what [he] might say in his presence." The court determined that Lee obeyed these instructions, that he "at no time asked any questions with respect to the crime," and that he "only listened to [respondent] and made notes regarding what [respondent] had to say." The trial court also found that respondent's statements to Lee were "spontaneous" and "unsolicited." Under state precedent, a defendant's volunteered statements to a police agent were admissible in evidence because the police were not required to prevent talkative defendants from making incriminating statements. The trial court accordingly denied the suppression motion. . . .

. . . In United States v. Henry, the Court applied the *Massiah* test to incriminating statements made to a jailhouse informant. The Court of Appeals in that case found a violation of *Massiah* because the informant had engaged the defendant in conversations and "had developed a relationship of trust and confidence with [the defendant] such that [the defendant] revealed incriminating information." This Court affirmed, holding that the Court of Appeals reasonably concluded that the Government informant "deliberately used his position to secure incriminating information from [the defendant] when counsel was not present." Although the informant had not questioned the defendant, the informant had "stimulated" conversations with the defendant in order to "elicit" incriminating information. The Court emphasized that those facts, like the facts of *Massiah*, amounted to "indirect and surreptitious interrogatio[n]" of the defendant.

[T]he primary concern of the *Massiah* line of decisions is secret interrogation by investigatory techniques that are the equivalent of direct police interrogation. Since "the Sixth Amendment is not violated whenever — by luck or happenstance — the State obtains incriminating statements from the accused after the right to counsel has attached," a defendant does not make out a violation of that right simply by showing that an informant, either through prior arrangement or voluntarily, reported his incriminating statements to the police. Rather, the defendant must demonstrate that the police and their informant took some action, beyond merely listening, that was designed deliberately to elicit incriminating remarks. . . .

Id., at 440, 458-459. Justice Brennan, joined by Justice Marshall, dissented:

In the instant case, as in *Henry*, the accused was incarcerated and therefore was "susceptible to the ploys of undercover Government agents." Like Nichols [the informant in *Henry*], Lee was a secret informant, usually received consideration for the services he rendered the police, and therefore had an incentive to produce the information which he knew the police hoped to obtain. Just as Nichols had done, Lee obeyed instructions not to question respondent and to report to the police any statements made by the respondent in Lee's presence about the crime in question. And, like Nichols, Lee encouraged respondent to talk about his crime by conversing with him on the subject over the course of several days and by telling respondent that his exculpatory story would not convince anyone without more work. However, unlike the situation in *Henry*, a disturbing visit from respondent's brother, rather than a conversation with the informant, seems to have been the immediate catalyst for respondent's confession to Lee. While it might appear from this sequence of events that Lee's comment regarding respondent's story and his general willingness to converse with respondent about the crime were not the immediate causes of respondent's admission, I think that the deliberate-elicitation standard requires consideration of the entire course of government behavior.

The State intentionally created a situation in which it was foreseeable that respondent would make incriminating statements without the assistance of counsel — it assigned respondent to a cell overlooking the scene of the crime and designated a secret informant to be respondent's cellmate. The informant, while avoiding direct questions, nonetheless developed a relationship of cellmate camaraderie with respondent and encouraged him to talk about his crime. While the coup de grace was delivered by respondent's brother, the groundwork for respondent's confession was laid by the State. Clearly the State's actions had a sufficient nexus with respondent's admission of guilt to constitute deliberate elicitation within the meaning of *Henry*. I would affirm the judgment of the Court of Appeals.

Id., at 475-476.

3. Why the differences between *Innis* on the one hand and *Henry* and *Kuhlmann* on the other? For a discussion, see Welsh S. White, Interrogation without Questions: Rhode Island v. Innis and United States v. Henry, 78 Mich. L. Rev. 1209 (1980).

4. In Kansas v. Ventris, 129 S. Ct. 1841 (2009), the Court held by 7-2 that statements obtained in violation of *Massiah* and its progeny can be used at trial for impeachment purposes. Justice Scalia, writing for the majority, explained:

Our opinion in *Massiah*, to be sure, was equivocal on what precisely constituted the violation. It quoted various authorities indicating that the violation occurred at the moment of the postindictment interrogation because such questioning "contravenes the basic dictates of fairness in the conduct of criminal causes." 377 U.S., at 205. But the opinion later suggested that the violation occurred only when the improperly obtained evidence was "used against [the defendant] at his trial." 377 U.S., at 206-207. That question was irrelevant to the decision in *Massiah* in any event. Now that we are confronted with the question, we conclude that the *Massiah* right is a right to be free of uncounseled interrogation, and is infringed at the time of the interrogation. That, we think, is when the "Assistance of Counsel" is denied.

This case does not involve, therefore, the prevention of a constitutional violation, but rather the scope of the remedy for a violation that has already occurred. Our precedents make clear that the game of excluding tainted evidence for impeachment purposes is not worth the candle. . . .

Once the defendant testifies in a way that contradicts prior statements, denying the prosecution use of "the traditional truth-testing devices of the adversary process" . . . is a high price to pay for vindication of the right to counsel at the prior stage.

On the other side of the scale, preventing impeachment use of statements taken in violation of *Massiah* would add little appreciable deterrence. Officers have significant incentive to ensure that they and their informants comply with the Constitution's demands, since statements lawfully obtained can be used for all purposes rather than simply for impeachment. And the *ex ante* probability that evidence gained in violation of *Massiah* would be of use for impeachment is exceedingly small. An investigator would have to anticipate both that the defendant would choose to testify at trial (an unusual occurrence to begin with) *and* that he would testify inconsistently despite the admissibility of his prior statement for impeachment. Not likely to happen — or at least not likely enough to risk squandering the opportunity of using a properly obtained statement for the prosecution's case in chief.

Id., at 1846-1847.

5. Should it matter if the state takes advantage, postindictment, of a codefendant's offer to assist the state's investigation? In other words, does "deliberate elicitation" extend to obtaining information as a result of a meeting between codefendants that was initiated by the noncooperating defendant? In addition, does it matter whether the reason prompting the state authorities to accept the codefendant's offer of assistance was the ongoing investigation of other crimes for which no indictments had yet been returned? In Maine v. Moulton, 474 U.S. 159 (1985), the Court held that *Massiah* controls in such a case, but that any information obtained may be used in the prosecution of those offenses for which an indictment had not been returned at the time the incriminating statements were made.

Compare *Moulton* to Arizona v. Roberson, supra, at page 824, in which the Court held that *Edwards* was violated where the police interrogate a suspect with respect to one crime if the suspect has already invoked his *Miranda* right to counsel with respect to some other crime. Why is it that the invocation of the *Miranda* right to counsel of a person in custody protects a suspect from any further state efforts to elicit information, but initiation of the Sixth Amendment right to counsel is limited to the particular charge with respect to which formal proceedings have begun?

6. Perhaps the best answer to this question is that the Fifth Amendment and Sixth Amendment are concerned with different matters, even if their concerns might overlap in the confession area. In Michigan v. Jackson, 475 U.S. 625 (1986), however, the Court temporarily lost sight of this. The *Jackson* Court held that, once a defendant's Sixth Amendment right to counsel has attached and has been "asserted" by the defendant, the authorities can no longer approach that defendant to seek a waiver of the right to counsel — even if *Miranda* warnings are properly given and the defendant responds by clearly expressing the desire to waive counsel. *Jackson* was based on a simple (or should we say simplistic?) analogy to *Edwards*; as with the Fifth Amendment right at issue in *Edwards*, the Court concluded that the Sixth Amendment right to counsel in *Jackson* requires protection by the same kind of prophylactic, "bright-line" rule prohibiting any further police-initiated interrogations.

The *Jackson* decision managed to survive for 23 years — and caused the Court numerous headaches; compare, e.g., McNeil v. Wisconsin, 501 U.S. 171 (1991) (Sixth Amendment *Jackson* rule is offense-specific) with Texas v. Cobb, 532 U.S. 162 (2001) (Sixth Amendment *Jackson* rule does not extend to "closely related" offenses) — before finally being overruled. In Montejo v. Louisiana, 129 S. Ct. 2079 (2009), the Court, per Justice Scalia, finally saw the light:

> What does the *Jackson* rule actually achieve by way of preventing unconstitutional conduct? Recall that the purpose of the rule is to preclude the State from badgering defendants into waiving their previously asserted rights. . . . The effect of this badgering might be to coerce a waiver, which would render the subsequent interrogation a violation of the Sixth Amendment. . . . [But] the Court has already taken substantial other, overlapping measures toward the same end. Under *Miranda*'s prophylactic protection of the right against compelled self-incrimination, any suspect subject to custodial interrogation has the right to have a lawyer present if he so requests, and to be advised of that right. . . . Under *Edwards*' prophylactic protection of the *Miranda* right, once such a defendant "has invoked his right to have counsel present," interrogation must stop. . . . And under *Minnick*'s prophylactic protection of the *Edwards* right, no subsequent interrogation may take place until counsel is present, "whether or not the accused has consulted with his attorney." . . . These three layers of prophylaxis are sufficient. Under the *Miranda-Edwards-Minnick* line of cases (which is not in doubt), a defendant who does not want to speak to the police without counsel present need only say as much when he is first approached and given the *Miranda* warnings. At that point, not only must the immediate contact end, but "badgering" by later requests is prohibited. If that regime suffices to protect the integrity of "a suspect's voluntary choice not to speak outside his lawyer's presence," . . . it is hard to see why it would not also suffice to protect that same choice after arraignment, when Sixth Amendment rights have attached. And if so, then *Jackson* is simply superfluous.
>
> It is true, as Montejo points out in his supplemental brief, that the doctrine established by *Miranda* and *Edwards* is designed to protect Fifth Amendment, not Sixth Amendment, rights. But that is irrelevant. What matters is that these cases, like *Jackson*, protect the right to have counsel during custodial interrogation — which right happens to be guaranteed (once the adversary judicial process has begun) by *two* sources of law. Since the right under both sources is waived using the same procedure, . . . doctrines ensuring voluntariness of the Fifth Amendment waiver simultaneously ensure the voluntariness of the Sixth Amendment waiver.
>
> Montejo also correctly observes that the *Miranda-Edwards* regime is narrower than *Jackson* in one respect: The former applies only in the context of custodial interrogation. If the defendant is not in custody then those decisions do not apply; nor do they govern other, noninterrogative types of interactions between the defendant and the State (like pretrial lineups). However, those uncovered situations are the *least* likely to pose a risk of coerced waivers. When a defendant is not in custody, he is in control, and need only shut his door or walk away to avoid police badgering. And noninterrogative interactions with the State do not involve the "inherently compelling pressures," *Miranda*, supra, at 467, that one might reasonably fear could lead to involuntary waivers.
>
> *Jackson* was policy driven, and if that policy is being adequately served through other means, there is no reason to retain its rule. *Miranda* and the cases that elaborate upon it already guarantee not simply noncoercion in the traditional sense, but what Justice Harlan referred to as "voluntariness with a vengeance," 384 U.S., at 505 (dissenting opinion). There is no need to take *Jackson*'s further step of requiring voluntariness on stilts.

Id., at 2089-2090.

7. Should the fact of representation alone matter for either Sixth or Fifth Amendment purposes? Consider one last aspect of Moran v. Burbine, 475 U.S. 412 (1986) (other aspects of which are discussed at page 829, supra):

Respondent also contends that the Sixth Amendment requires exclusion of his three confessions. It is clear, of course, that, absent a valid waiver, the defendant has the right to the presence of an attorney during any interrogation occurring after the first formal charging proceeding, the point at which the Sixth Amendment right to counsel initially attaches. And we readily agree that once the right has attached, it follows that the police may not interfere with the efforts of a defendant's attorney to act as a "'medium' between [the suspect] and the State" during the interrogation. Maine v. Moulton, 474 U.S. 159, 176 (1985). The difficulty for respondent is that the interrogation sessions that yielded the inculpatory statements took place before the initiation of "adversary judicial proceedings." He contends, however, that this circumstance is not fatal to his Sixth Amendment claim. At least in some situations, he argues, the Sixth Amendment protects the integrity of the attorney-client relationship regardless of whether the prosecution has in fact commenced "by way of formal charge, preliminary hearing, indictment, information or arraignment." Placing principal reliance on a footnote in *Miranda*, and on Escobedo v. Illinois, he maintains that *Gouveia*, *Kirby*, and our other "critical stage" cases, concern only the narrow question of when the right to counsel — that is, to the appointment or presence of counsel — attaches. The right to noninterference with an attorney's dealings with a criminal suspect, he asserts, arises the moment that the relationship is formed, or, at the very least, once the defendant is placed in custodial interrogation.

We are not persuaded. At the outset, subsequent decisions foreclose any reliance on *Escobedo* and *Miranda* for the proposition that the Sixth Amendment right, in any of its manifestations, applies prior to the initiation of adversary judicial proceedings. Although *Escobedo* was originally decided as a Sixth Amendment case, "the Court in retrospect perceived that the 'prime purpose' of *Escobedo* was not to vindicate the constitutional right to counsel as such, but, like *Miranda*, 'to guarantee full effectuation of the privilege against self-incrimination. . . .'" Kirby v. Illinois, at 689. Clearly then, *Escobedo* provides no support for respondent's argument. Nor, of course, does *Miranda*, the holding of which rested exclusively on the Fifth Amendment. Thus, the decision's brief observation about the reach of *Escobedo*'s Sixth Amendment analysis is not only dictum, but reflects an understanding of the case that the Court has expressly disavowed.

Questions of precedent to one side, we find respondent's understanding of the Sixth Amendment both practically and theoretically unsound. As a practical matter, it makes little sense to say that the Sixth Amendment right to counsel attaches at different times depending on the fortuity of whether the suspect or his family happens to have retained counsel prior to interrogation. More importantly, the suggestion that the existence of an attorney-client relationship itself triggers the protections of the Sixth Amendment misconceives the underlying purposes of the right to counsel. The Sixth Amendment's intended function is not to wrap a protective cloak around the attorney-client relationship for its own sake any more than it is to protect a suspect from the consequences of his own candor. Its purpose, rather, is to assure that in any "criminal prosecutio[n]," U.S. Const., Amdt. 6, the accused shall not be left to his own devices in facing the "prosecutorial forces of organized society." Maine v. Moulton, at 170 (quoting Kirby v. Illinois, 406 U.S., at 689). By its very terms, it becomes applicable only when the government's role shifts from investigation to accusation. For it is only then that the assistance of one versed in the "intricacies . . . of law," is needed to assure that the prosecution's case encounters "the crucible of meaningful adversarial testing." United States v. Cronic, 466 U.S. 648, 656 (1984).

Indeed, in Maine v. Moulton, decided this Term, the Court again confirmed that looking to the initiation of adversary judicial proceedings, far from being mere formalism, is fundamental to the proper application of the Sixth Amendment right to counsel. There, we considered the constitutional implications of a surreptitious investigation that yielded evidence pertaining to two crimes. For one, the defendant had been indicted; for the other, he had not. . . . The Court made clear . . . that the evidence concerning the crime for which the defendant had not been indicted — evidence obtained in precisely the same manner from the identical suspect — would be admissible at a trial limited to those charges. The clear implication of the holding . . . is that the Sixth Amendment right to counsel does not attach until after the initiation of formal charges. Moreover, because Moulton already had legal representation, the decision all but forecloses respondent's argument that the attorney-client relationship itself triggers the Sixth Amendment right.

Respondent contends, however, that custodial interrogations require a different rule. Because confessions elicited during the course of police questioning often seal a suspect's fate, he argues, the need for an advocate — and the concomitant right to noninterference with the attorney-client relationship — is at its zenith, regardless of whether the State has initiated the first adversary judicial proceeding. We do not doubt that a lawyer's presence could be of value to the suspect; and we readily agree that if a suspect confesses, his attorney's case at trial will be that much more difficult. But these concerns are no more decisive in this context than they were for the equally damaging preindictment lineup at issue in *Kirby*, or the statements pertaining to the unindicted crime elicited from the defendant in Maine v. Moulton. For an interrogation, no more or less than for any other "critical" pretrial event, the possibility that the encounter may have important consequences at trial, standing alone, is insufficient to trigger the Sixth Amendment right to counsel. As *Gouveia* made clear, until such time as the "government has committed itself to prosecute, and . . . the adverse positions of government and defendant have solidified" the Sixth Amendment right to counsel does not attach. 467 U.S., at 189.

Because, as respondent acknowledges, the events that led to the inculpatory statements preceded the formal initiation of adversary judicial proceedings, we reject the contention that the conduct of the police violated his rights under the Sixth Amendment.

Id., at 428-432.

What does *Burbine* suggest about the proper role of defense lawyers in criminal litigation? In civil litigation, the strong norm is not to talk to represented parties except with their attorneys present. See Model Code of Professional Responsibility DR 7-104(A)(1) (1980) (essentially barring uncounseled contact with represented parties by attorneys or their agents on any matter within the scope of the representation). Why doesn't the same norm exist in criminal investigation? For an explanation and defense of both the civil and the criminal practices, see William J. Stuntz, Lawyers, Deception, and Evidence Gathering, 79 Va. L. Rev. 1903 (1993).

Some defendants have tried to get around *Burbine* — at least in cases where a prosecutor was involved at some level in the interrogation of the defendant — by arguing that contact with represented defendants violates legal ethics, see DR 7-104(A), and that any resulting incriminating statements should be suppressed (in addition to any potential ethical sanctions imposed on the offending prosecutor). In United States v. Hammad, 858 F.2d 834 (2d Cir. 1988), the court seemed to adopt this argument in principle, though it declined to enforce the ethical prohibition with an exclusionary rule. See also United States v. Lopez, 4 F.3d 1455 (9th Cir. 1993) (adopting *Hammad* for postindictment contacts, but overturning the dismissal of an indictment due to a *Hammad* violation). In 1998, Congress confirmed the applicability of state ethical rules to federal prosecutors: "An attorney for the Government shall be subject to State laws and rules, and local Federal court rules, governing attorneys in each State where such attorney engages in that attorney's duties, to the same extent and in the same manner as other attorneys in that State." 28 U.S.C.A. §530B(a).

8. In its 2009 *Montejo* decision, after overruling *Jackson*, the Court remanded the case so that the defendant could litigate whether he had in fact asserted his *Miranda* rights, which (if true) would have triggered protection against any further police-initiated interrogation under *Edwards*. The Court then added:

> Montejo may also seek on remand to press any claim he might have that his Sixth Amendment waiver was not knowing and voluntary, e.g., his argument that the waiver was invalid because it was based on misrepresentations by police as to whether he had been appointed a lawyer, cf. Moran v. Burbine, 475 U.S., at 428-429. These matters have heightened importance in light of our opinion today.

129 S. Ct., at 2092. Does this mean that the Court — in light of its rejection of the *Jackson* rule — might now be willing to reconsider whether, at least in some cases, the fact of representation alone might be of constitutional significance? If the Court were to reconsider and ultimately overturn this important aspect of *Burbine*, what approach to the proper role of defense counsel should it substitute?

Chapter 7

Complex Investigations in the
Fourth Amendment's Shadow

Much of the law governing criminal investigations that we have looked at thus far has involved the investigation of street crimes — meaning offenses like homicide, robbery, and relatively low-level drug transactions. Most of the cases have grown out of simple investigations conducted for the most part by police. In many of these cases, the criminal investigation has been "reactive." It has begun in the aftermath of a particular crime, in response to a citizen's complaint, and has been directed at identifying and obtaining evidence to prosecute the perpetrator of the crime for the commission of that very offense. Many of the cases have also involved one or another form of "overt" investigation in which law enforcement agents *who are identified as such* have undertaken investigative steps that have included, among other things, conducting interviews, performing searches, and interrogating suspects. Not all of the cases we have addressed have had these characteristics. But neither have they tended to involve overly complicated crimes, sophisticated undercover investigations, or the search of computer records.

A significant number of criminal investigations, and particularly federal criminal investigations, deal with different types of crime, including public corruption, securities fraud, high-level drug distribution, and various forms of racketeering carried out by ongoing criminal associations. The investigation of such crimes is frequently long term and requires the commitment of substantial government resources. In such cases, law enforcement agents may select the targets of their investigation (or the subject matter) proactively, based on intelligence or leads from reliable sources rather than on complaints from identifiable victims or reports from contemporaneous witnesses. Certain of these cases are substantially different from more routine criminal cases because they involve sophisticated covert investigative techniques used relatively less frequently in the context of simpler crimes. Even when law enforcement agents identified as such conduct searches, moreover, these searches may be of computerized files and may implicate Fourth Amendment issues not generally seen in simpler contexts.

This chapter takes up some of the legal issues that can arise in cases of this sort. (Others are treated later, when we turn to the subject of grand jury investigations, which implicate a different set of legal problems.) The chapter begins by examining the law regulating the use of electronic surveillance and the search of electronic records. We then turn to the subject of undercover investigations and to the entrapment defense. These materials follow upon our treatment of the Fourth Amendment for good reason. With regard to the statutory frameworks governing electronic surveillance (not to mention the search of electronic files), the statutes themselves have been profoundly shaped by Fourth Amendment cases and cannot be fully understood without a background in Fourth Amendment law. The law of entrapment is included here for two reasons: It is an important limitation in the selection and pursuit of targets of undercover investigations, and, interestingly, it is a limitation on law enforcement action that has been judicially derived as a matter of statutory construction rather than from constitutional principles. (Recall here United States v. White, 401 U.S. 745 (1971), and our previous discussion on the question of whether it is reasonable to conclude that we bear the risk that the people we trust may be collecting evidence to prove we have committed or are committing crimes.) As you read the materials that follow, consider how these areas of law have grown up in the shadow of the Fourth Amendment — and how they might have looked, had Fourth Amendment jurisprudence developed along different lines.

A. *Electronic Surveillance and the Search of Electronic Data*

The electronic surveillance of communications and the search of computer and other electronic files is essential to the investigation of many complex crimes. In organized crime investigations, for example, witnesses and victims may be too intimidated to offer testimony, while it may be nearly impossible for undercover agents to infiltrate the criminal organization so as to obtain evidence sufficient to prosecute its principals. In such cases, the covert electronic surveillance of conversations among the members of criminal associations has proven to be an important investigative technique. Similarly, as people have increasingly turned to computers and the Internet to communicate, transfer information, and engage in commerce, computer crime and the use of computers in criminal activity have also expanded. The evidence of such crimes has frequently come to rest in computer files of one sort or another; the successful investigation of these crimes has often required the government to obtain access to data stored in electronic form on a single computer, on a network, or at a remote location.

The materials considered in this section raise many Fourth Amendment questions but are unlike the search and seizure materials you have already considered in an important way — namely, in this area, legislation has played an important role in setting out the procedures by which law enforcement may investigate crime. There are reasons to applaud legislative involvement of this type. Indeed, Professor Amsterdam argued over 30 years ago that, in general, the "great American vacuum" of such "subconstitutional" controls on police practices constitutes a significant barrier to the effective constraint of arbitrary police conduct. See Anthony G. Amsterdam, Perspectives on the Fourth Amendment, 58 Minn. L. Rev. 349, 380 (1974). At the same time, there may be a downside to legislatures playing a substantial role in the articulation of the rules that will regulate criminal investigations involving computers and electronic records. Consider the following general observation about the protection of constitutional values in cyberspace:

> My fear about cyberspace is that . . . the institutions most responsible for articulating constitutional values will simply stand back while issues of constitutional import are legislatively determined. The institutions most responsible for articulating constitutional values today are the courts. My sense is that they will step back because they feel . . . that these are new questions that cyberspace has raised. Their newness will make them feel political, and when a question feels political, courts step away from resolving it.

I fear this not because I fear legislatures, but because in our day constitutional discourse at the level of the legislature is a very thin sort of discourse. The philosopher Bernard Williams has argued that because the Supreme Court has taken so central a role in the articulation of constitutional values, legislatures no longer do. Whether Williams is correct or not, this much is clear: The constitutional discourse of our present Congress is far below the level it must be at to address the questions about constitutional values . . . raised by cyberspace.

Lawrence Lessig, Code and Other Laws of Cyberspace 120 (1999).

We begin our examination of this subject by stepping back from the newer issues involving criminal investigations in cyberspace to consider a decades-old legislative articulation of the procedures that police must employ in the conduct of traditional electronic surveillance. As you may recall from Chapter 5 (see supra, at page 384), Title III of the Omnibus Crime Control and Safe Streets Act of 1968 was enacted in the wake of the Supreme Court's decisions in Katz v. United States, 389 U.S. 347 (1967), and Berger v. New York, 388 U.S. 41 (1967), to address the constitutional concerns with electronic surveillance raised by those cases. The statute regulates the "nonconsensual" interception through use of any electronic, mechanical, or other device of the contents of any wire, oral, or electronic communications.[1] (An interception for law enforcement purposes is "consensual," and thus falls outside Title III, when any party to the communication consents to being overheard.) The statute sets forth circumstances in which federal law enforcement agencies may obtain court orders from federal judges authorizing interceptions; further, it empowers states to enact statutes permitting state law enforcement agencies to seek similar orders from state judges in keeping with Title III's provisions. Most states have enacted statutes pursuant to this authorization.

We start with Title III and its provisions for the interception of communications. In the next section, we turn to the search and seizure of stored electronic records, using this discussion to take up some broader Fourth Amendment questions associated with the advent of the Information Age. As you read the materials below, consider both the benefits and the potential problems associated with comprehensive legislative approaches to articulating the scope of police powers, and particularly in investigations involving computers, electronic communications and records, and future technologies.

1. Wiretapping and Related Electronic Surveillance

Title III's drafters sought to accomplish a number of things:

Congress enacted Title III with at least four specific goals in mind. First, in permitting investigators to obtain court authorization to wiretap or eavesdrop, it sought to provide law enforcement officials with a much-needed weapon in their fight against crime, particularly organized crime. Second, it sought to safeguard the privacy of . . .

---

1. Electronic communications, which include facsimile transmissions and electronic mail, were added to Title III's coverage only in 1986, with passage of the Electronic Communications Privacy Act. (Title III's definition of "wire communications" is limited to communications containing the human voice, so that without the 1986 amendment Title III would not apply to communications via wire that transfer only electronic data.) Electronic communications are in some respects treated differently from wire and oral communications in the amended Title III. Significant differences are noted in this discussion.

communications. Third, Congress endeavored to satisfy the procedural and substantive requirements previously enunciated by the . . . Supreme Court in Berger v. New York and Katz v. United States as constitutional prerequisites to lawful court-authorized interception of private communications. Finally, it attempted to "define on a uniform basis the circumstances and conditions under which the interception of . . . communications may be authorized."

Clifford S. Fishman, Interception of Communications in Exigent Circumstances: The Fourth Amendment, Federal Legislation, and the United States Department of Justice, 22 Ga. L. Rev. 1, 5-7 (1987). Title III is a detailed legislative scheme. In it, Congress sought to satisfy constitutional prerequisites to electronic surveillance, but also to do more: "The statute does [not] merely parallel the Fourth Amendment and Supreme Court decisions. Congress included within the statute several procedural and substantive safeguards that are not constitutionally mandated, many of which are not applicable to conventional search warrants." Id., at 25.

Title III requires law enforcement agents in most circumstances to obtain a judicial warrant before resorting to the nonconsensual electronic surveillance of wire, oral, or electronic communications. (A separate statute, the Pen Registers and Trap and Trace Devices Statute, 18 U.S.C. §§3121-3127, governs the surveillance of routing information for both wire and electronic communications.) Federal applications for the interception of wire or oral communications (though not for electronic communications) must also be authorized by specially designated high-ranking Justice Department officials; state applications similarly require the approval of the district attorney or an analogous high-ranking state officer. Applications for surveillance orders may only be made to seek evidence of statutorily enumerated offenses. The list of such offenses is very broad as it applies to federal criminal investigations. (Indeed, it includes any felony whatsoever when the application is to intercept electronic communications like e-mail or faxes, as opposed to voice communications.) The list of offenses that may be investigated using electronic surveillance is considerably narrower, however, in some state statutes.

Applications for interception orders must be in writing and under oath. They must include details regarding the particular offense under investigation; the type of communication sought to be intercepted; the identity of the person or persons, if known, committing the offense and whose communications are to be intercepted; and the facilities from which or the place where the communication is to be intercepted (unless the circumstances merit the issuance of a "roving" intercept order based on a showing that specification of a surveillance site is not practical with regard to oral communications or that the subject's actions could thwart interception from a specified facility in the case of wire or electronic communications). Applications must also include a "full and complete statement" as to whether or not other investigative techniques have been tried and failed or as to why they reasonably appear to be either unlikely to succeed or too dangerous to attempt. They must describe any previous applications for surveillance of the same persons or places.

An application must include a statement of the period of time for which the interception is required, not to exceed 30 days. When the nature of the investigation requires that the interception not automatically terminate when the described type of communication has been first obtained (for example, when the first drug-related conversation occurs in the investigation of a narcotics organization), the application must also include "a particular description of facts establishing probable cause to believe that additional communications of the same type will occur thereafter. . . ."

Extensions of wiretap orders are available, but only on a new showing of probable cause and compliance with the same procedures used in obtaining the initial order. Extension applications must also include a statement setting forth the results obtained from the prior interception or a reasonable explanation of the failure to obtain such results.

Interception orders are premised on multiple probable cause determinations: that a person is about to commit, is committing, or has committed an offense falling within Title III's coverage; that the proposed surveillance will result in the interception of particular communications concerning that offense; and (outside the context of roving intercept orders) that the particular facilities or place where communications are to be intercepted is being or is about to be used in connection with the offense (or is listed in the name of, leased to, or otherwise commonly used by the person or persons under suspicion). The order must contain "a particular description of the type of communication sought to be intercepted." The court must make a finding that other investigative techniques will be inadequate. As the Supreme Court said in United States v. Kahn, 415 U.S. 143, 153, n. 12 (1974), electronic surveillance pursuant to Title III should not be permitted if "traditional investigative techniques would suffice to expose the crime."

The statute also provides that within a reasonable period, but no later than 90 days after the denial of an interception application or the termination of a period of authorized surveillance, the judge who reviewed the Title III application must serve an "inventory" on the people named in the order or application and on such other parties to intercepted communications as the judge may determine is in the interest of justice. (The service of the inventory may be postponed for good cause.) The inventory notifies the parties served of the fact of an interception order or application; the dates of the application, the order, and the period of interception; and whether or not communications were obtained.

Intercept orders may require periodic reports to be made to the issuing judge showing what progress has been made toward intercepting the sought-after communications and explaining the need for continued interception. In addition, agents executing a surveillance order are required, where possible, to record on tape or other comparable device all the communications they intercept. Title III requires that immediately upon the termination of an interception order, recordings must be made available to the judge who issued the interception order and sealed under his direction.

Title III provides for both criminal and civil remedies against those who willfully intercept, use, or disclose information in violation of the statute. Violations of Title III are also enforced by a statutory exclusionary rule that applies to the interception of wire and oral (but not electronic) communications in violation of its terms. This rule, however, does not require suppression of evidence whenever there is a failure to comply with the statute's provisions. In United States v. Giordano, 416 U.S. 505, 528 (1974), the Supreme Court concluded that the law's exclusionary remedy extends to violations of those statutory provisions that play "a central role in the statutory scheme."

Finally, Title III contains a "minimization" requirement. This requirement addresses the reality that law enforcement agents executing an intercept order frequently gain access to communications unrelated to the crimes under investigation. Title III requires that surveillance "be conducted in such a way as to minimize the interception of communications not otherwise subject to interception under this chapter. . . ." 18 U.S.C. §2518(5). The primary way that officers intercepting conversations have satisfied this requirement is by listening to the conversations as they take place and stopping their interception (and listening) when they determine that a particular conversation is not pertinent to the investigation. Consider this obligation in light of the following case:

UNITED STATES v. YANNOTTI

Appeal to the United States Court of Appeals for the Second Circuit
541 F.3d 112 (2008)

PARKER, CIRCUIT JUDGE.

Michael Yannotti appeals from a judgment of conviction in the United States District Court for the Southern District of New York. The jury convicted him of conspiring to engage in racketeering in violation of the Racketeer Influenced and Corrupt Organizations ("RICO") Act. See 18 U.S.C. §1962(d). The district court sentenced Yannotti principally to 240 months' incarceration. . . .

On July 21, 2004, the government indicted Yannotti and his co-defendants, John Gotti Jr. and Louis Mariani, alleging that they were members of the Gambino Crime Family, a racketeering enterprise that engaged in, inter alia, extortion, extortionate extensions of credit, securities fraud, as well as violent conduct including murder. . . .

The government's proof at trial included testimony from several members and associates of the Gambino Crime Family, as well as from law enforcement officers. These witnesses described Yannotti's criminal activities as an associate of Family member Nicholas Corozzo, whose crew was based in the Canarsie section of Brooklyn. In addition to Yannotti's loansharking activity, the government offered proof, primarily thorough Gambino Family associate Andrew DiDonato, that Yannotti was involved in the 1987 shooting of Robert Tarantola, an associate of the Colombo Crime Family, a rival criminal enterprise. Gambino Family captain Michael DiLeonardo and soldier Joseph D'Angelo testified about Yannotti's involvement in a 1992 conspiracy to abduct and murder Curtis Sliwa, a radio host and founder of the Guardian Angels, in retaliation for his public criticism of John Gotti, Sr., then head of the Gambino Family. Finally, DiDonato and DiLeonardo testified that in 1996, Yannotti shot Robert Arena and Thomas Marenga as a result of a conflict between Yannotti's crew and members of the Lucchese Crime Family, a rival criminal enterprise. In addition to testimonial evidence, the government offered surveillance photographs, a beeper recovered at the scene of the Arena and Marenga murders, records indicating that the beeper belonging to Yannotti, recorded conversations between Yannotti and his loansharking customers, and additional loansharking records.

During trial, [an] evidentiary issue[ ] arose that figure[s] in this appeal . . . concern[ing] the admissibility of certain evidence secured as a result of a 1996 court authorized wiretap of a cellular phone used by Corozzo and his associates in Florida. The affidavit in support of the application averred that the phone was being used by Corozzo and "others yet unknown" in furtherance of a racketeering conspiracy that engaged in loansharking and money laundering, largely in New York. While the affidavit sought authorization to intercept conversations of Corozzo and several other named individuals, it did not identify Yannotti among the anticipated interceptees. It did, however, state that probable cause existed to suspect that "unknown others" used the phone while engaging in illegal activity.

On April 22, 1996, the day that the application was approved, Corozzo left the cell phone that was the subject of the application in Florida and returned to New York. The next day, the FBI intercepted its first phone call from Yannotti made on the target phone. The government's initial ten-day progress report to the judge supervising the wiretap described two phone calls made by Yannotti involving the collection of loansharking debts. The report explained that "Michael Yannotti will be identified as a named interceptee [on the wiretap application] if an extension affidavit is filed in this case." Finally, the government informed the judge that it believed that the phone would continue to be used by Yannotti, Corozzo, and unnamed others to discuss the offenses described in the initial authorizing order. The government never intercepted any phone calls from Corozzo or sought an extension of the wiretap, thus, Yannotti was never formally named in the authorization.

Before the start of the trial, Yannotti moved to suppress the two calls on the ground that the agents had exceeded their authority in continuing to intercept calls well after learning that Corozzo no longer possessed the phone. He argued that the agents were required to seek new authorization to intercept his conversations and that the continued interception converted the initial authorization into a general warrant proscribed by the Fourth Amendment. The district court disagreed, pointing to the fact that the initial order permitted the interception not only of Corozzo and others specifically named in the authorization, but also "others yet unknown," and consequently was not limited to the interception of calls placed by Corozzo himself. The court concluded that due to the easy mobility of cellular phones, the government was not required to seek a new authorization each time that a new person used the phone. Additionally, the government reasonably believed that the phone would continue to be used as an instrument of the charged conspiracy while in Yannotti's possession. For these reasons, the court concluded that the scope of the warrant and the reasonableness of the government's conduct posed no constitutional problems. . . .

Yannotti . . . complains that the district court improperly admitted his phone conversations because the government's original wiretap application did not specifically name him as a target. As previously noted, although the government was authorized to intercept communications on a cell phone belonging to Corozzo, that authorization did not specifically identify Yannotti. The government intercepted two calls in which Yannotti discussed his loansharking activities. . . .

Title III of the Omnibus Crime Control and Safe Streets Act of 1968 provides for court-ordered interceptions of communications. 18 U.S.C. §2518. The statute allows a court to authorize a wiretap "if it determines, on the basis of the facts submitted by the applicant, that there is probable cause to believe (1) that an individual was committing, had committed, or is about to commit a crime; (2) that communications concerning that crime will be obtained through the wiretap; and (3) that the premises to be wiretapped were being used for criminal purposes or are about to be used or owned by the target of the wiretap." United States v. Diaz, 176 F.3d 52, 110 (2d Cir. 1999). Intercepted communications are inadmissible if they were "unlawfully intercepted," intercepted pursuant to an authorization or approval that is "insufficient on its face," or intercepted not in conformity "with the order of authorization or approval." 18 U.S.C. §2518(10)(a). . . .

[W]e find no error in the admission of the conversations. The affidavit in support of the application did not solely request the interception of communications made to and by Corozzo. Instead, it named Corozzo, six alleged associates and members of the Gambino family, and "others as yet unknown." In authorizing the interceptions, the court determined that probable cause existed to believe that not only Corozzo, but also other unnamed targets, would use the cellular phone to engage in illegal activities. The government is not required to specify in the application each individual whose conversations may be intercepted. Where, as here, the government is investigating numerous members of an extensive criminal conspiracy, the government may not be able to identify in advance each person who will use the phone for criminal purposes. In United States v. Figueroa, we held that "[a]t the outset of a wiretap, surveillance under an order that authorizes interception of calls of 'others as yet unknown' is not strictly limited to only those who are specifically named in the authorizing order either as probable violators or as possible interceptees." Instead, "[t]he agents are required only to make reasonable efforts to minimize their interceptions in light of all the relevant circumstances." 757 F.2d 466, 473 (2d Cir. 1985). Here, the order limited interception to conversations which addressed conspiratorial activities and terminated "upon the attainment of authorized objectives" or at the end of the thirty days; thus, it did not, as Yannotti avers, give the government unfettered discretion to intercept phone calls unrelated to the alleged conspiracy. Moreover, the order also required the government to submit regular reports to the supervising judge "showing what progress has been made toward achievement of the authorized objectives and the need for continued interception." These restrictions were adequate safeguards that foreclosed the possibility that the order could be transformed into a general warrant.

Additionally, the government had no reason to believe that Yannotti would indefinitely maintain possession of the cell phone. Consequently, it acted reasonably in suspecting that Corozzo would return to Florida and re-claim his phone. Regardless, as the government stated in its progress report, it suspected that Yannotti's intercepted conversation indicated that he had used the phone in furtherance of the criminal activity identified in the initial application. Thus, as the district court reasonably found, "although Corozzo no longer possessed the phone, there was probable cause to believe that it remained an instrumentality of the alleged conspiracy." Under these circumstances, we agree with the district court's conclusion that the government did not exceed the wiretap authorization in its continued interception of Yannotti's calls. . . .

NOTES AND QUESTIONS

1. Why didn't the law enforcement agents in *Yannotti* have to stop intercepting telephone calls once they realized that Corozzo was not in possession of the cell phone? Is the intercept order here really consistent with the Fourth Amendment's requirement that "no Warrants shall issue, but upon probable cause . . . particularly describing the place to be searched, and the persons or things to be seized"? (Recall in this regard Justice Black's position in *Katz* that conversations not yet in existence can be neither seized nor adequately described for purposes of the Warrant Clause.) Isn't it a legitimate concern that Title III surveillance often involves court-authorized eavesdropping on communications involving people and places not mentioned in the warrant application?

2. Perhaps. Then again, Title III does put in place a number of safeguards — so many, in fact, that its use tends to be confined to a relatively modest number of criminal investigations in which law enforcement agencies presumably determine that interception is worth the trouble — and the cost. According to the 2009 Wiretap Report published by the Administrative Office of the U.S. Courts, there were 663 court-authorized orders for the interception of wire, oral, or electronic communications in 2009 in federal court, and 1703 such orders emanating from state courts, at an average cost of $52,200 per order. Given that some 63,592 felony cases were filed by federal prosecutors alone during the 12-month period ending March 31, 2009, see Federal Judicial Caseload Statistics (Administrative Office of the U.S. Courts, March 31, 2009), these figures would seem to suggest that (consistent with the statute's requirements), Title III is not the first investigative tool to which law enforcement turns.

3. Consider one such safeguard — the provision authorizing judges to require periodic reports to be made as to ongoing interception. In *Yannotti*, the Second Circuit observed in upholding the interception that the interception order "required the government to submit regular reports to the supervising judge 'showing what progress had been made toward achievement of the authorized objectives and the need for continued interception.'" Would this be a harder case if agents had not reported to a judge within ten days that they had intercepted Yannotti in conversation involving the collection of loansharking debts?

4. Title III also restricts the ability of criminal investigators to disseminate intercepted communications. (Setting aside disclosure in court or legitimate use in the course of performing her official duties, a law enforcement officer is authorized to disclose the contents of intercepted communications only "to another investigative or law enforcement officer to the extent that such disclosure is appropriate to the proper performance of the official duties of the officer making or receiving the disclosure." 18 U.S.C. §2517(1).) This statutory restriction contrasts with the Fourth Amendment law we have examined. In Fourth Amendment law, there are relatively few cases that touch upon the reasonable *use* of private information lawfully obtained by police: Thus, we have many cases about whether police can look inside a glove compartment, but very few implicating the question whether they can display the contents on the evening news. But there is a strong rationale for limitations on use:

> [A] limit [on the dissemination of evidence] serves to ensure that problematic search tactics will not be abused. If the police can disclose what they find, innocent but embarrassing discoveries can be the basis of a kind of blackmail. [If] there is no obvious law enforcement need for disclosure, this limit seems like a rare example of a nearly costless protection. Also one that nicely mirrors the solution our society has embraced for a whole host of necessary-but-potentially-problematic privacy intrusions: The IRS can find out a good deal of private information about my finances, but agents cannot leak that information to the local press or turn it over to just any government actor who asks for it. The consequence is that my privacy is reasonably well-protected, even while the government gets the information it needs to assess my tax liability.

William J. Stuntz, Local Policing After the Terror, 111 Yale L.J. 2137, 2185 (2002).

Note, however, that in the wake of the terrorist attacks of September 11, 2001, the restrictions on dissemination of intercepted communications have been loosened with regard to some material. Consider the following provision:

Any investigative or law enforcement officer, or attorney for the Government, who by any means authorized by [Title III], has obtained knowledge of the contents of any wire, oral, or electronic communications . . . may disclose such contents to any other Federal law enforcement, intelligence, protective, immigration, national defense, or national security official to the extent that such contents include foreign intelligence or counterintelligence . . . information . . . , to assist the official who is to receive that information in the performance of his official duties. Any Federal official who receives information pursuant to this provision may use that information only as necessary in the conduct of that person's official duties subject to any limitations on the unauthorized disclosure of such information.

18 U.S.C. §2517(6). The Act provides that disclosure may also be made to "any appropriate Federal, State, local, or foreign government official" to the extent that the contents of Title III surveillance reveal: (1) a threat of actual or potential attack or other grave hostile acts by foreign powers or their agents; (2) domestic or international sabotage; (3) domestic or international terrorism; or (4) certain clandestine intelligence gathering activities, for the purpose of preventing or responding to such threats.

5. You should also be aware that Title III does not regulate the collection of foreign intelligence information in the United States. This falls within the purview of the Foreign Intelligence Surveillance Act ("FISA"), 50 U.S.C. §§1801-1811. FISA surveillance is directed at obtaining "foreign intelligence information"—which includes information that relates to, and if concerning a United States citizen or lawful permanent resident alien, is necessary to, the ability of the United States to protect against international terrorism. 50 U.S.C. §1801(e).

The FISA statute creates a FISA court, the FISC, and an associated FISA Court of Review composed of specially designated Article III judges. Judges on the FISC issue surveillance orders, but on different terms than the ones contained in Title III. FISA orders generally issue on the basis of two principal findings: that there is "probable cause to believe that . . . the target of the electronic surveillance is a foreign power or an agent of a foreign power," and that "each of the facilities or places at which surveillance is directed is being used, or is about to be used, by a foreign power or its agent." 50 U.S.C. §1805(a)(3). (Foreign powers include not only states but also groups "engaged in international terrorism.")

FISA thus differs from Title III in the broad sense that it is status based, not evidence based. As you already know, investigators executing a Title III warrant generally listen in on a particular line when there is probable cause to believe that listening in on that line will uncover evidence of a specified crime. Once someone is a proper FISA target, in contrast, FISA authorizes something quite close to status-based surveillance of that person. In many electronic surveillances, the FBI may be authorized to conduct, simultaneously, telephone, cell phone, e-mail, and computer surveillance of a target's home, workplace, and vehicles. (Similar breadth is accorded in physical searches of a target's residence, office, automobiles, computers, safe deposit boxes, and mail.) Surveillance is authorized for 90 days and may continue for as long as a year when the target is not a U.S. person—meaning, for FISA, a U.S. citizen or lawful permanent resident alien. The Act does not require that notice be provided to the target of such surveillance unless the government intends to use FISA intercepts in the course of judicial or other official proceedings. Minimization relates only to U.S. persons, and is almost invariably done after the fact—in the most usual case, after communications have been recorded. It is also heavily weighted toward the retention of information — so that the communication of or information concerning a U.S. person is generally deleted only if *it could not be* foreign intelligence information or evidence of a crime.

2. The Search of Electronic Files

Title III's core provisions apply only to the interception of wire, oral, and electronic communications as they are being made or transmitted, and not to the search and seizure of electronic communications that have reached a destination and are held in electronic storage — for instance, the e-mail that has traveled to an Internet service provider and sits there until its addressee logs on and downloads it. The search and seizure by law enforcement of many communications of this latter type (like the copy of a friend's e-mail that you download from your online account to your personal home computer, where it is later retrieved by agents who conduct a search of that computer) is not governed by statute, but solely by the Fourth Amendment. The Stored Communications Act ("SCA"), 18 U.S.C. §§2701-2711, however, which was enacted in 1986 as part of the Electronic Communications Privacy Act, regulates government access to communications held by the providers of electronic communication services or remote computing services to the public. We begin with its provisions, and then turn more generally to consider the subject of searches for electronically stored information.

So let's begin with the SCA. Consider that when using the Internet, individuals typically have accounts consisting of a block of computer storage that is owned by an Internet service provider like America Online. Such Internet service providers

> . . . temporarily store e-mail communications. For example, suppose Doe sends an
> e-mail to Roe. The e-mail travels to Roe's ISP and sits there until Roe logs on and down-
> loads her e-mail. Under certain circumstances, a copy of that e-mail may even be kept
> by Roe's ISP after it is downloaded. With many ISPs, users can also keep copies of pre-
> viously read e-mail on the ISP's server. Maintaining copies of previously read e-mail
> with an ISP can be particularly useful, since this enables a person to access the e-mail
> from remote locations via the Internet. . . . Additionally, ISPs often maintain an out-
> box folder that contains copies of all the e-mail that a person has sent out.

Daniel J. Solove, Digital Dossiers and the Dissipation of Fourth Amendment Privacy, 75 S. Cal. L. Rev. 1083, 1141 (2002). The SCA regulates government access to the contents of electronic communications stored by "electronic communications service" providers — Internet service providers, telephone companies, or any others that provide to users the ability to send or receive wire or electronic communications. The Act also provides statutory protection to communications held by providers of "remote computing services" (for example, Internet companies that offer remote backup storage to businesses, or Internet payroll processing services to which small businesses might send (i.e., outsource) their employee data for computer processing).

The relevant provisions of the SCA apply to communications in electronic storage — meaning, with regard to electronic communications services, any temporary, intermediate storage of the communication incidental to its electronic transmission to its final recipient or any associated backup of this communication by the server. (In the case of remote computing services, the law protects data received by electronic transmission and maintained on the remote computing service provider's system.) The statute does not apply to stored communications such as an individual's word processing files or downloaded e-mails residing on an enduser's hard drive, even when these files were once transmitted via e-mail. Nor does the law generally apply to data maintained on internal corporate computer networks.

Subject to some statutory exceptions, the SCA generally prohibits providers that serve the public from disclosing the contents of stored communications — to law enforcement or to anyone else. It then articulates procedures by which the government may nevertheless obtain access to such communications. With regard to communications in temporary or backup storage, the government can obtain access to the contents during the first 180 days of electronic storage only by securing a search warrant based on probable cause. To obtain unretrieved communications that have been in storage for more than 180 days, or other files left in remote storage, the government may proceed either via search warrant based on probable cause or via simple subpoena. In the latter case, the customer or subscriber must receive prior notice of the disclosure; however, the SCA permits that notice to be delayed for 90 days upon the written certification of a supervisory official that notification may have certain undesirable consequences, and the government may extend the delay of notice on application to a court.

If the government seeks noncontent information about an account such as the subscriber's name, address, and the method the customer uses to pay for the account (including any credit card or bank account number), a subpoena will suffice. For most other transactional records, such as the e-mail addresses of individuals with whom the account holder has corresponded, the government must generally apply for a court order based on a showing of reasonable grounds to believe that the information sought is relevant and material to an ongoing criminal investigation. No notice to the subscriber is necessary in either case.

The statute provides for a civil damages remedy for persons aggrieved by its violation and for disciplinary action against federal government employees who intentionally violate its terms. The law contains no exclusionary remedy, however, and provides specifically that its specified remedies and sanctions "are the only judicial remedies and sanctions for nonconstitutional violations of this chapter." 18 U.S.C. §2708.

NOTES AND QUESTIONS

1. Why treat e-mail in transmission (covered by Title III) and e-mail in electronic storage with a provider (covered by the SCA) differently? To obtain e-mail while it is being transmitted, investigators must satisfy Title III's multiple probable cause requirements, including the requirement of showing that other investigative techniques will not suffice. For e-mail in storage at a service provider, however, a standard search warrant or, after some time, perhaps even a subpoena will do.[2] Consider the following:

---

2. Note that the Sixth Circuit has concluded that to the extent the SCA "purports to permit the government to obtain" the contents of a subscriber's e-mails from an ISP without a warrant, the Act is unconstitutional. See United States v. Warshak, ___ F.3d ___, 2010 WL 5071766 (6th Cir. 2010).

There is no logical reason to provide greater protection against covert police surveillance for an email in transmission than for the same email after it has reached the recipient's mailbox at his Internet Service Provider. In this regard, the statutory scheme lacks a coherent framework.

It seems that the drafters of the [SCA] were unable to anticipate a basic difference between telephone conversations and email messages. A telephone conversation can only be monitored while it is taking place since there is no permanent record left after the conversation ends. Similarly, an email message can be intercepted in transmission as it travels from sender to recipient. But the message can also be accessed while it is stored in the recipient's mailbox. In this respect, an email message shares some characteristics of a paper letter in that they both constitute a more permanent record than a phone call. . . .

Berger did not explain why the Supreme Court assumed that telephone conversations deserved greater protections against police wiretapping than are afforded to letters in the mail. Maybe the court assumed that the real-time nature of the interception of a telephone call was somehow more intrusive than [even] covert interception of letters in the mail. But the intrusive nature of the wiretap does not come from the fact that it is contemporaneous with the communication. Rather, the highly intrusive aspect of the telephone wiretap derives from the fact that the police surreptitiously intercept private communications. . . .

If so, then the constitutional protections for wire communications set out in *Berger* as codified and expanded by [Title III] should be equally applicable to the mail and [stored] electronic communications as well. It follows that the same safeguards against covert police surveillance should govern all media of communication. . . .

Robert A. Pikowsky, The Need for Revisions to the Law of Wiretapping and Interception of Email, 10 Mich. Telecomm. & Tech. L. Rev. 1, 49-51 (2003). Do you agree?

2. Orin Kerr has proffered an explanation for the relatively modest protections the SCA affords to e-mails left in electronic storage for more than 180 days. Consider the following:

The apparent thinking behind the lower thresholds for government access of both permanently stored files and unretrieved files stored for more than 180 days is that the lower thresholds track Supreme Court precedents interpreting the Fourth Amendment. For example, in Couch v. United States, [409 U.S. 322 (1973)], a defendant handed over records to her accountant so her accountant could process the data and complete the defendant's tax returns. The Court held that by giving her records to the accountant, Couch had relinquished her reasonable expectation of privacy. A provider acting as [a remote computing service] likely falls under this precedent: a person uses [a remote computing service] for outsourcing much like Couch used her accountant. Similarly, the strange "180 day rule" . . . may reflect the Fourth Amendment abandonment doctrine at work. Individuals lose the Fourth Amendment protection in property if they abandon the property, and the SCA's drafters may have figured that unretrieved files not accessed after 180 days have been abandoned.

Orin Kerr, A User's Guide to the Stored Communications Act, and a Legislator's Guide to Amending It, 72 Geo. Wash. L. Rev. 1208, 1234 (2004). Kerr goes on to argue that even assuming Fourth Amendment principles explain the statutory compromises of the SCA, "this tells us nothing about what standards the SCA should adopt. After all, the SCA was passed to bolster the weak Fourth Amendment privacy protections that applied to the Internet. Incorporating these weak Fourth Amendment principles into statutory law makes little sense." Do you agree?

3. But then, exactly what protection does the Fourth Amendment give to e-mail stored with a service provider? The Justice Department has, in the past, observed that network account holders may not possess a reasonable expectation of privacy in information sent to providers, citing United States v. Miller, 425 U.S. 435 (1976) (holding that bank records are not subject to Fourth Amendment protection), and Smith v. Maryland, 442 U.S. 735 (1979) (finding no reasonable expectation of privacy in dialed telephone numbers). See Searching and Seizing Computers and Obtaining Electronic Evidence in Criminal Investigations 94 (DOJ, July 2002). Does *this* sound right?

Some courts have said no, suggesting that at least the *contents* of stored e-mail (or text messages) are not like bank records or dialed telephone numbers, so that individuals maintain an expectation of privacy even when such communications are stored with, or transmitted through, a commercial ISP. See, e.g., United States v. Warshak, ___ F.3d ___, 2010 WL 5071766 (6th Cir. 2010) ("Given the fundamental similarities between e-mail and traditional forms of communication, it would defy common sense to afford e-mails lesser Fourth Amendment protection."). See also Quon v. Arch Wireless Operating Co., 520 F.3d 892, 905 (9th Cir. 2008) (noting that while "it is not reasonable to expect privacy in the information used to 'address' a text message . . . users do have a reasonable expectation of privacy in the content of their text messages vis-à-vis the service provider"), *reversed* and *remanded* on other grounds, 130 S. Ct. 2619 (2010). As previously noted, the Sixth Circuit has concluded that notwithstanding the SCA's 180-day rule, "[t]he government may not compel a commercial ISP to turn over the contents of a subscriber's e-mails without first obtaining a warrant based on probable cause." But as Professor Kerr has noted, "Case law on how the Fourth Amendment applies to Internet communications remains remarkably sparse." Orin S. Kerr, Applying the Fourth Amendment to the Internet: A General Approach, 62 Stan. L. Rev. 1005, 1025 (2010).

4. Perhaps the problem is the fact that changes in technology and in our modes of communication have at least partly outdistanced our existing legal frameworks. Consider the following:

> Electronic mail is a text-based message stored in digital form. It is like a transcribed telephone call. When sent from one person to another, e-mail is copied and transmitted from machine to machine; it sits on these different machines until removed either by routines — decisions by machines — or by people.
>
> The content of many e-mail messages is like the content of an ordinary telephone call — unplanned, unthinking, the ordinary chatter of friends. But unlike a telephone call, this content is saved, and once saved, it is monitorable, archivable, and searchable. . . .
>
> To be sure, in principle, such monitoring and searching are possible with telephone calls or letters. But in practice, they are not. To monitor telephones or regular mail requires time and money — that is, human intervention. . . . [T]he costs of control yield a certain kind of freedom.
>
> This freedom is reduced as the costs of searching fall. . . .

Lawrence Lessig, Code and Other Laws of Cyberspace 144-145 (1999). To restate the problem, changes in our modes of communication have generally rendered ordinary chatter both permanent and readily searchable. What implications should this have for statutory restrictions on government access to such chatter or for the Fourth Amendment analysis of questions involving the SCA? What about types of communication that have developed more recently, such as text messaging (Short Message Service), which are much less susceptible than e-mail to archiving and retrospective search?

5. Now consider more generally the subject of law enforcement searches for electronically stored information that constitutes evidence of crime. Computers, unlike homes, store only data, "but the amount of data is staggering. Computer hard drives sold in 2005 generally have storage capacities of about eighty gigabytes, roughly equivalent to forty million pages of text — about the information contained in the books on one floor of a typical academic library." Orin S. Kerr, Searches and Seizures in a Digital World, 119 Harv. L. Rev. 531, 542 (2005). This information often implicates the privacy interests of not one or a handful of people, but multitudes. What implications might this have for the conduct of law enforcement searches? Consider the following case:

UNITED STATES v. COMPREHENSIVE DRUG TESTING, INC.

Appeal to the United States Court of Appeals for the Ninth Circuit
579 F.3d 989 (2009)

KOZINSKI, CHIEF JUDGE (writing for the en banc panel)

This case is about a federal investigation into steroid use by professional baseball players. More generally, however, it's about the procedures and safeguards that federal courts must observe in issuing and administering search warrants . . . for electronically stored information. . . .

In 2002, the federal government commenced an investigation into the Bay Area Lab Cooperative (Balco), which it suspected of providing steroids to professional baseball players. That year, the Major League Baseball Players Association (the Players) also entered into a collective bargaining agreement with Major League Baseball providing for suspicionless drug testing of all players. Urine samples were to be collected during the first year of the agreement and each sample was to be tested for banned substances. The players were assured that the results would remain anonymous and confidential; the purpose of the testing was solely to determine whether more than five percent of players tested positive, in which case there would be additional testing in future seasons.

Comprehensive Drug Testing, Inc. (CDT), an independent business, administered the program and collected the specimens from the players; the actual tests were performed by Quest Diagnostics, Inc., a laboratory. CDT maintained the list of players and their respective test results. . . .

During the Balco investigation, federal authorities learned of ten players who had tested positive in the CDT program. The government secured a grand jury subpoena in the Northern District of California seeking *all* "drug testing records and specimens" pertaining to Major League Baseball in CDT's possession. CDT and the Players tried to negotiate a compliance agreement with the government but, when negotiations failed, moved to quash the subpoena.

The day that the motion to quash was filed, the government obtained a warrant in the Central District of California authorizing the search of CDT's facilities in Long Beach. Unlike the subpoena, the warrant was limited to the records of the ten players as to whom the government had probable cause. When the warrant was executed, however, the government seized and promptly reviewed the drug testing records for hundreds of players in Major League Baseball (and a great many other people). . . .

[W]e take the opportunity to guide our district and magistrate judges in the proper administration of search warrants . . . for electronically stored information, so as to strike a proper balance between the government's legitimate interest in law enforcement and the people's right to privacy and property in their papers and effects, as guaranteed by the Fourth Amendment. . . .

The affidavit supporting the . . . search warrant, the one that sought the drug testing records of the ten suspected baseball players, contains an extensive introduction that precedes any information specific to this case. The introduction seeks to justify a broad seizure of computer records from CDT by explaining the generic hazards of retrieving data that are stored electronically. In essence, the government explains, computer files can be disguised in any number of ingenious ways, the simplest of which is to give files a misleading name (pesto.recipe in lieu of blackmail-.photos) or a false extension (.doc in lieu of .jpg or .gz). In addition, the data might be erased or hidden; there might be booby traps that "destroy or alter data if certain procedures are not scrupulously followed," Warrant Affidavit at 3; certain files and programs might not be accessible at all without the proper software, which may not be available on the computer that is being searched; there may simply be too much information to be examined at the site; or data might be encrypted or compressed, requiring passwords, keycards or other external devices to retrieve. Id. at 4. The government also represented that "[s]earching computer systems requires the use of precise, scientific procedures which are designed to maintain the integrity of the evidence."

By reciting these hazards, the government made a strong case for off-site examination and segregation of the evidence seized. The government sought the authority to seize considerably more data than that for which it had probable cause, including various computers or computer hard drives and related storage media, and to have the information examined and segregated in a "controlled environment, such as a law enforcement laboratory." While the government did not point to any specific dangers associated with CDT, which is after all a legitimate business not suspected of any wrongdoing, it nevertheless made a strong generic case that the data in question could not be thoroughly examined or segregated on the spot.

Not surprisingly, the magistrate judge was persuaded by this showing and granted broad authority for seizure of data, including the right to remove pretty much any computer equipment found at CDT's Long Beach facility, along with any data storage devices, manuals, logs or related materials. The warrant also authorized government agents to examine all the data contained in the computer equipment and storage devices, and to attempt to recover or restore hidden or erased data. The magistrate, however, wisely made such broad seizure subject to certain procedural safeguards, roughly based on our . . . opinion [in United States v. Tamura, 694 F.2d 591 (9th Cir. 1982).] Thus, the government was first required to examine the computer equipment and storage devices at CDT to determine whether information pertaining to the ten identified players "c[ould] be searched on-site in a reasonable amount of time and without jeopardizing the ability to preserve the data."

The warrant also contained significant restrictions on how the seized data were to be handled. These procedures were designed to ensure that data beyond the scope of the warrant would not fall into the hands of the investigating agents. Thus, the initial review and segregation of the data was not to be conducted by the investigating case agents but by "law enforcement personnel trained in searching and seizing computer data ('computer personnel')," whose job it would be to determine whether the data could be segregated on-site. These computer personnel — not the case agents — were specifically authorized to examine all the data on location to determine how much had to be seized to ensure the integrity of the search. Moreover, if the computer personnel determined that the data did not "fall within any of the items to be seized pursuant to this warrant or is not otherwise legally seized," the government was to return those items "within a reasonable period of time not to exceed 60 days from the date of the seizure unless further authorization [was] obtained from the Court." Subject to these representations and assurances, Magistrate Judge Johnson authorized the seizure.

A word about *Tamura* is in order, and this seems as good a place as any for it. *Tamura*, decided in 1982, just preceded the dawn of the information age, and all of the records there were on paper. The government was authorized to seize evidence of certain payments received by Tamura from among the records of Marubeni, his employer. To identify the materials pertaining to the payments involved a three step procedure: Examining computer printouts to identify a transaction; locating the voucher that pertained to that payment; and finding the check that corresponded to the voucher. The government agents soon realized that this process would take a long time unless they got help from the Marubeni employees who were present. The employees, however, steadfastly refused, so the agents seized several boxes and dozens of file drawers to be sorted out in their offices at their leisure.

We disapproved the wholesale seizure of the documents and particularly the government's failure to return the materials that were not the object of the search once they had been segregated. However, we saw no reason to suppress the properly seized materials just because the government had taken more than authorized by the warrant. For the future, though, we suggested that "[i]n the comparatively rare instances where documents are so intermingled that they cannot feasibly be sorted on site, . . . the Government [should] seal[ ] and hold[ ] the documents pending approval by a magistrate of a further search, in accordance with the procedures set forth in the American Law Institute's Model Code of Pre-Arraignment Procedure." Id. at 595-596. "If the need for transporting the documents is known to the officers prior to the search," we continued, "they may apply for specific authorization for large-scale removal of material, which should be granted by the magistrate issuing the warrant only where on-site sorting is infeasible and no other practical alternative exists." Id. at 596.

No doubt in response to this suggestion in *Tamura*, the government here did seek advance authorization for sorting and segregating the seized materials off-site. But, as Judge Cooper[, the district court judge,] found, "[o]nce the items were seized, the requirement of the Warrant that any seized items not covered by the warrant be first screened and segregated by computer personnel was completely ignored." Brushing aside an offer by on-site CDT personnel to provide all information pertaining to the ten identified baseball players, the government copied from CDT's computer what the parties have called the "Tracey Directory" which contained, in Judge Cooper's words, "information and test results involving hundreds of other baseball players and athletes engaged in other professional sports."

Counsel for CDT, contacted by phone, pleaded in vain that "all material not pertaining to the specific items listed in the warrant be reviewed and redacted by a Magistrate or Special Master before it was seen by the Government." Instead, the case agent "himself reviewed the seized computer data and used what he learned to obtain the subsequent search warrants issued in Northern California, Southern California, and Nevada." Judge Cooper also found that, in conducting the seizure in the manner it did, "[t]he Government demonstrated a callous disregard for the rights of those persons whose records were seized and searched outside the warrant." . . .

The government argues that it *did* comply with the procedures articulated in *Tamura*, but was not required to return any data it found showing steroid use by other baseball players because that evidence was in plain view once government agents examined the Tracey Directory. Officers may lawfully seize evidence of a crime that is in plain view, the government argues, and thus it had no obligation under *Tamura* to return that property. The warrant even contemplated this eventuality, says the government, when it excluded from the obligation to return property any that was "otherwise legally seized."

[T]his argument . . . is . . . too clever by half. The point of the *Tamura* procedures is to maintain the privacy of materials that are intermingled with seizable materials, and to avoid turning a limited search for particular information into a general search of office file systems and computer databases. If the government can't be sure whether data may be concealed, compressed, erased or booby-trapped without carefully examining the contents of every file — and we have no cavil with this general proposition — then everything the government chooses to seize will, under this theory, automatically come into plain view. Since the government agents ultimately decide how much to actually take, this will create a powerful incentive for them to seize more rather than less: Why stop at the list of all baseball players when you can seize the entire Tracey Directory? Why just that directory and not the entire hard drive? Why just this computer and not the one in the next room and the next room after that? Can't find the computer? Seize the Zip disks under the bed in the room where the computer once might have been. Let's take everything back to the lab, have a good look around and see what we might stumble upon.

This would make a mockery of *Tamura* and render the carefully crafted safeguards in the Central District warrant a nullity. . . . One phrase in the warrant cannot be read as eviscerating the other parts, which would be the result if the "otherwise legally seized" language were read to permit the government to keep anything one of its agents happened to see while performing a forensic analysis of a hard drive. The phrase is more plausibly construed as referring to any evidence that the government is entitled to retain entirely independent of this seizure.

To avoid this illogical result, the government should, in future warrant applications, forswear reliance on the plain view doctrine or any similar doctrine that would allow it to retain data to which it has gained access only because it was required to segregate seizable from non-seizable data. If the government doesn't consent to such a waiver, the magistrate judge should order that the seizable and non-seizable data be separated by an independent third party under the supervision of the court, or deny the warrant altogether.

In addition, while it is perfectly appropriate for the warrant application to acquaint the issuing judicial officer with the theoretical risks of concealment and destruction of evidence, the government must also fairly disclose the *actual* degree of such risks in the case presented to the judicial officer. . . .

Finally, the process of sorting, segregating, decoding and otherwise separating seizable data (as defined by the warrant) from all other data must be designed to achieve that purpose and that purpose only. Thus, if the government is allowed to seize information pertaining to ten names, the search protocol must be designed to discover data pertaining to those names only, not to others, and not those pertaining to other illegality. For example, the government has sophisticated hashing tools at its disposal that allow the identification of well-known illegal files (such as child pornography) without actually opening the files themselves. These and similar search tools may not be used without specific authorization in the warrant, and such permission may only be given if there is probable cause to believe that such files can be found on the electronic medium to be seized.

The government also failed to comply with another important procedure specified in the warrant, namely that "computer personnel" conduct the initial review of the seized data and segregate materials not the object of the warrant for return to their owner. As noted, Judge Cooper found that these procedures were completely ignored; rather, the case agent immediately rooted out information pertaining to *all* professional baseball players and used it to generate additional warrants and subpoenas to advance the investigation. . . .

The government argues that it didn't violate the warrant protocol because the warrant didn't specify that *only* computer personnel could examine the seized files, and the case agent was therefore entitled to view them alongside the computer specialist. This, once again, is sophistry. It would make no sense to represent that computer personnel would be used to segregate data if investigatory personnel were also going to access all the data seized. What would be the point? . . . [T]he representation in the warrant that computer personnel would be used to examine and segregate the data was obviously designed to reassure the issuing magistrate that the government wouldn't sweep up large quantities of data in the hope of dredging up information it could not otherwise lawfully seize. . . .

To guard against such unlawful conduct in the future, the warrant application should normally include, or the issuing judicial officer should insert, a protocol for preventing agents involved in the investigation from examining or retaining any data other than that for which probable cause is shown. The procedure might involve, as in this case, a requirement that the segregation be done by specially trained computer personnel who are not involved in the investigation. It should be made clear that *only* those personnel may examine and segregate the data. The government must also agree that such computer personnel will not communicate any information they learn during the segregation process absent further approval of the court.

At the discretion of the issuing judicial officer, and depending on the nature and sensitivity of the privacy interests involved, the computer personnel in question may be government employees or independent third parties not affiliated with the government. . . . In a case such as this one, where the party subject to the warrant is not suspected of any crime, and where the privacy interests of numerous other parties who are not under suspicion of criminal wrongdoing are implicated by the search, the presumption should be that the segregation of the data will be conducted by, or under the close supervision of, an independent third party selected by the court.

Once the data has been segregated (and, if necessary, redacted), the government agents involved in the investigation may examine only the information covered by the terms of the warrant. Absent further judicial authorization, any remaining copies must be destroyed or, at least so long as they may be lawfully possessed by the party from whom they were seized, returned along with the actual physical medium that may have been seized (such as a hard drive or computer). The government may not retain copies of such returned data, unless it obtains specific judicial authorization to do so. Also, within a time specified in the warrant, which should be as soon as practicable, the government must provide the issuing officer with a return disclosing precisely what data it has obtained as a consequence of the search, and what data it has returned to the party from whom it was seized. The return must include a sworn certificate that the government has destroyed or returned all copies of data that it is not entitled to keep. If the government believes it is entitled to retain data as to which no probable cause was shown in the original warrant, it may seek a new warrant or justify the warrantless seizure by some means other than plain view. . . .

This case well illustrates both the challenges faced by modern law enforcement in retrieving information it needs to pursue and prosecute wrongdoers, and the threat to the privacy of innocent parties from a vigorous criminal investigation. At the time of *Tamura*, most individuals and enterprises kept records in their file cabinets or similar physical facilities. Today, the same kind of data is usually stored electronically, often far from the premises. Electronic storage facilities intermingle data, making them difficult to retrieve without a thorough understanding of the filing and classification systems used — something that can often only be determined by closely analyzing the data in a controlled environment. *Tamura* involved a few dozen boxes and was considered a broad seizure; but even inexpensive electronic storage media today can store the equivalent of millions of pages of information. Wrongdoers and their collaborators have obvious incentives to make data difficult to find, but parties involved in lawful activities may also encrypt or compress data for entirely legitimate reasons. . . . Law enforcement today thus has a far more difficult, exacting and sensitive task in pursuing evidence of criminal activities than even in the relatively recent past. . . .

[The] pressing need of law enforcement for broad authorization to examine electronic records . . . creates a serious risk that every warrant for electronic information will become, in effect, a general warrant, rendering the Fourth Amendment irrelevant. The problem can be stated very simply: There is no way to be sure exactly what an electronic file contains without somehow examining its contents — either by opening it and looking, using specialized forensic software, keyword searching or some other such technique. But electronic files are generally found on media that also contain thousands or millions of other files among which the sought-after data may be stored or concealed. By necessity, government efforts to locate particular files will require examining a great many other files to exclude the possibility that the sought-after data are concealed there.

Once a file is examined, however, the government may claim (as it did in this case) that its contents are in plain view and, if incriminating, the government can keep it. Authorization to search *some* computer files therefore automatically becomes authorization to search all files in the same subdirectory, and all files in an enveloping directory, a neighboring hard drive, a nearby computer or nearby storage media. Where computers are not near each other, but are connected electronically, the original search might justify examining files in computers many miles away, on a theory that incriminating electronic data could have been shuttled and concealed there.

The advent of fast, cheap networking has made it possible to store information at remote third-party locations, where it is intermingled with that of other users. For example, many people no longer keep their email primarily on their personal computer, and instead use a web-based email provider, which stores their messages along with billions of messages from and to millions of other people. Similar services exist for photographs, slide shows, computer code and many other types of data. As a result, people now have personal data that are stored with that of innumerable strangers. Seizure of, for example, Google's email servers to look for a few incriminating messages could jeopardize the privacy of millions.

It's no answer to suggest . . . that people can avoid these hazards by not storing their data electronically. To begin with, the choice about how information is stored is often made by someone other than the individuals whose privacy would be invaded by the search. Most people have no idea whether their doctor, lawyer or accountant maintains records in paper or electronic format, whether they are stored on the premises or on a server farm in Rancho Cucamonga, whether they are commingled with those of many other professionals or kept entirely separate. Here, for example, the Tracey Directory contained a huge number of drug testing records, not only of the ten players for whom the government had probable cause but hundreds of other professional baseball players, thirteen other sports organizations, three unrelated sporting competitions, and a non-sports business entity — thousands of files in all, reflecting the test results of an unknown number of people, most having no relationship to professional baseball except that they had the bad luck of having their test results stored on the same computer as the baseball players.

Second, there are very important benefits to storing data electronically. Being able to back up the data and avoid the loss by fire, flood or earthquake is one of them. Ease of access from remote locations while traveling is another. The ability to swiftly share the data among professionals, such as sending MRIs for examination by a cancer specialist half-way around the world, can mean the difference between death and a full recovery. Electronic storage and transmission of data is no longer a peculiarity or a luxury of the very rich; it's a way of life. Government intrusions into large private databases thus have the potential to expose exceedingly sensitive information about countless individuals not implicated in any criminal activity, who might not even know that the information about them has been seized and thus can do nothing to protect their privacy. . . .

Everyone's interests are best served if there are clear rules to follow that strike a fair balance between the legitimate needs of law enforcement and the right of individuals and enterprises to the privacy that is at the heart of the Fourth Amendment. . . . We believe it is useful, therefore, to update *Tamura* to apply to the daunting realities of electronic searches which will nearly always present the kind of situation that *Tamura* believed would be rare and exceptional — the inability of government agents to segregate seizable from non-seizable materials at the scene of the search, and thus the necessity to seize far more than is actually authorized.

We accept the reality that such over-seizing is an inherent part of the electronic search process and proceed on the assumption that, when it comes to the seizure of electronic records, this will be far more common than in the days of paper records. . . . The process of segregating electronic data that is seizable from that which is not must not become a vehicle for the government to gain access to data which it has no probable cause to collect. In general, we adopt *Tamura*'s solution to the problem of necessary over-seizing of evidence: When the government wishes to obtain a warrant to examine a computer hard drive or electronic storage medium in searching for certain incriminating files, or when a search for evidence could result in the seizure of a computer, magistrate judges must be vigilant in observing the guidance we have set out throughout our opinion, which can be summed up as follows:

1. Magistrates should insist that the government waive reliance upon the plain view doctrine in digital evidence cases.
2. Segregation and redaction must be either done by specialized personnel or an independent third party. If the segregation is to be done by government computer personnel, it must agree in the warrant application that the computer personnel will not disclose to the investigators any information other than that which is the target of the warrant.
3. Warrants and subpoenas must disclose the actual risks of destruction of information as well as prior efforts to seize that information in other judicial fora.
4. The government's search protocol must be designed to uncover only the information for which it has probable cause, and only that information may be examined by the case agents.
5. The government must destroy or, if the recipient may lawfully possess it, return non-responsive data, keeping the issuing magistrate informed about when it has done so and what it has kept. . . .

[Judge Callahan's opinion, in which Judge Ikuta joined, and Judge Bea's opinion, both concurring in part and dissenting in part, are omitted, as is Judge Ikuta's dissenting opinion, in which Judge Callahan joined.]

NOTES AND QUESTIONS

1. *Comprehensive Drug Testing*'s five-point guidance for issuing warrants for digital evidence generated substantial controversy and ultimately resulted in a revised en banc opinion: The court reaffirmed its holding that the government's review of the seized data had failed to comply with the long-established requirement of *Tamura* to segregate intermingled data where a search entailed large-scale removal of material. But this time, the majority refrained from adopting the five-point guidance for issuing warrants for digital evidence; those points were instead relegated to a concurring opinion by Chief Judge Kozinski. ___ F.3d ___ (9th Cir. 2010), 2010 WL 3529247.

Given ever-advancing technologies for storage and review of data, should courts — or even legislatures — attempt now to establish rules for the conduct of searches for digital evidence? Should magistrates issuing warrants define specific procedures for the execution of each warrant? Was *Comprehensive Drug Testing*, in fact, an example of a well-considered warrant that was simply not executed in the manner expected by the court?

2. Perhaps the Ninth Circuit's initial en banc decision was overly ambitious given the current state of technology and our understanding of how it might evolve. Professor Kerr has argued, however, that the "best way to neutralize dragnet searches"

in the context of digital evidence may be to rethink the plain view exception. Kerr, Searches and Seizures in a Digital World, 119 Harv. L. Rev., at 576. He discusses several alternative approaches. Perhaps courts might reject *Horton*, discussed supra, at page 471, in the digital evidence context and restore the inadvertence requirement. Proving that a forensic investigator intended to step beyond the scope of a warrant in conducting a thorough search, however — particularly when agencies "generally train[ ] . . . forensic analysts to conduct highly comprehensive examinations . . . to leave no digital stone unturned" — may be problematic. Id., at 578-579. Alternatively, if broad forensic searches must remain the norm, perhaps "the rule might be that the government could use evidence discovered in plain view only in specific types of prosecution. . . . in terrorism cases, or perhaps only in terrorism cases, homicide cases, and child pornography cases." Id., at 580. Professor Kerr concluded in 2005 that the plain view doctrine might one day need to be held inapplicable in the digital evidence context but that "[i]t [was] too early for courts or Congress to impose such a rule":

> Many of the characteristic dynamics of computer searches . . . are trends gradually becoming more significant with time. A decade ago, courts could simply and accurately analogize computers to other closed containers; today, the analogy seems a stretch, and a decade from now, it will probably seem obviously flawed. The need for new rules is emerging, but eliminating the plain view exception would be too severe at present.

Id., at 583. Do you agree?

B. *Undercover Agents and Entrapment*

In his study of undercover police practices in the United States, sociologist Gary Marx has observed that this country "once shared with England the fear of a centralized, permanently organized police force" that engaged in covert investigative tactics associated with despotism. Gary T. Marx, Undercover 22 (1988). Early police forces in nineteenth-century America, patterned after the London police, were organized on the theory that a visible police presence able to respond to citizen calls for assistance would deter would-be criminals and disorderly persons. Police, however, were not expected to act more proactively to discover law violations. And they were certainly not supposed to "'employ spies, resort to entrapment, or otherwise let their determination to stamp out crime carry them beyond the point at which decent and honorable men must stop.'" Id., at 23 (quoting an early Boston city councilman).

Marx identifies a number of reasons that this aversion to covert police practices gradually gave way — permitting the emergence of undercover policing as a principal tool of criminal investigation in this country today:

> The United States has moved far in a short period of time with respect to the acceptance of secret police practices. What once occurred infrequently and was viewed with disdain as a characteristic of continental despotism is now routine administrative practice. This is related to broad changes in social organization, the nature of crime, and the relation of police to the law. In its gradual embrace of covert practices over the past century, the U.S. has broken sharply with its earlier attitudes. There has been a move away from the early British notion of a clearly identifiable citizen- or community-based

police, where control agents do not have significant power beyond that of the ordinary citizen, toward the idea that police agents have much greater power than citizens and that policing is a function of the state, not of the citizen. . . .

Cultural images of social control have changed. Fear of crime has largely replaced fear of a militaristic police. . . . The secret agent, whether enshrined in film and television, literature, or song, has become something of a cultural hero. . . .

Broad processes of social transformation involving urbanization and industrialization created a context in which both crimes of deception and undercover means would increase. As the informal social controls associated with the small community and traditional family weakened and changed, formal control institutions grew in power. Large urban areas, rapid transportation, geographical and social mobility, and increased interaction with strangers, or interactions carried out electronically (by telegraph and later by telephone, teletypes, and computers) make deception easier. The impersonal relationships and anonymity associated with these conditions provide fertile ground for the projection of false selves, whether against or on behalf of the law.

The local bumbling gangs, street criminals, drunks, and relatively unorganized rioters who shocked upright citizens in the first half of the nineteenth century were supplemented in the last half of that century by skilled and inventive professionals using the latest technology and knowing how to manipulate the enforcement system.

. . . New forms of criminality appeared, and greater enforcement priority was given to types of crime for which evidence is not easily gathered by overt means, for example, counterfeiting and other monetary violations, fraud, and narcotics. The planned and conspiratorial nature of these lend themselves to secret means of discovery. . . .

The broad increase in covert means over the past century is part of a gradual shift in the United States from a largely rural, unpoliced society to an industrial, policed society. It is rooted in the rise of national and local police institutions. The significant increase in the number and power of the police is part of a broad trend involving the growth of the modern bureaucratic state.

Id., at 33-35. Marx also argues that changes in the relationship of police to law contributed to the expansion in covert practices:

At the turn of the [nineteenth] century, police, while formally engaged in law enforcement, were not oriented toward legal norms. As the twentieth century developed, law became increasingly important to the functioning of the criminal justice system, and legal norms have come to play a more prominent role in structuring and limiting police behavior. In the face of restrictions on traditional practices, undercover techniques have become more important as a means of gaining admissible evidence.

Id., at 35. Indeed, Marx contends that constitutional restrictions on overt search and seizure and interrogation tactics had the unintended consequence of promoting covert techniques: "[R]estrict police use of coercion, and the use of deception increases. Restrict investigative behavior after an offense, and increased attention will be paid to anticipating an offense." Id., at 47.

It is undeniable that undercover agents and informants operating in an undercover capacity play an important role in the investigation of crime in the United States today. Some "undercover" investigations are quite simple. (Consider the traditional "buy-and-bust" case, for example, in which an undercover police officer purchases a small quantity of narcotics from an individual selling on the street and this individual is arrested immediately after the transaction by the undercover's backup.) Other undercover investigations are extremely complex. They can require complicated ruses or protracted role-playing by an undercover agent. (Indeed, undercover agents sometimes operate over many months or even years to infiltrate a criminal organization or to close on negotiations with a suspect about a proposed criminal transaction.)

In the great majority of cases, neither kind of undercover investigation implicates the Fourth Amendment. Recall United States v. White, 401 U.S. 745 (1971), and the plurality's observation there that "one contemplating illegal activities must realize and risk that his companions may be reporting to the police." See supra, at page 380. In fact, the defense of entrapment, rather than any constitutional prohibition, represents the principal legal restriction on the way in which undercover investigations are conducted. The Supreme Court first recognized the defense in Sorrells v. United States, 287 U.S. 425 (1932), a case in which a government agent posing as a tourist befriended the defendant and, with repeated requests, persuaded him to supply the agent with liquor in violation of the National Prohibition Act. The Court adopted the defense as a matter of statutory construction, concluding that Congress could not have intended in enacting the criminal prohibition at issue to permit law enforcement officers to instigate criminal acts by otherwise innocent people and then to punish them for such acts.

There are two principal versions of the entrapment defense — the subjective and the objective. The majority of courts, including federal courts, employ the subjective defense. It focuses on the defendant's "predisposition" to commit crimes by affording a defense to an individual who commits a crime pursuant to government inducement and who cannot be shown to be otherwise predisposed in that direction.

The objective defense looks instead to the conduct of police. It asks whether police have offered inducements to commit the crime that are of a sort to which even normally law-abiding citizens would respond. If so, the defendant who committed a crime in response to these inducements cannot be convicted.

The entrapment defense is a difficult one and is unlikely to be successful in most cases involving the use of undercover agents or informants. Indeed, the defense is rarely successful at all. To the extent it does set limits on the conduct of undercover investigations, however, it generally plays a larger role in the second, more complex type of covert case. Consider why this might be so as you read the following case.

JACOBSON v. UNITED STATES

Certiorari to the United States Court of Appeals for the Eighth Circuit
503 U.S. 540 (1992)

JUSTICE WHITE delivered the opinion of the Court.

On September 24, 1987, petitioner Keith Jacobson was indicted for violating a provision of the Child Protection Act of 1984, which criminalizes the knowing receipt through the mails of a "visual depiction [that] involves the use of a minor engaging in sexually explicit conduct. . . ." Petitioner defended on the ground that the Government entrapped him into committing the crime through a series of communications from undercover agents that spanned the 26 months preceding his arrest. Petitioner was found guilty after a jury trial. The Court of Appeals affirmed his conviction, holding that the Government had carried its burden of proving beyond reasonable doubt that petitioner was predisposed to break the law and hence was not entrapped.

Because the Government overstepped the line between setting a trap for the "unwary innocent" and the "unwary criminal," *Sherman v. United States,* 356 U.S. 369, 372 (1958), and as a matter of law failed to establish that petitioner was independently predisposed to commit the crime for which he was arrested, we reverse the Court of Appeals' judgment affirming his conviction.

I

In February 1984, petitioner, a 56-year-old veteran-turned-farmer who supported his elderly father in Nebraska, ordered two magazines and a brochure from a California adult bookstore. The magazines, entitled Bare Boys I and Bare Boys II, contained photographs of nude preteen and teenage boys. The contents of the magazines startled petitioner, who testified that he had expected to receive photographs of "young men 18 years or older." On cross-examination, he explained his response to the magazines:

> [PROSECUTOR]:   [Y]ou were shocked and surprised that there were pictures of very young boys without clothes on, is that correct?
> [JACOBSON]:   Yes, I was.
> [PROSECUTOR]:   Were you offended?
> [JACOBSON]:   I was not offended because I thought these were a nudist type publication. Many of the pictures were out in a rural or outdoor setting. There was — I didn't draw any sexual connotation or connection with that.

The young men depicted in the magazines were not engaged in sexual activity, and petitioner's receipt of the magazines was legal under both federal and Nebraska law. Within three months, the law with respect to child pornography changed; Congress passed the Act illegalizing the receipt through the mails of sexually explicit depictions of children. In the very month that the new provision became law, postal inspectors found petitioner's name on the mailing list of the California bookstore that had mailed him Bare Boys I and II. There followed over the next 2½ years repeated efforts by two Government agencies, through five fictitious organizations and a bogus pen pal, to explore petitioner's willingness to break the new law by ordering sexually explicit photographs of children through the mail.

The Government began its efforts in January 1985 when a postal inspector sent petitioner a letter supposedly from the American Hedonist Society, which in fact was a fictitious organization. The letter included a membership application and stated the Society's doctrine: that members had the "right to read what we desire, the right to discuss similar interests with those who share our philosophy, and finally that we have the right to seek pleasure without restrictions being placed on us by outdated puritan morality." Petitioner enrolled in the organization and returned a sexual attitude questionnaire that asked him to rank on a scale of one to four his enjoyment of various sexual materials, with one being "really enjoy," two being "enjoy," three being "somewhat enjoy," and four being "do not enjoy." Petitioner ranked the entry "[p]re-teen sex" as a two, but indicated that he was opposed to pedophilia.

For a time, the Government left petitioner alone. But then a new "prohibited mailing specialist" in the Postal Service found petitioner's name in a file, and in May 1986, petitioner received a solicitation from a second fictitious consumer research company, "Midlands Data Research," seeking a response from those who "believe in the joys of sex and the complete awareness of those lusty and youthful lads and lasses of the neophite [*sic*] age." The letter never explained whether "neophite" referred to minors or young adults. Petitioner responded: "Please feel free to send me more information, I am interested in teenage sexuality. Please keep my name confidential."

Petitioner then heard from yet another Government creation, "Heartland Institute for a New Tomorrow" (HINT), which proclaimed that it was "an organization founded to protect and promote sexual freedom and freedom of choice. We believe that arbitrarily imposed legislative sanctions restricting *your* sexual freedom should be rescinded through the legislative process." The letter also enclosed a second survey. Petitioner indicated that his interest in "[p]reteen sex-homosexual" material was above average, but not high. In response to another question, petitioner wrote: "Not only sexual expression but freedom of the press is under attack. We must be ever vigilant to counter attack right wing fundamentalists who are determined to curtail our freedoms."

HINT replied, portraying itself as a lobbying organization seeking to repeal "all statutes which regulate sexual activities, except those laws which deal with violent behavior, such as rape. HINT is also lobbying to eliminate any legal definition of 'the age of consent.'" These lobbying efforts were to be funded by sales from a catalog to be published in the future "offering the sale of various items which we believe you will find to be both interesting and stimulating." HINT also provided computer matching of group members with similar survey responses; and, although petitioner was supplied with a list of potential "pen pals," he did not initiate any correspondence.

Nevertheless, the Government's "prohibited mailing specialist" began writing to petitioner, using the pseudonym "Carl Long." The letters employed a tactic known as "mirroring," which the inspector described as "reflect[ing] whatever the interests are of the person we are writing to." Petitioner responded at first, indicating that his interest was primarily in "male-male items." Inspector "Long" wrote back:

> My interests too are primarily male-male items. Are you satisfied with the type of VCR tapes available? Personally, I like the amateur stuff better if its [*sic*] well produced as it can get more kinky and also seems more real. I think the actors enjoy it more.

Petitioner responded:

> As far as my likes are concerned, I like good looking young guys (in their late teens and early 20's) doing their thing together.

Petitioner's letters to "Long" made no reference to child pornography. After writing two letters, petitioner discontinued the correspondence.

By March 1987, 34 months had passed since the Government obtained petitioner's name from the mailing list of the California bookstore, and 26 months had passed since the Postal Service had commenced its mailings to petitioner. Although petitioner had responded to surveys and letters, the Government had no evidence that petitioner had ever intentionally possessed or been exposed to child pornography. The Postal Service had not checked petitioner's mail to determine whether he was receiving questionable mailings from persons — other than the Government — involved in the child pornography industry.

At this point, a second Government agency, the Customs Service, included petitioner in its own child pornography sting, "Operation Borderline," after receiving his name on lists submitted by the Postal Service. Using the name of a fictitious Canadian company called "Produit Outaouais," the Customs Service mailed petitioner a brochure advertising photographs of young boys engaging in sex. Petitioner placed an order that was never filled.

The Postal Service also continued its efforts in the Jacobson case, writing to petitioner as the "Far Eastern Trading Company Ltd." The letter began:

> As many of you know, much hysterical nonsense has appeared in the American media concerning "pornography" and what must be done to stop it from coming across your borders. This brief letter does not allow us to give much comments; however, why is your government spending millions of dollars to exercise international censorship while tons of drugs, which makes yours the world's most crime ridden country are passed through easily.

The letter went on to say:

> [W]e have devised a method of getting these to you without prying eyes of U.S. Customs seizing your mail. . . . After consultations with American solicitors, we have been advised that once we have posted our material through your system, it cannot be opened for any inspection without authorization of a judge.

The letter invited petitioner to send for more information. It also asked petitioner to sign an affirmation that he was "not a law enforcement officer or agent of the U.S. Government acting in an undercover capacity for the purpose of entrapping Far Eastern Trading Company, its agents or customers." Petitioner responded. A catalog was sent, and petitioner ordered Boys Who Love Boys, a pornographic magazine depicting young boys engaged in various sexual activities. Petitioner was arrested after a controlled delivery of a photocopy of the magazine.

When petitioner was asked at trial why he placed such an order, he explained that the Government had succeeded in piquing his curiosity:

> Well, the statement was made of all the trouble and the hysteria over pornography and I wanted to see what the material was. It didn't describe the — I didn't know for sure what kind of sexual action they were referring to in the Canadian letter.

In petitioner's home, the Government found the Bare Boys magazines and materials that the Government had sent to him in the course of its protracted investigation, but no other materials that would indicate that petitioner collected, or was actively interested in, child pornography. . . .

II

There can be no dispute about the evils of child pornography or the difficulties that laws and law enforcement have encountered in eliminating it. Likewise, there can be no dispute that the Government may use undercover agents to enforce the law. . . .

In their zeal to enforce the law, however, Government agents may not originate a criminal design, implant in an innocent person's mind the disposition to commit a criminal act, and then induce commission of the crime so that the Government may prosecute. Where the Government has induced an individual to break the law and the defense of entrapment is at issue, as it was in this case, the prosecution must prove beyond reasonable doubt that the defendant was disposed to commit the criminal act prior to first being approached by Government agents.

Thus, an agent deployed to stop the traffic in illegal drugs may offer the opportunity to buy or sell drugs and, if the offer is accepted, make an arrest on the spot or later. In such a typical case, or in a more elaborate "sting" operation involving government-sponsored fencing where the defendant is simply provided with the opportunity to commit a crime, the entrapment defense is of little use because the ready commission of the criminal act amply demonstrates the defendant's predisposition. Had the agents in this case simply offered petitioner the opportunity to order child pornography through the mails, and petitioner — who must be presumed to know the law — had promptly availed himself of this criminal opportunity, it is unlikely that his entrapment defense would have warranted a jury instruction.

But that is not what happened here. By the time petitioner finally placed his order, he had already been the target of 26 months of repeated mailings and communications from Government agents and fictitious organizations. Therefore, although he had become predisposed to break the law by May 1987, it is our view that the Government did not prove that this predisposition was independent and not the product of the attention that the Government had directed at petitioner since January 1985.

The prosecution's evidence of predisposition falls into two categories: evidence developed prior to the Postal Service's mail campaign, and that developed during the course of the investigation. The sole piece of preinvestigation evidence is petitioner's 1984 order and receipt of the Bare Boys magazines. But this is scant if any proof of petitioner's predisposition to commit an illegal act, the criminal character of which a defendant is presumed to know. It may indicate a predisposition to view sexually oriented photographs that are responsive to his sexual tastes; but evidence that merely indicates a generic inclination to act within a broad range, not all of which is criminal, is of little probative value in establishing predisposition.

Furthermore, petitioner was acting within the law at the time he received these magazines. . . . Evidence of predisposition to do what once was lawful is not, by itself, sufficient to show predisposition to do what is now illegal, for there is a common understanding that most people obey the law even when they disapprove of it. . . . Hence, the fact that petitioner legally ordered and received the Bare Boys magazines does little to further the Government's burden of proving that petitioner was predisposed to commit a criminal act. This is particularly true given petitioner's unchallenged testimony that he did not know until they arrived that the magazines would depict minors.

The prosecution's evidence gathered during the investigation also fails to carry the Government's burden. Petitioner's responses to the many communications prior to the ultimate criminal act were at most indicative of certain personal inclinations, including a predisposition to view photographs of preteen sex and a willingness to promote a given agenda by supporting lobbying organizations. Even so, petitioner's responses hardly support an inference that he would commit the crime of receiving child pornography through the mails.[3] . . .

---

3. We do not hold, as the dissent suggests, that the Government was required to prove that petitioner knowingly violated the law. We simply conclude that proof that petitioner engaged in legal conduct and

On the other hand, the strong arguable inference is that, by waving the banner of individual rights and disparaging the legitimacy and constitutionality of efforts to restrict the availability of sexually explicit materials, the Government not only excited petitioner's interest in sexually explicit materials banned by law but also exerted substantial pressure on petitioner to obtain and read such material as part of a fight against censorship and the infringement of individual rights. . . .

Petitioner's ready response to these solicitations cannot be enough to establish beyond reasonable doubt that he was predisposed, prior to the Government acts intended to create predisposition, to commit the crime of receiving child pornography through the mails. The evidence that petitioner was ready and willing to commit the offense came only after the Government had devoted 2½ years to convincing him that he had or should have the right to engage in the very behavior proscribed by law. Rational jurors could not say beyond a reasonable doubt that petitioner possessed the requisite predisposition prior to the Government's investigation and that it existed independent of the Government's many and varied approaches to petitioner. As was explained in *Sherman*, where entrapment was found as a matter of law, "the Government [may not] pla[y] on the weaknesses of an innocent party and beguil[e] him into committing crimes which he otherwise would not have attempted." [356 U.S.] at 376.

Law enforcement officials go too far when they "implant in the mind of an innocent person the *disposition* to commit the alleged offense and induce its commission in order that they may prosecute." Sorrells [v. U.S., 287 U.S. 435, 442 (1932)] (emphasis added). Like the *Sorrells* Court, we are "unable to conclude that it was the intention of the Congress in enacting this statute that its processes of detection and enforcement should be abused by the instigation by government officials of an act on the part of persons otherwise innocent in order to lure them to its commission and to punish them." Id., at 448. When the Government's quest for convictions leads to the apprehension of an otherwise law-abiding citizen who, if left to his own devices, likely would have never run afoul of the law, the courts should intervene.

Because we conclude that this is such a case and that the prosecution failed, as a matter of law, to adduce evidence to support the jury verdict that petitioner was predisposed, independent of the Government's acts and beyond a reasonable doubt, to violate the law by receiving child pornography through the mails, we reverse the Court of Appeals' judgment. . . .

JUSTICE O'CONNOR, with whom THE CHIEF JUSTICE and JUSTICE KENNEDY join, and with whom JUSTICE SCALIA joins except as to Part II, dissenting.

Keith Jacobson was offered only two opportunities to buy child pornography through the mail. Both times, he ordered. Both times, he asked for opportunities to buy more. He needed no Government agent to coax, threaten, or persuade him; no one played on his sympathies, friendship, or suggested that his committing the crime would further a greater good. In fact, no Government agent even contacted him face to face. The Government contends that from the enthusiasm with which Mr. Jacobson responded to the chance to commit a crime, a reasonable jury could permissibly infer beyond a reasonable doubt that he was predisposed to commit the crime. I agree.

possessed certain generalized personal inclinations is not sufficient evidence to prove beyond a reasonable doubt that he would have been predisposed to commit the crime charged independent of the Government's coaxing.

The first time the Government sent Mr. Jacobson a catalog of illegal materials, he ordered a set of photographs advertised as picturing "young boys in sex action fun." He enclosed the following note with his order: "I received your brochure and decided to place an order. If I like your product, I will order more later." For reasons undisclosed in the record, Mr. Jacobson's order was never delivered.

The second time the Government sent a catalog of illegal materials, Mr. Jacobson ordered a magazine called "Boys Who Love Boys," described as: "11 year old and 14 year old boys get it on in every way possible. Oral, anal sex and heavy masturbation. If you love boys, you will be delighted with this." Along with his order, Mr. Jacobson sent the following note: "Will order other items later. I want to be discreet in order to protect you and me."

Government agents admittedly did not offer Mr. Jacobson the chance to buy child pornography right away. Instead, they first sent questionnaires in order to make sure that he was generally interested in the subject matter. Indeed, a "cold call" in such a business would not only risk rebuff and suspicion, but might also shock and offend the uninitiated, or expose minors to suggestive materials. Mr. Jacobson's responses to the questionnaires gave the investigators reason to think he would be interested in photographs depicting preteen sex. . . .

I

This Court has held previously that a defendant's predisposition is to be assessed as of the time the Government agent first suggested the crime, not when the Government agent first became involved. Sherman v. United States, 356 U.S. 369, 372-376 (1958). Until the Government actually makes a suggestion of criminal conduct, it could not be said to have "implant[ed] in the mind of an innocent person the disposition to commit the alleged offense and induce its commission. . . ." Sorrells v. United States, 287 U.S. 435, 442 (1932). Even in Sherman v. United States, supra, in which the Court held that the defendant had been entrapped as a matter of law, the Government agent had repeatedly and unsuccessfully coaxed the defendant to buy drugs, ultimately succeeding only by playing on the defendant's sympathy. The Court found lack of predisposition based on the Government's numerous unsuccessful attempts to induce the crime, not on the basis of preliminary contacts with the defendant.

Today, the Court holds that Government conduct may be considered to create a predisposition to commit a crime, even before any Government action to induce the commission of the crime. In my view, this holding changes entrapment doctrine. Generally, the inquiry is whether a suspect is predisposed before the Government induces the commission of the crime, not before the Government makes initial contact with him. There is no dispute here that the Government's questionnaires and letters were not sufficient to establish inducement; they did not even suggest that Mr. Jacobson should engage in any illegal activity. If all the Government had done was to send these materials, Mr. Jacobson's entrapment defense would fail. Yet the Court holds that the Government must prove not only that a suspect was predisposed to commit the crime before the opportunity to commit it arose, but also before the Government came on the scene.

The rule that preliminary Government contact can create a predisposition has the potential to be misread by lower courts as well as criminal investigators as requiring that the Government must have sufficient evidence of a defendant's predisposition *before it ever seeks to contact him.* Surely the Court cannot intend to impose such a requirement, for it would mean that the Government must have a reasonable suspicion of criminal activity before it begins an investigation, a condition that we have never before imposed. The Court denies that its new rule will affect run-of-the-mill sting operations, and one hopes that it means what it says. Nonetheless, after this case, every defendant will claim that something the Government agent did before soliciting the crime "created" a predisposition that was not there before. For example, a bribetaker will claim that the description of the amount of money available was so enticing that it implanted a disposition to accept the bribe later offered. A drug buyer will claim that the description of the drug's purity and effects was so tempting that it created the urge to try it for the first time. In short, the Court's opinion could be read to prohibit the Government from advertising the seductions of criminal activity as part of its sting operation, for fear of creating a predisposition in its suspects. That limitation would be especially likely to hamper sting operations such as this one, which mimic the advertising done by genuine purveyors of pornography. No doubt the Court would protest that its opinion does not stand for so broad a proposition, but the apparent lack of a principled basis for distinguishing these scenarios exposes a flaw in the more limited rule the Court today adopts.

The Court's rule is all the more troubling because it does not distinguish between Government conduct that merely highlights the temptation of the crime itself, and Government conduct that threatens, coerces, or leads a suspect to commit a crime in order to fulfill some other obligation. For example, in *Sorrells*, the Government agent repeatedly asked for illegal liquor, coaxing the defendant to accede on the ground that "one former war buddy would get liquor for another." 287 U.S., at 440. In *Sherman*, the Government agent played on the defendant's sympathies, pretending to be going through drug withdrawal and begging the defendant to relieve his distress by helping him buy drugs. 356 U.S., at 371.

The Government conduct in this case is not comparable. While the Court states that the Government "exerted substantial pressure on petitioner to obtain and read such material as part of a fight against censorship and the infringement of individual rights," one looks at the record in vain for evidence of such "substantial pressure." The most one finds are letters advocating legislative action to liberalize obscenity laws, letters which could easily be ignored or thrown away. Much later, the Government sent separate mailings of catalogs of illegal materials. Nowhere did the Government suggest that the proceeds of the sale of the illegal materials would be used to support legislative reforms. While one of the HINT letters suggested that lobbying efforts would be funded by sales from a catalog, the catalogs actually sent, nearly a year later, were from different fictitious entities . . . and gave no suggestion that money would be used for any political purposes. Nor did the Government claim to be organizing a civil disobedience movement, which would protest the pornography laws by breaking them. Contrary to the gloss given the evidence by the Court, the Government's suggestions of illegality may also have made buyers beware, and increased the mystique of the materials offered: "For those of you who have enjoyed youthful material . . . we have devised a method of getting these to you without prying eyes of U.S. Customs seizing your mail." Mr. Jacobson's curiosity to see what "all the trouble and the hysteria" was about, is certainly susceptible of more than one interpretation. And it is the jury that is charged with the obligation of interpreting it. In sum, the Court fails to construe the evidence in the light most favorable to the

Government, and fails to draw all reasonable inferences in the Government's favor. It was surely reasonable for the jury to infer that Mr. Jacobson was predisposed beyond a reasonable doubt, even if other inferences from the evidence were also possible.

II

The second puzzling thing about the Court's opinion is its redefinition of predisposition. The Court acknowledges that "[p]etitioner's responses to the many communications prior to the ultimate criminal act were . . . indicative of certain personal inclinations, including a predisposition to view photographs of preteen sex. . . ." If true, this should have settled the matter; Mr. Jacobson was predisposed to engage in the illegal conduct. Yet, the Court concludes, "petitioner's responses hardly support an inference that he would commit the crime of receiving child pornography through the mails."

The Court seems to add something new to the burden of proving predisposition. Not only must the Government show that a defendant was predisposed to engage in the illegal conduct, here, receiving photographs of minors engaged in sex, but also that the defendant was predisposed to break the law knowingly in order to do so. The statute violated here, however, does not require proof of specific intent to break the law; it requires only knowing receipt of visual depictions produced by using minors engaged in sexually explicit conduct. Under the Court's analysis, however, the Government must prove *more* to show predisposition than it need prove in order to convict.

. . . The elements of predisposition should track the elements of the crime. The predisposition requirement is meant to eliminate the entrapment defense for those defendants who would have committed the crime anyway, even absent Government inducement. Because a defendant might very well be convicted of the crime here absent Government inducement even though he did not know his conduct was illegal, a specific intent requirement does little to distinguish between those who would commit the crime without the inducement and those who would not. In sum, although the fact that Mr. Jacobson's purchases of Bare Boys I and Bare Boys II were legal at the time may have some relevance to the question of predisposition, it is not, as the Court suggests, dispositive.

The crux of the Court's concern in this case is that the Government went too far and "abused" the "processes of detection and enforcement" by luring an innocent person to violate the law. Consequently, the Court holds that the Government failed to prove beyond a reasonable doubt that Mr. Jacobson was predisposed to commit the crime. It was, however, the jury's task, as the conscience of the community, to decide whether Mr. Jacobson was a willing participant in the criminal activity here or an innocent dupe. . . . Because I believe there was sufficient evidence to uphold the jury's verdict, I respectfully dissent.

NOTES AND QUESTIONS

1. The subjective version of entrapment supposedly being applied in *Jacobson* holds that once a defendant has raised an entrapment defense by showing some government inducement to commit the crime, the government must demonstrate

that the defendant was predisposed. But was this really the test employed by the *Jacobson* majority? After all, the sole issue in this case was whether there was sufficient evidence to support the jury verdict. Can it really be maintained that reasonable jurors could not have concluded that Jacobson was predisposed to commit the crime? Does *Jacobson* mean that in complex cases where the government may have substantial contact with an individual before any crime occurs, the government must come forward with a strong showing of predisposition predating such contact in order to survive a motion for acquittal?

2. Of course, the preceding discussion assumes that we can define what it is we mean by predisposition. A standard federal jury instruction asks whether the defendant "'was ready and willing to commit crimes such as are charged in the indictment, whenever opportunity was afforded, and that government officers or their agents did no more than offer the opportunity.'" Louis Michael Seidman, The Supreme Court, Entrapment, and Our Criminal Justice Dilemma, 1981 Sup. Ct. Rev. 111 (quoting Edward J. Devitt & Charles B. Blackmar, Federal Jury Practice and Instructions §13.09, at 364 (3d ed. 1977)). But as Professor Seidman has pointed out,

> whether a person is "ready and willing" to break the law depends on what the person expects to get in return — that is, on the level of inducement. Like the rest of us, criminals do not generally work for free. . . .
>
> Consequently, so long as one equates "predisposition" with a readiness to commit crime, no definition of "predisposition" can be complete without an articulation of the level of inducement to which a "predisposed" defendant would respond. Furthermore, the "predisposed" cannot be distinguished from the "nondisposed" without focusing on the propriety of the government's conduct — the very factor that the subjective approach professes to ignore.

Id., at 118-119. Does this suggest that the distinction between the subjective and objective approaches to entrapment is less clear than might at first seem to be the case?

3. Some have suggested that *Jacobson* is an objective entrapment case posing as a subjective one — that the result in *Jacobson* is best understood as a reaction to what the Court may have seen as overbearing governmental tactics. Though most courts have adopted the subjective entrapment test, some 10 to 15 states have opted for the objective version, through either statutes or judicial rulings. The Model Penal Code also recommends an objective test — stating that police inducements should be deemed improper if they "create a substantial risk that an offense will be committed by persons other than those who are ready to commit it." See American Law Institute, Model Penal Code §2.13 (Official Draft 1962). Giving content to this test, however, may be as difficult as giving content to the subjective approach. Who are these people who would normally not be ready to commit a crime, but who can, at least occasionally, be induced to do so? Defining the "reasonable person" standard in tort may seem child's play when compared to defining the concept of the "sometimes criminal."

4. Ronald Allen, Melissa Luttrell, and Anne Kreeger have addressed these conundrums and have concluded as follows:

> There is a deeper difficulty with the controversy over the two tests for entrapment. The controversy is premised on the existence of a real something — state of mind,

character, whatever — that is referred to as "predisposition." This assumption is false. We assume that there are a few people who would not commit any criminal acts no matter what the provocation or enticement. . . . Everyone else, we assume, has a price. That price may be quite high, for example because a person puts a high value on her good name, but it exists. If this assumption is true, then everyone except saints is predisposed to commit crimes. But, that in turn means that "predisposition" cannot usefully distinguish anyone from anyone else. . . .

The discussion in the cases of whether the defendant was a willing participant, and whether the government implanted the criminal design in the defendant or created the crime verges on the silly. The defendant is always "willing" (otherwise there would be no need to rely on entrapment — duress would do) and to our knowledge, the government has never physically opened the brain of a defendant and "implanted" anything. Perhaps the government implants criminal designs psychologically, but again, if so, it is always so for the government always plays a causal role in the act. In all cases of police involvement, and thus of potential entrapment, the act would not have occurred as it did but for the involvement of the police — a tautology if ever there were one. Nor does the objective test avoid this point, just because it pragmatically operates upon the [same] assumption of the existence of predisposition as a real thing. Without predisposition as a sorting mechanism, the objective test is rootless.

Ronald J. Allen, Melissa Luttrell, & Anne Kreeger, Clarifying Entrapment, 89 J. Crim. L. & Criminology 407, 413-414 (1999). The authors argue that a more fruitful criterion for sorting out "those who have a plausible claim for exoneration" is whether the "inducements [offered to these individuals] exceeded real world market rates, which includes both financial and emotional markets." Id., at 415. They justify this conclusion in part with reference to the aims of the criminal law:

We assume, without regard to philosophical niceties, that the primary relevant objectives of the criminal law are to deter (general and specific), to incapacitate, and to rehabilitate (it is pointless to discuss retribution in this context). None of these objectives is likely to be accomplished by the punishment of an individual who accepted an extra-market inducement to act. The concern of deterrence surely is to reduce the occurrence of criminal acts in the world we actually inhabit, not some hypothetically different one. That a person responds to extra-market prices is uninformative of how he will respond to market prices, and thus is uninformative on the justification for incapacitation. A person who accepts extra-market prices provides evidence that indeed virtually everybody has a price, but not that this person is in need of rehabilitation, given the world we actually inhabit. The point generalized is that criminal acts occur in the real world, not an artificial one, and behavior in an artificial world is largely uninformative of behavior in this one.

Id., at 415-416. How would this approach to entrapment work in a case like *Jacobson*? Note that while they have not necessarily adopted a "market rate" limitation on permissible inducements, some courts in the wake of *Jacobson* have read that case to impose a requirement that the government's evidence demonstrate that a defendant would have responded affirmatively to an "ordinary" opportunity to commit the crime. See, e.g., United States v. Gendron, 18 F.3d 955, 962 (1st Cir. 1994).

5. In practice, procedural and evidentiary differences between the subjective and objective approaches to entrapment may be more important than substantive differences between the two defenses. Three principal differences of this type are worth mentioning. First, where the subjective test prevails, entrapment is generally

a question for the jury. Under the objective test, the defense is more likely to be a question of law for the judge. Second, by raising an entrapment defense in a subjective jurisdiction, the criminal defendant will generally open the door for the government to introduce evidence regarding the defendant's reputation, character, prior convictions, and prior bad acts — to show his predisposition to commit the crime. The objective defense does not usually involve this consequence. Finally, the allocations of burdens of proof may well be different in jurisdictions adopting one or the other version of the defense. In subjective jurisdictions, the prosecution normally has the burden of proving predisposition beyond a reasonable doubt. Then again, the burden of persuading a factfinder that a normally law-abiding person would likely have succumbed to the government's inducements may well rest with the defendant in jurisdictions employing the objective test. Note that these procedural and evidentiary features may not be necessary concomitants of the entrapment test normally associated with them. Would either of the entrapment defenses be improved by changing one or another of these features?

6. The Justice Department has issued guidelines on FBI undercover operations that go beyond the judicial controls we have thus far considered. These guidelines require that certain sensitive undercover investigations be authorized only after review by an Undercover Review Committee consisting of FBI personnel designated by the Director and Justice Department attorneys named by the Assistant Attorney General in charge of the Department's Criminal Division. These sensitive investigations include operations involving possible criminal conduct by elected officials, political or religious organizations, or foreign governments as well as investigations involving a reasonable expectation that an undercover agent will be involved in a serious crime, be arrested, or supply falsely sworn testimony. Attorney General's Guidelines on FBI Undercover Operations, ¶IV.C (2002). In addition, supervisory personnel at FBI headquarters must authorize all undercover operations expected to involve expenditures over $50,000 (or $100,000 in narcotics cases), or to last more than one year. Id. Other, more routine investigations may be authorized by the Special Agent in Charge of an FBI field office.

Undercover employees are specifically prohibited from participating in acts of violence, except in self-defense, or in conduct constituting unlawful investigative techniques — for example, illegal wiretapping, breaking and entering, or trespassing amounting to an illegal search. Id., at ¶IV.H.

With regard to entrapment, the guidelines provide that the supervisory officials authorizing undercover activity involving inducements must be satisfied that: (a) the illegal nature of the activity is reasonably clear to potential subjects; (b) the nature of the inducement is justifiable "in view of the character of the illegal transaction in which the individual is invited to engage"; (c) there is a reasonable expectation that offering the inducement will reveal illegal activities; and (d) there is some reasonable indication that the subject is engaging, has engaged, or is likely to engage in the proposed illegal activity or in similar illegal conduct or, alternatively, that the inducement has been structured so that there is reason to believe that any persons drawn by it are predisposed to engage in the contemplated illegal conduct. Id., at ¶IV.

Do these and other internal guidelines offer real checks on law enforcement — and particularly in the context of covert investigations? Professor Richman has argued that federal prosecutors and law enforcement agents, drawn as they are from two relatively distinct cultures, can operate as mutual monitors, promoting "more thoughtful decisionmaking, even in the absence of legislative or judicial oversight." Daniel Richman, Prosecutors and Their Agents, Agents and Their Prosecutors, 103 Colum. L. Rev. 749, 810 (2003). Internal guidelines, such as the ones regulating undercover operations, can help promote this "mutual monitoring." Consider his analysis:

> . . . Any FBI field office seeking to engage in an "undercover operation involving any sensitive circumstance" must first apply to FBI headquarters for approval. The application must contain a "letter from the appropriate Federal prosecutor indicating that he or she has reviewed the proposed operation, including the sensitive circumstances reasonably expected to occur, agrees with the proposal and its legality, and will prosecute any meritorious case that has developed." If favorably recommended by FBI headquarters, the proposal then goes to an "Undercover Review Committee," comprised of FBI personnel . . . and prosecutors. . . . Prosecutors from the relevant U.S. Attorney's Office and FBI agents from the field can attend the committee's meeting and, in practice, line assistants are "encouraged" to discuss the proposal with committee members before the meeting. Decisions within this committee are to be by consensus. If one of the prosecutors declines to join a favorable recommendation "because of legal, ethical, prosecutive, or departmental policy considerations," the Assistant Attorney General is consulted, and absent his approval or the approval of either the department's top two officials — the Deputy Attorney General or Attorney General — the operation will not proceed.
>
> The most salient operational feature of this administrative regime is the number of checkpoints it creates both at the local level and in Washington to ensure that as broad a variety of perspectives as the enforcement bureaucracy has to offer . . . are brought to bear on those operations most likely to spark allegations of government overreaching and targeting. An important by-product . . . is the colloboration it promotes at the field level, as prosecutors and agents become co-presenters of a joint proposal that each must sell up through his respective Washington hierarchy.

Id., at 815-816. Do these guidelines promote "mutual monitoring" by ensuring that both prosecutors and agents are part of the decision-making process — at least with regard to sensitive cases?

7. Finally, note that in the aftermath of the terrorist attack of September 11, 2001, some pertinent changes were made to the Attorney General's Guidelines on General Crimes, Racketeering Enterprise and Terrorism Enterprise Investigations, the guidelines governing the circumstances in which FBI criminal investigations may be begun, as well as the permissible scope, duration, subject matter, and objectives of these investigations. According to the Justice Department in a May 13, 2003, letter to the House Judiciary Committee:

> The old Guidelines did not clearly authorize agents to gather information for counterterrorism or other law enforcement purposes — for example, by visiting public places, or researching publicly available information — unless they were looking into particular crimes or criminal enterprises. In effect, agents had to wait for . . . some lead or evidence to come from others, before they could begin gathering information. The revised Guidelines were designed to enable law enforcement to proactively gather intelligence that could be useful to detecting and preventing terrorist attacks, by attending public events or collecting publicly available information.

First Amendment attorney Floyd Abrams has commented on the background of these guidelines and on the changes made after 9/11:

> [Should] FBI agents . . . be permitted to attend public meetings of a political or religious nature for the purpose of reporting upon what is said there[?] When [they] did so in the 1950s and 1960s, some of the worst abuses of the regime of J. Edgar Hoover occurred. The "chill" on speech was real; Hoover intended just that and achieved just that. It was a civil liberties disaster. After Hoover died, new guidelines, drafted by former Attorneys General Edward Levi and William French Smith, were adopted, effectively barring FBI agents from doing so in most circumstances. Those limits were hailed by civil libertarians — and they should have been.
>
> A quarter of a century has now passed, however, and we face new risks. Shall we now permit, as Attorney General Ashcroft has determined, FBI surveillance of such events? If the Bureau believes that public statements made in a particular mosque, say, may be of assistance in preventing future acts of terrorism, but it is short of proof sufficient to demonstrate the likelihood of criminal behavior, should surveillance of the event be permitted? I think so. Yet when we make that trade-off, we obviously risk the very governmental overreaching and misconduct that tends to accompany any broadening of governmental powers.

Floyd Abrams, The First Amendment and the War Against Terrorism, 5 U. Pa. J. Const. L. 1, 6 (2002). The revised guidelines provide that "[f]or the purpose of detecting or preventing terrorist activities, the FBI is authorized to visit any place and attend any event that is open to the public, on the same terms and conditions as members of the public generally." The FBI may do so even in the absence of any pre-existing lead or specific predication. The guidelines provide, however, that "[n]o information obtained from such visits shall be retained unless it relates to potential criminal or terrorist activity." They also prohibit the FBI from "maintaining files on individuals solely for the purpose of monitoring activities protected by the First Amendment. . . ."

PART FOUR

THE ADJUDICATION PROCESS

Chapter 8
Bail and Pretrial Detention

The practice of admission to bail, as it has evolved in Anglo-American law, is not a device for keeping persons in jail upon mere accusation until it is found convenient to give them a trial. On the contrary, the spirit of the procedure is to enable them to stay out of jail until a trial has found them guilty. Without this conditional privilege, even those wrongly accused are punished by a period of imprisonment while awaiting trial and are handicapped in consulting counsel, searching for evidence and witnesses, and preparing a defense.

Justice Robert Jackson

For defendants who have been taken into custody and charged with a crime, an immediate and potentially crucial concern is whether, and under what circumstances, they can obtain release from custody pending trial (or pending some other resolution of the charge). This decision is often made by a district judge or magistrate judge at the defendant's initial court appearance following an arrest, although sometimes a separate bail hearing is held.

Judges have broad discretion in making and shaping the pretrial release decision. The court may release the suspect based simply on a promise to show up for later court hearings (often called releasing the defendant on his "own recognizance," or "OR"), plus the suspect's promise not to commit any crimes while on release. Or the court may require the posting of bail — the pledging of money or a financial bond that the defendant will forfeit if he fails to show up as required, or if he otherwise violates the terms of his release. Whether the defendant is obligated to post bail or not, the court also may impose on the suspect a series of nonfinancial conditions, such as the requirement that the person observe a curfew, refrain from contacting the victim, or enter a drug treatment program.

The traditional purpose of imposing bail and other release conditions is to ensure that the defendant appears in court when required, not to punish or prejudge the merits of the case. Nonetheless, the type of crime a defendant is accused of committing undoubtedly plays a role in the bail decision. Most obviously, the more serious the charge, the higher the potential sentence, and thus the greater incentive for a defendant to flee rather than stand trial. For this reason, in cases of very serious crimes, pretrial release may be denied altogether, either by explicit judicial decision or by the less direct method of setting bail so high that the defendant is unable to post the necessary amount.

Even if a defendant is not a flight risk, judges also worry about the impact of releasing certain suspects back into the community. The fear that the accused will commit new crimes while awaiting trial is technically unrelated to whether the defendant will flee but is nonetheless widely believed to influence the judge's decision. As a result, over the past quarter century, Congress and many state legislatures have enacted statutes that grant judges the authority to order the preventive detention of defendants who are a flight risk *or* whose pretrial release may pose a danger to the community.

The Constitution speaks directly but vaguely to the question of bail in the Eighth Amendment, which says in part that "Excessive bail shall not be required." The first case in this section, Stack v. Boyle, deals with the interpretation of the "excessive bail clause." The second case, United States v. Salerno, resolves a constitutional challenge to the Bail Reform Act of 1984, 18 U.S.C. §§3141 et seq., the federal statute that authorizes federal judges to order preventive detention based on a prediction that the suspect will commit new crimes if released on bail.

A. Bail Amounts

STACK v. BOYLE

Certiorari to the United States Court of Appeals for the Ninth Circuit
342 U.S. 1 (1951)

CHIEF JUSTICE VINSON delivered the opinion of the Court.

Indictments have been returned in the Southern District of California charging the twelve petitioners with conspiring to violate the Smith Act, 18 U.S.C. (Supp. IV) §§371, 2385.* Upon their arrest, bail was fixed for each petitioner in the widely varying amounts of $2,500, $7,500, $75,000, and $100,000. On motion of petitioner Schneiderman following arrest in the Southern District of New York, his bail was reduced to $50,000 before his removal to California. On motion of the Government to increase bail in the case of other petitioners, and after several intermediate procedural steps not material to the issues presented here, bail was fixed in the District Court for the Southern District of California in the uniform amount of $50,000 for each petitioner.

Petitioners moved to reduce bail on the ground that bail as fixed was excessive under the Eighth Amendment.[1] In support of their motion, petitioners submitted statements as to their financial resources, family relationships, health, prior criminal records, and other information. The only evidence offered by the Government was a certified record showing that four persons previously convicted under the Smith Act in the Southern District of New York had forfeited bail. No evidence was produced relating those four persons to the petitioners in this case. At a hearing on the motion, petitioners were examined by the District Judge and cross-examined by an attorney for the Government. Petitioners' factual statements stand uncontroverted.

After their motion to reduce bail was denied, petitioners filed applications for habeas corpus in the same District Court. Upon consideration of the record on the motion to reduce bail, the writs were denied. The Court of Appeals for the Ninth Circuit affirmed. 192 F.2d 56. . . .

---

* The Smith Act of 1940 prohibited advocacy of forceful or violent overthrow of the United States government. During the "Red Scare" of the late 1940s and early 1950s, it was the basis for numerous prosecutions of persons with actual or suspected ties to the Communist Party. — EDS.

1. "Excessive bail shall not be required, nor excessive fines imposed, nor cruel and unusual punishments inflicted." U.S. Const., Amend. VIII.

. . . From the passage of the Judiciary Act of 1789, 1 Stat. 73, 91, to the present Federal Rules of Criminal Procedure, Rule 46(a)(1), federal law has unequivocally provided that a person arrested for a non-capital offense *shall* be admitted to bail. This traditional right to freedom before conviction permits the unhampered preparation of a defense, and serves to prevent the infliction of punishment prior to conviction. . . . Unless this right to bail before trial is preserved, the presumption of innocence, secured only after centuries of struggle, would lose its meaning.

The right to release before trial is conditioned upon the accused's giving adequate assurance that he will stand trial and submit to sentence if found guilty. . . . Like the ancient practice of securing the oaths of responsible persons to stand as sureties for the accused, the modern practice of requiring a bail bond or the deposit of a sum of money subject to forfeiture serves as additional assurance of the presence of an accused. Bail set at a figure higher than an amount reasonably calculated to fulfill this purpose is "excessive" under the Eighth Amendment. . . .

Since the function of bail is limited, the fixing of bail for any individual defendant must be based upon standards relevant to the purpose of assuring the presence of that defendant. The traditional standards as expressed in the Federal Rules of Criminal Procedure[3] are to be applied in each case to each defendant. In this case petitioners are charged with offenses under the Smith Act and, if found guilty, their convictions are subject to review with the scrupulous care demanded by our Constitution. . . . Upon final judgment of conviction, petitioners face imprisonment of not more than five years and a fine of not more than $10,000. It is not denied that bail for each petitioner has been fixed in a sum much higher than that usually imposed for offenses with like penalties and yet there has been no factual showing to justify such action in this case. The Government asks the courts to depart from the norm by assuming, without the introduction of evidence, that each petitioner is a pawn in a conspiracy and will, in obedience to a superior, flee the jurisdiction. To infer from the fact of indictment alone a need for bail in an unusually high amount is an arbitrary act. Such conduct would inject into our own system of government the very principles of totalitarianism which Congress was seeking to guard against in passing the statute under which petitioners have been indicted.

If bail in an amount greater than that usually fixed for serious charges of crimes is required in the case of any of the petitioners, that is a matter to which evidence should be directed in a hearing so that the constitutional rights of each petitioner may be preserved. In the absence of such a showing, we are of the opinion that the fixing of bail before trial in these cases cannot be squared with the statutory and constitutional standards for admission to bail.

. . . The Court concludes that bail has not been fixed by proper methods in this case and that petitioners' remedy is by motion to reduce bail, with right of appeal to the Court of Appeals. Accordingly, the judgment of the Court of Appeals is vacated and the case is remanded to the District Court. . . .

It is so ordered.

[The separate opinion of Justice Jackson is omitted.]

---

3. Rule 46(c). "AMOUNT. If the defendant is admitted to bail, the amount thereof shall be such as in the judgment of the commissioner or court or judge or justice will insure the presence of the defendant, having regard to the nature and circumstances of the offense charged, the weight of the evidence against him, the financial ability of the defendant to give bail and the character of the defendant." [NOTE — This rule has been amended substantially since the Bail Reform Act of 1984. See www.uscourts.gov/uscourts/RulesAndPolicies/rules/CR2009.pdf. — EDS.]

NOTES AND QUESTIONS

1. What does it mean to say that bail is "excessive" within the meaning of the Eighth Amendment after Stack v. Boyle? On the one hand, if a judge were to set bail at $200 for a homeless man charged with breaking into a store, is that "excessive" if the man has only $10 in assets? On the other hand, if a billionaire is charged with driving while intoxicated, is it excessive to set bail at $100 million? Courts would almost certainly conclude that bail was not excessive for the homeless man but was excessive for the billionaire. Can you articulate why this would be so?

2. Although the amount of bail set for a particular crime varies across jurisdictions, some statistics from the state courts provide a point of reference. A study of state felony criminal cases during 2006 in the 75 largest counties in America (where 37 percent of Americans live, but 49 percent of all reported serious violent crimes occur) found that the median amount of bail for all felony defendants in the study was $10,000. For murder, the median was $1,000,000; for weapons crimes, it was $15,000; and for property offenses, it was only $8,500. Among those defendants who could not (or did not) post bail, the median bail amount was $25,000, while for those defendants who posted bail and were released, the median bail amount was $5,000. See Thomas H. Cohen & Tracey Kyckelhahn, Felony Defendants in Large Urban Counties, 2006 (2010), available at http://bjs.ojp.usdoj.gov/index.cfm?ty=pbdetail&iid=2193.

3. Stack v. Boyle emphasized that bail for each defendant "must be based upon standards relevant to the purpose of assuring the presence of that defendant." The Bail Reform Act of 1984, discussed below, lists several factors that courts consider when evaluating the flight risk: the nature and circumstances of the crime charged; the weight of the evidence; and the defendant's character, physical and mental condition, family ties, employment, finances, length of residence in the community, community ties, past conduct, history of drug or alcohol abuse, criminal history, record of court appearances, and status as a probationer or parolee. 18 U.S.C. §3142(g).

Should it matter if some of these factors correlate with race and ethnicity? A three-year study in the Second Circuit found that for many such factors — including citizenship, home ownership, marital status, substance abuse, employment status, criminal history, time in the area, education, bail recommendations by pretrial service officers and Assistant U.S. Attorneys, and level of offense charged — "substantial differences between whites, African-Americans and Hispanics/Latinos were evident; for many of these factors, differences were also evident for Asian-Americans." See Report of the Working Committees to the Second Circuit Task Force on Gender, Racial and Ethnic Fairness in the Courts, 1997 Ann. Surv. Am. L. 124, 311-320.

Of course, some of these factors — such as criminal history and level of offense charged — are probably unassailable because they would also appear to correlate strongly with both the likelihood of flight and the risk that the defendant might commit more crimes if released. But the study found that other factors, such as home ownership (more than four times as many white arrestees as black arrestees owned a home) and marital status (almost twice as many white arrestees as black arrestees were married), may not be sufficiently predictive to justify their continued indiscriminate use, in light of the clear racial and ethnic correlations. "Care should be taken to determine whether [such factors] are in fact accurate predictors of whether a defendant presents a danger to the community and will return for trial." Id., at 317. The study concluded that, even after controlling for other factors, "race and ethnicity remained a statistically significant factor [in pretrial release decisions]." Id.

In contrast, a study commissioned by the Ninth Circuit's Task Force on Racial, Religious, and Ethnic Fairness, conducted by researchers from the Administrative Office of the U.S. Courts, concluded:

> The results of the [study and analyses] consistently reveal that race/ethnicity is not a strong predictor of the decision to detain or release. . . . [A]t the circuit level both Blacks and Hispanics are more likely than Whites to be detained. These differences, especially those between Blacks and Whites, substantially diminish when citizenship, offense seriousness, and rebuttable presumptions are taken into consideration. Although Hispanics continue to be detained at a higher rate than Whites even when these three factors are taken into account, the differences can be attributed to idiosyncratic policies and procedures in one or two districts. . . . The higher rate of detention for Hispanics at the circuit level is the result of pretrial procedures, a data coding problem, and the characteristics of the defendant population (especially illegal aliens) in the Southern District of California. . . .
>
> Without these . . . anomalies, the circuit-wide detention rates for Whites, Blacks, Native Americans, and Hispanics (controlling for citizenship, crime severity, and rebuttable presumption) would all be between ten and fifteen percent, with Asians detained at a rate of five percent.

See Thomas Bak, Pretrial Detention in the Ninth Circuit, 35 San Diego L. Rev. 993, 1033-1035 (1998).

4. Does the defendant have a Sixth Amendment right to counsel at a bail hearing? The answer is surprisingly unclear: Coleman v. Alabama, 399 U.S. 1 (1970), held that the right to counsel applies to preliminary hearings, but Gerstein v. Pugh, 420 U.S. 103 (1975), found the right inapplicable to the immediate post-arrest probable cause hearings, where bail determinations are now made in many states. The Federal Rules of Criminal Procedure provide for appointed counsel at "every stage of the proceeding," including the initial appearance where bail is often set, see Fed. R. Crim. P. 44(a), but one study revealed that only eight states and the District of Columbia currently guarantee counsel at bail hearings. See Douglas L. Colbert, Thirty-Five Years After *Gideon*: The Illusory Right to Counsel at Bail Proceedings, [1998] U. Ill. L. Rev. 1.

Would defense lawyers at bail hearings make any difference? In another study of defendants charged with nonviolent crimes in Baltimore, the researchers found that defendants who were represented by counsel were more likely to be released on their own recognizance and more likely to have bail set at a lower amount than unrepresented defendants. The net effect was that represented defendants spent a median time of only two days in jail, as compared with nine days for unrepresented defendants. See Douglas L. Colbert, Ray Paternoster, & Shawn Bushway, Do Attorneys Really Matter? The Empirical and Legal Case for the Right to Counsel at Bail, 23 Cardozo L. Rev. 1719 (2002).

5. Once the amount of bail is set, the defendant may be required to post the full amount with the court (a requirement called "full cash bond"), or may be required to post a "deposit bond" with the court, typically 10 percent of the bail amount, with the defendant being responsible for the full amount if he violates the terms of his release.

In some jurisdictions, however, a defendant may be required to obtain a surety bond from a third party — a bail bondsman — who will guarantee the payment of the full bail amount if the defendant fails to appear. The use of bail bondsmen is controversial. Once the defendant buys the bond and is released, his financial commitment is at an end: The cost of the surety bond is not refundable, and if the defendant fails to show up, it is the bondsman who is obligated to pay the full bail amount. So one argument is that bail bondsmen remove the financial incentive for defendant to appear — which is, of course, the purpose of setting bail in the first place.

But because bail bondsmen are now liable for the full bail amount, they have a great incentive to monitor the defendant while he is released and ensure the defendant appears at all court hearings. If the defendant flees, the bondsmen can hire "bounty hunters" (the subject of innumerable bad television shows) to track down the fugitives and return them to court. Bounty hunters have been frequently criticized for their harsh, even violent, tactics, but courts often turn a blind eye to the methods used to return a fleeing fugitive. For a useful discussion of these issues, as well as an interesting analysis of whether the Uniform Criminal Extradition Act supersedes the bounty hunter's common law authority, see Milton Hirsch, Midnight Run Re-run: Bail Bondsmen, Bounty Hunters, and the Uniform Criminal Extradition Act, 62 U. Miami L. Rev. 59 (2007).

Two law-and-economics scholars have concluded that, even after controlling for selection variables (i.e., the fact that trial judges make different decisions about release conditions based on individual case and defendant characteristics), bail bond companies do a much better job than the government at controlling the behavior of released defendants:

> Defendants released on surety bond are 28 percent less likely to fail to appear than similar defendants released on their own recognizance, and if they do fail to appear, they are 53 percent less likely to remain at large for extended periods of time. Deposit bonds perform only marginally better than release on own recognizance. Requiring defendants to pay their bonds in cash can reduce the [failure-to-appear] rate similar to that for those released on surety bond. Given that a defendant skips town, however, the probability of recapture is much higher for those defendants released on surety bond. As a result, the probability of being a fugitive is 64 percent lower for those released on surety bond compared with those released on cash bond. These findings indicate that bond dealers and bail enforcement agents (bounty hunters) are effective at discouraging flight and at recapturing defendants. Bounty hunters, not public police, appear to be the true long arms of the law.

Eric Helland & Alexander Tabarrok, The Fugitive: Evidence on Public Versus Private Law Enforcement From Bail Jumping, 47 J. Law & Econ. 93, 118 (2004).

6. One of the benefits of bail is that it reduces jail overcrowding, but releasing a large number of people on bail creates its own administrative problems. The Philadelphia Inquirer studied that city's bail system and found that a high volume of arrestees, coupled with low funding to monitor them, meant that more than 10 percent of all released suspects (almost 47,000 people) became long-term fugitives, one of the worst rates in the nation. And while, in theory, the failure to appear meant that the city was entitled to keep the bail money, in practice, no real effort was made to collect the $1 billion in forfeited bail. For an insightful and depressing look at the problems of a big-city bail system that one of its own prosecutors called "a

complete cartoon," see Dylan Purcell, Craig R. McCoy, & Nancy Phillips, Violent Criminals Flout Broken Bail System, Philly.com (Dec. 15, 2009), available at www.philly.com/inquirer/special/20091215_Violent_Criminals_Flout_Broken_Bail_System.html.

B.   Pretrial Detention

Although Stack v. Boyle discusses bail as if the only question is whether the defendant will flee, this has never been the only basis for denying pretrial release. Courts have long assumed that if they find that the accused is likely to intimidate witnesses or tamper with evidence in his pending case, the Court can either deny bail or set conditions on release that are unrelated to the risk of flight, such as ordering the suspect not to make contact with witnesses or victims. The reasoning is that courts have the ability to preserve the integrity of the pending case, and a court's exercise of this authority is uncontroversial.

Whether the court can detain someone prior to trial simply because the judge thinks the suspect is dangerous in general is another matter. On the one hand, keeping someone in custody who was not a flight risk simply because they might commit other crimes while on bail sounds uncomfortably like punishment without a trial (and without even a crime). On the other hand, there is a widespread belief that certain defendants are simply too dangerous to release, and as a result, some courts would set bail at extremely high levels, not because of the flight risk, but because the judge knew the suspect could not afford the bail and thus would remain locked up.

The fear that some suspects were continuing to commit new crimes while out on bail, coupled with the unfairness of judges using high bail amounts as a sub rosa method of pretrial detention, led Congress to pass the Bail Reform Act of 1984, 18 U.S.C. §3141 et seq. In general, the Act operates as follows:

- When an arrested defendant is brought before the court, the judicial officer (typically a magistrate judge) has four options:
  (1) Release the suspect on his own recognizance, or on a promise to pay money if he misses his court appearances. The simple promise to pay is often called an "unsecured bond," because it does not require the accused to post any money or collateral.
  (2) Release the person subject to financial conditions, nonfinancial conditions, or both. The conditions can include requiring that the suspect: post a percentage of the bail amount with the court or with a surety; agree to custodial supervision by a designated person; agree to keep or seek a job; participate in an educational program; agree to travel restrictions; agree not to contact witnesses or victims; report to designated authorities; abide by a curfew; agree not to possess weapons; abide by alcohol and drug restrictions; or seek medical or psychiatric treatment. 18 U.S.C. §3142(g). And of course, there is always a requirement that the accused not commit any crimes while out on bail.
  (3) Temporarily detain the suspect to allow the court to revoke the defendant's conditional release (if the defendant was already out on bail for another crime at the time of arrest, for example), or to permit the defendant to be deported.

(4)   Deny bail and order the suspect detained pending trial. 18 U.S.C. §3142(a).

- In determining whether the defendant is to be released or detained, the operative standard is whether the defendant is likely to appear at all required court appearances and whether his release will "endanger the safety of any other person or the community."

- Before a defendant can be detained, the court must hold a hearing, which may be called on motion of the prosecutor or by the court sua sponte. At the hearing, the accused has the right to counsel (including appointed counsel if he is indigent), has the right to testify, to present evidence, and to cross-examine the government's witnesses. For the accused to be detained, the court must find by clear and convincing evidence *either* that defendant is a flight risk *or* that no release conditions will ensure the safety of the community. 18 U.S.C. §3142(f).

- In some cases, a rebuttable presumption arises that the defendant should be detained. If the defendant has been arrested for certain serious drug crimes, for example, or if the defendant has previously been convicted of a serious crime while out on bail, the burden shifts to the accused to rebut the presumption that he should not be released. 18 U.S.C. §3142(e).

Not surprisingly, the notion that courts could detain a defendant based on the prediction that he would commit further crimes if released — that is, that he would "endanger the safety of the community" — was quickly challenged.

UNITED STATES v. SALERNO

Certiorari to the United States Court of Appeals for the Second Circuit
481 U.S. 739 (1987)

CHIEF JUSTICE REHNQUIST delivered the opinion of the Court.

The Bail Reform Act of 1984 (Act) allows a federal court to detain an arrestee pending trial if the Government demonstrates by clear and convincing evidence after an adversary hearing that no release conditions "will reasonably assure . . . the safety of any other person and the community." The United States Court of Appeals for the Second Circuit struck down this provision of the Act as facially unconstitutional, because, in that court's words, this type of pretrial detention violates "substantive due process." We granted certiorari because of a conflict among the Courts of Appeals regarding the validity of the Act. . . . We hold that, as against the facial attack mounted by these respondents, the Act fully comports with constitutional requirements. We therefore reverse.

I

Responding to "the alarming problem of crimes committed by persons on release," . . . Congress formulated the Bail Reform Act of 1984, 18 U.S.C. §3141 et seq. . . . , as the solution to a bail crisis in the federal courts. The Act represents the National Legislature's considered response to numerous perceived deficiencies in the federal bail process. By providing for sweeping changes in both the way federal courts consider bail applications and the circumstances under which bail is granted,

Congress hoped to "give the courts adequate authority to make release decisions that give appropriate recognition to the danger a person may pose to others if released." . . .

To this end, §3141(a) of the Act requires a judicial officer to determine whether an arrestee shall be detained. Section 3142(e) provides that "[i]f, after a hearing pursuant to the provisions of subsection (f), the judicial officer finds that no condition or combination of conditions will reasonably assure the appearance of the person as required and the safety of any other person and the community, he shall order the detention of the person prior to trial." Section 3142(f) provides the arrestee with a number of procedural safeguards. He may request the presence of counsel at the detention hearing, he may testify and present witnesses in his behalf, as well as proffer evidence, and he may cross-examine other witnesses appearing at the hearing. If the judicial officer finds that no conditions of pretrial release can reasonably assure the safety of other persons and the community, he must state his findings of fact in writing, §3142(i), and support his conclusion with "clear and convincing evidence," §3142(f).

The judicial officer is not given unbridled discretion in making the detention determination. Congress has specified the considerations relevant to that decision. These factors include the nature and seriousness of the charges, the substantiality of the Government's evidence against the arrestee, the arrestee's background and characteristics, and the nature and seriousness of the danger posed by the suspect's release. §3142(g). Should a judicial officer order detention, the detainee is entitled to expedited appellate review of the detention order. §§3145(b), (c).

Respondents Anthony Salerno and Vincent Cafaro were arrested on March 21, 1986, after being charged in a 29-count indictment alleging various Racketeer Influenced and Corrupt Organizations Act (RICO) violations, mail and wire fraud offenses, extortion, and various criminal gambling violations. The RICO counts alleged 35 acts of racketeering activity, including fraud, extortion, gambling, and conspiracy to commit murder. At respondents' arraignment, the Government moved to have Salerno and Cafaro detained pursuant to §3142(e), on the ground that no condition of release would assure the safety of the community or any person. The District Court held a hearing at which the Government made a detailed proffer of evidence. The Government's case showed that Salerno was the "boss" of the Genovese crime family of La Cosa Nostra and that Cafaro was a "captain" in the Genovese family. According to the Government's proffer, based in large part on conversations intercepted by a court-ordered wiretap, the two respondents had participated in wide-ranging conspiracies to aid their illegitimate enterprises through violent means. The Government also offered the testimony of two of its trial witnesses, who would assert that Salerno personally participated in two murder conspiracies. Salerno opposed the motion for detention, challenging the credibility of the Government's witnesses. He offered the testimony of several character witnesses as well as a letter from his doctor stating that he was suffering from a serious medical condition. Cafaro presented no evidence at the hearing, but instead characterized the wiretap conversations as merely "tough talk."

The District Court granted the Government's detention motion, concluding that the Government had established by clear and convincing evidence that no condition or combination of conditions of release would ensure the safety of the community or any person. . . .

Respondents appealed, contending that to the extent that the Bail Reform Act permits pretrial detention on the ground that the arrestee is likely to commit future crimes, it is unconstitutional on its face. Over a dissent, the United States Court of Appeals for the Second Circuit agreed. 794 F.2d 64 (1986). . . .

II

A facial challenge to a legislative Act is, of course, the most difficult challenge to mount successfully, since the challenger must establish that no set of circumstances exists under which the Act would be valid. The fact that the Bail Reform Act might operate unconstitutionally under some conceivable set of circumstances is insufficient to render it wholly invalid, since we have not recognized an "overbreadth" doctrine outside the limited context of the First Amendment. . . . We think respondents have failed to shoulder their heavy burden to demonstrate that the Act is "facially" unconstitutional.

Respondents present two grounds for invalidating the Bail Reform Act's provisions permitting pretrial detention on the basis of future dangerousness. First, they rely upon the Court of Appeals' conclusion that the Act exceeds the limitations placed upon the Federal Government by the Due Process Clause of the Fifth Amendment. Second, they contend that the Act contravenes the Eighth Amendment's proscription against excessive bail. We treat these contentions in turn.

A

The Due Process Clause of the Fifth Amendment provides that "No person shall . . . be deprived of life, liberty, or property, without due process of law. . . ." This Court has held that the Due Process Clause protects individuals against two types of government action. So-called "substantive due process" prevents the government from engaging in conduct that "shocks the conscience," Rochin v. California, 342 U.S. 165, 172 (1952), or interferes with rights "implicit in the concept of ordered liberty," Palko v. Connecticut, 302 U.S. 319, 325-326 (1937). When government action depriving a person of life, liberty, or property survives substantive due process scrutiny, it must still be implemented in a fair manner. Mathews v. Eldridge, 424 U.S. 319, 335 (1976). This requirement has traditionally been referred to as "procedural" due process.

Respondents first argue that the Act violates substantive due process because the pretrial detention it authorizes constitutes impermissible punishment before trial. . . . The Government, however, has never argued that pretrial detention could be upheld if it were "punishment." The Court of Appeals assumed that pretrial detention under the Bail Reform Act is regulatory, not penal, and we agree that it is.

As an initial matter, the mere fact that a person is detained does not inexorably lead to the conclusion that the government has imposed punishment. . . . To determine whether a restriction on liberty constitutes impermissible punishment or permissible regulation, we first look to legislative intent. . . . Unless Congress expressly intended to impose punitive restrictions, the punitive/regulatory distinction turns on "'whether an alternative purpose to which [the restriction] may rationally be connected is assignable for it, and whether it appears excessive in relation to the alternative purpose assigned [to it].'" [Schall v. Martin, 467 U.S. 253, 269 (1984)], quoting Kennedy v. Mendoza-Martinez, 372 U.S. 144, 168-169 (1963).

We conclude that the detention imposed by the Act falls on the regulatory side of the dichotomy. The legislative history of the Bail Reform Act clearly indicates that Congress did not formulate the pretrial detention provisions as punishment for dangerous individuals. . . . Congress instead perceived pretrial detention as a potential solution to a pressing societal problem. . . . There is no doubt that preventing danger to the community is a legitimate regulatory goal. . . .

Nor are the incidents of pretrial detention excessive in relation to the regulatory goal Congress sought to achieve. The Bail Reform Act carefully limits the circumstances under which detention may be sought to the most serious of crimes. See 18 U.S.C. §3142(f) (detention hearings available if case involves crimes of violence, offenses for which the sentence is life imprisonment or death, serious drug offenses, or certain repeat offenders). The arrestee is entitled to a prompt detention hearing, ibid., and the maximum length of pretrial detention is limited by the stringent time limitations of the Speedy Trial Act.[4] See 18 U.S.C. §3161 et seq. . . . Moreover, as in Schall v. Martin, the conditions of confinement envisioned by the Act "appear to reflect the regulatory purposes relied upon by the" Government. 467 U.S., at 270. As in *Schall*, the statute at issue here requires that detainees be housed in a "facility separate, to the extent practicable, from persons awaiting or serving sentences or being held in custody pending appeal." 18 U.S.C. §3142(i)(2). We conclude, therefore, that the pretrial detention contemplated by the Bail Reform Act is regulatory in nature, and does not constitute punishment before trial in violation of the Due Process Clause.

The Court of Appeals nevertheless concluded that "the Due Process Clause prohibits pretrial detention on the ground of danger to the community as a regulatory measure, without regard to the duration of the detention." 794 F.2d, at 71. Respondents characterize the Due Process Clause as erecting an impenetrable "wall" in this area that "no governmental interest — rational, important, compelling or otherwise — may surmount." . . .

We do not think the Clause lays down any such categorical imperative. We have repeatedly held that the Government's regulatory interest in community safety can, in appropriate circumstances, outweigh an individual's liberty interest. For example, in times of war or insurrection, when society's interest is at its peak, the Government may detain individuals whom the Government believes to be dangerous. . . . Even outside the exigencies of war, we have found that sufficiently compelling governmental interests can justify detention of dangerous persons. Thus, we have found no absolute constitutional barrier to detention of potentially dangerous resident aliens pending deportation proceedings. . . . We have also held that the government may detain mentally unstable individuals who present a danger to the public, Addington v. Texas, 441 U.S. 418 (1979), and dangerous defendants who become incompetent to stand trial, Jackson v. Indiana, 406 U.S. 715, 731-739 (1972). . . . We have approved of postarrest regulatory detention of juveniles when they present a continuing danger to the community. Schall v. Martin, supra. Even competent adults may face substantial liberty restrictions as a result of the operation of our criminal justice system. If the police suspect an individual of a crime, they may arrest and hold him until a neutral magistrate determines whether probable cause exists. Gerstein v. Pugh, 420 U.S. 103 (1975). Finally, respondents concede

---

4. We intimate no view as to the point at which detention in a particular case might become excessively prolonged, and therefore punitive, in relation to Congress' regulatory goal.

and the Court of Appeals noted that an arrestee may be incarcerated until trial if he presents a risk of flight, see Bell v. Wolfish, 441 U.S. [520], at 534 [(1979)], or a danger to witnesses.

Respondents characterize all of these cases as exceptions to the "general rule" of substantive due process that the government may not detain a person prior to a judgment of guilt in a criminal trial. Such a "general rule" may freely be conceded, but we think that these cases show a sufficient number of exceptions to the rule that the congressional action challenged here can hardly be characterized as totally novel. Given the well-established authority of the government, in special circumstances, to restrain individuals' liberty prior to or even without criminal trial and conviction, we think that the present statute providing for pretrial detention on the basis of dangerousness must be evaluated in precisely the same manner that we evaluated the laws in the cases discussed above.

The government's interest in preventing crime by arrestees is both legitimate and compelling. . . . In *Schall*, supra, we recognized the strength of the State's interest in preventing juvenile crime. This general concern with crime prevention is no less compelling when the suspects are adults. Indeed, "[t]he harm suffered by the victim of a crime is not dependent upon the age of the perpetrator." Schall v. Martin, supra, at 264-265. The Bail Reform Act of 1984 responds to an even more particularized governmental interest than the interest we sustained in *Schall*. The statute we upheld in *Schall* permitted pretrial detention of any juvenile arrested on any charge after a showing that the individual might commit some undefined further crimes. The Bail Reform Act, in contrast, narrowly focuses on a particularly acute problem in which the Government interests are overwhelming. The Act operates only on individuals who have been arrested for a specific category of extremely serious offenses. 18 U.S.C. §3142(f). Congress specifically found that these individuals are far more likely to be responsible for dangerous acts in the community after arrest. . . . Nor is the Act by any means a scattershot attempt to incapacitate those who are merely suspected of these serious crimes. The Government must first of all demonstrate probable cause to believe that the charged crime has been committed by the arrestee, but that is not enough. In a full-blown adversary hearing, the Government must convince a neutral decision-maker by clear and convincing evidence that no conditions of release can reasonably assure the safety of the community or any person. 18 U.S.C. §3142(f). While the Government's general interest in preventing crime is compelling, even this interest is heightened when the Government musters convincing proof that the arrestee, already indicted or held to answer for a serious crime, presents a demonstrable danger to the community. Under these narrow circumstances, society's interest in crime prevention is at its greatest.

On the other side of the scale, of course, is the individual's strong interest in liberty. We do not minimize the importance and fundamental nature of this right. But, as our cases hold, this right may, in circumstances where the government's interest is sufficiently weighty, be subordinated to the greater needs of society. We think that Congress' careful delineation of the circumstances under which detention will be permitted satisfies this standard. . . .

Finally, we may dispose briefly of respondents' facial challenge to the procedures of the Bail Reform Act. To sustain them against such a challenge, we need only find them "adequate to authorize the pretrial detention of at least some [persons] charged with crimes," *Schall*, supra, at 264, whether or not they might be insufficient in some particular circumstances. We think they pass that test. As we stated in

Schall, "there is nothing inherently unattainable about a prediction of future criminal conduct." 467 U.S., at 278. . . .

Under the Bail Reform Act, the procedures by which a judicial officer evaluates the likelihood of future dangerousness are specifically designed to further the accuracy of that determination. Detainees have a right to counsel at the detention hearing. 18 U.S.C. §3142(f). They may testify in their own behalf, present information by proffer or otherwise, and cross-examine witnesses who appear at the hearing. Ibid. The judicial officer charged with the responsibility of determining the appropriateness of detention is guided by statutorily enumerated factors, which include the nature and the circumstances of the charges, the weight of the evidence, the history and characteristics of the putative offender, and the danger to the community. §3142(g). The Government must prove its case by clear and convincing evidence. §3142(f). Finally, the judicial officer must include written findings of fact and a written statement of reasons for a decision to detain. §3142(i). The Act's review provisions, §3145(c), provide for immediate appellate review of the detention decision.

We think these extensive safeguards suffice to repel a facial challenge. The protections are more exacting than those we found sufficient in the juvenile context, see *Schall*, supra, at 275-281, and they far exceed what we found necessary to effect limited postarrest detention in Gerstein v. Pugh, 420 U.S. 103 (1975). Given the legitimate and compelling regulatory purpose of the Act and the procedural protections it offers, we conclude that the Act is not facially invalid under the Due Process Clause of the Fifth Amendment.

B

Respondents also contend that the Bail Reform Act violates the Excessive Bail Clause of the Eighth Amendment. The Court of Appeals did not address this issue because it found that the Act violates the Due Process Clause. We think that the Act survives a challenge founded upon the Eighth Amendment.

The Eighth Amendment addresses pretrial release by providing merely that "[e]xcessive bail shall not be required." This Clause, of course, says nothing about whether bail shall be available at all. Respondents nevertheless contend that this Clause grants them a right to bail calculated solely upon considerations of flight. They rely on Stack v. Boyle, 342 U.S. 1, 5 (1951), in which the Court stated that "[b]ail set at a figure higher than an amount reasonably calculated [to ensure the defendant's presence at trial] is 'excessive' under the Eighth Amendment." In respondents' view, since the Bail Reform Act allows a court essentially to set bail at an infinite amount for reasons not related to the risk of flight, it violates the Excessive Bail Clause. Respondents concede that the right to bail they have discovered in the Eighth Amendment is not absolute. A court may, for example, refuse bail in capital cases. And, as the Court of Appeals noted and respondents admit, a court may refuse bail when the defendant presents a threat to the judicial process by intimidating witnesses. . . . Respondents characterize these exceptions as consistent with what they claim to be the sole purpose of bail — to ensure the integrity of the judicial process.

While we agree that a primary function of bail is to safeguard the courts' role in adjudicating the guilt or innocence of defendants, we reject the proposition that the Eighth Amendment categorically prohibits the government from pursuing other admittedly compelling interests through regulation of pretrial release. The above-quoted dictum in Stack v. Boyle is far too slender a reed on which to rest this argument. The Court in *Stack* had no occasion to consider whether the Excessive Bail Clause requires courts to admit all defendants to bail, because the statute before the Court in that case in fact allowed the defendants to be bailed. Thus, the Court had to determine only whether bail, admittedly available in that case, was excessive if set at a sum greater than that necessary to ensure the arrestees' presence at trial. . . .

[W]e need not decide today whether the Excessive Bail Clause speaks at all to Congress' power to define the classes of criminal arrestees who shall be admitted to bail. For even if we were to conclude that the Eighth Amendment imposes some substantive limitations on the National Legislature's powers in this area, we would still hold that the Bail Reform Act is valid. Nothing in the text of the Bail Clause limits permissible Government considerations solely to questions of flight. The only arguable substantive limitation of the Bail Clause is that the Government's proposed conditions of release or detention not be "excessive" in light of the perceived evil. Of course, to determine whether the Government's response is excessive, we must compare that response against the interest the Government seeks to protect by means of that response. Thus, when the Government has admitted that its only interest is in preventing flight, bail must be set by a court at a sum designed to ensure that goal, and no more. Stack v. Boyle, supra. We believe that when Congress has mandated detention on the basis of a compelling interest other than prevention of flight, as it has here, the Eighth Amendment does not require release on bail.

III

In our society liberty is the norm, and detention prior to trial or without trial is the carefully limited exception. We hold that the provisions for pretrial detention in the Bail Reform Act of 1984 fall within that carefully limited exception. The Act authorizes the detention prior to trial of arrestees charged with serious felonies who are found after an adversary hearing to pose a threat to the safety of individuals or to the community which no condition of release can dispel. The numerous procedural safeguards detailed above must attend this adversary hearing. We are unwilling to say that this congressional determination, based as it is upon that primary concern of every government — a concern for the safety and indeed the lives of its citizens — on its face violates either the Due Process Clause of the Fifth Amendment or the Excessive Bail Clause of the Eighth Amendment.

The judgment of the Court of Appeals is therefore Reversed.

JUSTICE MARSHALL, with whom JUSTICE BRENNAN joins, dissenting.

This case brings before the Court for the first time a statute in which Congress declares that a person innocent of any crime may be jailed indefinitely, pending the trial of allegations which are legally presumed to be untrue, if the Government shows to the satisfaction of a judge that the accused is likely to commit crimes, unrelated to the pending charges, at any time in the future. Such statutes, consistent with the usages of tyranny and the excesses of what bitter experience teaches us to call the police state, have long been thought incompatible with the fundamental human rights protected by our Constitution. Today a majority of this Court holds otherwise. Its decision disregards basic principles of justice established centuries ago and enshrined beyond the reach of governmental interference in the Bill of Rights.

I

[This section, dealing with the procedural posture of the case, is omitted. — EDS.]

II

The majority approaches respondents' challenge to the Act by dividing the discussion into two sections, one concerned with the substantive guarantees implicit in the Due Process Clause, and the other concerned with the protection afforded by the Excessive Bail Clause of the Eighth Amendment. This is a sterile formalism, which divides a unitary argument into two independent parts and then professes to demonstrate that the parts are individually inadequate.

On the due process side of this false dichotomy appears an argument concerning the distinction between regulatory and punitive legislation. . . . The majority finds that "Congress did not formulate the pretrial detention provisions as punishment for dangerous individuals," but instead was pursuing the "legitimate regulatory goal" of "preventing danger to the community."[4] Concluding that pretrial detention is not an excessive solution to the problem of preventing danger to the community, the majority thus finds that no substantive element of the guarantee of due process invalidates the statute.

This argument does not demonstrate the conclusion it purports to justify. Let us apply the majority's reasoning to a similar, hypothetical case. After investigation, Congress determines (not unrealistically) that a large proportion of violent crime is perpetrated by persons who are unemployed. It also determines, equally reasonably, that much violent crime is committed at night. From amongst the panoply of "potential solutions," Congress chooses a statute which permits, after judicial proceedings, the imposition of a dusk-to-dawn curfew on anyone who is unemployed. Since this is not a measure enacted for the purpose of punishing the unemployed, and since the majority finds that preventing danger to the community is a legitimate regulatory goal, the curfew statute would, according to the majority's analysis, be a mere "regulatory" detention statute, entirely compatible with the substantive components of the Due Process Clause.

The absurdity of this conclusion arises, of course, from the majority's cramped concept of substantive due process. The majority proceeds as though the only substantive right protected by the Due Process Clause is a right to be free from punishment before conviction. The majority's technique for infringing this right is simple: merely redefine any measure which is claimed to be punishment as "regulation," and, magically, the Constitution no longer prohibits its imposition. Because, as I discuss in Part III, infra, the Due Process Clause protects other substantive rights which are infringed by this legislation, the majority's argument is merely an exercise in obfuscation.

4. . . . . The Bail Reform Act does not limit its definition of dangerousness to the likelihood that the defendant poses a danger to others through the commission of *federal* crimes. Federal preventive detention may thus be ordered under the Act when the danger asserted by the Government is the danger that the defendant will violate state law. The majority nowhere identifies the constitutional source of congressional power to authorize the federal detention of persons whose predicted future conduct would not violate any federal statute and could not be punished by a federal court. I can only conclude that the Court's frequently expressed concern with the principles of federalism vanishes when it threatens to interfere with the Court's attainment of the desired result.

The logic of the majority's Eighth Amendment analysis is equally unsatisfactory. The Eighth Amendment . . . states that "[e]xcessive bail shall not be required."

. . . If excessive bail is imposed the defendant stays in jail. The same result is achieved if bail is denied altogether. Whether the magistrate sets bail at $1 billion or refuses to set bail at all, the consequences are indistinguishable. It would be mere sophistry to suggest that the Eighth Amendment protects against the former decision, and not the latter. Indeed, such a result would lead to the conclusion that there was no need for Congress to pass a preventive detention measure of any kind; every federal magistrate and district judge could simply refuse, despite the absence of any evidence of risk of flight or danger to the community, to set bail. This would be entirely constitutional, since, according to the majority, the Eighth Amendment "says nothing about whether bail shall be available at all."

But perhaps, the majority says, this manifest absurdity can be avoided. Perhaps the Bail Clause is addressed only to the Judiciary. "[W]e need not decide today," the majority says, "whether the Excessive Bail Clause speaks at all to Congress' power to define the classes of criminal arrestees who shall be admitted to bail." The majority is correct that this question need not be decided today; it was decided long ago. Federal and state statutes which purport to accomplish what the Eighth Amendment forbids . . . may not stand. . . .

III

The essence of this case may be found, ironically enough, in a provision of the Act to which the majority does not refer. Title 18 U.S.C. §3142(j) . . . provides that "[n]othing in this section shall be construed as modifying or limiting the presumption of innocence." But the very pith and purpose of this statute is an abhorrent limitation of the presumption of innocence. The majority's untenable conclusion that the present Act is constitutional arises from a specious denial of the role of the Bail Clause and the Due Process Clause in protecting the invaluable guarantee afforded by the presumption of innocence.

"The principle that there is a presumption of innocence in favor of the accused is the undoubted law, axiomatic and elementary, and its enforcement lies at the foundation of the administration of our criminal law." Coffin v. United States, 156 U.S. 432, 453 (1895). Our society's belief, reinforced over the centuries, that all are innocent until the state has proved them to be guilty, like the companion principle that guilt must be proved beyond a reasonable doubt, is "implicit in the concept of ordered liberty," Palko v. Connecticut, 302 U.S. 319, 325 (1937), and is established beyond legislative contravention in the Due Process Clause. . . .

The statute now before us declares that persons who have been indicted may be detained if a judicial officer finds clear and convincing evidence that they pose a danger to individuals or to the community. The statute does not authorize the Government to imprison anyone it has evidence is dangerous; indictment is necessary. But let us suppose that a defendant is indicted and the Government shows by clear and convincing evidence that he is dangerous and should be detained pending a trial, at which trial the defendant is acquitted. May the Government continue to hold the defendant in detention based upon its showing that he is dangerous? The answer cannot be yes, for that would allow the Government to imprison someone for uncommitted crimes based upon "proof" not beyond a reasonable doubt. The result must therefore be that once the indictment has failed, detention cannot continue. But our fundamental principles of justice declare that the defendant is as innocent on the day before his trial as he is on the morning after his acquittal. Under this statute an untried indictment somehow acts to permit a detention, based on other charges, which after an acquittal would be unconstitutional. The conclusion is inescapable that the indictment has been turned into evidence, if not that the defendant is guilty of the crime charged, then that left to his own devices he will soon be guilty of something else. "'If it suffices to accuse, what will become of the innocent?'" Coffin v. United States, supra, at 455 (quoting Ammianus Marcellinus, Rerum Gestarum Libri Qui Supersunt, L. XVIII, c. 1, A.D. 359). To be sure, an indictment is not without legal consequences. It establishes that there is probable cause to believe that an offense was committed, and that the defendant committed it. Upon probable cause a warrant for the defendant's arrest may issue; a period of administrative detention may occur before the evidence of probable cause is presented to a neutral magistrate. See Gerstein v. Pugh, 420 U.S. 103 (1975). Once a defendant has been committed for trial he may be detained in custody if the magistrate finds that no conditions of release will prevent him from becoming a fugitive. But in this connection the charging instrument is evidence of nothing more than the fact that there will be a trial. . . . The finding of probable cause conveys power to try, and the power to try imports of necessity the power to assure that the processes of justice will not be evaded or obstructed. . . . [But the] detention purportedly authorized by this statute bears no relation to the Government's power to try charges supported by a finding of probable cause, and thus the interests it serves are outside the scope of interests which may be considered in weighing the excessiveness of bail under the Eighth Amendment.

It is not a novel proposition that the Bail Clause plays a vital role in protecting the presumption of innocence. . . . As Chief Justice Vinson wrote for the Court in Stack v. Boyle, supra: "Unless th[e] right to bail before trial is preserved, the presumption of innocence, secured only after centuries of struggle, would lose its meaning." 342 U.S., at 4.

IV

There is a connection between the peculiar facts of this case and the evident constitutional defects in the statute which the Court upholds today. Respondent Cafaro was originally incarcerated for an indeterminate period at the request of the Government, which believed (or professed to believe) that his release imminently threatened the safety of the community. That threat apparently vanished, from the Government's point of view, when Cafaro agreed to act as a covert agent of the Government. There could be no more eloquent demonstration of the coercive power of authority to imprison upon prediction, or of the dangers which the almost inevitable abuses pose to the cherished liberties of a free society.

"It is a fair summary of history to say that the safeguards of liberty have frequently been forged in controversies involving not very nice people." United States v. Rabinowitz, 339 U.S. 56, 69 (1950) (Frankfurter, J., dissenting). Honoring the presumption of innocence is often difficult; sometimes we must pay substantial social costs as a result of our commitment to the values we espouse. But at the end of the day the presumption of innocence protects the innocent; the shortcuts we take with those whom we believe to be guilty injure only those wrongfully accused and, ultimately, ourselves.

Throughout the world today there are men, women, and children interned indefinitely, awaiting trials which may never come or which may be a mockery of the word, because their governments believe them to be "dangerous." Our Constitution, whose construction began two centuries ago, can shelter us forever from the evils of such unchecked power. Over 200 years it has slowly, through our efforts, grown more durable, more expansive, and more just. But it cannot protect us if we lack the courage, and the self-restraint, to protect ourselves. Today a majority of the Court applies itself to an ominous exercise in demolition. Theirs is truly a decision which will go forth without authority, and come back without respect.

I dissent.

JUSTICE STEVENS, dissenting.

There may be times when the Government's interest in protecting the safety of the community will justify the brief detention of a person who has not committed any crime. . . .[1] To use Judge Feinberg's example, it is indeed difficult to accept the proposition that the Government is without power to detain a person when it is a virtual certainty that he or she would otherwise kill a group of innocent people in the immediate future. United States v. Salerno, 794 F.2d 64, 77 (CA2 1986) (dissenting opinion). Similarly, I am unwilling to decide today that the police may never impose a limited curfew during a time of crisis. These questions are obviously not presented in this case, but they lurk in the background and preclude me from answering the question that is presented in as broad a manner as Justice Marshall has. Nonetheless, I firmly agree with Justice Marshall that the provision of the Bail Reform Act allowing pretrial detention on the basis of future dangerousness is unconstitutional. Whatever the answers are to the questions I have mentioned, it is clear to me that a pending indictment may not be given any weight in evaluating an individual's risk to the community or the need for immediate detention.

If the evidence of imminent danger is strong enough to warrant emergency detention, it should support that preventive measure regardless of whether the person has been charged, convicted, or acquitted of some other offense. In this case, for example, it is unrealistic to assume that the danger to the community that was present when respondents were at large did not justify their detention before they were indicted, but did require that measure the moment that the grand jury found probable cause to believe they had committed crimes in the past. It is equally unrealistic to assume that the danger will vanish if a jury happens to acquit them. Justice Marshall has demonstrated that the fact of indictment cannot, consistent with the presumption of innocence and the Eighth Amendment's Excessive Bail Clause, be used to create a special class, the members of which are, alone, eligible for detention because of future dangerousness. . . .

---

1. "If the evidence overwhelmingly establishes that a skyjacker, for example, was insane at the time of his act, and that he is virtually certain to resume his violent behavior as soon as he is set free, must we then conclude that the only way to protect society from such predictable harm is to find an innocent man guilty of a crime he did not have the capacity to commit?" United States v. Greene, 497 F.2d [1068,] 1088 [(CA 7 1974)].

NOTES AND QUESTIONS

1. Recall in Stack v. Boyle the Court said that bail "serves to prevent the infliction of punishment prior to conviction." Tony Salerno claimed that to detain him based on a prediction of dangerousness amounted to punishment for crimes that had not yet occurred. Is he right? Or is the Court correct that pretrial detention is a "regulatory" measure rather than punishment?

As the Salerno majority points out, there are familiar examples of regulatory measures that can result in confinement of a person, often in quite undesirable conditions. Most notably, a mentally ill person can be involuntarily confined to a psychiatric institution based on a prediction of future dangerousness. See Addington v. Texas, 441 U.S. 418 (1979). If you disagree with the result in Salerno, how would you distinguish this example? Or are those committed to a psychiatric hospital also being improperly "punished?" Does the Court's focus on the intent of Congress in permitting the confinement help draw a distinction? See generally Marc Miller & Martin Guggenheim, Pretrial Detention and Punishment, 75 Minn. L. Rev. 335, 372 (1990), who claim that "the state cannot preventively detain a competent adult without making an implicit moral statement about the individual" and concluding that such a moral statement — when coupled with hard treatment, such as detention — constitutes "punishment."

2. It seems clear even after Salerno that there must be some triggering event that allows the government to make a prediction of dangerousness and then detain the person as a result. Before a person can be confined to a psychiatric institution, for example, there must be a finding of a mental illness. In the case of pretrial detention, the triggering event is the arrest — unless and until Tony Salerno is arrested, the government cannot detain him simply because they can confidently predict that he will commit future crimes. And of course, if Salerno were later acquitted, a court couldn't continue to hold him, even if it has overwhelming evidence that he likely to resume his criminal career on release. So there must be something about the arrest that moves Salerno into a different category, one that legitimizes the prediction of dangerousness and the resulting detention.

In the Court's view, what is it about an arrest that legitimizes the use of this power? An arrest can be based on probable cause, which is not a very exacting standard. One possible answer is found in a single line in the majority opinion: "Congress specifically found that these individuals [who are arrested for serious crimes] are far more likely to be responsible for dangerous acts in the community after arrest." Assuming the accuracy of this congressional finding, is this a sufficient basis for permitting preventive detention?

If so (or even if not), could Congress find that a *conviction* for a serious crime is sufficient to allow the preventive detention of someone, even after the person is released from prison? In other words, after Tony Salerno is convicted and serves his sentence, could Congress permit the government to seek his continued confinement based on a prediction of future criminality? If you think the answer should be no, consider Kansas v. Hendricks, 521 U.S. 346 (1997), and Kansas v. Crane, 534 U.S. 407 (2002), which upheld a Kansas statute that allowed for continued civil commitment of individuals who had already completed their sentence for sexual offenses based on a finding that they were likely to engage in future "predatory acts of sexual violence," as well as proof that the person currently has "serious difficulty in controlling behavior."

3. How confident should we be that trial courts can accurately predict the future dangerousness of a person? Empirical research is scarce because of the impossibility of conducting controlled experiments — defendants who are detained never get the chance to commit their predicted crimes pending trial, and it would be infeasible to release for study a randomly selected sample of those defendants determined by the courts to be dangerous.

One study, however, took advantage of a peculiar situation that arose in New York in 1981, when a federal judge issued an injunction against the preventive detention of juvenile offenders for dangerousness (defined as the risk that the juvenile would commit any crime during the pretrial period). Pursuant to the injunction (which remained in effect for three years), 74 juveniles were released pending trial despite the fact that a state judge had ordered them to be preventively detained for dangerousness. By comparing the 74 injunction-released juveniles with a control group of juveniles who possessed similar social and legal characteristics, but who had not been ordered preventively detained for dangerousness, the researchers were able to evaluate the accuracy of the state judges' predictions of dangerousness. See Jeffrey Fagan & Martin Guggenheim, Preventive Detention and the Judicial Prediction of Dangerousness for Juveniles: A Natural Experiment, 86 J. Crim. L. & Criminology 415 (1996).

Using a fixed 90-day period as the assumed length of time between release and trial, the researchers found that the 74 injunction-released juveniles were significantly more likely to be rearrested for a crime pending trial than the control group. As for violent crime, even though this was not the primary criterion for the preventive detention orders, 18.8 percent of the injunction-released juveniles were rearrested for a violent crime during the pretrial period, as compared with only 7.8 percent of the control group.

The researchers concluded: "The capacity to select from among a group of accused delinquents those who pose an elevated risk of criminality in the legally critical interval following arrest is clear from the study. These results are all the more impressive given the limited nature of the information available to the judge at the time of the detention decision." Id., at 445-446. Nevertheless, they termed the overall results of their study "ambiguous," mostly because of the high incidence of "false positives" (i.e., almost 60 percent of the juveniles who would have been preventively detained, absent the federal injunction, were not rearrested for any crimes during the pretrial period, and more than 80 percent were not rearrested for any violent crimes). The researchers found the presence of these "false positives" to be "at odds with constitutional concerns over false imprisonment and equal protection." Id., at 447.

4. In a post-*Salerno* world, how many defendants are released prior to trial and how many are detained? Among federal defendants in 2006, slightly more than one in three defendants (37 percent) were released at some point prior to trial, with the rest being detained. See http://bjs.ojp.usdoj.gov/content/pub/html/fjsst/2006/fjs06st.pdf (Table 3.1). This number reflects a steady decrease in the rate of released federal defendants from the earlier part of the decade, where in 2001, 46 percent were admitted to bail. See www.albany.edu/sourcebook/pdf/t513.pdf. These figures are, in turn, different from the statistics for state court felony defendants in the 75 largest counties in the United States, where between 1990 and 2004, 62 percent were released before the charges against them were resolved. See Thomas H. Cohen & Brian A. Reaves, Pretrial Release of Felony Defendants in State Courts, available at http://bjs.ojp.usdoj.gov/content/pub/pdf/prfdsc.pdf.

As Salerno notes, the concern that motivated the 1984 Bail Reform Act was not how many defendants were released, but rather, the behavior of those who were released. More than 30,000 federal defendants were released prior to trial in 2006, and 78 percent complied with all conditions of their release, while 22 percent committed at least one violation. Of all the federal defendants released, 5 percent failed to appear as required, and 9 percent had their release revoked. See http://bjs.ojp.usdoj.gov/content/pub/html/fjsst/2006/tables/fjs06st303.pdf.

On the state side, more than one-third of the released defendants (35 percent) engaged in some type of misconduct, with failure to appear (21 percent) being the most common violation. Of those who failed to appear, most returned to court eventually, voluntarily or otherwise, with only 5 percent remaining a fugitive. Twenty-one percent of the state defendants were rearrested for a new offense, two-thirds of those for a felony. See Tables 15-17, at http://bjs.ojp.usdoj.gov/content/pub/html/fdluc/2004/fdluc04st.pdf.

What should we make of these figures? Do they suggest that the bail system is working well, because a high percentage of defendants comply with all the conditions of release? Or do they show that too many dangerous defendants are still being released? For an insightful discussion of how we should calculate the full costs and the benefits of pretrial release, see Larry Laudan & Ronald J. Allen, Deadly Dilemmas II: Bail and Crime, 85 Chi.-Kent L. Rev. 23 (2010).

5. Academic commentary on the Bail Reform Act of 1984, and on the *Salerno* decision upholding it, has been almost uniformly critical. For example, Marc Miller and Martin Guggenheim (the coauthor of the New York dangerousness study cited above) argue that the high rate of "false positives" in making predictions of dangerousness means that "judges should not use them as an independent justification for major deprivations of liberty such as detention." See Marc Miller & Martin Guggenheim, Pretrial Detention and Punishment, 75 Minn. L. Rev. 335, 386 (1990). They conclude that "the modern trend toward increased detention based on inaccurate, unprovable predictions of dangerousness . . . is a subterfuge to undermine the presumption of innocence." Id., at 425.

Albert Alschuler disagrees with Miller and Guggenheim about the inability of judges to predict dangerousness, but agrees that the Bail Reform Act of 1984 should be found unconstitutional, primarily because it does not require strong proof that the detained defendant has committed a crime in the past. "Schemes of preventive detention that lack a predicate in past misconduct deny people the chance to turn around — the opportunity to choose. From the beginning, our history has treated this opportunity as an essential attribute of human dignity." Albert W. Alschuler, Preventive Detention and the Failure of Interest Balancing Approaches to Due Process, 85 Mich. L. Rev. 510, 557 (1986).

See also Paul H. Robinson, Commentary: Punishing Dangerousness: Cloaking Preventive Detention as Criminal Justice, 114 Harv. L. Rev. 1429 (2001). Professor Robinson claims that "in some respects, one can argue that pretrial preventive detention is less objectionable than [the increasingly prevalent] prevention-based expansions of criminal liability and punishment," such as "three strikes" and sexual-predator laws. This is because most pretrial detainees are, in fact, convicted at trial, and the convicted defendant then receives credit against his or her sentence for the time spent in pretrial detention; thus, "[a]t least theoretically, [the defendant] serves only the time deserved."

Chapter 9
The Charging Decision

A. *Prosecutorial Discretion*

Article II, Section 3 of the Constitution provides that the president "shall take Care that the Laws be faithfully executed." This clause, and those like it in state constitutions, has come to mean that the prosecutorial power is vested in the executive branch of government. In the federal system, prosecutions are conducted by 93 United States Attorneys, one for each judicial district,[1] and by the assistants who work for them. Unlike the lead prosecutors in most states, U.S. Attorneys are not elected; they are appointed by the president, and work under the direction of the Attorney General, the head of the Department of Justice.

It is hard to overstate the extent to which prosecutors control the initiation and direction of the criminal process. As the readings that follow show, decisions about whether to file criminal charges, which charges to file, and against whom charges should be brought, rest almost exclusively with the prosecutor, and normally are not subject to judicial review.

This discretion gives prosecutors enormous power to decide what the criminal law really means in their jurisdictions. There is more crime committed than there are resources to prosecute them, so an important threshold question is how prosecutors decide which defendants to charge and what types of crimes to pursue. Given this discretion, it is no surprise that once charges are filed, the government usually wins. In 2009, there were slightly more than 95,000 criminal defendants charged in federal district courts, 91 percent of whom eventually were convicted of something. Of the 9 percent who were not convicted, the vast majority had their charges dismissed for one reason or another; only one-half of 1 percent (.005) of all criminal defendants charged in federal court went to trial and were acquitted.

Not all of these convictions lead to a harsh sentence: In 2009, a full one-quarter of all convicted federal defendants either serve no jail time or are incarcerated for six months or less, often because the defense entered into a favorable plea bargain. See Sourcebook of Criminal Justice Statistics Online, Tables 5.24.2009, 5.25.2009, available at www.albany.edu/sourcebook. As these numbers show, prosecutorial decisions *not* to charge, or to charge for a lower offense than the facts might justify, are the primary way in which potential criminal defendants succeed in the federal system.

Control of the criminal process by professional prosecutors has not always been the norm. As recently as the early nineteenth century, a substantial fraction of criminal cases were litigated by private parties, usually crime victims or their families. At

---

1. There are actually 94 judicial districts, but the District of Guam and the District of the Northern Mariana Islands share a U.S. Attorney.

the founding of the republic, there were no professional police departments to investigate wrongdoing, not enough lawyers or money to staff even the judiciary, and most crimes in most places were relatively straightforward affairs. So if victims wanted to use the process to redress the wrongs against them, they needed to be self-starters, and sometimes brave as well.

There are many reasons why private control over criminal litigation gave way to public prosecution. In part, this development was a piece of a much larger phenomenon of growing professionalization (and bureaucratization) of criminal justice, a steady trend of the past 200 years. Police, judges, and prosecutors became full-time positions staffed by trained experts, leaving a diminished role for laypeople. Indeed, one might see the movement over the last two decades to protect the rights of crime victims, by giving them an official role in the plea negotiation or sentencing process, as a kind of rebellion against this professionalizing trend.

But two other reasons for the growth in power of professional prosecutors also deserve mention. The first is conceptual: Crime came to be seen, increasingly, not as a wrong to an individual victim but as a wrong to society as a whole. From this, it follows naturally that society's representative ought to act as the plaintiff, and ought to exercise the usual plaintiff's power of deciding whether to sue and what relief to seek. As Chief Justice Roberts has written, "Our entire criminal justice system is premised on the notion that a criminal prosecution pits the government against the governed, not one private citizen against another. . . . A basic step in organizing a civilized society is to take [the prosecution] sword out of private hands and turn it over to an organized government, acting on behalf of all the people." Robertson v. United States ex rel. Watson, 130 S. Ct. 2184, 2188, 2190 (2010) (Roberts, C.J., dissenting from dismissal of certiorari as improvidently granted).

The second reason is practical. Some modern crimes are so complex, and the trail of evidence so hard to follow, that only a full-time prosecutor can hope to devote the resources needed to uncover the wrongdoing. Just as important, in a world in which a large slice of criminal behavior creates no identifiable victim with an incentive to bring the criminal to justice, private prosecution might mean *no* prosecution. In 2008, for example, more than half of the federal criminal docket involved drug and immigration cases, two areas where private prosecutors would be hard to find.

Today, there is no dispute over the need for professional prosecutors, nor is there any serious question about the need for prosecutors to be vested with large amounts of discretion to manage their dockets — the size of the crime problem and institutional limits on the ability to process more cases require prioritizing scarce resources. Whether that discretion should be subject to some form of judicial oversight remains an important question, however, as the materials that follow show.

1. The Decision to Charge

INMATES OF ATTICA CORRECTIONAL FACILITY v. ROCKEFELLER

United States Court of Appeals for the Second Circuit
477 F.2d 375 (1973)

JUDGE MANSFIELD delivered the opinion of the court.

This appeal raises the question of whether the federal judiciary should, at the instance of victims, compel federal and state officials to investigate and prosecute persons who allegedly have violated certain federal and state criminal statutes. Plaintiffs in the purported class suit, which was commenced in the Southern District of New York against various state and federal officers, are certain present and former inmates of New York State's Attica Correctional Facility ("Attica"), the mother of an inmate who was killed when Attica was retaken after the inmate uprising in September 1971, and Arthur O. Eve, a New York State Assemblyman and member of the Subcommittee on Prisons. They appeal from an order of the district court, Lloyd F. MacMahon, Judge, dismissing their complaint. We affirm.

The complaint alleges that before, during, and after the prisoner revolt at and subsequent recapture of Attica in September 1971, which resulted in the killing of 32 inmates and the wounding of many others, the defendants, including the Governor of New York, the State Commissioner of Correctional Services, the Executive Deputy Commissioner of the State Department of Correctional Services, the Superintendent at Attica, and certain State Police, Corrections Officers, and other officials, either committed, conspired to commit, or aided and abetted in the commission of various crimes against the complaining inmates and members of the class they seek to represent. It is charged that the inmates were intentionally subjected to cruel and inhuman treatment prior to the inmate riot, that State Police, Troopers, and Correction Officers . . . intentionally killed some of the inmate victims without provocation during the recovery of Attica, that state officers . . . assaulted and beat prisoners after the prison had been successfully retaken and the prisoners had surrendered, . . . that personal property of the inmates was thereafter stolen or destroyed, and that medical assistance was maliciously denied to over 400 inmates wounded during the recovery of the prison.

The complaint further alleges that Robert E. Fischer, a Deputy State Attorney General specially appointed by the Governor . . . with a specially convened grand jury, to investigate crimes relating to the inmates' takeover of Attica and the resumption of control by the state authorities, . . . "has not investigated, nor does he intend to investigate, any crimes committed by state officers." . . .

With respect to the sole federal defendant, the United States Attorney for the Western District of New York, the complaint simply alleges that he has not arrested, investigated, or instituted prosecutions against any of the state officers accused of criminal violation of plaintiffs' federal civil rights, 18 U.S.C. §§241, 242, and he has thereby failed to carry out the duty placed upon him by 42 U.S.C. §1987, discussed below.

As a remedy for the asserted failure of the defendants to prosecute violations of state and federal criminal laws, plaintiffs request relief in the nature of mandamus (1) against state officials, requiring the State of New York to submit a plan for the independent and impartial investigation and prosecution of the offenses charged against the named and unknown state officers, and insuring the appointment of an impartial state prosecutor and state judge to "prosecute the defendants forthwith," and (2) against the United States Attorney, requiring him to investigate, arrest and prosecute the same state officers for having committed the federal offenses defined by 18 U.S.C. §§241 and 242. The latter statutes punish, respectively, conspiracies against a citizen's free exercise or enjoyment of rights secured by the Constitution and laws of the United States, . . . and the willful subjection of any inhabitant, under color of law, to the deprivation of such rights or to different punishment or penalties on account of alienage, color, or race than are prescribed for the punishment of citizens. . . .

The motions of the federal and state defendants to dismiss the complaint for failure to state claims upon which relief can be granted . . . were granted by Judge MacMahon without opinion. We agree that the extraordinary relief sought cannot be granted in the situation here presented. . . .

With respect to the defendant United States Attorney, plaintiffs seek mandamus to compel him to investigate and institute prosecutions against state officers, most of whom are not identified, for alleged violations of 18 U.S.C. §§241 and 242. Federal mandamus is, of course, available only "to compel an officer or employee of the United States . . . to perform a duty owed to the plaintiff." 28 U.S.C. §1361. And the legislative history of §1361 makes it clear that ordinarily the courts are "not to direct or influence the exercise of discretion of the officer or agency in the making of the decision," United States ex rel. Schonbrun v. Commanding Officer, 403 F.2d 371, 374 (2d Cir. 1968). More particularly, federal courts have traditionally and, to our knowledge, uniformly refrained from overturning, at the instance of a private person, discretionary decisions of federal prosecuting authorities not to prosecute persons regarding whom a complaint of criminal conduct is made. [There follows a long string of case citations.]

This judicial reluctance to direct federal prosecutions at the instance of a private party asserting the failure of United States officials to prosecute alleged criminal violations has been applied even in cases such as the present one where, according to the allegations of the complaint, which we must accept as true for purposes of this appeal, serious questions are raised as to the protection of the civil rights and physical security of a definable class of victims of crime and as to the fair administration of the criminal justice system. . . .

The primary ground upon which this traditional judicial aversion to compelling prosecutions has been based is the separation of powers doctrine.

> Although as a member of the bar, the attorney for the United States is an officer of the court, he is nevertheless an executive official of the Government, and it is as an officer of the executive department that he exercises a discretion as to whether or not there shall be a prosecution in a particular case. It follows, as an incident of the constitutional separation of powers, that the courts are not to interfere with the free exercise of the discretionary powers of the attorneys of the United States in their control over criminal prosecutions. United States v. Cox, 342 F.2d [167, 171 (5th Cir. 1965)].

. . . [In addition, in] the absence of statutorily defined standards governing reviewability, or regulatory or statutory policies of prosecution, the problems inherent in the task of supervising prosecutorial decisions do not lend themselves to resolution by the judiciary. The reviewing courts would be placed in the undesirable and injudicious posture of becoming "superprosecutors." In the normal case of review of executive acts of discretion, the administrative record is open, public and reviewable on the basis of what it contains. The decision not to prosecute, on the other hand, may be based upon the insufficiency of the available evidence, in which event the secrecy of the grand jury and of the prosecutor's file may serve to protect the accused's reputation from public damage based upon insufficient, improper, or even malicious charges. In camera review would not be meaningful without access by the complaining party to the evidence before the grand jury or U.S. Attorney. Such interference with the normal operations of criminal investigations, in turn, based solely upon allegations of criminal conduct, raises serious questions of potential abuse by persons seeking to have other persons prosecuted. Any person, merely by filing a complaint containing allegations in general terms (permitted by the Federal Rules) of unlawful failure to prosecute, could gain access to the prosecutor's file. . . .

Nor is it clear what the judiciary's role of supervision should be were it to undertake such a review. At what point would the prosecutor be entitled to call a halt to further investigation as unlikely to be productive? What evidentiary standard would be used to decide whether prosecution should be compelled? How much judgment would the United States Attorney be allowed? Would he be permitted to limit himself to a strong "test" case rather than pursue weaker cases? What collateral factors would be permissible bases for a decision not to prosecute, e.g., the pendency of another criminal proceeding elsewhere against the same parties? What sort of review should be available in cases like the present one where the conduct complained of allegedly violates state as well as federal laws? With limited personnel and facilities at his disposal, what priority would the prosecutor be required to give to cases in which investigation or prosecution was directed by the court?

These difficult questions engender serious doubts as to the judiciary's capacity to review and as to the problem of arbitrariness inherent in any judicial decision to order prosecution. On balance, we believe that substitution of a court's decision to compel prosecution for the U.S. Attorney's decision not to prosecute, even upon an abuse of discretion standard of review and even if limited to directing that a prosecution be undertaken in good faith, would be unwise.

Plaintiffs urge, however, that Congress withdrew the normal prosecutorial discretion for the kind of conduct alleged here by providing in 42 U.S.C. §1987[4] that the United States Attorneys are "authorized and required . . . to institute prosecutions against all persons violating any of the provisions of [18 U.S.C. §§241, 242]," and, therefore, that no barrier to a judicial directive to institute prosecutions remains. This contention must be rejected. The mandatory nature of the word "required" as it appears in §1987 is insufficient to evince a broad Congressional purpose to bar the exercise of executive discretion in the prosecution of federal civil rights crimes. . . .

With respect to the state defendants, plaintiffs also seek prosecution of named and unknown persons for the violation of state crimes. However, they have pointed to no statutory language even arguably creating any mandatory duty upon the state officials to bring such prosecutions. To the contrary, New York law reposes in its prosecutors a discretion to decide whether or not to prosecute in a given case, which is not subject to review in the state courts. . . . Yet the federal district court is asked to compel state prosecutions and appoint an "impartial" state prosecutor and state

---

4. §1987. Prosecution of violation of certain laws

The United States attorneys, marshals, and deputy marshals, the commissioners appointed by the district and territorial courts, with power to arrest, imprison, or bail offenders, and every other officer who is especially empowered by the President, are authorized and required, at the expense of the United States, to institute prosecutions against all persons violating any of the provisions of section 1990 of this title or of sections 5506 to 5516 and 5518 to 5532 of the Revised Statutes, and to cause such persons to be arrested, and imprisoned or bailed, for trial before the court of the United States or the territorial court having cognizance of the offense.

judge to conduct them, as well as to require the submission of a plan for impartial investigation and prosecution of the alleged offenses, . . . in the context of a continuing grand jury investigation into criminal conduct connected with the Attica uprising, and where the state itself on September 30, 1971, appointed a Special Commission on Attica which has now published its findings. The very elaborateness of the relief believed by plaintiffs to be required indicates the difficulties inherent in judicial supervision of prosecutions, federal or state, which render such a course inadvisable. . . .

The order of the district court is affirmed.

NOTES AND QUESTIONS

1. Few cases squarely address the legal issue in *Inmates of Attica*, in large part because the position the Second Circuit took is so well settled that few litigants bother to challenge it. Why is this so? Is it really self-evident, as the opinion suggests, that judges could not feasibly decide whether a given decision not to charge was fair?

The United States Attorney's Manual advises federal prosecutors that among the grounds for declining to file criminal charges is that "no substantial Federal interest would be served by prosecution." In assessing the federal interest in a case, the U.S. Attorney is to "weigh all relevant considerations, including: (1) Federal law enforcement priorities; (2) The nature and seriousness of the offense; (3) The deterrent effect of prosecution; (4) The person's culpability in connection with the offense; (5) The person's history with respect to criminal activity; (6) The person's willingness to cooperate in the investigation or prosecution of others; and (7) The probable sentence or other consequences if the person is convicted." U.S. Attorney's Manual §9-27.230.

How difficult would it be for a judge to evaluate these considerations? Note that courts now routinely review the decisions of administrative agencies, whose rulings often turn on highly technical and scientific evidence, as well as on the feasibility of the remedy and the opportunity costs of choosing one course of action over another. And while judicial review of administrative decisions is highly deferential, recall that *Inmates of Attica* rejected the notion of *any* such oversight, including a judicial check to ensure that prosecutors have made their decisions in good faith.

2. Suppose you were a chief prosecutor in the *Inmates of Attica* case, and one of your assistants made the following argument: "Any prosecution of the prison guards will very likely lead to an acquittal, because no upstate New York jury will convict prison guards for violence against prisoners who had already killed a guard. So any prosecution would be a waste of the taxpayers' money and the resources of this office." If you believed that the guards had in fact committed crimes and thought that you had enough evidence to prove it, would this risk of "jury nullification"—where the jury acquits despite its belief that the defendant committed the crime—influence your decision to prosecute? Should it? Would it matter if you were elected to your office rather than appointed? On the federal side, the U.S. Attorney's Manual provides: "The potential that—despite the law and the facts that create a sound, prosecutable case—the factfinder is likely to acquit the defendant because of the unpopularity of some factor involved in the prosecution or because of the overwhelming popularity of the defendant or his/her cause, is not a

factor prohibiting prosecution." §9-27.220 Comment. Notice that the U.S. Attorney's Manual does not say that the risk of nullification *may* not be considered; it only says that the risk does not prohibit a prosecution.

3. The separation of powers concerns that animated *Inmates of Attica* is more than a limit on the judicial power over the charging decision. Occasionally, a grand jury — the panel of citizens charged with reviewing the government's evidence and deciding if it is sufficient to proceed with a criminal charge (see Chapter 10) — will vote to return an indictment that the prosecutor believes is unjustified or unwise. The question then becomes whether the prosecutor must comply with the wishes of the grand jury and move the case forward, or whether she can ignore the grand jury and refuse to prosecute. Although the Supreme Court has observed that the grand jury "has not been textually assigned . . . to any of the branches described in the first three Articles" of the Constitution and is thus "a constitutional fixture in its own right," United States v. Williams, 504 U.S. 36, 47 (1992), courts have consistently refused to intervene and require the prosecutor to follow the grand jury's wishes. Stated differently, it now seems settled that neither the grand jury nor a court can compel a federal prosecutor to sign and return an indictment against her wishes. See United States v. Cox, 342 F.2d 167, 171 (5th Cir. 1965).

4. Separation of powers is not the only doctrine that prevents judicial review of charging decisions. A second obstacle is standing. As the Supreme Court put it in Linda R. S. v. Richard D., 410 U.S. 614, 619 (1973), ordinarily "a private citizen lacks a judicially cognizable interest in the prosecution or nonprosecution of another." See also Allen v. Wright, 468 U.S. 737 (1984) (applying this principle to bar a suit by black parents seeking to force the Internal Revenue Service to revoke the tax-exempt status of allegedly discriminatory private schools). On this theory, *no one* can challenge a decision not to prosecute because, by definition, no one is harmed by such a decision. Does that position make sense? Are crime victims really uninjured by decisions not to charge their injurers? In a part of the opinion not excerpted above, the court of appeals in *Inmates of Attica* noted that standing was at least problematic in that case, but it did not resolve the issue.

5. The lack of judicial oversight of charging decisions does not mean that these decisions are free from all scrutiny. Consider the following passage by Justice Scalia in Morrison v. Olson, 487 U.S. 654 (1988), a case challenging the constitutionality of the appointment of independent counsels:

> Under our system of government, the primary check against prosecutorial abuse is a political one. The prosecutors who exercise this awesome discretion are selected and can be removed by a President, whom the people have trusted enough to elect. Moreover, when crimes are not investigated and prosecuted fairly, nonselectively, with a reasonable sense of proportion, the President pays the cost in political damage to his administration. If federal prosecutors "pick people that [they think they] should get, rather than cases that need to be prosecuted," if they amass many more resources against a particular prominent individual, or against a particular class of political protesters, or against members of a particular political party, than the gravity of the alleged offenses or the record of successful prosecutions seems to warrant, the unfairness will come home to roost in the Oval Office. . . . That result, of course, was precisely what the Founders had in mind when they provided that all executive powers would be exercised by a *single* Chief Executive. . . . The President is directly dependent on the people, and since there is only *one* President, *he* is responsible. The people know whom to blame. . . .

Id., at 729-730 (Scalia, J., dissenting). Political checks are plainly a serious constraint on local district attorneys, who must run for election every few years. Are you persuaded that the political process also restrains appointed federal prosecutors?

2.   Selecting the Charge

Beyond the decision of whether to file charges, prosecutors also have broad authority to decide which charges to file. Criminal statutes are sometimes written in expansive language, with the result that a defendant's alleged behavior often meets the definition of more than one offense. Whether a prosecutor is free to decide whether to charge certain conduct as a more serious crime or the less serious crime is a matter of great strategic and systemic significance. As will been seen in Chapter 13, on guilty pleas, the unchecked ability to charge a defendant with a greater or lesser offense can give the government enormous leverage over the defendant during the plea bargaining process. The authority to charge identical conduct as a greater or lesser offense also raises concerns about unequal treatment of similarly situated defendants. Consider the Supreme Court's response to a defendant who challenged the prosecutor's exercise of the charge selection power.

UNITED STATES v. BATCHELDER

Certiorari to the United States Court of Appeals for the Seventh Circuit
442 U.S. 114 (1979)

MR. JUSTICE MARSHALL delivered the opinion of the Court.

At issue in this case are two overlapping provisions of the Omnibus Crime Control and Safe Streets Act of 1968 (Omnibus Act). Both prohibit convicted felons from receiving firearms, but each authorizes different maximum penalties. We must determine whether a defendant convicted of the offense carrying the greater penalty may be sentenced only under the more lenient provision when his conduct violates both statutes.

I

Respondent, a previously convicted felon, was found guilty of receiving a firearm that had traveled in interstate commerce, in violation of 18 U.S.C. §922(h).[2] The

___

2. In pertinent part, 18 U.S.C. §922(h) provides:

It shall be unlawful for any person —

(1) who is under indictment for, or who has been convicted in any court of, a crime punishable by imprisonment for a term exceeding one year;

(2) who is a fugitive from justice;

(3) who is an unlawful user of or addicted to marihuana or any depressant or stimulant drug . . . or narcotic drug . . . ; or

(4) who has been adjudicated as a mental defective or who has been committed to any mental institution;

to receive any firearm or ammunition which has been shipped or transported in interstate or foreign commerce.

District Court sentenced him under 18 U.S.C. §924(a) to five years' imprisonment, the maximum term authorized for violation of §922(h).[3]

The Court of Appeals affirmed the conviction but, by a divided vote, remanded for resentencing. The majority recognized that respondent had been indicted and convicted under §922(h) and that §924(a) permits five years' imprisonment for such violations. However, noting that the substantive elements of §922(h) and 18 U.S.C. App. §1202(a) are identical as applied to a convicted felon who unlawfully receives a firearm, the court interpreted the Omnibus Act to allow no more than the 2-year maximum sentence provided by §1202(a).[4] In so holding, the Court of Appeals relied on three principles of statutory construction. Because, in its view, the "arguably contradict[ory]" penalty provisions for similar conduct and the "inconclusive" legislative history raised doubt whether Congress had intended the two penalty provisions to coexist, the court first applied the doctrine that ambiguities in criminal legislation are to be resolved in favor of the defendant. Second, the court determined that since §1202(a) was "Congress' last word on the issue of penalty," it may have implicitly repealed the punishment provisions of §924(a). Acknowledging that the "first two principles cannot be applied to these facts without some difficulty," the majority also invoked the maxim that a court should, if possible, interpret a statute to avoid constitutional questions. Here, the court reasoned, the "prosecutor's power to select one of two statutes that are identical except for their penalty provisions" implicated "important constitutional protections."

We granted certiorari, and now reverse the judgment vacating respondent's 5-year prison sentence.

II

This Court has previously noted the partial redundancy of §§922(h) and 1202(a), both as to the conduct they proscribe and the individuals they reach. See United States v. Bass, 404 U.S. 336, 341-343, and n. 9 (1971). However, we find nothing in the language, structure, or legislative history of the Omnibus Act to suggest that because of this overlap, a defendant convicted under §922(h) may be imprisoned for no more than the maximum term specified in §1202(a). As we read the Act, each substantive statute, in conjunction with its own sentencing provision, operates independently of the other.

---

3. Title 18 U.S.C. §924(a) provides in relevant part:

Whoever violates any provision of this chapter . . . shall be fined not more than $5,000, or imprisoned not more than five years, or both, and shall become eligible for parole as the Board of Parole shall determine.

4. Section 1202(a) states:

Any person who—
    (1) has been convicted by a court of the United States or of a State or any political subdivision thereof of a felony, . . . or
    (2) has been discharged from the Armed Forces under dishonorable conditions, or
    (3) has been adjudged by a court of the United States or of a State or any political subdivision thereof of being mentally incompetent, or
    (4) having been a citizen of the United States has renounced his citizenship, or
    (5) being an alien is illegally or unlawfully in the United States,
and who receives, possesses, or transports in commerce or affecting commerce, after the date of enactment of this Act, any firearm shall be fined not more than $10,000 or imprisoned for not more than two years, or both.

While §§922 and 1202(a) both prohibit convicted felons such as petitioner from receiving firearms, each Title unambiguously specifies the penalties available to enforce its substantive proscriptions. Section 924(a) applies without exception to "[w]hoever violates any provision" of Title IV, and §922(h) is patently such a provision. See 18 U.S.C., ch. 44. Similarly, because Title VII's substantive prohibitions and penalties are both enumerated in §1202, its penalty scheme encompasses only criminal prosecutions brought under that provision. On their face, these statutes thus establish that §924(a) alone delimits the appropriate punishment for violations of §922(h).

In construing §1202(a) to override the penalties authorized by §924(a), the Court of Appeals relied, we believe erroneously, on three principles of statutory interpretation. First, the court invoked the well-established doctrine that ambiguities in criminal statutes must be resolved in favor of lenity. Although this principle of construction applies to sentencing as well as substantive provisions, in the instant case there is no ambiguity to resolve. Respondent unquestionably violated §922(h), and §924(a) unquestionably permits five years' imprisonment for such a violation. That §1202(a) provides different penalties for essentially the same conduct is no justification for taking liberties with unequivocal statutory language.

Nor can §1202(a) be interpreted as implicitly repealing §924(a) whenever a defendant's conduct might violate both Titles. For it is "not enough to show that the two statutes produce differing results when applied to the same factual situation." *Radzanower v. Touche Ross & Co.*, 426 U.S. 148, 155 (1976). Rather, the legislative intent to repeal must be manifest in the "positive repugnancy between the provisions." *United States v. Borden Co.*, 308 U.S. 188 (1939). In this case, however, the penalty provisions are fully capable of coexisting because they apply to convictions under different statutes.

Finally, the maxim that statutes should be construed to avoid constitutional questions offers no assistance here. This "'cardinal principle' of statutory construction . . . is appropriate only when [an alternative interpretation] is 'fairly possible'" from the language of the statute. *Swain v. Pressley*, 430 U.S. 372, 378, n. 11 (1977). We simply are unable to discern any basis in the Omnibus Act for reading the term "five" in §924(a) to mean "two."

III

In resolving the statutory question, the majority below expressed "serious doubts about the constitutionality of two statutes that provide different penalties for identical conduct." Specifically, the court suggested that the statutes might (1) be void for vagueness, (2) implicate "due process and equal protection interest[s] in avoiding excessive prosecutorial discretion and in obtaining equal justice," and (3) constitute an impermissible delegation of congressional authority. We find no constitutional infirmities.

A

It is a fundamental tenet of due process that "[n]o one may be required at peril of life, liberty or property to speculate as to the meaning of penal statutes." *Lanzetta v. New Jersey*, 306 U.S. 451, 453 (1939). A criminal statute is therefore invalid if it "fails to give a person of ordinary intelligence fair notice that his contemplated conduct is forbidden." United States v. Harriss, 347 U.S. 612, 617 (1954). So too, vague sentencing provisions may post constitutional questions if they do not state with sufficient clarity the consequences of violating a given criminal statute. See United States v. Evans, 333 U.S. 483 (1948).

The provisions in issue here, however, unambiguously specify the activity proscribed and the penalties available upon conviction. That this particular conduct may violate both Titles does not detract from the notice afforded by each. Although the statutes create uncertainty as to which crime may be charged and therefore what penalties may be imposed, they do so to no greater extent than would a single statute authorizing various alternative punishments. So long as overlapping criminal provisions clearly define the conduct prohibited and the punishment authorized, the notice requirements of the Due Process Clause are satisfied.

B

This Court has long recognized that when an act violates more than one criminal statute, the Government may prosecutes under either so long as it does not discriminate against any class of defendants. See United States v. Beacon Brass Co., 344 U.S. 43, 45-46 (1952); Rosenberg v. United States, 346 U.S. 273, 294 (1953) (Clark, J., concurring, joined by five Members of the Court); Oyler v. Boles, 368 U.S. 448, 456 (1962); SEC v. National Securities, Inc., 393 U.S. 453, 468 (1969). Whether to prosecute and what charge to file or bring before a grand jury are decisions that generally rest in the prosecutor's discretion. See Confiscation Cases, 7 Wall. 454, 19 L. Ed. 196 (1869); United States v. Nixon, 418 U.S. 683, 693 (1974); Bordenkircher v. Hayes, 434 U.S. 357 (1978).

The Court of Appeals acknowledged this "settled rule" allowing prosecutorial choice. Nevertheless, relying on the dissenting opinion in Berra v. United States, 351 U.S. 131 (1956), the court distinguished overlapping statutes with identical standards of proof from provisions that vary in some particular. In the court's view, when two statutes prohibit "exactly the same conduct," the prosecutor's "selection of which of two penalties to apply" would be "unfettered." Because such prosecutorial discretion could produce "unequal justice," the court expressed doubt that this form of legislative redundancy was constitutional. We find this analysis factually and legally unsound.

Contrary to the Court of Appeals' assertions, a prosecutor's discretion to choose between §§922(h) and 1202(a) is not "unfettered." Selectivity in the enforcement of criminal laws is, of course, subject to constitutional constraints.[9] And a decision to proceed under §922(h) does not empower the Government to predetermine ultimate criminal sanctions. Rather, it merely enables the sentencing judge to impose a longer prison sentence than §1202(a) would permit and precludes him from imposing the greater fine authorized by §1202(a). More importantly, there is no appreciable difference between the discretion a prosecutor exercises when deciding whether to charge under one of two statutes with different elements and the discretion he exercises when choosing one of two statutes with identical elements. In the former situation, once he determines that the proof will support conviction under

___

9. The Equal Protection Clause prohibits selective enforcement "based upon an unjustifiable standard such as race, religion, or other arbitrary classification." Oyler v. Boles, 368 U.S. 448, 456 (1962). Respondent does not allege that his prosecution was motivated by improper considerations.

either statute, his decision is indistinguishable from the one he faces in the latter context. The prosecutor may be influenced by the penalties available upon conviction, but this fact, standing alone, does not give rise to a violation of the Equal Protection or Due Process Clause. Just as a defendant has no constitutional right to elect which of two applicable federal statutes shall be the basis of his indictment and prosecution neither is he entitled to choose the penalty scheme under which he will be sentenced.

Approaching the problem of prosecutorial discretion from a slightly different perspective, the Court of Appeals postulated that the statutes might impermissibly delegate to the Executive Branch the Legislature's responsibility to fix criminal penalties. We do not agree. The provisions at issue plainly demarcate the range of penalties that prosecutors and judges may seek and impose. In light of that specificity, the power that Congress has delegated to those officials is no broader than the authority they routinely exercise in enforcing the criminal laws. Having informed the courts, prosecutors, and defendants of the permissible punishment alternatives available under each Title, Congress has fulfilled its duty.

Accordingly, the judgment of the Court of Appeals is

Reversed.

NOTES AND QUESTIONS

1. Justice Marshall's unanimous opinion for the Court seems to say that Congress is free to pass two statutes that punish identical conduct while providing for different sentences on conviction. Traditionally, it has been up to the legislature to decide on the range and contours of the sentence, and up to the judge to choose a more precise sentence within these limits. Doesn't *Batchelder* now give the prosecutor control over the potential sentencing range, at least in some cases? If so, on what basis should the prosecutor select a charge?

2. As the Court acknowledges in footnote 9, the prosecutor's charge-selecting power is still subject to the equal protection clause. Just as important, it is also subject to the Double Jeopardy Clause of the Fifth Amendment. A prosecutor may not, for example, spread several criminal charges over a series of trials if the crimes are related in a way that would make a second trial a relitigation of issues decided in the first trial. Thus, where a defendant is accused of robbing six men at a single poker game and the prosecution elected to hold six separate trials, an acquittal at the first trial precluded any further trials, because the first jury has already determined that the defendant was not guilty of robbing the poker players. See Ashe v. Swenson, 397 U.S. 436 (1970), which is discussed in detail in Chapter 16.

3. The prosecutor's broad authority over the selection of charges can create similar double jeopardy risks in drafting the indictment. A prosecutor might, for example, spread a single criminal charge over several counts in the indictment — charging a defendant who engaged in one fight with one person with simple assault, aggravated assault, assault with a deadly weapon, and assault with intent to kill. This is "multiplicitous" charging, and it creates a risk that a defendant will be punished more than once for a single crime.

A related but distinct problem occurs when a prosecutor charges multiple crimes in a single count of the indictment — charging a defendant with robbing two separate stores in a one-count indictment, for example. This is a "duplicitous" indictment, and it can harm the defendant because there is no way for the jury to convict of one count of robbery and acquit on another. A general verdict of guilt makes it appear (falsely) that the jury convicted on both, which can then prejudice the defendant at sentencing and on appeal.

Neither duplicity nor multiplicity is necessarily fatal to an indictment, but a court may require the government to choose a single criminal charge that is the basis of the prosecution and then tailor the evidence and jury instructions accordingly.

B. Limits on the Charging Power

Although the prosecutor's charging authority is extremely broad, it is not unlimited. The clearest restriction is that the government may not base its charging decision on race, ethnicity, political affiliation, or other constitutionally protected factors. But while this general point is obvious and uncontroversial, challenges to prosecutorial decision making on these grounds face significant practical and legal barriers.

Judge Mansfield's opinion in *Inmates of Attica* doesn't talk much about it, but race played a large role in that case. At the time of the riot, all but two members of the 500-plus-person prison staff were white, while more than 60 percent of the prisoners were black. See Leo Carroll, Race, Ethnicity and the Social Order of the Prison in The Pains of Imprisonment 184 (Robert Johnson & Hans Toch eds. 1982). Black prisoners believed, with reason, that white guards treated them with special brutality. Anger at such treatment was one of the causes of the prisoners' riot. The guards were angry too: During the riot itself, a number of guards were taken prisoner, several were physically abused, and one was killed. The extreme violence with which the prison was retaken was, in part, a response to the violence of the prisoners' takeover. And that response had a racial cast.

Claims like this sound in equal protection, and require, among other things, proof that the prosecutor engaged in intentional discrimination by consciously treating blacks and whites differently. Not surprisingly, evidence of official intent is hard for defendants to gather. In a related context, the Supreme Court rejected an argument that intentional discrimination can be inferred from a sophisticated statistical study that showed racial bias in the imposition of the death penalty, where the bias was correlated to the race of the murder victim. The Court noted that "Implementation of [the state's homicide] laws necessarily requires discretionary judgments. Because discretion is essential to the criminal justice process, we would demand exceptionally clear proof before we would infer that the discretion has been abused." The Court concluded that the statistical results were not the type "exceptionally clear proof" needed to create an inference of intentional discrimination. McCleskey v. Kemp, 481 U.S. 279 (1987).

A defendant who claims that the charges against him are tainted by racial considerations is raising a "selective prosecution" challenge. A person raising such a challenge has the usual problems of proving intentional discrimination, but as the next case shows, he also has the related problem of gaining access to the information needed to prove the claim or, at least, to shift the burden to the government to justify the charges.

UNITED STATES v. ARMSTRONG

Certiorari to the United States Court of Appeals for the Ninth Circuit
517 U.S. 456 (1996)

CHIEF JUSTICE REHNQUIST delivered the opinion of the Court.

In this case, we consider the showing necessary for a defendant to be entitled to discovery on a claim that the prosecuting attorney singled him out for prosecution on the basis of his race. We conclude that respondents failed to satisfy the threshold showing: They failed to show that the Government declined to prosecute similarly situated suspects of other races.

In April 1992, respondents were indicted in the United States District Court for the Central District of California on charges of conspiring to possess with intent to distribute more than 50 grams of cocaine base (crack) and conspiring to distribute the same, in violation of 21 U.S.C. §§841 and 846, and federal firearms offenses. For three months prior to the indictment, agents of the Federal Bureau of Alcohol, Tobacco, and Firearms and the Narcotics Division of the Inglewood, California, Police Department had infiltrated a suspected crack distribution ring by using three confidential informants. On seven separate occasions during this period, the informants had bought a total of 124.3 grams of crack from respondents and witnessed respondents carrying firearms during the sales. The agents searched the hotel room in which the sales were transacted, arrested respondents Armstrong and Hampton in the room, and found more crack and a loaded gun. The agents later arrested the other respondents as part of the ring.

In response to the indictment, respondents filed a motion for discovery or for dismissal of the indictment, alleging that they were selected for federal prosecution because they are black. In support of their motion, they offered only an affidavit by a "Paralegal Specialist," employed by the Office of the Federal Public Defender representing one of the respondents. The only allegation in the affidavit was that, in every one of the 24 §§841 or 846 cases closed by the office during 1991, the defendant was black. Accompanying the affidavit was a "study" listing the 24 defendants, their race, whether they were prosecuted for dealing cocaine as well as crack, and the status of each case.

The Government opposed the discovery motion, arguing, among other things, that there was no evidence or allegation "that the Government has acted unfairly or has prosecuted non-black defendants or failed to prosecute them." App. 150. The District Court granted the motion. It ordered the Government (1) to provide a list of all cases from the last three years in which the Government charged both cocaine and firearms offenses, (2) to identify the race of the defendants in those cases, (3) to identify what levels of law enforcement were involved in the investigations of those cases, and (4) to explain its criteria for deciding to prosecute those defendants for federal cocaine offenses.

The Government moved for reconsideration of the District Court's discovery order. With this motion it submitted affidavits and other evidence to explain why it had chosen to prosecute respondents and why respondents' study did not support the inference that the Government was singling out blacks for cocaine prosecution. The federal and local agents participating in the case alleged in affidavits that race played no role in their investigation. An Assistant United States Attorney explained in an affidavit that the decision to prosecute met the general criteria for prosecution, because there was over 100 grams of cocaine base involved, over twice the threshold necessary for a ten year mandatory minimum sentence; there were multiple sales involving multiple defendants, thereby indicating a fairly substantial crack cocaine ring; . . . there were multiple federal firearms violations intertwined with the narcotics trafficking; the overall evidence in the case was extremely strong, including audio and videotapes of defendants; . . . and several of the defendants had criminal histories including narcotics and firearms violations. Id., at 81.

The Government also submitted sections of a published 1989 Drug Enforcement Administration report which concluded that "large-scale, interstate trafficking networks controlled by Jamaicans, Haitians and Black street gangs dominate the manufacture and distribution of crack." J. Featherly & E. Hill, Crack Cocaine Overview 1989; App. 103.

In response, one of respondents' attorneys submitted an affidavit alleging that an intake coordinator at a drug treatment center had told her that there are "an equal number of caucasian users and dealers to minority users and dealers." Id., at 138. Respondents also submitted an affidavit from a criminal defense attorney alleging that in his experience many nonblacks are prosecuted in state court for crack offenses, id., at 141, and a newspaper article reporting that Federal "crack criminals . . . are being punished far more severely than if they had been caught with powder cocaine, and almost every single one of them is black," Newton, Harsher Crack Sentences Criticized as Racial Inequity, Los Angeles Times, Nov. 23, 1992, p. 1.

The District Court denied the motion for reconsideration. When the Government indicated it would not comply with the court's discovery order, the court dismissed the case.[2]

A divided three-judge panel of the Court of Appeals for the Ninth Circuit reversed, holding that, because of the proof requirements for a selective-prosecution claim, defendants must "provide a colorable basis for believing that 'others similarly situated have not been prosecuted'" to obtain discovery. 21 F.3d 1431, 1436 (1994) (quoting United States v. Wayte, 710 F.2d 1385, 1387 (CA9 1983), aff'd, 470 U.S. 598 (1985)). The Court of Appeals voted to rehear the case en banc, and the en banc panel affirmed the District Court's order of dismissal, holding that "a defendant is not required to demonstrate that the government has failed to prosecute others who are similarly situated." 48 F.3d 1508, 1516 (1995) (emphasis deleted). We granted certiorari to determine the appropriate standard for discovery for a selective-prosecution claim. . . .

A selective-prosecution claim is not a defense on the merits to the criminal charge itself, but an independent assertion that the prosecutor has brought the charge for reasons forbidden by the Constitution. Our cases delineating the necessary elements to prove a claim of selective prosecution have taken great pains to explain that the standard is a demanding one. . . .

A selective-prosecution claim asks a court to exercise judicial power over a "special province" of the Executive. Heckler v. Chaney, 470 U.S. 821, 832 (1985). The Attorney General and United States Attorneys retain "broad discretion" to enforce

---

2. We have never determined whether dismissal of the indictment, or some other sanction, is the proper remedy if a court determines that a defendant has been the victim of prosecution on the basis of his race. Here, "it was the government itself that suggested dismissal of the indictments to the district court so that an appeal might lie." 48 F.3d 1508, 1510 (CA9 1995).

the Nation's criminal laws. Wayte v. United States, 470 U.S. 598, 607 (1985). They have this latitude because they are designated by statute as the President's delegates to help him discharge his constitutional responsibility to "take Care that the Laws be faithfully executed." U.S. Const., Art. II, §3; see 28 U.S.C. §§516, 547. As a result, "the presumption of regularity supports" their prosecutorial decisions and "in the absence of clear evidence to the contrary, courts presume that they have properly discharged their official duties." United States v. Chemical Foundation, 272 U.S. 1, 14-15 (1926). In the ordinary case, "so long as the prosecutor has probable cause to believe that the accused committed an offense defined by statute, the decision whether or not to prosecute, and what charge to file or bring before a grand jury, generally rests entirely in his discretion." Bordenkircher v. Hayes, 434 U.S. 357, 364 (1978).

Of course, a prosecutor's discretion is "subject to constitutional constraints." United States v. Batchelder, 442 U.S. 114, 125 (1979). One of these constraints, imposed by the equal protection component of the Due Process Clause of the Fifth Amendment, is that the decision whether to prosecute may not be based on "an unjustifiable standard such as race, religion, or other arbitrary classification," Oyler v. Boles, 368 U.S. 448, 456 (1962). A defendant may demonstrate that the administration of a criminal law is "directed so exclusively against a particular class of persons . . . with a mind so unequal and oppressive" that the system of prosecution amounts to "a practical denial" of equal protection of the law. Yick Wo v. Hopkins, 118 U.S. 356, 373 (1886).

In order to dispel the presumption that a prosecutor has not violated equal protection, a criminal defendant must present "clear evidence to the contrary." *Chemical Foundation*, supra, at 14-15. We explained in *Wayte* why courts are "properly hesitant to examine the decision whether to prosecute." 470 U.S. at 608. Judicial deference to the decisions of these executive officers rests in part on an assessment of the relative competence of prosecutors and courts. "Such factors as the strength of the case, the prosecution's general deterrence value, the Government's enforcement priorities, and the case's relationship to the Government's overall enforcement plan are not readily susceptible to the kind of analysis the courts are competent to undertake." Id., at 607. It also stems from a concern not to unnecessarily impair the performance of a core executive constitutional function. "Examining the basis of a prosecution delays the criminal proceeding, threatens to chill law enforcement by subjecting the prosecutor's motives and decisionmaking to outside inquiry, and may undermine prosecutorial effectiveness by revealing the Government's enforcement policy." Ibid.

The requirements for a selective-prosecution claim draw on "ordinary equal protection standards." Id., at 608. The claimant must demonstrate that the federal prosecutorial policy "had a discriminatory effect and that it was motivated by a discriminatory purpose." Ibid. To establish a discriminatory effect in a race case, the claimant must show that similarly situated individuals of a different race were not prosecuted. This requirement has been established in our case law since Ah Sin v. Wittman, 198 U.S. 500 (1905). Ah Sin, a subject of China, petitioned a California state court for a writ of habeas corpus, seeking discharge from imprisonment under a San Francisco county ordinance prohibiting persons from setting up gambling tables in rooms barricaded to stop police from entering. Id., at 503. He alleged in his habeas petition "that the ordinance is enforced 'solely and exclusively against persons of the Chinese race and not otherwise.'" Id., at 507. We rejected his contention that this averment made out a claim under the Equal Protection Clause, because it did not allege "that the conditions and practices to which the ordinance was directed did not exist exclusively among the Chinese, or that there were other offenders against the ordinance than the Chinese as to whom it was not enforced." Id., at 507-508.

The similarly situated requirement does not make a selective-prosecution claim impossible to prove. Twenty years before *Ah Sin*, we invalidated an ordinance, also adopted by San Francisco, that prohibited the operation of laundries in wooden buildings. *Yick Wo*, 118 U.S. at 374. The plaintiff in error successfully demonstrated that the ordinance was applied against Chinese nationals but not against other laundry-shop operators. The authorities had denied the applications of 200 Chinese subjects for permits to operate shops in wooden buildings, but granted the applications of 80 individuals who were not Chinese subjects to operate laundries in wooden buildings "under similar conditions." Ibid.

Having reviewed the requirements to prove a selective-prosecution claim, we turn to the showing necessary to obtain discovery in support of such a claim. If discovery is ordered, the Government must assemble from its own files documents which might corroborate or refute the defendant's claim. Discovery thus imposes many of the costs present when the Government must respond to a prima facie case of selective prosecution. It will divert prosecutors' resources and may disclose the Government's prosecutorial strategy. The justifications for a rigorous standard for the elements of a selective-prosecution claim thus require a correspondingly rigorous standard for discovery in aid of such a claim.

The parties, and the Courts of Appeals which have considered the requisite showing to establish entitlement to discovery, describe this showing with a variety of phrases, like "colorable basis," "substantial threshold showing," "substantial and concrete basis," or "reasonable likelihood." However, the many labels for this showing conceal the degree of consensus about the evidence necessary to meet it. The Courts of Appeals "require some evidence tending to show the existence of the essential elements of the defense," discriminatory effect and discriminatory intent. United States v. Berrios, 501 F.2d 1207, 1211 (CA2 1974).

In this case we consider what evidence constitutes "some evidence tending to show the existence" of the discriminatory effect element. The Court of Appeals held that a defendant may establish a colorable basis for discriminatory effect without evidence that the Government has failed to prosecute others who are similarly situated to the defendant. 48 F.3d at 1516. We think it was mistaken in this view. The vast majority of the Courts of Appeals require the defendant to produce some evidence that similarly situated defendants of other races could have been prosecuted, but were not, and this requirement is consistent with our equal protection case law. . . .

The Court of Appeals reached its decision in part because it started "with the presumption that people of all races commit all types of crimes — not with the premise that any type of crime is the exclusive province of any particular racial or ethnic group." 48 F.3d at 1516-1517. It cited no authority for this proposition, which seems contradicted by the most recent statistics of the United States Sentencing Commission. Those statistics show that: More than 90% of the persons sentenced in 1994 for crack cocaine trafficking were black, United States Sentencing Commn., 1994 Annual Report 107 (Table 45); 93.4% of convicted LSD dealers were white, ibid.;

and 91% of those convicted for pornography or prostitution were white, id., at 41 (Table 13). Presumptions at war with presumably reliable statistics have no proper place in the analysis of this issue.

The Court of Appeals also expressed concern about the "evidentiary obstacles defendants face." 48 F.3d at 1514. But . . . . respondents could have investigated whether similarly situated persons of other races were prosecuted by the State of California, were known to federal law enforcement officers, but were not prosecuted in federal court. We think the required threshold — a credible showing of different treatment of similarly situated persons — adequately balances the Government's interest in vigorous prosecution and the defendant's interest in avoiding selective prosecution.

In the case before us, respondents' "study" did not constitute "some evidence tending to show the existence of the essential elements of "a selective-prosecution claim. The study failed to identify individuals who were not black, could have been prosecuted for the offenses for which respondents were charged, but were not so prosecuted. This omission was not remedied by respondents' evidence in opposition to the Government's motion for reconsideration. The newspaper article, which discussed the discriminatory effect of federal drug sentencing laws, was not relevant to an allegation of discrimination in decisions to prosecute. Respondents' affidavits, which recounted one attorney's conversation with a drug treatment center employee and the experience of another attorney defending drug prosecutions in state court, recounted hearsay and reported personal conclusions based on anecdotal evidence. The judgment of the Court of Appeals is therefore reversed, and the case is remanded for proceedings consistent with this opinion.

[The concurring opinions of Justices Souter, Ginsburg, and Breyer are omitted.]

JUSTICE STEVENS, dissenting.

. . . The Court correctly concludes that in this case the facts presented to the District Court in support of respondents' claim that they had been singled out for prosecution because of their race were not sufficient to prove that defense. Moreover, I agree with the Court that their showing was not strong enough to give them a right to discovery . . . [H]owever, I am persuaded that the District Judge did not abuse her discretion when she concluded that the factual showing was sufficiently disturbing to require some response from the United States Attorney's Office. Perhaps the discovery order was broader than necessary, but I cannot agree with the Court's apparent conclusion that no inquiry was permissible.

The District Judge's order should be evaluated in light of three circumstances that underscore the need for judicial vigilance over certain types of drug prosecutions. First, the Anti-Drug Abuse Act of 1986 and subsequent legislation established a regime of extremely high penalties for the possession and distribution of so-called "crack" cocaine. Those provisions treat one gram of crack as the equivalent of 100 grams of powder cocaine. The distribution of 50 grams of crack is thus punishable by the same mandatory minimum sentence of 10 years in prison that applies to the distribution of 5,000 grams of powder cocaine. The Sentencing Guidelines extend this ratio to penalty levels above the mandatory minimums: for any given quantity of crack, the guideline range is the same as if the offense had involved 100 times that amount in powder cocaine. These penalties result in sentences for crack offenders that average three to eight times longer than sentences for comparable powder offenders.[4]

Second, the disparity between the treatment of crack cocaine and powder cocaine is matched by the disparity between the severity of the punishment imposed by federal law and that imposed by state law for the same conduct. For a variety of reasons, often including the absence of mandatory minimums, the existence of parole, and lower baseline penalties, terms of imprisonment for drug offenses tend to be substantially lower in state systems than in the federal system. The difference is especially marked in the case of crack offenses. The majority of States draw no distinction between types of cocaine in their penalty schemes; of those that do, none has established as stark a differential as the Federal Government. For example, if respondent Hampton is found guilty, his federal sentence might be as long as a mandatory life term. Had he been tried in state court, his sentence could have been as short as 12 years, less worktime credits of half that amount.

Finally, it is undisputed that the brunt of the elevated federal penalties falls heavily on blacks. While 65% of the persons who have used crack are white, in 1993 they represented only 4% of the federal offenders convicted of trafficking in crack. Eighty-eight percent of such defendants were black. [United States Sentencing Commission, Special Report to Congress: Cocaine and Federal Sentencing Policy 39, 161 (Feb. 1995)]. During the first 18 months of full guideline implementation, the sentencing disparity between black and white defendants grew from preguideline levels: blacks on average received sentences over 40% longer than whites. See Bureau of Justice Statistics, Sentencing in the Federal Courts: Does Race Matter? 6-7 (Dec. 1993). Those figures represent a major threat to the integrity of federal sentencing reform, whose main purpose was the elimination of disparity (especially racial) in sentencing. The Sentencing Commission acknowledges that the heightened crack penalties are a "primary cause of the growing disparity between sentences for Black and White federal defendants." Special Report 145. . . .

Respondents submitted a study showing that of all cases involving crack offenses that were closed by the Federal Public Defender's Office in 1991, 24 out of 24 involved black defendants. To supplement this evidence, they submitted affidavits from two of the attorneys in the defense team. The first reported a statement from an intake coordinator at a local drug treatment center that, in his experience, an equal number of crack users and dealers were caucasian as belonged to minorities. App. 138. The second was from David R. Reed, counsel for respondent Armstrong. Reed was both an active court-appointed attorney in the Central District of California and one of the directors of the leading association of criminal defense lawyers who practice before the Los Angeles County courts. Reed stated that he did not recall "ever handling a [crack] cocaine case involving non-black defendants" in federal court, nor had he even heard of one. Id., at 140. He further stated that "there are many crack cocaine sales cases prosecuted in state court that do involve racial groups other than blacks." Id., at 141. . . .

The criticism that the affidavits were based on "anecdotal evidence" is . . . unpersuasive. I thought it was agreed that defendants do not need to prepare sophisticated statistical studies in order to receive mere discovery in cases like this one.

---

4. Under the guidelines, penalties increase at a slower rate than drug quantities. For example, 5 grams of heroin result in a base offense level of 14 (15-21 months) while 10 grams of heroin (double the amount) result in an offense level of 16 (21-27 months). USSG §§2D1.1(c)(13), (12). Thus, the 100-to-1 ratio does not translate into sentences that are 100 times as long.

Certainly evidence based on a drug counselor's personal observations or on an attorney's practice in two sets of courts, state and federal, can "tend to show the existence" of a selective prosecution.

Even if respondents failed to carry their burden of showing that there were individuals who were not black but who could have been prosecuted in federal court for the same offenses, it does not follow that the District Court abused its discretion in ordering discovery. There can be no doubt that such individuals exist, and indeed the Government has never denied the same. In those circumstances, I fail to see why the District Court was unable to take judicial notice of this obvious fact and demand information from the Government's files to support or refute respondents' evidence. The presumption that some whites are prosecuted in state court is not "contradicted" by the statistics the majority cites, which show only that high percentages of blacks are convicted of certain federal crimes, while high percentages of whites are convicted of other federal crimes. Those figures are entirely consistent with the allegation of selective prosecution. The relevant comparison, rather, would be with the percentages of blacks and whites who commit those crimes. But, as discussed above, in the case of crack far greater numbers of whites are believed guilty of using the substance. The District Court, therefore, was entitled to find the evidence before her significant and to require some explanation from the Government.[6]

In sum, I agree with the Sentencing Commission that "while the exercise of discretion by prosecutors and investigators has an impact on sentences in almost all cases to some extent, because of the 100-to-1 quantity ratio and federal mandatory minimum penalties, discretionary decisions in cocaine cases often have dramatic effects." Special Report 138.[7] The severity of the penalty heightens both the danger of arbitrary enforcement and the need for careful scrutiny of any colorable claim of discriminatory enforcement. In this case, the evidence was sufficiently disturbing to persuade the District Judge to order discovery that might help explain the conspicuous racial pattern of cases before her Court. I cannot accept the majority's conclusion that the District Judge either exceeded her power or abused her discretion when she did so. I therefore respectfully dissent.

---

6. Also telling was the Government's response to respondents' evidentiary showing. It submitted a list of more than 3,500 defendants who had been charged with federal narcotics violations over the previous 3 years. It also offered the names of 11 nonblack defendants whom it had prosecuted for crack offenses. All 11, however, were members of other racial or ethnic minorities. See 48 F.3d at 1511. The District Court was authorized to draw adverse inferences from the Government's inability to produce a single example of a white defendant, especially when the very purpose of its exercise was to allay the Court's concerns about the evidence of racially selective prosecutions. As another court has said: "Statistics are not, of course, the whole answer, but nothing is as emphatic as zero. . . ." United States v. Hinds County School Bd., 417 F.2d 852, 858 (CA5 1969) (per curiam).

7. For this and other reasons, the Sentencing Commission in its Special Report to Congress "strongly recommended against a 100-to-1 quantity ratio." Special Report 198. The Commission shortly thereafter, by a 4-to-3 vote, amended the guidelines so as to equalize the treatment of crack and other forms of cocaine, and proposed modification of the statutory mandatory minimum penalties for crack offenses. See Statement of Commission Majority in Support of Recommended Changes in Cocaine and Federal Sentencing Policy (May 1, 1995). In October 1995, Congress overrode the Sentencing Commission's guideline amendments. See Pub. L. 104-38, 109 Stat. 334. Nevertheless, Congress at the same time directed the Commission to submit recommendations regarding changes to the statutory and guideline penalties for cocaine distribution, including specifically "revision of the drug quantity ratio of crack cocaine to powder cocaine." §2(a).

NOTES AND QUESTIONS

1. *Armstrong* purports to be solely about the standard for determining when defendants are entitled to discovery on a claim of discriminatory charging. But given the Court's ruling that a defendant must show that similarly situated white defendants could have been prosecuted, but were not, it would seem that obtaining discovery will be crucial in virtually every case like this.

If a defendant sets out to prove that similarly situated defendants have not been prosecuted, how many such cases should he have to identify? If the answer is one or two, perhaps *Armstrong* does not matter much. But if that is the answer, it is hard to understand why this threshold requirement is so important, as the Court seems to believe. Then again, if the answer for claims such as Armstrong's is a substantial number, how likely is it that any defendant will be able to satisfy the Court's requirement of a credible preliminary showing in order to obtain discovery?

Moreover, what must the defendant show about these suspects who weren't charged? Justice Stevens seems to assume that it would be enough to point to state cases in which whites were prosecuted on crack offenses, the theory being that federal authorities could have found out about and pursued those cases. But one might imagine a very different requirement: that federal authorities actually knew about a given (white) suspect, had a strong case against him, and consciously decided not to pursue charges against him. That would, presumably, be much harder to show.

2. Reread footnote 2 in the majority opinion. What is the right remedy for a claim such as Armstrong's, assuming the claim is successful? Dismissal of charges has an obvious advantage: It rewards successful claimants. If Armstrong can prove race discrimination and *fails* to get the charges against him dismissed, how many future victims of discriminatory prosecution will go to the trouble of making the claim? The likely answer is "none." But dismissal has an equally obvious disadvantage: Guilty defendants escape punishment because the prosecutor's office misbehaved.

The alternative is the remedy that was sought and rejected in *Inmates of Attica*: Compel prosecution of the white suspects who *weren't* prosecuted by the U.S. Attorney for the Central District of California. That remedy avoids giving guilty defendants a windfall, but it has all the disadvantages that troubled the court in *Inmates of Attica*. Time is a scarce commodity in prosecutors' offices, and most offices charge as many cases as they can handle. It follows that compelling prosecution in one case means, as a practical matter, precluding prosecution somewhere else.

Suppose courts do dismiss charges against successful discriminatory prosecution claimants. What then? Should all black defendants in crack cases have a right to dismissal until the Central District's U.S. Attorney prosecutes a given number of whites for crack violations?

3. Perhaps the prosecutorial patterns at issue in *Armstrong* are the consequence not of *prosecutors'* decisions, but of *police* decisions — choices made both by local police officers and by federal agents. As Daniel Richman has noted, police and prosecutors constitute what antitrust lawyers would call a "bilateral monopoly": Each must deal with the other, and neither side of this relationship can achieve its goals without the other side's cooperation. Daniel C. Richman, Prosecutors and Their Agents, Agents and Their Prosecutors, 103 Colum. L. Rev. 749 (2003). Prosecutors cannot prosecute unless the police bring them cases, and the police, who want to see their suspects punished, cannot make that happen without a decision to prosecute.

In some classes of federal criminal cases — including drug cases like the ones in *Armstrong* — the relationship is more complicated. Federal prosecutors ordinarily get their cases from federal agents. But many federal drug cases begin with an arrest by local police; the case is turned over to federal prosecutors because the local district attorney lacks needed manpower, or because the arrest arose out of a local-federal task force, or because local police are trying to play off one prosecutor's office against the other, or for a variety of other reasons. In these cases, the bilateral monopoly does not hold.

But for most cases, it *does* hold, which means that the biggest check on the power of prosecutors may be the police officers with whom they must deal — and vice versa. Note, in this connection, that prosecutors decline to prosecute a large fraction of the cases police officers bring them. The same dynamic is at work in federal cases, even when the crimes are the subject of intense public interest: Richman's article noted that in the six months after the terrorist attacks on September 11, 2001, federal prosecutors declined to prosecute 61 percent of the terrorism cases federal agents brought them. Id., at 765.

In short, one of the largest effects of the legal doctrine we see in *Inmates of Attica* and *Armstrong* is that no one, save the prosecutors, knows why they pursue the cases they pursue and decline the ones they decline. The decision to file criminal charges, or not, is one of the most important ways government officials exercise power. It is also one of the least transparent.

4. Both *Inmates of Attica* and *Armstrong* bear on the scope of prosecutors' power to decline to charge for crimes that are both very serious and frequently enforced. At times, however, the defendant may raise a selective prosecution claim when he is charged with a crime that is virtually never enforced — typically a less serious offense — even though the number of violations is quite large.

The Supreme Court considered such a challenge in Wayte v. United States, 470 U.S. 598 (1985), where a defendant was prosecuted for failing to register for the draft. Rather than register as the law required, the defendant wrote letters to various government officials, including the president, stating that he had not registered and did not plan to do so. Several other young men who were required to register wrote similar letters, and after the government made several unsuccessful efforts to persuade these men to change their minds, the defendant and others were indicted for violating the Selective Service laws. Although a total of 674,000 young men failed to register for the draft, only 16 had been indicted at the time of Wayte's trial, all of whom had communicated their refusal to register to the government.

Wayte claimed that the decision to prosecute him was based on his First Amendment right to express his views, as shown by the fact that those who failed to register but remained silent were not prosecuted. The Supreme Court disagreed. After reaffirming the principles of broad prosecutorial charging authority, the Court concluded that the defendant had failed to show that the government's charging decisions were motivated by an improper purpose of punishing the defendant for protesting the registration requirement. The most the defendant could show, said the Court, was

> that the Government was aware that the passive enforcement policy would result in prosecution of vocal objectors and that they [the protestors] would probably make selective prosecution claims. As we have noted, however: "Discriminatory purpose . . . implies more than . . . intent as awareness of consequences. It implies that the

decisionmaker . . . selected or reaffirmed a particular course of action at least in part 'because of,' not merely 'in spite of,' its adverse effects upon an identifiable group."

470 U.S., at 610 (quotation marks and citation omitted). The Court also rejected the defendant's separate First Amendment claim.

Wayte suggests that the law requires no minimum threshold level of enforcement of criminal statutes — even if there were only *one* prosecution, that one defendant could not complain about the government's decision to single him out unless the decision was made on the basis of race, sex, religious conviction, or some other protected criterion. Is that proposition sensible? Is there any strong constitutional argument against it?

5. Sometimes defendants challenge prosecutors' charging decisions not on the ground that those decisions were selectively discriminatory, but on the ground that they were "vindictive." Vindictiveness has a special meaning here: It is not simply prosecutorial hostility; rather, it is prosecution aimed at punishing the exercise of a constitutional right. For a time in the 1970s, it appeared that "vindictive prosecution" claims would be both common and successful. Today, they are rarely made and even more rarely succeed. It is worth understanding why that is so.

Begin with Blackledge v. Perry, 417 U.S. 21 (1974). Perry, a state prisoner, was charged with misdemeanor assault for an altercation with another prisoner. After a bench trial at which he was convicted, Perry appealed; under North Carolina law at the time, the appeal entitled Perry to a new trial in a different state court. Perry's prosecutor responded to the appeal by charging Perry with felony assault with intent to kill. The Supreme Court invalidated the felony charges, stating: "[T]he Due Process Clause is not offended by all possibilities of increased punishment upon retrial after appeal, but only by those that pose a realistic likelihood of 'vindictiveness.'" Id., at 27. The Court explained:

> . . . A prosecutor clearly has a considerable stake in discouraging convicted misdemeanants from appealing and thus obtaining a trial de novo in the Superior Court, since such an appeal will clearly require increased expenditures of prosecutorial resources before the defendant's conviction becomes final, and may even result in a formerly convicted defendant's going free. And, if the prosecutor has the means readily at hand to discourage such appeals — by "upping the ante" through a felony indictment whenever a convicted misdemeanant pursues his statutory appellate remedy — the State can insure that only the most hardy defendants will brave the hazards of a de novo trial.
>
> . . . A person convicted of an offense is entitled to pursue his statutory right to a trial de novo, without apprehension that the State will retaliate by substituting a more serious charge for the original one, thus subjecting him to a significantly increased potential period of incarceration.
>
> Due process of law requires that such a potential for vindictiveness must not enter into North Carolina's two-tiered appellate process. We hold, therefore, that it was not constitutionally permissible for the State to respond to Perry's invocation of his statutory right to appeal by bringing a more serious charge against him prior to the trial de novo.

Id., at 27-29. *Blackledge* established a presumption of vindictiveness, but it did not make clear the range of cases to which the presumption would apply.

Potentially, the range was huge. Millions of defendants have pled guilty to some criminal charges in exchange for a prosecutor's promise not to bring, or to drop, other criminal charges. After *Blackledge*, some of those defendants started to claim that this ordinary plea bargaining practice amounted to vindictive prosecution, since prosecutors' bargaining position amounted to a threat to punish the exercise of the defendants' right to trial. The Supreme Court rejected that argument in Bordenkircher v. Hayes, 434 U.S. 357 (1978). Hayes was indicted in Kentucky state court for "uttering a forged instrument in the amount of $88.30," a crime for which the permissible sentence was two to ten years in prison. The prosecutor offered him a plea bargain with a recommended five-year sentence. Hayes declined the offer, whereupon the prosecutor charged him under Kentucky's "three strikes" statute — Hayes had two prior felony convictions — which carried an automatic life sentence. Hayes was convicted and sentenced to life in prison, and he argued that this sentence was, in effect, a prosecutorial punishment for his exercise of his constitutional right to trial. The Supreme Court disagreed, in an opinion that emphasized prosecutors' power to add or withdraw charges as part of the plea bargaining process.

Four years after *Bordenkircher*, the Court curtailed vindictive prosecution claims even more sharply. The defendant in United States v. Goodwin, 457 U.S. 368 (1982), was charged with several misdemeanors and scheduled for trial before a magistrate. He invoked his right to a jury trial, whereupon the case was transferred to another prosecutor, who promptly added a felony charge. The defendant claimed that the felony charge amounted to punishment for his exercise of his right to a jury trial. The Court disagreed:

> . . . [A] presumption of vindictiveness is not warranted. A prosecutor should remain free before trial to exercise the broad discretion entrusted to him to determine the extent of the societal interest in prosecution. An initial decision should not freeze future conduct. As we made clear in *Bordenkircher*, the initial charges filed by a prosecutor may not reflect the extent to which an individual is legitimately subject to prosecution. . . .

Id., at 381-382. The Court concluded that "[t]he possibility" that the charges against Goodwin were "not in the public interest" but were instead designed as a penalty for the exercise of a constitutional right was "so unlikely that a presumption of vindictiveness certainly is not warranted." Id., at 384.

The bottom line after *Goodwin* is this: In cases that are factually on point with *Blackledge* — where a defendant is convicted, is legally entitled to a new trial and exercises that right, after which the same prosecutor adds a more serious charge — prosecutorial vindictiveness is presumed. In all other cases, the presumption is that the prosecutor acted in good faith, and the defendant has the burden of proving an improper motive. In practice, that burden is rarely met. Unless prosecutors announce their own impermissible motive, proving vindictiveness is basically impossible, which is why successful vindictiveness claims are now rare.

For a good discussion of the Supreme Court's vindictiveness cases and the lower court cases they spawned, see Note, Breathing New Life into Prosecutorial Vindictiveness Doctrine, 114 Harv. L. Rev. 2074, 2076-2080 (2001). For a strong argument that prosecutors do indeed punish defense litigation by filing more serious charges and/or seeking harsher sentences, see id., at 2080-2086.

6. Sometimes the charges filed by the prosecutor have little to do with the criminal conduct that gives rise to an investigation. The best-known example of these "pretext prosecutions" involved mob boss Al Capone, perhaps the most famous gangster in the country's history. Capone made most of his money through the sale of beer and liquor (those were illegal drugs in 1931), though he was also responsible for many other crimes, including several murders. But the federal agents who were busy trying to nail Capone couldn't prove those crimes in court. So they charged him with nonpayment of his income taxes. Capone was convicted and received the maximum sentence; he later died in prison. There are countless other examples: The owner of a nightclub where drugs are allegedly sold may be arrested for liquor law violations, or a CEO suspected of corporate fraud may be charged with lying to the FBI during the investigation if the more serious crimes are too difficult to prove.

Shortly after the terrorist attacks of September 11, 2001, then-Attorney General John Ashcroft praised that strategy and vowed to use it against suspected terrorists:

Attorney General [Robert] Kennedy made no apologies for using all of the available resources in the law to disrupt and dismantle organized crime networks. Very often, prosecutors were aggressive, using obscure statutes to arrest and detain suspected mobsters. One racketeer and his father were indicted for lying on a federal home loan application. A former gunman for the Capone mob was brought to court on a violation of the Migratory Bird Act. Agents found 563 game birds in his freezer — a mere 539 birds over the limit. . . .

The American people face a serious, immediate and ongoing threat from terrorism. At this moment, American service men and women are risking their lives to battle the enemy overseas. It falls to the men and women of Justice and law enforcement to engage terrorism at home. History's judgment will be harsh — and the people's judgment will be sure — if we fail to use every available resource to prevent future terrorist attacks.

Attorney General John Ashcroft, Prepared Remarks for the U.S. Mayors' Conference, Oct. 25, 2001 (available at http://www.justice.gov/archive/ag/speeches/2001/agcrisisremarks10_25.htm).

Is this good law enforcement policy for suspected terrorists? For suspected mobsters? For anyone?

7. Defendants in these pretext prosecutions have often raised equal protection claims, arguing that it is irrational and arbitrary to enforce crime X based on whether a defendant is suspected of crime Y. Those claims have generally failed. For a representative decision, see People v. Mantel, 388 N.Y.S.2d 565 (1976). The government charged Mantel with building and health code violations as part of an effort to "clean up" midtown Manhattan and, in particular, to go after the area's "sex-related establishments." Mantel argued that this constituted impermissibly arbitrary enforcement. The court disagreed:

The city has found that efforts to curtail these illegal activities have been ineffective in the past because of fragmented efforts and serious manpower shortages in the various enforcement agencies. It was therefore determined to concentrate efforts on insuring compliance with safety and health related ordinances. . . . It is beyond doubt that health and building codes are well within the police power and necessary to regulate the public health, safety and welfare. Until the city has the financial, administrative and

manpower resources to vigorously prosecute all such offenses, the selective enforcement decided upon herein would seem to be both rational and permissible.

388 N.Y.S.2d, at 568-569.

There are only a few contrary authorities. In People v. Kail, 501 N.E.2d 979 (Ill.
App. 1986), local police were engaged in a crackdown on suspected prostitutes;
those who fell within the targeted class were arrested for any crime the police could
find. In the course of this crackdown, Kail was arrested for riding a bicycle without
a bell, in violation of a local criminal ordinance. The court found that the arrest violated Kail's right to the equal protection of the laws. The Second Circuit later came
out the other way in a factually similar case. The defendant in United States v.
McFadden, 238 F.3d 198 (2d Cir. 2001), was stopped for riding his bicycle on a sidewalk. He was searched "incident to arrest" (though it seems implausible that the
police actually planned to arrest him); the search turned up a gun, which, since
McFadden had a prior felony conviction, led to a federal charge and conviction
under the federal felon-in-possession statute. The Second Circuit affirmed the gun
conviction.

8. Sometimes a defendant seeks redress for an unfounded criminal charge by
suing the government actors who brought the charges; these civil actions are often
called "malicious prosecution" claims. Consider the following scenario. Defendant
does something to irritate an influential government official. That official, in turn,
lobbies police and prosecutors to undertake an investigation, to try to find some
crime they can pin on Defendant. (For fans of the HBO series The Wire, recall the
second-season story of how the investigation of the dockworkers union got started.)
After some investigation, Defendant is charged, but thereafter, the charges are
dropped or dismissed, or Defendant wins an acquittal. Now Defendant wants to sue.
After all, he has been criminally prosecuted because he irritated a powerful government official — not the sort of thing that is supposed to happen in a just system.
What happens?

That scenario describes Hartman v. Moore, 547 U.S. 250 (2006). Moore ran a
firm that had developed multiline scanning technology for sorting mail —
machines that could read addresses on letters and sort the letters properly. Moore
lobbied the Postal Service to buy his technology; instead, the Postal Service temporarily adopted nine-digit ZIP codes, because those longer ZIP codes could be read
without the equipment Moore was selling. Moore responded by turning his lobbying efforts to members of Congress and other government agencies. Eventually, in
part because of Moore's efforts, the nine-digit zip code program was abandoned,
and the Postal Service decided to purchase the multiline scanning technology — but
from one of Moore's competitors. To add insult to injury, postal inspectors began a
criminal investigation of Moore and his company; both were charged with criminal
fraud. After a six-week trial, a federal district judge dismissed the charges. See
United States v. Recognition Equipment Inc., 725 F. Supp. 587 (D.D.C. 1989).
Moore sued six postal inspectors and one federal prosecutor, claiming he had been
charged in retaliation for embarrassing the Postal Service.

After a litigation of Dickensian length — Justice Souter called it "a procedural
history portending another Jarndyce v. Jarndyce" — the postal inspectors successfully moved for summary judgment, on the ground that the underlying criminal
charges were supported by probable cause. By a vote of 5-2, the Supreme Court
agreed. Here is the key passage from Justice Souter's majority opinion:

In sum, the complexity of causation in a claim that prosecution was induced by an official bent on retaliation should be addressed specifically in defining the elements of the tort. Probable cause or its absence will be at least an evidentiary issue in practically all such cases. Because showing an absence of probable cause will have high probative force, and can be made mandatory with little or no added cost, it makes sense to require such a showing as an element of a plaintiff's case, and we hold that it must be pleaded and proven.

Justice Ginsburg's dissent, joined by Justice Breyer, began by stating:

The Court of Appeals, reviewing the record so far made, determined that "the evidence of retaliatory motive [came] close to the proverbial smoking gun." The record also indicated that the postal inspectors engaged in "unusual prodding," strenuously urging a reluctant U.S. Attorney's Office to press charges against Moore.

The dissenters went on to argue that plaintiffs like Moore should prevail if they could show that, but for the retaliatory motive, they would not have been prosecuted — a showing that Moore probably could have made.

Who has the better of the argument? Is the probable-cause requirement, as Justice Souter contends, little more than a matter of legal bookkeeping that will have only slight effects on case outcomes? Or does the Court's decision amount to a blank check for government officials inclined to use criminal charges to harass their critics? If state and federal criminal codes covered only core crimes — major thefts, violent felonies, plus prohibitions of distributing "hard" drugs like cocaine or heroin — *Hartman* would make little difference. Given how broad criminal codes really are, however, it comes close to absolute immunity not just for prosecutors, but for other government officials who may exert influence over them as well.

9. Although the prosecutor's decision to file one charge rather than another is an important one, note that in federal cases and in many states, even *uncharged* criminal conduct can influence a sentence following a conviction on other charges. In the federal system, if the defendant is convicted of crime A but the court is convinced by a preponderance of the evidence that the defendant also participated in crime B, an offense never charged in the indictment, the judge may consider crime B to be relevant conduct it can consider when setting the sentence for crime A. Thus, a prosecutor's decision not to charge a certain offense, or to drop a charge in return for a guilty plea, may still lead to the defendant facing an increased prison sentence. For a useful discussion on the use of uncharged and acquitted conduct as a basis for sentencing, see David Yellen, Reforming the Federal Sentencing Guidelines' Misguided Approach to Real-Offense Sentencing, 58 Stan. L. Rev. 267 (2005); Julie R. O'Sullivan, In Defense of the U.S. Sentencing Guidelines Modified Real Offense System, 91 Nw. U. L. Rev. 1342 (1997).

Chapter 10

Pretrial Screening and the Grand Jury

A grand jury serves two functions. First, working under the direction of the prosecutor the grand jury acts as a powerful investigative tool. It can require witnesses to appear before it and give testimony, and can compel those witnesses to produce documents and other physical evidence. The grand jury can exercise this power without having probable cause to believe that the compelled information will result in usable evidence — the subpoenas can issue without prior judicial approval, and as discussed below, challenges to a subpoena are likely to fail.

Second, the grand jury must approve the prosecutor's proposed criminal charges. Before the government can file an indictment formally accusing someone of a felony, it must persuade a jury of 23 citizens (or at least, must persuade a majority of them) that there is sufficient evidence to send a case forward to trial. Here the grand jury acts as a screen against unfounded prosecutions — if the government has insufficient evidence of a suspect's guilt, the grand jury is supposed to prevent the case from continuing.

How well the grand jury serves these two roles — often called the "sword" (i.e., investigative) and the "shield" (screening) function — is a source of debate, as the following materials show.

A. Background and Current Practice

The grand jury's English origins are commonly traced to the twelfth century, to the reign of Henry II. It began as an accusatory body of citizens drawn from local communities, whose task was to assist the Crown in instituting criminal cases. Local sheriffs had limited resources, and private criminal complaints were an unreliable way to ensure that bad behavior was detected, so the source of the incriminating information was often the jurors themselves; they were expected to bring to the jury room whatever evidence (or rumors and gossip) they possessed to help uncover criminality. The pressure on the grand jurors to inform on their neighbors was great, as fines could be imposed on panels that failed to indict those that the Crown considered guilty.

By the end of the seventeenth century, however, the grand jury had come to be viewed not as a convenient device for the lodging of criminal charges, but as a buffer between the state and the citizen, protecting the latter against oppressive and unwarranted accusations. Although it is far from clear that the grand jury routinely or even frequently resisted royal pressure to indict, there were enough famous cases of the jurors refusing to return charges against political opponents of the King to elevate the grand jury in the public mind to its role as a "bulwark against oppression."

It was this view of the institution that was transported to colonial America, where it took firm root, particularly in the years leading up to the Revolutionary War, when

tensions between England and the colonies would often play out through disagreements over enforcement of the criminal laws. The most famous example occurred
when the grand jury refused to indict the anti-royalist publisher John Peter Zenger
for seditious libel, but there were also other, more mundane cases involving the
Crown's frustrated efforts to enforce unpopular tax laws.

Grand juries were popular in early America for another reason. In many of the
colonies, they served as a kind of running town meeting, a device by which the local
population could ride herd on government officials of all sorts. Thus, a 1638 Massachusetts grand jury "rebuked the Town of Sandwich 'for not having their swine
ringed,' complained of the lack of surveyors for repairing the highway, and questioned the right of the governor and assistants to sell land to certain persons."
Richard D. Younger, The People's Panel 7 (1963). Late-seventeenth-century
Pennsylvania grand juries "supervised all county expenditures and tax levies." Id.,
at 15. Far from being under the thumb of a local prosecutor or other local official,
the very point of these grand juries was to serve as de facto local legislatures. The
combination of refusals to indict in perceived political cases and its more general
role as a watchdog over government officials helped pave the way for the inclusion
of the grand jury guarantee in the Constitution.

In the nineteenth and twentieth centuries, the grand jury's role as a shield
against oppression lost much of its luster. The increasing presence and professionalization of judges, prosecutors, and police, coupled with the increasing complexity
of the criminal law, led to a diminishing role for the grand jury as an independent
actor. There were still periodic stories of grand juries courageously pursuing organized crime, and occasional cases of "runaway" grand juries that defied the prosecutor and pursued their own investigative course. But while these stories helped
sustain the popular image of the "people's panel," in reality the grand jury had lost
its ability to act independently of the prosecution. In fact, today it is hard to find any
careful observer who will claim that the grand jury is truly an independent
body — except for the Supreme Court, which as this Chapter shows, continues to
insist that the grand jury is in control of, rather than controlled by, the prosecution.

The Fifth Amendment begins with the words, "No person shall be held to answer
for a capital, or otherwise infamous crime, unless on a presentment or indictment
of a Grand Jury, except in cases arising in the land or naval forces, or in the militia,
when in actual service in time of war or public danger. . . ." The Supreme Court has
assumed that the phrase "otherwise infamous crime" means felonies. See, e.g.,
Stirone v. United States, 361 U.S. 212, 215 (1961), and thus, the Constitution guarantees the grand jury screening process for all felonies.

The other mode of bringing charges mentioned in the Fifth Amendment, a "presentment," refers to a criminal charge brought directly by the grand jury and not by
the prosecutor. Today, presentments virtually never occur and the practice is considered obsolete, despite arguments that grand juries should still have this power.
See, e.g., Note, Renee B. Lettow, Reviving Federal Grand Jury Presentments, 103
Yale L.J. 1333 (1994). Indeed, should the grand jury vote to indict a defendant
against the prosecutor's wishes, it seems clear that it would have no effect: An indictment must be signed by the prosecutor, Fed. R. Crim. P. 7(f), and lower courts have
ruled that a judge may not force a prosecutor to proceed with a case. See Chapter 9,
supra (discussing the prosecutor's charging discretion).

In his article Why Grand Juries Do Not (and Cannot) Protect the Accused, 80
Cornell L. Rev. 260, 265-266 (1995), Andrew Leipold offers a capsule summary of
current grand jury procedure:

The operation of a typical federal grand jury is straightforward. A pool of citizens is summoned at random from the judicial district where the jury will sit. From the group of qualified people who appear, twenty-three are chosen to serve on the jury. The jurors sit for an indefinite period not to exceed eighteen months; the number of days per month when they must actually appear depends on the prosecutor's case load. A district court judge administers the oath and gives the jurors general instructions about their duties. This marks the end of the judge's formal involvement in the process. From that point forward, the prosecutor dictates the course of the proceedings.

The most striking feature of grand jury hearings is their secrecy. The press and public are barred from the proceedings, as are suspects and their counsel. Even judges are not allowed in the grand jury room; attendance is limited to the prosecutor, the jurors, the court reporter, and the single witness being questioned. Those who participate in the hearing are sworn to secrecy, and the court may use its contempt powers to ensure that this silence is maintained even after the case is resolved.

Once in session, the grand jury's primary task is to review the cases presented to it by the government. The prosecutor calls and questions witnesses, and presents documentary evidence related to the crime in question. Unlike trial jurors, grand jurors may ask questions of the witness and may discuss the case with the prosecutor as evidence is submitted. After the case is presented, the prosecutor asks the jurors to vote to return an indictment accusing the defendant of a specific crime that the prosecutor believes is supported by the evidence. The jurors then deliberate in private. If at least twelve agree that there is probable cause to believe that the suspect committed the crime, the grand jury returns a "true bill" that, when signed by the prosecutor, becomes the indictment. If the grand jury concludes that the evidence is insufficient, it returns a "no bill" (or "no true bill"), and any preliminary charges filed against the suspect are dismissed.

Two features about current grand jury practice warrant special emphasis. First, witnesses who are called before the grand jury are not permitted to bring a lawyer with them into the hearing. A person who receives a grand jury subpoena may consult with a lawyer in advance, and may even bring counsel with her to the hallway outside the grand jury room. But when it is time to enter the room and testify, the witness goes in alone.

For a system that makes the right to the assistance of counsel a core value, this exclusion is puzzling to say the least. As a formal matter, the Sixth Amendment does not apply, because witnesses are not the "accused" in a criminal prosecution. But this hardly explains why a witness is forbidden to bring a lawyer with her if she can afford one, especially given the potential risks that a witness may be running. A witness may be asked questions with answers that would implicate her in a crime, or would violate some other evidentiary privilege. And while the witness is always free to invoke a privilege and refuse to answer, this assumes that she will have both the presence of mind and the pluck to assert her right and remain silent. If a witness fails to assert the privilege and gives an incriminating answer, the prosecution is free to use the information later to prosecute the witness.

The situation in practice, however, is usually not as risky as the rules make it appear. Although the prosecution is not obligated to warn the witness in advance of the testimony of her right not to incriminate herself, it is the practice of the U.S. Attorneys to do so, just as it is considered ethical practice not to ask questions that obviously call for privileged information. In addition, if the witness is involved (or even may be involved) in criminal activity, a lawyer will advise the witness in advance to simply invoke the Fifth Amendment privilege in response to any questions the prosecutor asks. Finally, and most curiously, a witness who is unsure about a question is typically given the chance (with the prosecutor's/grand jurors' permission) to briefly leave the grand jury room, consult with her lawyer in the hallway, then return to the room and either answer or refuse to answer the question.

What explains this treatment of lawyers? Even if a lawyer in the grand jury room could not cross-examine a witness or object to a judge — there is no judge present — she could still provide valuable assistance by advising the client to invoke the Fifth Amendment or other privilege, much as lawyers do in police interrogations. Why should the grand jury room be different? Is it a fear that lawyers will complicate the proceedings, or is there something else at work? Note that many states with grand jury requirements allow counsel to be present, although their role is often limited. See, e.g., 725 Ill. Comp. Stat. 5/112-4.1 ("Any person appearing before the grand jury shall have the right to be accompanied by counsel who shall advise him of his rights but shall not participate in any other way.")

Historical inertia is undoubtedly part of the explanation, but another part may be skepticism that lawyers will always have the witness's best interest at heart. Consider a case where the grand jury is investigating a corporation and its CEO for possible fraud. The grand jury calls a staff accountant as a witness, and naturally the corporate lawyer wants to accompany the accountant into the grand jury room. The witness himself, however, might be chilled by having his employer's lawyer present because he knows that everything he says can be reported back to the CEO. By excluding all lawyers from the room, the witness still *may* report back to the lawyer what he told the grand jury, but he may also be freer to testify candidly and have his testimony remain at least temporarily secret.

The second feature worth considering is the limited reach of the constitutional grand jury clause: Unlike nearly every other provision of the Bill of Rights, the grand jury's protections do not apply to the States. In Hurtado v. California, 110 U.S. 516 (1884), the Supreme Court held that the grand jury clause of the Fifth Amendment is not incorporated into the Due Process Clause of the Fourteenth Amendment, and despite the wave of incorporation decisions in the last 50 years, Hurtado remains good law. As a result, more than half the states do not require a grand jury, or at least do not require it in many cases, and for those states that have the institution, their procedures need not and very often do not conform to federal practice. See 1 Sara Sun Beale & William C. Bryson, Grand Jury Law & Practice §§1.1, 1.5 (2d ed. 1997). So it is important to keep in mind that "grand jury law" differs widely between the state and federal systems and among the various states.

Its insistence that the grand jury clause is not incorporated against the states may shed light on the Supreme Court's views of the institution's importance. The Court recently ruled that the Second Amendment's right to keep and bear arms was incorporated because this right is "fundamental to a scheme of ordered liberty" and "deeply rooted in this Nation's history and tradition." McDonald v. City of Chicago, 130 S. Ct. 3020 (2010). It can hardly be disputed that the grand jury is deeply rooted in our country's history, so is it fair to assume that the Supreme Court does not find the grand jury a necessary part of ordered liberty? As you consider the material in the following sections, you should notice how often the Court speaks in glowing terms about the role of the grand jury in the criminal process, and ask yourself why, if the institution is so important, the grand jury is treated so differently from other constitutional protections.

The materials below explore the scope of both the grand jury's investigative powers and the extent to which grand juries screen the prosecutor's charging decisions.

The next section, however, looks in more detail at one of the defining features of the grand jury: the requirement that the proceedings remain secret.

B. *Grand Jury Secrecy*

1. The Scope of the Secrecy Rule

Grand jury practice is governed by Federal Rule of Criminal Procedure 6, which is set forth in the Supplement. The rules making the grand jury proceedings secret are set out indirectly in Rule 6(d) and directly in Rule 6(e).

Rule 6(d) describes who may be present while the grand jury is in session. Only the jurors, the prosecutor, the witness being questioned, a court reporter, and an interpreter, if needed, may be in the room during a hearing. Once the evidence is presented and it is time for the grand jury to deliberate and vote, everyone else must leave and only the jurors remain (plus an interpreter).

For those permitted in the grand jury room, most are sworn to secrecy pursuant to Rule 6(e), which provides, in part, that jurors, the prosecutor, and the court reporter "must not disclose a matter occurring before the grand jury." (This information is often referred to in practice as "6(e) material.") Violations of the secrecy provisions of Rule 6 can be punished as contempt, although, as the following material shows, what constitutes a "matter occurring before the grand jury" is hardly self-evident. The notable exception to this general rule is that witnesses are not required to keep confidential what they see and hear in the grand jury room, and they are free to discuss their grand jury testimony with anyone, including the target of the investigation.

At first blush, a secret proceeding seems antithetical to the American justice system, because so many parts of the judicial process are presumptively open for press and public scrutiny: Arrests are matters of public record; bail hearings, arraignments, preliminary hearings, and plea hearings take place in open court; and resulting documents presumptively are available for public review. And, of course, the Sixth Amendment guarantees that the actual trials will be public.

What justifies, or even explains, this insistence on a closed hearing? The origins of the rule are easy enough to explain: If the goal was to place ordinary citizens between the accused and an overreaching crown, secrecy would help protect the jurors from royal unhappiness if they failed to abide by the king's wishes. But today the historical explanation rings hollow, as the image of a truly independent grand jury is hard to maintain when the government's representative, the prosecutor, now dominates the grand jury room (more on the prosecutor's role in Section C, below). Instead, the Supreme Court in the modern era has given the following justifications for keeping grand jury hearings a secret:

> (1) To prevent the escape of those whose indictment may be contemplated; (2) to insure the utmost freedom to the grand jury in its deliberations, and to prevent persons subject to indictment or their friends from importuning the grand jurors; (3) to prevent subornation of perjury or tampering with the witness who may testify before the grand jury and later appear at the trial of those indicted by it; (4) to encourage free and untrammeled disclosures by persons who have information with respect to the commission of crimes; (5) to protect the innocent accused who is exonerated from disclosure of

the fact that he has been under investigation, and from the expense of standing trial where there was no probability of guilt.

Douglas Oil Co. v. Petrol Oil Stops Northwest, 441 U.S. 211, 219, n. 10 (1979) (quotation marks omitted).

As persuasive as these reasons may be while the investigation is in progress, they lose at least some of their force after an indictment is returned. Once a defendant is charged and arrested, there is no more risk of flight or of pressuring the grand jurors, and the desire to protect the innocent from a false charge is destroyed by the indictment itself. And while protecting witnesses from tampering and encouraging cooperation are worthy goals, presumably many of the critical witnesses may be called to testify at trial and thus will be publicly identified at that point. Given this, how persuasive is it to claim that grand jury secrecy is critical even after the indictment, or better yet, after the entire case is over?

Note that there is no time limit on grand jury secrecy. In U.S. v. McDougal, 559 F.3d 837 (8th Cir. 2009), for example, a defendant sought access to the grand jury material in her own case after the matter had ended and she had served her sentence, apparently because she wanted to write a novel or screenplay about the case. Although the woman argued that "[t]he reasons for sealing the record have now grown stale and disappeared," the court of appeals disagreed: "Although the interest in grand jury secrecy may be reduced after an investigation is completed, there is no provision in Rule 6(e) specifically authorizing disclosure at the conclusion of the proceedings." 559 F.3d, at 841.

Notice also that secrecy sometimes works against the interest of investigators. Selective disclosure of some investigative information "can place members of a targeted enterprise in a noncustodial 'prisoner's dilemma,' giving each person reason to fear that one of more of his comrades will race to the prosecutor's office to betray him in exchange for leniency, and therefore giving him reason to get there first." Daniel C. Richman, Grand Jury Secrecy: Plugging the Leaks in an Empty Bucket, 36 Am. Crim. L. Rev. 339, 346 (1999). So at least in some cases, prosecutors may wish they could reveal grand jury material because it could stimulate witnesses to come forward; stated differently, investigators might wish that they had a greater ability to barter such information to obtain access to evidence they do not have.

The law enforcement personnel participating in a grand jury investigation thus may have reasons either to adhere strictly to secrecy norms or to interpret those norms as narrowly as possible. Consider these conflicting incentives as you read the following case.

IN RE SEALED CASE NO. 99-3091

Appeal to the United States Court of Appeals for the D.C. Circuit
192 F.3d 995 (1999)

PER CURIAM:

The Office of Independent Counsel (OIC) seeks summary reversal of the district court's order to show cause why OIC should not be held in contempt for violating the grand jury secrecy rule, and its order appointing the United States Department of Justice as prosecutor of OIC in a criminal contempt proceeding. In the alternative,

OIC seeks a stay of those orders pending appeal. We conclude we have jurisdiction to consider the interlocutory appeal and grant the motion for summary reversal.

On January 31, 1999, while the Senate was trying President William J. Clinton on articles of impeachment, the New York Times published a front page article captioned "Starr is Weighing Whether to Indict Sitting President." As is relevant here, the article reported:

> Inside the Independent Counsel's Office, a group of prosecutors believes that not long after the Senate trial concludes, Mr. Starr should ask the grand jury of 23 men and women hearing the case against Mr. Clinton to indict him on charges of perjury and obstruction of justice, the associates said. The group wants to charge Mr. Clinton with lying under oath in his *Jones* deposition in January 1998 and in his grand jury testimony in August, the associates added.

The next day, the Office of the President (the White House) and Mr. Clinton jointly filed in district court a motion for an order to show cause why OIC, or the individuals therein, should not be held in contempt for disclosing grand jury material in violation of Federal Rule of Criminal Procedure 6(e). The White House and Mr. Clinton pointed to several excerpts from the article as evidence of OIC's violations of the grand jury secrecy rule.

OIC responded that the matters disclosed in the article merely rehashed old news reports and, in any event, did not fall within Rule 6(e)'s definition of "matters occurring before the grand jury." OIC also submitted a declaration from Charles G. Bakaly, III, then-Counselor to the Independent Counsel, regarding his communications with the author of the article, Don Van Natta, Jr. Bakaly declared, among other things, that in his conversations with Van Natta about whether the Independent Counsel could indict the President while still in office, "I refused to confirm or comment on what Judge Starr or the OIC was thinking or doing." According to OIC, the declaration was for the purpose of demonstrating that even if the matters disclosed were grand jury material, OIC was not the source of the information in the article.

Notwithstanding the foregoing, Independent Counsel Kenneth W. Starr asked the Federal Bureau of Investigation to provide OIC assistance in conducting an internal leak investigation. The Department of Justice authorized the FBI to do so, and as a result of the investigation, [ ].[2] Consequently, OIC took administrative action against Bakaly and referred the matter to the Department of Justice for a criminal investigation and decision. OIC informed the district court of these developments, withdrew Bakaly's declaration, and abandoned its argument that OIC was not the source of the information disclosed in the New York Times article. Although OIC noted that "the article regrettably discloses sensitive and confidential internal OIC information," it continued to maintain that the information was not protected by Rule 6(e).

Troubled by these developments, the district court ordered Bakaly and OIC to show cause why they should not be held in civil contempt for a violation of Rule 6(e), concluding that the portion of the New York Times article quoted above revealed grand jury material and constituted a prima facie violation of Rule 6(e). [ ] The district court scheduled a consolidated show cause hearing, ordered the FBI and OIC

---

2. Bold brackets signify sealed material.

to produce in camera all their relevant investigative reports, and required the FBI agents involved in the investigation to appear to testify. In accordance with this court's holding in In re Sealed Case No. 98-3077, 151 F.3d 1059, 1075-1076 (D.C. Cir. 1998), the district court ordered that the proceedings be closed and ex parte.

Convinced that the district court had misinterpreted this court's precedent, OIC and Bakaly asked the district court to certify for interlocutory appeal the question of the proper scope of Rule 6(e). The district court denied the request, referring only to its previous orders. . . .

One day later, on July 14th, the district court sua sponte issued an order appointing DOJ to serve as prosecutor of the contempt charges against Bakaly *and OIC*. The district court explained its unexpected inclusion of OIC in DOJ's prosecution: "DOJ's letter only refers to the contempt charges lodged against Mr. Bakaly. However, the Court also needs to resolve the closely related allegations against the OIC. The Court believes that these matters are best resolved through a single contempt proceeding involving both Mr. Bakaly and the OIC." Although the district court decided to afford Bakaly and OIC the protections of criminal law, it left open the possibility of civil, or a combination of civil and criminal, contempt sanctions. The district court also scheduled a pre-trial status conference for July 23. . . .

OIC filed an emergency motion to vacate the district court's July 14 order, [raising] numerous legal objections, including the argument that OIC is entitled to sovereign immunity from a criminal contempt proceeding. . . . To obtain an adversarial viewpoint on what we consider to be the dispositive issue in this case, we ordered Mr. Clinton and the White House, along with DOJ and OIC, to brief the question whether the alleged disclosures in the New York Times article relied upon by the district court in ordering a criminal contempt proceeding constitute a prima facie violation of Rule 6(e).

[Before reaching the Rule 6(e) issue, the court of appeals determined that by failing to respond to OIC's motion to vacate and allowing to stand its order requiring the OIC to appear as a criminal defendant at a status conference, the district court had conclusively rejected the OIC's claim of sovereign immunity. The court of appeals determined that this ruling was immediately appealable as a collateral order and that, in the circumstances of this case, taking pendent jurisdiction and disposing of the case on the merits of the Rule 6(e) issue was permissible and preferable to resolving the federal sovereign immunity issue.]

Turning . . . to the merits of this case, we conclude that the disclosures made in the New York Times article do not constitute a prima facie violation of Rule 6(e). A prima facie violation based on a news report is established by showing that the report discloses "matters occurring before the grand jury" and indicates that sources of the information include government attorneys. Because OIC has withdrawn its argument that none of its attorneys was the source of the disclosures in the New York Times article at issue here, the only remaining issue is whether those disclosures qualify as "matters occurring before the grand jury." Fed. R. Crim. P. 6(e)(2).[8]

The district court concluded that only one excerpt from the New York Times article constituted a prima facie violation of Rule 6(e). That excerpt . . . disclosed the desire of some OIC prosecutors to seek, not long after the conclusion of the

---

8. OIC contends that as an entity rather than an individual, it is not subject to Rule 6(e). It is unnecessary to decide this issue given our conclusion that there is no prima facie violation of Rule 6(e).

Senate trial, an indictment of Mr. Clinton on perjury and obstruction of justice charges, including lying under oath in his deposition in the Paula Jones matter and in his grand jury testimony. These statements, according to the district court, reveal a specific time frame for seeking an indictment, the details of a likely indictment, and the direction a group of prosecutors within OIC believes the grand jury investigation should take. Not surprisingly, Mr. Clinton and the White House agree with the district court's expansive reading of Rule 6(e). OIC takes a narrow view of the Rule's coverage, arguing that matters occurring outside the physical presence of the grand jury are covered only if they reveal grand jury matters. DOJ generally supports OIC with respect to the Rule's coverage, but emphasizes the importance of the context and concreteness of disclosures.

The key to the district court's reasoning is its reliance on this court's definition of "matters occurring before the grand jury." In In re Motions of Dow Jones & Co., 142 F.3d 496, 500 (D.C. Cir.), *cert. denied*, 525 U.S. 820 (1998), we noted that this phrase encompasses "not only what has occurred and what is occurring, but also what is likely to occur," including "the identities of witnesses or jurors, the substance of testimony as well as actual transcripts, the strategy or direction of the investigation, the deliberations or questions of jurors, and the like." Id. (internal quotation omitted). In the earlier contempt proceeding against Independent Counsel Starr, however, we cautioned the district court about "the problematic nature of applying so broad a definition, especially as it relates to the 'strategy or direction of the investigation,' to the inquiry as to whether a government attorney has made unauthorized disclosures." In re Sealed Case No. 98-3077, 151 F.3d at 1071 n. 12. Despite the seemingly broad nature of the statements in *Dow Jones*, we have never read Rule 6(e) to require that a "veil of secrecy be drawn over all matters occurring in the world that happen to be investigated by a grand jury." Securities & Exch. Commn. v. Dresser Indus., Inc., 628 F.2d 1368, 1382 (D.C. Cir. 1980) (en banc). Indeed, we have said that "[t]he disclosure of information 'coincidentally before the grand jury [which can] be revealed in such a manner that its revelation would not elucidate the inner workings of the grand jury' is not prohibited." Senate of Puerto Rico v. United States Dept. of Justice, 823 F.2d 574, 582 (D.C. Cir. 1987) (quoting Fund for Constitutional Govt. v. National Archives and Records Serv., 656 F.2d 856, 870 (D.C. Cir. 1981)). Thus, the phrases "likely to occur" and "strategy and direction" must be read in light of the text of Rule 6(e) — which limits the Rule's coverage to "matters occurring before the grand jury" — as well as the purposes of the Rule.

As we have recited on many occasions,

> Rule 6(e) . . . protects several interests of the criminal justice system: "First, if pre-indictment proceedings were made public, many prospective witnesses would be hesitant to come forward voluntarily, knowing that those against whom they testify would be aware of that testimony. Moreover, witnesses who appeared before the grand jury would be less likely to testify fully and frankly, as they would be open to retribution as well as to inducements. There also would be the risk that those about to be indicted would flee, or would try to influence individual grand jurors to vote against indictment. Finally, by preserving the secrecy of the proceedings, we assure that persons who are accused but exonerated by the grand jury will not be held up to public ridicule."

In re Sealed Case No. 98-3077, 151 F.3d 1059, 1070 (D.C. Cir. 1998) (quoting Douglas Oil Co. v. Petrol Stops Northwest, 441 U.S. 211, 219 (1979)). These purposes, as well as the text of the Rule itself, reflect the need to preserve the secrecy of the *grand jury* proceedings themselves. It is therefore necessary to differentiate between statements by a prosecutor's office with respect to its own investigation, and statements by a prosecutor's office with respect to a *grand jury*'s investigation, a distinction of the utmost significance. . . .

Information actually presented to the grand jury is core Rule 6(e) material that is afforded the broadest protection from disclosure. Prosecutors' statements about their investigations, however, implicate the Rule only when they directly reveal grand jury matters. To be sure, we have recognized that Rule 6(e) would be easily evaded if a prosecutor could with impunity discuss with the press testimony about to be presented to a grand jury, so long as it had not yet occurred. Accordingly, we have read Rule 6(e) to cover matters "likely to occur." And even a discussion of "strategy and direction of the investigation" could include references to not yet delivered but clearly anticipated testimony. But that does not mean that *any* discussion of an investigation is violative of Rule 6(e). Indeed, the district court's Local Rule 308(b)(2), which governs attorney conduct in grand jury matters, recognizes that prosecutors often have a legitimate interest in revealing aspects of their investigations "to inform the public that the investigation is underway, to describe the general scope of the investigation, to obtain assistance in the apprehension of a suspect, to warn the public of any dangers, or otherwise aid in the investigation."

It may often be the case, however, that disclosures by the prosecution referencing its own investigation should not be made for tactical reasons, or are in fact prohibited by other Rules or ethical guidelines. For instance, prosecutors may be prohibited by internal guidelines, see, e.g., United States Attorney Manual §1-7.530, from discussing the strategy or direction of their investigation before an indictment is sought.[9] This would serve one of the same purposes as Rule 6(e): protecting the reputation of innocent suspects. But a court may not use Rule 6(e) to generally regulate prosecutorial statements to the press. The purpose of the Rule is only to protect the secrecy of grand jury proceedings.

Thus, internal deliberations of prosecutors that do not directly reveal grand jury proceedings are not Rule 6(e) material. As the Fifth Circuit stated in circumstances similar to those presented here,

> [a] discussion of actions taken by government attorneys or officials — e.g., a recommendation by the Justice Department attorneys to department officials that an indictment be sought against an individual — does not reveal any information about matters occurring before the grand jury. Nor does a statement of opinion as to an individual's potential criminal liability violate the dictates of Rule 6(e). This is so even though the opinion might be based on knowledge of the grand jury proceedings, provided, of course, the statement does not reveal the grand jury information on which it is based.

[In re Grand Jury Investigation [*Lance*], 610 F.2d 202, 217 (5th Cir. 1980)]. It may be thought that when such deliberations include a discussion of whether an indictment

---

9. But see Eric H. Holder & Kevin A. Ohlson, Dealing with the Media in High-Profile White Collar Cases: The Prosecutor's Dilemma, in White Collar Crime, at B-1, B-1 to B-2 (1995) ("[I]n cases involving well-known people, the public has a right to be kept reasonably informed about what steps are being taken to pursue allegations of wrongdoing so that they can determine whether prosecutors are applying the law equally to all citizens. This point has become particularly pertinent in recent years because powerful figures increasingly seem to characterize criminal investigations of their alleged illegal conduct as 'political witch hunts.' This type of epithet only serves to unfairly impugn the motives of prosecutors and to undermine our legal system, and should not go unanswered.").

should be sought, or whether a particular individual is potentially criminally liable, the deliberations have crossed into the realm of Rule 6(e) material. This ignores, however, the requirement that the matter occur before the grand jury. Where the reported deliberations do not reveal that an indictment *has been* sought or *will be* sought, ordinarily they will not reveal anything definite enough to come within the scope of Rule 6(e).

For these reasons, the disclosure that a group of OIC prosecutors "believe" that an indictment should be brought at the end of the impeachment proceedings does not on its face, or in the context of the article as a whole, violate Rule 6(e).[10] We acknowledge, as did OIC, that such statements are troubling, for they have the potential to damage the reputation of innocent suspects. But bare statements that some assistant prosecutors in OIC wish to seek an indictment do not implicate the grand jury; the prosecutors may not even be basing their opinion on information presented to a grand jury.

The fact that the disclosure also reveals a time period for seeking the indictment of "not long after the Senate trial concludes" does not in any way indicate what is "likely to occur" before the grand jury within the meaning of Rule 6(e). That disclosure reflects nothing more than a desire on the part of some OIC prosecutors to seek an indictment at that time, not a decision to do so. The general uncertainty as to whether an indictment would in fact be sought (according to the article, only some prosecutors in OIC thought one should be) leads us to conclude that this portion of the article did not reveal anything that was "occurring before the grand jury."

Nor does it violate the Rule to state the general grounds for such an indictment — here, lying under oath in a deposition and before the grand jury — where no secret grand jury material is revealed. In ordinary circumstances, Rule 6(e) covers the disclosure of the names of grand jury witnesses. Therefore, the statement that members of OIC wished to seek an indictment based on Mr. Clinton's alleged perjury before a grand jury would ordinarily be Rule 6(e) material. In this case, however, we take judicial notice that the President's status as a witness before the grand jury was a matter of widespread public knowledge well before the New York Times article at issue in this case was written; the President himself went on national television the day of his testimony to reveal this fact. Where the general public is already aware of the information contained in the prosecutor's statement, there is no additional harm in the prosecutor referring to such information.[11] Therefore, it cannot be said that OIC "disclosed" the name of a grand jury witness, in violation of Rule 6(e), by referring to the President's grand jury testimony.

Similarly, it would ordinarily be a violation of Rule 6(e) to disclose that a grand jury is investigating a particular person. Thus, the statement that a grand jury is "hearing the case against Mr. Clinton" would be covered by Rule 6(e) if it were not for the fact that the New York Times article did not reveal any secret, for it was already common knowledge well before January 31, 1999, that a grand jury was investigating alleged perjury and obstruction of justice by the President. Once again, the President's appearance on national television confirmed as much.

In light of our conclusion that the excerpt from the New York Times article does not constitute a prima facie violation of Rule 6(e), we reverse and remand with

---

10. Indeed, the article stated that Independent Counsel Starr had not himself made any decision on whether to bring an indictment.

11. The prosecutor must still be careful, of course, when making such statements not to reveal some aspect of the grand jury investigation which is *itself* still cloaked in secrecy.

instructions to dismiss the Rule 6(e) contempt proceedings against OIC. Because we
have granted OIC's request for summary reversal, we dismiss as moot the alternative request for a stay. . . .

NOTES AND QUESTIONS

1. After the Rule 6(e) contempt proceeding against the OIC was dismissed,
Bakaly stood trial and was found not guilty of criminal contempt in connection with
the New York Times article. Given the ruling in In Re Sealed Case No. 99-3091 that
the information in the article did not constitute a prima facie violation of Rule 6(e),
the charges against Bakaly did not involve such a violation, but instead the allegation that Bakaly had lied in the court papers initially filed with the district court that
explained the extent of his role in providing information for the article. As a Wall
Street Journal article commented at the time of his acquittal, this created the
unusual situation where "Mr. Bakaly was prosecuted for allegedly lying about leak-
ing information that was legal to leak." Gary Fields, Starr Assistant Is Not Guilty of
Contempt, Wall Street Journal, Oct. 9, 2000, at A26.

2. Independent Counsel Kenneth Starr's investigation highlighted some confusion in the state of the law regarding grand jury secrecy. Do prosecutors violate Rule
6(e) when they reveal information about what witnesses have told FBI agents outside the grand jury? Are documents produced to the grand jury under compulsion
of subpoena "matters occurring before the grand jury" for the purpose of Rule 6(e)?
Professor Daniel Richman has proffered one explanation as to why Rule 6(e) doctrine is unsettled on these basic issues:

> Rule 6(e) does not establish a general regime of investigative secrecy for prosecu-
> tors and law enforcement agents. It addresses only what occurs "before the grand jury."
> As a matter of physical reality, however, the only thing that clearly occurs before a grand
> jury is testimony by a live witness, and sometimes the introduction of exhibits. Just
> about everything else generally occurs in a prosecutor's office or out in the field: delib-
> erations about what investigations the grand jury will pursue, and which witnesses and
> documents will be subpoenaed in its name; interviews of potential witnesses conducted
> with an eye to deciding whether they will actually be brought before the grand jury; and
> receipt and review of documents obtained via grand jury subpoena. Particularly when
> prosecutors simultaneously develop a case in the grand jury and pursue other investi-
> gative options without using the grand jury, the language of Rule 6(e) provides all too
> little guidance as to what the government's secrecy obligations are. . . .

Daniel C. Richman, Grand Jury Secrecy: Plugging the Leaks in an Empty Bucket,
36 Am. Crim. L. Rev. 339, 341 (1999).

3. Investigations into to the source of a leak of grand jury materials are notoriously difficult to bring to a successful resolution, in large measure because often
those most knowledgeable about the source of the leak — people in the
media — are not compelled to disclose *their* sources. In addition, because grand jury
witnesses are not generally bound by secrecy restrictions, there may be multiple ways
in which information about a grand jury investigation has legitimately entered the
public domain — making even the identification of a breach of secrecy very difficult.
In practice, this means that intentional leaks of grand jury material are virtually
impossible to prove. Does this fact draw into question Rule 6(e)'s entire regime for

grand jury secrecy? Or does Rule 6(e) serve its purpose by articulating a norm that will be at least partly internalized by investigative personnel?

4. If the articulation of a norm of investigative secrecy through a legal prohibition like Rule 6(e) is important, it's worth asking whether confining that norm to grand jury investigations can be justified. After all, the subject of a traditional FBI investigation certainly suffers reputational injury when that fact becomes widely known — whether or not a grand jury has been convened. Professor Richman has gone even further to note that to the extent Rule 6(e) is about limiting the harms suffered by those who are the subject of a criminal investigation, the Rule may have the effect of showing special concern for the type of suspect who needs it least — the often well-heeled, white-collar suspect who is implicated in the sort of complex case most likely to be pursued in a grand jury:

> Does it make sense to have a system that in effect shows a special solicitude for targets and witnesses in white collar cases? Aren't these, in fact, the cases where, in the face of efforts by well-financed lawyers to impede information collection, the government is most in need of options that might include the selective dissemination of investigative data? One can also argue that the need for prosecutors to defend an investigation to the public while it is on-going is likely to be greater in white collar than in other contexts. After all, white collar targets are far better able to marshal support in the press and elsewhere than other targets — support that may impede the progress of an investigation and/or sway the potential jury pool.

Daniel C. Richman, Grand Jury Secrecy, supra, at 355. Does Rule 6(e) reflect nothing more than the political clout of white-collar defendants? Or are there other reasons for the law's special concern with investigative leaks in the grand jury context?

5. As noted above, most participants in the grand jury process are covered by the obligation of secrecy, but grand jury witnesses are not. A witness who is asked a series of questions about Al Capone is free to tell Capone that he is the target of the investigation, and is even free to tell the press about what he learned during the course of his questioning about "matters occurring before the grand jury." This would seem to undermine several of the justifications for secrecy articulated above, particularly the need to prevent the target of an investigation from fleeing or tampering with the jurors or the evidence. Can you think of a reason why witnesses should not be subject to the same secrecy rules as everyone else?

2. Exceptions to the Secrecy Rule

Despite a strong presumption of secrecy, Rule 6(e)(3) permits limited disclosure of grand jury material, typically in situations that recognize the needs and reality of prosecutorial practice. For example, 6(e) material may be disclosed by the prosecutor to a different federal grand jury, or to another prosecutor if the disclosure will assist in enforcing the federal criminal law. The material may also be disclosed to people who work with the prosecutor — paralegals, expert witnesses, law enforcement, secretaries — although the prosecutor must provide the court with a list of those who have been given access. These are perfectly sensible exceptions, because the prosecutor in the grand jury room will normally have to call on a variety of nonprosecutors when putting a case together.

Beyond this narrow group, the list of exceptions is traditionally quite small. Consider the following situation: Suppose a U.S. Attorney, in the course of investigating a target for criminal fraud, uncovers information that would also give the government a strong claim for a civil action under the False Claims Act. The prosecutor would like to disclose the information to her civil counterparts at the Justice Department, and on examining Rule 6(e)(3), finds the following exceptions to the general secrecy rule:

> (A) Disclosure of a grand-jury matter — other than the grand jury's deliberations or any grand juror's vote — may be made to:
>> (i) an attorney for the government for use in performing that attorney's duty; [or]
>> (ii) any government personnel . . . that an attorney for the government considers necessary to assist in performing that attorney's duty to enforce federal criminal law.

The Rule goes on to say that if proposed disclosure is not covered by one of these two sections (or by other provisions not relevant here), then the U.S. attorney must seek leave of court before turning the information over. So the question for the U.S. Attorney is whether she can just disclose the information to her civil counterpart, or must she obtain court permission first?

This was the question presented in U.S. v. Sells Engineering, 463 U.S. 418 (1983). The government quite plausibly argued that while Rule 6(e)(3)(A)(ii) was limited to disclosures that were necessary to helping the prosecutor "enforce federal criminal law," Rule 6(e)(3)(A)(i) was not so limited — all it says is that disclosure can be made to "an attorney for the government for use in performing that attorney's duty." Since all lawyers in the Justice Department, civil as well as criminal, come within the definition of "attorneys for the government,"[1] the prosecutor in *Sells* argued that the plain language of the Rule allows disclosure to a civil government attorney for purposes of enforcing the civil law.

A divided Supreme Court disagreed, and held that even Rule 6(e)(3)(A)(i) "is limited to use by those attorneys who conduct the criminal matters to which the materials pertain," despite the absence of this restriction in the text of the Rule. The majority found that "[t]his conclusion is mandated by the general purposes and policies of grand jury secrecy, by the limited policy reasons why government attorneys are granted access to grand jury materials for criminal use, and by the legislative history of Rule 6(e)." 463 U.S., at 427.

This narrow interpretation of the disclosure Rule would not be very significant if district courts were to freely grant a government motion to disclose grand jury material, but *Sells* made it clear that judges should be slow to do so. Courts should only grant a request to disclose, said the majority, where the party seeking disclosure has shown a "strong showing of particularized need" for the information. Quoting from an earlier opinion, the Court elaborated on this standard:

> Parties seeking grand jury transcripts under Rule 6(e) must show that the material they seek is needed to avoid a possible injustice in another judicial proceeding, that the

---

1. Federal Rule of Criminal Procedure 1(b)(1)(B) defines "attorney for the government" to mean, in part, "a United States attorney or an authorized assistant."

need for disclosure is greater than the need for continued secrecy, and that their request is structured to cover only material so needed.

Id., at 443 (citation omitted). The Court in *Sells* added that even if the district court were to permit disclosure, the judge remained free to impose "protective limitations on the use of the disclosed material." Id.

There are other types of grand jury disclosure permitted by Rule 6(e)(3). The court may require disclosure at the request of a defendant who can show that grounds might exist for a motion to dismiss the indictment because of matters occurring before the grand jury. (Although as discussed below, the difficulties of making such a showing are considerable.) In addition, a court may order the disclosure of grand jury material in connection with some other judicial proceeding, or if the material shows a violation of state law, it may be given to state prosecutors. Importantly, however, these disclosures require judicial permission — the court continues to act as the gatekeeper and protector of grand jury information.

More recently, however, Congress has opened the disclosure door a bit wider, and has done so without requiring judicial approval. A few years after *Sells* was decided, Congress provided, as part of a sweeping financial legislation, that U.S. Attorneys could, as a matter of course, disclose grand jury material to civil attorneys within the Justice Department to assist those attorneys in enforcing certain civil banking and civil forfeiture laws. This change is now reflected in Rule 6(e)(3)(iii).

More significant, in response to the terrorist attacks of September 11, 2001, Congress passed the USA PATRIOT Act, Pub. L. No. 107-56, 115 Stat. 272. The Act amended Rule 6 to provide that disclosure of matters occurring before the grand jury may also be made to any federal law enforcement, intelligence, protective, immigration, national defense, or national security official when such matters involve foreign intelligence or counterintelligence, in order to assist the official receiving the information in the performance of his official duties. Critically, there is no provision for prior court authorization, although the amended rule does provide that "[w]ithin a reasonable time after such disclosure, an attorney for the government must file under seal a notice with the court stating the fact that such information was disclosed and the departments, agencies, or entities to which the disclosure was made."

Are these changes to the traditional regime justifiable? As Sara Sun Beale and James Felman have pointed out, concerns with grand jury secrecy would not, in all cases, outweigh the need for broader use of national security-related information that might emerge in the course of a grand jury investigation. They go on to assert, however, that the PATRIOT Act's reforms (particularly to the extent that these reforms downplay the role of the judiciary) raise concerns:

> The potential for a backdoor expansion of the grand jury's investigative jurisdiction is . . . problematic because it may increase the risk that the national defense and security institutions will be inappropriately involved in domestic affairs. Domestic law enforcement operates in a legal and constitutional culture that gives substantial weight to the rights of individuals. The relation of the government to its citizens is shaped by the constitutional requirement that the government respect each citizen's constitutional rights. The intelligence and military communities operate in a far different context than domestic law enforcement, and their institutional cultures and values have

been shaped by their roles. Foreign powers, their agents, and their armies have no constitutional rights comparable to the rights identified by the Fourth, Fifth, and Sixth Amendments. In general, therefore, federal law has precluded the military from taking part in domestic law enforcement, and has drawn a sharp distinction between domestic and foreign intelligence surveillance. These limitations have been intended to reduce the likelihood that the military and foreign intelligence communities will erode the rights of American citizens. Particularly in the absence of judicial review, and in a context where the process operates in secret, arming these communities with the powers of the grand jury is highly problematic.

Sara Sun Beale & James E. Felman, The Consequences of Enlisting Federal Grand Juries in the War on Terrorism: Assessing the USA Patriot Act's Changes to Grand Jury Secrecy, 25 Harv. J. L. & Pub. Pol'y 699, 717-718 (2002). Do you agree? Is it likely that the military and the intelligence community will find it convenient to draw upon the powers of the grand jury in their counterterrorism work? Doesn't this depend, in part, on what alternative authorities these communities possess?

C. The Investigative Power

In most cases, the suspect is arrested and a complaint is filed, and later the grand jury is asked to review the evidence to determine if there is enough evidence to indict. But as noted, there is another possible sequence of events, prototypically in a complex corporate matter or organized crime case. Here the government may believe that a crime has occurred or is ongoing, and may even know who the suspected criminals are. But because traditional law enforcement tools — witness interviews, gathering physical evidence, undercover police work — are sometimes insufficient to gather the necessary evidence, the prosecutor turns to the grand jury to assist in the investigation. In this sequence, the grand jury work occurs first, and the suspect is arrested only after the indictment is returned.

The grand jury carries out its investigation through the use of subpoenas — court orders directing a person to come before the grand jury and testify (subpoena ad testificandum) and to produce documents and other tangible items (subpoena duces tecum). The people receiving the subpoenas may be categorized by prosecutors as falling into one of three groups. The "target" is a person "as to whom the prosecutor or the grand jury has substantial evidence linking him or her to the commission of a crime and who, in the judgment of the prosecutor, is a putative defendant." A subpoenaed person is considered a "subject" of the investigation if his or her conduct comes within the scope of the grand jury's investigation, but the conduct is not enough to make the person a target. See U.S. Attorney's Manual 9-11.151. All others who are called before the grand jury are considered "witnesses."

In stark contrast to questioning by the police, the subpoenaed party need not be given the equivalent of *Miranda* warnings before testifying, see United States v. Mandujano, 425 U.S. 564 (1976) (plurality opinion). But like a police interrogation, the prosecutor need not inform the witness that she is the target of the investigation. See United States v. Washington, 431 U.S. 181 (1977). It is the policy of the Justice Department, however, to inform targets and subjects of their rights before they testify, and may, in certain circumstances, inform a person that he is the target of the investigation. U.S. Attorney's Manual 9-11.151, 9-11.153.

Once before the grand jury, the person is placed under oath and subject to questioning by the prosecutor. The rules of evidence do not apply (although as discussed, the privilege rules do apply), which means that the prosecutor is not required to ask questions that would be permitted if they were asked at trial. A person who appears once before the grand jury may be required to return and face later questioning as the investigation proceeds.

Although styled a "grand jury investigation," no one doubts that the prosecutor calls the shots. The prosecutor decides what matters to pursue, which targets to focus on, what witnesses to call, and what documents to request. During the hearing, the prosecutor leads the questioning, and while grand jurors may ask questions of the their own and may even seek additional information, at the end of the process it is the prosecutor who decides which charges will be part of the proposed indictment on which the grand jury will vote.

The prosecutor's control over the grand jury raises an interesting legal question. Every year for the last few decades, the Supreme Court has spent an enormous amount of time and effort defining, limiting, and fine-tuning the constitutional limits on police officers' ability to investigate crime. Which of these limits, if any, should apply to a grand jury investigation? Although the grand jury is not part of law enforcement proper, it nevertheless works under the prosecutor's direction, gathers information that is often similar to what the police gather, and is backed by the court's enforcement power. Do the search and seizure rules apply? How about the Fifth Amendment limits on questioning? As you read the following material, ask yourself why the Court takes such a different approach to grand jury investigations.

1. The Subpoena Power

UNITED STATES v. DIONISIO

Certiorari to the United States Court of Appeals for the Seventh Circuit
410 U.S. 1 (1973)

MR. JUSTICE STEWART delivered the opinion of the Court.

A special grand jury was convened in the Northern District of Illinois in February 1971, to investigate possible violations of federal criminal statutes relating to gambling. In the course of its investigation, the grand jury received in evidence certain voice recordings that had been obtained pursuant to court orders.

The grand jury subpoenaed approximately 20 persons, including the respondent Dionisio, seeking to obtain from them voice exemplars for comparison with the recorded conversations that had been received in evidence. . . . Dionisio and other witnesses refused to furnish the voice exemplars, asserting that these disclosures would violate their rights under the Fourth and Fifth Amendments. . . .

Following a hearing, the District Judge rejected the witnesses' constitutional arguments and ordered them to comply with the grand jury's request . . . When Dionisio persisted in his refusal to respond to the grand jury's directive, the District Court adjudged him in civil contempt and ordered him committed to custody until he obeyed the court order, or until the expiration of 18 months.

The Court of Appeals for the Seventh Circuit reversed . . . [holding] that the Fourth Amendment required a preliminary showing of reasonableness before a grand jury witness could be compelled to furnish a voice exemplar, and that in this case the proposed "seizures" of the voice exemplars would be unreasonable because of the large number of witnesses summoned by the grand jury and directed to produce such exemplars. We disagree. . . .

[T]he obtaining of physical evidence from a person involves a potential Fourth Amendment violation at two different levels — the "seizure" of the "person" necessary to bring him into contact with government agents, and the subsequent search for and seizure of the evidence. . . . The constitutionality of the compulsory production of exemplars from a grand jury witness necessarily turns on [a] dual inquiry — whether either the initial compulsion of the person to appear before the grand jury, or the subsequent directive to make a voice recording is an unreasonable "seizure" within the meaning of the Fourth Amendment.

It is clear that a subpoena to appear before a grand jury is not a "seizure" in the Fourth Amendment sense, even though that summons may be inconvenient or burdensome. Last Term we again acknowledged what has long been recognized, that "[c]itizens generally are not constitutionally immune from grand jury subpoenas. . . ." Branzburg v. Hayes, 408 U.S. 665, 682. We concluded that:

> Although the powers of the grand jury are not unlimited and are subject to the supervision of a judge, the longstanding principle that "the public . . . has a right to every man's evidence," except for those persons protected by a constitutional, common law, or statutory privilege, is particularly applicable to grand jury proceedings.

Id., at 688.

These are recent reaffirmations of the historically grounded obligation of every person to appear and give his evidence before the grand jury. "The personal sacrifice involved is a part of the necessary contribution of the individual to the welfare of the public." Blair v. United States, 250 U.S. 273, 281. . . .

The compulsion exerted by a grand jury subpoena differs from the seizure effected by an arrest or even an investigative "stop" in more than civic obligation. For, as Judge Friendly wrote for the Court of Appeals for the Second Circuit:

> The latter is abrupt, is effected with force or the threat of it and often in demeaning circumstances, and, in the case of arrest, results in a record involving social stigma. A subpoena is served in the same manner as other legal process; it involves no stigma whatever; if the time for appearance is inconvenient, this can generally be altered; and it remains at all times under the control and supervision of a court.

United States v. Doe (Schwartz) 457 F.2d [895, 898].

Thus the Court of Appeals for the Seventh Circuit correctly recognized in a case subsequent to the one now before us, that a "grand jury subpoena to testify is not that kind of governmental intrusion on privacy against which the Fourth Amendment affords protection once the Fifth Amendment is satisfied." Fraser v. United States, 452 F.2d 616, 620.

This case is thus quite different from Davis v. Mississippi, supra, on which the Court of Appeals primarily relied.[2] For in *Davis* it was the initial seizure — the

---

2. In Davis v. Mississippi, 394 U.S. 721 (1969), the Court held that it was error to admit the defendant's fingerprints into evidence at his trial for rape because they had been obtained in violation of the Fourth Amendment. The defendant was one of 25 young black men rounded up and detained for

lawless dragnet detention — that violated the Fourth and Fourteenth Amendments, not the taking of the fingerprints. We noted that "[i]nvestigatory seizures would subject unlimited numbers of innocent persons to the harassment and ignominy incident to involuntary detention," 394 U.S., at 726, and we left open the question whether, consistently with the Fourth and Fourteenth Amendments, narrowly circumscribed procedures might be developed for obtaining fingerprints from people when there was no probable cause to arrest them. *Davis* is plainly inapposite to a case where the initial restraint does not itself infringe the Fourth Amendment.

This is not to say that a grand jury subpoena is some talisman that dissolves all constitutional protections. The grand jury cannot require a witness to testify against himself. It cannot require the production by a person of private books and records that would incriminate him. See Boyd v. United States, 116 U.S. 616, 633-635. The Fourth Amendment provides protection against a grand jury subpoena duces tecum too sweeping in its terms "to be regarded as reasonable." Hale v. Henkel, 201 U.S. 43, 76.

But we are here faced with no such constitutional infirmities in the subpoena to appear before the grand jury or in the order to make the voice recordings. . . .

The Court of Appeals found critical significance in the fact that the grand jury had summoned approximately 20 witnesses to furnish voice exemplars. We think that fact is basically irrelevant to the constitutional issues here. The grand jury may have been attempting to identify a number of voices on the tapes in evidence, or it might have summoned the 20 witnesses in an effort to identify one voice. But whatever the case, "[a] grand jury's investigation is not fully carried out until every available clue has been run down and all witnesses examined in every proper way to find if a crime has been committed. . . ." United States v. Stone, 429 F.2d 138, 140. . . . The grand jury may well find it desirable to call numerous witnesses in the course of an investigation. It does not follow that each witness may resist a subpoena on the ground that too many witnesses have been called. Neither the order to Dionisio to appear nor the order to make a voice recording was rendered unreasonable by the fact that many others were subjected to the same compulsion.

But the conclusion that Dionisio's compulsory appearance before the grand jury was not an unreasonable "seizure" is the answer to only the first part of the Fourth Amendment inquiry here. Dionisio argues that the grand jury's subsequent directive to make the voice recording was itself an infringement of his rights under the Fourth Amendment. We cannot accept that argument.

In Katz v. United States, we said that the Fourth Amendment provides no protection for what "a person knowingly exposes to the public, even in his own home or office. . . ." 389 U.S. [347,] 351. The physical characteristics of a person's voice, its tone and manner, as opposed to the content of a specific conversation, are constantly exposed to the public. Like a man's facial characteristics, or handwriting, his voice is repeatedly produced for others to hear. No person can have a reasonable expectation that others will not know the sound of his voice, any more than he can reasonably expect that his face will be a mystery to the world. . . .

Since neither the summons to appear before the grand jury nor its directive to make a voice recording infringed upon any interest protected by the Fourth

---

fingerprinting in connection with the crime. These detentions were done without the authorization of a warrant and in the absence of any probable cause. The Court held that the fingerprints were the fruit of an unlawful seizure of the defendant's person. — Eds.

Amendment, there was no justification for requiring the grand jury to satisfy even the minimal requirement of "reasonableness" imposed by the Court of Appeals. A grand jury has broad investigative powers to determine whether a crime has been committed and who has committed it. The jurors may act on tips, rumors, evidence offered by the prosecutor, or their own personal knowledge. No grand jury witness is "entitled to set limits to the investigation that the grand jury may conduct." Blair v. United States, 250 U.S., at 282. . . . Since Dionisio raised no valid Fourth Amendment claim, there is no more reason to require a preliminary showing of reasonableness here than there would be in the case of any witness who, despite the lack of any constitutional or statutory privilege, declined to answer a question or comply with a grand jury request. Neither the Constitution nor our prior cases justify any such interference with grand jury proceedings.

The Fifth Amendment guarantees that no civilian may be brought to trial for an infamous crime "unless on a presentment or indictment of a Grand Jury." This constitutional guarantee presupposes an investigative body "acting independently of either prosecuting attorney or judge," Stirone v. United States, 361 U.S. 212, 218, whose mission is to clear the innocent, no less than to bring to trial those who may be guilty. Any holding that would saddle a grand jury with minitrials and preliminary showings would assuredly impede its investigation and frustrate the public's interest in the fair and expeditious administration of the criminal laws. The grand jury may not always serve its historic role as a protective bulwark standing solidly between the ordinary citizen and an overzealous prosecutor, but if it is even to approach the proper performance of its constitutional mission, it must be free to pursue its investigations unhindered by external influence or supervision so long as it does not trench upon the legitimate rights of any witness called before it.

Since the Court of Appeals found an unreasonable search and seizure where none existed, and imposed a preliminary showing of reasonableness where none was required, its judgment is reversed and this case is remanded to that court for further proceedings consistent with this opinion.

It is so ordered. [The opinion of Justice Brennan, concurring in part and dissenting in part, and the dissenting opinion of Justice Douglas are omitted.]

MR. JUSTICE MARSHALL, dissenting.

. . . [T]he present case[ ] involve[s] official investigatory seizures that interfere with personal liberty. The Court considers dispositive, however, the fact that the seizures were effected by the grand jury, rather than the police. I cannot agree.

First, in Hale v. Henkel, 201 U.S. 43, 76 (1906), the Court held that a subpoena duces tecum ordering "the production of books and papers [before a grand jury] may constitute an unreasonable search and seizure within the Fourth Amendment," and on the particular facts of the case, it concluded that the subpoena was "far too sweeping in its terms to be regarded as reasonable." Considered alone, *Hale* would certainly seem to carry a strong implication that a subpoena compelling an individual's personal appearance before a grand jury, like a subpoena ordering the production of private papers, is subject to the Fourth Amendment standard of reasonableness. The protection of the Fourth Amendment is not, after all, limited to personal "papers," but extends also to "persons," "houses," and "effects." It would seem a strange hierarchy of constitutional values that would afford papers more protection from arbitrary governmental interference than people.

The Court, however, offers two interrelated justifications for excepting grand jury subpoenas directed at "persons," rather than "papers," from the constraints of the Fourth Amendment. These are a "historically grounded obligation of every person to appear and give his evidence before the grand jury," and the relative unintrusiveness of the grand jury subpoena on an individual's liberty.

In my view, the Court makes more of history than is justified. The Court treats the "historically grounded obligation" which it now discerns as extending to all "evidence," whatever its character. Yet, so far as I am aware, the obligation "to appear and give evidence" has heretofore been applied by this Court only in the context of testimonial evidence, either oral or documentary. . . .

The Court seems to reason that the exception to the Fourth Amendment for grand jury subpoenas directed at persons is justified by the relative unintrusiveness of the grand jury process on an individual's liberty. . . .

It may be that service of a grand jury subpoena does not involve the same potential for momentary embarrassment as does an arrest or investigatory "stop." But this difference seems inconsequential in comparison to the substantial stigma that — contrary to the Court's assertion — may result from a grand jury appearance as well as from an arrest or investigatory seizure. Public knowledge that a man has been summoned by a federal grand jury investigating, for instance, organized criminal activity can mean loss of friends, irreparable injury to business, and tremendous pressures on one's family life. Whatever nice legal distinctions may be drawn between police and prosecutor, on the one hand, and the grand jury, on the other, the public often treats an appearance before a grand jury as tantamount to a visit to the station house. Indeed, the former is frequently more damaging than the latter, for a grand jury appearance has an air of far greater gravity than a brief visit "downtown" for a "talk." The Fourth Amendment was placed in our Bill of Rights to protect the individual citizen from such potentially disruptive governmental intrusion into his private life. . . .

Nor do I believe that the constitutional problems inherent in such governmental interference with an individual's person are substantially alleviated because one may seek to appear at a "convenient time." . . . No matter how considerate a grand jury may be in arranging for an individual's appearance, the basic fact remains that his liberty has been officially restrained for some period of time. . . .

Of course, the Fourth Amendment does not bar all official seizures of the person, but only those that are unreasonable and are without sufficient cause. With this in mind, it is possible, at least, to explain, if not justify, the failure to apply the protection of the Fourth Amendment to grand jury subpoenas requiring individuals to appear and *testify*. . . .

Certainly the most celebrated function of the grand jury is to stand between the Government and the citizen and thus to protect the latter from harassment and unfounded prosecution. The grand jury does not shed those characteristics that give it insulating qualities when it acts in its investigative capacity. Properly functioning, the grand jury is to be the servant of neither the Government nor the courts, but of the people. As such, we assume that it comes to its task without bias or self-interest. Unlike the prosecutor or policeman, it has no election to win or executive appointment to keep. The anticipated neutrality of the grand jury, even when acting in its investigative capacity, may perhaps be relied upon to prevent unwarranted interference with the lives of private citizens and to ensure that the grand jury's subpoena powers over the person are exercised in only a reasonable fashion.

Under such circumstances, it may be justifiable to give the grand jury broad personal subpoena powers that are outside the purview of the Fourth Amendment for — in contrast to the police — it is not likely that it will abuse those powers.

Whatever the present day validity of the historical assumption of neutrality which underlies the grand jury process, it must at least be recognized that if a grand jury is deprived of the independence essential to the assumption of neutrality — if it effectively surrenders that independence to a prosecutor — the dangers of excessive and unreasonable official interference with personal liberty are exactly those which the Fourth Amendment was intended to prevent. So long as the grand jury carries on its investigatory activities only through the mechanism of testimonial inquiries, the danger of such official usurpation of the grand jury process may not be unreasonably great. Individuals called to testify before the grand jury will have available their Fifth Amendment privilege against self-incrimination. . . .

But when we move beyond the realm of grand jury investigations limited to testimonial inquiries, as the Court does today, the danger increases that law enforcement officials may seek to usurp the grand jury process for the purpose of securing incriminating evidence from a particular suspect through the simple expedient of a subpoena . . . Thus, if the grand jury may summon criminal suspects [to obtain voice exemplars] without complying with the Fourth Amendment, it will obviously present an attractive investigative tool to prosecutor and police. . . .

. . . [B]y holding that the grand jury's power to subpoena these respondents for the purpose of obtaining exemplars is completely outside the purview of the Fourth Amendment, the Court fails to appreciate the essential difference between real and testimonial evidence in the context of these cases, and thereby hastens the reduction of the grand jury into simply another investigative device of law enforcement officials. By contrast, the Court of Appeals, in proper recognition of these dangers, imposed narrow limitations on the subpoena power of the grand jury that are necessary to guard against unreasonable official interference with individual liberty but that would not impair significantly the traditional investigatory powers of that body. . . .

NOTES AND QUESTIONS

1. In addition to the majority's arguments, *Dionisio*'s distinction between a grand jury subpoena and a police seizure might be justified because the subpoenaed person has the chance to challenge it in court before being required to comply. But what if the subpoena requires the witness to appear before the grand jury or to produce documents or other evidence before the grand jury "forthwith" — i.e., immediately? Several courts have upheld the use of such subpoenas (often served when there is a threat that evidence sought by the subpoena will be destroyed) while noting that they may be misused and do not confer on police the authority to seize either the person who is commanded to appear or any items the subpoena may seek. See, e.g., U.S. v. Triumph Capital Group, Inc. 211 F.R.D. 31 (D. Conn. 2002).

2. *Dionisio* states that the Fourth Amendment has little application to a grand jury subpoena seeking testimony from a witness. The situation is somewhat (but only somewhat) different for a subpoena duces tecum. In Hale v. Henkel, 201 U.S. 43 (1906), the Court considered a challenge to a grand jury subpoena demanding the production of corporate documents as part of an antitrust investigation. The Court observed:

> [A]n order for the production of books and papers may constitute an unreasonable search and seizure within the Fourth Amendment. While a search ordinarily implies a quest by an officer of the law, and a seizure contemplates a forcible dispossession of the owner, still, as was held in the *Boyd* [v. United States, 116 U.S. 616 (1886)] case, the substance of the offense is the compulsory production of private papers, whether under a search warrant or a subpoena duces tecum, against which the person, be he individual or corporation, is entitled to protection. Applying the test of reasonableness to the present case, we think the subpoena duces tecum is far too sweeping in its terms to be regarded as reasonable. It does not require the production of a single contract, or of contracts with a particular corporation, or a limited number of documents, but all understandings, contracts, or correspondence between the MacAndrews & Forbes Company, and no less than six different companies, as well as all reports made, and accounts rendered by such companies from the date of the organization of the MacAndrews & Forbes Company, as well as all letters received by that company since its organization from more than a dozen different companies, situated in seven different States in the Union.

Id., at 76-77.

The Court went on to note that "[d]oubtless many, if not all, of these documents may ultimately be required, but some necessity should be shown . . . or some evidence of their materiality produced, to justify an order for the production of such a mass of papers." Id., at 77.

Hale's language is somewhat misleading — over the course of the past century, the Court's bark on this issue has been a good deal worse than its bite. Today, subpoenas are rarely quashed because they are, in the language of the *Hale* Court, "too sweeping . . . to be regarded as reasonable." It would be an exaggeration to say that there is *no* Fourth Amendment regulation of subpoenas. But it would not be much of an exaggeration.

Subpoena recipients may, however, argue that a grand jury request for documents violates Federal Rule of Criminal Procedure 17(c), which states that "A subpoena may order the witness to produce any books, papers, documents, data, or other objects the subpoena designates." Rule 17(c)(2) then says: "On motion made promptly, the court may quash or modify the subpoena if compliance would be unreasonable or oppressive." One interpretation of this Rule is that there is a "reasonableness requirement" that attaches to the grand jury subpoena power. Consider the Court's interpretation of this requirement in the next case.

UNITED STATES v. R. ENTERPRISES, INC.

Certiorari to the U.S. Court of Appeals for the Fourth Circuit
498 U.S. 292 (1991)

JUSTICE O'CONNOR delivered the opinion of the Court.*

This case requires the Court to decide what standards apply when a party seeks to avoid compliance with a subpoena duces tecum issued in connection with a grand jury investigation.

---

* Justice Scalia joins in all but Part III-B of this opinion.

I

Since 1986, a federal grand jury sitting in the Eastern District of Virginia has been investigating allegations of interstate transportation of obscene materials. In early 1988, the grand jury issued a series of subpoenas to three companies — Model Magazine Distributors, Inc. (Model), R. Enterprises, Inc., and MFR Court Street Books, Inc. (MFR). Model is a New York distributor of sexually oriented paperback books, magazines, and videotapes. R. Enterprises, which distributes adult materials, and MFR, which sells books, magazines, and videotapes, are also based in New York. All three companies are wholly owned by Martin Rothstein. The grand jury subpoenas sought a variety of corporate books and records and, in Model's case, copies of 193 videotapes that Model had shipped to retailers in the Eastern District of Virginia. All three companies moved to quash the subpoenas, arguing that the subpoenas called for production of materials irrelevant to the grand jury's investigation and that the enforcement of the subpoenas would likely infringe their First Amendment rights.

The District Court, after extensive hearings, denied the motions to quash [on a variety of grounds]. . . . Notwithstanding these findings, the companies refused to comply with the subpoenas. The District Court found each in contempt and fined them $500 per day, but stayed imposition of the fine pending appeal.

The Court of Appeals for the Fourth Circuit upheld the business records subpoenas issued to Model, but remanded the motion to quash the subpoena for Model's videotapes. Of particular relevance here, the Court of Appeals quashed the business records subpoenas issued to R. Enterprises and MFR. In doing so, it applied the standards set out by this Court in United States v. Nixon, 418 U.S. 683, 699-700 (1974). The court recognized that *Nixon* dealt with a trial subpoena, not a grand jury subpoena, but determined that the rule was "equally applicable" in the grand jury context. Accordingly, it required the Government to clear the three hurdles that *Nixon* established in the trial context — relevancy, admissibility, and specificity — in order to enforce the grand jury subpoenas. The court concluded that the challenged subpoenas did not satisfy the *Nixon* standards, finding [in part that the subpoenas] . . . failed "to meet the requirements [*sic*] that any documents subpoenaed under [Federal] Rule [of Criminal Procedure] 17(c) must be admissible as evidence at trial." The Court of Appeals did not consider whether enforcement of the subpoenas duces tecum issued to respondents implicated the First Amendment.

We granted certiorari to determine whether the Court of Appeals applied the proper standard in evaluating the grand jury subpoenas issued to respondents. We now reverse.

II

The grand jury occupies a unique role in our criminal justice system. It is an investigatory body charged with the responsibility of determining whether or not a crime has been committed. Unlike this Court, whose jurisdiction is predicated on a specific case or controversy, the grand jury "can investigate merely on suspicion that the law is being violated, or even just because it wants assurance that it is not." United States v. Morton Salt Co., 338 U.S. 632, 642-643 (1950). The function of the grand jury is to inquire into all information that might possibly bear on its investigation until it has identified an offense or has satisfied itself that none has occurred. As a necessary consequence of its investigatory function, the grand jury paints with a broad brush. "A grand jury investigation 'is not fully carried out until every available clue has been run down and all witnesses examined in every proper way to find if a crime has been committed.'" Branzburg v. Hayes, 408 U.S. 665, 701 (1972), quoting United States v. Stone, 429 F.2d 138, 140 (CA2 1970).

A grand jury subpoena is thus much different from a subpoena issued in the context of a prospective criminal trial, where a specific offense has been identified and a particular defendant charged. "[T]he identity of the offender, and the precise nature of the offense, if there be one, normally are developed at the conclusion of the grand jury's labors, not at the beginning." Blair v. United States, 250 U.S. 273, 282 (1919). In short, the Government cannot be required to justify the issuance of a grand jury subpoena by presenting evidence sufficient to establish probable cause because the very purpose of requesting the information is to ascertain whether probable cause exists.

This Court has emphasized on numerous occasions that many of the rules and restrictions that apply at a trial do not apply in grand jury proceedings. This is especially true of evidentiary restrictions. The same rules that, in an adversary hearing on the merits, may increase the likelihood of accurate determinations of guilt or innocence do not necessarily advance the mission of a grand jury, whose task is to conduct an ex parte investigation to determine whether or not there is probable cause to prosecute a particular defendant. In Costello v. United States, 350 U.S. 359 (1956), this Court declined to apply the rule against hearsay to grand jury proceedings. Strict observance of trial rules in the context of a grand jury's preliminary investigation "would result in interminable delay but add nothing to the assurance of a fair trial." Id., at 364. In United States v. Calandra, 414 U.S. 338 (1974), we held that the Fourth Amendment exclusionary rule does not apply to grand jury proceedings. Permitting witnesses to invoke the exclusionary rule would "delay and disrupt grand jury proceedings" by requiring adversary hearings on peripheral matters, id., at 349, and would effectively transform such proceedings into preliminary trials on the merits, id., at 349-350. The teaching of the Court's decisions is clear: A grand jury "may compel the production of evidence or the testimony of witnesses as it considers appropriate, and its operation generally is unrestrained by the technical procedural and evidentiary rules governing the conduct of criminal trials," id., at 343.

This guiding principle renders suspect the Court of Appeals' holding that the standards announced in *Nixon* as to subpoenas issued in anticipation of trial apply equally in the grand jury context. The multifactor test announced in *Nixon* would invite procedural delays and detours while courts evaluate the relevancy and admissibility of documents sought by a particular subpoena. We have expressly stated that grand jury proceedings should be free of such delays. "Any holding that would saddle a grand jury with minitrials and preliminary showings would assuredly impede its investigation and frustrate the public's interest in the fair and expeditious administration of the criminal laws." United States v. Dionisio, 410 U.S. 1, 17 (1973). Additionally, application of the *Nixon* test in this context ignores that grand jury proceedings are subject to strict secrecy requirements. See Fed. Rule Crim. Proc. 6(e). Requiring the Government to explain in too much detail the particular reasons underlying a subpoena threatens to compromise "the indispensable secrecy of grand jury proceedings." United States v. Johnson, 319 U.S. 503, 513 (1943). Broad disclosure also affords the targets of investigation far more information about the grand jury's internal workings than the Federal Rules of Criminal Procedure appear to contemplate.

III

A

The investigatory powers of the grand jury are nevertheless not unlimited. Grand juries are not licensed to engage in arbitrary fishing expeditions, nor may they select targets of investigation out of malice or an intent to harass. In this case, the focus of our inquiry is the limit imposed on a grand jury by Federal Rule of Criminal Procedure 17(c), which governs the issuance of subpoenas duces tecum in federal criminal proceedings. The Rule provides that "[t]he court on motion made promptly may quash or modify the subpoena if compliance would be unreasonable or oppressive."

This standard is not self-explanatory. As we have observed, "what is reasonable depends on the context." New Jersey v. T.L.O., 469 U.S. 325, 337 (1985). In *Nixon*, this Court defined what is reasonable in the context of a jury trial. We determined that, in order to require production of information prior to trial, a party must make a reasonably specific request for information that would be both relevant and admissible at trial. 418 U.S., at 700. But, for the reasons we have explained above, the *Nixon* standard does not apply in the context of grand jury proceedings. In the grand jury context, the decision as to what offense will be charged is routinely not made until after the grand jury has concluded its investigation. One simply cannot know in advance whether information sought during the investigation will be relevant and admissible in a prosecution for a particular offense.

To the extent that Rule 17(c) imposes some reasonableness limitation on grand jury subpoenas, however, our task is to define it. In doing so, we recognize that a party to whom a grand jury subpoena is issued faces a difficult situation. As a rule, grand juries do not announce publicly the subjects of their investigations. A party who desires to challenge a grand jury subpoena thus may have no conception of the Government's purpose in seeking production of the requested information. Indeed, the party will often not know whether he or she is a primary target of the investigation or merely a peripheral witness. Absent even minimal information, the subpoena recipient is likely to find it exceedingly difficult to persuade a court that "compliance would be unreasonable." As one pair of commentators has summarized it, the challenging party's "unenviable task is to seek to persuade the court that the subpoena that has been served on [him or her] could not possibly serve any investigative purpose that the grand jury could legitimately be pursuing." 1 S. Beale & W. Bryson, Grand Jury Law and Practice §6:28 (1986).

Our task is to fashion an appropriate standard of reasonableness, one that gives due weight to the difficult position of subpoena recipients but does not impair the strong governmental interests in affording grand juries wide latitude, avoiding minitrials on peripheral matters, and preserving a necessary level of secrecy. We begin by reiterating that the law presumes, absent a strong showing to the contrary, that a grand jury acts within the legitimate scope of its authority. Consequently, a grand jury subpoena issued through normal channels is presumed to be reasonable, and the burden of showing unreasonableness must be on the recipient who seeks to avoid compliance. Indeed, this result is indicated by the language of Rule 17(c), which permits a subpoena to be quashed only "on motion" and "if *compliance* would be unreasonable" (emphasis added). To the extent that the Court of Appeals placed an initial burden on the Government, it committed error. Drawing on the principles articulated above, we conclude that where, as here, a subpoena is challenged on relevancy grounds, the motion to quash must be denied unless the district court determines that there is no reasonable possibility that the category of materials the Government seeks will produce information relevant to the general subject of the grand jury's investigation. Respondents did not challenge the subpoenas as being too indefinite nor did they claim that compliance would be overly burdensome.

B

It seems unlikely, of course, that a challenging party who does not know the general subject matter of the grand jury's investigation, no matter how valid that party's claim, will be able to make the necessary showing that compliance would be unreasonable. After all, a subpoena recipient "cannot put his whole life before the court in order to show that there is no crime to be investigated," Marston's, Inc. v. Strand, 114 Ariz. 260, 270, 560 P.2d 778, 788 (1977) (Gordon, J., specially concurring in part and dissenting in part). Consequently, a court may be justified in a case where unreasonableness is alleged in requiring the Government to reveal the general subject of the grand jury's investigation before requiring the challenging party to carry its burden of persuasion. We need not resolve this question in the present case, however, as there is no doubt that respondents knew the subject of the grand jury investigation pursuant to which the business records subpoenas were issued. In cases where the recipient of the subpoena does not know the nature of the investigation, we are confident that district courts will be able to craft appropriate procedures that balance the interests of the subpoena recipient against the strong governmental interests in maintaining secrecy, preserving investigatory flexibility, and avoiding procedural delays. For example, to ensure that subpoenas are not routinely challenged as a form of discovery, a district court may require that the Government reveal the subject of the investigation to the trial court *in camera*, so that the court may determine whether the motion to quash has a reasonable prospect for success before it discloses the subject matter to the challenging party.

IV

Applying these principles in this case demonstrates that the District Court correctly denied respondents' motions to quash. It is undisputed that all three companies — Model, R. Enterprises, and MFR — are owned by the same person, that all do business in the same area, and that one of the three, Model, has shipped sexually explicit materials into the Eastern District of Virginia. The District Court could have concluded from these facts that there was a reasonable possibility that the business records of R. Enterprises and MFR would produce information relevant to the grand jury's investigation into the interstate transportation of obscene materials. Respondents' blanket denial of any connection to Virginia did not suffice to render the District Court's conclusion invalid. A grand jury need not accept on faith the self-serving assertions of those who may have committed criminal acts. Rather, it is entitled to determine for itself whether a crime has been committed. . . .

The judgment is reversed insofar as the Court of Appeals quashed the subpoenas issued to R. Enterprises and MFR, and the case is remanded for further proceedings consistent with this opinion.

It is so ordered.

JUSTICE STEVENS, with whom JUSTICE MARSHALL and JUSTICE BLACKMUN join, concurring in part and concurring in the judgment.

Federal Rule of Criminal Procedure 17(c) authorizes a federal district court to quash or modify a grand jury subpoena duces tecum "if compliance would be unreasonable or oppressive." See United States v. Calandra, 414 U.S. 338, 346, n. 4 (1974). This Rule requires the district court to balance the burden of compliance, on the one hand, against the governmental interest in obtaining the documents on the other. A more burdensome subpoena should be justified by a somewhat higher degree of probable relevance than a subpoena that imposes a minimal or nonexistent burden. Against the procedural history of this case, the Court has attempted to define the term "reasonable" in the abstract, looking only at the relevance side of the balance. Because I believe that this truncated approach to the Rule will neither provide adequate guidance to the district court nor place any meaningful constraint on the overzealous prosecutor, I add these comments. . . .

The moving party has the initial task of demonstrating to the Court that he has some valid objection to compliance. This showing might be made in various ways. Depending on the volume and location of the requested materials, the mere cost in terms of time, money, and effort of responding to a dragnet subpoena could satisfy the initial hurdle. Similarly, if a witness showed that compliance with the subpoena would intrude significantly on his privacy interests, or call for the disclosure of trade secrets or other confidential information, further inquiry would be required. Or, as in this case, the movant might demonstrate that compliance would have First Amendment implications.

For the reasons stated by the Court, in the grand jury context the law enforcement interest will almost always prevail, and the documents must be produced. I stress, however, that the Court's opinion should not be read to suggest that the deferential relevance standard the Court has formulated will govern decision in every case, no matter how intrusive or burdensome the request.

I agree with the Court that what is "unreasonable or oppressive" in the context of a trial subpoena is not necessarily unreasonable or oppressive in the grand jury context. Although the same language of Rule 17(c) governs both situations, the teaching of United States v. Nixon, 418 U.S. 683 (1974), is not directly applicable to the very different grand jury context. Thus, I join in Parts I and II of the Court's opinion, and I am in accord with its decision to send the case back to the Court of Appeals.

NOTES AND QUESTIONS

1. *R. Enterprises* reaffirmed the view that "A grand jury investigation is not fully carried out until every available clue has been run down and all witnesses examined in every proper way to find if a crime has been committed," and that a grand jury "can investigate merely on suspicion that the law is being violated, or even just because it wants assurance that it is not." Is it troublesome that the grand jury has — at least in some respects — more sweeping investigative powers than the

police? Or, given that the prosecutor is in control of the grand jury process, is it desirable for an officer of the court to have this authority, to fill in the investigative gaps in the police power? Does the answer depend on the extent to which we trust prosecutors not to use this power simply to investigate disfavored people or groups?

2. What is the effect of *R. Enterprises'* relevance requirement? The Court says that one should start with a fairly strong presumption in favor of the subpoena and then ask whether "there is no reasonable possibility that the category of materials the Government seeks will produce information relevant to the general subject of the grand jury's investigation." How likely is a "reasonable possibility"? In light of this standard, can you hypothesize a case where the defendant will be able to show that the Court's standard is satisfied and the subpoena will be quashed?

3. Whatever the "reasonable possibility" standard means, it is plainly much less onerous than a probable cause standard. Why should that be so? Why should the standards for obtaining documents by subpoena be so much more lax than the standards that must be met to justify a police search for those same documents?

Two possible answers may be worth considering. The first bears on a good deal of the law of search and seizure; it is laid out in Louis Michael Seidman, The Problems with Privacy's Problem, 93 Mich. L. Rev. 1079 (1993). Seidman's claim is that police searches always involve "collateral damage" — the officer sees things other than the things he is looking for, and the encounter between the officer and citizen often involves substantial coercion — and a large part of what the probable cause requirement protects against is that collateral harm. Subpoenas, he says, are different:

> Subpoenas amount to self-searches. They involve no violence, no disruption, no public humiliation or embarrassment. Like the required completion of tax returns, subpoenas invade informational privacy but impose no collateral damage. For precisely this reason, the Court treats them no differently from tax returns. So long as the subpoena is "reasonable" and not unduly burdensome, a defendant has no . . . right not to comply.

Id., at 1092.

The second reason relates to the historical origins of the grand jury. A probable cause standard and warrant requirement might be necessary means of checking the ability of government officials to use their coercive power improperly, a means of protecting, in the words of the Fourth Amendment, "the right of the people to be secure in their persons, houses, papers, and effects." But the grand jury, in its classical conception, is not allied to government officials; it is *itself* "the people." This view of grand juries fits with a larger view of the original understanding of the Bill of Rights as a whole: not as a series of countermajoritarian rights, but as a series of *majoritarian* protections against official oppression. That understanding might explain the breadth of grand juries' power: Grand juries were a way that the people could check the power of government officials; they were not themselves in need of checking.

4. Are you persuaded by this reasoning? Perhaps Professor Seidman's argument can be turned on its head. After all, it's one thing when police obtain and look through my appointment book because they have probable cause to believe it will reflect the payment of bribes to a local official. It's quite another, isn't it, when my telephone records, bank records, and credit card receipts are perused by government prosecutors and laypeople who don't even know whether a crime has been committed? Consider the following analysis:

[T]he federal subpoena power [is] something akin to a blank check. Prosecutors can go after whomever they like; they can be as intrusive as they choose; they can fight as hard as they want. Federal criminal law covers enough ground that if prosecutors look hard enough, they can find nearly anyone to have violated it. And prosecutors decide how hard to look. . . . Some sort of serious regulation is needed. The real question is, what form should it take? . . .

An analogy to the civil process is useful. The rules for discovery in civil cases invite case-by-case adjustment based on the seriousness and scope of the case. Trial judges can give lawyers and litigants a lot of rope or a little. . . .

If rough judgments about the importance of a case and the need for intrusive investigation are possible in civil cases, they are possible in white-collar criminal investigations as well. Indeed, the idea that unreasonably burdensome subpoenas should be quashed already exists in the law, and on occasion that idea translates into legally enforceable limits. What does not presently exist is the idea that the line between reasonable and unreasonable burdens should track the line between serious and less-than-serious crimes. . . . And that judgment ought to be made by courts, not by the prosecutors conducting the investigation.

William J. Stuntz, O.J. Simpson, Bill Clinton, and the Transsubstantive Fourth Amendment, 114 Harv. L. Rev. 842, 864-868 (2001).

2. Limits on the Investigative Powers

Although the grand jury is a powerful investigative tool, there are some restrictions on its authority. The most obvious limit is a practical one: The grand jury is free to ask anyone, including suspects, to produce physical evidence, but if a person really has possession of the bloody knife used in the crime, he probably won't produce it. From the suspect's perspective, going to jail for contempt of the grand jury is better than proving your own guilt of a murder, so for this kind of physical evidence, a search warrant executed by the police is required. The subpoena power is thus only useful when there is reason to believe that the person served will diligently search for and faithfully produce the requested material.

The ability to gather physical evidence through a subpoena may also be limited by the type of crime under investigation. Murders and drug deals do not usually leave paper trails. Physical evidence and live witnesses tend to be the keys to solving those crimes, and police tend to gather that evidence through searches and seizures and interrogations. White-collar criminal investigations are different. The police cannot feasibly search through hundreds of file cabinets looking for a single piece of paper, even though that paper may be the key to proving that a crime occurred. So the government requires suspects (or witnesses, or custodians of relevant corporate documents) to do the work of searching through the file cabinets and assembling the relevant papers.

In addition, there are legal limits on the types of information that can be subpoenaed. Most important, the grand jury's subpoena power cannot compel the disclosure of privileged information. Although the rules of evidence generally do not apply to a grand jury proceeding, a grand jury witness need not disclose attorney-client communications, spousal communications, or information conveyed by the witness to a priest or physician. See Fed. R. Ev. 1101(d). And of course, the grand jury cannot compel a witness to testify or produce information in violation of the Fifth Amendment privilege against self-incrimination.

As discussed in Chapters 4 and 6, the Fifth Amendment privilege means that a grand jury witness cannot, by threat of contempt, be compelled to answer questions that would implicate him in a crime. The privilege allows the defendant to refuse to answer both direct questions ("Did you rob the bank?") and facially innocuous questions that might help the government to uncover evidence of the suspect's criminality ("Have you ever met Tony Salerno?"). As the Supreme Court has said, a suspect can refuse to provide information even if it would just provide a "link in the chain of evidence needed to prosecute" the speaker for a federal crime. Hoffman v. United States, 341 U.S. 479, 486 (1951). This standard is sufficiently broad that once a suspect invokes the privilege, it is very difficult for the government to convince a court that the fear of self-incrimination is a sham.

A grand jury witness can refuse to answer questions that might implicate himself but cannot refuse to answer simply because the answer is embarrassing, may cause the witness to lose his job, or might implicate some other person in a crime. Note that in this respect, the grand jury hearing is quite different from a suspect's refusal to answer questions during a police interrogation. In an interrogation, the suspect can refuse to answer any question for any reason, even a question that runs no risk of incriminating the speaker. Before the grand jury, however, the subpoena obligates the witness to speak unless the answer to a particular question is privileged.

The Fifth Amendment thus serves as a powerful protection for the individual defendant or, if you prefer, a significant limit on the government's investigative powers. The target of the investigation will almost certainly invoke the privilege rather than testify before the grand jury, so in a typical case, the target will not even be subpoenaed (although he might be invited to testify if he wishes to do so). Likewise, those who are involved in the transactions or who are part of the enterprise under investigation may well decide to stand on the privilege rather than testify, particularly since the grand jury hearings are secret and so no public stigma will attach to "taking the Fifth."

But critically, the prosecutor has a tool that allows her to overcome the suspect's privilege, albeit one that may come at a high cost. For the Fifth Amendment to apply, the testimony that the government is seeking to compel must incriminate the suspect in a crime *for which he can be prosecuted*. If there is no chance of prosecution, the suspect's privilege against self-incrimination disappears and a witness must testify, even about crimes that she committed, on pain of contempt. The next two sections discuss how a prosecutor might compel this testimony — through the power to immunize.

a. Immunizing Testimony

Assume that a grand jury is investigating a case of suspected corporate fraud. The corporate records do not reveal any wrongdoing, but the prosecutor believes that most of the relevant evidence was destroyed by someone inside the company. The problem is that no one who is willing to testify knows anything, and those who are in a position to know the truth have all asserted the Fifth Amendment privilege. What can a prosecutor do to break this impasse?

Federal statutes provide one answer: Consider 18 U.S.C. §§6002 and 6003.

§6002. Immunity generally

Whenever a witness refuses, on the basis of his privilege against self-incrimination, to testify or provide other information in a proceeding before or ancillary to —

(1) a court or grand jury of the United States,

(2) an agency of the United States, or

(3) either House of Congress, a joint committee of the two Houses, or a committee or a subcommittee of either House,

and the person presiding over the proceeding communicates to the witness an order issued under this title, the witness may not refuse to comply with the order on the basis of his privilege against self-incrimination; but no testimony or other information compelled under the order (or any information directly or indirectly derived from such testimony or other information) may be used against the witness in any criminal case, except a prosecution for perjury, giving a false statement, or otherwise failing to comply with the order.

§6003. Court and grand jury proceedings

(a) In the case of any individual who has been or may be called to testify or provide other information at any proceeding before or ancillary to a court of the United States or a grand jury of the United States, the United States district court for the judicial district in which the proceeding is or may be held shall issue, in accordance with subsection (b) of this section, upon the request of the United States attorney for such district, an order requiring such individual to give testimony or provide other information which he refuses to give or provide on the basis of his privilege against self-incrimination, such order to become effective as provided in section 6002 of this title.

(b) A United States attorney may, with the approval of the Attorney General, the Deputy Attorney General, the Associate Attorney General or any designated Assistant Attorney General or Deputy Assistant Attorney General, request an order under subsection (a) of this section when in his judgment —

(1) the testimony or other information from such individual may be necessary to the public interest; and

(2) such individual has refused or is likely to refuse to testify or provide other information on the basis of his privilege against self-incrimination.

There are several important features to notice about these statutes. First, notice the process Congress has prescribed for immunizing a witness. If a U.S. Attorney decides (with approval of the Justice Department) that obtaining a witness's testimony is in the public interest and that the witness is likely to invoke the Fifth Amendment privilege, the prosecutor simply requests a court order compelling the witness to testify, and the district court "shall issue" that order. In other words, the decision to obtain an immunity order requiring the witness to speak rests entirely with the prosecutor, with the court playing only an administrative role.

Why do you think that Congress entrusted the decision entirely to the executive branch? Shouldn't judges have at least some authority to decide what evidence should or should not be permitted in a trial or grand jury hearing? Or does the material on the prosecutor's charging discretion (see Chapter 9) provide an adequate justification for this process?

Second, there is nothing consensual or voluntary about a statutory immunity order; the witness must speak whether she wants to or not, and will be held in contempt if she refuses. Although earlier in the development of the Fifth Amendment the Court concluded that the privilege helped protect an individual's dignitary interest in not being forced to provide evidence against herself, see, e.g., Murphy v.

Waterfront Commission of New York Harbor, 378 U.S. 52 (1964) (Fifth Amendment privilege "reflects many of our fundamental values and most noble aspirations: . . . [including] our preference for an accusatorial rather than an inquisitorial system of criminal justice . . . [and] our respect for the inviolability of the human personality and of the right of each individual to a private enclave where he may lead a private life"), §6002 makes it clear that prosecutors can overcome this interest simply by imposing an immunity order on the witness. As a result, the Court has more recently concluded that the Fifth Amendment is entirely about ensuring that a witness is free from prosecution that is based on self-incriminating testimony. See U.S. v. Balsys, 542 U.S. 666 (1998).

Third, the government's ability to compel a witness to provide self-incriminating testimony comes at a price. Although the government may force a witness to speak, "no testimony or other information compelled under the order (or any information directly or indirectly derived from such testimony or other information) may be used against the witness in any criminal case," except for cases of perjury or failing to comply with the court's order to testify.

Is this tradeoff — the witness loses his right to invoke the Fifth Amendment protection, and in return the prosecutor can't use that testimony to prosecute the witness — sufficient to protect the constitutional privilege? Part of your answer may depend on how broadly the courts construe the immunity grant, and in particular, the meaning of the phrase "any information directly or indirectly derived from such testimony." The contours of this phrase have proven to be one of the most complex areas of criminal procedure, as the following material reveals.

NOTES AND QUESTIONS

1. Although the ability to immunize witnesses to obtain their testimony has been around a long time, the precise scope of an immunity grant remains a complex issue. For many years, it was believed that if the government was going to immunize a witness, it must provide "transactional" immunity — a blanket prohibition on later prosecuting the witness for the crime to which the testimony relates. Even if the police later learn about the witness's involvement in the bank robbery from a completely independent source, or even if the prosecutor already had enough information about the witness's involvement in the bank robbery to convict before granting the immunity, the witness is safe — the immunity makes the "transaction" (i.e., the bank robbery) off limits for prosecution.

Section 6002, however, only grants "use" immunity; it only prohibits the prosecutor from using the immunized testimony itself, directly or indirectly, to prosecute the testifying witness. If the prosecutor derives evidence from independent sources, the witness can still be prosecuted for the crime about which he was compelled to speak. This obviously provides less protection than transaction immunity, and so in Kastigar v. United States, 406 U.S. 441 (1972), the defendant challenged §6002 as being inconsistent with the Fifth Amendment. The Court disagreed, finding the "direct and indirect use" prohibition adequate to protect the defendant's interest. "[T]he immunity provided by 18 U.S.C. §6002 leaves the witness and the prosecutorial authorities in substantially the same position as if the witness had claimed the Fifth Amendment privilege," said the Court. "The immunity therefore is coextensive with the privilege and suffices to supplant it." Id., at 462.

2. *Kastigar* recognized, however, that the protection afforded by §6002 was only as good as the ability to ensure that immunized testimony was not used in a later prosecution. Preventing the direct use is easy — if the witness testified under a grant of immunity, the prosecutor cannot use that testimony to prove the witness's guilt in a later trial, or even to impeach the witness. "Indirect" use of the testimony has proven to be a more difficult concept. We know from *Kastigar* that it protects against "the use of compelled testimony as an 'investigatory lead,' and also bar[s] the use of any evidence obtained by focusing investigation on a witness as a result of his compelled disclosures." Id., at 460 (footnote omitted). What else is meant by the indirect use of immunized testimony is explored in more detail below in the *Hubbell* case, although even after that decision the answer is far from clear.

Because of this uncertainty, one of the risks that the prosecutor incurs in immunizing through §§6002 and 6003 is that he will later be effectively precluded from prosecuting the witness at all. As soon as the prosecution charges a previously immunized witness, the defense will move to dismiss, and the court will hold a "Kastigar hearing" to decide whether the prosecutor is attempting to make direct or indirect use of the immunized evidence. Critically, the government bears the burden at that hearing; as the Court explained:

> Once a defendant demonstrates that he has testified, under a state grant of immunity, to matters related to the federal prosecution, the federal authorities have the burden of showing that their evidence is not tainted by establishing that they had an independent, legitimate source for the disputed evidence. This burden of proof, which we reaffirm as appropriate, is not limited to a negation of taint; rather, it imposes on the prosecution the affirmative duty to prove that the evidence it proposes to use is derived from a legitimate source wholly independent of the compelled testimony.

Id. (internal quotation marks and citation omitted).

If you were a prosecutor, how would you try to establish that the evidence you plan to use against the defendant did *not* derive even indirectly from the immunized testimony? How would the timing and the identity of the law enforcement personnel involved in the evidence gathering affect your arguments?

3. Suppose Aaron and Betty are suspected of smuggling drugs from Canada into Maine. Believing that Aaron is the ringleader and that Betty is a peripheral player, the U.S. Attorney for Maine immunizes Betty under §§6002 and 6003 to obtain evidence against Aaron. Betty, however, refuses to testify, arguing that even if the federal prosecutors are barred from using her immunized testimony against her, she still faces a realistic threat of prosecution for drug possession by the Maine *state* prosecutor as well as by Canadian authorities, neither of whom are bound by the federal statutes and are thus free to use Betty's immunized admissions to prosecute her. (Recall also that under Criminal Rule 6(e)(3)(E), federal prosecutors may, with leave of court, disclose grand jury material to state or foreign prosecutors to assist with the enforcement of their respective criminal laws.) Thus, Betty argues, the scope of the immunity grant is *not* "substantially the same" as the Fifth Amendment privilege, *Kastigar* notwithstanding. Will this argument allow Betty to refuse to testify?

The Supreme Court has given a mixed answer to this question. In Murphy v. Waterfront Commission of New York Harbor, 378 U.S. 52, 78 (1964), the Court found that the Fifth Amendment privilege "protects a state witness against incrimination under federal as well as state law and a federal witness against incrimination under state as well as federal law." As a result, if a witness is immunized by a federal prosecutor in a federal case, a state prosecutor is barred from using that immunized testimony, directly or indirectly, against that witness to prosecute a state crime. Betty therefore cannot refuse to testify in the federal case, because the federal immunity protects against a state's use of the testimony. And while she still might be prosecuted under Maine law, the state district attorney will have to show that his evidence is not tainted by the immunized federal testimony.

Betty's worries about the Canadian prosecutors are a different matter. In U.S. v. Balsys, 542 U.S. 666 (1998), federal prosecutors issued an administrative subpoena to a resident alien, seeking to question him on whether he had lied in his immigration application about his activities during World War II. (The government suspected that Balsys had lied about working with the Nazis.) Balsys refused to answer, citing the Fifth Amendment privilege. Although the statute of limitations had run on any crimes arising from misstatements on the immigration forms — and thus any responses would not subject him to prosecution under U.S. law — Balsys claimed that his answers could subject him to prosecution under Israeli and Lithuanian law. The Court was unpersuaded, holding that the Fifth Amendment privilege did not protect against the threat of foreign prosecutions, and thus a witness could not refuse to comply with an immunity order on these grounds.

4. Statutory immunity under §§6002 and 6003 is not the only source of a prosecutor's power to immunize, and may not even be the most common way. A prosecutor and a witness might reach a separate agreement by which the witness will provide testimony, and, in return, the prosecutor will provide some level of immunity for that testimony. Under these "letter agreements" (sometimes called "pocket immunity"), the extent of the immunity will be whatever the parties agree to — if the witness has valuable information that is not otherwise available to the government, and if the witness is a relatively small player in a larger criminal enterprise, the prosecution might be willing to extend transaction immunity for the testimony. However, if the witness has relatively little bargaining power, the prosecutor might agree not to use the immunized testimony directly against the witness, but may reserve the right to use the testimony indirectly, say as a source of leads to other evidence. Because the immunity comes by way of agreement, the parties can include whatever terms they wish. But despite their nonstatutory and informal nature, courts will enforce these letter agreements just as they would a grant of immunity under §§6002 and 6003.

Letter agreements for immunity obviously offer the prosecutor a great deal of flexibility, but from the government's perspective, they have at least one significant drawback: Unlike statutory immunity, the witness has to agree to the terms of the immunity. The only way to truly "compel" the witness to testify is through the §§6002 and 6003 process.

5. Perhaps because of the flexibility of letter agreements, or perhaps because of the complexity of the legal doctrine, federal requests for immunity under §§6002 and 6003 have dropped dramatically in recent years. In 1987, federal prosecutors in the Criminal Division made over 2,300 requests to the Justice Department, seeking permission to immunize over 4,600 witnesses. By 2007, the number of requests had dropped to 665, seeking to immunize only 1,134 witnesses. Sourcebook of Criminal Justice Statistics, tbl. 5.1.2007, www.albany.edu/sourcebook/pdf/t512007.pdf.

6. Having the power to immunize is one thing, using it is another, and many prosecutors are very reluctant to immunize witnesses. Why do you think this is so? What risks does the prosecutor take in extending immunity? One obvious concern is that

the prosecutor might immunize the wrong person — the goal with immunity is to give something of value to the little fish in order to capture the big fish in the criminal scheme, but sometimes the prosecutor can't tell the size of the fish being immunized until after the evidence is gathered. So if he immunizes Betty to get Aaron, and the evidence later reveals that Betty is in fact the head of the smuggling ring, this is surely a bad day at the U.S. Attorney's office.

What other risks does the government run? In particular, ask yourself how an immunity order might affect the truthfulness of the witness's testimony as well as the jury's assessment of the witness's credibility.

b.   Documents and the Act of Production

Complications arise when a witness is asked not to testify directly but to produce documents or other information that might be incriminating. Consider a case of suspected corporate fraud. The grand jury subpoenas the corporation's financial records, meaning that someone at the company — perhaps the bookkeeper or chief financial officer — must cull through the documents, decide which ones are responsive, and produce them to the grand jury. Suppose the bookkeeper examines the relevant documents and realizes that they directly implicate him and the other officers in a scheme to defraud. Can the bookkeeper refuse to comply with the subpoena on Fifth Amendment grounds?

The answer can be complex. For over a century, the basic rule has been that corporations have no Fifth Amendment privilege, see Hale v. Henkel, 201 U.S. 43 (1906). As a result, corporate officers generally must produce corporate documents, whether or not those documents incriminate the corporation or even the officers themselves. So after *Hale*, it was easy to subpoena corporate documents, but still very hard to obtain documents from individual white-collar suspects.

Then came Fisher v. United States, 425 U.S. 391 (1976). *Fisher* involved a subpoena for documents related to the defendant's income taxes. The documents had been prepared by the defendant's accountant and were in the defendant's possession until he gave them to his lawyer for safekeeping. The question before the Court was whether the lawyer had to hand over the documents. The Court held that, if the defendant would have had a valid Fifth Amendment objection to turning over the documents himself, the lawyer could raise that objection on his client's behalf. So, in a roundabout way, *Fisher* raised the question of whether the Fifth Amendment allowed a defendant to refuse to hand over incriminating documents that he owned and possessed. This was the same issue the Court had decided in the defendant's favor 90 years earlier in Boyd v. United States, 116 U.S. 616 (1886) (discussed in Chapter 4).

In *Fisher*, the Court went the other way. The Court held that, since the government had not compelled the defendant to *create* the documents, the documents themselves were not covered by the privilege. As a result, the law is now settled that the *contents* of documents — the information contained in them — are not protected from disclosure. But even this principle is not as simple as it sounds.

Fisher went on to say that while the contents of the documents are not protected, the *act of producing* the documents might be. The physical act of producing the documents in response to a subpoena can itself be "testimonial," because it reveals to the government three things. First, the person producing the document "testifies" by his actions that the documents exist. Second, he testifies to the documents' authenticity — in effect, he says "these are the documents described in the subpoena." Third, he testifies to his possession of the documents. (If they were not in his control, he could not hand them over.) So under *Fisher*, this compelled testimony concerning the existence, authenticity, and possession of the subpoenaed documents is privileged, at least if it is incriminating. In such a case, the suspect can refuse to comply with a subpoena duces tecum, even though the information contained in the documents — which is what the prosecutor is really interested in — is not protected.

As if this formula were not complicated enough, *Fisher* introduced an additional qualification. Though the Court noted that every subpoena target "testifies" that the documents he hands over exist, are authentic, and were in his possession, the Court went on to say that, in some cases, one or more of those issues is a "foregone conclusion" — i.e., the government already knows and can prove that the documents exist, that they are what they purport to be, and that they were in the defendant's possession when the subpoena was issued. Where that is so, said *Fisher*, the Fifth Amendment "testimony" involved in handing over the documents is too insubstantial to merit constitutional protection.

Several commentators suggested that, in the wake of *Fisher*, the Court might hold that custodians of corporate documents can assert the privilege when asked to turn those documents over, as long as the act of production would incriminate the custodian personally. In Braswell v. United States, 487 U.S. 99 (1988), a five-vote Court majority held otherwise. In the Court's view, "the custodian's act of production is not . . . a personal act, but rather an act of the corporation. Any claim of Fifth Amendment privilege asserted by [the custodian] would be tantamount to a claim of privilege by the corporation — which of course possesses no such privilege." Id., at 110. Chief Justice Rehnquist's opinion for the Court closed with an odd paragraph suggesting that the government could not use the fact that the custodian turned over the documents against the custodian personally — but it could tell the jury that the corporation produced the documents. See id., at 117-118, and n. 11.

But even where the act of producing documents is protected by the Fifth Amendment, the government still has options. Under 18 U.S.C. §§6002 and 6003, the prosecutor can also immunize the "testimony" implicit in the act of production. Although this is sometimes called an "act of production immunity," in form and substance it is no different than the other types of immunity discussed above. If the government immunizes the act of production, it is then barred from making "direct or indirect" use of the statements that the documents exist, are authentic, and were within the control of the person producing them. The next case, involving a high-ranking official in the Justice Department under President Clinton, involves such an immunity grant, and shows the difficulty of determining the scope of the protection afforded to the person who turned over subpoenaed documents.

UNITED STATES v. HUBBELL

Certiorari to the United States Court of Appeals for the District of Columbia Circuit
530 U.S. 27 (2000)

JUSTICE STEVENS delivered the opinion of the Court.

The two questions presented concern the scope of a witness' protection against compelled self-incrimination: (1) whether the Fifth Amendment privilege protects a witness from being compelled to disclose the existence of incriminating documents that the Government is unable to describe with reasonable particularity; and (2) if the witness produces such documents pursuant to a grant of immunity, whether 18 U.S.C. §6002 prevents the Government from using them to prepare criminal charges against him.[3]

I

This proceeding arises out of the second prosecution of respondent, Webster Hubbell, commenced by the Independent Counsel appointed in August 1994 to investigate possible violations of federal law relating to the Whitewater Development Corporation. The first prosecution was terminated pursuant to a plea bargain. In December 1994, respondent pleaded guilty to charges of mail fraud and tax evasion arising out of his billing practices as a member of an Arkansas law firm from 1989 to 1992, and was sentenced to 21 months in prison. In the plea agreement, respondent promised to provide the Independent Counsel with "full, complete, accurate, and truthful information" about matters relating to the Whitewater investigation.

The second prosecution resulted from the Independent Counsel's attempt to determine whether respondent had violated that promise. In October 1996, while respondent was incarcerated, the Independent Counsel served him with a subpoena duces tecum calling for the production of 11 categories of documents before a grand jury sitting in Little Rock, Arkansas. On November 19, he appeared before the grand jury and invoked his Fifth Amendment privilege against self-incrimination. In response to questioning by the prosecutor, respondent initially refused "to state whether there are documents within my possession, custody, or control responsive to the Subpoena." Thereafter, the prosecutor produced an order, which had previously been obtained from the District Court pursuant to 18 U.S.C. §6003(a), directing him to respond to the subpoena and granting him immunity "to the extent allowed by law." Respondent then produced 13,120 pages of documents and records and responded to a series of questions that established that those were all of the documents in his custody or control that were responsive to the commands in the subpoena, with the exception of a few documents he claimed were shielded by the attorney-client and attorney work-product privileges.

The contents of the documents produced by respondent provided the Independent Counsel with the information that led to this second prosecution. On April 30, 1998, a grand jury in the District of Columbia returned a 10-count indictment charging respondent with various tax-related crimes and mail and wire fraud. The District Court dismissed the indictment relying, in part, on the ground that the Independent Counsel's use of the subpoenaed documents violated §6002 because all of the evidence he would offer against respondent at trial derived either directly or indirectly from the testimonial aspects of respondent's immunized act of producing those documents. Noting that the Independent Counsel had admitted that he was not investigating tax-related issues when he issued the subpoena, and that he had "learned about the unreported income and other crimes from studying the records' contents," the District Court characterized the subpoena as "the quintessential fishing expedition."

---

3. The text of §§6002 and 6003 are set forth supra in Section C.2.a of this chapter. — EDS.

The Court of Appeals vacated the judgment and remanded for further proceedings. The majority concluded that the District Court had incorrectly relied on the fact that the Independent Counsel did not have prior knowledge of the contents of the subpoenaed documents. The question the District Court should have addressed was the extent of the Government's independent knowledge of the documents' existence and authenticity, and of respondent's possession or control of them. It explained:

> On remand, the district court should hold a hearing in which it seeks to establish the extent and detail of the [G]overnment's knowledge of Hubbell's financial affairs (or of the paperwork documenting it) on the day the subpoena issued. It is only then that the court will be in a position to assess the testimonial value of Hubbell's response to the subpoena. Should the Independent Counsel prove capable of demonstrating with reasonable particularity a prior awareness that the exhaustive litany of documents sought in the subpoena existed and were in Hubbell's possession, then the wide distance evidently traveled from the subpoena to the substantive allegations contained in the indictment would be based upon legitimate intermediate steps. To the extent that the information conveyed through Hubbell's compelled act of production provides the necessary linkage, however, the indictment deriving therefrom is tainted.

In the opinion of the dissenting judge, the majority failed to give full effect to the distinction between the contents of the documents and the limited testimonial significance of the act of producing them. In his view, as long as the prosecutor could make use of information contained in the documents or derived therefrom without any reference to the fact that respondent had produced them in response to a subpoena, there would be no improper use of the testimonial aspect of the immunized act of production. In other words, the constitutional privilege and the statute conferring use immunity would only shield the witness from the use of any information resulting from his subpoena response "beyond what the prosecutor would receive if the documents appeared in the grand jury room or in his office unsolicited and unmarked, like manna from heaven."

On remand, the Independent Counsel acknowledged that he could not satisfy the "reasonable particularity" standard prescribed by the Court of Appeals and entered into a conditional plea agreement with respondent. In essence, the agreement provides for the dismissal of the charges unless this Court's disposition of the case makes it reasonably likely that respondent's "act of production immunity" would not pose a significant bar to his prosecution. The case is not moot, however, because the agreement also provides for the entry of a guilty plea and a sentence that will not include incarceration if we should reverse and issue an opinion that is sufficiently favorable to the Government to satisfy that condition. Despite that agreement, we granted the Independent Counsel's petition for a writ of certiorari in order to determine the precise scope of a grant of immunity with respect to the production of documents in response to a subpoena. We now affirm. . . .

IV

The Government correctly emphasizes that the testimonial aspect of a response to a subpoena duces tecum does nothing more than establish the existence, authenticity, and custody of items that are produced. We assume that the Government is also entirely correct in its submission that it would not have to advert to respondent's act of production in order to prove the existence, authenticity, or custody of any documents that it might offer in evidence at a criminal trial; indeed, the Government disclaims any need to introduce any of the documents produced by respondent into evidence in order to prove the charges against him. It follows, according to the Government, that it has no intention of making improper "use" of respondent's compelled testimony.

The question, however, is not whether the response to the subpoena may be introduced into evidence at his criminal trial. That would surely be a prohibited "use" of the immunized act of production. But the fact that the Government intends no such use of the act of production leaves open the separate question whether it has already made "derivative use" of the testimonial aspect of that act in obtaining the indictment against respondent and in preparing its case for trial. It clearly has.

It is apparent from the text of the subpoena itself that the prosecutor needed respondent's assistance both to identify potential sources of information and to produce those sources. See Appendix, infra. Given the breadth of the description of the 11 categories of documents called for by the subpoena, the collection and production of the materials demanded was tantamount to answering a series of interrogatories asking a witness to disclose the existence and location of particular documents fitting certain broad descriptions. The assembly of literally hundreds of pages of material in response to a request for "any and all documents reflecting, referring, or relating to any direct or indirect sources of money or other things of value received by or provided to" an individual or members of his family during a 3-year period, is the functional equivalent of the preparation of an answer to either a detailed written interrogatory or a series of oral questions at a discovery deposition. Entirely apart from the contents of the 13,120 pages of materials that respondent produced in this case, it is undeniable that providing a catalog of existing documents fitting within any of the 11 broadly worded subpoena categories could provide a prosecutor with a "lead to incriminating evidence," or "a link in the chain of evidence needed to prosecute."

Indeed, the record makes it clear that that is what happened in this case. The documents were produced before a grand jury sitting in the Eastern District of Arkansas in aid of the Independent Counsel's attempt to determine whether respondent had violated a commitment in his first plea agreement. The use of those sources of information eventually led to the return of an indictment by a grand jury sitting in the District of Columbia for offenses that apparently are unrelated to that plea agreement. What the District Court characterized as a "fishing expedition" did produce a fish, but not the one that the Independent Counsel expected to hook. It is abundantly clear that the testimonial aspect of respondent's act of producing subpoenaed documents was the first step in a chain of evidence that led to this prosecution. The documents did not magically appear in the prosecutor's office like "manna from heaven." They arrived there only after respondent asserted his constitutional privilege, received a grant of immunity, and — under the compulsion of the District Court's order — took the mental and physical steps necessary to provide the prosecutor with an accurate inventory of the many sources of potentially incriminating evidence sought by the subpoena. It was only through respondent's truthful reply to the subpoena[23] that the Government received the incriminating

---

23. See William J. Stuntz, Self-Incrimination and Excuse, 88 Colum. L. Rev. 1227, 1228-1229, 1256-1259, 1277-1279 (1988) (discussing the conceptual link between truth-telling and the privilege in the

documents of which it made "substantial use . . . in the investigation that led to the indictment." Brief for United States 3.

For these reasons, we cannot accept the Government's submission that respondent's immunity did not preclude its derivative use of the produced documents because its "possession of the documents [was] the fruit only of a simple physical act — the act of producing the documents." It was unquestionably necessary for respondent to make extensive use of "the contents of his own mind" in identifying the hundreds of documents responsive to the requests in the subpoena. The assembly of those documents was like telling an inquisitor the combination to a wall safe, not like being forced to surrender the key to a strongbox. The Government's anemic view of respondent's act of production as a mere physical act that is principally non-testimonial in character and can be entirely divorced from its "implicit" testimonial aspect so as to constitute a "legitimate, wholly independent source" (as required by *Kastigar*) for the documents produced simply fails to account for these realities.

In sum, we have no doubt that the constitutional privilege against self-incrimination protects the target of a grand jury investigation from being compelled to answer questions designed to elicit information about the existence of sources of potentially incriminating evidence. That constitutional privilege has the same application to the testimonial aspect of a response to a subpoena seeking discovery of those sources. Before the District Court, the Government arguably conceded that respondent's act of production in this case had a testimonial aspect that entitled him to respond to the subpoena by asserting his privilege against self-incrimination. See 167 F.3d, at 580 (noting District Court's finding that "Hubbell's compelled act of production required him to make communications as to the existence, possession, and authenticity of the subpoenaed documents"). On appeal and again before this Court, however, the Government has argued that the communicative aspect of respondent's act of producing ordinary business records is insufficiently "testimonial" to support a claim of privilege because the existence and possession of such records by any businessman is a "foregone conclusion" under our decision in Fisher v. United States. This argument both misreads *Fisher* and ignores our subsequent decision in United States v. Doe, 465 U.S. 605 (1984).

. . . *Fisher* involved summonses seeking production of working papers prepared by the taxpayers' accountants that the IRS knew were in the possession of the taxpayers' attorneys. In rejecting the taxpayers' claim that these documents were protected by the Fifth Amendment privilege, we stated:

> It is doubtful that implicitly admitting the existence and possession of the papers rises to the level of testimony within the protection of the Fifth Amendment. The papers belong to the *accountant*, were prepared by him, and are the kind usually prepared by an accountant working on the tax returns of his client. Surely the Government is in no way relying on the "truthtelling" of the *taxpayer* to prove the existence of or his access to the documents. . . . The existence and location of the papers are a foregone conclusion and the taxpayer adds little or nothing to the sum total of the Government's information by conceding that he in fact has the papers.

document production context); Samuel A. Alito, Jr., Documents and the Privilege Against Self-Incrimination, 48 U. Pitt. L. Rev. 27, 47 (1986); 8 J. Wigmore, Evidence §2264, p. 379 (J. McNaughton rev. 1961) (describing a subpoena duces tecum as "process relying on [the witness's] moral responsibility for truthtelling").

425 U.S., at 411 (emphases added).

Whatever the scope of this "foregone conclusion" rationale, the facts of this case plainly fall outside of it. While in *Fisher* the Government already knew that the documents were in the attorneys' possession and could independently confirm their existence and authenticity through the accountants who created them, here the Government has not shown that it had any prior knowledge of either the existence or the whereabouts of the 13,120 pages of documents ultimately produced by respondent. The Government cannot cure this deficiency through the over-broad argument that a businessman such as respondent will always possess general business and tax records that fall within the broad categories described in this subpoena. The *Doe* subpoenas also sought several broad categories of general business records, yet we upheld the District Court's finding that the act of producing those records would involve testimonial self-incrimination. Given our conclusion that respondent's act of production had a testimonial aspect, at least with respect to the existence and location of the documents sought by the Government's subpoena, respondent could not be compelled to produce those documents without first receiving a grant of immunity under §6003. As we construed §6002 in *Kastigar*, such immunity is co-extensive with the constitutional privilege. *Kastigar* requires that respondent's motion to dismiss the indictment on immunity grounds be granted unless the Government proves that the evidence it used in obtaining the indictment and proposed to use at trial was derived from legitimate sources "wholly independent" of the testimonial aspect of respondent's immunized conduct in assembling and producing the documents described in the subpoena. The Government, however, does not claim that it could make such a showing. Rather, it contends that its prosecution of respondent must be considered proper unless someone — presumably respondent — shows that "there is some substantial relation between the compelled testimonial communications implicit in the act of production (as opposed to the act of production standing alone) and some aspect of the information used in the investigation or the evidence presented at trial." Brief for United States 9. We could not accept this submission without repudiating the basis for our conclusion in *Kastigar* that the statutory guarantee of use and derivative-use immunity is as broad as the constitutional privilege itself. This we are not prepared to do.

Accordingly, the indictment against respondent must be dismissed. The judgment of the Court of Appeals is affirmed.

It is so ordered.

APPENDIX TO OPINION OF THE COURT

On October 31, 1996, upon application by the Independent Counsel, a subpoena was issued commanding respondent to appear and testify before the grand jury of the United States District Court for the Eastern District of Arkansas on November 19, 1996, and to bring with him various documents described in a "Subpoena Rider" as follows:

"A. Any and all documents reflecting, referring, or relating to any direct or indirect sources of money or other things of value received by or provided to Webster Hubbell, his wife, or children from January 1, 1993 to the present, including but not limited to the identity of employers or clients of legal or any other type of work.

"B. Any and all documents reflecting, referring, or relating to any direct or indirect sources of money or other things of value received by or provided to Webster Hubbell, his wife, or children from January 1, 1993 to the present, including but not limited to billing memoranda, draft statements, bills, final statements, and/or bills for work performed or time billed from January 1, 1993 to the present.

"C. Copies of all bank records of Webster Hubbell, his wife, or children for all accounts from January 1, 1993 to the present, including but not limited to all statements, registers and ledgers, cancelled checks, deposit items, and wire transfers.

"D. Any and all documents reflecting, referring, or relating to time worked or billed by Webster Hubbell from January 1, 1993 to the present, including but not limited to original time sheets, books, notes, papers, and/or computer records.

"E. Any and all documents reflecting, referring, or relating to expenses incurred by and/or disbursements of money by Webster Hubbell during the course of any work performed or to be performed by Mr. Hubbell from January 1, 1993 to the present.

"F. Any and all documents reflecting, referring, or relating to Webster Hubbell's schedule of activities, including but not limited to any and all calendars, daytimers, time books, appointment books, diaries, records of reverse telephone toll calls, credit card calls, telephone message slips, logs, other telephone records, minutes, databases, electronic mail messages, travel records, itineraries, tickets for transportation of any kind, payments, bills, expense backup documentation, schedules, and/or any other document or database that would disclose Webster Hubbell's activities from January 1, 1993 to the present.

"G. Any and all documents reflecting, referring, or relating to any retainer agreements or contracts for employment of Webster Hubbell, his wife, or his children from January 1, 1993 to the present.

"H. Any and all tax returns and tax return information, including but not limited to all W-2s, form 1099s, schedules, draft returns, work papers, and backup documents filed, created or held by or on behalf of Webster Hubbell, his wife, his children, and/or any business in which he, his wife, or his children holds or has held an interest, for the tax years 1993 to the present.

"I. Any and all documents reflecting, referring, or relating to work performed or to be performed or on behalf of the City of Los Angeles, California, the Los Angeles Department of Airports or any other Los Angeles municipal Governmental entity, Mary Leslie, and/or Alan S. Arkatov, including but not limited to correspondence, retainer agreements, contracts, time sheets, appointment calendars, activity calendars, diaries, billing statements, billing memoranda, telephone records, telephone message slips, telephone credit card statements, itineraries, tickets for transportation, payment records, expense receipts, ledgers, check registers, notes, memoranda, electronic mail, bank deposit items, cashier's checks, traveler's checks, wire transfer records and/or other records of financial transactions.

"J. Any and all documents reflecting, referring, or relating to work performed or to be performed by Webster Hubbell, his wife, or his children on the recommendation, counsel or other influence of Mary Leslie and/or Alan S. Arkatov, including but not limited to correspondence, retainer agreements, contracts, time sheets, appointment calendars, activity calendars, diaries, billing statements, billing memoranda, telephone records, telephone message slips, telephone credit card statements, itineraries, tickets for transportation, payment records, expense receipts, ledgers, check registers, notes, memoranda, electronic mail, bank deposit items, cashier's checks, traveler's checks, wire transfer records and/or other records of financial transactions.

"K. Any and all documents related to work performed or to be performed for or on behalf of Lippo Ltd. (formerly Public Finance (H.K.) Ltd.), the Lippo Group, the Lippo Bank, Mochtar Riady, James Riady, Stephen Riady, John Luen Wai Lee, John Huang, Mark W. Grobmyer, C. Joseph Giroir, Jr., or any affiliate, subsidiary, or corporation owned or controlled by or related to the aforementioned entities or individuals, including but not limited to correspondence, retainer agreements, contracts, time sheets, appointment calendars, activity calendars, diaries, billing statements, billing memoranda, telephone records, telephone message slips, telephone credit card statements, itineraries, tickets for transportation, payment records, expense receipts, ledgers, check registers, notes, memoranda, electronic mail, bank deposit items, cashier's checks, traveler's checks, wire transfer records and/or other records of financial transactions."

JUSTICE THOMAS, with whom JUSTICE SCALIA joins, concurring.

Our decision today involves the application of the act-of-production doctrine, which provides that persons compelled to turn over incriminating papers or other physical evidence pursuant to a subpoena duces tecum or a summons may invoke the Fifth Amendment privilege against self-incrimination as a bar to production only where the act of producing the evidence would contain "testimonial" features. I join the opinion of the Court because it properly applies this doctrine, but I write separately to note that this doctrine may be inconsistent with the original meaning of the Fifth Amendment's Self-Incrimination Clause. A substantial body of evidence suggests that the Fifth Amendment privilege protects against the compelled production not just of incriminating testimony, but of any incriminating evidence. In a future case, I would be willing to reconsider the scope and meaning of the Self-Incrimination Clause. . . .

This Court has not always taken the approach to the Fifth Amendment that we follow today. The first case interpreting the Self-Incrimination Clause — Boyd v. United States — was decided, though not explicitly, in accordance with the understanding that "witness" means one who gives evidence [whether in testimonial form or otherwise]. In *Boyd*, this Court unanimously held that the Fifth Amendment protects a defendant against compelled production of books and papers. And the Court linked its interpretation of the Fifth Amendment to the common-law understanding of the self-incrimination privilege.

But this Court's decision in Fisher v. United States rejected this understanding, permitting the Government to force a person to furnish incriminating physical evidence and protecting only the "testimonial" aspects of that transfer. In so doing, *Fisher* not only failed to examine the historical backdrop to the Fifth Amendment, it also required — as illustrated by extended discussion in the opinions below in this case — a difficult parsing of the act of responding to a subpoena duces tecum.

None of the parties in this case has asked us to depart from *Fisher*, but in light of the historical evidence that the Self-Incrimination Clause may have a broader reach than *Fisher* holds, I remain open to a reconsideration of that decision and its progeny in a proper case.

Chief Justice Rehnquist dissents and would reverse the judgment of the Court of Appeals in part, for the reasons given by Judge Williams in his dissenting opinion in that court, 167 F.3d 552, 597 (CADC 1999).

NOTES AND QUESTIONS

1. The critical question after *Hubbell* is much the same as it was beforehand: Under what circumstances can the grand jury subpoena records from a person and then use the contents of those documents to prosecute that person? Recall in *Fisher*, supra, the Court said that the act of production could implicate the Fifth Amendment, but because the existence of the documents was a foregone conclusion, the protection did not apply. *Hubbell* added another wrinkle — the government acknowledged that Mr. Hubbell could refuse to produce the documents on Fifth Amendment grounds, but then immunized the act of production. The question then became whether the government's reliance on the content of the documents to investigate and prosecute the defendant is the "direct or indirect use" of the three implicit statements Mr. Hubbell made when he turned over his boxes of documents.

The government rarely needs to make direct use of the three statements implicit in the act of production. Prosecutors in white-collar cases do not need to tell juries that the defendant handed over incriminating documents; they can authenticate documents through experts, and the documents prove their own existence. Thus, the government argued in *Hubbell*, as long as the prosecutor treats the documents as if they magically appeared in her office, with no use being made of where they came from, the government is free to use the contents of the documents.

Instead, the Court in *Hubbell* found that the prosecutors had made indirect use of the immunized statements, and did so in a way that tainted the contents of the documents. The Court's reasoning is deceptively simple: The government served a very broad subpoena on Mr. Hubbell, one that required a great deal of effort and thought to sort through a huge number of documents to find the ones that were responsive. When he produced the responsive documents under a grant of immunity — when he testified, in effect, that "these documents exist" — he was revealing information that had previously been unknown to prosecutors. As a result, when the government relied on the content of the documents to further its investigation, it was making indirect use of the immunized testimony — "but for" that implicit testimony, the prosecutor would have been unaware of the document's existence, and thus, its contents.

2. Although Mr. Hubbell's claim was upheld, applying the reasoning of the case is a challenge. The opinion emphasized that the act of production was not just a physical act, but instead, required Mr. Hubbell "to make extensive use of 'the contents of his own mind' in identifying the hundreds of documents responsive to the requests in the subpoena." Does it matter whether "extensive use" of the contents of the mind is required rather than only minimal use, or is it any use of the contents of the mind that matters? Suppose the subpoena requested a small and clearly defined group of documents, one that took little time or judgment to locate and produce. Could the government use the contents of the documents then?

In his opinion, Justice Stevens suggests that it is any use of the defendant's mind that matters when he says, "The assembly of those [subpoenaed] documents was like telling an inquisitor the combination to a wall safe, not like being forced to surrender the key to a strongbox." This suggests that physical acts are unprotected while any communicative aspects of those acts that require access to the defendant's thoughts are protected. In another part of the *Hubbell* opinion not excerpted above, the Court reaffirmed its previous cases that held certain incriminating actions were not protected by the Fifth Amendment:

[E]ven though the act may provide incriminating evidence, a criminal suspect may be compelled to put on a shirt, to provide a blood sample or handwriting exemplar, or to make a recording of his voice. The act of exhibiting such physical characteristics is not the same as a sworn communication by a witness that relates either express or implied assertions of fact or belief. Similarly, the fact that incriminating evidence may be the byproduct of obedience to a regulatory requirement, such as filing an income tax return, maintaining required records, or reporting an accident, does not clothe such required conduct with the testimonial privilege.

Is the act/statement distinction helpful? Is it clear, as the majority in *Hubbell* says, that the assembling of the documents called for by the subpoena was the "functional equivalent of the preparation of an answer to either a detailed written interrogatory or a series of oral questions at a discovery deposition" and therefore within the protections of the Fifth Amendment?

3. Going forward, the critical question would seem to be how certain the government must be of a subpoenaed document's existence before it can use the contents in a later prosecution. If the document's existence really is a "foregone conclusion," then *Fisher* holds that the Fifth Amendment doesn't apply at all, so there should be no occasion for the government to immunize the production. But the kind of sweeping subpoena at issue in *Hubbell* will frequently result in the contents of the documents being tainted. As noted in the Supreme Court opinion, the court of appeals in *Hubbell* said that the government must be able to identify the document with "reasonable particularity" before issuing the subpoena to avoid making improper use of the act of production. Perhaps because the government acknowledged that it could not meet this test, the Supreme Court did not have occasion to discuss the standard further.

D.   The Screening Function

As Chapter 9 shows, prosecutors have very broad power to decide whom to charge and for what. But how long are those decisions beyond the courts power to review? Does the authority to file charges entitle the government not only to file charges, but also to sustain a case until it is resolved at a trial or through a guilty plea? Or is the charging power qualified by some screening mechanism, some criminal procedure equivalent to summary judgment, by which bad charging decisions are separated from good ones?

The answer is layered. There is indeed a mechanism to review the prosecutor's charging decisions — in fact, there are two of them. In modern times, the preliminary hearing is often used as a judicial check on the charging decisions. In addition, both the historical and current function of the grand jury is to screen the charges, making sure that formal accusations are based on enough evidence to warrant a full trial. But as described in the materials that follow, sometimes the accused gets both a preliminary hearing and grand jury review; in many other cases, a defendant is not afforded a preliminary hearing but the grand jury reviews the case; and in still other matters, the defendant waives both the preliminary hearing and grand jury review, and so he gets neither. More important, even when one or both of these procedures occur, there remains great skepticism about how effective a screen they are.

1.   Preliminary Hearings

In a typical case, after the suspect is arrested the police or prosecutor will file a criminal complaint, which is defined in Criminal Rule of Procedure 3 as a "written statement of the essential facts constituting the offense charged." If the charge is a misdemeanor, the complaint may be the final charging instrument, but for felony charges, the complaint will, at some point, be replaced by a formal charging document, either an "information" or an "indictment." Each of these documents is prepared by the prosecutor and filed with the court, and each sets forth in some detail the crimes charged; the difference is that an indictment is a pleading approved by the grand jury, while an information is not subject to grand jury review.

Federal Rule 5.1 provides that after a suspect is arrested and has had his first appearance before a judge, he is entitled to a preliminary hearing on the charges set forth in the complaint. This hearing is to be held no more than 14 days after the first appearance if the defendant is in custody, within 21 days if he is not. The purpose of the preliminary hearing is for the court to determine if there is "probable cause to believe that an offense has been committed and the defendant committed it." Rule 5.1(e).

Note that a defendant who is entitled to a preliminary hearing has, by definition, already been arrested, which means that a judicial finding of probable cause has already been made. If the arrest was pursuant to a warrant, the judge necessarily found probable cause prior to the arrest to believe the defendant committed the crime; if the arrest was made without a warrant, the defendant was entitled to a probable cause determination within 48 hours after the arrest. See County of Riverside v. McLaughlin, 500 U.S. 44 (1991). We might wonder, then, why a second probable cause hearing — a couple of weeks later at a preliminary hearing — is needed.

The answer is that, unlike the earlier probable cause determination, the preliminary hearing is adversarial. The probable cause finding for an arrest warrant is ex parte and, at the finding at the first appearance, is often perfunctory and made without defense counsel being present. But at a preliminary hearing, the defendant has the right to cross-examine witnesses and introduce evidence of his own, so now the government's claim of probable cause can, in theory, be vigorously challenged. Most important, the defendant is now represented by counsel. The Supreme Court concluded in Coleman v. Alabama, 399 U.S. 1 (1970), that a preliminary hearing is a "critical stage" to which the Sixth Amendment right attaches. Justice Brennan's plurality opinion highlighted the importance of both the adversarial process and the presence of a lawyer:

> Plainly the guiding hand of counsel at the preliminary hearing is essential to protect the indigent accused against an erroneous or improper prosecution. First, the lawyer's skilled examination and cross-examination of witnesses may expose fatal weaknesses in the State's case that may lead the magistrate to refuse to bind the accused over. Second, in any event, the skilled interrogation of witnesses by an experienced lawyer can fashion a vital impeachment tool for use in cross-examination of the state's witnesses at the trial, or preserve testimony favorable to the accused of a witness who does not appear at the trial. Third, trained counsel can more effectively discover the case the State has against his client and make possible the preparation of a proper defense to meet that case at the trial. Fourth, counsel can also be influential at the preliminary hearing in making effective arguments for the accused on such matters as the necessity for an early psychiatric examination or bail.

399 U.S., at 9.

The government has the burden of persuasion at the preliminary hearing, and the prosecution presents its case through physical evidence and witnesses, much as it would at trial. The rules of evidence, however, are either relaxed or nonexistent, see Fed. R. Ev. 1101(d)(3), which means that hearsay information is likely to be freely admitted and heavily used. The ability to rely on hearsay is a great convenience for the government, because it means that it does not have to present the witnesses it will use at trial, and thus can avoid the possibility of cross-examination by the defense.

The defense can challenge the prosecutor's case, but whether it is wise to do so can raise hard strategic questions. On the one hand, the prosecutor's case will typically meet the probable cause threshold, and so defense counsel may be reluctant to cross-examine or introduce its own evidence that might reveal a defense strategy but is unlikely to change the result. Contesting the government's probable cause case might also reveal a hole in the prosecutor's case that, once revealed, can be fixed by the government prior to trial. On the other hand, discovery in criminal cases is often quite limited (see Chapter 12), and the defense may want to cross-examine a witness simply to learn something about the alleged facts and the government's theory of the case. Courts, however, are consistent in saying that preliminary hearings are not a discovery device, and so a judge may well cut off cross-examination if she believes the questions are irrelevant to the limited issue of probable cause.

But while courts are free to limit cross-examination in this way, lawyers on both sides need to be alert to the potential effect that such a decision can have. If the preliminary hearing witness later becomes unavailable to testify at trial, the inability of the defense to cross-examine fully may prevent the government from using the witness's preliminary hearing testimony as evidence. Under the Sixth Amendment Confrontation Clause, unless the defendant had a full chance to cross-examine the witness, the government is barred from using a transcript of the prior testimony as evidence at trial. See Crawford v. Washington, 541 U.S. 36 (2004) (testimonial evidence must be subject to confrontation to be admissible); Fed. R. Evid. 804(b)(1) (former testimony not excluded as hearsay if the opposing party had an "opportunity and similar motive" to cross-examine the declarant).

At the conclusion of the preliminary hearing, the magistrate judge will determine whether there is probable cause to move the case forward. If the judge finds no probable cause, she will dismiss the charges — but this does not prevent the government from filing new charges and putting the defendant through another preliminary hearing, or from seeking an indictment on the original charge from a grand jury. The bar on double jeopardy prevents the government from *trying* a defendant twice for the same crime, but not from *charging* him twice; this follows from the rule that "jeopardy" does not "attach" until either the trial jury is impanelled or the first witness is sworn. See Crist v. Bretz, 437 U.S. 28 (1978). But a preliminary hearing dismissal may, in practice, have more bite than that rule might suggest: Most prosecutors will be wary of "going back to the well" on the precise charge that had been rejected at a preliminary hearing.

If the magistrate judge finds that probable cause exists, the case is "bound over" to the grand jury, which will decide whether — you guessed it — there is probable cause to send the case forward to trial. If you wonder why there needs to be yet another probable cause determination, you need look no further than the Fifth Amendment, which, as noted, provides that in all felony cases the defendant has the right to grand jury review of the charges. So whether the defendant has a preliminary hearing or not, a federal prosecutor must present felony charges to the grand jury for a probable cause determination, unless the defendant waives that protection.

In contrast, the defendant has no constitutional right to a preliminary hearing; in fact, apart from the grand jury clause of the Fifth Amendment, there is no federal constitutional right to any review of a prosecutor's charging decision. See Gerstein v. Pugh, 420 U.S. 103, 119 (1975). And having still another proceeding to decide the same probable cause question really does seem duplicative. As a result, Federal Rule 5.1(a) provides that a defendant has a right to a preliminary hearing on felony charges *unless* the defendant waives that right *or* he is indicted by a grand jury before the preliminary hearing. Stated differently, the decision whether to afford the defendant a preliminary hearing rests largely in the prosecutor's hands — as long as there is a grand jury available that can return an indictment before the date of the preliminary hearing, the prosecutor can take the case directly to the grand jury and have the preliminary hearing canceled.

Why should this be so? If the purpose of the preliminary hearing is to review the prosecutor's charging decision, is it really appropriate to let that same prosecutor decide whether to let that review proceed? One response may be that the prosecutor is not avoiding a pretrial screen; he is just shifting the screening function from the preliminary hearing to the grand jury. But this, in turn, raises the obvious question of why there should be preliminary hearings at all.

At least superficially, the preliminary hearing would seem to offer a more effective method of screening charges. Preliminary hearings are open, adversarial, and the decision is made by a judge. Grand juries are secret, not adversarial, and decisions are made by the jurors. Recall also the discussion in Coleman v. Alabama, supra, about the importance of the guiding hand of counsel at the preliminary hearing, and recall that lawyers are not permitted to accompany their clients into the grand jury room. Given this, is it fair to view the two screening procedures as functional equivalents, as the rules do now?

Then again, if asked which procedure does a better job of eliminating weak charges, many observers would say "neither." Both procedures use the low "probable cause" threshold, both freely admit hearsay, and both fail to exclude illegally obtained evidence. In addition, experience has shown that both judges and grand juries approve the requested charges at very high rates, although judges are somewhat more likely to reject a proposed charge. A 1971 study of preliminary hearings in Los Angeles found a rate of dismissal of 8 percent,[4] and a 1984 study of two Arizona counties found dismissal rates of 3 and 6 percent.[5] In contrast, federal grand juries apparently return indictments on the request of the prosecutor well over 99 percent of the time.[6]

But it is important not to overread these last figures, because the number of times a court or grand jury rejects a proposed criminal charge may tell us little about

4. Kenneth Graham & Leon Letwin, The Preliminary Hearing in Los Angeles: Some Field Findings and Legal Policy Observations, 18 UCLA L. Rev. 635, 719-724 (1971).

5. Deborah Day Emerson & Nancy L. Ames, The Role of the Grand Jury and the Preliminary Hearing in Pretrial Screening 68 (1984).

6. See Andrew D. Leipold, Prosecutorial Charging Practices and Grand Jury Screening: Some Empirical Observations, in Grand Jury 2.0: Modern Perspectives on the Grand Jury (Roger A. Fairfax, Jr., ed. 2010); Thomas P. Sullivan & Robert D. Nachman, If It Ain't Broke, Don't Fix It: Why the Grand Jury's Accusatory Function Should Not Be Changed, 75 J. Crim. L. & Criminology 1047, 1050, n. 16 (1984) (99.6 percent of federal grand jury returns were true bills).

how often the prosecutor is deterred from bringing a weak charge. If the prosecutor knows that her proposed indictment or information will be rigorously tested, we would expect her not to even pursue the weak case in the first place, which, in turn, should result in a very high approval rate. In short, it should be the *existence* of the review process, not its workings, that prevents the unfounded charges.

One data point for measuring the effectiveness of preliminary hearings and/or grand juries might be gleaned from the frequency with which defendants waive these protections. One practicing lawyer claims that in his jurisdiction, 90 percent of felony defendants waive preliminary hearings. See Michael J. Malkiewicz, Preliminary Hearing Can Improve Final Results in Criminal Cases, Del. Law., Winter 1989-1990, at 9. Other estimates are lower, but waiver seems to be the rule rather than the exception. Of course, strength of the evidence is only one reason to waive; Malkeiwicz goes on to list others: Defense counsel lacks time or hasn't been paid, limits on defense presentation of evidence make the allegation hard to refute, the prosecutor has told defense counsel that an indictment will issue even if the defense wins at the preliminary hearing, and the prosecutor offers defense counsel a copy of the police report in return for waiving the hearing.

Grand jury review is waived less frequently, even though the rate at which the prosecutors' charges are approved is higher. In fiscal year 2007, there were over 77,000 federal felony defendants, and of this group, only 18 percent (fewer than 14,000) waived grand jury review. Interestingly, of those who waived review and proceeded by information, more than 97 percent eventually pled guilty, suggesting that many of those grand jury waivers were probably part of a plea agreement with the prosecutor.[7]

Whether or not the government is worried about having charges rejected by the judge or a grand jury, there is also a significant amount of prosecutorial screening that goes on outside these procedures. In The Screening/Bargaining Tradeoff, 55 Stan. L. Rev. 29 (2002), Ronald Wright and Marc Miller discuss a screening system used by the District Attorney's office in New Orleans. Roughly 20 percent of the lawyers in the New Orleans D.A.'s office work in part of the office known as the Screening Section. After the bail hearing, every case is reviewed by that Section:

> . . . [D]esignated cases such as homicide or rape get assigned to screeners with special expertise. Drug cases and a few other high-volume cases go to a subgroup known as Expedited Screening. Ordinary cases go to the Screening Attorney on duty for that day. The screener reviews the investigation file, speaks to all the key witnesses and the victims (often by telephone, but sometimes in person), and generally gauges the strength of the case. If the police report neglects to mention a factual issue that is likely to arise at trial, the screening attorney will speak directly with the police officer to resolve it. There is a powerful office expectation that the Screening Attorney will make a decision within ten days of receiving the folder.

Id., at 63. This screening process is ex parte: Neither the defendant nor defense counsel is present. (For a sharp criticism of the New Orleans system on this ground, see Gerard Lynch, Screening Versus Plea Bargaining: Exactly What Are We Trading

---

7. These figures are derived from a dataset maintained by the Federal Justice Statistics Resource Center (FJSRC), a project of the Bureau of Justice Statistics. See http://fjsrc.urban.org/index.cfm. The data comes from the case management files of the Administrative Office of the U.S. Courts. The file from which the data are taken is listed on the FJSRC Web page as "Defendants in Criminal Cases Terminated."

Off? 55 Stan. L. Rev. 1399 (2003).) In New Orleans, the Screening Section has largely taken the place of preliminary hearings and grand juries. It has also, according to Wright and Miller, taken the place of most plea bargaining — a great advantage, in their view. The weeding-out that, elsewhere, takes place in formal legal screens and bargaining sessions is now performed almost entirely by the screeners in the D.A.'s office.

Professors Wright and Miller may be right that the New Orleans system is a model that other jurisdictions should copy. Or it could be that paper screening systems would be more suitable. Or perhaps grand juries and preliminary hearings are better screens than the conventional wisdom would have it. Regardless, one point seems clear: In a system that resolves a huge majority of cases without trials, the choice of how best to screen prosecutors' charging decisions is critically important to the quality of justice the system delivers.

2. Grand Jury Review

Prosecutors may or may not have their charging decisions reviewed at a preliminary hearing, but unless the defendant waives, federal prosecutors must always subject their felony charges to grand jury review. How meaningful is this review likely to be?

Before turning to the substantive law, it is important to keep in mind the procedural setting in which the challenges to the grand jury arise. Because grand jury hearings are secret, defendants typically have no way of knowing what the prosecutor did or said in the grand jury room, making a motion to dismiss the indictment for irregularities in the process very difficult to sustain. Although Rule 6(e)(3)(E)(ii) says that a court can disclose grand jury material to "a defendant who shows that a ground may exist to dismiss the indictment because of a matter that occurred before the grand jury," it is often hard for the defendant to make even a preliminary showing of need without some access to the proceedings. In addition, a challenge to the grand jury process typically comes after the indictment is returned. As you read the cases, notice how often the procedural posture of the case affects the rules the Court adopts for regulating grand jury practice.

COSTELLO v. UNITED STATES

Certiorari to the United States Court of Appeals for the Second Circuit
350 U.S. 359 (1956)

JUSTICE BLACK delivered the opinion of the Court.

We granted certiorari in this case to consider a single question: "May a defendant be required to stand trial and a conviction be sustained where only hearsay evidence was presented to the grand jury which indicted him?"

Petitioner, Frank Costello, was indicted for wilfully attempting to evade payment of income taxes due the United States for the years 1947, 1948, and 1949. The charge was that petitioner falsely and fraudulently reported less income than he and his wife actually received during the taxable years in question. Petitioner promptly filed a motion for inspection of the minutes of the grand jury and for a dismissal of the indictment. His motion was based on an affidavit stating that he was firmly convinced there could have been no legal or competent evidence before the grand jury which indicted him since he had reported all his income and paid all taxes due. The motion was denied. At the trial which followed the Government offered evidence designed to show increases in Costello's net worth in an attempt to prove that he had received more income during the years in question than he had reported. To establish its case the Government called and examined 144 witnesses and introduced 368 exhibits. All of the testimony and documents related to business transactions and expenditures by petitioner and his wife. The prosecution concluded its case by calling three government agents. Their investigations had produced the evidence used against petitioner at the trial. They were allowed to summarize the vast amount of evidence already heard and to introduce computations showing, if correct, that petitioner and his wife had received far greater income than they had reported. We have held such summarizations admissible in a "net worth" case like this. United States v. Johnson, 319 U.S. 503.

Counsel for petitioner asked each government witness at the trial whether he had appeared before the grand jury which returned the indictment. This cross-examination developed the fact that the three investigating officers had been the only witnesses before the grand jury. After the Government concluded its case, petitioner again moved to dismiss the indictment on the ground that the only evidence before the grand jury was "hearsay," since the three officers had no firsthand knowledge of the transactions upon which their computations were based. Nevertheless the trial court again refused to dismiss the indictment, and petitioner was convicted. The Court of Appeals affirmed, holding that the indictment was valid even though the sole evidence before the grand jury was hearsay. Petitioner here urges: (1) that an indictment based solely on hearsay evidence violates that part of the Fifth Amendment providing that "No person shall be held to answer for a capital, or otherwise infamous crime, unless on a presentment or indictment of a Grand Jury . . ." and (2) that if the Fifth Amendment does not invalidate an indictment based solely on hearsay we should now lay down such a rule for the guidance of federal courts.

The Fifth Amendment provides that federal prosecutions for capital or otherwise infamous crimes must be instituted by presentments or indictments of grand juries. But neither the Fifth Amendment nor any other constitutional provision prescribes the kind of evidence upon which grand juries must act. The grand jury is an English institution, brought to this country by the early colonists and incorporated in the Constitution by the Founders. There is every reason to believe that our constitutional grand jury was intended to operate substantially like its English progenitor. The basic purpose of the English grand jury was to provide a fair method for instituting criminal proceedings against persons believed to have committed crimes. Grand jurors were selected from the body of the people and their work was not hampered by rigid procedural or evidential rules. In fact, grand jurors could act on their own knowledge and were free to make their presentments or indictments on such information as they deemed satisfactory. Despite its broad power to institute criminal proceedings the grand jury grew in popular favor with the years. It acquired an independence in England free from control by the Crown or judges. Its adoption in our Constitution as the sole method for preferring charges in serious criminal cases shows the high place it held as an instrument of justice. And in this country as in England of old the grand jury has convened as a body of laymen, free from technical rules, acting in secret, pledged to indict no one because of prejudice and to free no one because of special favor. As late as 1927 an English historian could say that English grand juries were still free to act on their own knowledge if they pleased to do so. And in 1852 Mr. Justice Nelson on circuit could say "No case has been cited, nor have we been able to find any, furnishing an authority for looking into and revising the judgment of the grand jury upon the evidence, for the purpose of determining whether or not the finding was founded upon sufficient proof. . . ." United States v. Reed, 27 Fed. Cas. 727, 738.

In Holt v. United States, 218 U.S. 245, this Court had to decide whether an indictment should be quashed because supported in part by incompetent evidence. Aside from the incompetent evidence "there was very little evidence against the accused." The Court refused to hold that such an indictment should be quashed, pointing out that "The abuses of criminal practice would be enhanced if indictments could be upset on such a ground." 218 U.S., at 248. The same thing is true where as here all the evidence before the grand jury was in the nature of "hearsay." If indictments were to be held open to challenge on the ground that there was inadequate or incompetent evidence before the grand jury, the resulting delay would be great indeed. The result of such a rule would be that before trial on the merits a defendant could always insist on a kind of preliminary trial to determine the competency and adequacy of the evidence before the grand jury. This is not required by the Fifth Amendment. An indictment returned by a legally constituted and unbiased grand jury, like an information drawn by the prosecutor, if valid on its face, is enough to call for trial of the charge on the merits. The Fifth Amendment requires nothing more.

Petitioner urges that this Court should exercise its power to supervise the administration of justice in federal courts and establish a rule permitting defendants to challenge indictments on the ground that they are not supported by adequate or competent evidence. No persuasive reasons are advanced for establishing such a rule. It would run counter to the whole history of the grand jury institution, in which laymen conduct their inquiries unfettered by technical rules. Neither justice nor the concept of a fair trial requires such a change. In a trial on the merits, defendants are entitled to a strict observance of all the rules designed to bring about a fair verdict. Defendants are not entitled, however, to a rule which would result in interminable delay but add nothing to the assurance of a fair trial.

Affirmed.

JUSTICE CLARK and JUSTICE HARLAN took no part in the consideration or decision of this case.

JUSTICE BURTON, concurring.

I agree with the denial of the motion to quash the indictment. In my view, however, this case does not justify the breadth of the declarations made by the Court. I assume that this Court would not preclude an examination of grand-jury action to ascertain the existence of bias or prejudice in an indictment. Likewise, it seems to me that if it is shown that the grand jury had before it no substantial or rationally persuasive evidence upon which to base its indictment, that indictment should be quashed. To hold a person to answer to such an empty indictment for a capital or otherwise infamous federal crime robs the Fifth Amendment of much of its protective value to the private citizen.

Here, . . . substantial and rationally persuasive evidence apparently was presented to the grand jury. We may fairly assume that the evidence before that jury included much of the testimony later given at the trial by the three government agents who said that they had testified before the grand jury. At the trial, they summarized financial transactions of the accused about which they were not qualified to testify of their own knowledge. To use Justice Holmes' phrase in [Holt v. United States, 218 U.S. 245], such testimony, standing alone, was "incompetent by circumstances" (supra, at 248), and yet it was rationally persuasive of the crime charged and provided a substantial basis for the indictment. At the trial, with preliminary testimony laying the foundation for it, the same testimony constituted an important part of the competent evidence upon which the conviction was obtained.

To sustain this indictment under the above circumstances is well enough, but I agree with Judge Learned Hand that "if it appeared that no evidence had been offered that rationally established the facts, the indictment ought to be quashed; because then the grand jury would have in substance abdicated." 221 F.2d 668, 677. . . .

NOTES AND QUESTIONS

1. Frank Costello, the petitioner in Costello v. United States, was a celebrity of sorts. The alleged head of the Gambino crime family, Costello was called in 1951 to testify before the Kefauver Committee, a Senate committee investigating organized crime. As this was in the early days of television, the networks were scrambling to find programming to fill daytime slots; they seized on the public hearings and televised them in full, and the hearings attracted a nationwide audience. Costello, unlike some of the other witnesses the committee called, agreed initially to testify (i.e., he agreed not to invoke his privilege against self-incrimination), but only on the condition that the television cameras not show his face. The cameras instead zeroed in on Costello's hands, which fidgeted nervously throughout his testimony; Costello's fingers drumming and fists clenching made for far better theater than showing his face would have done. For a good, brief account, see William Manchester, The Glory and the Dream 734-735 (1973). To millions of Americans, Costello — or at least Costello's hands — became the personification of the Mob.

The hearings made Estes Kefauver, the chair of the investigating committee and a previously unknown senator from Tennessee, a national figure; in both 1952 and 1956, Kefauver narrowly missed winning the Democratic presidential nomination, and in the latter year he was the vice presidential nominee. They also led to Costello's successful prosecution for income tax evasion. That prosecution, in turn, produced what is still the leading decision defining the scope of the grand jury's authority to indict and the limits of judicial authority to overturn indictments.

2. What exactly did the Court hold in Costello? The issue argued in the case was whether an indictment could be based wholly on evidence that would have been inadmissible hearsay at trial. (Remember that the agents' testimony in Costello was admissible at trial only because other witnesses with direct knowledge had testified to the facts the agents were summarizing, and those other witnesses didn't testify before the grand jury.) Obviously, the Court resolved that question in the government's favor, but that was hardly a surprise; existing case law made the answer fairly clear even before Costello. The more important aspect of the decision is what it says about judicial review of the *merits* of the indictment — whether, for example, a court can dismiss an indictment because the evidence was insufficient (not just inadmissible). On that question, the Court says very little, but what it says is very important: Reread the last two paragraphs of Justice Black's opinion, and note especially the declaration that indictments that are valid on their face are valid, period.

3. Despite Justice Burton's attempt to limit the reach of *Costello*, the case has come to stand for the proposition that grand jury decisions to indict are largely unreviewable on the merits. What justifies that proposition? The Court's opinion suggests two reasons: (1) Review of decisions to indict would turn into a minitrial prior to the real trial, and would thus be too administratively costly, and (2) review of decisions to indict would compromise the grand jury's independence.

How substantial are these justifications? As to the first, note that civil litigation has a fairly low-cost procedure for judicial resolution of clear cases without going through the trial process — summary judgment — and no one thinks *that* procedure is unadministrable. Why would review of decisions to indict be different? Isn't there something strange about the proposition that we take more seriously civil litigants' interest in being free from the burdens of civil trials than criminal defendants' interest in avoiding the costs and reputational harms associated with criminal trials? But then, if prosecutors knew that judges were likely to second-guess indictments, might that lead prosecutors to substantially expand the scope and extent of the evidence they present before grand juries, thereby lengthening and complicating grand jury proceedings? Besides, judicial review is unnecessary if grand juries already screen cases reasonably well. Certainly nothing in Costello's case suggests otherwise.

As for the need to protect grand juries' independence, the relevant question is, independence from whom? *Costello* makes grand juries' decisions to indict independent of *judicial* control. But those decisions are, in practice, far from independent of *prosecutorial* control. Grand jury proceedings are conducted with little or no judicial oversight, and *Costello* reaffirms that the laws of evidence do not limit what evidence or argument prosecutors can present. In these circumstances, it is hardly surprising that prosecutors generally find it easy to obtain indictments when they want them; as Sol Wachtler, then-chief judge of the New York Court of Appeals, famously put it, a grand jury will indict a ham sandwich if so instructed by the prosecutor. (It should be noted that Wachtler later had some experience of his own with grand juries: He was indicted, and convicted, of making threats by mail in 1993 and served 13 months in federal prison.)

4. The concept of the grand jury as a truly independent entity is more plausible if one looks at the institution's history. Recall from Section A of this chapter that grand juries in colonial America often served as a monitor of government action and as an informal local legislative body. In addition, colonial grand juries could not possibly be manipulated by professional prosecutors, because professional prosecutors did not exist. Indictments were regularly the product of the grand jurors' own information and their own investigation — and in a society where men tended to know a good deal about their neighbors, not much investigation was necessary. See Peter C. Hoffer & William B. Scott, Criminal Proceedings in Colonial Virginia xxvii-xxviii (1984).

Note the implication of this history for the kind of grand jury review at issue in *Costello*. The essence of the historical grand jury is the separation of charging from prosecution: Grand juries decided whom to charge and for what; prosecution was done by private parties, constables, or ad hoc public prosecutors. By the time of *Costello*, charging and prosecution were both jobs assigned to full-time professional prosecutors. Grand juries no longer seem to function as independent actors, but rather, serve as evaluators of the decisions that prosecutors make — a significantly different role. And the grand jury's sole source of information is the prosecutor whose decision it must evaluate.

Does that role make any sense? If not, why have grand juries survived so long?

UNITED STATES v. WILLIAMS

Certiorari to the United States Court of Appeals for the Tenth Circuit
504 U.S. 36 (1992)

JUSTICE SCALIA delivered the opinion of the Court.

The question presented in this case is whether a district court may dismiss an otherwise valid indictment because the Government failed to disclose to the grand jury "substantial exculpatory evidence" in its possession.

I

On May 4, 1988, respondent John H. Williams, Jr., a Tulsa, Oklahoma, investor, was indicted by a federal grand jury on seven counts of "knowingly making [a] false statement or report . . . for the purpose of influencing . . . the action [of a federally insured financial institution]," in violation of 18 U.S.C. §1014. According to the indictment, between September 1984 and November 1985 Williams supplied four Oklahoma banks with "materially false" statements that variously overstated the value of his current assets and interest income in order to influence the banks' actions on his loan requests.

Williams' misrepresentation was allegedly effected through two financial statements provided to the banks, a "Market Value Balance Sheet" and a "Statement of Projected Income and Expense." The former included as "current assets" approximately $6 million in notes receivable from three venture capital companies. Though it contained a disclaimer that these assets were carried at cost rather than at market value, the Government asserted that listing them as "current assets" — i.e., assets quickly reducible to cash — was misleading, since Williams knew that none of the venture capital companies could afford to satisfy the notes in the short term. The second document — the Statement of Projected Income and Expense — allegedly misrepresented Williams' interest income, since it failed to reflect that the interest payments received on the notes of the venture capital companies were funded entirely by Williams' own loans to those companies. The Statement thus falsely implied, according to the Government, that Williams was deriving interest income from "an independent outside source."

Shortly after arraignment, the District Court granted Williams' motion for disclosure of all exculpatory portions of the grand jury transcripts. See Brady v. Maryland, 373 U.S. 83 (1963). Upon reviewing this material, Williams demanded that the District Court dismiss the indictment, alleging that the Government had failed to fulfill its obligation under the Tenth Circuit's prior decision in United States v. Page, 808 F.2d 723, 728 (1987), to present "substantial exculpatory evidence" to the grand jury (emphasis omitted). His contention was that evidence which the Government had chosen not to present to the grand jury — in particular, Williams' general ledgers and tax returns, and Williams' testimony in his contemporaneous Chapter 11 bankruptcy proceeding — disclosed that, for tax purposes and otherwise, he had regularly accounted for the "notes receivable" (and the interest on them) in a manner consistent with the Balance Sheet and the Income Statement. This, he contended, belied an intent to mislead the banks, and thus directly negated an essential element of the charged offense.

The District Court initially denied Williams' motion, but upon reconsideration ordered the indictment dismissed without prejudice. It found, after a hearing, that the withheld evidence was "relevant to an essential element of the crime charged," created "a reasonable doubt about [respondent's] guilt," and thus "rendered the grand jury's decision to indict gravely suspect." Upon the Government's appeal, the Court of Appeals affirmed the District Court's order. . . . It . . . found that the Government's behavior "'substantially influenced'" the grand jury's decision to indict, or at the very least raised a "'grave doubt that the decision to indict was free from such substantial influence.'" 899 F.2d, at 903 (quoting Bank of Nova Scotia v. United States, 487 U.S. 250, 263 (1988)). Under these circumstances, the Tenth Circuit concluded, it was not an abuse of discretion for the District Court to require the Government to begin anew before the grand jury. . . .

III

Respondent does not contend that the Fifth Amendment itself obliges the prosecutor to disclose substantial exculpatory evidence in his possession to the grand jury. Instead, building on our statement that the federal courts "may, within limits, formulate procedural rules not specifically required by the Constitution or the Congress," United States v. Hasting, 461 U.S. 499, 505 (1983), he argues that imposition of the Tenth Circuit's disclosure rule is supported by the courts' "supervisory power." We think not. *Hasting*, and the cases that rely upon the principle it expresses, deal strictly with the courts' power to control their own procedures. See, e.g., Jencks v. United States, 353 U.S. 657, 667-668 (1957); McNabb v. United States, 318 U.S. 332 (1943). That power has been applied not only to improve the truth-finding process of the trial, but also to prevent parties from reaping benefit or incurring harm from violations of substantive or procedural rules (imposed by the Constitution or laws) governing matters apart from the trial itself, see, e.g., Weeks v. United States, 232 U.S. 383 (1914). [*Weeks* is the case that established the exclusionary rule as a remedy for Fourth Amendment violations. — EDS.] Thus, Bank of Nova Scotia v. United States, 487 U.S. 250 (1988), makes clear that the supervisory power can be used to dismiss an indictment because of misconduct before the grand jury, at least where that misconduct amounts to a violation of one of those "few, clear rules which were carefully drafted and approved by this Court and by Congress to ensure the integrity of the grand jury's functions," United States v. Mechanik, 475 U.S. 66, 74 (1986) (O'Connor, J., concurring in judgment).[6]

We did not hold in *Bank of Nova Scotia*, however, that the courts' supervisory power could be used, not merely as a means of enforcing or vindicating legally compelled standards of prosecutorial conduct before the grand jury, but as a means of prescribing those standards of prosecutorial conduct in the first instance — just as it may be used as a means of establishing standards of prosecutorial conduct before the courts themselves. It is this latter exercise that respondent demands. Because

---

6. Rule 6 of the Federal Rules of Criminal Procedure contains a number of such rules, providing, for example, that "no person other than the jurors may be present while the grand jury is deliberating or voting," Rule 6(d), and placing strict controls on disclosure of "matters occurring before the grand jury," Rule 6(e); see generally United States v. Sells Engineering, Inc., 463 U.S. 418 (1983). Additional standards of behavior for prosecutors (and others) are set forth in the United States Code. See 18 U.S.C. §§6002, 6003 (setting forth procedures for granting a witness immunity from prosecution); §1623 (criminalizing false declarations before grand jury); §2515 (prohibiting grand jury use of unlawfully intercepted wire or oral communications); §1622 (criminalizing subornation of perjury).

the grand jury is an institution separate from the courts, over whose functioning the courts do not preside, we think it clear that, as a general matter at least, no such "supervisory" judicial authority exists, and that the disclosure rule applied here exceeded the Tenth Circuit's authority.

A

"Rooted in long centuries of Anglo-American history," Hannah v. Larche, 363 U.S. 420, 490 (1960) (Frankfurter, J., concurring in result), the grand jury is mentioned in the Bill of Rights, but not in the body of the Constitution. It has not been textually assigned, therefore, to any of the branches described in the first three Articles. . . . In fact the whole theory of its function is that it belongs to no branch of the institutional Government, serving as a kind of buffer or referee between the Government and the people. Although the grand jury normally operates, of course, in the courthouse and under judicial auspices, its institutional relationship with the Judicial Branch has traditionally been, so to speak, at arm's length. Judges' direct involvement in the functioning of the grand jury has generally been confined to the constitutive one of calling the grand jurors together and administering their oaths of office. See United States v. Calandra, 414 U.S. 338, 343 (1974); Fed. Rule Crim. Proc. 6(a).

The grand jury's functional independence from the Judicial Branch is evident both in the scope of its power to investigate criminal wrongdoing and in the manner in which that power is exercised. "Unlike [a] court, whose jurisdiction is predicated upon a specific case or controversy, the grand jury can investigate merely on suspicion that the law is being violated, or even because it wants assurance that it is not." United States v. R. Enterprises, Inc., 498 U.S. 292, 297 (1991). It need not identify the offender it suspects, or even "the precise nature of the offense" it is investigating. Blair v. United States, 250 U.S. 273, 282 (1919). The grand jury requires no authorization from its constituting court to initiate an investigation, nor does the prosecutor require leave of court to seek a grand jury indictment. And in its day-to-day functioning, the grand jury generally operates without the interference of a presiding judge. It swears in its own witnesses, Fed. Rule Crim. Proc. 6(c), and deliberates in total secrecy.

True, the grand jury cannot compel the appearance of witnesses and the production of evidence, and must appeal to the court when such compulsion is required. And the court will refuse to lend its assistance when the compulsion the grand jury seeks would override rights accorded by the Constitution, see, e.g., Gravel v. United States, 408 U.S. 606 (1972) (grand jury subpoena effectively qualified by order limiting questioning so as to preserve Speech or Debate Clause immunity), or even testimonial privileges recognized by the common law, see In re Grand Jury Investigation of Hugle, 754 F.2d 863 (CA9 1985) (opinion of Kennedy, J.) (same with respect to privilege for confidential marital communications). Even in this setting, however, we have insisted that the grand jury remain "free to pursue its investigations unhindered by external influence or supervision so long as it does not trench upon the legitimate rights of any witness called before it." United States v. Dionisio, 410 U.S. 1, 17-18 (1973). Recognizing this tradition of independence, we have said that the Fifth Amendment's "constitutional guarantee *presupposes* an investigative body 'acting independently of either prosecuting attorney *or judge*.' . . ." Id., at 16 (emphasis added).

No doubt in view of the grand jury proceeding's status as other than a constituent element of a "criminal prosecution," U.S. Const., Amdt. 6, we have said that certain constitutional protections afforded defendants in criminal proceedings have no application before that body. The Double Jeopardy Clause of the Fifth Amendment does not bar a grand jury from returning an indictment when a prior grand jury has refused to do so. See Ex parte United States, 287 U.S. 241, 250-251 (1932). We have twice suggested, though not held, that the Sixth Amendment right to counsel does not attach when an individual is summoned to appear before a grand jury, even if he is the subject of the investigation. See United States v. Mandujano, 425 U.S. 564, 581 (1976) (plurality opinion); In re Groban, 352 U.S. 330, 333 (1957); see also Fed. Rule Crim. Proc. 6(d). And although "the grand jury may not force a witness to answer questions in violation of [the Fifth Amendment's] constitutional guarantee" against self-incrimination, our cases suggest that an indictment obtained through the use of evidence previously obtained in violation of the privilege against self-incrimination "is nevertheless valid." *Calandra,* supra, at 346; see Lawn v. United States, 355 U.S. 339, 348-350 (1958).

Given the grand jury's operational separateness from its constituting court, it should come as no surprise that we have been reluctant to invoke the judicial supervisory power as a basis for prescribing modes of grand jury procedure. Over the years, we have received many requests to exercise supervision over the grand jury's evidence-taking process, but we have refused them all, including some more appealing than the one presented today. In United States v. Calandra, supra, a grand jury witness faced questions that were allegedly based upon physical evidence the Government had obtained through a violation of the Fourth Amendment; we rejected the proposal that the exclusionary rule be extended to grand jury proceedings, because of "the potential injury to the historic role and functions of the grand jury." 414 U.S. at 349. In Costello v United States, 350 U.S. 359 (1956), we declined to enforce the hearsay rule in grand jury proceedings, since that "would run counter to the whole history of the grand jury institution, in which laymen conduct their inquiries unfettered by technical rules." Id., at 364.

These authorities suggest that any power federal courts may have to fashion, on their own initiative, rules of grand jury procedure is a very limited one, not remotely comparable to the power they maintain over their own proceedings. It certainly would not permit judicial reshaping of the grand jury institution, substantially altering the traditional relationships between the prosecutor, the constituting court, and the grand jury itself. As we proceed to discuss, that would be the consequence of the proposed rule here.

B

Respondent argues that the Court of Appeals' rule can be justified as a sort of Fifth Amendment "common law," a necessary means of assuring the constitutional right to the judgment "of an independent and informed grand jury." Respondent makes a generalized appeal to functional notions: Judicial supervision of the quantity and quality of the evidence relied upon by the grand jury plainly facilitates, he says, the grand jury's performance of its twin historical responsibilities, i.e., bringing to trial those who may be justly accused and shielding the innocent from unfounded accusation and prosecution. We do not agree. The rule would neither preserve nor enhance the traditional functioning of the institution that the Fifth

Amendment demands. To the contrary, requiring the prosecutor to present exculpatory as well as inculpatory evidence would alter the grand jury's historical role, transforming it from an accusatory to an adjudicatory body.

It is axiomatic that the grand jury sits not to determine guilt or innocence, but to assess whether there is adequate basis for bringing a criminal charge. That has always been so; and to make the assessment it has always been thought sufficient to hear only the prosecutor's side. As Blackstone described the prevailing practice in 18th-century England, the grand jury was "only to hear evidence on behalf of the prosecution[,] for the finding of an indictment is only in the nature of an enquiry or accusation, which is afterwards to be tried and determined." 4 W. Blackstone, Commentaries 300 (1769); see also 2 M. Hale, Pleas of the Crown 157 (1st Am. ed. 1847). So also in the United States. According to the description of an early American court, three years before the Fifth Amendment was ratified, it is the grand jury's function not "to enquire . . . upon what foundation [the charge may be] denied," or otherwise to try the suspect's defenses, but only to examine "upon what foundation [the charge] is made" by the prosecutor. Respublica v. Shaffer, 1 U.S. (1 Dall.) 236 (O. T. Phila. 1788); see also F. Wharton, Criminal Pleading and Practice §360, pp. 248-249 (8th ed. 1880). As a consequence, neither in this country nor in England has the suspect under investigation by the grand jury ever been thought to have a right to testify or to have exculpatory evidence presented.

Imposing upon the prosecutor a legal obligation to present exculpatory evidence in his possession would be incompatible with this system. If a "balanced" assessment of the entire matter is the objective, surely the first thing to be done — rather than requiring the prosecutor to say what he knows in defense of the target of the investigation — is to entitle the target to tender his own defense. To require the former while denying (as we do) the latter would be quite absurd. It would also be quite pointless, since it would merely invite the target to circumnavigate the system by delivering his exculpatory evidence to the prosecutor, whereupon it would have to be passed on to the grand jury — unless the prosecutor is willing to take the chance that a court will not deem the evidence important enough to qualify for mandatory disclosure. See, e.g., United States v. Law Firm of Zimmerman & Schwartz, P.C., 738 F. Supp. 407, 411 (D. Colo. 1990) (duty to disclose exculpatory evidence held satisfied when prosecution tendered to the grand jury defense-provided exhibits, testimony, and explanations of the governing law).

Respondent acknowledges (as he must) that the "common law" of the grand jury is not violated if the grand jury itself chooses to hear no more evidence than that which suffices to convince it an indictment is proper. Thus, had the Government offered to familiarize the grand jury in this case with the five boxes of financial statements and deposition testimony alleged to contain exculpatory information, and had the grand jury rejected the offer as pointless, respondent would presumably agree that the resulting indictment would have been valid. Respondent insists, however, that courts must require the modern prosecutor to alert the grand jury to the nature and extent of the available exculpatory evidence, because otherwise the grand jury "merely functions as an arm of the prosecution." We reject the attempt to convert a non-existent duty of the grand jury itself into an obligation of the prosecutor. The authority of the prosecutor to seek an indictment has long been understood to be "coterminous with the authority of the grand jury to entertain [the prosecutor's] charges." United States v. Thompson, 251 U.S. at 414. If the grand jury has no obligation to consider all "substantial exculpatory" evidence, we do not understand how the prosecutor can be said to have a binding obligation to present it.

There is yet another respect in which respondent's proposal not only fails to comport with, but positively contradicts, the "common law" of the Fifth Amendment grand jury. Motions to quash indictments based upon the sufficiency of the evidence relied upon by the grand jury were unheard of at common law in England, see, e.g., People v. Restenblatt, 1 Abb. Pr. 268, 269 (Ct. Gen. Sess. N.Y. 1855). And the traditional American practice was described by Justice Nelson, riding circuit in 1852, as follows:

> No case has been cited, nor have we been able to find any, furnishing an authority for looking into and revising the judgment of the grand jury upon the evidence, for the purpose of determining whether or not the finding was founded upon sufficient proof, or whether there was a deficiency in respect to any part of the complaint.

. . . United States v. Reed, 27 F. Cas. (2 Blatchf.) 727, 738 (No. 16,134) (CC NDNY 1852).

We accepted Justice Nelson's description in Costello v. United States, where we held that "it would run counter to the whole history of the grand jury institution" to permit an indictment to be challenged "on the ground that there was inadequate or incompetent evidence before the grand jury." 350 U.S. at 363-364. . . . It would make little sense, we think, to abstain from reviewing the evidentiary support for the grand jury's judgment while scrutinizing the sufficiency of the prosecutor's presentation. A complaint about the quality or adequacy of the evidence can always be recast as a complaint that the prosecutor's presentation was "incomplete" or "misleading." Our words in *Costello* bear repeating: Review of facially valid indictments on such grounds "would run counter to the whole history of the grand jury institution[,] [and] neither justice nor the concept of a fair trial requires [it]." 350 U.S. at 364.

Echoing the reasoning of the Tenth Circuit in United States v. Page, 808 F.2d at 728, respondent argues that a rule requiring the prosecutor to disclose exculpatory evidence to the grand jury would, by removing from the docket unjustified prosecutions, save valuable judicial time. That depends, we suppose, upon what the ratio would turn out to be between unjustified prosecutions eliminated and grand jury indictments challenged — for the latter as well as the former consume "valuable judicial time." We need not pursue the matter; if there is an advantage to the proposal, Congress is free to prescribe it. For the reasons set forth above, however, we conclude that courts have no authority to prescribe such a duty pursuant to their inherent supervisory authority over their own proceedings. The judgment of the Court of Appeals is accordingly reversed, and the cause is remanded for further proceedings consistent with this opinion.

JUSTICE STEVENS, with whom JUSTICE BLACKMUN, JUSTICE O'CONNOR, and JUSTICE THOMAS join, dissenting.

. . . Like the Hydra slain by Hercules, prosecutorial misconduct has many heads. Some are cataloged in Justice Sutherland's classic opinion for the Court in Berger v. United States, 295 U.S. 78 (1935):

That the United States prosecuting attorney overstepped the bounds of that propriety and fairness which should characterize the conduct of such an officer in the prosecution of a criminal offense is clearly shown by the record. He was guilty of misstating the facts in his cross-examination of witnesses; of putting into the mouths of such witnesses things which they had not said; of suggesting by his questions that statements had been made to him personally out of court, in respect of which no proof was offered; of pretending to understand that a witness had said something which he had not said and persistently cross-examining the witness upon that basis; of assuming prejudicial facts not in evidence; of bullying and arguing with witnesses; and in general, of conducting himself in a thoroughly indecorous and improper manner.

. . . The prosecuting attorney's argument to the jury . . . [contained] improper insinuations and assertions calculated to mislead the jury. Id., at 84-85.

. . . Nor has prosecutorial misconduct been limited to judicial proceedings: The reported cases indicate that it has sometimes infected grand jury proceedings as well. The cases contain examples of prosecutors presenting perjured testimony, United States v. Basurto, 497 F.2d 781, 786 (CA9 1974), questioning a witness outside the presence of the grand jury and then failing to inform the grand jury that the testimony was exculpatory, United States v. Phillips Petroleum, Inc., 435 F. Supp. 610, 615-617 (ND Okla. 1977), failing to inform the grand jury of its authority to subpoena witnesses, United States v. Samango, 607 F.2d 877, 884 (CA9 1979), operating under a conflict of interest, United States v. Gold, 470 F. Supp. 1336, 1346-1351 (ND Ill. 1979), misstating the law, United States v. Roberts, 481 F. Supp. 1385, 1389, and n. 10 (CD Cal. 1980), and misstating the facts on cross-examination of a witness, United States v. Lawson, 502 F. Supp. 158, 162, and nn. 6-7 (Md. 1980).

Justice Sutherland's identification of the basic reason why that sort of misconduct is intolerable merits repetition:

The United States Attorney is the representative not of an ordinary party to a controversy, but of a sovereignty whose obligation to govern impartially is as compelling as its obligation to govern at all; and whose interest, therefore, in a criminal prosecution is not that it shall win a case, but that justice shall be done. As such, he is in a peculiar and very definite sense the servant of the law, the twofold aim of which is that guilt shall not escape or innocence suffer. He may prosecute with earnestness and vigor — indeed, he should do so. But, while he may strike hard blows, he is not at liberty to strike foul ones. It is as much his duty to refrain from improper methods calculated to produce a wrongful conviction as it is to use every legitimate means to bring about a just one. Berger v. United States, 295 U.S. at 88.

It is equally clear that the prosecutor has the same duty to refrain from improper methods calculated to produce a wrongful indictment. Indeed, the prosecutor's duty to protect the fundamental fairness of judicial proceedings assumes special importance when he is presenting evidence to a grand jury. As the Court of Appeals for the Third Circuit recognized, "the costs of continued unchecked prosecutorial misconduct" before the grand jury are particularly substantial because there

the prosecutor operates without the check of a judge or a trained legal adversary, and virtually immune from public scrutiny. The prosecutor's abuse of his special relationship to the grand jury poses an enormous risk to defendants as well. For while in theory a trial provides the defendant with a full opportunity to contest and disprove the charges against him, in practice, the handing up of an indictment will often have a devastating personal and professional impact that a later dismissal or acquittal can never undo. Where the potential for abuse is so great, and the consequences of a mistaken indictment so serious, the ethical responsibilities of the prosecutor, and the obligation of the judiciary to protect against even the appearance of unfairness, are correspondingly heightened. United States v. Serubo, 604 F.2d 807, 817 (1979).

. . . In an opinion that I find difficult to comprehend, the Court today . . . seems to suggest that the court has no authority to supervise the conduct of the prosecutor in grand jury proceedings so long as he follows the dictates of the Constitution, applicable statutes, and Rule 6 of the Federal Rules of Criminal Procedure. The Court purports to support this conclusion by invoking the doctrine of separation of powers and citing a string of cases in which we have declined to impose categorical restraints on the grand jury. Needless to say, the Court's reasoning is unpersuasive.

Although the grand jury has not been "textually assigned" to "any of the branches described in the first three Articles" of the Constitution, it is not an autonomous body completely beyond the reach of the other branches. Throughout its life, from the moment it is convened until it is discharged, the grand jury is subject to the control of the court. As Judge Learned Hand recognized over 60 years ago, "a grand jury is neither an officer nor an agent of the United States, but a part of the court." Falter v. United States, 23 F.2d 420, 425 (CA2 1928). . . .

This Court has, of course, long recognized that the grand jury has wide latitude to investigate violations of federal law as it deems appropriate and need not obtain permission from either the court or the prosecutor. Correspondingly, we have acknowledged that "its operation generally is unrestrained by the technical procedural and evidentiary rules governing the conduct of criminal trials." *Calandra*, 414 U.S. at 343. But this is because Congress and the Court have generally thought it best not to impose procedural restraints on the grand jury; it is not because they lack all power to do so.

To the contrary, the Court has recognized that it has the authority to create and enforce limited rules applicable in grand jury proceedings. Thus, for example, the Court has said that the grand jury "may not itself violate a valid privilege, whether established by the Constitution, statutes, or the common law." Id., at 346. And the Court may prevent a grand jury from violating such a privilege by quashing or modifying a subpoena, id., at 346, n. 4, or issuing a protective order forbidding questions in violation of the privilege, Gravel v. United States, 408 U.S. 606, 628-629 (1972). Moreover, there are, as the Court notes, a series of cases in which we declined to impose categorical restraints on the grand jury. In none of those cases, however, did we question our power to reach a contrary result. . . .

We do not protect the integrity and independence of the grand jury by closing our eyes to the countless forms of prosecutorial misconduct that may occur inside the secrecy of the grand jury room. After all, the grand jury is not merely an investigatory body; it also serves as a "protector of citizens against arbitrary and oppressive governmental action." United States v. Calandra, 414 U.S. at 343. Explaining why the grand jury must be both "independent" and "informed," the Court wrote in Wood v. Georgia, 370 U.S. 375 (1962):

> Historically, this body has been regarded as a primary security to the innocent against hasty, malicious and oppressive persecution; it serves the invaluable function in our society of standing between the accuser and the accused, whether the latter be an

individual, minority group, or other, to determine whether a charge is founded upon reason or was dictated by an intimidating power or by malice and personal ill will. Id., at 390.

It blinks reality to say that the grand jury can adequately perform this important historic role if it is intentionally misled by the prosecutor — on whose knowledge of the law and facts of the underlying criminal investigation the jurors will, of necessity, rely. . . .

What, then, is the proper disposition of this case? I agree with the Government that the prosecutor is not required to place all exculpatory evidence before the grand jury. A grand jury proceeding is an ex parte investigatory proceeding to determine whether there is probable cause to believe a violation of the criminal laws has occurred, not a trial. Requiring the prosecutor to ferret out and present all evidence that could be used at trial to create a reasonable doubt as to the defendant's guilt would be inconsistent with the purpose of the grand jury proceeding and would place significant burdens on the investigation. But that does not mean that the prosecutor may mislead the grand jury into believing that there is probable cause to indict by withholding clear evidence to the contrary. I thus agree with the Department of Justice that "when a prosecutor conducting a grand jury inquiry is personally aware of substantial evidence which directly negates the guilt of a subject of the investigation, the prosecutor must present or otherwise disclose such evidence to the grand jury before seeking an indictment against such a person." U.S. Dept. of Justice, United States Attorneys' Manual 9-11.233, p. 88 (1988).

Although I question whether the evidence withheld in this case directly negates respondent's guilt, I need not resolve my doubts because the Solicitor General did not ask the Court to review the nature of the evidence withheld. Instead, he asked us to decide the legal question whether an indictment may be dismissed because the prosecutor failed to present exculpatory evidence. Unlike the Court and the Solicitor General, I believe the answer to that question is yes, if the withheld evidence would plainly preclude a finding of probable cause. I therefore cannot endorse the Court's opinion. . . .

NOTES AND QUESTIONS

1. Williams made two kinds of arguments for a rule requiring disclosure of at least some exculpatory evidence to grand juries. First, he argued that such a rule should be imposed under the Court's "supervisory power," its power to make common law governing the operation of the federal court system. Justice Scalia answers that argument by pointing to grand juries' independence of the court system (meaning that the supervisory power extends to grand juries only in a very limited way; recall Justice Scalia's statement that that power is "not remotely" as broad with respect to grand juries as it is with respect to ordinary court proceedings). Second, Williams argued that his proposed rule should be imposed as part of a "Fifth Amendment common law" that would define and limit grand juries' role. Justice Scalia responds in part by noting that grand juries have traditionally been permitted to indict based on whatever evidence satisfied them; he goes on to say that prosecutors surely cannot be obliged to inform grand juries of things that grand juries themselves are free to ignore. In other words, prosecutors' obligation cannot exceed the obligation of the grand jurors themselves.

Both of Justice Scalia's responses envision grand juries as independent entities, with prosecutors as the grand jurors' servant, not their master. That may well have been the historical relationship, but few people familiar with grand juries would so characterize them today. What sense does it make to place so much emphasis on grand jury independence *now*? More broadly, what do cases like *Williams* make you think about "original intent" methods of constitutional interpretation? If grand juries played a different role at the time of the Founding than they do now, how should the difference be taken into account in defining the law that governs grand juries today?

2. What about the more functional arguments offered by the Court? If prosecutors faced the obligation that Justice Stevens would impose, how would they behave? Might not Justice Stevens's regime invite a great deal of litigation about what evidence prosecutors did and didn't know about and how exculpatory it was? For that matter, under Justice Stevens's proposed standard, wouldn't prosecutors be worse off (in the sense that any indictment might now be threatened by future litigation) for knowing *more* about a given case? That certainly seems perverse.

3. But then, consider Justice Stevens's litany of different forms of prosecutorial manipulation of grand juries. How can grand juries do a decent job of screening prosecutorial charging decisions if prosecutors are free to mislead grand juries about the state of the evidence?

4. After *Williams* significantly narrowed the grounds for challenging an indictment, there remain only a few avenues available to the defense. Federal Rule 6 and its state counterparts still impose some obligations on prosecutors: They may not be present while the grand jury is voting, they must present only one witness at a time, and they must keep grand jury material secret, for example. In addition, a prosecutor obviously may not suborn perjury or present information known to be false to the grand jurors.

But even if a defendant learns of this type of prosecutorial misconduct, two barriers to obtaining relief remain. The first is the need to show prejudice. In Bank of Nova Scotia v. United States, 487 U.S. 250 (1988) (cited in *Williams*), the district court found that the prosecutor had, among other things, committed multiple violations of Rule 6(e), had presented misinformation to the grand jury, and had mistreated grand jury witnesses. Using his supervisory power, the district judge dismissed the indictment because of the government's misconduct. But the court of appeals reversed the dismissal and the Supreme Court affirmed, finding that, in the absence of demonstrated prejudice to the accused, grand jury errors are not a basis for dismissing the indictment. The Court pointed to Rule 52 of the Federal Rules, the "harmless error" provision, which provides that errors in the proceedings that do not affect the "substantial rights" of the accused are to be ignored, and said that judges may not avoid the harmless error rule simply to chastise prosecutorial overreaching. The Court noted that there were a few cases where prejudice was not required to be shown — racial bias in the selection of the grand jury, for example — but these were the exception and not the rule. In most cases, said the Court, including the one before it, "dismissal of the indictment is appropriate only if it is established that the violation substantially influenced the grand jury's decision to indict, or if there is grave doubt that the decision to indict was free from the substantial influence of such violations." Id., at 255 (internal quotation marks omitted). The Court did not explain how such a showing could be made, and it is fair to say that few defendants have succeeded in showing how alleged errors influenced the grand jury's thinking.

Bank of Nova Scotia involved a challenge to the indictment that was raised prior to trial; this distinction is important, because the second barrier to an indictment challenge is that once the criminal case is over, the challenge becomes effectively moot. If the defendant is acquitted, there is obviously no challenge remaining, and if the defendant is convicted via guilty plea or trial, the Court has said that generally the error is per se harmless. In U.S. v. Mechanik, 475 U.S. 66 (1986), the defendant learned during his trial that the government had presented two witnesses to the grand jury simultaneously, in violation of Rule 6(d). The defendant moved promptly to dismiss; the judge took the motion under advisement, and after the defendant was convicted, the motion was denied. The Supreme Court assumed the violation of the Rule but concluded that once the trial jury convicted, any errors before the grand jury became harmless. "In courtroom proceedings as elsewhere," said the Court, "the moving finger writes; and, having writ, moves on." Thus, a defendant has limited access to the information needed to challenge the indictment, a high standard of prejudice to overcome if he can get the information, and now a limited window of time within which the challenge can be brought.

The combination of *Costello*, *Williams*, *Bank of Nova Scotia*, and *Mechanik* eliminates nearly all challenges to the grand jury's work. The Supreme Court seems largely unconcerned by the structural barriers (many that it has built) that make it difficult for the grand jury to act as a shield; perhaps this is because most defendants will end up being convicted of something anyway, usually by a guilty plea, and perhaps because defendants retain the ability to force the case to trial, where the full range of procedural protections are available to protect them.

Given all this, is it realistic to think that the grand jury restrains the prosecutors in making their charging decisions? If not, does the grand jury still serve a useful purpose in the criminal system?

Chapter 11

The Scope of the Prosecution

Selecting the proper target for prosecution and the proper charges are not the only critical pretrial decisions a prosecutor must make. Even before the grand jury returns an indictment, there are important choices required about the timing, location, and scope of the criminal case being considered. In the first instance, these are the prosecutor's decisions to make, but now — unlike the decision of whether and what charges to bring — there are meaningful legal constraints on the government's discretion.

This chapter looks at the "when, where, what, and who" of the criminal case. Section A looks at the constraints on when the government files charges. Generally, law enforcement and prosecutors can investigate as long as necessary and bring criminal charges anytime, provided they don't run afoul of the applicable statute of limitations. But once the decision to prosecute is put into action, either by arrest or by indictment, a clock starts ticking and the government's time frame to investigate and prepare a case narrows. The defendant has both a constitutional and a statutory right to a speedy trial, one that puts pressure on both prosecutors and courts to move a case forward.

Section B.1 looks at where a case must be filed — the venue of the trial. A defendant has a constitutional right to stand trial in the judicial district where the crime was committed, but this simple test can quickly become complicated. If the defendant transports drugs across the country, where was the crime committed, and where should the charges be filed? Where the trip started? Where it ended? In any state through which the defendant drove? Suppose a defendant in Maine is in a conspiracy with a defendant in California, and neither one has been to the other's state. Can the California defendant be transported to Maine for trial there?

Section B.2 looks at venue from the other direction: When does the defendant have the right to a trial at some place *other* than where the crime was committed? Sometimes a crime is sufficiently notorious that the defendant fears he cannot get a fair trial in the district where the crime occurred, and will move for a change of venue. This section explores the competing interests at stake in such a motion, and asks how a judge should evaluate these interests.

Section C asks the "what" and the "who" — the issues of joinder and severance. If a defendant is accused of committing three bank robberies in three different towns on three different days, should all three charges be joined in a single indictment, and thus, be part of a single trial? Also, if more than one defendant is accused of robbing the same bank, should both defendants be considered in one trial, or should there be separate proceedings? Prosecutors and judges usually prefer a consolidated trial for efficiency reasons, but defendants will often argue that having a single jury hear about multiple charges and/or seeing multiple defendants in one case is highly prejudicial, and thus will move to sever the charges or defendants.

This section examines the circumstances under which trial judges should override the prosecutor's decision about the proper scope of the case.

A.   The Right to a Speedy Trial

When a defendant complains that his criminal trial has come too late, the claim may derive from several sources. In the case of delay between the crime and the commencement of formal legal proceedings, the defendant is protected primarily by the applicable state or federal statute of limitations. For a delay between the defendant's arrest or indictment and trial, the defendant is protected by: (1) the Speedy Trial Clause of the Sixth Amendment ("In all criminal prosecutions, the accused shall enjoy the right to a speedy and public trial. . . ."),[1] and similar speedy-trial provisions found in state constitutions; (2) state or federal statutes such as the federal Speedy Trial Act of 1974, 18 U.S.C. §§3161-3174 (1994) (comparable statutes have been enacted in most of the states); and (3) various court rules. Finally, delay that is both unjust and prejudicial to the defendant may violate the Due Process Clause, regardless of whether such delay precedes or follows the defendant's arrest or indictment.

In the cases that follow, the Supreme Court faced claims of inordinate delay arising in different factual settings. As you read the cases, try to distinguish the various legal bases for the defendant's claim, and try to determine what interests are protected by the constitutional or statutory provisions involved.

BARKER v. WINGO

Certiorari to the United States Court of Appeals for the Sixth Circuit
407 U.S. 514 (1972)

JUSTICE POWELL delivered the opinion of the Court. Although a speedy trial is guaranteed the accused by the Sixth Amendment to the Constitution, this Court has dealt with that right on infrequent occasions. . . .

[I]n none of [our prior] cases have we attempted to set out the criteria by which the speedy trial right is to be judged. . . . This case compels us to make such an attempt.

I

On July 20, 1958, in Christian County, Kentucky, an elderly couple was beaten to death by intruders wielding an iron tire tool. Two suspects, Silas Manning and Willie Barker, the petitioner, were arrested shortly thereafter. The grand jury indicted them on September 15. Counsel was appointed on September 17, and Barker's trial was set for October 21. The Commonwealth had a stronger case against Manning, and it believed that Barker could not be convicted unless Manning testified against him. Manning was naturally unwilling to incriminate himself. Accordingly, on October 23, the day Silas Manning was brought to trial, the Commonwealth sought and obtained the first of what was to be a series of 16 continuances of Barker's trial.

---

1. The Supreme Court has applied the Speedy Trial Clause to the states; see Klopfer v. North Carolina, 386 U.S. 213, 222-223 (1967).

Barker made no objection. By first convicting Manning, the Commonwealth would remove possible problems of self-incrimination and would be able to assure his testimony against Barker.

The Commonwealth encountered more than a few difficulties in its prosecution of Manning. The first trial ended in a hung jury. A second trial resulted in a conviction, but the Kentucky Court of Appeals reversed because of the admission of evidence obtained by an illegal search. Manning v. Commonwealth, 328 S.W.2d 421 (1959). At his third trial, Manning was again convicted, and the Court of Appeals again reversed because the trial court had not granted a change of venue. Manning v. Commonwealth, 346 S.W.2d 755 (1961). A fourth trial resulted in a hung jury. Finally, after five trials, Manning was convicted, in March 1962, of murdering one victim, and after a sixth trial, in December 1962, he was convicted of murdering the other.

The Christian County Circuit Court holds three terms each year — in February, June, and September. Barker's initial trial was to take place in the September term of 1958. The first continuance postponed it until the February 1959 term. The second continuance was granted for one month only. Every term thereafter for as long as the Manning prosecutions were in process, the Commonwealth routinely moved to continue Barker's case to the next term. When the case was continued from the June 1959 term until the following September, Barker, having spent 10 months in jail, obtained his release by posting a $5,000 bond. He thereafter remained free in the community until his trial. Barker made no objection, through his counsel, to the first 11 continuances.

When on February 12, 1962, the Commonwealth moved for the twelfth time to continue the case until the following term, Barker's counsel filed a motion to dismiss the indictment. The motion to dismiss was denied two weeks later, and the Commonwealth's motion for a continuance was granted. The Commonwealth was granted further continuances in June 1962 and September 1962, to which Barker did not object.

In February 1963, the first term of court following Manning's final conviction, the Commonwealth moved to set Barker's trial for March 19. But on the day scheduled for trial, it again moved for a continuance until the June term. It gave as its reason the illness of the ex-sheriff who was the chief investigating officer in the case. To this continuance, Barker objected unsuccessfully.

The witness was still unable to testify in June, and the trial, which had been set for June 19, was continued again until the September term over Barker's objection. This time the court announced that the case would be dismissed for lack of prosecution if it were not tried during the next term. The final trial date was set for October 9, 1963. On that date, Barker again moved to dismiss the indictment, and this time specified that his right to a speedy trial had been violated. The motion was denied; the trial commenced with Manning as the chief prosecution witness; Barker was convicted and given a life sentence.

Barker appealed his conviction to the Kentucky Court of Appeals, relying in part on his speedy trial claim. The court affirmed. Barker v. Commonwealth, 385 S.W.2d 671 (1964). In February 1970 Barker petitioned for habeas corpus in the United States District Court for the Western District of Kentucky. Although the District Court rejected the petition without holding a hearing, the Court granted petitioner leave to appeal in forma pauperis and a certificate of probable cause to appeal. On appeal, the Court of Appeals for the Sixth Circuit affirmed the District Court. 442 F.2d 1141 (1971). . . . We granted Barker's petition for certiorari.

II

The right to a speedy trial is generically different from any of the other rights enshrined in the Constitution for the protection of the accused. In addition to the general concern that all accused persons be treated according to decent and fair procedures, there is a societal interest in providing a speedy trial which exists separate from, and at times in opposition to, the interests of the accused. The inability of courts to provide a prompt trial has contributed to a large backlog of cases in urban courts which, among other things, enables defendants to negotiate more effectively for pleas of guilty to lesser offenses and otherwise manipulate the system. In addition, persons released on bond for lengthy periods awaiting trial have an opportunity to commit other crimes. It must be of little comfort to the residents of Christian County, Kentucky, to know that Barker was at large on bail for over four years while accused of a vicious and brutal murder of which he was ultimately convicted. Moreover, the longer an accused is free awaiting trial, the more tempting becomes his opportunity to jump bail and escape. Finally, delay between arrest and punishment may have a detrimental effect on rehabilitation.

If an accused cannot make bail, he is generally confined, as was Barker for 10 months, in a local jail. This contributes to the overcrowding and generally deplorable state of those institutions. Lengthy exposure to these conditions "has a destructive effect on human character and makes the rehabilitation of the individual offender much more difficult." At times the result may even be violent rioting. Finally, lengthy pretrial detention is costly. The cost of maintaining a prisoner in jail varies from $3 to $9 per day, and this amounts to millions across the Nation. In addition, society loses wages which might have been earned, and it must often support families of incarcerated breadwinners.

A second difference between the right to speedy trial and the accused's other constitutional rights is that deprivation of the right may work to the accused's advantage. Delay is not an uncommon defense tactic. As the time between the commission of the crime and trial lengthens, witnesses may become unavailable or their memories may fade. If the witnesses support the prosecution, its case will be weakened, sometimes seriously so. And it is the prosecution which carries the burden of proof. Thus, unlike the right to counsel or the right to be free from compelled self-incrimination, deprivation of the right to speedy trial does not per se prejudice the accused's ability to defend himself.

Finally, and perhaps most importantly, the right to speedy trial is a more vague concept than other procedural rights. It is, for example, impossible to determine with precision when the right has been denied. We cannot definitely say how long is too long in a system where justice is supposed to be swift but deliberate.[15] As a consequence, there is no fixed point in the criminal process when the State can put the defendant to the choice of either exercising or waiving the right to a speedy trial. If, for example, the State moves for a 60-day continuance, granting that continuance is not a violation of the right to speedy trial unless the circumstances of the case are such that further delay would endanger the values the right protects. It is impossible to do more than generalize about when those circumstances exist. There is nothing

15. "In large measure because of the many procedural safeguards provided an accused, the ordinary procedures for criminal prosecution are designed to move at a deliberate pace. A requirement of unreasonable speed would have a deleterious effect both upon the rights of the accused and upon the ability of society to protect itself." United States v. Ewell, 383 U.S. 116, 120 (1966).

comparable to the point in the process when a defendant exercises or waives his right to counsel or his right to a jury trial. Thus, . . . any inquiry into a speedy trial claim necessitates a functional analysis of the right in the particular context of the case. . . .

The amorphous quality of the right also leads to the unsatisfactorily severe remedy of dismissal of the indictment when the right has been deprived. This is indeed a serious consequence because it means that a defendant who may be guilty of a serious crime will go free, without having been tried. Such a remedy is more serious than an exclusionary rule or a reversal for a new trial, but it is the only possible remedy.

III

Perhaps because the speedy trial right is so slippery, two rigid approaches are urged upon us as ways of eliminating some of the uncertainty which courts experience in protecting the right. The first suggestion is that we hold that the Constitution requires a criminal defendant to be offered a trial within a specified time period. The result of such a ruling would have the virtue of clarifying when the right is infringed and of simplifying courts' application of it. Recognizing this, some legislatures have enacted laws, and some courts have adopted procedural rules which more narrowly define the right. . . .

But such a result would require this Court to engage in legislative or rulemaking activity, rather than in the adjudicative process to which we should confine our efforts. We do not establish procedural rules for the States, except when mandated by the Constitution. We find no constitutional basis for holding that the speedy trial right can be quantified into a specified number of days or months. The States, of course, are free to prescribe a reasonable period consistent with constitutional standards, but our approach must be less precise.

The second suggested alternative would restrict consideration of the right to those cases in which the accused has demanded a speedy trial. Most States have recognized what is loosely referred to as the "demand rule," although eight States reject it. It is not clear, however, precisely what is meant by that term. Although every federal court of appeals that has considered the question has endorsed some kind of demand rule, some have regarded the rule within the concept of waiver, whereas others have viewed it as a factor to be weighed in assessing whether there has been a deprivation of the speedy trial right. We shall refer to the former approach as the demand-waiver doctrine. The demand-waiver doctrine provides that a defendant waives any consideration of his right to speedy trial for any period prior to which he has not demanded a trial. Under this rigid approach, a prior demand is a necessary condition to the consideration of the speedy trial right. . . .

Such an approach, by presuming waiver of a fundamental right from inaction, is inconsistent with this Court's pronouncements on waiver of constitutional rights. The Court has defined waiver as "an intentional relinquishment or abandonment of a known right or privilege." Johnson v. Zerbst, 304 U.S. 458, 464 (1938). Courts should "indulge every reasonable presumption against waiver," . . . and they should "not presume acquiescence in the loss of fundamental rights." . . .

In excepting the right to speedy trial from the rule of waiver we have applied to other fundamental rights, courts that have applied the demand-waiver rule have relied on the assumption that delay usually works for the benefit of the accused and on the absence of any readily ascertainable time in the criminal process for a defendant to be given the choice of exercising or waiving his right. But it is not necessarily true that delay benefits the defendant. There are cases in which delay appreciably harms the defendant's ability to defend himself. Moreover, a defendant confined to jail prior to trial is obviously disadvantaged by delay as is a defendant released on bail but unable to lead a normal life because of community suspicion and his own anxiety.

The nature of the speedy trial right does make it impossible to pinpoint a precise time in the process when the right must be asserted or waived, but that fact does not argue for placing the burden of protecting the right solely on defendants. A defendant has no duty to bring himself to trial; the State has that duty as well as the duty of insuring that the trial is consistent with due process. Moreover, for the reasons earlier expressed, society has a particular interest in bringing swift prosecutions, and society's representatives are the ones who should protect that interest.

It is also noteworthy that such a rigid view of the demand-waiver rule places defense counsel in an awkward position. Unless he demands a trial early and often, he is in danger of frustrating his client's right. If counsel is willing to tolerate some delay because he finds it reasonable and helpful in preparing his own case, he may be unable to obtain a speedy trial for his client at the end of that time. Since under the demand-waiver rule no time runs until the demand is made, the government will have whatever time is otherwise reasonable to bring the defendant to trial after a demand has been made. Thus, if the first demand is made three months after arrest in a jurisdiction which prescribes a six-month rule, the prosecution will have a total of nine months — which may be wholly unreasonable under the circumstances. The result in practice is likely to be either an automatic, pro forma demand made immediately after appointment of counsel or delays which, but for the demand-waiver rule, would not be tolerated. Such a result is not consistent with the interests of defendants, society, or the Constitution.

We reject, therefore, the rule that a defendant who fails to demand a speedy trial forever waives his right. This does not mean, however, that the defendant has no responsibility to assert his right. We think the better rule is that the defendant's assertion of or failure to assert his right to a speedy trial is one of the factors to be considered in an inquiry into the deprivation of the right. Such a formulation avoids the rigidities of the demand-waiver rule and the resulting possible unfairness in its application. It allows the trial court to exercise a judicial discretion based on the circumstances, including due consideration of any applicable formal procedural rule. It would permit, for example, a court to attach a different weight to a situation in which the defendant knowingly fails to object from a situation in which his attorney acquiesces in long delay without adequately informing his client, or from a situation in which no counsel is appointed. It would also allow a court to weigh the frequency and force of the objections as opposed to attaching significant weight to a purely pro forma objection.

In ruling that a defendant has some responsibility to assert a speedy trial claim, we do not depart from our holdings in other cases concerning the waiver of fundamental rights, in which we have placed the entire responsibility on the prosecution to show that the claimed waiver was knowingly and voluntarily made. Such cases have involved rights which must be exercised or waived at a specific time or under clearly identifiable circumstances, such as the rights to plead not guilty, to demand a jury trial, to exercise the privilege against self-incrimination, and to have the assistance of counsel. We have shown above that the right to a speedy trial is unique in its uncertainty as to when and under what circumstances it must be asserted or may be deemed waived. But the rule we announce today, which comports with constitutional principles, places the primary burden on the courts and the prosecutors to assure that cases are brought to trial. We hardly need add that if delay is attributable to the defendant, then his waiver may be given effect under standard waiver doctrine, the demand rule aside.

We, therefore, reject both of the inflexible approaches — the fixed-time period because it goes further than the Constitution requires; the demand-waiver rule because it is insensitive to a right which we have deemed fundamental. The approach we accept is a balancing test, in which the conduct of both the prosecution and the defendant are weighed.[29]

IV

A balancing test necessarily compels courts to approach speedy trial cases on an ad hoc basis. We can do little more than identify some of the factors which courts should assess in determining whether a particular defendant has been deprived of his right. Though some might express them in different ways, we identify four such factors: Length of delay, the reason for the delay, the defendant's assertion of his right, and prejudice to the defendant.

The length of the delay is to some extent a triggering mechanism. Until there is some delay which is presumptively prejudicial, there is no necessity for inquiry into the other factors that go into the balance. Nevertheless, because of the imprecision of the right to speedy trial, the length of delay that will provoke such an inquiry is necessarily dependent upon the peculiar circumstances of the case. To take but one example, the delay that can be tolerated for an ordinary street crime is considerably less than for a serious, complex conspiracy charge.

Closely related to length of delay is the reason the government assigns to justify the delay. Here, too, different weights should be assigned to different reasons. A deliberate attempt to delay the trial in order to hamper the defense should be weighted heavily against the government. A more neutral reason such as negligence or overcrowded courts should be weighted less heavily but nevertheless should be considered since the ultimate responsibility for such circumstances must rest with the government rather than with the defendant. Finally, a valid reason, such as a missing witness, should serve to justify appropriate delay.

We have already discussed the third factor, the defendant's responsibility to assert his right. Whether and how a defendant asserts his right is closely related to the other factors we have mentioned. The strength of his efforts will be affected by the length of the delay, to some extent by the reason for the delay, and most particularly by the personal prejudice, which is not always readily identifiable, that he experiences. The more serious the deprivation, the more likely a defendant is to complain. The defendant's assertion of his speedy trial right, then, is entitled to strong evidentiary weight in determining whether the defendant is being deprived of the right. We emphasize that failure to assert the right will make it difficult for a defendant to prove that he was denied a speedy trial.

---

29. Nothing we have said should be interpreted as disapproving a presumptive rule adopted by a court in the exercise of its supervisory powers which establishes a fixed time period within which cases must normally be brought.

A fourth factor is prejudice to the defendant. Prejudice, of course, should be assessed in the light of the interests of defendants which the speedy trial right was designed to protect. This Court has identified three such interests: (i) to prevent oppressive pretrial incarceration; (ii) to minimize anxiety and concern of the accused; and (iii) to limit the possibility that the defense will be impaired. Of these, the most serious is the last, because the inability of a defendant adequately to prepare his case skews the fairness of the entire system. If witnesses die or disappear during a delay, the prejudice is obvious. There is also prejudice if defense witnesses are unable to recall accurately events of the distant past. Loss of memory, however, is not always reflected in the record because what has been forgotten can rarely be shown.

We have discussed previously the societal disadvantages of lengthy pretrial incarceration, but obviously the disadvantages for the accused who cannot obtain his release are even more serious. The time spent in jail awaiting trial has a detrimental impact on the individual. It often means loss of a job; it disrupts family life; and it enforces idleness. Most jails offer little or no recreational or rehabilitative programs. The time spent in jail is simply dead time. Moreover, if a defendant is locked up, he is hindered in his ability to gather evidence, contact witnesses, or otherwise prepare his defense.[35] Imposing those consequences on anyone who has not yet been convicted is serious. It is especially unfortunate to impose them on those persons who are ultimately found to be innocent. Finally, even if an accused is not incarcerated prior to trial, he is still disadvantaged by restraints on his liberty and by living under a cloud of anxiety, suspicion, and often hostility.

We regard none of the four factors identified above as either a necessary or sufficient condition to the finding of a deprivation of the right of speedy trial. Rather, they are related factors and must be considered together with such other circumstances as may be relevant. In sum, these factors have no talismanic qualities; courts must still engage in a difficult and sensitive balancing process. But, because we are dealing with a fundamental right of the accused, this process must be carried out with full recognition that the accused's interest in a speedy trial is specifically affirmed in the Constitution.

V

The difficulty of the task of balancing these factors is illustrated by this case, which we consider to be close. It is clear that the length of delay between arrest and trial — well over five years — was extraordinary. Only seven months of that period can be attributed to a strong excuse, the illness of the ex-sheriff who was in charge of the investigation. Perhaps some delay would have been permissible under ordinary circumstances, so that Manning could be utilized as a witness in Barker's trial, but more than four years was too long a period, particularly since a good part of that period was attributable to the Commonwealth's failure or inability to try Manning under circumstances that comported with due process.

Two counterbalancing factors, however, outweigh these deficiencies. The first is that prejudice was minimal. Of course, Barker was prejudiced to some extent by

---

35.   . . . There is statistical evidence that persons who are detained between arrest and trial are more likely to receive prison sentences than those who obtain pretrial release, although other factors bear upon this correlation. See Wald, Pretrial Detention and Ultimate Freedom: A Statistical Study, 39 N.Y.U. L. Rev. 631 (1964).

living for over four years under a cloud of suspicion and anxiety. Moreover, although he was released on bond for most of the period, he did spend 10 months in jail before trial. But there is no claim that any of Barker's witnesses died or otherwise became unavailable owing to the delay. The trial transcript indicates only two very minor lapses of memory — one on the part of a prosecution witness — which were in no way significant to the outcome.

More important than the absence of serious prejudice, is the fact that Barker did not want a speedy trial. Counsel was appointed for Barker immediately after his indictment and represented him throughout the period. No question is raised as to the competency of such counsel. Despite the fact that counsel had notice of the motions for continuances, the record shows no action whatever taken between October 21, 1958, and February 12, 1962, that could be construed as the assertion of the speedy trial right. On the latter date, in response to another motion for continuance, Barker moved to dismiss the indictment. The record does not show on what ground this motion was based, although it is clear that no alternative motion was made for an immediate trial. Instead the record strongly suggests that while he hoped to take advantage of the delay in which he had acquiesced, and thereby obtain a dismissal of the charges, he definitely did not want to be tried. Counsel conceded as much at oral argument: "Your honor, I would concede that Willie Mae Barker probably — I don't know this for a fact — probably did not want to be tried. I don't think any man wants to be tried. And I don't consider this a liability on his behalf. I don't blame him." Tr. of Oral Arg. 39.

The probable reason for Barker's attitude was that he was gambling on Manning's acquittal. The evidence was not very strong against Manning, as the reversals and hung juries suggest, and Barker undoubtedly thought that if Manning were acquitted, he would never be tried. Counsel also conceded this: "Now, it's true that the reason for this delay was the Commonwealth of Kentucky's desire to secure the testimony of the accomplice, Silas Manning. And it's true that if Silas Manning were never convicted, Willie Mae Barker would never have been convicted. We concede this." Id., at 15.[39]

That Barker was gambling on Manning's acquittal is also suggested by his failure, following the pro forma motion to dismiss filed in February 1962, to object to the Commonwealth's next two motions for continuances. Indeed, it was not until March 1963, after Manning's convictions were final, that Barker, having lost his gamble, began to object to further continuances. At that time, the Commonwealth's excuse was the illness of the ex-sheriff, which Barker has conceded justified the further delay.

We do not hold that there may never be a situation in which an indictment may be dismissed on speedy trial grounds where the defendant has failed to object to continuances. There may be a situation in which the defendant was represented by incompetent counsel, was severely prejudiced, or even cases in which the continuances were granted ex parte. But barring extraordinary circumstances, we would be reluctant indeed to rule that a defendant was denied this constitutional right on a

---

39. Hindsight is, of course, 20/20, but we cannot help noting that if Barker had moved immediately and persistently for a speedy trial following indictment, and if he had been successful, he would have undoubtedly been acquitted since Manning's testimony was crucial to the Commonwealth's case. It could not have been anticipated at the outset, however, that Manning would have been tried six times over a four-year period. Thus, the decision to gamble on Manning's acquittal may have been a prudent choice at the time it was made.

record that strongly indicates, as does this one, that the defendant did not want a speedy trial. We hold, therefore, that Barker was not deprived of his due process right to a speedy trial.

The judgment of the Court of Appeals is Affirmed.

[The concurring opinion of Justice White is omitted.]

NOTES AND QUESTIONS

1. In *Barker*, the defendant apparently did not want a speedy trial for almost four years. Are there reasons a defendant might prefer delay, even if he is in jail prior to trial? Of course, even if the accused would prefer a leisurely trial to a speedy one, as the Court noted, there remains an independent societal interest in a prompt trial. Are there other constitutional rights where the defendant's desire to forego a right will, at times, yield to society's interests in enforcement of the right, or is the speedy trial protection unique in this regard?

2. When discussing the four-part balancing test, the Court in *Barker* says "We regard none of the four factors identified above as *either a necessary or sufficient* condition to the finding of a deprivation of the right of speedy trial" (emphasis added). This statement should not be read too literally. The Court acknowledges that the length of delay "is to some extent a triggering mechanism," which really means that unless there is a significant time lag between the arrest and trial, even bad reasons for the delay and great prejudice will not support a constitutional speedy trial claim. Similarly, even if the length of the delay and the prejudice is great, if the delay is attributable to the accused, the claim will almost certainly not be upheld. With respect to the third factor, *Barker* "emphasize[d] that failure to assert the right will make it difficult for a defendant to prove that he was denied a speedy trial." And of course, if there is no prejudice caused by the delay, courts will rarely overturn a conviction simply because the trial was not speedy enough. And so while it remains true that for a speedy trial claim "courts must still engage in a difficult and sensitive balancing process," the absence of one or more of these factors will typically be sufficient to reject a Sixth Amendment challenge.

3. Suppose the "reasons for the delay" — the second *Barker* factor — are attributable, not to the defendant himself, but instead to defense *counsel*. Suppose further that defense counsel is appointed by, and paid by, the state, the entity that is responsible for bringing the defendant to trial promptly. Should these delays count heavily against a defendant who raises a constitutional speedy trial claim?

The Supreme Court has said that they do. In Vermont v. Brillon, 129 S. Ct. 1283 (2009), the Court considered a Vermont Supreme Court decision that had reversed a conviction on Sixth Amendment Speedy Trial grounds, in part because of "the failure of several assigned counsel . . . to move [the defendant's] case forward." In an opinion by Justice Ginsburg, the Court rejected this interpretation of *Barker*, relying on the usual rule that the lawyer is the defendant's agent, and that his or her actions (or inactions) are attributable to the accused. The fact that defense counsel is paid by the government does not change the analysis, said the Court, because "[u]nlike a prosecutor or the court, assigned counsel is ordinarily not considered a state actor." The Court noted that the speedy trial calculations might be different if the defendant could show a "systemic breakdown in the public defender system" that resulted in delay, but no such evidence was presented.

4. Shortly after the Court's decision in *Barker*, Congress enacted the Speedy Trial Act of 1974, 18 U.S.C. §§3161-3174. Unlike the Sixth Amendment analysis, the Speedy Trial Act gives specific time limits within which certain events must occur. First, once the defendant is arrested or served with a summons, the prosecution has 30 days to file indictment or information. Second, the trial must be commenced within 70 days of the filing and making public of the information or indictment or the defendant's first appearance — whichever event happens later. Third, if the defendant is continuously detained pending trial, then the trial must begin within 90 days of the detention.

This does not mean, however, that most federal trials actually take place within the 70-day and 90-day limits. The Act excludes from the time limits any delays caused by the unavailability of the defendant or a key witness, transportation needs, reasonable legal maneuvering by a codefendant, or "other proceedings" involving the defendant. The Act provides added flexibility by allowing trial courts to exclude delays caused by the granting of continuances based on the "ends of justice"; even delays caused by open-ended continuances are generally excluded. See Greg Ostfeld, Comment, Speedy Justice and Timeless Delays: The Validity of Open-Ended "Ends-of-Justice" Continuances Under the Speedy Trial Act, 64 U. Chi. L. Rev. 1037 (1997).

5. In the federal system the Speedy Trial Act of 1974 has largely supplanted the Sixth Amendment's Speedy Trial Clause as the basis for litigation about the defendant's right to a prompt disposition; in most cases, compliance with the statute will be interpreted as compliance with the constitutional provision. There remains, however, an important difference between the constitutional and the statutory right. As noted in *Barker*, if the defendant's Sixth Amendment right is violated, the "only possible remedy" is a dismissal of the charges with prejudice. In contrast, the remedy for a violation of the Speedy Trial Act of 1974 is dismissal of the charges, either with or without prejudice, based on the trial court's review of the seriousness of the crime charged, the circumstances surrounding the delay, and the potential effect of dismissal on the administration of justice. See United States v. Taylor, 487 U.S. 326 (1988) (reversing dismissal of charges because trial court was influenced primarily by government's "lackadaisical" attitude, instead of considering all relevant statutory factors).

Notice, however the potential oddity of the statutory remedy: A court finds that the government has taken too long to bring the defendant to trial and orders, as a remedy, that the case be dismissed without prejudice — meaning that the government is free to refile the case and begin again. The result, inevitably, is that it takes even longer to bring the defendant to trial, with all the negative consequences that can follow from that delay.

6. Like most protections, the speedy trial right can be waived. But how broad a waiver can the government obtain? In Zedner v. United States, 547 U.S. 489 (2006), in the midst of prolonged pretrial proceedings, the defendant agreed to waive "for all time" the application of the Speedy Trial Act. (He did so, in part, to buy himself time to try to prove that alleged counterfeit U.S. bonds, on which the charges against him were based, were actually authentic.) Thereafter, a 91-day delay ensued, and the defendant moved to dismiss the indictment for failure to comply with the Act. The district court denied the motion based on the earlier waiver, and the Second Circuit affirmed. But the Supreme Court reversed. According to the Court, the Act "comprehensively regulates the time within which a trial must begin," and makes no allowance for a "prospective" waiver of the kind purportedly signed by the

defendant. Although the Act itself provides that a defendant may waive a completed violation of the Act by failing to move for dismissal prior to the start of the trial (or the entry of a guilty plea), the Court noted that "prospective" and "retrospective" waivers raise quite different concerns:

> [T]here is no reason to think that Congress wanted to treat prospective and retrospective waivers similarly. Allowing prospective waivers would seriously undermine the Act because there are many cases — like the case at hand — in which the prosecution, the defense, and the court would all be happy to opt out of the Act, to the detriment of the public interest. The sort of retrospective waiver allowed by [the Act] does not pose a comparable danger because the prosecution and the court cannot know until the trial actually starts or the guilty plea is actually entered whether the defendant will forgo moving to dismiss. As a consequence, the prosecution and the court retain a strong incentive to make sure that the trial begins on time.

Id., at 502. The Court rejected the government's alternative arguments that (1) the defendant was estopped by his purported waiver from complaining about the Act's violation; (2) the trial court could still exclude the challenged 91-day delay, on remand, by making a post hoc finding that the "ends of justice" supported the delay; and (3) the violation of the Act could still be found, on remand, to be "harmless error." The Court held, therefore, that dismissal was required under the Act, and remanded the case solely for the purpose of allowing the trial court to determine whether the dismissal should be with or without prejudice. On remand, the district court ruled that the dismissal was without prejudice. U.S. v. Zedner, 2006 WL 6201406 (E.D.N.Y. 2006).

7. The Speedy Trial Clause and supporting legislation like the Speedy Trial Act apply only to delay occurring between the defendant's arrest or indictment and trial. But what about delay between the crime and the filing of charges? Accusing a defendant long after the alleged events occurred can raise some of the same problems that worried the Court in Barker v. Wingo: Memories fade, witnesses can disappear, and physical evidence can be lost, all of which can make it much more difficult for the accused to put on a defense. If a defendant is prejudiced by a lengthy preindictment delay, can he raise a constitutional challenge?

The Court considered this issue in U.S. v. Lovasco, 431 U.S. 783 (1977). The defendant was accused of possessing eight firearms that had been stolen from the U.S. mail. Although it appeared that the government had sufficient evidence of the defendant's guilt on five of the weapons within 1 month of the crime, charges were not filed for 18 months after the offense allegedly occurred. The defendant moved to dismiss for excessive preindictment delay, claiming that, among other things, the delay had caused the defense to lose the testimony of two witnesses, both of whom had died several months after the crime took place. The district court granted the defendant's motion to dismiss, finding that the delay in taking the case to the grand jury was "unnecessary and unreasonable," and the court of appeals affirmed.

The Supreme Court, in an opinion by Justice Marshall, reversed. It began by noting the irrelevance of the constitutional Speedy Trial right to claims such as this, observing that until there has been a formal criminal charge filed, there is no "accused" or a "criminal prosecution" to implicate the Sixth Amendment. On the other hand, while the primary protection against preindictment delay is found in statutes of limitations, said the Court, "the Due Process Clause has a limited role to play in protecting against oppressive delay." The Court went on to say:

[T]he Due Process Clause does not permit courts to abort criminal prosecutions simply because they disagree with a prosecutor's judgment as to when to seek an indictment. . . . We are to determine only whether the action complained of — here, compelling respondent to stand trial after the Government delayed indictment to investigate further — violates those "fundamental conceptions of justice which lie at the base of our civil and political institutions," Mooney v. Holohan, 294 U.S. 103, 112 (1935), and which define "the community's sense of fair play and decency," Rochin v. California, [342 U.S. 165, 173 (1952)].

[P]rosecutors are under no duty to file charges as soon as probable cause exists but before they are satisfied they will be able to establish the suspect's guilt beyond a reasonable doubt. To impose such a duty "would have a deleterious effect both upon the rights of the accused and upon the ability of society to protect itself." . . . From the perspective of potential defendants, requiring prosecutions to commence when probable cause is established is undesirable because it would increase the likelihood of unwarranted charges being filed, and would add to the time during which defendants stand accused but untried. . . . From the perspective of law enforcement officials, a requirement of immediate prosecution upon probable cause is equally unacceptable because it could make obtaining proof of guilt beyond a reasonable doubt impossible by causing potentially fruitful sources of information to evaporate before they are fully exploited. And from the standpoint of the courts, such a requirement is unwise because it would cause scarce resources to be consumed on cases that prove to be insubstantial, or that involve only some of the responsible parties or some of the criminal acts.

It might be argued that once the Government has assembled sufficient evidence to prove guilt beyond a reasonable doubt, it should be constitutionally required to file charges promptly, even if its investigation of the entire criminal transaction is not complete. Adopting such a rule, however, would have many of the same consequences as adopting a rule requiring immediate prosecution upon probable cause.

First, compelling a prosecutor to file public charges as soon as the requisite proof has been developed against one participant on one charge would cause numerous problems in those cases in which a criminal transaction involves more than one person or more than one illegal act. In some instances, an immediate arrest or indictment would impair the prosecutor's ability to continue his investigation, thereby preventing society from bringing lawbreakers to justice. . . .

Second, insisting on immediate prosecution once sufficient evidence is developed to obtain a conviction would pressure prosecutors into resolving doubtful cases in favor of early — and possibly unwarranted — prosecutions. . . .

Finally, requiring the Government to make charging decisions immediately upon assembling evidence sufficient to establish guilt would preclude the Government from giving full consideration to the desirability of not prosecuting in particular cases. . . .

We would be most reluctant to adopt a rule which would have these consequences absent a clear constitutional command to do so. We can find no such command in the Due Process Clause of the Fifth Amendment. In our view, investigative delay is fundamentally unlike delay undertaken by the Government solely "to gain tactical advantage over the accused," United States v. Marion, 404 U.S. [307, 324 (1971)], precisely because investigative delay is not so one-sided. Rather than deviating from elementary standards of "fair play and decency," a prosecutor abides by them if he refuses to seek indictments until he is completely satisfied that he should prosecute and will be able promptly to establish guilt beyond a reasonable doubt. . . . We therefore hold that to prosecute a defendant following investigative delay does not deprive him of due process, even if his defense might have been somewhat prejudiced by the lapse of time.

8. Under *Lovasco*, does prejudice to the defendant play a significant role in the resolution of due process challenges to pretrial delay? How does this compare to the role of prejudice under the Speedy Trial Clause? The next case addresses this issue.

DOGGETT v. UNITED STATES

Certiorari to the United States Court of Appeals for the Eleventh Circuit
505 U.S. 647 (1992)

JUSTICE SOUTER delivered the opinion of the Court. In this case we consider whether the delay of 8½ years between petitioner's indictment and arrest violated his Sixth Amendment right to a speedy trial. We hold that it did.

I

On February 22, 1980, petitioner Marc Doggett was indicted for conspiring with several others to import and distribute cocaine. See 84 Stat. 1265, 1291, as amended, 21 U.S.C. §§846, 963. Douglas Driver, the Drug Enforcement Administration's (DEA's) principal agent investigating the conspiracy, told the United States Marshal's Service that the DEA would oversee the apprehension of Doggett and his confederates. On March 18, 1980, two police officers set out under Driver's orders to arrest Doggett at his parents' house in Raleigh, North Carolina, only to find that he was not there. His mother told the officers that he had left for Colombia four days earlier.

To catch Doggett on his return to the United States, Driver sent word of his outstanding arrest warrant to all United States Customs stations and to a number of law enforcement organizations. He also placed Doggett's name in the Treasury Enforcement Communication System (TECS), a computer network that helps Customs agents screen people entering the country, and in the National Crime Information Center computer system, which serves similar ends. The TECS entry expired that September, however, and Doggett's name vanished from the system.

In September 1981, Driver found out that Doggett was under arrest on drug charges in Panama and, thinking that a formal extradition request would be futile, simply asked Panama to "expel" Doggett to the United States. Although the Panamanian authorities promised to comply when their own proceedings had run their course, they freed Doggett the following July and let him go to Colombia, where he stayed with an aunt for several months. On September 25, 1982, he passed unhindered through Customs in New York City and settled down in Virginia. Since his return to the United States, he has married, earned a college degree, found a steady job as a computer operations manager, lived openly under his own name, and stayed within the law.

Doggett's travels abroad had not wholly escaped the Government's notice, however. In 1982, the American Embassy in Panama told the State Department of his departure to Colombia, but that information, for whatever reason, eluded the DEA, and Agent Driver assumed for several years that his quarry was still serving time in a Panamanian prison. Driver never asked DEA officials in Panama to check into Doggett's status, and only after his own fortuitous assignment to that country in 1985 did he discover Doggett's departure for Colombia. Driver then simply assumed Doggett had settled there, and he made no effort to find out for sure or to track Doggett down, either abroad or in the United States. Thus Doggett remained lost to the American criminal justice system until September 1988, when the

Marshal's Service ran a simple credit check on several thousand people subject to outstanding arrest warrants and, within minutes, found out where Doggett lived and worked. On September 5, 1988, nearly 6 years after his return to the United States and 8½ years after his indictment, Doggett was arrested.

He naturally moved to dismiss the indictment, arguing that the Government's failure to prosecute him earlier violated his Sixth Amendment right to a speedy trial. The Federal Magistrate hearing his motion applied the criteria for assessing speedy trial claims set out in Barker v. Wingo, 407 U.S. 514 (1972). . . . The Magistrate found that the delay between Doggett's indictment and arrest was long enough to be "presumptively prejudicial," that the delay "clearly [was] attributable to the negligence of the government," and that Doggett could not be faulted for any delay in asserting his right to a speedy trial, there being no evidence that he had known of the charges against him until his arrest. The Magistrate also found, however, that Doggett had made no affirmative showing that the delay had impaired his ability to mount a successful defense or had otherwise prejudiced him. In his recommendation to the District Court, the Magistrate contended that this failure to demonstrate particular prejudice sufficed to defeat Doggett's speedy trial claim.

The District Court took the recommendation and denied Doggett's motion. Doggett then entered a conditional guilty plea under Federal Rule of Criminal Procedure 11(a)(2), expressly reserving the right to appeal his ensuing conviction on the speedy trial claim.

A split panel of the Court of Appeals affirmed. . . .

II

The Sixth Amendment guarantees that, "[i]n all criminal prosecutions, the accused shall enjoy the right to a speedy . . . trial. . . ." On its face, the Speedy Trial Clause is written with such breadth that, taken literally, it would forbid the government to delay the trial of an "accused" for any reason at all. Our cases, however, have qualified the literal sweep of the provision by specifically recognizing the relevance of four separate enquiries: whether delay before trial was uncommonly long, whether the government or the criminal defendant is more to blame for that delay, whether, in due course, the defendant asserted his right to a speedy trial, and whether he suffered prejudice as the delay's result. See Barker, supra, at 530.

The first of these is actually a double enquiry. Simply to trigger a speedy trial analysis, an accused must allege that the interval between accusation and trial has crossed the threshold dividing ordinary from "presumptively prejudicial" delay, 407 U.S. at 530-531, since, by definition, he cannot complain that the government has denied him a "speedy" trial if it has, in fact, prosecuted his case with customary promptness. If the accused makes this showing, the court must then consider, as one factor among several, the extent to which the delay stretches beyond the bare minimum needed to trigger judicial examination of the claim. See id., at 533-534. This latter enquiry is significant to the speedy trial analysis because, as we discuss below, the presumption that pretrial delay has prejudiced the accused intensifies over time. In this case, the extraordinary 8½-year lag between Doggett's indictment and arrest clearly suffices to trigger the speedy trial enquiry;[1] its further significance within that enquiry will be dealt with later.

---

1. Depending on the nature of the charges, the lower courts have generally found post accusation delay "presumptively prejudicial" at least as it approaches one year. . . . We note that, as the term is used

As for *Barker*'s second criterion, the Government claims to have sought Doggett with diligence. The findings of the courts below are to the contrary, however, and we review trial court determinations of negligence with considerable deference. . . . The Government gives us nothing to gainsay the findings that have come up to us, and we see nothing fatal to them in the record. For six years, the Government's investigators made no serious effort to test their progressively more questionable assumption that Doggett was living abroad, and, had they done so, they could have found him within minutes. While the Government's lethargy may have reflected no more than Doggett's relative unimportance in the world of drug trafficking, it was still findable negligence, and the finding stands.

The Government goes against the record again in suggesting that Doggett knew of his indictment years before he was arrested. Were this true, *Barker*'s third factor, concerning invocation of the right to a speedy trial, would be weighed heavily against him. But here again, the Government is trying to revisit the facts. At the hearing on Doggett's speedy trial motion, it introduced no evidence challenging the testimony of Doggett's wife, who said that she did not know of the charges until his arrest, and of his mother, who claimed not to have told him or anyone else that the police had come looking for him. . . .

III

The Government is left, then, with its principal contention: that Doggett fails to make out a successful speedy trial claim because he has not shown precisely how he was prejudiced by the delay between his indictment and trial.

A

We have observed in prior cases that unreasonable delay between formal accusation and trial threatens to produce more than one sort of harm, including "oppressive pretrial incarceration," "anxiety and concern of the accused," and "the possibility that the [accused's] defense will be impaired" by dimming memories and loss of exculpatory evidence. *Barker*, 407 U.S. at 532. . . . Of these forms of prejudice, "the most serious is the last, because the inability of a defendant adequately to prepare his case skews the fairness of the entire system." 407 U.S. at 532. Doggett claims this kind of prejudice, and there is probably no other kind that he can claim, since he was subjected neither to pretrial detention nor, he has successfully contended, to awareness of unresolved charges against him.

The Government answers Doggett's claim by citing language in three cases, United States v. Marion, 404 U.S. 307, 320-323 (1971), United States v. MacDonald, 456 U.S. 1, 8 (1982), and United States v. Loud Hawk, 474 U.S. 302, 312 (1986), for the proposition that the Speedy Trial Clause does not significantly protect a criminal defendant's interest in fair adjudication. In so arguing, the Government asks us, in effect, to read part of *Barker* right out of the law, and that we will not do. In context, the cited passages support nothing beyond the principle . . . that the Sixth

---

in this threshold context, "presumptive prejudice" does not necessarily indicate a statistical probability of prejudice; it simply marks the point at which courts deem the delay unreasonable enough to trigger the *Barker* enquiry. Cf. Uviller, Barker v. Wingo: Speedy Trial Gets a Fast Shuffle, 72 Colum. L. Rev. 1376, 1384-1385 (1972).

Amendment right of the accused to a speedy trial has no application beyond the confines of a formal criminal prosecution. Once triggered by arrest, indictment, or other official accusation, however, the speedy trial enquiry must weigh the effect of delay on the accused's defense just as it has to weigh any other form of prejudice that *Barker* recognized.[2] . . .

As an alternative to limiting *Barker*, the Government claims Doggett has failed to make any affirmative showing that the delay weakened his ability to raise specific defenses, elicit specific testimony, or produce specific items of evidence. Though Doggett did indeed come up short in this respect, the Government's argument takes it only so far: consideration of prejudice is not limited to the specifically demonstrable, and, as it concedes, . . . affirmative proof of particularized prejudice is not essential to every speedy trial claim. . . . *Barker* explicitly recognized that impairment of one's defense is the most difficult form of speedy trial prejudice to prove because time's erosion of exculpatory evidence and testimony "can rarely be shown." 407 U.S. at 532. And though time can tilt the case against either side, . . . one cannot generally be sure which of them it has prejudiced more severely. Thus, we generally have to recognize that excessive delay presumptively compromises the reliability of a trial in ways that neither party can prove or, for that matter, identify. While such presumptive prejudice cannot alone carry a Sixth Amendment claim without regard to the other *Barker* criteria, . . . it is part of the mix of relevant facts, and its importance increases with the length of delay.

B

This brings us to an enquiry into the role that presumptive prejudice should play in the disposition of Doggett's speedy trial claim. We begin with hypothetical and somewhat easier cases and work our way to this one.

Our speedy trial standards recognize that pretrial delay is often both inevitable and wholly justifiable. The government may need time to collect witnesses against the accused, oppose his pretrial motions, or, if he goes into hiding, track him down. We attach great weight to such considerations when balancing them against the costs of going forward with a trial whose probative accuracy the passage of time has begun by degrees to throw into question. . . . Thus, in this case, if the Government had pursued Doggett with reasonable diligence from his indictment to his arrest, his speedy trial claim would fail. Indeed, that conclusion would generally follow as a matter of course however great the delay, so long as Doggett could not show specific prejudice to his defense.

The Government concedes, on the other hand, that Doggett would prevail if he could show that the Government had intentionally held back in its prosecution of him to gain some impermissible advantage at trial. . . . That we cannot doubt. *Barker* stressed that official bad faith in causing delay will be weighed heavily against the government, 407 U.S. at 531, and a bad-faith delay the length of this negligent one would present an overwhelming case for dismissal.

---

2. Thus, we reject the Government's argument that the effect of delay on adjudicative accuracy is exclusively a matter for consideration under the Due Process Clause. We leave intact our earlier observation, see United States v. MacDonald, 456 U.S. 1, 7 (1982), that a defendant may invoke due process to challenge delay both before and after official accusation.

Between diligent prosecution and bad-faith delay, official negligence in bringing an accused to trial occupies the middle ground. While not compelling relief in every case where bad-faith delay would make relief virtually automatic, neither is negligence automatically tolerable simply because the accused cannot demonstrate exactly how it has prejudiced him. . . .

Barker made it clear that "different weights [are to be] assigned to different reasons" for delay. Ibid. Although negligence is obviously to be weighed more lightly than a deliberate intent to harm the accused's defense, it still falls on the wrong side of the divide between acceptable and unacceptable reasons for delaying a criminal prosecution once it has begun. And such is the nature of the prejudice presumed that the weight we assign to official negligence compounds over time as the presumption of evidentiary prejudice grows. Thus, our toleration of such negligence varies inversely with its protractedness, . . . and its consequent threat to the fairness of the accused's trial. Condoning prolonged and unjustifiable delays in prosecution would both penalize many defendants for the state's fault and simply encourage the government to gamble with the interests of criminal suspects assigned a low prosecutorial priority. The Government, indeed, can hardly complain too loudly, for persistent neglect in concluding a criminal prosecution indicates an uncommonly feeble interest in bringing an accused to justice; the more weight the Government attaches to securing a conviction, the harder it will try to get it.

To be sure, to warrant granting relief, negligence unaccompanied by particularized trial prejudice must have lasted longer than negligence demonstrably causing such prejudice. But even so, the Government's egregious persistence in failing to prosecute Doggett is clearly sufficient. The lag between Doggett's indictment and arrest was 8½ years, and he would have faced trial 6 years earlier than he did but for the Government's inexcusable oversights. The portion of the delay attributable to the Government's negligence far exceeds the threshold needed to state a speedy trial claim; indeed, we have called shorter delays "extraordinary." See *Barker*, supra, at 533. When the Government's negligence thus causes delay six times as long as that generally sufficient to trigger judicial review, see n. 1, supra, and when the presumption of prejudice, albeit unspecified, is neither extenuated, as by the defendant's acquiescence, e.g., 407 U.S. at 534-536, nor persuasively rebutted,[4] the defendant is entitled to relief.

IV

We reverse the judgment of the Court of Appeals and remand the case for proceedings consistent with this opinion.

So ordered. [The dissenting opinion of Justice O'Connor is omitted.]

JUSTICE THOMAS, with whom CHIEF JUSTICE REHNQUIST and JUSTICE SCALIA join, dissenting.

Just as "bad facts make bad law," so too odd facts make odd law. Doggett's 8½-year odyssey from youthful drug dealing in the tobacco country of North Carolina, through stints in a Panamanian jail and in Colombia, to life as a computer operations manager, homeowner, and registered voter in suburban Virginia is extraordinary.

---

4. While the Government ably counters Doggett's efforts to demonstrate particularized trial prejudice, it has not, and probably could not have, affirmatively proved that the delay left his ability to defend himself unimpaired. Cf. Uviller, 72 Colum. L. Rev., at 1394-1395.

But even more extraordinary is the Court's conclusion that the Government denied Doggett his Sixth Amendment right to a speedy trial despite the fact that he has suffered none of the harms that the right was designed to prevent. I respectfully dissent.

I

We have long identified the "major evils" against which the Speedy Trial Clause is directed as "undue and oppressive incarceration" and the "anxiety and concern accompanying public accusation." United States v. Marion, 404 U.S. 307, 320 (1971). The Court does not, and cannot, seriously dispute that those two concerns lie at the heart of the Clause, and that neither concern is implicated here. Doggett was neither in United States custody nor subject to bail during the entire 8½-year period at issue. Indeed, as this case comes to us, we must assume that he was blissfully unaware of his indictment all the while, and thus was not subject to the anxiety or humiliation that typically accompanies a known criminal charge.

Thus, this unusual case presents the question whether, independent of these core concerns, the Speedy Trial Clause protects an accused from two additional harms: (1) prejudice to his ability to defend himself caused by the passage of time; and (2) disruption of his life years after the alleged commission of his crime. The Court today proclaims that the first of these additional harms is indeed an independent concern of the Clause, and on that basis compels reversal of Doggett's conviction and outright dismissal of the indictment against him. As to the second of these harms, the Court remains mum — despite the fact that we requested supplemental briefing on this very point.

I disagree with the Court's analysis. In my view, the Sixth Amendment's speedy trial guarantee does not provide independent protection against either prejudice to an accused's defense or the disruption of his life. I shall consider each in turn.

A

As we have explained, "the Speedy Trial Clause's core concern is impairment of *liberty*." United States v. Loud Hawk, 474 U.S. 302, 312 (1986) (emphasis added). Whenever a criminal trial takes place long after the events at issue, the defendant may be prejudiced in any number of ways. But "[t]he Speedy Trial Clause does not purport to protect a defendant from all effects flowing from a delay before trial." Id., at 311. The Clause is directed not generally against delay-related prejudice, but against delay-related prejudice to a defendant's liberty. "The speedy trial guarantee is designed to minimize the possibility of lengthy incarceration prior to trial, to reduce the lesser, but nevertheless substantial, impairment of liberty imposed on an accused while released on bail, and to shorten the disruption of life caused by arrest and the presence of unresolved criminal charges." United States v. MacDonald, 456 U.S. 1, 8 (1982). Thus, "when defendants are not incarcerated or subjected to other substantial restrictions on their liberty, a court should not weigh that time towards a claim under the Speedy Trial Clause." Loud Hawk, supra, at 312.

A lengthy pretrial delay, of course, may prejudice an accused's ability to defend himself. But, we have explained, prejudice to the defense is not the sort of impairment of liberty against which the Clause is directed. . . .

[P]rejudice to the defense stems from the interval between *crime* and trial, which is quite distinct from the interval between *accusation* and trial. If the Clause were indeed aimed at safeguarding against prejudice to the defense, then it would presumably limit *all* prosecutions that occur long after the criminal events at issue. A defendant prosecuted 10 years after a crime is just as hampered in his ability to defend himself whether he was indicted the week after the crime or the week before the trial — but no one would suggest that the Clause protects him in the latter situation. . . .

Although being an "accused" is necessary to trigger the Clause's protection, it is not sufficient to do so. The touchstone of the speedy trial right, after all, is the substantial deprivation of liberty that typically accompanies an "accusation," *not* the accusation itself. That explains why a person who has been arrested but not indicted is entitled to the protection of the Clause, . . . even though technically he has not been "accused" at all. And it explains why the lower courts consistently have held that, with respect to sealed (and hence secret) indictments, the protections of the Speedy Trial Clause are triggered *not* when the indictment is *filed*, but when it is *unsealed*. . . .

. . . *Barker's* suggestion that preventing prejudice to the defense is a fundamental and independent objective of the Clause is plainly dictum. Never, until today, have we confronted a case where a defendant subjected to a lengthy delay after indictment nonetheless failed to suffer any substantial impairment of his liberty. I think it fair to say that *Barker* simply did not contemplate such an unusual situation. . . .

Just because the Speedy Trial Clause does not independently protect against prejudice to the defense does not, of course, mean that a defendant is utterly unprotected in this regard. To the contrary, "the applicable statute of limitations . . . is . . . the primary guarantee against bringing overly stale criminal charges," *Marion*, 404 U.S. at 322. . . .

Furthermore, the Due Process Clause always protects defendants against fundamentally unfair treatment by the government in criminal proceedings. See United States v. Lovasco, 431 U.S. 783 (1977). . . .

Therefore, I see no basis for the Court's conclusion that Doggett is entitled to relief under the Speedy Trial Clause *simply* because the Government was negligent in prosecuting him and because the resulting delay may have prejudiced his defense.

B

It remains to be considered, however, whether Doggett is entitled to relief under the Speedy Trial Clause because of the disruption of his life years after the criminal events at issue. In other words, does the Clause protect a right to repose, free from secret or unknown indictments? In my view, it does not, for much the same reasons set forth above.

The common law recognized no right of criminals to repose. "The maxim of our law has always been 'Nullum tempus occurrit regi,' ['time does not run against the king'], and as a criminal trial is regarded as an action by the king, it follows that it may be brought at any time." 2 J. Stephen, A History of the Criminal Law of England 1, 2 (1883) (noting examples of delays in prosecution ranging from 14 to 35 years). . . .

That is not to deny that our legal system has long recognized the value of repose, both to the individual and to society. But that recognition finds expression not in the sweeping commands of the Constitution, or in the common law, but in any number of specific statutes of limitations enacted by the federal and state legislatures. Such statutes not only protect a defendant from prejudice to his defense (as discussed above), but also balance his interest in repose against society's interest in the apprehension and punishment of criminals. . . . In general, the graver the offense, the longer the limitations period; indeed, many serious offenses, such as murder, typically carry no limitations period at all. . . . These statutes refute the notion that our society ever has recognized any general right of criminals to repose.

Doggett, however, asks us to hold that a defendant's interest in repose is a value independently protected by the Speedy Trial Clause. He emphasizes that at the time of his arrest he was "leading a normal, productive and law-abiding life," and that his "arrest and prosecution at this late date interrupted his life as a productive member of society and forced him to answer for actions taken in the distant past." . . . However uplifting this tale of personal redemption, our task is to illuminate the protections of the Speedy Trial Clause, not to take the measure of one man's life.

There is no basis for concluding that the disruption of an accused's life years after the commission of his alleged crime is an evil independently protected by the Speedy Trial Clause. Such disruption occurs *regardless* of whether the individual is under indictment during the period of delay. Thus, had Doggett been indicted shortly before his 1988 arrest rather than shortly after his 1980 crime, his repose would have been equally shattered — but he would not have even a colorable speedy trial claim. To recognize a constitutional right to repose is to recognize a right to be tried speedily *after the offense*. That would, of course, convert the Speedy Trial Clause into a constitutional statute of limitations — a result with no basis in the text or history of the Clause or in our precedents.

II

. . . The Court's error, in my view, lies not so much in its particular application of the *Barker* test to the facts of this case, but more fundamentally in its failure to recognize that the speedy trial guarantee cannot be violated — and thus *Barker* does not apply at all — when an accused is *entirely unaware* of a pending indictment against him. . . .

Today's opinion, I fear, will transform the courts of the land into boards of law enforcement supervision. For the Court compels dismissal of the charges against Doggett not because he was harmed in any way by the delay between his indictment and arrest,[6] but simply because the Government's efforts to catch him are found wanting. Indeed, the Court expressly concedes that "if the Government had pursued Doggett with reasonable diligence from his indictment to his arrest, his speedy trial claim would fail." . . . Our function, however, is not to slap the Government on the wrist for sloppy work or misplaced priorities, but to protect the legal rights of those individuals harmed thereby. By divorcing the Speedy Trial Clause from all considerations of prejudice to an accused, the Court positively invites the Nation's judges to indulge in ad hoc and result-driven second-guessing of the government's

---

6. It is quite likely, in fact, that the delay *benefited* Doggett. At the time of his arrest, he had been living an apparently normal, law-abiding life for some five years — a point not lost on the District Court Judge, who, instead of imposing a prison term, sentenced him to three years' probation and a $1,000 fine. . . . Thus, the delay gave Doggett the opportunity to prove what most defendants can only promise: that he no longer posed a threat to society. There can be little doubt that, had he been tried immediately after his cocaine-importation activities, he would have received a harsher sentence.

investigatory efforts. Our Constitution neither contemplates nor tolerates such a role. I respectfully dissent.

NOTES AND QUESTIONS

1. Why did Doggett win while Barker and Lovasco lost? Was the government's conduct somehow more reprehensible in Doggett's case? Did he suffer greater harm as a result of the lengthy delay in bringing him to trial? How important was the simple fact that Doggett, at the time of his trial, had become a respectable and law-abiding family man with a good job and education? Do you think the outcome of the case would have been the same had Doggett still been selling drugs at the time of his trial?

2. The dissent claims that "odd facts make odd law." Granting that *Doggett* presents odd facts, how does the case change the law on when the Sixth Amendment is violated? Consider the fourth Barker v. Wingo factor, prejudice to the accused from the delay. Did the majority adequately explain how Mr. Doggett was prejudiced? If he truly was unaware of the pending indictment, he could not have suffered the stress and public condemnation that comes from being accused of a crime, and the harm to the defendant's legal case was, as the Court recognized "unspecified." So what is the standard of prejudice after *Doggett*?

3. *Doggett* is also an unusual case in that he had a claim under the Speedy Trial Clause of the Sixth Amendment but not a claim under the Speedy Trial Act. Can you articulate why Doggett's statutory claim was not viable?

4. Defendants are not necessarily the only ones with an interest in a speedy trial. Victims (or their survivors) may also have a strong desire to see justice dispensed swiftly. Under the Crime Victims' Rights law, 18 U.S.C. §3771, federal crime victims have the "right to proceedings free from unreasonable delay," and the court has a duty to "ensure that the crime victim is afforded [this] right[]."

These provisions suggest that victims could object to continuances or other delays in the progression of a criminal case. Do you think the effect of these objections is to ensure a more responsive criminal system? Or is the process distorted by those victims with the knowledge and resources to make their voices heard? Notice that although the victims can assert this right in the appropriate proceedings, they have no cause of action if the court fails to comply.

B. Venue

1. Location of the Crime

Venue refers to the geographic location of the trial. Where the trial is held is set in the first instance by where the government files the criminal charge. So the initial, and usually final, decision of where a defendant will be tried rests with the prosecution. If challenged by the defense, the prosecutor must prove venue at trial, but only by a preponderance of the evidence.

Venue may sound like a technical, administrative detail in the processing of a criminal case — after all, in the federal system the applicable criminal laws and procedures are the same whether the trial takes place in New York or Alaska. But in fact, the venue of the case can have enormous importance to the accused. A defendant who is charged and must stand trial far from his home may be cut off from family, friends, and his job; he may not have ready access to his legal counsel, or may have difficulty retaining unfamiliar local counsel; and, he may have a more difficult time gathering evidence and interviewing witnesses.

The practice of moving colonists accused of crimes to England to stand trial was one of the grievances against the king enumerated in the Declaration of Independence: "For transporting us beyond Seas to be tried for pretended offenses." Thus, it was no surprise that the Framers included a provision in Article III Section 2 of the Constitution that "The trial of all crimes, except in cases of impeachment . . . shall be held in the state where the said crime shall have been committed." The drafters of the Bill of Rights also were concerned about this issue, specifying in the Sixth Amendment that "In all criminal prosecutions, the accused shall enjoy the right to a speedy and impartial trial, by an impartial jury of the State and district wherein the crime shall have been committed." The Sixth Amendment requirement is referred to as the "vicinage" provision, as it refers to the place where the jury shall be drawn from, rather than specifying the actual location of the trial. These requirements were later incorporated into Federal Rule of Criminal Procedure 18, which provides in part that "[u]nless a statute or these rules permit otherwise, the government must prosecute an offense in a district where the offense was committed."

So to determine whether venue is proper, prosecutors and reviewing courts must determine where the crime charged was committed. Note that this requirement does not necessarily relieve the accused of the burdens of defending himself in a location far from home. A California resident who commits a theft in Maine while on vacation will have to stand trial in Maine, regardless of the difficulties. (This type of fact pattern was much less common at the time of the country's founding, when most crimes were quite local.) A guilty defendant can hardly complain about the inconvenience, although an innocent person might, but on balance it seems that Maine's interest in protecting its residents is dominant, making it fair to hold the trial there.

Often the place where the crime committed is obvious, and leaves no choice to the prosecution. When a defendant robs a bank in Texas and is arrested in Texas, venue is proper in the Texas judicial district where the bank is located. But suppose the Texas bank robber flees to Oklahoma, where he is arrested after a violent confrontation and is charged with both bank robbery and assaulting a federal agent. Is venue for both charges proper in either state, or must there be two trials? Or suppose a kidnapper in Ohio drives his victim to Pennsylvania; is venue for the kidnapping charge proper in West Virginia, through which the getaway car briefly drove?

Hard venue questions usually arise in the context of "continuing crimes," that is, offenses where some of the elements are committed in one state or district and other elements occur in other states or districts. Congress has addressed this issue in 18 U.S.C. §3237, which provides in part:

> (a) Except as otherwise expressly provided by enactment of Congress, any offense against the United States begun in one district and completed in another, or committed

in more than one district, may be inquired of and prosecuted in any district in which such offense was begun, continued, or completed.

This broadly worded statute would appear to give prosecutors the maximum amount of flexibility in deciding where a case should be brought, but even this statute leaves room for ambiguity. Consider the next case and the notes that follow.

UNITED STATES v. RODRIGUEZ-MORENO

Certiorari to the United States Court of Appeals for the Third Circuit
526 U.S. 275 (1999)

JUSTICE THOMAS delivered the opinion of the Court.

This case presents the question whether venue in a prosecution for using or carrying a firearm "during and in relation to any crime of violence," in violation of 18 U.S.C. §924(c)(1), is proper in any district where the crime of violence was committed, even if the firearm was used or carried only in a single district.

I

During a drug transaction that took place in Houston, Texas, a New York drug dealer stole 30 kilograms of a Texas drug distributor's cocaine. The distributor hired respondent, Jacinto Rodriguez-Moreno, and others to find the dealer and to hold captive the middleman in the transaction, Ephrain Avendano, during the search. In pursuit of the dealer, the distributor and his henchmen drove from Texas to New Jersey with Avendano in tow. The group used Avendano's New Jersey apartment as a base for their operations for a few days. They soon moved to a house in New York and then to a house in Maryland, taking Avendano with them.

Shortly after respondent and the others arrived at the Maryland house, the owner of the home passed around a .357 magnum revolver and respondent took possession of the pistol. As it became clear that efforts to find the New York drug dealer would not bear fruit, respondent told his employer that he thought they should kill the middleman and end their search for the dealer. He put the gun to the back of Avendano's neck but, at the urging of his cohorts, did not shoot. Avendano eventually escaped through the back door and ran to a neighboring house. The neighbors called the Maryland police, who arrested respondent along with the rest of the kidnapers. The police also seized the .357 magnum, on which they later found respondent's fingerprint.

Rodriguez-Moreno and his codefendants were tried jointly in the United States District Court for the District of New Jersey. Respondent was charged with, inter alia, conspiring to kidnap Avendano, kidnaping Avendano, and using and carrying a firearm in relation to the kidnaping of Avendano, in violation of 18 U.S.C. §924(c)(1). At the conclusion of the Government's case, respondent moved to dismiss the §924(c)(1) count for lack of venue. He argued that venue was proper only in Maryland, the only place where the Government had proved he had actually used a gun. The District Court denied the motion, App. 54, and the jury found respondent guilty on the kidnaping counts and on the §924(c)(1) charge as well. He was sentenced to 87 months' imprisonment on the kidnaping charges, and was given a mandatory consecutive term of 60 months' imprisonment for committing the §924(c)(1) offense.

On a 2-to-1 vote, the Court of Appeals for the Third Circuit reversed respondent's §924(c)(1) conviction. A majority of the Third Circuit panel applied what it called the "verb test" to §924(c)(1), and determined that a violation of the statute is committed only in the district where a defendant "uses" or "carries" a firearm. Accordingly, it concluded that venue for the §924(c)(1) count was improper in New Jersey even though venue was proper there for the kidnaping of Avendano. The dissenting judge thought that the majority's test relied too much "on grammatical arcana," and argued that the proper approach was to "look at the substance of the statutes in question." In his view, the crime of violence is an essential element of the course of conduct that Congress sought to criminalize in enacting §924(c)(1), and therefore, "venue for a prosecution under [that] statute lies in any district in which the defendant committed the underlying crime of violence." The Government petitioned for review on the ground that the Third Circuit's holding was in conflict with a decision of the Court of Appeals for the Fifth Circuit. We granted certiorari, and now reverse.

II

Article III of the Constitution requires that "[t]he Trial of all Crimes . . . shall be held in the State where the said Crimes shall have been committed." Art. III, §2, cl. 3. Its command is reinforced by the Sixth Amendment's requirement that "[i]n all criminal prosecutions, the accused shall enjoy the right to a speedy and public trial, by an impartial jury of the State and district wherein the crime shall have been committed," and is echoed by Rule 18 of the Federal Rules of Criminal Procedure ("prosecution shall be had in a district in which the offense was committed").

As we confirmed just last Term, the "*locus delicti* [of the charged offense] must be determined from the nature of the crime alleged and the location of the act or acts constituting it." United States v. Cabrales, 524 U.S. 1, 6-7 (1998). In performing this inquiry, a court must initially identify the conduct constituting the offense (the nature of the crime) and then discern the location of the commission of the criminal acts.

At the time respondent committed the offense and was tried, 18 U.S.C. §924(c)(1) provided:

Whoever, during and in relation to any crime of violence . . . for which he may be prosecuted in a court of the United States, uses or carries a firearm, shall, in addition to the punishment provided for such crime of violence . . . be sentenced to imprisonment for five years . . . .

The Third Circuit, as explained above, looked to the verbs of the statute to determine the nature of the substantive offense. But we have never before held, and decline to do so here, that verbs are the sole consideration in identifying the conduct that constitutes an offense. While the "verb test" certainly has value as an interpretative tool, it cannot be applied rigidly, to the exclusion of other relevant statutory language. The test unduly limits the inquiry into the nature of the offense and thereby creates a danger that certain conduct prohibited by statute will be missed.

In our view, the Third Circuit overlooked an essential conduct element of the §924(c)(1) offense. Section 924(c)(1) prohibits using or carrying a firearm "during and in relation to any crime of violence . . . for which [a defendant] may be prosecuted in a court of the United States." That the crime of violence element of the statute is embedded in a prepositional phrase and not expressed in verbs does not dissuade us from concluding that a defendant's violent acts are essential conduct elements. To prove the charged §924(c)(1) violation in this case, the Government was required to show that respondent used a firearm, that he committed all the acts necessary to be subject to punishment for kidnaping (a crime of violence) in a court of the United States, and that he used the gun "during and in relation to" the kidnaping of Avendano. In sum, we interpret §924(c)(1) to contain two distinct conduct elements — as is relevant to this case, the "using and carrying" of a gun and the commission of a kidnaping.[4]

Respondent, however, argues that for venue purposes "the New Jersey kidnapping is completely irrelevant to the firearm crime, because respondent did not *use* or *carry* a gun *during* the New Jersey crime." In the words of one amicus, §924(c)(1) is a "point-in-time" offense that only is committed in the place where the kidnapping and the use of a gun coincide. We disagree. Several Circuits have determined that kidnapping is a unitary crime, and we agree with their conclusion. A kidnapping, once begun, does not end until the victim is free. It does not make sense, then, to speak of it in discrete geographic fragments. Section 924(c)(1) criminalized a defendant's use of a firearm "during and in relation to" a crime of violence; in doing so, Congress proscribed both the use of the firearm *and* the commission of acts that constitute a violent crime. It does not matter that respondent used the .357 magnum revolver, as the Government concedes, only in Maryland because he did so "during and in relation to" a kidnapping that was begun in Texas and continued in New York, New Jersey, and Maryland. In our view, §924(c)(1) does not define a "point-in-time" offense when a firearm is used during and in relation to a continuing crime of violence.

As we said in United States v. Lombardo, 241 U.S. 73 (1916), "where a crime consists of distinct parts which have different localities the whole may be tried where any part can be proved to have been done." Id., at 77. The kidnapping, to which the §924(c)(1) offense is attached, was committed in all of the places that any part of it took place, and venue for the kidnapping charge against respondent was appropriate in any of them. (Congress has provided that continuing offenses can be tried "in any district in which such offense was begun, continued, or completed," 18 U.S.C. §3237(a).) Where venue is appropriate for the underlying crime of violence, so too it is for the §924(c)(1) offense. As the kidnapping was properly tried in New Jersey, the §924(c)(1) offense could be tried there as well.

* * *

---

4. By way of comparison, last Term in United States v. Cabrales, 524 U.S. 1 (1998), we considered whether venue for money laundering was proper in Missouri, where the laundered proceeds were unlawfully generated, or rather, only in Florida, where the prohibited laundering transactions occurred. As we interpreted the laundering statutes at issue, they did not proscribe "the anterior criminal conduct that yielded the funds allegedly laundered." *Cabrales*, 524 U.S., at 7. The existence of criminally generated proceeds was a circumstance element of the offense but the proscribed conduct — defendant's money laundering activity — occurred "'after the fact' of an offense begun and completed by others." Here, by contrast, given the "during and in relation to" language, the underlying crime of violence is a critical part of the §924(c)(1) offense.

We hold that venue for this prosecution was proper in the district where it was brought. The judgment of the Court of Appeals is therefore reversed.

It is so ordered.

JUSTICE SCALIA, with whom JUSTICE STEVENS joins, dissenting.

I agree with the Court that in deciding where a crime was committed for purposes of the venue provision of Article III, §2, of the Constitution, and the vicinage provision of the Sixth Amendment, we must look at "the nature of the crime alleged and the location of the act or acts constituting it." I disagree with the Court, however, that the crime defined in 18 U.S.C. §924(c)(1) is "committed" either where the defendant commits the predicate offense or where he uses or carries the gun. It seems to me unmistakably clear from the text of the law that this crime can be committed only where the defendant *both* engages in the acts making up the predicate offense *and* uses or carries the gun.

[Section 924(c)(1)] prohibits the act of using or carrying a firearm "during" (and in relation to) a predicate offense. The provisions of the United States Code defining the particular predicate offenses already punish all of the defendant's alleged criminal conduct except his use or carriage of a gun; §924(c)(1) itself criminalizes and punishes such use or carriage "during" the predicate crime, because that makes the crime more dangerous. This is a simple concept, and it is embodied in a straightforward text. To answer the question before us we need only ask where the defendant's alleged act of using a firearm during (and in relation to) a kidnaping occurred. Since it occurred only in Maryland, venue will lie only there.

The Court, however, relies on United States v. Lombardo, 241 U.S. 73, 77 (1916), for the proposition that "where a crime consists of distinct parts which have different localities the whole may be tried where any part can be proved to have been done." The fallacy in this reliance is that the crime before us does *not* consist of "distinct" parts that can occur in different localities. Its two parts are bound inseparably together by the word "during." Where the gun is being used, the predicate act must be occurring as well, and vice versa. The Court quite simply reads this requirement out of the statute — as though there were no difference between a statute making it a crime to steal a cookie and eat it (which could be prosecuted either in New Jersey, where the cookie was stolen, or in Maryland, where it was eaten) and a statute making it a crime to eat a cookie while robbing a bakery (which could be prosecuted only where the ingestive theft occurred).

The Court believes its holding is justified by the continuing nature of the kidnaping predicate offense, which invokes the statute providing that "any offense against the United States begun in one district and completed in another, or committed in more than one district, may be inquired of and prosecuted in any district in which such offense was begun, continued, or completed." 18 U.S.C. §3237(a). To disallow the New Jersey prosecution here, the Court suggests, is to convert §924(c)(1) from a continuing offense to a "point-in-time" offense. That is simply not so. I in no way contend that the kidnaping, or, for that matter, the use of the gun, can occur only at one point in time. Each can extend over a protracted period, and in many places. But §924(c)(1) is violated only so long as, *and where*, both continuing acts are being committed simultaneously. That is what the word "during" means. . . .

The short of the matter is that this defendant, who has a constitutional right to be tried in the State and district where his alleged crime was "committed," U.S. Const., Art. III, §2, cl. 3; Amdt. 6, has been prosecuted for using a gun during a kidnaping in a State and district where all agree he did not use a gun during a kidnaping. If to state this case is not to decide it, the law has departed further from the meaning of language than is appropriate for a government that is supposed to rule (and to be restrained) through the written word.

NOTES AND QUESTIONS

1. Was *Rodriguez-Moreno* correctly decided? Is it consistent with the intent of the constitutional protection for venue to say that the crime of using a firearm during a crime of violence took place in New Jersey, where there is no evidence that anyone possessed a gun there?

2. If you agree with the dissent that the weapons crime only occurred in Maryland, how would you distinguish the following case: The defendant steals a painting in Illinois, flees to Indiana, and is later charged with interstate transportation of stolen property. If he is charged with the crime in Illinois, can it fairly be said that the crime "occurred" there, before the stolen art actually moved across state lines? 18 U.S.C. §3237, which is quoted in the introduction to this section and mentioned in *Rodriquez-Moreno*, seems to say that venue would be proper in Illinois, but if so, why is *Rodriguez-Moreno* different?

3. In footnote 4 of *Rodriguez-Moreno*, the court distinguishes a venue case it had decided the previous term. In U.S. v. Cabrales, 524 U.S. 1 (1998), the defendant was charged with money laundering, as she allegedly had engaged in financial transactions that were designed to avoid federal reporting requirements and that also involved criminally derived property. The "laundering" took place entirely in Florida; the money that was laundered came from cocaine sales that took place in Missouri. The question was whether venue for the money laundering charges was proper in Missouri.

The Court began by recognizing that where the crime occurred "must be determined from the nature of the crime alleged and the location of the act or acts constituting it." After examining the money laundering statutes, it concluded that they "interdict only the financial transactions (acts located entirely in Florida), not the anterior criminal conduct that yielded the funds allegedly laundered." The Court rejected the government's argument that these crimes were "continuing" offenses, ones that began with the accumulation of the illegal proceeds in Missouri. While the Court agreed that under the statutes "the money launderer must know she is dealing with funds derived from 'specified unlawful activity,' here, drug trafficking," it also concluded that the location of those unlawful activities was "of no moment" to the defendant. Under the statutes, the crime took place where the conduct occurred — the financial transactions themselves — not where the events giving rise to the circumstance element (the illegality of the funds) took place.

Is it possible to extract a consistent principle from *Rodriguez-Moreno* and *Cabrales*? Look again at the distinction between the two cases drawn in footnote 4 of *Rodriguez-Moreno*. Does the distinction between the circumstance element in *Cabrales* and the "critical part" of the statute in *Rodriguez-Moreno* provide some guidance?

4. One type of continuing crime that can easily raise venue questions is conspiracy. Because the essence of a conspiracy is simply the agreement to commit an offense, conspirators in large criminal enterprises can be scattered across the country. As will be seen in the section on joinder and severance (Section C, below), however, a conspiracy charge is one of the bases for joining multiple defendants into a single trial in a single location. So in a multistate conspiracy, where is venue proper?

The federal rule is quite expansive: Venue is proper in any jurisdiction where the agreement was made *or* where an overt act in furtherance of the conspiracy occurred. Thus, if *A* in Alaska, *B* in Idaho, and *C* in California agree by telephone to manufacture illegal drugs, and if *B* then goes to Montana to obtain a needed chemical, each of the three defendants could be required to stand trial for conspiracy in any of the four states.

Note, however, that the broad rule extends only to the conspiracy itself, and not necessarily to the crime that is the object of the conspiracy. In U.S. v. Walden, 464 F.2d 1015 (4th Cir. 1972), for example, the defendants were charged with both conspiracy to commit bank robbery and with the completed bank robbery. Both charges were filed in South Carolina, where overt acts in furtherance of the conspiracy had admittedly taken place. But the banks were located in other states, and the court found that venue for these robberies was proper only in those other states — that is, only in the states where the bank robbery actually occurred. Thus, a prosecutor who wants to bring both a conspiracy and a substantive charge in a single case must file the charges where venue is proper on the substantive counts.

5. 18 U.S.C. §3237 covers more than just venue for continuing offenses. The statute also provides:

> Any offense involving the use of the mails, transportation in interstate or foreign commerce, or the importation of an object or person into the United States is a continuing offense and, except as otherwise expressly provided by enactment of Congress, may be inquired of and prosecuted in any district from, through, or into which such commerce, mail matter, or imported object or person moves.

This provision is strikingly broad. Most notably, if an offense involves the use of the mails, venue is proper is any district from, *through*, or into which the mail travels. Taken literally, a package of drugs that is mailed from Georgia to an addressee in Oregon would make venue proper in Utah if the mail happened to pass through there, even though the people of Utah would otherwise be unaffected by (and unaware of) the offense. In what respect can it be said that the crime "occurred" in Utah simply because the package passed through there, unopened, on its trip to the West Coast?

There is some reason to think that the statute should not be taken at face value. In U.S. v. Brennan, 183 F.3d 139 (2d Cir. 1999), the defendants were charged with mail fraud under 18 U.S.C. §1341. The allegedly fraudulent mailings were sent from the defendant's offices in the Southern District of New York, but the case was filed in the Eastern District of New York. The government defended its venue choice by showing that the fraudulent mailings would have gone through either Kennedy or LaGuardia airports, both of which were located in the Eastern District, and that the mail would have thus moved "through" there within the meaning of §3237. The Second Circuit rejected the claim, holding that "the mail fraud statute does not proscribe conduct involving 'the use of the mails' *within the meaning of §3237(a)*" (emphasis added). Although the Court admitted that this conclusion was "perhaps surprising," it went on to find that the "history and purpose" of §3237(a), and more important, the constitutional protection of defendants' "venue rights" showed that venue was improper. The court therefore reversed the convictions.

Whatever the merits of the Second Circuit's statutory interpretation, it is probably fair to read *Brennan* as a cautionary tale for prosecutors who are tempted to use the statutory venue powers to their fullest extent.

2.   Changes of Venue

The Federal Rules provide two avenues for a defendant who wishes to change venue. Rule 21(b) states:

> Upon the defendant's motion, the court may transfer the proceeding, or one or more counts, against that defendant to another district for the convenience of the parties and witnesses and in the interest of justice.

Notice that while the court is to consider the convenience of both parties and the witnesses in ruling on a motion, only the defendant can initiate the process. At its core, the Rule is designed to help the defendant who is prejudiced by having to defend himself in a remote location, which is the concern that lies at the heart of the constitutional venue protection.

A second ground for changing venue is found in Rule 21(a), which provides:

> Upon the defendant's motion, the court must transfer the proceeding against that defendant to another district if the court is satisfied that so great a prejudice against the defendant exists in the transferring district that the defendant cannot obtain a fair and impartial trial there.

Here the court "must" transfer a case on request if keeping the case where it was filed would deprive the defendant of a fair trial. Again, the focus is on the defendant — because the protections of Article III and the Sixth Amendment run to the accused, only the defense can seek a change of venue for unfair prejudice. This is so even though courts have recognized that the government itself has a compelling interest in a fair criminal proceeding, and even though, in some cases, community sentiment may run strongly in favor of the accused (the popular politician caught taking a bribe, for example). But even if there is a risk that the government's case will not be given unbiased consideration in the district where the crime occurred, a case cannot be transferred against the defendant's wishes.

Cases where the defendant seeks a change of venue for pretrial publicity are relatively rare, but in high-profile cases, involving prominent victims or defendants, or gruesome or sordid facts, the risks of a biased jury pool can be significant. Consider the Supreme Court's latest word on what type of showing it takes to demonstrate that pretrial publicity deprived the defendant of a fair trial.

SKILLING v. UNITED STATES

Certiorari to the United States Court of Appeals for the
Fifth Circuit ___ U.S. ___ (2010)

JUSTICE GINSBURG delivered the opinion of the Court.

In 2001, Enron Corporation, then the seventh highest-revenue-grossing company in America, crashed into bankruptcy. We consider in this opinion two questions arising from the prosecution of Jeffrey Skilling, a longtime Enron executive, for crimes committed before the corporation's collapse. First, did pretrial publicity and community prejudice prevent Skilling from obtaining a fair trial? Second, did the jury improperly convict Skilling of conspiracy to commit "honest-services" wire fraud, 18 U.S.C. §§371, 1343, 1346?

Answering no to both questions, the Fifth Circuit affirmed Skilling's convictions. We conclude, in common with the Court of Appeals, that Skilling's fair-trial argument fails; Skilling, we hold, did not establish that a presumption of juror prejudice arose or that actual bias infected the jury that tried him. But we disagree with the Fifth Circuit's honest-services ruling. . . . We therefore affirm in part and vacate in part.[2]

I

Founded in 1985, Enron Corporation grew from its headquarters in Houston, Texas, into one of the world's leading energy companies. Skilling launched his career there in 1990 when Kenneth Lay, the company's founder, hired him to head an Enron subsidiary. Skilling steadily rose through the corporation's ranks, serving as president and chief operating officer, and then, beginning in February 2001, as chief executive officer. Six months later, on August 14, 2001, Skilling resigned from Enron.

Less than four months after Skilling's departure, Enron spiraled into bankruptcy. The company's stock, which had traded at $90 per share in August 2000, plummeted to pennies per share in late 2001. Attempting to comprehend what caused the corporation's collapse, the U.S. Department of Justice formed an Enron Task Force, comprising prosecutors and FBI agents from around the Nation. The Government's investigation uncovered an elaborate conspiracy to prop up Enron's short-run stock prices by overstating the company's financial well-being. In the years following Enron's bankruptcy, the Government prosecuted dozens of Enron employees who participated in the scheme. In time, the Government worked its way up the corporation's chain of command: On July 7, 2004, a grand jury indicted Skilling, Lay, and Richard Causey, Enron's former chief accounting officer. These three defendants, the indictment alleged,

engaged in a wide-ranging scheme to deceive the investing public, including Enron's shareholders, . . . about the true performance of Enron's businesses by: (a) manipulating Enron's publicly reported financial results; and (b) making public statements and representations about Enron's financial performance and results that were false and misleading.

Skilling and his co-conspirators, the indictment continued, "enriched themselves as a result of the scheme through salary, bonuses, grants of stock and stock options, other profits, and prestige."

In November 2004, Skilling moved to transfer the trial to another venue; he contended that hostility toward him in Houston, coupled with extensive pretrial publicity, had poisoned potential jurors. To support this assertion, Skilling, aided by media experts, submitted hundreds of news reports detailing Enron's downfall; he also presented affidavits from the experts he engaged portraying community attitudes in Houston in comparison to other potential venues.

The U.S. District Court for the Southern District of Texas, in accord with rulings in two earlier instituted Enron-related prosecutions, denied the venue-transfer motion. Despite "isolated incidents of intemperate commentary," the court

---

2. The "honest services" portion of the Court's opinion is omitted. — EDS.

observed, media coverage "ha[d] [mostly] been objective and unemotional," and the facts of the case were "neither heinous nor sensational." Moreover, "courts ha[d] commonly" favored "effective voir dire . . . to ferret out any [juror] bias." Pretrial publicity about the case, the court concluded, did not warrant a presumption that Skilling would be unable to obtain a fair trial in Houston.

In the months leading up to the trial, the District Court solicited from the parties questions the court might use to screen prospective jurors. Unable to agree on a questionnaire's format and content, Skilling and the Government submitted dueling documents. On venire members' sources of Enron-related news, for example, the Government proposed that they tick boxes from a checklist of generic labels such as "[t]elevision," "[n]ewspaper," and "[r]adio"; Skilling proposed more probing questions asking venire members to list the specific names of their media sources and to report on "what st[ood] out in [their] mind[s]" of "all the things [they] ha[d] seen, heard or read about Enron."

The District Court rejected the Government's sparer inquiries in favor of Skilling's submission. Skilling's questions "[we]re more helpful," the court said, "because [they] [we]re generally . . . open-ended and w[ould] allow the potential jurors to give us more meaningful information." The court converted Skilling's submission, with slight modifications, into a 77-question, 14-page document that asked prospective jurors about, inter alia, their sources of news and exposure to Enron-related publicity, beliefs concerning Enron and what caused its collapse, opinions regarding the defendants and their possible guilt or innocence, and relationships to the company and to anyone affected by its demise.

In November 2005, the District Court mailed the questionnaire to 400 prospective jurors and received responses from nearly all the addressees. The court granted hardship exemptions to approximately 90 individuals, and the parties, with the court's approval, further winnowed the pool by excusing another 119 for cause, hardship, or physical disability. The parties agreed to exclude, in particular, "each and every" prospective juror who said that a preexisting opinion about Enron or the defendants would prevent her from impartially considering the evidence at trial.

On December 28, 2005, three weeks before the date scheduled for the commencement of trial, Causey pleaded guilty. Skilling's attorneys immediately requested a continuance, and the District Court agreed to delay the proceedings until the end of January 2006. In the interim, Skilling renewed his change-of-venue motion, arguing that the juror questionnaires revealed pervasive bias and that news accounts of Causey's guilty plea further tainted the jury pool. If Houston remained the trial venue, Skilling urged that "jurors need to be questioned individually by both the Court *and* counsel" concerning their opinions of Enron and "publicity issues."

The District Court again declined to move the trial. Skilling, the court concluded, still had not "establish[ed] that pretrial publicity and/or community prejudice raise[d] a presumption of inherent jury prejudice." The questionnaires and voir dire, the court observed, provided safeguards adequate to ensure an impartial jury.

Denying Skilling's request for attorney-led voir dire, the court said that in 17 years on the bench:

> I've found . . . I get more forthcoming responses from potential jurors than the lawyers on either side. I don't know whether people are suspicious of lawyers — but I think if I ask a person a question, I will get a candid response much easier than if a lawyer asks the question.

But the court promised to give counsel an opportunity to ask follow-up questions, and it agreed that venire members should be examined individually about pretrial publicity. The court also allotted the defendants jointly 14 peremptory challenges, 2 more than the standard number prescribed by Federal Rule of Criminal Procedure 24(b)(2) and (c)(4)(B).

Voir dire began on January 30, 2006. The District Court first emphasized to the venire the importance of impartiality and explained the presumption of innocence and the Government's burden of proof. The trial, the court next instructed, was not a forum "to seek vengeance against Enron's former officers," or to "provide remedies for" its victims. "The bottom line," the court stressed, "is that we want . . . jurors who . . . will faithfully, conscientiously and impartially serve if selected." In response to the court's query whether any prospective juror questioned her ability to adhere to these instructions, two individuals indicated that they could not be fair; they were therefore excused for cause.

After questioning the venire as a group, the District Court brought prospective jurors one by one to the bench for individual examination. Although the questions varied, the process generally tracked the following format: The court asked about exposure to Enron-related news and the content of any stories that stood out in the prospective juror's mind. Next, the court homed in on questionnaire answers that raised a red flag signaling possible bias. The court then permitted each side to pose follow-up questions. Finally, after the venire member stepped away, the court entertained and ruled on challenges for cause. In all, the court granted one of the Government's for cause challenges and denied four; it granted three of the defendants' challenges and denied six. The parties agreed to excuse three additional jurors for cause and one for hardship.

By the end of the day, the court had qualified 38 prospective jurors, a number sufficient, allowing for peremptory challenges, to empanel 12 jurors and 4 alternates. Before the jury was sworn in, Skilling objected to the seating of six jurors. He did not contend that they were in fact biased; instead, he urged that he would have used peremptories to exclude them had he not exhausted his supply by striking several venire members after the court refused to excuse them for cause. The court overruled this objection. . . .

Following a 4-month trial and nearly five days of deliberation, the jury found Skilling guilty of 19 counts, including the honest-services-fraud conspiracy charge, and not guilty of 9 insider-trading counts. The District Court sentenced Skilling to 292 months' imprisonment, 3 years' supervised release, and $45 million in restitution.

On appeal, Skilling raised a host of challenges to his convictions, including the fair-trial and honest-services arguments he presses here. Regarding the former, the Fifth Circuit initially determined that the volume and negative tone of media coverage generated by Enron's collapse created a presumption of juror prejudice. 554 F.3d 529, 559 (2009). The court also noted potential prejudice stemming from Causey's guilty plea and from the large number of victims in Houston—from the "[t]housands of Enron employees . . . [who] lost their jobs, and . . . saw their 401(k) accounts wiped out," to Houstonians who suffered spillover economic effects.

The Court of Appeals stated, however, that "the presumption [of prejudice] is rebuttable," and it therefore examined the voir dire to determine whether "the District Court empanelled an impartial jury." The voir dire was, in the Fifth Circuit's view, "proper and thorough." Moreover, the court noted, Skilling had challenged only one seated juror — Juror 11 — for cause. Although Juror 11 made some troubling comments about corporate greed, the District Court "observed [his] demeanor, listened to his answers, and believed he would make the government prove its case." In sum, the Fifth Circuit found that the Government had overcome the presumption of prejudice and that Skilling had not "show[n] that any juror who actually sat was prejudiced against him."

Arguing that the Fifth Circuit erred in its consideration of these claims, Skilling sought relief from this Court. We granted certiorari, 558 U.S. ___ (2009).

II

Pointing to "the community passion aroused by Enron's collapse and the vitriolic media treatment" aimed at him, Skilling argues that his trial "never should have proceeded in Houston." And even if it had been possible to select impartial jurors in Houston, "[t]he truncated voir dire . . . did almost nothing to weed out prejudices," he contends, so "[f]ar from rebutting the presumption of prejudice, the record below affirmatively confirmed it." Skilling's fair-trial claim thus raises two distinct questions. First, did the District Court err by failing to move the trial to a different venue based on a presumption of prejudice? Second, did actual prejudice contaminate Skilling's jury?

A

1

The Sixth Amendment secures to criminal defendants the right to trial by an impartial jury. By constitutional design, that trial occurs "in the State where the . . . Crimes . . . have been committed." Art. III, §2, cl. 3. See also Amdt. 6 (right to trial by "jury of the State and district wherein the crime shall have been committed"). The Constitution's place-of-trial prescriptions, however, do not impede transfer of the proceeding to a different district at the defendant's request if extraordinary local prejudice will prevent a fair trial — a "basic requirement of due process," In re Murchison, 349 U.S. 133, 136 (1955).[11]

2

"The theory of our [trial] system is that the conclusions to be reached in a case will be induced only by evidence and argument in open court, and not by any outside influence, whether of private talk or public print." Patterson v. Colorado ex rel. Attorney General of Colo., 205 U.S. 454, 462 (1907) (opinion for the Court by Holmes, J.). When does the publicity attending conduct charged as criminal dim prospects that the trier can judge a case, as due process requires, impartially, unswayed by outside influence? Because most cases of consequence garner at least

---

11. Venue transfer in federal court is governed by Federal Rule of Criminal Procedure 21, which instructs that a "court must transfer the proceeding . . . to another district if the court is satisfied that so great a prejudice against the defendant exists in the transferring district that the defendant cannot obtain a fair and impartial trial there." . . . Skilling does not argue, distinct from his due process challenge, that the District Court abused its discretion under Rule 21 by declining to move his trial. We therefore review the District Court's venue-transfer decision only for compliance with the Constitution.

some pretrial publicity, courts have considered this question in diverse settings. We begin our discussion by addressing the presumption of prejudice from which the Fifth Circuit's analysis in Skilling's case proceeded. The foundation precedent is Rideau v. Louisiana, 373 U.S. 723 (1963).

Wilbert Rideau robbed a bank in a small Louisiana town, kidnaped three bank employees, and killed one of them. Police interrogated Rideau in jail without counsel present and obtained his confession. Without informing Rideau, no less seeking his consent, the police filmed the interrogation. On three separate occasions shortly before the trial, a local television station broadcast the film to audiences ranging from 24,000 to 53,000 individuals. Rideau moved for a change of venue, arguing that he could not receive a fair trial in the parish where the crime occurred, which had a population of approximately 150,000 people. The trial court denied the motion, and a jury eventually convicted Rideau. The Supreme Court of Louisiana upheld the conviction.

We reversed. "What the people [in the community] saw on their television sets," we observed, "was Rideau, in jail, flanked by the sheriff and two state troopers, admitting in detail the commission of the robbery, kidnapping, and murder." "[T]o the tens of thousands of people who saw and heard it," we explained, the interrogation "in a very real sense *was* Rideau's trial — at which he pleaded guilty." We therefore "d[id] not hesitate to hold, without pausing to examine a particularized transcript of the voir dire," that "[t]he kangaroo court proceedings" trailing the televised confession violated due process.

We followed *Rideau*'s lead in two later cases in which media coverage manifestly tainted a criminal prosecution. In Estes v. Texas, 381 U.S. 532, 538 (1965), extensive publicity before trial swelled into excessive exposure during preliminary court proceedings as reporters and television crews overran the courtroom and "bombard[ed] . . . the community with the sights and sounds of" the pretrial hearing. The media's overzealous reporting efforts, we observed, "led to considerable disruption" and denied the "judicial serenity and calm to which [Billie Sol Estes] was entitled."

Similarly, in Sheppard v. Maxwell, 384 U.S. 333 (1966), news reporters extensively covered the story of Sam Sheppard, who was accused of bludgeoning his pregnant wife to death. "[B]edlam reigned at the courthouse during the trial and newsmen took over practically the entire courtroom," thrusting jurors "into the role of celebrities." Pretrial media coverage, which we characterized as "months [of] virulent publicity about Sheppard and the murder," did not alone deny due process, we noted. But Sheppard's case involved more than heated reporting pretrial: We upset the murder conviction because a "carnival atmosphere" pervaded the trial.

In each of these cases, we overturned a "conviction obtained in a trial atmosphere that [was] utterly corrupted by press coverage"; our decisions, however, "cannot be made to stand for the proposition that juror exposure to . . . news accounts of the crime . . . alone presumptively deprives the defendant of due process." Murphy v. Florida, 421 U.S. 794, 798-799 (1975). See also, e.g., Patton v. Yount, 467 U.S. 1025 (1984).[13] Prominence does not necessarily produce prejudice, and juror *impartiality*,

---

13. In *Yount*, the media reported on Jon Yount's confession to a brutal murder and his prior conviction for the crime, which had been reversed due to a violation of Miranda v. Arizona, 384 U.S. 436 (1966). During voir dire, 77% of prospective jurors acknowledged they would carry an opinion into the jury box, and 8 of the 14 seated jurors and alternates admitted they had formed an opinion as to Yount's guilt.

we have reiterated, does not require *ignorance*. Irvin v. Dowd, 366 U.S. 717, 722 (1961) (Jurors are not required to be "totally ignorant of the facts and issues involved"; "scarcely any of those best qualified to serve as jurors will not have formed some impression or opinion as to the merits of the case. A presumption of prejudice, our decisions indicate, attends only the extreme case.")

3

Relying on *Rideau*, *Estes*, and *Sheppard*, Skilling asserts that we need not pause to examine the screening questionnaires or the voir dire before declaring his jury's verdict void. We are not persuaded. Important differences separate Skilling's prosecution from those in which we have presumed juror prejudice.[14]

First, we have emphasized in prior decisions the size and characteristics of the community in which the crime occurred. In *Rideau*, for example, we noted that the murder was committed in a parish of only 150,000 residents. Houston, in contrast, is the fourth most populous city in the Nation: At the time of Skilling's trial, more than 4.5 million individuals eligible for jury duty resided in the Houston area. Given this large, diverse pool of potential jurors, the suggestion that 12 impartial individuals could not be empaneled is hard to sustain. See Mu'Min v. Virginia, 500 U.S. 415, 429 (1991) (potential for prejudice mitigated by the size of the "metropolitan Washington [D.C.] statistical area, which has a population of over 3 million, and in which, unfortunately, hundreds of murders are committed each year").

Second, although news stories about Skilling were not kind, they contained no confession or other blatantly prejudicial information of the type readers or viewers could not reasonably be expected to shut from sight. Rideau's dramatically staged admission of guilt, for instance, was likely imprinted indelibly in the mind of anyone who watched it. Pretrial publicity about Skilling was less memorable and prejudicial. No evidence of the smoking-gun variety invited prejudgment of his culpability. See United States v. Chagra, 669 F.2d 241, 251-252, n. 11 (CA5 1982) ("A jury may have difficulty in disbelieving or forgetting a defendant's opinion of his own guilt but have no difficulty in rejecting the opinions of others because they may not be well-founded.").

Third, unlike cases in which trial swiftly followed a widely reported crime, over four years elapsed between Enron's bankruptcy and Skilling's trial. Although reporters covered Enron-related news throughout this period, the decibel level of media attention diminished somewhat in the years following Enron's collapse.

Finally, and of prime significance, Skilling's jury acquitted him of nine insider-trading counts. Similarly, earlier instituted Enron-related prosecutions yielded no overwhelming victory for the Government. In *Rideau*, *Estes*, and *Sheppard*, in marked contrast, the jury's verdict did not undermine in any way the supposition of juror bias. It would be odd for an appellate court to presume prejudice in a case in which jurors' actions run counter to that presumption.

Nevertheless, we rejected Yount's presumption-of-prejudice claim. The adverse publicity and community outrage, we noted, were at their height prior to Yount's first trial, four years before the second prosecution; time had helped "sooth[e] and eras[e]" community prejudice.

14. Skilling's reliance on *Estes* and *Sheppard* is particularly misplaced; those cases involved media interference with courtroom proceedings *during* trial. Skilling does not assert that news coverage reached and influenced his jury after it was empaneled.

4

Skilling's trial, in short, shares little in common with those in which we approved a presumption of juror prejudice. The Fifth Circuit reached the opposite conclusion based primarily on the magnitude and negative tone of media attention directed at Enron. But "pretrial publicity — even pervasive, adverse publicity — does not inevitably lead to an unfair trial." Nebraska Press Assn. v. Stuart, 427 U.S. 539, 554 (1976). In this case, as just noted, news stories about Enron did not present the kind of vivid, unforgettable information we have recognized as particularly likely to produce prejudice, and Houston's size and diversity diluted the media's impact.

Nor did Enron's "sheer number of victims" trigger a presumption of prejudice. Although the widespread community impact necessitated careful identification and inspection of prospective jurors' connections to Enron, the extensive screening questionnaire and follow-up voir dire were well suited to that task. And hindsight shows the efficacy of these devices; as we discuss infra, . . . , jurors' links to Enron were either nonexistent or attenuated.

Finally, although Causey's "well-publicized decision to plead guilty" shortly before trial created a danger of juror prejudice, the District Court took appropriate steps to reduce that risk. The court delayed the proceedings by two weeks, lessening the immediacy of that development. And during voir dire, the court asked about prospective jurors' exposure to recent publicity, including news regarding Causey. Only two venire members recalled the plea; neither mentioned Causey by name, and neither ultimately served on Skilling's jury. Although publicity about a codefendant's guilty plea calls for inquiry to guard against actual prejudice, it does not ordinarily — and, we are satisfied, it did not here — warrant an automatic presumption of prejudice.

Persuaded that no presumption arose,[18] we conclude that the District Court, in declining to order a venue change, did not exceed constitutional limitations.

B

We next consider whether actual prejudice infected Skilling's jury. Voir dire, Skilling asserts, did not adequately detect and defuse juror bias. "[T]he record . . . affirmatively confirm[s]" prejudice, he maintains, because several seated jurors "prejudged his guilt." We disagree with Skilling's characterization of the voir dire and the jurors selected through it.

1

No hard-and-fast formula dictates the necessary depth or breadth of voir dire. See United States v. Wood, 299 U.S. 123, 145-146 (1936) ("Impartiality is not a technical conception. It is a state of mind. For the ascertainment of this mental attitude of appropriate indifference, the Constitution lays down no particular tests and procedure is not chained to any ancient and artificial formula."). Jury selection, we have repeatedly emphasized, is "particularly within the province of the trial judge."

---

18. The parties disagree about whether a presumption of prejudice can be rebutted, and, if it can, what standard of proof governs that issue. Because we hold that no presumption arose, we need not, and do not, reach these questions.

When pretrial publicity is at issue, "primary reliance on the judgment of the trial court makes [especially] good sense" because the judge "sits in the locale where the publicity is said to have had its effect" and may base her evaluation on her "own perception of the depth and extent of news stories that might influence a juror." *Mu'Min*, 500 U.S., at 427.

Reviewing courts are properly resistant to second-guessing the trial judge's estimation of a juror's impartiality, for that judge's appraisal is ordinarily influenced by a host of factors impossible to capture fully in the record — among them, the prospective juror's inflection, sincerity, demeanor, candor, body language, and apprehension of duty. In contrast to the cold transcript received by the appellate court, the in-the-moment voir dire affords the trial court a more intimate and immediate basis for assessing a venire member's fitness for jury service.

2

Skilling deems the voir dire insufficient because, he argues, jury selection lasted "just five hours," "[m]ost of the court's questions were conclusory[,] high-level, and failed adequately to probe jurors' true feelings," and the court "consistently took prospective jurors at their word once they claimed they could be fair, no matter what other indications of bias were present." Our review of the record, however, yields a different appraisal.[21]

As noted, the District Court initially screened venire members by eliciting their responses to a comprehensive questionnaire drafted in large part by Skilling. That survey helped to identify prospective jurors excusable for cause and served as a springboard for further questions put to remaining members of the array. Voir dire thus was, in the court's words, the "culmination of a lengthy process."

The District Court conducted voir dire, moreover, aware of the greater-than-normal need, due to pretrial publicity, to ensure against jury bias. At Skilling's urging, the court examined each prospective juror individually, thus preventing the spread of any prejudicial information to other venire members. To encourage candor, the court repeatedly admonished that there were "no right and wrong answers to th[e] questions." The court denied Skilling's request for attorney-led voir dire because, in its experience, potential jurors were "more forthcoming" when the court, rather than counsel, asked the question. The parties, however, were accorded an opportunity to ask follow-up questions of every prospective juror brought to the bench for colloquy. Skilling's counsel declined to ask anything of more than half of the venire members questioned individually, including eight eventually selected for the jury, because, he explained, "the Court and other counsel have covered" everything he wanted to know.

Inspection of the questionnaires and voir dire of the individuals who actually served as jurors satisfies us that, notwithstanding the flaws Skilling lists, the selection process successfully secured jurors who were largely untouched by Enron's collapse.

---

21. In addition to focusing on the adequacy of voir dire, our decisions have also "take[n] into account . . . other measures [that] were used to mitigate the adverse effects of publicity." Nebraska Press Assn. v. Stuart, 427 U.S. 539, 565 (1976). We have noted, for example, the prophylactic effect of "emphatic and clear instructions on the sworn duty of each juror to decide the issues only on evidence presented in open court." Id., at 564. Here, the District Court's instructions were unequivocal. . . . Peremptory challenges, too, "provid[e] protection against [prejudice]," United States ex rel. Darcy v. Handy, 351 U.S. 454, 462 (1956); the District Court, as earlier noted, exercised its discretion to grant the defendants two extra peremptories.

Eleven of the seated jurors and alternates reported no connection at all to Enron, while all other jurors reported at most an insubstantial link. As for pretrial publicity, 14 jurors and alternates specifically stated that they had paid scant attention to Enron-related news. The remaining two jurors indicated that nothing in the news influenced their opinions about Skilling.

The questionnaires confirmed that, whatever community prejudice existed in Houston generally, Skilling's jurors were not under its sway. Although many expressed sympathy for victims of Enron's bankruptcy and speculated that greed contributed to the corporation's collapse, these sentiments did not translate into animus toward Skilling. When asked whether they "ha[d] an opinion about . . . Jeffrey Skilling," none of the seated jurors and alternates checked the "yes" box. And in response to the question whether "any opinion [they] may have formed regarding Enron or [Skilling] [would] prevent" their impartial consideration of the evidence at trial, every juror — despite options to mark "yes" or "unsure" — instead checked "no."

The District Court, Skilling asserts, should not have "accept[ed] *at face value* jurors' promises of fairness." In Irvin v. Dowd, 366 U.S., at 727-728, Skilling points out, we found actual prejudice despite jurors' assurances that they could be impartial. Justice Sotomayor, in turn, repeatedly relies on *Irvin*, which she regards as closely analogous to this case. We disagree with that characterization of *Irvin*.

The facts of *Irvin* are worlds apart from those presented here. Leslie Irvin stood accused of a brutal murder and robbery spree in a small rural community. In the months before Irvin's trial, "a barrage" of publicity was "unleashed against him," including reports of his confessions to the slayings and robberies. This Court's description of the media coverage in *Irvin* reveals why the dissent's "best case" is not an apt comparison:

[S]tories revealed the details of [Irvin's] background, including a reference to crimes committed when a juvenile, his convictions for arson almost 20 years previously, for burglary and by a court-martial on AWOL charges during the war. He was accused of being a parole violator. The headlines announced his police line-up identification, that he faced a lie detector test, had been placed at the scene of the crime and that the six murders were solved but [he] refused to confess. Finally, they announced [Irvin's] confession to the six murders and the fact of his indictment for four of them in Indiana. They reported [Irvin's] offer to plead guilty if promised a 99-year sentence, but also the determination, on the other hand, of the prosecutor to secure the death penalty, and that [Irvin] had confessed to 24 burglaries (the modus operandi of these robberies was compared to that of the murders and the similarity noted). One story dramatically relayed the promise of a sheriff to devote his life to securing [Irvin's] execution. . . . Another characterized [Irvin] as remorseless and without conscience but also as having been found sane by a court-appointed panel of doctors. In many of the stories [Irvin] was described as the "confessed slayer of six," a parole violator and fraudulent-check artist. [Irvin's] court-appointed counsel was quoted as having received "much criticism over being Irvin's counsel" and it was pointed out, by way of excusing the attorney, that he would be subject to disbarment should he refuse to represent Irvin. On the day before the trial the newspapers carried the story that Irvin had orally admitted [to] the murder of [one victim] as well as "the robbery-murder of [a second individual]; the murder of [a third individual]; and the slaughter of three members of [a different family]."

Id., at 725-726.

"[N]ewspapers in which the[se] stories appeared were delivered regularly to 95% of the dwellings in" the county where the trial occurred, which had a population of only 30,000; "radio and TV stations, which likewise blanketed that county, also carried extensive newscasts covering the same incidents." Id., at 725.

Reviewing Irvin's fair-trial claim, this Court noted that "the pattern of deep and bitter prejudice" in the community "was clearly reflected in the sum total of the voir dire": "370 prospective jurors or almost 90% of those examined on the point . . . entertained some opinion as to guilt," and "[8] out of the 12 [jurors] thought [Irvin] was guilty." Although these jurors declared they could be impartial, we held that, "[w]ith his life at stake, it is not requiring too much that [Irvin] be tried in an atmosphere undisturbed by so huge a wave of public passion and by a jury other than one in which two-thirds of the members admit, before hearing any testimony, to possessing a belief in his guilt."

In this case, as noted, news stories about Enron contained nothing resembling the horrifying information rife in reports about Irvin's rampage of robberies and murders. Of key importance, Houston shares little in common with the rural community in which Irvin's trial proceeded, and circulation figures for Houston media sources were far lower than the 95% saturation level recorded in Irvin, see App. to Brief for United States 15a ("The Houston Chronicle . . . reaches less than one-third of occupied households in Houston."). Skilling's seated jurors, moreover, exhibited nothing like the display of bias shown in Irvin. In light of these large differences, the District Court had far less reason than did the trial court in Irvin to discredit jurors' promises of fairness.

The District Court, moreover, did not simply take venire members who proclaimed their impartiality at their word. As noted, all of Skilling's jurors had already affirmed on their questionnaires that they would have no trouble basing a verdict only on the evidence at trial. Nevertheless, the court followed up with each individually to uncover concealed bias. This face-to-face opportunity to gauge demeanor and credibility, coupled with information from the questionnaires regarding jurors' backgrounds, opinions, and sources of news, gave the court a sturdy foundation to assess fitness for jury service. The jury's not-guilty verdict on nine insider-trading counts after nearly five days of deliberation, meanwhile, suggests the court's assessments were accurate. Skilling, we conclude, failed to show that his voir dire fell short of constitutional requirements.

3

Skilling also singles out several jurors in particular and contends they were openly biased. See United States v. Martinez-Salazar, 528 U.S. 304, 316 (2000) ("[T]he seating of any juror who should have been dismissed for cause . . . require[s] reversal."). In reviewing claims of this type, the deference due to district courts is at its pinnacle: "A trial court's findings of juror impartiality may be overturned only for manifest error." Mu'Min, 500 U.S., at 428. Skilling, moreover, unsuccessfully challenged only one of the seated jurors for cause, "strong evidence that he was convinced the [other] jurors were not biased and had not formed any opinions as to his guilt." Beck v. Washington, 369 U.S. 541, 557-558 (1962).

Skilling contends that Juror 11 — the only seated juror he challenged for cause — "expressed the most obvious bias." Juror 11 stated that "greed on Enron's part" triggered the company's bankruptcy and that corporate executives, driven by avarice, "walk a line that stretches sometimes the legality of something." But, as the Fifth Circuit accurately summarized, Juror 11

had "no idea" whether Skilling had "crossed that line," and he "didn't say that" every CEO is probably a crook. He also asserted that he could be fair and require the government to prove its case, that he did not believe everything he read in the paper, that he did not "get into the details" of the Enron coverage, that he did not watch television, and that Enron was "old news."

Despite his criticism of greed, Juror 11 remarked that Skilling "earned [his] salar[y]," and said he would have "no problem" telling his co-worker, who had lost 401(k) funds due to Enron's collapse, that the jury voted to acquit, if that scenario came to pass. The District Court, noting that it had "looked [Juror 11] in the eye and . . . . heard all his [answers]," found his assertions of impartiality credible. . . .[33]

Skilling also objected at trial to the seating of six specific jurors whom, he said, he would have excluded had he not already exhausted his peremptory challenges. . . .

[For example, Skilling points to] Juror 63, who, Skilling points out, wrote on her questionnaire "that [Skilling] 'probably knew [he] w[as] breaking the law.'" During voir dire, however, Juror 63 insisted that she did not "really have an opinion [about Skilling's guilt] either way"; she did not "know what [she] was thinking" when she completed the questionnaire, but she "absolutely" presumed Skilling innocent and confirmed her understanding that the Government would "have to prove" his guilt, id. In response to follow-up questions from Skilling's counsel, she again stated she would not presume that Skilling violated any laws and could "[a]bsolutely" give her word that she could be fair. "Jurors," we have recognized, "cannot be expected invariably to express themselves carefully or even consistently." *Yount*, 467 U.S., at 1039. From where we sit, we cannot conclude that Juror 63 was biased.

The [ ] remaining jurors Skilling said he would have excluded with extra peremptory strikes exhibited no sign of prejudice we can discern. . . .

In sum, Skilling failed to establish that a presumption of prejudice arose or that actual bias infected the jury that tried him. Jurors, the trial court correctly comprehended, need not enter the box with empty heads in order to determine the facts impartially. "It is sufficient if the juror[s] can lay aside [their] impression[s] or opinion[s] and render a verdict based on the evidence presented in court." *Irvin*, 366 U.S., at 723. Taking account of the full record, rather than incomplete exchanges selectively culled from it, we find no cause to upset the lower courts' judgment that Skilling's jury met that measure.

* * *

For the foregoing reasons, we affirm the Fifth Circuit's ruling on Skilling's fair-trial argument, vacate its ruling on his conspiracy conviction, and remand the case for proceedings consistent with this opinion.

It is so ordered.

[The opinions of Justice Scalia, concurring in the Court's opinion on the pretrial publicity issue, and Justice Alito, concurring in part and concurring in the judgment, are omitted.]

33. Skilling's trial counsel and jury consultants apparently did not regard Juror 11 as so "obvious[ly] bias[ed]," as to warrant exercise of a peremptory challenge.

JUSTICE SOTOMAYOR, with whom JUSTICE STEVENS and JUSTICE BREYER join, concurring in part and dissenting in part.

Under our relevant precedents, the more intense the public's antipathy toward a defendant, the more careful a court must be to prevent that sentiment from tainting the jury. In this case, passions ran extremely high. The sudden collapse of Enron directly affected thousands of people in the Houston area and shocked the entire community. The accompanying barrage of local media coverage was massive in volume and often caustic in tone. As Enron's one-time CEO, Skilling was at the center of the storm. Even if these extraordinary circumstances did not constitutionally compel a change of venue, they required the District Court to conduct a thorough voir dire in which prospective jurors' attitudes about the case were closely scrutinized. The District Court's inquiry lacked the necessary thoroughness and left serious doubts about whether the jury empaneled to decide Skilling's case was capable of rendering an impartial decision based solely on the evidence presented in the courtroom. Accordingly, I would grant Skilling relief on his fair-trial claim.

I

The majority understates the breadth and depth of community hostility toward Skilling and overlooks significant deficiencies in the District Court's jury selection process. The failure of Enron wounded Houston deeply. Virtually overnight, what had been the city's "largest, most visible, and most prosperous company," its "foremost social and charitable force," and "a source of civic pride" was reduced to a "shattered shell." Thousands of the company's employees lost their jobs and saw their retirement savings vanish. As the effects rippled through the local economy, thousands of additional jobs disappeared, businesses shuttered, and community groups that once benefited from Enron's largesse felt the loss of millions of dollars in contributions. Enron's community ties were so extensive that the entire local U.S. Attorney's Office was forced to recuse itself from the Government's investigation into the company's fall.

With Enron's demise affecting the lives of so many Houstonians, local media coverage of the story saturated the community. According to a defense media expert, the Houston Chronicle — the area's leading newspaper — assigned as many as 12 reporters to work on the Enron story full time. The paper mentioned Enron in more than 4,000 articles during the 3-year period following the company's December 2001 bankruptcy filing. Hundreds of these articles discussed Skilling by name. Skilling's expert, a professional journalist and academic with 30 years' experience, could not "recall another instance where a local paper dedicated as many resources to a single topic over such an extended period of time as the Houston Chronicle . . . dedicated to Enron." Local television news coverage was similarly pervasive and, in terms of "editorial theme," "largely followed the Chronicle's lead." Between May 2002 and October 2004, local stations aired an estimated 19,000 news segments involving Enron, more than 1600 of which mentioned Skilling.

While many of the stories were straightforward news items, many others conveyed and amplified the community's outrage at the top executives perceived to be responsible for the company's bankruptcy. A Chronicle report on Skilling's 2002 testimony before Congress is typical of the coverage. It began, "Across Houston, Enron employees watched former chief executive Jeffrey Skilling's congressional testimony on television, turning incredulous, angry and then sarcastic by turns, as a man they knew as savvy and detail-oriented pleaded memory failure and ignorance about critical financial transactions at the now-collapsed energy giant." "'He is lying; he knew everything,' said [an employee], who said she had seen Skilling frequently over her 18 years with the firm, where Skilling was known for his intimate grasp of the inner doings at the company. 'I am getting sicker by the minute.'"

Articles deriding Enron's senior executives were juxtaposed with pieces expressing sympathy toward and solidarity with the company's many victims. Skilling's media expert counted nearly a hundred victim-related stories in the Chronicle, including a "multi-page layout entitled 'The Faces of Enron,'" which poignantly described the gut-wrenching experiences of former employees who lost vast sums of money, faced eviction from their homes, could not afford Christmas gifts for their children, and felt "scared," "hurt," "humiliat[ed]," "helpless," and "betrayed."

When a federal grand jury indicted Skilling, Lay, and Richard Causey — Enron's former chief accounting officer — in 2004 on charges of conspiracy to defraud, securities fraud, and other crimes, the media placed them directly in its crosshairs. In the words of one article, "there was one thing those whose lives were touched by the once-exalted company all seemed to agree upon: The indictment of former Enron CEO Jeff Skilling was overdue." Scoffing at Skilling's attempts to paint himself as "a 'victim' of his subordinates," the Chronicle derided "the doofus defense" that Lay and Skilling were expected to offer.

Citing the widely felt sense of victimhood among Houstonians and the voluminous adverse publicity, Skilling moved in November 2004 for a change of venue. The District Court denied the motion, characterizing the media coverage as largely "objective and unemotional." Voir dire, it concluded, would provide an effective means to "ferret out any bias" in the jury pool.

To that end, the District Court began the jury selection process by mailing screening questionnaires to 400 prospective jurors in November 2005. The completed questionnaires of the 283 respondents not excused for hardship dramatically illustrated the widespread impact of Enron's collapse on the Houston community and confirmed the intense animosity of Houstonians toward Skilling and his codefendants. More than one-third of the prospective jurors indicated that they or persons they knew had lost money or jobs as a result of the Enron bankruptcy. Two-thirds of the jurors expressed views about Enron or the defendants that suggested a potential predisposition to convict. In many instances, they did not mince words, describing Skilling as "smug," "arrogant," "brash," "conceited," "greedy," "deceitful," "totally unethical and criminal," "a crook," "the biggest liar on the face of the earth," and "guilty as sin" (capitalization omitted). Only about 5 percent of the prospective jurors did not read the Houston Chronicle, had not otherwise "heard or read about any of the Enron cases," were not connected to Enron victims, and gave no answers suggesting possible antipathy toward the defendants. The parties jointly stipulated to the dismissal of 119 members of the jury pool for cause, hardship, or disability, but numerous individuals who had made harsh comments about Skilling remained.[6]

---

6. See, e.g., Juror 29 (Skilling is "[n]ot an honest man"); Juror 104 (Skilling "knows more than he's admitting"); Juror 211 ("I believe he was involved in wrong doings"); Juror 219 ("So many people lost their life savings because of the dishonesty of some members of the executive team"; Skilling was "[t]oo aggressive w[ith] accounting"); Juror 234 ("With his level of control and power, hard to believe that he was unaware and not responsible in some way"); Juror 240 (Skilling "[s]eems to be very much involved in criminal goings on"); Juror 255 ("[T]housands of people were taken advantage of by executives at

On December 28, 2005, shortly after the questionnaires had been returned, Causey pleaded guilty. The plea was covered in lead newspaper and television stories. A front-page headline in the Chronicle proclaimed that "Causey's plea wreaks havoc for Lay, Skilling." A Chronicle editorial opined that "Causey's admission of securities fraud . . . makes less plausible Lay's claim that most of the guilty pleas were the result of prosecutorial pressure rather than actual wrongdoing."

II

The Court of Appeals incorporated the concept of presumptive prejudice into a burden-shifting framework: Once the defendant musters sufficient evidence of community hostility, the onus shifts to the Government to prove the impartiality of the jury. The majority similarly envisions a fixed point at which public passions become so intense that prejudice to a defendant's fair-trial rights must be presumed.

This Court has never treated the notion of presumptive prejudice so formalistically. Our decisions instead merely convey the commonsense understanding that as the tide of public enmity rises, so too does the danger that the prejudices of the community will infiltrate the jury. The underlying question has always been this: Do we have confidence that the jury's verdict was "induced only by evidence and argument in open court, and not by any outside influence, whether of private talk or public print"? Patterson v. Colorado ex rel. Attorney General of Colo., 205 U.S. 454, 462 (1907).

At one end of the spectrum, this Court has, on rare occasion, confronted such inherently prejudicial circumstances that it has reversed a defendant's conviction "without pausing to examine . . . the voir dire examination of the members of the jury." Rideau v. Louisiana, 373 U.S. 723, 727 (1963). In *Rideau*, repeated television broadcasts of the defendant's confession to murder, robbery, and kidnaping so thoroughly poisoned local sentiment as to raise doubts that even the most careful voir dire could have secured an impartial jury. A change of venue, the Court determined, was thus the only way to assure a fair trial.

Irvin [v. Dowd, 366 U.S. 717, 722 (1961)] offers an example of a case in which the trial court's voir dire did not suffice to counter the "wave of public passion" that had swept the community prior to the defendant's trial. The local news media had "extensively covered" the crimes (a murder spree), "arous[ing] great excitement and indignation." Following Irvin's arrest, the press "blanketed" the community with "a barrage of newspaper headlines, articles, cartoons and pictures" communicating numerous unfavorable details about Irvin, including that he had purportedly

---

Enron"; Skilling is "arrogant"; "Skilling was Andrew Fastow's immediate superior. Fastow has plead[ed] guilty to felony charges. I believe Skilling was aware of Fastow's illegal behavior"); Juror 263 ("Nice try resigning 6 months before the collaps[e], but again, he had to know what was going on"); Juror 272 (Skilling "[k]new he was getting out before the [d]am [b]roke"); Juror 292 (Skilling "[b]ailed out when he knew Enron was going down"); Juror 315 ("[H]ow could they not know and they seem to be lying about some things"); Juror 328 ("They should be held responsible as officers of this company for what happened"); Juror 350 ("I believe he greatly misused his power and affected hundreds of lives as a result"; "I believe they are all guilty. Their 'doings' affected not only those employed by Enron but many others as well"); Juror 360 ("I seem to remember him trying to claim to have mental or emotional issues that would remove him from any guilt. I think that is deceitful. It seems as though he is a big player in the downfall"); Juror 378 ("I believe he knew, and certainly should have known as the CEO, that illegal and improper [activities] were rampant in Enron"; "I believe all of them were instrumental, and were co-conspirators, in the massive fraud perpetrated at Enron").

confessed. Nearly 90 percent of the 430 prospective jurors examined during the trial court's voir dire "entertained some opinion as to guilt-ranging in intensity from mere suspicion to absolute certainty." Of the 12 jurors seated, 8 "thought petitioner was guilty," although "each indicated that notwithstanding his opinion he could render an impartial verdict."

Despite the seated jurors' assurances of impartiality, this Court invalidated Irvin's conviction for want of due process. "It is not required," this Court declared, "that the jurors be totally ignorant of the facts and issues involved. . . . It is sufficient if the juror can lay aside his impression or opinion and render a verdict based on the evidence presented in court." The Court emphasized, however, that a juror's word on this matter is not decisive, particularly when "the build-up of prejudice [in the community] is clear and convincing."

III

A

Though the question is close, I agree with the Court that the prospect of seating an unbiased jury in Houston was not so remote as to compel the conclusion that the District Court acted unconstitutionally in denying Skilling's motion to change venue. Three considerations lead me to this conclusion. First, as the Court observes, the size and diversity of the Houston community make it probable that the jury pool contained a nontrivial number of persons who were unaffected by Enron's collapse, neutral in their outlook, and unlikely to be swept up in the public furor. Second, media coverage of the case, while ubiquitous and often inflammatory, did not, as the Court points out, contain a confession by Skilling or similar "smoking-gun" evidence of specific criminal acts. For many prospective jurors, the guilty plea of codefendant and alleged co-conspirator Causey, along with the pleas and convictions of other Enron executives, no doubt suggested guilt by association. But reasonable minds exposed to such information would not necessarily have formed an indelible impression that Skilling himself was guilty as charged. Third, there is no suggestion that the courtroom in this case became, as in *Estes* and *Sheppard*, a "carnival" in which the "calmness and solemnity" of the proceedings was compromised. It is thus appropriate to examine the voir dire and determine whether it instills confidence in the impartiality of the jury actually selected.

B

In conducting this analysis, I am mindful of the "wide discretion" owed to trial courts when it comes to jury-related issues. Trial courts are uniquely positioned to assess public sentiment and the credibility of prospective jurors. Proximity to events, however, is not always a virtue. Persons in the midst of a tumult often lack a panoramic view. In particular, reviewing courts are well qualified to inquire into whether a trial court implemented procedures adequate to keep community prejudices from infecting the jury. If the jury selection process does not befit the circumstances of the case, the trial court's rulings on impartiality are necessarily called into doubt.

1

As the Court of Appeals apprehended, the District Court gave short shrift to the mountainous evidence of public hostility. For Houstonians, Enron's collapse was an event of once-in-a-generation proportions. Not only was the volume of media coverage "immense" and frequently intemperate, but "the sheer number of victims" created a climate in which animosity toward Skilling ran deep and the desire for conviction was widely shared.

The level of public animus toward Skilling dwarfed that present in cases such as *Murphy* and *Mu'Min*. . . . The much closer analogy is thus to *Irvin*, which similarly featured a "barrage" of media coverage and a "huge . . . wave of public passion," although even that case did not, as here, involve direct harm to entire segments of the community.

Attempting to distinguish *Irvin*, the majority suggests that Skilling's economic offenses were less incendiary than Irvin's violent crime spree and that "news stories about Enron contained nothing resembling the horrifying information rife in reports about Irvin's rampage of robberies and murders." Along similar lines, the District Court described "the facts of this case [as] neither heinous nor sensational." The majority also points to the four years that passed between Enron's declaration of bankruptcy and the start of Skilling's trial, asserting that "the decibel level of media attention diminished somewhat" over this time. Neither of these arguments is persuasive.

First, while violent crimes may well provoke widespread community outrage more readily than crimes involving monetary loss, economic crimes are certainly capable of rousing public passions, particularly when thousands of unsuspecting people are robbed of their livelihoods and retirement savings. Indeed, the record in this case is replete with examples of visceral outrage toward Skilling and other Enron executives. Houstonians compared Skilling to, among other things, a rapist, an axe murderer, and an Al Qaeda terrorist. . . . The bad blood was so strong that Skilling and other top executives hired private security to protect themselves from persons inclined to take the law into their own hands.

Second, the passage of time did little to soften community sentiment. . . . The Enron story was a continuing saga, and "publicity remained intense throughout." Not only did Enron's downfall generate wall-to-wall news coverage, but so too did a succession of subsequent Enron-related events. Of particular note is the highly publicized guilty plea of codefendant Causey just weeks before Skilling's trial. If anything, the time that elapsed between the bankruptcy and the trial made the task of seating an unbiased jury more difficult, not less.

2

Given the extent of the antipathy evident both in the community at large and in the responses to the written questionnaire, it was critical for the District Court to take "strong measures" to ensure the selection of "an impartial jury free from outside influences." *Sheppard*, 384 U.S., at 362. As this Court has recognized, "[i]n a community where most veniremen will admit to a disqualifying prejudice, the reliability of the others' protestations may be drawn into question." *Murphy*, 421 U.S., at 803. Perhaps because it had underestimated the public's antipathy toward Skilling, the District Court's 5-hour voir dire was manifestly insufficient to identify and remove biased jurors.

As an initial matter, important lines of inquiry were not pursued at all. The majority accepts, for instance, that "publicity about a codefendant's guilty plea calls for inquiry to guard against actual prejudice." Implying that the District Court undertook this inquiry, the majority states that "[o]nly two venire members recalled [Causey's] plea." In fact, the court asked very few prospective jurors any questions directed to their knowledge of or feelings about that event. Considering how much news the plea generated, many more than two venire members were likely aware of it. The lack of questioning, however, makes the prejudicial impact of the plea on those jurors impossible to assess.

The topics that the District Court did cover were addressed in cursory fashion. Most prospective jurors were asked just a few yes/no questions about their general exposure to media coverage and a handful of additional questions concerning any responses to the written questionnaire that suggested bias. In many instances, their answers were unenlightening. Yet the court rarely sought to draw them out with open-ended questions about their impressions of Enron or Skilling and showed limited patience for counsel's followup efforts.

These deficiencies in the form and content of the voir dire questions contributed to a deeper problem: The District Court failed to make a sufficiently critical assessment of prospective jurors' assurances of impartiality. Although the Court insists otherwise, the voir dire transcript indicates that the District Court essentially took jurors at their word when they promised to be fair. Indeed, the court declined to dismiss for cause any prospective juror who ultimately gave a clear assurance of impartiality, no matter how much equivocation preceded it.

Worse still, the District Court on a number of occasions accepted declarations of impartiality that were equivocal on their face. Prospective jurors who "hope[d]" they could presume innocence and did "not necessarily" think Skilling was guilty were permitted to remain in the pool. Juror 61, for instance, wrote of Lay on her questionnaire, "Shame on him." Asked by the court about this, she stated that, "innocent or guilty, he was at the helm" and "should have known what was going on at the company." The court then asked, "can you presume, as you start this trial, that Mr. Lay is innocent?" She responded, "I hope so, but you know. I don't know. I can't honestly answer that one way or the other." Eventually, however, Juror 61 answered "Yes" when the court asked if she would be able to acquit if she had "a reasonable doubt that the defendants are guilty." Challenging her for cause, defense counsel insisted that they had not received "a clear and unequivocal answer" about her ability to be fair. The court denied the challenge, stating, "You know, she tried."

3

The majority suggests that the jury's decision to acquit Skilling on nine relatively minor insider trading charges confirms its impartiality. This argument, however, mistakes partiality with bad faith or blind vindictiveness. Jurors who act in good faith and sincerely believe in their own fairness may nevertheless harbor disqualifying prejudices. Such jurors may well acquit where evidence is wholly lacking, while subconsciously resolving closer calls against the defendant rather than giving him the benefit of the doubt.

* * *

Taken together, the District Court's failure to cover certain vital subjects, its superficial coverage of other topics, and its uncritical acceptance of assurances of impartiality leave me doubtful that Skilling's jury was indeed free from the deep-seated animosity that pervaded the community at large. "[R]egardless of the heinousness of the crime charged, the apparent guilt of the offender[,] or the station in life which he occupies," our system of justice demands trials that are fair in both appearance and fact. *Irvin*, 366 U.S., at 722. Because I do not believe Skilling's trial met this standard, I would grant him relief.

NOTES AND QUESTIONS

1. Who has the better of the argument in *Skilling*, the majority or the dissent? Both sides recognize that the collapse of Enron had far-reaching effects in Houston, and that the financial pain and accompanying anger caused by the event were deeply felt. In such a case, how realistic is it to think that a jury can close its ears and consider only the evidence presented in court?

Part of the majority's reasoning was that the Skilling publicity was not like cases such as *Rideau* and Sheppard v. Maxwell, cases from an earlier age, which involved violent crimes. But even acknowledging the differences in circumstances, isn't it fair to say that in modern times it is *easier* for potential jurors to be exposed to prejudicial pretrial publicity than it was when radio, television, and newspapers were the only credible sources of information?

More generally, why are courts so reluctant to grant a change of venue in high-profile cases? The convenience of the testifying witnesses and the need to transport potentially huge amounts of documents and physical evidence is part of the explanation, but is administrative efficiency an adequate answer? If you were a federal prosecutor arguing against Skilling's motion to transfer, what interests might you identify as to why the case should stay in Houston?

2. Then again, isn't the majority correct that prejudicial pretrial publicity claims are inherently fact-intensive questions, and that deference to the trial judge should be at its peak? Can the dissent realistically conclude, based on its reading of a paper record, that despite the district judge's factual findings based on his observations, the jurors were not credible in their claims of being able to put their prior knowledge and feelings about the case aside?

3. How should the problem of prejudicial pretrial publicity be remedied? Two psychology professors have evaluated the available options, based on the results of numerous empirical studies. See Christina Studebaker & Steven Penrod, Pretrial Publicity: The Media, the Law, and Common Sense, 3 Psychol. Pub. Pol'y. & L. 428 (1997). These options include (1) granting a continuance, in the hope that publicity will dissipate over time; (2) conducting extended voir dire to weed out prospective jurors who may have been influenced by publicity; (3) admonishing the jury not to be influenced by publicity; (4) encouraging the presentation of evidence at trial to counteract any impressions created by publicity; (5) relying on the jury's deliberations to overcome the effects of publicity; (6) changing the venire (i.e., bringing in jurors from another jurisdiction where there is less publicity); and (7) changing the venue (i.e., holding the trial in another jurisdiction).

Some of the findings collected by Studebaker and Penrod include the following: With respect to voir dire, "jurors who claimed that they could disregard the pretrial publicity simply did not — despite their apparent belief that they could." Id., at 441. With respect to judicial admonitions, "[t]he pre-trial publicity instruction did not reduce the biasing effect of exposure to either the 'factual' or 'emotional' pretrial publicity." Id., at 443. With respect to jury deliberations, "existing research on deliberation effects in the pretrial publicity arena is more supportive of the accentuation theory — jury deliberation appears to strengthen, not reduce, bias." Id., at 444. Studebaker and Penrod conclude that these three particular methods (voir dire, judicial admonitions, and jury deliberations) are especially unlikely to succeed because they "are based on removing bias after it has been developed" — indeed, they "require jurors to disregard pretrial publicity immediately after attention has been brought to it." Id., at 445. More promising are the approaches that seek "to select jurors who were never biased to begin with," such as a change of venire or change of venue. Id.

C. Joinder and Severance

Part of the prosecutor's job when drafting the indictment is to decide what the potential trial will look like; in particular, she must decide (a) how many charges to bring against a defendant and (b) how many defendants to join in a single case. These questions raise joinder and severance issues.

In general, prosecutors prefer to resolve all related charges against all related defendants in a single trial. If the defendant stole a car in June, a car in July, and a car in August, the government is likely to seek a single three-count indictment, and thus resolve all three counts in one case. Similarly, if Marlo and Chris agree to sell drugs, the prosecution naturally would want to charge both with conspiracy and try the two together. Trials are expensive and time consuming, not only for the parties and court but also for witnesses and jurors. From an efficiency standpoint, presenting the full set of evidence once is obviously superior to holding multiple trials on similar issues.

Efficiency is the main reason for joinder, but there are others. A single case where evidence is presented on all parties and all counts may help paint a more complete picture for the jury, a picture that allows the jurors to better understand each defendant's conduct and intent when evidence on these points is revealed as part of a larger story. Jurors, who are unfamiliar with complex criminal transactions (one hopes), may have a hard time understanding the "relevant" evidence unless that evidence is placed in a broader context, much of which the law would label irrelevant if the matters were tried separately. In this respect, joint trials can increase the accuracy of the verdict.

There may also be some advantages to the defendant from joinder. The accused may prefer to have all three car theft charges resolved against him at one time rather than stand trial three times. Not only can this save the wear and tear of repeated proceedings and repeated lawyer fees, it also might prevent the prosecutor from getting multiple chances to strengthen her case from one trial to the next.

But more often, a defendant will prefer a separate trial, and in particular, will frequently seek a separate proceeding when he is joined with other defendants — that is, he will file a motion to "sever" the different counts or the other defendants. Multiple charges can create an unfavorable "halo effect" in the minds of the jurors, leading them to assume that in a ten-count indictment the defendant surely must be guilty of *something*. Multiple counts that involve overlapping evidence also can confuse a jury, perhaps making it unclear whether there was sufficient evidence on each element of each count. (Was the handgun used in all three car thefts, or just in one?) Or, a defendant charged with two counts may face a dilemma on the question whether to testify on his own behalf. Perhaps he is not guilty of the first car theft, and even has an alibi to present, but he has no defense to the other two counts. In a single trial, he can't testify as to the first count without exposing himself to devastating cross-examination on the others.

The potential difficulties for an individual defendant in a multiparty trial are also significant. Consider the following description:

> An accused who sits at the defense table with other suspects risks being found guilty by association, especially if his co-defendants are charged with more serious crimes. In a joint trial the jury will be exposed to "spillover evidence," which might consist not only of information about co-defendant's crimes (which is bad enough), but also evidence of defendant's own other bad acts, which now come to the jury's attention through the case against the co-defendants. The risk of juror confusion about which evidence applies against which suspect is also present, growing worse as the number of defendants increases. Co-defendants may present antagonistic defenses, or may make different decisions about whether to testify, making distinctions among the defendants stark. Co-defendants who take the stand are often sorely tempted to point the fingers at others, confronting a defendant with an additional layer of accusation he would not have faced had he been tried separately.

Andrew D. Leipold & Hossein A. Abbasi, The Impact of Joinder and Severance on Federal Criminal Cases: An Empirical Study, 59 Vand. L. Rev. 349, 357-358 (2006).

Federal Rule of Criminal Procedure 8 sets forth the circumstances under which the government may join charges and defendants in an indictment. Rule 14(a) then permits the court, either sua sponte or on motion of a party (almost always the defense) to move to sever.[3]

Rule 8. Joinder of Offenses and of Defendants

(a) *Joinder of Offenses*. The indictment or information may charge a defendant in separate counts with 2 or more offenses if the offenses charged — whether felonies or misdemeanors or both — are of the same or similar character, or are based on the same act or transaction, or are connected with or constitute parts of a common scheme or plan.

(b) *Joinder of Defendants*. The indictment or information may charge 2 or more defendants if they are alleged to have participated in the same act or transaction, or in the same series of acts or transactions, constituting an offense or offenses. The defendants may be charged in one or more counts together or separately. All defendants need not be charged in each count.

---

3. Federal Rule 13 also addresses joinder. It provides: "The court may order that separate cases be tried together as though brought in a single indictment or information if all offenses and all defendants could have been joined in a single indictment or information." This simply allows the consolidation of cases that were originally filed separately. For the court to join cases under Rule 13, however, it first must determine that they could have properly been joined under Rule 8. Rule 13 is thus a timing provision, one that adds nothing to the substance of joinder or severance analysis.

Rule 14. Relief from Prejudicial Joinder

(a) *Relief.* If the joinder of offenses or defendants in an indictment, an information, or a consolidation for trial appears to prejudice a defendant or the government,
the court may order separate trials of counts, sever the defendants' trials, or provide
any other relief that justice requires. . . .

A defendant who objects to a consolidated trial thus has two avenues of attack.
Initially he can allege that the charges or defendants are not properly joined under
Rule 8; that is, he can claim there was "misjoinder." In addition, or in the alternative, he can argue that even if the charges are properly joined, the court should sever
the charges or defendants because of the risk of unfair prejudice. The courts' interpretation of these rules and standards follows.

UNITED STATES v. HAWKINS

United States Court of Appeals for the Fourth Circuit
589 F.3d 694 (2009)

AGEE, Circuit Judge:
Collin Hawkins was indicted on separate counts related to a carjacking and a subsequent arrest as a felon in possession of a firearm. Prior to trial, Hawkins timely
moved the court to sever the carjacking counts from the felon in possession charge
on the grounds of improper joinder. The district court denied the motion and
Hawkins was found guilty by a jury on all counts. For the reasons that follow, we
affirm the judgment of the district court, in part, and vacate the judgment, in part.

I.

Reuben King ("King") testified that on the evening of November 22, 2006, he was
employed as a driver for Sedan Service in Baltimore, Maryland. That night, King
received a phone call from a regular customer he knew as Warren, asking to be
picked up at an apartment complex parking lot. When King arrived three persons
entered his cab: Warren, the appellant Hawkins, and an unidentified female. At
trial, King testified that he instantly recognized Hawkins, who sat next to him on the
cab's front seat, from casual contact in the neighborhood over many years.

Warren instructed King that he needed to make three stops that night. During
the first two stops, King explained that Warren got out of the car, talked to unidentified individuals for roughly ten to fifteen minutes, returned to the car, and then
told King the intersection for the next stop. During the last stop, both Warren and
Hawkins got out of the car for about ten or fifteen minutes, and then returned. Warren then instructed King to return to the apartment complex parking lot.

Once back in the parking lot King turned on the overhead dome light to calculate the fare and saw Hawkins holding a .357 caliber revolver only a few inches from
his head, while Warren held a shotgun positioned to the back of King's head.
According to King, Warren stated that if King moved, Warren would shoot him.
King claimed that Hawkins then took two cell phones and roughly $400 in cash from
him, and pushed King out of the driver's side door. Hawkins then pushed King in
the direction of the trunk, during which time Hawkins emptied the remainder of
King's pockets while Warren kept the shotgun pointed at King. Once they reached

the trunk area, King testified that Hawkins told King to kneel down and keep his hands up. According to King, after he complied with the instruction, Hawkins then stated, "I'm not going to shoot you 'cause I know you."

King claimed he then heard footsteps going toward the car, the car doors closing, and the car pulling off. King testified that he then ran until he found police officers to whom he reported the carjacking.

On December 9, 2006, Baltimore City police officers were investigating an unrelated incident in the same area of Baltimore, which they had reason to believe involved Hawkins. Acting on information that Hawkins would be arriving at a convenience store officers watched Hawkins approach the entrance of the store and tug at his waistband, indicating that he might be armed.

Officers entered the store and ordered Hawkins to the ground, but he refused to comply and started to slide his right hand up under his waistband. This caused officers to order Hawkins to keep his hands where they could be seen, but Hawkins refused to comply until he was physically subdued. A 9 millimeter pistol was retrieved from Hawkins' waistband when he was arrested.

On March 7, 2007, a federal grand jury in the District of Maryland indicted Hawkins on four counts. Count I alleged a carjacking based on the robbery of King's vehicle, in violation of 18 U.S.C. §2119 (2000). Count II alleged that Hawkins "did knowingly possess and brandish a firearm in furtherance of a crime of violence," the carjacking, in violation of 18 U.S.C. §924(c)(1)(A)(ii). Count III alleged that Hawkins, "having been convicted of a crime punishable by imprisonment for a term exceeding one year, did knowingly and unlawfully possess a loaded firearm, to wit: a Bersa model Thunder 9 mm pistol" in violation of 18 U.S.C. §922(g)(1), the gun seized when he was arrested. Count IV alleged another felon in possession of a firearm charge, relating to a shotgun seized during a search of Hawkins' residence.

Prior to trial, Hawkins moved to sever Counts I and II (collectively the "carjacking counts") from Counts III and IV. Hawkins contended that Counts III and IV were improperly joined to Counts I and II under Federal Rule of Criminal Procedure 8(a). In the alternative, Hawkins argued severance was appropriate under Rule 14 because he "would be significantly prejudiced by a single trial" because "the jury may well conclude that Hawkins is guilty of one firearm count and then find him guilty of the others because of his criminal disposition." The district court denied Hawkins' motion because it could "discern no reason why a jury will not be able fairly and objectively to evaluate the evidence."

The Government elected not to proceed on Count IV and trial was held only on Counts I, II, and III. Hawkins pled not guilty to all three counts. However, as to Count III, Hawkins conceded his prior felony conviction and his possession of the 9 millimeter handgun at the time of his arrest both to the court prior to opening statements and again to the jury during opening statements.

Hawkins testified in his own defense and vigorously denied involvement in the carjacking. His counsel actively cross-examined King and elicited various inconsistencies from his testimony on direct examination.

During closing argument, counsel for the Government mentioned that the carjacking was not the first time Hawkins had committed a crime against a person he knew, stating, "You heard yesterday the defendant admitted to police that he stole the 9 millimeter he was caught with on December 9th from his cousin." While the Government acknowledged that Hawkins had conceded his guilt to the felon-in-possession charge, it argued to the jury that it was a tactical admission:

U.S. ATTORNEY: Now, why would the defendant rob someone he knew? Well, as I indicated, this was not the first time he did that. He robbed, stole a gun from [his] cousin around December 9th.

These statements prompted Hawkins to move for a mistrial maintaining that the Government was attempting to persuade the jury to conclude Hawkins committed the carjacking based on the fact that he robbed his own cousin. The district court denied the motion.

The jury found Hawkins guilty on all three counts. The district court sentenced Hawkins to 180 months for Count I, 120 months for Count II, and 120 months for Count III, for an aggregate term of incarceration of 360 months followed by three years of supervised release.

II.

Hawkins raises two primary issues on appeal. First, he contends that the district court erred in denying his motion to sever Counts I and II from Count III because Count III was improperly joined with Counts I and II under Rule 8. Alternatively, Hawkins argues that if all three counts were properly joined for a single trial, the district court abused its discretion in denying his motion to sever under Rule 14 because the joinder of Count III with Counts I and II was unduly prejudicial.

III.

Whether charges are properly joined in an indictment is a question of law that we review de novo. "If the initial joinder was not proper, however, we review this nonconstitutional error for harmlessness, and reverse *unless* the misjoinder resulted in no 'actual prejudice' to the defendant [ ] 'because it had [no] substantial and injurious effect or influence in determining the jury's verdict.'" United States v. Mackins, 315 F.3d 399, 412 (4th Cir. 2003). If misjoinder is found, the Government bears the burden of demonstrating that any error resulting from the misjoinder was harmless.

A.

Federal Rule of Criminal Procedure 8(a) provides:

Joinder of Offenses. The indictment or information may charge a defendant in separate counts with 2 or more offenses if the offenses charged — whether felonies or misdemeanors or both — are of the same or similar character, or are based on the same act or transaction, or are connected with or constitute parts of a common scheme or plan.

Rule 8(a) permits "very broad joinder," *Mackins*, 315 F.3d at 412, "because the prospect of duplicating witness testimony, impaneling additional jurors, and wasting limited judicial resources suggests that related offenses should be tried in a single proceeding." United States v. Mir, 525 F.3d 351, 357 (4th Cir. 2008). Thus, joinder is the "rule rather than the exception," United States v. Armstrong, 621 F.2d 951, 954 (9th Cir. 1980), "because of the efficiency in trying the defendant on related counts in the same trial." [U.S. v. Cardwell, 433 F.3d 378, 385 (4th Cir. 2005).]

The requirements of Rule 8(a), however, "are not infinitely elastic," *Mackins*, 315 F.3d at 412, "and so 'cannot be stretched to cover offenses . . . which are discrete and dissimilar.'" Id. Joinder of unrelated charges "create[s] the possibility that a defendant will be convicted based on considerations other than the facts of the charged offense." *Cardwell*, 433 F.3d at 385.

In this case, the Government contends that the carjacking counts and possession of a firearm by a felon (Count III) are all offenses of the "same or similar character." The Government did not argue on brief, nor provide a rationale at oral argument, that joinder was proper either because the counts "are based on the same act" or "constitute parts of a common scheme or plan." . . . Thus joinder rises and falls on whether Counts I and II are of a "same or similar character" to Count III.

Joinder of offenses that "are based on the same act or transaction or on two or more acts or transactions connected together or constituting parts of a common scheme or plan" presents the opportunity to submit evidence of one offense that ordinarily would be admissible at a separate trial for the other. United States v. Foutz, 540 F.2d 733, 737 (4th Cir. 1976). However, when offenses are joined based on their same or similar character, "admissibility at separate trials is not so clear." [Id.]

Hawkins admits that Counts I and II are properly joined because "they both related to the same carjacking that occurred on November 22, 200[6]." However, Hawkins argues that Count III "was entirely unrelated" to Counts I and II, in part because the felon-in-possession count "arose out of a distinct incident unrelated to the carjacking" and occurred seventeen days later. Hawkins emphasizes that there is no link between the carjacking counts and Count III because the handgun the police recovered from Hawkins' person on December 9 was *not* the same gun used in the carjacking.

The Government contends that all three counts were properly joined as offenses of the "same or similar character" for two reasons: first, because "all three were fire-arms offenses" and second, because "all these events occurred within a three-week period." In support of its argument, the government cites, inter alia, United States v. Cole, 857 F.2d 971 (4th Cir. 1988), and United States v. Rousseau, 257 F.3d 925 (9th Cir. 2001). These decisions, however, provide no help to the Government in this case.

In *Cole*, we held proper the joinder of various drug charges stemming from a large-scale cocaine distribution ring with the defendant's alien smuggling charges where the aliens smuggled into the country began to sell cocaine for his distribution ring after their arrival. We stated in *Cole* that "both the allegations in the indictment and the proof at trial were more than adequate to establish the connection between the drug conspiracy and the alien smuggling charges." . . . The Government alleges that this "analogous" case supports its argument because in *Cole*, we found "some connection" between the counts, and in balancing the possible prejudice in trying the counts together against the possible prejudice to the defendants, we found that the balance "tilted in favor of a joint trial."

However, the Government's argument fails to appreciate the extent of the connection we found in *Cole*. In *Cole*, the smuggled aliens worked in the drug distribution ring once they arrived in America. In effect, drug profits subsidized the illegal smuggling of aliens who, in turn, went to work in the drug conspiracy to generate further drug profits for the defendants. Indeed, there existed a logical and intimate connection between the offenses which made joinder proper.

[I]n the case at bar, the Government has proffered no evidence demonstrating a logical and close connection between the alleged carjacking and possession of a .357 caliber revolver on November 22, and Hawkins' possession of a 9 millimeter pistol on December 9.

Similarly, the Government's reliance on *Rousseau* is misplaced. In *Rousseau*, the defendant was charged with two counts of possession of a firearm by a convicted felon, although each arrest related to a different firearm. Prior to trial, Rousseau moved to sever the two felon-in-possession counts, but the court denied the motion. Based only upon its review of the face of the indictment, the Ninth Circuit found that both "incidents involved firearms charges," specifically felon-in-possession charges. Thus, the two offenses were of a "same or similar character."

The circumstances in *Rousseau* are easily distinguishable from the circumstances in the present case. In *Rousseau*, the defendant was charged with two counts of violating the *same* statute, 18 U.S.C. §922(g)(1), although the offenses occurred nearly six and a half months apart and the guns were different. But it is an unremarkable example of offenses of the "same or similar character" when the defendant is charged only with multiple violations of the same statute. See *Acker*, 52 F.3d at 514 ("Trial courts routinely allow joinder of different bank robbery counts against a single defendant in the same indictment.").

In the present case, however, Hawkins was charged with three *different* offenses: carjacking and possession of a firearm in furtherance of a crime of violence, and, about three weeks later, being a felon in possession of a different firearm. We perceive no similarity in the connection between these three *different* counts and the counts on the *same* offense found appropriate for joinder by the Ninth Circuit in *Rousseau*.

Moreover, the Government's reliance on the fact that all three offenses occurred during a three-week period will not sustain joinder, as we have held consistently that a mere temporal relationship is not sufficient to establish the propriety of joinder.

Accordingly, we conclude that the district court erred in allowing joinder of Counts I and II with Count III because the charges are not of a same or similar character. We therefore turn to the question of whether this error requires reversal.

B.

An error involving misjoinder "'affects substantial rights' and requires reversal *only* if the misjoinder results in actual prejudice because it 'had substantial and injurious effect or influence in determining the jury's verdict.'" United States v. Lane, 474 U.S. 438, 449 (1986). In assessing whether a misjoinder error results in actual prejudice, we are guided by the *Lane* Court's indicia of harmlessness:

> (1) whether the evidence of guilt was overwhelming and the concomitant effect of any improperly admitted evidence on the jury's verdict; (2) the steps taken to mitigate the effects of the error; and (3) the extent to which the improperly admitted evidence as to the misjoined counts would have been admissible at trial on the other counts.

Hawkins argues that if there had been separate trials, no evidence presented during a trial on Count III would have been admissible in the trial on Counts I and II, and vice versa. In particular, Hawkins avers that the Government's ability to present evidence on the unrelated charge of being a felon in possession to the same jury hearing the carjacking case "increase[d] the likelihood that . . . Hawkins would be convicted" of all three charges. Hawkins asserts that a jury hearing only Counts I and II would not hear evidence that Hawkins possessed a gun on December 9, 2006, that he had a prior felony conviction, that he sold drugs to support himself, and finally, that he had stolen the 9 millimeter gun from his cousin.

The Government responds that Hawkins suffered no undue prejudice from misjoinder because there was overwhelming evidence of Hawkins' guilt on each count, and because the evidence relating to Count III and the carjacking counts would have been mutually admissible under Rule 404(b). Furthermore, the Government contends "the district court took steps to eliminate any spillover effect as a result of the joinder." Br. of Appellee at 17.

The district court did provide a limiting instruction to the jury in its attempt to mitigate the effects of the joinder of all three counts. However, we conclude that, based on the other two indicia of harmlessness provided in *Lane*, the error in misjoinder affected Hawkins' substantial rights, and, furthermore, "had substantial and injurious effect or influence in determining the jury's verdict."

Although the Government argues to the contrary, we do not find that all of the evidence on Count III and that on Counts I and II would have been mutually admissible under Rule 404(b) if Hawkins had enjoyed the benefit of separate trials. Much of the evidence presented to the jury on Count III would have been only marginally relevant, if relevant at all, to Counts I and II. There was simply nothing about Hawkins being in possession of a different firearm in December that was related to any of the elements of the carjacking counts.

Additionally, under a proper balancing analysis pursuant to Federal Rules of Evidence 403 and 404(b), the probative value of the evidence would have been substantially outweighed by the danger of unfair prejudice to Hawkins. . . . Our point is illustrated by the district court's statement from the bench denying Hawkins' motion to exclude his admission that he had stolen the 9 millimeter pistol from his cousin:

> COURT: This is very interesting because it clearly suggests that if he's willing to steal his cousin's gun, he's willing to steal anything from anybody. If he's willing to steal his cousin's gun, why wouldn't he be willing to steal money? His cousin's gun, why wouldn't he be willing [to] steal a car or cash or cell phones from some guy he just knows casually from the neighborhood?

In response, Hawkins' attorney stated:

> DEFENSE COUNSEL: That's exactly why we think it's not admissible, Your Honor. You're sort of making my point. If he's willing to steal from his cousin, you're telling the jury, look, what a bad guy he is.

This exchange reflects how unrelated bad conduct (the felon-in-possession of a gun) offered in evidence on another charge (carjacking) to prove the defendant's general propensity to commit crimes can have a "substantial and injurious effect or influence in determining the jury's verdict," as with Counts I and II in the case at bar.

Additionally, . . . we are not persuaded that the evidence against Hawkins related to the carjacking counts was overwhelming. . . . The only evidence against Hawkins at trial on the carjacking counts was the testimony of the lone witness to the carjacking, King. Throughout the trial, counsel for Hawkins brought out multiple inconsistencies prevalent in King's story about the carjacking. . . . The Government produced no further corroborating evidence of Hawkins' guilt on that charge. The .357 caliber revolver and shotgun allegedly used in the carjacking were never found. Hawkins' accomplices, Warren and the unidentified female, were also never found.

While the evidence against Hawkins as to Count III was overwhelming, the Government's case against Hawkins on Counts I and II was not overwhelming and "it is possible that the jury found him guilty of that crime under the rationale that with so much smoke there must be fire." *Foutz*, 540 F.2d at 739. Had the three offenses not been joined for trial, Count Ill's prejudicial evidence would not have reached the jury, and Hawkins might well have been acquitted of Counts I and II.

IV.

For the foregoing reasons, we affirm Hawkins' conviction on Count III as a convicted felon in possession of a firearm, but vacate his sentence on that count as it was determined, in part, based on his convictions under Counts I and II. We vacate Hawkins' convictions under Counts I and II. We remand this case to the district court for retrial on Counts I and II and for resentencing on Count III.

[The opinion by Judge Motz, concurring in the judgment, is omitted.]

NOTES AND QUESTIONS

1. As *Hawkins* shows, one critical question that courts ask when faced with a severance request is the "cross admissibility" of evidence. If the evidence that would be presented on crime number three — here, the illegal gun possession at the convenience store — would be admissible for some reason in a separate trial on the first two crimes (the carjacking counts), then courts routinely conclude that there is no prejudice to the joinder, because the jury would hear the harmful evidence anyway.

Notice, however, that the opposite may not be true. Simply because evidence concerning count three (or concerning a codefendant) would be inadmissible in a separate trial does not itself compel severance. Many courts find that even if a jury is exposed to harmful evidence about other counts or other defendants, a joint trial is permitted if the evidence is simple and distinct enough that the jury can be trusted to keep straight which evidence relates to which counts or defendants. Moreover, judges put great faith in their own ability to instruct the jury on the proper and improper use of the evidence, and in jurors' ability to follow these instructions. See, e.g., U.S. v. Lazarenko, 564 F.3d 1026, 1043 (9th Cir. 2009) ("[I]n assessing the prejudice to a defendant from the 'spillover' of incriminating evidence, the primary consideration is whether the jury can reasonably be expected to compartmentalize the evidence as it relates to separate defendants, in view of its volume and the limited admissibility of some of the evidence. The trial court's instructions to the jury are a critical factor in this assessment" (internal quotation marks and citations omitted).). *Hawkins* is one of the relatively rare cases where, despite the trial court's limiting instructions, the appeals court found that the evidence on the misjoined count would not have been admissible in the carjacking case *and* that the jury might have been influenced by the spillover.

Is it realistic to believe that jurors segregate the evidence in this way during their deliberations? Or is Justice Jackson correct when he observed that in a joint conspiracy trial, "[t]here generally will be evidence of wrongdoing by somebody. It is difficult for the [defendant] to make his own case stand on its own merits in the minds of jurors who are ready to believe that birds of a feather are flocked together." *Krulewitch v. United States*, 336 U.S. 440, 454 (1949) (Jackson, J. concurring)?

2. The procedural posture of a joinder challenge matters a great deal. If the defendant shows *prior* to trial that the counts or defendants are not properly joined — and just as importantly, if the district judge finds that Rule 8 is not satisfied — the case should be severed, with no finding of prejudice required. But once the trial is held and the defendant is challenging the joinder on appeal, the appellate court will look for both a violation of Rule 8 and a showing of prejudice, as *Hawkins* shows. And while technically the prejudice showing for misjoinder (where the prosecution has the burden of persuasion) is different than the prejudice a defendant would have to show when claiming that the trial court erroneously failed to sever under Rule 14, in practice the inquiries are very similar.

3. Note that Rule 8 focuses on whether the criminal transactions at issue were "similar" (if the issue is joinder of offenses under 8(a)) or "the same" (joinder of defendants under 8(b)). Is that the right focus? Imagine a case in which three defendants — X, Y, and Z — are charged with robbery of a convenience store and conspiracy to commit robbery. The evidence against Y and Z is very strong; the evidence against X is shaky. And Y and Z are alleged to have actually robbed the store. X, at most, drove the car to and from the crime scene. There is no doubt that X, Y, and Z satisfy the "same act or transaction" test of Rule 8(b). Does X nevertheless have a good argument that joinder is improper? Does that argument say anything about how to read Rule 14? Consider the following case.

ZAFIRO v. UNITED STATES

Certiorari to the United States Court of Appeals for the Seventh Circuit
506 U.S. 534 (1993)

JUSTICE O'CONNOR delivered the opinion of the Court.

Rule 8(b) of the Federal Rules of Criminal Procedure provides that defendants may be charged together "if they are alleged to have participated in the same act or transaction or in the same series of acts or transactions constituting an offense or offenses." Rule 14 of the Rules, in turn, permits a district court to grant a severance of defendants if "it appears that a defendant or the government is prejudiced by a joinder."[4] In this case, we consider whether Rule 14 requires severance as a matter of law when codefendants present "mutually antagonistic defenses."

---

4. *Zafiro* was decided under an earlier version of Rules 8 and 14, but the differences in wording from the current rules version are purely stylistic, and have no effect on the substance of the analysis. The following is the text of Rule 14 that was in effect when *Zafiro* was decided:

Rule 14. Relief from Prejudicial Joinder

If it appears that a defendant or the government is prejudiced by a joinder of offenses or of defendants in an indictment or information or by such joinder for trial together, the court may order an election or separate trials of counts, grant a severance of defendants or provide whatever other relief justice requires. In ruling on a motion by a defendant for severance the court may order the attorney for the government to deliver to the court for inspection in camera any state-

I

Gloria Zafiro, Jose Martinez, Salvador Garcia, and Alfonso Soto were accused of distributing illegal drugs in the Chicago area, operating primarily out of Soto's bungalow in Chicago and Zafiro's apartment in Cicero, a nearby suburb. One day, government agents observed Garcia and Soto place a large box in Soto's car and drive from Soto's bungalow to Zafiro's apartment. The agents followed the two as they carried the box up the stairs. When the agents identified themselves, Garcia and Soto dropped the box and ran into the apartment. The agents entered the apartment in pursuit and found the four petitioners in the living room. The dropped box contained 55 pounds of cocaine. After obtaining a search warrant for the apartment, agents found approximately 16 pounds of cocaine, 25 grams of heroin, and 4 pounds of marijuana inside a suitcase in a closet. Next to the suitcase was a sack containing $22,960 in cash. Police officers also discovered 7 pounds of cocaine in a car parked in Soto's garage.

The four petitioners were indicted and brought to trial together. At various points during the proceeding, Garcia and Soto moved for severance, arguing that their defenses were mutually antagonistic. Soto testified that he knew nothing about the drug conspiracy. He claimed that Garcia had asked him for a box, which he gave Garcia, and that he (Soto) did not know its contents until they were arrested. Garcia did not testify, but his lawyer argued that Garcia was innocent: The box belonged to Soto and Garcia was ignorant of its contents.

Zafiro and Martinez also repeatedly moved for severance on the ground that their defenses were mutually antagonistic. Zafiro testified that she was merely Martinez's girlfriend and knew nothing of the conspiracy. She claimed that Martinez stayed in her apartment occasionally, kept some clothes there, and gave her small amounts of money. Although she allowed Martinez to store a suitcase in her closet, she testified, she had no idea that the suitcase contained illegal drugs. Like Garcia, Martinez did not testify. But his lawyer argued that Martinez was only visiting his girlfriend and had no idea that she was involved in distributing drugs.

The District Court denied the motions for severance. The jury convicted all four petitioners of conspiring to possess cocaine, heroin, and marijuana with the intent to distribute. 21 U.S.C. §846. In addition, Garcia and Soto were convicted of possessing cocaine with the intent to distribute, §841(a)(1), and Martinez was convicted of possessing cocaine, heroin, and marijuana with the intent to distribute, ibid.

Petitioners appealed their convictions. Garcia, Soto, and Martinez claimed that the District Court abused its discretion in denying their motions to sever. (Zafiro did not appeal the denial of her severance motion, and thus, her claim is not properly before this Court.) . . . Noting that "mutual antagonism . . . and other . . . characterizations of the effort of one defendant to shift the blame from himself to a codefendant neither control nor illuminate the question of severance," 945 F.2d at 886, the Court of Appeals found that the defendants had not suffered prejudice and affirmed the District Court's denial of severance. We granted the petition for certiorari, and now affirm the judgment of the Court of Appeals.

---

ments or confessions made by the defendants which the government intends to introduce in evidence at the trial. — EDS.

II

. . . In interpreting Rule 14, the Courts of Appeals frequently have expressed the view that "mutually antagonistic" or "irreconcilable" defenses may be so prejudicial in some circumstances as to mandate severance. See, e.g., United States v. Benton, 852 F.2d 1456, 1469 (CA6 1988); United States v. Smith, 788 F.2d 663, 668 (CA10 1986); United States v. Magdaniel-Mora, 746 F.2d 715, 718 (CA11 1984); United States v. Berkowitz, 662 F.2d 1127, 1133-1134 (CA5 1981); United States v. Halde-man, 559 F.2d 31, 71-72 (CADC 1976). Notwithstanding such assertions, the courts have reversed relatively few convictions for failure to grant a severance on grounds of mutually antagonistic or irreconcilable defenses. The low rate of reversal may reflect the inability of defendants to prove a risk of prejudice in most cases involving conflicting defenses.

Nevertheless, petitioners urge us to adopt a bright-line rule, mandating sever-ance whenever codefendants have conflicting defenses. We decline to do so. Mutu-ally antagonistic defenses are not prejudicial per se. Moreover, Rule 14 does not require severance even if prejudice is shown; rather, it leaves the tailoring of the relief to be granted, if any, to the district court's sound discretion. See, e.g., United States v. Lane, 474 U.S. 438, 449 (1986).

We believe that, when defendants properly have been joined under Rule 8(b), a district court should grant a severance under Rule 14 only if there is a serious risk that a joint trial would compromise a specific trial right of one of the defendants, or prevent the jury from making a reliable judgment about guilt or innocence. Such a risk might occur when evidence that the jury should not consider against a defen-dant and that would not be admissible if a defendant were tried alone is admitted against a codefendant. For example, evidence of a codefendant's wrongdoing in some circumstances erroneously could lead a jury to conclude that a defendant was guilty. When many defendants are tried together in a complex case and they have markedly different degrees of culpability, this risk of prejudice is heightened. See Kotteakos v. United States, 328 U.S. 750, 774-775 (1946). Evidence that is probative of a defendant's guilt but technically admissible only against a codefendant also might present a risk of prejudice. See Bruton v. United States, 391 U.S. 123 (1968). Conversely, a defendant might suffer prejudice if essential exculpatory evidence that would be available to a defendant tried alone were unavailable in a joint trial. The risk of prejudice will vary with the facts in each case, and district courts may find prejudice in situations not discussed here. When the risk of prejudice is high, a dis-trict court is more likely to determine that separate trials are necessary, but . . . less drastic measures, such as limiting instructions, often will suffice to cure any risk of prejudice.

Turning to the facts of this case, we note that petitioners do not articulate any spe-cific instances of prejudice. Instead they contend that the very nature of their defenses, without more, prejudiced them. Their theory is that when two defendants both claim they are innocent and each accuses the other of the crime, a jury will con-clude (1) that both defendants are lying and convict them both on that basis, or (2) that at least one of the two must be guilty without regard to whether the Government has proved its case beyond a reasonable doubt.

As to the first contention, it is well settled that defendants are not entitled to sev-erance merely because they may have a better chance of acquittal in separate trials. Rules 8(b) and 14 are designed "to promote economy and efficiency and to avoid a multiplicity of trials, [so long as] these objectives can be achieved without substantial prejudice to the right of the defendants to a fair trial." *Bruton*, 391 U.S. at 131, n. 6. . . . [A] fair trial does not include the right to exclude relevant and competent evidence. A defendant normally would not be entitled to exclude the testimony of a former codefendant if the district court did sever their trials, and we see no reason why relevant and competent testimony would be prejudicial merely because the witness is also a codefendant.

As to the second contention, the short answer is that petitioners' scenario simply did not occur here. The Government argued that all four petitioners were guilty and offered sufficient evidence as to all four petitioners; the jury in turn found all four petitioners guilty of various offenses. Moreover, even if there were some risk of prejudice, here it is of the type that can be cured with proper instructions, and "juries are presumed to follow their instructions." Richardson [v. Marsh, 481 U.S. 200, 211 (1987)]. The District Court properly instructed the jury that the Government had "the burden of proving beyond a reasonable doubt" that each defendant committed the crimes with which he or she was charged. The court then instructed the jury that it must "give separate consideration to each individual defendant and to each separate charge against him. Each defendant is entitled to have his or her case determined from his or her own conduct and from the evidence [that] may be applicable to him or to her." In addition, the District Court admonished the jury that opening and closing arguments are not evidence and that it should draw no inferences from a defendant's exercise of the right to silence. These instructions sufficed to cure any possibility of prejudice.

Rule 14 leaves the determination of risk of prejudice and any remedy that may be necessary to the sound discretion of the district courts. Because petitioners have not shown that their joint trial subjected them to any legally cognizable prejudice, we conclude that the District Court did not abuse its discretion in denying petitioners' motions to sever. The judgment of the Court of Appeals is affirmed.

[The opinion of Justice Stevens, concurring in the judgment, is omitted.]

NOTES AND QUESTIONS

1. *Zafiro* presents a common claim by defendants seeking to sever their trials, namely, that they have inconsistent and even antagonistic defenses. The Court clearly rejects the argument that antagonistic defenses are per se grounds for reversal, but goes on to describe the types of cases where severance would be proper: where "there is a serious risk that a joint trial would compromise a specific trial right of one of the defendants, or prevent the jury from making a reliable judgment about guilt or innocence."

Although the Court does not go into detail about the "specific trial right[s]" that are to be protected by severance, its citation to Bruton v. United States, 391 U.S. 123 (1968) is instructive. In a line of cases beginning with *Bruton*, the Court has said that a pretrial confession by a nontestifying codefendant (call him "A") cannot be admitted against A in a joint trial if the confession implicates another defendant ("B") standing trial in the same case. If the prosecutor wants to use A's confession against A at trial and A does not take the stand, the government generally must either redact the confession so it does not implicate B or must sever the cases. The *Bruton* doctrine is discussed in more detail in the material on the Confrontation Clause in Chapter 14.C.

2. One remarkable feature of joinder and severance decisions is the explicit tradeoff that courts make between fairness to the accused and efficiency of the trial process. This tradeoff is pervasive in the criminal system, of course, but courts are rarely as candid about it as they are when expressing a preference for joint trials. Thus, courts have said that Rule 8(a) "necessarily recognizes the adverse effect on the defendant by a joinder of counts, but considers this to be outweighed by gains in trial economy when one of the criteria of the rule are met," U.S. v. Werner, 620 F.2d 922, 929 (2d Cir. 1980), or that when charges or defendants are joined, "some prejudice almost necessarily results," but that "Rule 8(a) permits the first sort of prejudice and Rule 8(b) the second." Cupo v. United States, 359 F.2d 990, 993 (D.C. Cir. 1966). As a result, most courts seem to agree with Judge Richard Posner's statement: "The danger of prejudice to the least guilty, or perhaps prejudice to all from the sheer confusion of a multidefendant trial, is in all but the most unusual circumstances considered outweighed by the economies of a single trial in which all facets of the crime can be explored once and for all." U.S. v. Velasquez, 772 F.2d 1348 (7th Cir. 1985).

For the classic argument that this balance is wrong, see Robert O. Dawson, Joint Trials of Defendants in Criminal Cases: An Analysis of Efficiencies and Prejudices, 77 Mich. L. Rev. 1379 (1979):

> One supposed efficiency of joinder is a saving of the prosecutor's time because of the substantial overlap of evidence against the different defendants. But whether the trial is joint or individual affects only a small portion of the prosecutor's investment of time. It does not affect police investigation, which is usually completed before the prosecutor decides on charging and joinder. It should not affect plea bargaining — it is no more efficient for the prosecutor to plea bargain in a joined case than in one that has been severed. . . . It need not affect pretrial hearings, which may be held jointly, even when the trials are separate. It probably does not even make a substantial difference in the time the prosecutor spends preparing for trial. Whether trials are joint or separate, the prosecutor must review the evidentiary file and interview the witnesses. If separate trials are held, the prosecutor must review the file again, but would surely not need as much time as he would to prepare the case.
>
> A second presumed efficiency of joint trials is that they are more convenient for witnesses. In fact, however, the effect of joint trials on witnesses varies greatly from case to case and depends in part on whether the witness is a civilian or a professional. To involve lay witnesses in the prosecution of a case certainly forces real burdens upon them. They must leave work or home to testify, and an important witness may be required to remain at the courthouse throughout the trial. If the witness is a child or the victim of an alleged sex offense, we do not want him to repeat the trauma of testifying without excellent reasons. Most witnesses in criminal trials, however, are not civilians but professionals. The burden of presenting witnesses lies upon the government, whose witnesses are usually police officers, laboratory employees, prosecution investigators, and others whose jobs include testifying in court. While time away from the patrol beat or the laboratory is time away from important work, professional witnesses suffer little personal inconvenience or expense by testifying more than once. . . .
>
> Furthermore, the parties can protect witnesses from multiple appearances by stipulating necessary but undisputed noncritical testimony. . . . Under appropriate circumstances, the trial court could even condition severance on stipulations of such testimony.

A third justification alleged for joint trials is that they conserve limited judicial resources. . . . But joint trials do not necessarily save judicial energy. They are far more difficult to schedule than individual trials. . . . In addition, once begun, joint trials are more complicated to conduct and take longer to complete than individual trials.

Id., at 1383-1386. Dawson went on to note that jury selection, the order of presentation of witnesses, and the adjudication of evidentiary objections are all much more difficult and complicated enterprises in joint trials than in individual trials.

3. How serious is the prejudicial effect of joinder? One study looked at nearly 20,000 federal criminal trials over a five-year period and tried to measure the effect of joinder on the outcome. After controlling for a variety of variables — jury trial v. bench trial, type and seriousness of case, appointed or retained lawyer, and geographic location of the trial — the study reached the following conclusions: (a) Defendants who face more than one count at trial are about 10 percent more likely to be convicted of the most serious charge than defendants who stand trial on a single count; and (b) *in the aggregate*, joint trials have no impact on the outcome of cases. A defendant tried alone was just as likely to be convicted of the most serious charge as a defendant who stood trial with others. This latter finding was somewhat surprising, as it is frequently assumed that joinder of defendants creates a higher risk of prejudice than the joinder of counts, but the data show otherwise. The study recognizes, however, that the lack of demonstrated effect from joined defendants may mask an important effect in individual cases — it may be that in a trial with several defendants, the more guilty parties are worse off because of the joinder, while the relatively less guilty parties get a benefit from being charged with more culpable parties. Over the run of cases, this could result in a net effect of zero, without undermining the conventional wisdom that joint trials can have a prejudicial effect, at least on some defendants. See Leipold & Abbasi, supra, 59 Vand. L. Rev., at 383-384.

Chapter 12

Discovery and Disclosure

The discovery and disclosure rules that regulate a party's access to information about the other side's case are of great importance to the overall fairness of the criminal process and its ability to generate accurate verdicts:

> Information is what trials are about. Trials are not about law. Disputes may arise on questions of law, trial judges may be called upon to make some dicey initial calls on legal issues, but the heart of the trial is the determination of who did what to whom and in what frame of mind. . . .
>
> So, understandably, at the trial stage, the parties are vitally interested in the raw factual data that can be produced in court.

H. Richard Uviller, The Tilted Playing Field 73 (1999). Access to information influences not only the criminal trial and the manner in which it unfolds, but also the plea bargaining process that may ultimately lead to a negotiated settlement.

None of this is controversial. But just because there is widespread agreement on the importance of criminal discovery rules does not mean that there is comparable agreement on the appropriateness of any given discovery regime. Indeed, historically and today, the rules governing the exchange of information by parties in criminal cases in the United States have sparked considerable debate.

Denying a defense motion to inspect grand jury minutes (at a time when discovery was all but unheard of in criminal cases), Judge Learned Hand articulated one view of criminal discovery grounded in the prosecution's heavy burden at trial:

> Under our criminal procedure, the accused has every advantage. While the prosecution is held rigidly to the charge, he need not disclose the barest outline of his defense. He is immune from question or comment on his silence; he cannot be convicted when there is the least fair doubt in the minds of any one of the twelve. Why in addition he should in advance have the whole evidence against him to pick over at his leisure, and make his defense, fairly or foully, I have never been able to see.

United States v. Garsson, 291 F. 646, 649 (S.D.N.Y. 1923). Some 40 years later, Professor Abraham Goldstein took issue with Judge Hand in what has remained an influential article. He focused on the prosecution's superior ability to employ police, grand juries, and other state resources in the investigation of crime:

> [P]retrial discovery by the prosecution is far-reaching. And it cannot in any sense be said to be matched by what is available to the defendant or by what he can keep from the prosecution — even when his "immunity" from self-incrimination is thrown into the scales. While the possibility that the defendant may produce a hitherto undisclosed

witness or theory of defense is always present, the opportunity for surprise is rendered practically illusory by the government's broad investigatory powers. . . . The sum of the matter is that the defendant is not an effective participant in the pretrial criminal process. It is to the trial alone that he must look for justice. Yet the imbalance of the pretrial period may prevent him from making the utmost of the critical trial date.

Abraham S. Goldstein, The State and the Accused: Balance of Advantage in Criminal Procedure, 69 Yale L.J. 1149, 1192 (1960).

It is only in the last 50-plus years that discovery has emerged as a basic component of the criminal adjudicative process. And while the trend since the 1960s has clearly been in the direction of more liberal disclosure by both prosecution and defense, discovery in criminal cases is still considerably narrower than civil discovery. In fact, the criminal discovery rules have been shaped by a debate between those who believe that broader, "civil-style" discovery would facilitate fairer and more accurate outcomes in criminal cases and those who believe that criminal cases are fundamentally different, requiring an altogether different (and much more limited) discovery regime.

The proponents of liberal discovery have often argued that the criminal defendant, lacking the state's resources to conduct a thorough factual investigation, must be afforded full notice of the prosecution's evidence so that this evidence can be adequately challenged in the adversarial process. In recent years, some have also pointed to DNA exonerations — to conclusive evidence that factually innocent people have been convicted — to argue that fuller disclosure of material in the prosecution's hands is needed to avoid wrongful convictions.

Opponents of "civil-style" discovery frequently cite the possibility that defendants will misuse discovery — to intimidate witnesses, obstruct justice, or concoct plausible but perjurious defenses that result in false acquittals, given the state's heavy burden of proof. Complicating the debate is the question of reciprocity. Do the defendant's Fifth Amendment rights (or perhaps other constitutional protections afforded to him) limit the degree to which the prosecution can be granted reciprocal discovery from the defense? If so, how should this influence the overall shape of discovery rules?

Most discovery and disclosure rules have their basis in legislation or judicial rulings that vary substantially among jurisdictions in the United States. These rules are, however, shaped by limited but significant constitutional considerations. We begin by looking at disclosure by the defense, particularly at the major Supreme Court decisions that have found some types of required disclosure consistent with constitutional constraints. As a political matter, the slow but steady growth in criminal disclosure by the *prosecution* in recent decades probably could not have occurred absent the reciprocal defense disclosure that the Supreme Court has permitted. Next, we take up the prosecution's disclosure obligations — not only those obligations contained in discovery rules that differ from place to place, but also certain overarching constitutional requirements that are not discovery rules in the formal sense, but that bind all prosecutors to disclose certain critical information — whatever the federal or local rules might require. The entire discussion in this chapter, you will notice, is shaped by the still unresolved question with which we began: whether proponents of broad or more limited discovery in criminal cases have the better argument.

A.   *Disclosure by the Defense*

1.   Defense Disclosure and the Constitution

WILLIAMS v. FLORIDA

Certiorari to the District Court of Appeal of Florida, Third District
399 U.S. 78 (1970)

MR. JUSTICE WHITE delivered the opinion of the Court.

Prior to his trial for robbery in the State of Florida, petitioner filed a "Motion for a Protective Order," seeking to be excused from the requirements of Rule 1.200 of the Florida Rules of Criminal Procedure. That rule requires a defendant, on written demand of the prosecuting attorney, to give notice in advance of trial if the defendant intends to claim an alibi, and to furnish the prosecuting attorney with information as to the place where he claims to have been and with the names and addresses of the alibi witnesses he intends to use. In his motion petitioner openly declared his intent to claim an alibi, but objected to the further disclosure requirements on the ground that the rule "compels the Defendant in a criminal case to be a witness against himself" in violation of his Fifth and Fourteenth Amendment rights. The motion was denied. . . . Petitioner was convicted as charged. . . . The District Court of Appeal affirmed. . . . We granted certiorari.

Florida's notice-of-alibi rule is in essence a requirement that a defendant submit to a limited form of pretrial discovery by the State whenever he intends to rely at trial on the defense of alibi. In exchange for the defendant's disclosure of the witnesses he proposes to use to establish that defense, the State in turn is required to notify the defendant of any witnesses it proposes to offer in rebuttal to that defense. Both sides are under a continuing duty promptly to disclose the names and addresses of additional witnesses bearing on the alibi as they become available. The threatened sanction for failure to comply is the exclusion at trial of the defendant's alibi evidence — except for his own testimony — or, in the case of the State, the exclusion of the State's evidence offered in rebuttal of the alibi.

In this case, following the denial of his Motion for a Protective Order, petitioner complied with the alibi rule and gave the State the name and address of one Mary Scotty. Mrs. Scotty was summoned to the office of the State Attorney on the morning of the trial, where she gave pretrial testimony. At the trial itself, Mrs. Scotty, petitioner, and petitioner's wife all testified that the three of them had been in Mrs. Scotty's apartment during the time of the robbery. On two occasions during cross-examination of Mrs. Scotty, the prosecuting attorney confronted her with her earlier deposition in which she had given dates and times that in some respects did not correspond with the dates and times given at trial. Mrs. Scotty adhered to her trial story, insisting that she had been mistaken in her earlier testimony. The State also offered in rebuttal the testimony of one of the officers investigating the robbery who claimed that Mrs. Scotty had asked him for directions on the afternoon in question during the time when she claimed to have been in her apartment with petitioner and his wife.

We need not linger over the suggestion that the discovery permitted the State against petitioner in this case deprived him of "due process" or a "fair trial." Florida law provides for liberal discovery by the defendant against the State, and the notice-of-alibi rule is itself carefully hedged with reciprocal duties requiring state disclosure to the defendant. Given the ease with which an alibi can be fabricated, the State's interest in protecting itself against an eleventh-hour defense is both obvious and legitimate. Reflecting this interest, notice-of-alibi provisions, dating at least from 1927, are now in existence in a substantial number of States. The adversary system of trial is hardly an end in itself; it is not yet a poker game in which players enjoy an absolute right always to conceal their cards until played. We find ample room in that system, at least as far as "due process" is concerned, for the instant Florida rule. . . .

Petitioner's major contention is that he was "compelled . . . to be a witness against himself" contrary to the commands of the Fifth and Fourteenth Amendments because the notice-of-alibi rule required him to give the State the name and address of Mrs. Scotty in advance of trial and thus to furnish the State with information useful in convicting him. No pretrial statement of petitioner was introduced at trial; but armed with Mrs. Scotty's name and address and the knowledge that she was to be petitioner's alibi witness, the State was able to take her deposition in advance of trial and to find rebuttal testimony. Also, requiring him to reveal the elements of his defense is claimed to have interfered with his right to wait until after the State had presented its case to decide how to defend against it. We conclude, however, as has apparently every other court that has considered the issue, that the privilege against self-incrimination is not violated by a requirement that the defendant give notice of an alibi defense and disclose his alibi witnesses.

The defendant in a criminal trial is frequently forced to testify himself and to call other witnesses in an effort to reduce the risk of conviction. When he presents his witnesses, he must reveal their identity and submit them to cross-examination which in itself may prove incriminating or which may furnish the State with leads to incriminating rebuttal evidence. That the defendant faces such a dilemma demanding a choice between complete silence and presenting a defense has never been thought an invasion of the privilege against compelled self-incrimination. The pressures generated by the State's evidence may be severe but they do not vitiate the defendant's choice to present an alibi defense and witnesses to prove it, even though the attempted defense ends in catastrophe for the defendant. However "testimonial" or "incriminating" the alibi defense proves to be, it cannot be considered "compelled" within the meaning of the Fifth and Fourteenth Amendments.

Very similar constraints operate on the defendant when the State requires pretrial notice of alibi and the naming of alibi witnesses. Nothing in such a rule requires the defendant to rely on an alibi or prevents him from abandoning the defense; these matters are left to his unfettered choice.[15] That choice must be made, but the pressures that bear on his pretrial decision are of the same nature as those that would induce him to call alibi witnesses at the trial: the force of historical fact beyond both his and the State's control and the strength of the State's case built on these

15. . . . The mere requirement that petitioner disclose in advance his intent to rely on an alibi in no way "fixed" his defense as of that point in time. The suggestion that the State, by referring to petitioner's proposed alibi in opening or closing statements might have "compelled" him to follow through with the defense in order to avoid an unfavorable inference is a hypothetical totally without support in this record. The first reference to the alibi came from petitioner's own attorney in his opening remarks; the State's response did not come until after the defense had finished direct examination of Mrs. Scotty. . . . On these facts, then, we simply are not confronted with the question of whether a defendant can be compelled in advance of trial to select a defense from which he can no longer deviate. We do not mean to suggest, though, that such a procedure must necessarily raise serious constitutional problems.

facts. Response to that kind of pressure by offering evidence or testimony is not compelled self-incrimination transgressing the Fifth and Fourteenth Amendments.

In the case before us, the notice-of-alibi rule by itself in no way affected petitioner's crucial decision to call alibi witnesses or added to the legitimate pressures leading to that course of action. At most, the rule only compelled petitioner to accelerate the timing of his disclosure, forcing him to divulge at an earlier date information that the petitioner from the beginning planned to divulge at trial. Nothing in the Fifth Amendment privilege entitles a defendant as a matter of constitutional right to await the end of the State's case before announcing the nature of his defense, any more than it entitles him to await the jury's verdict on the State's case-in-chief before deciding whether or not to take the stand himself.

Petitioner concedes that absent the notice-of-alibi rule the Constitution would raise no bar to the court's granting the State a continuance at trial on the ground of surprise as soon as the alibi witness is called. Nor would there be self-incrimination problems if, during that continuance, the State was permitted to do precisely what it did here prior to trial: take the deposition of the witness and find rebuttal evidence. But if so utilizing a continuance is permissible under the Fifth and Fourteenth Amendments, then surely the same result may be accomplished through pretrial discovery, as it was here, avoiding the necessity of a disrupted trial. We decline to hold that the privilege against compulsory self-incrimination guarantees the defendant the right to surprise the State with an alibi defense. . . .

Affirmed.

MR. JUSTICE BLACKMUN took no part in the consideration or decision of this case.

MR. CHIEF JUSTICE BURGER, concurring.

I join fully in Mr. Justice White's opinion for the Court. I see an added benefit to the notice-of-alibi rule in that it will serve important functions by way of disposing of cases without trial in appropriate circumstances — a matter of considerable importance when courts, prosecution offices, and legal aid and defender agencies are vastly overworked. The prosecutor upon receiving notice will, of course, investigate prospective alibi witnesses. If he finds them reliable and unimpeachable he will doubtless re-examine his entire case and this process would very likely lead to dismissal of the charges. . . .

On the other hand, inquiry into a claimed alibi defense may reveal it to be contrived and fabricated and the witnesses accordingly subject to impeachment or other attack. In this situation defense counsel would be obliged to re-examine his case and, if he found his client has proposed the use of false testimony, either seek to withdraw from the case or try to persuade his client to enter a plea of guilty, possibly by plea discussions which could lead to disposition on a lesser charge.

In either case the ends of justice will have been served and the processes expedited. These are the likely consequences of an enlarged and truly reciprocal pretrial disclosure of evidence and the move away from the "sporting contest" idea of criminal justice.

MR. JUSTICE BLACK, with whom MR. JUSTICE DOUGLAS joins . . . , dissenting. . . .

The core of the majority's decision is an assumption that compelling a defendant to give notice of an alibi defense before a trial is no different from requiring a defendant, after the State has produced the evidence against him at trial, to plead alibi before the jury retires to consider the case. . . . That statement is plainly and simply wrong as a matter of fact and law, and the Court's holding based on that statement is a complete misunderstanding of the protections provided for criminal defendants by the Fifth Amendment and other provisions of the Bill of Rights.

When a defendant is required to indicate whether he might plead alibi in advance of trial, he faces a vastly different decision from that faced by one who can wait until the State has presented the case against him before making up his mind. Before trial the defendant knows only what the State's case might be. . . . At that time there is no certainty as to what kind of case the State will ultimately be able to prove at trial. Therefore any appraisal of the desirability of pleading alibi will be beset with guesswork and gambling far greater than that accompanying the decision at the trial itself. . . .

The Florida system, as interpreted by the majority, plays upon this inherent uncertainty in predicting the possible strength of the State's case in order effectively to coerce defendants into disclosing an alibi defense that may never be actually used. . . .

The Court apparently also assumes that a defendant who has given the required notice can abandon his alibi without hurting himself. Such an assumption is implicit in and necessary for the majority's argument that the pretrial decision is no different from that at the trial itself. I, however, cannot so lightly assume that pretrial notice will have no adverse effects on a defendant who later decides to forgo such a defense. Necessarily the defendant will have given the prosecutor the names of persons who may have some knowledge about the defendant himself or his activities. Necessarily the prosecutor will have every incentive to question these persons fully, and in doing so he may discover new leads or evidence. Undoubtedly there will be situations in which the State will seek to use such information — information it would probably never have obtained but for the defendant's coerced cooperation.

It is unnecessary for me, however, to engage in any such intellectual gymnastics concerning the practical effects of the notice-of-alibi procedure, because the Fifth Amendment itself clearly provides that "[n]o person . . . shall be compelled in any criminal case to be a witness against himself." If words are to be given their plain and obvious meaning, that provision, in my opinion, states that a criminal defendant cannot be required to give evidence, testimony, or any other assistance to the State to aid it in convicting him of crime. The Florida notice-of-alibi rule in my opinion is a patent violation of that constitutional provision because it requires a defendant to disclose information to the State so that the State can use that information to destroy him. It seems to me at least slightly incredible to suggest that this procedure may have some beneficial effects for defendants. . . . If a defendant thinks that making disclosure of an alibi before trial is in his best interests, he will obviously do so. And the only time the State needs the compulsion provided by this procedure is when the defendant has decided that such disclosure is likely to hurt his case.

It is no answer to this argument to suggest that the Fifth Amendment as so interpreted would give the defendant an unfair element of surprise, turning a trial into a "poker game" or "sporting contest," for that tactical advantage to the defendant is inherent in the type of trial required by our Bill of Rights. The Framers were well aware of the awesome investigative and prosecutorial powers of government and it was in order to limit those powers that they spelled out in detail in the Constitution the procedure to be followed in criminal trials. . . .

[The] constitutional right to remain absolutely silent cannot be avoided by superficially attractive analogies to any so-called "compulsion" inherent in the trial itself that may lead a defendant to put on evidence in his own defense. Obviously the

Constitution contemplates that a defendant can be "compelled" to stand trial, and obviously there will be times when the trial process itself will require the defendant to do something in order to try to avoid a conviction. But nothing in the Constitution permits the State to add to the natural consequences of a trial and compel the defendant in advance of trial to participate in any way in the State's attempt to condemn him. . . .

On the surface this case involves only a notice-of-alibi provision, but in effect the decision opens the way for a profound change in one of the most important traditional safeguards of a criminal defendant. The rationale of today's decision is in no way limited to alibi defenses, or any other type or classification of evidence. The theory advanced goes at least so far as to permit the State to obtain under threat of sanction complete disclosure by the defendant in advance of trial of all evidence, testimony, and tactics he plans to use at that trial. In each case the justification will be that the rule affects only the "timing" of the disclosure, and not the substantive decision itself. . . .

NOTES AND QUESTIONS

1. Justice Black's prediction that the implications of *Williams* would reach far beyond notice-of-alibi rules (based on a broad reading of the majority opinion) proved prophetic. While it remains the case that prosecution disclosure is uniformly broader than defense disclosure, a "revolutionary expansion" in criminal disclosure to the prosecution occurred in the wake of *Williams*. Robert P. Mosteller, Discovery Against the Defense: Tilting the Adversarial Balance, 74 Cal. L. Rev. 1567, 1567-1570 (1986).

Consider Rule 16(b) of the Federal Rules of Criminal Procedure, the basic federal rule governing disclosure by the defense. It requires a defendant to disclose: (1) books, papers, documents, data, photographs, and tangible objects and that are within his possession, custody, or control and that he intends to use in his case-in-chief at trial; (2) any results or reports of any physical or mental examinations, as well as any scientific tests or experiments, that are within his possession, custody, or control and that he intends to use in his case-in-chief or, with regard to reports, that were prepared by a witness he intends to call and that relate to the witness's testimony; and (3) a written summary of any expert testimony that he intends to use describing the opinions, bases, reasons for the opinions, and qualifications of the expert. (Note that the bulk of this disclosure is broadly conditioned on prior defense requests for the same type of discovery from the prosecution, and on the prosecution's compliance with these requests. In many states, however, the prosecution's entitlement to discovery into the defendant's case is automatic, and not conditioned on a prior defense request.)

In addition to Rule 16, the Federal Rules contain separate provisions providing for pretrial notice of alibi, insanity, and public authority defenses. See Rules 12.1, 12.2, and 12.3. Rule 26.2 also requires the defendant to provide certain witness statements to the government after a defense witness (excepting the defendant himself) has testified on direct examination at trial. See Rule 26.2.[1]

---

1. Note that Rule 16(b) does not authorize pretrial discovery into statements made by the defendant or by prospective government or defense witnesses to the defendant, his agents, or his attorneys. The Rule also provides that "[e]xcept for scientific or medical reports, Rule 16(b)(1) does not authorize

2. Defense disclosure in many states is broader than in the federal system, at times substantially so — some, for example, authorize the prosecution to obtain a specification of all defenses to be raised, the names and addresses of all defense witnesses to be called at trial, and all statements of defense witnesses, including memoranda of unsigned oral statements. Mosteller, supra, at 1570. Are such provisions consistent with the Fifth Amendment as merely examples of "accelerated disclosure"? Could the rules require the defense to tell the prosecutor prior to trial the order in which he intends to present his witnesses, or is this somehow different?

Setting aside items falling within the attorney-client or work product privilege, what about material the defense does *not* intend to introduce at trial? Are there any constitutional barriers to requiring the defendant to disclose scientific reports not intended to be used? What about documents or other physical evidence in the hands of the defense that are material to issues in the case? Or the identities of potential witnesses that the defendant does not intend to call? In other words, does the Fifth Amendment impose *any* constraints?

3. In Wardius v. Oregon, 412 U.S. 470, 474 (1973), the Court expanded on the summary due process analysis in *Williams*. The *Wardius* Court acknowledged that due process has little to say about the absolute amount of discovery provided in criminal cases. At the same time, however, the Court unanimously concluded that the Due Process Clause *does* "speak to the balance of forces between the accused and his accuser." The case invalidated a notice-of-alibi provision that did not provide for reciprocal discovery of the prosecution. Noting that the state "may not insist that trials be run as a 'search for truth' so far as defense witnesses are concerned, while maintaining 'poker game' secrecy for its own witnesses," the Court concluded that "[i]t is fundamentally unfair to require a defendant to divulge the details of his own case while at the same time subjecting him to the hazard of surprise concerning refutation of the very pieces of evidence which he disclosed to the State."

To comply with *Wardius*, rules providing for discovery into the defendant's case now commonly provide for reciprocal discovery from the prosecution. From the perspective of the criminal defendant, would it be fair to conclude that disclosure by the defense may be advantageous because it leads to broader government disclosure? Or are there reasons that a defense attorney might opt for *less* discovery from the government if also assured that the government could not seek disclosure into the defense case?

2. Sanctions for Defense Nondisclosure

TAYLOR v. ILLINOIS

Certiorari to the Appellate Court of Illinois, First District
484 U.S. 400 (1988)

JUSTICE STEVENS delivered the opinion of the Court. As a sanction for failing to identify a defense witness in response to a pretrial discovery request, an Illinois trial judge refused to allow the undisclosed witness to testify. The question presented is whether that refusal violated the petitioner's constitutional right to obtain the

---

discovery or inspection of . . . reports, memoranda, or other documents made by the defendant, or the defendant's attorney or agent, during the case's investigation or defense." Rule 16(b)(2).

testimony of favorable witnesses. We hold that such a sanction is not absolutely prohibited by the Compulsory Process Clause of the Sixth Amendment and find no constitutional error on the specific facts of this case.

A jury convicted petitioner in 1984 of attempting to murder Jack Bridges in a street fight on the south side of Chicago on August 6, 1981. The conviction was supported by the testimony of Bridges, his brother, and three other witnesses. They described a 20-minute argument between Bridges and a young man named Derrick Travis, and a violent encounter that occurred over an hour later between several friends of Travis, including petitioner, on the one hand, and Bridges, belatedly aided by his brother, on the other. The incident was witnessed by 20 or 30 bystanders. It is undisputed that at least three members of the group which included Travis and petitioner were carrying pipes and clubs that they used to beat Bridges. Prosecution witnesses also testified that petitioner had a gun, that he shot Bridges in the back as he attempted to flee, and that, after Bridges fell, petitioner pointed the gun at Bridges' head but the weapon misfired.

Two sisters, who are friends of petitioner, testified on his behalf. In many respects their version of the incident was consistent with the prosecution's case, but they testified that it was Bridges' brother, rather than petitioner, who possessed a firearm and that he had fired into the group hitting his brother by mistake. No other witnesses testified for the defense.

Well in advance of trial, the prosecutor filed a discovery motion requesting a list of defense witnesses.[2] In his original response, petitioner's attorney identified the two sisters who later testified and two men who did not testify. On the first day of trial, defense counsel was allowed to amend his answer by adding the names of Derrick Travis and a Chicago police officer; neither of them actually testified.

On the second day of trial, after the prosecution's two principal witnesses had completed their testimony, defense counsel made an oral motion to amend his "Answer to Discovery" to include two more witnesses, Alfred Wormley and Pam Berkhalter. In support of the motion, counsel represented that he had just been informed about them and that they had probably seen the "entire incident."

In response to the court's inquiry about defendant's failure to tell him about the two witnesses earlier, counsel acknowledged that defendant had done so, but then represented that he had been unable to locate Wormley. After noting that the witnesses' names could have been supplied even if their addresses were unknown, the trial judge directed counsel to bring them in the next day, at which time he would decide whether they could testify. The judge indicated that he was concerned about the possibility "that witnesses are being found that really weren't there."

The next morning Wormley appeared in court with defense counsel.[7] After further colloquy about the consequences of a violation of discovery rules, counsel was permitted to make an offer of proof in the form of Wormley's testimony outside the

---

2. Illinois Supreme Court Rule 413(d) provides in pertinent part:

Subject to constitutional limitations and within a reasonable time after the filing of a written motion by the State, defense counsel shall inform the State of any defenses which he intends to make at a hearing or trial and shall furnish the State with the following material and information within his possession or control:

   (i) *the names and last known addresses of persons he intends to call as witnesses* together with their relevant written or recorded statements, including memoranda reporting or summarizing their oral statements, any record of prior criminal convictions known to him . . . (emphasis added).

7. The record does not explain why Pam Berkhalter did not appear.

presence of the jury. It developed that Wormley had not been a witness to the incident itself. He testified that prior to the incident he saw Jack Bridges and his brother with two guns in a blanket, that he heard them say "they were after Ray [petitioner] and the other people," and that on his way home he "happened to run into Ray and them" and warned them "to watch out because they got weapons." On cross-examination, Wormley acknowledged that he had first met defendant "about four months ago" (i.e., over two years after the incident). He also acknowledged that defense counsel had visited him at his home on the Wednesday of the week before the trial began. Thus, his testimony rather dramatically contradicted defense counsel's representations to the trial court.

After hearing Wormley testify, the trial judge concluded that the appropriate sanction for the discovery violation was to exclude his testimony. The judge explained:

> THE COURT: All right, I am going to deny Wormley an opportunity to testify here. He is not going to testify. I find this is a blatent [*sic*] violation of the discovery rules, willful violation of the rules. I also feel that defense attorneys have been violating discovery in this courtroom in the last three or four cases blatantly and I am going to put a stop to it and this is one way to do so.
>
> Further, for whatever value it is, because this is a jury trial, I have a great deal of doubt in my mind as to the veracity of this young man that testified as to whether he was an eyewitness on the scene, sees guns that are wrapped up. He doesn't know Ray but he stops Ray.
>
> At any rate, Mr. Wormley is not going to testify, be a witness in this courtroom.

The Illinois Appellate Court affirmed petitioner's conviction. . . . The Illinois Supreme Court denied leave to appeal and we granted the petition for certiorari.

In this Court petitioner makes two arguments. He first contends that the Sixth Amendment bars a court from ever ordering the preclusion of defense evidence as a sanction for violating a discovery rule. Alternatively, he contends that even if the right to present witnesses is not absolute, on the facts of this case the preclusion of Wormley's testimony was constitutional error. Before addressing these contentions, we consider the State's argument that the Compulsory Process Clause of the Sixth Amendment is merely a guarantee that the accused shall have the power to subpoena witnesses and simply does not apply to rulings on the admissibility of evidence.

In the State's view, no Compulsory Process Clause concerns are even raised by authorizing preclusion as a discovery sanction. . . . The State's argument is supported by the plain language of the Clause, by the historical evidence that it was intended to provide defendants with subpoena power that they lacked at common law, by some scholarly comment, and by a brief excerpt from the legislative history of the Clause. We have, however, consistently given the Clause the broader reading. . . .

As we noted just last Term, "[o]ur cases establish, at a minimum, that criminal defendants have the right to the government's assistance in compelling the attendance of favorable witnesses at trial and the right to put before a jury evidence that might influence the determination of guilt." Pennsylvania v. Ritchie, 480 U.S. 39, 56 (1987). Few rights are more fundamental than that of an accused to present witnesses in his own defense. . . . The right to compel a witness' presence in the courtroom could not protect the integrity of the adversary process if it did not embrace the right to have the witness' testimony heard by the trier of fact. The right to offer testimony is thus grounded in the Sixth Amendment even though it is not expressly described in so many words. . . .

Petitioner's claim that the Sixth Amendment creates an absolute bar to the preclusion of the testimony of a surprise witness is just as extreme and just as unacceptable as the State's position that the Amendment is simply irrelevant. The accused does not have an unfettered right to offer testimony that is incompetent, privileged, or otherwise inadmissible under standard rules of evidence. The Compulsory Process Clause provides him with an effective weapon, but it is a weapon that cannot be used irresponsibly. . . .

The principle that undergirds the defendant's right to present exculpatory evidence is also the source of essential limitations on the right. The adversary process could not function effectively without adherence to rules of procedure that govern the orderly presentation of facts and arguments to provide each party with a fair opportunity to assemble and submit evidence to contradict or explain the opponent's case. The trial process would be a shambles if either party had an absolute right to control the time and content of his witnesses' testimony. Neither may insist on the right to interrupt the opposing party's case, and obviously there is no absolute right to interrupt the deliberations of the jury to present newly discovered evidence. The State's interest in the orderly conduct of a criminal trial is sufficient to justify the imposition and enforcement of firm, though not always inflexible, rules relating to the identification and presentation of evidence.

The defendant's right to compulsory process is itself designed to vindicate the principle that the "ends of criminal justice would be defeated if judgments were to be founded on a partial or speculative presentation of the facts." Rules that provide for pretrial discovery of an opponent's witnesses serve the same high purpose. Discovery, like cross-examination, minimizes the risk that a judgment will be predicated on incomplete, misleading, or even deliberately fabricated testimony. The "State's interest in protecting itself against an eleventh-hour defense" is merely one component of the broader public interest in a full and truthful disclosure of critical facts.

To vindicate that interest we have held that even the defendant may not testify without being subjected to cross-examination. Moreover, in United States v. Nobles, 422 U.S. 225 (1975), we upheld an order excluding the testimony of an expert witness tendered by the defendant because he had refused to permit discovery of a "highly relevant" report. . . .

Petitioner does not question the legitimacy of a rule requiring pretrial disclosure of defense witnesses, but he argues that the sanction of preclusion of the testimony of a previously undisclosed witness is so drastic that it should never be imposed. He argues, correctly, that a less drastic sanction is always available. Prejudice to the prosecution could be minimized by granting a continuance or a mistrial to provide time for further investigation; moreover, further violations can be deterred by disciplinary sanctions against the defendant or defense counsel.

It may well be true that alternative sanctions are adequate and appropriate in most cases, but it is equally clear that they would be less effective than the preclusion sanction and that there are instances in which they would perpetuate rather than limit the prejudice to the State and the harm to the adversary process. One of the purposes of the discovery rule itself is to minimize the risk that fabricated testimony will be believed. Defendants who are willing to fabricate a defense may also be willing to fabricate excuses for failing to comply with a discovery requirement. The risk of a contempt violation may seem trivial to a defendant facing the threat of imprisonment for a term of years. A dishonest client can mislead an honest attorney, and there are occasions when an attorney assumes that the duty of loyalty to the client outweighs elementary obligations to the court.

. . . It is . . . reasonable to presume that there is something suspect about a defense witness who is not identified until after the 11th hour has passed. If a pattern of discovery violations is explicable only on the assumption that the violations were designed to conceal a plan to present fabricated testimony, it would be entirely appropriate to exclude the tainted evidence regardless of whether other sanctions would also be merited.

In order to reject petitioner's argument that preclusion is never a permissible sanction for a discovery violation it is neither necessary nor appropriate for us to attempt to draft a comprehensive set of standards to guide the exercise of discretion in every possible case. . . .

A trial judge may certainly insist on an explanation for a party's failure to comply with a request to identify his or her witnesses in advance of trial. If that explanation reveals that the omission was willful and motivated by a desire to obtain a tactical advantage that would minimize the effectiveness of cross-examination and the ability to adduce rebuttal evidence, it would be entirely consistent with the purposes of the Compulsory Process Clause simply to exclude the witness' testimony.[20] . . .

The simplicity of compliance with the discovery rule is also relevant. As we have noted, the Compulsory Process Clause cannot be invoked without the prior planning and affirmative conduct of the defendant. Lawyers are accustomed to meeting deadlines. Routine preparation involves location and interrogation of potential witnesses and the serving of subpoenas on those whose testimony will be offered at trial. The burden of identifying them in advance of trial adds little to these routine demands of trial preparation.

It would demean the high purpose of the Compulsory Process Clause to construe it as encompassing an absolute right to an automatic continuance or mistrial to allow presumptively perjured testimony to be presented to a jury. We reject petitioner's argument that a preclusion sanction is never appropriate no matter how serious the defendant's discovery violation may be.

Petitioner argues that the preclusion sanction was unnecessarily harsh in this case because the voir dire examination of Wormley adequately protected the prosecution from any possible prejudice resulting from surprise. Petitioner also contends that it is unfair to visit the sins of the lawyer upon his client. Neither argument has merit.

More is at stake than possible prejudice to the prosecution. We are also concerned with the impact of this kind of conduct on the integrity of the judicial process itself. The trial judge found that the discovery violation in this case was both willful and blatant.[22] In view of the fact that petitioner's counsel had actually interviewed Wormley during the week before the trial began and the further fact that he

20. There may be cases in which a defendant has legitimate objections to disclosing the identity of a potential witness. Such objections, however, should be raised in advance of trial in response to the discovery request. . . . Under the Federal Rules of Criminal Procedure and under the rules adopted by most States, a party may request a protective order if he or she has just cause for objecting to a discovery request. In this case, there is no issue concerning the validity of the discovery requirement or petitioner's duty to comply with it. . . .

22. The trial judge also expressed concern about discovery violations in other trials. If those violations involved the same attorney, or otherwise contributed to a concern about the trustworthiness of Wormley's eleventh hour testimony, they were relevant. Unrelated discovery violations . . . would not,

amended his Answer to Discovery on the first day of trial without identifying Wormley while he did identify two actual eyewitnesses whom he did not place on the stand, the inference that he was deliberately seeking a tactical advantage is inescapable. Regardless of whether prejudice to the prosecution could have been avoided in this particular case, it is plain that the case fits into the category of willful misconduct in which the severest sanction is appropriate. . . . The pretrial conduct revealed by the record in this case gives rise to a sufficiently strong inference that "witnesses are being found that really weren't there," to justify the sanction of preclusion.

The argument that the client should not be held responsible for his lawyer's misconduct strikes at the heart of the attorney-client relationship. Although there are basic rights that the attorney cannot waive without the fully informed and publicly acknowledged consent of the client,[24] the lawyer has — and must have — full authority to manage the conduct of the trial. The adversary process could not function effectively if every tactical decision required client approval. Moreover, given the protections afforded by the attorney-client privilege and the fact that extreme cases may involve unscrupulous conduct by both the client and the lawyer, it would be highly impracticable to require an investigation into their relative responsibilities before applying the sanction of preclusion. . . . In this case, petitioner has no greater right to disavow his lawyer's decision to conceal Wormley's identity until after the trial had commenced than he has to disavow the decision to refrain from adducing testimony from the eyewitnesses who were identified in the Answer to Discovery. Whenever a lawyer makes use of the sword provided by the Compulsory Process Clause, there is some risk that he may wound his own client.

The judgment of the Illinois Appellate Court is affirmed.

JUSTICE BRENNAN, with whom JUSTICE MARSHALL and JUSTICE BLACKMUN join, dissenting.

Criminal discovery is not a game. It is integral to the quest for truth and the fair adjudication of guilt or innocence. Violations of discovery rules thus cannot go uncorrected or undeterred without undermining the truthseeking process. The question in this case, however, is not whether discovery rules should be enforced but whether the need to correct and deter discovery violations requires a sanction that itself distorts the truthseeking process by excluding material evidence of innocence in a criminal case. . . .

. . . The question at the heart of this case . . . is whether precluding a criminal defense witness from testifying bears an arbitrary and disproportionate relation to the purposes of discovery, at least absent any evidence that the defendant was personally responsible for the discovery violations. This question is not answered by merely pointing out that discovery, like compulsory process, serves truthseeking interests. . . .

The use of the preclusion sanction as a corrective measure — that is, as a measure for addressing the adverse impact a discovery violation might have on truth-seeking

---

however, normally provide a proper basis for curtailing the defendant's constitutional right to present a complete defense.

24. See, e.g., Brookhart v. Janis, 384 U.S. 1, 7-8 (1966) (defendant's constitutional right to plead not guilty and to have a trial where he could confront and cross-examine adversary witness could not be waived by his counsel without petitioner's consent); Doughty v. State, 470 N.E.2d 69, 70 (Ind. 1984) (record must show "personal communication of the defendant to the court that he chooses to relinquish the right [to a jury trial]"); Cross v. United States, 117 U.S. App. D.C. 56 (1963) (waiver of right to be present during trial).

in the case at hand — is asserted to have two justifications: (1) it bars the defendant from introducing testimony that has not been tested by discovery; and (2) it screens out witnesses who are inherently suspect because they were not disclosed until trial. The first justification has no bearing on this case because the defendant does not insist on a right to introduce a witness' testimony without giving the prosecution an opportunity for discovery. He concedes that the trial court was within its authority in requiring the witness to testify first out of the presence of the jury, and he concedes that the trial court could have granted the prosecution a continuance to give it sufficient time to conduct further discovery concerning the witness and the proffered testimony. He argues only that he should not be completely precluded from introducing the testimony. . . .

Nor, despite the Court's suggestions, is the preclusion at issue here justifiable on the theory that a trial court can exclude testimony that it presumes or finds suspect. . . .

[P]reventing a jury from hearing the proffered testimony based on its presumptive or apparent lack of credibility would be antithetical to the principles laid down in Washington v. Texas, 388 U.S. [14, 20-23 (1967) (invalidating a statute that disqualified accomplices from testifying for one another, but not for the state)], and reaffirmed in Rock v. Arkansas, 483 U.S. [44,] 53-55 [1987] [holding that a per se rule excluding all posthypnosis testimony impermissibly infringed on the defendant's right to testify]. . . . The Court in Washington v. Texas . . . concluded that "arbitrary rules that prevent whole categories of defense witnesses from testifying on the basis of a priori categories that presume them unworthy of belief " are unconstitutional. 388 U.S., at 22.

Although persons who are not identified as defense witnesses until trial may not be as trustworthy as other categories of persons, surely any presumption that they are so suspect that the jury can be prevented from even listening to their testimony is at least as arbitrary as presumptions excluding an accomplice's testimony, Washington v. Texas, supra, . . . or a defendant's posthypnosis testimony, Rock, supra. . . . The proper method, under Illinois law and Washington v. Texas, supra, for addressing the concern about reliability is for the prosecutor to inform the jury about the circumstances casting doubt on the testimony, thus allowing the jury to determine the credit and weight it wants to attach to such testimony. . . .

Of course, discovery sanctions must include more than corrective measures. They must also include punitive measures that can deter future discovery violations from taking place. . . .

In light of the availability of direct punitive measures, however, there is no good reason, at least absent evidence of the defendant's complicity, to countenance the arbitrary and disproportionate punishment imposed by the preclusion sanction. The central point to keep in mind is that witness preclusion operates as an effective deterrent only to the extent that it has a possible effect on the outcome of the trial. Indeed, it employs in part the possibility that a distorted record will cause a jury to convict a defendant of a crime he did not commit. Witness preclusion thus punishes discovery violations in a way that is both disproportionate — it might result in a defendant charged with a capital offense being convicted and receiving a death sentence he would not have received but for the discovery violation — and arbitrary — it might, in another case involving an identical discovery violation, result in a defendant suffering no change in verdict or, if charged with a lesser offense, being convicted and receiving a light or suspended sentence. In contrast, direct punitive measures (such as contempt sanctions or, if the attorney is responsible, disciplinary proceedings) can graduate the punishment to correspond to the severity of the discovery violation.

The arbitrary and disproportionate nature of the preclusion sanction is highlighted where the penalty falls on the defendant even though he bore no responsibility for the discovery violation. In this case, although there was ample evidence that the defense attorney willfully violated Rule 413(d), there was no evidence that the defendant played any role in that violation. . . .

Worse yet, the trial court made clear that it was excluding Wormley's testimony not only in response to the defense counsel's actions in this case but also in response to the actions of other defense attorneys in other cases. . . .

In the absence of any evidence that a defendant played any part in an attorney's willful discovery violation, directly sanctioning the attorney is not only fairer but *more* effective in deterring violations than excluding defense evidence. The threat of disciplinary proceedings, fines, or imprisonment will likely influence attorney behavior to a far greater extent than the rather indirect penalty threatened by evidentiary exclusion. . . .

The situation might be different if the defendant willfully caused the discovery violation because, as the Court points out, some defendants who face the prospect of a lengthy imprisonment are arguably impossible to deter with direct punitive sanctions such as contempt. But that is no explanation for allowing defense witness preclusion where there is no evidence that the defendant bore any responsibility for the discovery violation. . . . Deities may be able to visit the sins of the father on the son, but I cannot agree that courts should be permitted to visit the sins of the lawyer on the innocent client.

Nor is the issue resolved by analogizing to tactical errors an attorney might make such as failing to put witnesses on the stand that would have aided the defense. Although we have sometimes held a defendant bound by tactical errors his attorney makes that fall short of ineffective assistance of counsel, we have not previously suggested that a client can be punished for an attorney's *misconduct*. There are fundamental differences between attorney misconduct and tactical errors. . . . [T]he adversary system often cannot effectively deter attorney's tactical errors and does not want to deter tactical decisions. Thus, where a defense attorney makes a routine tactical decision not to introduce evidence at the proper time and the defense seeks to introduce the evidence later, deterrence measures may not be capable of preventing the untimely introduction of evidence from systemically disrupting trials, jury deliberations, or final verdicts. In those circumstances, treating the failure to introduce evidence at the proper time as a procedural default that binds the defendant is arguably the only means of systemically preventing such disruption — not because binding the defendant deters tactical errors any better than direct punitive sanctions but because binding the defendant to defense counsel's procedural default, by definition, eliminates the disruption. . . .

The rationales for binding defendants to attorneys' routine tactical errors do not apply to attorney misconduct. An attorney is never faced with a legitimate choice that includes misconduct as an option. Although it may be that "[t]he adversary process could not function effectively if every tactical decision required client approval," that concern is irrelevant here because a client has no authority to approve misconduct. Further, misconduct is not visible only with hindsight, as are many tactical errors. Consequently, misconduct is amenable to direct punitive sanctions against attorneys as a deterrent that can prevent attorneys from systemically engaging in misconduct that would disrupt the trial process. There is no need to take steps that will inflict the punishment on the defendant. . . .

In short, I can think of no scenario that does not involve a defendant's willful violation of a discovery rule where alternative sanctions would not fully vindicate the purposes of discovery without distorting the truthseeking process by excluding evidence of innocence. . . . Accordingly, absent evidence that the defendant was responsible for the discovery violation, the exclusion of criminal defense evidence is arbitrary and disproportionate to the purposes of discovery and criminal justice and should be per se unconstitutional. I thus cannot agree with the Court's case-by-case balancing approach or with its conclusion in this case that the exclusion was constitutional. . . .

NOTES AND QUESTIONS

1. Is it appropriate for a trial court to preclude the use of evidence at trial as the remedy for defense discovery violations based on the *suspicion* that proffered evidence has been fabricated? Isn't this precisely what *Taylor* says? If a continuance would permit the prosecutor adequately to challenge such evidence and would not otherwise prejudice her case, why should a trial court exclude the evidence on the ground that it is "presumptively" false? Aren't such questions for the jury?

2. The majority in *Taylor* suggests that regardless whether prejudice to the prosecution could have been avoided, the "willful misconduct" in the case justified precluding Wormley's testimony. Assuming preclusion is a more appropriate sanction in cases of intentional misconduct as opposed to negligent discovery violations, is a trial court likely to be able to distinguish between these cases? Suppose the misconduct is entirely the fault of defense counsel, and the defendant himself is blameless; is preclusion still an appropriate sanction, even if the exclusion of the evidence contributes to a conviction?

3. Though sanctions for discovery violations raise significant constitutional issues in the context of defense violations, Rule 16(d)(2) of the Federal Rules of Criminal Procedure, like most sanctions provisions in comparable discovery laws, speaks equally to the prosecution and defense. It provides that when a party has failed to comply with a discovery obligation, "the court may: (A) order that party to permit the discovery or inspection; specify its time, place, and manner; and prescribe other just terms and conditions; (B) grant a continuance; (C) prohibit that party from introducing the undisclosed evidence; or (D) enter any other order that is just under the circumstances." Many discovery violations result in the granting of continuances, but the case law recognizes other remedies — including not only the exclusion of evidence and various forms of contempt and disciplinary sanction, but also the granting of a mistrial and (in the case of a violation by the prosecution) dismissal of the case. In what sort of circumstances is a continuance unlikely to address the prejudice resulting from an untimely disclosure by the government or the defense?

4. One instance where a continuance will not solve the problem is when the other side has already acted on the assumption that the withheld evidence does not exist. Assume that a prosecutor has negligently failed to disclose discoverable material that proves that the defendant was present at the crime scene — say, a video from

the lobby of a bank that was robbed. The defendant, unaware of the video, takes the stand at trial and falsely testifies that he was in another city on the day in question. The prosecution seeks to use the video to expose the defendant's lie, and defense objects, correctly noting that the government improperly failed to disclose the video. Should the court permit the evidence, on the theory that the defense has no protected right to commit perjury? Or should it refuse to allow the jury to see the evidence, reasoning that this is the only effective sanction for the government's failure to comply with the discovery rules, and that the defendant never would have perjured himself if the government had made proper disclosure?

B.   *Disclosure by the Government*

1.   The Prosecutor's General Discovery Obligations

Rule 16(a) of the Federal Rules of Criminal Procedure sets forth the federal prosecutor's basic disclosure obligations. It is significantly narrower in its provisions for disclosure to the defense than the rules to be found in many jurisdictions. The federal model is still a good one to focus on in considering this topic, however, and not only because of the significant role of federal prosecutions: Rule 16(a) has also served as one pattern for comprehensive discovery laws around the country and is roughly equivalent to the discovery rules to be found in over a dozen states. See Wayne R. LaFave, Jerold H. Israel, Nancy J. King, & Orin S. Kerr, Criminal Procedure §20.2(b), at 959 (5th ed. 2009). How close does it come to providing for full disclosure of prosecution evidence? Does it afford the defendant with sufficient discovery to prepare adequately for trial? Consider these questions with particular reference to two subjects we will examine more closely: nonexpert government witnesses and scientific evidence.

FEDERAL RULES OF CRIMINAL PROCEDURE

Rule 16. Discovery and Inspection

(a) Government's Disclosure.

(1) Information Subject to Disclosure.

(A) Defendant's Oral Statement. Upon a defendant's request, the government must disclose to the defendant the substance of any relevant oral statement made by the defendant, before or after arrest, in response to interrogation by a person the defendant knew was a government agent if the government intends to use the statement at trial.

(B) Defendant's Written or Recorded Statement. Upon a defendant's request, the government must disclose to the defendant, and make available for inspection, copying, or photographing, all of the following:

(i) any relevant written or recorded statement by the defendant if:

— the statement is within the government's possession, custody, or control; and

— the attorney for the government knows — or through due diligence could know — that the statement exists;

(ii) the portion of any written record containing the substance of any relevant oral statement made before or after arrest if the defendant made the statement in response to interrogation by a person the defendant knew was a government agent; and

(iii) the defendant's recorded testimony before a grand jury relating to the charged offense.

(C) Organizational Defendant. Upon a defendant's request, if the defendant is an organization, the government must disclose to the defendant any statement described in Rule 16(a)(1)(A) and (B) if the government contends that the person making the statement:

(i) was legally able to bind the defendant regarding the subject of the statement because of that person's position as the defendant's director, officer, employee, or agent; or

(ii) was personally involved in the alleged conduct constituting the offense and was legally able to bind the defendant regarding that conduct because of that person's position as the defendant's director, officer, employee, or agent.

(D) Defendant's Prior Record. Upon a defendant's request, the government must furnish the defendant with a copy of the defendant's prior criminal record that is within the government's possession, custody, or control if the attorney for the government knows — or through due diligence could know — that the record exists.

(E) Documents and Objects. Upon a defendant's request, the government must permit the defendant to inspect and to copy or photograph books, papers, documents, data, photographs, tangible objects, buildings or places, or copies or portions of any of these items, if the item is within the government's possession, custody, or control and:

(i) the item is material to preparing the defense;

(ii) the government intends to use the item in its case-in-chief at trial; or

(iii) the item was obtained from or belongs to the defendant.

(F) Reports of Examinations and Tests. Upon a defendant's request, the government must permit a defendant to inspect and to copy or photograph the results or reports of any physical or mental examination and of any scientific test or experiment if:

(i) the item is within the government's possession, custody, or control;

(ii) the attorney for the government knows — or through due diligence could know — that the item exists; and

(iii) the item is material to preparing the defense or the government intends to use the item in its case-in-chief at trial.

(G) Expert Witnesses. At the defendant's request, the government must give to the defendant a written summary of any [expert] testimony that the government intends to use . . . during its case-in-chief at trial. . . . The summary provided under this subparagraph must describe the witness's opinions, the bases and reasons for those opinions, and the witness's qualifications.

(2) Information Not Subject to Disclosure. Except as Rule 16(a)(1) provides otherwise, this rule does not authorize the discovery or inspection of

reports, memoranda, or other internal government documents made by an attorney for the government or other government agent in connection with investigating or prosecuting the case. Nor does this rule authorize the discovery or inspection of statements made by prospective government witnesses except as provided in 18 U.S.C. §3500.[2] . . .

NOTES AND QUESTIONS

1. *Nonexpert witnesses.* Notice that Rule 16 does not require the prosecution to disclose before trial any prior statements by nonexpert government witnesses on the subject matter of the testimony they will offer. From one perspective, this is extraordinary. Consider Professor Uviller's analysis:

> From the defendant's perspective — especially the perspective of the innocent defendant, learning the details of the accuser's story or the supporting evidence well before the trial begins is probably the only opportunity to check them out. Does the witness harbor a grudge? Does anything in his background caution against credence? Is the story inconsistent with, or contradicted by the accounts of others? Did the witness have the vantage claimed? Does the paper trail support the live recitals? These are some of the vital clues to testimonial error — and the guideposts for the construction of a persuasive alternative scenario — that can make the difference when the case plays out before the jury. If not afforded pretrial, the information can rarely be drawn from the witness when he gets up to render his smooth, coached, and well-defended account from the stand.

H. Richard Uviller, The Tilted Playing Field 93-94 (1999). Without disclosure of prior statements, a criminal defendant may have no avenue for learning the content of a witness's expected trial testimony. A small number of jurisdictions permit the defendant generally to depose witnesses before trial. But in many jurisdictions, including the federal system, depositions in criminal cases are permitted only rarely, and usually to preserve the testimony of someone who is likely to be unavailable at trial; they are not available for routine discovery. In addition, witnesses frequently elect not to speak to the defense before testifying — thus often preventing defense counsel from obtaining the substance of a witness's testimony informally.

2. In contrast, both Federal Rule of Criminal Procedure 26.2 and the Jencks Act, 18 U.S.C. §3500, provide federal defendants the right to inspect certain witness statements following the testimony of a government witness on direct examination. (The law specifically provides that before this point, "no statement . . . in the possession of the United States which was made by a Government witness or prospective Government witness . . . shall be the subject of subpoena, discovery, or inspection. . . .") The law defines "statement" to mean those declarations relating to the subject matter of the witness's testimony and constituting: (1) a written statement made by the witness and signed or otherwise adopted or approved by him; (2) a recording or transcription of an oral statement, provided that it is substantially verbatim and was recorded contemporaneously; and (3) any statement, however taken or recorded, made to a grand jury.

---

2. For a description of §3500, see infra, Note 2 in the text. — EDS.

Despite the language of the statute, however, in many federal courts it is the practice of prosecutors to provide "3500" or "Jencks material" to the defense shortly before trial commences or shortly before the witness testifies rather than after the witness testifies on direct. See Ellen S. Podgor, Criminal Discovery of Jencks Witness Statements: Timing Makes a Difference, 15 Ga. St. U. L. Rev. 651, 681-683 (1999). Regardless of how sensible this practice might be, is it appropriate for the lawyers and the courts to follow a practice that Congress apparently intended to prohibit?

3. One rationale for not disclosing the prior statements of government witnesses earlier is witness safety. Because the successful investigation and prosecution of criminal cases depend heavily on the voluntary cooperation of witnesses, concerns with witness safety (and witness fears about safety) are important. Consider an extensive 1976 study based on interviews of witnesses in Brooklyn Criminal Court conducted by New York's Victim Services Agency and the Vera Institute of Justice. As recounted by Professor Graham, a full 39 percent of the witnesses interviewed were extremely fearful of retaliation by defendants; 26 percent of these witnesses said they had actually been threatened during the criminal process by the defendant or the defendant's family or friends. Michael H. Graham, Witness Intimidation 4 (1985). Don't these figures suggest that it may be helpful in some circumstances that a prosecutor is able to assure prospective government witnesses that their identities will not be disclosed until trial?

4. But on the other side (and there's always another side), in about half the states, pretrial discovery of witness statements *is* readily available. See LaFave, Israel, King, & Kerr, Criminal Procedure §20.3(i), at 969. Over half the states provide for defense discovery of the names of prospective government witnesses — with no apparent crippling of the criminal justice process. Does this suggest that the federal discovery rules on witnesses and their statements are too limited? It may strengthen this argument further to note that the disclosure requirement is not absolute — judges in a mandatory disclosure regime can issue protective orders restricting discovery in appropriate cases. See Nora V. Demleitner, Witness Protection in Criminal Cases: Anonymity, Disguise or Other Options? 46 Am. J. Comp. L. 641, 647 (1998) (noting that in states with expansive pretrial disclosure statutes, legislatures have generally afforded trial courts authority to issue protective orders to safeguard witnesses). Rule 16 itself provides for such orders: "At any time the court may, for good cause, deny, restrict, or defer discovery or inspection, or grant other appropriate relief. The court may permit a party to show good cause by a written statement that the court will inspect ex parte. If relief is granted, the court must preserve the entire text of the party's statement under seal." Rule 16(d)(1).

5. Perhaps the federal rules and similar state rules that limit disclosure into the identity or prior statements of government witnesses before trial stem from an implicit judgment that case-by-case assessments about witness safety and the attendant need to limit discovery into witness identity and testimony should normally be left to the prosecutor rather than to the judge. What arguments might support *this* conclusion?

6. *Scientific evidence.* A substantial majority of discovery regimes contain some version of Rule 16's provision for defense discovery into the results of specified scientific tests. Rule 16, as noted, also provides for disclosure of the substance of any expert testimony that the government intends to use during its case-in-chief. Do these provisions provide adequate discovery into the matters they regulate? Professor Giannelli thinks not:

> A discovery rule on scientific evidence should entail disclosure of all scientific reports. Rule 16 requires production only of reports by experts that the prosecution intends to call at trial, or reports that are material to the preparation of the defense. Consequently, if the prosecution receives an expert's report but does not intend to call that expert to the stand — the most intriguing situation from a defense perspective — the report is discoverable only if it is "material." The problem lies not with the materiality standard, but rather with the person who first applies that standard. Leaving the initial decision to the prosecutor to determine "materiality" is fraught with unnecessary risks, which often will lead to nondisclosure and needless litigation.

Paul C. Giannelli, Criminal Discovery, Scientific Evidence, and DNA, 44 Vand. L. Rev. 791, 808 (1991). Do you agree? Note that Rule 16(a)(1)(E), providing for the inspection of documents and objects, contains an analogous "materiality" provision.

7. Perhaps there *is* a problem with leaving it to the prosecutor to judge whether a scientific report — or any other item — is material to preparing a defense. Some prosecutors have adopted an "open file" discovery practice in which they grant defense counsel access to most material about the case within the prosecutor's possession or control. There are strong arguments in favor of such discovery: "The beauty of open-file discovery is obvious as a remedy for the difficulty of subjective choice in a competitive adversarial environment. It does not require a prosecutor to make difficult discretionary decisions." Robert P. Mosteller, Exculpatory Evidence, Ethics, and the Road to the Disbarment of Mike Nifong: The Critical Importance of Full Open-File Discovery, 15 Geo. Mason L. Rev. 257, 309 (2008). Even noting the "modest but steady movement" in the direction of liberalizing discovery over the years, however, so far, few jurisdictions could be characterized as having true open file discovery regimes. Id., at 274. Would such an approach to discovery be preferable? Might its utility for criminal defendants depend in part on just what prosecutors and police record and place in the official file?

8. Whatever the merits of open file discovery are more generally, the case for liberalizing discovery may be particularly powerful with regard to scientific evidence — and perhaps most particularly, the evidence emanating from forensic labs nationwide. Consider Strengthening Forensic Science in the United States — A Path Forward, the 2009 study by the National Academy of Sciences ("NAS") on the current state of forensic science in the United States. Forensic science, according to the NAS, encompasses a broad range of disciplines, including those that are "laboratory based" such as "nuclear and mitochondrial DNA analysis, toxicology and drug analysis," and those "based on expert interpretation of observed patterns" in the analysis of fingerprints, writing samples, toolmarks, bite marks, hair specimens, and the like. See id., at 7. The NAS reports that across these disciplines, "the integrity of crime laboratories [in the United States] increasingly has been called into question, with some highly publicized cases highlighting the sometimes lax standards of laboratories that have generated questionable or fraudulent evidence and that have lacked quality control measures that would have detected the questionable evidence." Id., at 44. The DNA exonerations helped provoke this scrutiny:

> The increased use of DNA analysis as a more reliable approach to matching crime scene evidence with suspects and victims has resulted in the reevaluation of older cases that retained biological evidence that could be analyzed by DNA. The number of exonerations resulting from the analysis of DNA has grown across the country in recent

years, uncovering a disturbing number of wrongful convictions — some for capital crimes — and exposing serious limitations in some of the forensic science approaches commonly used in the United States.

According to the Innocence Project, there have been 223 postconviction DNA exonerations in the United States since 1989 (as of November 2008). Some have contested the percentage of exonerated defendants whose convictions allegedly were based on faulty science. Although the Innocence Project figures are disputed by forensic scientists who have reexamined the data, even those who are critical of the conclusions of The Innocence Project acknowledge that faulty forensic science has, on occasion, contributed to the wrongful conviction of innocent persons.

The fact is that many forensic tests — such as those used to infer the source of toolmarks or bite marks — have never been exposed to stringent scientific scrutiny. Most of these techniques were developed in crime laboratories to aid in the investigation of evidence from a particular crime scene, and researching their limitations and foundations was never a top priority. . . . Before the first offering of the use of DNA in forensic science in 1986, no concerted effort had been made to determine the reliability of these tests, and some in the forensic science and law enforcement communities believed that scientists' ability to withstand cross-examination in court when giving testimony related to these tests was sufficient to demonstrate the tests' reliability. However, although the precise error rates of these forensic tests are still unknown, comparison of their results with DNA testing in some cases has revealed that some of these analyses, as currently performed, produce erroneous results. . . . Some non-DNA forensic tests do not meet the fundamental requirements of science, in terms of reproducibility, validity, and falsifiability.

Id., at 42. Would more liberal disclosure in criminal cases aid defense counsel in better exposing flaws in the forensic evidence offered against their clients?

9. Perhaps more liberal discovery would help, although changes to the discovery rules alone are probably inadequate to deal with the problems identified by the NAS. (Indeed, the NAS itself calls for reforms directed at improving the forensic science community and notes that "[f]or a variety of reasons . . . the legal system is ill-equipped to correct the problems of the . . . community.") Many attorneys "have neither the time nor the expertise to challenge scientific evidence." Paul Giannelli, Forensic Science: Scientific Evidence and Prosecutorial Misconduct in the Duke Lacross Rape Case, 45 Crim. L. Bull. 4 (2009). Still, counsel certainly can't challenge what they don't know about. Doesn't Professor Giannelli have a point that comprehensive (and comprehensible) discovery in cases involving scientific evidence may be important — even if not alone sufficient — to protect the interests of the innocent? See also Jim Dwyer, Peter Neufeld, & Barry Scheck, Actual Innocence 257 (2000) (advocating "[c]omplete discovery of underlying data from forensic tests" and "comprehensible explanations of the work performed" as needed reform to help avoid wrongful convictions).

Reconsider Judge Hand's famous statement that "the accused has every advantage" and "[w]hy in addition he should in advance have the whole evidence against him to pick over at his leisure, and make his defense, fairly or foully, I have never been able to see." Notably, Judge Hand also famously deemed "the ghost of the innocent man convicted . . . an unreal dream." *Garsson*, 291 F., at 649. Proponents of liberal discovery point to the set of postconviction exonerations from DNA to show that Judge Hand was wrong about the risk of wrongful conviction — and that, in fact, broad discovery is needed to protect the innocent. Does the argument on the other side amount, at least in part, to the claim that limited discovery is necessary so that the guilty can be convicted? And if so, is there any way to resolve *this* debate?

2. The Prosecutor's Constitutional Disclosure Obligations

KYLES v. WHITLEY

Certiorari to the United States Court of Appeals for the Fifth Circuit
514 U.S. 419 (1995)

JUSTICE SOUTER delivered the opinion of the Court. . . .

[A]t about 2:20 p.m. on Thursday, September 20, 1984, 60-year-old Dolores Dye left the Schwegmann Brothers' store (Schwegmann's) on Old Gentilly Road in New Orleans after doing some food shopping. As she put her grocery bags into the trunk of her red Ford LTD, a man accosted her and after a short struggle drew a revolver, fired into her left temple, and killed her. The gunman took Dye's keys and drove away in the LTD.

New Orleans police took statements from six eyewitnesses, who offered various descriptions of the gunman. They agreed that he was a black man, and four of them said that he had braided hair. The witnesses differed significantly, however, in their descriptions of height, age, weight, build, and hair length. Two reported seeing a man of 17 or 18, while another described the gunman as looking as old as 28. One witness described him as 5'4" or 5'5", medium build, 140-150 pounds; another described the man as slim and close to six feet. One witness said he had a mustache; none of the others spoke of any facial hair at all. One witness said the murderer had shoulder-length hair; another described the hair as "short."

Since the police believed the killer might have driven his own car to Schwegmann's and left it there when he drove off in Dye's LTD, they recorded the license numbers of the cars remaining in the parking lots around the store at 9:15 p.m. on the evening of the murder. . . .

At 5:30 p.m., on September 22, a man identifying himself as James Joseph called the police and reported that on the day of the murder he had bought a red Thunderbird from a friend named Curtis, whom he later identified as petitioner, Curtis Kyles. He said that he had subsequently read about Dye's murder in the newspapers and feared that the car he purchased was the victim's. He agreed to meet with the police.

A few hours later, the informant met New Orleans Detective John Miller, who was wired with a hidden body microphone, through which the ensuing conversation was recorded. The informant now said his name was Joseph Banks and that he was called Beanie. His actual name was Joseph Wallace.[3]

His story, as well as his name, had changed since his earlier call. In place of his original account of buying a Thunderbird from Kyles on Thursday, Beanie told Miller that he had not seen Kyles at all on Thursday, and had bought a red LTD the previous day, Friday. Beanie led Miller to the parking lot of a nearby bar, where he had left the red LTD, later identified as Dye's.

---

3. Because the informant had so many aliases, we will follow the convention of the court below and refer to him throughout this opinion as Beanie.

Beanie told Miller that he lived with Kyles's brother-in-law (later identified as Johnny Burns),[4] whom Beanie repeatedly called his "partner." Beanie described Kyles as slim, about 6-feet tall, 24 or 25 years old, with a "bush" hairstyle. When asked if Kyles ever wore his hair in plaits, Beanie said that he did but that he "had a bush" when Beanie bought the car.

During the conversation, Beanie repeatedly expressed concern that he might himself be a suspect in the murder. . . . Miller acknowledged that Beanie's possession of the car would have looked suspicious, but reassured him that he "didn't do anything wrong."

Beanie seemed eager to cast suspicion on Kyles, who allegedly made his living by "robbing people," and had tried to kill Beanie at some prior time. Beanie said that Kyles regularly carried two pistols, a .38 and a .32, and that if the police could "set him up good," they could "get that same gun" used to kill Dye. . . .

Beanie [said] that after he bought the car, he and his "partner" (Burns) drove Kyles to Schwegmann's about 9 p.m. on Friday evening to pick up Kyles's car, described as an orange four-door Ford.[5] When asked where Kyles's car had been parked, Beanie replied that it had been "[o]n the same side [of the lot] where the woman was killed at." [Miller and his supervisor, Sgt. James Eaton] later drove Beanie to Schwegmann's, where he indicated the space where he claimed Kyles's car had been parked. Beanie went on to say that when he and Burns had brought Kyles to pick up the car, Kyles had gone to some nearby bushes to retrieve a brown purse, which Kyles subsequently hid in a wardrobe at his apartment. Beanie said that Kyles had "a lot of groceries" in Schwegmann's bags and a new baby's potty "in the car." Beanie told Eaton that Kyles's garbage would go out the next day and that if Kyles was "smart" he would "put [the purse] in [the] garbage." Beanie made it clear that he expected some reward for his help, saying at one point that he was not "doing all of this for nothing." The police repeatedly assured Beanie that he would not lose the $400 he paid for the car.

After the visit to Schwegmann's, Eaton and Miller took Beanie to a police station where Miller interviewed him again on the record. . . . This statement, Beanie's third (the telephone call being the first, then the recorded conversation), repeats some of the essentials of the second one: that Beanie had purchased a red Ford LTD from Kyles for $400 on Friday evening; that Kyles had his hair "combed out" at the time of the sale; and that Kyles carried a .32 and a .38 with him "all the time."

Portions of the third statement, however, embellished or contradicted Beanie's preceding story and were even internally inconsistent. Beanie reported that after the sale, he and Kyles unloaded Schwegmann's grocery bags from the trunk and back seat of the LTD and placed them in Kyles's own car. Beanie said that Kyles took a brown purse from the front seat of the LTD and that they then drove in separate cars to Kyles's apartment, where they unloaded the groceries. Beanie also claimed that, a few hours later, he and his "partner" Burns went with Kyles to Schwegmann's, where they recovered Kyles's car and a "big brown pocket book" from "next to a building." Beanie did not explain how Kyles could have picked up his car and recovered the purse at Schwegmann's, after Beanie had seen Kyles with both just a few

---

4. Johnny Burns is the brother of a woman known as Pinky Burns. A number of trial witnesses referred to the relationship between Kyles and Pinky Burns as a common-law marriage (Louisiana's civil law notwithstanding). Kyles is the father of several of Pinky Burns's children.

5. . . . Kyles's car was actually a Mercury and . . . a two-door model.

hours earlier. The police neither noted the inconsistencies nor questioned Beanie about them.

Although the police did not thereafter put Kyles under surveillance, they learned about events at his apartment from Beanie, who went there twice on Sunday. According to a fourth statement by Beanie, this one given to the chief prosecutor in November . . . , he first went to the apartment about 2 p.m., after a telephone conversation with a police officer who asked whether Kyles had the gun that was used to kill Dye. Beanie stayed in Kyles's apartment until about 5 p.m., when he left to call Detective John Miller. Then he returned about 7 p.m. and stayed until about 9:30 p.m., when he left to meet Miller, who also asked about the gun. According to this fourth statement, Beanie "rode around" with Miller until 3 a.m. on Monday, September 24. Sometime during those same early morning hours, detectives were sent . . . to pick up the rubbish outside Kyles's building. As Sgt. Eaton wrote in an interoffice memorandum, he had "reason to believe the victims [*sic*] personal papers and the Schwegmann's bags will be in the trash."

At 10:40 a.m., Kyles was arrested as he left the apartment, which was then searched under a warrant. Behind the kitchen stove, the police found a .32-caliber revolver containing five live rounds and one spent cartridge. Ballistics tests later showed that this pistol was used to murder Dye. In a wardrobe in a hallway leading to the kitchen, the officers found a homemade shoulder holster that fit the murder weapon. In a bedroom dresser drawer, they discovered two boxes of ammunition, one containing several .32-caliber rounds of the same brand as those found in the pistol. Back in the kitchen, various cans of cat and dog food, some of them of the brands Dye typically purchased, were found in Schwegmann's sacks. No other groceries were identified as possibly being Dye's, and no potty was found. Later that afternoon at the police station, police opened the rubbish bags and found the victim's purse, identification, and other personal belongings wrapped in a Schwegmann's sack.

The gun, the LTD, the purse, and the cans of pet food were dusted for fingerprints. The gun had been wiped clean. Several prints were found on the purse and on the LTD, but none was identified as Kyles's. Dye's prints were not found on any of the cans of pet food. Kyles's prints were found, however, on a small piece of paper taken from the front passenger-side floorboard of the LTD. The crime laboratory recorded the paper as a Schwegmann's sales slip, but without noting what had been printed on it, which was obliterated in the chemical process of lifting the fingerprints. A second Schwegmann's receipt was found in the trunk of the LTD, but Kyles's prints were not found on it. Beanie's fingerprints were not compared to any of the fingerprints found.

The lead detective on the case, John Dillman, put together a photo lineup that included a photograph of Kyles (but not of Beanie) and showed the array to five of the six eyewitnesses who had given statements. Three of them picked the photograph of Kyles; the other two could not confidently identify Kyles as Dye's assailant.

Kyles was indicted for first-degree murder. Before trial, his counsel filed a lengthy motion for disclosure by the State of any exculpatory or impeachment evidence. The prosecution responded that there was "no exculpatory evidence of any nature," despite the government's knowledge of the following evidentiary items: (1) the six contemporaneous eyewitness statements taken by police following the murder; (2) records of Beanie's initial call to the police; (3) the tape recording of the Saturday conversation between Beanie and officers Eaton and Miller; (4) the typed and

signed statement given by Beanie on Sunday morning; (5) the computer print-out
of license numbers of cars parked at Schwegmann's on the night of the murder,
which did not list the number of Kyles's car; (6) the internal police memorandum
calling for the seizure of the rubbish after Beanie had suggested that the purse
might be found there; and (7) evidence linking Beanie to other crimes at Schwegmann's and to the unrelated murder of one Patricia Leidenheimer, committed in
January before the Dye murder.

At the first trial, in November, the heart of the State's case was eyewitness testimony from four people who were at the scene of the crime (three of whom had previously picked Kyles from the photo lineup). Kyles . . . supplied an alibi that he had
been picking up his children from school at the time of the murder. The theory of
the defense was that Kyles had been framed by Beanie, who had planted evidence
in Kyles's apartment and his rubbish for the purposes of shifting suspicion away
from himself, removing an impediment to romance with Pinky Burns, and obtaining reward money. Beanie did not testify as a witness for either the defense or the
prosecution.

[A]fter four hours of deliberation, the jury became deadlocked on the issue of
guilt, and a mistrial was declared.

After the mistrial, the chief trial prosecutor, Cliff Strider, interviewed Beanie.
Strider's notes show that Beanie again changed important elements of his story. He
said that he went with Kyles to retrieve Kyles's car from the Schwegmann's lot on
Thursday, the day of the murder, at some time between 5 and 7:30 p.m., not on
Friday, at 9 p.m., as he had said in his second and third statements. (Indeed, in his
second statement, Beanie said that he had not seen Kyles at all on Thursday.) He
also said, for the first time, that when they had picked up the car they were accompanied not only by Johnny Burns but also by Kevin Black, who had testified for the
defense at the first trial. Beanie now claimed that after getting Kyles's car they went
to Black's house, retrieved a number of bags of groceries, a child's potty, and a
brown purse, all of which they took to Kyles's apartment. Beanie also stated that on
the Sunday after the murder he had been at Kyles's apartment two separate times.
Notwithstanding the many inconsistencies and variations among Beanie's statements, neither Strider's notes nor any of the other notes and transcripts were given
to the defense.

In December 1984, Kyles was tried a second time. Again, the heart of the State's
case was the testimony of four eyewitnesses who positively identified Kyles in front
of the jury. The prosecution also offered a blown-up photograph taken at the crime
scene soon after the murder, on the basis of which the prosecutors argued that a
seemingly two-toned car in the background of the photograph was Kyles's. . . .
Once again, Beanie did not testify.

As in the first trial, the defense contended that the eyewitnesses were mistaken.
Kyles's counsel called several individuals, including Kevin Black, who testified to
seeing Beanie, with his hair in plaits, driving a red car similar to the victim's about
an hour after the killing. Another witness testified that Beanie, with his hair in
braids, had tried to sell him the car on Thursday evening, shortly after the murder.
Another witness testified that Beanie, with his hair in a "Jheri curl," had attempted
to sell him the car on Friday. One witness, Beanie's "partner," Burns, testified that
he had seen Beanie on Sunday at Kyles's apartment, stooping down near the stove
where the gun was eventually found, and the defense presented testimony that
Beanie was romantically interested in Pinky Burns. To explain the pet food found in

Kyles's apartment, there was testimony that Kyles's family kept a dog and cat and often fed stray animals in the neighborhood.

Finally, Kyles again took the stand. Denying any involvement in the shooting, he explained his fingerprints on the cash register receipt found in Dye's car by saying that Beanie had picked him up in a red car on Friday, September 21, and had taken him to Schwegmann's, where he purchased transmission fluid and a pack of cigarettes. He suggested that the receipt may have fallen from the bag when he removed the cigarettes.

On rebuttal, the prosecutor had Beanie brought into the courtroom. All of the testifying eyewitnesses, after viewing Beanie standing next to Kyles, reaffirmed their previous identifications of Kyles as the murderer. Kyles was convicted of first-degree murder and sentenced to death. . . .

The prosecution's affirmative duty to disclose evidence favorable to a defendant . . . is . . . most prominently associated with this Court's decision in Brady v. Maryland, 373 U.S. 83 (1963). *Brady* held "that the suppression by the prosecution of evidence favorable to an accused upon request violates due process where the evidence is material either to guilt or to punishment, irrespective of the good faith or bad faith of the prosecution." 373 U.S., at 87. . . .

In . . . United States v. Bagley, 473 U.S. 667 (1985), the Court disavowed any difference between exculpatory and impeachment evidence for *Brady* purposes, and it . . . held that regardless of request, favorable evidence is material, and constitutional error results from its suppression by the government, "if there is a reasonable probability that, had the evidence been disclosed to the defense, the result of the proceeding would have been different." 473 U.S., at 682 (opinion of Blackmun, J.); id., at 685 (White, J., concurring in part and concurring in judgment).

Four aspects of materiality under *Bagley* bear emphasis. Although the constitutional duty is triggered by the potential impact of favorable but undisclosed evidence, a showing of materiality does not require demonstration by a preponderance that disclosure of the suppressed evidence would have resulted ultimately in the defendant's acquittal (whether based on the presence of reasonable doubt or acceptance of an explanation for the crime that does not inculpate the defendant). *Bagley*'s touchstone of materiality is a "reasonable probability" of a different result, and the adjective is important. The question is not whether the defendant would more likely than not have received a different verdict with the evidence, but whether in its absence he received a fair trial, understood as a trial resulting in a verdict worthy of confidence. A "reasonable probability" of a different result is accordingly shown when the government's evidentiary suppression "undermines confidence in the outcome of the trial." *Bagley*, 473 U.S., at 678.

The second aspect of *Bagley* materiality bearing emphasis here is that it is not a sufficiency of evidence test. A defendant need not demonstrate that after discounting the inculpatory evidence in light of the undisclosed evidence, there would not have been enough left to convict. . . .

Third, we note that . . . once a reviewing court applying *Bagley* has found constitutional error there is no need for further harmless-error review. Assuming, arguendo, that a harmless-error enquiry were to apply, a *Bagley* error could not be treated as harmless, since "a reasonable probability that, had the evidence been disclosed to the defense, the result of the proceeding would have been different," necessarily entails the conclusion that the suppression must have had "'substantial and injurious effect or influence in determining the jury's verdict,'" Brecht v.

Abrahamson, 507 U.S. 619, 623 (1993), quoting Kotteakos v. United States, 328 U.S. 750, 776 (1946). . . .

The fourth and final aspect of *Bagley* materiality to be stressed here is its definition in terms of suppressed evidence considered collectively, not item by item. As Justice Blackmun emphasized in the portion of his opinion written for the Court, the Constitution is not violated every time the government fails or chooses not to disclose evidence that might prove helpful to the defense. 473 U.S., at 675 and n. 7. We have never held that the Constitution demands an open file policy (however such a policy might work out in practice), and the rule in *Bagley* (and, hence, in *Brady*) requires less of the prosecution than the ABA Standards for Criminal Justice, which call generally for prosecutorial disclosures of any evidence tending to exculpate or mitigate.

While the definition of *Bagley* materiality in terms of the cumulative effect of suppression must accordingly be seen as leaving the government with a degree of discretion, it must also be understood as imposing a corresponding burden. On the one side, showing that the prosecution knew of an item of favorable evidence unknown to the defense does not amount to a *Brady* violation, without more. But the prosecution, which alone can know what is undisclosed, must be assigned the consequent responsibility to gauge the likely net effect of all such evidence and make disclosure when the point of "reasonable probability" is reached. This in turn means that the individual prosecutor has a duty to learn of any favorable evidence known to the others acting on the government's behalf in the case, including the police. But whether the prosecutor succeeds or fails in meeting this obligation (whether, that is, a failure to disclose is in good faith or bad faith), the prosecution's responsibility for failing to disclose known, favorable evidence rising to a material level of importance is inescapable. . . .

[W]e were asked at oral argument to raise the threshold of materiality because the *Bagley* standard "makes it difficult . . . to know" from the "perspective [of the prosecutor at] trial . . . exactly what might become important later on." The State asks for "a certain amount of leeway in making a judgment call" as to the disclosure of any given piece of evidence.

Uncertainty about the degree of further "leeway" that might satisfy the State's request for a "certain amount" of it is the least of the reasons to deny the request. At bottom, what the State fails to recognize is that, with or without more leeway, the prosecution cannot be subject to any disclosure obligation without at some point having the responsibility to determine when it must act. . . .

This means, naturally, that a prosecutor anxious about tacking too close to the wind will disclose a favorable piece of evidence. This is as it should be. Such disclosure will serve to justify trust in the prosecutor as "the representative . . . of a sovereignty . . . whose interest . . . in a criminal prosecution is not that it shall win a case, but that justice shall be done." Berger v. United States, 295 U.S. 78, 88 (1935). And it will tend to preserve the criminal trial, as distinct from the prosecutor's private deliberations, as the chosen forum for ascertaining the truth about criminal accusations. . . .

In this case, disclosure of the suppressed evidence to competent counsel would have made a different result reasonably probable.

As the District Court put it, "the essence of the State's case" was the testimony of eyewitnesses, who identified Kyles as Dye's killer. Disclosure of their statements would have resulted in a markedly weaker case for the prosecution and a markedly stronger one for the defense. To begin with, the value of two of those witnesses would have been substantially reduced or destroyed.

The State rated Henry Williams as its best witness, who testified that he had seen the struggle and the actual shooting by Kyles. The jury would have found it helpful to probe this conclusion in the light of Williams's contemporaneous statement, in which he told the police that the assailant was "a black male, about 19 or 20 years old, about 5'4" or 5'5", 140 to 150 pounds, medium build" and that "his hair looked like it was platted." If cross-examined on this description, Williams would have had trouble explaining how he could have described Kyles, 6-feet tall and thin, as a man more than half a foot shorter with a medium build. Indeed, since Beanie was 22 years old, 5'5" tall, and 159 pounds, the defense would have had a compelling argument that Williams's description pointed to Beanie but not to Kyles.[13]

The trial testimony of a second eyewitness, Isaac Smallwood, was equally damning to Kyles. He testified that Kyles was the assailant, and that he saw him struggle with Dye. He said he saw Kyles take a ".32, a small black gun" out of his right pocket, shoot Dye in the head, and drive off in her LTD. When the prosecutor asked him whether he actually saw Kyles shoot Dye, Smallwood answered "Yeah."

Smallwood's statement taken at the parking lot, however, was vastly different. Immediately after the crime, Smallwood claimed that he had not seen the actual murder and had not seen the assailant outside the vehicle. "I heard a lound [sic] pop," he said. "When I looked around I saw a lady laying on the ground, and there was a red car coming toward me." Smallwood said that he got a look at the culprit, a black teenage male with a mustache and shoulder-length braided hair, as the victim's red Thunderbird passed where he was standing. When a police investigator specifically asked him whether he had seen the assailant outside the car, Smallwood answered that he had not; the gunman "was already in the car and coming toward me."

A jury would reasonably have been troubled by the adjustments to Smallwood's original story by the time of the second trial. The struggle and shooting, which earlier he had not seen, he was able to describe with such detailed clarity as to identify the murder weapon as a small black .32-caliber pistol, which, of course, was the type of weapon used. His description of the victim's car had gone from a "Thunderbird" to an "LTD" and he saw fit to say nothing about the assailant's shoulder-length hair and moustache, details noted by no other eyewitness. These developments would have fueled a withering cross-examination, destroying confidence in Smallwood's story and raising a substantial implication that the prosecutor had coached him to give it.

Since the evolution over time of a given eyewitness's description can be fatal to its reliability, the Smallwood and Williams identifications would have been severely

13. The defense could have further underscored the possibility that Beanie was Dye's killer through cross-examination of the police on their failure to direct any investigation against Beanie. If the police had disclosed Beanie's statements, they would have been forced to admit that their informant Beanie described Kyles as generally wearing his hair in a "bush" style (and so wearing it when he sold the car to Beanie), whereas Beanie wore his in plaits. There was a considerable amount of such *Brady* evidence on which the defense could have attacked the investigation as shoddy. The police failed to disclose that Beanie had charges pending against him for a theft at the same Schwegmann's store and was a primary suspect in the January 1984 murder of Patricia Leidenheimer, who, like Dye, was an older woman shot once in the head during an armed robbery. (Even though Beanie was a primary suspect in the Leidenheimer murder as early as September, he was not interviewed by the police about it until after Kyles's second trial in December. Beanie confessed his involvement in the murder, but was never charged in connection with it.) . . .

undermined by use of their suppressed statements. . . . Nor, of course, would the harm to the State's case on identity have been confined to their testimony alone. The fact that neither Williams nor Smallwood could have provided a consistent eyewitness description pointing to Kyles would have undercut the prosecution all the more because the remaining eyewitnesses called to testify (Territo and Kersh) had their best views of the gunman only as he fled the scene with his body partly concealed in Dye's car. . . .

Damage to the prosecution's case would not have been confined to evidence of the eyewitnesses, for Beanie's various statements would have raised opportunities to attack not only the probative value of crucial physical evidence and the circumstances in which it was found, but the thoroughness and even the good faith of the investigation, as well. . . . Beanie's statements to the police were replete with inconsistencies and would have allowed the jury to infer that Beanie was anxious to see Kyles arrested for Dye's murder. Their disclosure would have revealed a remarkably uncritical attitude on the part of the police. . . .

[T]he defense could have examined the police to good effect on their knowledge of Beanie's statements and so have attacked the reliability of the investigation in failing even to consider Beanie's possible guilt and in tolerating (if not countenancing) serious possibilities that incriminating evidence had been planted.

By demonstrating the detectives' knowledge of Beanie's affirmatively self-incriminating statements, the defense could have laid the foundation for a vigorous argument that the police had been guilty of negligence. In his initial meeting with police, Beanie admitted twice that he changed the license plates on the LTD. This admission enhanced the suspiciousness of his possession of the car; the defense could have argued persuasively that he was no bona fide purchaser. And when combined with his police record, evidence of prior criminal activity near Schwegmann's, and his status as a suspect in another murder, his devious behavior gave reason to believe that he had done more than buy a stolen car. There was further self-incrimination in Beanie's statement that Kyles's car was parked in the same part of the Schwegmann's lot where Dye was killed. Beanie's apparent awareness of the specific location of the murder could have been based, as the State contends, on television or newspaper reports, but perhaps it was not. . . . Since the police admittedly never treated Beanie as a suspect, the defense could thus have used his statements to throw the reliability of the investigation into doubt and to sully the credibility of Detective Dillman, who testified that Beanie was never a suspect, and that he had "no knowledge" that Beanie had changed the license plate.

The admitted failure of the police to pursue these pointers toward Beanie's possible guilt could only have magnified the effect on the jury of explaining how the purse and the gun happened to be recovered. In Beanie's original recorded statement, he told the police that "[Kyles's] garbage goes out tomorrow," and that "if he's smart he'll put [the purse] in [the] garbage." These statements, along with the internal memorandum stating that the police had "reason to believe" Dye's personal effects and Schwegmann's bags would be in the garbage, would have supported the defense's theory that Beanie was no mere observer, but was determining the investigation's direction and success. . . .

To the same effect would have been an enquiry based on Beanie's apparently revealing remark to police that "if you can set [Kyles] up good, you can get that same gun." While the jury might have understood that Beanie meant simply that if the police investigated Kyles, they would probably find the murder weapon, the jury could also have taken Beanie to have been making the more sinister suggestion that the police "set up" Kyles, and the defense could have argued that the police accepted the invitation. The prosecutor's notes of his interview with Beanie would have shown that police officers were asking Beanie the whereabouts of the gun all day Sunday, the very day when he was twice at Kyles's apartment and was allegedly seen by Johnny Burns lurking near the stove, where the gun was later found. Beanie's same statement, indeed, could have been used to cap an attack on the integrity of the investigation and on the reliability of Detective Dillman, who testified on cross-examination that he did not know if Beanie had been at Kyles's apartment on Sunday.

Next to be considered is the prosecution's list of the cars in the Schwegmann's parking lot at mid-evening after the murder. While its suppression does not rank with the failure to disclose the other evidence discussed here, it would have had some value as exculpation and impeachment, and it counts accordingly in determining whether *Bagley*'s standard of materiality is satisfied. On the police's assumption, argued to the jury, that the killer drove to the lot and left his car there during the heat of the investigation, the list without Kyles's registration would obviously have helped Kyles and would have had some value in countering an argument by the prosecution that a grainy enlargement of a photograph of the crime scene showed Kyles's car in the background. . . .

The State argues that the list was neither impeachment nor exculpatory evidence because Kyles could have moved his car before the list was created and because the list does not purport to be a comprehensive listing of all the cars in the Schwegmann's lot. Such argument, however, confuses the weight of the evidence with its favorable tendency. . . .

In assessing the significance of the evidence withheld, one must of course bear in mind that not every item of the State's case would have been directly undercut if the *Brady* evidence had been disclosed. It is significant, however, that the physical evidence remaining unscathed would . . . hardly have amounted to overwhelming proof that Kyles was the murderer. Ammunition and a holster were found in Kyles's apartment, but if the jury had suspected the gun had been planted the significance of these items might have been left in doubt. The fact that pet food was found in Kyles's apartment was consistent with the testimony of several defense witnesses that Kyles owned a dog and that his children fed stray cats. . . .

Similarly undispositive is the small Schwegmann's receipt on the front passenger floorboard of the LTD, the only physical evidence that bore a fingerprint identified as Kyles's. Kyles explained that Beanie had driven him to Schwegmann's on Friday to buy cigarettes and transmission fluid, and he theorized that the slip must have fallen out of the bag when he removed the cigarettes. This explanation is consistent with the location of the slip when found and with its small size. The State cannot very well argue that the fingerprint ties Kyles to the killing without also explaining how the 2-inch-long register slip could have been the receipt for a week's worth of groceries, which Dye had gone to Schwegmann's to purchase.

The inconclusiveness of the physical evidence does not, to be sure, prove Kyles's innocence, and the jury might have found the eyewitness testimony of Territo and Kersh sufficient to convict, even though less damning to Kyles than that of Smallwood and Williams. But the question is not whether the State would have had a case to go to the jury if it had disclosed the favorable evidence, but whether we can be confident that the jury's verdict would have been the same. . . .

"[F]airness" cannot be stretched to the point of calling this a fair trial. . . . The judgment of the Court of Appeals [affirming the denial of Kyles's petition for habeas corpus] is reversed, and the case is remanded for further proceedings consistent with this opinion. . . .

[The concurring opinion of Justice Stevens, joined by Justices Ginsburg and Breyer, is omitted.]

JUSTICE SCALIA, with whom the CHIEF JUSTICE, JUSTICE KENNEDY, and Justice Thomas join, dissenting. . . .

I am . . . forced to dissent . . . because, having improvidently decided to review the facts of this case, the Court goes on to get the facts wrong. Its findings are in my view clearly erroneous, and the Court's verdict would be reversed if there were somewhere further to appeal. . . .

[A] few general observations about the Court's methodology are appropriate. It is fundamental to the discovery rule of Brady v. Maryland, 373 U.S. 83 (1963), that the materiality of a failure to disclose favorable evidence "must be evaluated in the context of the entire record." United States v. Agurs, 427 U.S. 97, 112 (1976). It is simply not enough to show that the undisclosed evidence would have allowed the defense to weaken, or even to "destro[y]," the *particular* prosecution witnesses or items of prosecution evidence to which the undisclosed evidence relates. It is petitioner's burden to show that in light of all the evidence, including that untainted by the *Brady* violation, it is reasonably probable that a jury would have entertained a reasonable doubt regarding petitioner's guilt. . . .

In any analysis of this case, the desperate implausibility of the theory that petitioner put before the jury must be kept firmly in mind. The first half of that theory — designed to neutralize the physical evidence (Mrs. Dye's purse in his garbage, the murder weapon behind his stove) — was that petitioner was the victim of a "frame-up" by the police informer and evil genius, Beanie. Now, it is not unusual for a guilty person who knows that he is suspected of a crime to try to shift blame to someone else; and it is less common, but not unheard of, for a guilty person who is neither suspected nor subject to suspicion (because he has established a perfect alibi), to call attention to himself by coming forward to point the finger at an innocent person. But petitioner's theory is that the guilty Beanie, who *could* plausibly be accused of the crime . . . but who was *not* a suspect any more than Kyles was (the police as yet had no leads), injected both Kyles and himself into the investigation in order to get the innocent Kyles convicted. If this were not stupid enough, the wicked Beanie is supposed to have suggested that the police search his victim's premises *a full day before he got around to planting the incriminating evidence on the premises*.

The second half of petitioner's theory was that he was the victim of a quadruple coincidence, in which four eyewitnesses to the crime mistakenly identified him as the murderer — three picking him out of a photo array without hesitation, and all four affirming their identification in open court after comparing him with Beanie. The extraordinary mistake petitioner had to persuade the jury these four witnesses made was not simply to mistake the real killer, Beanie, for the very same innocent third party (hard enough to believe), but in addition to mistake him *for the very man Beanie had chosen to frame* — the last and most incredible level of coincidence. However small the chance that the jury would believe any one of those improbable scenarios, the likelihood that it would believe them all together is far smaller. . . .

[The] basic error of approaching the evidence piecemeal is . . . what accounts for the Court's obsessive focus on the credibility or culpability of Beanie, who did not even testify at trial and whose credibility or innocence the State has never once avowed. The Court's opinion reads as if either petitioner or Beanie must be telling the truth, and any evidence tending to inculpate or undermine the credibility of the one would exculpate or enhance the credibility of the other. But the jury verdict in this case said only that petitioner was guilty of the murder. That is perfectly consistent with the possibilities that Beanie repeatedly lied, that he was an accessory after the fact, or even that he planted evidence against petitioner. Even if the undisclosed evidence would have allowed the defense to thoroughly impeach Beanie and to suggest the above possibilities, the jury could well have believed *all* of those things and yet have condemned petitioner because it could not believe that *all four* of the eyewitnesses were similarly mistaken. . . .

The undisclosed evidence does not create a "'reasonable probability' of a different result." To begin with the eyewitness testimony. . . .

Territo, the first eyewitness called by the State, was waiting at a red light in a truck 30 or 40 yards from the Schwegmann's parking lot. He saw petitioner shoot Mrs. Dye, start her car, drive out onto the road, and pull up just behind Territo's truck. When the light turned green petitioner pulled beside Territo and stopped while waiting to make a turn. Petitioner looked Territo full in the face. . . . Territo also testified that a detective had shown him a picture of Beanie and asked him if the picture "could have been the guy that did it. I told him no." The second eyewitness, Kersh, also saw petitioner shoot Mrs. Dye. When asked whether she got "a good look" at him as he drove away, she answered "yes." . . . The third eyewitness, Smallwood, testified that he saw petitioner shoot Mrs. Dye, walk to the car, and drive away. Petitioner drove slowly by, within a distance of 15 or 25 feet, and Smallwood saw his face from the side. The fourth eyewitness, Williams, who had been working outside the parking lot, testified that "the gentleman came up the side of the car," struggled with Mrs. Dye, shot her, walked around to the driver's side of the car, and drove away. Williams not only "saw him before he shot her," but watched petitioner drive slowly by "within less than ten feet." When asked "[d]id you get an opportunity to look at him good?", Williams said, "I did."

The Court attempts to dispose of this direct, unqualified, and consistent eyewitness testimony in two ways. First, by relying on a theory so implausible that it was apparently not suggested by petitioner's counsel until the oral-argument-*cum*-evidentiary-hearing held before us, perhaps because it is a theory that only the most removed appellate court could love. This theory is that there is a reasonable probability that the jury would have changed its mind about the eyewitness identification because the *Brady* material would have permitted the defense to argue that the eyewitnesses only got a good look at the killer when he was sitting in Mrs. Dye's car, and thus could identify him, not by his height and build, but *only by his face*. Never mind, for the moment, that this is factually false, since the *Brady* material showed that only *one* of the four eyewitnesses, Smallwood, did not see the killer outside the car. And never mind, also, the dubious premise that the build of a man 6-feet tall (like petitioner) is indistinguishable, when seated behind the wheel, from that of a man less than 5½-feet tall (like Beanie). To assert that unhesitant and categorical identification by four witnesses who viewed the killer, close-up and with the sun high in the sky, would not eliminate reasonable doubt if it were based *only* on *facial* characteristics, and not on height and build, is quite simply absurd. Facial features are *the primary means* by which human beings recognize one another. That is why police departments distribute "mug" shots of wanted felons, rather than Ivy-League-type posture pictures; it is why bank robbers wear stockings over their faces instead of floor-length capes over their shoulders; it is why the Lone Ranger wears a mask instead of a poncho; and it is why a criminal defense lawyer who seeks to destroy an identifying witness by asking "You admit that you saw only the killer's face?" will be laughed out of the courtroom.

It would be different, of course, if there were evidence that Kyles's and Beanie's faces looked like twins, or at least bore an unusual degree of resemblance. That facial resemblance *would* explain why, if Beanie committed the crime, all four witnesses picked out Kyles at first (though not why they continued to pick him out when he and Beanie stood side-by-side in court), and would render their failure to observe the height and build of the killer relevant. . . . *No* court has found that Kyles and Beanie bear any facial resemblance. In fact, quite the opposite: *every* federal and state court that has reviewed the record photographs, or seen the two men, has found that they do not resemble each other in any respect. . . .

The Court's second means of seeking to neutralize the impressive and unanimous eyewitness testimony uses the same "build-is-everything" theory to exaggerate the effect of the State's failure to disclose the contemporaneous statement of Henry Williams. That statement would assuredly have permitted a sharp cross-examination, since it contained estimations of height and weight that fit Beanie better than petitioner. But I think it is hyperbole to say that the statement would have "substantially reduced or destroyed" the value of Williams' testimony. Williams saw the murderer drive slowly by less than 10 feet away, and unhesitatingly picked him out of the photo lineup. The jury might well choose to give greater credence to the simple fact of identification than to the difficult estimation of height and weight.

The Court spends considerable time showing how Smallwood's testimony could have been discredited to such a degree as to "rais[e] a substantial implication that the prosecutor had coached him to give it." Perhaps so, but that is all irrelevant to this appeal, since all of that impeaching material (except the "facial identification" point I have discussed above) was available to the defense independently of the *Brady* material [based on inconsistencies between Smallwood's testimony at the first and second trials]. In sum, the undisclosed statements, credited with everything they could possibly have provided to the defense, leave two prosecution witnesses (Territo and Kersh) totally untouched; one prosecution witness (Smallwood) barely affected (he saw "only" the killer's face); and one prosecution witness (Williams) somewhat impaired (his description of the killer's height and weight did not match Kyles). We must keep all this in due perspective, remembering that the relevant question in the materiality inquiry is not how many points the defense could have scored off the prosecution witnesses, but whether it is reasonably probable that the new evidence would have caused the jury to accept the basic thesis that all four witnesses were mistaken. I think it plainly is not. . . .

The physical evidence confirms the immateriality of the nondisclosures. In a garbage bag outside petitioner's home the police found Mrs. Dye's purse and other belongings. Inside his home they found, behind the kitchen stove, the .32-caliber revolver used to kill Mrs. Dye; hanging in a wardrobe, a homemade shoulder holster that was "a perfect fit" for the revolver; in a dresser drawer in the bedroom, two boxes of gun cartridges, one containing only .32-caliber rounds of the same brand found in the murder weapon, another containing .22, .32, and .38-caliber rounds; in a kitchen cabinet, eight empty Schwegmann's bags; and in a cupboard underneath that cabinet, one Schwegmann's bag containing 15 cans of pet food.

Petitioner's account at trial was that Beanie planted the purse, gun, and holster, that petitioner received the ammunition from Beanie as collateral for a loan, and that petitioner had bought the pet food the day of the murder. That account strains credulity to the breaking point.

The Court is correct that the *Brady* material would have supported the claim that Beanie planted Mrs. Dye's belongings in petitioner's garbage and (to a lesser degree) that Beanie planted the gun behind petitioner's stove. But we must see the whole story that petitioner presented to the jury. Petitioner would have it that Beanie did not plant the incriminating evidence until the day after he incited the police to search petitioner's home. Moreover, he succeeded in surreptitiously placing the gun behind the stove, and the matching shoulder holster in the wardrobe, while *at least 10 and as many as 19 people* were present in petitioner's small apartment. Beanie, who was wearing blue jeans and either a "tank-top" shirt or a short-sleeved shirt, would have had to be concealing about his person not only the shoulder holster and the murder weapon, but also a different gun with tape wrapped around the barrel that he showed to petitioner. Only appellate judges could swallow such a tale. Petitioner's only supporting evidence was Johnny Burns's testimony that he saw Beanie stooping behind the stove, presumably to plant the gun. Burns's credibility on the stand can perhaps best be gauged by observing that the state judge who presided over petitioner's trial stated, in a postconviction proceeding, that "[I] ha[ve] chosen to totally disregard everything that [Burns] has said." Burns, by the way, who repeatedly stated at trial that Beanie was his "best friend," has since been tried and convicted for killing Beanie.

Petitioner did not claim that the ammunition had been planted. The police found a .22-caliber rifle under petitioner's mattress and two boxes of ammunition, one containing .22, .32, and .38-caliber rounds, another containing only .32-caliber rounds of the same brand as those found loaded in the murder weapon. Petitioner's story was that Beanie gave him the rifle and the .32-caliber shells as security for a loan, but that he had taken the .22-caliber shells out of the box. Put aside that the latter detail was contradicted by the facts; but consider the inherent implausibility of Beanie's giving petitioner collateral in the form of a box containing *only* .32 shells, if it were true that petitioner did not own a .32-caliber gun. As the Fifth Circuit wrote, "[t]he more likely inference, apparently chosen by the jury, is that [petitioner] possessed .32 caliber ammunition because he possessed a .32-caliber firearm."

We come to the evidence of the pet food, so mundane and yet so very damning. Petitioner's confused and changing explanations for the presence of *15 cans* of pet food in a Schwegmann's bag under the sink must have fatally undermined his credibility before the jury. . . .

. . . Mr. and Mrs. Dye owned two cats and a dog, for which she regularly bought varying brands of pet food, several different brands at a time. Found in Mrs. Dye's home after her murder were the brands Nine Lives, Kalkan, and Puss n' Boots. Found in petitioner's home were eight cans of Nine Lives, four cans of Kalkan, and three cans of Cozy Kitten. Since we know that Mrs. Dye had been shopping that day and that the murderer made off with her goods, petitioner's possession of these items was powerful evidence that he was the murderer. Assuredly the jury drew that obvious inference. Pressed to explain why he just happened to buy 15 cans of pet food that very day (keep in mind that petitioner was a very poor man, who supported a common-law wife, a mistress, and four children), petitioner gave the reason that "it was on sale." The State, however, introduced testimony from the Schwegmann's advertising director that the pet food was not on sale that day. . . .

The State presented to the jury a massive core of evidence (including four eye-witnesses) showing that petitioner was guilty of murder, and that he lied about his guilt. The effect that the *Brady* materials would have had in chipping away at the edges of the State's case can only be called immaterial. . . .

I respectfully dissent.

NOTES AND QUESTIONS

1. How do the majority and the dissent reach such wildly different conclusions on the materiality of the prosecution's failure to disclose? Is it possible that they are addressing different questions? Justice Souter cites United States v. Bagley, 473 U.S. 667, 682 (1995), for the holding that the suppression of favorable evidence is material, for *Brady* purposes, "if there is a reasonable probability that, had the evidence been disclosed . . . the result of the proceeding would have been different." Is Justice Scalia asking this same question? Or is he asking whether there is a reasonable chance that the defendant did not commit the crime? Which is the better question on which to focus?

2. Kyles was tried for the murder three more times after the Supreme Court's decision. Each time, the jury hung. According to lawyers involved in the case, the number of votes for acquittal was substantially greater than for conviction on the first retrial. However, the votes for conviction rose with each subsequent retrial, with most of the jury voting for conviction in the final trial. Kyles was finally released in 1998 — almost 15 years after his arrest. Does this subsequent history cast any light on the question whether the suppressed evidence created a "reasonable probability" of a different result?

3. *Kyles* was read by some as an indication that the Court will apply the materiality standard strictly, that doubts will generally be resolved in the defendants' favor. The Court left a different impression four years later in Strickler v. Greene, 527 U.S. 263 (1999). *Strickler* arose out of the murder of Leanne Whitlock, a college student at James Madison University in Virginia. Whitlock was abducted from a shopping center near campus, after which she was robbed and murdered. Defendants Strickler and Henderson were both charged with the murder. Henderson was convicted of first-degree murder, which is not a capital offense in Virginia; Strickler was convicted of capital murder and sentenced to death.

The government had several witnesses linking the two defendants to the crime but — with one exception, to which we'll return — those witnesses didn't actually see any portion of the crime take place. A security guard at the shopping mall placed Henderson and Strickler there in the hours before Whitlock was abducted; the guard said she saw the two men trying to steal a car in the parking lot. Later that evening, another witness saw Henderson and Strickler driving Whitlock's car, a blue Mercury Lynx, about 25 miles from Harrisonburg, near where Whitlock's body was eventually found. Still later the same evening, the two defendants went dancing; Henderson gave one of the women with whom he danced Whitlock's watch. Strickler's girlfriend testified that he later gave her a pair of earrings that Whitlock had been seen wearing on the day of the murder; some of Whitlock's effects were later found in a search of Strickler's mother's house. And a few witnesses testified that, in the days following the crime, both defendants made veiled references to killing someone.

Physical evidence pointed in the defendants' direction, but offered little detailed information. Whitlock was killed by blows from a heavy rock found near her body; the nature of the killing suggested that there were at least two killers. A number of hair samples were found at the scene of the crime; three of them were "probably" Strickler's. 527 U.S., at 269. Notice that neither the testimony mentioned in the preceding paragraph nor any of the physical evidence distinguished among the defendants in a way that would allow a judge or jury to conclude that one of them was more culpable than the other.

One witness, Anne Stoltzfus, testified that she saw Whitlock's abduction. According to Stoltzfus, Strickler ran up to Whitlock's car as she was about to drive away from the mall parking lot, "pounded on the passenger window, shook the car, yanked the door open and jumped in." Stoltzfus testified that Whitlock "laid on the horn" in response, at which point Strickler "started hitting her . . . on the left shoulder, her right shoulder and then it looked like to me that he started hitting her on the head." Id., at 271-272. Stoltzfus then pulled her car up next to Whitlock's and asked if anything was wrong; she testified that Whitlock mouthed the word "help" in response. Id., at 272. Two other people got in the car (apparently Henderson and Strickler's girlfriend), after which Whitlock's car drove away. Before the car left, Stoltzfus wrote the license plate down on a small card. The card was later lost, but Stoltzfus remembered the plate, which matched Whitlock's car. At trial, Stoltzfus positively identified Strickler as the man she saw beating Whitlock, adding:

> [F]irst of all, I have an exceptionally good memory. I had very close contact with [petitioner] and he made an emotional impression with me because of his behavior and I, he caught my attention and I paid attention. So I have absolutely no doubt of my identification.

Id., at 272-273. Stoltzfus' testimony, unlike the rest of the government's evidence, allowed the jury to conclude that Strickler was the moving force in the murder, and that Henderson was (literally) along for the ride.

Strickler's *Brady* claim was based on the government's failure to disclose various notes concerning conversations police had with Stoltzfus shortly after the crime. After her initial conversation with a police detective, the detective wrote that Stoltzfus could identify neither Strickler nor Henderson. A few days later, Stoltzfus wrote a letter to the same detective saying that she initially hadn't recalled even being at the mall on the day of the crime; she added that "I have a very vague memory that I'm not sure of," and that her daughter, who was with her at the mall, didn't remember the incident at all. In another note to the detective, Stoltzfus described Whitlock's car, but made no mention of the license plate number. In still another note, Stoltzfus thanked the detective for his "patience with my sometime muddled memories." Id., at 273-274. None of these documents was made available to the defense. Taken together, they would seem to seriously undermine, perhaps destroy, Stoltzfus' testimony.

The Court found that the undisclosed notes did not meet the *Brady* materiality standard:

. . . Without a doubt, Stoltzfus' testimony was prejudicial in the sense that it made petitioner's conviction more likely than if she had not testified, and discrediting her testimony might have changed the outcome of the trial.

That, however, is not the standard that petitioner must satisfy in order to obtain relief. He must convince us that "there is a reasonable probability" that the result of the trial would have been different if the suppressed documents had been disclosed to the defense. As we stressed in *Kyles*: "[T]he adjective is important. The question is not whether the defendant would more likely than not have received a different verdict with the evidence, but whether in its absence he received a fair trial, understood as a trial resulting in a verdict worthy of confidence." 514 U.S., at 434. . . .

Given the record evidence involving Henderson, the District Court concluded that, without Stoltzfus' testimony, the jury might have been persuaded that Henderson, rather than petitioner, was the ringleader. He reasoned that a "reasonable probability of conviction" of first-degree, rather than capital, murder sufficed to establish the materiality of the undisclosed Stoltzfus materials and, thus, a *Brady* violation.

The District Court was surely correct that there is a reasonable *possibility* that either a total, or just a substantial, discount of Stoltzfus' testimony might have produced a different result, either at the guilt or sentencing phases. . . . As the District Court recognized, however, petitioner's burden is to establish a reasonable *probability* of a different result. *Kyles*, 514 U.S., at 434.

Even if Stoltzfus and her testimony had been entirely discredited, the jury might still have concluded that petitioner was the leader of the criminal enterprise because he was the one seen driving the car . . . near the location of the murder and the one who kept the car for the following week. . . .

More importantly, however, petitioner's guilt of capital murder did not depend on proof that he was the dominant partner: Proof that he was an equal participant with Henderson was sufficient under the judge's instructions. Accordingly, the strong evidence that Henderson was a killer is entirely consistent with the conclusion that petitioner was also an actual participant in the killing.

Furthermore, there was considerable forensic and other physical evidence linking petitioner to the crime. The weight and size of the rock, and the character of the fatal injuries to the victim, are powerful evidence supporting the conclusion that two people acted jointly to commit a brutal murder. . . .

The record provides strong support for the conclusion that petitioner would have been convicted of capital murder and sentenced to death, even if Stoltzfus had been severely impeached. . . .

Id., at 289-294. Justice Souter — the author of the majority opinion in *Kyles* — dissented (along with Justice Kennedy), arguing that the impeaching evidence was material, at least to the decision to impose the death penalty.

Based on a close examination of the record in *Strickler*, Professor Saltzburg has concluded that Justice Souter was right: "[I]t was Stoltzfus more than any other witness who established for the prosecution the fact of Strickler's control. . . . I have little doubt that the suppression of the Stoltzfus evidence might well have affected the jury's decision to convict Strickler of capital murder as opposed to non-capital murder, and might well have resulted in the death sentence that the jury recommended and the trial judge imposed." Stephen A. Saltzburg, Perjury and False Testimony: Should the Difference Matter So Much? 68 Fordham L. Rev. 1537, 1553-1554 (2000). Are you persuaded? Is *Strickler* consistent with *Kyles*?

At the level of doctrinal technicality, the answer to that last question is "yes." The *Strickler* Court didn't alter the test for *Brady* claims that *Kyles* articulated, and *Kyles* is cited and quoted throughout Justice Stevens' majority opinion in *Strickler*. But if the words are the same, the music seems different. *Strickler* shows a much greater deference to the trial outcome than does *Kyles*, and seems much more aware of the dangers of extending *Brady* doctrine too far — all of which makes one wonder if lower courts will be able to consistently apply the doctrine.

4. Notwithstanding ongoing debates as to whether *Brady*'s materiality standard is overly permissive vis-à-vis prosecutors or not generous enough, *Brady* and its progeny clearly established that due process requires prosecutors to turn over certain evidence in their possession in the interests of fair *trial*. That raises an obvious question. Should *Brady* material also be produced during plea negotiations in the interests of a fair *conviction*? Consider the next case.

UNITED STATES v. RUIZ

Certiorari to the United States Court of Appeals for the Ninth Circuit
536 U.S. 622 (2002)

JUSTICE BREYER delivered the opinion of the Court.

In this case we primarily consider whether the Fifth and Sixth Amendments require federal prosecutors, before entering into a binding plea agreement with a criminal defendant, to disclose "impeachment information relating to any informants or other witnesses." App. to Pet. for Cert. 46a. We hold that the Constitution does not require that disclosure.

After immigration agents found 30 kilograms of marijuana in Angela Ruiz's luggage, federal prosecutors offered her what is known in the Southern District of California as a "fast track" plea bargain. That bargain — standard in that district — asks a defendant to waive indictment, trial, and an appeal. In return, the Government agrees to recommend to the sentencing judge a two-level departure downward from the otherwise applicable United States Sentencing Guidelines sentence. In Ruiz's case, a two-level departure downward would have shortened the ordinary Guidelines-specified 18-to-24-month sentencing range by 6 months, to 12-to-18 months. 241 F.3d 1157, 1161 (2001).

The prosecutors' proposed plea agreement contains a set of detailed terms. Among other things, it specifies that "any [known] information establishing the factual innocence of the defendant" "has been turned over to the defendant," and it acknowledges the Government's "continuing duty to provide such information." App. to Pet. for Cert. 45a-46a. At the same time it requires that the defendant "waive the right" to receive "impeachment information relating to any informants or other witnesses" as well as the right to receive information supporting any affirmative defense the defendant raises if the case goes to trial. Id., at 46a. Because Ruiz would not agree to this last-mentioned waiver, the prosecutors withdrew their bargaining offer. The Government then indicted Ruiz for unlawful drug possession. And despite the absence of any agreement, Ruiz ultimately pleaded guilty.

At sentencing, Ruiz asked the judge to grant her the same two-level downward departure that the Government would have recommended had she accepted the "fast track" agreement. The Government opposed her request, and the District Court denied it, imposing a standard Guideline sentence instead.

. . . Ruiz appealed her sentence to the United States Court of Appeals for the Ninth Circuit. The Ninth Circuit vacated the District Court's sentencing determination. The Ninth Circuit pointed out that the Constitution requires prosecutors to make certain impeachment information available to a defendant before trial. It decided that this obligation entitles defendants to receive that same information before they enter into a plea agreement. [241 F.3d, at 1164.] The Ninth Circuit also decided that the Constitution prohibits defendants from waiving their right to that information. Id., at 1165-1166. And it held that the prosecutors' standard "fast track" plea agreement was unlawful because it insisted upon that waiver. Id., at 1167. . . .

The constitutional question concerns a federal criminal defendant's waiver of the right to receive from prosecutors exculpatory impeachment material — a right that the Constitution provides as part of its basic "fair trial" guarantee. See U.S. Const., Amdts. 5, 6. See also Brady v. Maryland, 373 U.S. 83, 87 (1963) (Due process requires prosecutors to "avoid . . . an unfair trial" by making available "upon request" evidence "favorable to an accused . . . where the evidence is material either to guilt or to punishment"); United States v. Agurs, 427 U.S. 97, 112-113 (1976) (defense request unnecessary); Kyles v. Whitley, 514 U.S. 419, 435 (1995) (exculpatory evidence is evidence the suppression of which would "undermine confidence in the verdict"); Giglio v. United States, 405 U.S. 150, 154 (1972) (exculpatory evidence includes "evidence affecting" witness "credibility," where the witness' "reliability" is likely "determinative of guilt or innocence").

When a defendant pleads guilty, he or she, of course, forgoes not only a fair trial, but also other accompanying constitutional guarantees. Given the seriousness of the matter, the Constitution insists, among other things, that the defendant enter a guilty plea that is "voluntary" and that the defendant must make related waivers "knowingly, intelligently, [and] with sufficient awareness of the relevant circumstances and likely consequences." Brady v. United States, 397 U.S. 742, 748 (1970).

In this case, the Ninth Circuit in effect held that a guilty plea is not "voluntary" (and that the defendant could not, by pleading guilty, waive his right to a fair trial) unless the prosecutors first made the same disclosure of material impeachment information that the prosecutors would have had to make had the defendant insisted upon a trial. We must decide whether the Constitution requires that preguilty plea disclosure of impeachment information. We conclude that it does not.

First, impeachment information is special in relation to the fairness of a trial, not in respect to whether a plea is voluntary ("knowing," "intelligent," and "sufficiently aware"). Of course, the more information the defendant has, the more aware he is of the likely consequences of a plea, waiver, or decision, and the wiser that decision will likely be. But the Constitution does not require the prosecutor to share all useful information with the defendant. And the law ordinarily considers a waiver knowing, intelligent, and sufficiently aware if the defendant fully understands the nature of the right and how it would likely apply in general in the circumstances — even though the defendant may not know the specific detailed consequences of invoking it. A defendant, for example, may waive his right to remain silent, his right to a jury trial, or his right to counsel even if the defendant does not know the specific questions the authorities intend to ask, who will likely serve on the jury, or the particular lawyer the State might otherwise provide.

It is particularly difficult to characterize impeachment information as critical information of which the defendant must always be aware prior to pleading guilty given the random way in which such information may, or may not, help a particular defendant. The degree of help that impeachment information can provide will depend upon the defendant's own independent knowledge of the prosecution's potential case — a matter that the Constitution does not require prosecutors to disclose.

Second, we have found no legal authority embodied either in this Court's past cases or in cases from other circuits that provide significant support for the Ninth Circuit's decision. To the contrary, this Court has found that the Constitution, in respect to a defendant's awareness of relevant circumstances, does not require complete knowledge of the relevant circumstances, but permits a court to accept a guilty plea, with its accompanying waiver of various constitutional rights, despite various forms of misapprehension under which a defendant might labor. See Brady v. United States, 397 U.S., at 757 (defendant "misapprehended the quality of the State's case"); ibid. (defendant misapprehended "the likely penalties"); ibid. (defendant failed to "anticipate a change in the law regarding" relevant "punishments"); McMann v. Richardson, 397 U.S. 759, 770 (1970) (counsel "misjudged the admissibility" of a "confession"); United States v. Broce, 488 U.S. 563, 573 (1989) (counsel failed to point out a potential defense); Tollett v. Henderson, 411 U.S. 258, 267 (1973) (counsel failed to find a potential constitutional infirmity in grand jury proceedings). It is difficult to distinguish, in terms of importance, a defendant's ignorance of grounds for impeachment of potential witnesses at a possible future trial from the varying forms of ignorance at issue in these cases.

Third, due process considerations, the very considerations that led this Court to find trial-related rights to exculpatory and impeachment information in *Brady* and *Giglio*, argue against the existence of the "right" that the Ninth Circuit found here. This Court has said that due process considerations include not only (1) the nature of the private interest at stake, but also (2) the value of the additional safeguard, and (3) the adverse impact of the requirement upon the Government's interests. Ake v. Oklahoma, 470 U.S. 68, 77 (1985). Here, as we have just pointed out, the added value of the Ninth Circuit's "right" to a defendant is often limited, for it depends upon the defendant's independent awareness of the details of the Government's case. And in any case, as the proposed plea agreement at issue here specifies, the Government will provide "any information establishing the factual innocence of the defendant" regardless. That fact, along with other guilty-plea safeguards, see Fed. Rule Crim. Proc. 11, diminishes the force of Ruiz's concern that, in the absence of impeachment information, innocent individuals, accused of crimes, will plead guilty.

At the same time, a constitutional obligation to provide impeachment information during plea bargaining, prior to entry of a guilty plea, could seriously interfere with the Government's interest in securing those guilty pleas that are factually justified, desired by defendants, and help to secure the efficient administration of justice. The Ninth Circuit's rule risks premature disclosure of Government witness information, which, the Government tells us, could "disrupt ongoing investigations" and expose prospective witnesses to serious harm. Brief for United States 25. And the careful tailoring that characterizes most legal Government witness disclosure requirements suggests recognition by both Congress and the Federal Rules Committees that such concerns are valid. See, e.g., 18 U.S.C. §3432 (witness list disclosure required in capital cases three days before trial with exceptions); §3500 (Government witness statements ordinarily subject to discovery only after testimony given); Fed. Rule Crim. Proc. 16(a)(2) (embodies limitations of 18 U.S.C. §3500).

Consequently, the Ninth Circuit's requirement could force the Government to abandon its "general practice" of not "disclosing to a defendant pleading guilty information that would reveal the identities of cooperating informants, undercover investigators, or other prospective witnesses." Brief for United States 25. It could require the Government to devote substantially more resources to trial preparation prior to plea bargaining, thereby depriving the plea-bargaining process of its main resource-saving advantages. Or it could lead the Government instead to abandon its heavy reliance upon plea bargaining in a vast number — 90% or more — of federal criminal cases. We cannot say that the Constitution's due process requirement demands so radical a change in the criminal justice process in order to achieve so comparatively small a constitutional benefit.

These considerations, taken together, lead us to conclude that the Constitution does not require the Government to disclose material impeachment evidence prior to entering a plea agreement with a criminal defendant.

In addition, we note that the "fast track" plea agreement requires a defendant to waive her right to receive information the Government has regarding any "affirmative defense" she raises at trial. We do not believe the Constitution here requires provision of this information to the defendant prior to plea bargaining — for most (though not all) of the reasons previously stated. That is to say, in the context of this agreement, the need for this information is more closely related to the fairness of a trial than to the voluntariness of the plea; the value in terms of the defendant's added awareness of relevant circumstances is ordinarily limited; yet the added burden imposed upon the Government by requiring its provision well in advance of trial (often before trial preparation begins) can be serious, thereby significantly interfering with the administration of the plea bargaining process.

For these reasons the decision of the Court of Appeals for the Ninth Circuit is reversed.

JUSTICE THOMAS, concurring in the judgment.

I agree with the Court that the Constitution does not require the Government to disclose either affirmative defense information or impeachment information relating to informants or other witnesses before entering into a binding plea agreement with a criminal defendant. The Court, however, suggests that the constitutional analysis turns in some part on the "degree of help" such information would provide to the defendant at the plea stage, a distinction that is neither necessary nor accurate. To the extent that the Court is implicitly drawing a line based on a flawed characterization about the usefulness of certain types of information, I can only concur in the judgment. The principle supporting *Brady* was "avoidance of an unfair trial to the accused." Brady v. Maryland, 373 U.S. 83, 87 (1963). That concern is not implicated at the plea stage. . . .

NOTES AND QUESTIONS

1. The holding in *Ruiz* is limited to the failure to disclose material impeachment evidence before entering into a plea agreement. Recall that in *Kyles*, however, the Court drew no distinction between information that might impeach government witnesses and other sorts of exculpatory evidence. Indeed, the Court had explicitly rejected this distinction in Giglio v. United States, 405 U.S. 150, 154 (1972), a case cited with approval in *Ruiz*. Does *Ruiz* nonetheless recognize such a distinction? If so, does this suggest that in the *trial* context, failures to disclose impeachment evidence should be viewed by courts as less serious than other types of *Brady* violations?

2. The Court in *Ruiz* apparently found it significant that the prosecutor had agreed to provide "any [known] information establishing the factual innocence of the defendant." It is hard to know what to make of this language; surely if the government "knows" of information that "establish[es]" the defendant's factual innocence, the proper course would be to dismiss the charge, not simply disclose the information and then press for a guilty plea. Is there another way to interpret the government's commitment? Does the language commit a prosecutor to disclose all *non*-impeachment *Brady* material prior to a guilty plea, or something less than that?

3. One way to read *Ruiz* is that *Brady* rights to receive material exculpatory evidence, like other constitutional rights, are waivable. Should they be? Most rights that defendants waive when pleading guilty fall into one of two categories. The first consists of rights to some future benefit — say, a jury trial — about which the defendant is informed at the plea colloquy. The second category consists of rights to litigate some claim of past government misconduct — say, an improper police search — about which the defendant already knows. Even when the defendant doesn't know the particulars of the claim, as with claims that the grand jury was discriminatorily selected, he generally knows that some such claim is possible, for he knows whether or not a grand jury has indicted him. *Brady* claims are different, because the defendant does not know about material exculpatory evidence in the government's possession unless and until such evidence is disclosed to him. Given this, is it appropriate to treat a defendant as having waived a right when, by definition, he could not have known of the violation?

4. *Brady*'s materiality standard is roughly analogous to the prejudice standard the Court uses for ineffective assistance claims under Strickland v. Washington, 466 U.S. 668 (1984). Could a defendant validly waive his right to raise a *Strickland* claim? (Recall that a defendant can waive his right to be represented by *any* lawyer, so why not a waiver of the right of an effective lawyer?) Could the government condition a plea bargain on such a waiver?

5. Suppose *Ruiz* had held that prior to a guilty plea, *Brady* requires disclosure of any material exculpatory evidence in the government's possession, and that the requirement cannot be waived. What effect would that ruling have on government evidence-gathering? One possibility is that the *Brady* right would make pre-plea investigation more expensive for the government; police or prosecutors might find evidence that would be helpful to the defense, in which case the evidence would have to be disclosed, possibly destroying any chance at reaching a plea bargain. At the margin, the government might decide to do less evidence-gathering prior to plea bargaining in order to reduce that risk. That does not sound like good news for innocent defendants, although it may help a guilty one if further investigation would have uncovered more criminal conduct. How should the law solve this problem?

6. Assume for a minute that, in at least some cases, *Brady* does require pre-guilty plea disclosure; how should a court articulate the materiality standard in guilty plea cases? In *Strickland* cases, defendants who plead guilty must show a reasonable probability that, but for defense counsel's errors, the defendant would not have pled guilty but would have insisted on going to trial. See Hill v. Lockhart, 474 U.S. 52 (1985). Should a similar standard apply to *Brady* claims? What if the nondisclosure only affected the terms of the defendant's sentence?

FINAL NOTES ON BRADY, INNOCENCE, AND THE ROLE OF CONSTITUTIONAL LAW

1. Consider again *Brady*'s materiality standard. Applying this standard prior to a trial "requires that prosecutors engage in a bizarre kind of anticipatory hindsight review." Alafair S. Burke, Improving Prosecutorial Decision Making: Some Lessons of Cognitive Science, 47 Wm. & Mary L. Rev. 1587, 1610 (2006). Professor Burke argues that due to cognitive bias, even the most conscientious prosecutor engaged in such review may prove unreliable in recognizing and producing *Brady* material:

> *Brady* requires a prosecutor who is determining whether to disclose a piece of evidence . . . to speculate first about how the remaining evidence will come together against the defendant at trial, and then about whether a reasonable probability exists that the piece of evidence at issue would affect the result of the trial. During the first step, a risk exists that prosecutors will engage in biased recall, retrieving from memory only those facts that tend to confirm the hypothesis of guilty. Moreover, because of selective information processing, the prosecutor will accept at face value the evidence she views as inculpatory, without subjecting it to the scrutiny that a defense attorney would encourage jurors to apply.
>
> Cognitive bias would also appear to taint the second speculative step of the *Brady* analysis. . . . Because of selective information processing, the prosecutor will look for weaknesses in evidence contradicting her existing belief in the defendant's guilt. In short, compared to a neutral decision maker, the prosecutor will overestimate the strength of the government's case against the defendant and underestimate the potential exculpatory value of the evidence whose disclosure is at issue. As a consequence, the prosecutor will fail to see materiality where it might in fact exist.

Id., at 1611-1612. The *Brady* rule treats the good or bad faith of the state as irrelevant to whether the failure to disclose exculpatory and impeachment evidence requires a reversal. Still, shouldn't we be troubled by this? As Professor Gianelli has argued, "If the prosecutor believed the accused was innocent, virtually all prosecutors would dismiss the case. Thus, *Brady* issues arise in cases where the prosecutor believes the defendant is guilty." Paul C. Giannelli, *Brady* and Jailhouse Snitches, 57 Case W. Res. L. Rev. 593, 601 (2007). He concludes that "[a]lthough many scrupulous prosecutors adhere to the *Brady* requirements, others have failed, and failed far too often." A better approach to avoiding miscarriages of justice, he argues, is "expanded discovery rules." Do you agree?

2. Professor Garrett studied 200 cases of persons found innocent through postconviction DNA testing. He found that "[t]he overwhelming number of convictions of the innocent involved eyewitness identification — 158 of 200 cases (79%)." Brandon L. Garrett, Judging Innocence, 108 Colum. L. Rev. 55, 78 (2008). Faulty forensic evidence was the second most common type of evidence supporting the convictions — in 113 cases, or 57 percent. Id., at 81. Note that reforms to the investigative process, rather than discovery rules, may be most important to the avoidance of wrongful conviction. And many such reforms — involving how identification procedures are conducted, how crime labs are organized, paid for, and the like — have been proposed and, in some places, implemented as a result of careful scrutiny of the DNA cases. See Dwyer, Neufeld, & Scheck, Actual Innocence, at 255-260 (proposing such reforms).

3. Let's return to the role of constitutional law. Surely one of the central values of due process in criminal cases is to protect the innocent against wrongful convictions. Is it the only one? Should constitutional disclosure requirements be seen principally as about protecting the innocent? Or are other values, including fairness to all who are accused and the state's interest in effective law enforcement, also at stake?

In this connection, consider Arizona v. Youngblood, 488 U.S. 51 (1988), a case involving the due process consequences of the state's failure to preserve evidence for trial. In *Youngblood*, police failed properly to preserve semen samples from the body and clothing of a ten-year-old victim of molestation and kidnapping. At trial, the defendant claimed that the child had erred in identifying him as the perpetrator and argued that if the evidence had been properly preserved, blood group tests performed on this evidence could have exonerated him. He was nevertheless convicted. The Court concluded that the state's failure to properly preserve this evidence for testing did not require reversal of the conviction in the absence of any showing that the police acted in bad faith:

> We think that requiring a defendant to show bad faith on the part of the police both limits the extent of the police's obligation to preserve evidence to reasonable bounds and confines it to that class of cases where the interests of justice most clearly require it, i.e., those cases in which the police themselves by their conduct indicate that the evidence could form a basis for exonerating the defendant. We therefore hold that unless a criminal defendant can show bad faith on the part of the police, failure to preserve potentially useful evidence does not constitute a denial of due process of law.

Id., at 58.

Youngblood's saga did not end with this holding. He served ten years in prison and was released in 1998, only to be rearrested the next year for failing to register a new address as required under Arizona's sex offender registration law. During this later period of incarceration, more sophisticated DNA tests were performed on the damaged evidence that was still in the possession of police. In August 2000, Youngblood was freed — the DNA tests exonerated him. See Laurie P. Cohen, DNA Tests Free Man Imprisoned 10 Years, Wall Street Journal, Aug. 10, 2000, at B12. Does Youngblood's story suggest that the Court should have held the prosecution to a different and more rigorous standard with regard to evidence preservation?

4. Now consider Illinois v. Fisher, 540 U.S. 544 (2004) (per curiam), which reaffirmed *Youngblood* in a different factual context. Fisher was arrested in September 1988 in the course of a traffic stop during which police observed him furtively attempt to conceal a plastic bag; lab testing confirmed the arresting officers' conclusion that the bag contained cocaine. Charged with possession, the defendant filed a discovery motion to inspect the physical evidence, but then fled before trial; he wasn't found until 1999, a decade later. The State of Illinois then informed the defense that earlier that year, the police, following established procedures, had destroyed the alleged cocaine. The Supreme Court, citing *Youngblood*, held that the trial court's refusal to dismiss the charges was proper, given the absence of bad faith. Do you think Fisher was entitled to some form of relief?

Chapter 13

Guilty Pleas and Plea Bargaining

A. *Guilty Pleas as a Substitute for Trials*

The criminal process that law students study, and movies and television shows celebrate, is formal, elaborate, and expensive. It involves detailed examination of witnesses and physical evidence, tough adversarial argument from attorneys for the prosecution and defense, and fair-minded decision making from an impartial judge and jury. The heart of that process, of course, is the criminal trial.

For the huge majority of cases, the criminal process includes none of these things. Trials are, to put it mildly, exceptional. Of the more than 1,132,000 defendants who were convicted of felony crimes in state courts during 2006, 94 percent pleaded guilty.[1] In federal cases, the plea rate was even higher; for the year ending September 30, 2007, more than 95.7 percent of all federal criminal convictions were obtained by guilty plea.[2] (Both of those numbers have risen steadily over time.) In jurisdictions with both high crime rates and strapped budgets — two characteristics shared by most American cities — plea rates are higher still. It follows that the huge majority of America's two-million-plus prison and jail inmates got where they are not by conviction at trial by a jury of their peers, but by pleading guilty. Even for the most serious crimes — remember that the state-court plea rates quoted above were for *felony* convictions — the heart of the real-world criminal process is the guilty plea.

That raises some fundamental questions. When is a guilty plea an adequate substitute for a formal decision by a qualified factfinder that, beyond a reasonable doubt, the defendant is guilty of the crime charged? In other words, what procedures are necessary to make guilty pleas sufficiently fair and accurate to justify dispensing with the trial process guaranteed by the Constitution? And what role do defense lawyers play in the plea process? Eighty percent of criminal defendants receive appointed defense counsel. And appointed defense counsel operate under serious resource constraints, meaning that they cannot afford to go to trial in more than a small number of cases. How does that fact shape the plea process?

Notice that all of these questions are quite separate from the question whether the state should be able to *induce* guilty pleas by making charging or sentencing concessions. To what extent should we tolerate (or perhaps even embrace) the pervasive practice known as plea bargaining — a practice that, for better or for worse, produces the vast majority of the guilty pleas represented by the aforementioned state and federal statistics?

---

1. See U.S. Bureau of Justice Statistics, Felony Sentences in State Courts — 2006, p. 1 (Dec. 2009), available online at http://bjs.ojp.usdoj.gov/content/pub/pdf/fssc06st.pdf.

2. See U.S. Bureau of Justice Statistics, Federal Justice Statistics — 2007, Table 4.2 (Aug. 2010), available online at http://bjs.ojp.usdoj.gov/content/pub/html/fjsst/2007/tables/fjs07st402.pdf.

The materials that immediately follow deal with the guilty plea process as a whole, including the consequences of entering a guilty plea — whether or not that guilty plea was induced by a plea bargain. We will then examine the dominant feature of the contemporary American criminal justice system: plea bargaining. In the final section of the chapter, we will discuss the role of defense counsel in guilty pleas and plea bargaining, a role that gives rise to one of the most important possible means by which a defendant who has pleaded guilty can subsequently challenge his plea.

1.   The Plea Process

FEDERAL RULES OF CRIMINAL PROCEDURE

Rule 11. Pleas

(a) Entering a Plea.

(1) *In General*. A defendant may plead not guilty, guilty, or (with the court's consent) nolo contendere.

(2) *Conditional Plea*. With the consent of the court and the government, a defendant may enter a conditional plea of guilty or nolo contendere, reserving in writing the right to have an appellate court review an adverse determination of a specified pretrial motion. A defendant who prevails on appeal may then withdraw the plea.

(3) *Nolo Contendere Plea*. Before accepting a plea of nolo contendere, the court must consider the parties' views and the public interest in the effective administration of justice.

(4) *Failure to Enter a Plea*. If a defendant refuses to enter a plea or if a defendant organization fails to appear, the court must enter a plea of not guilty.

(b) Considering and Accepting a Guilty or Nolo Contendere Plea.

(1) *Advising and Questioning the Defendant*. Before the court accepts a plea of guilty or nolo contendere, the defendant may be placed under oath, and the court must address the defendant personally in open court. During this address, the court must inform the defendant of, and determine that the defendant understands, the following:

(A) the government's right, in a prosecution for perjury or false statement, to use against the defendant any statement that the defendant gives under oath;

(B) the right to plead not guilty, or having already so pleaded, to persist in that plea;

(C) the right to a jury trial;

(D) the right to be represented by counsel — and if necessary have the court appoint counsel — at trial and at every other stage of the proceeding;

(E) the right at trial to confront and cross-examine adverse witnesses, to be protected from compelled self-incrimination, to testify and present evidence, and to compel the attendance of witnesses;

(F) the defendant's waiver of these trial rights if the court accepts a plea of guilty or nolo contendere;

(G) the nature of each charge to which the defendant is pleading;

(H) any maximum possible penalty, including imprisonment, fine, and term of supervised release;

(I) any mandatory minimum penalty;

(J) any applicable forfeiture;

(K) the court's authority to order restitution;

(L) the court's obligation to impose a special assessment;

(M) [the court's obligation to apply the U.S. Sentencing Guidelines, and the court's discretion to depart from those guidelines under some circumstances]; and

(N) the terms of any plea-agreement provision waiving the right to appeal or to collaterally attack the sentence.

(2) *Ensuring That a Plea Is Voluntary.* Before accepting a plea of guilty or nolo contendere, the court must address the defendant personally in open court and determine that the plea is voluntary and did not result from force, threats, or promises (other than promises in a plea agreement).

(3) *Determining the Factual Basis for a Plea.* Before entering judgment on a guilty plea, the court must determine that there is a factual basis for the plea.

(c) Plea Agreement Procedure.

(1) *In General.* An attorney for the government and the defendant's attorney, or the defendant when proceeding pro se, may discuss and reach a plea agreement. The court must not participate in these discussions. If the defendant pleads guilty or nolo contendere to either a charged offense or a lesser or related offense, the plea agreement may specify that an attorney for the government will:

(A) not bring, or will move to dismiss, other charges;

(B) recommend, or agree not to oppose the defendant's request, that a particular sentence or sentencing range is appropriate or that a particular provision of the Sentencing Guidelines, or policy statement, or sentencing factor does or does not apply (such a recommendation or request does not bind the court); or

(C) agree that a specific sentence or sentencing range is the appropriate disposition of the case, or that a particular provision of the Sentencing Guidelines, or policy statement, or sentencing factor does or does not apply (such a recommendation or request binds the court once the court accepts the plea agreement).

(2) *Disclosing a Plea Agreement.* The parties must disclose the plea agreement in open court when the plea is offered, unless the court for good cause allows the parties to disclose the plea agreement in camera.

(3) *Judicial Consideration of a Plea Agreement.*

(A) To the extent the plea agreement is of the type specified in Rule 11(c)(1)(A) or (C), the court may accept the agreement, reject it, or defer a decision until the court has reviewed the presentence report.

(B) To the extent the plea agreement is of the type specified in Rule 11(c)(1)(B), the court must advise the defendant that the defendant has no right to withdraw the plea if the court does not follow the recommendation or request.

(4) *Accepting a Plea Agreement.* If the court accepts the plea agreement, it must inform the defendant that to the extent the plea agreement is of the type specified in Rule 11(c)(1)(A) or (C), the agreed disposition will be included in the judgment.

(5) *Rejecting a Plea Agreement.* If the court rejects a plea agreement containing provisions of the type specified in Rule 11(c)(1)(A) or (C), the court must do the following on the record and in open court (or, for good cause, in camera):

(A) inform the parties that the court rejects the plea agreement;

(B) advise the defendant personally that the court is not required to follow the plea agreement and give the defendant an opportunity to withdraw the plea; and

(C) advise the defendant personally that if the plea is not withdrawn, the court may dispose of the case less favorably toward the defendant than the plea agreement contemplated.

(d) Withdrawing a Guilty or Nolo Contendere Plea. A defendant may withdraw a plea of guilty or nolo contendere:

(1) before the court accepts the plea, for any reason or no reason; or

(2) after the court accepts the plea, but before it imposes sentence if

(A) the court rejects a plea agreement under Rule 11(c)(5); or

(B) the defendant can show a fair and just reason for requesting the withdrawal.

(e) Finality of a Guilty or Nolo Contendere Plea. After the court imposes sentence, the defendant may not withdraw a plea of guilty or nolo contendere, and the plea may be set aside only on direct appeal or collateral attack.

(f) Admissibility or Inadmissibility of a Plea, Plea Discussions, and Related Statements. The admissibility or inadmissibility of a plea, a plea discussion, and any related statement is governed by Federal Rule of Evidence 410.

(g) Recording the Proceedings. The proceedings during which the defendant enters a plea must be recorded by a court reporter or by a suitable recording device. If there is a guilty plea or a nolo contendere plea, the record must include the inquiries and advice to the defendant required under Rule 11(b) and (c).

(h) Harmless Error. A variance from the requirements of this rule is harmless error if it does not affect substantial rights.

[SPECIAL NOTE — Rule 11 was amended in 2002, as part of a general restyling of the Federal Rules of Criminal Procedure. The current version of Rule 11 appears above. Many of the cases excerpted in this chapter refer to the older version of Rule 11, substantively the same as the current version but with different subsection headings and a slightly different organization. We have updated most of these old references, so that they refer to the relevant sections of the *current* Rule 11. All such updated references will appear in [brackets]. Wherever an old reference remains untouched, we will so specify. — EDS.]

NOTES ON RULE 11 AND THE GUILTY PLEA PROCESS

Rule 11 in General.   Rule 11 defines the basic shape of the guilty plea process in federal courts. Of course, most guilty pleas take place in state courts, where Rule 11 does not apply. Nevertheless, most states have similar rules, so the Federal Rule is a good place to begin study of the plea process.

The structure of the Rule is fairly simple. Subsection (a) deals with plea options and conditional pleas. Subsection (b), the heart of the Rule, has three parts. Subsection (b)(1) details the information the court must give the defendant as a prerequisite to a valid plea; the notes below deal with this issue.

Subsection (b)(2) requires that guilty pleas be voluntary. For most of American history, criminal defendants who pled guilty were asked to affirm in open court that their pleas were not the product of any threats or promises — notwithstanding that many pleas were bargained-for, and hence *were*, at least in part, the product of government threats ("we'll give you a more severe sentence if you go to trial and lose") and/or promises ("we'll drop some of the charges if you agree to plead guilty"). This gave guilty plea proceedings a strange quality; everyone in the courtroom knew that the plea was the product of a bargain, but everyone was supposed to deny that fact. In 1970, with Brady v. United States, 397 U.S. 742 (1970), the Supreme Court expressly held for the first time that plea bargaining did not itself render pleas involuntary; note how Rule 11(b)(2) now incorporates that idea by asking that the court "determine that the plea is voluntary and did not result from force, threats, or promises (other than promises in a plea agreement)." Since *Brady*, voluntariness challenges to guilty pleas have usually stemmed from claims that the government bargained improperly (for example, where the government made some impermissible threat in the course of bargaining for the plea). We will take up those claims below, at pages 1198-1231.

Subsection (b)(3) contains the interesting and potentially important requirement that a guilty plea have a "factual basis"; this requirement is explored in the notes after North Carolina v. Alford, at page 1185.

Subsection (c) deals explicitly with various procedural requirements for plea bargains. Subsections (d) and (e) govern withdrawal of guilty pleas. A defendant may of course withdraw his plea at any time before the court accepts it. Withdrawal is also permitted after the plea is accepted but before sentence is imposed, as long as the defendant "can show a fair and just reason for requesting the withdrawal." Subsection (e) bars withdrawal after sentence is imposed. Subsection (f) refers to Federal Rule of Evidence 410, which makes plea discussions presumptively inadmissible in later criminal proceedings. Defendants often waive the protections of Rule 410; the enforceability of those waivers is at issue in United States v. Mezzanatto, infra, at page 1223.

Subsection (g) requires the keeping of proper records — a small housekeeping matter, one might think, but historically most plea proceedings either were not transcribed or were very incompletely transcribed. Today, Rule 11(g) and its state counterparts occasion very little litigation. Last but not least, subsection (h) determines the standard of review for violations of the Rule.

Conditional Guilty Pleas. Notice the explicit approval given in Rule 11(a)(2) to the use of conditional guilty pleas. The basic idea is simple. Imagine a drug prosecution in which the defendant claims that the key evidence against him was seized illegally and hence is admissible. If the defendant's claim prevails, the drug charge will be dismissed. If not, the defendant will plead guilty. The norm in criminal procedure, as in civil procedure, is not to allow interlocutory appeals, so that cases must ordinarily proceed to judgment before issues can be fully litigated. The conditional guilty plea provides a means of isolating one or two issues for appellate review, while disposing of the rest of the case.

Interestingly, though this device has become much more common than it used to be, it is still very much the exception — only a small minority of guilty pleas are conditional. Why might that be so? Note that Rule 11(a)(2) requires both "the consent of the court and the government" in such cases. When, if ever, should a court *not* consent to a conditional plea? And why allow the government to veto one?

Required Warnings and the Plea Colloquy.   Rule 11(b)(1) requires that defendants be informed of a long list of legal rights and protections. One hopes that most of this information is conveyed through conversations between defendants and their attorneys. Even if that is so, judges must walk defendants through the relevant list, usually by reading a printed guilty plea colloquy. Plea colloquies appear in many form books and judges' manuals; the following example appears on the official website of the Honorable James P. Jones, U.S. District Court for the Western District of Virginia. See http://www.vawd.uscourts.gov/judges/Jones/documents/ GuiltyPleaColloquy.pdf (accessed October 22, 2010). Note that some optional items, applicable only to certain cases, are enclosed in brackets. A typical state plea proceeding would be similar, except for those items that refer to an indictment (not used in "information" states) and to the U.S. Sentencing Guidelines (state plea proceedings would substitute the corresponding state sentencing information).

GUILTY PLEA COLLOQUY

1. *Have Clerk call case.*

2. *To defense counsel*: Do I understand that the defendant wishes to enter a guilty plea pursuant to a written plea agreement?

3. *Ask defense counsel and defendant to stand before the bench.*

4. Before accepting your guilty plea, there are a number of questions I will ask you to assure that it is a valid plea. If you do not understand any of the questions, please say so since it is important that you fully understand my questions.

5. *Ask the Clerk to administer oath to defendant.*

6. Do you understand that you are now under oath, and if you do not answer my questions truthfully, your answers may later be used against you in another prosecution for perjury or making false statements?

7. How old are you? How far did you go in school? Can you read and write English? What jobs or occupations have you followed?

8. Have you ever been treated for mental or emotional issues or problems of any type?

9. Have you taken any drugs, medicine, or pills within the last 24 hours? Are you presently under the influence of alcohol?

10. What is the present state of your health today?

11. To defense counsel: Do you have any question or doubt as to the defendant's competence to plead at this time?

12. Have you received a copy of the indictment — that is, the written charges against you in this case? Have you had an adequate opportunity to discuss the indictment and your case in general with your attorney?

13. *Show defendant signed plea agreement.* Did you sign this agreement and initial each page to show that you read it?

14. Did you have an adequate opportunity to read and discuss the plea agreement with your lawyer before you signed it?

15. Are you fully satisfied with your attorney's representation?

16. *Ask the AUSA to summarize the terms of the plea agreement.*

17. Are those terms included in the plea agreement, as you understand it?

18. [Do you understand that under the plea agreement you waive or give up your right to appeal any sentence?]

19. [Do you understand that under the plea agreement you waive or give up your right to collaterally attack the sentence, meaning that in the future you could not try to set aside your conviction or sentence?]

20. Has anyone made any promise to you other than those made in the plea agreement that caused you to want to plead guilty?

21. Has anyone threatened you or attempted in any way to force you to plead guilty in this case?

22. Do you understand that the charge to which you are pleading guilty is a felony and that if your plea is accepted, you will be found guilty of that charge; that this may deprive you of valuable civil rights, such as the right to vote, to serve on a jury, to hold public office, and to possess any kind of firearm?

23. The maximum possible penalty for the offense is an imprisonment for _____ years plus a fine of up to $_____ plus a special assessment of $100 per count? [There is a mandatory minimum sentence of _____.] In addition, there will a period of supervised release after imprisonment of up to _____ years. Supervised release does not reduce the stated term of imprisonment, but rather is a term of supervision in addition to, and following, the term of imprisonment. If there is a violation of a condition of supervised release, the court may impose an additional prison term, regardless of how much time was served before the violation of the condition. In addition, there may be a further term of supervised release following imprisonment. Do you understand?] [The court may also order, or be required to order, you to make restitution to any victim of your offenses. Do you understand?] [The court may require you to forfeit certain property to the government. Do you understand?] [Since the offense involved fraud, the court may require you to give notice of the conviction to victims of the offense. Do you understand?]

24. Do you understand the possible consequences of your plea?

25. A. Do you understand that while the U.S. Sentencing Guidelines are not binding, the judge must consider those guidelines, as well as other factors, in fixing your sentence?

B. Do you understand that under these sentencing guidelines there will be a range of imprisonment and fine in your case, but that range will not be determined until after a presentence report has been completed and a sentencing hearing held?

C. Do you also understand that the judge has the authority to impose a sentence that is more severe or less severe than the sentencing range called for by these guidelines?

D. Do you also understand that under some circumstances [you or] the government may have the right to appeal your sentence?

E. Do you also understand that parole has been abolished, and that if you are sentenced to prison you will serve your full term less any good time credit earned?

[F. Do you understand that you will not be eligible for probation, since the offense carries a maximum sentence of 25 years or more?]

G. Do you understand that your sentence may be different from any estimate your attorney may have given you?

26. Do you understand that if I do not accept any recommendation or stipulation concerning your sentence as set forth in your plea agreement, you will still be bound by your plea of guilty and will have no right to withdraw it?

27. Please listen carefully to these rights that are given up when you plead guilty:

A. You have a right to plead not guilty to any offense charged against you, and to persist in that plea; that you would then have the right to a trial by jury, that at trial you would be presumed to be innocent and the government would have to prove your guilt beyond a reasonable doubt; that you would also have the right to be represented by a lawyer at trial and at every other stage of the proceeding, and if necessary have the court appoint a lawyer, the right to see and hear all witnesses and have them cross-examined in your defense, the right on your part not to testify unless you voluntarily elected to do so in your own defense, and the right to compel the attendance of witnesses to testify for you and to obtain other evidence on your behalf. Should you decide not to testify or put on any evidence, that could not be used against you. Do you understand all of these rights?

B. Do you further understand that by entering a plea of guilty, if that plea is accepted by the court, there will be no trial and you will have waived or given up your right to a trial as well as those other rights associated with a trial as I have just described?

28. *Read the charge(s) to which the defendant is pleading guilty and explain elements.*

29. Do you understand what the government would have to prove in order to find you guilty?

30. Are you pleading guilty because you are guilty?

31. *To government counsel:* Please make a representation or put on evidence concerning the facts the government would be prepared to prove at trial.

32. *To defendant:* Do you contest or dispute any of the facts just presented?

33. Before I ask you to enter your plea, do you have any questions of me? Do you wish to talk further with your lawyer?

34. How do you now plead to the charge(s) contained in count(s) _____, guilty or not guilty?

35. It is the finding of the court in the case of U. S. v. _____ that the defendant is fully competent and capable of entering an informed plea, that the defendant is aware of the nature of the charge and the consequences of the plea, and that the plea of guilty is a knowing and voluntary plea supported by an independent basis in fact as to each of the essential elements of the offense. The plea is therefore accepted and the defendant is now adjudged guilty of that offense.

36. *Inform the defendant:*

A. A written presentence report will be prepared by the probation office to assist me in sentencing;

B. You will be asked to give information for the report and your attorney may be present if you wish;

C. You and your attorney have the right to read the presentence report and file objections to the report;

D. I remind counsel that written objections to the presentence report must be made within 14 days after receiving the report.

[E. Since the plea agreement involves the dismissal of certain charges [an agreement not to pursue other charges], I will accept the plea, but defer acceptance of the plea agreement until after the presentence report has been prepared.]

37. *Set date for sentencing*.

38. *Determine possible release*.

39. *To defendant:* You are required to appear for sentencing on _____ at _____. Failure to appear as required is a criminal offense for which you can be sentenced to imprisonment, and the penalties of violating any of the conditions of release can be severe.

40. Adjourn.

Of what value is this process? Is substantial information actually being transmitted by a judge reading a list of written questions to a defendant responding as his lawyer instructs him? If not, what is the point of the exercise? One alternative would be simply to permit the defendant to enter his plea and rely on defense counsel to convey the necessary information. Are plea colloquies preferable to that? If so, why?

Recall that Rule 11(b) expressly requires that the judge "determine that the defendant understands" the information listed in that subsection. In practice, the plea colloquy makes that determination mechanical: Judges ask questions; defendants mostly say "yes." If that strikes you as inadequate, how could the inadequacy be corrected — or is this a problem that cannot be solved without turning the guilty plea process into a trial focused on the defendant's understanding?

Note another issue with the colloquy above. Parts of the colloquy seem to call for an accurate understanding on the defendant's part of his chances of successfully maneuvering through the legal system. Other parts seem to call for an accurate understanding of the charge to which the defendant is confessing, presumably to ensure that the confession is truthful. These are not inconsistent goals, but they do seem different. One seeks assurance that the defendant's decision to plead guilty is informed and intelligent — that it is the smart thing to do; the other seeks assurance that the decision to plead guilty is *accurate* — that the defendant really is guilty. Which is more important? Which can the law most successfully regulate?

Because the warnings required by Rule 11 *are* fairly mechanical, they are generally given correctly. Consequently, there isn't much litigation about them. But claims do arise occasionally — most often because the judge failed to say something that Rule 11 required her to say. In United States v. Dominguez Benitez, 542 U.S. 74 (2004), the Supreme Court held that defendants making such claims can prevail only if they can show that there is a reasonable probability that, but for the Rule 11 error, the defendant would have decided not to plead guilty:

> . . . [T]he burden of establishing entitlement to relief for plain error is on the defendant claiming it, and for several reasons, we think that burden should not be too easy for defendants in Dominguez's position. First, the standard should . . . encourage timely objections and reduce wasteful reversals by demanding strenuous exertion

to get relief for unpreserved error. Second, it should respect the particular importance of the finality of guilty pleas, which usually rest, after all, on a defendant's profession of guilt in open court, and are indispensable in the operation of the modern criminal justice system. See United States v. Timmreck, 441 U.S. 780, 784 (1979). And, in this case, these reasons are complemented by the fact . . . that the violation claimed was of Rule 11, not of due process.

We hold, therefore, that a defendant who seeks reversal of his conviction after a guilty plea, on the ground that the district court committed plain error under Rule 11, must show a reasonable probability that, but for the error, he would not have entered the plea. A defendant must thus satisfy the judgment of the reviewing court, informed by the entire record, that the probability of a different result is "sufficient to undermine confidence in the outcome" of the proceeding. Strickland [v. Washington, 466 U.S. 668, 694 (1984)]. . . .

542 U.S., at 82-83. This standard is generally hard to meet. Precisely because the plea colloquy is such a formal exercise, few defendants can argue with a straight face that that same exercise was the motivating force behind their guilty pleas.

Waiver of Constitutional Rights.   Rule 11(b)(1) contains a long list of rights that the defendant gives up by pleading guilty. But the list is not complete; criminal defendants have a host of constitutional rights, and the Rule does not mention all of them. What is the status of the unmentioned rights claims? And what about claims whose factual bases defendants do not know? Do defendants waive or forfeit all possible claims when pleading guilty, or only those they already know about? These questions prompted a great deal of litigation in the 1970s and early 1980s, but they have now mostly — albeit not entirely — been resolved in the government's favor, as the following case shows.

UNITED STATES v. BROCE

Certiorari to the United States Court of Appeals for the Tenth Circuit
488 U.S. 563 (1989)

JUSTICE KENNEDY delivered the opinion of the Court.

. . . Respondents, upon entering guilty pleas, were convicted of two separate counts of conspiracy, but contend now that only one conspiracy existed and that double jeopardy principles require the conviction and sentence on the second count to be set aside. . . . We hold that the double jeopardy challenge is foreclosed by the guilty pleas and the judgments of conviction. . . .

[Broce and a construction company Broce owned were charged with two conspiracies to rig bids and suppress competition in violation of the Sherman Antitrust Act. Both Broce and his company pled guilty to both charges; defendants did not challenge either the sufficiency of the plea colloquy or the adequacy of advice they received from counsel. In separate litigation that took place at about the same time, another local construction company and its head, Robert Beachner, were charged with participation in another bid-rigging conspiracy. Beachner and his company took their case to trial and were acquitted. The government then brought charges against Beachner for yet other bid-rigging conspiracies. Beachner moved to dismiss those new charges, on the ground that they were really part of the same conspiracy the government had charged earlier, and for which Beachner had been acquitted — the new charges thus violated double jeopardy. Beachner's double jeopardy argument was successful; his motion to dismiss was granted.

Broce at this point sought to raise the same argument in connection with his guilty plea. The Court assumed for purposes of the analysis that, like Beachner, Broce had a possibly winning double jeopardy claim — the double jeopardy clause bars two convictions for one crime, so if Broce was guilty of one conspiracy rather than two, one of his convictions would have to be overturned. The Court then turned to whether Broce had waived his double jeopardy claim when he pled guilty to both conspiracy charges. — EDS.]

. . . Respondents had the opportunity, instead of entering their guilty pleas, to challenge the theory of the indictments and to attempt to show the existence of only one conspiracy in a trial-type proceeding. They chose not to, and hence relinquished that entitlement. In light of Beachner['s litigation], respondents may believe that they made a strategic miscalculation. Our precedents demonstrate, however, that such grounds do not justify setting aside an otherwise valid guilty plea.

. . . [W]e held in McMann v. Richardson, 397 U.S. 759 (1970), that a counseled defendant may not make a collateral attack on a guilty plea on the allegation that he misjudged the admissibility of his confession. "Waiving trial entails the inherent risk that the good-faith evaluations of a reasonably competent attorney will turn out to be mistaken either as to the facts or as to what a court's judgment might be on given facts." Id., at 770. See also Tollett v. Henderson, 411 U.S. 258, 267 (1973) ("[J]ust as it is not sufficient for the criminal defendant seeking to set aside such a plea to show that his counsel in retrospect may not have correctly appraised the constitutional significance of certain historical facts, it is likewise not sufficient that he show that if counsel had pursued a certain factual inquiry such a pursuit would have uncovered a possible constitutional infirmity in the proceedings").

Respondents have submitted the affidavit of Kenneth F. Crockett, who served as their attorney when their pleas were entered. Crockett avers that he did not discuss double jeopardy issues with respondents prior to their pleas, and that respondents had not considered the possibility of raising a double jeopardy defense before pleading. Respondents contend that, under these circumstances, they cannot be held to have waived the right to raise a double jeopardy defense because there was no "intentional relinquishment or abandonment of a known right or privilege." Johnson v. Zerbst, 304 U.S. 458, 464 (1938).

Our decisions have not suggested that conscious waiver is necessary with respect to each potential defense relinquished by a plea of guilty. Waiver in that sense is not required. For example, the respondent in *Tollett* pleaded guilty to first-degree murder, and later filed a petition for habeas corpus contending that his plea should be set aside because black citizens had been excluded from the grand jury that indicted him. The collateral challenge was foreclosed by the earlier guilty plea. Although at the time of the indictment the facts relating to the selection of the grand jury were not known to respondent and his attorney, we held that to be irrelevant. . . .

The Crockett affidavit, as a consequence, has no bearing on whether respondents' guilty plea served as a relinquishment of their opportunity to receive a factual hearing on a double jeopardy claim. Relinquishment derives not from any inquiry into a defendant's subjective understanding of the range of potential defenses, but from the admissions necessarily made upon entry of a voluntary plea of guilty. The trial court complied with Rule 11 in ensuring that respondents were advised that, in pleading guilty, they were admitting guilt and waiving their right to a trial of any kind. A failure by counsel to provide advice may form the basis of a claim of ineffective assistance of counsel, but absent such a claim it cannot serve as the predicate for setting aside a valid plea. . . . Respondents have not called into question the voluntary and intelligent character of their pleas, and therefore are not entitled to the collateral relief they seek.

An exception to the rule barring collateral attack on a guilty plea was established by our decisions in Blackledge v. Perry, 417 U.S. 21 (1974), and Menna v. New York, supra, but it has no application to the case at bar.

The respondent in *Blackledge* had been charged in North Carolina with the state-law misdemeanor of assault with a deadly weapon. Pursuant to state procedures, he was tried in the county District Court without a jury, but was permitted, once he was convicted, to appeal to the county Superior Court and obtain a trial de novo. After the defendant filed an appeal, the prosecutor obtained an indictment charging felony assault with a deadly weapon with intent to kill and inflict serious bodily injury. The defendant pleaded guilty. We held that the potential for prosecutorial vindictiveness against those who seek to exercise their right to appeal raised sufficiently serious due process concerns to require a rule forbidding the State to bring more serious charges against defendants in that position. The plea of guilty did not foreclose a subsequent challenge because in *Blackledge* . . . the defendant's right was "the right not to be haled into court at all upon the felony charge. The very initiation of proceedings against him . . . thus operated to deny him due process of law." 417 U.S., at 30-31.

The petitioner in *Menna* had refused, after a grant of immunity, to obey a court order to testify before a grand jury. He was adjudicated in contempt of court and sentenced to a term in civil jail. After he was released, he was indicted for the same refusal to answer the questions. He pleaded guilty and was sentenced, but then appealed on double jeopardy grounds. The New York Court of Appeals concluded that Menna had waived his double jeopardy claim by pleading guilty. We reversed, citing *Blackledge* for the proposition that "[w]here the State is precluded by the United States Constitution from haling a defendant into court on a charge, federal law requires that a conviction on that charge be set aside even if the conviction was entered pursuant to a counseled plea of guilty." 423 U.S., at 62. We added, however, an important qualification:

> We do not hold that a double jeopardy claim may never be waived. We simply hold that a plea of guilty to a charge does not waive a claim that — judged on its face — the charge is one which the State may not constitutionally prosecute.

Id., at 63, n. 2.

In neither *Blackledge* nor *Menna* did the defendants seek further proceedings at which to expand the record with new evidence. In those cases, the determination that the second indictment could not go forward should have been made by the presiding judge at the time the plea was entered on the basis of the existing record. Both *Blackledge* and *Menna* could be (and ultimately were) resolved without any need to venture beyond that record. In *Blackledge*, . . . the constitutional infirmity in the proceedings lay in the State's power to bring any indictment at all. In *Menna*, the indictment was facially duplicative of the earlier offense of which the defendant had been convicted and sentenced so that the admissions made by Menna's guilty plea could not conceivably be construed to extend beyond a redundant confession to the earlier offense.

Respondents here, in contrast, pleaded guilty to indictments that on their face described separate conspiracies. They cannot prove their claim by relying on those indictments and the existing record. Indeed, . . . they cannot prove their claim without contradicting those indictments, and that opportunity is foreclosed by the admissions inherent in their guilty pleas. We therefore need not consider [the question whether the defendant's acceptance of] . . . a plea bargain [with] concessions by the Government . . . heightens the already substantial interest . . . in the finality of the plea. . . .

Based on the Court's discussions of Blackledge v. Perry and Menna v. New York, it would appear that by pleading guilty, defendants lose all claims other than those that both (1) suggest the government lacks the power to punish the defendant at all and (2) can be resolved without further factfinding. Does this distinction make sense, or is it just an effort to cabin *Blackledge* and *Menna* without overruling them?[3]

Even claims like Broce's are not necessarily lost. As we will see later, such claims simply must be converted into ineffective assistance of counsel claims — that is, someone in Broce's position would have to show that counsel's failure to raise the double jeopardy issue prior to the plea was constitutionally ineffective, and that this failure caused "prejudice" within the meaning of Strickland v. Washington, 466 U.S. 668 (1984); see pages 1250-1266.

2. The Special Problem of Innocence

NORTH CAROLINA v. ALFORD

Appeal from the United States Court of Appeals for the Fourth Circuit
400 U.S. 25 (1970)

JUSTICE WHITE delivered the opinion of the Court.

On December 2, 1963, Alford was indicted for first-degree murder, a capital offense under North Carolina law. The court appointed an attorney to represent him, and this attorney questioned all but one of the various witnesses who appellee said would substantiate his claim of innocence. The witnesses, however, did not support Alford's story but gave statements that strongly indicated his guilt. Faced with strong evidence of guilt and no substantial evidentiary support for the claim of innocence, Alford's attorney recommended that he plead guilty, but left the ultimate decision to Alford himself. The prosecutor agreed to accept a plea of guilty to a charge of second-degree murder, and on December 10, 1963, Alford pleaded guilty to the reduced charge.

---

3. Actually, there is one other category of claims that defendants retain after pleading guilty: claims that arise after the guilty plea is entered. In Mitchell v. United States, 526 U.S. 314 (1999), the defendant pled guilty, but refused to testify at her sentencing hearing; the sentencing judge ruled that she had waived her Fifth Amendment privilege against self-incrimination by pleading guilty. The Supreme Court disagreed, holding that Mitchell's guilty plea did not waive her Fifth Amendment right at the sentencing hearing.

Before the plea was finally accepted by the trial court, the court heard the sworn testimony of a police officer who summarized the State's case. Two other witnesses besides Alford were also heard. Although there was no eyewitness to the crime, the testimony indicated that shortly before the killing Alford took his gun from his house, stated his intention to kill the victim, and returned home with the declaration that he had carried out the killing. After the summary presentation of the State's case, Alford took the stand and testified that he had not committed the murder but that he was pleading guilty because he faced the threat of the death penalty if he did not do so.[2] In response to the questions of his counsel, he acknowledged that his counsel had informed him of the difference between second and first-degree murder and of his rights in case he chose to go to trial. The trial court then asked appellee if, in light of his denial of guilt, he still desired to plead guilty to second-degree murder and appellee answered, "Yes, sir. I plead guilty on — from the circumstances that he [Alford's attorney] told me." After eliciting information about Alford's prior criminal record, which was a long one,[4] the trial court sentenced him to 30 years' imprisonment, the maximum penalty for second-degree murder.

Alford sought post-conviction relief in the state court. Among the claims raised was the claim that his plea of guilty was invalid because it was the product of fear and coercion. After a hearing, the state court in 1965 found that the plea was "willingly, knowingly, and understandingly" made on the advice of competent counsel and in the face of a strong prosecution case. Subsequently, Alford petitioned for a writ of habeas corpus, first in the United States District Court for the Middle District of North Carolina, and then in the Court of Appeals for the Fourth Circuit. Both courts denied the writ on the basis of the state court's findings that Alford voluntarily and knowingly agreed to plead guilty. In 1967, Alford again petitioned for a writ of habeas corpus in the District Court for the Middle District of North Carolina. That court, without an evidentiary hearing, again denied relief on the grounds that the guilty plea was voluntary and waived all defenses and nonjurisdictional defects in any prior stage of the proceedings, and that the findings of the state court in 1965 clearly required rejection of Alford's claim that he was denied effective assistance of counsel prior to pleading guilty. On appeal, a divided panel of the Court of Appeals for the Fourth Circuit reversed on the ground that Alford's guilty plea was made involuntarily. 405 F.2d 340 (1968).

---

2. After giving his version of the events of the night of the murder, Alford stated:

I pleaded guilty on second degree murder because they said there is too much evidence, but I ain't shot no man, but I take the fault for the other man. We never had an argument in our life and I just pleaded guilty because they said if I didn't they would gas me for it, and that is all.

In response to questions from his attorney, Alford affirmed that he had consulted several times with his attorney and with members of his family and had been informed of his rights if he chose to plead not guilty. Alford then reaffirmed his decision to plead guilty to second-degree murder:

Q [by Alford's attorney]. And you authorized me to tender a plea of guilty to second degree murder before the court?
A. Yes, sir.
Q. And in doing that, that you have again affirmed your decision on that point?
A. Well, I'm still pleading that you all got me to plead guilty. I plead the other way, circumstantial evidence; that the jury will prosecute me on — on the second. You told me to plead guilty, right. I don't — I'm not guilty but I plead guilty.

4. Before Alford was sentenced, the trial judge asked Alford about prior convictions. Alford answered that, among other things, he had served six years of a ten-year sentence for murder, had been convicted nine times for armed robbery, and had been convicted for transporting stolen goods, forgery, and carrying a concealed weapon.

. . . We noted probable jurisdiction. We vacate the judgment of the Court of Appeals and remand the case for further proceedings.

We held in Brady v. United States, 397 U.S. 742 (1970), that a plea of guilty which would not have been entered except for the defendant's desire to avoid a possible death penalty and to limit the maximum penalty to life imprisonment or a term of years was not for that reason compelled within the meaning of the Fifth Amendment. . . . The standard was and remains whether the plea represents a voluntary and intelligent choice among the alternative courses of action open to the defendant. See Boykin v. Alabama, 395 U.S. 238, 242 (1969); Machibroda v. United States, 368 U.S. 487, 493 (1962); Kercheval v. United States, 274 U.S. 220, 223 (1927). That he would not have pleaded except for the opportunity to limit the possible penalty does not necessarily demonstrate that the plea of guilty was not the product of a free and rational choice, especially where the defendant was represented by competent counsel whose advice was that the plea would be to the defendant's advantage. . . .

As previously recounted, after Alford's plea of guilty was offered and the State's case was placed before the judge, Alford denied that he had committed the murder but reaffirmed his desire to plead guilty to avoid a possible death sentence and to limit the penalty to the 30-year maximum provided for second-degree murder. Ordinarily, a judgment of conviction resting on a plea of guilty is justified by the defendant's admission that he committed the crime charged against him and his consent that judgment be entered without a trial of any kind. The plea usually subsumes both elements, and justifiably so, even though there is no separate, express admission by the defendant that he committed the particular acts claimed to constitute the crime charged in the indictment. See Brady v. United States, supra, at 748. Here Alford entered his plea but accompanied it with the statement that he had not shot the victim.

If Alford's statements were to be credited as sincere assertions of his innocence, there obviously existed a factual and legal dispute between him and the State. Without more, it might be argued that the conviction entered on his guilty plea was invalid, since his assertion of innocence negatived any admission of guilt, which, as we observed last Term in *Brady*, is normally "central to the plea and the foundation for entering judgment against the defendant. . . ." 397 U.S., at 748.

In addition to Alford's statement, however, the court had heard an account of the events on the night of the murder, including information from Alford's acquaintances that he had departed from his home with his gun stating his intention to kill and that he had later declared that he had carried out his intention. Nor had Alford wavered in his desire to have the trial court determine his guilt without a jury trial. Although denying the charge against him, he nevertheless preferred the dispute between him and the State to be settled by the judge in the context of a guilty plea proceeding rather than by a formal trial. Thereupon, with the State's telling evidence and Alford's denial before it, the trial court proceeded to convict and sentence Alford for second-degree murder.

State and lower federal courts are divided upon whether a guilty plea can be accepted when it is accompanied by protestations of innocence and hence contains only a waiver of trial but no admission of guilt. Some courts, giving expression to the principle that "our law only authorizes a conviction where guilt is shown," Harris v. State, 76 Tex. Cr. R. 126, 131, 172 S.W. 975, 977 (1915), require that trial judges reject such pleas. But others have concluded that they should not "force any defense on a defendant in a criminal case," particularly when advancement of the defense might "end in disaster. . . ." Tremblay v. Overholser, 199 F. Supp. 569, 570 (DC 1961). They have argued that, since "guilt, or the degree of guilt, is at times uncertain and elusive," "an accused, though believing in or entertaining doubts respecting his innocence, might reasonably conclude a jury would be convinced of his guilt and that he would fare better in the sentence by pleading guilty. . . ." McCoy v. United States, 363 F.2d 306, 308 (CADC 1966). As one state court observed nearly a century ago, "reasons other than the fact that he is guilty may induce a defendant to so plead, . . . [and] he must be permitted to judge for himself in this respect." State v. Kaufman, 51 Iowa 578, 580, 2 N.W. 275, 276 (1879) (dictum).

This Court has not confronted this precise issue, but prior decisions do yield relevant principles. . . . The issue in Hudson v. United States, 272 U.S. 451 (1926), was whether a federal court has power to impose a prison sentence after accepting a plea of nolo contendere, a plea by which a defendant does not expressly admit his guilt, but nonetheless waives his right to a trial and authorizes the court for purposes of the case to treat him as if he were guilty.[8] The Court held that a trial court does have such power, and . . . the federal courts have uniformly followed this rule, even in cases involving moral turpitude. Implicit in the nolo contendere cases is a recognition that the Constitution does not bar imposition of a prison sentence upon an accused who is unwilling expressly to admit his guilt but who, faced with grim alternatives, is willing to waive his trial and accept the sentence.

These cases would be directly in point if Alford had simply insisted on his plea but refused to admit the crime. The fact that his plea was denominated a plea of guilty rather than a plea of nolo contendere is of no constitutional significance with respect to the issue now before us, for the Constitution is concerned with the practical consequences, not the formal categorizations, of state law. Thus, while most pleas of guilty consist of both a waiver of trial and an express admission of guilt, the latter element is not a constitutional requisite to the imposition of a

8. Courts have defined the plea of nolo contendere in a variety of different ways, describing it, on the one hand, as "in effect, a plea of guilty," United States v. Food & Grocery Bureau, 43 F. Supp. 974, 979 (SD Cal. 1942), aff'd, 139 F.2d 973 (CA9 1943), and on the other, as a query directed to the court to determine the defendant's guilt. State v. Hopkins, 27 Del. 306, 88 A. 473 (1913). As a result, it is impossible to state precisely what a defendant does admit when he enters a nolo plea in a way that will consistently fit all the cases.

Hudson v. United States, supra, was also ambiguous. In one place, the Court called the plea "an admission of guilt for the purposes of the case," id., at 455, but in another, the Court quoted an English authority who had defined the plea as one "where a defendant, in a case not capital, doth not directly own himself guilty. . . ." Id., at 453, quoting 2 W. Hawkins, Pleas of the Crown 466 (8th ed. 1824).

The plea may have originated in the early medieval practice by which defendants wishing to avoid imprisonment would seek to make an end of the matter (finem facere) by offering to pay a sum of money to the king. See 2 F. Pollock & F. Maitland, History of English Law 517 (2d ed. 1909). An early fifteenth-century case indicated that a defendant did not admit his guilt when he sought such a compromise, but merely "that he put himself on the grace of our Lord, the King, and asked that he might be allowed to pay a fine (petit se admittit per finem)." Anon., Y. B. Hil. 9 Hen. 6, f. 59, pl. 8 (1431). . . .

[A]n eighteenth-century case distinguished between a nolo plea and a jury verdict of guilty, noting that in the former the defendant could introduce evidence of innocence in mitigation of punishment, whereas in the latter such evidence was precluded by the finding of actual guilt. Queen v. Templeman, 1 Salk. 55, 91 Eng. Rep. 54 (K.B. 1702).

Throughout its history, that is, the plea of nolo contendere has been viewed not as an express admission of guilt but as a consent by the defendant that he may be punished as if he were guilty and a prayer for leniency. Fed. Rule Crim. Proc. 11 preserves this distinction in its requirement that a court cannot accept a guilty plea unless it ["determine[s] that there is a factual basis for the plea"]; there is no similar requirement for pleas of nolo contendere, since it was thought desirable to permit defendants to plead nolo without making any inquiry into their actual guilt. See Notes of Advisory Committee to Rule 11.

criminal penalty. An individual accused of crime may voluntarily, knowingly, and understandingly consent to the imposition of a prison sentence even if he is unwilling or unable to admit his participation in the acts constituting the crime.

Nor can we perceive any material difference between a plea that refuses to admit commission of the criminal act and a plea containing a protestation of innocence when, as in the instant case, a defendant intelligently concludes that his interests require entry of a guilty plea and the record before the judge contains strong evidence of actual guilt. Here the State had a strong case of first-degree murder against Alford. Whether he realized or disbelieved his guilt, he insisted on his plea because in his view he had absolutely nothing to gain by a trial and much to gain by pleading. Because of the overwhelming evidence against him, a trial was precisely what neither Alford nor his attorney desired. Confronted with the choice between a trial for first-degree murder, on the one hand, and a plea of guilty to second-degree murder, on the other, Alford quite reasonably chose the latter and thereby limited the maximum penalty to a 30-year term. When his plea is viewed in light of the evidence against him, which substantially negated his claim of innocence and which further provided a means by which the judge could test whether the plea was being intelligently entered,[10] its validity cannot be seriously questioned. In view of the strong factual basis for the plea demonstrated by the State and Alford's clearly expressed desire to enter it despite his professed belief in his innocence, we hold that the trial judge did not commit constitutional error in accepting it.[11]

. . . Alford now argues in effect that the State should not have allowed him this choice but should have insisted on proving him guilty of murder in the first degree. The States in their wisdom may take this course by statute or otherwise and may prohibit the practice of accepting pleas to lesser included offenses under any circumstances. But this is not the mandate of the Fourteenth Amendment and the Bill of Rights. The prohibitions against involuntary or unintelligent pleas should not be relaxed, but neither should an exercise in arid logic render those constitutional guarantees counterproductive and put in jeopardy the very human values they were meant to preserve. . . .

[The concurring statement of Justice Black is omitted.]

JUSTICE BRENNAN, with whom JUSTICE DOUGLAS and JUSTICE MARSHALL join, dissenting.

Last Term, this Court held, over my dissent, that a plea of guilty may validly be induced by [a] threat to subject the defendant to the risk of death, so long as the plea

10. Because of the importance of protecting the innocent and of insuring that guilty pleas are a product of free and intelligent choice, various state and federal court decisions properly caution that pleas coupled with claims of innocence should not be accepted unless there is a factual basis for the plea, see, e.g., Griffin v. United States, 405 F.2d 1378, 1380 (CADC 1968); Commonwealth v. Cottrell, 433 Pa. 177, 249 A.2d 294 (1969); and until the judge taking the plea has inquired into and sought to resolve the conflict between the waiver of trial and the claim of innocence. See, e.g., People v. Serrano, 15 N.Y.2d 304, 308-309, 206 N.E.2d 330, 332 (1965).

In the federal courts, Fed. Rule Crim. Proc. 11 expressly provides that ["[b]efore entering judgment on a guilty plea, the court must determine that there is a factual basis for the plea."]

11. Our holding does not mean that a trial judge must accept every constitutionally valid guilty plea merely because a defendant wishes so to plead. A criminal defendant does not have an absolute right under the Constitution to have his guilty plea accepted by the court, although the States may by statute or otherwise confer such a right. Likewise, the States may bar their courts from accepting guilty pleas from any defendants who assert their innocence. Cf. [former] Fed. Rule Crim. Proc. 11, which gives a trial judge discretion to "refuse to accept a plea of guilty. . . ." We need not now delineate the scope of that discretion.

is entered in open court and the defendant is represented by competent counsel who is aware of the threat . . . Brady v. United States, 397 U.S. 742, 745-758 (1970). Today the Court makes clear that its previous holding was intended to apply even when the record demonstrates that the actual effect of the unconstitutional threat was to induce a guilty plea from a defendant who was unwilling to admit his guilt.

. . . [W]ithout reaching the question whether due process permits the entry of judgment upon a plea of guilty accompanied by a contemporaneous denial of acts constituting the crime, I believe that at the very least such a denial of guilt is also a relevant factor in determining whether the plea was voluntarily and intelligently made. With these factors in mind, it is sufficient in my view to state that the facts set out in the majority opinion demonstrate that Alford was "so gripped by fear of the death penalty"[2] that his decision to plead guilty was not voluntary but was "the product of duress as much so as choice reflecting physical constraint." Haley v. Ohio, 332 U.S. 596, 606 (1948) (opinion of Frankfurter, J.). Accordingly, I would affirm the judgment of the Court of Appeals.

NOTES AND QUESTIONS

1. In cases in which a defendant is convicted at trial, the conviction rests on the judgment of a neutral factfinder that the government proved the defendant guilty of the crime charged beyond a reasonable doubt. In an ordinary guilty plea, the conviction rests on the defendant's confession in open court that he committed the crime charged. On what does Alford's conviction rest?

2. Although Alford professed to be factually innocent of the crime to which he pleaded guilty, the rest of the available evidence strongly suggested that he was, in fact, guilty. One persistent theme in the scholarly literature on guilty pleas and plea bargaining is the unquantifiable but generally perceived risk that at least some *truly* innocent defendants — especially those facing the possibility of serious prison time coupled with substantial offers of leniency from the prosecution — may plead guilty to crimes they did not commit. Part of the so-called "innocence problem" is related to the fact that it is difficult for truly innocent defendants to reliably "signal" — to the prosecution, the trial judge, and perhaps even their own defense lawyer — that they are, in fact, innocent. The "system" generally assumes that most, if not all, defendants are factually guilty, an assumption thought to be confirmed by the extremely high rates at which defendants plead guilty. As a matter of strategy, it is clearly in the best interests of *all* defendants, whether guilty or not, to feign innocence until a sufficiently attractive plea offer is made by the prosecution. So what can a truly innocent defendant do to "signal" that fact, and thereby avoid eventually being pushed (by better and better plea offers) into pleading guilty?

Some have argued that the signaling issue is largely insurmountable, given the strong incentives for guilty defendants to mimic the signaling behavior of truly innocent ones. See Robert E. Scott & William J. Stuntz, Plea Bargaining as Contract, 101 Yale L.J. 1909 (1992). Russell Covey asserts in response that effective signaling may be possible, but not necessarily within the plea negotiation process itself:

2. Brady v. United States, 397 U.S., at 750.

For signaling to occur, at least one party must have private information and an economic incentive to communicate it. Those conditions are typical of plea bargaining. Defendants usually know if they are innocent or guilty, and innocent defendants have powerful incentives to communicate their private information to prosecutors. The ease by which guilty defendants can mimic nonverifiable innocence claims made by innocent defendants, however, prevents prosecutors from taking those claims seriously. Observing this, Dean Robert Scott and Professor William Stuntz characterize plea bargaining's innocence problem as, at bottom, a signaling defect. . . .

Prosecutors cannot infer anything reliable about the defendant's private information based on their responses to plea offers because too many other factors influence plea evaluation. As Dean Scott and Professor Stuntz observe, the signal sent by innocent defendants through their higher price demands is indistinguishable from the comparatively higher price demands of those who heavily discount the future or who are less risk-averse. Since criminals likely are (almost by definition) less risk-averse and heavy discounters, the "innocence signal" implicit in the rejection of a plea offer is almost certain to be imperceptible to prosecutors. Accordingly, prosecutors cannot adjust plea prices based on unverified defendant signals of innocence. The plea bargaining "game" thus results in a "pooling equilibrium" in which defendant's private information is not incorporated into the price of the plea. . . .

I argue that the procedural mechanism best suited to perform the separating function necessary to achieve the goal of more accurate pleapricing is interrogation. Building on the insights of Seidmann and Stein's pathbreaking game-theoretic analysis of the privilege against self-incrimination,[144] the Article argues that the decision to cooperate or not cooperate in the pretrial investigation satisfies (in a partial way) the essential prerequisites of a signaling mechanism. Submitting to interrogation is costly to criminal suspects, and that cost is imposed differentially. Interrogation is not cost-free for innocent suspects, but innocent suspects' costs are less — sometimes far less — in submitting to interrogation than those of guilty suspects. Moreover, the signal produced in interrogation — cooperation in the interrogation room — is logically related to the subject of the signal: The suspect's guilt or innocence. And interrogation is, or at least can be, an economically rational move for innocent suspects. . . .

[P]lea bargain theory must be modified to account for the substantial likelihood that plea bargain prices are influenced by signaling. Pretrial interrogation creates an obvious dilemma for guilty suspects, and the defendant's response to interrogation generates a signal permitting some plea price differentiation to occur among guilty and innocent defendants, a prediction supported by the empirical data. Even apart from the substantive information obtained from interrogation, the choice to submit to interrogation serves as an important signal to police and prosecutors that is manifested in plea prices. In short, there is good reason to believe that plea bargains are negotiated not only in the shadows of trial, but also in the shadows of strategic choices made by suspects prior to trial and, especially, in the interrogation room.

Russell D. Covey, Signaling and Plea Bargaining's Innocence Problem, 66 Wash. & Lee L. Rev. 73 (2009).

3. The Court suggests that, though Alford's plea was technically guilty, it was functionally a plea of nolo contendere or no contest. It is worth noting that in an ordinary nolo plea, the defendant would not overtly claim innocence; he would simply refuse to acknowledge guilt. Footnote 8 in *Alford* offers a good short sketch of the history of the nolo plea.

---

144. See generally Daniel J. Seidmann & Alex Stein, The Right to Silence Helps the Innocent: A Game-Theoretic Analysis of the Fifth Amendment Privilege, 114 Harv. L. Rev. 430, 448-449 (2000).

An interesting article by Stephanos Bibas argues that nolo pleas and *Alford* pleas are a mistake, because they undermine the moral values on which the criminal justice system is based:

> . . . *Alford* and nolo contendere pleas are unwise and should be abolished. These procedures may be constitutional and efficient, but they undermine key values served by admissions of guilt in open court. They undermine the procedural values of accuracy and public confidence in accuracy and fairness by convicting innocent defendants and creating the perception that innocent defendants are being pressured into pleading guilty. More basically, they allow guilty defendants to avoid accepting responsibility for their wrongs. Guilty defendants' refusals to admit guilt impede their repentance, education, and reform, as well as victims' healing process. In addition, pleas without confessions muddy the criminal law's moral message. Both kinds of pleas, but especially *Alford* pleas, equivocate; one might call them "guilty-but-not-guilty" pleas. They permit equivocation and ambiguity when clarity is essential. This equivocation, in turn, undermines denunciation of the defendant and vindication of the victim and the community's moral norms. Sacrificing these substantive goals is too high a price for an efficient plea procedure. Procedures that undercut substance have little point, as the point of procedure is to serve substance. Yet substantive values for the most part are not even on the proceduralists' radar screens. Thus, guilty pleas should be reserved for those who confess. Jury trials should serve not only to acquit innocent defendants, but also to teach guilty defendants and vindicate their victims and the community's moral norms. They are morality plays. Because criminal law's norms include honesty and responsibility for one's actions, criminal procedure should not let guilty defendants dishonestly dodge responsibility and the truth.

Stephanos Bibas, Harmonizing Substantive-Criminal-Law Values and Criminal Procedure: The Case of *Alford* and Nolo Contendere Pleas, 88 Cornell L. Rev. 1361, 1363-1364 (2003). Bibas continues, id., at 1364-1366:

> Consider the prominent example of Kathleen Soliah, which illustrates why unequivocal guilty-plea confessions serve these values better than equivocal *Alford* and nolo pleas. In the 1970s, Soliah belonged to the Symbionese Liberation Army, a radical San Francisco group that kidnapped Patricia Hearst and tried to kill government officials. Soliah fled to Minnesota and changed her name to Sara Jane Olson. For years, she denied belonging to the Symbionese Liberation Army or taking part in an attempt to bomb two police cars in 1975. Her lawyer expressed interest in negotiating an *Alford* or nolo contendere plea, but the judge and prosecutors would not countenance such a plea. Finally, on October 31, 2001, Olson clearly and unequivocally pleaded guilty to taking part in an attempt to bomb the two cars. Immediately afterwards, however, Olson told reporters that she had pleaded guilty to crimes of which she was innocent. Prosecutors speculated that Olson had changed her story to please her friends and family who had maintained her innocence.
>
> Olson's judge, however, refused to countenance this express and instantaneous contradiction, noting that "the integrity of the criminal justice system is at stake." He called Olson in for another hearing and asked her whether she wanted her plea to stand. At that hearing, the judge confronted Olson and asked her, clearly and explicitly, if she was in fact guilty. She twice said yes and reaffirmed her plea. Five days later, Olson again publicly disavowed her guilt and moved to withdraw her plea. At the next court hearing, the judge noted that Olson found it psychologically very difficult to admit her crime to herself, her family, and her supporters. Relying on her previous admissions and pleas of guilt, the judge denied Olson's motion to withdraw her plea.

Only after this final ruling did Olson tremble with emotion and say she was sorry for harming others.

An *Alford* or nolo plea in this case would have undercut important procedural and substantive values and norms. If Olson had entered an *Alford* plea and never admitted guilt, it would have been wrong to punish her without an authoritative trial verdict. Instead of eventually apologizing, she might well have persisted in her denials to herself and to others. Continued denials would have led her friends, her family, and the public to doubt the justice of the system. Punishment in these circumstances would undercut the norm of punishing only those known to be blameworthy. In addition, consistent protestations of innocence would hinder closure for the victims and the community. Here, in contrast, Olson clearly admitted guilt in court, making her later denials less credible. The public could more easily believe that she had falsely protested her innocence to save face. In addition, the court could justify its ruling by pointing to Olson's earlier admissions, on the advice of counsel, in open court. The court's action vindicated the norm of not going back on one's word. Furthermore, after the judge confronted her with her earlier admissions, Olson took the first steps toward apology and reconciliation. In short, Olson's admissions of guilt in open court were much firmer bases for conviction, repentance, and closure than an *Alford* or nolo plea would have been.

What do you think? Does your response to Bibas's argument change depending on how many of the defendants who claim innocence actually *are* innocent?

4. Reread footnote 10 in *Alford*. Does the Court mean to establish a constitutional requirement of a "factual basis" for conviction in all cases in which conviction rests on a plea rather than on a trial? Rule 11(b)(3) establishes such a requirement for *guilty* pleas, at least in federal cases; in footnote 8, the *Alford* Court noted that that requirement traditionally was not applied to pleas of nolo contendere. Is the reason why convincing?

5. In Libretti v. United States, 516 U.S. 29 (1995), the defendant pled guilty to participation in a continuing criminal enterprise; as part of the plea agreement, he agreed to the forfeiture of a large amount of property. He then challenged the forfeiture portions of the plea agreement, arguing that they lacked a "factual basis," and hence that the plea violated Rule 11. The Supreme Court held that the factual basis requirement applies only to the substantive charge to which the defendant pleads guilty, not to the punishment the defendant receives. Forfeiture, the Court further held, is part of the punishment, not the charge.

6. There is very little case law on what an adequate "factual basis" is; in the large majority of cases, the requirement is satisfied by the defendant's admission that he committed the crime to which he pleads guilty. That admission carries weight only if the crime charged is accurately described to the defendant. Accordingly, the Supreme Court has held that an incorrect description of the crime charged in the guilty plea colloquy constitutes a denial of due process. See Henderson v. Morgan, 426 U.S. 637 (1976). The defendant in that case pled guilty to second-degree murder; at his plea proceeding, the trial judge failed to describe the intent term of that crime. The Supreme Court held that this error denied the defendant due process — regardless of whether the state could prove that the killing was intentional (the state claimed that the victim had been stabbed 45 times, which doesn't sound like an accidental death).

This right means little in practice. Defendants and their attorneys rarely object to errors in a guilty plea proceeding. Guilty pleas are consensual transactions; neither the government nor the defense has any interest in raising objections while the proceeding is taking place. So mistakes, like the one in Henderson v. Morgan, tend to pass unnoticed. For the same reason, guilty pleas are almost never challenged on direct appeal. When defendants raise arguments like the one in *Henderson*, they almost always do on habeas corpus — often years after the guilty plea proceeding took place.

Such claims must overcome a number of legal hurdles. The most important hurdles stem from the law of procedural default. All jurisdictions require that claims or challenges to criminal proceedings must be raised in a timely fashion — that defendants must object to a given legal error by the court at the time the error happens. If timely objections are not made, the claims are deemed procedurally defaulted. And procedurally defaulted claims cannot be raised later, on habeas corpus, unless the claimant can establish "cause" for the default and "prejudice" from it. See Wainwright v. Sykes, 433 U.S. 72 (1977). "Cause" means that the defendant has a good reason for not having raised the claim in a timely fashion. "Prejudice" means that the defendant was harmed by the failure to raise the relevant claim.

"Cause" and "prejudice" are defined very restrictively. Ineffective assistance of counsel constitutes "cause" and "prejudice." So does a valid claim that the government withheld material, exculpatory evidence under Brady v. Maryland, 373 U.S. 83 (1963). (See Chapter 12 for a detailed discussion of *Brady* doctrine.) Apart from ineffective assistance or *Brady* claims, however, showing "cause" and "prejudice" is virtually impossible.

Consider what all this means for guilty pleas. As we have noted, in the large majority of guilty pleas, neither side objects to anything. (It could hardly be otherwise, since the proceeding is not adversarial.) Consequently, all legal challenges to the guilty plea proceeding itself are procedurally defaulted. In order to raise those challenges later, the defendant must show "cause" and "prejudice" — meaning, as a practical matter, he must show that his counsel's failure to object at the proper time violated his right to the effective assistance of counsel.

B.   Plea Bargaining

1.   History and Practice

JOHN H. LANGBEIN, UNDERSTANDING THE SHORT HISTORY OF PLEA BARGAINING

13 Law & Soc'y Rev. 261, 261-270 (1979)

. . . [P]lea bargaining was unknown during most of the history of the common law. Only in the nineteenth century [is there] significant evidence of the practice in either England or America. These findings beckon to the legal historian for explanation. In modern times, plea bargaining has become the primary procedure through which we dispose of the vast proportion of cases of serious crime. How then could common law procedure function for so many centuries without a practice that is today so prevalent and seemingly so indispensable? . . .

The main historical explanation for the want of plea bargaining in former centuries is, I believe, simple and incontrovertible. When we turn back to the period before the middle of the eighteenth century, we find that common law trial procedure exhibited a degree of efficiency that we now expect only of our nontrial procedure. *Jury trial was a summary proceeding.* Over the intervening two centuries the rise of the adversary system and the related development of the law of evidence has caused the common law jury trial to undergo a profound transformation, robbing it of the wondrous efficiency that had characterized it for so many centuries.

The initial point to grasp . . . is how rapidly jury trials were conducted. The surviving sources show that well into the eighteenth century when the Old Bailey sat, it tried between twelve and twenty felony cases per day, and provincial assizes operated with similar dispatch. . . .

How could the Old Bailey of the 1730s process a dozen and more cases to full jury trial in one day, whereas in modern times the average jury trial requires several days of court time?

(1) The most important factor that expedited jury trial was the want of counsel. Neither prosecution nor defense was represented in ordinary criminal trials. The accused was forbidden counsel; the prosecution might be conducted by a lawyer, but in practice virtually never was. The victim or other complaining witness, sometimes aided by the law constable and the law justice of the peace, performed the role we now assign to the public prosecutor, gathering evidence and presenting it at trial. As a result, jury trial was not yet protracted by the motions, maneuvers, and speeches of counsel that afflict the modern trial.

(2) There was, for example, no voir dire of prospective jurors conducted by counsel. In practice the accused took the jury as he found it and virtually never employed his challenge rights. Indeed, at the Old Bailey only two twelve-man jury panels were used to discharge the entire caseload of as many as a hundred felony trials in a few days. Each jury usually heard several unrelated cases before deliberating on any. Often the juries rendered verdicts in these cases of life and death "at the bar," that is, so rapidly that they did not even retire from the courtroom to deliberate.

(3) The most efficient testimonial resource available to a criminal court is almost always the criminal defendant. He has, after all, been close enough to the events to get himself prosecuted. In modern Anglo-American procedure we have constructed the privilege against self-incrimination in a way that often encourages the accused to rely entirely upon the intermediation of counsel and say nothing in his own defense. But in the period before the accused had counsel, there could be no practical distinction between his roles as defender and as witness. The accused spoke continuously at the trial, replying to prosecution witnesses and giving his own version of the events.

(4) The presentation of evidence and the cross-examintion of witnesses and accused took place in a fashion that was businesslike but lacked the time-consuming stiffness of a modern adversary trial. . . .

(5) The common law of evidence, which has injected such vast complexity into modern criminal trials, was virtually nonexistent as late as the opening decades of the eighteenth century. The trial judge had an alternative system of jury control that was both swifter and surer than the subsequent resort to rules of admissibility and exclusion. He had unrestricted powers of comment on the merits of criminal cases; he could reject a verdict that displeased him and require the jury to deliberate

further; indeed, until 1670 he could fine a jury that persisted in acquitting against his wishes. . . .

(7) Finally, there was as yet virtually no appeal in criminal cases. Accordingly, the familiar modern machinations of counsel directed to provoking and preserving error for appeal were unknown.

It should surprise no one that in a system of trial as rough and rapid as this there was no particular pressure to develop nontrial procedure, or otherwise to encourage the accused to waive his right to jury trial. . . .

We should also not be surprised that this summary form of jury trial perished over the last two centuries. The level of safeguard against mistaken conviction was in several respects below what civilized people now require. The hard question, which remains unresearched, is why the pressure for greater safeguard led in the Anglo-American procedure to the common law of evidence and dominance of the trial by lawyers, reforms that ultimately destroyed the system in the sense that they rendered trials unworkable as an ordinary or routine dispositive procedure for cases of serious crime. Similar pressures for safeguard were being felt in the Continental legal systems in the same period, but they led to reforms in nonadversarial procedure that preserved the institution of trial.

We think that we understand why there was no plea bargaining while jury trial retained its character as a summary proceeding. And we have no difficulty seeing that once jury trial had been overlaid with the complexity that characterizes it today, it could no longer be used as the exclusive dispositive proceeding for cases of serious crime. But these insights leave us still a good distance from explaining why the particular adaptation that resulted was plea bargaining. . . . We may, however, indicate some features of the earlier system of jury trial that predisposed Anglo-American procedure to plea bargaining.

The tradition of private prosecution has been a feature of English criminal procedure nearly as striking and tenacious as the jury trial. . . . Although the English did place some limits upon the power of the private prosecutor to compromise criminal litigation, the prosecutorial function nevertheless grew up steeped in the conceptual forms of private discretion as opposed to official duty. Even in America, where the public prosecutor has a longer history than in the mother jurisdiction, the district attorney fell heir to the discretion of the citizen prosecutor whom he succeeded. When, therefore, the transformation of jury trial left the trial system clogged, the pressure of caseloads could find release in the exercise of prosecutorial discretion much more naturally than on the Continent, where the prosecutorial function has for so long been performed by officials and where there has been constant concern to regulate their discretion.

. . . For many centuries [the criminal defendant], too, has had the civil litigant's right to concede liability without trial, through the use of the guilty plea. This device, now familiar to us as the doctrinal basis of our nontrial plea bargaining procedure, also turns out to be an Anglo-American peculiarity. In Continental legal systems someone who is accused of a serious crime may confess, but he will nevertheless go to trial. . . . [T]he common law treated confession as a waiver of trial, by contrast with the Continental practice of viewing it as merely evidence of the most cogent kind. . . .

An adaptation seemingly less radical than the nontrial procedure of plea bargaining would have been to institute trial without jury, what we now call bench trial, in cases of serious crime. Although it has become a familiar via media between jury trial and the guilty plea in our own day, in the nineteenth century bench trial was resisted. . . .

In England the great political trials associated with the fall of Stuart aristocracy and the evolution of the eighteenth-century constitution had sanctified jury trial in political theory. . . . In America, where the judiciary's association with the excesses of English colonial administration had led the framers to make jury trial a constitutional right, bench trial was all the harder to envision. . . .

Not only was the nontrial solution of plea bargaining more rapid than bench trial, it also protected the weak, elective American trial bench from the moral responsibility for adjudication and from the political liability of unpopular decisions. In an ideological milieu in which the mounting defects of adversary jury trial could not have been admitted and discussed even if they had been correctly understood, it was easier for the judiciary to tolerate trial waivers than jury waivers — easier, that is, for the judges to allow the prosecutor to wring out a plea concession than to bring themselves to insist on adjudication before condemnation. [Citations and footnotes omitted.]

NOTES AND QUESTIONS

1. Professor Langbein's article appeared as part of a symposium on plea bargaining; two other articles in that symposium also addressed plea bargaining's strange history. See Albert W. Alschuler, Plea Bargaining and Its History, 13 Law & Soc'y Rev. 211 (1979); Lawrence M. Friedman, Plea Bargaining in Historical Perspective, 13 Law & Soc'y Rev. 247 (1979).

2. On Langbein's account, plea bargaining arose out of the intersection of three phenomena: elaborate jury trials, the use of lawyers to present the prosecution and defense cases, and prosecutorial discretion. Perhaps that means that if we are to do away with plea bargaining, we need to do away with at least one of its three causes. Which one? Each has substantial merit, does it not? Elaborate jury trials are designed to provide much more accurate adjudication than the kind of slapdash Old Bailey proceedings Langbein describes. The use of lawyers is likewise designed to ensure accuracy — especially accuracy on the defendant's side, the accuracy of guilty verdicts. Prosecutorial discretion offers the opportunity for mercy — no small thing in a world where criminal codes cover as much conduct as they do in the United States. If all those features of the criminal process are good and if plea bargaining follows from them, should we therefore keep plea bargaining?

3. The most detailed, and best, discussion of how plea bargaining came to dominate American criminal procedure is George Fisher, Plea Bargaining's Triumph, 109 Yale L.J. 857 (2000). Fisher focused his research on Middlesex County, Massachusetts; some of his conclusions may not be generalizable, though he maintains that most are. The following excerpt presents a rough sketch of his conclusions.

GEORGE FISHER, PLEA BARGAINING'S TRIUMPH

109 Yale L.J. 857, 864-868 (2000)

. . . [The] story of plea bargaining's rise begins in the opening decade of the nineteenth century. . . . Told chronologically, the story divides fairly neatly into two parts. During the first three-quarters or so of the nineteenth century, plea bargaining in Massachusetts advanced mainly in the realm of liquor-law prosecutions and murder cases, where . . . prosecutors had the power to negotiate pleas without any participation by the judge. These early deals took the form of *charge bargaining* — that is, in exchange for the defendant's plea to one or more of several charges, the prosecutor dropped the others or (in the case of murder) reduced the charge to a lesser offense. In the last quarter of the century, as judges converted to the cause, plea bargaining most often took the form of *sentence bargaining*, in which the defendant's plea won a reduced sentence. Backed by judges as well as prosecutors, plea bargaining now broke the narrow hold of liquor and murder prosecutions and conquered the whole penal territory — so that by century's close, guilty pleas accounted for some eighty-seven percent of criminal adjudications in Middlesex County. . . .

. . . My research in Middlesex County confirms earlier findings of a strikingly high rate of plea bargaining in Massachusetts liquor-law prosecutions in the early nineteenth century. Various . . . theories might explain a link between liquor prosecutions and plea bargaining, but the evidence overwhelmingly points to one — that the distinctive penalty scheme that the legislature created for the liquor laws, which assigned a fixed fine to almost every offense, deprived the judge of almost all sentencing discretion and put the prosecutor in a position to manipulate sentences by manipulating charges. Similarly, in capital [murder] cases, the prosecutor had the power to spare mandatory death by permitting them to plead guilty to a lesser charge. Prosecutors quickly exploited these narrow grants of sentencing authority and put in place a very modern practice of charge bargaining for pleas.

. . . [I]t is easy to see why prosecutors wanted to plea bargain. Prosecutors of the nineteenth century, like prosecutors today, plea bargained to ease their crushing workloads, made heavier in the nineteenth century both by their part-time status and utter lack of staff and by a caseload explosion perhaps set off by newly founded police forces and massive immigration. And of course they plea bargained to avoid the risk that wanton juries would spurn their painstakingly assembled cases. . . .

. . . Massachusetts legislators reacted sourly when they discovered how prosecutors were using the power unwittingly bestowed on them by the liquor law's rigid penalty scheme. At mid-century the legislature eliminated this power and very nearly succeeded in snuffing out prosecutorial plea bargaining in liquor cases. The legislature did not, however, disturb the prosecutor's power to conduct charge bargaining in murder cases, for there had been relatively few such bargains by mid-century. The result was that during the third quarter of the nineteenth century, plea bargaining advanced more dramatically in murder cases than in any other category. Even in liquor cases, the legislature's efforts to eradicate prosecutorial charge bargaining failed. After losing formal power to manipulate sentences in liquor cases, prosecutors retreated to the more covert and informal tactic of placing these cases "on file." This procedural maneuver, often done in exchange for a defendant's guilty plea, allowed prosecutors to elude altogether the legislature's sentencing provisions. The primitive device of *on-file plea bargaining* evolved directly into what we know today as probation. By the end of the century, probation had become one of plea bargaining's most dependable foot soldiers.

. . . [Now] consider the part played by defendants. It is not hard to see why defendants, given the chance, would plead guilty for a measure of leniency, but it is far less clear why their behavior on this score might change over time. Middlesex court records disclose that during the first half of the nineteenth century, decades before plea bargaining began its dramatic ascent, there had been a long decline in the proportion of non-liquor cases that ended in a plea. . . . [T]hese early guilty pleas were not plea bargains made in exchange for leniency, but rather the hopeless gestures of unrepresented defendants who properly saw that they had little chance of winning if they went to trial on their own. The gradual increase in the number of defendants who chose trial during the first part of the century therefore may mean that more and more defendants had counsel. Then, in the third quarter of the century, a sudden assault on the power of defendants to take their cases to trial may have reversed this course and helped to speed plea bargaining's rise. Laws passed in Massachusetts and elsewhere that gave defendants the right to testify at trial had the probably unintended effect of discouraging defendants with criminal pasts from going to trial. Seasoned criminals knew that if they took the stand to claim their innocence, the prosecutor could impeach their testimony with their old convictions and thereby destroy any real chance of acquittal. Yet if they failed to testify, defendants believed, juries would convict them for their silence. Together with the growing practice of probation, defendant-testimony laws confronted every defendant with a good reason to plea bargain. Defendant-testimony laws helped to persuade accomplished criminals to plead guilty, while the promise of probation, which was available almost exclusively to first offenders who pled guilty, served as an incentive for everyone else.

The combined willingness of all prosecutors and many defendants to bargain for pleas was not, however, enough for the practice to thrive outside the narrow context of liquor laws and murder cases. The statutory penalty structure for most crimes gave Massachusetts judges such great discretion in sentencing that the prosecutor typically could not unilaterally guarantee a low enough sentence to win the defendant's plea. Plea bargaining's sweeping triumph during the last quarter of the nineteenth century suggests, therefore, that judges had entered plea bargaining's ranks. . . . [A] caseload explosion on the civil side of Massachusetts courthouses helped force this change of judicial heart on the criminal side, for in Massachusetts, as in most American jurisdictions, the same judges sat on both civil and criminal cases. The industrial boom of the last part of the nineteenth century — and especially the spread of railroads and street cars — spawned a whole new strain of personal injury litigation that, case for case, absorbed far more time than the contractual nonpayment cases that once had filled the civil dockets. The figures in Massachusetts are clear: As judges devoted a hugely increasing proportion of their time to the civil caseload, they devoted a shrinking proportion to the criminal caseload, and they resolved more and more criminal cases by guilty plea. Judges apparently discovered that they had more power to spur pleas in criminal cases than to coerce settlements in civil cases. After all, a criminal court judge could credibly promise a reward in exchange for a plea or threaten a penalty for going to trial, but in civil court, the jury — not the judge — generally set the loser's penalty.

By century's end, all three of the courtroom's major actors — prosecutor, defendant, and judge — had found reasons to favor the plea-bargaining system. For prosecutor and judge, who together held most of the power that mattered, the spread of plea bargaining did not merely deliver marvelously efficient relief from a suffocating workload. It also spared the prosecutor the risk of loss and the judge the risk of reversal, and thereby protected the professional reputations of each. In fact, by erasing the possibility of either factual or legal error in the proceedings, plea bargains protected the reputation and hence the legitimacy of the system as a whole. . . .

. . . The power of the various actors who stood to gain from plea bargaining became, in a sense, plea bargaining's power. This collective, systemic interest in plea bargaining encouraged the rise of those institutions of criminal procedure that helped plea bargaining and hindered those that hurt it. In the nineteenth century, plea bargaining fostered probation's rise and thereby created a hugely versatile plea-bargaining tool. In the late nineteenth and early twentieth centuries, plea bargaining helped stave off the indeterminate sentence, which had threatened to halt plea bargaining's progress. And in the twentieth century, plea bargaining played a surprisingly direct role in assisting the creation of public defenders. In turn, these organizations for defense of the poor assured that in a majority of criminal cases, the defense lawyer would share the prosecutor's and judge's interests in maximizing systemic efficiency — and hence in plea bargaining. These examples of plea bargaining's influence over other institutions of criminal procedure are merely case studies within a larger trend. In fact, it is hard to think of a single enduring development in criminal procedure in the last 150 years that has not aided plea bargaining's cause.

Finally, [consider] how the power to plea bargain evolved in the late twentieth century. Before the advent of modern sentencing guidelines, both prosecutor and judge held some power to plea bargain without the other's cooperation. The result of their mutually independent bargaining strength was a certain balance of power, which to some degree protected defendants from abuses of power by either official. Today, however, sentencing guidelines have recast whole chunks of the criminal code in the mold of the old Massachusetts liquor laws. In the process, they have unsettled the balance of bargaining power by ensuring that the prosecutor, who always had the strongest interest in plea bargaining, now has the unilateral power to deal. . . . [Citations and footnotes omitted.]

NOTES AND QUESTIONS

1. Notice that while Professor Langbein emphasizes the role of jury trials and defense lawyers in plea bargaining's rise, Professor Fisher emphasizes the role of sentencing — Massachusetts prosecutors gained the power to bargain by gaining power over defendants' sentences, and that power has been reinforced by developments like probation and the rise of detailed sentencing guidelines. Who ought to have dominant power over sentencing? If prosecutors have the power to dismiss charges altogether — with judges effectively disabled from reviewing such decisions, see Chapter 9, supra — should they not also have the power to place a cap on the sentence a defendant can receive if he is convicted? If they can fix maximum sentences, why not minimum sentences? Is there a principled difference between ceilings and floors in this context?

2. Do you agree with the conclusion that "it is hard to think of a single enduring development in criminal procedure in the last 150 years that has not aided plea bargaining's cause"? What about the growth of a large and detailed body of search and seizure law enforced by the exclusionary rule (see Chapter 5, supra)? Assuming that development is "enduring" — it shows no signs of disappearing anytime soon — does it help plea bargaining or hinder it?

3. There is an enormous literature on plea bargaining, but very little of it seeks to describe what defense attorneys and prosecutors actually do, and what they think

about it. The best such description comes in an excellent short book by Milton Heumann, excerpted below. Heumann interviewed defense attorneys, prosecutors, and trial judges in three cities in Connecticut in the mid-1970s. Because the interviews took place decades ago, some of the examples are dated, and the sentences his interviewees discuss are lower than would be the case today, but the general picture still fits with the practice in many, probably most, jurisdictions.

The excerpt that follows begins with a discussion of how new criminal defense attorneys think about their job, then shifts to how they come to embrace plea bargaining, and finally closes with some discussion of how prosecutors think about and practice plea bargaining.

MILTON HEUMANN, PLEA BARGAINING: THE EXPERIENCES OF PROSECUTORS, JUDGES, AND DEFENSE ATTORNEYS

49-50, 57-59, 61-63, 76-78, 89, 100-103, 105-106
(University of Chicago Press 1978)

[New criminal defense attorneys] shared several general expectations about what working in the criminal justice system would be like. They assumed that most cases would be given lengthy and detailed consideration. In law school, they had been trained to dissect appellate cases; their briefs on legal cases were finely honed pieces undertaken only after extensive research and deliberation. As one judge put it, they had learned to have a "romance with each case."

> You have a romance with each case. You're interested in the legal aspects, you go up to the stacks, you go to this book, that book, the index of legal periodicals. . . . You rewrite, and each one means something. And as you write, you change your style, and you find that there is a phrase here, or a phrase there, it's creativity that you are in love with. Each appellate case, each line, each finding, each paragraph would mean something.

Because of both substantive and procedural concerns, newcomers expected that their criminal court cases would require comparable time and effort. They assumed that disputable legal questions would characterize many of those cases.

> *Q.* Did you think that legal issues would be more important in terms of the criminal cases you would be handling?
> *A.* Well, I suppose, coming out of law school, you thought that justice . . . you know, we had some really good teachers; they talked about justice and the great principles of the Constitution to be upheld, and the great Fourth Amendment, and the Fifth, and the Sixth, and such. . . . I anticipated that I would be working on constitutional cases much more than has been the case. . . .

In the process of handling their cases, new defense attorneys learn that the reality of the court differs from what they had expected; through rewards and sanctions, they are also taught to proceed in a certain fashion. . . .

The most important thing the new defense attorney learns is that most of his clients are factually guilty. His raw material is not typically the railroaded innocent defendant; instead, it is an individual who, in all likelihood, is guilty as charged, or at least is guilty of an offense related to the charge. . . .

[These attorneys] learn of the defendant's guilt in several ways. Attorneys with primarily circuit court practices handle mostly misdemeanants.[4] These clients often perceive their own cases to be relatively minor, and they frequently and freely admit their guilt during the first or second meeting with the attorney. . . . [T]hey are more concerned about "getting it over with" than with disputing their own guilt. . . .

In superior court cases, defendants are less likely to own up to the offense in their initial contact with the defense attorney. Experienced defense attorneys posit that the defendant's reluctance is based on the belief that a defense attorney will work harder for a client that he assumes innocent. Whatever the explanation, the defendant at first offers a story that exculpates him. The newer the defense attorney, the more likely he is to believe the defendant's version of what happened. It is only when he confronts the state's attorney with the defendant's story that he learns that there is more to the matter than the defendant first led him to believe. . . . Skepticism in evaluating the defendant's story, then, is something new attorneys learn. Over time they become veritable cynics.

> Yeah, well, you know . . . the first year you practice law you believe everything your client tells you. The second year you practice, you believe everything that the other side tells you. The third year you don't know who's telling the truth. Most people tend not to believe their clients that much, justifiably.

. . . At the same time that he is learning piecemeal about the factual culpability of most defendants and the futility of legal challenge, the new defense attorney is forced to decide how to proceed in given cases. His options are twofold: He can opt for an adversary posture (motions and trials), or he can engage in plea bargaining. . . . He is taught the risks of being an adversary and the benefits of being a plea bargainer.

His education begins almost immediately. In every case the defense attorney needs certain information that the prosecutor possesses. This material includes the police report, the defendant's record, the basic facts of the case, and so on.

. . . [T]here is a formal way to obtain some of this material — through filing a Motion for Discovery and a Bill of Particulars. The new defense attorney assumes that these motions are in order in every case. What he is taught, though, is that the prosecutors resent these motions. Prosecutors prefer to communicate the information orally and informally, thus relieving themselves of the burden of preparing typewritten responses in every case. Since they assume that the case will be settled by a plea bargain, they feel a formal response to be an unwarranted waste of time. . . . The following remarks, by circuit and superior court prosecutors respectively, illustrate the hostility to these motions, and the sanctions that are brought to bear.

> And then we have the open-file policy for public defenders. They can look at all the files they want. There was a time when some new public defenders started filing Bills of Particulars. Now, if I am going to show you all my notes, why would you file a Bill of Particulars? If they handle us like that, close the files to them. Let them file their bills, and we'll argue the Bill of Particulars. Don't forget, they've got ten cases here and ten cases

---

4. In Connecticut at the time of Heumann's study, circuit courts had jurisdiction over misdemeanors and some felonies; superior courts had jurisdiction over more serious felonies. — EDS.

upstairs, and they've got to run up and down those stairs. Me, I'm in this one court-room. I call the names, and I argue them. You know what I mean? So, they hassle you like that. . . . Same with private attorneys. There is an easy way and a hard way for them to get their fees. One way you can make the lawyer earn his fee; the other way you can have the lawyer come in, grab his thing, and run. If he wants to be a ball-breaker, I say, "File your motions, Pal." He has to file a Bill of Particulars, and then he'll have to come back to argue it. Then if he wants to put in a not-guilty plea to the jury, he comes back again. He comes back, and I say, "Oh, we have a case going on. You'll have to come back next week." So this guy is a private attorney, and he's running around trying to make money. He doesn't want to come to our court ten times for a lousy case. And with the public defenders, we control the docket in court, so you hassle them. You know, call one case, the guy upstairs runs downstairs, and back and forth. It's like a kid's game, but you know, I like to get along with people if I can, and I don't try to be obnoxious to people, but if a person hassles me, tries to make my life more difficult, I will make his more difficult.

. . . [W]hat I try to tell every new attorney who comes in . . . I try to "steer them straight." I'll call them in on the first case we're dealing with and say: "Look, there are two ways to practice law here. You can file all the motions you want, harass me any way you want, but you and your client in the long run are not going to gain anything. Or, do you want to come in, I'll tell you what my file has, I'll show you what my file has, and we can talk about the case. It's your choice." Now, he may give me a hard time the first or second time around, but, you know, the aggravations can be going both ways, and eventually most people come to the point where they'll prefer to sit down and see what I have rather than go into court and make a big production of everything.

. . . [In order to bargain successfully, defense attorneys] need to develop a sense of "what the case is worth." How are they to judge a prosecutor's offer which falls substantially below the maximum the charge allows? Is it a good deal? Could it be better? Is it in line with what other attorneys receive?

Newcomers learn to answer these questions through experience. All outside advice is sought and cherished. But, without exception, every attorney interviewed indicated the necessity of developing his own "feel for a case." . . . Essentially, it is an impressionistic multiple regression model carried in the attorney's head. It is a way of sorting and weighing the sundry factors that enter into a disposition. Attorneys believe it can be learned only through experience in negotiating cases. Once an attorney has a feel for cases, he knows whether to try or plea bargain a case; if he chooses plea bargaining, he knows how to weigh factors as diverse as the defendant's record, the facts of the case, the prosecutor's personality, the prosecutor's willingness to go to trial, the judge's reactions to specific types of crimes, the precedents in terms of prior dispositions for this type of offense, and so on. He is confident that he can predict early what disposition is obtainable. . . .

You know, I think I know what I'm doing. . . . I've been a lawyer for a few years; I've specialized in criminal law. I can analyze a case; I can tell a defendant in a few minutes just what's going to happen, what should be done and all.

I look at a file and I know I can beat it. So I know that maybe I'll have it continued, with a plea, and file motions, maybe one or two or three times, but I'm going to get it [dismissed]. Then on the other hand, you know, this guy has to plead to something. You know that after you talk to him and read the sheet. You know he'll have to plead to something.

I can take twenty-five files and look them over and, maybe without even speaking to the defendant, predict what is likely to happen. It's difficult to think that you could do that, but you can read a police report and the facts of the case, and because you have read so many and know that this guy should do this, and the prosecutor should do that. You have a good idea completely ahead of time.

Q. How does a new attorney learn what a case is worth?

A. Well, the new guy is in trouble. He's got to learn the hard way, get battered around. . . . You've got to put together a lot of things. You got to start off with the offense and the circumstances surrounding the events, naturally. Then you got to take the defendant, his record, . . . his family situation, anything good that you have going for you. These are the textbook things to look for. Then you got things that aren't in the textbooks. The month of the year. I've always made it a practice to do great things in December. The courts are closing; you want to get people out of the jails. It's the season, to a certain extent. I always save some of my real problems for the last day of court before Christmas recess. Nobody's going to turn me down. One of the things you'll also acquire a feel for, you get to know the people that you're dealing with. We all have our hang-ups. Some prosecutors get very upset with certain types of crimes, certain types of defendants. Sometimes they had the guy before, so they know him too well. . . .

Q. How did you learn to plea bargain? How did you learn what a case is worth and what you could get?

A. Well, there are no courses given on it. It's like . . . Well, I guess you could analogize it to making love. You know, it's something you can't teach; you can't put it in a book; you can't give a lecture on it. But, like making love, you do it enough times, you learn to like it, and you'll get good at it. . . .

Q. So generally you'd opt for plea bargaining?

A. Well . . . let me say this. It isn't so much that I'm going to get screwed at trial . . . it's just that I can do so much without going to trial. It isn't even the fear of what happens to you after trial so much as the fact that it's almost an irrelevant consideration. The fact is that in the plea bargaining system — which is not so much an alternative to trial as the system — you get good results by plea bargaining.

. . . Prosecutors and state's attorneys learn that their roles primarily entail the processing of factually guilty defendants. Contrary to their expectations that problems of establishing factual guilt would be central to their job, they find that in most cases the evidence in the file is sufficient to conclude (and prove) that the defendant is factually guilty. For those cases where there is a substantial question as to factual guilt, the prosecutor has the power — and is inclined to exercise it — to . . . dismiss the case. . . .

Furthermore, [the prosecutor] finds that defense attorneys only infrequently contest the prosecutor's own conclusion that the defendant is guilty. In their initial approach to the prosecutor they may raise the possibility that the defendant is factually innocent, but in most subsequent discussions their advances focus on disposition and not on the problem of factual guilt. Thus, from the prosecutor's own reading of the file . . . and from comments of his "adversary," he learns that he begins with the upper hand. . . .

In addition to learning of the factual culpability of most defendants, the prosecutor also learns that defendants would be hard pressed to raise legal challenges to the state's case. . . . [M]ost cases are simply barren of any contestable legal issue, and nothing in the prosecutor's file or the defense attorney's arguments leads the prosecutor to conclude otherwise. . . . What remains problematic is the sentence the defendant will receive. . . .

Prosecutors and state's attorneys draw sharp distinctions between serious and nonserious cases. In both instances, they assume the defendant guilty, but they are looking for different types of dispositions, dependent upon their classification of the case. If it is a nonserious matter, they are amenable to defense requests for a small fine in the circuit court, some short, suspended sentence, or some brief period of probation; similarly, in a nonserious superior court matter the state's attorney is willing to work out a combination suspended sentence and probation. The central concern with these nonserious cases is to dispose of them quickly. . . .

On the other hand, if the case is serious, the prosecutor and state's attorney are likely to be looking for time. The serious case cannot be quickly disposed of by a no-time alternative. These are cases in which we would expect more involved and lengthy plea bargaining negotiations.

Whether the case is viewed as serious or nonserious depends on factors other than the formal charge(s) the defendant faces. For example, these non-formal considerations might include the degree of harm done the victim, the amount of violence employed by the defendant, the defendant's prior record, the characteristics of the victim and defendant, the defendant's motive; all are somewhat independent of formal charge, and yet all weigh heavily in the prosecutor's judgment of the seriousness of the case. Defendants facing the same formal charges, then, may find that prosecutors sort their cases into different categories. . . .

> After a matter of time you just see so much that you really . . . You must always remember there are always two sides to the story, even though somebody might've gotten belted with a pipe, and it is a serious offense, but there might be something in mitigation to that. You know, there are some statutes that are mandatory minimum time. Assault in the third degree with a dangerous weapon is mandatory time of one year. Now if we stuck to that statute and subsection, if we stuck to that, we'd be trying everything out there; there'd be a lot of people going away for a minimum of one year. But a lot of times we allow a little flexibility; we give them assault in the third but not with a dangerous weapon, and then we or the judge look at the facts. This kid today was an example, the kid who hit the guy on the wrist with a pipe. Now technically he was guilty of assault with a dangerous weapon; he could have been charged with assault in the third with a dangerous weapon, and the mandatory minimum one year in jail. But the kid had a clean record, the fight was no big thing, so I gave him assault in the third, under subsection one, which is not with a dangerous weapon, and we were looking for a suspended sentence. That's what the judge did, thirty days suspended.

. . . In some serious cases, the prosecutor or state's attorney may not be looking for time. Generally, these are the cases in which the prosecutor has a problem establishing either the factual or legal guilt of the defendant, and thus is willing to settle for a plea to the charge and offer a recommendation of a suspended sentence. The logic is simple: The prosecutor feels the defendant is guilty of the offense but fears that if he insists on time, the defense attorney will go to trial and uncover the factual or legal defects of the state's case. Thus, the prosecutor "sweetens the deal" to extract a guilty plea and to decrease the likelihood that the attorney will gamble on complete vindication. . . .

NOTES ON PLEA BARGAINING IN PRACTICE

1. Heumann's book is a rich source of information about how lawyers and judges see plea bargaining; those interested in further study of the subject should read the book in its entirety.

If Heumann's picture is accurate, to what degree should we call plea bargaining "bargaining"? The label implies exchange, with each side giving something valuable to the other. It is easy to see what prosecutors give defendants. What do ordinary defendants — those who lack strong legal or factual claims — give prosecutors?

2. Defense attorneys and prosecutors alike seem convinced that the vast majority of defendants are guilty. Presumably, though, at least a few defendants are innocent of the charges brought against them. Who identifies those few defendants? How likely is it that this sorting process proceeds accurately?

3. Both prosecutors and defense attorneys regularly talk about customary "prices" for particular sorts of crime — the "feel" for what sentence a case would bring that lawyers acquired over time. Where do those customary prices come from? Who decides them, and how? What political or legal checks limit them?

4. The major point of Heumann's book is that the large majority of defense attorneys, prosecutors, and judges come to their jobs skeptical of plea bargaining but, over time, come to endorse the practice. One might argue that the breadth of that endorsement is itself a strong defense of plea bargaining — that if all the relevant actors (Heumann also notes that most *defendants* seem to embrace plea bargaining) find the practice acceptable and even a positive feature of the system, the rest of us should be untroubled by it. Are you persuaded? If not, why should the opinions of those who engage in this practice be disregarded?

5. The following sections deal with the law that surrounds plea bargaining. That law concerns three basic issues: the limits (if any) on the government's ability to threaten a defendant with serious adverse consequences for taking a case to trial; the limits (if any) on the subject matter of the bargain offered; and the manner in which the bargain is interpreted and enforced, both against the government and against the defense. As you read these materials, ask yourself whether, and if so how, these rules are likely to affect real-world behavior by the kind of lawyers Heumann interviewed.

2. Voluntariness

BRADY v. UNITED STATES

Certiorari to the United States Court of Appeals for the Tenth Circuit
397 U.S. 742 (1970)

JUSTICE WHITE delivered the opinion of the Court.

In 1959, petitioner was charged with kidnaping in violation of 18 U.S.C. §1201(a).[1] Since the indictment charged that the victim of the kidnaping was not

---

1. "Whoever knowingly transports in interstate or foreign commerce, any person who has been unlawfully seized, confined, inveigled, decoyed, kidnaped, abducted, or carried away and held for ransom or reward or otherwise, except, in the case of a minor, by a parent thereof, shall be punished (1) by

liberated unharmed, petitioner faced a maximum penalty of death if the verdict of the jury should so recommend. Petitioner, represented by competent counsel throughout, first elected to plead not guilty. . . . Upon learning that his codefendant, who had confessed to the authorities, would plead guilty and be available to testify against him, petitioner changed his plea to guilty. His plea was accepted after the trial judge twice questioned him as to the voluntariness of his plea.[2] Petitioner was sentenced to 50 years' imprisonment, later reduced to 30.

In 1967, petitioner sought relief under 28 U.S.C. §2255, claiming that his plea of guilty was not voluntarily given because §1201(a) operated to coerce his plea, because his counsel exerted impermissible pressure upon him, and because his plea was induced by representations with respect to reduction of sentence and clemency. . . .

That a guilty plea is a grave and solemn act to be accepted only with care and discernment has long been recognized. Central to the plea and the foundation for entering judgment against the defendant is the defendant's admission in open court that he committed the acts charged in the indictment. He thus stands as a witness against himself and he is shielded by the Fifth Amendment from being compelled to do so — hence the minimum requirement that his plea be the voluntary expression of his own choice. But the plea is more than an admission of past conduct; it is the defendant's consent that judgment of conviction may be entered without a trial — a waiver of his right to trial before a jury or a judge. Waivers of constitutional rights not only must be voluntary but must be knowing, intelligent acts done with sufficient awareness of the relevant circumstances and likely consequences. On neither score was Brady's plea of guilty invalid.

The trial judge in 1959 found the plea voluntary before accepting it; the District Court in 1968, after an evidentiary hearing, found that the plea was voluntarily made; the Court of Appeals specifically approved the finding of voluntariness. We see no reason on this record to disturb the judgment of those courts. Petitioner, advised by competent counsel, tendered his plea after his codefendant, who had already given a confession, determined to plead guilty and became available to testify against petitioner. . . .

The voluntariness of Brady's plea can be determined only by considering all of the relevant circumstances surrounding it. One of these circumstances was the possibility

---

death if the kidnaped person has not been liberated unharmed, and if the verdict of the jury shall so recommend, or (2) by imprisonment for any term of years or for life, if the death penalty is not imposed." [NOTE — The death penalty provision in this statute was held unconstitutional by the Supreme Court in *United States v. Jackson*, 390 U.S. 570 (1968), two years before the Court's decision in *Brady*. See Note 3 following *Brady*. — EDS.]

2. Eight days after petitioner pleaded guilty, he was brought before the court for sentencing. At that time, the court questioned petitioner for a second time about the voluntariness of his plea:

> *The Court*:   . . . Having read the presentence report and the statement you made to the probation officer, I want to be certain that you know what you are doing and you did know when you entered a plea of guilty the other day. Do you want to let that plea of guilty stand, or do you want to withdraw it and plead not guilty?
> *Defendant Brady*:   I want to let that plea stand, sir.
> *The Court*:   You understand that in doing that you are admitting and confessing the truth of the charge contained in the indictment and that you enter a plea of guilty voluntarily, without persuasion, coercion of any kind? Is that right?
> *Defendant Brady*:   Yes, your Honor.
> *The Court*:   And you do do that?
> *Defendant Brady*:   Yes, I do.
> *The Court*:   You plead guilty to the charge?
> *Defendant Brady*:   Yes, I do. [App. 29-30.]

of a heavier sentence following a guilty verdict after a trial. It may be that Brady, faced with a strong case against him and recognizing that his chances for acquittal were slight, preferred to plead guilty and thus limit the penalty to life imprisonment rather than to elect a jury trial which could result in a death penalty. But even if we assume that Brady would not have pleaded guilty except for the death penalty provision of §1201(a), this assumption merely identifies the penalty provision as a "but for" cause of his plea. That the statute caused the plea in this sense does not necessarily prove that the plea was coerced and invalid as an involuntary act.

The State to some degree encourages pleas of guilty at every important step in the criminal process. For some people, their breach of a State's law is alone sufficient reason for surrendering themselves and accepting punishment.

For others, apprehension and charge, both threatening acts by the Government, jar them into admitting their guilt. In still other cases, the post-indictment accumulation of evidence may convince the defendant and his counsel that a trial is not worth the agony and expense to the defendant and his family. All these pleas of guilty are valid in spite of the State's responsibility for some of the factors motivating the pleas; the pleas are no more improperly compelled than is the decision by a defendant at the close of the State's evidence at trial that he must take the stand or face certain conviction.

Of course, the agents of the State may not produce a plea by actual or threatened physical harm or by mental coercion overbearing the will of the defendant. But nothing of the sort is claimed in this case; nor is there evidence that Brady was so gripped by fear of the death penalty or hope of leniency that he did not or could not, with the help of counsel, rationally weigh the advantages of going to trial against the advantages of pleading guilty. Brady's claim is of a different sort: that it violates the Fifth Amendment to influence or encourage a guilty plea by opportunity or promise of leniency and that a guilty plea is coerced and invalid if influenced by the fear of a possibly higher penalty for the crime charged if a conviction is obtained after the State is put to its proof.

Insofar as the voluntariness of his plea is concerned, there is little to differentiate Brady from (1) the defendant, in a jurisdiction where the judge and jury have the same range of sentencing power, who pleads guilty because his lawyer advises him that the judge will very probably be more lenient than the jury; (2) the defendant, in a jurisdiction where the judge alone has sentencing power, who is advised by counsel that the judge is normally more lenient with defendants who plead guilty than with those who go to trial; (3) the defendant who is permitted by prosecutor and judge to plead guilty to a lesser offense included in the offense charged; and (4) the defendant who pleads guilty to certain counts with the understanding that other charges will be dropped. In each of these situations, as in Brady's case, the defendant might never plead guilty absent the possibility or certainty that the plea will result in a lesser penalty than the sentence that could be imposed after a trial and a verdict of guilty. We decline to hold, however, that a guilty plea is compelled and invalid under the Fifth Amendment whenever motivated by the defendant's desire to accept the certainty or probability of a lesser penalty rather than face a wider range of possibilities extending from acquittal to conviction and a higher penalty authorized by law for the crime charged.

The issue we deal with is inherent in the criminal law and its administration because guilty pleas are not constitutionally forbidden, because the criminal law characteristically extends to judge or jury a range of choice in setting the sentence in individual cases, and because both the State and the defendant often find it advantageous to preclude the possibility of the maximum penalty authorized by law. For a defendant who sees slight possibility of acquittal, the advantages of pleading guilty and limiting the probable penalty are obvious — his exposure is reduced, the correctional processes can begin immediately, and the practical burdens of a trial are eliminated. For the State there are also advantages — the more promptly imposed punishment after an admission of guilt may more effectively attain the objectives of punishment; and with the avoidance of trial, scarce judicial and prosecutorial resources are conserved for those cases in which there is a substantial issue of the defendant's guilt or in which there is substantial doubt that the State can sustain its burden of proof. It is this mutuality of advantage that perhaps explains the fact that at present well over three-fourths of the criminal convictions in this country rest on pleas of guilty, a great many of them no doubt motivated at least in part by the hope or assurance of a lesser penalty than might be imposed if there were a guilty verdict after a trial to judge or jury.

Of course, that the prevalence of guilty pleas is explainable does not necessarily validate those pleas or the system which produces them. But we cannot hold that it is unconstitutional for the State to extend a benefit to a defendant who in turn extends a substantial benefit to the State and who demonstrates by his plea that he is ready and willing to admit his crime and to enter the correctional system in a frame of mind that affords hope for success in rehabilitation over a shorter period of time than might otherwise be necessary.

A contrary holding would require the States and Federal Government to forbid guilty pleas altogether, to provide a single invariable penalty for each crime defined by the statutes, or to place the sentencing function in a separate authority having no knowledge of the manner in which the conviction in each case was obtained. In any event, it would be necessary to forbid prosecutors and judges to accept guilty pleas to selected counts, to lesser included offenses, or to reduced charges. The Fifth Amendment does not reach so far.

Bram v. United States, 168 U.S. 532 (1897), held that the admissibility of a confession depended upon whether it was compelled within the meaning of the Fifth Amendment. To be admissible, a confession must be "free and voluntary: that is, must not be extracted by any sort of threats or violence, nor obtained by any direct or implied promises, however slight, nor by the exertion of any improper influence." 168 U.S., at 542-543. . . .

Bram is not inconsistent with our holding that Brady's plea was not compelled even though the law promised him a lesser maximum penalty if he did not go to trial. *Bram* dealt with a confession given by a defendant in custody, alone and unrepresented by counsel. In such circumstances, even a mild promise of leniency was deemed sufficient to bar the confession, not because the promise was an illegal act as such, but because defendants at such times are too sensitive to inducement and the possible impact on them too great to ignore and too difficult to assess. But *Bram* and its progeny did not hold that the possibly coercive impact of a promise of leniency could not be dissipated by the presence and advice of counsel, any more than Miranda v. Arizona, 384 U.S. 436 (1966), held that the possibly coercive atmosphere of the police station could not be counteracted by the presence of counsel or other safeguards.

Brady's situation bears no resemblance to Bram's. Brady first pleaded not guilty; prior to changing his plea to guilty he was subjected to no threats or promises in face-to-face encounters with the authorities. He had competent counsel and full opportunity to assess the advantages and disadvantages of a trial as compared with those attending a plea of guilty; there was no hazard of an impulsive and improvident response to a seeming but unreal advantage. His plea of guilty was entered in open court and before a judge obviously sensitive to the requirements of the law with respect to guilty pleas. Brady's plea, unlike Bram's confession, was voluntary.

The standard as to the voluntariness of guilty pleas must be essentially that defined by Judge Tuttle of the Court of Appeals for the Fifth Circuit:

> A plea of guilty entered by one fully aware of the direct consequences, including the actual value of any commitments made to him by the court, prosecutor, or his own counsel, must stand unless induced by threats (or promises to discontinue improper harassment), misrepresentation (including unfulfilled or unfulfillable promises), or perhaps by promises that are by their nature improper as having no proper relationship to the prosecutor's business (e.g., bribes).

[Shelton v. United States, 246 F.2d 571, 572 n, 2 (5th Cir. 1957) (en banc), *rev'd* on other grounds, 356 U.S. 26 (1958).]

Under this standard, a plea of guilty is not invalid merely because entered to avoid the possibility of a death penalty.

The record before us also supports the conclusion that Brady's plea was intelligently made. He was advised by competent counsel, he was made aware of the nature of the charge against him, and there was nothing to indicate that he was incompetent or otherwise not in control of his mental faculties; once his confederate had pleaded guilty and became available to testify, he chose to plead guilty, perhaps to ensure that he would face no more than life imprisonment or a term of years. Brady was aware of precisely what he was doing when he admitted that he had kidnaped the victim and had not released her unharmed. . . .

We would have serious doubts about this case if the encouragement of guilty pleas by offers of leniency substantially increased the likelihood that defendants, advised by competent counsel, would falsely condemn themselves. But our view is to the contrary and is based on our expectations that courts will satisfy themselves that pleas of guilty are voluntarily and intelligently made by competent defendants with adequate advice of counsel and that there is nothing to question the accuracy and reliability of the defendants' admissions that they committed the crimes with which they are charged. In the case before us, nothing in the record impeaches Brady's plea or suggests that his admissions in open court were anything but the truth.

Although Brady's plea of guilty may well have been motivated in part by a desire to avoid a possible death penalty, we are convinced that his plea was voluntarily and intelligently made and we have no reason to doubt that his solemn admission of guilt was truthful. . . .

JUSTICE BLACK, while adhering to his belief that United States v. Jackson, 390 U.S. 570, was wrongly decided, concurs in the judgment and in substantially all of the opinion in this case.

[The opinion of Justice Brennan, joined by Justices Douglas and Marshall, concurring in the result, is omitted.]

NOTES AND QUESTIONS

1. *Brady* is the case in which the Supreme Court for the first time approved the constitutionality of plea bargaining. Prior to this time, the practice went forward, but mostly under the table, with defendants proclaiming in open court that their pleas were the product of neither promises nor threats and with courts declining to inquire into the presence or absence of charging or sentencing concessions. *Brady*'s significance is thus twofold: First, the decision validates the legitimacy of bargaining for guilty pleas, and second, the decision brings that bargaining process into the open, and hence potentially under legal regulation. Plea bargaining is a market, but it is today a regulated market. Before *Brady*, it was mostly a black market.

2. Brady makes two arguments. First, he contends that his guilty plea was involuntary, because it was made out of fear that a worse penalty (death) might be imposed on him if he took his case to trial. In response to this claim, Justice White repeatedly emphasizes the fact that Brady was represented by counsel (see, for example, the discussion distinguishing Brady's situation from *Bram*). This suggests a strong link between *Gideon* and the permissibility of plea bargaining. Is the link persuasive? Is counsel's presence an adequate answer to Brady's claim?

3. Brady's second argument is that the plea was not "intelligent." This claim requires some explanation. In United States v. Jackson, 390 U.S. 570 (1968), the Supreme Court invalidated the death penalty provision of §1201, the statute under which Brady was convicted. Thus, the threatened penalty that prompted Brady's plea — a death sentence — could not have been legally imposed on him for reasons that became apparent only after the plea was entered. Brady argued, naturally enough, that this made his plea unintelligent, because it was based on incorrect legal assumptions. In a portion of the opinion not excerpted above, the Court responded to this claim as follows:

> Often the decision to plead guilty is heavily influenced by the defendant's appraisal of the prosecution's case against him and by the apparent likelihood of securing leniency should a guilty plea be offered and accepted. Considerations like these frequently present imponderable questions for which there are no certain answers; judgments may be made that in the light of later events seem improvident, although they were perfectly sensible at the time. The rule that a plea must be intelligently made to be valid does not require that a plea be vulnerable to later attack if the defendant did not correctly assess every relevant factor entering into his decision. A defendant is not entitled to withdraw his plea merely because he discovers long after the plea has been accepted that his calculus misapprehended the quality of the State's case or the likely penalties attached to alternative courses of action. More particularly, absent misrepresentation or other impermissible conduct by state agents, cf. Von Moltke v. Gillies, 332 U.S. 708 (1948), a voluntary plea of guilty intelligently made in the light of the then applicable law does not become vulnerable because later judicial decisions indicate that the plea rested on a faulty premise. A plea of guilty triggered by the expectations of a competently counseled defendant that the State will have a strong case against him is not subject to later attack because the defendant's lawyer correctly advised him with respect to the then existing law as to possible penalties but later pronouncements of the courts, as in this case, hold that the maximum penalty for the crime in question was less than was reasonably assumed at the time the plea was entered.

> The fact that Brady did not anticipate United States v. Jackson, supra, does not impugn the truth or reliability of his plea. We find no requirement in the Constitution that a defendant must be permitted to disown his solemn admissions in open court that

he committed the act with which he is charged simply because it later develops that the State would have had a weaker case than the defendant had thought or that the maximum penalty then assumed applicable has been held inapplicable in subsequent judicial decisions.

Notice the emphasis on the accuracy of Brady's plea. This line of argument suggests that the permissibility of plea bargaining is closely linked to those aspects of the guilty plea process — perhaps the requirement of a "factual basis" for the plea under North Carolina v. Alford, 400 U.S. 25 (1970), see supra, page 1177, and Federal Rule of Criminal Procedure 11(b)'s requirement of an adequate plea colloquy — that aim to ensure factual correctness. Again, is the link persuasive? Is there a sense in which plea bargaining itself might make pleas *less* accurate? Is there any way to solve that problem, short of abolishing bargaining?

4. In United States v. Ruiz, 536 U.S. 622 (2002), the Court rejected a defendant's claim that he was constitutionally entitled to receive information from the prosecution, during plea bargaining, about material impeachment evidence or affirmative defense evidence known to the prosecution. The Court, citing *Brady*, noted that the Constitution "permits a court to accept a guilty plea, with its accompanying waiver of various constitutional rights, despite various forms of misapprehension under which a defendant might labor," and found the particular kinds of evidence in *Ruiz* to be indistinguishable from other missing information that had previously been held not to invalidate an otherwise voluntary guilty plea.

5. The link between the accuracy of the criminal process and plea bargaining is complicated. As noted previously, allowing the government to "pay" defendants to plead guilty, in the form of sentencing or charging concessions, might lead innocent defendants to plead guilty. But forbidding such inducements would presumably reduce the number of guilty pleas, and hence increase the number of trials. That might put pressure on the system to alter the trial process in ways that might not be accuracy enhancing.

Consider, in this regard, the consequences of the practice in Philadelphia in the 1970s and 1980s of forbidding plea bargaining. Stephen Schulhofer studied the Philadelphia experience (which Schulhofer regarded as definitely preferable to the alternative of plea bargaining); he reported his findings in Stephen Schulhofer, Is Plea Bargaining Inevitable? 97 Harv. L. Rev. 1037 (1984). He found that the guilty plea rate in Philadelphia was 45 percent, roughly half the rate found in other large cities. Most remaining defendants waived their right to jury trial, based on a more or less tacit system of sentencing concessions; that is, defendants believed that sentences following jury convictions were much more severe than sentences following convictions at bench trials. The consequence was that the large majority of Philadelphia's trials were bench trials — bench trials accounted for 49 percent of cases in the Philadelphia Court of Common Pleas and jury trials only 6 percent. These bench trials were shorter and somewhat more casual than ordinary criminal trials. Schulhofer's description of them follows:

Bench trials always began with a colloquy designed to ensure that the defendant's waiver of his jury trial right was knowing and voluntary . . .

After the colloquy and the acceptance of the jury waiver, the prosecution immediately called its first witness; we never observed an opening statement. Trial procedure followed the usual course, with cross-examination (if any), demurrers at the close of the Commonwealth's case, and testimony by defense witnesses (if any). Attorneys presented closing arguments in virtually every case, though the judge sometimes limited argument to one or two issues or heard argument only from the defense. The judge then announced a decision and — sometimes — a brief reason for it . . .

The time consumed by such proceedings was typically rather short . . . 64% of the Calendar trials in our sample were completed in less than two hours. List program trials tended to be even shorter; the typical List room trial lasted about forty-five minutes, and 69% were completed in less than one hour. [Calendar cases included the most serious criminal charges plus relatively complex cases regardless of the charge; List cases were regarded as relatively uncomplicated. — EDS.] Allowing for the waiting time attributable to each disposition, the total courtroom time consumed by the typical List program bench trial was approximately one hour and twenty minutes . . .

Id., at 1065-1066. Compare with the Philadelphia experience the following account of the likely consequences of forbidding plea bargaining:

First, the number of trials would increase sharply. Something in the neighborhood of ninety percent of cases now lead to pleas; if even one-third of those are the result of bargaining, prohibiting plea bargaining would quadruple the number of criminal trials. Second, the error rate of trials would rise. This follows from the first assumption. Trials are elaborate and costly affairs. Any reform that involves a several hundred percent increase in their number must necessarily involve economizing on the process, at least as long as one assumes a constant level of expenditures on the system. Reducing the process, in turn, logically implies increasing the rate of error. Third, the total number of convictions would fall, probably substantially. Abolition of plea bargaining would raise the average cost of prosecution because it would increase the percentage of cases that go to trial (and even slimmed-down, cheaper trials will be more expensive than bargained pleas). Given constant resources, this would mean a drop in the number of convictions. . . .

. . . [I]n a world without plea bargaining the average defendant would depend more heavily on his lawyer's expertise: the percentage of trials would sharply increase, and lawyers' skill surely matters more in a trial than in a plea bargaining session, particularly since the latter is likely to be constrained, to some extent, by customary "market" prices. This effect would be particularly pronounced in a trial system with a higher error rate than the current one, and with quicker, more slapdash preparation by the attorneys — a necessary consequence of vastly increasing the number of trials. The increased impact of skill differences among attorneys would adversely affect poor defendants, since they tend to have the worst lawyers. Thus, there is some ground for believing that a world without plea bargaining would disproportionately harm both the innocent and the poor, hardly a recipe for a more distributionally just system . . .

Robert E. Scott & William J. Stuntz, Plea Bargaining as Contract, 101 Yale L.J. 1909, 1932-1934 (1992).

6. Stephanos Bibas sharply challenges the prevailing wisdom that plea bargains typically reflect an appropriately modified version of the result that would most likely obtain at a full-blown trial:

[M]any plea bargains diverge from the shadows of trials. By "the shadows of trials," I mean the influence exerted by the strength of the evidence and the expected punishment after trial. Structural forces and psychological biases sometimes inefficiently prevent mutually beneficial bargains or induce harmful ones. Even when they do not harm efficiency, these legally irrelevant factors sometimes skew the fair allocation of punishment. As a result, some defendants strike skewed bargains. Other defendants plead when they would otherwise go to trial, or go to trial (and usually receive heavier sentences) when they would otherwise plead. Furthermore, some defendants' plea bargains diverge from trial shadows much more than others'. These divergent outcomes produce substantial sentencing inequities. Rather than basing sentences on the need for deterrence, retribution, incapacitation, or rehabilitation, plea bargaining effectively bases sentences in part on wealth, sex, age, education, intelligence, and confidence. Though trials allocate punishment imperfectly, plea bargaining adds another layer of distortions that warp the fair allocation of punishment. The shadow-of-trial model thus needs many refinements and nuances to make it more realistic. Plea-bargaining practices need many reforms to conform more closely to the shadows of trials and to iron out inequities.

Stephanos Bibas, Plea Bargaining Outside the Shadow of Trial, 117 Harv. L. Rev. 2463 (2004).

6. Rule 11(b)(2) of the Federal Rules of Criminal Procedure requires, as a precondition to acceptance of a guilty plea, that courts "determine that the plea is voluntary and did not result from force, threats, or promises (other than promises in a plea agreement)." With respect to the plea bargaining process, Rule 11(c) specifies three kinds of plea bargains. Subsection (c)(1)(A) deals with charge bargains: In exchange for the defendant's guilty plea, the prosecutor promises to drop or not to add specified charges. In theory, trial judges may reject these bargains, but that almost never happens. Subsection (c)(1)(B) describes bargains in which the prosecution promises "to recommend, or agree not to oppose" a particular sentence or sentencing range. Judges may (and sometimes do) decline to follow these recommendations, and must warn defendants of that fact. Finally, subsection (c)(1)(C) covers cases in which the prosecutor guarantees a particular sentence or sentencing range. Judges are free to accept or reject these bargains.

Charge bargains and sentencing recommendation bargains are common, in federal and state courts alike. (Remember, most states have rules resembling Rule 11.) Guaranteed sentence bargains are *not* common; in some jurisdictions, they are unknown, no doubt because most judges dislike such bargains, which seem to usurp their power to decide the defendant's sentence.

Rule 11 leaves power over sentencing split. Plea bargains (and the prosecutors who draft them) plainly affect sentences, but trial judges retain ultimate authority, until the rise of sentencing guidelines. Today, in most guidelines jurisdictions, the prosecutor's charging decision goes far toward determining the defendant's sentence. The result is that many charge bargains and sentencing recommendation bargains become, in practice, guaranteed-sentence bargains. Prosecutors end up with more power. Judges have less.

BORDENKIRCHER v. HAYES

Certiorari to the United States Court of Appeals for the Sixth Circuit
434 U.S. 357 (1978)

JUSTICE STEWART delivered the opinion of the Court.

The question in this case is whether the Due Process Clause of the Fourteenth Amendment is violated when a state prosecutor carries out a threat made during plea negotiations to reindict the accused on more serious charges if he does not plead guilty to the offense with which he was originally charged.

The respondent, Paul Lewis Hayes, was indicted by a Fayette County, Ky., grand jury on a charge of uttering a forged instrument in the amount of $88.30, an offense then punishable by a term of 2 to 10 years in prison. Ky. Rev. Stat. §434.130 (1973) (repealed 1975). After arraignment, Hayes, his retained counsel, and the Commonwealth's Attorney met in the presence of the Clerk of the Court to discuss a possible plea agreement. During these conferences the prosecutor offered to recommend a sentence of five years in prison if Hayes would plead guilty to the indictment. He also said that if Hayes did not plead guilty and "saved the court the inconvenience and necessity of a trial," he would return to the grand jury to seek an indictment under the Kentucky Habitual Criminal Act, then Ky. Rev. Stat. §431.190 (1973) (repealed 1975), which would subject Hayes to a mandatory sentence of life imprisonment by reason of his two prior felony convictions.[2] Hayes chose not to plead guilty, and the prosecutor did obtain an indictment charging him under the Habitual Criminal Act. . . .

A jury found Hayes guilty on the principal charge of uttering a forged instrument and, in a separate proceeding, further found that he had twice before been convicted of felonies. As required by the habitual offender statute, he was sentenced to a life term in the penitentiary. The Kentucky Court of Appeals rejected Hayes' constitutional objections to the enhanced sentence, holding in an unpublished opinion that imprisonment for life with the possibility of parole was constitutionally permissible in light of the previous felonies of which Hayes had been convicted,[3] and that the prosecutor's decision to indict him as a habitual offender was a legitimate use of available leverage in the plea bargaining process.

On Hayes' petition for a federal writ of habeas corpus, the United States District Court for the Eastern District of Kentucky agreed that there had been no constitutional violation in the sentence or the indictment procedure, and denied the writ. The Court of Appeals for the Sixth Circuit reversed. . . .

It may be helpful to clarify at the outset the nature of the issue in this case. While the prosecutor did not actually obtain the recidivist indictment until after the plea conferences had ended, his intention to do so was clearly expressed at the outset of the plea negotiations. Hayes was thus fully informed of the true terms of the offer when he made his decision to plead not guilty. This is not a situation, therefore, where the prosecutor without notice brought an additional and more serious charge after plea negotiations relating only to the original indictment had ended with the defendant's insistence on pleading not guilty. As a practical matter, in short, this case would be no different if the grand jury had indicted Hayes as a recidivist from

2. At the time of Hayes' trial the statute provided that "[a]ny person convicted a . . . third time of felony . . . shall be confined in the penitentiary during his life." Ky. Rev. Stat. §431.190 (1973) (repealed 1975). That statute has been replaced by Ky. Rev. Stat. §532.080 (Supp. 1977) under which Hayes would have been sentenced to, at most, an indeterminate term of 10 to 20 years. §532.080(6)(b). In addition, under the new statute a previous conviction is a basis for enhanced sentencing only if a prison term of one year or more was imposed, the sentence or probation was completed within five years of the present offense, and the offender was over the age of 18 when the offense was committed. At least one of Hayes' prior convictions did not meet these conditions. See n. 3, infra.

3. According to his own testimony, Hayes had pleaded guilty in 1961, when he was 17 years old, to a charge of detaining a female, a lesser included offense of rape, and as a result had served five years in the state reformatory. In 1970 he had been convicted of robbery and sentenced to five years' imprisonment, but had been released on probation immediately.

the outset, and the prosecutor had offered to drop that charge as part of the plea bargain. . . .

This Court held in North Carolina v. Pearce, 395 U.S. 711, 725, that the Due Process Clause of the Fourteenth Amendment "requires that vindictiveness against a defendant for having successfully attacked his first conviction must play no part in the sentence he receives after a new trial." The same principle was later applied to prohibit a prosecutor from reindicting a convicted misdemeanant on a felony charge after the defendant had invoked an appellate remedy, since in this situation there was also a "realistic likelihood of 'vindictiveness.'" Blackledge v. Perry, 417 U.S. [21,] 27.

In those cases the Court was dealing with the State's unilateral imposition of a penalty upon a defendant who had chosen to exercise a legal right to attack his original conviction — a situation "very different from the give-and-take negotiation common in plea bargaining between the prosecution and defense, which arguably possess relatively equal bargaining power." Parker v. North Carolina, 397 U.S. 790, 809 (opinion of Brennan, J.). The Court has emphasized that the due process violation in cases such as *Pearce* and *Perry* lay not in the possibility that a defendant might be deterred from the exercise of a legal right, but rather in the danger that the State might be retaliating against the accused for lawfully attacking his conviction. See Blackledge v. Perry, supra, at 26-28.

To punish a person because he has done what the law plainly allows him to do is a due process violation of the most basic sort. . . . . But in the "give-and-take" of plea bargaining, there is no such element of punishment or retaliation so long as the accused is free to accept or reject the prosecution's offer.

Plea bargaining flows from "the mutuality of advantage" to defendants and prosecutors, each with his own reasons for wanting to avoid trial. Brady v. United States, supra, at 752. Defendants advised by competent counsel and protected by other procedural safeguards are presumptively capable of intelligent choice in response to prosecutorial persuasion, and unlikely to be driven to false self-condemnation. Indeed, acceptance of the basic legitimacy of plea bargaining necessarily implies rejection of any notion that a guilty plea is involuntary in a constitutional sense simply because it is the end result of the bargaining process. By hypothesis, the plea may have been induced by promises of a recommendation of a lenient sentence or a reduction of charges, and thus by fear of the possibility of a greater penalty upon conviction after a trial.

While confronting a defendant with the risk of more severe punishment clearly may have a "discouraging effect on the defendant's assertion of his trial rights, the imposition of these difficult choices [is] an inevitable" — and permissible — "attribute of any legitimate system which tolerates and encourages the negotiation of pleas." Chaffin v. Stynchcombe, [412 U.S. 17, 31 (1973)]. It follows that, by tolerating and encouraging the negotiation of pleas, this Court has necessarily accepted as constitutionally legitimate the simple reality that the prosecutor's interest at the bargaining table is to persuade the defendant to forgo his right to plead not guilty.

It is not disputed here that Hayes was properly chargeable under the recidivist statute, since he had in fact been convicted of two previous felonies. In our system, so long as the prosecutor has probable cause to believe that the accused committed an offense defined by statute, the decision whether or not to prosecute, and what charge to file or bring before a grand jury, generally rests entirely in his discretion.[8] Within the limits set by the legislature's constitutionally valid definition of chargeable offenses, "the conscious exercise of some selectivity in enforcement is not in itself a federal constitutional violation" so long as "the selection was [not] deliberately based upon an unjustifiable standard such as race, religion, or other arbitrary classification." Oyler v. Boles, 368 U.S. 448, 456. To hold that the prosecutor's desire to induce a guilty plea is an "unjustifiable standard," which, like race or religion, may play no part in his charging decision, would contradict the very premises that underlie the concept of plea bargaining itself. Moreover, a rigid constitutional rule that would prohibit a prosecutor from acting forthrightly in his dealings with the defense could only invite unhealthy subterfuge that would drive the practice of plea bargaining back into the shadows from which it has so recently emerged.

There is no doubt that the breadth of discretion that our country's legal system vests in prosecuting attorneys carries with it the potential for both individual and institutional abuse. And broad though that discretion may be, there are undoubtedly constitutional limits upon its exercise. We hold only that the course of conduct engaged in by the prosecutor in this case, which no more than openly presented the defendant with the unpleasant alternatives of forgoing trial or facing charges on which he was plainly subject to prosecution, did not violate the Due Process Clause of the Fourteenth Amendment. . . .

[The dissenting opinion of Justice Blackmun, joined by Justices Brennan and Marshall, is omitted.]

JUSTICE POWELL, dissenting.

. . . Respondent was charged with the uttering of a single forged check in the amount of $88.30. Under Kentucky law, this offense was punishable by a prison term of from 2 to 10 years, apparently without regard to the amount of the forgery. During the course of plea bargaining, the prosecutor offered respondent a sentence of five years in consideration of a guilty plea. I observe, at this point, that five years in prison for the offense charged hardly could be characterized as a generous offer. Apparently respondent viewed the offer in this light and declined to accept it; he protested that he was innocent and insisted on going to trial. Respondent adhered to this position even when the prosecutor advised that he would seek a new indictment under the State's Habitual Criminal Act which would subject respondent, if convicted, to a mandatory life sentence because of two prior felony convictions.

The prosecutor's initial assessment of respondent's case led him to forgo an indictment under the habitual criminal statute. The circumstances of respondent's prior convictions are relevant to this assessment and to my view of the case. Respondent was 17 years old when he committed his first offense. He was charged with rape but pleaded guilty to the lesser included offense of "detaining a female." One of the other participants in the incident was sentenced to life imprisonment. Respondent was sent not to prison but to a reformatory where he served five years. Respondent's second offense was robbery. This time he was found guilty by a jury and was sentenced to five years in prison, but he was placed on probation and served no time. Although respondent's prior convictions brought him within the terms of the

---

8. This case does not involve the constitutional implications of a prosecutor's offer during plea bargaining of adverse or lenient treatment for some person other than the accused, see ALI Model Code of Pre-Arraignment Procedure, Commentary to §350.3, pp. 614-615 (1975), which might pose a greater danger of inducing a false guilty plea by skewing the assessment of the risks a defendant must consider.

Habitual Criminal Act, the offenses themselves did not result in imprisonment; yet the addition of a conviction on a charge involving $88.30 subjected respondent to a mandatory sentence of imprisonment for life. Persons convicted of rape and murder often are not punished so severely.

No explanation appears in the record for the prosecutor's decision to escalate the charge against respondent other than respondent's refusal to plead guilty. The prosecutor has conceded that his purpose was to discourage respondent's assertion of constitutional rights, and the majority accepts this characterization of events.

It seems to me that the question to be asked under the circumstances is whether the prosecutor reasonably might have charged respondent under the Habitual Criminal Act in the first place. The deference that courts properly accord the exercise of a prosecutor's discretion perhaps would foreclose judicial criticism if the prosecutor originally had sought an indictment under that Act, as unreasonable as it would have seemed.[2] But here the prosecutor evidently made a reasonable, responsible judgment not to subject an individual to a mandatory life sentence when his only new offense had societal implications as limited as those accompanying the uttering of a single $88 forged check and when the circumstances of his prior convictions confirmed the inappropriateness of applying the habitual criminal statute. I think it may be inferred that the prosecutor himself deemed it unreasonable and not in the public interest to put this defendant in jeopardy of a sentence of life imprisonment.

There may be situations in which a prosecutor would be fully justified in seeking a fresh indictment for a more serious offense. The most plausible justification might be that it would have been reasonable and in the public interest initially to have charged the defendant with the greater offense. In most cases a court could not know why the harsher indictment was sought, and an inquiry into the prosecutor's motive would neither be indicated nor likely to be fruitful. In those cases, I would agree with the majority that the situation would not differ materially from one in which the higher charge was brought at the outset.

But this is not such a case. Here, any inquiry into the prosecutor's purpose is made unnecessary by his candid acknowledgment that he threatened to procure and in fact procured the habitual criminal indictment because of respondent's insistence on exercising his constitutional rights. . . . I would affirm the opinion of the Court of Appeals on the facts of this case.

NOTES AND QUESTIONS

1. What do you make of Justice Powell's dissent? Should it really matter whether the prosecutor first charged Hayes with being a habitual offender and then offered to drop the charge, as opposed to charging him with "uttering a forged instrument"

2. The majority suggests that this case cannot be distinguished from the case where the prosecutor initially obtains an indictment under an enhancement statute and later agrees to drop the enhancement charge in exchange for a guilty plea. I would agree that these two situations would be alike only if it were assumed that the hypothetical prosecutor's decision to charge under the enhancement statute was occasioned not by consideration of the public interest but by a strategy to discourage the defendant from exercising his constitutional rights. In theory, I would condemn both practices. In practice, the hypothetical situation is largely unreviewable. The majority's view confuses the propriety of a particular exercise of prosecutorial discretion with its unreviewability. In the instant case, however, we have no problem of proof.

and then threatening to add the habitual offender charge if he refused to plead? Don't both scenarios amount to the same thing? Indeed, doesn't Justice Powell concede as much?

2. The voluntariness standard for guilty pleas was not at issue in *Bordenkircher* because Hayes did not plead guilty, but rather went to trial. Suppose he *had* pled guilty. Would Hayes then have an argument that his plea was involuntary — that the gap between a five-year sentence and a life sentence constitutes too great a threat to permit as the basis of a plea bargain? Presumably, that would be a very hard argument to make *after Brady*, where the Supreme Court explicitly validated a guilty plea based on the threat of a death sentence if the defendant went to trial.

But the prosecutor's offer (or threat, depending on how you look at it) in *Bordenkircher* may be worse in some respects than the choice Brady faced:

> Suppose that Hayes' earlier convictions were fairly low-level felonies, a possibility that would tend to explain the relatively light sentences he had received. Suppose further that Kentucky's habitual criminal law had authorized a sentence of anywhere from ten years to life. The judge's sentence for the forgery charge would surely have fallen closer to the minimum than the maximum. And that conclusion is consistent with the decision the legislature made when it passed the habitual criminal statute. Felonies encompass a wide range of criminal behavior; the legislature made, at best, a roughly accurate categorical judgment. If the same legislators who passed the statute were to vote on sentences case by case, many defendants who qualify for habitual criminal sentencing would get far less than life in prison. . . . [T]he key point is that the legislature did not intend for the statute to be applied to every offender who might fall within its terms. Rather, the legislature implicitly relied on prosecutors to separate the wheat from the chaff — to exercise their discretion *not* to pursue habitual criminal sentencing for offenders who fell within the statute but seemed not to deserve such harsh treatment. *Bordenkircher* may well be such a case; that is, the legislature may have expected that prosecutors would not charge people like Hayes under the statute, though no enforcement mechanism backed up that expectation (because judicial review of charging decisions would be too costly).
>
> The Kentucky statute thus gave the prosecutor a good deal of bargaining power over people like Hayes because it allowed him to threaten a sentence that, absent the statute, would have been implausible. . . . In a discretionary [sentencing] system, the choice might have been between a recommended five-year sentence and a likely ten or twelve years if the case went to trial. Given the statute, the choice was much more stark: five years or life. Hayes might not have accepted that deal, but every future defendant is likely to do so and do so quickly.

Scott & Stuntz, Plea Bargaining as Contract, 101 Yale L.J., at 1963-1964. Scott and Stuntz go on to argue that the government's bargaining strategy in *Bordenkircher* amounts to the equivalent of duress. Do you agree?

3. If there is a problem with the prosecutor's threat in *Bordenkircher*, the problem is closely tied to the presence of a mandatory sentence that no court can mitigate. At the time *Bordenkircher* was decided, mandatory sentences were unusual; sentencing, in state and federal cases alike, was overwhelmingly discretionary with the court, with the governing statutes fixing very broad ranges within which sentences could permissibly fall.

That is not so today. Mandatory sentences have multiplied, at both state and federal levels. These contemporary mandatory sentences take two forms. The first is like the habitual offender statute at issue in *Bordenkircher*: A growing number of states have mandatory recidivist sentencing statutes (some of which are popularly known as "three strikes" laws because, as with the Kentucky statute in *Bordenkircher*, they require some long sentence as a consequence of a third felony conviction). A popular variant is the so-called mandatory minimum statutes that require some high minimum sentence for, say, crimes involving the use of a gun or for possession or sale of a given quantity of drugs.

How do you suppose such sentencing statutes affect the plea bargaining process? The rest of the criminal process? The effects may be different than one would initially suppose:

> Research on mandatory sentencing laws during the 1970s and 1980s reveals a number of avoidance strategies. Boston police avoided application of a 1975 Massachusetts law calling for mandatory one-year sentences for persons convicted of carrying a gun by decreasing the number of arrests made for that offense and increasing (by 120 percent between 1974 and 1976) the number of weapons seizures without arrest. Prosecutors often avoid application of mandatory sentencing laws simply by filing charges for different, but roughly comparable, offenses that are not subject to mandatory sentences. Judges too can circumvent such laws. Detroit judges sidestepped a 1977 law requiring a two-year sentence for persons convicted of possession of a firearm in the commission of a felony by acquitting defendants of the gun charge (even though the evidence would support a conviction) or by decreasing the sentence they would otherwise impose by two years to offset the mandatory two-year term.
>
> Considerable recent research taken together . . . supports the following generalizations:
>
> 1. lawyers and judges will take steps to avoid application of laws they consider unduly harsh;
> 2. dismissal rates typically increase at early stages of the criminal justice process after effectuation of a mandatory penalty as practitioners attempt to shield some defendants from the law's reach;
> 3. defendants whose cases are not dismissed or diverted make more vigorous efforts to avoid conviction and to delay sentencing, which results in increased trial rates and case processing times increase;
> 4. defendants who are convicted of the target offense are often sentenced more severely than they would have been in the absence of the mandatory penalty provision; and
> 5. because declines in conviction rates for those arrested tend to offset increases in imprisonment rates for those convicted, often the overall probability that defendants will be incarcerated remains about the same after enactment of a mandatory sentence law.

Michael Tonry, Sentencing Matters 147-148 (1996) (citations omitted). Tonry's book offers an excellent summary and critical analysis of developments in American sentencing over the course of the past three decades.

A second kind of innovation in sentencing law that has flourished in recent years involves the use of sentencing guidelines. The federal system and a number of states now use such guidelines; they typically establish fairly narrow sentencing ranges for particular crimes, with limited flexibility for judicial departures from those ranges. (Mandatory sentencing guidelines, including the original version of the Federal Sentencing Guidelines, have been held unconstitutional; see Blakely v. Washington, 542 U.S. 296 (2004), and United States v. Booker, 543 U.S. 220 (2005). See Chapter

15, infra.) Guidelines systems sometimes incorporate "real offense" factors that are not easily subject to prosecutorial manipulation — for example, a state might have a guideline requiring a minimum sentence for robbery with a gun whether or not the gun element is part of the charged offense. But most sentences are anchored to the charged offense. The result is to give prosecutors a great deal more power over the ultimate sentence than in discretionary systems. Consider the following example, drawn from the Federal Sentencing Guidelines:

> Suppose an officer of a publicly held corporation has committed a course of insider trading over a period of years, involving numerous stock purchases by the officer based on nonpublic, material information. The officer has secreted his profits of $105,000 by a series of small transfers of monies through a domestic bank account. This offender might be indicted for mail fraud, securities fraud, racketeering, some type of money laundering, conspiracy to commit any one of these substantive offenses, or any combination of these charges.
>
> Under the sentencing guidelines, the ultimate sentence is a precise function of which of these charges, singularly or in combination, form the count or counts of conviction. Assume first that the sentence of conviction is on the count of mail fraud. Under the applicable sentencing guideline, the likely guidelines penalty for this first-time offender would be level 14, or a range of 15 to 21 months' imprisonment. If securities fraud forms the count of conviction, the sentencing outcome would not change. Even if the securities fraud count is added to the mail fraud conviction the sentencing outcome would not change because these counts would be "grouped" together. Thus, the guidelines are apparently somewhat sensitive to the power of prosecutors and appear to alleviate the effects of some charging discretion.
>
> Assume next, however, that the prosecutor wishes to avoid plea bargaining within the range established by a charge of fraud, even with multiple counts. The prosecutor need only seek an indictment on a count of racketeering. If the racketeering charge forms the likely count of conviction, then the probable punishment is level 19, or 30 to 37 months' imprisonment. . . .
>
> Assume next that the prosecutor wishes to substitute a charge of money laundering, which can be charged under several different statutes, each receiving different treatment under the guidelines. Specifically, the prosecutor could choose to expose the defendant to a sentencing level of 24 (51 to 63 months), 20 (33 to 41 months), or 18 (27 to 33 months). The choice to use one of these money laundering counts in lieu of a fraud count gives the prosecutor access to a possible penalty of 63 months, three times the maximum penalty under a single fraud count. . . .

Jeffrey Standen, Plea Bargaining in the Shadow of the Guidelines, 81 Cal. L. Rev. 1471, 1506-1508 (1993) (citations omitted). In theory, this prosecutorial power over sentence is constrained by federal judges' ability to "depart" from the applicable sentencing range, something the Guidelines themselves authorize. But departures are rare, in part because they create a risk of appellate reversal. See generally Kevin R. Reitz, Sentencing Guidelines Systems and Sentence Appeals: A Comparison of Federal and State Experiences, 91 Nw. U. L. Rev. 1441 (1997).

How does this increased prosecutorial power over sentencing affect plea bargaining? Professor Standen offers the following answer:

> [T]he prosecutor is no longer the price taker but the price setter. Within the broad constraint of filing a charge upon which a jury will probably convict, the prosecutor may set the bargaining parameters as high or low as the facts permit, unrestricted by the

prospect of a judge re-examining the same course of conduct and making an independent determination. The bargaining that follows will not take place in light of the broad range of possible outcomes from sentences set independently by judges but instead according to the narrow, legislatively created sentencing range that attaches to the prosecutor's charge.

81 Cal. L. Rev., at 1513. Does this greater prosecutorial power undermine the voluntariness of guilty pleas? Or is all this simply a matter of sentencing policy to which the law of plea bargaining should be indifferent?

3.   The Subject Matter of Plea Bargaining

Brady and *Bordenkircher* both involved situations in which the defendant was faced with the choice of pleading guilty and receiving a lenient sentence, or going to trial and (if convicted) receiving a harsher sentence. The two cases might be seen as flip sides of the same coin: In *Brady*, the defendant chose the plea and later challenged the plea as involuntary, whereas in *Bordenkircher*, the defendant chose the trial and later challenged the imposition of the harsher sentence as vindictive. The end result of the two decisions is that the basic concept of plea bargaining is constitutionally unassailable, because such bargaining does not inherently undermine either the voluntariness of the resulting plea or the validity of the harsher sentence imposed after trial.

The fact that plea bargaining itself is constitutional, however, does not end the discussion. Defendants may (and occasionally do) still challenge their bargain-induced guilty plea on the ground that the plea was invalid under the facts and circumstances of the particular case. Occasionally, this argument is based, as in *Brady*, on the sheer magnitude of the offer of leniency made by the prosecutor. (Overwhelmingly, as in *Brady*, this argument loses.) Sometimes the argument is based on the particular tactics used by the prosecutor in inducing the plea. (If the prosecutor used physical coercion, for example, the resulting plea almost certainly would be involuntary.) But often, the argument goes to the subject matter of the bargain — the defendant argues (after the fact) that certain subjects, not directly related to the defendant's guilt or punishment, should be viewed as "off-limits" in plea negotiations.

In footnote 8 in *Bordenkircher*, the Supreme Court hinted at one possible limit on the subject matter of plea bargaining, noting that the case before it did *not* involve an offer of lenient treatment (or a threat of harsh treatment) for a third party. Although the Court itself has never returned to the subject, lower courts have routinely upheld such so-called "wired" pleas. For example, in United States v. Pollard, 959 F.2d 1011 (1992), the D.C. Circuit affirmed the denial of habeas corpus relief for convicted spy Jonathan Pollard, who argued that he had been pressured into pleading guilty (and cooperating with the government) by the desire to protect his wife, who was seriously ill at the time, from a possible life sentence as his alleged accomplice:

> We agree with our sister circuits that plea wiring does not violate the Constitution. The question, of course, is whether the practice of plea wiring is so coercive as to risk inducing false guilty pleas. See *Bordenkircher*, 434 U.S. at 364 n. 8. To say that a practice

is "coercive" or renders a plea "involuntary" means only that it creates improper pressure that would be likely to overbear the will of some innocent persons and cause them to plead guilty. . . .

We can understand how it might be thought that a threat of long imprisonment for a loved one, particularly a spouse, would constitute even greater pressure on a defendant than a direct threat to him. Whether one could generalize as to that proposition depends, we suppose, on one's view of human nature. But it does not seem to be the sort of widely-shared intuition upon which a constitutional rule should be based. We must be mindful, moreover, that if the judiciary were to declare wired pleas unconstitutional, the consequences would not be altogether foreseeable and perhaps would not be beneficial to defendants. Would Pollard, for instance, have been better off had he not been able to bargain to aid his wife? Would his wife have been better off? Would the bargaining take place in any event, but with winks and nods rather than in writing?

Nor do we believe that Mrs. Pollard's medical condition makes an otherwise acceptable linkage of their pleas unconstitutional. The appropriate dividing line between acceptable and unconstitutional plea wiring does not depend upon the physical condition or personal circumstances of the defendant; rather, it depends upon the conduct of the government. Where, as here, the government had probable cause to arrest and prosecute both defendants in a related crime, and there is no suggestion that the government conducted itself in bad faith in an effort to generate additional leverage over the defendant, we think a wired plea is constitutional. Once the government had probable cause to prosecute Mrs. Pollard and had obtained a valid indictment, it was entitled, despite her illness, to prosecute her fully — or to offer lenience for her in exchange for Pollard's plea. See United States v. Clark, 931 F.2d 292, 294-295 (5th Cir. 1991) (plea offered by man, who maintains his innocence, in order to help his "sick, pregnant and innocent" wife held not involuntary); Bontkowski v. United States, 850 F.2d 306, 313 (7th Cir. 1988) (threat to prosecute validly indicted pregnant woman does not constitute unconstitutional coercion of her husband).

At minimum, Pollard argues, wired pleas raise special dangers of coercion, so that a district court faced with such a plea must undertake a more searching inquiry into the voluntariness of the plea than would normally be required. Even if that were so, we are satisfied that the district court adequately discharged its obligations here. The colloquy between the court and Pollard was so extensive that there could be little doubt about Pollard's willingness to plead. Pollard had several opportunities to confess any misgivings to the judge, but he never gave the slightest hint that his plea was anything other than voluntary. . . .

Id., at 1021-1022.

Are there any subjects that should be treated as "off-limits" in plea bargaining?

NEWTON v. RUMERY

Certiorari to the United States Court of Appeals for the First Circuit
480 U.S. 386 (1987)

JUSTICE POWELL delivered the opinion of the Court with respect to Parts I, II, III-A, IV, and V, and an opinion with respect to Part III-B, in which CHIEF JUSTICE REHNQUIST, JUSTICE WHITE, and JUSTICE SCALIA joined.

The question in this case is whether a court properly may enforce an agreement in which a criminal defendant releases his right to file an action under 42 U.S.C. §1983 in return for a prosecutor's dismissal of pending criminal charges.

I

In 1983, a grand jury in Rockingham County, New Hampshire, indicted David Champy for aggravated felonious sexual assault. Respondent Bernard Rumery, a friend of Champy's, read about the charges in a local newspaper. Seeking information about the charges, he telephoned Mary Deary, who was acquainted with both Rumery and Champy. Coincidentally, Deary had been the victim of the assault in question and was expected to be the principal witness against Champy. The record does not reveal directly the date or substance of this conversation between Rumery and Deary, but Deary apparently was disturbed by the call. On March 12, according to police records, she called David Barrett, the Chief of Police for the town of Newton. She told him that Rumery was trying to force her to drop the charges against Champy. Rumery talked to Deary again on May 11. The substance of this conversation also is disputed. Rumery claims that Deary called him and that she raised the subject of Champy's difficulties. According to the police records, however, Deary told Chief Barrett that Rumery had threatened that, if Deary went forward on the Champy case, she would "end up like" two women who recently had been murdered in Lowell, Massachusetts. App. 49. Barrett arrested Rumery and accused him of tampering with a witness in violation of N.H. Rev. Stat. Ann. §641:5(I)(b) (1986), a Class B felony.

Rumery promptly retained Stephen Woods, an experienced criminal defense attorney. Woods contacted Brian Graf, the Deputy County Attorney for Rockingham County. He warned Graf that he "had better [dismiss] these charges, because we're going to win them and after that we're going to sue." App. 11. After further discussions, Graf and Woods reached an agreement, under which Graf would dismiss the charges against Rumery if Rumery would agree not to sue the town, its officials, or Deary for any harm caused by the arrest. All parties agreed that one factor in Graf's decision not to prosecute Rumery was Graf's desire to protect Deary from the trauma she would suffer if she were forced to testify. . . .

Woods drafted an agreement in which Rumery agreed to release any claims he might have against the town, its officials, or Deary if Graf agreed to dismiss the criminal charges (the release-dismissal agreement). After Graf approved the form of the agreement, Woods presented it to Rumery. Although Rumery's recollection of the events was quite different, the District Court found that Woods discussed the agreement with Rumery in his office for about an hour and explained to Rumery that he would forgo all civil actions if he signed the agreement. Three days later, on June 6, 1983, Rumery returned to Woods' office and signed the agreement. The criminal charges were dropped.

Ten months later, on April 13, 1984, Rumery filed an action under §1983 in the Federal District Court for the District of New Hampshire. He alleged that the town and its officers had violated his constitutional rights by arresting him, defaming him, and imprisoning him falsely. The defendants filed a motion to dismiss, relying on the release-dismissal agreement as an affirmative defense. Rumery argued that the agreement was unenforceable because it violated public policy. The court rejected Rumery's argument and concluded that a "release of claims under section 1983 is valid . . . if it results from a decision that is voluntary, deliberate and informed." . . . The court then dismissed Rumery's suit.

On appeal, the Court of Appeals for the First Circuit reversed. It adopted a per se rule invalidating release-dismissal agreements. . . . We reverse.

II

We begin by noting the source of the law that governs this case. The agreement purported to waive a right to sue conferred by a federal statute. The question whether the policies underlying that statute may in some circumstances render that waiver unenforceable is a question of federal law. We resolve this question by reference to traditional common-law principles, as we have resolved other questions about the principles governing §1983 actions. . . . The relevant principle is well established: A promise is unenforceable if the interest in its enforcement is outweighed in the circumstances by a public policy harmed by enforcement of the agreement.

III

The Court of Appeals concluded that the public interests related to release-dismissal agreements justified a per se rule of invalidity. . . . [A]lthough we agree that in some cases these agreements may infringe important interests of the criminal defendant and of society as a whole, we do not believe that the mere possibility of harm to these interests calls for a per se rule.

A

Rumery's first objection to release-dismissal agreements is that they are inherently coercive. He argues that it is unfair to present a criminal defendant with a choice between facing criminal charges and waiving his right to sue under §1983. We agree that some release-dismissal agreements may not be the product of an informed and voluntary decision. The risk, publicity, and expense of a criminal trial may intimidate a defendant, even if he believes his defense is meritorious. But this possibility does not justify invalidating all such agreements. In other contexts criminal defendants are required to make difficult choices that effectively waive constitutional rights. For example, it is well settled that plea bargaining does not violate the Constitution even though a guilty plea waives important constitutional rights. See Brady v. United States, 397 U.S. 742, 752-753 (1970).[3] . . . We see no reason to believe that release-dismissal agreements pose a more coercive choice than other situations we have accepted. . . .

In many cases a defendant's choice to enter into a release-dismissal agreement will reflect a highly rational judgment that the certain benefits of escaping criminal prosecution exceed the speculative benefits of prevailing in a civil action. Rumery's voluntary decision to enter this agreement exemplifies such a judgment. Rumery is a sophisticated businessman. He was not in jail and was represented by an experienced criminal lawyer, who drafted the agreement. Rumery considered the agreement for three days before signing it. The benefits of the agreement to Rumery are

---

3. We recognize that the analogy between plea bargains and release-dismissal agreements is not complete. The former are subject to judicial oversight. Moreover, when the State enters a plea bargain with a criminal defendant, it receives immediate and tangible benefits, such as promptly imposed punishment without the expenditure of prosecutorial resources, see Brady v. United States, 397 U.S., at 752. Also, the defendant's agreement to plead to some crime tends to ensure some satisfaction of the public's interest in the prosecution of crime and confirms that the prosecutor's charges have a basis in fact. The benefits the State may realize in particular cases from release-dismissal agreements may not be as tangible, but they are not insignificant.

obvious: He gained immunity from criminal prosecution in consideration of abandoning a civil suit that he may well have lost.

Because Rumery voluntarily waived his right to sue under §1983, the public interest opposing involuntary waiver of constitutional rights is no reason to hold this agreement invalid. Moreover, we find that the possibility of coercion in the making of similar agreements insufficient by itself to justify a per se rule against release-dismissal bargains. If there is such a reason, it must lie in some external public interest necessarily injured by release-dismissal agreements.

B

[T]he Court of Appeals held that all release-dismissal agreements offend public policy because it believed these agreements "tempt prosecutors to trump up charges in reaction to a defendant's civil rights claim, suppress evidence of police misconduct, and leave unremedied deprivations of constitutional rights." 778 F.2d, at 69. We can agree that in some cases there may be a substantial basis for this concern. It is true, of course, that §1983 actions to vindicate civil rights may further significant public interests. But it is important to remember that Rumery had no public duty to institute a §1983 action merely to further the public's interest in revealing police misconduct. . . .

We also believe the Court of Appeals misapprehended the range of public interests arguably affected by a release-dismissal agreement. The availability of such agreements may threaten important public interests. They may tempt prosecutors to bring frivolous charges, or to dismiss meritorious charges, to protect the interests of other officials. But a per se rule of invalidity fails to credit other relevant public interests and improperly assumes prosecutorial misconduct.

The vindication of constitutional rights and the exposure of official misconduct are not the only concerns implicated by §1983 suits. No one suggests that all such suits are meritorious. Many are marginal and some are frivolous. Yet even when the risk of ultimate liability is negligible, the burden of defending such lawsuits is substantial. . . . To the extent release-dismissal agreements protect public officials from the burdens of defending such unjust claims, they further this important public interest.

A per se rule invalidating release-dismissal agreements also assumes that prosecutors will seize the opportunity for wrongdoing. . . . [C]ourts normally must defer to prosecutorial decisions as to whom to prosecute. . . . Because these decisions "are not readily susceptible to the kind of analysis the courts are competent to undertake," we have been "properly hesitant to examine the decision whether to prosecute." [Wayte v. United States, 470 U.S. 598,] 607-608 [(1985)].

Against this background of discretion, the mere opportunity to act improperly does not compel an assumption that all — or even a significant number of — release-dismissal agreements stem from prosecutors abandoning "the independence of judgment required by [their] public trust," Imbler v. Pachtman, 424 U.S. 409, 423 (1976). Rather, tradition and experience justify our belief that the great majority of prosecutors will be faithful to their duty. Indeed, the merit of this view is illustrated by this case, where the only evidence of prosecutorial misconduct is the agreement itself.

Because release-dismissal agreements may further legitimate prosecutorial and public interests, we reject the Court of Appeals' holding that all such agreements are invalid per se.[8]

IV

Turning to the agreement presented by this case, we conclude that the District Court's decision to enforce the agreement was correct. As we have noted, ... it is clear that Rumery voluntarily entered the agreement. Moreover, in this case the prosecutor had an independent, legitimate reason to make this agreement directly related to his prosecutorial responsibilities. The agreement foreclosed both the civil and criminal trials concerning Rumery, in which Deary would have been a key witness. She therefore was spared the public scrutiny and embarrassment she would have endured if she had had to testify in either of those cases. Both the prosecutor and the defense attorney testified in the District Court that this was a significant consideration in the prosecutor's decision.

In sum, we conclude that this agreement was voluntary, that there is no evidence of prosecutorial misconduct, and that enforcement of this agreement would not adversely affect the relevant public interests.[10]

V

We reverse the judgment of the Court of Appeals and remand the case to the District Court for dismissal of the complaint.

It is so ordered.

JUSTICE O'CONNOR, concurring in part and concurring in the judgment.

I join in Parts I, II, III-A, IV, and V of the Court's opinion. . . . I write separately, however, in order to set out the factors that lead me to conclude that this covenant should be enforced and to emphasize that it is the burden of those relying upon such covenants to establish that the agreement is neither involuntary nor the product of an abuse of the criminal process. . . .

[T]he defendants in a §1983 suit may establish that a particular release executed in exchange for the dismissal of criminal charges was voluntarily made, not the product of prosecutorial overreaching, and in the public interest. But they must prove that this is so; the courts should not presume it as I fear portions of Part III-B of the plurality opinion may imply.

---

8. Justice Stevens' evaluation of the public interests associated with release-dismissal agreements relies heavily on his view that Rumery is a completely innocent man. He rests this conclusion on the testimony Rumery and his attorney presented to the District Court, but fails to acknowledge that the District Court's factual findings gave little credence to this testimony. Justice Stevens also gives great weight to the fact that Rumery "must be presumed to be innocent." But this is not a criminal case. This is a civil case, in which Rumery bears the ultimate burden of proof.

10. We note that two Courts of Appeals have applied a voluntariness standard to determine the enforceability of agreements entered into after trial, in which the defendants released possible §1983 claims in return for sentencing considerations. See Bushnell v. Rossetti, 750 F.2d 298 (CA4 1984); Jones v. Taber, 648 F.2d 1201 (CA9 1981). We have no occasion in this case to determine whether an inquiry into voluntariness alone is sufficient to determine the enforceability of release-dismissal agreements. We also note that it would be helpful to conclude release-dismissal agreements under judicial supervision. Although such supervision is not essential to the validity of an otherwise-proper agreement, it would help ensure that the agreements did not result from prosecutorial misconduct.

Many factors may bear on whether a release was voluntary and not the product of overreaching, some of which come readily to mind. The knowledge and experience of the criminal defendant and the circumstances of the execution of the release, including, importantly, whether the defendant was counseled, are clearly relevant. The nature of the criminal charges that are pending is also important, for the greater the charge, the greater the coercive effect. The existence of a legitimate criminal justice objective for obtaining the release will support its validity. And, importantly, the possibility of abuse is clearly mitigated if the release-dismissal agreement is executed under judicial supervision.

Close examination of all the factors in this case leads me to concur in the Court's decision that this covenant not to sue is enforceable. There is ample evidence in the record concerning the circumstances of the execution of this agreement. Testimony of the prosecutor, defense counsel, and Rumery himself leave little doubt that the agreement was entered into voluntarily. While the charge pending against Rumery was serious — subjecting him to up to seven years in prison, N.H. Rev. Stat. Ann. §641:5(I)(b) (1986) — it is one of the lesser felonies under New Hampshire law, and a long prison term was probably unlikely given the absence of any prior criminal record and the weaknesses in the case against Rumery. Finally, as the Court correctly notes, the prosecutor had a legitimate reason to enter into this agreement directly related to his criminal justice function. . . . Mary Deary's emotional distress, her unwillingness to testify against Rumery, presumably in later civil as well as criminal proceedings, and the necessity of her testimony in the pending sexual assault case against David Champy all support the prosecutor's judgment that the charges against Rumery should be dropped if further injury to Deary, and therefore the Champy case, could thereby be avoided.

Against the convincing evidence that Rumery voluntarily entered into the agreement and that it served the public interest, there is only Rumery's blanket claim that agreements such as this one are inherently coercive. While it would have been preferable, and made this an easier case, had the release-dismissal agreement been concluded under some form of judicial supervision, I concur in the Court's judgment, and all but Part III-B of its opinion, that Rumery's §1983 suit is barred by his valid, voluntary release.

JUSTICE STEVENS, with whom JUSTICE BRENNAN, JUSTICE MARSHALL, and JUSTICE BLACKMUN join, dissenting.

The question whether the release-dismissal agreement signed by respondent is unenforceable is much more complex than the Court's opinion indicates. . . .

I

Respondent is an innocent man. As a matter of law, he must be presumed to be innocent. As a matter of fact, the uncontradicted sworn testimony of respondent, and his lawyer, buttressed by the circumstantial evidence, overwhelmingly attest to his innocence. There was no written statement by the alleged victim, sworn or unsworn, implicating respondent in any criminal activity. . . . Respondent was never indicted, and the warrant for his arrest was issued on the basis of a sketchy statement by Chief Barrett. . . . Prior to the arrest, and prior to the police chief's press conference concerning it, respondent was a respected member of a small community who had never been arrested, even for a traffic offense.

A few days before respondent was scheduled for a probable-cause hearing on the charge of witness tampering, respondent's attorney advised him to sign a covenant not to sue the town of Newton, its police officers, or the witness Deary in exchange for dismissal of the charge against him. The advice was predicated on the lawyer's judgment that the value of a dismissal outweighed the harmful consequences of an almost certain indictment on a felony charge together with the risk of conviction in a case in which the outcome would depend on the jury's assessment of the relative credibility of respondent and his alleged victim. The lawyer correctly advised respondent that even if he was completely innocent, there could be no guarantee of acquittal. He therefore placed a higher value on his client's interest in terminating the criminal proceeding promptly than on the uncertain benefits of pursuing a civil remedy against the town and its police department. After delaying a decision for three days, respondent reluctantly followed his lawyer's advice.

From respondent's point of view, it is unquestionably true that the decision to sign the release-dismissal agreement was, as the Court emphasizes, "voluntary, deliberate, and informed." I submit, however, that the deliberate and rational character of respondent's decision is not a sufficient reason for concluding that the agreement is enforceable. Otherwise, a promise to pay a state trooper $20 for not issuing a ticket for a traffic violation, or a promise to contribute to the police department's retirement fund in exchange for the dismissal of a felony charge, would be enforceable. Indeed, I would suppose that virtually all contracts that courts refuse to enforce nevertheless reflect perfectly rational decisions by the parties who entered into them. There is nothing irrational about an agreement to bribe a police officer, to enter into a wagering arrangement, to pay usurious rates of interests, or to threaten to indict an innocent man in order to induce him to surrender something of value.

The "voluntary, deliberate, and informed" character of a defendant's decision generally provides an acceptable basis for upholding the validity of a plea bargain. But it is inappropriate to assume that the same standard determines the validity of a quite different agreement to forgo a civil remedy for the violation of the defendant's constitutional rights in exchange for complete abandonment of a criminal charge.

The net result of every plea bargain is an admission of wrongdoing by the defendant and the imposition of a criminal sanction with its attendant stigma. Although there may be some cases in which an innocent person pleads guilty to a minor offense to avoid the risk of conviction on a more serious charge, it is reasonable to presume that such cases are rare and represent the exception rather than the rule. . . . Like a plea bargain, an agreement by the suspect to drop §1983 charges and to pay restitution to the victim in exchange for the prosecutor's termination of criminal proceedings involves an admission of wrongdoing by the defendant. The same cannot be said about an agreement that completely exonerates the defendant. Not only is such a person presumptively innocent as a matter of law; as a factual matter the prosecutor's interest in obtaining a covenant not to sue will be strongest in those cases in which he realizes that the defendant was innocent and was wrongfully accused. Moreover, the prosecutor will be most willing — indeed, he is ethically obligated — to drop charges when he believes that probable cause as established by the available, admissible evidence is lacking.

. . . A defendant entering a release-dismissal agreement is forced to waive claims based on official conduct under color of state law, in exchange merely for the assurance that the State will not prosecute him for conduct for which he has made no admission of wrongdoing. The State is spared the necessity of going to trial, but its willingness to drop the charge completely indicates that it might not have proceeded with the prosecution in any event. No social interest in the punishment of wrongdoers is satisfied; the only interest vindicated is that of resolving once and for all the question of §1983 liability.

Achieving this result has no connection with the give-and-take over the defendant's wrongdoing that is the essence of the plea-bargaining process, and thus cannot be justified by reference to the principles of mutual advantage that support plea bargaining. . . .

Thus, even though respondent's decision in this case was deliberate, informed, and voluntary, this observation does not address two distinct objections to enforcement of the release-dismissal agreement. The prosecutor's offer to drop charges if the defendant accedes to the agreement is inherently coercive; moreover, the agreement exacts a price unrelated to the character of the defendant's own conduct.

II

When the prosecutor negotiated the agreement with respondent, he represented three potentially conflicting interests. His primary duty, of course, was to represent the sovereign's interest in the evenhanded and effective enforcement of its criminal laws. In addition, as the covenant demonstrates, he sought to represent the interests of the town of Newton and its Police Department in connection with their possible civil liability to respondent. Finally, as the inclusion of Mary Deary as a covenantee indicates, the prosecutor also represented the interest of a potential witness who allegedly accused both respondent and a mutual friend of separate instances of wrongdoing. . . .

If we view the problem from the standpoint of the prosecutor's principal client, the State of New Hampshire, it is perfectly clear that the release-dismissal agreement was both unnecessary and unjustified. . . . The public is entitled to have the prosecutor's decision to go forward with a criminal case, or to dismiss it, made independently of his concerns about the potential damages liability of the Police Department. . . . At bottom, the Court's holding in this case seems to rest on concerns related to the potential witness, Mary Deary. . . . Arguably a special rule should be fashioned for witnesses who are victims of sexual assaults. The trauma associated with such an assault leaves scars that may make it especially difficult for a victim to press charges or to testify publicly about the event. It remains true, however, that uncorroborated, unsworn statements by persons who claim to have been victims of any crime, including such an assault, may be inaccurate, exaggerated, or incomplete — and sometimes even malicious. It is even more clear that hearsay descriptions of statements by such persons may be unreliable. Rather than adopting a general rule that upholds a release-dismissal agreement whenever the criminal charge was based on a statement by the alleged victim of a sexual assault, I believe the Court should insist upon a "close examination" of the facts that purportedly justified the agreement. . . .

Deary's unwillingness to testify against Rumery is perfectly obvious. That fact unquestionably supports the prosecutor's decision to dismiss the charge against respondent, but it is not a sufficient reason for exonerating police officers from the consequences of actions that they took when they must have known that Deary was unwilling to testify. . . . The need for Deary's testimony in the pending sexual assault case against Champy simply cannot justify denying this respondent a remedy for a violation of his Fourth Amendment rights. . . .

III

Because this is the first case of this kind that the Court has reviewed, I am hesitant to adopt an absolute rule invalidating all such agreements. I am, however, persuaded that the federal policies reflected in the enactment and enforcement of §1983 mandate a strong presumption against the enforceability of such agreements and that the presumption is not overcome in this case by the facts or by any of the policy concerns discussed by the plurality. . . .

Accordingly, although I am not prepared to endorse all of the reasoning of the Court of Appeals, I would affirm its judgment.

NOTES AND QUESTIONS

1. Because Justice O'Connor provided the crucial fifth vote for the outcome, her concurring opinion defines the enforceability of plea bargains containing release-dismissal agreements. What, exactly, is her position? How, exactly, does it differ from the positions of Justice Powell and Justice Stevens? Why?

2. Justice O'Connor and the *Rumery* dissenters apparently agree that release-dismissal agreements are problematic. Why? Are they more problematic than "wired" pleas like the one in *Pollard*? At least in *Rumery*, the defendant was bargaining about his own interests, albeit in two different (potential) cases. Pollard bargained about his wife's interest as well as his own. Which is worse?

3. Release-dismissal agreements are obviously a problem if the potential criminal charge is designed to be used solely as a bargaining chip. Was that the case in *Rumery*? Imagine a §1983 claim for police brutality, a criminal charge of disorderly conduct, and a release-dismissal agreement. Does that situation sound more problematic than *Rumery*? Less so?

UNITED STATES v. MEZZANATTO

Certiorari to the United States Court of Appeals for the Ninth Circuit
513 U.S. 196 (1995)

JUSTICE THOMAS delivered the opinion of the Court.

Federal Rule of Evidence 410 and Federal Rule of Criminal Procedure 11(e)(6)[5] provide that statements made in the course of plea discussions between a criminal defendant and a prosecutor are inadmissible against the defendant. The court below held that these exclusionary provisions may not be waived by the defendant. . . . [W]e now reverse. . . .

[Mezzanatto was arrested and charged with possession of methamphetamine with intent to distribute after an undercover officer purchased a pound of

---

5. This reference is to the prior version of Rule 11(e)(6), which contained language essentially identical to that of Federal Rule of Evidence 410. In 2002, Rule 11(e)(6) was replaced by new Rule 11(f), which simply provides that admissibility of plea discussions "is governed by Federal Rule of Evidence 410." — EDS.

methamphetamine from him. The undercover buy was set up with the cooperation of one Shuster, whom the authorities believed ran a large distribution operation and at whose house agents discovered a methamphetamine laboratory.]

On October 17, 1991, respondent and his attorney asked to meet with the prosecutor to discuss the possibility of cooperating with the Government. . . . At the beginning of the meeting, the prosecutor informed respondent that he had no obligation to talk, but that if he wanted to cooperate he would have to be completely truthful. As a condition to proceeding with the discussion, the prosecutor indicated that respondent would have to agree that any statements he made during the meeting could be used to impeach any contradictory testimony he might give at trial if the case proceeded that far. Respondent conferred with his counsel and agreed to proceed under the prosecutor's terms.

Respondent then admitted knowing that the package he had attempted to sell to the undercover police officer contained methamphetamine, but insisted that he had dealt only in "ounce" quantities of methamphetamine prior to his arrest. Initially, respondent also claimed that he was acting merely as a broker for Shuster and did not know that Shuster was manufacturing methamphetamine at his residence, but he later conceded that he knew about Shuster's laboratory. Respondent attempted to minimize his role in Shuster's operation by claiming that he had not visited Shuster's residence for at least a week before his arrest. At this point, the Government confronted respondent with surveillance evidence showing that his car was on Shuster's property the day before the arrest, and terminated the meeting on the basis of respondent's failure to provide completely truthful information.

Respondent eventually was tried on the methamphetamine charge and took the stand in his own defense. He maintained that he was not involved in methamphetamine trafficking and that he had thought Shuster used his home laboratory to manufacture plastic explosives for the CIA. He also denied knowing that the package he delivered to the undercover officer contained methamphetamine. Over defense counsel's objection, the prosecutor cross-examined respondent about the inconsistent statements he had made during the October 17 meeting. Respondent denied having made certain statements, and the prosecutor called one of the agents who had attended the meeting to recount the prior statements. The jury found respondent guilty, and the District Court sentenced him to 170 months in prison.

A panel of the Ninth Circuit reversed, . . . [holding] that respondent's agreement to allow admission of his plea statements for purposes of impeachment was unenforceable and that the District Court therefore erred in admitting the statements for that purpose. . . .

Federal Rule of Evidence 410 and Federal Rule of Criminal Procedure 11(e)(6) (Rules or plea-statement Rules) are substantively identical. Rule 410 provides:

> Except as otherwise provided in this rule, evidence of the following is not, in any civil or criminal proceeding, admissible against the defendant who . . . was a participant in the plea discussions: . . . (4) any statement made in the course of plea discussions with an attorney for the prosecuting authority which do not result in a plea of guilty. . . .

The Ninth Circuit noted that these Rules are subject to only two express exceptions,[1] neither of which says anything about waiver, and thus concluded that

---

1. A statement made by a criminal defendant in the course of plea discussions is "admissible (i) in any proceeding wherein another statement made in the course of the same . . . plea discussions has been

Congress must have meant to preclude waiver agreements such as respondent's. . . .

The Ninth Circuit's analysis is directly contrary to the approach we have taken in the context of a broad array of constitutional and statutory provisions. Rather than deeming waiver presumptively unavailable absent some sort of express enabling clause, we instead have adhered to the opposite presumption. . . . A criminal defendant may knowingly and voluntarily waive many of the most fundamental protections afforded by the Constitution. See, e.g., Ricketts v. Adamson, 483 U.S. 1, 10 (1987) (double jeopardy defense waivable by pretrial agreement); Boykin v. Alabama, 395 U.S. 238, 243 (1969) (knowing and voluntary guilty plea waives privilege against compulsory self-incrimination, right to jury trial, and right to confront one's accusers); Johnson v. Zerbst, 304 U.S. 458, 465 (1938) (Sixth Amendment right to counsel may be waived). Likewise, absent some affirmative indication of Congress' intent to preclude waiver, we have presumed that statutory provisions are subject to waiver by voluntary agreement of the parties. See, e.g., Evans v. Jeff D., 475 U.S. 717, 730-732 (1986) (prevailing party in civil-rights action may waive its statutory eligibility for attorney's fees). . . . The presumption of waivability has found specific application in the context of evidentiary rules. Absent some "overriding procedural consideration that prevents enforcement of the contract," courts have held that agreements to waive evidentiary rules are generally enforceable even over a party's subsequent objections. 21 C. Wright & K. Graham, Federal Practice and Procedure §5039, pp. 207-208 (1977) (hereinafter Wright & Graham). . . .

Because the plea-statement Rules were enacted against a background presumption that legal rights generally, and evidentiary provisions specifically, are subject to waiver by voluntary agreement of the parties, we will not interpret Congress' silence as an implicit rejection of waivability. Respondent bears the responsibility of identifying some affirmative basis for concluding that the plea-statement Rules depart from the presumption of waivability.

Respondent offers three potential bases for concluding that the Rules should be placed beyond the control of the parties. . . .

Respondent first suggests that the plea-statement Rules establish a "guarantee [to] fair procedure" that cannot be waived. We agree with respondent's basic premise: There may be some evidentiary provisions that are so fundamental to the reliability of the factfinding process that they may never be waived without irreparably "discrediting the federal courts." See 21 Wright & Graham §5039, at 207-208; see also Wheat v. United States, 486 U.S. 153, 162 (1988) (court may decline a defendant's waiver of his right to conflict-free counsel); United States v. Josefik, 753 F.2d 585, 588 (CA7 1985) ("No doubt there are limits to waiver; if the parties stipulated to trial by 12 orangutans the defendant's conviction would be invalid notwithstanding his consent, because some minimum of civilized procedure is required by community feeling regardless of what the defendant wants or is willing to accept"). But enforcement of agreements like respondent's plainly will not have that effect. The admission of plea statements for impeachment purposes enhances the truth-seeking function of trials and will result in more accurate verdicts. . . .

introduced and the statement ought in fairness be considered contemporaneously with it, or (ii) in a criminal proceeding for perjury or false statement if the statement was made by the defendant under oath, on the record and in the presence of counsel." Fed. Rule Evid. 410. Accord, Fed. Rule Crim. Proc. 11(e)(6).

Under any view of the evidence, the defendant has made a false statement, either to the prosecutor during the plea discussion or to the jury at trial; making the jury aware of the inconsistency will tend to increase the reliability of the verdict without risking institutional harm to the federal courts. . . .

Respondent also contends that waiver is fundamentally inconsistent with the Rules' goal of encouraging voluntary settlement. See Advisory Committee's Notes on Fed. Rule Evid. 410 (purpose of Rule is "promotion of disposition of criminal cases by compromise"). Because the prospect of waiver may make defendants "think twice" before entering into any plea negotiation, respondent suggests that enforcement of waiver agreements acts "as a brake, not as a facilitator, to the plea-bargain process." The Ninth Circuit expressed similar concerns. . . . According to the Ninth Circuit, the plea-statement Rules "permit the plea bargainer to maximize what he has 'to sell'" by preserving "the ability to withdraw from the bargain proposed by the prosecutor without being harmed by any of his statements made in the course of an aborted plea bargaining session." [998 F.2d, at 1455.]

We need not decide whether and under what circumstances substantial "public policy" interests may permit the inference that Congress intended to override the presumption of waivability, for in this case there is no basis for concluding that waiver will interfere with the Rules' goal of encouraging plea bargaining. The court below focused entirely on the defendant's incentives and completely ignored the other essential party to the transaction: the prosecutor. Thus, although the availability of waiver may discourage some defendants from negotiating, it is also true that prosecutors may be unwilling to proceed without it. Prosecutors may be especially reluctant to negotiate without a waiver agreement during the early stages of a criminal investigation, when prosecutors are searching for leads and suspects may be willing to offer information in exchange for some form of immunity or leniency in sentencing. In this "cooperation" context, prosecutors face "painfully delicate" choices as to "whether to proceed and prosecute those suspects against whom the already produced evidence makes a case or whether to extend leniency or full immunity to some suspects in order to procure testimony against other, more dangerous suspects against whom existing evidence is flimsy or nonexistent." Hughes, Agreements for Cooperation in Criminal Cases, 45 Vand. L. Rev. 1, 15 (1992). Because prosecutors have limited resources and must be able to answer "sensitive questions about the credibility of the testimony" they receive before entering into any sort of cooperation agreement, id., at 10, prosecutors may condition cooperation discussions on an agreement that the testimony provided may be used for impeachment purposes. If prosecutors were precluded from securing such agreements, they might well decline to enter into cooperation discussions in the first place and might never take this potential first step toward a plea bargain.

Indeed, as a logical matter, it simply makes no sense to conclude that mutual settlement will be encouraged by precluding negotiation over an issue that may be particularly important to one of the parties to the transaction. A sounder way to encourage settlement is to permit the interested parties to enter into knowing and voluntary negotiations without any arbitrary limits on their bargaining chips. To use the Ninth Circuit's metaphor, if the prosecutor is interested in "buying" the reliability assurance that accompanies a waiver agreement, then precluding waiver can only stifle the market for plea bargains. A defendant can "maximize" what he has to "sell" only if he is permitted to offer what the prosecutor is most interested in buying. And while it is certainly true that prosecutors often need help from the small fish in a conspiracy in order to catch the big ones, that is no reason to preclude waiver altogether. If prosecutors decide that certain crucial information will be gained only by preserving the inadmissibility of plea statements, they will agree to leave intact the exclusionary provisions of the plea-statement Rules. . . .

Finally, respondent contends that waiver agreements should be forbidden because they invite prosecutorial overreaching and abuse. Respondent asserts that there is a "gross disparity" in the relative bargaining power of the parties to a plea agreement and suggests that a waiver agreement is "inherently unfair and coercive." . . . The plea bargaining process necessarily exerts pressure on defendants to plead guilty and to abandon a series of fundamental rights, but we have repeatedly held that the government "may encourage a guilty plea by offering substantial benefits in return for the plea." Corbitt v. New Jersey, 439 U.S. 212, 219 (1978). "While confronting a defendant with the risk of more severe punishment clearly may have a 'discouraging effect on the defendant's assertion of his trial rights, the imposition of these difficult choices [is] an inevitable' — and permissible — 'attribute of any legitimate system which tolerates and encourages the negotiation of pleas.'" Bordenkircher v. Hayes, 434 U.S. 357, 364 (1978) (quoting Chaffin v. Stynchcombe, 412 U.S. 17, 31 (1973)). The mere potential for abuse of prosecutorial bargaining power is an insufficient basis for foreclosing negotiation altogether.

. . . Instead, the appropriate response to respondent's predictions of abuse is to permit case-by-case inquiries into whether waiver agreements are the product of fraud or coercion. We hold that absent some affirmative indication that the agreement was entered into unknowingly or involuntarily, an agreement to waive the exclusionary provisions of the plea-statement Rules is valid and enforceable.

Respondent conferred with his lawyer after the prosecutor proposed waiver as a condition of proceeding with the plea discussion, and he has never complained that he entered into the waiver agreement at issue unknowingly or involuntarily. The Ninth Circuit's decision was based on its per se rejection of waiver of the plea-statement Rules. Accordingly, the judgment of the Court of Appeals is reversed.

JUSTICE GINSBURG, with whom JUSTICE O'CONNOR and JUSTICE BREYER join, concurring.

The Court holds that a waiver allowing the Government to impeach with statements made during plea negotiations is compatible with Congress' intent to promote plea bargaining. It may be, however, that a waiver to use such statements in the case in chief would more severely undermine a defendant's incentive to negotiate, and thereby inhibit plea bargaining. As the Government has not sought such a waiver, we do not here explore this question.

JUSTICE SOUTER, with whom JUSTICE STEVENS joins, dissenting.

. . . [T]he fact of which all congressional and judicial action must take account in dealing with the possible evidentiary significance of plea discussions, is that the federal judicial system could not possibly litigate every civil and criminal case filed in the courts. The consequence of this is that plea bargaining is an accepted feature of the criminal justice system, and, "properly administered, it is to be encouraged." Santobello v. New York, 404 U.S. 257, 260 (1971). Thus the Advisory Committee's Notes on Rule 410 explained that "exclusion of offers to plead guilty or nolo has as its purpose the promotion of disposition of criminal cases by compromise." 28 U.S.C. App., p. 750. "As with compromise offers generally, . . . free communication is needed, and security against having an offer of compromise or related statement admitted in evidence effectively encourages it." Ibid. The Advisory Committee's Notes on Rule 11(e)(6) drew the same conclusion about the purpose of that Rule. . . .

These explanations show with reasonable clarity that Congress probably made two assumptions when it adopted the Rules: Pleas and plea discussions are to be encouraged, and conditions of unrestrained candor are the most effective means of encouragement. The provisions protecting a defendant against use of statements made in his plea bargaining are thus meant to create something more than a personal right shielding an individual from his imprudence. Rather, the Rules are meant to serve the interest of the federal judicial system (whose resources are controlled by Congress), by creating the conditions understood by Congress to be effective in promoting reasonable plea agreements. Whether Congress was right or wrong that unrestrained candor is necessary to promote a reasonable number of plea agreements, Congress assumed that there was such a need and meant to satisfy it by these Rules. Since the zone of unrestrained candor is diminished whenever a defendant has to stop to think about the amount of trouble his openness may cause him if the plea negotiations fall through, Congress must have understood that the judicial system's interest in candid plea discussions would be threatened by recognizing waivers under Rules 410 and 11(e)(6). . . .

. . . The majority may be right that a better balance could have been struck than the one Congress intended. The majority may also be correct as a matter of policy that enough pleas will result even if parties are allowed to make their own rule of admissibility by agreement, with prosecutors refusing to talk without a defendant's waiver (unless such refusal overloads the system beyond its capacity for trials) and defendants refusing to waive (unless they are desperate enough to forgo their option to be tried without fear of compromising statements if the plea negotiations fail). But whether the majority is right or wrong on either score is beside the point; the policy it endorses is not the policy that Congress intended when it enacted the Rules. . . .

The unlikelihood that Congress intended the modest default rule that the majority sees in Rules 11(e)(6) and 410 looms all the larger when the consequences of the majority position are pursued. The first consequence is that the Rules will probably not even function as default rules, for there is little chance that they will be applied at all. Already, standard forms indicate that many federal prosecutors routinely require waiver of Rules 410 and 11(e)(6) rights before a prosecutor is willing to enter into plea discussions. [See] United States v. Stevens, 935 F.2d 1380, 1396 (CA3 1991) ("Plea agreements . . . commonly contain a provision stating that proffer information that is disclosed during the course of plea negotiations is . . . admissible for purposes of impeachment"). As the Government conceded during oral argument, defendants are generally in no position to challenge demands for these waivers, and the use of waiver provisions as contracts of adhesion has become accepted practice. Today's decision can only speed the heretofore illegitimate process by which the exception has been swallowing the Rules. . . . [I]t is probably only a matter of time until the Rules are dead letters.

The second consequence likely to emerge from today's decision is the practical certainty that the waiver demanded will in time come to function as a waiver of trial itself. It is true that many (if not all) of the waiver forms now employed go only to admissibility for impeachment. But although the erosion of the Rules has begun with this trickle, the majority's reasoning will provide no principled limit to it. The Rules draw no distinction between use of a statement for impeachment and use in the Government's case in chief. If objection can be waived for impeachment use, it can be waived for use as affirmative evidence, and if the Government can effectively demand waiver in the former instance, there is no reason to believe it will not do so just as successfully in the latter. When it does, there is nothing this Court will legitimately be able to do about it. . . . [T]he majority opinion sanctions a demand for waiver of such scope that a defendant who gives it will be unable even to acknowledge his desire to negotiate a guilty plea without furnishing admissible evidence against himself then and there. In such cases, the possibility of trial if no agreement is reached will be reduced to fantasy. The only defendant who will not damage himself by even the most restrained candor will be the one so desperate that he might as well walk into court and enter a naked guilty plea. It defies reason to think that Congress intended to invite such a result, when it adopted a Rule said to promote candid discussion in the interest of encouraging compromise.

NOTES AND QUESTIONS

1. In United States v. Burch, 156 F.3d 1315 (D.C. Cir. 1998), the court considered the question raised by Justice Ginsburg's concurrence — whether a waiver of former Rule 11(e)(6) (now replaced by Rule 11(f)) can permit the government to use statements made during plea negotiations as part of the government's case-in-chief. In an opinion by Judge Wald, the court decided that question in the government's favor:

> [W]hile it is conceivable that sanctioning waivers for the use of statements made during plea proceedings in the prosecution's case-in-chief, as opposed to impeachment or rebuttal, could have a markedly greater impact on the willingness of defendants to participate in such negotiations, the three-Justice concurrence in *Mezzanatto* presents no reason why that would be the case. Nor has the appellant. Lacking any evidence to the contrary, it seems unlikely to us that most defendants would draw fine distinctions as to whether statements made in the course of or after the plea proceeding could be used in the government's case-in-chief or only in rebuttal. . . . [A]llowing the government to bargain for a waiver during plea negotiations certainly does not undermine the reliability of the fact-finding process, the only institutional concern cited by *Mezzanatto* as a potential counterweight to the presumption in favor of waivability. See [513 U.S.] at 204 (some evidentiary provisions are so fundamental that permitting their waiver would discredit the integrity of the federal judicial process; "if the parties stipulated to trial by 12 orangutans the defendant's conviction would be invalid notwithstanding his consent"). . . .

Is *Burch* right? Note that in *Burch*, the government did not insist on the waiver as a precondition to entering into plea negotiations; instead, the waiver was itself the subject of negotiation. Does that matter?

2. As Eric Rasmusen notes, plea agreements with cooperating defendants "seem unconscionably one-sided." Eric Rasmusen, *Mezzanatto* and the Economics of Self-Incrimination, 19 Cardozo L. Rev. 1541, 1551 (1998). Rasmusen offers the following example, excerpted from the plea agreement in United States v. Stirling, 571 F.2d 708 (7th Cir. 1978):

It is further understood that Mr. Schulz must at all times give complete, truthful and accurate information and testimony and must not commit any further crime whatsoever. Should Mr. Schulz commit any further crimes or should it be judged by this Office that Mr. Schulz has given false, incomplete or misleading testimony or information, or has otherwise violated any provision of this agreement, this agreement shall be null and void and Mr. Schulz shall thereafter be subject to prosecution for any federal criminal violation of which this Office has knowledge, including, but not limited to, perjury and obstruction of justice. Any such prosecutions may be premised upon any information provided by Mr. Schulz, and such information may be used against him.

The problem with such an agreement seems obvious:

The agreement allows one of the two parties to be the judge of whether it has been violated, and if that is so judged, the judging party is free to keep all of its benefits from the bargain and make even fuller use of them. The Government can say that Schulz gave incomplete testimony regardless of what he actually gives, and then use what he said against him. If the market for plea bargains leads to such one-sided contracts, how can they be allowed?

19 Cardozo L. Rev., at 1552. The answer, Rasmusen says, goes to "the quality of the defendant's performance":

. . . The prosecutor can be pinned down to a quite specific promise — a particular charge, or a specific sentence. The defendant, however, is providing "cooperation." At its most specific, this might just involve repeating in court under oath the story that the defendant told the prosecutor earlier in the negotiations. More often, however, the prosecutor wants the defendant to answer additional questions, to perform credibly under cross-examination, and to be available to cooperate in other matters that arise during investigations, pretrial preparation, sentencing proceedings, appeals, and so forth. Even if the performance were limited to repeating an earlier story, the defendant might effectively breach by adopting an unbelievable demeanor on the stand. Thus, we are left with the problem of performance quality.

It is helpful to view the situation as similar to when a seller wishes to guarantee the quality of his product to a buyer, but is not legally required to do so. Many sellers thus offer money-back guarantees, even though a dishonest consumer could take advantage of such a guarantee to return products after use even when the quality is satisfactory. Defendants are in a similar position. . . .

. . . This resolves the puzzle of why plea agreements so often seem to give enormous advantages to the prosecutor. It also explains why waivers [of former Rule 11(e)(6) and Rule 410] became so common in cooperation bargaining: It is because they increased the total benefits from the agreements to the advantage of both buyer and seller of cooperation. Waivers became common in the plea bargaining marketplace because the waiverless cooperation agreement was a product that did not sell.

Id., at 1559-1561. Are you persuaded? Should the government therefore be able to write, and enforce, one-sided agreements?

3. One of the provisions commonly seen in modern plea bargains is an agreement by the defendant not to appeal either his conviction or some particular legal issue subsumed therein, such as an issue of evidentiary suppression or the validity of

the sentence. Are such "waiver-of-appeal" provisions appropriate? Should they generally be enforced? In United States v. Navarro-Botello, 912 F.2d 318 (1990), the Ninth Circuit said yes:

> Navarro-Botello argues that his plea was involuntary because it is logically impossible to make a knowing and intelligent waiver of unknown rights, and a defendant cannot know or understand what appellate issues may arise until after sentencing. We reject this argument. . . .
>
> The rationale in *Rumery* applies here. Whatever appellate issues might have been available to Navarro-Botello were speculative compared to the certainty derived from the negotiated plea with a set sentence parameter. He knew he was giving up possible appeals, even if he did not know exactly what the nature of those appeals might be. In exchange, he gained a set sentence. Just because the choice looks different to Navarro-Botello with the benefit of hindsight, does not make the choice involuntary. . . .
>
> The Supreme Court has found that knowing and voluntary constitutional waivers do not violate due process. *Rumery*, 480 U.S. at 393. Accordingly, if it is not a due process violation for a defendant to waive constitutional rights as part of a plea bargain, then a defendant's waiver of a nonconstitutional right, such as the statutory right to appeal a sentence, is also waivable. . . . We note, however, that a waiver of the right to appeal would not prevent an appeal where the sentence imposed is not in accordance with the negotiated agreement or other sentencing error occurs.

Id., at 320-321; see also Note, An Unjust Bargain: Plea Bargains and Waiver of the Right to Appeal, 51 B.C. L. Rev. 871 (2010).

4. Plea Bargains as Contracts

It is often said that plea bargaining is a uniquely American institution. This statement, however, requires some important clarification. Virtually all systems of criminal justice throughout the world regularly provide defendants with a significant benefit (usually, more lenient punishment) if they concede, or at least do not contest, their guilt. And virtually all systems of criminal justice reserve the most elaborate kind of adjudicative proceeding available in such a system (e.g., a full-blown criminal trial) for a small subset of criminal cases, including those in which the defendants forego the aforementioned benefit and actively contest their guilt. These two key features of plea bargaining — encouragement for defendants to concede (or at least not to contest) their guilt, and corresponding conservation of systemic resources — may be said to be almost universal.

What is virtually unique about American-style plea bargaining, however, is the contract-like manner in which this incentive structure is implemented. In most other countries, it would be unthinkable (and often illegal) for the prosecution to engage in explicit negotiations with the defense for the purpose of entering into a binding agreement to trade favorable treatment for the defendant's trial rights.

As you read the following cases, you should think about the similarities — and the differences — between traditional contract law and the law and practice of plea bargaining.

a.   Contract Formation

MABRY v. JOHNSON

Certiorari to the United States Court of Appeals for the Eighth Circuit
467 U.S. 504 (1984)

JUSTICE STEVENS delivered the opinion of the Court.

The question presented is whether a defendant's acceptance of a prosecutor's proposed plea bargain creates a constitutional right to have the bargain specifically enforced.

In the late evening of May 22, 1970, three members of a family returned home to find a burglary in progress. Shots were exchanged resulting in the daughter's death and the wounding of the father and respondent — one of the burglars. Respondent was tried and convicted on three charges: burglary, assault, and murder. The murder conviction was set aside by the Arkansas Supreme Court. Thereafter, plea negotiations ensued.

At the time of the negotiations respondent was serving his concurrent 21- and 12-year sentences on the burglary and assault convictions. On Friday, October 27, 1972, a deputy prosecutor proposed to respondent's attorney that in exchange for a plea of guilty to the charge of accessory after a felony murder, the prosecutor would recommend a sentence of 21 years to be served concurrently with the burglary and assault sentences. On the following day, counsel communicated the offer to respondent who agreed to accept it. On the next Monday the lawyer called the prosecutor "and communicated [respondent's] acceptance of the offer." App. 10. The prosecutor then told counsel that a mistake had been made and withdrew the offer. He proposed instead that in exchange for a guilty plea he would recommend a sentence of 21 years to be served consecutively to respondent's other sentences.

Respondent rejected the new offer and elected to stand trial. On the second day of trial, the judge declared a mistrial and plea negotiations resumed, ultimately resulting in respondent's acceptance of the prosecutor's second offer. In accordance with the plea bargain, the state trial judge imposed a 21-year sentence to be served consecutively to the previous sentences.

After exhausting his state remedies, respondent filed a petition for a writ of habeas corpus under 28 U.S.C. §2254. The District Court dismissed the petition, finding that respondent had understood the consequences of his guilty plea, that he had received the effective assistance of counsel, and that because the evidence did not establish that respondent had detrimentally relied on the prosecutor's first proposed plea agreement, respondent had no right to enforce it. The Court of Appeals reversed. . . . The [court] concluded that "fairness" precluded the prosecution's withdrawal of a plea proposal once accepted by respondent. . . . We now reverse.

Respondent can obtain federal habeas corpus relief only if his custody is in violation of the Federal Constitution. A plea bargain standing alone is without constitutional significance; in itself it is a mere executory agreement which, until embodied in the judgment of a court, does not deprive an accused of liberty or any other constitutionally protected interest.[5] It is the ensuing guilty plea that

---

5. Under Arkansas law, there is no entitlement to have the trial court impose a recommended sentence since a negotiated sentence recommendation does not bind the court, see Varnedare v. State, 264 Ark. 596, 599, 573 S.W.2d 57, 60 (1978); Marshall v. State, 262 Ark. 726, 561 S.W.2d 76 (1978); Ark. Rule

implicates the Constitution. Only after respondent pleaded guilty was he convicted, and it is that conviction which gave rise to the deprivation of respondent's liberty at issue here.

It is well settled that a voluntary and intelligent plea of guilty made by an accused person, who has been advised by competent counsel, may not be collaterally attacked. It is also well settled that plea agreements are consistent with the requirements of voluntariness and intelligence — because each side may obtain advantages when a guilty plea is exchanged for sentencing concessions, the agreement is no less voluntary than any other bargained-for exchange. It is only when the consensual character of the plea is called into question that the validity of a guilty plea may be impaired. [See] Brady v. United States, 397 U.S. 742 (1970). . . .

Thus, only when it develops that the defendant was not fairly apprised of its consequences can his plea be challenged under the Due Process Clause. . . . It follows that when the prosecution breaches its promise with respect to an executed plea agreement, the defendant pleads guilty on a false premise, and hence his conviction cannot stand. . . .

. . . Respondent's plea was in no sense induced by the prosecutor's withdrawn offer; . . . at the time respondent pleaded guilty he knew the prosecution would recommend a 21-year consecutive sentence. Respondent does not challenge the District Court's finding that he pleaded guilty with the advice of competent counsel and with full awareness of the consequences — he knew that the prosecutor would recommend and that the judge could impose the sentence now under attack. Respondent's plea was thus in no sense the product of governmental deception; it rested on no "unfulfilled promise" and fully satisfied the test for voluntariness and intelligence.

Thus, because it did not impair the voluntariness or intelligence of his guilty plea, respondent's inability to enforce the prosecutor's offer is without constitutional significance. Neither is the question whether the prosecutor was negligent or otherwise culpable in first making and then withdrawing his offer relevant. The Due Process Clause is not a code of ethics for prosecutors; its concern is with the manner in which persons are deprived of their liberty. Here respondent was not deprived of his liberty in any fundamentally unfair way. Respondent was fully aware of the likely consequences when he pleaded guilty; it is not unfair to expect him to live with those consequences now. . . .

NOTES AND QUESTIONS

1. *Mabry* remains good law on the main legal issue presented, which involves the conditions under which a plea bargain becomes an enforceable agreement (more specifically, whether a defendant's unilateral acceptance of a plea bargain, without detrimental reliance thereupon, creates an obligation binding on the prosecution). In Puckett v. United States, 129 S. Ct. 1423 (2009), the Court held that — notwithstanding *Mabry* — a defendant whose defense lawyer failed to object at the time could not thereafter obtain a remedy for a breach of the prosecution's (otherwise enforceable) plea-bargain promise.

Crim. Proc. 25.3(c); there is a critical difference between an entitlement and a mere hope or expectation that the trial court will follow the prosecutor's recommendation, see Olim v. Wakinekona, 461 U.S. 238, 248-251 (1983).

2. If *Mabry* were an ordinary contracts case, how would it be decided? The standard contracts rule is that an executory contract is enforceable from the time the parties exchange promises. Once the government's offer to recommend concurrent sentences was accepted, that exchange had taken place — the government had promised a particular sentencing recommendation, and the defendant had promised to plead guilty. Then the government reneged. Why was the deal not enforceable?

3. Suppose the *defendant* had reneged: Suppose that, the day of the plea, the defendant announced that he had changed his mind and no longer wished to plead guilty. Could the government hold him to his promise? If not, why not? Do your answers help resolve the question in the preceding note?

4. In United States v. Traynoff, 53 F.3d 168 (7th Cir. 1995), a federal prosecutor promised, in a status hearing in open court, to dismiss federal charges against the defendant if the defendant received a 12-year sentence on pending state charges. The 12-year state sentence was imposed, but the federal charges were never dismissed. The court of appeals declined to enforce the prosecutor's promise, citing *Mabry*:

> [I]n Mabry v. Johnson, 467 U.S. 504 (1984), the Court reiterated its concern over only those offers that had induced defendants to act to their detriment, not every rescinded governmental promise. *Mabry* involved a prosecutor who withdrew a formal plea offer and a defendant who subsequently pleaded guilty pursuant to a second plea proposal. On appeal, the defendant sought to enforce the original offer against the government. The Court rejected the defendant's argument and upheld the plea as voluntary because it "was in no sense induced by the prosecution's withdrawn offer."
>
> . . . *Mabry* indicate[s] that the government must fulfill promises that induce a defendant to plead guilty. We assume that we must also hold the government to its agreements that reasonably cause criminal defendants to take other damaging actions.
>
> . . . Reasonable and detrimental reliance on behalf of a defendant is thus a necessity; without it we will not compel the government to discharge a withdrawn agreement.

Id., at 170-171. The court went on to conclude that Traynoff had shown no detrimental reliance.

Suppose Johnson had detrimentally relied on the government's sentencing promise in *Mabry*. The court of appeals' decision in *Traynoff*, quoted in the preceding note, suggests that reneging on the sentencing promise would then constitute breach. What would be the remedy? Johnson would, of course, seek specific performance. Should he get it?

5. Most plea bargains involve a fairly simple exchange — the defendant agrees to plead guilty, and the government agrees to some charging or sentencing concessions. The chief issues in those bargains are of the sort that arise for any class of contracts: determining whether a bargain has been struck, interpreting the contract terms, and choosing a remedy in case of breach.

There is another class of bargains that raise a somewhat different set of issues. In many cases, the government is "buying" not only a guilty plea but also information (and typically courtroom testimony). That kind of bargain necessarily involves a good deal more uncertainty, on both sides, than is often the case with more conventional plea bargains. Consider the following discussion, taken from Daniel C. Richman, Cooperating Clients, 56 Ohio St. L.J. 69, 94-101 (1995):

In contrast to the defendant choosing simply between plea and trial, the defendant who has testimony or information to "sell" must consider a leap into uncertainty. Everyone knows that, as a class, cooperators get big sentencing breaks. However, at the time he is contemplating whether to cooperate, a defendant typically will not know how large a discount he can expect, nor can he be sure that, were he to satisfy his part of the bargain, he would get a discount at all.

Nothing about cooperation inherently compels this state of affairs. One can imagine a scheme in which a defendant interested in cooperating would give the government a summary of the information he has to sell, protected by a side agreement that would bar the government from using the information against him if negotiations break down. Alternatively, the defendant's lawyer could make a proffer of this information. Were the government willing to deal, an agreement could be struck obliging the defendant to plead guilty to certain charges and to testify or give information truthfully at the government's request; in exchange, the government would agree to make a sentencing presentation designed to give the defendant a precise discount commensurate with the value of his information. The defendant could then be sentenced before he actually testified in a single trial. If, thereafter, he reneged on his obligations, he could be prosecuted anew, for perjury in his trial testimony, for any charge dropped in consideration of his promise to cooperate, or for both.

Such arrangements . . . are rarely available, because they do not serve the government's interests — and may not even serve most defendants' interests. Above all, the government's fear is that a defendant who has received his reward up front will perjure himself — give an account at odds with the "true" account that led the government to enter the cooperation agreement — when it comes time to testify against his former criminal associates. To deter defendants from "recanting," the government needs a mechanism . . . that promises swift and certain punishment for such conduct. An agreement that requires the government to pursue a defector in a separate criminal trial — and, for those charges dismissed pursuant to the agreement, to prove breach of the agreement before even getting before a jury — does not fit this bill. The most efficient way for the government to keep some hold over the defendant is to postpone sentencing until after his cooperation.

A similar concern that a defendant have an incentive to testify "at his best" also leads the government to prefer an agreement that does not specify how much leniency a defendant can expect for his cooperation. Such vagueness allows . . . the government to avoid a stark choice between rewarding the defendant whose cooperation has been grudging and ripping up his agreement. . . .

The uncertainty that the government prefers in its cooperation agreements also reflects the fact that the document is designed to be seen not just by the parties but by the jury considering the cooperator's testimony. A vague agreement permits a witness who has admitted his involvement in heinous crimes to say, "I honestly don't know what sentence I will receive. I hope for leniency, but it's up to the judge." While defense counsel will try to educate the jury about the likelihood that the witness will receive exceptional lenience — and that the government will have considerable control over the extent of that lenience — the expectation is that jurors will be less likely to be put off by the "deal" than if the agreement set out a precise discount.

. . . Special circumstances or the demands of a particular defendant with . . . bargaining power may lead to a different arrangement. Michael Milken's agreement, for example, first had him sentenced and then allowed him to seek a reduction in his sentence once he had cooperated. Payouts may also need to be made up front in those jurisdictions where a cooperator's sentence . . . will primarily be determined by the nature of the charges he has pleaded to. . . . The point is simply that the government will seek to keep the payout as uncertain as it can. Indeed, the government's risk aversion may lead defendants to prefer uncertainty as well, because if forced to commit himself . . . , a prosecutor would be less likely to be lenient, for fear that a defendant would renege or that the agreement would play badly before a jury.

The consequence of this convergence of interests is that cooperation agreements will typically be quite clear in setting out the charges a defendant will have to plead to and the scope of his immunity, but will often be quite vague as to what leniency the defendant can expect in exchange for his cooperation. . . . Typically, the defendant will broadly promise to testify truthfully, and to truthfully disclose all information concerning matters covered by the government's inquiries. Any effort to bind a cooperator to a particular "story" would be unseemly, and probably illegal. The government will reserve for itself the right to determine, prior to sentencing, whether the defendant has in fact cooperated fully and told the truth. Ordinarily, this reservation might simply mean that the government would retain control over what it tells the sentencing judge about the defendant's cooperation. Given that a judge would be likely to rely heavily on a prosecutor's assessment of such matters, this would be a substantial enforcement mechanism.

Richman goes on to explain that in federal cases, the Federal Sentencing Guidelines "have strengthened the government's hand even more" by authorizing downward departures for cooperating defendants only when the prosecutor certifies that the defendant has rendered "substantial assistance." Id., at 101.

From the government's point of view, the great difficulty in dealing with potential "cooperators" is dealing with cases where defendants seek to welsh on their end of the bargain by failing to provide the information or testimony the government expects. The next case deals with a variation on that problem — and with the question of what limits the law places on the government's ability to enforce compliance.

b.   Contract Interpretation

RICKETTS v. ADAMSON

Certiorari to the United States Court of Appeals for the Ninth Circuit
483 U.S. 1 (1987)

JUSTICE WHITE delivered the opinion of the Court.

. . . In 1976, Donald Bolles, a reporter for the Arizona Republic, was fatally injured when a dynamite bomb exploded underneath his car. Respondent was arrested and charged with first-degree murder in connection with Bolles' death. Shortly after his trial had commenced, while jury selection was underway, respondent and the state prosecutor reached an agreement whereby respondent agreed to plead guilty to a charge of second-degree murder and to testify against two other individuals — Max Dunlap and James Robison — who were allegedly involved in Bolles' murder. Specifically, respondent agreed to "testify fully and completely in any Court, State or Federal, when requested by proper authorities against any and all parties involved in the murder of Don Bolles. . . ." The agreement provided that "[s]hould the defendant refuse to testify or should he at any time testify untruthfully . . . then this entire agreement is null and void and the original charge will be automatically reinstated."[1] The parties agreed that respondent would receive a

---

1. The agreement further provided that, in the event respondent refused to testify, he "will be subject to the charge of Open Murder, and if found guilty of First Degree Murder, to the penalty of death or

prison sentence of 48-49 years, with a total incarceration time of 20 years and 2 months. In January 1977, the state trial court accepted the plea agreement and the proposed sentence, but withheld imposition of the sentence. Thereafter, respondent testified as obligated under the agreement, and both Dunlap and Robison were convicted of the first-degree murder of Bolles. While their convictions and sentences were on appeal, the trial court, upon motion of the State, sentenced respondent. In February 1980, the Arizona Supreme Court reversed the convictions of Dunlap and Robison and remanded their cases for retrial. State v. Dunlap, 125 Ariz. 104, 608 P.2d 41. This event sparked the dispute now before us.

The State sought respondent's cooperation and testimony in preparation for the retrial of Dunlap and Robison. On April 3, 1980, however, respondent's counsel informed the prosecutor that respondent believed his obligation to provide testimony under the agreement had terminated when he was sentenced. Respondent would again testify against Dunlap and Robison only if certain conditions were met, including, among others, that the State release him from custody following the retrial. 789 F.2d, at 733.[2] The State then informed respondent's attorney on April 9, 1980, that it deemed respondent to be in breach of the plea agreement. On April 18, 1980, the State called respondent to testify in pretrial proceedings. In response to questions, and upon advice of counsel, respondent invoked his Fifth Amendment privilege against self-incrimination. The trial judge, after respondent's counsel apprised him of the State's letter of April 9 indicating that the State considered respondent to be in breach of the plea agreement, refused to compel respondent to answer questions. The Arizona Supreme Court declined to accept jurisdiction of the State's petition for special action to review the trial judge's decision.

On May 8, 1980, the State filed a new information charging respondent with first-degree murder. Respondent's motion to quash the information on double jeopardy grounds was denied. Respondent challenged this decision by a special action in the Arizona Supreme Court. That court, after reviewing the plea agreement, the transcripts of the plea hearing and the sentencing hearing, respondent's April 3 letter to the state prosecutor, and the prosecutor's April 9 response to that letter, held with "no hesitation" that "the plea agreement contemplates availability of [respondent's] testimony whether at trial or retrial after reversal," Adamson v. Superior Court of Arizona, 125 Ariz. 579, 583, 611 P.2d 932, 936 (1980), and that respondent "violated the terms of the plea agreement." Ibid.[3] The court also rejected

---

life imprisonment requiring mandatory twenty-five years actual incarceration, and the State shall be free to file any charges, not yet filed as of the date of this agreement."

2. Respondent's other conditions — which he characterized as "demands" — included that he be held in a nonjail facility with protection during the retrials, that he be provided with new clothing, that protection be afforded his ex-wife and son, that a fund be provided for his son's education, that he be given adequate resources to establish a new identity outside Arizona following his release from custody, and that he be granted "full and complete immunity for any and all crimes in which he may have been involved."

3. The Arizona Supreme Court noted that at oral argument respondent explained for the first time the basis for his refusal to testify. Respondent relied on Paragraph 8 of the plea agreement, which provides: "All parties to this agreement hereby waive the time for sentencing and agree that the defendant will be sentenced at the conclusion of his testimony in all of the cases referred to in this agreement. . . ." In rejecting respondent's contention that this provision relieved him from his obligation to testify after he had already been sentenced, the court referred to the colloquy that occurred at the sentencing hearing. At that hearing, the prosecuting attorney stated that he had discussed with respondent's counsel the fact "that it may be necessary in the future to bring [respondent] back after sentencing for further testimony." 125 Ariz., at 583, 611 P.2d, at 936. Respondent's counsel indicated that they understood that future testimony may be necessary. The court concluded that whatever doubt was created by Paragraph

respondent's double jeopardy claim, holding that the plea agreement "by its very terms waives the defense of double jeopardy if the agreement is violated." Id., at 584, 611 P. 2d, at 937. Finally, the court held that under state law and the terms of the plea agreement, the State should not have filed a new information, but should have merely reinstated the initial charge. Accordingly, the court vacated respondent's second-degree murder conviction, reinstated the original charge, and dismissed the new information.

After these rulings, respondent offered to testify at the retrials, but the State declined his offer. . . . Respondent was then convicted of first-degree murder and sentenced to death. The judgment was affirmed on direct appeal. . . . Respondent sought federal habeas corpus . . . asserting a number of claims relating to his trial and sentence. The District Court dismissed the petition; a Court of Appeals panel affirmed. 758 F.2d 441 (1985). The Court of Appeals went en banc, held that the State had violated respondent's rights under the Double Jeopardy Clause, and directed the issuance of a writ of habeas corpus. . . .

. . . Assuming . . . that under Arizona law second-degree murder is a lesser included offense of first-degree murder, the Double Jeopardy Clause, absent special circumstances, would have precluded prosecution of respondent for the greater charge on which he now stands convicted. Brown v. Ohio, 432 U.S. 161, 168 (1977). The State submits, however, that respondent's breach of the plea arrangement to which the parties had agreed removed the double jeopardy bar to prosecution of respondent on the first-degree murder charge. We agree with the State.

Under the terms of the plea agreement, both parties bargained for and received substantial benefits. The State obtained respondent's guilty plea and his promise to testify against "any and all parties involved in the murder of Don Bolles" and in certain specified other crimes. 789 F.2d, at 731. Respondent, a direct participant in a premeditated and brutal murder, received a specified prison sentence accompanied with a guarantee that he would serve actual incarceration time of 20 years and 2 months. He further obtained the State's promise that he would not be prosecuted for his involvement in certain other crimes.

The agreement specifies in two separate paragraphs the consequences that would flow from respondent's breach of his promises. Paragraph 5 provides that if respondent refused to testify, "this entire agreement is null and void and the original charge will be *automatically* reinstated." Ibid. (emphasis added). Similarly, Paragraph 15 of the agreement states that "in the event this agreement becomes null and void, then the parties shall be returned to the positions they were in before this agreement." Id., at 732. Respondent unquestionably understood the meaning of these provisions. At the plea hearing, the trial judge read the plea agreement to respondent, line by line, and pointedly asked respondent whether he understood the provisions in Paragraphs 5 and 15. Respondent replied "Yes, sir," to each question. App. 23-24, 28-29. On this score, we do not find it significant, as did the Court

---

8 regarding respondent's obligation to testify after sentencing, the colloquy at the sentencing hearing evinced a "clear understanding" that respondent would be so obligated. Ibid. Respondent argued in the Court of Appeals — and renews the argument here — that the "further testimony" mentioned by the prosecutor at the sentencing hearing referred to testimony in a wholly separate prosecution that had yet to be tried. We will not second-guess the Arizona Supreme Court's construction of the language of the plea agreement. While we assess independently the plea agreement's effect on respondent's double jeopardy rights, the construction of the plea agreement and the concomitant obligations flowing therefrom are, within broad bounds of reasonableness, matters of state law, and we will not disturb the Arizona Supreme Court's reasonable disposition of those issues. . . .

of Appeals, that "double jeopardy" was not specifically waived by name in the plea agreement. . . . The terms of the agreement could not be clearer: in the event of respondent's breach occasioned by a refusal to testify, the parties would be returned to the status quo ante, in which case respondent would have no double jeopardy defense to waive. And, an agreement specifying that charges may be reinstated given certain circumstances is, at least under the provisions of this plea agreement, precisely equivalent to an agreement waiving a double jeopardy defense. . . .

We are also unimpressed by the [claim] that there was a good-faith dispute about whether respondent was bound to testify a second time and that until the extent of his obligation was decided, there could be no knowing and intelligent waiver of his double jeopardy defense. But respondent knew that if he breached the agreement he could be retried, and it is incredible to believe that he did not anticipate that the extent of his obligation would be decided by a court. Here he sought a construction of the agreement in the Arizona Supreme Court, and that court found that he had failed to live up to his promise. The result was that respondent was returned to the position he occupied prior to execution of the plea bargain: He stood charged with first-degree murder. Trial on that charge did not violate the Double Jeopardy Clause. United States v. Scott, 437 U.S. 82 (1978), supports this conclusion.

At the close of all the evidence in *Scott*, the trial judge granted defendant's motion to dismiss two counts of the indictment against him on the basis of pre-indictment delay. This Court held that the Double Jeopardy Clause did not bar the Government from appealing the trial judge's decision, because "in a case such as this the defendant, by deliberately choosing to seek termination of the proceedings against him on a basis unrelated to factual guilt or innocence of the offense of which he was accused, suffers no injury cognizable under the Double Jeopardy Clause. . . ." Id., at 98-99. . . . The respondent in this case had a similar choice. He could submit to the State's request that he testify at the retrial, and in so doing risk that he would be providing testimony that pursuant to the agreement he had no obligation to provide, or he could stand on his interpretation of the agreement, knowing that if he were wrong, his breach of the agreement would restore the parties to their original positions and he could be prosecuted for first-degree murder. Respondent chose the latter course, and the Double Jeopardy Clause does not relieve him from the consequences of that choice.

Respondent cannot escape the Arizona Supreme Court's interpretation of his obligations under the agreement. The State did not force the breach; respondent chose, perhaps for strategic reasons or as a gamble, to advance an interpretation of the agreement that proved erroneous. And, there is no indication that respondent did not fully understand the potential seriousness of the position he adopted. In the April 3 letter, respondent's counsel advised the prosecutor that respondent "is fully aware of the fact that your office may feel that he has not completed his obligations under the plea agreement . . . and, further, that your office may attempt to withdraw the plea agreement from him, [and] that he may be prosecuted for the killing of Donald Bolles on a first degree murder charge." 789 F.2d, at 733. This statement of respondent's awareness of the operative terms of the plea agreement only underscores that which respondent's plea hearing made evident: Respondent clearly appreciated and understood the consequences were he found to be in breach of the agreement.

Finally, it is of no moment that following the Arizona Supreme Court's decision respondent offered to comply with the terms of the agreement. At this point, respondent's second-degree murder conviction had already been ordered vacated and the original charge reinstated. The parties did not agree that respondent would be relieved from the consequences of his refusal to testify if he were able to advance a colorable argument that a testimonial obligation was not owing. The parties could have struck a different bargain, but permitting the State to enforce the agreement the parties actually made does not violate the Double Jeopardy Clause.

The judgment of the Court of Appeals is reversed.

JUSTICE BRENNAN, with whom JUSTICE MARSHALL, JUSTICE BLACKMUN, and JUSTICE STEVENS join, dissenting.

The critical question in this case is whether Adamson ever breached his plea agreement. Only by demonstrating that such a breach occurred can it plausibly be argued that Adamson waived his rights under the Double Jeopardy Clause. By simply assuming that such a breach occurred, the Court ignores the only important issue in this case. . . .

Without disturbing the conclusions of the Arizona Supreme Court as to the proper construction of the plea agreement, one may make two observations central to the resolution of this case. First, the agreement does not contain an explicit waiver of all double jeopardy protection. Instead, the Arizona Supreme Court found in the language of paras. 5 and 15 of the agreement only an implicit waiver of double jeopardy protection which was conditional on an act by Adamson that breached the agreement, such as refusing to testify as it required. Therefore, any finding that Adamson lost his protection against double jeopardy must be predicated on a finding that Adamson breached his agreement.

Second, Adamson's interpretation of the agreement — that he was not required to testify at the retrials of Max Dunlap and James Robison — was reasonable. Nothing in the plea agreement explicitly stated that Adamson was required to provide testimony should retrials prove necessary. Moreover, the agreement specifically referred in two separate paragraphs to events that would occur only after the conclusion of all testimony that Adamson would be required to give. Paragraph 8 stated that Adamson "will be sentenced at the conclusion of his testimony in all of the cases referred to in this agreement and Exhibits A and B, which accompany it." 789 F.2d 722, 732 (CA9 1986). At the time that the State demanded that Adamson testify in the retrials, he had been sentenced. Paragraph 18 stated that "the defendant is to remain in the custody of the Pima County Sheriff from the date of the entry of his plea until the conclusion of his testimony in all of the cases in which the defendant agrees to testify as a result of this agreement." Ibid. At the time the State demanded that Adamson testify in the retrials, Adamson had been transferred from the custody of the Pima County Sheriff. Adamson therefore could reasonably conclude that he had provided all the testimony required by the agreement, and that, as he communicated to the State by letter of April 3, 1980, the testimony demanded by the State went beyond his duties under the agreement. The Arizona Supreme Court rejected Adamson's construction. But even deferring to the state court's view that Adamson's interpretation was erroneous, one must also agree with the en banc Court of Appeals that Adamson's interpretation of the agreement was "reasonabl[e]," and was supported by the plain language of the agreement, "logic, and common sense." Id., at 729.

In sum, Adamson could lose his protection against double jeopardy only by breaching his agreement, and Adamson's interpretation of his responsibilities under the agreement, though erroneous, was reasonable. The next step in the analysis is to determine whether Adamson ever breached his agreement.

This Court has yet to address in any comprehensive way the rules of construction appropriate for disputes involving plea agreements. Nevertheless, it seems clear that the law of commercial contract may in some cases prove useful as an analogy or point of departure in construing a plea agreement, or in framing the terms of the debate. It is also clear, however, that commercial contract law can do no more than this, because plea agreements are constitutional contracts. The values that underlie commercial contract law, and that govern the relations between economic actors, are not coextensive with those that underlie the Due Process Clause, and that govern relations between criminal defendants and the State. Unlike some commercial contracts, plea agreements must be construed in light of the rights and obligations created by the Constitution.

The State argues and the Arizona Supreme Court seems to imply that a breach occurred when Adamson sent his letter of April 3, 1980, to the prosecutor in response to the State's demand for his testimony at the retrials of Dunlap and Robison. In this letter, Adamson stated that, under his interpretation of the agreement, he was no longer obligated to testify, and demanded additional consideration for any additional testimony.

Neither the State, the state courts, nor this Court has attempted to explain why this letter constituted a breach of the agreement. Of course, it could not plausibly be argued that merely sending such a letter constituted a breach by nonperformance, for nothing in the plea agreement states that Adamson shall not disagree with the State's interpretation of the plea agreement, or that Adamson shall not send the State a letter to that effect. But one might argue that, in the language of commercial contract law, the letter constituted a breach by anticipatory repudiation. Such a breach occurs when one party unequivocally informs the other that it no longer intends to honor their contract. "Where the contract is renounced before performance is due, and the renunciation goes to the whole contract, is absolute and unequivocal, the injured party may treat the breach as complete and bring his action at once." Roehm v. Horst, 178 U.S. 1, 7 (1900).[7] The reason for the rule is plain: "announcing [one's] purpose to default" destroys the assurance of future performance that is central to a commercial contract.[8]

In the conventional case of anticipatory repudiation, therefore, the announcement of an intention to default on the contract constitutes a breach.[9] In his letter of April 3, however, Adamson did not announce such an intention. To the contrary, Adamson invoked the integrity of that agreement as a defense to what he perceived to be an unwarranted demand by the prosecutor that he testify at the retrials of

7. See Restatement (Second) of Contracts §250 (1981); Uniform Commercial Code §2-610, 1A U. L. A. 321 (1976 and Supp. 1987); J. White & R. Summers, Uniform Commercial Code 212-214 (1980); 4 A. Corbin, Contracts §973 (1951); 2 S. Williston, Contracts §§1322, 1323 (3d ed. 1968).

8. Equitable Trust Co. v. Western Pacific R. Co., 244 F. 485, 502 (SDNY 1917) (L. Hand, J.), *aff'd*, 250 F. 327 (CA2 1918).

9. The classic case is Hochster v. De la Tour, 2 El. & Bl. 678, 118 Eng. Rep. 922 (Q.B. 1853), from which the doctrine of breach by anticipatory repudiation evolved. In that case, De la Tour first contracted to hire Hochster, then prior to the starting date of employment sent Hochster a letter stating that his services would not be needed. The court held that the letter constituted a breach of the contract, and that Hochster did not need to wait until after the starting date to bring suit. In Roehm v. Horst, this Court discussed *Hochster* at length, and concluded that it provided "a reasonable and proper rule to be applied in this case and in many others." 178 U.S., at 20. Commentators continue to draw on *Hochster* to illustrate the principle. E.g., C. Fried, Contract as Promise 128-130, and n. 25 (1981).

Dunlap and Robison. And in insisting that he had no obligation to perform as the State demanded, Adamson advanced an objectively reasonable interpretation of his contract. . . .

. . . Even if one assumes, arguendo, that Adamson breached his plea agreement by offering an erroneous interpretation of that agreement, it still does not follow that the State was entitled to retry Adamson on charges of first-degree murder. As the Court acknowledges, immediately following the decision of the Arizona Supreme Court adopting the State's construction of the plea agreement, Adamson sent a letter to the State stating that he was ready and willing to testify. At this point, there was no obstacle to proceeding with the retrials of Dunlap and Robison; each case had been dismissed without prejudice to refiling, and only about one month's delay had resulted from the dispute over the scope of the plea agreement. Thus, what the State sought from Adamson — testimony in the Dunlap and Robison trials — was available to it.

The State decided instead to abandon the prosecution of Dunlap and Robison, and to capitalize on what it regarded as Adamson's breach by seeking the death penalty against him. . . . [E]ven in the world of commercial contracts it has long been settled that the party injured by a breach must nevertheless take all reasonable steps to minimize the consequent damage. . . .

Here it is macabre understatement to observe that the State needlessly exacerbated the liability of its contractual partner. The State suffered a 1-month delay in beginning the retrial of Dunlap and Robison, and incurred litigation costs. For these "losses," the State chose to make Adamson pay, not with a longer sentence, but with his life. A comparable result in commercial law, if one could be imagined, would not be enforced. The fundamental unfairness in the State's course of conduct here is even less acceptable under the Constitution. . . .

NOTES AND QUESTIONS

1. *Adamson*'s subsequent history is complicated but interesting. On remand, the Ninth Circuit decided that Adamson's death sentence was unconstitutionally arbitrary and hence a violation of due process; in the court's words, "Adamson was sentenced to death because he violated a contract." Adamson v. Ricketts, 865 F.2d 1011, 1022 (9th Cir. 1988) (en banc). The Ninth Circuit also decided that Arizona's death penalty statute, under which Adamson was sentenced, (1) was unconstitutionally vague and (2) gave the sentencing judge authority that, under the Sixth Amendment, belonged to the jury. Id., at 1023-1038. Not surprisingly, the state again sought Supreme Court review.

In the meantime, the Supreme Court had granted certiorari in another case raising similar challenges to Arizona's death penalty statute. See Walton v. Arizona, 497 U.S. 639 (1990). As it usually does in such circumstances, the Court "held" the state's cert petition in Adamson's case — meaning that the Court simply left the petition undecided — until after it issued its decision in *Walton*. And in *Walton*, the Court upheld Arizona's death penalty statute and specifically rejected the arguments on which Adamson had prevailed in the Ninth Circuit. Ordinarily, the Court would have granted the state's petition in *Adamson*, vacated the Ninth Circuit's decision, and remanded for reconsideration in light of *Walton*. Three justices — Chief Justice Rehnquist and Justices White and Scalia — voted to do just that. But the other two justices in the *Walton* majority — Justices O'Connor and Kennedy — recused themselves (without explanation, per standard practice) in *Adamson*, and the *Walton* dissenters — Justices Brennan, Marshall, Blackmun, and Stevens (the same four who dissented in Ricketts v. Adamson) — voted to deny certiorari and let the Ninth Circuit's decision stand. Lewis v. Adamson, 497 U.S. 1031 (1990). So by a 4-3 vote, Adamson prevailed; his death penalty was overturned, even though all his arguments had just been rejected by a 5-4 decision of the Supreme Court. Technically, Arizona's death penalty statute was unconstitutional on its face as to Adamson (That sounds like a contradiction in terms, does it not?), but not as to anyone else.

The decision in *Walton* was later overruled, and the Arizona death penalty statute held unconstitutional (under the Sixth Amendment) as to all defendants, in Ring v. Arizona, 536 U.S. 584 (2002).

2. As the Court notes, the dispute in Ricketts v. Adamson arose when the convictions of Adamson's coconspirators, Dunlap and Robison, were reversed. At that point, Adamson refused to testify against them at their retrial, the state declared the plea agreement breached, and Adamson was tried for and convicted of capital murder.

If the state's reaction to Adamson's behavior seems surprisingly extreme, as Justice Brennan suggests and as the Ninth Circuit clearly believed, consider why Dunlap's and Robison's convictions were reversed. In Dunlap's and Robison's trials, Adamson was the key government witness; on direct examination, he testified quite extensively to their involvement in the Don Bolles murder. On cross-examination, defense counsel sought to explore a number of points from Adamson's direct testimony, but Adamson refused to answer, invoking his privilege against self-incrimination. For example, in his direct testimony, Adamson had testified at one point about $8,000 he had been given in connection with the killing; his testimony was that $6,000 had been given him by Dunlap. When asked on cross-examination where the other $2,000 came from, Adamson took the Fifth. The Arizona Supreme Court noted:

> Had defense counsel been able to delve into the sources of the $2,000, he might have uncovered ties with individuals who the defense claimed were responsible for the murder. For example, Dunlap admitted delivering the $6,000 to Adamson, but claimed he did so as a favor to Phoenix attorney Neal Roberts. If Adamson had testified that Roberts had given him the $2,000, Dunlap's testimony would have been bolstered.

State v. Dunlap, 608 P.2d 41, 44 (Ariz. 1980). Because of this and other invocations of the privilege by Adamson — again, the state's key witness — Dunlap and Robison claimed that they were denied their Sixth Amendment right to confront the witnesses against them. The Arizona Supreme Court agreed. See id.; State v. Robison, 608 P.2d 44 (Ariz. 1980).

Thus, Adamson's testimony, or lack thereof, was actually the cause of the reversals, which in turn were the cause of the retrials at which the state wanted Adamson to testify (no doubt with immunity the second time). Does that change your view of the legal issues in the case? If so, how?

3. What is the proper relationship between federal constitutional law and the law of contract in a case like *Ricketts*? The Court appears to hold that Arizona can permissibly define Adamson's conduct as breach and can permissibly allow the

government to rescind the plea agreement as a remedy. But Arizona is not *required* to define either breach or remedies in this way. What are the limits federal law places on states' definition of the parties' obligations under plea agreements?

4. Put federalism issues to one side for the moment. Why is specific performance not an adequate remedy for Adamson's breach (assuming there was a breach)? Adamson could be directed to testify again, the government could immunize him for the relevant crimes, and Dunlap and Robison could presumably be convicted again, this time in a way that would be immune to appellate reversal. Doesn't that give the government the benefit of its bargain? Or is there something else the government has lost in this transaction?

5. *Ricketts* is clearly a case about contract interpretation. Adamson and the prosecution differed about the meaning of the contract; in the end, the Court holds that Adamson pursued his own interpretation at his peril, since "it is incredible to believe that he did not anticipate that the extent of his obligation would be decided by a court." What *should* Adamson have done, instead of essentially refusing to follow the prosecution's interpretation (a decision that was later construed, much to Adamson's dismay, as an anticipatory breach)? How could Adamson have signaled his disagreement with the prosecution's interpretation, and obtained a ruling on the issue, without risking a breach? Should defendants specifically reserve the right to contest the interpretation of a plea agreement? Would prosecutors likely agree to such terms?

6. Contract interpretation questions arise frequently in plea bargaining cases. The nature of the government's promise in Mabry v. Johnson was clear, although the Court ultimately held that the promise was unenforceable. But that is not always the case. Should the government be permitted to say anything at sentencing if the plea agreement states that the prosecutor will "stand silent"? What if the defendant or defense counsel makes statements that the prosecutor believes are factually or legally incorrect? What can the prosecutor say if the agreement promises not silence but only that the government "will make no recommendation as to sentence"? Can the prosecutor offer every negative piece of evidence and argument at her disposal as long as she stops short of recommending a sentence? For discussions of lower court cases raising these and related issues, see 5 Wayne R. LaFave, Jerold H. Israel, & Nancy J. King, Criminal Procedure §21.2(d) (2d ed. 1999).

In this connection, consider United States v. Benchimol, 471 U.S. 453 (1985). In that case, the government agreed to recommend probation if the defendant pled guilty to one count of mail fraud and made restitution to his victims. The defendant duly pled guilty, and at sentencing, defense counsel stated that the government endorsed a sentence of probation with restitution. The prosecutor said only, "That is an accurate representation." The court ignored this less-than-enthusiastic recommendation and sentenced the defendant to 6 years, of which he served 18 months before being paroled. The defendant claimed breach, but the Court was unimpressed:

> It may well be that the Government in a particular case might commit itself to "enthusiastically" make a particular recommendation to the court, and it may be that the Government in a particular case might agree to explain to the court the reasons for the Government's making a particular recommendation. But respondent does not contend . . . that the Government had in fact undertaken to do either of these things here.

Id., at 455.

In all these settings, the defendant has a plausible claim that ambiguities in the plea agreement ought to be resolved in the defendant's favor, since the plea agreement is usually drafted by the government; the idea is the same as the familiar principle that ambiguities in insurance contracts are to be resolved in favor of the insured. Should that principle apply to plea bargains?

7. One of the most common and important issues in the interpretation of plea agreements is the question of the scope of immunity from prosecution the defendant enjoys by virtue of having pled guilty to the specified offenses. Many, perhaps most, plea bargains involve a guilty plea to some charges and the dismissal of others; presumably, the charges dismissed cannot be reinstated once the guilty plea is entered, at least not unless the plea agreement so specifies. How broadly does the immunity extend? Only to crimes listed in the agreement? To anything related to the criminal transaction that is the subject of the guilty plea? To any other crimes?

For a thorough and interesting discussion of this issue, see Daniel C. Richman, Bargaining About Future Jeopardy, 49 Vand. L. Rev. 1181 (1996). Richman summarizes the cases as follows:

> Some courts impose on prosecutors a reasonably narrow good faith obligation that bars sandbagging. These courts hold that the government may not intentionally nullify the explicit protections of a plea agreement by bringing a charge that it could easily have brought before and that is related to the offenses the agreement did address.[114] Other courts go beyond this focus on intent, extending default immunity to all charges that stem from the transactions referred to in the indictment and that the prosecution could have anticipated making when it entered into the agreement. Where a defendant pleads guilty pursuant to an agreement that makes no reference to possible murder charges and the victim later dies, for example, these courts bar the successive murder prosecution that could not even have been brought at the time of the defendant's plea.[115] At least one state court has gone further, presumptively barring any future charges that arise out of the transactions referenced in the charges to which the defendant pled.[116] Whether or not a prosecutor should have been able to anticipate making the successive charges does not appear to be relevant in this analysis.

114. See United States v. Burns, 990 F.2d 1426, 1435 (4th Cir. 1993) (concluding that the government would have violated Due Process Clause if, in the first case, it had deliberately delayed charging defendant with offense that it later brought in the second case, "in order to reap the benefits of his bargained guilty plea while denying him the opportunity to seek a concurrent sentence for related offenses"). See also United States v. Alessi, 544 F.2d 1139, 1154 (2d Cir. 1976) (having first determined that defendant's agreement with the U.S. Attorney in the Eastern District of New York did not bar the subsequent Southern District of New York prosecution, the court noted: "We would, of course, have a different case if there were evidence to show that the Eastern District was attempting to evade its own obligations by transferring a prosecution across the East River; but there is none"); United States v. Laskow, 688 F. Supp. 851, 855 (E.D.N.Y.) (reaching same conclusion), aff'd, 867 F.2d 1425 (2d Cir. 1988). . . .

115. See State v. Carpenter, 68 Ohio St. 3d 59, 623 N.E.2d 66, 68 (1993) (barring prosecution on greater charges following victim's death noting that all parties anticipated risk of this contingency); State v. Nelson, 23 Conn. App. 215, 579 A.2d 1104, 1106-1107 (1990) (same). But see People v. Latham, 609 N.Y.S.2d 141, 631 N.E.2d 83, 86 (1994) (finding no immunity for murder charges in absence of evidence that "both the defendant and the prosecution intended the plea to close the matter forever"). Long-established double jeopardy doctrine holds that even where [double jeopardy analysis] would otherwise bar the bringing of homicide charges after a defendant's conviction of a lesser included offense, the second prosecution can go forward if the victim was still alive when the defendant was first convicted. . . .

116. State v. Lordan, 116 N.H. 479, 363 A.2d 201, 203 (1976) ("Where the defendant commits several offenses in a single transaction and the prosecutor has knowledge of and jurisdiction over all these offenses and the defendant disposes of all charges then pending by a guilty plea to one or more of the charges, the prosecutor may not prefer additional charges arising from the same transaction unless

Id., at 1211-1212. Which of these various approaches makes the most sense? Richman argues that, unlike other settings in which ambiguities in plea agreements must be resolved, when it comes to liability for uncharged crimes, the default rule should probably favor the government:

> An approach that declines to extend protection to defendants who could have paid for it, but did not, has a particular allure in the context of uncharged crimes. Consider, by way of contrast, a dispute over a common provision in plea agreements: the government's explicit promise to remain silent at sentencing. In the absence of any explicit provision to the contrary, should the government also be required to remain silent during post-conviction proceedings in which the defendant moves for a reduction of sentence? In this context, a default rule obliging the government to remain silent would simply compensate for a lapse in the imagination of defense counsel. The defendant would have risked nothing in asking for an explicit commitment to such silence, and the government would likely not even have "charged" the defendant for such a provision, since the essence of the deal is to leave the sentence in the judge's hands. A very different story, however, might lie behind an agreement's failure to address explicitly whether a charge that is not jeopardy-barred can be brought in the future. Because this "lapse" might well reflect a defendant's decision to minimize his sentence by concealing the full extent of his criminal liability, expansive default immunity rules may be harder to justify.

Id., at 1215. Do you agree?

c.   *Remedies for Breach of Contract*

SANTOBELLO v. NEW YORK

Certiorari to the Appellate Division of the Supreme Court of New York
404 U.S. 257 (1971)

CHIEF JUSTICE BURGER delivered the opinion of the Court.

We granted certiorari in this case to determine whether the State's failure to keep a commitment concerning the sentence recommendation on a guilty plea required a new trial.

The facts are not in dispute. The State of New York indicted petitioner in 1969 on two felony counts, Promoting Gambling in the First Degree, and Possession of Gambling Records in the First Degree, N.Y. Penal Law §§225.10, 225.20. Petitioner first entered a plea of not guilty to both counts. After negotiations, the Assistant District Attorney in charge of the case agreed to permit petitioner to plead guilty to a lesser-included offense, Possession of Gambling Records in the Second Degree, N.Y.

---

either he has given notice on the record at the time of the plea of the possibility that he may prefer further charges or the defendant otherwise knows or ought reasonably to expect that further charges may be brought."). I am assuming that the *Lordan* court did not believe that a defendant's knowledge of his own conduct gave sufficient notice of the risk of future prosecution; a contrary assumption would render its rule virtually meaningless. See also United States v. Bouthot, 878 F.2d 1506, 1512 & n. 5 (1st Cir. 1989) (noting that the state prosecutor had no duty to tell defendant that the federal prosecutor was planning to bring charges based on the same transaction, but reserving judgment as to whether such a duty would arise had both prosecu[tions] been instituted under the same sovereign).

Penal Law §225.15, conviction of which would carry a maximum prison sentence of one year. The prosecutor agreed to make no recommendation as to the sentence.

On June 16, 1969, petitioner accordingly withdrew his plea of not guilty and entered a plea of guilty to the lesser charge. Petitioner represented to the sentencing judge that the plea was voluntary and that the facts of the case, as described by the Assistant District Attorney, were true. The court accepted the plea and set a date for sentencing. A series of delays followed, owing primarily to the absence of a presentence report, so that by September 23, 1969, petitioner had still not been sentenced. By that date petitioner acquired new defense counsel.

Petitioner's new counsel moved immediately to withdraw the guilty plea. In an accompanying affidavit, petitioner alleged that he did not know at the time of his plea that crucial evidence against him had been obtained as a result of an illegal search. The accuracy of this affidavit is subject to challenge since petitioner had filed and withdrawn a motion to suppress, before pleading guilty. In addition to his motion to withdraw his guilty plea, petitioner renewed the motion to suppress and filed a motion to inspect the grand jury minutes.

These three motions in turn caused further delay until November 26, 1969, when the court denied all three and set January 9, 1970, as the date for sentencing. On January 9 petitioner appeared before a different judge, the judge who had presided over the case to this juncture having retired. Petitioner renewed his motions, and the court again rejected them. The court then turned to consideration of the sentence.

At this appearance, another prosecutor had replaced the prosecutor who had negotiated the plea. The new prosecutor recommended the maximum one-year sentence. In making this recommendation, he cited petitioner's criminal record and alleged links with organized crime. Defense counsel immediately objected on the ground that the State had promised petitioner before the plea was entered that there would be no sentence recommendation by the prosecution. He sought to adjourn the sentence hearing in order to have time to prepare proof of the first prosecutor's promise. The second prosecutor, apparently ignorant of his colleague's commitment, argued that there was nothing in the record to support petitioner's claim of a promise, but the State, in subsequent proceedings, has not contested that such a promise was made.

The sentencing judge ended discussion with the following statement, quoting extensively from the presentence report:

> Mr. Aronstein [Defense Counsel], I am not at all influenced by what the District Attorney says, so that there is no need to adjourn the sentence, and there is no need to have any testimony. It doesn't make a particle of difference what the District Attorney says he will do, or what he doesn't do.
>
> I have here, Mr. Aronstein, a probation report. I have here a history of a long, long serious criminal record. I have here a picture of the life history of this man. . . .
>
> "He is unamenable to supervision in the community. He is a professional criminal." This is in quotes. "And a recidivist. Institutionalization" — that means, in plain language, just putting him away — "is the only means of halting his anti-social activities," and protecting you, your family, me, my family, protecting society. "Institutionalization." Plain language, put him behind bars.
>
> Under the plea, I can only send him to the New York City Correctional Institution for men for one year, which I am hereby doing.

The judge then imposed the maximum sentence of one year.

Petitioner sought and obtained a certificate of reasonable doubt and was admitted to bail pending an appeal. The Supreme Court of the State of New York, Appellate Division, First Department, unanimously affirmed petitioner's conviction, and petitioner was denied leave to appeal to the New York Court of Appeals. Petitioner then sought certiorari in this Court. . . .

Disposition of charges after plea discussions is not only an essential part of the process but a highly desirable part for many reasons. It leads to prompt and largely final disposition of most criminal cases; it avoids much of the corrosive impact of enforced idleness during pretrial confinement for those who are denied release pending trial; it protects the public from those accused persons who are prone to continue criminal conduct even while on pretrial release; and, by shortening the time between charge and disposition, it enhances whatever may be the rehabilitative prospects of the guilty when they are ultimately imprisoned. See Brady v. United States, 397 U.S. 742, 751-752 (1970).

However, all of these considerations presuppose fairness in securing agreement between an accused and a prosecutor. It is now clear, for example, that the accused pleading guilty must be counseled, absent a waiver. Moore v. Michigan, 355 U.S. 155 (1957). Fed. Rule Crim. Proc. 11, governing pleas in federal courts, now makes clear that the sentencing judge must develop, on the record, the factual basis for the plea, as, for example, by having the accused describe the conduct that gave rise to the charge. The plea must, of course, be voluntary and knowing and if it was induced by promises, the essence of those promises must in some way be made known. There is, of course, no absolute right to have a guilty plea accepted. Lynch v. Overholser, 369 U.S. 705, 719 (1962); Fed. Rule Crim. Proc. 11. A court may reject a plea in exercise of sound judicial discretion.

This phase of the process of criminal justice, and the adjudicative element inherent in accepting a plea of guilty, must be attended by safeguards to insure the defendant what is reasonably due in the circumstances. Those circumstances will vary, but a constant factor is that when a plea rests in any significant degree on a promise or agreement of the prosecutor, so that it can be said to be part of the inducement or consideration, such promise must be fulfilled.

On this record, petitioner "bargained" and negotiated for a particular plea in order to secure dismissal of more serious charges, but also on condition that no sentence recommendation would be made by the prosecutor. It is now conceded that the promise to abstain from a recommendation was made, and at this stage the prosecution is not in a good position to argue that its inadvertent breach of agreement is immaterial. The staff lawyers in a prosecutor's office have the burden of "letting the left hand know what the right hand is doing" or has done. That the breach of agreement was inadvertent does not lessen its impact.

We need not reach the question whether the sentencing judge would or would not have been influenced had he known all the details of the negotiations for the plea. He stated that the prosecutor's recommendation did not influence him and we have no reason to doubt that. Nevertheless, we conclude that the interests of justice and appropriate recognition of the duties of the prosecution in relation to promises made in the negotiation of pleas of guilty will be best served by remanding the case to the state courts for further consideration. The ultimate relief to which petitioner is entitled we leave to the discretion of the state court, which is in a better position to decide whether the circumstances of this case require only that there be specific performance of the agreement on the plea, in which case petitioner should be resentenced by a different judge, or whether, in the view of the state court, the circumstances require granting the relief sought by petitioner, i.e., the opportunity to withdraw his plea of guilty. We emphasize that this is in no sense to question the fairness of the sentencing judge; the fault here rests on the prosecutor, not on the sentencing judge.

The judgment is vacated and the case is remanded for reconsideration not inconsistent with this opinion.

JUSTICE DOUGLAS, concurring.

. . . I join the opinion of the Court and favor a constitutional rule for this as well as for other pending or oncoming [plea bargaining] cases. Where the "plea bargain" is not kept by the prosecutor, the sentence must be vacated and the state court will decide in light of the circumstances of each case whether due process requires (a) that there be specific performance of the plea bargain or (b) that the defendant be given the option to go to trial on the original charges. One alternative may do justice in one case, and the other in a different case. In choosing a remedy, however, a court ought to accord a defendant's preference considerable, if not controlling, weight inasmuch as the fundamental rights flouted by a prosecutor's breach of a plea bargain are those of the defendant, not of the State.

JUSTICE MARSHALL, with whom JUSTICE BRENNAN and JUSTICE STEWART join, concurring in part and dissenting in part.

I agree with much of the majority's opinion, but conclude that petitioner must be permitted to withdraw his guilty plea. This is the relief petitioner requested, and, on the facts set out by the majority, it is a form of relief to which he is entitled.

There is no need to belabor the fact that the Constitution guarantees to all criminal defendants the right to a trial by judge or jury, or, put another way, the "right not to plead guilty," United States v. Jackson, 390 U.S. 570, 581 (1968). This and other federal rights may be waived through a guilty plea, but such waivers are not lightly presumed and, in fact, are viewed with the "utmost solicitude." Boykin v. Alabama, 395 U.S. 238, 243 (1969). Given this, I believe that where the defendant presents a reason for vacating his plea and the government has not relied on the plea to its disadvantage, the plea may be vacated and the right to trial regained, at least where the motion to vacate is made prior to sentence and judgment. In other words, in such circumstances I would not deem the earlier plea to have irrevocably waived the defendant's federal constitutional right to a trial.

Here, petitioner never claimed any automatic right to withdraw a guilty plea before sentencing. Rather, he tendered a specific reason why, in his case, the plea should be vacated. His reason was that the prosecutor had broken a promise made in return for the agreement to plead guilty. When a prosecutor breaks the bargain, he undercuts the basis for the waiver of constitutional rights implicit in the plea. This, it seems to me, provides the defendant ample justification for rescinding the plea. Where a promise is "unfulfilled," Brady v. United States, 397 U.S. 742, 755 (1970), specifically denies that the plea "must stand." Of course, where the prosecutor has broken the plea agreement, it may be appropriate to permit the defendant to enforce the plea bargain. But that is not the remedy sought here. Rather, it seems to me that a breach of the plea bargain provides ample reason to permit the plea to be vacated. . . .

NOTES AND QUESTIONS

1. In a sense, *Santobello* is a companion case to Brady v. United States. *Brady* held that promising a defendant some charging or sentencing concession did not automatically render a guilty plea involuntary. *Santobello* holds that if the government promises such concessions, it has to keep its promises.

2. What is the legal source of *Santobello*'s holding? If the bargain between Santobello and the prosecutor is governed by the law of contract, the Supreme Court would appear to have no authority to determine either the presence of a breach or the range of appropriate remedies. Those matters would be determined by New York law. There is no federal rule or statute that governs such matters — Rule 11, recall, applies only to federal guilty pleas. So *Santobello* must be a constitutional decision, presumably a piece of law of due process. For an argument along these lines, see Peter Westen & David Westin, A Constitutional Law of Remedies for Broken Plea Bargains, 66 Cal. L. Rev. 471 (1978). Is that the right approach to developing a law of plea bargaining? Is there any alternative if the voluntariness requirement is to have any meaning?

3. Why not give Santobello the right to choose his remedy — to choose between requiring the government to specifically perform the agreement and rescinding his guilty plea? If the goal of the remedy is to put Santobello in the position he would have been in but for the wrong, what remedy will best do that? Suppose the state of the evidence has changed in the meantime — some of the witnesses are no longer available, or physical evidence has been lost or mislaid. Will rescinding the plea fairly compensate for the breach? Will specific performance?

4. In a footnote in Mabry v. Johnson not reproduced above, the Court pointed out that *Santobello*'s remedial holding provided yet another reason to reject Johnson's claim that his constitutional rights were violated by the prosecutor's failure to carry out his end of the plea bargain:

> Indeed, even if respondent's plea were invalid, *Santobello* expressly declined to hold that the Constitution compels specific performance of a broken prosecutorial promise as the remedy for such a plea; the Court made it clear that permitting Santobello to replead was within the range of constitutionally appropriate remedies. See 404 U.S., at 262-263; see also id., at 268-269 (Marshall, J., concurring in part and dissenting in part). It follows that respondent's constitutional rights could not have been violated. Because he pleaded after the prosecution had breached its "promise" to him, he was in no worse position than Santobello would have been had he been permitted to replead.

Mabry v. Johnson, 467 U.S., at 510, n. 11.

C.   The Role of Defense Counsel

As noted previously, most defendants who enter guilty pleas based upon a plea bargain do not thereafter seek to challenge their resulting convictions. The primary reason is that most such defendants believe that the plea bargain they struck represents a good deal for them. An important secondary reason is that even the few defendants who regret their guilty plea and decide to try to get the plea overturned — either because of a spontaneous change of heart, or because of new information learned after imposition of sentence — generally make that decision too late to preserve their appellate remedies, which in turn generally bars them from obtaining habeas corpus relief as well.

We have already learned that most legal issues (such as the admissibility of evidence) that could have been raised on an appeal from a conviction at trial are waived by the entry of a guilty plea. See supra, page 1174. However, defendants can still appeal (or collaterally attack) their guilty pleas based on the grounds that (1) the plea was involuntary (including the claim that it was induced by an improper promise or threat); (2) the plea lacked a "factual basis" (but the very fact that they pled guilty will tend to undermine that claim); or (3) some other legal issue, unrelated to guilt and not requiring further factual development, survived the entry of the guilty plea under *Broce* and thus can still be litigated. Are there any other possible legal grounds on which a defendant might seek to challenge his guilty plea?

HILL v. LOCKHART

Certiorari to the United States Court of Appeals for the Eighth Circuit
474 U.S. 52 (1985)

JUSTICE REHNQUIST delivered the opinion of the Court.

Petitioner William Lloyd Hill pleaded guilty in the Arkansas trial court to charges of first-degree murder and theft of property. More than two years later he sought federal habeas relief on the ground that his court-appointed attorney had failed to advise him that, as a second offender, he was required to serve one-half of his sentence before becoming eligible for parole. The United States District Court for the Eastern District of Arkansas denied relief without a hearing, and the en banc Court of Appeals for the Eighth Circuit affirmed by an equally divided court. . . . We affirm the judgment of the Court of Appeals . . . because we conclude that petitioner failed to allege the kind of prejudice from the allegedly incompetent advice of counsel that would have entitled him to a hearing.

Under Arkansas law, the murder charge to which petitioner pleaded guilty carried a potential sentence of 5 to 50 years or life in prison, along with a fine of up to $15,000. Petitioner's court-appointed attorney negotiated a plea agreement pursuant to which the State, in return for petitioner's plea of guilty to both the murder and theft charges, agreed to recommend that the trial judge impose concurrent prison sentences of 35 years for the murder and 10 years for the theft. Petitioner signed a written "plea statement" indicating that he understood the charges against him and the consequences of pleading guilty, that his plea had not been induced "by any force, threat, or promise" apart from the plea agreement itself, that he realized that the trial judge was not bound by the plea agreement and retained the sole "power of sentence," and that he had discussed the plea agreement with his attorney and was satisfied with his attorney's advice. The last two lines of the "plea statement," just above petitioner's signature, read: "I am aware of everything in this document. I fully understand what my rights are, and I voluntarily plead guilty because I am guilty as charged."

Petitioner appeared before the trial judge at the plea hearing, recounted the events that gave rise to the charges against him, affirmed that he had signed and understood the written "plea statement," reiterated that no "threats or promises" had been made to him other than the plea agreement itself, and entered a plea of guilty to both charges. The trial judge accepted the guilty plea and sentenced petitioner in accordance with the State's recommendations. The trial judge also granted petitioner credit for the time he had already served in prison, and told petitioner that "[you] will be required to serve at least one-third of your time before you are eligible for parole."

More than two years later petitioner filed a federal habeas corpus petition alleging, inter alia, that his guilty plea was involuntary by reason of ineffective assistance of counsel because his attorney had misinformed him as to his parole eligibility date. According to petitioner, his attorney had told him that if he pleaded guilty he would become eligible for parole after serving one-third of his prison sentence. In fact, because petitioner previously had been convicted of a felony in Florida, he was classified under Arkansas law as a "second offender" and was required to serve one-half of his sentence before becoming eligible for parole. Ark. Stat. Ann. §43-2829B(3) (1977). Petitioner asked the United States District Court for the Eastern District of Arkansas to reduce his sentence to a term of years that would result in his becoming eligible for parole in conformance with his original expectations.

The District Court denied habeas relief without a hearing. The court noted that neither Arkansas nor federal law required that petitioner be informed of his parole eligibility date prior to pleading guilty, and concluded that, even if petitioner was misled by his attorney's advice, parole eligibility "is not such a consequence of [petitioner's] guilty plea that such misinformation renders his plea involuntary." The court also held that "even if an attorney's advice concerning such eligibility is not wholly accurate, such advice does not render that attorney's performance constitutionally inadequate."

A divided panel of the Court of Appeals for the Eighth Circuit affirmed, holding that parole eligibility is a collateral rather than a direct consequence of a guilty plea, of which a defendant need not be informed, and that the District Court did not err in declining to hold a hearing on petitioner's claims. . . .

The longstanding test for determining the validity of a guilty plea is "whether the plea represents a voluntary and intelligent choice among the alternative courses of action open to the defendant." North Carolina v. Alford, 400 U.S. 25, 31 (1970). Here petitioner does not contend that his plea was "involuntary" or "unintelligent" simply because the State through its officials failed to supply him with information about his parole eligibility date. We have never held that the United States Constitution requires the State to furnish a defendant with information about parole eligibility in order for the defendant's plea of guilty to be voluntary, and indeed such a constitutional requirement would be inconsistent with the current rules of procedure governing the entry of guilty pleas in the federal courts. See Fed. Rule Crim. Proc. 11[(b)]; Advisory Committee's Notes on 1974 Amendment to Fed. Rule Crim. Proc. 11 (federal courts generally are not required to inform defendant about parole eligibility before accepting guilty plea). Instead, petitioner relies entirely on the claim that his plea was "involuntary" as a result of ineffective assistance of counsel because his attorney supplied him with information about parole eligibility that was erroneous. Where, as here, a defendant is represented by counsel during the plea process and enters his plea upon the advice of counsel, the voluntariness of the plea depends on whether counsel's advice "was within the range of competence demanded of attorneys in criminal cases." McMann v. Richardson, 397 U.S. 759, 771 (1970). . . .

Our concern in McMann v. Richardson with the quality of counsel's performance in advising a defendant whether to plead guilty stemmed from the more general principle that all "defendants facing felony charges are entitled to the effective assistance of competent counsel." 397 U.S., at 771, and n. 14. Two Terms ago, in Strickland v. Washington, 466 U.S. 668 (1984), we adopted a two-part standard for evaluating claims of ineffective assistance of counsel. There, citing *McMann*, we reiterated that "[when] a convicted defendant complains of the ineffectiveness of counsel's assistance, the defendant must show that counsel's representation fell below an objective standard of reasonableness." 466 U.S., at 687-688. We also held, however, that "[the] defendant must show that there is a reasonable probability that, but for counsel's unprofessional errors, the result of the proceeding would have been different." Id., at 694. This additional "prejudice" requirement was based on our conclusion that "[an] error by counsel, even if professionally unreasonable, does not warrant setting aside the judgment of a criminal proceeding if the error had no effect on the judgment." Id., at 691.

Although our decision in Strickland v. Washington dealt with a claim of ineffective assistance of counsel in a capital sentencing proceeding, and was premised in part on the similarity between such a proceeding and the usual criminal trial, the same two-part standard seems to us applicable to ineffective-assistance claims arising out of the plea process. Certainly our justifications for imposing the "prejudice" requirement in Strickland v. Washington are also relevant in the context of guilty pleas: "The government is not responsible for, and hence not able to prevent, attorney errors that will result in reversal of a conviction or sentence. Attorney errors come in an infinite variety and are as likely to be utterly harmless in a particular case as they are to be prejudicial. They cannot be classified according to likelihood of causing prejudice. Nor can they be defined with sufficient precision to inform defense attorneys correctly just what conduct to avoid. Representation is an art, and an act or omission that is unprofessional in one case may be sound or even brilliant in another. Even if a defendant shows that particular errors of counsel were unreasonable, therefore, the defendant must show that they actually had an adverse effect on the defense." Id., at 693.

In addition, we believe that requiring a showing of "prejudice" from defendants who seek to challenge the validity of their guilty pleas on the ground of ineffective assistance of counsel will serve the fundamental interest in the finality of guilty pleas we identified in United States v. Timmreck, 441 U.S. 780 (1979):

> Every inroad on the concept of finality undermines confidence in the integrity of our procedures; and, by increasing the volume of judicial work, inevitably delays and impairs the orderly administration of justice. The impact is greatest when new grounds for setting aside guilty pleas are approved because the vast majority of criminal convictions result from such pleas. Moreover, the concern that unfair procedures may have resulted in the conviction of an innocent defendant is only rarely raised by a petition to set aside a guilty plea.

Id., at 784 (quoting United States v. Smith, 440 F.2d 521, 528-529 (CA7 1971) (Stevens, J., dissenting)).

We hold, therefore, that the two-part Strickland v. Washington test applies to challenges to guilty pleas based on ineffective assistance of counsel. In the context of guilty pleas, the first half of the Strickland v. Washington test is nothing more than a restatement of the standard of attorney competence already set forth in Tollett v. Henderson, supra, and McMann v. Richardson, supra. The second, or "prejudice," requirement, on the other hand, focuses on whether counsel's constitutionally ineffective performance affected the outcome of the plea process. In other words, in order to satisfy the "prejudice" requirement, the defendant must show that there is a reasonable probability that, but for counsel's errors, he would not have pleaded guilty and would have insisted on going to trial.

In many guilty plea cases, the "prejudice" inquiry will closely resemble the inquiry engaged in by courts reviewing ineffective-assistance challenges to convictions obtained through a trial. For example, where the alleged error of counsel is a failure to investigate or discover potentially exculpatory evidence, the determination whether the error "prejudiced" the defendant by causing him to plead guilty rather than go to trial will depend on the likelihood that discovery of the evidence would have led counsel to change his recommendation as to the plea. This assessment, in turn, will depend in large part on a prediction whether the evidence likely would have changed the outcome of a trial. Similarly, where the alleged error of counsel is a failure to advise the defendant of a potential affirmative defense to the crime charged, the resolution of the "prejudice" inquiry will depend largely on whether the affirmative defense likely would have succeeded at trial. . . . As we explained in Strickland v. Washington, supra, these predictions of the outcome at a possible trial, where necessary, should be made objectively, without regard for the "idiosyncrasies of the particular decisionmaker." Id., at 695.

In the present case the claimed error of counsel is erroneous advice as to eligibility for parole under the sentence agreed to in the plea bargain. We find it unnecessary to determine whether there may be circumstances under which erroneous advice by counsel as to parole eligibility may be deemed constitutionally ineffective assistance of counsel, because in the present case we conclude that petitioner's allegations are insufficient to satisfy the Strickland v. Washington requirement of "prejudice." Petitioner did not allege in his habeas petition that, had counsel correctly informed him about his parole eligibility date, he would have pleaded not guilty and insisted on going to trial. He alleged no special circumstances that might support the conclusion that he placed particular emphasis on his parole eligibility in deciding whether or not to plead guilty. Indeed, petitioner's mistaken belief that he would become eligible for parole after serving one-third of his sentence would seem to have affected not only his calculation of the time he likely would serve if sentenced pursuant to the proposed plea agreement, but also his calculation of the time he likely would serve if he went to trial and were convicted.

Because petitioner in this case failed to allege the kind of "prejudice" necessary to satisfy the second half of the Strickland v. Washington test, the District Court did not err in declining to hold a hearing on petitioner's ineffective assistance of counsel claim. The judgment of the Court of Appeals is therefore Affirmed.

[The opinion of Justice White, joined by Justice Stevens, concurring in the judgment, is omitted.]

NOTES ON INEFFECTIVE ASSISTANCE OF COUNSEL AND GUILTY PLEAS

1. *Strickland*'s prejudice prong asks whether there was a reasonable probability that, but for counsel's errors, the outcome would have been different. In *Hill*, the

inquiry is whether "there is a reasonable probability that, but for counsel's errors, [the defendant] would not have pleaded guilty and would have insisted on going to trial." Note the difference: *Strickland*'s test looks for outcome effects. *Hill*'s test is explicitly limited to a *particular kind* of outcome effect.

Why would this be so? In *Strickland*, the defendant was either going to receive a death sentence or not; in the more typical ineffective assistance case where the defendant challenges the way his attorney conducted his trial, the defendant would be either convicted or acquitted. In those circumstances, the "reasonable probability" standard, though perhaps hard to apply in practice, is straightforward in theory: It asks whether, had counsel performed competently, the defendant might well have won rather than lost.

Where a guilty plea is the result of bargaining (and perhaps sometimes even where it isn't), the picture is different: The defendant faces not victory or defeat, but a range of intermediate outcomes — perhaps a guilty plea to a serious felony, a guilty plea to a lesser felony, or a guilty plea to a misdemeanor, each with a range of different possible sentences or sentencing recommendations. *Hill* is itself a good example: A proper understanding of parole eligibility on Hill's part (and on the part of Hill's lawyer) might have led to a more favorable deal — still a guilty plea, but with a lighter sentence or to a lesser charge. Why isn't that "prejudice" for Sixth Amendment purposes?

The problem is that in a case involving a plea bargain, everything defense counsel does or fails to do has some potential effect on the precise contours of the deal. Thus, claims of Sixth Amendment "prejudice" would always be plausible, for there would so often be a reasonable probability that *some aspect* of the outcome, including the specified charge and the sentence, would have been different but for counsel's alleged errors. The result might be to put an enormous amount of pressure on the "performance" prong of ineffective assistance analysis in guilty plea cases. Ineffective assistance doctrine might become a general regulator of the wisdom of defense attorney behavior in all plea bargaining cases.

That may explain why the Court framed the inquiry in *Hill* as whether, but for counsel's errors, Hill would have declined to plead guilty and insisted on going to trial. Notice what sort of errors tend to satisfy *that* prejudice standard: attorney errors that suggest not only that the defendant would have gone to trial, but that he would have *won* at trial.

2. Recall that 94 percent of state felony convictions are by guilty plea, and the percentage in many jurisdictions is higher still — percentages of 96 percent and above are common in large cities. Don't such numbers suggest a presumption that any given defendant would very probably have pled guilty in any given case?

3. *Hill*'s prejudice standard may be at odds with a subsequent ineffective-assistance decision. In Glover v. United States, 531 U.S. 198 (2001), a unanimous Court concluded that a sentencing error that added between 6 and 21 months to the defendant's sentence — the defendant was sentenced to 84 months in prison — satisfied *Strickland*'s prejudice prong. (The Solicitor General agreed with this conclusion. Thus, the *Glover* Court reached its decision without adversarial argument.) *Glover* is not a guilty plea case; the defendant in *Glover* was convicted at a jury trial, which presumably means that *Hill*'s prejudice standard for guilty pleas survives. But why? Isn't there something odd about saying that sentencing errors lead to valid ineffective-assistance claims for defendants who go to trial and lose but not for defendants who plead guilty?

Of course, *Glover* does apply to some guilty pleas — at the least, to those cases where defense counsel erred at the sentencing proceeding itself. Might it also apply to cases where counsel gave the defendant bad advice in the course of bargaining for a plea? Are errors that lead to unfavorable bargains (and thus to unfavorable sentences) prejudicial, even if the defendant was overwhelmingly likely to plead guilty? If the answer is yes, ineffective-assistance litigation in guilty pleas may see some dramatic changes in the next few years.

4. What about the reverse situation: a case in which a defense attorney's unprofessional errors lead a defendant to *reject* a highly desirable plea offer and go to trial, only to be convicted at trial and thereafter receive a much more severe sentence? Can such a defendant argue that he was prejudiced under *Strickland* and Hill v. Lockhart? This particular issue has vexed the lower courts for years, as exemplified by the following case.

WILLIAMS v. JONES

United States Court of Appeals for the Tenth Circuit
571 F.3d 1086 (2009)

PER CURIAM.

Petitioner-Appellant Michael Williams appeals from the district court's denial of his habeas corpus petition brought pursuant to 28 U.S.C. §2254. The only issue before us is whether, having determined that Mr. Williams received ineffective assistance of counsel in rejecting a plea offer, the Oklahoma Court of Criminal Appeals ("OCCA") fashioned a constitutionally permissible remedy. Our jurisdiction arises under 28 U.S.C. §1291, and we reverse and remand. On remand, the district court should impose a remedy that comes as close as possible to remedying the constitutional violation, and is not limited by state law.

BACKGROUND

Prior to trial for first-degree murder, an assistant district attorney offered Mr. Williams a ten-year sentence in exchange for a guilty plea to second-degree murder. Mr. Williams wanted to accept the offer, but his attorney, believing that Mr. Williams was innocent, threatened to withdraw from the case if the offer was accepted. The case proceeded to trial, the jury returned a guilty verdict, and Mr. Williams was sentenced to life imprisonment without the possibility of parole.

On direct appeal, the OCCA remanded the case back to the trial court for an evidentiary hearing on whether Mr. Williams's trial counsel rendered ineffective assistance during the plea process. After that hearing, the trial court found that trial counsel had rendered deficient performance but also found that Mr. Williams suffered no prejudice. On review, the OCCA held that Mr. Williams's trial counsel rendered deficient performance and that Mr. Williams was prejudiced thereby because he lost the opportunity to pursue the plea offer with trial counsel. As a remedy, the OCCA modified Mr. Williams's sentence to life imprisonment with the possibility of parole, which is the lowest punishment for first-degree murder. See Okla. Stat. tit. 21, §701.9; see also Okla. Stat. tit. 22, §1066.

Mr. Williams unsuccessfully sought habeas relief in federal district court, contending that the remedy for the ineffective assistance of counsel was inadequate. . . .

DISCUSSION

We must decide only whether the remedy imposed for the Sixth Amendment violation identified by the OCCA is constitutionally adequate. . . . The State does not contest the OCCA's finding of ineffective assistance of counsel in this context. . . .

. . . [E]ven under a deferential standard of review the remedy was objectively unreasonable. In fashioning the appropriate remedy for ineffective assistance of counsel, the remedy "should be tailored to the injury suffered from the constitutional violation and should not unnecessarily infringe on competing interests." [United States v. Morrison, 449 U.S. 361, 364 (1981).] We think it axiomatic that the remedy for a properly presented constitutional violation should not be frustrated by the sentencing options available under state law, but rather should be consistent with federal law. We proceed to consider the nature of the violation, any resulting prejudice, and the other interests involved.

The plea bargaining process is a critical stage of a criminal prosecution. [S]ee Iowa v. Tovar, 541 U.S. 77, 81 (2004) (entry of the guilty plea is a critical stage of the criminal process); Burger v. Kemp, 483 U.S. 776, 803-804 (1987) (pretrial plea negotiations are a critical stage of the criminal process). Accordingly, the Sixth Amendment applies to representation during the plea process. Hill v. Lockhart, 474 U.S. 52, 57 (1985).

Mr. Williams established deficient performance and prejudice. See Strickland [v. Washington], 466 U.S. [668,] 687 [(1984)]. The deficient performance was counsel's advice concerning the plea agreement — advising Mr. Williams he would be committing perjury by accepting the plea offer and insisting that Mr. Williams proceed to trial or find new counsel if he wanted to accept it. As the OCCA no doubt recognized, the prejudice Mr. Williams identified was that, had he been adequately counseled, there is a reasonable probability that he would have accepted the plea offer and limited his exposure to ten years. The fact that Mr. Williams subsequently received a fair trial (with a much greater sentence) simply does not vitiate the prejudice from the constitutional violation.

The State reminds us that plea offers are discretionary and the assistant district attorney was not required to extend one or keep an offer open. This would be a very different case had the assistant district attorney declined to extend an offer or revoked it prior to trial. See Mabry v. Johnson, 467 U.S. 504, 507-508 (1984), abrogated on other grounds by Puckett v. United States, 129 S. Ct. 1423 (2009); Weatherford v. Bursey, 429 U.S. 545, 561 (1977). However, the OCCA found that the ineffective assistance occurred when the plea offer was available. The evidence credited by the OCCA suggests a reasonable probability that the plea offer would have been accepted but for defense counsel's ineffective assistance. Accordingly, we are not dealing with the government's discretion to make or withdraw a plea offer. Rather, we are dealing with an offer that was rejected because of defense counsel's ineffective assistance, with disastrous results for Mr. Williams. In the end, this ineffective assistance and the resulting prejudice is attributable to the State. See Kimmelman v. Morrison, 477 U.S. 365, 379 (1986); Cuyler v. Sullivan, 446 U.S. 335, 343-345 (1980).

The result in this case is unchanged by the fact that the Supreme Court has commented, in the context of a Sixth Amendment choice of counsel case, United States v. Gonzalez-Lopez, 548 U.S. 140, 147 (2006), that effective assistance serves the purpose of protecting the right to a fair trial. *Gonzalez-Lopez* recognizes that counsel can be ineffective where "his mistakes have harmed the defense." Id. Surely, the plea process is part of the defense. See *Hill*, 474 U.S., at 57. The Court has rejected the idea that "the guarantee of effective assistance of counsel belongs solely to the innocent or that it attaches only to matters affecting the determination of actual guilt." *Kimmelman*, 477 U.S., at 380 (ineffective assistance claims may include failure to seek suppression of evidence even though such claims are barred on collateral review). Moreover, effective assistance is guaranteed for the whole plea process, not just in connection with accepting (but not rejecting) a plea agreement.

Much of the State's argument on appeal is that what remedy is afforded by the OCCA is solely a matter of State law and no due process violation occurs when the OCCA exercises that power. See Okla. Stat. tit. 22, §1066 ("The appellate court may reverse, affirm or modify the judgment or sentence. . . ."); Clemons v. Mississippi, 494 U.S. 738, 745 (1990). The short answer to that is that any correction for a federal constitutional violation must be consistent with federal law; Mr. Williams is not seeking habeas relief for errors of State law, but rather for a Sixth Amendment violation. . . .

The State certainly has an efficiency interest in upholding the modified sentence resulting from a fair trial and partially successful appeal. The State will have incurred the costs of prosecution, and Mr. Williams has defended and tested the State's case; yet he now will be able to obtain the benefits of the plea offer. Yet the OCCA recognized the obvious merit of reinstating the plea offer were it possible — it would address the prejudice Mr. Williams suffered. In the end, no remedy may restore completely the parties' original positions. Still, the OCCA was required to adopt the one that comes closest, without being constrained by state law. See *Morrison*, 449 U.S. at 365 ("Our approach has thus been to identify and then neutralize the taint by tailoring relief appropriate in the circumstances to assure the defendant the effective assistance of counsel and a fair trial."). . . .

Recognizing the discretion to resolve this issue "as law and justice require," 28 U.S.C. §2243, we will remand the case with instructions to the district court to entertain briefing and impose a remedy that comes as close as possible to remedying the constitutional violation, and is not limited by state law. The district court has the power to grant the writ conditionally to allow the State to comply.

We have carefully considered Judge Gorsuch's dissent. There is some common ground — the panel is unanimous that (1) Mr. Williams's right to counsel attached at the time of plea negotiations, (2) he had a right to effective representation during those negotiations, (3) his counsel rendered deficient performance, and (4) the OCCA's remedy is insufficient for the federal constitutional violation it found.[6] We reject the conclusion expressed in the dissent that Mr. Williams cannot demonstrate prejudice because he received a fair trial subsequent to plea negotiations and was not entitled to a plea offer. . . .

No one contests the rule that plea offers are executory in nature and that, under *Mabry* and *Weatherford*, a prosecutor may, consistent with due process, decline to

---

6. Of course, the dissent contends that there is no constitutional violation hence any remedy was unnecessary.

offer or withdraw an offer. But here, the assistant district attorney made an offer that Mr. Williams had a right to accept, as long as it was open, with effective assistance of counsel. See *Hill*, 474 U.S. at 56 (noting that the voluntariness of any plea depends upon effective assistance of counsel); *Strickland*, 466 U.S. at 688 (part of counsel's duty is to assist the defendant and consult with him on important decisions); Bordenkircher v. Hayes, 434 U.S. 357, 362 (1978) (discussing the importance of counsel during plea negotiations). Likewise, this is not a situation where Mr. Williams is claiming ineffective assistance of counsel based upon something to which he had no right, i.e., an objection by counsel based upon an erroneous interpretation of the law. See Lockhart v. Fretwell, 506 U.S. 364, 372-373 (1993). Though the dissent may well be right that the options in this case are limited to specific performance or a new trial, in an abundance of caution we would prefer the parties explore any alternatives under a backdrop of the applicable law. Thereafter, the district court may exercise its discretion.

REVERSED and REMANDED.

GORSUCH, J., dissenting.

The Sixth Amendment right to effective assistance of counsel is an instrumental right designed to ensure a fair trial. By his own admission, Michael Williams received just such a trial, at the end of which he was convicted of first degree murder by a jury of his peers. We have no authority to disturb this outcome. The majority says that counsel's deficient performance in the plea bargain process denied Mr. Williams a lesser second degree murder conviction, and that this justifies voiding the result of Mr. Williams's fair trial. But the due process clauses of the Constitution's Fifth and Fourteenth Amendments do not encompass a right to receive or accept plea offers. As the Supreme Court has repeatedly held, plea bargains are matters of executive discretion, not judicially enforceable entitlement; due process guarantees a fair trial, not a good bargain.

Without challenging any of this, the majority nonetheless recognizes a constitutional right to accept a plea offer grounded in the Sixth Amendment's guarantee of effective assistance of counsel, creating indirectly what the Supreme Court's precedents preclude it from recognizing directly as a matter of due process under the Fifth and Fourteenth Amendments. The practical upshot? So long as a defendant can claim his lawyer mishandled a plea offer, he can take his chances at a fair trial and, if dissatisfied with the result, still demand and receive the benefit of the forgone plea. . . .

[F]irst things first, what exactly is the right allegedly violated here? Mr. Williams argues that he was entitled by the Sixth Amendment to effective representation by counsel during his plea negotiations with the prosecution; that his lawyer provided grossly deficient performance when he threatened to withdraw unless Mr. Williams rejected the proffered plea; and that this deficient performance resulted in prejudice to Mr. Williams because he was unable to accept a plea bargain offered him by the prosecution. I accept, at least for argument's sake, all but the last link in this chain. . . .

Prejudice is the critical question in this case. Mr. Williams argues that, once the State made a plea offer, he had a right, emanating from the Sixth Amendment's right to effective representation, to be appropriately counseled about the consequences of accepting or rejecting the plea. Counsel's failure to advise him properly,

Mr. Williams submits, amounts to prejudice within the meaning of the Sixth Amendment. At least one court, People v. Curry, 687 N.E.2d 877 (Ill. 1997), has adopted this line of reasoning. In *Curry*, the Supreme Court of Illinois held that the Sixth Amendment contains a right "to be reasonably informed as to the direct consequences of accepting or rejecting that offer," id. at 888, and that the loss of this right qualifies as prejudice within the meaning of *Strickland*. In concluding that Mr. Williams had suffered a Sixth Amendment violation, the OCCA seemed to take much the same view.

This logic, however, collapses deficient performance and prejudice. Under *Curry*'s rationale and the OCCA's, a violation of the Sixth Amendment is complete the moment a lawyer fails to advise his client adequately about the consequences of a plea. That is, the lawyer's bad advice (deficient performance) deprives the client of a right to good advice (prejudice). The Supreme Court has repeatedly warned against this fallacy, reminding us that some *independent* showing of prejudice must be made. . . . Put differently, bad advice isn't enough. Some harm to the defense must follow. Calling a lawyer's incompetence both deficient performance *and* prejudice misconstrues the Supreme Court's test.

Given that the OCCA's prejudice analysis is not defensible, we might ask whether there is some other basis for finding prejudice in Mr. Williams's case that warrants remedy. The usual ineffective assistance claim in the plea bargaining context involves a defendant who has pled guilty as a result of poor legal advice. In such cases, we readily find prejudice because the waiver of the right to trial must be a "voluntary . . . knowing, intelligent act[] done with sufficient awareness of the relevant circumstances and likely consequences." *Brady*, 397 U.S. at 748. . . .

This case is different. Mr. Williams pled *not* guilty to the charge against him. And a not-guilty plea is a waiver of nothing; it is an *invocation* of the constitutional right to a trial, and it is effective whether or not it is made knowingly and voluntarily. So Mr. Williams cannot and does not challenge the validity of his not-guilty plea; he must identify some other source of prejudice. What might that be?

Mr. Williams argues that prejudice can be shown from the fact that he lost a good chance at a ten-year sentence, and instead received a life sentence. Though at first blush this sounds like a complaint that his *sentence* is the result of ineffective assistance, that isn't quite right. It is undisputed that the ten-year sentence Mr. Williams desires is unavailable for a person convicted of first degree murder in Oklahoma; life with the possibility of parole is the statutory minimum for that offense. Thus, it would have been unlawful for the Oklahoma court to convict Mr. Williams of first degree murder, as it did, and then impose a sentence less than life with the possibility of parole. Because Mr. Williams cannot legally obtain a ten-year sentence for first degree murder, he cannot complain that his attorney was ineffective for failing to secure such a result. . . .

Mr. Williams's claim of prejudice must begin with his *conviction* for first degree murder. His argument is and has to be that his lawyer's ineffectiveness rendered his first degree murder conviction invalid; that it should be vacated; and that he should be permitted to plead to a second degree murder charge instead — only that way would he become eligible for the ten-year sentence he seeks. But here, too, there is a twist. In the ordinary *Strickland* challenge to a conviction, the defendant argues that, because of counsel's incompetent acts or omissions, he did not get a fair or reliable trial; therefore, the resulting conviction is unlawful. Mr. Williams's claim is just the opposite. He claims that because of his lawyer's incompetence, he *did* get a fair and reliable trial leading to his first degree murder conviction. So the question Mr. Williams poses now becomes clear: Can a defendant be prejudiced, in the Sixth Amendment sense, by the loss of a plea bargain if he is later convicted only after an entirely fair trial?

I think not. . . . When, as here, "a defendant challenges a conviction, the question is whether there is a reasonable probability that, absent [counsel's] errors, the factfinder would have had a reasonable doubt respecting guilt." [*Strickland*, 466 U.S.,] at 695.

Mr. Williams cannot show prejudice under this standard. . . . Put in *Strickland*'s terms, he does not suggest that anything his lawyer could have done would have induced the jury to have "a reasonable doubt respecting [his] guilt" for first degree murder. Id. Rather, he says the jury would never have been empaneled in the first place.

No doubt that would have been better for Mr. Williams, but it has nothing to do with the question posed by *Strickland*. Prejudice is not established simply because, but for some accident or misfortune, the fair trial leading to a conviction would have been somehow averted. . . .

Put differently, rather than have us review the fairness of the trial that did deprive him of liberty, as *Strickland* requires, Mr. Williams's claim would have us examine the plea negotiation that did not. But that is not the relevant inquiry. In fact, Mr. Williams's attempt to shift our focus from the fairness of the trial that took place to an abandoned plea deal is foreclosed by the Supreme Court's decisions in Mabry v. Johnson, 467 U.S. 504 (1984), abrogated on other grounds by Puckett v. United States, 129 S. Ct. 1423 (2009), and Weatherford v. Bursey, 429 U.S. 545.

In *Mabry*, the government offered a plea on a Friday and the defendant pondered it over the weekend. When defense counsel called on Monday to accept the deal, the prosecutor said the offer was a mistake and withdrew it. In its place, the government offered a new bargain with a harsher sentence, which the defendant accepted. The defendant later sought the benefit of the original bargain in court, arguing that due process principles precluded the government from reneging on its deal. The Sixth Circuit agreed, holding that "fairness" prevented the government from withdrawing the original plea offer after it had been accepted. *Mabry*, 467 U.S. at 506. But the Supreme Court reversed, stressing that it was not the original, abandoned plea bargain that deprived the defendant of his liberty; it was the guilty plea he actually entered. . . .

The story of *Weatherford* is similar. There, the defendant complained that government misconduct (an undercover government agent, pretending to be a co-defendant, sat in on discussions with defense counsel) prevented him from having even the *opportunity* to bargain for a plea. This court agreed that due process was offended, but the Supreme Court again reversed. While the prosecution likely engaged in misconduct, and while its misconduct may have denied the defendant the opportunity to engage in plea bargaining, the defendant "was not denied a fair trial." *Weatherford*, 429 U.S. at 560. A lost opportunity to pursue a negotiated plea was of no moment.

The majority says our case is distinguishable because the prosecutor here neither declined to extend an offer nor revoked an offer already extended — that is, a different sort of problem kept Mr. Williams's plea deal from being embodied in a court's judgment. But the question we face isn't whether the particular accident befalling Mr. Williams is the same particular accident that befell Mr. Mabry and Mr.

Weatherford. That one petitioner has brown eyes and another blue usually makes no difference in the eyes of the law. Our job isn't to ask whether cases are factually identical but whether, by their terms, the *rules of law* set forth by the Supreme Court do or do not apply to our case. And the rule of *Mabry* and *Weatherford* — that constitutional scrutiny is applied only to the procedure that deprives the defendant of his liberty, and that executory plea bargains do not — is no less applicable to Mr. Williams than it was to the defendants in those cases. The historical happenstance of why Mr. Williams's plea remained executory is neither here nor there. . . .

One might ask why *Mabry* and *Weatherford* hold as they do. Why do we care about trials that deprive defendants of their liberty but not botched plea deals that don't? The most obvious answer of course is that the latter don't result in incarceration, and the Constitution cares only about processes that do. But there is even more to it than that. As both *Mabry* and *Weatherford* intimate, a lost plea deal implicates neither *Strickland*'s concern with ensuring a reliable result nor its concern with ensuring fair treatment. A fair trial's outcome is as reliable an outcome as we can hope to achieve. And because the plea bargain is a matter of prosecutorial grace, not a matter of legal entitlement, a defendant who loses the chance for a deal cannot be said to have been treated unfairly.

In the terms of *Strickland*'s prejudice prong, the loss of a plea bargain does not "undermine confidence" in the outcome of a subsequent fair trial. The American Constitution, our Bill of Rights, and our common law tradition place faith in the trial as the best means of protecting a defendant's rights, testing the government's case, and ensuring a reliable result. It is a foundational principle of our system of justice that a fair trial, imperfect though it and all human affairs surely are, offers the greatest assurance we have yet devised of a reliable resolution of a criminal charge. The guarantee of a fair trial is the bulwark of our national liberty.

This isn't to say plea bargaining has no place. But unlike a trial, plea bargaining is not designed to subject the prosecution's case to testing or to ensure that a defendant goes to jail only if no reasonable doubt remains about his or her guilt. In fact, plea bargains guarantee that some persons who would have been acquitted never receive a trial at all and instead serve time in prison. In part for this reason, the common law was hostile even to the uncompensated guilty plea, fearing that the innocent (and perhaps especially the innocent) would feel pressured to convict themselves either out of fear or hope of mercy.[3] The Supreme Court, in more recent years, has acknowledged the value of plea bargains in efficiently disposing of criminal cases. . . . But notably missing from the Court's recitation of the plea bargain's virtues is any suggestion that, compared to the trial as evolved through history and guaranteed by law, plea bargaining enhances the reliability of the outcome. When it comes to that — when it comes to the confidence we repose in the outcome of a criminal proceeding — the trial remains our gold standard.[4]

---

3. See Albert W. Alschuler, Plea Bargaining and Its History, 13 Law & Soc'y Rev. 211, 223 (1979) ("[T]he poor, friendless, helpless man is most apt to become the one who helps swell the record of convictions.") (internal quotation marks omitted). Mr. Williams's counsel was, of course, convinced that Mr. Williams's wish to plead guilty represented an example of just this phenomenon.

4. On one famous account, plea bargains remain nothing more than coerced guilty pleas. See generally John H. Langbein, Torture and Plea Bargaining, 46 U. Chi. L. Rev. 3 (1978). Others respond that the plea bargain reflects the probability of conviction and various possible sentences, each discounted for their likelihood, in a sort of net present value analysis. See Frank H. Easterbrook, Criminal Procedure as a Market System, 12 J. Leg. Stud. 289, 316-317 (1983). On either account, however, the rational plea bargain combines two things the law keeps separate: the risk of conviction at trial and the probable sentence

. . . Mr. Williams cannot claim any substantive or procedural right to accept or enforce the prosecutor's plea offer. To the contrary, because the plea was never embodied in the court's judgment, it remained a matter of pure executive discretion and could be withdrawn at whim. Without any entitlement to the plea, Mr. Williams cannot complain that the loss of it was unfair. . . .

. . . Mr. Williams was deprived of his liberty only after a proceeding in which, in the words of the Magna Carta, "the judge or jury acted according to law." *Strickland*, 466 U.S. at 694. The outcome of his trial was not just reliable but also fair, according him all protections to which he was entitled by law. The Sixth Amendment requires no more. As Justice White explained for the Supreme Court, "[i]t is a novel argument that constitutional rights are infringed by trying the defendant rather than accepting his plea of guilty." *Weatherford*, 429 U.S. at 561. . . .

Having found a violation of Mr. Williams's constitutional rights, and having held the OCCA's remedy inadequate to remedy that violation, the majority stops short of imposing a remedy of its own, instead telling the district court to devise one "that comes as close as possible to remedying the constitutional violation." But there should be no confusion, the part of this case that matters is over, finished, done. According to the majority, the Constitution is offended, a right guaranteed by the Sixth Amendment is infringed, when an attorney's deficient performance costs his client a plea bargain that appears in hindsight, after the trial's results are known, to have been a good one. The question that has divided lower courts for a decade is irrevocably decided in this circuit and binding on future panels. . . .

Rightly dissatisfied with the OCCA's remedy rejected by the majority, Mr. Williams urges us to order specific performance of the lost plea bargain, which would involve vacating his first degree murder conviction and give him a ten-year sentence for second degree murder. Some of the courts to have preceded us down this road have offered such a remedy. But they must be wrong, and wrong in a way that shows the absence of any constitutional right at stake. Even if Mr. Williams had managed to accept the plea offer, under Supreme Court precedent the prosecutor would have been free to withdraw it on a whim, and the state trial judge would have been free to reject it or to impose a different sentence than the one contemplated by the parties' plea. So ordering specific performance of plea agreement would not restore Mr. Williams to his original position; it would confer on him something he never had to begin with: a *legal entitlement*, as opposed to a *chance*, to obtain a ten-year sentence on a charge for second degree murder never brought by the State. Ordering such a remedy would effectively permit Mr. Williams to use the rubric of ineffective assistance to upend the plea bargaining process, transforming it from its historic role as an act of executive discretion to one of judicially enforceable right. We, rather than the State, would assume the job of selecting charges and offering plea terms.

. . . *Strickland* seeks to assure defendants of reliable and fair criminal proceedings, conducted according to law; that is what Mr. Williams received. Mr. Williams would have us follow him through the looking glass, to a world where a fair trial is

---

upon conviction. As the length of possible sentences increases, the number of guilty pleas goes up as well — even though the number of acquittals at trial presumably would stay the same. This is why whatever degree of reliability is produced by plea bargaining will always be less than that produced by a trial. And it is why the loss of a plea bargain can never undermine confidence in the result produced by a more reliable procedure.

called "prejudice"; where the results of a fair trial are void because of a lost opportunity rather than an infringed legal entitlement; and where a lawyer's incompetence transforms the executive plea bargain prerogative into a judicially enforceable entitlement. I do not believe the Sixth Amendment permits us to accompany him there. Respectful of my colleagues' contrary conclusion, I must dissent.

NOTES AND QUESTIONS

1. Williams v. Jones, like Hill v. Lockhart, is another case about *Strickland* prejudice. How should courts apply *Strickland*'s *performance* prong in the guilty plea context? United States v. Barnes, 83 F.3d 934 (7th Cir. 1996), involved a factual error that led to incorrect attorney advice about the likely sentence. Barnes's lawyer failed to recognize that, under the Guidelines, Barnes qualified as a career offender, which substantially altered his sentencing range. Before Barnes entered his guilty plea, counsel advised him he would face a sentence of between 46 and 57 months; given his career offender status, the correct range was 262 to 327 months. At his plea hearing,

> [T]he court informed [Barnes] that the statutorily defined maximum sentence for his offense was life imprisonment, and it reminded him that he would be sentenced according to the guidelines. [The court] also told him that he would be bound to his plea regardless of how the guidelines calculated his sentence. [Barnes] speculated that the relevant factors would give him a base offense level of 16 and a criminal history score of VI [which produced the estimate of 46 to 57 months]. Both the court and the prosecutor refused to confirm Mr. Barnes' speculation, pointing out that they did not have all of the information required to calculate his sentence under the guidelines. Mr. Barnes' attorney posited that he was certain that Mr. Barnes was correct in his estimate. Mr. Barnes then went forward with his plea.

After the presentence report was prepared and Barnes realized the mistake, he sought to withdraw his guilty plea, but the district court refused to permit withdrawal and sentenced him to 210 months (having made allowance for Barnes's acceptance of responsibility for his crime). Barnes then claimed counsel's advice had been constitutionally ineffective. The court rejected the claim, though not without some hesitation:

> Several circumstances of the plea suggest that Mr. Barnes' counsel may not have taken the utmost care in advising his client. At the time of the plea hearing, counsel did not know about a parole revocation on Mr. Barnes' record. That revocation made a 1973 robbery conviction relevant to determining his status under the guidelines, and that conviction qualified Mr. Barnes as a career offender. The existence of this revocation should have been relatively easy to discover, although the gravity of its implications for Mr. Barnes' guidelines score might not have been immediately apparent. It might have been appropriate for a defense attorney to pause before a plea hearing to carefully analyze his client's criminal record in light of the offered plea. Given that Mr. Barnes' change-of-plea hearing [where he entered his guilty plea] occurred immediately after plea bargaining ended, it is possible that counsel did not or could not undertake this kind of careful analysis. Counsel might not have been thorough in considering the sentencing consequences of Mr. Barnes' plea. But the circumstances of Mr. Barnes' plea only suggest this possibility; they do not demonstrate it. Nothing in the trial record

proves that Mr. Barnes' counsel did not undertake a good faith investigation earlier. With our study confined to the trial record, we cannot find either deficient performance or prejudice.

Successful ineffective assistance challenges to criminal convictions are rare in general, but they are especially rare — indeed, almost unheard of — in cases in which the defendant pled guilty. Why? Does *Barnes* suggest an answer?

2. In Padilla v. Kentucky, 130 S. Ct. 1473 (2010), the Court held that a defense attorney's failure to inform the defendant — a noncitizen who had resided lawfully in the United States for 40 years and had served with honor in Vietnam — that a guilty plea to a drug charge would render him automatically removable from the country constituted ineffective performance under *Strickland*. The Court did not address *Strickland* prejudice, leaving that issue to the Kentucky courts on remand.

3. As noted previously, defendants who have pled guilty rarely appeal their pleas, and they are usually barred by the procedural default doctrine from challenging their pleas in habeas. Ineffective assistance is one of the few ways to satisfy the "cause" and "prejudice" requirement, and thereby avoid the bar of procedural default, but Hill v. Lockhart shows how difficult it can be to establish ineffective assistance in the context of a guilty plea.

Actually, there is one more way around a procedurally defaulted challenge to a guilty plea: The defendant may assert his defaulted claim, without showing "cause" and "prejudice," if he can "establish that the constitutional error . . . has probably resulted in the conviction of one who is actually innocent. To establish actual innocence, petitioner must demonstrate that, in light of all the evidence, it is more likely than not that no reasonable juror would have convicted him." Bousley v. United States, 523 U.S. 614 (1998) (citations omitted). The constitutional error in *Bousley* was the same as in Henderson v. Morgan: The defendant was misinformed about the elements of the crime to which he pled guilty. Bousley pled guilty to "using" a firearm "during and in relation to a drug trafficking crime." He was told that "using" meant essentially the same thing as "possessing"; later, the Supreme Court construed the relevant statute to require proof that the defendant had actively employed the weapon, which Bousley claimed he had not done. Even though neither Bousley nor his lawyer objected at the plea proceeding (or appealed his conviction afterward), the Court held that he could raise his Henderson v. Morgan claim if he could prove his innocence.

The defendant in Bradshaw v. Stumpf, 545 U.S. 175 (2005), raised a similar claim but with less success. Stumpf and an accomplice named Wesley robbed and shot an elderly couple, leaving the husband wounded and the wife dead. Both men were charged with capital murder. Stumpf pled guilty. At his sentencing proceeding, the government argued that he had fired the shot that killed the victim; Stumpf maintained that Wesley had fired the fatal shot. In the alternative, the government contended that Stumpf deserved execution even if Wesley was the triggerman. Stumpf was sentenced to death. When Wesley was later tried for the same murder, the prosecution argued that *he* had fired the fatal shot, not Stumpf. Wesley was allowed to introduce evidence that the government had taken an inconsistent position in his accomplice's case; the jury convicted, but imposed a life sentence. Stumpf then sought relief on habeas corpus, maintaining that he had pled guilty under a false understanding of Ohio's capital murder statute, and that the government's use of inconsistent arguments in the two cases invalidated both his guilty plea and sentence.

The Supreme Court rejected Stumpf's challenge to his guilty plea, and remanded for consideration of the challenge to his death sentence. Justice O'Connor's opinion for a unanimous Court noted that, even if the trial judge in the plea colloquy had failed to describe the intent term of the crime to which Stumpf pled guilty, defense counsel had correctly described that term in previous conversations with the defendant. Due process required no more, the Court held. As for the government's inconsistent arguments in the two cases: The Court noted that it was difficult to see how the government's subsequent argument could undermine Stumpf's prior plea. Moreover, the accuracy of Stumpf's guilty plea did not depend on his having fired the fatal shot; the relevant state statute provides for liability for an accomplice who intends to kill but does not commit the act that directly causes the victim's death. And the requisite intent could be inferred from the defendant's other actions — including shooting the husband.

After *Bousley* and *Stumpf*, it is not clear how much additional work "actual innocence" actually does. If a defendant can show he is probably innocent of the crime to which he pled guilty, he can likely also show under Hill v. Lockhart that his lawyer was constitutionally ineffective for advising him to so plead. Thus, in most cases, ineffective assistance and actual innocence will travel together. Actual innocence adds something only in the rare case, like *Bousley*, in which the legal definition of the relevant crime has changed after the guilty plea. In all other cases, the defendant is, basically, stuck with having to show ineffective assistance if he wishes to undo his plea.

NOTE ON DEFENSE RESOURCE CONSTRAINTS AND THE GUILTY PLEA PROCESS

About 80 percent of criminal defendants receive appointed counsel. Steven K. Smith & Carol J. DeFrances, Indigent Defense, Bureau of Justice Statistics Selected Findings, February 1996, at 1, 4. Of the other 20 percent, a substantial number are only slightly above the indigency line — they may be able to hire their own counsel, but counsel are paid at levels roughly comparable to the pay received by appointed counsel. For both groups of defendants — both the large number who qualify as indigent and the smaller but significant number who do not so qualify, but come close — the nature and quality of legal representation may depend as much on attorney resource constraints as on anything else. What are those constraints, and how do they affect the decision to plead guilty?

The constraints themselves are severe. Between 1979 and 1990, felony filings in state court more than doubled; meanwhile, during roughly the same time period, the percentage of cases in which defendants receive appointed counsel rose from about half to 80 percent. See William J. Stuntz, The Uneasy Relationship Between Criminal Procedure and Criminal Justice, 107 Yale L.J. 1, 9 and nn. 18-19 (1997), and sources cited therein. These numbers suggest that, at least for serious crimes, the demand for appointed counsel rose very substantially. If budgets for indigent defense had *trebled* in real (i.e., inflation-adjusted) dollars, they would still have fallen short of keeping up with that increased demand. In fact, between 1979 and 1990, spending on indigent defense rose only 60 percent in real dollars — meaning that real-dollar spending per case fell dramatically. See Bureau, U.S. Department of Justice, Sourcebook of Criminal Justice Statistics — 1993, at 3, tbl. 3.[6]

> The predictable result is public defenders' offices with very large ratios of cases to lawyers. One recent study found a jurisdiction in which some public defenders represented over four hundred felony defendants in an eight-month span, and the average representation was more than half that number. In another jurisdiction, some lawyers represented over one thousand misdemeanor defendants in one year; again the averages were not vastly different. These numbers are, of course, extreme; more typical ratios are no doubt lower. . . . Still, those familiar with the system agree that the story these numbers tell is generally true: Public defenders are terribly overburdened.
>
> The story is essentially the same in jurisdictions that use separately appointed defense counsel rather than public defenders. Such counsel are usually paid according to statutory fee schedules that fix hourly amounts, sometimes varying the amount for pretrial preparation, trial, and appeal. Often the hourly fees are quite low: In Alabama, defense counsel receive $20 per hour for out-of-court time; in New York, the figure is $25. Not all the hourly rates are so stingy[;] . . . rates of $40 per hour are not unusual. The real key to the statutory fee schedules, however, is not the hourly amounts but the caps on total fees. Most states have such caps; they range as low as $265 and go no higher than $3500 for noncapital felonies. The typical range is $500 to $1000. These caps can be waived for good cause, but the governing statutes seem designed to ensure that waiver is exceptional, typically requiring a finding that the waiver was "necessary" or the circumstances "extraordinary." Thus, a typical appointed defense lawyer faces something like the following pay scale: $30 or $40 per hour for the first twenty to thirty hours, and zero thereafter.

Stuntz, supra, at 10-11 (footnotes omitted). In high-crime, big-city criminal courts, these constraints can be staggering. Lisa McIntyre's study of the Chicago public defenders' office reports one lawyer describing his early experience in the office as follows: "I had a partner for one week and then I was put on my own. It was crazy, we used to do fifteen bench trials a day and I had, on the average, forty clients a day." Lisa J. McIntyre, The Public Defender: The Practice of Law in the Shadows of Repute 103 (1987). A mid-1980s study of one subset of appointed defense counsel (not public defenders) in New York City found that the lawyers visited the crime scene in only 12 percent of homicide cases and 4 percent of other felony cases, interviewed witnesses in 21 percent of homicide cases and, again, only 4 percent of other felony cases, and consulted expert witnesses of some sort in 17 percent of homicide cases and only 2 percent of other felony cases. Michael McConville & Chester L. Mirsky, Criminal Defense of the Poor in New York City, 15 N.Y.U. Rev. L. & Soc. Change 581, 762-764 (1986-1987). These figures suggest that detailed investigation as a prerequisite to a guilty plea is exceptional, presumably because counsel do not have the time to take any other course of action.

One implication of these resource constraints is that defense counsel are engaged in a kind of triage — separating the few cases that will be the subject of significant attorney investment from the many that will not — because there simply is not enough time to invest in all or even most cases. That, in turn, would suggest a need for a high rate of guilty pleas, and there is some evidence that defense counsel do push defendants to plead guilty. McIntyre's study, among others, reports some such

---

6. The figure stated in the text is adjusted for inflation, based on the consumer price index figures in U.S. Department of Commerce, Statistical Abstract of the United States — 1996, at 483.

behavior. See McIntyre, supra, at 154-156. Note that plea bargaining facilitates this process — it is no doubt easier to talk clients into guilty pleas when the government can offer explicit concessions — but it is not the source of the pressure to plead guilty. Rather, that pressure comes from the limited time and money defense lawyers have.

In short, most criminal defendants are represented by lawyers who must carefully ration their time across a large number of cases, and who simply cannot afford to invest heavily in most of those cases. There is evidence that most cases receive very little factual investigation, and evidence that some defense counsel press their clients to plead guilty, presumably in order to free up time for other cases — all of which paints a picture of defense attorneys as case processors, not advocates.

Yet that picture may be wrong. There is a growing literature about the work of appointed criminal defense attorneys, and much of it argues that defense counsel are not case processors — that, notwithstanding the serious resource constraints they face, counsel do indeed function as aggressive advocates. Consider Lisa McIntyre's criticism of descriptions of public defenders as bureaucratic case processors:

> Today, some twenty years after [the leading critiques of public defenders], it might be argued that [the critics' views] have been discredited. There is some evidence that this is so. . . . [S]ociologist Jerome Skolnick's own study of a public defender's office led him to conclude that "critics of the public defender have tended to underestimate the quality of defense provided by the public defender." After Skolnick's came numerous empirical studies that failed to find any evidence that clients represented in court by public defenders fared worse (at least in terms of case outcomes) than defendants who had private lawyers.
>
> Other scholarly accounts of the criminal justice process and the public defender's role in that process have offered persuasive evidence that [the critics'] portrayals are simply inadequate characterizations of what actually takes place in criminal courts. Malcolm Feeley, for example, reported the interesting finding that in the jurisdictions he studied, public defenders, far from pushing assembly line-quick justice, often had to rein in . . . clients [impatient to plead guilty and get their cases over with]. . . .

McIntyre, supra, at 46-47 (citations omitted). For similar criticisms, see Roger A. Hanson et al., Indigent Defenders Get the Job Done and Done Well (1992); John B. Mitchell, Redefining the Sixth Amendment, 67 S. Cal. L. Rev. 1215 (1994). The true picture is no doubt complicated. As McIntyre and others have argued, public defenders plainly function as genuine, aggressive advocates sometimes, and they may achieve overall results similar to privately retained counsel. (Though this last point is unclear given the present state of the empirical literature, and it is worth bearing in mind that most privately retained counsel may operate under resource constraints as severe as do many public defenders' offices.) Still, resource constraints must have a powerful effect on their behavior.

It may be worth noting that even very severe budget constraints do not give rise to an ineffective assistance claim. Why would that be so? Consider the standard the Supreme Court articulated in Hill v. Lockhart, and think about how that standard would likely apply in a case where counsel did little or no investigating but instead recommended a guilty plea, the defendant accepted the plea recommendation, and the defendant later sought to claim ineffective assistance. What would the defendant have to show to succeed, and how would the size of counsel's caseload help him show it?

Though most courts have not been receptive to resource-related ineffective assistance claims, a few have. In State v. Peart, 621 So. 2d 780 (1993), the Louisiana Supreme Court held that appointed counsel in New Orleans were presumptively ineffective:

> Leonard Peart was charged with armed robbery, aggravated rape, aggravated burglary, attempted armed robbery, and first degree murder. He is indigent.
>
> In New Orleans, the Indigent Defender Board ("IDB") has created the Orleans Indigent Defender Program ("OIDP"). OIDP operates under a public defender model. The trial court appointed Rick Teissier . . . to defend Peart against all the above charges except first degree murder.
>
> In response to Teissier's "Motion for Relief to Provide Constitutionally Mandated Protection and Resources," the trial court held a series of hearings on the defense services being provided Peart and other defendants in Section E of Criminal District Court. At the hearings, the court found the following facts. At the time of his appointment, Teissier was handling 70 active felony cases. His clients are routinely incarcerated 30 to 70 days before he meets with them. In the period between January 1 and August 1, 1991, Teissier represented 418 defendants. Of these, he entered 130 guilty pleas at arraignment. He had at least one serious case set for trial for every trial date during that period. OIDP has only enough funds to hire three investigators. They are responsible for rendering assistance in more than 7,000 cases per year in the ten sections of Criminal District Court, plus cases in Juvenile Court, Traffic Court, and Magistrates' Court. In a routine case Teissier receives no investigative support at all. There are no funds for expert witnesses. OIDP's library is inadequate. . . .
>
> [After a discussion of the state constitutional requirement of adequate funding for indigent criminal defense, the court concluded as follows.]
>
> Acting pursuant to the established sources of authority noted above, and having found that evidence in the record before us shows that the provision of indigent defense services in Section E of Orleans Criminal District Court is in many respects so lacking that defendants who must depend on it are not likely to be receiving the reasonably effective assistance of counsel the constitution guarantees, we find that a rebuttable presumption arises that indigents in Section E are receiving assistance of counsel not sufficiently effective to meet constitutionally required standards. This presumption is to apply prospectively only; it is to apply to those defendants who were represented by attorney Teissier when he filed the original "Motion for Relief" who have not yet gone to trial; and it will be applicable to all indigent defendants in Section E who have OIDP attorneys appointed to represent them hereafter, so long as there are no changes in the workload and other conditions under which OIDP assigned defense counsel provide legal services in Section E. If legislative action is not forthcoming and indigent defense reform does not take place, this Court, in the exercise of its constitutional and inherent power and supervisory jurisdiction, may find it necessary to employ the more intrusive and specific measures it has thus far avoided to ensure that indigent defendants receive reasonably effective assistance of counsel. . . .

Id., at 784, 791. Note that *Peart* was based on *state* constitutional law.

Consider, in light of *Peart*, the way the various protections to which defendants are entitled in the guilty plea process are enforced. The basic answer is that, just as in cases that go to trial, individual defendants must raise any claims they may have, and courts will adjudicate those claims, case by case. *Peart* seems to rest on the proposition that that process does not work in the guilty plea setting, that the only way to enforce defendants' rights in that setting is for courts to entertain more

global challenges, and to consider issuing the kinds of broad injunctions for indigent defense services that federal courts have issued in cases challenging school segregation and prison conditions. (Notice the threat in the last sentence of the quoted
passage in the Louisiana Supreme Court's opinion.)

What do you think of that choice? Does the law governing guilty pleas ensure that
defendants who enter such pleas are treated fairly? Does it ensure that those defendants are guilty?

Chapter 14

The Jury and the Criminal Trial

A. The Right to a Trial by Jury

> I consider trial by jury as the only anchor ever yet imagined by man, by which a government can be held to the principles of its constitution.
>
> *Thomas Jefferson (1788)*

The right to a trial by jury in criminal cases, enshrined in Article III[1] and in the Sixth Amendment,[2] is one of the most revered civil liberties guaranteed by the United States Constitution. The jury trial (in a form that we might recognize as a direct predecessor to the modern jury trial) originated in England many centuries ago, with some scholars tracing its history back to Magna Carta or before[3] and a few finding analogues even in ancient Egypt[4] and Greece.[5] In any event, the right to jury trial in criminal cases was well established in the American colonies long before the Revolution. In fact, it was the only right that appeared in all 12 of the written state constitutions predating the Declaration of Independence.[6]

Two prominent pre-Revolution jury trials — one in England and the other in the colonies — helped lay the foundation for the Revolution itself. In 1670, 12 jurors who had refused to convict Quakers William Penn and William Mead for the crime of disturbing the peace by holding an unlawful assembly were themselves imprisoned under a writ of attaint, a procedure used at the time in England to punish jurors who "perjured" themselves by rendering a false verdict. One of the 12, Edward Bushell, challenged his imprisonment. In Bushell's Case, 124 Eng. Rep. 1006 (C.P. 1670), the Court of Common Pleas ordered Bushell's release, holding that no one has the right to question or second-guess a criminal jury's general verdict. Sixty-five years later, publisher John Peter Zenger was placed on trial in New York for the crime of seditious libel, based on newspaper stories critical of the royal governor. Andrew Hamilton volunteered in the middle of the trial to help defend Zenger. Hamilton argued successfully that the jury should acquit because the stories

---

1. "[T]he trial of all crimes, except in the cases of impeachment, shall be by jury; and such trial shall be held in the state where the said crimes shall have been committed." U.S. Const., Art. III, §2.

2. "In all criminal prosecutions, the accused shall enjoy the right to a speedy and public trial, by an impartial jury of the state and district wherein the crime shall have been committed." U.S. Const., Amdt. VI.

3. On the history of the jury trial in England, see generally 1 Sir Frederick Pollock & Frederic William Maitland, The History of English Law (1895); 1 W. C. Holdsworth, History of English Law (1922); 1 Winston Churchill, History of the English-Speaking People (1956).

4. See, e.g., J. Kendall Few, In Defense of Trial by Jury 12 (1993).

5. See, e.g., John Guinther, The Jury in America 2 (1988).

6. On the history of the jury trial in America, see generally Albert Alschuler & Andrew Deiss, A Brief History of the Criminal Jury in the United States, 61 U. Chi. L. Rev. 867 (1994).

were true, even though English libel law at the time did not recognize truth as a defense, citing Bushell's Case to the jurors as authority for their unreviewable power to do so. The widely publicized prosecution of Zenger, and his ultimate acquittal, served to underscore the deepening split between England and the colonies over freedom of speech and other civil liberties and became a catalyst for the Revolution.

Today it is well established that the proper role of the jury in a criminal trial is to determine the facts and apply the law — pursuant to instructions given by the trial judge — to those facts. In Sparf v. United States, 156 U.S. 51 (1895), the Supreme Court rejected the broad proposition that juries are free to "nullify" the law, i.e., to ignore the judge's instructions and proceed on their own view about what the law should be:

> We must hold firmly to the doctrine that in the courts of the United States it is the duty of juries in criminal cases to take the law from the court and apply that law to the facts as they find them to be from the evidence. Upon the court rests the responsibility of declaring the law; upon the jury, the responsibility of applying the law so declared to the facts as they, upon their conscience, believe them to be. Under any other system, the courts, although established in order to declare the law, would for every practical purpose be eliminated from our system of government as instrumentalities devised for the protection equally of society and of individuals in their essential rights. When that occurs our government will cease to be a government of laws, and become a government of men.

Id., at 102-103.

The *Sparf* Court carefully distinguished Bushell's Case, explaining that "the fundamental proposition decided [there] was that, in view of the different functions of court and jury, and because a general verdict of necessity resolves 'both law and fact complicately, and not the fact by itself,' it could never be proved, where the case went to the jury upon both law and facts, that the jurors did not proceed upon their view of the evidence." Id., at 90-91. In other words, the Court acknowledged that juries occasionally may refuse to convict guilty defendants[7] and that such verdicts are nonreviewable because the basis for them cannot be determined from the face of the verdict. But the practice of jury nullification is neither encouraged nor legally approved. Thus, prospective jurors who identify themselves, during jury selection, as potential nullifiers may be excluded from jury service. See, e.g., United States v. Thomas, 116 F.3d 606 (2d Cir. 1997). Trial judges routinely preclude defense lawyers from arguing (as Andrew Hamilton did in the *Zenger* case) that jurors should exercise their nullification power to acquit guilty defendants, as well as from presenting evidence to support a nullification defense. And jurors are universally instructed that it is their duty and obligation to obey the law as articulated by the judge.[8] See generally Nancy J. King, Silencing Nullification Advocacy Inside the

---

7. For example, before the Civil War, some Northern antislavery juries refused to convict defendants charged with violations of the Fugitive Slave Law. After the war, it was Southern white juries that nullified the law, in cases involving prosecution of whites for the mistreatment of blacks. Similar situations have arisen during Prohibition (nullification of liquor laws), in pre- and poststatehood Utah (nullification, by Mormon juries, of bigamy and polygamy laws), and during the Vietnam War (refusal to convict draft dodgers and war protestors).

8. The Fully Informed Jury Association (FIJA) is a nonprofit organization that attempts to inform prospective jurors (and the public) about jury nullification through distribution of pamphlets and other methods. The activities of the FIJA have been most noticeable in the West and South, where antigovernment sentiment often tends to run higher than in the East or Midwest. For more information, see the FIJA website: http://www.fija.org.

Jury Room and Outside the Courtroom, 65 U. Chi. L. Rev. 433 (1998). Perhaps the best explanation for this apparent conundrum was provided by Judge Leventhal of the U.S. Court of Appeals for the D.C. Circuit, who argued that jurors do not need formal instruction about their "freedom in an occasional case to depart from what the judge says"; instead, they learn about the nullification power through "informal communication from the total culture," including literature, movies, television, newspapers, magazines, and conversation. Anything more, Judge Leventhal claimed, would run an unacceptable risk of turning the jury into "a wildcat or run-away institution." See United States v. Dougherty, 473 F.2d 1113 (D.C. Cir. 1972).

The Sixth Amendment right to jury trial was applied to the states, by means of incorporation through the Fourteenth Amendment's Due Process Clause, in Duncan v. Louisiana, 391 U.S. 145 (1968). The Duncan case appears in Chapter 2, at page 97; at this point, you should read (or reread) it there. Notably, the Court in Duncan identified several reasons for believing that the right to jury trial in criminal cases is a "fundamental right" that must be recognized by the states: (1) It serves "to prevent oppression by the Government," protecting defendants against "unfounded criminal charges brought to eliminate enemies" and "judges too responsive to the voice of higher authority"; (2) it provides "an inestimable safe-guard against the corrupt or overzealous prosecutor and against the compliant, biased, or eccentric judge"; (3) it gives defendants the opportunity to seek "the common-sense judgment of a jury" rather than "the more tutored but perhaps less sympathetic reaction of the single judge"; and (4) it reflects "a reluctance to entrust plenary powers over the life and liberty of the citizen to one judge or to a group of judges." Id., at 155-156.

The Court in Duncan acknowledged that there must be "a category of petty crimes or offenses which is not subject to the Sixth Amendment jury trial provision," see id., at 159; it declined, however, to fix the line between "serious" and "petty" crimes, holding only that Duncan's crime—which carried a possible two-year prison sentence—was nonpetty. In Baldwin v. New York, 399 U.S. 117 (1970), the Court rejected the view that the line should be drawn between felonies and misde-meanors. Three justices (White, Brennan, and Marshall) concluded that "no offense can be deemed 'petty' for purposes of the right to trial by jury where imprisonment for more than six months is authorized." Id., at 69. Two other justices (Black and Douglas) wanted to go even further and apply the right to jury trial to all crimes. Id., at 74-76 (Black, J., concurring in the judgment).

What if the crime charged carries a maximum punishment of six months or less in prison? Can the defendant nevertheless claim a Sixth Amendment right to jury trial? There is a strong presumption against such claims unless the crime also involves "additional statutory penalties so severe as to indicate that the legislature considered the offense serious." See Lewis v. United States, 518 U.S. 322, 326 (1996). Thus, the Court has rejected jury-trial claims made by a defendant who received a mandatory two-day jail term for an otherwise petty crime, see Blanton v. City of North Las Vegas, 489 U.S. 538 (1989), and by a defendant who was charged in a single indictment with multiple petty crimes carrying an aggregate possible prison sentence of one year, see Lewis, supra. When the criminal statute does not provide a maximum sentence, however, the actual sentence imposed becomes important, and aggregation is permitted. See Codispoti v. Pennsylvania, 418 U.S.

506 (1974) (jury trial applies to multiple contempt charges resulting in more than six months' imprisonment); Taylor v. Hayes, 418 U.S. 488 (1974) (jury trial does not apply to multiple contempt charges resulting in exactly six months' imprisonment).

Note that the existence of a right to jury trial does not mean that a jury trial necessarily will occur. In addition to the strong likelihood of a plea bargain, see supra, Chapter 10, the defendant may waive his right to jury trial and request a bench trial. See Patton v. United States, 281 U.S. 276 (1930). The defendant does not, however, have the constitutional right to insist on a bench trial. In Singer v. United States, 380 U.S. 24 (1965), involving a challenge to a provision in the Federal Rules of Criminal Procedure requiring prosecutorial and judicial approval before a defendant could waive jury trial, the Court explained: "We find no constitutional impediment to conditioning a waiver of [the jury-trial] right on the consent of the prosecuting attorney and the trial judge when, if either refuses to consent, the result is simply that the defendant is subject to an impartial trial by jury — the very thing that the Constitution guarantees him." Id., at 36.

Once it has been determined that the right to jury trial applies to a particular case (and assuming that the defendant has not waived that right), then the next question becomes, what is the content of the right? What exactly is a "jury," within the meaning of the Sixth Amendment? This question involves several dimensions, including jury size, unanimity, and vicinage. The next case deals with the first dimension, size.

BALLEW v. GEORGIA

Certiorari to the Court of Appeals of Georgia
435 U.S. 223 (1978)

JUSTICE BLACKMUN announced the judgment of the Court and delivered an opinion in which JUSTICE STEVENS joined.

This case presents the issue whether a state criminal trial to a jury of only five persons deprives the accused of the right to trial by jury guaranteed to him by the Sixth and Fourteenth Amendments. Our resolution of the issue requires an application of principles enunciated in Williams v. Florida, 399 U.S. 78 (1970), where the use of a six-person jury in a state criminal trial was upheld against similar constitutional attack.

I

In November 1973 petitioner Claude Davis Ballew was the manager of the Paris Adult Theatre at 320 Peachtree Street, Atlanta, Ga. On November 9 two investigators from the Fulton County Solicitor General's office viewed at the theater a motion picture film entitled "Behind the Green Door." . . . After they had seen the film, they obtained a warrant for its seizure, returned to the theater, viewed the film once again, and seized it. . . . Petitioner and a cashier were arrested. Investigators returned to the theater on November 26, viewed the film in its entirety, secured still another warrant, and on November 27 once again viewed the motion picture and seized a second copy of the film. . . .

On September 14, 1974, petitioner was charged in a two-count misdemeanor accusation with [distributing obscene materials]. ...

Petitioner was brought to trial in the Criminal Court of Fulton County. After a jury of 5 persons had been selected and sworn, petitioner moved that the court impanel a jury of 12 persons. ... That court, however, tried its misdemeanor cases before juries of five persons. ... Petitioner contended that for an obscenity trial, a jury of only five was constitutionally inadequate to assess the contemporary standards of the community. ... He also argued that the Sixth and Fourteenth Amendments required a jury of at least six members in criminal cases. ...

The motion for a 12-person jury was overruled, and the trial went on to its conclusion before the 5-person jury that had been impaneled. At the conclusion of the trial, the jury deliberated for 38 minutes and returned a verdict of guilty on both counts of the accusation. ... The court imposed a sentence of one year and a $1,000 fine on each count, the periods of incarceration to run concurrently and to be suspended upon payment of the fines. ... After a subsequent hearing, the court denied an amended motion for a new trial.

Petitioner took an appeal to the Court of Appeals of the State of Georgia. There he argued[, inter alia, that] the use of the five-member jury deprived him of his Sixth and Fourteenth Amendment right to a trial by jury. ...

The Court of Appeals rejected petitioner's contentions. ... In its consideration of the five-person-jury issue, the court noted that Williams v. Florida had not established a constitutional minimum number of jurors. Absent a holding by this Court that a five-person jury was constitutionally inadequate, the Court of Appeals considered itself bound by Sanders v. State, 234 Ga. 586, 216 S.E.2d 838 (1975), ... where the constitutionality of the five-person jury had been upheld. ...

In his petition for certiorari here, petitioner raised[, inter alia,] the unconstitutionality of the five-person jury. ... We granted certiorari. 429 U.S. 1071 (1977). Because we now hold that the five member jury does not satisfy the jury trial guarantee of the Sixth Amendment, as applied to the States through the Fourteenth, we do not reach the other issues.

II

The Fourteenth Amendment guarantees the right of trial by jury in all state nonpetty criminal cases. Duncan v. Louisiana, 391 U.S. 145, 159-162 (1968). The Court in *Duncan* applied this Sixth Amendment right to the States because "trial by jury in criminal cases is fundamental to the American scheme of justice." Id., at 149. The right attaches in the present case because the maximum penalty for violating §26-2101, as it existed at the time of the alleged offenses, exceeded six months' imprisonment. ...

In Williams v. Florida, 399 U.S., at 100, the Court reaffirmed that the "purpose of the jury trial, as we noted in *Duncan*, is to prevent oppression by the Government. 'Providing an accused with the right to be tried by a jury of his peers gave him an inestimable safeguard against the corrupt or overzealous prosecutor and against the compliant, biased, or eccentric judge.' Duncan v. Louisiana, [391 U.S.,] at 156." ... This purpose is attained by the participation of the community in determinations of guilt and by the application of the common sense of laymen who, as jurors, consider the case. Williams v. Florida, 399 U.S., at 100.

Williams held that these functions and this purpose could be fulfilled by a jury of six members. As the Court's opinion in that case explained at some length, id., at 86-90, common-law juries included 12 members by historical accident, "unrelated to the great purposes which gave rise to the jury in the first place." Id., at 89-90. The Court's earlier cases that had *assumed* the number 12 to be constitutionally compelled were set to one side because they had not considered history and the function of the jury. Id., at 90-92. Rather than requiring 12 members, then, the Sixth Amendment mandated a jury only of sufficient size to promote group deliberation, to insulate members from outside intimidation, and to provide a representative cross-section of the community. Id., at 100. Although recognizing that by 1970 little empirical research had evaluated jury performance, the Court found no evidence that the reliability of jury verdicts diminished with six-member panels. Nor did the Court anticipate significant differences in result, including the frequency of "hung" juries. Id., at 101-102, and nn. 47 and 48. Because the reduction in size did not threaten exclusion of any particular class from jury roles, concern that the representative or cross-section character of the jury would suffer with a decrease to six members seemed "an unrealistic one." Id., at 102. As a consequence, the six-person jury was held not to violate the Sixth and Fourteenth Amendments.

III

When the Court in *Williams* permitted the reduction in jury size — or, to put it another way, when it held that a jury of six was not unconstitutional — it expressly reserved ruling on the issue whether a number smaller than six passed constitutional scrutiny. Id., at 91 n. 28.[9] The Court refused to speculate when this so-called "slippery slope" would become too steep. We face now, however, the two-fold question whether a further reduction in the size of the state criminal trial jury does make the grade too dangerous, that is, whether it inhibits the functioning of the jury as an institution to a significant degree, and, if so, whether any state interest counterbalances and justifies the disruption so as to preserve its constitutionality.

Williams v. Florida and Colgrove v. Battin, 413 U.S. 149 (1973) (where the Court held that a jury of six members did not violate the Seventh Amendment right to a jury trial in a civil case), generated a quantity of scholarly work on jury size.[10] These writings do not draw or identify a bright line below which the number of jurors would not be able to function as required by the standards enunciated in *Williams*. On the other hand, they raise significant questions about the wisdom and constitutionality of a reduction below six. We examine these concerns:

9. In the cited footnote the Court said: "We have no occasion in this case to determine what minimum number can still constitute a 'jury,' but we do not doubt that six is above that minimum."

Respondent picks up the last phrase with absolute literalness here when it argues: "If six is above the minimum, five cannot be below the minimum. There is no number in between." . . . We, however, do not accept the proposition that by stating the number six was "above" the constitutional minimum the Court, by implication, held that at least the number five was constitutional. Instead, the Court was holding that six passed constitutional muster but was reserving judgment on any number less than six.

10. [Here the Court cited 19 separate books and articles reporting various social scientific studies of jury size conducted between 1971 and 1977.]

We have considered [these studies] carefully because they provide the only basis, besides judicial hunch, for a decision about whether smaller and smaller juries will be able to fulfill the purpose and functions of the Sixth Amendment. Without an examination about how juries and small groups actually work, we would not understand the basis for the conclusion of Mr. Justice Powell that a "line has to be drawn somewhere." . . .

First, recent empirical data suggest that progressively smaller juries are less likely to foster effective group deliberation. At some point, this decline leads to inaccurate factfinding and incorrect application of the common sense of the community to the facts. Generally, a positive correlation exists between group size and the quality of both group performance and group productivity. A variety of explanations have been offered for this conclusion. Several are particularly applicable in the jury setting. The smaller the group, the less likely are members to make critical contributions necessary for the solution of a given problem. Because most juries are not permitted to take notes, . . . memory is important for accurate jury deliberations. As juries decrease in size, then, they are less likely to have members who remember each of the important pieces of evidence or argument. Furthermore, the smaller the group, the less likely it is to overcome the biases of its members to obtain an accurate result. When individual and group decisionmaking were compared, it was seen that groups performed better because prejudices of individuals were frequently counterbalanced, and objectivity resulted. Groups also exhibited increased motivation and self-criticism. All these advantages, except, perhaps, self-motivation, tend to diminish as the size of the group diminishes. Because juries frequently face complex problems laden with value choices, the benefits are important and should be retained. In particular, the counterbalancing of various biases is critical to the accurate application of the common sense of the community to the facts of any given case.

Second, the data now raise doubts about the accuracy of the results achieved by smaller and smaller panels. Statistical studies suggest that the risk of convicting an innocent person (Type I error) rises as the size of the jury diminishes. Because the risk of not convicting a guilty person (Type II error) increases with the size of the panel, an optimal jury size can be selected as a function of the interaction between the two risks. Nagel and Neef concluded that the optimal size, for the purpose of minimizing errors, should vary with the importance attached to the two types of mistakes. After weighting Type I error as 10 times more significant than Type II, perhaps not an unreasonable assumption, they concluded that the optimal jury size was between six and eight. As the size diminished to five and below, the weighted sum of errors increased because of the enlarging risk of the conviction of innocent defendants. [See Nagel & Neef, Deductive Modeling to Determine an Optimum Jury Size and Fraction Required to Convict, [1975] Wash. U. L.Q. 933, 946-948, 956, 975.]

Another doubt about progressively smaller juries arises from the increasing inconsistency that results from the decreases. Saks argued that the "more a jury type fosters consistency, the greater will be the proportion of juries which select the correct (i.e., the same) verdict and the fewer 'errors' will be made." [M. Saks, Jury Verdicts 86-87 (1977).] . . . Working with statistics described in H. Kalven & H. Zeisel, The American Jury 460 (1966), Nagel and Neef tested the average conviction propensity of juries, that is, the likelihood that any given jury of a set would convict the defendant. [See Nagel & Neef, supra, at 952, 971.] They found that half of all 12-person juries would have average conviction propensities that varied by no more than 20 points. Half of all six-person juries, on the other hand, had average conviction propensities varying by 30 points, a difference they found significant in both real and percentage terms. Lempert reached similar results when he considered the likelihood of juries to compromise over the various views of their members, an important phenomenon for the fulfillment of the common-sense function. . . . [See Lempert, Undiscovering "Nondiscernible" Differences:

Empirical Research and the Jury-Size Cases, 73 Mich. L. Rev. 643, 680 (1975).] And he predicted that compromises would be more consistent when larger juries were employed. For example, 12-person juries could be expected to reach extreme compromises in 4% of the cases, while 6-person panels would reach extreme results in 16%. All three of these post-*Williams* studies, therefore, raise significant doubts about the consistency and reliability of the decisions of smaller juries.

Third, the data suggest that the verdicts of jury deliberation in criminal cases will vary as juries become smaller, and that the variance amounts to an imbalance to the detriment of one side, the defense. Both Lempert and Zeisel found that the number of hung juries would diminish as the panels decreased in size. Zeisel said that the number would be cut in half — from 5% to 2.4% with a decrease from 12 to 6 members. [See Zeisel, . . . And Then There Were None: The Diminution of the Federal Jury, 38 U. Chi. L. Rev. 710, 720 (1971).] Both studies emphasized that juries in criminal cases generally hang with only one, or more likely two, jurors remaining unconvinced of guilt. Also, group theory suggests that a person in the minority will adhere to his position more frequently when he has at least one other person supporting his argument. . . . As the numbers [on the jury] diminish below six, . . . fewer panels would have one member with the minority viewpoint and still fewer would have two. The chance for hung juries would decline accordingly.

Fourth, what has just been said about the presence of minority viewpoint as juries decrease in size foretells problems not only for jury decisionmaking, but also for the representation of minority groups in the community. The Court repeatedly has held that meaningful community participation cannot be attained with the exclusion of minorities or other identifiable groups from jury service. . . . Although the Court in *Williams* concluded that the six-person jury did not fail to represent adequately a cross-section of the community, the opportunity for meaningful and appropriate representation does decrease with the size of the panels. Thus, if a minority group constitutes 10% of the community, 53.1% of randomly selected six-member juries could be expected to have no minority representative among their members, and 89% not to have two. Further reduction in size will erect additional barriers to representation.

Fifth, several authors have identified in jury research methodological problems tending to mask differences in the operation of smaller and larger juries. . . . Studies that aggregate data also risk masking case-by-case differences in jury deliberations. . . .

IV

While we adhere to, and reaffirm our holding in Williams v. Florida, these studies, most of which have been made since *Williams* was decided in 1970, lead us to conclude that the purpose and functioning of the jury in a criminal trial is seriously impaired, and to a constitutional degree, by a reduction in size to below six members. We readily admit that we do not pretend to discern a clear line between six members and five. But the assembled data raise substantial doubt about the reliability and appropriate representation of panels smaller than six. Because of the fundamental importance of the jury trial to the American system of criminal justice, any further reduction that promotes inaccurate and possibly biased decisionmaking, that causes untoward differences in verdicts, and that prevents juries from truly representing their communities, attains constitutional significance.

Georgia here presents no persuasive argument that a reduction to five does not offend important Sixth Amendment interests. First, its reliance on Johnson v. Louisiana, 406 U.S. 356 (1972), for the proposition that the Court previously has approved the five-person jury is misplaced. In *Johnson* the petitioner . . . contended that requiring only nine members of a 12-person panel to convict in a felony case was a deprival of equal protection when a unanimous verdict was required from the 5-member panel used in a misdemeanor trial. The Court held merely that the classification was not invidious. Id., at 364. Because the issue of the constitutionality of the five-member jury was not then before the Court, it did not rule upon it.

Second, Georgia argues that its use of five-member juries does not violate the Sixth and Fourteenth Amendments because they are used only in misdemeanor cases. If six persons may constitutionally assess the felony charge in *Williams*, the State reasons, five persons should be a constitutionally adequate number for a misdemeanor trial. The problem with this argument is that the purpose and functions of the jury do not vary significantly with the importance of the crime. . . . In the present case the possible deprivation of liberty is substantial. . . . We cannot conclude that there is less need for the imposition and the direction of the sense of the community in this case than when the State has chosen to label an offense a felony. The need for an effective jury here must be judged by the same standards announced and applied in Williams v. Florida.

Third, the retention by Georgia of the unanimity requirement does not solve the Sixth and Fourteenth Amendment problem. Our concern has to do with the ability of the smaller group to perform the functions mandated by the Amendments. That a five-person jury may return a unanimous decision does not speak to the questions whether the group engaged in meaningful deliberation, could remember all the important facts and arguments, and truly represented the sense of the entire community. . . .

Fourth, Georgia submits that the five-person jury adequately represents the community because there is no arbitrary exclusion of any particular class. We agree that it has not been demonstrated that the Georgia system violates the Equal Protection Clause by discriminating on the basis of race or some other improper classification. . . . But the data outlined above raise substantial doubt about the ability of juries truly to represent the community as membership decreases below six. . . . Not only is the representation of racial minorities threatened in such circumstances, but also majority attitude or various minority positions may be misconstrued or misapplied by the smaller groups. . . .

Fifth, the empirical data cited by Georgia do not relieve our doubts. . . . Methodological problems prevent reliance on the three studies that do purport to bolster Georgia's position. The reliability of the two Michigan studies cited by the State has been criticized elsewhere. [See Saks, supra, at 43-46; Zeisel & Diamond, "Convincing Empirical Evidence" on the Six Member Jury, 41 U. Chi. L. Rev. 281, 286-290 (1974); Diamond, A Jury Experiment Reanalyzed, 7 U. Mich. J.L. Reform 520 (1974).] The Davis study . . . also presented an extreme set of facts so that none of the panels rendered a guilty verdict. [See Saks, supra, at 49-51.] None of these three reports, therefore, convinces us that a reduction in the number of jurors below six will not affect to a constitutional degree the functioning of juries in criminal trials.

V

With the reduction in the number of jurors below six creating a substantial threat to Sixth and Fourteenth Amendment guarantees, we must consider whether any interest of the State justifies the reduction. We find no significant state advantage in reducing the number of jurors from six to five.

The States utilize juries of less than 12 primarily for administrative reasons. Savings in court time and in financial costs are claimed to justify the reductions. The financial benefits of the reduction from 12 to 6 are substantial; this is mainly because fewer jurors draw daily allowances as they hear cases. On the other hand, the asserted saving in judicial time is not so clear. . . . [In one study,] [t]otal trial time did not diminish, and court delays and backlogs improved very little. [See Pabst, Statistical Studies of the Costs of Six-Man Versus Twelve-Man Juries, 14 Wm. & Mary L. Rev. 326 (1972).] The point that is to be made, of course, is that a reduction in size from six to five or four or even three would save the States little. . . . Perhaps this explains why only two States, Georgia and Virginia, have reduced the size of juries in certain nonpetty criminal cases to five. In short, the State has offered little or no justification for its reduction to five members.

Petitioner, therefore, has established that his trial on criminal charges before a five-member jury deprived him of the right to trial by jury guaranteed by the Sixth and Fourteenth Amendments.

VI

The judgment of the Court of Appeals is reversed, and the case is remanded for further proceedings not inconsistent with this opinion.

It is so ordered. [Justice Brennan, in an opinion joined by Justices Stewart and Marshall, joined Justice Blackmun's lead opinion "insofar as it holds that the Sixth and Fourteenth Amendments require juries in criminal trials to contain more than five persons," but argued that the defendant should not undergo a new trial because the Georgia obscenity statute was unconstitutionally overbroad. The opinions of Justice Stevens, concurring, and Justice White, concurring in the judgment, are omitted.]

JUSTICE POWELL, with whom CHIEF JUSTICE BURGER and JUSTICE REHNQUIST join, concurring in the judgment.

I concur in the judgment, as I agree that use of a jury as small as five members, with authority to convict for serious offenses, involves grave questions of fairness. As the opinion of Mr. Justice Blackmun indicates, the line between five-and six-member juries is difficult to justify, but a line has to be drawn somewhere if the substance of jury trial is to be preserved.

I do not agree, however, that every feature of jury trial practice must be the same in both federal and state courts. . . . Also, I have reservations as to the wisdom — as well as the necessity — of Mr. Justice Blackmun's heavy reliance on numerology derived from statistical studies. Moreover, neither the validity nor the methodology employed by the studies cited was subjected to the traditional testing mechanisms of the adversary process. The studies relied on merely represent unexamined findings of persons interested in the jury system. . . .

NOTES AND QUESTIONS

1. With one exception, all of the empirical studies cited by the Court in *Ballew* involved a comparison between 6-member juries and 12-member juries. As noted by the Court, the studies established that 6-member juries are inferior, in almost every respect, to 12-member juries. Why, then, did the Court "adhere to, and reaffirm" its decision in Williams v. Florida, upholding the use of 6-member juries? Would it not have made much more sense for the Court simply to overrule *Williams* and hold that any jury with *6 or fewer* members — including Ballew's 5-member jury — violates the Sixth Amendment?

As for the specific question before the Court in *Ballew* — namely, whether five-member juries can function as well as the six-member juries that had been upheld in Williams v. Florida — only one cited study even touched on that subject. On what basis, then, did the Court conclude that there is a significant difference — of constitutional stature — between five-member and six-member juries? Did the Court have sufficient empirical evidence to support that proposition? Was the Court justified in simply extrapolating the results of the studies of six-member juries? Even if hard lines must sometimes be drawn, shouldn't the Court draw those lines in a logical and empirically supportable manner?

2. *Ballew* is a rare example of a case in which the Supreme Court relied on empirical evidence (or, as Justice Powell dismissively described it, "numerology") to establish constitutional doctrine. Social scientists tend to view *Ballew* with a combination of pride and outrage — pride that empirical social-science research, for once, made a difference to the Court, coupled with outrage that the Court so obviously missed (or ignored) the entire message of the studies. See, e.g., sources collected in Myron Jacobstein & Roy M. Mersky, Jury Size: Articles and Bibliography from the Literature of Law and the Social and Behavioral Sciences (1998).

The Court's almost universal reluctance to rely on empirical social-science research is itself a subject worthy of study. Why is empirical evidence relatively rare in Court opinions? Is it because the Court does not understand such evidence? Because the Court feels incompetent to weigh and evaluate it? Because the Court does not want to rely on such evidence, based on fear of losing control over the legal outcome? Or because the Court generally knows where it wants to go with a case and does not want to be bothered with empirical evidence that might point in the opposite direction? See J. Alexander Tanford, The Limits of a Scientific Jurisprudence: The Supreme Court and Psychology, 66 Ind. L.J. 137 (1990).

Given the presence of important empirical issues in so many of the constitutional cases that come before the Court, and the unavoidable necessity to resolve such empirical issues in the course of making a decision, what generally takes the place of empirical evidence in the Court's analysis? Professor Richard Lempert has suggested the following:

> . . . Courts are influenced . . . by popular knowledge, and judges as part of an edu-
> cated elite are influenced by social science learning to the extent it penetrates their elite
> culture. . . .
>
> It is . . . likely that appellate judges are most influenced by freelance research pub-
> lished in popular publications read by the educated elite or in publications specifically
> designed for lawyers, and to a lesser extent by the kinds of summary talks that social
> scientists sometimes give at bar association meetings, judicial conferences, continuing
> education programs for judges and the like.

Richard Lempert, "Between Cup and Lip": Social Science Influences on Law and Policy, 10 Law & Pol'y 167, 188, 190-191. In other words, instead of relying on empirical evidence that might be submitted by the parties, or by an amicus curiae, the justices may be more likely to base their empirical judgments on whatever social science they have read about in the New York Times or have seen on The NewsHour with Jim Lehrer.

3. Note that the justifications given for trial by jury do not include accurate adjudication, although perhaps a right to see the "common-sense judgment of the jury" edges up to the point. In fact, there is reason to believe that group decision making may have epistemological advantages in certain circumstances. Long ago, the Marquis de Condorcet proved, interestingly in the context of justifying jury decision making in capital cases, "that if the probable truth of an enlightened voter's opinion is greater than one-half when choosing between one of two alternatives, then the larger the group of such voters, the greater the probability that a majority decision will be true." Ronald J. Allen & Sarah A. Jehl, Burdens of Persuasion in Civil Cases: Algorithms v. Explanations, 4 Mich. St. L. Rev. 893, 906. The modern heir to Condorcet is a body of research commonly known as "the wisdom of the crowd," in honor of the book that brought the issue into public awareness, James Surowiecki, The Wisdom of Crowds: Why the Many Are Smarter Than the Few and How Collective Wisdom Shapes Business, Economies, Societies, and Nations (2004). The conditions under which these effects occur are stringent, however, including well-informed, independent, and unbiased voters, for example. Recent work has begun exploring how often those conditions are met in real work decision context and the detrimental consequences for accurate decision making when they are not. See, e.g., Vassilis Kostakos: Is the Crowd's Wisdom Biased? A Quantitative Analysis of Three Online Communities, 4 Computational Science & Engineering 251-255 (2009), and the MIT Technology Review: http://www.technologyreview.com/web/23477/?a=f. Nonetheless, jurors, and thus juries, may often meet these conditions, although majority voting is not the decision rule.

Other recent empirical work may also bear on the wisdom of jury decision making, but less optimistically so. Group deliberation seems, in many instances, to have a polarizing effect, moving bodies that deliberate toward more extreme positions than their initial starting points would suggest. This effect is discussed in Cass Sunstein, The Law of Group Polarization, 10 J. Pol. Phil. 175 (2002). Some jury trials may well reflect this phenomenon, such as death penalty cases involving controversial issues and, literally, life or death.

Should any of this matter to constitutional adjudication?

4. In Apodaca v. Oregon, 406 U.S. 404 (1972), the Court addressed the issue of jury unanimity in the context of the traditional 12-member jury. Four justices took the position that the Sixth Amendment requirement must be the same for both state and federal criminal cases and that jury unanimity is required in both contexts. Four other justices agreed that the Sixth Amendment requirement must be the same for both state and federal criminal cases, but felt that jury unanimity is not required in either context. The ninth justice, Justice Powell, claimed (reminiscent of the earlier views of Justice Harlan) that due process incorporation does not require imposition of the same Sixth Amendment rule in both state and federal criminal cases. Justice Powell concluded that, even though the Sixth Amendment guarantees a unanimous jury in federal criminal cases, the states may dispense with unanimity without violating due process. The confusing end result: Eight justices agreed that the Sixth

Amendment must mean the same thing in both state and federal criminal cases, and five justices agreed that the Sixth Amendment requires jury unanimity. Yet, because of Justice Powell's idiosyncratic view about due process incorporation, the states nevertheless were permitted to dispense with unanimity.

If a state chooses to reduce the size of its juries to six members, pursuant to Williams v. Florida, then unanimity is required. See Burch v. Louisiana, 441 U.S. 130 (1979).

Kim Taylor-Thompson defends the unanimity requirement because it forces the jury to reach "complete consensus," which "at least provide[s] an impetus to stretch beyond group experiences and loyalties" and thus helps to ensure that minority voices on the jury will be heard. In contrast, with nonunanimous juries "the majority could ignore minority views by simply outvoting dissenters." Kim Taylor-Thompson, Empty Votes in Jury Deliberations, 113 Harv. L. Rev. 1261, 1264 (2000). Interestingly, very few states have instituted nonunanimity voting rules for juries. One reason is the perception that the unanimity requirement does not lead too frequently to hung juries, and thus there is no good reason to jettison it. See, e.g., the empirical study done for the National Center for State Courts: Paula L. Hannaford-Agor, Valerie P. Hans, Nicole L. Mott, & G. Thomas Munsterman, Are Hung Juries a Problem? (2002). The rate for hung juries fluctuates around 5-6 percent in both state and federal felony courts, although there are numerous difficulties in obtaining and classifying the date (e.g., how does one classify a case in which a jury hangs on one but not another count?). As the authors point out, the implications of hung jurors may have been even less than meets the eye: "The limited data we were able to obtain suggest that juror deadlock often forces prosecutors and defense counsel to reassess the relative strengths and weaknesses of their cases and agree on a nontrial disposition. Over half of the cases that originally hung ultimately resulted in a plea agreement or a dismissal. Only one-third of trials that resulted in a hung jury were retried to a new jury. Dispositions in the retrials mirrored the original distribution of jury trial outcomes almost perfectly — a fact which belies the popular contention that these cases would have resulted in a conviction but for the unreasonable behavior of one or two holdout jurors." Id., at 82-83.

5. Article III of the Constitution contains a venue clause, requiring that "the trial of all crimes . . . shall be held in the state where the said crimes shall have been committed." In addition, the Sixth Amendment requires that juries be "of the state and district wherein the crime shall have been committed," a requirement usually referred to as vicinage. Application of these two constitutional requirements depends on an analysis of the elements of the particular crime involved. See, e.g., United States v. Rodriguez-Moreno, 526 U.S. 275 (1999) (defendant charged with using or carrying a firearm "during and in relation to any crime of violence," in violation of 18 U.S.C. §924(c)(1), may be tried, consistently with vicinage and venue requirements, in any district where the crime of violence was committed, even if no firearm was used therein); United States v. Cabrales, 524 U.S. 1 (1998) (defendant charged with money laundering offenses, in violation of 18 U.S.C. §§1956(a)(1)(B)(ii) and 1957, may not be tried in Missouri because, although the money allegedly derived from illegal sales of cocaine in Missouri, the alleged acts of money laundering by the defendant occurred entirely in Florida). Venue and vicinage are discussed in Chapter 11, supra.

B. *Jury Composition*

There are three central issues concerning the composition of a criminal jury: (1) Was the jury impartial, within the meaning of the Sixth Amendment? (2) Was the jury selected from a venire that represented a "fair cross section" of the community, an implied requirement under the Sixth Amendment? (3) Was the jury selected in a nondiscriminatory way in compliance with the requirements of the Equal Protection Clause of the Fourteenth Amendment (or, in federal cases, the equivalent requirements imposed under the Fifth Amendment's Due Process Clause. The first stage of jury selection, and thus the first step toward vindicating these requirements, involves the compilation by the jury commissioner (or equivalent official) of a large *master list* of prospective jurors. In the (not so distant) past, many jurisdictions employed a "key man" system, under which community leaders would identify those thought qualified to serve on a jury. Today, however, master lists are usually derived from a combination of voter registration lists, telephone books, drivers' license lists, lists of public utility customers, and even welfare rolls.

From the master list, random processes are used to select a subset of names for the *venire*, a smaller list from which prospective jurors will be called (again, on a random basis) to serve in an individual case (or, in some jurisdictions, for a term of weeks or months, during which the same venire remains subject to being called for jury duty). When members of the venire are contacted by the jury commissioner for possible jury service, they are asked to supply basic information about themselves. This information may result in the prospective juror being disqualified or exempted. *Disqualifications* are based on such matters as lack of citizenship, under-age status, illiteracy, or the existence of a prior felony conviction. *Exemptions* are based largely on occupation; in most jurisdictions, for example, doctors and members of the clergy are exempted.[9]

Many prospective jurors who are neither disqualified nor exempted claim that jury service would be a personal hardship for them. This claim, if persuasive, may lead to the granting of an excuse, either by the jury commissioner or (at a later stage of the selection process) by the trial judge. *Excuses* are often based on advanced age, physical infirmity, financial hardship, transportation problems, or the need to care for young children. Even within a particular jurisdiction, the likelihood of obtaining an excuse may vary with the receptivity of the trial judge to the prospective juror's particular claim of hardship.

After the venire has been culled by disqualifications, exemptions, and excuses, the next stage of jury selection consists of voir dire. During *voir dire* (from the French, "to see, to speak"), prospective jurors are asked questions, in person, so that the trial judge, prosecutor, and defense attorney can listen to their answers and thereby learn more about them. Depending on the jurisdiction, voir dire may be conducted by the lawyers, by the judge, or by both the lawyers and the judge. Even where the judge conducts voir dire, often the lawyers will be allowed to submit questions to be asked by the judge. The scope of voir dire questioning is determined, in general, by the local legal culture (i.e., in some areas, prolonged and probing voir

---

9. Not all exemptions, in all jurisdictions, are so logical; in Indiana, for example, doctors are not exempted, but licensed veterinarians and dentists are. Also exempted are school board members from the City of Indianapolis — but not from any other cities in the state. See Burns Ind. Code Ann. §33-28-4-8(7), (8), (9) (2004).

dire is a routine occurrence, while in others, the customary practice is to ask only a few brief questions) and, in specific cases, by limits set by the judge.

Voir dire serves at least three important purposes. First, the Sixth Amendment guarantees every defendant the right to be tried by an impartial jury, and voir dire provides the lawyers and the judge with information that allows for the *exclusion* of prospective jurors who may be disinterested for one reason or another. For example, if a prospective juror, in response to voir dire questioning, states that she is closely related to a police officer and, as a result, cannot fairly and impartially evaluate the defendant's claim that a police officer fabricated evidence against him, then that prospective juror would likely be subject to exclusion. The potential sources of lack of impartiality are as wide ranging as humanity is complex — financial interest, emotional attachment or its opposite, ideological commitments, and so on.

The primary mechanism for the exclusion of potential jurors lacking impartiality is the *challenge for cause*. During or after voir dire, the prosecutor and defense attorney have an unlimited opportunity to make challenges for cause against prospective jurors they believe to be biased. These challenges must be resolved by the trial judge, based on information obtained from the prospective juror. Even in the absence of a challenge for cause, however, the judge must exclude, on her own motion, any prospective juror whom the judge believes to be biased.

A second purpose for voir dire is to provide the lawyers with information that can be used in the exercise of another means of excluding potential jurors, called the *peremptory challenge*. These challenges are granted in limited number, according to the law of the particular jurisdiction (usually the same number for both sides, although sometimes the defense is granted more than the prosecution), and — subject to narrow exceptions discussed below — can be exercised for any reason at all (or even without any stated reason). The idea behind the peremptory challenge is that a lawyer may sometimes feel that a prospective juror would be adverse to her side of the case, yet be unable to establish that the prospective juror is biased; indeed, it may be impossible (or impolitic, in the presence of other prospective jurors) for the lawyer even to state the basis for her feelings. The peremptory challenge allows the lawyer to act on such feelings, and to exclude such prospective jurors, without the need to explain. For example, if a prospective juror, in response to voir dire questioning, states that he often got into trouble as a teenager, this would probably be insufficient to show bias but might provide the basis for the exercise of a peremptory challenge by the prosecutor, who might fear that such a prospective juror would be more likely than others to sympathize with the defendant.

The third purpose for voir dire, especially in those jurisdictions where lawyers play a prominent role in voir dire, is to provide prospective jurors with their first exposure to the issues in the particular case. Often, prosecutors and defense attorneys will use voir dire as an opportunity to begin the process of educating the jury about the case — from their own respective perspectives, of course. For example, a defense lawyer who plans to contest an eyewitness account of the crime may ask prospective jurors at voir dire if they have ever known of an instance where an eyewitness to an event turned out to be mistaken about the identity of the parties involved. It has been estimated that such attempts to sensitize the jury may occur in 40 to 80 percent of criminal trials. See R. W. Balch, Curt Taylor Griffiths, Edwin L. Hall, & L. Thomas Winfree, The Socialization of Jurors, 4 J. Crim. Just. 271-283 (1976).

At the conclusion of voir dire, after all challenges for cause have been ruled upon and all peremptory challenges have been exercised (or waived), what remains is the jury that will be sworn to decide the case. In the Notes and Questions that follow, we first examine more carefully the requirement of impartiality. We then turn to the remaining two issues. The *Duren* case and the materials following it examine the meaning of a "fair cross section of the community" for purposes of the right to trial by jury, and *Batson* and the related material examine the potential discriminatory use of peremptory challenges.

NOTES AND QUESTIONS ON THE IMPARTIALITY REQUIREMENT

1. The impartiality requirement does not mean that prospective jurors must be completely uninformed about the facts of the case; in modern society, it might not be possible to find jurors (at least ones with minimal intelligence) who have not heard something about a high-profile case from television, newspapers, or other media. The impartiality requirement also does not mean that prospective jurors must be completely without opinions or must start out precisely evenhanded in their views about the case. Rather, it is only "those strong and deep impressions which close the mind against the testimony that may be offered in opposition to them, which will combat that testimony and resist its force, [that] constitute a sufficient objection." Reynolds v. United States, 98 U.S. 145, 155 (1879). To put it another way, a prospective juror lacks impartiality only if he or she has views about the case strong enough to "prevent or substantially impair the performance of his [or her] duties as a juror" in accordance with the law. See Wainwright v. Witt, 469 U.S. 412, 424 (1985).

2. Several leading Supreme Court impartiality cases have involved claims that jurors were biased because of racial prejudice. Instructive in this regard are Ham v. South Carolina, 409 U.S. 524 (1973), and Ristaino v. Ross, 424 U.S. 589 (1976). In *Ham*, the defendant was a young, bearded black man who was active in the civil rights movement in Florence, South Carolina. He was charged with marijuana possession, and he claimed to have been framed by the police because of his race and his civil rights activism. His lawyer asked the trial judge to question the prospective jurors at voir dire about their possible racial biases, but the request was denied, and Ham was convicted. The Court found a constitutional violation; although "the trial judge was not required to put the question in any particular form," the defendant must be "permitted to have the jurors interrogated on the issue of racial bias." Id., at 527.

In *Ross*, the defendant was a black man from Massachusetts charged with armed robbery, assault, and battery by means of a dangerous weapon, and assault and battery with intent to murder, in connection with an attack on a white Boston University security guard. His lawyer sought to have the trial judge ask the prospective jurors the following voir dire question: "Are there any of you who believe that a white person is more likely to be telling the truth than a black person?" The trial judge refused, and Ross was convicted. The Court affirmed the conviction, explaining that *Ham* "did not announce a requirement of universal applicability. Rather, it reflected an assessment of whether under all circumstances presented there was a constitutionally significant likelihood that, absent questioning about racial prejudice, the jurors would not be [impartial]." Id., at 596.

As the Court has acknowledged, "[I]t is plain that there is some risk of racial prejudice influencing a jury whenever there is a crime involving interracial violence." Turner v. Murray, 476 U.S. 28, 36, n. 8 (1986) (plurality opinion of Justice White). What, then, is the constitutional distinction between *Ham* and *Ross*?

The critical factor present in *Ham*, but not present in [*Ross*], was that racial issues were "inextricably bound up with the conduct of the trial," and the consequent need, under all the circumstances, specifically to inquire into possible racial prejudice in order to assure an impartial jury. . . . Although [*Ross*] involved an alleged criminal confrontation between a black assailant and a white victim, that fact pattern alone did not create a need of "constitutional dimensions" to question the jury concerning racial prejudice. . . . There is no constitutional presumption of juror bias for or against members of any particular racial or ethnic groups. . . . Only when there are more substantial indications of the likelihood of racial or ethnic prejudice affecting the jurors in a particular case does the trial court's denial of a defendant's request to examine the jurors' ability to deal impartially with this subject amount to an unconstitutional abuse of discretion.

Rosales-Lopez v. United States, 451 U.S. 182, 190 (plurality opinion of Justice White).

See also Turner v. Murray, supra, where the Court applied *Ham*, not *Ross*, to hold that "a *capital* defendant accused of an interracial crime is entitled to have prospective jurors informed of the race of the victim and questioned on the issue of racial bias," id., at 36-37 (emphasis added). In a separate, plurality portion of Justice White's lead opinion in *Turner*, he reiterated that "[t]he fact of interracial violence alone is not a 'special circumstance' entitling the defendant to have prospective jurors questioned about racial prejudice," id., at 35, n. 7 (plurality opinion of Justice White). Nevertheless, Turner's death sentence (but not his guilty verdict) had to be overturned because of the combination of three such "special circumstances": (1) that "the crime charged involved interracial violence," (2) "the broad discretion given the jury at the death-penalty hearing," and (3) "the special seriousness of the risk of improper sentencing in a capital case." Id., at 37 (plurality opinion of Justice White).

3. Another important line of Supreme Court impartiality decisions involves juror attitudes about the death penalty. In Witherspoon v. Illinois, 391 U.S. 510 (1968), the Court declared that persons opposed to the death penalty could be excluded, on impartiality grounds, from juries in capital cases only if they made it "unmistakably clear (1) that they would *automatically* vote against the imposition of capital punishment without regard to any evidence that might be developed at the trial of the case before them, or (2) that their attitude toward the death penalty would prevent them from making an impartial decision as to the defendant's *guilt*." Id., at 522, n. 21 (emphasis in original).

In Wainwright v. Witt, 469 U.S. 412 (1985), however, the Court modified the *Witherspoon* standard, explaining that — in capital and noncapital cases alike — "the quest is for jurors who will conscientiously apply the law and find the facts." Id., at 423. The Court held:

[T]he proper standard for determining when a prospective juror may be excluded for cause because of his or her views on capital punishment . . . is whether the juror's views would "prevent or substantially impair the performance of his [or her] duties as a juror in accordance with his [or her] instructions and his [or her] oath." We note that, in addition to dispensing with *Witherspoon*'s reference to "automatic" decisionmaking, this standard likewise does not require that a juror's bias be proved with "unmistakable clarity." This is because determinations of juror bias cannot be reduced to question-and-answer sessions which obtain results in the manner of a catechism. What common sense should have realized experience has proved: many veniremen simply cannot be asked enough questions to reach the point where their bias has been made "unmistakably clear"; these veniremen may not know how they will react when faced with imposing the death sentence, or may be unable to articulate, or may wish to hide their true feelings. Despite this lack of clarity in the printed record, however, there will be situations where the trial judge is left with the definite impression that a prospective juror would be unable to faithfully and impartially apply the law. . . . [T]his is why deference must be paid to the trial judge who sees and hears the juror.

Id., at 424-426. See also Uttecht v. Brown, 551 U.S. 1 (2007), where the Court, by 5-4, held that the *Witt* standard must be applied by federal habeas courts with a kind of "double" deference: deference to the trial court that had the chance to judge the demeanor of the prospective juror in the first instance, as well as the mandatory deference owed to state courts by all federal habeas courts.

One year later, in Lockhart v. McCree, 476 U.S. 162 (1986), the Court faced a novel twist on the impartiality argument. The defendant in *McCree* claimed, inter alia, that the exclusion, prior to the start of his capital trial, of prospective jurors who would have been impartial as to guilt or innocence but who were biased as to capital sentencing (under the old *Witherspoon* standard) violated his right to an impartial jury. The claim was based on extensive empirical research concerning the impact of such exclusion on the guilt-innocence determination. As the *McCree* dissenters put it:

> The perspectives on the criminal justice system of jurors who survive death qualification are systematically different from those of the excluded jurors. Death-qualified jurors are, for example, more likely to believe that a defendant's failure to testify is indicative of his guilt, more hostile to the insanity defense, more mistrustful of defense attorneys, and less concerned about the danger of erroneous convictions. . . . This proprosecution bias is reflected in the greater readiness of death-qualified jurors to convict or to convict on more serious charges.

Id., at 188 (Marshall, J., dissenting).

The Court "assume[d] for purposes of this opinion that the studies are both methodologically valid and adequate to establish that 'death qualification' in fact produces juries somewhat more 'conviction-prone' than 'non-death-qualified' juries." Id., at 173. Nevertheless, the Court rejected the impartiality claim:

> McCree concedes that the individual jurors who served at his trial were impartial, as that term [has been] defined by this Court. . . . Instead, McCree argues that his jury lacked impartiality because the absence of "*Witherspoon*-excludables" "slanted" the jury in favor of conviction.
>
> We do not agree. McCree's "impartiality" argument apparently is based on the theory that, because all individual jurors are to some extent predisposed towards one result or another, a constitutionally impartial *jury* can be constructed only by "balancing" the various predispositions of the individual *jurors*. Thus, according to McCree, when the State "tips the scales" by excluding prospective jurors with a particular viewpoint, an impermissibly partial jury results. We have consistently rejected this view of jury impartiality, including as recently as last Term when we squarely held that an impartial *jury* consists of nothing more than "*jurors* who will conscientiously apply the law and find the facts." Wainwright v. Witt, 469 U.S. 412, 423 (1985) (emphasis added). . . .

The view of jury impartiality urged upon us by McCree is both illogical and hopelessly impractical. . . . McCree admits that exactly the same 12 individuals could have ended up on his jury through the "luck of the draw," without in any way violating the constitutional guarantee of impartiality. Even accepting McCree's position that we should focus on the *jury* rather than the individual *jurors*, it is hard for us to understand the logic of the argument that a given jury is unconstitutionally partial when it results from a state-ordained process, yet impartial when exactly the same jury results from mere chance. On a more practical level, if it were true that the Constitution required a certain mix of individual viewpoints on the jury, then trial judges would be required to undertake the Sisyphean task of "balancing" juries, making sure that each contains the proper number of Democrats and Republicans, young persons and old persons, white-collar executives and blue-collar laborers, and so on. Adopting McCree's concept of jury impartiality would also likely require the elimination of peremptory challenges, which are commonly used by both the State and the defendant to attempt to produce a jury favorable to the challenger. . . .

In our view, it is simply not possible to define jury impartiality, for constitutional purposes, by reference to some hypothetical mix of individual viewpoints. . . . [T]he Constitution presupposes that a jury selected from a fair cross section of the community is impartial, regardless of the mix of individual viewpoints actually represented on the jury, so long as the jurors can conscientiously and properly carry out their sworn duty to apply the law to the facts of the particular case.

Id., at 177-179, 183-184.

Are you persuaded by the Court's reasoning in *McCree*? Does it seem fair to you that the defendant — in a capital case, no less — was convicted by a jury that the empirical studies showed, and that the Court admitted (for purposes of its opinion), was more prone to convict than the average, non-death-qualified jury? Even if, as the Court noted, the same conviction-prone jury could have occurred by chance, should it not matter that in McCree's case it was the product of a deliberate prosecution strategy to exclude death-penalty opponents from the jury? Would it affect your view to know that at least some prosecutors are alleged to seek the death penalty in at least some murder cases mostly so that they will be able to "death-qualify" the jury, only to drop the request for the death penalty later in the case? See *McCree*, 476 U.S., at 176, n. 16 (declining to address this argument because the prosecutor did not waive the death penalty in McCree's case); id., at 188, n. 4 (Marshall, J., dissenting) (citing examples of this practice).

Is the problem simply that McCree's argument did not fit into the Court's existing case law on jury impartiality? Maybe what McCree needed was a new constitutional doctrine designed to prohibit the prosecution from systematically skewing juries in its favor. Could this doctrine be implied in the Sixth Amendment? Or could it be derived from more general notions of "fundamental fairness" under the Due Process Clause?

What other common practices might be affected by such a doctrine? What about the now-pervasive use of jury-selection experts — at least in a context where the prosecutor has superior resources to hire such experts, as compared with the defense lawyer? What about the practice, common in many prosecutors' offices, of keeping records about the verdicts rendered by past juries, so that such records can be used in the future to exclude (usually through peremptories) jurors who previously voted in favor of acquitting a defendant? Note that defense lawyers usually do not have an equal opportunity to maintain such jury records because they are not "repeat players" to the same extent as the prosecutor; in any given jurisdiction, the prosecutor is involved in every criminal case, whereas even the public defender will be involved in only a smaller subset of the cases.

Although they derive from separate constitutional sources, the remaining two issues — the "fair cross section" and the equal protection requirements — combine to serve the single goal of ensuring that juries reflect the diversity of the American people. In reading the cases and notes that follow, you should ask yourself several questions: Does diversity matter? If so, why does it matter? What is the proper role of the jury in a diverse (and often divided) society? Finally, and most controversially, should jurors represent their diverse genders, races, ethnicities, religions, and/or sexual orientations, or should they strive to overcome their differences and become a "melting pot" jury?

1. The Requirement of a Fair Cross Section

DUREN v. MISSOURI

Certiorari to the Supreme Court of Missouri
439 U.S. 357 (1979)

JUSTICE WHITE delivered the opinion of the Court.

In Taylor v. Louisiana, 419 U.S. 522 (1975), this Court held that systematic exclusion of women during the jury-selection process, resulting in jury pools not "reasonably representative" of the community, denies a criminal defendant his right, under the Sixth and Fourteenth Amendments, to a petit jury selected from a fair cross section of the community.[1] Under the system invalidated in Taylor, a woman could not serve on a jury unless she filed a written declaration of her willingness to do so. As a result, although 53% of the persons eligible for jury service were women, less than 1% of the 1,800 persons whose names were drawn from the jury wheel during the year in which appellant Taylor's jury was chosen were female. Id., at 524.

At the time of our decision in Taylor, no other State provided that women could not serve on a jury unless they volunteered to serve. However, five States, including Missouri, provided an automatic exemption from jury service for any women requesting not to serve. Subsequent to Taylor, three of these States eliminated this exemption. Only Missouri, respondent in this case, and Tennessee continue to exempt women from jury service upon request. Today we hold that such systematic exclusion of women that results in jury venires averaging less than 15% female violates the Constitution's fair-cross-section requirement.

I

Petitioner Duren was indicted in 1975 in the Circuit Court of Jackson County, Mo., for first-degree murder and first-degree robbery. In a pretrial motion to quash his petit jury panel, and again in a post-conviction motion for a new trial, he contended

---

1. See Taylor v. Louisiana, 419 U.S., at 526-531, 538; Duncan v. Louisiana, 391 U.S. 145 (1968). A criminal defendant has standing to challenge exclusion resulting in a violation of the fair-cross-section requirement, whether or not he is a member of the excluded class. See Taylor, supra, at 526.

that his right to trial by a jury chosen from a fair cross section of his community was denied by provisions of Missouri law granting women who so request an automatic exemption from jury service. Both motions were denied.

At hearings on these motions, petitioner established that the jury-selection process in Jackson County begins with the annual mailing of a questionnaire to persons randomly selected from the Jackson County voter registration list. Approximately 70,000 questionnaires were mailed in 1975. The questionnaire contains a list of occupations and other categories which are the basis under Missouri law for either disqualification or exemption from jury service. Included on the questionnaire is a paragraph prominently addressed "TO WOMEN" that states in part:

> Any woman who elects not to serve will fill out this paragraph and mail this questionnaire to the jury commissioner at once.

A similar paragraph is addressed "TO MEN OVER 65 YEARS OF AGE," who are also statutorily exempt upon request.

The names of those sent questionnaires are placed in the master jury wheel for Jackson County, except for those returning the questionnaire who indicate disqualification or claim an applicable exemption. Summonses are mailed on a weekly basis to prospective jurors randomly drawn from the jury wheel. The summons, like the questionnaire, contains special directions to men over 65 and to women, this time advising them to return the summons by mail if they desire not to serve. The practice also is that even those women who do not return the summons are treated as having claimed exemption if they fail to appear for jury service on the appointed day. Other persons seeking to claim an exemption at this stage must make written or personal application to the court.

Petitioner established that according to the 1970 census, 54% of the adult inhabitants of Jackson County were women. He also showed that for the periods June-October 1975 and January-March 1976, 11,197 persons were summoned and that 2,992 of these, or 26.7%, were women. Of those summoned, 741 women and 4,378 men appeared for service. Thus, 14.5% (741 of 5,119) of the persons on the post-summons weekly venires during the period in which petitioner's jury was chosen were female. In March 1976, when petitioner's trial began, 15.5% of those on the weekly venires were women (110 of 707). Petitioner's jury was selected from a 53-person panel on which there were 5 women; all 12 jurors chosen were men. None of the foregoing statistical evidence was disputed.

In affirming petitioner's conviction, the Missouri Supreme Court questioned two aspects of his statistical presentation. First, it considered the census figures inadequate because they were six years old and might not precisely mirror the percentage of women registered to vote. Second, petitioner had not unequivocally demonstrated the extent to which the low percentage of women appearing for jury service was due to the automatic exemption for women, rather than to sex-neutral exemptions such as that for persons over age 65.

The court went on to hold, however, that even accepting petitioner's statistical proof, "the number of female names in the wheel, those summoned and those appearing were well above acceptable constitutional standards." . . .[19] We granted

---

19. The decision below also rejected petitioner's challenge under the Equal Protection Clause of the Fourteenth Amendment. This challenge has not been renewed before this Court.

certiorari, . . . because of concern that the decision below is not consistent with our decision in *Taylor*.

II

We think that in certain crucial respects the Missouri Supreme Court misconceived the nature of the fair-cross-section inquiry set forth in Taylor. In holding that "petit juries must be drawn from a source fairly representative of the community," 419 U.S., at 538, we explained that "jury wheels, pools of names, panels, or venires from which juries are drawn must not systematically exclude distinctive groups in the community and thereby fail to be reasonably representative thereof." Ibid.[20]

In order to establish a prima facie violation of the fair-cross-section requirement, the defendant must show (1) that the group alleged to be excluded is a "distinctive" group in the community; (2) that the representation of this group in venires from which juries are selected is not fair and reasonable in relation to the number of such persons in the community; and (3) that this underrepresentation is due to systematic exclusion of the group in the jury-selection process.

A

With respect to the first part of the prima facie test, *Taylor* without doubt established that women "are sufficiently numerous and distinct from men" so that "if they are systematically eliminated from jury panels, the Sixth Amendment's fair-cross-section requirement cannot be satisfied." Id., at 531.

B

The second prong of the prima facie case was established by petitioner's statistical presentation. Initially, the defendant must demonstrate the percentage of the community made up of the group alleged to be underrepresented, for this is the conceptual benchmark for the Sixth Amendment fair-cross-section requirement. In *Taylor*, the State had stipulated that 53% of the population eligible for jury service was female, while petitioner Duren has relied upon a census measurement of the actual percentage of women in the community (54%). In the trial court, the State of Missouri never challenged these data. Although the Missouri Supreme Court speculated that changing population patterns between 1970 and 1976 and unequal voter registration by men and women rendered the census figures a questionable frame of reference, there is no evidence whatsoever in the record to suggest that the 1970 census data significantly distorted the percentage of women in Jackson County at the time of trial. Petitioner's presentation was clearly adequate prima facie evidence of population characteristics for the purpose of making a fair-cross-section violation.

---

20. We further explained that this requirement does not mean "that petit juries actually chosen must mirror the community," 419 U.S., at 538.

Given petitioner's proof that in the relevant community slightly over half of the adults are women, we must disagree with the conclusion of the court below that jury venires containing approximately 15% women are "reasonably representative" of this community. If the percentage of women appearing on jury pools in Jackson County had precisely mirrored the percentage of women in the population, more than one of every two prospective jurors would have been female. In fact, less than one of every six prospective jurors was female; 85% of the average jury was male. Such a gross discrepancy between the percentage of women in jury venires and the percentage of women in the community requires the conclusion that women were not fairly represented in the source from which petit juries were drawn in Jackson County.

C

Finally, in order to establish a prima facie case, it was necessary for petitioner to show that the underrepresentation of women, generally and on his venire, was due to their systematic exclusion in the jury-selection process. Petitioner's proof met this requirement. His undisputed demonstration that a large discrepancy occurred not just occasionally, but in every weekly venire for a period of nearly a year manifestly indicates that the cause of the underrepresentation was systematic — that is, inherent in the particular jury-selection process utilized.

Petitioner Duren's statistics and other evidence also established when in the selection process the systematic exclusion took place. There was no indication that underrepresentation of women occurred at the first stage of the selection process — the questionnaire canvass of persons randomly selected from the relevant voter registration list. The first sign of a systematic discrepancy is at the next stage — the construction of the jury wheel from which persons are randomly summoned for service. Less than 30% of those summoned were female, demonstrating that a substantially larger number of women answering the questionnaire claimed either ineligibility or exemption from jury service. Moreover, at the summons stage women were not only given another opportunity to claim exemption, but also were presumed to have claimed exemption when they did not respond to the summons. Thus, the percentage of women at the final, venire, stage (14.5%) was much lower than the percentage of women who were summoned for service (26.7%).

The resulting disproportionate and consistent exclusion of women from the jury wheel and at the venire stage was quite obviously due to the system by which juries were selected. Petitioner demonstrated that the underrepresentation of women in the final pool of prospective jurors was due to the operation of Missouri's exemption criteria — whether the automatic exemption for women or other statutory exemptions — as implemented in Jackson County. Women were therefore systematically underrepresented within the meaning of *Taylor*.

III

The demonstration of a prima facie fair-cross-section violation by the defendant is not the end of the inquiry into whether a constitutional violation has occurred. We have explained that "States remain free to prescribe relevant qualifications for their jurors and to provide reasonable exemptions so long as it may be fairly said that the jury lists or panels are representative of the community." *Taylor*, 419 U.S., at 538.

However, we cautioned that "[t]he right to a proper jury cannot be overcome on merely rational grounds," id., at 534. Rather, it requires that a significant state interest be manifestly and primarily advanced by those aspects of the jury-selection process, such as exemption criteria, that result in the disproportionate exclusion of a distinctive group.

The Supreme Court of Missouri suggested that the low percentage of women on jury venires in Jackson County may have been due to a greater number of women than of men qualifying for or claiming permissible exemptions, such as those for persons over 65, teachers, and government workers. . . . Respondent further argues that petitioner has not proved that the exemption for women had "any effect" on or was responsible for the underrepresentation of women on venires. . . .

However, once the defendant has made a prima facie showing of an infringement of his constitutional right to a jury drawn from a fair cross section of the community, it is the State that bears the burden of justifying this infringement by showing attainment of a fair cross section to be incompatible with a significant state interest. See *Taylor*, 419 U.S., at 533-535. Assuming, arguendo, that the exemptions mentioned by the court below would justify failure to achieve a fair community cross section on jury venires, the State must demonstrate that these exemptions caused the underrepresentation complained of. The record contains no such proof, and mere suggestions or assertions to that effect are insufficient.

The other possible cause of the disproportionate exclusion of women on Jackson County jury venires is, of course, the automatic exemption for women. Neither the Missouri Supreme Court nor respondent in its brief has offered any substantial justification for this exemption. In response to questioning at oral argument, counsel for respondent ventured that the only state interest advanced by the exemption is safeguarding the important role played by women in home and family life. But exempting all women because of the preclusive domestic responsibilities of some women is insufficient justification for their disproportionate exclusion on jury venires. What we stated in *Taylor* with respect to the system there challenged under which women could "opt in" for jury service is equally applicable to Missouri's "opt out" exemption:

> It is untenable to suggest these days that it would be a special hardship for each and every woman to perform jury service or that society cannot spare *any* women from their present duties. This may be the case with many, and it may be burdensome to sort out those who should be exempted from those who should serve. But that task is performed in the case of men, and the administrative convenience in dealing with women as a class is insufficient justification for diluting the quality of community judgment represented by the jury in criminal trials. . . .
>
> If it was ever the case that women were unqualified to sit on juries or were so situated that none of them should be required to perform jury service, that time has long since passed.

419 U.S., at 534-535, 537 (footnote omitted).

We recognize that a State may have an important interest in assuring that those members of the family responsible for the care of children are available to do so. An exemption appropriately tailored to this interest would, we think, survive a fair-cross-section challenge. We stress, however, that the constitutional guarantee to a jury drawn from a fair cross section of the community requires that States exercise proper caution in exempting broad categories of persons from jury service. Although most occupational and other reasonable exemptions may inevitably involve some degree of overinclusiveness or underinclusiveness, any category expressly limited to a group in the community of sufficient magnitude and distinctiveness so as to be within the fair-cross-section requirement — such as women — runs the danger of resulting in underrepresentation sufficient to constitute a prima facie violation of that constitutional requirement. We also repeat the observation made in *Taylor* that it is unlikely that reasonable exemptions, such as those based on special hardship, incapacity, or community needs, "would pose substantial threats that the remaining pool of jurors would not be representative of the community." Id., at 534.

The judgment of the Missouri Supreme Court is reversed, and the case is remanded for further proceedings not inconsistent with this opinion.

So ordered.

JUSTICE REHNQUIST, dissenting.

. . . The Constitution does not require, and our jurisprudence is ill served, by a hybrid doctrine such as that developed in *Taylor*, and in this case.*

Even if I were able to reconcile the Court's agile amalgamation of the Due Process Clause and the Equal Protection Clause of the Fourteenth Amendment in deciding this case and *Taylor*, I have no little concern about where the road upon which the Court has embarked will ultimately lead. . . .

Eventually the Court either will insist that women be treated identically to men for purposes of jury selection . . . , or in some later sequel to this line of cases will discover some peculiar magic in the number 15 that will enable it to distinguish between such a percentage and a higher percentage less than 50. But whichever of these routes the Court chooses to travel when the question is actually presented, its decision today puts state legislators and local jury commissioners at a serious disadvantage wholly unwarranted by the constitutional provisions upon which it relies. If the Court ultimately concludes that men and women must be treated exactly alike for purposes of jury service, it will have imposed substantial burdens upon many

---

* . . . If . . . men and women are essentially fungible for purposes of jury duty, the question arises how underrepresentation of either sex on the jury or the venire infringes on a defendant's right to have his fate decided by an impartial tribunal. Counsel for petitioner, when asked at oral argument to explain the difference, from the defendant's point of view, between men and women jurors, offered: "It is that indefinable something — . . . I think that we perhaps all understand it when we see it and when we feel it, but it is not that easy to describe; yes, there is a difference." . . . But close analysis of the fair-cross-section doctrine demonstrates that the Court itself does not really believe in such mysticism. For if "that indefinable something" were truly an essential element of the due process right to trial by an impartial jury, a defendant would be entitled to a jury composed of men and women in perfect proportion to their numbers in the community. Yet in *Taylor*, supra, at 538, the majority stressed: "Defendants are not entitled to a jury of any particular composition, . . . but the jury wheels, pools of names, panels, or venires from which juries are drawn must not systematically exclude distinctive groups in the community and thereby fail to be reasonably representative thereof." Thus, a defendant's constitutional right to an impartial jury is protected so long as "that indefinable something" supposedly crucial to impartiality is adequately represented on the jury venire; that the petit jury ultimately struck is composed of one sex is irrelevant.

The Sixth and Fourteenth Amendments guarantee a criminal defendant the right to be tried by an impartial jury. If impartiality is not lost because a particular class or group represented in the community is unrepresented on the petit jury, it is certainly not lost because the class or group is underrepresented on the jury venire. It is therefore clear that the majority's fair-cross-section rationale is not concerned with the defendant's due process right to an impartial jury at all. Instead, the requirement that distinct segments of the community be represented on jury venires is concerned with the equal protection right of the excluded class to participate in the judicial process through jury service. . . .

women, particularly in less populated areas, without necessarily producing any corresponding increase in the representative character of jury panels. If it ultimately concludes that a percentage of women on jury panels greater than 15 but substantially less than 50 is permissible even though the State's jury selection system permits women but not men to "opt out" of jury service, it is simply playing a constitutional numbers game. . . .

The probability, then, is that today's decision will cause States to abandon not only gender-based but also occupation-based classifications for purposes of jury service. Doctors and nurses, though virtually irreplaceable in smaller communities, may ultimately be held by the Court to bring their own "flavor" or "indefinable something" to a jury venire. . . . If so, they could then be exempted from jury service only on a case-by-case basis, and would join others with skills much less in demand whiling away their time in jury rooms of countless courthouses.

No one but a lawyer could think that this was a managerially sound solution to an important problem of judicial administration, and no one but a lawyer thoroughly steeped in the teachings of cases such as *Taylor* [and the Court's recent Equal Protection decisions] could think that such a solution was mandated by the United States Constitution. . . .

NOTES AND QUESTIONS

1. Why must a jury be drawn from a fair cross section of the community? In *Taylor*, the Court identified three primary reasons: (1) "guard[ing] against the exercise of arbitrary power," (2) preserving "public confidence in the fairness of the criminal justice system," and (3) implementing the belief that "sharing in the administration of justice is a phase of civic responsibility." 419 U.S., at 530-531. The Court emphasized, however, that "in holding that petit juries must be drawn from a source fairly representative of the community we impose no requirement that petit juries actually chosen must mirror the community and reflect the various distinctive groups in the population." Id., at 538.

2. In Lockhart v. McCree, discussed supra in the context of impartiality, the defendant also claimed that the "death qualification" of his jury violated the fair-cross-section requirement. The Court rejected this claim as well, on two grounds. First, "[w]e have never invoked the fair-section principle to invalidate the use of either for-cause or peremptory challenges to prospective jurors, or to require petit juries, as opposed to jury panels or venires, to reflect the composition of the community at large." 476 U.S., at 173. Second, "groups defined solely in terms of shared attitudes that would prevent or substantially impair members of the group from performing one of their duties as jurors, such as the '*Witherspoon*-excludables' at issue here, are not 'distinctive groups' for fair-cross-section purposes." Id., at 174. The Court asserted that the exclusion of "*Witherspoon*-excludables" — unlike the exclusion of blacks, women, or Latinos — does not contravene any of the three purposes of the fair-cross-section requirement identified in *Taylor*: (1) Because "*Witherspoon*-excludables" are excluded for a legally valid reason (i.e., their bias with respect to capital sentencing), there is little danger of "arbitrarily skew[ing]" the jury; (2) because they are excluded for a reason arguably within their control, there is no "appearance of unfairness"; and (3) because they may serve as jurors in other, noncapital cases, there is no "substantial deprivation of their basic rights of citizenship." Id., at 175-176.

3. The Court has also, on occasion, addressed similar claims of jury nonrepresentativeness under the Equal Protection Clause. See, e.g., Castaneda v. Partida, 430 U.S. 482 (1977) (finding equal protection violation when Texas "key man" system for selecting grand juries produced only 39 percent Mexican-Americans, compared to county population of 79.1 percent Mexican-Americans); Vasquez v. Hillery, 474 U.S. 254 (1986) (finding equal protection violation when no black had ever served on grand jury in Kings County, California, from 1900 to 1962, the year when defendant was indicted).

2. Equal Protection and the Peremptory Challenge

In the early 1980s, numerous constitutional attacks were made against the common practice of prosecutors using their peremptory challenges to remove all or most prospective black jurors in cases involving black defendants. These attacks were based primarily on the fair-cross-section requirement because most defendants believed that they could not satisfy the tougher burden of proof for establishing an equal protection violation. See, e.g., Booker v. Jabe, 775 F.2d 762 (6th Cir. 1985); McCray v. Abrams, 750 F.2d 1113 (2d Cir. 1984). In the next case, however, the Supreme Court — over the defendant's objection — recharacterized the claim as one based on equal protection and proceeded to make peremptory challenges a little less "peremptory."

BATSON v. KENTUCKY

Certiorari to the Supreme Court of Kentucky
476 U.S. 79 (1986)

JUSTICE POWELL delivered the opinion of the Court. This case requires us to reexamine that portion of Swain v. Alabama, 380 U.S. 202 (1965), concerning the evidentiary burden placed on a criminal defendant who claims that he has been denied equal protection through the State's use of peremptory challenges to exclude members of his race from the petit jury.

I

Petitioner, a black man, was indicted in Kentucky on charges of second-degree burglary and receipt of stolen goods. On the first day of trial in Jefferson Circuit Court, the judge conducted voir dire examination of the venire, excused certain jurors for cause, and permitted the parties to exercise peremptory challenges. The prosecutor used his peremptory challenges to strike all four black persons on the venire, and a jury composed only of white persons was selected. Defense counsel moved to discharge the jury before it was sworn on the ground that the prosecutor's removal of the black veniremen violated petitioner's rights under the Sixth and Fourteenth Amendments to a jury drawn from a cross section of the community, and under the Fourteenth Amendment to equal protection of the laws. Counsel requested a hearing on his motion. Without expressly ruling on the request for a hearing, the trial judge observed that the parties were entitled to use their peremptory challenges to "strike anybody they want to." The judge then denied petitioner's motion, reasoning that the cross-section requirement applies only to selection of the venire and not to selection of the petit jury itself.

The jury convicted petitioner on both counts. On appeal to the Supreme Court of Kentucky, petitioner pressed, among other claims, the argument concerning the prosecutor's use of peremptory challenges. Conceding that Swain v. Alabama, supra, apparently foreclosed an equal protection claim based solely on the prosecutor's conduct in this case, petitioner urged the court . . . to hold that such conduct violated his rights under the Sixth Amendment and §11 of the Kentucky Constitution to a jury drawn from a cross section of the community. Petitioner also contended that the facts showed that the prosecutor had engaged in a "pattern" of discriminatory challenges in this case and established an equal protection violation under *Swain*.

The Supreme Court of Kentucky affirmed. . . . We granted certiorari . . . and now reverse.

II

In Swain v. Alabama, this Court recognized that a "State's purposeful or deliberate denial to Negroes on account of race of participation as jurors in the administration of justice violates the Equal Protection Clause." 380 U.S., at 203-204. This principle has been "consistently and repeatedly" reaffirmed, id., at 204, in numerous decisions of this Court both preceding and following *Swain*. We reaffirm the principle today.[4]

A

More than a century ago, the Court decided that the State denies a black defendant equal protection of the laws when it puts him on trial before a jury from which members of his race have been purposefully excluded. Strauder v. West Virginia, 100 U.S. 303 (1880). That decision laid the foundation for the Court's unceasing efforts to eradicate racial discrimination in the procedures used to select the venire from which individual jurors are drawn. In *Strauder*, the Court explained that the central concern of the recently ratified Fourteenth Amendment was to put an end to governmental discrimination on account of race. Id., at 306-307. Exclusion of black citizens from service as jurors constitutes a primary example of the evil the Fourteenth Amendment was designed to cure.

In holding that racial discrimination in jury selection offends the Equal Protection Clause, the Court in *Strauder* recognized, however, that a defendant has no right to a "petit jury composed in whole or in part of persons of his own race." Id., at 305. . . .[6] But the defendant does have the right to be tried by a jury whose

4. In this Court, petitioner has argued that the prosecutor's conduct violated his rights under the Sixth and Fourteenth Amendments to an impartial jury and to a jury drawn from a cross section of the community. Petitioner has framed his argument in these terms in an apparent effort to avoid inviting the Court directly to reconsider one of its own precedents. On the other hand, the State has insisted that petitioner is claiming a denial of equal protection and that we must reconsider *Swain* to find a constitutional violation on this record. We agree with the State that resolution of petitioner's claim properly turns on application of equal protection principles and express no view on the merits of any of petitioner's Sixth Amendment arguments.

6. Similarly, though the Sixth Amendment guarantees that the petit jury will be selected from a pool of names representing a cross section of the community, Taylor v. Louisiana, 419 U.S. 522 (1975), we have

members are selected pursuant to non-discriminatory criteria. . . . The Equal Protection Clause guarantees the defendant that the State will not exclude members of his race from the jury venire on account of race, *Strauder*, supra, at 305, or on the false assumption that members of his race as a group are not qualified to serve as jurors. . . .

Purposeful racial discrimination in selection of the venire violates a defendant's right to equal protection because it denies him the protection that a trial by jury is intended to secure. "The very idea of a jury is a body . . . composed of the peers or equals of the person whose rights it is selected or summoned to determine; that is, of his neighbors, fellows, associates, persons having the same legal status in society as that which he holds." *Strauder*, supra, at 308. . . . The petit jury has occupied a central position in our system of justice by safeguarding a person accused of crime against the arbitrary exercise of power by prosecutor or judge. Duncan v. Louisiana, 391 U.S. 145, 156 (1968). Those on the venire must be "indifferently chosen," to secure the defendant's right under the Fourteenth Amendment to "protection of life and liberty against race or color prejudice." *Strauder*, supra, at 309.

Racial discrimination in selection of jurors harms not only the accused whose life or liberty they are summoned to try. Competence to serve as a juror ultimately depends on an assessment of individual qualifications and ability impartially to consider evidence presented at a trial. . . . A person's race simply "is unrelated to his fitness as a juror." . . . As long ago as *Strauder*, therefore, the Court recognized that by denying a person participation in jury service on account of his race, the State unconstitutionally discriminated against the excluded juror. 100 U.S., at 308. . . .

The harm from discriminatory jury selection extends beyond that inflicted on the defendant and the excluded juror to touch the entire community. Selection procedures that purposefully exclude black persons from juries undermine public confidence in the fairness of our system of justice. . . . Discrimination within the judicial system is most pernicious because it is "a stimulant to that race prejudice which is an impediment to securing to [black citizens] that equal justice which the law aims to secure to all others." *Strauder*, 100 U.S., at 308.

B

In *Strauder*, the Court invalidated a state statute that provided that only white men could serve as jurors. Id., at 305. We can be confident that no State now has such a law. The Constitution requires, however, that we look beyond the face of the statute defining juror qualifications and also consider challenged selection practices to afford "protection against action of the State through its administrative officers in effecting the prohibited discrimination." . . . Thus, the Court has found a denial of equal protection where the procedures implementing a neutral statute operated to exclude persons from the venire on racial grounds, and has made clear that the Constitution prohibits all forms of purposeful racial discrimination in selection of

---

never held that the Sixth Amendment requires that "petit juries actually chosen must mirror the community and reflect the various distinctive groups in the population," id., at 538. Indeed, it would be impossible to apply a concept of proportional representation to the petit jury in view of the heterogeneous nature of our society. Such impossibility is illustrated by the Court's holding that a jury of six persons is not unconstitutional. Williams v. Florida, 399 U.S. 78, 102-103 (1970).

jurors. While decisions of this Court have been concerned largely with discrimination during selection of the venire, the principles announced there also forbid discrimination on account of race in selection of the petit jury. Since the Fourteenth Amendment protects an accused throughout the proceedings bringing him to justice, . . . the State may not draw up its jury lists pursuant to neutral procedures but then resort to discrimination at "other stages in the selection process." . . .

Accordingly, the component of the jury selection process at issue here, the State's privilege to strike individual jurors through peremptory challenges, is subject to the commands of the Equal Protection Clause.[12] Although a prosecutor ordinarily is entitled to exercise permitted peremptory challenges "for any reason at all, as long as that reason is related to his view concerning the outcome" of the case to be tried, . . . the Equal Protection Clause forbids the prosecutor to challenge potential jurors solely on account of their race or on the assumption that black jurors as a group will be unable impartially to consider the State's case against a black defendant.

III

The principles announced in *Strauder* never have been questioned in any subsequent decision of this Court. Rather, the Court has been called upon repeatedly to review the application of those principles to particular facts. A recurring question in these cases, as in any case alleging a violation of the Equal Protection Clause, was whether the defendant had met his burden of proving purposeful discrimination on the part of the State. . . . That question also was at the heart of the portion of Swain v. Alabama we reexamine today.

A

Swain required the Court to decide, among other issues, whether a black defendant was denied equal protection by the State's exercise of peremptory challenges to exclude members of his race from the petit jury. 380 U.S., at 209-210. The record in *Swain* showed that the prosecutor had used the State's peremptory challenges to strike the six black persons included on the petit jury venire. Id., at 210. While rejecting the defendant's claim for failure to prove purposeful discrimination, the Court nonetheless indicated that the Equal Protection Clause placed some limits on the State's exercise of peremptory challenges. Id., at 222-224.

The Court sought to accommodate the prosecutor's historical privilege of peremptory challenge free of judicial control, id., at 214-220, and the constitutional prohibition on exclusion of persons from jury service on account of race, id., at 222-224. While the Constitution does not confer a right to peremptory challenges, id., at 219 . . . those challenges traditionally have been viewed as one means of assuring the selection of a qualified and unbiased jury, 380 U.S., at 219. To preserve the peremptory nature of the prosecutor's challenge, the Court in *Swain* declined to scrutinize his actions in a particular case by relying on a presumption that he properly exercised the State's challenges. Id., at 221-222.

---

12. We express no views on whether the Constitution imposes any limit on the exercise of peremptory challenges by defense counsel. . . .

The Court went on to observe, however, that a State may not exercise its challenges in contravention of the Equal Protection Clause. . . . For example, an inference of purposeful discrimination would be raised on evidence that a prosecutor, "in case after case, whatever the circumstances, whatever the crime and whoever the defendant or the victim may be, is responsible for the removal of Negroes who have been selected as qualified jurors by the jury commissioners and who have survived challenges for cause, with the result that no Negroes ever serve on petit juries." Id., at 223. . . .

B

Since the decision in *Swain*, we have explained that our cases concerning selection of the venire reflect the general equal protection principle that the "invidious quality" of governmental action claimed to be racially discriminatory "must ultimately be traced to a racially discriminatory purpose." Washington v. Davis, 426 U.S. 229, 240 (1976). As in any equal protection case, the "burden is, of course," on the defendant who alleges discriminatory selection of the venire "to prove the existence of purposeful discrimination." . . . Circumstantial evidence of invidious intent may include proof of disproportionate impact. Washington v. Davis, 426 U.S., at 242. We have observed that under some circumstances proof of discriminatory impact "may for all practical purposes demonstrate unconstitutionality because in various circumstances the discrimination is very difficult to explain on nonracial grounds." Ibid. For example, "total or seriously disproportionate exclusion of Negroes from jury venires," ibid., "is itself such an 'unequal application of the law . . . as to show intentional discrimination,'" id., at 241. . . .

Moreover, since *Swain*, we have recognized that a black defendant alleging that members of his race have been impermissibly excluded from the venire may make out a prima facie case of purposeful discrimination by showing that the totality of the relevant facts gives rise to an inference of discriminatory purpose. Washington v. Davis, supra, at 239-242. Once the defendant makes the requisite showing, the burden shifts to the State to explain adequately the racial exclusion. . . . The State cannot meet this burden on mere general assertions that its officials did not discriminate or that they properly performed their official duties. . . . Rather, the State must demonstrate that "permissible racially neutral selection criteria and procedures have produced the monochromatic result." . . .

The showing necessary to establish a prima facie case of purposeful discrimination in selection of the venire may be discerned in this Court's decisions. . . . The defendant initially must show that he is a member of a racial group capable of being singled out for differential treatment. . . . In combination with that evidence, a defendant may then make a prima facie case by proving that in the particular jurisdiction members of his race have not been summoned for jury service over an extended period of time. . . . Proof of systematic exclusion from the venire raises an inference of purposeful discrimination because the "result bespeaks discrimination." . . .

Since the ultimate issue is whether the State has discriminated in selecting the defendant's venire, however, the defendant may establish a prima facie case "in other ways than by evidence of long-continued unexplained absence" of members of his race "from many panels." . . .

Thus, since the decision in *Swain*, this Court has recognized that a defendant may make a prima facie showing of purposeful racial discrimination in selection of the venire by relying solely on the facts concerning its selection in *his* case. These decisions are in accordance with the proposition, articulated in Arlington Heights v. Metropolitan Housing Development Corp., 429 U.S. 252, 266 (1977), that "a consistent pattern of official racial discrimination" is not "a necessary predicate to a violation of the Equal Protection Clause. A single invidiously discriminatory governmental act" is not "immunized by the absence of such discrimination in the making of other comparable decisions." 429 U.S., at 266, n. 14. For evidentiary requirements to dictate that "several must suffer discrimination" before one could object, . . . would be inconsistent with the promise of equal protection to all.

C

. . . These principles support our conclusion that a defendant may establish a prima facie case of purposeful discrimination in selection of the petit jury solely on evidence concerning the prosecutor's exercise of peremptory challenges at the defendant's trial. To establish such a case, the defendant first must show that he is a member of a cognizable racial group, . . . and that the prosecutor has exercised peremptory challenges to remove from the venire members of the defendant's race. Second, the defendant is entitled to rely on the fact, as to which there can be no dispute, that peremptory challenges constitute a jury selection practice that permits "those to discriminate who are of a mind to discriminate." . . . Finally, the defendant must show that these facts and any other relevant circumstances raise an inference that the prosecutor used that practice to exclude the veniremen from the petit jury on account of their race. This combination of factors in the empaneling of the petit jury, as in the selection of the venire, raises the necessary inference of purposeful discrimination.

In deciding whether the defendant has made the requisite showing, the trial court should consider all relevant circumstances. For example, a "pattern" of strikes against black jurors included in the particular venire might give rise to an inference of discrimination. Similarly, the prosecutor's questions and statements during voir dire examination and in exercising his challenges may support or refute an inference of discriminatory purpose. These examples are merely illustrative. We have confidence that trial judges, experienced in supervising voir dire, will be able to decide if the circumstances concerning the prosecutor's use of peremptory challenges creates a prima facie case of discrimination against black jurors.

Once the defendant makes a prima facie showing, the burden shifts to the State to come forward with a neutral explanation for challenging black jurors. Though this requirement imposes a limitation in some cases on the full peremptory character of the historic challenge, we emphasize that the prosecutor's explanation need not rise to the level justifying exercise of a challenge for cause. . . . But the prosecutor may not rebut the defendant's prima facie case of discrimination by stating merely that he challenged jurors of the defendant's race on the assumption — or his intuitive judgment — that they would be partial to the defendant because of their shared race. . . . Just as the Equal Protection Clause forbids the States to exclude black persons from the venire on the assumption that blacks as a group are unqualified to serve as jurors, . . . so it forbids the States to strike black veniremen on the assumption that they will be biased in a particular case simply because the defendant is black. The core guarantee of equal protection, ensuring citizens that their State will not discriminate on account of race, would be meaningless were we to approve the exclusion of jurors on the basis of such assumptions, which arise solely from the jurors' race. Nor may the prosecutor rebut the defendant's case merely by denying that he had a discriminatory motive or "affirm[ing] [his] good faith in making individual selections." . . . If these general assertions were accepted as rebutting a defendant's prima facie case, the Equal Protection Clause "would be but a vain and illusory requirement." . . . The prosecutor therefore must articulate a neutral explanation related to the particular case to be tried.[20] The trial court then will have the duty to determine if the defendant has established purposeful discrimination[21] . . . .

V

In this case, petitioner made a timely objection to the prosecutor's removal of all black persons on the venire. Because the trial court flatly rejected the objection without requiring the prosecutor to give an explanation for his action, we remand this case for further proceedings. If the trial court decides that the facts establish, prima facie, purposeful discrimination and the prosecutor does not come forward with a neutral explanation for his action, our precedents require that petitioner's conviction be reversed. . . .

It is so ordered. [The concurring opinions of Justice White, Justice Stevens (with whom Justice Brennan joined), and Justice O'Connor are omitted.]

JUSTICE MARSHALL, concurring.

. . . The decision today will not end the racial discrimination that peremptories inject into the jury-selection process. That goal can be accomplished only by eliminating peremptory challenges entirely.

I . . .

Misuse of the peremptory challenge to exclude black jurors has become both common and flagrant. . . .

The Court's discussion of the utter unconstitutionality of that practice needs no amplification. . . . [T]he Equal Protection Clause prohibits a State from taking any action based on crude, inaccurate racial stereotypes — even an action that does not serve the State's interests. Exclusion of blacks from a jury, solely because of race, can no more be justified by a belief that blacks are less likely than whites to consider fairly or sympathetically the State's case against a black defendant than it can be justified by the notion that blacks lack the "intelligence, experience, or moral integrity" . . . to be entrusted with that role.

---

20. The Court of Appeals for the Second Circuit [has] observed . . . that "[t]here are any number of bases" on which a prosecutor reasonably may believe that it is desirable to strike a juror who is not excusable for cause. As we explained in another context, however, the prosecutor must give a "clear and reasonably specific" explanation of his "legitimate reasons" for exercising the challenges. . . .

21. In a recent Title VII sex discrimination case, we stated that "a finding of intentional discrimination is a finding of fact" entitled to appropriate deference by a reviewing court. . . . Since the trial judge's findings in the context under consideration here largely will turn on evaluation of credibility, a reviewing court ordinarily should give those findings great deference. . . .

II

I wholeheartedly concur in the Court's conclusion that use of the peremptory challenge to remove blacks from juries, on the basis of their race, violates the Equal Protection Clause. I would go further, however, in fashioning a remedy adequate to eliminate that discrimination. Merely allowing defendants the opportunity to challenge the racially discriminatory use of peremptory challenges in individual cases will not end the illegitimate use of the peremptory challenge.

. . . First, defendants cannot attack the discriminatory use of peremptory challenges at all unless the challenges are so flagrant as to establish a prima facie case. This means, in those States, that where only one or two black jurors survive the challenges for cause, the prosecutor need have no compunction about striking them from the jury because of their race. . . . Prosecutors are left free to discriminate against blacks in jury selection provided that they hold that discrimination to an "acceptable" level.

Second, when a defendant can establish a prima facie case, trial courts face the difficult burden of assessing prosecutors' motives. . . . Any prosecutor can easily assert facially neutral reasons for striking a juror, and trial courts are ill equipped to second-guess those reasons. How is the court to treat a prosecutor's statement that he struck a juror because the juror had a son about the same age as defendant, . . . or seemed "uncommunicative," . . . or "never cracked a smile" and, therefore "did not possess the sensitivities necessary to realistically look at the issues and decide the facts in this case" . . . ? If such easily generated explanations are sufficient to discharge the prosecutor's obligation to justify his strikes on non-racial grounds, then the protection erected by the Court today may be illusory. . . .

I applaud the Court's holding that the racially discriminatory use of peremptory challenges violates the Equal Protection Clause, and I join the Court's opinion. However, only by banning peremptories entirely can such discrimination be ended.

[The dissenting opinion of Chief Justice Burger is omitted.]

JUSTICE REHNQUIST, with whom CHIEF JUSTICE BURGER joins, dissenting. . . .

In *Swain*, this Court carefully distinguished two possible scenarios involving the State's use of its peremptory challenges to exclude blacks from juries in criminal cases. In Part III of the majority opinion, the *Swain* Court concluded that the first of these scenarios, namely, the exclusion of blacks "for reasons wholly unrelated to the outcome of the particular case on trial . . . to deny the Negro the same right and opportunity to participate in the administration of justice enjoyed by the white population," 380 U.S., at 224, might violate the guarantees of equal protection. See id., at 222-228. The Court felt that the important and historic purposes of the peremptory challenge were not furthered by the exclusion of blacks "in case after case, whatever the circumstances, whatever the crime *and whoever the defendant or the victim may be*." Id., at 223 (emphasis added). Nevertheless, the Court ultimately held that "the record in this case is not sufficient to demonstrate that [this] rule has been violated. . . . Petitioner has the burden of proof and he has failed to carry it." Id., at 224, 226. Three Justices dissented, arguing that the petitioner's evidentiary burden was satisfied by testimony that no black had ever served on a petit jury in the relevant county. See id., at 228-247 (Goldberg, J., joined by Warren, C.J., and Douglas, J., dissenting).

Significantly, the *Swain* Court reached a very different conclusion with respect to the second kind of peremptory-challenge scenario. In Part II of its opinion, the

Court held that the State's use of peremptory challenges to exclude blacks from a particular jury based on the assumption or belief that they would be more likely to favor a black defendant does not violate equal protection. . . .

Even the *Swain* dissenters did not take issue with the majority's position that the Equal Protection Clause does not prohibit the State from using its peremptory challenges to exclude blacks based on the assumption or belief that they would be partial to a black defendant. . . .

The Court today asserts, however, that "the Equal Protection Clause forbids the prosecutor to challenge potential jurors solely . . . on the assumption that black jurors as a group will be unable impartially to consider the State's case against a black defendant." . . . Later, in discussing the State's need to establish a nondiscriminatory basis for striking blacks from the jury, the Court states that "the prosecutor may not rebut the defendant's prima facie case of discrimination by stating merely that he challenged jurors of the defendant's race on the assumption — or his intuitive judgment — that they would be partial to the defendant because of their shared race." . . . [B]oth statements are directly contrary to the view of the Equal Protection Clause shared by the majority and the dissenters in *Swain*. . . .

I cannot subscribe to the Court's unprecedented use of the Equal Protection Clause to restrict the historic scope of the peremptory challenge, which has been described as "a necessary part of trial by jury." *Swain*, 380 U.S., at 219. In my view, there is simply nothing "unequal" about the State's using its peremptory challenges to strike blacks from the jury in cases involving black defendants, so long as such challenges are also used to exclude whites in cases involving white defendants, Hispanics in cases involving Hispanic defendants, Asians in cases involving Asian defendants, and so on. This case-specific use of peremptory challenges by the State does not single out blacks, or members of any other race for that matter, for discriminatory treatment. Such use of peremptories is at best based upon seat-of-the-pants instincts, which are undoubtedly crudely stereotypical and may in many cases be hopelessly mistaken. But as long as they are applied across-the-board to jurors of all races and nationalities, I do not see — and the Court most certainly has not explained — how their use violates the Equal Protection Clause.

Nor does such use of peremptory challenges by the State infringe upon any other constitutional interests. The Court does not suggest that exclusion of blacks from the jury through the State's use of peremptory challenges results in a violation of either the fair-cross-section or impartiality component of the Sixth Amendment. . . . And because the case-specific use of peremptory challenges by the State does not deny blacks the right to serve as jurors in cases involving non-black defendants, it harms neither the excluded jurors nor the remainder of the community. . . .

The use of group affiliations, such as age, race, or occupation, as a "proxy" for potential juror partiality, based on the assumption or belief that members of one group are more likely to favor defendants who belong to the same group, has long been accepted as a legitimate basis for the State's exercise of peremptory challenges. See *Swain*, supra. . . . Indeed, given the need for reasonable limitations on the time devoted to voir dire, the use of such "proxies" by both the State and the defendant may be extremely useful in eliminating from the jury persons who might be biased in one way or another. The Court today holds that the State may not use its peremptory challenges to strike black prospective jurors on this basis without violating the Constitution. But I do not believe there is anything in the

Equal Protection Clause, or any other constitutional provision, that justifies such a departure from the substantive holding contained in Part II of *Swain*. . . .

NOTES AND QUESTIONS

1. What is the rationale for the Court's decision in *Batson*? Justice Powell's majority opinion seems to equate (for purposes of applying the Equal Protection Clause) two situations: (1) the use of peremptories (in *Batson*) to remove all blacks from the jury in a particular criminal case involving a black defendant, on the assumption that they would tend to favor the black defendant more than white jurors would, and (2) the previous practice (prior to *Swain*) of excluding all blacks from the venire in all cases, on the assumption that they were unqualified as a class to serve as jurors. Are the two situations really analogous?

Surely there is simply no correlation between race and qualification to serve as a juror, but is the use of race-based peremptories in particular cases similarly irrational? Do you think that jury verdicts are unaffected by the racial composition of the juries that render those verdicts? Are black jurors and white jurors fungible? In a society that continues to be plagued by serious racial disparities, it seems highly unlikely that this would be so. Certainly, there have been a number of prominent recent examples (including the two trials of the Los Angeles police officers who beat Rodney King and perhaps the O. J. Simpson case as well) suggesting that, at least in some cases, the race of the jurors *does* make a difference. Would Batson have litigated his appeal all the way to the Supreme Court if he truly believed that being tried by an all-white jury did not have any effect on the outcome of his case?

Empirical evidence lends support to the conclusion that, at least sometimes, race does matter. See, e.g., Deborah Ramirez, Affirmative Jury Selection: A Proposal to Advance Both the Deliberative Ideal and Jury Diversity, 1998 U. Chi. Legal F. 161, 165-166 (citing studies) ("[I]t is not surprising that the empirical evidence shows in some close cases, where small differences in perspective matter, the racial composition of the jury affects substantive outcomes and verdicts. . . . [I]n those close cases where the verdict is properly in doubt when the deliberations begin, the different perspectives and dynamics of a racially mixed jury can generate results that are different from those reached by homogenous juries.")

If, in fact, black jurors and white jurors sometimes *do* tend to have different perspectives about the same case and if, in fact, racially mixed juries sometimes *do* reach different results than racially homogeneous juries, then we must return to the original question: What is the rationale for the Court's decision in *Batson*? Was there an alternative approach in *Batson* that would have allowed the Court to recognize the existence of a correlation between race and juror behavior, but nevertheless prohibit prosecutors from using such a correlation as the basis for exercising peremptories?

2. Why does the rationale matter? The answer to this question requires consideration of traditional equal protection analysis. This analysis often depends heavily on the Court's choice of a review standard for the challenged government action: Under the "strict scrutiny" standard generally applicable to race-based government action, the government usually loses, whereas under the "rational basis" standard applicable to most non-race-based government action, the government usually wins. What equal protection standard is used by the Court in *Batson*? Does Justice Powell ever identify the applicable standard?

If *Batson* is based on the notion that the prosecutor's race-based use of peremptories is irrational and contrary to fact (because black jurors and white jurors are fungible), then, of course, the result of the case would be the same under either the "rational basis" or the "strict scrutiny" standard. But what about other possible constitutional challenges to peremptories? If the Court in *Batson* is saying that race-based peremptories fail to meet even the "rational basis" standard, then how can age-based peremptories (which are presumably no more "rational" than race-based ones) survive a constitutional challenge? Or occupation-based peremptories? Or any other use of peremptories based on loose correlations rather than provable biases of an individual prospective juror—a category that basically includes all peremptories? Does *Batson* effectively lead to the abolition of all peremptories?

What about gender-based use of peremptories? In J. E. B. v. Alabama ex rel. T. B., 511 U.S. 127 (1994), the Court—in a paternity case where nine out of the ten male prospective jurors were removed by state peremptory challenges—held that gender-based use of peremptories violates the Equal Protection Clause:

> Under our equal protection jurisprudence, gender-based classifications require "an exceedingly persuasive justification" in order to survive constitutional scrutiny. See Personnel Administrator of Mass. v. Feeney, 442 U.S. 256, 273 (1979).[10] . . . Thus, the only question is whether discrimination on the basis of gender in jury selection substantially furthers the State's legitimate interest in achieving a fair and impartial trial. . . .
>
> Far from proffering an exceptionally persuasive justification for its gender-based peremptory challenges, respondent maintains that its decision to strike virtually all the males from the jury in this case "may reasonably have been based upon the perception, supported by history, that men otherwise totally qualified to serve upon a jury in any case might be more sympathetic and receptive to the arguments of a man alleged in a paternity action to be the father of an out-of-wedlock child, while women equally qualified to serve upon a jury might be more sympathetic and receptive to the arguments of the complaining witness who bore the child." . . .
>
> We shall not accept as a defense to gender based-peremptory challenges "the very stereotype the law condemns." . . . Respondent's rationale, not unlike those regularly expressed for gender-based strikes, is reminiscent of the arguments advanced to justify the total exclusion of women from juries. Respondent offers virtually no support for the conclusion that gender alone is an accurate predictor of juror's attitudes; yet it urges this Court to condone the same stereotypes that justified the wholesale exclusion of women from juries and the ballot box. Respondent seems to assume that gross generalizations that would be deemed impermissible if made on the basis of race are somehow permissible when made on the basis of gender. . . .
>
> . . . Striking individual jurors on the assumption that they hold particular views simply because of their gender is "practically a brand upon them, affixed by the law, an assertion of their inferiority." Strauder v. West Virginia, 100 U.S., at 308. It denigrates the dignity of the excluded juror, and, for a woman, reinvokes a history of exclusion from political participation. The message it sends to all those in the courtroom, and all those who may later learn of the discriminatory act, is that certain individuals, for no reason other than gender, are presumed unqualified by state actors to decide important questions upon which reasonable persons could disagree. . . .

---

10. This equal protection standard for gender-based classifications, falling somewhere between "strict scrutiny" and "rational basis," is often referred to as "intermediate scrutiny." — EDS.

In light of *Batson*, the result in *J. E. B.* was perhaps not surprising. What *was* interesting, however, was the apparent ambivalence of the *J. E. B.* majority on the question of whether or not gender-based peremptories are inevitably irrational or contrary to fact. Just after denigrating the state for failing to demonstrate that "gender alone is an accurate predictor of juror's attitudes," see supra, Justice Blackmun, writing for the majority, added the following important words in a footnote:

> Even if a measure of truth can be found in some of the gender stereotypes used to justify gender-based peremptory challenges, that fact alone cannot support discrimination on the basis of gender in jury selection. We have made abundantly clear in past cases that gender classifications that rest on impermissible stereotypes violate the Equal Protection Clause, even when some statistical support can be conjured up for the generalization. . . . The generalization advanced by Alabama in support of its asserted right to discriminate on the basis of gender is, at the least, overbroad, and serves only to perpetuate the same "outmoded notions of the relative capabilities of men and women" . . . that we have invalidated in other contexts. . . . The Equal Protection Clause, as interpreted by decisions of this Court, acknowledges that a shred of truth may be contained in some stereotypes, but requires that state actors look beyond the surface before making judgments about people that are likely to stigmatize as well as to perpetuate historical patterns of discrimination.

Id., at 139, n. 11. Justice O'Connor, who provided the crucial fifth vote for Justice Blackmun's majority opinion, made the same point, but much more emphatically, in her separate opinion:

> . . . We know that like race, gender matters. A plethora of studies make clear that in rape cases, for example, female jurors are somewhat more likely to vote to convict than male jurors. See R. Hastie, S. Penrod, & N. Pennington, Inside the Jury 140-141 (1983) (collecting and summarizing empirical studies). Moreover, though there have been no similarly definitive studies regarding, for example, sexual harassment, child custody, or spousal or child abuse, one need not be a sexist to share the intuition that in certain cases a person's gender and resulting life experience will be relevant to his or her view of the case. "Jurors are not expected to come into the jury box and leave behind them all that their human experience has taught them." . . . Individuals are not expected to ignore as jurors what they know as men — or women.
>
> Today's decision severely limits a litigant's ability to act on this intuition, for the import of our holding is that any correlation between a juror's gender and attitudes is irrelevant as a matter of constitutional law. But to say that gender makes no difference as a matter of law is not to say that gender makes no difference as a matter of fact. I previously have said with regard to *Batson*: "That the Court will not tolerate prosecutors' racially discriminatory use of the peremptory challenge, in effect, is a special rule of relevance, a statement about what this Nation stands for, rather than a statement of fact." . . . Today's decision is a statement that, in an effort to eliminate the potential discriminatory use of the peremptory, . . . gender is now governed by the special rule of relevancy formerly reserved for race. . . . In extending *Batson* to gender we have . . . diminished the ability of litigants to act on sometimes accurate gender-based assumptions about juror attitudes.

Id., at 149-150 (O'Connor, J., concurring).

Do these remarks by Justice Blackmun (for the majority) and Justice O'Connor signify a subtle yet significant shift in the rationale for invalidating certain peremptories under the Equal Protection Clause? Do they suggest that the state's gender-based use of peremptories might be rational, yet nevertheless unconstitutional — under the "intermediate scrutiny" given to gender-based classifications? In light of *J. E. B.*, should *Batson* be interpreted as a "strict scrutiny" rather than a "rational basis" case? And, if so, can the Court hold the line on *Batson* in the future by limiting its application to those few classifications (like race and gender) that trigger heightened levels of equal protection scrutiny, while refusing to extend it to other situations (such as age-based and occupation-based peremptories) that would have to be evaluated under the lower, "rational basis" standard?

3. If the underlying premise of the fair-cross-section cases, and of *Batson*, is that race sometimes does matter and if we are serious about ensuring that black defendants receive a fair trial, then should we recognize a black defendant's affirmative right to have blacks on the actual jury? After all, even after *Batson*, and based on the racial demographics of most jurisdictions, it is unlikely that — absent such an affirmative right — the usual random process of jury selection will produce a jury with significant black representation. This idea has been advocated by Deborah Ramirez, Affirmative Jury Selection: A Proposal to Advance Both the Deliberative Ideal and Jury Diversity, 1998 U. Chi. Legal F. 161. Professor Ramirez argues that "a racially diverse jury is more likely to render a race-neutral verdict, because it is more likely to suppress racial bias in deliberations and to challenge inferences based on thoughtless racial stereotypes." Id., at 161. She acknowledges "the danger that jurors who are chosen in part because of their racial, religious, or ethnic affiliation may come to believe that they have a duty to represent their particular group in some fashion," id., at 162, but suggests that the particular procedures used to achieve racially mixed juries could help to minimize this danger (e.g., using "affirmative peremptory choices," through which the inclusion of prospective jurors of different races would be achieved by means of secret decisions by the litigants, as opposed to using open racial quotas). For a contrary view, see Jeffrey Abramson, Two Ideals of Jury Deliberation, 1998 U. Chi. Legal F. 125; see also Hiroshi Fukurai & Darryl Davies, Affirmative Action in Jury Selection: Racially Representative Juries, Racial Quotas, and Affirmative Juries of the Hennepin Model and the Jury De Medietatae Linguae, 4 Va. J. Soc. Pol'y & L. 645 (1997); Nancy J. King, Racial Jurymandering: Cancer or Cure? A Contemporary Review of Affirmative Action in Jury Selection, 68 N.Y.U. L. Rev. 707 (1993).

An even more controversial suggestion has been made by Professor Paul Butler. He argues that black jurors should, at least in some cases, use the nullification power to find guilty black defendants not guilty:

> . . . Let us assume that there is a black defendant who, the evidence suggests, is guilty of the crime with which he has been charged, and a black juror who thinks that there are too many black men in prison. The black juror has two choices: She can vote for conviction, thus sending another black man to prison and implicitly allowing her presence to support public confidence in the system that puts him there, or she can vote "not guilty," thereby acquitting the defendant, or at least causing a mistrial. In choosing the latter, the juror makes a decision not to be a passive symbol of support for a system for which she has no respect. Rather than signaling her displeasure with the system by breaching "community peace," the black juror invokes the political nature of her role in the criminal justice system and votes "no." In a sense, the black juror engages in

an act of civil disobedience, except that her choice is better than civil disobedience because it is lawful. Is the black juror's race-conscious act moral? Absolutely. It would be farcical for her to be the sole color-blind actor in the criminal process, especially when it is her blackness that advertises the system's fairness. At this point, every African-American should ask herself whether the operation of the criminal law in the United States advances the interests of black people. If it does not, the doctrine of jury nullification affords African-American jurors the opportunity to control the authority of the law over some African-American criminal defendants. In essence, black people can "opt out" of American criminal law.

Paul Butler, Racially Based Jury Nullification: Black Power in the Criminal Justice System, 105 Yale L.J. 677, 714 (1995). For a contrary view, see Andrew D. Leipold, The Dangers of Race-Based Jury Nullification: A Response to Professor Butler, 44 UCLA L. Rev. 109 (1996); see also Elissa Krauss & Martha Schulman, The Myth of Black Juror Nullification: Racism Dressed Up in Jurisprudential Clothing, 7 Cornell J.L. & Pub. Pol'y 57 (1997).

What do you think of these proposals? Is it possible to select a neutral jury without taking account of the race of the jurors? Is it possible to use race in jury selection without fostering even greater race-consciousness within the jury? If not, then what is the future of the jury in our racially diverse society?

4. *Batson* left numerous other important questions unanswered:

A. Can a white defendant challenge the prosecutor's use of peremptories to strike black prospective jurors? In Holland v. Illinois, 493 U.S. 474 (1990), the white defendant, concerned that he might lack standing to raise a *Batson* equal protection claim, argued instead that the prosecutor's striking of black prospective jurors violated his Sixth Amendment fair-cross-section right. The Court disagreed, reiterating its view that the fair-cross-section right applies only to the venire, and not to the actual jury. Just one year later, in Powers v. Ohio, 499 U.S. 400 (1991), the Court held that a white defendant indeed has standing to raise a *Batson* equal protection claim. Such standing was based on (1) the view (expressed for the first time in *Powers*) that the *Batson* right belongs not only to the defendant, but also to the excluded prospective jurors, see id., at 406-409, and (2) the holding that, under traditional rules of standing to raise constitutional claims, defendants can assert jus tertii (third-party) standing to raise the *Batson* rights of excluded prospective jurors of a different race, see id., at 410-415.

B. Does *Batson* apply to peremptories exercised by defendants? The Court addressed this question in Georgia v. McCollum, 505 U.S. 42 (1992), but the answer was already largely predetermined by two earlier decisions. One was Powers v. Ohio, where (as noted above) the Court recognized the concept of third-party standing (in a white defendant) to assert the *Batson* rights of black prospective jurors. The other was Edmonson v. Leesville Concrete Co., 500 U.S. 614 (1991), where the Court held that *Batson* applies to civil cases on the ground that "state action" (a requirement for an equal protection claim) can be found in the judicial system's close supervision of jury selection and peremptory challenges (even if both litigants are private parties). After *Powers* and *Edmonson*, *McCollum* was an easy case — there was "state action" even if the defendant was the party exercising the peremptory challenges, and the prosecutor could claim third-party standing to raise the *Batson* rights of the excluded prospective jurors.

In *J. E. B.*, supra, Justice O'Connor, who had dissented in *Edmonson* and *McCollum*, repeated her assertion that "the Equal Protection Clause does not limit the exercise of peremptory challenges by private civil litigants and criminal defendants." 511 U.S., at 151 (O'Connor, J., concurring). She added:

> Will we, in the name of fighting gender discrimination, hold that the battered wife — on trial for wounding her abusive husband — is a state actor? Will we preclude her from using her peremptory challenges to ensure that the jury of her peers contains as many women members as possible? I assume we will, but I hope we will not.

Ibid.

What if a defendant seeks to exercise a peremptory challenge against a juror who would not be subject to a for-cause challenge, and the peremptory challenge is erroneously denied by the trial judge based on *Batson* and *McCollum*? Does the seating of such a challenged juror violate the constitutional rights of the defendant, and if so, does it require automatic reversal of the resulting conviction? In Rivera v. Illinois, 129 S. Ct. 1446 (2009), the Court unanimously held that such an error does not require automatic reversal as a matter of federal law. The Court noted that peremptory challenges are not themselves of constitutional status; moreover, because the challenged juror was unbiased, there was no violation of the defendant's constitutional right to an impartial jury. In the end, the Court held that it was up to each state to decide — as a matter of state law — whether the erroneous denial of a peremptory challenge should lead to automatic reversal or be subjected to harmless-error analysis.

C. Perhaps the key issue, in terms of *Batson*'s significance to the real world of criminal jury trials, is how the lower courts should interpret and apply the *Batson* standard to prosecutorial (and, after *McCollum*, defense) peremptory challenges. Justice Marshall, in his *Batson* dissent, argued that the standard would not limit prosecutors who wished to discriminate because it would be all too easy to come up with "race-neutral" explanations for any contested challenges. The *Batson* majority, however, placed its faith in the lower courts to police the prosecutorial abuse of peremptories. Subsequent developments seemed to indicate that perhaps Marshall was right. In Hernandez v. New York, 500 U.S. 352 (1991), the prosecutor used peremptories in a manner that disproportionately excluded Latinos. The offered reason for the strikes was that they were based not on ethnicity, but instead on the prosecutor's perception (derived from voir dire) that the challenged individuals, who were English-Spanish bilingual, would find it difficult to accept the court translator's official English version of the Spanish-language testimony to be given during the trial. The trial judge rejected the defendant's *Batson* claim, and the Supreme Court affirmed. Justice Kennedy, writing for a four-justice plurality, found the offered reason to be "race neutral." He concluded that "the challenges rested neither on the intention to exclude Latino or bilingual jurors, nor on stereotypical assumptions about Latinos or bilinguals. . . . While the prosecutor's criterion might well result in the disproportionate removal of prospective Latino jurors, that disproportionate impact does not turn the prosecutor's actions into a per se violation of the Equal Protection Clause." Justice Kennedy added, however, that trial judges may consider such disproportionate impact as evidence that the offered reason might be a pretext for racial discrimination. Justice O'Connor, joined by Justice Scalia, concurred on the ground that the trial judge had made a factual finding, not clearly erroneous, that the offered reason was race neutral and thus satisfied *Batson*.

In Purkett v. Elem, 514 U.S. 765 (1995), the prosecutor used peremptories to strike two black prospective jurors. When the trial judge requested an explanation, the prosecutor answered that he struck the first juror because of his long, curly, "unkempt" hair and the second because of his mustache and goatee-type beard. The trial judge found these answers satisfactory under *Batson*, but a federal appeals court, sitting in habeas, later concluded that they were pretextual because the prosecutor never explained why hair length or facial hair should matter to a juror's qualifications. A per curiam Supreme Court reversed. The Court found that the prosecutor's explanations, whether reasonable or not, were race neutral and thus satisfied step two of the *Batson* inquiry. Turning to step three of the inquiry, the habeas court never offered any valid basis for overturning the trial judge's factual finding of "no racial motive" for the peremptories. The Court emphasized that, in step three, the proper focus is on the *genuineness* of the proponent's alleged race-neutral motive rather than its *reasonableness*.

After *Hernandez* and *Purkett*, many believed that *Batson*'s promise would go unfulfilled. If it was really so easy for prosecutors to explain their peremptories in race-neutral terms, and thereby avoid a *Batson* reversal, then what was the point of the whole exercise in the first place?

Possibly for this reason, some lower courts began to screen *Batson* claims more aggressively at the initial stage of the three-stage inquiry, eliminating many claims before ever reaching the second, "race-neutral explanation" stage. These courts (utilizing the flexibility that the Supreme Court appeared to grant them in implementing *Batson*'s mandate) held that, at the initial stage of the inquiry, the defendant must meet a prima facie burden of proving, by a preponderance of the evidence, that the prosecutor's use of peremptories gives rise to an inference of racial discrimination. Otherwise, there is nothing for the prosecutor to rebut at the second stage.

In Johnson v. California, 545 U.S. 162 (2005), the Supreme Court, by 8-1, soundly rejected this interpretation of *Batson*. According to the Court:

> [W]e assumed in *Batson* that the trial judge would have the benefit of all relevant circumstances, including the prosecutor's explanation, before deciding whether it was more likely than not that the challenge was improperly motivated. We did not intend the first step to be so onerous that a defendant would have to persuade the judge on the basis of all the facts, some of which are impossible for the defendant to know with certainty — that the challenge was more likely than not the product of purposeful discrimination. Instead, a defendant satisfies the requirements of *Batson*'s first step by producing evidence sufficient to permit the trial judge to draw an inference that discrimination has occurred.

In a footnote, the Court pointed out what perhaps should have been obvious — that even if a defendant's *Batson* claim is relatively weak, there might nevertheless be some value in requiring the prosecution to respond. The clear message of *Johnson* seems to be that most *Batson* claims (i.e., all those that are not facially implausible) should survive the first stage of the *Batson* analysis and proceed to the second and third stages. But that may still beg the question. What happens when those claims get to the later stages of the analysis? How aggressive should the lower courts be, in reviewing the prosecutor's asserted race-neutral reasons for the challenged peremptory strikes?

Two recent Supreme Court decisions — in the same case — seem, at least on the surface, to suggest that such review should be fairly aggressive. In the first decision, Miller-El v. Cockrell, 537 U.S. 322 (2003), the Court (with only Justice Thomas dissenting) overturned the Fifth Circuit's denial of a "certificate of appealability" to review a *Batson* claim made by a Dallas County, Texas, death-row inmate in a federal habeas corpus petition. The Court concluded that Miller-El's evidence was more than adequate to raise an inference of prosecutorial race discrimination, and thus met the test of habeas appealability, which requires a "substantial showing of the denial of a constitutional right." The Court also found the lower court's reliance on the prosecution's alleged race-neutral reasons unwarranted, especially given that "the application of these rationales to the venire might have been selective and based on racial considerations." Id., at 343.

The Fifth Circuit, on remand, issued the "certificate of appealability," but then (somewhat inexplicably, given the Supreme Court's tone in Miller-El v. Cockrell) rejected Miller-El's underlying *Batson* claim on the merits. The case then returned to the Supreme Court.

MILLER-EL v. DRETKE

Certiorari to the U.S. Court of Appeals for the Fifth Circuit
545 U.S. 231 (2005)

JUSTICE SOUTER delivered the opinion of the Court.

Two years ago, we ordered that a certificate of appealability, under 28 U.S.C. §2253(c), be issued to habeas petitioner Miller-El, affording review of the District Court's rejection of the claim that prosecutors in his capital murder trial made peremptory strikes of potential jurors based on race. Today we find Miller-El entitled to prevail on that claim and order relief under §2254.

I

In the course of robbing a Holiday Inn in Dallas, Texas in late 1985, Miller-El and his accomplices bound and gagged two hotel employees, whom Miller-El then shot, killing one and severely injuring the other. During jury selection in Miller-El's trial for capital murder, prosecutors used peremptory strikes against 10 qualified black venire members. Miller-El objected that the strikes were based on race and could not be presumed legitimate, given a history of excluding black members from criminal juries by the Dallas County District Attorney's Office. The trial court received evidence of the practice alleged but found no "systematic exclusion of blacks as a matter of policy" by that office, and therefore no entitlement to relief under Swain v. Alabama, 380 U.S. 202 (1965), the case then defining and marking the limits of relief from racially biased jury selection. The court denied Miller-El's request to pick a new jury, and the trial ended with his death sentence for capital murder.

While an appeal was pending, this Court decided Batson v. Kentucky, 476 U.S. 79 (1986), which replaced *Swain*'s threshold requirement to prove systemic discrimination under a Fourteenth Amendment jury claim, with the rule that discrimination by the prosecutor in selecting the defendant's jury sufficed to establish the constitutional violation. The Texas Court of Criminal Appeals then remanded the matter to the trial court to determine whether Miller-El could show that prosecutors in his case peremptorily struck prospective black jurors because of race. Miller-El v. State, 748 S.W.2d 459 (1988).

The trial court found no such demonstration. After reviewing the voir dire record of the explanations given for some of the challenged strikes, and after hearing one of the prosecutors, Paul Macaluso, give his justification for those previously unexplained, the trial court accepted the stated race-neutral reasons for the strikes, which the judge called "completely credible [and] sufficient" as the grounds for a finding of "no purposeful discrimination." The Court of Criminal Appeals affirmed, stating it found "ample support" in the voir dire record for the race-neutral explanations offered by prosecutors for the peremptory strikes.

Miller-El then sought habeas relief under 28 U.S.C. §2254, again pressing his *Batson* claim, among others not now before us. The District Court denied relief, and the Court of Appeals for the Fifth Circuit precluded appeal by denying a certificate of appealability, Miller-El v. Johnson, 261 F.3d 445 (2001). We granted certiorari to consider whether Miller-El was entitled to review on the *Batson* claim, Miller-El v. Cockrell, 534 U.S. 1122 (2002), and reversed the Court of Appeals. After examining the record of Miller-El's extensive evidence of purposeful discrimination by the Dallas County District Attorney's Office before and during his trial, we found an appeal was in order, since the merits of the *Batson* claim were, at the least, debatable by jurists of reason. Miller-El v. Cockrell, 537 U.S. 322 (2003). After granting a certificate of appealability, the Fifth Circuit rejected Miller-El's *Batson* claim on the merits. 361 F.3d 849 (2004). We again granted certiorari, and again we reverse.

II

A

"It is well known that prejudices often exist against particular classes in the community, which sway the judgment of jurors, and which, therefore, operate in some cases to deny to persons of those classes the full enjoyment of that protection which others enjoy." Strauder v. West Virginia, 100 U.S. 303, 309 (1880). . . .

The rub has been the practical difficulty of ferreting out discrimination in selections discretionary by nature, and choices subject to myriad legitimate influences, whatever the race of the individuals on the panel from which jurors are selected. . . . The *Swain* court tried to relate peremptory challenge to equal protection by presuming the legitimacy of prosecutors' strikes except in the face of a longstanding pattern of discrimination. . . . [380 U.S.,] at 223-224.

Swain's demand to make out a continuity of discrimination over time, however, turned out to be difficult to the point of unworkable, and in Batson v. Kentucky, we . . . held that a defendant could make out a prima facie case of discriminatory jury selection by "the totality of the relevant facts" about a prosecutor's conduct during the defendant's own trial. 476 U.S., at 94, 96. . . .

Although the move from *Swain* to *Batson* left a defendant free to challenge the prosecution without having to cast *Swain*'s wide net, the net was not entirely consigned to history, for *Batson*'s individualized focus came with a weakness of its own, owing to its very emphasis on the particular reasons a prosecutor might give. If any facially neutral reason sufficed to answer a *Batson* challenge, then *Batson* would not amount to much more than *Swain*. Some stated reasons are false, and although some false reasons are shown up within the four corners of a given case, sometimes a court may not be sure unless it looks beyond the case at hand. Hence *Batson*'s explanation that a defendant may rely on "all relevant circumstances" to raise an inference of purposeful discrimination. 476 U.S., at 96-97.

B

This case comes to us on review of a denial of habeas relief sought under 28 U.S.C. §2254, following the Texas trial court's prior determination of fact that the State's race-neutral explanations were true, see Purkett v. Elem, 514 U.S. 765, 769 (1995) (per curiam); Batson v. Kentucky, supra, at 98, n. 21.

Under the Antiterrorism and Effective Death Penalty Act of 1996, Miller-El may obtain relief only by showing the Texas conclusion to be "an unreasonable determination of the facts in light of the evidence presented in the State court proceeding." 28 U.S.C. §2254(d)(2). Thus we presume the Texas court's factual findings to be sound unless Miller-El rebuts the "presumption of correctness by clear and convincing evidence." §2254(e)(1). The standard is demanding but not insatiable; as we said the last time this case was here, "deference does not by definition preclude relief." Miller-El v. Cockrell, 537 U.S., at 340.

III

A

The numbers describing the prosecution's use of peremptories are remarkable. Out of 20 black members of the 108-person venire panel for Miller-El's trial, only 1 served. Although 9 were excused for cause or by agreement, 10 were peremptorily struck by the prosecution. Id., at 331. "The prosecutors used their peremptory strikes to exclude 91% of the eligible African-American venire members. . . . Happenstance is unlikely to produce this disparity." Id., at 342.

More powerful than these bare statistics, however, are side-by-side comparisons of some black venire panelists who were struck and white panelists allowed to serve. If a prosecutor's proffered reason for striking a black panelist applies just as well to an otherwise similar nonblack who is permitted to serve, that is evidence tending to prove purposeful discrimination to be considered at *Batson*'s third step. . . . While we did not develop a comparative juror analysis last time, we did note that the prosecution's reasons for exercising peremptory strikes against some black panel members appeared equally on point as to some white jurors who served. Miller-El v. Cockrell, supra, at 343. The details of two panel member comparisons bear this out.

The prosecution used its second peremptory strike to exclude Billy Jean Fields, a black man who expressed unwavering support for the death penalty. On the questionnaire filled out by all panel members before individual examination on the stand, Fields said that he believed in capital punishment, and during questioning he disclosed his belief that the State acts on God's behalf when it imposes the death penalty. "Therefore, if the State exacts death, then that's what it should be." App. 174. He testified that he had no religious or philosophical reservations about the death penalty and that the death penalty deterred crime. Id., at 174-175. He twice averred, without apparent hesitation, that he could sit on Miller-El's jury and make a decision to impose this penalty. Id., at 176-177.

Although at one point in the questioning, Fields indicated that the possibility of rehabilitation might be relevant to the likelihood that a defendant would commit future acts of violence, id., at 183, he responded to ensuing questions by saying that although he believed anyone could be rehabilitated, this belief would not stand in the way of a decision to impose the death penalty:

Based on what you [the prosecutor] said as far as the crime goes, there are only two things that could be rendered, death or life in prison. If for some reason the testimony didn't warrant death, then life imprisonment would give an individual an opportunity to rehabilitate. But, you know, you said that the jurors didn't have the opportunity to make a personal decision in the matter with reference to what I thought or felt, but it was just based on the questions according to the way the law has been handed down.

Id., at 185 (alteration omitted).

Fields also noted on his questionnaire that his brother had a criminal history. During questioning, the prosecution went into this, too:

Q.   Could you tell me a little bit about that?
A.   He was arrested and convicted on [a] number of occasions for possession of a controlled substance.
Q.   Was that here in Dallas?
A.   Yes.
Q.   Was he involved in any trials or anything like that?
A.   I suppose of sorts. I don't really know too much about it.
Q.   Was he ever convicted?
A.   Yeah, he served time.
Q.   Do you feel that that would in any way interfere with your service on this jury at all?
A.   No.

App. 190.

Fields was struck peremptorily by the prosecution, with prosecutor James Nelson offering a race-neutral reason:

We . . . have concern with reference to some of his statements as to the death penalty in that he said that he could only give death if he thought a person could not be rehabilitated and he later made the comment that any person could be rehabilitated if they find God or are introduced to God and the fact that we have a concern that his religious feelings may affect his jury service in this case.

Id., at 197 (alteration omitted).

Thus, Nelson simply mischaracterized Fields's testimony. He represented that Fields said he would not vote for death if rehabilitation was possible, whereas Fields unequivocally stated that he could impose the death penalty regardless of the possibility of rehabilitation. Perhaps Nelson misunderstood, but unless he had an ulterior reason for keeping Fields off the jury we think he would have proceeded differently. In light of Fields's outspoken support for the death penalty, we expect the prosecutor would have cleared up any misunderstanding by asking further questions before getting to the point of exercising a strike.

If, indeed, Fields's thoughts on rehabilitation did make the prosecutor uneasy, he should have worried about a number of white panel members he accepted with no evident reservations. Sandra Hearn said that she believed in the death penalty "if a criminal cannot be rehabilitated and continues to commit the same type of crime." Id., at 429. Hearn went so far as to express doubt that at the penalty phase of a capital case she could conclude that a convicted murderer "would probably commit some criminal acts of violence in the future." Id., at 440. "People change," she said, making it hard to assess the risk of someone's future dangerousness. "The evidence would have to be awful strong." Ibid. But the prosecution did not respond to Hearn the way it did to Fields, and without delving into her views about rehabilitation with any further question, it raised no objection to her serving on the jury. White panelist Mary Witt said she would take the possibility of rehabilitation into account in deciding at the penalty phase of the trial about a defendant's probability of future dangerousness, 6 Record of *Voir Dire* 2433 (hereinafter Record), but the prosecutors asked her no further question about her views on reformation, and they accepted her as a juror. Id., at 2464-2465.[4] Latino venireman Fernando Gutierrez, who served on the jury, said that he would consider the death penalty for someone who could not be rehabilitated, App. 777, but the prosecutors did not question him further about this view. In sum, nonblack jurors whose remarks on rehabilitation could well have signaled a limit on their willingness to impose a death sentence were not questioned further and drew no objection, but the prosecution expressed apprehension about a black juror's belief in the possibility of reformation even though he repeatedly stated his approval of the death penalty and testified that he could impose it according to state legal standards even when the alternative sentence of life imprisonment would give a defendant (like everyone else in the world) the opportunity to reform.[5]

The unlikelihood that his position on rehabilitation had anything to do with the peremptory strike of Fields is underscored by the prosecution's response after Miller-El's lawyer pointed out that the prosecutor had misrepresented Fields's responses on the subject. A moment earlier the prosecutor had finished his misdescription of Fields's views on potential rehabilitation with the words, "Those are our reasons for exercising our . . . strike at this time." Id., at 197. When defense counsel called him on his misstatement, he neither defended what he said nor withdrew the strike. Id., at 198. Instead, he suddenly came up with Fields's brother's prior conviction as another reason for the strike. Id., at 199.

It would be difficult to credit the State's new explanation, which reeks of afterthought. While the Court of Appeals tried to bolster it with the observation that no seated juror was in Fields's position with respect to his brother, 361 F.3d, at 859-860, the court's readiness to accept the State's substitute reason ignores not only its pretextual timing but the other reasons rendering it implausible. Fields's testimony indicated he was not close to his brother, App. 190 ("I don't really know too much about it"), and the prosecution asked nothing further about the influence his brother's history might have had on Fields, as it probably would have done if the family history had actually mattered. See, e.g., Ex parte Travis, 776 So. 2d 874, 881 (Ala. 2000) ("The State's failure to engage in any meaningful voir dire examination on a subject the State alleges it is concerned about is evidence suggesting that the explanation is a sham and a pretext for discrimination"). There is no good reason to doubt that the State's afterthought about Fields's brother was anything but makeweight. . . .

---

4. Witt ultimately did not serve because she was peremptorily struck by the defense. 6 Record 2465. The fact that Witt and other venire members discussed here were peremptorily struck by the defense is not relevant to our point. For each of them, the defense did not make a decision to exercise a peremptory until after the prosecution decided whether to accept or reject, so each was accepted by the prosecution before being ultimately struck by the defense. . . .

5. Prosecutors did exercise peremptory strikes on Penny Crowson and Charlotte Whaley, who expressed views about rehabilitation similar to those of Witt and Gutierrez. App. 554, 715.

In sum, when we look for nonblack jurors similarly situated to Fields, we find strong similarities as well as some differences.[6] But the differences seem far from significant, particularly when we read Fields's voir dire testimony in its entirety. Upon that reading, Fields should have been an ideal juror in the eyes of a prosecutor seeking a death sentence, and the prosecutors' explanations for the strike cannot reasonably be accepted. See Miller-El v. Cockrell, 537 U.S., at 339 (the credibility of reasons given can be measured by "how reasonable, or how improbable, the explanations are; and by whether the proffered rationale has some basis in accepted trial strategy").

The prosecution's proffered reasons for striking Joe Warren, another black venireman, are comparably unlikely. Warren gave this answer when he was asked what the death penalty accomplished:

> I don't know. It's really hard to say because I know sometimes you feel that it might help to deter crime and then you feel that the person is not really suffering. You're taking the suffering away from him. So it's like I said, sometimes you have mixed feelings about whether or not this is punishment or, you know, you're relieving personal punishment.

App. 205; 3 Record 1532.

The prosecution said nothing about these remarks when it struck Warren from the panel, but prosecutor Paul Macaluso referred to this answer as the first of his reasons when he testified at the later *Batson* hearing:

> I thought [Warren's statements on voir dire] were inconsistent responses. At one point he says, you know, on a case-by-case basis and at another point he said, well, I think — I got the impression, at least, that he suggested that the death penalty was an easy way out, that they should be made to suffer more.

App. 909.

On the face of it, the explanation is reasonable from the State's point of view, but its plausibility is severely undercut by the prosecution's failure to object to other panel members who expressed views much like Warren's. [For example,] Sandra Jenkins, whom the State accepted (but who was then struck by the defense) testified that she thought "a harsher treatment is life imprisonment with no parole." Id., at 542. Leta Girard, accepted by the State (but also struck by the defense) gave her opinion that "living sometimes is a worse — is worse to me than dying would be." Id., at 624. The fact that Macaluso's reason also applied to these other panel members, most of them white, none of them struck, is evidence of pretext.

The suggestion of pretext is not, moreover, mitigated much by Macaluso's explanation that Warren was struck when the State had 10 peremptory challenges left and

6. The dissent contends that there are no white panelists similarly situated to Fields and to panel member Joe Warren because "'similarly situated' does not mean matching any one of several reasons the prosecution gave for striking a potential juror — it means matching *all* of them." Post, at 19 (quoting Miller-El v. Cockrell, 537 U.S., at 362-363 (Thomas, J., dissenting)). None of our cases announces a rule that no comparison is probative unless the situation of the individuals compared is identical in all respects, and there is no reason to accept one. Nothing in the combination of Fields's statements about rehabilitation and his brother's history discredits our grounds for inferring that these purported reasons were pretextual. A per se rule that a defendant cannot win a *Batson* claim unless there is an exactly identical white juror would leave *Batson* inoperable; potential jurors are not products of a set of cookie cutters.

could afford to be liberal in using them. Id., at 908. If that were the explanation for striking Warren and later accepting panel members who thought death would be too easy, the prosecutors should have struck Sandra Jenkins, whom they examined and accepted before Warren. . . . Yet the prosecutors accepted the white panel member Jenkins and struck the black venireman Warren.

Macaluso's explanation that the prosecutors grew more sparing with peremptory challenges as the jury selection wore on does, however, weaken any suggestion that the State's acceptance of [Troy] Woods, the one black juror, shows that race was not in play. Woods was the eighth juror, qualified in the fifth week of jury selection. Joint Lodging 125. When the State accepted him, 11 of its 15 peremptory strikes were gone, 7 of them used to strike black panel members. The juror questionnaires show that at least three members of the venire panel yet to be questioned on the stand were opposed to capital punishment, Janice Mackey, id., at 79; Paul Bailey, id., at 63; and Anna Keaton, id., at 55. With at least three remaining panel members highly undesirable to the State, the prosecutors had to exercise prudent restraint in using strikes. This late-stage decision to accept a black panel member willing to impose a death sentence does not, therefore, neutralize the early-stage decision to challenge a comparable venireman, Warren. In fact, if the prosecutors were going to accept any black juror to obscure the otherwise consistent pattern of opposition to seating one, the time to do so was getting late. . . .

[T]he rule in Batson provides an opportunity to the prosecutor to give the reason for striking the juror, and it requires the judge to assess the plausibility of that reason in light of all evidence with a bearing on it. 476 U.S., at 96-97; Miller-El v. Cockrell, 537 U.S., at 339. It is true that peremptories are often the subjects of instinct, Batson v. Kentucky, 476 U.S., at 106 (Marshall, J., concurring), and it can sometimes be hard to say what the reason is. But when illegitimate grounds like race are in issue, a prosecutor simply has got to state his reasons as best he can and stand or fall on the plausibility of the reasons he gives. A Batson challenge does not call for a mere exercise in thinking up any rational basis. If the stated reason does not hold up, its pretextual significance does not fade because a trial judge, or an appeals court, can imagine a reason that might not have been shown up as false. The Court of Appeals's and the dissent's substitution of a reason for eliminating Warren does nothing to satisfy the prosecutors' burden of stating a racially neutral explanation for their own actions.

The whole of the voir dire testimony subject to consideration casts the prosecution's reasons for striking Warren in an implausible light. Comparing his strike with the treatment of panel members who expressed similar views supports a conclusion that race was significant in determining who was challenged and who was not.

B

The case for discrimination goes beyond these comparisons to include broader patterns of practice during the jury selection. The prosecution's shuffling of the venire panel, its enquiry into views on the death penalty, its questioning about minimum acceptable sentences: all indicate decisions probably based on race. Finally, the appearance of discrimination is confirmed by widely known evidence of the general policy of the Dallas County District Attorney's Office to exclude black venire members from juries at the time Miller-El's jury was selected.

The first clue to the prosecutors' intentions, distinct from the peremptory challenges themselves, is their resort during voir dire to a procedure known in Texas as
the jury shuffle. In the State's criminal practice, either side may literally reshuffle
the cards bearing panel members' names, thus rearranging the order in which
members of a venire panel are seated and reached for questioning. Once the order
is established, the panel members seated at the back are likely to escape voir dire
altogether, for those not questioned by the end of the week are dismissed. . . .

In this case, the prosecution and then the defense shuffled the cards at the beginning of the first week of voir dire; the record does not reflect the changes in order.
App. 113-114. At the beginning of the second week, when a number of black members were seated at the front of the panel, the prosecution shuffled. 2 Record 836-
837. At the beginning of the third week, the first four panel members were black.
The prosecution shuffled, and these black panel members ended up at the back.
Then the defense shuffled, and the black panel members again appeared at the
front. The prosecution requested another shuffle, but the trial court refused. App.
124-132. Finally, the defense shuffled at the beginning of the fourth and fifth weeks
of voir dire; the record does not reflect the panel's racial composition before or after
those shuffles. Id., at 621-622; 9 Record 3585.

The State notes in its brief that there might be racially neutral reasons for shuffling the jury, and we suppose there might be. But no racially neutral reason has ever
been offered in this case, and nothing stops the suspicion of discriminatory intent
from rising to an inference.

The next body of evidence that the State was trying to avoid black jurors is the
contrasting voir dire questions posed respectively to black and nonblack panel
members, on two different subjects. First, there were the prosecutors' statements
preceding questions about a potential juror's thoughts on capital punishment.
Some of these prefatory statements were cast in general terms, but some followed
the so-called graphic script, describing the method of execution in rhetorical and
clinical detail. It is intended, Miller-El contends, to prompt some expression of hesitation to consider the death penalty and thus to elicit plausibly neutral grounds for
a peremptory strike of a potential juror subjected to it, if not a strike for cause. If the
graphic script is given to a higher proportion of blacks than whites, this is evidence
that prosecutors more often wanted blacks off the jury, absent some neutral and
extenuating explanation.

As we pointed out last time, for 94% of white venire panel members, prosecutors
gave a bland description of the death penalty before asking about the individual's
feelings on the subject. Miller-El v. Cockrell, 537 U.S., at 332. . . . Only 6% of white
venire panelists, but 53% of those who were black, heard [the much more graphic]
description of the death penalty before being asked their feelings about it. . . .

The State concedes that this disparate questioning did occur but argues that use
of the graphic script turned not on a panelist's race but on expressed ambivalence
about the death penalty in the preliminary questionnaire. Prosecutors were trying,
the argument goes, to weed out noncommittal or uncertain jurors, not black jurors.
And while some white venire members expressed opposition to the death penalty
on their questionnaires, they were not read the graphic script because their feelings
were already clear. The State says that giving the graphic script to these panel members would only have antagonized them. Brief for Respondent 27-32.

This argument, however, first advanced in dissent when the case was last here,
Miller-El v. Cockrell, supra, at 364-368 (opinion of Thomas, J.), and later adopted

by the State and the Court of Appeals, simply does not fit the facts. Looking at the answers on the questionnaires, and at voir dire testimony expressly discussing answers on the questionnaires, we find that black venire members were more likely than nonblacks to receive the graphic script regardless of their expressions of certainty or ambivalence about the death penalty, and the State's chosen explanation for the graphic script fails in the cases of four out of the eight black panel members who received it. Two of them, Janice Mackey and Anna Keaton, clearly stated opposition to the death penalty but they received the graphic script, while the black panel members Wayman Kennedy and Jeannette Butler were unambiguously in favor but got the graphic description anyway. The State's explanation does even worse in the instances of the five nonblacks who received the graphic script, missing the mark four times out of five: Vivian Sztybel and Filemon Zablan received it, although each was unambiguously in favor of the death penalty, while Dominick Desinise and Clara Evans unambiguously opposed it but were given the graphic version. . . .

The State's attempt at a race-neutral rationalization thus simply fails to explain what the prosecutors did. But if we posit instead that the prosecutors' first object was to use the graphic script to make a case for excluding black panel members opposed to or ambivalent about the death penalty, there is a much tighter fit of fact and explanation. Of the 10 nonblacks whose questionnaires expressed ambivalence or opposition, only 30% received the graphic treatment. But of the seven blacks who expressed ambivalence or opposition, 86% heard the graphic script. As between the State's ambivalence explanation and Miller-El's racial one, race is much the better, and the reasonable inference is that race was the major consideration when the prosecution chose to follow the graphic script.

The same is true for another kind of disparate questioning, which might fairly be called trickery. The prosecutors asked members of the panel how low a sentence they would consider imposing for murder. Most potential jurors were first told that Texas law provided for a minimum term of five years, but some members of the panel were not, and if a panel member then insisted on a minimum above five years, the prosecutor would suppress his normal preference for tough jurors and claim cause to strike [on the ground of protecting defendants from overzealous jurors — EDS.]. Two Terms ago, we described how this disparate questioning was correlated with race:

> Ninety-four percent of whites were informed of the statutory minimum sentence, compared [with] only twelve and a half percent of African-Americans. No explanation is proffered for the statistical disparity. . . . Indeed, while petitioner's appeal was pending before the Texas Court of Criminal Appeals, that court found a *Batson* violation where this precise line of disparate questioning on mandatory minimums was employed by one of the same prosecutors who tried the instant case. Chambers v. State, 784 S.W.2d 29, 31 (Tex. Crim. App. 1989).

Miller-El v. Cockrell, 537 U.S., at 345.

The State concedes that the manipulative minimum punishment questioning was used to create cause to strike, but now it offers the extenuation that prosecutors omitted the 5-year information not on the basis of race, but on stated opposition to the death penalty, or ambivalence about it, on the questionnaires and in the voir dire testimony. . . . But the State's rationale flatly fails to explain why most white panel members who expressed similar opposition or ambivalence were not subjected to it. . . . [O]nly 27% of nonblacks questioned on the subject who expressed these views were subjected to the trick question, as against 100% of black members. Once again, the implication of race in the prosecutors' choice of questioning cannot be explained away.

There is a final body of evidence that confirms this conclusion. We know that for decades leading up to the time this case was tried prosecutors in the Dallas County office had followed a specific policy of systematically excluding blacks from juries, as we explained the last time the case was here.

> . . . [T]he defense presented evidence that the District Attorney's Office had adopted a formal policy to exclude minorities from jury service. . . . A manual entitled 'Jury Selection in a Criminal Case' [sometimes known as the Sparling Manual] was distributed to prosecutors. It contained an article authored by a former prosecutor (and later a judge) under the direction of his superiors in the District Attorney's Office, outlining the reasoning for excluding minorities from jury service. Although the manual was written in 1968, it remained in circulation until 1976, if not later, and was available at least to one of the prosecutors in Miller-El's trial.

Miller-El v. Cockrell, 537 U.S., at 334-335.

Prosecutors here "marked the race of each prospective juror on their juror cards." Id., at 347.[38]

The Court of Appeals concluded that Miller-El failed to show by clear and convincing evidence that the state court's finding of no discrimination was wrong, whether his evidence was viewed collectively or separately. 361 F.3d, at 862. We find this conclusion as unsupportable as the "dismissive and strained interpretation" of his evidence that we disapproved when we decided Miller-El was entitled to a certificate of appealability. See Miller-El v. Cockrell, supra, at 344. It is true, of course, that at some points the significance of Miller-El's evidence is open to judgment calls, but when this evidence on the issues raised is viewed cumulatively its direction is too powerful to conclude anything but discrimination.

In the course of drawing a jury to try a black defendant, 10 of the 11 qualified black venire panel members were peremptorily struck. At least two of them, Fields and Warren, were ostensibly acceptable to prosecutors seeking a death verdict, and Fields was ideal. The prosecutors' chosen race-neutral reasons for the strikes do not hold up and are so far at odds with the evidence that pretext is the fair conclusion, indicating the very discrimination the explanations were meant to deny.

The strikes that drew these incredible explanations occurred in a selection process replete with evidence that the prosecutors were selecting and rejecting potential jurors because of race. At least two of the jury shuffles conducted by the State make no sense except as efforts to delay consideration of black jury panelists to the end of the week, when they might not even be reached. The State has in fact never offered any other explanation. Nor has the State denied that disparate lines of questioning were pursued: 53% of black panelists but only 3% of nonblacks were questioned with a graphic script meant to induce qualms about applying the death penalty (and thus explain a strike), and 100% of blacks but only 27% of nonblacks were subjected to a trick question about the minimum acceptable penalty for murder, meant to induce a disqualifying answer. The State's attempts to explain the

---

38. The State claimed at oral argument that prosecutors could have been tracking jurors' races to be sure of avoiding a *Batson* violation. Tr. of Oral Arg. 44. *Batson*, of course, was decided the month after Miller-El was tried.

prosecutors' questioning of particular witnesses on nonracial grounds fit the evidence less well than the racially discriminatory hypothesis.

If anything more is needed for an undeniable explanation of what was going on, history supplies it. The prosecutors took their cues from a 20-year-old manual of tips on jury selection, as shown by their notes of the race of each potential juror. By the time a jury was chosen, the State had peremptorily challenged 12% of qualified nonblack panel members, but eliminated 91% of the black ones.

It blinks reality to deny that the State struck Fields and Warren, included in that 91%, because they were black. The strikes correlate with no fact as well as they correlate with race, and they occurred during a selection infected by shuffling and disparate questioning that race explains better than any race-neutral reason advanced by the State. The State's pretextual positions confirm Miller-El's claim, and the prosecutors' own notes proclaim that the Sparling Manual's emphasis on race was on their minds when they considered every potential juror.

The state court's conclusion that the prosecutors' strikes of Fields and Warren were not racially determined is shown up as wrong to a clear and convincing degree; the state court's conclusion was unreasonable as well as erroneous. The judgment of the Court of Appeals is reversed, and the case is remanded for entry of judgment for petitioner together with orders of appropriate relief.

JUSTICE BREYER, concurring.

In Batson v. Kentucky, 476 U.S. 79 (1986), the Court adopted a burden-shifting rule designed to ferret out the unconstitutional use of race in jury selection. In his separate opinion, Justice Thurgood Marshall predicted that the Court's rule would not achieve its goal. The only way to "end the racial discrimination that peremptories inject into the jury-selection process," he concluded, was to "eliminate peremptory challenges entirely." Id., at 102-103 (concurring opinion). Today's case reinforces Justice Marshall's concerns.

I

To begin with, this case illustrates the practical problems of proof that Justice Marshall described. . . .

At *Batson*'s first step, litigants remain free to misuse peremptory challenges as long as the strikes fall *below* the prima facie threshold level. . . . At *Batson*'s second step, prosecutors need only tender a neutral reason, not a "persuasive, or even plausible" one. . . . And most importantly, at step three, *Batson* asks judges to engage in the awkward, sometime hopeless, task of second-guessing a prosecutor's instinctive judgment — the underlying basis for which may be invisible even to the prosecutor exercising the challenge. . . .

Given the inevitably clumsy fit between any objectively measurable standard and the subjective decision making at issue, I am not surprised to find studies and anecdotal reports suggesting that, despite *Batson*, the discriminatory use of peremptory challenges remains a problem. See, e.g., Baldus, Woodworth, Zuckerman, Weiner, & Broffitt, The Use of Peremptory Challenges in Capital Murder Trials: A Legal and Empirical Analysis, 3 U. Pa. J. Const. L. 3, 52-53, 73, n. 197 (2001) (in 317 capital trials in Philadelphia between 1981 and 1997, prosecutors struck 51% of black jurors and 26% of nonblack jurors; defense counsel struck 26% of black jurors and 54% of nonblack jurors; and race-based uses of prosecutorial peremptories declined by only 2% after *Batson*); Rose, The Peremptory Challenge Accused of Race or Gender Discrimination? Some Data from One County, 23 Law & Hum. Behav. 695, 698-699 (1999) (in one North Carolina county, 71% of excused black jurors were removed by the prosecution; 81% of excused white jurors were removed by the defense); Tucker, In Moore's Trials, Excluded Jurors Fit Racial Pattern, Washington Post, Apr. 2, 2001, p. A1 (in a D. C. murder case spanning four trials, prosecutors excused 41 blacks or other minorities and 6 whites; defense counsel struck 29 whites and 13 black venire members); Mize, A Legal Discrimination; Juries Are Not Supposed to be Picked on the Basis of Race and Sex, But It Happens All the Time, Washington Post, Oct. 8, 2000, p. B8 (authored by judge on the D.C. Superior Court); see also Melilli, *Batson* in Practice: What We Have Learned About *Batson* and Peremptory Challenges, 71 Notre Dame L. Rev. 447, 462-464 (1996) (finding *Batson* challenges' success rates lower where peremptories were used to strike black, rather than white, potential jurors); Brand, The Supreme Court, Equal Protection and Jury Selection: Denying That Race Still Matters, 1994 Wis. L. Rev. 511, 583-589 (examining judicial decisions and concluding that few *Batson* challenges succeed); Note, Batson v. Kentucky and J. E. B. v. Alabama ex rel. T. B.: Is the Peremptory Challenge Still Preeminent? 36 Boston College L. Rev. 161, 189, and n. 303 (1994) (same); Montoya, The Future of the Post-*Batson* Peremptory Challenge: Voir Dire by Questionnaire and the "Blind" Peremptory Challenge, 29 U. Mich. J.L. Reform 981, 1006, nn. 126-127, 1035 (1996) (reporting attorneys' views on the difficulty of proving *Batson* claims).

II

Practical problems of proof to the side, peremptory challenges seem increasingly anomalous in our judicial system. On the one hand, the Court has widened and deepened *Batson*'s basic constitutional rule [by applying it to criminal defendants, private litigants, cases in which defendants and excluded jurors are of different races, and peremptory challenges based on gender].

On the other hand, the use of race- and gender-based stereotypes in the jury-selection process seems better organized and more systematized than ever before. See, e.g., Post, A Loaded Box of Stereotypes: Despite "Batson," Race, Gender Play Big Roles in Jury Selection., Nat'l L.J., Apr. 25, 2005, pp. 1, 18 (discussing common reliance on race and gender in jury selection). For example, one jury-selection guide counsels attorneys to perform a "demographic analysis" that assigns numerical points to characteristics such as age, occupation, and marital status — in addition to race as well as gender. See V. Starr & A. McCormick, Jury Selection 193-200 (3d ed. 2001). Thus, in a hypothetical dispute between a white landlord and an African-American tenant, the authors suggest awarding two points to an African-American venire member while subtracting one point from her white counterpart. Id., at 197-199.

For example, a bar journal article counsels lawyers to "rate" potential jurors "demographically (age, gender, marital status, etc.) and mark who would be under stereotypical circumstances [their] natural *enemies* and *allies*." Drake, The Art of Litigating: Deselecting Jurors Like the Pros, 34 Md. Bar J. 18, 22 (Mar.-Apr. 2001) (emphasis in original).

For example, materials from a legal convention, while noting that "nationality" is less important than "once was thought," and emphasizing that "the answers a prospective juror gives to questions are much more valuable," still point out that "stereotypically" those of "Italian, French, and Spanish" origin "are thought to be pro-plaintiff as well as other minorities, such as Mexican and Jewish[;] persons of German, Scandinavian, Swedish, Finnish, Dutch, Nordic, British, Scottish, Oriental, and Russian origin are thought to be better for the defense"; African-Americans "have always been considered good for the plaintiff," and "more politically conservative minorities will be more likely to lean toward defendants." Blue, Mirroring, Proxemics, Nonverbal Communication and Other Psychological Tools, Advocacy Track — Psychology of Trial, Association of Trial Lawyers of America Annual Convention Reference Materials, 1 Ann. 2001 ATLA-CLE 153, available at WESTLAW, ATLACLE database (June 8, 2005). . . .

These examples reflect a professional effort to fulfill the lawyer's obligation to help his or her client. Cf. *J. E. B.*, supra, at 148-149 (O'Connor, J., concurring) (observing that jurors' race and gender may inform their perspective). Nevertheless, the outcome in terms of jury selection is the same as it would be were the motive less benign. And as long as that is so, the law's antidiscrimination command and a peremptory jury-selection system that permits or encourages the use of stereotypes work at cross-purposes.

Finally, a jury system without peremptories is no longer unthinkable. Members of the legal profession have begun serious consideration of that possibility. See, e.g., Allen v. Florida, 596 So. 2d 1083, 1088-1089 (Fla. App. 1992) (Hubbart, J., concurring). . . . And England, a common-law jurisdiction that has eliminated peremptory challenges, continues to administer fair trials based largely on random jury selection. See Criminal Justice Act, 1988, ch. 33, §118(1), 22 Halsbury's Statutes 357 (4th ed. 2003 reissue) (U.K.); see also 2 Jury Service in Victoria, Final Report, ch. 5, p. 165 (Dec. 1997) (1993 study of English barristers showed majority support for system without peremptory challenges).

III

I recognize that peremptory challenges have a long historical pedigree. They may help to reassure a party of the fairness of the jury. But long ago, Blackstone recognized the peremptory challenge as an "arbitrary and capricious species of [a] challenge." 4 W. Blackstone, Commentaries on the Laws of England 346 (1769). . . .

. . . In light of the considerations I have mentioned, I believe it necessary to reconsider *Batson*'s test and the peremptory challenge system as a whole. With that qualification, I join the Court's opinion.

JUSTICE THOMAS, with whom CHIEF JUSTICE REHNQUIST and JUSTICE SCALIA join, dissenting.

. . . Miller-El's cumulative evidence does not come remotely close to clearly and convincingly establishing that the state court's factual finding was unreasonable. [This case involves] four types of evidence: (1) the alleged disparate treatment and (2) disparate questioning of black and white veniremen; (3) the prosecution's jury shuffles; and (4) historical discrimination by the D.A.'s Office in the selection of juries. Although each type of evidence "is open to judgment calls," supra, the majority finds that a succession of unpersuasive arguments amounts to a compelling case.

In the end, the majority's opinion is its own best refutation: It strains to demonstrate what should instead be patently obvious.

The majority devotes the bulk of its opinion to a side-by-side comparison of white panelists who were allowed to serve and two black panelists who were struck, Billy Jean Fields and Joe Warren. Ante, at 7-19. The majority argues that the prosecution's reasons for striking Fields and Warren apply equally to whites who were permitted to serve, and thus those reasons must have been pretextual. The voir dire transcript reveals that the majority is mistaken.

It is worth noting at the outset, however, that Miller-El's and the Court's claims have always been a moving target. Of the 20 black veniremen at Miller-El's trial, 9 were struck for cause or by the parties' agreement, and 1 served on the jury. Miller-El claimed at the *Batson* hearing that all 10 remaining black veniremen were dismissed on account of race. That number dropped to 7 on appeal, and then again to 6 during his federal habeas proceedings. . . .

The majority now focuses exclusively on Fields and Warren. But Warren was obviously equivocal about the death penalty. In the end, the majority's case reduces to a single venireman, Fields, and its reading of a 20-year-old voir dire transcript that is ambiguous at best. This is the antithesis of clear and convincing evidence.

From the outset of questioning, Warren did not specify when he would vote to impose the death penalty. When asked by prosecutor Paul Macaluso about his ability to impose the death penalty, Warren stated, "There are some cases where I would agree, you know, and there are others that I don't." 3 Record 1526. Macaluso then explained at length the types of crimes that qualified as capital murder under Texas law, and asked whether Warren would be able to impose the death penalty for those types of heinous crimes. Id., at 1527-1530. Warren continued to hedge: "I would say it depends on the case and the circumstances involved at the time." Id., at 1530. He offered no sense of the circumstances that would lead him to conclude that the death penalty was an appropriate punishment.

Macaluso then changed tack and asked whether Warren believed that the death penalty accomplished any social purpose. Id., at 1531-1532. Once again, Warren proved impossible to pin down: "Yes and no. Sometimes I think it does and sometimes I think it don't. Sometimes you have mixed feelings about things like that." Id., at 1532. Macaluso then focused on what the death penalty accomplished in those cases where Warren believed it useful. Ibid. Even then, Warren expressed no firm view:

"I don't know. It's really hard to say because I know sometimes you feel that it might help to deter crime and then you feel that the person is not really suffering. You're taking the suffering away from him. So it's like I said, sometimes you have mixed feelings about whether or not this is punishment or, you know, you're relieving personal punishment." Ibid.

While Warren's ambivalence was driven by his uncertainty that the death penalty was severe enough, that is beside the point. Throughout the examination, Warren gave no indication whether or when he would prefer the death penalty to other forms of punishment, specifically life imprisonment. 3 Record 1532-1533. To prosecutors seeking the death penalty, the reason for Warren's ambivalence was irrelevant. . . .

According to the majority, Macaluso testified that he struck Warren for his statement that the death penalty was "an easy way out," ante, at 14 (quoting App. 909), and not for his ambivalence about the death penalty, ante, at 17. This grossly mischaracterizes the record. Macaluso specifically testified at the *Batson* hearing that he was troubled by the *"inconsistency"* of Warren's responses. App. 909 (emphasis added). Macaluso was speaking of Warren's ambivalence about the death penalty, a reason wholly unrelated to race. This was Macaluso's "stated reason," and Macaluso ought to "stand or fall on the plausibility" of this reason — not one concocted by the majority. Ante, at 18.

The majority points to four other panel members — Kevin Duke, Troy Woods, Sandra Jenkins, and Leta Girard — who supposedly expressed views much like Warren's, but who were not struck by the State. According to the majority, this is evidence of pretext. But the majority's premise is faulty. None of these veniremen was as difficult to pin down on the death penalty as Warren. For instance, Duke supported the death penalty. App. 373 ("I've always believed in having the death penalty. I think it serves a purpose"); ibid. ("I mean, it's a sad thing to see, to have to kill someone, but they shouldn't have done the things that they did. Sometimes they deserve to be killed"); id., at 394 ("If I feel that I can answer all three of these [special-issue] questions yes and I feel that he's done a crime worthy of the death penalty, yes, I will give the death penalty"). By contrast, Warren never expressed a firm view one way or the other. . . .

Nevertheless, even assuming that any of these veniremen expressed views similar to Warren's, Duke, Woods, and Girard were questioned much later in the jury selection process, when the State had fewer peremptories to spare. Only Sandra Jenkins was questioned early in the voir dire process, and thus only Jenkins was even arguably similarly situated to Warren. However, Jenkins and Warren were different in important respects. Jenkins expressed no doubt whatsoever about the death penalty. She testified that she had researched the death penalty in high school, and she said in response to questioning by both parties that she strongly believed in the death penalty's value as a deterrent to crime. 3 Record 1074-1075, 1103-1104. This alone explains why the State accepted Jenkins as a juror, while Miller-El struck her. In addition, Jenkins did not have a relative who had been convicted of a crime, but Warren did. At the *Batson* hearing, Macaluso testified that he struck Warren both for Warren's inconsistent responses regarding the death penalty and for his brother's conviction.

The majority thinks it can prove pretext by pointing to white veniremen who match only one of the State's proffered reasons for striking Warren. This defies logic. "'Similarly situated' does not mean matching any one of several reasons the prosecution gave for striking a potential juror — it means matching *all* of them." *Miller-El I*, 537 U.S., at 362-363 (Thomas, J., dissenting). Given limited peremptories, prosecutors often must focus on the potential jurors most likely to disfavor their case. By ignoring the totality of reasons that a prosecutor strikes any particular venireman, it is the majority that treats potential jurors as "products of a set of cookie cutters" — as if potential jurors who share only some among many traits must be treated the same to avoid a *Batson* violation. Of course jurors must not be "identical in all respects" to gauge pretext, but to isolate race as a variable, the jurors must be comparable in all respects that the prosecutor proffers as important. This does not mean "that a defendant cannot win a *Batson* claim unless there is an exactly identical white juror." It means that a defendant cannot support a *Batson* claim by comparing veniremen of different races unless the veniremen are truly similar. . . .

The second black venireman on whom the majority relies is Billy Jean Fields. Fields expressed support for the death penalty, App. 174-175, but Fields also expressed views that called into question his ability to impose the death penalty. Fields was a deeply religious man, id., at 173-174, 192-194, and prosecutors feared that his religious convictions might make him reluctant to impose the death penalty. Those fears were confirmed by Fields' view that all people could be rehabilitated if introduced to God, a fear that had special force considering the special-issue questions necessary to impose the death penalty in Texas. One of those questions asked whether there was a probability that the defendant would engage in future violence that threatened society. When they reached this question, Macaluso and Fields had the following exchange:

[MACALUSO:]   What does that word probability mean to you in that connotation?
[FIELDS:]   Well, it means is there a possibility that [a defendant] will continue to lead this type of life, will he be rehabilitated or does he intend to make this a life-long ambition.
[MACALUSO:]   Let me ask you, Mr. Fields, do you feel as though some people simply cannot be rehabilitated?
[FIELDS:]   No.
[MACALUSO:]   You think everyone can be rehabilitated?
[FIELDS:]   Yes.

Id., at 183-184.

Thus, Fields indicated that the possibility of rehabilitation was ever-present and relevant to whether a defendant might commit future acts of violence. In light of that view, it is understandable that prosecutors doubted whether he could vote to impose the death penalty.

Fields did testify that he could impose the death penalty, even on a defendant who could be rehabilitated. Id., at 185. For the majority, this shows that the State's reason was pretextual. But of course Fields said that he could fairly consider the death penalty — if he had answered otherwise, he would have been challengeable *for cause*. The point is that Fields' earlier answers cast significant doubt on whether he could impose the death penalty. The very purpose of peremptory strikes is to allow parties to remove potential jurors whom they suspect, but cannot prove, may exhibit a particular bias. See *Swain*, 380 U.S., at 220, 202; J. E. B. v. Alabama ex rel. T. B., 511 U.S. 127, 148 (1994) (O'Connor, J., concurring). Based on Fields' voir dire testimony, it was perfectly reasonable for prosecutors to suspect that Fields might be swayed by a penitent defendant's testimony. The prosecutors may have been worried for nothing about Fields' religious sentiments, but that does not mean they were instead worried about Fields' race. . . .

Miller-El's claims of disparate questioning [involving use of the so-called "graphic script"] also do not fit the facts. . . . The State questioned panelists differently when their questionnaire responses indicated ambivalence about the death penalty. Any racial disparity in questioning resulted from the reality that more non-black veniremen favored the death penalty and were willing to impose it.

Miller-El also alleges that the State employed two different scripts on the basis of race when asking questions about imposition of the minimum sentence. This disparate-questioning argument is even more flawed than the last one. The evidence confirms that, as the State argues, prosecutors used different questioning on minimum sentences to create cause to strike veniremen who were ambivalent about or opposed to the death penalty. . . .

Miller-El's argument that prosecutors shuffled the jury to remove blacks is pure speculation. At the *Batson* hearing, Miller-El did not raise, nor was there any discussion of, the topic of jury shuffling as a racial tactic. The record shows only that the State shuffled the jury during the first three weeks of jury selection, while Miller-El shuffled the jury during each of the five weeks. This evidence no more proves that prosecutors sought to eliminate blacks from the jury, than it proves that Miller-El sought to eliminate whites even more often. *Miller-El I*, 537 U.S., at 360 (Thomas, J., dissenting).

Miller-El notes that the State twice shuffled the jury (in the second and third weeks) when a number of blacks were seated at the front of the panel. According to the majority, this gives rise to an "inference" that prosecutors were discriminating. But Miller-El should not be asking this Court to draw "inferences"; he should be asking it to examine clear and convincing proof. And the inference is not even a strong one. We do not know if the nonblacks near the front shared characteristics with the blacks near the front, providing race-neutral reasons for the shuffles. We also do not know the racial composition of the panel during the first week when the State shuffled, or during the fourth and fifth weeks when it did not.

More important, any number of characteristics other than race could have been apparent to prosecutors from a visual inspection of the jury panel. Granted, we do not know whether prosecutors relied on racially neutral reasons, but that is because Miller-El never asked at the *Batson* hearing. It is Miller-El's burden to prove racial discrimination, and the jury-shuffle evidence itself does not provide such proof.

The majority's speculation would not be complete, however, without its discussion (block-quoted from *Miller-El I*) of the history of discrimination in the D.A.'s Office. This is nothing more than guilt by association that is unsupported by the record. Some of the witnesses at the *Swain* hearing did testify that individual prosecutors had discriminated. However, no one testified that the prosecutors in Miller-El's trial — Norman Kinne, Paul Macaluso, and Jim Nelson — had ever been among those to engage in racially discriminatory jury selection.

The majority then tars prosecutors with a manual entitled Jury Selection in a Criminal Case (hereinafter Manual or Sparling Manual), authored by John Sparling, a former Dallas County prosecutor. There is no evidence, however, that Kinne, Macaluso, or Nelson had ever read the Manual — which was written in 1968, almost two decades before Miller-El's trial. The reason there is no evidence on the question is that Miller-El never asked. During the entire *Batson* hearing, there is no mention of the Sparling Manual. Miller-El never questioned Macaluso about it, and he never questioned Kinne or Nelson at all. The majority simply assumes that all Dallas County prosecutors were racist and remained that way through the mid-1980's.

Nor does the majority rely on the Manual for anything more than show. The Manual contains a single, admittedly stereotypical line on race: "Minority races almost always empathize with the Defendant." App. 102. Yet the Manual also tells prosecutors not to select "anyone who had a close friend or relative that was prosecuted by the State." Id., at 112. That was true of both Warren and Fields, and yet the majority cavalierly dismisses as "makeweight" the State's justification that Warren and Fields were struck because they were related to individuals convicted of crimes. . . .

Finally, the majority notes that prosecutors "marked the race of each prospective juror on their juror cards." Ante, at 31 (quoting *Miller-El I*, supra, at 347). This suffers from the same problems as Miller-El's other evidence. Prosecutors did mark the juror cards with the jurors' race, sex, and juror number. We have no idea — and even the majority cannot bring itself to speculate — whether this was done merely for identification purposes or for some more nefarious reason. The reason we have no idea is that the juror cards were never introduced before the state courts, and thus prosecutors were never questioned about their use of them.

* * *

. . . Miller-El has not established, much less established by clear and convincing evidence, that prosecutors racially discriminated in the selection of his jury — and he certainly has not done so on the basis of the evidence presented to the Texas courts. On the basis of facts and law, rather than sentiments, Miller-El does not merit the writ. I respectfully dissent.

———————————————

What message can be drawn from the *Miller-El* saga? Is the Supreme Court trying to signal to the lower courts that *Batson* review, especially at stages two and three, should be conducted more aggressively than perhaps *Hernandez* and *Purkett* suggested? The outcome of *Miller-El* would seem to so indicate.

But what, exactly, is the nature of *Batson* review, as contemplated by the Court? One of the most striking aspects of *Miller-El* is the extent to which both the majority and the dissent become caught up in lengthy and complicated arguments over the myriad particular facts of the case. (Indeed, in its original form, *Miller-El* is far more lengthy and complicated than the version that appears above; radical editing was necessary in order to fit the case into the casebook.) It is far from clear that, on balance, the majority has the better of the factual argument.

Why spend so much time and energy arguing about the meaning of specific words used by each prospective juror during voir dire? Or about subtle comparisons of one juror's views with another's? Or about the nuances of the prosecutor's explanations for challenged peremptory strikes? Can these fact-based arguments ever really settle the question whether the prosecutor's strikes were motivated by discrimination?

From an epistemological point of view, the problem is that, in the absence of such things as direct admission of racist motivation, such particular facts acquire meaning only when viewed in the context of patterns of behavior. Such patterns emerge only from analyzing behavior in the aggregate. To put it bluntly, without the evidence provided by the raw numbers in *Miller-El* (11 qualified black venire members, 10 of whom were eliminated by prosecution peremptory challenges) — together with the racially disparate use of different questioning "scripts," *and* the apparently long-standing prosecutorial abuse of the bizarre Texas "jury-shuffling" procedure, *and* the long history of racial discrimination by Dallas County prosecutors — would the peremptory strikes of Fields and Warren have been enough to prove discrimination in the case? The answer is almost certainly no, especially in light of the fact that, with even slightly more plausible race-neutral explanations, the prosecutors might well have prevailed *despite* such evidence.

Consider the data from the studies Justice Breyer cites to in his concurrence, supra. The single most striking thing is that the parties are discriminating in mirror image ways. In one study, in 317 capital trials in Philadelphia between 1981 and 1997, prosecutors struck 51 percent of black jurors and 26 percent of nonblack jurors; defense counsel struck 26 percent of black jurors and 54 percent of nonblack jurors; in another, 71 percent of excused black jurors were removed by the prosecution; 81 percent of excused white jurors were removed by the defense; and in yet another, in a D.C. murder case spanning four trials, prosecutors excused 41 blacks or other minorities and 6 whites; defense counsel struck 29 whites and 13 black venire members. If entering into voir dire both black and whites have about an equal chance of being stricken "because of their color," then how is a member of either race being discriminated against? What about the correlates of race such as education, social standing, income, and the like? How can one sort these out in the causal chain from a racial animus? One answer may be that, in cases such as *Miller-El*, those other variables seemed to be applied only with respect to one race but not other, but how can one even know that? Any particular variable will be in almost infinitely complex relationships with a large number of other variables, and their interaction may be the cause of any particular outcome.

This leads us (and the Court) back to the basic issue: How does one prove discrimination in a particular case? *Batson* was designed to free defendants (and, after *McCollum*, prosecutors as well) from the necessity of conducting sophisticated statistical studies to identify patterns of discriminatory behavior. The *Batson* Court apparently believed that discrimination could be proved simply by examining the facts of a particular case. *Miller-El* (together with its predecessors, *Hernandez* and *Purkett*) demonstrates, however, that such fact-based inquiry is destined to be meaningless without context — the very kind of context provided by statistical studies. Absent the statistical studies, the Court is forced to rely on "statistics-lite" (some raw numbers, a little history) as a weak substitute.

Two recent post-*Miller-El* decisions reveal the kind of judicial confusion that can result whenever such "statistics-lite" are absent, or when context is similarly lacking. In Rice v. Collins, 546 U.S. 333 (2006), a unanimous Court overturned the Ninth Circuit's decision to find a *Batson* violation on habeas review. The Ninth Circuit's ruling was based on its rejection of the race-neutral reasons offered by the prosecutor for striking a particular prospective juror. Those reasons (which had been accepted by all previous state and federal courts to review the case) included that the prospective juror was young, single, lacked ties to the community, and had "rolled her eyes" in response to a voir dire question. The Court explained: "The panel majority's attempt to use a set of debatable inferences to set aside the conclusion reached by the state court does not satisfy [the] requirements for granting a writ of habeas corpus." Id., at 342. In a separate concurrence, Justice Breyer, joined by Justice Souter, reiterated his view (first expressed in *Miller-El II*) that *Batson* itself might need to be revisited, and peremptory challenges might need to be abolished, because of the "unresolvable tension between, on the one hand, what Blackstone called an inherently 'arbitrary and capricious' peremptory challenge system, . . . and, on the other hand, the Constitution's nondiscrimination command." Id., at 344 (Breyer, J., concurring).

The second case was Snyder v. Louisiana, 128 S. Ct. 1203 (2008). There, the defendant complained about the peremptory strike of two black prospective jurors, Mr. Brooks and Ms. Scott. The Court noted that *Miller-El* "made it clear that in considering a *Batson* objection, or in reviewing a ruling claimed to be *Batson* error, all of the circumstances that bear upon the issue of racial animosity must be consulted. . . . Here, as just one example, if there were persisting doubts as to the outcome, a court would be required to consider the strike of Ms. Scott for the bearing it might have upon the strike of Mr. Brooks." But the Court ultimately ruled (by 7-2, with Justices Scalia and Thomas dissenting) that the strike of Mr. Brooks failed on its own, because it was based on an asserted rationale (the prosecutor's claim that Mr. Brooks was a student-teacher who might be "nervous" about the impact of a lengthy jury trial on his teaching job) that could equally have applied to numerous white prospective jurors who were not struck. The Court acknowledged that the trial judge, who had rejected the *Batson* challenge, usually would be in the best position to evaluate the credibility of the rationale proffered by the prosecutor, but explained that in the instant case, the trial judge made no findings on the record about Mr. Brooks's demeanor. Thus, the Court reversed Snyder's conviction.

In the end, can the *Batson/Miller-El* approach — well-intentioned though it may be — ever produce a truly satisfying conclusion about the existence (or nonexistence) of discrimination in a particular case?

C. The Defendant's Rights to Be Present, to Testify, to Obtain Evidence, to Confront His Accusers, and to Present a Defense at Trial

Although neither the Constitution nor any provision of the Bill of Rights says so explicitly, the Supreme Court has rendered a series of decisions essentially generalizing various specific rights into a right to present a defense. For example, in Illinois v. Allen, 397 U.S. 337 (1970), the Court concluded that a defendant has the right to be present during the trial. In *Allen*, the defendant argued with the trial judge "in a most abusive and disrespectful manner," used vile and abusive language, and engaged in disruptive behavior (including throwing papers on the floor). After being warned by the judge that another outburst would lead to his removal from the courtroom, Allen continued to behave badly. The judge ordered him removed, and the trial proceeded without him up to the conclusion of the prosecution's case. At that point, Allen agreed to settle down, and he was allowed to stay in the courtroom for the remainder of the trial. The Court held that "trial judges confronted with disruptive, contumacious, stubbornly defiant defendants must be given sufficient discretion to meet the circumstances of each case." Id., at 343. The Court cited with approval three possible remedies: (1) binding and gagging the unruly defendant, (2) holding him in contempt, and (3) removing him from the courtroom until he agrees to behave properly. The Court affirmed Allen's conviction, finding that the trial judge did not abuse his discretion. See also Holbrook v. Flynn, 475 U.S. 560 (1986), holding that due process was not violated when the defendant was surrounded for security purposes, in the courtroom, by numerous uniformed state troopers and other police officers. The *Flynn* Court distinguished strong police presence, which "need not be interpreted [by jurors] as a sign that [the defendant] is particularly dangerous or culpable," id., at 569, from the constitutionally disapproved practice of forcing a defendant to wear prison clothes before the jury, which serves as a "constant reminder of the accused's condition" and thus "may affect a juror's judgment," id., at 568, citing Estelle v. Williams, 425 U.S. 501 (1976).

The Court revisited the right to be present in Kentucky v. Stincer, 482 U.S. 730 (1987). There the defendant was excluded from a witness-competency hearing, held in the trial judge's chambers, for two young girls who were scheduled to testify against him on sodomy charges. The Court held that the right to be present, which is protected by the Due Process Clause, is limited to "any stage of the criminal proceeding that is critical to its outcome if [the defendant's] presence would contribute to the fairness of the procedure." Id., at 745. Because the girls would not give any substantive testimony at the hearing, but only would answer questions designed to determine their ability to testify factually and truthfully, and because the defendant "has given no indication that his presence . . . would have been useful in ensuring a more reliable determination as to whether the witnesses were competent to testify," the Court rejected the defendant's claim. Id., at 745-747. See also Carey v. Musladin, 549 U.S. 70 (2006), where the Court found no error warranting federal habeas corpus relief when a state court allowed members of a murder victim's family to wear buttons, while seated in the front row of the courtroom during the defendant's murder trial, displaying the victim's image.

Again, although nothing says so explicitly, the Court has concluded that a defendant has the right to testify in one's own behalf. Rock v. Arkansas, 483 U.S. 44 (1987), reached this conclusion through the combined effects of Due Process, the Compulsory Process Clause, and the Fifth Amendment right to be free from self-incrimination implying an opportunity to testify. On the related right to obtain evidence, consider Arizona v. Youngblood, 488 U.S. 51 (1988), in which the defendant was charged with molesting and sodomizing a ten-year-old boy. After the assault, the victim had been taken to a hospital where semen samples were collected from his rectum and refrigerated for later analysis. The victim's clothing was also collected, but was not stored in a refrigerator or freezer; the police did not notice semen stains on the clothing until more than a year after the crime. At trial, the defendant claimed mistaken identity, but the semen samples from the victim's rectum were too small to permit meaningful blood testing, and the stains on the clothing could not be tested because the clothing had not been properly preserved. The defendant was convicted, but the Arizona Court of Appeals reversed on due process grounds. The Supreme Court reinstated the conviction. According to the Court:

> The Due Process Clause of the Fourteenth Amendment, as interpreted in Brady [v. Maryland, 373 U.S. 83 (1963)], makes the good or bad faith of the State irrelevant when the State fails to disclose to the defendant material exculpatory evidence. But we think the Due Process Clause requires a different result when we deal with the failure of the State to preserve evidentiary material of which no more can be said than that it could have been subjected to tests, the results of which might have exonerated the defendant. . . . We think that requiring a defendant to show bad faith on the part of the police both limits the extent of the police's obligation to preserve evidence to reasonable bounds and confines it to the class of cases where the interests of justice most clearly require it, i.e., those cases in which the police themselves by their conduct indicate that the evidence could form a basis for exonerating the defendant. We therefore hold that unless a criminal defendant can show bad faith on the part of the police, failure to preserve potentially useful evidence does not constitute a denial of due process.

Id., at 57-58; see also California v. Trombetta, 467 U.S. 479 (1984) (refusing to suppress results of blood-alcohol tests because State had failed to preserve breath samples used in tests).

The Youngblood story did not end with the Supreme Court's decision. On August 8, 2000, all charges against Youngblood were dismissed when DNA testing — which could be conducted even on the tiny samples of semen that had been preserved by the police — proved conclusively that he was not the person who had molested and sodomized the victim. See Thomas Stauffer & Jim Erickson, DNA Test Clears Tucsonan Convicted in Molestation, Arizona Daily Star, Aug. 9, 2000, §1, at 1.

Criminal cases are not like civil cases in two critical respects, which can create difficulties. First, the defendant cannot be called to the stand by the government (in civil cases, anyone can call anyone), see Griffin v. California, 380 U.S. 609 (1965), discussed below; and second, as discussed in Chapter 12, discovery rights are quite limited in criminal cases. This creates the possibility, or at least fear, that defendants will try to manipulate matters either by not disclosing information, surprising the government at trial, or tailoring their testimony to that of the other witnesses in the case. This, in turn, has led to a number of efforts to limit their ability to do so. Based on concern about perjured testimony, Georgia law forbad a defendant's lawyer from guiding the defendant on direct examination, which the Court struck down as violating the right to counsel. Ferguson v. Georgia, 365 U.S. 570 (1961). Tennessee required that a defendant testify before any other defense witnesses are called, out of a concern that the defendant would tailor the testimony in light of the testimony of the other witness. Finding that such a requirement violated both the defendant's right to remain silent (he had to choose whether to testify at an inopportune time) and the right to counsel (the decision had to be made without counsel having full knowledge of the evidence), the Court struck down the statute in Brooks v. Tennessee, 406 U.S. 605 (1972).

Other efforts to restrict defense proffers have met similar fates. In Holmes v. South Carolina, 547 U.S. 319 (2006), the defendant was precluded from introducing evidence that another man possibly had committed the crime with which he was charged. The exclusion was based on an odd South Carolina rule stating that evidence of third-party guilt is admissible only if it raises a "reasonable inference" of the defendant's innocence. The South Carolina Supreme Court held that such an inference could not be raised in the instant case because the prosecution's evidence of Holmes's guilt was strong; the court therefore did not even consider the probative value of Holmes's proffered third-party-guilt evidence in making its admissibility decision. The U.S. Supreme Court unanimously reversed. In an opinion by Justice Alito, the Court held that the South Carolina rule was "arbitrary" and "does not rationally serve the end" of excluding non-probative evidence. Therefore, the rule denied Holmes his right to "a meaningful opportunity to present a complete defense." Id., at 331. In Rock v. Illinois, mentioned above, a per se exclusion of the defendant's hypnotically refreshed testimony was held to violate the due process rights to be heard and to offer testimony, Sixth Amendment right to compulsory process, and Fifth Amendment Self-Incrimination Clause, under which the defendant's "opportunity to testify is a necessary corollary to the . . . guarantee against compelled testimony."

One should not conclude that the state is powerless to enforce reasonable rules governing evidence, however. In Taylor v. Illinois, 484 U.S. 400 (1988), the Court upheld the refusal to allow a witness to testify as a sanction for the defendant having failed to identify the witness in a pretrial discovery request. In United States v. Nobles, 422 U.S. 225 (1975), the exclusion of a defense expert was upheld where the defense refused to disclose his report, and in Michigan v. Lucas, 500 U.S. 145 (1991), the Court concluded that the Constitution did not necessarily forbid exclusion as a sanction for failure to put the government on notice of the defendant's intent to introduce past sexual behavior of a rape complainant, as required by state law.

As the holdings discussed above suggest, there is almost an infinite variety of ways in which questions of evidentiary proffers can raise constitutional questions. The best generalization is that the probability of upholding a state's exclusion of evidence as a sanction for a defendant's failure to abide by procedural requirements increases as the evidence gets further away from the defendant and as the defendant's (or lawyer's) behavior is increasingly obstreperous. There is one other evidentiary matter that has systematically caused difficulties, and that is whether juries should be precluded from drawing certain inferences and the associated question whether the government should be precluded from arguing those inferences in closing. In *Griffin*, supra, the prosecutor, at closing, made several disparaging comments to the jury about the fact that the defendant had failed to take the stand to explain his presence in the alley where the murder victim's body was found. The trial judge's instructions lent support to the prosecutor's comments, stating that "if [the defendant] does not testify . . . the jury may take that failure into consideration as tending to indicate . . . that among the inferences that may be reasonably drawn therefrom those unfavorable to the defendant are the more probable." Id., at 610. The Court held that any such comment on the defendant's silence, by either the prosecutor or the judge, violates the Self-Incrimination Clause of the Fifth Amendment because "[i]t is a penalty imposed by courts for exercising a constitutional privilege." Id., at 614. The Court acknowledged that juries might draw negative inferences from a defendant's silence at trial, even without improper comments, but nevertheless found it unacceptable for the trial judge to "solemnize[] the silence of the accused into evidence against him." Id. See also Carter v. Kentucky, 450 U.S. 288 (1981), holding that the trial judge must, upon the defendant's request, instruct the jury not to draw any adverse inferences from the defendant's silence.

Following *Griffin*, the Court used similar reasoning to invalidate other practices that imposed burdens on the exercise of defendants' constitutional rights. For example, in United States v. Jackson, 390 U.S. 570 (1968), the Federal Kidnapping Act provided for the possibility of a death sentence for defendants who were convicted at a jury trial, but only a maximum sentence of life imprisonment for defendants who pleaded guilty or were convicted in a bench trial. The Court, citing *Griffin*, found that the statute "needlessly encouraged" waivers of the constitutional rights to jury trial and to remain silent, and therefore invalidated the death-penalty provision contained in the statute. In Doyle v. Ohio, 426 U.S. 610 (1976), the Court relied on *Griffin* to hold that a defendant's postarrest silence, after receiving *Miranda* warnings, cannot be used against the defendant in the prosecution's case-in-chief at trial. See also Brooks v. Tennessee, 406 U.S. 605 (1972) (cited and discussed in *Agard*, supra).

The *Griffin* doctrine has come under significant pressure. In Mitchell v. United States, 526 U.S. 314 (1999), the defendant pleaded guilty to several drug crimes, but reserved the right to contest the amount of the drugs attributable to her. At the sentencing hearing, the trial judge found, based on the testimony of several witnesses, that the defendant had sold enough cocaine to qualify for a ten-year mandatory minimum sentence. The judge told the defendant, "I held it against you that you didn't come forward today and tell me that you really only did this a couple of times. . . . I'm taking the position that you should come forward and explain your side of this issue." Id., at 319. The Court held that such use of the defendant's silence, at sentencing, violates the Fifth Amendment under *Griffin*. But Justice

Scalia, in a strongly worded dissent joined by three other justices, argued that *Griffin* was unsupportable by logic or history:

> The illogic of the *Griffin* line is plain, for it runs exactly counter to normal evidentiary inferences: If I ask my son whether he saw a movie I had forbidden him to watch, and he remains silent, the import of his silence is clear. . . . And as for history, *Griffin's* pedigree is equally dubious. . . . [T]he text and history of the Fifth Amendment give no indication that there is a federal *constitutional* prohibition on the use of the defendant's silence as demeanor evidence. . . . To my mind, *Griffin* was a wrong turn — which is not cause enough to overrule it, but is cause enough to resist its extension.

Id., at 332, 335-336 (Scalia, J., dissenting).

The *Griffin* rule was reconsidered in Portuondo v. Agard, 529 U.S. 61 (2000), where the court considered "whether it was constitutional for a prosecutor, in her summation, to call the jury's attention to the fact that the defendant had the opportunity to hear all other witnesses testify and to tailor his testimony accordingly." The Court concluded this did not violate the Constitution:

> Lacking any historical support for the constitutional rights that he asserts, respondent must rely entirely upon our opinion in *Griffin*. That case is a poor analogue, however, for several reasons. What we prohibited the prosecutor from urging the jury to do in *Griffin* was something *the jury is not permitted to do*. The defendant's right to hold the prosecution to proving its case without his assistance is not to be impaired by the jury's counting the defendant's silence at trial against him — and upon request the court must instruct the jury to that effect. See Carter v. Kentucky, 450 U.S. 288 (1981). It is reasonable enough to expect a jury to comply with that instruction since, as we observed in *Griffin*, the inference of guilt from silence is not always "natural or irresistible." 380 U.S., at 615. A defendant might refuse to testify simply out of fear that he will be made to look bad by clever counsel, or fear "that his prior convictions will prejudice the jury." Ibid. . . . By contrast, it *is* natural and irresistible for a jury, in evaluating the relative credibility of a defendant who testifies last, to have in mind and weigh in the balance the fact that he heard the testimony of all those who preceded him. It is one thing (as *Griffin* requires) for the jury to evaluate all the *other* evidence in the case without giving any effect to the defendant's refusal to testify; it is something else (and quite impossible) for the jury to evaluate the credibility of the defendant's testimony while blotting out from its mind the fact that before giving the testimony the defendant had been sitting there listening to the other witnesses. Thus, the principle respondent asks us to adopt here differs from what we adopted in *Griffin* in one or the other of the following respects: It either prohibits inviting the jury to do what the jury is perfectly entitled to do; or it requires the jury to do what is practically impossible.
>
> Second, *Griffin* prohibited comments that suggest a defendant's silence is "evidence of *guilt*." 380 U.S., at 615 (emphasis added). . . . The prosecutor's comments in this case, by contrast, concerned respondent's *credibility as a witness*, and were therefore in accord with our longstanding rule that when a defendant takes the stand, "his credibility may be impeached and his testimony assailed like that of any other witness." . . .
>
> Respondent points to our opinion in Geders v. United States, 425 U.S. 80, 87-91 (1976), which held that the defendant must be treated differently from other witnesses insofar as sequestration orders are concerned, since sequestration for an extended period of time denies the Sixth Amendment right to counsel. With respect to issues of

credibility, however, no such special treatment has been accorded. Jenkins v. Anderson, 447 U.S. 231 (1980), illustrates the point. There the prosecutor in a first-degree murder trial, during cross-examination and again in closing argument, attempted to impeach the defendant's claim of self-defense by suggesting that he would not have waited two weeks to report the killing if that was what had occurred. In an argument strikingly similar to the one presented here, the defendant in *Jenkins* claimed that commenting on his prearrest silence violated his Fifth Amendment privilege against self-incrimination because "a person facing arrest will not remain silent if his failure to speak later can be used to impeach him." Id., at 236. The Court noted that it was not clear whether the Fifth Amendment protects prearrest silence, id., at 236, n. 2, but held that, *assuming it does*, the prosecutor's comments were constitutionally permissible. "[T]he Constitution does not forbid 'every government-imposed choice in the criminal process that has the effect of discouraging the exercise of constitutional rights.'" Id., at 236. . . . Once a defendant takes the stand, he is "subject to cross-examination impeaching his credibility just like any other witness." *Jenkins*, 447 U.S., at 235-236. . . .

Indeed, in Brooks v. Tennessee, 406 U.S. 605 (1972), the Court suggested that arguing credibility to the jury — which would include the prosecutor's comments here — is the preferred means of counteracting tailoring of the defendant's testimony. . . . The Court expressed its awareness, however, of the danger that tailoring presented. The antidote, it said, was not Tennessee's heavy-handed rule, but the more nuanced "adversary system[, which] reposes judgment of the credibility of all witnesses in the jury." Id., at 611. The adversary system surely envisions — indeed, it requires — that the prosecutor be allowed to bring to the jury's attention the danger that the Court was aware of.

Respondent and the dissent also contend that the prosecutor's comments were impermissible because they were "generic" rather than based upon any specific indication of tailoring. Such comment, the dissent claims, is unconstitutional because it "does not serve to distinguish guilty defendants from innocent ones." . . . But this Court has approved of such "generic" comment before. In Reagan [v. United States, 157 U.S. 301 (1895)], for example, the trial court instructed the jury that "[t]he deep personal interest which [the defendant] may have in the result of the suit should be considered . . . in weighing his evidence and in determining how far or to what extent, if at all, it is worthy of credit." [Id.,] at 304. The instruction did not rely on any specific evidence of actual fabrication for its application; nor did it, directly at least, delineate the guilty and the innocent. Like the comments in this case, it simply set forth a consideration the jury was to have in mind when assessing the defendant's credibility, which, *in turn*, assisted it in determining the guilt of the defendant. We deemed that instruction perfectly proper. Thus, that the comments before us here did not, of their own force, demonstrate the guilt of the defendant, or even distinguish among defendants, does not render them infirm. . . .

Justice Ginsburg, in dissent, argued that

The Court today transforms a defendant's presence at trial from a Sixth Amendment right into an automatic burden on his credibility. . . .

The burden today's decision imposes on the exercise of Sixth Amendment rights is justified, the Court maintains, because "the central function of the trial . . . is to discover the truth." . . . A trial ideally is a search for the truth, but I do not agree that the

Court's decision advances that search. The generic accusation that today's decision permits the prosecutor to make on summation does not serve to distinguish guilty defendants from innocent ones. Every criminal defendant, guilty or not, has the [Sixth Amendment] right to attend his trial. . . . Indeed, as the Court grants, . . . New York law *requires* defendants to be present when tried. It follows that every defendant who testifies is equally susceptible to a generic accusation about his opportunity for tailoring. The prosecutorial comment at issue, tied only to the defendant's presence in the courtroom and not to his actual testimony, tarnishes the innocent no less than the guilty.

NOTES AND QUESTIONS

1. Portuondo v. Agard involves several rights: the right to testify in one's own behalf (protected by the Fifth and Sixth Amendments), the right to be present (protected by the Sixth Amendment), and the right to confront one's accusers (protected by the Sixth Amendment), as well as the general right to due process of law (protected by the Fifth and Fourteenth Amendments). In the notes that follow, we will take up the subject of these various trial rights, along with others that were not at issue in *Agard*.

2. One of the most interesting, and potentially important, aspects of *Agard* is its impact on the doctrine of "unconstitutional burdens" that originated with Griffin v. California, 380 U.S. 609 (1965). *Agard*, decided just a year after *Mitchell* — reaffirms *Griffin*, although refuses to extend it to bar prosecutorial comment on the defendant's choice to testify last at trial. But does *Agard* manage to undermine *Griffin* in the course of reaffirming it?

3. Notice that there has always been a latent ambiguity in *Griffin*. Is *Griffin* based on the idea that the inference of guilt from the defendant's silence is unfair because there exist other *equally likely* reasons (i.e., other than guilt) for a defendant to remain silent at trial? Or is the inference improper *even if it accurately reflects the most likely reason* for the defendant to remain silent? Under the first interpretation, only empirically unsupportable burdens on constitutional rights would be invalid, whereas under the second, all burdens would be invalid unless strictly necessary, whether or not they are based on empirically accurate assumptions. The potential scope of the *Griffin* doctrine, of course, is much broader under the second interpretation than under the first.

Does *Agard* suggest that the Court may now be edging toward adopting the narrower, first interpretation of *Griffin*? Is that not precisely why the Court refuses to extend *Griffin* to the situation presented in *Agard* — i.e., because the inference in *Agard* is empirically supportable and therefore not "unfair"?

4. The Court in *Agard* was arguing, in part, over empirical reality — facts, as it were. This happens frequently in Supreme Court cases, and you saw it in our discussion of the right to an impartial jury. "Facts" are often slippery entities, though, and both how one draws reasonable inferences about them and what "facts" may justify some further "inference" are more complicated concepts than they appear to be at first glance. There are, in short, difficulties lurking here of which you should be aware. For example, what does it mean for an inference to be "empirically supportable"? Does it mean that, in some relevant reference class such as those who testify in their own defense, the statement is true of more than half of those in the reference class? If not, what? How does one go about making such a determination in

the absence of empirical studies? What about Justice Ginsburg's lament that the inference here "undermines all defendants equally"? Is that the proper question, or should it be whether or not the jury is likely to know what the baseline is? A jury could just as easily make a mistake by misapplying a general proposition as it could by being unaware of the proper baseline. Actually, all evidentiary proffers at trial are subject to these and analogous questions, and this note barely scratches the surface of the pertinent problems. This may lead one reasonably to wonder to what extent the Supreme Court should enter into the thicket of judging evidentiary proffers, in part, on the basis of their factual implications. Perhaps the regulation of such matters should, for the most part, be left to evidentiary rules and rulings, absent a very good reason to intervene on a constitutional basis. Perhaps the essential problem here was the constitutionalizing of what should have been a run-of-the-mill evidentiary matter. Keep this thought in mind throughout this chapter, and at various other places in the materials as well.

5. The approach taken by the Court in *Agard* leads to the following provocative question: If a prosecutor promises a defendant that prior convictions will not be introduced against him, can the prosecutor then comment on the defendant's silence at trial — because, having eliminated the most likely nonguilt reason for the defendant's silence, such adverse comment will no longer be "unfair"?

NOTES ON THE CONFRONTATION CLAUSE

There are three major lines of Supreme Court decisions dealing with the Confrontation Clause. The first involves the specific procedures that must be followed when a witness testifies at trial, in order to ensure that the defendant's right of confrontation is vindicated. The second involves the admission, at trial, of prior statements of witnesses who do not testify at trial and thus are not subject to confrontation and cross-examination. The third involves the special problems posed by the admission, at a joint trial, of prior statements by nontestifying codefendants.

1. With respect to in-court procedures, Maryland v. Craig, 497 U.S. 836 (1990), and Coy v. Iowa, 487 U.S. 1012 (1988), together stand for the proposition that "a defendant's right to confront accusatory witnesses may be satisfied absent a physical, face-to-face confrontation at trial only where denial of such confrontation is necessary to further an important public policy and only where the reliability of the testimony is otherwise assured," *Craig*, 497 U.S., at 850. Thus, in *Coy*, where a child witness testified from behind a screen and no necessity for this particular procedure was shown, the right of confrontation was violated; but in *Craig*, where a child witness testified on closed-circuit television after a showing of necessity, the right was not violated.

2. With respect to the general issue of prior statements, the Supreme Court has signaled a major change from its previous approach, as represented by cases such as White v. Illinois, 502 U.S. 346 (1992); Idaho v. Wright, 497 U.S. 805 (1990); Bourjaily v. United States, 483 U.S. 171 (1987); Lee v. Illinois, 476 U.S. 530 (1986); United States v. Inadi, 475 U.S. 387 (1986); and Ohio v. Roberts, 448 U.S. 56 (1980). The previous rule, as outlined in *Roberts*, was that a prior statement of a witness who did not testify at trial (and therefore was not subject to cross-examination by the defendant) nevertheless could be introduced at trial if (1) the witness was

"unavailable" to testify at trial, and (2) the prior statement bore adequate "indicia of reliability" to substitute for the missing cross-examination. *Roberts*, 448 U.S., at 66. Such reliability, in turn, could be inferred if (1) the prior statement fell within a "firmly rooted" hearsay exception, such as spontaneous declarations or statements made in the course of receiving medical care, see *White*, 502 U.S., at 355, n. 8, or coconspirator statements, see *Bourjaily*, 483 U.S., at 183, or if (2) the prior statement was supported by "particularized guarantees of trustworthiness," see *Roberts*, 448 U.S., at 66. *Inadi* and *White* later softened the "unavailability" requirement by holding it inapplicable to at least some out-of-court prior statements, such as excited utterances, that would tend to be even more probative than similar statements made by the same witness in court. See *White*, 502 U.S., at 356.

The approach of *Roberts*, and the entire line of cases following it, was squarely rejected by the Court in the following recent case:

CRAWFORD v. WASHINGTON

Certiorari to the Supreme Court of Washington
541 U.S. 36 (2004)

Petitioner Michael Crawford stabbed a man who allegedly tried to rape his wife, Sylvia. At his trial, the State played for the jury Sylvia's tape-recorded statement to the police describing the stabbing, even though he had no opportunity for cross-examination. The Washington Supreme Court upheld petitioner's conviction after determining that Sylvia's statement was reliable. The question presented is whether this procedure complied with the Sixth Amendment's guarantee that, "[i]n all criminal prosecutions, the accused shall enjoy the right . . . to be confronted with the witnesses against him."

I

On August 5, 1999, Kenneth Lee was stabbed at his apartment. Police arrested petitioner later that night. After giving petitioner and his wife *Miranda* warnings, detectives interrogated each of them twice. Petitioner eventually confessed that he and Sylvia had gone in search of Lee because he was upset over an earlier incident in which Lee had tried to rape her. The two had found Lee at his apartment, and a fight ensued in which Lee was stabbed in the torso and petitioner's hand was cut. Petitioner gave the following account of the fight:

> Q. Okay. Did you ever see anything in [Lee's] hands?
> A. I think so, but I'm not positive.
> Q. Okay, when you think so, what do you mean by that?
> A. I coulda swore I seen him goin' for somethin' before, right before everything happened. He was like reachin', fiddlin' around down here and stuff . . . and I just . . . I don't know, I think, this is just a possibility, but I think, I think that he pulled somethin' out and I grabbed for it and that's how I got cut . . . but I'm not positive. I, I, my mind goes blank when things like this happen. I mean, I just, I remember things wrong, I remember things that just doesn't, don't make sense to me later.

App. 155 (punctuation added).

Sylvia generally corroborated petitioner's story about the events leading up to the fight, but her account of the fight itself was arguably different — particularly with respect to whether Lee had drawn a weapon before petitioner assaulted him:

Q.   Did Kenny do anything to fight back from this assault?

A.   (pausing) I know he reached into his pocket . . . or somethin' . . . I don't know what.

Q.   After he was stabbed?

A.   He saw Michael coming up. He lifted his hand . . . his chest open, he might [have] went to go strike his hand out or something and then (inaudible).

Q.   Okay, you, you gotta speak up.

A.   Okay, he lifted his hand over his head maybe to strike Michael's hand down or something and then he put his hands in his . . . put his right hand in his right pocket . . . took a step back . . . Michael proceeded to stab him . . . then his hands were like . . . how do you explain this . . . open arms . . . with his hands open and he fell down . . . and we ran (describing subject holding hands open, palms toward assailant).

Q.   Okay, when he's standing there with his open hands, you're talking about Kenny, correct?

A.   Yeah, after, after the fact, yes.

Q.   Did you see anything in his hands at that point?

A.   (pausing) um um (no).

Id., at 137 (punctuation added).

The State charged petitioner with assault and attempted murder. At trial, he claimed self-defense. Sylvia did not testify because of the state marital privilege, which generally bars a spouse from testifying without the other spouse's consent. See Wash. Rev. Code §5.60.060(1) (1994). In Washington, this privilege does not extend to a spouse's out-of-court statements admissible under a hearsay exception, . . . so the State sought to introduce Sylvia's tape-recorded statements to the police as evidence that the stabbing was not in self-defense. Noting that Sylvia had admitted she led petitioner to Lee's apartment and thus had facilitated the assault, the State invoked the hearsay exception for statements against penal interest, Wash. Rule Evid. 804(b)(3) (2003).

[Petitioner objected on Confrontation Clause grounds, but the trial court admitted Sylvia's statement pursuant to Ohio v. Roberts, 448 U.S. 56 (1980), on the grounds that (1) the wife was "unavailable" (due to the defendant's invocation of the spousal privilege), and (2) the prior statement bore "particularized guarantees of trustworthiness," specifically, it interlocked in several respects with the defendant's own statements. Petitioner was convicted of assault. — EDS.]

II

The Sixth Amendment's Confrontation Clause provides that, "[i]n all criminal prosecutions, the accused shall enjoy the right . . . to be confronted with the witnesses against him." We have held that this bedrock procedural guarantee applies to both federal and state prosecutions. Pointer v. Texas, 380 U.S. 400, 406 (1965). As noted above, *Roberts* says that an unavailable witness's out-of-court statement may be admitted so long as it has adequate indicia of reliability — i.e., falls within a "firmly rooted hearsay exception" or bears "particularized guarantees of trustworthiness." 448 U.S., at 66. Petitioner argues that this test strays from the original meaning of the Confrontation Clause and urges us to reconsider it.

[Here, Justice Scalia reviewed the original intent behind the Confrontation Clause, and the relation between the Clause and the common law of hearsay. — EDS.]

III

This history supports two inferences about the meaning of the Sixth Amendment.

A

First, the principal evil at which the Confrontation Clause was directed was the civil-law mode of criminal procedure, and particularly its use of ex parte examinations as evidence against the accused. . . . The Sixth Amendment must be interpreted with this focus in mind.

Accordingly, we once again reject the view that the Confrontation Clause applies of its own force only to in-court testimony. . . . Leaving the regulation of out-of-court statements to the law of evidence would render the Confrontation Clause powerless to prevent even the most flagrant inquisitorial practices. . . . This focus also suggests that not all hearsay implicates the Sixth Amendment's core concerns. An off-hand, overheard remark might be unreliable evidence and thus a good candidate for exclusion under hearsay rules, but it bears little resemblance to the civil-law abuses the Confrontation Clause targeted. On the other hand, ex parte examinations might sometimes be admissible under modern hearsay rules, but the Framers certainly would not have condoned them.

The text of the Confrontation Clause reflects this focus. It applies to "witnesses" against the accused — in other words, those who "bear testimony." 1 N. Webster, An American Dictionary of the English Language (1828). "Testimony," in turn, is typically "[a] solemn declaration or affirmation made for the purpose of establishing or proving some fact." Ibid. An accuser who makes a formal statement to government officers bears testimony in a sense that a person who makes a casual remark to an acquaintance does not. The constitutional text, like the history underlying the common-law right of confrontation, thus reflects an especially acute concern with a specific type of out-of-court statement.

Various formulations of this core class of "testimonial" statements exist: "ex parte in-court testimony or its functional equivalent — that is, material such as affidavits, custodial examinations, prior testimony that the defendant was unable to cross-examine, or similar pretrial statements that declarants would reasonably expect to be used prosecutorially," Brief for Petitioner 23; "extrajudicial statements . . . contained in formalized testimonial materials, such as affidavits, depositions, prior testimony, or confessions," White v. Illinois, 502 U.S. 346, 365 (1992) (Thomas, J., joined by Scalia, J., concurring in part and concurring in judgment); "statements that were made under circumstances which would lead an objective witness reasonably to believe that the statement would be available for use at a later trial," Brief for National Association of Criminal Defense Lawyers et al. as Amici Curiae 3. These formulations all share a common nucleus and then define the Clause's coverage at various levels of abstraction around it. Regardless of the precise articulation, some statements qualify under any definition — for example, ex parte testimony at a preliminary hearing.

Statements taken by police officers in the course of interrogations are also testimonial under even a narrow standard. Police interrogations bear a striking resemblance to examinations by justices of the peace in England. The statements are not *sworn* testimony, but the absence of oath was not dispositive. . . .

That interrogators are police officers rather than magistrates does not change the picture either. Justices of the peace conducting examinations under the Marian statutes were not magistrates as we understand that office today, but had an essentially investigative and prosecutorial function. See 1 Stephen, Criminal Law of England, at 221; Langbein, Prosecuting Crime in the Renaissance, at 34-45. England did not have a professional police force until the 19th century, see 1 Stephen, supra, at 194-200, so it is not surprising that other government officers performed the investigative functions now associated primarily with the police. The involvement of government officers in the production of testimonial evidence presents the same risk, whether the officers are police or justices of the peace.

In sum, even if the Sixth Amendment is not solely concerned with testimonial hearsay, that is its primary object, and interrogations by law enforcement officers fall squarely within that class.[4]

B

The historical record also supports a second proposition: that the Framers would not have allowed admission of testimonial statements of a witness who did not appear at trial unless he was unavailable to testify, and the defendant had had a prior opportunity for cross-examination. The text of the Sixth Amendment does not suggest any open-ended exceptions from the confrontation requirement to be developed by the courts. Rather, the "right . . . to be confronted with the witnesses against him," Amdt. 6, is most naturally read as a reference to the right of confrontation at common law, admitting only those exceptions established at the time of the founding. See Mattox v. United States, 156 U.S. 237, 243 (1895). . . .

[T]he common law in 1791 conditioned admissibility of an absent witness's examination on unavailability and a prior opportunity to cross-examine. The Sixth Amendment therefore incorporates those limitations. The numerous early state decisions applying the same test confirm that these principles were received as part of the common law in this country.

We do not read the historical sources to say that a prior opportunity to cross-examine was merely a sufficient, rather than a necessary, condition for admissibility of testimonial statements. They suggest that this requirement was dispositive, and not merely one of several ways to establish reliability. This is not to deny . . . that "[t]here were always exceptions to the general rule of exclusion" of hearsay

4. We use the term "interrogation" in its colloquial, rather than any technical legal, sense. Cf. Rhode Island v. Innis, 446 U.S. 291, 300-301 (1980). Just as various definitions of "testimonial" exist, one can imagine various definitions of "interrogation," and we need not select among them in this case. Sylvia's recorded statement, knowingly given in response to structured police questioning, qualifies under any conceivable definition.

evidence. Several had become well established by 1791. See 3 Wigmore §1397, at 101; Brief for United States as Amicus Curiae 13, n 5. But there is scant evidence that exceptions were invoked to admit *testimonial* statements against the accused in a *criminal* case.[6] Most of the hearsay exceptions covered statements that by their nature were not testimonial — for example, business records or statements in furtherance of a conspiracy. We do not infer from these that the Framers thought exceptions would apply even to prior testimony. Cf. Lilly v. Virginia, 527 U.S. 116, 134 (1999) (plurality opinion) ("[A]ccomplices' confessions that inculpate a criminal defendant are not within a firmly rooted exception to the hearsay rule").

IV

Our case law has been largely consistent with these two principles. . . .

[Here, Justice Scalia reviewed the case law back to the late 1800s, to show that the results in the cases generally conformed to the two historical principles described above. He noted only one exception: White v. Illinois, 502 U.S. 346 (1992), in which the Court approved the admission, under the "spontaneous declaration" hearsay exception, of prior statements by a child victim to an investigating police officer. He described *White* as being "arguably in tension with the rule requiring a prior opportunity for cross-examination when the proffered statement is testimonial." — EDS.]

Our cases have thus remained faithful to the Framers' understanding: Testimonial statements of witnesses absent from trial have been admitted only where the declarant is unavailable, and only where the defendant has had a prior opportunity to cross-examine.[9]

V

Although the results of our decisions have generally been faithful to the original meaning of the Confrontation Clause, the same cannot be said of our rationales. *Roberts* conditions the admissibility of all hearsay evidence on whether it falls under a "firmly rooted hearsay exception" or bears "particularized guarantees of trustworthiness." 448 U.S., at 66. This test departs from the historical principles identified above in two respects. First, it is too broad: It applies the same mode of analysis whether or not the hearsay consists of ex parte testimony. This often results in close constitutional scrutiny in cases that are far removed from the core concerns of the Clause. At the same time, however, the test is too narrow: It admits statements that

---

6. The one deviation we have found involves dying declarations. The existence of that exception as a general rule of criminal hearsay law cannot be disputed. See, e.g., Mattox v. United States, 156 U.S. 237, 243-244 (1895); King v. Reason, 16 How. St. Tr. 1, 24-38 (K.B. 1722). . . . Although many dying declarations may not be testimonial, there is authority for admitting even those that clearly are. . . . We need not decide in this case whether the Sixth Amendment incorporates an exception for testimonial dying declarations. If this exception must be accepted on historical grounds, it is sui generis.

9. . . . [W]e reiterate that, when the declarant appears for cross-examination at trial, the Confrontation Clause places no constraints at all on the use of his prior testimonial statements. See California v. Green, 399 U.S. 149, 162 (1970). It is therefore irrelevant that the reliability of some out-of-court statements "'cannot be replicated, even if the declarant testifies to the same matters in court.'" . . . (quoting United States v. Inadi, 475 U.S. 387, 395 (1986)). The Clause does not bar admission of a statement so long as the declarant is present at trial to defend or explain it. (The Clause also does not bar the use of testimonial statements for purposes other than establishing the truth of the matter asserted. See Tennessee v. Street, 471 U.S. 409, 414 (1985).)

do consist of ex parte testimony upon a mere finding of reliability. This malleable standard often fails to protect against paradigmatic confrontation violations. . . .

A

Where testimonial statements are involved, we do not think the Framers meant to leave the Sixth Amendment's protection to the vagaries of the rules of evidence, much less to amorphous notions of "reliability." Certainly none of the authorities discussed above acknowledges any general reliability exception to the common-law rule. Admitting statements deemed reliable by a judge is fundamentally at odds with the right of confrontation. To be sure, the Clause's ultimate goal is to ensure reliability of evidence, but it is a procedural rather than a substantive guarantee. It commands, not that evidence be reliable, but that reliability be assessed in a particular manner: by testing in the crucible of cross-examination. The Clause thus reflects a judgment, not only about the desirability of reliable evidence (a point on which there could be little dissent), but about how reliability can best be determined. Cf. 3 Blackstone, Commentaries, at 373 ("This open examination of witnesses . . . is much more conducive to the clearing up of truth"); M. Hale, History and Analysis of the Common Law of England 258 (1713) (adversarial testing "beats and bolts out the Truth much better").

The *Roberts* test allows a jury to hear evidence, untested by the adversary process, based on a mere judicial determination of reliability. It thus replaces the constitutionally prescribed method of assessing reliability with a wholly foreign one. . . .

Dispensing with confrontation because testimony is obviously reliable is akin to dispensing with jury trial because a defendant is obviously guilty. This is not what the Sixth Amendment prescribes.

B

The legacy of *Roberts* in other courts vindicates the Framers' wisdom in rejecting a general reliability exception. The framework is so unpredictable that it fails to provide meaningful protection from even core confrontation violations.

Reliability is an amorphous, if not entirely subjective, concept. There are countless factors bearing on whether a statement is reliable; the nine-factor balancing test applied by the Court of Appeals below is representative. . . . Whether a statement is deemed reliable depends heavily on which factors the judge considers and how much weight he accords each of them. Some courts wind up attaching the same significance to opposite facts. For example, . . . [t]he Virginia Court of Appeals found a statement more reliable because the witness was in custody and charged with a crime (thus making the statement more obviously against her penal interest), see Nowlin v. Commonwealth, 40 Va. App. 327, 335-338, 579 S.E. 2d 367, 371-372 (2003), while the Wisconsin Court of Appeals found a statement more reliable because the witness was *not* in custody and *not* a suspect, see State v. Bintz, 2002 WI App. 204, P13, 257 Wis. 2d 177, 187, 650 N.W.2d 913, 918. . . .

The unpardonable vice of the *Roberts* test, however, is not its unpredictability, but its demonstrated capacity to admit core testimonial statements that the Confrontation Clause plainly meant to exclude. Despite the plurality's speculation in *Lilly*, 527 U.S., at 137, that it was "highly unlikely" that accomplice confessions implicating the accused could survive *Roberts*, courts continue routinely to admit them. . . . One recent study found that, after *Lilly*, appellate courts admitted accomplice statements to the authorities in 25 out of 70 cases — more than one-third of the time. Kirst, Appellate Court Answers to the Confrontation Questions in Lilly v. Virginia, 53 Syracuse L. Rev. 87, 105 (2003). Courts have invoked *Roberts* to admit other sorts of plainly testimonial statements despite the absence of any opportunity to cross-examine. See United States v. Aguilar, 295 F.3d 1018, 1021-1023 (CA9 2002) (plea allocution showing existence of a conspiracy); United States v. Papajohn, 212 F.3d 1112, 1118-1120 (CA8 2000) (grand jury testimony); *Bintz*, supra, PP15-22, 257 Wis. 2d, at 188-191, 650 N.W. 2d, at 918-920 (prior trial testimony).

To add insult to injury, some of the courts that admit untested testimonial statements find reliability in the very factors that *make* the statements testimonial. As noted earlier, one court relied on the fact that the witness's statement was made to police while in custody on pending charges — the theory being that this made the statement more clearly against penal interest and thus more reliable. *Nowlin*, supra, at 335-338, 579 S.E. 2d, at 371-372. Other courts routinely rely on the fact that a prior statement is given under oath in judicial proceedings. . . . That inculpating statements are given in a testimonial setting is not an antidote to the confrontation problem, but rather the trigger that makes the Clause's demands most urgent. It is not enough to point out that most of the usual safeguards of the adversary process attend the statement, when the single safeguard missing is the one the Confrontation Clause demands.

C

Roberts' failings were on full display in the proceedings below. Sylvia Crawford made her statement while in police custody, herself a potential suspect in the case. Indeed, she had been told that whether she would be released "depend[ed] on how the investigation continues." App. 81. In response to often leading questions from police detectives, she implicated her husband in Lee's stabbing and at least arguably undermined his self-defense claim. Despite all this, the trial court admitted her statement, listing several reasons why it was reliable. In its opinion reversing, the Court of Appeals listed several *other* reasons why the statement was *not* reliable. Finally, the State Supreme Court relied exclusively on the interlocking character of the statement and disregarded every other factor the lower courts had considered. The case is thus a self-contained demonstration of *Roberts'* unpredictable and inconsistent application.

Each of the courts also made assumptions that cross-examination might well have undermined. . . . We readily concede that we could resolve this case by simply reweighing the "reliability factors" under *Roberts* and finding that Sylvia Crawford's statement falls short. But we view this as one of those rare cases in which the result below is so improbable that it reveals a fundamental failure on our part to interpret the Constitution in a way that secures its intended constraint on judicial discretion. Moreover, to reverse the Washington Supreme Court's decision after conducting our own reliability analysis would perpetuate, not avoid, what the Sixth Amendment condemns. The Constitution prescribes a procedure for determining the reliability of testimony in criminal trials, and we, no less than the state courts, lack authority to replace it with one of our own devising.

We have no doubt that the courts below were acting in utmost good faith when they found reliability. The Framers, however, would not have been content to indulge this assumption. They knew that judges, like other government officers, could not always be trusted to safeguard the rights of the people . . . They were loath to leave too much discretion in judicial hands. Cf. U.S. Const., Amdt. 6 (criminal jury trial); Amdt. 7 (civil jury trial); Ring v. Arizona, 536 U.S. 584, 611-612 (2002) (Scalia, J., concurring). By replacing categorical constitutional guarantees with open-ended balancing tests, we do violence to their design. Vague standards are manipulable, and, while that might be a small concern in run-of-the-mill assault prosecutions like this one, the Framers had an eye toward politically charged cases . . . — great state trials where the impartiality of even those at the highest levels of the judiciary might not be so clear. It is difficult to imagine *Roberts* providing any meaningful protection in those circumstances. . . .

Where nontestimonial hearsay is at issue, it is wholly consistent with the Framers' design to afford the States flexibility in their development of hearsay law — as does *Roberts*, and as would an approach that exempted such statements from Confrontation Clause scrutiny altogether. Where testimonial evidence is at issue, however, the Sixth Amendment demands what the common law required: unavailability and a prior opportunity for cross-examination. We leave for another day any effort to spell out a comprehensive definition of "testimonial."[10] Whatever else the term covers, it applies at a minimum to prior testimony at a preliminary hearing, before a grand jury, or at a former trial; and to police interrogations. These are the modern practices with closest kinship to the abuses at which the Confrontation Clause was directed. In this case, the State admitted Sylvia's testimonial statement against petitioner, despite the fact that he had no opportunity to cross-examine her. That alone is sufficient to make out a violation of the Sixth Amendment. *Roberts* notwithstanding, we decline to mine the record in search of indicia of reliability. Where testimonial statements are at issue, the only indicium of reliability sufficient to satisfy constitutional demands is the one the Constitution actually prescribes: confrontation.

The judgment of the Washington Supreme Court is reversed, and the case is remanded for further proceedings not inconsistent with this opinion.

[Chief Justice Rehnquist and Justice O'Connor concurred in the judgment, agreeing that the wife's statement should have been excluded, but finding that result to be properly dictated by *Roberts*, and expressing the view that adoption of a new approach "is not backed by sufficiently persuasive reasoning to overrule long-established precedent."]

Crawford, although subsequently held *not* to apply retroactively to convicted defendants whose criminal cases were already final, see Whorton v. Bockting, 549 U.S. 406 (2006), nevertheless impacted the world of criminal trials like a bombshell, not least because of the singular lack of guidance provided by Justice Scalia about the meaning of the crucial term, "testimony." Does the following case help?

---

10. We acknowledge the Chief Justice's objection, that our refusal to articulate a comprehensive definition in this case will cause interim uncertainty. But it can hardly be any worse than the status quo. . . . The difference is that the *Roberts* test is *inherently*, and therefore *permanently*, unpredictable.

DAVIS v. WASHINGTON

Certiorari to the Supreme Court of Washington
547 U.S. 813 (2006)

JUSTICE SCALIA delivered the opinion of the Court. These cases require us to determine when statements made to law enforcement personnel during a 911 call or at a crime scene are "testimonial" and thus subject to the requirements of the Sixth Amendment's Confrontation Clause.

I

A

The relevant statements in Davis v. Washington, No. 05-5224, were made to a 911 emergency operator on February 1, 2001. When the operator answered the initial call, the connection terminated before anyone spoke. She reversed the call, and Michelle McCottry answered. In the ensuing conversation, the operator ascertained that McCottry was involved in a domestic disturbance with her former boyfriend Adrian Davis, the petitioner in this case:

> 911 Operator: Hello.
> Complainant: Hello.
> 911 Operator: What's going on?
> Complainant: He's here jumpin' on me again.
> 911 Operator: Okay. Listen to me carefully. Are you in a house or an apartment?
> Complainant: I'm in a house.
> 911 Operator: Are there any weapons?
> Complainant: No. He's usin' his fists.
> 911 Operator: Okay. Has he been drinking?
> Complainant: No.
> 911 Operator: Okay, sweetie. I've got help started. Stay on the line with me, okay?
> Complainant: I'm on the line.
> 911 Operator: Listen to me carefully. Do you know his last name?
> Complainant: It's Davis.
> 911 Operator: Davis? Okay, what's his first name?
> Complainant: Adran.
> 911 Operator: What is it?
> Complainant: Adrian.
> 911 Operator: Adrian?
> Complainant: Yeah.
> 911 Operator: Okay. What's his middle initial?
> Complainant: Martell. He's runnin' now.

App. in No. 05-5224, pp. 8-9.

As the conversation continued, the operator learned that Davis had "just run out the door" after hitting McCottry, and that he was leaving in a car with someone else.

McCottry started talking, but the operator cut her off, saying, "Stop talking and answer my questions." She then gathered more information about Davis (including his birthday) and learned that Davis had told McCottry that his purpose in coming to the house was "to get his stuff," since McCottry was moving. McCottry described the context of the assault, after which the operator told her that the police were on their way. "They're gonna check the area for him first," the operator said, "and then they're gonna come talk to you." Id., at 12-13.

The police arrived within four minutes of the 911 call and observed McCottry's shaken state, the "fresh injuries on her forearm and her face," and her "frantic efforts to gather her belongings and her children so that they could leave the residence." 154 Wash. 2d 291, 296, 111 P. 3d 844, 847 (2005) (en banc).

The State charged Davis with felony violation of a domestic no-contact order. "The State's only witnesses were the two police officers who responded to the 911 call. Both officers testified that McCottry exhibited injuries that appeared to be recent, but neither officer could testify as to the cause of the injuries." Ibid. McCottry presumably could have testified as to whether Davis was her assailant, but she did not appear. Over Davis's objection, based on the Confrontation Clause of the Sixth Amendment, the trial court admitted the recording of her exchange with the 911 operator, and the jury convicted him. The Washington Court of Appeals affirmed, 116 Wash. App. 81, 64 P. 3d 661 (2003). The Supreme Court of Washington, with one dissenting justice, also affirmed, concluding that the portion of the 911 conversation in which McCottry identified Davis was not testimonial, and that if other portions of the conversation were testimonial, admitting them was harmless beyond a reasonable doubt. 154 Wash. 2d, at 305, 111 P. 3d, at 851. We granted certiorari.

B

In Hammon v. Indiana, No. 05-5705, police responded late on the night of February 26, 2003, to a "reported domestic disturbance" at the home of Hershel and Amy Hammon. 829 N.E.2d 444, 446 (Ind. 2005). They found Amy alone on the front porch, appearing "somewhat frightened," but she told them that "nothing was the matter," id., at 446, 447. She gave them permission to enter the house, where an officer saw "a gas heating unit in the corner of the living room" that had "flames coming out of the . . . partial glass front. There were pieces of glass on the ground in front of it and there was flame emitting from the front of the heating unit." App. in No. 05-5705, p. 16.

Hershel, meanwhile, was in the kitchen. He told the police "that he and his wife had 'been in an argument' but 'everything was fine now' and the argument 'never became physical.'" 829 N.E.2d, at 447. By this point Amy had come back inside. One of the officers remained with Hershel; the other went to the living room to talk with Amy, and "again asked [her] what had occurred." Ibid. Hershel made several attempts to participate in Amy's conversation with the police, but was rebuffed. The officer later testified that Hershel "became angry when I insisted that [he] stay separated from Mrs. Hammon so that we can investigate what had happened." After hearing Amy's account, the officer "had her fill out and sign a battery affidavit." Amy handwrote the following: "Broke our Furnace & shoved me down on the floor into the broken glass. Hit me in the chest and threw me down. Broke our lamps &

phone. Tore up my van where I couldn't leave the house. Attacked my daughter."
[App. in No. 05-5705,] at 2.

The State charged Hershel with domestic battery and with violating his probation. Amy was subpoenaed, but she did not appear at his subsequent bench trial.
The State called the officer who had questioned Amy, and asked him to recount what
Amy told him and to authenticate the affidavit. Hershel's counsel repeatedly
objected to the admission of this evidence. At one point, after hearing the prosecutor defend the affidavit because it was made "under oath," defense counsel said,
"That doesn't give us the opportunity to cross examine [the] person who allegedly
drafted it. Makes me mad." Nonetheless, the trial court admitted the affidavit as a
"present sense impression," and Amy's statements as "excited utterances" that "are
expressly permitted in these kinds of cases even if the declarant is not available to
testify." The officer thus testified that Amy

> informed me that she and Hershel had been in an argument. That he became irrate
> [*sic*] over the fact of their daughter going to a boyfriend's house. The argument
> became . . . physical after being verbal and she informed me that Mr. Hammon, dur-
> ing the verbal part of the argument was breaking things in the living room and I believe
> she stated he broke the phone, broke the lamp, broke the front of the heater. When it
> became physical he threw her down into the glass of the heater. . . .
>
> She informed me Mr. Hammon had pushed her onto the ground, had shoved her
> head into the broken glass of the heater and that he had punched her in the chest twice
> I believe.

Id., at 17-18.

The trial judge found Hershel guilty on both charges, and the Indiana Court of
Appeals affirmed in relevant part, 809 N.E.2d 945 (2004). The Indiana Supreme
Court also affirmed, concluding that Amy's statement was admissible for state-law
purposes as an excited utterance, 829 N.E. 2d, at 449; that "a 'testimonial' statement is one given or taken in significant part for purposes of preserving it for potential future use in legal proceedings," where "the motivations of the questioner and
declarant are the central concerns," id., at 456, 457; and that Amy's oral statement
was not "testimonial" under these standards, id., at 458. It also concluded that,
although the affidavit was testimonial and thus wrongly admitted, it was harmless
beyond a reasonable doubt, largely because the trial was to the bench. Id., at 458-
459. We granted certiorari.

II

The Confrontation Clause of the Sixth Amendment provides: "In all criminal prosecutions, the accused shall enjoy the right . . . to be confronted with the witnesses
against him." In Crawford v. Washington, 541 U.S. 36, 53-54 (2004), we held that
this provision bars "admission of testimonial statements of a witness who did not
appear at trial unless he was unavailable to testify, and the defendant had had a
prior opportunity for cross-examination." A critical portion of this holding, and the
portion central to resolution of the two cases now before us, is the phrase "testimonial statements." Only statements of this sort cause the declarant to be a "witness"
within the meaning of the Confrontation Clause. See id., at 51. It is the testimonial
character of the statement that separates it from other hearsay that, while subject to

traditional limitations upon hearsay evidence, is not subject to the Confrontation Clause.

Our opinion in *Crawford* set forth "various formulations" of the core class of "testimonial" statements, ibid., but found it unnecessary to endorse any of them, because "some statements qualify under any definition," id., at 52. Among those, we said, were "statements taken by police officers in the course of interrogations," ibid.; see also id., at 53. The questioning that generated the deponent's statement in *Crawford* — which was made and recorded while she was in police custody, after having been given *Miranda* warnings as a possible suspect herself — "qualifies under any conceivable definition" of an "interrogation," 541 U.S., at 53, n. 4. We therefore did not define that term, except to say that "we use [it] . . . in its colloquial, rather than any technical legal, sense," and that "one can imagine various definitions . . . , and we need not select among them in this case." Ibid. The character of the statements in the present cases is not as clear, and these cases require us to determine more precisely which police interrogations produce testimony.

Without attempting to produce an exhaustive classification of all conceivable statements — or even all conceivable statements in response to police interrogation — as either testimonial or nontestimonial, it suffices to decide the present cases to hold as follows: Statements are nontestimonial when made in the course of police interrogation under circumstances objectively indicating that the primary purpose of the interrogation is to enable police assistance to meet an ongoing emergency. They are testimonial when the circumstances objectively indicate that there is no such ongoing emergency, and that the primary purpose of the interrogation is to establish or prove past events potentially relevant to later criminal prosecution.[1]

III

A

In *Crawford*, it sufficed for resolution of the case before us to determine that "even if the Sixth Amendment is not solely concerned with testimonial hearsay, that is its primary object, and interrogations by law enforcement officers fall squarely within that class." Id., at 53. Moreover, as we have just described, the facts of that case spared us the need to define what we meant by "interrogations." The *Davis* case today does not permit us this luxury of indecision. The inquiries of a police operator in the course of a 911 call[2] are an interrogation in one sense, but not in a sense that "qualifies under any conceivable definition." We must decide, therefore,

---

1. Our holding refers to interrogations because, as explained below, the statements in the cases presently before us are the products of interrogations — which in some circumstances tend to generate testimonial responses. This is not to imply, however, that statements made in the absence of any interrogation are necessarily nontestimonial. The Framers were no more willing to exempt from cross-examination volunteered testimony or answers to open-ended questions than they were to exempt answers to detailed interrogation. (Part of the evidence against Sir Walter Raleigh was a letter from Lord Cobham that was plainly not the result of sustained questioning. Raleigh's Case, 2 How. St. Tr. 1, 27 (1603).) And of course even when interrogation exists, it is in the final analysis the declarant's statements, not the interrogator's questions, that the Confrontation Clause requires us to evaluate.

2. If 911 operators are not themselves law enforcement officers, they may at least be agents of law enforcement when they conduct interrogations of 911 callers. For purposes of this opinion (and without deciding the point), we consider their acts to be acts of the police. As in Crawford v. Washington, 541 U.S. 36 (2004), therefore, our holding today makes it unnecessary to consider whether and when statements made to someone other than law enforcement personnel are "testimonial."

whether the Confrontation Clause applies only to testimonial hearsay; and, if so, whether the recording of a 911 call qualifies.

The answer to the first question was suggested in *Crawford*, even if not explicitly held:

> The text of the Confrontation Clause reflects this focus [on testimonial hearsay]. It applies to "witnesses" against the accused — in other words, those who "bear testimony." 1 N. Webster, An American Dictionary of the English Language (1828). "Testimony," in turn, is typically "a solemn declaration or affirmation made for the purpose of establishing or proving some fact." Ibid. An accuser who makes a formal statement to government officers bears testimony in a sense that a person who makes a casual remark to an acquaintance does not.

541 U.S., at 51.

A limitation so clearly reflected in the text of the constitutional provision must fairly be said to mark out not merely its "core," but its perimeter.

[Justice Scalia next cited numerous early and modern cases to show that the Confrontation Clause has — with one exception, White v. Illinois, 502 U.S. 346 (1992), discussed and implicitly criticized in *Crawford* — been applied by the Court only in cases that "clearly involve testimony." — EDS.]

Most of the American cases applying the Confrontation Clause or its state constitutional or common-law counterparts involved testimonial statements of the most formal sort — sworn testimony in prior judicial proceedings or formal depositions under oath — which invites the argument that the scope of the Clause is limited to that very formal category. But the English cases that were the progenitors of the Confrontation Clause did not limit the exclusionary rule to prior court testimony and formal depositions, see *Crawford*, supra, at 52, and n. 3. In any event, we do not think it conceivable that the protections of the Confrontation Clause can readily be evaded by having a note-taking policeman *recite* the unsworn hearsay testimony of the declarant, instead of having the declarant sign a deposition. Indeed, if there is one point for which no case — English or early American, state or federal — can be cited, that is it.

The question before us in *Davis*, then, is whether, objectively considered, the interrogation that took place in the course of the 911 call produced testimonial statements. When we said in *Crawford*, supra, at 53, that "interrogations by law enforcement officers fall squarely within [the] class" of testimonial hearsay, we had immediately in mind (for that was the case before us) interrogations solely directed at establishing the facts of a past crime, in order to identify (or provide evidence to convict) the perpetrator. The product of such interrogation, whether reduced to a writing signed by the declarant or embedded in the memory (and perhaps notes) of the interrogating officer, is testimonial. It is, in the terms of the 1828 American dictionary quoted in *Crawford*, "[a] solemn declaration or affirmation made for the purpose of establishing or proving some fact." 541 U.S., at 51. (The solemnity of even an oral declaration of relevant past fact to an investigating officer is well enough established by the severe consequences that can attend a deliberate falsehood. See, e.g., United States v. Stewart, 433 F.3d 273, 288 (CA2 2006) (false statements made to federal investigators violate 18 U.S.C. §1001); State v. Reed, 2005 WI 53, ¶30, 280 Wis. 2d 68, 695 N.W.2d 315, 323 (state criminal offense to "knowingly give false information to [an] officer with [the] intent to mislead the officer in the performance of his or her duty").) A 911 call, on the other hand, and at least the initial interrogation conducted in connection with a 911 call, is ordinarily not designed primarily to "establish or prove" some past fact, but to describe current circumstances requiring police assistance.

The difference between the interrogation in *Davis* and the one in *Crawford* is apparent on the face of things. In *Davis*, McCottry was speaking about events *as they were actually happening*, rather than "describing past events," Lilly v. Virginia, 527 U.S. 116, 137 (1999) (plurality opinion). Sylvia Crawford's interrogation, on the other hand, took place hours after the events she described had occurred. Moreover, any reasonable listener would recognize that McCottry (unlike Sylvia Crawford) was facing an ongoing emergency. Although one *might* call 911 to provide a narrative report of a crime absent any imminent danger, McCottry's call was plainly a call for help against bona fide physical threat. Third, the nature of what was asked and answered in *Davis*, again viewed objectively, was such that the elicited statements were necessary to be able to *resolve* the present emergency, rather than simply to learn (as in *Crawford*) what had happened in the past. That is true even of the operator's effort to establish the identity of the assailant, so that the dispatched officers might know whether they would be encountering a violent felon. See, e.g., Hiibel v. Sixth Judicial Dist. Court of Nev., Humboldt Cty., 542 U.S. 177, 186 (2004). And finally, the difference in the level of formality between the two interviews is striking. Crawford was responding calmly, at the station house, to a series of questions, with the officer-interrogator taping and making notes of her answers; McCottry's frantic answers were provided over the phone, in an environment that was not tranquil, or even (as far as any reasonable 911 operator could make out) safe.

We conclude from all this that the circumstances of McCottry's interrogation objectively indicate its primary purpose was to enable police assistance to meet an ongoing emergency. She simply was not acting as a *witness*; she was not *testifying*. What she said was not "a weaker substitute for live testimony" at trial, United States v. Inadi, 475 U.S. 387, 394 (1986), like Lord Cobham's statements in Raleigh's Case, 2 How. St. Tr. 1 (1603), or Jane Dingler's ex parte statements against her husband in King v. Dingler, 2 Leach 561, 168 Eng. Rep. 383 (1791), or Sylvia Crawford's statement in *Crawford*. In each of those cases, the ex parte actors and the evidentiary products of the ex parte communication aligned perfectly with their courtroom analogues. McCottry's emergency statement does not. No "witness" goes into court to proclaim an emergency and seek help.

Davis seeks to cast McCottry in the unlikely role of a witness by pointing to English cases. None of them involves statements made during an ongoing emergency. In King v. Brasier, 1 Leach 199, 168 Eng. Rep. 202 (1779), for example, a young rape victim, "immediately on her coming home, told all the circumstances of the injury" to her mother. Id., at 200, 168 Eng. Rep., at 202. The case would be helpful to Davis if the relevant statement had been the girl's screams for aid as she was being chased by her assailant. But by the time the victim got home, her story was an account of past events.

This is not to say that a conversation which begins as an interrogation to determine the need for emergency assistance cannot, as the Indiana Supreme Court put it, "evolve into testimonial statements," 829 N.E. 2d, at 457, once that purpose has been achieved. In this case, for example, after the operator gained the information needed to address the exigency of the moment, the emergency appears to have ended (when Davis drove away from the premises). The operator then told

McCottry to be quiet, and proceeded to pose a battery of questions. It could readily be maintained that, from that point on, McCottry's statements were testimonial, not unlike the "structured police questioning" that occurred in *Crawford*, 541 U.S., at 53, n. 4. This presents no great problem. Just as, for Fifth Amendment purposes, "police officers can and will distinguish almost instinctively between questions necessary to secure their own safety or the safety of the public and questions designed solely to elicit testimonial evidence from a suspect," New York v. Quarles, 467 U.S. 649, 658-659 (1984), trial courts will recognize the point at which, for Sixth Amendment purposes, statements in response to interrogations become testimonial. Through in limine procedure, they should redact or exclude the portions of any statement that have become testimonial, as they do, for example, with unduly prejudicial portions of otherwise admissible evidence. Davis's jury did not hear the *complete* 911 call, although it may well have heard some testimonial portions. We were asked to classify only McCottry's early statements identifying Davis as her assailant, and we agree with the Washington Supreme Court that they were not testimonial. That court also concluded that, even if later parts of the call were testimonial, their admission was harmless beyond a reasonable doubt. Davis does not challenge that holding, and we therefore assume it to be correct.

B

Determining the testimonial or nontestimonial character of the statements that were the product of the interrogation in *Hammon* is a much easier task, since they were not much different from the statements we found to be testimonial in *Crawford*. It is entirely clear from the circumstances that the interrogation was part of an investigation into possibly criminal past conduct — as, indeed, the testifying officer expressly acknowledged, App. in No. 05-5705, at 25, 32, 34. There was no emergency in progress; the interrogating officer testified that he had heard no arguments or crashing and saw no one throw or break anything. When the officers first arrived, Amy told them that things were fine, and there was no immediate threat to her person. When the officer questioned Amy for the second time, and elicited the challenged statements, he was not seeking to determine (as in *Davis*) "what is happening," but rather "what happened." Objectively viewed, the primary, if not indeed the sole, purpose of the interrogation was to investigate a possible crime — which is, of course, precisely what the officer *should* have done.

It is true that the *Crawford* interrogation was more formal. It followed a *Miranda* warning, was tape-recorded, and took place at the station house, see 541 U.S., at 53, n. 4. While these features certainly strengthened the statements' testimonial aspect — made it more objectively apparent, that is, that the purpose of the exercise was to nail down the truth about past criminal events — none was essential to the point. It was formal enough that Amy's interrogation was conducted in a separate room, away from her husband (who tried to intervene), with the officer receiving her replies for use in his "investigation." App. in No. 05-5705, at 34. What we called the "striking resemblance" of the *Crawford* statement to civil-law ex parte examinations, 541 U.S., at 52, is shared by Amy's statement here. Both declarants were actively separated from the defendant — officers forcibly prevented Hershel from participating in the interrogation. Both statements deliberately recounted, in response to police questioning, how potentially criminal past events began and progressed. And both took place some time after the events described were over. Such statements under official interrogation are an obvious substitute for live testimony, because they do precisely *what a witness does* on direct examination; they are inherently testimonial.[5]

Both Indiana and the United States as amicus curiae argue that this case should be resolved much like *Davis*. For the reasons we find the comparison to *Crawford* compelling, we find the comparison to *Davis* unpersuasive. The statements in *Davis* were taken when McCottry was alone, not only unprotected by police (as Amy Hammon was protected), but apparently in immediate danger from Davis. She was seeking aid, not telling a story about the past. McCottry's present-tense statements showed immediacy; Amy's narrative of past events was delivered at some remove in time from the danger she described. And after Amy answered the officer's questions, he had her execute an affidavit, in order, he testified, "to establish events that have occurred previously." App. in No. 05-5705, at 18.

Although we necessarily reject the Indiana Supreme Court's implication that virtually any "initial inquiries" at the crime scene will not be testimonial, see 829 N.E. 2d, at 453, 457, we do not hold the opposite — that *no* questions at the scene will yield nontestimonial answers. We have already observed of domestic disputes that "officers called to investigate . . . need to know whom they are dealing with in order to assess the situation, the threat to their own safety, and possible danger to the potential victim." *Hiibel*, 542 U.S., at 186. Such exigencies may *often* mean that "initial inquiries" produce nontestimonial statements. But in cases like this one, where Amy's statements were neither a cry for help nor the provision of information enabling officers immediately to end a threatening situation, the fact that they were given at an alleged crime scene and were "initial inquiries" is immaterial. Cf. *Crawford*, supra, at 52, n. 3.[6]

IV

Respondents in both cases, joined by a number of their amici, contend that the nature of the offenses charged in these two cases — domestic violence — requires

---

5. The dissent criticizes our test for being "neither workable nor a targeted attempt to reach the abuses forbidden by the [Confrontation] Clause," post, at 9 (opinion of Thomas, J.). As to the former: We have acknowledged that our holding is not an "exhaustive classification of all conceivable statements — or even all conceivable statements in response to police interrogation," supra, at 7, but rather a resolution of the cases before us and those like them. For those cases, the test is objective and quite "workable."

As for the charge that our holding is not a "targeted attempt to reach the abuses forbidden by the [Confrontation] Clause," which the dissent describes as the depositions taken by Marian magistrates, characterized by a high degree of formality, see post, at 2-3: We do not dispute that formality is indeed essential to testimonial utterance. But we no longer have examining Marian magistrates; and we do have, as our 18th-century forebears did not, examining police officers, see L. Friedman, Crime and Punishment in American History 67-68 (1993) — who perform investigative and testimonial functions once performed by examining Marian magistrates, see J. Langbein, The Origins of Adversary Criminal Trial 41 (2003). It imports sufficient formality, in our view, that lies to such officers are criminal offenses. Restricting the Confrontation Clause to the precise forms against which it was originally directed is a recipe for its extinction. Cf. Kyllo v. United States, 533 U.S. 27 (2001).

6. Police investigations themselves are, of course, in no way impugned by our characterization of their fruits as testimonial. Investigations of past crimes prevent future harms and lead to necessary arrests. While prosecutors may hope that inculpatory "nontestimonial" evidence is gathered, this is essentially beyond police control. Their saying that an emergency exists cannot make it be so. The Confrontation Clause in no way governs police conduct, because it is the trial use of, not the investigatory *collection* of, ex parte testimonial statements which offends that provision. But neither can police conduct govern the Confrontation Clause; testimonial statements are what they are.

greater flexibility in the use of testimonial evidence. This particular type of crime is notoriously susceptible to intimidation or coercion of the victim to ensure that she does not testify at trial. When this occurs, the Confrontation Clause gives the criminal a windfall. We may not, however, vitiate constitutional guarantees when they have the effect of allowing the guilty to go free. Cf. Kyllo v. United States, 533 U.S. 27 (2001) (suppressing evidence from an illegal search). But when defendants seek to undermine the judicial process by procuring or coercing silence from witnesses and victims, the Sixth Amendment does not require courts to acquiesce. While defendants have no duty to assist the State in proving their guilt, they *do* have the duty to refrain from acting in ways that destroy the integrity of the criminal-trial system. We reiterate what we said in *Crawford*: that "the rule of forfeiture by wrongdoing . . . extinguishes confrontation claims on essentially equitable grounds." 541 U.S., at 62 (citing *Reynolds*, 98 U.S., at 158-159). That is, one who obtains the absence of a witness by wrongdoing forfeits the constitutional right to confrontation.

We take no position on the standards necessary to demonstrate such forfeiture, but federal courts using Federal Rule of Evidence 804(b)(6), which codifies the forfeiture doctrine, have generally held the Government to the preponderance-of-the-evidence standard, see, e.g., United States v. Scott, 284 F.3d 758, 762 (CA7 2002). State courts tend to follow the same practice, see, e.g., Commonwealth v. Edwards, 444 Mass. 526, 542, 830 N.E.2d 158, 172 (2005). Moreover, if a hearing on forfeiture is required, *Edwards*, for instance, observed that "hearsay evidence, including the unavailable witness's out-of-court statements, may be considered." Id., at 545, 830 N.E.2d, at 174. . . .

We have determined that, absent a finding of forfeiture by wrongdoing, the Sixth Amendment operates to exclude Amy Hammon's affidavit. The Indiana courts may (if they are asked) determine on remand whether such a claim of forfeiture is properly raised and, if so, whether it is meritorious.

***

We affirm the judgment of the Supreme Court of Washington in No. 05-5224. We reverse the judgment of the Supreme Court of Indiana in No. 05-5705, and remand the case to that Court for proceedings not inconsistent with this opinion.

JUSTICE THOMAS, concurring in the judgment in part and dissenting in part.

In Crawford v. Washington, 541 U.S. 36 (2004), we abandoned the general reliability inquiry we had long employed to judge the admissibility of hearsay evidence under the Confrontation Clause, describing that inquiry as "*inherently*, and therefore *permanently*, unpredictable." Id., at 68, n. 10 (emphasis in original). Today, a mere two years after the Court decided *Crawford*, it adopts an equally unpredictable test, under which district courts are charged with divining the "primary purpose" of police interrogations. Besides being difficult for courts to apply, this test characterizes as "testimonial," and therefore inadmissible, evidence that bears little resemblance to what we have recognized as the evidence targeted by the Confrontation Clause. Because neither of the cases before the Court today would implicate the Confrontation Clause under an appropriately targeted standard, I concur only in the judgment in Davis v. Washington, No. 05-5224, and dissent from the Court's resolution of Hammon v. Indiana, No. 05-5705.

I

A

The Confrontation Clause provides that "in all criminal prosecutions, the accused shall enjoy the right . . . to be confronted with the witnesses against him . . . ." U.S. Const., Amdt. 6. We have recognized that the operative phrase in the Clause, "witnesses against him," could be interpreted narrowly, to reach only those witnesses who actually testify at trial, or more broadly, to reach many or all of those whose out-of-court statements are offered at trial. *Crawford*, supra, at 42-43; White v. Illinois, 502 U.S. 346, 359-363 (1992) (Thomas, J., concurring in part and concurring in judgment). Because the narrowest interpretation of the Clause would conflict with both the history giving rise to the adoption of the Clause and this Court's precedent, we have rejected such a reading. See *Crawford*, supra, at 50-51; *White*, supra, at 360 (opinion of Thomas, J.).

Rejection of the narrowest view of the Clause does not, however, require the broadest application of the Clause to exclude otherwise admissible hearsay evidence. The history surrounding the right to confrontation supports the conclusion that it was developed to target particular practices that occurred under the English bail and committal statutes passed during the reign of Queen Mary, namely, the "civil-law mode of criminal procedure, and particularly its use of ex parte examinations as evidence against the accused." *Crawford*, supra, at 43, 50; *White*, supra, at 361-362 (opinion of Thomas, J.); Mattox v. United States, 156 U.S. 237, 242 (1895). "The predominant purpose of the [Marian committal] statute was to institute *systematic* questioning of the accused and the witnesses." J. Langbein, Prosecuting Crime in the Renaissance 23 (1974) (emphasis added). The statute required an oral examination of the suspect and the accusers, transcription within two days of the examinations, and physical transmission to the judges hearing the case. Id., at 10, 23. These examinations came to be used as evidence in some cases, in lieu of a personal appearance by the witness. *Crawford*, supra, at 43-44; 9 W. Holdsworth, A History of English Law 223-229 (1926). Many statements that would be inadmissible as a matter of hearsay law bear little resemblance to these evidentiary practices, which the Framers proposed the Confrontation Clause to prevent. See, e.g., *Crawford*, supra, at 51 (contrasting "an off-hand, overheard remark" with the abuses targeted by the Confrontation Clause). Accordingly, it is unlikely that the Framers intended the word "witness" to be read so broadly as to include such statements. Cf. Dutton v. Evans, 400 U.S. 74, 94 (1970) (Harlan, J., concurring in result) (rejecting the "assumption that the core purpose of the Confrontation Clause of the Sixth Amendment is to prevent overly broad exceptions to the hearsay rule").

In *Crawford*, we recognized that this history could be squared with the language of the Clause, giving rise to a workable, and more accurate, interpretation of the Clause. "Witnesses," we said, are those who "'bear testimony.'" 541 U.S., at 51 (quoting 1 N. Webster, An American Dictionary of the English Language (1828)). And "'testimony'" is "'[a] solemn declaration or affirmation made for the purpose of establishing or proving some fact.'" Ibid. (quoting Webster, supra). Admittedly, we did not set forth a detailed framework for addressing whether a statement is "testimonial" and thus subject to the Confrontation Clause. But the plain terms of the "testimony" definition we endorsed necessarily require some degree of solemnity before a statement can be deemed "testimonial."

This requirement of solemnity supports my view that the statements regulated by the Confrontation Clause must include "extrajudicial statements . . . contained in formalized testimonial materials, such as affidavits, depositions, prior testimony, or confessions." *White*, supra, at 365 (opinion of Thomas, J.). Affidavits, depositions, and prior testimony are, by their very nature, taken through a formalized process. Likewise, confessions, when extracted by police in a formal manner, carry sufficient indicia of solemnity to constitute formalized statements and, accordingly, bear a "striking resemblance," *Crawford*, supra, at 52, to the examinations of the accused and accusers under the Marian statutes.[1] See generally Langbein, supra, at 21-34.

Although the Court concedes that the early American cases invoking the right to confrontation or the Confrontation Clause itself all "clearly involved testimony" as defined in *Crawford*, it fails to acknowledge that all of the cases it cites fall within the narrower category of formalized testimonial materials I have proposed.[2] Interactions between the police and an accused (or witnesses) resemble Marian proceedings — and these early cases — only when the interactions are somehow rendered "formal." In *Crawford*, for example, the interrogation was custodial, taken after warnings given pursuant to Miranda v. Arizona, 384 U.S. 436 (1966). 541 U.S., at 38. *Miranda* warnings, by their terms, inform a prospective defendant that "'anything he says can be used against him in a court of law.'" Dickerson v. United States, 530 U.S. 428, 435 (2000) (quoting *Miranda*, supra, at 479). This imports a solemnity to the process that is not present in a mere conversation between a witness or suspect and a police officer.[3]

The Court all but concedes that no case can be cited for its conclusion that the Confrontation Clause also applies to informal police questioning under certain circumstances. Instead, the sole basis for the Court's conclusion is its apprehension that the Confrontation Clause will "readily be evaded" if it is only applicable to formalized testimonial materials. But the Court's proposed solution to the risk of evasion is needlessly overinclusive. Because the Confrontation Clause sought to regulate prosecutorial abuse occurring through use of ex parte statements as evidence against the accused, it also reaches the use of technically informal statements when used to evade the formalized process. That is, even if the interrogation itself is not formal, the production of evidence by the prosecution at trial would resemble the abuses targeted by the Confrontation Clause if the prosecution attempted to use out-of-court statements as a means of circumventing the literal right of confrontation, see Coy v. Iowa, 487 U.S. 1012 (1988). In such a case, the Confrontation Clause could fairly be applied to exclude the hearsay statements offered by the prosecution, preventing evasion without simultaneously excluding evidence offered by the prosecution in good faith.

The Court's standard is not only disconnected from history and unnecessary to prevent abuse; it also yields no predictable results to police officers and prosecutors attempting to comply with the law. Cf. *Crawford*, supra, at 68, n. 10 (criticizing

---

1. Like the Court, I presume the acts of the 911 operator to be the acts of the police. Accordingly, I refer to both the operator in *Davis* and the officer in *Hammon*, and their counterparts in similar cases, collectively as "the police."

2. Our more recent cases, too, nearly all hold excludable under the Confrontation Clause materials that are plainly highly formal. . . .

3. The possibility that an oral declaration of past fact to a police officer, if false, could result in legal consequences to the speaker, may render honesty in casual conversations with police officers important. It does not, however, render those conversations solemn or formal in the ordinary meanings of those terms.

unpredictability of the pre-*Crawford* test); *White*, 502 U.S., at 364-365 (Thomas, J., concurring in part and concurring in judgment) (limiting the Confrontation Clause to the discrete category of materials historically abused would "greatly simplify" application of the Clause). In many, if not most, cases where police respond to a report of a crime, whether pursuant to a 911 call from the victim or otherwise, the purposes of an interrogation, viewed from the perspective of the police, are *both* to respond to the emergency situation *and* to gather evidence. See New York v. Quarles, 467 U.S. 649, 656 (1984) ("Undoubtedly most police officers [deciding whether to give *Miranda* warnings in a possible emergency situation] would act out of a host of different, instinctive, and largely unverifiable motives — their own safety, the safety of others, and perhaps as well the desire to obtain incriminating evidence from the suspect"). Assigning one of these two "largely unverifiable motives," primacy requires constructing a hierarchy of purpose that will rarely be present — and is not reliably discernible. It will inevitably be, quite simply, an exercise in fiction.

The Court's repeated invocation of the word "objective" to describe its test, however, suggests that the Court may not mean to reference purpose at all, but instead to inquire into the function served by the interrogation. Certainly such a test would avoid the pitfalls that have led us repeatedly to reject tests dependent on the subjective intentions of police officers.[4] It would do so, however, at the cost of being even more disconnected from the prosecutorial abuses targeted by the Confrontation Clause. Additionally, it would shift the ability to control whether a violation occurred from the police and prosecutor to the judge, whose determination as to the "primary purpose" of a particular interrogation would be unpredictable and not necessarily tethered to the actual purpose for which the police performed the interrogation.

B

Neither the 911 call at issue in *Davis* nor the police questioning at issue in *Hammon* is testimonial under the appropriate framework. Neither the call nor the questioning is itself a formalized dialogue.[5] Nor do any circumstances surrounding the taking of the statements render those statements sufficiently formal to resemble the Marian examinations; the statements were neither Mirandized nor custodial, nor accompanied by any similar indicia of formality. Finally, there is no suggestion that the prosecution attempted to offer the women's hearsay evidence at trial in order to evade confrontation. See 829 N.E.2d 444, 447 (Ind. 2005) (prosecution subpoenaed Amy Hammon to testify, but she was not present); 154 Wash. 2d 291, 296, 111 P. 3d 844, 847 (2005) (en banc) (State was unable to locate Michelle

---

4. See New York v. Quarles, 467 U.S. 649, 655-656, and n. 6 (1984) (subjective motivation of officer not relevant in considering whether the public safety exception to Miranda v. Arizona, 384 U.S. 436 (1966), is applicable); Rhode Island v. Innis, 446 U.S. 291, 301 (1980) (subjective intent of police officer to obtain incriminatory statement not relevant to whether an interrogation has occurred); Whren v. United States, 517 U.S. 806, 813 (1996) (refusing to evaluate Fourth Amendment reasonableness in light of the officers' actual motivations).

5. Although the police questioning in *Hammon* was ultimately reduced to an affidavit, all agree that the affidavit is inadmissible per se under our definition of the term "testimonial." Brief for Respondent in No. 05-5705, p. 46; Brief for United States as Amicus Curiae in No. 05-5705, p. 14.

McCottry at the time of trial). Accordingly, the statements at issue in both cases are nontestimonial and admissible under the Confrontation Clause.

The Court's determination that the evidence against Hammon must be excluded extends the Confrontation Clause far beyond the abuses it was intended to prevent. When combined with the Court's holding that the evidence against Davis is perfectly admissible, however, the Court's *Hammon* holding also reveals the difficulty of applying the Court's requirement that courts investigate the "primary purposes" of the investigation. The Court draws a line between the two cases based on its explanation that *Hammon* involves "no emergency in progress," but instead, mere questioning as "part of an investigation into possibly criminal past conduct," and its explanation that *Davis* involves questioning for the "primary purpose" of "enabling police assistance to meet an ongoing emergency." But the fact that the officer in *Hammon* was investigating Mr. Hammon's past conduct does not foreclose the possibility that the primary purpose of his inquiry was to assess whether Mr. Hammon constituted a continuing danger to his wife, requiring further police presence or action. It is hardly remarkable that Hammon did not act abusively towards his wife in the presence of the officers, and his good judgment to refrain from criminal behavior in the presence of police sheds little, if any, light on whether his violence would have resumed had the police left without further questioning, transforming what the Court dismisses as "past conduct" back into an "ongoing emergency."[6] Nor does the mere fact that McCottry needed emergency aid shed light on whether the "primary purpose" of gathering, for example, the name of her assailant was to protect the police, to protect the victim, or to gather information for prosecution. In both of the cases before the Court, like many similar cases, pronouncement of the "primary" motive behind the interrogation calls for nothing more than a guess by courts.

II

Because the standard adopted by the Court today is neither workable nor a targeted attempt to reach the abuses forbidden by the Clause, I concur only in the judgment in Davis v. Washington, No. 05-5224, and respectfully dissent from the Court's resolution of Hammon v. Indiana, No. 05-5705.

NOTES AND QUESTIONS

1. Who's got the better of the argument here? Justice Scalia, whose definition of "testimony" seems to depend mostly on whether the statements at issue dealt with contemporaneous or past events? Or Justice Thomas, whose test would depend on the "formality" of the circumstances under which the statements were made? What, if anything, do either of these competing approaches have to do with the underlying purpose of the Confrontation Clause, which is (presumably) to help ensure that

6. Some of the factors on which the Court relies to determine that the police questioning in *Hammon* was testimonial apply equally in *Davis*. For example, while Hammon was "actively separated from the [victim]" and thereby "prevented . . . from participating in the interrogation," Davis was apart from McCottry while she was questioned by the 911 operator and thus unable to participate in the questioning. Similarly, "the events described [by McCottry] were over" by the time she recounted them to the 911 operator. See 154 Wash. 2d 291, 295-296, 111 P.3d 844, 846-847 (2005) (en banc).

trial testimony is adequately tested and, therefore, can be trusted as reasonably reliable? In particular, isn't it a little strange that, under both tests, most 911 calls (which are usually made under highly stressful, if not downright dangerous, circumstances that seem very likely to affect the witness's perceptions) will turn out to be nonproblematic under the Confrontation Clause (and thus admissible without cross-examination, assuming all other requirements for admissibility are met)?

2. There is an interesting tension in the majority opinion in *Davis*. Why does Justice Scalia spend so much time discussing the behavior and purposes of the relevant government agents, if as he states, see fn. 1, it's the nature of the declarant's statements that matters to the application of the Confrontation Clause, and not the nature of the interrogator's questions? For example, if the 911 operator in *Davis* had asked no questions at all, but simply had listened quietly and patiently while Michelle McCottry blurted out her statements, would the result in the case have been any different? Wouldn't the Confrontation Clause have kicked in at exactly the same point — i.e., the moment when McCottry stated that "[h]e's runnin' now," thus indicating that the immediate emergency had passed? Why should the "primary purpose of the interrogation" matter at all, given that (to use Justice Scalia's own words, in footnote 6) "police conduct [cannot] govern the Confrontation Clause; testimonial statements are what they are"?

3. Perhaps temporality is a necessary but not sufficient condition. Near the end of his lead opinion in Giles v. California, 128 U.S. 2678 (2008), in a portion joined by a majority of the Court, Justice Scalia penned the following interesting passage:

> The dissent closes by pointing out that a forfeiture rule which ignores *Crawford* would be particularly helpful to women in abusive relationships — or at least particularly helpful in punishing their abusers. Not as helpful as the dissent suggests, since only *testimonial* statements are excluded by the Confrontation Clause. Statements to friends and neighbors about abuse and intimidation, and statements to physicians in the course of receiving treatment would be excluded, if at all, only by hearsay rules. . . .

What does this mean? Recall that in *Davis*, Scalia's majority opinion cited — as an apparent example of "testimony" — the English case of King v. Brasier, 1 Leach 199, 168 Eng. Rep. 202 (1779), in which a young girl, immediately after being raped, reported the facts of the crime to her mother. If the *Brasier* case involved "testimony," because it was (in Scalia's words from *Davis*) "an account of past events," then how could "[s]tatements to friends and neighbors about abuse and intimidation" not also involve "testimony"? Aren't they all equally "account[s] of past events"? Is Scalia now going back on his position in *Davis*?

Does it help to note that, earlier in *Davis*, Scalia had stated, in a footnote, that "our holding today makes it unnecessary to consider whether and when statements made to someone other than law enforcement personnel are testimonial"? Perhaps the true meaning of "testimony" depends on *both* (1) the temporal dimension (i.e., whether the statement is given in "real time" or is made about "past events") *and* (2) the identity of the person or persons to whom the statement is made. And perhaps as well (3) the apparent purpose of the exchange. We will have to wait and see.

4. In *Davis*, the Court noted that a defendant can lose his Confrontation Clause protection through the equitable doctrine of "forfeiture by wrongdoing." Does the

act of "wrongdoing" have to be for the purpose of preventing the witness from testifying? Or is any act of "wrongdoing" sufficient, as long as it has the effect of preventing the witness from testifying?

In Giles v. California, 128 U.S. 2678 (2008), the case notes in the previous note that the defendant was accused of murdering his wife, and the prosecution was allowed to use the "forfeiture by wrongdoing" exception to introduce prior unconfronted testimonial statements, made by the wife, accusing her husband of domestic violence. A fractured Court (in a lead opinion by Justice Scalia that garnered majority support for all but one section) held that the forfeiture exception applies "only when the defendant engaged in conduct *designed* to prevent the witness from testifying." Although this required reversal of the conviction, Scalia noted that on remand, an inquiry could be made into whether there might be evidence sufficient to show that the defendant did, indeed, murder his wife for the purpose of silencing her. Such evidence might include, for example, "[e]arlier abuse, or threats of abuse, intended to dissuade the victim from resorting to outside help," as well as "evidence of ongoing criminal proceedings at which the victim would have been expected to testify," all of which would be "highly relevant" to the key issue of whether the defendant's crime "expressed the intent to isolate the victim and to stop her from reporting abuse to the authorities or cooperating with a criminal prosecution." Justices Thomas and Alito joined the lead opinion, but wrote separately to express the view that, although not an issue properly before the Court, the contested statements might not even be "testimonial" in the first place (since they were not closely analogous to in-court witness statements). Justices Souter and Ginsburg joined all but one section of the lead opinion (a section that contained exceptionally strong rhetoric about the role of history and original intent in interpreting the Confrontation Clause, and correspondingly strong denigration of the dissenters' policy-oriented jurisprudence). Justices Breyer, Stevens, and Kennedy dissented, largely on the grounds that the Court's decision would allow domestic abusers to benefit from the violent results of their abuse.

5. In more general terms, doesn't the Court's fundamental approach to the Confrontation Clause in *Crawford* and *Davis* seem rather sterile? In particular, note Justice Scalia's back-of-the-hand dismissal of the concern that *Davis* will undermine the factual accuracy of criminal adjudication, especially in domestic violence cases: "When this occurs, the Confrontation Clause gives the criminal a windfall. We may not, however, vitiate constitutional guarantees when they have the effect of allowing the guilty to go free."

How can such a view be squared with, for example, the Court's decision during the same Term in House v. Bell, 547 U.S. 518 (2006), discussed at page 1397, infra, a decision clearly motivated by the desire to improve factual accuracy in criminal cases (or, more specifically, to remedy factual *in*-accuracy)? How can it be squared with Holmes v. South Carolina, discussed at page 1334, supra? Should constitutional criminal procedure rules be designed and applied with a primary focus on enhancing factual accuracy, or are some procedural rules an end in themselves — even when they may sometimes work *against* accuracy, as in *Crawford* and *Davis*?

It is undoubtedly true that procedural justice and factual accuracy often complement each other. But when these two values come into conflict, how should the Court choose between them? Does an absolutist statement like the one quoted in the preceding paragraph seem like the best way to resolve such a conflict? Do you think Justice Scalia really meant what he said?

6. Apparently Justice Scalia was quite serious. In an astonishing elevation of form over both substance and good sense, the same five-person majority, with Scalia writing the opinion, held in Melendez-Diaz v. Massachusetts, 129 S. Ct. 2527 (2009), that a certificate from a state laboratory after chemical testing certifying the contents and quantity of a seized substance was a "testimonial" statement, and thus within the rule in *Crawford* requiring the opportunity to cross-examine the maker of the statement.

To the majority, the "case involves little more than the application of our holding in *Crawford*. . . . The Sixth Amendment does not permit the prosecution to prove its case via ex parte out-of-court affidavits. . . ." In a biting and powerful dissent, however, Justice Kennedy pointed out that, regardless whether *Crawford* may stand for that proposition, the Sixth Amendment does not. It does not prohibit "ex parte affidavits"; it provides a right to confront the witnesses against you. The question is not what is "testimonial"; the question is who are the witnesses the Sixth Amendment refers to? As the dissent pointed out, there is virtually nothing in the constitutional language, history, precedent, or good sense justifying the majority's reworking of long-settled procedural and evidentiary rules that exempted such people as lab technicians from being called by the state in order to admit their lab results. The concern of the Sixth Amendment, according to the dissent, is the key factual witnesses against a defendant, with respect to whom face-to-face confrontation may make a difference. Face-to-face confrontation with lab technicians is highly unlikely to be of any benefit to the defense and will impose serious costs on the state. To be sure, errors are made by lab technicians, and it is not inconceivable that, in a small number of cases, cross-examining the lab technician may point out a problem. However, defendants now have the right under the Compulsory Process Clause to subpoena whomever they like, including lab technicians, and examine them at trial.

Against the minimal benefits to factual accuracy of the Court's approach, consider the costs. As the dissent argued in passages to which the majority did not respond:

> The Court says that, before the results of a scientific test may be introduced into evidence, the defendant has the right to confront the "analyst." One must assume that this term, though it appears nowhere in the Confrontation Clause, nevertheless has some constitutional substance that now must be elaborated in future cases. There is no accepted definition of analyst, and there is no established precedent to define that term.
> Consider how many people play a role in a routine test for the presence of illegal drugs. One person prepares a sample of the drug, places it in a testing machine, and retrieves the machine's printout — often, a graph showing the frequencies of radiation absorbed by the sample or the masses of the sample's molecular fragments. . . . A second person interprets the graph the machine prints out — perhaps by comparing that printout with published, standardized graphs of known drugs. Meanwhile, a third person — perhaps an independent contractor — has calibrated the machine and, having done so, has certified that the machine is in good working order. Finally, a fourth person — perhaps the laboratory's director — certifies that his subordinates followed established procedures.
> It is not at all evident which of these four persons is the analyst to be confronted under the rule the Court announces today. If all are witnesses who must appear for in-court confrontation, then the Court has, for all practical purposes, forbidden the use of scientific tests in criminal trials . . . . [R]equiring even one of these individuals to

testify threatens to disrupt if not end many prosecutions where guilt is clear but a newly found formalism now holds sway.

The Federal Government may face even graver difficulties than the States because its operations are so widespread. For example, the FBI laboratory at Quantico, Virginia, supports federal, state, and local investigations across the country. Its 500 employees conduct over one million scientific tests each year. . . . The Court's decision means that before any of those million tests reaches a jury, at least one of the laboratory's analysts must board a plane, find his or her way to an unfamiliar courthouse, and sit there waiting to read aloud notes made months ago.

The Court purchases its meddling with the Confrontation Clause at a dear price, a price not measured in taxpayer dollars alone. Guilty defendants will go free, on the most technical grounds, as a direct result of today's decision, adding nothing to the truth-finding process. The analyst will not always make it to the courthouse in time. He or she may be ill; may be out of the country; may be unable to travel because of inclement weather; or may at that very moment be waiting outside some other courtroom for another defendant to exercise the right the Court invents today. If for any reason the analyst cannot make it to the courthouse in time, then, the Court holds, the jury cannot learn of the analyst's findings (unless, by some unlikely turn of events, the defendant previously cross-examined the analyst). The result, in many cases, will be that the prosecution cannot meet its burden of proof, and the guilty defendant goes free on a technicality that, because it results in an acquittal, cannot be reviewed on appeal.

7. To what, exactly, does this new rule apply? Suppose a lab technician is called to testify. Can he or she explain the chain of custody that led to the substance being brought to the lab for testing, or does every single person in the chain of custody have to be produced? If the latter, isn't that a bit ridiculous?

8. If the costs are as dear as the dissent in *Melendez-Diaz* seems to think, the results may not be quite what the dissent predicts but instead become the incentive for creative reengineering by the states and federal government. Recall that *Crawford* is satisfied with the right to confront and cross-examine at some point, and that point does not need to be at the trial on the merits. A pretrial process involving notice to the defendant and the opportunity to cross-examine the relevant witnesses under oath suffices. Could a state thus satisfy *Melendez-Diaz* through largely pro forma pretrial hearings, with notice to defendants, where lab technicians are sworn and made available for cross-examination? If the defendant appears in person or through counsel, the Confrontation Clause would be satisfied, and if the defendant does not appear, any such right would be waived. A state could likely conduct hundreds of such hearings in a few hours, and could thus preserve, at relatively little cost, the benefits of the previous way of doing business that the Court has now ruled unconstitutional. Do you think such possibilities support what the Court has done, or emphasize its curiousness?

9. What is the extension of the rule in *Crawford*? Consider the case of expert testimony. Typically, an expert can rely on inadmissible evidence to form an opinion. Suppose an expert, offered by the state, relies on out-of-court statements about a defendant to draw an inference about the competence of the defendant at the time he committed a criminal act. Those statements may refer, for example, to the everyday functioning of the individual, and so on, and are only pertinent to competence if true. Can an expert testify on such a basis? Who is actually "testifying against the defendant" in such cases? Can the expert explain the basis of his opinion, or will each of the persons making a statement that the expert relied upon have to be called as a witness?

Take the matter one step further. Many forensic experts learn their discipline from books written by individuals who fully expect that the books will be used in the education of individuals who will testify, in part, on the basis of what they learn in those books. Indeed, most knowledge is transmitted through such forms of "testimony." When, say, a ballistics expert or a fingerprint expert who learned his field, in part, through the use of such books testifies, who is "testifying against the defendant"? The in-court expert is testifying, in part, on what the out-of-court expert asserted in the educational material relied upon, and in some ways is simply repeating the out-of-court statements that the author of the book fully expected would lead to in-court testimony. Does that violate *Crawford*? If not, why not?

If so, are we hovering over an abyss?

10. Note two interesting aspects of the Court's opinions in this area. First, they were prompted, in part, by the ambiguities in the *Roberts* line of cases, suggesting at a minimum that the *Crawford* replacement should be easier to apply. Second, they consistently refuse to take account of the implications of modern-day social, economic, scientific, and justice system realities and insist on the application of a formal test mandated by the constitutional text as "the Framers" understood it. On the first issue, it is fair to say that, rather than calming the waters disturbed by *Roberts*, *Crawford* threw the criminal justice process into turmoil. Within two years of the cases, over 6,000 cases had cited to it, and now tens of thousands have. See, e.g., Jennifer A. Lindt, Protecting the Most Vulnerable Victims: Prosecution of Child Sex Offenses in Illinois Post Crawford v. Washington, 27 N. Ill. U. L. Rev. 95 (2006). As to the second, the Court's history has systematically been shown to be in error, which calls into question a form of constitutional interpretation so dependent on historical analysis. Consider the following from Thomas Y. Davies, Not "The Framers' Design": How the Framing-Era Ban Against Hearsay Evidence Refutes the *Crawford-Davis* "Testimonial" Formulation of the Scope of the Original Confrontation Clause, 15 J.L. & Pol'y 349-350 (2007):

> According to proponents, an originalist approach to constitutional interpretation injects discipline into constitutional decision-making. At least in criminal procedure, this claim is unrealistic. Instead, the originalist claims that have appeared in recent criminal procedure decisions have usually reflected the ideological proclivities of the justices who made them, but have rarely resembled the historical legal doctrines that actually shaped the Framers' understanding.
>
> The divergence between originalist claims and historical doctrine has been particularly apparent in two recent decisions that construed the Sixth Amendment Confrontation Clause with regard to the admission of hearsay evidence in criminal trials. In the 2004 decision Crawford v. Washington, and again in the 2006 decision Davis v. Washington, Justice Scalia asserted in opinions for the Court that "the Framers' design" for the scope of the confrontation right was that the right should regulate the admission as evidence in criminal trials of only "testimonial" out-of-court statements, but not apply at all to less formal, "nontestimonial" hearsay evidence.
>
> As a practical matter, it seems likely that the narrow scope accorded to the confrontation right in *Crawford* will allow prosecutors considerable room to use hearsay evidence in criminal cases rather than produce the person who made the out-of-court statement as a trial witness, even when the person who made the hearsay statement is readily available to be called. Thus, the *Crawford* formulation of the limited scope of the right appears to mean that criminal defendants will often be deprived of meeting face to face the available declarant who made the out-of-court statement and will also be deprived of cross-examining the declarant in the view of the jury. Is that outcome really

consistent with the framing-era doctrine that shaped the Framers' understanding of the confrontation right?

Plainly not. Although Justice Scalia endorsed formulating the Confrontation Clause to permit "only those [hearsay] exceptions established at the time of the founding," he did not follow through on identifying such exceptions in *Crawford* or *Davis*. If he had actually canvassed the framing-era evidence authorities, he would have discovered that framing-era evidence doctrine imposed a virtually total ban against using unsworn hearsay evidence to prove a criminal defendant's guilt. Although framing-era law did permit some hearsay evidence to be admitted regarding certain specific issues in civil lawsuit trials, those exceptions were not understood to apply to criminal trials. Instead, as of 1789, a dying declaration of a murder victim was the only kind of unsworn out-of-court statement that could be admitted in a criminal trial to prove the guilt of the defendant. Otherwise, the hearsay "exceptions" that now constitute a prominent feature of criminal evidence law had not yet been invented. Instead, nineteenth-century judges invented the hearsay exceptions that now apply to criminal trials only after the framing. Hence, it is clear that the Framers did not design the Confrontation Clause so as to accommodate the admission of unsworn hearsay statements.

Indeed, the framing-era authorities indicate that admission of hearsay statements would have violated basic principles of common-law criminal evidence. In particular, the framing-era sources indicate that the confrontation right itself prohibited the use of hearsay statements as evidence of the defendant's guilt. The condemnations of hearsay that appeared in prominent and widely used framing-era authorities typically recognized that the admission of a hearsay statement would deprive the defendant of the opportunity to cross-examine the speaker in the presence of the trial jury, and that opportunity to cross-examine was understood to be a salient aspect of the confrontation right. Thus, the framing-era sources actually suggest that the Framers would not have approved of the hearsay exceptions that were later invented because the Framers would have perceived such exceptions to violate a defendant's confrontation right.

Hence, *Crawford*'s testimonial formulation of the scope of the confrontation right does not reflect "the Framers' design." Rather, *Crawford*'s permissive allowance of unsworn hearsay is inconsistent with the basic premises that shaped the Framers' understanding of the right. Thus, whatever might be said for or against *Crawford*'s formulation as a matter of contemporary constitutional policy, the fictional character of the historical claims made in that opinion constitute further evidence that originalism is a defective approach to constitutional decision-making. . . .

11. Given the turmoil introduced into the criminal justice system by decisions such as *Crawford*, and the controversial nature of cases such as *Agard*, one is inclined to wonder if there are things to learn from how other countries handle similar matters in particular, and operate their criminal justice systems in particular. Unfortunately, there are at least four limitations on such inquires. First, it is difficult, if not impossible, to abstract the criminal justice system from the entire range of governmental activity and appraise just it. Perhaps in some country, the criminal justice system works just great, measured by crime rates for example, but it turns out that it is because the government is investing too many resources in crime prevention and not much in other social welfare areas. For a interesting discussion of this issue, see Ronald J. Allen & Larry Laudan, Deadly Dilemmas, 41 Texas Tech. L. Rev. 65-92 (2008). Second, simply comparing the operation of two different systems is enormously complicated, involving not just crime rates, for example, but also their interaction with conviction rates, treatment of suspects, levels of surveillance in the society as a whole, and so on. Third, most of the rest of the world does not have the American appetite for self-criticism that results in large expenditures of resources

on critical empirical studies or funding things like innocence projects. Fourth, the criminal justice process of each country is unique, even within large areas such as Western Europe that are often thought of as having similar, inquisitorial systems. For a sense of just how wide-ranging the differences are, see Craig M. Bradley (ed.), Criminal Procedure: A Worldwide Study (1999), and Diane Marie Amann, Harmonic Convergence? Constitutional Criminal Procedure in an International Context, 75 Ind. L.J. 809 (2000).

Keeping the difficulties noted above in mind, consider the following two excerpts comparing American and European practice, the first dealing with the rights to silence and counsel, and the second focusing on the hearsay rule:

Europeans recognize a right to silence and to counsel, while still encouraging suspects to participate as a testimonial resource. In Europe today, there is universal recognition of a right to silence and of a privilege against self-incrimination, although vast differences remain with respect to the nature and scope of these rights. While it is accepted that they prohibit coercion and inhumane practices, including compulsion by legal mandate to give testimony under oath which could be used in a criminal prosecution, there is a general understanding that rules implementing the right to silence should not present substantial barriers to testimonial evidence from defendants. This perspective is reflected in the limited right to counsel during police interrogation and in the permissive approach to waiver rules that allow continued questioning in the face of assertions of silence or expressions of a desire for counsel. With a culture of cooperation and compromise and a criminal defense bar that generally advises suspects to cooperate and give their side of the case at an early stage in the proceedings, it is not surprising that on the Continent the vast bulk of suspects do not remain silent during pretrial questioning by the police or the investigating magistrate.

At trial, European systems encourage suspects to speak by limiting the dangers of testifying and increasing the cost of silence. Continental and English procedures reduce the harm from speaking by rules that do not condition use of prior convictions on whether the accused agrees to speak. Continental systems increase the cost of refusing to speak by procedural devices and expectations, while England accomplishes similar objectives by explicitly authorizing the fact-finder to draw adverse inferences from silence.

In America, on the other hand, as a matter of both practice and principle, *Miranda* and *Griffin* seem to have won the day. Suspects in this country tend to speak to police less frequently and to testify at trial less often than their Continental or English counterparts. Furthermore, we have come to accept the proposition that the more one is suspected of criminal activity, the less we should look to that person for an explanation of his conduct. As a result, we have defendants like O. J. Simpson and Terry Nichols, who make pretrial statements but do not testify, and Timothy McVeigh, who does neither, leaving the fact-finders and the public either uncertain as to what the defendant did or at a loss as to why he did it and speculating about the possible involvement of others.

European perspectives suggest that recognition of a right to silence and a right to counsel is not incompatible with learning what happened from the accused. Modern, civilized justice systems can recognize a right to silence and to counsel while still encouraging suspects to speak and actively participate in the fact-finding enterprise. Provided such rights are viewed in proper perspective, they need not require sacrificing the most important witness in order to have fair trials.

With respect to the question of "proper perspective," I offer some alternatives to conventional views of the nature and status of the right to silence. First, from an historical perspective, the right to silence and the privilege against self-incrimination protections afforded by American and European systems of justice in important respects go far beyond what modern scholars have identified as the scope of such rights follow-ing their adoption in England and in America. When the privilege was first advocated and eventually accepted in Seventeenth Century England, it protected only against unjustified compulsory inquires. Compelled testimony was acceptable if based on probable cause. When the privilege was adopted in America as part of the Fifth Amend-ment, it went beyond England's original version and prohibited even justified compul-sion of incriminating testimony, but it did not require warnings and permitted adverse inferences from silence during pretrial questioning by the justice of the peace as long as the accused remained unsworn.

Second, the silence right should be viewed in relation to the speaking right. Cur-rently, we seem to regard the right to silence as akin to the basic right to trial counsel recognized as an essential aspect of a fair trial in Gideon v. Wainwright. We assume that unless the right is available and frequently exercised, defendants will not have a fair trial, and thus believe that it should be applied broadly and that defendants should be encouraged to claim it. However, the right to silence might better be seen as similar to Gideon's counterpart, the right of self-representation, which is controversial and more narrowly drawn because it often leads to disruption and injustice. Better harmonizing the silence right with the speaking right would lead to accepting procedures designed to encourage the exercise of the right to testify — a Constitutional guarantee more essential to a fair trial than the right to silence.

Finally, we might recognize that the American justice system is even more depen-dent than European systems on forcing admissions of guilt from defendant's mouth. Both Continental and common law systems apply pressures on defendants to speak, but in America the pressures are applied later during the plea bargaining process, which disposes of ninety to ninety-five percent of criminal cases. Furthermore, in the bargaining process coercive pressures are allowed that would never be accepted in the context of asking a defendant for his story. Most significantly, the goal of the prosecu-tor in plea bargaining is not merely gaining defendant's story, but his confession, and the focus of the process is not so much on finding the truth, but on settling cases and clearing dockets. Perhaps we should consider shifting our efforts from pressuring defendants to confess and waive their trial rights to encouraging them to give their ver-sion of the events so that the fact-finder is better able to determine what happened and why. European perspectives demonstrate that systems of justice can recognize silence and counsel rights while fairly distinguishing between inducements and coercion and permitting procedures that encourage defendants to speak and meaningfully partici-pate in the fact-finding process.

Gordon Van Kessel, European Perspectives on the Accused as a Source of Testimo-nial Evidence, 100 W. Va. L. Rev. 799, 802 (1998).

[Although the conventional view is that modern Continental legal systems permit the widespread use of hearsay and do not enforce a robust right of confrontation, they] have, in fact, erected barriers to certain uses of derivative proof. These barriers have two sources: the principle of "immediacy" embraced by Continental legal systems since the nineteenth century, and the fair trial guarantee in the European Human Rights Convention. The principle of immediacy requires that witnesses testify orally at trial. As a formal matter, it bars only the medieval practice of having witnesses testify before one official, with another official then deciding the case. . . . Nonetheless the prin-ciple of immediacy is occasionally invoked in support of a broader disapproval of rely-ing on hearsay when the original witnesses are available to testify.

Even this broader, intermittently applied version of the principle, though, does not amount to a ban on hearsay; it is strictly a rule of preference. This is true even in Italy, often said to have adopted a version of the hearsay rule closely approximating the traditional common-law rule, along with other elements of "adversarial" criminal trials. Recent amendments to the Italian constitution do in fact restrict the admissibility of out-of-court statements, but the restrictions do not apply when "examination of the witness is impossible for objective reasons independent of the parties' will."[1]

The same may be said of the limitations imposed on hearsay by the fair trial provisions of the European Human Rights Convention. Adopted in the aftermath of World War II, the Convention provides, among other things, that every criminal defendant "is entitled to a fair and public hearing" and "to examine or have examined witnesses against him." Over the past two decades, the European Court of Human Rights (ECHR) — charged with implementing the Convention — has interpreted these provisions to require, as a general matter, that evidence "be produced at a public hearing, in the presence of the accused" and that "the accused . . . be given an adequate and proper opportunity to challenge and question a witness against him, either when he makes his statement or at a later stage." These are procedural requirements, not rules of admissibility. The ECHR has repeatedly stressed that "the admissibility of evidence is primarily a matter for regulation by national law"; the court understands its task as "not to give a ruling on whether statements of witnesses were properly admitted as evidence, but rather to ascertain whether the proceedings as a whole, including the way in which evidence was taken, were fair." Accordingly, the ECHR has found violations of the Convention when informants have been questioned but their identities not disclosed to the defense, and when alleged victims of child sexual abuse have been questioned by police officers but not by magistrates.

It has also ruled, more recently, that Convention does not permit government depositions of witnesses who do not testify at trial to be the "sole or decisive basis" for a criminal conviction, even if the witness' absence is beyond the prosecution's control. The "sole or decisive" rule is currently under challenge, and it operates, in any event, as a rule of sufficiency, not a rule of admissibility. The ECHR has never disapproved the mere introduction of hearsay statements by witnesses who are dead or otherwise unavailable at the time of trial. Nor is it clear whether the European Human Rights Convention imposes any restrictions at all on the introduction of hearsay evidence through "intermediaries" other than government officials.

David Sklansky, Hearsay's Last Hurrah, [2009] Sup. Ct. Rev. 1 (2010).

12. Prior statements by a codefendant that are *not* admissible against the defendant as coconspirator statements, but that *are* admissible against the codefendant himself (in a joint trial), create special problems because of their potentially devastating impact on the jury with respect to the guilt of both defendants. This has led the Court to develop a special prophylactic rule generally barring the admission of such statements. The next case deals with the scope of this rule.

---

1. Michele Panzavolta, Reforms and Counter-Reforms in the Italian Struggle for an Accusatorial Criminal Law System, 30 N.C. J. Int'l L. & Com. Reg. 577, 611-612 (2005); see also William T. Pizzi & Mariangela Montagna, The Battle to Establish an Adversarial Trial System in Italy, 25 Mich. J. Int'l L. 429, 462 (2004).

GRAY v. MARYLAND

Certiorari to the Court of Appeals of Maryland
523 U.S. 185 (1998)

JUSTICE BREYER delivered the opinion of the Court. The issue in this case concerns the application of Bruton v. United States, 391 U.S. 123 (1968). *Bruton* involved two defendants accused of participating in the same crime and tried jointly before the same jury. One of the defendants had confessed. His confession named and incriminated the other defendant. The trial judge issued a limiting instruction, telling the jury that it should consider the confession as evidence only against the codefendant who had confessed and not against the defendant named in the confession. *Bruton* held that, despite the limiting instruction, the Constitution forbids the use of such a confession in the joint trial.

The case before us differs from *Bruton* in that the prosecution here redacted the codefendant's confession by substituting for the defendant's name in the confession a blank space or the word "deleted." We must decide whether these substitutions make a significant legal difference. We hold that they do not and that *Bruton*'s protective rule applies.

I

In 1993, Stacy Williams died after a severe beating. Anthony Bell gave a confession, to the Baltimore City police, in which he said that he (Bell), Kevin Gray, and Jacquin "Tank" Vanlandingham had participated in the beating that resulted in Williams' death. Vanlandingham later died. A Maryland grand jury indicted Bell and Gray for murder. The State of Maryland tried them jointly.

The trial judge, after denying Gray's motion for a separate trial, permitted the State to introduce Bell's confession into evidence at trial. But the judge ordered the confession redacted. Consequently, the police detective who read the confession into evidence said the word "deleted" or "deletion" whenever Gray's name or Vanlandingham's name appeared. Immediately after the police detective read the redacted confession to the jury, the prosecutor asked, "after he gave you that information, you subsequently were able to arrest Mr. Kevin Gray; is that correct?" The officer responded, "That's correct." . . . The State also introduced into evidence a written copy of the confession with those two names omitted, leaving in their place blank white spaces separated by commas. . . . The State produced other witnesses, who said that six persons (including Bell, Gray, and Vanlandingham) participated in the beating. Gray testified and denied his participation. Bell did not testify.

When instructing the jury, the trial judge specified that the confession was evidence only against Bell; the instructions said that the jury should not use the confession as evidence against Gray. The jury convicted both Bell and Gray. Gray appealed.

Maryland's intermediate appellate court accepted Gray's argument that *Bruton* prohibited use of the confession and set aside his conviction. . . . Maryland's highest court disagreed and reinstated the conviction. . . . We granted certiorari in order to consider *Bruton*'s application to a redaction that replaces a name with an obvious blank space or symbol or word such as "deleted."

II

In deciding whether *Bruton*'s protective rule applies to the redacted confession before us, we must consider both *Bruton*, and a later case, Richardson v. Marsh, 481 U.S. 200 (1987), which limited *Bruton*'s scope. We shall briefly summarize each of these two cases.

Bruton, as we have said, involved two defendants — Evans and Bruton — tried jointly for robbery. Evans did not testify, but the Government introduced into evidence Evans' confession, which stated that both he (Evans) and Bruton together had committed the robbery. 391 U.S., at 124. The trial judge told the jury it could consider the confession as evidence only against Evans, not against Bruton. Id., at 125.

This Court held that, despite the limiting instruction, the introduction of Evans' out-of-court confession at Bruton's trial had violated Bruton's right, protected by the Sixth Amendment, to cross-examine witnesses. Id., at 137. The Court recognized that in many circumstances a limiting instruction will adequately protect one defendant from the prejudicial effects of the introduction at a joint trial of evidence intended for use only against a different defendant. Id., at 135. But it said that

[T]here are some contexts in which the risk that the jury will not, or cannot, follow instructions is so great, and the consequences of failure so vital to the defendant, that the practical and human limitations of the jury system cannot be ignored. Such a context is presented here, where the powerfully incriminating extrajudicial statements of a codefendant, who stands accused side-by-side with the defendant, are deliberately spread before the jury in a joint trial. Not only are the incriminations devastating to the defendant but their credibility is inevitably suspect. . . . The unreliability of such evidence is intolerably compounded when the alleged accomplice, as here, does not testify and cannot be tested by cross-examination.

Id., at 135-136 (citations omitted).

The Court found that Evans' confession constituted just such a "powerfully incriminating extrajudicial statemen[t]," and that its introduction into evidence, insulated from cross-examination, violated Bruton's Sixth Amendment rights. Id., at 135.

In Richardson v. Marsh, . . . the Court considered a redacted confession. The case involved a joint murder trial of Marsh and Williams. The State had redacted the confession of one defendant, Williams, so as to "omit all reference" to his codefendant, Marsh — "indeed, to omit all indication that *anyone* other than . . . Williams" and a third person had "participated in the crime." [481 U.S.], at 203 (emphasis in original). The trial court also instructed the jury not to consider the confession against Marsh. Id., at 205. As redacted, the confession indicated that Williams and the third person had discussed the murder in the front seat of a car while they traveled to the victim's house. Id., at 203-204, n. 1. The redacted confession contained no indication that Marsh — or any other person — was in the car. Ibid. Later in the trial, however, Marsh testified that she was in the back seat of the car. Id., at 204. For that reason, in context, the confession still could have helped convince the jury that Marsh knew about the murder in advance and therefore had participated knowingly in the crime.

The Court held that this redacted confession fell outside *Bruton*'s scope and was admissible (with appropriate limiting instructions) at the joint trial. The Court distinguished Evans' confession in *Bruton* as a confession that was "incriminating on

its face," and which had "expressly implicate[d]" Bruton. 481 U.S. 200, at 208. By
contrast, Williams' confession amounted to "evidence requiring linkage" in that it
"became" incriminating in respect to Marsh "only when linked with evidence introduced later at trial." Ibid. The Court held

> that the Confrontation Clause is not violated by the admission of a nontestifying code-
> fendant's confession with a proper limiting instruction when, as here, the confession is
> redacted to eliminate not only the defendant's name, but any reference to his or her
> existence.

Id., at 211.

The Court added: "We express no opinion on the admissibility of a confession in
which the defendant's name has been replaced with a symbol or neutral pronoun."
Id., at 211, n. 5.

III

Originally, the codefendant's confession in the case before us, like that in *Bruton*,
referred to, and directly implicated another defendant. The State, however,
redacted that confession by removing the nonconfessing defendant's name. Nonetheless, unlike *Richardson*'s redacted confession, this confession refers directly to the
"existence" of the nonconfessing defendant. The State has simply replaced the nonconfessing defendant's name with a kind of symbol, namely the word "deleted" or a
blank space set off by commas. The redacted confession, for example, responded to
the question "Who was in the group that beat Stacey," with the phrase, "Me, _____,
and a few other guys." . . . And when the police witness read the confession in court,
he said the word "deleted" or "deletion" where the blank spaces appear. We therefore must decide a question that *Richardson* left open, namely whether redaction
that replaces a defendant's name with an obvious indication of deletion, such as a
blank space, the word "deleted," or a similar symbol, still falls within *Bruton*'s protective rule. We hold that it does.

Bruton, as interpreted by *Richardson*, holds that certain "powerfully incriminating
extrajudicial statements of a codefendant" — those naming another defendant —
considered as a class, are so prejudicial that limiting instructions cannot work. *Richardson*, 481 U.S., at 207; *Bruton*, 391 U.S., at 135. Unless the prosecutor wishes to
hold separate trials or to use separate juries or to abandon use of the confession, he
must redact the confession to reduce significantly or to eliminate the special prejudice that the *Bruton* Court found. Redactions that simply replace a name with an
obvious blank space or a word such as "deleted" or a symbol or other similarly obvious indications of alteration, however, leave statements that, considered as a class,
so closely resemble *Bruton*'s unredacted statements that, in our view, the law must
require the same result.

For one thing, a jury will often react similarly to an unredacted confession and a
confession redacted in this way, for the jury will often realize that the confession
refers specifically to the defendant. This is true even when the State does not blatantly link the defendant to the deleted name, as it did in this case by asking whether
Gray was arrested on the basis of information in Bell's confession as soon as the
officer had finished reading the redacted statement. Consider a simplified but typical example, a confession that reads "I, Bob Smith, along with Sam Jones, robbed

the bank." To replace the words "Sam Jones" with an obvious blank will not likely fool anyone. A juror somewhat familiar with criminal law would know immediately that the blank, in the phrase "I, Bob Smith, along with _____, robbed the bank," refers to defendant Jones. A juror who does not know the law and who therefore wonders to whom the blank might refer need only lift his eyes to Jones, sitting at counsel table, to find what will seem the obvious answer, at least if the juror hears the judge's instruction not to consider the confession as evidence against Jones, for that instruction will provide an obvious reason for the blank. A more sophisticated juror, wondering if the blank refers to someone else, might also wonder how, if it did, the prosecutor could argue the confession is reliable, for the prosecutor, after all, has been arguing that Jones, not someone else, helped Smith commit the crime.

For another thing, the obvious deletion may well call the jurors' attention specially to the removed name. By encouraging the jury to speculate about the reference, the redaction may overemphasize the importance of the confession's accusation — once the jurors work out the reference. . . .

Finally, *Bruton*'s protected statements and statements redacted to leave a blank or some other similarly obvious alteration, function the same way grammatically. They are directly accusatory. Evans' statement in *Bruton* used a proper name to point explicitly to an accused defendant. And *Bruton* held that the "powerfully incriminating" effect of what Justice Stewart called "an out-of-court accusation," 391 U.S., at 138 (concurring opinion), creates a special, and vital, need for cross-examination — a need that would be immediately obvious had the codefendant pointed directly to the defendant in the courtroom itself. The blank space in an obviously redacted confession also points directly to the defendant, and it accuses the defendant in a manner similar to Evans' use of Bruton's name or to a testifying codefendant's accusatory finger. By way of contrast, the factual statement at issue in *Richardson* — a statement about what others said in the front seat of a car — differs from directly accusatory evidence in this respect, for it does not point directly to a defendant at all.

We concede certain differences between *Bruton* and this case. A confession that uses a blank or the word "delete" (or, for that matter, a first name or a nickname) less obviously refers to the defendant than a confession that uses the defendant's full and proper name. Moreover, in some instances the person to whom the blank refers may not be clear: Although the follow-up question asked by the State in this case eliminated all doubt, the reference might not be transparent in other cases in which a confession, like the present confession, uses two (or more) blanks, even though only one other defendant appears at trial, and in which the trial indicates that there are more participants than the confession has named. Nonetheless, as we have said, we believe that, considered as a class, redactions that replace a proper name with an obvious blank, the word "delete," a symbol, or similarly notify the jury that a name has been deleted are similar enough to *Bruton*'s unredacted confessions as to warrant the same legal results.

IV

. . . We concede that *Richardson* placed outside the scope of *Bruton*'s rule those statements that incriminate inferentially. 481 U.S., at 208. We also concede that the jury must use inference to connect the statement in this redacted confession with the defendant. But inference pure and simple cannot make the critical difference, for if it did, then *Richardson* would also place outside *Bruton*'s scope confessions that use shortened first names, nicknames, descriptions as unique as the "redhaired, bearded, one-eyed man-with-a-limp," United States v. Grinnell Corp., 384 U.S. 563, 591 (1966) (Fortas, J., dissenting), and perhaps even full names of defendants who are always known by a nickname. This Court has assumed, however, that nicknames and specific descriptions fall inside, not outside, *Bruton*'s protection. . . .

That being so, *Richardson* must depend in significant part upon the *kind* of, not the simple *fact* of, inference. *Richardson*'s inferences involved statements that did not refer directly to the defendant himself and which became incriminating "only when linked with evidence introduced later at trial." 481 U.S., at 208. The inferences at issue here involve statements that, despite redaction, obviously refer directly to someone, often obviously the defendant, and which involve inferences that a jury ordinarily could make immediately, even were the confession the very first item introduced at trial. Moreover, the redacted confession with the blank prominent on its face, in *Richardson*'s words, "*facially* incriminat[es]" the codefendant. Id., at 209 (emphasis added). Like the confession in *Bruton* itself, the accusation that the redacted confession makes "is more vivid than inferential incrimination, and hence more difficult to thrust out of mind." 481 U.S., at 208.

Nor are the policy reasons that *Richardson* provided in support of its conclusion applicable here. *Richardson* expressed concern lest application of *Bruton*'s rule apply where "redaction" of confessions, particularly "confessions incriminating by connection," would often "not [be] possible," thereby forcing prosecutors too often to abandon use either of the confession or of a joint trial. 481 U.S., at 209. Additional redaction of a confession that uses a blank space, the word "delete," or a symbol, however, normally is possible. Consider as an example a portion of the confession before us: The witness who read the confession told the jury that the confession (among other things) said,

> *Question*:   Who was in the group that beat Stacey?
> *Answer*:   Me, deleted, deleted, and a few other guys. . . .

Why could the witness not, instead, have said:

> *Question*:   Who was in the group that beat Stacey?
> *Answer*:   Me and a few other guys.

The *Richardson* Court also feared that the inclusion, within *Bruton*'s protective rule, of confessions that incriminated "by connection" too often would provoke mistrials, or would unnecessarily lead prosecutors to abandon the confession or joint trial, because neither the prosecutors nor the judge could easily predict, until after the introduction of all the evidence, whether or not *Bruton* had barred use of the confession. 481 U.S., at 209. To include the use of blanks, the word "delete," symbols, or other indications of redaction, within *Bruton*'s protections, however, runs no such risk. Their use is easily identified prior to trial and does not depend, in any special way, upon the other evidence introduced in the case. We also note that several Circuits have interpreted *Bruton* similarly for many years, . . . yet no one has told us of any significant practical difficulties arising out of their administration of that rule.

For these reasons, we hold that the confession here at issue, which substituted blanks and the word "delete" for the respondent's proper name, falls within the class of statements to which *Bruton*'s protections apply.

The judgment of the Court of Appeals is vacated, and the case is remanded for further proceedings not inconsistent with this opinion.

It is so ordered.

JUSTICE SCALIA, with whom CHIEF JUSTICE REHNQUIST, JUSTICE KENNEDY, and JUSTICE THOMAS join, dissenting.

In Richardson v. Marsh, 481 U.S. 200 (1987), we declined to extend the "narrow exception" of Bruton v. United States, 391 U.S. 123 (1968), beyond confessions that facially incriminate a defendant. Today the Court "concede[s] that *Richardson* placed outside the scope of *Bruton*'s rule those statements that incriminate inferentially," . . . "concede[s] that the jury must use inference to connect the statement in this redacted confession with the defendant," . . . but nonetheless extends *Bruton* to confessions that have been redacted to delete the defendant's name. Because I believe the line drawn in *Richardson* should not be changed, I respectfully dissent.

The almost invariable assumption of the law is that jurors follow their instructions. . . . This rule "is a pragmatic one, rooted less in the absolute certitude that the presumption is true than in the belief that it represents a reasonable practical accommodation of the interests of the state and the defendant in the criminal justice process." *Richardson*, 481 U.S., at 211. . . . The same applies to codefendant confessions: "[A] witness whose testimony is introduced at a joint trial is not considered to be a witness 'against' a defendant if the jury is instructed to consider that testimony only against a codefendant." *Richardson*, supra, at 206. In *Bruton*, we recognized a "narrow exception" to this rule. . . .

We declined in *Richardson*, however, to extend *Bruton* to confessions that incriminate only by inference from other evidence. . . . Today the Court struggles to decide whether a confession redacted to omit the defendant's name is incriminating on its face or by inference. On the one hand, the Court "concede[s] that the jury must use inference to connect the statement in this redacted confession with the defendant," . . . but later asserts, on the other hand, that "the redacted confession with the blank prominent on its face . . . *'facially* incriminat[es]'" him. . . . The Court should have stopped with its concession: the statement "Me, deleted, deleted, and a few other guys" does not facially incriminate anyone but the speaker. The Court's analogizing of "deleted" to a physical description that clearly identifies the defendant . . . does not survive scrutiny. By "facially incriminating," we have meant incriminating independent of other evidence introduced at trial. *Richardson*, supra, 481 U.S. 200, at 208-209. Since the defendant's appearance at counsel table is not evidence, the description "red-haired, bearded, one-eyed man-with-a-limp," . . . would be facially incriminating — unless, of course, the defendant had dyed his hair black and shaved his beard before trial, and the prosecution introduced evidence concerning his former appearance. Similarly, the statement "Me, Kevin Gray, and a few other guys" would be facially incriminating, unless the defendant's name set forth in the indictment was not Kevin Gray, and evidence was introduced to the effect that he sometimes used "Kevin Gray" as an alias. By contrast, the person to whom "deleted" refers in "Me, deleted, deleted, and a few other guys" is not apparent from anything the jury knows independent of the evidence at trial. Though the jury may speculate, the statement expressly implicates no one but the speaker.

Of course the Court is correct that confessions redacted to omit the defendant's name are more likely to incriminate than confessions redacted to omit any reference to his existence. But it is also true — and more relevant here — that confessions redacted to omit the defendant's name are *less* likely to incriminate than confessions that expressly state it. The latter are "powerfully incriminating" as a class, *Bruton,* supra, at 124, n. 1, 135; the former are not so. . . . The issue [here] is not whether the confession incriminated petitioner, but whether the incrimination is so "powerful" that we must depart from the normal presumption that the jury follows its instructions. *Richardson,* supra, at 208, n. 3. I think it is not — and I am certain that drawing the line for departing from the ordinary rule at the *facial identification* of the defendant makes more sense than drawing it anywhere else.

The Court's extension of *Bruton* to name-redacted confessions "as a class" will seriously compromise "society's compelling interest in finding, convicting, and punishing those who violate the law." Moran v. Burbine, 475 U.S. 412, 426 (1986) (citation omitted). . . . The Court minimizes the damage that it does by suggesting that "[a]dditional redaction of a confession that uses a blank space, the word 'delete,' or a symbol . . . normally is possible." In the present case, it asks, why could the police officer not have testified that Bell's answer was "Me and a few other guys"? . . . The answer, it seems obvious to me, is because that is not what Bell said. Bell's answer was "Me, Tank, Kevin and a few other guys." Introducing the statement with full disclosure of deletions is one thing; introducing as the complete statement what was in fact only a part is something else. And of course even concealed deletions from the text will often not do the job that the Court demands. For inchoate offenses — conspiracy in particular — redaction to delete all reference to a confederate would often render the confession nonsensical. If the question was "Who agreed to beat Stacey?" and the answer was "Me and Kevin," we might redact the answer to "Me and [deleted]," or perhaps to "Me and somebody else," but surely not to just "Me" — for that would no longer be a confession to the conspiracy charge, but rather the foundation for an insanity defense. To my knowledge we have never before endorsed — and to my strong belief we ought not endorse — the redaction of a statement by some means other than the deletion of certain words, with the fact of the deletion shown.[1] The risk to the integrity of our system (not to mention the increase in its complexity) posed by the approval of such free-lance editing seems to me infinitely greater than the risk posed by the entirely honest reproduction that the Court disapproves.

The United States Constitution guarantees, not a perfect system of criminal justice (as to which there can be considerable disagreement), but a minimum standard of fairness. Lest we lose sight of the forest for the trees, it should be borne in mind that federal and state rules of criminal procedure — which can afford to seek perfection because they can be more readily changed — exclude nontestifying codefendant confessions even where the Sixth Amendment does not. Under the Federal Rules of Criminal Procedure (and Maryland's), a trial court may order separate trials if joinder will prejudice a defendant. See Fed. Rule Crim. Proc. 14; Md. Crim. Rule 4-253(c) (1998). . . . The federal rule expressly contemplates that in ruling on a severance motion the court will inspect "in camera any statements or confessions

---

1. The Court is mistaken to suggest that in Richardson v. Marsh, 481 U.S. 200 (1987), we endorsed rewriting confessions as a proper method of redaction. . . . There the parties agreed to the method of redaction, . . . and we had no occasion to address the propriety of editing confessions without showing the nature of the editing.

made by the defendants which the government intends to introduce in evidence at the trial." Fed. Rule Crim. Proc. 14. Federal and most state trial courts (including Maryland's) also have the discretion to exclude unfairly prejudicial (albeit probative) evidence. Fed. Rule Evid. 403; Md. Rule Evid. 5-403 (1998). Here, petitioner moved for a severance on the ground that the admission of Bell's confession would be unfairly prejudicial. The trial court denied the motion, explaining that where a confession names two others, and the evidence is that five or six others participated, redaction of petitioner's name would not leave the jury with the "unavoidable inference" that Bell implicated Gray. . . .

I do not understand the Court to disagree that the redaction itself left unclear to whom the blank referred.[2] . . . That being so, the rule set forth in *Richardson* applies, and the statement could constitutionally be admitted with limiting instruction. This remains, insofar as the Sixth Amendment is concerned, the most "reasonable practical accommodation of the interests of the state and the defendant in the criminal justice process." *Richardson*, 481 U.S., at 211. For these reasons, I would affirm the judgment of the Court of Appeals of Maryland.

NOTES AND QUESTIONS

1. Keep in mind that the issue in *Gray* is not whether the codefendant statement should be admissible against the defendant — everyone agrees that it should not be — but rather how the courts should address and remedy this recurring problem. Does it seem strange that the Court should rely so heavily on the (probably overrated) power of curative instructions to solve similar problems in other contexts, as we have already seen, yet adopt a strict prophylactic rule against admissibility of codefendant statements based on a lack of confidence in curative instructions? Does the Court have any empirical evidence to support the implicit conclusion that codefendant statements are uniquely prejudicial, so much so that they deserve to be treated as a special exception to the usual rule about curative instructions?

2. What about the not uncommon situation of "interlocking confessions," where the confession of the codefendant overlaps in significant respects with a statement made by the defendant himself? In Parker v. Randolph, 442 U.S. 62 (1979), a plurality of the Court suggested that such confessions need not be excluded under *Bruton*, on the ground that they "will seldom, if ever, be of the 'devastating' character referred to in *Bruton* when the incriminated defendant has admitted his own guilt." See *Randolph*, 442 U.S., at 73. Thus, impeaching the codefendant "would likely yield small advantage." Id.

But in Cruz v. New York, 481 U.S. 186 (1987), a majority of the Court came out the other way on the issue. In *Cruz*, the defendant, Eulogio Cruz, was under investigation along with his brother, Benjamin Cruz, for the murder of Jerry Cruz (who was not related to Eulogio and Benjamin). During the investigation, Norberto Cruz,

---

2. The Court does believe, however, that the answer to a "follow-up question" — "All right, now, officer, after he gave you that information, you subsequently were able to arrest Mr. Kevin Gray; is that correct?" ("That's correct") — "eliminated all doubt" as to the subject of the redaction. Ante, at 2, 8. That is probably not so, and is certainly far from clear. . . . But if the question *did* bring the redaction home to the defendant, surely that shows the impropriety of the question rather than of the redaction — *and the question was not objected to*. The failure to object deprives petitioner of the right to complain. . . . Of course the Court's reliance upon this testimony belies its contention that name-redacted confessions are powerfully incriminating "as a class." . . .

Jerry's brother, told the police about incriminating statements that Eulogio and Benjamin had previously made to him, concerning the murder of a Bronx gas-station attendant. When the police questioned Benjamin about Jerry's murder, he denied any involvement in it. But he confessed, on videotape, to the gas-station murder. Eulogio and Benjamin were charged with the gas-station murder. At a joint trial, the prosecution introduced Benjamin's confession and also called Norberto as a witness to testify about the statements made by Eulogio and Benjamin. Eulogio's lawyer argued that Norberto's testimony was false and stemmed from Norberto's belief that Eulogio had killed his brother, Jerry. Both Eulogio and Benjamin were convicted.

The Court reversed the convictions. In an opinion by Justice Scalia, the Court explained:

> [I]t seems to us that "interlocking" bears a positively inverse relationship to devastation. A codefendant's confession will be relatively harmless if the incriminating story it tells is different from that which the defendant himself is alleged to have told, but enormously damaging if it confirms, in all essential respects, the defendant's alleged confession. It might be otherwise if the defendant were *standing by* his confession, in which case it could be said that the codefendant's confession does no more than support the defendant's very own case. But in the real world of criminal litigation, the defendant is seeking to *avoid* his own confession — on the ground that it was not accurately reported, or that it was not really true when made. In the present case, for example, [Eulogio] sought to establish that Norberto had a motive for falsely reporting a confession that never in fact occurred. In such circumstances a codefendant's confession that corroborates the defendant's confession significantly harms the defendant's case, whereas one that is positively incompatible gives credence to the defendant's assertion that his own alleged confession was nonexistent or false.

Id., at 192.

3. As noted by the *Gray* dissent, the *Bruton* problem is one reason why trial courts sometimes grant severance motions under Federal Rule of Criminal Procedure 14. See also Chapter 9, supra. One prominent recent example was the Oklahoma City bombing case, where the trial court granted a motion to sever the trials of Timothy McVeigh and Terry Nichols on the ground that the admission of out-of-court statements by Nichols (which could not effectively be redacted), at a joint trial, would "profoundly prejudice[]" McVeigh. See United States v. McVeigh, 169 F.R.D. 362 (1996).

D.   Influences upon the Jury

Although jury trials may be revered in American history, juries are not perfect. Indeed, the use of juries in criminal cases creates special problems — problems that would not arise if the system relied on bench trials exclusively. Precisely because of the jury's amateur status, it is peculiarly susceptible to certain improper influences that would be less likely to affect the decisions of a professionally trained and experienced trial judge. In Chapter 11, we consider the effect of pretrial publicity on the location of the trial. Here we address the issues of improper prosecutorial argument.

DARDEN v. WAINWRIGHT

Certiorari to the United States Court of Appeals for the Eleventh Circuit
477 U.S. 168 (1986)

JUSTICE POWELL delivered the opinion of the Court. This case presents three questions concerning the validity of petitioner's criminal conviction and death sentence: (i) whether the exclusion for cause of a member of the venire violated the principles announced in Wainwright v. Witt, 469 U.S. 412 (1985); (ii) whether the prosecution's closing argument during the guilt phase of a bifurcated trial rendered the trial fundamentally unfair and deprived the sentencing determination of the reliability required by the Eighth Amendment; and (iii) whether petitioner was denied effective assistance of counsel at the sentencing phase of his trial.

I

Petitioner was tried and found guilty of murder, robbery, and assault with intent to kill in the Circuit Court for Citrus County, Florida, in January 1974. Pursuant to Florida's capital sentencing statute, the same jury that convicted petitioner heard further testimony and argument in order to make a nonbinding recommendation as to whether a death sentence should be imposed. The jury recommended a death sentence, and the trial judge followed that recommendation. On direct appeal, the Florida Supreme Court affirmed the conviction and the sentence. Petitioner made several of the same arguments in that appeal that he makes here. With respect to the prosecutorial misconduct claim, the court disapproved of the closing argument, but reasoned that the law required a new trial "only in those cases in which it is reasonably evident that the remarks might have influenced the jury to reach a more severe verdict of guilt . . . or in which the comment is unfair." . . . It concluded that the comments had not rendered petitioner's trial unfair. . . . This Court granted certiorari, . . . limited the grant to the claim of prosecutorial misconduct, . . . heard oral argument, and dismissed the writ as improvidently granted, 430 U.S. 704 (1977).

Petitioner then sought federal habeas corpus relief, raising the same claims he raises here. The District Court denied the petition. . . . A divided panel of the Court of Appeals for the Eleventh Circuit affirmed. . . . The Court of Appeals granted rehearing en banc, and affirmed the District Court by an equally divided court. . . . Following a second rehearing en banc the Court of Appeals reversed on the claim of improper excusal of a member of the venire. . . . This Court granted the State's petition for certiorari on that claim, vacated the Court of Appeals' judgment, and remanded for reconsideration in light of Wainwright v. Witt. 469 U.S. 1202 (1985). On remand, the en banc court denied relief. . . . Petitioner filed an application for a stay of his execution that this Court treated as a petition for certiorari and granted, at the same time staying his execution. . . . We now affirm.

II

Because of the nature of petitioner's claims, the facts of this case will be stated in more detail than is normally necessary in this Court. On September 8, 1973, at about 5:30 p.m., a black adult male entered Carl's Furniture Store near Lakeland, Florida. The only other person in the store was the proprietor, Mrs. Turman, who lived with her husband in a house behind the store. Mr. Turman, who worked nights at a juvenile home, had awakened at about 5 p.m., had a cup of coffee at the store with his wife, and returned home to let their dogs out for a run. Mrs. Turman showed the man around the store. He stated that he was interested in purchasing about $600 worth of furniture for a rental unit, and asked to see several different items. He left the store briefly, stating that his wife would be back to look at some of the items.

The same man returned just a few minutes later asking to see some stoves, and inquiring about the price. When Mrs. Turman turned toward the adding machine, he grabbed her and pressed a gun to her back, saying "Do as I say and you won't get hurt." He took her to the rear of the store and told her to open the cash register. He took the money, then ordered her to the part of the store where some box springs and mattresses were stacked against the wall. At that time Mr. Turman appeared at the back door. Mrs. Turman screamed while the man reached across her right shoulder and shot Mr. Turman between the eyes. Mr. Turman fell backwards, with one foot partially in the building. Ordering Mrs. Turman not to move, the man tried to pull Mr. Turman into the building and close the door, but could not do so because one of Mr. Turman's feet was caught in the door. The man left Mr. Turman faceup in the rain, and told Mrs. Turman to get down on the floor approximately five feet from where her husband lay dying. While she begged to go to her husband, he told her to remove her false teeth. He unzipped his pants, unbuckled his belt, and demanded that Mrs. Turman perform oral sex on him. She began to cry "Lord, have mercy." He told her to get up and go towards the front of the store.

Meanwhile, a neighbor family, the Arnolds, became aware that something had happened to Mr. Turman. The mother sent her 16-year-old son Phillip, a part-time employee at the furniture store, to help. When Phillip reached the back door he saw Mr. Turman lying partially in the building. When Phillip opened the door to take Turman's body inside, Mrs. Turman shouted "Phillip, no, go back." Phillip did not know what she meant and asked the man to help get Turman inside. He replied, "Sure, buddy, I will help you." As Phillip looked up, the man was pointing a gun in his face. He pulled the trigger and the gun misfired; he pulled the trigger again and shot Phillip in the mouth. Phillip started to run away, and was shot in the neck. While he was still running, he was shot a third time in the side. Despite these wounds, Phillip managed to stumble to the home of a neighbor, Mrs. Edith Hill. She had her husband call an ambulance while she tried to stop Phillip's bleeding. While she was helping Phillip, she saw a late model green Chevrolet leave the store and head towards Tampa on State Highway 92. Phillip survived the incident; Mr. Turman, who never regained consciousness, died later that night.

Minutes after the murder petitioner was driving towards Tampa on Highway 92, just a few miles away from the furniture store. He was out on furlough from a Florida prison, and was driving a car borrowed from his girl friend in Tampa. He was driving fast on a wet road. Petitioner testified that as he came up on a line of cars in his lane, he was unable to slow down. He attempted to pass, but was forced off the road to avoid a head-on collision with an oncoming car. Petitioner crashed into a telephone pole. The driver of the oncoming car, John Stone, stopped his car and went to petitioner to see if he could help. Stone testified that as he approached the car, petitioner was zipping up his pants and buckling his belt. Police at the crash site later identified petitioner's car as a 1969 Chevrolet Impala of greenish golden brown color. Petitioner paid a bystander to give him a ride to Tampa. Petitioner later returned with a wrecker, only to find that the car had been towed away by the police.

By the time the police arrived at the scene of the accident, petitioner had left. The fact that the car matched the description of the car leaving the scene of the murder, and that the accident had occurred within three and one-half miles of the furniture store and within minutes of the murder, led police to suspect that the car was driven by the murderer. They searched the area. An officer found a pistol — a revolver — about 40 feet from the crash site. The arrangement of shells within the chambers exactly matched the pattern that should have been found in the murder weapon: one shot, one misfire, followed by three shots, with a live shell remaining in the next chamber to be fired. A specialist for the Federal Bureau of Investigation examined the pistol and testified that it was a Smith & Wesson .38 special revolver. It had been manufactured as a standard .38; it later was sent to England to be rebored, making it a much rarer type of gun than the standard .38. An examination of the bullet that killed Mr. Turman revealed that it came from a .38 Smith & Wesson special.

On the day following the murder petitioner was arrested at his girl friend's house in Tampa. A few days later Mrs. Turman identified him at a preliminary hearing as her husband's murderer. Phillip Arnold selected petitioner's picture out of a spread of six photographs as the man who had shot him.[1] By that time, a Public Defender had been appointed to represent petitioner.

As petitioner's arguments all relate to incidents in the course of his trial, they will be taken up, together with the relevant facts, in chronological order.

III

[This section of the Court's opinion, rejecting the defendant's claim of improper exclusion of a prospective juror, is omitted.]

IV

Petitioner next contends that the prosecution's closing argument at the guilt-innocence stage of the trial rendered his conviction fundamentally unfair and

---

1. There are some minor discrepancies in the eyewitness identification. Mrs. Turman first described her assailant immediately after the murder while her husband was being taken to the emergency room. She told the investigating officer that the attacker was a heavy-set man. . . . When asked if he was "neat in his appearance, clean-looking, clean-shaven," she responded "[a]s far as I can remember, yes, sir." Ibid. She also stated to the officer that she thought that the attacker was about her height, 5' 6" tall, and that he was wearing a pullover shirt with a stripe around the neck. . . . The first time she saw petitioner after the attack was when she identified him at the preliminary hearing. She had not read any newspaper accounts of the crime, nor had she seen any picture of petitioner. When she was asked if petitioner was the man who had committed the crimes, she said yes. She also repeatedly identified him at trial.

Phillip Arnold first identified petitioner in a photo lineup while in the hospital. He could not speak at the time, and in response to the written question whether petitioner had a mustache, Phillip wrote back "I don't think so." . . . Phillip also testified at trial that the attacker was a heavy-set man wearing a dull, light color knit shirt with a ring around the neck. . . . He testified that the man was almost his height, about 6' 2" tall.

A motorist who stopped at the scene of the accident testified that petitioner was wearing a white or off-grey button-down shirt and that he had a slight mustache. . . . In fact, the witness stated that he "didn't know it was that [the mustache] or the raindrops on him or not. I couldn't really tell that much to it, it was real thin, that's all." . . . Petitioner is about 5' 10" tall, and at the time of trial testified that he weighed about 175 pounds.

deprived the sentencing determination of the reliability that the Eighth Amendment requires.

It is helpful as an initial matter to place these remarks in context. Closing argument came at the end of several days of trial. Because of a state procedural rule petitioner's counsel had the opportunity to present the initial summation as well as a rebuttal to the prosecutors' closing arguments. The prosecutors' comments must be evaluated in light of the defense argument that preceded it, which blamed the Polk County Sheriff 's Office for a lack of evidence,[5] alluded to the death penalty,[6] characterized the perpetrator of the crimes as an "animal,"[7] and contained counsel's personal opinion of the strength of the State's evidence.[8]

The prosecutors then made their closing argument. That argument deserves the condemnation it has received from every court to review it, although no court has held that the argument rendered the trial unfair. Several comments attempted to place some of the blame for the crime on the Division of Corrections, because Darden was on weekend furlough from a prison sentence when the crime occurred.[9] Some comments implied that the death penalty would be the only guarantee against a future similar act.[10] Others incorporated the defense's use of the word "animal."[11] Prosecutor McDaniel made several offensive comments reflecting an emotional reaction to the case.[12] These comments undoubtedly were improper. But as both the District Court and the original panel of the Court of Appeals (whose opinion on this issue still stands) recognized, it "is not enough that the prosecutors' remarks were undesirable or even universally condemned." . . . The relevant question is whether the prosecutors' comments "so infected the trial with unfairness as to make the

---

5. "The Judge is going to tell you to consider the evidence or the lack of evidence. We have a lack of evidence, almost criminally negligent on the part of the Polk County Sheriff 's Office in this case. You could go on and on about it." . . .

6. "They took a coincidence and magnified that into a capital case. And they are asking you to kill a man on coincidence." . . .

7. "The first witness that you saw was Mrs. Turman, who was a pathetic figure; who worked and struggled all of her life to build what little she had, the little furniture store; and a woman who was robbed, sexually assaulted, and then had her husband slaughtered before her eyes, by what would have to be a vicious animal." . . . "And this murderer ran after him, aimed again, and this poor kid with half his brains blown away. . . . It's the work of an animal, there's no doubt about it." . . .

8. "So they come on up here and ask Citrus County people to kill the man. You will be instructed on lesser included offenses. . . . The question is, do they have enough evidence to kill that man, enough evidence? And I honestly do not think they do." . . .

9. "As far as I am concerned, there should be another Defendant in this courtroom, one more, and that is the division of corrections, the prisons. . . . Can we expect him to stay in a prison when they go there? Can't we expect them to stay locked up once they go there? Do we know that they're going to be out on the public with guns, drinking?" . . . "Yes, there is another Defendant, but I regret that I know of no charges to place upon him, except the public condemnation of them, condemn them." . . .

10. "I will ask you to advise the Court to give him death. That's the only way that I know that he is not going to get out on the public. It's the only way I know. It's the only way I can be sure of it. It's the only way that anybody can be sure of it now, because the people that turned him loose — ." . . .

11. "As far as I am concerned, and as Mr. Maloney said as he identified this man, this person as an animal, this animal was on the public for one reason." . . .

12. "He shouldn't be out of his cell unless he has a leash on him and a prison guard at the other end of that leash." . . . "I wish [Mr. Turman] had had a shotgun in his hand when he walked in the back door and blown his [Darden's] face off. I wish that I could see him sitting here with no face, blown away by a shotgun." . . . "I wish someone had walked in the back door and blown his head off at that point." . . . "He fired in the boy's back, number five, saving one. Didn't get a chance to use it. I wish he had used it on himself." . . . "I wish he had been killed in the accident, but he wasn't. Again, we are unlucky that time." . . . "[D]on't forget what he has done according to those witnesses, to make every attempt to change his appearance from September the 8th, 1973. The hair, the goatee, even the moustache and the weight. The only thing he hasn't done that I know of is cut his throat." . . . After this, the last in a series of such comments, defense counsel objected for the first time.

resulting conviction a denial of due process." Donnelly v. DeChristoforo, 416 U.S. 637 (1974). . . .

Under this standard of review, we agree with the reasoning of every court to consider these comments that they did not deprive petitioner of a fair trial.[13] The prosecutors' argument did not manipulate or misstate the evidence, nor did it implicate other specific rights of the accused such as the right to counsel or the right to remain silent. . . . Much of the objectionable content was invited by or was responsive to the opening summation of the defense. As we explained in United States v. Young, 470 U.S. 1 (1985), the idea of "invited response" is used not to excuse improper comments, but to determine their effect on the trial as a whole. Id., at 13. The trial court instructed the jurors several times that their decision was to be made on the basis of the evidence alone, and that the arguments of counsel were not evidence. The weight of the evidence against petitioner was heavy; the "overwhelming eyewitness and circumstantial evidence to support a finding of guilt on all charges," . . . reduced the likelihood that the jury's decision was influenced by argument. Finally, defense counsel made the tactical decision not to present any witness other than petitioner. This decision not only permitted them to give their summation prior to the prosecution's closing argument, but also gave them the opportunity to make a final rebuttal argument. Defense counsel were able to use the opportunity for rebuttal very effectively, turning much of the prosecutors' closing argument against them by placing many of the prosecutors' comments and actions in a light that was more likely to engender strong disapproval than result in inflamed passions against petitioner.[14] For these reasons, we agree with the District Court below that "Darden's trial was not perfect — few are — but neither was it fundamentally unfair." . . .[15]

V

[This section of the Court's opinion, rejecting the defendant's claim of ineffective assistance of counsel based on failure to develop mitigating evidence at the capital sentencing phase of the trial, is omitted.]

---

13. Justice Blackmun's dissenting opinion argues that because of prosecutorial misconduct petitioner did not receive a fair trial. The dissent states that the Court is "willing to tolerate not only imperfection but a level of fairness and reliability so low it should make conscientious prosecutors cringe." . . . We agree that the argument was, and deserved to be, condemned. . . . Conscientious prosecutors will recognize, however, that *every court* that criticized the argument went on to hold that the *fairness* of petitioner's trial was not affected by the prosecutors' argument. . . .

14. "Mr. McDaniel made an impassioned plea . . . how many times did he repeat [it]? I wish you had been shot, I wish they had blown his face away. My God, I get the impression he would like to be the man that stands there and pulls the switch on him." . . .

One of Darden's counsel testified at the habeas corpus hearing that he made the tactical decision not to object to the improper comments. Based on his long experience with prosecutor McDaniel, he knew McDaniel would "get much more vehement in his remarks if you allowed him to go on." By not immediately objecting, he hoped to encourage the prosecution to commit reversible error. . . .

15. Justice Blackmun's dissenting opinion mistakenly argues that the Court today finds, in essence, that any error was harmless, and then criticizes the Court for not applying the harmless-error standard. . . . We do not decide the claim of prosecutorial misconduct on the ground that it was harmless error. In our view of the case, that issue is not presented. Rather, we agree with the holding of every court that has addressed the issue, that the prosecutorial argument, in the context of the facts and circumstances of this case, did not render petitioner's trial unfair — i.e., that it was not constitutional error.

VI

The judgment of the Court of Appeals is affirmed, and the case is remanded for proceedings consistent with this opinion.

It is so ordered. [The concurring opinion of Chief Justice Burger and the dissenting opinion of Justice Brennan are omitted.]

JUSTICE BLACKMUN, with whom JUSTICE BRENNAN, JUSTICE MARSHALL, and JUSTICE STEVENS join, dissenting.

Although the Constitution guarantees a criminal defendant only "a fair trial [and] not a perfect one," . . . this Court has stressed repeatedly in the decade since Gregg v. Georgia, 428 U.S. 153 (1976), that the Eighth Amendment requires a heightened degree of reliability in any case where a State seeks to take the defendant's life. Today's opinion, however, reveals a Court willing to tolerate not only imperfection but a level of fairness and reliability so low it should make conscientious prosecutors cringe.

I

A

The Court's discussion of Darden's claim of prosecutorial misconduct is noteworthy for its omissions. Despite the fact that earlier this Term the Court relied heavily on standards governing the professional responsibility of defense counsel in ruling that an attorney's actions did not deprive his client of any constitutional right, see Nix v. Whiteside, 475 U.S. 157, 166-171 (1986), today it entirely ignores standards governing the professional responsibility of prosecutors in reaching the conclusion that the summations of Darden's prosecutors did not deprive him of a fair trial. . . .

The prosecutors' remarks in this case reflect behavior as to which "virtually all the sources speak with one voice," Nix v. Whiteside, supra, at 166, that is, a voice of strong condemnation. The following brief comparison of established standards of prosecutorial conduct with the prosecutors' behavior in this case merely illustrates, but hardly exhausts, the scope of the misconduct involved:

1. "A lawyer shall not . . . state a personal opinion as to . . . the credibility of a witness . . . or the guilt or innocence of an accused." Model Rules of Professional Conduct, Rule 3.4(e) (1984); see also Code of Professional Responsibility, DR 7-106(C)(4) (1980); ABA Standards for Criminal Justice 3-5.8(b) (2d ed. 1980). Yet one prosecutor, White, stated: "I am convinced, as convinced as I know I am standing before you today, that Willie Jasper Darden is a murderer, that he murdered Mr. Turman, that he robbed Mrs. Turman and that he shot to kill Phillip Arnold. I will be convinced of that the rest of my life." . . . And the other prosecutor, McDaniel, stated, with respect to Darden's testimony: "Well, let me tell you something: If I am ever over in that chair over there, facing life or death, life imprisonment or death, I guarantee you I will lie until my teeth fall out." . . .

2. "The prosecutor should refrain from argument which would divert the jury from its duty to decide the case on the evidence, by injecting issues broader than the guilt or innocence of the accused under the controlling law, or by making predictions of the consequences of the jury's verdict." ABA Standards for Criminal Justice

3-5.8(d) (2d ed. 1980); cf. Model Rules of Professional Conduct, Rule 3.4(e); Code of Professional Responsibility, DR 7-106(C)(7); ABA Standards for Criminal Justice 3-6.1(c) (2d ed. 1980). Yet McDaniel's argument was filled with references to Darden's status as a prisoner on furlough who "shouldn't be out of his cell unless he has a leash on him." . . . Again and again, he sought to put on trial an absent "defendant," the State Department of Corrections that had furloughed Darden. . . . He also implied that defense counsel would use improper tricks to deflect the jury from the real issue. . . . Darden's status as a furloughed prisoner, the release policies of the Department of Corrections, and his counsel's anticipated tactics obviously had no legal relevance to the question the jury was being asked to decide: whether he had committed the robbery and murder at the Turmans' furniture store. Indeed, the State argued before this Court that McDaniel's remarks were harmless precisely because he "failed to discuss the issues, the weight of the evidence, or the credibility of the witnesses." . . .

3. "The prosecutor should not use arguments calculated to inflame the passions or prejudices of the jury." ABA Standards for Criminal Justice 3-5.8(c) (2d ed. 1980). . . . Yet McDaniel repeatedly expressed a wish "that I could see [Darden] sitting here with no face, blown away by a shotgun." . . . Indeed, I do not think McDaniel's summation, taken as a whole, can accurately be described as anything but a relentless and single-minded attempt to inflame the jury.

B

The Court . . . relies on the standard established in Donnelly v. DeChristoforo, 416 U.S. 637, 643 (1974), for deciding when a prosecutor's comments at a state trial render that trial fundamentally unfair. It omits, however, any discussion of the facts, so different from those in this case, that led the Court to conclude in *DeChristoforo* that that defendant had not been deprived of a fair trial.

DeChristoforo concerned "two remarks made by the prosecutor during the course of his rather lengthy closing argument to the jury." Id., at 640. One remark was "but one moment of an extended trial." Id., at 645. And even the more objectionable remark was so "ambiguous," ibid., that it provided no basis for inferring either that the prosecutor "intend[ed] [it] to have its most damaging meaning or that a jury, sitting through lengthy exhortation, [would] draw that meaning from the plethora of less damaging interpretations," id., at 647. Finally, the trial judge in *DeChristoforo* expressly instructed the jury to disregard the improper statements. Id., at 645. This Court's holding thus rested on its conclusion that the prosecutor's comments were neither so extensive nor so improper as to violate the Constitution.

Far from involving "ambiguous" statements that "might or might not" affect the jury, id., at 647, the remarks at issue here were "focused, unambiguous, and strong." Caldwell v. Mississippi, 472 U.S. 320, 340 (1985). It is impossible to read the transcript of McDaniel's summation without seeing it as a calculated and sustained attempt to inflame the jury. Almost every page contains at least one offensive or improper statement; some pages contain little else. The misconduct here was not "slight or confined to a single instance, but . . . was pronounced and persistent, with a probable cumulative effect upon the jury which cannot be disregarded as inconsequential." . . .

C

The Court presents what is, for me, an entirely unpersuasive one-page laundry list of reasons for ignoring this blatant misconduct. First, the Court says that the summations "did not manipulate or misstate the evidence [or] . . . implicate other specific rights of the accused such as the right to counsel or the right to remain silent." . . . With all respect, that observation is quite beside the point. The "solemn purpose of endeavoring to ascertain the truth . . . is the sine qua non of a fair trial," Estes v. Texas, 381 U.S. 532, 540 (1965), and the summations cut to the very heart of the Due Process Clause by diverting the jury's attention "from the ultimate question of guilt or innocence that should be the central concern in a criminal proceeding." . . .

Second, the Court says that "[m]uch of the objectionable content was invited by or was responsive to the opening summation of the defense." . . . The Court identifies four portions of the defense summation that it thinks somehow "invited" McDaniel's sustained barrage. The State, however, did not object to any of these statements, and, to my mind, none of them is so objectionable that it would have justified a tactical decision to interrupt the defense summation and perhaps irritate the jury. . . .

The Court begins by stating that defense counsel "blamed" the Sheriff's Office for a lack of evidence. . . . The Court does not identify which, if any, of McDaniel's remarks represented a response to this statement. I cannot believe that the Court is suggesting, for example, that defense counsel's one mention of the "almost crimina[l] negligen[ce] on the part of the Polk County Sheriff 's Office," . . . justified McDaniel's express and repeated wish that he could try the Department of Corrections for murder. . . .

Next, the Court notes that defense counsel "alluded" to the death penalty. . . . While this allusion might have justified McDaniel's statement that "you are merely to determine his innocence or guilt, nothing else," . . . it could hardly justify, for example, McDaniel's expressions of his personal wish that Darden be "blown away by a shotgun." . . .

Moreover, the Court says, defense counsel twice referred to the perpetrator as an "animal." . . . It is entirely unclear to me why this characterization called for any response from the prosecutor at all. Taken in context, defense counsel's statements did nothing more than tell the jury that, although everyone agreed that a heinous crime had been committed, the issue on which it should focus was whether Darden had committed it.

Finally, the Court finds that Darden brought upon himself McDaniel's tirade because defense counsel gave his "personal opinion of the strength of the State's evidence." . . . Again, the Court gives no explanation of how the statement it quotes — a single, mild expression of defense counsel's overall assessment of the evidence — justified the "response" that followed, which consisted, to the extent it represented a comment on the evidence at all, of accusations of perjury, . . . and personal disparagements of opposing counsel. . . . In sum, McDaniel went so far beyond "respond[ing] substantially in order to 'right the scale,'" *Young*, 470 U.S., at 13, that the reasoning in *Young* provides no basis at all for the Court's holding today.

The third reason the Court gives for discounting the effects of the improper summations is the supposed curative effect of the trial judge's instructions: The judge had instructed the jury that it was to decide the case on the evidence and that the arguments of counsel were not evidence. . . . But the trial court overruled Darden's objection to McDaniel's repeated expressions of his wish that Darden had been killed, . . . thus perhaps leaving the jury with the impression that McDaniel's comments were somehow relevant to the question before them. The trial judge's instruction that the attorneys were "trained in the law," and thus that their "analysis of the issues" could be "extremely helpful," . . . might also have suggested to the jury that the substance of McDaniel's tirade was pertinent to their deliberations.

Fourth, the Court suggests that because Darden enjoyed the tactical advantage of having the last summation, he was able to "tur[n] much of the prosecutors' closing argument against them." . . . Since Darden was ultimately convicted, it is hard to see what basis the Court has for its naked assertion that "[d]efense counsel were able to use the opportunity for rebuttal very effectively." . . .

Fifth, the Court finds, in essence, that any error was harmless . . . but it does not identify the standard it [uses] to decide the harmlessness of the error. . . .

Regardless of which test is used, I simply do not believe the evidence in this case was so overwhelming that this Court can conclude, on the basis of the written record before it, that the jury's verdict was not the product of the prosecutors' misconduct. The three most damaging pieces of evidence — the identifications of Darden by Phillip Arnold and Helen Turman and the ballistics evidence — are all sufficiently problematic that they leave me unconvinced that a jury not exposed to McDaniel's egregious summation would necessarily have convicted Darden.

Arnold first identified Darden in a photo array shown to him in the hospital. The trial court suppressed that out-of-court identification following a long argument concerning the reliability and constitutionality of the procedures by which it was obtained. . . .

Mrs. Turman's initial identification was made under even more suggestive circumstances. She testified at trial that she was taken to a preliminary hearing at which Darden appeared in order "[t]o identify him." . . . Instead of being asked to view Darden in a lineup, Mrs. Turman was brought into the courtroom, where Darden apparently was the only black man present. . . . Over defense counsel's objection, after the prosecutor asked her whether "this man sitting here" was "the man that shot your husband," . . . she identified Darden.[5] . . .

---

5. Mrs. Turman's identification took place after the following colloquy between the court, the prosecutor (Mr. Mars), and the defense attorney (Mr. Hill):

> *The Court:* Ask her to identify.
> *Mr. Mars:* Yes, sir.
> *Q:* Can you see this man sitting here?
> *Mr. Hill:* Your Honor, I am going to object to that type of identification.
> *The Court:* I am not. Sit down.
> *Mr. Hill:* Judge —
> *The Court:* Not under these circumstances, Mr. Hill.
> *Mr. Hill:* Judge, even as a defense attorney, that shows no respect in court, much less for the Court, and I —
> *The Court:* I appreciate —
> *Mr. Hill:* And the objection, I want on the record.
> *The Court:* I appreciate that. It's on the record. This woman has had a traumatic experience and she —
> *Mr. Hill:* Judge, I appreciate that. I still have an obligation to my client.
> *The Court:* I appreciate that. Now if you want to be held in contempt, you pardon me. Alright, go ahead.
> *Q:* Is this the man that shot your husband?
> *A:* Yes, sir. . . .

Finally, the ballistics evidence is hardly overwhelming. The purported murder weapon was tied conclusively neither to the crime nor to Darden. Special Agent Cunningham of the Federal Bureau of Investigation's Firearms Identification Unit testified that the bullets recovered at the scene of the crime "could have been fired" from the gun, but he was unwilling to say that they in fact had come from that weapon. . . . He also testified, contrary to the Court's assertion, that rebored Smith & Wessons were fairly common. . . . Deputy Sheriff Weatherford testified that the gun was discovered in a roadside ditch adjacent to where Darden had wrecked his car on the evening of the crime. But the gun was discovered the next day, . . . and the ditch was also next to a bar's parking lot. . . .

Darden testified at trial on his own behalf and denied any involvement in the robbery and murder. . . . His account of his actions on the day of the crime was contradicted only by Mrs. Turman's and Arnold's identifications. Indeed, a number of the State's witnesses corroborated parts of Darden's account. The trial judge who had seen and heard Darden testify found that he "emotionally and with what appeared on its face to be sincerity, proclaimed his innocence." . . . In setting sentence, he viewed the fact that Darden "repeatedly professed his complete innocence of the charges" as a mitigating factor. . . .

Thus, at bottom, this case rests on the jury's determination of the credibility of three witnesses — Helen Turman and Phillip Arnold, on the one side, and Willie Darden, on the other. I cannot conclude that McDaniel's sustained assault on Darden's very humanity did not affect the jury's ability to judge the credibility question on the real evidence before it. Because I believe that he did not have a trial that was fair, I would reverse Darden's conviction; I would not allow him to go to his death until he has been convicted at a fair trial.

II

[This section of the dissenting opinion, addressing the defendant's claim of improper exclusion of a prospective juror, is omitted.]

III

Twice during the past year — in United States v. Young, 470 U.S. 1 (1985), and again today — this Court has been faced with clearly improper prosecutorial misconduct during summations. Each time, the Court has condemned the behavior but affirmed the conviction. Forty years ago, Judge Jerome N. Frank, in dissent, discussed the Second Circuit's similar approach in language we would do well to remember today:

> This court has several times used vigorous language in denouncing government counsel for such conduct as that of the [prosecutor] here. But, each time, it has said that, nevertheless, it would not reverse. Such an attitude of helpless piety is, I think, undesirable. It means actual condonation of counsel's alleged offense, coupled with verbal disapprobation. If we continue to do nothing practical to prevent such conduct, we should cease to disapprove it. For otherwise it will be as if we declared in effect, "Government attorneys, without fear of reversal, may say just about what they please in addressing juries, for our rules on the subject are pretend-rules. If prosecutors win verdicts as a result of 'disapproved' remarks, we will not deprive them of their victories; we will merely go through the form of expressing displeasure. The deprecatory words we use

in our opinions on such occasions are purely ceremonial." Government counsel, employing such tactics, are the kind who, eager to win victories, will gladly pay the small price of a ritualistic verbal spanking. The practice of this court — recalling the bitter tear shed by the Walrus as he ate the oysters — breeds a deplorably cynical attitude towards the judiciary (footnote omitted).

United States v. Antonelli Fireworks Co., 155 F.2d 631, 661 . . . (1946).

I believe this Court must do more than wring its hands when a State uses improper legal standards to select juries in capital cases and permits prosecutors to pervert the adversary process. I therefore dissent.

NOTES AND QUESTIONS

1. On the general subject of prosecutorial misconduct, consider the following famous words from Berger v. United States, 295 U.S. 78 (1935), on the prosecutor as "servant of the law":

> He may prosecute with earnestness and vigor — indeed, he should do so. But while he may strike hard blows, he is not at liberty to strike foul ones. It is as much his duty to refrain from improper methods calculated to produce a wrongful conviction as it is to use every legitimate means to bring about a just one. . . . It is fair to say that the average jury, in a greater or lesser degree, has confidence that these obligations, which so plainly rest upon the prosecuting attorney, will be faithfully observed. Consequently, improper suggestions, insinuations, and, especially, assertions of personal knowledge are apt to carry much weight against the accused when they should properly carry none.

Notice the *Berger* Court's special concern about the potential impact of prosecutorial misconduct on the jury.

2. *Darden* relied heavily on three previous Court decisions involving challenges to prosecutorial arguments before the jury.

In Donnelly v. DeChristoforo, 416 U.S. 637, 643 (1974), the defendant and a codefendant were charged with first-degree murder. In the midst of the joint trial, the codefendant pleaded guilty to second-degree murder, and the jury was so informed. In closing argument, the prosecutor told the jury, "I honestly and sincerely believe that there is no doubt in this case, none whatsoever." In addition, the prosecutor stated: "[The defendant and his lawyer] said they hope that you find him not guilty. I quite frankly think that they hope that you find him guilty of something a little less than first-degree murder." The defendant was convicted of first-degree murder, and the Supreme Court affirmed. The Court noted that the trial judge acted quickly to inform the jury that the prosecutor's comments were not evidence, and concluded that the overall impact of the comments was insufficient to make out a due process violation.

In United States v. Young, 470 U.S. 1 (1985), the defense lawyer, in summation, intimated that the prosecution had deliberately withheld exculpatory evidence, charged the prosecution with "reprehensible" conduct, and stated, "I submit to you that there's not a person in this courtroom including [the prosecution] who think that [the defendant] intended to defraud [the victim]." The prosecutor did not object, but in his rebuttal argument responded by expressing his own opinion about the defendant's guilt and telling the jurors that, if they acquitted the defendant, "I don't think you're doing your job as jurors. . . ." The defense did not object, and the defendant was convicted. The Supreme Court affirmed, despite lamenting that "[t]he kind of advocacy shown by this record has no place in the administration of justice." The Court noted that the prosecutor's comments were a form of "invited response" to the defense lawyer's prior improper comments. However, the Court stressed that "the issue is not the prosecutor's license to make otherwise improper arguments, but whether the prosecutor's 'invited response,' taken in context, unfairly prejudiced the defendant." The Court concluded that the prosecutor's comments "went beyond what was necessary to 'right the scale' in the wake of defense counsel's misconduct." Nevertheless, the prosecutor's error "was not 'plain error' warranting the court to overlook the absence of any objection by the defense."

In Caldwell v. Mississippi, 472 U.S. 320 (1985), the prosecutor, in the sentencing phase of a capital case, responded to the defense lawyer's plea for mercy by telling the jury at closing:

> Now, they would have you believe that you're going to kill this man and they know — they know that your decision is not the final decision. My God, how unfair can you be? Your job is reviewable. . . . They said, "Thou shalt not kill," If that applies to him, it applies to you, insinuating that your decision is the final decision and that they're gonna take [the defendant] out in front of this Courthouse in moments and string him up and that is terribly, terribly unfair. For they know, as I know, and as Judge Baker has told you, that the decision you render is automatically reviewable by the Supreme Court. Automatically, and I think it's unfair and I don't mind telling them so.

Id., at 325-326. The Supreme Court held that this argument violated the Eighth Amendment's Cruel and Unusual Punishment Clause because it led the jury to believe "that the responsibility for determining the appropriateness of the defendant's death rests elsewhere." The Court rejected the contention that the prosecutor's comments about appellate review were an "invited response," noting that they had little to do directly with the defense lawyer's mercy plea. Justice O'Connor, in concurrence, emphasized that the prosecutor's comments were not only potentially highly prejudicial, but also inaccurate, because appellate review in capital cases is limited and cannot revisit the merits of the jury's verdict.

3. In addition to publicity and improper prosecutorial argument, similar concerns about jury influence arise in the context of admission of tainted evidence. This is yet another area in which judges and lawyers tend to follow the traditional legal approach, which consists of giving a curative instruction to tell the jury not to rely on the improper evidence. Empirical research, however, demonstrates that such curative instructions do not usually have the desired effect on jury behavior — perhaps lending credence to the folk wisdom about what happens if you tell someone not to think about pink elephants:

> [P]eople find it very difficult to actively suppress a thought upon instruction, particularly when that thought is vivid or emotionally arousing. Indeed, the harder people try to control a thought, the less likely they are to succeed.

Christina Studebaker & Steven Penrod, Pretrial Publicity: The Media, the Law, and Common Sense, 3 Psychol. Pub. Pol'y & Law 428, 446 (1997), citing D. M. Wegner,

White Bears and Other Unwanted Thoughts: Suppression, Obsession, and the Psychology of Mental Control (1989); see also Thompson, Fong, & Rosenhan, Inadmissible Evidence and Juror Verdicts, 40 J. Personality & Soc. Psychol. 453, 461 (1981) (jurors tend to ignore curative instructions to disregard inadmissible evidence); Brooks & Doob, Justice and the Jury, J. Soc. Issues, Summer 1975, at 176-177 (jurors tend to ignore curative instructions limiting use of previous convictions to impeach defendant's credibility); cf. Tanford & Penrod, Social Inference Processes in Juror Judgments of Multiple Offense Trials, 47 J. Personality & Soc. Psychol. 749 (1984) (joinder of charges increases likelihood of conviction on particular charge, and curative instructions do not remedy problem).

E. Proof and Verdict Issues

At the close of the trial, the case will be submitted to the factfinder for a decision. In a jury trial, the trial judge will instruct the jury in a detailed manner about the law pertaining to the case, and the jury will then retire to deliberate in secrecy about the defendant's guilt or innocence. Several important procedural issues relate to the standards by which the jury (or trial judge, in a bench trial) must make this decision, the nature and form of the verdict by which the decision is announced, and permissible challenges to the verdict.

1. The Burden of Proof

In the landmark case of In Re Winship, 397 U.S. 358 (1970), the Supreme Court held that, under the Due Process Clause, a criminal conviction cannot be based on any standard less than proof of every element of the crime "beyond a reasonable doubt." "Reasonable doubt" has never been clearly defined by the Court. In Cage v. Louisiana, 498 U.S. 39 (1990) (per curiam), the Court rejected (as too pro-prosecution) jury instructions defining "reasonable doubt" as "a grave uncertainty" and "an actual substantial doubt," and describing the proper standard as one of "moral certainty." In the companion cases of Victor v. Nebraska and Sandoval v. California, 511 U.S. 1 (1994), however, the Court approved jury instructions stating that a "reasonable doubt" exists whenever, after "consideration of all the evidence," the juror lacks "an abiding conviction, to a moral certainty," of the defendant's guilt. The Court reiterated its displeasure with such phrases as "substantial doubt" and "moral certainty," but concluded that the instructions, in their entirety, provided sufficient context to explain to the jurors the true meaning of "reasonable doubt" — which, the Court suggested, is doubt "that would cause a reasonable person to hesitate to act." Id., at 20. See also Jackson v. Virginia, 443 U.S. 307, 317, n. 9 (1979) (describing "reasonable doubt" as doubt "based on reason which arises from the evidence or lack of evidence").

Under *Winship*, it is clear that the prosecution must bear the burden of proving all elements of a crime beyond a reasonable doubt. See also Sandstrom v. Montana, 442 U.S. 510 (1979), holding that *Winship* prohibits a jury instruction creating a presumption with respect to an element of a crime; Francis v. Franklin, 471 U.S. 307 (1985), holding that *Winship* and *Sandstrom* prohibit not only conclusive, but also rebuttable, presumptions. But what are the elements of a crime?

In Mullaney v. Wilbur, 421 U.S. 684 (1975), a unanimous Court held that *Winship* prohibits a legislature from placing on the defendant in a homicide case the burden of proving by a preponderance of the evidence, in order to reduce the crime from murder to manslaughter, that the killing had occurred in the heat of passion. The Court explained that *Winship* cannot be "limited to those facts that constitute a crime as defined by state law"; otherwise, the legislature could "undermine many of the interests that decision sought to protect" by "redefin[ing] the elements that constitute different crimes, characterizing them [instead] as factors that bear solely on the extent of punishment." Id., at 698.

Just two years after *Mullaney*, however, in Patterson v. New York, 432 U.S. 197 (1977), the Court upheld a similar statute placing on the defendant the burden of proving, in a second-degree murder case, the "affirmative defense" that the killing was the result of "extreme emotional disturbance for which there was a reasonable explanation or excuse"; such proof had the effect of reducing the crime from second-degree murder to manslaughter. The Court distinguished *Mullaney* on the ground that the statute in *Patterson* did not make the absence of "extreme emotional disturbance" an element of second degree murder, but instead provided only that the existence of such a factor would serve as an "affirmative defense" to the crime. The Court drew an analogy to the insanity defense, which previously had been held by the Court to be an "affirmative defense" that the defendant could constitutionally be required to prove, and noted that a contrary result might cause legislatures to eliminate such defenses entirely. The Court concluded:

> . . . [E]ven if we were to hold that a State must prove sanity to convict once that fact is put in issue, it would not necessarily follow that a State must prove beyond a reasonable doubt every fact, the existence or nonexistence of which it is willing to recognize as an exculpatory or mitigating circumstance affecting the degree of culpability or the severity of the punishment. . . .
>
> We thus decline to adopt as a constitutional imperative, operative countrywide, that a State must disprove beyond a reasonable doubt every fact constituting any and all affirmative defenses related to the culpability of an accused. . . .
>
> This view may seem to permit state legislatures to reallocate burdens of proof by labeling as affirmative defenses at least some of the elements of the crimes now defined in their statutes. But there are obviously constitutional limits beyond which the States may not go in this regard. . . .

Id., at 207, 210.

What are these "constitutional limits" on legislative reshaping of the elements of a crime? The *Patterson* Court identified only one — that the legislature cannot "declare an individual guilty or presumptively guilty of a crime." Id., at 210. In Martin v. Ohio, 480 U.S. 228 (1987), the Court upheld a statute placing on the defendant the burden of proving by a preponderance of the evidence, as an "affirmative defense" to a murder charge, that the killing was committed in self-defense — even though 48 out of the 50 states treated the absence of self-defense as an element of the crime of murder.

The Court's burden-of-proof cases — and especially *Patterson* — have been sharply criticized by commentators on the ground that they elevate form over substance in determining exactly what are the "elements" of a crime. The best of these commentaries have suggested that, at a minimum, the prosecution should be required to prove beyond a reasonable doubt any facts that would be necessary in order for the statutorily authorized range of punishments to satisfy the Eighth Amendment's proportionality requirement. See, e.g., Ronald J. Allen, Foreword: Montana v. Egelhoff — Reflections on the Limits of Legislative Imagination and Judicial Authority, 87 J. Crim. L. & Criminology 633 (1997); John C. Jeffries & Paul B. Stephan, Defenses, Presumptions, and Burden of Proof in the Criminal Law, 88 Yale L.J. 1325 (1979); Ronald J. Allen, Mullaney v. Wilbur, the Supreme Court, and the Substantive Criminal Law — An Examination of the Limits of Legitimate Intervention, 55 Tex. L. Rev. 269 (1977).

The *Winship/Mullaney/Patterson* problem has recently recurred with a vengeance, in the different context of burdens of proof with respect to so-called "sentencing factors." See infra, Chapter 15. In fact, the problem is ubiquitous in criminal litigation. It affects statutory inferences, presumptions, comment on the evidence, judicial notice, instructions on defenses and lesser-included counts, and affirmative defenses, because each of these intersects with burdens of persuasion in one manner or another. This leads to very strange results. For example, a legislature may not create a "presumption" of an element upon proof of some other fact, because that would adversely affect proof beyond reasonable doubt, yet the legislature almost surely could eliminate the "presumed" element entirely, or make it into an affirmative defense. The Court has never noticed the interconnectedness of the various categories noted above that intersect the burden of persuasion, and thus it has never addressed the somewhat internally inconsistent, if not paradoxical, jurisprudence it has created in this area. For a thorough discussion, see Ronald J. Allen, Structuring Jury Decisionmaking in Criminal Cases: A Unified Constitutional Analysis of Evidentiary Devices, 94 Harv. L. Rev. 321-368 (1980).

2. Unanimity of the Verdict

As noted at the beginning of this chapter, the Sixth Amendment has been held not to require unanimous verdicts, at least in the context of 12-member juries. Nevertheless, unanimity is still a requirement in the federal system, as well as in most states. Does the unanimity requirement, where it exists, mean that the jurors must all agree on one particular theory of the case? Or on one particular way of establishing one of the elements of the crime?

In Schad v. Arizona, 501 U.S. 624 (1991), the Court affirmed a state conviction for first-degree murder despite the fact that the jury may not have been unanimous on the question whether the required level of culpability for the crime was proven by means of premeditation or felony-murder. But in Richardson v. United States, 526 U.S. 813 (1999), the Court reversed a federal conviction because the jury was not required to reach a unanimous verdict with respect to the defendant's commission of numerous specific violations of federal drug laws that were alleged to be part of a "series of violations" needed to establish the larger crime of operating a "continuing criminal enterprise." The *Richardson* Court explained that resolution of such an issue requires close examination of the statutory elements of the crime charged:

. . . Where, for example, an element of robbery is force or the threat of force, some jurors might conclude that the defendant used a knife to create the threat; others might conclude he used a gun. But that disagreement — a disagreement about means — would not matter as long as all 12 jurors unanimously concluded that the Government had proved the necessary related element, namely that the defendant has threatened force. . . .

In this case, we must decide whether the statute's phrase "series of violations" refers to one element, namely, a "series," in respect to which the "violations" constitute the underlying brute facts or means, or whether the words create several elements, namely the several "violations," in respect to *each* of which the jury must agree unanimously and separately.

Id., at 817-818. Ultimately, the Court's statutory analysis led it to conclude that each alleged violation constituted a separate element of the "continuing criminal enterprise" crime and thus had to be found unanimously. Id., at 818-820.

What can the trial judge do to prod the jury to reach a unanimous verdict? In Allen v. United States, 164 U.S. 492 (1896), the Court upheld the giving of an instruction, in the midst of a prolonged period of jury deliberation, designed to encourage any jurors still in the minority to reconsider the reasonableness of their views. The Court explained that "[i]t certainly cannot be the law that each juror should not listen with deference to the arguments and with a distrust of his own judgment, if he finds a large majority of the jury taking a different view of the case from what he does himself." Id., at 501. But in Jenkins v. United States, 380 U.S. 445 (1965) (per curiam), the Court found a due process violation when the trial judge instructed the jury that "[y]ou have got to reach a decision in this case." Id., at 446.

The constitutionality of the so-called dynamite charge was also at issue in Lowenfield v. Phelps, 484 U.S. 231 (1988). There the trial judge gave an instruction not specifically addressed to jurors who were in the minority, but urging all of the jurors to rethink their views. The judge also polled the jury, twice, to see whether the jurors believed that further deliberations would be productive. The Court concluded that, on the facts, "the combination of the polling of the jury and the supplemental instruction was not 'coercive' in such a way as to deny [the defendant] any constitutional right." Id., at 241.

On the empirical effects of "dynamite charges," see Vicki Smith & Saul Kassin, Effects of the Dynamite Charge on the Deliberations of Deadlocked Mock Juries, 17 Law & Hum. Behav. 625 (1993) (concluding that the "dynamite charge" moved deadlocked juries toward unanimity by increasing pressure on jurors in the minority, but not on those in the majority, to change their votes).

3. Consistency of the Verdict; General Verdicts

The general rule is that no constitutional issue is created by the return of inconsistent verdicts because such verdicts may be simply the product of permissible leniency. See, e.g., Harris v. Rivera, 454 U.S. 339 (1981) (per curiam) (upholding conviction by inconsistent verdicts in bench trial in state court); United States v. Powell, 469 U.S. 57 (1984) (same result, in jury trial in federal court).

Although the almost universal practice in America is for criminal cases to be decided by general verdict, without any indication of the reasons underlying the verdict, such practice is currently under attack in Europe as a possible violation of human rights. Article 6 of the European Convention on Human Rights (ECHR) provides that all criminal defendants are entitled to a trial before an independent and impartial tribunal, whose judgments must be delivered in public. Some have argued that general jury verdicts are not the kind of reasoned judgments contemplated by the ECHR. This argument may have serious implications for the British jury system. See Robert Verkaik, New Law Will Force Juries to Give Reasons for Verdicts, The Independent, Aug. 25, 2000.

Andrew Leipold has recently argued that defendants who are acquitted of a crime should have a statutory right to ask the jury (or the judge, in a bench trial) to determine, in addition to his *legal* guilt or innocence, whether or not he is *factually* innocent. According to Leipold, the "innocent, acquitted defendant" — although obviously far less deserving of society's sympathy than an innocent, convicted defendant — nevertheless suffers several demonstrable harms:

> My thesis is that while innocent people who are arrested, charged, and acquitted of crimes have far fewer problems than the wrongfully convicted, their burdens are still substantial and still worthy of attention. Many of these problems, such as cost and the risk of an erroneous outcome, are faced by every party in any legal proceeding, but others are unique. In particular, a factually innocent defendant confronts the problem of being publicly accused by the government of criminal behavior with no real prospect of ever being officially vindicated. An innocent suspect may have the charges dismissed or may be acquitted, but the sequella of an indictment may leave the defendant's reputation, personal relationships, and ability to earn a living so badly damaged that he may never be able to return to the life he knew before being accused. More subtly, a person who was once charged with a crime is put on a different (and far less desirable) track in the legal system than someone who has never been arrested. A later acquittal or dismissal does surprisingly little to relieve an innocent defendant of the resulting burdens.

Andrew D. Leipold, The Problem of the Innocent, Acquitted Defendant, 94 Nw. U. L. Rev. 1297, 1299 (2000). Leipold acknowledges numerous practical problems with his proposal, including the nature and allocation of the burden of proof with respect to factual innocence, but concludes that "[l]eaving the most important decision that courts make, and the most important decision in some defendants' lives, shrouded in mystery can hardly be the right outcome for a system that prizes fair and equal treatment under the law." Id., at 1356.

4. Impeachment of the Verdict

Once the jury has reached its verdict, the rule is that no impeachment of the verdict by a juror will be allowed, except for the rare case in which a juror testifies that some *external* influence affected the jury's deliberations. This rule is strictly applied. In Tanner v. United States, 483 U.S. 107 (1987), a juror in a federal fraud trial volunteered, after the conclusion of the trial, information that several of the jurors consumed alcohol during lunch breaks, causing them to sleep through the afternoon sessions of the trial. Later, another juror volunteered that "the jury was on one big party"; he stated that seven of the jurors drank alcohol during lunch breaks, that four of the jurors (including himself) often drank from one to three pitchers of beer, that several other jurors also consumed mixed drinks, that four of the jurors (again, including himself) smoked marijuana regularly during the trial, that one juror ingested cocaine five times and another juror did so two or three times, and that one juror sold a quarter-pound of marijuana to another juror during the trial and brought drug paraphernalia into the courthouse. The Court held that this information was of no legal consequence:

> There is little doubt that postverdict investigation into juror misconduct would in some instances lead to the invalidation of verdicts reached after irresponsible or improper juror behavior. It is not at all clear, however, that the jury system could survive such efforts to perfect it. Allegations of juror misconduct, incompetency, or inattentiveness, raised for the first time days, weeks, or months after the verdict, seriously disrupt the finality of the process. . . . Moreover, full and frank discussion in the jury room, jurors' willingness to return an unpopular verdict, and the community's trust in a system that relies on the decisions of laypeople would all be undermined by a barrage of postverdict scrutiny of juror conduct. . . .

Id., at 120-121.

Does this remind you, just a little bit, of the adage about ostriches who bury their heads in the sand? Is there no possibility of an alternative approach that would insulate jury decision making from review in most cases, but allow for correction of the most egregious instances of juror (or, apparently, in the *Tanner* case, jury) misconduct?

The United Kingdom's House of Lords recently addressed whether traditional jury secrecy might violate Article 6 of the ECHR. The cases were Regina v. Connor and another, Regina v. Mirze, [2004] UKHL 2. Both cases involved defendants who claimed misconduct by the juries that convicted them. In one case, a juror allegedly held the use of an interpreter against the defendant; in the other case, a juror accused other jurors of not giving proper consideration to the verdict. A majority of the Lords declined to abrogate the common-law rule of secrecy of jury deliberations on the alleged facts of the two cases. But the Lords acknowledged that modern human-rights law, as expressed in the ECHR, might require abrogation of jury secrecy in exceptional cases, especially if the allegations of jury misconduct were made before the verdict was reached. The Lords also recommended improvements to the British jury system, including better jury instructions and better factual reporting about trials from trial judges to appellate courts.

5. Postverdict Motions

After the jury's verdict has been announced, and assuming that the defendant has been convicted, there are several procedural routes by which the defendant may seek to overturn the verdict in the trial court. The defendant may file a motion for a judgment of acquittal, on the ground that the evidence presented during the trial was legally insufficient for a conviction (i.e., the evidence did not meet the legal standard of proof of guilt "beyond a reasonable doubt"). The trial judge has the authority to enter a judgment of acquittal notwithstanding the jury's verdict, if the judge finds the evidence legally insufficient — although the fact that the jury reached the opposite conclusion will inevitably weigh heavily on the judge's mind. (This is one reason why many defendants file an initial motion for a judgment of acquittal immediately after the conclusion of the prosecution's case-in-chief, before the jury has a chance to render its verdict.) In addition, the trial judge must view the evidence in the light most favorable to the prosecution, further reducing the likelihood of the defendant's success.

The defendant may also file a motion for a new trial, either on the ground of newly discovered evidence or on some other ground (often including the "interests of justice"). In the case of newly discovered evidence, most states and the federal system limit the time period after judgment during which such evidence can be used to seek a new trial. See, e.g., Fed. R. Crim. P. 33 (3-year limit); Ariz. Rule Crim. Proc. 24.2(a) (60-day limit); Minn. Rule Crim. Proc. 26.04(3) (15-day limit). Moreover, to qualify as "newly discovered," such evidence generally must have been unavailable to the defendant, even assuming the exercise of "due diligence," at the time of the trial.

In the case of a motion for a new trial based on grounds other than newly discovered evidence, the defendant may raise any number of procedural trial errors; some states actually require the filing of such a motion in order to preserve procedural issues for appeal. The defendant may also ask the trial judge to order a new trial on the ground that the jury's verdict was contrary to the weight of the evidence; because the remedy of a new trial is less disruptive than the remedy of a court-directed acquittal, the standard for granting such a motion is somewhat more favorable to the defendant, as compared to the aforementioned motion for a judgment of acquittal. A motion for a new trial based on grounds other than newly discovered evidence, however, is often subject to very strict time limits, see, e.g., Fed. R. Crim. P. 33 (14-day time limit).

F. Criminal Trials and Factual Accuracy

To what extent should criminal trials (and, more generally, criminal justice — including the full range of pretrial proceedings, trials, direct appeals, and postconviction proceedings) be designed to ensure, as much as humanly possible, factually accurate results? Should our choices about the structure and procedural rules of the criminal justice system be made mostly, or even exclusively, on the basis of whether those choices will further both the conviction of the guilty and the acquittal of the innocent (which are, after all, two sides of the very same coin)? Or are there other important values — such as autonomy, privacy, equality, fairness, respect for the individual — that deserve equal treatment?

In recent years, the Supreme Court has seemed increasingly ambivalent about where the primary emphasis should lie. On the one hand, the Court has manifested a growing discomfort about the number of criminal cases in which potentially innocent defendants have been found guilty of serious, and sometimes even capital, crimes. This concern about factual inaccuracy can clearly be seen in such decisions as Holmes v. South Carolina, 547 U.S. 319 (2006) (reversing a conviction because the defendant was precluded from introducing evidence at trial that pointed to a different suspect); Youngblood v. West Virginia, 547 U.S. 867 (2006) (reversing and remanding a potentially meritorious *Brady* claim to the state courts for further review); and especially House v. Bell, 547 U.S. 518 (2006).

In *House*, the Court (by 5-3, with Justice Alito not participating) reversed the Sixth Circuit, and allowed a Death-Row inmate's habeas corpus action to proceed despite the petitioner's failure to follow the applicable procedural rules in state court, because the Court found that the petitioner's newly discovered evidence of factual innocence (specifically, DNA test results) was strong enough that "it is more likely than not that no reasonable juror would have found petitioner guilty beyond a reasonable doubt" if the evidence had been available at trial. The Court's emphatic conclusion was based not only on the new DNA evidence itself, but also on the "evidentiary disarray" (which was described in great detail, and at great length, in Justice Breyer's majority opinion) surrounding the prosecution's forensic evidence at trial. Upon consideration of all of the evidence (including the new DNA evidence), the Court held that although the case was not one of "conclusive exoneration," it nevertheless qualified as one of those "rare case[s]" meriting habeas review despite the petitioner's procedural default.

On the other hand, the Court has also decided several recent cases in ways that seemingly ignored or downplayed the issue of factual accuracy in favor of something else. For example, in Davis v. Washington, 547 U.S. 813 (2006), the Court continued its development of a brand new Confrontation Clause approach that elevates the Framers' views about what kinds of evidence must be subjected to cross-examination (specifically, evidence resembling that which was introduced under certain English statutes passed during the reign of Queen Mary) over more functional considerations about whether, and to what extent, cross-examination might actually contribute to the reliability of evidence (and thus the factual accuracy of trials). Along somewhat similar lines, see Oregon v. Guzek, 546 U.S. 517 (2006) (holding that a capital defendant has no constitutional right to introduce evidence of his innocence at a capital sentencing hearing, once he has been found guilty at the trial stage of the case); United States v. Ruiz, 536 U.S. 622 (2002) (holding that prosecutors need not disclose to defendants, prior to accepting a guilty plea, evidence that would impeach prosecution informants or witnesses).

Is there a way to reconcile these apparent inconsistencies in approach? Is this a simple case of two different factions on the Court disagreeing about what matters most in criminal cases? Or does this confusing situation possibly reflect, instead, a gradual shift from the largely procedural emphasis of the Court during much of the 1960s and 1970s to a new substantive approach — perhaps motivated by the recent, highly publicized spate of DNA exonerations (especially in capital cases)? Will we see in the near future, perhaps, additional decisions by the Court along the lines of House v. Bell, opening up new avenues of opportunity for defendants with claims of factual innocence to challenge their convictions?

Any perception of a trend in this direction may have been dashed, at least temporarily, by the Court's ruling in District Attorney's Office for the Third Judicial District v. Osborne, 129 S. Ct. 2308 (2009). Osborne was convicted of kidnapping, sexual assault, and assault (but acquitted of attempted murder) in connection with a brutal 1993 attack on a prostitute, and was sentenced to 26 years in prison. Although Osborne's conviction and sentence were affirmed on appeal, and also in state and federal postconviction review, he continued to profess his innocence. Osborne eventually filed a §1983 petition in federal court, seeking access to physical evidence in the state's possession so that he could have it tested by advanced DNA methods. His petition was premised on the argument that such access should be guaranteed by the Due Process Clause — in either the procedural sense, by analogy to the defendant's right to be notified of material exculpatory evidence under Brady v. Maryland, 373 U.S. 83 (1969), or in the substantive sense.

The Court, in a 5-4 decision, rejected both versions of the argument. According to the Court, claims of factual innocence made after conviction entitle the claimant to less stringent procedural protections than would attach to such claims made at trial, thus making *Brady* inapposite. "The State accordingly has more flexibility in deciding what procedures are needed in the context of postconviction relief. . . . Federal courts may upset a State's postconviction relief procedures only if they are fundamentally inadequate to vindicate the substantive rights provided. . . . We see nothing inadequate about the procedures Alaska has provided to vindicate its state right to postconviction relief in general, and nothing inadequate about how those procedures apply to those who seek access to DNA evidence." The Court also rejected Osborne's substantive due process argument, based on both the argument's "novelty" as well as the fact that it would embroil the Court in difficult policy choices (such as whether, and for how long, states should be required to preserve evidence for possible future testing). In the end, the Court concluded:

> DNA evidence will undoubtedly lead to changes in the criminal justice system. It has done so already. The question is whether further change will primarily be made by legislative revision and judicial interpretation of the existing system, or whether the Federal Judiciary must leap ahead — revising (or even discarding) the system by creating a new constitutional right and taking over responsibility for refining it.

PART FIVE

POSTTRIAL PROCEEDINGS

Chapter 15

Sentencing

A. *Introduction to Sentencing*

1. Sentencing Options

A defendant who has been convicted of a crime may be sentenced to a variety of different punishments. Almost all felony crimes are punishable by a sentence of confinement in a state or federal prison, or in a local jail, and/or by a period of probation. At the extreme, in many jurisdictions, some murders are punishable by a sentence of death. Monetary punishments, such as fines, orders of restitution, and criminal forfeitures, are common, either separately or in combination with other punishments. Between incarceration and probation lie intermediate sanctions including house arrest, inpatient treatment programs, "boot camps," electronic monitoring, day-reporting programs, furlough programs, and community service.

In 2006, more than 1.2 million American adults were convicted and sentenced for felony crimes, an increase of almost 40 percent since 1990.[1] About 94 percent were convicted of state crimes, while the other 6 percent were convicted of federal crimes. The number of felons convicted and sentenced in state court represented 503 out of every 100,000 adult U.S. residents, as compared with a rate of 447 per 100,000 in 1990. Among those convicted of state felony crimes in 2006, 69 percent were sentenced to a period of confinement — 41 percent for longer periods in a state or federal prison, and 28 percent for shorter periods in a local jail. The average maximum sentence length for those incarcerated for state felony crimes was 38 months; for federal felonies, the average maximum sentence was almost 65 months.

Over the past two decades, both incarceration rates and average maximum sentence lengths have increased substantially, imposing a severe strain on America's correctional resources. Despite a relative leveling-off of the growth in the incarceration rate after 1998, at the end of 2008 some 2,304,115 persons were incarcerated in state or federal prisons or local jails in America, or about 754 per 100,000 adult U.S. residents; this was a slight decline in the incarceration rate from 756 per 100,000 in 2007, but an increase of more than 10 percent since 2000. About

---

1. The statistics in this section are reported in various publications by the U.S. Department of Justice, Bureau of Justice Statistics, available online at http://bjs.ojp.usdoj.gov/, including Heather C. West, Prisoners at Yearend 2009 — Advance Counts (NCJ 230189, June 2010); Heather C. West, Prison Inmates at Midyear 2009 — Statistical Tables (NCJ 230113, June 2010); William J. Sabol, Heather C. West, & Matthew Cooper, Prisoners in 2008 (NCJ 228417, December 2009); Sean Rosenmerkel, Matthew Durose, & Donald Farole, Felony Sentences in State Courts, 2006 (NCJ 226846, December 2009); Mark Motivans, Federal Justice Statistics, 2006 (NCJ 225711, May 2009); and Thomas P. Bonczar & Lauren E. Glaze, Probation and Parole in the United States, 2008 (NCJ 228230, December 2009). The death penalty statistics at the end of this section are reported in NAACP Legal Defense Fund, Death Row U.S.A., January 1, 2010, available online at http://www.deathpenaltyinfo.org/documents/DRUSA_Winter_2010.pdf.

4,271,000 persons were on probation, and about 828,000 persons were on parole, meaning that 1 in every 45 American adults was under community supervision. At the end of 2008, the total number of persons subject to the supervision of the correctional system was estimated to be about 7.3 million, or 3.2 percent of the entire U.S. adult population — roughly 1 out of every 31.5 Americans. This represented an increase of almost 40 percent from 1990, when the supervision rate was only 2.3 percent of the adult population.

Recent statistical snapshots reveal both the diversity of sentencing practices for different kinds of crimes and significant disparities in the characteristics of those sentenced. For example, at the end of 2008, there were 3,161 black men in prison for every 100,000 black men in the United States. By far, the highest incarceration rates were for young black men — more than 7 percent of all black non-Hispanic men between 25 and 29 (and more than 8 percent of all those between 30 and 34) were in either prison or jail at year-end 2008, as compared with 2.5 percent of all Hispanic men and only 1 percent of all white men. The total incarceration rate for all men was 952 per 100,000; for women, only 68 per 100,000.

In 2006, 77 percent of persons convicted in state court of violent crimes, including murder, sexual assault, robbery, and aggravated assault, were sentenced to confinement. The average maximum sentence length was just under five years. Within the category of violent crimes, the harshest sentences were for murder or manslaughter — 95 percent of persons convicted of such crimes were sentenced to confinement, for an average of more than 20 years. Robbery was punished by confinement in 85 percent of the cases, for an average of more than six years; sexual assault in 81 percent of the cases, for an average of almost nine years; and aggravated assault in 72 percent of the cases, for an average of just over three years. For nonviolent crimes, the percentage of convicted persons sentenced to confinement ranged from highs of 83 percent and 73 percent for motor vehicle theft and burglary, respectively, to a low of 59 percent for fraud and forgery. For drug trafficking, the confinement rate was 67 percent. Sentence length also varied, from a high of over three years for burglary, to a low of only one and a half years for motor vehicle theft.[2] In every category, almost all convicted felons who did not receive sentences of confinement were sentenced to probation.

There are no comparable comprehensive studies of intermediate sanctions, but the available evidence suggests that — especially as prison capacities are more frequently exceeded — such punishments are becoming increasingly popular with tax-conscious legislatures and sentencing judges. "Intermediate sanctions have been seen as a way both to reduce the need for prison beds and to provide a continuum of sanctions that satisfies the just deserts concern for proportionality in punishment." See Michael Tonry, Intermediate Sanctions in Sentencing Reform, 2 U. Chi. L. Sch. Roundtable 391 (1995). Although occasional notorious failures (like the Willie Horton prison-furlough debacle that contributed to the downfall of Democratic presidential candidate Michael Dukakis in 1988) have led public officials to underutilize such sanctions, or to limit their use to offenders who would not have

2. In the case of drug crimes, the maximum sentence length was significantly affected by whether the defendant was convicted in state or federal court. For drug traffickers convicted in state court, the average sentence was just over three years; for those convicted in federal court, the average was more than seven years. For drug possessors, the comparison was 23 months in state court and 48 months in federal court. These dramatic differences likely resulted from the numerous federal statutes defining tough mandatory minimum prison sentences for drug trafficking.

been imprisoned anyway, nevertheless such sanctions "can be used to save money and prison use, without significant sacrifices in public safety." See Michael Tonry, Intermediate Sanctions in Sentencing Guidelines, 23 Crime & Just. 199 (1998).

At the apex of the sentencing pyramid lies the most extreme punishment — the death penalty. Prior to 1972, the death penalty was imposed by juries that were given virtually no guidance as to how the decision should be made. In Furman v. Georgia, 408 U.S. 238 (1972), the Supreme Court held that such open-ended discretion in death sentencing violates the Eighth Amendment's "cruel and unusual punishment" clause, because it tends to produce arbitrary, capricious, and often discriminatory results. All death sentences imposed prior to Furman were therefore reversed. After Furman, however, many states enacted new death-penalty statutes designed to guide the jury's exercise of sentencing discretion, primarily through statutory lists of "aggravating circumstances" (that weighed in favor of a death sentence) and "mitigating circumstances" (that weighed against it). In Gregg v. Georgia, 428 U.S. 153 (1976), the Court held that these new "guided discretion" statutes complied with the Eighth Amendment, and allowed capital punishment to resume. In Lockett v. Ohio, 438 U.S. 586 (1978), the Court clarified that defendants cannot be limited to the "mitigating circumstances" listed in the relevant statute; rather, the Eighth Amendment requires that all relevant mitigating evidence must be considered by the jury.

Despite the Court's efforts in Furman and Gregg to bring rationality and fairness to capital sentencing, the problem of disparate application persists. In McCleskey v. Kemp, 481 U.S. 279 (1987), the death penalty in Georgia was challenged on equal protection and Eighth Amendment grounds, based on a landmark study by Professor David Baldus establishing that defendants who killed white victims were significantly more likely to receive the death penalty than those who killed black victims. The Court, in a 5-4 decision, rejected the challenge, finding that the discrepancies identified in the Baldus study were the inevitable result of necessary discretion in capital sentencing, and did not rise to the level of "the major systemic defects identified in Furman." Id., at 313. Subsequent empirical studies have found similar race-of-the-victim disparity in other death penalty jurisdictions.

In the United States today, the death penalty is effectively limited to intentional murders or felony murders during which the defendant exhibited a "reckless disregard for human life." See Kennedy v. Louisiana, 554 U.S. 407 (2008) (death penalty for rape of child held unconstitutional); Tison v. Arizona, 481 U.S. 137 (1987) (death penalty permitted for some felony murderers); Coker v. Georgia, 433 U.S. 584 (1977) (death penalty for rape of adult woman held unconstitutional).[3] Thirty-five states and the federal government currently authorize the imposition of the death penalty for some murders.[4] As of January 1, 2010, a total of 3,261 persons were on death row, and 1,188 persons had been executed since the resumption of capital punishment in 1976. Of those on death row in January 2010, 44.4 percent were white, 41.4 percent were black, and 11.7 percent were of Hispanic origin. Death row populations steadily increased from 1976 through the end of 2002, but have slightly decreased since then. Much of this decrease occurred in January 2003,

---

3. Federal law continues to authorize the death penalty for certain crimes of treason or espionage, but these statutes have not been tested in the Supreme Court, and their constitutional validity remains unanswered.

4. New Mexico has prospectively abolished the death penalty, but two men previously sentenced to death remained on death row as of January 2010.

when the lame-duck Governor of Illinois, George Ryan, commuted all of the death sentences in that state. California has the largest current death row, at nearly 700 persons, followed by Florida (398) and Texas (337). Texas, however, has executed far more persons than any other state since 1976 — a total of 447 executions as of January 2010, or more than one-third of the entire national total. Other states with relatively large numbers of executions include Virginia (105) and Oklahoma (91); by contrast, California — despite its huge death row — has executed only 13 persons since 1976. In recent years, perhaps due to the national publicity surrounding several high-profile exonerations of death-row inmates in Illinois and elsewhere, or perhaps due to the extremely high cost of litigating a capital case to conclusion, the numbers of both new death sentences and executions have declined. In 2009, slightly more than 100 new death sentences were imposed in America, down from several hundred per year a decade ago. After reaching the high-water mark of 98 executions in 1999, the number of executions dropped steadily to a low of 37 in 2008, before jumping back up to 52 in 2009.

2. Sentencing Considerations

The Supreme Court has addressed several constitutional challenges to the consideration of particular kinds of information at sentencing. Some of the most important rulings include the following.

Past Criminal Conduct.   Such information generally may be considered at sentencing. On the one hand, sentences may not be increased on the basis of prior felony convictions obtained in violation of the Sixth Amendment right to appointed counsel under Gideon v. Wainwright, 372 U.S. 335 (1963). See United States v. Tucker, 404 U.S. 443 (1972); Burgett v. Texas, 389 U.S. 109 (1967). On the other hand, uncounseled misdemeanor convictions, in cases where the defendant had no Sixth Amendment right to appointed counsel in the first place, may be considered at sentencing. See Nichols v. United States, 511 U.S. 738 (1994).

Future Dangerousness.   Psychiatric testimony about the defendant's future dangerousness may be considered at sentencing, even in a death penalty case where the need for reliability is greatest. See Barefoot v. Estelle, 463 U.S. 880 (1983); Jurek v. Texas, 428 U.S. 262 (1976).

False Testimony at Trial.   The fact that the defendant committed perjury at trial may be considered at sentencing, and such consideration does not place an unconstitutional burden on the defendant's right to testify at trial. See United States v. Dunnigan, 507 U.S. 87 (1993); United States v. Grayson, 438 U.S. 41 (1978).

Silence at Sentencing.   The fact that the defendant chose not to testify at a sentencing hearing may not be considered in determining the defendant's sentence, because such use would violate the defendant's Fifth Amendment privilege against self-incrimination. This is true even if the defendant pleaded guilty to the crime. See Mitchell v. United States, 526 U.S. 314 (1999).

Racial Bias.   The fact that a defendant was motivated by racial hatred to commit a crime may be considered at sentencing. See Wisconsin v. Mitchell, 508 U.S. 476

(1993); Barclay v. Florida, 463 U.S. 939 (1983). But a defendant's abstract beliefs, including membership in a racist group, are protected by the First Amendment and may not be considered unless directly relevant to the sentencing proceeding. See Dawson v. Delaware, 503 U.S. 159 (1992).

Judicial Vindictiveness. A defendant's sentence may not be increased after a retrial simply because the defendant chose to challenge his conviction by means of an appeal or postconviction proceeding. And, in order to protect defendants against the fear of such judicial vindictiveness, any trial judge who wishes to impose a harsher sentence after a retrial must set forth, on the record, the legitimate reasons supporting such a sentence. See North Carolina v. Pearce, 395 U.S. 711 (1969). These legitimate reasons may include information about the defendant's conduct occurring after the time of the original sentencing hearing, see *Pearce*, or other information that is similarly not susceptible to judicial manipulation, such as the fact that the defendant was later convicted on charges that were pending at the time of the original sentencing hearing, see Wasman v. United States, 468 U.S. 559 (1984). Moreover, the prophylactic protection of *Pearce* is quite limited in scope. It does not apply to resentencing at a trial de novo following a challenge to a misdemeanor conviction, see Colten v. Kentucky, 407 U.S. 104 (1972); to resentencing by a second jury, in a case involving jury sentencing, see Chaffin v. Stynchcombe, 412 U.S. 17 (1973); to resentencing by a trial judge after an original sentence that was imposed by a jury, see Texas v. McCullough, 475 U.S. 134 (1986); or to resentencing by a trial judge after the vacation of a guilty plea, see Alabama v. Smith, 490 U.S. 794 (1989). In each of these situations, the Court found that the circumstances generally did not warrant an inference of likely judicial vindictiveness.

Victim Impact Statements. Statements from crime victims (or their survivors) about the impact of the crime generally may be considered at sentencing, even in a death penalty case, as long as those statements are not so prejudicial as to violate either the general rules of evidence or the Due Process Clause. In a death penalty case, however, such statements may not include the opinions of the survivors about whether or not the defendant should receive a death sentence. See Payne v. Tennessee, 501 U.S. 808 (1991).

3. Substantive Limits on Sentencing — Eighth Amendment Proportionality

The Eighth Amendment provides: "Excessive bail shall not be required, nor excessive fines imposed, nor cruel and unusual punishments inflicted." Although it is generally agreed that the Eighth Amendment absolutely prohibits certain kinds of "cruel and unusual" punishments (e.g., in modern American society, drawing and quartering would be unconstitutional), there is far less agreement about whether, and to what extent, the Eighth Amendment also regulates the *relationship* between crimes and punishments. Does the Eighth Amendment contain an implied requirement of proportionality (i.e., that the punishment must fit the particular crime)? Under such a view, a punishment that is constitutional for one crime might be unconstitutional for another, less serious crime. Can life imprisonment, even if it is a constitutional punishment for the crime of murder, be imposed for the crime of driving without a valid driver's license? Or for an overtime parking violation?

In the special context of capital punishment, the Supreme Court has long acknowledged — and continues to acknowledge — the existence of an Eighth Amendment proportionality requirement. Thus, in Coker v. Georgia, 433 U.S. 584 (1977), the Court held that the death penalty was disproportionate to the crime of rape of an adult woman. In Tison v. Arizona, 481 U.S. 137 (1987), the Court held that the death penalty was disproportionate for the crime of felony murder, unless the defendant exhibited at least "reckless disregard for human life."

Outside the capital punishment context, however, the Court has been much less willing to engage in extended Eighth Amendment proportionality review of sentences.

EWING v. CALIFORNIA

Certiorari to the Court of Appeal of California, Second Appellate District
538 U.S. 11 (2003)

JUSTICE O'CONNOR announced the judgment of the Court and delivered an opinion in which CHIEF JUSTICE REHNQUIST and JUSTICE KENNEDY join.

In this case, we decide whether the Eighth Amendment prohibits the State of California from sentencing a repeat felon to a prison term of 25 years to life under the State's "Three Strikes and You're Out" law.

I

A

California's three strikes law reflects a shift in the State's sentencing policies toward incapacitating and deterring repeat offenders who threaten the public safety. The law was designed "to ensure longer prison sentences and greater punishment for those who commit a felony and have been previously convicted of serious and/or violent felony offenses." Cal. Penal Code Ann. §667(b) (West 1999). [In early 1993, the bill that would later become the three strikes law was defeated in a legislative committee.] Public outrage over the defeat sparked a voter initiative to add Proposition 184, based loosely on the bill, to the ballot in the November 1994 general election.

On October 1, 1993, while Proposition 184 was circulating, 12-year-old Polly Klaas was kidnaped from her home in Petaluma, California. Her admitted killer, Richard Allen Davis, had a long criminal history that included two prior kidnaping convictions. Davis had served only half of his most recent sentence (16 years for kidnaping, assault, and burglary). Had Davis served his entire sentence, he would still have been in prison on the day that Polly Klaas was kidnaped.

Polly Klaas' murder galvanized support for the three strikes initiative. Within days, Proposition 184 was on its way to becoming the fastest qualifying initiative in California history. [It passed both houses of the legislature by wide margins, and was signed into law on March 7, 1994.] California voters approved Proposition 184 by a margin of 72 to 28 percent on November 8, 1994.

California thus became the second State to enact a three strikes law. In November 1993, the voters of Washington State approved their own three strikes law, Initiative 593, by a margin of 3 to 1. U.S. Dept. of Justice, National Institute of Justice, J. Clark, J. Austin, & D. Henry, "Three Strikes and You're Out": A Review of State Legislation 1 (Sept. 1997) (hereinafter Review of State Legislation). Between 1993 and 1995, 24 States and the Federal Government enacted three strikes laws. Ibid. Though the three strikes laws vary from State to State, they share a common goal of protecting the public safety by providing lengthy prison terms for habitual felons.

B

California's current three strikes law [(which is at Cal. Penal Code Ann. §§667 and 1170)] consists of two virtually identical statutory schemes "designed to increase the prison terms of repeat felons." When a defendant is convicted of a felony, and he has previously been convicted of one or more prior felonies defined as "serious" or "violent" in Cal. Penal Code Ann. §§667.5 and 1192.7 (West Supp. 2002), sentencing is conducted pursuant to the three strikes law. Prior convictions must be alleged in the charging document, and the defendant has a right to a jury determination that the prosecution has proved the prior convictions beyond a reasonable doubt. §1025; §1158 (West 1985).

If the defendant has one prior "serious" or "violent" felony conviction, he must be sentenced to "twice the term otherwise provided as punishment for the current felony conviction." If the defendant has two or more prior "serious" or "violent" felony convictions, he must receive "an indeterminate term of life imprisonment." Defendants sentenced to life under the three strikes law become eligible for parole on a date calculated by reference to a "minimum term," which is the greater of (a) three times the term otherwise provided for the current conviction, (b) 25 years, or (c) the term determined by the court pursuant to §1170 for the underlying conviction, including any enhancements.

Under California law, certain offenses may be classified as either felonies or misdemeanors. These crimes are known as "wobblers." Some crimes that would otherwise be misdemeanors become "wobblers" because of the defendant's prior record. . . . Other crimes, such as grand theft, are "wobblers" regardless of the defendant's prior record. . . . Both types of "wobblers" are triggering offenses under the three strikes law only when they are treated as felonies. Under California law, a "wobbler" is presumptively a felony and "remains a felony except when the discretion is actually exercised" to make the crime a misdemeanor. . . .

In California, prosecutors may exercise their discretion to charge a "wobbler" as either a felony or a misdemeanor. Likewise, California trial courts have discretion to reduce a "wobbler" charged as a felony to a misdemeanor either before preliminary examination or at sentencing to avoid imposing a three strikes sentence. . . . In exercising this discretion, the court may consider [the same factors that influence criminal sentencing generally].

California trial courts can also vacate allegations of prior "serious" or "violent" felony convictions, either on motion by the prosecution or sua sponte. . . . In ruling whether to vacate allegations of prior felony convictions, courts consider whether, "in light of the nature and circumstances of [the defendant's] present felonies and prior serious and/or violent felony convictions, and the particulars of his background, character, and prospects, the defendant may be deemed outside the [three strikes'] scheme's spirit, in whole or in part." People v. Williams, 17 Cal. 4th 148, 161, 948 P.2d 429, 437, 69 Cal. Rptr. 2d 917 (1998). Thus, trial courts may avoid imposing a three strikes sentence in two ways: first, by reducing "wobblers" to misdemeanors (which do not qualify as triggering offenses), and second, by vacating allegations of prior "serious" or "violent" felony convictions.

C

On parole from a 9-year prison term, petitioner Gary Ewing walked into the pro shop of the El Segundo Golf Course in Los Angeles County on March 12, 2000. He walked out with three golf clubs, priced at $399 apiece, concealed in his pants leg. A shop employee, whose suspicions were aroused when he observed Ewing limp out of the pro shop, telephoned the police. The police apprehended Ewing in the parking lot.

Ewing is no stranger to the criminal justice system. [Here, Justice O'Connor reviewed Ewing's criminal history *prior* to the specific crimes that triggered the three strikes law in the instant case. This history included convictions for felony grand theft auto (later dismissed), theft (twice), petty theft, battery, burglary, possession of drug paraphernalia, appropriating lost property, unlawful possession of a firearm, and trespassing. — EDS.]

In October and November 1993, Ewing committed three burglaries and one robbery at a Long Beach, California, apartment complex over a 5-week period. He awakened one of his victims, asleep on her living room sofa, as he tried to disconnect her video cassette recorder from the television in that room. When she screamed, Ewing ran out the front door. On another occasion, Ewing accosted a victim in the mailroom of the apartment complex. Ewing claimed to have a gun and ordered the victim to hand over his wallet. When the victim resisted, Ewing produced a knife and forced the victim back to the apartment itself. While Ewing rifled through the bedroom, the victim fled the apartment screaming for help. Ewing absconded with the victim's money and credit cards.

On December 9, 1993, Ewing was arrested [at the same apartment complex]. A jury convicted Ewing of first-degree robbery and three counts of residential burglary. Sentenced to nine years and eight months in prison, Ewing was paroled in 1999.

Only 10 months later, Ewing stole the golf clubs at issue in this case. He was charged with, and ultimately convicted of, one count of felony grand theft of personal property in excess of $400. As required by the three strikes law, the prosecutor formally alleged, and the trial court later found, that Ewing had been convicted previously of four serious or violent felonies for the three burglaries and the robbery in the Long Beach apartment complex.

At the sentencing hearing, Ewing asked the court to reduce the conviction for grand theft, a "wobbler" under California law, to a misdemeanor so as to avoid a three strikes sentence. . . . Ewing also asked the trial court to exercise its discretion to dismiss the allegations of some or all of his prior serious or violent felony convictions, again for purposes of avoiding a three strikes sentence. . . . Before sentencing Ewing, the trial court took note of his entire criminal history, including the fact that he was on parole when he committed his latest offense. The court also heard arguments from defense counsel and a plea from Ewing himself.

In the end, the trial judge determined that the grand theft should remain a felony. The court also ruled that the four prior strikes for the three burglaries and the robbery in Long Beach should stand. As a newly convicted felon with two or more "serious" or "violent" felony convictions in his past, Ewing was sentenced under the three strikes law to 25 years to life.

The California Court of Appeal affirmed in an unpublished opinion. Relying on our decision in Rummel v. Estelle, 445 U.S. 263 (1980), the court rejected Ewing's claim that his sentence was grossly disproportionate under the Eighth Amendment. Enhanced sentences under recidivist statutes like the three strikes law, the court reasoned, serve the "legitimate goal" of deterring and incapacitating repeat offenders. The Supreme Court of California denied Ewing's petition for review, and we granted certiorari. We now affirm.

II

A

The Eighth Amendment, which forbids cruel and unusual punishments, contains a "narrow proportionality principle" that "applies to noncapital sentences." Harmelin v. Michigan, 501 U.S. 957, 996-997 (1991) (Kennedy, J., concurring in part and concurring in judgment). . . . We have most recently addressed the proportionality principle as applied to terms of years in a series of cases beginning with Rummel v. Estelle, supra.

In *Rummel*, we held that it did not violate the Eighth Amendment for a State to sentence a three-time offender to life in prison with the possibility of parole. Like Ewing, Rummel was sentenced to a lengthy prison term under a recidivism statute. Rummel's two prior offenses were a 1964 felony for "fraudulent use of a credit card to obtain $80 worth of goods or services," and a 1969 felony conviction for "passing a forged check in the amount of $28.36." His triggering offense was a conviction for felony theft — "obtaining $120.75 by false pretenses."

This Court ruled that "having twice imprisoned him for felonies, Texas was entitled to place upon Rummel the onus of one who is simply unable to bring his conduct within the social norms prescribed by the criminal law of the State." [445 U.S.,] at 284. The recidivism statute "is nothing more than a societal decision that when such a person commits yet another felony, he should be subjected to the admittedly serious penalty of incarceration for life, subject only to the State's judgment as to whether to grant him parole." Id., at 278. We noted that this Court "has on occasion stated that the Eighth Amendment prohibits imposition of a sentence that is grossly disproportionate to the severity of the crime." Id., at 271. But "outside the context of capital punishment, successful challenges to the proportionality of particular sentences have been exceedingly rare." Id., at 272. Although we stated that the proportionality principle "would . . . come into play in the extreme example . . . if a legislature made overtime parking a felony punishable by life imprisonment," id., at 274, n. 11, we held that "the mandatory life sentence imposed upon this petitioner does not constitute cruel and unusual punishment under the Eighth and Fourteenth Amendments" id., at 285.

In Hutto v. Davis, 454 U.S. 370 (1982) (per curiam), the defendant was sentenced to two consecutive terms of 20 years in prison for possession with intent to distribute nine ounces of marijuana and distribution of marijuana. We held that such a sentence was constitutional: "In short, *Rummel* stands for the proposition that federal courts should be reluctant to review legislatively mandated terms of imprisonment, and that successful challenges to the proportionality of particular sentences should be exceedingly rare." Id., at 374 (citations and internal quotation marks omitted).

Three years after *Rummel*, in Solem v. Helm, 463 U.S. 277, 279 (1983), we held that the Eighth Amendment prohibited "a life sentence without possibility of parole for a seventh nonviolent felony." The triggering offense in *Solem* was "uttering a 'no account' check for $100." We specifically stated that the Eighth Amendment's ban on cruel and unusual punishments "prohibits . . . sentences that are disproportionate to the crime committed," and that the "constitutional principle of proportionality has been recognized explicitly in this Court for almost a century." Id., at 284, 286. The *Solem* Court then explained that three factors may be relevant to a determination of whether a sentence is so disproportionate that it violates the Eighth Amendment: "(i) the gravity of the offense and the harshness of the penalty; (ii) the sentences imposed on other criminals in the same jurisdiction; and (iii) the sentences imposed for commission of the same crime in other jurisdictions." Id., at 292.

Applying these factors in *Solem*, we struck down the defendant's sentence of life without parole. We specifically noted the contrast between that sentence and the sentence in *Rummel*, pursuant to which the defendant was eligible for parole. 463 U.S., at 297. . . . Indeed, we explicitly declined to overrule *Rummel*. . . .

Eight years after *Solem*, we grappled with the proportionality issue again in *Harmelin*, supra. *Harmelin* was not a recidivism case, but rather involved a first-time offender convicted of possessing 672 grams of cocaine. He was sentenced to life in prison without possibility of parole. A majority of the Court rejected Harmelin's claim that his sentence was so grossly disproportionate that it violated the Eighth Amendment. The Court, however, could not agree on why his proportionality argument failed. Justice Scalia, joined by Chief Justice Rehnquist, wrote that the proportionality principle was "an aspect of our death penalty jurisprudence, rather than a generalizable aspect of Eighth Amendment law." Id., at 994. He would thus have declined to apply gross disproportionality principles except in reviewing capital sentences.

Justice Kennedy, joined by two other Members of the Court, concurred in part and concurred in the judgment. Justice Kennedy specifically recognized that "the Eighth Amendment proportionality principle also applies to noncapital sentences." Id., at 997. He then identified four principles of proportionality review — "the primacy of the legislature, the variety of legitimate penological schemes, the nature of our federal system, and the requirement that proportionality review be guided by objective factors" — that "inform the final one: The Eighth Amendment does not require strict proportionality between crime and sentence. Rather, it forbids only extreme sentences that are 'grossly disproportionate' to the crime." Id., at 1001 (citing *Solem*, supra, at 288). Justice Kennedy's concurrence also stated that *Solem* "did not mandate" comparative analysis "within and between jurisdictions." 501 U.S., at 1004-1005.

The proportionality principles in our cases distilled in Justice Kennedy's concurrence guide our application of the Eighth Amendment in the new context that we are called upon to consider.

B

For many years, most States have had laws providing for enhanced sentencing of repeat offenders. See, e.g., U.S. Dept. of Justice, Bureau of Justice Assistance, National Assessment of Structured Sentencing (1996). Yet between 1993 and 1995, three strikes laws effected a sea change in criminal sentencing throughout the Nation.[1] These laws responded to widespread public concerns about crime by targeting the class of offenders who pose the greatest threat to public safety: career criminals. As one of the chief architects of California's three strikes law has explained: "Three Strikes was intended to go beyond simply making sentences tougher. It was intended to be a focused effort to create a sentencing policy that would use the judicial system to reduce serious and violent crime." Ardaiz, California's Three Strikes Law: History, Expectations, Consequences 32 McGeorge L. Rev. 1, 12 (2000) (hereinafter Ardaiz).

Throughout the States, legislatures enacting three strikes laws made a deliberate policy choice that individuals who have repeatedly engaged in serious or violent criminal behavior, and whose conduct has not been deterred by more conventional approaches to punishment, must be isolated from society in order to protect the public safety. Though three strikes laws may be relatively new, our tradition of deferring to state legislatures in making and implementing such important policy decisions is longstanding. . . .

Our traditional deference to legislative policy choices finds a corollary in the principle that the Constitution "does not mandate adoption of any one penological theory." Id., at 999 (Kennedy, J., concurring in part and concurring in judgment). A sentence can have a variety of justifications, such as incapacitation, deterrence, retribution, or rehabilitation. . . . Some or all of these justifications may play a role in a State's sentencing scheme. Selecting the sentencing rationales is generally a policy choice to be made by state legislatures, not federal courts.

When the California Legislature enacted the three strikes law, it made a judgment that protecting the public safety requires incapacitating criminals who have already been convicted of at least one serious or violent crime. Nothing in the Eighth Amendment prohibits California from making that choice. . . . Recidivism has long been recognized as a legitimate basis for increased punishment. . . .

California's justification is no pretext. Recidivism is a serious public safety concern in California and throughout the Nation. According to a recent report, approximately 67 percent of former inmates released from state prisons were charged with at least one "serious" new crime within three years of their release. See U.S. Dept. of Justice, Bureau of Justice Statistics, P. Langan & D. Levin, Special Report: Recidivism of Prisoners Released in 1994, p. 1 (June 2002). In particular, released property offenders like Ewing had higher recidivism rates than those released after committing violent, drug, or public-order offenses. Id., at 8. Approximately 73 percent of the property offenders released in 1994 were arrested again within three years, compared to approximately 61 percent of the violent offenders, 62 percent of the public-order offenders, and 66 percent of the drug offenders.

---

1. It is hardly surprising that the statistics relied upon by JUSTICE BREYER show that prior to the enactment of the three strikes law, "*no* one like Ewing could have served more than *10* years in prison." Profound disappointment with the perceived lenity of criminal sentencing (especially for repeat felons) led to passage of three strikes laws in the first place. See, e.g., Review of State Legislation 1.

In 1996, when the Sacramento Bee studied 233 three strikes offenders in California, it found that they had an aggregate of 1,165 prior felony convictions, an average of 5 apiece. . . . The Sacramento Bee concluded, based on its investigation, that "in the vast majority of the cases, regardless of the third strike, the [three strikes] law is snaring [the] long-term habitual offenders with multiple felony convictions. . . ."[See Furillo, Three Strikes — The Verdict's In: Most Offenders Have Long Criminal Histories, Sacramento Bee, Mar. 31, 1996, p. A1.]

The State's interest in deterring crime also lends some support to the three strikes law. We have long viewed both incapacitation and deterrence as rationales for recidivism statutes. . . . Four years after the passage of California's three strikes law, the recidivism rate of parolees returned to prison for the commission of a new crime dropped by nearly 25 percent. California Dept. of Justice, Office of the Attorney General, "Three Strikes and You're Out" — Its Impact on the California Criminal Justice System After Four Years 10 (1998). Even more dramatically:

> an unintended but positive consequence of 'Three Strikes' has been the impact on parolees leaving the state. More California parolees are now leaving the state than parolees from other jurisdictions entering California. This striking turnaround started in 1994. It was the first time more parolees left the state than entered since 1976. This trend has continued and in 1997 more than 1,000 net parolees left California.

Ibid.

To be sure, California's three strikes law has sparked controversy. Critics have doubted the law's wisdom, cost-efficiency, and effectiveness in reaching its goals. See, e.g., Zimring, Hawkins, & Kamin, Punishment and Democracy: Three Strikes and You're Out in California (2001); Vitiello, Three Strikes: Can We Return to Rationality? 87 J. Crim. L. & Criminology. 395, 423 (1997). This criticism is appropriately directed at the legislature, which has primary responsibility for making the difficult policy choices that underlie any criminal sentencing scheme. We do not sit as a "superlegislature" to second-guess these policy choices. It is enough that the State of California has a reasonable basis for believing that dramatically enhanced sentences for habitual felons "advances the goals of [its] criminal justice system in any substantial way." See *Solem*, 463 U.S., at 297, n. 22.

III

Against this backdrop, we consider Ewing's claim that his three strikes sentence of 25 years to life is unconstitutionally disproportionate to his offense of "shoplifting three golf clubs." We first address the gravity of the offense compared to the harshness of the penalty. At the threshold, we note that Ewing incorrectly frames the issue. The gravity of his offense was not merely "shoplifting three golf clubs." Rather, Ewing was convicted of felony grand theft for stealing nearly $1,200 worth of merchandise after previously having been convicted of at least two "violent" or "serious" felonies. Even standing alone, Ewing's theft should not be taken lightly. His crime was certainly not "one of the most passive felonies a person could commit." *Solem*, supra, at 296 (internal quotation marks omitted). . . .

That grand theft is a "wobbler" under California law is of no moment. Though California courts have discretion to reduce a felony grand theft charge to a misdemeanor, it remains a felony for all purposes "unless and until the trial court imposes a misdemeanor sentence." . . . In Ewing's case, however, the trial judge justifiably exercised her discretion not to extend such lenient treatment given Ewing's long criminal history.

In weighing the gravity of Ewing's offense, we must place on the scales not only his current felony, but also his long history of felony recidivism. . . . In imposing a three strikes sentence, the State's interest is not merely punishing the offense of conviction, or the "triggering" offense: "It is in addition the interest . . . in dealing in a harsher manner with those who by repeated criminal acts have shown that they are simply incapable of conforming to the norms of society as established by its criminal law." See *Rummel*, 445 U.S., at 276; *Solem*, supra, at 296. To give full effect to the State's choice of this legitimate penological goal, our proportionality review of Ewing's sentence must take that goal into account.

Ewing's sentence is justified by the State's public-safety interest in incapacitating and deterring recidivist felons, and amply supported by his own long, serious criminal record.[2] Ewing has been convicted of numerous misdemeanor and felony offenses, served nine separate terms of incarceration, and committed most of his crimes while on probation or parole. His prior "strikes" were serious felonies including robbery and three residential burglaries. To be sure, Ewing's sentence is a long one. But it reflects a rational legislative judgment, entitled to deference, that offenders who have committed serious or violent felonies and who continue to commit felonies must be incapacitated. . . . Ewing's is not "the rare case in which a threshold comparison of the crime committed and the sentence imposed leads to an inference of gross disproportionality." *Harmelin*, 501 U.S., at 1005 (Kennedy, J., concurring in part and concurring in judgment).

We hold that Ewing's sentence of 25 years to life in prison, imposed for the offense of felony grand theft under the three strikes law, is not grossly disproportionate and therefore does not violate the Eighth Amendment's prohibition on cruel and unusual punishments. The judgment of the California Court of Appeal is affirmed.

JUSTICE SCALIA, concurring in the judgment.

. . . Out of respect for the principle of stare decisis, I might [accept the] holding of Solem v. Helm, 463 U.S. 277 (1983) — that the Eighth Amendment contains a narrow proportionality principle — if I felt I could intelligently apply it. This case demonstrates why I cannot.

Proportionality — the notion that the punishment should fit the crime — is inherently a concept tied to the penological goal of retribution. . . . In the present case, the game is up once the plurality has acknowledged that "the Constitution does not mandate adoption of any one penological theory," and that a "sentence can have a variety of justifications, such as incapacitation, deterrence, retribution, or rehabilitation." That acknowledgment having been made, it no longer suffices merely to assess "the gravity of the offense compared to the harshness of the penalty"; that classic description of the proportionality principle (alone and in itself quite resistant to policy-free, legal analysis) now becomes merely the "first" step of

---

2. . . . As we have explained, the overarching objective of the three strikes law is to prevent serious or violent offenders like Ewing from repeating their criminal behavior. . . . The California legislature therefore made a "deliberate policy decision . . . that the gravity of the new felony should not be a determinative factor in 'triggering' the application of the Three Strikes Law." Ardaiz 9. Neither the Eighth Amendment nor this Court's precedent forecloses that legislative choice.

the inquiry. Having completed that step (by a discussion which, in all fairness, does not convincingly establish that 25-years-to-life is a "proportionate" punishment for stealing three golf clubs), the plurality must then *add* an analysis to show that "Ewing's sentence is justified by the State's public-safety interest in incapacitating and deterring recidivist felons."

Which indeed it is — though why that has anything to do with the principle of proportionality is a mystery. Perhaps the plurality should revise its terminology, so that what it reads into the Eighth Amendment is not the unstated proposition that all punishment should be reasonably proportionate to the gravity of the offense, but rather the unstated proposition that all punishment should reasonably pursue the multiple purposes of the criminal law. That formulation would make it clearer than ever, of course, that the plurality is not applying law but evaluating policy.

Because I agree that petitioner's sentence does not violate the Eighth Amendment's prohibition against cruel and unusual punishments, I concur in the judgment.

JUSTICE THOMAS, concurring in the judgment.

I agree with Justice Scalia's view that the proportionality test announced in Solem v. Helm, 463 U.S. 277 (1983), is incapable of judicial application. Even were *Solem*'s test perfectly clear, however, I would not feel compelled by stare decisis to apply it. In my view, the Cruel and Unusual Punishments Clause of the Eighth Amendment contains no proportionality principle. . . .

JUSTICE STEVENS, with whom JUSTICE SOUTER, JUSTICE GINSBURG, and JUSTICE BREYER join, dissenting.

Justice Breyer has cogently explained why the sentence imposed in this case is both cruel and unusual.[1] The concurrences prompt this separate writing to emphasize that proportionality review is not only capable of judicial application but also required by the Eighth Amendment.

. . . [T]his Court has held that the Constitution directs judges to apply their best judgment in determining the proportionality of fines, see, e.g., United States v. Bajakajian, 524 U.S. 321, 334-336 (1998), bail, see, e.g., Stack v. Boyle, 342 U.S. 1, 5 (1951), and other forms of punishment, including the imposition of a death sentence, see, e.g., Coker v. Georgia, 433 U.S. 584, 592 (1977). It "would be anomalous indeed" to suggest that the Eighth Amendment makes proportionality review applicable in the context of bail and fines but not in the context of other forms of punishment, such as imprisonment. . . . Rather, by broadly prohibiting excessive sanctions, the Eighth Amendment directs judges to exercise their wise judgment in assessing the proportionality of all forms of punishment.

The absence of a black-letter rule does not disable judges from exercising their discretion in construing the outer limits on sentencing authority that the Eighth Amendment imposes. . . .

Throughout most of the Nation's history — before guideline sentencing became so prevalent — federal and state trial judges imposed specific sentences pursuant to

---

1. I agree with Justice Breyer that Ewing's sentence is grossly disproportionate even under *Harmelin*'s narrow proportionality framework. However, it is not clear that this case is controlled by *Harmelin*, which considered the proportionality of a life sentence imposed on a drug offender who had no prior felony convictions. Rather, the three-factor analysis established in Solem v. Helm, 463 U.S. 277, 290-291 (1983), which specifically addressed recidivist sentencing, seems more directly on point.

grants of authority that gave them uncabined discretion within broad ranges. See K. Stith & J. Cabranes, Fear of Judging: Sentencing Guidelines in the Federal Courts 9 (1998) (hereinafter Stith & Cabranes). . . . In exercising their discretion, sentencing judges wisely employed a proportionality principle that took into account all of the justifications for punishment — namely, deterrence, incapacitation, retribution and rehabilitation. See Stith & Cabranes 14. Likewise, I think it clear that the Eighth Amendment's prohibition of "cruel and unusual punishments" expresses a broad and basic proportionality principle that takes into account all of the justifications for penal sanctions. . . .

Accordingly, I respectfully dissent.

JUSTICE BREYER, with whom JUSTICE STEVENS, JUSTICE SOUTER, and JUSTICE GINSBURG join, dissenting.

The constitutional question is whether the "three strikes" sentence imposed by California upon repeat-offender Gary Ewing is "grossly disproportionate" to his crime. The sentence amounts to a real prison term of at least 25 years. The sentence-triggering criminal conduct consists of the theft of three golf clubs priced at a total of $1,197. The offender has a criminal history that includes four felony convictions arising out of three separate burglaries (one armed). In Solem v. Helm, 463 U.S. 277 (1983), the Court found grossly disproportionate a somewhat longer sentence imposed on a recidivist offender for triggering criminal conduct that was somewhat less severe. In my view, the differences are not determinative, and the Court should reach the same ultimate conclusion here.

I

. . . I believe that the case before us is a "rare" case — one in which a court can say with reasonable confidence that the punishment is "grossly disproportionate" to the crime.

II

Ewing's claim crosses the gross disproportionality "threshold." First, precedent makes clear that Ewing's sentence raises a serious disproportionality question. Ewing is a recidivist. Hence the two cases most directly in point are those in which the Court considered the constitutionality of recidivist sentencing: *Rummel* and *Solem*. Ewing's claim falls between these two cases. It is stronger than the claim presented in *Rummel*, where the Court upheld a recidivist's sentence as constitutional. It is weaker than the claim presented in *Solem*, where the Court struck down a recidivist sentence as unconstitutional.

Three kinds of sentence-related characteristics define the relevant comparative spectrum: (a) the length of the prison term in real time, i.e., the time that the offender is likely actually to spend in prison; (b) the sentence-triggering criminal conduct, i.e., the offender's actual behavior or other offense-related circumstances; and (c) the offender's criminal history. . . .

In *Rummel*, the Court held constitutional (a) a sentence of life imprisonment *with parole available within 10 to 12 years*, (b) for the offense of obtaining $120 by false pretenses, (c) committed by an offender with two prior felony convictions (involving small amounts of money). In *Solem*, the Court held unconstitutional (a) a sentence of life imprisonment *without parole*, (b) for the crime of writing a $100 check on a nonexistent bank account, (c) committed by an offender with six prior felony convictions (including three for burglary). Which of the three pertinent comparative factors made the constitutional difference?

The third factor, prior record, cannot explain the difference. The offender's prior record was *worse* in *Solem*, where the Court found the sentence too long, than in *Rummel*, where the Court upheld the sentence. The second factor, offense conduct, cannot explain the difference. The nature of the triggering offense — viewed in terms of the actual monetary loss — in the two cases was about the same. The one critical factor that explains the difference in the outcome is the length of the likely prison term measured in real time. In *Rummel*, where the Court upheld the sentence, the state sentencing statute authorized parole for the offender, Rummel, after 10 or 12 years. In *Solem*, where the Court struck down the sentence, the sentence required the offender, Helm, to spend the rest of his life in prison.

Now consider the present case. The third factor, *offender characteristics* — i.e., prior record — does not differ significantly here from that in *Solem*. . . . The second factor, *offense behavior*, is worse than that in *Solem*, but only to a degree. . . . [T]he difference lies in the *value* of the goods obtained. That difference, measured in terms of the most relevant feature (loss to the victim, i.e., wholesale value) and adjusted for the irrelevant feature of inflation, comes down (in 1979 values) to about $379 here compared with $100 in *Solem*, or (in 1973 values) to $232 here compared with $120.75 in *Rummel*. . . .

The difference in *length* of the real prison term — the first, and critical, factor in *Solem* and *Rummel* — is considerably more important. Ewing's sentence here amounts, in real terms, to at least 25 years without parole or good-time credits. That sentence is considerably shorter than Helm's sentence in *Solem*, which amounted, in real terms, to life in prison. Nonetheless Ewing's real prison term is more than twice as long as the term at issue in *Rummel*, which amounted, in real terms, to at least 10 or 12 years. And, Ewing's sentence, unlike Rummel's (but like Helm's sentence in *Solem*), is long enough to consume the productive remainder of almost any offender's life. (It means that Ewing himself, seriously ill when sentenced at age 38, will likely die in prison.)

The upshot is that the length of the real prison term — the factor that explains the *Solem/Rummel* difference in outcome — places Ewing closer to *Solem* than to *Rummel*, though the greater value of the golf clubs that Ewing stole moves Ewing's case back slightly in *Rummel*'s direction. Overall, the comparison places Ewing's sentence well within the twilight zone between *Solem* and *Rummel* — a zone where the argument for unconstitutionality is substantial, where the cases themselves cannot determine the constitutional outcome.

Second, Ewing's sentence on its face imposes one of the most severe punishments available upon a recidivist who subsequently engaged in one of the less serious forms of criminal conduct. I do not deny the seriousness of shoplifting, which an amicus curiae tells us costs retailers in the range of $30 billion annually. . . . [But] the sentence-triggering behavior here ranks well toward the bottom of the criminal conduct scale. . . .

Third, some objective evidence suggests that many experienced judges would consider Ewing's sentence disproportionately harsh. The United States Sentencing Commission . . . does not include shoplifting (or similar theft-related offenses) among the crimes that might trigger especially long sentences for recidivists, see USSG §4B1.1 (Nov. 2002). . . .

Taken together, these three circumstances make clear that Ewing's "gross disproportionality" argument is a strong one. That being so, his claim *must* pass the "threshold" test. If it did not, what would be the function of the test? . . . A threshold test that blocked every ultimately invalid constitutional claim — even strong ones — would not be a *threshold* test but a *determinative* test. And, it would be a *determinative* test that failed to take account of highly pertinent sentencing information, namely, comparison with other sentences. . . .

III

Believing Ewing's argument a strong one, sufficient to pass the threshold, I turn to the comparative analysis. A comparison of Ewing's sentence with other sentences requires answers to two questions. First, how would other jurisdictions (or California at other times, i.e., without the three strikes penalty) punish the *same offense conduct*? Second, upon what other conduct would other jurisdictions (or California) impose the *same prison term*? Moreover, since hypothetical punishment is beside the point, the relevant prison time, for comparative purposes, is real prison time, i.e., the time that an offender must *actually serve*. . . .

As to California itself, we know the following: First, between the end of World War II and 1994 (when California enacted the three strikes law), *no one* like Ewing could have served more than *10* years in prison. . . .

Second, statistics suggest that recidivists *of all sorts* convicted during that same time period in California served a small fraction of Ewing's real-time sentence. On average, recidivists served three to four additional (recidivist-related) years in prison, with 90 percent serving less than an additional real seven to eight years. . . .

Third, we know that California has reserved, and still reserves, Ewing-type prison time, i.e., at least 25 real years in prison, for criminals convicted of crimes far worse than was Ewing's. Statistics for the years 1945 to 1981, for example, indicate that typical (nonrecidivist) male first-degree murderers served between 10 and 15 real years in prison, with 90 percent of all such murderers serving less than 20 real years. . . . Moreover, California, which has moved toward a real-time sentencing system (where the statutory punishment approximates the time served), still punishes far less harshly those who have engaged in far more serious conduct. . . . It reserves the sentence that it here imposes upon (former-burglar-now-golf-club-thief) Ewing, for nonrecidivist, first-degree murderers. See §190(a) (West Supp. 2003) (sentence of 25 years to life for first-degree murder).

As to other jurisdictions, we know the following: The United States, bound by the federal Sentencing Guidelines, would impose upon a recidivist, such as Ewing, a sentence that, in any ordinary case, would not exceed 18 months in prison. USSG §2B1.1(a) (Nov. 1999). . . .

. . . [T]he law would make it legally impossible for a Ewing-type offender to serve more than 10 years in prison in 33 jurisdictions, as well as the federal courts, more than 15 years in 4 other States, and more than 20 years in 4 additional States. In nine other States, the law *might* make it legally possible to impose a sentence of 25 years or more — though that fact by itself, of course, does not mean that judges have actually done so. . . .

The upshot is that comparison of other sentencing practices, both in other jurisdictions and in California at other times (or in respect to other crimes), validates what an initial threshold examination suggested. . . . Outside the California three strikes context, Ewing's recidivist sentence is virtually unique in its harshness for his offense of conviction, and by a considerable degree.

IV

[In this section, Justice Breyer rejected the argument that California's three strikes law might nevertheless be justified on grounds of administrative efficiency, because the law could have specified the triggering crimes and thereby avoided the anomaly of including persons like Ewing. He also rejected the claim that the law might be justified by deterrence, concluding that it "amounts to overkill." — EDS.]

V

Justice Scalia and Justice Thomas argue that we should not review for gross disproportionality a sentence to a term of years. . . . I concede that a bright-line rule would give legislators and sentencing judges more guidance. But application of the Eighth Amendment to a sentence of a term of years requires a case-by-case approach. And, in my view, like that of the plurality, meaningful enforcement of the Eighth Amendment demands that application — even if only at sentencing's outer bounds.

A case-by-case approach can nonetheless offer guidance through example. Ewing's sentence is, at a minimum, 2 to 3 times the length of sentences that other jurisdictions would impose in similar circumstances. That sentence itself is sufficiently long to require a typical offender to spend virtually all the remainder of his active life in prison. These and the other factors that I have discussed, along with the questions that I have asked along the way, should help to identify "gross disproportionality" in a fairly objective way — at the outer bounds of sentencing.

In sum, even if I accept for present purposes the plurality's analytical framework, Ewing's sentence (life imprisonment with a minimum term of 25 years) is grossly disproportionate to the triggering offense conduct — stealing three golf clubs — Ewing's recidivism notwithstanding.

For these reasons, I dissent.

NOTES AND QUESTIONS

1. Do you agree with the conclusion reached by a majority of the Justices in *Ewing* that the Eighth Amendment is not offended by a sentence of 25 years to life in prison for a "triggering crime" of stealing three golf clubs? How is your analysis affected by the knowledge that — even with the recent trend toward increased criminal punishments — no other state would appear to allow such severe punishment for a defendant like Ewing? Or that California generally reserves such punishment exclusively for murderers? How, if at all, is your analysis affected by the fact that Ewing was "seriously ill" at the time of his sentencing, and would "likely die in prison"?

Does Justice Breyer's alternative, highly detailed (and, at points, highly mathematical) analysis seem like a better way for the Court to apply the Eighth Amendment? Or would it simply produce a flood of costly and time-consuming appellate litigation?

2. After *Harmelin* and *Ewing*, what is left of the Eighth Amendment proportionality requirement in noncapital cases? According to Justice Kennedy's *Harmelin* concurrence (which controls, given the fragmented Court lineup — remember that three Justices in Ewing adopted Justice Kennedy's *Harmelin* position, while two other Justices would have gone even further and eliminated all proportionality review), no comparative analysis need be performed unless "a threshold comparison of the crime committed and the sentence imposed leads to an inference of gross disproportionality." Based on the results in *Harmelin* and *Ewing*, however, would any sentence of imprisonment, no matter how long, ever be likely to cross this threshold?

3. The Supreme Court's decision in *Harmelin* turned out not to be the last word on that particular statute. One year later, the Michigan Supreme Court held that the mandatory-life-without-parole statute, as applied to simple possession of narcotics, violated a provision in the Michigan state constitution prohibiting "cruel *or* unusual" punishments. See People v. Bullock, 485 N.W. 2d 866 (Mich. 1992). But the statute remained in effect for those convicted of manufacture, distribution, or possession with intent to manufacture or distribute narcotics. By 1997, 205 prisoners in Michigan were serving life sentences without parole under the statute involved in *Harmelin* and *Bullock*. Of these, 173 had no prior criminal record.

In July 1998, the Michigan legislature enacted an amendment to the statute allowing for the possibility of parole, after 15 years, for first-time, nonviolent offenders who agreed to cooperate fully with the prosecutor. See Brian M. Thomas, Note, Recent Legislation: Criminal Procedure — Parole Eligibility — Michigan Eliminates Mandatory Drug Sentences and Allows Parole for Possession of 650 or More Grams of Cocaine or Heroin, 76 U. Det. Mercy L. Rev. 679 (1999).

4. What about the excessive fines clause of the Eighth Amendment? How does the analysis of a monetary punishment under that provision compare with the *Harmelin/Ewing* analysis of prison sentences under the cruel and unusual punishments clause?

In United States v. Bajakajian, 524 U.S. 321 (1998), the Supreme Court — for the first time — applied the excessive fines clause to invalidate a monetary punishment. The defendant was convicted of willfully violating the law that requires anyone leaving the United States to report if they are carrying more than $10,000 in currency, see 31 U.S.C. §§5316(a)(1)(A) and 5322(a). In fact, the defendant was carrying a total of $357,144. The government sought forfeiture of the entire amount, as authorized by 18 U.S.C. §982(a)(1), but the defendant claimed that such a forfeiture would violate the excessive fines clause.

The Court agreed with the defendant that forfeiture of the entire $357,144 would violate the excessive fines clause. Justice Thomas, writing for the majority, explained:

The touchstone of the constitutional inquiry under the Excessive Fines Clause is the principle of proportionality: The amount of the forfeiture must bear some relationship to the gravity of the offense that it is designed to punish. . . . Until today, however, we have not articulated a standard for determining whether a punitive forfeiture is constitutionally excessive. We now hold that a punitive forfeiture violates the Excessive Fines Clause if it is grossly disproportional to the gravity of a defendant's offense.

The text and history of the Excessive Fines Clause demonstrate the centrality of proportionality to the excessiveness inquiry; nonetheless, they provide little guidance as to how disproportional a punitive forfeiture must be to the gravity of an offense in order to be "excessive." . . .

We must therefore rely on other considerations in deriving a constitutional excessiveness standard, and there are two that we find particularly relevant. The first . . . is that judgments about the appropriate punishment for an offense belong in the first instance to the legislature. See, e.g., Solem v. Helm, 463 U.S. 277 (1983). . . . The second is that any judicial determination regarding the gravity of a particular criminal offense will be inherently imprecise. Both of these principles counsel against requiring strict proportionality between the amount of a punitive forfeiture and the gravity of a criminal offense, and we therefore adopt the standard of gross disproportionality articulated in our Cruel and Unusual Punishments Clause precedents. . . .

Under this standard, the forfeiture of respondent's entire $357,144 would violate the Excessive Fines Clause. Respondent's crime was solely a reporting offense. It was permissible to transport the currency out of the country so long as he reported it. . . . Furthermore, as the District Court found, respondent's violation was unrelated to any other illegal activities. . . . Whatever his other vices, respondent does not fit into the class of persons for whom the statute was principally designed: He is not a money launderer, a drug trafficker, or a tax evader. . . .

Comparing the gravity of respondent's crime with the $357,144 forfeiture the Government seeks, we conclude that such a forfeiture would be grossly disproportionate to the gravity of his offense. . . . [I]t bears no articulable correlation to any injury suffered by the Government.

524 U.S., at 334-340.

Note that the *Bajakajian* Court purported to apply the same "gross disproportionality" standard as in *Harmelin* and *Ewing*. Yet the result reached was different. The *Bajakajian* dissenters argued that "[t]he crime of smuggling or failing to report cash is more serious than the Court is willing to acknowledge. The drug trade, money laundering, and tax evasion all depend in part on smuggled and unreported cash. . . . Money launderers will rejoice to know they face forfeitures of less than 5% of the money transported, provided they hire accomplished liars to carry their money for them." 524 U.S., at 351, 354 (Kennedy, J., dissenting). Shouldn't the *Bajakajian* Court have granted more deference to the judgment of Congress about the seriousness of the crime, as well as about the appropriate level of monetary punishment?

5. In *Harmelin* and *Ewing*, the Court basically declined the invitation to engage in meaningful substantive review of noncapital prison sentences. This reluctance may have its roots in legitimacy concerns related to the Court's basic counter-majoritarian dilemma, which may be intensified in the particular legal and historical context of the Eighth Amendment. See Joseph L. Hoffmann, "The 'Cruel and Unusual Punishment' Clause: A Significant Limit on the Government's Power to Punish, or Mere Constitutional Rhetoric?" in The Bill of Rights in Modern America (D. Bodenhamer & J. Ely, Jr., eds. 1993). Or it may stem from the realization that the Court has few, if any, anchors to prevent substantive review of criminal sentences from devolving into standardless pronouncements of the Justices' own personal moral beliefs. Or it may reflect simply the Court's relative lack of experience, and thus lack of expertise, in such substantive review. See Ronald J. Allen & Ethan A.

Hastert, From *Winship* to *Apprendi* to *Booker*: Constitutional Command or Constitutional Blunder? 58 Stan. L. Rev. 195-216 (2005).

In any event, it is hard not to be struck by the stark contrast between the Court's cautious approach to Eighth Amendment substantive review of noncapital sentences and its much more aggressive approach to substantive review of capital sentences.

ROPER v. SIMMONS

Certiorari to the Supreme Court of Missouri
543 U.S. 551 (2005)

JUSTICE KENNEDY delivered the opinion of the Court.

This case requires us to address, for the second time in a decade and a half, whether it is permissible under the Eighth and Fourteenth Amendments to the Constitution of the United States to execute a juvenile offender who was older than 15 but younger than 18 when he committed a capital crime. In Stanford v. Kentucky, 492 U.S. 361 (1989), a divided Court rejected the proposition that the Constitution bars capital punishment for juvenile offenders in this age group. We reconsider the question.

I

[This section, detailing the brutal facts of the murder that was planned by Simmons, and that was committed by him and two younger accomplices, is omitted. — EDS.]

II

The Eighth Amendment provides: "Excessive bail shall not be required, nor excessive fines imposed, nor cruel and unusual punishments inflicted." The provision is applicable to the States through the Fourteenth Amendment. As the Court explained in Atkins [v. Virginia, 536 U.S. 304 (2002)], the Eighth Amendment guarantees individuals the right not to be subjected to excessive sanctions. The right flows from the basic "'precept of justice that punishment for crime should be graduated and proportioned to [the] offense.'" 536 U.S., at 311 (quoting Weems v. United States, 217 U.S. 349, 367 (1910)). By protecting even those convicted of heinous crimes, the Eighth Amendment reaffirms the duty of the government to respect the dignity of all persons.

The prohibition against "cruel and unusual punishments," like other expansive language in the Constitution, must be interpreted according to its text, by considering history, tradition, and precedent, and with due regard for its purpose and function in the constitutional design. To implement this framework we have established the propriety and affirmed the necessity of referring to "the evolving standards of decency that mark the progress of a maturing society" to determine which punishments are so disproportionate as to be cruel and unusual. Trop v. Dulles, 356 U.S. 86, 100-101 (1958) (plurality opinion).

In Thompson v. Oklahoma, 487 U.S. 815 (1988), a plurality of the Court determined that our standards of decency do not permit the execution of any offender under the age of 16 at the time of the crime. . . . With Justice O'Connor concurring in the judgment on narrower grounds, id., at 848-859, the Court set aside the death sentence that had been imposed on the 15-year-old offender.

The next year, in Stanford v. Kentucky, 492 U.S. 361 (1989), the Court, over a dissenting opinion joined by four Justices, referred to contemporary standards of decency in this country and concluded the Eighth and Fourteenth Amendments did not proscribe the execution of juvenile offenders over 15 but under 18. The Court noted that 22 of the 37 death penalty States permitted the death penalty for 16-year-old offenders, and, among these 37 States, 25 permitted it for 17-year-old offenders. These numbers, in the Court's view, indicated there was no national consensus "sufficient to label a particular punishment cruel and unusual." . . .

The same day the Court decided *Stanford*, it held that the Eighth Amendment did not mandate a categorical exemption from the death penalty for the mentally retarded. Penry v. Lynaugh, 492 U.S. 302 (1989). . . .

Three Terms ago the subject was reconsidered in *Atkins*. We held that standards of decency have evolved since *Penry* and now demonstrate that the execution of the mentally retarded is cruel and unusual punishment. The Court noted objective indicia of society's standards, as expressed in legislative enactments and state practice with respect to executions of the mentally retarded. When *Atkins* was decided only a minority of States permitted the practice, and even in those States it was rare. On the basis of these indicia the Court determined that executing mentally retarded offenders "has become truly unusual, and it is fair to say that a national consensus has developed against it." [536 U.S.,] at 316.

The inquiry into our society's evolving standards of decency did not end there. . . . Mental retardation, the Court said, diminishes personal culpability even if the offender can distinguish right from wrong. The impairments of mentally retarded offenders make it less defensible to impose the death penalty as retribution for past crimes and less likely that the death penalty will have a real deterrent effect. Based on these considerations and on the finding of national consensus against executing the mentally retarded, the Court ruled that the death penalty constitutes an excessive sanction for the entire category of mentally retarded offenders. . . .

Just as the *Atkins* Court reconsidered the issue decided in *Penry*, we now reconsider the issue decided in *Stanford*. The beginning point is a review of objective indicia of consensus, as expressed in particular by the enactments of legislatures that have addressed the question. This data gives us essential instruction. We then must determine, in the exercise of our own independent judgment, whether the death penalty is a disproportionate punishment for juveniles.

III

A

The evidence of national consensus against the death penalty for juveniles is similar, and in some respects parallel, to the evidence *Atkins* held sufficient to demonstrate a national consensus against the death penalty for the mentally retarded. When *Atkins* was decided, 30 States prohibited the death penalty for the mentally retarded. This number comprised 12 that had abandoned the death penalty altogether, and 18 that maintained it but excluded the mentally retarded from its reach. By a similar calculation in this case, 30 States prohibit the juvenile death penalty, comprising 12 that have rejected the death penalty altogether and 18 that maintain it but, by express provision or judicial interpretation, exclude juveniles from its reach. *Atkins* emphasized that even in the 20 States without formal prohibition, the practice of executing the mentally retarded was infrequent. Since *Penry*, only five States had executed offenders known to have an IQ under 70. In the present case, too, even in the 20 States without a formal prohibition on executing juveniles, the practice is infrequent. Since *Stanford*, six States have executed prisoners for crimes committed as juveniles. In the past 10 years, only three have done so: Oklahoma, Texas, and Virginia. See V. Streib, The Juvenile Death Penalty Today: Death Sentences and Executions for Juvenile Crimes, January 1, 1973-December 31, 2004, No. 76, p. 4 (2005), available at http://www.law.onu.edu/faculty/streib/documents/JuvDeathDec2004.pdf (last updated Jan. 31, 2005) (as visited Feb. 25, 2005, and available in the Clerk of Court's case file). . . .

. . . The number of States that have abandoned capital punishment for juvenile offenders since *Stanford* is smaller than the number of States that abandoned capital punishment for the mentally retarded after *Penry*; yet we think the same consistency of direction of change has been demonstrated. Since *Stanford*, no State that previously prohibited capital punishment for juveniles has reinstated it. This fact, coupled with the trend toward abolition of the juvenile death penalty, carries special force in light of the general popularity of anticrime legislation, *Atkins*, supra, at 315, and in light of the particular trend in recent years toward cracking down on juvenile crime in other respects. . . . Any difference between this case and *Atkins* with respect to the pace of abolition is thus counterbalanced by the consistent direction of the change.

The slower pace of abolition of the juvenile death penalty over the past 15 years, moreover, may have a simple explanation. When we heard *Penry*, only two death penalty States had already prohibited the execution of the mentally retarded. When we heard *Stanford*, by contrast, 12 death penalty States had already prohibited the execution of any juvenile under 18, and 15 had prohibited the execution of any juvenile under 17. If anything, this shows that the impropriety of executing juveniles between 16 and 18 years of age gained wide recognition earlier than the impropriety of executing the mentally retarded. . . .

As in *Atkins*, the objective indicia of consensus in this case — the rejection of the juvenile death penalty in the majority of States; the infrequency of its use even where it remains on the books; and the consistency in the trend toward abolition of the practice — provide sufficient evidence that today our society views juveniles, in the words *Atkins* used respecting the mentally retarded, as "categorically less culpable than the average criminal." 536 U.S., at 316.

B

A majority of States have rejected the imposition of the death penalty on juvenile offenders under 18, and we now hold this is required by the Eighth Amendment.

Because the death penalty is the most severe punishment, the Eighth Amendment applies to it with special force. *Thompson*, 487 U.S., at 856 (O'Connor, J., concurring in judgment). Capital punishment must be limited to those offenders who commit "a narrow category of the most serious crimes" and whose extreme culpability makes them "the most deserving of execution." *Atkins*, supra, at 319. . . .

Three general differences between juveniles under 18 and adults demonstrate that juvenile offenders cannot with reliability be classified among the worst offenders. First, as any parent knows and as the scientific and sociological studies respondent and his amici cite tend to confirm, "[a] lack of maturity and an underdeveloped sense of responsibility are found in youth more often than in adults and are more understandable among the young. These qualities often result in impetuous and ill-considered actions and decisions." Johnson [v. Texas, 509 U.S. 350,] 367 [(1993)]. . . . It has been noted that "adolescents are overrepresented statistically in virtually every category of reckless behavior." Arnett, Reckless Behavior in Adolescence: A Developmental Perspective, 12 Developmental Review 339 (1992). In recognition of the comparative immaturity and irresponsibility of juveniles, almost every State prohibits those under 18 years of age from voting, serving on juries, or marrying without parental consent. . . .

The second area of difference is that juveniles are more vulnerable or susceptible to negative influences and outside pressures, including peer pressure. . . . This is explained in part by the prevailing circumstance that juveniles have less control, or less experience with control, over their own environment. See Steinberg & Scott, Less Guilty by Reason of Adolescence: Developmental Immaturity, Diminished Responsibility, and the Juvenile Death Penalty, 58 Am. Psychologist 1009, 1014 (2003) (hereinafter Steinberg & Scott) ("[A]s legal minors, [juveniles] lack the freedom that adults have to extricate themselves from a criminogenic setting").

The third broad difference is that the character of a juvenile is not as well formed as that of an adult. The personality traits of juveniles are more transitory, less fixed. See generally E. Erikson, Identity: Youth and Crisis (1968).

These differences render suspect any conclusion that a juvenile falls among the worst offenders. The susceptibility of juveniles to immature and irresponsible behavior means "their irresponsible conduct is not as morally reprehensible as that of an adult." *Thompson*, supra, at 835 (plurality opinion). Their own vulnerability and comparative lack of control over their immediate surroundings mean juveniles have a greater claim than adults to be forgiven for failing to escape negative influences in their whole environment. See *Stanford*, 492 U.S., at 395 (Brennan, J., dissenting). The reality that juveniles still struggle to define their identity means it is less supportable to conclude that even a heinous crime committed by a juvenile is evidence of irretrievably depraved character. From a moral standpoint it would be misguided to equate the failings of a minor with those of an adult, for a greater possibility exists that a minor's character deficiencies will be reformed. Indeed, "[t]he relevance of youth as a mitigating factor derives from the fact that the signature qualities of youth are transient; as individuals mature, the impetuousness and recklessness that may dominate in younger years can subside." *Johnson*, supra, at 368; see also Steinberg & Scott 1014 ("For most teens, [risky or antisocial] behaviors are fleeting; they cease with maturity as individual identity becomes settled. Only a relatively small proportion of adolescents who experiment in risky or illegal activities develop entrenched patterns of problem behavior that persist into adulthood").

In *Thompson*, a plurality of the Court recognized the import of these characteristics with respect to juveniles under 16, and relied on them to hold that the Eighth Amendment prohibited the imposition of the death penalty on juveniles below that age. We conclude the same reasoning applies to all juvenile offenders under 18.

Once the diminished culpability of juveniles is recognized, it is evident that the penological justifications for the death penalty apply to them with lesser force than to adults. We have held there are two distinct social purposes served by the death penalty: "retribution and deterrence of capital crimes by prospective offenders." *Atkins*, 536 U.S., at 319. . . .

Whether viewed as an attempt to express the community's moral outrage or as an attempt to right the balance for the wrong to the victim, the case for retribution is not as strong with a minor as with an adult. Retribution is not proportional if the law's most severe penalty is imposed on one whose culpability or blameworthiness is diminished, to a substantial degree, by reason of youth and immaturity.

As for deterrence, it is unclear whether the death penalty has a significant or even measurable deterrent effect on juveniles, as counsel for the petitioner acknowledged at oral argument. Tr. of Oral Arg. 48. In general we leave to legislatures the assessment of the efficacy of various criminal penalty schemes, see Harmelin v. Michigan, 501 U.S. 957, 998-999 (1991) (Kennedy, J., concurring in part and concurring in judgment). Here, however, the absence of evidence of deterrent effect is of special concern because the same characteristics that render juveniles less culpable than adults suggest as well that juveniles will be less susceptible to deterrence. . . . To the extent the juvenile death penalty might have residual deterrent effect, it is worth noting that the punishment of life imprisonment without the possibility of parole is itself a severe sanction, in particular for a young person.

In concluding that neither retribution nor deterrence provides adequate justification for imposing the death penalty on juvenile offenders, we cannot deny or overlook the brutal crimes too many juvenile offenders have committed. Certainly it can be argued, although we by no means concede the point, that a rare case might arise in which a juvenile offender has sufficient psychological maturity, and at the same time demonstrates sufficient depravity, to merit a sentence of death. . . . A central feature of death penalty sentencing is a particular assessment of the circumstances of the crime and the characteristics of the offender. The system is designed to consider both aggravating and mitigating circumstances, including youth, in every case. Given this Court's own insistence on individualized consideration, petitioner maintains that it is both arbitrary and unnecessary to adopt a categorical rule barring imposition of the death penalty on any offender under 18 years of age.

We disagree. The differences between juvenile and adult offenders are too marked and well understood to risk allowing a youthful person to receive the death penalty despite insufficient culpability. An unacceptable likelihood exists that the brutality or cold-blooded nature of any particular crime would overpower mitigating arguments based on youth as a matter of course, even where the juvenile offender's objective immaturity, vulnerability, and lack of true depravity should require a sentence less severe than death. In some cases a defendant's youth may even be counted against him. In this very case, as we noted above, the prosecutor argued Simmons' youth was aggravating rather than mitigating. While this sort of overreaching could be corrected by a particular rule to ensure that the mitigating force of youth is not overlooked, that would not address our larger concerns.

It is difficult even for expert psychologists to differentiate between the juvenile offender whose crime reflects unfortunate yet transient immaturity, and the rare juvenile offender whose crime reflects irreparable corruption. See Steinberg & Scott 1014-1016. As we understand it, this difficulty underlies the rule forbidding psychiatrists from diagnosing any patient under 18 as having antisocial personality disorder, a disorder also referred to as psychopathy or sociopathy, and which is characterized by callousness, cynicism, and contempt for the feelings, rights, and suffering of others. American Psychiatric Association, Diagnostic and Statistical

Manual of Mental Disorders 701-706 (4th ed. text rev. 2000); see also Steinberg & Scott 1015. If trained psychiatrists with the advantage of clinical testing and observation refrain, despite diagnostic expertise, from assessing any juvenile under 18 as having antisocial personality disorder, we conclude that States should refrain from asking jurors to issue a far graver condemnation — that a juvenile offender merits the death penalty. When a juvenile offender commits a heinous crime, the State can exact forfeiture of some of the most basic liberties, but the State cannot extinguish his life and his potential to attain a mature understanding of his own humanity.

Drawing the line at 18 years of age is subject, of course, to the objections always raised against categorical rules. The qualities that distinguish juveniles from adults do not disappear when an individual turns 18. By the same token, some under 18 have already attained a level of maturity some adults will never reach. For the reasons we have discussed, however, a line must be drawn. . . . The age of 18 is the point where society draws the line for many purposes between childhood and adulthood. It is, we conclude, the age at which the line for death eligibility ought to rest. . . .

IV

Our determination that the death penalty is disproportionate punishment for offenders under 18 finds confirmation in the stark reality that the United States is the only country in the world that continues to give official sanction to the juvenile death penalty. This reality does not become controlling, for the task of interpreting the Eighth Amendment remains our responsibility. Yet at least from the time of the Court's decision in *Trop*, the Court has referred to the laws of other countries and to international authorities as instructive for its interpretation of the Eighth Amendment's prohibition of "cruel and unusual punishments."

As respondent and a number of amici emphasize, Article 37 of the United Nations Convention on the Rights of the Child, which every country in the world has ratified save for the United States and Somalia, contains an express prohibition on capital punishment for crimes committed by juveniles under 18. United Nations Convention on the Rights of the Child, Art. 37, Nov. 20, 1989, 1577 U.N.T.S. 3, 28 I.L.M. 1448, 1468-1470 (entered into force Sept. 2, 1990); Brief for Respondent 48; Brief for European Union et al. as Amici Curiae 12-13; Brief for President James Earl Carter, Jr., et al. as Amici Curiae 9; Brief for Former U.S. Diplomats Morton Abramowitz et al. as Amici Curiae 7; Brief for Human Rights Committee of the Bar of England and Wales et al. as Amici Curiae 13-14. No ratifying country has entered a reservation to the provision prohibiting the execution of juvenile offenders. Parallel prohibitions are contained in other significant international covenants.

Respondent and his amici have submitted, and petitioner does not contest, that only seven countries other than the United States have executed juvenile offenders since 1990: Iran, Pakistan, Saudi Arabia, Yemen, Nigeria, the Democratic Republic of Congo, and China. Since then each of these countries has either abolished capital punishment for juveniles or made public disavowal of the practice. Brief for Respondent 49-50. In sum, it is fair to say that the United States now stands alone in a world that has turned its face against the juvenile death penalty.

Though the international covenants prohibiting the juvenile death penalty are of more recent date, it is instructive to note that the United Kingdom abolished the juvenile death penalty before these covenants came into being. The United Kingdom's experience bears particular relevance here in light of the historic ties between our countries and in light of the Eighth Amendment's own origins. The Amendment was modeled on a parallel provision in the English Declaration of Rights of 1689, which provided: "[E]xcessive Bail ought not to be required nor excessive Fines imposed; nor cruel and unusual Punishments inflicted." 1 W. & M., ch. 2, §10, in 3 Eng. Stat., at Large 441 (1770). As of now, the United Kingdom has abolished the death penalty in its entirety; but, decades before it took this step, it recognized the disproportionate nature of the juvenile death penalty; and it abolished that penalty as a separate matter. . . .

It is proper that we acknowledge the overwhelming weight of international opinion against the juvenile death penalty, resting in large part on the understanding that the instability and emotional imbalance of young people may often be a factor in the crime. See Brief for Human Rights Committee of the Bar of England and Wales et al. as Amici Curiae 10-11. The opinion of the world community, while not controlling our outcome, does provide respected and significant confirmation for our own conclusions.

Over time, from one generation to the next, the Constitution has come to earn the high respect and even, as Madison dared to hope, the veneration of the American people. See The Federalist No. 49, p. 314 (C. Rossiter ed. 1961). The document sets forth, and rests upon, innovative principles original to the American experience, such as federalism; a proven balance in political mechanisms through separation of powers; specific guarantees for the accused in criminal cases; and broad provisions to secure individual freedom and preserve human dignity. These doctrines and guarantees are central to the American experience and remain essential to our present-day self-definition and national identity. Not the least of the reasons we honor the Constitution, then, is because we know it to be our own. It does not lessen our fidelity to the Constitution or our pride in its origins to acknowledge that the express affirmation of certain fundamental rights by other nations and peoples simply underscores the centrality of those same rights within our own heritage of freedom.

* * *.

The Eighth and Fourteenth Amendments forbid imposition of the death penalty on offenders who were under the age of 18 when their crimes were committed. The judgment of the Missouri Supreme Court setting aside the sentence of death imposed upon Christopher Simmons is affirmed.

JUSTICE STEVENS, with whom JUSTICE GINSBURG joins, concurring.

Perhaps even more important than our specific holding today is our reaffirmation of the basic principle that informs the Court's interpretation of the Eighth Amendment. If the meaning of that Amendment had been frozen when it was originally drafted, it would impose no impediment to the execution of 7-year-old children today. See Stanford v. Kentucky, 492 U.S. 361, 368 (1989) (describing the common law at the time of the Amendment's adoption). The evolving standards of decency that have driven our construction of this critically important part of the Bill of Rights foreclose any such reading of the Amendment. In the best tradition of the common law, the pace of that evolution is a matter for continuing debate; but that our understanding of the Constitution does change from time to time has been settled since John Marshall breathed life into its text. If great lawyers of his day — Alexander Hamilton, for example — were sitting with us today, I would expect them to join Justice Kennedy's opinion for the Court. In all events, I do so without hesitation.

JUSTICE O'CONNOR, dissenting.

The Court's decision today establishes a categorical rule forbidding the execution of any offender for any crime committed before his 18th birthday, no matter how deliberate, wanton, or cruel the offense. Neither the objective evidence of contemporary societal values, nor the Court's moral proportionality analysis, nor the two in tandem suffice to justify this ruling.

. . . [T]he rule decreed by the Court rests, ultimately, on its independent moral judgment that death is a disproportionately severe punishment for any 17-year-old offender. I do not subscribe to this judgment. . . .

It is beyond cavil that juveniles as a class are generally less mature, less responsible, and less fully formed than adults, and that these differences bear on juveniles' comparative moral culpability. But even accepting this premise, the Court's proportionality argument fails to support its categorical rule.

First, the Court adduces no evidence whatsoever in support of its sweeping conclusion . . . that it is only in "rare" cases, if ever, that 17-year-old murderers are sufficiently mature and act with sufficient depravity to warrant the death penalty. The fact that juveniles are generally *less* culpable for their misconduct than adults does not necessarily mean that a 17-year-old murderer cannot be *sufficiently* culpable to merit the death penalty. . . . Similarly, the fact that the availability of the death penalty may be *less* likely to deter a juvenile from committing a capital crime does not imply that this threat cannot *effectively* deter some 17-year-olds from such an act. Surely there is an age below which no offender, no matter what his crime, can be deemed to have the cognitive or emotional maturity necessary to warrant the death penalty. But at least at the margins between adolescence and adulthood . . . the relevant differences between "adults" and "juveniles" appear to be a matter of degree, rather than of kind. . . .

The Court's proportionality argument suffers from a second and closely related defect: It fails to establish that the differences in maturity between 17-year-olds and young "adults" are both universal enough and significant enough to justify a bright-line prophylactic rule against capital punishment of the former. The Court's analysis is premised on differences *in the aggregate* between juveniles and adults, which frequently do not hold true when comparing individuals. Although it may be that many 17-year-old murderers lack sufficient maturity to deserve the death penalty, some juvenile murderers may be quite mature. Chronological age is not an unfailing measure of psychological development, and common experience suggests that many 17-year-olds are more mature than the average young "adult." In short, the class of offenders exempted from capital punishment by today's decision is too broad and too diverse to warrant a categorical prohibition. Indeed, the age-based line drawn by the Court is indefensibly arbitrary — it quite likely will protect a number of offenders who are mature enough to deserve the death penalty and may well leave vulnerable many who are not.

For purposes of proportionality analysis, 17-year-olds as a class are qualitatively and materially different from the mentally retarded. "Mentally retarded" offenders, as we understood that category in *Atkins*, are *defined* by precisely the characteristics which render death an excessive punishment. A mentally retarded person is, "by definition," one whose cognitive and behavioral capacities have been proven to fall below a certain minimum. . . . Accordingly, for purposes of our decision in *Atkins*, the mentally retarded are not merely *less* blameworthy for their misconduct or *less* likely to be deterred by the death penalty than others.

Rather, a mentally retarded offender is one whose demonstrated impairments make it so highly unlikely that he is culpable enough to deserve the death penalty or that he could have been deterred by the threat of death, that execution is not a defensible punishment. There is no such inherent or accurate fit between an offender's chronological age and the personal limitations which the Court believes make capital punishment excessive for 17-year-old murderers. . . .

The proportionality issues raised by the Court clearly implicate Eighth Amendment concerns. But these concerns may properly be addressed not by means of an arbitrary, categorical age-based rule, but rather through individualized sentencing in which juries are required to give appropriate mitigating weight to the defendant's immaturity, his susceptibility to outside pressures, his cognizance of the consequences of his actions, and so forth. In that way the constitutional response can be tailored to the specific problem it is meant to remedy. . . .

Because I do not believe that a genuine *national* consensus against the juvenile death penalty has yet developed, and because I do not believe the Court's moral proportionality argument justifies a categorical, age-based constitutional rule, I can assign no . . . *confirmatory* role to the international consensus described by the Court. In short, the evidence of an international consensus does not alter my determination that the Eighth Amendment does not, at this time, forbid capital punishment of 17-year-old murderers in all cases.

Nevertheless, I disagree with Justice Scalia's contention that foreign and international law have no place in our Eighth Amendment jurisprudence. Over the course of nearly half a century, the Court has consistently referred to foreign and international law as relevant to its assessment of evolving standards of decency. This inquiry reflects the special character of the Eighth Amendment, which, as the Court has long held, draws its meaning directly from the maturing values of civilized society. Obviously, American law is distinctive in many respects, not least where the specific provisions of our Constitution and the history of its exposition so dictate. But this Nation's evolving understanding of human dignity certainly is neither wholly isolated from, nor inherently at odds with, the values prevailing in other countries. On the contrary, we should not be surprised to find congruence between domestic and international values, especially where the international community has reached clear agreement — expressed in international law or in the domestic laws of individual countries — that a particular form of punishment is inconsistent with fundamental human rights. At least, the existence of an international consensus of this nature can serve to confirm the reasonableness of a consonant and genuine American consensus. The instant case presents no such domestic consensus, however, and the recent emergence of an otherwise global consensus does not alter that basic fact.

* * *

. . . Reasonable minds can differ as to the minimum age at which commission of a serious crime should expose the defendant to the death penalty, if at all. Many jurisdictions have abolished capital punishment altogether, while many others have determined that even the most heinous crime, if committed before the age of 18, should not be punishable by death. Indeed, were my office that of a legislator, rather than a judge, then I, too, would be inclined to support legislation setting a minimum age of 18 in this context. But a significant number of States, including Missouri, have decided to make the death penalty potentially available for 17-year-old capital murderers such as respondent. Without a clearer showing that a genuine national consensus forbids the execution of such offenders, this Court should not substitute its own "inevitably subjective judgment" on how best to resolve this difficult moral question for the judgments of the Nation's democratically elected legislatures. I respectfully dissent.

JUSTICE SCALIA, with whom CHIEF JUSTICE REHNQUIST and JUSTICE THOMAS join, dissenting.

In urging approval of a constitution that gave life-tenured judges the power to nullify laws enacted by the people's representatives, Alexander Hamilton assured the citizens of New York that there was little risk in this, since "[t]he judiciary . . . ha[s] neither FORCE nor WILL but merely judgment." The Federalist No. 78, p. 465 (C. Rossiter ed. 1961). But Hamilton had in mind a traditional judiciary, "bound down by strict rules and precedents which serve to define and point out their duty in every particular case that comes before them." Id., at 471. Bound down, indeed. What a mockery today's opinion makes of Hamilton's expectation, announcing the Court's conclusion that the meaning of our Constitution has changed over the past 15 years — not, mind you, that this Court's decision 15 years ago was *wrong*, but that the Constitution *has changed*. The Court reaches this implausible result by purporting to advert, not to the original meaning of the Eighth Amendment, but to "the evolving standards of decency" of our national society. It then finds, on the flimsiest of grounds, that a national consensus which could not be perceived in our people's laws barely 15 years ago now solidly exists. Worse still, the Court says in so many words that what our people's laws say about the issue does not, in the last analysis, matter. The Court thus proclaims itself sole arbiter of our Nation's moral standards — and in the course of discharging that awesome responsibility purports to take guidance from the views of foreign courts and legislatures. Because I do not believe that the meaning of our Eighth Amendment, any more than the meaning of other provisions of our Constitution, should be determined by the subjective views of five Members of this Court and like-minded foreigners, I dissent.

I

In determining that capital punishment of offenders who committed murder before age 18 is "cruel and unusual" under the Eighth Amendment, the Court first considers, in accordance with our modern (though in my view mistaken) jurisprudence, whether there is a "national consensus" that laws allowing such executions contravene our modern "standards of decency." . . . As in Atkins v. Virginia, 536 U.S. 304, 312 (2002), the Court dutifully recites this test and claims halfheartedly that a national consensus has emerged since our decision in *Stanford*, because 18 States — or 47% of States that permit capital punishment — now have legislation prohibiting the execution of offenders under 18, and because all of four States have adopted such legislation since *Stanford*.

Words have no meaning if the views of less than 50% of death penalty States can constitute a national consensus. Our previous cases have required overwhelming opposition to a challenged practice, generally over a long period of time. . . .

In an attempt to keep afloat its implausible assertion of national consensus, the Court throws overboard a proposition well established in our Eighth Amendment jurisprudence. . . . *None* of our cases dealing with an alleged constitutional limitation upon the death penalty has counted, as States supporting a consensus in favor of that limitation, States that have eliminated the death penalty entirely. And with good reason. Consulting States that bar the death penalty concerning the necessity of making an exception to the penalty for offenders under 18 is rather like including old-order Amishmen in a consumer-preference poll on the electric car. Of *course* they don't like it, but that sheds no light whatever on the point at issue. That 12 States favor *no* executions says something about consensus against the death penalty, but nothing — absolutely nothing — about consensus that offenders under 18 deserve special immunity from such a penalty. . . . What might be relevant, perhaps, is how many of those States permit 16- and 17-year-old offenders to be treated as adults with respect to noncapital offenses. (They all do; indeed, some even *require* that juveniles as young as 14 be tried as adults if they are charged with murder.) The attempt by the Court to turn its remarkable minority consensus into a faux majority by counting Amishmen is an act of nomological desperation.

Recognizing that its national-consensus argument was weak compared with our earlier cases, the *Atkins* Court found additional support in the fact that 16 States had prohibited execution of mentally retarded individuals since Penry v. Lynaugh, 492 U.S. 302 (1989). . . . Now, the Court says a legislative change in four States is "significant" enough to trigger a constitutional prohibition. It is amazing to think that this subtle shift in numbers can take the issue entirely off the table for legislative debate.

I also doubt whether many of the legislators who voted to change the laws in those four States would have done so if they had known their decision would (by the pronouncement of this Court) be rendered irreversible. After all, legislative support for capital punishment, in any form, has surged and ebbed throughout our Nation's history. . . .

Relying on such narrow margins is especially inappropriate in light of the fact that a number of legislatures and voters have expressly affirmed their support for capital punishment of 16- and 17-year-old offenders since *Stanford*. Though the Court is correct that no State has lowered its death penalty age, both the Missouri and Virginia Legislatures — which, at the time of *Stanford*, had no minimum age requirement — expressly established 16 as the minimum. Mo. Rev. Stat. §565.020.2 (2000); Va. Code Ann. §18.2-10(a) (Lexis 2004). The people of Arizona and Florida have done the same by ballot initiative. Thus, even States that have not executed an under-18 offender in recent years unquestionably favor the possibility of capital punishment in some circumstances. . . .

II

Of course, the real force driving today's decision is not the actions of four state legislatures, but the Court's "own judgment" that murderers younger than 18 can never be as morally culpable as older counterparts. . . . If the Eighth Amendment set forth an ordinary rule of law, it would indeed be the role of this Court to say what the law is. But the Court having pronounced that the Eighth Amendment is an ever-changing reflection of "the evolving standards of decency" of our society, it makes no sense for the Justices then to *prescribe* those standards rather than discern them from the practices of our people. On the evolving-standards hypothesis, the only legitimate function of this Court is to identify a moral consensus of the American people. By what conceivable warrant can nine lawyers presume to be the authoritative conscience of the Nation?[8]

. . . Today's opinion provides a perfect example of why judges are ill equipped to make the type of legislative judgments the Court insists on making here. To support its opinion that States should be prohibited from imposing the death penalty on anyone who committed murder before age 18, the Court looks to scientific and sociological studies, picking and choosing those that support its position. It never explains why those particular studies are methodologically sound; none was ever entered into evidence or tested in an adversarial proceeding. . . .

That "almost every State prohibits those under 18 years of age from voting, serving on juries, or marrying without parental consent," is patently irrelevant. . . . As we explained in *Stanford*, 492 U.S., at 374, it is "absurd to think that one must be mature enough to drive carefully, to drink responsibly, or to vote intelligently, in order to be mature enough to understand that murdering another human being is profoundly wrong, and to conform one's conduct to that most minimal of all civilized standards." Serving on a jury or entering into marriage also involve decisions far more sophisticated than the simple decision not to take another's life.

. . . In other contexts where individualized consideration is provided, we have recognized that at least some minors will be mature enough to make difficult decisions that involve moral considerations. For instance, we have struck down abortion statutes that do not allow minors deemed mature by courts to bypass parental notification provisions. See, e.g., Bellotti v. Baird, 443 U.S. 622, 643-644 (1979) (opinion of Powell, J.); Planned Parenthood of Central Mo. v. Danforth, 428 U.S. 52, 74-75 (1976). It is hard to see why this context should be any different. Whether to obtain an abortion is surely a much more complex decision for a young person than whether to kill an innocent person in cold blood.

The Court concludes, however, that juries cannot be trusted with the delicate task of weighing a defendant's youth along with the other mitigating and aggravating factors of his crime. This startling conclusion undermines the very foundations of our capital sentencing system. . . . The Court says that juries will be unable to appreciate the significance of a defendant's youth when faced with details of a brutal crime. This assertion is based on no evidence; to the contrary, the Court itself acknowledges that the execution of under-18 offenders is "infrequent" even in the States "without a formal prohibition on executing juveniles," suggesting that juries take seriously their responsibility to weigh youth as a mitigating factor. . . .

8. Justice O'Connor agrees with our analysis that no national consensus exists here. She is nonetheless prepared (like the majority) to override the judgment of America's legislatures if it contradicts her own assessment of "moral proportionality." She dissents here only because it does not. The votes in today's case demonstrate that the offending of selected lawyers' moral sentiments is not a predictable basis for law — much less a democratic one.

III

Though the views of our own citizens are essentially irrelevant to the Court's decision today, the views of other countries and the so-called international community take center stage.

. . . [T]he basic premise of the Court's argument — that American law should conform to the laws of the rest of the world — ought to be rejected out of hand. In fact the Court itself does not believe it. In many significant respects the laws of most other countries differ from our law — including not only such explicit provisions of our Constitution as the right to jury trial and grand jury indictment, but even many interpretations of the Constitution prescribed by this Court itself. The Court-pronounced exclusionary rule, for example, is distinctively American. When we adopted that rule in Mapp v. Ohio, 367 U.S. 643, 655 (1961), it was "unique to American Jurisprudence." Bivens v. Six Unknown Fed. Narcotics Agents, 403 U.S. 388, 415 (1971) (Burger, C.J., dissenting). Since then a categorical exclusionary rule has been "universally rejected" by other countries, including those with rules prohibiting illegal searches and police misconduct, despite the fact that none of these countries "appears to have any alternative form of discipline for police that is effective in preventing search violations." Bradley, *Mapp* Goes Abroad, 52 Case W. Res. L. Rev. 375, 399-400 (2001). . . .

The Court has been oblivious to the views of other countries when deciding how to interpret our Constitution's requirement that "Congress shall make no law respecting an establishment of religion. . . ." Amdt. 1. Most other countries — including those committed to religious neutrality — do not insist on the degree of separation between church and state that this Court requires. . . .

And let us not forget the Court's abortion jurisprudence, which makes us one of only six countries that allow abortion on demand until the point of viability. See Larsen, Importing Constitutional Norms from a "Wider Civilization": *Lawrence* and the Rehnquist Court's Use of Foreign and International Law in Domestic Constitutional Interpretation, 65 Ohio St. L.J. 1283, 1320 (2004); Center for Reproductive Rights, The World's Abortion Laws (June 2004), http://www.reproductiverights.org/pub_fac_abortion_laws.html. Though the Government and amici in cases following Roe v. Wade, 410 U.S. 113 (1973), urged the Court to follow the international community's lead, these arguments fell on deaf ears. . . .

The Court's special reliance on the laws of the United Kingdom is perhaps the most indefensible part of its opinion. It is of course true that we share a common history with the United Kingdom, and that we often consult English sources when asked to discern the meaning of a constitutional text written against the backdrop of 18th-century English law and legal thought. If we applied that approach today, our task would be an easy one. As we explained in Harmelin v. Michigan, 501 U.S. 957, 973-974 (1991), the "Cruell and Unusuall Punishments" provision of the English Declaration of Rights was originally meant to describe those punishments "out of [the Judges'] Power" — that is, those punishments that were not authorized by common law or statute, but that were nonetheless administered by the Crown or the Crown's judges. Under that reasoning, the death penalty for under-18 offenders would easily survive this challenge. The Court has, however — I think wrongly — long rejected a purely originalist approach to our Eighth Amendment, and that is certainly not the approach the Court takes today. Instead, the Court undertakes the majestic task of determining (and thereby prescribing) *our* Nation's *current* standards of decency. It is beyond comprehension why we should look, for that purpose, to a country that has developed, in the centuries since the Revolutionary War — and with increasing speed since the United Kingdom's recent submission to the jurisprudence of European courts dominated by continental jurists — a legal, political, and social culture quite different from our own. If we took the Court's directive seriously, we would also consider relaxing our double jeopardy prohibition, since the British Law Commission recently published a report that would significantly extend the rights of the prosecution to appeal cases where an acquittal was the result of a judge's ruling that was legally incorrect. See Law Commission, Double Jeopardy and Prosecution Appeals, LAW COM No. 267, Cm 5048, p. 6, P 1.19 (Mar. 2001); J. Spencer, The English System in European Criminal Procedures 142, 204, and n. 239 (M. Delmas-Marty & J. Spencer eds. 2002). We would also curtail our right to jury trial in criminal cases since, despite the jury system's deep roots in our shared common law, England now permits all but the most serious offenders to be tried by magistrates without a jury. See D. Feldman, England and Wales, in Criminal Procedure: A Worldwide Study 91, 114-115 (C. Bradley ed. 1999).

The Court should either profess its willingness to reconsider all these matters in light of the views of foreigners, or else it should cease putting forth foreigners' views as part of the *reasoned basis* of its decisions. To invoke alien law when it agrees with one's own thinking, and ignore it otherwise, is not reasoned decisionmaking, but sophistry.

. . . I do not believe that approval by "other nations and peoples" should buttress our commitment to American principles any more than (what should logically follow) disapproval by "other nations and peoples" should weaken that commitment. More importantly, however, the Court's statement flatly misdescribes what is going on here. Foreign sources are cited today, *not* to underscore our "fidelity" to the Constitution, our "pride in its origins," and "our own [American] heritage." To the contrary, they are cited *to set aside* the centuries-old American practice — a practice still engaged in by a large majority of the relevant States — of letting a jury of 12 citizens decide whether, in the particular case, youth should be the basis for withholding the death penalty. What these foreign sources "affirm," rather than repudiate, is the Justices' own notion of how the world ought to be, and their diktat that it shall be so henceforth in America. The Court's parting attempt to downplay the significance of its extensive discussion of foreign law is unconvincing. "Acknowledgment" of foreign approval has no place in the legal opinion of this Court *unless it is part of the basis for the Court's judgment* — which is surely what it parades as today.

IV

To add insult to injury, the Court affirms the Missouri Supreme Court without even admonishing that court for its flagrant disregard of our precedent in *Stanford*. Until today, we have always held that "it is this Court's prerogative alone to overrule one of its precedents." State Oil Co. v. Khan, 522 U.S. 3, 20 (1997). That has been true even where "'changes in judicial doctrine' ha[ve] significantly undermined" our prior holding, United States v. Hatter, 532 U.S. 557, 567 (2001), and even where our prior holding "appears to rest on reasons rejected in some other line of decisions," Rodriguez de Quijas v. Shearson/American Express, Inc., 490 U.S. 477, 484 (1989).

Today, however, the Court silently approves a state-court decision that blatantly rejected controlling precedent.

One must admit that the Missouri Supreme Court's action, and this Court's indulgent reaction, are, in a way, understandable. In a system based upon constitutional and statutory text democratically adopted, the concept of "law" ordinarily signifies that particular words have a fixed meaning. Such law does not change, and this Court's pronouncement of it therefore remains authoritative until (confessing our prior error) we overrule. The Court has purported to make of the Eighth Amendment, however, a mirror of the passing and changing sentiment of American society regarding penology. The lower courts can look into that mirror as well as we can; and what we saw 15 years ago bears no necessary relationship to what they see today. Since they are not looking at the same text, but at a different scene, why should our earlier decision control their judgment?

However sound philosophically, this is no way to run a legal system. We must disregard the new reality that, to the extent our Eighth Amendment decisions constitute something more than a show of hands on the current Justices' current personal views about penology, they purport to be nothing more than a snapshot of American public opinion at a particular point in time (with the timeframes now shortened to a mere 15 years). We must treat these decisions just as though they represented *real* law, *real* prescriptions democratically adopted by the American people, as conclusively (rather than sequentially) construed by this Court. Allowing lower courts to reinterpret the Eighth Amendment whenever they decide enough time has passed for a new snapshot leaves this Court's decisions without any force — especially since the "evolution" of our Eighth Amendment is no longer determined by objective criteria. To allow lower courts to behave as we do, "updating" the Eighth Amendment as needed, destroys stability and makes our case law an unreliable basis for the designing of laws by citizens and their representatives, and for action by public officials. The result will be to crown arbitrariness with chaos.

NOTES AND QUESTIONS

1. Other than the recognized fact that "death is different," see Gregg v. Georgia, 428 U.S. 153, 188 (1976), is there any way to explain the dramatic divergence, in both result and Eighth Amendment methodology, between *Harmelin* and *Ewing*, on the one hand, and *Simmons*, on the other? Even if "death is different," is that a satisfactory explanation for the divergence? Why is a marginal "national consensus" of either 30 states (per Justice Kennedy) or 18 states (per Justice Scalia) sufficient to establish a categorical Eighth Amendment rule in *Simmons*, whereas a consensus of 49 states was held insufficient in both *Harmelin* and *Ewing*? (Recall that, in both of those cases, the relevant states stood alone in the harshness of the prison sentences they imposed.) Why are the views of the United Kingdom and the European Union relevant to the Eighth Amendment issue in *Simmons*, but not even mentioned in *Harmelin* and *Ewing*? Isn't there a consistency problem with the Court's view that 17-year-olds, as a class, are insufficiently "mature" and "responsible" to commit crimes that might justify capital punishment, but sufficiently "mature" and "responsible" to exercise the right to an abortion without parental consent?

Might the result in *Simmons* simply reflect the Court's seemingly growing concern with the morality of capital punishment itself? If so, then wouldn't it be better for the Court to 'fess up and address the problem in a more direct and honest manner?

2. Do the above questions, and apparent inconsistencies, provide further evidence in support of Justice Scalia's claim that the Court should (as it seemed to do in *Harmelin* and *Ewing*) get out of the business of Eighth Amendment proportionality review entirely? Is this one of those areas of constitutional adjudication — like substantive due process — in which the Court's decisions are destined, at least much of the time, to appear arbitrary and lawless? Or is there another possible approach to proportionality review that would offer greater predictability and doctrinal stability?

3. In Kennedy v. Louisiana, 554 U.S. 407 (2008), the Court, by 5-4, struck down the death penalty as a punishment for the rape of a child that does not result in the victim's death. The majority opinion acknowledged that, since 1995, six states (including Louisiana) had enacted legislation authorizing the death penalty for child rape, while five others were considering similar legislation, but found this trend insufficient to outweigh the fact that — at least as of the time of the decision — 44 states (including the 12 states that had no death penalty at all) would not allow a defendant to be executed for such a crime. The Court also emphasized that the Eighth Amendment is measured by the "evolving standards of human decency," and expressed the view that "decency, in its essence, presumes respect for the individual and thus moderation or restraint in the application of capital punishment."

4. Just how "different" *is* death, anyway, in Eighth Amendment proportionality terms? The Court injected more than a little bit of uncertainty into the answer to this question in Graham v. Florida, 130 S. Ct. 2011 (2010). There, the Court held, per Justice Kennedy, that juveniles who are convicted of a nonhomicide crime may not be sentenced to life in prison without possibility of parole, but instead must be provided with "some meaningful opportunity to obtain release based on demonstrated maturity and rehabilitation." Id., at 2030. The decision was based on a categorical analysis of crime and punishment essentially identical to that employed in the capital cases of *Atkins*, *Roper*, and *Kennedy*, and drew heavily on similar "objective" indicia of an emerging "national consensus." The *Graham* Court, like the *Roper* Court, also engaged in a detailed and lengthy discussion of the reduced maturity and moral responsibility of juveniles, and cited extensively the views of other nations.

Justice Thomas, joined by Justices Scalia and Alito, sharply dissented:

> The question of what acts are "deserving" of what punishments is bound so tightly with questions of morality and social conditions as to make it, almost by definition, a question for legislative resolution. It is true that the Court previously has relied on the notion of proportionality in holding certain classes of offenses categorically exempt from capital punishment. But never before today has the Court relied on its own view of just deserts to impose a categorical limit on the imposition of a lesser punishment. Its willingness to cross that well-established boundary raises the question whether any democratic choice regarding appropriate punishment is safe from the Court's ever-expanding constitutional veto.

Id., at 2056.

Does *Graham* indicate that the kind of aggressive Eighth Amendment review seen in *Atkins* and *Roper* will soon become the norm for noncapital cases as well, supplanting the more cautious approach of *Harmelin* and *Ewing*? Or is *Graham*, instead, a unique case narrowly limited to the special context of juveniles and life without parole?

B.   *Discretion and Rules in Sentencing*

In the middle of the twentieth century, American trial judges were vested with broad discretion to determine the appropriate sentence for a defendant who was convicted of a crime, and the exercise of this discretion — within the limits set by the legislature in the relevant crime statute — was virtually unreviewable. There was no requirement for the judge to state publicly the reasons for imposing a particular sentence. In short, traditional discretionary sentencing operated in a virtual "black box"; information about the crime and about the defendant would enter on one side, and the sentence would emerge from the other side, usually without explanation.

By the 1960s, virtually every state had also adopted a system of indeterminate sentences, meaning that a defendant's release date was determined not by the trial judge, but through the further exercise of discretion by a parole board or probation agency. Such indeterminate sentences were thought to be more consistent with the rehabilitative ideal that generally prevailed at the time in American penological theory.

One of the most prominent critics of discretionary and indeterminate sentencing, Judge Marvin Frankel, wrote about some of the problems with the traditional approach.

LAWLESSNESS IN SENTENCING

Marvin Frankel, United States District Judge for the Southern District of New York
41 U. Cin. L. Rev. 1, 4-6, 29-31, 51 (1972)

The common form of criminal penalty provision confers upon the sentencing judge an enormous range of choice. The scope of what we call "discretion" permits imprisonment for anything from a day to one, five, 10, 20, or more years. . . .

The statutes granting such powers characteristically say nothing about the factors to be weighed in moving to either end of the spectrum or to some place between. It might be supposed by some stranger arrived in our midst that the criteria for measuring a particular sentence would be discoverable outside the narrow limits of the statutes and would be known to the judicial experts rendering the judgments. But the supposition would lack substantial foundation. Even the most basic sentencing principles are not prescribed or stated with persuasive authority. . . .

Moving upward from what should be the philosophical axioms of a rational scheme of sentencing law, we have no structure of rules, or even guidelines, affecting other elements arguably pertinent to the nature or severity of the sentence. . . .

What factors should be assessed — and where, if anywhere, are comparisons to be sought — in gauging the relative seriousness of the specific offense and offender as against the spectrum of offenses by others in the same legal category? . . .

With the delegation of power so unchanneled, it is surely no overstatement to say that "the new penology has resulted in vesting in judges and parole and probation agencies the greatest degree of uncontrolled power over the liberty of human beings that one can find in the legal system." The process would be totally unruly even if judges were superbly and uniformly trained for the solemn work of sentencing. As everyone knows, however, they are not trained at all. . . .

The basic premise of the indeterminate sentence is the modern conception that rehabilitation is the paramount goal in sentencing. . . . I do not argue that the indeterminate sentence is always and everywhere inappropriate. I believe, however, that its unqualified use rests upon undemonstrated premises; that the premises, even if sound, should not have the sweeping application they are given; and that the excessive extension of indeterminacy has probably resulted in much cruelty and injustice, rather than the great goods its proponents envisage. . . .

. . . I propose that there be established a National Commission charged with permanent responsibility for (1) the study of sentencing, corrections, and parole; (2) the formulation of laws and rules to which the results of such study may lead; and (3) the actual enactment of rules subject to congressional veto. . . .

. . . [T]he stakes of everyone in a system of rational sentencing are too great for contentment with the disheveled status quo. The improvements needed will not be achieved through fitful bursts of activity. The task requires the continuous attention of a respected agency. . . .

Within a few years, Judge Frankel's proposal for the creation of a national "sentencing commission" began to take root. Meanwhile, by the late 1970s, with crime rates rising and empirical studies documenting the inability of penological experts to rehabilitate most offenders, the rehabilitative ideal began to fade from the American penological scene. See generally Francis A. Allen, The Decline of the Rehabilitative Ideal: Penal Policy and Social Purpose (1981). In 1976, Andrew von Hirsch wrote an influential book, Doing Justice, advocating a retributive theory of punishment based on Kantian "just deserts." The book, together with Judge Frankel's proposal, served as the catalyst for many of the sentencing reforms that followed.

SPECIAL REPORT: "TRUTH IN SENTENCING IN STATE PRISONS"

U.S. Department of Justice, Bureau of Justice Statistics
January 1999

Sentencing reform policies have paralleled the mood of the country on crime and punishment, shifting between requiring a fixed prison time prior to release or allowing discretionary release of offenders by judges, parole boards, or corrections officials. Over the last two decades, sentencing requirements and release policies have become more restrictive, primarily in response to widespread "get tough on crime" attitudes in the Nation. . . .

In the early 1970s, States generally permitted parole boards to determine when an offender would be released from prison. In addition, good-time reductions for satisfactory prison behavior, earned-time incentives for participation in work or educational programs, and other time reductions to control prison crowding resulted in the early release of prisoners. These policies permitted officials to individualize the amount of punishment or leniency an offender received and provided means to manage the prison population.

Such discretion in sentencing and release policies led to criticism that some offenders were punished more harshly than others for similar offenses and to complaints that overall sentencing and release laws were too soft on criminals. By the late 1970s and early 1980s, States began developing sentencing guidelines, enacting mandatory minimum sentences and adopting other sentencing reforms to reduce disparity in sentencing and to toughen penalties for certain offenses, specifically drug offenses (as part of the "war on drugs"), offenses with weapons, and offenses committed by repeat or habitual criminals.

States continued to increase the severity of sentencing laws (primarily for violent offenders) by enacting restrictions on the possibility of early release, which became known as truth in sentencing. Truth-in-sentencing laws require offenders to serve a substantial portion of the prison sentence imposed by the court before being eligible for release. Previous policies which reduced the amount of time an offender served on a sentence, such as good-time, earned-time and parole board release, are restricted or eliminated under truth-in-sentencing laws. The definition of truth in sentencing varies among the States, as do the percent of sentence required to be served and the crimes covered by the laws. Most States have targeted violent offenders under truth in sentencing. . . .

Fourteen States have abolished early release by discretion of a parole board for all offenders. Seven States abolished parole board release within the last 10 years. Eight States abolished parole board release during the same year a truth-in-sentencing law was passed. . . . Parole boards still have discretion over inmates who were sentenced for crimes committed prior to the effective date of the law that eliminated parole board release. . . .

A few other States have abolished parole board release for certain violent or felony offenders . . . or for certain crimes against a person. . . . California allows discretionary release by a parole board only for offenders with indeterminate life sentences. In general, States restrict the possibility of parole board release based on the offender's criminal history or the circumstances of the offense. . . .

The first legislatively created sentencing commission was formed in Minnesota in 1978. At the federal level, in 1984, Congress enacted the Sentencing Reform Act, 18 U.S.C. §3551 et seq., and 28 U.S.C. §§991-998, thereby transferring much of the control over federal criminal sentencing from trial judges to a newly created Federal Sentencing Commission.

SERVING THIS TIME: EXAMINING THE FEDERAL SENTENCING GUIDELINES AFTER A DECADE OF EXPERIENCE

Deanell Reece Tacha, Circuit Judge, United States Court of Appeals for
the Tenth Circuit; Commissioner, U.S. Sentencing Commission
62 Mo. L. Rev. 471 (1997)

In 1984, after more than ten years of study and debate, Congress overwhelmingly passed the Sentencing Reform Act, which brought about the most farreaching reforms in federal sentencing that this nation has ever seen. The Sentencing Reform Act abolished parole and introduced a comprehensive new sentencing scheme to ensure that federal sentencing satisfied the goals of certainty, uniformity and fairness, while furthering the traditional purposes of criminal punishment: deterrence, incapacitation, just punishment and rehabilitation.

To achieve these goals, the Sentencing Reform Act created the United States Sentencing Commission, which in turn created the federal sentencing guidelines. The guidelines went into effect in 1987 and, although they have been amended more than 500 times, the basic structure and operation has remained intact. The guidelines are designed so that a judge measures the seriousness of a defendant's offense and the extent of his criminal history in order to select the sentence he should receive. The seriousness of the offense is based on a combination of factors, including:

— the offense of conviction (e.g., robbery, drug trafficking, fraud);
— specific aggravating or mitigating conduct that occurs during the offense of conviction (e.g., the amount of money taken, use of a gun, bodily injury); and
— other adjustments for factors that are relevant regardless of the type of offense involved (e.g., the victim's vulnerability, the defendant's role in the offense, obstruction of justice, acceptance of responsibility). A defendant's criminal history score reflects the number, seriousness and recency of his prior offenses.

These two considerations — offense seriousness and criminal history — are represented along the two axes of the sentencing table, which judges use to select a final sentence. The table is a grid with the offense levels running along the vertical axis and the criminal history levels running along the horizontal axis. The point at which a given offense level and criminal history score intersect on the grid shows the range of months from which the judge can choose a specific sentence.

The judge may depart from the sentencing range and impose a higher or lower sentence only if there are aggravating or mitigating circumstances that have not been adequately taken into account by the Commission in formulating the guidelines. On the rationale that it would undermine the principal goals of the Sentencing Reform Act, a judge may not depart simply because she thinks the final sentencing range is too harsh or too lenient. However, she is given flexibility to depart when faced with an extraordinary or atypical case.

Finally, the judge must determine whether the guideline sentence is consistent with the statutory maximum and minimum sentences mandated by Congress. The guidelines were drafted to achieve some parity with mandatory sentences, but if the guideline sentence is inconsistent with a mandatory sentence, the mandatory sentence will trump the guidelines.

The Federal Sentencing Guidelines, together with their counterparts in the roughly one-half of the states that have adopted similar guidelines, were designed primarily to reduce disparity in sentencing. But the federal guidelines achieved this goal by shifting sentencing discretion from trial judges to prosecutors, whose discretionary charging decisions now largely determine (together with the guidelines themselves and the relevant facts about the crime and the defendant) the sentence that a defendant will receive upon conviction. This led to sharp criticism of the federal guidelines by numerous judges and scholars; see, e.g., Kate Stith & Jose Cabranes, Fear of Judging: Sentencing Guidelines in the Federal Courts (1998); Michael Tonry, Sentencing Matters (1996); Doris Marie Provine, Too Many Black Men: The Sentencing Judge's Dilemma, 23 Law & Soc. Inquiry 823 (1998); Daniel J. Freed, Federal Sentencing in the Wake of Guidelines: Unacceptable Limits on the Discretion of Sentencers, 101 Yale L.J. 1681 (1992); Donald P. Lay, Rethinking the Guidelines: A Call for Cooperation, 101 Yale L.J. 1755 (1992); Gerald W. Heaney, The Reality of Guidelines Sentencing: No End to Disparity, 28 Am. Crim. L. Rev. 161 (1991).

One unanticipated consequence of the federal guidelines has been a dramatic increase in sentencing litigation. Sentencing issues that previously were nonreviewable, in the era of "black-box" discretionary sentencing, have now emerged into the light of day to become the basis for sentencing appeals and petitions to vacate sentences. Between 1987 (when the Federal Sentencing Guidelines first went into effect) and 1999, while the overall number of case filings in the federal appellate courts grew by about 50 percent, the number of petitions in those same courts seeking to vacate a sentence grew by almost 500 percent. During fiscal 1999, more than 60 percent of all federal criminal appeals involved at least one sentencing issue, and 37.5 percent involved *only* sentencing issues.[5]

C. *Do the Rules of Constitutional Criminal Procedure Apply to Sentencing?*

The single most important procedural issue in sentencing law today is whether, and to what extent, sentencing proceedings are subject to the rules of constitutional criminal procedure that apply to the determination of a defendant's guilt or innocence at trial. Until recently, the answer was relatively clear. Traditional discretionary sentencing has long been viewed as sufficiently distinct from the guilt-innocence determination to warrant different constitutional treatment. Thus, although a few constitutional rules, such as the right to counsel, have been applied equally to trials and sentencing proceedings, other rules, such as the right to confrontation, have not. The next case, although predating the constitutionalization of most criminal procedure rules, still represents the leading exposition of the reasoning behind the traditional approach.

5. These percentages may be even higher today; during the one-year period ending September 30, 2006, more than 82.8 percent of all criminal appeals terminated in the federal courts included a sentencing issue. See Mark Motivans, Federal Justice Statistics, 2006 (NCJ 225711, May 2009).

WILLIAMS v. NEW YORK

Appeal from the Court of Appeals of New York
337 U.S. 241 (1949)

JUSTICE BLACK delivered the opinion of the Court. A jury in a New York state court found appellant guilty of murder in the first degree. The jury recommended life imprisonment, but the trial judge imposed sentence of death. In giving his reasons for imposing the death sentence the judge discussed in open court the evidence upon which the jury had convicted stating that this evidence had been considered in the light of additional information obtained through the court's "Probation Department, and through other sources." Consideration of this additional information was pursuant to §482 of New York Criminal Code which provides:

> . . . Before rendering judgment or pronouncing sentence the court shall cause the defendant's previous criminal record to be submitted to it, including any reports that may have been made as a result of a mental, phychiatric [*sic*] or physical examination of such person, and may seek any information that will aid the court in determining the proper treatment of such defendant.

The Court of Appeals of New York affirmed the conviction and sentence over the contention that as construed and applied the controlling penal statutes are in violation of the due process clause of the Fourteenth Amendment of the Constitution of the United States "in that the sentence of death was based upon information supplied by witnesses with whom the accused had not been confronted and as to whom he had no opportunity for cross-examination or rebuttal. . . ." Because the statutes were sustained over this constitutional challenge the case is here on appeal under 28 U.S.C. §1257 (2).

The narrow contention here makes it unnecessary to set out the facts at length. The record shows a carefully conducted trial lasting more than two weeks in which appellant was represented by three appointed lawyers who conducted his defense with fidelity and zeal. The evidence proved a wholly indefensible murder committed by a person engaged in a burglary. The judge instructed the jury that if it returned a verdict of guilty as charged, without recommendation for life sentence, "The Court must impose the death penalty," but if such recommendation was made, "the Court may impose a life sentence." The judge went on to emphasize that "the Court is not bound to accept your recommendation."

About five weeks after the verdict of guilty with recommendation of life imprisonment, and after a statutory pre-sentence investigation report to the judge, the defendant was brought to court to be sentenced. Asked what he had to say, appellant protested his innocence. After each of his three lawyers had appealed to the court to accept the jury's recommendation of a life sentence, the judge gave reasons why he felt that the death sentence should be imposed. He narrated the shocking details of the crime as shown by the trial evidence, expressing his own complete belief in appellant's guilt. He stated that the pre-sentence investigation revealed many material facts concerning appellant's background which though relevant to the question of punishment could not properly have been brought to the attention of the jury in its consideration of the question of guilt. He referred to the experience appellant "had had on thirty other burglaries in and about the same vicinity" where the murder had been committed. The appellant had not been convicted of these burglaries although the judge had information that he had confessed to some and had been identified as the perpetrator of some of the others. The judge also referred to certain activities of appellant as shown by the probation report that indicated appellant possessed "a morbid sexuality" and classified him as a "menace to society." The accuracy of the statements made by the judge as to appellant's background and past practices was not challenged by appellant or his counsel, nor was the judge asked to disregard any of them or to afford appellant a chance to refute or discredit any of them by cross-examination or otherwise.

The case presents a serious and difficult question. The question relates to the rules of evidence applicable to the manner in which a judge may obtain information to guide him in the imposition of sentence upon an already convicted defendant. Within limits fixed by statutes, New York judges are given a broad discretion to decide the type and extent of punishment for convicted defendants. Here, for example, the judge's discretion was to sentence to life imprisonment or death. To aid a judge in exercising this discretion intelligently the New York procedural policy encourages him to consider information about the convicted person's past life, health, habits, conduct, and mental and moral propensities. The sentencing judge may consider such information even though obtained outside the courtroom from persons whom a defendant has not been permitted to confront or cross-examine. It is the consideration of information obtained by a sentencing judge in this manner that is the basis for appellant's broad constitutional challenge to the New York statutory policy.

Appellant urges that the New York statutory policy is in irreconcilable conflict with the underlying philosophy of a second procedural policy grounded in the due process of law clause of the Fourteenth Amendment. That policy . . . is in part that no person shall be tried and convicted of an offense unless he is given reasonable notice of the charges against him and is afforded an opportunity to examine adverse witnesses. That the due process clause does provide these salutary and time-tested protections where the question for consideration is the guilt of a defendant seems entirely clear from the genesis and historical evolution of the clause. . . .

Tribunals passing on the guilt of a defendant always have been hedged in by strict evidentiary procedural limitations. But both before and since the American colonies became a nation, courts in this country and in England practiced a policy under which a sentencing judge could exercise a wide discretion in the sources and types of evidence used to assist him in determining the kind and extent of punishment to be imposed within limits fixed by law. Out-of-court affidavits have been used frequently, and of course in the smaller communities sentencing judges naturally have in mind their knowledge of the personalities and backgrounds of convicted offenders. A recent manifestation of the historical latitude allowed sentencing judges appears in Rule 32 of the Federal Rules of Criminal Procedure. That rule provides for consideration by federal judges of reports made by probation officers containing information about a convicted defendant, including such information "as may be helpful in imposing sentence or in granting probation or in the correctional treatment of the defendant. . . ."

In addition to the historical basis for different evidentiary rules governing trial and sentencing procedures there are sound practical reasons for the distinction. In a trial before verdict the issue is whether a defendant is guilty of having engaged in certain criminal conduct of which he has been specifically accused. Rules of evidence have been fashioned for criminal trials which narrowly confine the trial contest to evidence that is strictly relevant to the particular offense charged. These rules rest in part on a necessity to prevent a time-consuming and confusing trial of collateral issues. They were also designed to prevent tribunals concerned solely with the issue of guilt of a particular offense from being influenced to convict for that offense by evidence that the defendant had habitually engaged in other misconduct. A sentencing judge, however, is not confined to the narrow issue of guilt. His task within fixed statutory or constitutional limits is to determine the type and extent of punishment after the issue of guilt has been determined. Highly relevant — if not essential — to his selection of an appropriate sentence is the possession of the fullest information possible concerning the defendant's life and characteristics. And modern concepts individualizing punishment have made it all the more necessary that a sentencing judge not be denied an opportunity to obtain pertinent information by a requirement of rigid adherence to restrictive rules of evidence properly applicable to the trial.

Undoubtedly the New York statutes emphasize a prevalent modern philosophy of penology that the punishment should fit the offender and not merely the crime. . . . The belief no longer prevails that every offense in a like legal category calls for an identical punishment without regard to the past life and habits of a particular offender. This whole country has traveled far from the period in which the death sentence was an automatic and commonplace result of convictions — even for offenses today deemed trivial. Today's philosophy of individualizing sentences makes sharp distinctions for example between first and repeated offenders. Indeterminate sentences the ultimate termination of which are sometimes decided by non-judicial agencies have to a large extent taken the place of the old rigidly fixed punishments. The practice of probation which relies heavily on non-judicial implementation has been accepted as a wise policy. Execution of the United States parole system rests on the discretion of an administrative parole board. . . . Retribution is no longer the dominant objective of the criminal law. Reformation and rehabilitation of offenders have become important goals of criminal jurisprudence.

Modern changes in the treatment of offenders make it more necessary now than a century ago for observance of the distinctions in the evidential procedure in the trial and sentencing processes. For indeterminate sentences and probation have resulted in an increase in the discretionary powers exercised in fixing punishments. In general, these modern changes have not resulted in making the lot of offenders harder. On the contrary a strong motivating force for the changes has been the belief that by careful study of the lives and personalities of convicted offenders many could be less severely punished and restored sooner to complete freedom and useful citizenship. This belief to a large extent has been justified.

Under the practice of individualizing punishments, investigational techniques have been given an important role. Probation workers making reports of their investigations have not been trained to prosecute but to aid offenders. Their reports have been given a high value by conscientious judges who want to sentence persons on the best available information rather than on guesswork and inadequate information. To deprive sentencing judges of this kind of information would undermine modern penological procedural policies that have been cautiously adopted throughout the nation after careful consideration and experimentation. We must recognize that most of the information now relied upon by judges to guide them in the intelligent imposition of sentences would be unavailable if information were restricted to that given in open court by witnesses subject to cross-examination. And the modern probation report draws on information concerning every aspect of a defendant's life.[15] The type and extent of this information make totally impractical if not impossible open court testimony with cross-examination. Such a procedure could endlessly delay criminal administration in a retrial of collateral issues.

The considerations we have set out admonish us against treating the due process clause as a uniform command that courts throughout the Nation abandon their age-old practice of seeking information from out-of-court sources to guide their judgment toward a more enlightened and just sentence. New York criminal statutes set wide limits for maximum and minimum sentences. Under New York statutes a state judge cannot escape his grave responsibility of fixing sentence. In determining whether a defendant shall receive a one-year minimum or a twenty-year maximum sentence, we do not think the Federal Constitution restricts the view of the sentencing judge to the information received in open court. The due process clause should not be treated as a device for freezing the evidential procedure of sentencing in the mold of trial procedure. So to treat the due process clause would hinder if not preclude all courts — state and federal — from making progressive efforts to improve the administration of criminal justice.

It is urged, however, that we should draw a constitutional distinction as to the procedure for obtaining information where the death sentence is imposed. We cannot accept the contention. Leaving a sentencing judge free to avail himself of out-of-court information in making such a fateful choice of sentences does secure to him a broad discretionary power, one susceptible of abuse. But in considering whether a rigid constitutional barrier should be created, it must be remembered that there is possibility of abuse wherever a judge must choose between life imprisonment and death. And it is conceded that no federal constitutional objection would have been possible if the judge here had sentenced appellant to death because appellant's trial manner impressed the judge that appellant was a bad risk for society, or if the judge had sentenced him to death giving no reason at all. We cannot say that the due process clause renders a sentence void merely because a judge gets additional out-of-court information to assist him in the exercise of this awesome power of imposing the death sentence.

Appellant was found guilty after a fairly conducted trial. His sentence followed a hearing conducted by the judge. Upon the judge's inquiry as to why sentence should not be imposed, the defendant made statements. His counsel made extended arguments. The case went to the highest court in the state, and that court had power to reverse for abuse of discretion or legal error in the imposition of the sentence. That court affirmed. We hold that appellant was not denied due process of law.

Affirmed.

[The dissenting opinion of Justice Murphy is omitted.]

15. A publication circulated by the Administrative Office of the United States Courts contains a suggested form for all United States probation reports and serves as an example of the type of information contained in the reports. This form consists of thirteen "marginal headings." (1) Offense; (2) Prior Record; (3) Family History; (4) Home and Neighborhood; (5) Education; (6) Religion; (7) Interests and Activities; (8) Health (physical and mental); (9) Employment; (10) Resources; (11) Summary; (12) Plan; and (13) Agencies Interested. Each of the headings is further broken down into subheadings. The form represents a framework into which information can be inserted to give the sentencing judge a composite picture of the defendant. Administrative Office of the United States Courts, The Presentence Investigation Report, Pub. No. 101 (1943).

NOTES AND QUESTIONS

1. In Gardner v. Florida, 430 U.S. 349 (1977), the Court held that modern capital sentencing — where the sentencer's discretion must, in order to comply with the Eighth Amendment, be guided by statutory "aggravating circumstances" — requires a higher level of procedural protection for the defendant than does traditional discretionary sentencing under *Williams*. Thus, in a post-*Furman* capital case, the defendant was denied due process "when the death sentence was imposed, at least in part, on the basis of information which he had no opportunity to deny or explain." Id., at 362.

In Ring v. Arizona, 536 U.S. 584 (2002), the Court went even further in applying the constitutional rules of criminal procedure to capital sentencing, holding that "aggravating circumstances" are the functional equivalents of elements of a crime, and thus must be found beyond reasonable doubt by a jury. *Ring* is discussed infra, at page 1453.

2. Does the decision in *Williams* represent a normative statement by the Court that criminal sentencing *should not* be subject to all of the same procedural rules that apply to criminal trials? Or does the decision reflect merely the Court's recognition of the practical reality that — in a world of "black box" discretionary sentencing — much of what happens *cannot* effectively be governed by such procedural rules, since in most cases there will be no practical way to determine whether those rules have been followed?

3. The Supreme Court in *Williams* held that at least some of the constitutional rules of criminal procedure applicable to criminal trials — specifically, in that case, the right to confront adverse witnesses — do not apply to traditional discretionary criminal sentencing. But what about nontraditional forms of criminal sentencing? In the late twentieth century, the legislatures of many states and the federal government — wanting to be seen as "tough on crime" — began to experiment with "mandatory minimum" sentencing. Under such statutes, all defendants convicted of certain designated crimes (or of crimes committed under certain designated factual circumstances, such as the defendant's use of a gun) must serve a fixed minimum prison term before becoming eligible for parole or other release.

In Chapter 14, at page 1391, you first encountered the *Winship/Mullaney/Patterson* line of cases dealing with burdens of proof and the elements of a crime. In McMillan v. Pennsylvania, 477 U.S. 79 (1986), the Court squarely addressed, for the first time, the potential implications of the *Winship/Mullaney/Patterson* line of cases for "mandatory minimum" sentencing. *McMillan* involved a Pennsylvania statute that mandated a minimum five-year prison sentence for any defendant who "visibly possessed a firearm" during the commission of certain enumerated felonies. Under the statute, the presence of this special sentencing factor was determined by the sentencing judge, on a "preponderance of the evidence" standard, based on all of the evidence introduced either at trial or during a separate sentencing hearing. The defendant, McMillan, received the mandatory five-year prison sentence; on appeal, he argued that because the "visible firearm possession" sentencing factor was the functional equivalent of an element of the crime for which he was ultimately sentenced, due process — as interpreted by *Winship* and its progeny — required proof "beyond a reasonable doubt" (or, at least, some standard of proof more rigorous than mere "preponderance of the evidence").

The Supreme Court, in a 5-4 majority opinion by Justice Rehnquist, upheld the constitutionality of the statute. The Court relied heavily on *Patterson*, where it had explained that "the state legislature's definition of the elements of the offense is usually dispositive." While noting — as it had in *Patterson* — that "there are obviously constitutional limits beyond which the States may not go in this regard," the Court found Pennsylvania's statute to fall within those still-undefined limits: The statute did not create any impermissible presumptions, it did not change the definitions of any existing crimes (but merely "dictated the precise weight" to be given one particular sentencing factor), and — perhaps most important — it did not provide for a mandatory minimum sentence larger than the sentences already authorized for the underlying substantive crimes to which the statute applied. In the Court's words, "The statute gives no impression of having been tailored to permit the visible possession finding to be a tail which wags the dog of the substantive offense." Having found no constitutional defect in the statute's treatment of "visible possession" as a sentencing factor (rather than an element of the crime), the Court handily dismissed McMillan's objections to the preponderance standard, citing *Williams* for the proposition that "[s]entencing courts have traditionally heard evidence and found facts without any prescribed burden of proof at all." Finally, the Court noted a logical flaw in McMillan's argument:

> Petitioners apparently concede that Pennsylvania's scheme would pass constitutional muster if only it did not remove the sentencing court's discretion, i.e., if the legislature had simply directed the court to *consider* visible possession in passing sentence. . . . We have some difficulty fathoming why the due process calculus would change simply because the legislature has seen fit to provide sentencing courts with additional guidance.

Id., at 92.

Justice Stevens dissented,[6] pointing out that the majority's position suffered from its own logical flaw:

> It would demean the importance of the reasonable-doubt standard — indeed, it would demean the Constitution itself — if the substance of the standard could be avoided by nothing more than a legislative declaration that prohibited conduct is not an "element" of a crime. A legislative definition of an offense named "assault" could be broad enough to encompass every intentional infliction of harm by one person upon another, but surely the legislature could not provide that only that fact must be proved beyond a reasonable doubt and then specify a range of increased punishments if the prosecution could show by a preponderance of the evidence that the defendant robbed, raped, or killed his victim "during the commission of the offense."
>
> . . . . I submit . . . that if a State provides that a specific component of a prohibited transaction shall give rise both to a special stigma and to a special punishment, that component must be treated as a "fact necessary to constitute the crime" within the meaning of our holding in In re Winship.

Id., at 102-103.

---

6. There was also a separate dissent by Justice Marshall, which was joined by Justices Brennan and Blackmun.

4. In Walton v. Arizona, 497 U.S. 639 (1990), the Court — in another 5-4 decision, with virtually the same lineup as in *McMillan*[7] upheld the Arizona death penalty statute against, inter alia, a challenge that it violated the Sixth Amendment's right to trial by jury by giving to the trial judge (instead of a jury) the responsibility of finding the "aggravating circumstances" that could lead to imposition of a death sentence.

The majority, in an opinion by Justice White, explained that under Arizona law "[a]ggravating circumstances are not separate penalties or offenses, but are 'standards to guide the making of [the] choice' between the alternative verdicts of death and life imprisonment. Thus, . . . the judge's finding of any particular aggravating circumstance does not of itself 'convict' a defendant (i.e., require the death penalty), and the failure to find any particular aggravating circumstance does not 'acquit' a defendant (i.e., preclude the death penalty)." *Walton*, 497 U.S., at 648.

In dissent on this issue, Justice Stevens[8] pointed out that "under Arizona law, . . . a first-degree murder is not punishable by a death sentence until at least one statutory aggravating circumstance has been proved," and argued that such aggravating circumstances thus "operate as statutory 'elements' of capital murder," id., at 709, and n. 1. He concluded — in language that now seems all too prescient:

> By stretching the limits of sentencing determinations that are made by judges . . . , these decisions have encroached on the factfinding function that has so long been entrusted to the jury. Further distorting the sentencing function to encompass findings of factual elements necessary to establish a capital offense is the unhappy product of the gradual "increase and spread" of these precedents, "to the utter disuse of juries in questions of the most momentous concern." . . . [I]t is not too late to change our course. . . .

Id., at 713-714.

NOTES ON DETERMINATE SENTENCING AND THE CONSTITUTION

Does the recent shift from traditional discretionary sentencing to determinate sentencing, as described above at pages 1439-1443, necessitate reexamination of the basic principles underlying *Williams* and *McMillan*? The answer, perhaps surprisingly, turns out to be yes. In Apprendi v. New Jersey, 530 U.S. 466 (2000), the Supreme Court rocked the world of criminal sentencing by holding that at least some of the factors relied upon in determinate sentencing are the functional equivalents of elements of a new crime, and thus must be found by a jury beyond a reasonable doubt. This holding, if extended by the Court to its logical limits, may bring about the demise of determinate sentencing altogether — or at least of the particular form of determinate sentencing that has been implemented in most jurisdictions over the past 20 years. To understand *Apprendi* and its potential

---

7. The only difference was that Justice Scalia replaced the retired Justice Powell on the winning side of the case.

8. Justices Brennan, Marshall, and Blackmun dissented on other grounds.

consequences, however, we must first survey the pre-*Apprendi* jurisprudential landscape.

1. The Supreme Court's first major constitutional encounter with determinate sentencing came in Mistretta v. United States, 488 U.S. 361 (1989). *Mistretta* involved a broad claim that the Sentencing Reform Act of 1984, which created the United States Sentencing Commission and charged that body with the responsibility to draft sentencing guidelines for federal crimes, violated the constitutional doctrine of separation of powers and involved excessive delegation of legislative powers to a nonlegislative body. The Court, by 8-1, disagreed. In an opinion by Justice Blackmun, the Court carefully reviewed the Act and the Guidelines promulgated thereunder, and held that the Act's delegation of Congressional powers was "sufficiently specific and detailed" to meet constitutional requirements. Although the *Mistretta* Court did not decide any particular constitutional issues relating to the operation of the Guidelines, neither did it signal any serious concerns about how those Guidelines operated.

2. During the next decade or so, the Court addressed — and mostly rejected — a series of narrower and more specific constitutional challenges to particular aspects or applications of the Federal Sentencing Guidelines. In Witte v. United States, 515 U.S. 389 (1995), for example, the Court rejected a claim that reliance on uncharged condut to enhance a defendant's sentence under the Guidelines precluded, under the Double Jeopardy Clause, a subsequent criminal prosecution based on that same conduct. In United States v. Watts, 519 U.S. 148 (1997), the Court held, in a per curiam opinion, that even alleged crimes for which the defendant previously was acquitted could be used, without violating due process, to enhance his sentence for a later crime under the Guidelines. Although neither *Witte* nor *Watts* dealt with the constitutional right to jury trial, both cases seemed to signify that the Constitution generally did not prohibit judges from increasing defendants' sentences based on judicial findings of facts that were never found by the jury.

Perhaps more significant, in Edwards v. United States, 523 U.S. 511 (1998), the Court flatly rejected a statutory and constitutional challenge to the imposition of a higher Guideline sentence for conspiracy to possess crack cocaine, despite the fact that the jury's general verdict might have been based solely on a conspiracy involving powder cocaine (which would have produced a lower sentence). The defendant in *Edwards* argued unsuccessfully that the trial judge should have been limited to sentencing him for the kind of conspiracy that necessarily was found by the jury. According to Justice Breyer's opinion for a unanimous Court: "The Sentencing Guidelines instruct *the judge* in a case like this one to determine both the amount and the kind of 'controlled substances' for which a defendant should be held accountable — and then to impose a sentence that varies depending upon amount and kind."[9]

3. In another case decided the same Term as *Edwards*, however, the constitutional worm began to turn. In Almendarez-Torres v. United States, 523 U.S. 224 (1998), the Court faced for the first time a claim that one of the factors identified in the

---

9. Note that Justice Breyer, before being appointed to the Supreme Court (i.e., when he was still a Circuit Judge), served as one of the original members of the United States Sentencing Commission that drafted the Federal Sentencing Guidelines.

Federal Sentencing Guidelines as the basis for an increased sentence — specifically, the defendant's prior criminal convictions — should be viewed as the functional equivalent of an element of a new crime. The defendant argued that, under the Fifth Amendment, his prior criminal convictions (to which he had admitted at his plea hearing) were required to be alleged in the indictment. The Court rejected this claim, but the case was close (5-4), and the four dissenters — Justices Stevens, Scalia, Souter, and Ginsburg — expressed "serious doubt as to whether the statute as interpreted by the Court in the present case is constitutional." In the prophetic words of Justice Scalia: "[I]t is genuinely doubtful whether the Constitution permits a judge (rather than a jury) to determine by a mere preponderance of the evidence (rather than beyond a reasonable doubt) a fact that increases the maximum penalty to which a criminal defendant is subject. . . ."

One year later, in Jones v. United States, 526 U.S. 227 (1999), the Court considered the Government's contention that the federal carjacking statute did not require a jury finding, beyond a reasonable doubt, on the factual issue whether the defendant's crime caused "serious bodily injury" to the victim (a fact that increased the defendant's maximum sentence from 15 years to 25 years in prison). Justice Thomas joined the four *Almendarez-Torres* dissenters to produce the *Jones* majority, which concluded: "[U]nder the Due Process Clause of the Fifth Amendment and the notice and jury trial guarantees of the Sixth Amendment, any fact (other than prior conviction) that increases the maximum penalty for a crime must be charged in an indictment, submitted to a jury, and proven beyond a reasonable doubt. Because our prior cases suggest rather than establish this principle, our concern about the Government's reading of the statute rises only to the level of doubt, not certainty." In order to avoid this "constitutional doubt," the *Jones* Court, in an opinion by Justice Souter, construed the statute to require "serious bodily injury" to be alleged in the indictment, and found by a jury at trial beyond a reasonable doubt.

4. That led directly to the momentous decision in Apprendi v. New Jersey, 530 U.S. 466 (2000). In *Apprendi*, the defendant was convicted of possessing a firearm for an unlawful purpose, a crime carrying a statutory sentence of between 5 and 10 years in prison. During the defendant's sentencing hearing, however, the trial judge found, by a preponderance of the evidence, that the crime was committed for the purpose of intimidation based on the race of the victim. This judicial finding triggered the New Jersey "hate crime" statute, which provided for an "extended term" of imprisonment — doubling the normal sentencing range — for any such "hate crime." Under the "hate crime" statute, the judge was authorized to impose a sentence of up to 20 years, and sentenced the defendant to 12 years in prison.

In an opinion by Justice Stevens (the author of the primary dissent in *McMillan*), joined by Justices Scalia, Souter, Thomas, and Ginsburg, the Court held that this situation violated the Constitution by depriving the defendant of his right to have pretrial notice of all elements of the crime with which he was charged, and to have those elements found at trial by a jury beyond a reasonable doubt. According to the Court: "Other than the fact of a prior conviction [as in *Almendarez-Torres*], any fact that increases the penalty for a crime beyond the prescribed statutory maximum must be submitted to a jury, and proved beyond a reasonable doubt. . . ." Rejecting New Jersey's argument that the "hate crime" enhancement was a "sentencing factor" under *McMillan*, rather than an "element" of a new crime, the Court described the proffered distinction as "constitutionally novel and elusive," and explained: "[T]he relevant inquiry is one not of form, but of effect — does the required finding expose the defendant to a greater punishment than that authorized by the jury's guilty verdict?"

5. *Apprendi* was a significant enough decision in its own right; for example, it led some federal courts to begin invalidating sentences imposed for drug crimes where the jury did not make factual findings about the amount of drugs sold or possessed. See, e.g., Nordby v. United States, 225 F.3d 1053 (9th Cir. 2000). But even more significant were the questions left unanswered by *Apprendi*.

For example, what did *Apprendi* mean for capital sentencing? In Ring v. Arizona, 536 U.S. 584 (2002), the Court held that the prior *Walton* decision (upholding judicial factfinding of the aggravating circumstances necessary to impose a death sentence) was incompatible with *Apprendi*. In response to Arizona's contention that *Apprendi* did not apply because the statutory range of punishment for first-degree murder in Arizona included death (and thus the defendant was not sentenced above the statutory maximum), the *Ring* Court explained: "In effect, 'the required finding [of an aggravating circumstance] expose[d] [Ring] to a greater punishment than that authorized by the jury's guilty verdict.' The Arizona first-degree murder statute 'authorizes a maximum punishment of death only in a formal sense.' . . . Because Arizona's enumerated aggravating factors operate as 'the functional equivalent of a greater offense,' . . . the Sixth Amendment requires that they be found by a jury."

Another unanswered question was whether *McMillan* itself could survive *Apprendi*. On this question, in Harris v. United States, 536 U.S. 545 (2002), the Court — by 5-4, and without a complete majority opinion — reaffirmed the validity of *McMillan*. According to the plurality opinion of Justice Kennedy:

> . . . *McMillan* and *Apprendi* are consistent because there is a fundamental distinction between the factual findings that were at issue in those two cases. *Apprendi* said that any fact extending the defendant's sentence beyond the maximum authorized by the jury's verdict [is] an element of an aggravated crime. . . . The same cannot be said of a fact increasing the mandatory minimum (but not extending the sentence beyond the statutory maximum), for the jury's verdict has authorized the judge to impose the minimum with or without the finding. As *McMillan* recognized, a statute may reserve this type of factual finding for the judge without violating the Constitution.
>
> The Court has recognized that . . . [j]udicial factfinding in the course of selecting a sentence within the authorized range does not implicate the indictment, jury-trial, and reasonable-doubt components of the Fifth and Sixth Amendments. . . .
>
> Read together, *McMillan* and *Apprendi* mean that those facts setting the outer limits of a sentence, and of the judicial power to impose it, are the elements of the crime for purposes of the constitutional analysis. Within the range authorized by the jury's verdict, however, the political system may channel judicial discretion — and rely on judicial expertise — by requiring defendants to serve minimum terms after judges make certain factual findings. It is critical not to abandon that understanding at this late date. Legislatures and their constituents have relied upon *McMillan* to exercise control over sentencing through dozens of statutes like the one the Court approved in that case. . . . We see no reason to overturn those statutes or cast uncertainty upon the sentences imposed under them.

Justice Breyer did not join this portion of Justice Kennedy's lead opinion, because he felt that "in terms of logic," *Apprendi* could not be distinguished from *Harris*. Moreover, he believed that mandatory minimum sentences "are fundamentally inconsistent with Congress' simultaneous effort to create a fair, honest, and rational sentencing system through the use of Sentencing Guidelines." Nevertheless, because he disagreed so strongly with *Apprendi* itself, Justice Breyer joined in the result, refusing to apply *Apprendi* to mandatory minimum sentences.

6. The "big question" that loomed after *Apprendi*, however, was whether that decision would lead to the invalidation of the Federal Sentencing Guidelines and similar state-law determinate-sentencing schemes — none of which required jury determination of all facts that triggered increases in guideline sentences. In *Apprendi*, both Justice Stevens's majority opinion and Justice Thomas's concurrence explicitly declined to discuss the possible impact of *Apprendi* on the Guidelines, while Justice O'Connor's dissent suggested that, in light of *Apprendi*, the Guidelines must be viewed as constitutionally suspect. Meanwhile, Justice Breyer (one of the drafters of the original Guidelines) wrote a separate dissent in *Apprendi* for the sole purpose of defending the Guidelines against what he perceived to be a thinly veiled threat to their constitutionality. This provoked Justice Scalia to accuse Justice Breyer of succumbing to the "erroneous and all-too-common assumption that the Constitution means what we think it ought to mean."

On June 24, 2004, after four years of significant uncertainty in the lower courts (and, no doubt, significant anxiety in Justice Breyer as well), the Court — in a majority opinion by Justice Scalia — took a big step toward answering the "big question."

BLAKELY v. WASHINGTON, 542 U.S. 296 (2004): Petitioner Ralph Howard Blakely, Jr., pleaded guilty to the kidnaping of his estranged wife. The facts admitted in his plea, standing alone, supported a maximum sentence of 53 months. Pursuant to state law, the court imposed an "exceptional" sentence of 90 months after making a judicial determination that he had acted with "deliberate cruelty." We consider whether this violated petitioner's Sixth Amendment right to trial by jury. . . .

This case requires us to apply the rule we expressed in Apprendi v. New Jersey, 530 U.S. 466, 490 (2000): "Other than the fact of a prior conviction, any fact that increases the penalty for a crime beyond the prescribed statutory maximum must be submitted to a jury, and proved beyond a reasonable doubt." This rule reflects two longstanding tenets of common-law criminal jurisprudence: that the "truth of every accusation" against a defendant "should afterwards be confirmed by the unanimous suffrage of twelve of his equals and neighbours," 4 W. Blackstone, Commentaries on the Laws of England 343 (1769), and that "an accusation which lacks any particular fact which the law makes essential to the punishment is . . . no accusation within the requirements of the common law, and it is no accusation in reason," 1 J. Bishop, Criminal Procedure §87, p. 55 (2d ed. 1872). These principles have been acknowledged by courts and treatises since the earliest days of graduated sentencing; we compiled the relevant authorities in *Apprendi*, see 530 U.S., at 476-483, 489-490, n. 15; id., at 501-518, (Thomas, J., concurring), and need not repeat them here.[6] . . .

[In both *Apprendi* and Ring v. Arizona, 536 U.S. 584 (2002),] we concluded that the defendant's constitutional rights had been violated because the judge had imposed a sentence greater than the maximum he could have imposed under state law without the challenged factual finding.

---

6. [In dissent,] Justice O'Connor does not even provide a coherent alternative meaning for the jury-trial guarantee, unless one considers "whatever the legislature chooses to leave to the jury, so long as it does not go too far" coherent.

In this case, petitioner was sentenced to more than three years above the 53 month statutory maximum of the standard range because he had acted with "deliberate cruelty." The facts supporting that finding were neither admitted by petitioner nor found by a jury. The State nevertheless contends that there was no *Apprendi* violation because the relevant "statutory maximum" is not 53 months, but the 10-year maximum for class B felonies in §9A.20.021(1)(b). . . . Our precedents make clear, however, that the "statutory maximum" for *Apprendi* purposes is the maximum sentence a judge may impose solely on the basis of the facts reflected in the jury verdict or admitted by the defendant. See *Ring*, supra, at 602 ("'the maximum he would receive if punished according to the facts reflected in the jury verdict alone'" (quoting *Apprendi*, supra, at 483)) . . . In other words, the relevant "statutory maximum" is not the maximum sentence a judge may impose after finding additional facts, but the maximum he may impose without any additional findings. When a judge inflicts punishment that the jury's verdict alone does not allow, the jury has not found all the facts "which the law makes essential to the punishment," Bishop, supra, §87, at 55, and the judge exceeds his proper authority. . . .

[T]he State tries to distinguish *Apprendi* and *Ring* by pointing out that the enumerated grounds for departure in its regime are illustrative rather than exhaustive. This distinction is immaterial. Whether the judge's authority to impose an enhanced sentence depends on finding a specified fact (as in *Apprendi*), one of several specified facts (as in *Ring*), or any aggravating fact (as here), it remains the case that the jury's verdict alone does not authorize the sentence. The judge acquires that authority only upon finding some additional fact.[8]

Because the State's sentencing procedure did not comply with the Sixth Amendment, petitioner's sentence is invalid.[9]

Our commitment to *Apprendi* in this context reflects not just respect for longstanding precedent, but the need to give intelligible content to the right of jury trial. That right is no mere procedural formality, but a fundamental reservation of power in our constitutional structure. Just as suffrage ensures the people's ultimate control in the legislative and executive branches, jury trial is meant to ensure their control in the judiciary. . . . *Apprendi* carries out this design by ensuring that the judge's authority to sentence derives wholly from the jury's verdict. Without that restriction, the jury would not exercise the control that the Framers intended.

Those who would reject *Apprendi* are resigned to one of two alternatives. The first is that the jury need only find whatever facts the legislature chooses to label elements of the crime, and that those it labels sentencing factors—no matter how much they may increase the punishment—may be found by the judge. This would mean, for example, that a judge could sentence a man for committing murder even if the jury convicted him only of illegally possessing the firearm used to commit it—or of making an illegal lane change while fleeing the death scene. Not even *Apprendi*'s critics would advocate this absurd result. . . . The jury could not function as circuitbreaker in the State's machinery of justice if it were relegated to making a

8. Nor does it matter that the judge must, after finding aggravating facts, make a judgment that they present a compelling ground for departure. He cannot make that judgment without finding some facts to support it beyond the bare elements of the offense. Whether the judicially determined facts require a sentence enhancement or merely allow it, the verdict alone does not authorize the sentence.

9. The United States, as amicus curiae, urges us to affirm. It notes differences between Washington's sentencing regime and the Federal Sentencing Guidelines but questions whether those differences are constitutionally significant. See Brief for United States as Amicus Curiae 25-30. The Federal Guidelines are not before us, and we express no opinion on them.

determination that the defendant at some point did something wrong, a mere preliminary to a judicial inquisition into the facts of the crime the State actually seeks to punish.[10]

The second alternative is that legislatures may establish legally essential sentencing factors within limits — limits crossed when, perhaps, the sentencing factor is a "tail which wags the dog of the substantive offense." *McMillan*, 477 U.S., at 88. What this means in operation is that the law must not go too far — it must not exceed the judicial estimation of the proper role of the judge.

The subjectivity of this standard is obvious . . . Whether the Sixth Amendment incorporates this manipulable standard rather than *Apprendi*'s bright-line rule depends on the plausibility of the claim that the Framers would have left definition of the scope of jury power up to judges' intuitive sense of how far is too far. We think that claim not plausible at all, because the very reason the Framers put a jury-trial guarantee in the Constitution is that they were unwilling to trust government to mark out the role of the jury.

Justice O'Connor argues that, because determinate sentencing schemes involving judicial factfinding entail less judicial discretion than indeterminate schemes, the constitutionality of the latter implies the constitutionality of the former. This argument is flawed on a number of levels. First, the Sixth Amendment by its terms is not a limitation on judicial power, but a reservation of jury power. It limits judicial power only to the extent that the claimed judicial power infringes on the province of the jury. Indeterminate sentencing does not do so. It increases judicial discretion, to be sure, but not at the expense of the jury's traditional function of finding the facts essential to lawful imposition of the penalty. . . .

But even assuming that restraint of judicial power unrelated to the jury's role is a Sixth Amendment objective, it is far from clear that *Apprendi* disserves that goal. Determinate judicial-factfinding schemes entail less judicial power than indeterminate schemes, but more judicial power than determinate jury-factfinding schemes. Whether *Apprendi* increases judicial power overall depends on what States with determinate judicial-factfinding schemes would do, given the choice between the two alternatives. Justice O'Connor simply assumes that the net effect will favor judges, but she has no empirical basis for that prediction. . . .

Justice Breyer argues that *Apprendi* works to the detriment of criminal defendants who plead guilty by depriving them of the opportunity to argue sentencing factors to a judge. But nothing prevents a defendant from waiving his *Apprendi* rights. When a defendant pleads guilty, the State is free to seek judicial sentence enhancements so long as the defendant either stipulates to the relevant facts or consents to judicial factfinding. . . .

Nor do we see any merit to Justice Breyer's contention that *Apprendi* is unfair to criminal defendants because, if States respond by enacting "17-element robbery crimes," prosecutors will have more elements with which to bargain. . . . [G]iven the sprawling scope of most criminal codes, and the power to affect sentences by making (even nonbinding) sentencing recommendations, there is already no shortage of in terrorem tools at prosecutors' disposal. See King & Klein, *Apprendi* and Plea

10. Justice O'Connor believes that a "built-in political check" will prevent lawmakers from manipulating offense elements in this fashion. But the many immediate practical advantages of judicial factfinding . . . suggest that political forces would, if anything, pull in the opposite direction. In any case, the Framers' decision to entrench the jury-trial right in the Constitution shows that they did not trust government to make political decisions in this area.

Bargaining, 54 Stan. L. Rev. 295, 296 (2001) ("Every prosecutorial bargaining chip mentioned . . . existed pre-*Apprendi* exactly as it does post-*Apprendi*").

Justice Breyer's more general argument — that *Apprendi* undermines alternatives to adversarial factfinding — is not so much a criticism of *Apprendi* as an assault on jury trial generally. His esteem for "non-adversarial" truth-seeking processes . . . supports just as well an argument against either. Our Constitution and the common-law traditions it entrenches, however, do not admit the contention that facts are better discovered by judicial inquisition than by adversarial testing before a jury. See 3 Blackstone, Commentaries, at 373-374, 379-381. Justice Breyer may be convinced of the equity of the regime he favors, but his views are not the ones we are bound to uphold.

Ultimately, our decision cannot turn on whether or to what degree trial by jury impairs the efficiency or fairness of criminal justice. One can certainly argue that both these values would be better served by leaving justice entirely in the hands of professionals; many nations of the world, particularly those following civil-law traditions, take just that course. There is not one shred of doubt, however, about the Framers' paradigm for criminal justice: not the civil-law ideal of administrative perfection, but the common-law ideal of limited state power accomplished by strict division of authority between judge and jury. As *Apprendi* held, every defendant has the right to insist that the prosecutor prove to a jury all facts legally essential to the punishment. Under the dissenters' alternative, he has no such right. That should be the end of the matter.

Notwithstanding the careful language of footnote 9 in *Blakely*, the potential import of the decision for the Federal Sentencing Guidelines (and all state guideline systems other than Washington's) was readily apparent to all. Most observers stubbornly refused to believe that the Court would, after 20 years, throw out the Federal Guidelines, and predicted instead that relevant distinctions with the Washington state guideline system would be found. A few sages warned of looming chaos and disaster. On January 12, 2005, the Court finally addressed the uncertainty over the application of *Apprendi* and *Blakely* to the Federal Sentencing Guidelines. But the Court's decision may have managed to create even more uncertainty than it resolved.

UNITED STATES v. BOOKER

Certiorari to the United States Court of Appeals for the Seventh Circuit
543 U.S. 220 (2005)

JUSTICE STEVENS delivered the opinion of the Court in part.[10]

The question presented in each of these cases[11] is whether an application of the Federal Sentencing Guidelines violated the Sixth Amendment. In each case, the courts below held that binding rules set forth in the Guidelines limited the severity of the sentence that the judge could lawfully impose on the defendant based on the facts found by the jury at his trial. In both cases the courts rejected, on the basis of

-----

10. Justice Stevens was joined in this part by Justices Scalia, Souter, Thomas, and Ginsburg. — EDS.
11. *Booker* was decided together with United States v. Fanfan, on certiorari before judgment to the United States Court of Appeals for the First Circuit. — EDS.

our decision in Blakely v. Washington, 542 U.S. 296 (2004), the Government's recommended application of the Sentencing Guidelines because the proposed sentences were based on additional facts that the sentencing judge found by a
preponderance of the evidence. We hold that both courts correctly concluded that
the Sixth Amendment as construed in *Blakely* does apply to the Sentencing Guidelines. In a separate opinion authored by Justice Breyer, the Court concludes that in
light of this holding, two provisions of the Sentencing Reform Act of 1984 (SRA) that
have the effect of making the Guidelines mandatory must be invalidated in order to
allow the statute to operate in a manner consistent with congressional intent.

I

[In this section, Justice Stevens reviewed the facts of the two cases. Booker was
found, by a jury, to have possessed with intent to distribute 92.5 grams of crack
cocaine, which authorized a Guideline sentence of 210 to 262 months. At sentencing, the judge found by a preponderance that Booker actually possessed an additional 566 grams of crack, raising the Guideline sentence to 360 months to life in
prison. Booker received a sentence of 360 months. The Seventh Circuit, relying on
Blakely, reversed.

Fanfan was convicted by a jury of conspiracy to distribute more than 500 grams
of cocaine, which authorized a maximum Guideline sentence of 78 months. At sentencing, the judge found by a preponderance that Fanfan actually controlled a much
greater quantity of various illegal drugs, and that he was a leader of the operation,
raising the Guideline maximum to 16 years. Relying on *Blakely*, however, the judge
imposed the lower Guideline sentence authorized by the jury's verdict. The government appealed and also filed a petition for certiorari before judgment, which the
Supreme Court granted. — Eds.]

II

It has been settled throughout our history that the Constitution protects every
criminal defendant "against conviction except upon proof beyond a reasonable
doubt of every fact necessary to constitute the crime with which he is charged." In re
Winship, 397 U.S. 358, 364 (1970). It is equally clear that the "Constitution gives a
criminal defendant the right to demand that a jury find him guilty of all the elements of the crime with which he is charged." United States v. Gaudin, 515 U.S. 506,
511 (1995). These basic precepts, firmly rooted in the common law, have provided
the basis for recent decisions interpreting modern criminal statutes and sentencing
procedures. . . .

[T]here is no distinction of constitutional significance between the Federal Sentencing Guidelines and the Washington procedures at issue in [*Blakely*]. . . . This
conclusion rests on the premise, common to both systems, that the relevant sentencing rules are mandatory and impose binding requirements on all sentencing judges.

If the Guidelines as currently written could be read as merely advisory provisions
that recommended, rather than required, the selection of particular sentences in
response to differing sets of facts, their use would not implicate the Sixth Amendment. We have never doubted the authority of a judge to exercise broad discretion
in imposing a sentence within a statutory range. See Apprendi [v. New Jersey,] 530
U.S. [466,] 481; Williams v. New York, 337 U.S. 241, 246 (1949). . . .

The Guidelines as written, however, are not advisory; they are mandatory and binding on all judges. . . . [18 U.S.C. §3553] (b) directs that the court "*shall* impose a sentence of the kind, and within the range" established by the Guidelines, subject to departures in specific, limited cases. . . .

The availability of a departure in specified circumstances does not avoid the constitutional issue . . . . At first glance, one might believe that the ability of a district judge to depart from the Guidelines means that she is bound only by the statutory maximum. Were this the case, there would be no *Apprendi* problem. Importantly, however, departures are not available in every case, and in fact are unavailable in most. In most cases, as a matter of law, the Commission will have adequately taken all relevant factors into account, and no departure will be legally permissible. In those instances, the judge is bound to impose a sentence within the Guidelines range. . . .

In his dissent, Justice Breyer . . . points to traditional judicial authority to increase sentences to take account of any unusual blameworthiness in the manner employed in committing a crime, an authority that the Guidelines require to be exercised consistently throughout the system. This tradition, however, does not provide a sound guide to enforcement of the Sixth Amendment's guarantee of a jury trial in today's world.

In 1986, [we] first recognized a new trend in the legislative regulation of sentencing when we considered the significance of facts selected by legislatures that not only authorized, or even mandated, heavier sentences than would otherwise have been imposed, but increased the range of sentences possible for the underlying crime. See McMillan v. Pennsylvania, 477 U.S. 79, 87-88 (1986). Provisions for such enhancements of the permissible sentencing range reflected growing and wholly justified legislative concern about the proliferation and variety of drug crimes and their frequent identification with firearms offences.

The effect of the increasing emphasis on facts that enhanced sentencing ranges, however, was to increase the judge's power and diminish that of the jury. It became the judge, not the jury, that determined the upper limits of sentencing, and the facts determined were not required to be raised before trial or proved by more than a preponderance.

As the enhancements became greater, the jury's finding of the underlying crime became less significant. And the enhancements became very serious indeed. . . .

As it thus became clear that sentencing was no longer taking place in the tradition that Justice Breyer invokes, the Court was faced with the issue of preserving an ancient guarantee under a new set of circumstances. The new sentencing practice forced the Court to address the question how the right of jury trial could be preserved, in a meaningful way guaranteeing that the jury would still stand between the individual and the power of the government under the new sentencing regime. And it is the new circumstances, not a tradition or practice that the new circumstances have superseded, that have led us to the answer. . . . It is an answer not motivated by Sixth Amendment formalism, but by the need to preserve Sixth Amendment substance.

III

[Here, Justice Stevens considered, and rejected, arguments made by the government that *Blakely* should not apply to the Federal Guidelines because (1) they were drafted by a commission, rather than by the legislature itself; (2) prior Court decisions had upheld the constitutionality of the Guidelines; and (3) doing so would violate the principle of separation of powers, because it would effectively convert the Guidelines (which were not written by Congress) into new criminal statutes. — EDS.]

IV

All of the foregoing support our conclusion that our holding in *Blakely* applies to the Sentencing Guidelines. We recognize . . . that in some cases jury factfinding may impair the most expedient and efficient sentencing of defendants. But the interest in fairness and reliability protected by the right to a jury trial — a common-law right that defendants enjoyed for centuries and that is now enshrined in the Sixth Amendment — has always outweighed the interest in concluding trials swiftly. *Blakely*, 542 U.S. 296. As Blackstone put it:

> However *convenient* these [new methods of trial] may appear at first (as doubtless all arbitrary powers, well executed, are the most *convenient*) yet let it be again remembered, that delays, and little inconveniences in the forms of justice, are the price that all free nations must pay for their liberty in more substantial matters; that these inroads upon this sacred bulwark of the nation are fundamentally opposite to the spirit of our constitution; and that, though begun in trifles, the precedent may gradually increase and spread, to the utter disuse of juries in questions of the most momentous concerns.

4 Commentaries on the Laws of England 343-344 (1769).

Accordingly, we reaffirm our holding in *Apprendi*: Any fact (other than a prior conviction) which is necessary to support a sentence exceeding the maximum authorized by the facts established by a plea of guilty or a jury verdict must be admitted by the defendant or proved to a jury beyond a reasonable doubt.

JUSTICE BREYER delivered the opinion of the Court in part.[12]

. . . We answer the question of remedy by finding the provision of the federal sentencing statute that makes the Guidelines mandatory, 18 U.S.C. §3553(b)(1), incompatible with today's constitutional holding. We conclude that this provision must be severed and excised, as must one other statutory section, §3742(e), which depends upon the Guidelines' mandatory nature. So modified, the Federal Sentencing Act makes the Guidelines effectively advisory. It requires a sentencing court to consider Guidelines ranges, but it permits the court to tailor the sentence in light of other statutory concerns as well.

I

We answer the remedial question by looking to legislative intent. . . . We seek to determine what "Congress would have intended" in light of the Court's constitutional holding. Denver Area Ed. Telecommunications Consortium, Inc. v. FCC, 518 U.S. 727, 767 (1996) (plurality opinion). . . . In this instance, we must determine which of the two following remedial approaches is the more compatible with the legislature's intent as embodied in the 1984 Sentencing Act.

---

12. Justice Breyer was joined in this part by Chief Justice Rehnquist and Justices O'Connor, Kennedy, and Ginsburg. — EDS.

One approach, that of Justice Stevens' dissent, would retain the Sentencing Act (and the Guidelines) as written, but would engraft onto the existing system today's Sixth Amendment "jury trial" requirement. The addition would change the Guidelines by preventing the sentencing court from increasing a sentence on the basis of a fact that the jury did not find (or that the offender did not admit).

The other approach, which we now adopt, would (through severance and excision of two provisions) make the Guidelines system advisory while maintaining a strong connection between the sentence imposed and the offender's real conduct — a connection important to the increased uniformity of sentencing that Congress intended its Guidelines system to achieve.

Both approaches would significantly alter the system that Congress designed. But today's constitutional holding means that it is no longer possible to maintain the judicial factfinding that Congress thought would underpin the mandatory Guidelines system that it sought to create . . . . Hence we must decide whether we would deviate less radically from Congress' intended system (1) by superimposing the constitutional requirement announced today or (2) through elimination of some provisions of the statute. . . .

In today's context — a highly complex statute, interrelated provisions, and a constitutional requirement that creates fundamental change — we cannot assume that Congress, if faced with the statute's invalidity in key applications, would have preferred to apply the statute in as many other instances as possible. Neither can we determine likely congressional intent mechanically. We cannot simply approach the problem grammatically, say, by looking to see whether the constitutional requirement and the words of the Act are linguistically compatible.

Nor do simple numbers provide an answer. It is, of course, true that the numbers show that the constitutional jury trial requirement would lead to additional decisionmaking by juries in only a minority of cases. . . . Prosecutors and defense attorneys would still resolve the lion's share of criminal matters through plea bargaining, and plea bargaining takes place without a jury. Many of the rest involve only simple issues calling for no upward Guidelines adjustment. And in at least some of the remainder, a judge may find adequate room to adjust a sentence within the single Guidelines range to which the jury verdict points, or within the overlap between that range and the next highest.

But the constitutional jury trial requirement would nonetheless affect every case. It would affect decisions about whether to go to trial. It would affect the content of plea negotiations. It would alter the judge's role in sentencing. Thus we must determine likely intent not by counting proceedings, but by evaluating the consequences of the Court's constitutional requirement in light of the Act's language, its history, and its basic purposes.

While reasonable minds can, and do, differ about the outcome, we conclude that the constitutional jury trial requirement is not compatible with the Act as written and that some severance and excision are necessary. . . . [I]n light of today's holding, we compare maintaining the Act as written with jury factfinding added (the dissenters' proposed remedy) to the total invalidation of the statute, and conclude that Congress would have preferred the latter. We then compare our own remedy to the total invalidation of the statute, and conclude that Congress would have preferred our remedy.

II

[Here, Justice Breyer explained that Congress relied heavily on judicial factfinding in the Sentencing Reform Act, especially for the purpose of ensuring that sentences would uniformly reflect the defendant's "real conduct," and not merely what was charged and proved at trial. Engrafting a jury-trial requirement onto the Guideline system (as the dissenters would do) would make it impossible to achieve this goal, and Congress thus would have preferred to have no Guidelines at all. — EDS.]

III

We now turn to the question of *which* portions of the sentencing statute we must sever and excise as inconsistent with the Court's constitutional requirement. Although, as we have explained, we believe that Congress would have preferred the total invalidation of the statute to the dissenters' remedial approach, we nevertheless do not believe that the entire statute must be invalidated. . . . Most of the statute is perfectly valid. . . . And we must "refrain from invalidating more of the statute than is necessary." . . . Indeed, we must retain those portions of the Act that are (1) constitutionally valid, (2) capable of "functioning independently," and (3) consistent with Congress' basic objectives in enacting the statute. [See Alaska Airlines, Inc. v. Brock, 480 U.S. 678 (1987); Regan v. Time, Inc., 468 U.S. 641 (1984) (plurality opinion).]

Application of these criteria indicates that we must sever and excise two specific statutory provisions: the provision that requires sentencing courts to impose a sentence within the applicable Guidelines range (in the absence of circumstances that justify a departure), see 18 U.S.C. §3553(b)(1), and the provision that sets forth standards of review on appeal, including de novo review of departures from the applicable Guidelines range, see §3742(e). With these two sections excised . . . , the remainder of the Act satisfies the Court's constitutional requirements.

As the Court today recognizes in its first opinion in these cases, the existence of §3553(b)(1) is a necessary condition of the constitutional violation. . . .

The remainder of the Act "functions independently." Without the "mandatory" provision, the Act nonetheless requires judges to take account of the Guidelines together with other sentencing goals. See 18 U.S.C. §3553 (a). The Act nonetheless requires judges to consider the Guidelines "sentencing range established for . . . the applicable category of offense committed by the applicable category of defendant," the pertinent Sentencing Commission policy statements, the need to avoid unwarranted sentencing disparities, and the need to provide restitution to victims. And the Act nonetheless requires judges to impose sentences that reflect the seriousness of the offense, promote respect for the law, provide just punishment, afford adequate deterrence, protect the public, and effectively provide the defendant with needed educational or vocational training and medical care. . . .

Moreover, despite the absence of §3553(b)(1), the Act continues to provide for appeals from sentencing decisions (irrespective of whether the trial judge sentences within or outside the Guidelines range in the exercise of his discretionary power under §3553(a)). See §3742(a) (appeal by defendant); §3742(b) (appeal by Government). We concede that the excision of §3553(b)(1) requires the excision of a different, appeals-related section, namely §3742(e), which sets forth standards of review on appeal. That section contains critical cross-references to the (now-excised) §3553(b)(1) and consequently must be severed and excised for similar reasons.

Excision of §3742(e), however, does not pose a critical problem for the handling of appeals. That is because, as we have previously held, a statute that does not *explicitly* set forth a standard of review may nonetheless do so *implicitly*. See Pierce v. Underwood, 487 U.S. 552, 558-560 (1988) (adopting a standard of review, where "neither a clear statutory prescription nor a historical tradition" existed, based on the statutory text and structure, and on practical considerations). . . . We infer appropriate review standards from related statutory language, the structure of the statute, and the "sound administration of justice." *Pierce*, supra, at 559-560. And in this instance those factors . . . imply a practical standard of review already familiar to appellate courts: review for "unreasonableness." 18 U.S.C. §3742(e)(3).

. . . Section 3553(a) remains in effect, and sets forth numerous factors that guide sentencing. Those factors in turn will guide appellate courts, as they have in the past, in determining whether a sentence is unreasonable.

Taking into account the factors set forth in *Pierce*, we read the statute as implying this appellate review standard . . . . Justice Scalia believes that only in "Wonderland" is it possible to infer a standard of review after excising §3742(e). But our application of *Pierce* does not justify that characterization. *Pierce* requires us to judge the appropriateness of our inference based on the statute's language and basic purposes. We believe our inference a fair one linguistically, and one consistent with Congress' intent to provide appellate review. . . .

Nor do we share the dissenters' doubts about the practicality of a "reasonableness" standard of review. "Reasonableness" standards are not foreign to sentencing law. The Act has long required their use in important sentencing circumstances — both on review of departures, . . . and on review of sentences imposed where there was no applicable Guideline . . . . Together, these cases account for about 16.7% of sentencing appeals. . . . That is why we think it fair . . . to assume judicial familiarity with a "reasonableness" standard. And that is why we believe that appellate judges will prove capable of facing with greater equanimity than would Justice Scalia what he calls the "daunting prospect" of applying such a standard across the board.

Neither do we share Justice Scalia's belief that use of a reasonableness standard "will produce a discordant symphony" leading to "excessive sentencing disparities," and "wreak havoc" on the judicial system. The Sentencing Commission will continue to collect and study appellate court decisionmaking. It will continue to modify its Guidelines in light of what it learns, thereby encouraging what it finds to be better sentencing practices. It will thereby promote uniformity in the sentencing process. . . .

Regardless, in this context, we must view fears of a "discordant symphony," "excessive disparities," and "havoc" (if they are not themselves "gross exaggerations") with a comparative eye. We cannot and do not claim that use of a "reasonableness" standard will provide the uniformity that Congress originally sought to secure. Nor do we doubt that Congress wrote the language of the appellate provisions to correspond with the mandatory system it intended to create. . . . But, as by now should be clear, that mandatory system is no longer an open choice. And the remedial question we must ask here (as we did in respect to §3553(b)(1)) is, which alternative adheres more closely to Congress' original objective: (1) retention of sentencing appeals, or (2) invalidation of the entire Act, including its appellate provisions? The former, by providing appellate review, would tend to iron out sentencing differences; the latter would not. Hence we believe Congress would have preferred the former to the latter — even if the former means that some provisions will apply differently from the way Congress had originally expected. . . .

. . . Congress sought to "provide certainty and fairness in meeting the purposes of sentencing, [while] avoiding unwarranted sentencing disparities . . . [and] maintaining sufficient flexibility to permit individualized sentences when warranted." 28 U.S.C. §991 (b)(1)(B). . . . The system remaining after excision, while lacking the mandatory features that Congress enacted, retains other features that help to further these objectives.

As we have said, the Sentencing Commission remains in place, writing Guidelines, collecting information about actual district court sentencing decisions, undertaking research, and revising the Guidelines accordingly. . . . The district courts, while not bound to apply the Guidelines, must consult those Guidelines and take them into account when sentencing. But compare post, at 4 (Scalia, J., dissenting) (claiming that the sentencing judge has the same discretion "he possessed before the Act was passed"). The courts of appeals review sentencing decisions for unreasonableness. These features of the remaining system, while not the system Congress enacted, nonetheless continue to move sentencing in Congress' preferred direction, helping to avoid excessive sentencing disparities while maintaining flexibility sufficient to individualize sentences where necessary. . . . We can find no feature of the remaining system that tends to hinder, rather than to further, these basic objectives. Under these circumstances, why would Congress not have preferred excision of the "mandatory" provision to a system that engrafts today's constitutional requirement onto the unchanged pre-existing statute — a system that, in terms of Congress' basic objectives, is counterproductive?

We do not doubt that Congress, when it wrote the Sentencing Act, intended to create a form of mandatory Guidelines system. But, we repeat, given today's constitutional holding, that is not a choice that remains open. Hence we have examined the statute in depth to determine Congress' likely intent *in light of today's holding*. . . . And we have concluded that today's holding is fundamentally inconsistent with the judge-based sentencing system that Congress enacted into law. In our view, it is more consistent with Congress' likely intent in enacting the Sentencing Reform Act (1) to preserve important elements of that system while severing and excising two provisions (§§3553(b)(1) and 3742(e)) than (2) to maintain all provisions of the Act and engraft today's constitutional requirement onto that statutory scheme.

Ours, of course, is not the last word: The ball now lies in Congress' court. The National Legislature is equipped to devise and install, long-term, the sentencing system, compatible with the Constitution, that Congress judges best for the federal system of justice.

IV

[Here, Justice Breyer considered, and rejected, arguments made by the parties for other remedies, including (1) rendering the Guidelines advisory in any case where their mandatory application would violate the Sixth Amendment (but retaining them as mandatory otherwise), and (2) excising only the provisions of the statute that require judicial factfinding. — EDS.]

V

In respondent Booker's case, . . . [w]e affirm the judgment of the Court of Appeals and remand the case. On remand, the District Court should impose a sentence in accordance with today's opinions, and, if the sentence comes before the Court of Appeals for review, the Court of Appeals should apply the review standards set forth in this opinion.

. . . Fanfan's sentence does not violate the Sixth Amendment. Nonetheless, the Government (and the defendant should he so choose) may seek resentencing under the system set forth in today's opinions. Hence we vacate the judgment of the District Court and remand the case for further proceedings consistent with this opinion.

As these dispositions indicate, we must apply today's holdings — both the Sixth Amendment holding and our remedial interpretation of the Sentencing Act — to all cases on direct review. See Griffith v. Kentucky, 479 U.S. 314, 328 (1987). . . . That fact does not mean that we believe that every sentence gives rise to a Sixth Amendment violation. Nor do we believe that every appeal will lead to a new sentencing hearing. That is because we expect reviewing courts to apply ordinary prudential doctrines, determining, for example, whether the issue was raised below and whether it fails the "plain-error" test. It is also because, in cases not involving a Sixth Amendment violation, whether resentencing is warranted or whether it will instead be sufficient to review a sentence for reasonableness may depend upon application of the harmless-error doctrine.

It is so ordered.

JUSTICE STEVENS, dissenting in part.

Neither of the two Court opinions that decide these cases finds any constitutional infirmity inherent in any provision of the Sentencing Reform Act of 1984 (SRA) or the Federal Sentencing Guidelines. Specifically, neither 18 U.S.C. §3553(b)(1), which makes application of the Guidelines mandatory, nor §3742(e), which authorizes appellate review of departures from the Guidelines, is even arguably unconstitutional. Neither the Government, nor the respondents, nor any of the numerous amici has suggested that there is any need to invalidate either provision in order to avoid violations of the Sixth Amendment in the administration of the Guidelines. The Court's decision to do so represents a policy choice that Congress has considered and decisively rejected. While it is perfectly clear that Congress has ample power to repeal these two statutory provisions if it so desires, this Court should not make that choice on Congress' behalf. I respectfully dissent from the Court's extraordinary exercise of authority. . . .

JUSTICE SCALIA, dissenting in part.

. . . I write separately mainly to add some comments regarding the change that the remedial majority's handiwork has wrought (or perhaps — who can tell? — has not wrought) upon appellate review of federal sentencing.

The remedial majority takes as the North Star of its analysis the fact that Congress enacted a "judge-based sentencing system." That seems to me quite misguided. Congress did indeed expect judges to make the factual determinations to which the Guidelines apply, just as it expected the Guidelines to be mandatory. But which of those expectations was central to the congressional purpose is not hard to determine. No headline describing the Sentencing Reform Act of 1984 (Act) would have read "Congress reaffirms judge-based sentencing" rather than "Congress prescribes standardized sentences." Justice Breyer's opinion for the Court repeatedly acknowledges that the primary objective of the Act was to reduce sentencing disparity. Inexplicably, however, the opinion concludes that the *manner* of achieving uniform sentences was more important to Congress than actually achieving uniformity — that Congress was so attached to having *judges* determine "real conduct" on the basis of bureaucratically prepared, hearsay-riddled presentence reports that it would rather lose the binding nature of the Guidelines than adhere to the old-fashioned process of having *juries* find the facts that expose a defendant to increased prison time. The majority's remedial choice is thus wonderfully ironic: In order to rescue from nullification a statutory scheme designed to eliminate discretionary sentencing, it discards the provisions that eliminate discretionary sentencing.

That is the plain effect of the remedial majority's decision to excise 18 U.S.C. §3553(b)(1). . . . District judges will no longer be told they "shall impose a sentence . . . within the range" established by the Guidelines. §3553(b)(1). Instead, under §3553(a), they will need only to "consider" that range as one of many factors, including "the need for the sentence . . . to provide just punishment for the offense," "to afford adequate deterrence to criminal conduct," and "to protect the public from the further crimes of the defendant." The statute provides no order of priority among all those factors, but since the three just mentioned are the fundamental criteria governing penology, the statute — absent the mandate of §3553(b)(1) — authorizes the judge to apply his own perceptions of just punishment, deterrence, and protection of the public even when these differ from the perceptions of the Commission members who drew up the Guidelines. Since the Guidelines are not binding, in order to comply with the (oddly) surviving requirement that the court set forth "the specific reason for the imposition of a sentence different from that described" in the Guidelines, §3553(c)(2), the sentencing judge need only state that "this court does not believe that the punishment set forth in the Guidelines is appropriate for this sort of offense." That is to say, . . . the sentencing judge, after considering the recited factors (including the Guidelines), has full discretion, as full as what he possessed before the Act was passed, to sentence anywhere within the statutory range. If the majority thought otherwise — if it thought the Guidelines not only had to be "considered" (as the amputated statute requires) but had generally to be followed — its opinion would surely say so.

As frustrating as this conclusion is to the Act's purpose of uniform sentencing, it at least establishes a clear and comprehensible regime — essentially the regime that existed before the Act became effective. That clarity is eliminated, however, by the remedial majority's surgery on 18 U.S.C. §3742, the provision governing appellate review of sentences. Even the most casual reading of this section discloses that its purpose — its *only* purpose — is to enable courts of appeals to enforce conformity with the Guidelines. . . . If the Guidelines are no longer binding, one would think that the provision designed to ensure compliance with them would, in its totality, be inoperative. The Court holds otherwise. Like a black-robed Alexander cutting the Gordian knot, it simply severs the purpose of the review provisions from their text, holding that only subsection (e), which sets forth the determinations that the court of appeals must make, is inoperative, whereas all the rest of §3742 subsists . . . . This is rather like deleting the ingredients portion of a recipe and telling the cook to proceed with the preparation portion.

The Court claims that "a statute that does not *explicitly* set forth a standard of review may nonetheless do so *implicitly*." Perhaps so. But we have before us a statute that *does* explicitly set forth a standard of review. The question is, when the Court has *severed* that standard of review (contained in §3742(e)), does it make any sense to look for some congressional "implication" of a *different* standard of review in the remnants of the statute that the Court has left standing? Only in Wonderland. (This may explain in part why . . . *none* of the numerous persons and organizations filing briefs as parties or amici in these cases — all of whom filed this side of the looking-glass — proposed, or I think even imagined, the remedial majority's wonderful disposition.) . . . The Court's need to create a new, "implied" standard of review — however "linguistically" "fair" — amounts to a confession that it has exceeded its powers. . . .

There can be no doubt that the Court's severability analysis has produced a scheme dramatically different from anything Congress has enacted since 1984. Sentencing courts are told to "provide just punishment" (among other things), and appellate courts are told to ensure that district judges are not "unreasonable." The worst feature of the scheme is that no one knows — and perhaps no one is meant to know — how advisory Guidelines and "unreasonableness" review will function in practice. . . .

[A]ny system which held it per se unreasonable (and hence reversible) for a sentencing judge to reject the Guidelines is indistinguishable from the mandatory Guidelines system that the Court today holds unconstitutional. But the remedial majority's gross exaggerations (it says that the "practical standard of review" it prescribes is "already familiar to appellate courts" . . .) may lead some courts of appeals to conclude — may indeed be designed to lead courts of appeals to conclude — that little has changed . . . ([i.e.,] within the correct Guidelines range, affirm; outside the range without adequate explanation, vacate and remand). . . . At the other extreme, a court of appeals might . . . approv[e] virtually any sentence within the statutory range . . . , so long as the district judge goes through the appropriate formalities, such as expressing his consideration of and disagreement with the Guidelines sentence. What I anticipate will happen is that "unreasonableness" review will produce a discordant symphony of different standards, varying from court to court and judge to judge . . . .

. . . Will appellate review for "unreasonableness" preserve de facto mandatory Guidelines by discouraging district courts from sentencing outside Guidelines ranges? Will it simply add another layer of unfettered judicial discretion to the sentencing process? Or will it be a mere formality, used by busy appellate judges only to ensure that busy district judges say all the right things when they explain how they have exercised their newly restored discretion? Time may tell, but today's remedial majority will not.

I respectfully dissent.

[Justice Thomas, dissenting in part, argued that 18 U.S.C. §3553(b)(1), and related portions of the Federal Guidelines, should be invalidated as applied to *Booker* (and all similar cases involving Guideline sentences based on judicial fact-finding), but should be upheld as constitutional in all other cases (including *Fanfan*), where application of the Guidelines as written would not violate the Sixth Amendment. — EDS.]

JUSTICE BREYER, dissenting in part.

. . . The Court holds that the Sixth Amendment requires a jury, not a judge, to find sentencing facts — facts about the *way* in which an offender committed the crime — where those facts would move an offender from lower to higher Guidelines ranges. I disagree with the Court's conclusion. I find nothing in the Sixth Amendment that forbids a sentencing judge to determine (as judges at sentencing have traditionally determined) the *manner* or *way* in which the offender carried out the crime of which he was convicted. . . .

NOTES AND QUESTIONS

1. The combined effects of *Blakely* and *Booker* reverberated like shock waves through the federal and state criminal justice systems. Some jurisdictions decided to completely rewrite their sentencing laws in an attempt to conform to *Blakely/Booker*; others took the position (perhaps just wishful thinking?) that their sentencing schemes could still be distinguished from those at issue in *Blakely* and *Booker*, and thus could be spared from the *Blakely/Booker* avalanche. See, e.g., Cunningham v. California, 549 U.S. 270 (2007), in which California's determinate sentencing law was struck down by 6-3 (with Justices Kennedy, Breyer, and Alito dissenting); the Court, in a majority opinion written by Justice Ginsburg, rejected California's claim that its sentencing law could survive *Blakely/Booker* because it did not specify the particular "aggravating" facts necessary for a trial judge to move a defendant up from the "middle term" sentence to the "upper term" sentence for the crime of conviction, but instead left such factual findings to the "broad discretion" of the trial judge. Still other jurisdictions took a "wait and see" attitude, apparently waiting for the next shoe to drop from the Supreme Court. For a helpful summary account of the post-*Booker* landscape, see Joshua Dressler, Understanding Criminal Procedure: Adjudication 366-375 (2006); for a set of insightful scholarly contributions on the subject, see the aptly titled special issue The *Booker* Aftershock, 17 Fed. Sent. Rep., 231-290 (2005).

At least two important subsidiary questions were helpfully answered by the Court. On the same day as *Blakely*, the Court also held (by a 5-4 vote) that Ring v. Arizona — and thus, by extension, *Apprendi*, *Blakely*, and *Booker* (all three of which derived from the same source) — did *not* apply retroactively to cases litigated on federal habeas corpus review. The Court's decision in Schriro v. Summerlin, 542 U.S. 348 (2004), helped to keep *Blakely/Booker* from impacting literally hundreds of thousands of determinate sentences previously imposed in the federal and state criminal justice systems.

Moreover, *Blakely/Booker* errors *can* be held "harmless." In Washington v. Recuenco, 548 U.S. 212 (2006), the Court, in a 7-2 majority opinion written by Justice Thomas (with Justices Stevens and Ginsburg dissenting), rejected the defendant's argument that failure to submit a sentencing factor to a jury determination, under a "beyond reasonable doubt" standard, is the kind of "structural error" that automatically requires reversal in every case. The Court relied heavily on the case of Neder v. United States, 527 U.S. 1 (1999), which held that a trial court's erroneous failure to submit an element of a crime (in that case, the "materiality" of an alleged mail and wire fraud) to the jury could be subjected to "harmless error" review, because such an error "does not *necessarily* render a criminal trial fundamentally unfair or an unreliable vehicle for determining guilt or innocence." Id., at 9. The Court in *Recuenco* concluded that *Blakely/Booker* errors are "indistinguishable" from the kind of error involved in *Neder*, and thus require the same result with respect to "harmless error" analysis.

2. Within the context of "mandatory" determinate sentencing systems to which *Blakely* and *Booker* apply, what kinds of judicial factfinding can survive? There are only two of which we can be reasonably sure: (1) judicial findings about a defendant's prior crimes, which are still permissible under *Almendarez-Torres*; and (2) judicial findings that lead to the imposition of a mandatory minimum sentence, which are still permissible under *McMillan*, as reaffirmed by *Harris*. But *why* should these two kinds of judicial factfinding survive *Blakely* and *Booker*?

As for *Almendarez-Torres*, is it only stare decisis that keeps that particular case alive? Does stare decisis really seem to matter very much in this context, given the way that the Court has completely reversed its course on the more important constitutional question within the past several years?

As for *McMillan* and *Harris*, does it make sense for mandatory minimums to be treated so differently from maximum sentences, for *Apprendi/Blakely* purposes? Which is more important to a criminal defendant — the maximum sentence (which most judges are unlikely to impose anyway) or a mandatory minimum sentence (which no judge, even a lenient one, can ignore)? Which one should be left in the control of the jury, if we are concerned primarily about protecting defendants from governmental overreaching? Isn't the Court's distinction between *Apprendi/Blakely* and *McMillan/Harris* precisely the kind of "form over substance" distinction that the Court rejected in *Apprendi* and *Blakely*?

3. Does *Booker* reflect well on the Court? Consider the Justices' handiwork: Two majority opinions — both of whose authors also authored *dissenting* opinions. A right and a remedy that eight of the nine Justices find utterly inconsistent — and not a single word from the one Justice who believes in both. A major federal statute rewritten to require a standard of review that Congress has repeatedly rejected — all justified by the need to defer to Congress's wishes. These are not characteristics one would generally associate with wise judging. Does *Booker* seem wise to you? Does Justice Ginsburg's position?

Justice Scalia appears to be exercised about his colleagues' lack of deference to Congress. How deferential is Justice Scalia? Had his position prevailed, some sentencing factors — but only some — would have shifted from the sentencing proceeding to the trial, with a different decision maker and a different burden of proof. Facts that triggered a rise in the maximum sentence would be treated very differently than facts that triggered a fall, or (under *Harris*, see supra, at page 1453) that triggered a mandatory minimum sentence. No one in Congress ever proposed such a system. It does seem fair to charge Justice Breyer with rewriting the federal sentencing laws; at the same time, Justices Stevens and Scalia seemed bent on doing some considerable rewriting of their own. No one in *Booker* can fairly claim to have shown much deference to the legislative branch.

4. *Booker* took yet another step down the path the Supreme Court first trod with its decision in Apprendi v. New Jersey, see supra, at page 1452. Where does that path lead? *Apprendi* and *Blakely* were written as ringing defenses of the right to trial by jury. Sentencing guidelines and other mandatory sentencing rules supposedly threatened that right, by basing the defendant's punishment on facts found not by a jury but by a trial judge. *Apprendi* and its progeny were supposed to block that

threat, to right the balance of power between judge and jury by shifting facts that bear on the defendant's culpability from the judge-controlled sentencing proceeding to the trial, where the jury would rule.

How does that balance of power look after *Booker*? Under Justice Breyer's newly voluntary Guidelines, judges will do just as much factfinding as they did before the Court's decision. Indeed, they will probably do even *more* factfinding, since judges can now base their sentences on facts other than those the Guidelines deemed relevant: yet more facts for judges to consider, as long as their sentencing decisions are "reasonable" (whatever that means). The scope of jury power does not seem any greater the day after *Booker* than it was the day before. If anything, juries are less powerful. Judges appear to be the real winners: trial judges who now have a great deal more sentencing discretion than they had before, and federal Court of Appeals judges who may now, in the guise of fleshing out Breyer's "reasonableness" standard of review, create something like a common law of sentencing.

5. Whatever the long-term practical effects of *Apprendi/Blakely/Booker* prove to be, the fact remains that the most important initiative in the realm of constitutional criminal procedure over the past two decades is the Court's expansion into sentencing law of the right to a jury trial. Is that the right that most needs expanding? The idea behind constitutional protections for criminal defendants is that minorities need protection from the majority. That idea seems especially powerful given the hugely disproportionate number of African Americans in our 2-million-plus inmate population — and the long history of abuse of black suspects and defendants by white-dominated law enforcement agencies. If ever there were a place for strong constitutional protection of minority rights, it would seem to be America's criminal justice system.

But the jury is a very odd way to protect those rights. Juries are fundamentally majoritarian. At the time of the Founding (which, needless to say, was not a time when anyone was particularly worried about protecting the rights of black Americans), juries were seen as a way that the people — the *majority* of the people — could rein in the power of distant rulers, not a means by which discrete and insular minorities would be protected from a majority bent on locking them up. (For the classic discussion, see Akhil Reed Amar, The Bill of Rights as a Constitution, 100 Yale L.J. 1131 (1991).) Throughout the long reign of Jim Crow, the criminal jury was one of the bulwarks of white supremacy, a story well told in Michael J. Klarman, From Jim Crow to Civil Rights: The Supreme Court and the Struggle for Racial Equality (2004). Robert Caro's biography of Lyndon Johnson offers a telling example. In 1957, Congress looked likely to pass major voting rights legislation. Southern Senators could not block the legislation, so they sought a means of rendering it toothless. They found what they were looking for: The bill was amended to require a right to jury trial for any officials charged with violating black voting rights. The Southern Senators understood that no white Southern jury (blacks were kept off juries at the time) would convict in such a case. The bill was passed with the jury provision, and Southern blacks continued to be denied the right to vote. Robert A. Caro, The Years of Lyndon Johnson: Master of the Senate 944-989 (2002). Given that history, isn't it more than a little strange that the jury would wind up at the center of constitutional regulation of American criminal justice?

6. Consider another angle on the problem. Juries are supposed to be a democratic check on the criminal justice system. But why, exactly, is the criminal justice system in need of more democracy? America is the only country in the developed

world that elects its prosecutors. (The vast majority of criminal prosecutions are brought by local district attorneys, nearly all of whom are elected by the counties in which they work.) That is not all: A large proportion of local trial judges are elected too, as are most of the appellate judges who review criminal convictions. The system hardly seems to suffer from a lack of democratic checks.

Given the breadth of American criminal codes and the range of the sentencing options those codes offer, it is, for the most part, relatively easy for prosecutors to convict the people they want, and to put them away for as long as they want. Or, rather, it is easy to convict and punish the people the *voters* want convicted and punished. The danger in such a system is that the voters will want to punish the wrong people, and will want to punish the right people too severely. How is that danger best addressed? Juries? Better procedural rules? Perhaps the real need is for better *substantive* rules — criminal codes and sentencing rules that define the worst and most harmful conduct and assign fair sentences. *Apprendi/Blakely/Booker* does nothing to advance *that* goal.

How is the goal best advanced? How can we make sentencing more fair? How can we make criminal justice more just?

7. If *Booker* truly authorizes the creation of a judicial "common law" of sentencing, what will that common law look like? To what extent will it be influenced by the newly "voluntary" Guidelines? The answers may depend heavily on how the federal appellate courts respond to Justice Breyer's remarkably opaque invitation for those courts to review sentences, post-*Booker*, for "unreasonableness." Consider the following:

(a) What if a particular federal district judge believes (as many do) that certain personal characteristics of the defendant (e.g., the defendant's age, education, mental and physical condition, employment record, family ties, and socioeconomic status) — which the Guidelines *specifically exclude* from sentencing consideration, see U.S.S.G. §5H1 — are, in fact, relevant to the goals of criminal sentencing? Justice Breyer says that judges "must consult th[e] Guidelines and take them into account when sentencing." If a judge requests, and considers, the Guideline-prohibited information at sentencing, and imposes a sentence based on such information, has she complied with Breyer's opinion? Does she have to explain (in every such case) why she is disobeying the clear mandate of the Guidelines? How should the appellate court respond?

A few days after *Booker* was decided, U.S. District Judge Lynn Adelman imposed a sentence less than one-third of what the Guidelines would have required, based on information that the defendant was a 50-year-old "devoted family man," with a solid employment history, who was responsible for the care and support of his elderly parents — all information that was excluded from consideration by the Guidelines. Judge Adelman went so far as to say that she was *required* to consider this information, because the underlying statute (18 U.S.C. §3553 (a) — note that this is the very same statute upon which Breyer bases his "unreasonableness" standard of review), which remains binding, identifies "the history and characteristics of the defendant" as relevant to the goals of federal sentencing, whereas the exclusionary Guidelines provision, after *Booker*, is no longer binding. See United States v. Ranum, No. 04-CR-31 (E.D. Wisc. Jan. 19, 2005).

(b) What if a particular federal district judge believes (as many do) that the Guidelines are simply too harsh (or, as is less frequently the case, too lenient) for some crime or category of crimes? Can the judge ignore the Guidelines? Does she have to explain (in every such case) why she believes the Guidelines are wrong? Is this what Breyer means by "consult[ing] the Guidelines and tak[ing] them into account"? How should the appellate court respond?

(c) What if a particular federal district judge believes (as at least some do) that sentences should be based solely on criminal conduct that is charged and proven, beyond a reasonable doubt, at trial, and should not be based on uncharged criminal conduct proven by a preponderance of the evidence at sentencing? Despite the Guidelines' central reliance on "real conduct" factors, can the judge refuse to consider any such factors offered by the prosecution at sentencing, and sentence the defendant based solely on the criminal conduct that was charged and proven at trial? Does the judge have to explain (in every such case) why she is unwilling to consider such factors? Wouldn't this be a mortal blow to the sentencing uniformity that Breyer is so desperately trying to preserve? How should the appellate court respond?

The answers to the above questions about appellate review will help determine the real impact of *Booker*. If federal appellate courts exercise their review authority aggressively to ensure conformity with the Guidelines, and with the various procedural and substantive policy choices contained therein, then federal district judges will quickly get the message, and the Guidelines — whether formally designated as mandatory or advisory — will continue to constrain judicial sentencing discretion. In an opinion written the day after *Booker* was decided, U.S. District Judge Paul Cassell wrote: "[T]he court will only depart from th[e] Guidelines in unusual cases for clearly identified and persuasive reasons." See United States v. Wilson, Case No. 2:03-CR-00882 (D. Utah Jan. 13, 2005).

If, however, federal appellate courts exercise their review authority deferentially in cases like those described above, then we really *do* seem to be heading right back to the old days of unfettered judicial sentencing discretion. Federal sentencing may revert to something resembling the situation before the Guidelines existed — at least for those federal district judges who *choose* to reclaim such discretion. It is in this sense that *Booker* actually introduces a new kind of uncertainty into the old world of discretionary sentencing. In the old days, the problem was sentencing variation based on differing judicial views about sentencing policy; after *Booker*, we will also have sentencing variation based on differing judicial views about the binding-ness of the newly "voluntary" Guidelines.

In the end, Justice Breyer seems perfectly willing to let Congress resolve the standard of review issue: "The ball now lies in Congress' court." Does this mean that Congress could enact a new statute imposing a more rigorous standard of review than "reasonableness" — e.g., "clear and convincing evidence justifying a departure from the sentence that the Guidelines would require" — and thereby re-create (in effect) the mandatory Guideline system? If so, then hasn't the five-year run-up to *Booker* been a colossal waste of time and energy? Or would such a new statute be barred because it would not be, in Breyer's words, "compatible with the Constitution"?

Congress, by the way, so far has not taken up Justice Breyer's suggestion in any meaningful way, shape, or form. Indeed, the silence from Capitol Hill on the issue has been deafening. Does that make you feel more, or less, sanguine about what the Court did in *Booker*?

8. Unlike Justice Breyer, who (perhaps deliberately) supplies almost no content to his "unreasonableness" standard of review, Justice Scalia has a clear answer for the questions raised in the preceding note. Scalia says: "[T]he sentencing judge,

after considering the recited factors (including the Guidelines), has full discretion, as full as what he possessed before the Act was passed, to sentence anywhere within the statutory range." In Scalia's view of the post-*Booker* world, in other words, the federal appellate court has no meaningful role to play, and the Guidelines are basically dead.

Aggressive appellate review, according to Scalia, would effectively re-create a quasi-mandatory Guideline system flatly inconsistent with the *other* part of the majority opinion in *Booker* (the part written by Stevens, and joined by Scalia): "[A]ny system which held it per se unreasonable (and hence reversible) for a sentencing judge to reject the Guidelines is indistinguishable from the mandatory Guidelines system that the Court today holds unconstitutional." Of course, Scalia is exactly right about this — automatic appellate reversals *would* mean the Guidelines remain binding in effect — and it will therefore be exceedingly difficult, if not impossible, for appellate judges *both* to exert meaningful pressure on trial judges to conform to the new advisory Guidelines, *and* at the same time to avoid converting those Guidelines into unconstitutional, quasi-mandatory ones.

Is it possible for a federal district judge to have complete sentencing discretion (as apparently required by the Stevens majority opinion), but yet not to have it (as apparently required by the Breyer majority opinion)? Or is discretion like an on-off switch — you either have it, or you don't?

Note that even discretionary decisions traditionally are subject to the deferential "abuse of discretion" standard of review. Would it have been more acceptable, under Scalia's view, for Breyer's majority opinion to adopt the "abuse of discretion" standard for appellate review of sentences, rather than the "unreasonableness" one? Would this have made any difference? Don't all of the same tough questions from the preceding note inevitably arise, even under an "abuse of discretion" standard? Does this mean Scalia's position is ultimately untenable?

9. So, in the end, what does "reasonableness" in appellate review really mean? Does it mean a presumption in favor of within-Guidelines sentences, and against outside-Guideline sentences? If so, doesn't that essentially re-create the constitutional problem the Court faced in *Blakely* and *Booker*? But if not, aren't we right back to the "old days" of unfettered sentencing discretion, which led to the Guidelines in the first place?

GALL v. UNITED STATES

Certiorari to the United States Court of Appeals for the Eighth Circuit
552 U.S. 38 (2007)

JUSTICE STEVENS delivered the opinion of the Court.

In two cases argued on the same day last Term we considered the standard that courts of appeals should apply when reviewing the reasonableness of sentences imposed by district judges. The first, Rita v. United States, 551 U.S. 338 (2007), involved a sentence *within* the range recommended by the Federal Sentencing Guidelines; we held that when a district judge's discretionary decision in a particular case accords with the sentence the United States Sentencing Commission deems appropriate "in the mine run of cases," the court of appeals may presume that the sentence is reasonable. Id., at 347, 351.

The second case, Claiborne v. United States, involved a sentence *below* the range recommended by the Guidelines, and raised the converse question whether a court of appeals may apply a "proportionality test," and require that a sentence that constitutes a substantial variance from the Guidelines be justified by extraordinary circumstances. We did not have the opportunity to answer this question because the case was mooted by Claiborne's untimely death. Claiborne v. United States, 549 U.S. 1016 (2007) (per curiam). We granted certiorari in the case before us today in order to reach that question, left unanswered last Term. We now hold that, while the extent of the difference between a particular sentence and the recommended Guidelines range is surely relevant, courts of appeals must review all sentences — whether inside, just outside, or significantly outside the Guidelines range — under a deferential abuse-of-discretion standard. We also hold that the sentence imposed by the experienced District Judge in this case was reasonable.

I

In February or March 2000, petitioner Brian Gall, a second-year college student at the University of Iowa, was invited by Luke Rinderknecht to join an ongoing enterprise distributing a controlled substance popularly known as "ecstasy." Gall — who was then a user of ecstasy, cocaine, and marijuana — accepted the invitation. During the ensuing seven months, Gall delivered ecstasy pills, which he received from Rinderknecht, to other conspirators, who then sold them to consumers. He netted over $30,000.

A month or two after joining the conspiracy, Gall stopped using ecstasy. A few months after that, in September 2000, he advised Rinderknecht and other co-conspirators that he was withdrawing from the conspiracy. He has not sold illegal drugs of any kind since. He has, in the words of the District Court, "self-rehabilitated." App. 75. He graduated from the University of Iowa in 2002, and moved first to Arizona, where he obtained a job in the construction industry, and later to Colorado, where he earned $18 per hour as a master carpenter. He has not used any illegal drugs since graduating from college.

After Gall moved to Arizona, he was approached by federal law enforcement agents who questioned him about his involvement in the ecstasy distribution conspiracy. Gall admitted his limited participation in the distribution of ecstasy, and the agents took no further action at that time. On April 28, 2004 — approximately a year and a half after this initial interview, and three and a half years after Gall withdrew from the conspiracy — an indictment was returned in the Southern District of Iowa charging him and seven other defendants with participating in a conspiracy to distribute ecstasy, cocaine, and marijuana, that began in or about May 1996 and continued through October 30, 2002. The Government has never questioned the truthfulness of any of Gall's earlier statements or contended that he played any role in, or had any knowledge of, other aspects of the conspiracy described in the indictment. When he received notice of the indictment, Gall moved back to Iowa and surrendered to the authorities. While free on his own recognizance, Gall started his own business in the construction industry, primarily engaged in subcontracting for the installation of windows and doors. In his first year, his profits were over $2,000 per month.

Gall entered into a plea agreement with the Government, stipulating that he was "responsible for, but did not necessarily distribute himself, at least 2,500 grams of [ecstasy], or the equivalent of at least 87.5 kilograms of marijuana." Id., at 25. In the agreement, the Government acknowledged that by "on or about September of 2000," Gall had communicated his intent to stop distributing ecstasy to Rinderknecht and other members of the conspiracy. Ibid. The agreement further provided that recent changes in the Guidelines that enhanced the recommended punishment for distributing ecstasy were not applicable to Gall because he had withdrawn from the conspiracy prior to the effective date of those changes.

In her presentence report, the probation officer concluded that Gall had no significant criminal history; that he was not an organizer, leader, or manager; and that his offense did not involve the use of any weapons. The report stated that Gall had truthfully provided the Government with all of the evidence he had concerning the alleged offenses, but that his evidence was not useful because he provided no new information to the agents. The report also described Gall's substantial use of drugs prior to his offense and the absence of any such use in recent years. The report recommended a sentencing range of 30 to 37 months of imprisonment.

The record of the sentencing hearing held on May 27, 2005, includes a "small flood" of letters from Gall's parents and other relatives, his fiance, neighbors, and representatives of firms doing business with him, uniformly praising his character and work ethic. . . . The [federal prosecutor] did not contest any of the evidence concerning Gall's law-abiding life during the preceding five years, but urged that "the Guidelines are appropriate and should be followed," and requested that the court impose a prison sentence within the Guidelines range. Id., at 93. He mentioned that two of Gall's co-conspirators had been sentenced to 30 and 35 months, respectively, but upon further questioning by the District Court, he acknowledged that neither of them had voluntarily withdrawn from the conspiracy.

The District Judge sentenced Gall to probation for a term of 36 months. In addition to making a lengthy statement on the record, the judge filed a detailed sentencing memorandum explaining his decision, and provided the following statement of reasons in his written judgment:

> The Court determined that, considering all the factors under 18 U.S.C. 3553(a), the Defendant's explicit withdrawal from the conspiracy almost four years before the filing of the Indictment, the Defendant's post-offense conduct, especially obtaining a college degree and the start of his own successful business, the support of family and friends, lack of criminal history, and his age at the time of the offense conduct, all warrant the sentence imposed, which was sufficient, but not greater than necessary to serve the purposes of sentencing.

Id., at 117.

At the end of both the sentencing hearing and the sentencing memorandum, the District Judge reminded Gall that probation, rather than "an act of leniency," is a "substantial restriction of freedom." Id., at 99, 125. In the memorandum, he emphasized:

> [Gall] will have to comply with strict reporting conditions along with a three-year regime of alcohol and drug testing. He will not be able to change or make decisions about significant circumstances in his life, such as where to live or work, which are prized liberty interests, without first seeking authorization from his Probation Officer or, perhaps, even the Court. Of course, the Defendant always faces the harsh consequences that await if he violates the conditions of his probationary term.

Id., at 125.

Finally, the District Judge explained why he had concluded that the sentence of probation reflected the seriousness of Gall's offense and that no term of imprisonment was necessary:

> Any term of imprisonment in this case would be counter effective by depriving society of the contributions of the Defendant who, the Court has found, understands the consequences of his criminal conduct and is doing everything in his power to forge a new life. The Defendant's post-offense conduct indicates neither that he will return to criminal behavior nor that the Defendant is a danger to society. In fact, the Defendant's post-offense conduct was not motivated by a desire to please the Court or any other governmental agency, but was the pre-Indictment product of the Defendant's own desire to lead a better life.

Id., at 125-126.

II

The Court of Appeals reversed and remanded for resentencing. Relying on its earlier opinion in United States v. Claiborne, 439 F.3d 479 (8th Cir. 2006), it held that a sentence outside of the Guidelines range must be supported by a justification that "'"is proportional to the extent of the difference between the advisory range and the sentence imposed."'" 446 F.3d 884, 889 (8th Cir. 2006) (quoting Claiborne, 439 F.3d, at 481, in turn quoting United States v. Johnson, 427 F.3d 423, 426-427 (7th Cir. 2005)). Characterizing the difference between a sentence of probation and the bottom of Gall's advisory Guidelines range of 30 months as "extraordinary" because it amounted to "a 100% downward variance," 446 F.3d, at 889, the Court of Appeals held that such a variance must be — and here was not — supported by extraordinary circumstances.

Rather than making an attempt to quantify the value of the justifications provided by the District Judge, the Court of Appeals identified what it regarded as five separate errors in the District Judge's reasoning: (1) He gave "too much weight to Gall's withdrawal from the conspiracy"; (2) given that Gall was 21 at the time of his offense, the District Judge erroneously gave "significant weight" to studies showing impetuous behavior by persons under the age of 18; (3) he did not "properly weigh" the seriousness of Gall's offense; (4) he failed to consider whether a sentence of probation would result in "unwarranted" disparities; and (5) he placed "too much emphasis on Gall's post-offense rehabilitation." Id., at 889-890. As we shall explain, we are not persuaded that these factors, whether viewed separately or in the aggregate, are sufficient to support the conclusion that the District Judge abused his discretion. As a preface to our discussion of these particulars, however, we shall explain why the Court of Appeals' rule requiring "proportional" justifications for departures from the Guidelines range is not consistent with our remedial opinion in United States v. Booker, 543 U.S. 220 (2005).

III

In Booker we invalidated both the statutory provision, 18 U.S.C. §3553(b)(1), which made the Sentencing Guidelines mandatory, and §3742(e), which directed appellate courts to apply a de novo standard of review to departures from the Guidelines.

As a result of our decision, the Guidelines are now advisory, and appellate review of sentencing decisions is limited to determining whether they are "reasonable." Our explanation of "reasonableness" review in the *Booker* opinion made it pellucidly clear that the familiar abuse-of-discretion standard of review now applies to appellate review of sentencing decisions. See 543 U.S., at 260-262; see also *Rita*, 551 U.S., at 360 (Stevens, J., concurring).

It is also clear that a district judge must give serious consideration to the extent of any departure from the Guidelines and must explain his conclusion that an unusually lenient or an unusually harsh sentence is appropriate in a particular case with sufficient justifications. For even though the Guidelines are advisory rather than mandatory, they are, as we pointed out in *Rita*, the product of careful study based on extensive empirical evidence derived from the review of thousands of individual sentencing decisions. Id., at 349.

In reviewing the reasonableness of a sentence outside the Guidelines range, appellate courts may therefore take the degree of variance into account and consider the extent of a deviation from the Guidelines. We reject, however, an appellate rule that requires "extraordinary" circumstances to justify a sentence outside the Guidelines range. We also reject the use of a rigid mathematical formula that uses the percentage of a departure as the standard for determining the strength of the justifications required for a specific sentence.

As an initial matter, the approaches we reject come too close to creating an impermissible presumption of unreasonableness for sentences outside the Guidelines range. See id. ("The fact that we permit courts of appeals to adopt a presumption of reasonableness does not mean that courts may adopt a presumption of unreasonableness"). Even the Government has acknowledged that such a presumption would not be consistent with *Booker*. See Brief for United States in Rita v. United States, O. T. 2006, No. 06-5754, pp. 34-35.

The mathematical approach also suffers from infirmities of application. On one side of the equation, deviations from the Guidelines range will always appear more extreme — in percentage terms — when the range itself is low, and a sentence of probation will always be a 100% departure regardless of whether the Guidelines range is 1 month or 100 years. Moreover, quantifying the variance as a certain percentage of the maximum, minimum, or median prison sentence recommended by the Guidelines gives no weight to the "substantial restriction of freedom" involved in a term of supervised release or probation. App. 95.

We recognize that custodial sentences are qualitatively more severe than probationary sentences of equivalent terms. Offenders on probation are nonetheless subject to several standard conditions that substantially restrict their liberty. . . . Probationers may not leave the judicial district, move, or change jobs without notifying, and in some cases receiving permission from, their probation officer or the court. They must report regularly to their probation officer, permit unannounced visits to their homes, refrain from associating with any person convicted of a felony, and refrain from excessive drinking. USSG §5B1.3. Most probationers are also subject to individual "special conditions" imposed by the court. Gall, for instance, may not patronize any establishment that derives more than 50% of its revenue from the sale of alcohol, and must submit to random drug tests as directed by his probation officer. App. 109.

On the other side of the equation, the mathematical approach assumes the existence of some ascertainable method of assigning percentages to various justifications. Does withdrawal from a conspiracy justify more or less than, say, a 30% reduction? Does it matter that the withdrawal occurred several years ago? Is it relevant that the withdrawal was motivated by a decision to discontinue the use of drugs and to lead a better life? What percentage, if any, should be assigned to evidence that a defendant poses no future threat to society, or to evidence that innocent third parties are dependent on him? The formula is a classic example of attempting to measure an inventory of apples by counting oranges.

Most importantly, both the exceptional circumstances requirement and the rigid mathematical formulation reflect a practice — common among courts that have adopted "proportional review" — of applying a heightened standard of review to sentences outside the Guidelines range. This is inconsistent with the rule that the abuse-of-discretion standard of review applies to appellate review of all sentencing decisions — whether inside or outside the Guidelines range.

As we explained in *Rita*, a district court should begin all sentencing proceedings by correctly calculating the applicable Guidelines range. See 551 U.S., at 351. As a matter of administration and to secure nationwide consistency, the Guidelines should be the starting point and the initial benchmark. The Guidelines are not the only consideration, however. Accordingly, after giving both parties an opportunity to argue for whatever sentence they deem appropriate, the district judge should then consider all of the §3553(a) factors to determine whether they support the sentence requested by a party.[6] In so doing, he may not presume that the Guidelines range is reasonable. See id. He must make an individualized assessment based on the facts presented. If he decides that an outside-Guidelines sentence is warranted, he must consider the extent of the deviation and ensure that the justification is sufficiently compelling to support the degree of the variance. We find it uncontroversial that a major departure should be supported by a more significant justification than a minor one. After settling on the appropriate sentence, he must adequately explain the chosen sentence to allow for meaningful appellate review and to promote the perception of fair sentencing. Id., at 356-358.

Regardless of whether the sentence imposed is inside or outside the Guidelines range, the appellate court must review the sentence under an abuse-of-discretion standard. It must first ensure that the district court committed no significant procedural error, such as failing to calculate (or improperly calculating) the Guidelines range, treating the Guidelines as mandatory, failing to consider the §3553(a) factors, selecting a sentence based on clearly erroneous facts, or failing to adequately explain the chosen sentence — including an explanation for any deviation from the Guidelines range. Assuming that the district court's sentencing decision is procedurally sound, the appellate court should then consider the substantive reasonableness of the sentence imposed under an abuse-of-discretion standard. When conducting this review, the court will, of course, take into account the totality of the circumstances, including the extent of any variance from the Guidelines range. If the sentence is within the Guidelines range, the appellate court may, but is not required to, apply a presumption of reasonableness. Id., at 347. But if the sentence is outside the Guidelines range, the court may not apply a presumption of unreasonableness. It may consider the extent of the deviation, but must give due

6. . . . . The fact that §3553(a) explicitly directs sentencing courts to consider the Guidelines supports the premise that district courts must begin their analysis with the Guidelines and remain cognizant of them throughout the sentencing process.

deference to the district court's decision that the §3553(a) factors, on a whole, justify the extent of the variance. The fact that the appellate court might reasonably have concluded that a different sentence was appropriate is insufficient to justify reversal of the district court.

Practical considerations also underlie this legal principle. "The sentencing judge is in a superior position to find facts and judge their import under §3553(a) in the individual case. The judge sees and hears the evidence, makes credibility determinations, has full knowledge of the facts and gains insights not conveyed by the record." Brief for Federal Public and Community Defenders et al. as Amici Curiae 16. "The sentencing judge has access to, and greater familiarity with, the individual case and the individual defendant before him than the Commission or the appeals court." *Rita*, 551 U.S., at 357-358. Moreover, "district courts have an institutional advantage over appellate courts in making these sorts of determinations, especially as they see so many more Guidelines sentences than appellate courts do." Koon v. United States, 518 U.S. 81, 98 (1996).[7]

"It has been uniform and constant in the federal judicial tradition for the sentencing judge to consider every convicted person as an individual and every case as a unique study in the human failings that sometimes mitigate, sometimes magnify, the crime and the punishment to ensue." Id., at 113.[8] The uniqueness of the individual case, however, does not change the deferential abuse-of-discretion standard of review that applies to all sentencing decisions. As we shall now explain, the opinion of the Court of Appeals in this case does not reflect the requisite deference and does not support the conclusion that the District Court abused its discretion.

IV

As an initial matter, we note that the District Judge committed no significant procedural error. He correctly calculated the applicable Guidelines range, allowed both parties to present arguments as to what they believed the appropriate sentence should be, considered all of the §3553(a) factors, and thoroughly documented his reasoning. The Court of Appeals found that the District Judge erred in failing to give proper weight to the seriousness of the offense, as required by §3553(a)(2)(A), and failing to consider whether a sentence of probation would create unwarranted disparities, as required by §3553(a)(6). We disagree.

. . . The Court of Appeals concluded that "the district court did not properly weigh the seriousness of Gall's offense" because it "ignored the serious health risks ecstasy poses." 446 F.3d, at 890. Contrary to the Court of Appeals' conclusion, the District Judge plainly did consider the seriousness of the offense. . . . It is true that the District Judge did not make specific reference to the (unquestionably significant) health risks posed by ecstasy, but the prosecutor did not raise ecstasy's effects at the sentencing hearing. Had the prosecutor raised the issue, specific discussion

---

7. District judges sentence, on average, 117 defendants every year. Administrative Office of United States Courts, 2006 Federal Court Management Statistics 167. . . .

8. It is particularly revealing that when we adopted an abuse-of-discretion standard in *Koon*, we explicitly rejected the Government's argument that "de novo review of departure decisions is necessary 'to protect against unwarranted disparities arising from the differing sentencing approaches of individual district judges.'" 518 U.S., at 97 (quoting Brief for United States in O. T. 1995, No. 94-1664, p. 12). Even then we were satisfied that a more deferential abuse-of-discretion standard could successfully balance the need to "reduce unjustified disparities" across the Nation and "consider every convicted person as an individual." 518 U.S., at 113.

of the point might have been in order, but it was not incumbent on the District Judge to raise every conceivably relevant issue on his own initiative.

The Government's legitimate concern that a lenient sentence for a serious offense threatens to promote disrespect for the law is at least to some extent offset by the fact that seven of the eight defendants in this case have been sentenced to significant prison terms. Moreover, the unique facts of Gall's situation provide support for the District Judge's conclusion that, in Gall's case, "a sentence of imprisonment may work to promote not respect, but derision, of the law if the law is viewed as merely a means to dispense harsh punishment without taking into account the real conduct and circumstances involved in sentencing." Id., at 126.

Section 3553(a)(6) requires judges to consider "the need to avoid unwarranted sentence disparities among defendants with similar records who have been found guilty of similar conduct." . . . [A]voidance of unwarranted disparities was clearly considered by the Sentencing Commission when setting the Guidelines ranges. Since the District Judge correctly calculated and carefully reviewed the Guidelines range, he necessarily gave significant weight and consideration to the need to avoid unwarranted disparities.

Moreover, . . . it seems that the judge gave specific attention to the issue of disparity when he inquired about the sentences already imposed by a different judge on two of Gall's codefendants. . . . [I]t is perfectly clear that the District Judge considered the need to avoid unwarranted disparities, but also considered the need to avoid unwarranted *similarities* among other co-conspirators who were not similarly situated. The District Judge regarded Gall's voluntary withdrawal as a reasonable basis for giving him a less severe sentence than the three codefendants . . . , who neither withdrew from the conspiracy nor rehabilitated themselves as Gall had done. We also note that neither the Court of Appeals nor the Government has called our attention to a comparable defendant who received a more severe sentence.

Since the District Court committed no procedural error, the only question for the Court of Appeals was whether the sentence was reasonable — i.e., whether the District Judge abused his discretion in determining that the §3553(a) factors supported a sentence of probation and justified a substantial deviation from the Guidelines range. As we shall now explain, the sentence was reasonable. The Court of Appeals' decision to the contrary was incorrect and failed to demonstrate the requisite deference to the District Judge's decision.

V

The Court of Appeals gave virtually no deference to the District Court's decision that the §3553(a) factors justified a significant variance in this case. Although the Court of Appeals correctly stated that the appropriate standard of review was abuse of discretion, it engaged in an analysis that more closely resembled de novo review of the facts presented and determined that, in its view, the degree of variance was not warranted.

The Court of Appeals thought that the District Court "gave too much weight to Gall's withdrawal from the conspiracy because the court failed to acknowledge the significant benefit Gall received from being subject to the 1999 Guidelines."[10] 446

---

10. The Court of Appeals explained that under the current Guidelines, which treat ecstasy more harshly, Gall's base offense level would have been 32, eight levels higher than the base offense level imposed under the 1999 Guidelines.

F.3d, at 889. This criticism is flawed in that it ignores the critical relevance of Gall's voluntary withdrawal, a circumstance that distinguished his conduct not only from that of all his codefendants, but from the vast majority of defendants convicted of conspiracy in federal court. The District Court quite reasonably attached great weight to the fact that Gall voluntarily withdrew from the conspiracy after deciding, on his own initiative, to change his life. This lends strong support to the District Court's conclusion that Gall is not going to return to criminal behavior and is not a danger to society. See 18 U.S.C. §§3553(a)(2)(B), (C). Compared to a case where the offender's rehabilitation occurred after he was charged with a crime, the District Court here had greater justification for believing Gall's turnaround was genuine, as distinct from a transparent attempt to build a mitigation case.

The Court of Appeals thought the District Judge "gave significant weight to an improper factor" when he compared Gall's sale of ecstasy when he was a 21-year-old adult to the "impetuous and ill-considered" actions of persons under the age of 18. 446 F.3d, at 890. The appellate court correctly observed that the studies cited by the District Judge do not explain how Gall's "specific behavior in the instant case was impetuous or ill-considered." Ibid.

In that portion of his sentencing memorandum, however, the judge was discussing the "character of the defendant," not the nature of his offense. App. 122. He noted that Gall's criminal history included a ticket for underage drinking when he was 18 years old and possession of marijuana that was contemporaneous with his offense in this case. In summary, the District Judge observed that all of Gall's criminal history "including the present offense, occurred when he was twenty-one-years old or younger" and appeared "to stem from his addictions to drugs and alcohol." Id., at 123. . . .

Given the dramatic contrast between Gall's behavior before he joined the conspiracy and his conduct after withdrawing, it was not unreasonable for the District Judge to view Gall's immaturity at the time of the offense as a mitigating factor, and his later behavior as a sign that he had matured and would not engage in such impetuous and ill-considered conduct in the future. Indeed, his consideration of that factor finds support in our cases. See, e.g., Johnson v. Texas, 509 U.S. 350, 367 (1993) (holding that a jury was free to consider a 19-year-old defendant's youth when determining whether there was a probability that he would continue to commit violent acts in the future and stating that "'youth is more than a chronological fact. It is a time and condition of life when a person may be most susceptible to influence and to psychological damage'" (quoting Eddings v. Oklahoma, 455 U.S. 104, 115 (1982))).

Finally, the Court of Appeals thought that, even if Gall's rehabilitation was dramatic and permanent, a sentence of probation for participation as a middleman in a conspiracy distributing 10,000 pills of ecstasy "lies outside the range of choice dictated by the facts of the case." 446 F.3d, at 890. If the Guidelines were still mandatory, and assuming the facts did not justify a Guidelines-based downward departure, this would provide a sufficient basis for setting aside Gall's sentence because the Guidelines state that probation alone is not an appropriate sentence for comparable offenses. But the Guidelines are not mandatory, and thus the "range of choice dictated by the facts of the case" is significantly broadened. Moreover, the Guidelines are only one of the factors to consider when imposing sentence, and §3553(a)(3) directs the judge to consider sentences other than imprisonment.

We also note that the Government did not argue below, and has not argued here, that a sentence of probation could never be imposed for a crime identical to Gall's. Indeed, it acknowledged that probation could be permissible if the record contained different — but in our view, no more compelling — mitigating evidence. Tr. of Oral Arg. 37-38 (stating that probation could be an appropriate sentence, given the exact same offense, if "there are compelling family circumstances where individuals will be very badly hurt in the defendant's family if no one is available to take care of them").

The Court of Appeals clearly disagreed with the District Judge's conclusion that consideration of the §3553(a) factors justified a sentence of probation; it believed that the circumstances presented here were insufficient to sustain such a marked deviation from the Guidelines range. But it is not for the Court of Appeals to decide de novo whether the justification for a variance is sufficient or the sentence reasonable. On abuse-of-discretion review, the Court of Appeals should have given due deference to the District Court's reasoned and reasonable decision that the §3553(a) factors, on the whole, justified the sentence. Accordingly, the judgment of the Court of Appeals is reversed.

It is so ordered.

JUSTICE SCALIA, concurring.

I join the opinion of the Court.

In Rita v. United States, 551 U.S. 338 (2007), I wrote separately to state my view that any appellate review of sentences for substantive reasonableness will necessarily result in a sentencing scheme constitutionally indistinguishable from the mandatory Guidelines struck down in United States v. Booker, 543 U.S. 220 (2005). Whether a sentencing scheme uses mandatory Guidelines, a "proportionality test" for Guidelines variances, or a deferential abuse-of-discretion standard, there will be some sentences upheld only on the basis of additional judge-found facts.

Although I continue to believe that substantive-reasonableness review is inherently flawed, I give stare decisis effect to the statutory holding of *Rita*. The highly deferential standard adopted by the Court today will result in far fewer unconstitutional sentences than the proportionality standard employed by the Eighth Circuit. Moreover, as I noted in *Rita*, the Court has not foreclosed as-applied constitutional challenges to sentences. The door therefore remains open for a defendant to demonstrate that his sentence, whether inside or outside the advisory Guidelines range, would not have been upheld but for the existence of a fact found by the sentencing judge and not by the jury.

JUSTICE SOUTER, concurring.

I join the Court's opinion here, as I do in today's companion case of Kimbrough v. United States, 552 U.S. 85 (2007), which follow United States v. Booker, 543 U.S. 220 (2005), and Rita v. United States, 551 U.S. 338 (2007). My disagreements with holdings in those earlier cases are not the stuff of formally perpetual dissent, but I see their objectionable points hexing our judgments today, see id., at 384 (Souter, J., dissenting), and *Booker*, supra, at 272 (Stevens, J., dissenting in part). After *Booker*'s remedial holding, I continue to think that the best resolution of the tension between substantial consistency throughout the system and the right of jury trial would be a new Act of Congress: reestablishing a statutory system of mandatory sentencing guidelines (though not identical to the original in all points of detail), but providing for jury findings of all facts necessary to set the upper range of sentencing discretion. See *Rita*, supra, at 392.

JUSTICE THOMAS, dissenting.

Consistent with my dissenting opinion in Kimbrough v. United States, 552 U.S. 85 (2007), I would affirm the judgment of the Court of Appeals because the District Court committed statutory error when it departed below the applicable Guidelines range.

JUSTICE ALITO, dissenting.

The fundamental question in this case is whether, under the remedial decision in United States v. Booker, 543 U.S. 220 (2005), a district court must give the policy decisions that are embodied in the Sentencing Guidelines at least some significant weight in making a sentencing decision. I would answer that question in the affirmative and would therefore affirm the decision of the Court of Appeals.

I

In *Booker*, . . . the lower federal courts were instructed that the Guidelines must be regarded as "effectively advisory," *Booker*, 543 U.S., at 245, and that individual sentencing decisions are subject to appellate review for "reasonableness." Id., at 262. The *Booker* remedial opinion did not explain exactly what it meant by a system of "advisory" guidelines or by "reasonableness" review, and the opinion is open to different interpretations.

It is possible to read the opinion to mean that district judges, after giving the Guidelines a polite nod, may then proceed essentially as if the Sentencing Reform Act had never been enacted. This is how two of the dissents interpreted the Court's opinion. . . .

While this is a possible understanding of the remedial opinion, a better reading is that sentencing judges must still give the Guidelines' policy decisions some significant weight and that the courts of appeals must still police compliance. . . . [Under such a reading], district courts are still required to give some deference to the policy decisions embodied in the Guidelines and . . . appellate review must monitor compliance. District courts must not only "consult" the Guidelines, they must "take them into account." Id., at 264. In addition, the remedial majority [in *Booker* distanced itself] from Justice Scalia's position that, under an advisory Guidelines scheme, a district judge would have "discretion to sentence anywhere within the ranges authorized by statute" so long as the judge "stated that 'this court does not believe that the punishment set forth in the Guidelines is appropriate for this sort of offense.'" Id., at 305 (opinion dissenting in part).

[I]n the remedial opinion, the Court expressed confidence that appellate review for reasonableness would help to avoid "excessive sentencing disparities" and "would tend to iron out sentencing differences." Id., at 263. Indeed, a major theme of the remedial opinion, as well as our decision last Term in Rita v. United States, 551 U.S. 338 (2007), was that the post-*Booker* sentencing regime would still promote the Sentencing Reform Act's goal of reducing sentencing disparities. . . .

It is unrealistic to think this goal can be achieved over the long term if sentencing judges need only give lip service to the Guidelines. The other sentencing factors set out in §3553(a) are so broad that they impose few real restraints on sentencing judges. See id., at 305 (Scalia, J., dissenting in part). Thus, if judges are obligated to do no more than consult the Guidelines before deciding upon the sentence that is, in their independent judgment, sufficient to serve the other §3553(a) factors, federal sentencing will not "move . . . in Congress' preferred direction." Id., at 264 (opinion of the Court). On the contrary, sentencing disparities will gradually increase. Appellate decisions affirming sentences that diverge from the Guidelines (such as the Court's decision today) will be influential, and the sentencing habits developed during the pre-*Booker* era will fade.

Finally, in reading the *Booker* remedial opinion, we should not forget the decision's constitutional underpinnings. *Booker* and its antecedents are based on the Sixth Amendment right to trial by jury. . . . It is telling that the rules set out in the Court's opinion in the present case have nothing to do with juries or factfinding and, indeed, that not one of the facts that bears on petitioner's sentence is disputed. What is at issue, instead, is the allocation of the authority to decide issues of substantive sentencing policy, an issue on which the Sixth Amendment says absolutely nothing. The yawning gap between the Sixth Amendment and the Court's opinion should be enough to show that the *Blakely/Booker* line of cases has gone astray. . . .

I recognize that the Court is committed to the *Blakely/Booker* line of cases, but we are not required to continue along a path that will take us further and further off course. Because the *Booker* remedial opinion may be read to require sentencing judges to give weight to the Guidelines, I would adopt that interpretation and thus minimize the gap between what the Sixth Amendment requires and what our cases have held.

II

[In this last section, which is omitted, Justice Alito found "no evidence that the District Court deferred to the Guidelines to any significant degree," but instead simply "determined what it thought was appropriate under the circumstances and sentenced petitioner accordingly." He noted that "abuse-of-discretion review is not toothless," and ultimately agreed with the Eighth Circuit that "the District Court did not properly exercise its discretion." — EDS.]

NOTES AND QUESTIONS

1. Does *Gall* resolve the conflict between Justice Breyer and Justice Scalia over the proper standard of review for Guideline cases? Or does it leave the issue still unsettled? Does the fact that both Breyer and Scalia joined the majority opinion help you to answer these questions?

2. In Kimbrough v. United States, 552 U.S. 85 (2007), the companion case to *Gall*, the Supreme Court upheld as "reasonable" a district judge's decision to deviate from the Guidelines based on the judge's disagreement with the wide sentencing disparity between crimes involving crack cocaine and powder cocaine. The Court, in a majority opinion by Justice Ginsburg, explained that "closer review may be in order when the sentencing judge varies from the Guidelines based solely on the judge's view that the Guidelines range 'fails properly to reflect §3553(a) considerations' even in a mine-run case," but concluded that the instant case "presents no occasion for elaborative discussion of this matter," because the Guidelines for crack

cocaine crimes "do not exemplify the Commission's exercise of its characteristic institutional role." Instead, those Guidelines, according to the Court, were more or less forced upon the Sentencing Commission by Congress's failure properly to address the crack/powder distinction in several statutes creating mandatory minimum sentences. Justice Scalia joined the majority opinion, but also added, in concurrence, that nothing in *Kimbrough* should be read as inconsistent with prior Court decisions holding that "the district court is free to make its own reasonable application of the §3553(a) factors, and to reject (after due consideration) the advice of the Guidelines."

For a helpful analysis of *Kimbrough* and its confusing consequences in the federal appellate courts, see Carissa Byrne Hessick, Appellate Review of Sentencing Policy Decisions After *Kimbrough*, 93 Marq. L. Rev. 717 (2009). As Professor Hessick explains:

> In light of the ambiguous language contained in the *Kimbrough* decision and the criticism that can be leveled at the opinion, it may come as no surprise that the circuits have taken several different approaches to reviewing district court policy determinations after *Kimbrough*. Indeed, the Court has already decided an additional case in order to clarify some ambiguous dicta from *Kimbrough* that led several circuits to permit district courts to vary from the crack cocaine Guidelines based only on individual case or defendant characteristics, rather than based on categorical policy disagreements. Spears v. United States[, 129 S. Ct. 840 (2009),] confirmed that "district courts are entitled to reject and vary categorically from the crack-cocaine Guidelines based on a policy disagreement with those Guidelines," as opposed to case-specific criteria. But several other points of contention remain, including whether to follow the closer review dictum, what effect *Kimbrough* had on prior circuit precedent, and whether certain Guidelines represent policy choices by the Commission or by Congress. The circuits disagree on each of these questions. . . .
>
> The Court's decision in *Kimbrough* was designed to clarify uncertainty surrounding the new form of appellate sentencing review established in *Booker*. It appears, however, that *Kimbrough* may have actually resulted in more appellate uncertainty. Some of this uncertainty is attributable to the Court's dicta suggesting the level of appellate scrutiny of district court disagreement with Guidelines' policy may depend on whether a particular Guideline is the product of "empirical data and national experience." But, even without such dicta, appellate review of district court sentencing decisions is likely to occur differently in different circuits. That is because the *Booker* remedy — solving the Sixth Amendment problem by restoring district court discretion while, at the same time, seeking to preserve some adherence to the Guidelines through appellate review — is internally inconsistent and thus inherently unstable. Some circuits are inevitably going to prioritize one facet of the *Booker* remedy over the other, and thus circuit conflict is likely to continue.

Id., at 733, 749. For another helpful article examining the impact of *Blakely/Booker* in the state courts, see John F. Pfaff, The Future of Appellate Sentencing Review: *Booker* in the States, 93 Marq. L. Rev. 683 (2009).

3. In the first significant empirical study to compare the actual sentencing behavior of federal district judges before and after the Court's decisions in *Gall* and *Kimbrough*, Professor Ryan W. Scott examined a unique data set of federal criminal cases from the District of Massachusetts, the only federal district in the United States that reports publicly the "Statement of Reasons" for almost all sentencing

decisions[13] including the offense level, criminal history, Guideline range, any statutory minimum sentence, and the basis for any departure from the Guidelines. Scott was able to match this case-specific sentencing information with corresponding information from public docket entries, thereby identifying the specific judges who rendered each particular sentence. After limiting the study to those judges who (1) drew their cases randomly from the same shared pool and (2) imposed at least 25 sentences between October 1, 2001, and September 30, 2008, Scott ended up with a data set of 2,262 sentences imposed by 10 district judges. Comparing individual judicial sentencing behavior during three separate time periods — before *Booker*, between *Booker* and *Gall/Kimbrough*, and after *Gall/Kimbrough* — Scott reports:

> Analysis of the Boston data reveals a clear increase in inter-judge sentencing disparity, both in sentence length and in guideline sentencing patterns. The effect of the judge on sentence length has doubled in strength since *Kimbrough* and *Gall*. And in their guideline sentencing patterns, judges have responded in starkly different ways to *Booker*, with some following a "free at last" pattern and others a "business as usual" pattern. . . .
>
> Among Boston judges as a whole, average sentence length has increased since *Booker*. . . . Average sentence length climbed from 47.7 months before *Booker*, to 58.3 months in the years following *Booker*, to 63.7 months after *Kimbrough* and *Gall*. Excluding cases subject to a mandatory minimum, the increase is more gradual, from 30.8 months before *Booker*, to 33.7 months after *Booker*, to 35.5 months after *Kimbrough* and *Gall*.
>
> But average sentence length for the district as a whole masks significant variation among individual judges. . . . Although the difference between the highest and lowest averages remains essentially unchanged between periods, the distribution of averages has widened compared to the pre-*Booker* period. After *Kimbrough* and *Gall*, in particular, two clusters of judges are readily apparent: one cluster following the trend toward higher sentences with averages around 70 months, and another cluster splitting off with averages around 45 months.
>
> Statistical analysis confirms that the effect of the judge on sentence length has grown stronger since *Kimbrough* and *Gall*. . . . [T]he regression models indicate a delayed reaction, but ultimately a sharp uptick in inter-judge sentencing disparity since *Booker*. In the years before the decision, the percentage of variance in sentence length explained by the identity of the judge stood at 2.9%. Immediately after *Booker*, the rate actually declined slightly to 2.5%. But in the *Kimbrough/Gall* period, it rose sharply to 6.1%. That means the effect of the judge on sentence length is now more than twice as strong as in the three years before *Booker*.
>
> The increase in inter-judge disparity is even clearer in cases not governed by a mandatory minimum sentence. . . . For cases not subject to a mandatory minimum, the trend is unmistakable. The distribution of average sentences among judges has grown substantially wider since *Booker*: from a total spread of 15 months before *Booker*, to almost 30 months after *Booker*, to almost 40 months in the wake of *Kimbrough* and *Gall*.
>
> The stark differences between judges have real consequences for criminal defendants. Before *Booker*, regardless of the judge, a defendant in Boston not facing a mandatory minimum could expect that the judge's average sentence would fall between 25.9 months and 40.2 months. Today, after *Kimbrough* and *Gall*, three judges on the court are imposing average sentences of 25.5 months or less, while two other judges on the court are imposing average sentences of 51.4 months or more. That is an average

---

13. The "Statement of Reasons" is not made public if the presiding judge orders it sealed.

difference of more than two years in prison, depending on which judge is assigned to the case. . . .

Statistical analysis of how far, on average, each judge has sentenced from the guideline range confirms an increase in inter-judge disparity in guideline sentencing. . . . Under the mandatory Guidelines in 2002-2003, average distance from the guideline range was tightly clustered within a range of 4.5 months. . . . But after *Booker*, the distribution has widened dramatically and grown broader in every period. In the most recent period, following *Kimbrough* and *Gall*, average distances from the Guidelines span 20.0 months, ranging from 4.2 months to a remarkable 24.2 months.

As expected, the trend is even more pronounced for "discretionary" sentences in which the sentencing judge was free, as a legal and practical matter, to sentence outside the guideline range. . . . For criminal defendants in the 80% of cases where the judge has full discretion to sentence outside the guideline range, [i.e., those that did not involve the constraints of a mandatory minimum, time already served that exceeded the Guideline minimum sentence, or a Guideline recommendation of probation,] the difference between judges has serious consequences. Under the mandatory Guidelines in 2002-2003, regardless of the judge assigned to the case, a criminal defendant could expect an average sentence 7.8 months or less [in terms of distance] from the Guidelines. Today, in the wake of *Kimbrough* and *Gall*, three judges in Boston continue to sentence on average 6.1 months or less from the guideline range. But a different group of three Boston judges sentences, on average, 24.6 months or more from the guideline range. That is an average difference of more than a year and a half in prison, depending on the judge.

Ryan W. Scott, Inter-Judge Sentencing Disparity After *Booker*: A First Look, 63 Stan. L. Rev. 1 (2010), available online at http://papers.ssrn.com/sol3/papers.cfm?abstract_id=1446744.

Does Professor Scott's study suggest that Justice Breyer's attempt to keep the Guidelines "semi-binding" has proved at least partially effective, because at least some district judges continue to sentence mostly according to the Guidelines? Or does Justice Scalia get the last laugh, because other district judges now feel "free at last" to disobey the Guidelines? Does adding a brand new source of sentencing disparity — i.e., the extent to which a particular district judge, after *Booker*, *Gall*, and *Kimbrough*, now views the Guidelines as "semi-binding" (per Breyer) or "advisory only" (per Scalia) — to all of the traditional sources of sentencing disparity seem like a move in the right direction?

4. *Booker*, *Gall*, and *Kimbrough* might be viewed as calling into question the fundamental premises underlying *Apprendi* and *Blakely*, because they approved a remedial scheme that (at least in the view of Justice Scalia, the author of *Blakely* and thus the chief architect of the prevailing doctrine) seems incompatible with those premises. But those cases did not directly challenge the *Apprendi/Blakely/Booker* doctrine itself. The first such direct challenge might be the case of Oregon v. Ice, 129 S. Ct. 711 (2009). Under Oregon law, Ice — who was convicted of multiple crimes in a single trial — was subject to consecutive rather than concurrent sentences only if the trial judge made a factual finding that the crimes involved separate incidents, or if (in the same incident) the defendant manifested a "willingness to commit more than one criminal offense" or the crimes created a risk of "greater or qualitatively different loss, injury or harm to the victim." The judge made such findings in Ice's case, and Ice was given consecutive sentences that totaled 340 months in prison.

The Court held that Ice's consecutive sentencing did not violate *Apprendi* or *Blakely/Booker*. In a majority opinion by Justice Ginsburg, joined by Justices Stevens, Kennedy, Breyer, and Alito, the Court explained:

> This case concerns the scope of the Sixth Amendment's jury-trial guarantee, as construed in Apprendi v. New Jersey, 530 U.S. 466 (2000), and Blakely v. Washington, 542 U.S. 296 (2004). Those decisions are rooted in the historic jury function — determining whether the prosecution has proved each element of an offense beyond a reasonable doubt. They hold that it is within the jury's province to determine any fact (other than the existence of a prior conviction) that increases the maximum punishment authorized for a particular offense. Thus far, the Court has not extended the *Apprendi* and *Blakely* line of decisions beyond the offense-specific context that supplied the historic grounding for the decisions. The question here presented concerns a sentencing function in which the jury traditionally played no part: When a defendant has been tried and convicted of multiple offenses, each involving discrete sentencing prescriptions, does the Sixth Amendment mandate jury determination of any fact declared necessary to the imposition of consecutive, in lieu of concurrent, sentences?
>
> Our application of *Apprendi*'s rule must honor the "long-standing common-law practice" in which the rule is rooted. . . . The rule's animating principle is the preservation of the jury's historic role as a bulwark between the State and the accused at the trial for an alleged offense. See *Apprendi*, 530 U.S., at 477. Guided by that principle, our opinions make clear that the Sixth Amendment does not countenance legislative encroachment on the jury's traditional domain. See id., at 497. We accordingly considered whether the finding of a particular fact was understood as within "the domain of the jury . . . by those who framed the Bill of Rights." Harris v. United States, 536 U.S. 545, 557 (2002) (plurality opinion). In undertaking this inquiry, we remain cognizant that administration of a discrete criminal justice system is among the basic sovereign prerogatives States retain. See, e.g., Patterson v. New York, 432 U.S. 197, 201 (1977).
>
> These twin considerations — historical practice and respect for state sovereignty — counsel against extending *Apprendi*'s rule to the imposition of sentences for discrete crimes. The decision to impose sentences consecutively is not within the jury function that "extends down centuries into the common law." *Apprendi*, 530 U.S., at 477. Instead, specification of the regime for administering multiple sentences has long been considered the prerogative of state legislatures.
>
> Members of this Court have warned against "wooden, unyielding insistence on expanding the *Apprendi* doctrine far beyond its necessary boundaries." Cunningham [v. California], 549 U.S. [270], 295 (Kennedy, J., dissenting). The jury-trial right is best honored through a "principled rationale" that applies the rule of the *Apprendi* cases "within the central sphere of their concern." 549 U.S., at 295. Our disposition today — upholding an Oregon statute that assigns to judges a decision that has not traditionally belonged to the jury — is faithful to that aim.

Justice Scalia, predictably, was not amused:

> [T]he Court attempts to distinguish Oregon's sentencing scheme by reasoning that the rule of *Apprendi* applies only to the length of a sentence for an individual crime and not to the total sentence for a defendant. I cannot understand why we would make such a strange exception to the treasured right of trial by jury. Neither the reasoning of the *Apprendi* line of cases, nor any distinctive history of the factfinding necessary to imposition of consecutive sentences, nor (of course) logic supports such an odd rule. . . .

To support its distinction-without-a-difference, the Court puts forward the same (the *very* same) arguments regarding the history of sentencing that were rejected by *Apprendi*. Here, it is entirely irrelevant that common-law judges had discretion to impose either consecutive or concurrent sentences, just as there it was entirely irrelevant that common-law judges had discretion to impose greater or lesser sentences (within the prescribed statutory maximum) for individual convictions. . . . Our concern here is precisely the same as our concern in *Apprendi*: What happens when a State breaks from the common-law practice of discretionary sentences and permits the imposition of an elevated sentence only upon the showing of extraordinary facts? In such a system, the defendant "is *entitled* to" the lighter sentence "and by reason of the Sixth Amendment[,] the facts bearing upon that entitlement must be found by a jury." *Blakely*, 542 U.S., at 309. . . .

Today's opinion muddies the waters, and gives cause to doubt whether the Court is willing to stand by *Apprendi*'s interpretation of the Sixth Amendment's jury-trial guarantee.

Might *Ice* truly represent the beginning of the end for the *Apprendi/Blakely/Booker* doctrine? Or is it a one-off exception that will leave the core of the rule unscathed? Only time will tell.

Chapter 16

Double Jeopardy

The double jeopardy clause of the Fifth Amendment provides, "[N]or shall any person be subject for the same offence to be twice put in jeopardy of life or limb." That simple phrase has produced a varied set of legal doctrines of astonishing complexity. While most of the doctrines themselves are settled — few issues in double jeopardy law are up for grabs at the present time — there is no agreed-upon theory that unites them. As you work through the doctrinal tangles below, ask yourself two questions: (1) What is the purpose of the ban on double jeopardy in this context? (2) How does this legal rule further that purpose?

Begin with the fact that the ban on double jeopardy "consist[s] of three separate constitutional protections. It protects against a second prosecution for the same offense after acquittal. It protects against a second prosecution for the same offense after conviction. And it protects against multiple punishments for the same offense." North Carolina v. Pearce, 395 U.S. 711, 717 (1969). Actually, there is a fourth protection: The double jeopardy clause also protects the defendant's interest in having his case decided by a particular judge or jury. The need to protect that interest explains the rule banning retrial after a mistrial, unless the mistrial was justified by what the Court calls "manifest necessity." None of these protections is absolute; each exists within a network of exceptions and conditions — the rationales for which are often obscure.

The material below is divided into four sections. First, in Section A, we take up the meaning of the phrase "twice put in jeopardy," and the two major doctrines that phrase has spawned: double jeopardy's "acquittal rule" and the presumptive ban on prosecution after a mistrial. Next, in Section B, the chapter turns to the meaning of the other key phrase of the double jeopardy clause: "for the same offence." That has been the locus of most double jeopardy litigation over the past two decades. Section C discusses the "dual sovereignty" doctrine, which holds that multiple prosecutions for the same crime by different sovereigns — different states, or a state and the federal government — are permissible. Section D concludes with an important boundary question: What counts as a criminal prosecution for purposes of double jeopardy law?

A. *"Twice Put in Jeopardy"*

1. Acquittals

FONG FOO v. UNITED STATES

Certiorari to the United States Court of Appeals for the First Circuit
369 U.S. 141 (1962)

Per Curiam.

The petitioners, a corporation and two of its employees, were brought to trial before a jury in a federal district court upon an indictment charging a conspiracy and the substantive offense of concealing material facts in a matter within the jurisdiction of an agency of the United States, in violation of 18 U.S.C. §§371 and 1001. After seven days of what promised to be a long and complicated trial, three government witnesses had appeared and a fourth was in the process of testifying. At that point the district judge directed the jury to return verdicts of acquittal as to all the defendants, and a formal judgment of acquittal was subsequently entered.

The record shows that the district judge's action was based upon one or both of two grounds: supposed improper conduct on the part of the Assistant United States Attorney who was prosecuting the case, and a supposed lack of credibility in the testimony of the witnesses for the prosecution who had testified up to that point.

The Government filed a petition for a writ of mandamus in the Court of Appeals for the First Circuit, praying that the judgment of acquittal be vacated and the case reassigned for trial. The court granted the petition, upon the ground that under the circumstances revealed by the record the trial court was without power to direct the judgment in question. Judge Aldrich concurred separately, finding that the directed judgment of acquittal had been based solely on the supposed improper conduct of the prosecutor, and agreeing with his colleagues that the district judge was without power to direct an acquittal on that ground. 286 F.2d 556. We granted certiorari to consider a question of importance in the administration of justice in the federal courts.

In holding that the District Court was without power to direct acquittals under the circumstances disclosed by the record, the Court of Appeals relied primarily upon two decisions of this Court, Ex parte United States, 242 U.S. 27, and Ex parte United States, 287 U.S. 241. In the first of these cases it was held that a district judge had no power to suspend a mandatory prison sentence, and that a writ of mandamus would lie to require the judge to vacate his erroneous order of suspension. In the second case the Court issued a writ of mandamus ordering a district judge to issue a bench warrant which he had refused to do, in the purported exercise of his discretion, for a person under an indictment returned by a properly constituted grand jury.

Neither of those decisions involved the guaranty of the Fifth Amendment that no person shall "be subject for the same offence to be twice put in jeopardy of life or limb." That constitutional provision is at the very root of the present case, and we cannot but conclude that the guaranty was violated when the Court of Appeals set aside the judgment of acquittal and directed that the petitioners be tried again for the same offense.

The petitioners were tried under a valid indictment in a federal court which had jurisdiction over them and over the subject matter. The trial did not terminate prior to the entry of judgment, as in Gori v. United States, 367 U.S. 364. It terminated with the entry of a final judgment of acquittal as to each petitioner. The Court of Appeals thought, not without reason, that the acquittal was based upon an egregiously erroneous foundation. Nevertheless, "[t]he verdict of acquittal was final, and could not be reviewed . . . without putting [the petitioners] twice in jeopardy, and thereby violating the Constitution." United States v. Ball, 163 U.S. 662, 671. . . .

MR. JUSTICE HARLAN, concurring.

Were I able to find, as Judge Aldrich did, that the District Court's judgment of acquittal was based solely on the Assistant United States Attorney's *alleged* misconduct, I would think that a retrial of the petitioners would not be prevented by the Double Jeopardy Clause of the Fifth Amendment. Even assuming that a trial court may have power, in extreme circumstances, to direct a judgment of acquittal, instead of declaring a mistrial, because of a prosecutor's misconduct — a proposition which I seriously doubt — I do not think that such power existed in the circumstances of this case. But since an examination of the record leaves me unable, as it did the majority of the Court of Appeals, to attribute the action of the District Court to this factor alone, I concur in the judgment of reversal.

MR. JUSTICE CLARK, dissenting.

The Court speaks with such expanse that I am obliged to dissent. It says that because "a final judgment of acquittal" was entered pursuant to a directed verdict the propriety of such "acquittal" cannot be reviewed even though the Government had not concluded its main case at the time the verdict was directed. The District Court under the circumstances here clearly had no power to direct a verdict of acquittal or to enter a judgment thereon. In my view when a trial court has no power to direct such a verdict, the judgment based thereon is a nullity. The word "acquittal" in this context is no magic open sesame freeing in this case two persons and absolving a corporation from serious grand jury charges of fraud upon the Government.

On the record before us it matters not whether the so-called acquittal was pursuant to the trial court's conclusion that the Government's witnesses up to that point lacked credibility or was based on the alleged misconduct of the prosecution.

On the first point, the Government had only examined three of its witnesses and was in the process of examining a fourth when the acquittal was entered. The first and third witnesses were merely preliminary, offered to identify documents and explain the functions performed by the individual defendants for the corporate defendant. The second was offered to give the jury an explanation of radiosondes, devices for gathering weather data, which petitioners were furnishing the Government under contracts totaling several million dollars. It was during the latter's testimony — entirely explanatory — that the court called a recess for the stated purpose of requiring the United States Attorney to "consider whether the public interest is served by a further prosecution of this case." Upon the vigorous insistence of the United States Attorney himself, the trial was resumed and the Government called its third and fourth witnesses. The fourth witness was the first to testify as to the fraud upon the Government which related to a deliberate scheme to conceal from government inspectors defects in the devices. During direct examination the fourth witness was "not sure" as to the date of a certain conference at which representatives of the corporate defendant were present. Thereafter at a recess period his memory was refreshed during a conversation with one of the Assistant United States Attorneys. Upon resuming the stand he corrected his previous testimony as to the date, placing it a few months earlier. On cross-examination he admitted that the error had been called to his attention by the Assistant. The court then excused the jury and after excoriating the Assistant called the jury back into session and directed the verdict of acquittal.

It is fundamental in our criminal jurisprudence that the public has a right to have a person who stands legally indicted by a grand jury publicly tried on the charge. No judge has the power before hearing the testimony proffered by the Government or at least canvassing the same to enter a judgment of acquittal and thus frustrate the Government in the performance of its duty to prosecute those who violate its law.

Here, as the United States Attorney advised the court, only three witnesses of the "many . . . to be heard from . . ." had testified. The court had only begun to hear what promised to be a protracted conspiracy case involving many witnesses. The Government had not rested. As the majority of the Court of Appeals observed, the District Court:

> abruptly terminated the Government's case . . . long before the Government had had an opportunity to show whether or not it had a case; and, moreover, he did so in ignorance of either the exact nature or the cogency of the specific evidence of guilt which Government's counsel said he had available and was ready to present. 286 F.2d, at 562-563.

At such a stage of the case the District Court had no power to prejudge the Government's proof — find it insufficient or unconvincing — and set the petitioners free.

On the second point, even if there were misconduct, the court still had no power to punish the Government because of the indiscretion of its lawyer. As this Court said in McGuire v. United States, 273 U.S. 95, 99 (1927), "A criminal prosecution is more than a game in which the Government may be checkmated and the game lost merely because its officers have not played according to rule." At most, if there had been misconduct, the remedy would have been to declare a mistrial and impose appropriate punishment upon the Assistant United States Attorney, rather than upon the public. In my view the judgment of the Court of Appeals should, therefore, be affirmed.

NOTES ON THE SPECIAL STATUS OF ACQUITTALS

Fong Foo stands for the proposition that acquittals are final, even when clearly mistaken. This proposition is as much of an absolute as you are likely to find anywhere in the law. There is only one scenario that has ever been held (and only by an intermediate appellate court, not by the Supreme Court) to be an exception to that proposition: when the acquittal was obtained by bribing or coercing the decision maker. Consider the highly unusual case of Aleman v. Judges of the Circuit Court of Cook County, 138 F.3d 302 (7th Cir. 1998). Harry Aleman — also known as the "Pizza Guy" (don't you love Mafia aliases?) — was charged with murdering a local Teamsters official. Aleman was tried by a Cook County, Illinois judge (no jury); the defendant paid the judge $10,000 to acquit him, which the judge then did. (When he received his payment, the bribed judge said, in classic Chicago style: "That's all I get is ten thousand dollars? I think I deserve more.") The government discovered the bribe, re-charged Aleman with the same murder, and argued that double jeopardy did not apply because Aleman was never really in "jeopardy" of a conviction at the original trial, because it was rigged. The Court of Appeals for the Seventh Circuit agreed; the Supreme Court denied Aleman's writ of certiorari. Is *Aleman* consistent with *Fong Foo*?

Bribery aside, the proposition that acquittals are final entails another proposition: The government "has no right of appeal in a criminal case, absent explicit statutory authority." United States v. Scott, 437 U.S., at 84-85. A federal statute, 18 U.S.C. §3731, permits a government appeal in a federal criminal case except "where the double jeopardy clause of the United States Constitution prohibits further prosecution." Many states have similar statutes. As you read the notes that follow, remember that the definition of "acquittal" also determines the boundaries of the government's right to appeal adverse judgments.

Identity of the Decision Maker — Jury or Judge.   Juries are, of course, free to acquit in criminal cases, even when the evidence justifies a conviction. That power is generally discouraged: Jurors are not told they may acquit for any reason — frequently they are told the opposite — and the literature on jury nullification is largely critical of the practice. See, e.g., Andrew D. Leipold, Rethinking Jury Nullification, 82 Va. L. Rev. 253 (1996). Yet *Fong Foo* seems to give trial judges the same nullification power that criminal juries have. Why? One can readily imagine arguments for giving 12 ordinary citizens the right to decide that a given criminal statute is too harsh to be applied in a given context. But why should *judges* have that right?

Whatever its merits, the authority *Fong Foo* establishes was reaffirmed in Sanabria v. United States, 437 U.S. 54 (1978). *Sanabria*'s facts are unusually complicated. Along with a number of codefendants, Sanabria was charged with conducting an illegal gambling business in violation of 18 U.S.C. §1955; the federal crime was defined to include only gambling businesses that were unlawful in the state in which they took place. As to Sanabria, the government's evidence tended to establish his participation in a numbers business but not his participation in a business involving gambling on horse races (the latter was the business most of Sanabria's codefendants allegedly operated). During the course of the trial, defense counsel moved for a judgment of acquittal as to Sanabria, on the ground that the indictment referred to a Massachusetts statute that forbade gambling on horse races but not numbers businesses. (Another state statute covered numbers businesses; that is, the error in the indictment was apparently technical only. See 437 U.S., at 58-59.) The trial court struck all evidence concerning the numbers operation, and then granted the motion for judgment of acquittal.

The government appealed, arguing that the ruling in *Sanabria* was not really an acquittal but merely a dismissal for error in the indictment. The Supreme Court disagreed. In an opinion by Justice Marshall, the Court held that even assuming the trial judge's decision was erroneous, the judgment was final. The Court called the rule barring any appeal of acquittals "the most fundamental rule of double jeopardy jurisprudence," id., at 64 (quotation omitted), and, quoting *Fong Foo*, added: "The fundamental nature of this rule is manifested by its explicit extension to situations where an acquittal is 'based upon an egregiously erroneous foundation.'" Id.

With *Fong Foo* and *Sanabria*, compare Wilson v. United States, 420 U.S. 332 (1975). Wilson was charged with illegally converting union funds to his personal use; his case went to trial before a jury. The jury convicted. The trial judge then granted a defense motion to dismiss the charges against Wilson due to excessive preindictment delay by the government. The government appealed, and the defense argued that the trial judge's ruling was an acquittal and was therefore final and unchallengeable. The Supreme Court, once again speaking through Justice Marshall, concluded otherwise:

> . . . [W]here there is no threat of either multiple punishment or successive prosecutions, the Double Jeopardy Clause is not offended. . . . Although review of any ruling of law discharging a defendant obviously enhances the likelihood of conviction and subjects him to continuing expense and anxiety, a defendant has no legitimate claim to benefit from an error of law when that error could be corrected without subjecting him to a second trial before a second trier of fact.

Id., at 344-345. Note the Court's emphasis on the fact that no second trial would be necessary; presumably, the idea is that if the government's appeal were successful, Wilson would stand convicted based on the jury verdict. Note too that the Court did not address the subject matter of the trial judge's ruling; it appears that the *Wilson* result would hold even if the judge had found the defendant factually innocent of the charges against him. Does that make sense?

Finally, consider United States v. Martin Linen Supply Co., 430 U.S. 564 (1977). Two corporations and their individual owner were tried for criminal contempt. The jury deadlocked and was dismissed. At that point, the defendant filed a motion for judgment of acquittal, which the district judge granted. As in the cases discussed above, the issue before the Supreme Court was whether the government could appeal this ruling. The Court held it could not, in an opinion that relied heavily on *Fong Foo*. Justice Brennan's majority opinion emphasized the impermissibility of a second trial following an acquittal — and the district judge's order unquestionably qualified as an acquittal.

What is the point of these cases? It is often said that they are designed to protect the defendant's interest in finality — hence the emphasis in *Wilson* and *Martin Linen Supply* on whether a retrial would be necessary if the government's appeal were successful. But as Peter Westen noted in a famously interesting article, this argument fails to explain why the finality interest is protected *absolutely* — why acquittals are deemed final "even where the prosecution is acknowledged to have acted in good faith and even where the acquittals are known to be 'egregiously erroneous.'" Peter Westen, The Three Faces of Double Jeopardy: Reflections on Government Appeals of Criminal Sentences, 78 Mich. L. Rev. 1001, 1006-1007 (1980) (quoting *Fong Foo*). As Westen further notes (and as the materials below explore), the finality interest is not deemed powerful enough to bar retrials after an appellate reversal or (at least in some circumstances) a mistrial.

The better argument, Westen contends, is that the finality of acquittals is tied to the jury's right to nullify:

> To say that a verdict is erroneous means that it is the end product of a trial that did not conform to the rules governing opening statements, evidence, jury instructions, closing statements, and so forth. The purpose of such rules is to insure that a case is tried

in accord with the legislative standard governing guilt or innocence. Yet as long as the criminal jury has authority to acquit against the evidence, viz., authority to alter legislative standards in favor of more lenient standards of its own, trial errors of that kind may be immaterial. One cannot tell whether an "erroneous" acquittal is the product of legal error, or whether it is the fruit of the jury's desire to nullify the law by which the case was tried. Since the jury verdict itself is opaque, and since the jury cannot be easily examined about its verdict without skewing its deliberations, two alternatives remain: either to reject all "erroneous" jury verdicts, knowing full well that some of them will be based on the jury's desire to nullify, or to accept all such verdicts, knowing that some of them will be the product of legal errors. As between the two alternatives, the jury-acquittal rule opts for the latter, reflecting the judgment that it is ultimately better to err in favor of nullification than against it.

Id., at 1018. Of course, as Westen recognizes, that explains the jury's prerogative, not the judge's. But as Westen and coauthor Richard Drubel argue in another article,

> [T]here are . . . good reasons to vest trial judges with the authority to acquit against the evidence. It enables the judicial system to temper the legislature's generalized standards of criminal responsibility with lenity in particular cases. It also places bench trials on an equal footing with jury trials. . . .

Peter Westen & Richard Drubel, Toward a General Theory of Double Jeopardy, [1978] Sup. Ct. Rev. 81, 134 (1979). Are those reasons powerful enough to justify constitutionally protecting nullification from the bench? (Westen and Drubel think not. See id., at 134-135.)

One way to reconcile the cases discussed above is to say that criminal defendants are entitled to one potential "nullifier" — the jury if the jury comes to a final decision, but the judge if the trial is to the bench or if the jury deadlocks. Is that a sensible entitlement? Is it important that criminal defendants have some opportunity to make nonlegal arguments (e.g., whatever the law says, this conduct does not deserve to be criminally punished)? Are judges likely to do a good job of evaluating such arguments?

Timing.   The constitutional bar on defendants' being "twice put in jeopardy" for the same crime is, in part, a rule about timing. For a defendant to be "twice put in jeopardy," (1) he must be "in jeopardy," (2) he must have been in some *other* "jeopardy" — i.e., there must be more than one "jeopardy," and (3) these multiple "jeopardies" must be "for the same offence." The first two of these three conditions depend in large part on when a given "jeopardy" begins and when it ends.

In Crist v. Bretz, 437 U.S. 28 (1978), the Court held that in jury trials, jeopardy begins or "attaches" when the jury is impanelled and sworn. The Court justified its conclusion by

> the need to protect the interest of an accused in retaining a chosen jury. That interest was described in Wade v. Hunter, [336 U.S. 684, 689,] as a defendant's "valued right to have his trial completed by a particular tribunal." It is an interest with roots deep in the historic development of trial by jury in the Anglo-American system of criminal justice. Throughout that history there ran a strong tradition that once banded together a jury should not be discharged until it had completed its solemn task of announcing a verdict.

Id., at 35-36. Note that this conclusion bars the use of double jeopardy doctrine as a vehicle to prevent multiple or harassing criminal investigations, since a mere investigation does not constitute "jeopardy." Consider Serfass v. United States, 420 U.S. 377 (1975). There, the defendant was charged with criminal draft evasion; the district court granted a pretrial motion to dismiss the charge on the ground that the defendant had established conscientious objector status — seemingly the equivalent of a ruling that the government lacked sufficient evidence to prosecute. The Supreme Court held that the government could appeal from the district court's ruling, even though the appeal could lead to a trial, because jeopardy had not yet attached when the district court's ruling was made.

When does a given jeopardy end? Obviously, it ends with an acquittal — *Fong Foo* holds as much. Does it end with the reversal of a conviction? In Ball v. United States, 163 U.S. 662, 672 (1896), the Court held that "it is quite clear that a defendant, who procures a judgment against him upon an indictment to be set aside, may be tried anew upon the same indictment . . . for the same offence of which he had been convicted." Under *Ball*, a second trial is permitted following the reversal of the defendant's conviction because the second trial does not constitute a new "jeopardy," but simply a continuation of the same jeopardy that began with the first trial. See also United States v. Tateo, 377 U.S. 463 (1964), holding the *Ball* rule applicable to reversals on collateral review.

Appellate "Acquittals."   The *Ball* rule establishes that at least some appellate reversals do not bar retrial. In Burks v. United States, 437 U.S. 1 (1978), the Court held that an appellate holding that the evidence was insufficient to convict *does* bar retrial:

> [S]uch an appellate reversal means that the government's case was so lacking that it should not have even been *submitted* to the jury. Since we necessarily afford absolute finality to a jury's *verdict* of acquittal — no matter how erroneous its decision — it is difficult to conceive how society has any greater interest in retrying a defendant when, on review, it is decided as a matter of law that the jury could not properly have returned a verdict of guilty.

Id., at 16 (emphasis in original). Suppose an intermediate appellate court finds the evidence insufficient, and the government wishes to appeal that ruling to the state supreme court. Is the appeal permissible? In other words, does the appellate acquittal have the same standing as a jury acquittal? Recall Wilson v. United States, 420 U.S. 332 (1975), where the Court upheld an appeal from a trial court dismissal after a jury verdict of guilty had been returned. *Wilson* might suggest that judicial acquittals are less final than jury acquittals. But then, the trial court in Wilson did not squarely find that the evidence was insufficient to convict, so maybe the court's ruling was not an "acquittal" after all.

In some jurisdictions, appellate judges have the authority to order new trials when they disagree with the jury's verdict, even if the verdict was legally supportable. These "thirteenth juror" reversals do not bar retrial under *Burks*. See Tibbs v. Florida, 457 U.S. 31 (1982).

Acquittals and Dismissals.   As the preceding note suggests, double jeopardy doctrine places a great deal of emphasis on whether a given appellate ruling was or was not the equivalent of an acquittal. The same is true of trial court rulings. In United

States v. Scott, 437 U.S. 82 (1978), the defendant was charged with three counts of drug distribution. The defense moved to dismiss two of the three counts for prejudicial preindictment delay by the government. At the close of the evidence, the district judge granted the defense motion. (The third count went to the jury, which acquitted.) The government sought to appeal the district judge's ruling; the defendant argued that that ruling was final, since a reversal would necessarily require another trial. The Court held that appeal from dismissals of this sort were permissible, even if they might result in a second trial. The Court analogized the issue to the cases involving appellate reversal:

> The successful appeal of a judgment of conviction, on any ground other than the insufficiency of the evidence to support the verdict, Burks v. United States, [437 U.S. 1 (1978),] poses no bar to further prosecution on the same charge. A judgment of acquittal, whether based on a jury verdict of not guilty or on a ruling by the court that the evidence is insufficient to convict, may not be appealed and terminates the prosecution when a second trial would be necessitated by a reversal. What may seem superficially to be a disparity in the rules governing a defendant's liability to be tried again is explainable by reference to the underlying purposes of the Double Jeopardy Clause. As . . . Fong Foo illustrate[s], the law attaches particular significance to an acquittal. To permit a second trial after an acquittal, however mistaken the acquittal may have been, would present an unacceptably high risk that the Government, with its vastly superior resources, might wear down the defendant so that "even though innocent he may be found guilty." Green [v. United States, 355 U.S. 184, 188 (1957)]. On the other hand, to require a criminal defendant to stand trial again after he has successfully invoked a statutory right of appeal to upset his first conviction is not an act of governmental oppression of the sort against which the Double Jeopardy Clause was intended to protect. . . .
>
> . . . [Here], the dismissal of an indictment for preindictment delay represents a legal judgment that a defendant, although criminally culpable, may not be punished because of a supposed constitutional violation.
>
> We think that in a case such as this the defendant, by deliberately choosing to seek termination of the proceedings against him on a basis unrelated to factual guilt or innocence of the offense of which he is accused, suffers no injury cognizable under the Double Jeopardy Clause if the Government is permitted to appeal from such a ruling of the trial court in favor of the defendant.

Id., at 90-91, 98-99. Elsewhere in its opinion, the Court sought to define which trial court rulings would constitute an acquittal:

> [A] defendant is acquitted only when the ruling of the judge, whatever its label, actually represents a resolution in the defendant's favor, correct or not, of some or all of the factual elements of the offense charged. Where the court, before the jury returns a verdict, enters a judgment of acquittal pursuant to Fed. Rule Crim. Proc. 29, appeal will be barred only when it is plain that the District Court evaluated the Government's evidence and determined that it was legally insufficient to sustain a conviction.

Id., at 97 (quotations and citations omitted). Review the statement of facts in Fong Foo; does the trial judge's acquittal in that case satisfy the standard in Scott?

In Smith v. Massachusetts, 543 U.S. 462 (2005), the defendant was charged with three separate crimes related to a shooting incident. One of those crimes, unlawful possession of a firearm, required proof that the weapon had a barrel of "less than 16 inches" in length. At trial, the shooting victim testified that the defendant shot him with "a pistol," which was further described as "a revolver" that "appeared to be a .32 or .38." The prosecution introduced no other testimony concerning the firearm. At the close of the prosecution's evidence, the defendant moved for a required finding of "not guilty" on the firearm count because, he claimed, the prosecution had failed to prove the length of the gun barrel. The trial judge granted the motion, and the ruling was entered on the docket. The prosecution rested its case. After the defense presented its witnesses, and before closing arguments, the prosecution informed the judge about a Massachusetts precedent indicating that the firearm count could be sustained based on descriptive testimony like that of the victim. The judge announced that she was "reversing" her ruling and allowing the firearm count to go to the jury. The jury convicted on all three counts, and the defendant was also convicted on a recidivist charge; he received a concurrent sentence of 10 to 12 years on the firearms charge. On appeal, the defendant raised a double jeopardy claim premised in part on Massachusetts Rule of Criminal Procedure 25(a), which provides: "The judge . . . shall enter a finding of not guilty . . . if the evidence is insufficient as a matter of law to sustain a conviction. If a defendant's motion for a required finding of not guilty is made at the close of the Commonwealth's evidence, it shall be ruled upon at that time." The Appeals Court of Massachusetts held that Rule 25(a) prohibited a trial judge from reserving a decision on such a motion, but did not preclude the judge from reconsidering a decision previously made.

The Supreme Court, in a 5-4 decision, reversed. All nine Justices agreed that the finding made by the trial judge was based on insufficiency of the evidence, and thus was tantamount to an acquittal. All nine Justices also agreed that the states possess the power to authorize — by statute, court rule, or judicial decision — trial judges to reconsider midtrial insufficiency-of-the-evidence rulings, and that such reconsideration itself would not violate double jeopardy. Writing for the majority, however, Justice Scalia emphasized that before the appellate decision in Smith's case, no such authorization had been clearly granted in Massachusetts. Scalia continued:

> It may suffice for an appellate court to announce the state-law rule that midtrial acquittals are tentative in a case where reconsideration of the acquittal occurred at a stage in the trial where the defendant's justifiable ignorance of the rule could not possibly have caused him prejudice. But when, as here, the trial has proceeded to the defendant's presentation of his case, the possibility of prejudice arises. The seeming dismissal may induce a defendant to present a defense to the undismissed charges when he would be better advised to stand silent. Many jurisdictions still follow the traditional rule that after trial or on appeal, sufficiency-of-the-evidence challenges are reviewed on the basis of the *entire* trial record, even if the defendant moved for acquittal when the prosecution rested and the court erroneously denied that motion. In these jurisdictions, the defendant who puts on a case runs "the risk that . . . he will bolster the Government case enough for it to support a verdict of guilty." McGautha v. California, 402 U.S. 183, 215 (1971). The defendant's evidence "may lay the foundation for otherwise inadmissible evidence in the Government's initial presentation or provide corroboration for essential elements of the Government's case." United States v. Calderon, 348 U. S. 160, 164, n. 1 (1954). In all jurisdictions, moreover, false assurance of acquittal on one count may induce the defendant to present defenses to the remaining counts that are inadvisable — for example, a defense that entails admission of guilt on the acquitted count.
>
> The Double Jeopardy Clause's guarantee cannot be allowed to become a potential snare for those who reasonably rely upon it. If, after a facially unqualified midtrial

dismissal of one count, the trial has proceeded to the defendant's introduction of evidence, the acquittal must be treated as final, unless the availability of reconsideration has been plainly established by pre-existing rule or case authority expressly applicable to midtrial rulings on the sufficiency of the evidence. . . .

Massachusetts argues that if the Double Jeopardy Clause does not allow for reconsideration, every erroneous grant of a directed-verdict motion will be unremediable, even one attributable to mistaken expression that is promptly corrected. We think not. Double-jeopardy principles have never been thought to bar the immediate repair of a genuine error in the announcement of an acquittal, even one rendered by a jury. See M. Friedland, Double Jeopardy 61 (1969); King v. Parkin, 1 Mood. 45, 46-47, 168 Eng. Rep. 1179, 1180 (1824). And of course States can protect themselves still further against the "occasional errors" of law that the dissent thinks "inevitabl[e]" in the course of trial, by rendering midtrial acquittals nonfinal. . . .

Id., at 471-474. Justice Ginsburg, joined in dissent by Chief Justice Rehnquist and Justices Kennedy and Breyer, argued that Smith's claim should properly be viewed as arising under the Due Process Clause, not the Double Jeopardy Clause, and that the claim should fail because Smith suffered no prejudice. In a footnote, Scalia responded:

The dissent goes to great lengths to establish that there was no prejudice here, since the acquittal was legally wrong and the defendant was deprived of no available defense. But the Double Jeopardy Clause has never required prejudice beyond the very exposure to a second jeopardy. To put it differently: requiring someone to defend against a charge of which he has already been acquitted is prejudice per se for purposes of the Double Jeopardy Clause — even when the acquittal was erroneous because the evidence was sufficient. See, e.g., Sanabria v. United States, 437 U.S. 54, 77-78 (1978). . . .

Id., at 473, n. 7.

Should federal double jeopardy claims turn on the clarity (or lack thereof) of state law? Suppose Massachusetts law, prior to Smith's case, had clearly authorized reconsideration of midtrial insufficiency rulings. Now suppose the trial judge in *Smith* had dismissed the firearm charge and said "this decision is final and irrevocable. I will not, under any circumstances, entertain a motion for reconsideration." Later in the trial, the prosecution moves to reconsider, points out the relevant state law, and the judge corrects her mistake. Would Smith have a valid double jeopardy claim? Does *Fong Foo* bear on this question?

Consider one more hypothetical. Suppose *Smith* were a bench trial, not a jury trial; suppose further that, at the trial's conclusion, the trial judge acquitted Smith, after which the prosecution immediately moved for reconsideration. Finally, suppose the judge granted the prosecutor's motion (concluding that she had simply been wrong about the evidence on the length of the gun barrel), vacated her own judgment of acquittal, and entered a new judgment of conviction. Assuming that Massachusetts law clearly authorized such a procedure, would Smith have a valid double jeopardy claim? Should he?

Implied Acquittals. In Green v. United States, 355 U.S. 184 (1957), the defendant was charged with arson and murder in the first degree. At trial, the judge also instructed the jury on the lesser-included offense of murder in the second degree. The jury found Green guilty of arson and second-degree murder, but its verdict was silent on the first-degree murder charge. Green successfully appealed the murder conviction on the ground that the evidence did not support the charge of second-degree murder, and the case was remanded for a new trial. At the second trial, Green was once again prosecuted for first-degree murder; this time, he was convicted, and he received a death sentence.

The Supreme Court held that the second trial on the charge of first-degree murder was a violation of Green's double jeopardy rights:

> Green was in direct peril of being convicted and punished for first degree murder at his first trial. He was forced to run the gantlet once on that charge and the jury refused to convict him. When given the choice between finding him guilty of either first or second degree murder it chose the latter. In this situation the great majority of cases in this country have regarded the jury's verdict as an implicit acquittal on the charge of first degree murder. But the result in this case need not rest alone on the assumption, which we believe legitimate, that the jury for one reason or another acquitted Green of murder in the first degree. For here, the jury was dismissed without returning any express verdict on that charge and without Green's consent. Yet it was given a full opportunity to return a verdict and no extraordinary circumstances appeared which prevented it from doing so. Therefore it seems clear, under established principles of former jeopardy, that Green's jeopardy for first degree murder came to an end when the jury was discharged so that he could not be retried for that offense. In brief, we believe this case can be treated no differently, for purposes of former jeopardy, than if the jury had returned a verdict which expressly read: "We find the defendant not guilty of murder in the first degree but guilty of murder in the second degree."

Id., at 190-191. The Court also held that Green did not waive his double jeopardy rights by appealing his conviction on the charge of second-degree murder.

Protecting Acquittals. An acquittal represents a judgment that the defendant should not be convicted of a particular crime. The most obvious way to undermine that judgment is to prosecute the defendant a second time for the same crime — a course of action barred, quite plainly, by the double jeopardy clause. But suppose the government's behavior is more subtle. Suppose it charges the defendant with another crime that, though different, turns on facts common to the charge for which the defendant was acquitted. If the second charge stands, the government can, in effect, relitigate the case that it lost — the very thing cases like *Fong Foo* purport to forbid. Consider the next case.

ASHE v. SWENSON

Certiorari to the United States Court of Appeals for the Eighth Circuit
397 U.S. 436 (1970)

Mr. Justice Stewart delivered the opinion of the Court.

. . . Sometime in the early hours of the morning of January 10, 1960, six men were engaged in a poker game in the basement of the home of John Gladson at Lee's Summit, Missouri. Suddenly three or four masked men, armed with a shotgun and pistols, broke into the basement and robbed each of the poker players of money and various articles of personal property. The robbers — and it has never been clear whether there were three or four of them — then fled in a car belonging to one of the victims of the robbery. Shortly thereafter the stolen car was discovered in a field, and later that morning three men were arrested by a state trooper while they were walking on a highway not far from where the abandoned car had been found. The petitioner was arrested by another officer some distance away.

The four were subsequently charged with seven separate offenses — the armed robbery of each of the six poker players and the theft of the car. In May 1960 the petitioner went to trial on the charge of robbing Donald Knight, one of the participants in the poker game. At the trial the State called Knight and three of his fellow poker players as prosecution witnesses. Each of them described the circumstances of the holdup and itemized his own individual losses. The proof that an armed robbery had occurred and that personal property had been taken from Knight as well as from each of the others was unassailable. The testimony of the four victims in this regard was consistent both internally and with that of the others. But the State's evidence that the petitioner had been one of the robbers was weak. Two of the witnesses thought that there had been only three robbers altogether, and could not identify the petitioner as one of them. Another of the victims, who was the petitioner's uncle by marriage, said that at the "patrol station" he had positively identified each of the other three men accused of the holdup, but could say only that the petitioner's voice "sounded very much like" that of one of the robbers. The fourth participant in the poker game did identify the petitioner, but only by his "size and height, and his actions."

The cross-examination of these witnesses was brief, and it was aimed primarily at exposing the weakness of their identification testimony. Defense counsel made no attempt to question their testimony regarding the holdup itself or their claims as to their losses. Knight testified without contradiction that the robbers had stolen from him his watch, $250 in cash, and about $500 in checks. His billfold, which had been found by the police in the possession of one of the three other men accused of the robbery, was admitted in evidence. The defense offered no testimony and waived final argument.

The trial judge instructed the jury that if it found that the petitioner was one of the participants in the armed robbery, the theft of "any money" from Knight would sustain a conviction. He also instructed the jury that if the petitioner was one of the robbers, he was guilty under the law even if he had not personally robbed Knight. The jury — though not instructed to elaborate upon its verdict — found the petitioner "not guilty due to insufficient evidence."

Six weeks later the petitioner was brought to trial again, this time for the robbery of another participant in the poker game, a man named Roberts. The petitioner filed a motion to dismiss, based on his previous acquittal. The motion was overruled, and the second trial began. The witnesses were for the most part the same, though this time their testimony was substantially stronger on the issue of the petitioner's identity. For example, two witnesses who at the first trial had been wholly unable to identify the petitioner as one of the robbers, now testified that his features, size, and mannerisms matched those of one of their assailants. Another witness who before had identified the petitioner only by his size and actions now also remembered him by the unusual sound of his voice. The State further refined its case at the second trial by declining to call one of the participants in the poker game whose identification testimony at the first trial had been conspicuously negative. The case went to the jury on instructions virtually identical to those given at the first trial. This time the jury found the petitioner guilty, and he was sentenced to a 35-year term in the state penitentiary. . . .

"Collateral estoppel" is an awkward phrase, but it stands for an extremely important principle in our adversary system of justice. It means simply that when an issue
of ultimate fact has once been determined by a valid and final judgment, that issue
cannot again be litigated between the same parties in any future lawsuit. Although
first developed in civil litigation, collateral estoppel has been an established rule of
federal criminal law at least since this Court's decision more than 50 years ago in
United States v. Oppenheimer, 242 U.S. 85. As Mr. Justice Holmes put the matter in
that case, "It cannot be that the safeguards of the person, so often and so rightly
mentioned with solemn reverence, are less than those that protect from a liability in
debt." 242 U.S., at 87. As a rule of federal law, therefore, "[i]t is much too late to suggest that this principle is not fully applicable to a former judgment in a criminal
case, either because of lack of 'mutuality' or because the judgment may reflect only
a belief that the Government had not met the higher burden of proof exacted in
such cases for the Government's evidence as a whole although not necessarily as to
every link in the chain." United States v. Kramer, 289 F.2d 909, 913.

The federal decisions have made clear that the rule of collateral estoppel in
criminal cases is not to be applied with the hypertechnical and archaic approach of
a 19th century pleading book, but with realism and rationality. Where a previous
judgment of acquittal was based upon a general verdict, as is usually the case, this
approach requires a court to "examine the record of a prior proceeding, taking into
account the pleadings, evidence, charge, and other relevant matter, and conclude
whether a rational jury could have grounded its verdict upon an issue other than
that which the defendant seeks to foreclose from consideration." The inquiry "must
be set in a practical frame and viewed with an eye to all the circumstances of the proceedings." Sealfon v. United States, 332 U.S. 575, 579. Any test more technically
restrictive would, of course, simply amount to a rejection of the rule of collateral
estoppel in criminal proceedings, at least in every case where the first judgment was
based upon a general verdict of acquittal.

Straightforward application of the federal rule to the present case can lead to but
one conclusion. For the record is utterly devoid of any indication that the first jury
could rationally have found that an armed robbery had not occurred, or that Knight
had not been a victim of that robbery. The single rationally conceivable issue in dispute before the jury was whether the petitioner had been one of the robbers. And
the jury by its verdict found that he had not. The federal rule of law, therefore, would
make a second prosecution for the robbery of Roberts wholly impermissible.

The ultimate question to be determined, then, in the light of Benton v. Maryland, [395 U.S. 784],[1] is whether this established rule of federal law is embodied in
the Fifth Amendment guarantee against double jeopardy. We do not hesitate to hold
that it is. For whatever else that constitutional guarantee may embrace, it surely protects a man who has been acquitted from having to "run the gantlet" a second time.
Green v. United States, 355 U.S. 184, 190.

The question is not whether Missouri could validly charge the petitioner with six
separate offenses for the robbery of the six poker players. It is not whether he could
have received a total of six punishments if he had been convicted in a single trial of
robbing the six victims. It is simply whether, after a jury determined by its verdict

---

1. In Benton v. Maryland, 395 U.S. 784 (1969), the Supreme Court held that the Double Jeopardy
Clause applied to the states through the Due Process Clause of the Fourteenth Amendment. — EDS.

that the petitioner was not one of the robbers, the State could constitutionally hale him before a new jury to litigate that issue again.

After the first jury had acquitted the petitioner of robbing Knight, Missouri could certainly not have brought him to trial again upon that charge. Once a jury had determined upon conflicting testimony that there was at least a reasonable doubt that the petitioner was one of the robbers, the State could not present the same or different identification evidence in a second prosecution for the robbery of Knight in the hope that a different jury might find that evidence more convincing. The situation is constitutionally no different here, even though the second trial related to another victim of the same robbery. For the name of the victim, in the circumstances of this case, had no bearing whatever upon the issue of whether the petitioner was one of the robbers.

In this case the State in its brief has frankly conceded that following the petitioner's acquittal, it treated the first trial as no more than a dry run for the second prosecution: "No doubt the prosecutor felt the state had a provable case on the first charge and, when he lost, he did what every good attorney would do — he refined his presentation in light of the turn of events at the first trial." But this is precisely what the constitutional guarantee forbids.

The judgment is reversed, and the case is remanded to the Court of Appeals for the Eighth Circuit for further proceedings consistent with this opinion.

[The concurring opinions of Justice Black, Justice Harlan, and Justice Brennan are omitted.]

MR. CHIEF JUSTICE BURGER, dissenting.

. . . The collateral-estoppel concept . . . ordinarily applies to parties on each side of the litigation who have the same interest as or who are identical with the parties in the initial litigation. Here the complainant in the second trial is not the same as in the first even though the State is a party in *both* cases. . . . [C]ourts that have applied the collateral-estoppel concept to criminal actions would certainly not apply it to both parties, as is true in civil cases, i.e., here, if Ashe had been convicted at the first trial, presumably no court would then hold that he was thereby foreclosed from litigating the identification issue at the second trial.

Perhaps, then, it comes as no surprise to find that the only expressed rationale for the majority's decision is that Ashe has "run the gantlet" once before. This is not a doctrine of the law or legal reasoning but a colorful and graphic phrase, which, as used originally in an opinion of the Court written by Mr. Justice Black, was intended to mean something entirely different. The full phrase is "run the gantlet once *on that charge* . . ." (emphasis added); it is to be found in Green v. United States, 355 U.S. 184, 190 (1957), where no question of multiple crimes against multiple victims was involved. Green, having been found guilty of second-degree murder on a charge of first degree, secured a new trial. This Court held nothing more than that Green, once put in jeopardy — once having "run the gantlet . . . *on that charge*" — of first degree murder, could not be compelled to defend against that charge again on retrial.

Today's step in this area of constitutional law ought not be taken on no more basis than casual reliance on the "gantlet" phrase lifted out of the context in which it was originally used. This is decision by slogan. . . .

NOTES AND QUESTIONS

1. What do you think of Chief Justice Burger's argument? Both the dissent and the majority seem to assume that collateral estoppel couldn't possibly be applied in the *government's* favor. Is that sensible?

In fact, in a few cases, criminal defendants *have* been precluded from litigating an issue resolved against them in an earlier criminal trial. In United States v. Rangel-Perez, 179 F. Supp. 619 (S.D. Cal. 1959), the defendant was charged with being a deported alien found in the United States; the court barred relitigation by the defense of the defendant's alien status, based on an earlier conviction for a similar offense where that element had been proved. In United States v. Levasseur, 699 F. Supp. 965 (D. Mass.), *rev'd* on other grounds, 846 F.2d 786 (1st Cir. 1988), the court barred several defendants from relitigating the legality of a police search, where the defendants had lost a suppression motion in another criminal case based on the same search. At least one state supreme court has gone farther, albeit in dicta: In People v. Ford, 416 P.2d 132 (Cal. 1966), the California Supreme Court stated that it was proper to instruct the jury in a felony murder prosecution that the defendant had already been convicted of the underlying felony. These and other cases are collected in Richard B. Kennelly, Jr., Note, Precluding the Accused: Offensive Collateral Estoppel in Criminal Cases, 80 Va. L. Rev. 1379 (1994).

2. Notwithstanding the cases in the preceding note, the general assumption remains that collateral estoppel in criminal cases is asymmetric — that it bars the government from relitigation but does not apply to the defense. That is a strong disincentive to litigating a crime like the one in *Ashe* serially: "If a prosecutor wins the first trial, she will have to prove everything all over again in a second criminal case; but if she loses on any issue, she loses that issue forever . . . ." Akhil Reed Amar, Double Jeopardy Law Made Simple, 106 Yale L.J. 1807, 1828 (1997). Actually, even without *Ashe*, serial prosecutions would be rare. Recall the discussion of joinder in Chapter 9. In joinder cases, the usual assumption is that prosecutors gain from bringing as many charges (and as many defendants) as possible in *one* proceeding. If that gain is real, the risk of serial prosecution must be small.

3. In Yeager v. United States, 129 S. Ct. 2360 (2009), the Court held that acquittals that otherwise qualify for *Ashe*'s preclusive effect do not become disqualified simply because the jury also became hung on other related counts:

> A hung count is not a "relevant" part of the "record of [the] prior proceeding." See *Ashe*, 397 U.S., at 444. Because a jury speaks only through its verdict, its failure to reach a verdict cannot — by negative implication — yield a piece of information that helps put together the trial puzzle. A mistried count is therefore nothing like the other forms of record material that *Ashe* suggested should be part of the preclusion inquiry. . . . A host of reasons — sharp disagreement, confusion about the issues, exhaustion after a long trial, to name but a few — could work alone or in tandem to cause a jury to hang. To ascribe meaning to a hung count would presume an ability to identify which factor was at play in the jury room. But that is not reasoned analysis; it is guesswork. Such conjecture about possible reasons for a jury's failure to reach a decision should play no part in assessing the legal consequences of a unanimous verdict that the jurors did return.
>
> A contrary conclusion would require speculation into what transpired in the jury room. Courts properly avoid such explorations into the jury's sovereign space, see United States v. Powell, 469 U.S. 57, 66 (1984); Fed. Rule Evid. 606(b), and for good reason. The jury's deliberations are secret and not subject to outside examination. If

there is to be an inquiry into what the jury decided, the "evidence should be confined to the points in controversy on the former trial, to the testimony given by the parties, and to the questions submitted to the jury for their consideration." Packet Co. v. Sickles, 72 U.S. 580, 5 Wall. 580, 593 (1866); see also Vaise v. Delaval, 99 Eng. Rep. 944 (K. B. 1785) (Lord Mansfield, C.J.) (refusing to rely on juror affidavits to impeach a verdict reached by a coin flip); J. Wigmore, Evidence §2349, pp 681-690, and n 2.

    . . . [W]e hold that the consideration of hung counts has no place in the issue-preclusion analysis. Indeed, if it were relevant, the fact that petitioner has already survived one trial should be a factor cutting in favor of, rather than against, applying a double jeopardy bar. To identify what a jury necessarily determined at trial, courts should scrutinize a jury's decisions, not its failures to decide.

Ashe imposes an almost insurmountable burden on a defendant seeking preclusion, in the sense that the defendant must demonstrate that the previous jury's acquittal verdict (which, of course, generally carries no explanation) necessarily was based on the same factual issue that he now seeks to treat as resolved. *Yeager* represents a decision by the Court not to make that burden any more insurmountable than it already is: After *Yeager*, at least the defendant does not *also* have to overcome speculation about why the jury *didn't* reach a verdict on some of the other charges against him.

4. Does *Ashe* affect the way the law ought to construe plea bargains? Many, perhaps most, plea bargains involve an agreement by the defendant to plead guilty in return for an agreement by the government to forgo pressing certain charges. Should the defendant be treated as having been "impliedly acquitted" of the forgone charges? Compare Green v. United States, 355 U.S. 184 (1957) (cited in *Ashe*, and discussed supra, at page 1501). Why or why not? For an insightful analysis of the relationship between double jeopardy doctrine and plea bargaining, especially with respect to defendants who may face future prosecutions for crimes not yet charged, see Daniel C. Richman, Bargaining About Future Jeopardy, 49 Vanderbilt L. Rev. 1181 (1996).

2. Mistrials

OREGON v. KENNEDY

Certiorari to the Court of Appeals of Oregon
456 U.S. 667 (1982)

JUSTICE REHNQUIST delivered the opinion of the Court.

The Oregon Court of Appeals decided that the Double Jeopardy Clause of the Fifth Amendment to the United States Constitution barred respondent's retrial after his first trial ended in a mistrial granted on his own motion. 49 Ore. App. 415, 619 P.2d 948 (1980). The Court of Appeals concluded that retrial was barred because the prosecutorial misconduct that occasioned the mistrial in the first instance amounted to "overreaching." Because that court took an overly expansive view of the application of the Double Jeopardy Clause following a mistrial resulting from the defendant's own motion, we reverse its judgment.

Respondent was charged with the theft of an oriental rug. During his first trial, the State called an expert witness on the subject of Middle Eastern rugs to testify as to the value and the identity of the rug in question. On cross-examination, respondent's attorney apparently attempted to establish bias on the part of the expert witness by asking him whether he had filed a criminal complaint against respondent. The witness eventually acknowledged this fact, but explained that no action had been taken on his complaint. On redirect examination, the prosecutor sought to elicit the reasons why the witness had filed a complaint against respondent, but the trial court sustained a series of objections to this line of inquiry.[1] The following colloquy then ensued:

> *Prosecutor*:   Have you ever done business with the Kennedys?
> *Witness*:   No, I have not.
> *Prosecutor*:   Is that because he is a crook?

The trial court then granted respondent's motion for a mistrial.

When the State later sought to retry respondent, he moved to dismiss the charges because of double jeopardy. After a hearing at which the prosecutor testified, the trial court[2] found as a fact that "it was not the intention of the prosecutor in this case to cause a mistrial." 49 Ore. App., at 418, 619 P.2d, at 949. On the basis of this finding, the trial court held that double jeopardy principles did not bar retrial, and respondent was then tried and convicted.

Respondent then successfully appealed to the Oregon Court of Appeals, which sustained his double jeopardy claim. . . . The Court of Appeals accepted the trial court's finding that it was not the intent of the prosecutor to cause a mistrial. Nevertheless, the court held that retrial was barred because the prosecutor's conduct in this case constituted what it viewed as "overreaching." . . . [T]he Court of Appeals expressed the view that [the prosecutor's] personal attack left respondent with a "Hobson's choice — either to accept a necessarily prejudiced jury, or to move for a mistrial and face the process of being retried at a later time." Id., at 418, 619 P.2d, at 950. . . .

Where the trial is terminated over the objection of the defendant, the classical test for lifting the double jeopardy bar to a second trial is the "manifest necessity" standard first enunciated in Justice Story's opinion for the Court in United States v. Perez, 9 Wheat. 579, 580 (1824). *Perez* dealt with the most common form of "manifest necessity": a mistrial declared by the judge following the jury's declaration that it was unable to reach a verdict. While other situations have been recognized by our cases as meeting the "manifest necessity" standard, the hung jury remains the prototypical example. See, e.g., Arizona v. Washington, 434 U.S. 497, 509 (1978); Illinois v. Somerville, 410 U.S. 458, 463 (1973). The "manifest necessity" standard provides sufficient protection to the defendant's interests in having his case finally decided by the jury first selected while at the same time maintaining "the public's interest in fair trials designed to end in just judgments." Wade v. Hunter, [336 U.S. 684, 689 (1949)].

But in the case of a mistrial declared at the behest of the defendant, quite different principles come into play. Here the defendant himself has elected to terminate the proceedings against him, and the "manifest necessity" standard has no place in

---

1. The Court of Appeals later explained that respondent's "objections were not well taken, and the judge's rulings were probably wrong." 49 Ore. App. 415, 417, 619 P.2d 948, 949 (1980).

2. These proceedings were not conducted by the same trial judge who presided over respondent's initial trial.

the application of the Double Jeopardy Clause. United States v. Dinitz, [424 U.S. 600, 607-610 (1976)]. . . .

Our cases, however, have indicated that even where the defendant moves for a mistrial, there is a narrow exception to the rule that the Double Jeopardy Clause is no bar to retrial. The circumstances under which respondent's first trial was terminated require us to delineate the bounds of that exception more fully than we have in previous cases.

Since one of the principal threads making up the protection embodied in the Double Jeopardy Clause is the right of the defendant to have his trial completed before the first jury empaneled to try him, it may be wondered as a matter of original inquiry why the defendant's election to terminate the first trial by his own motion should not be deemed a renunciation of that right for all purposes. We have recognized, however, that there would be great difficulty in applying such a rule where the prosecutor's actions giving rise to the motion for mistrial were done "in order to goad the [defendant] into requesting a mistrial." United States v. Dinitz, supra, at 611. In such a case, the defendant's valued right to complete his trial before the first jury would be a hollow shell if the inevitable motion for mistrial were held to prevent a later invocation of the bar of double jeopardy in all circumstances. But the precise phrasing of the circumstances which *will* allow a defendant to interpose the defense of double jeopardy . . . have been stated with less than crystal clarity in our cases. . . . In United States v. Dinitz, 424 U.S., at 611, we said:

> The Double Jeopardy Clause does protect a defendant against governmental actions intended to provoke mistrial requests and thereby to subject defendants to the substantial burdens imposed by multiple prosecutions.

. . . But immediately following the quoted language we went on to say:

> [The Double Jeopardy Clause] bars retrials where "bad-faith conduct by judge or prosecutor," threatens the "[harassment]" of an accused by successive prosecutions or declaration of a mistrial so as to afford the prosecution a more favorable opportunity to convict" the defendant. United States v. Dinitz, 424 U.S., at 611 (citation omitted).

The language just quoted would seem to broaden the test from one of *intent* to provoke a motion for a mistrial to a more generalized standard of "bad faith conduct" or "harassment" on the part of the judge or prosecutor. . . .

The difficulty with the more general standards which would permit a broader exception than one merely based on intent is that they offer virtually no standards for their application. Every act on the part of a rational prosecutor during a trial is designed to "prejudice" the defendant by placing before the judge or jury evidence leading to a finding of his guilt. Given the complexity of the rules of evidence, it will be a rare trial of any complexity in which some proffered evidence by the prosecutor or by the defendant's attorney will not be found objectionable by the trial court. Most such objections are undoubtedly curable by simply refusing to allow the proffered evidence to be admitted, or in the case of a particular line of inquiry taken by counsel with a witness, by an admonition to desist from a particular line of inquiry.

More serious infractions on the part of the prosecutor may provoke a motion for mistrial on the part of the defendant, and may in the view of the trial court warrant the granting of such a motion. The "overreaching" standard applied by the court below . . . , however, would add another classification of prosecutorial error, one requiring dismissal of the indictment, but without supplying any standard by which to assess that error.

By contrast, a standard that examines the intent of the prosecutor, though certainly not entirely free from practical difficulties, is a manageable standard to apply. It merely calls for the court to make a finding of fact. Inferring the existence or non-existence of intent from objective facts and circumstances is a familiar process in our criminal justice system. When it is remembered that resolution of double jeopardy questions by state trial courts are reviewable not only within the state court system, but in the federal court system on habeas corpus as well, the desirability of an easily applied principle is apparent.

Prosecutorial conduct that might be viewed as harassment or overreaching, even if sufficient to justify a mistrial on defendant's motion, therefore, does not bar retrial absent intent on the part of the prosecutor to subvert the protections afforded by the Double Jeopardy Clause. A defendant's motion for a mistrial constitutes "a deliberate election on his part to forgo his valued right to have his guilt or innocence determined before the first trier of fact." United States v. Scott, 437 U.S. 82, 93 (1978). Where prosecutorial error even of a degree sufficient to warrant a mistrial has occurred, "[the] important consideration, for purposes of the Double Jeopardy Clause, is that the defendant retain primary control over the course to be followed in the event of such error." United States v. Dinitz, supra, at 609. Only where the governmental conduct in question is intended to "goad" the defendant into moving for a mistrial may a defendant raise the bar of double jeopardy to a second trial after having succeeded in aborting the first on his own motion.

Were we to embrace the broad and somewhat amorphous standard adopted by the Oregon Court of Appeals, we are not sure that criminal defendants as a class would be aided. Knowing that the granting of the defendant's motion for mistrial would all but inevitably bring with it an attempt to bar a second trial on grounds of double jeopardy, the judge presiding over the first trial might well be more loath to grant a defendant's motion for mistrial. If a mistrial were in fact warranted under the applicable law, of course, the defendant could in many instances successfully appeal a judgment of conviction on the same grounds that he urged a mistrial, and the Double Jeopardy Clause would present no bar to retrial. But some of the advantages secured to him by the Double Jeopardy Clause — the freedom from extended anxiety, and the necessity to confront the government's case only once — would be to a large extent lost in the process of trial to verdict, reversal on appeal, and subsequent retrial. . . .

. . . We do not by this opinion lay down a flat rule that where a defendant in a criminal trial successfully moves for a mistrial, he may not thereafter invoke the bar of double jeopardy against a second trial. But we do hold that the circumstances under which such a defendant may invoke the bar of double jeopardy in a second effort to try him are limited to those cases in which the conduct giving rise to the successful motion for a mistrial was intended to provoke the defendant into moving for a mistrial.

Since the Oregon trial court found, and the Oregon Court of Appeals accepted, that the prosecutorial conduct culminating in the termination of the first trial in this case was not so intended by the prosecutor, that is the end of the matter for purposes of the Double Jeopardy Clause of the Fifth Amendment to the United States Constitution. . . .

[A concurring opinion by Justice Powell and opinions concurring in the judgment by Justice Brennan and Justice Stevens are omitted.]

NOTES AND QUESTIONS

1. What is the proper standard to adopt in a case like *Kennedy*? Here as elsewhere, intentional misconduct can be very hard to establish. Perhaps, then, *Kennedy* comes close in practice to a rule that mistrials sought by the defense always permit retrial. That seems insufficiently protective of the defendant's interest in being tried by *this* jury. But what is the alternative? Is this a matter best left to the judgment of trial judges?

2. Why does the defendant have such a strong interest in being tried by a particular jury (or a particular judge) in the first place? As long as the jury that convicts or acquits him is properly selected and impartial, why does it matter which jury it is? Perhaps it doesn't. The problem in mistrial cases may be not protecting the defendant's interest in a particular decision maker, but guarding against both sides' efforts to relitigate jury selection, by prompting mistrial motions when the selection process has gone badly. Does *Kennedy* adequately guard against that problem?

3. *Kennedy* deals with mistrials prompted by prosecutorial conduct, but the issue can arise from defense conduct as well. In Arizona v. Washington, 434 U.S. 497 (1978), the defendant was convicted of murder, but his conviction was overturned on appeal on the ground that the government had improperly withheld exculpatory evidence. In his opening statement at the defendant's second trial, defense counsel stated to the jury:

> You will hear testimony that notwithstanding the fact that we had a trial in May of 1971 in this matter, that the prosecutor hid those statements and . . . didn't give those statements at all, hid them.
>
> You will hear that that evidence was suppressed and hidden by the prosecutor in that case. You will hear that that evidence was purposely withheld. You will hear that because of the misconduct of the County Attorney at that time and because he withheld evidence, that the Supreme Court of Arizona granted a new trial in this case.

Id., at 499. After opening statements were completed, the prosecutor sought and was granted a mistrial. The Supreme Court held that retrial was permissible — that the mistrial had satisfied the "manifest necessity" standard — though the Court stressed that the case was a close one:

> We recognize that the extent of the possible bias cannot be measured, and that the District Court was quite correct in believing that some trial judges might have proceeded with the trial after giving the jury appropriate cautionary instructions. In a strict, literal sense, the mistrial was not "necessary." Nevertheless, the overriding interest in the evenhanded administration of justice requires that we accord the highest degree of respect to the trial judge's evaluation of the likelihood that the impartiality of one or more jurors may have been affected by the improper comment.

Id., at 511. Is *Washington* consistent with *Kennedy*?

4. In the "prototypical" scenario described in *Kennedy*, where the trial judge finds "manifest necessity" and declares a mistrial due to a "hung" or deadlocked jury,

under what standard should that decision be reviewed? In Renico v. Lett, 130 S. Ct. 1855 (2010), the Court made clear that the standard is both flexible and highly deferential:

> We have expressly declined to require the "mechanical application" of any "rigid formula" when trial judges decide whether jury deadlock warrants a mistrial. . . . We have also explicitly held that a trial judge declaring a mistrial is not required to make explicit findings of "manifest necessity" nor to "articulate on the record all the factors which informed the deliberate exercise of his discretion." [Arizona v.] Washington, [434 U.S. 497,] 517 [(1978)]. And we have never required a trial judge, before declaring a mistrial based on jury deadlock, to force the jury to deliberate for a minimum period of time, to question the jurors individually, to consult with (or obtain the consent of) either the prosecutor or defense counsel, to issue a supplemental jury instruction, or to consider any other means of breaking the impasse. In 1981, then-Justice Rehnquist noted that this Court had never "overturned a trial court's declaration of a mistrial after a jury was unable to reach a verdict on the ground that the 'manifest necessity' standard had not been met." Winston v. Moore, 452 U.S. 944, 947 (opinion dissenting from denial of certiorari). The same remains true today, nearly 30 years later.

Id., at 1863-1864.

B. "For the Same Offence"

The Double Jeopardy Clause bars prosecuting or punishing someone twice for a single crime. What that clause means depends critically on what counts as a single crime — or, to use the constitutional language, "the same offence." The issue arises in three settings: (1) The defendant is acquitted, and the government tries to prosecute him again for the same crime. (2) The defendant is convicted, and the government tries to prosecute him again for the same crime. (3) The government tries to punish the defendant twice for the same crime in a single proceeding.

Most of this section is devoted to the second scenario, but we begin with a few comments on the first and the third. The first scenario, acquittal followed by reprosecution, is governed by Ashe v. Swenson, 397 U.S. 436 (1970). In practice, it rarely arises — perhaps because the government feels politically constrained not to challenge jury verdicts. The third scenario likewise produces little litigation, because the relevant double jeopardy rule is so lax. In "multiple punishment" cases — the government brings two charges against a defendant in one proceeding, and the defendant claims the two charges are the same — double jeopardy is a rule of legislative intent. As the Supreme Court put it in Missouri v. Hunter, 459 U.S. 359, 366 (1983): "With respect to cumulative sentences imposed in a single trial, the Double Jeopardy Clause does no more than prevent the sentencing court from prescribing greater punishment than the legislature intended." The defendant in *Hunter* was charged, in the same proceeding, with robbing a supermarket and with "armed criminal action" (he used a gun in the robbery). The Missouri legislature created the latter crime in order to raise the sentence of anyone who used a dangerous weapon to commit a crime: precisely what happened in *Hunter*. Consequently, the Court found no double jeopardy violation. That is the usual bottom line in "multiple punishment" cases. See Anne Bowen Poulin, Double Jeopardy and Multiple Punishment: Cutting the Gordian Knot, 77 U. Colo. L. Rev. 595 (2006).

The doctrine is both more demanding and much more complicated in the second scenario: A defendant is prosecuted and convicted, and the government wants to prosecute him again for (the defendant claims) "the same offence." Consider the following simple hypothetical: Suppose the defendant assaults the victim with a knife. The government prosecutes and convicts the defendant of simple assault; the defendant is sentenced to six months in the local jail. Then, the same prosecutor's office charges the defendant with assault with a deadly weapon, based on the same incident; the sentencing range for that crime is two to five years in the state penitentiary. The defendant challenges the second charge on double jeopardy grounds; as we shall see, the defendant's claim succeeds on these facts. Before taking up the doctrine, however, it helps to think about two questions: (1) Why does the government want to prosecute a defendant again for the same crime, after having already convicted him once? (2) What interest of the defendant does the law of double jeopardy protect in this situation?

There are several reasons why a prosecutor's office might wish to proceed in this way. The prosecutor might be unhappy with the sentence the judge imposed in the first proceeding. The prosecutor may not have correctly understood the facts before the first trial; given a better understanding now, she may believe the more severe charge is appropriate. The first charge may have been a bureaucratic error: Office policy required a more severe charge, but the assistant district attorney handling the case misunderstood the policy. All these possibilities (and there are others) are variations on a single theme: The government wishes to relitigate the defendant's sentence.

Of course, the defendant has an obvious interest in *not* relitigating his sentence. A large part of that interest is captured by the term "repose": At some point, the defendant needs to know that the incident in question is closed — that he has received his punishment, and there will be no more. Double jeopardy law protects this interest in repose with a constitutional finality rule. Another possibility is more substantive: Nancy King has suggested that *successive* prosecution tends to produce excessive punishment — that, for example, two assault sentences in the hypothetical above will be harsher than a single sentence for the more severe assault charge. See Nancy J. King, Portioning Punishment: Constitutional Limits on Successive and Excessive Penalties, 144 U. Pa. L. Rev. 101 (1995). If King is right, double jeopardy serves as an adjunct to the Eighth Amendment's ban on "cruel and unusual punishment."

The double jeopardy case law does not embrace any of these theories, or any other theory for that matter. For the most part, double jeopardy doctrine is fairly stable (though that has not always been the case). But the doctrine is not well theorized; courts agree on the correct outcomes, but pay surprisingly little attention to the reasons behind those outcomes. As you read the cases that follow, ask yourself what theory best explains the doctrine — and what theory makes the most sense.

NOTES ON THE RISE, FALL, AND RISE OF THE *BLOCKBURGER* TEST

1. The defendant in Blockburger v. United States, 284 U.S. 299 (1932), was charged under the old Harrison Act, the first major federal drug legislation. The Harrison Act didn't ban drug sales altogether, but it did impose strict licensing and

tax requirements that, in practice, functioned as a prohibition. Blockburger was charged with selling morphine outside the original stamped package in violation of the Act, and also with selling the drug without a written order from the buyer, which violated another provision of the Act. Blockburger argued that the two charges were "the same" for double jeopardy purposes.

The Supreme Court disagreed. Writing for a unanimous Court, Justice Sutherland concluded:

> The applicable rule is that where the same act or transaction constitutes a violation of two distinct statutory provisions, the test to be applied to determine whether there are two offenses or only one, is whether each provision requires proof of a fact which the other does not.

Id., at 304. Applying that formula to Blockburger's claim, the Court concluded that the two crimes were different. The first required proof that the morphine was outside the original stamped package, while the second didn't. The second crime required proof that the sale was not pursuant to a buyer's written order; the first crime didn't. Consequently, Blockburger could be prosecuted for both — in the same proceeding or in two separate trials.

Blockburger turns double jeopardy law into an exercise in high-school algebra. Imagine a defendant charged and convicted of a crime with elements A, B, C, and D. Now imagine that the prosecutor wants to bring a new charge against this same defendant, arising out of the same incident. The new crime has elements B, C, D, and E. Under *Blockburger*, the new charge is permissible: The first crime required proof of element A and the second one did not, while the second required proof of element E, which was outside the scope of the first crime. If the government had instead brought a second charge with elements B, C, and D only, that charge *would* be barred by double jeopardy: One of the two crimes has a unique element (A) but the other one doesn't; B, C, and D are common to both crimes. This conclusion is important: It means that lesser-included offenses are barred by the prosecution of greater offenses — and vice versa.

So, under *Blockburger*, if a defendant is convicted of manslaughter, he may not then be prosecuted for murdering the same victim. If the defendant is convicted of assault with a deadly weapon, he may not then be prosecuted for simple assault (again assuming the victim and date of the crime remain the same). But the same defendant *may* be charged with, say, assault with a deadly weapon and assault with intent to kill in separate proceedings — even though the time, place, victim, and perpetrator are all the same. The first crime requires proof that a deadly weapon was used and the second doesn't (one can intend to kill without using a deadly weapon); the second crime requires proof of intent to kill and the first doesn't (one can use a deadly weapon without intending to kill).

Notice three features of this exercise. First, the double jeopardy issue can be decided on the face of the charging document — no evidence need be taken; it does not matter how the government intends to prove the second charge. The question is resolved based on the elements of the two crimes. Second, the size of the overlap between the two crimes makes no difference. In the first algebraic example, three of the four elements of each crime were common to both crimes, and both crimes happened at the same time and were committed by the same person. It could easily be the case that both crimes were proved by precisely the same evidence. Under *Block-burger*, the government still wins. Third, the sentencing consequences of the two crimes are irrelevant. Successive prosecution and multiple punishment cases arise in the first place because prosecutors wish to impose a different sentence than a single charge would yield. One would think that double jeopardy law would therefore pay some attention to sentencing: It is, after all, the point of the exercise. Under *Blockburger*, though, sentencing consequences are beside the point. Double jeopardy is a matter of form, not substance.

One more aspect of *Blockburger* deserves mention: The defendant's claim was multiple punishment, not successive prosecution; the two drug charges were both brought in the same case. Most of the cases discussed in the notes that follow involve defendants who were prosecuted twice, and who claim that the second prosecution was barred by the first. It is worth remembering that throughout the relevant time period, most courts applied *Blockburger*'s test to multiple punishment cases — where the two charges are brought in a single prosecution — as well as to successive prosecution cases. There is an important difference, however: Under Missouri v. Hunter, 459 U.S. 359 (1983), *Blockburger* is nothing more than a rule of statutory interpretation in the multiple punishment context. In the successive prosecution cases, *Blockburger* is a constitutional requirement.

2. *Blockburger*'s algebraic approach governed the "same offence" issue for the next several decades. For most of that time, the issue did not attract much litigation, because the Double Jeopardy Clause only applied to the federal government, and most criminal prosecutions happened in state courts. Benton v. Maryland, 395 U.S. 784 (1969), held that the ban on double jeopardy applied to state cases, because that ban was one of the fundamental liberties incorporated into the Due Process Clause in the Fourteenth Amendment. After *Benton*, *Blockburger*'s boundaries were frequently tested — and the Court's commitment to the algebraic approach wavered, as the following cases show.

3. One of the most important tests came in Brown v. Ohio, 432 U.S. 161 (1977). The facts in *Brown* were as follows:

> On November 29, 1973, the petitioner, Nathaniel Brown, stole a 1965 Chevrolet from a parking lot in East Cleveland, Ohio. Nine days later, on December 8, 1973, Brown was caught driving the car in Wickliffe, Ohio. The Wickliffe police charged him with "joyriding" — taking or operating the car without the owner's consent — in violation of Ohio Rev. Code Ann. §4549.04(D). . . . Brown pleaded guilty to this charge and was sentenced to 30 days in jail and a $1,000 fine.
>
> Upon his release from jail on January 8, 1974, Brown was returned to East Cleveland to face further charges, and on February 5 he was indicted by the Cuyahoga County grand jury. The indictment was in two counts, the first charging the theft of the car "on or about the 29th day of November 1973," in violation of Ohio Rev. Code Ann. §4549.04(A) (1973), and the second charging joyriding on the same date in violation of §4549.04(D).

Id., at 162-163. The joyriding prohibition read: "No person shall purposely take, operate, or keep any motor vehicle without the consent of its owner." The auto theft statute was simpler: "No person shall steal any motor vehicle." According to the Ohio Court of Appeals, auto theft was joyriding plus the intent to permanently deprive the owner of his car. Thus, joyriding was a lesser-included version of auto theft, meaning the two crimes were "the same offence" under *Blockburger*. The state nevertheless claimed they *weren't* the same offense as far as Brown was concerned, because the first joyriding charge was based on Brown's behavior on December 8, 1973, while the auto theft charge was based on his conduct on November 29, 1973 — the day Brown took the car. The different dates meant that each crime required proof of a fact that the other didn't.

The Supreme Court rejected the state's argument:

> After correctly holding that joyriding and auto theft are the same offense under the Double Jeopardy Clause, the Ohio Court of Appeals nevertheless concluded that Nathaniel Brown could be convicted of both crimes because the charges against him focused on different parts of his 9-day joyride. We hold a different view. The Double Jeopardy Clause is not such a fragile guarantee that prosecutors can avoid its limitations by the simple expedient of dividing a single crime into a series of temporal or spatial units. The applicable Ohio statutes, as written and as construed in this case, make the theft and operation of a single car a single offense. Although the Wickliffe and East Cleveland authorities may have had different perspectives on Brown's offense, it was still only one offense under Ohio law. Accordingly, the specification of different dates in the two charges on which Brown was convicted cannot alter the fact that he was placed twice in jeopardy for the same offense in violation of the Fifth and Fourteenth Amendments.

Id., at 169-170. Justice Powell, author of the *Brown* majority opinion, dropped a footnote qualifying the language just quoted:

> We would have a different case if the Ohio Legislature had provided that joyriding is a separate offense for each day in which a motor vehicle is operated without the owner's consent. We also would have a different case if in sustaining Brown's second conviction the Ohio courts had construed the joyriding statute to have that effect. . . . .

Id., at 169, n. 8. Doesn't this mean that prosecutors *can* avoid double jeopardy "by the simple expedient of dividing a single crime into a series of temporal . . . units" — as long as the state legislature drafts or the state appellate courts construe the relevant statutes to do just that?

4. Harris v. Oklahoma, 433 U.S. 682 (1977) (per curiam), was decided two weeks after *Brown*. The Court's opinion was brief, but important:

> A clerk in a Tulsa, Oklahoma grocery store was shot and killed by a companion of petitioner in the course of a robbery of the store by the two men. Petitioner was convicted of felony murder in Oklahoma State court. The opinion of the Oklahoma Court of Criminal Appeals in this case states that "[i]n a felony murder case, the proof of the underlying felony [here robbery with firearms] is needed to prove the intent necessary for a felony murder conviction." 555 P.2d 76, 80-81 (1976). Petitioner nevertheless was thereafter brought to trial and convicted on a separate information charging the robbery with firearms, after denial of his motion to dismiss on the ground that this prosecution violated the Double Jeopardy Clause of the Fifth Amendment because he had been already convicted of the offense in the felony-murder trial. The Oklahoma Court of Criminal Appeals affirmed.
>
> When, as here, conviction of a greater crime, murder, cannot be had without conviction of the lesser crime, robbery with firearms, the Double Jeopardy Clause bars

prosecution for the lesser crime after conviction of the greater one.* In re Nielsen, 131 U.S. 176 (1889); cf. Brown v. Ohio, 432 U.S. 161 (1977). "[A] person [who] has been tried and convicted for a crime which has various incidents included in it, . . . cannot be a second time tried for one of those incidents without being twice put in jeopardy for the same offence." In re Nielsen, supra, at 188.

Id., at 682-683.

At first blush, *Harris* seems squarely at odds with *Blockburger*. Felony murder does not require proof of robbery, and armed robbery does not require proof that the defendant caused the victim's death, so the two crimes cannot be "the same" for double jeopardy purposes. But perhaps the cases are consistent after all. Felony murder is a crime that incorporates a set of other crimes. It could be expressed as a list: murder during the course of a robbery, murder during the course of a rape, murder during the course of a kidnapping, and so on. When deciding double jeopardy cases under *Blockburger*, perhaps such crimes should be considered *as if the legislature had enacted the relevant list* rather than a single criminal statute. *Harris* then becomes an easy case — for the defense. After all, armed robbery is plainly a lesser-included offense relative to murder during the course of an armed robbery.

As the cases in the notes that follow indicate, there are a number of crimes like felony murder — crimes that incorporate a list of other crimes; sometimes the list is specified, sometimes not. Should all such criminal statutes be read the way the Court read the felony murder law in *Harris*? If not, how are courts supposed to know when to follow *Harris* and when to ignore it?

5. *Harris* had disturbing implications for enterprise crimes like RICO (Racketeer Influenced and Corrupt Organizations Act, 18 U.S.C. §§1961-1968) and CCE (the "continuing criminal enterprise" statute, 21 U.S.C. §848). (Both of the statutes just cited are federal, but similar statutes exist in many state codes.) These statutes have two goals. First, as the label suggests, they aim to define criminal enterprises and punish those who operate them. The second goal is related: to punish career criminals by identifying various "predicate crimes" that such criminals typically commit. RICO is the classic example of an enterprise crime. The most commonly used provision in the RICO statute covers anyone who operates a criminal enterprise "through a pattern of racketeering activity." 18 U.S.C. §1962(c). "Pattern" basically means two or more acts of "racketeering activity," which the statute defines by giving a long list of predicate crimes — ranging from drugs to violent crimes to white-collar offenses. Similarly, the CCE statute seeks to punish "drug kingpins." The statute does this by listing qualifying drug crimes; anyone who commits such crimes is, by definition, a "drug kingpin," and may be punished for a CCE violation. As these examples suggest, enterprise crimes bear some similarity to status offenses: a famous article by Judge (then Professor) Gerard Lynch labeled RICO "the crime of being a criminal." Gerard E. Lynch, RICO: The Crime of Being a Criminal, Parts I and II, 87 Colum. L. Rev. 661 (1987). Lynch's title is apt because of the huge role predicate crimes play in RICO (or CCE) analysis.

Often, defendants prosecuted for enterprise crimes have already been charged and convicted for one or more of the predicate crimes on which the government relies for the enterprise charge. If enterprise crimes are treated as felony murder

---

* The State conceded in its response to the petition for certiorari that "in the Murder case, it was necessary for all the ingredients of the underlying felony of Robbery with Firearms to be proved. . . ."

was treated in *Harris*, those prosecutions would all be invalid. *Harris* held that felony murder statutes should be read as lists: murder during the course of a rape, murder during the course of a robbery, and so forth. Enterprise crimes could plausibly be read the same way: a continuing enterprise that combined drug crimes A, B, and C; a continuing enterprise that combined drug crimes B, C, and D; a continuing enterprise that combined drug crimes A, B, and D; and so on. On that construction, any one predicate crime would be a lesser-included offense (just as armed robbery was in *Harris*), and prosecution for the greater offense — the enterprise crime — would be barred.

The Supreme Court found that result unacceptable. The defendant in Garrett v. United States, 471 U.S. 773 (1985), was charged and convicted of importing marijuana; the charge involved a large shipment that Garrett helped unload from a ship at Neah Bay, Washington. Two months after that conviction, Garrett was charged in a federal CCE indictment in Florida; the Washington marijuana importation was one of three predicate crimes charged in the Florida indictment. The Court found no double jeopardy bar to the second charge. Then-Justice Rehnquist's majority opinion noted that there was a "good deal of difference" between the "classic" lesser-included-offense situation and the one presented in *Garrett*, because — unlike joyriding and automobile theft, where each moment of criminal conduct simultaneously violates both statutes — CCE defines an ongoing crime; Garrett's CCE offense was not complete when he imported marijuana in Washington. (In fact, as the Court noted, the CCE offense was still not complete when the indictment was returned for the Washington crime.) As Rehnquist artfully put it: "One who insists that the music stop and the piper be paid at a particular point must at least have stopped dancing himself before he may seek such an accounting." Id., at 790.

The Court's analysis in *Garrett* was consistent with *Blockburger* itself: The CCE statute did not require proof of marijuana importation — that was just one of a list of predicate crimes — and marijuana importation obviously did not require proof of a "continuing criminal enterprise." But *Garrett* could not easily be squared with *Harris*. At the least, *Garrett* stands for the proposition that *Harris* does not apply to enterprise crimes. The upshot is that such crimes almost never raise serious double jeopardy problems.

That last sentence applies to conspiracy prosecutions as well. Criminal defendants are often charged with both a particular substantive crime and with conspiracy to commit that crime, sometimes in a single prosecution and sometimes in separate prosecutions. In United States v. Felix, 503 U.S. 378 (1992), the Court held that "a substantive crime and a conspiracy to commit that crime are not the 'same offence' for double jeopardy purposes." The majority opinion in *Felix*, again authored by Chief Justice Rehnquist, explained that holding as follows:

> In a related context, we recently cautioned against the "ready transposition of the 'lesser included offense' principles of double jeopardy from the classically simple situation presented in Brown v. Ohio to the multilayered conduct, both as to time and to place, involved in [CCE prosecutions]." [Garrett v. United States, 441 U.S.,] at 789. The great majority of conspiracy prosecutions involve similar allegations of multi-layered conduct as to time and place; the conspiracy charge against Felix is a perfect example. Reliance on the lesser included offense analysis, however useful in the context of a "single course of conduct," is therefore much less helpful in analyzing subsequent conspiracy prosecutions that are supported by previously prosecuted overt acts, just as it

falls short in examining CCE offenses that are based on previously prosecuted predicate acts. Id., at 788-789.

503 U.S., at 389-390. As the passage just quoted indicates, the *Felix* Court cited *Garrett* extensively.

6. Even before *Felix*, the *Blockburger* test seemed unstable. Cases like *Brown*, *Harris*, and *Garrett* suggested that the Court was looking for a better approach to "same offence" cases. So it did not come as a complete surprise when, in Grady v. Corbin, 495 U.S. 508 (1990), the Court decided simply to do away with *Blockburger*.

Grady arose out of a miscommunication. Corbin was a drunk driver; he drove his car across the double yellow line of a state highway in upstate New York, and struck two cars traveling in the other direction. The driver of one of those two cars was killed, and a passenger in that same car was seriously injured. A blood alcohol test showed that Corbin had nearly twice the legal limit of alcohol in his blood. On these facts, the local district attorney's office could be expected to seek an indictment for manslaughter and felony assault — which shortly happened. In the meantime, though, Corbin was served with two traffic tickets, charging him with driving while intoxicated and "failing to keep right of the median." Three weeks after the accident, Corbin pled guilty to those charges — with no one from the District Attorney's office present. Three weeks after the guilty plea, Corbin received his sentence: a $350 fine and a six-month revocation of his driver's license. An Assistant District Attorney did show up for Corbin's sentencing, but she had not read the file, was not aware that anyone had been killed or injured in the accident, and did not know that a grand jury would soon be investigating the relevant events.

Two months later, Corbin was indicted for manslaughter, reckless assault, and driving while intoxicated. The prosecution "filed a bill of particulars that identified the three reckless or negligent acts on which it would rely to prove the homicide and assault charges":

> (1) operating a motor vehicle on a public highway in an intoxicated condition, (2) failing to keep right of the median, and (3) driving approximately 45 to 50 miles per Comprehensive hour in heavy rain, "which was a speed too fast for the weather and road conditions then pending." App. 20. Respondent moved to dismiss the indictment on . . . double jeopardy grounds.

Id., at 514.

On a straightforward application of *Blockburger*, Corbin seemed to have a weak case. Manslaughter and assault did not require proof that Corbin had failed to keep his car on the right side of the road, and the traffic charge did not require proof of injury or death. The New York Court of Appeals nevertheless found Corbin's double jeopardy claim valid — and, by a 5-4 vote in an opinion by Justice Brennan, the Supreme Court agreed:

> [A] subsequent prosecution must do more than merely survive the Blockburger test. . . . [T]he Double Jeopardy Clause bars any subsequent prosecution in which the government, to establish an essential element of an offense charged in that prosecution, will prove conduct that constitutes an offense for which the defendant has already

been prosecuted.[11] This is not an "actual evidence" or "same evidence" test. The critical inquiry is what conduct the State will prove, not the evidence the State will use to prove that conduct. As we have held, the presentation of specific evidence in one trial does not forever prevent the government from introducing that same evidence in a subsequent proceeding. See Dowling v. United States, 493 U.S. 342 (1990). On the other hand, a State cannot avoid the dictates of the Double Jeopardy Clause merely by altering in successive prosecutions the evidence offered to prove the same conduct. For example, if two bystanders had witnessed Corbin's accident, it would make no difference to our double jeopardy analysis if the State called one witness to testify in the first trial that Corbin's vehicle crossed the median (or if nobody testified in the first trial because Corbin, as he did, pleaded guilty) and called the other witness to testify to the same conduct in the second trial.

495 U.S., at 521-522. Having articulated a new constitutional test for successive prosecutions, Justice Brennan then proceeded to apply that test to the facts of Corbin's case. Because of the filing of the bill of particulars, it was relatively easy for the Court to determine exactly what the state intended to prove in order to obtain a conviction on the manslaughter and assault charges — and to conclude that those charges, under the state's current theory of the case, were barred by double jeopardy.

Justice Brennan's opinion noted that Corbin could be prosecuted for manslaughter and assault by using a different theory of the case: "This holding would not bar a subsequent prosecution on the homicide and assault charges if the bill of particulars revealed that the State would not rely on proving the conduct for which Corbin had already been convicted (i.e., if the State relied solely on Corbin's driving too fast in heavy rain to establish recklessness or negligence)." Justice Brennan stressed that the Court was *not* adopting a "same transaction" test — i.e., a requirement that all crimes related to a given transaction or incident be charged in a single prosecution. Still, *Grady* was a sharp departure from previous double jeopardy cases — and a major expansion of the meaning of "the same offence."[2]

Justice Scalia wrote the chief dissent in *Grady*. (He was joined by Chief Justice Rehnquist and Justice Kennedy; Justice O'Connor dissented separately.) After defending the *Blockburger* test, Scalia opined that the effect of the Court's ruling in *Grady* would be to force the states into adopting the "same transaction" approach — because otherwise, they would be barred from using, in a later prosecution, potentially persuasive evidence of substantive crimes that were proved in a prior prosecution, even if those earlier crimes were not elements of the later crime. Justice Scalia also noted some practical difficulties in applying Justice Brennan's

---

11. Similarly, if in the course of securing a conviction for one offense the State necessarily has proved the conduct comprising all of the elements of another offense not yet prosecuted (a "component offense"), the Double Jeopardy Clause would bar subsequent prosecution of the component offense. See Harris v. Oklahoma, 433 U.S. 682 (1977) ("When, as here, conviction of a greater crime, murder, cannot be had without conviction of the lesser crime, robbery with firearms, the Double Jeopardy Clause bars prosecution for the lesser crime after conviction of the greater one") (footnote omitted); cf. *Brown*, 432 U.S., at 168 (noting that it is irrelevant for the purposes of the Double Jeopardy Clause whether the conviction of the greater offense precedes the conviction of the lesser offense or vice versa).

2. Technically, Justice Brennan's opinion in *Grady* did not overrule *Blockburger* — rather, the Court added a new double jeopardy requirement in addition to the *Blockburger* test. The effect, however, was the same as if *Blockburger* had been overruled. On the one hand, in any case in which the state satisfies *Grady*'s requirements, *Blockburger* will be satisfied as well. On the other hand, there are a great many cases that satisfy *Blockburger* but flunk *Grady*. The upshot is that, as long as *Grady* was good law, *Blockburger* did not work.

new rule — especially the bar on introduction, during a second prosecution, of evidence that would "prove conduct that constitutes an offense for which the defendant has already been prosecuted":

> Apart from the lack of rational basis for this latter limitation, I am greatly perplexed (as will be the unfortunate trial court judges who must apply today's rootless decision) as to what precisely it means. It is not at all apparent how a court is to go about deciding whether the evidence that has been introduced (or that will be introduced) at the second trial "proves conduct" that constitutes an offense for which the defendant has already been prosecuted. Is the judge in the second trial supposed to pretend that he is the judge in the first one, and to let the second trial proceed only if the evidence would not be enough to go to the jury on the earlier charge? Or (as the language of the Court's test more readily suggests) is the judge in the second trial supposed to decide on his own whether the evidence before him really "proves" the earlier charge (perhaps beyond a reasonable doubt)? Consider application of the Court's new rule in the unusually simple circumstances of the present case: Suppose that, in the trial upon remand, the prosecution's evidence shows, among other things, that when the vehicles came to rest after the collision they were located on what was, for the defendant's vehicle, the wrong side of the road. The prosecution also produces a witness who testifies that prior to the collision the defendant's vehicle was "weaving back and forth" — *without* saying, however, that it was weaving back and forth over the center line. Is this enough to meet today's requirement of "proving" the offense of operating a vehicle on the wrong side of the road? If not, suppose in addition that defense counsel asks the witness on cross-examination, "When you said the defendant's vehicle was 'weaving back and forth,' did you mean weaving back and forth across the center line?" — to which the witness replies "yes." Will this self-inflicted wound count for purposes of determining what the prosecution has "proved"? If so, can the prosecution then seek to impeach its own witness by showing that his recollection of the vehicle's crossing the center line was inaccurate? Or can it at least introduce another witness to establish that fact? There are many questions here, and the answers to all of them are ridiculous. Whatever line is selected as the criterion of "proving" the prior offense — enough evidence to go to the jury, more likely than not, or beyond a reasonable doubt — the prosecutor in the second trial will presumably seek to introduce as much evidence as he can without crossing that line; and the defense attorney will presumably seek to provoke the prosecutor into (or assist him in) proving the defendant guilty of the earlier crime. This delicious role reversal, discovered to have been mandated by the Double Jeopardy Clause lo these 200 years, makes for high comedy but inferior justice. . . . Even if we had no constitutional text and no prior case law to rely upon, rejection of today's opinion is adequately supported by the modest desire to protect our criminal legal system from ridicule.

Id., at 540-542 (Scalia, J., dissenting).

The opinions in *Grady* contain a great deal of discussion of the merits of different double jeopardy rules. But there is very little discussion of the justice of Corbin's claim. Suppose the state had been allowed to proceed with the manslaughter and assault charges. Would Corbin have been the victim of an injustice? Certainly not by reference to the results in factually similar cases. The only way any defendant could walk away with a modest fine on facts like those in *Grady* was through the kind of bureaucratic mistake that characterized Corbin's first "prosecution." Why should Corbin benefit from the government's error? Corbin seems more the beneficiary of official ineptitude than the victim of government oppression.

Consider another angle on the case. Suppose Corbin was indeed prosecuted twice — once for the traffic offenses, once for manslaughter and assault; suppose further that that course of action is indeed unjust. How can the injustice best be remedied? The Court assumes the only possible remedy is to dismiss the indictment for manslaughter and assault. But there is another possibility: Why not give Corbin his $350 back, rescind the license revocation, and let the prosecution for manslaughter and assault go forward? In other words, why not eliminate punishment for the traffic offense, rather than for manslaughter and assault? The answer is that, traditionally, double jeopardy law does not work that way; once one "jeopardy" is complete, the only available remedy is dismissal of charges that produce a second "jeopardy" for the same crime. Still, tradition is not much of an answer. Grady v. Corbin may be a case in which the defendant's interest in being punished once — not twice — for his crime *and* the state's interest in punishing homicides could have been protected. But that could only happen if the courts focused attention not just on the scope of the double jeopardy right, but on the proper remedy for its violation.

7. In the three years following *Grady*, the Supreme Court saw two personnel changes. Justice Brennan retired and was replaced by Justice Souter; and Justice Marshall retired and was replaced by Justice Thomas. In 1993, the Court revisited *Grady* — only this time, Justice Thomas lined up with the *Grady* dissenters. The *Blockburger* test rose from the ashes.

The case was United States v. Dixon, 509 U.S. 688 (1993). *Dixon* was actually two companion cases — Alvin Dixon and Michael Foster were both convicted of criminal contempt; in both cases, the government proceeded to indict the defendants for the same conduct that formed the basis of the contempt charges. Foster's case required the Court either to apply *Grady* or overrule it; the Court chose the latter path, and reinstated the *Blockburger* test as governing double jeopardy law. Dixon's case raised questions about the nature and meaning of the *Blockburger* test. Though the Court dealt with the two cases in a single set of opinions, they are best understood separately. We excerpt the Court's discussion of Dixon's case below. But first, consider Foster's double jeopardy claim.

Michael Foster was an abusive husband; his repeated assaults led his wife, Ana Foster, to obtain a civil protection order (CPO) against him. That order required that Foster not "molest, assault, or in any manner threaten or physically abuse" Ana. After repeatedly violating the CPO, Foster was charged with criminal contempt — the elements of which were the same as the crime of simple assault plus knowing violation of the CPO. He was convicted, and received a total sentence of 600 days of incarceration. Later, Foster was indicted for, inter alia, "threatening to injure another" and assault with intent to kill.

All nine Justices agreed that, on these facts, Foster did not have a valid double jeopardy claim under *Blockburger*. Eight of the nine agreed that Foster *did* have a valid claim under Grady v. Corbin. (Justice Blackmun disagreed: He thought there was no double jeopardy violation even under *Grady*, because of the special status of contempt proceedings.) Thus, Foster's case squarely posed the question whether *Grady* should remain good law. Justice Scalia wrote for a five-vote majority — the four *Grady* dissenters plus Justice Thomas:

> . . . We have concluded . . . that *Grady* must be overruled. Unlike *Blockburger* analysis, whose definition of what prevents two crimes from being the "same offence" has deep historical roots and has been accepted in numerous precedents of this Court,

Grady lacks constitutional roots. The "same-conduct" rule it announced is wholly inconsistent with earlier Supreme Court precedent and with the clear common-law understanding of double jeopardy. . . .

. . . *Grady* was not only wrong in principle; it has already proved unstable in application. Less than two years after it came down, in United States v. Felix, 503 U.S. 378 (1992), we were forced to recognize a large exception to it. There we concluded that a subsequent prosecution for conspiracy to manufacture, possess, and distribute methamphetamine was not barred by a previous conviction for attempt to manufacture the same substance. We offered as a justification for avoiding a "literal" (i.e., faithful) reading of *Grady* "longstanding authority" to the effect that prosecution for conspiracy is not precluded by prior prosecution for the substantive offense. *Felix*, supra, at 388-391. Of course the very existence of such a large and longstanding "exception" to the *Grady* rule gave cause for concern that the rule was not an accurate expression of the law. . . .

. . . [W]e think it time to acknowledge what is now, three years after *Grady*, compellingly clear: The case was a mistake. We do not lightly reconsider a precedent, but, because *Grady* contradicted an "unbroken line of decisions," contained "less than accurate" historical analysis, and has produced "confusion," we do so here. Solorio v. United States, 483 U.S. 435, 439, 442, 450 (1987). . . .

Dixon, 509 U.S., at 703-711. Justice Souter was *Grady*'s chief defender:

. . . [W]hile the government may punish a person separately for each conviction of at least as many different offenses as meet the *Blockburger* test, we have long held that it must sometimes bring its prosecutions for these offenses together. If a separate prosecution were permitted for every offense arising out of the same conduct, the government could manipulate the definitions of offenses, creating fine distinctions among them and permitting a zealous prosecutor to try a person again and again for essentially the same criminal conduct. . . .

An example will show why this [position is correct]. Assume three crimes: robbery with a firearm, robbery in a dwelling, and simple robbery. The elements of the three crimes are the same, except that robbery with a firearm has the element that a firearm be used in the commission of the robbery while the other two crimes do not, and robbery in a dwelling has the element that the robbery occur in a dwelling while the other two crimes do not.

If a person committed a robbery in a dwelling with a firearm and was prosecuted for simple robbery, all agree he could not be prosecuted subsequently for either of the greater offenses of robbery with a firearm or robbery in a dwelling. Under the lens of *Blockburger*, however, if that same person were prosecuted first for robbery with a firearm, he could be prosecuted subsequently for robbery in a dwelling, even though he could not subsequently be prosecuted on the basis of that same robbery for simple robbery. This is true simply because neither of the crimes, robbery with a firearm and robbery in a dwelling, is either identical to or a lesser-included offense of the other. But since the purpose of the Double Jeopardy Clause's protection against successive prosecutions is to prevent repeated trials in which a defendant will be forced to defend against the same charge again and again, . . . it should be irrelevant that the second prosecution would require the defendant to defend himself not only from the charge that he committed the robbery, but also from the charge of some additional fact, in this case, that the scene of the crime was a dwelling. If, instead, protection against successive prosecution were as limited as it would be by *Blockburger* alone, the doctrine would be as striking for its anomalies as for the limited protection it would provide. . . .

Id., at 747-749 (Souter, J., concurring in the judgment in part and dissenting in part). Justice Scalia responded to Souter's argument as follows:

The centerpiece of Justice Souter's analysis is an appealing theory of a "successive prosecution" strand of the Double Jeopardy Clause that has a different meaning from its supposed "successive punishment" strand. We have often noted that the Clause serves the function of preventing both successive punishment and successive prosecution, but there is no authority, except *Grady*, for the proposition that it has different meanings in the two contexts. That is perhaps because it is embarrassing to assert that the single term "same offence" (the words of the Fifth Amendment at issue here) has two different meanings — that what is the same offense is yet not the same offense. Justice Souter provides no authority whatsoever (and we are aware of none) for the bald assertion that "we have long held that [the government] must sometimes bring its prosecutions for [separate] offenses together." The collateral-estoppel effect attributed to the Double Jeopardy Clause, see Ashe v. Swenson, 397 U.S. 436 (1970), may bar a later prosecution for a separate offense where the Government has lost an earlier prosecution involving the same facts. But this does not establish that the Government "must . . . bring its prosecutions . . . together." It is entirely free to bring them separately, and can win convictions in both. Of course the collateral-estoppel issue is not raised in this case. . . .

Id., at 704-705.

Who has the better of this debate?

8. Given the Court's decision to abandon *Grady*, *Blockburger* is once again binding law. The precise boundaries of the *Blockburger* test are now a matter of great doctrinal importance. Consider what *Dixon* says about *that* issue.

UNITED STATES v. DIXON

Certiorari to the District of Columbia Court of Appeals
509 U.S. 688 (1993)

JUSTICE SCALIA announced the judgment of the Court and delivered the opinion of the Court with respect to Parts I, II, and IV. . . .

I

Respondent Alvin Dixon was arrested for second-degree murder and was released on bond. Consistent with the District of Columbia's bail law authorizing the judicial officer to impose any condition that "will reasonably assure the appearance of the person for trial or the safety of any other person or the community," D.C. Code Ann. §23-1321(a) (1989), Dixon's release form specified that he was not to commit "any criminal offense," and warned that any violation of the conditions of release would subject him "to revocation of release, an order of detention, and prosecution for contempt of court." See §23-1329(a) (authorizing those sanctions).

While awaiting trial, Dixon was arrested and indicted for possession of cocaine with intent to distribute, in violation of D.C. Code Ann. §33-541(a)(1) (1988). The court issued an order requiring Dixon to show cause why he should not be held in contempt or have the terms of his pretrial release modified. At the show-cause hearing, four police officers testified to facts surrounding the alleged drug offense; Dixon's counsel cross-examined these witnesses and introduced other evidence. The court concluded that the Government had established "beyond a reasonable doubt that [Dixon] was in possession of drugs and that those drugs were possessed with the intent to distribute." 598 A.2d 724, 728 (D.C. 1991). The court therefore found Dixon guilty of criminal contempt under §23-1329(c), which allows contempt sanctions after expedited proceedings without a jury and "in accordance with principles applicable to proceedings for criminal contempt." For his contempt, Dixon was sentenced to 180 days in jail. D.C. Code §23-1329(c) (maximum penalty of six months' imprisonment and $1000 fine). He later moved to dismiss the cocaine indictment on double jeopardy grounds; the trial court granted the motion. . . .

The Government appealed the double jeopardy ruling in *Dixon*. . . . The District of Columbia Court of Appeals . . . , relying on our recent decision in Grady v. Corbin, 495 U.S. 508 (1990), ruled that [the second prosecution for cocaine possession was] barred by the Double Jeopardy Clause. 598 A.2d, at 725. In its petition for certiorari, the Government presented the sole question "whether the Double Jeopardy Clause bars prosecution of a defendant on substantive criminal charges based upon the same conduct for which he previously has been held in criminal contempt of court." . . .

II

[Justice Scalia began by reviewing the history of the contempt power, noting that the specific kinds of contempt orders issued herein would have been impossible at common law, or in the nineteenth century American judicial system.]

We have held that constitutional protections for criminal defendants other than the double jeopardy provision apply in nonsummary criminal contempt prosecutions just as they do in other criminal prosecutions. See, e.g., Gompers v. Bucks Stove & Range Co., 221 U.S. 418, 444 (1911) (presumption of innocence, proof beyond a reasonable doubt, and guarantee against self-incrimination); Cooke v. United States, 267 U.S. 517, 537 (1925) (notice of charges, assistance of counsel, and right to present a defense); In re Oliver, 333 U.S. 257, 278 (1948) (public trial). We think it obvious, and today hold, that the protection of the Double Jeopardy Clause likewise attaches.

In both the multiple punishment and multiple prosecution contexts, this Court has concluded that where the two offenses for which the defendant is punished or tried cannot survive the "same-elements" test, the double jeopardy bar applies. See, e.g., Brown v. Ohio, 432 U.S. 161, 168-169 (1977); Blockburger v. United States, 284 U.S. 299, 304 (1932) (multiple punishment); Gavieres v. United States, 220 U.S. 338, 342 (1911) (successive prosecutions). The same-elements test, sometimes referred to as the "Blockburger" test, inquires whether each offense contains an element not contained in the other; if not, they are the "same offence" and double jeopardy bars additional punishment and successive prosecution. In a case such as [State v. Yancy, 4 N.C. 133 (1814)], for example, in which the contempt prosecution was for disruption of judicial business, the same-elements test would not bar subsequent prosecution for the criminal assault that was part of the disruption, because the contempt offense did not require the element of criminal conduct, and the criminal offense did not require the element of disrupting judicial business. . . .

III

. . . The statute applicable in Dixon's contempt prosecution provides that "[a] person who has been conditionally released . . . and who has violated a condition of release shall be subject to . . . prosecution for contempt of court." §23-1329(a). Obviously, Dixon could not commit an "offence" under this provision until an order setting out conditions was issued. The statute by itself imposes no legal obligation on anyone. Dixon's cocaine possession, although an offense under [the D.C. Code], was not an offense under §23-1329 until a judge incorporated the statutory drug offense into his release order.

In this situation, in which the contempt sanction is imposed for violating the order through commission of the incorporated drug offense, the later attempt to prosecute Dixon for the drug offense resembles the situation that produced our judgment of double jeopardy in Harris v. Oklahoma, 433 U.S. 682 (1977) (per curiam). There we held that a subsequent prosecution for robbery with a firearm was barred by the Double Jeopardy Clause, because the defendant had already been tried for felony murder based on the same underlying felony. We have described our terse per curiam in *Harris* as standing for the proposition that, for double jeopardy purposes, "the crime generally described as felony murder" is not "a separate offense distinct from its various elements." Illinois v. Vitale, 447 U.S. 410, 420-421 (1980). So too here. . . . The Dixon court order incorporated the entire governing criminal code in the same manner as the *Harris* felony-murder statute incorporated the several enumerated felonies. Here, as in *Harris*, the underlying substantive criminal offense is "a species of lesser-included offense." *Vitale*, supra, at 420. . . .

. . . Because Dixon's drug offense did not include any element not contained in his previous contempt offense, his subsequent prosecution violates the Double Jeopardy Clause . . .

IV

[This part of Justice Scalia's opinion, joined by a majority of the Justices, discussed Michael Foster's claims. The Court concluded that those claims failed under the *Blockburger* test, but would succeed under Grady v. Corbin. The Court then went on to explain why *Grady* should be overruled.]

CHIEF JUSTICE REHNQUIST, with whom JUSTICE O'CONNOR and JUSTICE THOMAS join, concurring in part and dissenting in part.

. . . I do not join Part III of Justice Scalia's opinion because I think that none of the criminal prosecutions in this case were barred under *Blockburger*. I must then confront the expanded version of double jeopardy embodied in *Grady*. For the reasons set forth in the *Grady* dissent (Scalia, J., dissenting), . . . I, too, think that *Grady* must be overruled. I . . . write separately to express my disagreement with Justice Scalia's application of Blockburger in Part III.

In my view, *Blockburger*'s same-elements test requires us to focus not on the terms of the particular court orders involved, but on the elements of contempt of court in the ordinary sense. Relying on Harris v. Oklahoma, 433 U.S. 682 (1977), a three-paragraph per curiam in an unargued case, Justice Scalia concludes otherwise today, and thus incorrectly finds in Part III of his opinion that the subsequent prosecution[] of Dixon for drug distribution . . . violated the Double Jeopardy Clause. In so doing, Justice Scalia rejects the traditional view — shared by every federal court of appeals and state supreme court that addressed the issue prior to *Grady* — that, as a general matter, double jeopardy does not bar a subsequent prosecution based on conduct for which a defendant has been held in criminal contempt. I cannot subscribe to a reading of *Harris* that upsets this previously well-settled principle of law. Because the generic crime of contempt of court has different elements than the substantive criminal charges in this case, I believe that they are separate offenses under *Blockburger*. I would therefore limit *Harris* to the context in which it arose: where the crimes in question are analogous to greater and lesser-included offenses. The crimes at issue here bear no such resemblance. . . .

Close inspection of the crimes at issue in *Harris* reveals, moreover, that our decision in that case was not a departure from *Blockburger*'s focus on the statutory elements of the offenses charged. In *Harris*, we held that a conviction for felony murder based on a killing in the course of an armed robbery foreclosed a subsequent prosecution for robbery with a firearm. Though the felony-murder statute in *Harris* did not require proof of armed robbery, it did include as an element proof that the defendant was engaged in the commission of some felony. We construed this generic reference to some felony as incorporating the statutory elements of the various felonies upon which a felony-murder conviction could rest. The criminal contempt provision involved here, by contrast, contains no such generic reference which by definition incorporates the statutory elements of assault or drug distribution.

Unless we are to accept the extraordinary view that the three-paragraph per curiam in *Harris* was intended to overrule sub silentio our previous decisions that looked to the statutory elements of the offenses charged in applying *Blockburger*, we are bound to conclude . . . that the ratio decidendi of our *Harris* decision was that the two crimes there were akin to greater and lesser included offenses. The crimes at issue here, however, cannot be viewed as greater and lesser included offenses, either intuitively or logically. A crime such as possession with intent to distribute cocaine is a serious felony that cannot easily be conceived of as a lesser included offense of criminal contempt, a relatively petty offense as applied to the conduct in this case. See D.C. Code Ann. §33-541(a)(2)(A) (Supp. 1992) (the maximum sentence for possession with intent to distribute cocaine is 15 years in prison). Indeed, to say that criminal contempt is an aggravated form of that offense defies common sense. . . .

But there is a more fundamental reason why the offenses in this case are not analogous to greater and lesser included offenses. A lesser included offense is defined as one that is "necessarily included" within the statutory elements of another offense. See Fed. Rule Crim. Proc. 31(c). Taking the facts of *Harris* as an example, a defendant who commits armed robbery necessarily has satisfied one of the statutory elements of felony murder. The same cannot be said, of course, about this case: A defendant who is guilty of possession with intent to distribute cocaine or of assault has not necessarily satisfied any statutory element of criminal contempt. Nor, for that matter, can it be said that a defendant who is held in criminal contempt has necessarily satisfied any element of those substantive crimes. In short, the offenses for which Dixon [was] prosecuted in this case cannot be analogized to greater and lesser included offenses; hence, they are separate and distinct for double jeopardy purposes.

The following analogy, raised by the Government at oral argument, helps illustrate the absurd results that Justice Scalia's *Harris/Blockburger* analysis could in theory produce. Suppose that the offense in question is failure to comply with a lawful order of a police officer, see, e.g., Ind. Code §9-21-8-1 (Supp. 1992), and that the police officer's order was, "Don't shoot that man." Under Justice Scalia's flawed reading of *Harris*, the elements of the offense of failure to obey a police officer's lawful order would include, for purposes of *Blockburger*'s same-elements test, the elements of, perhaps, murder or manslaughter, in effect converting those felonies into a lesser included offense of the crime of failure to comply with a lawful order of a police officer. . . .

JUSTICE WHITE, with whom JUSTICE STEVENS joins, concurring in the judgment in part and dissenting in part.

. . . [M]y view is that the subsequent prosecutions in both *Dixon* and *Foster* were impermissible as to *all* counts. I reach this conclusion because the offenses at issue in the contempt proceedings were either identical to, or lesser included offenses of, those charged in the subsequent prosecutions. . . .

The contempt orders in *Foster* and *Dixon* referred in one case to the District's laws regarding assaults and threats, and, in the other, to the criminal code in its entirety. The prohibitions imposed by the court orders, in other words, duplicated those already in place by virtue of the criminal statutes. Aside from differences in the sanctions inflicted, the distinction between being punished for violation of the criminal laws and being punished for violation of the court orders, therefore, is simply this: Whereas in the former case "the entire population" is subject to prosecution, in the latter such authority extends only to "those particular persons whose legal obligations result from their earlier participation in proceedings before the court." [Young v. United States ex rel. Vuitton et Fils, 481 U.S. 787, 800, n. 10 (1987).] But the *offenses* that are to be sanctioned in either proceeding must be similar, since the contempt orders incorporated, in full or in part, the criminal code.

Thus, in this case, the offense for which Dixon was held in contempt was possession with intent to distribute drugs. Since he previously had been indicted for precisely the same offense, the double jeopardy bar should apply. . . .[8]

JUSTICE SOUTER, with whom JUSTICE STEVENS joins, concurring in the judgment in part and dissenting in part.

. . . I would . . . apply our successive prosecution decisions . . . to conclude that the prosecutions below were barred by the Double Jeopardy Clause. Dixon was prosecuted for violating a court order to "[r]efrain from committing any criminal offense." The contempt prosecution proved beyond a reasonable doubt that he had possessed cocaine with intent to distribute it. His prosecution, therefore, for possession with intent to distribute cocaine based on the same incident is barred. It is of course true that the elements of the two offenses can be treated as different. In the contempt conviction, the government had to prove knowledge of the court order as well as Dixon's commission of some criminal offense. In the subsequent prosecution, the government would have to prove possession of cocaine with intent to distribute. In any event, because the government has already prosecuted Dixon for the

8. Therefore, I obviously disagree with the Chief Justice's Blockburger v. United States, 284 U.S. 299 (1932), analysis which would require overruling not only Grady v. Corbin, 495 U.S. 508 (1990), but, as Justice Scalia explains, Harris v. Oklahoma, 433 U.S. 682 (1977), as well. At the very least, where conviction of the crime of contempt cannot be had without conviction of a statutory crime forbidden by court order, the Double Jeopardy Clause bars prosecution for the latter after acquittal or conviction of the former.

possession of cocaine at issue here, Dixon cannot be tried for that incident a second time. . . .

[The opinion of Justice Blackmun, concurring in part and dissenting in part, is omitted.]

NOTES AND QUESTIONS

1. Where does the law stand after *Dixon*? The answer is complicated, because *Dixon* produced two different, overlapping majorities. First, one majority of the Justices decided that Dixon's two crimes — contempt of court and possession of cocaine — were "the same." Justices Scalia and Kennedy see those crimes as "the same" because the contempt charge, in their view, is analogous to the felony murder law in Harris v. Oklahoma, 433 U.S. 682 (1977). Justices White and Stevens agree; notice footnote 8 in Justice White's opinion. That amounts to four votes for the *Blockburger* test coupled with a broad reading of *Harris*. Justice Souter, the fifth vote to bar Dixon's drug charge, has a different view: He sees the contempt charge and the cocaine charge as "the same" because they were based on the same conduct and would be proved by the same evidence — the approach mandated by Grady v. Corbin, 495 U.S. 508 (1990), which *Dixon* overrules.

That is the first *Dixon* majority. Then there is the second *Dixon* majority, the one that overruled *Grady*. Justices Scalia and Kennedy belong to that majority, as do the Chief Justice and Justices O'Connor and Thomas. These five Justices believe *Blockburger* and not *Grady* defines the meaning of "same offence." But they do not agree about what *Blockburger* means, nor about whether Dixon should win. Scalia and Kennedy take a broad view of *Harris* and vote to strike down Dixon's drug charge; Rehnquist, O'Connor, and Thomas would limit *Harris* to its facts and would permit the drug charge to go forward. As this confusing head count indicates, the key to the disagreement is the legal status of *Harris*. The Court has given that case a narrow reading in Garrett v. United States, 471 U.S. 773 (1985), and United States v. Felix, 503 U.S. 378 (1992) — the cases that apply double jeopardy analysis to enterprise crimes and conspiracy cases. Now, a four-Justice plurality has given that case a broad reading in *Dixon*. What the proper reading of *Harris* is today is anyone's guess.

2. Professor Erin Murphy notes that *Dixon* seems to have had little effect on the growing popularity, at least in the states, of contempt charges as a means to enforce conformity with legal and social norms:

Although *Dixon* might have stalled the use of contempt charges in state courts, that does not seem to be the case. In ruling that double jeopardy precluded only charges based on identical elements, the Court left open a fairly wide swath of terrain. One of the defendants discussed in *Dixon*, for instance, could not be tried for simple assault after having been convicted for contempt on that basis, but he could still be tried for the more serious offenses of assault with intent to kill and several counts of threats. Moreover, in many cases, bringing contempt charges may be appealing as a means of inducing plea bargaining with regard to other substantive counts.

For instance, domestic violence prosecutors have increasingly used contempt charges in order to secure convictions in otherwise difficult to prosecute cases. . . .

But contempt prosecutions are not confined only to the realm of domestic violence. Perhaps in response to the widespread formation of pretrial services agencies across the nation, conditions of release such as drug testing, job or educational training, and rehabilitative programs have become standard parts of release. In some jurisdictions, imposition of a "stay away" from a block or area has become a regular bail term.

And, of course, as release conditions have proliferated, so too have reported violations of those conditions. In 2000, for instance, 32% of released felony defendants in the seventy-five most populous counties committed some misconduct while in a release status, including failure to appear, arrest for a new offense, or [another violation of release conditions]. And, in general, the use of contempt as a means of enforcing such release conditions has become quite common.

Erin Murphy, Manufacturing Crime: Process, Pretext, and Criminal Justice, 97 Georgetown L.J. 1435 (2009); see also Jeannie Suk, Criminal Law Comes Home, 116 Yale L.J. 2 (2006) (discussing prevalence of protective orders, and associated criminal contempt prosecutions, as a means of addressing the problem of domestic violence).

3. *Dixon* involves successive prosecution claims. What rules apply to multiple punishment claims? Recall that in Missouri v. Hunter, 459 U.S. 359 (1983), the Court held that the Double Jeopardy Clause does not limit legislatures' ability to punish a defendant more than once for the same crime in the same proceeding. In multiple punishment cases, *Hunter* holds, double jeopardy law functions as a rule of statutory interpretation: We presume the legislature does not intend double punishment, but it is only a presumption. Then, in *Dixon*, Justice Scalia (in the portion of his opinion that was joined by a majority) writes that "there is no authority, except *Grady*, for the proposition that" the Double Jeopardy Clause means something different in multiple punishment cases than in successive prosecution cases. "[I]t is embarrassing to assert that the single term 'same offence' . . . has two different meanings — that what is the same offense is yet not the same offense." 509 U.S., at 704. It sounds like *Hunter* and *Dixon* are at odds.

The Court addressed this issue in a backhanded way in Rutledge v. United States, 517 U.S. 292 (1996). Rutledge was charged with conspiracy to distribute cocaine; he was also charged with operating a continuing criminal enterprise (CCE). The "enterprise" was cocaine distribution. One of the elements of the CCE charge was that Rutledge acted "in concert with" others — i.e., that Rutledge conspired with others. The Court held that that made CCE and conspiracy greater- and lesser-included offenses under *Blockburger*. The Court stated the relevant double jeopardy rule as follows: "[W]e presume that where two statutory provisions proscribe the 'same offense,' a legislature does not intend to impose two punishments for that offense." Id., at 297 (citation omitted). So "same offence" means the same thing in multiple punishment and successive prosecution cases; the governing test is *Blockburger*. But that test operates as a rule of statutory construction in multiple punishment cases. It is a constitutional requirement in successive prosecution cases.

4. What is the point of the *Blockburger* test? If the goal is to limit excessive punishment, the law surely fails: No attention is paid in these cases to the fairness (or not) of the aggregate sentence the defendants receive. If the goal is to guarantee finality, so that when a defendant once faces prosecution for a criminal incident, he can know that he will not face it again (at least not for that same incident), again the law fails. *Blockburger* makes charge-stacking easy. Most criminal codes have multiple versions of every major crime; those different prohibitions generally share most elements, but each has at least one unique element. Thus, a single criminal incident can easily yield a half-dozen criminal charges, either in one prosecution or spread across multiple prosecutions. *Blockburger* does nothing to prevent that. None of this

is to say that defendants never prevail under *Blockburger*. Clearly, they do. But when they do, it is usually a sign that the prosecution made a foolish mistake, charged crimes *A* and *B* when they should have charged crimes *B* and *C* instead — or that one part of the district attorney's office failed to inform another part of the same office about a pending case: the scenario that produced Grady v. Corbin.

In short, "same offence" doctrine is not merely an instance of placing form over substance, though it is surely that. The larger problem with the doctrine is that the form bears no relation to the substance. Charge-stacking and prosecutorial harassment may be large problems in America's criminal justice system. If they are, there is no reason to believe that double jeopardy law does anything to make those problems smaller.

NOTES ON SENTENCING AND THE MEANING OF "THE SAME OFFENCE"

1. The traditional view about sentencing and double jeopardy was that the latter had nothing to do with the former. Double jeopardy applied to prosecutions, not to sentences. Therefore, relitigation of issues resolved in previous sentencing proceedings was fine — regardless of what the issue was or who won in the earlier proceeding. Neither *Blockburger* nor Ashe v. Swenson nor any of the doctrines surrounding double jeopardy's "acquittal rule" applied to sentencing.

That was the traditional rule. That rule began to bend in Bullington v. Missouri, 451 U.S. 430 (1981). Bullington was convicted of capital murder. At the close of the sentencing proceeding that followed, the jury determined that he should be sentenced to life in prison rather than death. Bullington's conviction was later overturned due to an error in jury selection, and he was again tried for capital murder. Bullington objected that he had been "acquitted" of the death penalty, and consequently could not be placed in jeopardy of receiving it again. By a 5-4 vote, the Supreme Court agreed. In several more recent cases, the Court has explained the *Bullington* rule. "[A]n acquittal on the merits by the sole decision-maker in the [capital sentencing] proceeding is final and bars retrial on the same charge." Arizona v. Rumsey, 467 U.S. 203, 211 (1984). A capital murder defendant wins an "acquittal on the merits" with respect to the death penalty when the sentencer (judge or jury) "decides that the prosecution has not proved its case that the death penalty is appropriate." Poland v. Arizona, 476 U.S. 147, 155 (1986) (emphasis deleted). Absent an "acquittal on the merits" — if, for example, the sentencing jury hangs, see Sattazahn v. Pennsylvania, 537 U.S. 101 (2003) — relitigation of the death penalty is permissible.

These rules apply to the death penalty. Until recently, it was taken for granted that noncapital sentencing did not implicate the double jeopardy guarantee. The defendant in Witte v. United States, 515 U.S. 389 (1995), was charged and convicted of conspiring to distribute marijuana. Under the Federal Sentencing Guidelines, Witte's sentence was raised considerably based on other, uncharged drug violations, including a conspiracy to import a large quantity of cocaine. (His ultimate sentence on the marijuana charge was 12 years in prison.) While Witte was serving his sentence, another federal grand jury indicted him for importing that same large quantity of cocaine. Naturally, Witte claimed that this chain of events violated double jeopardy, since he had already been punished for the cocaine

violation. The Supreme Court decided otherwise — the Court held that his entire
12-year sentence constituted "punishment" only for the marijuana charge. Since
the cocaine charge was plainly not "the same" as the marijuana charge, the second
prosecution was permissible.

2. Then came the Court's decisions in Apprendi v. New Jersey, 530 U.S. 466
(2000) and, more recently, Blakely v. Washington, 542 U.S. 296 (2004), and United
States v. Booker, 543 U.S. 220 (2005). *Apprendi* held that any fact that increases the
defendant's sentence beyond the statutory maximum functions as an element of an
aggravated crime, and must therefore be found beyond a reasonable doubt by a
jury. *Blakely* and *Booker* held that the *Apprendi* rule applies as well to any fact that is
necessary in order to increase the defendant's maximum lawful sentence under a
particular jurisdiction's sentencing guidelines (*Booker* involved the Federal
Sentencing Guidelines, while *Blakely* dealt with the guidelines in the state of
Washington).

If *Apprendi*, *Blakely*, and *Booker* hold that certain sentencing facts are to be
treated as elements of crimes for purposes of the Sixth Amendment's jury trial
guarantee and the Due Process Clause's standard of proof beyond a reasonable
doubt, are they also elements of crimes for purposes of the Fifth Amendment's ban
on double jeopardy? If so, the *Blockburger* test will be even more forgiving than it
was before. *Apprendi/Blakely/Booker* means that ordinary crimes in guidelines
jurisdictions now have many more "elements" than they once did. The *Blockburger*
test says that any two crimes are different as long as each has at least one "element"
that the other lacks. In a world where crimes have not three or four elements but a
dozen or more, it will presumably be easier to find those unique elements — and it
was already fairly easy.

The story may be the same in capital murder cases — or it may be different. The
Court has not yet spoken, but Justice Scalia — *Blakely*'s author — offered his view of
the matter in a plurality opinion in Sattazahn v. Pennsylvania, 537 U.S. 101 (2003):

. . . Our decision in Apprendi v. New Jersey, 530 U.S. 466 (2000), clarified what constitutes an "element" of an offense for purposes of the Sixth Amendment's jury-trial
guarantee. Put simply, if the existence of any fact (other than a prior conviction)
increases the maximum punishment that may be imposed on a defendant, that
fact — no matter how the State labels it — constitutes an element, and must be found
by a jury beyond a reasonable doubt.

Just last Term we recognized the import of *Apprendi* in the context of capital-
sentencing proceedings. In Ring v. Arizona, [536 U.S. 584] (2002), we held that aggravating circumstances that make a defendant eligible for the death penalty "operate as
'the functional equivalent of an element of a *greater offense*.'" Id., at [608] (emphasis
added). That is to say, for purposes of the Sixth Amendment's jury-trial guarantee, the
underlying offense of "murder" is a distinct, lesser included offense of "murder plus
one or more aggravating circumstances": Whereas the former exposes a defendant to
a maximum penalty of life imprisonment, the latter increases the maximum permissible sentence to death. Accordingly, we held that the Sixth Amendment requires that
a jury, and not a judge, find the existence of any aggravating circumstances, and that
they be found, not by a mere preponderance of the evidence, but beyond a reasonable
doubt. We can think of no principled reason to distinguish, in this context, between
what constitutes an offense for purposes of the Sixth Amendment's jury-trial guarantee and what constitutes an "offence" for purposes of the Fifth Amendment's Double
Jeopardy Clause. . . . If a jury unanimously concludes that a State has failed to meet its

burden of proving the existence of one or more aggravating circumstances, double-jeopardy protections attach to that "acquittal" on the offense of "murder plus aggravating circumstance(s)." . . .

For purposes of the Double Jeopardy Clause, then, "first-degree murder" under Pennsylvania law — the offense of which petitioner was convicted during the guilt phase of his proceedings — is properly understood to be a lesser included offense of "first-degree murder plus aggravating circumstance(s)." Thus, if petitioner's first sentencing jury had unanimously concluded that Pennsylvania failed to prove any aggravating circumstances, that conclusion would operate as an "acquittal" of the greater offense — which would bar Pennsylvania from retrying petitioner on that greater offense (and thus, from seeking the death penalty) on retrial.

Id., at 111-112. Notice that Justice Scalia characterizes the crime of capital murder as "murder plus one or more aggravating circumstances." There is another way that crime might be defined for double jeopardy purposes, consistent with *Apprendi*: murder plus the *particular* aggravating circumstance that the prosecution seeks to prove in each particular case. Suppose, as is common, that a given state's capital murder statute says that the prosecution must prove at least one aggravating factor in order for the defendant to receive the death penalty; suppose further that the statute lists a dozen different aggravating factors. Can the state now prosecute a single capital murder a dozen times, as long as it alleges a different aggravating factor in each prosecution? Stay tuned.

C. Double Jeopardy and the "Dual Sovereignty" Doctrine

HEATH v. ALABAMA

Certiorari to the Supreme Court of Alabama
474 U.S. 82 (1985)

JUSTICE O'CONNOR delivered the opinion of the Court.

The question before the Court is whether the Double Jeopardy Clause of the Fifth Amendment bars Alabama from trying petitioner for the capital offense of murder during a kidnaping after Georgia has convicted him of murder based on the same homicide. In particular, this case presents the issue of the applicability of the dual sovereignty doctrine to successive prosecutions by two States.

I

In August 1981, petitioner, Larry Gene Heath, hired Charles Owens and Gregory Lumpkin to kill his wife, Rebecca Heath, who was then nine months pregnant, for a sum of $2,000. On the morning of August 31, 1981, petitioner left the Heath residence in Russell County, Alabama, to meet with Owens and Lumpkin in Georgia, just over the Alabama border from the Heath home. Petitioner led them back to the Heath residence, gave them the keys to the Heaths' car and house, and left the premises in his girlfriend's truck. Owens and Lumpkin then kidnaped Rebecca Heath from her home. The Heath car, with Rebecca Heath's body inside, was later found on the side of a road in Troup County, Georgia. The cause of death was a gunshot wound in the head. The estimated time of death and the distance from the Heath residence to the spot where Rebecca Heath's body was found are consistent with the theory that the murder took place in Georgia, and respondent does not contend otherwise.

Georgia and Alabama authorities pursued dual investigations in which they cooperated to some extent. On September 4, 1981, petitioner was arrested by Georgia authorities. Petitioner waived his *Miranda* rights and gave a full confession admitting that he had arranged his wife's kidnaping and murder. In November 1981, the grand jury of Troup County, Georgia, indicted petitioner for the offense of "malice" murder under Ga. Code Ann. §16-5-1 (1984). Georgia then served petitioner with notice of its intention to seek the death penalty, citing as the aggravating circumstance the fact that the murder was "caused and directed" by petitioner. See Ga. Code Ann. §17-10-30(b)(6) (1982). On February 10, 1982, petitioner pleaded guilty to the Georgia murder charge in exchange for a sentence of life imprisonment, which he understood could involve his serving as few as seven years in prison.

On May 5, 1982, the grand jury of Russell County, Alabama, returned an indictment against petitioner for the capital offense of murder during a kidnaping. See Ala. Code §13A-5-40(a)(1) (1982). Before trial on this indictment, petitioner entered pleas of autrefois convict and former jeopardy under the Alabama and United States Constitutions, arguing that his conviction and sentence in Georgia barred his prosecution in Alabama for the same conduct. Petitioner also entered a plea contesting the jurisdiction of the Alabama court on the ground that the crime had occurred in Georgia.

After a hearing, the trial court rejected petitioner's double jeopardy claims. It assumed, arguendo, that the two prosecutions could not have been brought in succession by one State but held that double jeopardy did not bar successive prosecutions by two different States for the same act. The court postponed a ruling on petitioner's plea to jurisdiction until the close of the State's case in chief.

At the close of the State's case, petitioner argued that Alabama did not have jurisdiction under state law because there had been no evidence of kidnaping and all the evidence showed that Rebecca Heath was killed in Georgia. The State responded that a kidnaping had been proved, and that under Ala. Code §15-2-3 (1982), if a crime commences in Alabama it may be punished in Alabama regardless of where the crime is consummated. The court rejected both petitioner's jurisdictional plea and his renewed double jeopardy claims.

On January 12, 1983, the Alabama jury convicted petitioner of murder during a kidnaping in the first degree. After a sentencing hearing, the jury recommended the death penalty. Pursuant to Alabama law, a second sentencing hearing was held before the trial judge. The judge accepted the jury's recommendation, finding that the sole aggravating factor, that the capital offense was "committed while the defendant was engaged in the commission of a kidnaping," outweighed the sole mitigating factor, that the "defendant was convicted of the murder of Rebecca Heath in the Superior Court of Troup County, Georgia, . . . and received a sentence of life imprisonment in that court." See Ala. Code §§13A-5-49(4), 13A-5-50 (1982).

On appeal, the Alabama Court of Criminal Appeals rejected petitioner's pleas of autrefois convict and former jeopardy under the Alabama and United States Constitutions and affirmed his conviction. 455 So. 2d 898 (1983). Petitioner then filed a petition for writ of certiorari with the Alabama Supreme Court, stating the sole issue to be "whether or not the prosecution in the State of Alabama constituted double jeopardy in violation of the 5th Amendment of the United States Constitution." The court granted his petition, and unanimously affirmed his conviction. Ex parte Heath, 455 So. 2d 905 (1984).

The Alabama Supreme Court noted that "[p]rosecutions under the laws of separate sovereigns do not improperly subject an accused twice to prosecutions for the same offense," citing this Court's cases applying the dual sovereignty doctrine. Id., at 906. The court acknowledged that this Court has not considered the applicability of the dual sovereignty doctrine to successive prosecutions by different States. It reasoned, however, that "[i]f, for double jeopardy purposes, Alabama is considered to be a sovereign entity vis-à-vis the federal government then surely it is a sovereign entity vis-à-vis the State of Georgia." Ibid.

Petitioner sought a writ of certiorari from this Court, raising double jeopardy claims and claims based on Alabama's exercise of jurisdiction. No due process objections were asserted. We granted certiorari limited to the question whether petitioner's Alabama conviction was barred by this Court's decision in Brown v. Ohio, 432 U.S. 161 (1977), and requested the parties to address the question of the applicability of the dual sovereignty doctrine to successive prosecutions by two States. 470 U.S. 1026 (1985). For the reasons explained below, we affirm the judgment of the Alabama Supreme Court.

II

Successive prosecutions are barred by the Fifth Amendment only if the two offenses for which the defendant is prosecuted are the "same" for double jeopardy purposes. Respondent does not contravene petitioner's contention that the offenses of "murder during a kidnaping" and "malice murder," as construed by the courts of Alabama and Georgia respectively, may be considered greater and lesser offenses and, thus, the "same" offense under Brown v. Ohio, supra, absent operation of the dual sovereignty principle. See id., at 169; Illinois v. Vitale, 447 U.S. 410 (1980). We therefore assume, arguendo, that, had these offenses arisen under the laws of one State and had petitioner been separately prosecuted for both offenses in that State, the second conviction would have been barred by the Double Jeopardy Clause.

The sole remaining question upon which we granted certiorari is whether the dual sovereignty doctrine permits successive prosecutions under the laws of different States which otherwise would be held to "subject [the defendant] for the same offence to be twice put in jeopardy." Although we have not previously so held, we believe the answer to this query is inescapable. The dual sovereignty doctrine, as originally articulated and consistently applied by this Court, compels the conclusion that successive prosecutions by two States for the same conduct are not barred by the Double Jeopardy Clause.

The dual sovereignty doctrine is founded on the common-law conception of crime as an offense against the sovereignty of the government. When a defendant in a single act violates the "peace and dignity" of two sovereigns by breaking the laws of each, he has committed two distinct "offences." United States v. Lanza, 260 U.S. 377, 382 (1922). As the Court explained in Moore v. Illinois, 14 How. 13, 19 (1852), "[an] offence, in its legal signification, means the transgression of a law." Consequently, when the same act transgresses the laws of two sovereigns, "it cannot be truly averred that the offender has been twice punished for the same offence; but only that by one act he has committed two offences, for each of which he is justly punishable." Id., at 20.

In applying the dual sovereignty doctrine, then, the crucial determination is whether the two entities that seek successively to prosecute a defendant for the same course of conduct can be termed separate sovereigns. This determination turns on whether the two entities draw their authority to punish the offender from distinct sources of power. See, e.g., United States v. Wheeler, 435 U.S. 313, 320 (1978); Waller v. Florida, 397 U.S. 387, 393 (1970); Puerto Rico v. Shell Co., 302 U.S. 253, 264-265 (1937); *Lanza*, supra, at 382; Grafton v. United States, 206 U.S. 333, 354-355 (1907). Thus, the Court has uniformly held that the States are separate sovereigns with respect to the Federal Government because each State's power to prosecute is derived from its own "inherent sovereignty," not from the Federal Government. *Wheeler*, supra, at 320, n. 14. See Abbate v. United States, 359 U.S. 187, 193-194 (1959) (collecting cases); *Lanza*, supra. As stated in *Lanza*, supra, at 382:

> Each government in determining what shall be an offense against its peace and dignity is exercising its own sovereignty, not that of the other.
>
> It follows that an act denounced as a crime by both national and state sovereignties is an offense against the peace and dignity of both and may be punished by each.

See also Bartkus v. Illinois, 359 U.S. 121 (1959); Westfall v. United States, 274 U.S. 256, 258 (1927) (Holmes, J.) (the proposition that the State and Federal Governments may punish the same conduct "is too plain to need more than statement").

The States are no less sovereign with respect to each other than they are with respect to the Federal Government. Their powers to undertake criminal prosecutions derive from separate and independent sources of power and authority originally belonging to them before admission to the Union and preserved to them by the Tenth Amendment. See *Lanza*, supra, at 382. The States are equal to each other "in power, dignity and authority, each competent to exert that residuum of sovereignty not delegated to the United States by the Constitution itself." Coyle v. Oklahoma, 221 U.S. 559, 567 (1911). See Skiriotes v. Florida, 313 U.S. 69, 77 (1941). Thus, "[e]ach has the power, inherent in any sovereign, independently to determine what shall be an offense against its authority and to punish such offenses, and in doing so each 'is exercising its own sovereignty, not that of the other.'" *Wheeler*, supra, at 320 (quoting *Lanza*, supra, at 382).

The cases in which the Court has applied the dual sovereignty principle outside the realm of successive federal and state prosecutions illustrate the soundness of this analysis. United States v. Wheeler, supra, is particularly instructive because there the Court expressly refused to find that only the State and Federal Governments could be considered distinct sovereigns with respect to each other for double jeopardy purposes, stating that "so restrictive a view of [the dual sovereignty] concept . . . would require disregard of the very words of the Double Jeopardy Clause." Id., at 330. Instead, the *Wheeler* Court reiterated the principle that the sovereignty of two prosecuting entities for these purposes is determined by "the ultimate source of the power under which the respective prosecutions were undertaken." Id., at 320. On the basis of this reasoning, the Court held that the Navajo Tribe, whose power to prosecute its members for tribal offenses is derived from the Tribe's "primeval sovereignty" rather than a delegation of federal authority, is an independent sovereign from the Federal Government for purposes of the dual sovereignty doctrine. Id., at 328.

In those instances where the Court has found the dual sovereignty doctrine inapplicable, it has done so because the two prosecuting entities did not derive their powers to prosecute from independent sources of authority. Thus, the Court has held that successive prosecutions by federal and territorial courts are barred because such courts are "creations emanating from the same sovereignty." *Puerto Rico*, 302 U.S., at 264. See id., at 264-266. See also *Grafton*, supra (the Philippine Islands). Similarly, municipalities that derive their power to try a defendant from the same organic law that empowers the State to prosecute are not separate sovereigns with respect to the State. See, e.g., *Waller*, supra. These cases confirm that it is the presence of independent sovereign authority to prosecute, not the relation between States and the Federal Government in our federalist system, that constitutes the basis for the dual sovereignty doctrine.

Petitioner argues that Nielsen v. Oregon, 212 U.S. 315 (1909), indicates, albeit in dicta, that where States have concurrent jurisdiction over a criminal offense, the first State to prosecute thereby bars prosecution by any other State. We find that *Nielsen* is limited to its unusual facts and has continuing relevance, if at all, only to questions of jurisdiction between two entities deriving their concurrent jurisdiction from a single source of authority. In *Nielsen*, the Court set aside a conviction obtained by the State of Oregon against a resident of the State of Washington for his operation of a purse net for fish in the Columbia River pursuant to a valid license to do so from the State of Washington. The Court noted: "By the legislation of Congress the Columbia River is made the common boundary between Oregon and Washington, and to each of those States is given concurrent jurisdiction on the waters of that river." Id., at 319. "[T]he grant of concurrent jurisdiction may bring up from time to time . . . some curious and difficult questions, so we properly confine ourselves to the precise question presented. . . . It is enough to decide, as we do, that for an act done within the territorial limits of the State of Washington under authority and license from that State one cannot be prosecuted and punished by the State of Oregon." Id., at 320-321. It is obvious that the *Nielsen* Court did not attempt to decide or even to consider the double jeopardy effect of successive state prosecutions for offenses proscribed by both States; the case, therefore, has no bearing on the issue of the applicability of the dual sovereignty doctrine presented in this case.

III

Petitioner invites us to restrict the applicability of the dual sovereignty principle to cases in which two governmental entities, having concurrent jurisdiction and pursuing quite different interests, can demonstrate that allowing only one entity to exercise jurisdiction over the defendant will interfere with the unvindicated interests of the second entity and that multiple prosecutions therefore are necessary for the satisfaction of the legitimate interests of both entities. This balancing of interests approach, however, cannot be reconciled with the dual sovereignty principle. This Court has plainly and repeatedly stated that two identical offenses are *not* the "same offence" within the meaning of the Double Jeopardy Clause if they are prosecuted by different sovereigns. See, e.g., United States v. Lanza, 260 U.S. 377 (1922) (same conduct, indistinguishable statutes, same "interests"). If the States are separate sovereigns, as they must be under the definition of sovereignty which the Court consistently has employed, the circumstances of the case are irrelevant. . . .

It is axiomatic that "[i]n America, the powers of sovereignty are divided between the government of the Union, and those of the States. They are each sovereign, with respect to the objects committed to it, and neither sovereign with respect to the objects committed to the other." McCulloch v. Maryland, 4 Wheat. 316, 410 (1819). It is as well established that the States, "as political communities, [are] distinct and sovereign, and consequently foreign to each other." Bank of United States v. Daniel, 12 Pet. 32, 54 (1838). See also Skiriotes v. Florida, 313 U.S., at 77; Coyle v. Oklahoma, 221 U.S., at 567. The Constitution leaves in the possession of each State "certain exclusive and very important portions of sovereign power." The Federalist No. 9, p. 55 (J. Cooke ed. 1961). Foremost among the prerogatives of sovereignty is the power to create and enforce a criminal code. See, e.g., Alfred L. Snapp & Son, Inc. v. Puerto Rico ex rel. Barez, 458 U.S. 592, 601 (1982); McCulloch, supra, at 418. To deny a State its power to enforce its criminal laws because another State has won the race to the courthouse "would be a shocking and untoward deprivation of the historic right and obligation of the States to maintain peace and order within their confines." Bartkus, 359 U.S., at 137.

Such a deprivation of a State's sovereign powers cannot be justified by the assertion that under "interest analysis" the State's legitimate penal interests will be satisfied through a prosecution conducted by another State. A State's interest in vindicating its sovereign authority through enforcement of its laws by definition can never be satisfied by another State's enforcement of its own laws. Just as the Federal Government has the right to decide that a state prosecution has not vindicated a violation of the "peace and dignity" of the Federal Government, a State must be entitled to decide that a prosecution by another State has not satisfied its legitimate sovereign interest. In recognition of this fact, the Court consistently has endorsed the principle that a single act constitutes an "offence" against each sovereign whose laws are violated by that act. The Court has always understood the words of the Double Jeopardy Clause to reflect this fundamental principle, and we see no reason why we should reconsider that understanding today.

The judgment of the Supreme Court of Alabama is affirmed.

[The dissenting opinion of Justice Brennan is omitted.]

JUSTICE MARSHALL, with whom JUSTICE BRENNAN joins, dissenting.

Seizing upon the suggestion in past cases that every "independent" sovereign government may prosecute violations of its laws even when the defendant has already been tried for the same crime in another jurisdiction, the Court today gives short shrift to the policies underlying those precedents. The "dual sovereignty" doctrine, heretofore used to permit federal and state prosecutions for the same offense, was born of the need to accommodate complementary state and federal concerns within our system of concurrent territorial jurisdictions. It cannot justify successive prosecutions by different States. Moreover, even were the dual sovereignty doctrine to support successive state prosecutions as a general matter, it simply could not legitimate the collusion between Georgia and Alabama in this case to ensure that petitioner is executed for his crime.

I

On August 31, 1981, the body of Rebecca Heath was discovered in an abandoned car in Troup County, Georgia. Because the deceased was a resident of Russell

County, Alabama, members of the Russell County Sheriff's Department immediately joined Troup County authorities in investigating the causes and agents of her death. This cooperative effort proved fruitful. On September 4, petitioner Larry Heath, the deceased's husband, was arrested and brought to the Georgia State Patrol barracks in Troup County, where he confessed to having hired other men to murder his wife. Shortly thereafter, petitioner was indicted by the grand jury of Troup County for malice murder. The prosecution's notice to petitioner that it was seeking the death penalty triggered the beginning of the Unified Appeals Procedure that Georgia requires in capital cases. But while these pretrial proceedings were still in progress, petitioner seized the prosecution's offer of a life sentence in exchange for a guilty plea. Upon entry of his plea in February 1982, petitioner was sentenced in Troup County Superior Court to life imprisonment. His stay in the custody of Georgia authorities proved short, however. Three months later, a Russell County, Alabama, grand jury indicted him for the capital offense of murdering Rebecca Heath during the course of a kidnaping in the first degree.

The murder of Rebecca Heath must have been quite noteworthy in Russell County, Alabama. By petitioner's count, of the 82 prospective jurors questioned before trial during voir dire, all but 7 stated that they were aware that petitioner had pleaded guilty to the same crime in Georgia. The voir dire responses of almost all of the remaining 75 veniremen can only be characterized as remarkable. When asked whether they could put aside their knowledge of the prior guilty plea in order to give petitioner a fair trial in Alabama, the vast majority answered in the affirmative. These answers satisfied the trial judge, who denied petitioner's challenges for cause except as to those jurors who explicitly admitted that the Georgia proceedings would probably affect their assessment of petitioner's guilt.

With such a well-informed jury, the outcome of the trial was surely a foregone conclusion. Defense counsel could do little but attempt to elicit information from prosecution witnesses tending to show that the crime was committed exclusively in Georgia. The court having rejected petitioner's constitutional and jurisdictional claims, the defense was left to spend most of its summation arguing that Rebecca Heath may not actually have been kidnaped from Alabama before she was murdered and that petitioner was already being punished for ordering that murder. Petitioner was convicted and, after sentencing hearings, was condemned to die. The conviction and sentence were upheld by the Alabama Court of Criminal Appeals, 455 So. 2d 898 (1983), and the Alabama Supreme Court. Ex parte Heath, 455 So. 2d 905 (1984).

II

Had the Georgia authorities suddenly become dissatisfied with the life sentence petitioner received in their courts and reindicted petitioner in order to seek the death penalty once again, that indictment would without question be barred by the Double Jeopardy Clause of the Fifth Amendment, as applied to the States by the Fourteenth Amendment, Benton v. Maryland, 395 U.S. 784 (1969). Whether the second indictment repeated the charge of malice murder or instead charged murder in the course of a kidnaping, it would surely, under any reasonable constitutional standard, offend the bar to successive prosecutions for the same offense. See Brown v. Ohio, 432 U.S. 161, 166 (1977); id., at 170 (Brennan, J., concurring).

The only difference between this case and such a hypothetical volte-face by Georgia is that here Alabama, not Georgia, was offended by the notion that petitioner might not forfeit his life in punishment for his crime. The only reason the Court gives for permitting Alabama to go forward is that Georgia and Alabama are separate sovereigns.

The dual sovereignty theory posits that where the same act offends the laws of two sovereigns, "it cannot be truly averred that the offender has been twice punished for the same offence; but only that by one act he has committed two offences, for each of which he is justly punishable." Moore v. Illinois, 14 How. 13, 20 (1852). Therefore, "prosecutions under the laws of separate sovereigns do not, in the language of the Fifth Amendment, 'subject [the defendant] for the same offence to be twice put in jeopardy.'" United States v. Wheeler, 435 U.S. 313, 317 (1978). Mindful of the admonitions of Justice Black, we should recognize this exegesis of the Clause as, at best, a useful fiction and, at worst, a dangerous one. See Bartkus v. Illinois, 359 U.S. 121, 158 (1959) (Black, J., dissenting). No evidence has ever been adduced to indicate that the Framers intended the word "offence" to have so restrictive a meaning.

This strained reading of the Double Jeopardy Clause has survived and indeed flourished in this Court's cases not because of any inherent plausibility, but because it provides reassuring interpretivist support for a rule that accommodates the unique nature of our federal system. Before this rule is extended to cover a new class of cases, the reasons for its creation should therefore be made clear.

Under the constitutional scheme, the Federal Government has been given the exclusive power to vindicate certain of our Nation's sovereign interests, leaving the States to exercise complementary authority over matters of more local concern. The respective spheres of the Federal Government and the States may overlap at times, and even where they do not, different interests may be implicated by a single act. See, e.g., Abbate v. United States, 359 U.S. 187 (1959) (conspiracy to dynamite telephone company facilities entails both destruction of property and disruption of federal communications network). Yet were a prosecution by a State, however zealously pursued, allowed to preclude further prosecution by the Federal Government for the same crime, an entire range of national interests could be frustrated. The importance of those federal interests has thus quite properly been permitted to trump a defendant's interest in avoiding successive prosecutions or multiple punishments for the same crime. See Screws v. United States, 325 U.S. 91, 108-110, and n. 10 (1945) (plurality opinion). Conversely, because "the States under our federal system have the principal responsibility for defining and prosecuting crimes," Abbate v. United States, supra, at 195, it would be inappropriate — in the absence of a specific congressional intent to pre-empt state action pursuant to the Supremacy Clause — to allow a federal prosecution to preclude state authorities from vindicating "the historic right and obligation of the States to maintain peace and order within their confines," Bartkus v. Illinois, supra, at 137.

The complementary nature of the sovereignty exercised by the Federal Government and the States places upon a defendant burdens commensurate with concomitant privileges. Past cases have recognized that the special ordeal suffered by a defendant prosecuted by both federal and state authorities is the price of living in a federal system, the cost of dual citizenship. Every citizen, the Court has noted, "owes allegiance to the two departments, so to speak, and within their respective spheres must pay the penalties which each exacts for disobedience to its laws. In return, he can demand protection from each within its own jurisdiction." United States v.

Cruikshank, 92 U.S. 542, 551 (1876). See Moore v. Illinois, supra, at 20 ("Every citizen . . . may be said to owe allegiance to two sovereigns, and may be liable to punishment for an infraction of the laws of either").

. . . Where two States seek to prosecute the same defendant for the same crime in two separate proceedings, the justifications found in the federal-state context for an exemption from double jeopardy constraints simply do not hold. Although the two States may have opted for different policies within their assigned territorial jurisdictions, the sovereign concerns with whose vindication each State has been charged are identical. Thus, in contrast to the federal-state context, barring the second prosecution would still permit one government to act upon the broad range of sovereign concerns that have been reserved to the States by the Constitution. The compelling need in the federal-state context to subordinate double jeopardy concerns is thus considerably diminished in cases involving successive prosecutions by different States. Moreover, from the defendant's perspective, the burden of successive prosecutions cannot be justified as the quid pro quo of dual citizenship.

To be sure, a refusal to extend the dual sovereignty rule to state-state prosecutions would preclude the State that has lost the "race to the courthouse" from vindicating legitimate policies distinct from those underlying its sister State's prosecution. But as yet, I am not persuaded that a State's desire to further a particular policy should be permitted to deprive a defendant of his constitutionally protected right not to be brought to bar more than once to answer essentially the same charges.

III

Having expressed my doubts as to the Court's ill-considered resolution of the dual sovereignty question in this case, I must confess that my quarrel with the Court's disposition of this case is based less upon how this question was resolved than upon the fact that it was considered at all. Although, in granting Heath's petition for certiorari, this Court ordered the parties to focus upon the dual sovereignty issue, I believe the Court errs in refusing to consider the fundamental unfairness of the process by which petitioner stands condemned to die.

Even where the power of two sovereigns to pursue separate prosecutions for the same crime has been undisputed, this Court has barred both governments from combining to do together what each could not constitutionally do on its own. See Murphy v. Waterfront Comm'n, 378 U.S. 52 (1964); Elkins v. United States, 364 U.S. 206 (1960).[3] And just as the Constitution bars one sovereign from facilitating another's prosecution by delivering testimony coerced under promise of immunity

---

3. To be sure, *Murphy*, which bars a State from compelling a witness to give testimony that might be used against him in a federal prosecution, and *Elkins*, which bars the introduction in a federal prosecution of evidence illegally seized by state officers, do not necessarily undermine the basis of the rule allowing successive state and federal prosecutions. It is one thing to bar a sovereign from using certain evidence and quite another to bar it from prosecuting altogether. But these cases can be read to suggest that despite the independent sovereign status of the Federal and State Governments, courts should not be blind to the impact of combined federal-state law enforcement on an accused's constitutional rights. See Note, Double Prosecution by State and Federal Governments: Another Exercise in Federalism, 80 Harv. L. Rev. 1538, 1547 (1967). Justice Harlan's belief that *Murphy* "abolished the 'two sovereignties' rule," Stevens v. Marks, 383 U.S. 234, 250 (1966) (Harlan, J., concurring in part, dissenting in part), was thus well founded.

or evidence illegally seized, I believe that it prohibits two sovereigns from combining forces to ensure that a defendant receives only the trappings of criminal process as he is sped along to execution.

While no one can doubt the propriety of two States cooperating to bring a criminal to justice, the cooperation between Georgia and Alabama in this case went far beyond their initial joint investigation. Georgia's efforts to secure petitioner's execution did not end with its acceptance of his guilty plea. Its law enforcement officials went on to play leading roles as prosecution witnesses in the Alabama trial. Indeed, had the Alabama trial judge not restricted the State to one assisting officer at the prosecution's table during trial, a Georgia officer would have shared the honors with an Alabama officer. Although the record does not reveal the precise nature of the assurances made by Georgia authorities that induced petitioner to plead guilty in the first proceeding against him, I cannot believe he would have done so had he been aware that the officials whose forbearance he bought in Georgia with his plea would merely continue their efforts to secure his death in another jurisdiction. Cf. Santobello v. New York, 404 U.S. 257, 262 (1971).

Even before the Fourteenth Amendment was held to incorporate the protections of the Double Jeopardy Clause, four Members of this Court registered their outrage at "an instance of the prosecution being allowed to harass the accused with repeated trials and convictions on the same evidence, until it [achieved] its desired result of a capital verdict." Ciucci v. Illinois, 356 U.S. 571, 573 (1958). Such "relentless prosecutions," they asserted, constituted "an unseemly and oppressive use of a criminal trial that violates the concept of due process contained in the Fourteenth Amendment, whatever its ultimate scope is taken to be." Id., at 575. The only differences between the facts in *Ciucci* and those in this case are that here the relentless effort was a cooperative one between two States and that petitioner sought to avoid trial by pleading guilty. Whether viewed as a violation of the Double Jeopardy Clause or simply as an affront to the due process guarantee of fundamental fairness, Alabama's prosecution of petitioner cannot survive constitutional scrutiny. I therefore must dissent.

NOTES AND QUESTIONS

1. Notice Justice Marshall's account of jury selection in Heath's case: Not only was Heath prosecuted twice for the same crime, but news coverage of the first prosecution may have had a great deal to do with the second conviction. Was the Court right to ignore that possibility? Isn't that precisely the kind of scenario double jeopardy doctrine should aim to prevent?

2. The history of double jeopardy doctrine does not support the Court's position in *Heath*. In English law, the principle that no one should be prosecuted twice for the same crime dates to the twelfth century:

In the twelfth century a major element of the conflict between Thomas Becket and Henry II was the king's desire to have clerics who had been convicted in ecclesiastical courts turned over to civil tribunals for further prosecution. Henry conceded the point in 1176 following Becket's martyrdom. The king's concession is significant because the royal and ecclesiastical courts obviously did not draw their power from the same sovereign. The application of the double jeopardy bar to successive religious and secular prosecutions demonstrates that the focus of the prohibition was the defendant, not the prosecutor.

Ronald J. Allen & John P. Ratnaswamy, Heath v. Alabama: A Case Study of Doctrine and Rationality in the Supreme Court, 76 J. Crim. L. & Criminology 801, 807 (1985). Allen and Ratnaswamy go on to note that the dual-sovereignty concept entered American law in the mid-nineteenth century, at a time when conflict between state and federal governments was at its height; the focus was on state-federal coordination, not on state-state prosecutions as in *Heath*:

> In the middle of the nineteenth century the conception of the double jeopardy clause as prohibiting successive prosecutions by any prosecuting authority was questioned by dicta in a series of [Supreme Court] cases. These cases were not motivated by mystical conceptions of "sovereignty"; instead, they were motivated by concerns about the different roles of the two levels of American government and by a growing realization that something had to be done to prevent conflict between the states and the national government. Those considerations led to the discussion in these cases of a dual sovereignty exception to the double jeopardy clause, and it is those concerns, along with the individual interests protected by the clause, that should control the scope of any such exception. . . .

> [The key case was] Moore v. Illinois, [55 U.S. 13 (1852),] [where] the Court for the first time directly discussed the problem of duplicate state and federal prosecutions for the same crime. Moore was convicted under an Illinois statute proscribing the harboring or secreting of fugitive slaves. Moore's principal argument was preemption of the state law by the federal Fugitive Slave Act, but he also objected to the possible double jeopardy problem of prosecution under both the state and federal statutes. The Supreme Court found that the Illinois and federal statutes were dissimilar in their essential underlying purpose, in their definition of the offense, and in the nature of the punishment which they authorized. The purpose of the federal government was protection of the property interests of slave owners, while the state's goal was to bar black persons, whether slave or free, from the state's territory. Despite these differences, the Court nevertheless proceeded to articulate for the first time the dual sovereignty theory. . . .

> The decision was an inevitable consequence of its historical context. In *Moore*, the Court was asked to strike down a type of state statute that was at the heart of a dispute over the scope of states' rights, a dispute so serious that it would lead to the Civil War. The Court was being asked to do so not only where the laws of neither "sovereign" impinged upon the legitimate interests of the other, but where the Court was beginning to realize that state and federal criminal statutes were going to overlap and intersect in unpredictable ways. Moreover, none of the alternatives available to the Court were feasible, except for the creation of a dual sovereignty exception to the double jeopardy prohibition. . . .

> "Dual sovereignty," in short, arose as an exception to the normal rules of double jeopardy for certain fundamental reasons related to the structure of American government. Unless there is some other justification for the theory, it should apply only where the reasons which gave rise to it are present: where two governmental entities pursuing quite diverse interests share substantially overlapping territorial jurisdictions, where there is a substantial risk of interference by one governmental entity in the affairs of another, and where multiple prosecutions are necessary for the satisfaction of the legitimate purposes of each governmental unit. The Court in *Heath* virtually ignored these considerations . . .

76 J. Crim. L. & Criminology, at 811-814.

3. There are few cases like *Heath*. Double prosecution by state and federal officials is more common. The prosecutions of the police officers who beat Rodney King in March 1991 offer a famous example. King, a black man, was apprehended after a high-speed chase through Los Angeles. Four police officers beat him brutally; a nearby civilian captured the beating on videotape. The officers were charged with felony assault in California state court. Before trial, the case was moved to Simi Valley — a nearly all-white community with one of the highest concentrations of retired police officers in the United States. The jury acquitted three of the four defendants on all charges; a single charge against one defendant produced a hung jury. There were no convictions. The verdict triggered massive rioting in Los Angeles; at least 40 people died in the course of the riots and the police efforts to quell them.

The federal government then prosecuted the four officers for willfully depriving King of his constitutional rights (in particular, his right to be free from excessive police use of force under the Fourth Amendment). Two of the officers — Timothy Wind and Ted Briseno — were again acquitted. The other two — Stacey Koon and Lawrence Powell — were convicted. Their convictions were affirmed on appeal; the case went up to the Supreme Court, though not on any issues related to double jeopardy. See Koon v. United States, 518 U.S. 81 (1996) (discussing standard of review in sentencing decisions under the Federal Sentencing Guidelines).

What about Terry Nichols? Nichols was Timothy McVeigh's codefendant in the Oklahoma City bombing case. The federal government prosecuted both Nichols and McVeigh in federal court; the government sought the death penalty as to both defendants. McVeigh was convicted and sentenced to death. Nichols was convicted and sentenced to life in prison. Oklahoma wanted another shot at the death penalty for Nichols, so he was tried again in state court, for capital murder. (Once again, he escaped a death sentence.) Does that process sound fair? Are your reactions to the Rodney King and Oklahoma City bombing cases consistent?

4. There is an obvious functional concern underlying the dual prosecutions in *Koon*. The federal government has a strong interest in protecting its citizens from deprivations of constitutional rights by state and local officials — that, after all, was one of the driving forces behind the Fourteenth Amendment. If federal prosecution is barred by a state prosecution, local district attorneys might prosecute halfheartedly or even purposely try to produce an acquittal, thereby insulating defendants from criminal punishment. Is that problem serious enough to justify dual sovereignty doctrine? Keep in mind that there is also a troubling scenario on the other side of the scale: A defendant is prosecuted in state court and wins; the federal government then prosecutes him again in response to political pressure. Is *that* problem serious enough to suggest that dual sovereignty doctrine is a mistake?

For insightful analyses of these and other questions, see Akhil Reed Amar & Jonathan L. Marcus, Double Jeopardy after Rodney King, 95 Colum. L. Rev. 1 (1995); Paul Cassell, The Rodney King Trials and the Double Jeopardy Clause: Some Observations on Original Meaning and the ACLU's Schizophrenic Views of the Dual Sovereignty Doctrine, 41 UCLA L. Rev. 693 (1994); Susan Herman, Double Jeopardy All Over Again: Dual Sovereignty, Rodney King, and the ACLU, 41 UCLA L. Rev. 609 (1994).

D. *Double Jeopardy and the Criminal-Civil Divide*

The government sometimes fights crime in proceedings that are, at least nominally, civil rather than criminal. Civil fines, forfeitures of personal and real property, punitive damages, and even some kinds of taxes are used to deter and, at least in the popular sense of the word, punish crime. These practices raise a host of issues, some deeply philosophical. For a fascinating exploration of those issues, see generally Carol S. Steiker, Punishment and Procedure: Punishment Theory and the Criminal-Civil Procedural Divide, 85 Geo. L.J. 775 (1997) (seeking to develop philosophical basis for determining whether particular sanctions are "civil" or "criminal").

These not-quite-criminal proceedings can raise double jeopardy concerns. The Supreme Court has followed a meandering path in dealing with those concerns. The defendant in United States v. Halper, 490 U.S. 435 (1989) was the manager of a New York medical laboratory that served Medicare patients. He was charged under the criminal false-claims statute, 18 U.S.C. §287, with 65 separate counts of filing falsely inflated claims for Medicare reimbursement of patient expenses. The total amount of the overbilling was $585. Halper was convicted on all counts, sentenced to two years in prison, and fined $5,000. The government then filed a lawsuit against Halper under the civil False Claims Act, 31 U.S.C. §§3729-3731, seeking the maximum statutory remedy of $2,000 per violation, plus twice the amount of actual damages sustained by the government and litigation costs. The district court entered summary judgment against Halper on liability, on the basis of the prior criminal proceeding. But the court ultimately concluded that a civil sanction of more than $130,000 against Halper would constitute a second "punishment" for the "same offense" for which he had already been punished, in violation of the Double Jeopardy Clause, and thus reduced the government's award to double-damages plus costs.

A unanimous Supreme Court agreed. The Court saw the question as "[w]hether and under what circumstances a civil penalty may constitute punishment for the purpose of the Double Jeopardy Clause." The Court rejected the government's contention that "whether proceedings are criminal or civil is a matter of statutory construction," finding such a view "not well suited to the context of the 'humane interests' safeguarded by the Double Jeopardy Clause's proscription of multiple punishments." Instead, the Court explained:

> What we announce now is a rule for the rare case, the case such as the one before us, where a fixed-penalty provision subjects a prolific but small-gauge offender to a sanction overwhelmingly disproportionate to the damages he has caused. The rule is one of reason: Where a defendant previously has sustained a criminal penalty and the civil penalty sought in the subsequent proceeding bears no rational relation to the goal of compensating the Government for its loss, but rather appears to qualify as "punishment" in the plain meaning of the word, then the defendant is entitled to an accounting of the Government's damages and costs to determine if the penalty sought in fact constitutes a second punishment.

490 U.S., at 449-450. The Court concluded that the statutorily authorized award of more than $130,000 would be so excessive, compared to the government's actual

damages, as to constitute "punishment" for double jeopardy purposes, but remanded the case for additional findings on the amount of those actual damages.

In Department of Revenue of Montana v. Kurth Ranch, 511 U.S. 767 (1994), the Court faced a different configuration of criminal and civil proceedings. In 1987, Montana enacted a "Dangerous Drug Tax Act," which imposed a tax on the "possession and storage of dangerous drugs," defined as drugs whose possession can lead to criminal prosecution and seizure under Montana law. The tax was set at a relatively high rate — 10 percent of the assessed market value of the drugs, or a specified amount (e.g., $100 per ounce for marijuana), whichever is greater.[3] Two weeks after this new tax law became effective, six members of the Kurth family were charged with conspiracy to possess drugs with intent to sell, based on accusations that they were cultivating marijuana on their family farm. All pled guilty. In addition, the government filed a civil forfeiture action seeking recovery of all cash and equipment used in the Kurth's marijuana operation; this action was settled when the Kurths agreed to the forfeiture of $18,016.83 in cash and equipment. Shortly after the conclusion of the criminal case and civil forfeiture proceeding, the state Department of Revenue assessed almost $900,000 in tax liability against the Kurths under the new tax law. The Kurths filed for bankruptcy and objected to the DOR's claim for unpaid drug taxes. The bankruptcy court held the Montana tax law unconstitutional under the double jeopardy clause and *Halper*, and the district and appellate courts affirmed.

The Supreme Court, in a 5-4 decision, likewise ruled in the Kurths' favor, although for somewhat different reasons. Justice Stevens' majority opinion noted that *Halper* dealt with a civil penalty and not a tax, and explained that *Halper*'s "method of determining whether the exaction was remedial or punitive" — i.e., a method that focuses on the costs of investigation and prosecution, and on other actual damages suffered by the government — "simply does not work in the case of a tax statute," where the purposes of the law (e.g., raising revenue) are so different. In this instance, the high rate of taxation and the obvious deterrent purpose did not "automatically" render the legislation punitive. But the fact that the drug tax was assessed only against "persons who have been arrested" for a crime, combined with the further fact that it was levied on "goods that the taxpayer neither owns nor possesses when the tax is imposed," led the Court to conclude that "this drug tax is a concoction of anomalies, too far-removed in crucial respects from a standard tax assessment to escape characterization as punishment for the purpose of Double Jeopardy analysis." The Court expressly limited its constitutional holding to the situation where such a punitive tax is levied after the conclusion of the criminal case, reserving the reverse situation (as well as the situation of criminal and tax sanctions imposed in the same proceeding) for another day.

There were three dissenting opinions. Chief Justice Rehnquist, joined by Justices O'Connor and Scalia, agreed with the Court that the *Halper* test did not apply to tax statutes, but disagreed with the Court's conclusion that the "anomalies" in the Montana statute made it unconstitutional. Justice O'Connor found the *Halper* test applicable and would have upheld the Montana statute based on the government's need

---

3. For some components of a marijuana plant, such as the stems, leaves, and other loose parts known collectively as "shake," the minimum tax of $100 per ounce amounted to approximately eight times the market value of the drug itself.

for funds to offset the high costs of drug interdiction and prosecution. Finally, Justice Scalia, joined by Justice Thomas, took a broader approach:

> The difficulty of applying *Halper*'s analysis to Montana's Dangerous Drug Tax has prompted me to focus on the antecedent question whether there is a multiple-punishments component of the Double Jeopardy Clause. As indicated above, I have concluded . . . that there is not. Instead, the Due Process Clause keeps punishment within the bounds established by the legislature, and the Cruel and Unusual Punishments and Excessive Fines Clauses place substantive limits upon what those legislated bounds may be. . . .
>
> It is time to put the *Halper* genie back in the bottle, and to acknowledge what the text of the Constitution makes perfectly clear: the Double Jeopardy Clause prohibits successive prosecution, not successive punishment. Multiple punishment is of course restricted by the Cruel and Unusual Punishments Clause insofar as its nature is concerned, and by the Excessive Fines Clause insofar as its cumulative extent is concerned. Its multiplicity qua multiplicity, however, is restricted only by the Double Jeopardy Clause's requirement that there be no successive criminal prosecution, and by the Due Process Clause's requirement that the cumulative punishments be in accord with the law of the land, i.e., authorized by the legislature.

511 U.S., at 802-805 (Scalia, J., dissenting).

Having dispensed with the "multiple punishment" aspect of double jeopardy, Justice Scalia then turned his attention to the "successive prosecution" aspect, which the majority had also found to be implicated by the combination of the criminal prosecution of the Kurths and the subsequent civil proceedings growing out of the tax assessment:

> Although a few of our cases include statements to the effect that a proceeding in which punishment is imposed is criminal, see, e.g., Kennedy v. Mendoza-Martinez, 372 U.S. 144, 167 (1963), the criterion of "punishment" for that purpose is significantly different (and significantly more deferential to the government) than the criterion applied in *Halper*. United States v. Ward, 448 U.S. 242 (1980), put it this way:
>
>> Where Congress has indicated an intention to establish a civil penalty, we have inquired further whether the statutory scheme was so punitive either in purpose or effect as to negate that intention. In regard to this latter inquiry, we have noted that "only the clearest proof could suffice to establish the unconstitutionality of a statute on such a ground."
>
> Id., at 248-249, quoting Flemming v. Nestor, 363 U.S. 603, 617 (1960) (citation omitted).
>
> *Halper*'s focus on whether the sanction serves the goals of "retribution and deterrence" is just one factor in the *Kennedy-Ward* test, see 372 U.S., at 168-169, and one factor alone is not dispositive, see *Ward*, 448 U.S., at 250-251. . . .

511 U.S., at 805-806. Justice Scalia concluded that, under the *Kennedy-Ward* test, the Montana drug tax law did not impose "punishment" in a manner violative of the "successive prosecution" aspect of double jeopardy. Though that position did not carry the day in *Kurth Ranch*, it did a good deal better in the next case.

UNITED STATES v. URSERY

Certiorari to the United States Court of Appeals for the Sixth Circuit
518 U.S. 267 (1996)

[This case was decided together with United States v. $405,089.23 in United States Currency et al., on certiorari to the United States Court of Appeals for the Ninth Circuit. — EDS.]

CHIEF JUSTICE REHNQUIST delivered the opinion of the Court.

In separate cases, the United States Court of Appeals for the Sixth Circuit and the United States Court of Appeals for the Ninth Circuit held that the Double Jeopardy Clause prohibits the Government from both punishing a defendant for a criminal offense and forfeiting his property for that same offense in a separate civil proceeding. We consolidated those cases for our review, and now reverse. These civil forfeitures (and civil forfeitures generally), we hold, do not constitute "punishment" for purposes of the Double Jeopardy Clause.

I

No. 95-345: Michigan Police found marijuana growing adjacent to respondent Guy Ursery's house, and discovered marijuana seeds, stems, stalks, and a growlight within the house. The United States instituted civil forfeiture proceedings against the house, alleging that the property was subject to forfeiture under 84 Stat. 1276, as amended, 21 U.S.C. §881(a)(7) because it had been used for several years to facilitate the unlawful processing and distribution of a controlled substance. Ursery ultimately paid the United States $13,250 to settle the forfeiture claim in full. Shortly before the settlement was consummated, Ursery was indicted for manufacturing marijuana, in violation of §841(a)(1). A jury found him guilty, and he was sentenced to 63 months in prison.

The Court of Appeals for the Sixth Circuit by a divided vote reversed Ursery's criminal conviction, holding that the conviction violated the Double Jeopardy Clause of the Fifth Amendment of the United States Constitution. 59 F.3d 568 (1995). The court based its conclusion in part upon its belief that our decisions in United States v. Halper, 490 U.S. 435 (1989), and Austin v. United States, 509 U.S. 602 (1993), meant that any civil forfeiture under §881(a)(7) constitutes punishment for purposes of the Double Jeopardy Clause. Ursery, in the court's view, had therefore been "punished" in the forfeiture proceeding against his property, and could not be subsequently criminally tried for violation of 21 U.S.C. §841(a)(1).

No. 95-346: Following a jury trial, Charles Wesley Arlt and James Wren were convicted of: conspiracy to aid and abet the manufacture of methamphetamine, in violation of 21 U.S.C. §846; conspiracy to launder monetary instruments, in violation of 18 U.S.C. §371; and numerous counts of money laundering, in violation of §1956. The District Court sentenced Arlt to life in prison and a 10-year term of supervised release, and imposed a fine of $250,000. Wren was sentenced to life imprisonment and a 5-year term of supervised release.

Before the criminal trial had started, the United States had filed a civil in rem complaint against various property seized from, or titled to, Arlt and Wren, or Payback Mines, a corporation controlled by Arlt. The complaint alleged that each piece of property was subject to forfeiture both under 18 U.S.C. §981(a)(1)(A), which provides that "[a]ny property . . . involved in a transaction or attempted transaction in violation of" §1956 (the money-laundering statute) "is subject to forfeiture to the United States"; and under 21 U.S.C. §881(a)(6), which provides for the forfeiture of (i) "[a]ll . . . things of value furnished or intended to be furnished by any person in exchange for" illegal drugs, (ii) "all proceeds traceable to such an exchange," and (iii) "all moneys, negotiable instruments, and securities used or intended to be used to facilitate" a federal drug felony. The parties agreed to defer litigation of the forfeiture action during the criminal prosecution. More than a year after the conclusion of the criminal trial, the District Court granted the Government's motion for summary judgment in the civil forfeiture proceeding.

Arlt and Wren appealed the decision in the forfeiture action, and the Court of Appeals for the Ninth Circuit reversed, holding that the forfeiture violated the Double Jeopardy Clause. 33 F.3d 1210 (1994). The court's decision was based in part upon the same view as that expressed by the Court of Appeals for the Sixth Circuit in Ursery's case — that our decisions in *Halper* and *Austin* meant that, as a categorical matter, forfeitures under §§981(a)(1)(A) and 881(a)(6) always constitute "punishment."

We granted the Government's petition for certiorari in each of the two cases, and we now reverse. 516 U.S. 1070 (1996).

II

The Double Jeopardy Clause provides: "[N]or shall any person be subject for the same offence to be twice put in jeopardy of life or limb." U.S. Const., Amdt. 5. The Clause serves the function of preventing both "successive punishments and . . . successive prosecutions." United States v. Dixon, 509 U.S. 688, 696 (1993), citing North Carolina v. Pearce, 395 U.S. 711 (1969). The protection against multiple punishments prohibits the Government from "'punishing twice, or attempting a second time to punish criminally for the same offense.'" Witte v. United States, 515 U.S. 389, 396 (1995) (emphasis deleted), quoting Helvering v. Mitchell, 303 U.S. 391, 399 (1938).

In the decisions that we review, the Courts of Appeals held that the civil forfeitures constituted "punishment," making them subject to the prohibitions of the Double Jeopardy Clause. The Government challenges that characterization of the forfeitures, arguing that the courts were wrong to conclude that civil forfeitures are punitive for double jeopardy purposes.

A

Since the earliest years of this Nation, Congress has authorized the Government to seek parallel in rem civil forfeiture actions and criminal prosecutions based upon the same underlying events. See, e.g., Act of July 31, 1789, ch. 5, §12, 1 Stat. 39 (goods unloaded at night or without a permit subject to forfeiture and persons unloading subject to criminal prosecution); §25, id., at 43 (persons convicted of buying or concealing illegally imported goods subject to both monetary fine and in rem forfeiture of the goods); §34, id., at 46 (imposing criminal penalty and in rem forfeiture where person convicted of relanding goods entitled to drawback); see also The Palmyra, 25 U.S. 1, 12 Wheat. 1, 14-15 (1827) ("Many cases exist, where there is both a forfeiture in rem and a personal penalty"). . . . And, in a long line of cases, this Court has considered the application of the Double Jeopardy Clause to civil forfeitures, consistently concluding that the Clause does not apply to such actions because they do not impose punishment.

[The Court then discussed two of its earlier cases involving the relationship between the double jeopardy clause and civil forfeiture. The first case, Various Items of Personal Property v. United States, 282 U.S. 577 (1931), held that the clause was inapplicable to civil forfeiture actions because the forfeiture proceeding was in rem and thus not any part of the punishment imposed against the individual for the criminal offense. The second case, One Lot Emerald Cut Stones v. United States, 409 U.S. 232 (1972) (per curiam), reaffirmed the rule of *Various Items*, emphasizing that the statutory forfeiture provision was codified separately from the parallel criminal provisions and thus constituted a civil sanction rather than a second punishment. The Court also noted that the decisions in *Various Items* and *Emerald Cut Stones* were consistent with the long-standing common law rule that civil forfeiture *could not* proceed until *after* the offender was convicted of the parallel crime. — EDS.]

In our most recent decision considering whether a civil forfeiture constitutes punishment under the Double Jeopardy Clause, we again affirmed the rule of *Various Items*. In United States v. One Assortment of 89 Firearms, 465 U.S. 354 (1984), the owner of the defendant weapons was acquitted of charges of dealing firearms without a license. The Government then brought a forfeiture action against the firearms under 18 U.S.C. §924(d), alleging that they were used or were intended to be used in violation of federal law.

In another unanimous decision, we held that the forfeiture was not barred by the prior criminal proceeding. We began our analysis by stating the rule for our decision:

> Unless the forfeiture sanction was intended as punishment, so that the proceeding is essentially criminal in character, the Double Jeopardy Clause is not applicable. The question, then, is whether a §924(d) forfeiture proceeding is intended to be, or by its nature necessarily is, criminal and punitive, or civil and remedial. *89 Firearms*, supra, at 362 (citations omitted).

Our inquiry proceeded in two stages. In the first stage, we looked to Congress' intent, and concluded that "Congress designed forfeiture under §924(d) as a remedial civil sanction." 465 U.S., at 363. This conclusion was based upon several findings. First, noting that the forfeiture proceeding was in rem, we found it significant that "[a]ctions in rem have traditionally been viewed as civil proceedings, with jurisdiction dependent upon the seizure of a physical object." *89 Firearms*, id., at 363, citing Calero-Toledo v. Pearson Yacht Leasing Co., 416 U.S. [663,] 684 [(1974)]. Second, we found that the forfeiture provision, because it reached both weapons used in violation of federal law and those "intended to be used" in such a manner, reached a broader range of conduct than its criminal analogue. Third, we concluded that the civil forfeiture "further[ed] broad remedial aims," including both "discouraging unregulated commerce in firearms," and "removing from circulation firearms that have been used or intended for use outside regulated channels of commerce." *89 Firearms*, supra, at 364.

In the second stage of our analysis, we looked to "'whether the statutory scheme was so punitive either in purpose or effect as to negate' Congress' intention to establish a civil remedial mechanism," 465 U.S., at 365, quoting United States v. Ward, 448 U.S. 242, 248-249 (1980). Considering several factors that we had used previously in order to determine whether a civil proceeding was so punitive as to require application of the full panoply of constitutional protections required in a criminal trial, see id., at 248, we found only one of those factors to be present in the §924(d) forfeiture. By itself, however, the fact that the behavior proscribed by the forfeiture was already a crime proved insufficient to turn the forfeiture into a punishment subject to the Double Jeopardy Clause. Hence, we found that the petitioner had "failed to establish by the 'clearest proof' that Congress has provided a sanction so punitive as to 'transfor[m] what was clearly intended as a civil remedy into a criminal penalty.'" 89 Firearms, supra, at 366, quoting Rex Trailer Co. v. United States, 350 U.S. 148, 154 (1956). We concluded our decision by restating that civil forfeiture is "not an additional penalty for the commission of a criminal act, but rather is a separate civil sanction, remedial in nature." 89 Firearms, supra, at 366.

B

Our cases reviewing civil forfeitures under the Double Jeopardy Clause adhere to a remarkably consistent theme. Though the two-part analytical construct employed in 89 Firearms was more refined, perhaps, than that we had used over 50 years earlier in Various Items, the conclusion was the same in each case: In rem civil forfeiture is a remedial civil sanction, distinct from potentially punitive in personam civil penalties such as fines, and does not constitute a punishment under the Double Jeopardy Clause. See Gore v. United States, 357 U.S. 386, 392 (1958) ("In applying a provision like that of double jeopardy, which is rooted in history and is not an evolving concept . . . a long course of adjudication in this Court carries impressive authority").

In the case that we currently review, the Court of Appeals for the Ninth Circuit recognized as much, concluding that after 89 Firearms, "the law was clear that civil forfeitures did not constitute 'punishment' for double jeopardy purposes." 33 F.3d, at 1218. Nevertheless, that court read three of our decisions to have "abandoned" 89 Firearms and the oft-affirmed rule of Various Items. According to the Court of Appeals for the Ninth Circuit, through our decisions in United States v. Halper, 490 U.S. 435 (1989), Austin v. United States, 509 U.S. 602 (1993), and Department of Revenue of Mont. v. Kurth Ranch, 511 U.S. 767 (1994), we "changed [our] collective mind," and "adopted a new test for determining whether a nominally civil sanction constitutes 'punishment' for double jeopardy purposes." 33 F.3d, at 1218-1219. The Court of Appeals for the Sixth Circuit shared the view of the Ninth Circuit, though it did not directly rely upon Kurth Ranch. We turn now to consider whether Halper, Austin, and Kurth Ranch accomplished the radical jurisprudential shift perceived by the Courts of Appeals. . . .

We think that the Court of Appeals for the Sixth Circuit and the Court of Appeals for the Ninth Circuit misread Halper, Austin, and Kurth Ranch. None of those decisions purported to overrule the well-established teaching of Various Items, Emerald Cut Stones, and 89 Firearms. Halper involved not a civil forfeiture, but a civil penalty. That its rule was limited to the latter context is clear from the decision itself, from the historical distinction that we have drawn between civil forfeiture and civil penalties, and from the practical difficulty of applying *Halper* to a civil forfeiture. . . .

The narrow focus of *Halper* followed from the distinction that we have drawn historically between civil forfeiture and civil penalties. Since at least *Various Items*, we have distinguished civil penalties such as fines from civil forfeiture proceedings that are in rem. While a "civil action to recover . . . penaltie[s], is punitive in character," and much like a criminal prosecution in that "[i]t is the wrongdoer in person who is proceeded against . . . and punished," in an in rem forfeiture proceeding, "[i]t is the property which is proceeded against, and by resort to a legal fiction, held guilty and condemned." *Various Items*, 282 U.S., at 580-581. Thus, though for Double Jeopardy purposes we have never balanced the value of property forfeited in a particular case against the harm suffered by the Government in that case, we have balanced the size of a particular civil penalty against the Government's harm. See, e.g., Rex Trailer Co. v. United States, 350 U.S. 148, 154 (1956) (fines not "so unreasonable or excessive" as to transform a civil remedy into a criminal penalty); United States ex rel. Marcus v. Hess, 317 U.S. 537 (1943) (fine of $315,000 not so disproportionate to Government's harm of $101,500 as to transform the fine into punishment). Indeed, the rule set forth in *Halper* developed from the teaching of *Rex Trailer* and *Hess*. See *Halper*, supra, at 445-447.

It is difficult to see how the rule of *Halper* could be applied to a civil forfeiture. Civil penalties are designed as a rough form of "liquidated damages" for the harms suffered by the Government as a result of a defendant's conduct. See *Rex Trailer*, supra, at 153-154. The civil penalty involved in *Halper*, for example, provided for a fixed monetary penalty for each false claim count on which the defendant was convicted in the criminal proceeding. Whether a "fixed-penalty provision" that seeks to compensate the Government for harm it has suffered is "so extreme" and "so divorced" from the penalty's nonpunitive purpose of compensating the Government as to be a punishment may be determined by balancing the Government's harm against the size of the penalty. Civil forfeitures, in contrast to civil penalties, are designed to do more than simply compensate the Government. Forfeitures serve a variety of purposes, but are designed primarily to confiscate property used in violation of the law, and to require disgorgement of the fruits of illegal conduct. Though it may be possible to quantify the value of the property forfeited, it is virtually impossible to quantify, even approximately, the nonpunitive purposes served by a particular civil forfeiture. Hence, it is practically difficult to determine whether a particular forfeiture bears no rational relationship to the nonpunitive purposes of that forfeiture. Quite simply, the case-by-case balancing test set forth in *Halper*, in which a court must compare the harm suffered by the Government against the size of the penalty imposed, is inapplicable to civil forfeiture.

We recognized as much in *Kurth Ranch*. In that case, the Court expressly disclaimed reliance upon *Halper*, finding that its case-specific approach was impossible to apply outside the context of a fixed civil-penalty provision. . . . This is not to say that there is no occasion for analysis of the Government's harm. *89 Firearms* makes clear the relevance of an evaluation of the harms alleged. The point is simply that *Halper*'s case-specific approach is inapplicable to civil forfeitures.

In the cases that we review, the Courts of Appeals did not find *Halper* difficult to apply to civil forfeiture because they concluded that its case-by-case balancing approach had been supplanted in *Austin* by a categorical approach that found a civil sanction to be punitive if it could not "fairly be said solely to serve a remedial purpose." See *Austin*, 509 U.S., at 610; see also *Halper*, supra, at 448. But *Austin*, it must be remembered, did not involve the Double Jeopardy Clause at all. *Austin* was decided solely under the Excessive Fines Clause of the Eighth Amendment, a constitutional provision which we never have understood as parallel to, or even related to, the Double Jeopardy Clause of the Fifth Amendment. The only discussion of the Double Jeopardy Clause contained in *Austin* appears in a footnote that acknowledges our decisions holding that "[t]he Double Jeopardy Clause has been held not to apply in civil forfeiture proceedings . . . where the forfeiture could properly be characterized as remedial." *Austin*, supra, at 608, n. 4. And in *Austin* we expressly recognized and approved our decisions in *Emerald Cut Stones* and *89 Firearms*.

We acknowledged in *Austin* that our categorical approach under the Excessive Fines Clause was wholly distinct from the case-by-case approach of *Halper*, and we explained that the difference in approach was based in a significant difference between the purposes of our analysis under each constitutional provision. See *Austin*, supra, at 622, n. 14. It is unnecessary in a case under the Excessive Fines Clause to inquire at a preliminary stage whether the civil sanction imposed in that particular case is totally inconsistent with any remedial goal. Because the second stage of inquiry under the Excessive Fines Clause asks whether the particular sanction in question is so large as to be "excessive," see *Austin*, 509 U.S., at 622-623 (declining to establish criteria for excessiveness), a preliminary-stage inquiry that focused on the disproportionality of a particular sanction would be duplicative of the excessiveness analysis that would follow. See id., at 622, n. 14 ("[I]t appears to make little practical difference whether the Excessive Fines Clause applies to all forfeitures . . . or only to those that cannot be characterized as purely remedial," because the Excessive Fines Clause "prohibits only the imposition of 'excessive' fines, and a fine that serves purely remedial purposes cannot be considered 'excessive' in any event"). Forfeitures effected under 21 U.S.C. §§881(a)(4) and (a)(7) are subject to review for excessiveness under the Eighth Amendment after *Austin*; this does not mean, however, that those forfeitures are so punitive as to constitute punishment for the purposes of double jeopardy. The holding of *Austin* was limited to the Excessive Fines Clause of the Eighth Amendment, and we decline to import the analysis of *Austin* into our double jeopardy jurisprudence.

In sum, nothing in *Halper*, *Kurth Ranch*, or *Austin*, purported to replace our traditional understanding that civil forfeiture does not constitute punishment for the purpose of the Double Jeopardy Clause. Congress long has authorized the Government to bring parallel criminal proceedings and civil forfeiture proceedings, and this Court consistently has found civil forfeitures not to constitute punishment under the Double Jeopardy Clause. It would have been quite remarkable for this Court both to have held unconstitutional a well-established practice, and to have overruled a long line of precedent, without having even suggested that it was doing so. *Halper* dealt with in personam civil penalties under the Double Jeopardy Clause; *Kurth Ranch* with a tax proceeding under the Double Jeopardy Clause; and *Austin* with civil forfeitures under the Excessive Fines Clause. None of those cases dealt with the subject of this case: in rem civil forfeitures for purposes of the Double Jeopardy Clause.

C

We turn now to consider the forfeitures in these cases under the teaching of *Various Items*, *Emerald Cut Stones*, and *89 Firearms*. Because it provides a useful analytical tool, we conduct our inquiry within the framework of the two-part test used in *89 Firearms*. First, we ask whether Congress intended proceedings under 21 U.S.C. §881 and 18 U.S.C. §981 to be criminal or civil. Second, we turn to consider whether the proceedings are so punitive in fact as to "persuade us that the forfeiture proceeding[s] may not legitimately be viewed as civil in nature," despite Congress' intent. *89 Firearms*, 465 U.S., at 366.

There is little doubt that Congress intended these forfeitures to be civil proceedings. As was the case in *89 Firearms*, "Congress' intent in this regard is most clearly demonstrated by the procedural mechanisms it established for enforcing forfeitures under the statute[s]." 465 U.S., at 363. Both 21 U.S.C. §881 and 18 U.S.C. §981, which is entitled "Civil forfeiture," provide that the laws "relating to the seizure, summary and judicial forfeiture, and condemnation of property for violation of the customs laws . . . shall apply to seizures and forfeitures incurred" under §§881 and 981. See 21 U.S.C. §881(d); 18 U.S.C. §981(d). Because forfeiture proceedings under the customs laws are in rem, see 19 U.S.C. §1602 et seq., it is clear that Congress intended that a forfeiture under §881 or §981, like the forfeiture reviewed in *89 Firearms*, would be a proceeding in rem. Congress specifically structured these forfeitures to be impersonal by targeting the property itself. "In contrast to the in personam nature of criminal actions, actions in rem have traditionally been viewed as civil proceedings, with jurisdiction dependent upon seizure of a physical object." *89 Firearms*, 465 U.S., at 363, citing *Calero-Toledo*, 416 U.S., at 684. Other procedural mechanisms governing forfeitures under §§981 and 881 also indicate that Congress intended such proceedings to be civil. Forfeitures under either statute are governed by 19 U.S.C. §1607, which provides that actual notice of the impending forfeiture is unnecessary when the Government cannot identify any party with an interest in the seized article, and by §1609, which provides that seized property is subject to forfeiture through a summary administrative procedure if no party files a claim to the property. And 19 U.S.C. §1615, which governs the burden of proof in forfeiture proceedings under §881 and §981, provides that once the Government has shown probable cause that the property is subject to forfeiture, then "the burden of proof shall lie upon [the] claimant." In sum, "[b]y creating such distinctly civil procedures for forfeitures under [§§881 and 981], Congress has 'indicate[d] clearly that it intended a civil, not a criminal sanction.'" *89 Firearms*, supra, at 363, quoting Helvering v. Mitchell, 303 U.S., at 402.

Moving to the second stage of our analysis, we find that there is little evidence, much less the "clearest proof" that we require, see *89 Firearms*, supra, at 365, quoting *Ward*, 448 U.S., at 249, suggesting that forfeiture proceedings under 21 U.S.C. §§881(a)(6) and (a)(7), and 18 U.S.C. §981(a)(1)(A), are so punitive in form and effect as to render them criminal despite Congress' intent to the contrary. The statutes involved in this case are, in most significant respects, indistinguishable from those reviewed, and held not to be punitive, in *Various Items*, *Emerald Cut Stones*, and *89 Firearms*.

Most significant is that §981(a)(1)(A), and §§881(a)(6) and (a)(7), while perhaps having certain punitive aspects, serve important nonpunitive goals. Title 21 U.S.C. §881(a)(7), under which Ursery's property was forfeited, provides for the forfeiture of "all real property . . . which is used or intended to be used, in any manner or part, to commit, or to facilitate the commission of " a federal drug felony. Requiring the forfeiture of property used to commit federal narcotics violations encourages property owners to take care in managing their property and ensures that they will not permit that property to be used for illegal purposes. See Bennis v. Michigan, 516 U.S. 442, 452 (1996) ("Forfeiture of property prevents illegal uses . . . by imposing an economic penalty, thereby rendering illegal behavior unprofitable"); *89 Firearms*, supra, at 364 (forfeiture "discourages unregulated commerce in firearms"); *Calero-Toledo*, supra, at 687-688. In many circumstances, the forfeiture may abate a nuisance. See, e.g., United States v. 141st Street Corp., 911 F.2d 870 (CA2 1990) (forfeiting apartment building used to sell crack cocaine); see also *Bennis*, supra, at 452 (affirming application of Michigan statute abating car as a nuisance; forfeiture "prevent[s] further illicit use of " property). . . .

The forfeiture of the property claimed by Arlt and Wren took place pursuant to 18 U.S.C. §981(a)(1)(A), and 21 U.S.C. §881(a)(6). Section 981(a)(1)(A) provides for the forfeiture of "[a]ny property" involved in illegal money-laundering transactions. Section 881(a)(6) provides for the forfeiture of "[a]ll . . . things of value furnished or intended to be furnished by any person in exchange for " illegal drugs; "all proceeds traceable to such an exchange"; and "all moneys, negotiable instruments, and securities used or intended to be used to facilitate" a federal drug felony. The same remedial purposes served by §881(a)(7) are served by §§881(a)(6) and 981(a)(1)(A). Only one point merits separate discussion. To the extent that §881(a)(6) applies to "proceeds" of illegal drug activity, it serves the additional non-punitive goal of ensuring that persons do not profit from their illegal acts.

Other considerations that we have found relevant to the question whether a proceeding is criminal also tend to support a conclusion that §981(a)(1)(A) and §§881(a)(6) and (a)(7) are civil proceedings. See *Ward*, supra, at 247-248, n. 7, 249 (listing relevant factors and noting that they are neither exhaustive nor dispositive). First, in light of our decisions in *Various Items*, *Emerald Cut Stones*, and *89 Firearms*, and the long tradition of federal statutes providing for a forfeiture proceeding following a criminal prosecution, it is absolutely clear that in rem civil forfeiture has not historically been regarded as punishment, as we have understood that term under the Double Jeopardy Clause. Second, there is no requirement in the statutes that we currently review that the Government demonstrate scienter in order to establish that the property is subject to forfeiture; indeed, the property may be subject to forfeiture even if no party files a claim to it and the Government never shows any connection between the property and a particular person. See 19 U.S.C. §1609. Though both §§881(a) and 981(a) contain an "innocent owner" exception, we do not think that such a provision, without more indication of an intent to punish, is relevant to the question whether a statute is punitive under the Double Jeopardy Clause. Third, though both statutes may fairly be said to serve the purpose of deterrence, we long have held that this purpose may serve civil as well as criminal goals. See, e.g., *89 Firearms*, supra, at 364; *Calero-Toledo*, supra, at 677-678. We recently reaffirmed this conclusion in Bennis v. Michigan, supra, at 452, where we held that "forfeiture . . . serves a deterrent purpose distinct from any punitive purpose." Finally, though both statutes are tied to criminal activity, as was the case in *89 Firearms*, this fact is insufficient to render the statutes punitive. See *89 Firearms*, 465 U.S., at 365-366. It is well settled that "Congress may impose both a criminal and a civil sanction in respect to the same act or omission," *Helvering*, 303 U.S., at 399. By itself, the fact that a forfeiture statute has some connection to a criminal violation is far from the "clearest proof" necessary to show that a proceeding is criminal.

We hold that these in rem civil forfeitures are neither "punishment" nor criminal for purposes of the Double Jeopardy Clause. The judgments of the Court of Appeals for the Sixth Circuit, in No. 95-345, and of the Court of Appeals for the Ninth Circuit, in No. 95-346, are accordingly reversed.

It is so ordered.

[The concurring opinion of Justice Kennedy is omitted.]

JUSTICE SCALIA, with whom JUSTICE THOMAS joins, concurring in the judgment.

In my view, the Double Jeopardy Clause prohibits successive prosecution, not successive punishment. See Department of Revenue of Mont. v. Kurth Ranch, 511 U.S. 767, 798 (1994) (Scalia, J., dissenting). Civil forfeiture proceedings of the sort at issue here are not criminal prosecutions, even under the standard of Kennedy v. Mendoza-Martinez, 372 U.S. 144, 164 (1963), and United States v. Ward, 448 U.S. 242, 248-251 (1980).

JUSTICE STEVENS, concurring in the judgment in part and dissenting in part.

The question the Court poses is whether civil forfeitures constitute "punishment" for purposes of the Double Jeopardy Clause. Because the numerous federal statutes authorizing forfeitures cover such a wide variety of situations, it is quite wrong to assume that there is only one answer to that question. For purposes of analysis it is useful to identify three different categories of property that are subject to seizure: proceeds, contraband, and property that has played a part in the commission of a crime. The facts of these two cases illustrate the point.

In No. 95-346 the Government has forfeited $405,089.23 in currency. Those funds are the proceeds of unlawful activity. They are not property that respondents have any right to retain. The forfeiture of such proceeds, like the confiscation of money stolen from a bank, does not punish respondents because it exacts no price in liberty or lawfully derived property from them. I agree that the forfeiture of such proceeds is not punitive and therefore I concur in the Court's disposition of No. 95-346.

None of the property seized in No. 95-345 constituted proceeds of illegal activity. Indeed, the facts of that case reveal a dramatically different situation. Respondent Ursery cultivated marijuana in a heavily wooded area not far from his home in Shiawassee County, Michigan. The illegal substance was consumed by members of his family, but there is no evidence, and no contention by the Government, that he sold any of it to third parties. Acting on the basis of the incorrect assumption that the marijuana plants were on respondent's property, Michigan police officers executed a warrant to search the premises. In his house they found marijuana seeds, stems, stalks, and a growlight. I presume those items were seized, and I have no difficulty concluding that such a seizure does not constitute punishment because respondent had no right to possess contraband. Accordingly, I agree with the Court's opinion insofar as it explains why the forfeiture of contraband does not constitute punishment for double jeopardy purposes.

The critical question presented in No. 95-345 arose, not out of the seizure of contraband by the Michigan police, but rather out of the decision by the United States Attorney to take respondent's home. There is no evidence that the house had been purchased with the proceeds of unlawful activity and the house itself was surely not contraband. Nonetheless, 21 U.S.C. §881(a)(7) authorized the Government to seek forfeiture of respondent's residence because it had been used to facilitate the manufacture and distribution of marijuana. Respondent was then himself prosecuted for and convicted of manufacturing marijuana. In my opinion none of the reasons supporting the forfeiture of proceeds or contraband provides a sufficient basis for concluding that the confiscation of respondent's home was not punitive. . . .

In recent years, both Congress and the state legislatures have armed their law enforcement authorities with new powers to forfeit property that vastly exceed their traditional tools. In response, this Court has reaffirmed the fundamental proposition that all forfeitures must be accomplished within the constraints set by the Constitution. See, e.g., Austin v. United States, 509 U.S. 602 (1993); United States v. James Daniel Good Real Property, 510 U.S. 43 (1993). This Term the Court has begun dismantling the protections it so recently erected. In Bennis v. Michigan, 516 U.S. 442 (1996), the Court held that officials may confiscate an innocent person's automobile. And today, for the first time it upholds the forfeiture of a person's home. On the way to its surprising conclusion that the owner is not punished by the loss of his residence, the Court repeatedly professes its adherence to tradition and time-honored practice. As I discuss below, however, the decision shows a stunning disregard not only for modern precedents but for our older ones as well.

In the Court's view, the seminal case is Various Items of Personal Property v. United States, 282 U.S. 577 (1931), which approved the forfeiture of an illegal distillery by resort to the "legal fiction" that the distillery rather than its owner was being punished "as though it were conscious instead of inanimate and insentient." Id., at 581. Starting from that fanciful premise, the Court was able to conclude that confiscating the property after the owner was prosecuted for the underlying violations of the revenue laws did not offend the Double Jeopardy Clause.

According to the Court, *Various Items* established a categorical rule that the Double Jeopardy Clause was "inapplicable to civil forfeiture actions." . . . The Court asserts that this rule has received "remarkably consistent" application and was "reaffirmed" by a pair of cases in 1972 and 1984. . . . In reality, however, shortly after its announcement, *Various Items* simply disappeared from our jurisprudence. We cited that case in only two decisions over the next seven years, and never again in nearly six decades. Neither of the two cases that supposedly "affirmed" *Various Items* — One Lot Emerald Cut Stones v. United States, 409 U.S. 232 (1972) (per curiam), and United States v. One Assortment of 89 Firearms, 465 U.S. 354 (1984) — even mentioned it. More important, neither of those cases endorsed the asserted categorical rule that civil forfeitures never give rise to double jeopardy rights. Instead, each carefully considered the nature of the particular forfeiture at issue, classifying it as either "punitive" or "remedial," before deciding whether it implicated double jeopardy. . . .

The majority, surprisingly, claims that Austin v. United States, 509 U.S. 602 (1993), "expressly recognized and approved" those decisions. . . . But the Court creates the appearance that we endorsed its interpretation of *89 Firearms* and *Emerald Cut Stones* by quoting selectively from *Austin*. We actually stated the following:

> The Double Jeopardy Clause has been held not to apply in civil forfeiture proceedings, *but only in cases where the forfeiture could properly be characterized as remedial.* See United States v. One Assortment of 89 Firearms, 465 U.S. 354, 364 (1984); One Lot Emerald Cut Stones v. United States, 409 U.S. 232, 237 (1972); see generally United States v.

> Halper, 490 U.S. 435, 446-449 (1989) (Double Jeopardy Clause prohibits second sanc-
> tion that may not be fairly characterized as remedial). 509 U.S., at 608, n. 4 (emphasis
> added).

In reality, both cases rejected the monolithic view that all in rem civil forfeitures
should be treated the same, and recognized the possibility that other types of forfeitures that could not "properly be characterized as remedial" might constitute "an
additional penalty for the commission of a criminal act." 465 U.S., at 366. . . .

Read properly, therefore, *89 Firearms* and *Emerald Cut Stones* are not inconsistent
with, but set the stage for the modern understanding of how the Double Jeopardy
Clause applies in nominally civil proceedings. That understanding has been developed in a trio of recent decisions: United States v. Halper, 490 U.S. 435 (1989), Austin v. United States, 509 U.S. 602 (1993), and Department of Revenue of Montana
v. Kurth Ranch, 511 U.S. 767 (1994). The court of appeals found that the combined
effect of two of those decisions — *Halper* and *Austin* — established the proposition
that forfeitures under 21 U.S.C. §881(a)(7) implicated double jeopardy. This Court
rejects that conclusion, asserting that none of these cases changed the "oft-affirmed
rule" of *Various Items*. . . .

It is the majority, however, that has "misread" *Halper, Austin,* and *Kurth Ranch* by
artificially cabining each to a separate sphere, . . . and treating the three as if they
concerned unrelated subjects. In fact, all three were devoted to the common enterprise of giving meaning to the idea of "punishment," a concept that plays a central
role in the jurisprudence of both the Excessive Fines Clause and the Double Jeopardy Clause. *Halper* laid down a general rule for applying the Double Jeopardy
Clause to civil proceedings:

> [A] civil sanction that cannot fairly be said solely to serve a remedial purpose, but rather
> can only be explained as also serving either retributive or deterrent purposes, is pun-
> ishment, as we have come to understand the term. . . . We therefore hold that under
> the Double Jeopardy Clause a defendant who already has been punished in a criminal
> prosecution may not be subjected to an additional civil sanction to the extent that the
> second sanction may not fairly be characterized as remedial, but only as a deterrent or
> retribution. 490 U.S., at 448-449.

In the past seven years, we have applied that same rule to three types of sanctions:
civil penalties, civil forfeitures, and taxes. . . .

The claim that *Halper*'s "case-by-case" method is "impossible to apply" to
forfeitures or taxes . . . misses the point. It is true that since fixed penalties can
serve only one remedial end (compensation), it is easy to determine whether a
particular fine is punitive in application. Forfeitures and taxes, generally speaking,
may have a number of remedial rationales. But to decide if a sanction is punitive,
one need only examine each claimed remedial interest and determine whether the
sanction actually promotes it. Many of our cases have followed just such an approach, regardless of whether any nonpunitive purpose can be "quantif[ied]."
. . . See, e.g., *Austin*; One 1958 Plymouth Sedan [v. Pennsylvania, 380 U.S. 693
(1965)]. . . . Furthermore, even in the context of forfeitures and taxes, nothing prevents a court from deciding that although a sanction is designed to be remedial,
its application in a particular case is so extreme as to constitute punishment.
Austin, 509 U.S., at 608, n. 4.

In reaching the conclusion that the civil forfeiture at issue yielded punishment, the Austin Court surveyed the history of civil forfeitures at some length. That history is replete with expressions of the idea that forfeitures constitute punishment. But it was not necessary in *Austin*, strictly speaking, to decide that all in rem forfeitures are punitive. As Justice Scalia emphasized in his separate opinion, it was only necessary to characterize the specific "in rem forfeiture in *this* case." Id., at 626 (opinion concurring in part and concurring in judgment). The punitive nature of §§881(a)(4) and (a)(7) was accepted by every Member of the *Austin* Court. The majority offered several reasons for its holding. The applicable provisions expressly provided an "innocent owner" defense, indicating that culpability was a requirement for forfeiture. Further, the provisions tied forfeiture directly to the commission of narcotics offenses. Id., at 620. Finally, the legislative history indicated that the provisions were necessary because traditional criminal sanctions were "'inadequate to deter or punish.'" Ibid. (quoting S. Rep. No. 98-225, p. 191 (1983)). In sum, it was unanimously agreed that "[s]tatutory forfeitures under §881(a) are certainly *payment* (in kind), *to a sovereign* as *punishment* for an *offense*." 509 U.S., at 626-627 (Scalia, J., concurring in part and concurring in judgment) (emphasis in original).

Remarkably, the Court today stands *Austin* on its head—a decision rendered only three years ago, with unanimity on the pertinent points—and concludes that §881(a)(7) is remedial rather than punitive in character. Every reason *Austin* gave for treating §881(a)(7) as punitive—the Court rejects or ignores. Every reason the Court provides for treating §881(a)(7) as remedial—*Austin* rebuffed. The Court claims that its conclusion is consistent with decisions reviewing statutes "indistinguishable" "in most significant respects" from §881(a)(7), . . . but ignores the fact that *Austin* reached the opposite conclusion as to the *identical* statute under review here. . . .

Even if the point had not been settled by prior decisions, common sense would dictate the result in this case. There is simply no rational basis for characterizing the seizure of this respondent's home as anything other than punishment for his crime. The house was neither proceeds nor contraband and its value had no relation to the Government's authority to seize it. Under the controlling statute an essential predicate for the forfeiture was proof that respondent had used the property in connection with the commission of a crime. The forfeiture of this property was unquestionably "a penalty that had absolutely no correlation to any damages sustained by society or to the cost of enforcing the law." United States v. Ward, 448 U.S., at 254. As we unanimously recognized in *Halper*, formalistic distinctions that obscure the obvious practical consequences of governmental action disserve the "'humane interests'" protected by the Double Jeopardy Clause. 490 U.S., at 447, quoting United States ex rel. Marcus v. Hess, 317 U.S. 537, 554 (1943) (Frankfurter, J., concurring). Fidelity to both reason and precedent dictates the conclusion that *this forfeiture* was "punishment" for purposes of the Double Jeopardy Clause. . . .

One final example may illustrate the depth of my concern that the Court's treatment of our cases has cut deeply into a guarantee deemed fundamental by the Founders. The Court relies heavily on a few early decisions that involved the forfeiture of vessels whose entire mission was unlawful and on the Prohibition-era precedent sustaining the forfeiture of a distillery—a property that served no purpose other than the manufacture of illegal spirits. Notably none of those early cases involved the forfeiture of a home as a form of punishment for misconduct that occurred therein. Consider how drastic the remedy would have been if Congress in 1931 had authorized the forfeiture of every home in which alcoholic beverages were consumed. Under the Court's reasoning, I fear that the label "civil," or perhaps "in rem," would have been sufficient to avoid characterizing such forfeitures as "punitive" for purposes of the Double Jeopardy Clause. Our recent decisions in *Halper*, *Austin*, and *Kurth Ranch*, dictate a far different conclusion. I remain persuaded that those cases were correctly decided and should be followed today.

Accordingly, I respectfully dissent from the judgment in No. 95-345.

NOTES AND QUESTIONS

1. What is the right result in cases like *Ursery*? Should congressional intent control? If it does, why would Congress ever label such penalties "criminal" or "punitive"? But if the size of the penalty or forfeiture determines the outcome, a host of civil proceedings will have to comply with the many rules of constitutional criminal procedure. Would that be a bad thing?

2. To the extent that *Ursery* began to undermine the doctrinal foundations of *Halper* and *Kurth Ranch*, the Court completed the demolition job in Hudson v. United States, 522 U.S. 93 (1997). In *Hudson*, the three defendants — officers and directors of two small Oklahoma banks — were assessed civil penalties of $100,000, $50,000, and $50,000, respectively, pursuant to 12 U.S.C. §§84(a)(1) and 375b, for causing illegal loans to be made by their banks. The notice of violation, sent by the Office of the Comptroller of the Currency (OCC), made no mention of any specific harm to the government as a result of the defendants' actions. The defendants ultimately paid $16,500, $15,000, and $12,500, respectively, to settle the claims against them, and also agreed not to become involved with any banks in the future unless authorized by the OCC. Three years later, however, the defendants were indicted on charges of conspiracy, misapplication of bank funds, and making false bank entries, based on the same loans that had been involved in the earlier civil proceedings; they sought dismissal of the indictments, complaining that the subsequent criminal proceedings violated the Double Jeopardy Clause under *Halper*.

Chief Justice Rehnquist, writing for a five-member Court majority, rejected the defendants' double jeopardy claims, and in the process discarded the *Halper* test for determining whether a particular punishment is criminal or civil:

> Whether a particular punishment is criminal or civil is, at least initially, a matter of statutory construction. *Helvering*, supra, at 399. A court must first ask whether the legislature, "in establishing the penalizing mechanism, indicated either expressly or impliedly a preference for one label or the other." *Ward*, 448 U.S., at 248. Even in those cases where the legislature "has indicated an intention to establish a civil penalty, we have inquired further whether the statutory scheme was so punitive either in purpose or effect," id., at 248-249, as to "transfor[m] what was clearly intended as a civil remedy into a criminal penalty," Rex Trailer Co. v. United States, 350 U.S. 148, 154 (1956).
>
> In making this latter determination, the factors listed in Kennedy v. Mendoza-Martinez, 372 U.S. 144, 168-169 (1963), provide useful guideposts, including: (1) "[w]hether the sanction involves an affirmative disability or restraint"; (2) "whether it has historically been regarded as a punishment"; (3) "whether it comes into play only on a finding of *scienter*"; (4) "whether its operation will promote the traditional aims of punishment — retribution and deterrence"; (5) "whether the behavior to which it applies is already a crime"; (6) "whether an alternative purpose to which it may

rationally be connected is assignable for it"; and (7) "whether it appears excessive in relation to the alternative purpose assigned." It is important to note, however, that "these factors must be considered in relation to the statute on its face," id., at 169, and "only the clearest proof" will suffice to override legislative intent and transform what has been denominated a civil remedy into a criminal penalty, *Ward*, supra, at 249 (internal quotation marks omitted). . . .

We believe that *Halper*'s deviation from long-standing double jeopardy principles was ill considered. As subsequent cases have demonstrated, *Halper*'s test for determining whether a particular sanction is "punitive," and thus subject to the strictures of the Double Jeopardy Clause, has proved unworkable. We have since recognized that all civil penalties have some deterrent effect. See Department of Revenue of Montana v. Kurth Ranch, 511 U.S. 767, 777, n. 14 (1994); United States v. Ursery, 518 U.S. 267, 284-285, n. 2 (1996).[6] If a sanction must be "solely" remedial (i.e., entirely non-deterrent) to avoid implicating the Double Jeopardy Clause, then no civil penalties are beyond the scope of the Clause. Under *Halper*'s method of analysis, a court must also look at the "sanction actually imposed" to determine whether the Double Jeopardy Clause is implicated. Thus, it will not be possible to determine whether the Double Jeopardy Clause is violated until a defendant has proceeded through a trial to judgment. But in those cases where the civil proceeding follows the criminal proceeding, this approach flies in the face of the notion that the Double Jeopardy Clause forbids the government from even "*attempting* a second time to punish criminally." *Helvering*, 303 U.S., at 399 (emphasis added).

Finally, it should be noted that some of the ills at which *Halper* was directed are addressed by other constitutional provisions. The Due Process and Equal Protection Clauses already protect individuals from sanctions which are downright irrational. Williamson v. Lee Optical of Okla., Inc., 348 U.S. 483 (1955). The Eighth Amendment protects against excessive civil fines, including forfeitures. Alexander v. United States, 509 U.S. 544 (1993); Austin v. United States, 509 U.S. 602 (1993). The additional protection afforded by extending double jeopardy protections to proceedings heretofore thought to be civil is more than offset by the confusion created by attempting to distinguish between "punitive" and "nonpunitive" penalties.

522 U.S., at 99-100, 101-103.

3. After *Ursery* and *Hudson*, what is left of the Court's decision in *Halper*? Or *Kurth Ranch*? Clearly, the so-called "*Halper* test" is no longer useful as a means for determining whether a civil sanction is "punitive" enough to trigger the protection of the double jeopardy clause; henceforth, the *Hudson* Court has declared, the list of factors first identified in Kennedy v. Mendoza-Martinez, 372 U.S. 144, 168-169 (1963), will govern that question. But does the *result* in *Halper* survive? What about *Kurth Ranch*? Are there any cases in which the sheer size of the disparity between the civil sanction and the damage that is allegedly being compensated will make the civil sanction punitive?

4. Halper was assessed a civil penalty of $130,000 for Medicare fraud, after a prison sentence for the same conduct. The Kurths pled guilty to conspiracy to possess marijuana with intent to distribute and were sentenced for that crime, after which they were charged a "tax" of $900,000 on the marijuana they possessed.

___

6. In *Kurth Ranch*, we held that the presence of a deterrent purpose or effect is not dispositive of the double jeopardy question. 511 U.S., at 781. Rather, we applied a *Kennedy*-like test, see 511 U.S., at 780-783, before concluding that Montana's dangerous drug tax was "the functional equivalent of a successive criminal prosecution." Similarly, in *Ursery*, we rejected the notion that civil in rem forfeitures violate the Double Jeopardy Clause. 518 U.S., at 270-271. We upheld such forfeitures, relying on the historical support for the notion that such forfeitures are civil and thus do not implicate double jeopardy. Id., at 292.

Police found drugs in Ursery's house, leading to a government civil forfeiture proceeding against the house. Ursery was later convicted of a drug offense, for which he was sentenced to more than five years in prison. Federal bank regulators imposed civil fines of $200,000 on Hudson and his codefendants. Later, a federal grand jury indicted those same defendants for crimes based on the same conduct that had given rise to the civil fines.

In all of these cases, the government sought to incarcerate the defendants for their crimes, and also sought to impose some financial penalty for the same conduct. The question in each case was whether the financial penalty was, in essence, another criminal punishment. The Supreme Court has struggled mightily with this question. But is it really so difficult? People are regularly sued and assessed huge damages bills, including punitive damages, and no one thinks those damages bills preclude criminal prosecution. Nor does criminal prosecution preclude a private tort claim: Remember O. J. Simpson, who famously won his criminal trial for murder, and equally famously lost his subsequent civil trial for wrongful death. Why should civil claims by the government be handled differently? Perhaps they shouldn't, as long as the government's civil penalty can be reduced to dollars.

5. But the reasoning in *Ursery* and *Hudson* extends beyond financial penalties. Kansas v. Hendricks, 521 U.S. 346 (1997), involved a state statute that authorized the civil commitment of persons who, due to a "mental abnormality" or "personality disorder," have a tendency to commit "predatory acts of sexual violence." Hendricks was convicted of child molestation; after serving ten years in prison, he was about to be released to a halfway house, when the state charged him under the civil commitment statute. Hendricks claimed this "civil" proceeding violated both double jeopardy and the ban on ex post facto laws. The Court disagreed, noting that civil commitment proceedings are, after all, civil — and using the same analysis as in *Ursery* and *Hudson*. The Kansas statute passed muster because the legislature's expressed goal was "to create a civil proceeding," and because the statute's characteristics were not so similar to those of a typical criminal statute as to establish "the clearest proof" of punitive purpose or effect. Absent such proof, the legislature's "manifest intent" that the statute be treated as civil rather than criminal was dispositive. 521 U.S., at 361-369.

Hendricks meant that laws like the Kansas sexual predator statute were not facially invalid. The defendant in Seling v. Young, 531 U.S. 250 (2001), challenged Washington's similar statute as applied to his case. Young claimed that the state failed to provide the mental-health treatment that was mandated by the statute, and generally treated those confined as if they were convicted criminals serving a prison sentence, not sick patients in need of treatment. All of which, Young argued, meant that the allegedly civil commitment was actually criminal for purposes of double jeopardy law; Young also made an ex post facto claim on the same grounds. The Court rejected both claims:

> Since deciding *Hendricks*, this Court has reaffirmed the principle that determining the civil or punitive nature of an Act must begin with reference to its text and legislative history. Hudson v. United States, 522 U.S. 93 (1997). In *Hudson*, . . . this Court expressly disapproved of evaluating the civil nature of an Act by reference to the effect that Act has on a single individual. Instead, courts must evaluate the question by reference to a variety of factors "considered in relation to the statute on its face" . . . Id., at 100 (quoting Kennedy v. Mendoza-Martinez, 372 U.S. 144, 169 (1963)). . . .

> We hold that respondent cannot obtain release through an "as-applied" challenge to the Washington Act on double jeopardy and ex post facto grounds. We agree with petitioner that an "as-applied" analysis would prove unworkable. Such an analysis would never conclusively resolve whether a particular scheme is punitive and would thereby prevent a final determination of the scheme's validity under the Double Jeopardy and Ex Post Facto Clauses . . . . Unlike a fine, confinement is not a fixed event. As petitioner notes, it extends over time under conditions that are subject to change. The particular features of confinement may affect how a confinement scheme is evaluated to determine whether it is civil rather than punitive, but it remains no less true that the query must be answered definitively. The civil nature of a confinement scheme cannot be altered based merely on vagaries in the implementation of the authorizing statute.

531 U.S., at 262-263.

Are you persuaded? Should the government be able to incarcerate its citizens twice for the same conduct? Isn't that what the laws at issue in *Hendricks* and *Seling* authorize? Given the breadth of the civil commitment power, what is to stop the government from transferring a large portion of the criminal code to the civil side of the legal ledger? Can the law of constitutional criminal procedure be evaded so easily?

Chapter 17

Appellate and Collateral Review

A. Appellate Review

1. The Defendant's Right to Appeal

In every state and the federal system, a defendant who has been convicted of a crime has a right to appeal that conviction. It might surprise you to learn that this right is not grounded in the United States Constitution; for more than 100 years, the Supreme Court has consistently maintained that the defendant's right to appeal in a criminal case is purely a creature of statute, not a component of due process, and thus presumably can be eliminated if the legislature chooses to do so. See, e.g., Jones v. Barnes, 463 U.S. 745 (1983); McKane v. Durston, 153 U.S. 684 (1894). Today, however, it seems unthinkable that a convicted defendant would be denied the right to appeal. Why might the Court refuse to recognize a constitutional right to appeal, despite the fact that such a right is seemingly taken for granted in every American jurisdiction? Is the Court worried about some further consequence — e.g., concerning the right to the effective assistance of counsel on appeal — that might follow from the recognition of such a constitutional right to appeal?

Most states and the federal government provide for a statutory "right" to appeal only to the level of the intermediate appellate court (where one exists); further appellate review by the highest court in the jurisdiction is available only if that court agrees to accept the case. The right to appeal is generally viewed as waivable; many (if not most) plea bargains include an explicit agreement by the defendant not to appeal his conviction. See Note, An Unjust Bargain: Plea Bargains and Waiver of the Right to Appeal, 51 B.C. L. Rev. 871 (2010). For further discussion of the effect of guilty pleas on the right to appeal, see supra, Chapter 13, page 1230.

2. The Prosecution's Right to Appeal

Like defense appeals, the prosecution's right to appeal in a criminal case is also purely a creature of statute. But the prosecution's right to appeal is necessarily far more limited than that of the defendant. This is primarily because of the double jeopardy clause, which absolutely bars prosecution appeals from verdicts of acquittal by the factfinder (or their functional equivalent, see Chapter 16, supra). Thus, statutes granting the prosecution the right to appeal in criminal cases apply mostly in three special contexts: (1) interlocutory appeals from certain pretrial orders, such as suppression orders or orders dismissing an indictment; (2) appeals from posttrial rulings that set aside a guilty verdict rendered by the factfinder (in such situations, reinstatement of the guilty verdict, on appeal, does not violate double jeopardy); and (3) sentencing appeals, which were virtually nonexistent under traditional discretionary sentencing systems but have become commonplace under determinate or guideline sentencing systems. See, e.g., 18 U.S.C. §3731, authorizing prosecution appeals, in federal criminal cases, from all final orders except when the appeal would be barred by double jeopardy, as well as from certain kinds of suppression orders (even though not final); 18 U.S.C. §3742(b), authorizing prosecution appeals of sentences in federal criminal cases, to the extent those sentences were imposed "in violation of law" or in contravention of the Federal Sentencing Guidelines. In short, the right to appeal in criminal cases is far from symmetrical. See Kate Stith, The Risk of Legal Error in Criminal Cases: Some Consequences of the Asymmetry in the Right to Appeal, 57 U. Chi. L. Rev. 1 (1990).

In determinate sentencing jurisdictions, sentencing appeals — filed by both sides — have become a dominant feature of appellate litigation. For example, during the year ending September 30, 2006, the U.S. Courts of Appeals resolved 13,642 appeals in criminal cases that were subject to the Federal Sentencing Guidelines. Of those, more than 92.6 percent involved at least one sentencing issue, and more than one out of three (4,556) involved *only* sentencing issues. See Mark Motivans, Federal Justice Statistics, 2006 (NCJ 225711, May 2009), published by the U.S. Department of Justice, Bureau of Justice Statistics, and available online at http://bjs.ojp.usdoj.gov/.

3. Interlocutory Appeals

In Flanagan v. United States, 465 U.S. 259 (1984), the Supreme Court held that, under 28 U.S.C. §1291, the federal statute that generally governs appeals from final orders of federal district courts, a pretrial order disqualifying defense counsel in a criminal case is not a "final collateral order" subject to interlocutory appeal by the defendant. The Court explained that three conditions must be met for the so-called "collateral order" doctrine to apply: (1) the order "must conclusively determine the disputed question"; (2) the order must "resolve an important issue completely separate from the merits of the action"; and (3) the order must "be effectively unreviewable on appeal from a final judgment." The Court noted that these conditions have been interpreted "with the utmost strictness in criminal cases"; indeed, the only kinds of orders previously found to satisfy the test were those (1) denying a motion to reduce bail, (2) denying a motion to dismiss an indictment on double jeopardy grounds, and (3) denying a motion to dismiss an indictment for violation of the speech or debate clause. An order disqualifying counsel, according to the Court, "lacks the critical characteristics that make [such orders] immediately appealable. Unlike a request for bail reduction, a constitutional objection to counsel's disqualification is in no danger of becoming moot upon conviction and sentence. Moreover, it cannot be said that the right petitioners assert . . . is a right not to be tried. Double jeopardy and Speech or Debate rights are sui generis in this regard."

See also Midland Asphalt Corp. v. United States, 489 U.S. 794 (1989), holding that an order denying a claim of violation of Fed. R. Crim. P. 6(e), in connection with a grand jury proceeding, is not subject to interlocutory appeal by the defendant because the issues involved in the claim are "enmeshed in the merits of the dispute." The rub here is that such orders are *also* not generally reviewable *after* conviction, because the conviction itself establishes conclusively that the alleged defect in the indictment was "harmless error." Cf. United States v. Mechanik, 475 U.S. 66 (1986) (involving alleged Rule 6(d) violation). In many jurisdictions, prosecutors are granted somewhat greater leeway than defendants to file interlocutory appeals from pretrial orders, largely because of the aforementioned asymmetry that prevents the prosecutor from appealing most adverse trial verdicts. See, e.g., 18 U.S.C. §3731, authorizing interlocutory appeals by the prosecution, in federal criminal cases, from certain kinds of suppression orders.

4. What Law Applies?

In general, of course, an appellate court must review the decision of the court below on the basis of all of the relevant state and/or federal law. But what if the relevant law has changed since the time when the court below rendered its decision? Under what circumstances should a new legal rule apply "retroactively," to require the reversal of a decision that might have been proper under the law that was applicable at the time?

For more than two decades, beginning with the decision in Linkletter v. Walker, 381 U.S. 618 (1965), the Supreme Court held that the retroactivity of new constitutional rules was to be determined separately for each new rule, based on an analysis of three factors: "(a) the purpose to be served by the new standards, (b) the extent of the reliance by law enforcement authorities on the old standards, and (c) the effect on the administration of justice of a retroactive application of the new standards." See Stovall v. Denno, 388 U.S. 293, 297 (1967).

In Griffith v. Kentucky, 479 U.S. 314 (1987), however, the Court discarded the *Linkletter* approach, holding instead that, henceforth, all new constitutional rules must be applied retroactively to all cases still pending on direct appeal:

> [F]ailure to apply a newly declared constitutional rule to criminal cases pending on direct review violates basic norms of constitutional adjudication. . . . [I]t is a settled principle that this Court adjudicates only "cases" and "controversies." See U.S. Const., Art. III, §2. Unlike a legislature, we do not promulgate new rules of constitutional criminal procedure on a broad basis. Rather, the nature of judicial review requires that we adjudicate specific cases, and each case usually becomes the vehicle for announcement of a new rule. But after we have decided a new rule in the case selected, the integrity of judicial review requires that we apply that rule to all similar cases pending on direct review.

Id., at 322-323. The Court further held that no exception would be recognized for new constitutional rules that make a "clear break" with past precedent — even in such situations, the new rule would be applied retroactively, for two reasons:

> First, the principle that this Court does not disregard current law, when it adjudicates a case pending before it on direct review, applies regardless of the specific characteristics of the particular new rule announced. . . .
> Second, the use of a "clear break" exception creates the same problem of not treating similarly situated defendants the same. . . .

Id., at 326-327.

On the related issue of retroactivity in the context of collateral review, see Teague v. Lane, 489 U.S. 288 (1989), discussed at page 1584, infra.

5. Prejudice and Harmless Error

When a defendant seeks to overturn a criminal conviction on appeal, it is not always enough to persuade the appellate court that a legal (or even a constitutional) error occurred during the trial. Most of the time, the court also must decide whether any prejudice, or harm, resulted from the error. Depending on the particular kind of error involved, and on the procedural posture of the particular case, different rules with respect to prejudice will apply.

First, some relatively rare kinds of errors — including ineffective assistance of counsel under Strickland v. Washington, or prosecutorial failure to disclose material exculpatory evidence under Brady v. Maryland — contain a prejudice requirement as an inherent part of the definition of what constitutes error in the first place. For such kinds of errors, the appellate court cannot find error at all without first finding prejudice. Second, other relatively rare kinds of errors — such as denial of counsel under Gideon v. Wainwright, or denial of the right to self-representation under Faretta v. California — always lead to reversal (assuming they are preserved at trial and presented on appeal in the proper manner), even if the defendant cannot show any prejudice. This is either because such errors are presumed to be prejudicial, or because they are so fundamental that no prejudice is required. Third, for most kinds of errors, reversal on appeal is automatic (again, assuming proper preservation at trial and presentation on appeal), unless the *government* can prove that the error was "harmless." Finally, if an error is not preserved properly at trial (such as by failing to make a contemporaneous objection), then reversal on appeal depends on whether the defendant can persuade the appellate court that the error constituted "plain error," which — at least in the federal courts — requires a showing that it "affect[ed] substantial rights."

The following case and notes explore various aspects of these different prejudice rules.

CHAPMAN v. CALIFORNIA

Certiorari to the Supreme Court of California
386 U.S. 18 (1967)

JUSTICE BLACK delivered the opinion of the Court.

Petitioners, Ruth Elizabeth Chapman and Thomas LeRoy Teale, were convicted in a California state court upon a charge that they robbed, kidnaped, and murdered a bartender. She was sentenced to life imprisonment and he to death. At the time of the trial, Art. I, §13, of the State's Constitution provided that "in any criminal case, whether the defendant testifies or not, his failure to explain or to deny by his testimony any evidence or facts in the case against him may be commented upon by the court and by counsel, and may be considered by the court or the jury." Both petitioners in this case chose not to testify at their trial, and the State's attorney prosecuting them took full advantage of his right under the State Constitution to comment upon their failure to testify, filling his argument to the jury from beginning to end with numerous references to their silence and inferences of their guilt resulting therefrom. The trial court also charged the jury that it could draw adverse inferences from petitioners' failure to testify. Shortly after the trial, but before petitioners' cases had been considered on appeal by the California Supreme Court, this Court decided Griffin v. California, 380 U.S. 609 [(1965)], in which we held California's constitutional provision and practice invalid on the ground that they put a penalty on the exercise of a person's right not to be compelled to be a witness against himself, guaranteed by the Fifth Amendment to the United States Constitution and made applicable to California and the other States by the Fourteenth Amendment. . . . On appeal, the State Supreme Court, . . . admitting that petitioners had been denied a federal constitutional right by the comments on their silence, nevertheless affirmed, applying the State Constitution's harmless-error provision, which forbids reversal unless "the court shall be of the opinion that the error complained of has resulted in a miscarriage of justice." . . .

I

Before deciding the two questions here — whether there can ever be harmless constitutional error and whether the error here was harmless — we must first decide whether state or federal law governs. The application of a state harmless-error rule is, of course, a state question where it involves only errors of state procedure or state law. But the error from which these petitioners suffered was a denial of rights guaranteed against invasion by the Fifth and Fourteenth Amendments. . . . We have no hesitation in saying that the right of these petitioners not to be punished for exercising their Fifth and Fourteenth Amendment right to be silent — expressly created by the Federal Constitution itself — is a federal right which, in the absence of appropriate congressional action, it is our responsibility to protect by fashioning the necessary rule.

II

We are urged by petitioners to hold that all federal constitutional errors, regardless of the facts and circumstances, must always be deemed harmful. Such a holding, as petitioners correctly point out, would require an automatic reversal of their convictions and make further discussion unnecessary. We decline to adopt any such rule. All 50 states have harmless-error statutes or rules, and the United States long ago through its Congress established for its courts the rule that judgments shall not be reversed for "errors or defects which do not affect the substantial rights of the parties." 28 U.S.C. §2111. None of these rules on its face distinguishes between federal constitutional errors and errors of state law or federal statutes and rules. All of these rules, state or federal, serve a very useful purpose insofar as they block setting aside convictions for small errors or defects that have little, if any, likelihood of having changed the result of the trial. We conclude that there may be some constitutional errors which in the setting of a particular case are so unimportant and insignificant that they may, consistent with the Federal Constitution, be deemed harmless, not requiring the automatic reversal of the conviction.

III

In fashioning a harmless-constitutional-error rule, we must recognize that harmless-error rules can work very unfair and mischievous results when, for example, highly important and persuasive evidence, or argument, though legally forbidden, finds its way into a trial in which the question of guilt or innocence is a close one. What harmless-error rules all aim at is a rule that will save the good in harmless-error practices while avoiding the bad, so far as possible.

. . . . We prefer the approach of this Court in deciding what was harmless error in our recent case of Fahy v. Connecticut, 375 U.S. 85 [(1963)]. There we said: "The question is whether there is a reasonable possibility that the evidence complained of might have contributed to the conviction." . . . Although our prior cases have indicated that there are some constitutional rights so basic to a fair trial that their infraction can never be treated as harmless error,[8] this statement in *Fahy* itself belies any belief that all trial errors which violate the Constitution automatically call for reversal. At the same time, however, like the federal harmless-error statute, it emphasizes an intention not to treat as harmless those constitutional errors that "affect substantial rights" of a party. An error in admitting plainly relevant evidence which possibly influenced the jury adversely to a litigant cannot, under *Fahy*, be conceived of as harmless. Certainly error, constitutional error, in illegally admitting highly prejudicial evidence or comments, casts on someone other than the person prejudiced by it a burden to show that it was harmless. It is for that reason that the original common-law harmless-error rule put the burden on the beneficiary of the error either to prove that there was no injury or to suffer a reversal of his erroneously obtained judgment. There is little, if any, difference between our statement in Fahy v. Connecticut about "whether there is a reasonable possibility that the evidence complained of might have contributed to the conviction" and requiring the beneficiary of a constitutional error to prove beyond a reasonable doubt that the error complained of did not contribute to the verdict obtained. We, therefore, do no more than adhere to the meaning of our *Fahy* case when we hold, as we now do, that before a federal constitutional error can be held harmless, the court must be able to declare a belief that it was harmless beyond a reasonable doubt. While appellate courts do not ordinarily have the original task of applying such a test, it is a familiar standard to all courts, and we believe its adoption will provide a more workable standard, although achieving the same result as that aimed at in our *Fahy* case.

IV

Applying the foregoing standard, we have no doubt that the error in these cases was not harmless to petitioners. . . .

. . . . [T]he state prosecutor's argument and the trial judge's instruction to the jury continuously and repeatedly impressed the jury that from the failure of petitioners to testify, to all intents and purposes, the inferences from the facts in evidence had to be drawn in favor of the State — in short, that by their silence petitioners had served as irrefutable witnesses against themselves. And though the case in which this occurred presented a reasonably strong "circumstantial web of evidence" against petitioners . . . , it was also a case in which, absent the constitutionally forbidden comments, honest, fair-minded jurors might very well have brought in not-guilty verdicts. Under these circumstances, it is completely impossible for us to say that the

8. See, e.g., Payne v. Arkansas, 356 U.S. 560 [(1958)] (coerced confession); Gideon v. Wainwright, 372 U.S. 335 [(1963)] (right to counsel); Tumey v. Ohio, 273 U.S. 510 [(1927)] (impartial judge).

State has demonstrated, beyond a reasonable doubt, that the prosecutor's comments and the trial judge's instruction did not contribute to petitioners' convictions. Such a machine-gun repetition of a denial of constitutional rights, designed and calculated to make petitioners' version of the evidence worthless, can no more be considered harmless than the introduction against a defendant of a coerced confession. See, e.g., Payne v. Arkansas, 356 U.S. 560 [(1958)]. Petitioners are entitled to a trial free from the pressure of unconstitutional inferences. . . .

JUSTICE STEWART, concurring in the result. . . .

. . . [C]onstitutional rights are not fungible goods. The differing values which they represent and protect may make a harmless-error rule appropriate for one type of constitutional error and not for another. I would not foreclose the possibility that a harmless-error rule might appropriately be applied to some constitutional violations.[2] Indeed, one source of my disagreement with the Court's opinion is its implicit assumption that the same harmless-error rule should apply indiscriminately to all constitutional violations.

. . . The adoption of any harmless-error rule . . . , commits this Court to a case-by-case examination to determine the extent to which we think unconstitutional comment on a defendant's failure to testify influenced the outcome of a particular trial. This burdensome obligation is one that we here are hardly qualified to discharge. . . .

For these reasons I believe it inappropriate to inquire whether the violation of Griffin v. California that occurred in this case was harmless by any standard, and accordingly I concur in the reversal of the judgment.

[The dissenting opinion of Justice Harlan is omitted.]

NOTES AND QUESTIONS

1. What is the source of the Court's authority to develop a harmless-error rule for constitutional errors in *Chapman*? Is this an example of "constitutional common law"? See Daniel Meltzer, Harmless Error and Constitutional Remedies, 61 U. Chi. L. Rev. 1 (1994).

Does the existence of a harmless-error rule subvert the normal relationship between trial and appellate courts? What about the special role of the jury in our criminal justice system? How is it possible for an appellate court to determine that a particular constitutional error was harmless, without intruding on the domain of the jury?

The Court in *Chapman* pointed out that harmless-error rules exist everywhere, for all kinds of errors. Why, then, was the Court so cautious in the articulation of its new harmless-error rule for federal constitutional violations? What kinds of problems might the Court have been trying to anticipate — and avoid? If enough instances of a particular constitutional error are found to be harmless, what are the

---

2. For example, quite different considerations are involved when evidence is introduced which was obtained in violation of the Fourth and Fourteenth Amendments. The exclusionary rule in that context balances the desirability of deterring objectionable police conduct against the undesirability of excluding relevant and reliable evidence. The resolution of these values with interests of judicial economy might well dictate a harmless-error rule for such violations. . . .

consequences for the viability of the underlying constitutional rule? In such a situation, is it not likely that the wisdom of the rule itself might someday be revisited? See Steven Goldberg, Harmless Error: Constitutional Sneak Thief, 71 J. Crim. L. & Criminology 421 (1980).

2. In *Chapman*, the Court referred to Payne v. Arkansas, 356 U.S. 560 (1958), involving the introduction of a coerced confession, as an example of a case *not* subject to harmless-error review. See footnote 8, supra. In Arizona v. Fulminante, 499 U.S. 279 (1991), however, Chief Justice Rehnquist, writing for a majority on the issue, reached the opposite conclusion — and, in the process, developed a new approach for determining whether particular constitutional errors are subject to *Chapman* analysis:

> Since this Court's landmark decision in Chapman v. California, 386 U.S. 18 (1967), in which we adopted the general rule that a constitutional error does not automatically require reversal of a conviction, the Court has applied harmless-error analysis to a wide range of errors and has recognized that most constitutional errors can be harmless. See, e.g., Clemons v. Mississippi, 494 U.S. 738, 752-754 (1990) (unconstitutionally overbroad jury instructions at the sentencing stage of a capital case); Satterwhite v. Texas, 486 U.S. 249 (1988) (admission of evidence at the sentencing stage of a capital case in violation of the Sixth Amendment Counsel Clause); Carella v. California, 491 U.S. 263, 266 (1989) (jury instruction containing an erroneous conclusive presumption); Pope v. Illinois, 481 U.S. 497, 501-504 (1987) (jury instruction misstating an element of the offense); Rose v. Clark, 478 U.S. 570 (1986) (jury instruction containing an erroneous rebuttable presumption); Crane v. Kentucky, 476 U.S. 683, 691 (1986) (erroneous exclusion of defendant's testimony regarding the circumstances of his confession); Delaware v. Van Arsdall, 475 U.S. 673 (1986) (restriction on a defendant's right to cross-examine a witness for bias in violation of the Sixth Amendment Confrontation Clause); Rushen v. Spain, 464 U.S. 114, 117-118, and n. 2 (1983) (denial of a defendant's right to be present at trial); United States v. Hasting, 461 U.S. 499 (1983) (improper comment on defendant's silence at trial, in violation of the Fifth Amendment Self-Incrimination Clause); Hopper v. Evans, 456 U.S. 605 (1982) (statute improperly forbidding trial court's giving a jury instruction on a lesser included offense in a capital case in violation of the Due Process Clause); Kentucky v. Whorton, 441 U.S. 786 (1979) (failure to instruct the jury on the presumption of innocence); Moore v. Illinois, 434 U.S. 220, 232 (1977) (admission of identification evidence in violation of the Sixth Amendment Confrontation Clause); Brown v. United States, 411 U.S. 223, 231-232 (1973) (admission of the out-of-court statement of a nontestifying codefendant in violation of the Sixth Amendment Confrontation Clause); Milton v. Wainwright, 407 U.S. 371 (1972) (confession obtained in violation of Massiah v. United States, 377 U.S. 201 (1964)); Chambers v. Maroney, 399 U.S. 42, 52-53 (1970) (admission of evidence obtained in violation of the Fourth Amendment); Coleman v. Alabama, 399 U.S. 1, 10-11 (1970) (denial of counsel at a preliminary hearing in violation of the Sixth Amendment Counsel Clause).
>
> The common thread connecting these cases is that each involved "trial error" — error which occurred during the presentation of the case to the jury, and which may therefore be quantitatively assessed in the context of other evidence presented in order to determine whether its admission was harmless beyond a reasonable doubt. In applying harmless-error analysis to these many different constitutional violations, the Court has been faithful to the belief that the harmless-error doctrine is essential to preserve the "principle that the central purpose of a criminal trial is to decide the factual question of the defendant's guilt or innocence, and promotes public

respect for the criminal process by focusing on the underlying fairness of the trial rather than on the virtually inevitable presence of immaterial error." . . .

The admission of an involuntary confession — a classic "trial error" — is markedly different from the other two constitutional violations referred to in the *Chapman* footnote as not being subject to harmless-error analysis. One of those violations, involved in Gideon v. Wainwright, 372 U.S. 335 (1963), was the total deprivation of the right to counsel at trial. The other violation, involved in Tumey v. Ohio, 273 U.S. 510 (1927), was a judge who was not impartial. These are structural defects in the constitution of the trial mechanism, which defy analysis by "harmless-error" standards. The entire conduct of the trial from beginning to end is obviously affected by the absence of counsel for a criminal defendant, just as it is by the presence on the bench of a judge who is not impartial. Since our decision in *Chapman*, other cases have added to the category of constitutional errors which are not subject to harmless error the following: unlawful exclusion of members of the defendant's race from a grand jury, Vasquez v. Hillery, 474 U.S. 254 (1986); the right to self-representation at trial, McKaskle v. Wiggins, 465 U.S. 168, 177-178, n. 8 (1984); and the right to public trial, Waller v. Georgia, 467 U.S. 39, 49, n. 9 (1984). Each of these constitutional deprivations is a similar structural defect affecting the framework within which the trial proceeds, rather than simply an error in the trial process itself. "Without these basic protections, a criminal trial cannot reliably serve its function as a vehicle for determination of guilt or innocence, and no criminal punishment may be regarded as fundamentally fair." . . .

It is evident from a comparison of the constitutional violations which we have held subject to harmless error, and those which we have held not, that involuntary statements or confessions belong in the former category. The admission of an involuntary confession is a "trial error," similar in both degree and kind to the erroneous admission of other types of evidence. . . . When reviewing the erroneous admission of an involuntary confession, the appellate court, as it does with the admission of other forms of improperly admitted evidence, simply reviews the remainder of the evidence against the defendant to determine whether the admission of the confession was harmless beyond a reasonable doubt.

Nor can it be said that the admission of an involuntary confession is the type of error which "transcends the criminal process." This Court has applied harmless-error analysis to the violation of other constitutional rights similar in magnitude and importance and involving the same level of police misconduct. . . .

Of course an involuntary confession may have a more dramatic effect on the course of a trial than do other trial errors — in particular cases it may be devastating to a defendant — but this simply means that a reviewing court will conclude in such a case that its admission was not harmless error; it is not a reason for eschewing the harmless-error test entirely. . . .

Id., at 306-312.

Justice White, in dissent on the same issue in *Fulminante*, argued that "a coerced confession is fundamentally different from other types of erroneously admitted evidence to which the [*Chapman*] rule has been applied. . . . The inability to assess its effect on a conviction causes the admission at trial of a coerced confession to 'defy analysis by "harmless-error" standards,' just as certainly as do deprivation of counsel and trial before a biased judge." Id., at 289-290. On the separate issue of the application of the *Chapman* standard to the facts of the case, however, Justice White carried a majority, concluding that the erroneous introduction of the coerced confession was not harmless. See id., at 295-302.

3. Are you confident that you can recognize the distinction between "trial errors" and "structural errors"? What about errors in the jury instructions concerning the

prosecution's burden of proof at trial? How do such errors fit into the *Fulminante* scheme? The Court has addressed this subject in several cases.

In Rose v. Clark, 478 U.S. 570 (1986), the Court — pre-*Fulminante* — held that a jury instruction that created an unconstitutional presumption about an element of the crime was subject to *Chapman* harmless-error analysis. Reviewing numerous harmless-error cases, the Court concluded that "harmless-error analysis . . . presupposes a trial, at which the defendant, represented by counsel, may present evidence and argument before an impartial judge and jury." Because the presumption instruction neither denied the defendant such a trial, nor operated as the equivalent of a directed verdict for the prosecution, the Court held *Chapman* applicable. The case was remanded to allow the lower court to decide, in the first instance, whether the error was harmless under *Chapman*.

Yates v. Evatt, 500 U.S. 391 (1991), involved a similar challenge — post-*Fulminante* — to an unconstitutional presumption instruction. This time, however, the lower court had previously tried, and failed, to apply the *Chapman* harmless-error standard properly. The Court, in a majority opinion by Justice Souter, thus felt compelled to provide the lower court with more guidance than it had in Rose v. Clark:

> To say that an error did not contribute to the verdict is, rather, to find that error unimportant in relation to everything else the jury considered on the issue in question, as revealed in the record. Thus, to say that an instruction to apply an unconstitutional presumption did not contribute to the verdict is to make a judgment about the significance of the presumption to reasonable jurors, when measured against the other evidence considered by those jurors independently of the presumption.
>
> Before reaching such a judgment, a court must take two quite distinct steps. First, it must ask what evidence the jury actually considered in reaching its verdict. If, for example, the fact presumed is necessary to support the verdict, a reviewing court must ask what evidence the jury considered as tending to prove or disprove that fact. Did the jury look at only the predicate facts, or did it consider other evidence bearing on the fact subject to the presumption? In answering this question, a court does not conduct a subjective enquiry into the jurors' minds. The answer must come, instead, from analysis of the instructions given to the jurors and from application of that customary presumption that jurors follow instructions and, specifically, that they consider relevant evidence on a point in issue when they are told that they may do so.
>
> Once a court has made the first enquiry into the evidence considered by the jury, it must then weigh the probative force of that evidence as against the probative force of the presumption standing alone. To satisfy *Chapman*'s reasonable-doubt standard, it will not be enough that the jury considered evidence from which it could have come to the verdict without reliance on the presumption. Rather, the issue under *Chapman* is whether the jury actually rested its verdict on evidence establishing the presumed fact beyond a reasonable doubt, independently of the presumption. Since that enquiry cannot be a subjective one into the jurors' minds, a court must approach it by asking whether the force of the evidence presumably considered by the jury in accordance with the instructions is so overwhelming as to leave it beyond a reasonable doubt that the verdict resting on that evidence would have been the same in the absence of the presumption. It is only when the effect of the presumption is comparatively minimal to this degree that it can be said, in *Chapman*'s words, that the presumption did not contribute to the verdict rendered.

Id., at 403-405.

Finally, in Sullivan v. Louisiana, 508 U.S. 275 (1993), the Court, in a majority opinion by Justice Scalia, held that a constitutionally deficient "reasonable doubt" instruction cannot be harmless error. The Court explained that "[t]he inquiry . . . is not whether, in a trial that occurred without the error, a guilty verdict would surely have been rendered, but whether the guilty verdict actually rendered in *this* trial was surely unattributable to the error. That must be so, because to hypothesize a guilty verdict that was never in fact rendered — no matter how inescapable the findings to support that verdict might be — would violate the jury-trial guarantee." Id., at 279. Because the deficient instruction wholly deprived the defendant of a jury verdict of "guilty-beyond-a-reasonable-doubt," "[t]here is no *object*, so to speak, upon which the harmless-error scrutiny can operate. . . . The Sixth Amendment requires more than appellate speculation about a hypothetical jury's action, or else directed verdicts for the State would be sustainable on appeal; it requires an actual jury finding of guilty." Id., at 280.

The *Sullivan* Court distinguished the defective "reasonable doubt" instruction from an unconstitutional presumption: "A reviewing court may . . . be able to conclude that the presumption played no significant role in the finding of guilt beyond a reasonable doubt. *Yates*, supra, at 402-406. But the essential connection to a 'beyond a reasonable doubt' factual finding cannot be made where the instructional error consists of a misdescription of the burden of proof, which vitiates *all* the jury's findings. A reviewing court can only engage in pure speculation — its view of what a reasonable jury would have done. And when it does that, 'the wrong entity judge[s] the defendant guilty.'" Id., at 281.

Do you agree that there is a significant difference between Rose v. Clark and Yates v. Evatt on the one hand, and *Sullivan* on the other? Didn't all three cases involve similar failures by the prosecution to satisfy the constitutionally mandated burden of proof?

4. Six years after Sullivan, the Court further complicated the matter. In Neder v. United States, 527 U.S. 1 (1999), the defendant was prosecuted for tax fraud. The trial judge determined that the defendant's false statements were "material." This was error, because under United States v. Gaudin, 515 U.S. 506 (1995), materiality is an element of the crime of tax fraud, and thus should have been submitted to the jury for determination. On appeal, the defendant claimed, inter alia, that the error could not be harmless, because — under the rationale of *Sullivan* — there was no jury verdict on the issue of materiality to which harmless-error analysis could be applied.

The Court, in a majority opinion by Chief Justice Rehnquist, disagreed: "Unlike such defects as the complete deprivation of counsel or trial before a biased judge, an instruction that omits an element of the offense does not necessarily render a criminal trial fundamentally unfair or an unreliable vehicle for determining guilt or innocence." *Neder*, 527 U.S., at 9. The Court explained that, contrary to the "reasonable doubt" instruction error in *Sullivan*, the error in *Neder* did not "vitiate[] *all* the jury's findings"; instead, only one particular finding (materiality) was affected. Id., at 11. Moreover, according to the Court, many past harmless-error cases, such as Yates v. Evatt and Rose v. Clark, likewise involved defective jury instructions on one or more of the elements of the crime charged. The Court frankly conceded that "[i]t would not be illogical to extend the reasoning of *Sullivan* from a defective 'reasonable doubt' instruction to a failure to instruct on an element of the crime," but ultimately concluded that the sheer weight of precedent (such as Yates v. Evatt and

Rose v. Clark), coupled with the fact that the defendant in *Neder* never seriously contested the materiality of his false statements, militated in favor of applying the *Chapman* harmless-error standard. Id., at 15. Under that standard, the Court held the error to be harmless beyond a reasonable doubt, and affirmed the tax fraud conviction.

Justice Scalia, joined by Justices Souter and Ginsburg in dissent on the harmless-error issue, responded: "A court cannot, no matter how clear the defendant's culpability, direct a guilty verdict. . . . The question that this raises is why, if denying the right to conviction by jury is structural error, taking one of the elements of the crime away from the jury should be treated differently from taking all of them away — since failure to prove one, no less than failure to prove all, utterly prevents conviction." Id., at 32-33.

Justice Stevens, in concurrence, also disagreed with the majority's harmless-error analysis but found that the jury had implicitly and necessarily decided the materiality issue and hence the error was, indeed, harmless "under any test of harmlessness." Id., at 26.

Can *Neder* be squared with *Sullivan*? Why was the defendant's failure to contest the issue of materiality relevant to the threshold question whether *Chapman* harmless-error analysis applies? What is the constitutional difference, if any, between directing a verdict for the prosecution in general, and doing so with respect to one element of the crime charged?

In Washington v. Recuenco, 548 U.S. 212 (2006), the Court relied on *Neder* to hold that *Blakely/Booker* errors (involving the failure to submit to a jury, under a "beyond reasonable doubt" standard, the existence of certain sentencing factors that operate functionally as elements of a new, enhanced crime — see Chapter 15, at page 1451) are subject to "harmless error" review.

5. In Kotteakos v. United States, 328 U.S. 750 (1946), the Court discussed the proper application of the federal harmless-error statute, which applies to most federal criminal cases involving nonconstitutional error: "[T]he question is, not were [the jurors] right in their judgment, regardless of the error or its effect upon the verdict. It is rather what effect the error had or reasonably may be taken to have had upon the jury's decision. . . . If, when all is said and done, the conviction is sure that the error did not influence the jury, or had but very slight effect, the verdict and the judgment should stand, except perhaps where the departure is from a constitutional norm or a specific command of Congress. But if one cannot say, after pondering all that happened without stripping the erroneous action from the whole, that the judgment was not substantially swayed by the error, it is impossible to conclude that substantial rights were not affected." *Kotteakos* returned to prominence when the Court relied upon it in Brecht v. Abrahamson, 507 U.S. 619 (1993), to define the appropriate harmless-error standard for federal habeas review of state convictions. See page 1617, infra.

6. As previously mentioned, an error that is not properly preserved at trial generally will not lead to reversal on appeal, unless the error is held to be "plain error." The Federal Rules of Criminal Procedure provide:

Rule 52. Harmless and Plain Error

   (a) Harmless Error. Any error, defect, irregularity, or variance that does not affect substantial rights must be disregarded.

(b) Plain Error. A plain error that affects substantial rights may be considered even though it was not brought to the court's attention.

In United States v. Olano, 507 U.S. 725 (1993), the Court elaborated on the meaning of "plain error," and its relationship with "harmless error," under Rule 52. The case involved a violation of Rule 24(c), which at the time provided that alternate jurors must be dismissed after the jury has retired for deliberation.[1] The defendant, however, did not object to the error. The Court, in an opinion by Justice O'Connor, explained:

> The first limitation on appellate authority under Rule 52(b) is that there indeed be an "error." . . . If a legal rule was violated during the district court proceedings, and if the defendant did not waive the rule, then there has been an "error" within the meaning of Rule 52(b) despite the absence of a timely objection.
>
> The second limitation on appellate authority under Rule 52(b) is that the error be "plain." "Plain" is synonymous with "clear" or, equivalently, "obvious." See [United States v. Young, 470 U.S. 1, 17, n. 14 (1985).] . . . We need not consider the special case where the error was unclear at the time of trial but becomes clear on appeal because the applicable law has been clarified. At a minimum, a court of appeals cannot correct an error pursuant to Rule 52(b) unless the error is clear under current law.
>
> The third and final limitation on appellate authority under Rule 52(b) is that the plain error "affec[t] substantial rights." This is the same language employed in Rule 52(a), and in most cases it means that the error must have been prejudicial: It must have affected the outcome of the district court proceedings. See, e.g., . . . Kotteakos v. United States, 328 U.S. 750, 758-765 (1946). When the defendant has made a timely objection to an error and Rule 52(a) applies, a court of appeals normally engages in a specific analysis of the district court record — a so-called "harmless error" inquiry — to determine whether the error was prejudicial. Rule 52(b) normally requires the same kind of inquiry, with one important difference: It is the defendant rather than the Government who bears the burden of persuasion with respect to prejudice. In most cases, a court of appeals cannot correct the forfeited error unless the defendant shows that the error was prejudicial. See *Young*, supra, at 17, n. 14 ("Federal courts have consistently interpreted the plain-error doctrine as requiring an appellate court to find that the claimed error . . . had [a] prejudicial impact on the jury's deliberations"). This burden shifting is dictated by a subtle but important difference in language between the two parts of Rule 52: While Rule 52(a) precludes error correction only if the error "does *not* affect substantial rights" (emphasis added), Rule 52(b) authorizes no remedy unless the error *does* "affec[t] substantial rights." . . .
>
> We need not decide whether the phrase "affect[ing] substantial rights" is always synonymous with "prejudicial." See generally Arizona v. Fulminante, 499 U.S. 279, 310 (1991) (constitutional error may not be found harmless if error deprives defendant of the "basic protections [without which] a criminal trial cannot reliably serve its function as a vehicle for determination of guilt or innocence, and no criminal punishment may be regarded as fundamentally fair") (quoting Rose v. Clark, 478 U.S. 570, 577-578 (1986)). There may be a special category of forfeited errors that can be corrected regardless of their effect on the outcome, but this issue need not be addressed. Nor need we address those errors that should be presumed prejudicial if the defendant cannot make a specific showing of prejudice. Normally, although perhaps not in every

---

1. Rule 24 was amended in 1999, and now permits alternate jurors to be retained during jury deliberation, so long as they do not discuss the case with anyone.

case, the defendant must make a specific showing of prejudice to satisfy the "affect[ing] substantial rights" prong of Rule 52(b).

Rule 52(b) is permissive, not mandatory. If the forfeited error is "plain" and "affects substantial rights," the court of appeals has authority to order correction, but is not required to do so. . . .

We previously have explained that the discretion conferred by Rule 52(b) should be employed "in those circumstances in which a miscarriage of justice would otherwise result." *Young*, 470 U.S., at 15. . . . In our collateral-review jurisprudence, the term "miscarriage of justice" means that the defendant is actually innocent. . . . The court of appeals should no doubt correct a plain forfeited error that causes the conviction or sentencing of an actually innocent defendant, . . . but we have never held that a Rule 52(b) remedy is *only* warranted in cases of actual innocence.

Rather, the standard that should guide the exercise of remedial discretion under Rule 52(b) was articulated in United States v. Atkinson, 297 U.S. 157 (1936). The court of appeals should correct a plain forfeited error affecting substantial rights if the error "seriously affect[s] the fairness, integrity or public reputation of judicial proceedings[," id., at 160, which may be] independent of the defendant's innocence. Conversely, a plain error affecting substantial rights does not, without more, satisfy the *Atkinson* standard, for otherwise the discretion afforded by Rule 52(b) would be illusory.

With these basic principles in mind, we turn to the instant case. . . . The presence of alternate jurors during jury deliberations is not the kind of error that "affects substantial rights" independent of its prejudicial impact. Nor have respondents made a specific showing of prejudice. Finally, we see no reason to presume prejudice here. . . .

. . . In sum, respondents have not met their burden of showing prejudice under Rule 52(b). Whether the Government could have met its burden of showing the absence of prejudice, under Rule 52(a), if respondents had not forfeited their claim of error, is not at issue here. This is a plain-error case, and it is respondents who must persuade the appellate court that the deviation from Rule 24(c) was prejudicial.

Because the conceded error in this case did not "affec[t] substantial rights," the Court of Appeals had no authority to correct it. We need not consider whether the error, if prejudicial, would have warranted correction under the *Atkinson* standard as "seriously affecting the fairness, integrity or public reputation of judicial proceedings." The judgment of the Court of Appeals is reversed. . . .

Justice Stevens, joined by Justices White and Blackmun, dissented on the ground that (1) Rule 24(c) errors implicate "substantial rights" even without a case-specific showing of prejudice, because they "undermin[e] the structural integrity of the criminal tribunal itself," and (2) the appellate court — which retained the discretion to reverse, or not to reverse, under Rule 52(b) — did not abuse its discretion.

7. In Johnson v. United States, 520 U.S. 461 (1997), the trial judge, in a perjury case, decided the issue of the "materiality" of the defendant's alleged false statement. This was error, because materiality was an element of the crime of perjury and thus should have been submitted to the jury for determination. Compare Neder v. United States, 527 U.S. 1 (1999) (involving a similar error with respect to the issue of materiality in a tax fraud prosecution), page 1575, supra. In *Johnson*, however, the defendant failed to object. Reviewing the defendant's conviction under the *Olano* "plain error" standard, the Court concluded that the error did not require reversal because the evidence of materiality was "overwhelming" and "uncontroverted." The Court emphasized that, under *Olano*, the determination whether an error "seriously affect[s] the fairness, integrity or public reputation of judicial proceedings" must be made on a case-by-case basis.

8. What is the standard for determining whether an error, to which the defendant did not contemporaneously object, "affect[ed] substantial rights"? The Court declined to answer that question with precision in *Olano*, but returned to it in United States v. Dominguez Benitez, 542 U.S. 74 (2004). *Dominguez Benitez* involved a failure by the trial court to warn the defendant, before he entered a guilty plea, that he could not withdraw the plea if the trial court did not accept the prosecutor's sentencing stipulations and recommendations. The failure to so warn the defendant violated Federal Rule of Criminal Procedure 11(c)(3)(B). For obvious reasons (specifically, because he was unaware of the Rule's requirements), the defendant did not object to the trial court's mistake at the time of the plea. Nevertheless, according to the Court's previous decision in United States v. Vonn, 535 U.S. 55 (2002), the defendant's failure to object meant that he could obtain relief on appeal only if he could show that the violation constituted "plain error" under Rule 52(b).

The *Dominguez Benitez* Court, in an opinion by Justice Souter, held as follows: "[A] defendant who seeks reversal of his conviction after a guilty plea, on the ground that the district court committed plain error under Rule 11, must show a reasonable probability that, but for the error, he would not have entered the plea. A defendant must thus satisfy the judgment of the reviewing court, informed by the entire record, that the probability of a different result is 'sufficient to undermine confidence in the outcome' of the proceeding."

9. Does it make sense for the issue of prejudice, or harm, to be handled in so many different ways, depending on the particular legal issue involved and the procedural context of the particular case? Do you think that appellate courts are capable of making meaningful distinctions between the several different applicable legal standards?

Justice Scalia, for one, does not think so. In *Dominguez Benitez*, he wrote the following provocative opinion, concurring in the judgment:

> . . . By my count, this Court has adopted no fewer than four assertedly different standards of probability relating to the assessment of whether the outcome of trial would have been different if error had not occurred, or if omitted evidence had been included. See Chapman v. California, 386 U.S. 18, 24 (1967) (adopting "harmless beyond a reasonable doubt" standard for preserving, on direct review, conviction obtained in a trial where constitutional error occurred); Brecht v. Abrahamson, 507 U.S. 619, 637 (1993) (rejecting *Chapman* in favor of the less defendant-friendly "substantial and injurious effect or influence" standard of Kotteakos v. United States, 328 U.S. 750 (1946), for overturning conviction on collateral review); United States v. Agurs, 427 U.S. 97, 111-113 (1976) (rejecting *Kotteakos* for overturning conviction on the basis of *Brady* violations, in favor of an even less defendant-friendly standard later described in Strickland v. Washington, 466 U.S. 668, 694 (1984), as a "reasonable probability"); id., 466 U.S., at 693-694 (distinguishing the "reasonable probability" standard from the *still yet* less defendant-friendly "more likely than not" standard applicable to claims of newly discovered evidence). Such ineffable gradations of probability seem to me quite beyond the ability of the judicial mind (or any mind) to grasp, and thus harmful rather than helpful to the consistency and rationality of judicial decisionmaking. That is especially so when they are applied to the hypothesizing of events that never in fact occurred. Such an enterprise is not factfinding, but closer to divination.
>
> For purposes of estimating what *would* have happened, it seems to me that the only serviceable standards are the traditional "beyond a reasonable doubt" and "more likely

than not." We should not pretend to a higher degree of precision. I would not, there-fore, extend our "reasonable probability" standard to the plain-error context. I would hold that, where a defendant has failed to object at trial, and thus has the burden of proving that a mistake he failed to prevent had an effect on his substantial rights, he must show that effect to be probable, that is, more likely than not.

542 U.S., at 86-87. Do you agree with Justice Scalia that the Court's four different prejudice standards should be simplified? Does his opinion in *Dominguez Benitez* sig-nify the start of a new period of instability in the law relating to appellate review?

B. Collateral Review

A defendant's conviction becomes final when it has been affirmed on appeal (or cer-tiorari review has been declined) by the highest court available to review the case (including the United States Supreme Court), or when the defendant has failed to file an appeal (or a certiorari petition) from an adverse decision below within the allotted time. Even after the conviction has become final, however, that is not nec-essarily the end of the story. Today, in every American jurisdiction, there exists at least one opportunity for a convicted defendant to seek so-called "collateral review" of his conviction.

There are three kinds of collateral review: (1) state-court collateral review for defendants who were convicted in state court (usually called a state postconvic-tion or state habeas corpus proceeding); (2) federal-court collateral review for defendants who were convicted in federal court (usually called a "Section 2255 proceeding," after the federal statute authorizing such review, 28 U.S.C. §2255); and (3) federal-court collateral review for defendants who were convicted in state court (usually called a federal habeas corpus proceeding). All three kinds of collateral review should be distinguished from the so-called "Great Writ" of habeas corpus, which (as explained below) serves a different purpose altogether.

State postconviction review, or state habeas, was created by the states largely in response to the expanded scope of federal habeas review of state convictions during the second half of the twentieth century. It was believed that making such review available in the state courts might help to minimize the need for habeas review in the federal courts—either by resolving any constitutional issues that might be present in the case, or at least by defining the factual contours of those issues more clearly before the start of federal habeas review. As a practical matter, state habeas today serves primarily as a procedure for posttrial litigation, especially of certain kinds of fact-based claims that are not easily litigated on direct appeal, such as inef-fective assistance, *Brady*, and newly discovered evidence claims.

Section 2255 review, for persons convicted in federal court, serves many of the same functions as state and federal habeas do for those convicted in state court. The federal statute, 28 U.S.C. §2255, provides that a person convicted in federal court who claims "the right to be released upon the ground that the sentence was imposed in violation of the Constitution or laws of the United States, or that the court was without jurisdiction to impose such sentence, or that the sentence was in excess of the maximum authorized by law, or is otherwise subject to collateral attack," may file a petition in federal district court for collateral review. The Court has held that "an error of law does not provide a basis for habeas relief under 28 U.S.C. §2255 unless it constitutes 'a fundamental defect which inherently results in a complete miscarriage of justice.'" See Brecht v. Abrahamson, 507 U.S. 619, 634, n. 8 (1993) (quoting United States v. Timmreck, 441 U.S. 780, 783 (1979), and Hill v. United States, 368 U.S. 424, 428 (1962)).

Because the rules governing state postconviction review vary widely from state to state, and because the rules governing §2255 proceedings for federal prisoners often tend to mirror those governing federal habeas for state prisoners, we will focus our attention for the remainder of this section exclusively on the third kind of collateral review: federal habeas corpus review of state convictions.

1. The "Great Writ" of Habeas Corpus

The writ of habeas corpus, often called the "Great Writ," traces its roots back to Magna Carta in 1215. "Executive imprisonment has been considered oppressive and lawless since John, at Runnymede, pledged that no free man should be imprisoned, dispossessed, outlawed, or exiled save by the judgment of his peers or by the law of the land. The judges of England developed the writ of habeas corpus largely to preserve these immunities from executive restraint." Shaughnessy v. United States ex rel. Mezei, 345 U.S. 206, 218-219 (Jackson, J., dissenting). "Habeas corpus," which means literally "you may have the body," is a writ addressed to the person who has custody of a prisoner, requiring the production of the prisoner so that the judge may inquire into the fundamental justice of the detention. Throughout its long and storied history, habeas corpus has preserved individual liberty, protected the governmental balance of powers, and vindicated the rule of law.[2]

The Framers placed great stock in the "Great Writ." In Federalist No. 84, Hamilton cited it as a crucial protection against "the practice of arbitrary imprisonments . . . in all ages, [among] the favourite and most formidable instruments of tyranny." The writ was included in the first congressional statute granting jurisdiction to the federal courts, the Judiciary Act of 1789, and is codified today at 28 U.S.C. §2241, which authorizes a federal court to issue a writ of habeas corpus on behalf of a prisoner "in custody under or by color of the authority of the United States . . . ," or "in custody in violation of the Constitution or laws or treaties of the United States." The "Great Writ" also is enshrined in the American Constitution, which prohibits suspension of "the Privilege of the Writ of Habeas Corpus . . . unless when in Cases of Rebellion or Invasion the public Safety may require it." Art. I, §9, cl. 2.

An excellent example of the "Great Writ," as the traditional judicial remedy for allegedly unjust executive detention, can be seen in the recent terrorism cases of Hamdi v. Rumsfeld, 542 U.S. 507 (2004), and Rasul v. Bush, 542 U.S. 466 (2004). In *Hamdi*, the Court ruled that a U.S. citizen who had been detained for more than two years without criminal charges (initially in Afghanistan and later at the Naval Brigs in Norfolk, Virginia, and Charleston, South Carolina) is entitled under due process to some kind of independent review of his alleged status as an "enemy combatant" in the war against "forces hostile to the United States or coalition partners" in

---

2. For the definitive history of the Great Writ in England and America, see Paul D. Halliday, Habeas Corpus: From England to Empire (Belknap Press of Harvard University 2010).

Afghanistan. Under the Court's ruling, if the military does not provide such independent review, then Hamdi can obtain such review in a federal court by means of a writ of habeas corpus.[3] In *Rasul*, the Court held that the statutory habeas jurisdiction of the federal courts extends to the review of the detention of more than 600 non-U.S. citizens held (again, without criminal charges) at Guantanamo Bay, Cuba, in connection with the ongoing "war on terrorism."[4] In both cases, the Court squarely rejected the argument that judicial review by means of the "Great Writ" would be incompatible with the needs of the government in general, and of the military in particular. For more on *Hamdi*, see supra, Chapter 2, at page 114.

Despite the historical importance of the "Great Writ," and its protection in the text of the American Constitution, this traditional version of habeas corpus offered no prospect of collateral review or relief to persons who had been convicted of crimes. This is because a facially valid criminal conviction, demonstrating that the prisoner was held in confinement as the result of judicial proceedings, traditionally served as a complete defense to a petition for a writ of habeas corpus. To provide for collateral review of criminal convictions, Congress needed to pass new legislation extending the writ of habeas corpus beyond its common-law origins. We next turn our attention to the statutory version of federal habeas corpus that was enacted by Congress, after the Civil War, to authorize federal collateral review of state criminal convictions.

2.   The Nature and Purposes of Federal Habeas

Federal habeas for state prisoners has been available in one form or another since 1867, when the post-Civil War Congress enacted the Habeas Corpus Act. The original purpose of the Act was to extend the writ of habeas corpus in order to provide a federal forum for individuals — often either newly freed slaves or federal Reconstruction officials — who were wrongly convicted of crimes in state courts in violation of their federal constitutional rights. However, the nature of federal habeas, as well as its primary purposes, have changed substantially over the years.[5]

3. There was no majority opinion in *Hamdi*, but Justice O'Connor's plurality opinion — which took a position between the two extremes expressed by Justice Thomas (no judicial review required) and Justice Scalia (the government must either suspend habeas corpus, file criminal charges, or release the prisoner) — effectively establishes the legal basis for the Court's decision.

4. As a general matter, habeas cases must be filed in the federal district court in which the habeas petitioner is being held in custody. See, e.g., Rumsfeld v. Padilla, 542 U.S. 426 (2004) (Padilla's habeas petition, which challenges his current confinement, must name as defendant the person with immediate custody over him, and must be filed in the district court in which he is confined (and which, by definition, also has jurisdiction over his immediate custodian)). Note that this is slightly different from the jurisdictional rule under the federal habeas statute authorizing collateral review of state criminal convictions, which — for states comprising more than one federal district — allows such a habeas petition to be filed either in the district of confinement or in the district where the criminal conviction was obtained. See 28 U.S.C. §2241(d).

According to the *Rasul* Court, in a habeas case involving persons held outside the sovereign territory of the United States, jurisdiction lies in any federal district court that has jurisdiction over the person or persons with custody of the habeas petitioner. Given that Rasul's effective custodians include the President of the United States, in his role as Commander-in-Chief of the Armed Forces, as well as the Secretary of Defense, the District Court for the District of Columbia (together with many other district courts as well) has jurisdiction over Rasul's habeas petition.

5. For an excellent account of the history and significance of habeas in America, see Eric M. Freedman, Habeas Corpus: Rethinking the Great Writ of Liberty (NYU Press 2003).

For almost 100 years after the Act's adoption, the scope of federal habeas review of state convictions was relatively narrow, primarily because the scope of federal constitutional rights applicable to state criminal cases was also relatively narrow. Hence, the statements by the Court in two prominent early twentieth-century federal habeas cases, Frank v. Mangum, 237 U.S. 309, 327 (1915), and Moore v. Dempsey, 261 U.S. 86, 91-92 (1923), that "the writ of habeas corpus [is available] . . . only in case the judgment under which the prisoner is detained is shown to be absolutely void."

In the second half of the twentieth century, however, federal habeas became much more important, for two related reasons. First, beginning in the 1950s, and accelerating rapidly in the 1960s, the scope of federal constitutional rights applicable to state criminal cases increased dramatically, as a result of due process incorporation and the Warren Court's criminal procedure revolution. Second, at about the same time, federal habeas jurisdiction was also significantly expanded, by the Court itself, as a means to empower the lower federal courts (who, unlike the Court, were unable to review state criminal cases directly) to assist the Court in the enforcement of these newly created federal constitutional rights. The defining purpose of federal habeas, during this period, was to provide an unrestricted federal forum for the litigation of federal constitutional claims.

The two leading cases in this expansion were Brown v. Allen, 344 U.S. 443 (1953), and Fay v. Noia, 372 U.S. 391 (1963). In Brown v. Allen, the Court rejected the view that prior determinations, in state court, of legal or mixed law-and-fact issues relating to federal constitutional claims should be given res judicata effect by federal habeas courts. "Although there is no need for the federal judge, if he could, to shut his eyes to the State consideration of such issues, no binding weight is to be attached to the State determination. . . . The State court cannot have the last say when it, though on fair consideration . . ., may have misconceived a federal constitutional right." 344 U.S., at 508 (opinion of Justice Frankfurter for the Court). In Fay v. Noia, one of several key federal habeas decisions authored by Justice Brennan, the Court held that a state prisoner's failure to present his federal constitutional claims properly in state court did not bar subsequent federal habeas review of the merits of his claims, unless he "deliberately by-passed" the state forum. "[T]he doctrine under which state procedural defaults are held to constitute an adequate and independent state law ground barring direct Supreme Court review is not to be extended to limit the power granted the federal courts under the federal habeas statute." 372 U.S., at 399.

Starting in the 1970s, as the criminal procedure revolution began to wane, a new Court majority — led by Justices Rehnquist, Powell, and O'Connor — began to impose new restrictions on the availability of federal habeas. In a series of decisions, the Court gradually made it much more difficult for state prisoners to obtain federal habeas review of the merits of their federal constitutional claims. One important rationale behind these decisions was that federal habeas — an equitable remedy designed to serve the "ends of justice" — should be used primarily to protect innocent defendants. See, e.g., Henry J. Friendly, Is Innocence Irrelevant? Collateral Attack on Criminal Judgments, 38 U. Chi. L. Rev. 142 (1970). Another was that Justice Brennan's view of federal habeas was insufficiently respectful of state courts, who, like their federal judicial counterparts, are sworn to obey and defend the federal constitution. The Court's changing views about federal habeas prompted numerous scholars to search for a new theory that might explain what habeas was all about. See, e.g., Joseph L. Hoffmann & William J. Stuntz, Habeas after the Revolution, [1993] Sup. Ct. Rev. 65 (1994); Evan Tsen Lee, The Theories of Federal Habeas Corpus, 72 Wash. U. L.Q. 151 (1994); Daniel J. Meltzer, Habeas Corpus Jurisdiction: The Limits of Models, 66 S. Cal. L. Rev. 2507 (1993); Jordan Steiker, Innocence and Federal Habeas, 41 UCLA L. Rev. 303 (1993); Ann Woolhandler, Demodeling Habeas, 45 Stan. L. Rev. 575 (1993); James S. Liebman, Apocalypse Next Time?: The Anachronistic Attack on Habeas Corpus/Direct Review Parity, 92 Colum. L. Rev. 1997 (1992); Larry W. Yackle, Form and Function in the Administration of Justice: The Bill of Rights and Federal Habeas Corpus, 23 U. Mich. J.L. Reform 685 (1990); Barry Friedman, A Tale of Two Habeas, 73 Minn. L. Rev. 247 (1988).

At the end of the 1980s, the Court handed down a decision — relatively little-noticed when it was first issued — that eventually turned out to be crucial to the development of a new understanding about the nature and purposes of federal habeas. In Teague v. Lane, 489 U.S. 288 (1989), one of the issues before the Court was whether a habeas petitioner should be entitled to claim the benefit of a "new rule" of constitutional criminal procedure that was declared after his state criminal conviction became "final" on direct appeal. Recall that in Griffith v. Kentucky, 479 U.S. 314 (1987), the Court had held that all such "new rules" should apply retroactively to all cases pending on direct appeal at the time the "new rule" was declared. See supra, at page 1567. In *Teague*, Justice O'Connor, writing for a plurality of the Court,[6] decided that, as a general matter, "new rules" — defined as any rule that "breaks new ground or imposes a new obligation on the States or the Federal Government," or in which "the result was not *dictated* by precedent existing at the time the defendant's conviction became final" — should not apply retroactively to habeas cases. The plurality acknowledged only two narrow exceptions in which a new rule should apply retroactively in habeas: (1) "if it places 'certain kinds of primary, private individual conduct beyond the power of the criminal law-making authority to proscribe'" and (2) "if it requires the observance of 'those procedures that . . . are "implicit in the concept of ordered liberty,"'" and "without which the likelihood of an accurate conviction is seriously diminished." With respect to this second exception, the plurality found it "unlikely that many such components of basic due process have yet to emerge."

The *Teague* plurality based its new habeas non-retroactivity rule on the following restatement of the goals of habeas:

With regard to the nature of habeas corpus, Justice Harlan wrote:

> Habeas corpus always has been a *collateral* remedy, providing an avenue for upsetting judgments that have become otherwise final. It is not designed as a substitute for direct review. The interest in leaving concluded litigation in a state of repose, that is, reducing the controversy to a final judgment not subject to further judicial revision, may quite legitimately be found by those responsible for defining the scope of the writ to outweigh in some, many, or most instances the competing interest in readjudicating convictions according to all legal standards in effect when a habeas petition is filed. . . .

---

6. The plurality's view in *Teague* was later adopted by a majority of the Court in Penry v. Lynaugh, 492 U.S. 302 (1989), and Saffle v. Parks, 494 U.S. 484 (1990). The 1996 AEDPA amendments to the federal habeas corpus statute slightly modified, but did not substantially affect, the holding in *Teague*. See Terry Williams v. Taylor, infra, at page 1587.

[As Justice Harlan explained,] "the threat of habeas serves as a necessary additional incentive for trial and appellate courts throughout the land to conduct their proceedings in a manner consistent with established constitutional standards. In order to perform this deterrence function, . . . the habeas court need only apply the constitutional standards that prevailed at the time the original proceedings took place." . . . See also [Solem v.] Stumes, 465 U.S. [638], 653 [(1984)] (Powell, J., concurring in judgment) ("Review on habeas to determine that the conviction rests upon correct application of the law in effect at the time of the conviction is all that is required to 'forc[e] trial and appellate courts . . . to toe the constitutional mark'") [quoting Mackey v. United States, 401 U.S. 667, 687 (1971) (Harlan, J., concurring in judgments in part and dissenting in part)]. . . .

We agree with Justice Harlan's description of the function of habeas corpus. "[T]he Court never has defined the scope of the writ simply by reference to a perceived need to assure that an individual accused of crime is afforded a trial free of constitutional error." . . . Rather, we have recognized that interests of comity and finality must also be considered in determining the proper scope of habeas review. . . .

. . . Application of constitutional rules not in existence at the time a conviction became final seriously undermines the principle of finality which is essential to the operation of our criminal justice system. Without finality, the criminal law is deprived of much of its deterrent effect. The fact that life and liberty are at stake in criminal prosecutions "shows only that 'conventional notions of finality' should not have *as much* place in criminal as in civil litigation, not that they should have *none*." Friendly, Is Innocence Irrelevant? Collateral Attacks on Criminal Judgments, 38 U. Chi. L. Rev. 142, 150 (1970). "[I]f a criminal judgment is ever to be final, the notion of legality must at some point include the assignment of final competence to determine legality." Bator, Finality in Criminal Law and Federal Habeas Corpus for State Prisoners, 76 Harv. L. Rev. 441, 450-451 (1963) (emphasis omitted). . . .

The plurality also agreed with Justice Harlan that a second purpose of habeas was "to assure that no man has been incarcerated under a procedure which creates an impermissibly large risk that the innocent will be convicted."

On a theoretical level, *Teague* represented a clear shift from the earlier view (expressed most forcefully by Justice Brennan) that federal habeas exists to provide a remedy to individuals for violations of their federal constitutional rights, to the view (expressed most forcefully by Justice Harlan, and ultimately adopted in *Teague* and its progeny) that federal habeas exists primarily to deter state courts from committing federal constitutional errors. This shift was important, because it set the stage for the conclusion that federal habeas review is not needed unless the state courts have behaved badly. See Joseph L. Hoffmann, The Supreme Court's New Vision of Federal Habeas Corpus for State Prisoners, [1989] Sup. Ct. Rev. 165 (1990); Robert Weisberg, A Great Writ While It Lasted, 81 J. Crim. L. & Criminology 9 (1990).

Another hidden dimension of *Teague* was its impact on the development of federal constitutional law. *Teague* certainly did not deprive the Supreme Court of the opportunity to declare new federal constitutional rights in state criminal cases, because the Court can always do so on direct certiorari review. But *Teague* did effectively take the lower federal courts out of the business of declaring new federal constitutional rights in state criminal cases — after *Teague*, such courts can only apply "old law" to such cases. In other words, the ongoing judicial dialogue about the proper scope of federal constitutional law in state criminal cases, post-*Teague*, was limited to the Supreme Court and the state courts, and no longer included the lower federal courts. Cf. Robert Cover & Alexander Aleinikoff, Dialectical Federalism: Habeas Corpus and the Court, 86 Yale L.J. 1035 (1977) (describing judicial dialogue between state courts and lower federal courts sitting in habeas).

What is a "new rule" under *Teague*? That is a tricky question. You must try to keep in mind that, under *Teague*, the broader the definition of "new law," or a "new rule," the more difficult it is to obtain federal habeas relief (because "new rules" cannot be applied to habeas cases). Thus, when Butler v. McKellar, 494 U.S. 407 (1990), explained that "[t]he 'new rule' principle . . . validates reasonable, good-faith interpretations of existing precedents made by state courts even though they are shown to be contrary to later decisions," and described the *Teague* "new rule" inquiry as asking whether the rule sought by the petitioner "was susceptible to debate among reasonable minds," such formulations — which narrowed the definition of "old law," and thus expanded the scope of "new law" — represented bad news for habeas petitioners. See also Lambrix v. Singletary, 520 U.S. 518 (1997), holding that a rule is "old law" only if it "was dictated by precedent" (i.e., "no other interpretation was reasonable").

Long before *Teague*, the federal habeas statute already provided that factual determinations made by state courts, in connection with the litigation of federal constitutional claims, must be presumed correct by federal habeas courts. See former 28 U.S.C. §2254(d) (providing for presumption of correctness, and defining narrow circumstances in which state-court factual findings may be revisited by federal habeas courts). And, as a direct result of *Teague* and its progeny, legal determinations (on federal constitutional issues) made by state courts cannot be overturned by federal habeas courts unless they were contrary to clearly established federal law at the time of the state-court decision. What, then, should be the proper habeas standard of review for mixed fact-and-law determinations (involving the application of federal law to the particular facts of a case) made by state courts — such as whether the defendant's counsel was constitutionally ineffective? After *Teague*, many observers thought that federal habeas review of such mixed issues would be governed by a similarly deferential standard.

But in Wright v. West, 505 U.S. 277 (1992), a majority of the Supreme Court — without a majority opinion — declined to decide this issue, preserving (at least temporarily) the tradition of de novo review of such mixed issues in federal habeas. In *West*, the U.S. Court of Appeals for the Fourth Circuit had ruled that the evidence against the defendant at trial was legally insufficient under the rule of Jackson v. Virginia, 443 U.S. 307 (1979) ("whether, after viewing the evidence in the light most favorable to the prosecution, any rational trier of fact could have found the essential elements of the crime beyond a reasonable doubt"). All nine justices agreed that the conviction should not have been overturned by the Fourth Circuit, but only the opinion of Justice Thomas (writing for three justices) suggested that federal habeas courts perhaps should defer to state court applications of federal law to the facts of a particular case. Justice O'Connor (also writing for three justices) flatly rejected the idea of deferring to such state court decisions.

The Antiterrorism and Effective Death Penalty Act of 1996 (AEDPA), enacted in a wave of anticrime sentiment following the 1995 bombing of the Murrah Federal Building in Oklahoma City, dramatically altered many of the statutory provisions governing federal habeas. One of the most important changes was in the habeas standard of review, as set forth in 28 U.S.C. §2254(d)(1). In AEDPA, Congress weighed in heavily on the same subject that had split the Court in Wright v. West. The next case represents the Court's first look at the new standard.

Please note that, with respect to the habeas standard of review under 28 U.S.C. §2254(d)(1), it was Part II of Justice O'Connor's opinion — and *not* Part II of Justice Stevens's opinion — that expressed the view of a majority of the Supreme Court.

TERRY WILLIAMS v. TAYLOR

Certiorari to the United States Court of Appeals for the Fourth Circuit
529 U.S. 362 (2000)

JUSTICE STEVENS announced the judgment of the Court and delivered the opinion of the Court with respect to Parts I, III, and IV, and an opinion with respect to Parts II and V.*

The questions presented are whether Terry Williams' constitutional right to the effective assistance of counsel as defined in Strickland v. Washington, 466 U.S. 668 (1984), was violated, and whether the judgment of the Virginia Supreme Court refusing to set aside his death sentence "was contrary to, or involved an unreasonable application of, clearly established Federal law, as determined by the Supreme Court of the United States," within the meaning of 28 U.S.C. §2254(d)(1). . . .

I

[The underlying facts of the case are as follows: Terry Williams was convicted of robbery and murder in connection with the death of Harris Stone. At the hearing to decide whether Williams should be sentenced to death, the prosecution introduced Williams's prior convictions for armed robbery, burglary, and grand larceny, and also told the jury about two auto thefts and two violent assaults committed by Williams after the Stone murder. One of these assaults, to which Williams had confessed, left an elderly woman in a "vegetative state" from which she was not expected to recover. Two expert witnesses testified that there was a "high probability" that Williams would be dangerous in the future. The only mitigating evidence presented on Williams's behalf came from his mother and two neighbors, all of whom briefly described Williams as a "nice boy" who was not violent, and from a psychiatrist who reported that Williams had removed the bullets from a gun prior to a robbery so that he would not injure anyone. In closing argument, Williams's defense lawyer talked about how difficult it was to find a reason to spare Williams's life. The jury sentenced Williams to death. — EDS.]

STATE HABEAS CORPUS PROCEEDINGS

In 1988 Williams filed for state collateral relief. . . . [T]he same judge who had presided over Williams' trial and sentencing . . . held an evidentiary hearing on Williams' claim that trial counsel had been ineffective. Based on the evidence

---

*Justice Souter, Justice Ginsburg, and Justice Breyer join this opinion in its entirety. Justice O'Connor and Justice Kennedy join Parts I, III, and IV of this opinion.

adduced after two days of hearings, Judge Ingram found that Williams' conviction was valid, but that his trial attorneys had been ineffective during sentencing. Among the evidence reviewed that had not been presented at trial were documents prepared in connection with Williams' commitment when he was 11 years old that dramatically described mistreatment, abuse, and neglect during his early childhood, as well as testimony that he was "borderline mentally retarded," had suffered repeated head injuries, and might have mental impairments organic in origin. . . . The habeas hearing also revealed that the same experts who had testified on the State's behalf at trial believed that Williams, if kept in a "structured environment," would not pose a future danger to society. . . .

Counsel's failure to discover and present this and other significant mitigating evidence was "below the range expected of reasonable, professional competent assistance of counsel." . . . Counsel's performance thus "did not measure up to the standard required under the holding of Strickland v. Washington . . . , and [if it had,] there is a reasonable probability that the result of the sentencing phase would have been different." . . . Judge Ingram therefore recommended that Williams be granted a rehearing on the sentencing phase of his trial.

The Virginia Supreme Court did not accept that recommendation. . . . Although it assumed, without deciding, that trial counsel had been ineffective, . . . it disagreed with the trial judge's conclusion that Williams had suffered sufficient prejudice to warrant relief. Treating the prejudice inquiry as a mixed question of law and fact, the Virginia Supreme Court accepted the factual determination that available evidence in mitigation had not been presented at the trial, but held that the trial judge had misapplied the law in two respects. First, relying on our decision in Lockhart v. Fretwell, 506 U.S. 364 (1993), the court held that it was wrong for the trial judge to rely "on mere outcome determination" when assessing prejudice. . . . Second, it construed the trial judge's opinion as having "adopted a per se approach" that would establish prejudice whenever any mitigating evidence was omitted. . . .

The court then reviewed the prosecution evidence. . . . [I]t found that the excluded mitigating evidence — which it characterized as merely indicating "that numerous people, mostly relatives, thought that defendant was nonviolent and could cope very well in a structured environment," . . . — "barely would have altered the profile of this defendant that was presented to the jury." . . . On this basis, the court concluded that there was no reasonable possibility that the omitted evidence would have affected the jury's sentencing recommendation, and that Williams had failed to demonstrate that his sentencing proceeding was fundamentally unfair.

FEDERAL HABEAS CORPUS PROCEEDINGS

Having exhausted his state remedies, Williams sought a federal writ of habeas corpus pursuant to 28 U.S.C. §2254. . . . After reviewing the state habeas hearing transcript and the state courts' findings of fact and conclusions of law, the federal trial judge agreed with the Virginia trial judge: The death sentence was constitutionally infirm.

After noting that the Virginia Supreme Court had not addressed the question whether trial counsel's performance at the sentencing hearing fell below the range of competence demanded of lawyers in criminal cases, the judge began by addressing that issue in detail. He identified five categories of mitigating evidence that counsel had failed to introduce,[4] and he rejected the argument that counsel's failure to conduct an adequate investigation had been a strategic decision. . . .

Turning to the prejudice issue, the judge determined that there was "'a reasonable probability that, but for counsel's unprofessional errors, the result of the proceeding would have been different.' *Strickland.* . . ." . . . He found that the Virginia Supreme Court had erroneously assumed that *Lockhart* had modified the *Strickland* standard for determining prejudice, and that it had made an important error of fact in discussing its finding of no prejudice.[5] . . . [T]he judge concluded that those errors established that the Virginia Supreme Court's decision "was contrary to, or involved an unreasonable application of, clearly established Federal law" within the meaning of §2254(d)(1).

The Federal Court of Appeals reversed. . . .

We granted certiorari, . . . and now reverse.

II

In 1867, Congress enacted a statute providing that federal courts "shall have power to grant writs of habeas corpus in all cases where any person may be restrained of his or her liberty in violation of the constitution, or of any treaty or law of the United States. . . ." . . . It is, of course, well settled that the fact that constitutional error occurred in the proceedings that led to a state-court conviction may not alone be sufficient reason for concluding that a prisoner is entitled to the remedy of habeas. See, e.g., Stone v. Powell, 428 U.S. 465 (1976); Brecht v. Abrahamson, 507 U.S. 619 (1993). On the other hand, errors that undermine confidence in the fundamental fairness of the state adjudication certainly justify the issuance of the federal writ. See, e.g., Teague v. Lane, 489 U.S. 288, 311-314 (1989). . . . The deprivation of the right to the effective assistance of counsel recognized in *Strickland* is such an error. . . .

The warden here contends that federal habeas corpus relief is prohibited by the amendment to 28 U.S.C. §2254 . . . , enacted as a part of the Antiterrorism and Effective Death Penalty Act of 1996 (AEDPA). The relevant portion of that amendment provides:

> (d) An application for a writ of habeas corpus on behalf of a person in custody pursuant to the judgment of a State court shall not be granted with respect to any claim that was adjudicated on the merits in State court proceedings unless the adjudication of the claim —

4. "(i) Counsel did not introduce evidence of the Petitioner's background. . . . (ii) Counsel did not introduce evidence that Petitioner was abused by his father. (iii) Counsel did not introduce testimony from correctional officers who were willing to testify that defendant would not pose a danger while incarcerated. Nor did counsel offer prison commendations awarded to Williams for his help in breaking up a prison drug ring and for returning a guard's wallet. (iv) Several character witnesses were not called to testify. . . . The testimony of Elliott, a respected CPA in the community, could have been quite important to the jury. . . . (v) Finally, counsel did not introduce evidence that Petitioner was borderline mentally retarded, though he was found competent to stand trial." . . .

5. ". . . The Virginia Supreme Court ignored or overlooked the evidence of Williams' difficult childhood and abuse and his limited mental capacity. It is also unreasonable to characterize the additional evidence as coming from 'mostly relatives.' . . . Bruce Elliott, a respected professional in the community, and several correctional officers offered to testify on Williams' behalf." . . .

> (1) resulted in a decision that was contrary to, or involved an unreasonable
> application of, clearly established Federal law, as determined by the Supreme Court
> of the United States; . . .

In this case, the Court of Appeals applied the construction of the amendment that it had adopted in its earlier opinion in Green v. French, 143 F.3d 865 (CA4 1998). It read the amendment as prohibiting federal courts from issuing the writ unless:

> (a) the state court decision is in "square conflict" with Supreme Court precedent that
> is controlling as to law and fact or (b) if no such controlling decision exists, "the state
> court's resolution of a question of pure law rests upon an objectively unreasonable
> derivation of legal principles from the relevant [S]upreme [C]ourt precedents, or if its
> decision rests upon an objectively unreasonable application of established principles to
> new facts." . . .

Accordingly, it held that a federal court may issue habeas relief only if "the state courts have decided the question by interpreting or applying the relevant precedent in a manner that reasonable jurists would all agree is unreasonable." . . .

We are convinced that that interpretation of the amendment is incorrect. It would impose a test for determining when a legal rule is clearly established that simply cannot be squared with the real practice of decisional law. It would apply a standard for determining the "reasonableness" of state-court decisions that is not contained in the statute itself, and that Congress surely did not intend. And it would wrongly require the federal courts, including this Court, to defer to state judges' interpretations of federal law. . . .

The inquiry mandated by the amendment relates to the way in which a federal habeas court exercises its duty to decide constitutional questions; the amendment does not alter the underlying grant of jurisdiction in §2254(a). . . . When federal judges exercise their federal-question jurisdiction under the "judicial Power" of Article III of the Constitution, it is "emphatically the province and duty" of those judges to "say what the law is." Marbury v. Madison, 5 U.S. 137, 1 Cranch 137, 177 (1803). At the core of this power is the federal courts' independent responsibility — independent from its coequal branches in the Federal Government, and independent from the separate authority of the several States — to interpret federal law. A construction of AEDPA that would require the federal courts to cede this authority to the courts of the States would be inconsistent with the practice that federal judges have traditionally followed in discharging their duties under Article III of the Constitution. If Congress had intended to require such an important change in the exercise of our jurisdiction, we believe it would have spoken with much greater clarity than is found in the text of AEDPA.

This basic premise informs our interpretation of both parts of §2254(d)(1): first, the requirement that the determinations of state courts be tested only against "clearly established Federal law, as determined by the Supreme Court of the United States," and second, the prohibition on the issuance of the writ unless the state court's decision is "contrary to, or involved an unreasonable application of," that clearly established law. We address each part in turn.

THE "CLEARLY ESTABLISHED LAW" REQUIREMENT

In Teague v. Lane, 489 U.S. 288 (1989), we held that the petitioner was not entitled to federal habeas relief because he was relying on a rule of federal law that had not been announced until after his state conviction became final. The anti-retroactivity rule recognized in *Teague*, which prohibits reliance on "new rules," is the functional equivalent of a statutory provision commanding exclusive reliance on "clearly established law." . . . It is perfectly clear that AEDPA codifies *Teague* to the extent that *Teague* requires federal habeas courts to deny relief that is contingent upon a rule of law not clearly established at the time the state conviction became final.

Teague's core principles are therefore relevant to our construction of this requirement. . . . *Teague* established some guidance for making this determination, explaining that a federal habeas court operates within the bounds of comity and finality if it applies a rule "dictated by precedent existing at the time the defendant's conviction became final." . . . A rule that "breaks new ground or imposes a new obligation on the States or the Federal Government," . . . falls outside this universe of federal law.

To this, AEDPA has added, immediately following the "clearly established law" requirement, a clause limiting the area of relevant law to that "determined by the Supreme Court of the United States." 28 U.S.C. §2254(d)(1). . . . If this Court has not broken sufficient legal ground to establish an asked-for constitutional principle, the lower federal courts cannot themselves establish such a principle with clarity sufficient to satisfy the AEDPA bar . . . . In this respect, . . . this clause "extends the principle of *Teague* by limiting the source of doctrine on which a federal court may rely in addressing the application for a writ." . . .

It has been urged, in contrast, that we should read *Teague* and its progeny to encompass a broader principle of deference requiring federal courts to "validat[e] 'reasonable, good-faith interpretations' of the law" by state courts. . . . This presumption of deference was in essence the position taken by three Members of this Court in Wright [v. West], 505 U.S. [277,] 290-291 [(1992)] (opinion of Thomas, J.) ("[A] federal habeas court 'must defer to the state court's decision rejecting the claim unless that decision is patently unreasonable'"). . . .

Teague, however, does not extend this far. The often repeated language that *Teague* endorses "reasonable, good-faith interpretations" by state courts is an explanation of policy, not a statement of law. The *Teague* cases reflect this Court's view that habeas corpus is not to be used as a second criminal trial, and federal courts are not to run roughshod over the considered findings and judgments of the state courts that conducted the original trial and heard the initial appeals. On the contrary, we have long insisted that federal habeas courts attend closely to those considered decisions, and give them full effect when their findings and judgments are consistent with federal law. . . . But as Justice O'Connor explained in *Wright*:

> [T]he duty of the federal court in evaluating whether a rule is 'new' is not the same as deference; . . . Teague does not direct federal courts to spend less time or effort scrutinizing the existing federal law, on the ground that they can assume the state courts interpreted it properly.
>
> [T]he maxim that federal courts should 'give great weight to the considered conclusions of a coequal state judiciary' . . . does not mean that we have held in the past that federal courts must presume the correctness of a state court's legal conclusions on

habeas, or that a state court's incorrect legal determination has ever been allowed to stand because it was reasonable. We have always held that federal courts, even on habeas, have an independent obligation to say what the law is.

505 U.S., at 305.

We are convinced that in the phrase, "clearly established law," Congress did not intend to modify that independent obligation.

THE "CONTRARY TO, OR AN UNREASONABLE APPLICATION OF," REQUIREMENT

The message that Congress intended to convey by using the phrases, "contrary to" and "unreasonable application of" is not entirely clear. The prevailing view in the Circuits is that the former phrase requires de novo review of "pure" questions of law and the latter requires some sort of "reasonability" review of so-called mixed questions of law and fact. . . .

We are not persuaded that the phrases define two mutually exclusive categories of questions. Most constitutional questions that arise in habeas corpus proceedings — and therefore most "decisions" to be made — require the federal judge to apply a rule of law to a set of facts, some of which may be disputed and some undisputed. . . . In constitutional adjudication, as in the common law, rules of law often develop incrementally as earlier decisions are applied to new factual situations. . . . But rules that depend upon such elaboration are hardly less lawlike than those that establish a bright-line test.

Indeed, our pre-AEDPA efforts to distinguish questions of fact, questions of law, and "mixed questions," and to create an appropriate standard of habeas review for each, generated some not insubstantial differences of opinion as to which issues of law fell into which category of question, and as to which standard of review applied to each. . . .

Even though we cannot conclude that the phrases establish "a body of rigid rules," they do express a "mood" that the federal judiciary must respect. . . . In this respect, it seems clear that Congress intended federal judges to attend with the utmost care to state-court decisions, including all of the reasons supporting their decisions, before concluding that those proceedings were infected by constitutional error sufficiently serious to warrant the issuance of the writ. . . . AEDPA plainly sought to ensure a level of "deference to the determinations of state courts," provided those determinations did not conflict with federal law or apply federal law in an unreasonable way. . . . Congress wished to curb delays, to prevent "retrials" on federal habeas, and to give effect to state convictions to the extent possible under law. When federal courts are able to fulfill these goals within the bounds of the law, AEDPA instructs them to do so.

On the other hand, it is significant that the word "deference" does not appear in the text of the statute itself. Neither the legislative history, nor the statutory text, suggests any difference in the so-called "deference" depending on which of the two phrases is implicated.[13] Whatever "deference" Congress had in mind with respect

---

13. As Judge Easterbrook has noted, the statute surely does not require the kind of "deference" appropriate in other contexts: "It does not tell us to 'defer' to state decisions, as if the Constitution means one thing in Wisconsin and another in Indiana. Nor does it tell us to treat state courts the way we treat federal administrative agencies. Deference [to agencies] depends on delegation. . . . Congress did not delegate interpretive or executive power to the state courts. They exercise powers under their domestic

to both phrases, it surely is not a requirement that federal courts actually defer to a state-court application of the federal law that is, in the independent judgment of the federal court, in error. . . .

Our disagreement with Justice O'Connor about the precise meaning of the phrase "contrary to," and the word "unreasonable," is, of course, important, but should affect only a narrow category of cases. The simplest and first definition of "contrary to" as a phrase is "in conflict with." Webster's Ninth New Collegiate Dictionary 285 (1983). In this sense, we think the phrase surely capacious enough to include a finding that the state-court "decision" is simply "erroneous" or wrong. . . . And there is nothing in the phrase "contrary to" . . . that implies anything less than independent review by the federal courts.

Moreover, state-court decisions that do not "conflict" with federal law will rarely be "unreasonable" under either her reading of the statute or ours. We all agree that state-court judgments must be upheld unless, after the closest examination of the state-court judgment, a federal court is firmly convinced that a federal constitutional right has been violated. Our difference is as to the cases in which, at first-blush, a state-court judgment seems entirely reasonable, but thorough analysis by a federal court produces a firm conviction that that judgment is infected by constitutional error. In our view, such an erroneous judgment is "unreasonable" within the meaning of the act even though that conclusion was not immediately apparent.

In sum, the statute directs federal courts to attend to every state-court judgment with utmost care, but it does not require them to defer to the opinion of every reasonable state-court judge on the content of federal law. If, after carefully weighing all the reasons for accepting a state court's judgment, a federal court is convinced that a prisoner's custody — or, as in this case, his sentence of death — violates the Constitution, that independent judgment should prevail. Otherwise the federal "law as determined by the Supreme Court of the United States" might be applied by the federal courts one way in Virginia and another way in California. In light of the well-recognized interest in ensuring that federal courts interpret federal law in a uniform way, we are convinced that Congress did not intend the statute to produce such a result.

III

In this case, Williams contends that he was denied his constitutionally guaranteed right to the effective assistance of counsel when his trial lawyers failed to investigate and to present substantial mitigating evidence to the sentencing jury. The threshold question under AEDPA is whether Williams seeks to apply a rule of law that was clearly established at the time his state-court conviction became final. That question is easily answered because the merits of his claim are squarely governed by our holding in Strickland v. Washington. . . .

It is past question that the rule set forth in *Strickland* qualifies as "clearly established Federal law, as determined by the Supreme Court of the United States." That the *Strickland* test "of necessity requires a case-by-case examination of the evidence," . . . obviates neither the clarity of the rule nor the extent to which the

---

law, constrained by the Constitution of the United States. 'Deference' to the jurisdictions bound by those constraints is not sensible." Lindh v. Murphy, 96 F.3d 856, 868 (CA7 1996) (en banc), *rev'd* on other grounds, 521 U.S. 320 (1997).

rule must be seen as "established" by this Court. This Court's precedent "dictated" that the Virginia Supreme Court apply the *Strickland* test at the time that court entertained Williams' ineffective-assistance claim. . . . Williams is therefore entitled to relief if the Virginia Supreme Court's decision rejecting his ineffective-assistance claim was either "contrary to, or involved an unreasonable application of," that established law. It was both.

IV

The Virginia Supreme Court erred in holding that our decision in Lockhart v. Fretwell, 506 U.S. 364 (1993), modified or in some way supplanted the rule set down in *Strickland*. It is true that while the *Strickland* test provides sufficient guidance for resolving virtually all ineffective-assistance-of-counsel claims, there are situations in which the overriding focus on fundamental fairness may affect the analysis. Thus, on the one hand, as *Strickland* itself explained, there are a few situations in which prejudice may be presumed. . . . And, on the other hand, there are also situations in which it would be unjust to characterize the likelihood of a different outcome as legitimate "prejudice." Even if a defendant's false testimony might have persuaded the jury to acquit him, it is not fundamentally unfair to conclude that he was not prejudiced by counsel's interference with his intended perjury. Nix v. Whiteside, 475 U.S. 157, 175-176 (1986).

Similarly, in *Lockhart*, we concluded that, given the overriding interest in fundamental fairness, the likelihood of a different outcome attributable to an incorrect interpretation of the law should be regarded as a potential "windfall" to the defendant rather than the legitimate "prejudice" contemplated by our opinion in *Strickland*. . . .

Cases such as Nix v. Whiteside . . . and Lockhart v. Fretwell . . . do not justify a departure from a straightforward application of *Strickland* when the ineffectiveness of counsel *does* deprive the defendant of a substantive or procedural right to which the law entitles him. In the instant case, it is undisputed that Williams had a right — indeed, a constitutionally protected right — to provide the jury with the mitigating evidence that his trial counsel either failed to discover or failed to offer.

Nevertheless, the Virginia Supreme Court read our decision in *Lockhart* to require a separate inquiry into fundamental fairness even when Williams is able to show that his lawyer was ineffective and that his ineffectiveness probably affected the outcome of the proceeding. . . .

Unlike the Virginia Supreme Court, the state trial judge omitted any reference to *Lockhart* and simply relied on our opinion in *Strickland* as stating the correct standard for judging ineffective-assistance claims. . . . The trial judge analyzed the ineffective-assistance claim under the correct standard; the Virginia Supreme Court did not.

We are likewise persuaded that the Virginia trial judge correctly applied both components of that standard to Williams' ineffectiveness claim. Although he concluded that counsel competently handled the guilt phase of the trial, he found that their representation during the sentencing phase fell short of professional standards — a judgment barely disputed by the State in its brief to this Court. . . .

[A]s the Federal District Court correctly observed, the failure to introduce the comparatively voluminous amount of evidence that did speak in Williams' favor was not justified by a tactical decision to focus on Williams' voluntary confession.

Whether or not those omissions were sufficiently prejudicial to have affected the outcome of sentencing, they clearly demonstrate that trial counsel did not fulfill their obligation to conduct a thorough investigation of the defendant's background. . . .

We are also persuaded, unlike the Virginia Supreme Court, that counsel's unprofessional service prejudiced Williams within the meaning of Strickland. After hearing the additional evidence developed in the postconviction proceedings, the very judge who presided at Williams' trial and who once determined that the death penalty was "just" and "appropriate," concluded that there existed "a reasonable probability that the result of the sentencing phase would have been different" if the jury had heard that evidence. . . .

The Virginia Supreme Court's own analysis of prejudice reaching the contrary conclusion was thus unreasonable in at least two respects. First, as we have already explained, the State Supreme Court mischaracterized at best the appropriate rule, made clear by this Court in *Strickland*, for determining whether counsel's assistance was effective within the meaning of the Constitution. . . .

Second, the State Supreme Court's prejudice determination was unreasonable insofar as it failed to evaluate the totality of the available mitigation evidence — both that adduced at trial, and the evidence adduced in the habeas proceeding — in reweighing it against the evidence in aggravation. . . .

V

In our judgment, the state trial judge was correct both in his recognition of the established legal standard for determining counsel's effectiveness, and in his conclusion that the entire postconviction record, viewed as a whole and cumulative of mitigation evidence presented originally, raised "a reasonable probability that the result of the sentencing proceeding would have been different" if competent counsel had presented and explained the significance of all the available evidence. It follows that the Virginia Supreme Court rendered a "decision that was contrary to, or involved an unreasonable application of, clearly established Federal law." Williams' constitutional right to the effective assistance of counsel as defined in Strickland v. Washington was violated.

Accordingly, the judgment of the Court of Appeals is reversed, and the case is remanded for further proceedings consistent with this opinion. . . .

JUSTICE O'CONNOR delivered the opinion of the Court with respect to Part II (except as to the footnote), concurred in part, and concurred in the judgment.*

. . . The Court holds today that the Virginia Supreme Court's adjudication of Terry Williams' application for state habeas corpus relief resulted in just such a decision. I agree with that determination and join Parts I, III, and IV of the Court's opinion. Because I disagree, however, with the interpretation of §2254(d)(1) set forth in Part II of Justice Stevens' opinion, I write separately to explain my views.

---

* Justice Kennedy joins this opinion in its entirety. Chief Justice Rehnquist and Justice Thomas join this opinion with respect to Part II. Justice Scalia joins this opinion with respect to Part II, except as to the footnote. . . .

I

Before 1996, this Court held that a federal court entertaining a state prisoner's application for habeas relief must exercise its independent judgment when deciding both questions of constitutional law and mixed constitutional questions (i.e., application of constitutional law to fact). . . . In other words, a federal habeas court owed no deference to a state court's resolution of such questions of law or mixed questions. . . . [I]n the case of Wright v. West, [505 U.S. 277 (1992)], we revisited our prior holdings by asking the parties to address the following question in their briefs:

> In determining whether to grant a petition for writ of habeas corpus by a person in custody pursuant to the judgment of a state court, should a federal court give deference to the state court's application of law to the specific facts of the petitioner's case or should it review the state court's determination de novo? . . .

Although our ultimate decision did not turn on the answer to that question, our several opinions did join issue on it. . . .

Justice Thomas, announcing the judgment of the Court, acknowledged that our precedents had "treated as settled the rule that mixed constitutional questions are 'subject to plenary federal review' on habeas." . . . He contended, nevertheless, that those decisions did not foreclose the Court from applying a rule of deferential review for reasonableness in future cases. . . . Justice Thomas suggested that the time to revisit our decisions may have been at hand, given that our more recent habeas jurisprudence in the nonretroactivity context, see, e.g., Teague v. Lane, 489 U.S. 288 (1989), had called into question the then-settled rule of independent review of mixed constitutional questions. . . .

I wrote separately in *Wright* because I believed Justice Thomas had "understate[d] the certainty with which Brown v. Allen rejected a deferential standard of review of issues of law." . . . I also explained that we had considered the standard of review applicable to mixed constitutional questions on numerous occasions and each time we concluded that federal habeas courts had a duty to evaluate such questions independently. . . . With respect to Justice Thomas' suggestion that Teague and its progeny called into question the vitality of the independent-review rule, I noted that "Teague did not establish a 'deferential' standard of review" because "[i]t did not establish a standard of review at all." . . . While *Teague* did hold that state prisoners could not receive "the retroactive benefit of new rules of law," it "did *not* create any deferential standard of review with regard to old rules." . . . (emphasis in original).

Finally, and perhaps most importantly for purposes of today's case, I stated my disagreement with Justice Thomas' suggestion that de novo review is incompatible with the maxim that federal habeas courts should "give great weight to the considered conclusions of a coequal state judiciary." . . . Our statement . . . signified only that a state-court decision is due the same respect as any other "persuasive, well-reasoned authority." . . . "But this does not mean that we have held in the past that federal courts must presume the correctness of a state court's legal conclusions on habeas, or that a state court's incorrect legal determination has ever been allowed to stand because it was reasonable. We have always held that federal courts, even on habeas, have an independent obligation to say what the law is." . . . Under the federal habeas statute as it stood in 1992, then, our precedents dictated that a federal court should grant a state prisoner's petition for habeas relief if that court were to conclude in its independent judgment that the relevant state court had erred on a question of constitutional law or on a mixed constitutional question.

If today's case were governed by the federal habeas statute prior to Congress' enactment of AEDPA in 1996, I would agree with Justice Stevens that Williams' petition for habeas relief must be granted if we, in our independent judgment, were to conclude that his Sixth Amendment right to effective assistance of counsel was violated. . . .

II

A

Williams' case is *not* governed by the pre-1996 version of the habeas statute. Because he filed his petition in December 1997, Williams' case is governed by the statute as amended by AEDPA. Section 2254 now provides:

> (d) An application for a writ of habeas corpus on behalf of a person in custody pursuant to the judgment of a State court shall not be granted with respect to any claim that was adjudicated on the merits in State court proceedings unless the adjudication of the claim —
>> (1) resulted in a decision that was contrary to, or involved an unreasonable application of, clearly established Federal law, as determined by the Supreme Court of the United States.

Accordingly, for Williams to obtain federal habeas relief, he must first demonstrate that his case satisfies the condition set by §2254(d)(1). That provision modifies the role of federal habeas courts in reviewing petitions filed by state prisoners.

Justice Stevens' opinion in Part II essentially contends that §2254(d)(1) does not alter the previously settled rule of independent review. Indeed, the opinion concludes its statutory inquiry with the somewhat empty finding that §2254(d)(1) does no more than express a "'mood' that the federal judiciary must respect." . . .

That Justice Stevens would find the new §2254(d)(1) to have no effect on the prior law of habeas corpus is remarkable given his apparent acknowledgment that Congress wished to bring change to the field. . . . That acknowledgment is correct and significant to this case. It cannot be disputed that Congress viewed §2254(d)(1) as an important means by which its goals for habeas reform would be achieved.

Justice Stevens arrives at his erroneous interpretation by means of one critical misstep. He fails to give independent meaning to both the "contrary to" and "unreasonable application" clauses of the statute. . . . By reading §2254(d)(1) as one general restriction on the power of the federal habeas court, Justice Stevens manages to avoid confronting the specific meaning of the statute's "unreasonable application" clause and its ramifications for the independent-review rule. It is, however, a cardinal principle of statutory construction that we must "give effect, if possible, to every clause and word of a statute." . . .

The Court of Appeals for the Fourth Circuit properly accorded both the "contrary to" and "unreasonable application" clauses independent meaning. The Fourth Circuit's interpretation of §2254(d)(1) in Williams' case relied, in turn, on that court's previous decision in Green v. French, 143 F.3d 865 (CA4 1998). . . . With respect to the first of the two statutory clauses, the Fourth Circuit held in *Green* that a state-court decision can be "contrary to" this Court's clearly established precedent in two ways. First, a state-court decision is contrary to this Court's precedent if the state court arrives at a conclusion opposite to that reached by this Court on a question of law. Second, a state-court decision is also contrary to this Court's precedent if the state court confronts facts that are materially indistinguishable from a relevant Supreme Court precedent and arrives at a result opposite to ours. . . .

The word "contrary" is commonly understood to mean "diametrically different," "opposite in character or nature," or "mutually opposed." Webster's Third New International Dictionary 495 (1976). The text of §2254(d)(1) therefore suggests that the state court's decision must be substantially different from the relevant precedent of this Court. The Fourth Circuit's interpretation of the "contrary to" clause accurately reflects this textual meaning. A state-court decision will certainly be contrary to our clearly established precedent if the state court applies a rule that contradicts the governing law set forth in our cases. Take, for example, our decision in Strickland v. Washington. . . . If a state court were to reject a prisoner's claim of ineffective assistance of counsel on the grounds that the prisoner had not established by a preponderance of the evidence that the result of his criminal proceeding would have been different, that decision would be "diametrically different," "opposite in character or nature," and "mutually opposed" to our clearly established precedent because we held in Strickland that the prisoner need only demonstrate a "reasonable probability that . . . the result of the proceeding would have been different." . . . A state-court decision will also be contrary to this Court's clearly established precedent if the state court confronts a set of facts that are materially indistinguishable from a decision of this Court and nevertheless arrives at a result different from our precedent. Accordingly, in either of these two scenarios, a federal court will be unconstrained by §2254(d)(1) because the state-court decision falls within that provision's "contrary to" clause.

On the other hand, a run-of-the-mill state-court decision applying the correct legal rule from our cases to the facts of a prisoner's case would not fit comfortably within §2254(d)(1)'s "contrary to" clause. Assume, for example, that a state-court decision on a prisoner's ineffective-assistance claim correctly identifies Strickland as the controlling legal authority and, applying that framework, rejects the prisoner's claim. Quite clearly, the state-court decision would be in accord with our decision in Strickland as to the legal prerequisites for establishing an ineffective-assistance claim, even assuming the federal court considering the prisoner's habeas application might reach a different result applying the Strickland framework itself. It is difficult, however, to describe such a run-of-the-mill state-court decision as "diametrically different" from, "opposite in character or nature" from, or "mutually opposed" to Strickland, our clearly established precedent. Although the state-court decision may be contrary to the federal court's conception of how Strickland ought to be applied in that particular case, the decision is not "mutually opposed" to Strickland itself.

Justice Stevens would instead construe §2254(d)(1)'s "contrary to" clause to encompass such a routine state-court decision. That construction, however, saps the "unreasonable application" clause of any meaning. If a federal habeas court can, under the "contrary to" clause, issue the writ whenever it concludes that the state court's application of clearly established federal law was incorrect, the "unreasonable application" clause becomes a nullity. . . .

The Fourth Circuit's interpretation of the "unreasonable application" clause of §2254(d)(1) is generally correct. That court held in Green that a state-court decision can involve an "unreasonable application" of this Court's clearly established precedent in two ways. First, a state-court decision involves an unreasonable application of this Court's precedent if the state court identifies the correct governing legal rule from this Court's cases but unreasonably applies it to the facts of the particular state prisoner's case. Second, a state-court decision also involves an unreasonable application of this Court's precedent if the state court either unreasonably extends a legal principle from our precedent to a new context where it should not apply or unreasonably refuses to extend that principle to a new context where it should apply. . . .

A state-court decision that correctly identifies the governing legal rule but applies it unreasonably to the facts of a particular prisoner's case certainly would qualify as a decision "involving an unreasonable application of . . . clearly established Federal law." . . .*

The Fourth Circuit also held in *Green* that state-court decisions that unreasonably extend a legal principle from our precedent to a new context where it should not apply (or unreasonably refuse to extend a legal principle to a new context where it should apply) should be analyzed under §2254(d)(1)'s "unreasonable application" clause. . . . Although that holding may perhaps be correct, the classification does have some problems of precision. Just as it is sometimes difficult to distinguish a mixed question of law and fact from a question of fact, it will often be difficult to identify separately those state-court decisions that involve an unreasonable application of a legal principle (or an unreasonable failure to apply a legal principle) to a new context. Indeed, on the one hand, in some cases it will be hard to distinguish a decision involving an unreasonable extension of a legal principle from a decision involving an unreasonable application of law to facts. On the other hand, in many of the same cases it will also be difficult to distinguish a decision involving an unreasonable extension of a legal principle from a decision that "arrives at a conclusion opposite to that reached by this Court on a question of law." . . . Today's case does not require us to decide how such "extension of legal principle" cases should be treated under §2254(d)(1). For now it is sufficient to hold that when a state-court decision unreasonably applies the law of this Court to the facts of a prisoner's case, a federal court applying §2254(d)(1) may conclude that the state-court decision falls within that provision's "unreasonable application" clause.

B

There remains the task of defining what exactly qualifies as an "unreasonable application" of law under §2254(d)(1). The Fourth Circuit held in Green that a state-court decision involves an "unreasonable application of . . . clearly established Federal law" only if the state court has applied federal law "in a manner that reasonable jurists would all agree is unreasonable." . . . The placement of this additional overlay on the "unreasonable application" clause was erroneous. It is difficult to fault the Fourth Circuit for using this language given the fact that we have employed nearly

---

* The legislative history of §2254(d)(1) also supports this interpretation. See, e.g., 142 Cong. Rec. 7799 (1996) (remarks of Sen. Specter) ("[U]nder the bill deference will be owed to State courts' decisions on the application of Federal law to the facts. Unless it is unreasonable, a State court's decision applying the law to the facts will be upheld"); 141 Cong. Rec. 14666 (1995) (remarks of Sen. Hatch) ("[W]e allow a Federal court to overturn a State court decision only if it is contrary to clearly established Federal law or if it involves an 'unreasonable application' of clearly established Federal law to the facts").

identical terminology to describe the related inquiry undertaken by federal courts in applying the nonretroactivity rule of *Teague*. . . .

Defining an "unreasonable application" by reference to a "reasonable jurist," however, is of little assistance to the courts that must apply §2254(d)(1) and, in fact, may be misleading. Stated simply, a federal habeas court making the "unreasonable application" inquiry should ask whether the state court's application of clearly established federal law was objectively unreasonable. The federal habeas court should not transform the inquiry into a subjective one by resting its determination instead on the simple fact that at least one of the Nation's jurists has applied the relevant federal law in the same manner the state court did in the habeas petitioner's case. The "all reasonable jurists" standard would tend to mislead federal habeas courts by focusing their attention on a subjective inquiry rather than on an objective one. . . .

The term "unreasonable" is no doubt difficult to define. That said, it is a common term in the legal world and, accordingly, federal judges are familiar with its meaning. For purposes of today's opinion, the most important point is that an *unreasonable* application of federal law is different from an *incorrect* application of federal law. Our opinions in *Wright*, for example, make that difference clear. . . . In §2254(d)(1), Congress specifically used the word "unreasonable," and not a term like "erroneous" or "incorrect." Under §2254(d)(1)'s "unreasonable application" clause, then, a federal habeas court may not issue the writ simply because that court concludes in its independent judgment that the relevant state-court decision applied clearly established federal law erroneously or incorrectly. Rather, that application must also be unreasonable.

Justice Stevens turns a blind eye to the debate in *Wright* because he finds no indication in §2254(d)(1) itself that Congress was "directly influenced" by Justice Thomas' opinion in *Wright*. . . . As Justice Stevens himself apparently recognizes, however, Congress need not mention a prior decision of this Court by name in a statute's text in order to adopt either a rule or a meaning given a certain term in that decision. . . . In any event, whether Congress intended to codify the standard of review suggested by Justice Thomas in *Wright* is beside the point. *Wright* is important for the light it sheds on §2254(d)(1)'s requirement that a federal habeas court inquire into the reasonableness of a state court's application of clearly established federal law. The separate opinions in *Wright* concerned the very issue addressed by §2254(d)(1)'s "unreasonable application" clause — whether, in reviewing a state-court decision on a state prisoner's claims under federal law, a federal habeas court should ask whether the state-court decision was correct or simply whether it was reasonable. . . . The *Wright* opinions confirm what §2254(d)(1)'s language already makes clear — that an *unreasonable* application of federal law is different from an *incorrect* or *erroneous* application of federal law.

Throughout this discussion the meaning of the phrase "clearly established Federal law, as determined by the Supreme Court of the United States" has been put to the side. That statutory phrase refers to the holdings, as opposed to the dicta, of this Court's decisions as of the time of the relevant state-court decision. In this respect, the "clearly established Federal law" phrase bears only a slight connection to our *Teague* jurisprudence. With one caveat, whatever would qualify as an old rule under our *Teague* jurisprudence will constitute "clearly established Federal law, as determined by the Supreme Court of the United States" under §2254(d)(1). . . . The one caveat, as the statutory language makes clear, is that §2254(d)(1) restricts the source of clearly established law to this Court's jurisprudence.

In sum, §2254(d)(1) places a new constraint on the power of a federal habeas court to grant a state prisoner's application for a writ of habeas corpus with respect to claims adjudicated on the merits in state court. Under §2254(d)(1), the writ may issue only if one of the following two conditions is satisfied — the state-court adjudication resulted in a decision that (1) "was contrary to . . . clearly established Federal law, as determined by the Supreme Court of the United States," or (2) "involved an unreasonable application of . . . clearly established Federal law, as determined by the Supreme Court of the United States." Under the "contrary to" clause, a federal habeas court may grant the writ if the state court arrives at a conclusion opposite to that reached by this Court on a question of law or if the state court decides a case differently than this Court has on a set of materially indistinguishable facts. Under the "unreasonable application" clause, a federal habeas court may grant the writ if the state court identifies the correct governing legal principle from this Court's decisions but unreasonably applies that principle to the facts of the prisoner's case.

III

Although I disagree with Justice Stevens concerning the standard we must apply under §2254(d)(1) in evaluating Terry Williams' claims on habeas, I agree with the Court that the Virginia Supreme Court's adjudication of Williams' claim of ineffective assistance of counsel resulted in a decision that was both contrary to and involved an unreasonable application of this Court's clearly established precedent. . . .

Accordingly, although I disagree with the interpretation of §2254(d)(1) set forth in Part II of Justice Stevens' opinion, I join Parts I, III, and IV of the Court's opinion and concur in the judgment of reversal.

CHIEF JUSTICE REHNQUIST, with whom JUSTICE SCALIA and JUSTICE THOMAS join, concurring in part and dissenting in part.

I agree with the Court's interpretation of 28 U.S.C. §2254(d)(1) . . . , but disagree with its decision to grant habeas relief in this case. . . .

I, like the Virginia Supreme Court and the Federal Court of Appeals below, will assume without deciding that counsel's performance fell below an objective standard of reasonableness. As to the prejudice inquiry, I agree with the Court of Appeals that evidence showing that petitioner presented a future danger to society was overwhelming. As that court stated:

> The murder of Mr. Stone was just one act in a crime spree that lasted most of Williams's life. Indeed, the jury heard evidence that, in the months following the murder of Mr. Stone, Williams savagely beat an elderly woman, stole two cars, set fire to a home, stabbed a man during a robbery, set fire to the city jail, and confessed to having strong urges to choke other inmates and to break a fellow prisoner's jaw. . . .

In *Strickland*, . . . we said that both the performance and prejudice components of the ineffectiveness inquiry are mixed questions of law and fact. . . . It is with this kind of a question that the "unreasonable application of" clause takes on meaning.

While the determination of "prejudice" in the legal sense may be a question of law, the subsidiary inquiries are heavily factbound.

Here, there was strong evidence that petitioner would continue to be a danger to society, both in and out of prison. It was not, therefore, unreasonable for the Virginia Supreme Court to decide that a jury would not have been swayed by evidence demonstrating that petitioner had a terrible childhood and a low IQ. . . . The potential mitigating evidence that may have countered the finding that petitioner was a future danger was testimony that petitioner was not dangerous while in detention. . . . But, again, it is not unreasonable to assume that the jury would have viewed this mitigation as unconvincing upon hearing that petitioner set fire to his cell while awaiting trial for the murder at hand and has repeated visions of harming other inmates.

Accordingly, I would hold that habeas relief is barred by 28 U.S.C. §2254(d). . . .

NOTES AND QUESTIONS

1. In *Terry Williams*, Justice O'Connor (writing for the majority on this issue) interpreted AEDPA's new standard of review to mean that "a federal habeas court may not issue the writ simply because that court concludes in its independent judgment that the relevant state-court decision applied clearly established federal law erroneously or incorrectly. Rather, that application must also be unreasonable." What does this mean in practice? If you were a federal habeas judge, how would you decide whether a challenged state-court decision was not merely "erroneous" or "incorrect," but also "unreasonable"? Note that even the Supreme Court itself is limited by AEDPA's new standard of review. Is this result compatible with the Supremacy Clause and the proper constitutional role of the federal courts?

2. As mentioned in both Justice Stevens's and Justice O'Connor's opinions, AEDPA's new standard of review provides that federal habeas courts may reverse the decisions of state courts *only* if those decisions are contrary to, or involve an unreasonable application of, existing *Supreme Court* precedent. This was a change from the *Teague* standard, which allowed federal habeas courts to reverse the decisions of state courts on the basis of existing federal law as established in the decisions of the federal circuit and district courts. Why do you think that Congress enacted such a change? Are state courts and lower federal courts in the same federal circuit or district now free to disagree, for extended periods of time (i.e., unless and until the Supreme Court decides to resolve the dispute), over the proper interpretation of federal constitutional provisions? If so, is this a good thing?

3. What do you think Justice O'Connor meant when she wrote that AEDPA's "'clearly established federal law' phrase bears only a slight connection to our *Teague* jurisprudence"? Did she mean that the scope of "clearly established federal law" is somehow broader than the scope of "old law" under *Teague*? For an interesting argument that she may have meant exactly this, see Larry W. Yackle, Habeas: The Figure in the Carpet, 78 Tex. L. Rev. 1731 (2000).

4. To what extent do significant changes to the federal habeas statute (such as AEDPA) potentially implicate the Suspension Clause?

In Boumediene v. Bush, 553 U.S. 723 (2008), the Supreme Court, in a hotly contested 5-4 decision, ruled that aliens held as "enemy combatants" at Guantanamo Bay have the constitutional right, protected by the Suspension Clause, to file a habeas corpus petition in federal court challenging their status as an "enemy combatant" and thus their continued detention. The Court also held that the procedures set forth by Congress, in the Detainee Treatment Act of 2005 (DTA), for reviewing such challenges to alleged "enemy combatant" status before so-called Combatant Status Review Tribunals (CSRTs) are not an "adequate substitute" for a traditional habeas corpus action, and thus cannot suffice to satisfy the Suspension Clause.

Although the situation of aliens held in executive detention at Guantanamo Bay is not entirely analogous to that of prisoners convicted of crimes in judicial proceedings, and although Lakhdar Boumediene did not rely on the same statutory version of federal habeas that applies to state criminal cases, the *Boumediene* case is nonetheless of some significance in the context of a criminal procedure course. For one thing, *Boumediene* extensively reviews the historical role and significance of the writ of habeas corpus — a habeas primer well worth reading. For another, *Boumediene* represents the latest word on the meaning and scope of the Suspension Clause — although, in the end, that word turns out not to be very illuminating:

> The Court has been careful not to foreclose the possibility that the protections of the Suspension Clause have expanded along with post-1789 developments that define the present scope of the writ. See INS v. St. Cyr, 533 U.S. 289, 300-301 (2001). But the analysis may begin with precedents as of 1789, for the Court has said that "at the absolute minimum" the Clause protects the writ as it existed when the Constitution was drafted and ratified. Id., at 301.

553 U.S., at 746. In other words, *Boumediene* leaves unresolved the question whether the Suspension Clause protects the statutory version of federal habeas, originally enacted in 1867, that applies to state criminal cases and that is the primary focus of this chapter.

On the related question of what qualifies as an "adequate substitute" for habeas, although the Court did not purport to set forth a comprehensive guide, it did note that, at a minimum:

> [T]he privilege of habeas corpus entitles the prisoner to a meaningful opportunity to demonstrate that he is being held pursuant to "the erroneous application or interpretation" of relevant law. *St. Cyr*, 533 U.S. [289], at 302 [(2001)]. And the habeas court must have the power to order the conditional release of an individual unlawfully detained — though release need not be the exclusive remedy and is not the appropriate one in every case in which the writ is granted.

553 U.S., at 779. Because the CSRTs, as provided under the DTA, could not meet these minimum requirements, the Court concluded that the denial of access to habeas corpus would violate the Suspension Clause.

3.   Procedural Issues in Federal Habeas

a.   Timing

AEDPA, for the first time, sets a time limit for the filing of a federal habeas petition. In 28 U.S.C. §2244(d), the Act provides:

(d)(1) A 1-year period of limitation shall apply to an application for a writ of habeas corpus by a person in custody pursuant to the judgment of a State court. The limitation period shall run from the latest of —

(A) the date on which the judgment became final by the conclusion of direct review or the expiration of the time for seeking such review;

(B) the date on which the impediment to filing an application created by State action in violation of the Constitution or laws of the United States is removed, if the applicant was prevented from filing by such State action;

(C) the date on which the constitutional right asserted was initially recognized by the Supreme Court, if the right has been newly recognized by the Supreme Court and made retroactively applicable to cases on collateral review; or

(D) the date on which the factual predicate of the claim or claims presented could have been discovered through the exercise of due diligence.

(d)(2) The time during which a properly filed application for State post-conviction or other collateral review with respect to the pertinent judgment or claim is pending shall not be counted toward any period of limitation under this subsection.

b. Exhaustion

AEDPA changes the rules with respect to the long-standing requirement that a petitioner must exhaust available state remedies before seeking federal habeas relief. See Rose v. Lundy, 455 U.S. 509 (1982) (interpreting exhaustion requirement under pre-AEDPA federal habeas law). In 28 U.S.C. §2254(b), the Act provides:

(b)(1) An application for a writ of habeas corpus on behalf of a person in custody pursuant to the judgment of a State court shall not be granted unless it appears that —

(A) the applicant has exhausted the remedies available in the courts of the State, or

(B)(i) there is an absence of available State corrective process; or

(B)(ii) circumstances exist that render such process ineffective to protect the rights of the applicant.

(b)(2) An application for a writ of habeas corpus may be denied on the merits, notwithstanding the failure of the applicant to exhaust the remedies available in the courts of the State.

(b)(3) A State shall not be deemed to have waived the exhaustion requirement or be estopped from reliance upon the requirement unless the State, through counsel, expressly waives the requirement.

In O'Sullivan v. Boerckel, 526 U.S. 838 (1999), the Court held that a habeas petitioner, in order to meet the exhaustion requirement, must file a petition for discretionary review in the state's highest appellate court, so long as such review is part of the state's "established, normal appellate review procedure." Id., at 845. In Slack v. McDaniel, 529 U.S. 473 (2000), the Court held inter alia that AEDPA's general prohibition on "second or successive" habeas petitions does not apply when the initial petition was dismissed without an adjudication on the merits because of the petitioner's failure, under 28 U.S.C. §2254(b), to exhaust state remedies.

c. *Procedural Default*

It is axiomatic that the federal courts "will not review judgments of state courts that rest on adequate and independent state grounds." Michigan v. Long, 463 U.S. 1032, 1041 (1982). The "adequate and independent state ground" doctrine has given rise to a special — and controversial — procedural rule that often bars federal habeas courts from reaching the merits of a habeas petitioner's federal constitutional claims.

WAINWRIGHT v. SYKES, 433 U.S. 72 (1977): We granted certiorari to consider the availability of federal habeas corpus to review a state convict's claim that testimony was admitted at his trial in violation of his rights under Miranda v. Arizona, 384 U.S. 436 (1966), a claim which the Florida courts have previously refused to consider on the merits because of noncompliance with a state contemporaneous-objection rule. . . .

[I]t is a well-established principle of federalism that a state decision resting on an adequate foundation of state substantive law is immune from review in the federal courts. . . . The application of this principle in the context of a federal habeas proceeding has therefore excluded from consideration any questions of state *substantive* law, and thus effectively barred federal habeas review where questions of that sort are either the only ones raised by a petitioner or are in themselves dispositive of his case. The area of controversy which has developed has concerned the reviewability of federal claims which the state court has declined to pass on because not presented in the manner prescribed by its *procedural* rules. . . .

The contemporaneous-objection rule itself is by no means peculiar to Florida, and deserves greater respect than [Fay v. Noia, 372 U.S. 391 (1963),[7]] gives it, both for the fact that it is employed by a coordinate jurisdiction within the federal system and for the many interests which it serves in its own right. A contemporaneous objection enables the record to be made with respect to the constitutional claim when the recollections of witnesses are freshest, not years later in a federal habeas proceeding. It enables the judge who observed the demeanor of those witnesses to make the factual determinations necessary for properly deciding the federal constitutional question. While . . . §2254 requires deference to be given to such determinations made by state courts, the determinations themselves are less apt to be made in the first instance if there is no contemporaneous objection to the admission of the evidence on federal constitutional grounds.

A contemporaneous-objection rule may lead to the exclusion of the evidence objected to, thereby making a major contribution to finality in criminal litigation. Without the evidence claimed to be vulnerable on federal constitutional grounds, the jury may acquit the defendant, and that will be the end of the case; or it may nonetheless convict the defendant, and he will have one less federal constitutional claim to assert in his federal habeas petition. If the state trial judge admits the evidence in question after a full hearing, the federal habeas court pursuant to . . . §2254 will gain significant guidance from the state ruling in this regard. Subtler considerations as well militate in favor of honoring a state contemporaneous-objection rule. An objection on the spot may force the prosecution to take a hard look at its hole card, and even if the prosecutor thinks that the state trial judge will admit the evidence he must contemplate the possibility of reversal by the state

---

7. See supra, at page 1583. — EDS.

appellate courts or the ultimate issuance of a federal writ of habeas corpus based on the impropriety of the state court's rejection of the federal constitutional claim.

We think that the rule of Fay v. Noia, broadly stated, may encourage "sandbagging" on the part of defense lawyers, who may take their chances on a verdict of not guilty in a state trial court with the intent to raise their constitutional claims in a federal habeas court if their initial gamble does not pay off. The refusal of federal habeas courts to honor contemporaneous-objection rules may also make state courts themselves less stringent in their enforcement. Under the rule of Fay v. Noia, state appellate courts know that a federal constitutional issue raised for the first time in the proceeding before them may well be decided in any event by a federal habeas tribunal. Thus, their choice is between addressing the issue notwithstanding the petitioner's failure to timely object, or else face the prospect that the federal habeas court will decide the question without the benefit of their views.

The failure of the federal habeas courts generally to require compliance with a contemporaneous-objection rule tends to detract from the perception of the trial of a criminal case in state court as a decisive and portentous event. A defendant has been accused of a serious crime, and this is the time and place set for him to be tried by a jury of his peers and found either guilty or not guilty by that jury. . . . Any procedural rule which encourages the result that those proceedings be as free of error as possible is thoroughly desirable, and the contemporaneous-objection rule surely falls within this classification.

. . . The "cause"-and-"prejudice" exception . . . will afford an adequate guarantee, we think, that the rule will not prevent a federal habeas court from adjudicating for the first time the federal constitutional claim of a defendant who in the absence of such an adjudication will be the victim of a miscarriage of justice. Whatever precise content may be given those terms by later cases, we feel confident in holding without further elaboration that they do not exist here. . . .

NOTES AND QUESTIONS

1. Under Wainwright v. Sykes, a federal habeas petitioner is generally held responsible for the errors and omissions of his defense lawyer that lead to the procedural default of his claims — errors that, in a capital case, could potentially cost the defendant his life. Does this seem fair? This is another area in which the shift in the theoretical focus of federal habeas, from providing an individual remedy to deterring state-court misconduct, turns out to be quite important. Under the deterrence theory, if the state court was never given a chance to resolve the federal constitutional claim, then no misconduct occurred, and federal habeas relief is unwarranted.

Note, by the way, that the prevailing standard for ineffective assistance of counsel under Strickland v. Washington makes it extremely unlikely that a petitioner whose federal habeas claim is lost by a single isolated episode of procedural default will be able to convert that claim into one of ineffective assistance. See generally John C. Jeffries & William J. Stuntz, Ineffective Assistance and Procedural Default in Federal Habeas Corpus, 57 U. Chi. L. Rev. 679 (1990); Daniel J. Meltzer, State Court Forfeiture of Federal Rights, 99 Harv. L. Rev. 1128 (1986).

2. The doctrine of procedural default in Wainwright v. Sykes was a creation of the Court, not Congress. AEDPA contains no statutory provisions addressing

procedural default, thus presumably leaving Wainwright v. Sykes unaffected. In Edwards v. Carpenter, 529 U.S. 446, (2000), a post-AEDPA decision, the Court applied Wainwright v. Sykes to hold that a procedural default may be excused by ineffective assistance of counsel — but only if the ineffective assistance claim itself was not procedurally defaulted, or if such procedural default was, in turn, excused by its own showing of "cause" and "prejudice." (At this point, you may find yourself consoled by Justice Breyer's frank admission, in a concurring opinion, that "few lawyers, let alone unrepresented state prisoners, will readily understand" the Court's decision in Edwards v. Carpenter.)

3. In Wainwright v. Sykes, the Court declined to overrule Fay v. Noia on its own facts (i.e., where the particular procedural default involved was the defense lawyer's failure to file the documents necessary to preserve an appeal). In Coleman v. Thompson, 501 U.S. 722 (1991), the Court completed the dismantling of Fay v. Noia, holding that the Wainwright v. Sykes "cause" and "prejudice" standard applied to defense counsel's failure to file a notice of appeal within the state's 30-day jurisdictional time limit. (This was a capital case, and the mistake was made by a lawyer from a respected Washington law firm. Coleman was subsequently executed. See Peter Applebome, Execution Stirs Up Troubling Questions, N.Y. Times, p. A14 (May 22, 1992).)

4. On the definition of "cause" for failing to pursue a claim in state court, compare Murray v. Carrier, 477 U.S. 478 (1986) (ignorance or inadvertence of defense lawyer is not "cause," unless it satisfies Strickland v. Washington standard for ineffective assistance of counsel) with Amadeo v. Zant, 486 U.S. 214 (1988) (state concealment of memorandum documenting discrimination in jury selection is "cause"); Reed v. Ross, 468 U.S. 1 (1984) (novelty of legal claim, so that it was not "reasonably available" to defense lawyer, is "cause").

5. On the definition of "prejudice," see United States v. Frady, 456 U.S. 152 (1982) (no "prejudice" where there was "no substantial likelihood" that petitioner would have prevailed absent the constitutional error that was procedurally defaulted).

6. *Successive Petitions and Abuse of the Writ.* Under AEDPA, 28 U.S.C. §2244(b):

> (b)(1) A claim presented in a second or successive habeas corpus application under section 2254 that was presented in a prior application shall be dismissed.
>
> (b)(2) A claim presented in a second or successive habeas corpus application under section 2254 that was not presented in a prior application shall be dismissed unless—
>
> (A) the applicant shows that the claim relies on a new rule of constitutional law, made retroactive to cases on collateral review by the Supreme Court, that was previously unavailable; or
>
> (B)(i) the factual predicate for the claim could not have been discovered previously through the exercise of due diligence; and
>
> (B)(ii) the facts underlying the claim, if proven and viewed in light of the evidence as a whole, would be sufficient to establish by clear and convincing evidence that, but for the constitutional error, no reasonable factfinder would have found the applicant guilty of the underlying offense.

AEDPA also requires petitioners who seek to file a second or successive petition to obtain permission from the court of appeals before filing with the district court, see 28 U.S.C. §2244(b)(3), and requires the district court to dismiss any claims in such a petition unless the petitioner can show that the claim satisfies the statutory requirements, see 28 U.S.C. §2244(b)(4).

With respect to claims that were contained in a prior habeas petition (usually called a "successive petition"), AEDPA forecloses any realistic possibility of relief. But cf. Calderon v. Thompson, 523 U.S. 538 (1998) (Court allows lower court to recall mandate with respect to first habeas petition, in order to avoid AEDPA's ban on "successive petitions"); compare Kuhlmann v. Wilson, 477 U.S. 436 (1986) (treatment of "successive petitions" under pre-AEDPA law).

With respect to claims that were not contained in a prior habeas petition (usually called an "abuse of the writ"), AEDPA's new requirements, while not completely foreclosing habeas relief, are certainly much tougher than the requirements under pre-AEDPA law; compare McCleskey v. Zant, 499 U.S. 467 (1991) (treatment of "abuse of the writ" under pre-AEDPA law).

7. *"Fundamental Miscarriage of Justice" Exception.* Prior to AEDPA, most procedural bars to federal habeas relief contained an exception for cases representing a "fundamental miscarriage of justice." See, e.g., Schlup v. Delo, 513 U.S. 298 (1995) (finding "fundamental miscarriage of justice" sufficient to avoid "abuse of the writ" procedural bar). Under AEDPA, the only exceptions to the "successive petition" and "abuse of the writ" bars are those expressed in the statute, see Note 6, supra. The "fundamental miscarriage of justice" exception remains available, however, in cases involving procedural default bar under Wainwright v. Sykes, see Note 8, infra.

8. The Wainwright v. Sykes procedural default doctrine applies even to cases involving a guilty plea. This is highly significant because, in almost all such cases, the defendant fails to contest his plea on direct appeal, thereby procedurally defaulting any possible subsequent constitutional challenges to the plea. In Bousley v. United States, 523 U.S. 614 (1998), the Court applied Wainwright v. Sykes to such a case, but ultimately held that the defendant (who was challenging his plea on a §2255 motion, based on the Court's later reinterpretation of the federal criminal statute under which he pleaded guilty) would be entitled to relief if he could make a sufficient showing of "actual innocence" to satisfy the "fundamental miscarriage of justice" exception.

d. Evidentiary Hearings

AEDPA also changes the rules with respect to the requirements for obtaining an evidentiary hearing in connection with a federal habeas petition. See Keeney v. Tamayo-Reyes, 504 U.S. 1 (1992) (interpreting requirements for evidentiary hearing under pre-AEDPA federal habeas law). In 28 U.S.C. §2254(e), the Act provides:

> (e)(1) In a proceeding instituted by an application for a writ of habeas corpus by a person in custody pursuant to a judgment of a State court, a determination of a factual issue made by a State court shall be presumed to be correct. The applicant shall have the burden of rebutting the presumption of correctness by clear and convincing evidence.
>
> (e)(2) If the applicant has failed to develop the factual basis of a claim in State court proceedings, the court shall not hold an evidentiary hearing on the claim unless the applicant shows that —
>
>> (A) the claim relied on —

(i) a new rule of constitutional law, made retroactive to cases on collateral review by the Supreme Court, that was previously unavailable; or

(ii) a factual predicate that could not have been previously discovered through the exercise of due diligence; and

(B) the facts underlying the claim would be sufficient to establish by clear and convincing evidence that but for constitutional error, no reasonable factfinder would have found the applicant guilty of the underlying offense.

See Michael Williams v. Taylor, 529 U.S. 420 (2000) (under AEDPA, petitioner did not "fail to develop the factual basis of a claim in State court" unless petitioner or his counsel exhibited a lack of diligence or some greater degree of fault).

4. What Law Applies?

We have already seen that under AEDPA the federal habeas courts, as a general matter, can apply only federal constitutional law that was clearly established, by decisions of the U.S. Supreme Court, as of the time of the state court's final decision. New rules of constitutional law do not apply, unless they fall within one of the two narrow exceptions created by Teague v. Lane (and reaffirmed by the Court under AEDPA). See supra, at page 1584. But this is not the only limitation on the law that applies to a federal habeas case.

STONE v. POWELL

Certiorari to the United States Court of Appeals for the Eighth Circuit
428 U.S. 465 (1976)

JUSTICE POWELL delivered the opinion of the Court.

Respondents in these cases were convicted of criminal offenses in state courts, and their convictions were affirmed on appeal. The prosecution in each case relied upon evidence obtained by searches and seizures alleged by respondents to have been unlawful. Each respondent subsequently sought relief in a Federal District Court by filing a petition for a writ of federal habeas corpus under 28 U.S.C. §2254. The question presented is whether a federal court should consider, in ruling on a petition for habeas corpus relief filed by a state prisoner, a claim that evidence obtained by an unconstitutional search or seizure was introduced at his trial, when he has previously been afforded an opportunity for full and fair litigation of his claim in the state courts. The issue is of considerable importance to the administration of criminal justice.

I

[This section summarized the facts and procedural history of each case. In each case, the petitioner moved to suppress certain evidence, claiming a violation of the Fourth Amendment, but the state court rejected the claim. In each case, the petitioner was convicted, subsequently renewed the Fourth Amendment claim in a federal habeas corpus petition, and ultimately obtained relief from the habeas court. — EDS.]

II

[This section began with a review of the history of federal habeas corpus review of state convictions, up to and including the expansions of federal habeas jurisdiction in Brown v. Allen, 344 U.S. 443 (1953), and Fay v. Noia, 372 U.S. 391 (1963). — EDS.]

During the period in which the substantive scope of the writ was expanded, the Court did not consider whether exceptions to full review might exist with respect to particular categories of constitutional claims. Prior to the Court's decision in Kaufman v. United States, 394 U.S. 217 (1969), however, a substantial majority of the Federal Courts of Appeals had concluded that collateral review of search-and-seizure claims was inappropriate on motions filed by federal prisoners under 28 U.S.C. §2255, the modern postconviction procedure available to federal prisoners in lieu of habeas corpus. The primary rationale advanced in support of those decisions was that Fourth Amendment violations are different in kind from denials of Fifth or Sixth Amendment rights in that claims of illegal search and seizure do not "impugn the integrity of the fact-finding process or challenge evidence as inherently unreliable; rather, the exclusion of illegally seized evidence is simply a prophylactic device intended generally to deter Fourth Amendment violations by law enforcement officers." . . .

Kaufman rejected this rationale and held that search-and-seizure claims are cognizable in §2255 proceedings. The Court noted that "the federal habeas remedy extends to state prisoners alleging that unconstitutionally obtained evidence was admitted against them at trial," . . . and concluded, as a matter of statutory construction, that there was no basis for restricting "access by federal prisoners with illegal search-and-seizure claims to federal collateral remedies, while placing no similar restriction on access by state prisoners." . . . Although in recent years the view has been expressed that the Court should re-examine the substantive scope of federal habeas jurisdiction and limit collateral review of search-and-seizure claims "solely to the question of whether the petitioner was provided a fair opportunity to raise and have adjudicated the question in state courts," . . . the Court, without discussion or consideration of the issue, has continued to accept jurisdiction in cases raising such claims . . .

The discussion in Kaufman of the scope of federal habeas corpus rests on the view that the effectuation of the Fourth Amendment, as applied to the States through the Fourteenth Amendment, requires the granting of habeas corpus relief when a prisoner has been convicted in state court on the basis of evidence obtained in an illegal search or seizure since those Amendments were held in Mapp v. Ohio, 367 U.S. 643 (1961), to require exclusion of such evidence at trial and reversal of conviction upon direct review. Until these cases we have not had occasion fully to consider the validity of this view. . . . Upon examination, we conclude, in light of the nature and purpose of the Fourth Amendment exclusionary rule, that this view is unjustified. We hold, therefore, that where the State has provided an opportunity for full and fair litigation of a Fourth Amendment claim, the Constitution does not require that a state prisoner be granted federal habeas corpus relief on the ground that evidence obtained in an unconstitutional search or seizure was introduced at his trial.

III

The Fourth Amendment assures the "right of the people to be secure in their persons, houses, papers, and effects, against unreasonable searches and seizures." The Amendment was primarily a reaction to the evils associated with the use of the general warrant in England and the writs of assistance in the Colonies, . . . and was intended to protect the "sanctity of a man's home and the privacies of life," Boyd v. United States, 116 U.S. 616, 630 (1886), from searches under unchecked general authority. . . .

The exclusionary rule was a judicially created means of effectuating the rights secured by the Fourth Amendment. Prior to the Court's decisions in Weeks v. United States, 232 U.S. 383 (1914), and Gouled v. United States, 255 U.S. 298 (1921), there existed no barrier to the introduction in criminal trials of evidence obtained in violation of the Amendment. . . . Thirty-five years after *Weeks* the Court held in Wolf v. Colorado, 338 U.S. 25 (1949), that the right to be free from arbitrary intrusion by the police that is protected by the Fourth Amendment is . . . enforceable against the States. . . . The Court concluded, however, that the *Weeks* exclusionary rule would not be imposed upon the States. . . . The full force of *Wolf* was eroded in subsequent decisions, . . . and a little more than a decade later the exclusionary rule was held applicable to the States in Mapp v. Ohio, 367 U.S. 643 (1961).

. . . The *Mapp* majority justified the application of the rule to the States on several grounds, but relied principally upon the belief that exclusion would deter future unlawful police conduct. . . .

Although our decisions often have alluded to the "imperative of judicial integrity," . . . they demonstrate the limited role of this justification in the determination whether to apply the rule in a particular context. . . . While courts, of course, must ever be concerned with preserving the integrity of the judicial process, this concern has limited force as a justification for the exclusion of highly probative evidence. The force of this justification becomes minimal where federal habeas corpus relief is sought by a prisoner who previously has been afforded the opportunity for full and fair consideration of his search-and-seizure claim at trial and on direct review.

The primary justification for the exclusionary rule then is the deterrence of police conduct that violates Fourth Amendment rights. Post-*Mapp* decisions have established that the rule is not a personal constitutional right. It is not calculated to redress the injury to the privacy of the victim of the search or seizure, for any "[r]eparation comes too late." . . . Instead, "the rule is a judicially created remedy designed to safeguard Fourth Amendment rights generally through its deterrent effect. . . ."

Mapp involved the enforcement of the exclusionary rule at state trials and on direct review. The decision in *Kaufman*, as noted above, is premised on the view that implementation of the Fourth Amendment also requires the consideration of search-and-seizure claims upon collateral review of state convictions. But despite the broad deterrent purpose of the exclusionary rule, it has never been interpreted to proscribe the introduction of illegally seized evidence in all proceedings or against all persons. As in the case of any remedial device, "the application of the rule has been restricted to those areas where its remedial objectives are thought most efficaciously served." . . . [Here, Justice Powell noted that the exclusionary rule does not apply to grand jury proceedings, nor does it prohibit the use of illegally seized evidence to impeach a defendant who testifies at trial. — EDS.]

The balancing process at work in these cases also finds expression in the standing requirement. Standing to invoke the exclusionary rule has been found to exist only when the Government attempts to use illegally obtained evidence to incriminate the victim of the illegal search. . . . The standing requirement is premised on the view that the "additional benefits of extending the . . . rule" to defendants other than the victim of the search or seizure are outweighed by the "further encroachment upon the public interest in prosecuting those accused of crime and having them acquitted or convicted on the basis of all the evidence which exposes the truth." . . .

IV

We turn now to the specific question presented by these cases. Respondents allege violations of Fourth Amendment rights guaranteed them through the Fourteenth Amendment. The question is whether state prisoners — who have been afforded the opportunity for full and fair consideration of their reliance upon the exclusionary rule with respect to seized evidence by the state courts at trial and on direct review — may invoke their claim again on federal habeas corpus review. The answer is to be found by weighing the utility of the exclusionary rule against the costs of extending it to collateral review of Fourth Amendment claims.

The costs of applying the exclusionary rule even at trial and on direct review are well known: The focus of the trial, and the attention of the participants therein, are diverted from the ultimate question of guilt or innocence that should be the central concern in a criminal proceeding. Moreover, the physical evidence sought to be excluded is typically reliable and often the most probative information bearing on the guilt or innocence of the defendant. . . . Application of the rule thus deflects the truth-finding process and often frees the guilty. The disparity in particular cases between the error committed by the police officer and the windfall afforded a guilty defendant by application of the rule is contrary to the idea of proportionality that is essential to the concept of justice. Thus, although the rule is thought to deter unlawful police activity in part through the nurturing of respect for Fourth Amendment values, if applied indiscriminately it may well have the opposite effect of generating disrespect for the law and administration of justice. These long-recognized costs of the rule persist when a criminal conviction is sought to be overturned on collateral review on the ground that a search-and-seizure claim was erroneously rejected by two or more tiers of state courts.

Evidence obtained by police officers in violation of the Fourth Amendment is excluded at trial in the hope that the frequency of future violations will decrease. Despite the absence of supportive empirical evidence, we have assumed that the immediate effect of exclusion will be to discourage law enforcement officials from violating the Fourth Amendment by removing the incentive to disregard it. More importantly, over the long term, this demonstration that our society attaches serious consequences to violation of constitutional rights is thought to encourage those who formulate law enforcement policies, and the officers who implement them, to incorporate Fourth Amendment ideals into their value system.

We adhere to the view that these considerations support the implementation of the exclusionary rule at trial and its enforcement on direct appeal of state-court convictions. But the additional contribution, if any, of the consideration of search-and-seizure claims of state prisoners on collateral review is small in relation to the costs.

To be sure, each case in which such claim is considered may add marginally to an awareness of the values protected by the Fourth Amendment. There is no reason to believe, however, that the overall educative effect of the exclusionary rule would be appreciably diminished if search-and-seizure claims could not be raised in federal habeas corpus review of state convictions. Nor is there reason to assume that any specific disincentive already created by the risk of exclusion of evidence at trial or the reversal of convictions on direct review would be enhanced if there were the further risk that a conviction obtained in state court and affirmed on direct review might be overturned in collateral proceedings often occurring years after the incarceration of the defendant. The view that the deterrence of Fourth Amendment violations would be furthered rests on the dubious assumption that law enforcement authorities would fear that federal habeas review might reveal flaws in a search or seizure that went undetected at trial and on appeal.[35] Even if one rationally could assume that some additional incremental deterrent effect would be present in isolated cases, the resulting advance of the legitimate goal of furthering Fourth Amendment rights would be outweighed by the acknowledged costs to other values vital to a rational system of criminal justice.

In sum, we conclude that where the State has provided an opportunity for full and fair litigation of a Fourth Amendment claim, a state prisoner may not be granted federal habeas corpus relief on the ground that evidence obtained in an unconstitutional search or seizure was introduced at his trial.[37] In this context the contribution of the exclusionary rule, if any, to the effectuation of the Fourth Amendment is minimal and the substantial societal costs of application of the rule persist with special force.

Accordingly, the judgments of the Courts of Appeals are reversed.

[The concurring opinion of Chief Justice Burger is omitted.]

JUSTICE BRENNAN, with whom JUSTICE MARSHALL concurs, dissenting.

The Court today holds "that where the State has provided an opportunity for full and fair litigation of a Fourth Amendment claim, a state prisoner may not be granted federal habeas corpus relief on the ground that evidence obtained in an unconstitutional search or seizure was introduced at his trial." . . . To be sure, my

35. The policy arguments that respondents marshal in support of the view that federal habeas corpus review is necessary to effectuate the Fourth Amendment stem from a basic mistrust of the state courts as fair and competent forums for the adjudication of federal constitutional rights. . . . Despite differences in institutional environment and the unsympathetic attitude to federal constitutional claims of some state judges in years past, we are unwilling to assume that there now exists a general lack of appropriate sensitivity to constitutional rights in the trial and appellate courts of the several States. State courts, like federal courts, have a constitutional obligation to safeguard personal liberties and to uphold federal law. . . . Moreover, the argument that federal judges are more expert in applying federal constitutional law is especially unpersuasive in the context of search-and-seizure claims, since they are dealt with on a daily basis by trial level judges in both systems. In sum, there is "no intrinsic reason why the fact that a man is a federal judge should make him more competent, or conscientious, or learned with respect to the [consideration of Fourth Amendment claims] than his neighbor in the state courthouse." [Paul Bator, Finality in Criminal Law and Federal Habeas Corpus for State Prisoners, 76 Harv. L. Rev. 441, 509 (1963).]

37. . . . With all respect, the hyperbole of the dissenting opinion is misdirected. Our decision today is *not* concerned with the scope of the habeas corpus statute as authority for litigating constitutional claims generally. . . . [W]e hold only that a federal court need not apply the exclusionary rule on habeas review of a Fourth Amendment claim absent a showing that the state prisoner was denied an opportunity for a full and fair litigation of that claim at trial and on direct review. Our decision does not mean that the federal court lacks jurisdiction over such a claim, but only that the application of the rule is limited to cases in which there has been both such a showing and a Fourth Amendment violation.

Brethren are hostile to the continued vitality of the exclusionary rule as part and parcel of the Fourth Amendment's prohibition of unreasonable searches and seizures. . . . But these cases, despite the veil of Fourth Amendment terminology employed by the Court, plainly do not involve any question of the right of a defendant to have evidence excluded from use against him in his criminal trial when that evidence was seized in contravention of rights ostensibly secured by the Fourth and Fourteenth Amendments. Rather, they involve the question of the availability of a federal forum for vindicating those federally guaranteed rights. Today's holding portends substantial evisceration of federal habeas corpus jurisdiction, and I dissent. . . .

I

. . . The Court, assuming without deciding that respondents were convicted on the basis of unconstitutionally obtained evidence erroneously admitted against them by the state trial courts, acknowledges that respondents had the right to obtain a reversal of their convictions on appeal in the state courts or on certiorari to this Court. . . . It is simply inconceivable that that constitutional deprivation suddenly vanishes after the appellate process has been exhausted. And as between this Court on certiorari, and federal district courts on habeas, it is for *Congress* to decide what the most efficacious method is for enforcing *federal* constitutional rights and asserting the primacy of federal law. . . . The Court, however, simply ignores the settled principle that for purposes of adjudicating constitutional claims Congress, which has the power to do so under Art. III of the Constitution, has effectively cast the district courts sitting in habeas in the role of surrogate Supreme Courts.[10]

. . . [B]y conceding that today's "decision does not mean that the federal [district] court lacks jurisdiction over [respondents'] claim[s]," . . . the Court admits that respondents have sufficiently alleged that they are "in custody in violation of the Constitution" within the meaning of §2254 and that there is no "constitutional" rationale for today's holding. Rather, the constitutional "interest balancing" approach to this case is untenable, and I can only view the constitutional garb in which the Court dresses its result as a disguise for rejection of the longstanding principle that there are no "second class" constitutional rights for purposes of federal habeas jurisdiction; it is nothing less than an attempt to provide a veneer of respectability for an obvious usurpation of Congress' Art. III power to delineate the jurisdiction of the federal courts.

10. The failure to confront this fact forthrightly is obviously a core defect in the Court's analysis. For to the extent Congress has accorded the federal district courts a role in our constitutional scheme functionally equivalent to that of the Supreme Court with respect to review of state-court resolutions of federal constitutional claims, it is evident that the Court's direct/collateral review distinction for constitutional purposes simply collapses. . . .

The Court's arguments respecting the cost/benefit analysis of applying the exclusionary rule on collateral attack also have no merit. For all of the "costs" of applying the exclusionary rule on habeas *should already have been incurred* at the trial or on direct review if the state court had not misapplied federal constitutional principles. As such, these "costs" were evaluated and deemed to be outweighed when the exclusionary rule was fashioned. . . .

II

Therefore, the real ground of today's decision — a ground that is particularly troubling in light of its portent for habeas jurisdiction generally — is the Court's novel reinterpretation of the habeas statutes. . . . Much in the Court's opinion suggests that a construction of the habeas statutes to deny relief for non-"guilt-related" constitutional violations, based on this Court's vague notions of comity and federalism, . . . is the actual premise for today's decision, and although the Court attempts to bury its underlying premises in footnotes, those premises mark this case as a harbinger of future eviscerations of the habeas statutes that plainly does violence to congressional power to frame the statutory contours of habeas jurisdiction. . . . [T]he groundwork is being laid today for a drastic withdrawal of federal habeas jurisdiction, if not for all grounds of alleged unconstitutional detention, then at least for claims — for example, of double jeopardy, entrapment, self-incrimination, *Miranda* violations, and use of invalid identification procedures —that this Court later decides are not "guilt related." . . .

Federal habeas corpus review of Fourth Amendment claims of state prisoners was merely one manifestation of the principle that "conventional notions of finality in criminal litigation cannot be permitted to defeat the manifest federal policy that federal constitutional rights of personal liberty shall not be denied without the fullest opportunity for plenary federal judicial review." Fay v. Noia, 372 U.S. 391, 424 (1963). . . . In effect, habeas jurisdiction is a deterrent to unconstitutional actions by trial and appellate judges, and a safeguard to ensure that rights secured under the Constitution and federal laws are not merely honored in the breach. . . .

At least since Brown v. Allen, detention emanating from judicial proceedings in which constitutional rights were denied has been deemed "contrary to fundamental law," and all constitutional claims have thus been cognizable on federal habeas corpus. There is no foundation in the language or history of the habeas statutes for discriminating between types of constitutional transgressions. . . . Today's opinion, however, marks the triumph of those who have sought to establish a hierarchy of constitutional rights, and to deny for all practical purposes a federal forum for review of those rights that this Court deems less worthy or important. . . .

I would address the Court's concerns for effective utilization of scarce judicial resources, finality principles, federal-state friction, and notions of "federalism" only long enough to note that such concerns carry no more force with respect to non-"guilt-related" constitutional claims than they do with respect to claims that affect the accuracy of the fact-finding process. Congressional conferral of federal habeas jurisdiction for the purpose of entertaining petitions from state prisoners necessarily manifested a conclusion that such concerns could not be controlling, and any argument for discriminating among constitutional rights must therefore depend on the nature of the constitutional right involved.

The Court, focusing on Fourth Amendment rights as it must to justify such discrimination, thus argues that habeas relief for non-"guilt-related" constitutional claims is not mandated because such claims do not affect the "basic justice" of a defendant's detention . . . ; this is presumably because the "ultimate goal" of the criminal justice system is "truth and justice." . . . Even if punishment of the "guilty" were society's highest value — and procedural safeguards denigrated to this end — in a constitution that a majority of the Members of this Court would prefer, that is not the ordering of priorities under the Constitution forged by the Framers, and this Court's sworn duty is to uphold that Constitution and not to frame its own. The procedural safeguards mandated in the Framers' Constitution are not admonitions to be tolerated only to the extent they serve functional purposes that ensure that the "guilty" are punished and the "innocent" freed; rather, every guarantee enshrined in the Constitution, our basic charter and the guarantor of our most precious liberties, is by it endowed with an independent vitality and value, and this Court is not free to curtail those constitutional guarantees even to punish the most obviously guilty. . . . To sanction disrespect and disregard for the Constitution in the name of protecting society from lawbreakers is to make the government itself lawless and to subvert those values upon which our ultimate freedom and liberty depend. . . . Enforcement of *federal* constitutional rights that redress constitutional violations directed against the "guilty" is a particular function of *federal* habeas review, lest judges trying the "morally unworthy" be tempted not to execute the supreme law of the land. State judges popularly elected may have difficulty resisting popular pressures not experienced by federal judges given lifetime tenure designed to immunize them from such influences, and the federal habeas statutes reflect the congressional judgment that such detached federal review is a salutary safeguard against *any* detention of an individual "in violation of the Constitution or laws . . . of the United States." . . .

. . . It is one thing to assert that state courts, as a general matter, accurately decide federal constitutional claims; it is quite another to generalize from that limited proposition to the conclusion that, despite congressional intent that federal courts sitting in habeas must stand ready to rectify any constitutional errors that are nevertheless committed, federal courts are to be judicially precluded from ever considering the merits of whole categories of rights that are to be accorded less procedural protection merely because the Court proclaims that they do not affect the accuracy or fairness of the fact-finding process. . . . To the extent state trial and appellate judges faithfully, accurately, and assiduously apply federal law and the constitutional principles enunciated by the federal courts, such determinations will be vindicated on the merits when collaterally attacked. But to the extent federal law is erroneously applied by the state courts, there is no authority in this Court to deny defendants the right to have those errors rectified by way of federal habeas; indeed, the Court's reluctance to accept Congress' desires along these lines can only be a manifestation of this Court's mistrust for federal judges. Furthermore, some might be expected to dispute the academic's dictum seemingly accepted by the Court that a federal judge is not necessarily more skilled than a state judge in applying federal law. . . . For the Supremacy Clause of the Constitution proceeds on a different premise, and Congress, as it was constitutionally empowered to do, made federal judges (and initially federal district court judges) "the *primary* and powerful reliances for vindicating every right given by the Constitution, the laws, and treaties of the United States." . . .

. . . Employing the transparent tactic that today's is a decision construing the Constitution, the Court usurps the authority — vested by the Constitution in the Congress — to reassign federal judicial responsibility for reviewing state prisoners' claims of failure of state courts to redress violations of their Fourth Amendment rights. Our jurisdiction is eminently unsuited for that task, and as a practical matter the only result of today's holding will be that denials by the state courts of claims by state prisoners of violations of their Fourth Amendment rights will go unreviewed by a federal tribunal. I fear that the same treatment ultimately will be accorded state prisoners' claims of violations of other constitutional rights; thus the potential ramifications of this case for federal habeas jurisdiction generally are ominous. The Court, no longer content just to restrict forthrightly the constitutional rights of the citizenry, has embarked on a campaign to water down even such constitutional rights as it purports to acknowledge by the device of foreclosing resort to the federal habeas remedy for their redress.

I would affirm the judgments of the Courts of Appeals.

[The dissenting opinion of Justice White is omitted.]

NOTES AND QUESTIONS

1. Despite Justice Brennan's fears, Stone v. Powell has not turned out to be the vanguard for wholesale substantive restrictions of federal habeas corpus jurisdiction. Indeed, the Court has rejected several calls to extend Stone v. Powell to other categories of claims. See, e.g., Jackson v. Virginia, 443 U.S. 307 (1979) (Fourteenth Amendment claim of insufficient evidence to support a conviction); Rose v. Mitchell, 443 U.S. 545 (1979) (Fourteenth Amendment claim of racial discrimination in selection of grand-jury foreman); Kimmelman v. Morrison, 477 U.S. 365 (1986) (Sixth Amendment ineffective-assistance-of-counsel claim, based on counsel's failure to pursue Fourth Amendment search-and-seizure claim); Withrow v. Williams, 507 U.S. 680 (1993) (Fifth Amendment *Miranda* claim).

2. Can a federal habeas petitioner challenge his sentence on the ground that it was enhanced on the basis of a prior conviction that was allegedly unconstitutionally obtained? In Lackawanna County District Attorney v. Coss, 532 U.S. 394 (2001), the Court answered this question squarely in the negative, unless (1) the challenge to the prior conviction was based on a failure to appoint counsel for the defendant in violation of the Sixth Amendment, see Custis v. United States, 511 U.S. 485, 496-497 (1994); or (2) the defendant, through no fault of his own, never had a fair opportunity to challenge the prior conviction, so that the new petition represents "the first and only forum available for review of the prior conviction." See also Daniels v. United States, 532 U.S. 374 (2001), applying the same general rule and exceptions to a federal prisoner seeking collateral review under 28 U.S.C. §2255.

5.   Prejudice and Harmless Error

BRECHT v. ABRAHAMSON

Certiorari to the United States Court of Appeals for the Seventh Circuit
507 U.S. 619 (1993)

CHIEF JUSTICE REHNQUIST delivered the opinion of the Court.

In this case we must decide whether the *Chapman* harmless-error standard applies in determining whether the prosecution's use for impeachment purposes of petitioner's post-*Miranda* silence, in violation of due process under Doyle v. Ohio, 426 U.S. 610 (1976), entitles petitioner to habeas corpus relief. We hold that it does not. Instead, the standard for determining whether habeas relief must be granted is whether the *Doyle* error "had substantial and injurious effect or influence in determining the jury's verdict." Kotteakos v. United States, 328 U.S. 750, 776 (1946). The

Kotteakos harmless-error standard is better tailored to the nature and purpose of collateral review than the *Chapman* standard, and application of a less onerous harmless-error standard on habeas promotes the considerations underlying our habeas jurisprudence. Applying this standard, we conclude that petitioner is not entitled to habeas relief.

[Petitioner Brecht fatally shot his brother-in-law in Alma, Wisconsin. Attempting to flee in his sister's car, he drove the car into a ditch. A police officer (unaware of the shooting) offered assistance, but petitioner refused. He hitchhiked to Winona, Minnesota, where he was stopped by the police. After initially concealing his identity, he later identified himself and was arrested. He was returned to Wisconsin, and was given *Miranda* warnings at his arraignment. At petitioner's trial for first-degree murder, he admitted the shooting, but claimed it was an accident. Over defense objections, petitioner was cross-examined about whether he had ever told anyone, at any time before trial, that the shooting was an accident, and he replied, "no." At closing argument, the prosecutor made several references to the fact that petitioner had never mentioned, prior to trial, that the shooting was an accident. Petitioner was convicted and sentenced to life imprisonment. — EDS.]

. . . The Wisconsin Court of Appeals set the conviction aside on the ground that the State's references to petitioner's post-*Miranda* silence . . . violated due process under Doyle v. Ohio . . . and that this error was sufficiently "prejudicial" to require reversal. The Wisconsin Supreme Court reinstated the conviction. Although it agreed that the State's use of petitioner's post-*Miranda* silence was impermissible, the court determined that this error "'was harmless beyond a reasonable doubt.'" . . . (quoting *Chapman* . . .). In finding the *Doyle* violation harmless, the court noted that the State's "improper references to Brecht's silence were infrequent," in that they "comprised less than two pages of a 900 page transcript, or a few minutes in a four day trial in which twenty-five witnesses testified," and that the State's evidence of guilt was compelling.

Petitioner then sought a writ of habeas corpus under 28 U.S.C. §2254, reasserting his *Doyle* claim. The District court agreed that the State's use of petitioner's post-*Miranda* silence violated *Doyle*, but disagreed with the Wisconsin Supreme Court that this error was harmless beyond a reasonable doubt, and set aside the conviction. . . .

The Court of Appeals held that the *Chapman* harmless-error standard does not apply in reviewing *Doyle* error on federal habeas. Instead, . . . the Court of Appeals held that the standard for determining whether petitioner was entitled to habeas relief was whether the *Doyle* violation "'had substantial and injurious effect or influence in determining the jury's verdict,'" . . . (quoting *Kotteakos* . . .). Applying this standard, the Court of Appeals concluded that petitioner was not entitled to relief. . . .

We granted certiorari . . . and now affirm. . . .

In Doyle v. Ohio, . . . we held that "the use for impeachment purposes of [a defendant's] silence, at the time of arrest and after receiving *Miranda* warnings, violate[s] the Due Process Clause of the Fourteenth Amendment." This rule "rests on 'the fundamental unfairness of implicitly assuring a suspect that his silence will not be used against him and then using his silence to impeach an explanation subsequently offered at trial.'" . . .

The Court of Appeals characterized *Doyle* as "a prophylactic rule." . . . It reasoned that, since the need for Doyle stems from the implicit assurance that flows from *Miranda* warnings, and "the warnings required by *Miranda* are not themselves part of the Constitution," "*Doyle* is . . . a prophylactic rule designed to protect another prophylactic rule from erosion or misuse." . . . But *Doyle* was not simply a further extension of the *Miranda* prophylactic rule. Rather, . . . it is rooted in fundamental fairness and due process concerns. However real these concerns, Doyle does not "overprotec[t]" them . . . Under the rationale of *Doyle*, due process is violated whenever the prosecution uses for impeachment purposes a defendant's post-*Miranda* silence. *Doyle* thus does not bear the hallmarks of a prophylactic rule.

Instead, we think *Doyle* error fits squarely into the category of constitutional violations which we have characterized as "trial error." See Arizona v. Fulminante, 499 U.S. 279, 307 (1991). Trial error "occur[s] during the presentation of the case to the jury," and is amenable to harmless-error analysis because it "may . . . be quantitatively assessed in the context of other evidence presented in order to determine [the effect it had on the trial]." . . . At the other end of the spectrum of constitutional errors lie "structural defects in the constitution of the trial mechanism, which defy analysis by 'harmless-error' standards." . . . The existence of such defects — deprivation of the right to counsel, for example — requires automatic reversal of the conviction because they infect the entire trial process. . . . Since our landmark decision in Chapman v. California, 386 U.S. 18 (1967), we have applied the harmless-beyond-a-reasonable-doubt standard in reviewing claims of constitutional error of the trial type.

. . . *Chapman* reached this Court on direct review, as have most of the cases in which we have applied its harmless-error standard. Although we have applied the *Chapman* standard in a handful of federal habeas cases, see, e.g., Yates v. Evatt, 500 U.S. 391 (1991); Rose v. Clark, 478 U.S. 570 (1986) . . ., we have yet squarely to address its applicability on collateral review. . . .

The federal habeas corpus statute is silent on this point. It permits federal courts to entertain a habeas petition on behalf of a state prisoner "only on the ground that he is in custody in violation of the Constitution or laws or treaties of the United States," 28 U.S.C. §2254(a), and directs simply that the court "dispose of the matter as law and justice require," §2243. The statute says nothing about the standard for harmless-error review in habeas cases. Respondent urges us to fill this gap with the *Kotteakos* standard, under which an error requires reversal only if it "had substantial and injurious effect or influence in determining the jury's verdict." . . . This standard is grounded in the federal harmless-error statute, 28 U.S.C. §2111 ("On the hearing of any appeal or writ of certiorari in any case, the court shall give judgment after an examination of the record without regard to errors or defects which do not affect the substantial rights of the parties"). On its face §2111 might seem to address the situation at hand, but to date we have limited its application to claims of non-constitutional error in federal criminal cases. . . .

. . . In the absence of any express statutory guidance from Congress, it remains for this Court to determine what harmless-error standard applies on collateral review of petitioner's *Doyle* claim. We have filled the gaps of the habeas corpus statute with respect to other matters, . . . and find it necessary to do so here. As always, in defining the scope of the writ, we look first to the considerations underlying our habeas jurisprudence, and then determine whether the proposed rule would advance or inhibit these considerations by weighing the marginal costs and benefits of its application on collateral review.

The principle that collateral review is different from direct review resounds throughout our habeas jurisprudence. . . . Direct review is the principal avenue for challenging a conviction. "When the process of direct review — which, if a federal question is involved, includes the right to petition this Court for a writ of certiorari — comes to an end, a presumption of finality and legality attaches to the conviction and sentence. The role of federal habeas proceedings, while important in assuring that constitutional rights are observed, is secondary and limited. Federal courts are not forums in which to relitigate state trials." . . .

In keeping with this distinction, the writ of habeas corpus has historically been regarded as an extraordinary remedy, "a bulwark against convictions that violate 'fundamental fairness.'" . . . "Those few who are ultimately successful [in obtaining habeas relief] are persons whom society has grievously wronged and for whom belated liberation is little enough compensation." Fay v. Noia, 372 U.S. 391, 440-441 (1963). . . . Accordingly, it hardly bears repeating that "'an error that may justify reversal on direct appeal will not necessarily support a collateral attack on a final judgment.'" . . .

The reason most frequently advanced in our cases for distinguishing between direct and collateral review is the State's interest in the finality of convictions that have survived direct review within the state court system. . . . We have also spoken of comity and federalism. . . . Finally, we have recognized that "[l]iberal allowance of the writ . . . degrades the prominence of the trial itself," . . . and at the same time encourages habeas petitioners to relitigate their claims on collateral review. . . .

In light of these considerations, we must decide whether the same harmless-error standard that the state courts applied on direct review of petitioner's *Doyle* claim also applies in this habeas proceeding. We are the sixth court to pass on the question whether the State's use for impeachment purposes of petitioner's post-*Miranda* silence in this case requires reversal of his conviction. Each court that has reviewed the record has disagreed with the court before it as to whether the State's *Doyle* error was "harmless." State courts are fully qualified to identify constitutional error and evaluate its prejudicial effect on the trial process under *Chapman*, and state courts often occupy a superior vantage point from which to evaluate the effect of trial error. . . . For these reasons, it scarcely seems logical to require federal habeas courts to engage in the identical approach to harmless-error review that *Chapman* requires state courts to engage in on direct review.

Petitioner argues that application of the *Chapman* harmless-error standard on collateral review is necessary to deter state courts from relaxing their own guard in reviewing constitutional error and to discourage prosecutors from committing error in the first place. Absent affirmative evidence that state-court judges are ignoring their oath, we discount petitioner's argument that courts will respond to our ruling by violating their Article VI duty to uphold the Constitution. . . . Federalism, comity, and the constitutional obligation of state and federal courts all counsel against any presumption that a decision of this Court will "deter" lower federal or state courts from fully performing their sworn duty. . . . In any event, we think the costs of applying the *Chapman* standard on federal habeas outweigh the additional deterrent effect, if any, that would be derived from its application on collateral review.

Overturning final and presumptively correct convictions on collateral review because the State cannot prove that an error is harmless under *Chapman* undermines the States' interest in finality and infringes upon their sovereignty over criminal matters. Moreover, granting habeas relief merely because there is a "reasonable possibility" that trial error contributed to the verdict, see Chapman v. California, 386 U.S., at 24 . . . , is at odds with the historic meaning of habeas corpus — to afford relief to those whom society has "grievously wronged." Retrying defendants whose convictions are set aside also imposes significant "social costs," including the expenditure of additional time and resources for all the parties involved, the "erosion of memory" and "dispersion of witnesses" that accompany the passage of time and make obtaining convictions on retrial more difficult, and the frustration of "society's interest in the prompt administration of justice." . . . And since there is no statute of limitations governing federal habeas,[8] and the only laches recognized is that which affects the State's ability to defend against the claims raised on habeas, retrials following the grant of habeas relief ordinarily take place much later than do retrials following reversal on direct review.

The imbalance of the costs and benefits of applying the *Chapman* harmless-error standard on collateral review counsels in favor of applying a less onerous standard on habeas review of constitutional error. The *Kotteakos* standard, we believe, fills the bill. The test under *Kotteakos* is whether the error "had substantial and injurious effect or influence in determining the jury's verdict." 328 U.S., at 776. Under this standard, habeas petitioners may obtain plenary review of their constitutional claims, but they are not entitled to habeas relief based on trial error unless they can establish that it resulted in "actual prejudice." . . . The *Kotteakos* standard is thus better tailored to the nature and purpose of collateral review and more likely to promote the considerations underlying our recent habeas cases. Moreover, because the *Kotteakos* standard is grounded in the federal harmless-error rule, 28 U.S.C. §2111, federal courts may turn to an existing body of case law in applying it. Therefore, contrary to the assertion of petitioner, application of the *Kotteakos* standard on collateral review is unlikely to confuse matters for habeas courts.

For the foregoing reasons, then, we hold that the *Kotteakos* harmless-error standard applies in determining whether habeas relief must be granted because of constitutional error of the trial type.[9] All that remains to be decided is whether petitioner is entitled to relief under this standard based on the State's Doyle error. Because the Court of Appeals applied the *Kotteakos* standard below, we proceed to this question ourselves rather than remand the case for a new harmless-error determination. . . . At trial, petitioner admitted shooting Hartman, but claimed it was an accident. The principal question before the jury, therefore, was whether the State met its burden in proving beyond a reasonable doubt that the shooting was intentional. Our inquiry here is whether, in light of the record as a whole, the State's improper use for impeachment purposes of petitioner's post-*Miranda* silence . . . "had substantial and injurious effect or influence in determining the jury's verdict." We think it clear that it did not.

---

8. This has changed, of course, since the enactment of AEDPA. See page 1603, supra. — EDS.

9. Our holding does not foreclose the possibility that in an unusual case, a deliberate and especially egregious error of the trial type, or one that is combined with a pattern of prosecutorial misconduct, might so infect the integrity of the proceeding as to warrant the grant of habeas relief, even if it did not substantially influence the jury's verdict. . . . We, of course, are not presented with such a situation here.

The State's references to petitioner's post-*Miranda* silence were infrequent, comprising less than two pages of the 900-page trial transcript in this case. And in view of the State's extensive and permissible references to petitioner's pre-*Miranda* silence — i.e., his failure to mention anything about the shooting being an accident to the officer who found him in the ditch, the man who gave him a ride to Winona, or the officers who eventually arrested him — its references to petitioner's post-*Miranda* silence were, in effect, cumulative. Moreover, the State's evidence of guilt was, if not overwhelming, certainly weighty. The path of the bullet through Mr. Hartman's body was inconsistent with petitioner's testimony that the rifle had discharged as he was falling. The police officers who searched the Hartmans' home found nothing in the downstairs hallway that could have caused petitioner to trip. The rifle was found outside the house (where Hartman was shot), not inside where petitioner claimed it had accidently fired, and there was a live round rammed in the gun's chamber, suggesting that petitioner had tried to fire a second shot. Finally, other circumstantial evidence, including the motive proffered by the State, also pointed to petitioner's guilt.

In light of the foregoing, we conclude that the *Doyle* error that occurred at petitioner's trial did not "substantial[ly] . . . influence" the jury's verdict. Petitioner is therefore not entitled to habeas relief. . . .

JUSTICE STEVENS, concurring. . . .

To apply the *Kotteakos* standard properly, the reviewing court must . . . make a de novo examination of the trial record. The Court faithfully engages in such de novo review today. . . .

The purpose of reviewing the entire record is, of course, to consider all the ways that error can infect the course of a trial. . . . [W]e would misread *Kotteakos* itself if we endorsed only a single-minded focus on how the error may (or may not) have affected the jury's verdict. The habeas court cannot ask only whether it thinks the petitioner would have been convicted even if the constitutional error had not taken place. *Kotteakos* is full of warnings to avoid that result. It requires a reviewing court to decide that "the error did not influence the jury," . . . and that "the judgment was not substantially swayed by the error." . . .

The *Kotteakos* standard that will now apply on collateral review is less stringent than the Chapman v. California, 386 U.S. 18 (1967), standard applied on direct review. Given the critical importance of the faculty of judgment in administering either standard, however, that difference is less significant than it might seem. . . . In the end, the way we phrase the governing standard is far less important than the quality of the judgment with which it is applied.

Although our adoption of *Kotteakos* does impose a new standard in this context, it is a standard that will always require "the discrimination . . . of judgment transcending confinement by formula or precise rule. . . ." . . . In my own judgment, for the reasons explained by the Chief Justice, the *Doyle* error that took place in petitioner's trial did not have a substantial and injurious effect or influence in determining the jury's verdict. . . .

JUSTICE WHITE, with whom JUSTICE BLACKMUN joins, and with whom JUSTICE SOUTER joins in part, dissenting.

Assuming that petitioner's conviction was in fact tainted by a constitutional violation that, while not harmless beyond a reasonable doubt, did not have "substantial and injurious effect or influence in determining the jury's verdict," Kotteakos v. United States, 328 U.S. 750, 776 (1946), it is undisputed that he would be entitled to reversal in the state courts on appeal or in this Court on certiorari review. If, however, the state courts erroneously concluded that no violation had occurred or (as is the case here) that it was harmless beyond a reasonable doubt, and supposing further that certiorari was either not sought or not granted, the majority would foreclose relief on federal habeas review. As a result of today's decision, in short, the fate of one in state custody turns on whether the state courts properly applied the Federal Constitution as then interpreted by decisions of this Court, and on whether we choose to review his claim on certiorari. Because neither the federal habeas corpus statute nor our own precedents can support such illogically disparate treatment, I dissent.

I

A

Chapman v. California, 386 U.S. 18 (1967), established the federal nature of the harmless-error standard to be applied when constitutional rights are at stake. . . . Under *Chapman*, federal law requires reversal of a state conviction involving a constitutional violation that is not harmless beyond a reasonable doubt. A defendant whose conviction has been upheld despite the occurrence of such a violation certainly is "in custody in violation of the Constitution or laws . . . of the United States," 28 U.S.C. §2254(a), and therefore is entitled to habeas relief. Although we have never explicitly held that this was the case, our practice before this day plainly supports this view, as the majority itself acknowledges. . . .

B

[This subsection is omitted.]

II

The majority's decision . . . is far from inconsequential. Under *Chapman*, the State must prove beyond a reasonable doubt that the constitutional error "did not contribute to the verdict obtained." . . . In contrast, the Court now invokes Kotteakos v. United States, 328 U.S. 750 (1946) — a case involving a non-constitutional error of trial procedure — to impose on the defendant the burden of establishing that the error "resulted in 'actual prejudice.'" . . . Moreover, . . . the Court extends its holding to all "constitutional error[s] of the trial type." . . . Given that all such "trial errors" are now subject to harmless-error analysis, see Arizona v. Fulminante, 499 U.S. 279, 307-308 (1991), and that "most constitutional errors" are of this variety, . . . the Court effectively has ousted *Chapman* from habeas review of state convictions. In other words, a state court determination that a constitutional error — even one as fundamental as the admission of a coerced confession, see *Fulminante* . . . — is harmless beyond a reasonable doubt has in effect become unreviewable by lower federal courts by way of habeas corpus.

I believe this result to be at odds with the role Congress has ascribed to habeas review, which is, at least in part, to deter both prosecutors and courts from disregarding their constitutional responsibilities. "[T]he threat of habeas serves as a necessary additional incentive for trial and appellate courts throughout the land to conduct their proceedings in a manner consistent with established constitutional standards." . . . Either state courts are faithful to federal law, in which case there is no cost in applying the *Chapman* as opposed to the *Kotteakos* standard on collateral review; or they are not, and it is precisely the role of habeas corpus to rectify that situation.

Ultimately, the central question is whether States may detain someone whose conviction was tarnished by a constitutional violation that is not harmless beyond a reasonable doubt. *Chapman* dictates that they may not; the majority suggests that, so long as direct review has not corrected this error in time, they may. If state courts remain obliged to apply *Chapman*, and in light of the infrequency with which we grant certiorari, I fail to see how this decision can be reconciled with Congress' intent.

III

Our habeas jurisprudence is taking on the appearance of a confused patchwork in which different constitutional rights are treated according to their status, and in which the same constitutional right is treated differently depending on whether its vindication is sought on direct or collateral review. I believe this picture bears scant resemblance either to Congress' design or to our own precedents. . . .

JUSTICE O'CONNOR, dissenting.

I have no dispute with the Court's observation that "collateral review is different from direct review." . . . But decisions concerning the Great Writ "warrant restraint," . . . for we ought not take lightly alteration of that fundamental safeguard against unlawful custody. . . .

In my view, restraint should control our decision today. . . . [W]e are asked to alter a standard that not only finds application in virtually every case of error but that also may be critical to our faith in the reliability of the criminal process. Because I am not convinced that the principles governing the exercise of our habeas powers — federalism, finality, and fairness — counsel against applying *Chapman*'s harmless-error standard on collateral review, I would adhere to our former practice of applying it to cases on habeas and direct review alike. . . .

A repudiation of the application of *Chapman* to *all* trial errors asserted on habeas should be justified, if at all, based on the nature of the *Chapman* rule itself. Yet, . . . one searches the majority opinion in vain for a discussion of the basis for *Chapman*'s harmless-error standard. We are left to speculate whether *Chapman* is the product of constitutional command or a judicial construct that may overprotect constitutional rights. More important, the majority entirely fails to discuss the effect of the *Chapman* rule. If there is a unifying theme to this Court's habeas jurisprudence, it is that the ultimate equity on the prisoner's side — the possibility that an error may have caused the conviction of an actually innocent person — is sufficient by itself to permit plenary review of the prisoner's federal claim. . . . Whatever the source of the *Chapman* standard, the equities may favor its application on habeas if it substantially promotes the central goal of the criminal justice system — accurate determinations of guilt and innocence. . . .

In my view, the harmless-error standard often will be inextricably intertwined with the interest of reliability. By now it goes without saying that harmless-error review is of almost universal application; there are few errors that may not be forgiven as harmless. . . . When such an error is detected, the harmless-error standard is crucial to our faith in the accuracy of the outcome: The absence of full adversary testing, for example, cannot help but erode our confidence in a verdict; a jury easily may be misled by such an omission. Proof of harmlessness beyond a reasonable doubt, however, sufficiently restores confidence in the verdict's reliability that the conviction may stand despite the potentially accuracy impairing error. Such proof demonstrates that, even though the error had the *potential* to induce the jury to err, in fact there is no reasonable possibility that it did. Rather, we are confident beyond a reasonable doubt that the error had no influence on the jury's judgment at all. . . .

At least where errors bearing on accuracy are at issue, I am not persuaded that the *Kotteakos* standard offers an adequate assurance of reliability. Under the Court's holding today, federal courts on habeas are barred from offering relief unless the error "had substantial and injurious effect or influence in determining the jury's verdict." . . . By tolerating a greater probability that an error with the potential to undermine verdict accuracy was harmful, the Court increases the likelihood that a conviction will be preserved despite an error that actually affected the reliability of the trial. . . .

. . . The Court does offer a glimmer of hope by reserving in a footnote the possibility of an exception: *Chapman* may remain applicable, it suggests, in some "unusual" cases. But the Court's description of those cases suggests that its potential exception would be both exceedingly narrow and unrelated to reliability concerns. . . .

. . . [T]he Court's decision buys the federal courts a lot of trouble. From here on out, prisoners undoubtedly will litigate — and judges will be forced to decide — whether each error somehow might be wedged into the narrow potential exception the Court mentions in a footnote today. Moreover, since the Court only mentions the *possibility* of an exception, all concerned must also address whether the exception exists at all. I see little justification for imposing these novel and potentially difficult questions on our already overburdened justice system.

Nor does the majority demonstrate that the *Kotteakos* standard will ease the burden of conducting harmless-error review in those cases to which it does apply. Indeed, . . . *Kotteakos* is unlikely to lighten the load of the federal judiciary at all. The courts still must review the entire record in search of conceivable ways the error may have influenced the jury; they still must conduct their review de novo; and they still must decide whether they have sufficient confidence that the verdict would have remained unchanged even if the error had not occurred. . . . The only thing the Court alters today is the degree of confidence that suffices. But *Kotteakos*'s threshold is no more precise than *Chapman*'s; each requires an exercise of judicial judgment that cannot be captured by the naked words of verbal formulae. *Kotteakos*, it is true, is somewhat more lenient; it will permit more errors to pass uncorrected. But that simply reduces the number of cases in which relief will be granted. It does not decrease the burden of identifying those cases that warrant relief.

. . . [I]t seems to me that the Court's decision cuts too broadly and deeply to comport with the equitable and remedial nature of the habeas writ. . . .

[The dissenting opinions of Justices Blackmun and Souter are omitted.]

NOTES AND QUESTIONS

1. Will the shift, from the *Chapman* standard to the *Kotteakos* standard, make much of a difference in the way that federal habeas courts analyze questions of harmless error? Or is the decision in *Brecht* more about tone setting than about the actual legal standard to be used?

2. In O'Neal v. McAninch, 513 U.S. 432 (1995), in a majority opinion by Justice Breyer, the Court placed an important gloss on the holding in *Brecht*:

> This case asks us to decide whether a federal habeas court should consider a trial error harmless when the court (1) reviews a state-court judgment from a criminal trial, (2) finds a constitutional error, and (3) is in *grave doubt* about whether or not that error is harmless. We recognize that this last mentioned circumstance, "grave doubt," is unusual. Normally a record review will permit a judge to make up his or her mind about the matter. And indeed a judge has an obligation to do so. But we consider here the legal rule that governs the special circumstance in which record review leaves the conscientious judge in grave doubt about the likely effect of an error on the jury's verdict. (By "grave doubt" we mean that, in the judge's mind, the matter is so evenly balanced that he feels himself in virtual equipoise as to the harmlessness of the error.) We conclude that the uncertain judge should treat the error, not as if it were harmless, but as if it affected the verdict (i.e., as if it had a "substantial and injurious effect or influence in determining the jury's verdict"). . . . We repeat our conclusion: When a federal judge in a habeas proceeding is in grave doubt about whether a trial error of federal law had "substantial and injurious effect or influence in determining the jury's verdict," that error is not harmless. And, the petitioner must win.

Id., at 434-435, 436. In short, *O'Neal* makes clear that the harmless-error rule of *Kotteakos/Brecht*, like the harmless-error rule of *Chapman*, places the ultimate burden of persuasion on the prosecutor to establish "harmlessness."

6.   Innocence and the Future of Federal Habeas

In the 1960s, Justice Brennan expanded the scope of federal habeas as a way to ensure that individual state criminal defendants would have their federal constitutional rights vindicated. In the 1970s, Judge Friendly argued that federal habeas should be more concerned with protecting innocent defendants. In the 1980s, Justices Rehnquist, Powell, and O'Connor took the position that federal habeas is less about correcting errors on a case-by-case basis, and more about deterring misconduct by state courts. In the 1990s, Congress significantly amended the federal habeas statute in the hopes of making it more efficient and less of a burdensome intrusion into the criminal justice systems of the states.

But what do we know about how federal habeas review of state criminal cases actually works today? A recent empirical study led by Professor Nancy J. King — the first major study of its kind since AEDPA — found that, with the exception of capital cases (where federal habeas review is generally quite vigorous and many defendants obtain relief, at least from their death sentences), habeas is a complete waste of time that benefits almost no one:

> It is taking longer for habeas petitioners to reach federal court. The average period from conviction to habeas filing before AEDPA was about five years. The same average for prisoners in the [study] was 6.3 years — an increase of over a year. . . .
>
> It is also taking more time for federal courts to resolve the habeas petitions that are filed. Of the noncapital habeas cases filed in 2003 and 2004, almost one in ten were still pending as of October 2006. Disposition time for cases that courts managed to terminate increased from a median of six months in the early 1990s to a median of 7.1 months for cases filed in 2003 and 2004. On average, the slowest 25% of cases dragged on for more than 412 days. When one includes cases filed in 2003 or 2004 and still pending as of December 1, 2006, habeas cases are averaging at least 11.5 months to complete.
>
> The prolonged time required to satisfy the prerequisites for filing a habeas petition, and then to obtain a decision on that petition from a habeas court, dramatically skews the distribution of habeas cases among the overall population of state prison inmates. The [study] found that almost 30% of all noncapital habeas petitions were filed by inmates serving life sentences, even though only 1% of all prison sentences are for life. On the other hand, only 12% of all noncapital habeas petitions were filed by those serving sentences of five years or less, even though that group represents the majority of all those who are sent to prison. Because most federal habeas cases will not be resolved until years after the original conviction and sentencing, only inmates who receive life or other very long prison sentences will be in custody long enough even to file. For the vast majority of the more than two million people now incarcerated in America, the Great Writ is a pipe dream.
>
> Moreover, except in capital cases, those inmates who do manage to obtain federal habeas review can expect to lose. Although federal judges are taking longer to resolve petitions, they ultimately reject almost all of them. The chances that a petitioner will obtain any relief are even more miniscule now than they were before AEDPA. The grant rate for noncapital cases has dropped from 1% in the early 1990s to only 0.34% today. Only eight of the 2384 noncapital habeas filings the study examined resulted in a grant of habeas relief, and one of those eight grants was later reversed on appeal. At this rate, we estimate that fewer than sixty-five of the more than 18,000 petitions filed each year by noncapital petitioners will eventually be granted by district courts. Efforts to improve the efficiency of habeas litigation only appear to have exacerbated this trend.
>
> Today, the necessary prelude in the state courts to a first federal habeas filing is so lengthy, the habeas review process itself so prolonged, and habeas relief so unlikely that post-AEDPA federal habeas in noncapital cases is approaching a lottery for lifers.

Joseph L. Hoffmann & Nancy J. King, Rethinking the Federal Role in State Criminal Justice, 84 N.Y.U. L. Rev. 791, 806-810 (2009).

Does it make sense to continue to perpetuate a costly and time-consuming system of duplicative federal collateral review of state criminal cases when only 0.34 percent of all noncapital habeas petitioners — only 65 out of 18,000 per year — will ever obtain relief? Whatever Congress may have believed when it enacted AEDPA, the legislative effort to streamline and improve federal habeas clearly has failed. Given that failure, and assuming that the federal government still wants to try to improve the quality of state criminal justice and protect federal constitutional rights, is there a better way?

Hoffmann and King argue that there is:

We should redirect the resources that are currently spent on ineffective federal habeas litigation to where they will have a chance to make a bigger difference — to the beginning, not the end, of the criminal justice process. Our primary goal should be to avoid problems before they arise, not to try to find and correct them afterwards. The resources now wasted on reviewing and rejecting claims of constitutional error in habeas litigation should be redeployed to help prevent constitutional violations from occurring in the first place: They should be invested in the reform of state systems of defense representation.

. . . We propose first that Congress amend the federal habeas statute so that . . . an application for a writ of habeas corpus on behalf of a person in custody pursuant to a judgment of conviction entered by a state court shall not be granted unless the court finds that: (1) the petitioner is in custody in violation of the Constitution or laws or treaties of the United States and has established by clear and convincing new evidence, not previously discoverable through the exercise of due diligence, that no reasonable factfinder would have found him guilty of the underlying offense in light of the evidence as a whole; (2) the petitioner is in custody in violation of a new rule of constitutional law, made retroactive to cases on collateral review by the Supreme Court; or (3) the petitioner is under a sentence of death, and either (a) his death sentence was imposed in violation of the Constitution or laws or treaties of the United States or (b) he is legally ineligible to be executed.

. . . Whatever can be saved by cutting back on habeas review — and additional funds — should be devoted to a new federal initiative aimed at helping the states prevent and correct constitutional violations in their own courts.

. . . Congress [should] authorize a new federal initiative to help states provide competent defense representation . . . . In 1979, the House of Delegates of the American Bar Association (ABA) adopted a resolution from the Standing Committee on Legal and Indigent Defendants calling for "the establishment of an independent federally funded Center for Defense Services for the purpose of assisting and strengthening state and local governments in carrying out their constitutional obligations to provide effective assistance of counsel for the defense of poor persons in state and local criminal proceedings."

. . . We believe that the time has come for Congress to acknowledge not only that effective criminal defense at the trial and appellate levels is a far better means of guaranteeing constitutional rights in criminal cases than post hoc habeas litigation but also that state criminal defense systems are in crisis and require federal support. Our adversarial system relies on defense counsel to protect individual rights in criminal cases. Yet case-by-case litigation under Strickland v. Washington has failed, and will continue to fail, as a means of ensuring the right to counsel in noncapital cases. Systematic underfunding of criminal defense representation in the state courts persists, resulting in repeated and widespread breakdowns in defense representation in many states. As a chorus of commentators has observed, the scant postconviction reversals under *Strickland* have had little or no impact on the pervasive pressures on state and county legislative bodies to limit funding for defense services. This is a systemic problem that habeas is woefully inadequate to address.

Hoffmann & King, supra, at 818-827.

The proposal offered by Hoffmann and King would limit federal habeas review to the three special categories of (1) strong claims of innocence based on new evidence, (2) new federal constitutional rules held retroactive, and (3) capital cases. The general issue of factual innocence as a possible ground for either appellate or habeas relief has long been controversial. See generally Brandon L. Garrett,

Judging Innocence, 108 Colum. L. Rev. 55 (2008) (reporting and analyzing the results of an empirical study of DNA exonerations and how those cases were previously handled in the appellate and habeas courts).

In Herrera v. Collins, 506 U.S. 390 (1993), the Court addressed — but did not resolve — the novel claim that a habeas petitioner, despite having been convicted at a concededly fair trial, was nevertheless entitled to federal habeas review based on the allegation that he was factually innocent of the capital crime of which he had been convicted. The Court, in a majority opinion written by Chief Justice Rehnquist, noted:

> [P]etitioner does not come before this Court as an innocent man, but rather as one who has been convicted by due process of law of two capital murders. The question before us, then, is not whether due process prohibits the execution of an innocent person, but rather whether it entitles petitioner to judicial review of his "actual innocence" claim.

Id., at 408, n. 6. Treating the claim as arising under procedural (rather than substantive) due process, the Court concluded:

> [W]e cannot say that Texas' refusal to entertain petitioner's newly discovered evidence eight years after his conviction transgresses a principle of fundamental fairness "rooted in the traditions and conscience of our people." . . . . This is not to say, however, that petitioner is left without a forum to raise his actual innocence claim. For under Texas law, petitioner may file a request for executive clemency. . . . Clemency is deeply rooted in our Anglo-American tradition of law, and is the historic remedy for preventing miscarriages of justice where judicial process has been exhausted.

Id., at 411-412. Finally, the Court acknowledged:

> We may assume, for the sake of argument in deciding this case, that in a capital case a truly persuasive demonstration of "actual innocence" made after trial would render the execution of a defendant unconstitutional, and warrant federal habeas relief if there were no state avenue open to process such a claim. But because of the very disruptive effect that entertaining claims of actual innocence would have on the need for finality in capital cases, and the enormous burden that having to retry cases based on often stale evidence would place on the States, the threshold showing for such an assumed right would necessarily be extraordinarily high. The showing made by petitioner in this case falls far short of any such threshold.

Id., at 417. Herrera was executed shortly after the Court handed down its decision in his case. See generally Joseph L. Hoffmann, Is Innocence Sufficient? An Essay on the U.S. Supreme Court's Continuing Problems with Federal Habeas Corpus and the Death Penalty, 68 Ind. L.J. 817 (1993).

Herrera may have been the first so-called "naked innocence" habeas case to reach the Court, but it was not the last. In 1985, Paul Gregory House was convicted of murdering a neighbor's wife and was sentenced to death. For more than two decades, House doggedly proclaimed his innocence. After unsuccessfully pursuing his state remedies, House filed a federal habeas petition arguing that his trial lawyer failed to conduct a proper factual investigation in violation of Strickland v. Washington, and that the prosecutor hid exculpatory evidence in violation of Brady v. Maryland. The claims were initially held to be procedurally defaulted under Wainwright v. Sykes, due to a different defense lawyer's strategic decision not to raise them in the state appellate courts. In February 1999, a federal district judge nevertheless decided to grant House an evidentiary hearing. At the hearing, House introduced persuasive new evidence of his innocence, eventually leading six judges of the U.S. Court of Appeals for the Sixth Circuit to conclude that it was "highly probable that [House] is completely innocent of any wrongdoing whatever." See House v. Bell, 386 F.3d 668, 708 (6th Cir. 2004) (en banc). The New York Times, the National Law Journal, and 60 Minutes reported extensively on the case, noting the strong likelihood that the victim's abusive husband, and not House, was the real killer.

On June 12, 2006, the Supreme Court held that, notwithstanding the prior procedural default, House should no longer be barred from litigating the merits of his *Strickland* and *Brady* claims. See House v. Bell, 547 U.S. 518 (2006). The Court reviewed House's new evidence in detail and concluded that — "had the jury heard all the conflicting testimony — it is more likely than not that no reasonable juror viewing the record as a whole would lack reasonable doubt [about House's guilt]." See Schlup v. Delo, 513 U.S. 298 (1995), (establishing "fundamental miscarriage of justice" exception to Wainwright v. Sykes procedural default), discussed supra, at page 1608. The Court held that House's new evidence so undermined the strength of the prosecution's case against him that he should be entitled to habeas review of his procedural claims. But the Court also ruled that House failed to meet the (still-undefined) Herrera v. Collins "actual innocence" standard, and therefore could not obtain immediate habeas relief on that basis. Instead, the case was remanded to the lower courts for further consideration of the *Strickland* and *Brady* claims. House, who had contracted multiple sclerosis in prison and was confined to a wheelchair, remained on Death Row for two additional years before the federal district court finally found his trial lawyer to have been constitutionally ineffective and he gained his release.

As one commentator has noted:

> Compelling post-trial claims of innocence, like House's, pose the most excruciating dilemmas. Such claims have the potential to destroy our faith in a legal system that often represents our best hope for achieving a better society. They strike at the heart of the jury system, the foundation of American democracy. They force appellate judges into fact-finding roles with which they may be intensely uncomfortable, and produce conflicts between state and federal courts. They unsettle our notions of finality, creating cognitive dissonance by challenging what we have already accepted as true. The very thought of such an enormous injustice may be so intolerable that almost everyone associated with the legal system — including judges, jurors, prosecutors, police, and even defense attorneys — may prove vulnerable to cognitive biases that prevent them from concluding that a wrongful conviction actually has occurred.
>
> All of this may explain why it is so hard for the courts to remedy an erroneous conviction, but the problem is one that simply must be solved. The case of Paul Gregory House is the kind that gives law, lawyers, and the death penalty a bad name. As one of House's Death Row guards, in late 2007, asked . . . a minister visiting the prison: "The Supreme Court has said any reasonable juror would find this man innocent, right? Then why is he still here?"

Joseph L. Hoffmann, House v. Bell and the Death of Innocence, in Death Penalty Stories 449-451, John H. Blume & Jordan M. Steiker eds. 2009).

Are federal habeas courts the best forum for addressing postconviction claims of factual innocence? The prolonged legal saga of Paul Gregory House would seem to suggest that they are not. In 2006, North Carolina created an Innocence Inquiry Commission for the purpose of reviewing claims of factual innocence in individual criminal cases. The Commission can hold hearings and refer a case of likely innocence to a special three-judge court, which holds the ultimate power to set aside the conviction. On February 17, 2010, Gregory F. Taylor, who had served 16 years in prison for the murder of a prostitute in 1991, became the first person to be freed by the three-judge court, which found "clear and convincing evidence" that Taylor was innocent of the crime. Taylor's case was only the third to gain a hearing before the Commission, and only the second to be referred to the three-judge court. See Robbie Brown, Judges Free Inmate on Recommendation of Special Innocence Panel, N.Y. Times, Feb. 17, 2010, available online at http://www.nytimes.com/2010/02/18/us/18innocent.html.

As the track record of the North Carolina Innocence Inquiry Commission would tend to indicate, the number of criminal cases in which factually innocent defendants are convicted is undoubtedly miniscule in comparison to the total number of criminal convictions. See also http://www.innocenceproject.org/know/ (reporting that, as of late 2010, "[t]here have been 261 post-conviction DNA exonerations in United States history"). But such cases do occur. The big problem with federal habeas is that the same procedural rules that have been developed in an effort to prevent abuses and frivolous claims also serve to block access even for those very few defendants who might actually deserve substantive relief.

On August 17, 2009, the Supreme Court — faced with a potentially innocent Death Row inmate whose "regular" federal habeas petition had already been denied — ordered a new evidentiary hearing in connection with a so-called "original writ" of habeas corpus filed directly with the Court itself under 28 U.S.C. §2241. See In re Troy Anthony Davis, 130 S. Ct. 1 (2009). This was the first such action by the Court in an "original writ" habeas case since 1962. Justice Scalia, joined by Justice Thomas, dissented:

> Today this Court takes the extraordinary step — one not taken in nearly 50 years — of instructing a district court to adjudicate a state prisoner's petition for an original writ of habeas corpus. The Court proceeds down this path even though every judicial and executive body that has examined petitioner's stale claim of innocence has been unpersuaded, and (to make matters worst) even though it would be impossible for the District Court to grant any relief. Far from demonstrating, as this Court's Rule 20.4(a) requires, "exceptional circumstances" that "warrant the exercise of the Court's discretionary powers," petitioner's claim is a sure loser. Transferring his petition to the District Court is a confusing exercise that can serve no purpose except to delay the State's execution of its lawful criminal judgment. . . .
>
> [T]his Court sends the District Court for the Southern District of Georgia on a fool's errand. That court is directed to consider evidence of actual innocence which has been reviewed and rejected at least three times, and which, even if adequate to persuade the District Court, cannot (as far as anyone knows) form the basis for any relief. I truly do not see how the District Court can discern what is expected of it. If this Court thinks it possible that capital convictions obtained in full compliance with law can never be final, but are always subject to being set aside by federal courts for the reason of "actual innocence," it should set this case on our own docket so that we can (if necessary) resolve that question.

Id., at 2-4 (Scalia, J., dissenting). After holding the required evidentiary hearing, the federal district court ultimately rejected the innocence claim on the merits, finding that "while Mr. Davis's new evidence casts some additional, minimal doubt on his conviction, it is largely smoke and mirrors. The vast majority of the evidence at trial remains intact, and the new evidence is largely not credible or lacking in probative value." See In re Troy Anthony Davis, 2010 U.S. Dist. LEXIS 87340 (S.D. Ga. August 24, 2010), at 216.

United States Constitution (Selected Provisions)

ARTICLE I

Section 9. . . . . The Privilege of the Writ of Habeas Corpus shall not be suspended, unless when in Cases of Rebellion or Invasion the public Safety may require it.

No Bill of Attainder or ex post facto Law shall be passed. . . .

ARTICLE III

Section 1. The judicial Power of the United States, shall be vested in one supreme Court, and in such inferior Courts as the Congress may from time to time ordain and establish. . . .

Section 2. The judicial Power shall extend to all Cases, in Law and Equity, arising under this Constitution, the Laws of the United States, and Treaties made, or which shall be made, under their Authority; — to all Cases affecting Ambassadors, other public Ministers and Consuls; — to all Cases of admiralty and maritime Jurisdiction; — to Controversies to which the United States shall be a Party; — to Controversies between two or more States; — between a State and Citizens of another State; — between Citizens of different States; — between Citizens of the same State claiming Lands under Grants of different States, and between a State, or the Citizens thereof, and foreign States, Citizens or Subjects.

In all Cases affecting Ambassadors, other public Ministers and Consuls, and those in which a State shall be Party, the supreme Court shall have original Jurisdiction. In all the other Cases before mentioned, the supreme Court shall have appellate Jurisdiction, both as to Law and Fact, with such Exceptions, and under such Regulations as the Congress shall make.

The Trial of all Crimes, except in Cases of Impeachment, shall be by Jury; and such Trial shall be held in the State where the said Crimes shall have been committed; but when not committed within any State, the Trial shall be at such Place or Places as the Congress may by Law have directed. . . .

ARTICLE IV

Section 2. The Citizens of each State shall be entitled to all Privileges and Immunities of Citizens in the several States.

A Person charged in any State with Treason, Felony, or other Crime, who shall flee from Justice, and be found in another State, shall on Demand of the executive Authority of the State from which he fled, be delivered up, to be removed to the State having Jurisdiction of the Crime. . . .

ARTICLE VI

. . . This Constitution, and the Laws of the United States which shall be made in Pursuance thereof; and all Treaties made, or which shall be made, under the Authority of the United States, shall be the supreme Law of the Land; and the Judges in every State shall be bound thereby, any Thing in the Constitution or Laws of any State to the Contrary notwithstanding. . . .

AMENDMENT I

Congress shall make no law respecting an establishment of religion, or prohibiting the free exercise thereof; or abridging the freedom of speech, or of the press; or the right of the people peaceably to assemble, and to petition the Government for a redress of grievances.

AMENDMENT II

A well regulated Militia, being necessary to the security of a free State, the right of the people to keep and bear Arms, shall not be infringed.

AMENDMENT III

No Soldier shall, in time of peace be quartered in any house, without the consent of the Owner, nor in time of war, but in a manner to be prescribed by law.

AMENDMENT IV

The right of the people to be secure in their persons, houses, papers, and effects, against unreasonable searches and seizures, shall not be violated, and no Warrants shall issue, but upon probable cause, supported by Oath or affirmation, and particularly describing the place to be searched, and the persons or things to be seized.

AMENDMENT V

No person shall be held to answer for a capital, or otherwise infamous crime, unless on a presentment or indictment of a Grand Jury, except in cases arising in the land or naval forces, or in the Militia, when in actual service in time of War or public danger; nor shall any person be subject for the same offence to be twice put in jeopardy of life or limb; nor shall be compelled in any criminal case to be a witness against himself, nor be deprived of life, liberty, or property, without due process of law; nor shall private property be taken for public use, without just compensation.

AMENDMENT VI

In all criminal prosecutions, the accused shall enjoy the right to a speedy and public trial, by an impartial jury of the State and district wherein the crime shall have been committed, which district shall have been previously ascertained by law, and to be informed of the nature and cause of the accusation; to be confronted with the witnesses against him; to have compulsory process for obtaining witnesses in his favor, and to have the Assistance of Counsel for his defence.

AMENDMENT VII

In Suits at common law, where the value in controversy shall exceed twenty dollars, the right of trial by jury shall be preserved, and no fact tried by a jury, shall be otherwise re-examined in any Court of the United States, than according to the rules of the common law.

AMENDMENT VIII

Excessive bail shall not be required, nor excessive fines imposed, nor cruel and unusual punishments inflicted.

AMENDMENT IX

The enumeration in the Constitution, of certain rights, shall not be construed to deny or disparage others retained by the people.

AMENDMENT X

The powers not delegated to the United States by the Constitution, nor prohibited by it to the States, are reserved to the States respectively, or to the people.

AMENDMENT XIII

Section 1. Neither slavery nor involuntary servitude, except as a punishment for crime whereof the party shall have been duly convicted, shall exist within the United States, or any place subject to their jurisdiction.

Section 2. Congress shall have power to enforce this article by appropriate legislation.

AMENDMENT XIV

Section 1. All persons born or naturalized in the United States, and subject to the jurisdiction thereof, are citizens of the United States and of the State wherein they reside. No State shall make or enforce any law which shall abridge the privileges or immunities of citizens of the United States; nor shall any State deprive any person of life, liberty, or property, without due process of law; nor deny to any person within its jurisdiction the equal protection of the laws. . . .

Section 5. The Congress shall have power to enforce, by appropriate legislation, the provisions of this article.

Table of Cases

Principal cases are indicated by italics. Alphabetization is letter-by-letter
(e.g., "Martinez" precedes "Martin Linen Supply Co.").

1637

Table of Authorities

Easterbrook, Frank H., Criminal Procedure as a Market System, 12 J. Leg. Stud. 289 (1983), 1263

Ellickson, Robert C., Controlling Chronic Misconduct in City Spaces: Of Panhandlers, Skid Rows, and Public-Space Zoning, 105 Yale L.J. 1165 (1996), 584

Elliott, Rogers, Expert Testimony about Eyewitness Identification, 17 L. & Hum. Behav. 423 (1993), 168

Emerson, Deborah Day, & Nancy L. Ames, The Role of the Grand Jury and the Preliminary Hearing in Pretrial Screening (1984), 1037

Erikson, E., Identity: Youth and Crisis (1968), 1426

Fagan, Jeffrey, & Martin Guggenheim, Preventive Detention and the Judicial Prediction of Dangerousness for Juveniles: A Natural Experiment, 86 J. Crim. L. & Criminology 415 (1996), 958

Fairman, Charles, Does the Fourteenth Amendment Incorporate the Bill of Rights? The Original Understanding, 2 Stan. L. Rev. 5 (1949), 91

Farkas, K., Training Health Care and Human Services Personnel in Perinatal Substance Abuse, in Drug & Alcohol Abuse Reviews, Substance Abuse During Pregnancy and Childhood (R. Watson ed., 1995), 623

Featherly, J., & E. Hill, Crack Cocaine Overview 1989, 975

Federal Bureau of Prisons, National Prisoner Statistics: Prisoners in State and Federal Institutions — 1950 (1954), 101

The Federalist
    No. 9, 1538
    No. 49, 1429
    No. 78, 1432
    No. 84, 124

Feldman, D., England and Wales, in Criminal Procedure: A Worldwide Study 91 (C. Bradley ed., 1999), 1436

Fell, Ferguson, Williams, & Fields, Why Aren't Sobriety Checkpoints Widely Adopted as an Enforcement Strategy in the United States? 35 Accident Analysis & Prevention 897 (Nov. 2003), 610

Few, J. Kendall, In Defense of Trial by Jury (1993), 1271

Fisher, George, The Birth of the Prison Retold, 104 Yale L.J. 1235 (1994), 82

———, Plea Bargaining's Triumph, 109 Yale L.J. 857 (2000), 82, 1189

Fishman, Clifford S., Interception of Communications in Exigent Circumstances: The Fourth Amendment, Federal Legislation, and the United States Department of Justice, 22 Ga. L. Rev. 1 (1987), 902

Fourteenth Amendment and the Bill of Rights, 18 J. of Cont. Legal Issues (2009), 92

Frankel, Marvin, United States District Judge for the Southern District of New York, 41 U. Cin. L. Rev. 1 (1972), 1439

Frankfurter, Felix, & Thomas G. Corcoran, Petty Offenses and the Constitutional Guaranty of Trial by Jury, 39 Harv. L. Rev. 917 (1926), 143

Freed, Daniel J., Federal Sentencing in the Wake of Guidelines: Unacceptable Limits on the Discretion of Sentencers, 101 Yale L.J. 1681 (1992), 1443

Freedman, Eric M., Habeas Corpus: Rethinking the Great Writ of Liberty (2003), 1582

Fried, C., Contract as Promise (1981), 1241

———, Privacy, 77 Yale L.J. 475 (1968), 328

———, Reflections on Crime and Punishment, 30 Suffolk U. L. Rev. 681 (1997), 51

Friedman, Barry, A Tale of Two Habeas, 73 Minn. L. Rev. 247 (1988), 1584

Friedman, Lawrence M., Crime and Punishment in American History (1993), 1355

———, Plea Bargaining in Historical Perspective, 13 Law & Soc'y Rev. 247 (1979), 1189

Friendly, Henry J., The Bill of Rights as a Code of Criminal Procedure, 53 Cal. L. Rev. 929 (1965), 81

———, The Fifth Amendment Tomorrow: The Case for Constitutional Change, 37 U. Cin. L. Rev. 671 (1968), 330, 711

———, Is Innocence Irrelevant? Collateral Attack on Criminal Judgments, 38 U. Chi. L. Rev. 142 (1970), 1583, 1585

Fukurai, Hiroshi, & Darryl Davies, Affirmative Action in Jury Selection: Racially Representative Juries, Racial Quotas, and Affirmative Juries of the Hennepin Model and the Jury De Medietatae Linguae, 4 Va. J. Soc. Pol'y & L. 645 (1997), 1309

Fyfe, James J., The Split-Second Syndrome and Other Determinants of Police Violence, in Violent Transactions (Anne Campbell & John Gibbs eds., 1986), 640

Galloway, Russell W., Jr., The Intruding Eye: A Status Report on the Constitutional Ban against Paper Searches, 25 How. L.J. 367 (1982), 296, 320

Garrett, Brandon L., Judging Innocence, 108 Colum. L. Rev. 55 (2008), 1162, 1629

Geller, William A., & Michael S. Scott, Deadly Force: What We Know, in Thinking About Police (Carl B. Klockars & Stephen D. Mastrofski eds., 1991), 635

Gerstein, Robert S., The Demise of *Boyd*: Self-Incrimination and Private Papers in the Burger Court, 27 UCLA L. Rev. 343 (1979), 329, 727

———, Privacy and Self-Incrimination, 80 Ethics 87 (1970), 729

Gianelli, Paul, *Brady* and Jailhouse Snitches, 57 Case W. Res. L. Rev. 593 (2007), 1162

———, Criminal Discovery, Scientific Evidence, and DNA, 44 Vand. L. Rev. 791 (1991), 1139

———, Forensic Science: Scientific Evidence and Prosecutorial Misconduct in the Duke Lacross Rape Case, 45 Crim. L. Bull. 4 (2009), 1140

Goldberg, Steven, Harmless Error: Constitutional Sneak Thief, 71 J. Crim. L. & Crimonology 421 (1980), 1572

Goldstein, Abraham S., The State and the Accused: Balance of Advantage in Criminal Procedure, 69 Yale L.J. 1149 (1960), 1120

Goldstein, Herman, Policing a Free Society (1977), 359

Goodman, James, Stories of Scottsboro (1994), 93, 94

Goodpaster, Gary, The Trial for Life: Effective Assistance of Counsel in Death Penalty Cases, 58 N.Y.U. L. Rev. 299 (1983), 205

Graham, Kenneth, & Leon Letwin, The Preliminary Hearing in Los Angeles: Some Field Findings and Legal Policy Observations, 18 UCLA L. Rev. 635 (1971), 1037

Graham, Michael H., Witness Intimidation (1985), 1138

Grano, Joseph D., Ascertaining the Truth, 77 Cornell L. Rev. 1061 (1992), 29

———, Confessions, Truth and the Law (1993), 856

———, *Kirby*, *Biggers*, and *Ash*: Do Any Constitutional Safeguards Remain Against the Danger of Convicting the Innocent? 72 Mich. L. Rev. 717 (1974), 171

———, The Right to Counsel: Collateral Issues Affecting Due Process, 54 Minn. L. Rev. 1175 (1970), 230

———, Truth and the Law (1993), 856

———, "Through a Glass, Darkly": How the Court Sees Motions to Disqualify Criminal Defense Lawyers, 89 Colum. L. Rev. 1201 (1989), 255

Greenawalt, R. Kent, Silence as a Moral and Constitutional Right, 23 Wm. & Mary L. Rev. 15 (1981), 727, 729

Griffiths, Ideology in Criminal Procedure, or a Third "Model" of the Criminal Process, 79 Yale L.J. 359 (1970), 27

Griswold, Erwin N., The Fifth Amendment Today (1955), 722, 727

Gross, Samuel R., & Katherine Y. Barnes, Road Work: Racial Profiling and Drug Interdiction on the Highway, 101 Mich. L. Rev. 651 (2002), 570

Gross, Samuel R., & Debra Livingston, Racial Profiling Under Attack, 102 Colum. L. Rev. 1413 (2002), 572

Guinther, John, The Jury in America (1988), 1271

Hale, M., History and Analysis of the Common Law of England (1713), 1345

———, Pleas of the Crown (1st Am. ed. 1847), 107, 497, 1048

Halliday, Paul D., Habeas Corpus: From England to Empire (2010), 1582

Halsbury's Laws of England (3d ed. 1955), 497

Halsbury's Statutes (4th ed. 2003 reissue), 1325

Hannaford-Agor, Paula L., Valerie P. Has, Nicole L. Mott, & G. Thomas Munsterman, Are Hung Juries a Problem? (2002), 1283

Hanson, Roger A., et al., Indigent Defenders Get the Job Done and Done Well (1992), 1268

Harcourt, Bernard, Illusion of Order: The False Promise of Broken Windows Policing (2001), 583

Harris, David A., The Constitution and Truth Seeking: A New Theory on Expert Services for Indigent Defendants, 83 J. Crim. L. & Criminology 469 (1992), 172

———, Particularized Suspicion, Categorical Judgments: Supreme Court Rhetoric Versus Lower Court Reality under *Terry v. Ohio*, 72 St. John's L. Rev. 975 (1998), 558, 569

———, The Stories, the Statistics, and the Law: Why "Driving While Black" Matters, 84 Minn. L. Rev. 265 (1999), 581

Hastie, R., S. Penrod, & N. Pennington, Inside the Jury 140 (1983), 1308

Hawkins, W., Pleas of the Crown (8th ed. 1824), 1180

Heaney, Gerald W., The Reality of Guidelines Sentencing: No End to Disparity, 28 Am. Crim. L. Rev. 161 (1991), 1443

Heffernan, William C., Fourth Amendment Privacy Interests, 92 J. Crim. L. & Criminology 1 (2001), 371, 389, 390

Heidt, Robert, The Fifth Amendment Privilege and Documents — Cutting *Fisher*'s Tangled Line, 49 Mo. L. Rev. 439 (1984), 332

President's Commission on Law Enforcement and Administration of Justice
  The Challenge of Crime in a Free Society (1967), 3
    Task Force Report: The Courts (1967), 60
    Task Force Report: The Police (1967), 542, 566
Priar and Martin, Searching and Disarming Criminals, 45 J. Crim. L.C. & P.S. 481 (1954), 543
Provine, Doris Marie, Too Many Black Men: The Sentencing Judge's Dilemma, 23 Law & Soc. Inquiry
  823 (1998), 1443

Ramirez, Deborah, Affirmative Jury Selection: A Proposal to Advance Both the Deliberative Ideal and
  Jury Diversity, 1998 U. Chi. Legal F. 161, 1306
Ramusen, Eric, *Mezzanatto* and the Economics of Self-Incrimination, 19 Cardoza L. Rev. 1541 (1998),
  1229, 1230
Read, Frank T., Lawyers at Lineups: Constitutional Necessity or Avoidable Extravagance? 17 UCLA L.
  Rev. 339 (1969), 168
Reik, T., The Compulsion to Confess (1972), 888
Reiner, Robert, The Politics of the Police (1985), 55, 56
Reitz, Kevin R., Lawyers and the Fifth Amendment: The Need for a Projected Privilege, 41 Duke L.J. 572
  (1991), 332
———, Sentencing Guidelines Systems and Sentence Appeals: A Comparison of Federal and State
  Experiences, 91 Nw. U. L. Rev. 1441 (1997), 1213
Report of Attorney General's Committee on Poverty and the Administration of Federal Criminal Justice
  (1963), 184, 773
Report of the Working Committees to the Second Circuit Task Force on Gender, Racial and Ethnic
  Fairness in the Courts, 1997 Ann. Surv. Am. L. 124, 942, 943
Ribton-Turner, C., A History of Vagrants and Vagrancy and Beggars and Begging (reprint 1972), 594
Richman, Daniel C., Bargaining About Future Jeopardy, 49 Vand. L. Rev. 1181 (1996), 1245, 1507
———, Cooperating Clients, 56 Ohio St. L.J. 69 (1995), 1234, 1236
———, Grand Jury Secrecy: Plugging the Leaks in an Empty Bucket, 36 Am. Crim. L. Rev. 339 (1999),
  994, 1000, 1001
———, Prosecutors and Their Agents, Agents and Their Prosecutors, 103 Colum. L. Rev. 749 (2003),
  935, 981, 982
Roberts, Dorothy E., Crime, Race and Reproduction, 67 Tul. L. Rev. 1945 (1993), 30
———, Foreword: Race, Vagueness, and the Social Meaning of Order-Maintenance Policing, 89 J. Crim.
  L. & Criminology 775 (1999), 596
Robinson, Paul H., Commentary: Punishing Dangerousness: Cloaking Preventive Detention as Criminal
  Justice, 114 Harv. L. Rev. 1429 (2001), 959
Rogers, O.A., Jr., The Elaine Race Riots of 1919, 19 Ark. Hist. Q. 142 (1960), 93
Rose, The Peremptory Challenge Accused of Race or Gender Discrimination? Some Data from One
  County, 23 Law & Hum. Behav. 5695 (1999), 1324
Rosen, Jeffrey, The Naked Crowd (2004), 397
Rothman, David J., Perfecting the Prison: United States, 1789-1865, in The Oxford History of the Prison
  (Norval Morris & David J. Rothman eds., 1998), 82
Ruess-Ianni, Elizabeth, The Two Cultures of Policing: Street Cops and Management Cops (1983), 57
Russell on Crimes (6th ed.), 761

Saks, M., Jury Verdicts (1977), 1277
Saltzburg, Stephen A., Perjury and False Testimony: Should the Difference Matter So Much? 68 Fordham
  L. Rev. 1537 (2000), 1156
———, *Terry v. Ohio*, A Practically Perfect Doctrine, 72 St. John's L. Rev. 911 (1998), 550, 558
Schnapper, Eric, Unreasonable Searches and Seizures of Papers, 71 Va. L. Rev. 869 (1985), 321
Schroeder, William A., Warrantless Misdemeanor Arrests and the Fourth Amendment, 58 Mo. L. Rev.
  771 (1993), 496
Schulhofer, Stephen J., Is Plea Bargaining Inevitable? 97 Harv. L. Rev. 1037 (1984), 1204, 1205
———, *Miranda's* and Clearance Rates, 91 Nw. U. L. Rev. 278 (1996), 859
———, *Miranda's* Practical Effect: Substantial Benefits and Vanishingly Small Social Costs, 90 Nw. U. L.
  Rev. 500 (1996), 859
———, Some Kind Words for the Privilege against Self-Incrimination, 26 Val. U. L. Rev. 311 (1991), 729
Schwartz, Adina, "Just Take Away Their Guns": The Hidden Racism of *Terry v. Ohio*, 23 Fordham Urb.
  L.J. 317 (1996), 551
Schwartz, B., The Roots of the Bill of Rights (1980), 679

————, IVHS, Legal Privacy, and the Legacy of Dr. Faustus, 11 Santa Clara Computer & High Tech. L.J. 75 (1995), 396

Weisselberg, Charles D., In the Stationhouse After *Dickerson*, 99 Mich. L. Rev. 1121 (2001), 870

Wells, Gary L., & E. A. Olson, Eyewitness Identification: Information Gain From Incriminating and Exonerating Behaviors, 8 J. Exp. Psychol. Appl. 155 (2002), 170

Wells, Gary L., Mark Small, Steven Penrod, Roy S. Malpass, Solomon M. Fulero, & C.A.E. Brimacombe, Eyewitness Identification Procedures: Recommendations for Lineups and Photospreads, 22 Law & Hum. Behav. 603 (1998), 169

Westen, Peter, The Empty Idea of Equality, 95 Harv. L. Rev. 537 (1982), 188

————, The Three Faces of Double Jeopardy: Reflections on Government Appeals of Criminal Sentences, 78 Mich. L. Rev. 1001 (1980), 1496, 1497

Westen, Peter, & Richard Drubel, Toward A General Theory of Double Jeopardy [1978] Sup. Ct. Rev. 81 (1979), 1497

Westen, Peter, & David Westin, A Constitutional Law of Remedies for Broken Plea Bargains, 66 Cal. L. Rev. 471 (1978), 1250

Wharton, F., Criminal Pleading and Practice (8th ed. 1880), 1048

Wharton Com. on Amer. Law, 298

White, J., & R. Summers, Uniform Commercial Code (1980), 1241

White, Welsh S., Effective Assistance of Counsel in Capital Cases: The Evolving Standard of Care, [1993] U. Ill. L. Rev. 323, 240

————, Interrogation without Questions: *Rhode Island v. Innis* and *United States v. Henry*, 78 Mich. L. Rev. 1209 (1980), 892

————, Police Trickery in Inducing Confessions, 127 U. Pa. L. Rev. 581 (1979), 809, 810

————, Regulating Prison Informers under the Due Process Clause, [1991] Sup. Ct. Rev. 4, 810

————, *Rhode Island v. Innis*: The Significance of a Suspect's Assertion of His Right to Counsel, 17 Am. Crim. L. Rev. 53 (1979), 803

Whitebread, The Burger Court's Counter-Revolution in Criminal Procedure: The Recent Criminal Decisions of the United States Supreme Court, 24 Washburn L.J. 471 (1985), 76

Wice, Paul B., Chaos in the Courthouse: The Inner Workings of the Urban Criminal Courts (1985), 60

————, Criminal Lawyers: An Endangered Species (1978), 61

Wigmore, J., 3 Evidence, 1344

————, 8 Evidence (3d ed. 1940), 772

————, 8 Evidence (McNaughton rev. 1961), 306, 323, 727, 785, 1029

————, Evidence, 1507

Wilgus, Horace L., Arrest Without a Warrant, 22 Mich. L. Rev. 541 (1924), 497

————, Identification Parades, Part I, [1963] Crim. L. Rev. 479, 161

Williston, S., Contracts (3d ed. 1968), 1241

Wilson, James Q., and George L. Kelling, Broken Windows, Atlantic Monthly, 29 (Mar. 1982), 583

Winzeler, Zack L., Whoa, Whoa, Whoa . . . One at a Time: Examining the Responses to the Illinois Study on Double-Blind Sequential Lineup Procedures, 2008 Utah L. Rev. 1595, 170

Woolhandler, Ann, Demodeling Habeas, 45 Stan. L. Rev. 575 (1993), 1584

Wright, C., & K. Graham, Federal Practice and Procedure (1977), 1225

Wright, Ronald, & Marc Miller, The Screening/Bargaining Tradeoff, 55 Stan. L. Rev. 29 (2002), 47, 1038

Yackle, Larry W., Form and Function in the Administration of Justice: The Bill of Rights and Federal Habeas Corpus, 23 U. Mich. J.L. Reform 685 (1990), 1584

————, Habeas: The Figure in the Carpet, 78 Tex. L. Rev. 1731 (2000), 1602

Yellen, David, Reforming the Federal Sentencing Guidelines Misguided Approach to Real-Offense Sentencing, 58 Stan. L. Rev. 267 (2005), 987

Younger, Richard D., The People's Panel (1963), 990

Zeisel, And Then There Were None: The Diminution of the Federal Jury, 38 U. Chi. L. Rev. 710 (1971), 1278

Zeisel & Diamond, "Convincing Empirical Evidence" on the Six Member Jury, 41 U. Chi. L. Rev. 281 (1974), 1279

Zimring, Hawkins, & Kamin, Punishment and Democracy: Three Strikes and You're Out in California (2001), 1414

Zulawski, D., & D. Wicklander, Practical Aspects of Interview and Interrogation (2d ed. 2002), 849

Table of Statutes and Rules

Federal Rules of Civil Procedure

Federal Rules of Criminal Procedure

Index